THE WORKS OF JOHN BUNYAN

Drawn by E. Walker

Engraved by T Fleming

Bunyan's Tomb.

Bunhill Fields Burning Ground, London.

BLACKIE & SON, GLASGOW, EDINBURGH & LONDON.

THE

WORKS OF JOHN BUNYAN.

WITH AN

INTRODUCTION TO EACH TREATISE, NOTES,

AND A

SKETCH OF HIS LIFE, TIMES, AND CONTEMPORARIES.

VOLUME SECOND.

EXPERIMENTAL, DOCTRINAL, AND PRACTICAL.

EDITED BY

GEORGE OFFOR, Esq.

THE BANNER OF TRUTH TRUST

THE BANNER OF TRUTH TRUST
3 Murrayfield Road, Edinburgh EH12 6EL
PO Box 621, Carlisle, Pennsylvania 17013, USA

*

Reprinted from the edition of 1854
published by W.G. Blackie and Son, Glasgow

*

First Banner of Truth Trust Edition 1991
ISBN 0 85151 598 3 the set of three volumes

*

Printed and bound in Great Britain by
The Bath Press, Avon

The Works of John Bunyan

Vol ii.

Drawn by W. L. Leitch.

Engraved by W. Forrest.

Bedford.

From the London Road.

Blackie and Son.

Glasgow Edinburgh and London.

CONTENTS OF THE SECOND VOLUME.

ILLUSTRATIONS

THE SAINTS' KNOWLEDGE OF CHRIST'S LOVE;

OR,

THE UNSEARCHABLE RICHES OF CHRIST.

BY JOHN BUNYAN.

PREFATORY REMARKS BY THE EDITOR.

THIS Treatise is one of those ten distinct works, which the author had prepared for the press, when he was so suddenly summoned to the Celestial City. Well did his friends in the ministry, Ebenezer Chandler and John Wilson, call it 'an excellent manuscript, calculated to assist the Christian that would grow in grace, and to win others over to Jesus Christ.'

It was first published, with a selection of Bunyan's Works in a folio volume, in 1692, about four years after the author's decease; and although it is a treatise exhibiting very deep research and calculated for extensive usefulness, it does not appear ever to have been published as a separate volume. Like all other of his works, it is *original*; no one before him treated this subject with such profound depth of thought, nor with such clear Christian philosophy.

The revered John Bunyan proves in this, as in all other of his works, that he was a *real* and not a *pretended* descendant from the apostles,—he breathes their spirit—he knew his Master's work, and faithfully discharged his solemn requirements. His object was as pure as it was apparent; to preach not himself, but Christ Jesus his Lord. One desire appears to have influenced him in writing all his works—that of shrinking back and hiding himself behind his Master, while exhibiting the unsearchable, Divine, eternal riches of His grace.

This treatise is admirably adapted to warn the thoughtless—break the stony heart—convince the wavering—cherish the young inquirer—strengthen the saint in his pilgrimage, and arm him for the good fight of faith—and comfort the dejected, doubting, despairing Christian. It abounds with ardent sympathy for the broken-hearted, a cordial suited to every wounded conscience; while, at the same time, it thunders in awful judgment upon the impenitent and the hypocritical professor: wonders of grace to God belong, for all these blessings form but a small part of the unsearchable riches.

The reader should keep in his recollection, that this treatise was originally conceived for the pulpit; and afterwards, probably with great additions, written for the press. This will account for the divisions and sub-divisions, intended to assist a hearer's memory; or to enable a ready writer, by taking notes of each part, to digest prayerfully in private, what he had heard in the public ministry of the word,—a practice productive of great good to individuals, and by which families may be much profited while conversing upon the truths publicly taught in the church; instead of what Bunyan would have justly called, frothy conversation about the dress or appearances of their fellow-worshippers.

This discourse has been published in every edition of the works of our great author, but, most strangely, the references to Scripture are omitted in all the editions since that of 1737. Bunyan's anxiety at every step of this momentous inquiry is to shew a 'thus saith the Lord,' in proof of every assertion. In this treatise only, there are nearly *four hundred and forty* distinct references to the holy oracles. These are all carefully restored, and have been collated with the standard text, for want of which some imperfections had crept in, even to the old editions; and where the author preferred the Genevan or Puritan version, it is shewn by a note at the foot of the page.

To point out beauties in such a discourse, is to point to the whole treatise—it is all admirable; a solemn earnestness is found in every sentence; even where Bunyan modestly differs with many excellent divines, when treating upon the sufferings of the Saviour, between the period of his crucifixion and of his resurrection: this is worthy of our prayerful consideration; ever keeping in remembrance those deeply impressive—those awfully triumphant words of our Lord, 'It is finished.'

The catholic spirit, which so pervaded the mind of Bunyan, appears conspicuously in this discourse; and whatever bitter controversy this spirit occasioned him, it ought to be impressed upon the heart of every Christian professor. It is a liberality which shines more brightly, as reflected by one, whose religious education was drawn *solely* from the pure fountain of truth—the holy oracles; and however unlettered he was, as to polite literature or the learned languages, his Christian liberality can no more be enlightened by the niggard spirit of learned sectarians, than the sun could be illuminated by a rush-light. The inquiry was then, as, alas, it is too frequent now, Are there many that be saved? forgetful of the Saviour's answer and just rebuke, What is that to *thee*, follow *thou* me, seek thine *own* salvation. The inquiry is pursued a step farther, 'Can those who differ with *me* be saved?' Hear the reply of one so honest and so fully embued with the Scriptures, into the truths of which his spirit had been baptized, 'A man, through unbelief, may think that Christ has no love to him; and yet Christ may love him, with a love that passeth knowledge. But when men, in the common course of their profession, will be always terminating here, that they know how, and how far, Christ can love; and will thence be bold to conclude of their own safety, and of the loss and ruin of all that are not in the same *notions*, *opinions*, *formalities*, or *judgment*, as they. This is the *worst* [pride] and *greatest* of all [delusions]. The text, therefore, to rectify those false and erroneous conclusions, says, [the love of Christ] is a love that passeth knowledge.' Page 33.

Throughout the whole, there is a continued effort to comfort the sincere, but doubting, Christian. 'Does Satan suggest that God will not hear your stammering and chattering prayers? Does Satan suggest that thy trials, and troubles, and afflictions, are so many that you shall never get beyond them? —relief is at hand, for Christ loves thee with a love that passeth knowledge. This is a weapon that will baffle the devil, when all other weapons fail.' Page 33, 34.

The practical application of these soul-encourag-ing truths is, 'To walk in love—filled with all the fulness of God.' Bunyan has, in enforcing this duty, a very remarkable expression, 'these are the men that *sweeten* the churches, and bring glory to God and to religion. Why should anything have my heart but God, but Christ? He loves me, he loves me with love that passeth knowledge, and I will love him. His love stripped him of all for my sake; Lord, let my love strip me of all for thy sake. I am a son of love, an object of love, a monument of love; of free love, of distinguishing love, of peculiar love, and of love that passeth knowledge: and why should not I walk in love— in love to God, in love to man, in holy love, in love unfeigned?' Page 39.

And will our ministering elders bear with me in respectfully and affectionately commending to them John Bunyan, as an example of devotedness to his Master's service; of humble walking with God, of tender faithfulness to the souls of men, of holy fervour? Under such a course of sermons as this treatise would make, how attentively would our children listen with reverence to the voice of truth, and with a Divine blessing our earthen vessels would be replenished with heavenly treasure. It is delightful to read the testimony of Bunyan's ministerial friends, of various denominations, when recording his extensive usefulness. His works do follow him. And upon reading of them, we cannot wonder when we hear, that on a week-day morning, in the depth of winter, long before daylight, the inclemency of frost and snow was braved by crowded assemblies of hungry and thirsty souls, who eagerly listened to hear him proclaim 'The Saints' Knowledge of Christ's Love, or the unsearchable riches of Christ—which passeth knowledge.'

May the effectual blessing of the Holy Spirit attend the reading, as it did the preaching, of these soul-saving truths.

Hackney, Oct., 1848.   Geo. Offor.

THE SAINTS' KNOWLEDGE OF CHRIST'S LOVE.

'THAT YE - - - MAY BE ABLE TO COMPREHEND WITH ALL SAINTS, WHAT *IS* THE BREADTH, AND LENGTH, AND DEPTH, AND HEIGHT; AND TO KNOW THE LOVE OF CHRIST, WHICH PASSETH KNOWLEDGE.'—EPH. III. 18, 19.

The Apostle having, in the first chapter, treated of the doctrine of election, and in the second, of the reconciling of the Gentiles with the Jews to the Father, by his Son, through the preaching of the gospel; comes in the third chapter to shew that *that* also was, as that of election, determined before the world began. Now lest the afflictions that attend the gospel should, by its raging among these Ephesians, darken the glory of these things unto them; therefore he makes here a brief repetition and explanation, to the end they might be supported and made live above them. He also joins thereto a fervent prayer for them, that God would let them see in the spirit and faith, how they, by God and by Christ, are secured from the evil of the worst that might come upon them. 'For this cause I bow my knees unto the Father of our Lord Jesus Christ, of whom the whole family in heaven and earth is named; that he would grant you, according to the riches of his glory, to be strengthened with might by his Spirit in the inner man; that Christ may dwell in your hearts by faith; that ye, being rooted and grounded in love, may be able to comprehend with all saints, what *is* the breadth, and length, and depth, and height; and to know the love of Christ, which passeth knowledge,' &c. Knowing, that their deep understanding what good by these were reserved for them, they would never be discouraged, whatever troubles should attend their profession.

BREADTH, and LENGTH, and DEPTH, and HEIGHT, are words that in themselves are both ambiguous, and to wonderment; ambiguous, because unexplained, and to wonderment, because they carry in them an unexpressible something; and *that* something that which far out-goes all those things that can be found in this world. The Apostle here was under a spiritual surprize, for while meditating and writing, he was caught: The strength and glory of the truths that he was endeavouring to fasten upon the people to whom he wrote, took him away into their glory, beyond what could to the full be uttered. Besides, many times things are thus expressed, on purpose to command attention, a stop and pause in the mind about them; and to divert, by their greatness, the heart from the world, unto which they naturally are so inclined. Also, truths are often delivered to us, like wheat in full ears, to the end we should rub them out before we eat them, and take pains *about* them, before we have the comfort of them.

BREADTH, LENGTH, DEPTH, and HEIGHT. In my attempting to open these words, I will give you, some that are of the same kind. And then show you, First, The reasons of them; and then also, Secondly, Something of their fulness.

Those of the same kind, are used sometimes to shew us the power, force, and subtilty of the enemies of God's church, Dan. iv. 11. Rom. viii. 38, 39. But, [Sometimes] Most properly to shew us the infinite and unsearchable greatness of God, Job xi. 7, 8, 9. Rom. xi. 33.

They are here to be taken in this second sense, that is, to suggest unto us the unsearchable and infinite greatness of God; who is a *breadth*, beyond all breadths; a *length*, beyond all lengths; a *depth*, beyond all depths; and a *height*, beyond all heights, and that in all his attributes: He is an eternal being, an everlasting being, and in that respect he is beyond all measures, whether they be of breadth, or length, or depth, or height. In all his attributes he is beyond all measure: whether you measure by words, by thoughts, or by the most

enlarged and exquisite apprehension; His greatness is unsearchable; His judgments are unsearchable: Job v. 9. He is infinite in wisdom. 'O! the depth of the riches both of the wisdom and knowledge of God!' Rom. xi. 33. 'If I speak of strength, lo, he is strong;' Job ix. 19. yea, 'the thunder of his power who can understand?' Job xxvi. 14. 'There is none holy as the Lord:' 1 Sa. ii. 2. 'and his mercy is from everlasting to everlasting, upon them that fear him.' Ps. ciii. 17. The *greatness* of God, of the God and Father of our Lord Jesus Christ, is that, if rightly considered, which will support the spirits of those of his people that are frighted with the greatness of their adversaries. For here is a greatness against a greatness. Pharaoh was great, but God more great, more great in power, more great in wisdom, more great every way for the help of his people; wherein they dealt proudly, he was above them. These words therefore take in for this people, the great God who in his immensity and infinite greatness is beyond all beings. But, to come

FIRST, *to the reason of the words.* They are made use of to shew to the Ephesians, that God with what he is in himself, and with what he hath in his power, is all for the use and profit of the believers. Else no great matter is held out to them thereby. 'But this God is our God!' there is the comfort: For this cause therefore he presenteth them with this description of him. To wit, by breadth, and length, and depth, and height: As who should say, the High God is yours; the God that fills heaven and earth is yours; the God whom the heaven of heavens cannot contain, is yours; yea, the God whose works are wonderful, and whose ways are past finding out, is yours. Consider therefore the greatness that is for you, that taketh part with you, and that will always come in for your help against them that contend with you. It is my support, it is my relief; it [is] my comfort in all my tribulations, and I would have it yours, and so it will when we live in the lively faith thereof. Nor should we admit of distrust in this matter from the consideration of our own unworthiness, either taken from the finiteness of our state, or the foulness of our ways. Ps. xlvi. For now, though God's attributes, several of them in their own nature, are set against sin and sinners; yea, were we righteous, are so high that needs they must look over us, for 'tis to him a condescension to behold things in heaven: How much more then to open his eyes upon such as we: yet by the passion of Jesus Christ, they harmoniously agree in the salvation of our souls. Hence God is said to be *love*, 1 Jo. iv. God is *love*; might some say, and *justice* too: but his justice is turned with wisdom, power, holiness and truth, to love; yea, to love those that be found in his Son: forasmuch as there is nothing fault-worthy in his righteousness which is put upon us. So then, as there is in God's nature a *length*, and *breadth*, and *depth*, and *height*, that is beyond all that we can think: So we should conclude that all this is *love* to us, for Christ's sake; and then dilate with it thus in our minds, and enlarge it thus in our meditations; saying still to our low and trembling spirits: 'It is high as heaven; what canst thou do? deeper than hell; what canst thou know? the measure thereof *is* longer than the earth, and *broader than the sea.' Job xi. 8, 9. But we will pass generals, and more particularly speak

SECONDLY, *something of their fulness,* as they are fitted to suit and answer to the whole state and condition of a christian in this life. The words are boundless; we have here a breadth, a length, a depth, and height made mention of; but *what* breadth, *what* length, *what* depth, *what* height is not so much as hinted. It is therefore infiniteness suggested to us, and that has engaged for us. For the Apostle conjoins therewith, *And to know the love of Christ which passeth knowledge.* Thus therefore it suits and answers a Christian's condition, while in this world, let that be what it will. If his afflictions be broad, here is a breadth; if they be long, here is a length; and if they be deep, here is a depth; and if they be high, here is a height. And I will say, there is nothing that is more helpful, succouring, or comfortable to a christian while in a state of trial and temptation, than to know that there is a *breadth* to answer a breadth, a *length* to answer a length, a *depth* to answer a depth, and a *height* to answer a height. Wherefore this is it that the Apostle prayeth for, namely, that the Ephesians might have understanding in these things, 'That ye may know what is the breadth, and length, and depth, and height.'

Of the largeness of the Apostle's heart in praying for this people, to wit, 'That they might be able to comprehend with all saints, what,' &c. of that we shall speak afterwards.

But first, to speak to these four expressions, breadth, length, depth, and height.

First, What is the BREADTH. This word is to shew, that God is all over, everywhere, spreading of his wings, stretching out his goodness to the *utmost bounds,* for the good of those that are his people. De. xxxii. 11, 12. Ge. xlix. 26.

In the sin of his people there is a *breadth;* a breadth that spreadeth *over all,* wheresoever a man shall look. The sin of the saints is a spreading leprosy. Le. xiii. 12. Sin is a scab that spreadeth; it is a spreading plague; it knows no bounds: Le. xiii.

---

* In the first edition of this treatise, which was published four years after Bunyan's death, this is quoted 'deeper than the sea,' probably a typographical error. It is afterwards quoted correctly.—ED.

8, and 57. or, as David saith, 'I have seen the wicked spreading himself.' Ps. xxxvii. 35. Hence it is compared to a cloud, to a thick cloud, that covereth or spreadeth over the face of all the sky. Wherefore here is a breadth called for, a *breadth* that can cover all, or else what is done is to no purpose. Therefore to answer this, here we have a *breadth,* a spreading breadth; 'I spread my skirt over thee:' But how far? Even so far as to cover all. 'I spread my skirt over thee, and covered thy nakedness.' Eze. xvi. 8. Here now is a breadth according to the spreading nature of the sin of this wretched one; yea, a super-abounding spreading; a spreading *beyond;* a spreading to cover. 'Blessed *is he whose* sin *is* covered,' Ps. xxxii. 1. whose spreading sin is covered by the mercy of God through Christ. Ro. iv. 4-7. This is the spreading cloud, whose spreadings none can understand. Job xxxvi. 29. 'He spread a cloud for a covering, and fire to give light in the night.' Ps. cv. 39.

This breadth that is in God, it also overmatcheth that spreading and overspreading rage of men, that is sometimes as if it would swallow up the whole church of God. You read of the rage of the king of Assyria, that there was a *breadth* in it, an *overflowing* breadth, to the filling of 'the breadth of thy land, O Immanuel.' Is. viii. 8. But what follows? 'Associate yourselves, O ye people, (ye Assyrians) and ye shall be broken in pieces; and give ear, all ye of far countries; gird yourselves and ye shall be broken in pieces. Take counsel together, and it shall come to nought; speak the word, and it shall not stand, for God is with us;' Is. viii. 8-10. God will over-match and go beyond you.

Wherefore this word, *breadth, and what is the breadth:* It is here expressed on purpose to succour and relieve, or to shew what advantage, for support, the knowledge of the overspreading grace of God by Christ yieldeth unto those that have it, let their trials be what they will. Alas! the sin of God's children seemeth sometimes to overspread not only their flesh, and the face of their souls, but the whole face of heaven. And what shall he do now, that is a stranger to *this breadth,* made mention of in the text? Why he must despair, lie down and die, and shut up his heart against all comfort, unless he, with his fellow-christians, can, at least, apprehend what is *this* breadth, or the breadth of mercy intended in this place. Therefore Paul for the support of the Ephesians, prays, that they may know 'what is the breadth.'

This largeness of the heart and mercy of God towards his people, is also signified by the *spreading* out of his hand to us in the invitations of the gospel. 'I said,' saith he, 'Behold me, behold me, - - - I have spread out my hands all the day unto a rebellious people, - - - to a people that provoketh me continually.' Is. lxv. 1-3.

I have spread out my hands, that is, opened my arms as a mother affectionately doth, when she stoopeth to her child in the warm workings of her bowels, and claspeth it up in them, and kisseth, and putteth it into her bosom.

For, by spreading out the hands or arms to embrace, is shewed the breadth or largeness of God's affections; as by our spreading out our hands in prayer, is signified the great sense that we have of the spreading nature of our sins, and of the great desires that are in us, that God would be merciful to us. Ezr. ix. 5-7, &c.

This word also answereth to, or may fitly be set against the wiles and temptations of the devil, who is that great and dogged Leviathan, that spreadeth his 'sharp-pointed things upon the mire:' Job xli. 30. For, be the spreading nature of our corruptions never so broad, he will find sharp-pointed things enough to stick in the mire *of them*, for our affliction. These sharp-pointed things are those that in another place are called 'fiery darts,' Ep. vi. 16. and he has abundance of them, with which he can and will sorely prick and wound our spirits: Yea, so sharp some have found these things to their souls, that they have pierced beyond expression. 'When,' said Job, 'I say, my bed shall comfort me, my couch shall ease my complaint; then thou scarest me with dreams, and terrifiest me through visions; so that my soul chooseth strangling, *and* death rather than my life.' Job vii. 13-15. But now, answerable to the spreading of these sharp-pointed things, there is a super-abounding breadth in the sovereign grace of God, the which whoso seeth and understandeth, as the Apostle doth pray we should, is presently helped: for he seeth that this grace spreadeth itself, and is broader than can be, either our mire, or the sharp-pointed things that he spreadeth thereupon for our vexation and affliction: 'It is broader than the sea.' Job xi. 9.

This therefore should be that upon which those that see the spreading nature of sin, and the leprosy and contagion thereof, should meditate, to wit, The *broadness* of the grace and mercy of God in Christ. This will poise and stay the soul; this will relieve and support the soul in and under those many misgiving and desponding thoughts unto which we are subject when afflicted with the apprehensions of sin, and the abounding nature of it.

Shall *another* man pray for this, one that knew the goodness and benefit of it, and shall not I meditate upon it? and shall not I exercise my mind about it? Yes surely, for it is *my* duty, it is *my* privilege and mercy so to do. Let this therefore, when thou seest the spreading nature of thy sin be a *memento* to thee, to the end thou may'st not sink and die in thy soul.

Secondly, What is the breadth and LENGTH. As there is a *breadth* in this mercy and grace of God

by Christ, so there is a LENGTH therein, and this *length* is as *large* as the *breadth*, and as much suiting the condition of the child of God, as the other is. For, though sin sometimes is most afflicting to the conscience, while the soul beholdeth the overspreading nature of it, yet here it stoppeth not, but oft-times through the power and prevalency of it, the soul is driven with it, as a ship by a mighty tempest, or as a rolling thing before the whirlwind: driven, I say, from God, and from all hopes of his mercy, *as far* as the east is from the west, or as the ends of the world are asunder. Hence it is supposed by the prophet, that for and by sin they may be driven from God to the utmost part of heaven; De. xxx. 4. and that is a sad thing, a sad thing, I say, to a gracious man. 'Why,' saith the prophet to God, '*Art thou so* far from helping me, *and from* the words of my roaring?' Ps. xxii. 1. Sometimes a man, yea, a man of God, is, as he apprehends, so *far* off from God, that he can neither *help* him, nor *hear* him, and this is a dismal state. 'And thou hast removed my soul,' said the church, 'far off from peace: I forgat prosperity.' La. iii. 17. This is the state sometimes of the godly, and that not only with reference to their being removed by persecutors, from the appointments and gospel-seasons, which are their delight, and the desire of their eyes; but also with reference to their faith and hope in their God. They think themselves beyond the reach of his mercy. Wherefore in answer to this conceit it is, that the Lord asketh, saying, 'Is my hand shortened at all that it cannot redeem?' Is. l. 2. And again, 'Behold, the Lord's hand is not shortened, that it cannot save; neither his ear heavy, that it cannot hear.' Is. lix. 1. Wherefore he saith again, 'If any of them be driven out unto the outmost parts of heaven, from thence will the Lord thy God gather thee, and from thence will he fetch thee.' De. xxx. 4. God has a *long* arm, and he can *reach* a great way further than we can conceive he can: Ne. i. 9. When we think his mercy is *clean* gone, and that ourselves are *free* among the dead, and of the number that he remembereth no more, *then* he can reach us, and cause that again we stand before him. He *could* reach Jonah, tho' in the belly of hell; Jon. ii. and reach thee, even then, when thou thinkest thy way is hid from the Lord, and thy judgment passed over from thy God. There is a *length* to admiration, beyond apprehension or belief, in the arm of the strength of the Lord; and this is that which the Apostle intended by this word, *Length*; namely, To insinuate what a *reach* there is in the mercy of God, how *far* it can extend itself. '*If* I take the wings of the morning,' said David, '*and* dwell in the uttermost parts of the sea; even there shall thy hand lead me, and thy right hand shall hold me.' Ps. cxxxix. 9, 10. I will gather them from the east, and from the west, and from the north, and from the south, saith he: That is, from the utmost corners.

This therefore should encourage them that for the present cannot stand, but that do fly before their guilt: Them that feel no help nor stay, but that go, as to their thinking, every day by the power of temptation, driven yet farther off from God, and from the hope of obtaining of his mercy to their salvation; poor creature, I will not now ask thee how thou camest into this condition, or how long this has been thy state; but I will say before thee, and I prithee hear me, *O the length of the saving arm of God!* As yet thou art within the reach thereof; do not thou go about to measure arms with God, as some good men are apt to do: I mean, do not thou conclude, that because thou canst not reach God by thy short stump, therefore he cannot reach thee with his long arm. Look again, 'Hast thou an arm like God,' Job xl. 9, an arm like his for length and strength? It becomes thee, when thou canst not perceive that God is within the reach of *thy* arm, then to believe that thou art within the reach of *his;* for it is long, and none knows how long.

Again, is there such a *length?* such a length in the arm of the Lord, that he can reach those that are gone away, as far as they could? then this should encourage us to pray, and hope for the salvation of any one of our backslidden relations, that God would reach out his arm after them: Saying, ' Awake, - - O arm of the Lord, - art thou not it that hath cut Rahab, *and* wounded the dragon? *Art* thou not it which hath dried the sea, the waters of the great deep, that hath made the depths of the sea a way for the ransomed to pass over?' Is. li. 9, 10. Awake, O arm of the Lord, and be stretched out as far as to where my poor husband is, where my poor child, or to where my poor backslidden wife or dear relation is, and lay hold, fast hold; they are gone from thee, but, O thou the hope of Israel, fetch them again, and let them stand before thee. I say, here is in this word LENGTH matter of encouragement for us thus to pray; for if the length of the reach of mercy is *so great,* and if also this length is for the benefit of those that may be gone off *far* from God, (for they at present have no need thereof that are near) then improve this advantage at the throne of grace for such, that they may come to God again.

Thirdly, As there is a *breadth* and *length* here, so there is a DEPTH. What is the breadth, and length, and depth? And this depth is also put in here, on purpose to help us under a trial that is diverse from the two former. I told you, that by the *breadth* the apostle insinuates a remedy and succour to us, when we see our corruptions spread like a leprosy; and by *length* he would shew us, that when sin has driven God's elect to the far-

thest distance from him, yet his arm is long enough to reach them, and fetch them back again.

But, I say, as we have here a *breadth,* and a *length,* so we have also a *depth.* That ye may know what is the DEPTH. Christians have sometimes their sinking fits, and are as if they were always descending: or as Heman says, 'counted with them that go down into the pit.' Ps. lxxxviii. 4. Now guilt is not to such so much a wind and a tempest, as a load and burthen. The *devil,* and *sin,* and the *curse* of the law, and *death,* are gotten upon the shoulders of this poor man, and are treading of him down, that he may sink into, and be swallowed up of *his* miry place.

' I sink,' says David, ' in deep mire, where *there is* no standing. I am come into DEEP waters, where the floods overflow me.' Ps. lxix. 2. Yea, there is nothing more common among the saints of old, than this complaint: ' Let neither the water flood overflow me, neither let the deep swallow me up, neither let the pit shut her mouth upon me.' Ps. lxix. 14, 15. Heman also saith, ' Thou hast laid me in the lowest pit, in darkness, in the deeps. Thy wrath lieth hard upon me, and thou hast afflicted *me* with all thy waves.' Ps. lxxxviii. 6, 7. Hence it is again that the Psalmist says : ' Deep calleth unto deep, at the noise of thy water spouts: all thy waves, and thy billows are gone over me.' Ps. xlii. 7. *Deep* calleth unto *deep:* What's that? Why, it is expressed in the verse before: ' O God,' says he, ' My soul is cast down within me.' ' Down,' that is, *deep* into the jaws of distrust and fear. And, Lord, my soul in this *depth* of sorrow calls for help to thy *depth* of mercy. For though I am sinking and going down, yet not so low, but that thy mercy is yet underneath me: Do of thy compassions open those everlasting arms, De. xxxiii. 27, and catch him that has no help or stay in himself: For so it is with one that is falling into a *well* or a *dungeon.*

Now mark, as there is in these texts, the sinking condition of the godly man set forth, of a man whom sin and Satan is treading down into the *deep;* so in our text which I am speaking to at this time, we have a *depth* that can more than counterpoise these *deeps,* set forth with a hearty prayer, that we may know it. And although the deeps, or depths of calamity into which the godly may fall, may be as *deep* as Hell, and methinks they should be no deeper: yet *this* is the comfort, and for the comfort of them of the godly that are thus a sinking: The mercy of God for them lies *deeper.* ' It is deeper than hell, what canst thou know?' Job xi. 8. And this is that which made Paul that he was not afraid of this *depth,* ' I am persuaded,' saith he, ' that neither - - height nor depth shall be able to separate us from the love of God, which is in Christ Jesus our Lord.' Ro. viii.

38, 39. But of this he could by no means have been persuaded, had he not believed that mercy lieth deeper for the godly to help them, than can all other depths be to destroy them: This is it at which he stands and wonders, saying, ' O the depth of the riches both of the wisdom and knowledge of God,' Ro. xi. 33. that is to find out a way to save his people, notwithstanding all the deep contrivances that the enemy hath, and may invent to make us come short [of] home.

This is also that, as I take it, which is wrapped up in the blessing, wherewith Jacob blessed his son Joseph. ' God shall bless thee,' saith he, ' with blessings of heaven above,' and with the ' blessings of the deep that lieth under.' Ge. xlix. 25. A blessing which he had ground to pronounce, as well from his observation of God's good dealing with Joseph, as in a spirit of prophecy: For he saw that he lived and was become a flourishing bough, by a wall, after that the archers had done their worst to him. Ge. xlix. 22—24. Moses also blesseth God for blessing of Joseph thus, and blessed his portion to him, as counting of it sufficient for his help in all afflictions. ' Blessed,' saith he, ' of the Lord, be his land, for the precious things of heaven, for the dew, and for the deep that coucheth beneath.' De. xxxiii. 13.

I am not of belief that these blessings are confined to things temporal, or carnal, but to things spiritual and divine; and that they have most chiefly respect to soul, and eternal good. Now mark, he tells us here, that the blessings of the *deep*, do *couch* beneath. *Couch*, that is, lie close, so as hardly to be discerned by him that willingly would see that himself is not below these arms that are beneath him. But that as I said, is hard to be discerned by him that thus is sinking, and that has as he now smartingly feels, all God's waves, and his billows rolling over him. However, whether he sees or not, for this blessing lieth *couched;* yet there it is, and there will be, though one should sink as deep as hell: And hence they are said to be ' everlasting arms' that are ' underneath:' De. xxxiii. 27. That is, arms that are *long* and *strong*, and that can reach to the bottom, and also beyond, of all misery and distress, that Christians are subject to in this life. Indeed mercy seems to be asleep, when we are sinking: for then we are as if all things were careless of us, but it is but as a *lion couchant*, it will awake in time for our help. Ps. xliv. 22, 26; Mar. iv. 36—39. And forasmuch as this term is it, which is applicable to the lion in his den; it may be to shew that as a lion, so will God at the fittest season, arise for the help and deliverance of a sinking people. Hence when he is said to address himself to the delivering of his people, it is that he comes as a roaring lion. ' The Lord shall go forth as a mighty man, he shall stir up jealousy like a man of war: he shall cry, yea, roar; he shall prevail against his enemies.' Is. xlii. 13. However here is a depth against the depth that's against us, let *that* depth be what it will. As let it be the depth of misery, the depth of mercy is sufficient. If it be the depth of hellish policy, the depth both of the wisdom and knowledge of God shall go beyond it, and prevail.

This therefore is worthy of the consideration of all sinking souls; of the souls that feel themselves descending into the pit. There is such a thing as this experienced among the godly. Some come to them (when tempted) when you will, they will tell you, they have no ground to stand on, their feet have slipped, their foundation is removed, and they feel themselves sinking, as into a pit that has no bottom. Ps. xi. 3. They inwardly sink, not for want of something to relieve the body, but for want of some spiritual cordial to support the mind. ' I went down to the bottoms of the mountains,' said Jonas, ' the earth with her bars *was* about me for ever; - - - my soul fainted within me.' Jonah ii. 6, 7.

Now for such to consider that *underneath* them, even at the *bottom* there lieth a blessing, or that in this deep whereinto they are descending, there lieth a delivering mercy couching to catch them, and to save them from sinking for ever, this would be relief unto them, and help them to hope for good.

Again, As this, were it well considered by the sinking ones, would yield them stay and relief, so this is it by the virtue whereof, they that have been sinking heretofore, have been lifted up, and above their castings down again. There are of those that have been in the *pit*, now upon mount *Sion*, with the harps of God in their hands, and with the song of the Lamb in their mouths. But how is it that they are there? why, David, by his own deliverance shews you the reason. ' For great *is* thy mercy towards me,' saith he, ' and thou hast delivered my soul from the lowest hell.' Ps. lxxxvi. 13. And again, ' He brought me up also out of an horrible pit,' (a pit of noise, a pit wherein was the noise of devils, and of my heart answering them with distrust and fear) ' out of the miry clay,' (into which I did not only sink, but was by it held from getting up: but he brought me up) ' and set my feet upon a rock, and established my goings. And he hath put a new song in my mouth, even praise to our God.' Ps. xl. 2, 3.

But let me here give, if it may be, a timely caution to them that think they stand upon their feet. Give not way to falling because everlasting arms are underneath, take heed of that: God can let thee fall into mischief, he can let thee fall, and not help thee up. Tempt not God, lest he cast thee away indeed. I doubt there are many that have presumed upon this mercy, that thus do couch beneath, and have cast themselves down from their pinnacles into vanity, of a vain conceit that they shall be lifted up again: whom yet God will leave to die there, because their fall was rather of *willfulness*, than *weakness*, and of stubborness, and desperate resolutions, than for want of means and helps to preserve them from it.

Fourthly, As there is a *breadth*, and *length*, and *depth*, in this mercy and grace of God through Christ towards his people: So there is also a HEIGHT, 'That ye may comprehend with all saints, what is the breadth and length, and depth, and HEIGHT.' There are things that are *high*, as well as things that are *low*; things that are *above* us, as well as things that are *under*, that are distressing to God's people. It is said when Noah was a preacher of righteousness, there were *giants* in the earth in those days. Ge. vi. 4. And these, as I conceive, were some of the heights that were set against Noah; yea, they were the very *dads* and fathers of all that monstrous brood that followed in the world in that day. Of this sort were they who so frighted, and terrified Israel, when they were to go to inherit the land of promise. The men that were *tall* as the cedars, and *strong* as the oaks, frighted them: they were in their own sight, when compared with these high ones, but as grasshoppers. This therefore was their discouragement. Nu. xiii. 31—33, and De. ii. 10, and ix. 2.

Besides, together with these, they had *high walls*, walls as high as heaven; and these walls were of purpose to keep Israel out of his possession. See how it is expressed: The people *is* greater and taller than we, the cities *are* great and walled up to heaven : and moreover, we have seen the sons of the Anakims there. De. i. 28. One of these, to wit, Goliah by name, how did he fright the children of Israel in the days of Saul! How did the appearance of him, make them scuttle together on heaps before him. 1 Sa. xvii. By these *giants*, and by these *high walls*, God's children to this day are sorely distressed, because they stand in the cross ways to cut off Israel from his possession.

But now to support us against all these, and to encourage us to take heart notwithstanding all these things; there is for us, a height in God. He hath made his Son higher than the kings of the earth : Ps. lxxxix. 26, 28. His word also is settled for ever in heaven, and therefore must needs be higher than their walls: Ps. cxix. 89. He also saith in another place, 'If thou seest the oppression of the poor, and violent perverting of judgment and justice in a province, marvel not at the matter; for *he that is* higher than the highest, regardeth, and *there be* higher than they.' Ec. v. 8. 'Twas this that made Paul, that he feared not the height: not things present, nor things to come. Ro. viii. 39.

But again, As there are these things standing, or lying in our way: So there are another sort of heights that are more mischievous than these: And they are the fallen angels. These are called spiritual wickedness, *or wicked spirits*, in high places: Eph. vi. 12. For God has suffered them for a time to take to themselves principality and power, and so they are become the rulers of the darkness of this world. By these we are tempted, sifted, threatened, opposed, undermined: also by these there are snares, pits, holes, and what not made and laid for us, if peradventure by something we may be destroyed. Yea, and we should most certainly be so, were it not for the rock that is *higher* than they. 'But he that cometh from heaven is above all!' Jn iii. 31. These are they that our king has taken captive, and hath rid (in his chariots of salvation) in triumph over their necks. These are they, together with all others, whose most devilish designs he can wield, and turn and make work together for his ransomed's advantage, Ro. viii. 28. There is a height, an infinitely overtopping height in the mercy and goodness of God for us, against them.

There are heights also that build up themselves *in* us, which are not but to be taken notice of: Yea, there are a *many* of them, and they place themselves directly so, that if possible they may keep the saving knowledge of God out of our hearts. These high things therefore are said to exalt themselves against the knowledge of God: 2 Cor. x. 5; and do ofttimes more plague, afflict, and frighten Christian men and women, than any thing besides. It is from these that our faith and spiritual understanding of God and his Christ is opposed and contradicted, and from these also that we are so inclinable to swerve from right doctrine into destructive opinions. 'Tis from these that we are so easily persuaded to call into question our former experience of the goodness of God towards us, and from these that our minds are so often clouded and darkened that we cannot see afar off. These would betray us into the hands of fallen angels, and men, nor should we by any means help or deliver ourselves, were it not for one that is higher. These are the dark mountains at which our feet would certainly stumble, and upon which we should fall, were it not for one who can *leap* and *skip* over these mountains of division, and come in to us. Song ii. 8 and 17.

Further, There is a height also that is obvious to our senses, the which when it is dealt withal by our corrupted reason, proves a great shaking to our mind, and that is the height, and exceeding distance that heaven is off of us, and we off it. '*Is* not God in the height of heaven? and behold the height of the stars, how high they are?' Job xxii. 12. Hence heaven is called the place for height, Pr. xxv. 3. Also when Ahaz is bid to ask with reference to heaven, he is bid to ask it, In the height, the height above. Is. vii. 11. Now saith reason, how shall I come thither? especially when a good man is at his furthest distance therefrom: which is, when he is in the grave. Now I say, every height is a difficulty to him that is loaden with a burden, especially the heaven of heavens, where God is, and where is the resting-place of his, to them that are oppressed with the guilt of sin. And besides, the dispensation which happeneth to us last, to wit, death, as I said before, makes this heaven, in my thoughts while I live so much the more unaccessible. Christ indeed could mount up, Ac. i. 9, but *me, poor me*, how shall I get thither? Elias indeed had a chariot sent him to ride in thither, and went up by it into that holy place: 2 Ki. ii. 11. but I, poor I, how shall I get thither? Enoch is there, because God took him, Ge. v. 24: but as for *me*, how shall I get thither? Thus some have mourningly said. And although distrust of the power of God, as to the accomplishing of this thing, is by no means to be smiled upon, yet methinks the unconcernedness of professors thereabout, doth argue that considering thoughts about that, are wanting.

I know the answer is ready. *Get Christ and go to heaven.* But methinks the height of the place, and the glory of the state that we are to enjoy therein, should a little concern us, at least so as to make us wonder in our thinking, that the time is coming that we must mount up thither. And since there are so many heights between *this* place, between us, and *that*; it should make us admire at the heights of the grace and mercy of God, by which, means is provided to bring us thither. And I believe that this thing, this very thing, is included here by the Apostle when he prays for the Ephesians, that they might know the height.

Methinks, *How shall we get thither* will still stick in my mind. 'I will ascend,' says one, 'above the height of the clouds, I will be like the most High.' Is. xiv. 14. And I, says another, will set my nest among the stars of heaven. Ob. 4. Well, but what of all this? If heaven has gates, and they shall be shut, how wilt thou go in thither? Though such should climb up to heaven, from thence will God bring them down, Am. ix. 2. Still I say, therefore, how shall we get in thither? Why, for them that are godly, there is the power of God, the merits of Christ, the help of angels, and the testimony of a good conscience to bring them thither; and he that has not the help of all these, let him do what he can, shall never come thither. Not that all these go to the making up of the height that is intended in the text: for the height there, is what is in God through Christ to us alone. But the angels are the servants of God for that end:

Lu. xvi. 32, and He. i. 14. and none with ill consciences enter in thither, Ps. xv. 1, and xxiv. 3, 4. What, 'know ye not that the unrighteous shall not inherit the kingdom of God? be not deceived,' 1 Cor. vi. 9. such have none inheritance in the kingdom of Christ and of God, Ep. v. 5.

This then should teach us that in God is a power that is able to subdue all things to himself. In the completing of many things, there seems to be an utter impossibility, as that a virgin should conceive in her womb, as a virgin, and bring a Son into the world; that the body that is turned into dust, should arise and ascend into the highest heaven. Ph. iii. 21. These things with many more seem to be utterly impossible: but there is that which is called the power of God, by the which he is able to make all things bend to his will, and to make all obstructions give place to what he pleases. God is high above all things and can do whatever it pleaseth him. But since he can do so, why doth he suffer this, and that thing to appear, to act, and do so horribly repugnant to his word? I answer, he admits of many things, to the end he may shew his wrath, and make his power known; and that all the world may see how he checks and overrules the most vile and unruly things, and can make them subservient to his holy will. And how would the *breadth* and the *length*, and the *depth*, and the *height* of the love and mercy of God in Christ to us-ward, be made to appear, so as in all things it doth, were there not admitted that there should be *breadths*, and *lengths*, and *depths* and *heights*, to oppose. Wherefore these oppositions are therefore suffered, that the greatness of the wisdom, the power, the mercy, and grace of God to us in Christ might appear and be made manifest unto us.

This calls therefore upon christians, wisely to consider of the doings of their God. How many opposite breadths, and lengths, and depths, and heights did Israel meet with in their journey from Egypt to Canaan, and all to convince them of their own weakness, and also of the power of their God. And they that did wisely consider of his doings there, did reap the advantage thereof. Come, behold the works of the Lord towards me, may every christian say. He hath set a Saviour against sin; a heaven against a hell; light against darkness; good against evil, and the *breadth*, and *length*, and *depth*, and *height* of the grace that is in himself, for my good, against all the power, and strength, and force, and subtilty, of every enemy.

This also, as I hinted but just before, shews both the power of them that hate us, and the inability of us to resist. The power that is set against us none can crush, and break, but God: for it is the power of devils, of sin, of death, and hell But we for our parts are crushed before the moth: being a shadow, a vapour, and a wind that passes away. Job iv. 19. Oh! how should we, and how would we, were but our eyes awake, stand and wonder at the preservations, the deliverances, the salvations and benefits with which we are surrounded daily: while so many mighty evils seek daily to swallow us up, as the grave. See how the golden psalm of David reads it. 'Be merciful unto me, O God; for man would swallow me up; he fighting daily oppresseth me. Mine enemies would daily swallow *me* up: for *they be* many that fight against me, O thou most high.' Ps. lvi. 1, 2. This is at the beginning of it. And he concludes it thus, 'Thou hast delivered my soul from death: *wilt* not *thou deliver* my feet from falling, that I may walk before God in the light of the living.' ver. 13.

By this also we see the reason why it is so impossible for man or angel to persuade unbelievers to come in to, and close *with* Christ; why there is a *breadth* that they cannot get over, a *length* that they cannot get beyond, a *depth* that they cannot pass, and *heights* that so hinder them of the prospect of glory, and the way thereto, that they cannot be allured thither. And that nothing can remove these; but *those* that are in God, and that are opposite thereto; even the *breadth*, and *length*, and *depth* and *height* that is in the text expressed, is to all awakened men an undoubted truth.*

One item I would here give to him that loveth his own soul, and then we will pass on in pursuance of what is to come. Since there is an height obvious to sense, and that that height must be overcome ere a man can enter into life eternal: let thy heart be careful that thou go the right way to overpass this height, that thou mayest not miss of the delectable plains, and the pleasures that are above. Now, there is nothing so *high*, as to overtop this *height;* but Jacob's ladder, and that can do it: that ladder, when the foot thereof doth stand upon the earth, reacheth with its top to the gate of heaven. This is the ladder by which angels ascend thither: and this is the ladder by which thou mayest ascend thither. 'And he dreamed, and behold a ladder set up on the earth, and the top of it reached to heaven: and behold the angels of God ascending and descending on it.' Ge. xxviii. 12.

This ladder is Jesus Christ, the son of man, as is clear by the evangelist John. Jn. i. 51. And in that it is said to stand upon the earth, that is to shew that he took hold of man who is of the earth,

and therein laid a foundation for his salvation: in that it is said the top reached up to heaven, that is to shew that the divine nature was joined to the human, and by that means he was every way made a Saviour complete. Now concerning this ladder, 'tis said, *Heaven* was open where it stood, to shew that by him there is entrance into life: 'tis said also concerning this ladder, that the Lord stood there, at the top, above it: saying, 'I am the Lord God of Abraham,' Ge. xxviii. 13, to shew his hearty and willing reception of those that ascend the height of his sanctuary this way. All which Christ further explains by saying, 'I am the way, and the truth, and the life, no man cometh unto the father, but by me.' Jn. xiv. 6. Look to thyself then, that thou do truly and after the right manner embrace this ladder, so will he *draw* thee up thither after him. Jn. xii. 32. All the *rounds* of this ladder are sound and fitly placed, not one of them is set further than that by faith thou mayest ascend step by step unto, even until thou shalt come to the highest step thereof, from whence, or by which thou mayest step in at the celestial gate where thy soul desireth to dwell.

Take my caution then, and be wary, no man can come thither but by him. Thither I say to be accepted: thither, there to dwell, and there to abide with joy for ever.

'That ye - - - may be able to comprehend with all saints, what *is* the breadth, and length, and depth, and height; and to know the love of Christ which passeth knowledge.'

Having thus spoke of the breadth, and length, and depth, and height, that is in God's mercy by Christ to us-ward; we will now come more directly to

THE PRAYER OF THE APOSTLE FOR THESE EPHESIANS, WITH REFERENCE THEREUNTO; to wit, that they might be able to comprehend with all saints what they are. And

FIRST, As to THE ABILITY that he prays for, to the end that they may be capable to do this thing.

First, That ye may *be able.* The weakness that is here supposed to hinder their thus comprehending, &c., did doubtless lie in their grace, as well as their nature: for in both, with reference to *them* that are Christians, there is great disability, unless they be strengthened mightily by the Holy Ghost. Nature's ability depends upon graces, and the ability of graces, depends upon the mighty help of the spirit of God. Hence as nature itself, where grace is not, sees nothing; so nature by grace sees but weakly, if that grace is not strengthened with all might by the spirit of grace. The breadths, lengths, depths and heights here made mention of, are mysteries, and in all their operations, do work wonderfully mysteriously: insomuch that many times, though they are all of them busily engaged for this and the other child

---

* How admirably does Bunyan bring *home* to the christian's heart these solemn truths. The breadth and length and depth and height of our guilt and misery, requires a remedy beyond all human power. This can only be found in the love of God in Christ: this extends beyond all bounds. It is divine, unsearchable, eternal mercy, swallowing up all our miseries. —ED.

of God, yet they themselves see nothing of them. As Christ said to Peter, 'What I do thou knowest not now;' Jn. xiii. 7; so may it be said to many where the grace and mercy of God in Christ is working: they do not know, they understand not what it is, nor what will be the end of such dispensations of God towards them. Wherefore they also say as Peter to Christ, 'Dost thou wash my feet? - - thou shalt never wash my feet;' Jn. xiii. 6—8. Yea, and when some light to convince of this folly breaks in upon them, yet if it be not very distinct and clear; causing the person to know the true cause, nature, and end of God's doing of this or that, they swerve with Peter, *as much on the other side.* Jn. xiii. 9, 10. They have not known my ways, and my methods with them in this world, were that that caused Israel always to err in their hearts, He. iii. 10. and lie cross to all, and each of these breadths, lengths, depths, and heights, whenever they were under the exercise of any of them in the wilderness.

And the reason is, as I said before, for that they are very mysterious in their workings. For they work by, upon, and against oppositions; for, and in order to the help and salvation of his people. Also (as was hinted a while since) that the power and glory of *this* breadth, and length, &c. of the mercy and grace of God, may the more shew its excellency and sufficiency as to our deliverance; we by him seem quite to be delivered up to the breadths, lengths, and depths, and heights that oppose, and that utterly seek our ruin: wherefore at such times, nothing of breadths, lengths, depths, or heights can be seen, save by those that are very well skilled in those mysterious methods of God, in his gracious actings towards his people. 'Who will bring me *into* the strong city,' and '*wilt* not thou, O God, *which* hadst cast us off? and thou, O God, *which* didst not go out with our armies?' Ps. lx. 9, 10. is a lesson too hard for every Christian man to say over believingly. And what was it that made Jonah say, when he was in the belly of hell, 'Yet I will look again toward thy holy temple,' Jonah ii. 4. but the good skill that he had in understanding of the mystery of these breadths, and lengths, and depths, and heights of God, and of the way of his working by them. Read the text at large. 'Thou hadst cast me into the deep, in the midst of the seas, and the floods compassed me about. All thy billows and thy waves passed over me. Then I said, I am cast out of thy sight; yet I will look again toward thy holy temple.' Jonah ii. 3, 4.

These, and such like sentences, are easily played with by a preacher, when in the pulpit, specially if he has a little of the notion of things, but of the *difficulty* and *strait*, that those are brought into, out of whose mouth such things, or words are extorted, by reason of the force of the labyrinths they are fallen into: of *those* they experience nothing, wherefore to those they are utterly strangers.

He then that is able to comprehend with all saints what is the breadth, and length, and depth, and height; must be a good expositor of *providences,* and must see the way, and the workings of God by *them.* Now there are providences of two sorts, seemingly good, and seemingly bad, and those do usually as Jacob did, when he blessed the sons of Joseph, cross hands; and lay the blessing where *we* would not. 'And when Joseph saw that his father laid his right hand upon the head of Ephraim, it displeased him.' Ge. xlviii. 17. I say there are providences unto which we would have the blessings entailed, but they are not. And they are providences that smile upon the flesh; to wit, such as cast into the lap, health, wealth, plenty, ease, friends, and abundance of this world's good: because these, [Manasseh, as his name doth signify,] have in them an aptness to make us forget our toil, our low estate, and from whence we were: Ge. xli. 51. but the great blessing is not in them. There are providences again, that take away from us whatever is desirable to the flesh; such is the sickness, losses, crosses, persecution and affliction; and usually in these, though they make us *shuck whenever they come upon us, blessing coucheth, and is ready to help us. For God, as the name of Ephraim signifies, makes us 'fruitful in the land of our affliction.' Ge. xli. 52. He therefore, in blessing of his people, lays his hands across, guiding them wittingly, and laying the chiefest blessing on the head of Ephraim, or in that providence, that sanctifies affliction. Abel! what, to the reason of Eve was he, in comparison of Cain. Rachel called Benjamin the son of her sorrow: but Jacob knew how to give him a better name. Ge. xxxv. 18. Jabez also, though his mother so called him, because, as it seems, she brought him forth with more than ordinary sorrow, was yet more honourable, more godly, than his brethren. 1 Ch. iv. 9, 10. He that has skill to judge of providences aright, has a great ability in him to comprehend with other saints, what is the breadth, and length, and depth, and height: but he that has not skill as to discerning of them, is but a child in his judgment in those *high* and mysterious things. And hence it is, that some shall suck honey out of that, at the which others tremble for fear it should poison them, I have often been made to say, 'Sorrow is better than laughter; and the house of mourning better than the house of mirth.' Ec. vii. 3–5. And I have more often seen, that the afflicted are always the best sort of Christians. There is a man, never well, never prospering, never

---

* *Shuck,* a corruption of shrug, to express horror by motions of the body.

but under afflictions, disappointments and sorrows: why this man, if he be a Christian, is one of the best of men. 'They that go down to the sea, - - that do business in great waters, these see the works of the Lord, and his wonders in the deep.* Ps. cvii. 23, 24. And it is from hence, for aught I know, that James admonishes the brother of high degree to rejoice in that he is made low. And he renders the reason of it, to wit, for that the fashion of the world perisheth, the rich man fadeth away in his way; but the tempted, and he that endureth temptation is blessed. Ja. i. 10-12. Now, I know these things are not excellent in themselves, nor yet to be desired for any profit that they can yield, but God doth use by these, as by a tutor or instructor, to make known to them that are exercised with them, so much of himself as to make them understand *that* riches of his goodness that is seldom by other means broken up to the sons of men. And hence 'tis said, that the afterwards of affliction doth yield the peaceable fruits of righteousness unto them which are exercised thereby. He. xii. 11.

The sum is, *these* breadths, and lengths, and depths, and heights of God, are to be discerned; and some that are good, do more, and some do less discern them, and how they are working, and putting forth themselves in every providence, in every change, in every turn of the wheel that passeth by us in this world. I do not question but that there are some that are alive that have been able to say, the days of affliction have been the best unto them; and that could, if it were lawful, pray that they might always be in affliction, if God would but do to them as he did when his hand was last upon them. For by them he caused his light to shine: Or as Job has it, 'Thou huntest me as a fierce lion: and again thou shewest thyself marvellously upon me.' Job x. 16. See also the writing of Hezekiah, and read what profit he found in afflictions. Is. xxxviii.

But again, these breadths, lengths, depths, and heights, have in themselves naturally that glory, that cannot be so well discerned, or kept in view by weak eyes. He had need have an eye like an eagle, that can look upon the sun, that can look upon these great things, and not be stricken blind therewith. You see how Saul was served when he was going to Damascus: Ac. ix. But Stephen could

* This is a very striking application of these words of David, which so fearfully describe the agitation of those who are exposed to a hurricane at sea. We too generally limit this passage to its literal sense. To Bunyan, who had passed through such a deep experience of the "terrors of the Lord," when he came out of tribulation and anguish, he must have richly enjoyed the solemn imagery of these words, depicting the inmost feelings of his soul when in the horrible deeps of doubt and despair. But young Christians must not be distressed because they have never experienced such tempests: thousands of vessels of mercy get to heaven, without meeting with hurricanes in their way.—Ed.

stand and look up stedfastly into heaven; and that too when with Jonas he was going into the deep. Ac. vii. But I have done with this, and proceed.

Second—That ye may be able to comprehend. Although apprehending is included in comprehending; yet to comprehend is more. To comprehend is to know a thing fully; or, to reach it all. But here we must distinguish, and say, that there is a comprehending that is absolute, and a comprehending that is comparative. Of comprehending absolutely, or perfectly, we are not here to speak; for that the Apostle could not, in this place, as to the thing prayed for, desire: For it is utterly impossible perfectly to know whatsoever is in the breadths, lengths, depths, and heights here spoken of. Whether you call them mercies, judgments, or the ways of God with men. 'How unsearchable *are* his judgments, and his ways past finding out!' Ro. xi. 33. Or, if you take them to signify his love, unto which you see I am inclined; why, that you read of in the same place, to be it 'which passes knowledge.' Wherefore should the Apostle by this term, conclude, or insinuate, that what he calls here breadths, lengths, depths, or heights, might be fully, or perfectly understood and known, he would not only contradict other scriptures, but himself, in one and the self same breath. Wherefore it must be understood comparatively; that is, and that he says, with, or as much as others, as any, even with all saints. *That ye may be able to comprehend with all saints, what is the breadth, and length, and depth, and height.* I would ye were as able to understand, to know, and to find out these things, as ever any were; and to know with the very best of saints, *The love of Christ, which passeth knowledge.* There are, as has before been hinted, degrees of knowledge of these things; some know more, some less; but the Apostle prays that these Ephesians might see, know, and understand as much thereof as the best, or as any under heaven.

1. And this, in the *first* place, shews us the love of a minister of Jesus Christ. A minister's love to his flock is seen in his praying for them: wherefore Paul, commonly, by his epistles, either first or last, or both, gives the churches to understand, That he did often heartily pray to God for them: Ro. xvi. 20, 24. 1 Co. xvi. 23. Ga. vi. 18. Ep. i. 16. Phil. i. 4. Col. i. 3. 1 Th. i. 2. 1 Ti. vi. 21. 2 Ti. iv. 22. And not only so, but also specifies the mercies, and blessings, and benefits which he earnestly begged for them of God. 2 Co. xiii. 7. 2 Th. i. 11.

2. But, *secondly*, This implies that there are great benefits accrue to Christians by the comprehending of these things: Yea, it implies that something very special is ministered to us by this knowledge of these; and here to touch upon a few of them.

(1.) He that shall arrive to some competent knowledge of these things, shall understand more thoroughly the greatness, the wisdom, the power, &c. of the God that is above. For by these expressions are the attributes of God set forth unto us: And although I have discoursed of them hitherto under the notion of grace and mercy, yet it was not for that I concluded, they excluded the expressing of his other attributes, but because they all, as it were, turn into loving methods in the wheel of their heavenly motion towards the children of God. Hence it is said, 'God is love,' 1 Jn. iv. 16. 'God is light,' 1 Jn. i. 5. God is what He is for His own glory, and the good of them that fear Him. God! Why God in the breadth, length, depth, height, that is here intended, comprehends the whole world. Col. i. 17. The whole world is *in* him: for he is before, above, beyond, and round about all things. Hence it is said, The heavens for breadth, are but his span: That he gathereth the wind in his fists, Pr. xxx. 4. measureth the waters in the hollow of his hand, weigheth the mountains in scales, and the hills in a balance. Is. xl. 12. Yea, that 'all nations before him *are* as nothing, and they are counted to him less than nothing, and vanity.' ver. 17. Hence we are said to live and move in him, Ac. xvii. 28. and that He is beyond all search.

I will add one word more, notwithstanding there is such a revelation of Him in his word, in the book of creatures, and in the book of providences; yet the scripture says, 'Lo, these *are* parts of his ways: but how little a portion is heard of him?' Job xxvi. 14. So great is God above all that we have read, heard, or seen of Him, either in the bible, in heaven, or earth, the sea, or what else is to be understood. But now, That a poor mortal, a lump of sinful flesh, or, as the scripture-phrase is, poor *dust and ashes*, should be in the favour, in the heart, and wrapped up in the compassions of SUCH a God! O amazing! O astonishing consideration! And yet 'This God *is* our God for ever and ever; and He will be our guide *even* unto death.' Ps. xlviii. 14.

It is said of our God, 'That he humbleth himself when he beholds things in heaven.' How much more then when he openeth his eyes upon man; but most of all when he makes it, as one may say, his business to visit him every morning, and to try him every moment, having set His heart upon him, being determined to set him also among his princes. 'The Lord *is* high above all nations, *and* his glory above the heavens. Who *is* like unto the Lord our God, who dwelleth on high, Who humbleth *himself* to behold *the things that are* in heaven, and in the earth! He raiseth up the poor out of the dust, *and* lifteth the needy out of the dunghill; that he may set *him* with princes, *even* with the princes of his people.' Ps. cxiii. 3–8.

(2.) IF *this* God be our God; or if our God be such a God, and could we but attain to *that* knowledge of the breadth, and length, and depth, and height that is in him, as the Apostle here prays, and desires we may, we should never be afraid of anything we shall meet with, or that shall assault us in this world. The great God, the former of all things, taketh part with them that fear Him, and that engage themselves to walk in His ways, of love, and respect, they bear unto him; so that such may boldly say, 'The Lord *is* my helper, and I will not fear what man shall do unto me.' He. xiii. 6. Would it not be amazing, should you see a man encompassed with chariots and horses, and weapons for his defence, yet afraid of being sparrow blasted, or over-run by a grasshopper! Why '*It is* he that sitteth upon the circle of the earth, and' to whom 'the inhabitants thereof are as grasshoppers:' Is. xl. 22. that is the God of the people that are lovers of Jesus Christ; therefore we should not fear them. To fear man, is to forget God; and to be careless in a time of danger, is to forget God's ordinance. What is it then? Why, let us fear God, and diligently keep his way, with what prudence and regard to our preservation, and also the preservation of what we have, we may: And if, we doing this, our God shall deliver us, and what we have, into the hands of them that hate us, let us laugh, be fearless and careless, not minding *now* to do anything else but to stand up for Him against the workers of iniquity; fully concluding, that both we, and our enemies, are in the hand of him that loveth his people, and that will certainly render a reward to the wicked, after that he has sufficiently tried us by their means. 'The great God that formed all *things*, both rewardeth the fool, and rewardeth transgressors.' Pr. xxvi. 10.*

(3.) Another thing that the knowledge of what is prayed for of the Apostle, if we attain it, will minister to us, is, *An holy fear and reverence of this great God in our souls;* both because he is great, and because he is wise and good. Je. x. 7. 'Who shall not fear thee, O Lord, and glorify thy name?' Re. xv. 4.

Greatness should beget fear, greatness should beget reverence: Now who so great as our God; and so, who to be feared like him! He also is wise, and will not be deceived by any. 'He will bring evil, and not call back his words, but will rise against the house of evil-doers, and against

---

* How thankful should *we* be, for the great spread of gospel light in this country, since Bunyan's days. He for refusing to attend, what he considered, an unscriptural church; suffered above *twelve* years' incarceration in a miserable den; while all his friends were either imprisoned or plundered. It was a dreadful attempt to root out Christianity from this country; but was overruled to make it take deeper root. How long will Antichrist still hold up his head in this country? He has had some hard knocks of late.—ED.

the help of them that work iniquity. Is. xxxi. 2.   Most men deal with God as if he were not wise; as if he either knew not the wickedness of their hearts and ways, or else knew not how to be even with them for it: When, alas! he is *wise* in heart, and *mighty* in power; and although he will not, without cause, afflict, yet he will not let wickedness go unpunished. This therefore should make us fear. He also is *good*, and this should make us serve him with fear. Oh! that a great God should be a good God; a good God to an unworthy, to an undeserving, and to a people that continually do what they can to provoke the eyes of his glory; this should make us tremble. He is fearful in service, fearful in praises.

The *breadth*, and *length*, and *depth*, and *height* of his out-going towards the children of men, should also beget in us a very great fear and dread of his majesty. When the prophet saw the height of the wheels, he said they were *dreadful*, Eze. i. 18. and cried out unto them, *O wheel!* ch. x. 13. His judgments also are a great deep; Ps. xxxvi. 6. nor is there any 'searching of his understanding.' Is. xl. 28. He can tell how to bring his *wheel* upon us; and to make our table a snare, a trap, and a stumbling-block unto us. Is. viii. 14; and Ro. xi. 8-10. He can tell how to make his Son to us a rock of offence, and his gospel to be a savour of death unto death, unto us. 2 Co. ii. 15, 16. He can tell how to choose delusions for us, Is. lxvi. 4; 2 Th. ii. 11,12. and to lead us forth with the workers of iniquity, Ps. cxxv. 5. He can out-wit, and out-do us, and prevail against us for ever; Job xiv. 20. and therefore we should be afraid and fear before Him, for our good, and the good of ours for ever: Yea, it is for these purposes, with others, that the Apostle prayeth thus for this people: For the comprehending of these things, do poise and keep the heart in an even course. This yields comfort; this gives encouragement; this begets fear and reverence in our hearts of God.

(4.) This knowledge will make us willing that he should be our God; yea, will also make us abide by that willingness. Jacob said with a vow, 'If God will be with me, and will keep me in this way that I go, and will give me bread to eat, and raiment to put on, so that I come again to my father's house in peace; then shall the LORD be my God: And this stone, which I have set *for* a pillar, shall be God's house: and of all that thou shalt give me I will surely give the tenth unto thee.' Ge. xxviii. 20-22. Thus he considered the greatness of God, and from a supposition that he was what he had heard him, of his father, to be; he concluded to choose him for his God, and that he would worship him, and give him that honour that was due to him as God. How did the king of Babylon set him above all gods, when but some sparkling rays from him did light upon him: he calls

him 'a God of gods,' Da. ii. 47. prefers him above all gods, charges all people and nations that they do nothing amiss against him: Da. iii. 28, 29. he calls him 'the most high' God, the God ' that liveth for ever;' and confesses, that he doth whatsoever he will in heaven and earth; and concludes with praising and extolling of him. Da. iv. We naturally love greatness; and when the glorious beauty of the King of glory shall be manifest to us, and we shall behold it, we shall say as Joshua did; Let all men do as seems them good; but I, and my house will serve the Lord. Jos. xxiv. 15.

When the Apostle Paul sought to win the Athenians to him, he sets Him forth before them with such terms as bespeaks his greatness; calling of him (and that rightly) 'God that made the world, and all things: - - the Lord of heaven and earth; - - One that giveth to all life and breath, and all things;' One that is nigh to every one; 'he in whom we live, and move, and have our being:' God that hath made of one blood all nations of men, and that hath determined the times before appointed, and the bounds of their habitation, &c. Ac. xvii. 24-28. These things bespeak the greatness of God, and are taking to considering men. Yea, these very Athenians, while ignorant of him, from those dark hints that they had by natural light concerning him, erected an altar to him, and put this singular inscription upon it, 'To the unknown God:' to shew, that according to their mode, they had some kind of reverence for him: but how much more when they came to know him? and to believe that God, in all his greatness, had engaged himself to be theirs; and to bring them to himself, that they might in time be partakers of his glory.

(5.) The more a man knows, or understands of the greatness of God towards him, expressed here by the terms of unsearchable breadth, length, depth, and height; the better will he be able in his heart to conceive of the excellent glory and greatness of the things that are laid up in the heavens for them that fear him. They that know nothing of this greatness, know nothing of them; they that think amiss of this greatness, think amiss of them; they that know but little of this greatness, know but little of them: But he that is able to comprehend with all saints what is the *breadth*, and *length*, and *depth*, and *height*; he is best able to conceive of, and, consequently to make a judgment concerning the due worth, and blessed glory of them.

This is both evident to reason; also experience confirmeth the same. For, as for those *dark souls* that know nothing of his greatness, they have in derision those who are, through the splendor of the glory, captivated and carried away after God. Also, those whose judgments are corrupted, and themselves thereby made as drunkards, to judge of things foolishly, they, as it were, step in the same steps with the other, and vainly imagine thereabout. Moreover, we shall see those little spirited Christians, though Christians indeed, that are but in a small measure acquainted with this God, with the breadths, and lengths, and depths, and heights that are in him, taken but little with the glory and blessedness that they are to go to when they die: wherefore they are neither so mortified to this world, so dead to sin, so self-denying, so delighted in the book of God, nor so earnest in desires to be acquainted with the heights, and depths that are therein. No, this is reserved only for those who are devoted thereto; who have been acquainted with God in a measure beyond that which your narrow-spirited Christians understand. There doth want as to these things, enlargings in the hearts of the most of saints, as there did in those of Corinth, and also in those at Ephesus: Wherefore, as Paul bids the one, and prays that the other may be enlarged, and have great knowledge thereabout: so we should, to answer such love, through desire, separate ourselves from terrene things that we may seek and intermeddle with all wisdom. Pr. xviii. 1. Christ says, 'If any man will do his will, he shall know of the doctrine.' Jo. vii. 7; Is. xxviii. 9. Oh! that we were *indeed* enlarged as to these breadths, and lengths, and depths, and heights of God, as the Apostle desired the Ephesians might.

(6.) THEN those great truths; the coming of Christ, the resurrection of the dead, and eternal judgment, would neither seem so like fables, nor be so much off our hearts as they do, and are. 1 Co xv. 35. For the thorough belief of them depends upon the knowledge of the abilities that are in God to perform what he has said thereabout: And hence it is that your inferior sort of Christians live so like, as if none of these things were at hand; and hence it is again, that they so soon are shaken in mind about them, when tempted of the devil, or briskly assaulted by deceivers. But this cometh to pass that there may be fulfilled what is written: 'And while the bridegroom tarried, they all slumbered and slept.' Mat. xxv. 1-7. Surely, the meaning is, they were asleep about his coming, the resurrection and the judgment; and, consequently had lost much of that knowledge of God, the which if they had retained; these truths, with power, would have been upon their hearts. The Corinthians were horribly decayed here, though some more than others: Hence Paul, when he treats of this doctrine, bids them 'awake to righteousness,' and not sin, telling them, that some among them had not the knowledge of God. 1 Co. xv. 34. To be sure, they had not such a knowledge of God as would keep them steady in the faith of these things. ver. 51.

Now, the knowledge of the things above-mentioned, to wit, 'this comprehending knowledge;' will greaten these things, bring them near, and

make them to be credited as are the greatest of God's truths: and the virtue of the faith of them is, to make one die daily. Therefore,

(7.) Another advantage that floweth from this knowledge, is, that it makes the next world desirable, not simply as it is with those *lean souls*, that desire it only as the thief desireth the judge's favour, that he may be saved from the halter; but out of love such have to God and to the beauties of the house he dwells in; and that they may be rid of this world, which is to such as a dark dungeon. The knowledge of God that men pretend they have, may easily be judged of, by the answerable or unanswerableness of their hearts and lives thereto. Where is the man that groans earnestly to be gone to God, that counts this life a strait unto him: that saith as a sick man of my acquaintance did, when his friend at his bed-side prayed to God to spare his life, *No, no*, said he, *pray not so; for it is better to be dissolved and be gone.* Christians should shew the world how they believe; not by words on paper, not by gay and flourishing notions: Ja. ii. 18. but by those desires they have to be gone, and the proof that these desires are true, is a life in heaven while we are on earth. Phil. iii. 20, 21. I know words are cheap, but a dram of grace is worth all the world. But where, as I said, shall it be found, not among carnal men, not among weak Christians, but among those, and those only, that enjoy a great measure of Paul's wish here. But to come to the

SECOND PART OF THE TEXT,

AND TO KNOW THE LOVE OF CHRIST WHICH PASSETH KNOWLEDGE. These words are the second part of the text, and they deal mainly about the love of Christ, who is the Son of God. We have spoken already briefly of God, and therefore now we shall speak also of his Son. These words are a part of the prayer afore-mentioned, and have something of the same strain in them. In the first part, he prays that they might comprehend that which cannot absolutely by any means be comprehended: and here he prays that that might be known, which yet in the same breath he saith, *passeth knowledge*, to wit, the love of Christ. *And to know the love of Christ, which passeth knowledge.* In the words we are to take notice of three things:

FIRST, Of the love of Christ.

SECOND, Of the exceeding greatness of it.

THIRD, Of the knowledge of it.

FIRST, We will begin with the first of these, to wit, *Of the love of Christ*. Now for the explication of this we must inquire into three things, *First*, Who Christ is. *Second*, What love is. *Third*, What the love of Christ is.

First, Christ is a person of no less quality than he is of whom we treated before: to wit, *very God*.

So I say, not *titularly*, not *nominally*, not so *counterfeitly*, but the self-same in *nature* with the Father. Jn. i. 1, 2; 1 Jn. v. 7; Phi. ii. 6. Wherefore what we have under consideration, is so much the more to be taken notice of; namely, that a person so great, so high, so glorious, as this Jesus Christ was, should have love for us, that passes knowledge. It is common for equals to love, and for superiors to be beloved; but for the King of princes, for the Son of God, for Jesus Christ to love *man* thus: this is amazing, and that so much the more, for that man the object of this love, is so low, so mean, so vile, so undeserving, and so inconsiderable, as by the scriptures, everywhere he is described to be.

But to speak a little more particularly of this person. He is called God. Jn. i. 1. The King of glory, Ps. xxiv. 10. and Lord of glory. 1 Co. ii. 8. The brightness of the glory of his Father. He. i. 3. The head over all things. Ep. i. 22. The Prince of life. Ac. iii. 15. The Creator of all things. Col. i. 16. The upholder of all things. He. i. 3. The disposer of all things. Mat. xxviii. 18. The only beloved of the Father. Mat. xi.

But the persons of him beloved, are called transgressors, sinners, enemies, dust and ashes, fleas, 1 Sa. xxiv. 14, worms, shadows, vapours: vile, sinful, filthy, unclean, ungodly fools, madmen. And now is it not to be wondered at, and are we not to be affected herewith, saying, And wilt thou set thine eye upon such a one? But how much more when *He* will set his *heart* upon us. And yet this great, this high, this glorious person, verily, verily loveth such.

Second, We now come to the second thing, namely, *to shew what is love;* not in a way of nice distinction of words, but in a plain and familiar discourse, yet respecting the love of the person under consideration.

Love ought to be considered with reference to the subject as well as to the object of it.

The subject of love in the text, is Christ; but forasmuch as love *in him* is diverse from the love that is *in us ;* therefore it will not be amiss, if a little [of] the difference be made appear.

Love in us is a passion of the soul, and being such, is subject to *ebb* and *flow*, and to be extreme both ways. For whatever is a passion of the soul, whether love or hatred, joy or fear, is more apt to exceed, or come short, than to keep within its due bounds. Hence, oft-times that which is loved to-day is hated to-morrow; 2 Sa. xiii. 15. yea, and that which should be loved with bounds of moderation, is loved to the drowning of both soul and body in perdition and destruction. 1 Ti. vi. 9, 10.

Besides, love in us is apt to choose to itself undue and unlawful objects, and to reject those, that with leave of God, we may embrace and enjoy; so unruly, as to the laws and rules of divine government, oft-times is this passion of love in us.

Love in us, requires, that something pleasing and delightful be in the object loved, at least, so it must appear to the lust and fancy of the person loving; or else love cannot act; for the love that is in us, is not of power to set itself on work, where no allurement is in the thing to be beloved.

Love in us decays, though once never so warm and strongly fixed, if the object falls off, as to its first alluring provocation; or disappointeth our expectation with some unexpected reluctancy to our fancy or our mind.

All this we know to be true from nature, for every one of us are thus; nor can we refuse, or choose as to love, but upon, and after the rate, and the working thus of our passions. Wherefore our love, as we are natural, is weak, unorderly, fails and miscarries, either by being too much or too little; yea, though the thing which is beloved be allowed for an object of love, both by the law of nature and grace. We therefore must put a vast difference betwixt love, as found in us, and love as found in Christ, and that, both as to the nature, principle, or object of love.

Love in Christ is not love of the same nature, as is love in us; love in him is essential to his being; 1 Jn. iv. 16. but in us it is not so, as has been already shewed. God is love; Christ is God; therefore Christ is love, *love naturally.* Love therefore is essential to His being. He may as well cease to *be*, as cease to *love*. Hence therefore it follows, that love in Christ floweth not from so low and beggarly a principle, as doth love in man; and consequently is not, nor can be attended with those infirmities or defects, that the love of man is attended with.

It is not attended with those unruly or uncertain motions that ours is attended with: here is no ebbing, no flowing, no going beyond, no coming short; and so nothing of uncertainty. 'Having loved his own which were in the world, he loved them unto the end.' Jn. xiii. 1.

True, there is a way of manifesting of this love, which is suited to our capacities, as men, and by that we see it sometimes more, sometimes less: Song vii. 11, 12. also it is manifested to us as we *do*, or do *not* walk with God in this world. Jn. xiv. 23. I speak now of saints.

Love in Christ pitcheth not itself upon undue or unlawful objects; nor refuseth to embrace what by the eternal covenant is made capable thereof. It always acteth according to God; nor is there at any time the least shadow of swerving as to this.

Love in Christ requireth no taking beauteousness in the object to be beloved, as not being able to put forth itself without such attracting allurements. Eze. xvi. 6—8. It can act *of* and *from* itself, without all such kind of dependencies. This is manifest to all who have the least true knowledge of what that object is in itself, on which the Lord Jesus has set his heart to love them.

Love in Christ decays not, nor can be tempted so to do by anything that happens, or that shall happen hereafter, in the object so beloved. But as this love at first acts by, and from itself, so it continueth to do until all things that are imperfections, are completely and everlastingly subdued. The reason is, because Christ loves to make us comely, *not* because we *are* so. Eze. xvi. 9—14.

Object. But all along Christ compareth his love to ours; now, why doth he so, if they be so much alike?

Answ. Because we know not love but by the passions of love that work in our hearts; wherefore he condescends to our capacities, and speaketh of His love to us, according as we find love to work in ourselves to others. Hence he sets forth his love to us, by borrowing from us instances of our love to wife and children. Ep. v. 25. Yea, he sometimes sets forth his love to us, by calling to our mind how sometimes a man loves a woman that is a whore, ' Go,' (saith God to the prophet) ' love a woman beloved of *her* friend, yet an adultress, according to the word of the Lord toward the children of Israel, who look to other gods, and love flagons of wine.' Ho. iii. 1. But then, these things must not be understood with respect to the nature, but the dispensations and manifestations of love; no, nor with reference to these neither, any further than by making use of such suitable similitudes, thereby to commend his love to us, and thereby to beget in us affections to him for the love bestowed upon us.

Wherefore Christ's love must be considered both with respect to the essence, and also as to the divers workings of it. For the essence thereof, it is as I said, natural with himself, and as such, it is the root and ground of all those actions of his, whereby he hath shewed that himself is loving to sinful man. But now, though the love that is in him is essential to his nature, and can vary no more than God himself: yet we see not this love but by the fruits of it, nor can it otherwise be discerned. ' Hereby perceive we the love *of God*, because he laid down his life for us.' 1 Jn. iii. 16. We must then betake ourselves to the discoveries of this love, of which there are two sorts; [namely,] such as are the foundations, and such as are the consequences of those fundamental acts. Those which I call the foundations, are they upon which all other discoveries of his goodness depend, and they are two. 1. His dying for us. 2. His improving of his death for us at the right hand of God.

Third, And this leads me to the third particular, to wit, to shew you *what the love of Christ is;* namely, in the discovery of it. *And to know the love of Christ.*

The love of Christ is made known unto us, as I said, First, By his dying for us. Second, By his improving of his dying for us.

1. His dying for us appears, (1.) To be wonderful in itself. (2.) In his preparations for that work.

(1.) It appears to be *wonderful in itself*, and that both with respect to the nature of that death, as also, with respect to the persons for whom he so died.

The love of Christ appears to be wonderful by the death he died: In that *he* died, in that he died *such* a death. 'Twas strange love in Christ that moved him to die for us: strange, because not according to the custom of the world. Men do not use, in cool blood, deliberately to come upon the stage or ladder, to lay down their lives for others; but this did Jesus Christ, and that too for such, whose qualification, if it be duly considered, will make this act of his, far more amazing, *He laid down his life for his enemies*, Ro. v. and for those that could not abide him; yea, for those, even for those that brought him to the cross: not accidentally, or because it happened so, but knowingly, designedly, Ze. xii. 10. he knew it was for those he died, and yet his love led him to lay down his life for them. I will add, That those very people for whom he laid down his life, though they by all sorts of carriages did what they could to provoke him to pray to God his Father, that he would send and cut them off by the flaming sword of angels, Mat. xxvi. 53. would not be provoked, but would lay down his life for them. Nor must I leave off here: We never read that Jesus Christ was more chearful in all his life on earth, than when he was going to lay down his life for them, now he thanked God, Lu. xxii. 19. now he sang. Mat. xxvi. 30.

But this is not all. He did not only die, but died *such a death*, as indeed cannot be expressed. He was content to be counted the *sinner:* yea, to be counted the *sin* of the sinner, nor could this but be odious to so holy a Lamb as he was, yet willing to be *this* and *thus* for that love that he bare to men.

This being thus, it follows, that his sufferings must be unconceivable; for that, what in justice was the proper wages of sin and sinners, he must undergo; and what that was can no man so well know as he himself and damned spirits; for the proper wages of sin, and of sinners for their sin, is that death which layeth pains, *such* pains which it deserveth upon the man that dieth so: But Christ died so, and consequently was seized by those pains not only in body but in soul. His tears, his cries, his bloody sweat, Lu. xxii. 44. the hiding of his Father's face; yea, God's forsaking of him in his extremity, Mat. xxvii. 46. plainly enough declares the nature of the death he died. Mar. xv. 39.

For my part, I stand amazed at those that would not have the world believe, that the death of Jesus Christ was, in itself, so terrible as it was.

I will not stand here to discourse of the place called *Hell*, where the spirits of the damned are, we are discoursing of the nature of Christ's sufferings: and I say, if Christ was put into the very capacity of one that must suffer what in justice ought to be inflicted for sin; then, how we can so diminish the greatness of his sufferings, as some do, without undervaluing of the greatness of his love, I know not; and how they will answer it, I know not. And on the contrary, what if I should say, that the soul of Christ suffered as long as his body lay in the grave, and that God's loosing of the pains of death at Christ's resurrection, must not so much be made mention of with reference to his body, as to his soul, if to his body at all. For what pain of death was his body capable of, when his soul was separate from it? Ac. ii. 24. And yet God's loosing the pains of death, seems to be but an immediate antecedent to his rising from the dead. And this sense Peter doth indeed seem to pursue, saying, ' For David speaketh concerning him; I foresaw the Lord always before my face, for he is on my right hand, that I should not be moved. Therefore did my heart rejoice, and my tongue was glad; moreover also my flesh shall rest in hope, because thou wilt not leave my soul in hell, neither wilt thou suffer thine holy one to see corruption.' Ac. ii. 25—27. This, saith Peter, was not spoken of David, but he being a prophet, and knowing that God had sworn with an oath, that of the fruit of his loins according to the flesh he would raise up Christ to sit on his throne: ver. 29, 30. He seeing this before, spake of the resurrection of Christ, that his soul was not left in hell, neither did his flesh see corruption. ver. 31. ' Thou wilt not leave my soul in hell;' his soul was not left in hell. Of what use are these expressions, if the soul of Christ suffered not, if it suffered not when separated from the body? for of that time the Apostle Peter seems to treat. Besides, if it be not improper to say, that soul was not left there, that never was there, I am at a loss. *Thou wilt not* leave, his soul was *not left there; ergo,* It was there, seems to be the natural conclusion. If it be objected, that by *hell* is meant the grave, 'tis foolish to think that the soul of Christ lay there while his body lay dead therein. But again, the Apostle seems clearly to distinguish between the places where the soul and body of Christ was; counting his body to be in the grave, and his soul, for the time, in hell. If there be objected what was said by him to the thief upon the cross, La. xxiii. 43. I can answer, Christ might speak that with reference to his God-head, and if so, that lies as no objection to what hath been insinuated. And

why may not that be so understood, as well as where he said, when on earth, ' The Son of man which is in heaven,' Jn. iii. 13. meaning himself. For the personality of the Son of God, call him Son of man, or what other term is fitting, resideth not in the human, but divine nature of Jesus Christ. However, since hell is sometimes taken for the place, Ac. i. 25. sometimes for the grave, sometimes for the state, Ps. cxvi. 3. and sometimes but for a figure of the place where the damned are tormented; Jonah ii. 2. I will not strictly assign to Christ the place, the prison where the damned spirits are, 1 Pe. iii. 19. but will say, as I said before, that he was put into the place of sinners, into the sins of sinners, and received what by justice was the proper wages of sin both in body and soul: As is evident from that fifty-third of Isaiah. ver. 10, 11. This soul of his I take to be that which the *inwards* and the *fat* of the burnt sacrifices was a figure, or shadow of. ' And the fat and the inwards were burnt upon the altar, whilst the body was burned for sin without the camp.' Ex. xxix. 13, 14; Le. viii. 14—17.

And now having said this much, wherein have I derogated from the glory and holiness of Christ? Yea, I have endeavoured to set forth something of the greatness of his sorrows, the odiousness of sin, the nature of justice, and the love of Christ. And be sure, by how much the sufferings of the Son of God abounded for us, by so much was this unsearchable love of Christ made manifest. Nor can they that would, before the people, pare away, and make but little these infinite sufferings of our Lord, make his love to be so great as they ought, let them use what rhetoric they can. For their objecting the odious names and place of hell, accounting it not to be fit to say, That so holy a person as the Son of God was there. I answer, though I have not asserted it, yet let me ask, which is more odious, hell or sin? Or whether such think that Christ Jesus was subject to be tainted by the badness of the place, had he been there? Or whether, when the scripture says, God is in hell, it is any disparagement to him? Ps. cxxxix. 8. Or if a man should be so bold as to say so, Whether by so saying, he confineth Christ to that place for ever? And whether by so thinking he has contradicted that called the *Apostles' creed?**

---

* The descent of Christ into hell has been the subject of much controversy, and the question is as far from solution now as it was in the dark ages, when it was first propounded, and then arbitrarily decreed to be an article of faith. Those who explain hell as *hades*, the place of departed souls, or of the dead generally, fortify themselves with Psalm cxxxix. 8, and also Psalm xvi. 10; and yet the first passage may only imply the omnipresence of God, and the second, the resurrection of the incorruptible body of Christ from the grave. The descent of Christ into the place of torment is a figment, a monkish fable, in which Bible incidents and heathen myths are woven

(2.) Having thus spoken of the death and sufferings of Christ, I shall in the next place speak of *his preparations for his so suffering* for us; and by so doing, yet shew you something more of the greatness of his love.

Christ, as I have told you, was even before his sufferings, a person of no mean generation, being the Son of the eternal God: Neither had his Father any more *such* sons but he; consequently he of right was heir of all things, and so to have dominion over all worlds. For, 'for him were all things created.' Col. i. 16. And hence all creatures are subject to him; yea the angels of God worship him. He. i. Wherefore as *so* considered, he augmented not his state by becoming lower than the angels for us, for what can be added to him, that is naturally God. Indeed he did take, for our sakes, the human nature into union with himself, and so began to manifest his glory; and the kindness that he had for us before all worlds, began now eminently to shew itself. Had this Christ of God, our friend, given all he had to save us, had not his love been wonderful? But when he shall give for us *himself*, this is more wonderful. But this is not all, the case was so betwixt God and man, that this Son of God could not, as he was before the world was, give himself a ransom for us, he being altogether incapable so to do, being such an one as could not be subject to death, the condition that we by sin had put ourselves into.

Wherefore that by which would have been a death to some, to wit, the laying aside of glory and becoming, of the King of princes, a servant of the meanest form; this he of his own good-will, was heartily content to do. Wherefore, he that once was the object of the fear of angels, is now become a *little* creature, a worm, an inferior one, Ps. xxii. 6. born of a woman, brought forth in a stable, laid in a manger, Lu. ii. 7. scorned of men, tempted of devils, Lu. iv. 2. was beholden to his creatures for food, for raiment, for harbour, and a place wherein to lay his head when dead. In a word, he 'made himself of no reputation, took upon him the form of a servant, and was made in the likeness of men,' Phi. ii. 7. that he might become capable to do this kindness for us. And it is worth your noting, that all the while that he was in the world, putting himself upon those other preparations which were to be antecedent to his being made a sacrifice for us, no man, though he told what he came about to many, had, as we read of, an heart once to thank him for what he came about. Is. liii. 3. No, they railed on him, they degraded him, they called

him devil, they said he was mad, and a deceiver, a blasphemer of God, and a rebel against the state: They accused him to the governor; yea, one of his disciples sold him, another denied him, and they all forsook him, and left him to shift for himself in the hands of his horrible enemies; who beat him with their fists, spat on him, mocked him, crowned him with thorns, scourged him, made a gazing stock of him, and finally, hanged him up by the hands and the feet alive, and gave him vinegar to increase his affliction, when he complained that his anguish had made him thirsty. And yet all this could not take his heart off the work of our redemption. To die he *came*, die he *would*, and die he *did* before he made his return to the Father, for our sins, that we might live through him.*

Nor may what we read of in the word concerning those *temporal* sufferings that he underwent be over-looked, and passed by without serious consideration; they being a part of the curse that our sin had deserved! For all temporal plagues are due to our sin while we live, as well as the curse of God to everlasting perdition, when we die. Wherefore this is the reason why the whole life of the Lord Jesus was such a life of affliction and sorrow, he therein bare our sicknesses, and took upon him our deserts: So that now the curse *in* temporals, as well as the curse in spirituals, and of everlasting malediction, is removed by him away from God's people; and since he overcame them, and got to the cross, it was by reason of the worthiness of the humble obedience that he yielded to his Father's law in our flesh. For his whole life (as well as his death) was a life of merit and purchase, and desert. Hence it is said, 'he increased in favour with God.' Lu. ii. 52. For his works made him still more acceptable to him: For he standing in the room of man, and becoming our reconciler to God; by the heavenly majesty he was counted as such, and so got for us what he earned by his mediatory works; and also partook thereof as he was our head himself. And was there not in all these things love, and love that was infinite? Love which was not essential to his divine nature, could never have carried him through so great a work as this: Passions here would a failed, would a retreated, and have given the recoil; yea, his very humanity would here have flagged and fainted, had it not been managed, governed, and strengthened by his

---

together to delude a credulous and ignorant laity. The formulary designated the apostles' creed, has, beyond question, a high claim to antiquity, but none whatever to be the work of the apostles themselves. The 'descent into hell' was an after interpolation, and its rejection has been suggested.

* This is one of those strikingly solemn passages, which abound in Bunyan's works. It almost irresistibly brings to our imagination his expressive countenance, piercing eyes and harmonious voice; pressed on by his rapid conceptions and overpowering natural eloquence. How must it have rivetted the attention of a great congregation. It is a rush of words, rolling on like the waves of the sea; increasing in grandeur and in force as they multiply in number.—Ed.

eternal Spirit. Wherefore it is said, that 'through the eternal Spirit he offered himself without spot to God.' He. ix. 14. And that he was declared to be the Son of God, with so doing, and by the resurrection from the dead. Ro. i. 4.

2. We come now to the second thing propounded, and by which his love is discovered, and that is *his improving of his dying for us.* But I must crave pardon of my reader, if he thinks that I can discover the ten hundred thousandth part thereof, for it is impossible; but my meaning is, to give a few hints what beginnings of improvement he made thereof, in order to his further progress therein.

(1.) Therefore, This his death for us, was so virtuous, that in the space of three days and three nights, it reconciled to God in the body of his flesh as a common person, all, and every one of God's elect. Christ, when he addressed himself to die, presented himself to the justice of the law, as a *common* person; standing in the stead, place, and room of all that he undertook for; He gave 'his life a ransom for many.' Mat. xx. 28. 'He came into the world to save sinners.' 1 Ti. i. 15. And as he thus presented himself, so God, his Father, admitted him to this work; and therefore it is said, 'The Lord laid upon him the iniquity of us all:' And again, 'Surely he hath borne our griefs, and carried our sorrows.' Is. liii. 4, 6, 12. Hence it unavoidably follows, that whatever he felt, and underwent in the manner, or nature, or horribleness of the death he died, he felt and underwent all as a common person; that is, as he stood in the stead of others: Therefore it is said, 'He *was* wounded for our transgressions, and bruised for our iniquities;' and that 'the chastisement of our peace was upon him.' Is. liii. 5. And again 'the just died for the unjust.' 1 Pe. iii. 18.

Now then, if he presented himself as a common person to justice, if God so admitted and accounted him, if also he laid the sins of the people, whose persons he represented, upon him, and under that consideration punishes him with those punishments and death, that he died. Then Christ in life and death is concluded by the Father to live and die as a common or public person, representing all in this life and death, for whom he undertook *thus* to live, and *thus* to die. So then, it must needs be, that what next befalls this common person, it befalls him with respect to them in whose room and place he stood and suffered. Now, the next that follows, is, 'that he is justified of God:' That is, acquitted and discharged from this punishment, for the sake of the worthiness of his death and merits; for that must be before he could be raised from the dead: Ac. ii. 24. God raised him not up as guilty, to justify him afterwards: His resurrection was the declaration of his precedent

justification. He was raised from the dead, because it was neither in equity or justice possible that he should be holden longer there, his merits procured the contrary.

Now he was condemned of God's law, and died by the hand of justice, he was acquitted by God's law, and justified of justice; and all as a common person; so then, in his acquitting, we are acquitted, in his justification we are justified; and therefore the apostle applieth God's justifying of Christ to himself; and that rightly. Is. l. 8. and Ro. ii. 33, 34. For if Christ be my undertaker, will stand in my place, and do for me, 'tis but reasonable that I should be a partaker: Wherefore we are also said to be 'quickened together with him:' Ep. ii. 5. That is, when he was quickened in the grave; raised up together, and made to sit together in heavenly places *in* Christ Jesus. Therefore another scripture saith, 'Hath He quickened you - - together with him, having forgiven you all trespasses.' Col. ii. 13. *This quickening*, must not be understood of the renovation of our hearts, but of the restoring of Jesus Christ to life after he was crucified; and we are said to be quickened together with him, because we were quickened in him at his death, and were to fall or stand by him quite through the three days and three nights work; and were to take therefore our lot with him: Wherefore it is said again, That his resurrection is our justification. Ro. iv. 25. That by one offering he has purged our sins for ever; He. x. 12. and that by his death he hath 'delivered us from the wrath to come.' 1 Th. i. 10. But I say, I would be understood aright: This life resideth yet in the Son, and is communicated from him to us, as we are called to believe his word; mean while we are secured from wrath and hell, being justified in his justification, quickened in his quickening, raised up in his resurrection; and made to sit already together in heavenly places in Christ Jesus ! *

And is not this a glorious improvement of his death, that after two days the whole body of the elect, in him, should be revived, and that in the third day we should live in the sight of God, in and by him. He. vi. 18-20.

(2.) Another improvement of his death for us, was this, By that he slew for us, our infernal foes; by it he abolished death; 2 Ti. i. 1. by death he destroyed him that had the power of death: He. ii. 14. By death he took away the sting of death; 1 Co. xv. 55, 56. by death he made death a pleasant sleep to saints, and the grave for a while, an easy house and home

---

* The reader must not misunderstand the word *common* as here applied to the Saviour. It has the same meaning that is applied to a piece of land, to which *many* persons have an equal or *common* right; but which none but those, who have *a right* or title, can use. It strikingly illustrates the union of Christ and his church.—ED.

for the body. By death he made death such an advantage to us, that it is become a means of translating of the souls of them that believe in him, to life. And all this is manifest, for that death is ours, a blessing to us, as well as Paul and Apollos, the world and life itself. 1 Co. iii. 22. And that all this is done for us by his death, is apparent, for that his person is where it is, and that by himself as a common person he has got the victory for us. For though as yet all things are not put under our feet, yet we see Jesus crowned with honour and glory, who by the grace of God tasteth death for every man. 'For it became God, for whom *are* all things, and by whom *are* all things, to make the captain of their salvation perfect through sufferings.' He. ii. 7-10. *It became him;* that is, it was but just and right, he should do so, if there was enough in the virtuousness of his death and blood to require such a thing. But there was so. Wherefore God has exalted him, and us in him, above these infernal foes. Let us therefore see ourselves delivered from death first, by the exaltation of our Jesus, let us behold him I say as crowned with glory and honour, as, or because, he tasted death for us. And then we shall see ourselves already in heaven by our head, our undertaker, our Jesus, our Saviour.

(3.) Another improvement that has already been made of his death for us, is thus, he hath at his entrance into the presence of God, for his worthiness sake, obtained that the Holy Ghost should be given unto him for us, that we by that might in all things, yet to be done, be made meet to be partakers *personally*, in ourselves, as well as *virtually* by our head and forerunner, of the inheritance of the saints in light. Wherefore the abundant pourings out of that was forborn until the resurrection, and glorification of our Lord Jesus. 'For the Holy Ghost was not yet *given*, because that Jesus was not yet glorified.' Jn. vii. 39. Nor was it given so soon as received: for he received it upon his entering into the holy place, when he had sprinkled the mercy seat with the blood of sprinkling, but it was not given out to us till sometime after: Ac. iv. however it was obtained before. Ac. ii. 32, 33. And it was meet that it should in that infinite immeasurableness in which he received it, first abide upon him, that his human nature, which was the first fruits of the election of God, might receive by its abidings upon him, that glory for which it was ordained; and that we might receive,' as we receive all other things, first by our head and undertaker, sanctification in the fulness of it. Hence it is written, that as he is made unto us of God, wisdom, and righteousness, and redemption, so *sanctification* too: 1 Co. i. 30. For first we are sanctified *in* his flesh, as we are justified by his righteousness. Wherefore he is that holy one that setteth us, in himself, a holy lump before God, not only with reference to justification and life, but with reference to sanctification and holiness: For we that are elect, are all considered in him as he has received that, as well as in that he has taken possession of the heaven for us. I count not this all the benefit that accrueth to us by Jesus his receiving the Holy Ghost, at his entrance into the presence of God for us: For we also are to receive it ourselves from him, according as by God we are placed in the body at the times appointed of the Father. That we, as was said, may receive personal quickening, personal renovation, personal sanctification; and in conclusion, glory. But I say, for that he hath received this holy Spirit to himself, he received it as the effect of his ascension, which was the effect of his resurrection, and of the merit of his death and passion. And he received it as a common person, as a head and undertaker for the people.

(4.) Another improvement that has been made of his death, and of the merits thereof for us, is that he has obtained to be made of God, the chief and high Lord of heaven and earth, for us, (All this while we speak of the exaltation of the human nature, in, by, and with which, the Son of God became capable to be our reconciler unto God) 'All things,' saith he, 'are delivered unto me of my Father. And all power in heaven and earth is given unto me;' and all this because he died. 'He humbled himself, and became obedient unto death, even the death of the cross; wherefore God hath highly exalted him, and given him a name above every name, that at the name of Jesus every knee should bow, of things in heaven, of things in earth, or things under the earth: and that every tongue shall confess that Jesus Christ is Lord, to the glory of God the Father.' Phil. ii. And all this is, as was said afore, for our sakes. He has given him to be head over all things to the church. Ep. i. 22.

Wherefore, whoever is set up on earth, they are set up by our Lord. 'By me,' saith he, 'kings reign, and princes decree justice. By me princes rule, and nobles, *even* all the judges of the earth.' Pr. viii. 15, 16. Nor are they when set up, left to do, though they should desire it, their own will and pleasure. The *Metheg-Ammah,** the bridle, is in his own hand, and he giveth reins, or check, even as it pleaseth him, 2 Sa. viii. 1. He has this power, for the well-being of his people. Nor are the fallen angels exempted from being put under his rebuke: He is the 'only potentate,' 1 Ti. vi. 15. and in his times will shew it, Peter tells us, he 'is gone into heaven, and is on the right hand of God; angels, and authorities, and powers being made subject unto him.' 1 Pe. iii. 22.

* There is no affectation of learning in Bunyan's giving the meaning of the Hebrew words, מתג, Metheg; it is translated in the margin of our Bibles, 'the bridle' of Ammah.—ED.

This power, as I said, he has received for the sake of his church on earth, and for her conduct and well-being among the sons of men. Hence, as he is called the king of nations, in general; Je. x. 7. so the King of saints, in special: Re. xv. 3. and as he is said to be head *over* all things in general; so to his church in special.

(5.) Another improvement that he hath made of his death for us, is, he hath obtained, and received into his own hand sufficiency of gifts to make ministers for his church withal. I say, to make and maintain, in opposition to all that would hinder, a sufficient ministry. 1 Co. xii. 28-30. Wherefore he saith, 'When he ascended on high, he led captivity captive, and gave gifts unto men. And he gave some apostles, some prophets, some evangelists, some pastors and teachers; for the perfecting of the saints, for the work of the ministry, for edifying of the body of Christ. Until we all come in the unity of the faith, and knowledge of the Son of God, unto a perfect man, unto the measure of the stature of the fulness of Christ.' Ep. iv. 8-14. Many ways has Satan devised to bring into contempt this blessed advantage that Christ has received of God for the benefit of his church; partly while he stirs up persons to revile the sufficiency of the Holy Ghost, as to this thing: partly, while he stirs up his own limbs and members, to broach his delusions in the world, in the name of Christ, and as they blasphemously call it by the assistance of the Holy Ghost;* partly while he tempteth novices in their faith, to study and labour in nice distinctions, and the affecting of uncouth expressions, that vary from the form of sound words, thereby to get applause, and a name, a forerunner of their own destruction. Jn. iii. 6.

But, notwithstanding all this, 'Wisdom is justified of her children:' Mat. xi. 19. and at the last day, when the *outside*, and *inside* of all things shall be seen and compared, it will appear that the Son of God has so managed his own servants in the ministry of his word, and so managed his word, while they have been labouring in it, as to put in his blessing by *that*, upon the souls of sinners, and has blown away all other things as chaff. Ja. i. 18.

6. Another improvement that the Lord Christ has made of his death, for his, is the obtaining, and taking possession of heaven for them. 'By his own blood he entered in once into the holy place, having obtained eternal redemption *for us.*' He. ix. 12. This heaven! who knows what it is?

Mat. xxii. 23. This glory! who knows what it is? It is called God's throne, God's house, Jn. xiv. 2. God's habitation; paradise, 2 Co. xii. 4. the kingdom of God, the high and holy place. Is. lvii. 15. Abraham's bosom, Lu. xvi. 22. and the place of heavenly pleasures; Ps. xvi. 11. in this heaven is to be found, *the face of God for ever:* Ps. xli. 12. Immortality, the person of Christ, the prophets, the angels, the revelation of all mysteries, the knowledge of all the elect, ETERNITY.

Of this heaven, as was said afore, we are possessed already, we are in it, we are set down in it, and partake already of the benefits thereof, but all by our head and undertaker; and 'tis fit that we should believe this, rejoice in this, talk of this, tell one another of this, and live in the expectation of our own personal enjoyment of it. And as we should do all this, so we should bless and praise the name of God who has put over this house, this kingdom, and inheritance into the hand of so faithful a friend. Yea, a brother, a Saviour and blessed undertaker for us. And lastly, since all these things already mentioned, are the fruit of the sufferings of our Jesus, and his sufferings the fruit of that love of his that *passeth knowledge:* how should we bow the knee before him, and call him tender Father; yea, how should we love and obey him, and devote ourselves unto his service, and be willing to be also sufferers for his sake, to whom be honour and glory for ever. And thus much of the love of Christ in general.

I might here add many other things, but as I told you before, we would under the head but now touched upon, treat about the fundamentals or great and chief parts thereof, [Christ's love] and then,

SECOND, *Of the exceeding greatness of it* more particularly: Wherefore of that we must say something now.

And to know the love of Christ, which passeth knowledge. In that it is said to pass knowledge, 'tis manifest it is exceeding great, or greatly going beyond what can be known; for to exceed, is to go beyond, be above, or to be out of the reach of what would comprehend that which is so. And since the expression is absolutely indefinite, and respecteth not the knowledge of *this* or the *other* creature only: it is manifest, that Paul by his thus saying, challengeth all creatures in heaven and earth to find out the bottom of this love if they can. *The love of Christ which passeth knowledge.* I will add, that forasmuch as he is indefinite also about the *knowledge*, as well as about the *persons* knowing, it is out of doubt that he here engageth all knowledge, in what enlargements, attainments, improvements, and heights soever it hath, or may for ever attain unto. *It passeth knowledge.* Ep. iii. 8.

Of the same import also is that other passage of the apostle a little above in the self-same chap-

---

* Bunyan seems here evidently to refer to the case of unregenerate and worldly men entering into the ministry, and making a public and solemn declaration that they 'are inwardly moved thereto by the Holy Ghost,' and 'truly called according to the will of our Lord Jesus Christ.' See form and manner of ordaining deacons and priests in the Church of England. —ED.

ter. I preach, saith he, among the Gentiles *the unsearchable riches of Christ:* or those riches of Christ that cannot by searching, be found out in the *all* of them: *The riches,* the riches of his love and grace. The riches of his love and grace *towards us.* 'For ye know the grace of our Lord Jesus Christ, that, though he was rich, yet for your sakes he became poor, that ye through his poverty might be made* rich.' 2 Co. viii. 9. Ye know the grace, that is so far, and so far every believer knows it: for that his leaving heaven and taking upon him flesh, that he might bring us thither, is manifest to all. But yet, all the grace that was wrapped up in that amazing condescension, knoweth none, nor can know: for if that might be, that possibility would be a flat contradiction to the text: 'The love of Christ which passeth knowledge.' Wherefore the riches of this love in the utmost of it, is not, cannot be known by any: let their understanding and knowledge, be heightened and improved what it may. Yea, and being heightened and improved, let what search there can by it be made into this love and grace. 'That which is afar off, and exceeding deep, who can find out?' Ecc. vii. 24. And that this love of Christ is so, shall anon be made more apparent. But at present we will proceed to particular challenges for the making out of this, and then we will urge those reasons that will be for the further confirmation of the whole.

First, This love passes the knowledge of *the wisest saint,* we now single out the greatest proficient in this knowledge; and to confirm this, I need go no further than to the man that spake these words; to wit, Paul, for in his conclusion he includes himself. The love of Christ which passeth knowledge, even my knowledge. As who should say; though I have waded a great way in the grace of Christ, and have as much experience of his love as any *he* in all the world, yet I confess myself short, as to the fulness that is therein, nor will I stick to conclude of any other, That 'he knows nothing yet as he ought to know.' 1 Co. viii. 2. and xiii. 12.

Second, This love passeth the knowledge of *all the saints,* were it all put together, we, we all, and every one, did we each of us contribute for the manifesting of this love, what it is, the whole of what we know, it would amount but to a broken knowledge; we know but in part, we see darkly, 1 Co. xiii. 9-12. we walk not by sight, but faith. 2 Co. v. 7. True, now we speak of saints on earth.

Third, But we will speak of *saints in heaven;* they cannot *to the utmost,* know this love of Christ. For though they know more thereof than saints on earth, because they are more in the open visions of it, and also are more enlarged, being spirits per-

fect, than we on earth. Yet, to say no more now, they do not see the rich and unsearchable runnings out thereof unto sinners here on earth. Nor may they there measure that, to others, by what they themselves knew of it here. For sins, and times and persons and other circumstances, may much alter the case, but were all the saints on earth, and all the saints in heaven to contribute all that they know of this love of Christ, and to put it into one sum of knowledge, they would greatly come short of knowing the utmost of this love, for that there is an infinite deal of this love, yet unknown by them. 'Tis said plainly, that they on earth do not *yet* know what they shall be. 1 Jn. iii. 2. And as for them in heaven, they are not yet made perfect *as they shall be.* He. xi. 39, 40. Besides, we find the souls under the altar, how perfect now soever, when compared with that state they were in when with the body; Is. lxiii. 16. yet are not able in all points, though in glory, to know, and so to govern themselves there without directions. Re. vi. 9-11. I say, they are not able, without directions and instructions, to know the kinds and manner of workings of the love of Christ towards us that dwell on earth.

Fourth, We will join with these, *the angels,* and when all of them, with men, have put all and every whit of what they know of this love of Christ together, they must come far short of reaching to, or of understanding the utmost bound thereof. I grant, that angels do know, in some certain parts of knowledge of the love of Christ, more than saints on earth can know while here; but then again, I know that even they do also learn many things of saints on earth, which shews that themselves know also but in part; Ep. iii. 10. so then, *all,* as yet, as to this love of Christ, and the utmost knowledge of it, are but as so many imperfects, 1 Pe. i. 12. nor can they all, put all their imperfects together, make up a perfect knowledge of this love of Christ; for the texts do yet stand where they did, and say, *his riches are unsearchable,* and his love that *which passeth knowledge.* We will come now to shew you, besides what has been already touched on,

THE REASON *why this riches is unsearchable, and that love such as passeth knowledge;* and the

Reason First is, Because *It is eternal.* All that is eternal, has attending of it, as to the utmost knowledge of it, a fourfold impossibility. 1. It is without beginning. 2. It is without end. 3. It is infinite. 4. It is incomprehensible.

1. It is without beginning: That which was before the world was, is without a beginning, but the love of Christ was before the world.

This is evident from Proverbs the eighth, 'his delights,' before God had made the world, are there said to be, 'with the sons of men.' Not that we

---

* Bunyan quotes this passage from the puritan version; vulgarly called 'The Breeches Bible.' The present authorized translation is 'might be rich.'

then had being, for we were as yet uncreated; but though we had not beings created, we had being in the love and affections of Jesus Christ. Now this love of Christ must needs, as to the fulness of it, as to the utmost of it, be absolutely unknown to man. Who can tell how many heart-pleasing thoughts Christ had of us before the world began? Who can tell how much he *then* was delighted in that being we had in his affections; as also, in the consideration of our beings, believings, and being with him afterwards.

In general we may conclude, it was great; for there seems to be a parallel betwixt his Father's delights in *him*, and *his* delights in *us*. ' I was daily his delight, - - and my delights *were* with the sons of men.' Pr. viii. 22, 30, 31. But I say, who can tell, who can tell altogether, *what* and *how much* the Father delighted in his Son before the world began? Who can tell what *kind* of delight the Father had in the Son before the world began? Why there seems to be a parallel betwixt the Father's *love* to Christ, and Christ's *love* to us; the Father's *delight* in Christ, and his *delight* in us. Yea, Christ confirms it, saying, ' As the Father hath loved me, so have I loved you, continue ye in my love.' Jn. xv. 9. I know that I am not yet upon the nature of the word *eternal*; yet since, by eternal, we understand, before the world began, as well as forward, to an endless for-ever: We may a little enquire of folks as they may read, if they can tell the kind or measure of the love wherewith Christ then loved us. I remember the question that God asked Job, ' Where,' saith he, ' wast thou when I laid the foundation of the earth? declare if thou hast understanding:' Job xxxviii. 4. Thereby insinuating that because it was done before he had his being, therefore he could not tell how it was done. Now, if a work so visible, as the creation is, is yet as to the manner of the workmanship thereof wholly unknown to them that commenced in their beings afterwards: How shall that which has, in all the circumstances of it, been more hidden and inward, be found out by them that have intelligence thereof by the ear, and but in part, and that in a mystery, and long afterwards. But to conclude this, That which is eternal is without all beginning. This was presented to consideration before, and therefore it cannot to perfection be known.

2. That which is eternal is without end, and how can an endless thing be known, that which has no end has no middle, wherefore it is impossible that the one half of the love that Christ has for his church should ever by them be known. I know that those visions that the saved shall have in heaven of this love, will far transcend our utmost knowledge here, even as far as the light of the sun at noon, goes beyond the light of a blinking candle at midnight; and hence it is, that when

the days of those visions are come, the knowledge that we *now* have, shall be swallowed up. ' When that which is perfect is come, then that which is in part shall be done away.' 1 Co. xiii. 10. And although he speaks here of perfections, ' when that which is perfect is come,' &c., yet even that perfection must not be thought to be such as is the perfection of God; for then should all that are saved be so many *eternals* and so many *infinites*, as he is infinite. But the meaning is, we shall then be with the eternal, shall immediately enjoy him with all the perfection of knowledge, as far as is possible for a creature, when he is wrought up to the utmost height that his created substance will bear to be capable of. But for all that, this perfection will yet come short of the perfection of him that made him, and consequently, short of knowing the utmost of his love; since that in the root is his very essence and nature. I know it says also, *that we shall know even as we are known.* But yet this must not be understood, as *if* we should know God as fully as he knows us. It would be folly and madness so to conclude; but the meaning is, we are known *for* happiness; we are known of God, *for* heaven and felicity; and when that which is perfect is come, then shall we perfectly know, and enjoy that for which we are now known of God. And this is that which the Apostle longed for, namely, If by any means, he might apprehend that for which he was also apprehended of Christ Jesus. Phi. iii. 12. That is, know, and see that, unto the which he was appointed of God and apprehended of Christ Jesus. 'Tis said again, ' We shall be like him, for we shall see him as he is.' 1 Jn. iii. 2. This text has respect to the Son, as to his humanity, and not as to his divinity. And not as to his divinity, simply, or distinctly considered; for as to that it is as possible for a spirit to drink up the sea, as for the most enlarged saint that is, or ever shall be in glory, so to see God as to know him altogether, to the utmost, or throughout. But the humanity of the Son of God, we shall see throughout, in all the beauty and glory that is upon him; and that was prepared for him before the foundation of the world. And Christ will that we see this glory, when he takes us up in glory to himself; Jn. xvii. 24. but the utmost boundlessness of the divine majesty, the eternal deity of the Son of God, cannot be known to the utmost or altogether. I do not doubt, but that there will then in him, I mean in Christ, and in us, break forth these glorious rays and beams of the eternal majesty, as will make him in each of us admirable one to another; 2 Th. i. 10. and that then, that of God shall be known of us, that now never entered into our hearts to think of. But the whole, is not, cannot, shall never be fully known of any. And therefore the love of Christ, it being essential to himself, cannot be known because of the endlessness that is in it. I said before, that which has no end, has no middle, how then shall those that shall be in heaven eternally, ever pass over half the breadth of eternity. True, I know that all enjoyments there will be enjoyments eternal. Yea, that whatever we shall there embrace, or what embraces we shall be embraced with, shall be eternal; but I put a difference betwixt that which is eternal, as to the *nature*, and that which is so as to the durableness thereof. The *nature* of eternal things we shall enjoy, so soon as ever we come to heaven, but the *duration* of eternal things, them we shall never be able to pass through, for they are endless. So then, the eternal love of Christ, as to the nature of it, will be perfectly known of saints, when they shall dwell in heaven; but the endlessness thereof they shall never attain unto. And this will be their happiness. For could it be, that we should in heaven ever reach the end of our blessedness: (as we should, could we reach to the end of this love of Christ) why then, as the saying is, We should be at the land's end, and feel the bottom of all our enjoyments. Besides, whatsoever has an end, has a time to decay, and to cease to be, as well as to have a time to shew forth its highest excellencies. Wherefore, from all these considerations it is most manifest, that the love of Christ is unsearchable, and that it passes knowledge.

3. and 4. Now the other two things follow of course, to wit, That *this* love is *infinite* and *incomprehensible*. Wherefore here is that that still is above and beyond even those that are arrived to the utmost of their perfections. And this, if I may so say, will keep them in an employ, even when they are in heaven; though not an employ that is laboursome, tiresome, burthensome, yet an employ that is dutiful, delightful and profitable; for although the work and worship of saints in heaven is not particularly revealed as yet, and so ' it doth not yet appear what we shall be,' yet in the general we may say, there will be that for them to do, that has not yet by them been done, and by that work which they shall do there, their delight will be delight unto them. The law was the shadow and not the very image of heavenly things. He. x. 1. The image is an image, and not the heavenly things themselves He. ix. 23. (the heavenly things they are saints) there shall be worship in the heavens. Nor will this at all derogate from their glory. The angels now wait upon God and serve him; Ps. ciii. 20. the Son of God, is now a minister, and waiteth upon his service in heaven; He. viii. 1, 2, some saints have been employed about service for God after they have been in heaven; Lu. ix. 29—32. and why we should be idle spectators, when we come thither, I see not reason to believe.

It may be said, ' They there rest from their labours.' True, but not from their delights. All things then that once were burthensome, whether in suffering or service, shall be done away, and that which is delightful and pleasureable shall remain. *But then will be a time to receive*, and not to work. True, if by work you mean such as we now count work; but what if our work be there, to receive and bless. The fishes in the sea do drink, swim and drink. But for a further discourse of this, let that alone till we come thither. But to come down again into the world, for now we are talking of things aloft:

Reason Second, This love of Christ must needs be beyond our knowledge, because we cannot possibly know the *utmost of our sin*. Sin is that which sets out, and off, the knowledge of the love of Christ. There are four things that must be spoken to for the clearing of this. 1. The nature of sin. 2. The aggravations of sin. 3. The utmost tendencies of sin. 4. And the perfect knowledge of all this.

1. Before we can know this love of Christ, as afore, we must necessarily know the *nature* of sin, that is, what sin is, what sin is in itself. But no man knows the nature of sin to the full; not what sin in itself is to the full. The Apostle saith, ' That sin, (that is in itself) is exceeding sinful.' Ro. vii. 13. That is, exceeding it as to its filthiness, goes beyond our knowledge: But this is seen by the commandment. Now the reason why none can, to the full, know the horrible nature of sin, is because none, to the full, can know the blessed nature of the blessed God. For sin is the opposite to God. There is nothing that seeketh absolutely, and in its own nature to overcome, and to annihilate God, but sin, and sin doth so. Sin is worse than the devil; he therefore that is more afraid of the devil than of sin, knows not the badness of sin as he ought; nor but little of the love of Jesus Christ. He that knows not what sin would have done to the world, had not Christ stept betwixt those harms and it. How can he know so much as the extent of the love of Christ in common? And he that knows not what sin would have done to him in particular, had not Christ the Lord, stept in and saved, cannot know the utmost of the love of Christ to him in particular. Sin therefore in the utmost evil of it, cannot be known of us: so consequently the love of Christ in the utmost goodness of it, cannot be known of us.

Besides, there are many sins committed by us, dropping from us, and that pollute us, that we are not at all aware of; how then should we know that love of Christ by which we are delivered from them? Lord, ' who can understand *his* errors?' said David. Ps. xix. 12. Consequently, who can understand the love that saves him from them? moreover, he that knows the love of Christ to the full, must also know to the full that wrath and anger of God, that like hell itself, burneth against sinners for the sake of sin: but this knows none. Lord, 'who knoweth the power of thine anger?' said Moses. Ps. xc. 11. Therefore none knows this love of Christ to the full. The nature of sin is to get into our good, to mix itself with our good, to lie lurking many times under the formality and shew of good; and that so close, so cunningly, and invisibly, that the party concerned, embraces it for virtue, and knows not otherwise to do; and yet from this he is saved by the love of Christ; and therefore, as was hinted but now, if a man doth not know the nature of his wound, how should he know the nature and excellency of the balsam that hath cured him of his wound.

2. There are the due *aggravations* that belong to sin, which men are unacquainted with; it was one of the great things that the prophets were concerned with from God towards the people, Je. ii. (as to shew them their sins, so) to shew them what aggravations did belong thereto. Je. iii. and Eze. xvi.

There are sins against light, sins against knowledge, sins against love, sins against learning, sins against threatenings, sins against promises, vows and resolutions, sins against experience, sins against examples of anger, and sins that have great, and high, and strange aggravations attending of them; the which we are ignorant of, though not altogether, yet in too great a measure. Now if these things be so, how can the love that saveth us from them be known or understood to the full?

Alas! our ignorance of these things is manifest by our unwillingness to abide affliction, by our secret murmuring under the hand of God; by our wondering why we are so chastised as we are, by our thinking long that the affliction is no sooner removed.

Or, if our ignorance of the vileness of our actions is not manifest this way, yet it is in our lightness under our guilt, our slight thoughts of our doings, our slovenly doing of duties, and asking of forgiveness after some evil or unbecoming actions. 'Tis to no boot to be particular, the whole course of our lives doth too fully make it manifest, that we are wonderful short in knowing both the nature, and also the aggravations of our sins: and how then should we know that love of Christ in its full dimensions, by which we are saved and delivered therefrom?

3. Who knows the utmost *tendencies* of sin? I mean, what the least sin driveth at, and what it would unavoidably run the sinner into. There is not a plague, a judgment, an affliction, an evil under heaven, that the least of our transgressions has not called for at the hands of the great God! nay, the least sin calleth for all the distresses that are under heaven, to fall upon the soul and body of the sinner at once. This is plain, for that the least sin deserveth hell; which is worse than all the plagues that are on earth. But I say, who understandeth this? And I say again, if one sin, the least sin deserveth all these things, what thinkest thou do all thy sins deserve? how many judgments! how many plagues! how many lashes with God's iron whip dost thou deserve? besides there is hell itself, the place itself, the fire itself, the nature of the torments, and the durableness of them, who can understand?

But this is not all, the tendencies of thy sins are to kill others. Men, good men little think how many of their neighbours one of their sins may kill. As, how many good men and good women do unawares, through their uncircumspectness, drive their own children down into the deep? Ps. cvi. 6, 7. We will easily count them very hardhearted sinners, that used to offer their children in sacrifice to devils; when 'tis easy to do worse ourselves: they did but kill the body, but we body and soul in hell, if we have not a care.

Do we know how our sins provoke God? how they grieve the Holy Ghost? how they weaken our graces? how they spoil our prayers? how they weaken faith? how they tempt Christ to be ashamed of us? and how they hold back good from us? And if we know not every one of all these things to the full, how shall we know to the full the love of Christ which saveth us from them all?

4. Again, But who has the perfect knowledge of *all* these things? I will grant that some good souls may have waded a great way in some one, or more of them; but I know that there is not any that thoroughly know them *all*. And yet the love of Christ doth save us from *all*, notwithstanding all the vileness and soul-damning virtue* that is in them. Alas! how short are we of the knowledge of ourselves, and of what is in us. How many are there that do not know that man consisteth of a body made of dust, and of an immortal soul? Yea, and how many be there of those that confess it, that know not the constitution of either. I will add, how many are there that profess themselves to be students of those two parts of man, that have oftentimes proved themselves to be but fools as to both? and I will conclude that there is not a man under heaven that knoweth it all together: For man is 'fearfully *and* wonderfully made:' Ps. cxxxix. 14. nor can the manner of the *union* of these two parts be perfectly found out. How much more then must we needs be at loss as to the fulness of the knowledge of the love of Christ? But,

Reason Third, He that altogether knoweth the

---

* 'Virtue,' secret agency: efficacy without visible or material action. 'Walker's Dictionary.'—ED.

love of Christ, must, precedent to that, know not only all the wiles of the devil; but also all the plottings, contrivings and designs and attempts of that wicked one; yea, he must know, all the times that he hath been with God, together with all the motions that he has made that he might have leave to fall upon us, as upon Job and Peter, to try if he might swallow us up. Job i. and ii. Lu. xxii. 31. But who knows all this? no man, no angel. For, if the heart of man be so deep, that none, by all his actions, save God, can tell the utmost secrets that are therein; how should the heart of angels, which in all likelihood are deeper, be found out by any mortal man. And yet this must be found out before we can find out the utmost of the love of Christ to us. I conclude therefore from all these things, that the love of Christ passeth knowledge: or that by no means, the bottom, the utmost bounds thereof can be understood.

Reason Fourth, He that will presume to say, this love of Christ can be to the utmost known by us, must presume to say that he knoweth the utmost of the merits of his blood, the utmost exercise of his patience, the utmost of his intercession, the utmost of the glory that he has prepared and taken possession of for us. But I presume that there is none that can know all this, therefore I may without any fear assert, there is none that knows, that is, that knows to the full, the other.

We come now more particularly to speak of the knowledge of the love of Christ; we have spoken of the *love* of Christ; and of the *exceeding greatness* of it: and now we come,

THIRD, To speak *of the knowledge of it;* that is to say, we will shew

WHAT KNOWLEDGE OF CHRIST'S LOVE IS ATTAINABLE IN THIS WORLD,

under these three heads. As to this, *First,* It may be known as to the nature of it. *Second,* It may be known in many of the degrees of it. *Third,* But the greatest knowledge that we can have of it here, is to know that it passes knowledge.

First, We may know it in the *nature* of it. That is, that it is love *free, divine, heavenly, everlasting, incorruptible.* And this no love is but the love of Christ; all other love is either love corruptible, transient, mixed, or earthly. It is *divine,* for 'tis the love of the holy nature of God. It is *heavenly,* for that it is from above: it is *everlasting,* for that it has no end: it is *immortal,* for that there is not the appearance of corruptibleness in it, or likelihood of decay.

This is general knowledge, and this is common among the saints, at leastwise in the notion of it. Though I confess, it is hard in time of temptation, practically to hold fast the soul to all these things. But, as I have said already, this love of Christ *must* be such, because love in the root of it, is essential to his nature, as also I have proved now, as is the root, such are the branches; and as is the spring, such are the streams, unless the channels in which those streams do run, should be corrupted, and so defile it; but I know no channels through which this love of Christ is conveyed unto us, but those made in his *side,* his *hands,* and his *feet,* &c. Or those gracious promises that dropt like honey from his holy lips, in the day of his love, in which he spake them: and seeing his love is conveyed to us, as through those channels, and so by the conduit of the holy and blessed spirit of God, to our hearts, it cannot be that it should hitherto be corrupted. I know the *cisterns,* to wit, our hearts, into which it is conveyed, are unclean, and may take away much, through the damp that they may put upon it, of the native savour and sweetness thereof. I know also, that there are those that tread down, and muddy those streams with their feet; Eze. xxxiv. 18, 19. but yet neither the love nor the channels in which it runs, should bear the blame of this. And I hope those that are saints indeed, will not only be preserved to eternal life, but nourished with this that is incorruptible unto the day of Christ.

I told you before, that in the hour of temptation, it will be hard for the soul to hold fast to these things; that is, to the true definition of this love; for then, or at such seasons, it will not be admitted that the love of Christ is either transient, or mixed; but we count that we cannot be loved long, unless something better than yet we see in us, be found there, as an inducement to Christ to love, and to continue to love our poor souls. Is. lxiv. 6. But these the Christian at length gets over; for he sees, by experience, he hath no such inducement; De. ix. 5. also, that Christ loves freely, and not for, or because of such poor, silly, imaginary enticements. Eze. xvi. 60—62. Thus therefore the love of Christ may be known, that is, in the nature of it: it *may,* I say, but not easily. Eze. xxxvi. 25—33. For this knowledge is neither easily got, though got, nor easily retained, though retained. There is nothing that Satan setteth himself more against, than the breaking forth of the love of Christ in its own proper *native* lustre. For he knows it destroys his kingdom, which standeth in profaneness, in errors and delusions, the only destruction of which is the knowledge of this love of Christ. 2 Co. v. 14. What mean those swarms of opinions that are in the world? what is the reason that some are carried about as clouds, with a tempest? what mean men's waverings, men's changing, and interchanging truth for error, and one error for another? why, this is the thing, the devil is in it. This work is his, and he makes this a-do, to make a dust; and a dust to darken the light of the gospel withal.

And if he once attaineth to that, then farewell the true knowledge of the love of Christ.

Also he will assault the spirits of Christians with divers and sundry cogitations, such as shall have in them a tendency to darken the judgment, delude the fancy, to abuse the conscience. He has an art to metamorphose all things. He can make God seem to be to us, a most fierce and terrible destroyer; and Christ a terrible exactor of obedience, and most amazingly pinching of his love. He can make supposed sins unpardonable; and unpardonable ones, appear as virtues. He can make the law to be received for gospel, and cause that the gospel shall be thrown away as a fable. He can persuade, that faith is fancy, and that fancy is the best faith in the world. Besides, he can tickle the heart with false hope of a better life hereafter, even as if the love of Christ were there. But, as I said before, from all these things the true love of Christ in the right knowledge of it, delivereth those that have it shed abroad in the heart by the Holy Ghost that he hath given. Ro. v. Wherefore it is for this purpose that Christ biddeth us to *continue in his love*; Jn. xv. 9. because the right knowledge, and faith of that to the soul, disperseth and driveth away all such fogs, and mists of darkness; and makes the soul to sit fast in the promise of eternal life by him; yea, and to grow up into him who is, the head, 'in all things.'

Before I leave this head, I will present my reader with these things, as helps to the knowledge of the love of Christ. I mean the knowledge of the *nature* of it, and as HELPS to retain it.

Help First, Know thy self, what a vile, horrible, abominable sinner thou art: For thou canst not know the love of Christ, before thou knowest the badness of thy nature. 'O wretched man that I am,' Ro. vii. 24. must be, before a man can perceive the *nature* of the love of Christ. He that sees himself *but little,* will hardly know *much* of the love of Christ: he that sees of himself *nothing at all,* will hardly ever see *any thing* of the love of Christ. But he that sees *most* of what an abominable wretch he is, he is like to see *most* of what is the love of Christ. All errors in doctrine take their rise from the want of this (I mean errors in doctrine as to justification.) All the idolizing of men's virtues, and human inventions, riseth also from the want of this. So then if a man would be kept sure and stedfast, let him labour before all things to know his own wretchedness. People naturally think that the knowledge of their sins is the way to destroy them; when in very deed, it is the first step to salvation. Now if thou wouldest know the badness of thy self, begin in the first place to study the law, *then* thy heart, and *so* thy life. The law thou must look into, for that's *the glass;* thy *heart* thou must look upon, for that's *the face;* thy

life thou must look upon, for that's the *body* of a man, as to religion. Ja. i. 25. And without the wary consideration of these three, 'tis not to be thought that a man can come at the knowledge of himself, and consequently to the knowledge of the love of Christ. Ja. i. 26, 27.

Help Second, Labour to see the emptiness, shortness, and the pollution that cleaveth to a man's own righteousness. This also must in some measure be known, before a man can know the *nature* of the love of Christ. They that see nothing of the loathsomeness of man's best things, will think, that the love of Christ is of *that* nature as to be procured, or won, obtained or purchased by man's good deeds. And although so much gospel light is broke forth as to stop men's mouths from *saying* this, yet 'tis nothing else but sound conviction of the vileness of man's righteousness, that will enable men to see that the love of Christ is of that nature, as to save a man without it; as to see that it is of that nature as to justify him without it: I say, without it, or not at all. There is *shortness,* there is *hypocrisy,* there is a desire of *vain glory,* there is *pride,* there is *presumption* in man's own righteousness: nor can it be without these wickednesses, when men know not the *nature* of the love of Christ. Now these defile it, and make it abominable. Yea, if there were no imperfection in it, but that which I first did mention, to wit, *shortness;* how could it cover the nakedness of him that hath it, or obtain for the man, in whole or in part, that Christ should love, and have respect unto him.

Occasions many thou hast given thee to see the emptiness of man's own righteousness, but all will not do unless thou hast help from heaven: wherefore thy wisdom will be, if thou canst tell where to find it, to lie in the way of God, that when he comes to visit the men that wait upon him in the means of his own appointing, thou mayest be there; if perhaps he may cast an eye of pity upon thy desolate soul, and make thee see the things abovementioned. That thou mayest know the *nature* of the love of Christ.

Help Third, If thou wouldest know the *nature* of *this* love, be much in acquainting of thy soul with the nature of the law, and the nature of the gospel. Ga. iii. 21. The which though they are not diametrically opposite one to another, yet do propound things so differently to man, that if he knows not where, when, and how to take them, 'tis impossible but that he should confound them, and in confounding of them, lose his own soul. Ro. ix. 31, 32. The law is a servant, both first and last, to the gospel: Ro. x. 3, 4. when therefore it is made a Lord, it destroyeth: and then to be sure it is made a Lord and Saviour of, when its dictates and commands are depended upon for life.

Thy wisdom therefore will be to study these

things distinctly, and thoroughly; for so far as thou art ignorant of the true knowledge of the nature of these, so far thou art ignorant of the true knowledge of the nature of the love of Christ. Read Paul to the Galatians, that epistle was indicted by the Holy Ghost, on purpose to direct the soul, in, and about this very thing.

Help Fourth, The right knowledge of the *nature* of the love of Christ, is obtained, and retained, by keeping of these two doctrines at an everlasting distance as to the conscience; to wit, not suffering the law to rule but over my outward man, not suffering the gospel to be removed one hair's breadth from my conscience. When Christ dwells in my heart by faith, Ep. iii. 17. and the moral law dwells in my members, Col. iii. 5. the one to keep up peace with God, the other to keep my conversation in a good decorum: then am I right, and not till then.

But this will not be done without much experience, diligence, and delight in Christ. For there is nothing that Satan more desireth, than that the law may abide in the conscience of an awakened Christian, and there take up the place of Christ, and faith; for he knows if this may be obtained, the vail is presently drawn over the face of the soul, and the heart darkened as to the knowledge of Christ; and being darkened, the man is driven into despair of mercy, or is put upon it to work for life. 2 Co. iii. 13—15. There is therefore, as I say, much diligence required of him that will keep these two in their places assigned them of God. I say much diligent study of the word, diligent prayer; with diligence to walk with God in the world. But we will pass this, and come to the second head.

Secondly, As the love of Christ may be known in the *nature* of it, so it may be known in many *degrees* of it. That which is knowable, admits of degrees of knowledge: the love of Christ is knowable. Again, that which is not possible to be known to the utmost, is to be known, we know not how much; and therefore they that seek to know it, should never be contented or satisfied to what degree of the knowledge of it soever they attain; but still should be reaching forward, because there is more to be known of it before them. 'Brethren,' said Paul, 'I count not myself to have apprehended, (that is to the utmost) but *this* one thing *I do*, forgetting those things which are behind, and reaching forth unto those things which are before, I press towards the mark for the prize of the high calling of God in Christ Jesus,' Phi. iii. 13, 14.

I might here discourse of many things, since I am upon this head of reaching after the knowledge of the love of Christ in many of the degrees of it. But I shall content myself with few.

1. He that would know the love of Christ in several degrees of it, must begin at his person, for in him *dwells* all the treasures of wisdom and knowledge. Nay, more: In him 'are hid all the treasures of wisdom and knowledge.' Col. ii. 3. In him, that is, in his person: For, for the godhead of Christ, and our nature to be united in one person, is the highest mystery, and the first appearance of the love of Christ by himself, to the world. 1 Ti. iii. 16. Here I say, *lie* hid the treasures of wisdom, and here, to the world, *springs* forth the riches of his love. Jn. i. 14. That the eternal word, for the salvation of sinners, should come down from heaven and be made flesh, is an act of such condescension, a discovery of such love, that can never to the full be found out. Only here we may see, love in him was deep, was broad, was long, and high: let us therefore first begin here to learn to know the love of Christ, in the high degrees thereof.

(1.) Here, in the first place, we perceive love, in that the *human* nature, the nature of man, not of angels, is taken into union with God. Who so could consider this, as it is possible for it to be considered, would stand amazed till he died with wonder. By this very act of the heavenly wisdom, we have an unconceivable pledge of the love of Christ to man: for in that he hath taken into union with himself our *nature*, what doth it signify, but that he intendeth to take into union with himself our persons. For, for this very purpose did he assume our nature. Wherefore we read that in the flesh he took upon him, in *that* flesh, he died for us, the just for the unjust, that he might bring us to God. 1 Pe. iii. 18.

(2.) As he was made *flesh*, so as was said afore, he became a public or common person for us: and hereby is perceived another degree of his love; undertaking to do for his, what was not possible they should do for themselves, perfecting of righteousness to the very end of the law, and doing for us, to the reconciling of us unto his Father, and himself. Ro. x. 3, 4. and iii. 24.

(3.) Herein also we may attain to another degree of knowledge of his love, by understanding that he has conquered, and so disabled our foes, that they cannot now accomplish their designed enmity upon us: Ro. v. and Ep. v. 26, 27. but that when Satan, death, the grave and sin have done to his people, whatever can by them be done, we shall be still more than conquerors, (though on our side be many disadvantages,) through him that has loved us, over them. Ro. viii. 37.

(4.) By this also we may yet see more of his love, in that as a forerunner, he is gone into heaven to take possession thereof for us: He. vi. 20. there to make ready, and to prepare for us our summerhouses, our mansion, dwelling-places. As if we were the *lords*, and *he* the *servant!* Jn. xiv. 2, 3. Oh this love!

(5.) Also we may see another degree of his love, in this, that *now* in his absence, he has sent the third person in the Trinity to supply his place as another comforter of us, Jn. xvi. 7. and xv. 26. that we may not think he has forgot us, not be left destitute of a revealer of truth unto us. Jn. xiv. 16. Yea, he has sent him to fortify our spirits, and to strengthen us under all adversity; and against our enemies of what account, or degree soever. Lu. xxi. 15.

(6.) In this also we may see yet more of the love of Christ, in that though he is in heaven and we on earth: Nothing can happen to his people to hurt them, but he *feels* it, is *touched* with it, and *counteth* it as done unto himself: Yea, *sympathizes* with them, and is afflicted, and grieved in their griefs, and their afflictions.

(7.) Another thing by which also yet more of the love of Christ is made manifest, and so may by us be known, is this: He is now, and has been ever since his ascension into glory, laying out himself as high-priest for us, He. vii. 24-26. that by the improving* of his merits before the throne of grace, in way of intercession, he might preserve us from the ruins that our daily infirmities would bring upon us: He. viii. 12. yea, and make our persons and performances acceptable in his Father's sight. Ro. v. 10. 1 Pe. ii. 5.

(8.) We also see yet more of his love by this, that he will have us where himself is, that we may behold and be partakers of his glory. Jn. xvii. 24. And in this degree of his love, there are *many* loves.

Then he will come for us, as a bridegroom for his bride. Mat. xxv. 6-10. Then shall a public marriage be solemnized, and eternized betwixt him and his church. Re. xix. 6, 7. Then she shall be wrapped up in his mantles and robes of glory. Col. iii. 4. Then they shall be separated, and separated from other sinners, and all things that offend shall be taken away from among them. Mat. xxv. 31. and xiii. 41. Then shall they be exalted to thrones, and power of judgment; and shall also sit in judgment on sinful men and fallen angels, acquiescing, by virtue of authority, with their king and head, upon them. 1 Co. vi. 2, 3. Then or from thenceforth for ever, there shall be no more death, sorrow, hidings of his face, or eclipsing of their glory for ever. Lu. xx. 36. And thus you may see what *rounds* this our Jacob's ladder hath, and how by them we may climb, and climb, even until we are climbed up to heaven: but now we are set again; for *all* the glories, *all* the benefits, *all* the blessings, and *all* the good things that are laid up in heaven for these; Who can understand?

2. A second thing whereby the love of Christ in *some degrees* of it may be known, is this:

That he should pass by *angels* and take hold of *us.* Who so considereth the nature of spirits, as they are God's workmanship, must needs confess, that as such, they have a pre-eminency above that which is made of dust: This then was the disparity 'twixt us and them; they being, by birth, far more noble than we. But now, when both are fallen, and by our fall, both in a state of condemnation, that Jesus Christ should choose to take up us, the most inconsiderable, and pass by them, to their eternal perdition and destruction: O love! love in a high degree to man: For verily he took not hold of angels, but of the seed of Abraham he took hold. He. ii. 16. Yet this is not all: In all probability this Lord Jesus has ten times as much to do now he has undertaken to be our Saviour, as he would have had, had he stepped over us and taken hold on them.

(1.) He needed not to have stooped so low as to take flesh upon him; theirs being a more noble nature.

(2.) Nor would he in all likelihood, have met with those contempts, those scorns, those reproaches and undervaluings from them, as he has all-along received in this his undertaking, and met with from sinful flesh. For they were more noble than we, and would sooner have perceived the design of grace, and so one would think more readily have fallen in therewith, than [creatures in] such darkness as we were, and still by sin are.

(3.) They would not have had those disadvantages as we, for that they would not have had a tempter, a destroyer, so strong and mighty as ours is. Alas! had God left us, and taken them, though we should have been ever so full of envy against their salvation; yet being but flesh, what could we have done to them to have laid obstacles in the way of their faith and hope, as they can and do in ours?

(4.) They, it may fairly be presumed, had they been taken, and we left, and made partakers in our stead, while we had been shut out, as they are, would not have put Christ so to it, now in heaven (pray bear with the expression, because I want a better) as we by our imperfections have done and do. Sin, methinks, would not have so hanged in their natures as it doth in ours: their reason, and sense, and apprehensions being more quick, and so more apt to have been taken with this love of Christ, and by it more easily have been sanctified.

(5.) The law which they have broken, being not so intricate, as that against which we have offended, theirs being a commandment with faithfulness to abide in the place in which their Creator had set them; methinks, considering also the aptness of their natures as angels, would not have made their complete obedience so difficult.

---

* 'Improving,' not in quality but by extending the benefits. employing to good purpose; turning to profitable account.—ED.

(6.) Nor can I imagine, but had they been taken, they, as creatures excelling in strength, would have been more capable of rendering these praises and blessings to God for eternal mercies, than such poor sorry creatures as we are, could. But! 'behold what manner of love the Father hath bestowed upon us, that we should be called the children of God.' 1 Jn. iii. 1. That *we*, not they, that *we* notwithstanding all that they have, or could have done to hinder it, should be called the children of God.

This therefore is an high degree of the love of Jesus Christ to us, that when we and they were fallen, he should stoop and take up us, the more ignoble, and leave so mighty a creature in his sins to perish.

3. A third thing whereby the love of Christ in *some* of the degrees of it may be known, will be to consider more particularly the way, and unwearied work that he hath with man to bring him to that kingdom, that by his blood he hath obtained for him.

(1.) Man, when the Lord Jesus takes him in hand to make him partaker of the benefit, is found an enemy to his redeemer; nor doth all the intelligence that he has had of the grace and love of Christ to such, mollify him at all, to wit, before the day of God's power comes. Ro. iv. 5. and v. 7-10. And this is a strange thing. Had man, though he could not have come to Christ, been willing that Christ should have come to him, it had been something; it would have shewn that he had taken his grace to heart, and considered of it: yea, and that he was willing to be a sharer in it. But verily here is no such thing; man, though he has free will, yet is willing by no means to be saved God's way, to wit, by Jesus Christ, before (as was said before) the day of God's power comes upon him. When the good shepherd went to look for his sheep that was lost in the wilderness, and had found it: did it go one step homewards upon its own legs? did not the shepherd take her and lay her upon his shoulder, and bring her home rejoicing. Lu. xv. This then is not love only, but love to a degree.

(2.) When man is taken, and laid under the day of God's power: When Christ is opening his ear to discipline, and speaking to him that his heart may receive instruction; many times that poor man is, as if the devil had found him, and not God. How frenzily he imagines? how crossly he thinks? How ungainly he carries it under convictions, counsels, and his present apprehension of things? I know some are more powerfully dealt withal, and more strongly bound at first by the world; but others more in an ordinary manner, that the flesh, and reason may be seen, to the glory of Christ. Yea, and where the will is made more quickly to comply with its salvation, 'tis no thanks to the

sinner at all. Job iv. 18. 'Tis the day of the power of the Lord that has made the work so soon to appear. Therefore count this an act of love, *in the height of love;* Love in a great degree. Jn. xv. 16.

(3.) When Christ Jesus has made this *mad* man to come to himself, and persuaded him to be willing to accept of his salvation: yet he may not be trusted, nor left alone, for then the corruptions that still lie scattering up and down in his flesh will tempt him to it, and he will be gone; yea, so desperately wicked is the flesh of saints, that should they be left to themselves but a little while, none knows what horrible transgressions would break out. Proof of this we have to amazement, plentifully scattered here and there in the word. Hence we have the patience of God, and his gentleness so admired: 2 Ch. xxxii. 21. for through that it is that they are preserved. He that keepeth Israel neither slumbers nor sleeps, Ps. cxxi. 4. but watches for them, and over them every moment, for he knows else they will be hurt. Is. xxvii. 3.

(4.) Yea, notwithstanding this, how often are saints found playing *truant*, and lurking like thieves in one hole or other. Now, in the guilt of backsliding by the power of this, and then in filth by the power of that corruption. Je. ii. 26. Yea, and when found in such decayings, and under such revoltings from God, how commonly do they hide their sin with Adam, and David, even until their Saviour fireth out of their mouths a confession of the truth of their naughtiness. 'When I keep silence,' said David, (and yet he chose to keep silence after he had committed his wickedness) 'my bones waxed old through my roaring all the day long. For day and night thy hand was heavy upon me, my moisture is turned into the drought of summer.' Ps. xxxii. 3, 4. But why didst thou not confess what thou hadst done *then?* So I did, saith he, at last, and thou forgavest the iniquity of my sin. ver. 5.

(5.) When the sins of saints are so visible and apparent to others, that God for the vindication of his name and honour must punish them in the sight of others; yea, must do it, as he is just: Yet then for Christ's sake, he waveth such judgments, and refuseth to inflict such punishments as naturally tend to their destruction, and chooseth to chastise them with such rods and scourges, as may do them good in the end; and that they may not be condemned with the world. 1 Co. xi. 31, 32. Wherefore the Lord loves them, and they are blessed, whom he chasteneth and teacheth out of his law. He. xii. 5—8. and Ps. xciv. 12. And these things are love to a degree.

(6.) That Christ should supply out of his fulness the beginnings of grace in our souls, and carry on that work of so great concern, and that which at times we have so little esteem of, is none of the least of the aggravations of the love of Christ to his people. And this work is as *common as any of the works of Christ, and as *necessary* to our *salvation*, as is his righteousness, and the *imputation thereof* to our *justification:* For else how could we hold out to the end; Mat. xxiv. 13. and yet none else can be saved.

(7.) And that the love of Christ should be such to us that he will thus act, thus do to, and for us, with gladness; (as afore is manifest by the parable of the lost sheep) is another degree of his love towards us: And such an one too, as is none of the lowest rate. I have seen hot love, soon cold; and love that has continued to act, yet act towards the end, as the man that by running, and has run himself off his legs, *pants*, and can hardly run any longer: but I never saw love like the love of Christ, who as a giant, and bridegroom coming out of his chamber, and as a strong man, *rejoiceth to run his race.* Ps. xix. 5. Loving higher and higher, stronger and stronger, I mean as to the lettings out of love, for he reserveth the best wine even till the last. Jn. ii. 10.

(8.) I will conclude with this, that his love may be known in many degrees of it, by that sort of sinners whose salvation he *most* rejoiceth in, and that is, in the salvation of the sinners that are of the biggest size: Great sinners, *Jerusalem* sinners, *Samaritan* sinners, publican sinners. I might urge moreover, how he hath proportioned invitations, promises and examples of his love, for the encouragement and support of those whose souls would trust in him: By which also great degrees of his love may be understood. But we will come now to the third thing that was propounded.

Thirdly, But the greatest attainment that as to the understanding of the love of Christ, we can arrive to here, is to *know* that it passes *knowledge: And to know the love of Christ that passeth knowledge.* This truth discovereth itself,

1. By the text itself, for the apostle here, in this prayer of his for the Ephesians, doth not only desire that they may know, but describeth that thing which he prays they may know, by this term, *It passeth knowledge.* And to know the love of Christ which passeth knowledge. As our reason and carnal imagination will be rudely, and unduly tampering with any thing of Christ, so more especially with the love and kindness of Christ: Judging and concluding that just such it is, and none other, as may be apprehended by them; Yea, and will have a belief that just so, and no otherwise are the dimensions of this love; nor can it save beyond our carnal conceptions of it. Saying to the soul as Pharaoh once did to Israel in another

case: ' Let the Lord be with you as I shall ' (judge it meet he should) 'let you go.' We think Christ loves us no more than *we* do think he can, and so conclude that his love is such as may by us be comprehended, or known to the utmost bounds thereof. But these are false conceptions, and this love of Christ that we think is such, is indeed none of the love of Christ, but a false image thereof, set before our eyes. I speak not now of weak knowledge, but of foolish and bold conclusions. A man through unbelief may think that Christ has no love for him, and yet Christ may love him with a love that passeth knowledge. But when men in the common course of their profession, will be always terminating here, that they know how, and how far Christ can love, and will thence be bold to conclude of their own safety, and of the loss and ruin of all that are not in the same notions, opinions, formalities, or judgments as they: this is the worst and greatest of all. The text therefore, to rectify those false and erroneous conclusions, says, *It is a love that passeth knowledge.*

And it will be worth our observation to take notice that men, erroneous men, do not put these limits so commonly to the Father and his love, as [to] the Son and his. Hence you have some that boast that God can save some who have not the knowledge of the person of the mediator Jesus Christ the righteous; as the heathens that have, and still do make a great improvement of the law and light of nature: crying out with disdain against the narrowness, rigidness, censoriousness, and pride of those that think the contrary. Being not ashamed all the while to eclipse, to degrade, to lessen and undervalue the love of Jesus Christ; making of him and his undertakings, to offer himself a sacrifice to appease the justice of God for our sins, but a thing indifferent, and in its own nature but as other smaller matters.

But all this while the devil knows full well at what game he plays, for he knows that without Christ, without faith in his blood, there is no remission of sins. Wherefore, saith he, let these men talk what they will of the greatness of the love of God as *creator*, so they slight and undervalue the love of Christ as *mediator*. And yet it is worth our consideration, that the greatness of the love of God is most expressed in his giving of Christ to be a Saviour, and in bestowing his benefits upon us that we may be happy through him.

But to return, The love of Christ that is so indeed, is love that passeth knowledge: and the best and highest of our knowledge of it is, that we know it to be such.

2. Because I find that at this point, the *great men of God*, of old, were wont to stop, be set, and beyond which they could not pass. 'Twas this that made Moses wonder. De. iv. 31—34. 'Twas

---

this that made David cry out, How great and wonderful are the works of God? ' Thy thoughts to usward: they cannot be reckoned up in order unto thee: *If* I would declare and speak *of them*, they are more than can be numbered.' Ps. xl. 5. And again, ' How precious also are thy thoughts unto me, O God! how great is the sum of them! *If* I should count them, they are more in number than the sand.' Ps. cxxxix. 17, 18. And a little before, ' *such* knowledge *is* too wonderful for me.' ver. 6. Isaiah saith, there hath not entered into the heart of man what God has prepared for them that wait for him. Is. lxiv. 4. Ezekiel says, this is the river that cannot be passed over: chap. xlvii. 5. And Micah to the sea, [chap. vii. 19.] and Zechariah to a fountain, hath compared this unsearchable love. chap. xiii. 1. Wherefore the Apostle's position, *That the love of Christ is that which passeth knowledge*, is a truth not to be doubted of: Consequently, to know this, *and that it is such*, is the farthest that we can go. This is to justify God, who has said it, and to magnify the Son, who has loved us with such a love: And the contrary is to dishonour him, to lessen him, and to make him a *deficient* Saviour. For suppose this should be true, that thou couldest to the utmost comprehend this love; yet unless, by thy knowledge thou canst comprehend beyond all evil of sin, or beyond what any man sins, who shall be saved, can spread themselves or infect: Thou must leave some pardonable man in an unpardonable condition. For that thou canst comprehend this love, and yet canst not comprehend that sin. This makes Christ a deficient Saviour. Besides, if thou comprehendest truly; the word that says, it passeth knowledge, hast lost its sanctity, its truth.

It must therefore be, that this love passeth knowledge; and that the highest pitch that a man by knowledge can attain unto, as to this, is to *know* that *it passeth knowledge*. My reason is, for that all degrees of love, be they never so high, or many, and high, yet, if we can comprehend them, rest in the bowels of our knowledge, for that only which is beyond us, is that which passeth knowledge. That which we can reach, cannot be the highest: And if a man thinks there is nothing beyond what he can reach, he has no more knowledge as to that: but if he knows that together with what he hath already reached, there is that which he cannot reach, before [him]; then he has a knowledge for that also, even a knowledge, that it *passeth* knowledge. 'Tis true a man that thus knoweth may have divers conjectures about that thing that is beyond his knowledge. Yea, in reason it will be so, because he knows that there is something yet before him: But since the thing itself is truly beyond his knowledge, none of his conjectures about that thing may be counted knowledge. Or

suppose a man that thus conjectureth, should hit right as to what he now conjectures; his right hitting about that thing may not be called *knowledge*: It is as yet *to him* but as an uncertain guess, and is still beyond his knowledge.

Quest. But, may some say, what good will it do a man to know that the love of Christ passeth knowledge? one would think that it should do one more good to believe that the knowledge of the whole love of Christ might be attainable.

Answ. That there is an advantage in knowing that the love of Christ passeth knowledge; must not be questioned, for that the Apostle saith it doth. 2 Ti. iii. 16. For to *know* what the holy word affirms, is profitable: nor would he pray that we might *know* that which passeth *knowledge*, were there not by our knowing of it, some help to be administered. But to shew you some of the advantages that will come to us by knowing that the love of Christ passeth knowledge.

(1.) By knowing of this a child of God has in *reserve* for himself, at a day, when all that he otherwise knows, may be taken from him through the power of temptation. Sometimes a good man may be so put to it, that all that he knows comprehensively may be taken from him: to wit, the knowledge of the truth of his faith, or that he has the grace of God in him, or the like, this I say may be taken from him. Now if at this time, *he knows the love of Christ that passeth knowledge*, he knows a way in all probability to be recovered again. For if Christ Jesus loves with a love that passeth knowledge: then, saith the soul, that is thus in the dark, he may love me yet, for ought I know, for I know that he loves with a love that passeth knowledge; and therefore I will not utterly despond. Yea, if Satan should attempt to question whether ever Christ Jesus will look upon me or no: the answer is, if I know the love that passes knowledge: But he may look upon me, (O, Satan) yea, and love, and save me too, for ought I poor sinner know; for he loves with a love that passeth knowledge. If I be fallen into sin that lies hard upon me, and my conscience fears, that for this there is no forgiveness. The help for a stay from utter despair is at hand: but there may, say I, for Christ loves, with a love that passeth knowledge. If Satan would dissuade me from praying to God, by suggesting as if Christ would not regard the stammering, and chattering prayer of mine. The answer is ready, but he may regard for ought I know; for he loves with a love that passeth knowledge. If the tempter doth suggest that thy trials, and troubles, and afflictions, are so many, that it is to be thought thou shall never get beyond them. The answer is near, but for ought we know, Christ may carry me through them all, for he loves with a love that passeth knowledge.

Thus I say, is relief at hand, and a help in reserve for the tempted, let their temptations be what they will. This therefore is the weapon that will baffle the devil when all other weapons fail; for ought I know, Christ may save me, for he loves with a love that passeth knowledge. Yea, suppose he should drive me to the worst of fears, and that is to doubt that I neither have nor shall have for ever the grace of God in my soul. The answer is at hand, but I have or may have it, for Christ loves with a love that passeth knowledge. Thus therefore you may see that in this prayer of Paul, there is a great deal of good. He prays, when he prays that we might know the love of Christ that passeth knowledge: that we may have a help at hand, and relief against all the horrible temptations of the devil. For this is a help at hand, a help that is ready to fall in with us, if there be yet remaining with us, but the least grain of right reasoning according to the nature of things. For if it be objected against a man that he is poor, because he has but a groat in his pocket; yet if he has an unknown deal of money in his trunks, how easy is it for him to recover himself from that slander, by returning the knowledge of what he has, upon the objector. This is the case, and thus it is, and will be with them that know the love of Christ that passeth knowledge. Wherefore,

(2.) By this knowledge, room is made for a christian, and liberty is ministered unto him, to turn himself every way in all spiritual things. This is the Christian's rehoboth, that well for which the Philistines have no heart to strive, and that which will cause that we be fruitful in the land. Ge. xxvi. 22.

If Christians know not with this knowledge, they walk in the world as if they were *pinioned*; or as if fetters were hanged on their heels. But this enlarges their steps under them: 2 Sa. xxii. 37. by the knowledge of *this* love they may walk at liberty, and their steps shall not be straitened. This is that which Solomon intends when he saith, 'Get wisdom, and get understanding.' Pr. iv. 5. Then 'when thou goest, thy steps shall not be straitened, and when thou runnest, thou shalt not stumble.' Pr. iv. 12. A man that has only from hand to mouth, is oft put to it to know how to use his penny, and comes off also, many times, but with an hungry belly; but he that has, not only that, but always over and to spare, he is more at liberty, and can live in fulness, and far more like a gentleman. There is a man has a cistern, and that is full of water: there is another also, that has his cistern full, and withal, his spring in his yard; but a great drought is upon the land in which they dwell: I would now know, which of these two have the most advantage to live in their own minds at liberty, without fear of wanting water? Why this is the case in hand. There is a Christian that knows Christ in all those degrees

of his love that are knowable, but he knoweth Christ nothing in his love that passeth knowledge. There is another Christian, and he knows Christ, as the first, but withal, he also knows him as to his love that passeth knowledge. Pray now tell me, which of these two are likeliest to live most like a Christian, that is, like a spiritual prince, and like him that possesseth all things? which has most advantage to live in godly largeness of heart, and is most at liberty in his mind? which of these two have the greatest advantage to believe, and the greatest engagements laid upon him to love the Lord Jesus? which of these have also most in readiness to resist the wiles of the devil, and to subdue the power and prevalency of corruptions? 'Tis *this*, that makes men fathers in Christianity. 'I write unto you, fathers, because ye have known; - - I have written unto you, fathers, because ye have known,' 1 Jn. ii. 13—14. why, have not others known, not so as the fathers? The fathers have *known* and *known*. They have known the love of Christ in those degrees of love which are *knowable*, and have also known the love of Christ to be such which *passeth knowledge*. In my father's house is bread enough and to spare, was that that fetched the prodigal home. Lu. xv. 17. And when Moses would speak an endless all to Israel, for the comfort and stay of their souls, he calls their God, 'The fountain of Jacob upon a land of corn and wine.' De. xxxiii. 28.

(3.) By this knowledge, or knowing of the love of Christ which passeth knowledge, there is begot in Christians a greater desire to press forwards to that which is before them. Phi. iii. 12—21. What is the reason of all that sloth, carnal contentedness, and listlessness of spirit in Christians, more than the ignorance of this. For he that thinks he *knows* what can be *known*, is beyond all reason that should induce him to seek yet after more. Now the love of Christ may be said, not to be *knowable*, upon a threefold account: [namely.] For that my knowledge is *weak*. For that my knowledge is *imperfect*. Or for that, though my knowledge be never so perfect, because the love of Christ is *eternal*.

There is love that is not to be apprehended by weak knowledge. Convince a man of this, and then, if the knowledge of what he already has, be truly sweet to his soul, Pr. ii. 10. it will stir him up with great heartiness to desire to know what more of this is possible.

There is love beyond what he knows already, who is indued with the most perfect knowledge, that man here may have. Now if what this man knows already of this love is indeed sweet unto him; then it puts him upon hearty desires that his soul may yet know more. And because there is no bound set to man, how much he may *know* in this life thereof; therefore his desires, notwith-standing what he has attained, are yet *kept alive*, and in the pursuit after the knowledge of more of the love of Christ. And God in old time has taken it so well at the hands of some of his, that their desires have been so great, that when, as I may say, they have known as much on earth as is possible for them to know; (that is by ordinary means) he has come down to them in visions and revelations; or else taken them up to him for an hour or two into paradise, that they might *know*, and then let them down again.

But this is not all, There is a knowledge of the love of Christ, that we are by no means capable of until we be possessed of the heavens. And I would know, if a man indeed loveth Christ, whether the belief of this be not one of the highest arguments that can be urged, to make such an one weary of this world, that he may be with him. To such an one, 'to live is Christ, and to die is gain.' Phi. i. 21—23. And to such an one, it is difficult to bring his mind to be content to stay here a longer time; except he be satisfied that Christ has still work for him here to do.

I will yet add, There is a love of Christ, I will not say, that cannot be *known*, but I will say, that cannot be *enjoyed*; no, not by them now in heaven (in soul) until the day of judgment. And the knowledge of this, when it has possessed even men on earth, has made them choose a day of judgment, before a day of death, that they might know what is beyond that state and knowledge which even the spirits of just men made perfect, now do enjoy in heaven. 2 Co. v. 4. Wherefore, as I said at first, *To know the love of Christ that passeth knowledge*, is advantageous upon this account: it begetteth in Christians a great desire to reach, and press forward to that which is before.

One thing more, and then, as to this reason, I have done. Even that love of Christ that is absolutely unknowable, as to the utmost bound thereof because it is eternal, will be yet in the *nature* of it sweet and desirable, because we shall enjoy or be possessed of it *so*. This therefore, if there were no more, is enough, when known, to draw away the heart from things that are below, to itself.

(4.) The *love that passeth knowledge*. The knowledge of that is a very fruitful knowledge. It cannot be, but it must be fruitful. Some knowledge is empty, and alone, not attended with that good, and with those blessings wherewith this knowledge is attended. Did I say, it is fruitful? I will add, it is attended with the best fruit; it yieldeth the best wine: It fills the soul with all the fulness of God. '*And to know the love of Christ which passeth knowledge*, that ye may be filled with all the fulness of God.' God is in Christ, and makes himself known to us by the love of

Christ. 'Whosoever transgresseth, and abideth not in the doctrine of Christ, hath not God,' for God is not to be found nor enjoyed, but in him, consequently, he that hath, and abideth in the doctrine of Christ, 'hath both the Father and the Son.' 2 Jn. 9. Now, since there are degrees of knowledge of this doctrine, and since the highest degree of the knowledge of him, is to know that he has a *Love that passeth knowledge*, it follows, that if he that has the least saving knowledge of this doctrine, hath God; he that hath the largest knowledge of it, has God much more, or, according to the text, is filled with all the fulness of God. What this fulness of God should be, is best gathered from such sayings of the Holy Ghost, as come nearest to this, in language, filled,

Full of goodness. Ro. xv. 14.

Full of faith. Ac. vi. 5.

Full of the Holy Ghost. Ac. vii. 55.

Full of assurance of faith. He. x. 22.

Full of assurance of hope. He. vi. 11.

Full of joy unspeakable, and full of glory. 1 Pe. i. 8.

Full of joy. 1 Jn. i. 4.

Full of good works. Ac. xi. 36.

Being filled with the knowledge of his will. Col. i. 9.

Being filled with the spirit. Ep. v. 18.

Filled with the fruits of righteousness, which are by Jesus Christ unto the glory and praise of God. Phi. iv. 11.

These things to be sure are included either for the cause or effect of this *fulness*. The cause they cannot be, for that is God's, by his Holy Spirit. The effects therefore they are, for wherever God dwells in the degree intended in the text, there is shewn in an eminent manner, by these things, 'what *is* the riches of the glory of his inheritance in the saints.' Ep. i. 18. But these things dwell not in that measure specified by the text, in any, but those who *know the love of Christ which passeth knowledge*.

But what a man is he that is filled with all these things! or that is, as we have it in the text, 'filled with all the fulness of God!' Such men are, at this day, wanting in the churches. These are the men that *sweeten* churches, and that bring glory to God and to religion. And knowledge will make us such, such *knowledge* as the Apostle here speaketh of.*

I have now done, when I have spoken something by way of USE unto you, from what hath been said. And,

Use First, Is there such breadth, and length, and

---

* How delightfully has Bunyan brought forth the marrow of this important text. He felt that those who were filled with all the fulness of God, *sweetened* the churches in his day; they were wanted then; are they not equally wanted now? —ED.

depth, and height in God, for us? And is there toward us love in Christ that passeth knowledge? Then this shews us, not only the greatness of the majesty of the Father and the Son, but the great good will that is in their heart to them that receive their word.

God has engaged the breadth, and length and depth, and height of the love, the wisdom, the power, and truth that is in himself, for us; and Christ has loved us with a love that passeth knowledge. We may well say, 'Who is like thee, O Lord, among the gods?' Ex. xv. 11. Or, as another prophet has it, 'Who *is* a God like unto thee, that pardoneth iniquity, and passeth by the transgression of the remnant of his heritage? he retaineth not his anger for ever: because he delighteth *in* mercy.' Mi vii. 18. Yea, no words can sufficiently set forth the greatness of this love of God and his Son to us poor miserable sinners.

Use Second, Is there so great a heart for love, towards us, both in the Father and in the Son? Then let us be much in the study and search after the greatness of this love. This is the sweetest study that a man can devote himself unto; because it is the study of the love of God and of Christ to man. Studies that yield far less profit than this, how close are they pursued, by some who have adapted themselves thereunto? Men do not use to count telling over of their money burthensome to them, nor yet the recounting of their grounds, their herds, and their flocks, when they increase. Why? the study of the unsearchable love of God in Christ to man, is better in itself, and yields more sweetness to the soul of man, than can ten thousand such things as but now are mentioned. I know the wise men of this world, of whom there are many, will say as to what I now press you unto; Who can shew us any good in it? But Lord, lift thou up the light of thy countenance upon us. Thou hast put gladness in my heart, more than in the time that their corn and their wine increaseth. Ps. iv. 6, 7. David also said that his meditation on the Lord should be sweet. Oh, there is in God and in his Son, that kindness for the sons of men, that, did they know it, they would like to retain the knowledge of it in their hearts. They would cry out as she did of old; 'Set me as a seal upon thy heart, as a seal upon thine arm: For love is strong as death.' Song viii. 6, 7. Every part, crumb, grain, or scrap of this knowledge, is to a Christians, as drops of honey are to sweet-palated children, worth the gathering up, worth the putting to the taste to be relished. Yea, David says of the word which is the ground of knowledge: 'It is sweeter than honey or the honey-comb. More,' saith he, 'to be desired *are they* than gold; yea, than much fine gold; sweeter also than honey or the honey-comb.' Ps. xix. 10. Why then do not

Christians devote themselves to the meditation of this so heavenly, so goodly, so sweet, and so comfortable a thing, that yieldeth such advantage to the soul? The reason is, these things are talked of, but not believed: did men believe what they say, when they speak so largely of the love of God, and the love of Jesus Christ, they would, they could not but meditate upon it. There are so many wonders in it, and men love to think of wonders. There is so much profit in it, and men love to think of that which yields them profit. But, as I said, the belief of things is wanting. Belief of a thing will have strong effects, whether the ground for it be true, or false. As suppose one of you should, when you are at a neighbour's house, believe that your own house is on fire, whilst your children are fast asleep in bed, though indeed there were no such thing; I will appeal to any of you if this belief would not make notable work with and upon your hearts. Let a man believe he shall be damned, though afterwards it is evident he believed a lie, yet what work did that belief make in that man's heart; even so, and much more, the belief of heavenly things will work, because true and great, and most good; also, where they are indeed believed, their evidence is managed upon their spirit, by the power and glory of the Holy Ghost it self: Wherefore let us study these things.

Use Third, Let us cast ourselves upon this love. No greater encouragement can be given us, than what is in the text and about it. It is great, it is love that passeth knowledge. Men that are sensible of danger, are glad when they hear of such helps upon which they may boldly venture for escape. Why such an help and relief, the text helpeth trembling and fearful consciences to. Fear and trembling as to misery hereafter, can flow but from what we know, feel, or imagine: but the text speaks of a love that is beyond that we can know, feel, or imagine, even of a love that passeth knowledge; consequently of a love that goes beyond all these. Besides, the Apostle's conclusion upon this subject, plainly makes it manifest that this meaning which I have put upon the text, is the mind of the Holy Ghost. 'Now unto him,' saith he, 'that is able to do exceeding abundantly above all that we ask or think, according to the power that worketh in us, unto him *be* glory in the church by Christ Jesus, throughout all ages, world without end. Amen.' Ep. iii. 20, 21. What can be more plain? what can be more full? What can be more suitable to the most desponding spirit in any man? He can do more than thou knowest he will. He can do more than thou thinkest he can. What dost thou think? why, I think, saith the sinner, *that I am cast away.* Well, but there are worse thoughts than these, therefore think again. Why, saith the sinner, *I think that my sins are as many as the sins of all the world.* Indeed this is a very black thought, but there are worse thoughts than this, therefore prithee think again. Why, *I think,* saith the sinner, *that God is not able to pardon all my sins.* Ay, now thou hast thought indeed. For this thought makes thee look more like a devil than a man, and yet because thou art a man and not a devil, see the condescension and the boundlessness of the love of thy God. *He is able to do above all that we think!* Couldest thou (sinner) if thou hadst been allowed, thyself express what thou wouldest have expressed, the greatness of the love thou wantest, with words that could have suited thee better? for 'tis not said he can do above what we think, meaning our thinking at present, but above all we can think, meaning above the worst and most soul-dejecting thoughts that we have at any time. Sometimes the dejected have worse thoughts than at other times they have. Well, take them at their worst times, àt times when they think, and think, till they think themselves down into the very pangs of hell; yet this word of the grace of God, is above them, and shews that he can yet recover and save these miserable people. And now I am upon this subject, I will a little further walk and travel with the desponding ones, and will put a few words in their mouths for their help against temptations that may come upon them hereafter. For as Satan follows such now, with charges and applications of guilt, so he may follow them with interrogatories and appeals: for he can tell how by appeals, as well as by charging of sin, to sink and drown the sinner whose soul he has leave to engage. Suppose therefore that some distressed man or woman, should after this way be engaged, and Satan should with his interrogatories, and appeals be busy with them to drive them to desperation; the text last mentioned, to say nothing of the subject of our discourse, yields plenty of help for the relief of such a one. Says Satan, dost thou not know that thou hast horribly sinned? yes, says the soul, I do. Says Satan, dost thou not know, that thou art one of the vilest in all the pack of professors? yes, says the soul, I do. Says Satan, doth not thy conscience tell thee that thou art and hast been more base than any of thy fellows can imagine thee to be? Yes, says the soul; my conscience tells me so. Well, saith Satan, now will I come upon thee with my appeals. Art thou not a graceless wretch? Yes. Hast thou an heart to be sorry for this wickedness? No, not as I should. And albeit, saith Satan, thou prayest sometimes, yet is not thy heart possessed with a belief that God will not regard thee? yes, says the sinner. Why then despair, and go hang thyself, saith the devil. And now we are at the end of the thing designed and driven at by Satan. But what shall I now do, saith the sinner; I answer, take up the words of the text against him, Christ loves with a love that passeth knowledge, and answereth him farther, saying Satan, though I cannot think that God loves me; though I cannot think that God will save me; yet I will not yield to thee: for God can do more than I think he can. And whereas thou appealedst unto me, if whether when I pray, my heart is not possessed with unbelief that God will not regard me; that shall not sink me neither: for God can do abundantly above what I ask or think. Thus this text helpeth, where obstructions are put in against our believing, and thereby casting ourselves upon the love of God in Christ for salvation.

And yet this is not all, for the text is yet more full: 'He is able to do abundantly more,' yea, 'exceeding abundantly more,' or 'above all that we ask or think.' It is a text made up of words *picked* and *packed* together by the wisdom of God, *picked* and *packed* together on purpose for the succour and relief of the tempted, that they may when in the midst of their distresses, cast themselves upon the Lord their God. He can do abundantly more than we *ask.* Oh! says the soul, that he would but do *so* much for me as I could *ask* him to do! How happy a man should I then be. Why, what wouldest thou *ask* for, sinner? you may be sure, says the soul, I would ask *to be saved* from my sins; I would ask for *faith* in, and *love* to, Christ; I would ask to be preserved in this evil world, and ask to be glorified with Christ in heaven. He that *asketh* for all this, doth indeed *ask* for much, and for more than Satan would have him believe that God is able or willing to bestow upon him; but mark, the text doth not say, that God is able to do *all* that we can *ask or think,* but that he is able to do *above* all, yea, *abundantly* above all, yea, *exceeding* abundantly above all that we ask or think. What a text is this! What a God have we! God foresaw the sins of his people, and what work the devil would make with their hearts about them, and therefore to prevent their ruin by his temptation, he has thus largely, as you see, expressed his love by his word. Let us therefore, as has been bidden us, make this good use of this doctrine of grace, as to cast ourselves upon this love of God in the times of distress and temptation.

Use Fourth, Take heed of abusing this love. This exhortation seems needless; for love is such a thing, that one would think none could find in their heart to abuse. But for all that, I am of opinion, that there is nothing that is more abused among professors this day, than is this love of God. There has of late more light about the love of Christ broke out, than formerly: every boy now can *talk* of the love of Christ; but this love of Christ has not been rightly applied by preachers, or else not rightly received by professors. For never was this grace of Christ so turned into lasciviousness, as now. Now it is a practice among professors to learn to be vile, of the profane. Yea, and to plead for that vileness: Nay, we will turn it the other way, now it is so that the profane do learn to be vile of those that profess (They teach the wicked ones their ways:) Je. ii. 33: a thing that no good man should think on but with blushing cheeks.*

Jude speaketh of these people, and tells us that they, notwithstanding their profession, deny the only Lord God, and our Saviour Jesus Christ. ver. 4. ' They profess,' saith Paul, ' that they know God; but in works they deny *him*, being abominable, and disobedient, and unto every good work reprobate.' Tit. i. 16.

But I say, let not this love of God and of Christ, be abused. 'Tis unnatural to abuse love, to abuse love is a villany condemned of all, yea, to abuse love, is the most inexcusable sin of all. It is next the sin of devils to abuse love, the love of God and of Christ.

And what says the Apostle? ' Because they received not the love of the truth, that they might be saved, therefore God shall send them strong delusion that they should believe a lie, that they all might be damned, who believed not the truth, but had pleasure in unrighteousness.' 2 Th. ii. 10—12. And what can such an one say for himself in the judgment, that shall be charged with the *abuse of love?* Christians, deny yourselves, deny your lusts, deny the vanities of this present life, devote yourselves to God; become lovers of God, lovers of his ways, and 'a people zealous of good works;' then shall you show one to another, and to all men, that you have not received the grace of God in vain. 2 Co. vi. 1. Renounce therefore the hidden things of dishonesty, walk not in craftiness, nor handle God's word deceitfully, but by manifestation of the truth, commend yourselves to every man's conscience in the sight of God. Do this, I say, yea, and *so* endeavour such a closure with this love of God in Christ, as may graciously constrain you to do it, because, when all proofs of the right receiving of this love of Christ shall be produced, none will be found of worth enough to justify the simplicity of our profession, but that which makes us 'zealous of good works.' Tit. ii. 14. And what a thing will it be to be turned off at last, as one that abused the love of Christ! as one that presumed upon his lusts, this world, and all manner of naughtiness, because the love of Christ to pardon

* Bunyan lived in singularly eventful times. Under the Commonwealth the strictest outward morality was enforced. But when a licentious monarch was placed upon the throne, a flood of the grossest debauchery was let loose; and those hypocrites, who had put on a cloak of religion to serve a temporary purpose, threw it off and became ringleaders in the vilest iniquities. See Matt. xii. 43—45.—ED.

sins was so great! What an unthinking, what a disingenuous one wilt thou be counted at that day! yea, thou wilt be found to be the man that made a *prey* of love, that made a stalking-horse of love, that made of love a slave to sin, the devil and the world, and will not that be bad? Read Eze. xvi.

Use Fifth, Is the love of God and of Christ so great? let us then labour to improve it to the utmost for our advantage, against all the hindrances of faith.

To what purpose else is it revealed, made mention of, and commended to us? We are environed with many enemies, and faith in the love of God and of Christ, is our only succour and shelter. Wherefore our duty and wisdom and privilege is, to improve this love for our own advantage. Improve it against daily infirmities, improve it against the wiles of the devil; improve it against the threats, rage, death, and destruction, that the men of this world continually with their terror set before you. But how must that be done? why, set this love and the safety that is in it, before thine eyes; and behold it while these things make their assaults upon thee. These words, the faith of this, *God loves me*, will support thee in the midst of what dangers may assault thee. And this is that which is meant, when we are exhorted to rejoice in the Lord, Phi. iii. 1. to make our boast in the Lord; Ps. xliv. 51. to triumph in Christ; 2 Co. ii. 14. and to set the Lord always before our face. Ps. xvi. 8. For he that can do this thing stedfastly, cannot be overcome. For in God there is more than can be in the world, either to help or hinder; wherefore if God be my helper, if God loves me, if Christ be my redeemer, and has bestowed his love that passeth knowledge upon me, who can be against me? He. xiii. 6, and Ro. viii. 31. and if they be against me, what disadvantage reap I thereby; since even all this also, worketh for my good? This is improving the love of God and of Christ for my advantage. The same course should Christians also take with the degrees of this love, even set it against all the degrees of danger; for here *deep calleth unto deep.* There cannot be wickedness and rage wrought up to such or such a degree, as of which it may be said, there are not degrees in the love of God and of Christ to match it. Wherein Pharaoh dealt proudly against God's people, the Lord was above him, Ex. xviii. 11. did match and overmatch him; he came up to him, and went beyond him; he collared with him, overcame him, and cast him down. 'The Lord *is* a man of war, the Lord *is* his name. Pharaoh's chariots and his host hath he cast into the sea - - - they sank into the bottom as a stone.' Ex. xv. 5. There is no striving against the Lord that hath loved us; there is none that strive against him can prosper. If the shields of the earth be the Lord's, Ps. xlvii. 9 then he can wield them for the safeguard of his body the church; or if they are become incapable of being made use of any longer in that way, and for such a thing, can he not lay them aside, and make himself new ones? Men can do after this manner, much more God. But again, if the miseries, or afflictions which thou meetest with, seem to thee to overflow, and to go beyond measure, above measure, and so to be above strength, and begin to drive thee to despair of life; 2 Co. i. 8. then thou hast also, in the love of God, and of Christ, that which is above, and that goes beyond all measure also, to wit, love unsearchable, unknown, and 'that can do exceeding abundantly above all that we ask or think.' Now God hath set them one against the other, and 'twill be thy wisdom to do so too, for this is the way to improve this love. But, though it be easy, thus to admonish you to do, yet you shall find the practical part more difficult; wherefore, here it may not be amiss, if I add to these, another head of COUNSEL.

Counsel First, Then, Wouldst thou *improve* this love of God and of Christ to thy advantage, Why then *thou must labour after the knowledge of it*. This was it that the Apostle prayed for, for these Ephesians, as was said before, and this is that that thou must labour after, or else thy *reading* and my *writing*, will, as to thee, be fruitless. Let me then say to thee, as David to his son Solomon, 'And thou Solomon, my son, know thou the God of thy father.' 1 Ch. xxviii. 9. Empty *notions* of this love will do nothing but harm, wherefore, they are not empty notions that I press thee to rest in, but that thou labour after the knowledge of the favour of this good ointment, Song i. 3. which the Apostle calleth the *favour* of the knowledge of this Lord Jesus. 2 Co. ii. 14. Know it, until it becometh *sweet* or pleasant to thy soul, and then it will *preserve* and keep thee. Pr. ii. 10, 11. Make this love of God and of Christ *thine own*, and not another's. Many there are that can talk largely of the love of God to Abraham, to David, to Peter and Paul. But that is not the thing, give not over until this love be made thine own; until thou *find* and *feel* it to run warm in thy heart by the shedding of it abroad there, by the spirit that God hath given thee. Ro. v. 5. Then thou wilt know it with an obliging and engaging knowledge; yea, then thou wilt know it with a soul-strengthening, and soul-encouraging knowledge.

Counsel Second, Wouldst thou improve this love? then set it against the love of all other things whatsoever, even until this love shall conquer thy soul from the love of them to itself.

This is christian. Do it therefore, and say, why should any thing have my heart but God, but Christ? He loves me, he loves me with love that passeth knowledge. He loves me, and he shall have me: he loves me, and I will love him: his love stripped him of all for my sake; Lord let my love strip me of all for thy sake. I am a son of love, an object of love, a monument of love, of *free* love, of *distinguishing* love, of *peculiar* love, and of love that passeth knowledge: and why should not I walk in love? In love to God, in love to men, in holy love, in love unfeigned? This is the way to improve the love of God for thy advantage, for the subduing of thy passions, and for sanctifying of thy nature. 'Tis an odious thing to hear men of base lives talking of the love of God, of the death of Christ, and of the glorious grace that is presented unto sinners by the word of the truth of the gospel. Praise is comely for the upright, not for the profane. Therefore let him speak of love that is *taken* with love, that is *captivated* with love, that is *carried away* with love. If this man speaks of it, his speaking signifies something; the powers, and bands of love are upon him, and he shews to all that he knows what he is speaking of. But the very mentioning of love, is in the mouth of the profane, like a parable in the mouth of fools, or as salt unsavory. Wherefore, Christian, improve this love of God as thou *shouldest*, and that will improve thee as thou *wouldest*. Wherefore,

Counsel Third, If thou wouldest improve this love, keep thyself in it. 'Keep yourselves in the love of God.' Jude 21. This text looks as if it favoured the Socinians, but there is nothing of that in it. And so doth that, 'If ye keep my commandments, ye shall abide in my love: even as I have kept my Father's commandments and abide in his love.' Jn. xv. 10. The meaning then is this, that living a holy life is the way, after a man has believed unto justification, to keep himself in the savour and comfort of the love of God. And Oh, that thou wouldest indeed so do. And that because, if thou shall want the savour of it, thou wilt soon want tenderness to the commandment, which is the rule by which thou must walk, if thou wilt do good to thyself, or honour God in the world. 'To him that ordereth *his* conversation *aright*, will I shew the salvation of God.' Ps. l. 23. He that would live a sweet, comfortable, joyful life, must live a very holy life. This is the way to improve this love to thyself indeed.

Counsel Fourth, To this end, you must take root and be grounded in love; that is, you must be well settled, and stablished in this love, if indeed you would improve it. You must not be shaken as to the doctrine and grounds of it. Ep. iii. 17. These you must be well acquainted with: for he that is but a child in this doctrine, is not capable as yet, of falling in with these exhortations: For such waver, and fear when tempted; and 'he that feareth is not made perfect in love,' 1 Jn. iv. 18. nor can he so improve it for himself and soul's good as he should.

Counsel Fifth, and lastly, Keep, to this end,

those grounds, and evidences that God hath given you of your call to be partakers of this love, with all clearness upon your hearts, and in your minds. For he that wants a sight of them, or a proof that they are true and good, can take but little comfort in this love. There is a great mystery in the way of God with his people. He will justify them without their works, he will pardon them for his Son's sake: but they shall have but little comfort of what he hath done, doth, and will do for them that are careless, carnal, and not holy in their lives. Nor shall they have their evidences for heaven at hand, nor out of doubt with them, yea, they shall walk without the sun, and have their comforts by bits and knocks;* while others sit at their father's table, have liberty to go into the wine-cellar, rejoice at the sweet and pleasant face of their heavenly Father towards them; and know it shall go well with them at the end.

Something now for a conclusion should be spoken to the carnal world, who have heard me tell of all this love. But what shall I say unto them? If I should speak to them, and they should not hear; or if I should testify unto them, and they should not believe; or intreat them, and they should scorn me; all will but aggravate, and greaten their sin, and tend to their further condemnation. And therefore I shall leave the obstinate where I found him, and shall say to him that is willing to be saved, Sinner, thou hast the advantage of thy neighbour, not only because thou art willing to live, but because there are [those] that are willing thou shouldest; to wit, those unto whom the issues from death do belong, and they are the Father and the Son, to whom be glory with the blessed Spirit of grace, world without end. Amen.

---

* 'Bits and knocks;' this phrase is now obsolete: it alludes to a dog at table, who while picking up the crumbs, often gets a bite and a buffet or knock with it, but still perseveres.—ED.

OF ANTICHRIST, AND HIS RUIN:

AND OF

THE SLAYING THE WITNESSES.

By JOHN BUNYAN.

PREFATORY REMARKS BY THE EDITOR.

This important treatise was prepared for the press, and left by the author, at his decease, to the care of his surviving friends for publication. It first appeared in a collection of his works in folio, 1691; and although a subject of universal interest; most admirably elucidated; no edition has been published in a separate form.

Antichrist has agitated the christian world from the earliest ages; and his craft has been to mislead the thoughtless, by fixing upon the humble followers of the Lamb his own opprobrious proper name. The mass of professed Christians, whose creed and mode of worship have been provided by human laws, has ever been opposed to the sincere disciples of Christ. To imbibe every principle from investigation and conviction of the holy oracles—to refuse submission to any authority in the spiritual kingdom of God, except it is to Christ, the supreme head and only lawgiver in his church—to refuse obedience to human laws in the great concern of salvation and of worship; whether those laws or decrees emanate from a Darius, a Nebuchadnezzar, a Bourbon, a Tudor, or a Stuart—to be influenced by the spirit which animated Daniel, the three Hebrew youths, and the martyrs, brought down denunciations upon them, and they were called Antichristian: but alas! the sincere disciples of Jesus have ever known and FELT who and what is Antichrist. They have been robbed—incarcerated in dungeons—racked and tormented—transported—drowned—hung or burned. The most frightful atrocities have been committed upon the most peaceful and valuable members of society; because they valued their soul's peace in preference to temporal advantages. These cruelties are THY cursed deeds, O Antichrist! The hand writing against thee is exhibited in blood-stained and indelible characters. The Great God has decreed thy downfall and ruin—" That wicked - - whom the Lord shall consume with the spirit of his mouth," 2 Th. ii. 8. All who are found partakers in his community, must be consumed with *an everlasting destruction.* No "*paper-winkers*"* can hide

this truth from the enlightened regenerated mind. " O my soul, come not thou into their secret, unto their assembly, mine honour, be not thou united: for in their anger they slew a man. Cursed be their anger, for *it was* fierce; and their wrath, for it was cruel!"

In Bunyan's time great cruelties were practised to compel uniformity. To that absurd shrine many thousand invaluable lives were sacrificed. Blessed be God, that happier days have dawned upon us. Antichrist can no longer put the Christian to a cruel death. It very rarely sends one to prison for refusing obedience to human laws that interfere with religious worship. " My kingdom is not of this world," said the Redeemer: and his followers dare not render unto Cæsar, or temporal governments, that which belongs exclusively to God. Human coercion, in anything connected with religion, whether it imposes creeds, liturgies, or modes of worship, is Antichrist: whom to obey, is spiritual desolation, and if knowingly persevered in, leads to death.

On the contrary, the kingdom of Christ is love, meekness, forbearance, persuasion, conviction, and holy faith. The Christian who dares not obey Antichrist may still, in some countries, suffer personal violence; but the olden cruelties have given way to the spread of the gospel. Should the wicked spirit of persecution still light its unhallowed fire in any sect; may heaven forgive and convert such misguided men, before the divine wrath shall consume all that pertains to Antichrist. "Come out from among them and be ye separate, saith the Lord."

Bunyan conceives that previous to the universal triumphs of the Saviour, Antichrist will spread his influence over the whole earth; and the church be hidden from outward observation, in the hearts of believers. This idea, which was also cherished by Dr. Gill, and others, deserves careful consideration; while we keep in mind, *that* leaven which must spread, however invisible in its operation, until the whole earth shall be leavened.

The dread enemy may yet appear in a different

---

* Bunyan's expression, see the last page.

F

shape to any that he has hitherto assumed. When mankind, by the spread of knowledge, shall throw off the absurdities and disgraceful trammels of hypocrisy, fanaticism, and tyranny, which has so long oppressed them; there may be experienced a vast overflowing of infidelity, and perverted *reason* assume the place of Antichrist. Through this and all other opposing systems, Christianity must make its irresistible progress: all that opposes is doomed to ruin by the *Great God.* Every heart will be subdued by that blessed knowledge, which has the promise of the life that now is as well as of that which is to come. Bloodless victory! The ark being exhibited, every Dagon must fall before it, *then* shall be realized the heavenly anthem, " Glory to God in the highest, and on earth peace, good will towards men."

GEORGE OFFOR.

A PREMONITION TO THE READER.

AFTER that God had delivered Babylon and her king into the hands of the kings of the Medes and Persians, then began the liberty of the Jews, from their long and tedious captivity: For though Nebuchadnezzar and his sons did tyrannically enslave, and hold them under; yet so wrought God with the hearts of those kings that succeeded them, that they made proclamation to them to go home, and build their city, temple, &c., and worship their *own* God according to *his own* law. 2 Ch. xxx. 6; & Ezr. i. But because I would not be tedious in enumerating instances for the clearing of this, therefore I will content myself with one, and with a brief note upon it. It is that in the seventh of Ezra 26: ' And whosoever will not do the law of thy God, and the law of the king, let judgment be executed speedily upon him, whether *it be* to death, or to banishment, or to confiscation of goods, or to imprisonment.' This is the conclusion of a letter that king Artaxerxes gave to Ezra the priest and scribe, when he granted his petition, and gave him leave to go to Jerusalem to build the temple, and to offer sacrifice there to the God whose house is in Jerusalem. And a conclusion it was, both comfortable and sharp; comfortable to Ezra and his companions, but sharp unto his enemies. I shall here present you with a copy of the letter at large.

' Artaxerxes, king of kings, unto Ezra the priest, a scribe of the law of the God of heaven, perfect *peace,* and at such a time. I make a decree, that all they of the people of Israel, and of his priests and levites, in my realm, which are minded of their own free-will to go up to Jerusalem, go with thee. Forasmuch as thou art sent of the king, and of his seven counsellors, to inquire concerning Judah and Jerusalem, according to the law of thy God which is in thine hand; And to carry the silver and gold, which the king and his counsellors have freely offered unto the God of Israel, whose habitation *is* in Jerusalem. And all the silver and gold that thou canst find in all the province of Babylon, with the free-will-offering of the people, and of the priests, offering willingly for the house of their God which *is* in Jerusalem: That thou mayst buy speedily with this money bullocks, rams, lambs, with their meat-offerings and their drink-offerings, and offer them upon the altar of the house of your God which *is* in Jerusalem. And whatsoever shall seem good to thee, and to thy brethren, to do with the rest of the silver and the gold, that do after the will of your God. The vessels also that are given thee for the service of the house of thy God, *those* deliver thou before the God of Jerusalem. And whatsoever more shall be needful for the house of thy God, which thou shalt have occasion to bestow, bestow *it* out of the king's treasure-house. And I, *even* I Artaxerxes the king, do make a decree to all the treasurers which *are* beyond the river, that whatsoever Ezra the priest, the scribe of the law of the God of heaven, shall require of you, it be done speedily. Unto an hundred talents of silver, and to an hundred measures of wheat, and to an hundred baths of wine, and to an hundred baths of oil, and salt without prescribing *how much.* Whatsoever is commanded by the God of heaven, let it be diligently done for the house of the God of heaven: for why should there be wrath against the realm of the king and his sons? Also we certify you, that touching any of the priests and levites, singers, porters, nethinims, or ministers of this House of God, it shall not be lawful to impose toll, tribute, or custom, upon them. And thou, Ezra, after the wisdom of thy God, that *is* in thine hand, set magistrates and judges, which may judge all the people that *are* beyond the river, all such as know the laws of thy God; and teach ye them that know *them* not. And whosoever will not do the law of thy God, and the law of the king, let judgment be executed speedily upon him, whether *it be* unto death, or to banishment, or to confiscation of goods, or to imprisonment.' [Ezr. vii. 11–26.]

This is the letter; and now for the scope thereof. *First,* Generally. *Secondly,* Particularly.

GENERALLY. The general scope of the letter is this: A grant given by the king to Ezra the scribe, to go to Jerusalem, and build there the temple of God, and offer sacrifice in it according to the law: With commissions annexed thereunto, to the king's lieutenants, treasurers and governors on that side the river, to further the work with such things as by the king was commanded they should.

PARTICULARLY. But we will consider the matter particularly. 1. As to the *manner* of the grant which the king gave to Ezra and his brethren to go thither. 2. As to the king's grant, with reference to their building, and way of worship. 3. With reference to the king's liberality and gifts towards the building of the temple, and by what rules it was to be bestowed. 4. As to the way that the king concluded they should be governed in their own land. 5. With reference to the king's charge to his officers that were thereabout, not to hinder Ezra in his work. 6. And lastly, with reference to the king's threat and commandment to do judgment if they should hinder it.

First, As to the *manner* of the grant that the king gave to Ezra and his brethren to go to build, it was such an one as forced none, but left every Jew to his own choice, whether he would go, or forbear. The words are these: ' Artaxerxes, king of kings, unto Ezra the priest, a scribe of the law of the God of heaven, perfect *peace*, and at such a time. I make a decree, that all they of the people of Israel, and *of* his priests and levites, in my realm, which are minded of their own free-will to go up to Jerusalem, go with thee.' ver. 12, 13.

Thus gracious then was the king: He made a decree, That all they of the captive Jews, their priests and levites, that would return to their own land, to build their temple, and to sacrifice there, might: He would hinder none, force none, but left them free, to do as they would.

Secondly, As to the king's grant, with reference to their building, and way of worship there, nothing was to be done therein, *but according to the law of the God of Ezra, which was in his hands.* ver. 14. Hence, when he was come to Jerusalem, he was to inquire concerning Judah and Jerusalem; to wit, what was wanting in order to the temple and worship of God there, according to the law of his God, which was in his hand. Also when they went about to build, and to sacrifice, all was to be done according as was commanded by the God of heaven: ver. 23. Yea, this was granted by the king, and his seven counsellors.

Thirdly, As to the king's liberality towards the building of this house, &c. it was large: He gave silver, gold, bullocks, rams, lambs; with wheat, wine, oil, and salt; ver. 17, 22. but would by his royal power, give no orders how in particular things should be bestowed, but left all *that* to Ezra the priest, to do with it according to the will, word, or law of his God. ver. 18.

Fourthly, As to the way that the king concluded they should be governed in their own land, it was by their own laws; yea, he did bid Ezra the priest, after the wisdom of his God that was in his hand, set magistrates and judges, which might judge all the people, &c. only he bid him make them such, which did know the law of his God: Also the king added, That they should teach it to them that knew it not.

Fifthly, As to the king's officers, he gave them a charge not to *hinder*, but *further* this work. To *further* this work, not by putting their hand thereto, (that was to be left to the Jews alone, especially to Ezra, according to the law of his God,) but that they should speedily give him such things which the king had commanded, to wit, silver, and wheat, and wine, and oil, and salt, for their encouragement; and to do therewith, as by the law of their God they should. Further, That they should not impose toll, tribute, or custom, upon the priests, levites, singers, porters, nethinims, or ministers. ver. 20—22.

Sixthly, And now we come to the conclusion, to wit, the king's threat and command to do judgment on them that obeyed not the law of Ezra's God, and the king.

Considering what hath been said before, I conclude,

1. That this king imposed no law, no priest, no people upon these Jews; but left them wholly to their own law, their own ministers, and their own people: All which were the laws of God, the priests of God, the people of God, as to their building of their temple, and the worship of their God.

2. He forced not THIS people, no, not to their land, their temple, nor their worship, by his or their law; but left them free to their own mind, to do thereabout as they would.

3. He added not any law therefore of his own, either to prescribe worship, or to enforce it upon the Jews.

But you will say, upon what then was the threatening and the command to punish grounded? I answer, upon a supposed breach of two laws. He of the Jews, that in Jerusalem, rebelled against the law of the Lord, was in his own land left by the king to be punished by the same law, according to the penalties thereof: And he of the king's officers, that refused to do the king's laws, that refused to give the Jews such things as the king commanded, and that would yet exact such customs and tributes as the king forbade, should be punished by the king's laws, whether unto death or unto banishment, or unto confiscation of goods, or to imprisonment.

And if all kings would but give such liberty, to wit, that God's people should be directed in their temple-building, and temple worship, as they find it in the law of their God, without the additions of man's inventions: And if all kings did but lay the same penalty upon them of their pretended servants, that should hinder this work, which this brave king Artaxerxes laid upon his ; how many of the enemies of the Jews, before this time, would have been hanged, banished, had their goods confiscated to the king, or their bodies shut up in prison! The which we desire not; we desire only that this letter of the king might be considered of, and we left to do as is there licensed and directed: And when we do the contrary, let us be punished by the law of God, as we are his servants, and by the law of the king, as we are his subjects; and we shall never complain.

Only I cannot but observe how prettily it is done of some, who urge this text to colour their malice, ignorance and revenge withal, while they cry, *The law of God*, and *The law of the king*, when they will neither let, according to *this* scripture, the law of God, nor the law of the king take place: Not the law of God; for that they will not leave us to that, to square and govern ourselves in temple-work, and sacrificing by. Nor will they do the law of the king, which has made void, *ipso facto*, whatever law is against the word of God; but because themselves can do, they will force us to do so too.*

Before I leave this, I would touch once again upon the *candour* of this king Artaxerxes, who thus did: Because he gave this leave and license to the Jews, contrary (if he had any) to his own national worship ; yea, and also to the impairing of his own incomes. Methinks he should have a religion of his own ; and that, not that of the Jews, because he was a Gentile ; and not, as we read of, proselyted to the Jews religion. Indeed, he spake reverently of the God of Israel, and of his temple-worship, and sacrifices, as did also several other kings; but that will not prove that he was adapted to that religion.

That his incomes were impaired, 'tis evident; because he took off toll, tribute, and custom from them, of whom mention is made before ; nor is it, I think, to be believed, that he did exact it of their brethren. But we may see what the Lord can do ; for thus to do, was put into the heart of the king by the God of heaven. ver. 27. This therefore ariseth not of nature: no more did the kindness of Cyrus or Darius, of whom we read in the beginning of this history. As God therefore did

put it into the hearts of the wicked kings of Babylon, to distress his church and people for their sins; so he put it into the hearts of the kings of the Medes and Persians, who were to be, in a sense, their saviours ; to ease them of those distresses, to take off the yoke, and let them go free. Indeed, there was an Artaxerxes that put a stop to this work of God, chap. iv. and he also was of the kings that had destroyed the Babylonians ; for it doth not follow, because God hath begun to deliver his people, that therefore their deliverance must be completed without stop or let. The protestants in France had more favour formerly, than from their prince they at this time have ; yet I doubt not but that God will make that horn also one of them (in his time) that (indeed) shall hate the whore. As the sins of God's people brought them into captivity ; so their sins can hold them there ; yea, and when the time comes that grace must fetch them out, yet the oxen that draw this cart may stumble ; and the way through roughness, may shake it sorely. However, heaven rules and over-rules ; and by one means and another, as the captivity of Israel did seem to linger, so it came out at the time appointed ; in the way that best pleased God, most profited them, and that most confounded those that were their implacable enemies. This therefore should instruct those that yet dwell where the woman sitteth, to quietness and patience.

To *quietness:* For God rules, and has the dispose of things. Besides, it is a kind of arraigning of his wisdom, to be discontent at that which at present is upon the wheel. Above all, it displeases him that any should seek, or go about to revenge their own injuries, or to work their own deliverances; for that is the work of God, and he will do it by the kings: Nor is he weak, nor has he missed the opportunity ; nor doth he sleep but waketh, and waiteth to be gracious.

This also should teach them to be *patient*, and put them upon bearing what at present they may undergo, patiently. Let them wait upon God; patiently let them wait upon men, and patiently let them bear the *fruits* of their own transgressions; which though they should be none other but a deferring of the mercy wished for, is enough to try, and crack, and break their patience, if a continual supply, and a daily increase thereof be not given by the God of heaven.

And before I do conclude this, let me also add one word more ; to wit, to exhort them to look that they may see that which God at present may be doing among the Babylonians.

When God had his people into Babylon of old, he presented them with such rarities there, as he never shewed them in their own country. And is there nothing now to be seen by them that are not yet delivered from that oppression, that may

---

* The absurd act to compel uniformity in modes of worship, xiv. Charles II., had then recently passed; and when this treatise was written, it desolated the country. An amazing number of godly ministers were driven from their pulpits—proscribed from preaching or teaching, and by the Five Mile Act, driven as prisoners to houses and villages five miles from a market-town, upon pain of imprisonment, transportation, and death ! ! !—Ed.

give them occasion to stay themselves and wonder! What, is preservation nothing? What, is baffling and befooling the enemies of God's church nothing? In the Maryan days here at home, there was such sweet songs sung in the fire, such sweet notes answering them from prison, and such providences, that coals of burning fire still dropped here and there upon the heads of those that hated God; that it might, and doubtless did make those that did wisely consider of God's doings, to think God was yet near, with, and for, a despised and afflicted people.*

I conclude then, first with a word of counsel, and then with a word of caution.

First, Let us mend our pace in the way of reformation, that is the way to hasten the downfall of Antichrist, ministers need reforming, particular congregations need reforming, there are but few church-members but need reforming. This twenty years we have been degenerating, both as to principles, and as to practice; and have grown at last into an amazing likeness to the world, both as to religion and civil demeanour: Yea, I may say, so remiss have churches been in instructing those that they have *received* into fellowship with them; and so careless have the *received* been, of considering the grounds of their coming into churches, that most members, in some places, seem now to be at a loss; yea, and those churches stand with their fingers in their mouths, and are as if they would not, durst not, or could not help it.

My *Second* is, A word of caution.

1. Take heed of over-looking, or of shutting your eyes upon your own guilt: 'He that covereth his sins, shall not prosper.' It is incident to some men, when they find repentance is far from them, to shut their eyes upon their own guilt, and to please themselves with such notions of deliverance from present troubles, as will stand with that course of sin which is got into their families, per-

* When seven members of the first dissenting church in London were burned, a proclamation was made that no one should pray for them, speak to them, nor once say, 'God help them.' But the church pressed through the officers,—embraced and prayed for and with the martyrs; and all the people with one consent said, Amen; to the astonishment of the officers. And so these godly martyrs, praying and praising God, sweetly ended their lives in the flames at Smithfield.— *Clarke's Martyrology,* p. 500 and 516.—Ed.

sons, and professions, and with a state of impenitence: But I advise you to take heed of this.

2. Take heed in laying the cause of your troubles in the badness of the temper of governors. I speak not now with reflection upon any, excepting those concerned in this caution: God is the chief, and has the hearts of all, even of the worst of men, in his hand. *Good tempered* men have sometimes brought trouble; and *bad tempered* men have sometimes brought enlargement to the churches of God: Saul brought enlargement, 1 Sa. xiv. 28. David brought trouble: 2 Sa. xii. 10. Ahab brought enlargement, 1 Ki. xxi. 29. Jehoshaphat and Hezekiah did both sometimes bring trouble: 2 Ch. xix. 2. and xv. 35. and xxxii. 25. Therefore, the good or bad tempers of men sway nothing with God in this matter; they are the sins or repentances of his people, that make the church either happy or miserable upon earth.

Take heed, I say therefore, of laying of the trouble of the church of God at the doors of governors; especially at the doors of kings, who seldom trouble churches of their own inclinations; (I say, *seldom;* for some have done so, as Pharaoh:) But I say, lay not the cause of your trouble there; for oftentimes they *see* with other men's eyes, *hear* with other men's ears, and *act* and *do* by the judgments of others: (Thus did Saul, when he killed the priests of the Lord; 1 Sa. xxii. 18. and thus did Darius, when he cast Daniel into the lions' den: Da. vi. 7.) But rather labour to see the true cause of trouble, which is sin; and to attain to a fitness to be delivered out thence, and that is by repentance, and amendment of life. If any object, That God oft-times delivers his of mere grace: I answer, That's no thanks to them; besides, we must mind our duty. Further, When God comes to save his people, he can cut off such objectors, if they be impenitent, as the sinners of his people; and can save his church, without letting of them be sharers in that salvation: So he served many in the wilderness; and 'tis to be feared, so he will serve many at the downfall of Antichrist.

I shall say no more, but to testify my loyalty to my king, my love to my brethren, and service for my country, has been the cause of this my present scribble. Farewell.

Thine in the Lord, J. BUNYAN.

OF ANTICHRIST.

ANTICHRIST is the adversary of Christ; an adversary *really,* a friend *pretendedly:* So then, Antichrist is one that is *against* Christ; one that is *for* Christ, and one that is *contrary* to him: (And this is that mystery of iniquity. 2 Th. ii. 7.) Against him in *deed;* for him in *word,* and contrary to him in *practice.* Antichrist is so *proud* as to go before Christ; so *humble* as to pretend to come after him, and so *audacious* as to say that himself is *he.* Antichrist will cry *up* Christ ; Antichrist will cry *down* Christ: Antichrist will proclaim that himself is one above Christ. Antichrist is the *man of sin,* the *son of perdition;* a beast, [that] hath two horns like a lamb, but speaks as a dragon. Re. xiii. 11.

Christ is the Son of God ; Antichrist is the son of Hell.

Christ is holy, meek, and forbearing : Antichrist is wicked, outrageous, and exacting.

Christ seeketh the good of the soul: Antichrist seeks his own avarice and revenge.

Christ is content to rule by his word : Antichrist saith, The word is not sufficient.

Christ preferreth his Father's will above heaven and earth : Antichrist preferreth himself and his traditions above all that is written, or that is called God, or worshipped.

Christ has given us such laws and rules as are helpful and healthful to the soul: Antichrist seeketh to abuse those rules to our hurt and destruction.

Antichrist may be considered either more particularly, or more generally. 1. More particularly: And so there are many Antichrists. 1 Jn. ii. 18. 2. More generally: And so the *many* maketh but *one* great Antichrist, one man of sin, one enemy, one great whore, one son of perdition. 2 Th. ii. 3. Re. xix. 2.

Again, Antichrist must be distinguished, with respect to his more *internal* and *external* parts ; and so there is the *spirit, soul,* or *life* ; 1 Jn. iv. 3. and also the *body* and *flesh* of Antichrist. 2 Th. ii. 7. The spirit, or soul, or life of Antichrist, is *that* spirit of error, *that* wicked, *that* mystery of iniquity, that under colour and pretence of verity, draweth men from truth to falsehood. The *body* or flesh of Antichrist, is that heap of men, that assembly of the wicked, that synagogue of Satan that is acted and governed by that spirit. But God will destroy both soul and body ; He 'shall consume the glory of his forest, and of his fruitful field, both soul and body : (or from the soul, even to the flesh) and they shall be (both soul and body) as when a standard-bearer fainteth.' Is. x. 18.

A PARTICULAR DESCRIPTION OF ANTICHRIST.

Antichrist therefore is a mystical man, so made, or begotten of the devil, and sent into the world, himself being the chief and highest of him. Three things therefore go to the making up of Antichrist, the head, body, and soul. The devil *he* is the head ; the synagogue of Satan, *that* is the body ; that wicked spirit of iniquity, *that* is the soul of Antichrist. Christ then is the head of his church ; the devil is the head of Antichrist ; the elect are the body of Christ ; the reprobate professors are the body of Antichrist ; the Holy Ghost is the spirit of life that act[uat]eth Christ's body ; that wicked spirit of iniquity, is that which act[uat]eth the body of Antichrist. Thus therefore are the two great mighties set forth before us, who are the heads of those two bodies ; and thus are these two bodies set before us, who are to be act[uat]ed by these two spirits.

The reason why Christ came into the world, was, That he might destroy all the works of the head of Antichrist, and they which he endeavoureth to complete by his wicked spirit working in his body. 1 Jn. iii. 8. And the reason why Antichrist came into the world, was, That the church, which is the body of Christ, might be tried, and made white by suffering under his tyranny, and by bearing witness against his falsehoods. For, for the trial of the faithful, and for the punishment of the world, Antichrist was admitted to come : But when he came, he first appeared there where one would have thought there had been no place nor corner for his reception.

WHERE ANTICHRIST FIRST APPEARED.

The devil then, made use of the church of God to midwife this monster into the world, as the Apostle plainly shews, there he first sat, *shewing himself.* 2 Th. ii. 4. Here therefore was his first appearance, even in the church of God: Not that the church of God did willingly admit him there to sit *as such* ; he had *covered* his cloven-foot ; he had *plumbs* in his dragon's mouth, and so came in by flatteries ; promising to do for Christ and his church, that which he never meant to perform. For he shewed himself that he was God, and in appearance, set his heart to do as the heart of God. Eze. xxviii 2—6. And who could have found in their hearts to shut the door upon such an one ? True, he came, when he came thither, out of the bottomless-pit ; but there came such a smoke out thence with him, and that smoke so darkened the light of the sun, of the moon, of the stars, and of the day, that had they [the church] been upon their watch, as they were not, they could not have perceived him from another man. Besides, there came with him so many *locusts* to usher him into the house of God, Re. ix. 2, 3. and they so suited the flesh and reason of the godly of that day, that with good words and fair speeches, by their crafty and cunning sleights, whereby they lay in wait to deceive, they quite got him in, and set him up, and made him a *great one,* even the chief, before they were aware. Further, He quickly got him a *beast* to ride on, far, for sumptuous glory, beyond (though as to nature, as assish a creature as) that on which Balaam was wont to ride : And by this exaltation he became not only more stately, but the *horns* of the beast would push for him. Re. xvii. 3—6.

OF ANTICHRIST, AND HIS RUIN.

Again, This man of sin, when he came into the world, had the art of metamorphosing, and could change himself, both in form and shape, into the likeness of a beast, a man, or woman; and the kings of the earth, with the inhabitants of the world, began then to love such women dearly; wherefore they went to her into the bed of love, and defiled themselves with the filthiness of her fornications, gave her their troth, and became her husbands, and beloved sons; took up helmet and shield, and stood to defend her; yea, though Christ himself, and some of the chief of his followers, cried out of *her* shame, and of the evil of *their* doings; yet would she be audacious.

Also this woman had now arrayed herself in *flesh-taking* ornaments, of the colour of purple and scarlet, and was decked with gold, and precious stones, and pearls, after the manner or attire of harlots. Thus came she to them, and lay in their bosoms, and gave them out of her golden cup of the wine of her fornication; of the which they bibbed till they were drunken; and then, in requital, they also gave her of such liquors as they could, to wit, to drink of the blood of saints, and of martyrs of Jesus, till she, like these beasts, was drunken also.

Now when they were drunken, they did as drunkards do, revel, roar, and belch out their own shame, in the sight of them that were *sober:* Wherefore *they* cried out upon such doings, and chose rather to die, than to live with such company. And so 'tis still with them where she yet sitteth, and so will be till she shall fall into the hands of the strong Lord, who will judge her according to her ways. And that she must do, as is implied by this, That her fornications are in a cup; she has therefore but her cup to be drank out; wherefore when it is empty, then, whether she will or no, the Lord God will call her to such a reckoning, that all the clothes on her back, with what pearls and jewels she has, shall not be able to pay the shot.

OF THE RUIN OF ANTICHRIST.

Antichrist, as was said, had a time to come into the world, and so must have a time to go out again: For although he saith that he is a God, yet must he be subject to the will of God, and must go as well as come according to that will. Nor can all the fallen angels, with all the members and limbs of Antichrist, cause that this their brat should abide so much as one day longer than our God's prefixed time. And this the head of Antichrist understandeth very well: Wherefore the Holy Ghost saith, 'Woe to the inhabiters of the earth, and of the sea! for the devil is come down unto you, having great wrath, because he knoweth that he hath but a short time.' Re. xii. 12.

Besides, the text says plainly, The Lord shall destroy him, 2 Th. ii. 8. and that he goeth into perdition: Re. xvii. 11. and xix. 26. Also the church of God believes it, and the limbs of Antichrist fear it.

Now when, or as his time shall come to be destroyed, so he shall be made a hand of; and that with such instruments and weapons of God's indignation, as best shall be suited to his several parts.

Such weapons as are best for the destroying of his *soul*, shall be used for the destroying of it; and such weapons as are best for the destroying of his *body*, shall be made use of for the destroying of it.

THE SOUL OF IT DESTROYED, AND HOW.

And therefore, as to his *soul*, or that spirit of error that governs him in all his works of mischief; this must be consumed by the spirit of Christ's mouth, and be destroyed by the brightness of his coming.

This we have in the words of Paul: 'For (saith he) the mystery of iniquity (the spirit of Antichrist) doth already work: only he who now letteth, *will let*, until he be taken out of the way. And then shall that wicked be revealed, whom the Lord shall consume with the spirit of his mouth, and shall destroy with the brightness of his coming.' 2 Th. ii. 7, 8. The Apostle here treateth of Antichrist, with reference to his more subtil and spiritual part, since that indeed is the chiefest of Antichrist: Wherefore he calls it that *wicked*; not, that wicked *one*, as referring to the whole; but that *wicked*, as referring to the *mystery* or *spirit of iniquity*, the heart and soul of Antichrist; and tells us, that the Lord shall ' consume him with the spirit of his mouth, and shall destroy him with the brightness of his coming.'

Now, by the *spirit of his mouth*, I understand his *holy word*, which is called ' The word and breath of his lips :' Is. xi. 4. And also, ' The sword of his mouth.' Re. ii. 16. By 'the brightness of his coming,' I also understand, not *only* his presence, but an *increase* of light by his presence; not only to help Christians to begin to bear witness against some parts and pieces of the errors of Antichrist, but until the *whole* is rooted out of the world. By this, I say, must the soul, spirit, or life of Antichrist be taken away. But how shall Christ by this rod, sword, or spirit of his mouth, consume this wicked, this *mystery of iniquity*? Not by himself immediately, but by his *spirit* and *word* in his church; the which he will use, and so manage in this work, that they shall not rest till he by them has brought this beast to his grave. This beast is compared to the wild boar, and the beast that comes out of the wood to devour the church of God, (as we read in the book of Psalms: lxxx. 13.)

But Christ, with the dogs that eat the crumbs of his table, will so hunt and scour him about, that albeit he may let out some of their bowels with the tushes of his chaps, yet they will not let him alone till they have his life: For the church shall single him out from *all* beasts, and so follow him with cries, and pinch him with their voices, that he alone shall perish by their means.* Thus shall Christ consume and wear him out by the spirit of his mouth, and destroy him with the brightness of his coming.

Hence you find again, That this *wicked*, is to melt and consume away as grease: For the Lord Jesus shall consume him, and cause him to melt away; not all at once, but *now* this part, and *then* that; now his *soul*, and after that his *body*, even until soul and body are both destroyed.

And that you may be convinced of the truth of this thing, do but look back and compare Antichrist four or five hundred years ago, with Antichrist as he is now, and you shall see what work the Lord Jesus has begun to make with him, even with the spirit and soul, and life of Antichrist; both in confounding and blasting of it by this spirit of his mouth, as also by forcing of it to dishonourable retreats, and by making of it give up to him, as the conqueror, not only some of his superstitious and diabolical rites and ceremonies, to be destroyed, but many a goodly truth, which this vile one had taken from his church, to be renewed to them: Nay, further, he hath also already began to take from him both kingdoms and countries, though as to some not so absolutely as he shall do by and by. And in the meantime, this is the plague wherewith the Lord shall plague or smite the people that have fought against Jerusalem: 'Their flesh shall consume away while they stand upon their feet, and their eyes shall consume away in their holes, and their tongue shall consume away in their mouth.' Zec. xiv. 12. And how has this long ago been fulfilled here in England! as also in Scotland, Holland, Germany, France, Sweden, Denmark, Hungary, and other places! Is. xvii. 4—6. Nor hath this spirit of Antichrist, with all his art and artificers, been able to reduce to Antichrist again, those people, nations, or parts of nations, that by the spirit of Christ's mouth, and 'the brightness of his coming,' have been made to forsake him, and

to turn from him to Christ: The reason is, for that the Lord has not retreated, but is still going on in the spirit of his mouth, and his brightness, to make that conquest over him that is determined, in the way that is determined: Of which more shall be spoken afterward; for the path-way that he goeth, is as the shining light, which shines more and more unto noon. True, the fogs of Antichrist, and the smoke that came with him out of the bottomless-pit, has darkened and eclipsed the glorious light of the gospel: But you know, in eclipses, when they are on the recovering hand, all the creatures upon the face of the earth cannot put a stop to that course, until the sun or the moon have recovered their glory. And thus it shall be now, the Lord is returned to visit the earth, and his people with his primitive lustre; he will not go back, nor slack his hand, until he has recovered what Antichrist has darkened of his. 'The anger of the Lord shall not return, until he have executed, and till he have performed the thoughts of his heart: in the latter days ye shall consider it perfectly.' Je. xxiii. 20. Therefore he saith again, 'The light of the moon shall be as the light of the sun (was in her eclipse;) and the light of the sun shall be sevenfold, as the light of seven days, in the day that the Lord bindeth up the breach of his people, and healeth the stroke of their wound, ' &c. as the verse before has it: 'In the day when the towers fall.'

For (as was said before) as to the recovery of the light of the gospel from under Antichristian mists, and fogs of darkness; Christ will do that, not by might nor power, but by the spirit of his mouth, and the brightness of his coming: Wherefore the *soul* of Antichrist, or that spirit of wickedness by which this gospel-light hath been diminished, must be consumed and destroyed by that spirit also. Nor can any other way of conquest over that be thorough, and lasting; because that spirit can by no other means be slain. The *body* of Antichrist may be destroyed by other instruments, but spirits cannot be killed but by spirits. The temporal sword then may kill the body, but after that it hath no more that it can do, wherefore, the other must be dealt with by another kind of weapon: And *here* is one sufficient, the spirit against the spirit; the spirit and face of Christ, against the spirit, that wicked, of Antichrist. And by this spirit of Christ's mouth, all the spirit that is in all the *trinkets* and *wash* of Antichrist shall also be destroyed; so that those trinkets, those rites, ceremonies, and ordinances of this man of sin, shall be left as carrion upon the face of the earth, and shall stink in the noses of men, as doth the corrupted blood of a dead man.

* Christian, read in these words *your* duty. Bunyan felt the tusks of the wild boar, even to the peril of his life. He bore with resignation all his sufferings, and was blest. Pity those whose souls are under the yoke. Antichrist, if cruel to the body, is more dangerous to the souls of men. Your prayers and exertions should be redoubled until it is delivered up to the just judgment of the Almighty. Come out, O Christian, and be separate from every system which is stained with the blood and defiled with the soul-harrowing groans of the saints of God.—Ed.

THE ORDINANCES OF ANTICHRIST.

Now therefore will the beauty of Antichrist fade like a flower, and fall as doth a leaf when the sap of the tree has left it; or as the beauty departeth from the body, when the soul, or life, or spirit is gone forth. And as the body cannot be but unpleasant and unsavoury when under such a state; so the body of Antichrist will be to beholders, when the Lord has slain the spirit thereof. It is the spirit of Antichrist that puts life into the body; and that puts lustre into the ordinances of Antichrist, as the light of the sun, and of the moon, and of the stars, do put lustre upon the things of this visible world: Wherefore, when this spirit, and soul, and life of Antichrist is slain, then it will be with *him* as 'twould be with the *world*, had it no light of the sun, of the moon, or of the stars.

And hence, as the loss of our natural life is compared to the loss of *these* lights; Ec. xii. 2. so the loss of the life, soul and spirit of Antichrist is compared to these things also. For, the soul of Antichrist is compared to a heaven; and her ordinances and rites, to the ordinances of heaven: Wherefore, when the Lord comes to fight against her with the spirit of his mouth, he saith, ' The stars of heaven [shall be darkened], and the constellations thereof shall not give their light;' Is. xiii. 10. because he will slay that spirit of Antichrist that is in them. Is. xxxiv. Re. vi. 13, 14.

Take things therefore more distinctly, thus: The Antichristians spirit, is the heaven of Antichristians; their sun, moon and stars, are their superstitious ordinances; their earth is the body or flesh of Antichrist, otherwise called the church and synagogue of Satan. Now as the earth cannot live, and be desirable, without the influences of the spirit of the heavens; so neither can Antichrist live, when the Lord shall darken the light of his heaven, and shall slay the spirit thereof. Hence you read, as I touched before, that when his heaven shall be rolled together as a scroll, ' all the host thereof,' unto which I compare the ordinances of Antichrist, ' shall fall down, as the leaf falleth off from the vine, and as a falling *fig* from the fig-tree.' Is. xxxiv. 4. But how, or why doth the leaf, or the fig fall from the tree? Why, because the spirit, or sap of the tree, is gone from them.

Therefore, the first and chief proceeding of the Lord with the man of sin, is *to slay his soul*, that his *body* may also be consumed: And when the spirit of Antichrist shall be made to leave both the body and ordinances of Antichrist, 'twill be easy to deal both with the one and the other. And first, for the ordinances of Antichrist; because the spirit of error is in them, as well as in the body itself. When that spirit, as I said, has left them,

they will of themselves even moulder away, and not be: As we have seen by experience here in England, as others also have seen in other countries. For as concerning his masses, prayers for the dead, images, pilgrimages, monkish vows, sinful fasts, and the beastly single life of their priests, though when the spirit of Antichrist was in them, they did bear some sway in the world; yet now, of what esteem are they? or who has reverence for them? They are now blown together under hedges, as the dry leaves, for the mice and frogs to harbour in: yea, the locusts too, camp in the hedges among the dry leaves, in the cold day, and ' when the sun ariseth they flee away:' Na. iii. 15—17. When 'tis a cold day for them in a nation, then they lurk in the hedges, though their ordinances lie there, as leaves that are dry, and fallen down from the tree; but when the sun ariseth, and waxeth warm, they abide not, but betake them to their wings, and fly away. But one would think that fallen leaves should have no great nourishment in them: True, if you have respect to men, but with vermin any thing will do: We speak then of them with reference to *men*, not with respect to the very members of Antichrist: And I say, as to *them*, when the spirit of Antichrist is gone out of these ordinances, they will be with them as dry leaves that no body seeketh after. The ordinances therefore of Antichrist are not able to bear up themselves in the world, as the ordinances of the Lord Jesus are, for even the ordinances of Christ, where the spirit of Christ is not, are yet in some esteem with men: But THESE, when the spirit of delusion has left them, are abhorred, both skin and bones: For in themselves they are without any sense, or rationality; Eze. xx. 25, 26. yea, they look as parts of things which are used to conjure up devils with: These were prefigured by the ordinances that were NOT good, and by the judgments whereby one *should not live*. For what is there, or can there be of the least dram of truth or profit in the things that are without the word, that being the only stamp by which one is distinguished from the other? I say, What is there in any of them, to the man whose eyes are open, but delusion and deceit! Wherefore, as has been expressed already, when the Lord Christ, by the spirit of his mouth, &c. shall drive this mystery of iniquity from them, and strip them of that spirit of delusion that now by its craft puts bewitching excellency upon them, they will of themselves become such stinking rivers, ponds and pools, that flesh and blood will loathe to drink of them; yea, as it was with the ponds and pools of Egypt, they will be fit for nought but to breed and hatch up frogs in.

Wherefore these ordinances shall be rejected, not one of them shall find favour with men on earth; when the Lord, ' by the spirit of his mouth, and the brightness of his coming,' shall have separated their spirit from them.

Now, by *ordinances* of Antichrist, I do not intend things that *only* respect matters of worship in Antichrist's kingdom, but those *civil laws* that impose and enforce *them* also; yea, that enforce THAT worship with pains and penalties, as in the Spanish inquisition: For these must, as the other, be overthrown by Christ, by the spirit of his mouth, and the brightness of his coming: For these laws, as the other, took their being, and have their soul and life by the spirit of Antichrist; yea, as long as there is life in them, 'tis because the spirit of that man of sin yet remaineth in them. Wherefore, these are also great ordinances, though of another nature than those mentioned before: *Great*, I say, are they; forasmuch as neither the church of Antichrist, nor his instruments of worship, can either live or stand without them. Wherefore, it was admitted to the image of the beast, not only to *speak*, but to *cause*. To speak out his laws of worship, 'and cause that as many as would not worship the image of the beast, should be killed.' Re. xiii. 15. And mark, This is because *that* the life that was communicated to the image of the beast, was by him also communicated to his word and authority. Wherefore, these laws must not be separated from those in which the spirit of Antichrist is; yea, they are the very pillars and sinews by which Antichristianism remains: And were these dis-spirited, the whole building would quickly become a ruinous heap.

What could the king of Babylon's golden image have done, had it not been for the burning fiery furnace that stood within view of the worshippers? Da. iii. Yea, what could that horrible command, to pray, for thirty days, to neither God nor man, but to the king, have done, had it not been for the dark den, and the roaring lions there in readiness to devour those that disobeyed it? Da. vi. As therefore the burning fiery furnace, and the den of lions, were the support of the horrible religion of the Babylonians of old; so popish edicts are the support of the religion of Antichrist now; and as long as there is spirit, that is, *authority*, in them, they are like to those now mentioned; the spirit of such laws is that that makes them dreadful: For as the furnace would have been next to nothing, if void of fire; and the den as little frightful, if destitute of lions; so these laws will be as insignificant, when Christ has slain that spirit that is in them; that spirit that causes that as many as will not worship the image of the beast, should be killed.

Nor can any sword reach *that* life of Antichrist that is in these, but the sword of Christ's mouth: Therefore, as all the religious rites and ceremonies of Antichrist are overthrown by his spirit working in *his*, as Christians; so those Antichristian laws will have their soul and their life taken from them also by this spirit of his mouth working in some of his, as magistrates, and no otherwise; for before kings and princes, &c. come to be enlightened about the evils that are in *such* edicts, by the spirit of the living God, they will let this image of the beast both *speak* and *cause*, &c. But when they shall *see*, they will say, let it be decreed that this prop of Antichrist be taken down. It was decreed by Darius, that they that prayed, for thirty days, to any God but him, should be cast into the den of lions: Da. vi. 9. but this was *before he saw*; but when he came to see, then he decreed again; a decree that quite took away the power of that which he had decreed before. Da. vi. 26.

Nor are we without instances of this kind nearer home: who is now afraid of the act for burning of those that papists call heretics, since by the king and parliament, as by the finger of God, the life and soul is taken out of it. I bring this to shew you, that as there is life in wicked Antichristian penal laws, as well as in those that are superstitiously religious; so the life of these, of all these, must be destroyed by the same spirit working in those that are Christ's, though in a diverse way.

Nor will the life of these sinews, as I have called them, be taken away; but as God shall enlighten men to see the abominable filthiness of that which is Antichristian worship: as would easily be made appear, if some that dwell in those countries where the beast and his image have been worshipped, would but take the pains to inquire into antiquity about it. As the noble king, king Henry VIII. did cast down the Antichristian worship; so he cast down the laws that held it up: so also did the good king Edward his son. The brave queen, queen Elizabeth also, the sister to king Edward, hath left of things of this nature, to her lasting fame behind her. And if one such law of Antichrist hath escaped the hand of one, another hath taken it, and done that execution on it that their zeal and piety prompted them to.

There is yet another thing that the spirit of Antichrist is immediately concerned in; and that is, the Antichristian names of the men that worship the beast: the names, I mean, that Antichrist hath baptized them into: for those names are breathed upon them by the very spirit of Antichrist; and are such as are absolutely names of blasphemy, or such as do closely border thereupon; some such as Elihu durst not for his life give unto men, only he calls them 'flattering titles.' Job xxxii. 21, 22. Now therefore, of the danger (though not of the names themselves) you read sufficiently in the scripture; and perhaps the Holy Ghost has contented himself with giving of items that are general, that men might, as to them, be the more cautious of what names they give one to another: Re. xvii. 5. but this is clear, they are worn by men of spiritual employ: but since they are but mentioned, and are not distinctly nominated, how should we know which are they, and which not? Verily, by searching the word of God, and by seeing by that what names we are allowed to give unto men, with reference to their offices, dignities, and places: for God has a quarrel with the *names*, as well as with the *persons* that wear them; and when his Son shall down with Antichrist, he will slay seven thousand names of men, as well as the persons of the worshippers of the beast. Re. xi. 13. Margin.

But there are things, as well as men; Job xxii. 28. and these also have been baptized into those names by the very spirit of Antichrist, and must be destroyed by Christ, the spirit of his mouth, and the brightness of his coming: 'The idols he shall utterly abolish;' Is. ii. 18. and there are *men* that are idols as well as *things:* Zec. xi. 17. wherefore, let men have a care, as to shun the worship of idols, so that they bare not the name, or stand in the place of one: and the reason of this caution is, because *name* and *thing* are both abominable unto God.

To give you the number of these names that the spirit of Antichrist has baptized men into, (besides the *things* that do also wear such blasphemies upon them,) would be a task too great for me, and too wearisome for you. It shall satisfy then, that I give you notice that there are such *things* and *men* and *names ;* and that I put you upon search to find out what they be. But whatsoever of the spirit, or soul, or life of Antichrist is in these names, men, or things, must be consumed by Christ, by the spirit of his mouth, and the brightness of his coming.*

Another thing that I would touch upon is this; to wit, The lying legends, and false miracles that Antichrist cries up: *These*, by the means of which such as dwell upon the earth are deceived, and made to adore and worship the beast: these have their life and soul (as had those mentioned before) from the spirit of wickedness; and must be destroyed as they, namely, by Christ, the spirit of his mouth, and the brightness of his coming: for these are not of the body of Antichrist, but rather such implements, or whatever you will call them, by which the spirit and soul of Antichrist is conveyed into, and kept also alive in the body of Antichrist, which is the church and synagogue of Sa-

tan; you may call them organs and means by which that *wicked* worketh in the mysteries of iniquity, for the begetting of, and maintaining a lying and false belief of the religion of the beast: nor can it be thought, but that, as the antichristian statists† of Antichrist, mentioned before, do put a dread and fear upon men that are worshippers of the beast, and his image, to the holding of them still to his service; so these legends and miracles do, on the other hand, abridge and bind their consciences to that worship; but all because of that spirit of Antichrist that is in them.‡

So then, here is the spirit of Antichrist diffusing itself into all the things pertaining to the kingdom of the beast; for it dwells in the body of Antichrist; it dwells in the matters and things of worship of Antichrist; it dwells in the titles and names that are antichristian; and it dwells in the laws, legends and miracles of Antichrist. And as it is the spirit of Antichrist, so it must be destroyed; not by sword, nor by bow, but by Christ, as fighting against it with the spirit of his mouth, and as conquering of it by the brightness of his coming.

THE BODY OF ANTICHRIST DESTROYED, AND HOW.

We come now to discourse of the *body* or flesh of Antichrist, and of the destruction of *that ;* for that must be destroyed also. Now the body of Antichrist, is that church or synagogue in which the spirit of Antichrist dwells, or unto which the spirit of Antichrist is become a soul and life.

And this is to be destroyed, either as it is a body mystical, or under the more gross consideration.

First, As it is a body mystical, and so it is to be destroyed absolutely.

Secondly, As it is to be considered more grossly, and so it is to be destroyed conditionally. That is, if repentance doth not save the men that have gone to the making up of this body, and to the rejoicing in it.

As she is a body mystical, so she is to be destroyed the same way that the things of Antichrist, of which we discoursed before, were to be destroyed; to wit, by Christ, the spirit of his mouth, and the brightness of his coming.

This then is the sum, as to this: *That the church of Antichrist, as a church, shall be destroyed by the word and spirit of Christ.* Nor can anything in

---

* No man of the most refined education could have manifested greater delicacy than Bunyan has in treating this subject, leaving his reader to imagine whether the **names** 'Reverend,' 'Very Reverend,' 'Right Reverend,' Venerable Father in God, or His Holiness, are all or any of them applicable as titles given by Antichrist: so of *things*, whether 'The body of Christ,' in a wafer, or 'Church,' a building of stone brick, or timber, are or are not Antichristian.—Ed.

† Antichristian statists of Antichrist. Those who weigh things to place them in their relative order in the kingdom of Antichrist, as the decree followed by the lion's den, &c.

‡ The homilies read in the Church of England prior to the Reformation, called 'The Festival,' contains the pith of these lying legends and pretended miracles. Omitting the obscene parts, it ought to be republished, to exhibit the absurdities of Popery and of the then Established religion.—Ed.

heaven prevent it, because the strong God has decreed it: 'And a mighty angel took up a stone, like a great mill-stone, and cast *it* into the sea, saying, Thus with violence shall that great city Babylon be thrown down, and shall be found no more at all.' Re. xviii.21. This city, Babylon, is here sometimes considered in the *whole*, and sometimes as to the *parts* of it; but always, whether in whole, or in part, as *some*, or else as the *whole* of the antichristian church; and as such, it must not be destroyed, but by the means aforesaid. By which means her witchcrafts, spiritual whoredoms, spiritual murders, thefts, and blasphemies, shall be so detected and made manifest, so laid open, and so discovered, that the nations shall abhor her, flee from her, and buy her merchandise no more. Re. xviii. 11. Hence her tempting things rot, and moulder away; for these will not keep, they are things not lasting, but that perish in the using: what then will they do when they are laid by? Therefore it follows, 'All things which were (thy) dainty and goodly (ones) are departed from thee, and thou shalt find them no more at all.' Re. xviii. 14. Now, if when she had things to trade with, her dealers left her; how shall she think of a trade, when she has nothing to traffic with? Her things are slain, and stink already, by the weapons that are made mention of before; what then will her carcase do? It follows then, that as to her church-state, she must of necessity tumble: wherefore, from Rev. xviii. 22 to 24, you have the manner of her total ruin as a church, and something of the cause thereof.

But as she must, with reference to her body, be considered mystically as a church; so also she must be considered as a body of men, (this is that which I called more *grossly*,) and as such, against whom the wrath of God will burn, and against whom, if repentance prevent not, he will have indignation for ever. These, I say are them; to wit, as they are the body of the people, that have been seduced by this spirit of Antichrist, that have been made use of to do all the mischiefs that have been done both to true religion, and to the professors of it, for this many hundred years, wherefore these must not escape. Wherefore you find, that after Antichrist, as to the spirit and mystery of Antichrist, is slain, that the body of Antichrist, or the heap of people that became her vassals, come next to be dealt withal.

Therefore, the angel that standeth in the sun, makes a proclamation to all the fowls that fly in the midst of heaven, to gather themselves, and to come unto the supper of the great God; that they may eat the flesh of the several sorts of the men that have been the lovers, the countenancers, the upholders and defenders of her antichristian state, worship, and falsehoods: Re. xix. 17, 18. for abun-

dance of their hearts shall be hardened, and made yet more obdurate, that they may be destroyed for the wickedness that they have done.

Wherefore, you find (as did the enemies of the church of old,) that they might revenge themselves for the loss of their idol, or antichristian state, begin a new war with the king, whose name is the Lord of hosts: 'And I saw the beast, and the kings of the earth, and their armies, gathered together to make war against him that sat on the horse, and against his army.' Re. xix. 19.

Their implacable malice remained when their church-state was gone; wherefore they will now at last make another attempt upon the men that had been the instruments in Christ's hand to torment them that dwelt on the earth; of which more hereafter.

Now therefore is the last stroke of the batter,* with reference to the destroying the body of Antichrist; only the head of this monster remains, and that is SATAN himself: wherefore, the next news that we hear, is, that he is taken also: 'And I saw an angel come down from heaven, having the key of the bottomless pit and a great chain in his hand. And he laid hold on the Dragon, that old serpent, which is the devil, and Satan, and bound him a thousand years, and cast him into the bottomless pit, and shut him up, and set a seal upon him, that he should deceive the nations no more, till the thousand years should be fulfilled,' &c. Re. xx. 1–3.

BRAVE DAYS WHEN ANTICHRIST IS DEAD.

Now therefore there will be nothing of Antichrist to be seen throughout the nations, but ruinous heaps, and desolate places. It is said of the army of the man of sin, when he came into the land of God's people, though it was before him 'as the garden of Eden,' yet behind him 'twould be as 'a desolate wilderness;' Joel ii. 3. such ruins would he make of the flock of God, and of all their ordinances, and heavenly dainties. But when the days that I have spoken of, shall come, it will be to him a time of retaliation: for it shall then be done unto Antichrist, as he hath done to the church of God: As he hath made women childless, so shall he be made childless; as he has made Zion sit upon the ground, so now must this wicked one come down and sit in the dust; yea, as he has made many churches desolations, so now shall he be also made a desolation. Wherefore, whoso will find his body, they must look for it in the side of the pit's mouth; and whoso will find his friends and companions, they must look for them there

---

* 'The last stroke of the batter,' probably alludes to an engine of war used by the ancients, called a battering-ram. —ED.

likewise. 'They have set her a bed in the midst of the slain with all her multitude : her graves *are* round about him : all of them uncircumcised, slain by the sword : though their terror was caused in the land of the living, yet have they borne their shame with them that go down to the pit, he is put in the midst of *them that be* slain. There *is* Meshech, Tubal, and all her multitude : - - - There is Edom, her king, and all her princes, &c. - - There be the princes of the north, all of them, - - which - - with their - - might ' are laid with them that are ' slain by the sword, and bare their shame with them that go down to the pit.' Eze. xxxii. 25—30. For 'as Babylon *hath caused* the slain of Israel to fall, so at Babylon shall fall the slain of all the earth.' Je. li. 49. The margin reads it thus : Both Babylon is to fall, O ye slain of Israel ! And with Babylon the slain of all the earth. Now then she is gone down, when all these things shall be fulfilled ; and what remains now, but to talk of her, as folk use to do of them that are dead : for the day will come that the church of God shall have no more of Antichrist, Babylon, or the mother of harlots, than only the remembrance of her ; to wit, that there was such an enemy of God in the world ; that there was such a superstitious, idolatrous, bloody people in the world. Wherefore the people that shall be born, that shall live to serve God in these happy days, they shall see Antichrist only in its ruins ; they shall, like the sparrows, the little robins, and the wren, sit and sing, and chirrup one to another, while their eyes behold this dead hawk. ' Here (shall they say) did once the lion dwell; and there was once a dragon inhabited : here did they live that were the murderers of the saints ; and there another, that did use to set his throat against the heavens ; but now in the places where these ravenous creatures lay, grows grass, with reeds and rushes, Is. xxxv. 7. (or else, now their habitation is cursed, nettles grow, and so do thorns and brambles, where their palaces were wont to be.) And as no good was with them while they lived, so their name stinketh now they are dead : yea, as they wrought mischiefs, and lived like the wild beasts when they enjoyed their abundance ; so now the wild beasts of the desert, yea, they of the desert, shall meet with the wild beasts of the island : and the satyr shall cry to his fellows. Their houses shall be full of doleful creatures, even as devils and wicked spirits do haunt the desolate houses of the wicked, when they are dead.' Is. xxxiv. ' And Babylon, the glory of kingdoms, the beauty of the Chaldees excellency, shall be as when God overthrew Sodom and Gomorrah. It shall never be inhabited, neither shall it be dwelt in from generation to generation : neither shall the Arabian pitch tent there : neither shall the shepherds make their folds there.' Is. xiii. 19, 20.

A while after this, as was hinted before, the Christians will begin with detestation to ask what Antichrist was ? Where Antichrist dwelt ? Who were his members ? And, What he did in the world ? and it shall be answered by them that shall have skill to consider his features by the word, by way of taunt and scorn, ' *Is* this the man that made the earth to tremble, that did shake kingdoms ; *that* made the world as a wilderness, and destroyed the cities thereof ; *that* opened not the house of his prisoners ? All the kings of the nations, *even* all of them, lie in glory, every one in his own house. But thou art cast out of thy grave like an abominable branch ; *and* as the raiment of those that are slain, thrust through with a sword, that go down to the stones of the pit, as a carcass trodden under feet.' Is. xiv. 16—19.

There will be a strange alteration when Antichrist is dead, and that both in the church, and in the world. The church and the members of it then, shall wear the name of their God in their foreheads ; that is, they shall be bold in the profession of their king, and their God ; yea, it shall be their glory to be godly ; and carnal men shall praise them for it : the praise of the whole earth shall the church of God be in those days.

Then there shall no more be a Canaanite in the house of the Lord : no lion shall be there ; the unclean shall no more tread in the paths of God's people, but the ransomed of the Lord shall walk there.

Glory that has not been seen nor heard of by the people that used to walk in sackcloth, shall now be set in the land of the living. For as it was said of Christ, with reference to his day ; so it shall be said of saints, with reference to *this* day : many kings and righteous men have desired to see the things that will be seen then, and shall not see them : but without all doubt, the men that shall be born at this time, will consider that these glories, and liberties, and privileges of theirs, cost the people that walked in the king of Babylon's fiery furnace, or that suffered the trials, troubles and tyranny of the antichristian generation, more groans and hearty wishes, than they did them that shall enjoy them. Thus then it will go ; the afflicted prayed for them, and the possessors bless God for the enjoyment of them.

Oh ! now shall the church walk in the light of the Lord, and sit every man under his vine, and under his fig-tree, and none shall make him afraid !

' For the Lord will have mercy on Jacob, and will yet choose Israel, and set them in their own land : and the strangers shall be joined with them, and they shall cleave to the house of Jacob. And the people shall take them, and bring them to their place : and the house of Israel shall possess them in the land of the Lord for servants and handmaids : And they shall take them captives, whose captives they were ; and they shall rule over their oppressors. And it shall come to pass in the day that the Lord shall give thee rest from thy sorrow, and from thy fear, and from the hard bondage wherein thou wast made to serve, that thou shalt take up this proverb against the king of Babylon, and say, How hath the oppressor ceased ! the golden city, (or the exactress of gold) ceased ! The Lord hath broken the staff of the wicked, *and* the sceptre of the rulers. He who smote the people in wrath with a continual stroke, he that ruled the nations in anger, is persecuted, *and* none hindereth. The whole earth is at rest, *and* is quiet: they break forth into singing. Yea, the fir trees rejoice at thee, *and* the cedars of Lebanon, *saying*, Since thou art laid down, no seller is come up against us.' Is. xiv. 1—8.

Also the world will now be (as it were) another thing than it was in the days of Antichrist: now will kings, and princes, and nobles, and the whole commonalty be rid of that servitude and bondage which in former times (when they used to carry Bell and the dragon upon their shoulders) they were subjected to. They were then a burthen to them, but now they are at ease. 'Tis with the world, that are the slaves of Antichrist now, as it is with them that are slaves and captives to a whore: they must come when she calls, run when she bids, fight with and beat them that she saith miscall her, and spend what they can get by labour or fraud upon her, or she will be no more their whore, and they shall be no more her bosom ones. But now ! Now it will be otherwise ! Now they will have no whore to please ! Now they will have none to put them upon persecuting of the saints ! Now they shall not be made, as before, guilty of the blood of those against whom this gentleman shall take a pet ! Now the world shall return and discern between the righteous and the wicked ; yea, they shall cleave to, and countenance the people of God, being persuaded, as Laban was of Jacob, that the Lord will bless them for his people's sakes : for at this day, ' the remnant of Jacob shall be (among the Gentiles) in the midst of many people, as a dew from the Lord, as the showers upon the grass, that tarrieth not for man, nor waiteth for the sons of men.' Mi. v. 7.

Also in these days men shall come flocking into the house of God, both kings and princes, and nobles, and the common people, as the doves do to their windows : and for that cause it is spoken to the church, with reference to the latter days, saying, ' Enlarge the place of thy tent, and let them stretch forth the curtains of thy habitations : spare not, lengthen thy cords, and strengthen thy stakes ; for thou shalt break forth on the right hand, and on the left ; and thy seed shall inherit the Gentiles, and make the desolate cities to be inhabited.' Is. liv. 2, 3.

Now will be broken up those prophecies and promises that to this day lie as under lock and key, and that cannot be opened until they be fulfilled. Now will the Spirit of God be poured forth abundantly ; and our rivers shall be in high places, that is, shall break forth from the hearts of great ones ; yea, then shall our waters be made deep : ' And I will cause their rivers to run like oil, saith the Lord God.' Eze. xxxii. 14. Then shall the differences, the divisions and debates that are among the godly, cease : for men ' shall see eye to eye, when the Lord shall bring again Zion : ' Is. lii. 8. yea, the watchmen of God's people shall do so ; for it is for want of light *in them*, that the lambs have so butted one another.

Now the church of God shall read with great plainness the depths of providence, and the turnings and windings of all God's dark and intricate dispensations, through which she hath waded in the cloudy and dark day : now, I say, they shall see there was an harmony in them ; and that if one of them had been wanting, the work and way of her deliverance could not have been so full of the wisdom, and justice, and goodness of God : Wherefore now will that song be sung with clearer notes than ever : ' Great and marvellous *are* thy works, Lord God Almighty ; just and true *are* thy ways, thou king of Saints. Who shall not fear thee, O Lord, and glorify thy name ? for *thou* only *art* holy : for all nations shall come and worship before thee ; for thy judgments are made manifest.' Re. xv. 3, 4. And again, ' For true and righteous *are* his judgments : For he hath judged the great whore, which did corrupt the earth with her fornication, and hath avenged the blood of his servants at her hand.' Re. xix. 2.

OF THE MANNER OF THE RUIN OF ANTICHRIST.

What Antichrist is, I have told you ; and that as to his soul and body. I have also told you where, or in what things the spirit and life of Antichrist lieth, and how he shall reign for a time. I have moreover shewed you that he shall be destroyed, and by what, and that with reference both to his soul and body. Wherefore, waving other things, I shall here only present you with a few short hints concerning the *manner* of his downfall.

There is the *downfall*, the *time* of the downfall, and the *manner* of the downfall of Antichrist.

The manner of the downfall of Antichrist, may be considered, either with respect to the *suddenness, unexpectedness. terribleness*, or *strangeness* thereof. It may also be considered with respect to the way of God's procedure with her, as to the *gradualness* thereof. As to the suddenness thereof, 'tis said to be in an *hour*. It is also to be, *when* by her *unexpected*; for then she saith, 'I sit a queen.' Re. xviii. 7, 8. For the *terribleness* of it, The nations shall shake at the sound of her fall. Eze xxxi. 16, 17. And for the strangeness thereof, it shall be to the wonder of the world, Is. xiv. 12. it will be as when God overthrew Sodom.

But I shall not enlarge upon this method in my discourse, but shall shew you the *manner* of the ruin of Antichrist, with respect to the *gradualness* thereof. Eze. xvi. 36—43; Re. xviii. 8; Is. xlvii. 9.

Antichrist then shall be brought to ruin gradually; that is, by degrees: A part after a part; *here* a fenced city, and *there* a high tower, even until she is made to lie even with the ground. And yet all shall be within the compass of God's days, hours, or moments; for within the compass of these *limited* times Antichrist shall be destroyed.*

Now, (as I said) He, she, Sodom, Egypt, Babylon, Antichrist, shall be destroyed, not all at once, after the way of our counting of time; but by step after step, piece after piece. And perhaps there may be in the words now following, something that signifies this: They shall 'shew the king of Babylon that his city is taken at *one* end.' Je. li. 31. This is also shewed by the vessels in which is contained the wrath of God for her, together with the manner of pouring it out. The vessels in which it is contained are called VIALS; Now a *vial* is that which letteth out what is contained in it by degrees, and not all at once.

There are also two things to be considered, as to the manner of its being poured out of them. The first respecteth the nature of the vial. The other, the *order* of the angels that poured forth this wrath.

For the First: The vial, as it letteth out what is in it by degrees; so it doth it with certain *gusts*, that are mixed with strength and violence, bolting it out with noise, &c.

As for the *order* of the angels, or that order that they observe, they plainly shew that this enemy must come down by degrees; for that these vials are by them poured out one after another, each one working something of their own effects, before another is poured forth. The first is poured forth upon the antichristian *earth*: The second, upon her *sea*: The third is poured forth upon her *rivers*: And the fourth, upon her *sun*: The fifth is poured forth upon the *seat of the beast*: The sixth,

upon her *euphrates*: And the seventh, into her *air*. Re. xvi. 2—17. And, I say, they are poured forth not all at one time, but now one, and then another. Now, since by these vials Antichrist must fall; and since also they are poured forth successively: 'Tis evident that this *man of sin*, this *son of perdition*, is to fall and die by degrees. He would not die at all, as is manifest by his wrestling with it; but he is a strong God that judges, and therefore he must come down: His friends also, with what cordials they can, will labour to lengthen out his tranquillity; but God hath set his bounds, and he cannot go beyond the time appointed.

We must also put a difference betwixt her being fought withal and wounded, and that of her dying the death. Michael and his angels have been holding of her in play a long season; but yet she is not dead: Re. xii. But, as I said, she shall descend in battle and perish, and shall be found no more for ever.

A TENTH PART FALLS FIRST.

To speak then to the manner of the ruin of this Antichrist, with respect to the gradualness thereof: It must piece after piece be overthrown, until at last every whit thereof is rolled down from the rocks as a burnt mountain.

And hence we read that this city falls first in a *tenth part* thereof, even while nine parts remain yet standing: Nor doth this tenth part, notwithstanding the faith and faithful testimony of the two witnesses, quite fall, until they are slain, and also raised again: For 'tis said, The same *hour* that the witnesses were raised, the tenth part of the city fell: Re. xi. 13. The tenth part of that city that reigneth over the kings of the earth, which city is Sodom, Ægypt, Babylon, or the great whore. Re. xvii. 18.

By the city then, I understand the church of Antichrist in its utmost bounds; and so it reacheth as far as the beast with seven heads and ten horns hath dominion. Hence this city is also called cities, as one universe is called by the name of several countries, &c. And them cities also are called 'the cities of the nations:' Re. xvi. 19. For as when they are put together, they all make but one; so when they are considered apart, they are found in number ten, and answer to the ten horns upon the heads of the (seven headed) beast that carries her, and do give her protection.

This then I take to be the meaning: That the antichristian church is divided into ten parts, and each part is put under one of the horns of the beast for protection: But that aid and protection shall not help, when God shall come to execute judgment upon her: For it saith, 'A tenth part of the city fell;' that is, first, and as a forerunner of the fall of all the rest: Now where this tenth part

---

* Upon the Sunday sports being authorized, and pious ministers persecuted for refusing to wear popish vestments in the reign of James I., that godly puritan, Mr. Carter, exclaimed, 'I have had a longing desire to see or hear of the fall of Antichrist: but I check myself. I shall go to heaven, and there news will come, thick, thick, thick.'—*Life by his Son*, p. 13.

is, or which of the ten parts must fall first, or whether indeed a tenth part is already fallen, that I will leave to those that are wiser than myself to determine.

But since I am speaking of the fall of a tenth part of Antichrist; a word or two about the means of the fall thereof.

The means of the fall of this tenth part, is an earthquake ; yet not such as is universal, over the face of all, but an earthquake in that tenth part where that city stood that should fall. Now by earthquakes here, cannot be meant any thing but such a shaking as unsettleth the foundations of this tenth part : But whether it shall be in this tenth part as a city, or in it as a state, that I shall not determine ; only my thoughts are, That it shall be an earthquake in that kingdom where this tenth part shall happen to be : An earthquake not to overthrow further than is appointed ; and that is the city which is called the tenth part of the great Antichrist. So far as *that* state is a state, so far then it is shaken for reformation, not for destruction ; for in the earthquake were slain seven thousand (names of) men ; and the remnant were affrighted, and gave glory to the God of heaven. But thus much for the first: Great Babylon falleth first, in a tenth part of it.

THE NINE PARTS FALL.

Again, The next step that the strong God taketh towards the utter overthrow of Antichrist, will be more sore upon the whole, though not at first universal neither, yet in conclusion, it shall throw down the nine parts that are left : For thus it is recorded : ' And the cities of the nations fell :' The *cities of the nations*, the antichristian churches, otherwise called the daughters of the mother of harlots, and abominations of the earth.

Now to shew you the hand of God in this second stroke, wherewith the Lord will smite this enemy.

1. Here we have a great earthquake.

2. And then, The fall of the cities of the nations.

For the earthquake, it is said to be such as never was, ' so mighty an earthquake, and so great;' Re. xvi. 18. for it extended itself as far as the other nine cities had any ground to stand on ; for it shook the foundations of them all.

The fall of the cities, was not immediately upon the shake that was made, but the earthquake produced an eruption, an eruption in the nine remaining parts of this city : And such an eruption as is of the worser sort, for it divided them into a three-headed division : ' And the great city was divided into three parts :' The great city, to wit, the powers by which they were upheld.   The meaning then is this ; when God shall strike this man of sin the second time, he will not be so

sparing as he was at first, when he struck but a tenth part to the ground; but now he will so shake, so confound, so divide, so raise up Antichrist against himself, to wit, in the body and members of him, that they shall set to fighting, and to tearing one another in pieces, until they have consumed the whole of these nine parts. It was, saith the text, divided into three parts, which divisions are the worst of all : It will be therefore such a division as will bring them all to ruin. Hence it follows, ' And the cities of the nations fell.'

Wherefore, this three-cornered eruption will be the most dreadful to Antichrist that ever was : It will be like that that was in Jerusalem when she came to be laid even with the ground ; and like that that came upon the armies of the Gentiles, when they came up to fight against Jehosaphat.

' For the children of Ammon and Moab stood up against the inhabitants of Mount Seir, utterly to slay and destroy *them:* And when they had made an end of the inhabitants of Seir, every one helped to destroy another.' 2 Ch. xx. 23. This, I say, is the division that this mighty earthquake shall make betwixt the horns that are left to these nine parts that remained, when the tenth part of the city fell.   And this will come to pass through the increase of the heat of God's anger : For he is angry with the waters where the woman sitteth, because they have delivered up his beloved to the bloody whore ; wherefore, he now will give them blood to drink in fury.

Hence his beginning to deal with Antichrist, is called, the beginning of revenges: ' I will make (saith God) mine arrows drunk with blood, and my sword shall devour flesh ; *and that* with the blood of the slain and of the captives, from the beginning of revenges upon the enemy.' De. xxxii. 42.   And therefore it is said again, that when God comes to do this work upon this Antichrist, it is because '*it is* the day of the Lord's vengeance, *and* the year of recompences for the controversy of Zion.' Is. xxxiv. 8. ' For the day of vengeance is in mine heart, and the year of my redeemed is come.' Is. lxiii. 4.

A peace therefore cannot be made among these cities when God has forbidden it : Wherefore the effect of all, is, *The cities of the nations fall.* There is therefore like to be no more good days for Antichrist after this earthquake has begun to shake her : No, nothing now is to be expected of her, but rumours, tumults, stirs, and uproars: ' One post shall run to meet another, - - to shew the king of Babylon that his city is taken at *one* end:' And again, ' A rumour shall both come *one* year ; and after that in *another* year *shall come* a rumour, and violence in the land, ruler against ruler,' &c. Je. li. 31, 46.   So that this earthquake has driven away peace, shaken the foundations, and will cast the nine cities down to the ground.

GREAT BABEL FALLS.

And this is a second stroke that God will give this man of sin, and a third cometh quickly. Wherefore it follows upon the downfall of these cities of the nations, that ' great Babylon came into remembrance before God, to give unto her the cup of the wine of the fierceness of his wrath.' Now then, have at great Babylon. *Great Babylon!* What is that? Why, I take it to be the *mother*, the *metropolitan*, the *great whore* herself: For though sometimes, by the great whore, or great Babylon, we may understand, the church of Antichrist in general; yet by it is meant more properly, the mother of the daughters, of whose overthrow we have spoken before. We are now then come to the threshold of the door of the house of the OLD one; to the door of the mother of harlots, and abomination of the earth. This then that but now is said to come into remembrance with God, is that which gave being to the cities destroyed before; to wit, the mistress, the queen, the mother-church, as she calleth herself.

And this is the wisdom of God concerning her, that she should not be the first that should die; but that she should live to see the destruction of her daughters, and pine away under the sight and sense of that, even until judgment also shall overtake herself.

Thus Pharaoh and his chief ones did live to see the greatest part of Egypt destroyed before judgment overtook them, but at last it came to their doors also.

Zedekiah lived to see his children slain before his face, before judgment overtook him to his own personal destruction. Je. lii. 8—11.

Babylon also, when God sent the cup of his fury unto her, yet was to live to see the nations drink before her: ' Take the wine cup of my fury (said God to the prophet,) and cause all the nations to whom I send thee, to drink it.' Je. xxv. 15. To wit, All the kingdoms of the world which are upon the face of the earth. 'And Sheshach shall drink after them.' ver. 26. But what was Sheshach? may some say. I answer, It was Babylon, the princess of the world, and at that time the head of all those nations, Da. iv. 22. (as this queen is now the mother of harlots.) Wherefore, the same prophet, speaking of the destruction of the same Sheshach, saith, ' How is Sheshach taken? and how is the praise of the whole earth surprised! How is Babylon become an astonishment among the nations!' Je. li. 41.

Now, if this was the method of God's proceeding with his enemies in the way of his judgments of old, why may we not suppose that he will go the same way with his great enemy now: especially

since those judgments mentioned before, were executed upon those, which, in some things, were figures of the great whore. Besides, we read here plainly, that when the cities of the nations were fallen, great Babylon came into remembrance before God, to give her to drink of the cup.

From all which I conclude, as I did before, that the mother, the metropolitan, the lady of kingdoms, shall live to see her daughters executed before her face: After which she shall come into consideration herself; for she must assuredly drink of the cup.*

This destruction therefore must be last, for the reasons urged before, and also because she most deserves the bottom of the cup. The bottom is the dregs, the most bitter part, and that where the most heat, and fiercest wrath of God doth lie: Ps. lxxv. 8. Wherefore, although you find that by the first earthquake a great slaughter was made, and that a tenth part of the city fell; yet from that judgment some did escape: 'And the remnant were affrighted, and gave glory to the God of heaven.' Re. xi. 13. But now, this *earthquake*, by virtue of which the cities of the nations fall, and as an effect of which great Babylon is come into ' remembrance before God,' neither spares one of the daughters of this whore, nor any man that is a lover of them; but it so is seconded by a 'hail-storm,' and that hail-storm worketh so in wrath, that not one escapes by repentance. Every hail-stone was the weight of a talent, which some say is six pounds above half an hundred weight:† By this therefore God shews, that now his anger was wrought up to the height. I know not wherewith so to compare these hailstones, as with the talent of lead that was laid over the mouth of the ephah, which was prepared to hold the woman, whose name was *wickedness*, this very whore of Babylon: For that talent of lead was to keep down this mistress, that she might get no more out of the ephah, and these hail-stones are to banish her out of the world: Ze. v. 5—11. Therefore it follows, that she must have the most heavy judgment, even the bottom of the cup.

'And great Babylon came into remembrance before God.' To *remember* with God, is to visit

---

* How remarkably has this come to pass since Bunyan's time; a slow but sure progression. That darling ugly daughter, Intolerance, was executed by the Act of Toleration. The impious Test by the repeal of the Sacramental Test Act, &c., &c.—ED.

† There is great difficulty in estimating the weight of a talent. Dr. Gill considers it about sixty pounds; this was the lesser Roman talent. Michaelis estimates the Jewish talent at thirty-two pounds and a half. The attic talent of gold used in Greece in the time of Homer is estimated at less than an ounce. The safest conclusion as to the weight of the hail-stones is, that they were enormous, and fell with a velocity to crush all animals to instant death.—ED.

either with grace or wrath, God is said to remember Rachel, when he visited her with the blessing of a fruitful womb. Ge. xxx. 22. It is said also that God *remembered* Noah, when the time came on that he was to be delivered from the flood. Ge. viii. 1. Here also he is said to *remember* Babylon, that is, to visit her with his anger for the wickedness that she had committed: 'To give unto her the cup of the wine of the fierceness of his wrath.'

Now then is the time of iniquity, when it will be come to the full; and now also is the time of God's anger, when it will be come to the full: Now therefore must the murders, Re. xviii. 24. and thefts, and blasphemies, and fornications, &c., belonging to this mother of harlots, be recompensed to the full, to wit, with the dregs of this cup: Yet since the *hail-stones* come by *weight*, and the wrath comes by *measure*, (for so a talent and a cup imports) it follows, that the Almighty God, even in the midst of the heat of all this anger, will keep to the rules of justice and judgment while he is dealing with this enemy: He has not *passions,* to carry him beyond rules of judgment; nor *weakness,* to cause him to fall short of doing justice: Therefore he has (as was said) his judgments for her by weight, and his indignation by measure: But yet this weight and measure is not suited to her constitution, not with an intent to purge or refine her; but it is disposed according to the measure and nature of her iniquity, and comes to sweep her, as with the besom of destruction, until she is swept off from the face of all the earth.

And thus I have shewed you the manner of the ruin of Antichrist; that is, That it will be gradual, part after part, until the whole be overthrown. And this truth may be applied both to the soul, as well as to the body of Antichrist: For the soul, spirit, or life of Antichrist must also after this manner be destroyed. And hence it is said to be consumed, that is, by degrees: For to consume, is to destroy by degrees: Only this caution I would have the reader remember, That much of the soul of Antichrist may be destroyed, when none of her daughters are; and that the destruction of her spirit is a certain forerunner of the destruction of her body in the manner that we have related.

Now since she is dying, let us ring her passing-bell; for when she is dead, we that live to see it, intend to *ring out.*

'For thus saith the Lord God; When I shall make thee a desolate city, like the cities that are not inhabited; when I shall bring up the deep upon thee, and great waters shall cover thee; when I shall bring thee down with them that descend into the pit, with the people of old time, and shall set thee in the low parts of the earth, in places desolate of old, with them that go down to the pit, that thou be not inhabited; and I shall

set glory in the land of the living; I will make thee a terror, and thou *shalt be* no *more :* though thou be sought for, yet shalt thou never be found again, saith the Lord GOD.' Eze. xxvi. 19—21.

OF THE SIGNS OF THE APPROACH OF THE DOWNFALL OF ANTICHRIST.

Having in the foregoing discourse spoken of Antichrist his ruin, and the manner thereof, I now come to speak of the signs of the approach of her destruction. And whether I shall hit right, as to these, *that* I must leave to time to make manifest; and in the mean while to the wise in heart to judge.

That she shall fall, there is nothing more certain; and when she is fallen, that she never shall rise again, is also as firmly decreed; yea, and shewed too by him that cast the millstone into the sea, and said, 'Thus with violence shall that great city Babylon be thrown down, and shall be found no more at all.' Re. xviii. 21. This is therefore her fate and destiny, from the mouth of the holy one; and is sealed up in the scriptures of truth, for the comfort of the people that have been afflicted by her.

True, the time of her fall is not certainly known by the saints, nor *at all believed by her;* wherefore, her plagues must come unlooked for by her. And as to the saints, their guesses, as to the *time* of her ruin, must needs be *conjectural* and uncertain. For her part, she shall say, and that when she stands where she must suddenly fall, 'I shall be a lady for ever.' Is. xlvii. 7—9. And as to the saints that would very willingly see her downfall, how often have they been mistaken as to the set time thereof.

Nor have I been without thought, but that this mistake of the godly may become a snare to Antichrist, and a trap to her upholders. For what can be a greater judgment, or more effectually harden the hearts of the wicked, than for them to behold that the predictions, prophecies, expectation and hopes of their enemies (as to their ruin) should quite (as to the time) be frustrate, and made void.

Moses prophesied, and the people hoped that God would give Israel 'the land of Canaan ;' and yet the Canaanites beat them. Nu. xiv. 40; Jos. vii. 5—9.

Jeremiah prophesied that the enemy should come and take the city [of] Jerusalem; but because he came once, and went back without doing it, how stout and hardened were the hearts of that people against all the rest of his prophetic sayings, as to such a thing. Je. xxxvii. Now the error lay not in these prophets, but in the people's mistaking the times: and if mistakes do so much harden the heart of the wicked, what will they do to such of them who make it their business to blind and harden their hearts against God, by abusing all truths? Surely, when men seek to harden their hearts by abusing of truth, they will do it to purpose, when they have also the advantage of the weakness of their professed enemies to do it by: especially when their enemies shall say they speak by the word of the Lord, and time shall manifest it to be both a mistake and a falsehood.

It is to be bewailed, namely, the forwardness of some in this matter, who have predicted concerning the *time* of the downfall of Antichrist, to the shame of them and their brethren: nor will the wrong that such by their boldness have done to the church of God, be ever repaired by them nor their works. But the judgments of God are a great deep; and therefore who can tell, since the enemy of God would not be convinced by the power of truth, and the virtuous lives of some, but that God might leave them to be snared, hardened and emboldened to run upon their unavoidable destruction, by the lies and lightness of others. They begin to vaunt it already, and to say, Where is the word of the Lord, as to this, let it come now. But when Agag said, 'surely the bitterness of death is past,' then was the time for him to be hewn in pieces. 1 Sa. xv. 32, 33. I shall not therefore meddle with the times and seasons which the Father hath put in his own power; no, though they as to Antichrist's ruin are revealed; because by the Holy Ghost there is a challenge made, notwithstanding the time is set, and by the word related to the man of wisdom, to find it out if he can. Re. xiii. 18.

If Samson's riddle was so puzzling, what shall we think of this? and though the angel hath intimated, that this sealed matter shall be opened towards the time of the end; Da. xii. 9. yet 'tis evident, some have either been so hasty, or presumed too much upon their own abilities: for I am sure they have missed the mark, hardened the heart of the enemy, stumbled the weak, and shamed them that loved them.

But since the most high hath irreversibly determined her downfall also, let us see if we can have better success in discoursing upon the *signs*, than others have had who have meddled with the *timing* thereof.

FIRST SIGN.

First then. The downfall and ruin of Antichrist draws near, *when the church and people of God are driven from all those hiding-places that God has prepared for them in the wilderness*. The church of God, when the dragon did his worst, had an hiding-place prepared her of God, that she might not utterly be devoured by him; and so shall have till the time of his end shall come.

Of this you read in the 12th of the Revelations,

a place worthy to be noted for this. But now, when the time of the ruin of Antichrist draws on, then is the church deprived of her shelter, and laid open, as one would think, to be utterly swallowed up for ever, having no more place in the wilderness, that is, among the nations, to hide herself from the face of the serpent. But how comes this to be a SIGN of the approach of the ruin of Antichrist? why thus. The *time* of this beast's war with the church of God, and the time that the church shall have an hiding-place in the wilderness, are both of a length, the one continuing *forty-two months*, the other *a thousand two hundred and threescore days*. Now since the war that this beast makes with the woman and her seed, and the woman's hiding-place in the wilderness from his face, are, for length of time, the same; what hindereth but that when the woman and her seed can find no more shelter in the nations, the time that the beast hath allotted him to make war against her, should be finished also? when we therefore shall see that plots and conspiracies, that designs for utter ruin, are laid against God's church all the world over; and that none of the kings, princes, or mighty states of the world, will open their doors, or give them a city for refuge; then is the ruin of Antichrist at hand: for Haman's plot, though the most universal that ever yet was hatching, (being laid in an hundred twenty-seven provinces,) did but presage the deliverance and exaltation of the Jews, and the hanging of Haman and his sons: yea, and I take it, that the very day that this great enemy had set for the utter overthrow of the church, God made the day in which their deliverance began, and that from whence it was completed; and I take *that* to be a type of *this*.

There is but one thing that I can think of that can give matter of a shew of doubt about this thing; and that is, though the time of this war against the saints, and that of the woman's shelter in the wilderness as to length, be one and the same; yet whether they did commence together, and begin to take their rise, as men do that begin to run a race? a word therefore to this. I suppose they did commence much together; for else with whom should this beast make war, and how should the church escape? Or, if the beast began his war before the woman began to have a hiding place, why was she not swallowed up, since in the wilderness was her only place of shelter? Again, what needed the woman to have a place of shelter in the wilderness, when there was no war made against her? And yet this must be, if her thousand two hundred and threescore days, began before the beast's forty-two months: but they ended both together; for the *beast* could not kill the *witnesses* before they had finished their testimony; which testimony of theirs lasted this full time that the beast had granted him to make war with them, to wit, one thousand two hundred and threescore days: Re. xi. 3. therefore their times went out together, as will be made appear, if you consider also that the witnesses were slain, by virtue, not of the old, but of a new war levied against them; and that, as it should seem, at the very time when her hiding place was taken from her; for then indeed, for a little season, will the church of God be overcome, as I shall shew by and by.

Wherefore, let God's people consider and remember that when God's church is absolutely forlorn, and has no hiding place any longer in the world, the kingdom of Antichrist will quickly begin to tumble. Nor is this the alone place from whence we may gather these conclusions.

The time of Pharaoh's tyranny, of his life, and of the deliverance of the children of Israel, came out much together; as any will discern that shall consider the history of them. Ge. xv. 13.

David, when Saul did sorely prosecute him, fled last into the wilderness to Achish the king of Gath, *a Philistine*, for shelter; and he gave him Ziklag for his refuge. 1 Sa. xxvii. 5, 6. And that place so continued to David, 'till just about the time in which Saul must die; and then behold, David's Ziklag is burnt with fire, and himself stript naked of harbour! 1 Sa. xxx. 1. But what matter! The time of Saul's life, as well as of David's Ziklag, was now upon expiring; for within three or four days after, David became the king of Israel. 1 Sa. xxxi. 1—6.

And thus also it was with the Babel-beast: His time expired, when the captivity of Israel was upon the finishing: then was the time of his land come, and 'in that' very 'night was Belshazzar the king of the Chaldeans slain.' Da. v. 25—30.

Thus therefore it will happen to the church in the latter days: her place of shelter in the wilderness; her Ziklag will be taken from her, about the time that the war that the beast has to make upon the woman and her seed shall be finished. But now the church is not therefore immediately delivered, when her Ziklag is taken from her; for after that, the beast levieth a new war, to the overcoming and killing of the church: I say therefore, that this is a sign, not of the downfall of Antichrist, but of the approach thereof: for the church's bondage shall continue but three days, and a little after this [shall be her deliverance]. Much like to this was that of David; for after he had lost his Ziklag, for two or three days he had sore distress: but lo, then came the kingdom to him.

Indeed, sense and reason saith, it is a fearful thing for the church of God to be exposed to the rage of her enemy all over the world at once; and that all nations should shut up their gates, let

down their portcullises, bolt up their doors, and set open their flood-gates to destroy them: but so will be the dispensation of God, to the end deliverance may be the sweeter, and the enemies fall the more headlong, and the arm of God the more manifest, both *for* the one, and *against* the other. And in this will that scripture be fulfilled: 'And there shall be a time of trouble, such as never was since there was a nation - - and at that time thy people shall be delivered, every one that shall be found written in the book.' Da. xii. 1.

Let us gather up what has been said again; namely, that it is a sign of the approach of the ruin of Antichrist, when God's church can find no more shelter in the wilderness; because when her Ziklag is burned, the time of the war that the beast is to make against her, is finished. Wherefore, when she hath given one desperate struggle more, and laid the church of God, or his witnesses, for dead, in the street of his great city, for three days and an half, then comes the kingdom, and the long, long-looked-for rest and glory. Wherefore it remains, that an angel should stand in the sun, and make proclamation to all the fowls that fly in the midst of heaven, to gather themselves together to the supper of the great God: 'That ye may eat the flesh of kings, and the flesh of captains, and the flesh of mighty men, and the flesh of horses, and of them that sit on them; and the flesh of all *men*, *both* free and bond, both small and great.' Re. xix. 18. This is to be after the forty-two months of the beast; and consequently, after the thousand two hundred and threescore days that the church was to be in sackcloth; yea, after the resurrection of the witnesses, as is evident by that which follows: 'And the beast was taken, (that is, after the second year) and with him the false prophet that wrought miracles before him, with which he deceived them that had received the mark of the beast, and them that worshipped his image. These both were cast alive into a lake of fire burning with brimstone.' v. 20.

Secondly, Another sign of the approach of the ruin of Antichrist, is this: towards the end of her reign, the nations will be made to see her baseness, and to abhor her and her ways. They will, I say, be made to see these things, in order to her ruin: also, when they shall be made to see, her ruin will not be far off. For so long as the nations and their rulers shall continue in that dead sleep that she hath bewitched them into, by their drinking of the wine of her fornication; so long we have no ground to think that her ruin is at the door: but when God shall lay her before kings, and shall discover her nakedness to the nations, then be sure her destruction is at hand. Hence you read, that precedent to her downfall: An angel comes down from heaven, and enlightens the earth with his glory. Re. x. 1. [*The earth;*] that is, the kingdoms, countries, and nations where the woman sitteth, or they that border thereupon. [*Enlightened;*] to let them see the filthiness of the whore. [*With his glory;*] with the doctrine that he had commission to preach against her, for the discovering of her lewdness to the earth. This also was the way that God took with backsliding Israel of old, (and she was a type of our religious Babel) when he intended to bring her to judgment for her sins; Eze. xvi. 37. and this is the way that God will take to destroy our religious Antichrist, when he comes to deliver his people out of her hand.

For though the people that suffer at her hand, can do nothing against her, but lay, in prayers and tears against her before the God of heaven, and bear their witness against her before the gods of the earth; yet when kings shall come to be concerned, and they will count themselves concerned when they shall see how they have been deceived by her; then let her look to it. 'Behold, I *am* against thee, saith the LORD of Hosts; and 1 will discover thy skirts upon thy face, and I will shew the nations thy nakedness, and the kingdoms thy shame. And I will cast abominable filth upon thee, and make thee vile, and will set thee as a gazing-stock.' And what follows? 'And it shall come to pass, *that* all they that look upon thee, shall flee from thee, and say, Nineveh is laid waste: who will bemoan her? whence shall I seek comforters for thee?' Na. iii. 5—7.

Wherefore, there wants nothing but that she be discovered to the nations and their kings; for did they but see her, though they lay yet in her bosom, they would rise up against her, that she must die: wherefore it is written again, I will 'bring forth a fire from the midst of thee, it shall devour thee, and I will bring thee to ashes upon the earth in the sight of all them that behold thee.' Eze. xxviii. 18.

The chief of the wisdom of Antichrist this day is laid out, if perhaps by it she may cover her nakedness, and keep it from the eyes of kings and their people. But God has said it shall not avail: 'Thy nakedness shall be uncovered, yea, thy shame shall be seen: I will take vengeance, and I will not meet *thee as* a man.' Is. xlvii. 3. But how will he make her naked? Verily, by kings. But how shall kings do it? Why, by virtue of the glory of the angel: yea, they 'shall make her desolate and naked, and shall eat her flesh, and burn her with fire.' Re. xvii. 16.

Let this, I pray, be considered, That Antichrist shall not down, but by the hand of kings. The preacher then kills her soul, and the king kills her body. And why should not the kings have it

granted unto them, that she should fall by their hand? the kings are those that she has abused, that she has in the grossest manner abused, and has served herself of them: but the time of the end of Antichrist, mystery Babylon is coming, 'and then many nations and great kings shall serve themselves of him.' Je. xxvii. 7. *

Nor shall all the tricks, lies, and deceit under which formerly she used to shroud herself, be able to prove a balm to her any longer: No, 'in vain shalt thou use many medicines;' for no cure shall be unto thee; 'the nations have heard of thy shame.' Je. xlvi. 11, 12.

Babylon has for a long time been 'a lady of kingdoms,' and 'a golden cup in the Lord's hand:' the nations also have largely drank of her cup, and the kings have committed fornication with her Re. xviii. 3. But now the angel is come down, and hath *enlightened the earth with his glory.* Wherefore now it follows immediately, 'Babylon is fallen! is fallen!' That is, in the eyes and esteem of the nations, as well as otherwise.

True, some of the kings will bewail her fall, and will cry, Alas! Alas! when they see that they cannot help her; for that they shall see, as is evident, because they stand afar off to lament her, 'afar off for the fear of her torment.' The kings therefore into whose hands God shall deliver her, and who shall execute his judgments upon her, shall be more mighty and powerful to bring her down, than shall be the whole world besides to uphold her.

The Protestant Kings.

And this observe further, That as the kings that shall hate her, shall hate her because in the light of the glory of the angel they are made able to see her filthiness; so the kings that shall bewail her, are such as in judgment are left in the dark, and that shall be bewitched by her to the end. This therefore will let us see something of the meaning of God, in that he has drawn off from her some of the kings already; to wit, that he might train them up by the light of the gospel, that they may be expert, like men of war, to scale her walls, when the king of kings shall give out the commandment to them so to do.

There has been a great deal of talk in the countries about the ruin and destruction of Babylon;

---

* The reader must not misunderstand the words, 'The king kills her body.' Bunyan does not in the slightest degree concede to kings or nations a right to interfere with 'the soul' or religious principles or practices—these are to be slain, if false, by persecution of the preacher. Kings and nations will restore to the people the immense property and revenue of which they have been plundered, under the hollow knavish pretence of curing souls and forgiving sins. THUS will human laws kill the body of Antichrist. Every motive for professing to believe absurdities and contradictions will be at an end, when neither rule nor honour, nor pelf is to be gained by hypocrisy.—ED.

but could we see more of the kings engaged against her, we should hope groundedly that her fall was at the door. Well, blessed be God for what kings there are, and the Lord turn the hearts of many more to hate her.

Some, as I said before, have adventured to foretell the *time* of her downfall; but give me the *signs* thereof. This therefore is a sign, a sign that her downfall approaches, when God shall lay her nakedness before the nations, and put it into the hearts of kings to abhor her. The signs of the times the Lord Jesus would have us mind; and because the Jews neglected them, though as to the time they hit pretty right, yet they missed of the thing that the time brought forth.

THIRD SIGN.

Thirdly, A third sign of the approach of the ruin of Antichrist, is this: 'When Babylon is become the habitation of devils, &c.,' then the downfall thereof is upon us. True, Babylon was always an habitation for devils; but not an habitation *only* for them; Israel once dwelt there, and *our* Antichrist was sometimes a place of residence for good men. The meaning then, is, When you shall see the church and people of God *so* forsake her that she is left in a manner to herself, and to her disciples, then she is to fall quickly. When you hear it proclaimed by them that are yet in her, of God's people, 'We would have healed Babylon, but she is not healed: forsake her, and let us go every one into his own country:' Je. li. 9. Then she will soon be hissed out of the world: for this is the way of the wisdom of God; namely, to bring his people out of a city or place, when he intends the ruin of that place. When God was about to destroy the *old* world, he put his Noah into an ark: when God was about to destroy Sodom, he sent his Lot away thence to Zoar: when Christ was about to destroy Jerusalem, he bid his disciples flee from the midst of that: and when there shall be by God a hissing for his people; and when they shall hear him, and obey, and gather to him, then you shall see what will become of this enemy of Christ: 'I will hiss for them, and gather them; for I have redeemed them.' Ze. x. 8—12.

I say therefore, when Babylon shall become the habitation of devils, a hold for all foul spirits, and a cage for every unclean and hateful bird, then Babylon is fallen.

And thus the angel that lightened the earth with his glory, proclaimed, 'Babylon the great is fallen! is fallen! and is become the habitation of devils, and a hold for every foul spirit, and a cage for every unclean and hateful bird.' Wherefore it must be, that by that her time is come that she should fall, God will have gleaned his people from the midst of her. And when God shall have gleaned his people from the midst of her, those that are left

behind will appear more than ever to be what they are, to wit, devils, foul spirits, and hateful birds; wherefore, now will Antichrist appear in his own most proper colours.

But to comment a little upon the words.

Babylon 'Mystery Babylon.' Re. xvii. 5. The antichristian church.

'Is fallen! Is fallen!' In the eyes and faith of the godly, by her dropping into the dregs of degeneracy, and so is become the habitation of devils, &c., in order to her falling into utter and unavoidable destruction for ever.

'Is become.' That is, through the labour of the fanners and winnowers that God hath sent to fan Babylon, and to fetch out his people, that she might be left to her chaff: 'I will send (saith God to Babylon) fanners, that shall fan her, and shall empty her land (of good men;) for in the day of trouble they shall be against her round about.' Je. li. 2.

'An habitation of devils.' Devils: not such by *nature*, but by *practice*. Incarnate devils. For when the time is come that Babylon must be destroyed, she shall be found to be an habitation for the most vile of the sons of men. For as devils have acted towards the world, so shall the sons of this sorceress, and this whore, act towards Christ and his members in the latter days. And, perhaps, the departing of Zion from the midst of her, will blow her up into this spirit of devilism. Let God's people therefore, when Antichrist is towards her end, look for nothing from her, but what the devil, in times past, used to do; to wit, all sinful subtilty, malice, wrath, fraud, deceit, lying, murder, false accusings, and implacable madness of spirit to do them mischief. (But Lord God! think I, what will become of good men! and where will they be safe in such days? Only I comfort myself, by saying to myself again, this a sign that the ruin of Antichrist is at the door.) But this I say, he must needs be a *tuneable* man, that shall be able in those days to sing this song to himself at all seasons: for this is to drive reason backward, and to set the cart before the horse. For what will the good man's reason say, when it seeth all Babylonians are become devils, but that the church of God will certainly be torn in pieces? But behold! the text and the Holy Ghost runs counter. 'Babylon is fallen! is fallen! and (or, for it) is become the habitation of devils.' These words for certain are the words of an holy angel; for it could not have entered into the heart of mere man to have conceived them.

'An habitation.' To be an habitation (for devils) is to be their house, their dwelling-place, their place of privilege, their place of rest and abode, or thither whither they have right to go. And thus will Babylon be; that is, an house, an habitation, a dwelling-place, and a place of rest, only for devilish-minded men; thither may such men come; for such her doors stand open, and there may such inhabit. When therefore you see good men come out thence, and all sorts of wicked men flock in thither, then know that Babylon is near her end.

'And a hold for every foul spirit.' Understand by spirit, either those that are devils by nature, or such as are such otherwise. But I think that the angel chiefly intends all manner of unclean and filthy spirits; and so the church and members of Babylon, their only place of safety: Or if you understand it of the uncleanness of the spirits and minds of men, then the meaning is, that they are called foul spirits, in allusion to those of devils which go by the same name. Ma. ix. 25. But however, or which way soever taken, it seems Babylon is their *hold*; that is, their place of defence: For by an hold, we often understand a place of strength, a castle, a fort, a tower; so that these devils, these foul-spirited men, these Babylonians, will not only find house-room and harbour in Babel, but shelter, defence and protection, when she is near her ruin: yea, they will find her an upholder to them, and a countenancer of them, in all their foul and devilish pranks; yea, such an hold shall she be to such foul spirits in such foul acts, that it shall not be possible that they should be driven from her, or from them: For an *hold* is often taken in the scriptures for a place that is impregnable, and must be so taken here. This intimates then, that some faint opposition by the kings and nations will be made against these inhabiters, foul spirits, but to little purpose, until the time of her land shall come; Je. xxvii. 7. for in their hold they still will be secured and defended from what reason, law and scripture can or would do unto them. Thus then we see how Babel, towards her end, will be filled, and with what, to wit, with devils and foul spirits; yea, and that she will not only be an habitation, but a place of defence for such.

'And a cage for every unclean and hateful bird.' Those that before are called devils, and foul spirits, are also here called 'birds, unclean and hateful beasts.' By the term [*Birds*,] he may allude to that of the prophet Isaiah, where these unclean birds are mentioned. xxxiv. 11—17. And by *cage*, he may allude to the prophet Jeremiah, from whom, as I think, the Holy Ghost takes those words; but then we must put *men* in the place of *birds*, and the *Babylonian kingdom* for the *cage*. Je. v. 27.

'Every unclean bird.' As was said before, a hold for *every* foul spirit. These unclean birds therefore are not all of one feather, or kind, but of *all* and *every* kind; and it intimates, that the worst act of all professions, shall be, as in a cage, in Babylon, a little before her downfall. But I say, if they will not be all of one feather, yet in their temper they will somewhat agree, being either in

shape, monstrous; of *appetite*, ravenous; or, of *inclination*, lovers of the night. For of all these sorts were the forbidden, or unclean birds among the Jews. Now since these unclean birds are not all of one feather, or kind, it intimates that the basest of all sorts, sects, professions and degrees, shall take shelter in Babylon towards her end; and that they shall there, in their temper, unanimously agree to show themselves monstrous, to devour and eat up the poor and needy, and to blow out the light of the gospel.

'A cage.' Not to imprison them in, but for them to sit and sing in, to confer their notes in, to make melodious music in; I mean, melodious to their own thinking; for the ass thinks that he sings full favouredly, and the owl endeavours to lift up her voice above all the birds of the wood: But it will be a prediction of her fall, and that her ruin is at the door.

Of these birds Zephaniah speaks, when he prophecies of the downfall of Nineveh, saying, 'The cormorant and the bittern [shall] lodge in the uppermost lintels of it, *their* voice shall sing in the windows; (when) desolation *shall be* in the thresholds.' Zep. ii. 14. An unseasonable time to sing in; for when *death* is coming in at the door, *mourning* should be in the chambers. But this is the judgment of God, That she should be a cage for every unclean bird to sing in, even then when her destruction and desolation cometh upon her.

To sing, as in a cage, doth also denote security, and that the heart is far from fear; for she saith, 'I shall see no sorrow, in that hour in which her judgment comes.'

But is this a sign of the approach of the ruin of Antichrist? And must those that shall live to see those days, rejoice when these things begin to come to pass? Are not these things rather a sign that the utter overthrow of the church of God is at the door? Indeed, to *sense* it is, and *reason* will be apt to say so: But hark what the Holy Ghost saith! 'She is fallen! is fallen now!'

When therefore we shall see men like devils; yea, every foul spirit, and hateful bird, flock to, and take shelter in Babylon; let us not be frighted or dejected, but pluck up our hearts, and say, This is one of the signs that the downfall of Babylon is near. Wherefore it follows, after that the prophet had told us that these birds should dwell in the land of the people of God's curse, Is. xxxiv. That 'the wilderness and the solitary place shall be glad for them; (for that they are there) and the desert shall rejoice, and blossom as the rose: It shall blossom, (saith he) abundantly, and rejoice even with joy and singing: The glory of Lebanon shall be given unto it, the excellency of Carmel and Sharon, they shall see the glory of the Lord, *and* the excellency of our God.' And to support the weak from those fears that in those days will be pulling of them down, he adds, 'Strengthen ye the weak hands, and confirm the feeble knees. Say to them *that are* of a fearful heart, Be strong, fear not: behold, your God will come *with* vengeance, *even* God *with* a recompence; he will come and save you. Then the eyes of the blind shall be opened, and the ears of the deaf shall be unstopped. Then shall the lame *man* leap as an hart, and the tongue of the dumb sing: for in the wilderness shall waters break out, and streams in the desert. And the parched ground shall become a pool, and the thirsty land springs of water: In the habitation of dragons, where each lay, *shall be* grass with reeds and rushes. And an highway shall be there, and a way, and it shall be called, The way of holiness; the unclean shall not pass over it; but it *shall be* for those: the wayfaring men, though fools, shall not err *therein*. No lion shall be there, nor *any* ravenous beast shall go up thereon, it shall not be found there; but the redeemed shall walk *there*. And the ransomed of the Lord shall return, and come to Zion with songs and everlasting joy upon their heads: They shall obtain joy and gladness, and sorrow and sighing shall flee away.' Is. xxxv.

What say ye now, ye sons of God! Will you learn to make a judgment of things according to the mystery of the wisdom of God, or will ye longer conclude according to sense and reason: 'He turneth the shadow of death into the morning:' Am. v. 8. And commands oft-times, that the *fairest* day should succeed the *foulest* night. Wherefore, when we see these devils, foul spirits, and unclean birds in Babylon; yea, when we see good men leave her, and the vilest run in to her, then let us sing the angels' song, and say, 'Babylon the great is fallen! is fallen! and is become the habitation of devils, and a hold for every foul spirit, and a cage for every unclean and hateful bird.'

FOURTH SIGN.

Fourthly, Another sign of the approach of the ruin of Antichrist, is, 'The Slaying of the Witnesses:' For the witnesses are to be slain before the fall of Antichrist; and that by the hand of the beast, who shall manage the members of Antichrist, having qualified them before that work, with those qualifications of which you read in the sign foregoing. For what can better fit a generation for such a work, than to be themselves all turned *devils*, and also succourers of all foul spirits. Wherefore, they must be the wickedest of men that shall do this: the very scum of the nations, and the very vilest of people. Nor is this a new notion: God threatened to give his sanctuary 'into the hands of strangers for a prey, and to the wicked

of the earth for a spoil;' Eze. vii. 21. To robbers, burglars, and they should defile it. ver. 22. Again, saith God of his people, 'I will bring the worst of the heathen, and they shall possess their houses.' ver. 24. For the truth is, this work is too bad for men either of reason or conscience to be found in the practice of. The hangman is usually none of the best: The witnesses are also to be slain; but not a man, but a beast must slay them, 'a den of thieves, a hold of foul spirits,' must do it.

That the witnesses must be slain before the fall of Babylon, has been hinted already. Also, that their death is a forerunner of the ruin of Antichrist, has before been touched upon; but in this place I shall a little enlarge.

And therefore I proceed: 'And when they shall have finished their testimony, the beast that ascendeth out of the bottomless pit shall make war against them, and shall overcome them, and kill them. And their dead bodies *shall lie* in the street of the great city, which spiritually is called Sodom and Egypt, where also our Lord was crucified. And they of the people, and kindreds and tongues and nations shall see their dead bodies three days and an half, and shall not suffer their dead bodies to be put into graves.' 'And after three days and an half, the spirit of life from God entered into them, and they stood upon their feet; and great fear fell upon them which saw them. And they heard a great voice from heaven, saying unto them, Come up hither: And they ascended up to heaven in a cloud; and their enemies beheld them.' Re. xi. 7—12.

Thus you see their *death* is before their *deliverance*. Also their death is to be by the hand of the beast; to wit by the men that have and hold his mark, and that of his image, and that are of the number of his name. You see also that their death is not only a fore-runner of their deliverance, but a *sign* that their deliverance is at the door; since the one is but three days and a half before the other.

And if a short comment upon this text will give a little light to the reader, I shall not count my labour lost.

'And when they shall have finished their testimony, when, or about the time they have done their work of witness-bearing for God in the world: When they have made or are making an end of giving their testimony for Christ, and against the witchcrafts, idolatries, sorceries, fornications, thefts, murders, and wickedness of Antichrist: Then and not till then.

'The beast that ascended out of the bottomless pit.' The *beast*: The power that carrieth and beareth up Antichrist, the mother of harlots: The beast upon which the woman sitteth, and by the heads and horns of which she is protected and defended; he is said to ascend out of the bottomless pit; for that he manifesteth by his doings, that he was born there, and came to [do] the work of the king thereof.

'Shall make war against them.' We read that he made war against them all the time of their prophesying in sackcloth, while they were bearing their testimony against his doing; and that his commission was, That he should have leave to make war *so long*. Re. xii. 6. But here we read again, that when they had finished their testimony, and so consequently he had run out the time of his first commission for war, he makes war again. So that *this* war which now he raiseth against them, seems to be another, a new war, and such as is grounded upon other, to wit, new arguments, besides those upon which his first war stood. By his first war, he sought to beat down and overthrow *their testimony*. Re. xiii. 4. By this war he seeketh to overthrow *themselves*. The first war he made, was grounded upon a vain *confidence* of his ability to destroy their faith; but this last was grounded upon *madness* against them, because their testimony had prevailed against him: Wherefore, *Torment*, wherewith these witnesses by their testimony tormented him and his followers, was the cause of this last war. And this is insinuated when he saith, 'They make merry for their victory over them, because these two prophets,' (to wit, by their testimony,) 'tormented them that dwelt on the earth.' Re. xi. 10.

The beast therefore will make a war against the witnesses all the time of their prophesying in sackcloth, which will be a thousand two hundred and threescore days. Re. xii. 6. In all which time they shall give him the foil, and overcome him by their faith and testimony; and be proclaimed more than conquerors over him, through the Christ that loved them. But now in this second war he overcomes them, 'he overcomes them, and kills them.'

Jezebel for a long time made war against Elias the prophet, seeking to overthrow the worship of God which he maintained, and to establish the religion of Baal: But when she saw that by all she could do she got nothing, but that the prophet got the day of her worship, priests and worshippers, 1 Ki. xviii. 30—40. she breaks out into a rage, as one tormented almost to death, and raises a new war; not now against his religion, but his person, and desperately swears by all the gods that she had, That by to-morrow that time the life of the prophet should be as the life of one of her priests whom he had slain for an idolator. 1 Ki. xix. 2. When the devil sees that he cannot do by argument, he will try if he can by blows.

When Zedekiah, the son of Chenanah, saw that with argument he could not overcome Micaiah, he steps to him, and takes him a box of the ear. 1 Ki. xxii. 24. This new war, is a box of the ear which

the beast will give the witnesses, because they overcame him by their faith and testimony, all the time that the first war lasted.

Now how long this second war will last, and what strugglings the witnesses will make before he shall overcome them, I know not: This I know, that the text saith, 'By this war he shall overcome them.'

'And shall overcome them.' Saints are not said to be overcome, when they are imprisoned, banished, and killed for their faithful testimony: No, by these things *they overcome*. To overcome then, is to get the mastery, to subdue, to turn out of possession, to take and hold captive, to strip the subdued of power and privilege, as is sufficiently manifest both by scripture and reason: 'For of whom a man is overcome, of the same he is brought in bondage.' 2 Pe. ii. 19.

So then, when he is said to overcome them, it is meant, he shall get the mastery of them, they shall grow faint before him, have no heart or spirit to bear up in their profession against him: *Against him*, I say, as she did the thousand two hundred and threescore days' war with him; for then they were overcomers, and did bear away the garland.

Nor do I, for my part, wonder at this, when I consider that these witnesses are a succession of good men; and that when Israel came out of Egypt of old, the feeble and weak-handed did come behind. De. xxv. 17—19. It will be the lot therefore of the church, in the latter end of the reign of the beast, to be feeble and weak in their profession, the valiant ones having gone before: *These* will come, when those that were able have bravely borne their testimony, or when they are upon finishing of that: In comparison of whom, they that come after will be but like *eggs* to the cocks of the game: wherefore they must needs be crushed, cowed, and overcome. And then will the beast boast himself, as did his type of old, and say, 'My hand hath found as a nest the riches of the people: and as one gathereth eggs *that are* left, have I gathered all the earth; and there was none that moved the wing, or opened the mouth, or peeped.' Is. x. 14.

A sad time, and it is to happen to the people that are left, to the latter end of the witness-bearers; and that too when they shall have finished their testimony.

Of this tyranny the cruelty of Amalek was a type; who, as was hinted before, smote the hindermost, the weak: But his judgment is, That 'he shall perish for ever.'

'And shall overcome them.' There are two ways of overcoming; to wit, by power and policy: And perhaps by *both* these ways they may be overcome. However, overcome they shall be; for so saith the holy word of God; yea, the beast shall overcome them. Wherefore the church of God, at that day, will be under such a cloud as she never was since Christ's day. Now how long they shall thus be held captive before they are brought to execution; whether the beast will ride in triumph while they are in his bonds; or whether he will suddenly kill them; that time, and observation, and experience, must make manifest: But kill them he shall, that's most certain, for so says the Holy Ghost.

'And shall overcome them, *and kill them.*' In this method therefore God will suffer the beast to proceed with the church of God, after she has sufficiently borne her testimony for him in the world. He shall 'war against them,' but that is not all: He shall overcome them, but that is not all; he 'shall overcome them, and kill them.'

'And kill them.' Of their slaughter also I shall speak a word or two. But first I would note, as all know, that there is a difference to be put betwixt killing and overcoming: For though every one that is killed, is overcome: yet every one that is overcome, is not killed: Ac. xxi 32. men may be overcome, and yet live; Je. xii. 11. but when they are killed, it is otherwise: There may be a cry heard from the mouth of them that are overcome, but not from the mouth of them that are killed: Ex. xxxii. 18; Ac. vii. 34. They that are overcome, may consult their own enlargement and deliverance; but they that are killed, cannot do so. I do therefore distinguish between *killed* and *overcome*, because the text doth so: 'He shall make war against them, and shall overcome them, and kill them.'

'And kill them.' From these words therefore I will take occasion to inquire,

1. How they are to be considered as to this slaughter.

2. What death they must die to accomplish this prophecy.

FIRST, How they are to be considered?

I answer: Not in a carnal or natural, but in a mystical sense. For, first, they are called witnesses. Secondly, They are put under the number of two: 'My two witnesses.' Re. xi. 3. Both which are to be mystically taken.

First, Because their testimony standeth not in their words only, but in their conversation; yea, in their suffering also: and that is a mystical witness-bearing.

Secondly, They go under the number of *two*: Not because there were indeed two such men in the world, but because *two* are a sufficient number to bear witness; Nu. xxxv. 30; De. xvii. 6. & xix. 15. and God's church, in the most furious heat and rage of Antichrist, has been at least of such a number of professing saints, to proclaim against the beast and his worship in the name of God. To think that there have been two such men in the world, is ridi-

culous; for these witnesses must continue to give their testimony for God against Antichrist, a thousand two hundred and threescore years. Nor can they scripturally bear this title, *My two witnesses*, but with respect to their prophesying so long. The witnesses therefore are nothing else but a successive church, or the congregation of God abiding for him against Antichrist, by reason of a continual succession of men that is joined by the special blessing of God unto it.

SECONDLY, What death they must die? I answer, Not a corporeal one, but that which is mystically such. And I choose to understand it thus, because this suiteth best with their state and condition, which is mystical. Besides, thus did they (when they did overcome,) slay their enemies, even with the fire or sword of their mouth: 'If any man will hurt them, fire proceedeth out of their mouth, and devoureth their enemies: and *if* any man will hurt them, he must in this manner be killed.' Re. xi. 5. As therefore they went about to kill their enemies, so their enemies will kill them: But they sought to kill their enemies by their testimony, as to their antichristian spirit, and church state; and their enemies will kill them, as to their Christian heat and fervency of mind; and also as to their Christian church state. So that, (at least so I think,) there will be such ruins brought both upon the spirit of Christianity, and the true Christian church state, before this Antichrist is destroyed, that there will for a time scarce be found a Christian spirit, or a true visible living church of Christ in the world: Nothing but the dead bodies of these will be to be seen of the nations; nor them neither, otherwise than as so many ruinous heaps. For the love that I bear to the church of Christ, I wish, as to this, I may prove a false prophet: But this looks so like the text, and also so like the dispensations of God with his church of old, that I cannot but think it will be so. For the text, I have spoken to that already; wherefore I will now present you with some things that look like parallel cases.

First, When the church was coming out of Egypt, just before they were delivered from Pharaoh, they were in their own eyes, and in the eyes of their enemies, none other than dead: '*It had been* better (said they to Moses) for us to serve the Egyptians, than that we should die in the wilderness.' Ex. xiv. 12 The people said so, Moses feared, and Pharaoh concluded they were all dead men. Ex. xii. 33. Also Paul tells us, 'that they were baptized (that is, buried) unto Moses in the cloud, and in the sea.' They were, for the time, to use the expression, *a dead church* both in the eyes of Pharaoh, in the eyes of Moses, and also in their own.

And 'tis to be taken notice of: As the witnesses

in the text were slain but a little before the ruin of Antichrist began; so this church was *baptized* in the sea but a little before great Pharaoh was *drowned* there.

Secondly, In the time of Elias, which time also was typical of this, what church was there to be seen in Israel? None but what was under ground, buried in dens, and in caves of the earth: Yea, the prophet could see none, and therefore he cried to God, and said, Lord, they have ' digged down thine altars,' and slain thy prophets, ' and I am left alone, and they seek my life.' 1 Ki. xix. 14; Ro. xi 3. What visible living church was now in the land, I mean, either with reference to a godly spirit for it, or the form and constitution of it? What was, was known to God, but dead to every man alive.

Thirdly, What was the *dry bones* that we read of in the 37th of Ezekiel, but the church of God, and also a figure of what we are treating of? And why called *dry bones*, since the people were alive, with their substance, wives, and children; but to shew, that that church of God was now, as to their spirit and church-state, accounted as *dead*, not only by themselves, but by the king of Babylon, and the nations round about? Babylon then was the valley, and the grave; and the church of God were the bones: Bones without flesh, sinews, or skin; bones exceeding dry; yea so dry and dead were they, that the prophet himself could not tell whether ever they should live again. Eze. xxxvii. 1—3.

Now this, as I said, was a state that was not to end with the church of Israel, but to be acted over once again by the beast with the church of the new testament: Yea, it is an easy matter to make their witnesses in this their death, and the church of Israel in this their grave, in many things to symbolize.

Fourthly, Take another instance, or rather comparison, into which the church of God compared herself, when under the king of Babylon's tyranny: And that is, she counted herself as the dung that the beast lets fall to the ground from behind him. And doth this look like a visible church-state? Or has it the smell or savour of such a thing? Nebuchadnezzar (said she) ' hath swallowed me up like a dragon, he hath filled his belly with my delicates, he hath cast me out.' Je. li. 34. Pray, what would you think of a man, of whom one should tell you, That he was eaten up of a dragon; made to fill the belly of a dragon; and cast out as the dung of a dragon? Would you think that such an one did all this while retain the shape, form, or similitude of a man? Why, thus the church said she was, and thus the church shall be again: For she is once more to be overcome, to be overcome and killed; and that by the beast, the dragon's whelp, of which the king of Babylon was a type. And therefore I conclude the premises; that is,

That the beast will kill the church that shall be in the latter days, as to her Christian spiritedness, and her church-state. And I could further add, That if we hold they die corporeally, we must conclude, that their natural body being slain, shall lie three years and a half in the street; yea, that their resurrection shall be corporeal, &c. But why we should think thus, as yet I can see no reason, since the persons are such mystically; the beast mystically so; the street in which they be, mystically such; and the days of their unburied state, to be taken mystically likewise. But we will pass this, and descend to other things.

Fifthly, I will yet add another thing. When Israel was coming out of Babylon; yea, while they were building of the temple of God, which was a figure of our church-state now under the Gospel; they were not only troubled, hindered and molested in their work, but were made for a time to cease, and let the work lie still.

' Now (says the text) when the copy of king Artaxerxes letter (which he sent to forbid the Jews in their work) *was* read before Rehum and Shimshai the scribe, and their companions, they went up in haste to Jerusalem unto the Jews, and made them to cease by force and power. Then ceased the work of the house of God which *is* at Jerusalem. So it ceased unto the second year of the reign of Darius king of Persia.' Ezr. iv. 23, 24.

And I pray, since their temple-worship was a type of a new-testament church state and worship, what doth their causing of that work to cease signify to us, but that we must have a time also to cease as they? And since their temple-work was caused to cease before the house was finished, what face could there be at present thereupon, but that, to look to, it was like some deformed, battered, broken building, or as such an one that was begun by foolish builders? Yea, and since the Jews left off to build God's house at the command of the heathens, what did that bespeak, but that they had lost their spirit, were quashed, and so as to their temple-work, killed, as it were, to all intents and purposes? And thus it will be, a little before the church of God shall be set free from the beast, and all his angels: For these things were writ for our admonition, to show us what shall be done hereafter; yea, and whether we believe or disbelieve hereabout, time will bring it to pass.

I do not question but many good men have writ more largely of this matter: but as I have not seen their books, so I walk not by their rules. If I mistake, the mistakes are only mine; and if I shall merit shame, I alone must bear it.

Some may think they have said enough, when they assert, that for the witnesses to be *killed*, is, To be *dead in law*. But I answer, That is not *to be overcome*. They are here said to be overcome:

and that is more than to be dead in law: For a man may be dead in law, and yet not be overcome; and if so, then far enough off from being killed. So then, for as much as they are said to be *overcome* and *killed*, it must be more than to be *dead in law*. Besides, the text supposeth that they had yielded up, as dying men do, their souls, their spirit of life into the hands of God: For it saith concerning them, That at their resurrection, the spirit of life from God entered *again* into them: Into them, antecedent thereunto. 'And after three days and an half the spirit of life from God entered into them, and they stood upon their feet.' Re. xi. 11. Thus it was concerning the dry bones, of which mention was made before: 'Then said he unto me, Prophesy unto the wind, prophesy, son of man, and say to the wind, Thus saith the Lord GOD; Come from the four winds, O breath, and breathe upon these slain, that they may live.' Eze. xxxvii. 9. And thus much concerning their killing.

Now, as I said, since in death, the body doth not only lie dead, but the spirit of life departs therefrom; it is to shew, that not only their bodies, their church-state, shall die, (for *churches* are called *bodies*, 1 Co. xii. 27; Ep. iii. 6. iv. 12. v. 23. & Col. i. 18.) but that spirit of life that acted those bodies, shall be taken up to God. There shall, for a time, be no living visible church of Christ in the world: A church, but no *living* church, as to church-state: A church in ruins, but not a church in order: Even as there was once a Christ, but no living Christ in the grave; yet the gates of hell shall not prevail to an utter overthrow thereof, no more than they prevailed to an utter overthrow of Christ; but as one did, so shall the other, revive, and rise again, to the utter confusion and destruction of their enemies: Yea, and as Christ, after his resurrection, was, as to his body, more glorious than he was before; so the witnesses, after their resurrection, shall be more spiritual, heavenly, and exact in all their ways, than they were before they were killed. *Resurrections* are always attended with new additions of glory; and so shall the church of God, as to her church-state, be in the latter days.

But yet the beast shall not altogether have his will, (if that at all was his will) that these witnesses, in this second war, should be conquered to a compliance with Antichrist in his foolish and vain religion: For it is not with dead men to comply; but as they are dead to their own church-state, so they are to his. When the Jews had killed Christ, it was beyond all the art of hell to cause that his body should see corruption; so when the beast has killed the witnesses, he shall not be able to corrupt them with any of his vices.

Hence you find, that not the witnesses, but the dwellers upon the earth were them that danced after the devil's pipe, when he had fulfilled their murder.

Nor doth this murder, as to the fulfilling of it in those nations where the woman sitteth, seem to be a great way off, if all be true that from foreign parts some have said: For what a withdrawing of God and of his Spirit is there already in some of the churches of God! The word worketh not that sound repentance which it was wont to do: Preachers preach for little, but to spend themselves, as men that are wounded do when with groans they let out their life. Where (say some) is the spirit and life of communion? And where that practical holiness that formerly used to be seen in the houses, lives and conversations of professors? The whole head is sick, and the whole heart faint already; and how long will it be before churches die of the wound that the beast has given them, time must make appear: But die I perceive they must; for if the wound already given will not kill, repeated blows shall.

By all that I have said, I do not deny but that many of the people of God may die corporeally, by the hand of the beast, in this second war that shall be made by him against the witnesses. But should as many more die, that will not prove that that death will be that that by the killing of the witnesses is intended.

Some thing I would bestow upon the reader, for him to carry with him as a memorandum, while he reads this account of things: As,

First, This victory of the beast, is not to be until the witnesses have finished their testimony; and so by all that he shall do, he shall not hinder the revelation of any of the truths that they either were to bring to light, or to confirm by their witness-bearing.

Witnesses are not always bound to speak: There is a time 'to keep silence,' Ec. iii. 7. and 'thou shalt be dumb.' Eze. iii. 26. But how shall we know when this time is come?

1. When a sufficient testimony has been given for Christ, and against Antichrist, before the God of heaven; for he must be the judge.

2. When her enemies forbear to plead against her by argument, and rather betake themselves to blows. Mat. x. 19.

3. When the spirit of testimony-bearing is taken from the church; for that is not essential to Christianity, but is given and taken away as there is occasion.

4. When testimony-bearing becomes a vain or needless repetition, when they have heard sufficiently of things before. Jn. ix. 27.

Secondly, This victory of the beast shall not invalidate or weaken their testimony; no, not in the eyes of the world; for they will still remember, and have a reverence for it: This is intimated by this, That 'they of the people and kindreds and tongues and nations—(that are neither the witnesses, nor they that in the next verse are called the inhabiters, or they that dwell upon the earth,) —shall not suffer their dead bodies to be [buried, or be] put in graves.' Re. xi. 9.

Thirdly, This shall not lengthen the reign and tranquillity of the antichristian kingdom; nor frustrate, drive back (or cause to tarry) the glorious freedom and liberty of the saints.

But some may say, This will be a SAD day.

So it will, and gloomy; but it will be but short, and 'the righteous shall have dominion over them next morning.' 'Twill last but three days and an half; nor shall it come, but for the sins of churches and saints, and to hasten the downfall of the kingdom of the beast, and for the sweetening to the church her future mercies. Christ Jesus, our Lord, in answer to the question of his disciples, about the destruction of Jerusalem, presented them with a relation of many sad things; but when he was come even to the hearts of men, and had told them 'that they should fail for fear:' He said, 'when these things begin to come to pass, then look up, and lift up your heads; for your redemption draweth nigh.' Lu. xxi. 25—28.

'Tis as ordinary as for the light to shine, for God to make black and dismal dispensations, to usher in bright and pleasing [ones]; yea, and the more frightful that is which goes before, the more comforting is that which follows after. Instances in abundance might be given as to this, but at present let this suffice that is here upon the paper before us; namely, the state of the witnesses, with their glorious resurrection.

Fifthly, Another *sign* of the approach of the ruin of Antichrist, will be this: The great joy that will be in her, and among her disciples, when they shall see that the witnesses are slain, and lie dead upon the spot: 'And they that dwell upon the earth shall rejoice over them, and make merry, and shall send gifts one to another; because these two prophets tormented them that dwell on the earth.' Re. xi. 10. Babylon has been always a merry city, and her disciples merry men; but the poor church of Christ has been solitary, and as a wife forsaken; her tears upon her cheeks bear her witness, and so doth her sackcloth-weed.

Hence our Babylon, under the name of Nineveh, is called, 'the rejoicing city.' Zep. ii. 15. Only her joy is distinguished from that which is the joy of God's people, by these two things.

First, Either she rejoiceth in outward and carnal glory, or else in the ruin of the church of God. This last, to wit, the *supposed* ruin of the church of God, is that which will be now the cause of her glorying. And this is the joy that God complaineth

of, and for the which he said that he would punish Babylon: 'Chaldea shall be a spoil: All that spoil her shall be satisfied, saith the LORD. Because ye were glad, because ye rejoiced, O ye destroyers of mine heritage,' &c. Je. l. 10, 11. The joy therefore of Babylon, Antichrist; the joy that she shall conceive in her heart upon the slaughter of the witnesses, is a sure sign of her unavoidable ruin and destruction. These two prophets tormented her; they were to Babylon as Mordecai was to Haman, a continual plague and eye-sore: As also was David to the wretched Saul: But now they are overcome, now they are killed; now she rejoiceth, and maketh merry. And this her joy was of old prefigured by them that in her spirit have gone before her: As,

First, When the Philistines had, as they thought, for ever overcome Samson, that Nazarite of God, how joyful were they of the victory! 'Then the lords of the Philistines gathered them together for to offer a great sacrifice unto Dagon their god, and to rejoice: for they said, Our god hath delivered Samson our enemy into our hand. And when the people saw him, (saw him in chains) they praised their god: for they said, Our god hath delivered into our hands our enemy, and the destroyer of our country, which slew many of us.' Ju. xvi. 23, 24. Poor Samson! While thou hadst thy locks, thy liberty, and thine eyes, thou didst shake the pillar that did bear up their kingdom! But now they have conquered thee, how great is their joy! How great is their joy, and how near their downfall! This therefore is a joy that is like that we have under consideration, to wit, the joy of them that dwell upon the earth; for that the witnesses that did bear up the name of God in the world, were overcome and killed.

Secondly, Like to this, is that which you read of in the first book of Samuel, concerning the men that had burnt David's Ziklag. Ziklag was poor David's place of safety; nor had he any else but that under the whole heaven: But the children of the east came upon it, and took it; set it on fire, and carried thence all David's substance, with his wives and his children. (Very ill done to a man in affliction; to a man that went always in fear of his life, because of the rage of his master Saul.) But how were they that had got the victory? Oh! joyful, and glad, and merry at heart at the thoughts of the richness of the booty? 'Behold, *they were* spread abroad upon all the earth, eating and drinking, and dancing, because of all the great spoil that they had taken out of the land of the Philistines (from Ziklag) and out of the land of Judah.' 1 Sa. xxx. 16. Here again you find a joy and merriment like these that we have under consideration, and that upon such like accounts. Nothing pleases the wicked more, than to see the godly go down the wind; for their words, and lives, and actions are a plague and a torment to them: As 'tis said of these two prophets, 'They tormented them that dwelt on the earth.'

Thirdly, While the church of God lay dead in Babylon, and as bones exceeding dry; what a trampling upon them was there by Belshazzar a little before his death! He called for his golden and silver vessels that his father Nebuchadnezzar had taken out of the temple of God that was at Jerusalem, (those holy vessels once dedicated to the worship and service of God) that his princes, his wives and his concubines might drink therein. An high affront to heaven: 'They drank wine, and praised the gods of gold, and of silver, of brass, of iron, of wood, and of stone.' Da. v. 4. And all to shew what a conquest, as he thought, he had got over the God of heaven, and over his people that dwelt in Jerusalem, and over his ordinances and vessels used in his worship and service: Yea, this he did with such joy that was not usual, as is intimated by his doing of it before 'a thousand of his lords,' and that till he had drank himself drunken. But all this while, as was hinted before, the church of God, as it were, lay dead at his feet; or as the phrase is, 'as bones exceeding dry.' This too will be the joy of the beast and his followers in the latter days; they will make war with the witnesses; they shall overcome them, and kill them; and when that is done, they shall rejoice over them, and make merry. But as Belshazzar soon after this, saw the hand-writing that made his *knees knock together;* and as he lived not to see the light of another day; so 'twill be with the beast and his followers; the next news that we hear upon this mirth and jollity, is, the tenth part of his kingdom falls, and so on till the whole is ruined.

Thirdly, Moab also, in the day that Israel was taken captive by their enemies, could not forbear but *skip for joy,* so glad was he in his heart thereat. But what saith the jealous Lord? 'Make ye him drunken: for he magnified *himself* against the Lord: Moab also shall - - be in derision: For was not Israel (saith God) a derision unto thee? was he found among thieves? for since thou spakest of him, thou skippedst for joy.' Je. xlviii. 26, 27. Of all things, God cannot away with this: For when the wicked would rejoice that they have been suffered to make havoc of the church of God, they deny the wisdom and power by which they were permitted to do this, and offer sacrifice to their own net and drag; Hab. i. 16. which provoketh the holiness of Israel: 'Shall the axe boast itself against him that heweth therewith? or shall the saw magnify itself against him that shaketh it? As if the rod should shake *itself* against them that lift it up, or as if the staff should lift up *itself, as if it were* no wood.' But what follows? Why, burning and consuming of soul and body of them that do such

a thing. Is. x. 15—18. And this text I the rather bring, because 'tis to be the portion of Antichrist.

And therefore let this be a caution to the men that wonder after the beast, to caution them to repentance, for he will assuredly go into perdition. What! shall the witnesses of God be killed! Shall the beast stand glorying over them while they are dead, with his feet in their neck? and shall none be angry at it? Let them that *love* themselves *look* to themselves: God will be concerned, and will assuredly for this quickly put a period to the kingdom and reign of Antichrist. Je. l. 13.

And although this glorying mistress of iniquity, this Antichrist and Babylon, may say that her power is the hammer of the whole earth; yet God will cut him in sunder, and break him in pieces with his *bout-hammers,** with the kings† of the earth, that he will use to do this work withal; that is, when this last sign is fulfilled: I call it the *last* sign; I find none that doth intervene betwixt the slaying of the witnesses, and the beginnings of the ruin of Antichrist but this.

But a little to comment upon their joy, as the Holy Ghost doth set it forth. The cause of their joy we have touched already; which was, for that they had slain their tormentors. For, as was shewed you, the witnesses had been their tormentors: But when they shall overcome them, and kill them, they rejoice, make merry, and send gifts one to another.

This *repeating,* and *repeating* with aggravation, doth manifest, and at that day their joy will be exceeding great: 'They shall rejoice, and make merry,' &c. They shall rejoice over *them,* over their slain, their enemies, their tormenting enemies. This joy therefore, is a joy that flows from victory, from victory after a war that has lasted a thousand two hundred and threescore years. They shall rejoice, as they do that have a most potent, vexatious, and tormenting enemy lying dead at their foot, and as those that ride in triumph over them. They shall therefore rejoice as conquerors use to do, who make the slaughters of their spoiled enemies the *trophy* of their joy.

For the devil, that great deceiver of mankind, will so flush up and bewitch the men that wonder after the beast, with the victory that they shall get over the faithful witnesses for God and his Son, that they will think ('twill never be day) that the victory is so complete, so universal, so thorough, that the conquest must be lasting. And from sense and reason they will have ground to think so; for

---

* This is a very expressive term, but better understood by Bunyan the brazier than by many of his readers. It is well known to those who live near a coppersmith's, when three or four athletic men are keeping up, bout and bout, incessant blows upon a rivet, until their object is accomplished.—Ed.

† Protestant kings.

who now is left in the world any more to make head against them? but here comes in that which will utterly spoil this joy; these conquered, killed, dead men must come to life again, and then what's become of their joy? 'And great fear fell upon them which saw them.' Re. xi. 11. Wherefore, this joy must fade and vanish: But, I say, the followers of the beast will be far from thinking so; for they will 'rejoice over them, make merry, and send gifts one to another,' concluding that these tormentors shall never torment them more. But Jacob's blessing upon his son Gad, shall be fulfilled upon these witnesses: 'Gad (saith he) a troop shall overcome him: but he shall overcome at the last.' Ge. xlix. 19. So then these conquerors must not always rejoice, though they will suppose they shall, and also make merry too.

'And make merry.' To make merry, is more than to rejoice. To rejoice, doth shew the present act of the soul; but to make merry, is to use the means as will keep this joy alive, and on foot. Joy is one thing, and the continuance of it is another. 1 Sa. xxv. 36. Joy may be begotten by a conceit, a thought; but it cannot be maintained so; because deliberation will come in and spoil it, Es. v. 4. if sufficient means is not used to continue it: wherefore he adds, They rejoiced over them, 'And made merry.'

And there are five things that are usually made use of to keep up wicked joy. 1. There is the merriment of music. Lu. xv. 25, 32. 2. The merriment of feasting. Ju. xix. 6, 9. 3. The merriment of laughter. Ec. x. 19. 4. The merriment of fleshly solace. Je. xxxi. 4. 5. Revenge upon a supposed enemy. 2 Sa. xiii. 28. So then, by these five things we see what is the way that sinful joy is maintained in the hearts of wicked men; and also by what means the limbs and brats of Antichrist will keep up that joy that at first will be conceived in their hearts at the thought that now they have killed their tormentors. They shall have music. They shall have feasting. They shall have laughter. They shall have fleshly solace. And they shall have their fill, for the time, of revenge. Thus therefore shall they rejoice over them, and make merry, all the time of that little, *short everlasting* that they are to live in the world.

'And make merry.' To make merry, to make wicked mirth, there must be a continual fraternity, or brotherhood in iniquity, maintained among them, and that where none may come to interrupt; and that they will be capable of doing any where then, for that their tormentors will be dead. Wickedness shall walk with open face in those days; for then there will be none alive for God and his ways; wherefore, the beast and his train may do what they will: now will be the time for men to live carelessly and wantonly, and to make their wantonness their joy, (after the manner of the Zidonians) for there will be none to put them to shame.

'And shall send gifts one to another.' This is another token of their gladness, and also a means to buoy them up still. And it will be a sign that they have joined hand in hand to do this wickedness, not dreaming of the punishment that must follow. This sending of gifts to each other, and that after they have slain these two prophets, doth also declare that they will be far from repentance, for the commission of so great an offence. Nay, it signifies further, that they were resolved, and determined to quench all manner of convictions one in another, that might arise in their hearts for the sin which they had committed: for a gift blinds the eyes of the wise, and perverts the judgment of the righteous; how much more then will it stifle and choke appearances of such upon the spirits of wicked men! I question not at all but many have been, by the favours and gifts of wicked men, drawn down into the belly of hell.

Now what these gifts will be, either as to kind or quantity, that I can say nothing to: but probably, whatever they will be, there will be but little of their own cost in them. Victors and conquerors do use to visit their friends with their spoils won in battle, with the spoil of the enemies of their God. Ezr. x. 7.

And this was David's way, after he had recovered the loss that he had sustained at the burning of his Ziklag; he sent to his friends of what he had taken from his enemies, as token of victory: 'David sent of the spoil (says the text) unto the elders of Judah, *even* to his friends, saying, Behold a present for you of the spoils of the enemies of the LORD;' 1 Sa. xxx. 26. And why may not those we have now under consideration, do so to their god, and their friends also? Spoiling is like to be one of the last of the mischiefs that Antichrist shall do to the church of God in this world: And methinks, since the beast will have power to overcome, and to kill, he should also have power to take away: Da. xi. 33. 'Hast thou killed, and also taken possession?' said the prophet to wicked Ahab.

However, whatever their gifts may be, and at whose cost soever bought, 'tis a sign their hearts will be open, they shall send gifts one to another: their merry days will then be come, and their enemies will then be dead at their feet; wherefore, now they will have nothing to do but to rejoice over them, and to make merry, and to send gifts one to another.

Thus as to sense and reason, all shall be hush, all shall be quiet and still: the followers of the *Lamb* shall be down; the followers of the *Beast* be up, cry peace and safety, and shall be as secure as an hard heart, false peace, and a deceitful devil can make them. But behold! While they thus 'sing in the windows,' death is stradling over the threshold! Zep. ii. 14. While they are crying peace and safety, sudden destruction cometh: By that they have well settled themselves at their table with Adonijah, 1 Ki. i. they shall hear it proclaimed with sound of trumpet, the witnesses are risen again.

Now the Christians' pipes will go again, and surely the earth will be rent with the sound of their shouts and acclamations, while they cry with joyful sound, 'The kingdoms of this world are become *the kingdoms* of our Lord, and of his Christ ; and he shall reign for ever and ever.' Re. xi. 15.

But woe to the wicked, it shall be ill with them; for the Lord Jesus will now begin to shew his jealousy, and to make known his indignation towards those that have thus cruelly slain his prophets, digged down his altars, and made such havoc of the afflicted church of God. Is. lxvi. 14. Now will he whet his *glittering sword*, and his hand shall take hold on vengeance, that he may render a recompence to his enemies, and repay them that hate him. De. xxxii. 41.

But this he will not do immediately by himself, but by such instruments as have been spoken of before: of which more particularly to treat, shall be that I shall next take in hand.

OF THE INSTRUMENTS THAT GOD WILL USE TO BRING ANTICHRIST TO HIS RUIN.

Although I have hinted at this before, yet it may be convenient briefly to touch it again. Antichrist, as I have told you, consisteth of soul and body, and must be destroyed by such instruments as may most properly be applied to each. Further, As to the soul, spirit or life of Antichrist, and its destruction, of that we have also spoken already : It remains then that now we discourse of the ruin of his body and flesh.

I then take it, That the destruction of her flesh shall come by the sword, as managed in the hands of kings, who are God's ministers for the punishment of evil deeds, and the praise of them that do well. Ro. xiii. Not that the church, even as a church, shall be quite exempt and have therein no hand at all; for she, even as such, shall with her faith and prayers help forward that destruction.

The church therefore, as a church, must use such weapons as are proper to her as such; and the magistrate, as a magistrate, must use such weapons as are proper to him as such. When the church of Israel were prisoners in Babylon, they did not fight their way through their foes, and the countries to Jerusalem; but waited in their captivated state with patience, until the kings of the Medes and Persians came to deliver them. Nor is it to be slighted, but to be thought on seriously, that before there was an Israelite captive in Babylon, their deliverer Cyrus was prophesied of : which Cyrus did afterwards come and take Babylon, and deliver the captives, as it was foretold he should. He saith unto Cyrus, '*He is* my shepherd, and shall perform all my pleasure : even saying to Jerusalem, Thou shalt be built ; and to the temple, Thy foundation shall be laid.' Is. xliv. 28. And again, 'Thus saith the Lord to his anointed, to Cyrus, whose right hand I have holden to subdue nations before him, &c. I have raised him up in righteousness, and I will direct all his ways: he shall build my city, and he shall let go my captives, not for price nor reward, saith the LORD of Hosts.' Is. xlv. 1, 13. And this accordingly he did, to wit, when the time was come ; as may be seen in those holy records where these things are made mention of. Indeed, as I said, the church is not excluded : 2 Ch. xxxvi. 2. she may, and ought, with her faith and prayer, and holy life, to second this work of kings. Ezr. i. 2, 3. Wherefore, when God speaks of bringing down the lofty city and of laying it low in the dust by the church, he saith, they shall do it by their feet, and with their steps : 'The foot shall tread it down, *even* the feet of the poor, *and* the steps of the needy.' Is. xxvi. 6.

By feet and steps, I understand the good lives of the children of God : but now, when kings come to deal with her, as kings, they serve her as Samuel served Agag, as a judge, 'cut her in pieces with their swords:' or as you have it elsewhere, 'They make her desolate and naked ; they eat her flesh, and burn her with fire.' The sword will be put into their hands for this very purpose. Thus therefore must their deliverance be begun.

It is also to be considered, That after these first kings of the Medes and Persians had broken the yoke of the king of Babylon from off the neck of the captive church, and had given her license to go to her place to build her temple and city, and to sacrifice there according to the law of their God, (as both in Ezra and Nehemiah we read;) and when their work was hindered by under-officers, or they endeavoured so to do, they pleaded the license that they received to build and sacrifice by the decree of the first kings, and so finished their deliverance: They went not on in headstrong manner, as if they regarded neither king nor Cæsar: 'But Zerubbabel, and Joshua, and the rest of the chief of the fathers of Israel, said unto them,' that sought to hinder their work, 'Ye have nothing to do with us to build an house unto our God ; but we ourselves will build unto the LORD God of Israel, as king Cyrus the king of Persia hath commanded us.' Ezr. iv. 3. And as they said, so also they did: 'The elders of the Jews builded, and they prospered through the prophesying of Haggai the prophet and Zechariah the son of Iddo. And they builded, and finished *it*, according to the commandment of the God of Israel, and according to the commandment of Cyrus, and Darius, and Artaxerxes king of Persia.' Ezr. vi. 14. Yea, they did not only accept of the kindness of kings, but did acknowledge that kindness with thanksgiving, as a gift of the God of heaven: for the kings had commanded and given leave to the Jews to go to Jerusalem, to build their temple, and to do sacrifice there, according to the counsel of the priests that were at Jerusalem, and according to the law of God that they had in their hand. Ezr. vii. 13, 14. For Artaxerxes sent Ezra the priest to enquire after the condition that Jerusalem and Judah was in, according to, or by the law of God that was in his hand. ver. 14. And he had license also further to do with the king's silver and gold, which he gave for the service of the house of the Lord, 'according to the will, word or law of HIS God.' 'And thou, Ezra, (says the king) after the wisdom of thy God, (that is, after his word) that *is* in thine hand, set magistrates and judges, which may judge all the people that *are* beyond the river, all such as know the laws of thy God; and teach ye them that know *them* not. And whosoever will not do the law of thy God, (that is, worship, and walk by the rule of his testament,) and the law of the king, (that is, shall refuse to give Ezra such things as by the king was appointed for Ezra's help in the furthering of the worship of God, according to the law of his God,) let judgment be executed speedily upon him, whether *it be* unto death, or to banishment, or to confiscation of goods, or to imprisonment.' Ezr. vii. 25, 26. This was therefore a wonderful gracious license that the king now gave to Ezra: he imposed nothing upon him or the Jews in matters of religion and worship, but left him and them wholly to the law, will, and word of God, only he laid check upon wicked and ungodly people: that if they did things contrary to the laws of Ezra's God, or did slight the king's law, as aforesaid, that then such penalties and pains should be inflicted upon them.

To the same purpose was the decree of Cyrus, and that of Darius, to put it in execution. Also the penalty enacted against such offenders, was full as sharp and severe: 'Also I have made a decree (said the king,) that whosoever shall alter this word, let timber be pulled down from his house, and being set up, let him be hanged thereon; and let his house be made a dunghill for this.— And the God that hath caused his name to dwell there destroy all kings and people, that shall put to their hand to alter *and* to destroy this house of God which *is* at Jerusalem. I Darius have made a decree; let it be done with speed.' Ezr. vi. 11, 12.

Indeed, sometimes a stop was put to this work

by the kings, and the Jews were made to cease by force and power, ch. iv. 23, 24. the which the good people did bear with patience: Ezr. iv. 11—21. also they waited to see their God go before them among the kings, who at length took away Artaxerxes, who for a time had put a stop to the work, and brought in another, who gave leave that with speed it should be set on foot again. Ezr. v.

The Jews did also in these vacancies, or times in the which hinderances were put, carry it very tenderly and lovingly to those kings that at present they were under, submitting of their bodies and their goods to their will, and meekly endured the trial and affliction, serving them with all faithfulness, watching to save their lives from the hands of bloody men. Also when the king's laws, and the law of their God, did at any time come in competition, they would indeed adhere to, and do the law of their God; yet with that tenderness to the king, his crown and dignity, that they could at all times appeal to the righteous God about it. Da. vi. 22. Nor did they lose by so doing; yea, they prospered; for by this means Mordecai was made a great man, and a saviour of his people. Es. ii. 21—23. By this means also was Daniel made a great man, and helpful to his brethren. Da. v. 29.

Kings, I say, must be the men that must down with Antichrist, and they shall down with her in God's time.

God hath begun to draw the hearts of some of them from her already, and he will set them, in time, against her round about. If therefore they do not that work so fast as we would have them, let us exercise patience and hope in God: 'tis a wonder that they go so fast as they do, since the concerns of whole kingdoms lie upon their shoulders, and that there are so many Sanballats and Tobias's to flatter with them and misinform them concerning the people that are delivered but in part. See what an ugly account was given of Jerusalem by the enemies of the Jews, even then when they were in the hands of their deliverers: 'Be it known unto the king, that the Jews which came up from thee to us, are come unto Jerusalem, building the rebellious and bad city, and have set up the walls *thereof*, and joined the foundations.— Be it known now unto the king, that, if this city be builded, and the walls set up *again, then* will they not pay toll, tribute, and custom, and *so* thou shalt endamage the revenue of the kings.' Ezr. iv. 12, 13. Oh! what a *be it known, be it known*, is here! But were not these gentlemen more afraid of losing their own places and preferments, than of the king's losing of his toll and custom? But the whole was a lie, though it hindered the work for a time, and the patience of the people, and their loyalty to the king, did conquer and overcome all.

I speak the more to this, because, (as I have

said) I believe that by magistrates and powers we shall be delivered and kept from Antichrist; and because God has already begun to do it by such, by which also she shall be destroyed : and I have a few things to present to good men, to be conversant in, in such a day as this.

Let the king have verily a place in your hearts, and with heart and mouth give God thanks for him; he is a better saviour of us than we may be aware of, and may have delivered us from more deaths than we can tell how to think. We are bidden to 'give thanks to God for all men, and in the first place, for kings, and all that are in authority.' 1 Ti. ii. 1, 2.

Be not angry with them, no, not in thy thought; but consider, if they go not on in the work of reformation so fast as thou wouldest they should, the fault may be thine; know that thou also hast thy cold and chill frames of heart, and sittest still when thou shouldest be up and doing.

Pray for kings to the God of heaven, who has the hearts of kings in his hand : and do it ' without wrath, and doubting;' without *wrath*, because thy self is not perfect; and without *doubting*, because God governeth them, and has promised to bring down Antichrist by them.

Pray for the long life of the king.

Pray that God would always give wisdom and judgment to the king.

Pray that God would discover all plots and conspiracies against his person and government.

Pray also that God would make him able to drive away all evil and evil men from his presence; and that he may be a greater countenancer than ever, of them that are holy and good, and wait and believe, that God that has begun his quarrel with Babylon, Antichrist, the mother of Antichrist, the whore; would in his own time, and in his own way, bring her down by the means which he has appointed.

I do confess myself one of the old-fashion professors, that covet ' to fear God, and honour the king.' I also am for *blessing* of them that *curse* me, for *doing good* to them that *hate* me, and for *praying* for them that *despitefully use me, and persecute me*. And have had more peace in the practice of these things, than all the world are aware of. I only drop this, because I would shew my brethren that I also am one of them; and to set them right that have wrong thoughts of me, as to so weighty matters as these.*

Now these kings whose hearts God shall set to destroy Antichrist, shall do it without those inward reluctancies that will accompany inferior men : they shall be stript of all pity and compassion. Hence they are compared to the mighty waves of the sea, Je. li. 42. which saith, when the wrecked and dying mariners cry out for mercy for themselves, and for their children, I am a sea; ' I travail not, nor bring forth children, neither do I nourish up young men, *nor* bring up virgins:' Isa. xxiii. 4, 5. I have therefore no pity for these, or any of them. Therefore they must be swallowed up of this sea, and sink like a stone in the midst of these mighty waters.

And thus much for the *means* by which God will destroy the body and flesh of Antichrist.

OF THE CAUSES OF THE RUIN OF ANTICHRIST.

Although the causes of the ruin of Antichrist be to some conspicuous enough, yet to some they may be otherwise; yea, and will to all kings and people whose eyes shall be held, that they may not see the judgment, in the reasonableness and equitableness thereof; and these shall wail when they see 'the smoke of her - - torment;' and these shall cry, Alas! Alas! Re. xviii. 10. Wherefore, for further edification, as I have treated of the *man of sin* already; so will I now, of the *causes* of his downfall. And,

FIRST CAUSE.

First, He must down, *for that he hath usurped, and taken the name and attributes of God upon himself:* He hath said, ' I am God:' He hath set in the temple of God, ' shewing himself that he is God;' yea, and that in contempt and scorn of any other, ' exalting himself above all that is called God, or that is worshipped;' 2 Th. ii. yea, hath cried down all gods but himself. Wherefore it must needs be, that he be brought to judgment, that the truth of his saying may be proved. And for this cause he is threatened, under the name of the prince of Tyrus: ' Because thine heart *is* lifted up (saith the Lord) and thou hast said, I am a god, - - therefore I will bring strangers upon thee, the terrible of the nations : and they shall draw their swords against the beauty of thy wisdom, and they shall defile thy brightness. They shall bring thee down to the pit, and thou shalt die the deaths of *them that are* slain in the midst of the seas. Wilt thou yet say before him that slayeth thee, I *am* god? but thou *shalt be* a man, and no god, in the hand of him that slayeth thee.' Eze. xxviii. 2, 7—9.

If God will not give his *name* or *glory* to another,

---

* This Christian temper of Bunyan certainly saved him from much suffering while under persecution. It probably saved his invaluable life. But how deeply it increases the guilt of his persecutors, to send *such* a man to a damp wretched prison, for more than twelve years, because he dared not join in the worship established by law; and after all this, to hear his prayers and good wishes to his persecutors, ought to have cut them to the quick.—ED.

be sure he will not be *under* another; but *this* to have, and *thus* to do, Antichrist has attempted. But how? In that he has been so bold as to prescribe and impose a worship besides, and without reverence of that which God has prescribed and imposed: For to do this, is, to make one's self a God. 'Thou shalt have no other Gods before me,' is the first command: And the first, to enforce the second, 'Thou shalt not make unto thee any graven image, or the likeness *of any thing* that *is* in heaven above, or that *is* in the earth beneath, or that *is* in the water under the earth: thou shalt not bow down thyself to them, nor serve them:' For he that thus doth, is an idolater; and he that these things doth impose, is one that shews himself a God. But this doth Antichrist do: And 'tis worth the noting, That God forbids not only images, but the *likeness of any thing;* books, altars, fancies, imaginations, or any thing in heaven above, or in the earth beneath, to bow down to, or to make them a means to worship or come to God by, if he hath not commanded nor tolerated them in his holy word.

Thus saith the Lord: And, *I am the Lord*, is the *stamp*, the *seal*, and *sign* of all true rules of worship; and therefore it is so often repeated both in Moses, and in the prophets, where God commandeth worship to be performed, and imposeth the means and methods of it. Now this, *Thus saith the Lord*, Antichrist has rejected; and *I am the Lord*, he hath assumed to himself: and therefore without the law, the word and commandment, hath framed and imposed a worship, exalting himself in the temple of God, although he is but the man of sin, above all that is called God, or that is worshipped.

Nor is he in this his so foul a fact, without them that adore, worship his image, and wonder after him; yea, he hath got by this means almost the whole world to himself, who say, 'Who *is* like unto the beast? Who is able to make war with him?' Re. xiii. 4. And that they might shew their resolvedness to stand by him, they receive his mark in their forehead, or in their hand; His *mark;* that is, they either openly or seriously become his disciples, and worship him according to the rules, methods, and ways that he hath prescribed. Wherefore, these with him, are also to drink of the fierceness of the wrath of almighty God: 'If any man worship the beast and his image, and receive *his* mark in his forehead, or in his hand, the same shall drink of the wine of the wrath of God, which is poured out without mixture into the cup of his indignation; and he shall be tormented with fire and brimstone in the presence of the holy angels, and in the presence of the Lamb:' Re. xiv. 9, 10.

But, I say, for that Antichrist hath thus taken the *place of God*, prescribed and imposed a worship *as a God*, got the world to worship and wonder after him as *after a God*. Therefore shall he die the death of the uncircumcised, both in the soul, spirit, body, or flesh of Antichrist; therefore will God enlighten, and gather, and set the kings and nations against him, that both he and his may be buried, and have their dolesome withdrawing-rooms from the world in the sides of the pit's mouth.

SECOND CAUSE.

Secondly, Antichrist must be destroyed, because *he hath set himself against the* Son *of God;* against the Father, and against the Son. He had a spite against the Son betimes, even then when he came forth but in little *bits*, when he attempted to deny that he was come in the flesh. 1 Jn. iv. 1—4. But seeing he could make no earnings of that, he hath changed his methods, and seeks to run him out and down by other means and ways: Because therefore he hath set himself against the Son of God, the king, therefore he must die. That he hath set himself against the Son of God, is also evident; for he hath his name from thence: He is therefore called Antichrist. That he hath set himself against him, is yet further evident; for that he hath endeavoured to take from him his headship *over*, and his offices *for* and *in* the church, which is his body. He hath plainly endeavoured to be head, for that he hath striven to take his wife from him, and to cause that she should be called HIS: Yea, he hath endeavoured by all inventions to prostrate her to his lusts, to deflower her, and to make her an adulteress. He has been worse than Pharaoh, who took Abraham's wife; Ge. xii. and worse than Abimelech, who lusted after Isaac's: Ge. xxvi. Yea, worse than Phalti, who run away with David's; 1 Sa. xxv. 44. forasmuch as she is higher, beloved better, and cost more than did any of these. Would it not be counted an high affront, for a base inferior fellow, to call himself the head of the queen? Yet thus has Antichrist done, and worse; he has called himself the head of the universal church of God.

And as he has attempted to be head in his stead, so to be king, priest, and prophet.

[1.] He has attempted to wrest his sceptre and kingdom from him, in that he hath endeavoured to thrust himself into his throne, which is the heart and conscience of his people. The *heart* and *conscience* is that which Christ claimeth for his own proper and peculiar seat: 'My son, give me thy heart.' 'That Christ may dwell in your hearts by faith.' Ep. iii. 17. In this therefore the church is not to be for another man, so will he be for her; but this throne Antichrist has lusted for, attempted to take, and made war with Christ and his church, because they would not yield up to him this glorious throne of his, and therefore he must die.

[2.] He hath intruded upon the priestly office of Christ, hath called himself *high-priest;* though the Lord hath said, 'Because thou hast rejected knowledge, I will also reject thee, that thou shalt be no priest to me: seeing thou hast forgotten the law of thy God, I will also forget thy children.' Ho. iv. 6. But he will make himself a *priest;* he hath invented sacrifices for the *quick* and the *dead:* he hath put, as he presumes, merit and worth into these sacrifices; he hath commanded that those that worship, should have faith in, and expect benefit by these sacrifices, although he offereth to his God nought else but the flesh of the *hog,* and of the *mouse,* with the *broth* of his abominable things. Is. lxvi. 17. Many and sundry ways he hath set himself up to be high-priest, though God knows no high-priest but one, though the church ought to know no high-priest but one; yea, though no high-priest but one can approach God's mercy-seat, to do for us the necessary and desired work.

[3.] He hath intruded upon the prophetical office of Jesus Christ. What else means his pretences to *infallibility?** And that too when he imposes unwritten verities, abominable traditions, blasphemous rites and ceremonies; and forbids or dispenseth with the holy commands of God: Yea, when he enforceth these his *Omrian* statutes, and doth impose the works of the house of Ahab, Mi. vi. 16. he doth all in the name of the Lord Christ, when himself hath set himself in his place, and in his room. This is mystery Babylon, *the mystery of iniquity:* This is Antichrist's soul and body, and as such, must be destroyed. But,

THIRD CAUSE.

Thirdly, Antichrist must be destroyed, because *he hath blasphemed against the Holy Ghost,* and so set himself above the Father, the Son, the Spirit; against ALL that is called God. The Holy Ghost is that Spirit of truth that Christ has promised to give unto his church, to help her in the understanding of his holy word, and to enable her to believe, and walk humbly and holily before God and man. The spirit of Antichrist is that spirit of error that hath puffed up the false church into a conceit of herself, and unscriptural worship; and that hath made this false church, which is his body, to ascribe all the horrible things and acts thereof, to

the wisdom, guidance, directions or operations of the Holy Ghost: As,

1. In all her unscriptural councils, assemblies and convocations, they blasphemously father what they do upon the Holy Ghost, and make him the inventor and approver thereof.

2. She also blasphemeth the Holy Ghost, in accusing and condemning the holy scriptures of insufficiency, for that she saith, though it is a rule, yet but an imperfect one; one deficient, one that is not able to make the man of God perfect in all things, without the traditions, inventions, and blasphemous helps of antichristian wisdom.

3. She hath also blasphemed the Holy Ghost, in that she hath set up her own church-government, offices, officers and discipline: None of all which is the church of Christ directed to by the wisdom of the Spirit of God in his testament.

4. She hath also sinned against the Holy Ghost, in that she hath, as it were, turned the Holy Ghost out of doors, in concluding that he, without the works of the flesh, is not sufficient to govern the hearts of worshippers, in the service and worship of God.

5. She hath also thus sinned, in that *she hath wrought many lying miracles* in the face of the world, and imposed them upon her disciples for the confirming of her errors and blasphemous opinions, to the confronting of the true miracles wrought by the Holy Ghost; and also to the concluding, that there was an insufficiency in those that were true, to confirm the truth, without the addition of hers; which she has wrought by the power of Satan, and the spirit of delusion, only to confirm her lies.

6. She hath sinned against the Holy Ghost, in that she hath, with Jeroboam the son of Nebat, striven against the judgments wherewith God hath punished her; to call her back from her wicked way; and persisted therein, to the effectual proving of herself to be the lewd woman. 2 Ki. xiii. 4—7, 23, 24.

7. She hath sinned, by labouring to hide all her wickedness, by lies, dissimulations, and filthy equivocations of her priests, friars, Jesuits, &c. I say, her labouring to hide the wickedness that she hath committed against kings, countries, nations, kingdoms and people. She hath hid these things by the means or persons made mention of before; as by the tail; for they indeed are the tail of the beast, that cover his most filthy parts:† The prophet that speaketh lies, he is the tail. Is. ix. 15. But,

FOURTH CAUSE.

Fourthly, Antichrist must be destroyed, *for the horrid outrage, and villanous murders that she hath*

---

* What are Acts of Uniformity, compelling all persons, under pains and penalties, to conform to National Liturgies, or alluring them by honours and emoluments, but pretended infallibilities? All laws interfering with the solemn duty of *personal* investigation and decision, in all things connected with religion, are pretences to infallibility.—ED.

† See note on page 78.

committed upon the bodies of the saints. For there is none, as to these things, for cruelty, to be compared with the church of Antichrist, and her followers: For upon whom hath not her cruelty been shewed; have they never so little stood in her way, though never so innocently and honestly by so doing, stood to the truth and verity of God? Yea, the promoting of her own superstition, idolatry, and blasphemous rites and ceremonies, have been so pursued by her, that she has waded through a sea of innocent blood for the accomplishment thereof.

The poor church of God is a sensible bleeding witness of this, and so has been for hundreds of years together; witness the chronicles of all nations where she hath had to do; yea, and the sackcloth and ashes, and tears, and widows, and fatherless children, and their cries, of all which the holy word of God is a sufficient confirmation; 'And in her,' when God shall come to make inquisition for blood, 'will be found the blood of prophets and of saints, and of all that were slain upon the earth.' Re. xviii. 24. And yet has she such a whore's forehead, such a blindness in her judgment, and such an hard and obdurate heart, that it is not possible she should ever repent. Murders have been so natural to her, and in them her hand has been so exercised, that it is now become a custom, a trade, a pastime to her, to be either in the act, or laying some foundation for murders: Witness those plots, designs, conspiracies, and frequent attempts that are, one or other of them, continually on foot in the world for the commission of murders.

Nay, the text last mentioned seems to import, that blood is so natural to her, that she sticketh not at any condition, sex, age, or degree, so she may imbrue her hands in blood. In her was found the blood of saints and prophets, and of *all* other carnal, natural, ignorant, graceless men that have been slain upon the earth. It is she that sets kings and kingdoms at variance: It is she that sets parents and children at variance, by her abuse of the word of our Lord and Christ. And besides, is it not easy, if we do but consider those bloody massacres that have been committed by her hand, both in France, Ireland, Piedmont, and in several places besides, without wronging of her, to conclude, that the blood of thousands, that have not known their right hand from their left in religion, hath been shed, to quench, if it might have been, her insatiate thirst after blood. Therefore, for these things shall she be judged, as women that shed blood are judged; because she is an adulteress, and blood is in her hands. Eze. xxiii. 45. She hath been as a beast of prey: Nay, worse; for they do but kill and tear for the hunger of themselves, and of their whelps: but she, to satisfy her wanton and beastly lusts. 'They have

cast lots for my people; (saith God) and have given a boy for an harlot, and sold a girl for wine, that they might drink:' Joel iii. 3. and therefore must Antichrist be destroyed. Forbearance is no payment, God's patience is not a sign that he *forgetteth* to take vengeance; but rather, that he waiteth till his own are come out of her, and until her iniquity is filled up: For then he will execute the judgment written, and will remember, as has been said, the Babylonians, and all their ways.*

FIFTH CAUSE.

Fifthly, Antichrist must be destroyed, *because she hath put out of order, and confounded the rule and government that God has set up in the world.* I say, she has put it out of order, and confounded it in all places where she rules; so that it cannot accomplish the design of him that ordained it, To wit, To be a terror to evil works, and a praise to them that do well.

Wherefore we read, That those *horns* or *kings* where Mystery Babylon sitteth, are upon the heads of that beast that carrieth her, which beast is her protector. Magistracy is God's ordinance, appointed for the good of society, and for the peace and safety of those that are good. But this Antichrist has, where she rules, put all out of order; and no wonder, for she has *bepuddled* the word of God; no wonder, then, I say, if the foundations of the world be out of course. 'Tis she that hath turned the sword of the magistrate against those that keep God's law: 'Tis she that has made it the ruin of the good and virtuous, and a protection to the vile and base. Wherefore, when the Holy Ghost tells us, that the time is coming in which God will count with the bloody-minded, for the murders that they have committed; he in a manner doth quite excuse the magistrate, saying, 'Woe to the bloody city! it *is* all full of lies *and* robbery; the prey departeth not: The noise of a whip, and the noise of the rattling of the wheels, and of the prancing horses, and of the jumping chariots. The horseman lifteth up both the bright sword, and the glittering spear: and *there is* a multitude of slain, and a great number of carcases; and *there is*

---

* These bloody massacres, to which Bunyan here alludes, were attended with atrocities at which nature shudders. In France, under a Bourbon and a Guise, the murder of hundreds of thousands of pious men and women, with helpless infants, threw down every barrier to the spread of infidelity, and a frightful reaction took place at the Revolution. In Ireland, under a Stuart and a Bourbon, still *more frightful* atrocities were perpetrated, and which were severely punished by Cromwell and his Roundheads. Under a second Stuart, awful wholesale murders were again committed, and punished by William III.; and the voice of the blood that was shed by Antichrist, and the voices of people enslaved by a national religion, which it considers heresy—these voices cry for vengeance, and desolate that unhappy country.—ED.

none end of *their* corpses; they stumble upon their corpses.' Na. iii. 1—3. But what is the cause of all this slaying, and the reason of this abundance of corpses? Why, it is because of the unsatiable thirst of the bloody city after blood: and, 'Because of the multitude of the whoredoms of the well-favoured harlot, the mistress of witchcrafts, that selleth nations through her whoredoms, and families through her witchcrafts.' ver. 4. But doth this bloody city spill this blood by herself simply, as she is the adulterated whore? No, this church has found out a trick; that is to say, to quarrel with Christ in his members; and to persuade the powers where she rules to set ensnaring laws to catch them, and to execute the same upon them.

Thus when the synagogue of Satan, of old, had taken Christ, and accused him, they made Pontius Pilate to condemn and hang him. But God has begun to shew to some of the kings this wickedness, and has prevailed with them to PROTEST against her. And in the mean time, for those that are yet in the bed of love with her, the Holy Ghost doth, in the text last mentioned, and in Re. xviii. 24. much excuse them for the blood that they have shed, and for the injuries that they have done to his people; because they have not done it of their mere inclinations, nor in the prosecution of their office, but through the whoredoms and witchcrafts of this well-favoured harlot, who hath with false doctrines, false promises, and causeless curses, prevailed on them to do it. And they have done it, rather of *fear* than *favour*. Some indeed have more doted upon her beauty, and have more thoroughly been devoted to her service: But they also had not that aptness to do so of themselves, but have been forced to it by the power of her enchantments: Therefore, I say, the main guilt shall be laid at her door, for that she in chief has deserved it. 'Son of man (says God) take up a lamentation for the princes of Israel.' Why? Because their mother, the church, was at that time adulterated, and become a lioness, had lain down with the heathen, and so brought forth young lions, that is, rulers: 'And she brought up one of her whelps: it became a young lion, and it learned to catch the prey; it devoured men.' Eze. xix. 1—3. It *learnt*, It *learnt*: But of *who* but of its *dam*, or of the lioness to whom she had put it to learn to do such things? Therefore they are to be lamented and pitied, rather than condemned, and their mother made to bear the blame. Wherefore it follows, 'She was plucked up in fury, she was cast down to the ground, and the east wind dried up her fruit: her strong rods were broken and withered; the fire consumed them. And now she *is* planted in the wilderness, (in the provinces of Babylon,) in a dry and thirsty ground. And fire is gone out of a rod of her branches, *which* hath devoured her fruit, so that he hath no strong rod *to be* a sceptre to rule. This *is* a lamentation, and shall be for a lamentation.' Eze. xix. 12—14.

Sixthly, Antichrist must be destroyed, because of *her exceeding covetousness.* Religion, such as it is, is the thing pretended to: But the great things of this world, are the things really intended by her in all her seeming self-denials and devotions. And for this covetousness also it is that this destruction is to fall upon her: 'Woe to him that coveteth an evil covetousness to his house, (to his church) that he may set his nest on high;' Hab. ii. 9. (for he could not do the one, before he had obtained the other:) for then indeed they began to be high, when they had so inveigled Constantine, that he bestowed upon them much riches and honour; and then it was cried by an angel, and the cry was heard in the city, Constantinople! 'Woe! woe! woe! this day is venom poured into the church of God!' (as both my Lord Cobham and Mr. Fox witness in the book of Acts and Monuments.)*

Nor has any generation since the world began, been so insatiably greedy of gain, as these poor people have been: They have got kingdoms, they have got crowns, they have got, —— What have they not got? They have got everything but grace and pardon. Did I say before, that *religion* is their pretence? Doth not the whole course of their way declare it to their face? Every one of them, from the least even to the greatest, is given to covetousness, from the prophet even to the priest, every one dealeth falsely: Je. vi. 13. and viii. 10. *Money, money*, as the pedlar cries,† broken or whole, is the sinews of their religion: And it is for that they set kingdoms, crowns, principalities, places, preferments, sacraments, pardons, prayers, indulgences, liberty; yea, and souls and bodies of men, women and children, to sale. Yea, it is for this that they have invented so many places, offices, names, titles, orders, vows, &c. It is to get money, to rob countries, that they may make their nests on high. And indeed they have done it, to the amazement of all the world. They are clam-

---

* In the first examination of Lord Cobham, (Fox, vi. p. 732, edit. 1632,) the gallant knight was asked by his bitter persecutor, what he meant by 'the venom shed over the church;' his reply was, 'Your possessions and lordships.' For then cried an angel in the air—'Wo! Wo! Wo! this day is venom shed into the church of God. - - Rome is the very nest of Antichrist—prelates, priests and monks are the body; and these pild (bald, but query, pillaging) friars are the tail, which covereth his most filthy part.' How peaceful and blessed will be the church when ALL her ministers can glory with Paul, in Acts xx. 33, 34.—ED.

† The principal cry of the travelling pedlars was for broken or light money, to exchange for their wares: now obsolete. —ED

bered up above *kings* and *princes*, and *emperors:**
They wear the *triple-crown:* They have made
kings bow at their *feet*, and *emperors*, stand bare-
foot at their *gates:* They have *kicked* the crowns
of princes from their heads, and *set* them on again
with their *toes*.† Thus their covetousness has set
them high, even above the suns, moons and stars
of this world: but to what end? That they may
be cast down to hell.

SEVENTH CAUSE.

Seventhly, Antichrist must be destroyed, because
*he standeth in the way of the setting up of the king-
dom of Christ in the world.* Many princes were in
Edom before there was a king in Israel; and
Christ has suffered Antichrist to set up before him.
And he standeth in his way, and has so overspread
the world in all places, with that which is directly
contrary to him, that he cannot set up his kingdom, until that which is Antichrist's is tumbled
down to the ground; even as a man whose ground
is full of thorns, and briars, and weeds, cannot
sow in expectation of a crop, until he hath
removed them. And these seeds has Antichrist
sown where the kingdom of Christ should stand:
'Upon the land of my people shall come up thorns
and briars; yea, upon all the houses of joy *in* the
joyous city: Because the palaces shall be forsaken;
the multitude of the city shall be left; the forts
and towers shall be for dens for ever, a joy of wild
asses, a pasture of flocks, (this is to happen to the
church of God,) Until the Spirit be poured upon
us from on high, and the wilderness be a fruitful
field, and the fruitful field be counted for a forest.'
Is. xxxii. 13—15. And the antichristian synagogue be
turned into a wilderness.

When God came from Egypt with his people, to
set up his kingdom in Canaan, he cast out the
heathen before them in order thereunto; 'Thou
hast brought a vine out of Egypt: thou hast cast
out the heathen, and planted it.' Ps. lxxx. 8. Wherefore, Antichrist must be removed and destroyed
for this: For Antichrist is in flat opposition to
Christ, as Tibni was to Omri: 1 Ki. xvi. 21, 22. Wherefore Antichrist must die. The reason is, because
Christ's kingdom shall be peaceable, without molestation; and glorious, without the fumes and fogs
of Antichristian darkness: Because also, as the
world hath seen the manner of the reign of Antichrist, and how tyrannical and outrageous a kingdom his is: so they shall see the reign of Christ,

by his word and spirit in his people, how peaceable, how fruitful in blessedness and prosperity his
kingdom is. And hence it is that God purposeth
to bury Antichrist, before he sets 'glory in the land
of the living.' Eze. xxvi. 20, 21. As also you read in
the book of Revelations; for there you find the
kingdom of Antichrist was destroyed before the
new Jerusalem was set up. When men intend to
build a new house, if in the place where the old one
stood, they first pull down the old one, raze the
foundation, and then they begin their new. Now
God, as I said, will have his primitive church state
set up in this world, (even where Antichrist has set
up his;) wherefore, in order to this, Antichrist
must be pulled down, down stick and stone; and then
they that live to see it, will behold the new Jerusalem come down from heaven, *as a bride* adorned
for her husband.

New wine is not put into old bottles, nor a new
piece into an old garment; nor shall any of the old
anti-scriptural ordinances, ceremonies, rites, or
vessels of the man of sin, be made use of, or accounted anything worth, in this day of the kingdom of Jesus Christ. And thus I have shewed
you something of Antichrist, of his ruin, and of
the manner and signs of the approach thereof; together with the means and causes of his ruin.
All which I leave to the judgment of the godly,
and beg their instruction where they see me to be
out; and shall conclude, after a short word of
application.

First, Must Antichrist be destroyed? Then this
informs us, that a time is coming wherein there
shall be no Antichrist to afflict God's church any
more. 'Tis Antichrist, Antichristians, and Antichristianism, that is the cause of the troubles of
Christians, *for being Christians.* And therefore 'tis
from the consideration of this that it is said, men
'shall beat their swords into plough-shares, and
their spears into pruning-hooks,' and that they
'shall learn war no more:' Is. ii. 4. Yea it is from
the consideration of this, that it is said the child
shall play with venomous and destroying beasts,
and that *a little child* shall lead the *wolf*, the *leopard*,
and the *young lion*, and that the weaned child shall
put his hand into the cockatrice's den, and catch
no hurt thereby. Is. xi. 6—9. For as was said before,
'tis through the instigation of this spirit of error,
that the governors of the world have heretofore
done hurt to Zion, and I say now again, all things
shall turn to their right course, and occupy their
places, as do the bodies in the higher orbs.

Secondly, Is Antichrist to be destroyed, and
must she have an end? Then this gives us to understand, that a day is coming when Antichrist
shall be unknown, not seen, nor felt by the church
of God. There are men to be born who shall not
know Antichrist, but as they read in the word that

---

* Such has been the tendency of the Antichristian church
in all ages; witness the cases of the Emperor Henry IV.,
Henry II. of England, and many others. The spirit and precept of Christianity, on the contrary, is, while fearing God, to
honour the king; and that we be subject to principalities and
powers, Tit. iii. 1; see also Mat. xxii. 21; Ro. xiii. 1-7.—ED.

† See Fox's Martyr., folio, vol. i., last leaf.—ED.

such a thing has been. These shall talk of her, as Israel's childrens' children were to talk of Pharaoh, of his cruelty; of his tasks, of his pride, of the Red Sea, and how he was drowned there: They shall talk of them, as of those that have been long dead; as of those who for their horrible wickedness, are laid in the pit's mouth. This will be some of that sweet chat that the saints shall, at their spare hours, have in time to come. When God has pulled this dragon out of the sea, this leviathan out of his river, and cast his dead carcase upon the open field, then shall those whose ancestors have been put into terrors by him, come flocking to see the monster; and shall rejoice for all the mercy. In that day, the church of God shall say, ' O Lord I will praise thee: though thou wast angry with me, thine anger is turned away, and thou comfortest me.—In that day shall ye say, Praise the Lord, call upon his name, declare his doings among the people,' &c. Is. xii. 1, 4. O how sweetly did David, and the church in his day, sing of the ruins of the Egyptians, and the deliverances of their fathers, which had been in times of old! Ps. lxviii. to wit, what God did in Egypt, what he did at the Red Sea; what he did to Sihon, to Og, and to the remnant of the giants: How he divided the waters of Jordan, and gave the land of Canaan in its fruitfulness among his people: Ps. cv. How that though Pharaoh and his horsemen and chariots were terrible *then*, yet *now* there is nothing left but their souls, their feet, and the palms of their hands; nothing but that which can do no hurt; nothing but what may minister an occasion of joyful remembrance of them. Ps. cvi. and cxxxii.

Thirdly, Is Antichrist to be destroyed? *Then this calls aloud to God's people to make haste to come out of her.* ' Ho, ho,' says the prophet: He cries out as if the people were asleep: ' *Come forth*, and flee from the land of the north.' Zec. ii. 6. The people of God in the latter days will want a heart to come out of her, with that fear of her plagues as they should: Wherefore another says, ' Come out of her, my people, that ye be not partakers of her sins and that ye receive not of her plagues.' Re. xviii. 4. When Israel was carried into Babylon, 'twas not that they should dwell there for ever: Though they were bid to build them houses, and beget them children there. But when they had built, planted vineyards, and got wives and children there, 'twas hard getting them from thence again: For now they were as it were naturalized to the country, and to the manners of it. Je. xxix. 4—7. But God will have them out, (but they must not think to carry thence their houses and vineyards on their backs,) or he will destroy them with those destructions wherewith he hath threatened to destroy Babylon itself. Flesh will hang behind, because it

favoureth the things of the flesh, plenty of which there is in that country: But they that will live after the flesh must die. ' Wherefore come out from among them, and be ye separate, - - and touch not the unclean *thing;* and I will receive you, and will be a father unto you, and ye shall be my sons and daughters, saith the Lord Almighty.' 2 Co. vi. 17, 18. But why (some may say) *must we come out?* I answer, because God has *temple-work* to do, *temple-worship* to do, *temple-sacrifices* to offer, and none of these things can by any means be done, but at Jerusalem. But if you still object and say, ' The Lord has raised us up prophets in Babylon,' and we will not come out; you must not murmur if you feel what is to follow. And that such may know upon what bottom they stand, let them read the 29th chapter of Jer. 15 —19.

Fourthly, Must Antichrist be destroyed? *Then what mean they, who were to appearance once come out, but now are going thither again?* If it cost Lot's wife dear for but *looking* back, shall not it cost them much dearer, that are *going* back, that are *gone* back again? and that, AFTER the angel had fled through the midst of heaven, preaching the gospel to those that dwell on the earth? Re. xiv. 6—10. They that received the mark of the beast at first, *before* this angel came forth, are when compared with these, excusable: Re. xiii. 16, 17. Wherefore, they are not threatened with that smoking wrath, as are these which are here under consideration.

You dread, that which is like to become of them that will be so mad to run into an house, when fire is putting to the gunpowder barrel, in order to its blowing up: Why thus do they, let their pretended cause be what it will, that are returning again to Babel. Are her plagues pleasant or easy to be borne? Or dost thou think that God is at play with thee, and that he threateneth but in jest? Her plagues are *death*, and *mourning*, and *famine*, and *fire;* Re. xviii. 8. are these things to be overlooked? And they that, as before is hinted, shall receive the mark of the beast in their forehead, or in their hand, and shall worship him, they, ' the same shall drink of the wine of the wrath of God:' Re. xiv. 10. And will this be a delightsome draught? Remember how ill God took it, that his people of old, in their hearts, though but in their hearts, went back again into Egypt. You may say, but I have *friends, relations,* and *concerns* in Babylon. And, I answer, so had Lot in Sodom; Ge. xix. 14—16. but for all that, he must either quickly come out, or run the hazard of being burned there with them. But methinks, a people that belong to God, should be willing to leave all to follow him: Besides, his presence is promised at Jerusalem, there also will he accept thy offerings.

Fifthly, Is Antichrist to be destroyed? *Then let them that love God, his Son, and his Zion, cry to God that it may be hastened in its time.* One of the songs of Zion is, that Babylon shall be destroyed. The cries of the souls of them that were slain for the witness of Jesus is, that Babylon may be counted with, and that their blood may be revenged upon her. The promise is, that Babylon shall be destroyed: And do we hold our tongues? The church of God will not flourish as it should, until Babylon is destroyed: The world will never be in its right wits, until Babylon is destroyed: The kingdom of Christ will never be set up, in and by his church, as it ought, and shall, until Antichrist is destroyed: There will never be peace upon earth till Antichrist is destroyed: And God has promised that there shall be peace and truth, and glory, when Babylon is destroyed: And do we hold our peace? Besides, your innocency in suffering; your honesty towards God, in your testimony for his truth; the substantial ground which you have for the bottom of your faith, as to things controverted betwixt Antichrist and you, will never be manifested as it will then; and so consequently, you never so brought out to the light, and your enemies never so put to shame as then. 'Then shame shall cover her that said unto thee, Where is the Lord thy God?' Wherefore, as I said, cry unto the Lord, keep not silence, give him no rest, let him not alone, until he has delivered his miserable people out of the mouth of this lion, and from the paw of this bear.

Sixthly, Is Antichrist to be destroyed? *Then let us live in the expectation of it;* and let this be one of our songs in the house of our pilgrimage. God bids his people, while in Babylon, to let Jerusalem come into their mind, Je. li. 50. and writes to them that then were in her, to acquaint them that he remembered them still, and would assuredly deliver them from that *place* and *state.* And wherefore doth he thus, but to beget an expectation in them of their salvation and deliverance? Je. xxix. 13, 14. The Lord is so pleased with the faith and expectation of his people, as to this, that they seldom are herein concerned as they should, but he steps in with them, and warms their hearts. The reason is, because the faith of God's people, as to the downfall of Babylon, stands upon as sure a foundation as doth the salvation of their souls; and that next to that, God is as much delighted in what he has purposed to do against Babylon, as in anything else in the earth: And therefore, if you consider it well, the great and glorious promises that are to be fulfilled on earth, are to be fulfilled when Antichrist is dead and buried: These *bits* are too good even for his children to have, so long as this dog is by, lest he should snatch at the crumbs thereof; wherefore they are reserved until he is

VOL. II.

gone: For thus saith the Lord, 'That after seventy years be accomplished at Babylon, I will visit you, and perform my good word towards you, in causing you to return to this place: For I know the thoughts that I think toward you, saith the Lord; thoughts of peace, and not of evil, to give you an expected end.' This is in Jeremiah the twenty-ninth, ver. 10, 11. and in chapter the thirty-first he adds, 'Therefore they shall come and sing in the height of Zion, and shall flow together to the goodness of the LORD, for wheat, and for wine, and for oil, and for the young of the flock and of the herd: and their soul shall be as a watered garden; and they shall not sorrow any more at all. Then shall the virgin rejoice in the dance, both young men and old together: for I will turn their mourning into joy, and will comfort them, and make them rejoice from their sorrow. And I will satiate the soul of the priests with fatness, and my people shall be satisfied with my goodness, saith the Lord.' ver. 12—14. Again, in the thirty-second chapter, still speaking of the same thing, he saith, 'Yea, I will rejoice over them to do them good, and I will plant them in this land assuredly with my whole heart and with my whole soul.' ver. 41.

I conclude this with that which I find in chapter the thirty-third: 'And I will cleanse them from all their iniquity, whereby they have sinned against me; and I will pardon all their iniquities, whereby they have sinned, and whereby they have transgressed against me. And it shall be to me a name of joy, a praise, and an honour before all the nations of the earth, which shall hear all the good that I do unto them: and they shall fear and tremble, for all the goodness and for all the prosperity that I procure unto it.' ver. 8, 9.

Seventhly, Must Antichrist be destroyed? *Then this should make us glad, when we see the signs of his fall presenting themselves to our view.* Indeed, the signs of his fall, or those that forerun it, are terrible, and amazing to behold. But what of that, since the wrinkles that are in their faces threaten not us but them? A man is angry, and will punish; yea, and whets his sword, makes his rod, and he speaks not a word, but *blood, blood,* is in it. Indeed, this should make them that are concerned in this anger, be afraid; (but the judgment is, they are fast asleep,) but what is in all this of terror to them, for the pleading whose cause he is *so* angry with the other? Nothing whereat the innocent should be afraid. Cold blasts in November are not received with that gentleness as are colder in March and April; for that these last cold ones are but the farewell notes of a piercing winter; they also bring with them the signs and tokens of a comfortable summer. Why, the church is now at the rising of the year; let then the blasts at present, or to come, be what they will, Anti-

L

christ is assuredly drawing towards his downfall: And though the devil, knowing what is to be done to him, and to his kingdom, shall so blind his disciples, and fright the godly, do something like it upon the church of Christ; yet we should look through these *paper-winkers*,* and espy in all this, that fear, yea, certain terrible judgments are following of him at the heels, by which not only the soul, spirit, and life of Antichrist, but the body thereof; yea, body, and soul, and head, are quickly to go down thither; from whence they, as such, shall not arise again.   Amen.

* '*Paper-winkers*,' in every edition, except the first, which was from the author's manuscript, has been altered to 'paper-windows.' Bunyan's allusion is to the winkers, called by many 'blinkers,' put by the side of a horse's eyes, to keep him under the *complete control* of his driver—and by '*paper*-winkers' the flimsy attempts of Antichrist to *hood-wink* mankind by printed legends, miracles, and absurd assumptions—it is one of the almost innumerable sparks of wit, which render all the writings of Bunyan so entertaining and strikingly instructive. —ED.

THE RESURRECTION OF THE DEAD,

AND

ETERNAL JUDGMENT:

OR, THE TRUTH OF THE *RESURRECTION* OF THE *BODIES*, BOTH OF GOOD AND BAD AT THE
LAST DAY: ASSERTED, AND PROVED BY GOD'S WORD.

ALSO, THE MANNER AND ORDER OF THEIR COMING FORTH OF THEIR GRAVES; AS ALSO, WITH WHAT BODIES
THEY DO ARISE. TOGETHER, WITH A DISCOURSE OF THE LAST JUDGMENT, AND THE
FINAL CONCLUSION OF THE WHOLE WORLD.

By JOHN BUNYAN, A SERVANT OF THE LORD'S CHRIST.

' *Behold, I shew you a mystery; We shall not all sleep, but we shall all be changed, in a moment, in the twinkling of an eye, at the last trump: for the trumpet shall sound, and the dead shall be raised incorruptible, and we shall be changed.* —1 COR. xv. 51, 52.

' *Marvel not at this: for the hour is coming, in the which all that are in the graves shall hear his voice, and shall come forth; they that have done good, unto the resurrection of life; and they that have done evil, unto the resurrection of damnation.*'—JOHN v. 28, 29.

London: Printed for Francis Smith, at the Elephant and Castle, without Temple-Barre. [No date.]

ADVERTISEMENT BY THE EDITOR.

THIS very important treatise, judging from the style in which it is written, was, probably, one of the first books composed by Bunyan. The form in which it is prepared, with minute divisions to assist the memory, and its colloquial language, indicate that it was first intended for the pulpit and then enlarged to form a more complete treatise; while the frequent recurrence of the words 'I say,' shew the unpolished style in which he was in the habit of committing his thoughts to paper, when he became an author.

A good copy of what appears to be the first edition, is in the British Museum, a small 8vo, without date—and from this, collated with the reprint by C. Doe in Bunyan's works, 1691, the present edition is published. Doe, in his catalogue of all Mr. Bunyan's books, appended to the Heavenly Footman, 1690, states that 'The resurrection of the Dead, and eternal Judgment by John Bunyan, a servant of the Lord's Christ, was first published in 1665.' I have not been able to discover any subsequent edition in a separate volume.

The resurrection of the body is a subject of universal and deep importance. It defies our reasoning powers, while it exalts our ideas of the divine omnipotence. With God, all things revealed in his word are not only possible, but certain of accomplishment. The bodies of the saints, which are a part of the Redeemer's purchase will be raised in heavenly and wondrous perfection; like to the Saviour's glorious body. That body, which being transfigured ' did shine as the sun, and his raiment became as the light.' That body which, after his resurrection, might be touched, but which could appear and disappear to mortal eyes; in the room at Emmaus, or in a closed room filled with his disciples; could be touched, yet vanish away; could eat with them on the sea shore, and could ascend to heaven from the mount. Thus it was foretold by the prophet and reiterated by the apostle— 'Eye hath not seen, nor ear heard, neither have entered into the heart of man, the things which God hath prepared for them that love him.' Is. lxiv. 4; 1 Co. ii. 9. Not one atom of our dust can be lost; a bright, a glorious anticipation to the saints; but how solemn and awful a thought to those who die without hope. Among Christians it is common to think and talk of the happiness of the *spirits* of the just made perfect; but alas, how seldom do we think or speak of the perfect bliss of our whole nature, body, soul, and spirit—incorruptible, undefiled, glorified—every part equally the object of the Saviour's purchase and of his care.

This treatise, which will be *ever new*, and *ever important*, was peculiarly required in Bunyan's early days. Under the protectorate, the minds of men, which had been kept in slavery, became suddenly emancipated from human creeds and formularies of public worship. The personal attention of every one was then directed to the Bible—the Lord's day was observed, men were chosen as ministers not from high connections, but from deep and humble piety. Tens of thousands became happy in a personal knowledge of divine truth. At such a period, it must have happened that some evil spirits would exalt themselves, and that even some serious inquirers would draw strange conclusions from a misconception of divine truth; and dimly see 'men as trees walking.' Among these there appeared teachers, who, unable to comprehend how that body, which had gone to dust, or in some cases had been reduced by fire to its primary elements, and dispersed to the winds or waves, could be again produced. They revived an ancient error, That the new birth was the only resurrection from death; and consequently, that to those who were born again, the resurrection was passed. The individuals who promulgated these opinions, do not appear to have been associated together as a sect, or a church. The greater number were called in derision 'ranters,' and some 'quakers.' It is very probable, that this treatise was intended as an antidote to these delusions. We must not infer from the opinions of a few unworthy individuals, who justly deserved censure, that Bunyan meant to reflect upon the Society of Friends. This treatise was printed in 1665: but it was not until 1675 that the Quakers' rules of discipline were first published, and they from that time as a sect have been, in a high degree, conformable to the morality and heavenly influences of the gospel. But even before this, Fox, Crisp, Penn, Barclay, and others, who afterwards formed the Society of Friends, had declared their full belief in this doctrine. ' The resurrection of the just and unjust—the last judgment—heaven and hell as future rewards—we believe and confess.' ' We believe the holy manhood of Christ to be in heavenly glory.' ' We acknowledge a resurrection in order to eternal recompence, and rest contented with that body which it shall please God to give us.' ' We do firmly believe that *besides* the resurrection of the soul from the death of sin, to a life of righteousness while here, *there will be* a resurrection of the dead hereafter, and that we must *all* appear before the judgment seat of Christ.' Barclay, in his catechism, 1673, clearly asserts Bunyan's own ideas of the resurrection. But in the face of these, and a thousand similar declarations, the grossest calumnies were asserted by a fanatic clergyman, Alexr. Ross, in his View of all Religions:—' The Ranters are a sect of beasts that neither divide the hoof, nor chew the cud; that is to say, very unclean ones. They, like the Quakers,

oppose forms and order (the form and order of Common Prayer). To anatomize this monster: 1st, They hold that God, Devils, Angels, Heaven, and Hell, are fictions. 2d, That Moses, the Baptist, and Christ were impostors. 3d, That preaching and praying is lying.' 8vo., 1696, p. 273. And such wild slanders were uttered occasionally against all dissenters, until a much later period. Happily they are now better known, and the truths of Christianity are more appreciated. I have been careful to guard the reader upon this subject, lest it should be thought that Bunyan had in any degree manifested the spirit of those, who even to the present day misrepresent the opinions of the Quakers. This may be occasioned by their distinguishing tenet—That the work of the ministry is purely a labour of love, and ought not to be performed for hire — derived from the command of Christ to his disciples, ' Freely ye have received, freely give.' This, however, is no reason that they should be, as to their general views of divine truth, misrepresented and traduced.

Bunyan, at all times solemn and impressive, is peculiarly earnest and searching in this treatise. The dead will arise involuntarily and irresistibly —conscience uncontrolled, *must* testify the truth, yea, *all* the truth to the condemnation of the soul and body, unless cleansed from sin by faith in the Redeemer and the sacred influences of the Holy Spirit. The books will be opened, and every thought and word and action be seen inscribed in characters legible to all. Every soul will be able to read and clearly to understand those mysterious books—God's omniscient, his penetrating, his universal sight of all things from the creation of the world to the final consummation; and his perfect remembrance of all that he saw—*are one and the same*. There is *then* no refuge, no escape—the word depart *impels* obedience, and the sinner plunges into eternal woe!! O that the living may lay these awful realities to heart, and fly for refuge to the bosom of the Redeemer—he only is able— he is willing to save to the uttermost all that come unto God by him. And they who find in him a refuge from the storms of life, shall hear his voice irresistibly impelling them to heaven, ' Come, ye blessed of my Father, inherit the kingdom prepared for you from the foundation of the world.'

> O glorious hour! O blest abode!
> I shall be like and near my God!
> And flesh and sin no more control
> The sacred pleasures of the soul.

May the divine blessing abundantly attend the reading of these awful or joyful realities.

GEO. OFFOR.

PREFACE.

Courteous Reader,

Though this be a small treatise, yet it doth present thee with things of the greatest and most weighty concernment, even with a discourse of life and death to eternity: opening, and clearing, by the scriptures of God, that the time is at hand, when, *there shall be a resurrection of the dead, both of the just and unjust; even of the bodies of both, from the graves where they are, or shall be, at the approach of that day.*

Thou hast also in these few lines, the order and manner of the rising of these two sorts of people, wherein is shewed thee with what *body* they shall then rise, as also their states and condition at this day, with great clearness.

For here thou shalt see the truth, and manner of the terrible judgment, the opening of the books, the examining of witnesses, with a final conclusion upon good and bad. Which, I hope will be profitable to thy soul that shall read it. For if thou art godly, then here is that which will, through God's blessing, encourage thee to go on in the faith of the truth of the gospel; but if thou art ungodly, then here thou mayst meet with conviction: yea, and that of what will be, without fail, thy end, at the end of the world: whether thou continue in thy sins, or repent. If thou continue in them, blackness, and darkness, and everlasting destruction; but if thou repent, and believe the gospel, then light, and life, and joy, and comfort, and glory, and happiness, and that to eternity.

Wherefore let me here beg these things at thy hand,

First, That thou take heed of that spirit of mockery that saith, 'Where is the promise of his coming?' 2 Pe. iii. 4, 5.

Secondly, Take heed that thy heart be not over-charged with surfeiting and drunkenness, and the cares of this life, and so that day come upon thee unawares. Lu. xxi. 34, 35.

Thirdly, But be diligent in making thy calling and election sure; that thou in the day, of which thou shalt read more in this book, be not found without that glorious righteousness that will then stand thee in stead, and present thee before his glorious presence, with exceeding joy. To him be glory in the church by Christ Jesus, world without end. Amen.   John Bunyan.

OF THE RESURRECTION OF THE DEAD.

'But this I confess unto thee, that after the way which they call heresy, so worship I the God of my fathers, believing all things which are written in the law and in the prophets: and have hope toward God, which they themselves also allow, that there shall be a resurrection of the dead, both of the just and unjust.' —Acts xxiv. 14, 15.

My discourse upon this text, will chiefly concern the resurrection of the dead: wherefore to that I shall immediately apply myself, not meddling with what else is couched in the words.

You see here, that Paul, being upon his arraignment, accused of many things, by some that were violent for his blood; and being licensed to speak for himself by the then heathen magistrate; he doth in few words tell them, that as touching the crimes wherewith they charged him, he was utterly faultless, only this he confessed, that after that way which they call heresy, so he worshipped the God of his fathers; believing all things that are written in the law and the prophets, and that he had the same hope towards God, which they themselves did allow, that there should be a resurrection of the dead, both of the just and unjust.

Whence note by the way, that a hypocritical people, will persecute the power of those truths in others, which themselves in words profess. I have hopes towards God, and that, such a hope which themselves do allow, and yet I am this day, and that for this very thing, persecuted by them.

But to come to my purpose, 'There shall be a resurrection of the dead,' &c. By these words, the apostle sheweth us what was the substance of his doctrine, to wit, that there should be 'a resurrection of the dead;' and by these words also, what was the great argument with his soul, to carry him through these temptations, afflictions, reproaches, and necessities he met with in this world, even the doctrine of a *resurrection*. I have hope towards God, saith he, and there is my mind fixed; for there shall be 'a resurrection of the dead, both of the just and unjust.' The reason why I cannot do what these Jews would have me; also why I cannot live as do the Gentiles, it is, because I have in my soul, the faith of the resurrection. This is the doctrine I say, which makes me fear to offend, and that is as an undergirder to my soul, whereby I am kept from destruction and confusion, under all the storms and tempests I here go through. In a word, this is it that hath more awe upon my conscience than all the laws of men, with all the penalties they inflict. 'And herein do I exercise myself, to have always a conscience void of offence toward God and *toward* men.' ver. 16.

Now here, seeing this doctrine of the resurrection of the dead hath that power, both to bear up and to awe; both to encourage and to keep within compass, the spirit and body of the people of God; it will be requisite, and profitable for us, to inquire into the true meaning and nature of this word, 'the resurrection of the dead.'

And for the better compassing of this matter, I shall briefly enquire,

First, What in this place is meant by *the dead*.

Secondly, What is meant by *the resurrection*.

Thirdly, Why the apostle doth here speak of the resurrection of the dead as *of a thing yet to come* —'There shall be a resurrection of the dead, both of the just and unjust.'

First. The *dead* in scripture go under a fivefold consideration; as,

1. Such as die a natural death, or as when a man ceaseth to be any more in this world, as David, whom Peter tells us 'is both dead and buried, and his sepulchre is with us to this day.' Ac. ii. 29.

2. There is a people that are reckoned dead in trespasses and sins, as those are, who never yet were translated from darkness to light, and from the power of Satan to God. Such, I say, who yet never felt the power of the Word and Spirit of God, to raise them from that state, to walk with him in the regeneration; making a life out of Christ, and his present benefits. Ep. ii. 1, 2; Jn. v. 25.

3. There is a death seizeth men often after some measure of light received from God, and some profession of the gospel of Christ. These, for the certainty of their damnation, are said to be dead —dead, twice dead, and plucked up by the roots. Jude 12.

4. There is in scripture mention made of a death *to sin*, and the lusts of the flesh; this death is the beginning of true life and happiness, and is a certain forerunner of a share in Christ, and with him in another world. Ro. vi. 6—8; 2 Ti. ii. 11.

5. Lastly. There is also in the word, a relation of eternal death. This is the death that those are in, and swallowed up of, that go out of this world Godless, Christless, and graceless; dying in sin, and so under the curse of the dreadful God; who, I say, because they have missed of the Lord Jesus Christ, the Saviour in this day of grace: are fallen into the gulf and jaws of eternal death and misery, in the fire that never shall be quenched. Mar. ix. 43, 44; Lu. xvi. 23—26.

Now then, seeing there is death, or to be dead, taken under so many considerations in the scripture; it is evident, that to be dead in Christ, the text is not meant of them all: I then must distinguish, and inquire which of these deaths it is, that here the apostle did look for a resurrection from. (1.) then, It cannot be meant a resurrection from eternal death, for from that there is no redemption. Ps. xlix. 8. (2.) Neither is it a resurrection from that double death; for they that are in that, are past recovery also. (3.) And as for those that are dead to sin, it is nonsense to say there shall, or can be a resurrection from that: for that itself is a resurrection; which resurrection also, the apostle had then passed through: and also all the brethren, as he saith, You hath he quickened, who were dead in trespasses and sins. Col. ii. 12, 13, 20. And again, 'If ye then be risen with Christ,' Col. iii. 1. And again, 'Wherein also ye are risen with *him*, through the faith of the operation of God, who hath raised him from the dead.' Col. ii. 12. (4.) The dead therefore in this scripture, must be understood of those that have departed this life, that have body and soul separated each from the other; and so the resurrection, a resurrection of the body out of the grave; as Daniel saith, 'Many of them that sleep in the dust of the earth shall awake.' Da. xii 2. And again, 'The hour is coming, in the which all that are in the graves shall hear his voice, and shall come forth,' &c. Jn. v. 28, 29.

Second. [What is meant by *the resurrection*.] The resurrection of the just, then, is the rising of the bodies of the just, and the resurrection of the unjust, the rising of their bodies, at the last judgment. This also is the meaning of that saying of Paul to Agrippa, 'I stand,' saith he, 'and am judged for the hope of the promise made of God unto our fathers,' Ac. xxvi. 6. which promise at first began to be fulfilled in the resurrection of the body of Christ, Ac. xiii. 32, 33. and hath its accomplishment, when the dead, small and great, are raised out of their graves. Wherefore, though Paul saith in the 13th of the Acts, it is already fulfilled; yet here he saith, he hopes it shall come. 'Which *promise*,' saith he, 'our twelve tribes, instantly serving *God* day and night, hope to come.' [Ac. xxvi. 7.] As God told Daniel, saying, 'go thy way, till the end *be*: for thou shalt rest and stand in thy lot at the end of the days.' Da. xii. 13.

Christ is already risen, and therefore so far the promise is fulfilled; but his saints are yet in their graves, and therefore that part of the fulfilling of it is yet to come, as he saith, 'Why should it be thought a thing incredible with you, that God should raise the dead?' Ac. xxvi. 8.

Again, That it is the resurrection of the dead bodies of both saints and sinners that is here inserted, it is further evident; because the apostle saith, it is the resurrection, that the *very Pharisees themselves allowed.* I have hope towards God, saith he, which themselves also allow; then what that hope is, he in the next words sheweth, namely, *that there shall be a resurrection of the dead,* &c. Now we know, that the Pharisees did not allow of a resurrection from a state of nature, to a state of grace, which is the same with the new birth; but did confidently allow and teach, that they were the children of Abraham, according to the flesh. Yea, when any of them began to adhere, or incline to Christ's doctrine in some things, yet the doctrine of the new birth, or of being raised from a state of nature, to a state of grace, they would very much stick at; though in the meantime, they utterly were against the doctrine of the Sadducees, which denied the resurrection of the body. Jn. iii. 1—9; viii. 51—56; Ac. xxiii. 6—8.

Further, the resurrection here spoken of, must needs be the resurrection of the body, because it is called, ' a resurrection of the dead, both of the just and unjust'—that is, of both saints and sinners, according to the saying of Christ, 'The hour is coming, in the which all that are in the graves shall hear his voice, and shall come forth; they that have done good, unto the resurrection of life; and they that have done evil, unto the resurrection of damnation.' Jn. v. 28, 29.

Third. [The resurrection spoken of *is a thing yet to come;*] the resurrection here mentioned, is a resurrection *to come,* not already enjoyed, either by saints or sinners—'There shall be a resurrection of the dead, both of the just and unjust.' Now, I say, the resurrection here being yet deferred by the just, and counted also the resurrection of the dead, both of the just and unjust: it must needs be the same resurrection that is spoken of by Job, who saith, ' So man lieth down, and riseth not: till the heavens *be* no more, they shall not awake, nor be raised out of their sleep.' Job xiv. 12.

Having thus, in few words, opened this scripture unto you, I shall in the next place, for the further satisfaction of those that are yet wavering, and for the refreshment of those that are strong and steadfast, lay down before you, several undeniable scripture demonstrations *of the resurrection of the dead, both of the just, and unjust.*

FIRST, I shall first begin with,

THE RESURRECTION OF THE JUST.

First, The just must arise, because Christ is risen from the dead. Christ is the head of the just, and they are the members of his body; and because of this union, therefore the just must arise. This is the apostle's own argument—' If Christ,' saith he, 'be preached that he rose from the dead, how say some among you that there is no resurrection of the dead? But if there be no resurrection of the dead, then is Christ not risen.' 1 Co. xv. 12, 13. Now, I say, the reason why the apostle thus argueth the resurrection from the dead, by the resurrection of Christ, it is, because the saints, of whose resurrection he here chiefly discourseth, are in their bodies, as well as in their souls, the members of Christ; 'Know ye not,' saith he, 'that your bodies are the members of Christ.' 1 Co. vi. 15. A very weighty argument; for if a good man be a member of Christ, then he must either be raised out of his grave, or else sin and death must have power over a member of Christ. I say again, if this body be not raised, then also Christ is not a complete conqueror over his enemies; forasmuch as death and the grave have still power over his members. ' The last enemy that shall be destroyed is death.' 1 Co. xv. 26. Now, though Christ in his own person hath a complete conquest over death, &c., yet death hath still power over the bodies of all that are in their graves: now, I say, Christ being considered with relation to his members, then he hath not yet a complete conquest over death, neither will he, until they every one be brought forth of their graves; for then, and not till then, shall that saying be every way fulfilled, ' Death is swallowed up in victory.' 1 Co. xv. 53, 54.

Second, As there must be a resurrection of the just, because Christ is their head, and they his members: so also, because the body of the saints, as well as their soul, is the purchase of Christ's blood. ' Ye are bought with a price:' saith Paul; ' therefore glorify God in your body, and in your spirit, which are God's.' 1 Co. vi. 20. Christ will not lose the purchase of his blood. O death, saith Christ, I will have them; O grave, I will make thee let them go; I will ransom them from the power of the grave, I will redeem them from death. I have bought them, and they shall be mine. ' O death, I will be thy plagues; O grave, I will be thy destruction:' Ho. xiii. 14. I say, though the power of the grave be invincible, and death be ' the king of terrors,' Job xviii. 14. yet he who hath the keys of hell and of death at his girdle, Re. i. 18. to him belongeth the issues from death. ' *He that is* our God *is* the God of salvation; and unto God the Lord *belong* the issues from death,' Ps. lxviii. 20. and we, the price of his blood, shall be delivered.

Third, As the body is the member of Christ, and the price of his blood: so it is the temple of the Holy Ghost, which is in us. ' What ? know ye not that your body is the temple of the Holy Ghost *which is* in you, - - and ye are not your own?' 1 Co. vi. 19. The body is no such ridiculous thing in the account of Christ as it was in the account of the Sadducees. ' The body *is* not for fornication, but for the Lord; and the Lord for the body,' ver. 13. and that not only in this world, but that which is to come ; wherefore he saith, ' God hath both raised up the Lord [Jesus,] and will also raise us up by his own power '—that is, as he hath raised up the body of Christ, so will he raise up ours also by Christ.

Fourth, The bodies of the just must arise again, because of that similitude, that must be betwixt the body of the Lord Jesus Christ and the bodies of the saints. ' When he shall appear, we shall be like him.' 1 Jn. iii. 2. Now we have it abundantly manifest in scripture, that the body of the Lord Jesus, was raised out of the grave, caught up into heaven, and that it ever remaineth in the holiest of all, a glorified body. Lu. xxiv. 3—7, 36—43; Jn. xx. 24—28; Ac. i. 2—11; ii. 31; xvii. 30—32; Mar. xvi. 6, 7, 19; He. vii. 24—26; viii. 1—3; x. 12.

Now, I say, it would be very strange to me if Christ should be raised, ascended, and glorified in that body; and yet that his people should be with him, no otherwise than in their spirits ; especially, seeing that he in his resurrection, is said to be but ' the first-born from the dead, and the first-fruits of them that sleep.' Col. i. 18; 1 Co. xv. 23. For we know, that a first-begotten doth imply more sons, and that first-fruits do foreshew an after-crop ; wherefore we conclude, that ' as in Adam all die, even so in Christ shall all be made alive. But every man in his own order: Christ the first-fruits; afterward they that are Christ's at his coming.' 1 Co. xv. 22, 23.

And hence it is that the scripture saith, He ' shall change our vile body, that it may be fashioned like unto his glorious body.' Phi. iii. 21. And hence it is again, that the day of Christ is said to be the day of the manifestation of the sons of God, and of the redemption of our body, Ro. viii. 21—24; for then shall the saints of God not only be, but appear as their Saviour, being delivered from their graves, as he is from his, and glorified in their bodies, as he is in his.

Fifth, There must be a resurrection of the body of the saints, because the body, as well as the mind, hath been a deep sharer in the afflictions that we meet with for the gospel's sake. Yea, the body is ofttimes the greater sufferer, in all the calamities, that for Christ's sake we here undergo; it is the body that feels the stocks, the whip, hunger and cold, the fire and rack, and a thousand calamities; it is the body in which we have the dying marks of the Lord Jesus, ' that the life also of Jesus might be made manifest in our mortal * flesh.' Ga. vi. 17; 2 Co. iv. 11. God is so just a God, and so merciful to his people, that though the bodies of his saints should, through the malice of the enemy,

be never so dishonourably tortured, killed, and sown in the grave : yet he will, as further will be shewn anon, raise it again in incorruption, glory, and honour: as he saith also in another place, that we who have continued with Christ in his temptations, that have for his sake underwent the reproach and malice of the world, to you, saith Christ. ' I appoint a kingdom, as my Father hath appointed unto me.' Lu. xxii. 28, 29. If we suffer, we shall also reign with *him:* 2 Ti. ii. 12. ' and he that hateth his life in this world shall keep it unto life eternal.' Jn. xii. 25. All this is to be enjoyed, especially at the resurrection of the just. But,

Sixth, There must be a resurrection of the just, otherwise, there will be the greatest disappointment on all sides that ever was, since man had a being on the earth. A disappointment, I say,

1. Of the *will* of God—' And this is the Father's will which hath sent me,' saith Christ, ' that of all which he hath given me I should lose nothing, [not a dust,] but should raise it up again at the last day.' Jn. vi. 39.

2. A disappointment of the *power* of God ; for he that hath raised up the Lord Jesus, doth also intend to raise us up by his power, even our bodies; as Paul saith, ' The body *is* not for fornication, but for the Lord; and the Lord for the body. And God hath both raised up the Lord, and will also raise up us by his power.' 1 Co. vi. 13, 14.

3. If there should be no resurrection of the just, Christ also would be wonderfully disappointed of the fruits of all his sufferings. As I told you before, his people are the price of his blood, and the members of his body, and he is now at the right hand of God, ' far above all principalities and powers, and every name that is named,' expecting till his enemies be made his footstool, He. i. 13. and brought under the foot of the weakest saint; which will not be, until the last enemy *death* is destroyed. We know that he said, when he went away, that he would come again, and fetch all his people to himself, even up into heaven, that where he is, there we may be also. Jn. xii. 26; xiv. 1—3; xvii. 24. But, I say, how will he be disappointed, if when he comes, the grave and death should prevent and hinder him, and with its bars, keep down those, whom he hath ransomed with his blood, from the power thereof.

4. If the bodies of the just arise [not] from the dead, then *they* also will be disappointed. 'Tis true, the saints departed, have far more fellowship and communion with God and the Lord Jesus, than we have, or are not yet capable of having, they being in paradise, and we in this world ; Lu. xxiii. 43. but yet, I say for all that, they are, though there, very much longing for the day of the Lord's vengeance, which will be the day in which they will, and must arise from the dead. This, I say, is the

---

* Bunyan quotes this from the Genevan or Puritan version; our present translation has ' in our body.'—Ed.

time that they long for, when they cry under the altar, 'How long, O Lord, holy and true, dost thou not judge and avenge our blood on them that dwell on the earth?' Re. vi. 10, 11. When they died, they died in hope to 'obtain a better resurrection,' He. xi. 35. and now they are gone, they long till that day be come; till the day come, I say, when the dead, even all the enemies of Christ, shall be judged; for then will he give rewards to his servants the prophets, and to his saints, and to all that fear his name, small and great. Re. xi. 18.

5. If the just arise not, great disappointment also will be to the saints yet alive in this world; for, notwithstanding they have already received the first-fruits of the Spirit, yet they wait, not only for more of that, but also for the resurrection, redemption, and changing of this vile body. 'For our conversation is in heaven,' saith Paul, 'from whence also we look for the Saviour, the Lord Jesus Christ, who shall change our vile body, that it may be fashioned like to his glorious body.' Ro. viii. 20—23; Phi. iii. 20, 21. But now, I say, if the body riseth not, then how can it be made like to the glorious body of Christ Jesus: yea, what a sad disappointment, infatuation, and delusion, are those poor creatures under, that look, and *that* by scripture warrant, for such a thing? They look for good, but behold evil; they expect to be delivered in their whole man from every enemy; but lo, both death and the grave, their great enemies, do swallow them up for ever. But, beloved, be not deceived. 'The needy shall not alway be forgotten, the expectation of the poor shall *not* perish for ever.' Ps. ix. 18. Saith Christ, He that seeth the Son, and believeth on him that sent him, hath everlasting life, and I will raise him up at the last day. Jn. vi. 40.

6. If the just arise not out of their graves, then also is every grace of God in our souls defeated; for though the spirit of devotion can put forth a feigned show of holiness with the denial of the resurrection, yet every grace of God in the elect doth prompt them forward to live as becomes the gospel, by pointing at this day; as, (1.) 'Tis this that faith looks at, according as it is written, 'I believed, and therefore have I spoken; we also believe, and therefore speak; knowing that he which raised up the Lord Jesus shall raise up us also by Jesus, and shall present *us* with you.' 2 Co. iv. 13, 14. (2.) Hope looks at this. 'We,' saith Paul, 'which have the first-fruits of the Spirit, even we ourselves groan within ourselves, waiting for the adoption, *to wit*, the redemption of our body'—that is, we expect this by hope; 'but hope that is seen is not hope: for what a man seeth,' or hath in present possession, 'why doth he yet hope for?' Ro. viii. 23, 24. (3.) The grace of self-denial also worketh by this doctrine—'If after the manner of

men I have fought with beasts at Ephesus, what advantageth it me, if the dead rise not?' 1 Co. xv. 32. As who should say, Wherefore do I deny myself of those mercies and privileges that the men of this world enjoy? Why do not I also, as well as they, shun persecution for the cross of Christ? If the dead rise not, what shall I be the better for all my trouble that here I meet with for the gospel of Christ? (4.) Both zeal and patience, with all other the graces of the Spirit of God in our hearts, are much, yea, chiefly encouraged, animated, and supported by this doctrine; as James saith, 'Be patient, therefore, brethren, unto the coming of the Lord,' for then shall the dead be raised. 1 Th. iv. 16, 17. 'Behold, the husbandman waiteth for the precious fruit of the earth, and hath long patience for it, until he receive the early and latter rain. Be ye also patient; stablish your hearts; for the coming of the Lord draweth nigh.' Ja. v. 7, 8.

Seventh, The doctrine of the resurrection of the just, must needs be a certain truth of God, if we consider the devilish, and satanical errors and absurdities that must unavoidably follow the denial thereof; as, he that holdeth no resurrection of our body, he denieth the resurrection of the body of Christ. This is the Spirit's own doctrine—'For if the dead rise not, then is not Christ raised.' 1 Co. xv. 16. He that denieth the resurrection of the members, denieth the resurrection of the head; for seeing the resurrection of the saints is proved by the resurrection of Christ, he that doth deny the resurrection of the saints, must needs deny the resurrection of Christ, that proves it. Now this error, as it is in itself destructive to all Christian religion: so it, like an adder, carrieth within its bowels, many other alike devilish and filthy; as,

1. He that denieth the resurrection of the saints, he concludeth, that to preach deliverance from sin and death, it is vain preaching; for how can he be freed of sin, that is swallowed up for ever of death and the grave? as he most certainly is, that is always contained therein, as Paul saith, 'If Christ be not risen,' whose resurrection is the ground of ours, 'then *is* our preaching vain, and your faith *is* also vain,' 1 Co. xv. 14. then we preach fables, and you receive them for truth.

2. This error, casteth the lie in the face of God, of Christ, and the Scriptures—'Yea, and we,' saith Paul, 'are found false witnesses of God; because we have testified of God that he raised up Christ: - - - if so be that the dead rise not.' 1 Co. xv. 15. Mark, before he said, Christ in his resurrection, doth prove our resurrection; but now he saith, that our resurrection will prove the truth of his; and indeed both are true; for as by Christ's rising, ours is affirmed; so by ours, his is demonstrated.

3. The denial of the resurrection, it also damneth

all those that have departed this world in the faith of this doctrine. 'If Christ be not raised,' (as if he is not, we rise not, then is not only) your faith vain, ye are yet in your sins (that are alive,) but 'then they also which are fallen asleep in Christ are perished.' 1 Co. xv. 17, 18.

4. He that denieth the resurrection of the just, he concludeth, that the Christian is of all men the most miserable. Mark the words: ' If in this life only we have hope in Christ, we are of all men most miserable.' 1 Co. xv. 19. First of all, men the most miserable, because we let go present enjoyments for those that will never come, ' if the dead rise not.' Of all men most miserable, because our faith, our hope, our joy, and peace, are all but a lie, 'if the dead rise not.' But you will say, he that giveth up himself to God shall have comfort in this life. Ah! but 'if the dead rise not,' all our comfort that now we think we have from God, will then be found presumption and madness, because we believe, that God hath so loved us, as to have us in his day, in body and soul, to heaven: which will be nothing so, if the dead rise not. If in this life only, we have hope in Christ, we are of all men most miserable. Poor Christian! thou that lookest for the blessed hope of the resurrection of the body, at the glorious appearing of the great God, and our Saviour Jesus Christ, how wilt thou be deceived, if the dead rise not! ' But now is Christ risen from the dead, *and* become the first-fruits of them that slept. For since by man *came* death, by man *came* also the resurrection of the dead.' 1 Co. xv. 20, 21.

5. But again; he that denieth the resurrection of the dead, he setteth open a flood-gate to all manner of impiety; he cutteth the throat of a truly holy life, and layeth the reins upon the neck of the most outrageous lusts; for if the dead rise not, let us eat and drink; that is, do anything, though never so diabolical and hellish; ' let us eat and drink, for to-morrow we die,' 1 Co. xv. 32. and there is an end of us; we shall not arise again, to receive either evil or good.

6. To deny this resurrection, nay, if a man do but say, it is past either with him or any Christian: his so saying tendeth directly to the destruction and overthrow of the faith of them that hear him; and is so far from being according to the doctrine of God, that it eateth out good and wholesome doctrine even as cankers eat the face and flesh of a man. How ill-favouredly do they look, that have their nose and lips eaten off with the canker? Even so badly doth the doctrine of no resurrection of the dead, look in the eyes of God, Christ, saints, and scripture. 2 Ti. ii. 18.

7. I conclude then, that to deny the resurrection of the bodies of the just, it argueth,

(1.) Great ignorance of God, ignorant of his power to raise, ignorant of his promise to raise, ignorant of his faithfulness to raise; and that both to himself, Son, and saints, as I shewed before. Therefore saith Paul to those that were thus deluded, ' Awake to righteousness, and sin not; for some have not the knowledge of God. I speak *this* to your shame.' 1 Co. xv. 34. As if he had said, Do you profess Christianity? and do you question the resurrection of the body? Do you not know, that the resurrection of the body, and glory to follow, is the very quintessence of the gospel of Jesus Christ? Are you ignorant of the resurrection of the Lord Jesus, and do you question the power and faithfulness of God, both to his Son and his saints; because you say, there shall be no resurrection of the dead? You are ignorant of God; of what he can do, of what he will do, and of what he will by doing glorify himself.

(2.) As it argueth very great ignorance of God's power, faithfulness, &c., so it argueth gross ignorance of the tenor and current of the scriptures; for ' as touching the dead, that they rise: have ye not read in the book of Moses (saith Christ) how in the bush, God spake unto him, saying, ' I *am* the God of Abraham, and the God of Isaac, and the God of Jacob? He is not the God of the dead, but the God of the living: ye therefore do greatly err.' Mar. xii. 26, 27.

To be the God of Abraham, Isaac, and Jacob, it is to be understood of his being their God under a new covenant consideration; as he saith, ' I will be their God, and they shall be my people.' Now, thus he is not the God of the dead—that is, of those that perish, whether they be angels or men. He. viii. 10, 11; Jn. viii. 42; 1 Jn. iii. 8—10; Ho. vi. 2; Col. iii. 4; Ep. i. 4.

Now, I say, they that are the children of God, as Abraham, Isaac, and Jacob, they are counted the living under a threefold consideration—(a.) In their Lord and head, and thus all the elect may be said to live; for they are from eternity chosen in him, who also is their life, though possibly many of them yet unconverted. I say, yet Christ is their life, by the eternal purpose of God. (b.) The children of the new covenant, do live both in their spirits in glory, by open vision, and here by faith and the continual communication of grace from Christ into their souls. Ga. ii. 20. (c.) They live also with respect to their rising again; for God ' calleth those things which be not as though they were.' Ro. iv. 17. To be born, dead, buried, risen, and ascended, are all present with God, he liveth not by time, as we do—a thousand years to him are but as the day that is past. And again, ' One day is as a thousand years.' 2 Pe. iii. 8. Eternity, which is God himself, admitteth of no first, second, and third; all things are naked and bare before him, and present with him; He. iv. 13; Is. xlvi. 9, 10. all *his* live unto him.

There shall be a resurrection of the dead, both of the just and unjust. Ro. viii. 29—34.

A resurrection—of what? Of that which is sown, or of that which was never sown? If of that which is sown, then it must be either of that nature that was sown, or else of the corruption that cleaveth to it; but it is the nature, and not the corruption that cleaveth unto it, that riseth again. And verily, the very term 'resurrection' is a forcible argument to prove the dead shall come forth of their graves; for the Holy Ghost hath always spoken more properly than to say, 'There shall be a resurrection of the dead, both of the just and unjust;' when yet neither the good nor the bad shall come forth of their graves, but rather something else to delude the world withal.

Having thus in few words, shewed you the truth of the resurrection of the dead, I now come,

SECOND—To the manner of their rising.

THE MANNER OF THE RESURRECTION OF THE JUST.

And FIRST of the just.

The apostle, when he had in the fifteenth of the 1st of the Corinthians proved the truth and certainty of the resurrection, he descends to the discovery of the manner of it; and to the end, he might remove those foolish scruples that attend the hearts of the ignorant, he begins with one of their questions—'But some *man* will say,' saith he, 'How are the dead raised up? and with what body do they come?' ver. 35. To which he answereth,

First, By a similitude of seed, that is sown in the earth. In which similitude, he inserteth three things—

1. That our reviving or rising, must be after death—'That which thou sowest is not quickened except it die.' ver. 36.

2. That at our rising, we shall not only revive and live, but be changed into a far more glorious state than when we were sown. 'That which thou sowest, thou sowest not that body that shall be,' &c. 'But God giveth it a body as it hath pleased him,' ver. 38.—that is, he giveth the body more splendour, lustre, and beauty at its resurrection. But,

3. Neither its quickening, not yet its transcendent splendour, shall hinder it from being the same body—as to the nature of it—that was sown in the earth; for as God giveth it a body, for honour and splendour as it pleaseth him, so 'to every seed his own body.' ver. 38.

And, indeed, this similitude by which he here reasoneth the manner of the resurrection of the just, is very natural, and fitly suiteth each particular; for, as to its burial—(1.) The corn of wheat is first dead, and after sown and buried in the earth; and so is the body of man. (2.) After the corn is thus dead and buried, then it quickeneth

and reviveth to life: so also shall it be with our body; for after it is laid in the grave and buried, it shall then quicken, rise, and revive.

Again, as to the manner of its change in its rising, this similitude also doth fitly suit; as,

It is sown a dead corn; it is raised a living one. It is sown dry, and without comeliness; it riseth green and beautiful. It is sown a single corn; it riseth a full ear. It is sown in its husk; but in its rising it leaveth that husk behind it.

Further, though the kernel thus die, be buried, and meet with all this change and alteration in these things, yet none of them can cause the nature of the kernel to cease—it is wheat still. Wheat was sown and wheat ariseth; only it was sown dead, dry, and barren wheat; and riseth living, beautiful, and fruitful wheat. It hath this alteration, then, that it doth greatly change its resemblance, though yet it hath this power, as still to retain its own nature. God giveth it a body as it pleaseth him, 'but to every seed his own body.'

The apostle having thus presented the *manner of the resurrection of the saints* by the nature of seed sown and rising again; he proceedeth,

Second, for further illustration, *to three more similitudes*—The first is, to shew us the variety and glory of flesh. The second is, to shew us the difference of glory that is between heavenly bodies, and those that are earthy. The third is, to shew us the difference that is between the glory of the light of the sun, from that of the moon; and also how one star differeth from another in glory: and then concludeth, 'so is the resurrection of the dead.' 1 Co. xv. 39—43. As who should say, at the resurrection of the bodies, they will be abundantly more altered and changed, than if the flesh of beasts and fowls were made as noble as the flesh of men; or the bodies of earth, were made as excellent as the heavenly bodies, or as if the glory of the moon should be made as bright, and as clear as the glory of the sun; or as if the glory of the least star was as glorious, and as shining, as the biggest in the firmament of heaven.

It is a *resurrection* indeed, a resurrection every way. The body ariseth, as to the nature of it, the self-same nature; but as to the manner of it; how far transcendent is it! There is a poor, dry, wrinkled kernel cast into the ground, and there it lieth, and swelleth, breaketh, and, one would think, perisheth; but behold, it receiveth life, it chitteth,* it putteth forth a blade, and groweth into a stalk, there also appeareth an ear; it also sweetly blossoms, with a full kernel in the ear: it is the same wheat, yet behold how the form and fashion of that

---

* From the verb 'to chit,' to sprout—to shoot at the end of the grain; provincial and almost obsolete.—ED.

which now ariseth, doth differ from that which then was sown; its glory also when 'twas sown, is no glory, when compared with that in which it riseth. And yet it is the same that riseth that was sown, and no other; though the same after a far more glorious manner; not the same with its *husk*, but without it. Our *bran* shall be left behind us when we rise again. The comparison also between the bodies heavenly and bodies earthly holds forth the same—' The glory of the celestial is one, and the glory of the terrestrial is another.' Now mark it; he doth not speak here of the natures of each of these bodies; but of the transcendent glory of one above another. 'The glory of the heavenly is one, and the glory of the earthly is another.' Wherefore I say, at our rising, we shall not change our *nature*, but our *glory;* we shall be equal to the angels, Lu. xx. 36, not with respect to their *nature*, but glory. The nature also of the moon is one thing, and the glory of the moon is another; and so one star also differeth from another in glory.

A beggar hath the same nature as a king, and gold in the ore, the same nature with that which is best refined; but the beggar hath not the same glory with the king, nor yet the gold in ore, the same glory with that which is refined. But our state will be far more altered than any of these in the days when we, like so many suns in the firmament of heaven, arise out of the heart and bowels of the earth.

These things thus considered do shew you how vainly they argue, that say, our human nature consisting of body and soul, shall not inherit the kingdom of God, and also how far from their purpose, that saying of the apostle is, which saith, that ' flesh and blood shall not inherit the kingdom of God.' And now also, because I am fallen upon the objection itself, I shall not pass it, but with a short dash at it. Wherefore reader, whoever thou art, consider that frequently in scripture the words ' flesh' and ' blood,' as also in the place alleged, are not to be understood of that matter which God made; which flesh cleaveth to our bones, and blood runs in 'our veins: but is taken for that corruption, weakness, mortality, and evil that cleaveth to it; which weakness and corruption, because it possesseth all men, and also wholly ruleth where the soul is unconverted; therefore it beareth the name of that which is ruled and acted by it—to wit, our whole man, consisting of body and soul; yet, I say, is a thing distinct from that flesh and blood which is essential to our being, and without which we are no men. As, for instance, he that is Christ's, saith Paul, ' hath crucified the flesh, with the affections and lusts,' Ga. v. 24. Who is so vain as to think that the apostle by these words, should mean our material flesh that hangeth cn our bones, and

that is mixed with our natural blood, sinews, and veins; and not rather of that *inward* fountain of sin, corruption, and wickedness, which in another place he calleth ' the old man,' with his ' deceitful lusts.' Ep. iv. 22. Again, ' The flesh lusteth against the spirit, and the spirit against the flesh.' Is it our flesh that hangeth on our bones, which lusteth against the spirit? and that also against which the spirit lusteth? Certainly, if the spirit lusteth against our material flesh, then it is our duty not to nourish it at all, because, by nourishing of it we nourish that against which the Spirit of God fighteth, and warreth. Nay, if the spirit lust against the flesh on our bones simply considered as flesh; and if it be our duty to follow the Spirit, as it is, then we must needs kill ourselves, or cut our flesh from our bones. For whatever the Spirit of God lusteth against, it must be destroyed; yea, it is our duty with all speed to destroy it. But wilt thou know, O vain man, that by flesh here is to be understood, not the nature that God hath made, but the corrupt apprehension, and wisdom, with those inclinations to evil, that lodge within us, which in another place are called the ' wisdom of the flesh,' yea, in plain terms, ' flesh and blood,' where Christ saith, ' Flesh and blood hath not revealed [this] unto thee, but my Father which is in heaven.' Mat. xvi. 17.

Nay, observe it, all these places, with many others, do rather point at a corrupt soul, than a corrupt body; for, indeed, sin and all spiritual wickedness, they have their seat in the heart and soul of a man, and by their using this or that member of the body, so defile the man; the weaknesses of the body, or that attend our material flesh and blood, they are weaknesses of another kind, as sickness, aches, pains, sores, wounds, defection of members, &c. Wherefore, where you read of flesh and blood, as rejected of God; especially, when it speaks of the flesh and blood of saints, you are not to understand it as meant of the flesh, which is their proper human nature, but of that *weakness* which cleaveth to it.

Paul in another place, reckoneth up the works of the flesh, in many things, as in witchcraft, hatred, variance, strife, emulation, fornication, and many others. But can any imagine, that he there should strike at that flesh which hangeth on our bones, or rather at that malignity and rebellion that is in the mind of man against the Lord, by reason of which the members of the body are used this way, and also sometimes that, to accomplish its most filthy and abusive deeds. Ga. v. 17—21. ' They were - - enemies in [their] mind by wicked works,' Col. i. 21.

Thus you see that ' flesh and blood' is not to be taken always for the flesh that is upon our hands, and feet, and other parts of our body; but for that sin, weakness, and infirmity, that cleaveth to our whole man.

Further then, touching our real substantial flesh, it may be either considered as God's creature purely, or as corrupted with sin and infirmity. Now if you consider it as corrupted, so it shall not inherit the kingdom of God: but yet consider it as God's creature, and so all that God hath converted to himself, through Jesus Christ, shall, even with that body when changed, inherit the kingdom of God. The woman whose clothes are foul, can yet distinguish between the dirt and the cloth on which it hangeth; and so deals God with us. 'Tis true, there is not one saint, but while he liveth here, his body is arrayed and infected with many corrupt and filthy things, as touching bodily weaknesses; yea, and also with many sinful infirmities, by reason of that body of sin and death that yet remains in us: but yet God, I say, distinguisheth between our weaknesses, and his workmanship, and can tell how to save the whole man of his people, while he is destroying the corruption and weakness that cleaveth to them.

And now to return to the place objected—'Flesh and blood shall not inherit the kingdom of God.' It cannot be truly understood, that that flesh which is man's nature shall not enter the kingdom; for then, as I said before, Christ must lose his members, the purchase of his blood, the vessels and temples of his Spirit; for all this is our body. Again, then Christ also, in that his body, which is also our flesh and blood, is not in glory, contrary to the whole current of the New Testament. He. ii. 14, 15. vii. 24, 25. viii. 3, 4. x. 10—12. Re. i. 18. ii. 8.

Yea, it would be nonsense to say, there should be a resurrection, and that *our* vile body shall be *changed*, 'and made like to the glorious body of the Son of God;' if this body do not at all rise again, but some other thing, which is not in us, and our nature. But to be short; the apostle here, when he saith, 'Flesh and blood cannot inherit,' &c., speaks properly of that mortality and weakness, that now attends our whole man, and not of our real substantial body itself. For after he had said, 'Flesh and blood cannot inherit the kingdom of God,' he adds, 'neither doth corruption inherit incorruption,' which two sayings are answerable to what he presently adds, saying, 'Behold, I shew you a mystery; we shall not all sleep, but we shall all be changed. in a moment, in the twinkling of an eye, at the last trump: for the trumpet shall sound, and the dead '—mark, 'the dead shall be raised incorruptible '—that is, the dead shall be so raised as that in their rising, incorruption shall possess them instead of corruption, and immortality instead of that mortality that descended to the grave with them,—'for this corruptible '—mark, this corruptible—'must put on in-

corruption, and this mortal *must* put on immortality.' Mark, I say, it is this corruptible, and this mortal, that must be raised, though not corruptible and mortal, as it was buried; but immortal and incorruptible; it shall leave its grave-clothes of corruption and mortality behind it. 1 Co. xv. 50—53.

THIRD. The manner of which their rising, the apostle doth more distinctly branch out a little above in four particulars, which particulars are these that follow—1. It is sown in corruption; *it is raised in incorruption*. 2. It is sown in dishonour, *it is raised in glory*. 3. It is sown in weakness, *it is raised in power*. 4. It is sown a natural body, *it is raised a spiritual body*. 1 Co. xv.

1. *It is raised in incorruption*. We are brought into this world by sin and corruption; corruption is our father, and in sin did our mother conceive us. Job xvii. 14. Ps. li. 5. And hence it is that we have our life, not only like a span, shadow, or post, for shortness, but also, that it is attended with so much vanity and vexation of spirit. But now being raised from the dead incorruptible, which is also called a begetting and birth, these things that now in our life annoy us, and at last take away our life, are effectually destroyed; and therefore we live for ever, as saith the Spirit—'And there shall be no more death, neither sorrow, nor crying, neither shall there be any more pain: for the former things,' that is, all our corruptibleness, 'are passed away.' Re. xxi. 4.

There shall be in our resurrection no corruption, either of body or of soul; no weakness, nor sickness, nor anything tending that way; as he saith, He will present us 'to himself a glorious church, not having spot, or wrinkle, or any such thing.' Ep. v. 27. Therefore, when he saith it is raised in incorruption, it is as if he had said, It is impossible that they should ever sin more, be sick more, sorrow more, or die more. 'They which shall be counted worthy to obtain that world, and the resurrection from the dead, neither marry, nor are given in marriage;' though 'twas thus with them in this world; 'neither can they die any more, for they are equal unto the angels; and are the children of God, being the children of the resurrection.' Lu. xx. 35, 36.

2. *It is raised in glory*. The dishonour that doth attend the saint at his departing this world, it is very great—'he is sown in dishonour;' he is so loathsome at his death, that his dearest friends are weary of him, stop their noses at him, see no beauty in him, nor set any price upon him, (I speak nothing here how some of them are hanged, starved, banished, and so die, torn to pieces, and not suffered to be put into graves,) but it is raised in glory. Glory is the sweetness, comeliness, purity,

and perfection of a thing. The light is the glory of the sun, strength is the glory of youth, and grey hairs are the glory of old age—that is, it is the excellency of these things, and that which makes them shine. 1 Co. xv. 40, 41. Pr. xx. 29.

Therefore, to arise in glory, it is first to arise in all the beauty, and utmost completeness that is possible to possess a human creature; I say, in all its features and members, inconceivably beautiful. Sin and corruption have made *mad* work in our bodies as well as in our souls. 'Tis sin commonly that is the cause of all that deformity and ill-favouredness that now cleaveth to us, and that also rendereth us so dishonourable at our death; but now at our rising, we being raised incorruptible, we shall appear in such perfections, and that of all sorts, belonging to the body, that all the beauty and comeliness, sweetness and amiableness, that hath at any time been in this world, it shall be swallowed up a thousand times told with this glory. The Psalmist saith of Christ that ' he was fairer than the children of men,' Ps. xlv. 2. and that, as I believe, in his outward man, as well as in his inward part. He was the exactest, purest, completest, and beautifulest creature that ever God made, *till his visage was so marred by his persecutions;* for in all things he had and shall have the pre-eminence. Is. lii. 14. Col. i. 18. Why, our bodies at our resurrection will not only be as free from sin, as his was before he died, but also as free from all other infirmities as he was after he was raised again. In a word, if incorruptibleness can put a beauty upon our bodies when they arise, we shall have it. There shall be no lame legs, nor crump shoulders, no bleared eyes, nor yet wrinkled faces—He ' shall change our vile body, that it may be fashioned like unto his glorious body.' Phi. iii. 21.

Again, all the glory that a glorified soul can help this body to, it at this day shall enjoy. That soul that hath been these hundreds or thousands of years in the heavens, soaking in the bosom of Christ, it shall in a moment come spangling into the body again, and inhabit every member and vein of the body, as it did before its departure. That Spirit of God also that took its leave of the body when it went to the grave, shall now in all perfection dwell in this body again; I tell you, the body at this day will shine brighter than the face of Moses or Stephen, even as bright as the sun, the stars, and angels. ' When Christ *who is* our life, shall appear, then shall ye also appear with him in glory.' Ex. xxxiv. 29, 35. Ac. vi. 15. Da. xii. 3. Mat. xiii. 43. Lu. xx. 36. Col. iii. 3, 4.

3. *It is raised in power.* While we are here, we are attended with so many weaknesses and infirmities, that in time the least sin or sickness is too hard for us, and taketh away both our strength,

our beauty, our days, our breath, and life, and all. Job xxxviii. 17. But behold, we are raised in power, in that power that all these things are as far below us as a grasshopper is below a giant; at the first appearance of us the world will tremble.

Behold, the gates of death and the bars of the grave are now carried away on our shoulders, as Samson carried away the gates of the city. Ju. xvi. 3. Death quaketh, and destruction falleth down dead at our feet: What, then, can stand before us ? We shall then carry that grace, majesty, terror, and commanding power in our souls that our countenances shall be like lightning.* Compare Lu. xx. 16 with Mat. xxviii. 2, 3. ' For this corruptible must put on incorruption, and this mortal *must* put on immortality. So when this corruptible shall have put on incorruption, and this mortal shall have put on immortality, then shall be brought to pass the saying that is written, Death is swallowed up in victory.' 1 Co. xv. 53, 54.

4. *It is raised a spiritual body.* This is the last particular, and is indeed the reason of the other three; it is an incorruptible body, because it is a spiritual one; it is a glorious body, because it is a spiritual one; it doth rise in power, because it is a spiritual body. When the body is buried, or sown in the earth, it is a body corruptible, dishonourable, weak, and natural; but when it ariseth, it doth rise incorruptible, glorious, powerful, and spiritual; so that so far as incorruption is above corruption, glory above dishonour, power above weakness, and spiritual above natural; so great an alteration will there be in our body, when raised again. And yet it is this body and not another; this in nature, though changed into a far more glorious state, a thousand times further than if a †hoggard was changed to be an emperor. Mark, ' it is sown a natural body;' a very fit word; for though there dwell never so much of the Spirit and grace of God in it while it liveth, yet so soon as the soul is separate from it, so soon also doth the Spirit of God separate from it, and so will continue while the day of its rising be come. Therefore, it is laid into the earth a mere lump of man's nature—' It is sown a natural body;' but now at the day when ' the heavens *be* no more,' as Job saith, xiv. 12. then

---

* These ideas are as new as they are striking and splendid. Our vile bodies, when raised from the dust, shall be *spiritual* —*like that of Christ*—with him *in glory;* ' bright as the sun and stars and angels.' How amazingly superior is our preaching mechanic, to all the fathers (so called) and dignitaries of state churches that ever wrote upon this subject. Bunyan proves his apostolic descent in the right line; he breathes the spirit—the holy fire of the inspired writers.—ED.

† I have continued this word as Bunyan spelt it, but he probably meant hog-herd, a keeper or driver of swine, one of the dirtiest and lowest employments.

    ' No boorish hog-herd fed his rooting swine.'
                          Browne's Pastorals.—ED.

the trump shall sound, even the trump of God, and, in a moment, the dead shall be raised incorruptible, glorious, and spiritual. 1 Co. xv. 52. 1 Th. iv. 16, 17. So that I say, the body when it ariseth, will be so swallowed up of life and immortality, that it will be, as if it had lost its own human nature; though, in truth, the same substantial real nature is every whit there still. 'Tis the same *it* that riseth, that was sown; '*It* is sown,' '*it* is raised;' '*it* is sown,' '*it* is raised,' saith the apostle. You know, that things which are candied, by the art of the apothecary, they are so swallowed up with the sweetness and virtue of that in which they are candied, that they are now, as though they had no other nature, than that in which they are boiled: when yet, in truth, the thing candied doth still retain its own proper nature and essence; though by virtue of its being candied, it loseth its former sourness, bitterness, stinking, smell, or the like. Just thus, at the last day, it will be with our bodies: we shall be so candied, by being swallowed up of life, as before is shewed, that we shall be, as if we were all spirit, when in truth, it is but this body that is swallowed up of life. And it must needs be, that our nature still remain, otherwise it cannot be *us* that shall be in heaven, but *something besides us*. Let us lose our proper human nature, and we lose absolutely our being, and so are annihilated into nothing. Wherefore *it*, the same *it*, that is sown a natural body, it shall rise a spiritual body.

But again, as I said, concerning things that are candied; our body, when thus risen, it shall lose all that sourness and stink, that now, by reason of sin and infirmity, cleaveth to it: neither shall its lumpishness, or unwieldiness, be any impediment to its acting after the manner of angels. Christ hath shewed us, what our body at our resurrection shall be, by shewing of us, in his word, what his body was, at and after, his resurrection. We read, that his body, after he was risen from the dead, though it yet retained the very *same flesh and bones* that did hang upon the cross, yet how angelical was it at all times, upon all occasions! He could come in to his disciples with that very body, when the doors were shut upon them: He could, at pleasure, to their amazement, appear in the twinkling of an eye, in the midst of them: he could be visible and invisible as he pleased, when he sat at meat with them: in a word, he could pass and repass, ascend and descend in that body, with far more pleasure and ease, than the bird by the art of her wing. Lu. xxiv. 31, 32, 36—42, 50, 51. Jn. xx. 19, 24—26. Ac. i. 1—12. Mar. xvi. 19. Ep. iv. 7—10.

Now, I say, as we have in this world borne the image of our first father; so, at that day, we shall have the image of Jesus Christ, and be as he is— 'As *is* the earthy, such *are* they also that are earthy: and as *is* the heavenly, such *are* they also

that are heavenly. And as we have borne the image of the earthy, we shall also, (at our resurrection,) bear the image of the heavenly.' 1 Co. xv. 48, 49. It is so in part now, but shall so be in perfection then.

To mount up to heaven, and to descend again at pleasure, shall, with us, in that day, be ordinary. If there were ten thousand bars of iron, or walls of brass, to separate between us, and our pleasure and desire, at that day, they should as easily be pierced by us, as is the cobweb, or air by the beams of the sun: And the reason is, because to *the Spirit*, wherewith we shall be inconceivably filled at that day, *nothing is impossible;* Mat. xvii. 20. and the working of it at that day, shall be in that nature and measure as to swallow up all impossibilities. He 'shall change our vile body, that it may be fashioned like unto his glorious body,'—now mark, 'according to the working whereby he is able even to subdue all things unto himself.' Phi. iii. 21. As who should say, I know that there are many things, that in this world hinder us from having our bodies like the body of Christ; but when God shall raise us from the dead, because he will then have our body like the body of his Son; He will stretch forth such a power to work upon, and in our body, that he will remove all impossibilities and hindrances.

Nay, further, we do not only see what operation the Spirit will have in our body, by the carriage of Christ, after his resurrection; but even by many a saint before their death. The Spirit used to catch Elijah away, no man could tell whither. It carried Ezekiel hither and thither: It carried Christ from the top of the pinnacle of the temple into Galilee; through it he walked on the sea; the Spirit caught away Philip from the eunuch, and carried him as far as Azotus. 1 Ki. xviii. 11, 12. 2 Ki. ii. 11. Eze. iii. 14. Lu. iv. 14. Mat. xiv. 25. Ac. viii. 39, 40.

Thus the great God hath given us a taste of the power and glory that is in himself, and how easily it will help us, by its possessing* of us at the resurrection, to act and do like angels; as Christ saith, They that shall be counted worthy of that world, and of the resurrection from the dead, they shall not die, but be equal to the angels. Lu. xxi. 36.

Further, as the body by being thus spiritualized, shall be as I have said; so again it must needs be, that hereby all the service of the body, and faculties of the soul, must be infinitely enlarged also. Now 'we shall see him as he is,' and now we shall know even as we are known. 1 Jn. iii. 2. 1 Co. xiii. 12.

First, Now we shall see him; to wit, Christ in

---

* 'Its possessing of us,' or to give us possession. 'This possesses us of the most valuable blessing of human life, friendship.' *Gov. of Tongue.*—ED.

his glory; not by revelation only, as we do now, but then *face to face;* and he will have us with him *to this very end.* Jn. xvii. 24. Though John was in the Spirit when he had the vision of Christ, yet it made him fall at his feet as dead; Re. i. 17. and also turned Daniel's beauty into corruption. Da. x. 8. It was so glorious, and so overweighing a glory, that he appeared in; but we shall, at the day of our resurrection, be so furnished, that we shall with the eagle, be able to look upon the sun in his strength: we shall then, I say, 'see Him as he is,' who now is in the light, that no eye hath seen, nor any man can see till that day. 1 Ti. vi. 16.

Now we shall see into all things; there shall not be anything hid from us; there shall not be a saint, a prophet, or saved soul, small or great, but we shall then perfectly know them. Also, all the works of creation, election, and redemption, and shall see and know as thoroughly, all the things of heaven, and earth, and hell, even as perfectly, as now we know our A, B, C. For the Spirit, with which we shall in every cranny of soul and body be filled, I say, 'searcheth all things, yea, the deep things of God.' 1 Co. ii. 10. We see what strange things have been known by the prophets and saints of God, and that when they knew but 'in part.'

Abraham could, by it, tell to a day, how long his seed should be under persecution in Egypt; Ge. xv. 13. Elisha, by it, could tell what was done in the king of Assyria's bed-chamber; 2 Ki. vi. 12. Ahijah could know by this, Jeroboam's wife, so soon, yea before her feet entered within his door, though he saw her not. 1 Ki. xiv. 1—6.

The prophet of Judah could tell by this, what God would do to Bethel, for the idolatry there committed; and could also point out the man by name that should do the execution, long before he was born 1 Ki. xiii. 2. What shall I say, Enoch by it could tell what should be done at the end of the world. Jude 14, 15. How did the prophets, to a circumstance, prophesy of Christ's birth, his death, his burial, of their giving him gall and vinegar, of their parting his raiment, and piercing his hands and feet! Is. liii. Of his riding on an ass also; all this they saw, when they spake of him. Jn. xii. 41. Peter also, though half asleep, could at the very first word, call Moses and Elias by their names, when they appeared to Christ in the holy mount. Lu. ix. 33. He is very ignorant of the operation of the Spirit of God, that scrupleth these things. But now, I say, if these things have been done, seen, and known, by spiritual men, while their knowledge hath been but in part, how shall we know, see, and discern, when that which is perfect is come? Which will be at the resurrection; 'It is raised a spiritual body.'

Thus, in few words, have I shewed you the truth of the resurrection of the just, and also the manner of their rising. Had I judged it convenient, I might have much enlarged on each particular, and have added many more; for the doctrine of the resurrection, however questioned by heretics, and erroneous persons; yet is such a truth, that almost all the holy scriptures of God point at, and centre in it.

God hath, from the beginning of the world, shewed to us, that our body must be with him, as well as our soul, in the kingdom of heaven. I say, he hath shewed us, how he will deal with those that are alive at Christ's coming, by his translating of Enoch, Ge. v. 24. and by taking him body and soul to himself; He. xi. 5. As also, by his catching of Elias up body and soul into heaven, in a fiery chariot, 2 Ki. ii. 11. and,

Secondly, He hath often put us in remembrance of the rising of those that are dead, at that day, as, (1.) By the faith he gave Abraham, concerning the offering of his son: for when he offered him, he accounted 'that God *was* able to raise *him* up, even from the dead; from whence also he received him in a figure.' He. xi. 19. In a figure of the resurrection of Christ, for Abraham's justification; and of Abraham's resurrection by Christ at the last day, for his glorification. (2.) By the faith he gave Joseph concerning his bones; which charge, the godly in Egypt, did diligently observe, and to that end, did keep them four hundred years; and at length, carried them, I say, from Egypt to Canaan, which was a type of our being carried in our body, from this world to heaven. He. xi. 22.

Besides, how oft did God give power to his prophets, servants, and Christ Jesus, to raise some that were now dead, and some that had been long so; and all, no doubt, to put the present generations, as also the generations yet unborn, in mind of the resurrection of the dead. To this end, I say, how was the Shunammite's son raised from the dead? 2 Ki. iv. The man also at the touching of the bones of Elisha? 2 Ki. xiii. 20, 21. together with the body of Lazarus, with Jairus's daughter, and Tabitha, and many others, who, after their souls were departed from them, Lazarus lying in his grave four days, were all raised to life again, and lived with that very body out of which the soul, at their death, had departed. Lu. viii. 53—56. Jn. xi. 43, 44. Ac. ix. 40, 41.

But above all, that notable place in Matthew, at the resurrection of the Lord Jesus, gives us a notable fore-word of the resurrection of the just. Saith the text, 'And the graves were opened; and many bodies of the saints which slept arose, and came out of the graves after his resurrection, and went into the holy city, and appeared unto many.' Mat. xxvii. 52, 53.

When the author to the Hebrews had given us a catalogue of the worthies of the Old Testament, he saith at last, 'These all died in faith.' In the faith of what? That they should lie and rot in their graves eternally? No, verily; this is the faith of Ranters, not of Christians. They all died in faith, that they should rise again; and therefore counted this world not worth the living in, upon unworthy terms, that after death 'they might obtain a better resurrection.' He. xi. 13, 35.

It is also worth the considering, that of Paul to the Philippians, where he saith that he was confident that that God that had begun a good work in them would 'perform it until the day of Jesus Christ.' Phi. i. 6. Which day of Christ, was not the day of their conversion, for that was passed with them already, they were now the children of God; but this day of Christ, it is the same which in other places is called the day when he shall come with the sound of the last trump to raise the dead. For you must know, that the work of salvation is not at an end with them that are now in heaven; no, nor ever will, until (as I shewed you before) their bodies be raised again. God, as I have told you, hath made our bodies the members of Christ, and God doth not count us thoroughly saved, until our bodies be as well redeemed and ransomed out of the grave and death, as our souls from the curse of the law, and dominion of sin.

Though God's saints have felt the power of much of his grace, and have had many a sweet word fulfilled on them; yet one word will be unfulfilled on their particular person, so long as the grave can shut her mouth upon them: but, as I said before, when the gates of death do open before them, and the bars of the grave do fall asunder; then shall be brought to pass that saying that is written, 'Death is swallowed up of victory;' and then will they hear that most pleasant voice, 'Awake and sing, ye that dwell in dust: for thy dew is as the dew of herbs, and the earth shall cast out the dead.' Is. xxvi. 19. Thus much touching the truth of the resurrection of the just, with the manner of their rising.

Now you must know, that the time of the rising of these just, will be at the coming of the Lord: for when they arise, nay, just before they are raised, the Lord Jesus Christ will appear in the clouds in flaming fire, with all his mighty angels; the effect of which appearing will be the rising of the dead, &c. 'For the Lord himself shall descend from heaven with a shout,' saith Paul, 'and with the voice of the archangel, and with the trump of God, and the dead shall rise.' 2 Th. i. 8. 1 Th. iv. 16. 1 Co. xv. 52.

Now at the time of the Lord's coming, there will be found in the world alive both saints and sinners. As for the saints that then shall be found alive, they shall, so soon as all the saints are raised out of their graves, not die, but be changed, and swal-

lowed up of incorruption, immortality, and glory; and have the soul-spiritual translation, as the raised saints shall have; as he saith, 'We shall not all [die, or] sleep, but we shall all be changed, in a moment, in the twinkling of an eye, - - for the trumpet shall sound, and the dead shall be raised incorruptible, and we shall be changed.' 1 Co. xv. 51, 52. And again, 'For the Lord himself shall descend from heaven with a shout, with the voice of the archangel, and with the trump of God: and the dead in Christ shall rise first: then we which are alive and remain shall be caught up together with them in the clouds, to meet the Lord in the air: and so shall we ever be with the Lord.' 1 Th. iv. 16, 17. As he saith also in another place, he 'shall judge the quick and the dead at his appearing and his kingdom.' 2 Ti. iv. 1.

Now when the saints that sleep shall be raised thus incorruptible, powerful, glorious, and spiritual; and also those that then shall be found alive, made like them: then forthwith, before the unjust are raised, the saints shall appear before the judgment-seat of the Lord Jesus Christ, there to give an account to their Lord the Judge, of all things they have done; and to receive a reward for their good according to their labour.

They shall rise, I say, before the wicked, they being themselves the proper *children of the resurrection*; that is, Those that must have all the glory of it, both as to pre-eminence and sweetness; and therefore they are said, when they rise, to *rise from the dead*; that is, in their rising, they leave the reprobate world behind them. Lu. xx. 35, 36. Ac. iii. 15; iv. 10; xiii. 30. Jn. xii. 1, 9, 17. And it must be so, because also the saints will have done their account, and be set upon the throne with Christ, as kings and princes with him, to judge the world, when the wicked world are raised. The saints shall judge the world; they shall judge angels; yea, they shall sit upon the thrones of judgment to do it. 1 Co. vi. 2, 3. Ps. cxxii. 5. But to pass that, [we come

THIRD, to the examination the just must undergo, and the account they must give to the Lord the Judge; or,]

THE JUDGMENT OF THE JUST.

Now when the saints are raised, as ye have heard, they must give an account of all things, in general, that they have done while they were in the world; of all things, I say, whether they be good or bad.

FIRST, *Of all their bad*; but mark, not under the consideration of vagabonds, slaves and sinners, but as sons, stewards, and servants of the Lord Jesus. That this shall be, it is evident from divers places of the holy Scriptures:

First, Paul saith, 'We shall all stand before the judgment-seat of Christ,'—we saints—'For it is written, *As* I live, saith the Lord, every knee shall bow to me, and every tongue shall confess to God. So then every one of us shall give account of himself to God.' Ro. xiv. 10—12. Again, 'Wherefore we labour, that, whether present or absent, we may be accepted of him. For we must all appear before the judgment-seat of Christ; that every one [of us] may receive the things *done* in *his* body, according to what he hath done, whether *it be* good or bad.' 2 Co. v. 9, 10.

It is true, God loveth his people, but yet he loveth not their sins, nor anything they do, though with the greatest zeal for him, if he be contrary to his word; wherefore as truly as God will give a reward to his saints and children for all that they have indeed well done; so truly will he at this day distinguish their good and bad: and when both are manifest by the righteous judgment of Christ; he will burn up their bad, with all their labour, travel, and pains in it for ever. He can tell how to save his people, and yet take vengeance on their inventions. Ps. xcix. 8.

That is an observable place, in the first epistle of Paul to the Corinthians, and the third chapter, 'If any man build,' saith he, 'upon this foundation (Christ) gold, silver, precious stones, wood, hay, stubble; every man's work shall be made manifest: for the day shall declare it, because it shall be revealed by fire; and the fire shall try every man's work of what sort it is. If any man's work abide which he hath built thereupon, he shall receive a reward. If any man's work shall be burned, he shall suffer loss; but he himself shall be saved; yet so as by fire.' 1 Co. iii. 12 —15. Now observe,

1. As I said before, the *foundation* is Christ. ver. 11.

2. The gold, silver, and precious stones that here are said to be built upon him, are all the actings in faith and love, according to the word, that the saints are found doing for his sake in the world. 1 Pe. i. 7; Re. iii. 18.

3. To build on him wood, hay, and stubble, it is to build, together with what is right in itself, human inventions and carnal ordinances, fathering them still on God and his allowance.

4. The fire that here you read of, it is the pure word and law of God. Je. xxiii. 29. Jn. xii. 48.

5. The day that here you read of, it is the day of Christ's coming to judgment, to reveal the hidden things of darkness, and to make manifest the counsels of the heart. 1 Co. iv. 5.

6. At this day, the gold, silver, precious stones, wood, hay, and stubble, and that of every man, shall be tried by this fire, that it may be manifest of what sort it is; the wind, the rain, and floods, beat now as vehemently against the house upon the rock, as against that on the sand. Lu. vi. 48, 49.

Observe again,

(1.) That the apostle speaks here of the saved, not of the reprobate—'He himself shall be saved.'

(2.) That this saved man may have wood, hay, and stubble; that is, things that will not abide the trial.

(3.) That neither this man's goodness, nor yet God's love to him, shall hinder all his wood, hay, or stubble from coming on the stage, 'Every man's work shall be manifest: the fire shall try every man's work, of what sort it is.'

(4.) Thus, a good man shall see all his wood, hay, and stubble burnt up in the trial before his face.

(5.) That good man then shall suffer loss, or, the loss of all things that are not then according to the word of God—'If any man's works shall be burnt,' or any of them, 'he shall suffer loss; but he himself shall be saved; yet so as by fire'—that is, yet so as that all that ever he hath done, shall be tried, and squared by the word of God.

From all which, it must be unavoidably concluded, that the whole body of the elect must count with their Lord for all things they have done, whether good or bad, and that he will destroy all their bad, with the purity of his word, yea, and all their pains, travel, and labour that they have spent about it. I am persuaded that there are now many things done by the best of saints, that then they will gladly disown and be ashamed of; yea, which they have and do still do with great devotion. Alas, what gross things do some of the saints in their devotion father upon God, and do reckon him the author thereof; and that he also prompts them forward to the doing thereof, and doth give them his presence in the performance of them! Yea, and as they father many superstitions and scriptureless things upon him; so they die in the same opinion, and never come in this world, to the sight of their evil and ignorance herein.* But now the judgment-day is the principal time wherein everything shall be set in its proper place; that which is of God in its place, and that which is not, shall now be discovered, and made manifest. In many things now we offend all; and then we shall see the many offences we have committed, and shall ourselves judge them as they are. The Christian, is in this world, so candid a creature, that take him when he is not under some great temptation,

---

* This is an awful state of delusion; to imagine that God is the author of *gross* things, such as worshipping a wafer, or applying to a priest to forgive sins; and that a holy God prompts them to the doing thereof, and sanctions them by his presence!! 'Every man is tempted, when he is drawn away of his own lust, and enticed,' James i. 14. *Christian*, take care that you receive not any doctrine, nor conform to any practice in religion, without prayerful investigation, and a 'thus saith the Lord' for its sanction.—ED.

and he will ingeniously confess to his God, before all men, how he hath sinned and transgressed against his Father; and will fall down at the feet of God, and cry, *Thou art righteous, for I have sinned;* and thou art gracious, that, notwithstanding my sin, thou shouldest save me. Now, I say, if the Christian is so simple and plain-hearted with God, in the days of his imperfection, when he is accompanied with many infirmities and temptations; how freely will he confess and acknowledge his miscarriages, when he comes before his Lord and Saviour; absolutely stript of all temptation and imperfection. 'As I live, saith the Lord, every knee shall bow to me, and every tongue shall confess to God.' Ro. xiv. 11. Phi. ii. 10. 11. Every knee shall bow, and reverence God the Creator, and Christ the Redeemer of the world; and every tongue shall confess, that his will alone ought by them to have been obeyed in all things; and shall confess also, and that most naturally and freely —I mean, the saints shall—in how many things they were deceived, mistaken, deluded, and drawn aside in their intended devotion and honour to God.

[*Second.*] But yet take notice, that in this day, when the saints are thus counting for their evil before their Saviour and Judge; they shall not then, as now, at the remembrance and confession of sin, be filled with that guilt, confusion, and shame that now through the weakness of faith attendeth their souls; neither shall they in the least be grieved or offended, that God hath before the angels and the rest of their holy brethren, laid open to a tittle their infirmities, from the least and first, to the biggest and last. For,

1. The God to whom they confess all, they will now more perfectly than ever see he doth love them, and free them from all, even when and before they confess and acknowledge them to him; and they shall, I say, have their soul so full of the ravishing raptures of the life and glory that now they are in, that they shall be of it swallowed up in that measure and manner, that neither fear, nor guilt, nor confusion can come near them, or touch them. Their Judge is their Saviour, their Husband, and Head; who, though he will bring every one of them for all things to judgment, yet he will keep them for ever out of condemnation, and anything that tendeth that way. 'Perfect love casteth out fear,' even while we are here; much more then, when we are with our Saviour, our Jesus, being passed from death to life, Jn. v. 24. 1 Jn. iv. 18.

2. The saints at this day, shall have their hearts and souls so wrapped up in the pleasure of God their Saviour, that it shall be their delight, to see all things, though once never so near and dear unto them; yet now to perish, if not according to his word and will. 'Thy will be done,' is to be always our language here; Mat. vi. 10. but to delight to see it done in all things, though it tend never so much to the destruction of what we love; to delight, I say, to see it done in the height and perfection of delight; it will be when we come to heaven, or when the Lord shall come to judge the world. But,

3. The sole end of the counting of the saints at the day of God, it will be, not only for the vindication of the righteousness, holiness, and purity of the word, neither will it centre only in the manifestation of the knowledge and heart-discerning nature of Christ (though both these will be in it, Re. ii. 22, 23.) But their very remembrances and sight of the sin and vanity that they have done while here; it shall both set off, and heighten the tender affections of their God unto them; and also increase their joy and sweetness of soul, and clinging of heart to their God. Saints while here, are sweetly sensible that the sense of sin, and the assurance of pardon, will make famous work in their poor hearts. Ah, what meltings without guilt! what humility without casting down! and what a sight of the creature's nothingness, yet without fear, will this sense of sin work in the soul! The sweetest frame, the most heart-endearing frame, that possibly a Christian can get into while in this world, is to have a warm sight of sin, and of a Saviour upon the heart at one time. Now it weeps not for fear and through torment, but by virtue of constraining grace and mercy, and is at this very time, so far off of disquietness of heart, by reason of the sight of its wickedness, that it is driven into an ecstasy, by reason of the love and mercy that is mingled with the sense of sin in the soul.

The heart never sees so much of the power of mercy as now, nor of the virtue, value, and excellency of Christ in all his offices as now, and the tongue so sweetly enlarged to proclaim and cry up grace as now; now will Christ 'come to be glorified in his saints, and to be admired in all them that believe,' 2 Th. i. 10.

Wherefore, though the saints receive by faith the forgiveness of sins in this life, and so are passed from death to life; yet again, Christ Jesus, and God his Father, will have every one of these sins reckoned up again, and brought fresh upon the stage in the day of judgment, that they may see and be sensible for ever, what grace and mercy hath laid hold upon them. And this I take to be the reason of that remarkable saying of the apostle Peter, 'Repent ye therefore, and be converted, that your sins may be blotted out, when the times of refreshing shall come from the presence of the Lord; and he shall send Jesus Christ, which before was preached unto you: whom the heaven must receive until the times of restitution of all things, which God hath spoken by the mouth of all his holy prophets since the world began.' Ac. iii. 19—21.

If a sense of some sin, (for who sees all? Ps. xix. 12.) and a sight of the love of God, will here so work upon the spirit of the godly : what will a sight of all sin do, when together with it they are personally present with their Lord and Saviour ?

Yea, if a sight of some sins, with a possibility of pardon, will make the heart love, reverence, and fear with guiltless and heart-affecting fears ; what will a general sight of all sin, and together with them an eternal acquittance from them, work on the heart of the saint for ever ?

Yea, I say again, if a sight of sin, and the love of God, will make such work in that soul where yet there is unbelief, blindness, mistrust, and forgetfulness: what will a sight of sin do in that soul, who is swallowed up of love, who is sinless, and temptationless ; who hath all the faculties of soul and body strained by love and grace, to the highest pin of perfection, that is possible to be in glory enjoyed and possessed ?   Oh the wisdom and goodness of God, that he at this day, should so cast about the worst of our things, even those that naturally tend to sink us, and damn us, for our great advantage !   ' All things shall work together for good,' indeed, ' to them that love God.' Ro. viii. 28.   Those sins that brought a curse upon the whole world, that spilt the heart-blood of our dearest Saviour, and that laid his tender soul under the flaming wrath of God, shall by his wisdom and love, tend to the exaltation of his grace, and the inflaming of our affections to him for ever and ever. Re. v. 9—14.

It will not be thus with devils ; it will not be thus with reprobates ; the saved only have this privilege peculiar to themselves.   Wherefore, to vary a little from the matter in hand : will God make that use of sin, even in our counting for it, that shall in this manner work for our advantage ? Why then, let saints also make that advantage of their sin, as to glorify God thereby, which is to be done, not by saying, ' Let us do evil, that good may come;' or, ' Let us sin, that grace may abound;' but by taking occasion by the sin that is past to set the crown upon the head of Christ for our justification; continually looking upon it, so as to press us, to cleave close to the Lord Jesus, to grace and mercy through him, and to the keeping of us humble for ever, under all his dispensations and carriages to us.

Now, having counted for all their evil, and confessed to God's glory, how they fell short, and did not the truth in this, or that, or other particulars, and having received their eternal acquittance from the Lord and Judge, in the sight of both angels and saints ; forthwith the Lord Jesus will make inquiry,

SECOND, into all the *good and holy actions and deeds they did do in the world*.   Now here shall all things be reckoned up, from the very first good thing that was done by Adam or Abel, to the last that will fall out to be done in the world.   The good of all the holy prophets, of all apostles, pastors, teachers, and helps in the church; here also will be brought forth and to light, all the good carriages of masters of families, of parents, of children, of servants, of neighbours, or whatever good thing any man doth.   But to be general and short,

First, here will be a recompense for all that have sincerely laboured in the word and doctrine—I say, a recompense for all the souls they have saved by their word, and watered by the same.   Now shall Paul the planter, and Apollos the waterer, with every one of their companions, receive the reward that is according to their works. 1 Co. iii. 6—8.

Now, all the preaching, praying, watching, and labour thou hast been at, in thy endeavouring to catch men from Satan to God, shall be rewarded with spangling glory.   Not a soul thou hast converted to the Lord Jesus, nor a soul thou hast comforted, strengthened, or helped by thy wholesome counsel, admonition, and comfortable speech, but it shall stick as a pearl in that crown ' which the Lord the righteous Judge, shall give thee at that day.' 2 Ti. iv. 7, 8.   That is, if thou dost it willingly, delighting to lift up the name of God among men; if thou doest it with love, and longing after the salvation of sinners, otherwise thou wilt have only thy labour for thy pains, and no more.   'If I do this thing willingly, I have a reward : but if against my will, a dispensation *of the gospel* is committed to my charge.' 1 Co. ix. 17; & Phi. i. 15.   But, I say, if thou do it graciously, then a reward followeth ; ' For what is our hope, or joy, or crown of rejoicing ? *Are* not even ye,' saith Paul, 'in the presence of our Lord Jesus Christ at his coming ?   For ye are our glory and joy.' 1 Th. ii. 19, 20.   Let him therefore that Christ hath put into his harvest, take comfort in the midst of all his sorrow, and know that God acknowledgeth, that he that converteth a sinner from the error of his way, doth even save that soul from death, 'and covereth a multitude of sins.' Ja. v. 20.   Wherefore labour to convert, labour to water, labour to build up, and to ' Feed the flock of God which is among you, taking the oversight *thereof*, not by constraint, but willingly; not for filthy lucre, but of a ready mind;—and when the chief Shepherd shall appear, ye shall receive a crown of glory that fadeth not away.' 1 Pe. v. 2, 4.

Secondly, And as the ministers of Christ's gospel shall at this day be recompensed; so shall also those more private saints be with tender affections, and love looked on, and rewarded for all their work and labour of love, which they have shewed to the name of Christ, in ministering to his saints, and suffering for his sake. He. vi. 10. 'Whatsoever good thing any man doeth, the same shall he receive of the Lord, whether *he be* bond or free.' Ep. vi. 8. Ah! little do the people of God think, how largely and thoroughly, God will at that day, own and recompense all the good and holy acts of his people. Every bit, every drop, every rag, and every night's harbour, though but in a wisp of straw, shall be rewarded in that day before men and angels —'Whosoever shall give to drink unto one of these little ones a cup of cold *water* only in the name of a disciple, verily I say unto you,' saith Christ, 'he shall in no wise lose his [a disciple's] reward.' Mat. x. 42. Therefore 'When thou makest a feast,' saith he, 'call the poor, the maimed, the lame, the blind: And thou shalt be blessed; for they cannot recompense thee: for thou shalt be recompensed at the resurrection of the just.' Lu. xiv. 13, 14. If there be any repentance among the godly at this day, it will be, because the Lord Jesus, in his person, members, and word, was no more owned, honoured, entertained, and provided for by them, when they were in this world: For it will be ravishing to all, to see what notice the Lord Jesus will then take of every widow's mite. He, I say, will call to mind, even all those acts of mercy and kindness, which thou hast shewed to him, when thou wast among men. I say, he will remember, cry up, and proclaim before angels and saints, those very acts of thine, which thou hast either forgotten, or, through bashfulness wilt not at that day count worth the owing. He will reckon them up so fast, and so fully, that thou wilt cry, Lord, *when* did I do this? and *when* did I do the other? 'When saw we thee an hungered, and fed *thee?* or thirsty, and gave *thee* drink? When saw we thee a stranger, and took *thee* in? or naked, and clothed *thee?* Or when saw we thee sick, or in prison, and came unto thee? And the King shall answer and say unto them, Verily I say unto you, inasmuch as ye have done *it* unto one of the least of these my brethren, ye have done *it* unto me.' Mat. xxv. 37—40. 'The good works of *some* are manifest beforehand; and they that are otherwise cannot be hid.' 1 Ti. v. 25. Whatever thou hast done to one of the least of these my brethren, thou hast done it unto me. I felt the nourishment of thy food, and the warmth of thy fleece. I remember thy loving and holy visits when my poor members were sick, and in prison, and the like. When they were strangers, and wanderers in the world, thou tookest them in. 'Well done, *thou* good and faithful servant; - - - enter thou into the joy of thy Lord.' Mat. xxv. 21—23, 34—37.

Thirdly, Here also will be a reward for all that hardness, and Christian enduring of affliction that thou hast met with for thy Lord, while thou wast in the world. Here now will Christ begin from the greatest suffering, even to the least, and bestow a reward on them all: from the blood of the suffering saint, to the loss of a hair: nothing shall go unrewarded. He. xi. 36—40. 2 Co. viii. 8—14. 'For our light affliction, which is but for a moment, worketh for us a far more exceeding *and* eternal weight of glory.' 2 Co. iv. 17. Behold by the scriptures how God hath recorded the sufferings of his people, and also how he hath promised to reward them—'Blessed *are* they which are persecuted for righteousness' sake: for theirs is the kingdom of heaven. Blessed are ye, when *men* shall revile you,' and speak 'all manner of evil against you falsely, for my sake. Rejoice,' leap for joy, 'and be exceeding glad: for great *is* your reward in heaven.' Mat. v. 11,12. Lu. vi. 22,23. 'And every one that hath forsaken houses, or brethren, or sisters, or father, or mother, or wife, or children, or lands, for my name's sake, shall receive an hundred-fold, and shall inherit everlasting life.' Mat. xix. 29.

Fourthly, There is also a reward at this day, for all the more secret, and more retired works of Christianity. 1. There is not now one act of faith in thy soul, either upon Christ, or against the Devil, and Antichrist; but it shall in this day be found out, and praised, honoured and glorified, in the face of heaven. 1 Pe. i. 7. 2. There is not one groan to God in secret, against thy own lusts, and for more grace, light, spirit, sanctification, and strength to go through this world like a Christian; but it shall even at the coming of Christ be rewarded openly. Mat. vi. 6. 3. There hath not one tear dropped from thy tender eye against thy lusts, the love of this world, or for more communion with Jesus Christ, but as it is now in the bottle of God; so then it shall bring forth such plenty of reward, that it shall return upon thee with abundance of increase. 'Blessed *are ye* that weep now: for ye shall laugh.' Lu. vi. 21. 'Thou tellest my wanderings: put thou my tears into thy bottle; *are they* not in thy book?' Ps. lvi. 8. 'They that sow in tears shall reap in joy. He that goeth forth and weepeth, bearing precious seed, shall doubtless come again with rejoicing, bringing his sheaves *with him.*' Ps. cxxvi. 5, 6.

Having thus in brief shewed you something concerning *the resurrection of the saints*, and that they shall count with their Lord at his coming, both for the burning up what was not according to the truth, and rewarding them for all their good. It remains, that I now in few words,

FOURTH, Shew you something also of that with which *they shall be rewarded.*

THE REWARD OF THE JUST.

First then, those that shall be found in the day

of their resurrection, when they shall have all their good things brought upon the stage; they I say, that then shall be found the people most laborious for God while here; they shall at that day enjoy the greatest portion of God, or shall be possessed with most of the glory of the Godhead then. For that is the portion of saints in general. Ro. viii. 17. La. iii. 24. And why shall he that doth most for God in this world, enjoy most of him in that which is to come? But because by doing and acting, the heart, and every faculty of the soul is enlarged, and more capacitated, whereby more room is made for glory. Every vessel of glory shall at that day be full of it; but every one will not be capable to contain a like measure; and so if they should have it communicated to them, would not be able to stand under it; for there is 'an eternal weight in the glory that saints shall then enjoy,' 2 Co. iv. 17. and every vessel must be at that day filled—that is, have its heavenly load of it.

All Christians have not the same enjoyment of God in this life, neither indeed were they able to bear it if they had it. 1 Co. iii. 2. But those Christians that are most laborious for God in this world, they have already most of him in their souls, and that not only because diligence in God's ways, is the means whereby God communicates himself; but also because thereby the senses are made more strong, and able, by reason of use, to understand God, and to discern both good and evil. He. v. 13, 14. To him that hath, to him shall be given, and he shall have more abundance. Mat. xiii. 11, 12. He that laid out his pound for his master, and gained ten therewith, he was made ruler over ten cities; but he that by his pound gained but five, he was made ruler over but five. Lu. xix. 16—19. Often, he that is best bred in his youth, he is best able to manage most, when he is a man, touching things of this life; Da. i. 3, 4. but always he that is best bred, and that is most in the bosom of God, and that so acts for him here; he is the man that will be best able to enjoy most of God in the kingdom of heaven. It is observable that Paul saith, 'Our - affliction - - worketh for us a far more exceeding *and* eternal weight of glory.' 2 Co. iv. 17. Our afflictions do it, not only because there is laid up a reward for the afflicted, according to the measure of affliction; but because afflictions, and so every service of God, doth make the heart more deep, more experimental, more knowing and profound; and so more able to hold, contain, and bear more. Ps. cxix. 71. 'Every man shall receive his own reward, according to his own labour.' 1 Co. iii. 8. And this is the reason of such sayings as these—Lay up for yourselves a good foundation against the time to come, that you may lay hold on eternal life, 1 Ti. vi. 19. which eternal life, is not the matter of our justification from sin in the sight of God; for that is done freely by grace,

through faith in Christ's blood; (but here the apostle speaks of giving of alms) but it is the same that in the other place he calls 'the far more exceeding and eternal weight of glory.' And hence it is that he in his stirring them up to be diligent in good works, doth tell them, that he doth not exhort them to it because he wanted, but because he would have 'fruit that might abound to their account;' Phi. iv. 17. as he saith also in another place, 'Beloved brethren, be ye stedfast, unmoveable, always abounding in the work of the Lord, forasmuch as ye know that your labour is not in vain in the Lord.' 1 Co. xv. 58. Therefore I say, the reward that the saints shall have at this day for all the good they have done, it is the enjoyment of God, according to their works: though they shall be freely justified and glorified without works.

Second, As the enjoyment of God at that day, will be to the saints, according to their works and doings—I speak not now of justification from sin —so will their praise and commendations at that day, be according to the same, and both of them their degrees of glory; for I say, as God by communicating of himself unto us at that day, will thereby glorify us, so also he will for the adding all things that may furnish with glory every way, cause to be proclaimed in the face of heaven, and in the presence of all the holy angels; everything that hath for God, his ways, and people, been done by us while here we have been. 'Whatsoever ye have spoken in darkness shall be heard in the light; and that which ye have spoken in the ear in closets shall be proclaimed upon the housetops.' Lu. xii. 2, 3. Again, He that 'shall confess me,' saith Christ, 'before men, him will I confess also before my Father which is in heaven.' Mat. x. 32.

Now as he of whom Christ is ashamed when he comes in his glory, and in the glory of the holy angels, will then lie under inconceivable disgrace, shame, dishonour, and contempt: so he whom Christ shall confess, own, commend, and praise at that day, must needs have very great dignity, honour, and renown, 'for then shall every man have praise of God'—to wit, according to his works. 1 Co. iv. 5. Now will Christ proclaim before thee and all others what thou hast done, and what thou hast suffered, what thou hast owned, and what thou hast withstood for his name. Mar. viii. 38. This is he that forsook his goods, his relations, his country, and life for me: this is the man that overcame the flatteries and threats, allurements and enticings, of a whole world for me; behold him, he is an Israelite indeed, Jn. i. 47. the top man in his generation, 'none like him in all the earth.' Job i. 8. It is said, that when king Ahasuerus had understanding of how good service Mordecai the Jew had done to and for him, he commanded that the royal apparel and the crown, with the horse that the king did ride on, should be given to him, and that he should with that crown, apparel, and horse, be had through the city, in the presence of all his nobles, and that proclamation should be made before him, 'Thus shall it be done unto the man whom the king delighteth to honour.' Es. vi. 9—11.

Ahasuerus in this was a type to hold forth to the children of God, how kindly he will take all their labour and service of love, and how he will honour and dignify the same; as Christ saith, 'Let your loins be girded about, and *your* lights burning; And ye yourselves like unto men that wait for their lord, when he will return from the wedding; that when he cometh and knocketh, they may open unto him immediately. Blessed *are* those servants, whom the lord when he cometh shall find watching: verily I say unto you, that he shall gird himself, and make them sit down to meat, and will come forth and serve them.' Lu. xii. 35—37. The meaning is, that those souls that shall make it their business to honour the Lord Jesus Christ, in the day of their temptation ; he will make it his business to honour and glorify them in the day of his glorification. Jn. xii. 26. 'Verily, I say unto you, that he will make them sit down to meat, and shall come forth and serve them. If any man will serve me,' saith he, 'him will my Father honour.' It hath been God's way in this world to proclaim the acts and doings of his saints in his word before all in this world, and he will do it in that which is to come. Mar. xiv. 9. Re. iii. 4; xiv. 1—6.

Third, Another thing that shall be yet added to the glory of the saints, in the kingdom of their Saviour, at his coming is, they shall every one of them then have his throne and place of degree on Christ's right hand, and on his left, in his glorious kingdom, according to the relation they stand in to Christ, as the members of his body; for as Christ will have a special eye on us, and a tender and affectionate heart, to recompense to the full every good thing that any man doth for his name in this world: so also he will have as great regard, that there be to every member of his body, the place, and state that is comely for every such member. When the mother of Zebedee's children petitioned our Saviour that he would grant to her, that her two sons might sit, the one on his right hand, and the other on his left, in his kingdom: though he did not grant to her the request for her children, yet he affirmed that there would be places of degrees and honour in heaven, saying, 'To sit on my right hand, and on my left, is not mine to give, but *it shall be given to them* for whom it is prepared of my Father.' Mat. xx. 20—23. In the temple, there were chambers bigger and lesser, higher and lower, more inward and more outward: which chambers were types of the mansions that

our Lord when he went away, told us he went to prepare for us. 'In my Father's house are many mansions: if *it were* not *so,* I would have told you. I go to prepare a place for you.' Jn. xiv. 2, 3. The foot here, shall not have the place prepared for the eye, nor yet the hand, that which is prepared for the ear, but every one shall have his own place in the body of Christ, and the glory also prepared for such a relation. Order, as it is comely in earth, so much more in the kingdom of the God of order, in heaven; where all things shall be done in their utmost perfections. Here shall Enoch, Noah, Abraham, Moses, Joshua, David, with the prophets, have every one his place, according to the degree of Old Testament saints. As God said to Daniel, 'Go thou thy way till the end *be:* for thou shalt rest, and stand in thy lot at the end of the days.' Da. xii. 13. And here also shall Peter, Paul, Timothy, and all other the church officers have their place, and heavenly state, according as God hath set them in the church in the New Testament. As Paul saith of the deacons, 'They that have used the office of a deacon well, purchase to themselves a good degree, and great boldness in the faith which is in Christ Jesus.' 1 Ti. iii. 13. And so of all other saints, be they here of what rank, quality, or place in the church soever, they shall have every one his state, his heavenly state, according as he standeth in the body. As he saith, seeing those members that are most feeble are necessary, to them shall be given 'more abundant honour.' 1 Co. xii. 22, 23. Of this heavenly order in the kingdom of Christ, when his saints are risen from the dead, was Solomon a notable type in his family, and among his servants and officers, who kept such exactness in the famous order in which he had placed all about him, that it did amaze and confound beholders. For 'when the queen of Sheba had seen the wisdom of Solomon, and the house that he had built, and the meat of his table, and the sitting of his servants, and the attendance of his ministers, and their apparel; his cup-bearers also, and their apparel; and his ascent by which he went up into the house of the Lord, there was no more spirit in her.' 2 Ch. ix. 3, 4. 'Glorious things are spoken of thee, O city of God.' Ps. lxxxvii. 3. Having gone thus far, I shall now come to

THE SECOND PART OF THE TEXT,

To wit, that there shall be a resurrection of the wicked. 'There shall be a resurrection of the dead, both of the just and unjust;' for as the just go before the unjust, in name and dignity, and honour, so they shall in the last day, go before them in the resurrection.

Now, then, when the saints have thus risen out of their graves, given up their accounts, received their glory, and are set upon the thrones, 'for there are set thrones of judgment, the thrones of the house of David.' Ps. cxxii. 5. When, I say, they are all of them in their royal apparel, with crowns of glory, every one presenting the person of a king, then come the unjust out of their graves, to receive their judgment for what they have done in the body. As Paul saith, 'We must all appear before the judgment-seat of Christ, that every one,' both saints and sinners, 'may receive the things done in the body, whether it be good, or whether it be bad.'

But now, because I would prove by the word, whatever I would have others receive for a truth, therefore I shall in few particulars,

FIRST, prove *the resurrection of the wicked*.

THE RESURRECTION OF THE WICKED.

First, then, it is evident, that the wicked shall rise, from the very *terms and names that the raised shall then go under*, which are the very same names that they did go under when they lived in this world. They are called the heathen, the nations, the world, the wicked, and those that do iniquity; they are called men, women, [of] Sodom, Sidon, Bethsaida, Capernaum, and Tyre. The men of Nineveh shall rise up in judgment; Lu. x. 12—14. the queen of the south shall rise up in the judgment; Mat. xii. 41, 42. and it shall be more tolerable for Sodom in the day of judgment than for other sinners that have resisted more light. Mat. xi. 21—24. 'The heavens and the earth, which are now, - - are kept in store, reserved unto fire against the day of judgment and perdition of ungodly men.' 2 Pe. iii. 7. Joel iii. 12—14. Now these terms, or names, are not given to the spirits of the wicked only, but to them as consisting of body and soul. Further, Christ tells his adversaries, when they had apprehended him, and shamefully entreated him, that yet they should see him sit on the right hand of power, and coming in the clouds of heaven, Mat. xxv. 31, 32; xxvi. 64. Jude 14, 15. as John also doth testify, saying, 'Behold, he cometh with clouds; and every eye shall see him, and they *also* which pierced him : and all kindreds of the earth shall wail because of him.' Re. i. 7. Now none of these sayings are yet fulfilled, neither shall they, until his second coming; for though the Jews did many of them see him, when he did hang upon the cross, yet then he was not coming in the clouds of heaven, neither did then all kindreds of the earth wail because of him. No, this is reserved till he comes to judge the world; for then shall the ungodly be so put to it, that gladly they would creep into the most invincible rock or mountain under heaven, to hide themselves from his face, and the majesty of his heavenly presence. Re. vi. 14—17. There shall

therefore, that this may be brought to pass, be a resurrection of the dead, both of the just and unjust. For though an opinion of no resurrection may now lull men asleep, in security and impiety, yet the Lord when he comes will rouse them, and cause them to awake; not only out of their security, but out of their graves, to their doom, that they may receive for their error, the recompense that is meet.

Second, The body of the ungodly must, at the last, arise out of the grave, because that body and their soul, while they lived in the world, were co-partners in their lusts and wickedness. 'The Lord *is* a God of knowledge, and by him actions are weighed.' 1 Sa. ii. 3. He will therefore bring every work into judgment, 'with every secret thing.' Ec. xii. 14. And as he will bring into judgment every work, so will he also the worker thereof, 'even the dead, small and great.' Re. xx. 12—14. It is not in God to lay the punishment where the fault is not, neither to punish a part of the damned for the whole. 'With righteousness shall he judge the world, and the people with equity.' Ps. xcviii. 9. 'Shall not the Judge of all the earth do right?' Ge. xviii. 25. As therefore the body was co-partner with the soul in sinning, so shall every man receive the things done in his body, according to what he hath done. Wherefore he saith in another place, 'Behold, I come quickly; and my reward *is* with me, to give every man according as his work shall be.' Re. xxii. 12. There shall therefore be a resurrection of the dead, *both of the just and unjust*.

Third, The body of the wicked must rise again, because as the whole man of the just also that is the vessel of mercy and glory; so the whole man of the unjust is the vessel of wrath and destruction. There are, saith Paul, in a great house not only vessels of gold and of silver, but also of wood and of earth, and some to honour and some to dishonour. Now, as he sheweth us, these vessels to honour, they are good men, and the vessels to dishonour are the bad. 2 Ti. ii. 20, 21. Now as these vessels to dishonour, are called the vessels of wrath: so it is said, that God with much long-suffering, doth suffer them to be fitted to destruction. Ro. ix. 22. How they are thus fitted, he also further sheweth, where he saith, They do 'after thy hardness and impenitent heart treasure up unto thyself wrath against the day of wrath and revelation of the righteous judgment of God,' Ro. ii. 5. which treasures of wickedness, James saith, it is treasured up against the last days (which is the time of judgment), and observe it, he saith, that then it shall eat their flesh as it were fire. Ja. v. 2, 3. Now then, their bodies being the vessels of the wrath of God, and again, seeing with this wrath they must be possessed at the last day, that their flesh must with it be eaten, it is evident, that their body must rise again out of their graves, and before the judgment-seat appear; for it is from thence, that each of them must go with his full load to their long and eternal home, 'where their worm dieth not, and the fire is not quenched.' Mar. ix. 47, 48.

Fourth, The severity of the hand of God towards his children, with his forbearance of his enemies, doth clearly bespeak a resurrection of the ungodly, that they may receive the reward for their wickedness which they have committed in this world. We know, that while the eyes of the wicked start out with fatness, the godly are plagued all the day long, and chastened every morning, Ps. lxxiii. 3—15. wherefore it is evident, that the place and time of the punishment of the ungodly, it is another world. If 'judgment must begin at the house of God, - - what shall the end *be* of them that obey not the gospel of God? And if the righteous scarcely be saved, where shall the ungodly and the sinner appear?' 1 Pe. iv. 17, 18. Alas, poor creatures! they now plot against the righteous, and gnash upon them with their teeth; but 'the Lord shall laugh at him, for he seeth that his day is coming;' Ps. xxxvii. 13. for as he saith, the wicked is reserved, or let alone in his wickedness, to the day of destruction, and shall then be brought forth to the day of wrath, though in the meantime, he may go to his grave in his banner, and rest within his tomb.* Job xxi. 29—32. As Peter saith again, 'The Lord knoweth how to deliver the godly out of temptations, and to reserve the unjust unto the day of judgment to be punished:' 2 Pe. ii. 9. And Jude saith, For them ' is reserved the blackness of darkness for ever.' Jude 13. The punishment of the ungodly, it is reserved till the day of judgment, which will be the time of their resurrection. Observe,

1. The wicked must be punished.

2. The time of their punishment is not now, but at the day of judgment.

3. This day of judgment, must be the same with the *resurrection of the dead*, at the end of this world. 'As therefore the tares are gathered and burned in the fire; so shall it be in the end of this world. The Son of man shall send forth his angels, and they shall gather out of his kingdom all things that offend, and them which do iniquity; And shall cast them into a furnace of fire: there shall be wailing and gnashing of teeth.' Mat. xiii. 40, 41. There shall then be resurrection of the dead, both of the just and unjust.

4. The sovereignty of the Lord Jesus over all creatures, doth plainly foreshew a resurrection of the bad, as well as of the good. Indeed, the unjust shall not arise, by virtue of any relation they

stand in to the Lord Jesus, as the saints shall; but yet, because all are delivered into his hand, and he made sovereign Lord over them; therefore by an act of his sovereign power, they that are ungodly, shall arise; this is Christ's own argument, 'The Father judgeth no man,' saith he, 'but hath committed all judgment unto the Son '—that is, count him, and fall before him as their sovereign Lord, even as they honour the Father, and he hath given him authority to execute judgment also, because he is the Son of man. And then he adds, 'Marvel not at this: for the hour is coming, in the which all that are in the graves shall hear his voice, And shall come forth; they that have done good, unto the resurrection of life; and they that have done evil, unto the resurrection of damnation.' Jn. v. 22—29. From hence also Paul argueth, saying, 'For to this end Christ both died, and rose, and revived, that he might be Lord both of the dead and living,' and then adds, 'We shall all stand before the judgment-seat of Christ.' Ro.xiv.9,10.

Pray mind these words, Jesus Christ by his death and resurrection, did not only purchase grace, and remission of sins, for his elect, with their eternal glory; but did thereby also obtain of the Father to be Lord, and head over all things, whether they be things in heaven, or things on earth, or things under the earth. 'All power,' saith he, 'is given unto me, in heaven and in earth, and I have the keys of hell and of death,' Mat. xxviii. 18; Re. i. 18. So that all things, I say, whether they be visible, or invisible, whether they be thrones or dominions, or principalities or powers; all things were created by him, and for him, Col. i. 16. This being thus, 'at the name of Jesus every knee should bow, - - - and *that* every tongue should confess that Jesus Christ *is* Lord, to the glory of God the Father,' Phil. ii. 10, 11. Now, that this may be done, He hath his resolutions upon a judgment-day, in which he, to shew himself his people, his way, and word in their glory, will have all his enemies raised out of their graves, and brought before him, where he will sit upon them in the throne of his glory, and will shew them then, '*who is* the blessed and only potentate, the King of kings, and Lord of lords;' Mat. xxv. 31, 32; 1 Ti. vi. 14, 15.

Behold, He comes, 'with ten thousand of his saints, to execute judgment upon all, and to convince all that are ungodly among them of all their ungodly deeds which they have ungodly committed, and of all their hard *speeches* which ungodly sinners have spoken against him,' Jude 14, 15.

Fifth, The great preparation that God hath made for the judgment of the wicked, doth clearly demonstrate their rising forth out of their graves. 1. He hath appointed the day of their rising. 2. He hath appointed their judge, to judge them. 3. He hath recorded all their acts and doings against

---

* 'Go to his grave in his banner,' alluding to splendid funerals, the hearse being ornamented with banners captured in war, or armorial bearings.—Ed.

that day. 4. He hath also already appointed the witnesses to come in against them. 5. The instruments of death and misery, are already prepared for them.

1. He hath appointed the day of their rising, which day John calleth the *time* of the dead, that they should be judged, Re. xi. 18; which time, Paul saith, is a time fixed; ' He hath appointed a day in which he will judge the world,' &c., Ac. xvii. 31. This *time* and *day* Christ brings down to an *hour*, saying, ' The hour is coming, in the which all that are in the graves shall hear his voice, and shall come forth;' &c., Jn. v. 28, 29.

2. As he hath appointed the day, so he hath appointed the judge, ' He hath appointed a day in the which he will judge the world in righteousness, by *that* man whom he hath ordained, *whereof* he hath given assurance to all *men*, in that he hath raised him from the dead.' Ac. xvii. 31. This man is Jesus Christ; for it is he that is ' ordained of God *to be* the judge of quick and dead.' Ac. x. 42.

3. All their deeds and works, to a word and thought, are every one already recorded and enrolled in the books of the laws of heaven against that day. ' The sin of Judah *is* written with a pen of iron, *and* with the point of a diamond: - - - upon the table of their heart,' Je. xvii. 1. And again saith God, ' Write it - - in a table, and note it in a book, that it may be for the time to come, even for ever and ever, that this *is* a rebellious people,' &c., Is. xxx. 8, 9.

4. God hath prepared his witnesses against this day. Ja. v. 1–3. Job xx. 27. Mat. xxiv. 14. Ro. ii. 14, 15. Mal. iii. 5.

5. The instruments of death, and eternal misery, are already prepared. ' He hath also prepared for him the instruments of death; he ordaineth his arrows against the persecutors.' Ps. vii. 13. Ps. xxi. 12. Hell is of old prepared, he hath made it deep and large, the fire, the everlasting fire, is also now of a long time prepared; Is. xxx. 33. Mat. xxv. 41; the heavy weights of God's curse are also ready, De. xxix. 20, and their ' damnation now of a long time slumbereth not.' 2 Pe. ii. 3. But now I say, how ridiculous a business would all this be, if these things should be all prepared of the only wise God, and there should be none to be judged; or if he that is ordained judge, should not, either through want of power or will, command these rebels, and force them before his judgment-seat. Glad indeed, would the sinners be, if these things might be true; glad I say, at very heart, if they might be in their secret places of darkness, and the grave for ever; but it must not be; the day of their rising is set; the judge is appointed; their deeds are written; the deep dungeon is with open mouth ever waiting for them; wherefore at the day appointed, neither earth, nor death, nor hell can hinder: There *shall* be a resurrection of the dead, both of the just and unjust.

Sixth and *Lastly*, Besides what hath been said, I cannot but believe, there shall be a resurrection of the wicked at the last day, because of the ungodly consequences, and errors that do most naturally follow the denial thereof. For,

1. He that taketh away the doctrine of the resurrection of the wicked; he taketh away one of the main arguments that God hath provided for to convince a sinner of the evil of his ways; for how shall a sinner be convinced of the evil of sin, if he be not convinced of the certainty of eternal judgment? and how shall he be convinced of eternal judgment, if you persuade him, that when he is dead, he shall not at all rise? especially seeing the *resurrection* of the dead and eternal *judgment* must unavoidably be one the forerunner of the other. He. vi. 2. It was Paul's reasoning of righteousness, temperance, and judgment to come that made Felix tremble. Ac. xxiv. 25. It is this also he calleth the argument of terror, wherewith he persuaded men. 2 Co. v. 10, 11. This was Solomon's argument; Ec. xi. 9. and Christ's also, where he saith, ' that every idle word that men shall speak, they shall give account thereof in the day of judgment.' Mat. xii. 36.

2. They that deny the resurrection of the wicked, they do both allow and maintain the chief doctrine of the ranters, with most of the debauched persons in the world. For the ranters deny it both in principle and practice, and the other in practice at least. Now to me it is very strange, that these men above all other, should both know and live* in the doctrines of the kingdom of God: especially seeing the denial hereof is an evident token of one appointed to wrath and destruction. 2 Ti. ii. 18. But to be plain; there *shall* be a resurrection of the dead, both of the just and unjust: wherefore, whatever others may say or profess, being beguiled by Satan, and their own hearts, yet do thou fear him that can ' destroy both soul and body in hell.' Mat. x. 28.

There *shall* be a resurrection of the dead, both of the just and unjust. 'And the sea gave up the dead which were in it, and death and hell delivered up the dead which were in them.' Re. xx. 13.

Having in the first place shewed you, that the wicked must arise; I shall in the next place,

SECOND, Shew you the manner of their rising. And observe it, as the very title of the *just* and *unjust*, are opposites, so they are in all other matters, and in their resurrections.

MANNER OF THE RESURRECTION OF THE WICKED.

First then, as the just in their resurrection do come forth in incorruption: the unjust in their resurrection, shall come forth in their corruptions;

---

* Unsanctified knowledge, accompanied by a degree of conformity in conduct, may be the portion of some who indulge soul-destroying heresies.—ED.

for though the ungodly at their resurrection, shall for ever after, be incapable of having body and soul separate; or of their being annihilated into nothing, yet it shall be far from them to rise in incorruption; for if they arise in incorruption, they must arise to life, and also must have the conquest over sin and death, 1 Co. xv. 45. but that they shall not; for it is the righteous only, that put on incorruption, that are swallowed up of life. The wicked's resurrection, it is called the resurrection of damnation. Jn. v. 28. These in their very resurrection, shall be hurt of the second death. They shall arise in death, and shall be under it, under the gnawings, and terrors of it, all the time of their arraignment. As it were, a living death shall feed upon them; they shall never be spiritually alive, nor yet absolutely dead; but much after that manner, that natural death, and hell, by reason of guilt, doth feed on him, that is going before the judge, to receive his condemnation to the gallows. You know, though a felon go forth of the jail, when he is going to the bar for his arraignment, yet he is not out of prison, or out of his irons for that; his fetters are still making a noise on his heels,* and the thoughts of what he is to hear by and by from the judge, is still frighting and afflicting his heart; death, like some evil spirit or ghost, doth continually haunt him, and playeth the butcher continually in his soul and conscience, with frights and fears about the thoughts of the sudden, and insupportable after-clap, by and by he is to meet withal.

Thus I say, will the wicked come out of their graves, having yet the chains of eternal death hanging on them, and the talons of that dreadful ghost fastened in their souls; so that life will be far from them, even as far as heaven is from hell. This morning to them, is even as the shadow of death. They will then be in the very terrors of the shadow of death. Job xxiv. 17. As Christ saith, 'Their worm dieth not and the fire is not quenched.' Mar. ix. 44. From death to eternity, it never shall be quenched, their bed is now among the flames; and when they rise, they will rise in flames; while they stand before the judge, it will be in flames, even in the flames of a guilty conscience; they will in their coming before the judge, be within the very jaws of death and destruction. Thus I say, the ungodly shall be far off from rising as the saints; for they will be even in the region and shadow of death. The first moment of their rising, death will be ever over them, ever feeding on their souls;

and ever presenting to their hearts, the heights and depths, of the misery that now must seize them, and, like a bottomless gulf, must swallow them up. 'They shall move out of their holes like worms of the earth: They shall be afraid of the LORD our God.' Mi. vii. 17.

Second, As the resurrection of the godly shall be a resurrection in glory: so the resurrection of the wicked, it will be a resurrection in dishonour. Yea, as the glory of saints, at the day of their rising, will be glory unspeakable; so the dishonour of the ungodly at that day, it will be dishonour beyond expression. As Daniel saith, the good shall rise to everlasting life, but the wicked to shame and everlasting contempt. Da. xii. 2. And again, 'O Lord, when thou awakest,' that is, to judge them, 'thou shalt despise their image.' Ps. lxxiii. 20. Never was toad or serpent more loathsome to any, than these will be in the eyes of God, in their rising forth of their graves. When they go to their graves, saith Job, 'His bones are full *of the sin* of his youth, which shall lie down with him in the dust.' Job xx. 11. And arise they shall, in the same noisome and stinking condition; for as death leaves, so judgment finds them. At the resurrection then of these ungodly, they will be in a very loathsome condition.

The ungodly at their death are like the thistle seed, but at their rising, they will be like the thistle grown; more noisome, offensive, and provoking to rejection abundance.* Then such dishonour, shame, and contempt will appear in them, that neither God nor Christ, saints nor angels, will so much as once regard them, or vouchsafe once to come near them. 'He beholdeth the wicked afar off;' because in the day of grace, they would not come to hand, and be saved, therefore now they shall, all as thorns, be thrust away, as with fences of iron, 2 Sa. xxiii. 6, 7. Their rising, is called the resurrection of the unjust, and so they at that day will appear, and will more stink in the nostrils of God, and all the heavenly hosts, than if they had the most irksome plague-sores in the world running on them. If a man at his birth, be counted as one cast forth to the loathing of his person; how loathsome, and irksome, dishonourable, and contemptible, will those be that shall arise Godless, Christless, Spiritless, and graceless, when the trumpet sounds to their judgment, they coming out of their graves, far more loathsome, and filthy, than if they should ascend out of the most filthy hole on earth.

Third, As the just shall arise in power, so the wicked and unjust, in weakness and astonishment. Sin and guilt bringeth weakness, and faintness in this life; how much more, when both with all their power and force, like a giant, fasten on them; as

* 'Abundance,' exuberance, more than enough.—ED.

God saith, 'Can thine heart endure, or can thine hands be strong, in the days that I shall deal with thee?' Eze. xxii. 14. Now will the ghastly jaws of despair gape upon thee, and now will condemnings of conscience, like thunder-claps, continually batter against thy weary spirit. It is the godly that have boldness in the day of judgment; 1 Jn. iv. 17. but the wicked will be like the chaff which the wind driveth away. Ps. i. 4. Oh the fear, and the heart-aching that will seize them in their rising! the frightful thoughts that then will fill their throbbing hearts! Now must that soul that hath been in hell-fire among the devils possess the body again. Possess it, I say, with the hot scalding stink of hell upon it. They shall not be able to lift up the head for ever; pangs shall take hold on them, all their hands shall faint, and every man's heart shall melt; 'They shall be amazed one at another, their faces shall be as flames.' Is. xiii. 6—8. Everything they see, hear, or think of, shall tend to their discomfort. They must needs be weak, whom God hath left, whom guilt hath seized, and whom death is swallowing up for ever.

Fourth, As the just shall arise spiritual bodies, so the unjust shall arise only as mere and naked lumps of sinful nature; not having the least help from God, to bear them up under this condition. Wherefore, so soon as ever they are risen out of their graves; they will feel a continual sinking under every remembrance of every sin, and thoughts of judgment; in their rising they fall—fall, I say, from thenceforth, and for ever. And for this reason the dungeon into which they fall is called 'bottomless.' Re. xx. 1. Because, as there will be no end of their misery, so there will be no stay or prop to bear them up in it. Only, as I said before, they shall not now, as afore, be separate body from soul; but both together, be bound in the cords of sin and iniquity, in which they shall now tremble as thieves and murderers, &c., as they go before the Judge, to hear what he will say unto them.

[THIRD—*The examination and judgment of the wicked.*]—Now, when the wicked are thus raised out of their graves, they shall, together with all the angels of darkness, their fellow-prisoners, be brought up, being shackled in their sins, to the place of judgment; where there shall sit upon them Jesus Christ, the King of kings and Lord of lords, the Lord Chief Judge of things in heaven, and things in earth, and things under the earth. On whose right hand, and left, shall sit all the princes, and heavenly nobles; the saints and prophets, the apostles and witnesses of Jesus; every one in his kingly attire, upon the throne of his glory. Joel iii. 11—14. Then shall be fulfilled that which is written, 'But those mine enemies, which would not that I should reign over them, bring hither, and slay *them.*' Lu. xix. 27.

[THE JUDGMENT OF THE WICKED.]

When every one is thus set in his proper place, the Judge on his throne, with his attendants, and the prisoners coming up to judgment, forthwith there shall issue forth a mighty fire and tempest from before the throne, which shall compass it round about; which fire, shall be as bars and bounds to the wicked, to keep them at a certain distance from the heavenly Majesty. As David saith, 'Our God shall come, and shall not keep silence; a fire shall devour before him, and it shall be very tempestuous round about him.' Ps. l. 3. And again, 'His throne *was like* the fiery flame, *and* his wheels *as* burning fire. A fiery stream issued and came forth from before him:' &c. Da. vii. 9, 10.

This preparation being made, to wit, the Judge with his attendants, on the throne; the bar for the prisoners, and the rebels all standing with ghastly jaws, to look for what comes after: presently the books are brought forth, to wit, the books both of death and life; and every one of them opened before the sinners, now to be judged and condemned. For after that he had said before, 'A fiery stream issued and came forth from before him:' he adds, 'Thousand thousands ministered unto him, and ten thousand times ten thousand stood before him: the judgment was set, and the book was opened.' Da. vii. 10. And again, 'I saw a great white throne, and him that sat on it, from whose face the earth and the heaven fled away; and there was found no place for them. And I saw the dead, small and great, stand before God; and the books were opened: and another book was opened, which is *the book* of life: and the dead were judged out of those things which were written in the books, according to their works.' Re. xx. 11, 12.

He doth not say, the book was opened, as of one, but the books, as of many. And indeed, they are more than one, two, or three, out of which the dead shall in the judgment be proceeded against.

First then, there is the book of *the creatures* to be opened. *Second,* The book of God's *remembrance.* *Third,* The book of the *law.* And *fourth,* the book of *life.* For by every one of these, that is, out of what is written in them, shall the world of the ungodly be judged.

'And the books were opened.'

First, The book of *the creatures* The first Book shall be opened, and that first, it con- opened in its cerns man's nature; and next, as it relates to all first part. other creatures.

I. He will shew in what the principles of nature were, as they were God's creation; and how contrary to these principles, the world have walked, acted, and done. The principles of nature are concluded under three general heads.

1. That man by his own natural reason and judgment may gather, that there is a God, a Deity, a chief, or first, or principal Being, who is over all, and supreme above all. This instinct, I say, man merely as he is a rational creature findeth in himself; and hence it is, that all heathens that mind their own natural reason, do conclude, that we are his offspring; that is, His creation and workmanship. That He made heaven and earth, and hath made of one blood, all nations of men; that 'in him we live, and move, and have our being;' &c. Ac. xvii. 24—29.

It appears further, that man by his own nature, doth know that there is such a God.

(1.) By his being able to judge by nature, that there is such a thing as sin; as Christ saith, 'Why even of yourselves judge ye not what is right?' Lu. xii. 57. As if he had said, You are degenerated even from the principles of nature, and right reason; as Paul saith in another place, 'Doth not even nature itself teach you?' 1 Co. xi. 14. Now he that can judge, that there is such a thing as sin, it must of necessity be, that he understandeth that there is a God, to whom sin is opposite; for if there be no God, there is no sin against him; and he that knows not the one, knows not the other.

(2.) It is evident further, that man by nature knows that there is a God, by those fits of fear, and dread that are often begotten in themselves, even in every man that breatheth in this world; for they are by their own consciences, and thoughts, convicted and reproved, though they know neither Moses nor Christ—For the Gentiles which have not the law, these are a law to themselves, and shew the work of the law written in their hearts, Ro. ii. 14, 15.—that is, by this very thing, they hold forth to all men, that God created them in that state and quality, that they might in and by their own nature, judge and know that there is a God. And it further sheweth itself, saith he, by those workings of heart, convictions of conscience, and accusations, that every thought maketh within them, together with the fear that is begotten in them, when they transgress, or do those things that are irrational, or contrary to what they see they shall do. I might add further, that the natural proneness that is in all men to devotion and religion, that is, of one kind or another, doth clearly tell us, that they by the book of nature, which book is themselves, do read that there is one great and eternal God.

Man's nature is a Book, or law to itself.

2. The second principle of nature is, that this God should by man be sought after, that they might enjoy communion with him for ever. As I said before, the light of nature sheweth man, that there is a great God, even God that made the world; and the end of its shewing him this is, that 'they should seek the Lord, if haply they might feel after him, and find him, though he be not far from every one of us.' Ac. xvii. 27.

3. This light of nature teacheth, that men between themselves, should do that which is just and equal. As Moses said, and that long before the law was given, 'Sirs, ye are brethren, why do ye wrong one another?' Ac. vii. 26. Ex. ii. 13. as who should say, You are of equal creation, you are the same flesh; you *both* judge, that it is not equally done of any, to do you wrong, and therefore ought to judge by the same reason, that ye ought not to wrong one another.

Now against every one of these three principles, hath every man in the whole world transgressed; as Paul saith, 'For both Jews and Gentiles - - are all under sin.' Ro. iii. 9. For as touching *the first*, (1.) who is he that hath honoured, reverenced, worshipped, and adored the living God, to the height, both of what they saw in him, and also according to the goodness and mercy they have as men received from him? All have served and worshipped the creature more than the Creator, who is blessed for ever, Ro. i. 25. and so have walked contrary to, and have sinned against, this bond of nature, in this first principle of it.

(2.) Men, instead of minding their own future happiness, as nature teacheth, they have, through their giving way to sin and Satan, minded nothing less; for though reason teacheth all men to love that which is good and profitable, yet they, contrary to this, have loved that which is hurtful and destructive. Yea, though sense teacheth to avoid the danger that is manifest; yet man, contrary to reason and sense both, even all men, have both against light and feeling, rejected their own happiness; as Paul saith, 'Who knowing the judgment of God, that they which commit such things are worthy of death, not only do the same, but have pleasure in them that do them.' Ro. i. 31.

(3.) Man, instead of doing equity, and as he would be done by, which nature itself teacheth: he hath given up himself to vile affections, being filled, by refusing the dictates of nature, 'with all unrighteousness, fornication, wickedness, covetousness, maliciousness: full of envy, murder, debate, deceit, malignity; whisperers, backbiters, haters of God, despiteful, proud, boasters, inventors of evil things, disobedient to parents, without understanding, covenant-breakers, without natural affection, implacable, unmerciful.' Ro. i. 29—31.

And observe it, he doth not say, that all these things are by every man put into practice; but every man hath all these in his heart, which there defile the soul, and make it abominable in the sight of God. They are *filled* with all unrighteousness, which also appears, as occasion serveth, sometimes one of them, sometimes more. Now, man having sinned against that natural light, judgment, reason, and conscience, that God hath given him; therefore, though as I said before, he neither knew Moses nor Christ, yet he shall perish. ' As many,' saith Paul, ' as have sinned without law, shall also perish without law.' Ro. ii. 12.

Yea, here will man be found not only a sinner against God, but an opposer of himself, a contradictor of his own nature, and one that will not do that which he judgeth even of himself to be right. 2 Ti. ii. 25. Their sin is written upon the tables of their own heart, Je. xvii. 1. and their own wickedness and backsliding shall both correct and reprove them. Je. ii. 19.

It is marvellous, if we consider, how curious a creature man was made of God; to behold how much below, besides, and against that state and place, man acts and does in this state of sin and degeneracy. Man in his creation was made in the image of God, Ge. i. 26. but man, by reason of his yielding to the tempter, hath made himself the very figure and image of the devil. Man by creation was made upright and sinless ; but man by sin, hath made himself crooked and sinful. Ec. vii. 29. Man by creation had all the faculties of his soul at liberty to study God his creator, and his glorious attributes and being; but man by sin, hath so bound up his own senses and reason ; and hath given way for blindness and ignorance of God, so to reign in his soul; that now he is captivated and held bound in alienation and estrangedness both from God, and all things truly spiritually good ; ' Because,' saith he, ' that when they knew God, they glorified him not as God, - - but became vain in their imaginations, and their foolish heart was darkened.' Ro. i. 21. And again, ' Having the understanding darkened, being alienated from the life of God, through the ignorance that is in them, because of the blindness of their hearts.' Ep. iv. 18.

Now, for this abuse of the workmanship of God, shall man be brought forth to the judgment, shall be convicted, cast, and condemned as a rebel, against both God and his own soul, as Paul affirmeth, and that when he reasoned but as a man. Ro. iii. 5, 6.

When this part of the book touching man's nature is opened, and man convicted and cast by it, by reason of his sinning against the three general principles thereof :

II. Then forthwith is the second part of the book opened, which is the *mystery* of the creatures; for the whole creation, that is before thee, are not only made to shew the power of God in themselves ; but also to teach thee, and to preach unto thee, both much of God and thyself; as also the righteousness, and justice of God against sin ; ' For the wrath of God is revealed from heaven against all

ungodliness and unrighteousness of men, who hold the truth in unrighteousness ; Because that which may be known of God is manifest in them ; for God hath shewed *it* unto them. For the invisible things of him from the creation of the world are clearly seen, being understood by the things that are made, *even* his eternal power and Godhead ; so that they are without excuse.' Ro. i. 18—20.

1. The creation then of the world, namely, of the heavens, earth, sun, moon, stars, with all other the creatures of God : they preach aloud to all men, the eternal power and Godhead of their Creator. Ps. viii. 3. In wisdom he hath made them all : Ps. civ. 24. to be teachable, and carrying instruction in them ; and he that is wise, and will understand these things, even he shall understand the lovingkindness of the Lord ; for ' the works of the LORD *are* great, sought out of all them that have pleasure therein.' Ps. cvii. ; cxi. 2.

2. As the creation in general preacheth to every man something of God ; so they do hold forth, how man should behave himself both to God, and one to another ; and will assuredly come in, in the judgment, against all those that shall be found crossers, and thwarters of what God by the creatures doth hold forth to us.

(1.) As *First*, The obedience of the creatures, both to God and thee. (*a.*) To God, they are all in subjection (set devils and men aside) even the very dragons, and all deeps, fire, hail, snow, and vapours, Ps. cxlviii. 7, 8. fulfilling his word. Yea, the winds and seas obey him. Mar. iv. 41. Thus, I say, by their obedience to God they teach thee obedience, and by their obedience shall thy disobedience be condemned in the judgment. Ps. cxlvii. 15—18. (*b.*) Their obedience to thee, also teacheth thee obedience to all superiors ; for every kind of beasts, and of birds, and serpents, and things in the sea, is tamed, and hath been tamed, and brought into obedience by mankind. Man only remains untamed and unruly, and therefore by these is condemned. Ja. iii. 7, 8.

(2.) The fruitfulness of all the creatures in their kind, doth teach and admonish thee to a fruitful life to Godward, and in the things of his holy word. God did but say in the beginning, Let the earth bring forth fruit, grass, herbs, trees, beasts, creeping things, and cattle after their kind ; and it was so. Ge. i. 24. But to man, he hath sent his prophets, rising early, and sending them, saying, ' O do not this abominable thing that I hate.' Je. xliv. 4. but they will not obey. For if the Gentiles, which have not the law, do, by some acts of obedience, condemn the wickedness of those who do by the letter and circumcision, break the law : how much more shall the fruitfulness of all the creatures come in, in the judgment, against the whole world! As Job saith, By the obedience and fruitfulness of the creatures he judgeth, and so will judge, the people. Job xxxvi. 27—32.

(3.) The knowledge and wisdom of the creatures, do with a check, command thee to be wise, and do teach thee wisdom. The stork in the heaven, the swallow and the crane, by observing the time and season of their coming, do admonish thee to learn the time of grace, and of the mercy of God. Je. viii. 7. The ox and the ass, by the knowledge they have of their master's crib, do admonish thee to know the bread and table of God, and both do and shall condemn thy ignorance of the food of heaven. Is. i. 3.

(4.) The labour and toil of the creatures doth convict thee of sloth and idleness. 'Go to the ant, thou sluggard; consider her ways, and be wise;' for she provideth her food in the summer, and layeth up against the day of trial. Pr. vi. 6, 7. But thou spendest the whole summer of thy life in wasting both time and soul. All things are full of labour, saith Solomon, Ec. i. 8, only man spendeth all the day idle, Mat. xx. 6. and his years like a tale that is told. Ps. xc. 9. Ro. x. 21. The coney is but a feeble folk, yet laboureth for a house in the rock, to be safe from the rage of the hunter. Pr. xxx. 26.

The spider also, taketh hold with her hands, and is in king's palaces. Pr. xxx. 28. It is man only that turneth himself upon the bed of sloth, as the door doth itself upon the hinges. 'Tis man, I say, that will neither lay hold on the rock Christ, as the coney doth teach, nor lay hold on the kingdom of heaven, as the spider doth bid him. Jn. v. 40.

(5.) The fear that is in all creatures, when they perceive that danger is near, it teacheth men to fly from the wrath to come, 'In vain the net is spread in the sight of any bird,' Pr. i. 17. but man, man only is the fool-hardy creature, that lieth wait for his own blood, and that lurketh privily for his own life. How I say, will every creature fly, run, strive, and struggle to escape the danger it is sensible of! 'Tis man only that delighteth to dance about the mouth of hell, and to be knowingly smitten with Satan's snare. Ro. i. 32.

(6.) The dependence that all the creatures have upon God; they teach thee to depend on him that made thee; yea, and will in the judgment condemn thee for thy unlawful practices, and dealings for thy preservation. The young ravens seek their food from God, Ps. cxlvii. 9. Job xxxviii. 41. and will condemn thy lying, cheating, overreaching, defrauding, and the like. They provide neither storehouse, nor barn; Lu. xii. 24. but thou art so greedy of these things, that thou for them shuttest thyself out of the kingdom of heaven. Pr. xvii. 16.

(7.) The love and pity that is in their hearts to their young, and one another: will judge and condemn the hard-heartedness that is in thee to thy own soul. What shall I say? 'The heaven shall reveal his iniquity; and the earth shall rise up against him.' Job xx. 27. That is, all the creatures of God, they will, by their fruitfulness and subjection to the will of their Creator, judge and condemn thee for thy disobedience, and rebellion against him.

3. Now, as these creatures do every day call unto thee, and lay before thee these things: so he hath for thy awakening, in case thou be asleep, and senseless, creatures of another nature; as,

(1.) Thy bed, when thou liest down in it, preacheth to thee thy grave; thy sleep, thy death; and thy rising in the morning, thy resurrection to judgment. Job xiv. 12. xvii. 13. Is. xxvi. 19.

(2.) The jail that thou seest with thine eyes, and the felons that look out at the grate, they put thee in mind of the prison of hell, and of the dreadful state of those that are there. Lu. xii. 58, 59.

(3.) The fire that burns in thy chimney, it holds forth the fire of hell unto thee. Is. x. 16. Re. xx. 14.

(4.) The ugly smell, stench, and steam, of the burning brimstone, it shews thee the loathsome, odious, and dreadful torments of hell. Re. xix. 20.

(5.) The darkness of the night in solitary places, and the fears that do commonly haunt those that walk therein: it preacheth to thee the fears and frights, the scares and amazements, that will for ever attend all damned souls. Mat. viii. 12. De. xxviii. 65—67.

(6.) By thy delighting, when thou art cold, to lay sticks on the fire to warm thyself, not caring how fiercely they flame therein, so thou canst be warm and be refreshed thereby, by this, I say, God preacheth to thee, with what delight he will burn sinners in the flames of hell, for the easing of his mind, and the satisfaction of his justice. 'Ah,' saith he, 'I will ease me of mine adversaries, and avenge me of mine enemies.' Is. i. 24.

(7.) Yea, by thy blowing the fire, that it may fasten upon the wood the better; thou preachest to thyself how God will blow the fire of hell by the rigour of his law, to the end, it may by its flames, to purpose, kindle upon damned sinners. Is. xxx. 33.

All these things, as inconsiderable and unlikely as they may appear to you now, yet in the judgment will be found the items, and warning words of God to your souls. And know, that he who could overthrow the land of Egypt with frogs, lice, flies, locusts, &c., will overthrow the world, at the last day, by the book of the creatures; and that by the least and most inconsiderable of them, as well as by the rest. This book of the creatures, it is so excellent, and so full, so easy, and so suiting the capacity of all, that there is not one man in the world but is catched, convicted, and cast by it. This is the book, that he who knows no letters may read in; yea, and that he who neither saw New

Testament, nor Old, may know both much of God, and himself by. 'Tis this book, out of which generally, both Job and his friends did so profoundly discourse of the judgments of God; and that out of which God himself did so convincingly answer Job. Job was as perfect in this book, as we are, many of us in the scriptures; yea, and could see further by it, than many now adays do see by the New Testament and Old. This is the book out of which, both Christ, the prophets, and apostles, do so frequently discourse by their similitudes, proverbs, and parables, as being the most easy way to convince the world, though by reason of their ignorance, nothing will work with them, but what is set on their heart by the Holy Ghost.

One word further, and I have done with this, and that is, God hath sealed the judgment of the world by the book of the creatures; even by man's own carriage unto such of them, which, through any impediment, have disappointed his expectations. As thus: if thou hast but a tree in thy orchard, that neither beareth fruit, nor aught else that is good; why, thou art for hewing it down, and for appointing it, as fuel for the fire. Now thou little thinkest that by thy thus judging thou shouldst pass sentence upon thy own fruitless soul; but it is so; 'And now also the axe is laid unto the root of the trees, therefore every tree which bringeth not forth good fruit is hewn down, and cast into the fire.' For as truly as thou sayest of thy fruitless tree, Cut it down, why doth it cumber the ground? so truly doth thy voice cause heaven to echo again upon thy head, Cut him down; why doth he cumber the ground? Mat. iii. 10; Lu. xiii. 6—8; Eze. xv. 1—6.*

Further, the inclination of thy heart towards fruitless and unprofitable creatures, doth fore-preach to thee, the inclination of the heart of God towards thee in the judgment. If thou hast either cow, or any other beast, that is now unprofitable to thee, though thou mayst suffer them for some time to be with thee, as God suffereth sinners in the world, yet all this while thy heart is not with them, but thou wilt take thy time to clear thy hands of them. Why, just so shall thy judgment be, as God saith, 'Though Moses and Samuel stood before me,' that is, to pray me to spare this people, 'yet my mind *could* not *be* towards this people: cast *them* out of my sight, and let them go forth.' Je. xv. 1; Eze. xiv. 13, 14.

Thus I say, will God judge the world at the last day; he will open before them, how they have degenerated and gone back from the principles of nature in which he created them. Also how they have-slighted all the instructions that he hath given them, even by the obedience, fruitfulness, wisdom, labour, fear, and love of the creatures; and he will tell them, that as to their judgment, they themselves have decided it, both by their cutting down that which was fruitless, and by the withdrawing of their hearts from those things, which to them were unprofitable, 'As therefore the tares are gathered, and burned in the fire, so shall it be in the end of the world.' As men deal with weeds, and rotten wood: so will God deal with sinners in the day of judgment: and will bring in, I say, all the counsels and warnings he hath given men by these things, both to clear up and to aggravate their judgment to them.

Second. The *second* book that will be opened at this day, it will be the book of *God's remembrance.* Mal. iii. 16. For as God hath in his remembrance, recorded all and every particular good thing that his own The book of God's remembrance opened. people hath done to, and for his name while they were in this world; so he hath in his remembrance, recorded all the evil and sin of his adversaries; even everything. Ec. xii. 14. Now God's remembrance is so perfect every way, that it is impossible that anything should be lost, that is committed to it to be kept, and brought forth to the judgment at the time appointed; for as a thousand years are but as yesterday, with his eternity: so the sins that have been committed thousands of years since, they are all so firmly fixed in the remembrance of the eternal God, that they are always as fresh and clear in his sight, as if they were but just now in committing. He calleth again the things that are past, Ec. iii. 15. and hath set 'our [most] secret sins in the light of his countenance.' Ps. xc. 8. As he also saith in another place, 'Hell [itself] *is* naked before him, and destruction hath no covering,' Job xxvi. 6. that is, the most secret, cunning, and hidden contrivances of the most subtle of the infernal spirits, which yet are far more slethy,† than men, to hide their wickedness; yet, I say, all their ways, hearts, and most secret doings, are clear, to the very bottom of them, in the eyes of the great God. All things are open and bare before the eyes of him with whom we have to do; who will bring to light the hidden things of darkness, and will make manifest the counsels of the heart. He. iv. 13; 1 Co. iv. 5.

'Ye that say, The Lord shall not see, neither

shall the God of Jacob regard it. Understand, [O] ye brutish among the people: and *ye* fools, when will ye be wise? He that planted the ear, shall he not hear? he that formed the eye, shall he not see? he that chastiseth the heathen, shall not he correct? he that teacheth man knowledge, *shall not he know?*' Ps. xciv. 8—10; see also Ho. vii. 2. and viii. 13. ' Can any hide himself in secret places that I shall not see him?'—that is, when he is committing wickedness—'saith the LORD: Do not I fill heaven and earth? saith the LORD,' Je. xxiii. 24.

Now to know and see things, it is the cause among men of their remembrance. Wherefore, God to shew us, that he will remember all our sins if we die out of Christ, he tells us, that he knoweth, and seeth them all, and therefore must needs remember them; for as is his sight and knowledge, so is his remembrance of all things.

When this book of his remembrance therefore is opened, as it shall be, in the judgment, then shall be brought forth of their hidden holes, all things, whatsoever hath been done since the world began, whether by kingdoms in general, or persons in particular. Now also shall be brought forth to open view, all the transactions of God and his Son, among the sons of men, and everything shall be applied to every particular person, in equity and justice, to whom they belong: the sins that thou hast committed shall be thy own, and thou thyself shalt bear them. ' The Lord *is* a God of knowledge, and by him actions are weighed.' 1 Sa. ii. 3.

It will be marvellous to behold how by thousands, and ten thousands, God will call from their secret places, those sins, that one would have thought, had been dead, and buried, and forgotten; yea, how he will shew before the sun, such things, so base and so horrid, that one would think, it was not in the hearts of any to commit; for all is recorded in the book of God's remembrance. While men are here, they have a thousand tricks to present themselves one to another, far more fair, and honest than they are, or ever were. As Christ said to the Pharisees, ' Ye are they which justify yourselves before men; but God knoweth your hearts:' Lu. xvi. 15. Ay, God knoweth, indeed, what a nest, what a heap, what swarms; yea, what legions of hellish wickednesses, there are with power lurking, like cockatrices, in those men, that one would swear a thousand times, are good and honest men. The way of men in their sins, it is like ' an eagle in the air, the way of a serpent upon a rock, the way of a ship in the midst of the sea; and the way of a man with a maid,' saith Solomon, Pr. xxx. 19. that is, hiddenly, closely, covertly, burying all under fair pretences, wipeth their mouths in the close of their evil, saying, ' I have done [no] wickedness.' Pr. xxx. 20.

But this, though it may serve for the time present, and no longer, God will not be deluded, nor

blinded, nor mocked, nor put off. Ga. vi. 7. ' They consider not - - that I remember all their wickedness;' Ho. vii. 2. saith he, '*but* I will reprove thee, and set *them* in order before thine eyes.' Ps.l.21. Here will be laid open the very heart of Cain the murderer, of Judas the traitor, of Saul the adversary of David, and of those that under pretences of holiness have persecuted Christ, his word, and people. Now shall every drunkard, whoremaster, thief, and other wicked person, be turned their inside outward; their hearts right open, and every sin, with every circumstance of place, time, person with whom, with the causes also that drew them to the commission of every evil, be discovered to all. Here will be no hiding yourselves behind curtains, nor no covering yourselves with the black and dark night. ' If I say, Surely the darkness shall cover me; even the night shall be light about me: Yea,' O God, ' darkness hideth not from thee; but the night shineth as the day: the darkness and the light *are* both alike *to thee*.' Ps. cxxxix. 11, 12.

The piercing eye of God, beholds all places, persons, and things; the holy hand of his justice writeth them down in the book of his remembrance; and by his power and wisdom, will he open and read to all men exactly, distinctly, and convincingly, whatever hath passed from them, or been done by them, in their whole life; for, ' For all these *things* God will bring thee into judgment.' Ec. xi. 9. Again, as God will bring out of the book of his remembrance, whatever hath passed from thee against him; so also will he then bring forth by the same book, all things and carriages of his towards thee.

Here will he bring to thy mind, every sermon thou hast heard, every chapter thou hast read; every conviction thou hast had on thy conscience; and every admonition that hath been given thee in all thy life, when thou wast in the land of the living.

Now will God lay open before thee, what patience he extended to thee, how he let thee live one year, two years, ten, yea, twenty and twenty years,* and all to try thee. Yea, now also will he bring to thy view, how many times he warned, rebuked, threatened, and chastised thee for thy wickedness; how many awakening providences and judgments he continually laid before thy face; yea, how many a time thou didst, like Balaam, run upon the point of the sword of justice, and how he gave back, as being loath to kill thee. Nu. xxii. 23—34.

Now also again, shall be brought before thee and all men, how many strugglings God had with thy heart, on thy sick-bed, to do thee good; yea,

---

* ' Twenty and twenty years,' a singular mode of expression, probably alluding to the forty years' trial of the Israelites in the wilderness.— ED.

and at such times, how many vows, promises, engagements, and resolutions thou madest before God, to turn, if he would release thee from thy affliction, and take off his rod from thy back; and yet, how thou didst, like the man possessed, Mar. v. 1—5. break and snap in twain all these chains of iron, with which thou hadst bound thy soul, and that for a very lust and sin.   Here also, will be opened before thee, how often thou hast sinned against thy light and knowledge; how often thou hast laid violent hands on thy own conscience; how often thou hast laboured to put out that light that hath stood in thy way to hinder thee from sinning against thy soul.   Ah, Lord, what a condition will the Christless soul be in at this day! how will every one of these things afflict the damned soul! They will pierce like arrows, and bite like serpents, and sting like an adder.   With what shame, will that man stand before the judgment-seat of Christ who must have all things he hath done against God, to provoke the eyes of his glory to jealousy, laid open before the whole host of the heavenly train!   It would make a man blush to have his pockets searched, for things that are stolen in the midst of a market, especially, if he stand upon his reputation and honour.   But thou must have thy heart searched, the bottom of thy heart searched; and that, I say, before thy neighbour whom thou hast wronged, and before the devils whom thou hast served; yea, before God, whom thou hast despised, and before the angels, those holy and delicate creatures, whose holy and chaste faces will scarce forbear blushing, while God is making thee vomit up, all thou hast swallowed; for God shall bring it out of thy belly. Job xx. 12—15.

For as for God to forget iniquity, is one of the chief heads of the covenant of grace, and is an argument of the highest nature, to beget and to continue consolation in the godly: so the remembrance of iniquity, by the Lord, it is one of the heaviest loads and judgments, that can befal any poor creature. 'Lord,' saith the prophet, 'remember not against us former inquities.' And again, 'If thou, LORD, shouldst mark iniquities, O LORD, who shall stand?' Ps. cxxx. 3. And the reason is, because, that which the Lord forgetteth, is forgiven for ever; He. viii. 12; Ro. iv. 6—8. but that which he remembereth, it is charged for ever, and nothing can take it away—'Though thou wash thee with nitre, and take thee much soap, *yet* thine iniquity is marked before me, saith the Lord GOD.' Je. ii. 22.

Third. The *third* book that will at this day be opened, and out of which God will judge the world: it is *the book of the law,* or ten words given forth on the Mount Sinai. But this book will more specially concern those that have received it, or that have had knowledge

The book of the law opened.

thereof. Every one shall not be judged by this book, as there delivered, though they shall be judged by the works of it, which are written in their hearts. 'As many as have sinned without law, shall also perish without law: and as many as have sinned in the law, shall be judged by the law.' Ro. ii. 12. That is, the heathens that never knew the law, as delivered on Sinai, they shall be judged by the law, as it was written in man's heart in his creation, which is comprised within the book of the creatures, but those that have knowledge of the law, as delivered on Sinai: they shall be judged by the law as there given.

Now then, this book when it is opened at the day of judgment, it will to those to whom it especially relates, be a most terrible law, far surpassing the two afore-mentioned. This law, as I may so say, it is the chief and most pure resemblance of the justice and holiness of the heavenly majesty, and doth hold forth to all men the sharpness and keenness of his wrath above the other two that I have before mentioned. I say, both because it hath been delivered more plain and open, both as to the duty enjoined, and the sin prohibited; and therefore must of necessity, fall with the more violence upon the head of all that shall be found within the compass of it. This law, it hath in it to be opened at this day, these two general heads:

1. A discovery of the evil of sin, that is so, against plain light and truth; and, secondly, a discovery of the vanity of all things, that will at this day be brought by sinners for their help and plea at the judgment. Alas, who can but imagine, that the poor world, at the day of their arraignment, should muster up all that ever they can think of, as arguments to shelter them from the execution of that fierce wrath, that then, with sinking souls, they will see prepared for them.

As to the first of these, the apostle tells us that 'the law entered, that the offence might abound,' Ro. v. 20. or be discovered what it is. As he saith again, 'I had not known sin, but by the law.' Ro. vii. 7, 13. Thus it is in this life, and thus it will be in the day of judgment, that is, those that see sin, and that in its abounding nature, and in its exceeding sinfulness, they must see it by the law, for that is indeed the glass by which God discovereth sin, and the filthy spots of leprosy, that are in the soul. Ja. i. 22—25. Now those that have not the *happiness* to see their sin by the law in this life, while there is a fountain of grace to wash in, and be clean; they must have the *misery* to see it at the judgment, when nothing is left but misery and pain, as the punishment for the same. At which day, those little tittles of this holy law, that now men so easily look over, and sin against with ease, they will every one of them appear with such dread, and with such flaming justice against every offence committed; that if heaven and earth itself, should step in to shelter the sinner from the justice and wrath due to sin, it would turn them up by the roots. 'It is easier for heaven and earth to pass, than one tittle of the law to fail.' Lu. xvi. 17. If there appeared such flames, such thunderings, and tempests, as there were at the giving of the law; what flames and blackness will there appear at the execution thereof! And if at the giving of the law there appeared so much holiness and justice, that it made all Israel fly; yea, holy Moses 'exceedingly fear and quake,' what will become of these that God shall judge by the rigour of this law in the day of judgment? Ex. xix. 16; He. xii. 21.

O what thunderings and lightnings, what earthquakes and tempests, will there be in every damned soul, at the opening of this book ? Then, indeed, will God visit them ' with thunder, and with earthquake, and great noise, with storm and tempest, and the flame of devouring fire.' Is. xxix. 6 ' For behold,' saith the prophet, ' the Lord will come with fire, and with his chariots like a whirlwind, to render his anger with fury, and his rebuke with flames of fire.' chap. lxvi. 15.

The Lord will come with fire, that is, in the flaming heat of his justice and holiness against sin, and sinners, to execute the rigour of his threatenings upon their perishing souls.

2. The second general head, that is contained in this law, to be opened at this day is, its exactness, and purity, and strictness as to all acts of good that any poor creature hath done in this life, whereby he in the judgment will think to shelter, or secure himself from the wrath of God. This is the rule, and line, and plummet, whereby every act of every man shall be measured; Ro. iii. 21, 22. and he whose righteousness is not found every way answerable to this law, which all will fall short of, but they that have the righteousness of God by faith in Jesus Christ: he must perish, as he saith, ' Judgment also will I lay to the line, and righteousness to the plummet: and the hail shall sweep away the refuge of lies, and the waters shall overflow the hiding place.' Is. xxviii. 17. That is, though men may now shelter themselves under legal repentance, cold profession, good meaning, thinkings, and doings: yet all these things must be measured, and weighed in the balance of God's most righteous law: and, as I said, whatever in that day is not found the righteousness of God, it will be found a refuge of lies, and will be drowned by the overflowing of the wrath of God, as the waters of Noah overflowed the world. And hence it is that all the ungodly will at this day, be found as stubble, and the law as fire. Mal. iv. 1. As it saith, ' From his right hand went a fiery law.' De. xxxiii. 2. And again, 'His lips are full of indignation, and his tongue as a devouring fire.' Is. xxx. 27. For as fire,

where it seizeth, doth burn, eat, destroy, devour and consume: so will the law, all those that at this day, shall be found under the transgression of the least tittle of it. It will be with these souls at the day of judgment, as it is with those countries that are overrun with most merciless conquerors, who leave not anything behind them, but swallow up all with fire and sword. ' For by fire, and by his sword, will the LORD plead with all flesh: and the slain of the LORD shall be many.' Is. lxvi. 16. There are two things at the day of judgment, will meet in their height and utmost strength, and they are *sin* and the *law;* for the judgment will not be, till the iniquity of the world be full ripe. Joel iii. 13. Re. xiv. 15—20.

Now then, when sin is come to its full, having played all its pranks, and done all the mischief it can against the Lord of glory : then God brings forth the law, his holy and righteous law, one of which will now reign for ever, that is, either the law or sin: wherefore sin and sinners, they must tremble, with all that help, and hold them up; for God 'will magnify the law, and make *it* honourable.' Is. xlii. 21. That is, will give it the victory over the world for ever; for that is holy, just, and good; they are unholy, unjust, and bad. Therefore by this law ' the Lord shall rain snares, fire, and brimstone, and an horrible tempest: *this shall be* the portion of their cup.' Ps. xi. 6. Let no man say then, that because God is so famous in his mercy and patience, in this day of his grace, that therefore he will not be fierce, and dreadful in his justice, in the day of judgment; for judgment and justice, are the last things that God intends to bring upon the stage, which will then be to the full, as terrible, as now his goodness and patience, and long-sufferance are admirable. Lord, ' who knoweth the power of thine anger ? even according to thy fear, *so is* thy wrath.' Ps. xc. 11.

You may see, if you will, a few of the sparks of the justice of God against sin and sinners. By his casting off angels for sin, from heaven to hell; by his drowning the old world; by his burning of Sodom and Gomorrah, to ashes ; condemning them with an overthrow, making them an example to those that after should live ungodly. 2 Pe. ii. 4—6. Jude 6, 7.

For ' what things soever the law saith, it saith to them who are under the law; that every mouth may be stopped, and all the world may become guilty before God.' Ro. iii. 19.

Moses seems to wonder, that the children of Israel could continue to live, when they did but hear the law delivered on the mountain—'Did *ever* people,' saith he, ' hear the voice of God speaking out of the midst of the fire, as thou hast heard, and live ?' De. iv. 33. O that ye did but know the law, and the wondrous things that are written therein, before the Lord cause that fearful voice to be heard—' Cursed *is* every one that continueth not in all things that are written in the book of the law to do them;' Ga. iii. 10. which curse must fall on all that walk not in all the commandments of God *without iniquity*; Eze. xxxiii. 15. which none do, I say, but they that walk in Christ, who hath alone fulfilled them all. Col. ii. 10.

The law is that which standeth at the entrance of the paradise of God, as a flaming sword, turning every way to keep out those that are not righteous with the righteousness of God; Ge. iii. 24. that have not skill to come to the throne of grace by that new and living way which he hath consecrated for us through the veil; that is to say, his flesh, He. x. 20. for though this law, I say, be taken away by Christ Jesus, for all that truly and savingly believe; Col. ii. 14. yet it remains in full force and power, in every tittle of it, against every soul of man, that now shall be found in his tabernacle, that is, in himself, and out of the Lord Jesus; Ro. iii. 19. it lieth, I say, like a lion rampant at the gates of heaven, and will roar upon every unconverted soul, fiercely accusing every one that now would gladly enter in through the gates into this city. Job xviii. 14. Jn. v. 45. So, then, he that can answer all its most perfect and legal commands, and that can live in the midst of devouring fire, and there enjoy God and solace himself, he shall dwell on high, and shall not be hurt by this law— ' His place of defence *shall be* the munitions of rocks: bread shall be given him ; his waters *shall be* sure. Thine eyes shall see the king in his beauty: they shall behold the land that is very far off.' Is. xxxiii. 16, 17. Blessed then is he whose righteousness doth answer every point of the law of God, according to 1 Co. i. 30. he shall be able to escape all those things that shall come to pass, and to stand before the Son of man; for in himself, our God is a consuming fire, and man out of Christ, is but as stubble, chaff, thorns, briars, and fuel for the wrath of this holy and sinner-consuming God to seize upon for ever. He. xii. 29. Mal. iv. 1. Mat. iii. 12. He. vi. 8. Is. xxvii. 4. 2 Sa. xxiii. 6, 7. ' Who can stand before his indignation ? And who can abide the fierceness of his anger ? His fury is poured out like fire, and the rocks are thrown down by him.' Na. i. 6.

Now when these three books are thus opened, there will without doubt, be sad throbbing and pricking, in every heart that now stands for his life, before the judgment-seat of Christ, the righteous Judge ; and without all question, they will be studying a thousand ways to evade and shift the stroke, that by the sin that these three books do charge them with, will immediately fall upon them.

But now to cut off all these at a blow, forthwith appear the witnesses, who are ready to evince, and

make full and soul-killing proof of every particular charged against them.

[*First Witness.*]—And the first is God himself. 'I,' saith he, 'will be a swift witness against the sorcerers, The Witnesses give in their evidence. and against the adulterers, and against false swearers, and against those that oppress the hireling in *his* wages, the widow, and the fatherless, and that turn aside the stranger *from his right*, and fear not me, saith the Lord of hosts.' Mal. iii. 5.

This must needs be of great sway with every soul, that God should now come in. I will witness, saith God, that these things of which you are accused before the Judge are true. I have seen all, know all, and write down all. There hath not been a thought in your heart, nor a word in your tongue, but I have known it altogether ; *all things have always been open and naked to mine eye.* He. iv. 13. Yea, my eyelids try the children of men. Ps. xi. 4. I have known your down-sitting, and your up-rising ; and have understood your thoughts afar off. I have compassed your path, and am well acquainted with all your ways. Ps. cxxxix. 1—3.

1. You have not continued in that state of nature in which I did at first create you ; Ec. vii. 29. you have not liked to retain that knowledge and understanding of God, that you had, and might have had, by the very book of the creatures. Ro. i. You gave way to the suggestions of fallen angels, and so your foolish hearts were darkened and alienated, and estranged from God.

2. All the creatures that were in the world, have even condemned you ; they have been fruitful, but you fruitless ; they have been fearful of danger, but you foolhardy ; they have taken the fittest opportunity for their own preservation, but thou hast both blindly, and confidently gone on to thy punishment. Pr. xxii. 3.

3. Touching the book of my remembrance, who can contradict it ? *Do not I fill heaven and earth?* saith the Lord. Was not I in all places to behold, to see, and to observe thee in all thy ways ? My eye saw the thief, and the adulterer, and I heard every lie and oath of the wicked. I saw the hypocrisy of the dissembler. 'They have committed villany in Israel, and have committed adultery with their neighbours' wives, and have spoken lying words in my name, which I have not commanded them ; even I know, and *am* a witness, saith the Lord.' Je. xxix. 23.

4. God will also come in against them for their transgressing his law, even the law which he delivered on Mount Sinai ; he will, I say, open every tittle thereof in such order and truth: and apply the breach of each particular person with such convincing argument, that they will fall down silenced for ever—' Every mouth shall be stopped, and all the world shall become guilty before God.' Ro. iii. 19.

[*Second Witness.*]—There is yet another witness, for the condemning the transgressors of these laws, and that is, conscience—'Their conscience also bearing witness,' saith the apostle. Ro. ii. 15. Conscience is a thousand witnesses. Conscience, it will cry amen to every word that the great God doth speak against thee. Conscience is a terrible accuser, it will hold pace with the witness of God as to the truth of evidence, to a hair's breadth. The witnesses of conscience, it is of great authority, it commands guilt,* and fasteneth it on every soul which it accuseth; and hence it is said, 'If our heart [or conscience] condemn us.' 1 Jn. iii. 20. Conscience will thunder and lighten at this day; even the consciences of the most pagan sinners in the world, will have sufficiently wherewith to accuse, to condemn, and to make paleness appear in their faces, and breaking in their loins, by reason of the force of its conviction. Oh, the mire and dirt, that a guilty conscience, when it is forced to speak, will cast up, and throw out before the judgment-seat! It must out, none can speak peace, nor health, to that man upon whom God hath let loose his own conscience. Cain will now cry, 'My punishment is greater than I can bear;' Judas will hang himself; and both Belshazzar and Felix will feel the joints of their loins to be loosened, and their knees to smite one against another, when conscience stirreth. Ge. iv. 13. Mat. xxvii. 3. Da. v. 6. Ac. xxiv. 23. When conscience is once thoroughly awakened, as it shall be before the judgment-seat: God need say no more to the sinner than Solomon said to filthy Shimei, 'Thou knowest all the wickedness which thine heart is privy to.' 1 Ki. ii. 44. As who should say, Thy conscience knoweth, and can well inform thee of all the evil, and sin that thou art guilty of. To all which it answereth, even as face answereth to face in a glass; or as an echo answereth the man that speaketh; as fast, I say, as God chargeth conscience will cry out, Guilty, guilty; Lord, guilty of all, of every whit; I remember clearly all the crimes thou layest before me. Thus, I say, will conscience be a witness against the soul, in the day of God.

[*Third Witness.*]—As God and conscience will at this day be most dreadful witnesses against the sinful man; so also will those several thoughts that have passed through man's heart, be a witness also against him. As he said before, 'Their conscience also bearing witness, and *their* thoughts the meanwhile accusing, or else excusing one another; In the day when God shall judge the secrets of men by Jesus Christ according to my gospel.' Ro. ii. 15, 16.

The thoughts come in as a witness for God against the sinner upon the account of that unsteadiness and variety that were in them, both touching God, and their ownselves. Sometimes the man thinks there is no God, but that everything hath its rise of itself, or by chance, or fortune—'The fool hath said in his heart, *There is* no God.' Ps. xiv. 1.

Sometimes, again, they think there is a God, but yet they think and imagine of him falsely. 'Thou thoughtest that I was altogether *such an one* as thyself,' saith God; '*but* I will reprove thee.' Ps. l. 21.

Men think, that because they can sin with delight: that therefore God can let them escape without punishment. Nay, oftentimes they think, that God doth either quite forget their wickedness, or else that he will be pleased with such satisfaction as they are pleased to give him, even a few howling prayers, Ho. vii. 14. feigned and hypocritical tears, and weepings, which pass from them more for fear of the punishment of hell-fire, than because they have offended so holy, so just, and so glorious a God, and so loving and so condescending a Jesus. Mal. ii. 13.

Sometimes again, they have had right thoughts of something of God, but not of him together; either thinking so of his justice, as to drive them from him, and also cause them to put him out of their mind. Job xxi. 14. Or else so thinking of his mercy as that they quite forget his holiness and justice. Now both these are but base thoughts of God, and so erroneous, and sinful thoughts.

Sometimes also, they have pretty right thoughts of God, both as to justice and mercy, but then, through the wretchedness of their unsatisfied nature, they, against this light and knowledge, do, with shut eyes, and hardened hearts, rush fiercely, knowingly, and willingly again into their sins and wickedness. He. vi. 4—6; x. 26. 2 Pe. ii. 20.

As men have these various thoughts of God, so also their thoughts are not steady about themselves.

Sometimes they think they are sinners, and therefore they have need of mercy.

Sometimes again, they think they are righteous, and so have not so much need; mark, and yet both alike rotten and base; because, as the last is altogether senseless, so the first is not at all savingly sensible. Mar. x. 17—22. Lu. xviii. 11, 12.

Sometimes again, they think they are gods; Eze. xxviii. 1—6. that they shall never die; or that if they do die, yet they shall never rise again; 1 Co. xv. 12. or if they do rise again, yet they shall be saved, though they have lived vilely and in their sins all the days of their life. De. xxix. 18—20. Now, I say, every one of these thoughts, with ten thousand

---

* Conscience, at the day of judgment, will imperatively '*command guilt*,' which had been committed, to appear, and will fasten it upon the soul, which it accuseth. This is a most impressive and solemn appeal;—there can then be no concealment, no subterfuge.—ED.

more of the like nature, will God bring in against the rebels in the judgment-day. Which thoughts shall every one of them be brought forth in their distinct order. He sheweth to man what is his thought. Am. iv. 13. And, again, ' I know that thou canst do every *thing*, and *that* no thought can be with-holden from thee.' Job xlii. 2. We read, that when the strangers at Jerusalem did but hear the apostles speak to every one of them in their own language, how it amazed and confounded them. Ac. ii. 6—8. But, I say, how will they look and be amazed when God shall evidently, clearly, and fully speak out all their hearts, and every thought they have had before them !

Now the reason and strength of this witness will lie here, that God will by the variety and crossness that their thoughts had one to another, and by the contradiction that was in them, prove them sinners and ungodly; because that, I say, sometimes they thought there was a God, sometimes again, they thought there was none. Sometimes they thought, that he was such a God, and sometimes again, they thought of him quite contrary; sometimes they thought he was worth regarding, and sometimes they thought he was not; as also, sometimes they thought he would be faithful, both to mercy, and justice, and sinners; and sometimes again, they thought he would not.

What greater argument now can there be, to prove men, vanity, froth, a lie, sinners, deluded by the devil, and such as had false apprehensions of God, his ways, his word, his justice, his holiness, of themselves, their sins, and every action?

Now they will indeed appear a very lump of confusion, a mass of sin, a bundle of ignorance, of atheism, of unbelief, and of all things that should lay them obnoxious to the judgments of God. This will God, I say, by mustering up the thoughts of man, and by shewing of them, that every imagination and thought of their heart was only evil, and that continually, (by shewing of them what staggering, drunken, wild, and uncomely thoughts they have had, both of him, and of themselves,) convince them, cast them, and condemn them for sinners, and transgressors against the book of creatures, the book of his remembrance, and the book of the law. By the variety of their thoughts, they shall be proved unstable, ignorant, wandering stars, clouds carried with a tempest, without order or guidance, and taken captive of the devil at his will.

Now, while the wicked are thus standing upon their trial and lives before the judgment-seat, and that in the view of heaven and hell, they, I say, hearing and seeing such dreadful things, both written and witnessed against every one of them, and that by such books and such witnesses as do not only talk, but testify, and that with the whole

strength of truth against them: they will then begin, though poorly, and without any advantage, to plead for themselves, which plea will be to this effect.

Lord, we did find in the scriptures, that thou didst send a Saviour into the world, to deliver us from these sins and miseries. We heard this Saviour also published, and openly proffered to such poor sinners as we are. Lord, Lord, we also made profession of this Saviour, and were many of us frequenters of his holy ordinances. We have eaten and drank in thy presence, and thou hast taught in our streets. Lord, we have also some of us, been preachers ourselves, we have prophesied in thy name, and in thy name have we cast out devils, and done many wondrous works. Nay, Lord, we did herd among thy people; we forsook the profane and wicked world, and carried our shining lamps before us in the face of all men ; *Lord, Lord, open to us.* Mat. vii. 21—23 ; xxv. 1, 2, 10, 11 ; Lu. xiii. 24—28. *The sinner's plea for himself at the judgment-seat.*

And all the while they are thus pleading, and speaking for themselves: behold, how earnestly they groan, how ghastly they look, and how now the brinish tears flow down like rivers from their eyes, ever redoubling their petition, Lord, Lord, Lord, Lord: first thinking of this thing, and then of that, ever contending, seeking, and striving to enter in at this strait gate. As Christ saith, ' When once the master of the house is risen up,' that is, when Christ hath laid aside his mediation for sinners, and hath taken upon him only to judge and condemn ; then will the wicked begin to stand without, and to knock and contend for a portion among them that are the blessed. Ah, how will their hearts twitter while they look upon the kingdom of glory ! and how will they ache and throb at every view of hell, their proper place ! still crying, O that we might inherit life, and O that we might escape eternal death !

Fourth, But now, to take away all cavils and objections, that of this nature will arise in the hearts of these men: forthwith *the book of life* is brought out for a conclusion, and a final end of eternal judgment. As John saith, ' The books were opened ; and another book was opened, which is *the book* of life : and the dead were judged out of those things which were written in the books, according to their works.' Re. xx. 12. *The book of Life opened.*

But this book of life, it is not at this time opened, because there are not any godly to be tried; for as I have shewed before, their judgment is past and over, before the wicked rise. The book of life, then, is now opened for further conviction of damned reprobates, that their mouths may be stopped for ever, as touching all their cavils, contendings, and arguments against God's proceeding in judgment with them. For believe it, while God is judging them, they will fall to judging him again; but he will be justified in his sayings, and will overcome when he is judged at this day. Ro. iii. 4—6. Yet not by a hasty and angry casting them away, but by a legal and convincing proceeding against them, and overthrowing all their cavils by his manifest and invincible truth. Wherefore, to cut off all that they can say, he will now open the book of life before them, and will shew them what is written therein, both as to election, conversion, and a truly gospel conversation. And will convince them that they neither are of the number of his elect, neither were they ever regenerate, neither had they ever a truly gospel conversation in the world.

By these three things, then, out of this book, thou, who art not saved, must at last be judged and overcome.

1. Here will be tried, whether thou art within that part of this book wherein all the elect are recorded; for all the elect are written here, as Christ saith, 'Rejoice, because your names are written in heaven;' Lu. x. 20. and again, 'In thy book,' saith he to his Father, 'all my members were written.' Ps. cxxxix. 16. He. xii. 22, 23.

Now, then, if thy name be not found, either among the prophets, apostles, or the rest of saints, thou must be put by, as one that is cast away, as one polluted, and as an abominable branch; Isa. xiv. 19. thy name is wanting in the genealogies and rolls of heaven, Ezr. ii. 62. thou art not *pricked for everlasting life, therefore thou must not be delivered from that soul-amazing misery; for there are no souls can, though they would give a thousand worlds, be delivered at the day of God but such that are found written in this book. Every one of those that are written, though never an one of those that are not written, shall in that day be delivered from the wrath to come. Da. xii. 1.

But, O methinks, with what careful hearts will the damned now begin to look for their names in this book. Those that, when once the long-suffering of God waited on them, made light of all admonition, and slighted the counsel of making their calling and election sure: would now give thousands of treasures, that they could but spy their names, though last and least among the sons of God. But, I say, how will they fail? how will they faint? how will they die and languish in their souls? when they shall still as they look, see their names wanting. What a pinch will it be to Cain to see his brother there recorded, and he himself left out. Absalom will now swoon, and be as one that giveth up the ghost, when he shall see David his father, and Solomon his brother written here, while he withal is written in the earth,

among the damned. Thus, I say, will sadness be added to sadness, in the soul of the perishing world when they fail of finding their names in this part of 'the book of life of the Lamb slain from the foundation of the world.' Re. xiii. 8.

2. The second part of this book, is that in which is recorded, the nature of conversion, of faith, love, &c. And those that have not had the effectual word of God upon them, and the true and saving operation of grace in their hearts, which is indeed the true life which is begun in every Christian, they will be found still not written in this book; for the living, the holy living souls, are they only that are written therein; as the prophet saith, 'And he that remaineth in Jerusalem, shall be called holy, even every one that is written among the living in Jerusalem:' Is. iv. 3. Eternal life is already in this life, begun in every soul that shall be saved; as Christ saith, 'He that believeth in me hath everlasting life.' And again, 'Whoso eateth my flesh, and drinketh my blood, hath eternal life; and I will raise him up at the last day.' Jn. vi. 54. And hence they are called the living, that are written in this book. Here then, the Lord will open before thee, what conversion is, in the true and simple nature of it, which when thou beholdest, thou wilt then be convinced, that this thou hast missed of; for it must needs be, that when thou beholdest by the records of heaven, what a change what a turn; what an alteration the work of regeneration maketh on every soul, and in every heart, where the effectual call, or the call according to his purpose, is; that thou who hast lived a stranger to this, or that hast contented thyself with the notion only, or a formal, and feigned profession thereof: I say, it cannot be but that thou must forthwith fall down, and with grief conclude, that thou hast no share in this part of the book of life neither, the living only are written herein. There is not one dead, carnal, wicked man recorded here. No; but when the Lord shall at this day make mention of Rahab, of Babylon, of Philistia, and Ethiopia: that is, of all the cursed rabble and crew of the damned: then he will say, that this man was born there—that is, amongst them, and so hath his name where they have theirs; namely, under the black rod, in the king's black book, where he hath recorded all his enemies and traitors. It shall be said of this man, of this ungodly man, that he was born there, Ps. lxxxvii. 4. that he lived and died in the state of nature, and so under the curse of God, even as others: for as he said of wicked Coniah, 'Write ye this man childless,' Je. xxii. 30. so he saith of every ungodly man that so departeth out of this world, Write this man graceless.

Wherefore, I say, among the Babylonians and Philistines; among the unbelieving Moors and pagans, his name will be found in the day when it

---

* 'Pricked,' nominated by a puncture or mark, as our sheriffs are pricked.—ED.

will be inquired where every man was born; for God at this day, will divide the whole world into these two ranks—the children of the world, and the children of Zion. Wherefore here is the honour, the privilege, and advantage that the godly above the wicked will have at the day of their counting, when the Lord maketh mention of Zion, it shall be then acknowledged that this and that (good) man was born in her. 'The Lord shall count,' saith the prophet, 'when he writeth up the people, *that* this *man* was born there.' Ps. lxxxvii. 6. This man had the work of conversion, of faith, and grace in his soul. This man is a child of Zion, of the heavenly Jerusalem, which is also written in heaven. Ga. iv. 26. He. xii. 23. Blessed is the people that is in such a case. Ps. cxliv. 15.

But, poor soul, counters* will not go for gold now; for though so long as thou didst judge thyself by the crooked rule of thy own reason, fancy, and affection, thou wast pure in thine own eyes: yet now thou must be judged alone by the words and rule of the Lord Jesus: which word shall not now, as in times past, be wrested and wrung, both this way and that, to smooth thee up in thy hypocrite's hope and carnal confidence; but be thou king or keser,† be thou who thou wilt, the word of Christ, and that with this interpretation only, it shall judge thee in the last day. Jn. xii. 48.

Now will sinners begin to cry with loud and bitter cries, Oh! ten thousand worlds for a saving work of grace. Crowns and kingdoms for the least measure of saving faith, and for the love, that Christ will say, is the love of his own Spirit.

Now they will begin also to see the work of a broken and a contrite spirit, and of walking with God, as living stones, in this world. But alas! these things appear in their hearts to the damned too late; as also do all things else. This will be but like the repentance of the thief, about whose neck is the halter, and he turning off the ladder; for the unfortunate hap of the damned will be, that the glory of heavenly things will not appear to them till out of season. Christ must now indeed be shewed to them, as also the true nature of faith and all grace; but it will be, when the door is shut, and mercy gone. They will pray, and repent most earnestly; but it will be in the time of *great waters* of the floods of eternal wrath, when they cannot come nigh him. 1 Ti. vi. 15; Mat. xxv. 10, 11; Ps. xxxii. 6.

Well, then, tell me, sinner, if Christ should now come to judge the world, canst thou abide the trial of the book of life? art thou confident that thy

profession, that thy conversion, thy faith, and all other graces thou thinkest thou hast, will prove gold, silver, and precious stones in this day? Behold, he comes as a refiner's fire, and as fuller's soap. Shalt thou indeed abide the melting and washing of this day? Examine, I say, beforehand, and try thyself unfeignedly; for every one 'that doth truth cometh to the light, that his deeds may be made manifest, that they are wrought in God.' Jn. iii. 21.

Thou sayest thou art a Christian, that also thou hast repented, dost believe, and love the Lord Jesus; but the question is, whether these things will be found of equal length, height, and breadth with the book of life, or whether, when thou art weighed in the balance, thou wilt yet be found wanting. Da. v. 27. How if, when thou comest to speak for thyself before God, thou shouldst say Sibboleth instead of Shibboleth: that is, though almost, yet not rightly and naturally the language of the Christians. Ju. xii. 6.

If thou miss but one letter in thy evidence, thou art gone; for though thou mayest deceive thy own heart with brass, instead of gold, and with tin instead of silver, yet God will not be so put off. Ga. vi. 7. You know how confident the foolish virgins were, and yet how they were deceived. They herded with the saints, they went forth from the gross pollutions of the world, they every one had shining lamps, and all went forth to meet the bridegroom, and yet they missed the kingdom; they were not written among the living at Jerusalem; they had not the true, powerful, saving work of conversion, of faith, and grace in their souls: they that are foolish take their lamps, but take no oil, no saving grace, with them. Mat. xxv. 1—4. Thus you see how sinners will be put to it before the judgment-seat from these two parts of this book of life. But,

3. There is yet another part of this book to be opened, and that is, that part of it in which are recorded those noble and Christian acts, that they have done since the time of their conversion and turning to Christ. Here, I say, are recorded the testimony of the saints against sin and antichrist; their suffering for the sake of God, their love to the members of Christ, their patience under the cross, and their faithful frequenting the assemblies of the saints, and their encouraging one another to bear up in his ways in the worst of times; even when the proud were called happy, and when they that wrought wickedness were even set up. As he there saith, 'Then they that feared the Lord spake often one to another: and the Lord hearkened, and heard *it*, and a book of remembrance was written before him for them that feared the Lord, and that thought upon his name.' Mal. iii.

---

* 'Counters,' false coin—

'Will you with *counters* sum
The vast proportion of his infinite.'
                              Shakspeare.—Ed.

† 'Keser,' Cæsar or emperor.—Ed.

16.

For indeed, as truly as any person hath his name found in the first part of this book of life, and his conversion in the second; so there is a third part, in which there are his noble, spiritual, and holy actions recorded and set down. As it is said by the Spirit to John, concerning those that suffered martyrdom for the truth of Jesus, 'Write, Blessed *are* the dead which die in the Lord: - - Yea, saith the Spirit, that they may rest from their labours; and their works do follow them.' Re. xiv. 13.

And hence it is that the labours of the saints and the book of life, are mentioned together, signifying that the travels, and labours, and acts of the godly, are recorded therein. Phi. iv. 3.

And hence it is again, that the Lord doth tell Sardis, that those among them that stood it out to the last gasp, in the faith and love of the gospel, should not be blotted out of the book of life; but they, with the work of God on their soul, and their labour for God in this world; should be confessed before his Father, and before his angels. Re. iii. 5.

This part of this book, is in another place called, 'The book of the wars of the LORD,' Nu. xxi. 14. because in it, I say, are recorded these famous acts of the saints against the world, flesh, and the devil.

You find also, how exact the Holy Ghost is, in recording the travels, pains, labour, and goodness of any of the children of Israel, in their journey from Egypt to Canaan, which was a representation of the travels of the saints, from nature to grace, and from grace to glory. King Ahasuerus, kept in his library a book of records, wherein was written, the good service that his subjects did for him at any time, which was a type also of the manner and order of heaven. And as sure as ever Mordecai, when search was made in the rolls, was found there to have done such and such service for the king and his kingdom: Es. vi. 1, 2. so surely will it be found, what every saint hath done for God, at the day of inquiry. You find in the Old Testament also, still as any of the kings of Judah died, there was surely a record in the book of Chronicles, of their memorable acts and doings for their God, the church, and the *commonwealth* of Israel, which still doth further hold forth unto the children of men, this very thing, that all the kings of the New Testament, which are the saints of God, have all their acts, and what they have done for their God, &c., recorded in the book of Chronicles in the heavenly Jerusalem.

Now, I say, when this part of the book of life shall be opened, what can be found in it, of the good deeds and heaven-born actions of wicked men? Just nothing; for as it is not to be expected that thorns should bring forth grapes, or that thistles should bear figs: so it cannot be imagined, that ungodly men should have anything to their com-

mendations, recorded in this part of the book of life. What hast thou done, man, for God in this world? Art thou one of them that hast set thyself against those strong strugglings of pride, lust, covetousness, and secret wickedness, that remain in thy heart, like Job and Paul? Job i. 8; 2 Co. x. 4, 5. And do these strugglings against these things, arise from pure love to the Lord Jesus, or from some legal terrors and conviction for sin. Ga. v. 6. Dost thou, I say, struggle against thy lusts, because thou dost in truth, love the sweet, holy, and blessed leadings of the Spirit of the Lord Jesus; its leadings of thee, I say, into his blood and death, for thy justification and deliverance from wrath to come. Phi. iii. 6—8; 2 Co. v. 14.

What acts of self-denial, hast thou done for the name of the Lord Jesus, among the sons of men? I say, what house, what friend, what wife, what children, and the like, hast thou lost, or left for the word of God, and the testimony of his truth in the world? Mat. xix. 27, 28. Re. xii. 11. Wast thou one of them, that didst sigh, and afflict thyself for the abominations of the times? and that Christ hath marked and recorded for such an one? Eze. ix. 4. Zep. iii. 18.

In a word, art thou one of them, that wouldst not be won, neither by fear, frowns, nor flatteries, to forsake the ways of God, or wrong thy conscience? or art thou one of them that slightest those opportunities that Satan and this world did often give thee to return to sin in secret. He. xi. 15. These be the men whose praise is in the gospel, and whose commendable and worthy acts are recorded before the Judge of all the world. Alas, alas, these things are strange things to a carnal and wicked man. Nothing of this hath been done by him in this life, and therefore how can any such be recorded for him in the book of life? wherefore he must needs be shut out of this part also. As David saith, 'Let them be blotted out of the book of the living, and not be written with the righteous.' Ps. lxix. 28.

Thus I say, the wicked will find nothing for their comfort, either in the first part of this book, where all the names of the elect are, neither will they find anything in the second part thereof, where are recorded the true nature and operation of effectual conversion, of faith, or love, or the like; and I say, neither can anything be found in this third part, wherein are recorded the worthy acts, and memorable deeds of the saints of the Lord Jesus. Thus, when Christ therefore hath opened before them this book of life, and convinced the ungodly at this day out of it, he will then shut it up again, saying, I find nothing herein that will do you good; you are none of my elect, you are the sons of perdition. For as these things will be found clear and full in the book of life, so they will be found

Q

effectually wrought in the hearts of the elect, all whose conversion and perseverance shall now be opened before thine eyes, as a witness, I say, of the truth of what thou here seest opened before thee, and also of thy unregenerate estate. Now, thou wilt see what a turn, what a change, and what a clinging to God, to Christ, and his word and ways; there was found in the souls of the saved ones! Here shall be seen also how resolvedly, unfeignedly, and heartily the true child of God did oppose, resist, and war against his most dear and darling lusts and corruptions. Now the saints are hidden ones, but then they shall be manifest; this is the *morrow* in which the Lord will shew who are his, and who they are that fear the Lord, and who that fear him not. Ps. lxxxiii. 3; 1 Sa. viii. 19. Nu. xvi. 5. Mal. iii. 18. Now you shall see how Abraham left his country; He. xi. 8. how close good Lot did stick to God in profane and wicked Sodom; 2 Pe. ii. 7, 8. how the apostles left all to follow Jesus Christ; Mat. xix. 29. and how patiently they took all crosses, afflictions, persecutions, and necessities for the kingdom of heaven's sake; how they endured burning, striving, stoning, hanging, and a thousand calamities; how they manifested their love to their Lord, his cause, and people in the worst of times, and in the days when they were most rejected, slighted, abused, and abased; 'then shall the King say to them on his right hand, (and that when all the devils and damned sinners stand by,) Come, ye blessed of my Father, inherit the kingdom prepared for you from the foundation of the world: (you are indeed the truly converted souls, as appears by the grace that was in your hearts) for I was an hungered, and ye gave me meat: I was thirsty, and ye gave me drink: I was a stranger, and ye took me in: Naked, and ye clothed me: I was sick, and ye visited me: I was in prison, and ye came unto me.' Mat. xxv. 34—36. You owned me, stood by me, and denied yourselves to nourish me and my poor members, in our low, and weak, and most despised condition. This, I say, the world shall see, hear, and be witnesses of, against themselves and their souls for ever; for how can it be, but these poor damned sinners should be forced to confess, that they were both Christless and graceless, when they shall find, both in the book of life, and in the hearts of the holy and beloved souls, that which themselves are quite barren of, and greatest strangers to. The saints, by the fruits of regeneration, even in this world, do testify to the world, not only the truth of conversion in themselves, but also that they are yet Christless, and so heavenless, and salvationless, that are not converted. 1 Ti. vi. 12; 1 Th. ii. 10; 2 Ti. ii. 2. But alas! while we are here, they will evade this testimony, both of our happiness, by calling our faith, phantasy; our communion with God, delusion; and the sincere

profession of his word before the world, hypocrisy, pride, and arrogancy: yet, I say, when they see us on the right hand of Christ, commingled among the angels of light, and themselves on his left hand, and commingled with the angels of darkness; and, I say, when they shall see our hearts and ways opened before their eyes, and owned by the Judge for honest hearts and good ways, and yet the same ways that they hated, slighted, disowned and contemned, what will they, or what can they say, but thus—We fools counted their lives madness, and their end to be without honour; but how are they numbered with the saints, and owned by God and Christ!

And truly, was it not that the world might, by seeing the turn that is wrought on the godly at their conversion, be convinced of the evil of their ways, or be left without excuse the more in the day of God, (with some other reasons) they should not, I am persuaded, stay so long from heaven as they do, nor undergo so much abuse and hardship as frequently befals them. God, by the lengthening out the life of his people that are scattered here and there among men in this world, is making work for the day of judgment, and the overthrow of the implacable, for ever and ever; and, as I have said, will by the conversion, life, patience, self-denial, and heavenly-mindedness of his dear children, give them a heavy and most dreadful blow. Now, when God hath thus laid open the work of grace, both by the book of life and the Christian's heart: then, of itself will fall to the ground, their pleading what gifts and abilities they had in this world; they will now see that gifts, and grace, are two things: and also, that whosoever is graceless, let their gifts be never so excellent, they must perish and be lost for ever; wherefore, for all their gifts, they shall be found the workers of iniquity, and shall so be judged and condemned. Mat. vii. 22, 23. That is a notable place in the prophecy of Ezekiel, 'Thus saith the Lord GOD,' saith he, 'If the prince,' the Prince of Life, 'give a gift to any of his sons,'—that is, to any that are truly gracious —'the inheritance,' or the profit that he gets thereby, 'shall be his son's'—that is, for the exercise of his gift he shall receive a reward; 'but if he give a gift of his inheritance to one of his servants,' that is not a son, 'then it shall be his' but 'to the year of liberty; after, it shall return to the prince,' &c. Eze. xlvi. 16, 17. This day of liberty it is now, when the Judge is set upon the throne to judgment, even the glorious liberty of the children of God, Ro. viii. 21. wherefore then will Christ say to them that stand by, 'Take from him the pound, and give it to him that hath ten pounds. This servant must not abide in the house for ever, though with the son it shall be so.' Jn. viii. 35. Lu. xix. 24. A man may be used as a servant in the church of

God, and may receive many gifts, and much knowledge of the things of heaven, and yet at last himself be no more than a very bubble and nothing. 1 Co. xiii. 1—3.

But now, I say, at this day, they shall clearly see the difference between gifts and grace, even as clearly, as now they that have eyes can see the difference between gifts and ignorance, and very foolishness. This our day doth indeed abound with gifts; many sparkling wits are seen in every corner; men have the word and truths of Christ at their fingers' ends; but alas, with many, yea, a great many, there is nought but wits and gifts; they are but words, all their religion lieth in their tongues and heads, the power of what they say and know, it is seen in others, not in themselves. These are like the lord on whom the king of Israel leaned, they shall see the plenty, the blessed plenty that God doth provide, and will bestow upon his church, but they shall not taste thereof. 2 Ki. vii. 17—20.

Obs. First. Before I conclude this matter, observe, [first,] that among all the objections and cavils that are made, and will be made, by the ungodly, in the day of the Lord Jesus, they have not one *hump** about election and reprobation; they murmur not at all that they were not predestinated to eternal life; and the reason is, because then they shall see, though now they are blind, that God could in his prerogative royal, without prejudice to them that are damned, choose and refuse at pleasure; and besides, they at that day shall be convinced, that there was so much reality and downright willingness in God, in every tender of grace and mercy to the worst of men; and also so much goodness, justness, and reasonableness in every command of the gospel of grace, which they were so often entreated and beseeched to embrace, that they will be drowned in the conviction of this, that did refuse love, grace, reason, &c.: love, I say, for hatred, grace for sin, and things reasonable, for things unreasonable and vain. Now they shall see they left glory for shame, God for the devil, heaven for hell, light for darkness. Now they shall see that though they made themselves beasts, yet God made them reasonable creatures, and that he did with reason expect that they should have adhered to, and have delighted in, things that are good, and according to God; yea, now they shall see, that though God did not determine to bring them to heaven against their hearts and wills, and the love that they had to their sins: yet then they shall be convinced, that God was far from infusing anything into their souls, that should in the

least hinder, weaken, obstruct, or let them in seeking the welfare of their souls. Now men will tattle and prattle at a mad rate, about election and reprobation, and conclude, that because all are not elected, therefore God is to blame that any are damned: but then they will see, that they are not damned because they were not elected, but because they sinned; and also that they sinned, not because God put any weakness into their souls, but because they gave way, and that wilfully, knowingly, and desperately, to Satan and his suggestions; and so turned away from the holy commandment delivered unto them; yea, then they will see, that though God at some times did fasten his cords about their heads, and heels, and hands, both by godly education, and smarting convictions, yet they rushed away with violence from all, saying, ' Let us break their bands asunder, and cast away their cords from us.' Ps. ii. 3. God will be justified in his sayings, and clear when he judgeth, Ps. li. 4; though thy proud ignorance thinks to have, and to multiply, cavils against him.

Obs. Second. But secondly, as the whole body of the elect, by the nature of conversion in their hearts, shall witness a non-conversion in the hearts of the wicked; and as the ungodly shall fall under the conviction of this cloud of witnesses: so, to increase their conviction, there will also be opened before them all the labours of the godly, both ministers and others, and the pains that they have taken, to save, if it had been possible, these damned wretches; and now will it come burning hot upon their souls, how often they were forewarned of this day; now they shall see, that there was never any quarter-sessions, nor general jail-delivery more publicly foretold of, than this day. You know that the judges before they begin their assizes, do give to the country in charge, that they take heed to the laws and statutes of the king. Why rebel, thou shalt be at this day convicted, that every sermon thou hast heard, and that every serious debate thou hast been at about the things of God, and laws of eternity, they were to thee as the judge's charge before the assizes and judgment began. Every exhortation of every minister of God, it is as that which Paul gave to Timothy, and commanded him to give in charge to others—' I charge *thee* before God, and the Lord Jesus Christ, and the elect angels,' saith he, ' that thou observe these things;' and again, ' I give thee charge in the sight of God, who quickeneth all things, and *before* Jesus Christ, who before Pontius Pilate witnessed a good confession; That thou keep *this* commandment without spot, unrebukeable, until the appearing of our Lord Jesus Christ.' 1 Ti. v. 21; vi. 13, 14. These things give in charge, saith he, that they may be blameless. This, I say, hast thou heard and seen, and yet thou hast not held fast, but hast cast away

* ' Hump;' or ' hump-back' is a deformity in nature, so Bunyan uses the word ' hump' as a deformity in judgment.—Ed.

the things that thou hast heard, and hast been warned of: alas! God will multiply his witnesses against thee.

1. Thy own vows and promises shall be a witness against thee, that thou hast, contrary to thy light and knowledge, destroyed thy soul, as Joshua said to the children of Israel, when they said the Lord should be their God. Well, saith he, ' Ye *are* witnesses against yourselves that ye have chosen you the Lord, to serve him.' That is, if now you turn back again, even this covenant and resolution of yours will in the great day be a witness against you—'And they said, *We are* witnesses.' Jos. xxiv. 22.

2. Every time you have with your mouth said well of godliness, and yet gone on in wickedness; or every time you have condemned sin in others, and yet have not refrained it yourselves; I say, every such word and conclusion that hath passed out of thy mouth, sinner, it shall be as a witness against thee in the day of God, and the Lord Jesus Christ; as Christ saith, ' By thy words thou shalt be justified, and by thy words thou shalt be condemned.' Mat. xii. 37. I observe, that talk with who you will, they will with their mouth say, serving of God, and loving of Christ, and walking in ways of holiness, are best, and best will come of them. I observe again, that men that are grossly wicked themselves, will yet, with heavy censures and judgments, condemn drunkenness, lying, covetousness, pride, and whoring, with all manner of abominations in others; and yet, in the meantime, continue to be neglecters of God, and embracers of sin and the allurements of the flesh themselves. Why, such souls, every time they speak well of godliness, and continue in their sins; they do pass judgment upon themselves, and provide a witness, even their own mouth, against their own soul, at the judgment-seat—' Out of thy own mouth,' saith Christ, ' will I judge thee, thou wicked servant;' thou knewest what I was, and that I loved to see all my servants zealous, and active for me, that at my coming, I might have received again what I gave thee, with increase; thou oughtest therefore to have been busying thyself in my work, for my glory, and thy own good; but seeing thou hast, against thy own light and mouth gone contrary: Angels, take this unprofitable servant, and cast ye him into utter darkness, there shall be weeping and gnashing of teeth ; he sinned against his light, he shall go to hell against his will. Mat. xxv. 26—31.

The very same I say, will befall all those that have used their mouth to condemn the sins of others, while they themselves live in their sins. Saith God, O thou wicked wretch, thou didst know that sin was bad, thou didst condemn it in others, thou didst also condemn, and pass judgment upon them for their sin, ' Therefore thou art inexcusable, O man, whosoever thou art that judgest: for '

thou that judgest dost the same thing; wherefore, ' wherein thou hast judged another, thou condemnest thyself.' I must therefore, saith Christ, look upon thee to be no other but a sinner against thy own mouth, and cannot but judge thee as a despiser of my goodness, and the riches of my forbearance ; by which means, thou hast treasured up wrath against this day of wrath, and revelation of the righteous judgment of God. Ro. ii. 1—5. *He that knoweth to do good, and doth it not, to him it is sin.* Thus will God, I say, judge and condemn poor sinners, even from and by themselves, to the fire, that lake of brimstone and fire.

3. God hath said in his word, that rather than there shall want witness at the day of judgment, against the workers of iniquity: the very dust of their city, that shall cleave to his messengers that publish the gospel shall itself be a witness against them; and so Christ bid his servants say—' Into whatsoever city ye enter, and they receive you not, go your ways out into the streets of the same, and say, Even the very dust of your city, which cleaveth on us, we do wipe off against you:' &c. ' But I say unto you,' saith he to his ministers, 'it shall be more tolerable for Sodom' at the judgment 'than for that city.' Lu. x. 10—12.

It may be, that when thou hearest that the dust of the street, (that cleaveth to a minister of the gospel, while thou rejectest his word of salvation,) shall be a witness against thee at the day of judgment: thou wilt be apt to laugh, and say, The dust a witness ! Witnesses will be scarce where *dust* is forced to come in to plead against a man. Well sinner, mock not; God doth use to confound the great and mighty by things that are not, and that are despised. And how sayest thou ? If God had said by a prophet to Pharoah, but two years before the plague, that he would shortly come against him with one army of lice, and a second army of frogs, and with a third army of locusts, &c., and would destroy his land, dost thou think it had been wisdom in Pharaoh, now to have laughed such tidings to scorn ? ' Is anything too hard for the Lord ? Hath he said it, and shall he not bring it to pass ?' You shall see in the day of judgment, of what force all these things will be, as witnesses against the ungodly.

Many more witnesses might I here reckon up, but these at this time shall suffice to be nominated; for out of the mouth of two or three witnesses, every word shall be established. 2 Co. xiii. 1. ' And at the mouth of two or three witnesses, shall he that is worthy of death, be put to death.' De. xvii. 6. Jn. viii. 17.

[*Fourth—the sentence of the ungodly.*] Thus then, the books being opened, the laws read, the witnesses heard, and the ungodly convicted; forthwith the Lord and Judge proceeds to execution.

[THE SENTENCE AND PUNISHMENT OF THE WICKED.]

And to that end doth pass the sentence of eternal death upon them, saying, 'Depart from me, ye cursed, into everlasting fire, prepared for the devil and his angels.' Mat. xxv. 41. You are now by the book of the creatures, by the book of God's remembrance, by the book of the law, and by the book of life, adjudged guilty of high treason against God and me; and as murderers of your own souls, as these faithful and true witnesses here have testified, every one of them appearing in their most upright testimony against you. Also, you never had a saving work of conversion, and faith, passed upon you, you died in your sins; neither can I find anything in the last part of this book that will serve your turn, no worthy act is here recorded of you— When ' I was an hungered, and ye gave me no meat:' when ' I was thirsty, ye gave me no drink: when I was a stranger, ye took me not in: I was naked, but ye clothed me not: I was sick and in prison, but ye visited me not:' I have made a thorough search among the records of the living, and find nothing of you, or of your deeds, therein— ' Depart from me, ye cursed,' &c. Mat. xxv. 42, 43.

Thus will these poor ungodly creatures be stripped of all hope and comfort, and therefore must need fall into great sadness and wailing, before the Judge; yea, crying out, as being loth to let go all for lost; and even as the man that is fallen into the river, will catch hold of anything when he is struggling for life, though it tend to hold him faster under the water to drown him: so, I say, while these poor creatures, as they lie struggling and twining under the ireful countenance of the Judge; they will bring out yet one more faint and weak groan, and there goes life and all; their last sigh is this—Lord, when saw we thee an hungered, and gave thee no meat? or when saw we thee thirsty, and gave thee no drink? when saw we thee a stranger, and took thee not in? or naked, and clothed thee not? or when wast thou sick, or in prison, and we did not minister unto thee? Mat. xxv. 44.

Thus you see, how loath the sinner is now to take a 'nay' of life everlasting. He that once would not be persuaded to close with the Lord Jesus, though one should have persuaded him with tears of blood: behold how fast he now hangs about the Lord, what arguments he frames with mournful groans; how with shifts and words he seeks to gain the time, and to defer the execution: Lord, open unto us! Lord, Lord, open unto us! Mat. xxv. 11. Lord, thou hast taught in our streets, and we have both taught in thy name and in thy name have we cast out devils. Mat. vii. 22. We have eaten and drank in thy presence. Lu. xiii. 26. And

when did we see thee an hungry, or thirsty, or a stranger, or naked, or sick, or in prison, and did not minister to thee? Mat. xxv. 10, 11. O poor hearts! how loth, how unwillingly do they turn away from Christ! How loth are they to partake of the fruit of their ungodly doings! Christ must say, Depart once, and depart twice, before they will depart. When he hath shut the door upon them, yet they knock, and cry, 'Lord, open unto us;' when he hath given them their answer, 'that he knows them not,' yet they plead and mourn. Wherefore he is fain to answer again, 'I tell you, I know you not whence you are; depart.' Lu. xiii. 25 —27.

'DEPART.' O this word, Depart! How dreadful is it! with what weight will it fall on the head of every condemned sinner! For you must note, that while the ungodly stand thus before the Judge; they cannot choose but have a most famous view both of the kingdom of heaven, and of the damned wights in hell. Now they see the God of glory, the King of glory, the saints of glory, and the angels of glory; and the kingdom in which they have their eternal abode. Now, they also begin to see the worth of Christ, and what it is to be smiled upon by him; from all which they must depart; and as I say, they shall have the view of this; so they will most famously* behold the pit, the bottomless pit, the fire, the brimstone, and the flaming beds that justice hath prepared for them of old. Jude 4. Their associates also, will be very conspicuous, and clear before their watery eyes. They will see now, what and which are devils, and who are damned souls; now their great-grandfather Cain, and all his brood, with Judas and his companions, must be their fellow-sighers in the flames and pangs for ever. O heavy day! O heavy word!

This word 'depart,' therefore, it looketh two ways, and commands the damned to do so too. Depart from heaven, depart to hell; depart from life, depart to death: 'depart from me'—now the ladder doth turn from under them indeed.† The Saviour turns them off, the Saviour throws them down. He hath given him authority to execute judgment also, because he is the Son of man. Jn. v. 27. Depart from me: I would come to have done you good; but then you would not. Now then, though you would have it never so willingly, yet you shall not.

---

* 'Famously,' plainly, openly; in this sense obsolete. Tillotson used the words 'famous malefactors.' Sermon on 1 John iv. 9.—ED.

† Bunyan here alludes to men convicted of crime; but how many innocent, nay, pious servants of Christ, have been compelled to go up the ladder to the gibbet, and when the rope has been adjusted and the ladder turned, have been ignominiously murdered by the sanction of wicked laws.—ED.

'Depart from me, ye cursed.' You lie open to the stroke of justice for your sins ; ye forsaken, and left of God, ye vessels of wrath, ye despisers of God and goodness, you must now have vengeance feed on you; for you did, when you were in the world, feed on sin, and treasure up wrath against this day of wrath, and revelation of the righteous judgment of God. Ro. ii. 3—6.

'Depart, ye cursed, into everlasting fire.' Fire is that which of all things is the most insufferable and insupportable. Wherefore, by fire, is shewed the grievous state of the ungodly, after judgment. Who can eat fire, drink fire, and lie down in the midst of flames of fire? Yet this must the wicked do. Again; not only fire, but everlasting fire. 'Behold how great a fire a little matter kindleth.' A little sin, a little pleasure, a little unjust dealing and doing; what preparation is made for the punishment thereof. And hence it is, that the fire into which the damned fall, is called the lake, or sea of fire—' And whosoever,' saith John, ' was not found written in the book of life was cast into the lake of fire and brimstone.' Re. xx. 15. Little did the sinner seriously think, that when he was sinning against God, he was making such provision for his poor soul; but now 'tis too late to repent, his worm must never die, and his fire never shall be quenched. Mar. ix. 48. Though the time in which men commit sin is short, yet the time of God's punishing of them for their sin, is long.

'Depart from me, ye cursed, into everlasting fire, prepared for the devil and his angels. In that he saith, 'prepared for the devil and his angels:' he insinuates a further conviction upon the consciences of the damned. As if he had said, As for this fire and lake that you must go to, though you thought but little of it, because you were careless, yet I did betimes put you in mind of what would be the fruits of sin ; even by preparing of this judgment for the devil and his angels. The devil in his creation is far more noble than you ; yet when he sinned, I spared him not. He sinned also before man ; and I, upon his sinning, did cast him down from heaven to hell, and did hang the chains of everlasting darkness upon him, Jude 6. which might, yea, ought to have been a fair item to you to take heed, but you would not. Ge. iii. 2—5. Wherefore, seeing you have sinned as he hath done, and that too, after he had both sinned, and was bound over to eternal punishment; the same justice that layeth hold on these more noble creatures, must surely seize on you. Re. xx. 1. The world should be convinced of judgment then, ' because the prince of this world is judged. Jn. xvi. 8. And that before they came to this condition of hearing the eternal sentence rattle in their ears ; but seeing they did not regard it then, they must and shall feel the smart of it now. ' Depart from

me, ye cursed, into everlasting fire, prepared for the devil and his angels.'

God would have men learn both what mercy and justice is to them, by his shewing it to others; but if they be sottish and careless in the day of forbearance, they must learn by smarting in the day of rebukes and vengeance. Thus it was with the old world; God gave them one hundred and twenty years' warning, by the preparation of Noah, for the flood that should come; but forasmuch as they then were careless, and would not consider the works of the Lord, nor his threatening them by this preparation: therefore he brought in the flood upon the world of the ungodly, as he doth here the last judgment upon the workers of iniquity, and sweeps them all away in their wilful ignorance. Mat. xxiv. 37—39.

Wherefore, I say, the Lord Chief Judge by these words, 'Prepared for the devil and his angels,' doth as good as say, This fire into which now I send you, it did of itself, even in the preparation of it, had you considered it, forewarn you of this that now is come upon you. Hell-fire is no new, or unheard-of thing ; you cannot now plead, that you heard not of it in the world, neither could you with any reason judge, that seeing I prepared it for angels, for noble, powerful, and mighty angels; that you, poor dust and ashes, should escape the vengeance.

'Depart from me, ye cursed, into everlasting fire, prepared for the devil and his angels:' The sentence being thus passed, it remains now, the work being done, that every one goeth to his eternal station. Wherefore, forthwith this mighty company, do now with heavy heart, return again from before the judgment-seat : and that full hastily, God knoweth, for their proper centre, is the hell of hell; into which they descend like a stone into a well, or like Pharaoh into the bottom of the Red Sea. Ex. xv. 10. For all hope being now taken from them, they must needs fall with violence, into the jaws of eternal desperation, which will deal far worse with the souls of men, and make a greater slaughter in their tortured consciences, than the lions in the den with Daniel, could possibly do with the men that were cast in among them. Da. vi. 24.

This is that which Paul calleth eternal judgment, He. vi. 2. because it is that which is last and final. Many are the judgments that God doth execute among the sons of men, some after this manner, and some after that; divers of which, continue but for awhile, and none of them are eternal; no, the very devils and damned spirits in hell, though *there*, is the longest and most terrible of all the judgments of God, yet on foot: yet I say, they must pass under another judgment, even this last, great, and final judgment—' The angels which kept not their first estate, but left their own habi-tation, he hath reserved in everlasting chains under darkness, unto the judgment of the great day.' Jude 6. And so also it is with damned souls; for both Sodom and Gomorrah, with all other, though already in hell in their souls; yet they must, as I have before shewed, all arise to this judgment, which will be their final judgment. Other of the judgments of God, as they have an end, so the end of many of them prove the profit of those on whom they are inflicted, being I say, God's instru-ments of conversion to sinners; and so may fitly be compared to those petty judgments among men, as putting in the stocks, whipping, or burning in the hand: which punishments, and judgments, do often prove profitable to those that are punished with them; but eternal judgment, it is like those more severe judgments among men, as beheading, shooting to death, hanging, drawing and quarter-ing, which swoop* all, even health, time, and the like, and cut off all opportunity of good, leaving no place for mercy or amendment—' These shall go away into everlasting punishment,' &c. Mat. xxv. 46. This word, 'depart,' &c., is the last word the damned for ever are like to hear—I say, it is the last voice, and therefore will stick longest, and with most power, on their slaughtered souls; there is no calling of it back again; it is the very wind-up of eternal judgment.

Thus then, the judgment being over, the king-dom ceaseth to be any longer in the hand of the *man* Christ Jesus; for as the judges here among men, when they have gone their circuit, do deliver up their commission to the king; so Christ the judge, doth now deliver up his kingdom to his Father, Mat. xxi. 8. and now, all is swallowed up of eternity. The damned are swallowed up of eternal justice and wrath; the saved, of eternal life and felicity; and the Son also delivereth up, I say, the kingdom to the Father, and subjects himself under him that did put all things under him, that God may be all in all. 1 Co. xv. 24—28.

For now is the end come, and not before, even the end of the reign of death itself; for death, and hell, and sinners, and devils, must now [fall] to-gether into the lake, that burns with fire and brim-stone. Re. xx. 14, 15. And now is the end of Christ's reign, as the Son of man; and the end of the reign of the saints with him, in this his kingdom, which he hath received of his Father for his work sake, which he did for him, and for his elect. 'Then *cometh* the end,' saith Paul, 'when he shall have delivered up the kingdom to God, even the Father;' But when shall that be? Why, he

answers, saying, 'When he shall have put down all rule and all authority and power. For he must reign,' saith he, 'till he hath put all enemies under his feet,' which will not be until the final sentence and judgment be over; for 'the last enemy *that* shall be destroyed *is* death. For he (God) hath put all things under his feet. But when he saith, All things are put under *him, it is* manifest that he is excepted which did put all things under him. And when all things shall be subdued unto him, then shall the Son also himself be subject unto him that put all things under him, that God may be all in all.' 1 Co. xv. 24—28.

All things being now at this pass—to wit, every one being in its proper place, God in his, Christ in his, the saint in his, and the sinner in his; I shall conclude with this brief touch upon both the state of the good and bad after this eternal judg-ment—

The righteous now shall never fear death, the devil, and hell more; and the wicked shall never hope of life.

The just shall ever have the victory over these things: but the wicked shall everlastingly be swal-lowed up of them.

The holy shall be in everlasting light: but the sinner in everlasting darkness. Without light, I say, yet in fire ever burning, yet not consumed; always afraid of death and hell, vehemently desiring to be annihilated to nothing. Continually fearing to stay long in hell, and yet certainly sure they shall never come out of it. Ever desiring the saints' happiness, and yet always envying their felicity. They would have it, because it is easy and comfortable; yet cannot abide to think of it, because they have lost it for ever. Ever laden with the delight of sin; and yet that is the greatest torture; always desiring to put it out of their mind, and yet assuredly know they must for ever abide the guilt and torment thereof.

The saints are always inflamed with the consi-deration of the grace that once they embraced; but the wicked, most flamingly tormented with the thoughts of rejecting and refusing it.

The just, when they think of their sins, they are comforted with the thoughts of their being delivered from them; but the ungodly, when they think of their righteousness, will gnaw themselves, to think that this would not deliver them from hell.

When the godly think of hell, it will increase their comfort; but when the wicked think of heaven, it will twinge them like a serpent. Oh, this eternal judgment! What would a damned soul give that there might be, though after thousands and hun-dreds of thousands of millions of years, an end put to this eternal judgment. But their misery is, they have sinned against a God that is eternal; they have offended that justice that will never be

---

* The physician looks with another eye on the medicinal herb than the grazing ox, which *swoops* it in with the com-mon grass. *Glanville.*—Ed.

satisfied; and therefore they must abide the fire that never shall be quenched. Here is judgment, just and sad.

Again; as it will be thus with good and bad in general, so again, more particularly, when the wicked are thus adjudged and condemned, and also received of the fiery gulf, then they shall find, That as he that busieth himself to do good, shall have more glory than others; so they that have been more busy and active in sin than others, they shall have more wrath and torment than others. For as doing good abundantly, doth enlarge the heart to receive and hold more glory: so doing evil abundantly, doth enlarge the heart and soul to receive punishment so much the more. And hence it is that you have such sayings as these— It shall be more tolerable in the judgment for Sodom than for others—Lu. x. 12. that is, than for those that had sinned against much greater light and mercy. 'For these,' as he saith in another place, 'shall receive greater damnation.' Lu. xx. 47. Yea, it standeth to reason, that he who had most light, most conviction, most means of conversion, and that was highest towards heaven, he must needs have the greatest fall, and so sink deepest into the jaws of eternal misery. As one star— that is, as one saint—differeth from another in heaven; so one damned soul shall differ from another in hell. It is so among the devils themselves; they are some worse than others; Beelzebub is the prince, or chief of the devils. Mat. ix. 34. Mar. iii. 22.

That is, one that was most glorious in heaven; chief among the reprobate angels before his fall, Is. xiv. 12. and therefore sinned against the greater light, mercy, and goodness; and so became the chief for wickedness, and will also have as the wages thereof, the chief of torments. For that will be true of the damned in hell, which is prayed for against Babylon.—'How much she hath glorified herself, and lived deliciously, so much torment and sorrow give her.' Re. xviii. 7. Can it be imagined that Judas should have no more torment, who betrayed the Prince of life and Saviour of the world, than others who never came near his wickedness by ten thousand degrees? He that knew his master's will, and prepared not himself, neither did according to his will, shall be beaten with many stripes; with many more stripes, than others that through ignorance did commit sin worthy of many stripes. But what should I thus discourse of the degrees of the torments of the damned souls in hell? For he that suffers least, will the waters of a full cup be wrung out to him; the least measure of wrath, it will be the wrath of God, eternal and fiery wrath, insupportable wrath; it will lay the soul in the gulf of that second death, which will for ever have the mastery over the poor damned perishing sinner. 'And death and hell were cast into the lake of fire. This is the second death. And whosoever was not found written in the book of life was cast into the lake of fire.' Re. xx. 14, 15.

SOME GOSPEL TRUTHS OPENED,

ACCORDING TO THE SCRIPTURES;

OR,

THE DIVINE AND HUMAN NATURE OF CHRIST JESUS;

HIS COMING INTO THE WORLD; HIS RIGHTEOUSNESS, DEATH, RESURRECTION, ASCENSION, INTERCESSION, AND SECOND COMING TO JUDGMENT, PLAINLY DEMONSTRATED AND PROVED.

AND ALSO,

Answers to several Questions, with profitable Directions to stand fast in the Doctrine of Jesus the SON of MARY, against those blustering Storms of the Devil's Temptations, which do at this Day, like so many Scorpions, break loose from the bottomless Pit, to bite and torment those that have not tasted the Vertue of Jesus, by the Revelation of the Spirit of God.

Published for the good of God's chosen ones, by that unworthy servant of CHRIST,
JOHN BUNYAN, of BEDFORD,
By the grace of GOD, preacher of the GOSPEL of his dear SON.

'*Jesus saith,* - - *I am the way, and the truth, and the life: no man cometh unto the Father but by me.*'—JOHN xiv. 6.
'*Neither is there salvation in any other.*'—ACTS iv. 12.

EDITOR'S ADVERTISEMENT.

THIS was the first work published by the indefatigable servant of Christ, John Bunyan; and he modestly sought the patronage of his brethren in the ministry, and Messrs. Burton, Spencly and Child wrote prefatory recommendations. The latter of these, Mr. John Child, for some temporal advantages afterwards conformed; and became notorious for having, in a fit of despair, destroyed himself.

Well might Bunyan in this treatise, call the early period of his ministry 'distracted and dangerous times,' in which many a poor sincere inquirer stood 'tottering and shaking,' bewildered with the new din of sectaries, each boldly declaring his divine authority. In the midst of this storm of contending opinions, Bunyan stood forth conspicuously to declare 'Gospel Truths;' and to open and vindicate them these discourses were written. To enable the reader to understand and appreciate them, it will be needful to take a rapid glance at the state of society which then prevailed. The frivolities of dress and laxity of morals introduced by James the First, increased by the mixture of French fashions under the popish wife of Charles the First, had spread their debauching influence throughout the kingdom. George Fox, the founder of the Society of Friends, in an address 'To such as follow the world's fashions,' gives an almost incredible description of the tomfooleries of dress which prevailed. 'How doth the devil garnish

himself, and the people are carried away with vanity—women plaiting their hair—men and women powdering it, making their backs like bags of meal. The men having store of ribbands of divers colours about their waists, and at their knees, and in their hats. The women with their spots on their noses, cheeks, and foreheads—rings on their fingers—cuffs double, like a butcher in his white sleeves — ribbands about their arms, hands, back, waists, knees—and hats like unto fidlers' bags—is not this the devil's adorning?'*

At this period the iron hand of tyranny and oppression over the worship of God had been suddenly paralyzed. The ruinous penalties, and even capital punishments, which had enforced attendance on a form of common prayer, and a pretence to believe articles, creeds, and catechisms, ordained by Acts of Parliament, were removed. Man, by nature averse to religious inquiries, was now stimulated, under a threat of eternal ruin, personally and individually, to seek for truth and salvation. At this time a little persecuted band of puritans had directed every inquirer after salvation to the sacred Scriptures, which alone were able to make wise unto salvation, by the aid of the Holy Spirit enlightening their minds to understand, and subduing their wills to receive those eternal truths. But a new light was now discovered—that which lighteneth every

---

* George Fox's Journal, folio, p. 144.

man that cometh into the world; and which, it was alleged, would alone, if cherished and followed, lead the honest inquirer into all truth. National religion, so called, had been propagated at an incredible expense of treasure, and by the sacrifice of the best blood in the country, to the shrine of infallibility—called uniformity. A hireling priesthood had limited to themselves the right to teach men how to be Christians. The result of all this was clearly seen, when the people were driven to think and choose for themselves. Their minds were in darkness and confusion, which quickly produced the most whimsical, mischievous, and even ludicrous opinions, mixed with truth.

National establishments, whether Pagan, Mohamedan, or Christian—be this latter either Greek, Roman, or Protestant—have a direct and natural tendency to repress and prevent personal inquiries, lest they should interfere with uniformity in faith and worship; which is a presumed incapability of error on the part of those who impose them. Systems, which IN FACT, although not in words, claim infallibility, by requiring implicit and absolute submission, must have had a direct tendency to hoodwink and blind the people; nor can we be surprised, that when their eyes were first opened, they saw indistinctly; or, to use a scripture phrase, 'men as trees walking.' They utterly failed in preparing the mind to receive divine truth, or in furnishing an antidote to extravagant speculations in religion.

The state of the millions can hardly be conceived; they had paid a priest to think on religion for them— to read the Bible for them—and to pray for them. They had paid the church to make them Christians —to confirm them—to forgive their sins—and to bury their bodies in sure and certain hope of heaven. From this fatal sleep of ignorance and error, they were aroused by itinerant preachers; many of whom were men of education, of irreproachable morals, and most benevolent habits. They went forth upon their mission at a fearful sacrifice of comfort, property, health, and even of life; calling all to repentance, and to obey the light within— to follow on to perfection in this life—and, at the same time, denouncing all hireling ministers. They were called in derision, Familists, Ranters, Quakers, New Lights, &c. The old leaven, which had led the people without inquiry to follow the priests, now operated on multitudes to follow those ardent and self-denying leaders. The Familists, or family of love, were consistent in their lives;— considered every day a sabbath, and baptized none under thirty years of age. The Ranters mingled a little truth with much error—abused their Christian liberty—and lived licentiously, and were a scandal to religion. The Quakers—so called from their trembling agitation when under a powerful

sense of eternal realities, and because, in preaching, they admonished their hearers to tremble and quake at the word of God—considered the sacraments as mere ceremonies, inconsistent with spiritual worship—lived and dressed with the utmost simplicity, and took the lead in attacking error at all risks.

These itinerants went through the whole length and breadth of the land, and in every place of public resort they made proclamation. In fairs, markets, meetings, assizes, and steeple-houses, their voice was heard denouncing evil and exhorting to righteousness. Short weights and deceit were declared an abomination to the Lord, in fairs and markets. Every religious delusion was exposed in meetings and parish churches. The journals of George Fox, and others, are exceedingly interesting in recounting their hazardous adventures, zeal, and no ordinary degree of ready wit and talent. Some of these itinerants came to Bedford, and in the parish church, called 'the steeple-house,' in Bedford town, on the 23d of May, 1656, they met John Bunyan, probably after he had been ministering there. With him they held a public disputation or controversy, to which allusions are made by both parties,* and in Bunyan they met a master spirit who confounded them. The subjects in dispute were of the deepest importance—the work of the Holy Spirit in conversion—the authority of the Bible—the perfection of holiness in this life—and whether it was lawful to perform the work of the ministry for hire.

After a very careful perusal of E. Burrough's answers to Bunyan, it is gratifying to find that the whole truth is set forth in the following pages;— some of the facts are worthy of a careful notice. The Baptists and Independents had long existed in this country, and had published confessions of faith. The Ranters and Familists existed not as sects but in name, and soon disappeared. The Quakers, who were confounded with the Ranters and Familists, were not at this time formed into a society; nor had they published any book of discipline. The Society of Friends were some years after united, and have been one of the most useful as well as the brightest ornaments to this kingdom. The works of Fox, Penn, Barclay, and others, with their books of discipline, and yearly epistles, shew that they, to a very great extent, agree with Bunyan in his sentiments; and it is well worthy of notice that, in the latter part of his life, when he wrote his admirable treatise on the resurrection of the dead, he does not accuse the Society of Friends with holding any false opinions. Bunyan is clear and scriptural upon the 'Light within,' or that conscience of right and wrong which all possess to

---

* See Burrough's Works, p. 304.

their condemnation—as distinguished from the indwelling of the Holy Spirit, the gift of God to his people, revealing in them the pardon of sin and hope of glory, by opening their understandings to receive the truths of the Bible. When Ann Blakeley bid Bunyan 'throw away the Scriptures,' he replied, 'No, for then the devil would be too hard for me.'* And when accused of being a hireling priest, how triumphant was the reply—it ought to be printed in letters of gold. He was charged with making merchandize of souls, and he answered— 'Friend, dost thou speak this from thy own knowledge, or did any other tell thee so? However, that spirit that led thee out this way is a lying spirit. For though I be poor, and of no repute in the world, as to outward things; yet through grace I have learned by the example of the apostle, to preach the truth; and also to work with my hands, both for my own living, and for those that are with me, when I have opportunity. And I trust that the Lord Jesus, who hath helped me to reject the wages of unrighteousness hitherto, will also help me still, so that I shall distribute that which God hath given me FREELY, and not for filthy lucre's sake.'† How does this contrast with the description of the state clergy, before the triers were appointed.‡

Favoured by the kind assistance of Charles Bowden, the secretary to the Society of Friends, access was afforded me to the extensive library in Devonshire House, and upon collation of Bunyan's quotations with the original editions of Burrough's exceedingly rare tracts, my gratification was great to find that every extract made by John Bunyan was perfectly faithful.

Edward Burrough, called a son of thunder and of consolation, answered both these treatises of Bunyan's,—denying, on the part of the Quakers, many of the charges made against them, as connected with the Ranters. He was a man of great talent—fearless, devoted, and pious. He became extensively useful; and like thousands of most excellent men, was sacrificed at the shrine of that fanatical church over which the profligate and debauched Charles the Second was the supreme head. He died in the prime of life, receiving the crown of martyrdom, when his happy spirit ascended from Newgate in 1662: aged 28 years.

* Page 201.   † Page 201.   ‡ Page 178.

No sect was so severely tormented as the Quakers. A fanatical clergyman, Edward Lane, in a book called 'Look unto Jesus,' 1663, thus pours forth his soul, breathing out cruelty—' I hope and pray the Lord to incline the heart of his majesty our religious King, to suppress the Quakers, that none of them may be suffered to abide in the land.' A prayer as full of cruelty against a most peaceful and valuable part of the community, as it was hypocritical in calling a debauched and profligate man [Charles the Second] 'our religious king.'

Controversy was carried on in those days with extreme virulence; learned and unlettered men alike used violent language, which, in this enlightened and comparatively happy age, is read with wonder. Burrough called his answer 'The Gospel of Peace contended for in the spirit of meekness and of love.' He meekly commences with—'How long, ye crafty fowlers, will ye prey upon the innocent; how long shall the righteous be a prey to your teeth, ye subtile foxes; your dens are in darkness, and your mischief is hatched upon your beds of secret whoredoms.' He says, 'I own the words but I deny thy voice.' Such was the unhallowed spirit of controversy in that age. A harsh epithet was called faithful dealing: thus, a learned clergyman, writing upon Baptism, entitled his work— 'The Anabaptists ducked and plunged over head and ears—washed and shrunk in the washing;' to which an equally learned Baptist replied, in his 'Baby Baptism mere Babyism.' All this unseemly violence has passed away, and with it much of the virulence of persecution; soon may it pass away altogether, only to be pointed at as the evidence of a barbarous age. We now look back to cruelties perpetrated in the times of Bunyan by the national religion, as a stigma upon human nature. 'What a church is this of yours, to be defended by gaols, and prisons, and whips, and stocks, and violent dealing.' 'Let us fairly try our spiritual weapons, and not carnal cruel tortures.' 'Let us not hurt or imprison each other, nor put in the stocks, nor cruelly whip and lacerate each others' bodies; but let us thrash deceit, whip and beat that and all false doctrines:' these were the breathings of our pilgrim forefathers,—it is the language of common sense and of real religion. May such sentiments spread, and soon cover the earth!—GEO. OFFOR.

THE AUTHOR TO THE READER.

SEEING the Lord hath been pleased to put it into my heart, to write a few things to thee (Reader) touching those things which are *most surely believed* by all those that are, or shall be saved. Lu. i. 1. Ac. xiii. 38. I think it meet also, to stir up thy heart by way of remembrance, touching those things that are the *hindrances* of thy believing the things that are necessary to the welfare of thine immortal soul. And indeed, this is the only thing necessary; it is better to lose all that ever thou hast, than to have thy soul and body for ever cast into hell; And therefore, I beseech thee to consider with me a few things touching the stratagems, or subtle temptations of the devil, whereby he lieth in wait, if by any means he may, to make thee fall short of eternal life. 1 Pe. v. 8.

And first of all, he doth endeavour by all means to keep thee in love with thy sins and pleasures, knowing that he is sure of thee, if he can but bewitch thee to live and die in them. 1 Co. vi. 9, 10; 2 Th. ii. 12. Yea, he knows that he is as sure of thee, as if he had thee in hell already. Jn. iii. 19. And that he might accomplish his design on thee in this particular, he laboureth by all means possible to keep thy conscience asleep in security and self-conceitedness, keeping thee from all things that might be a means to awaken and rouse up thine heart. As first, he will endeavour to keep thee from hearing of the word, by suggesting unto [thee] this and the other worldly business which must be performed; so that thou wilt not want excuse to keep thee from the ordinances of Christ, in hearing, reading, meditation, &c., or else, he seeks to disturb, and distract thy mind when thou art conversant in these things, that thou canst not attend to them diligently, and so they become unprofitable; or else if thou art a little more stirred, he labours to rock thee asleep again, by casting thee upon, and keeping thee in evil company, as among rioters, drunkards, *jesters*, and other of his instruments, which he employeth on purpose to keep thee secure, and so ruin thy soul and body for ever and ever.

If not thus, then peradventure he will seek to persuade thee it is but a melancholy fit, and will put thee upon the works of thy calling, or thy pleasures, or phys ; or some other trick he will invent, such as best agreeth with thy nature. And thus thy heart is again deaded, and thou art kept in carnal security, that thou mightest perish for ever. But if notwithstanding these, and many cunning slights more which might be named, he cannot so blind, and benumb thy conscience, but that it doth see and feel sin to be a burden, intolerable and exceeding sinful; Then in the second place, his design is to drive thee to *despair*, by persuading thee that thy sins are too big to be pardoned; he will seek by all means possible to aggravate them by all the circumstances of time, place, person, manner, nature, and continuance of thy sins, he will object in thy soul, thou hast outsinned grace, by rejecting so many exhortations, and admonitions, so many reproofs, so many tenders of grace; hadst thou closed in with them it had been well with thee, but now thou hast stood it out so long, that there is no hope for thee: thou mightest have come sooner, if thou didst look to be saved, but now it is too late. And withal, that he might carry on his design upon thee to purpose, he will be sure to present to thy conscience, the most sad sentences of the scripture; yea, and set them home with such cunning arguments, that, if it be possible, he will make thee despair, and make away thyself, as did Judas.

But if he be prevented in this his intended purpose; the next thing he doth beset thee with, is to make thee rest upon thine own righteousness, telling thee, that if thou wilt needs be saved, thou must earn heaven with thy fingers' ends; and it may be, he represents to thy soul such a scripture; 'If thou doest well, shalt thou not be accepted ?' And thou having (but in the strength of nature) kept thyself from thy former grosser pollutions, and it may be from some more secret sins, are ready to conclude, now thou *dost well*; now God accepts thee; now he will pardon, yea, hath pardoned thee; now thy condition is good, and so goest on till thou meetest with a searching word, and ministry, which tells thee, and discovers plainly unto thee, that thou doest all this while deceive thyself, by a vain hope and confidence; for tho' thou seek after the law of righteousness, thou hast not yet attained to the law of righteousness, nor yet canst, because thou seekest it 'not by faith, but as it were, by the works of the law.' Ro. ix. 31, 32. Here again, thou art left in the mire, and now peradventure thou seest, that thou art not profited by the works of the law, nor thy own righteousness: And this makes thee stir a little, but in process of time, (through the subtil sleights of the devil, and the wickedness of thine own heart;) thou forgettest thy trouble of conscience, and slippest into a notion of the gospel, and the grace thereof, and now thou thinkest thyself cock-sure: Now thou art able to say, 'He that lives and dies in his sins, shall be damned for them: He that trusts in his own righteousness, shall not be saved:' Now thou canst cry, 'grace, grace, it's freely by grace, it's through

THE AUTHOR TO THE READER. 133

the death of the man Christ Jesus, that sinners do attain unto eternal life.' He. ix. 14. This, I say, thou hast in the notion, and hast not the power of the same in thine heart, and so it may be thine head is full of the knowledge of the scriptures, though thine heart be empty of sanctifying grace. And thus thou dost rejoice for a time. Yet because thou hast not the root of the matter within thee, in time of temptation thou fallest away. Lu. viii. 13.

Now being in this condition, and thinking thyself to be wondrous well, because of that notion of the truth, and that notion thou hast in the things of God: I say, being in this state, thou art liable to these dangers.

First, Thou art like to perish if thou die with this notion in thine head, except God out of his rich grace do work a saving work of grace and knowledge in thy heart; for know this, thou mayest understand glorious mysteries, and yet be a cast-away. 1 Co. xiii. 1–3. Or else,

Secondly, Thou art liable to the next damnable heresy that the devil sendeth into the world. See and consider Lu. viii. 13. 2 Ti. ii. 18. I say, thou dost lie liable to be carried away with it, and to be captivated by it; so that at last, through the delusions of the devil, thou mayest have thy conscience seared as with an hot iron, so hard, that neither law, nor gospel, can make any entrance thereinto, to the doing of thee the least good. And indeed, who are the men that at this day are so deluded by the quakers, and other pernicious doctrines; but those who thought it enough to be talkers of the gospel, and grace of God, without seeking and giving all diligence to make it sure unto themselves? 'And for this cause God' [shall send] hath sent 'them strong delusion, that they should believe a lie: That they all might be damned, who believed not the truth, but had pleasure in unrighteousness,' as it is written. 2 Th. ii. 11, 12. And indeed if you mark it, you shall see, that they be such kind of people, who at this day are so carried away with the quakers' delusions; namely, a company of loose *ranters,* and light notionists, with here and there a legalist, which were shaking in their principles from time to time, sometimes on this religion, sometimes on that.* And thus these *unstable souls* are deluded and beguiled at last. 2 Pe. ii. 14. So that these who before (as one would have thought) had something of God in them, are now turned such enemies to the glorious truths of the gospel, that there are none so obstinately erroneous as they. And indeed it is just with God, to give them over to 'believe a lie,' 2 Th. ii. 11. who before were

---

* The word 'quakers' must not be misunderstood as referring to the society of *friends,* but to some deluded individuals calling themselves quakers; the friends were not formed into a society for some years after this was written.—ED.

so idle that they would not receive the truth of God into their hearts, *in the love of it.* And to be bewitched by the devil to obey his temptations, and be damned, who would not obey the truth, that they might be saved. Ga. iii. 1.

But you will say, what lies are those, that the devil beguileth poor souls withal? I shall briefly tell you some of them, but having before said, that they especially are liable to the danger of them, who slip into high notions, and rest there; taking that for true faith which is not. I shall desire thee seriously to consider this one character of a NOTIONIST. Such an one, whether he perceives it or not, is puffed up in his fleshly mind, and advanceth himself above others, thinking but few may compare with him for religion and knowledge in the scriptures, but are ignorant and foolish in comparison of him: (Thus knowledge puffeth up, 1 Cor. viii. 1.) whereas when men receive truth in the love of the truth, the more the head and heart is filled with the knowledge of the mystery of godliness, the more it is emptied of its own things, and is more sensible of its own vileness, and so truly humbled in its own eyes.

And further, a notionist, though he fall from his former strictness and seeming holiness, and appear more loose, and vain in his practices, yet speaks as confidently of himself, as to *assurance* of salvation, the love of God, and union with God, as ever. But now to return, and declare some of those lies which the devil persuades some of these men to believe.

I. That salvation was not fully, and completely wrought out for poor sinners by the man Christ Jesus, though he did it gloriously, Ac. xiii. 38, 39. by his death upon the cross, without the gates of Jerusalem, Heb. xiii. 12. compared with Jn. xix. 19, 20.

II. This is another of his lies wherewith he doth deceive poor sinners, bidding them follow the light that they brought into the world with them, telling them, that light will lead them to the kingdom; for (say they) it will convince of sin, as swearing, lying, stealing, covetousness, and the rest of the sins against the law. Ro. iii. 20. But 'the law is not of faith.' Ga. iii. 13. And then I am sure, that it, with all its motions and convictions, is never able to justify the soul of any poor sinner. 'For as many as are of the works of the law are under the curse: for it is written, Cursed is every one that continueth not in all things which are written in the book of the law to do them,' Ga. iii. 10. but that no man is justified by the law is evident, 'for, The just shall live by faith,' ver. 11. Now because I am not altogether ignorant of the delusion of the devil touching this grace of faith also, I shall therefore in short give thee (reader) a brief, yet true description from the scripture. 1. What true justifying faith is, and what it lays hold upon. 2. I shall shew who it doth come from. 3. That every one hath it not. 4. What are the fruits of it.

1. First therefore, *true faith is* a fruit, work, or gift of the Spirit of God, Ga. v. 22. 2 Th. i. 11. and 1 Co. xii. 9. whereby a poor soul is enabled through the mighty operation of God, Col. ii. 12. in a sense of its sins and wretched estate to lay hold on the righteousness, blood, death, resurrection, ascension, intercession, and coming again of the Son of God which was crucified without the gates of Jerusalem, for eternal life; Jn. iii. 16—18. compared with Mat. iii. 17. Ga. ii. 20. Ro. v. 8—10. Ro. iii. 25. Ac. xvi. 31. He. xiii. 12. according to that saying in He. xi. 1. 'Now faith is the substance of things hoped for,' and 'the evidence of things not seen,' that is, the things that are hoped for faith sees, lays hold upon, and embraces them, He. xi. 13. as if they were present; yea, it seals up the certainty of them to the soul. Therefore saith the Apostle, it is the evidence, or testimony, or witness, of those things that are not seen as yet with a bodily eye; which are obtained by the blood of the man Christ Jesus, He. ix. 14. compared with He. x. 12, 19, 20. by which the soul sees as in a glass the things that God hath laid up for them that fear him. 1 Co. xiii. 12. 2 Co. iii. 18.

2. If you would know *who this faith comes from,* read Ep. ii. 8. 'For by grace ye are saved (saith the scripture) through faith; and that not of yourselves: *it is* the gift of God.' Again, in Phil. i. 29. it is thus written: ' For unto you (that are believers) it is given in the behalf of Christ, not only to believe on him, but also to suffer for his sake;' And thus much do the Apostles hold forth to us in their prayer, or request to the Lord Jesus, when they say, ' Lord increase our faith,' Lu. xvii. 5. and he is therefore called ' the author and finisher of *our* faith.' He. xii. 2. Also we find in Ja. i. 17. that 'Every good gift and every perfect gift is from above, and cometh down from the Father of lights,' &c., and therefore faith comes from God, for true justifying faith is a good gift, and perfect in respect of the author God, in respect of its object, Christ; and in respect of the nature, though not in respect of the degree, and measure of it in us: even as a grain of gold, is as perfect gold, as a pound of gold, though not so much.

3. *All men have not faith,* this the Apostle witnesseth in so many words as we find, 2 Th. iii. 2. and De. xxxii. 20. Also in Ti. i. 15. 'Unto them that are defiled and unbelieving *is* nothing pure,' &c. It appeareth also in this, that all do not attain salvation, which they must needs do if they had true justifying faith; compare Lu. xiii. 24. and 1 Jn. v. 19. with Mark xvi. 16. And He. iv. 3. with ver. 6. and 11. 'they that believe shall be saved.'

4. *The fruits of it are,* (1.) to purify the heart, Ac. xv. 9. and 1 Jn. iii. 3. and that, as I said before, by

laying hold on what Jesus Christ had done and suffered for sinners. Ac. xiii. 38, 39. (2.) It fills the soul with peace and joy, in that it lays hold on the things that are obtained for it. Ro. v. 1. 2 Ti. i. 9, 10. 1 Pe i. 8. (3.) It makes the soul to wait patiently, for the glory that is to be revealed at the second appearing of the man Christ Jesus, whom God hath raised from the dead, which hath also delivered it from the wrath to come, as in Ti. ii. 13, 14. 1 Pe. iv. 13. and v. 1, 4. 1 Th. i. 10.

Quest.—But how (may some say) doth the devil make his delusions take place in the hearts of poor creatures?

Answ. 1.—Why, first, He labours to render the doctrine of the Lord Jesus, and salvation by him alone, very odious and low: and also his ordinances, as hearing, reading, meditation, use of the scriptures, &c. telling poor sinners that these things are but poor, low, carnal, beggarly, empty notions; preached up by the clergymen, who are the scribes and pharisees of this generation; who have the letter, but not the Spirit of God in them; which lead men into the form, but not into the power of the Lord Jesus: And with this persuasion, he also represents the ungodly and base carriage, or behaviour, of some, who have taken in hand to preach the doctrine of the Lord Jesus Christ, and thereby he doth render the gospel of our Lord Jesus the more contemptible and base. But woe, woe, woe, be to them by whom such offences come. Mat. xviii. 7. Lu. xvii. 1, 2.

Answ. 2. He pretends to lead them up into some higher light, mysteries, and revelations of the Spirit, into which a very few have attained or can attain, also bewitching their affections, and taking them with an earnest pursuit after these his pretended truths; persuading them, that they shall be as God himself, able to discern between good and evil. Ge. iii. 5. And in this he is exceeding subtil and expert, as having practised it ever since the days of Adam. These things being thus considered, and in some measure hungered after, and the rather because they are good (as they think) to make one wise. Ge. iii. 6. The poor soul is all on the sudden possessed with a desperate spirit of delusion, which carries it away headlong with some high, light, frothy notions, and spiritual wickedness (which drown it in perdition and destruction) that doth feed and tickle the heart a while, to the end it may make way for a farther manifestation of itself in the poor deluded soul; which when it hath attained to, it doth then begin to bring the soul into a clearer sight of those things, which it was loth it should know at the first; but having fitted the soul by degrees for a further possession of itself, at last it begins to hold forth its new gospel; shewing the soul a new Christ, and new scriptures. The new and false Christ, is a Christ crucified within, dead within, risen again within, and ascended within, in opposition to the Son of Mary, who was crucified without, dead without, risen again without, and ascended in a cloud away from his disciples into heaven without them. Ac. i. 9—11.

Now this new and false Christ, hath a new and false faith belonging to his gospel, which faith is this, to apprehend this Christ crucified within, dead within, risen again within, and ascended within: But ask them for a scripture that doth positively prove their doctrine, they also have a scripture, but it is within, it doth bear witness within, and if they had not that, (though that be of the devil's making) I am sure they would have none out of God's holy scriptures, for they will allow of no crucified Christ, but he that was crucified without the gates of Jerusalem. He. xiii. 12. Jn. xix. 17, 18. Dead and buried in the sepulchre of Joseph of Arimathea. Jn. xix. 38—41. Was raised again out of that sepulchre into which Joseph had laid him. Jn. xx. 1—12. Who went before his disciples into Galilee. Mar. xvi. 7. And to Emmaus. Lu. xxiv. 15. Shewed them his hands and his feet, where the nails had gone through. Lu. xxiv. 39, 40. Did eat and drink with them after his resurrection: Was seen of them on earth forty days after his resurrection. Ac. i. 3. And after that ascended away in a cloud, out of the sight of his disciples into heaven. Ac. i. 9—11. Which Christ ever lives to make intercession for us. He. vii. 25. Who will come again also at the end of the world to judgment. Ac. x. 42; xvii. 31; 2 Pe. iii. 10, 11. Who also is the same that hath obtained eternal redemption for us. Ac. xiii. 37—39. Ro. iii. 25. Ep. i. 7. Re. i. 5. He. i. 2; ix. 14. This I say, or rather the scriptures say, is God's Christ. Mat. xvi. 16. In whom he is well pleased. Mat. iii. 17. Neither doth God own any other, or allow of any other: For there is none other name under heaven given among men, whereby we must be saved, than the name of Jesus of Nazareth, Ac. iv. 10. compared with ver. 11, 12. But as I told you before, the way to be thus deluded, is first to render God's Christ odious and low, with a pretence of some further light and revelations; and thus professing themselves to be wise, they became fools. Ro. i. 22.

Quest.—But you will say, doth not the scripture make mention of a Christ within? Col. i. 27; 2 Co. xiii. 5. Ro. viii. 10.

Though I shall go seemingly about in answer to the question, yet it will be very profitable to them who shall weigh and consider the several sentences hereof.

Answ.—I answer, God's Christ was, and is, true God and true man; he was born of the Virgin Mary, true God, and true man. Mat. i. 23. 'And they shall call his name Emmanuel, which being interpreted is, God with us,' or God in our nature, according to 1 Ti. iii. 16. 'God was manifested in the flesh:' And Jn. i. 14. 'The word was made flesh, and dwelt among us, and we beheld his glory, the glory as of the only begotten of the Father, full of grace and truth.' And in He. ii. 14. 'Forasmuch then as the children are partakers of flesh and blood, he,' that is, God, He. i. 8. 'also himself likewise took part of the same, that through death he might destroy him that had the power of death, that is, the devil.' Now as he was thus true God, and true man, so he became our redeemer and Saviour. Compare the first and second chapters to the Hebrews together, and you may clearly see that this is a glorious truth, that he who is the ·first and the last, Re. i. 17, 18; ii. 8. humbled himself, and made himself of no reputation, and took upon him the form of a servant, and was made in the likeness of men: And was this all? No. He humbled himself unto death, even the death of the cross. Phi. ii. 7, 8. compared with Re. i. 17, 18. and Re. ii. 8. with Ga. i. 4. Now after this Christ of God, true God and true man, had wrought out eternal redemption for us poor miserable sinners, He. ix. 14. compared with 1 Ti. i. 15. I say, after he had done this, he ascended up into heaven, and there ever lives to make intercession for us. Now this Christ, having thus completely wrought out our salvation, sends his disciples abroad to preach the same to poor sinners, Ac. ii. 2 Co. v. 19, 20. and so many as were ordained to eternal life, when they heard the word, or the gospel preached by the Apostles, which gospel was this Christ, 1 Co. i. 17. compared with ver. 23. I say, so many as were ordained to eternal life, when they heard the word, the Holy Ghost or Spirit of Christ, fell upon them, Ac. x. 44. compared with Ac. xiii. 48. which did lead them into the redemption and glorious things that the Lord Jesus had laid up and prepared for them. Jn. xvi. 13—15; 1 Co. ii. 9. Which Spirit was the earnest of their inheritance, until the redemption of the purchased possession, to the praise of his glory. Ep. i. 13, 14. The earnest of their inheritance was a glorious encouragement to them that had it, to hope for the glory that was to be revealed at the appearing of Jesus Christ, which is the meaning of that place in Col. i. 27. And that will be seen clearly, if we compare it with Ep. i. 13, 14. before recited. Now this Spirit, which sometimes is called the Spirit of Christ. 2 Co. xiii. 5. This Spirit, I say, being given to all those that were ordained to eternal life, it must needs follow, that those that had not this Spirit, *The Spirit of Christ is the earnest of that inheritance, that Christ, as he was God and man, did obtain.* but did live and die without it, were not ordained to eternal life, and so were none of Christ's; but were reprobates, Ro. viii. 9. for the Spirit of Christ is the distinguishing character betwixt a believer and an unbeliever, he that hath it, and is led by it, is a child of God, Ro. vii. 4. but he that hath it not is none of Christ's.

So then, the answer that I give to the question, is this. The Spirit of *The objection answered.*

Christ that is given to believers, is the *earnest* or hope of that inheritance that Christ hath already purchased, and is now preparing for so many as he hath given, or shall give this holy spirit unto. And for the proof hereof, read Ep. i. 13, 14. In whom (saith the scripture) ye also trusted, after that ye heard the word of truth, the gospel of your salvation. In whom also, after that ye believed, ye were sealed with the holy Spirit of promise, which is the earnest of our inheritance; (which inheritance is the eternal redemption that was purchased by Christ for poor sinners, He. ix. 15.) until the redemption of the purchased possession, unto the praise of his glory. Again, Ga. v. 5. 'For ye through the Spirit, wait for the hope of righteousness by faith.' And Col. i. 27. the Apostle speaking of this great mystery, saith, 'To whom God would make known what *is* the riches of the glory of this mystery among the Gentiles; which is Christ in you the hope of glory;' which glory was then revealed to the saints no otherwise than by faith, as the Apostle saith, 'We rejoice in hope of the glory of God.' Ro. v. 2. Which hope is begotten by the Spirit's shedding abroad the love of God in our hearts, ver. 5. which hope is not yet seen, that is, not yet actually enjoyed; 'For we are saved by hope: But hope that is seen is not hope: for what a man seeth, why doth he yet hope for? But if we hope for that we see not, *then* do we with patience wait for *it*.' Ro. viii. 24, 25. And as I say, the cause of believers' hope is this, Christ, or the Spirit of Christ, in them, the hope of glory. And indeed he may well hope for glory to come, who hath already an earnest thereof given him of God, and that earnest no less than the Spirit of the Lord Jesus. Ro. viii. 16, 17.

But now, this Spirit, which is the cause of a believer's hope, all men have not. Jude 19. Ep. ii. 12. Ro. viii. 9. Jn. xiv. 16, 17. Therefore what a sad doctrine is that which saith, follow the *light* that Christ hath enlightened every man withal, which cometh into the world; which light is the conscience, that convinceth of sins against the law; and that you may see clearly if you mind that scripture, Jn. viii. 9. which saith, That the Pharisees, [which had neither the love of God, nor his word, abiding in them, Jn. v. 38, 43.] when they had heard Christ speaking thus to them, He that is without sin among you, &c. being convicted by their own consciences, went out one by one, beginning at the eldest, even to the least. But the devil, that he might be sure not to miss of his design, labours by all means to render the scriptures also odious and low, telling them of the *scriptures* within; which Christ never taught, nor yet his disciples: But they being given up of God to a reprobate mind, have given themselves over, rather

It is the spirit of the devil that doth render the Scriptures contemptible and low.

to follow the suggestions of the devil, than the holy scriptures which God hath commanded us to betake ourselves to, Is. viii. 20. compared with Jn. v. 39. which scripture is called the sword of the Spirit, Ep. vi. 17. which weapon our Lord Jesus himself held up, to overcome the devil withal. Mat. iv. 4, 7, 10. Lu. iv. 4. 8, 12. But this design (as I told you) the devil carries on, by pretending to shew them a more excellent way which they may attain to, if they be but wise, and follow what is made known unto them from the light within them.

But, reader, that thou mayest be able to escape the snare of this cunning hunter, I shall lay thee down some few directions, which if the Lord give thee grace to follow, thou shalt escape these WICKED DELUSIONS.

Direct. 1. And first of all, I do admonish thee to be very serious touching thine estate and condition; and examine thine own heart by the rule of the word of God, whether or no, thou hast as yet any beginnings of desiring after religion: and if thou findest that thou hast lived until now in ignorance, and hast not set thyself to remember thy Creator as thou art commanded, Ec. xii. 1. then I beseech thee consider that thou art under the wrath of Almighty God, and hast been so ever since thou camest into the world, Ep. ii. 1, 2. being then in thy first parents, those didst transgress against thy maker, Ro. v. 18. 'Therefore as by the offence of one,' that is, of Adam, ver. 14. '*judgment came* upon all men to condemnation.' Besides the many SINS thou hast committed ever since thou wast born: sins against the law of God, and sins against the gospel of the grace of God; sins against the long-suffering and forbearance of God, and sins against his judgments; sins of omission, and sins of commission, in thoughts, words, and actions: consider, I say, thy condition; yea, get a very great sense of thy sins that thou hast committed; and that thou mayest so do, beg of God to convince thee by his Holy Spirit, not only of sins against law, but also of that damning sin, the sin of unbelief.

Direct. 2. If thou by grace, art but brought into such an estate as to see thyself in a lost condition because of sin, without the Lord Jesus; then in the next place, have a care of resting on any DUTY done, though it be never so specious; I say, have a care of making any stay anywhere on this side the Lord Jesus Christ: but above all strive to believe, that that very Man that was born of the Virgin Mary, did come into the world on purpose to save thee, as well as other poor sinners: I say, thou must not be content till thou art enabled to say, 'He loved me, and gave himself for me.' Ga. ii. 20. And that thou mayest be sure to attain to this most precious faith, (for so it is) be much in applying the freest promises to thy own soul; yea, those that have no conditions annexed to them, as these, or other like, Re. xxii. 17. Je. xxxi. 3; iii. Jn. vi. 37. also xiv. 19. Ho. xiv. 3. I say, labour to apply to thy own soul in particular, the most glorious and freest promises in the book of God. And if at any time the devil besets thee by his *temptations*, (for so is his wonted manner to do, and so much the more, as he sees thee labour to get out of his reach) I say, when he assails thee with his fiery darts, be sure to act faith on the most free promises, and have a care that thou dost not enter into any dispute with him, but rather resist him by those blessed promises that are laid down in the word of God: And withal, be sure to meditate upon the blood of the man Christ Jesus, who also is the true God, and read those scriptures that do most fully and clearly speak of it; as, 1 Jn. i. 7. Ep. i. 7. He. ix. 14. Ro. iii. 25.

Direct. 3. But if thou say (as it is often the speech of poor souls lying under a sense of sin, and the apprehensions of wrath due to it) I cannot apply the promises to mine own soul; and the reason is, because my SINS are so great, and so many. Consider, and know it for a truth, that the more and greater thou seest thy sins to be, the more cause hast thou to believe; yea, thou must therefore believe because thy sins are great: David made it an encouragement to himself, or rather the Spirit of the Lord made it his encouragement, to crave, yea to hope for pardon, because he had greatly transgressed. Ps. xxv. 11. 'For thy name's sake, O Lord, (saith he) pardon mine iniquity; for it *is* great.' As if he had said, O Lord, thy name will be more glorified, the riches of thy grace will be more advanced, thy mercy and goodness will more shine, and be magnified in pardoning me who am guilty of great iniquity, than if thou pardonest many others who have not committed such heinous offences. And I dare say, the reason why thou believest not, is not because thy sins are great, but because thou dost reason too much with that wicked enemy of man's salvation, and givest way too much to the fleshly reasoning of thine own heart. For Christ hath said, 'He that cometh unto me, I will in no wise cast out.' Jn. vi. 37. And again, 'Though your sins be as scarlet, they shall be as white as snow.' Is. i. 18. And Christ calleth those that labour, and are heavy laden, to come to him, with promise to give them rest. Mat. xi. 28. Wherefore thou must not say, my sins are too big; but thou must say, because I am a great sinner; yea, because I have sinned above many of my companions, and am nearer to hell, and eternal damnation than they, because of my sins, therefore will I cry unto the Lord, and say, O Lord, pardon my sins, for they are great.

Now that thou mayest not be deceived in a matter of so great concernment, have a special care of these three things.

Caution 1. First, Have a care of putting off thy *trouble* of spirit the *wrong way*, which thou mayest do three ways; (1.) When thy conscience flieth in thy face, and tells thee of thy sins, thou dost put off convictions the wrong way, if thou dost stop thy conscience by promising to reform thyself, and lead a new life, and gettest off thy guilt by so doing: for though thou mayest by this means still and quiet thy conscience for a time, yet thou canst not hereby satisfy and appease the wrath of God: yea, saith God to such, 'Though thou wash thee with nitre, and take thee much soap, *yet* thine iniquity is marked before me.' Je. ii. 22.

(2.) If when thou art under the guilt of thy sins, thou puttest off convictions by thy performances of DUTIES, and so satisfiest thy conscience, then also thou dost put off thy convictions the wrong way: for God will not be satisfied with anything less than the blood, righteousness, resurrection, and intercession of his own Son. Ac. iv. 12. And thou shouldest not satisfy thyself with any less than God would have thee to satisfy thyself withal, and that is the water of life, Is. lv. 1, 2. which water of life thy duties, and all thy righteousness, is not; for they are as filthy rags. Is. lxiv. 6.

(3.) Have a care that when thou art under conviction, thou dost not satisfy thyself with a *notion* of the free grace of the gospel; my meaning is, do not content thyself with any measure of knowledge that thou canst attain unto, or bottom thy peace upon it, thinking thou art now well enough, because thou canst speak much of the grace of God, and his love in Christ to poor sinners. For this thou mayest have, and do; and yet be but a companion for Demas, yea, for Judas and the rest of the damned multitude: As the Apostle saith, For all this thou mayest be but as sounding brass, and as a tinkling cymbal; that is, nothing but a sound. 1 Co. xiii. 1—3.

Caution 2. But Secondly. If thou wouldest not be deceived, then have a care to avoid *false doctrines*, which are according to the spirit of the devil, and not after Christ. As,

(1.) If any doctrine doth come unto thee, that tells thee, except thou art circumcised after the manner of Moses, thou canst not be saved: that is, if any man come unto thee, and tell thee, thou must do such and such works of the *law*, to the end thou mayest present thyself the better before God, do not receive him: For 'to him that worketh not, but believeth on him that justifieth the ungodly, his faith is counted for righteousness.' Ro. iv. 5.

(2.) If any come unto thee, and bring such a doctrine as this; That thou mayest be saved by *grace*, though thou walk in the imaginations of thy own wicked heart: His doctrine also is devilish, do not receive him. De. xxix. 19—23.

Nothing can make us accepted with God, but the merits of Jesus Christ. The *Ranters'* doctrine is false.

s

(3.) But if any come unto thee, and doth in truth advance the *blood, righteousness, resurrection, intercession*, and *second coming* of that very Man in the clouds of heaven, that was born of the virgin Mary; and doth press thee to believe on what he hath done (shewing thee thy lost condition without him) and to own it as done for thee in particular, and withal doth admonish thee, not to trust in a bare notion of it, but to receive it into thy heart, so really, that thy very heart and soul may burn in *love* to the Lord Jesus Christ again: and doth also teach thee, that the love of Christ should and must constrain thee, not to live to thyself: But to him that loved thee, and gave himself for thee. 2 Co. v. 14, 15. Ep. iv. 21—24. 1 Co. vii. 23. ' Ye are bought with a price; be not ye the servants of men.' If his conversation be also agreeable to his doctrine, a believing, honest, loving, self-denying,

The doctrine is courteous conversation, (he also is a
true, and of God,
whatever the true Christian.) Receive that doctrine
man be.
and receive it really; for it is the doctrine of God, and of Christ. Ga. iv. 4; i. 4. Ep. i. 7. Re. i. 5. Ac. xiii. 38. Jn. i. 29. Ac. iv. 12; x. 40—42. and 1 Th. i. 10. Mar. xiii. ult. 2 Pe. i. 5—10. Considering the end of their conversation Jesus Christ, yesterday, and to-day, and the same for ever. He. xiii. 7, 8.

Caution 3. Again, If thou wouldest not be deceived, then beware of slighting any known truth that thou findest revealed, or made known to thee in the gospel; but honour and obey it in its place, be it (as thou thinkest) never so low. Jn. xiv. 15.

(1.) Have a care that thou do not undervalue, or entertain low thoughts of God, Christ the Son of Mary, and the holy scriptures, but search them. Jn. v. 39. And give attendance to the reading of them. 1 Ti. iv. 13. For, I will tell thee, he that slights the scriptures, doth also slight him of whom they testify. And I will tell thee also, that for this cause God hath given up many to strong delusions, that they might believe a lie: ' that they all might be damned who believed not the truth, but had pleasure in unrighteousness.' 2 Th. ii. 11, 12.

(2.) Therefore I say unto thee, In the name of the Lord Jesus, the Son of Mary, the Son of God, the very creator of heaven and earth, and all things that are therein; have a care of thyself; for the devil doth watch for thee day and night. 1 Pe. v. 8. Thine own heart also doth labour to deceive thee, if by any means it may. Je. xvii. 9. Therefore do not thou trust it; for if thou do, thou wilt not do wisely. Pr. xxviii. 26. I say therefore, have a care that thou labour in the strength of the Lord Jesus, to escape all these things; for if thou fall into any one of them, it will make way for a farther income of sin and the devil, through whose deceitfulness thy heart will be hardened, and thou wilt be more incapable of receiving instruction, or

reaping advantage, by and from the ordinances of Jesus Christ: the rather therefore, give all diligence to believe in the Christ of God, which is the Son of Mary, and be sure to apply all that he hath done, and is doing, unto thyself, as for thee in particular; which thing if thou dost, thou shalt *never* fall.

And now, reader, I shall also give thee some few *considerations*, and so I shall commit thee to the Lord.

Consider, 1. That God doth hold out his grace, and mercy freely, and that to every one. Re. xxii. 17. Is. lv. 1—7.

Consider, 2. That there is no way to attain to this free mercy and grace, but by him that was born of the Virgin Mary; for he himself saith, ' I am the way, and the truth, and the life: no man cometh unto the Father but by me.' Jn. xiv. 6. compared with Mat. i. 20, 21.

Consider, 3. If thou strivest to go over any other way, thou wilt be but a thief and a robber. Jn. x. 1. compared with 9. And know that none of these (so continuing) shall enter into the kingdom of heaven. 1 Co. vi. 9, 10.

Consider, 4. That if the devil should be too hard for thee, and deceive thee, by persuading thee to embrace, or entertain a new gospel, which neither Christ nor his disciples did allow of, it would make thee gnash teeth when it is too late.

Consider, 5. That though thou hast been deluded by Satan to this day, yet if now thine eyes be opened to see and acknowledge it, though as yet thou hast been either exceedingly wicked, 1 Ti. i. 13. or an idle, Mat. xx. 6, 7. lukewarm, hypocritical professor; Re. iii. 17—19. and hast stood it out to the last; Eze. xviii. 20—22. for all this there is hope; and if now thou receive the truth in the love of the truth, being as willing to be rid of the filth of sin, as the guilt of it, thou shalt be saved.

Consider, 6. That the Lord will call thee to judgment for all thy sins past, present, and what else thou shalt practise hereafter, especially for thy rejecting and trampling on the blood of his Son, the Man Christ Jesus: And if thou dost not agree with thine adversary, now, while thou art in the way, ' Lest he hale thee to the judge, and the judge deliver thee to the officer, and the officer cast thee into prison. I tell thee, thou shalt not depart thence, till thou hast paid the very last mite.' Lu. xii. 58, 59.

And therefore I beseech thee to consider; Here is at this time *life* and *death, heaven* and *hell*, everlasting joy, and everlasting torment set before thee. Here is also the way to have the one, and the way to escape the other. Now if the Lord shall do thee any good by what I have spoken, I hope it will be a means to stir me up to thank the Lord that ever he did use such a sinner as I am, in the work of his gospel. And here I shall close up what I have said, desiring thee (if thou be a christian) to pray for him who desires to continue

Thy servant in the Lord Jesus Christ, though less than the least of all saints,

JOHN BUNYAN.

THE EPISTLE WRIT BY MR. BURTON, MINISTER AT BEDFORD.

TO THE READER,

READER, thou hast in this small treatise, set before thee, the several pieces of that great and glorious mystery, Jesus Christ, God manifested in the flesh: And if thou art enlightened by the Spirit of Christ, here thou mayest see by that Spirit how Jesus Christ the Son of God, the Son of Mary, is both true God and true Man, both natures making but one Christ, one Jesus, as Phi. ii. 5—9. where speaking first of his being God, and then of his taking upon him the nature of man; afterwards in the 8th and 9th verses, he saith, he (meaning this Jesus) humbled himself, &c., and God (meaning the Father) hath highly exalted him, &c. speaking of both natures God and man as together making but one Christ; who is the Saviour, and is to be believed and trusted in for salvation not only as God, but as man also; and those who do not thus make him the object of their faith, will surely fall short of pardon of sin, and of salvation; 'through this man (speaking of Christ as crucified at Jerusalem) is preached unto you the forgiveness of sins:' Ac. xiii. 38. And saith he, there is 'one mediator between God and men, the man Christ Jesus;' 1 Ti. ii. 5. and this discovers the damnable errors of those commonly called Socinians, who on the one hand deny him that was born of the Virgin Mary to be true God as well as true Man: And this is also quite contrary to those commonly called Familists, Ranters, Quakers, or others, who on the other hand either deny Christ to be a real Man *without* them, blasphemously fancying him to be only God manifest *in their* flesh; or else make his human nature with the fulness of the godhead in it, to be but a type of God, to be manifest in the saints, and so according to their wicked imagination, his human nature was to be laid aside after he had offered it up on the cross without the gate at Jerusalem, contrary to Ac. i. 1 —3, 9—11. compared with the last chapter of Luke, ver. 39, 40, 50, 51. where it is clearly held forth, that the man Christ rose again out of the grave, with the same body which was crucified and laid in the grave, and was taken up above the clouds into heaven with the same real body, and that he shall again descend from heaven in that same glorious body of flesh, as Ac. i. 9—11. And this sure truth of Christ being the Saviour and Mediator, as Man,

and not only as God, will also shew serious believers what to think of some, who though they will not (it may be) deny that Christ is a real man without them in the heavens as well as God, yet do own him to be the Saviour only as God, first dwelling in that flesh that was born of the Virgin, and then dwelling in saints, and thus both beginning and perfecting their salvation within them, and so indeed do hold Christ as Man, to be only (I say to be only) the saved or glorified one of God, together with the saints his members, only something in another and more glorious manner and measure than the saints; and these high-flown people are in this very like to Familists and Quakers, undervaluing the Lord Jesus Christ, God-man, and though they may speak much of Christ, yet they do not rightly and savingly lay him for their foundation.

Now as a help against all these dangerous things, thou hast here the main things of Christ laid down before thee briefly, and fully proved by the scriptures:

First, Of his being true God out of flesh from eternity, and then of his taking flesh, or the nature of man upon him in the womb of the Virgin, and so his fulfilling the law, his dying for sins at Jerusalem, his rising again without, his ascending into heaven without, and not into a fancied heaven only within, as some say; his interceding in heaven for all his, and his coming again in his body of flesh to judge the world. And if thou art yet in a state of nature, though covered over with an outside profession, here thou mayest find something (if the Spirit of Christ meet thee in reading) to convince thee of the sad condition thou art in, and to shew thee the righteousness thou art to fly to by faith, and to trust in for salvation, when convinced of sin; which is a righteousness wrought by that God-man Jesus Christ without thee, dying without thee at Jerusalem for sinners: here also thou mayest see the difference between true and false faith. If thou art a true believer, as these things are the foundation of thy faith, so they may be of great use for thee to meditate upon, and to exercise thy faith in, particularly in meditation, and in this way to seek daily for a higher faith in these truths, to be given into thy heart from heaven; and there is a great need of this, for though these truths be commonly known amongst professors to the notion of them, yet very few know or believe them aright: nay, it may well be said in this age, that, if the faith of the true saints was well sifted, and tradition, notion, and the apprehensions of their own reason and fancy was sifted out, most of them would be found to have very little knowledge of, and faith in, these common truths.

Secondly, These truths being put thus together, and plainly proved by the scriptures, may be a great help (through the Spirit concurring) to strengthen thee against all those damnable heresies which are spread abroad, which deny the Lord Jesus Christ either plainly, or more cunningly and mysteriously. And

Thirdly, The more thou art rooted and set down from heaven in the faith of these truths of Christ, to believe fully the glorious reality of them, and their interest in them, the more heavenly peace and joy thou wilt have, 1 Pe. i. 7, 8. and also thou wilt hereby attain the more true holiness and purity of heart and life, ' purifying their hearts by faith.' Ac. xv. 9. And then the more thou hast of the right faith of Christ, and of his things in thy heart, the more strong and valiant wilt thou be in spirit, to do any work private or public for Jesus Christ, like Stephen, who being full of faith, and of the Holy Spirit, was also full of power. Ac. vi. 8.

In this book thou hast also laid down from the scriptures, how Jesus Christ is *without* the saints as Man, and yet dwelleth *within* them, that is, something of his divine nature or his blessed Spirit dwells within them, which Spirit is sometime called, The Spirit of Christ. Ro. viii. 9. He that hath not the Spirit of Christ, &c. and sometime called Christ, ' If Christ *be* in you.' &c. Ro. viii. 10. And also how we may know whether it be Christ and the Spirit of Christ within, or a false spirit calling itself Christ, and that is thus: If it be indeed Christ *within*, that is, the Spirit of Christ God-man; why then it teaches that man or woman in whom it is, to apply, and trust in Christ *without* for salvation; Christ as born of the Virgin Mary, as fulfilling the law *without* them, as dying without the gate of Jerusalem as a sacrifice for sin; it teaches them to trust in the Man Christ as rising again out of the grave *without* them, as ascending into, and interceding in heaven *without* for them; and as to come from that heaven again in his flesh to judge the world. Thus the man Christ himself saith, ' When he (the Spirit of truth) is come, &c. he shall glorify me.' Jn. xvi. 13, 14. He shall make you more to prize, admire and glorify me, who am both God and man, and who shall be absent from you touching my body. Then follows, for he shall take of mine (of my glorious things) and shew them to you; he shall take my divine and human nature, my birth, my person and offices, my obedience, death, satisfaction, my resurrection,

ascension and intercession, and of my second coming in the clouds with my mighty angels to judgment, and shall shew them, or clear them up to you: He shall take of my salvation, which I have wrought for you in my own person without you: And he shall take of my glory and exaltation in the heavens, and shew to you. Now to mind this one thing, and to be set down in a right understanding of it, by the Spirit, from the scriptures, will be of great concernment to thee and me; for, for want of this, many professors have split themselves, some looking only on what Christ hath done and suffered *without* them, resting in an historical, traditional, and indeed a fancied faith of it, without looking for the Spirit of Jesus Christ to come with power into their hearts, without which they cannot rightly know, nor rightly believe in Christ the Son of God *without* them, so as to have any share or interest in him, ' If any man have not the Spirit of Christ, he is none of his.' Ro. viii. 9. Others have been depending too much upon something they call Christ, and the righteousness of Christ *within* them, in opposition to Christ and his righteousness *without* them, from which all true saints have their justification and comfort, it being received through the operation of the Spirit which dwells in them; and however these may talk much of Christ within them, yet it is manifest, that it is not the Spirit of Christ, but the spirit of the devil; in that it doth not glorify, but slight and reject the man Christ and his righteousness which was wrought *without* them: Reader, in this book thou wilt not meet with high flown airy notions, which some delight in, counting them high mysteries, but the sound, plain, common, (and yet spiritual and mysterious) truths of the gospel, and if thou art a believer, thou must needs reckon them so, and the more, if thou hast not only the faith of them in thy heart, but art daily living in the spiritual sense and feeling of them, and of thy interest in them. Neither doth this treatise offer to thee doubtful controversial things, or matters of opinion, as some books chiefly do, which when insisted upon, the weightier things of the gospel have always done more hurt than good: But here thou hast things certain, and necessary to be believed, which thou canst not too much study. Therefore pray, that thou mayest receive this word which is according to the scriptures in faith and love, not as the word of man, but as the word of God, without respect of persons, and be not offended because Christ holds forth the glorious treasure of the gospel to thee in a poor earthen vessel, by one who hath neither the greatness nor the wisdom of this world to commend him to thee; for as the scripture, saith Christ, (who was low and contemptible in the world himself) ordinarily chooseth such for himself, and for the doing of his work. 1 Co. i. 26—28.

Not many wise men after the flesh, not many mighty, not many noble are called: But God hath chosen the foolish things of the world, &c. This man is not chosen out of an earthly, but out of the heavenly university, the church of Christ, which church, as furnished with the Spirit, gifts, and graces of Christ, was in the beginning, and still is, and will be to the end of the world, that out of which the word of the Lord, and so all true gospel ministers must proceed, whether learned or unlearned, as to human learning. 1 Co. xii. 27, 28. And though this man hath not the learning or wisdom of man, yet, through grace he hath received the teaching of God, and the learning of the Spirit of Christ, which is the thing that makes a man both a Christian and a minister of the gospel. 'The Lord God hath given me the tongue of the learned,' &c. Is. l. 4. compared with Lu. iv. 18. where Christ, as man, saith, 'The Spirit of the Lord *is* upon me, because he hath anointed me to preach the gospel to the poor,' &c. He hath, through grace taken these three heavenly degrees, to wit, union with Christ, the anointing of the Spirit, and experience of the temptations of Satan, which do more fit a man for that mighty work of preaching the gospel, than all university learning and degrees that can be had.

My end in writing these few lines is not to set up man, but having had experience with many other saints of this man's soundness in the faith, of his godly conversation, and his ability to preach the gospel, not by human art, but by the Spirit of Christ, and that with much success in the conversion of sinners when there are so many carnal empty preachers, both learned and unlearned; I say having had experience of this, and judging this book may be profitable to many others, as well as to myself: I thought it my duty upon this account (though I be very unfit for it) to bear witness with my brother to the plain and simple (and yet glorious) truths of our Lord Jesus Christ. And now reader, the Lord give thee and me a right understanding in these things, that we may live and die not with a traditional notional dead faith, but with a right spiritual lively faith of Christ in our heart, wrought by the mighty power of God; such a faith as may make Jesus Christ more real and precious to us than any thing in the world, as may purify our hearts, and make us new creatures, that so we may be sure to escape the wrath to come, and after this life enjoy eternal life and glory through the Lord Jesus Christ, to whom be glory for ever and ever. Amen.

Farewell, thine to serve thee in the Lord Jesus,

JOHN BURTON.

SOME GOSPEL TRUTHS OPENED, &c.

FORASMUCH as many have taken in Hand to set forth their several Judgments concerning the Son of the Virgin MARY, the Lord JESUS CHRIST; and some of those many having most grossly erred from the simplicity of the Gospel, it seemed good to me, having had some Knowledge of these things, to write a few words, to the end, if the Lord will, Souls might not be so horribly deluded by those several corrupt Principles that are gone into the World concerning him.

Now, that there is such a thing as a Christ, I shall not spend much time in proving of; only I shall shew you, that he was first promised to the fathers, and afterwards expected by their children: But before I do that, I shall speak a few words concerning GOD'S FORE-ORDAINING AND PURPOSING, THAT A CHRIST, A SAVIOUR, SHOULD BE, AND THAT BEFORE THE WORLD BEGAN. Now God in his own wisdom and counsel, knowing what would come to pass, as if it were already done. Ro. iv. 17. He knowing that man would break his commandments, and so throw himself under eternal destruction, did in his own purpose *fore-ordain* such a thing as the rise of him that should fall, and that by a *Saviour*, ' According as he hath chosen us in him, (meaning the Saviour) before the foundation of the world.' Ep. i. 4. That is, God seeing that we would transgress, and break his commandment, did before *choose* some of those that would fall, and give them to him that should afterward purchase them actually, though in the account of God, his blood was shed before the world was. Re. xiii. 8. I say, in the account of God, his Son was slain! that is, according to God's purpose and conclusion, which he purposed in himself before the would was; as it is written, 2 Ti. i. 9. 'Who hath saved us, and called *us* with an holy calling, according to his own purpose and grace, which was given us in Christ Jesus before the world began.' As also, in 1 Pe. i. 20. Where the Apostle speaking of Christ, and the redemption purchased by him for sinners, saith of him, 'Who verily was fore-ordained before the foundation of the world, but was manifest in these last days for you, who by him do believe in God, that raised him up from the dead.' God having thus purposed in himself, that he would save some of them that by transgression had destroyed themselves, did with the everlasting Son of his love, make an agreement, or bargain, that upon such and such terms, he would give him a company of such poor souls as had by transgression fallen from their own innocency and uprightness, into those wicked inventions that they themselves had sought out. Ec. vii. 29. The agreement also how this should be, was made before the foundation of the world was laid. Tit. i. 2. The Apostle, speaking of the promise, or covenant made between God and the Saviour (for that is his meaning,) saith on this wise; ' In hope of eternal life, which God that cannot lie, promised before the world began.' Now this promise, or covenant was made with none but with the Son of God, the Saviour. And it must needs be so; for there was none with God before the world began, but he by whom he made the world, as in Pr. viii. from ver. 22 to ver. 31. which was and is, the Son of his love.

This covenant, or bargain, had these conditions in it.

First, That the Saviour should take upon him flesh and blood, the same nature that the sons of men were partakers of (sin only excepted) He. ii. 14. He. iv. 15. And this was the will or agreement that God had made with him: And therefore when he speaks of doing the will of God, He. x. 5. he saith, ' a body hast thou prepared me,' (as according to thy promise, Ge. iii. 15. which I was to take of a woman,) and in it I am come to do thy will, O God, as it is written of me in the volume of thy book. ver. 7.

Second, The Saviour was to bring *everlasting* righteousness to justify sinners withal. Da. ix. 24, 25. The Messias, or Saviour, shall bring in everlasting righteousness, and put an end to iniquity, as it is there written, ' To make an end of sins, and to make reconciliation for iniquity, and to bring in everlasting righteousness.' This, I say, was to be brought into the world by the Saviour, according to the covenant, or agreement, that was between God and Christ before the world began, which God, that cannot lie, promised at that time. Tit. i. 2.

Third, He was to accomplish this everlasting righteousness by spilling his most precious blood, according to the terms of the covenant, or bargain; and therefore when God would shew his people what the agreement was that he and the Saviour had made, even before the covenant was accomplished and sealed actually. See for this Zec. ix. (where he is speaking of him that should be the Saviour,) v. 11. ' As for thee also (meaning the Saviour) by the blood of thy covenant,' or as some render it, whose covenant is by blood (which is all to one purpose) ' I (meaning God) have sent forth thy prisoners out of the pit wherein *is* no water.' The meaning is this: As for thee also, seeing the covenant, or bargain that was made between me and thee before the world was, is accomplished in

When these words were spoken the covenant was not actually sealed, for that was done when the blood of Christ was let out upon the cross.

my account, as if it were actually and really done, with all the conditions that were agreed upon by me and thee; I have therefore, according to that agreement that was on my part, sent forth the prisoners, and those that were under the curse of my law, out of the pit wherein there is no water; seeing thou also hast completely fulfilled in my account whatsoever was on thy part to be done, according to our agreement. And thus is that place to be understood in Jn. xvii. 9. ' I pray for them: I pray not for the world, but for them which thou hast given me' (which I covenanted with thee for) 'thine they were and thou gavest them me,' (but on such and such conditions as are beforementioned, Zec. ix.) And again, ' According as he hath chosen us in him, (that is, in Christ,) before the foundation of the world, that we should be holy and without blame before him in love.' Ep. i. 4.

Now, seeing this was thus concluded upon by those that did wish well to the souls and bodies of poor sinners, after the world was made by them, and after they had said, ' let us make man in our image, after our likeness.' Ge. i. 26. And after

To be holy and without blame is that which God intended for us in that glorious covenant; and by it alone we are holy and without blame before him in love; for we are complete in him alone, with whom the covenant was made. Col. ii. 10; Tit. i. 2.

man, whom God had made upright, had by transgression fallen from that state into which God at first placed him, and thrown himself into a miserable condition by his transgression, then God brings out of his love that which he and his Son had concluded upon, and begins now to make forth that to the world, which he had purposed in himself before the world began, Ep. i. 4, 9; 2 Ti. i. 9.

1. Now the *first* discovery that was made to a lost creature of the love of God, was made to fallen Adam. Ge. iii. 15. Where it is said, ' I will put enmity between thee and the woman, and between thy seed and her seed;' which is the Saviour, Ga. iv. 4. ' It shall bruise thy head, and thou shalt bruise his heel.' This was the first discovery of the love of God to lost man: This was the gospel which was preached to Adam in his generation; in these words was held forth to them in that generation, that which should be farther accomplished in after generations.

2. Another discovery of the love of God in the gospel, was held forth to Noah, in that he would have him to prepare an ark to save himself withal; which ark did type out the Lord that was to come, and be the Saviour of those whom he before had covenanted for with God the Father. ' And God said unto Noah, The end of all flesh is come before me; - - make thee an ark of gopher wood.' Ge. vi. 13, 14. and ch. vii. 1. ' The Lord said unto Noah, Come thou and all thy house into the ark; for thee have I seen righteous before me in this generation.'

3. God breaks out with a farther discovery of himself in love to that generation in which Abraham lived, Where he saith, 'And in thee, (that is, from thee shall Christ come through, in whom) shall all families of the earth be blessed.' Ge. xii. 3. This was also a farther manifestation of the good will of God to poor lost sinners; and through this discovery of the gospel, did Abraham see that which made him rejoice. Jn viii. 56.

4. When the time was come that Moses was to be a prophet to the people of his generation, then God did more gloriously yet break forth with one type after another, as the blood of bulls, and lambs, and goats: Also sacrifices of divers manners, and of several things, which held forth that Saviour more clearly which God had in his own purpose and decree determined to be sent; for these things (the types) were a shadow of that which was to come, which was the substance. He. ix. 9, 10. He. x. 1, 5—7. Now when these things were thus done, when God had thus signified to the world, what he intended to do in after times, presently all that had faith to believe that God would be as good as his word, began to look for, and to expect that the Lord should accomplish and bring to pass what he had promised, what his hand and counsel had before determined to be done.

(1.) Now Abraham begins to look for what God had promised and signified; namely, that he would send a Saviour into the world in his appointed time, which thing being promised, Abraham embraces, being persuaded of the certainty of it; as in He. xi. 13. And this did fill his heart with joy and gladness, as I said before; for 'he saw it, and was glad.' Jn. viii. 56.

(2.) Jacob also, while he was blessing his sons, concerning things to come, breaks forth with these words, 'I have waited for thy salvation.' Ge. xlix. 18. He was also put in expectation of salvation to come by this Saviour.

(3.) David was in earnest expectation of this, which was held forth by types and shadows in the law; for as yet the Saviour was not come, which made him cry out with a longing after it, 'O that the salvation of Israel were come out of Sion.' Ps. liii. 6. And again, 'O that the salvation of Israel were come out of Sion!' Ps. xiv. 7. The thing that David waited for, was not in his time come, though before his time it was promised; which makes him cry out, O that it were come, that it were come out of Sion! Where, by the way, take notice, that the true salvation and Saviour of Israel was to come out of Sion, that is, out of the church of God, touching the flesh, as it is written; A prophet shall the Lord your God raise up unto you of your brethren like unto me. De. xviii. 15, 18. And again, 'I have laid help upon one that is mighty; I have exalted one chosen out of the people.' Ps. lxxxix. 19.

and Ro. ix. 5. 'Whose are the fathers, and of whom as concerning the flesh Christ came, who is over all, God blessed for ever.' Christ, as concerning the flesh, did come of the fathers.

(4.) Isaiah did prophesy of this, that God would thus save his people; yea, he breaks forth with these words, 'But Israel shall be saved in the LORD with an everlasting salvation.' Is. xlv. 17. He also tells them how it shall be accomplished in that 53d chapter. Yea, he had such a glorious taste of the reality of it, that he speaks as though it had been actually done.

(5.) In the days of Jeremiah, this that God had promised to the fathers, was not yet accomplished; in ch. xxiii. 5. he saith, 'Behold, the days come, saith the Lord, that I will (mark, it was not yet done) but I will (saith God) raise unto David a righteous branch, and a king shall reign and prosper. - - In his days Judah shall be saved, and Israel shall dwell safely; and this is his name wherewith he shall be called, THE LORD OUR RIGHTEOUSNESS.'

(6.) He was also to come in Zechariah's time, Zec. iii. 8. Where he saith, 'for, behold, I will bring forth my servant the BRANCH.'

(7.) He was not come in the time of Malachi neither, though he was indeed at that time near his coming. For he saith himself, 'Behold, I will send my messenger, (meaning John the baptist,) and he shall prepare the way before me: and the Lord whom ye seek, shall suddenly come to his temple, even the messenger of the covenant, whom ye delight in: behold he shall come, saith the Lord of hosts.' Mal. iii. 1; see also Is. xl. 3; Lu. i. 76.

(8.) Old Simeon did also wait for the consolation of Israel a long time. Lu. ii. 25. Where it is said, 'And, behold, there was a man in Jerusalem, whose name was Simeon; and the same man was just and devout, waiting for the consolation of Israel.' That is, waiting for him that was to be the Saviour, as is clear, if you read with understanding a little farther: 'And it was revealed unto him by the Holy Ghost, that he should not see death, before he had seen the Lord's Christ.' ver. 26.

God has a Christ, one distinct from all other things whatsoever that is called Christ, whether they be spirit or body, or both spirit and body, and this is signified, where he saith, the Lord's Christ.

And thus have I in brief shewed you, 1. That there is such a thing as Christ. 2. That this Christ was promised and signified out by many things before he did come. 3. How he was waited for, and expected before the time that God had appointed in the which he should come.

The SECOND THING that I will (through the strength of Christ) prove, is this, THAT HE THAT WAS OF THE VIRGIN, IS HE THAT IS THE SAVIOUR.

FIRST, And first, I shall lay down this for a truth; That it is not any Spirit only by, and of itself, without it do take the nature of man, that can be a Saviour of man from eternal vengeance.

Or thus: That that [which] will be a Saviour of man, must in the nature of man satisfy and appease the justice and wrath of God.   And the arguments that I do bring to prove it by, are these.

First, Because it was man that had offended; and justice required that man must give the satisfaction: And therefore, when he that should be the Saviour, was come, he ' took upon him the form of a servant, and was made in the likeness of men:' Phi. ii. 7. and in He. ii. 14. Because 'the children are partakers of flesh and blood; he also himself likewise took part of the same;' To what end? 'that through death he might destroy him that had the power of death, that is, the devil.' And is that all? No; but also that he might 'deliver them who through fear of death, were all their lifetime subject to bondage.' ver. 15.

Second, The second argument is this; because, if a spirit only could have made satisfaction for the sin of mankind, and have subdued Satan for man, without the nature of man, either there had been weakness in God when he made that promise to fallen Adam, That the seed of the woman should break the serpent's head; (for there hath been no need of and so no room for that promise) or else God having made it, would have appeared unfaithful, in not fulfilling his promise, by redeeming the world without it.

Third, If a spirit only could have made satisfaction, and so have saved man; then Christ needed not to have come into the world, and to have been born of a woman. Ga. iv. 4. But in that he must come into the world, and must be born of a woman, it is clear, that without this, he could not have been a Saviour: For he was made of a woman, made under the law, to this end, that he might redeem them that were under the law; implying, No subjection to this, (viz. the taking of the nature of man) no redemption from the curse of the law. But Christ hath delivered from the curse of the law (all that believe in his name) being in their nature made a curse for them.

And this is the reason, why the fallen angels are not recovered from their damnable estate, because, he did not take hold of their nature, ' For verily he took not on *him the nature of* angels; but he took on *him* the seed of Abraham. He. ii. 16.

They that are redeemed, must have *redemption* wrought out for them through their natures; for except that nature that sinned do bring in recovery from the curse that is due to it for its sin, that nature that sinned must suffer for its own sin. Ga. iii. 16.

SECOND, Now then, seeing this is the very truth of God, I shall next prove, that Jesus that was born of the virgin, to be the Saviour.   And,

First, I shall prove it by comparing some places of the Old and New testament together, and by some arguments drawn from the scriptures.

1. And first, see Ge. iii. 15. where he is called the seed of the woman, saying, ' I will put enmity between thee and the woman, and between thy seed and her seed;' and so was Jesus, Ga. iv. 4. where it is said, ' God sent forth his Son, made of a woman,' or born of a woman.

2. This woman must be a virgin, Is. vii. 14. where it is said, ' A virgin shall conceive, and bear a son, and shall call his name Imanuel.'   And Jesus is he that was the fulfilling of this scripture, Mat. i. 22, 23. ' Now all this was done, that it might be fulfilled which was spoken of the Lord by the prophet, saying, Behold, a virgin shall be with child, and shall bring forth a Son, and they shall call his name Imanuel.'

3. The Saviour must be of the tribe of Judah. And this Jacob prophesied of on his death-bed, saying, ' Judah, thou *art he* whom thy brethren shall praise,' or honour, ' thy hand *shall be* in the neck of thine enemies; thy father's children shall bow down before thee.' Ge. xlix. 8.

And again, Mi. v. 2. ' But thou, Bethlehem Ephratah, *though* thou be little among the thousands of Judah, *yet* out of thee shall he come forth unto me *that is* to be ruler in Israel.'   Jesus also came of the tribe of Judah, and that will clearly appear, if you read. Mat. i.   Matthew, he begins first with Abraham, ver. 2. and thence to Judah ver. 3. from Judah to David, ver. 6. from David to Zorobabel, ver. 13. then to Jacob the father of Joseph, the husband of Mary, of whom was born Jesus, ver. 16.

Now Mary was one of the same house also, and for this consider, Jesus came from the loins of David; see Mat. i. but that he could not do, if Mary had not been of the seed of David: For Christ came from her, not from him, for Joseph ' knew her not till she had brought forth her first-born.' Mat. i. 25.   Again, the angel told her, that he was the son of David, saying, ' And the Lord God shall give unto him the throne of his father David.' Lu. i. 32.

And again, The Jews knew this very well, or else they would have been sure to have laid it open before all the world; for they sought by all means to disown him.   And though they did through the devilishness of their unbelief disown him, yet could they find no such thing as to question the right of his birth from Mary.   If it had been to be done, they would no doubt have done it; they did not want malice to whet them on; neither did they want means so far as might help forward their malice; without manifest and apparent injury; for they had exact registers, or records of their genealogies, so that, if they had had any colour for it, they would sure have denied him to have been the son of David.   There was reasoning concerning him when he was with them, Jn. vii. 27, 43. and I do believe, part of it was about the generation of which he came,

And this was so commonly known, that the blind man that sat by the way-side could cry out, ' Jesus *thou* Son of David, have mercy on me.—*Thou* Son of David, have mercy on me.' Lu. xviii. 38, 39. It was so common, that he came from the loins of his father David according to the flesh, that it was not so much as once questioned. ' And when' Herod ' demanded of the chief priests and scribes of the people where Christ should be born. They said unto him, in Bethlehem of Judea: For thus it is written by the prophet, And thou Bethlehem, *in* the land of Juda, art not the least among the princes of Juda, for out of thee shall come a governor, that shall rule my people Israel.' Mat. i. 4—6. (For out of thee) mark that; if Mary had not been of Judah, Christ had not come out of Judah, but Christ came out of Judah; therefore Mary is also a daughter of Judah. And this is evident, as saith the scripture, ' for - - our Lord sprang out of Judah.' He. vii. 14.

Again, when Christ the Saviour was to come into the world, at that time the sceptre was to depart from Judah, according to the prophecy of Jacob. ' The sceptre shall not depart from Judah, nor a law-giver from between his feet, until Shiloh come.' Ge. xlix. 10.

Now the sceptre was then departed from those that were Jews by nature, and also the law-giver, and Herod who was a stranger, and not of Judea, was king over them, as Cæsar's deputy; and Cæsar Augustus imposed laws on them.

The stubborn Jews also confessed the sceptre to be departed, when before Pontius Pilate a Roman governor of Judea, they cried out against Christ: ' We have no king but Cesar.' Jn. xix. 15.

Nay farther, the Jews from that day to this, have been without a king of their own nation to govern them: they never had the sceptre swayed since by any of themselves, but have been a scattered despised people, and have been as it were liable to all dangers, and for a long time driven out from their country, and scattered over all the nations of the earth, as was prophesied concerning them. Je. xiv. 10. Zec. vi. 14, 15. And yet these poor souls are so horribly deluded by the devil, that though they see these things come to pass, yet they will not believe. And one reason among many, of their being thus deluded, is this, they say that the word sceptre in Ge. xlix. is not meant of a kingly government; but the meaning is, (say they) a rod, or persecutions shall not depart from Judah till Shiloh come. Now they do most grossly mistake that place; for though I am not skilled in the Hebrew tongue, yet through grace, I am enlightened into the scriptures; whereby I find that the meaning is not persecutions, nor the rod of afflictions, but a governor or sceptre of the kingdom shall not depart from Judah till Shiloh

come. And that this is the meaning of the place, weigh but the very next words of the same verse, and you will find it to be the sceptre of a king that is meant; for he addeth, ' nor a law-giver from between his feet.' Mark it, The sceptre, nor a law-giver; the legislative power depending on the sceptre of the kingdom, shall not depart from Judah till Shiloh come. According to that scripture, written in Is. vii. 16. ' For before the child shall know to refuse the evil, and choose the good, the land that thou abhorrest shall be forsaken of both her kings.' Which scripture hath been fulfilled from that same time.

But a word to the Jews' exposition of the sceptre to be a rod, or persecutions; saying, that persecutions shall not depart from Judah till Shiloh come. This cannot be the meaning of the place; for the Jews have had rest oftentimes, and that before Shiloh did come; at one time they ' had rest fourscore years.' Ju. iii. 30. Again, ' And the land had rest from war.' Jos. xiv. 15. And again, ' And the Lord gave them rest round about, according to all that he sware unto their fathers, and there stood not a man of all their enemies before them.' Jos. xxi. 44. ' And the land had rest forty years.' Ju. iii. 11. There was rest many a time from persecution and from the rod, though it were but for a season; but the sceptre, or kingdom, did not depart from Judah, and a law-giver from between his feet till Shiloh came.

Second, Again, To prove that Jesus is the Christ, it is clear from the hand of God against the Jews, for putting him to death. What was the reason why they did put him to death, but this, He did say that he was the Christ the Son of God? Lu. xxii. 70. ' Then said they all, Art thou then the Son of God? And he said unto them, Ye say that I am.' That is, I am he as you say, I am the Son of God; yea, the only begotten Son of the Father, and I was with him before the world was. Jn. ix. 37. and xvii. 5.

Now the Jews did put him to death for his thus owning his own; that is, for not denying of his Sonship, but making himself equal with God, therefore did they put him to death. Jn. xix. 7.

Now God did, and doth most miserably plague them to this very day, for their crucifying of him: But I say, had he not been the Christ of God, God's Son, he would not have laid sin to their charge, for crucifying him; but rather have praised them for their zeal, and for taking him out of the way, who did rob God of his honour, in that he made himself equal with God, and was not. He would have praised them for doing the thing that was right, as he did Phineas the son of Eleazar, for executing judgment in his time, on the adulterer and adulteress. Nu. xxv. 8.

But in that he said he was the Son of God, and

accounted it no robbery so to call himself. Phi. ii. 6. And seeing that they did put him to death, because he said he was the Son of God; and in that God doth so severely charge them with, and punish them for their sin in putting him to death, for saying that he was the Son of God, it is evident that he was and is the Son of God, and that Saviour that should come into the world. For his blood hath been upon them to this very day for their hurt, according to their desire. Mat. xxvii. 25.

Again, Jesus himself doth in this day hold forth that he is the Christ, where he saith, 'The time is fulfilled, and the kingdom of God is at hand.' Mar. i. 15. What time is this that Jesus speaks of? Surely, 'tis that of Daniel's seventy weeks, spoken of in chap. ix. 24. where he saith, ' Seventy weeks are determined upon thy people - - - to finish the transgression, and to make an end of sins, and to make reconciliation' or satisfaction 'for iniquity, and to bring in everlasting righteousness, - - and to anoint the most Holy.' This time, that here Daniel speaks of, is it that Christ saith hath an end; and the argument that he brings to persuade them to believe the gospel, is this, ' The kingdom of God is at hand,' (according as was prophesied of it by Daniel) ' repent, and believe the gospel.' Repent, and believe that this is the gospel; and that this is the truth of God; consider, that Daniel had a revelation of these days from the angel of God, and also the time in which it should be accomplished: namely, Seventy weeks was the determined time of the Messias his coming, from the time when the angel spake these words to Daniel: Seventy weeks, that is, about 490 years, if you reckon every day in the said seventy weeks for a year: A day for a year, a day for a year; for so is the Holy Spirit's way sometimes to reckon days. Eze. iv. 6. And this the Jews were convinced of, when Christ saith to them, ' Ye hypocrites, ye can discern the face of the sky; but can ye not *discern* the signs of the times?' Mat. xvi. 3. Do you not see that those things that are spoken of as forerunners of my coming, are accomplished? Do you not see that the sceptre is departed from Judah? Do you not see the time that Daniel spake of is accomplished also? There shall no sign be given unto it, but the sign of the prophet Jonas: O ye hypocritical generation! ver. 4.

Third, Another argument to prove that Jesus is the Christ, is this, By his power the blind see, the lame walk, the deaf hear, the dumb speak, the dead are raised up, the devils are dispossessed. In Is. xxxv. 4. it is thus prophesied of him, ' Behold your God will come *with* vengeance, *even* God *with* a recompense; he will come and save you;' But how shall we know when he is come? Why, ' Then the eyes of the blind shall be opened, and the ears of the deaf shall be unstopped. Then shall the lame *man* leap as an hart, and the tongue of the dumb sing; for in the wilderness shall waters break out, and streams in the desert.' ver. 5, 6. Now when John would know whether he were the Christ or no, Jesus sends him this very answer, ' Go, and shew John (saith he) again those things which you do hear and see: the blind receive their sight, and the lame walk, the lepers are cleansed, and the deaf hear, the dead are raised up, and the poor have the gospel preached to them. Mat. xi. 3—5.

Fourth, Another argument that doth prove this Jesus to be the Christ, is this, namely, he to whom it was revealed, that he should see him, though he waited long for him. So soon as ever he did but see that sweet babe that was born of the virgin Mary, he cried out, ' Lord now lettest thou thy servant depart in peace, according to thy word: For mine eyes have seen thy salvation, which thou hast prepared before the face of all people;' as it is in Lu. ii. 26—31. The prophetess Anna also, so soon as she had seen him, ' gave thanks to the Lord, and spake of him to all them that looked for redemption in Jerusalem.' ver. 36—38.

Fifth, Another argument is, the sign of the prophet Jonah. He, even Jonah, was three days and three nights in the whale's belly, Jonah i. 17. and Jesus makes this very thing an argument to the Jews, that he was the true Messias, where he saith, ' An evil and adulterous generation seeketh after a sign;' that is, they would have me to show them a sign, to prove that I am the Saviour, ' And there shall no sign be given to it, but the sign of the prophet Jonas: For as Jonas was three days and three nights in the whale's belly; so shall the Son of man be three days and three nights in the heart of the earth.' Mat. xii. 39, 40. And this, the Apostle makes mention of to be accomplished, where he says, The Jews slew Jesus, and hanged him on a tree, Ac. x. 39. and laid him in a sepulchre. Mat. xxvii. But God raised him up the third day, and shewed him openly. Ac. x. 40.

Sixth, Another scripture argument to prove that Jesus is the Christ, is this, that there was not one of his bones broken; which thing was foretold and typed out by the Paschal Lamb, where he saith, ' They shall leave none of it unto the morning, nor break any bone of it,' Ex. xii. 46. Nu. ix. 12. which thing was fulfilled in the Son of the virgin, (though contrary to the customs of that nation,) as it is written, ' Then came the soldiers, and brake the legs of the first, and of the other which was crucified with him. But when they came to Jesus, and saw that he was dead already, they break not his legs:' Jn. xix. 32, 33. ' that the scripture should be fulfilled, A bone of him shall not be broken.' ver. 36.

Seventh, Another scripture demonstration is, in that they did fulfil the saying that was written, ' They part my garments among them, and cast lots upon my vesture.' Ps. xxii. 18. But this was also fulfilled in Jesus, as it is written; 'Then the soldiers, when they had crucified Jesus, took his garments, and made four parts, to every soldier a part; and also his coat: now the coat was without seam, - - They said therefore among themselves, let us not rend it, but cast lots for it whose it shall be: that the scripture might be fulfilled, which saith, They parted my raiment among them, and for my vesture they did cast lots.' Jn. xix. 23, 24.

Eighth, Again, The scripture saith, 'they shall look upon me, whom they have pierced.' Zec. xii. 10. But the soldier thrust a spear into his side, That it might be fulfilled which was written, 'they shall look on him whom they pierced.' Jn. xix. 34—37.

Error 1. Now then, seeing this is the truth of God, that Jesus that was born of the virgin, is the Christ of God; how horribly are those deceived who look on Jesus the Son of Mary, to be but a shadow or type, of something that was afterward to be revealed; whereas the scriptures most lively hold him forth to be the Christ of God, and not a shadow of a spirit, or of a body afterwards to be revealed, but himself was the very substance of all things that did any way type out Christ to come; and when he was indeed come, then was an end put to the law for righteousness, or justification to every one that believeth; 'Christ *is* the end of the law for righteousness to every one that believeth,' as it is written. Ro. x. 4. That is, he was the end of the ceremonial law, and of that commonly called the moral law, the substance of which is laid down, Ex. xx. from the first to the 17th verse, though that law, as handed out by Christ, still remains of great use to all believers, which they are bound to keep for sanctification, as Christ saith, Mat. v. 19th verse, to the end of the chapter. But Christ Jesus hath obtained everlasting righteousness, having fulfilled all the law of God in the body of his flesh, wherein he also suffered on the cross without the gates, and doth impute this righteousness to poor man, having accomplished it for him in the body of his flesh, which he took of the virgin. Gal. iv. 4. 'God sent forth his Son, made of a woman, [that is, born of the virgin] made under the law,' that is, to obey it, and to bear the curse of it, 'being made a curse for us;' Ga. iii. 13. to redeem them that were under the law, that is, to redeem such as were ordained to life eternal, from the curse of the law. And this he did by his birth, being made or born of a woman; by his obedience, yea, by his perfect obedience 'he became the author of eternal salvation unto all them that obey him;' He. v. 8, 9. and by his doing and suffering, did completely satisfy the law and the justice of God, and bring in that glorious

A believer hath no law to fulfil for justification; only to believe on what the man Christ Jesus hath done and be saved.

and everlasting salvation, without which we had all eternally been undone, and that without remedy; for without shedding of his blood there was no remission.

See He. ix. 22, and compare it with He. viii. 3, where he saith, 'it is of necessity that this man have somewhat also to offer.' Which man was Jesus. ch. vii. 22.

Error 2. Seeing Jesus Christ, the Son of the virgin Mary, was and is the Christ of God: and that salvation came in alone by him, for there is salvation in no other, Ac. iv. 12. then how are they *deceived,* that think to obtain salvation by following the convictions of the law, which they call Christ (though falsely) when alas, let them follow those convictions that do come from the law, and conscience set on work by it; I say, let them follow all the convictions that may be hinted in upon their spirits from that law, they shall never be able to obtain salvation by their obedience to it, 'for by the law *is* the knowledge of sin.' Ro. iii. 20. Ga. iii. 10. Jn. x. 15. He. ix. 12. And 'It is not of works least any man should boast,' as those fond hypocrites called Quakers would do. And again, 'If righteousness *come* by the law, then Christ is dead in vain.' Ga. ii. 21. 'But that no man is justified by the works of the law, in the sight of God, *it is* evident: for, The just shall live by faith.' Ga. iii. 11. Which living by faith, is to apply the Lord Jesus Christ his benefits, as birth, righteousness, death, blood, resurrection, ascension, and intercession, with the glorious benefits of his second coming to me, as mine, being given to me, and for me, and thus much doth the Apostle signify, saying; 'The life which I now live in the flesh I live by the faith of the Son of God, who loved me, and gave himself for me.' Ga. ii. 20.

Error 3. Again, Seeing God's Christ, which was with him before the world was, Jn. xvii. 5. took upon him flesh and blood from the virgin Mary, (who was espoused to Joseph the carpenter) and in that human nature yielded himself an offering for sin, (for it was the body of his flesh by which sin was purged, Col. i. 22.) I say, seeing the Son of God, as he was in a body of flesh, did bring in salvation for sinners, and by this means, as I said before, we are saved, even by faith in his blood, righteousness, resurrection, &c. How are they then deceived who own Christ no otherwise than as he was before the world began, who was then without flesh and blood (for he took that in time of the virgin. Ga. iv. 4. He. ii. 14.) I say, they are wickedly deluded, who own him no otherwise but as he was before the world was: For in their owning of him thus and no otherwise, they do directly deny him to be come in the flesh, and are of that antichristian party which John speaks of, 1 Jn. iv. 3. 'Every spirit that confesseth not that Jesus Christ is come in the flesh, is not of God: and this is that *spirit* of antichrist, whereof ye have heard that it should come, and even now already is it in the world.' Now because the enemy doth most notably wrest this scripture, as they do others, to their own damnation, I shall speak something to it; and therefore, when he saith, every spirit that confesseth not that Jesus Christ is come in the flesh, is not of God, his meaning is, Every spirit that doth not confess that that Christ that was with the Father before the world was, did in the appointed time of the Father come into the world, took on him a body from the virgin, and was very man as well as very God, and in that body of flesh did do and suffer whatsoever belonged to the sons of men for the breach of the holy law of God, and impute his glorious righteousness which he fulfilled in that body of his flesh, to the souls that shall believe on what he hath done, and is adoing in the same body.

Consider 1. And that this is the mind of the Spirit of God, consider, *first*, he himself saith, handle me and see, for a spirit hath not flesh and bones, as ye see me have, when his disciples had thought he had been but a spirit. Lu. xxiv. 39, 40.

Consider 2. Now that in this flesh he died for sins: consider, *secondly*, that scripture which saith, ' Who his own self, (that is, the Christ that was born of the Virgin) bare our sins in his own body on the tree.' 1 Pe. ii. 24. See Col. i. 22. ' in the body of his flesh,' saith he, ' to present you holy and unblameable, and unreprovable in his sight.' Now that he arose again from the dead, with the body of flesh wherewith he was crucified, consider, that forenamed scripture, Lu. xxiv. 39, 40. spoken after his resurrection.

Now that he went away with the same body from them into heaven, consider that it is said, ' And he led them out as far as to Bethany, and he lifted up his hands, and blessed them. And it came to pass, while he blessed them, he was parted from them, and carried up into heaven,' Lu. xxiv. 50, 51. This is the meaning of those words therefore ; Jesus Christ is come into the flesh, that is, Jesus Christ hath come in the flesh that he took of the Virgin, hath brought us who were enthralled to the law, the devil, and sin, to liberty; and that by his obedience and death. ' Forasmuch then as the children are partakers of flesh and blood, (saith the scripture) he, (Christ) also himself likewise took part of the same ;' wherefore ? ' That through death he might destroy him that had the power of death, that is, the devil; and deliver them who through fear of death were all their life-time subject to bondage.' He. ii. 14, 15. For he 'was delivered for our offences, and was raised again for our justification.' Ro. iv. 25. For he, even that man, through the power of the eternal Spirit, did offer up himself without spot to God, and thereby, or by that offering, ' obtained eternal redemption for us.' He. ix. 12, 14. And therefore I say again and again, look to yourselves, that you receive no Christ except

God's Christ: For he is like to be deceived that will believe every thing that calls itself a Christ. ' For many, [saith he] shall come in my name, - - and shall deceive many.' Mat. xxiv. 5.

Now having spoken thus much touching the Saviour, the Lord Jesus Christ, I shall, according to the assistance of the Lord Jesus, proceed, and shall speak something of his godhead, birth, death, resurrection, ascension, *and* intercession; *together with* his most glorious and personal appearing the second time, *which will be* to raise the dead, and bring every work to judgment. Ec. xii. 14.

And FIRST I shall shew you that he (Christ) is very God, co-eternal, and also co-equal with his Father. SECOND, That by this Son of Mary (which is equal with his Father) the world was made. THIRD, That he in the fulness of time, was made of a woman, made under the law, to redeem them that were (or are) under the law ; that is, was born of a woman : and in our nature (for he made himself of no reputation, and took on him the form of a servant, and was made in the likeness of men) and in our stead he did fulfil the law in point of justification, Ro. x. 4. and was crucified for our transgressions. 1 Co. i. 23—25. FOURTH, That very body of the Son of Mary which was crucified, did rise again from the dead, after he had been buried in Joseph's sepulchre ; that he in that very body ascended up into heaven ; and in that very body shall come again to these ends, 1. To judge the quick and the dead. 2. To receive his saints to himself. 3. To pass eternal condemnation on his enemies. These things in brief I shall touch upon, according to the wisdom given me.

FIRST, And therefore that Christ is very God, I shall *first* prove by plain texts of scripture. *Second*, From the testimony of God, angels, and men, witnessed by the scriptures. *Third*, By several arguments drawn from scripture, which will prove the same clearly.

First, Then to prove it by the scriptures ; tho' indeed the whole book of God's holy scripture, testify these things plainly to be most true, yet there be some places more pregnant and pertinent to the thing than others ; and therefore I shall mention some of them : as that in Pr. viii. 22, &c. and there you shall find him spoken of under the name of *Wisdom*, the same name that is given him in 1 Co. i. 24. I say in that place of the Proverbs above mentioned, you shall find these expressions from his own mouth. ' The Lord possessed me in the beginning of his way, before his works of old. I was set up from everlasting, from the beginning, or ever the earth was. When *there were* no depths, I was brought forth ; when *there were* no fountains abounding with water. Before the mountains were settled, before the hills was I brought forth : While as yet he had not made the earth, nor the fields, nor the highest part of the dust of the world. When he prepared the heavens, I *was* there: when he set a compass upon the face of the depth : When he established the clouds above: when he strengthened the fountains of the deep: When he gave to the sea his decree, that the waters should not pass his commandment : when he appointed the foundations of the earth: Then I was by him, as one brought up *with him :* and I was daily *his* delight, rejoicing always before him; rejoicing in the habitable part of his earth; and my delights were with the sons of men.' Also in Jn. i. 1, 2. you have these words spoken of Christ, ' In the beginning was the Word, and the Word was with God, and the Word was God. The same was in the beginning with God.' As also in He. i. 2. the Apostle being about to prove the Son of Mary to be very God, saith ; He ' hath in these last days spoken unto us by *his* Son ;' which Son is the Son of Mary, as in Mat. iii. ' But (saith the Apostle He. i. 8.) unto the Son *he saith*, Thy throne, O God, *is* for ever and ever, a sceptre of righteousness *is* the sceptre of thy kingdom.' Again, in Jn. xvii. 5. you have the words of the Son of Mary for it, saying, ' And now, O Father, glorify thou me with thine own self, with the glory which I had with thee before the world was.' Again, he himself saith, before Abraham was, I am: And again, I and my Father are one. And in Phi. ii. 5. the Apostle saith, ' Let this mind be in you which was also in Christ Jesus : who, being in the form of God, thought it not robbery to be equal with God: But made himself of no reputation, and took upon him the form of a servant, and was made in the likeness of men.' Also Re. ii. 8. Christ himself saith, I am 'the first and the last, which was dead, and is alive.' And thus have I quoted some few scriptures to prove that the Son of Mary is the true God.

Second, I shall give you the testimony of God himself touching the truth of this, viz. That Christ, the Son of the Virgin, is the true God:

1. And first see Zec. xiii. 7. and there you shall find these words, 'Awake, O sword, against my shepherd, and against the man *that is* my fellow, saith the Lord of hosts.' In this place the Lord doth call that *Man* his fellow, which he doth not do to any mere creature. Again, in Mat. iii. 17. he calls him his beloved Son, saying, ' This is my beloved Son, in whom I am well pleased.' And in the aforesaid place of the Hebrews, ch. i. the Apostle advancing the Lord Jesus, brings in this question. ' To which of the angels said he at any time, Thou art my Son ?' ver. 5. ' But unto the Son *he saith*, ver. 8. Thy throne, O God, *is* for ever and ever:' And thus far of the testimony that God himself hath given of the Son of Mary, Jesus Christ.

2. The angels do shew that he is God: (1.) In that they do obey him. (2.) In that they worship him.

(1.) That they obey him, is clear, if we compare Re. xxi. 9. with xxii. 6. In the first of these places we find, that there came one of the angels of the seven vials, which had the seven last plagues, and talked with John. He came not of himself ; for in that xxii. ch. ver. 6. he saith, ' The Lord - - sent his angel to shew unto his servants, the things which must shortly be done.' Now in the 16th ver. you may see who this Lord God is: He saith there, 'I Jesus have sent mine angel to testify - - these things in the churches. [compare Re. i. 1.] I am the root and (as well as) the offspring of David, *and* the bright and morning star.' I say this obedience of the angels doth testify that Jesus, which is the Son of Mary, is the true and very God; for they do obey God only.

(2.) The angels do shew that the Son of Mary, is the true God, in that they do not only obey him, but worship him also; yea, they are commanded so to do, He. i. 6. where it is written, ' When he bringeth in the first begotten into the world, he (*i. e.* God,) saith, And let all the angels of God worship him,' viz. the Son of Mary. Now the angels themselves command that we worship none but God, Re. xxii. 8, 9. When John fell down to worship the angel, the angel said, ' See *thou do it* not: for I am thy fellow servant, - - worship God.' Now if the angels should command to worship God, and they themselves should worship him that by nature is no god, they should overthrow themselves, in commanding one thing, and doing another, and so lose their own habitations, and be shut up in chains of darkness, to be punished with everlasting destruction from God himself at the great day. And thus much concerning the testimony of angels touching Jesus the Son of Mary, the Son of God, yea, very and true God. Is. ix. 6.

3. [The testimony of men witnessed by the scriptures do shew that Christ is very God.] Now followeth David his testimony among other of the saints, who witness Jesus the Son of Mary to be true God; and that you may find in Ps. cx. 1. where he saith, ' The Lord said unto my Lord, Sit thou at my right hand, until I make thine enemies thy footstool.' Also Isaiah in the 9th. ch. ver. 6. saith, ' For unto us a child is born, unto us a son is given ; and the government shall be upon his shoulder : and his name shall be called Wonderful, Counsellor, The mighty God, The everlasting Father, the Prince of Peace. Of the increase of *his* government and peace *there shall be* no end, upon the throne of David, (which is not, nor ever was the heart of any believer) and upon his kingdom, to order it, and to establish it with judgment and with justice from henceforth even for ever.

The zeal of the LORD of hosts will perform this.' Again, see Peter's testimony of this Son of Mary; When Jesus asked his disciples, whom say ye that I am? Peter, as the mouth of the rest, said, 'Thou art the Christ, the Son of the living God.' Mat. xvi. 16. Also when Thomas, one of Christ's disciples, would not be persuaded by the others that they had seen the Lord, except he did also see in his hands the print of the nails, and put his fingers into the print of the nails, and thrust his hand into his side, he would not believe. Saith the Son of Mary, 'Reach hither thy finger, and behold my hands; and reach hither thy hand, and thrust it into my side; and be not faithless but believing.' And then Thomas breaks out with a mighty faith, and a glorious testimony for his master, and saith, 'My Lord, and my God.' Jn. xx. 27, 28. Again, See Paul's testimony of him, Ro. ix. 5. where speaking of the Son of Mary, he saith, That Christ came of the Fathers, 'who is over all, God blessed for ever, Amen.' And the apostle John doth also witness as much, 1 Jn. v. 20. where speaking of Jesus Christ, he saith on this wise, 'And we know that the Son of God is come, and hath given us an understanding, that we may know him that is true, and we are in him that is true, (Who is that? why, saith John) even in his Son Jesus Christ.' Who is he? Why, 'This is the true God, and eternal life.'

I could here also bring in the testimony of the very devils themselves, as Lu. iv. 41; viii. 28. where he is by them acknowledged to be the Son of the living God: But it is needless so to do; for we have plainly proved it already.

Third, Now followeth the several scripture arguments, which will prove that Jesus the Son of Mary is very God.

1. There is none but he that is the true God, can satisfy the justice of the true God, for the breach of his holy law; but if you compare Is. liii. 6. with Mat. iii. 17. you shall find, that Jesus the Son of Mary did give God a full and complete satisfaction for the breach of his holy law; therefore Jesus the Son of Mary must needs be the great and true God.

2. He that hath power of his own to lay down his life, and hath power of his own to take it up again, must needs be the true God: but this did Jesus the Son of Mary the virgin; therefore he must needs be the true God. Jn. x. 17. Ro. i. 4.

3. There was never any able to bear the sins of all the believers in the world, that ever were, now are, or hereafter shall be, but the true God: But Jesus, the Son of the Virgin Mary, did bear them all, 'in his own body on the tree.' 1 Pe. ii. 24. Is. liii. 6. Therefore Jesus the Son of Mary must needs be the true God as well as man.

4. There was never any mere man able, by his own power, to overcome the devil in all his temptations, but he that is also the true God. (for Adam in his state of innocency was overcome by them, and fell under them:) But Jesus the Son of the Virgin did overcome them all by his own power; therefore he is very God, as well as very Man. See Ge. iii. 15. Is. li. 9; lxiii. 5. Mat. iv. 24. Lu. iv. 12.

If all the Quakers and Ranters in the world, were but under the guilt of one sinful thought, it would make them to cry out with Cain, My punishment is greater than I can bear, Ge. iv. 13.

5. There was never any that did call himself the true God (and was not) which did *please* God in so doing. But Jesus the Son of Mary did call himself the true God, or account himself equal with God (which is all one) yet God was well pleased with him. Mat. iii. 17. Phi. ii. 6, 7. Jn. viii. 29. And therefore Jesus the Son of Mary must needs be true God as well as man.

6. There was never any that had all power in heaven and in earth, but the true God. Jesus the Son of the Virgin Mary, who was espoused to Joseph, hath all power in heaven and in earth in his own hand. Therefore he is the true and great God. Mat. xxviii. 18.

7. There was never any able to keep poor souls from falling from God, saving he that is the true God. Jesus the Son of Mary did, and doth this. Jn. x. 27—30; xvii. 12. Therefore he is the true and great God.

8. Never could any justly call himself the first and the last, except the true God, nor truly (as the Lord did say) I AM. But these did Jesus the Son of Mary. Re. i. 1. compared with ver. 17, 18; Re. ii. 8. and Jn. viii. 58. Therefore Jesus must needs be true God as well as man.

9. Never was there any that could absolutely forgive sins but God. Mar. ii. 7. Lu. v. 21. But Jesus the Son of the Virgin Mary, can forgive sins. Lu. v. 20. Mar. ii. 5. Therefore Jesus the Son of Mary must needs be true God, as well as man.

10. The scriptures never call any the true and living God; but he that is the true God. The scriptures call Jesus, the Son of the Virgin, the true God. Is. ix. 6. 1 Jn. v. 20. Therefore he is the true and great God.

11. He that made all things, whether they be visible, or invisible, whether be they thrones or dominions, or principalities, or powers, must needs be the true God. But Jesus the Son of the Virgin Mary did make all these. Col. i. 14—18. Jn. i. 1—16. He. i. 2, 3. And therefore he is the true God as well as man.

12. The blood of a mere finite creature could never obtain eternal redemption for sinners. But the blood of Jesus, the Son of the Virgin Mary, hath obtained eternal redemption for sinners. Ro. iii. 25; v. 9. He. ix. 12, 14; x. 19, 20. Therefore the blood of the Son of the Virgin, must needs be the blood of God. And so the Apostle calleth it, saying to

the pastors of the churches, ' Feed the church of God, which he hath purchased with his own blood.' Ac. xx. 28. 1 Jn. iii. 16.

13. Never was there any that could overcome death in his own power, but the true God. Ho. xiii. 14; 2 Ti. i. 10. He. i. 2. Jesus the Son of the Virgin Mary did overcome death by himself. He. iii. 14. Therefore he is the true God as well as man.

14. He that searcheth the *hearts*, and knoweth the thoughts of men, must needs be the true God. Je. xvii. 10. But Jesus the Son of the Virgin doth. Lu. v. 22; ix. 47. Jn. ii. 24, 25. Therefore he is the true God.

15. He that by his own power commandeth the raging sea, must needs be the true God. Job xxxviii. 10, 11. Pr. viii. 29. But this did Jesus the Son of Mary. Mar. iv. 39—41. Lu. viii. 24. Therefore, he is the true God.

16. He that is the WISDOM, power, and glory of God, must needs be the true God. But Jesus the Son of the Virgin is all these, as 1 Co. i. 24. He. i. 3. Therefore Jesus the Son of the Virgin must needs be true God as well as man.

SECOND.—The next thing that I am to prove, is this; namely, That by this Jesus Christ, the Son of the Virgin, the world was made: And here I shall be brief, having touched on it already. Only I shall lay down some of the scriptures, that hold forth this to be a truth, and so pass to the next things that I intend to speak of.

And therefore in the *first* place, see He. i. 2. where the Apostle is speaking of the Son of God, which Son was born of the Virgin Mary, according to these scriptures mentioned before, Mat. i. 18—23. Lu. ii. Mat. iii. 17. where God himself saith, This is my beloved Son, &c. This Son of God, saith the Apostle, by whom God hath spoken to us, by him also he made the worlds. And Col. i. the Apostle speaking of the deliverance of the saints, saith, ' who hath delivered us from the power of darkness, and translated *us* into the kingdom of his dear Son: In whom we have redemption through his blood, *even* the forgiveness of sins:' And is that all ? No, but he is (also) 'the image of the invisible God, the first born of every creature.' ver. 15. And in ver. 16, 17. ' By him were all things created that are in heaven, and that are in earth, visible and invisible, whether *they be* thrones, or dominions, or principalities, or powers: all things were created by him, and for him: And he is before all things, and by him all things consist.' Also He. i. 10. it is thus written of this Son of God, Christ Jesus the Son of Mary, 'And, Thou, Lord, in the beginning hast laid the foundation of the earth: and the heavens are the works of thine hands.' And again, John i. and the first 9 verses, the Evangelist, or Apostle, speaking of the Son, saith, ' In the beginning was the Word,' which

Word was the Son. Re. xix. 13. This Word, or Son, was with God, and the Word was God. All things were made by him, and without him was not any thing made that was made. 'In him was life; and the life was the light of men. And the light shineth in darkness; and the darkness comprehended it not.' But in the ninth verse of this first chapter of John, it is written, ' *That* was the true light, which lighteth every man that cometh into the world.' Now seeing the Lord hath brought me thus far; and because the Quakers by wresting this scripture, do not only split themselves upon it, but endeavour also to split others, I shall therefore, before I proceed any further, speak a few words to it; and they are these that follow.

The Apostle in these nine first verses, or most of them, is speaking of the divinity or godhead of the Son of Mary, and shewing that he made the world: Now in this ninth verse he speaketh of man as he is in his coming into the world, and not as he is a regenerate person. Now every man as he comes into the world, receives a light from Christ, as he is God, which light is the conscience, that some call Christ though falsely. This light, or conscience, will shew a man that there is a God, and that this God is eternal. Ro. i. 20. This light doth discover this eternal God by his works in the world; for saith the scripture before named, 'The invisible things of him (meaning God) from the creation of the world are clearly seen, being understood by the things that are made, *even* his eternal power and godhead;' This light also will reprove of sin, or convince of, and make manifest sins against the law of this eternal God: so that man, before he is regenerate, is able by that light to know that sins against the law, are sins against God, as is manifested in the unconverted Pharisees, who, (as Christ told them) had neither the love of God, nor the word of God abiding in them, Jn. v. 38, 42. yet knew sins against the law, to be sins; for they were offended at a woman for committing adultery, which act was forbidden, by the law; Mat. v. 27, 28. and it is said also, they were convicted of sin by their own consciences. Jn. viii. 7—10.

Again, The Apostle writing to the Corinthians, and admonishing them to walk orderly, 1 Co. xi. 14. turns them to nature itself, saying, 'Doth not even nature itself teach you ?' &c. This light surely is that, wherewith Christ, as he is God, hath enlightened every man that cometh into the world, which doth convince of sins against the law of God. Therefore, as the Apostle saith, Ro. i. 20. They are left without excuse. That is, they have their own conscience, that doth shew them there is a God, and that this God is to be served and obeyed; and the neglect of this will be sure to damn them, though the obedience to the law will not save them, because they are not able to make a full recompense to God for the sins that are past; neither are they able for the time to come,

If works would do it, what need is there of faith? But it is evident that works will not save, because there must be faith in the blood of Jesus the Son of Mary. to yield a full, continual, and complete obedience to the law of this almighty, infinite, and eternal God. For as many as are of the works of the law, are under the curse; for it is written, 'Cursed *is* every one that continueth not in all things which are written in the book of the law to do them. But that no man is justified by the [works of the] law, - - *it is* evident: for, The just shall live by faith.' Ga. iii. 10, 11.

But now, though Christ, as he is God, doth give a light to every one that cometh into the world, which light is the conscience, (as they themselves confess;) yet it doth not therefore follow that this conscience is the Spirit of Christ, or the work of grace, wrought in the heart of any man whatsoever; for every one hath conscience, yet every one hath not the Spirit of Christ: For Jude speaks of a company of men in his days, who had not the Spirit of Christ, Jude 19. 'These be they who separate themselves, (saith he) sensual, having not the spirit.' Yea, Heathens, Turks, Jews, Pagans, Athiests, have that also that doth convince of sin, and yet are so far from having the Spirit of Christ in them, that it is their great delight to serve their lusts, this world, their sins; whereas the Apostle saith plainly, 'If Christ *be* in you, the body is dead because of sin; but the Spirit *is* life for righteousness sake.' Ro. viii. 10. * So that those who are alive to their sins, have not the Spirit of Christ. Nay, let me tell you, the very devils themselves, who were thrown from their first state by sin, Jude 6. have such a taste of their horrible sins, 2 Pe. ii. 4. that when they did but suppose that Jesus was come to put an end to their tyrannical dealing with the world, and to bring them to judgment for their sins, (to which they know they shall be brought,) it made them cry out, 'Art thou come hither to torment us before the time?' Mat. viii. 29. James doth also signify this much unto us, where he saith, 'The devils also believe and tremble.' Ja. ii. 19. Which belief of theirs is not a believing in Christ to save them; for they know he did not take hold on their nature, He. ii. 16. But they do believe that Christ will come to their everlasting torment; and the belief of this doth make these proud spirits to tremble.

Again, Man at his coming into the world, hath his conscience given him, which doth convince of sin, Jn. ii. 9. and viii. 9. yet man, as he cometh into the world, hath not the Spirit of Christ in him; for that must be received afterward, by the preaching of the word, which is preached by the ministers and servants of Jesus Christ. This is God's usual way to communicate of his Spirit into the hearts of his elect; and this is clear in so many words, where Peter preaching to a certain number, the scripture saith, 'While Peter yet spake these words, the Holy Ghost, [or Holy Spirit,] fell on all them which heard the word.' Ac. x. 44. And again, Ga. iii. ver. 2 and 5. compared together, 'Received ye the Spirit by the works of the law, (saith the Apostle) or by the hearing of faith?' or the Gospel, which is the word of faith preached by us? Which Spirit, as Christ saith, the world cannot receive, because it seeth him not, neither knoweth him, though his children shall have fellowship with him to the great comfort of their own souls. Jn. xiv. 16, 17.

But now, this merciless butcherer of men, the devil, that he might be sure to make the soul fall short of glory, if possible, endeavours to persuade the soul that its state is good; that it hath the Spirit of Christ in it; and for a proof of the same, saith he, turn thy mind inward, and listen within, and see if there be not that within thee that doth convince of sin: Now the poor soul; finding this to be so, all on haste (if it be willing to profess) through ignorance of the Gospel, claps in with these motions of its own conscience, which doth command to abstain from this evil, and to practise that good; which, if neglected, will accuse and torment for the same neglect of others, both now and hereafter. Ro. ii. 15.

Now the soul seeing that there is something within that convinceth of sin, doth all on a sudden close with that, supposing it is the Spirit of Christ, and so through this mistake, is carried away with the teachings and convictions of its own conscience, (being misinformed by the devil) unto the works of the law; under which, though it work all its days, and labour with its might and main, yet it never will be able to appease the wrath of God, nor get from under the curse of the law, nor get from under the guilt of one sinful thought the right way, which is to be done by believing what another man hath done by himself, without us, on the cross, without the gates of Jerusalem. He. i. 2, 3. Ro. v. 15. See also for this, 1 Pe. ii. 24. He. xiii. 12. The one saith, He bare our sins in his own body on the tree; the other saith, It was done without the gate.

And thus the poor soul is most horribly carried away headlong, and thrown down violently under the curse of the law, under which it is held all its days, if God of his mere mercy prevent not; and at the end of its life doth fall into the very belly of hell.

Again, That the devil might be sure to carry on his design, he now begins to counterfeit the work of grace: Here he is very subtil, and doth transform himself into an angel of light. 2 Co. xi. 14. Now he makes the soul believe that he is its friend, and that he is a gospel minister; and if the soul will be led by what shall be made known unto it by the light (or conscience) within, it shall not need to fear but it shall do well.

Now he counterfeits the new birth, persuading them, that it is wrought by following the light that they brought into the world with them. Now he begins also to make them run through difficulties: and now, like Baal's priests, they must lance themselves with knives, &c. Now, 1656, quakers are changed to the laws of the world. Now they must wear no hatbands; now they must live with bread and water; now they must give heed to seducing spirits, and doctrines of devils, which bids them abstain from marriage, and commands them to abstain from meats, which God hath created to be received with thanksgiving, of them which love and know the truth, as in 1 Ti. iv. 1—3. Now they must not speak, except their spirit moves them, (I do not say the Spirit of Christ) though when it moves, they will speak such sad blasphemies, and vent such horrible doctrines, that it makes me wonder to see the patience of God, in that he doth not command, either the ground to open her mouth, and swallow them up, or else suffer the devil to fetch them away alive, to the astonishment of the whole world.

Object. But you will say, doth not the scripture say, that it is the Spirit of Christ that doth make manifest or convince of sin? Jn. xvi. 8.

Answ. Yes, it doth so. But for the better understanding of this place, I shall lay down this; namely, That there are two things spoken of in the scriptures, which do manifest sin, or convince of sin. *First,* The law, as saith the Apostle. Ro. iii. 20. 'Therefore by the deeds of the law there shall no flesh be justified in his sight: [viz., God's sight:] for by the law *is* the knowledge of sin.' *Secondly,* The Spirit of Christ doth make manifest, or reprove of sin, as it is written. Jn. xvi. 8, 9. 'And when he (the Spirit) is come, he will reprove the world of sin, and of righteousness, and of judgment: Of sin, because they believe not on me;' saith the Son of Mary, which is Christ.

Now the law doth sometimes by its own power manifest sin without the Spirit of Christ; as in the case of Judas, who was convinced of the sin of murder, which made him cry out, 'I have sinned;' yet at that time he was so far from having the Spirit of Christ in him, that he was most violently possessed of the devil. Lu. xxii. 3, 4.

He hanged himself immediately after, Mat. xxvii. 3—5.

Again, Sometimes the Spirit of Christ takes the law, and doth effectually convince of sin, of righteousness, and judgment to come.

Query. But you will say, How should I know whether I am convinced by the law alone, or that the law is set home effectually by the Spirit of the Lord Jesus upon my conscience?

Ans. 1. Unto this I answer. *First,* When the law doth convince by its own power, without the help of the Spirit of Christ, it doth only convince of sins against the law, as of swearing, lying, stealing, murdering, adultery, covetousness, and the like. I say, it doth only make manifest sins against the law, pronouncing a horrible curse, against thee, if thou fulfil it not, and so leaves thee; but it gives thee no strength to fulfil it completely, and continually, (which thou must do, if thou wilt be saved thereby). Now thy own strength being insufficient for these things, having lost it in Adam, thou art a breaker of the law. Here the law finds thee in thy sins, and condemns thee for thy sins: But gives thee no power to come wholly out of them; neither doth it shew thee thy right Saviour, to save thee from them (which is the Son of the Virgin Mary, the man Christ Jesus) but commands thee upon pain of eternal damnation, to continue in all things that are written in the book of the law to do them. Ga. iii. 10. And therefore if thou hast been convinced of no other sins, but what are against the law, for all thy convictions and horror of conscience, thou mayest be but a natural man, at the best, and so under the curse.

For a (farther) proof hereof take the carriage of the Pharisees towards our Saviour, who, while they trusted in Moses, crucified Jesus. 1 Co. ii. 8.

(*Obj.*) But, perhaps thou wilt say, I am not only convinced of my sins against the law, but I have also some power against my sins, so that I do in some considerable measure abstain from those things that are forbidden in the law.

(*Ans.*) This thou mayest have, and do, as thou thinkest, perfectly, as those blind Pharisees called quakers, do think that they also do, and yet be but a natural man: And therefore I pray consider that place, in Ro. ii. 14, 15. the Apostle there speaks on this wise, concerning the Gentiles' obedience to the law, 'For when the Gentiles, which have not the law, do by nature the things contained in the law, these, having not the law, are a law unto themselves: Which shew the work of the law written in their hearts.' Which work of the law, Christ as he is God, hath enlightened every one withal, that cometh into the world, Jn. i. 9. which, as the quakers say, doth convince of sin, yet of no other than sins against the law: and therefore must needs be all one light or law; for 'the law *is* light,' Pr. vi. 23. and gives 'the knowledge of sin.' Ro. iii. 20. And therefore, as I said before, so say I now again, if thy convictions are no other than for the sins against the law, though thy obedience be the strictest that ever was wrought by any man, (except the Lord Jesus the Son of Mary) thou art at the best but under the law, and so consequently under the curse, and under the wrath of God, whether thou believest it or not. Ga. iii. 10. Jn. iii. 36.

Ans. 2. But now the second thing, how thou shouldest know, whether the Spirit of Christ doth effectually set home the law upon thy conscience, or not; and therefore to speak directly to it, if the Spirit of the Lord Jesus, the Son of God, doth set home the law effectually; then the same Spirit of Christ shews thee more sin than the sins against the law. For,

(1.) It shews thee, that 'all our righteousnesses *are* as filthy rags.' Is. lxiv. 6. Thou seest all thy praying, meditation, hearing, reading, alms-deeds, fasting, reformation, and whatsoever else thou hast done, doest, or canst do, being an unbeliever, deserves at the hands of God his curse and condemnation, and that for ever: And therefore thou art so far from trusting to it, that in some measure thou even loathest it, and art ashamed of it, as being a thing abominable, both in God's sight and thine own. Phil. iii. 8. Thou countest thy own performances, when at best, and thine own righteousness, A bed too short to stretch thyself upon, and a covering too narrow to wrap thyself in. Is. xxviii. 20. And these things thou seest not *overly, or slightly, and as at a great distance, but really and seriously, and the sense of them sticks close unto thee.

(2.) It shews thee that thou hast no faith in the man Christ Jesus by nature, and that though thou hadst no other sins, yet thou art in a perishing state because of unbelief, according to that 16th of John, ver. 9, 'Of sin, because they believe not on me.' If therefore thou hast been convinced aright by the Spirit, thou hast seen that thou hadst no faith in Christ the Son of Mary, the Son of God, before conversion. It shews thee also, that thou canst not believe in thine own strength, though thou wouldest never so willingly; yea, though thou wouldest give all the world (if thou hadst it) to believe, thou couldest not.

(3.) In the next place it will shew thee, that if thou doest not believe in the man Christ Jesus, and that with 'the faith of the operation of God,' Col. ii. 12. thou wilt surely perish, and that without remedy; Also it shews thee, that if thou hast not that righteousness, which the man Christ Jesus accomplished in his own person for sinners; I say, if thou be not clothed with that instead of thine own, thou art gone for ever; and therefore saith Christ, (speaking of the Spirit) 'When he is come he will reprove the world of sin, and of righteousness' too. Jn. xvi. 8. That is, the Spirit shall convince men and women of the sufficiency of that righteousness that Christ, in his human nature,

Because faith is the gift of God. Ep. ii. 8. Phil. i. 29.

hath fulfilled: So that they need not run to the law for righteousness: 'For Christ is the end of the law for righteousness, to every one that believeth. Ro. x. 4. Again, if the Spirit of Jesus setteth home the law upon thy conscience, thou wilt freely confess, that although the law curseth, and condemneth thee for thy sins, and gives thee no power either to fulfil it, or to come out of thy sins: Yet God is just in giving that law, and 'the law *is* holy, and the commandment holy, and just, and good.' Ro. vii. 12.

(4.) Lastly, It also convinceth of judgment to come: He (viz. the Spirit) shall reprove the world of sin, of righteousness, yea, and of judgment too. Ac. xxiv. 25. Then doth the soul see, that that very man that was born of the Virgin Mary, crucified upon the cross without the gates of Jerusalem, shall so come again; even that same Jesus, in like manner as he was seen to go up from his disciples. Ac. i. 11. Yea, they that are thus convinced by the Spirit of Christ, know that God 'hath appointed a day, in the which he will judge the world in righteousness, by *that* man whom he hath ordained: Ac. xvii. 31. which is the man Christ Jesus: For 'it is he which was ordained of God *to be* the judge of quick and dead.' Ac. x. 42.

And now, O man, or woman, whoever thou art, that art savingly convinced by the Spirit of Christ, thou hast such an endless desire after the Lord Jesus Christ, that thou canst not be satisfied or content with anything below the blood of the Son of God to purge thy conscience withal; even that blood that was shed without the gate. He. xiii. 12. and ix. 14. Also thou canst not be at quiet, till thou dost see by true faith, that the righteousness of the Son of Mary is imputed unto thee, and put upon thee. Ro. iii. 21—23. Then also thou canst not be at quiet, till thou hast power over thy lusts, and corruptions, till thou hast brought them into subjection to the Lord Jesus Christ. Then thou wilt never think that thou hast enough faith. No, thou wilt be often crying out, Lord, give me more precious faith: Lord, more faith in thy righteousness; more faith in thy blood and death; more faith in thy resurrection: And Lord, more faith in this, that thou art now at the right hand of thy father in thy human nature, making intercession for me a miserable sinner. Jn. xvi. 5—7. 1 Ti. ii. 5. He. vii. 24, 25. And then, O poor soul, if thou comest but hither, thou wilt never have an itching ear after another gospel. Nay, thou wilt say, if a presbyter, or anabaptist, or independent, or ranter, or quaker, or papist, or pope, or an angel from heaven, preach any other doctrine, let him be accursed, again and again. Ga. i. 8. And thus have I briefly shewed you.

First, How Christ, as he is God, doth enlighten every man that comes into the world.

---

* 'Overly,' carelessly, negligently, inattentively.—Ed.

Secondly, What this light will do, viz. shew them that there is a God, by the things that are made; and that this God must be worshipped. Ro. i. 20.

Thirdly, I have shewed you the difference between that *light* and the Spirit of Christ the Saviour.

Fourthly, I have also shewed you, how you should know the one from the other, by their several effects.

The first light convinces of sins, but of none other than sins against the law; neither doth it shew the soul a Saviour, or deliver (for that is the work of the Spirit) from the curse wherewith it doth curse it. But I shewed you, that when the Spirit of Christ comes and works effectually, it doth not only shew men their sins against the law, but also shews them their lost condition, if they believe not in the righteousness, blood, death, resurrection, and intercession of Jesus Christ, the Son of Mary, the Son of God. Jn. vi. 44. and xvi. 24. Mat. iii. 17. He. i. 9. And thus much I thought necessary to be spoken at this time, touching the nature of conviction.

THIRD. Now in the Third Place. Though I have spoken something to this thing already, namely, concerning our Lord the Saviour, yet again, in few words, through grace, I shall shew, that he was made, that is, born of a woman, and made under the law, to redeem them that are under the law. My meaning is, That God is our Saviour.

First, And for this, see Is. xlv. 15. where you have these words, 'Verily, thou *art* a God that hidest thyself, O God of Israel, the Saviour:' And ver. 21, 22. you have these words, '*Who* hath declared this from ancient time? - - *Have* not I the LORD? And *there is* no God else beside me; a just God and a Saviour; *there is* none beside me. Look unto me, and be ye saved, all the ends of the earth:' Why, who art thou? 'For I *am* God, and *there is* none else.' Also in Is. liv. 5. 'For thy Maker *is* thine husband; the LORD of hosts *is* his name; and thy Redeemer the Holy One of Israel; the God of the whole earth shall he be called.' Read also ver. 6-8. of that chapter. I could abundantly multiply scriptures to prove this to be truth, but I shall only mind you of two or three, and so pass on; the first is in Jude, ver. 25. 'To the only wise God our Saviour *be* glory.' And Ac. xx. 23. Jn. iii. 16; 1 Jn. v. 20.

Object. But you will say, How is God a Saviour of sinners, seeing his eyes are so pure that he cannot behold iniquity; Hab. i. 13.

Answ. For answer hereunto. · When the fulness of the time was come' wherein the salvation of sinners should be actually wrought out, 'God sent forth his Son, (which Son is equal with the Father, Jn. i. 1. xvii. 5. and x. 30.) made of a woman, made under the law,' (that is, he was subject to the power and curse of the law) to this end, 'to redeem them that (are, or) were under the law,' Ga. iv. 4, 5. that is, to deliver us 'from the curse of the law, being made a curse for us.' Ga. iii. 13. From whence take notice, that when the salvation of sinners was to be actually wrought out, then God sent forth the everlasting Son of his love into the world, clothed with the human nature, according to that in Jn. i. 14. He. ii. 14. and 1 Ti. iii. 16. which saith, 'God was manifest in the flesh,' that is, took flesh upon him.

Second, This Son of God, which is equal with the Father, did in that flesh, which he took upon him, completely fulfil the whole law: So that the Apostle saith, 'Christ *is* the end of the law for righteousness to every one that believeth.' Ro. x. 4. This righteousness which this Christ did accomplish, is called, 'The righteousness of God.' Ro. iii. 22. This righteousness of God, is by the faith of Jesus Christ, unto all, and upon all them that believe: My meaning is, it is imputed to so many as shall by faith lay hold on it. This is also part of the meaning of that speech of the Apostle: 'As many of you as have been baptized into Christ, have put on Christ.' Ga. iii. 27. That is, by faith have put on the righteousness of Christ, with the rest of that which Christ hath bestowed upon you, having accomplished it for you. This is also the meaning of the Apostle, Co. ii. 9, 10. where he saith, 'for in him (that is the Son of Mary, chap. i. 13, 14.) dwelleth all the fulness of the godhead bodily. And ye are complete in him.' That is, in his obedience and righteousness; which also the Apostle himself doth so hard press after, Phil. iii. 8, 9. saying, 'doubtless, and I count all things *but* loss, for the excellency of the knowledge of Christ Jesus my Lord;' which Lord was crucified by the Jews, as it is in 1 Co. ii. 8. 'for whom, (that is for Christ,) I have suffered the loss of all things (as well the righteousness of the law, in which I was blameless, Phil. iii. 6. as all other things) and do count them *but* dung, that I may win Christ: And be found in him, not having mine own righteousness, which is of the law, but that which is through the faith of Christ, the righteousness which is of God by faith:' which is 'unto all, and upon all them that believe.' Ro. iii. 22. That place also in the ninth of Daniel, ver. 24, 25, holdeth forth as much where prophesying of the Messias, he saith, that it is he that came 'to finish the transgression, and to make an end of sins, and to make reconciliation for iniquity, and to bring in everlasting righteousness.' Now that the righteousness of the Son of Mary is it, mind the 26th verse, where he saith thus, 'And after threescore and two weeks shall Messiah be cut off,' that is, Christ shall be crucified, 'but not for himself,' that is, not for any sin that he hath committed; for he committed none. Then surely, it must be for the sins of the people, Jn. xi. 50. as the high priest said, 'It is expedient for us that one man should die for the people,' which man was the true Messias, Da. ix. 24. which also is the Son of Mary. Mat. i. 18—23. And the Son of God, Mat. iii. 17. And also the true God, 1 Jn. v. 20. And this Messias, this Son of the Virgin, this Son of God, this true God, did not die for himself, for he had not offended; neither did he fulfil the law or finish transgression, and bring in everlasting righteousness for himself, for he had not sinned, 1 Pe. ii. 22. therefore it must of necessity follow, that this righteousness of God, this everlasting righteousness, is imputed to all, and upon all them that believe. Ro. iii. 22; 2 Co. v. 19—21. But,

Thirdly, this Messias, this Son of Mary, this Son of God, this true God, he was put to death for the sins that his children had committed, according to that saying, 'Herein perceive we the love *of God*, because he laid down his life for us.' 1 Jn. iii. 16. Also in Ac. xx. 28. the apostle speaking to the pastors of the churches, saith, 'feed the church of God, which he hath purchased with his own blood.' See also Zec. xii. 10.

Now, I would not be mistaken. I do not think, or say, that he died in his divine nature, but as it is written, he in his own body on the tree did bear our sins; 1 Pe. ii. 24. which tree was the cross. Col. ii. 14. And as the apostle saith again, who ' when he had by himself purged our sins, sat down on the right hand of the majesty on high.' He. i. 3. And again, the apostle speaking of this glorious God, saith on this wise, (being before speaking of his godhead) in Col. i. 19—22. ' For it pleased *the Father* that in him should all fulness dwell; and having made peace through the blood of his cross by him to reconcile all things to himself: by him, *I say*, whether *they be* things in earth, or things in heaven. And you, who were sometime alienated and enemies in *your* mind by wicked works, yet now hath he reconciled.' But how? Why in ver. 22. he tells you, that it is ' in the body of his flesh through death, to present you holy and unblameable and unreprovable in his sight.' That is, Christ, who is the true God, after that he had finished all actual obedience on earth, did in the power and strength of his godhead, Jn. xix. 30 and x. 18. yield up himself to the wrath of his Father, which was due to poor sinners (and that willingly) Is. lxiii. 3. [see He. ix. 14. and read that verse with understanding] according to that saying in 1 Pe. iii. 18. ' For Christ also hath once suffered for sins, the just for the unjust:' That is, the Son of God for poor sinners: ' that he might bring us to God, being put to death in the flesh, but quickened by the Spirit.' Again, 1 Pe. iv. 1. ' Forasmuch then as Christ hath suffered for us (not for himself Da. ix. 26.) in the flesh, (in his own body which he took of the Virgin, 1 Pe. ii. 24.) arm

yourselves likewise with the same mind: ' That is, let us die to sin as he did, that we might live to God as he did, and doth. Ro. vi. 10. And thus have I briefly showed you,

I. That the Son of Mary is very God.

II. That he made the world.

III. That he is our Saviour, and how.

IV. That he died for sinners, and how, namely, not in his divine nature, but in his human, in his own body, and in his own flesh, Col. i. 22. redeeming his church with his own blood, Ac. xx. 28. and with his own life. 1 Jn. iii. 16. Jn. x. 18.

We shall now pass on to some other things (the Lord willing) touching his burial, resurrection, ascension, intercession, second coming, resurrection of the body, and eternal judgment.

HIS BURIAL PROVED.—I shall prove by several scriptures that *he was buried*, and so pass on. Therefore see that place, Mat. xxvii. ver. 57. and so forward. After that Jesus the Son of God had been crucified a while, he gave up the ghost; that is, he died; and after he had been awhile dead, Joseph of Arimathea went in to Pilate, and begged the body of Jesus, and Pilate gave consent thereto. And Joseph took the body of Jesus and wrapped it in clean linen, and laid it (viz. the body of Jesus) in his own tomb, and rolled a stone upon the mouth of the sepulchre, and departed. Also in Lu. xxiii. 51—53. The apostle Paul also teacheth so much, 1 Cor. xv. 3, 4. where he saith, ' For I delivered unto you first of all that which I also received, how that Christ died for our sins according to the scripture; And that he was buried.' Again, in Ac. xiii. 29. the apostle speaking there of Jesus Christ, saith, ' And when they had fulfilled all that was written of him, they took *him* down from the tree, and laid *him* in a sepulchre.' And so much touching the burial of Jesus Christ the Son of God.

RESURRECTION. In the next place, I am to prove, That that very man, whom the Jews did crucify between two thieves, called Jesus Christ, *did rise again*. That very man, with that very body wherewith he was crucified upon the cross, did rise again out of the grave in which he was laid. And this I shall prove 1. by scripture, 2. by the testimony of angels, 3. by Christ's own words after he was risen, and 4. by the testimony of the apostles in the scripture.

First therefore consider, Ps. xvi. verse 10. where the prophet speaks on this wise of Christ's resurrection; ' For thou wilt not leave my soul in hell; neither wilt thou suffer thine Holy One to see corruption.' Which words the Apostle Peter cites in Ac. ii. from ver. 22 to 32. also Is. xxvi. 19. in the person of Christ saith, ' Thy dead *men* shall live, *together with* my dead body shall they arise.' See also Jn. xx. 15, 16. where mention is made of his appearing unto Mary Magdalen, and he called her Mary, and she called him master; which signifies that he was risen, and that she knew him after his resurrection; for he was come out of the grave, see ver. 6, 7, 8. Again, another scripture is that in Lu. xxiv. 1—3. The disciples of Jesus coming to the sepulchre, thinking to anoint the body of Jesus, found the stone that was on the mouth of the sepulchre rolled away; and when they went in, they found not the body of the Lord Jesus; and at this they were troubled and perplexed. ver. 4. But as two of them went up to Emmaus, and were talking of what had befallen to Jesus, Jesus himself drew near, and went with them, ver. 15. Another scripture is that in Mar. xvi. ver. 9. which saith on this wise, ' Now when *Jesus* was risen early the first *day* of the week, he appeared first to Mary Magdalen, out of whom he had cast seven devils.' Where take notice how the Holy Ghost lays it down in these words, out of whom he had cast seven devils. To intimate to us the certainty, that it was the same Jesus that was born of the virgin Mary, who did many miracles, and cured many diseases, who did also cast seven devils out of Mary Magdalen, that did rise again. Yea, saith the Holy Ghost, it was the same Jesus that did work such a wonderful miracle on Mary, he appeared to her first, out of whom he had cast seven devils. And let these scriptures suffice to prove the resurrection of the Son of God.

Second, you shall have the testimony of the holy angels also by the scriptures. And first look into Mar. xvi. 3—7. the words are these, ' And they (viz. the disciples) said among themselves, Who shall roll us away the stone?' They had a good mind to see their Lord, but they could not, as they thought, get away the stone which covered the mouth of the sepulchre. ' And when they looked (that is, towards the sepulchre) they saw that the stone was rolled away: for it was very great. And entering into the sepulchre, they saw a young man (that is, an angel) sitting on the right side, clothed in a long white garment; And they (the disciples) were affrighted. And he saith unto them, Be not affrighted (you have no cause for it) Ye seek Jesus of Nazareth, which was crucified: he is risen, he is not here; behold the place where they laid him.' What scripture can be plainer spoken than this? Here is an angel of the Lord ready to satisfy the disciples of Jesus, that he was risen from the dead. And lest they should think it was not the right Jesus he spoke of, Yes, saith he, it is the same Jesus that you mean; you seek Jesus of Nazareth, do you not ? Why he is risen, he is not here. But do you speak seriously, and in good earnest? Yea surely, if you will not believe me, behold the place where they laid him. This scripture, or testimony is very clear to our purpose. But again, the next place is in Mat. xxviii. ver. 3—7. In the third verse

there is an angel (as before) bearing witness of the resurrection of Jesus. ' His countenance was like lightning, and his raiment white as snow: And for fear of him the keepers did shake, and became as dead *men*. And the angel answered and said unto them, (viz. to the women who came to seek Jesus) Fear not ye:' but let them that seek to keep the Lord in his grave fear if they will; for you have no ground of fear, who seek Jesus who was crucified; He is not here, for he is risen; he cannot be in body here and risen too: If you will not believe me, come, see where the Lord lay, and go quickly and tell his disciples that he is risen from the dead; and behold, he goeth before you into Galilee, there shall you see him. But shall we be sure of it? Yea, saith the angel, Lo, it is I that have told you. See how plainly this scripture also doth testify of Christ his resurrection. Here, saith the angel, you seek a Saviour and none will content you but he, even the same that was crucified: Well you shall have him, but he is not here. Why, where is he then? He is risen from the dead. But are you sure it is the same that we look for? Yea, it is the same that was crucified. ver. 5. But where should we find him? Why, he goeth before you into Galilee, where he used to be in his life-time, before he was crucified: And that you might be sure of it, there to find him, know that he is an angel of God that hath told you. ver. 7. And thus have you in brief the testimony of the angels of God, to witness that Jesus the Son of the virgin, the Son of God, is risen from the dead.

They are they that had need to fear and tremble, for they deny the faith of the Son of God.

Object. But you will say, might they not be deceived? Might not their eyes dazzle, and they might think they did see such a thing, when indeed there was no such matter?

Ans. Well, because it is so difficult a matter, to be persuaded of the truth of this thing, that Christ is raised again out of the grave, that very man, with that very body; though these things that have been already spoken, might be enough (through grace) to satisfy, yet because of the unbelief of some, we shall turn to some more of those infallible proofs that are spoken of in Ac. i. 3. to prove the point yet more clear.

Third, Do but see how the Lord doth deal with an unbelieving disciple. Jn. xx. ver. 23—29. You shall see in the 23d verse, Christ after his resurrection is talking with his disciples, but Thomas was not with them. But when the disciples saw him again, they said unto him, We have seen the Lord, ver. 25. but Thomas would not believe them. Another time Jesus comes to his disciples again, and then Thomas was with them; then so soon as the Lord had said, ' Peace be unto you,' he turned himself to Thomas, and said to him; ' Thomas, reach hither thy finger, and behold my hands; and reach hither thy hand, and thrust *it* into my side: and be not faithless, but believing.' ver. 27.   As much as if the Lord should have said, Come Thomas, thou hast doubted of the truth of my resurrection very much; thou sayest that thou wilt not believe, except thou do feel with thy fingers the print of the nails, and do thrust thy hand into my side.   Come Thomas, reach hither thy finger, and behold my hands, and see if there were not the nails driven through them; and reach hither thy hands and thrust them into my side, and feel if I have not the very hole in it still, that was

O how doth the Lord condescend, to the end he might strengthen the faith of one that is weak. made with the spear that the soldier did thrust into it, and be not so full of unbelief, but believe that my resurrection is a glorious truth.

Another infallible proof, is that in Lu. xxiv. from the 36th, to the end of the 44th verse.   In ver. 30. it is said that the Lord, (even while they were talking) 'stood in the midst of them and saith unto them, Peace be unto you:' But they were so far from being at peace, that they were terrified, and supposed that they had seen a spirit.   And Jesus said to them, 'Why are ye troubled, and why do thoughts arise in your hearts?' What, do you think that I am a spirit?   Do you think your eyes dazzle?   'Behold my hands and my feet.'   Look well upon me, and see my hands, and the holes in them, and likewise my feet, and the holes in them, and know that it is I myself, and not a spirit, as you suppose.   Know, that it is I myself, and not another.   Doth your hearts fail you?   Then take hold of me with your hands, yea, 'handle me, and see; for a spirit hath not flesh and bones, as ye see me have.   And when he had thus spoken he shewed them *his* hands and *his* feet.'   As if he had said, Come my disciples, take special notice of me, do not be daunted, nor affrighted, but consider that it is I myself.   Well, they could not believe as yet, but wondered that such a thing as this should be: And while they were thus wondering he will give them another infallible proof: And 'he said unto them, have you here any meat?' ver. 41.   As if the Lord had said, Come my disciples, I see that you are very full of unbelief, if you have here any meat, you shall see me eat before you all.   And they gave him a piece of a broiled fish, and of an honey-comb, 'And he took it, and did eat before them.'   Again, ver. 42. the Lord strives with another infallible proof against their doubting, saying, My disciples, do you not remember what discourse you and I had before I was crucified, how that I told you, that all things must be fulfilled which were written in the law of Moses, and in the prophets concerning me. Mar. viii. 31; xiv. 21.   Another infallible proof was, that appearance of his at the sea of Tiberias,

where he came to them on the shore, and called them, and provided for them a dinner, and wrought a notable miracle while he was there with them at that time, namely, the catching of 153 great fishes, and yet their net break not.   (Jn. xxi. read that whole chapter, and Ac. x. 41.)   Which as it was a great miracle, so it did also show his power and authority over his creatures.   Besides his eating and drinking with his disciples after his resurrection; and also his preaching to them. Ac. i. 3.   This is not the least, viz. that he was with his disciples on earth forty days, which was almost six weeks, speaking to them the things concerning his kingdom: which was a mighty confirmation of their faith in his resurrection.

Fourth, I shall now briefly touch two or three scriptures, the which hold forth his disciples' testimony of his resurrection.   And the first is in Ac. x. 40, 41.   In which place the Apostle speaking of the Lord Jesus, saith, 'Him God raised up the third day, and shewed him openly,' yet 'Not to all the people, but unto witnesses chosen before of God, *even* to us (saith the Apostle) who did eat and drink with him after he rose from the dead.'   Again, Ac. iv. 10; and xiii. 29—31.   The words run thus (the Apostle speaking of Jesus, saith) 'And when they had fulfilled all that was written of him, they took *him* down from the tree, and laid *him* in a sepulchre.   But God raised him from the dead: And he was seen many days of them which came up with him from Galilee to Jerusalem, who are his witnesses unto the people.'   See 1 Co. xv. 1—8.   And thus far touching his resurrection from the dead.

Ascension. In the next place I am to prove that this very man, Christ Jesus, the Son of the virgin, in his very body, the same body that was crucified, is above the clouds and the heavens.   And though this is made light of by those men called quakers, and other infidels of this generation: Yet I am sure that it will prove true to their cost, who reject it as erroneous and vain.   But to prove it, *First*, I shall prove that he is ascended. *Secondly*, that he is ascended above the clouds, and the heaven.

First, that he is ascended, see Ep. iv. 8—10. 'Wherefore (saith the Apostle) When he ascended up on high, he led captivity captive, and gave gifts unto men.   Now that he ascended, what is it but that he also descended first into the lower parts of the earth, he that descended is the same also that ascended (again) up far above all heavens.'

Again, read Jn. xx. 17. where Christ after his resurrection from the dead, saith to Mary Magdalen, 'Touch me not; for I am not yet ascended to my Father:' That is, I have not yet ascended with this my body wherewith I was crucified on the cross.   'But go to my brethren, and say unto them (meaning his disciples) I ascend unto my

Father and your Father; and *to* my God and your God.'

Object. But in that place, (may some say) Ep. iv. 10. He that descended, is said to be the same that ascended. Now there was no human nature with God in heaven before the world was; Therefore if he be but the same that was with the Father from all eternity, then the humanity of the Son of Mary is not ascended into heaven.

Ans. For answer, It is clear from Jn. i. 1. that the Word or Son of God, as he was a Spirit, was with the Father before the world was. Tit. i. 2. But now, in the fulness of time, that is, when that time that the Father and he had concluded on, was come, ' God sent forth his Son (which was with him before the world was, Jn. xvii. 5.) made of a woman;' Ga. iv. 4. that is, born of a woman. ' And took upon him the form of a servant, and was made in the likeness of men.' Phi. ii. 6, 7. Now as he was born of a woman, as he was in the likeness of men, so he ascended to the right hand of his Father, in our nature. And for this, I pray turn to Ac. i. 9—11. and there you shall find, that he is the same that was born of the virgin, that very man that was crucified; if you compare ver. 3. with ver. 9, 10, 11. you will find it so to be. Now in ver. 9. after he had spoken many things while they beheld, that is, while his disciples looked on him, he was taken up, that is, he was taken up from them into heaven, as in ver. 11. and a cloud received him out of their sight. And while they looked up stedfastly towards heaven, as he went up (which heaven, was not within them; if it had, they needed not to have looked toward the clouds and the heaven without them) behold two men stood by them, not in them, in white apparel, which also said (that is, the two men, or angels which stood by them said) Ye men of Galilee, why stand ye gazing up into heaven? Here again, they did not look within them, but stood gazing or looking after the Lord Jesus, the Son of Mary, who was carried away from them in a cloud. ver. 9. But why (say the angels) do you stand gazing so much into heaven: your master will come again after a certain time. Mat. xxv. 19; Mar. xiii. 34. For, This same Jesus, namely, which was crucified, which rose again, and hath been with you these forty days, which also you see go into heaven, shall so come, (namely in a cloud) as ye have seen him go into heaven. Ac. i. 3. But shall he not lose his body before he come again? No say the angels, he shall so come, that is, as ye have seen him go; in like manner, that is, with the same body. Or else I am sure he cannot come in the same manner, if he lose his body before he comes again; for he went thither with that body. But that same Jesus that was crucified, is he that went, or ascended up into heaven. If you compare Luke xxiv. v. 39 to 44 with the 50th and 51st verses of the same chapter,

you may clearly find it so to be. And therefore if he come again in like manner, he must come again with the same body wherewith he was crucified.

Object. But you will say, The scripture saith, he that descended is the same that ascended, which to me (say you) implies, none but the Spirit's ascending?

Ans. For answer, we do not say, (as I said before) that it is another that ascended, but the very same: That is, the very same Christ, that was with the Father from everlasting did come down from heaven: That same Christ also that came down from heaven did ascend up thither again; only, he descended without a body from heaven, and took flesh and blood upon him from the virgin. And though he descended without a body, yet he, the very same Christ that descended without a body, the same did ascend again with a body, even that very body that he took of the virgin Mary. See Lu. xxiv. from 39th to 51st verses. Ac. ii. 30, 31; Jn. xv. 1; 1 Co. ix. 24, 25. Now let me give you a similitude, for it is warrantable; for both Christ and his apostles did sometimes use them, to the end, souls might be better informed. The similitude is this, Suppose there come into thine house a man that is naked, and without clothing, though he go out of thy house again well clothed, yet the same man that came in without clothing, is the same man also that goes out of thy house, though very well clothed. Even so it is in this case, The Lord Jesus came into the womb of the virgin, Spirit, Mat. i. 18. but he came out of the womb clothed with a body, and went up into heaven again clothed with a body. Compare Lu. xxiv. 39. with Ac. i. 11; and ii. 30, 31.

Now also I shall lay down some few things to be considered, for the better clearing of it.

Consider 1. That he did say to his disciples that he would go away from them. Jn. xiv. 3. and xvi. 7; Mat. xxv. 19. Yea, saith he, I go and prepare a place for you, and then I will, after a long time, come again, and take you to myself, that where I am, that is, whither I am going, there ye may be also. Now, I say, if Christ had not gone from his disciples (for that was his meaning) touching his bodily presence; I say, if he had not gone away from them, in respect of his bodily presence, he had said more than he had performed; which is horrible blasphemy once to assert; which going of his, is his going into heaven. See 1 Pe. iii. 22.

Consider 2. That there it was that he was to receive the *promise* of the Father, Lu. xxiv. 49, which promise was the shedding forth in an abundant manner the blessed Holy Ghost. And for this see Ac. ii. 33—36. 'Therefore being by the right hand of God (which is in heaven) exalted, and having received of the Father the promise of the Holy Ghost, he hath shed forth this, which ye now see and hear. For David is not ascended into the heavens: but he saith himself, the Lord said unto my Lord, Sit thou on my right hand, until I make thy foes thy footstool. Therefore let all the house of Israel know assuredly (for 'tis very true) that God hath made that same Jesus, whom ye have crucified, both Lord and Christ.'

Consider 3. That if he were on earth, he could not be a priest. He. viii. 4. Now the man Christ Jesus is a glorious priest, He. vii. 24. in the heavens. He. ix. 24. And therefore he is able to save to the uttermost, all that come to God by him, seeing he ever liveth to make intercession for them. (This *man,* vii. ver. 25.)

Consider 4. If he be not gone into heaven, both his own, and his Apostles' doctrine is false; yea, the witness of the angels also, which to think were damnable infidelity in any man. 1 Pe. iii. 22. Ac. i. 9—11.

Consider 5. Know that he is gone into heaven, because the scriptures say he is; which is the very truth of God, spoken by his holy Apostles and prophets: Yea, holy men of God, spake them as they were moved by the Holy Ghost. Ep. vi. 9; 1 Pe. iii. 22; He. ix. 24.

Consider 6. If thou sayest that that man is not gone into heaven, then thou must also conclude that he is still in the grave; and if so, then thou sayest that the prophets, apostles, angels, Christ, God, and all are liars, who have testified these things in the scriptures for glorious truths. Is. xxvi. 19; Ac. x. 40—43; xiii. 30—39; and i. 9—11; Re. i. 17, 18; and ii. 8. And as the Apostle saith of himself, and the rest of the Apostles and ministers of Jesus Christ, 'And we are found false witnesses of God; because we have testified of God that he raised up Christ: whom he raised not up, if so be that the dead rise not. - - - But now is Christ risen from the dead, *and* become the first fruits of them that slept. For as by man *came* death, by MAN *came* also the resurrection of the dead.' 1 Co. xv. 15, 20—22.

Second, Now I am to prove, that he is above the clouds and the heavens. My meaning is, he is above the lowest heavens. For there are three, as appears in 2 Co. xii. 1—4. I knew a man in Christ, (saith Paul there) caught up into the third heaven. Now,

The scripture speaking of the highest implies a lower.

Heaven in scripture, is taken sometimes metaphorically, and sometimes properly. *First,* Metaphorically it is taken for the church and people of God, as in Re. xii. 12. *Second,* Properly, it is taken for the material heaven, where the sun, moon, and stars are placed, as in Ge. i. ver. 8, 14, 15, 16. compared together: above which heaven, Jesus the Son of Mary is ascended. Therefore I pray you consider with me a little.

Consider 1. That when he went into this heaven into which he is gone, he went AWAY from his disciples, as it is written, If I go not away, the comforter will not come. Jn. xiv. 2, 3; Jn. xvi. 7; Ac. i. 9—11. So that he did not go into a heaven within them in his person and human nature. If so, he must needs go into that heaven without, above the clouds and the stars. Ge. i. 8, 5, 16.

Consider 2. He was caught away in a cloud; yea, and was caught upwards from them, as it is Ac. i. 9—11. and carried away into heaven; yea, and his disciples stood gazing or looking up after him into heaven, which heaven must needs be that above the clouds. (1.) If you consider the posture of the disciples, they looked upwards after the cloud that did take him away. (2.) Consider the manner of his going, it was in a cloud. (3.) He was received out of their sight. (4.) And so received up into heaven; which heaven must needs be above the clouds, where God is in his special presence. Job xxii. 12—14. But further,

Consider 3. That those believers that are alive at this day in the body, 'are absent from the Lord,' 2 Co. v. 6. but now, if the man Christ were ascended into that heaven within them, he would neither be 'absent from them,' nor they from him; but in that he is *absent* from them touching his bodily presence, and they from him touching the same, it is evident that that heaven into which he is ascended, must needs be without, above the clouds.

Consider 4. That that heaven into which the man Christ is ascended, must contain him till the time of the restitution of all things, as in Ac. iii. 21. into which heaven he hath been ascended above sixteen hundred years by computation. And I am sure there is not a saint that doth live in the world half so long, before he fall asleep, and be gathered to his fathers; so that that heaven into which he is ascended, is not within, but must needs be that above the clouds. But

Consider 5. That he that ascended from his disciples, was a man, with flesh and bones, not a spirit only; for handle me, and see, (saith he) for a spirit hath not flesh and bones, as ye see me have. Lu. xxiv. 39, 50, 51. Now let the adversaries show by the scriptures, that there is any place in them called heaven, that is able to contain a man of some four or five feet long, the space of fifteen or sixteen hundred years; besides that: therefore, it must needs be that heaven without, which is above the clouds and stars.

Consider 6. That heaven into which the Lord Jesus that man is ascended must not contain him always; for, saith the Apostle, 1 Th. iv. 16. 'The Lord himself shall descend from heaven with a shout, with the voice of the archangel.' So that there is another descending from that heaven into which he is ascended; and his descending from that heaven is to this end, namely, to take his people to himself, as it is ver. 17. so that it is clear that it is not any heaven *within* thee, into which the man Christ that was born of the Virgin Mary is ascended, but it must needs be that heaven without, which is above the clouds. He. xii. 22. If thou consider, that the place into which he ascended, even the heaven into which he is entered, is the same place where all the deceased saints are in their spirits: 'Therefore,' saith Paul, 'I desire to depart, and to be with Christ, which is far better.' Now Paul did not in this place, Ph. i. 23. mean the enjoying of Christ only in the Spirit; for that he enjoyed in great measure when he spake these words; but he spake of a dying, and being with Christ after this life is ended; as is clear if you compare the 20th to the 26th verses together, being absent from him while he was here in the body. 2 Co. v. 6. For 'whilst we are at home in the body, we are absent from the Lord.'

Consider 7. That that heaven into which the man Christ is ascended, is not into his church on earth; but into heaven without, above the clouds and the stars. Jn. xvi. 7; and xiv. 1—3; 1 Ti. ii. 5. And this David doth prophesy of, Ps. xlvii. 5. where he saith, 'God is gone up with a shout, the LORD with the sound of a trumpet.' Now Christ, as God merely, could not go up, being no less in one place than another; but as God-man, or in his human nature, he went up; as will clearly appear, Ep. iv. 8—10. where he speaketh of his triumph over all the enemies of his people at his resurrection and ascension into heaven above the clouds.

Consider 8. When Christ doth descend from that heaven into which he is now ascended, his saints and he will meet one another, just in the air, according to the scripture, 1 Th. iv. 16, 17. 'For,' (saith he) 'the Lord himself shall descend from heaven with a shout, with the voice of the archangel, and with the trump of God: and the dead in Christ shall rise first: (that is, they shall come out of their graves.) Then we which [shall be saved] are alive (at that day) and remain shall be caught up together with them in the clouds, to meet the Lord in the air, and so shall we ever be with the Lord.'

Pray mark here a little, and see what heaven the man Christ is ascended into, and see if it be not the heaven without, above the sun, moon, and stars.

When Christ and his saints do meet a second time together, the one ascends and the other descends; the one is caught up in the clouds towards the heaven, the other descends from heaven towards the earth, and they must needs meet one another just in the air, that is, between the heaven and the earth. So then, the one coming from heaven and the other from the earth, and their meeting being in the air, which is between heaven and earth, is an undeniable demonstration, that that heaven into which the man Christ is ascended, must needs be that heaven

without, above the sun, moon, and stars. Ph. iii. 20; 1 Th. i. 10. And thus much touching the Son of Mary, his ascending up into the heaven without above the clouds. Ac. i. 9—11; and iii. 21. and 1 Pe. iii. 22.

INTERCESSION. In the next place, now I shall prove the intercession of the man Christ Jesus to be in the heaven that I have been speaking of; though some have mocked at it, and others have called it juggling; which names here I shall not mention, only I shall admonish them, that they do not blaspheme the truth and Son of God in his intercession.

I shall quote some of the scriptures that hold out this truth, and so pass on.

First, And first of all, see Ps. xvi. 4. where David prophesying of the intercession of Christ, saith, 'Their sorrows shall be multiplied *that* hasten *after* another God, (speaking of the wicked) their drink-offerings of blood will I not offer, nor take up their names into my lips.' Now, compare this with He. viii. 4. where he saith, 'if he were on earth, he should not be a priest.' And He. ix. 24. 'For Christ is not entered into the holy places made with hands, (meaning the temple which Solomon built) *which are* the figures of the true; but into heaven itself, now to appear in the presence of God for us:' 'wherefore he is able also to save them to the uttermost, that come unto God by him, seeing he ever liveth to make intercession for them.' He. vii. 25.

Second, But you will say, is there a man made mention of here? Yes, for the scripture saith, '*There is* one God, and one mediator between God and men, the man Christ Jesus.' 1 Ti ii. 5. And in that 8th to the Hebrews made mention of before; where the Apostle is speaking of Christ's priestly office, as he is in the heavens, compared with other priests that are on earth; he saith ver. 3. 'For every high priest is ordained to offer gifts and sacrifices: wherefore (speaking of Christ) *it is* of necessity that this man have somewhat also to offer. For if he were on earth, he should not be a priest, seeing that there are priests that offer gifts according to the law,' which law was the law of Moses, ch. ix. from 19 to 23. where also he is speaking of the priesthood of the priests under the law, and their offering of the blood of bulls and goats (ver. 12 compared with ver. 19—21.) And of the Lord Jesus the high priests of saints, and of his blood (ver. 14 compared with ver. 24.) Now as men under the law did offer up the blood of bulls and goats, so the man Christ Jesus did offer up his own blood to his Father; and this you may clearly see, if you compare He. ix. 14. where he saith, 'How much more shall the blood of Christ, who through the eternal Spirit offered himself without spot to God, purge your consciences from dead works to serve the living God? [with] He. x. 12. where he saith, 'But this man (meaning the Son of the Virgin, ch. ii. 14 compared with Mat. i. 21.)

after he had offered one sacrifice for sins, for ever
sat down on the right hand of God;' again, He. 7.
the chapter I mentioned before, you shall find his
intercession plainly held forth, if you read ver. 22.
and so on, where the scripture saith, ' By so much
was Jesus made a surety of a better testament.
And they truly were many priests (meaning the
priests under the law) because they were not suffered to continue by reason of death:' (that is, the
high-priest under the law, could not live ever in
this world, because it was appointed to all men
once to die.) Re. ii. 8. But when he speaks of Christ
Jesus, he saith on this wise, ' But this *man*,
because he continueth ever, hath an unchangeable
priesthood. Re. i. 18. Wherefore he (this man) is
able also to save them to the uttermost that come
unto God by him, seeing he (this man) ever liveth
to make intercession for them. And thus in brief
have I proved through the assistance of the Lord,
the intercession of the Son of Mary, which is also
the Son of God. And this concerning Christ's
priestly office, might serve also for a proof of his
being in the heaven without, above the stars. But
all men may see (unless they be blind) that these
are the truths of our Lord Jesus Christ, and of
God his Father; and that those men that oppose
them (as the quakers do) are very violently possessed of the devil, and besides themselves; and
have neither the truth of God, nor his Spirit in
them. 2 Jn. ix. 10. Jn. v. 38, 42.

[CHRIST JUDGE OF QUICK AND DEAD.] And now
through the assistance of the Lord, I shall come
to the last that I promised, and that is to prove,
that this very man Christ, will come to judge the
quick and the dead. And *first*, I shall prove the
truth itself, viz., That that man shall come again
to judge the world, quick and dead. *Second*, I
shall shew you that his coming will be very shortly.
Third, What shall be done at his coming. *Fourth*,
Who shall stand when he shall come, and who not.

*First, That that man that was born of the
Virgin Mary shall come again to judge the quick
and the dead*, read 2 Ti. iv. 1. 'I, (saith Paul)
' charge *thee* therefore before God, (speaking to
him, even to Timothy, and so to all believers) ' and
the Lord Jesus Christ, who shall judge the quick
and the dead at his appearing and his kingdom.'
Now if you would know who this Lord Jesus is,
look into Ac. x. 28. and you shall see it was Jesus of
Nazareth; would you know who that was? read
Mat. ii. towards the end, and you shall see it was
the Son of Mary the Virgin, who was espoused to
Joseph the carpenter. But read Ac. x. ver. 38 to 42. you
shall find these words, 'God anointed Jesus of
Nazareth with the Holy Ghost and with the power:
who went about doing good, and healing all that
were oppressed of the devil; for God was with
him: And we are witnesses of all things which he

did both in the land of the Jews, and in Jerusalem;
whom they slew and hanged on a tree, (even Jesus
of Nazareth) Him God raised up the third day,
and shewed him openly; not to all the people, but
unto witnesses chosen before of God, *even* to us,
who did eat and drink with him after he rose from
the dead. And he commanded us to preach unto
the people, (that is, God commanded us) and to
testify (that is, to be bold in our preaching) that
it is he (namely, Jesus of Nazareth, whom the
Jews did thus crucify) which was ordained of God
to be the judge of quick and dead.' This is he
also that is spoken of in Ac. xvii. 30, 31. 'The times
of this ignorance God winked at; (meaning men's
being without the gospel) but now commandeth all
men everywhere to repent: Because he hath appointed a day (which day is the day of judgment,
Mat. xii. 36.) in the which he will judge the world in
righteousness, by *that* man (namely, Jesus of
Nazareth) whom he hath ordained, (compare this
with that in Ac. x. 38 to 42.) *whereof* he hath given
assurance unto all *men* (that is, hath given a sure
sign unto all men) in that he hath raised him, (that
is, in that he hath raised Jesus of Nazareth) from
the dead.' This also is Christ's own meaning,
Mat. xxiv. where speaking of his second coming, he
styleth himself the Son of man, saying; 'And then
shall appear the sign of the Son of man,' ver. 30.
and ' so shall also the coming of the Son of man
be.' ver. 27. So shall also the coming of the Son of
man be, ver. 37. So shall also the coming of the
Son of man be. ver. 39. Where, by the way, it is
observable to see how the Lord of life and glory
doth in this chapter, where he speaketh of his
second coming, for the most part style himself the
Son of man. Sure he doth it to this end, because
he will not have his humanity and the doctrine
thereof, to be razed out from under heaven: For
he knew, that in the last days, there would come
mockers 'walking after their own lusts, and saying,
Where is the promise of his coming.' 2 Pe. iii. 3. I
could multiply scriptures to prove this doctrine of
his second coming, as He. ix. ver. 28; 2 Pe. iii; 2 Th. i. 6—8.
Lu. xxi. Mat. xxiv. and xxv. Re. xxii. 7,12, and 20; 2 Co. v. 10. Ro. xiv. 10.
Ac. xxiv. 25. But,

*Secondly, I will shew you that his coming will be
shortly*. It is true, no man can tell neither the
day nor the hour, yet so far as the scriptures will
give us light into the nearness of his coming, so
far we may go. And if you read Mat. xxiv. you shall
see many *signs* of his coming spoken of.

1. There is falling away from the faith spoken
of. And that hath been fulfilled and is fulfilling
every day.

2. Wars and rumours of wars is another sign
that his coming doth draw nigh, even at the doors.

3. The love of many waxing cold, is another
sign that it is nigh, even the coming of Christ.

And how cold is the love of many at this day? They that were hot two or three years ago, are now grown lukewarm and cold. They are cold in the Lord's appearing. They are cold in the profession of the gospel. They are cold in love to the saints, they are cold in the worship of God; Yea, very cold, which is a notable demonstration that the coming of the Lord draweth nigh.

4. The stars falling from heaven; (That is professors falling from the faith which once they professed) is another sign that the coming of the Lord is at hand. And how many professors do you see now a-days, fall from the doctrine of God, and his Son Jesus Christ, as though there were no such thing as a world to come, and no such thing as a Lord Jesus Christ, and his second coming.

5. Many poor souls will go on in their profession with lamps without oil, just before his second coming. Mat. xxv. 1—7. And the Lord knows that most of the professors of this generation, are such kind of professors, yea, very foolish professors, which is another sure sign, that the coming of the Lord draws nigh. *These things I do but hint at, though I enlarge upon them. Lu. xviii. 8.*

6. When the time of Christ's second coming is at hand, there will be but a very little faith in the world. And the Lord knows, that there be many, who are now as high as lucifer, that at that day for want of faith will be thrown down to the sides of the pit : even in the very belly of hell. *Say 1 Jn. iii. 3 to thy heart, and compare thy condition with it, and thou wilt find this a glorious truth.*

7. Another sign of Christ's second coming, is the carnal mindedness of the most of the world; and the very carriages of almost all men now living do discover this truth to be at this day fulfilled, and know that when they shall say peace and safety, then sudden destruction comes, and they shall not escape. 1 Th. v. 1—4.

8. Before Christ's second coming, there shall come many false Christs and false prophets, and shall shew great signs, and wonders, to seduce if it were possible the elect. Mat. xxiv. 24. Mar. xiii. 22. And is not this more clearly fulfilled in our days than ever it was, especially among those men called quakers, who being as persons, whose consciences are seared with an hot iron, and they being sealed up unto destruction, do some of them call themselves Christ, and shew great signs, (as their quaking) and such a legal holiness, as makes the simple admire them, and wonder after them, which shews the coming of Christ to be very nigh.

9. Before Christ's second coming, there shall come scoffers in the world, walking after their own lusts, 2 Pe. iii. 3. and if ever this scripture was fulfilled, it is fulfilled on these men called quakers: For they are the men, that at this day make a mock at Christ's second coming, which shall be from heaven without; 1 Th. i. 10. Phi. iii. 20. and therefore saith the Holy Ghost, these mockers shall be such as shall say, where is the promise of his coming? For since the fathers fell asleep, all things continue as they were, see 2 Pe. iii. 3—7. And there you shall see their mocking and the reason of it. Read and the Lord give thee understanding. But I would not have thee think that I speak at random, in this thing, Know for certain, that I myself have heard them blaspheme; yea, with a grinning countenance, at the doctrine of that man's second coming from heaven above the stars, who was born of the Virgin Mary. Yea, they have told me to my face, that I have used conjuration, and witchcraft, because what I preached was according to the scriptures. I was also told to my face, that I preached up an idol, because I said, that the Son of Mary was in heaven, with the same body that was crucified on the cross; And many other things have they blasphemously vented against the Lord of life and glory, and his precious gospel. The Lord reward them according as their work shall be.

I could have hinted in many other things which Christ and his Apostles have shewed to be signs of his coming. But I shall commend the holy scriptures unto thee, which are able to make the man of God perfect in all things, through faith in the Lord Jesus. 2 Ti. iii. 17.

Now you have also *the manner* of his coming how it shall be, most notably laid down in the scriptures. I shall hint in a few things touching it.

1. He will come when there is but very few looking for his coming. 'When they shall say, peace and safety; then sudden destruction cometh.' 1 Th. v. 1—3. Which sudden destruction will be at his second coming, for that is it which the Apostle spake of in those three verses. Then will all the world be caught at such an unexpected time, that it will come upon them, even as a snare cometh upon those creatures that are caught in it. As it is written Lu. xxi. 35. 'For as a snare shall it come on all them that dwell on the face of the whole earth.' Which is all on a sudden, before they are aware.

2. He cometh with all his saints and angels. Then will the Lord descend from that heaven, into which he is now ascended, as it is written in 1 Th. iv. 16. Then will he come, and all his saints with him, as Jude saith in his Epistle, 15. Then shall Abel and Enoch, Noah and Abraham, David and Job, Peter and Paul: Together with all the saints which have been, now are, or hereafter shall be, and they shall sit on the throne with the Lord Jesus Christ, as in Mat. xix. 28. Before whom shall all the nations of the world be gathered, as it is written. Joel iii. 12. 'Let the heathen be wakened (or raised out of their graves, Da. xii. 2.) and come up to the valley of Jehoshaphat: for there will I sit

to judge the heathen round about.' Which never was yet accomplished, though it shall certainly be, in God's time: To the astonishment, and everlasting damnation of all those that shall continue mocking, or sinning against God and his Christ.

3. He shall come in a flaming fire, (when he doth come again: he will come in such a manner, as will make all that shall be found in their sins rather seek to creep under a mountain, than to meet the Lord of glory. Rev. vi. 15. As Isaiah saith, 'For, behold, the LORD will come with fire, and with his chariots like a whirlwind, to render his anger with fury, and his rebuke with flames of fire.' Is. lxvi. 15. 'To execute judgment upon all, and to convince all that are ungodly among them, of all their ungodly deeds which they have ungodly committed, and of all their hard *speeches*, which ungodly sinners have spoken against him,' Jude 15. as I shall shew farther by and by.

Third, And therefore in the next place, I shall shew you, *what shall be done when he is come.*

1. When Christ is come the second time, they that are in their graves shall arise, and come forth of their graves (as I said before) in which they have lain according to that in Jn. v. 28, 29. Where Christ saith, 'Marvel not at this: for the hour is coming, in the which all that are in the graves shall hear his voice, and shall come forth; they that have done good, unto the resurrection of life; and they that have done evil, unto the resurrection of damnation.' You will say, Are these graves spoken of here, the graves that are made in the earth? Yea, that they are, and for a further proof of the same, look into Da. xii. 2. Daniel there speaking of the same thing saith, 'And many of them that sleep in the dust of the earth shall awake, (or arise) some to everlasting life, and some to shame *and* everlasting contempt' (or damnation.)

I shall not stand here to dispute any distinctions of the resurrections, only prove that the dead shall arise; and that is a clear truth from the scriptures. Ac. x. 42. Re. xx. 11—14; and 1 Th. iv. 16. 1 Co. xv. 52. 'The dead shall be raised.'

2. He shall call all men and women to an account for all their *close sinful thoughts, words and actions; then will the secrets of all hearts be made manifest. Then shall all thy adulterous, and thievish, and covetous, idolatrous, and blasphemous thoughts be laid open, according to that saying, 'Their consciences also bearing witness, and *their* thoughts the mean (time, or) while accusing or else excusing one another.' Ro. ii. 15. But when? Why, 'In the day when God shall judge the secrets of men by Jesus Christ.' ver. 16. See also 1 Co. iv. 5. 'Therefore judge nothing before the time.' What time is that? Why, when the Lord comes; what

will he do? He 'will bring to light the hidden things of darkness,' that is, all those cunning, close, hidden wickednesses that thou in thy life-time hast committed; yea, he will 'make manifest the counsels of the hearts;' that is, the most hidden and secret things that are contrived and plotted by the sons of men. Then shall all the midnight whoremongers be laid open with all their sins; Then thou (it may be) who has committed such sins as thou wouldest not have thy neighbour, thy father, thy wife, thy husband, or any one else know of for thousands, then thou shalt have them all laid open, even upon the house tops. Lu. xii. 3. Then thou that hatest God's children; his ways, his word, his Spirit; then thou that makest a mock at Jesus of Nazareth's second coming, then thou that livest in open prophaneness, or secret hypocrisy, then I say, will be such a time of reckoning for you, as never was since the world began, then you that shall die in your sins, will cry to the mountains, Fall on us, and cover us from the face of him that sits on the throne, and from the wrath of the Lamb (which Lamb is the Man Christ Jesus. Jn. i. 29.) And ah, my friends! If the very looks of God be so terrible, what will his blows be, think you? Then if all thy idle words shall be accounted for, as it is written, 'But I say unto you, That every idle word that men shall speak, they shall give account thereof in the day of judgment, Mat. xii. 36. and also all thy filthy actions shall be then regarded in such sort, as thou shalt receive a just recompense for them. And know, saith the scripture, 'that for all these *things*, God will bring thee into judgment.' Ec. xi. 9. Then

Though sinners will be unwilling to come to judgment, yet this will be their misery, God will bring them. Mal. iv. 1.

Thou that art an unbeliever, shalt be sure to fall under the judgment for all thy sins. (1.) Thou must give an account. (2.) Thou must fall in the judgment. Oh my friends, there are hot days a-coming for all those that are found out of the Lord Jesus: Behold, saith Malachi, 'The day cometh, that shall burn as an oven; and all the proud, yea, and all that do wickedly, shall be stubble: and the day that cometh shall burn them up, saith the LORD of hosts, that it shall leave them neither root nor branch.' iv. 1. The day of judgment will burn like an oven, and all that have not the righteousness of Christ upon them shall be as stubble. Ah friends, put a red hot oven and stubble together, and what work will there be! Even the one will burn and destroy the other.

3. When Christ doth come the second time, another end of his coming will be to purge out all things that offended in this kingdom. Mat. xiii. 41, 42. 'The Son of Man shall send forth his angels, and they shall gather out of his kingdom all things that offend, and them which do iniquity; And shall cast

---

* 'Close,' secret, not *disclosed.*—Ed.

them into a furnace of fire; there shall be wailing and gnashing of teeth.' There are many things that do offend in his kingdom now: namely

(1.) The lukewarm professor, he doth offend, (*a.*) the Lord, (*b.*) his people. But then thou lukewarm offending *professor* shalt offend the church of God no more.

(2.) The loose professors do also offend God, Christ and his church. (*a.*) He scandals the gospel by his loose walking, and naughty carriages. (*b.*) He doth make the world blaspheme the name of God by the same. (*c.*) He grieves the hearts of God's people. Phi. iii. 18. But know that thou also shalt be taken away from offending any more, God, Christ, and his saints, and thou shalt have weeping and gnashing of teeth, for thy thus offending. Mat. xviii. 6, 7.

4. Another end of Christ's second coming, is to cut off all the *ignorant* persons that are in the world. There is a generation of poor souls that do think to be excused for their ignorance: Alas! saith one, I am a poor ignorant man, or woman; and therefore I hope that the Lord will have mercy upon me: we cannot, say others, do as such and such, and will the Lord condemn us? And thus poor souls, as they are in the broad way to destruction, lest they should miss of the way

Men seeking to get encouragement from their ignorance, do more harden themselves in sin, and so are in greater danger of eternal damnation.

to hell; do swallow down by clusters, that which will poison them, body and soul for ever and ever.

Quest. But you will say, What, will not the Lord have mercy on ignorant souls?

Answ. Not on those who live and die in their ignorance. He himself hath said, Is. xxvii. 11. ' For it is a people of no understanding: therefore he that made them will not have mercy on them, and he that formed them will shew them no favour.' Again, Paul also in that 2 Th. 1. 8. saith, that when Jesus Christ shall come to judge the world, he doth come to take vengeance on all ' them that know not God, and that obey not the gospel of our Lord Jesus Christ.'

But ye will say, Who are those ignorant persons, that shall find no favour at that day? or how doth the ignorance discover itself? I shall only mention

The xxvii. Is. 11th verse is a notable confutation of the ignorant's hypocritical hope, where he saith, ' He that made them will not have mercy on them, and he that formed them, will show them no favour.'

three or four sorts of men; and leave thee to the scriptures, which if thou read them diligently, will further lay them open before thee. And,

(1.) The profane scoffer, who makes a mock at the truths of God, and so goes on in his sins, for this see in 2 Pe. iii. 3. which the apostle attributes to their ignorance. ver. 5. And therefore he likens them to brute beasts, ch. ii. 10, 12. who ' walk after the flesh in the lust of uncleanness,' and ' speak

evil of the things that they understand not; and shall utterly perish in their own corruption;' who because they understand not the scripture, nor the power of God in them, speak evil of the truths therein contained, and think the Lord like unto themselves. Ps. l.

(2.) The formal professor, who hath only a notion of the gospel, and some seeming holiness, but wants gospel faith: such are called foolish virgins, Mat. xxv. 2, 3. to whom Christ will say in that day, Verily, ' I know you not.' Add hereto, those that think it enough to confess Christ with their mouths, and profess that they know God, but deny him in their works; such notwithstanding all their profession, shall, if they so continue, perish eternally, being abominable, disobedient, and to every good work reprobate, or void of judgment, that is, ignorant. Tit. i. 16.

(3.) The legal righteous man or woman, though they walk blameless, as touching the righteousness that is in the law: For they being ignorant of God's righteousness, go about to establish their own righteousness, as reading, hearing sermons, prayers, public or private, peaceableness with their neighbours, fasting, alms, good works as they count them, just dealings, abstinence from the grosser pollutions of the world, stricter obedience to the commandments of the first and second table; all which with many other things may be comprehended in their own righteousness, and it is grounded on their ignorance, and goes on in rebellion; and such ignorant persons shall in that day perish, not submitting through ignorance to the righteousness of God, Ro. x. 3. compared with Lu. xix. 27. where Christ saith, that when he shall come the second time, he will command those his enemies, who submitted not themselves to him, [who is called the righteousness of God, Is. xlvi. 13.] or would not have him to reign over them, to be slain before his face.

(4.) Those whose hearts are set upon the world, and follow the alluring persuasions of it; the Lord calls such fools, [Lu. xii. 20. and Pr. vii. 7.] who go after it (viz. the world, held forth by a similitude of a woman with the attire of an harlot) as an ox to the slaughter, or a fool to the correction of the stocks, till a dart strike through his liver, as a bird hasteth to the snare, and knoweth not that it is for his life: and *knows* not, mark, it is through ignorance. ver. 23.

5. A fit end of Christ's coming, is, that his righteous ones might shine as the sun in the glory, or kingdom of their father. Mat. xiii. 43. There are many things that do hinder the people of God from shining forth as the sun now.

As, They have a body of death, which makes them fetch many a groan in their journey to Canaan. Ro. vii. 24; 2 Co. v. 2. They meet with many a sad temptation, which also makes them in heaviness many a time. 1 Pe. i. 6. They have also many other things that do hinder their shining now; but then the body of death shall be left off. My meaning is, that sin shall be no more in the natures of God's people then: Their bodies that are now so vile, shall then be made like unto the glorious body of the Son of God, 'Who shall change our vile body, that it may be fashioned like unto his glorious body, according to the working whereby he is able even to subdue all things unto himself.' Ph. iii. 21.

6. Another end of Christ's coming shall be to take an account of his children, how they have laid out their talents, that he hath committed to their trust. Mat. xxv. 19; Ro. xiv. 12; 2 Co. v. 10.

7. Another end of his coming is, to set up his kingdom, which will be glorious indeed at his appearing. 2 Ti. iv. 1; Ro. viii. 19—21. I do but touch these things, because I would hasten towards a conclusion; many other things might have been spoken to, but at this time I shall forbear.

But you will say, Who shall stand when he appears? Why, I told you before, that 'the ungodly shall not stand in the judgment, nor sinners in the congregation of the righteous.' Ps. i. 5. Let him be close or profane, as I told you even now, all shall be laid open, all shall be made manifest, all shall come into judgment.

Ah poor soul! It is not then thy brave words will save thee; it is not thine eloquent tongue that will then do thee any good: if thou be without the wedding garment, thou wilt be speechless, as in Mat. xxii. 12. But thou that art a converted person, shalt stand in the judgment; thou that art born again shalt enter into the kingdom, and none else. Jn. iii. 5; Re. xxi. 27.

But how shall I know that I am born again?

(1.) Why, if thou art born again, then thou knowest that thou wast not born a Christian at first. Ep. ii. 1—3. 'You hath he quickened, who were dead in trespasses and sins.'

(2.) Thou knowest that once thou hadst no faith in the Lord Jesus; and wert convinced of sin because thou didst not believe in the Son of Mary. Jn. xvi. 9.

(3.) Thou seest all true joy through the blood and righteousness of the Son of Mary. 1 Co. xv. 57; Ro. vii. 25.

(4.) Art thou born again? Then thou canst not be quiet till thou seest God smile, and lift up the light of his countenance upon thee, 2 Co. iv. 6; Ps. iv. 6. and that through the face of the Son of Mary, the Son of God.

(5.) Thou knowest that God hath given thee thy faith. Phi. i. 29; Ep. ii. 8.

(6.) Art thou born again? Then thou knowest that the doctrine of the Son of Mary the Virgin, is a right doctrine. 2 Jn. 9.

(7.) Then also thou lookest for the personal appearing of the Son of Mary from heaven in the clouds, the second time. He. ix. 28. Re. i. 7.

These things, though plain, yet if the Lord set them home upon thy conscience, may be profitable both to thee and me. Therefore let us examine the matter a little. And

Examine 1. Thou thinkest that thou art a Christian; thou shouldest be sorry else: Well, But when did God shew thee that thou wert no Christian? When didst thou see that: And in the light of the Spirit of Christ, see that thou wert under the wrath of God because of original sin? Ro. v. 12. Nay, dost thou know what original sin means? Is it not the least in thy thoughts? And dost thou not rejoice in secret, that thou art the same that thou ever wert? If so, then know for certain that the wrath of God to this very day abideth on thee. Jn. iii. 36. And if so, then thou art one of those that will fall in the judgment, except thou art born again, and made a new creature. 2 Co. v. 17.

Exam. 2. Thou thinkest that thou hast been born again, ('tis well if thou hast) but least thou shouldest deceive thy poor soul, I pray thee consider, when did the Spirit of the Lord Jesus shew thee, that thou hadst no faith in thee by nature? And when did the Spirit of Christ convince thee of sin, because thou didst not believe in him? It may be thou hast been convinced of sins against the law, by the law, and thine own conscience, as the Pharisees were. Jn. viii. 9, and Ro. iii. 20. Ay, but when didst thou see thyself a lost creature for want of faith in the son of Mary? If not, thou hast not yet been savingly convinced by the Spirit of Christ; for that, when it convinceth effectually of sin, it convinceth of unbelief; though thou hast been never so much convinced of sins against the law, if thou hast not seen thyself under the power and dominion, guilt and punishment of sin, because thou didst not believe in Christ, thou hast not yet been savingly convinced; for that's one work of the Spirit to convince of sin, 'Because they believe not on me,' saith Jesus the Son of Mary, who was espoused to Joseph the carpenter: But on the contrary, dost thou not say in thy heart, thou never hadst thy faith to seek, but hast always believed with as good a faith as any one alive? If so, then know for certain that thou hast no faith of the operation of God in thee, according to God's ordinary working; and if so, then know, that if the Son of Man should come to judge the world at this moment of time, that thou with all thy faith (thou thinkest thou hast) wouldst fall in the judgment. 2 Th. ii. 12.

Exam. 3. Art thou born again? Then thou seest that thy great sin was want of faith in the Son of Mary. Then thou seest that it is he that was sent of God to die for the sins of the world, Jn. i. 29, and iii. 16—19. Ac. xiii. 38, 39. and that thou art complete in him, without any works of the law, Ro. iv. 5. then thou rejoicest in Christ Jesus, and puttest no confidence in the flesh, Phi. iii. 3. yet thou rejoicest in the flesh and blood of the Son of Mary, knowing that his flesh is meat indeed, and his blood is drink indeed, Jn. vi. 55. out of which thou wouldest very willingly make thy life all thy days; out of his birth, obedience, death, resurrection, ascension, and glorious intercession, now at the right hand of his Father, He. vii. 24, 25. but if thou art wavering in these things, know that thou art but a babe at the best, and for ought thou knowest, God may cut thee off in thy unbelief, and cast thee into utter darkness, where there shall be weeping and wailing and gnashing of teeth.

Exam. 4. Art thou born again? Then thou seest all true peace and joy comes through the blood of the Son of Mary, and his righteousness, as in Ro. vii. 25, and 1 Co. xv. 57. there are many poor souls that are taken with raptures of joy, and false conceited consolation, [Jn. xvi. 20.] which doth come from the devil, and their own deceitful hearts; but their joy shall be turned into mourning and sorrow of heart, Lu. vi. 24, 25. but thou that art a Christian in deed, and not in word only, rejoicest in Christ Jesus the Son of Mary; yea, though now you see him not, yet believing, you rejoice with joy unspeakable and full of glory. 1 Pe. i. 8. And these two things are the fruits of thy faith, and of thy joy.

(1.) The Lord Jesus Christ is very precious unto thee. 1 Pe. ii. 7.

(2.) Thou dost purify thine heart by this faith, and the power of the Spirit of Christ, which thou hast received into thy soul. Ro. viii. 13. Ac. xv. 9, 1 and Jn. iii. 3. But if thy guilt of sin goes off, and convictions go off any other way than by the blood and righteousness of the Man Christ Jesus, thy guilt goes off not right, but wrong, and thy latter end will be a very bitter end without faith and repentance; for it is his blood through which all true peace comes, Col. i. 20. and there is no other name under heaven given among men, whereby we should be saved, but by the Lord Jesus of Nazareth, Ac. iv. ver. 10—12. compared together.

Exam. 5. Art thou born again? Then thou canst not be quiet till thou doest see God lift up the light of his countenance upon thee; yea, thou hast such a desire after the light of God's countenance, that, all the glory, riches, honour, pleasure, profits, &c. of this world will not satisfy, till thou doest see God to be a reconciled Father to thee in the Lord Jesus Christ, as it is Ps. iv. 6. Jn. xiv. 8. Ps. xxxv. 3. Then thou wilt not be quiet till thou dost hear from the Son of Mary, which is the Lord of glory, such a voice as this, Son be of good cheer, thy sins are forgiven thee: And 'my grace is sufficient for thee.' 2 Co. xii. 9; 1 Co. ii. 8. But if thou canst content

thyself with anything below this, thou wilt, when all comes to all, be found but a rotten-hearted professor, who will have thy portion among the slothful ones, who will fall in the judgment of the Son of Man, when he comes in flaming fire with his mighty angels. 2 Th. i. 8.

Exam. 6. Art thou born again? Then thou knowest that God hath given thee thy faith that thou hast in his Son: Then thou art to say through grace, there was a time in which I had no faith; there was a time in which I could not believe in the Son of God for eternal life. ' But God, who is rich in mercy, for his great love wherewith he loved us, even when we were dead in sins (and unbelief; which is the greatest;) hath quickened us together with Christ, by grace ye are saved,' Ep. ii. 4, 5. 'through faith.' ver. 8.

Exam. 7. Art thou born again? Then thou knowest that the doctrine of the Son of God, the Son of Mary, is a right doctrine, which is this:

That the Son of God which was with his Father before the world was, (Jn. i. 1; xvii. 5.) came into the world in the fulness of time, and was made in the likeness of man. (Phi. ii. 7.) being made of a woman or virgin, made under the law, to redeem them that were under the law. Ga. iv. 4. And that was done in this wise. What the law could not do in that it was weak through the flesh; that is, through our flesh; God sending his own Son in likeness of sinful flesh, and for sin, condemned sin in the flesh, that is, condemned him in the flesh for the sins of poor sinners: For this, compare Ro. viii. 3. 2 Co. v. 21. with Ga. iii. 13. and it will appear clearly to be the truth of God: Also, that this Son of God, which is the true God, as well as the Son of Mary, did bear our sins in his own body on the tree, 1 Pe. ii. 24. and did spill his own blood, which is also the blood of God, Ac. xx. 28. that he died, and was laid in Joseph's sepulchre, Jn. xix. 38—42. and rose again the third day, Ac. x. 40. that very Man, Lu. xxiv. 39—45. and ascended up into heaven in a cloud, Ac. i. 9—11. and there ever lives to make intercession for us, *that very man.* He. vii. 24, 25; viii. 3; x. 12.

Exam. 8. And in the last place, If thou art a Christian, then thou lookest for that very Jesus again, whom the Jews did crucify, Jn. xix. whom God raised again, as it is 1 Th. i. 10. I say, thou lookest, thou waitest, thou hasteneth after the coming of this Lord Jesus, which doth deliver thee from the wrath to come. 2 Pe. iii. 10—12. He. ix. 26—28; 1 Th. i. 10. Yea, thou knowest, that this very man shall so come in like manner, as his disciples did see him go into heaven, which was a very man, Lu. xxiv. 39. compared with ver. 50, 51. of the same chapter. Yea, in a cloud he went away from his disciples, and in the clouds he shall come again, Re. i. 7. to judge all that are in their graves, Jn. v. 28, 29. Da. xii. 2. and shall receive all that look for, and love his second coming, to himself. He. ix. 27, 28. And they shall be for ever with him. 1 Th. iv. 16, 17. But the wicked shall be cast into eternal damnation. Mat. xxv. 46. These things, I say, if thou be a Christian indeed, thou believest, and ownest, and the faith of them doth purify thy heart, 1 Jn. iii. 3. and wean thee from this world, and the things thereof; and if it is not from this principle; that is, if thy obedience do not flow from this faith, which is the faith of God's elect, as I have proved at large, thy obedience, thy zeal, thy self-denial, thy holiness, righteousness ; yea, all that thou canst do, is but sin in the sight of the great God of heaven and earth. He. xi. 6. Ro. xiv. 23. For all true sanctification comes through the name of the Lord Jesus Christ, by the operation of the Spirit of God. 1 Co. vi. 11. 'But ye are washed, but ye are sanctified, but ye are justified in the name of the Lord Jesus, and by the Spirit of our God.' And in Ca. i. 3. 'Thy name *is as* ointment poured forth, therefore do the virgins love thee.'

Well then, seeing this is a truth of so great concernment, I beseech you, seek to be thoroughly rooted into it by faith. And that thou mayest so be, examine thy heart; yea, beg of God to help thee to examine it, and to throw out all that fancy that thou takest instead of faith; also throw away all thine own wisdom; yea, thy own righteousness also, and come to God in the name of the Son of Mary, which is the Son of God, and beg faith of him, true faith, the faith of the operation of God; such a faith as he gives to his own elect, which will shew thee clearly of these things; so that thou shalt not deceive thyself with a fancy of them; and the advantages will be many.

Advantage 1. It will comfort thy heart against persecutions, temptations, and cross providences, as also James saith to his persecuted brethren ; 'Be patient (my brethren, saith he), stablish your hearts, for the coming of the Lord draweth nigh.' Ja. v. 8.

Advantage 2. It will through grace, wean thy heart and affections abundantly from this world, and the things therein. 'Who is he that overcometh the world, (saith John) but he that believeth that Jesus is the Son of God ?' 1 Jn. v. 5. Who is he also that purifies his heart, but he that looketh for the second coming of Christ from heaven to judge the world ? as in 1 Jn. iii. 3. compared with 2 Pe. iii. 10, 11.

Advantage 3. Hereby thou wilt be able to judge of all doctrines whatsoever, though they come never so nigh the truth, yet if they be not indeed the very truth, thou wilt find them and their doctrine liars. Re. ii. 2. 1 Co. ii. 15.

Advantoge 4. If thou beest thoroughly set down in this doctrine, even in the faith of this doctrine which I have held forth unto thee, thou wilt not be taken with any other doctrine whatsoever. What is the reason I pray you, that there are so many giddy-headed professors in these days, that do stagger to and fro like a company of drunkards, but this, They were never sealed in the doctrine of the Father, and the Son ? They were never enabled to believe that that child that was born of the virgin Mary, was the mighty God. Is. ix. 6. No, saith Christ, he that is built upon this rock, (meaning the faith of himself, which is to believe that the Son of Mary is the Christ of God, Mat. xvi. 16,) the gates of hell shall not prevail against him. ver. 18.

Advantage 5. The faith of this doctrine, will make thee labour in the work of God in the world. Oh, it will liven thy heart in the work of the Lord ; especially, if thou livest in the faith of thy interest in Christ, it will make thee labour to be found watching when thy Lord shall return from the wedding ; that when he doth come, thou mayest open to him immediately. Lu. xii. 35, 36.

Now seeing the coming of the Lord Jesus Christ is so nigh, even at the doors, what doth this speak to all sorts of people (under heaven) but this?

Admonition 1. First, to see whether they have oil in their lamps or not; that is, to search and see, whether the Spirit of the Man Christ Jesus be in them or no ; for he that hath not the Spirit of Christ in him, is none of Christ's. Ro. viii. 9. Thou that hast not the Spirit of Christ in thee, why, at that day (let thy profession be what it will) he will say to thee, Depart, I know you not, Mat. xxv. and if so, then thy latter end will be worse than thy beginning, as in 2 Pe. ii. 20.

Admonition 2. Then what will become of all the profane, ignorant, scoffers, self-righteous, proud, bastard-professors in the world ? If the children of God shall 'scarcely be saved, where shall the ungodly, and the sinner appear ?' 1 Pe. iv. 18.

Admonition 3. Then what will become of all those that creep into the society of God's people without a wedding garment on ? Why, it will be said unto them, Friends, how came you hither ? Take them, and bind them hand and foot, and cast them into utter darkness; 'There shall be weeping and gnashing of teeth.' Mat. xxii. 11—13.

Admonition 4. Then what will become of all those that mock at the second coming of the Man Christ, as do the Ranters, Quakers, drunkards, and the like ? Why read their doom in Mat. xxiv. 50, 51. 'The Lord of that or these servants, shall come in a day when they look not for *him*, and in an hour that they are not aware of, and shall cut them asunder, and appoint them their portion with the hypocrites,' And 'there shall be weeping and gnashing of teeth.'

Admonition 5. Then what doth this speak to

the Lord's own people? Surely this, that they should be in a watchful posture. Mar. xiii. 37.

(1.) Watch therefore over your own hearts, least they should be over-charged with surfeiting and drunkenness, and the cares of this life, and so that day come upon you unawares; for as a snare shall it come upon all the dwellers upon the face of the earth, as it is in Lu. xxi. 34—36.

(2.) Watch over the devil's temptations. Oh, have a care in the first place, lest by any means, as the serpent beguiled Eve, so your minds should be corrupted from the simplicity that is in Christ: And the rather, because at this day he is very busy with his doctrines, and his ministers; trying all ways, if by any means he might deceive you with fair speeches, and enticing carriages; what a fair shew in the flesh, yet denying the Lord, and refusing to be justified by the blood of Jesus the Son of Mary, the Son of God. Watch I say over the devil touching doctrines, for he labours as much this way as any way, for he knows that if he can but get you to lay a rotten foundation, he is sure of you, live as godly in your conceit as you will, and therefore, it is worth your observation, in that xxivth of Mat. when Christ is speaking of the signs of his coming, he breaks forth with a warning word to his disciples, to beware of false teachers, ver. 4. the very first words that he answers to a question that his disciples put to him is this, 'Take heed that no man deceive you.' Again, ver. 11. 'And many false prophets shall rise, and shall deceive many.' And in ver. 24. he saith again, 'For there shall (come or) arise, false Christs, and false prophets, and shall shew great signs and wonders; insomuch that, if it were possible, they shall deceive the very elect.'

(3.) Take heed that he doth not deceive you in point of worship, that he make you not slight any of the ordinances of God; for if he do, he will quickly make way for another temptation.

(4.) Take heed also that you have not your lamps to trim when the bridegroom comes; if you have, you may peradventure be ashamed and blush before him at his coming. 1 Jn. ii. 28. Therefore content not yourselves with a profession of Christ, and no more, for the devil may deceive, yea, doth deceive a professing people many times. And if he will deceive a professing generation, he must come in this manner: Under the name of Christ. With a fair shew in the flesh of outward holiness. Ga. vi. 12. He must come 'with good words and fair speeches.' Ro. xvi. 18. Now though he come to drunkards, swearers, whoremongers, thieves, liars, murderers, and covetous persons, in his black colours; yet if he will come to deceive a professing party, he must appear like an angel of light. 2 Co. xi. 14. And the reason why souls are deceived by him in these his appearances, is, because they

are not able to distinguish betwixt the law and the gospel, the convictions of conscience by the law only, and convictions by the Spirit, but do (though they profess the Lord Jesus) give ear to every wind of doctrine, and being unstable, as Peter saith, do fall into the temptations of the devil, in wresting the scriptures to their own destruction. 2 Pe. iii. 16.

Admonition 6. In a word, you that have not yet laid hold on the Lord Jesus Christ, for eternal life, lay hold upon him; upon his righteousness, blood, resurrection, ascension, intercession, and wait for his second coming to 'judge the world in righteousness.' Ac. xvii. 31. And you that have laid hold, I say to you, lay faster hold on your Lord Jesus, 'Who hath ears to hear, let him hear.' Mat. xiii. 43.

Now, that thou mayest the more clearly understand my faith in the doctrine of God's dear Son, I have thought good to hold forth again the doctrine of the former treatise by way of question and answer, as followeth.

Quest. Seeing there are many false Christs gone out into the world, according as was prophesied of in former times by the Lord himself. Mat. xxiv. 5, 23. And seeing (if we be saved) we must be saved by a Christ; for he that misses of him (saith the scriptures) cannot be saved, because there is no way to come to the Father but by him, as it is written. Jn. xiv. 6. Ac. iv. 12. How therefore, is the knowledge of the true Christ to be attained unto, that we may be saved by him?

Ans. Indeed to know Christ, (God's Christ) is as the scripture saith, the one thing necessary, Lu. x. 42. without which all other things will avail nothing: And therefore I shall according to the scriptures, (1.) Tell you what God's Christ is. And, (2.) How the knowledge of him is attained unto. And therefore, God's Christ is true God, and true man. *That he is true God*, is manifest by that scripture, in Is. ix. 6. where it is said, 'unto us a child is born, unto us a Son is given: and the government shall be upon his shoulder: and his name shall be called Wonderful, Counsellor, the mighty God, the everlasting Father, the Prince of Peace.' Also 1 Jn. 5. 20. And we are in him that is true, (saith the apostle) *even* in his Son Jesus Christ. This is the true God, and eternal life. See He. i. 8. Jn. i. 12. Ro. ix. 5. Jn. xx. 28. *That he is true man*, see again, Is. ix. 6. where it is said, 'Unto us a child is born, unto us a Son is given; and compare it with Mat. i. 21. where it is said, 'And she shall bring forth a Son, and thou shalt call his name JESUS: for he shall save his people from their sins, see Jn. i. 14. 'And the word was made flesh.' 1 Ti. iii. 16. 'God was manifest in the flesh.' These two scriptures are expounded by He. ii. 14. where it is said, 'Forasmuch then as the children are partakers of flesh and blood, he also himself

Y

likewise took part of the same;' that is, of flesh and blood, see Ro. viii. 3. and compare it with Lu. xxiv. 39. where Christ saith, 'Behold my hands and my feet, that it is I myself: handle me, and see; for a spirit hath not flesh and bones, as ye see me have.' And he doth often call himself by the name of the Son of man to signify that he is very man, as well as very God. Mat. xxiv.; xvi 13.

Quest. But why was he true God and true man?

Ans. He was true man, because man had offended, and justice required that man should suffer and make satisfaction, and so it is written. 1 Co. xv. 21. 'For since by man *came* death, by man *came* also the resurrection of the dead.' And again, 'All we like sheep have gone astray; - - and the Lord hath laid on him the iniquity of us all.' And in 1 Pe. ii. 24. where that liii. of Is. is mentioned, he saith, 'Who his own self bare our sins in his own body on the tree, that we, being dead to sins, should live unto righteousness; by whose stripes ye were healed.' And again, God did prepare this body, the human nature of Christ, that it should be a sacrifice for sins, 'wherefore - - he saith, Sacrifice and offering (that is, such as were offered by the law of Moses) thou wouldest not, but a body hast thou prepared me. He. x. 5. In this body which God had prepared for him, which he took of the virgin, Ga. iv. 4. in this he did bear all the sins of all his elect. 1 Pe. ii. 24.

And he must needs be true God, because, it was an infinite God that was transgressed against, and justice required an infinite satisfaction, and therefore he must be infinite that must give this satisfaction, or else justice could not be satisfied, and so it was written, where the apostle is telling the pastors of the church of Ephesus, by what they were redeemed, he tells them, that God did purchase them 'with his own blood.' Ac. xx. 28. see 1 Jn. iii. 16. where he saith, 'Hereby perceive we the love *of God,* because he laid down his life for us.' Not in his divine, but in his human nature; for as I said before, God's Christ was of both natures, Esa. ix. 6. Ro. ix. 5. 1 Jn. v. 20. Jn. i. 1—14. True God, and true man, and the divine nature did enable him to undergo in his human nature, all that sin, curse, and wrath that was laid upon him for us; and to overcome, and obtain eternal redemption for us. He. ix. 24.

Quest. How did this Christ bring in redemption for man?

Ans. (1.) Why first, man broke the law of God; but this man did fulfil it again, and became the end of it 'for righteousness to every one that believeth.' Ro. x. 4.

(2.) Man was foiled and overcome by the devil; but this Man Christ did overcome him again, and that for us. Lu. iv. He. ii. 14, 15.

(3.) Man did lose the glory of God, but this Man hath obtained it again.

(4.) Man by sin lost eternal salvation; but this Man by his own blood hath obtained it again for him. He. ix. 12.

(5.) Man by sin brought death into the world. Ro. v. 12. But Jesus Christ, *that Man,* hath destroyed it again, He. ii. 14. compared with Ho. xiii. 14. and brought in life and immortality. 2 Ti. i. 10. Ro. v. 15.

Quest. But how are we *justified* by this man's obedience?

Ans. All our iniquities were laid upon him, Is. liii. 6, 8, 11, 12. And his righteousness is bestowed on us, if we believe, as it is written, 'Even the righteousness of God *which is* by faith of Jesus Christ unto all and upon all them that believe.' Ro. iii. 22. And this is it which Paul so much sought after, when he saith, 'Yea doubtless, and I count all things *but* loss, - - - and do count them *but* dung, that I may win Christ, and be found in him, not having mine own righteousness, which is of the law, but that which is through the faith of Christ, the righteousness which is of God by faith.' Phi. iii. 8, 9.

Quest. How do men come by this righteousness and everlasting life?

Ans. By faith men lay hold upon it, and apply it to their own souls in particular. Ga. ii. 20. For it is by faith they are justified, as also saith the scripture. Ro. v. 1. That his faith lays hold on and applies, that which this Christ of God hath done, and is a doing, and owns it as his own.

Quest. What is this faith that doth justify the sinner?

Ans. It is a gift, Ep. ii. 8. fruit, Ga. v. 22. or work, of the Spirit of God, whereby a soul is enabled, under a sight of its sins, and wretched estate, to lay hold on the birth, righteousness, blood, death, resurrection, ascension and intercession of the Lord Jesus Christ, 1 Th. ii. 7. and by the assistance of the Spirit, whereby it is wrought, to apply all the virtue, life and merit of what hath been done and suffered, or is a doing by the same Lord Jesus Christ, to its own self in particular, Ga. ii. 20. Ro. vii. 24, 25. as if itself had really done all that the Lord Jesus Christ hath done: I do not say that the soul doth any thing for justification, but it doth know, that whatsoever Jesus Christ hath done in point of justification, is given to, and bestowed upon it, Ro. iii. 22. and God finding the soul in him, that is in Christ, doth 'justify it from all things, from which it could not be justified by the law of Moses.' Ac. xiii. 39.

Quest. Well, but is there no way to come to the Father of mercies but by this man that was born of the virgin? Is there no way to come to God but by the faith of him?

Ans. No, 'there is none other name under heaven given among men, whereby we must be saved.' Ac. iv. 12. And Jesus himself, that was born of the virgin Mary, said, 'I am the way, and the truth, and the life: no man cometh unto the Father, but by me.' Jn. xiv. 6.

Quest. And where is this man, that was born of the virgin, that we may come to the Father by him?

Ans. He ascended away from his disciples in a cloud, into heaven, as we may read. Ac. i. 9—11.

Quest. What doth he there?

Ans. He ever lives to make intercession for all that come unto God by him. He. vii. 25. That is, they shall come out of themselves to him, and venture their souls on what he did and suffered when he was on earth, and is doing now in heaven; shall certainly be saved: For he ever lives to save them, that do thus come to the Father by him. And it is, because he spilt his blood for all that shall by the faith of God's elect lay hold upon him. And thus it is written where he saith, 'Being justified freely by his grace, through the redemption that is in Christ Jesus, [Mark this] whom God hath set forth *to be* a propitiation through faith in his blood, to declare his righteousness, (that is, to declare God's righteousness) for the remission of sins that are past, through the forbearance of God; to declare, *I say*, at this time his righteousness: that he might be just, and the justifier of him which believeth (or layeth hold) in Jesus.' Ro. iii. 24—26.

Quest. But did this man rise again from the dead, that very man, with that very body wherewith he was crucified? for you do seem, as I conceive, to hold forth so much by these your expressions.

Ans. Why do you doubt of it?

Quest. Do you believe it?

Ans. Yes, by the grace of the Lord Jesus Christ, for he hath enabled me so to do.

Quest. And can you prove it by the scripture?

Ans. Yes.

Quest. How?

Ans. First, From that scripture in Lu. xxiv. 39, 40. where Christ himself after he was crucified appeared to his disciples, (who having seen him) supposed they had seen a spirit. But he said, Why are ye troubled, and why do thoughts arise in your hearts? Behold my hands and my feet, that it is I myself, and do not think you see a spirit; handle me, and see, for a spirit hath not flesh and bones, as you see me have. This he spake after he was crucified, Lu. xxiii. 33. and buried, ver. 53. and rose again from the dead, ch. xxiv. 6, 7. many other scriptures could I give for the proof hereof, as Ac. x. 40, 41. And Ac. xiii. 30, 31. 1 Th. i. 10. only read Ac. ii. 29—32. where the apostle proveth the same, bringing in the words of the prophet David for a testimony thereof, saying, He 'being a pro-

phet, and knowing that God had sworn with an oath to him, that of the fruit of his loins, according to the flesh, he would raise up Christ to sit on his throne; (saith) he seeing this before, spake of the resurrection of Christ, that his soul was not left in hell, neither his flesh did see corruption.' Mark it, his flesh did see no corruption. ver. 31. But if he had not risen again, his flesh had seen corruption. But he rose again from the dead, that very man, that very body; for his flesh did see no corruption.

Quest. Why did he rise again from the dead, with that very body?

Answ. (1.) Because it was not possible he should be holden of death.

(2.) Because in his human nature he suffered for sin; and if he had not recovered himself from that very curse, even from under death, and all other things that lay on him, which he had through the sins of his children subjected himself unto, he had not overcome sin, hell, death, the law, and the devil: Ac. ii. 24. but had been overcome by them; and if so, then had not redemption been obtained for sinners; for it was at his resurrection from the dead, that God said unto him, 'Thou art my Son, this day have I begotten thee:' (As saith the Apostle) ' And we declare unto you glad tidings, how that the promise which was made unto the fathers, God hath fulfilled the same unto us their children, in that he hath raised up Jesus again;' as it is also written in the second psalm, 'Thou art my Son, this day have I begotten thee.' Ac. xiii. 30—36. And it is this, namely, the resurrection of that Man from the dead, that doth give us ground of hope; as in 1 Pe. i. 3. where he saith, He 'hath begotten us again unto a lively hope by the resurrection of Jesus Christ from the dead.'

(3.) Because God intends to redeem the bodies of his saints out of their graves in which they have lain many a year, Jn. v. 28, 29. Ro. viii. 23. 1 Co. xv. 52. and to possess them with his own glory; and when this comes to pass, then shall that scripture be fulfilled, that saith, He 'shall change our vile body, that it may be fashioned like unto his glorious body, according to the working (of his mighty power) whereby he is able even to subdue all things unto himself.' Phi. ii. 21. And he hath given us assurance thereof, in that he hath raised up Jesus our Lord again from the dead. Ac. xvii. 31.

Quest. But do you think, that these our bodies that we do carry about with us in this world, after that they are dead and buried, and rotten, shall rise again out of those graves into which they are laid; when the scripture saith, flesh and blood shall not inherit the kingdom of God? 1 Co. xv. 50.

Answ. Flesh in scripture is taken more ways than one: As,

It is taken for the works of the law; where the Apostle saith, 'Received ye the Spirit by the works of the law, or by the hearing of faith? Are ye so foolish? having begun in the Spirit, are ye now made perfect by the flesh?' Ga. iii. 2, 3. By flesh here, he means the law; as is clear, if you compare it with ver. 10—12. Again, sometimes flesh is taken for sins. Ro. viii. 1, 5. And sometimes it is taken for the bodies of the saints, as subject to distempers, to pain, sickness, corruptions, to death; by reason of sin. 2 Co. iv. 11; vii. 5. Now the Apostle in that place, where he saith, 'Flesh and blood cannot inherit the kingdom (of heaven, or) of God,' his meaning is, sinful flesh and blood, or the sin, with any imperfection that is in the bodies of the saints, shall not inherit the kingdom; and that you shall find to be the mind of the Holy Ghost, if you read with understanding the latter end of the same verse, where he saith, 'Neither doth corruption inherit incorruption.' That is, sin, or any imperfection of the body, shall not inherit eternal life; for, saith he, in ver. 53. 'This corruptible must put on incorruption, and this mortal *must* put on immortality.' Mark here, I pray you, though he saith, 'Flesh and blood cannot inherit the kingdom of God;' yet he saith, 'This corruptible must put on incorruption.' For the trump shall blow, and the dead shall be raised (as Christ saith) 'They that are in the graves shall hear his voice.' Jn. v. 28. And shall come forth of their graves incorruptible. 1 Co. xv. 52. And shall 'all appear before the judgment seat of Christ.' 2 Co. v. 10. Re. ii. 12, 13. See also that scripture, Phi. iii. 20, 21. where the Apostle saith, He waited for Christ the Saviour from heaven. And what shall he do when he comes? why, He 'shall change our vile body.' Mark it, it must be our vile body that must be changed. But if it be changed, then how can it be the same? not the same in respect of sin, or bodily infirmities, but the very same in respect of substance: For, saith he, It is our vile body that must be changed; and it is the very same, It shall be 'fashioned like unto his glorious body.' And if you ask, How is it possible that this should be done? He answers, 'According to the working whereby he is able even to subdue all things unto himself.'

Quest. But do you think this is certain? methinks the scriptures seemingly hold forth so much, yet I cannot believe it, for it is contrary to all reason.

Answ. Truly the scriptures do not only hold forth so much seemingly, but they do most really, and plainly, hold out these things to all those that have received the Spirit of the Lord Jesus Christ. For it is it, and it alone, that can reveal these things. 'For the things of God knoweth no man, but the Spirit of God.' 1 Co. ii. 11. Now if thou wouldest know these things, thou must first receive the Spirit of the Son of God, without which, thou canst not know so much as one of the fundamental truths of the gospel of our Lord Jesus Christ.

Quest. But there are those in our days, who reject this doctrine that you lay down, concerning the Lord Jesus Christ, as you lay it down, and they are for a Christ within, for a cross within, for a resurrection, and intercession within; and they do not hold as you do, a Christ without, and a resurrection of Christ without; and intercession of Christ without; Ay, and they have very much scripture for that which they say too: And therefore what shall such as we do, that stand tottering and shaking in these distracted and dangerous times? For our poor souls are in very much doubt what way to take.

Answ. Therefore I will speak a few words to you by way of discovery of the falsity of such opinions; and a word of direction, how you should understand the truth.

Therefore, he that cries up a Christ within, *in opposition* to a Christ without, that man instead of having the Spirit of Christ in him, is possessed with a spirit of delusion; for where the Spirit of Christ is in truth, that Spirit causeth the soul to look to the Christ that was born of the Virgin, for all justification; as it is written, 'Howbeit when he, the Spirit of truth, is come, he will guide you into all truth: for he shall not speak of himself; but whatsoever he shall hear, *that* shall he speak: and he will shew you things to come,' mark the next verse, 'He (saith the Son of the Virgin) shall receive of mine, and shall shew *it* unto you.' Jn. xvi. 13, 14. He shall take of mine; What is that? Why surely it is, he shall take of my Godhead, my humanity, my birth, my righteousness, my blood, my death, my resurrection, my ascension and intercession, my kingly, priestly, and prophetical offices, and shall shew you the life, merit, and value of them. And this was it which was revealed to Paul by the Holy Spirit, here spoken of. 1 Co. xv. 1—8. 'Moreover brethren, (saith he) I declare unto you the gospel which I preached unto you, which also ye have received, and wherein ye stand; By which also ye are saved, if ye keep in memory what I preached unto you, unless ye have believed in vain.' But what is this doctrine? why, 'I delivered unto you first of all that which I also received.' What was that? Why, 'How that Christ died for our sins according to the scriptures; And that he was buried, and that he rose again the third day according to the scriptures: (there is his death and resurrection preached.) And that he was seen of Cephas, then of the twelve; after that, he was seen of above five hundred brethren at once; of whom the greater part remain unto this present, but some are fallen asleep. After that, he was seen of James; then of all the Apostles. And last of all he was seen of me also, (saith Paul) as of one born out of due time.' This is it, I say, that the Spirit of Truth doth hold forth to poor sinners, a Christ crucified without the gates of Jerusalem, Lu. xxiii. 33. buried in Joseph's sepulchre, 53. risen again the third day, Lu. xxiv. 6. ascended away from his disciples in a cloud into heaven, as in Ac. i. 9—11. And there ever liveth, that very man, with that very body, to make intercession for all that receive him. He. vii. 24, 25. This is, I say, the doctrine of the Spirit of truth, whatsoever is the spirit of error.

Quest. But do not the scriptures make mention of a Christ within ? 2 Co. xiii. 5. Col. i. 27.

Answ. Yes, And he that hath not the Spirit of Christ, is none of his. Ro. viii. 9. But he that hath it, is led out of himself by it ; and as I said before, it shews the soul, what the blessed Son of the Virgin Mary hath done and suffered, and is a doing for it. Therefore hereby know we the Spirit of truth from the spirit of error. [2 Jn. 7.] ' Every spirit that doth confess that Jesus Christ is come in the flesh, is of God :' 1 Jn. iv. 2. That is, that spirit that doth confess, that Jesus Christ took flesh upon him, and in that flesh did bear our sins. 1 Pe. ii. 24. Col. i. 20—22. 1 Pe. iii. 18 ; iv. 1. And after he was taken down from the cross, and laid in a sepulchre, rose again from the dead ; that very Man with that very body, wherewith he was crucified : That spirit that doth believe and confess this, is of God, and is the blessed Spirit of Christ, whereof he spake, when he was yet with his disciples touching his bodily presence : For 'he (saith the Son of Mary) shall glorify me, for he shall receive of mine and shew *it* unto you.' Jn. xvi. 13, 14.

I have answered this already in my epistle to the first treatise. Therefore believe not every spirit, but try the spirits whether they be of God, for many false spirits and prophets are gone out into the world, therefore have a care how thou receivest the voice that speaks to thee, but try whether they are according to the truth of God's word as it is written, 'To the law and to the testimony : if they speak not according to this word, *it is* because *there is* no light in them.' Is. viii. 20.

(1.) Therefore try a little, Do they slight God's Christ, which is the Son of the Virgin ? that spirit is of the devil. 1 Co. xii. 3.

(2.) Do they say that that blood of his which was shed without the gates of Jerusalem, doth not wash away sin, yea, all sin from him that believes? That is a spirit of antichrist. 1 Jn. i. 7.

(3.) Do they say, that that Man that was crucified without the gates of Jerusalem, is not risen again (with that very body wherewith he was crucified) out of the sepulchre? Lu. xxiv. 38, 39. That is a spirit of antichrist.

(4.) Do they say that that very Man that was crucified with that very body, is not now in the presence of his Father, absent from his people touching his bodily presence, though present in Spirit ? I say whoever they be, that say he is not there, they are of the devil : for the proof of this see Ac. v. 30 and 31. and compare it with He. vii. 24, 25. 'The God of our fathers (saith the Apostle) raised up Jesus.' But what Jesus? 'he whom ye slew,' saith he to the Jews. ' Him (the very same whom ye slew) hath God exalted with his right hand *to be* a Prince and a Saviour, for to give repentance to Israel, and forgiveness of sins.'

And indeed, here is my LIFE, namely, the birth of this Man, the righteousness of this Man, the blood of this Man, the death and resurrection of this Man, the ascension and intercession of this Man for me ; and the second coming of this Man to judge the world in righteousness. Ac. xvii. 31. I say, here is my LIFE, if I see this by faith without me, through the operation of the Spirit within me : I am safe, I am at peace, I am comforted, I am encouraged, and I know that my comfort, peace, and encouragement is true, and given me from heaven, by the Father of mercies, through the Son of the Virgin Mary, Mat. i. 21. who is the way to the Father of mercies, Jn. xiv. 6. who is able to save to the uttermost, all that come to the Father by him. He. vii. 25. Because he, that very Man, with that very body wherewith he was crucified, is ascended into heaven, Ac. i. 9—11. and there ever lives to make intercession for them that come to God by him. This is the rock, sinner, upon which, if thou be built, the gates of hell, nor Ranter, Quaker, sin, law, death, no nor the devil himself, shall ever be able to prevail against thee. Mat. xvi. 16—18. And here I leave thee to the wisdom of the great God, who if he hath chosen thee in his Son, and brought thee to him ; and hath made thee by faith to lay hold on him, thou needest not fear the devil with his siftings, snares, wiles, and fiery darts, wherewith he doth destroy thousands ; but mayest with the Apostle (if thou live in the power and life of the love of God towards thee) cry out, ' I am persuaded, that neither death, nor life, nor angels, nor principalities, nor powers, nor things present, nor things to come, nor height, nor depth, nor any other creature, shall be able to separate us from the love of God which is in Christ Jesus our Lord.' Ro. viii. 38, 39.

And now reader, if thou be a true Christian, I am sure that these be the things that appear to be the glorious substantial truths to thy soul, and thou doest not care for that comfort that doth not make this Man, the Son of the Virgin, precious to thy soul, 1 Pe. ii. 7. for thou knowest, that it is he, that hath delivered thee from the wrath to come. 1 Th. i. 10. But as for you that are disobedient, except you mend your manners, you will stumble 'and fall backward, and be broken, and snared, and taken.'

Is. xxviii. 13. and wonder and perish because you believe not. Ac. xiii. 41.

A few words more, and so I shall have done, and they are words of counsel to thee. Have a care thou receive not every Christ that is proffered to thee, though it may appear very excellent to thy foolish heart: for under the name Christ, are men deceived, as it is written, 'many shall come in my name, saying, I am Christ; and shall deceive many.' Mat. xxiv. 5. But have a care that thou receive that Christ, that was born without thee, fulfilled the law in his human nature without thee; spilt his blood without thee, is risen again and ascended without thee, and maketh intercession without thee: And that he that very Man that was born of the Virgin, will come again in the clouds without thee; and this truth must thou receive by that Spirit that he hath promised to send and give to them that ask him: And that shall dwell in thy heart, and shall shew thee what the Son of Mary the virgin, the Son of man, the Son of God, the true God hath in his body done for thy soul. Jn. xvi. 13, 14. And if thou receive him in truth, then though thou do not boast, nor brag of thy holiness, as those painted hypocrites called Quakers do: yet thou wilt do more work for God in one hour, than they, even all of them, can do in all their lifetime.

Take my counsel, and the Lord Jesus Christ have mercy upon thy soul and body. Farewell.

SOME QUESTIONS TO THE QUAKERS,

OR A FEW QUERIES TO THOSE WHO ARE POSSESSED WITH A SPIRIT OF DELUSION IN THIS GENERATION.

' Be ready always to give an answer to every man that asketh you a reason of the hope that is in you,' 1 Pet. iii. 15. And
I beseech you do it in sincerity.

1. IF thou sayest that every one hath a measure of the Spirit of Jesus Christ within him, why say the scriptures that some are ' sensual having not the Spirit.' Jude 19. And when Christ tells his disciples of sending them the Spirit, he also saith, The world cannot receive it. Jn. xiv. 17.

2. What is the church of God redeemed by, from the curse of the law? Is it by something that is done within them, or by something done without them? If thou answer, it is redeemed from the curse of the law by something that worketh in them; then I ask, why did the Man Christ Jesus hang upon the cross on Mount Calvary, without the gates of Jerusalem, for the sins of the people? Ga. iii. 3. 1 Pe. ii. 24. And why do the scriptures say, that through this Man, is preached to us the forgiveness of sins. Ac. xiii. 38. That is, through his blood, Ep. i. 7. Col. i. 20. which was shed without the gates of Jerusalem. He. xiii. 12.

3. What scripture have you to prove, that Christ is, or was crucified *within* you, dead within you, risen within you, and ascended within you?

4. Is that very Man that was crucified on Mount Calvary between two thieves, whose name is Jesus, the Son of Mary, I say, is he the very Christ of God, yea, or no?

5. Is that very Man, with that very body, within you, yea, or no?

6. Was that Jesus, that was born of the Virgin Mary, a real Man of flesh and bones, after his resurrection from the dead, out of Joseph's sepulchre, yea, or no? For the scripture saith he was, as in Lu. xxiv. 39. If so, then did that Man that said handle me and see, for a spirit hath not flesh and bones as ye see me have; I say, did that Man go away from his disciples (and not into them, in his body) as these scriptures declare, Lu. xxiv. 39, 40. compared with 50, 51. also Ac. i. 9—11. or did he with that body of flesh go into his disciples, as some fond dreamers think?

7. Hath that Christ that was with God the Father before the world was, no other body but his church? If you say no, as it is your wonted course; then again I ask you, what that was in which he did bear the sins of his children? If you answer, It was ' in his own body on the tree,' for so saith the scripture. 1 Pe. ii. 24. Then I ask you further, whether that body in which he did bear our sins, (which is also called his own body) was, or is, the church of God, yea, or no? Again if you say he hath no body but the church, the saints, Then I ask, what that was that was taken down from the cross, and laid into Joseph's sepulchre. Lu. xxiii. 53.

Now I know, that as Christ is the head of his church, so the church is the body of the head, which is Christ. But as Christ is the mediator between God and man, I say, as he is mediator, so he is a man, 1 Ti. ii. 5. and absent from his saints in the world, as is clear. 2 Co. v. 6. Therefore as he is a mediator, and a Man, so he hath a body that is absent from his church, which body is ascended from his disciples, above the clouds into heaven. Lu. xxiv. 51. Ac. i. 9—11. If you say no, then I ask you, Did he leave the body behind him, which was born of the Virgin Mary, which walked up and down with his disciples in the world, was afterwards hanged upon the cross, Lu. xxiii. 26, 33, 53. buried, rose again from the dead, Mat. xxiv. 3, 6, 15, 41, 42, 39, 50. with which body he did eat, drink, and likewise walk with his disciples after his resurrection from the dead, Ac. x. 41. and did bid his disciples see if he were not flesh and bones, yea, or no?

JOHN BUNYAN.

A VINDICATION

OF

GOSPEL TRUTHS OPENED;

ACCORDING TO THE SCRIPTURES,

AND THE OPPOSITION MADE AGAINST IT BY EDWARD BORROUGH, A PROFESSED QUAKER, BUT PROVED
AN ENEMY TO THE TRUTH, EXAMINED AND CONFUTED BY THE WORD OF GOD.

AND ALSO,

The Things that were then laid down, and declared to the World by me, are a second Time borne witness to, according to truth: With the Answer of EDWARD BORROUGH to the Queries then laid down in my Book reproved. And also, a plain Answer to his Queries, given in Simplicity of Soul; and is now also presented to the World, or who else may read, or hear them; to the end (if God will) that Truth may be discovered thereby.

'*I have found David - - a man after mine own heart,*' (saith God, Acts xiii. 22.)

'*Of this man's seed hath God according to his promise raised unto Israel a Saviour, Jesus:*' (saith the Apostle) 23.

'*And when they had fulfilled all that was written of him, they took him down from the tree, and laid him in a sepulchre:*' 29.

'*But God raised him from the dead:*' 30.

'*And we declare unto you glad tidings, how that the Promise which was made unto the fathers, God hath fulfilled the same unto us their children, in that he hath raised up Jesus again:*' 32, 33.

'*Be it known unto you therefore, men and brethren, that through this man is preached unto you the forgiveness of sins:*' 38.

And by him all that believe are justified from all things, from which ye could not be justified by the law of Moses:' 39.

TO THE READER.

SINCE it hath pleased the Lord to work in my soul by his holy Spirit, and hath translated me in some measure from darkness to light, I have seen and heard, that such things have been done by those who did once pretend themselves to be the servants of Jesus Christ, that it hath made me marvel: Partly, while I have beheld the vile conversation of some, and also the seeming legal holiness of others, together with their damnable doctrine; which have, notwithstanding their professions, made shipwreck of the faith, both to themselves, and their followers. I having had some in-sight into such things as these, was provoked to publish a small treatise touching the fundamentals of religion, supposing that God might add his blessing thereto, both for the establishing of some, and the convincing of others; which things I doubt not but they have been accomplished; and will be still more and more. But, as it was in former days, so it is now: That is, some in all former ages have been on foot in the world, ready to oppose the truth: So it is now, there are certain men newly started up in our days, called quakers, who have set themselves against the truth of our Lord Jesus Christ, and do in very deed deny, that salvation was then obtained by him, when he did hang on the cross without Jerusalem's gate. Now these men do pretend, that they do verily and truly profess the Lord Jesus Christ; but when it comes to the trial, and their principles be thoroughly weighed, the best that they do, is to take one truth, and corrupt it, that they may thereby fight more stoutly against another. As for instance:

FIRST, They will own that salvation was obtained by Christ, this is truth, that salvation was obtained by Christ; but come close to the thing, and you will find, that they corrupt the word, and only mean thus much, That salvation is wrought out by Christ as he is within; and by it (though not warranted by the scripture) they will fight against the truth: Namely, that salvation was obtained for sinners, by the man that did hang on the cross on Mount Calvary, between two thieves, called Jesus Christ. I say, by what he did then for sinners in his own person or body, which he took from the Virgin Mary, according to the word of God.

SECOND, They will own the doctrine of Christ within. This is truth, that Christ is within his saints: But this doctrine they will take to fight against the doctrine of Christ without, ascended from his disciples into heaven, by whom salvation was obtained, 'neither is there salvation in any other.' Ac. iv. 12.

THIRD, They will own the resurrection of the saints, but their meaning is only thus much, That the saints are raised from the state of nature to a state of grace, and herewith they will fight against this truth; namely, the resurrection of the bodies of saints out of their graves, into which they were laid, some thousands, some hundreds of years before. And if they do say, they do own the resurrection of the saints out of their graves, they do mean out of the grave of sin only, and nothing else.

FOURTH, They will say, they do own the second coming of Christ to judge the world; but search them to the bottom, and you will find them only to own him in his coming in spirit, within, in opposition to the glorious coming of the Lord Jesus, the Son of Mary, from heaven in the clouds, with all his mighty angels, to raise the dead, and bring them to judgment, according to the scripture. And so for the intercession of Christ, and the truths of the gospel, they only own them to be within; in opposition to the glorious intercession, and mediation of the man Christ Jesus in his own person without, now in the presence of his Father, between us and him, pleading and making intercession for his children. These things, together with many more, I might mention, but now I forbear, knowing that none shall be lost, nor altogether carried away by them, nor any heretics, but the sons of perdition. Now that they might the better make their doctrine take place in the hearers, they endeavour to make a fair shew in the flesh, that thereby they might now, as did their fathers in time past, compel and constrain them who are not by the Lord's right hand planted into the truth of Jesus, to follow their covered errors, as it is written. Ga. vi. 12. 'As many as desire to make a fair shew in the flesh,' That is, according to works of the law; do 'by good words and fair speeches deceive the hearts of the simple.' Ro. xvi. 18. And indeed it doth clearly appear, that those that are carried away, are such as are not able to discern between fair speeches declared by heretics, and sound doctrine declared by the simple-hearted servants of Jesus.

First, Now I shall lay down several grounds, not only why errors are broached in the world; but also, why so many are carried away with them.

1. One ground, why so many errors do from time to time come into the world, is because those that are not indeed of the planting of the Lord's right hand, might be rooted out. Mat. xv. 13. Now these are many times carried away by deceivable doctrines: And truly in this our God hath both a care of his own glory, and of his church's welfare. For first, should they not be swept away by some heresy or other, there might be great dishonour brought to his name by their continuing among his people: And secondly, that he might take away such grievances as such may bring, had they continued still in the society of his children.

2. Another ground why the Lord doth suffer

These things I am an ear witness to.

such errors to come into the world is, because, those that are Christians indeed, might be approved and appear. 1 Co. xi. 19. 'For there must be also heresies among you, that they which are approved may be made manifest.' Should not the Lord go this way to work (sometimes) there would be many that would make people believe that they are Christians, and yet are not. And again, that he might make it appear, that though there be heretics, yet he hath a people, enabled by his Spirit, to contradict, and oppose them, and plead to the truth of our Lord Jesus Christ, and his glorious gospel against them.

3. Another ground why the Lord doth suffer, yea, even send delusions among the people, is, That those who were so idle and slothful, as not to seek after the Lord Jesus Christ in sincerity, might be taken away, and violently possessed with error, and be made to run greedily after the same; that they might smart the more for their neglect of the truth. For always, those who were lazy in seeking after the truth when it was proffered, and afterward hasty after the doctrine of devils, when that is declared to them, shall be sure to have their latter behaviour to rise up in judgment against them, in that when the truth was proffered to them they were idle and did not receive it, and yet when delusion did proffer itself, they were industrious, and labouring. Now mark, that they all might be damned who believed not the truth, but had pleasure in unrighteousness; because they received not the truth in the love of it, that they might be saved. And for this cause God shall send them strong delusions, that they might believe a lie, and be damned. 2 Th. ii. 10—12.

Second, Now in the second place, why so many are so easily carried away with errors in this day: The grounds are these that follow.

1. Because men count it enough to be professors of the truth, without seeking to be possessors of the same. Now because men are but only professors of the truth, not having it in their hearts in reality, they are carried away with an error, if it come in never so little power, more than the truth they profess. And this is the reason why so many are carried away with the errors that are broached in these days, because they have not indeed received the Lord Jesus by the revelation of the Spirit, and with power, but by the relation of others only; and so having no other witness to set them down withal, but the history of the word, and the relation of others concerning the truths contained therein, (though the knowledge of the truth this way shall abundantly aggravate their damnation) yet they having not had the Spirit of the Lord to confirm these things effectually unto them, they are carried away with delusions.

2. Another reason why so many are carried

away with delusions, is, those differences that are among the children of God about smaller matters. O Friends! how is the hand of the enemy strengthened by our carnality, while one saith, I am of Paul; and another, I am of Apollos; many a poor soul is carried away with delusion. And why so? They are not satisfied that this is the truth, because the children are at difference among themselves, about some outward things. And again, it makes those that are not so desperately possessed with a spirit of delusion, as are others, but are mere moral men: I say it makes them to say within themselves, and one to another; There are so many sects and judgments in the world, that we cannot tell which way to take. And therefore you that have the Spirit, pray that these things may cease, least you blush for your folly, at the appearing of Jesus our Lord.

3. The pride, covetousness, and impiety of hypocrites, and carnal professors, are great stumbling-blocks to the poor world; and the cause why many at this day do drink down so greedily a deluding doctrine, and especially if it come with a garment of pretended holiness. But as for these, they shall go to their place in their time, with the curse of the Almighty poured out upon them, for their casting of stumbling-blocks before the simple by their loose conversations, if they do not hastily repent of their wickedness, and close in reality with our blessed Lord Jesus.

4. Another reason why delusions do so easily take place in the hearts of the ignorant, is, because those that pretend to be their teachers, do behave themselves so basely among them. And indeed I may say of these, as our Lord said of the Pharisees in another case, all the blood of the ignorant, from the beginning of the world, shall be laid to the charge of this generation. They that pretend they are sent of the Lord, and come, saying, Thus saith the Lord; we are the servants of the Lord, our commission is from the Lord (by succession) and the like; I say, these pretending themselves to be the preachers of truth, (but are not) do by their loose conversation, render the doctrine of God, and his Son Jesus Christ, (by whom the saints are saved) contemptible, and do give the adversary mighty encouragement, to cry out against the truths of our Lord Jesus Christ, because of their wicked walking. Now shall not his soul be avenged on such a nation as this, who pretend to be teachers of the people in goodness, when, as for the most part of them, they are the men, that at this day do so harden their hearers in their sins by giving them, even their hearers, such ill examples, that none goeth beyond them for impiety. As for example; Would a parishioner learn to be proud? he or she need look no farther than to the priest, his wife and family; for there is a

notable pattern before them. Would the people learn to be wanton, they may also see a pattern among their teachers. Would they learn to be drunkards? they may also have that from some of their ministers; for indeed they are ministers in this, to minister ill example to their congregations. Again, would the people learn to be covetous, they need but look to their minister, and they shall have a lively, or rather a deadly resemblance set before them, in both riding and running after great benefices, and parsonages by night and by day. Nay, they among themselves will scramble for the same. I have seen, that so soon as a man hath but departed from his benefice as he calls it, either by death or out of covetousness of a bigger, we have had one priest from this town, and another from that, so run, for these tithe-cocks and handfuls of barley, as if it were their proper trade, and calling, to hunt after the same. O wonderful impiety and ungodliness! are you not ashamed of your doings? If you say no, it is (perhaps) because you are given over of God to a reprobate mind. Read Ro. i. towards the end. As it was with them, so (it is to be feared) it is with many of you, who knowing the judgments of God, that they who do such things are worthy of death, not only do the same, but have (as I may so say) pleasure also in them that do them. And now you that pretend to be the teachers of the people in verity and truth, though we know that some of you are not: Is it a small thing with you, to set them you say are your flock such an example as this. Were ever the Pharisees so profane; to whom Christ said, ye vipers, how can ye escape the damnation of hell; doth not the ground groan under you? surely, it will favour you no more than it favoured your fore-runners. Certainly the wrath of God lies heavy at your doors, it is but a very little while, and your recompense shall be upon your own head. And as for you that are indeed of God among them, though not of them; separate yourselves. ^{Eze. xiii.; read that whole chapter and you will find it as it was a looking glass by which thou mayest notably see them with their marks and discoveries.} Why should the righteous partake of the same plagues with the wicked? O ye children of the harlot! I cannot well tell how to have done with you, your stain is so odious, and you are so senseless, as appears by your practices. But I shall at this time forbear, having in some measure discharged my conscience according to the truth against you; hoping if God do give me opportunity, and a fair call, that I shall a second time in this world give testimony against your filthy conversations, though now I shall say no more, only thus much; Be ashamed of your earthly-mindedness, if you can; and be converted, or else you shall never be healed.

Here might I also aggravate your sin by its

several circumstances, but I shall rather forbear; supposing that you may entertain wrong and harsh thoughts of me, though I have spoken the truth; therefore I shall at this time rather keep silence, and wish you to amend, than to rake in your sores; for thereby would your stink go more abroad in the world, Therefore I say, I forbear. And now to the reader, I beseech thee to have a care of thy soul, and look well to the welfare of it: And that you may do so, have a care what doctrine it is that thou receivest. Be not contented until thou in deed and in truth, in the light of the Spirit of Christ, see thy sins washed away in the blood of that Lamb, who did offer up himself a ransom on the cross on Mount Calvary, for the sins of thy soul and body, together with the rest of the saints of God.

And let not the legal holiness of the one, nor the loose profane conversation of the other, beat thee off from pursuing after the truths of Jesus, as the truth is in Jesus, (and so laid down in this my discourse) neither let the plausibleness of the other beguile thy simple heart. And now to you that are carried away with the delusions at this day broached in the world, by the instruments of Satan, and that after a profession of the truth: I say to you, Turn again, (if you can) peradventure there may be hope, and that you may escape that wrath which justly you have deserved: But if you shall still refuse the Lord that speaks now from heaven in mercy to you, you shall not hereafter escape the Lord, that in his own time will speak to you in his wrath, and vex you in his sore displeasure.

And now a few words to you that have indeed closed in with the Lord Jesus Christ, the Son of Mary, and they are these that follow. (1.) Be of good cheer, all ' your sins are forgiven you for his name's sake.' 1 Jn. ii. 12. (2.) Know, he that hath begun the good work of his grace in you, will perfect it, even to the second coming of our Lord Jesus Christ. Phi. i. 6. (3.) Know that though your Lord Jesus, who is in you by his Spirit, be absent from you touching his bodily presence, yet he is not forgetful of you, but is preparing a place for you. Jn. xiv. 1—3. (4.) Consider, That he is also at this very present, in his very person in the presence of his Father now in the heavens, praying and making intercession for you, that you may be brought safe to glory. He. vii. 24. Father, I will (saith he) that they also, whom thou hast given me, be with me where I am; that they may behold my glory. Jn. xvii. 25. (5.) Know also, That he hath overcome in his own person (when he was in the world) devil, death, sin, hell, the curse of the law, the power of the grave, and and all other evils, in the body of his flesh for you. He. ii. 14. (6.) Believe also, that while you are in the world, all things

shall fall out for your good at the end, whether they be temptations, doctrines of devils, workings of corruptions, all things shall fall out for your good, who love our precious Lord Jesus. Ro. viii. 28. (7.) Be assured, that all your enemies shall very suddenly be under your feet, even Satan and all. Ro. xvi. 20. (8.) Consider, That there shall no temptation befall you in the days of your pilgrimage, but God will enable you to bear it; Ay, and make a way also for you to escape the destroying danger of it. 1 Co. x. 13. (9.) When the time of your dissolution shall come, your Jesus will deal with you, as he did with blessed Lazarus, that is, he will send his angels to fetch your souls away to glory. Lu. xvi. 22. (10.) Believe also, and know assuredly, that at the last day, he will also raise your bodies out of their graves, and make them also for ever vessels of his glory, Ro. viii. 23. compared with Jn. v. 28; 1 Th. iv. 14—18. (11.) And lastly, consider, That though now by the world, and heretics, you be counted as not worth the looking after; Yet you have your day a coming, when as the Dives's of this and all other ages, would be glad if they might have but the least favour from you, one drop of cold water on the tip of your fingers. O you despised begging Lazarus's (as in Lu. xvi. 24.) For the world, for all their stoutness, must be forced to come to judgment, before your Lord and you. 1 Co. vi. 2. 'This honour have all his saints.' Ps. cxlix. 9.

Now seeing that these things be so, I beseech you by (those) the mercies of God, (1.) That you do give up your bodies, as hands, tongue, strength, health, wealth, and all that you have and are, to the service of God, your God. Ro. xii. 1. (2.) 'Let your moderation [in every thing] be known unto all men. (for) The Lord is at hand.' Phi. iv. 5. (3.) Study to walk as like the Lord Jesus Christ, as ever you can, for your lives. Mat. xi. 29. (4.) Let that you strive for, be the faith of the gospel of your precious Lord Jesus. Phi. i. 27. And not any earthly advantages. (5.) 'Let your conversation be as it becometh the gospel.' Ph. i. 27. (6.) Let your hearts be always in heaven, where our Lord Jesus is. Col. iii. 1—3. (7.) Forbear and forgive one another, in love, and with all your hearts, as God for Christ sake hath forgiven you. Ep. iv. 2. (8.) Let your light so shine before men, that they may see your good works and glorify your Father which is in heaven. Mat. v. 16. (9.) You are the salt of the earth, have a care you lose not your savour. Mat. v. 13. (10.) Be forward to distribute to those that are in want, for this is well-pleasing to your most glorious loving Father. He. xiii. 16. (11.) Learn all one of another the things that are good, for this is the command of God, and also commendable in saints. Phi. iii. 17. (12.) And lastly, O brethren, consider what the Lord hath done for you; he hath bought you, and paid for you with his blood, and he doth now also make it his business to pray for your safe conduct to glory. He. vii. 25. He hath delivered you from those that would have been your ruin, and hath promised to you everlasting life. Let the love of Christ constrain you, let the love of God win upon your souls. What! he that spared not his own Son, but delivered him up for us all: How shall he not with him freely give us all things. Hold out my brethren, hold out, for you have but a little while to run: Hold fast unto the death, and Christ will give you a crown of life. Re. ii. 10. Farewell, dear brethren; the mighty God of Jacob preserve and deliver you from every evil work; and all the days of our pilgrimage let us pray one for another, that our God will count us worthy of this rich and glorious calling, and fulfil all the good pleasure of his goodness, and the work of faith with power, to whom be glory now and ever.

And now reader, before I make an end of this discourse, I think it meet to let thee understand, that though there hath been a book put forth by Edward Borrough, in seeming opposition to that of mine, called, 'Some Gospel-Truths opened according to the scripture.' Yet the substance of my discourse then published by me, standeth uncontrolled by scripture, as from him or others. I do not say he doth not wrangle with them, but I say, he doth not by any one plain scripture contradict them. As for instance:

1. The first great thing that I do hold forth in that discourse, is this: That that babe that was born of the virgin Mary, and that at that time did give satisfaction for sin, was the very Christ of God, and not a type of anything afterward to be revealed for the obtaining redemption for sinners within them. Which thing my adversary can find no ground in scripture to build an opposition upon, see his book, page 12. but is forced to confess it in word, though he do deny the very same in doctrine, see his book p. 29. at his 6th query. And p. 26. where in answer to this question of mine; Why did the Man Christ hang on the cross on Mount Calvary? All the answer he gives, is this; Because they wickedly judged him to be a blasphemer; and as in their account (saith he) he died as an evil doer. And this is all the ground he giveth: See his answer to my second query in this my book, taken word for word as he laid them down.

2. The next thing I do prove in that book is, That that light which every one hath, is not the Spirit of Christ; because the scripture saith, Some have it not. Jude 19. But Edward Borrough saith, It is given to every one; [p. 18. of his book:] And he saith, They have it within them too; [p. 26. of his book,] in answer to my first

question, though he hath no scripture to confirm the same, as I have had to contradict it. See his book.

3. The next thing I prove, is, That Jesus Christ did fulfil the law in his own person without us for justification, and that his blood then shed, hath washed away the sins of the children of God, as aforesaid. Which thing he would oppose, but finds no footing for his discourse. See his book, p. 12. where he saith, The law is not fulfilled: (read the latter end of that page) [which is] contrary to scripture. Col. ii. 14. Ro. x. 4. which saith, 'For Christ is the end of the law for righteousness to every one that believeth.' Another thing I prove in that book is, That Christ is ascended into that heaven without, above the clouds and stars; and that I prove by eight several scripture demonstrations, of which not one is confuted by scripture, though secretly in his book smitten against. Read his whole book.

4. The next thing I prove, is, That the same Jesus that was born of Mary, laid in the manger, who is the Saviour, is at this day making intercession in that body he then took of Mary; which thing also is not confuted by him, by the scripture; though cunningly smitten against in his discourse, where he saith, It is only necessary to salvation to preach Christ within, laying aside all that Christ did when he was in his own person in the world. See p. 29. of his book, Qu. 6.

5. Another truth I prove, is, That the very same Jesus that was born of Mary, that very Man (that was also hanged on the cross) will come the second time, and that shall be to save his children, and to judge the world at the last day, that great day of judgment. And though they will not own, that he shall so come as he went away, which was a very Man without; yet they could not at all by the scripture contradict it. But the very sum of his discourses is a wrangling with the thing laid down, as a dog with a bone; but hath not, nor cannot by scripture overcome the same. This have I written, that the reader into whose hand this book may come, may have the more certain information concerning the things before published by me, and also concerning the opposition made against them by the adversary. And here, because I am loath to be too tedious, I do conclude, and desire thy prayers to God for me (if thou be a Christian) that I may not only be preserved to the end in the faith of Jesus, but that God would enable me to be an earnest contender for the same, even to the last; and rest,

The servant of the Lord JESUS,

JOHN BUNYAN.

READER,

WE, whose names are here under-written, having (through grace) some blessed faith and experience of the truths declared in this book, and knowing them so to be; having tried them by the scriptures in the light of the Spirit, thought it our duty to bear witness thereunto, together with our brother, desiring the blessing of God may go along with these endeavours of his, for the doing good to our Christian brethren, or any other who may read it. Farewell.

Yours in the faith of our Lord Jesus Christ, for which faith we desire to contend,

RICHARD SPENCLY.
JOHN BURTON.
JOHN CHILD.

A VINDICATION OF GOSPEL TRUTHS, &c.

IT is very expedient that there should be heresies amongst us, that thereby those which are indeed of the truth might be made manifest; and also that the doctrine of God, and his Son Jesus Christ, might the more cast forth its lustre and glory. For the truth is of that nature, that the more it is opposed, the more glory it appears in; and the more the adversary objects against it, the more it will clear itself; which doth give me, and all that stand for it, and doth plead on its side in the wisdom of the Spirit, much boldness and encouragement, to venture without any slavish fear upon those that have already, or shall hereafter, stand up to oppose it. I did some few weeks past, put forth a small book, called, Some Gospel-Truths opened, and so forth; and the thing I looked for from them was, namely, opposition from the adversary, which hath been accomplished in that, namely, as I did look for it, so did it happen; not that it daunted me; for if it had so done, it might have made me kept those truths within my breast, which are now made manifest by me (as well as others) to the world. Now I have not only met with some opposition from others face to face in secret, but there is one Edward Burrough (as I heard his name is so, by some of themselves) that hath ventured to stand up against the truth, with the rest of his companions, and hath published a book, called, ' The true faith of the gospel of peace contended for, &c.' In which book of his there is a very great number of heresies cunningly vented by him, and also many things there falsely reported of me, which things in this my discourse I shall very plainly discover; and the way that I shall take, shall be by laying down some of thy expressions, and also some of mine; and by inquiring into the truth of one, and the error of the other, through the assistance of the Spirit of Christ, and according to the scriptures. Only by the way, I think good to mind thee of thy clothing thyself with the words of the prophets and apostles, against whom thou dost fight (as will appear in my following discourse) and also of thy endeavouring to wrest the sword out of the hands of the saints, and art fighting against them bitterly, with a parcel of scolding expressions. But I wish thee to learn, (if thou canst) to be sober, and to keep under thy unruly spirit; and do not so much appear, at least not so grossly, a railing Rabshakeh; but contrariwise, if you would be looked upon to be holy, which (we know and believe that) as yet, many of you are not. Let at the least some appearance of moderation be manifest among you. After many words that are flung into the wind by thee my adversary, in the first and second page of thy book, thou couldst not be contented therewith, as being too few to vent thyself withal; but thou breakest out in page 3. with a small testimony of John Burton, and his fellow, saying, ' They have joined themselves with the broken army of Magog.—And have shewed themselves in the defence of the dragon against the Lamb, in the day of war betwixt them.' When alas! poor soul we do know, and are bold to declare, in the name of the Lord Jesus the Son of Mary, that our God hath owned us, with others of his servants, in his own work against the devil's devices and false doctrine; as instruments both for the comforting and establishing of his own, and also for the convincing and converting of some of them, who aforetime was not converted. And friend, why dost thou say, that we join with Magog in the defence of the dragon against the Lamb, when thou seest the whole drift both of my brother's epistle, and also of my writing, is to exalt and advance the first-born of Mary, the Lord of glory, and to hold on his side, notwithstanding there are so many tempests go through the world. And the rather, because we know that it is he, and he alone, that did bear our sins in his own body on the tree, 1 Pe. ii. 24. for it is he that hath taken away the sins of the world. Now I say therefore, do not thou thus accuse the brethren, for speaking good of the name of Jesus, lest thou be troubled at thy end for thus spending thy beginning in taking part with the devil to accuse God's children.

Then in the same page thou sayest, thou hast numbered up part of our work, and the sum is, A

This is a lie, I bless God, spoken of the adversary against me.

corrupted grain of Babylon's treasure, &c.   Ans.
Friend, The sum of our discourse is of the birth,
righteousness, death, blood, resurrection, ascension, intercession, and second coming of the Son
of Mary the virgin, by which righteousness, blood,
death, burial, resurrection, ascension, and intercession we are saved.   And dost thou count this
a corrupted grain of Babylon's treasure?   Have
a care what thou sayest, least thou utter that with
thy mouth now, which will lie heavy on thy conscience for ever.

Then, as though this thy unwise speaking were
too little, thou breakest out with a taunt, or a jeer,
saying; A larger portion, and more to the purpose
might have been brought in, but with such as you
had, or could procure from your neighbours are
you come.   Ans. Friend, Who hath despised the
day of small things?   But again, we desire not to
bring to others, no nor to know ourselves, anything else but Jesus Christ (the Son of Mary) and
him crucified for our sins. 1 Co. ii. 2.   Then thou
sayest further in the same page, That though thou
hast not seen our faces, yet our spirit is tried, and
we are clearly described to thee, (sayest thou) to
be of the stock of Ishmael, and of the seed of
Cain, whose line reacheth to the murdering priests,
&c.   Ans. Friend, thou art very censorious, and
utterest many words without knowledge.   We
bless God, for the most part of our line, we do
labour to stretch it out, either in building up and
exhorting the saints of the most High, to cleave
close to their Jesus, or else as much as in us lies,
we labour to convince poor souls of their lost condition, according to the word of God, and not to
murder any.   Nay contrariwise, we desire through
grace, if at any time we chance to see any of
Christ's lambs in the teeth of any wolf or bear, be
they never so terrible in appearance; I say, we
desire, we labour, we strive, and lay out ourselves,
if it be possible, to recover the same, though with
the hazard of our lives, or whatsoever may befal
us in doing our duty.   And whereas thou sayest
Here is one false charge laid down by the adversary against me. in the 4th page, That we are found
enemies to Christ, revealed in his
saints.   Ans. Thou dost us wrong,
for we labour all that we may to countenance the same, where he doth indeed appear:
and if at any time we do see or discern, that any
soul hath any breathing after the knowledge of
the Lord Jesus Christ, we are so far from disown-
ing or discountenancing of the same, that we give
them all the encouragement we may: Nay, and we
are so far from discountenancing the doctrine of
God, and his Son Jesus Christ, that we say plainly,
some have not the Spirit of Christ in them, and
they are reprobates, according to that scripture,
Ro. viii. 9. 'If any man have not the Spirit of Christ,
he is none of his.'   And again, Some are 'sensual,

having not the Spirit.' Jude 19.   And again, we are
so far from being against the doctrine of the Spirit
of Christ in his saints, we bless God that we say,
It is the distinguishing character of a true believer,
from others: All which things do I also affirm in
my book, and hold forth, as doth also my brother
in his epistle.   Therefore, I marvel, that you should
be overseen, as to utter so many false things together, in less than four sides of paper, I wonder
what will be the end of your discourse.

Well, now thou dost come and fall a wrangling
with some of the words of my brother Burton,
which are to this purpose, (he speaking before of
the doctrine of Jesus) and this is quite contrary
(saith he) to those commonly called Familists,
Ranters, Quakers, and others, who on the other
hand either deny Christ to be a real man without
them, blasphemously fancying him to be only God
manifest in their flesh; or else make his human
nature with the fulness of the Godhead in it, to be
but a type of God to be manifested in the saints.
Now first of all, the great offence thou takest of
some of these words, is, because he doth join in
his discourse Familists, Ranters, and Quakers
together.   Friend, what harm is it to join a dog
and a wolf together?   A fawning dog and a wolf
in sheep's clothing; they differ a little in outward
appearance, but they can both agree to worry
Christ's lambs.   But again, friend, let us a little
compare the principles of a Ranter and a Quaker
together, and it will clearly appear, that in many
of their principles (at least) they agree, or jump
in one: As

1. The Ranters will own Christ no otherwise,
than only within; and this is also the principle of
the Quakers, they will not own Christ without them.
2. The Ranters, they cry down all teaching, but
the teaching within: and so do the Quakers (witness thousands) and yet condemn their principles
by their practice, as the Ranters also did and do.
Now the apostle saith the contrary, saying, 'He
that knoweth God heareth us; (meaning himself
with the rest of the apostles and servants of Christ.)
He that is not of God heareth not us.' 1 Jn. iv. 6.
Again, 3. The Ranters are neither for the ordinance of baptism with water, nor breaking of bread.
And are not you the same?   4. The Ranters would
profess that they were without sin: and how far
short of this opinion are the Quakers?   5. The
Ranters would not own the resurrection of the
bodies of the saints after they were laid in the
graves: And how say you, Do you believe that the
very bodies of the saints, as the very body of
Abraham, and the body of Isaac, with the bodies
of all the saints, notwithstanding some of them
have been in the graves thousands of years, others
hundreds, some less: I say, Do you believe the
resurrection of these very bodies again, which were

buried so long since; or do you hold, as the Ranters do, nothing but the resurrection from a sinful to an holy state in this life.

And really I tell thee (reader) plainly, that for the generality, the very opinions that are held at this day by the Quakers, are the same that long ago were held by the Ranters. Only the Ranters had made them threadbare at an alehouse, and the Quakers have set a new gloss upon them again, by an outward legal holiness, or righteousness. But again, Why should you be so angry with my brother, for joining of a sinner and a liar together? Is there any great harm in that? Surely no. And the joining Ranters and Quakers together, is but so. The Quakers themselves confess, the Ranters are to be disowned, page 4. Nay if they would not, yet God hath disowned them in the open view of the nations. Now that the Quakers are liars, I shall prove from their own mouth. As first, from the several things that I did oppose even now, page 1—4, of this book, called, 'The true Faith of the Gospel of Peace,' &c. Now lest they should be slighted and set at nought, I shall shew you clearly this man's lies manifestly laid down in his book against me. As first, he saith of me in his book, page 11, 12. That I said positively, the blood of Christ was shed before the world began. Whereas I said only this, *That in the account of God* (mark it, in the account of God) his blood was shed before the world was, according to that scripture, Re. xiii. 8. 'The Lamb slain from the foundation of the world,' in my book, page 3 [141]. Secondly, he saith, that I cry aloud against Christ within, in page 24. of his book. And again he saith, 'That all my work is an obscure shooting against the manifestation of Christ within.' Where he speaks very falsely of me, for I confess and own God's Christ within as well as without, as appears in my book, page 206. towards the end [173]. And in the epistle to my book you may find the same held out by me for two or three leaves together; besides, many other places of my book doth testify of the same; therefore, doth not he lie miserably in this also?

Again, he saith, that I am one of those that do preach for hire, through covetousness, making merchandise of souls, page 23. of his book, which is also an untruth, as I shall shew further when I come to the place.

Again he saith, in page 30, that I said 'Christ's coming in the Spirit was no coming.' Here also he uttereth falsehood. I never said so, as many of our brethren can witness. But of this also in its place, when I come to it, with many other things which he hath very untruly vented of me, which I fear not but they shall be cleared, both now, and also at the second appearance of the man Christ Jesus. And therefore friend (I say to thee) be not so pharisaical as to say within thine heart, 'I am not as this publican.' Why am I reckoned with the Ranters? Thou art, both thou and thy fellows, of the same mind with them in many things, and shall assuredly partake of the same plague with them, if they and you repent not speedily.

Again, in page 7, thou wouldest make us believe, that the Quakers do really and truly lay the Christ of God, God-man, for their foundation. Saying, 'We prize the Lord Jesus Christ, God-man, to be precious to us, and to all that do believe, and have owned him to be the foundation,' &c. Now friend, this is fairly spoken; but by words in general we may be deceived, because a man may speak one thing with his mouth, and mean another thing in his heart; especially it is so with those that use to utter themselves doubtfully; therefore we will a little enquire what it is to lay Christ, God-man for a foundation.

1. Then, To lay God's Christ, God-man, for a foundation, is to believe that man that was born of the Virgin Mary, to be the saviour.

How he was and is the saviour, and therefore if you do indeed lay him for your foundation, then you do believe that when the man Christ did hang on the cross on Mount Calvary, that then your sins were satisfied for at that time, as it is written, 'Who his ownself bare our sins in his own body on the tree.' 1 Pe. ii. 24.

2. If the Christ of God, God-man, be indeed your foundation, then you do believe, that that very man in that very body, did fulfil all the law, in the point of justification, as it is written, 'Christ *is* the end of the law for righteousness to every one that believeth.' Ro. x. 4. So that now, believe aright in what the Son of Mary hath done without on the cross, and be saved.

3. If you have laid Christ that man aright for your foundation, then you do believe, that when he was raised out of the sepulchre into which Joseph had laid him, then at that time was accomplished your justification. Ro. iv. 25. How say you to these things, Do you make an open profession of them without dissembling? Or do you not (notwithstanding your talk of Christ) in very deed deny the virtue of the death and blood of Christ without, as for justification and life? If so, you have not laid him for your foundation.

4. If you have indeed laid Christ, God-man, for your foundation, then you do lay the hope of your felicity and joy on this, That the Son of Mary is now absent from his children in his person and humanity, making intercession for them and for thee, in the presence of his Father. 2 Co. v. 6. And the reason that thou canst rejoice here-at is, because thou hast not only heard of it with thine ear only, but dost enjoy the sweet hope and faith

of them in thy heart; which hope and faith is begotten by the Spirit of Christ, which Spirit dwelleth in thee, (if thou be a believer) and sheweth those things to thee to be the only things. And God having shewn thee these things, thus without thee by the Spirit that dwelleth in thee, thou hast mighty encouragement to hope for the glory that shall be revealed at the coming again of the man Christ Jesus, of which glory thou hast also greater ground to hope for a share in, because that that Spirit that alone is able to discover to thee the truth of these things, is given to thee of God, as the first fruits of that glory which is hereafter to be revealed, being obtained for thee by the man Christ Jesus's death on Mount Calvary, and by his blood that was shed there, together with his resurrection from the dead, out of the grave where they had laid him. Also, thou believest that he is gone away from thee in the same body which was hanged on the cross, to take possession of that glory, which thou, through his obedience, shall at his (the very same man's) return from heaven the second time, have bestowed upon thee, having all this while prepared and preserved it for thee, as he saith himself: ' I go to prepare a place for you. And if I go and prepare a place for you, I will come again, and receive you unto myself, that where I am, *there* ye may be also.' Jn. xiv. 2, 3. Again,

5. If thou hast laid Christ, God-man, for thy foundation, though thou hast the Spirit of this man Christ within thee, yet thou dost not look that justification should be wrought out for thee, by that Spirit of Christ that dwelleth within thee, for thou knowest that salvation is already obtained for thee by the man Christ Jesus without thee, and is witnessed to thee by his Spirit which dwelleth within thee. And thus much doth this man Christ Jesus testify unto us where he saith he shall glorify me; mark, ' He shall glorify me;' (saith the Son of Mary) but how ? Why, ' he shall receive of mine (what I have done, and am doing in the presence of the Father) and shall shew *it* unto you.' Jn. xvi. 14. I have been a little the larger in this, because it is of weight.

But again, thou sayest further, The rest of this first epistle I shall say little to; only thus much is the mind of the penman's spirit, secretly smiting at the doctrine of true faith and salvation, (to wit) Christ within. Ans. My friend, by saying that my brother doth strike at the doctrine of true faith and salvation, thou dost him a great deal of wrong; for it is so far from him so to do, that he telleth souls plainly, that without true faith in the blood of the Son of Mary, who was crucified on Mount Calvary, there is no remission; for saith he, it is only through that one offering then given up to

Here again he speaks falsely.

the Father, that you must be justified. And that is according to the whole stream of scripture : For by one offering, What was that ? Why, the offering up of the body of Jesus once for all, (He. x. 10.) he hath perfected for ever them that are sanctified. ' But this man after he had offered one sacrifice for sins, for ever sat down.' Mark it : ' This man after he had offered one sacrifice for sins, for ever sat down on the right hand of God.' ver. 12.

And as for thy saying, that salvation is Christ within; if thou mean in opposition to Christ without; instead of pleading for Christ, thou wilt plead against him; for Christ, God-man, without on the cross. did bring in salvation for sinners. And the right believing of that, doth justify the soul. Therefore Christ within, or the Spirit of him who did give himself a ransom, doth not work out justification for the soul in the soul; but doth lead the soul out of. itself, and out of that that can be done within itself, to look for salvation in that man that is now absent from his saints on earth. 2 Co. v. 6. Why so? For [because] it knoweth that there is salvation in none other. Ac. iv. 12, And therefore I would wish thee to have a care what thou dost, for I tell thee, that man who is now jeered by some, because he is preached to be without them, will very suddenly come the second time, to the great overthrow of those, who have spoken, and shall still speak against him. Jude 14, 15.

Thou sayest also the next thing thou mindest, is this in the second epistle,* where a question is asked. Who are the men that at this day are so deluded by the Quakers, and other pernicious doctrines, but they that counted it enough to be talkers of the gospel, &c. This man, saith the Quaker, is of the same Spirit with his fellow, and will more abound in lies, &c. And why? because he saith the Quakers are those deceivers that at this day beguile poor souls by their doctrine. Alas poor man, why shouldest thou be angry for my speaking the truth, in saying: The Quakers are deceivers, this will easily appear.

1. They deny the man Christ to be without them, and own Christ no otherwise, but as he is within, contrary to that scripture, which saith, for 'while we are at home in the body we are absent from the Lord.' This is touching his bodily presence. And again, he was parted from them, ' and a cloud received him out of their sight.' And he was carried away from them, and so received up into heaven, Ac. i. 9—11. Now he that denieth this, is a deceiver, as is clear, in that he doth speak against the truth laid down in the scripture.

---

* Bunyan's epistle to " Some Gospel Truths Opened."

2. The Quakers are deceivers, in that they persuade souls that Christ is crucified in them, dead within them, and kept down with some thing within them, which was never taught by those that spoke the scripture from the Spirit of God. Shew me a scripture to confirm such a doctrine as this, which hath been avouched over and over by the Quakers.

3. The Quakers are deceivers, because they do persuade souls, that that man that was born of the Virgin Mary, is not above the clouds and the stars, when the scripture saith, 'a cloud received him out of the sight of his saints.' And again, that he is above the highest heavens, which must needs be above the stars, for they are not the highest.

4. The Quakers are deceivers, because they persuade souls not to believe, that that man that was crucified, and rose again flesh and bones, Lu. xxiv. 38—40. shall so come again, that very man, in the clouds of heaven to judgment as he went away; and at the very same time shall raise up all the men and women out of their graves, and cause them to come to the valley of Jehoshaphat; because there will he, that very man, sit to judge all the heathen round about. I say, they strive to beat souls off from believing this, though it be the truth of God witnessed by the scripture, Joel iii. 11, 12. as also Ac. i. 10, 11. 'This same Jesus, which is taken up from you into heaven, shall so come (mark, the very same) in like manner as ye have seen him go into heaven.' 'And his feet shall stand in that day (the day of his second coming) upon the Mount of Olives.' Zec. xiv. 4. Where is that? Not within thee, but that which is without Jerusalem, before, it on the east side. I say now, he that persuades souls not to believe this, but makes them believe there is no such thing, as the Quakers do, he is a deceiver. Again, the Quakers make no difference between that light wherewith Christ, as he is God, hath enlightened all; and the Spirit of Christ he gives not to all, which I shall show by and by to be a deceit.

5. The Quakers are deceivers, because they say, That every one hath that which is like the Spirit of Christ, even as good as the Spirit of Christ, page 10 of his book, which is desperate blasphemy. The scripture saith plainly, 'That some are sensual, having not the Spirit.' And yet though they have not that, they have, says the Quakers, that which is as good as that. O wonderful deceit, as I shall farther show by and by when I come to the place. But to cover himself, and so his deceit, he doth apply that to himself that should be applied for the encouragement of the children of God: saying, the children of God was always counted deceivers, we (saith

VOL. II.

he) have a cloud of witnesses. Answer, friend, they were called deceivers, and were not so; but you are rightly called so, as I have already showed, and shall show farther by and by. In the meantime know, that the devil knows how to take children's bread, and cast it to the dogs.

Then the next thing that he is grieved with, is, because I said, there are none but a company of light notionists, ranters, with here and there a legalist, that was shaking in their principles, that were carried away by the Quakers, &c. When this appears in all men's sight that can see, though you would not have it so (it is like.) And as for your saying, because all sorts of people are brought to God, I am offended therewith; I answer, No friend, I bless God my soul can rejoice that souls come in to Jesus Christ, though it grieves me to see, how some with a spirit of delusion are deceived, and destroyed, by its coming unto them as an angel of light. And whereas thou sayest I am like the Pharisees, who said, none believe, but a company of poor people, which know not the law. Answ. I bless God, I do know they are the poor that receive the gospel; but friend, I must tell you, that you and your fellows may seek for justification from the law, and yet have no better a recompense, than to be condemned by the law.

Another false thing spoken of me, by the Quakers.

Now passing many railings, I come to the next thing that thou dost stumble at, which is in that I say, some of those delusions the devil doth deceive poor souls withal, is first, in that he doth persuade them, that salvation was not completely wrought out for sinners by the man Christ Jesus, though he did it gloriously upon the cross without the gates of Jerusalem. Now these words, 'he did it gloriously on the cross, without the gates of Jerusalem,' thou leavest out. Therefore I ask, do you believe that at that time, when he did hang upon that cross on Mount Calvary, that he did by that death he died there, redeem all his elect from eternal vengeance? If not, whatever thou sayest, thou wilt certainly see, that Satan hath caught thee in his snare, notwithstanding thy railing against the Lord Jesus. And friend, thou mayest call thy conscience the man Christ Jesus, or the light (as thou callest it) in thy conscience the man Christ Jesus; which if thou do, this is a delusion, and a dangerous doctrine. For a Spirit hath not flesh and bones, and so hath the man Christ Jesus. Now it may be, you think farther that the church, with the Spirit of Christ, is the man Christ Jesus, which is also a damnable heresy. Therefore, speak plainly; Dost thou believe that the man Christ Jesus is ascended from his people in his person? And again, dost thou believe that he which ascended from his disciples, did bring in

2 A

everlasting salvation for them, in that his body which ascended from them ? An answer to this might give great satisfaction to souls, if also it might be made in words easily to be understood. Again,

Thou art also offended with the second deceit which I lay down in my epistle, which is (say I) for the devil to bid souls follow that light which they brought into the world with them, telling them, that that will lead them to the kingdom. Now thou seemest gravelled, because I said, which they brought into the world with them. If thou art offended at that, show me when, and at what time every soul receives a light from Christ after it comes into the world. Now this I say, That every man hath not the Spirit of Christ within him. Jude 19. And that there is nothing that can show the soul the things of Christ savingly, but the Spirit of Christ. 1 Co. ii. 11. Then will not you yourself confess, that he is deluded, that is persuaded to follow that light that cannot reveal Christ unto him ? But I must mind you of one filthy error also which thou layest down in page 10. Corrupting the scripture to make it good, but in vain ; where thou sayest, That light which every man is lightened withal, will lead unto the kingdom of peace and righteousness. And then thou addest, for saith Christ, ' I am the light of the world, he that followeth me shall not [abide in darkness, or] walk in darkness.' Pray mark. First, thou callest it the light of Christ, wherewith he hath lightened every one ; and here thou comest a step higher, and callest it, Christ himself; and then corruptest that scripture, where the Son of Mary saith, 'I am the light of the world,' &c. Here thou wouldest very willingly have room to broach thy folly, but it may not be ; for though Christ be the light of the world, yet he is not in every one in the world. But secondly, I pray where was Christ when he spake those words ? was he I say, within his disciples, or without them, when he said, ' I am the light of the world?' He was without them, and walked up and down in the world with them from place to place, a very man. Therefore, he did not mean at that time any light within, but himself who was without. And indeed, they who will follow Christ aright, must follow him without, to the cross without, for justification on Mount Calvary without, (that is, they must seek for justification by his obedience without.) To the grave without, and to his ascension and intercession in heaven without ; and this must be done through the operation of his own Holy Spirit, that he hath promised shall show these things unto them, being given within them for that purpose. Jn. xvi. 14. Now the Spirit of Christ *that* leads also, but whither ? It leads to Christ without, which said, being without, ' I am the light of the world:

he that followeth me shall not walk in darkness, but shall have the light of life.' Jn. viii. 12. Deny this, that Christ was without when he spake those words (I am the light of the world :) if you can.

But to come more close, to the thing. That light wherewith Christ, as he is God, hath lightened every one that cometh into the world, is the soul of man, which is the life of the body, and yet itself is but a creature, and made by the creator of all things, Is. lvii. 16. and is not the Spirit, as some do think it is. This creature hath one faculty of its own nature, called conscience, which hath its place in the soul, where it is as a judge to discern of things good or bad, and judge them accordingly, as the apostle saith, speaking of the heathens, ' Their conscience also bearing witness and their thoughts the meanwhile accusing or else excusing one another.' Ro. ii. 14. This conscience is that in which is the law of nature, 1 Co. xi. 14. which is able to teach the Gentiles, that sin against the law, is sin against God: And yet it is called but even nature itself, as he saith there, ' Doth not even nature itself teach you ? ' &c.

Now this conscience, this nature itself, because it can control, and chide them for sin, who give ear unto it, therefore must it be idolized, and made a God of. O wonderful ! that men should make a God and a Christ of their consciences, because they can convince of sin. But thou goest ramping on, and sayest, there is nothing but the light of Christ that will convince of sin, and thou biddest me, mind that. Now dost thou mean the Spirit of Christ ? dost thou say that that which thou callest the light of Christ, is the Spirit of Christ ? If so, then there is conscience which is not the Spirit of Christ, but a poor dunghill creature, in comparison of the Spirit of Christ ; yet will convince of sin, as is clear, from that 8th of John. Where the woman is mentioned, who was taken in adultery by the Pharisees, or others, who when they had brought her to Christ, and began to accuse her, Christ said, ' He that is without sin among you, let him first cast a stone at her.' And what then ? When they heard that, they were convicted by their own consciences. Mark, he doth not say, by the light of Christ in their consciences, as some would have it be ; No, but by their own consciences they were convinced, and went out one by one. And were they all served so ? Yea, from the eldest, even to the last; for they all had consciences, though not the Spirit of Christ. So that friend, here is something beside the Spirit of Christ, that can and doth convince of sin, even a man's own conscience, the law of nature ; nay nature itself, which no man will say is as good as the Spirit of Christ, except they are guided by a deluding Spirit. Again, thou sayest, He that convinceth of sins against the law, leads up to the fulfilling of the law. Friend, thy conscience convinceth of sins against the law, follow thy conscience, it may lead thee under the curse of the law, through its weakness; but it can never deliver thee from the curse of the law by its power. For if righteousness come by the obedience to the law, or by thy conscience either, then Christ is dead in vain. Ga. ii. 21.

Again thou sayest, 'That I and my generation would leap over the law.'

Answ. For justification we look beyond it to the Son of Mary; yet we know that the law is good, if it be used lawfully; but if it be used unlawfully, as those do use it, who seek to be justified by their obedience to it, it is made an idol of, and a saviour, though it were given to no such purpose: For if there had been a law given which could have given life, verily righteousness should have come by (thy obedience to) the law. Ga. iii. 21. Now at thy conclusions, sometimes thou dost utter thyself in this wise, Learn what this means.

Answ. Indeed thy words are dark, and enough to deceive the hearts of the simple; but blessed be God, he hath given me to understand, that thou dost all along in the drift of thy discourse, disown Christ without, by pretending to a Christ within; whereas hadst thou indeed the Spirit of Christ within thee, it would be thy great business to extol and magnify the Son of Mary, the Christ of God without thee, because it is the nature of the same Spirit so to do, even to glorify Christ without, who went away from his disciples into heaven, to prepare a place for them. Lu. xxiv. 50, 51.

Then thou further sayest (with a kind of disdaining spirit) 'Many things more thou passest by in my book, as being not pertinent to the thing in hand.' But I believe they are so pertinent, that neither thou, nor thy friends or fellows are able to contradict without blaspheming, in the view of all them that have eyes to see: for if they could, it should have been done by thee. And whereas thou sayest, 'Fools must be meddling.' Answer, It must needs be, that the saints of God should be called fools by the enemies of the man Christ Jesus without, because that the doctrine of the man Christ Jesus, crucified without for the sins of poor sinners, is also held to be foolishness by them; although it be the wisdom; and also the power of God, unto every one that believeth. 1 Co. i. 23, 24.

And further, thou sayest, that the Pope can speak as much of Christ without, as I. Answer, friend, dost thou put no difference betwixt the speaking of Christ without, and believing in Christ without? I tell thee, though there may be many that can speak of the Christ of God without, yet there are but very few that can, or do believe indeed in him without, by the mighty operation of his Holy Spirit within. Nay, you yourselves do testify this, who deny that the salvation of sinners was completely wrought out by that one offering of Jesus Christ without upon the cross on Mount Calvary, and that he is ascended from his disciples above the clouds, touching his bodily presence, as in 2 Co. v. 6. compared with Ac. i. 9—11.

Then again thou sayest, 'I do ask myself a question, and do also answer it myself deceitfully.' The question is, Do not the scriptures make mention of a Christ within? And thou sayest, I answer it deceitfully myself. But I answer again, that I am not ashamed of that answer I then gave, because I know it is truth; and whereas thou sayest it is deceitful, and yet canst not find fault with any point thereof, it confirms me, that had there been falsity in it, such an enemy to the truth, as thou art, would have taken that advantage, as to have discovered, that thereby thou mightest have rendered the truth the more odious. The answer I shall leave to the Christian reader, which is so indeed; yet am confirmed myself concerning it, and shall give thee an answer to thy question, which is, Doth not the scriptures say, or witness, that all that have not Christ within are reprobates? Answer: Yes, the scripture saith so, and it is true, they that have not the Spirit of Christ in them, are reprobates. But there are some that are reprobates, that you will confess. Then by your own argument you must grant, that some have not the Spirit of Christ in them. Pray take notice, they that have not the Spirit of Christ in them are reprobates. There are some who are reprobates; therefore there are some who are sensual, 'having not the Spirit of Christ in them.' (See thy folly how it is made manifest.) Ju. v. 19. The next thing thou art offended withal, is, because I say, the devil deceives poor souls by persuading them to follow the light within which all men have. Answer, friend, I say, again, and again, That there is nothing less than the Spirit of Christ, that can give a soul a sight of justification by the blood of the man Christ Jesus without, by following of it. Now as thou sayest thyself, some are reprobates, and have not the Spirit of Christ.

Then is it any heresy to say, that it is of the devil to persuade a soul to follow that light which is no better than conscience, or nature itself, Ro. ii. 14. which are not able to lead to Christ his things, being foolishness to it; or is conscience, which every one is lightened withal, the Spirit of Christ? give an answer in sincerity.

Then thou sayest, that my whole purpose is a secret smiting at the light wherewith Christ hath lightened every man. I answer, my whole design in my book, is, and was, these following things:—

1. To show souls, where salvation is to be had. Namely, in Christ without.

2. To show souls how they should lay hold of

this salvation; namely, by the operation of the Spirit of Christ, which must be given within.

3. To forewarn poor souls, that they should not deceive themselves, neither by conscience, nor the law; which are both inferior, and much below the Spirit of Christ; even as much as he that buildeth the house, hath more honour than the house. He. iii. 3.

4. To show how poor souls should know, whether they had the Spirit of Christ, or not, within them, or whether the Spirit of the devil had exalted himself above the Spirit of Christ, by transforming himself into an angel of light.

Farther, thou thinkest I contradict myself, because I admonish poor souls to beg of God to convince them by his Holy Spirit; and thou sayest, This is my confusion. When alas, confusion is of, and from thyself, who wouldst make a defiled conscience, the law and the Spirit of Christ to be all one; as I shall further clear to the reader by and by.

But I tell thee friend, there are many who have not the Spirit of Christ, and yet are convinced of sin by their own consciences, Ju. viii. 9. He doth not say, 'by the light of Christ in their consciences,' that is a saying of your own, without warrant from the word of God, but 'by their own consciences.' Mark that: Now I knowing, that a man may be convinced, and yet not by the Spirit of Christ (for he may be without that) but by nature itself. 1 Co. xi. 14. I do admonish every soul, if they love themselves, to beg of God for Jesus Christ his sake, that he would not only let them be convinced by these poor, low, empty, beggarly things (their consciences) in respect of the Spirit of Christ, but that he would convince them by that Spirit of his effectually, which is not only able to show their lost state because of sins against the law, but also, to lead them to the right Saviour, and plant them into him, which all other things are not able to do. And thus much in answer to thy scolding against my epistle the truth of which I bless God through the strength of Christ, I could be willing to seal with my blood.

And now friend, in love to thy soul, I say, have a care of thyself, that thou do not satisfy thyself with anything, until thou seest by the operation of the Spirit of Christ (which thou must have given thee from heaven, as being without it before conversion) that the blood of that man Christ Jesus that was crucified on Mount Calvary, did at that same time, when it was there shed, wash thee from all thy sins, and be not so stout, and so stern against the truth, because it suits not with thy beguiled conscience. (Bear with me in patience) and seriously inquire into the truth of things according to the scriptures. 'For they are they that testify of Christ,' and how salvation doth come by him.

In thy entering upon my book, the first thing I find thee wrangling with, is by corrupting my words, and then by calling me liar.

Thou corruptest my words saying, That I said, 'The blood of Christ was shed before the world began.' Whereas I said, that in the account of God, (mark, in the account of God) the blood of Christ was shed before the world began. Friend, art thou not able to distinguish, betwixt a thing being done in God's account, or according to his foreknowledge, and a thing that is really and actually done? Surely it was either thy folly to speak evil of the thing thou knowest not, or else thy madness doth much appear, in that though thou understandest these things, yet for to wrangle by corrupting my sayings here, as also in other places, as will afterwards appear. This is in page 11, of thine, page 3, of my book.

Then thou goest on, page 12, and quotest the place where I say, page 37. How horribly are those deceived who look on Jesus (but thou leavest out those words, the Son of Mary) to be but a type; which thing you say, you know none that do. And again thou sayest, that I say, he is of something afterwards to be revealed. My words thou corruptest; thou wouldst fain gather thus much out of my words, by corrupting them. That though I denied Christ Jesus the Son of Mary to be a type, yet I myself say, He was Here my words a type of something afterward to be are corrupted. revealed. Which thing, as there in my book, so here again I do most positively deny, and I quote the same words again, for a second confirmation of the same, saying as then I did; 'How horribly are those deceived, who look on Jesus the Son of Mary to be but a shadow, or type of something that was afterwards to be revealed.' Whereas the scriptures most lively hold him forth to be the Christ of God; and not a type or shadow of a Spirit, or body afterwards to be revealed, but himself was the very substance of all things that did any way hold forth, or type out, Christ to come: And when he was indeed come, then was an end put to the law for righteousness or justification to every one that believeth. Ro. x. 4. And therefore, friend, though thou hast, or wouldest corrupt my words, yet have a care of corrupting Christ's words, lest thou dost even heap up wrath against the day of wrath, and revelation of the righteous judgment of God. And whereas thou sayest, 'Thou deniest not but Jesus is the substance.' Answer, I doubt thou dost not speak thine heart plainly, but hidest thyself with so saying, as with an apron; if we inquire into what it is to hold forth Jesus the Son of Mary to be the substance. Therefore he that holds forth Jesus the Son of Mary to be indeed the substance, and not a type; holds forth and believes, that that Jesus that was born of the Virgin Mary, did in his own body of flesh fulfil the law, and impute the righteousness of his obedience unto them that he accomplished then without them; and that his blood that was shed without on the cross, doth, and hath washed away all sin past, present, and to come, from him that believeth this; as it is written, ' For what the law could not do, in that it was weak through the flesh, (that is, through our flesh:) God sending his own Son in the likeness of sinful flesh, and for sin, condemned sin in the flesh: ' That is, he was condemned in the flesh that he took on him of the Virgin Mary. Ro. viii. 3. And again, he bore our sins in his own body on the tree, which was the cross on Mount Calvary.

Jesus also (saith the apostle) that he might sanctify the people with his own blood, suffered: Where? Not in any believer, but without the gate of Jerusalem. He. xiii. 12. How say you, do you really believe that at that time when Jesus did hang on the cross without Jerusalem's gate, even at that time he did give the justice of God a full and complete satisfaction for all the sins of all believers, that have been formerly, or are now, or hereafter shall be? Or do you look upon Jesus at that time to be but a shadow, or type of somewhat that was afterwards to be done within? Answer plainly, yea, or no; that the simple may understand you.

Now I come to answer thy query laid down, page 12, in these words; ' Did Christ Jesus put an end to the law, for them who live yet in the transgression of the law? Or doth he justify that which the law condemned?' Indeed a right answer to this will be great satisfaction to some, though I think some trouble to others. And therefore in answer to thy question I shall lay down these following things:

Answ. 1. Christ Jesus did put an end to the law for righteousness, for all that the Father hath given him; as it is written, the body of Jesus was offered once for all, for all that shall be saved; for he shall not be offered a second time: No, ' but once for all.' He. x. 10. Once in the end of the world hath he appeared, to put away sin by the sacrifice of himself; and he hath done it once by himself for all. He. ix. 26. Otherwise he must have often suffered since the world began: But that must not be; for he ' dieth no more.' Ro. vi. 9. But say you, ' Did he put an end to the law for them who still live in transgression?'

Answ. 2. There are many poor souls that are given unto Christ, who yet live in their sins. But Christ did at that time, when he hanged on the cross, give a full and complete satisfaction for them. ' In due time Christ died for the ungodly: For scarcely for a righteous man will one die, yet peradventure for a good man some would even dare to die.' Ay, ' But God commendeth his love towards us, in that, while we were yet sinners, Christ died for us.' While we were yet sinners, yet ungodly. Ro. v. 6—8. Nay, he did not only die for those who still live in sin, but he also makes intercession now at the throne of his Father's grace for them. ' And he made intercession for the transgressors.' Is. liii. 12. ' Thou hast ascended on high, thou hast led captivity captive; - and received gifts for men.' For what men? Even ' for the rebellious also.' To what end? ' That the LORD God might dwell *among them.*' Ps. lxviii. 18.

And whereas thou askest; ' Doth he justify that which the law condemneth, before the work of the law be finished?' I answer:

Answ. 3. That at that very time when Jesus Christ did hang on the cross on Mount Calvary, was buried, rose again from the dead, and ascended above the clouds from his disciples, at that very time was all the law fulfilled for righteousness. He is the end of the law, mark; he is the end of the law for righteousness. But if there were anything yet to be done for justification, which was not then done; there could not be an end put to the law for righteousness, for every one that believeth. But in that there is an end put to the law for righteousness by Jesus for all the elect of God, Christ having once fulfilled it for them: It is manifest, that there was not anything then left undone by Christ at that time, which was afterward to be done by his own Spirit in his children for justification, only believe what the man Christ, at that time did do, and be saved; Ac. xiii. 29—39. and whereas thou asketh, whether Christ did justify that which the law condemneth?

Answ. 4. I answer, Fourthly, That though Christ Jesus did not justify sins of ungodliness, yet he justifieth the ungodly. ' Now to him that worketh is the reward [given, or] not reckoned of grace, but of debt. But to him that worketh not, but believeth on him that justifieth the ungodly, (mark the ungodly) his faith is counted for righteousness.' Ro. iv. 4. He is he that justifieth, having finished the righteousness of the law in his own person for them. ' Mine own arm brought salvation,' saith he, but how? Even by his bleeding on the cross; ' we have redemption through his blood,' Ep. i. 7. which was shed without the gate. He. xiii. 12. Ay, and though the law condemneth a sinner, yet let but that sinner believe in Christ, in what he hath done in his own person, and he shall be ' justified from all things, from which he could not be justified by the law of Moses.' Ac. xiii. 39.

And whereas thou asketh me the meaning of that scripture, ' not one tittle of the law shall fail till all be fulfilled.' I answer, That the law hath already been fulfilled for justification, for every one that believeth: And a believer is to do nothing for justification, only believe and be saved; though that law be a rule for every one that believeth to walk by, but not for justification. But if you do not put a difference between justification wrought by the man Christ without, and sanctification wrought by the Spirit of Christ, within; teaching believers their duty to their God, for his love in giving Christ; you are not able to divide the word aright: but contrariwise, you corrupt the word of God, and cast stumbling-blocks before the people; and will certainly one day most deeply smart for your folly, except you repent. Here is a plain answer that may satisfy the simple. The Lord God grant that they may lay it to heart effectually.

Now this I say further, that if God enable any to receive this doctrine aright (namely what I said even now) it will more engage the soul to God, than all the threatenings, thunder-claps, and curses that come from the law itself. And a soul will do more for God, seeing itself redeemed by the blood of the Lamb the Son of Mary, Jn. i. 29. than if he had all the conditions of the law to fulfil, and might be sure to have heaven for the fulfilling of them. Now as to the assurance thou speakest of at the end of thy question. I know in the first place, that though believers themselves do sin, yet they have ' an advocate with the Father, Jesus Christ the righteous:' 1 Jn. ii. 1. And though the doctrine of the gospel be to abstain from all appearance of evil, yet our Lord Jesus Christ is so pitiful, as not altogether to deprive his children of an assurance of their salvation,* though sometimes through weakness they do transgress. And whereas you would lay an assurance on our obedience to the law; I say, our assurance comes through our believing, and our obedience to the law is a fruit of our believing; for every one that hath this hope, that he is one of the children, or sons of God, by faith in Jesus, 1 Jn. iii. 3. ' purifieth himself, even as he is pure.' Holiness of life, if it be right, flows from an assurance of our being justified by Christ's death on the cross, on Mount Calvary; as it is written again, that he might sanctify his people with his own blood, he suffered without the gate.

But again, page 12. thou seemest offended, because I say, ' They are deceived, who think to obtain salvation by following the law, which they call Christ, though falsely.' Why shouldst thou be offended at this, when the scripture saith plainly, ' That by the deeds of the law there shall no flesh be justified in his sight: for by the law *is* the knowledge of sin.' Ro. iii. 20. But this is thy frothy argument, ' The law convinceth, and is our schoolmaster to bring us to Christ; therefore the law is not taken away,' sayest thou. Friend, what is this to the purpose? must we seek for justification

* For the proof of this, read the good love of God to David, Peter, and others, which did most woefully sin again after they were converted.

by the works of the law, because the law convinceth? you may as well say, we must seek for justification from our consciences, because they do convince: Now where the scripture saith, the law was our schoolmaster to bring us to Christ; do you think it means, we must be first fitted by purification of ourselves by, or according to the law, before we can be saved by Christ from the curse of the law? If you say, yea; then doth not this follow, that Christ Jesus did not come to save sinners, but to save the righteous; and if so, then you must say, that Christ, Peter, Paul, and all the servants of the Lord are liars, who have testified that Christ died not for the godly, but for the ungodly and sinners.

But where the scripture saith, The law was our schoolmaster to bring us to Christ: I ask again, is it the ceremonial law, or the moral law that is meant in this place? If you say the moral, or the ten commandments, I answer; That doth not lead to life and so not to Christ; but is properly the ministration of condemnation. 2 Co. iii. 6—11. That is, the proper work of the moral law, or ten commandments, is to condemn, if it be not obeyed; and yet not to bless, until it be every jot fulfilled, which is impossible to be done by any man for justification, in that exact and severe way which the law calls for; which makes the Apostle say, as many as are of the works of the law, are under the curse. Mark, he doth not say, as many as are of the works of sin, are under the curse, though that be true; but as many as are of the works of the law, are under the curse: ' for it is written, Cursed *is* every one that continueth not in all things which are written in the book of the law to do them. But that no man is justified by the law in the sight of God, *it is* evident: for, The just shall live by faith.' Ga. iii. 10, 11.

If it be meant of the ceremonial law, as I am most inclinable to believe, because he saith it was our schoolmaster; he doth not say it is, but it WAS our schoolmaster to bring us to Christ, being tutor or governor; holding and significations forth, Christ to come by its types until the time appointed of the Father, which appointed time (and so that law) was to have an end, when God sent forth his Son made of a woman, Jesus the Son of Mary, who was made under the law, to redeem those that were under the law.

Now the ceremonial law did bring or lead to Christ these two ways: First, In that it did continue in full force until he did come into the world, and had done that which was by it held out for him to do.

Secondly, In that the several types and shadows, as the blood of bulls and lambs, with diverse other services did lead to, or hold forth Christ that was to come: But the moral law, or ten commandments, is so far from leading us to Christ by our following it, that it doth even lead those that are led by it under the curse. Not because the law hath an evil end in it, but because of our weakness and inability to do it; therefore it is forced, as it is just, to pass a sentence of condemnation on every one, that in every particular fulfils it not.

In the next place, thou art offended because I said, ' It is not of works least any man should boast, as those fond hypocrites, called Quakers would do.'

Thou art offended it seems, because I call you boasters. You need not, for I do not know your fellows for boasting under heaven, in that you, (Pharisees like) do cry up yourselves to be the men, and condemns all others; when you are THE MEN that are the greatest enemies to the Christ of God without (who is the Saviour) of any men under heaven. And in that you pretend you are perfect, when you are the notablest liars and corrupters of the sayings of the people of God, yea, and of the scriptures also, that ever I came near in all the days of my life; and I doubt not but before I have done with you, I shall make it appear to them that read or hear my lines aright. The query in page 13. runs thus, ' Will that faith which is without works justify?' I answer, No, neither will those works which are without faith sanctify. What then, Is it faith and works together that doth justify? No, it is only faith in the blood of the man Christ, that did hang on the cross on Mount Calvary, that doth justify in the sight of God and the soul, and it is the fruits of faith, good works, which do justify in the sight of men. So that when it is said, we are justified by works; it is not meant that works will justify in the sight of God. No, but shew me (or shew men) thy faith, or justify thy faith to be true and right before men by thy works. Shew men thy faith by thy works, it is in the sight of men. So that we conclude a man is justified by faith without the works of the law in the sight of God, and so his own soul also, and his faith is justified, or made manifest to be indeed that which is right, both to believers, and to the world by its works. Though I must confess, that both Paul and Peter, and the rest of the saints, may sometimes be deceived in the truth of the faith of others by their works.

Again in page 17 thou seemest to be offended, because, I say ' living by faith, is to apply the Lord Jesus Christ, his benefits, as birth, righteousness, death, blood, resurrection, ascension, and intercession, together with the glorious benefits of his second coming to me, as mine, and for me, &c.' Ga. ii. 20.

Friend, methinks thou shouldest find no fault with this, but that the Man Christ Jesus, the Son of Mary, is not very pleasant to thee, because thou hast swallowed down secretly another doctrine; but friend, I speak of applying these things, and thou speakest of talking of them, I know that there are many who talk of Christ, that will fall short of heaven and glory.

But tell me, what sayest thou to him that doth apply all these things to his soul, is there not enough in them to justify him, that doth really and truly in the power of the Spirit, believe this to be true which I have said? or dost thou deny it and preach another gospel? and whereas thou sayest, the word of the gospel saith not, who shall ascend, to fetch Christ from above for salvation. Though there is never a scripture that saith these words, word for word; yet the scripture saith, ' The word is nigh thee, *even* in thy mouth, and in thy heart;' but mark, it is the word of faith, not the Man Christ Jesus, but faith which layeth hold on him, Ro. x. 8, read the 9th verse, which is this, ' That if thou shalt confess with thy mouth the Lord Jesus, (who was born of the Virgin, Mat. i. 21) and shalt believe in thine heart that God hath raised him from the dead, thou shalt be saved.' These great and precious scriptures, with which by corrupting of them, the Quakers have beguiled many, have this meaning, that if thou shalt confess with thy mouth the Lord Jesus; that is, in profession and practice, own him, and believe him to be the anointed Saviour. And shalt believe in thine heart, there is the word of faith, if thou shalt believe in thine heart, that God raised him from the dead, thou shalt be saved; ' for with the heart man believeth unto righteousness; and with the mouth confession is made unto salvation.' But what should men believe with the heart? Namely this, that God raised him (that is Christ) from the dead. ver. 10. And therefore, I wonder thou shouldest. so scold, as thou dost, against the truth: If this be not truth, blame the scriptures which do testify of these things for truth. For I am ruled and would be ruled by them through the Spirit.

But farther, thou art offended that I should say, ' They are deceived who own Christ no otherwise than as he was before the world began.' This question, I briefly ask thee, ' Had Christ a body of flesh before the world began?' If you say no, as you must, if you say true; then do not I say true, when I say, they are deceived who own Christ no otherwise than as he was before the world began? because they own him not with that body of flesh which he took of the Virgin Mary; and so are antichrists, as the scripture saith. And how say you? Do you believe that the same Christ who was before the world, without a body, did in time come into the world and take a body from the Virgin, and in that body did obtain everlasting redemption for sinners? and is gone with that very body into the presence of his Father above the clouds into heaven, from his saints on earth, though in them by his Spirit. A plain answer to this would unlock your double meanings. Again, thou sayest the saints drank of the spiritual rock that followed them.

Friend, I confess, that that spiritual rock that did follow the fathers, and long after, was from the same loins with them, even from the loins of Abraham, and the rest of the children of the promise, according to the promise, was the meat and drink of saints. Ro. ix. 4, 5. But to look upon Christ no otherwise than as he was before the world was, which was a Spirit only, and not to own him now clothed with a body, absent from his children touching the same body, I dare be bold to say, they are no Christians, but antichristians, yea antichrists. He that confesseth not that Jesus Christ is come in the flesh is antichrist, and of antichrist. Again,

At this also thou wranglest, because I said that ' every spirit that confesseth not that Jesus Christ, who was with the Father before the world was, did in the appointed time of the Father, come into the world, take a body upon him, and was very Man as well as very God: and did in that very body suffer what did belong to the sons of men, &c.' So my book, page 42, 43, 44. I answer, if thou didst indeed believe the truth, thou wouldest own these things. But being deceived, rather than thou wilt let this pass for truth, though thou darest not oppose it with open face, yet thou wilt put on a vail, and venture upon it thus, saying, ' If every spirit were of God, which doth confess in words this, then is not the Pope himself antichrist.'

Answ. Friend, it is one thing to confess the things in words and another thing to believe them, and to make a life out of them ; and therefore is thy life made out of Christ without thee, by the operation of his Spirit within thee, yea or no ?

Then in answer to my bidding people receive no Christ except God's Christ, thou sayest thus, ' That Christ is a mystery, and unto him is light, and shall be salvation where his person never came.' This question I ask thee, Did or doth Christ obtain salvation for any, without that body which he took of the Virgin ? And yet thou sayest, it cannot be said, here is the place where the Son is not.

I answer: As the Son of God is also very Man, so it may be said, here is the place where he is not, and there is the place where he hath not been, though as he is God it is otherwise: let him that reads understand.

And now passing by many things that I might justly examine, and also many unseemly expressions, I come to the next thing, and that is, where you say, you wrest not the scriptures in Jn. i. 9. But it is evident, that you do most horribly wrest it, in that you, though you seem to take it in the plain words, yet would hold, that that light is the Spirit of Christ, notwithstanding here is no such thing mentioned in that scripture. For mark, as I have sometimes said, and now also will say, that that light wherewith Christ, as he is God, hath lightened every one with, is not the Spirit of Christ, as is clear, in that some are sensual having not the Spirit, which they must needs have, if it were given to every one that comes into the world, and therefore, in that you say, I say you lay down that scripture false ; I say again, that you say many things which I do know to be blasphemy, as I shall prove clearly anon, as also I have already. And therefore, to take thee off from this, I shall say, that Christ as he is a mediator, a Man between God and man, so he doth not lighten every man that comes into the world, though as he is God he doth. And this is manifest, where he often, (as he was Man) saith, These things are spoken to them that are without in parables ; ' that seeing they might not see, and hearing they might not understand,' Lu. viii. 10. And again, where Judas (not Iscariot) said ; Lord, how is it, that thou wilt manifest thyself to us, and not unto the world ? He saith, ' If a man love me, he will keep my words : and my Father will love him, and we (I as mediator, and my Father as reconciled in me) will come unto him, and make our abode with him.' Jn. xiv. 23. And again, ' No man knoweth the Father but the Son:' That is no man knoweth him as a Father, but the Son, and he to whom the Son will reveal him. Mat. xi. 27. But above all, take that scripture where the Son saith, ' I thank thee O Father, Lord of heaven and earth, because thou hast hid these things from the wise and prudent, and hast revealed them unto babes.' ver. 25. Here the Son and the Father are speaking one to another; the Father he hides the glorious things of the gospel from the world, Mat. xi. 25—27. and the Son he rejoices in so doing. At the same hour Jesus rejoiced in Spirit, and said, ' I thank thee, O Father,' &c. Therefore understand thus much, that though Christ as he is God, doth give to every man a light, which is conscience, otherwise called nature, Ro. ii. 14. 1 Co. xi. 14. yet it doth not follow, that every man hath enlightening from Christ as he is mediator. No, Christ as he is mediator doth neither pray for the world, Jn. xvii. 9. neither doth he give his Spirit to all that are in the world ; for some are sensual, and have it not. But now the argument that thou dost bring to colour the contrary with, is this; for what the Father doth, sayest thou, the Son doth also. Answ. Though this be true, that the Son doth what the Father doth ; yet it doth not appear that either the Father or the Son hath given the Spirit to every one that comes into the world. Jude 19.

Again thou sayest, thou deniest those that say,

'That light which every one hath as he comes into the world, is conscience; though some call it Christ falsely.' Answ. Friend, What wilt thou have it called; Christ. No, if not conscience, then call it nature itself; for all have not the Spirit.

But another great argument thou bringest in page 15, is, 'The light of Christ doth convince of sin.' Now do you call conscience the light of Christ? that will convince of sin. Jn. viii. 9. And they being convinced by their own consciences, &c. if thou dost call the law the light of Christ, that also will convince of or make known sin; For by the law is the knowledge of sin. Ro. iii. 20. If thou dost call even nature itself, the light of Christ; That also doth shew, that sins are a shame, even those sins which some leap over, 1 Co. xi. 14. and ruffian-like they will wear long hair, which nature itself forbiddeth, and is commended for the same by the apostle. The Spirit of Christ also will convince of sin. What, because these several things will convince of sin, therefore will they needs be the Spirit of Christ? Or do they altogether make but one Spirit of Christ? Dost thou profess thyself to walk in the light, and art not able to know these things; Or, if thou dost know them, art thou so unfaithful as not to tell poor people of them, who are some of them at their wits end, by reason they are not enlightened into these things.

Another of thy arguments is, 'They saw the eternal power and Godhead, by that which was made manifest of God in them.'

[I reply] The scripture say not so word for word, but thus: 'Because that which might be known of God, was manifested in them.' But how? for he hath shewed it unto them. But how? why the invisible things of him from the creation of the world are clearly seen, being understood by the things that are made, (which words in thy charge against me thou didst leave out) but mark: The invisible things of God from the creation of the world are clearly seen, being understood by the things that are made. But how then doth it say, that the knowledge of God is manifested in them? Why, because God hath shewed it unto them by the things that are made, even by the creation of the world. So that this scripture holdeth forth thus much; that the invisible things of God, as his power, holiness, and common goodness to the sons of men are clearly seen, being understood by the things that are made. But how feeble an argument is this, to prove such a doctrine as this: That every one hath the Spirit when this light discovers God only by his works in the world. Friend, if they that know God, because he doth shew himself to them by his works in the world, have the Spirit of Christ, then the same argument will serve to speak thus much; that the devils

themselves have the Spirit of Christ, which would be wonderful blasphemy once to affirm. And friend, the very devils, both for the knowledge of sin, and also for the knowledge of God's eternal power and Godhead, have more experience than all the unregenerate men in the world; and yet have not the least spark of the Spirit of Christ in them.

Other lame arguments thou tumblest over, like a blind man in a thicket of bushes, which I pass by. But one thing more thou hast, and that is this,

Thou askest me 'whether I do know this light which God and Christ hath given to every man?' Ro. ii. 14. 1 Co. xi. 14. First, I deny that Christ as he is mediator, hath given to every man his Spirit. And Secondly, I deny, that Christ as he is God hath given to every one his Spirit; but this I say as I have often said, it is conscience of nature itself that every one hath, take it in either of these scripture terms, as I have proved at large. And whereas thou askest me, 'Whether that light, which Christ as he is God hath lightened every one with that comes into the world, be sufficient in itself for life and salvation. I answer plainly, no; for then Christ Jesus needed not to have come into the world to die for sinners; for every one had that light before Christ did come into the world.

2. And secondly I answer, it is not able, for then it would have been a needless thing for Christ to tell his disciples of sending them his Spirit, to lead them into all truth. They might have said, why dost thou talk of sending us thy Spirit, who have that that can do the deed already, if that could have done it.

3. Because the scripture saith, 'Some are sensual, not having the Spirit.' Now a man cannot lay hold on Christ, nor believe in him savingly without the Spirit, because faith is the work of the Spirit.

4. Because then it had been in vain for the Lord to have given the scriptures to teach men out of, either concerning himself or themselves: Why? because without it, they had a sufficient light to guide them: that thing must not be so.

And whereas thou askest, whether the fault be then in God, or in that thou callest his light, or in the creature? I answer; What if God willing to shew his wrath, and to make his power known, endured with much patience the vessels of wrath fitted to destruction; and that he might make known the riches of his glory on the vessels of mercy, which he had afore (before the world was, Ep. i. 4.) ordained unto glory? And secondly, O vain man! What is that to thee if God should make some vessels to dishonour: hath not the potter power over the clay, of the same lump to do therewith as he pleases. Ro. ix. 16—22.

And where I say, 'Christ as he is God hath lightened every one that cometh into the world:'

to it thou givest a glavering answer; but having touched on this before, I pass it by.

To the next thing, where I say, 'men's neglecting this light, or law, will be sure to damn them, though their obedience to the law will not save them.' Here thou sayest I have confessed truth, (and I know it is true by experience) and thou commentest on those things laid down by me thus: 'Then surely (sayest thou) It is good not to neglect it;' that is, not to neglect following the law. To which I answer, as their obedience to the law will not save them, so their neglect of obedience to the law will be sure to damn them; these things thou canst not deny. But is this all the wit thou hast? Because the neglect of the law will be sure to damn them; therefore wouldst thou put poor souls to follow that which will not save them? (O wonderful ignorance.) Nay, but thou shouldest have said, then surely the best course is, for a poor soul in this case, to fly to the Lord Christ, even the Man Christ Jesus, who was slain on Mount Calvary for the sins of poor sinners. And the rather, because he did so willingly, of his own accord lay down his life for them. Methinks, I say, thou shouldest rather have said, then let us follow the Son of Mary, the Man Christ Jesus, the Lamb of God that takest away the sins of the world, by his blood on the cross; who is now also at his Father's right hand making intercession for all those that do come to the Father by him; but they that are not for the truth, will advance anything but the truth. And as for that which thou callest the second clause, which is, The law (sayest thou) must be obeyed.

I answer, Christ Jesus hath done that in his own person, and justified me thereby, and for my part, I will not labour now to fulfil the law for justification, least I should undervalue the merits of the Man Christ Jesus, and what he hath done without me: and yet will I labour to fulfil, if it were possible, ten thousand laws, if there were so many: And O! let it be out of love to my sweet Lord Jesus (2 Co. v. 14) 'for the love of Christ constrains me.' And thus much to thy 16th page.

In the next place, thou art offended with this, because I say, though Christ doth give a light to every one that comes into the world, yet it doth not therefore follow, that this conscience, (or light) is the Spirit of Christ, or the work of grace wrought in the heart of any believer. This I shall pass also, as having spoken to it already, only mind thee of thy weakness, in that thou shouldest make this conscience, that Christ hath given to every man, to be the same with the Spirit of Christ. And thou sayest further, that the light, that Christ hath lightened every one with, is the same in nature with the Spirit of Christ. O wonderful! that a man should be so foolish, and so much

besides the truth, as to compare that nature, or conscience, that is given to every man; equal to the Spirit of Christ: nay, thou sayest that it is one with it in nature. Didst thou not blush when thou laidst it down? if thou didst not, thou mightest have done with shame enough. As I said before, because thy conscience will convince thee of sin, therefore thou wilt call it Christ, or as good as Christ. What! because the law will convince of sin, therefore the law must be called Christ. What ignorance is this? Nay, nature itself, that must have the pre-eminency, even as high as Christ Jesus, because it can tell a man that it is a shame for him to wear long hair.

Then thou askest me, can there be a surer thing for the creature to walk by, than by the light of Christ, which thou confessest every one hath, that cometh into the world. Answer, Friend, to the law, and to the testimony (sayeth the scriptures) for they testify of Christ. And if thou or any else, shall leave the scriptures, to follow the convictions of their own conscience; ye are not like to know Christ Jesus the Lord, for they may be defiled. And again, it is through the promises laid down in the scriptures, 'that we might be partakers of the divine nature,' 2 Pe. i. 4. and not by our following of the law, or conscience. Ga. iii. 1—4.

But again, where I say, Heathens, Turks, Jews, Atheists, &c. have that which doth convince of sin, and yet are so far from having the Spirit of Christ in them, that they delight to do iniquity; and to serve their lust. Upon this thou movest this query; Do they, or I, or any other, serve sin and lust, because Christ hath not given us light, or because we hate this light.

Ans. This I do really confess, that every Heathen, Turk, or Jew, in this world, hath a conscience within them, that doth convince of sin; for the Gentiles which have not the law, that is, not the law in tables of stone, or written as we have; these do by nature, the things contained in the law; these having not the law, are a law unto themselves; which shew the work of the law written in their hearts, their consciences also bearing them witness, &c. And all men and women shall be left without excuse, even by the convictions of their own consciences, or the law. But now that these things are the Spirit of Christ, that I deny. For conscience is but a creature, a faculty of the soul of man, which God hath made. Neither is the law the Spirit of Christ; for the law is not of faith. They that are of the works of the law, are under the curse, but they that have the spirit of Christ they are the children of God, and under grace, and delivered from the curse, as it is written Ga. iii. 10. 'As many as are of the works of the law are under the curse.' But what is it to be of the works of the law, or under the law? *Ans.* Why to seek to be justified by their obedience to the law. 'Israel which followed after the law of righteousness,' mark. They that follow after righteousness, do not attain to the law of righteousness; if they seek it not by faith: but as it were by the works of the law. Ro. ix. 30, 31. But 'Christ hath redeemed us from the curse of the law, being (in our nature) made a curse for us.' Ga. iii. 10—13.

But whereas thou sayest, this conscience or law, which you would fain have called the Spirit of Christ, works in all men either to justify, or condemn. I do plainly deny, that either conscience, or the law can justify, though they can condemn. Mark, The law is called the ministration of condemnation, but not of life.

The gospel is called the ministration of life, but not of condemnation. 2 Co. iii. 9. The law was given that sin might be discovered. The gospel was sent, that sin might be taken away. The law worketh wrath; but the gospel is a gospel of peace. Ro. x. 'The law made nothing perfect.' He. vii. 19. But Christ justifieth from all those things from which we could not be justified by the law of Moses. Ac. xiii. 39.

And whereas thou askest me whether any thing doth convince of sin contrary to, or besides the Spirit of Christ.

I answer. There is conscience, and the law, yea, and nature itself that doth convince of sin; as before I have proved at large. Yet neither is conscience, the law; or nature itself the Spirit of Christ; no, but are much inferior to it, as being things of no glory in respect of it.

And again, that something doth convince of sin besides the Spirit of Christ, it is evident, for the law saith, 'Cursed is every one that continueth not in all things which are written in it to do them.' Ga. iii. 10. But the Spirit convinceth men of their unbelief, together with other sins. Now mark, The law also convinceth to work for life, the Spirit convinceth to believe for life; the law saith, He that doth not fulfil me, shall be damned. The Spirit saith, He that believeth in Christ shall be saved. Now observe the terms of the law and of the gospel, are different one from another as to justification. If men seek for life by the law; then the law saith, Fulfil me perfectly, and thou shalt live. The Spirit saith, that Christ Jesus came into the world to save those that by transgression had broken the law. For, for this cause saith the Spirit 'He (Jesus the Son of Mary, the Man Christ between God and us. 1 Ti. ii. 5.) is the mediator of the New Testament.' For what? 'That by means of death, for the redemption of the transgressions *that were* under the first testament, they which are called might receive the promise of eternal inheritance.' He. ix. 15. Now I

would not be mistaken; I do not say, that the Spirit of Christ doth give the least liberty to sin; God forbid. But its convictions are of a more saving and refreshing nature than the convictions of the law, and do more constrain the soul to holiness than that.

The law saying, Work for life; the Spirit saying, 'Now to him that worketh not, (for life) but believeth on him that justifieth the ungodly, his faith is counted for righteousness,' Ro. iv. 5. as thus, if I should owe to two creditors ten thousand talents; the one should say unto me, thou owest me five thousand talents, pay that thou owest; the other should say, thou owest me five thousand talents, and I frankly and freely forgive thee all. Now these expressions are contrary one to another: even so is the end of the convictions of the law, not according to the end of the convictions of the Spirit of Christ; the one saying, pay me that thou owest, the other saying, thou art frankly and freely forgiven all.

The next thing thou utterest is, where I say, 'Those that are alive unto sins, have not the Spirit of Christ.' But sayest thou, it is given to every man. Mark, thou sayest, It is given to every man. The Apostle saith, some are sensual, having not the Spirit. Jude 19. Who must we now believe, the Apostle or you? Certainly your doctrine is not according to truth, but a lie; as is clear, in that you will affirm, that which the Apostle doth deny.

Then thou sayest, I bring other vain arguments to prove that every one hath not the Spirit of Christ. This one is enough to prove it, that the Apostle saith, Some men have it not. But that which thou callest vain, I am sure neither thou nor any of thy fellows, are able to answer. One is to this purpose; the devils are so convinced of sin, that they did fear the torment that was to come upon them for their sins; and did fear also that the Son of Man was come to torment them for their sins, and yet the devils have not the spirit of Christ. So that it is evident, that we may be convinced of sin, and yet not by the Spirit of Christ. A second argument which thou callest vain, is this, Man in his coming into the world, hath his conscience given him, which doth convince of sin, Jn. viii. 9. yet man in his coming into the world, or as he cometh into the world, hath not the Spirit of Christ given him, for that must be received ordinarily afterward by the preaching of the word, which is preached by the ministers and servants of Jesus Christ. Ac. x. 44. 'While Peter yet spake' to the people, 'the Holy Ghost fell on all them which heard the word.'

But farther, thou sayest, 'Until I prove the light of Christ contrary to the Spirit of Christ, thou wilt say, that every man hath that which is one in union, and like the Spirit of Christ, even as good as the Spirit of Christ in its measure.'

Answer. Friend, I have proved already that every man hath not the Spirit of Christ, though they have that which thou dost call the Spirit of Christ, which is conscience and nature itself. And this I say again, that thou hast laid open thy weakness very much, to say that every man hath that which is as good as the Spirit of Christ. Friend, seeing the scriptures say, some have not the Spirit of Christ, how durst thou so blaspheme, as to say, then it is as good as the Spirit of Christ in its measure. Was there ever such a deal of ignorance discovered at one time by man, as to say, that every man hath the Spirit, or that which is as good as the Spirit; though the Spirit saith plainly, that some have not the Spirit, as I have proved plainly. Jude 19. Friend, what is there besides the Spirit that is as good as the Spirit. Be silent, and say no more so, lest thou dost through ignorance, or presumption, set up thy conscience or nature, as high and as good as the Spirit of Christ, when indeed they are not worthy to be compared with it, being weak, and not able to do that which is and hath been done by the Spirit of Christ.

Then thou art offended, because I said the devil doth deceive poor souls by bidding them listen within, and see if there be not that which doth convince of sin. Friend, all men have not the Spirit, though they have that conscience that doth convince of sin. Jn. viii. 9. Now seeing all men have not the Spirit, is it not a great deceit of the devil to persuade poor souls, that because they are convinced for sin by their own consciences, therefore they have the Spirit of Christ: surely it is from the devil. Because he would make thee believe that conscience, which is but a creature, is the Spirit of Christ, by whom the world was made. Again, because the soul, being persuaded that it hath the Spirit (when it hath it not) as all men naturally are without it, Ep. v. 13, 14. it is kept off from seeking and begging for it, being already persuaded (falsely) that it hath it.

And whereas thou sayest, the voice of the gospel is to bid listen within the heart, as Paul preacheth. I deny that Paul biddeth listen within. But the scripture that you would fain make shelter for your error is this, where he saith, ' The word is nigh thee, *even* in thy mouth, and in thy heart.' Ro. x. 8. That is, The word of faith which we preach. Now, Friend, faith is that which layeth hold of, or believeth the gospel. And that this is the meaning read the next verse: That (saith he) ' If thou shalt confess with thy mouth the Lord Jesus, and shalt believe in thine heart that God hath raised him from the dead, thou shalt be saved.' So that it is clear that the word of faith, is to believe assuredly from the very heart, that God hath raised up Jesus from the dead, out of the grave

into which he was laid by Joseph; and that he was raised again for my justification, Ro. iv. 25. as it is written, 1 Co. xv. ' Moreover brethren (saith he,) I declare unto you the gospel which I preached unto you' at the first, 'which also you have received, and wherein ye stand, by which also ye are saved, if ye keep in memory, (or assuredly believe,) what I preached unto you, unless ye have believed in vain.' But what was that gospel you preached? why, saith he, ver. 3. ' I delivered unto you first of all, that which I also received, how that Christ died for our sins according to the scriptures ; and that he was buried, and that he rose again the third day according to the scriptures: and that he was seen of - - the brethren after his resurrection,' &c. The word of the gospel, my friend, is, Christ died for our sins according to the scriptures, and that he rose again according to the scriptures, and that he is ascended from his disciples, to prepare a place for them according to the scripture.

That he ever liveth to make intercession in his own person without, as mediator between God and man, according to the scripture. He. vii. 25.

That he will come again in the clouds with all his mighty angels, and before him shall all nations be gathered, according to the scriptures, 1 Th. iv. 16, 17. Mat. xxv. 31, 32. after which time, his saints shall be ever with him according to the scriptures.

Again, thou art offended in that I said, Now the poor soul finding this to be so (that it is convinced of sin) all in haste (if it be willing to profess) through ignorance Here my words are corrupted. of the gospel, claps in with the motions of its own conscience, which doth command to abstain from this evil, and to practise that good. Which words of mine thou corruptest, and wrestest, and layest down in another form, as are to be seen in thy book, page 18. But now, friend, is not he ignorant of the gospel, which thinks his own conscience will lead him to eternal life, by commanding to abstain from this evil, and practise that good? Surely, if salvation comes by our conscience, or by the convictions or commands thereof, Christ Jesus died for nothing. Ga. ii. 21.

And whereas thou askest, what, and how doth the light of the gospel work, if not in the conscience. I answer, Though the light of the Spirit of God and the gospel be in the hearts of the elect of God; yet the gospel light is hid, and doth not shine so much as unto, much less into the consciences of some of them that be lost, 2 Co. iv. 3, 4. that though the light of the gospel doth shine, and that gloriously too in the hearts of God's elect, yet it doth not follow, that the convictions of conscience is the gospel; no, nor the convictions of the law neither. And again, though every one of God's elect have the light of the glorious gospel shining in them, what argument is this to prove all men have the light of the gospel shining in them. No, saith Christ, ' I thank thee, O Father, because thou hast hid these things (the things of the gospel) from the wise and prudent, and hast revealed them unto babes.' Mat. xii. 25. And whereas thou sayest (as I gather by thy words) that I call conscience the light of Christ, I say, if thou meanest by these words (the light of Christ) the Spirit of Christ, I do deny that every man hath it: but if thou callest conscience the light of Christ, or the highest light that is in an unconverted man the light of Christ; then, I say, that the highest light that is in a natural or unconverted man (which you call the light of Christ) is not able by all its motions and convictions, nor yet by all the obedience that a man can yield to these convictions; I say, they are not able to deliver him from the wrath to come; for deliverance from that is obtained by the blood of Jesus, which was shed on the cross, without the gate of Jerusalem (as I have often said) Ep. i. 7. compared with He. xiii. 12. and not any light within a natural man.

And whereas thou sayest that I said, the devil counterfeits the new birth by persuading to follow the light of the world. I answer,
* Here is another of his false accusations of me.
* Thou hast most naughtily belied me. The words that I said (speaking of the devil before) are these; Now he counterfeits the new birth (said I) by persuading them that it is wrought by following the light that they brought into the world with them; as is clearly seen in my book, page 76. Friend, I wonder that you should so boldly profess yourself to be led by the Spirit of Christ, when you make it manifest that you are guided by the spirit of Satan. Was not he a liar? and hast not thou been led by a lying spirit also, in wresting of my words as thou hast done?

But I do freely declare again, that Satan doth deceive those souls, whom he persuades the new birth is wrought in, by following the light they brought into the world with them; for men as they come into the world, do not receive the Spirit, for it is given to the elect afterwards; neither have all men the Spirit. And he that hath the new birth, must have it by, and through the Spirit; as it is written, ' Except a man be born of water and of the Spirit, he cannot enter into the kingdom of God.' Therefore, if men do not bring the Spirit into the world with them; and if nothing without the Spirit, or nothing but the Spirit, will or can work the new birth in a man: it must needs follow, that they who think the new birth is wrought by that light or conscience which they brought into the world with them, must needs be beguiled by Satan.

I do pass by many of thy raging expressions, which I might justly charge with much unrighteousness; but I know the time is short, and then whatsoever thou hast done in secret, shall be laid open upon the house tops, therefore I forbear them.

Again, thou art offended because I said, now Satan makes the soul believe he is its friend, and that he is a gospel minister, 2 Co. xi. 14. and if the soul will be led by what shall be made known to it, from the light or conscience within, it shall not need to fear, but it shall do well, page 76. of my book [153]. I said it then, and I say it now; and I know that he that doth think to be born again by following his conscience, or any other light that is in an unregenerate man, will be deceived, and shall one day know, that there is a difference between conscience and Christ; between the light of nature, and the Spirit of God.

Quest. But you may say, how can you prove that conscience is not of the same nature, of the Spirit of Christ?

Answ. 1. They that are unbelieving, even their conscience is defiled. Tit. i. 15. But so cannot be the Spirit of Christ.

Answ. 2. Conscience is not of the same nature with the Spirit of Christ, for conscience may be hardened or seared with an hot iron: as it is written, 1 Ti. iv. 2. But so cannot be the Spirit of Christ.

Answ. 3. Our consciences naturally are evil, ' having (saith the scripture) our hearts sprinkled from an evil conscience.' He. x. 22. But so is not the Spirit of Christ.

But again whereas you said, that I said, they will not speak except the Spirit move them, &c. thou dost falsely speak of me, and again dost corrupt my words; for I said, How they will not speak except their spirit move them, (I do not say the Spirit of Christ) (said I) Friend; if you can be lead to life by your own spirit, if your own spirit will learn you the things of the Spirit of God; and if you can speak them with and in your own spirit, in that demonstration that they are spoken, when they are spoken in the Spirit of Christ; (which all men have not) then say that I speak false things; but till that time hold your peace. Thus I pass by thy 20. page, leaving many of thy scolding terms to thyself. The next thing thou sayest is, that I did run but Another false was not sent, like unto my forefathers: accusation. and therefore sayest thou, I do not profit the people at all. *Answ.* Which accusation of thine, I shall leave to be taken notice of by the people of God in the country where I dwell, who will testify the contrary for me, setting aside the carnal ministry, with their retinue; who are as mad against me as thyself.

But farther, thou art somewhat distempered, and discontented that I said, ' Many sad and horrible doctrines are vented by you.' And you said, I named nothing. *Answ.* I need not, thine own speech betrayeth thee, that thou art one of them, that do such things; and I need go no further than thy own mouth and doctrine. But if it will be more satisfaction to tell you wherein, they of your society do hold sad doctrine I shall.

1. Therefore your society do hold and affirm, that that man which was hanged on the cross between two thieves, called Jesus; in his person is within you, contrary to the scripture. Ac. i. 11.

2. You say that Christ is crucified within, dead within, risen and ascended within; which also you have no word of scripture to prove.

3. Your Society affirm, that the coming of the Spirit into the hearts of believers, is Christ his second coming, when the scriptures do plainly hold forth, that the coming of Christ in the Spirit was before his coming in the flesh; as in 1 Pe. i. 10, 11. where the apostle speaking of the prophets inquiring into the great salvation which was afterwards to be accomplished, saith, 'Searching what, or what manner of time the Spirit of Christ which was in them did signify, when it testified before hand the sufferings of Christ, and the glory that should follow.' Mark, here is the Spirit of Christ in the prophets, long before the first coming of Christ in the flesh, which was when he was born of Mary the Virgin, the Spirit of Christ, saith he, did testify before hand the suffering of Christ, to the prophets, which were before Christ came in the flesh, as the scriptures hold forth plentifully.

4. But again, you deny the second coming of that very Man, with that very body, which was born of the Virgin Mary; and say, his second coming is not his coming again personally, but his coming in the Spirit only; and that is all you look for, when the scripture saith; That same Jesus (who appeared to his disciples after his passion, Ac. i. 3.) shall so come, even as they did see him depart from them into heaven; which was a very Man, as well as very God. And will come again, a very Man, as well as very God, at the end of the world. For it is that Man; namely, he that was crucified, whom God raised again, must be the judge of quick and dead. Ac. x. 39—42. seriously compared.

5. Again, you say, that every man hath the Spirit of Christ, which is a sad doctrine, because contrary to the scripture. Jude 19. And you say, there is that in every man which is as good as the Spirit of Christ; which is a blasphemous doctrine. Besides many other things which they of your own spirit have most sadly spoken; which I shall not mention, being so commonly known to the saints of the Lord, before whom you have openly, and without fear (at least in shew) spoken. Which will doubtless be laid open to your sorrow and great amazement, at the appearing of our Lord Jesus Christ.

Then thou art offended because I said, I wonder that the Lord doth not either cause the ground to open her mouth and swallow you up: or else suffer the devil to fetch you away, to the astonishing the whole world. Certainly, Korah, Dathan, and Abiram did not so horribly transgress, as you have done. Yet his hand on them (no question) was as it were the astonishment of the world. Therefore I may well wonder that you are not served so. Only this I consider, it may be, you have not yet filled up the measure of your wickedness; therefore is not the hand of God as yet upon you.

The next thing I take notice of is, that thou findest fault with mine answer to this question. 'But doth not the scripture say, that it is the Spirit of Christ that doth convince of sin?' Thou sayest it is a good question, but I have confounded it in the answer, and not answered plainly. Wherefore I shall not at all stick at the pains, to give the reader in brief some of the heads of the answer I then gave to it word for word, or to the same purpose. The answer was, yes, the Spirit doth convince of sin; but for the better understanding of this place, I shall lay down this, said I, That there are two things spoken of in scripture, that do manifest or convince of sin. First, the law. Ro. iii. 20. 'For by the law is the knowledge of sin.' Secondly, the Spirit of Christ doth also the same, as it is written, 'And when he is come, he will *convince the world of sin.' Jn. xvi. 7—9. Now say I, sometimes the law itself, by its own power doth manifest sin, as in the case of Judas, who was so far from having the Spirit of Christ, that the devil had very great possession of him. Which things my adversary doth wrangle at, yet dares not affirm the contrary: only saith this, he had the righteous law of God written in his heart: which thing is not the Spirit of Christ. The law is not of faith. The law is not the comforter, but rather a tormentor: yet the Spirit of Christ is a comforter. Again say I, the Spirit of Christ doth take the law, and doth effectually convince of sin, &c. Then I put forth another question, saying, 'But how should I know whether I am convinced by the law alone, or whether the law be effectually set home by the Spirit?' To which I answer, when the law doth convince by its own power, it doth convince only of sins against the law; as lying, swearing, stealing, &c. pronouncing an horrible curse against thee if thou fulfil it not, and there leaves thee, but gives thee no power to fulfil it completely and continually, which thou must do, if thou be saved thereby. With which my adversary is much offended; also saying, that I am confounded in my discourse, and so leaves me, confuting none of my words by holy scripture,

---

* See margin of the bible.—Ed.

but falls a railing, because I reckon Pharisees and Quakers together.

Only this much he saith; That I make it a light thing to be convinced by the law, and then brings in that scripture; ' This is the condemnation, that light is come into the world, and men love darkness rather than light;' cunningly corrupting of it, and would fain have you understand it as spoken of the law, when the Son of Mary speaks it of himself, which was not the law, but the Saviour. And that he might the better go away undiscerned, he saith, and the law is light, therefore the light is the law (saith he). But I perceive that he doth not yet understand the difference between the light of the law, and the light of the gospel; but would fain make the law and Christ one Saviour: the one being but only a condemning light, and nothing else; the other a saving comfortable light. And whereas thou sayest, I make it a light thing to be convinced by the law, I answer; the law is good, if a man use it lawfully; and I honour it in its place; yet if they make a Saviour of it, they make an idol of it, and wrest it out of its proper place. Also, if they think that it is Christ, they are much deceived.

But farther, he put me to prove any such distinction in scripture as that there is anything made mention of therein that doth convince of sin, beside the Spirit of Christ: which thing I have already answered, where I said the scripture saith, ' By the law is the knowledge of sin.' Ro. iii. 20. And again, doth not even nature itself teach you, that it is a shame for a man to wear long hair, 1 Co. xi. 14, and also conscience, which are neither of them the Spirit of Christ, but much inferior to the same; yet this also convinceth of sin. Jn. viii. 9.

But to the other thing, which is the answer that I give in my book to this objection: But I am not only convinced of my sins (may some say) but have also some power against my sins; so that I do in some measure abstain from the sins forbidden in the law. And because I say, this thou mayest have and do, as thou thinkest, perfectly too [as thou thinks, mark that] as those fond hypocrites, called Quakers [think] that they also do, and yet be but a natural man. Here my adversary is very much offended, and calls me perverter of the right way of the Lord; and saith, Shew me any natural man in the scripture that hath done it. Whereas had he been but willing to have laid down the scripture I brought to prove it, he needed not to have looked for a second answer. But because he would have it again, I will therefore shew you, that natural men merely by nature may be convinced, and abstain from those things forbidden in the law, and think they do it perfectly, nay, they do the things contained in the law. For saith the apostle, Ro. ii. 14, ' When the Gentiles, which have

not the law, do by nature [mark, do by nature] the things contained in the law, these, [the Gentiles] having not the law, are a law unto themselves.' Mark; the Gentiles do by nature the things contained in, or held forth, or made mention of by the law; the light also that they have, it is themselves, being a law to themselves; that is, their consciences (being of themselves) bearing them witness and their thoughts the meanwhile accusing, or else excusing one another, ver. 15. though they cannot be saved thereby.

Again, when Paul was a natural man, and a persecutor of Jesus Christ, he saith of himself, that then he was, ' touching the righteousness which is in the law, blameless.' Phil. iii. 6. And whereas thou sayest, thou hadst rather choose to be one of those who abstain from those things forbidden in the law, and to have power over sin, than to live in the transgression of the law; this is fair spoken, and it doth shew that thou art under the convictions of the law; and if it be no worse, I fear thy state the less, though it be bad enough; yet this I say, If thy soul be not saved freely by the blood of that man who was crucified on Mount Calvary, and by his merits alone done by himself in his own person, thou, notwithstanding wilt fall short of eternal life. For by the works of the law, shall no flesh living be justified. Ro. iii. 20. Though by it be the knowledge of sin, and a command to abstain from the same. And thus have I spoken to thy 21 page.

But farther thou sayest, that thou fearest I worship the name Mary, because I mention her name so much.

[I reply] If thou hadst said, I worship her Son, thou hadst said truly (I hope) But is not thy spite more against her Son, than her? I doubt it is; for neither thou, nor thy companions There are more offended at this besides the Quakers. can endure that one should say, he is still the same that was born of Mary, flesh and bones, a very man, now absent from his people, though in them in his Spirit.

Again, thou sayest I said, ' That as he is God, Christ lighteneth every man that comes into the world;' which thing again I say. What then? Then say you, I will mind you of one scripture which you yourself have quoted, which saith ' The law is light.' Pr. vi. 23. Therefore sayest thou, ' The light is the law.' Give me leave here to take thy words in twain:—

First, if when thou sayest, then the law is light, thou mean, the light of the law is the light of the law, and no more, thou sayest right. But if thou mean the light of the law, is the light of the gospel, or the Spirit of Christ, I must needs reprove thee. For I tell thee again, the law is not of faith, the law makes nothing perfect. He. vii. 19. The law is but a weak and unprofitable thing, as to justification, He. vii. 13. though as I said before, it is good if it be used lawfully; which is, not to seek or look for justification thereby, nor yet to say, it is the Spirit of Christ.

Then farther thou art offended, because I said, when the Spirit of Christ convinceth, it convinceth of more sins than the sins against the law. Friend, will the law shew a man that his righteousness is sin and dung? No, for though the law will shew a man that his failing in the acts of righteousness is sin; yet I question, whether the law will shew, that a man's own righteousness is sin. For there is in scripture [that which] saith it doth, or can.

Secondly, shew me, if thou canst, that the sin of unbelief is spoken against in all the ten commandments, or that called the moral law. But now the Spirit of Christ convinceth of unbelief, that is, it sheweth, that if men do not believe, that they have redemption by the obedience of that man who was laid in the manger, hanged on the cross, &c. I say, it sheweth, that those who do not lay hold on what he hath done and suffered without them in his own body on the tree (through the operation of his Spirit, which he hath promised to give to them that ask him) or else they have not yet been convinced of the sin of unbelief, and so are still in a perishing condition; notwithstanding their strict obedience, to the light within them, or to the law. And now tell me, you that desire to mingle the law and the gospel together, and to make of both one and the same gospel of Christ: Did you ever see yourselves undone and lost, unless the righteousness, blood, death, resurrection and intercession of that man Christ Jesus (in his own person) was imputed to you? and until you could by faith own it as done for you, and counted yours by imputation, yea, or no? Nay rather, have you not set up your consciences, and the law, and counted your obedience to them better, and of more value, than the obedience of the Son of Mary without you, to be imputed to you? and if so, it is because you have not been savingly convinced by the Spirit of Christ, of the sin of unbelief.

Other things thou dost quarrel against, but seeing they are in effect the same with the former, I pass them by; and shall come to the next thing thou dost think to catch me withal, and that is; because I say, that 'God only is the Saviour, there is none besides him.' Therefore sayest thou, how contrary is this to that in p. 24, where I say, How wickedly are they deluded, who own Christ no otherwise than as he was before the world began. Now this is no contradiction as thou wouldest have it; for though I say there is none but God our Saviour, yet I did also then in my book shew how he was our Saviour, namely, 'in that he came into the world, being born of a virgin, made under the

law, that he might redeem them that were under the law, by his obedience in that nature, by suffering in that nature, by his rising again in that nature, and by carrying that nature into heaven with him,' as the scriptures at large declare; and therefore, though I say God is our Saviour, and none besides him; yet they that own him to be the Saviour no otherwise than as he was before the world began, are such as deny that he is come in the flesh, and so are of antichrist. 1 Jn. ii. For before God could actually be a Saviour, he must partake of another nature than the divine, even the nature of man. He. ii. 14, 15.

Again, thou sayest, it is a slander put upon the Quakers, to say, they slight the resurrection: Ans. What say you, Do you believe the resurrection of the body after it is laid in the grave? Do you believe that the saints that have been this four or five thousand years in their graves shall rise, and also the wicked, each one with that very body wherein they acted in this world; some to everlasting life, and some to everlasting contempt? Answer plainly, and clear yourselves, but I know you dare not, for you deny these things.

But if you speak doubtfully, or covertly in answer thereunto; I doubt not but God will help me to find you out, and lay open your folly; if I shall live till another cavil by you be put forth against the truth.

The next thing thou cavillest at is, that query raised from Ep. iv. 10. and thou sayest I have not answered it. You should have answered it better, or else have confuted that answer I gave unto it, and then you had done something: But the great thing that troubles thee is, because I say, (further in my book) he that ascended from his disciples, was a very man, 'Handle me and see; saith Christ, for a spirit hath not flesh and bones as ye see me have.' Now let the adversary shew by the scripture (said I) that there is in them any place called heaven, which is able to contain a man of some four or five foot long (or a competent man of flesh and bones) for the space of fifteen or sixteen hundred years, but that above the clouds, which troubles thee so, that it makes thy tongue run thou canst not tell how; but know, that when the Son of man shall come from heaven to judge the world in righteousness, that which thou callest foolishness now, thou wilt find a truth then to thy own wrong, if thou close not in with him, who said, 'Handle me and see, for a spirit hath not flesh and bones as ye see me have.' Lu. xxiv. 39.

Another thing that thou art troubled at, is, in that I do reckon the Quakers to be of the deluding party; when alas, all men that have eyes to see; may easily discern, that you are of that generation, as will appear in part by your own expressions, both now, and also at other times. But that you may take off the brand from yourselves, you say, that the false prophets and antichrist, were in the apostle days, as though there should be no false prophets now, when the very time we live in doth manifestly declare, and hold forth, that there are many, who at this day seek to beguile unstable souls, of which sort you are not the least, though for ought I can learn as yet, you are the last, (that are come into the world) but that you may the better shift it from yourselves, you say, that in those days there was not a Quaker heard of; namely, in the days of John. Friend, thou hast rightly said, there was not a Quaker heard of indeed, though there were many Christians heard of then. By this you yourselves do confess, that you are a new upstart sect, which was not at other times in the world, though Christian saints have been always in the world. Friend, here like a man in the dark, in seeking to keep thyself out of one ditch, thou art fallen into another; instead of proving yourselves no false prophets, you prove yourselves no Christians, saying, There was not a Quaker heard of then. But if Quakers had been Christians, then they would have been heard of to the glory of God, and his Christ.

Again to defend thyself thou throwest the dirt in my face, saying; If we should diligently trace thee, we should find thee in their steps, meaning false prophets, through fained words, through covetousness making merchandise of souls, loving the wages of unrighteousness.

Friend, dost thou speak this as from thy own knowledge, or did any other tell thee so? However, that spirit that led thee out this way, is a lying spirit. For though I be poor, and of no repute in the world, as to outward things; yet through grace I have learned by the example of the apostle to preach the truth; and also to work with my hands, both for mine own living, and for those that are with me, when I have opportunity. And I trust that the Lord Jesus, who hath helped me to reject the wages of unrighteousness hitherto, will also help me still, so that I shall distribute that which God hath given me freely, and not for filthy lucre's sake. Other things I might speak in vindication of my practice in this thing: but ask of others, and they will tell thee that the things I say are truth: and hereafter have a care of receiving anything by hearsay only, lest you be found a publisher of those lies which are brought to you by others, and so render yourself the less credible; but be it so.

And as for your thinking, that to drink water, *

Another of his false accusations.

and wear no hatbands, is not walking after your own lusts; I say, that whatsoever men do make a religion out of, having no warrant for it in the scripture, is but walking after their own lusts, and not after the Spirit of God. Thus have I passed thy 23d page.

And lest you should think that the Quakers are not such as condemned me and others for preaching according to the scriptures; as you would fain clear yourselves of this charge laid against you in my book, by your saying, you deny the accusation to be true upon any of the Quakers. I shall therefore tell you of your sister Anne Blackly, who did bid me in the audience of many, 'To throw away the scriptures.' To which I answered, ' No, for then the devil would be too hard for me.'

And again, because I said, The man Christ Jesus was above the clouds and the heavens, now absent from his people in the world, touching his bodily presence; she said, I preached up an idol, and used conjuration and witchcraft. Which things I should rather have desired her to repent of, than to make her a public example for others to take warning by; but that it is expedient that your folly be laid open, that others may fear to do as you have done.

But farther, thou chargest me with a loud crying out against Christ within. This is thy throwing of dirt in my face again, for I have said it often, that if any man have not the Spirit of Christ he is none of his.

This is another of his false accusations of me.

Again thou sayest that in page 203, I do take in hand to prove or discover that the doctrine of Christ within, is a false opinion.

Here is another lie made of me.

Thou dost also here speak falsely of me, for all that I take in hand to prove, is this, That they hold a false opinion (and principles too) who hold up a Christ within, in opposition to Christ without, who is the Saviour; as doth plainly appear by my following discourse, if you read from page 203 to the end of my book.

But in the next place, after much railing, thou comest to the place where I again ask this question, ' Doth not the scripture make mention of a Christ within ?'

To which I answer, Yes, and he that hath it not is none of his. But to lay open my folly at last thou sayest, Doth not the scripture say, Christ is within you, except ye be reprobates? and is not this thus much, are not all they reprobates (say you) but they in whom Christ is within?

Ans. They are indeed reprobates who have not Christ within them; but now, how is thy folly manifest? that in one place thou shouldest confess some are reprobates, who have not Christ within; and yet in page 18, of thy book thou sayest, it is given to every man. And in page 26, of thy

---

* There is nothing new under the sun. It appears from this that there was a tee-total movement in the time of the Commonwealth. For the meaning of hatband, see editor's advertisement.—ED.

book, thou sayest, that a measure of the Spirit is given to every man, and is given within him too, though the scripture declareth the contrary, and thyself also now at last. It is well thou dost recant so much, as to eat thy first words at the last, or at least to show thyself unstable in judgment: Friend, thou mayest see, the more thou dost fight against the truth, the more thou foilest thyself: Partly by helping of it, and partly by contradicting thyself.

One thing more thou dost befool thyself with; and that is, in that thou in the first place sayest thou ownest the words in my book, and yet hath spent some four sheets of paper to vent thy thoughts against them.

But peradventure thou wilt say; those words that I own are not those that I speak against, but the other. To which I answer, There are many things in my book spoken of by me that are truth, which if you own, you must leave professing yourself a Quaker. As,

1. That that man that was born of the virgin Mary, called Jesus (I say you will not own) that he in his own person, by himself without us, did completely bring in everlasting life for us, by offering up himself once for all upon the cross.

2. That Christ who wrought out redemption for his children, did after he had wrought it out, go away from them, and not into them in his person.

3. That he ever liveth, that very man to make intercession in his person, in the presence of his Father without, until the end of the world.

4. That that very man who did go away from his disciples into heaven, will come again personally the same man the second time, and before him shall be gathered all nations, and he shall judge them for their sins: and take his to himself, who shall soul and body be with him to all eternity; these things (I say) thou couldest not own, though they are the truth of God. But leaving thee to the great God, who will give thee according to thy works, in this as in other things: I shall come to thy answers to my queries.

Query 1. The first query that I propounded is, If thou sayest that every man hath a measure of the Spirit of Christ within him, why say the scriptures, ' Some are sensual, having not the Spirit.' And when Christ telleth his disciples, of sending them the Spirit, he saith, the world cannot receive it. Here in the first place thou hast not only answered deceitfully, but hast also corrupted my words in laying down the query, in that thou didst leave out some words, for thou didst lay it down thus : ' If thou sayest that every man hath a measure of the Spirit of Christ within him, why say the scriptures, some are sensual, having not the Spirit:' and Christ saith, ' The world cannot receive it.' (Reader, compare them both together.)

Now thy answer, is, ' Some are sensual, having not the Spirit, because they receive it not, and some cannot receive it, because they believe not on him from whence it comes.' Yet sayest thou, ' The measure of the Spirit is given to every man to profit withal,' as the scriptures say: when there is no scripture faith, a measure of the Spirit is given to every man to profit withal. But again, see here thy strange confusion. 1. To say, some have it not. 2. To say every man hath it. But you would make a difference between having and receiving: but I tell thee, he that hath it hath received it, Ga. iii. 2. and he that hath not received it, hath it not. Jude 19.

Query 2. My second query was, ' What is the church of God redeemed by from the curse of law ? Is it by something done within them, or by something done without them ?' If you say, it is redeemed by something that worketh in them, then why did the man Christ Jesus hang on the cross on Mount Calvary, without the gate of Jerusalem, for the sins of his children ? And why do the scriptures say, ' That through this man is preached to us the forgiveness of sins ?'

The answer thou givest is, ' The church of God is redeemed by Christ Jesus, which is revealed in all believers. And Christ Jesus wrought in them mightily; And it was he that wrought in them to will and to do.'

This is plain scripture, and the man Christ Jesus (sayest thou) hanged on the cross on Mount Calvary: because, they wickedly judged him to be a blasphemer, and through their envy persecuted him to death ; because he bare witness against them, and as in their account he died, and hanged on the cross, for an evil doer. And this is one ground (at least) why he hanged on the cross, &c.

Ha Friend ? I had thought thou hadst not been so much hardened ; art thou not ashamed thus to slight the death of the Man Christ Jesus on the cross ; and reckon it not effectually for salvation, but sayest, the church is redeemed by Christ Jesus which is revealed within. And to confirm it, thou dost also corruptly bring in two scriptures.

The one saith, ' Whereunto I also labour according to his working, which worketh in me mightily.' By which words Paul signifies thus much, ' That as God was with him in the ministry of the word, so did he also strive according to his working which wrought in him mightily.' What is this to the purpose ? See Col. i. 26—30. And also, the other scripture makes nothing to prove, that the church of God is redeemed by Christ within, as he is within. Only you must corrupt the scriptures, and be transformed (though ministers of darkness) into an angel of light, if you will do any mischief.

And now, that thy answer is false, I shall clearly prove. First, because thou deniest that redemption was wrought out for sinners by the Man Christ Jesus on the cross, or tree, on Mount Calvary; when the scripture saith plainly, that when he did hang on the tree, then did he bear all our sins there in his own body. 1 Pe. ii. 24. And secondly, In thy saying it is redeemed by Christ within, by being within; when the work of the Spirit of Christ in believers, is to make known to the soul by dwelling within, which way and how they were redeemed by the Man Christ Jesus on the cross. And this I prove farther, because when thou art forced to answer to these words, Why did the Man Christ Jesus hang on the cross on Mount Calvary for the sins of his children? Thou sayest, because they wickedly judged him to be a blasphemer. Friend, I did not ask thee why the Jews did put him to death? But why was he crucified there for the sins of his children? But thou willing to cover over thine error, goest on cunningly saying, and through their envy they persecuted him to death, for an evil doer. This is one ground at least, &c.

Friend, but that thou art ashamed to own the gospel of Jesus Christ, thou wouldest have said, he was crucified there for the sins of the world; and by his offering up of himself upon the cross, he did for ever perfect them that are sanctified. Nay, thou wouldest have studied to exalt his dying there; first, by shewing what a sad condition we were in without it; Secondly, by holding forth the manifold and great privileges that we have by his dying for us there. But thou art at enmity against the things of God, as is clearly seen by those that have indeed the Spirit of God in them, and are enabled thereby to discern you. And though you say, there is no other that can forgive sin, nor the blood of any other that can take away sin, but the blood of God. Yet thou deniest, that the blood of him, who was, and is truly God as well as Man, Christ Jesus: I say, thou deniest that his blood that was shed without Jerusalem Gates, doth wash away sin from the saints of God: and cunningly (though not at this time uttered) concluding that the blood of God was shed for sin on a cross within. If it be not so, then call me liar; but it will clearly appear so to be in your answer to my third query.

Query 3. What scripture have you to prove, that Christ is, or was crucified within you, dead within you, risen within you, ascended within you?

Thy answer is, There is no scripture that mentions every of our names in particular. And thy query (sayest thou) is raised from a misunderstanding of us, so I judge. But Christ is within us, that we do not deny, and he is the Lamb that was slain in the streets of the great city, which is spiritually called Sodom, and Egypt (mind spiritually) and he is now risen, and ascended; this we know, and leave thee to receive a further answer from them that are led by a spirit of delusion.

Friend, How dost thou run about the bush, seeking to scrabble up an answer, but findest not a right one, and wouldest also fain hold out, that Christ is, or was crucified within, dead within, risen and ascended within; but seeing thou canst not with or by the scriptures give an answer; then seeing thyself left of them, through the strength of carnal reason, thou goest about this way. Is there any of our names made mention of in scripture, or to that purpose, and wouldst fain infer from thence, that because we have names, though not mentioned in scripture, therefore, Christ is, and was crucified within, though not mentioned in the scriptures. Friend, Thy sophistry deceives thee.

The second Argument, which is like the first, is this, He is the Lamb slain in the streets of the great city, spiritually called Sodom and Egypt. Now from the word 'spiritually,' thou wouldest willingly infer also, that Christ is and was crucified within, dead within, and risen within you, and therefore thou sayest, mind spiritually. Friend, I may well mind thy spiritual wickedness, by which thou wouldest willingly cover thy heresy, but it will not be. Though thou dare not speak plainly in so many words, yet the thoughts of thy heart are made manifest, by the words that flow from thee.

Ah Friend! That thou couldest but close with the truth, and venture thy soul upon what was done by Jesus on the cross without the gates of Jerusalem, for it is by and through that blood that was there shed that we have redemption, (He. xiii. 12. compared with Col. i. 20.) and remission of sins, Ep. i. 7. and 1 Pe. ii. 24.

Query 4. My fourth query was, Is that very Man that was crucified between two thieves, whose name was Jesus the Son of Mary, is he the very Christ of God, yea, or nay?

Thy Answer is, Yes, he is the very Christ of God, which was before the world was, by whom the world was made, who was made manifest from Mary's womb, and was persecuted to death by the Scribes and Pharisees, in whose steps thou treadest in asking subtile questions to ensnare the innocent, as they did. Read thy example (sayest thou) and thyself to be an enemy to God's Christ.

This Answer is doubtfully given, I did not ask thee whether he was the Christ of God, that was before the world was; but I asked thee whether he was the Christ of God, that did hang between two thieves on Mount Calvary. Now I know the Christ of God was before the world was; but thou art afraid to look upon him, as suffering on the cross on Mount Calvary, between two thieves for our sins. But contrary-wise, wouldst willingly own him to be no otherwise, but as he was before the world, which thing is very dangerous; for he that doth so, doth lay aside all things, that in his own person he did in the flesh that he took from the Virgin Mary, as to justification and salvation; only supposing him to be but an example, and so bespatters all his merit and righteousness, by your false conclusions, which in his own person he accomplished for our justification.

And Friend, hadst thou not been afraid of thyself, thou wouldst have been so far from calling these my queries, subtil questions, that thou wouldst have owned them, and have given a sober Christian answer to them, instead of a railing accusation. But it matters not, it hath but made thee shew thyself the more, which peradventure for a time might otherwise have lien hid.

Query 5. My fifth query was, ' Is that very man with that very body within you, yea, or no?' To which thou answerest: ' The very Christ of God is within us, we dare not deny him; and we are members of his body, of his flesh, and of his bones, as the Ephesians were: They that are led with a spirit of delusion, shall answer the rest of this thy query, if they will.'

Thy answer is nothing to the question, for I did not ask, whether the Spirit of Christ was in thee? (though I question the truth of that) But I asked you whether that very Man, with that very body, (or the body of Christ that was hanged on the cross) be within you? But I see you are minded to famble,* and will not answer plainly. But thou answerest, saying, ' We are members of his body, of his flesh, and of his bones, as the Ephesians were.' This is nothing to the purpose neither; for it is one thing for a man to be a member of the flesh and bones of Christ, and another thing to have the flesh and bones of Christ within him. What, because believers are members one of another, must they therefore be also one in another? No. Even so, though a believer be a member of the body, flesh and bones of Christ; it doth not therefore follow, that Christ, flesh and bones is within him. But thou art loth to discover thyself in plain terms, though thou art made manifest full sore against thy will; for thou dost here also, though very cunningly, signify, that thou ownest Christ no otherwise, but as he is within. And to own him no otherwise, is still against the gospel and faith of the Apostles, who said, they were absent from him while they were at home in the body, or here below. 2 Co. v. 6.

Query 6. My sixth query was this, ' Was that very Jesus, that was born of the Virgin Mary, a real man of flesh and bones after his resurrection out of Joseph's sepulchre, yea, or nay. The scrip-

* ' To famble,' to falter, or stammer in speech; obsolete. —ED.

tures say he was; and if so, then did that man go away from his disciples, and not into them, as the scriptures declare; or did he with that body of flesh go into his disciples, as some fond dreamers think.

Thy answer is, What the scripture speaks of Christ, we own to be truth, and own him to be what the scriptures speak of him; and all men's imaginations of him we deny, and their false interpretations of the scripture concerning him. And let the fond dreamers, who err in their thoughts, be reproved; for we dare own nothing but what the Spirit of the Lord bears witness of according to the scriptures. And thus far I answer in behalf of the Quakers; and let them that are led with a spirit of delusion answer the rest, which concerns themselves.

This answer hath some pretended fairness in it. But yet we know you, that you can wrest the scriptures to your own destruction; and that is clear, in that though you say you own him as the scriptures speak of him, yet you deny him as the scriptures speak of him in part. And if at any time you plead one truth, it is that you might by your corrupt dealing with that, clash against another: as for instance: You profess you own Christ within, but withal, with that doctrine you will smite against the doctrine of Christ Jesus in his person without, and deny that, though that is a truth, as is also the other. You do use the truth of the resurrection of saints, from a state of nature, to a state of grace, to fight against that truth of the resurrection of the bodies of saints out of their graves; together with other things that I might add, as your holding forth the intercession of the Spirit of Christ within, in opposition to the intercession of Christ in his person without in the heavens. Which things being thus done, they shew forth a great deal either of ignorance or presumption, knowingly to fight against the truth. And in this that thou answerest so generally, and not particularly to the question, it is evident that thou dost not plainly declare thy mind, but dost keep that in thy bosom, which thou darest not manifest to the world.

Query 7. My seventh query was, ' Hath that Christ that was with God the Father before the world was, no other body but his church?' If you say No, as it is your wonted course; then again I ask you, ' What was that in which he did bear the sins of his children? If you say, in his own body on the tree; then I ask, Whether that body in which he did bear our sins, was, or is, the church of God, yea, or no?' Again, if you say he hath no other body but his church, then I ask, What that was that was taken down from the cross? But here thou puttest a stop to the rest of my words, with an &c.

Thy answer is, In this thou hast not only queried, but slandered; therefore thy slander (sayest thou) I do remove. It is our wonted course, sayest thou, to say, that Christ hath no other body but his church. Thou art here a false accuser. But we say, the church is Christ's body; and it is sufficient for salvation to know Christ Jesus to be head in us, and over us, and ourselves to be members of his body; which thou sayest is his church. And what thou intendest by making so many foldings in one query, sayest thou, it may be judged it is to insnare; and in that thou answerest, thou answerest thyself for us in some things, that thou mightest have a further ground to lay a deeper snare; we do deny thee and thy spirit, and see thee to be only feeding in thy imaginations upon the report of things, without the life: And thy religion stands in disputes and controversies, and queries, and many words. But our religion stands in the exercise of a pure conscience towards God, and towards man; whether we speak, or be silent: These are thy words.

Now in my query thou sayest I slander, in that I say, you Quakers allow of no other body of Christ; but the Church of Christ; yet dost thou not clear thyself at all, only thou wouldest say something to dazzle the eyes of the ignorant. But friend, if thou wouldest have made it appear that I slandered in saying, you own no other body but the church; you should have said yes, we do own this, That Christ hath a body that is now in glory, ascended from his disciples, according to the scripture. Ac. i. 3. compared with ver. 9—11. But thou dost only fling up a few words into the air, that thou mightest thereby puzzle thy simple reader. But I bless God, for my part I do see thee, that thou dost, like a beguiled man, seek by all means to beguile others. And whereas thou sayest, It is sufficient to salvation, to know Christ Jesus as head in us, and over us. To this I answer, whatsoever thy meaning is by these words, yet there are none shall be saved, but those who through the mighty operation of the Spirit of Christ, are enabled to apply what the man Christ Jesus the Son of Mary hath done and suffered, and is now a-doing for sinners and saints, (and for him) in the presence of his Father, now ascended in his body of flesh and bones, from his children which are alive in this world. I say, there are none shall be saved, but those that are thus established, or shall be so, as is clear from these (1 Pe. i. 18, 19. & ii. 24. & iii. 18, 22. & iv. 1. 2 Pe. i. 17. He. vii. 24, 25. & x. 7, 9. & xiii. 12. 1 Ti. ii. 5, 6. Ep. i. 7. Ac. xiii. 37—39.) with many other scriptures. And again, when you say, I answer you in something, if you mean, that the body in which he did bare the sins of his children, is his church (for that is partly my query,) then I do say, that your doctrine is desperate and devilish; and you do thereby undervalue the death, blood, resurrection and ascension, intercession and second coming again of that man for salvation; and therefore for a better satisfaction to all who may read your book, I entreat you to answer, 'Did he bear our sins in that body which is his church, or did he bear our sins in that body that did hang on the cross on Mount Calvary?' Answer plainly I beseech you.

And now friend, passing by the rest of thy brawlings, I shall come to thy several queries, and shall answer to them in the simplicity of my soul, not laying down any doubtful expressions, but in all plainness, and not as you do. For the better understanding of them, by those that read them.

These be the Quaker's Queries, and my Answers to them.

Query 1. 'Is any man justified in the sight of God, but he that followeth Christ; and is it not a work to follow Christ, yea or nay, and what is the sight of God.

Ans. He that followeth Christ aright, must first believe in Christ; for how shall they follow him, in whom they believe not. Now then the scripture saith, He that believeth on the Son hath everlasting life, Jn. iii. 16—18. so then we are justified by believing; and if so, then to follow Christ is rather a fruit of our believing, than justification itself. And whereas you ask, What is the sight of God? I answer, To be justified in the sight of God by Jesus Christ, is for God to look on such poor creatures as we are; as complete, without spot or wrinkle, in the obedience of the man Christ Jesus; who otherwise could not behold them in love, because of their iniquity. Hab. i. 3.

Query 2. 'Whether will that faith justify a man which hath not works, seeing the scripture, or the Apostle saith, faith without works is dead; and what is that which worketh faith; and where is it, within, or without?'

Ans. That faith that hath not works is dead, being alone. Yet it doth not follow, that all that have works, have faith. No; but contrary-wise, men may have works, yea, the works of the law of God too, and yet be under the curse; Ga. iii. 10—13. which they could not be if they had saving faith. So then, if faith without works is dead; and again, if men may have works, and yet no faith, no saving faith, I mean: Then it will be good to inquire, what it is to have a right faith, which doth bring forth right good works; and who have works without a right faith. And

(1.) A right saving faith, is, for a man to be enabled of God's holy Spirit, to lay hold on what the man Christ hath done in his own person, when he was in the world? as his birth, righteousness, death, blood, resurrection, ascension, and intercession; and to apply the virtue and merit thereof to himself, so as to see himself saved thereby. Ro. iv. 24, 25. Being justified freely by his grace: How? Even through the redemption that is in Christ Jesus. Whom God hath set forth to be a propitiation, or reconciler, through faith in his blood, &c. Again, 'Be it known unto you, - - that through this man is preached unto you the forgiveness of sins: And by him all that believe: (Mark, all that believe; namely, in his blood which was shed on Mount Calvary) are justified from all things, from which ye could not be justified by the law of Moses.' Ac. xiii. 38, 39. If the faith that applies these things be of the operation of God, it is very much accompanied with good works. 'For the love of Christ constraineth us; because we thus judge, that if one died for all, then were all dead. And *that* he died for all, that they which live (namely by the faith of this, that Christ died for all, Ga. ii. 20.) should not henceforth live unto themselves, but unto him which died for them.' 2 Co. v. 14, 15. But

(2.) They that deny the merits of the birth, death, righteousness, blood, &c. of the man that was born of Mary, which he fulfilled in his own person, by himself. He. i. 3. I say, they that do not venture their souls on these glorious, mysterious truths, but deny the belief of them to be sufficient of themselves to save from hell, and all other things, and doth expect that salvation should be obtained by something that worketh in them, by working in them. It is impossible that these, though they may be, touching the righteousness of the law blameless, (as Paul was while he was a persecutor, Phi. iii. 6.) to be saved hereby. Wherefore? because they seek it not by the faith of Christ, but as it were by the works of the law. Ro. ix. 30, 31.

And whereas you ask me, 'What is that which worketh faith? And where is it, within or without?' I answer, That which worketh saving faith, is the holy Spirit of God, which is renewed through the hearing of the word, preached by the Apostles or ministers of Jesus Christ: Now the Spirit when it doth work, it entereth into the soul, and as I said before, doth enable the soul to believe, and lay hold on the merits of the Son of Mary, Jesus Christ. For saith he, when he is come, he shall glorify me, for he shall take of mine, and shew it unto you. Jn. xvi. 14.

Query 3. 'Whether any be justified but he that is born of God? And whether doth he that is born of God commit sin? And is that within the creature, or without, that worketh the new birth?'

Ans. Justification may be taken two ways, (1.) either in the sight of God, or in the sight of the soul, or creature; my meaning is, that all that are or shall be saved, are justified in the sight and foreknowledge of God before the foundation of the world. Ep. i. 4. According as he hath chosen us in him before the foundation of the world, &c. Having predestinated us to the adoption of children by Jesus Christ unto himself. And again, 'Moreover whom he did predestinate, them he also called; and whom he called, them he also justified; and whom he justified, them he also glorified.' Ro. viii. 30. Mark, all these thing are spoken as being already done; predestinated, called, justified, glorified. He doth not say, they shall be, but he hath done it, that is, in and according to the foreordination of God. (2.) Saints are said to be justified in their own sight or knowledge, as when God doth make manifest to the soul, what he had determined before should be done. 'Be of good cheer, thy sins are forgiven thee.' This is justification in the sight of the creature. And whereas you ask me, 'Do they that are born of God commit sin?' To this I answer,

They shall never commit the sin against the Holy Ghost, as is the meaning of that place, 1 Jn. v. 16—18. There is a sin unto death, and there is a sin not unto death.—He that is born of God sinneth not, but keepeth himself; and that wicked one, (mark, that wicked one, the sin unto death,) toucheth him not: But they that are born of God notwithstanding, do daily sin, as it is evident. Ja. iii. 2. 'In many things we offend all,' saith he, I and you, all of us. And again, if we say that we have no sin we deceive ourselves, and (instead of having no sin) the truth is not in us. 1 Jn. i. 8. And who can say, my heart is clean? There is none righteous, no not one. And again, 'There is not a just man upon earth that doeth good, and sinneth not.' Ec. vii. 20. And I am confident, that while some would persuade others that they have no sin, their own consciences tell them they lie; and if it be not so in the rest, it is because they are hardened, and given to believe a lie.

As to the latter part of your query, I answer; The new birth is wrought through hearing of the word preached. And yet not by conscience, nor by the obedience to the law, or dictates of nature; but by the Spirit coming into the soul, and shewing its lost condition without the obedience of the Son of Mary, the Son of God; and his freeness and willingness to communicate, or give himself, and all his things unto it; which being done, the man is thereupon given up to God, and is become a new creature. I might spend much time in speaking to this, but I forbear, because of itself it is enough to fill up a small volume.

Query 4. 'If Christ hath enlightened all men as he is God (as thou confessest) then hath he not enlightened all men as he is the Son of God? and is not the light of God sufficient in itself, to lead to God all that follow it, yea, or nay?'

Ans. (1.) Christ as he is God, doth enlighten

every man that comes into the world, which light is conscience, or otherwise nature itself, which doth also convince of sin. Jn. viii. 9. Yet Christ as he is God; doth not give unto every man that spirit that doth lead to eternal life, for all men have it not. Jude 19. (2.) Christ as he was and is the Son of God before the world was, being one in power, and being with his Father, hath enlightened every one that comes into the world, as aforesaid; but hath not so neither given them his spirit. 'Some are sensual,' &c. (3.) Christ as God-man, or as he came into the world to die for those whom before as God he knew and loved; I say, he doth not in this way neither enlighten every man with the saving light of life, or give unto them his holy Spirit. No, they that have been, and now are believers, do know and can remember, that all the time of their unregenerate state, they were without Christ. Ep. ii. 12. So that here is no way or room for your doctrine, take it how you will, Christ hath not given to every one his Spirit.

Second Part of the Query. Is not the light of God sufficient in itself, to lead to God all that follow it, yea, or nay?

Ans. (1.) As I said before, some are sensual, and have not the Spirit of Christ. (2.) No man can come to God as a Father by adoption, but by Jesus Christ; then it must needs be that all men, though they do follow that light which is given to every man, it is not able to lead to God as a Father in the Lord Jesus Christ. Yet this light that every man hath, will shew a man there is a God, and that this God is eternal; and also will clear out something of him, to them, by the things that are made. But now, if this light would lead to everlasting life, then might the devils also be delivered from everlasting damnation; seeing they also do know God as a creator, and revenger of sin, more perfectly than any natural man in the world, though not as a Father by adoption.

But you say, Doth it not lead to God all that follow it? Answ. (1.) Not to be saved, though to be condemned, through the weakness and unprofitableness of that light, or conscience, or the law, call it either, and I clear it thus: Because, if that light that every man receives. were able by our following it, to save us, then Christ needed not to have suffered, seeing all men had that light. (2.) If that light that every man hath, which is conscience, were able to lead a man to justification by following it; that promise was made in vain by Jesus the Son of Mary, when he said, 'I will send you; [Mark, I will send you] the Spirit, and he shall lead you into all truth:' for they had a light before. But it is evident, that that was not sufficient, because they must have another sent them by Jesus Christ, and that must be the Spirit.

Query 5. 'Whether is not the same light in him that hates it, as it is in him that loves it, Jn. iii. If there be a difference in the light, show it wherein; whether in the nature, or otherwise?'

Answ. (1.) That scripture quoted in Jn. iii. 'Light is come into the world,' &c., is not meant of that light, or conscience, that every man hath; but the Man Christ Jesus is speaking there of himself, as God-man, come into the world, born of the Virgin, if thou compare 19—21. with 14—18. of the same chapter, it is clear, for they all do speak of the same thing; namely, the Son of Mary. And again, saith he, 'I am the light of the world.' Now the man Christ, though he was then in the world, and walked up and down in the same, yet he was not within any man in the world as man, (though he calls himself the light thereof) though he was in some; I say, in some, as God by his Spirit. Now the light, which was the Man Christ, was the very same, whether loved by some, or hated by others; but if you conclude every man hath Christ, or that light spoken of there, Jn. iii. within him; that I deny, having proved the contrary. But (2.) Whether is there a difference in the light? Answ. There are more lights than one, there is a light that may be suspected to be darkness, where he saith, 'if the light that is in thee be darkness,' &c. Again, there is the light of the law. Pr. vi. 23. Again, conscience also will convince of sin. Now there is none of these that can save a sinner from the evil of his ways. Take the best of them, which is the righteous law of God, that cannot. For had there been a law given, which might have given life, then verily righteousness had come by the law: But if you conclude that righteousness, or everlasting life cometh by the law, you must conclude this again; that Christ did die in vain. Ga. ii. 21. So then these things being not able to save the soul, the next thing is, the Son of God, the Son of righteousness arising with healing under his wings; he is also a light, and indeed the saving light, far surpassing all the other mentioned.

Now though Christ doth not differ in himself, yet there is a difference in the power of these lights; the law and Christ, the one not being able to save, the other being able. And again, there is also a difference in the nature of them; the one being a condemning light, the other a saving light. It is Moses that accuseth you (saith Christ) even Moses in whom ye trust: But do not think, saith Christ, that I will accuse you to the Father: No, saith he, it is Moses, or the law given by him. But again, where Christ speaks for himself as a Saviour, he saith 'God sent not his Son into the world to condemn the world; but that the world through him might be saved.' Jn. iii. 17. So that I say, (a) That light spoken of, Jn. iii. which is the Man Christ, is not in every man that comes into the world. (b)

That the Man Christ, or the light spoken of there, is not against himself. (c) There is the light of the law, conscience, and nature itself, which are in all men, which things are altogether insufficient to save a man from death, by his seeking of justification thereby. Again, there is Jesus Christ, he is the Saviour, but not in all men. And again, neither is the Man Christ Jesus the condemning light.

Query 6. 'Whether is it possible, that any can be saved, without Christ manifested within? If no, then whether is not the doctrine of salvation, which is only necessary, to preach Christ within: And is not the whole mystery of salvation, God manifest in the flesh?'

Answ. There can none be saved, but they that have the Spirit of Christ given unto them. But it is not the Spirit of Christ given to the elect, that doth work out the salvation of their souls within them, for that was obtained by the blood of the Man Christ Jesus on the cross. He. ix. 12. compared with He. xiii. 12.

Again, every one that is, or shall be saved, must, and shall have the Spirit of Christ within them; yet doth it not follow, that to preach Christ (only) within, is the only doctrine of salvation. For then also the preaching of the blood of Christ shed on the cross, as I said before, must be of none effect. But he that doth preach the doctrine of salvation aright, must first begin to preach that doctrine that Paul preached in 1 Co. xv. 3, 4. 'For I delivered unto you (saith he) first of all that which I also received, how that Christ died for our sins according to the scriptures; and that he was buried, and that he rose again the third day according to the scriptures.' Now Christ, or the Spirit of Christ, is received by such preaching as this is, as is clear from that scripture, Ac. x. 38—44. Where Peter speaking of the word that was published throughout all Judea: 'How God anointed Jesus of Nazareth (or which dwelt at Nazareth) with the Holy Ghost and with power: who went about doing good, and healing all that were oppressed of the devil; for God was with him. And we are witnesses of all things which he did both in the land of the Jews, and in Jerusalem; (saith Peter) whom they slew and hanged on a tree: Him God raised up the third day, and shewed him openly; Not to all the people, but unto witnesses chosen before of God, *even* to us, who did eat and drink with him, after he rose from the dead. And he commanded us to preach unto the people, and to testify that it is he which was ordained of God *to be* the Judge of quick and dead.' And is that all? No, But 'to him give all the prophets witness, (to him, even Jesus of Nazareth whom the Jews crucified on the tree) that through his name whosoever believeth in him shall receive remission (or for-

giveness) of sins.' Now mark. And 'while Peter yet spake these words, the Holy Ghost fell on all them which heard the word.' While Peter spake these words, that by Jesus of Nazareth forgiveness of sins was preached to them that believe in his name, 'the Holy Ghost fell on all them that heard the word.' Namely, which Peter spake: This is the way in which the Spirit is given? namely, by preaching a crucified Christ.

But now, no man can be saved without Christ, or the Spirit of Christ be given to him, because he cannot be able to lay hold savingly of, and to hope for that glory that Christ as he is God-man hath accomplished in his own person without, unless he have the Spirit. But farther, thou sayest; Is it not the whole mystery of salvation, God manifested in the flesh?

Answ. Truly, to know that God out of love to poor sinners, did in the fulness of time send forth his only begotten Son, who is equal with his Father, to be born of a woman, and made under the law, to redeem them that are under the law, that we might receive the adoption of sons; this is to know the mystery of godliness. Therefore, when the scriptures say, God was manifested in the flesh, they mean, God sent forth his Son, which was and is the word of God, God himself, and he was made flesh. Jn. i. 14. And so in the nature of man he did become the Lamb of God, or the sacrifice of God, that doth take away the sins of the world. ver. 29. Now here I might enlarge abundantly, but that I would not be tedious.

Query 7. 'Whether is it not possible, that many may profess as much of Christ without, as thou hast said of him, and yet be damned; and if this be the faith to profess him born, dead, risen and ascended without; then is there any unbeliever in England? seeing all in the outward sound believes, and professes as much as thou hast said. Yea, or nay?'

Answ. 1. I know there are many that do profess in word, that Christ was born, dead, risen, and ascended without, and yet may be damned. Yet he that doth really, with the faith of the operation of God, believe these things, and doth also apply the virtue and merit of the same to themselves for justification and life, shall be saved. 'If thou shalt confess with thy mouth the Lord Jesus, and shalt believe in thine heart that God hath raised him from the dead, thou shalt be saved.' Ro. x. 9. And also 1 Co. xv. 2. 'By which also ye are saved, if ye keep in memory what I preached unto you.' What was that? why, 'how that Christ died for our sins according to the scriptures; And that he was buried, and rose again,' &c.

(2.) It is not faith, only to talk of him with the mouth, but as I said before, to believe the same by the operation of the Spirit in our hearts. If this be faith, (sayest thou) to profess him born, dead, risen and ascended without, then is there any unbeliever in England? [I reply] All that profess this do not truly believe it; for to profess in word alone, and believe in heart, are two things. Secondly, If to profess this were the Faith, yet were there a good many Unbelievers in England, for the *Quakers* will not profess him ascended without, neither making intercession without, but contrarywise strike at this doctrine.

Query 8. 'Whether hath that man faith in Christ that is not changed in the nature, and is not the liar and slanderer an unbeliever, and of the cursed nature, yea or no?'

Answ. He that hath faith in Christ is a new creature: and the liar and slanderer is an unbeliever: and if he live and die in that condition, his state is very sad, though if he turn there is hope for him; therefore repent and turn quickly, or else look to yourselves, for you are the men, as is clear by your discourse.

Query 9. 'Whether [doth] any [man] receive Christ, who receives him not into him? if not, show how Christ can be received, and whether many professes him not which never received him.'

Answ. Christ as he is Man, as he was a sacrifice for sin, cannot be received really and personally into any, but yet, he that doth indeed receive the gospel, and believe that he was a sacrifice upon the cross for his sins, doth and hath also received his Spirit into him, which giveth him the comfort of these things. Jn. xiv. 26. And there are very many that profess him, that at the day of judgment will fall short of eternal life, notwithstanding all their profession; for as I said before; it is not the professor, but the sound believer that shall be saved by him. But let the reader mark, how thou condemnest thy own doctrine by this query, for thou grantest many profess Christ that never receive him. How then hath every man Christ, or the light of Christ within him? If it be within him, either he must receive it, or snatch it by force against the will of another, however the scripture saith, what is it that thou hast not received; (yet all men have not received that) Jude 19.

Query 10. 'Whether to preach for hire, for gifts and rewards, and to divine for money, and to make merchandise of the people for so much a year for preaching to them, be not true marks and signs of false prophets? or can any give truer signs of false prophets than Isaiah and Micah give, yea or nay?'

Answ. There are a company of dumb dogs that are crept into the nation, that love give ye, and desire to bear rule by their means; and they are every one for his gain from their quarter. There are a company of wolves crept out also, having wrapped themselves about with sheep's clothing,

and these are both alike abominable to the Lord. Neither can a man give a more right description of a false prophet, than the prophets and Christ with his apostles did give, therefore examine yourselves.

Query 11. 'Whether must not the devil be chained before Christ reign, and what is that which chains him, and whether art thou come to one of the days of the thousand years, yea, or no?'

Answ. Christ hath two several times wherein Satan must be bound by him, one is at the conversion of sinners, the other when he shall come the second time, and personally appear, and reign, in the world to come. Again, 'Whether I am come to one of the days of the thousand years?' [I reply] No, because he that doth reign with Christ one of these days, shall live and reign with Christ a thousand years. Re. xx. 4. But there is never a believer in the world, that doth, or in any likelihood shall live half so long, before they die or be changed at the coming of the Man Christ Jesus.

Query 12. 'Whether dost thou know any Christ, preach or profess any Christ who hath not lightened every man that comes into the world with the light of life, or of condemnation; And is he not a deceiver that exhorts people for salvation to any other thing than the light of Christ, yea, or no? And how hath Christ lightened every man if not within him?'

Answ. That Christ I preach, is the Christ of God, who as he is God hath enlightened every man that comes into the world with conscience, and the law, which is the light of condemnation, but not of life; For the law is the ministration of condemnation. 2 Co. iii. 7, 8. And all men have the law and conscience: but these will not save them. Again, there are some that do indeed enjoy the light of life. And whereas thou askest, is not he a deceiver, that exhorts people to anything else than the light of Christ? Answ. He that telleth any man that the ministration of condemnation will save him, which is the law, he is a liar, and a deceiver: but he that exhorts people to lay hold on what the Man Christ Jesus hath done in his own person for sinners, and presseth souls to venture upon that for salvation, preacheth the truth. Christ hath given to every one the law, and conscience within him: yet these are not able to save him, but let him follow the righteousness of the law never so much, yet if he be not directed of God to fly to Jesus the Son of Mary, and to what he hath done in his own person for them, he shall never be saved. Ac. iv. 12.

Friend, Thus have I with all plainness of speech answered thy queries, and I fear not at all, but I have spoken the truth as it is in Jesus. And as for committing them to the judgment of others, as thou wouldst have me; let others say what they will, I am sure I have spoken the truth of God; and I make no question but at the second coming of my Lord Jesus from heaven to judge the world, these things I shall not be ashamed of; neither am I now; but am ready, if God shall give me life, to speak the same things to any man, face to face; and I desire thee, and all, even as many as shall read or hear this treatise, to consider, and look to themselves, lest they sin against God so much in their lifetime by rejecting these truths, that it shall never be forgiven them to all eternity, though they repent them of their rejecting the same. There is one thing more to which I shall speak a few words, and that is to a few words written at the end of thy book, which is called the postscript, wherein is several charges against myself and some others, which I shall speak somewhat to.

The first is against John Burton, thus: John Burton said in a discourse with some friends, that Christ had two bodies, and one of them is out of the sight of the saints. My brother Burton being absent, I shall answer for him concerning the charge laid against him. And therefore, that Christ, who is and was before the world began, God equal with his Father, did in the fulness of time take upon him a body from the Virgin Mary, which was so prepared by God his Father, it is evident in scripture; and in it after he had lived a while in the world, he did hang on the cross, was taken down thence again, and laid in Joseph's sepulchre, was raised again, and ascended away from his disciples therewith into glory. Ac. i. 3, 9—11.

Again, he hath another body, and that is his church. Ep. i. 23. Now that he is out of the sight of his saints in one of the bodies; namely, that which did hang on the cross, it is also evident, 1 Ti. vi. where Paul speaking of that very Jesus, who did bear a faithful witness before Pontius Pilate, saith in ver. 16. 'Who only hath immortality, dwelling in the light which no man can approach unto; whom no man hath seen, nor can see.' That is, not with their mortal eyes, in that glory as yet. If you say still, notwithstanding this, that Christ as he was before the world began, hath but one body, and that to be his church. I ask you what that was that was taken down from the cross, and laid into Joseph's sepulchre. Lu. xxiii. 53.

The second charge is against myself, and is this; John Bunyan said, Christ's second coming is not his coming in Spirit, for his coming in Spirit is no coming.

The former part of the words, namely, Christ's second coming is not his coming in the Spirit, those I own. But the other, namely, For his coming in Spirit is no coming, is a lie, made of me by the Author, Edward Borrough.

The former words were spoken at a meeting in

This is a false thing spoken of me.

Bedford, some Quakers being present contradicting and blaspheming: And now they could not be content with that; but they must make up all with a lie, and publish it in print. A Quaker there and I had some discourse concerning Christ's second coming, and he would affirm, that his coming in Spirit, was his second coming spoken of in scripture. Then I asked him which was his first coming? He answered, when he was born of the Virgin, and took flesh upon him from her. Then said I, I shall easily prove, that his coming in the Spirit is not his second coming, for I will prove that his coming in the Spirit was before that which the scripture and you also do call his first coming; and proved it by that plain scripture, where Peter speaking of the prophets, saith, 'Searching what, or what manner of time the Spirit of Christ which was in them (the prophets) did signify, when it testified before-hand the sufferings of Christ, and the glory that should follow.' 1 Pe. i. 11. and iii. 19, where speaking of Christ's being put to death in the flesh, but quickened in the Spirit. 'By which Spirit also he went and preached unto the spirits (now) in prison;' but when was this, only 'when once the longsuffering of God waited in the days of Noah. ver. 20. Which was long before the first coming of Christ, so called in scripture, for that was, as I said, when he took a body from the Virgin Mary.

But it seems clearly by these words that you do look for no other coming but his coming in Spirit. O! how suddenly and unexpected of you, will the Son of Man break down from heaven, with all his mighty angels in flaming fire, and call you, together with all nations to judgment. And though now peradventure you are ready to slight the personal appearing of the Lord Jesus Christ, that Man to judgment, only looking for a judgment within, yet you will I am certain, very suddenly be made to pass under another judgment, which will be more exceeding great than any judgment you shall have here, and more terrible. As for the latter part of the charge, which is a very lie; though I shall not trouble myself to lay it to your charge (you have so manifestly declared yourselves already what you are) yet I beseech you, that hereafter you would not be so ready to receive lies from others, and publish them to the view of the world, least you appear to all men (as you do to some) to be such as are of an accusing lying spirit.

But farther, That Christ's coming in the Spirit is not his second coming, it is evident; partly, in that the coming of Christ in Spirit, was before that called in scripture, his first coming. Secondly, he that comes the second time is he that came the first time. Now he that came the first time was very God and very Man, and not a Spirit only; for handle me, saith he, a Spirit hath not flesh and bones, as you see me have. Lu. xxiv. 39. Now this same Jesus that was very God and very Man, so born of Mary, saith, 'I go and prepare a place for you; and I, (the very same as also Ac. i. 10, 11.) will come again, and receive you unto myself; that where I am, *there* ye may be also.' Jn. xiv. 3. Here I might spend many words, but it needs not; the whole current of scriptures do confirm this thing; and therefore I shall forbear, and content myself with this, He that will be filthy let him be filthy, for the day is at hand.

The Third Charge is also against me, saying, 'I said there was nothing in me, nor any man to be taken notice of.'

Though in some sense I do not deny these words, yet I know, and am sure, that directly in this form of words, I did never lay them down, but I pass that. Now in this sense I do not deny them, there was nothing in me, as I was in my unregenerate estate; nor in any man else in the same estate, that is worthy to be taken notice of for justification. Because every unregenerate man is without Christ, before he be converted. Ep. ii. 12. Wherefore remember, that ye being Gentiles in the flesh (unconverted) that at that time ye were without Christ. Now a man that is without Christ, and hath not his Spirit in him, as some, yea, most men are. Jude 19. What is there in that man, that is worth the taking notice of to justify him.

Also converted Paul saith, 'I know that in me, (that is, in my flesh,) dwelleth no good thing.' Ro. vii. 18.

As for others that are charged with things, because their names are not also mentioned, I shall pass them by; only thus much I shall say further to the last charge. That there is nothing in any man by nature, before he be converted, that is worth the taking notice of, as to seek justification thereby. And that that light which every man hath, being at the best but conscience, nature, or the law, let a man take notice of it, follow it, obey it never so much, it is not able to justify the soul: For if righteousness come by the law, then Christ is dead in vain. And as I said before, every man hath not Christ to take notice of, though every man hath conscience, or the light of nature in him, which is also able to convince of sins against the law of God, yet is not able to deliver from that curse pronounced by the Lord, against them that disobey the law. Nay the law itself is not able to save them that do follow it, being too weak for such a thing. And indeed God did not give it to that end, that saints should have life by it. No, compare Ga. iii. 21. with Ro. v. 20. you may clearly see why God gave the law, namely, that sins or offences might abound. But how? By discovering sin by its workings. Now then you that follow the law, and seek life by it, this is all you are

like to have of it: You shall see your transgression against it, made known to you by it, Ro. iii. 20. and an horrible curse pronounced against you, because you cannot give a complete continual obedience to every tittle of it.

And now friend to thee, who hast taken in hand to answer my queries laid down in the end of my book; I say, thou hast only wrangled and quarrelled at them; but hast not given one plain and right answer to any one of them. Therefore I shall leave them still to be answered by you, or others of your spirit. You will find them at the end of the foregoing discourse: And I beseech you to answer them in all plainness of heart, and with as moderate a spirit as you may. It is like there may be some addition to them: But as I have dealt plainly and sincerely with yours, so do you deal uprightly and plainly with mine, for the satisfaction of those who shall read them. And here I shall draw towards a conclusion, only speak some words to those who unawares to themselves may be carried away with the doctrines of the Quakers: And I shall be brief in speaking to it. The way that I shall take, shall be very plain to be understood; for I shall not lay down any doubtful sentence in my speech to them, nor others. *First*, I shall shew you that the doctrine of the Quakers is an error, and how. *Second*, Who they are that are carried away with it, and why. *Third*, The way Satan takes to make this delusion, or filthy doctrine to take place in the soul.

First, That the doctrine of the Quakers is false, or an error, I shall shew,

1. By discovering the doctrine itself. Now the doctrine of the Quakers is plainly this; namely, that every man that comes into the world, hath the Spirit of Christ in him. Now that this is an error is clear, because the word of God saith plainly, that some are 'sensual, having not the Spirit.' Jude 19. And again, The unregenerate man, in the time of his unregenerate state, is without Christ. Ep. ii. 12.

2. He that will but observe the motions of that light which every man hath within him (say they) so as to obey and close in with it to follow it, shall undoubtedly be saved from the wrath to come. Now this is clearly a gross error; for first, If all men have not Christ, as they have not, then is it not an error to press men to seek for life, by following that which is not able to give life. Yet this they do, who labour to persuade men, yea, the souls of men, that it is no less than the very Spirit of Christ in every man, that doth convince of sin, when the scriptures say plainly, 'the law.' Ro. iii. 20. 'Conscience,' Ro. ii. 15. and nature itself, Ro. ii. 14. 1 Co. xi. 14. will and doth convince of sin, yet none of these is the Spirit of Christ. And the great argument that they bring to prove that it is

the Spirit of Christ, is, because the Spirit doth also convince of sin. Now what a poor argument is this, to say, That because the Spirit of Christ doth convince of sin, therefore whatsoever doth convince of sin, must needs be the Spirit of Christ. As much as to say, because the saints are called ' the light of the world.' Mat. v. 14. Therefore the saints are the Saviour of the world, seeing Christ also doth call himself the light of the world, Jn. viii. 12. or because the moon hath, or is light, therefore the moon is the sun. This is but sophistical arguing, and doth beget most damnable errors and heresies in the world; but this is the way that they take, to entangle poor souls with their sad and erroneous doctrine, see page 22 of his book, lines 12 and 13. They say, that it must be Christ within them, that must within them work out justification for them; when it is evident from the whole current of scripture, that the Son of Mary was delivered to be crucified for our offences, and his resurrection, through faith in it, is our justification; as all along, through grace, I have declared and cleared. And the work that the Spirit doth in point of justification, is, to shew us what the Son of Mary hath done and suffered in his own body on the tree, and is now doing in the presence of his Father, in the highest heaven.

And to help us to apply this to our souls by faith now, for a preservative against these and the like delusions, observe, (1.) As I said before, all have not the Spirit of Christ. Jude 19. Ep. ii. 12. (2.) That the law, with all our obedience to it, is not able to save, or justify any poor soul. Ro. iii. 20. For by the works of the law shall no flesh living be justified, though it gives the knowledge of sin. (3.) That there is none other way to be justified in the sight of God, but by laying hold of what the Son of Mary (Jesus) did do and suffer in his own person, when he was in the world. For it is by him (and what he hath done in his own person by himself, He. i. 3.) that any man is justified from his sins, and the wrath of God due to the same, by believing that his blood was shed for their sins; as it is written, ' With his stripes we are healed,' Is. liii. 5. as if their own blood had been shed for their own sins ; and that his righteousness is theirs by imputation, as if they themselves had actually fulfilled all the law of God for their own justification. Ro. x. 4.

Second, The second thing is, who are they that are carried away with this delusion, and why?

1. Not one of God's elect whom he foreknew, shall be utterly destroyed thereby; (I do not say they shall not be led away for a time ; but they shall not be utterly destroyed) for they are kept by the mighty power of God through faith unto salvation. But they are such as are not indeed the elect of God, nor chosen in Christ before the

world began. Though Hymeneus and Philetus fall away, and overthrow the faith of some, yet ' the foundation of God stands sure, having this seal, The Lord knoweth them that are his.' 2 Ti. ii. 17—19.

2. They are such as in time past, for the generality of them were either but light, frothy professors, or else were shaken in their principles, and unstable therein, as saith the scriptures, They that are deceivers do beguile unstable souls. Or if they were such as were in appearance sober and serious in the account of others, it was either from those convictions they had from the law, or else from high notions they had of the gospel; which have both such influence at some time on the soul (though not savingly) that the soul will go very far in obedience to them ; as for example, Herod who was an enemy to the truth, yet for a time had such heart-workings, being convinced by the preaching of John the Baptist, that he feared him, and observed him, and when he heard him, he did many things, and heard him gladly. Mar. vi. 20.

Now the reason why such people are carried away with such heresies as these, or the like, is,

(1.) That as they were not of the elect of God, so God by suffering them to be carried away finally, may make it appear, that they were not of his elect. They went out from us, but they were not of us: for if they had been of us, they would no doubt have continued with us. But they went out from us, that it might be made manifest (or that men might see) that they were not all of us. 1 Jn. ii. 19.

(2.) Because God will not have his church so disturbed always with such as are not of the truth. Now there are some men that have their time to walk with the church of God by permission, and these men are ever and anon ready to broach their errors, even while they are among the saints, to their trouble. Now God having a care of his church, hath a time to suffer the devil to run through the world with some erroneous doctrine or other, which when these men taste, being spirited beforehand for that purpose, do presently close in with the same, to the purifying of the church, and the manifestation of themselves. And thus every branch which the Lord's right hand hath not planted, shall and must have a time to be rooted up. Mat. xv. 13.

(3.) Because others that are of the right graffing in, may notwithstanding not presume but fear, lest they also fall through the same example of others who are already fallen, or may fall hereafter. He. iv. 1, 2, 11.

(4.) Because others may see, that it is not by their own strength that they do stand, but freely by the grace of God, and his power and love towards them in the Lord Jesus Christ. God hath chosen some before the foundation of the world. Now to manifest this, though they are even as bad as the worst by nature, yet I say, because God will shew his power and his love, he doth preserve some to eternal life, though others fall into eternal damnation. Of all that thou hast given me, saith Christ, have I lost none but the son of perdition, that the scripture might be fulfilled. Jn. xvii. 12. Many other reasons might be given why these things must and shall be; but I rather choose to forbear. Only thus much I have spoken, because I know it is my duty to speak a few words unto you, that you may either close in with the truth, or else the more clearly be left without excuse at the great day.

Third. The third and last thing, is the way that Satan takes to make those delusions take place in the soul.

Now the way whereby he makes these or any other delusions to take place in the soul, is, 1. to persuade the soul that they are the truth; and 2. to stir up in the soul an enmity to any thing or person that shall declare the contrary.

1. They are given over to believe a lie; that is, to believe false doctrine to be the doctrine of God and of Christ. And that he might bring this to pass, he goeth about to change the names of things; and because the law, conscience, and nature itself can convince of sin, therefore he calleth them Christ, or the light of Christ; saying to a natural man, one that is not yet converted, 'Mind the light within you.' If they ask what light? say they, That which doth convince of sin. If they farther ask, why, what is that? They say, 'It is the light of Christ, the light of life, or Christ within.'

Now these things are nothing else but conscience, nature, or the law, for a natural man hath nothing else that dwelleth within him to convince him of sin; only these things have a new name put upon them. And poor creatures hearing the name Christ, being ignorant of the nature of Christ, do presently close in with these things, supposing, nay, verily believing that these are the Spirit of Christ. Which things being thus received, if at any time one come and oppose them, and tell them that it is an error that they have taken up, to think that that which is in an unregenerate man is the Spirit of Christ, and contrariwise telleth them plainly, that it is but their own conscience that doth convince them, or the law written in their hearts by nature. Nay, say they, it is the light of Christ in the conscience, when there is no scripture hath any such manner of expressions, only a fancy of their own, taken up without ground from the word.

2. But the soul being possessed with this doctrine, presently its heart riseth against anything that doth contradict it, and is filled with a secret enmity against it. Now the way that Satan takes to bring this about, is to persuade poor souls, that all these thoughts that do any wise contradict the principles received, is but a temptation of the devil. And if at any time there be the doctrine of Jesus held forth in truth, his death, burial, resurrection, ascension, and intercession; now without in the presence of his Father for sinners, and that there is salvation nowhere else but in the merits of the firstborn of Mary, which is Jesus Christ, without the works of the law, Ro. iii. 28. Presently with envy they are enraged and cry, 'Dost thou not know that every man hath a measure of the Spirit given to him? Follow that, listen to that, turn thy mind to that, and walk in the light of that.' When alas, there is no such thing as the Spirit of Christ in every man, as I said, and proved before at large; only the devil hath gotten this way to call conscience Christ, the law Christ; and hereby to entangle the soul with the name of a thing, without the thing itself.

But now the soul is set down in its principles, and he that doth any way confute that spirit, presently it falls a raging, and cries out, serpent, liar, wolf, dragon, devil, be silent with thy serpentine wisdom, and smoke of the bottomless pit. Now in this the devil is wonderfully cunning; for least he should indeed be discovered, he doth set the face hard against the truth, and counteth it such a deadly enemy, that he will not, cannot bear it; but lets fly against it all the hellish words and madness he can: And now he begins first to cry, avoid Satan. All which is only to harden him in whom he doth dwell, more and more against the truth. Now he doth also harden souls in delusions, by presenting the ugly and base conversations of a company of covetous wretches, who do profess themselves to be the ministers of the gospel, but are not; now poor creatures being shaking and doubtful what way to take, seeing the conversation of these men to be wicked, and the doctrine of these deluders covered with a seeming holiness; they presently embrace it, saying, surely these men are in the right way; they cry down the priests, whose lives we also see to be profane, they are very strict in their ways, and if such be not good men, who are? But yet that which is most taking is (through the corruption and pride that is naturally in the heart of man) these men propose such a way to salvation, as is in the compass of a man's own ability, even works of righteousness done by him, which is very agreeable to man's nature, which would willingly be saved, but would not be altogether beholden to God for it: and these works not being wrought by the priests or national ministers, but by the other, though in opposition to the righteousness of Christ, the

Messias God-man, poor souls not only suck in these erroneous principles, but are hardened in them against the doctrine of God and his Son Jesus Christ, by their ungodly conversation; and thus dishonour the Son of God. But come brethren, let us be patient, stablish our hearts, wait but a while, and I doubt not but you will see that those who dishonour our Jesus shall soon be brought down, both Ranters, Quakers, priests, and people also, that shall continue in opposing him either in doctrine or practice; for our God hath said, 'Ah! I will ease me of my adversaries.'

Now, a few words more to those who do believe in Christ aright, and lay him for their foundation.

First, Bless God that you are not carried away with the delusions that are on foot in this generation. *Secondly*, See that you are labourers after a more experimental knowledge of our Lord Jesus Christ; fly more to his birth, death, blood, resurrection, ascension and intercession; and fetch refreshing for your souls more and more from him without, through the operation of his Spirit within; and though the fruits of the Spirit be excellent, and to be owned where they are found; yet have a care you take not away the glory of the blood of Christ shed on the cross without the gates of Jerusalem, and give it them; which you will do, if you do content yourselves, and satisfy your consciences with this; that you find the fruits of the Spirit within you, and do not go for peace and consolation of conscience to the blood of Jesus shed on the cross.

Therefore learn of the saints, or rather of the Spirit, Re. v. 9. who teacheth to sing this song, 'Thou art worthy to take the book, and to open the seals thereof, for thou wast slain, and hast redeemed us to God by thy blood.'

And as for you that cannot yet well endure to think you should be justified by the blood of the Son of Mary shed on the cross without the gate, I say to you, 'Kiss the Son, lest he be angry, and ye perish *from* the way, when his wrath is kindled but a little. Blessed *are* all they that put their trust in him.' Ps. ii. 12.

ΙΡΩΔΗΣ

A DISCOURSE

UPON

THE PHARISEE AND THE PUBLICAN;

WHEREIN SEVERAL

GREAT AND WEIGHTY THINGS ARE HANDLED:

AS, THE NATURE OF PRAYER, AND OF OBEDIENCE TO THE LAW, WITH HOW FAR IT OBLIGES CHRISTIANS, AND WHEREIN IT CONSISTS.

WHEREIN IS ALSO SHEWED,

THE EQUALLY DEPLORABLE CONDITION OF THE PHARISEE, OR HYPOCRITICAL AND SELF-RIGHTEOUS MAN; AND OF THE PUBLICAN, OR SINNER THAT LIVES IN SIN, AND IN OPEN VIOLATION OF THE DIVINE LAWS. TOGETHER WITH THE WAY AND METHOD OF GOD'S FREE GRACE IN PARDONING PENITENT SINNERS; PROVING THAT HE JUSTIFIES THEM BY IMPUTING CHRIST'S RIGHTEOUSNESS TO THEM.

By JOHN BUNYAN, AUTHOR OF THE PILGRIM'S PROGRESS.

[The first edition is neatly printed in foolscap duodecimo, and ends on page 202. It is embellished with a frontispiece, the upper half a view of the Temple with the publican and pharisee, under which is a verse:—

See how ye Pharisee in the Temple stands
And justifies himself with lifted hands
Whilst ye poor publican with downcast eyes
Conscious of guilt to God for mercy cries.

The lower half is occupied with the Vera effigies Johanis Bunyan, Æt. sac 57. It is a small circle, apparently copied from the portrait by White, prefixed to the Holy War.]

ADVERTISEMENT BY THE EDITOR.

THIS important treatise unvails, in few but telling words, the nature of prayer, about which mankind has made most awful mistakes. Multitudes conceive that the heart-searching God can be influenced and propitiated by eloquent words and forms of prayer; whilst the few, who are taught by the Holy Spirit, feel and know that the ardent desire, the aspirations, the fervent wishes of the mind, can alone be accepted by the Eternal; and even then only through the merits of the Redeemer.

The first edition appeared in 1635, and it soon became a very popular book. The use and application announced at the end do not appear to have been published, unless the author meant one of his later productions to answer that purpose. The twelfth edition has no date on the title page; to it is added Bunyan's last Sermon, and his dying sayings,— 'Licensed, Sept. 10th, 1688;' but this announcement had been probably continued from some earlier edition. The number of cheap reprints of this little volume may account, in some measure, for the amazing errors which crept in and deformed the book; for with the exception of 'Grace Abounding,' 'The Pilgrim,' and 'The Holy War,' few books have been so carelessly and disgracefully printed. For more than a century Bunyan has been represented as saying, 'How did God deal with sinners before *his* righteousness was actually in being,' (p. 255). In fact, no reader can conceive the mutilated state in which this valuable treatise has been published, unless by actual comparison with those printed before the author's decease. Some considerable omissions, doubtless, arose from political causes. Bunyan died very shortly before the glorious revolution in 1688,— and in drawing a faithful portrait of a publican or tax gatherer, he supposed the country to be conquered by a foreign power. 'Would it not be an insufferable thing? yea, did not that man deserve hanging ten times over, that should, being *a Dutchman*, fall in with a French invader, and farm at his hands, those cruel and grievous taxations, which he, in barbarous wise, should at his conquest lay upon them; and exact and force them to be paid with an over, and above of what is appointed.' He goes on to argue, that if this would be a severe trial at the hand of a foreigner, how much more oppressive would it appear if exercised by a fellow-countryman. 'If these things are intolerable, what shall we think of such men as shall join to all this compliance with a foreign prince, to rob the church of God? yea, that shall become a man in power under them, to wring out of the hand of a brother, his estate; yea, his bread and livelihood.' These paragraphs, and much more, were omitted, probably, from a fear of giving offence to the new government, and, until the present edition, they had not been restored. In Bunyan's time, severe and awful persecutions fell upon the church of God in England, and he must have felt the utmost compassion, mingled with deep abhorrence, for those emissaries of Satan, the Informers, who plundered mercilessly all who refused obedience to the order of common prayer. These men, aided by fanatic justices and clergymen, reduced many pious families to the severest sufferings, while thousands fled to the wilds of America for that refuge among men called savages, which was denied them by their much more savage countrymen. It is distressing to read the narrative, published in 1670, of those proceedings in Bedford, while Bunyan was an inmate in its jail. The porters, charged to assist in carrying off the people's goods, ran away, saying, that 'they would be hanged, drawn, and quartered, before they would assist in that work;' two of them were sent to gaol for thus refusing to aid in this severe enforcement of impious laws. This populous town 'was so thin of people that it looked more like a country village than a corporation; and the shops being generally shut down, it seemed like a place visited with the pest, where usually is written upon the door—*Lord, have mercy upon us.*' When in the presence of the justice the officers took *all* his goods from Thomas Arthur, he appealed to the humane feelings of the magistrate on behalf of his children,—' Sir, shall my children starve,' to which he replied, ' yes, your children shall starve.' All these bitter sufferings were inflicted for worshipping God according to the directions of his holy word. Can we wonder then that Bunyan uses hard words. He felt that state hierarchies were anti-christian; their fruit declared that those who supported them by such cruelties were *aliens* and enemies to the church of Christ.

As a theological treatise, this of the Pharisee and Publican is invaluable. It is clear and perfectly intelligible to every candid and prayerful inquirer. When our author is proving the impossibility of a sinner's recommending himself to the divine favour by any imperfect good works of his own, he draws a vivid picture, (p. 239, 240). A lord invites his friends to a sumptous banquet, the provision is bountiful and in rich abundance, when some of the guests take a few mouldy crusts out of their pockets and lay them on their plates, lest the prince had not provided a sufficient repast for his friends; ' would it not be a high affront to, a great contempt of, and a distrust in, the goodness of the Lord.' We are bound to produce good works as a fruit of faith—a proof of love to him that hath redeemed us, but not to recommend us to his favour. The picture of such a feast drawn by John Bunyan must make upon every reader a deep, a lasting, an indelible impression. How bitter and how true is the irony, when the Pharisee is represented as saying, ' I came to thy feast out of civility, but for thy dainties I need them not, I have enough of my own; I thank thee for thy kindness, but I am not as those that stand in need of thy provisions, nor yet as this Publican.' And how excellent is the reasoning and the Christian philosophy of that paragraph which was suppressed after Bunyan's death, (p. 248). The language is bold and striking, but it exhibits the unvarnished truth; an inward change of nature is the only cause of good and acceptable works—good or evil actions are but the evidences of our state by grace or by nature—they do not work that change or produce that state. It is a soul-humbling view of our state of death by sin, or of life by the righteousness and obedience of Christ. Bunyan's train of reasoning on Ro. v. (p. 256) is worthy of our profound consideration,—' When we were enemies we were reconciled to God by the death of his Son.' What is a sinful man in himself, or in his approach to God, but as stubble fully dry in the presence of a consuming fire, unless he is washed and cleansed by the atoning sacrifice of Jesus.

May the glorified spirit of Bunyan rejoice among the angels of heaven, over souls converted by the instrumentality of this solemn and searching treatise.

GEORGE OFFOR.

TO THE READER.

Courteous Reader,

I HAVE made bold once again to present thee with some of my meditations; and they are now about the PHARISEE and the PUBLICAN: Two men in whose condition the whole world is comprehended, both as to their state now, and condition at the judgment.

Wherefore in reading this little book thou must needs read thyself. I do not say thou must understand thy condition; for it is the gift of God must make thee do that. Howbeit, if God will bless it to thee, it may be a means to bring thee to see whose steps thou art treading, and so at whose end thou art like to arrive.

And let me beg this at thy hand, now thou art about to read; reserve thy judgment or sentence as to me, until thou hast passed through the discourse.

Justification is treated of here, and the way for men to be saved.

I have also O PUBLICAN here, as my skill hath served me, for thy encouragement, set before thee the Pharisee and the Publican in their colours, and shewed thee, that though the Publican seemed to be far behind, yet in running he got the prize from the lofty Pharisee. I say, Art thou a Pharisee? Here is a Pharisee for thee! Art thou a Publican? Here is a Publican for thee!

God give thee the Publican's heart, if thou art in the Publican's sins, that thou mayest partake with the Publican, of mercy.—So wisheth thy friend,

JOHN BUNYAN.

A DISCOURSE UPON THE PHARISEE AND PUBLICAN.

'TWO MEN WENT UP INTO THE TEMPLE TO PRAY; THE ONE A PHARISEE, AND THE OTHER A PUBLICAN: THE PHARISEE STOOD AND PRAYED THUS WITH HIM-SELF, GOD, I THANK THEE, THAT I AM NOT AS OTHER MEN ARE, EXTORTIONERS, UNJUST, ADUL-TERERS, OR EVEN AS THIS PUBLICAN. I FAST TWICE IN THE WEEK, I GIVE TITHES OF ALL THAT I POSSESS. AND THE PUBLICAN, STANDING AFAR OFF, WOULD NOT LIFT UP SO MUCH AS HIS EYES UNTO HEAVEN, BUT SMOTE UPON HIS BREAST, SAYING, GOD BE MERCIFUL TO ME A SINNER.' LUKE XVIII. 10—13.

IN the beginning of this chapter you read of the reason of the parable of the unjust judge and the poor widow; namely, to encourage men to pray. He spake a parable to THIS END, that men ought always to pray and not to faint. And a most sweet parable for that purpose it is: For if through importunity, a poor widow-woman may prevail with an unjust judge; and so consequently with an un-merciful and hard-hearted tyrant; how much more shall the poor, afflicted, distressed, and tempted people of God, prevail with, and obtain mercy at the hands of a loving, just and merciful God? The unjust judge would not hearken to, nor regard, the cry of the poor widow for a while: 'But after-ward he said within himself, Though I fear not God, nor regard man; yet because this widow troubleth me, I will avenge her, lest by her con-tinual coming she weary me.' Hark, saith Christ, 'what the unjust judge saith. And shall not God avenge his own elect, which cry day and night unto him?' I tell you, that he will avenge them speedily.

This is therefore a very comfortable parable to such of the saints, that are under hard usages by reason of evil men, their might, and tyranny. For by it we are taught to believe and expect, that God, though for a while he seemeth not to regard, yet will, in due time and season, arise and set such in safety from them that puff at them. Ps. xii. 5.

Let the good Christian pray always; let him pray and not faint at seeming delays; for if the widow by importunity prevailed with the unjust

VOL. II.

judge, how much more shall he with his heavenly Father. 'I tell you, (says Christ,) that he will avenge them speedily.'

But now, forasmuch as this parable reacheth not (so directly) the poor publican in the text, therefore our Lord begins again, and adds to that another parable, this parable, which I have chosen for my text. By the which he designeth two things: First, The conviction of the proud and self-conceited Pharisee. Secondly, The raising up and healing of the cast down and dejected Publi-can. And observe it, as by the first parable he chiefly designeth the relief of those that are under the hand of cruel tyrants: So by this he designeth the relief of those that lie under the load and burden of a guilty and a disquieted conscience.

This therefore is a parable that is full of singu-lar comfort to such of the sinners in the world, that are clogged with guilt, and a sense of sin; and that lie under the apprehensions of, and that are driven to God by, the sense of the judgment, that for sin is due unto them.

In my handling of this text, I shall have respect to these things.

First, To the PERSONS in the text.

Secondly, To the CONDITION of the persons in the text.

Thirdly, To the CONCLUSION that Christ makes upon them both.

First, For the PERSONS. They were, as you see, far one from another in their own apprehension of themselves; one good, the other bad; but yet in the judgment of the law, both alike, both the same, both sinners; for they both stood in need of merit.* True, the first mentioned did not see it, as the other poor sinner did; but that altereth not the case. He that is in the judgment of the law a sinner, is in the judgment of the law for sin con-demned, though in his own judgment he be never so righteous.

Men must not be judged, or justified, according to what themselves do think, but according to the

_____

* The word 'merit' was changed for 'mercy' after the author's death.—ED.

verdict and sentence that cometh out of the mouth of God about them.* Now the sentence of God is, 'They are all under sin - - There is none righteous, no, not one:' Ro. iii. 'Tis no matter then what the Pharisee did think of himself, God by his word hath proclaimed him a sinner. A sinner, by reason of original sin. A sinner by reason of actual transgression. Personally therefore, with reference to the true nature of their state, they both were sinners, and both by the law under condemnation. True, the Publican's leprosy was outward; but the Pharisee's leprosy was inward: his heart, his soul, his spirit, was as foul, and had as much the plague of sin, as had the other in his life or conversation.

Secondly, As to their CONDITION. I do not mean by condition, so much a habit of mind, as the state that they had each of them put themselves into by that mind. The one, says the text, was a Pharisee, the other a Publican. A Pharisee: That is, one that hath chosen to himself *such* a course of life. A Publican: That is, one that hath chosen to himself *such* a course of life. These terms therefore shew, the divers courses of life that they had put themselves into. The Pharisee, as he thought, had put himself into a condition for heaven and glory; but the Publican was for this world, and his lusts. Wherefore when the Pharisee stands in the temple, he boasteth of himself and good condition; but condemneth the Publican, and bitterly inveigheth against him. But, as I said, their personal state by the law, was not at all changed. The Pharisee made himself never the better; the Publican also abode in his place.

Indeed the Publican is here found to recant, and repent of his condition; of the condition that he had put himself into; and the Pharisee to boast of his: But the Publican's repentance was not of himself, but of God; who can also, yea, and sometimes it is evident, Ac. ix. he doth make Pharisees also repent of that condition that they have chosen to be in themselves. Phi. iii. 3—8. The Pharisee, therefore in commending of himself, makes himself never the better. The Publican also, in condemning of himself, makes himself never the worse. Nay, contrariwise, the Pharisee by commending of himself makes himself much the worse (*v.* 14). And the Publican, by condemning of himself, makes himself much the better. 'I tell you, (says Christ) This man went down to his house justified *rather* than the other: For every one that exalteth himself shall be abased; and he that humbleth himself shall be exalted.'

But, I say, as to men's commending of themselves, yea, though others should commend them

also, that availeth, to Godward, nothing at all. 'For not he that commendeth himself is approved, but whom the Lord commendeth.' So then, men in 'measuring themselves by themselves, and comparing themselves among themselves, are not wise.' 2 Co. x. 18, 12.

Now this was the way of the Pharisee, I am not, saith he, as other men; I am no extortioner, nor unjust, no adulterer, nor yet as this Publican. TWO MEN WENT UP INTO THE TEMPLE TO PRAY. And they two, as I said, as opposite one to the other, as any two men that ever went thither to pray. One of them was *over* righteous, and the other wicked *over* much. Some would have thought, had they not by the word of Christ been otherwise described, that they had been both of the same religion; for they both went up into the temple to pray; yea, both to pray, and that at the same time, as if they did it by appointment, by agreement, but there was no such thing. The one was a Pharisee, the other a Publican; for so saith the after words: And therefore persons as opposite as light and darkness, as fire and water; I mean as to their apprehensions one of another. The Pharisee could not abide the Publican, nor could the Publican brook the Pharisee, and yet both went up into the temple to pray. It is strange to see, and yet it is seen, that men cross in their minds, cross in their principles, cross in their apprehensions; yea, and cross in their prayers too, should yet meet together in the temple to pray.

TWO MEN, Men not of the middle sort, as afore is shewed; but two, and them too, picked out of the best and worst that was: as shall now be a little more largely handled. Two men, a Pharisee and a Publican.

To be a Pharisee was in those days counted honourable for religion, and for holiness of life. A Pharisee was a man of esteem and repute among the Jews, though it is a term of reproach with us. Else Paul would not as he did, and at such a time as he did it, have said, 'Men *and* brethren, I am a Pharisee, the son of a Pharisee.' Ac. xxiii. 6. Phi. iii. 5. For now he stood upon his purgation and justification, especially it appears so by the place first named. And far be it from any to think, that Paul would make use of a colour of wickedness, to save, thereby, himself from the fury of the people.

A Publican was in those days counted one of the vilest of men, as is manifest; because when they are by the word, by way of discrimination, made mention of, they are ranked with the most vile and base. Therefore they are joined with sinners. 'He eateth and drinketh with publicans and sinners;' and with harlots. 'The publicans and the harlots go into the kingdom of God.' Yea, when our Lord Christ would have the rebellious professor stigmatized to purpose, he saith: ' Let him be unto thee as an heathen man, and a publican.'

We therefore can make no judgment of men upon the outward appearance of them. Who would have thought, but that the Pharisee had been a good man, for he was righteous; for he prayed. And who could have thought, that the other had been a good man? For he was a Publican: A man, by good men, and bad men, joined with the worst of men, to wit, with sinners, harlots, heathens.

The Pharisee was a sectarian; the Publican was an officer. The Pharisee even because he was a sectarian, was had the more in esteem; and the Publican because he was an officer, was had the more in reproach. To speak a little to both these.

The Pharisee was a sectarian, one that deviated, that turned aside in his worshipping from the way of God, both in matter and manner of worship; for such an one I count a sectarian. That he turned aside from the matter, which is the rule of worship, to wit, the written word, it is evident; for Christ saith, That they rejected the commandments of God, and made them of no effect, that they might keep their own traditions. Mar. vii. 9—14. That they turned aside also as to their manner of worship, and became sectarians there, is with no less authority asserted; For 'all their works they do for to be seen of men.' Ac. xxvi. 5. Mat. xxiii. 5.

Now this being none of the order or ordinance of Christ, and yet being chose by, and stuck to of these sort of men, and also made a singular and necessary part of worship, became a sect, or bottom for these hypocritical factious men to adhere unto, and to make of others, disciples to themselves. And that they might be admired, and rendered venerable by the simple people to their fellows, they loved to go in long robes; they loved to pray in markets, and in the corners of the streets; they shewed great zeal for the small things of the law, but had only great words for things that were substantial. ' They make broad their phylacteries, and enlarge the borders of their garments.' Mat. xxiii. 5.

When I say the Pharisee was a sectarian, I do not mean that every sectarian is a Pharisee. There was the sect of the Herodians, and of the Alexandrians, of the Sadducees, with many others; but to be a Pharisee, was to be of the straitest sect: After the most straitest sect of our religion I lived a Pharisee; that therefore of all the sects, was the most strait and strict. Therefore, saith he in another place, I was 'taught according to the perfect manner of the law of the fathers.' Ac. xxii. 3; xxvi. 4—6. And again, 'Touching the law a

Pharisee.' Phi. iii. 5. The Pharisees therefore did carry the bell,* and did wear the garland for religion; for he out-did, he went beyond all other sectarians in his day. He was the strictest, he was the most zealous; therefore Christ in his making of this parable, waveth all other sects then in being, and pitcheth upon the Pharisee as the man most meet, by whose rejection he might shew forth, and demonstrate the riches of his mercy in its extension to sinners: 'Two men went up into the temple to pray, the one a Pharisee.' The one such a brave man as you have heard.

The PUBLICAN also went up thither to pray. The Publican, I told you before, was an officer. An officer that served the Romans and themselves too; for the Romans at that time were possessors of the land of Jewry, the lot of Israel's inheritance, and the Emperor Tiberius Cæsar placed over that land four governors, to wit, Pilate, Herod, Philip, and Lysanias; Lu. iii. 1. all these were gentiles, heathens, infidels; and the Publicans were a sort of inferior men, to whom was let out to farm, and so men that were employed by these to gather up the taxes and customs, that the heathens had laid upon the Jews to be paid to the emperor. Lu. ii. 1; iii. 12, 13.

But they were a generation of men that were very injurious in the execution of their office. They would exact and demand more than was due of the people; yea, and if their demands were denied, they would falsely accuse those that so denied them to the governor, and by false accusation obtain the money of the people, and so wickedly enrich themselves. Lu. iii. 13; xix. 2, 8. This was therefore grievous to the Jews, who always counted themselves a free people, and could never abide to be in bondage to any. And this was something of the reason, that they were so generally, by all the Jews, counted so vile and base, and reckoned among the worst of men, even as our informers and bum bailiffs are with us at this day.

But that which heightened the spirit of the people against them, and that made them so odious and filthy in their eyes, was for that, at least so I think, these Publicans were not, as the other officers, aliens, heathens, and gentiles, but men of their own nation, Jews, and so the brethren of those that they so abused. Had they been gentiles, it had not been to be wondered at; that they abused, accused and by false accusations peeled and wasted the people; for that cannot but be expected at the hands of aliens and strangers.

The Publican then was a Jew, a kind of a rene-

---

* 'Carry the bell and wear the garland,' alluding to our old English races; the winner being rewarded with a silver bell, and crowned with a garland: or to the morris dance, in which the leader carried the garland and danced with bells fixed to his dress.—ED.

gade Jew, that through the love that he had to unjust gains, fell off in his affections from his brethren, adhered to the Romans, and became a kind of servant to them against their brethren, farming the heathenish taxations at the hand of strangers, and exacting of them upon their brethren with much cruelty, falsehood, and extortion. And hence, as I said, it was, that to be a Publican, was to be so odious a thing, so vile a sinner, and so grievous a man in the eyes of the Jews. And would it not be an insufferable thing? Yea, did not that man deserve hanging ten times over, that should, being a Dutchman, fall in with a French invader, and take place or farm at his hands, those cruel and grievous taxations, which he in barbarous wise should at his conquest lay upon them; and exact and force them to be paid him with an over and above of what is appointed.* Why this was the Publican, he was a Jew, and so should have abode with them, and have been content to share with his brethren in their calamities; but contrary to nature, to law, to religion, reason, and honesty, he fell in with the heathen, and took the advantage of their tyranny, to pole, to peel,† to rob and impoverish his brethren.

But for proof that the Publican was a Jew.

1. They are, even then, when compared with, yet distinguished from the heathen; *Let him be to thee as an heathen man and a Publican*, Mat. xviii. which two terms, I think, must not here be applied to one and the self-same man, as if the heathen was a Publican, or the Publican a heathen, but to men of two distinct nations; as that Publican and Harlot, is to be understood of sinners of both sexes. The Publican is not an harlot, for he is a man, &c. and such a man as has been described before. So by Publicans and Sinners, is meant Publicans, and such sinners as the Gentiles were; or such as, by the text, the Publican is distinguished from: Where the Pharisee saith he was not an extortioner, unjust, adulterer, or even as

this Publican. Nor can he by Heathen Man, intend the person, and by the term Publican, the office or place of the heathen man; but by Publican is meant the renegade Jew, in such a place, &c. as is yet further manifest by that which follows. For,

2. Those Publicans, even every one of them that by name are made mention of in the New Testament, have such names put upon them; yea, and other circumstances thereunto annexed, as doth demonstrate them to be Jews. I remember the names of no more but three, to wit, Matthew, Levi, and Zaccheus, and they were all Jews.

(1.) Matthew was a Jew, and the same Matthew was a Publican; yea, and also afterward an apostle. He was a Jew, and wrote his gospel in Hebrew; He was an apostle, and is therefore found among the twelve. That he was a Publican too, is as evident by his own words: For though Mark and Luke in their mentioning of his name and apostleship, do forbear to call him a Publican. (Mar. iii. 18. Lu. vi. 15.) Yet when this Matthew comes to speak of himself, he calls himself Matthew the Publican, Mat. x. 3. for I count this the self-same Matthew that Mark and Luke maketh mention of, because I find no other Matthew among the apostles but he: Matthew the Publican, Matthew the man so deep in apostacy, Matthew the man of that ill fame among his brethren. Love in Mark and Luke, when they counted him among the apostles, did cover with silence this his publican state; and it is meet for Peter to call Paul his beloved brother, when Paul himself shall call himself the chief of sinners; but faithfulness to the world, and a desire to be abased, that Christ thereby, and grace by him, might be advanced, made Matthew, in his evangelical writings, call himself by the name of Matthew the Publican. Nor has he lost thereby; for Christ again to exalt him, as he hath also done by the apostle Paul, hath set, by his special providence, the testimony that this Matthew hath given of his birth, life, death, doctrine, and miracles, in the front of all the New Testament.

(2.) The next Publican that I find by the testament of Christ, made mention of by name, is Levi, another of the apostles of Jesus Christ. This Levi also, by the Holy Ghost in holy writ, is called by the name of James. Not James the brother of John, for Zebedee was his father; but James the son of Alpheus. Now I take this Levi also to be another than Matthew; first, because Matthew is not called the son of Alpheus; and because Matthew and Levi, or James the son of Alpheus, are distinctly counted where the names of the apostles are mentioned, Mat. x. 3. for two distinct persons: And that this Levi, or James the apostle was a Publican, as was the apostle Matthew, whom we mentioned before, is evident; for both

---

* The glorious revolution, conducted by William, Prince of Orange, afterwards King William the 3rd, took place soon after Bunyan's decease. It was probably on this account that this paragraph was omitted from the edition of September, 1688, and all the subsequent ones to the present time. The popular opinion, in those times, was, that *Dutchman* and *extortioner* were nearly synonymous.

'We trade wid de Yankey, we deal wid de Scot.
And cheaten de tain and de teither:
We cheaten de Jew, aye and better dan dat,
We cheaten well ein aniether.'   *Old Song.*

† 'To pole, to peel,' to take off the top and branches of a tree, and then to peel off the bark; terms used to designate violent oppressions under pretended legal authority. 'Which pols and pils the poor in piteous wise.' *Fairy Queen.* 'Pilling and polling is grown out of request, since plain pilfering came into fashion.' *Winwood's Memorials.* 'They had rather pill straws than read the scriptures.' *Dent's Pathway.*—ED.

Mark and Luke do count him such. First, Mark saith, Christ found him when he called him, as he also found Matthew, sitting at the receipt of custom; yea, Luke words it thus: 'He went forth, and saw a publican, named Levi, sitting at the receipt of custom: and he said unto him, Follow me.' Mar. ii. 14. Lu. v. 27.

Now that this Levi, or James the son of Alpheus, was a Jew, his name doth well make manifest. Besides, had there been among the apostles any more Gentiles save Simon the Canaanite; or if this Levi James had been [one] here, I think the Holy Ghost would, to distinguish him, have included him in the same discriminating character as he did the other, when he called him Simon the Canaanite. Mat. x. 4.

Matthew, therefore, and Levi or James, were both Publicans, and, as I think, called both at the same time;* were both Publican-Jews, and made by grace the apostles of Jesus Christ.

(3.) The next Publican that I find by name, made mention of in the testament of Christ, is one Zaccheus. And he was a chief Publican; yea, for ought I know, the master of them all. 'There was a man, (saith Luke,) named Zaccheus, which was the chief among the Publicans, and he was rich.' Lu. xix. 2. This man, Christ saith, was a son of Abraham, that is, as other Jews were; for he spake that to stop the mouths of their pharisaical cavillations. Besides, the Publican shewed himself to be such an one, when under a supposition of wronging any man, he has respect to the Jewish law of restoring four-fold. Ex. xxii. 1. 2 Sa. xii. 6.

It is further manifest that he was a Jew, because Christ puts him among the lost; to wit, among the lost sheep of the house of Israel, Lu. xix. 8—10. and Mat. xv. 24. for Zaccheus was one that might properly be said to be lost, and that in the Jews account: Lost I say, and that not only in the most common sense, by reason of transgression against the law, but for that he was an apostate Jew; not with reference to heathenish religion, but as to heathenish, cruel, and barbarous actions; and therefore he was, as the other, by his brethren counted as bad as heathens, gentiles, and harlots. But salvation is come to this house, saith Christ, and that notwithstanding his Publican practices, forasmuch as he also is the son of Abraham.

3. Again, Christ by the parable of the lost sheep, doth plainly intimate, that the Publican was a Jew. 'Then drew near unto him all the Publicans and sinners for to hear him. And the Pharisees and Scribes murmured, saying, This man receiveth sinners, and eateth with them.' Lu. xv. 1, 2.

But by what answer doth Christ repel their objections? Why, he saith, 'What man of you, having an hundred sheep, if he lose one of them, doth not leave the ninety and nine in the wilderness, and go after that which is lost until he find it?' Doth he not here, by the lost sheep, mean the poor Publican? Plenty of whom, while he preached this sermon, were there, as objects of the Pharisees' scorn; but of the pity and compassion of Jesus Christ! he did without doubt mean them. For, pray, what was the flock, and who Christ's sheep under the law, but the house and people of Israel? Exe. xxxiv. 30, 31. So then, who could be the lost sheep of the house of Israel, but such as was Matthew, James, Zaccheus, and their companions in their, and such like transgressions.

4. Besides, had not the Publicans been of the Jews, how easy had it been for the Pharisees to have objected, that an impertinency was couched in that most excellent parable of the lost sheep? They might have said, We are offended, because thou receivest the Publicans, and thou for vindication of thy practice, propoundest a parable of lost sheep; but *they* are the sinners of the house of Israel, and the Publicans are aliens and Gentiles. I say, How easily might they thus have objected? But they knew full well, that the parable was pertinent, for that the Publicans were of the Jews, and not of the aliens. Yea, had they not been Jews, it cannot, it must not be thought, that Christ, in sum, should call them so; and yet he did do so, when he called them lost sheep.

Now that these Publicans were Jews, what follows, but that for this they were a great deal the more abominated of their brethren. And, as I have also hinted before, it is no marvel though they were; for a treacherous brother is worse than an open enemy. Ps. lv. 12, 13. For, if to be debauched in open and common transgressions is odious, how odious is it for a brother to be so? For a brother in nature and religion to be so? I say again, if these things are intolerable, what shall we think of such men, as shall join to all this compliance with a foreign prince to rob the church of God? Yea, that shall become a tenant, an officer, a man in power under them, to exact, force, and wring out of the hand of a brother his estate; yea, his bread and livelihood. Add to all this, What shall we say to him that shall do for an enemy against a brother in a way of injury and wrong, more than in strictness of law they were commanded by that same enemy to do? And yet all this they did, as both John insinuates, and Zaccheus confesses.†

---

* Immediately after the calling of Matthew and of James, our Lord sat at meat in Levi's [James!] house, and made that gracious declaration, 'I am not come to call the righteous but sinners to repentance;' compare Matt. ix. 10—13, with Mark ii. 14—17 and Luke v. 27—32.—ED.

† Nearly half this paragraph is omitted from every edition since 1688, probably from a fear lest it should be misinter-

The Pharisee therefore was not so good, but the Publican was as bad: Indeed, the Publican was a notorious wretch, one that had a way of transgressing by himself; one that could not be sufficiently condemned by the Jews, nor coupled with a viler than himself. 'Tis true, you find him here in the temple at prayer; not because he retained in his apostacy, conscience of the true religion, but God had awakened him, shewn him his sin, and bestowed upon him the grace of repentance, by which he was not only fetched back to the temple, and prayer, but to his God, and to the salvation of his soul.

The Pharisee, then, was a man of another complexion, and stood as to his own thoughts of himself; yea, and in the thoughts of others also, upon the highest and better ground by far. The Publican was a *notorious* sinner; the Pharisee was a *notorious* righteous man. The Publican was a sinner out of the ordinary way of sinning; and the Pharisee was a man for righteousness in a singular way also. The Publican pursued his villanies, and the Pharisee pursued his righteousness; and yet they both meet in the temple to pray. Yea, the Pharisee stuck to, and boasted in the law of God; but the Publican did forsake it, and hardened his heart against his way and people.

Thus diverse were they in their appearances; the Pharisee, very good; the Publican, very bad. But as to the law of God, which looked upon them with reference to the state of their spirits, and the nature of their actions, by that they were both found sinners; the Publican an open *outside* one, and the Pharisee a filthy *inside* one. This is evident, because the best of them was rejected, and the worst of them was received to mercy. Mercy standeth not at the Publican's badness, nor is it enamoured with the Pharisee's goodness: It suffereth not the law to take place on both, though it findeth them both in sin, but graciously embraceth the most unworthy, and leaveth the best to shift for himself. And good reason that both should be dealt with after this manner; to wit, that the word of grace should be justified upon the soul of the penitent, and that the other should stand or fall to that, which he had chosen to be his master.

There are three things that follow upon this discourse.

[Conclusion.] 1. That the righteousness of man is not of any esteem with God, as to Justification. It is passed by as a thing of naughtiness, a thing not worth the taking notice of. There was not so much as notice taken of the Pharisee's person, or prayer, because he came into the temple mantled up in his own good things.

[Conclusion.] 2. That the man that has nothing to commend him to God, but his own good doings, shall never be in favour with him. This also is evident from the text: The Pharisee had his own righteousness, but had nothing else to commend him to God; and therefore could not by that obtain favour with God, but abode still a rejected one, and in a state of condemnation.

[Conclusion.] 3. Wherefore, though we are bound by the law of charity to judge of men, according as in appearance they present themselves unto us: yet withal, to wit, though we do so judge, we must leave room for the judgment of God. Mercy may receive him that we have doomed to hell, and justice may take hold on him, whom we have judged to be bound up in the bundle of life. And both these things are apparent by the persons under consideration.

We, like Joseph, are for setting of Manasseh before Ephraim; but God, like Jacob, puts his hands across, and lays his right hand upon the worst man's head, and his left hand upon the best, to the amazement and wonderment even of the best of men. Ge. xlviii. 14.

[THE PHARISEE'S PRAYER.]

'Two men went up into the temple to pray; the one a Pharisee, and the other a Publican. The Pharisee stood and prayed thus with himself, God, I thank thee, that I am not as other men *are*, extortioners, unjust, adulterers, or even as this Publican. I fast twice in the week, I give tithes of all that I possess.'*

In these words many things are worth the noting. As,

FIRST. THE PHARISEE'S DEFINITION OF RIGHTEOUSNESS; the which standeth in two things: 1. In negatives. 2. In positives.

In negatives; to wit, what a man that is righteous must not be: I am no extortioner, no unjust man, no adulterer, nor yet as this publican.

In positives; to wit, what a man that is righteous must be: I fast twice a week, I give tithes of all that I possess, &c.

That righteousness standeth in negative and positive holiness is true; but that the Pharisee's definition is, notwithstanding, false, will be manifest by and by. But I will first treat of righteousness in the general, because the text leadeth me to it.

First then, A Man that is righteous, must have *negative holiness;* that is, he must not live in actual

* This proud beggar shews not his wounds but his worth; not his rags, but his robes; not his misery, but his stoutheartedness: he brings in God Almighty as a debtor to him for his services, and thanks God more that others were bad, than for his own fancied goodness.—*Ryland.*

transgressions: He must not be an extortioner, unjust, an adulterer, or, as the Publican was. And this the apostle intends, when he saith, 'Flee fornication, 2 Ti. ii. 22. flee also youthful lusts, 1 Co. vi. 18. flee from idolatry,' 1 Co. x. 14. and 'Little children, keep yourselves from idols.' 1 Jn. v. 21. For it is a vain thing to talk of righteousness, and that ourselves are righteous, when every observer shall find us in actual transgression. Yea, though a man shall mix his want of negative holiness, with some good actions, that will not make him a righteous man. As suppose, a man that is a swearer, a drunkard, an adulterer, or the like, should, notwithstanding this, be open handed to the poor, be a greater executor of justice in his place, be exact in his buying, selling, keep touch with his promise and with his friend, or the like. These things, yea, many more such, cannot make him a righteous man; for the beginning of righteousness is yet wanting in him, which is this negative holiness: For except a man shall leave off to do evil he cannot be a righteous man. Negative holiness is therefore of absolute necessity to make one in one's self a righteous man. This therefore condemns them, that count it sufficient if a man have some actions that in themselves, and by virtue of the command are good, to make him a righteous man, though negative holiness is wanting. This is as saying to the wicked, Thou art righteous, and a perverting of the right way of the Lord. Negative holiness therefore must be in a man before he can be accounted righteous.

Second. As negative holiness is required to declare one a righteous man; so also *positive holiness must be joined therewith*, or the man is unrighteous still. For it is not what a man is not, but what a man does, that declares him a righteous man. Suppose a man be no thief, no liar, no unjust man; or, as the Pharisee saith, no extortioner, no adulterer, &c., this will not make him a righteous man. But there must be joined to these, holy and good actions, before he can be declared a righteous man. Wherefore, as the apostle, when he pressed the Christians to righteousness, did put them first upon negative holiness, so he joineth thereto an exhortation to positive holiness; knowing, that where positive holiness is wanting, all the negative holiness in the whole world cannot declare a man a righteous man. When therefore he had said, 'But thou, O man of God, flee these things,' (sins and wickedness) he adds, 'and follow after righteousness, godliness, faith, love, patience, meekness.' 1 Ti. vi. 11. Here Timothy is exhorted to negative holiness, when he is bid to flee sin. Here also he is exhorted to positive holiness, when he is bid to follow after righteousness, &c., for righteousness can neither stand in negative nor positive holiness, as severed one from another. That

man then, and that man only, is, as to actions a righteous man, that hath left off to do evil, and hath learnt to do well, Is. i. 16, 17. that hath cast off the works of darkness, and put on the armour of light. Flee also youthful lusts, (said Paul,) but follow righteousness, faith, charity, peace, with them that call on the Lord out of a pure heart. 2 Ti. ii. 22.

The Pharisee therefore, as to the general description of righteousness, made his definition right; but as to his person and personal righteousness, he made his definition wrong. I do not mean, he defined his own righteousness wrong; but I mean, his definition of true righteousness, which standeth in negative and positive holiness, he made to stoop to justify his own righteousness, and therein he played the hypocrite in his prayer: For although it is true righteousness, that standeth in negative and positive holiness; yet that is not true righteousness, that standeth but in some pieces and ragged remnants of negative and positive righteousness. If then the Pharisee would in his definition of personal righteousness, have proved his own righteousness to be good, he must have proved, that both his negative and positive holiness had been universal: to wit, that he had left off to act in any wickedness, and that he had given up himself to the duty enjoined in every commandment. For so the righteous man is described, Job i. 8. As it is also said of Zacharias and Elizabeth his wife, 'They were both righteous before God, walking in all the commandments and ordinances of the Lord blameless.' Lu. i. 6. Here the perfection, that is, the universality of their negative holiness is implied, and the universality of their positive holiness is expressed: They walked in all the commandments of the Lord; but that they could not do, if they had lived in any unrighteous thing or way. They walked in all blamelessly, that is, sincerely with upright hearts. The Pharisee's righteousness therefore, even by his own implied definition of righteousness, was not good, as is manifest these two ways.

1. *His negative holiness was not universal.*

2. *His positive holiness was rather criminal* than moral.*

1. His *negative holiness* was *not universal.* He saith indeed, he was not an extortioner, nor unjust, no adulterer, nor yet as this Publican: but none of these expressions apart, nor all, if put together, do prove him to be perfect as to negative holiness; that is, they do not prove him, should it be granted, that he was as holy with this kind of holiness, as himself of himself had testified. For,

---

* The word 'criminal,' used by Bunyan, has been altered in modern editions to 'ceremonial;' but it was not only ceremonial but superstitious, and therefore more criminal than moral.

(1.) What though he was no extortioner, he might yet be a covetous man. Lu. xvi. 14.

(2.) What though, as to dealing, he was not unjust to others, yet he wanted honesty to do justice to his own soul. Lu. xvi. 15.

(3.) What, though he was free from the act of adultery, he might yet be made guilty by an adulterous eye, against which the Pharisee did not watch, of which the Pharisee did not take cognizance. Mat. v. 28.

(4.) What, though he was not like the publican, yet he was like, yea, was a downright hypocrite; he wanted in those things wherein he boasted himself, sincerity; but without sincerity no action can be good, or accounted of God as righteous. The Pharisee therefore, notwithstanding his boasts, was deficient in his righteousness, though he would fain have shrouded it under the right definition thereof.

2. Nor doth his *positive holiness help him at all*, forasmuch as it is grounded mostly, if not altogether, in ceremonial holiness. Nay, I will recollect myself, it was *grounded partly in ceremonial, and partly in superstitious holiness*, if there be such a thing as superstitious holiness in the world, this paying of tithes was ceremonial, such as came in and went out with the typical priesthood. But what is that to positive holiness, when it was but a small pittance by the by. Had the Pharisee argued plainly and honestly; I mean, had he so dealt with that law, by which now he sought to be justified, he should have brought forth positive righteousness in morals, and should have said and proved it too, that, as he was no wicked man with reference to the act of wickedness, he was indeed a righteous man in acts of moral virtues. He should, I say, have proved himself a true lover of God, no superstitious one, but a sincere worshipper of him; for this is contained in the first table, Ex. xx. and is so in sum expounded by the Lord Christ himself. Mar. xii. 30. He should also in the next place have proved himself truly kind, compassionate, liberal, and full of love and charity to his neighbour; for that is the sum of the second table, as our Lord also doth expound it, saying, 'Thou shalt love thy neighbour as thyself.' Mar. xii. 31.

True, he says, he did them no hurt; but did he do them good? To do no hurt is one thing; and to do good, is another; and it is possible for a man to do neither hurt nor good to his neighbour. What then, Is he a righteous man because he hath done him no hurt? No verily; unless, to his power, he hath also done him good.

It is therefore a very fallacious and deceitful arguing of the Pharisee, thus to speak before God in his prayer: I am righteous, because I have not hurt my neighbour, and because I have acted in ceremonial duties. Nor will that help him at all to say, he gave TITHES of all that he possessed. It had been more modest to say, that he had paid them; for they, being commanded, were a due debt; nor could they go before God for a free gift, because by the commandment they were made a payment; but proud men and hypocrites, love so to word it both with God and man, as at least to imply, that they are more forward to do, than God's commandment is to require them to do.

The second part of his positive holiness was superstitious; for God hath appointed no such set fasts, neither more nor less, but just twice a week: I fast twice a week. Ay, but who did command thee to do so;* commanded to fast when occasion required if thou wast, but that thou shouldest have any occasion to do so as thou doest, other than by thy being put upon it by a superstitious and erroneous conscience, doth not, nor canst thou make to appear. This part therefore of this positive righteousness, was positive superstition, an abuse of God's law, and a gratification of thy own erroneous conscience. Hitherto therefore, thou art defective in thy so seemingly brave and glorious righteousness.

Yet this let me say in commendation of the Pharisee: In my conscience he was better than many of our English Christians; for many of them are so far off from being at all partakers of positive righteousness, that all their ministers, bibles, good books, good sermons, nor yet God's judgments, can persuade them to become so much as negatively holy, that is, to leave off evil.

SECOND.—The second thing that I take notice of in this prayer of the Pharisee, is, HIS MANNER OF DELIVERY, as he stood praying in the temple. 'God, I thank thee (said he) that I am not as other men *are*. He seemed to be at this time, in more than an ordinary frame, while now he stood in the presence of the divine majesty: for a prayer made up of praise, is a prayer of the highest order, and is most like the way of them that are now in a state beyond prayer. Praise is the work of heaven; but we see here, that an hypocrite may get into that vein, even while an hypocrite, and while on earth below. Nor do I think that this prayer of his was a premeditated stinted form, but a prayer extempore, made on a sudden, according to what he felt, thought, or understood of himself.

Here therefore, we may see, that even prayer, as well as other acts of religious worship, may be performed in great hypocrisy; although, I think,

---

* It is singular that our modern pharisees continue the custom of fasting twice a week, on Wednesday and Friday. This is not so monstrous as pretending to do what 'God manifest in the flesh' alone could do—to fast for forty consecutive days.—ED.

that to perform prayer in hypocrisy, is one of the most daring sins that are committed by the sons of men. For by prayer, above all duties, is our most direct, and immediate personal approach into the presence of God: and as there is an uttering of things before him, especially a giving of him thanks for things received, or a begging, that such and such things might be bestowed upon me. But now to do these things in hypocrisy, and 'tis easy to do them so, when we go up into the temple to pray, must needs be intolerable wickedness, and it argueth infinite patience in God, that he should let such as do so, arise alive from their knees, or that he should suffer them to go away from the place where they stand, without some token or mark of his wrath upon them.

I also observe, That this extempore prayer of the Pharisee, was performed by himself, or in the strength of his own natural parts; for so the text implieth, 'The Pharisee,' saith the text, 'stood and prayed thus with himself,' with himself, or by himself, and may signify, either that he spoke softly, or that he made this prayer by reason of his natural parts. 'I will pray with the Spirit,' said Paul. 1 Co. xiv. 15. The Pharisee prayed with himself, said Christ. It is at this day wonderful common, for men to pray extempore also. To pray by a book, by a premeditated set form, is now out of fashion. He is counted no body now, that cannot at any time, at a minute's warning, make a prayer of half an hour long. I am not against extempore prayer, for I believe it to be the best kind of praying; but yet I am jealous, that there are a great many such prayers made, especially in pulpits and public meetings, without the breathing of the Holy Ghost in them: For if a Pharisee of old could do so, Why may not a Pharisee do the same now? Wit, and reason, and notion is now screwed up to a very great height; nor do men want words, or fancies, or pride, to make them do this thing. Great is the formality of religion this day, and little the power thereof. Now where there is a great form and little power, and such there was also among the Jews, in the time of our Saviour Jesus Christ, there men are most strangely under the temptation to be hypocrites; for nothing doth so properly and directly oppose hypocrisy, as the power and glory of the things we profess. And so on the contrary, nothing is a greater temptation to hypocrisy, than a form of knowledge of things without the savour thereof. Nor can much of the power and savour of the things of the gospel be seen at this day upon professors, I speak not now of all, if their notions and conversations be compared together. How proud, how covetous, how like the world in garb and guise, in words and actions, are most of the great professors of this our day! But when they come to divine worship, especially to

pray, by their words and carriages there, one would almost judge them to be angels in heaven. But such things must be done in hypocrisy, as also the Pharisee's were.

The Pharisee stood and prayed THUS WITH HIMSELF.

And, in that it is said, 'he prayed with himself;' it may signify, that he went in his prayer no further than his sense and reason, feeling and carnal apprehensions went. True, Christian prayer ofttimes leaves sense and reason, feeling, and carnal apprehensions behind it, and it goeth forth with faith, hope, and desires to know what at present we are ignorant of, and that unto which our sense, feeling, reason, &c., are strangers. The apostle indeed doth say, 'I will pray with the understanding,' 1 Co. xiv. 15. but then it must be taken for an understanding spiritually enlightened. I say, it must be so understood, because the natural understanding, properly as such, receiveth not the things of the Spirit of God when offered, and therefore cannot pray for them; for they to such, are foolish things. 1 Co. ii. 14.

Now a spiritually enlightened understanding may be officious in prayer these ways.

1. As it has received conviction of the truth of the being of the things that are of the Spirit of God; For to receive conviction of the truth and being of such things, comes from the Spirit of God, not from the law, sense, or reason. 1 Co. ii. 10 —12. Now the understanding having, by the Holy Ghost, received conviction of the truth of the being of such things, draweth out the heart to cry in prayer to God for them. Therefore he saith, he would pray with the understanding.

2. A spiritually enlightened understanding, hath also received by the Holy Ghost, conviction of the excellency and glory of the things that are of the Spirit of God, and so enflameth the heart with more fervent desires in this duty of prayer; for there is a supernatual excellency in the things that are of the Spirit; 'But if the ministration of death, (to which the Pharisee adhered) written and engraven in stones, was glorious, so that the children of Israel could not stedfastly behold the face of Moses for the glory of his countenance; which glory was to be done away: How shall not the ministration of the Spirit be rather glorious. For if the ministration of condemnation be glory, much more doth the ministration of righteousness exceed in glory. For even that which was made glorious had no glory in this respect, by reason of the glory that excelleth.' 2 Co. iii. 7—10. And the Spirit of God sheweth, at best, some things of that excellent glory of them to the understanding that it enlighteneth. Ep. i. 17—19.

3. The spiritually enlightened understanding hath also thereby received knowledge, that these

excellent supernatural things of the Spirit, are given by covenant in Christ to those that love God, that are beloved of him. ' Now we have received, (says Paul) not the Spirit of the world, (that the Pharisee had) but the Spirit which is of God, that we might know the things that are freely given to us of God.' 1 Co. ii. 12. And this knowledge, that the things of the Spirit of God are freely given to us of God, puts yet a greater edge, more vigour, and yet further confidence into the heart to ask for what is mine by gift, by a free gift of God in his Son.* But all these things the poor Pharisee was an utter stranger to; he knew not the Spirit, nor the things of the Spirit, and therefore must neglect faith, judgment, and the love of God, Mat. xxiii. 23. Lu. xi. 42. and follow himself, and himself only, as to his sense, feeling, reason, and carnal imagination in prayer.

He stood and prayed thus WITH HIMSELF. He prayed thus, talking to himself; for so also it may, I think, be understood. It is said of the unjust judge, ' he said within himself, Though I fear not God, nor regard man,' &c. Lu. xviii. 4. That is, he said it to himself. So the Pharisee is said to pray with himself. God and the Pharisee were not together, there was only the Pharisee and himself. Paul knew not what to pray for without the Holy Ghost joined himself with him, spake with him and helped him with groans unutterable. But the Pharisee had no need of that, it was enough that HE and HIMSELF were together at this work; for he thought without doubting that he and himself together could do. How many times have I heard ancient men, and ancient women, at it, with themselves, when all alone in some private room, or in some solitary path; and in their chat, they have been sometimes reasoning, sometimes chiding, sometimes pleading, sometimes praying, and sometimes singing; but yet all has been done by themselves when all alone: But yet so done, as one that has not seen them, must needs have concluded, that they were talking, singing, and praying with company, when all that they said, they did it with themselves, and had neither auditor nor regarder.

So the Pharisee was at it with himself, *he* and *himself* performed, at this time, the duty of prayer. Now I observe, that usually when men do speak to, or with themselves, they greatly strive to please themselves: Therefore it is said, there is a man, That ' flattereth himself in his own eyes, until his iniquity be found to be hateful.' Ps. xxxvi. 2. He flattereth himself in his own way, according as his sense and carnal reason dictates to him; and he

might do it as well in prayer, as in any other way. Some men will so hear sermons, and apply them that they may please themselves: And some men will pray, but will refuse such words and thoughts in prayer as will not please themselves.

Oh, how many men speak all that they speak in prayer, rather to themselves, or to their auditory, than to God that dwelleth in heaven! And this I take to be the manner, I mean something of the manner of the Pharisee's praying. Indeed, he made mention of God, as also others do; but he prayed with himself to himself, in his own spirit, and to his own pleasing, as the matter of his prayer doth manifest. For was it not pleasant to this hypocrite, think you, to speak thus well of himself at this time? doubtless it was. Also children and fools are of the same temper with hypocrites as to this; they also love without ground, as the Pharisee, to flatter themselves in their own eyes. But not he that commendeth himself is approved.

God, I thank thee, that I am not as other men *are*, extortioners, unjust, adulterers, or even as this Publican, &c.

Thus he begins his prayer; and it is, as was hinted before, a prayer of the highest strain. For to make a prayer all of thanksgiving, and to urge in that prayer, the cause of that thanksgiving, is the highest manner of praying, and seems to be done in the strongest faith, &c., in the greatest sense of things. And such was the Pharisee's prayer, only he wanted substantial ground for his thanksgiving; to wit, he wanted proof of that he said, ' he was not as other men were,' except he had meant, as he did not, that he was even of the worst sort of men: For even the best of men by nature, and the worst, are all alike. ' What, then? are we better *than they?*' said Paul, ' No, in no wise.' Ro. iii. 9. So then, he failed in the ground of his thankfulness, and therefore his thankfulness was grounded on an untruth, and so became feigned, and self-flattering, and could not be acceptable with the God of heaven.

Besides, in this high prayer of the Pharisee, he fathered that upon God which he could by no means own; to wit, that his being so good as he thought himself to be, was through distinguishing love and favour of God, 'God, I thank thee, that I am not as other men are.' I thank thee, that thou hast made me better than others. I thank thee that my condition is so good, and that I am so far advanced above my neighbour.

THERE ARE SEVERAL THINGS FLOW FROM THIS PRAYER OF THE PHARISEE, THAT ARE WORTH OUR OBSERVATION. As,

First, That the Pharisees and hypocrites, *do not love to count themselves sinners, when they stand before God.* They choose rather to commend

---

* God heareth the heart, without the mouth; but never heareth the mouth acceptably, without the heart. 1 Sa. i. 13, 15. *Puritan Saying.*

themselves before him for virtuous and holy persons, sometimes saying, and oftener thinking, that they are more righteous than others. Yea, it seems by the word, to be natural, hereditary, and so common for hypocrites to trust to themselves that they are righteous, and then to condemn others; this is the foundation upon which this very parable is built: 'He spake this parable, (saith Luke) unto certain which trusted in themselves that they were righteous;' or that they were so, 'and despised others.' ver. 9.

I say, hypocrites love not to think of their sins, when they stand in the presence of God; but rather to muster up, and to present him with their several good deeds, and to venture a standing or falling by them.

Second, This carriage of the Pharisee before God informs us, *that moral virtues,* and the ground of them, which is the law, *if trusted to, blinds the mind of man,* that he cannot for them perceive the way to happiness. While Moses is read, and his law, and the righteousness thereof trusted to, the vail is upon their heart. 'For until this day, (said Paul) remaineth the same vail untaken away in the reading of the old testament, which *vail* is done away in Christ. But even unto this day, when Moses is read, the vail is upon their heart.' 2 Co. iii. 14, 15. And this is the reason that so many moral men, that are adorned with civil and moral righteousness, are yet so ignorant of themselves, and the way of life by Christ.

The law of works, and the righteousness of the flesh, which is the righteousness of the law, blinds their minds, shuts up their eyes, and causeth them to miss of the righteousness that they are so hotly in the pursuit of. Their minds were blinded, saith the text: Whose minds? Why those that adhered to, that stood by, and that sought righteousness of the law. Now,

The Pharisee was such an one, he rested in the law, he made his boasts of God, and trusted to himself that he was righteous; And all this proceeded of that blindness and ignorance that the law had possessed his mind withal; for it is not granted to the law to be the ministration of life and light, but to be the ministration of death, when it speaks; and of darkness, when trusted unto, that the Son of God might have the pre-eminence in all things: Therefore 'tis said, 'When the heart shall turn to him, the vail shall be taken away.' 2 Co. iii. 16.

Third, We may see by this prayer, *the strength of vain confidence; it will embolden a man to stand in a lie before God;* it will embolden a man to trust to himself and to what he hath done; yea, to plead his own goodness instead of God's mercy before him. For the Pharisee was not only a man that justified himself before men, but one that justified himself before God. And what was the cause of

his so justifying of himself before God; but that vain confidence that he had in himself and his works, which were both a cheat and a lie to himself. But, I say, the boldness of the man was wonderful, for he stood to the lie that was in his right hand, and pleaded the goodness of it before him. But, besides these things, there are four things more that are couched in this prayer of the Pharisee.

Fourth, By this prayer the Pharisee *doth appropriate to himself conversion,* he challengeth it to himself and to his fellows. I am not, saith he, as other men; that is, in unconversion, in a state of sin, wrath, and death. And this must be his meaning; for the religion of the Pharisee was not grounded upon any particular natural privilege. I mean not singly, not only upon that, but upon a falling in with those principles, notions, opinions, decrees, traditions, and doctrines that they taught distinct from the true and holy doctrines of the prophets. And they made to themselves disciples by such doctrine, men, that they could captivate by those principles, laws, doctrines, and traditions: And therefore such are said to be of the sect of the Pharisees; that is, the scholars, and disciples of them, converted to them and to their doctrine. Oh! it is easy for souls to appropriate conversion to themselves, that know not what conversion is. It is easy, I say, for men to lay conversion to God, on a legal, or ceremonial, or delusive bottom, on such a bottom that will sink under the burden that is laid upon it; on such a bottom that will not stand when it is brought under the touch-stone of God, nor against the rain, wind, and floods that are ordained to put it to the trial, whether it is true or false. The Pharisee here stands upon a supposed conversion to God; 'I am not as other men;' but both he, and his conversion are rejected by the sequel of the parable: 'That which is highly esteemed among men is abomination in the sight of God.' Lu. xvi. 15. That is, that conversion, that men, as men, flatter themselves that they have, is such. But the Pharisee will be a converted man, he will have more to shew for heaven than his neighbour, 'I am not as other men are;' to wit, in a state of sin and condemnation, but in a state of conversion and salvation. But see how grievously this sect, this religion beguiled men. It made them two-fold worse the children of hell than they were before: And than their teachers were, Mat. xxiii. 15. that is, their doctrine begat such blindness, such vain confidence, and groundless boldness in their disciples, as to involve them in that conceit of conversion that was false, and so if trusted to, damnable.

Fifth, By these words, we find the Pharisee, not only appropriating conversion to himself, *but rejoicing in that conversion:* 'God, I thank thee,' saith he, 'that I am not as other men;' which saying of his, gives us to see that he gloried in his conversion; he made no doubt at all of his state, but lived in the joy of the safety that he supposed his soul by his conversion to be in. Oh! thanks to God, says he, I am not in the state of sin, death, and damnation, as the unjust, and this Publican is. But a strong delusion! to trust to the spider's web, and to think, that a few of the most fine of the works of the flesh, would be sufficient to bear up the soul in, at, and under the judgment of God. '*There is* a generation *that are* pure in their own eyes, and *yet is* not washed from their filthiness.' Pr. xxx. 12. This text can be so fitly applied to none, as to the Pharisee, and to those that tread in the Pharisee's steps, and that are swallowed up with his conceits, and with the glory of his own righteousness.

So again, 'There is a way (a way to heaven) which seemeth right unto a man, but the end thereof *are* the ways of death.' Pr. xiv. 12. This also is fulfilled in these kind of men; at the end of their way is death and hell, notwithstanding their confidence in the goodness of their state.

Again, 'There is that maketh himself rich, yet *hath* nothing.' Pr. xiii. 7. What can be more plain from all these texts, than that some men, that are out of the way think themselves in it; and that some men think themselves clean that are yet in their filthiness; and that think themselves rich for the next world, and yet are poor, and miserable, and wretched, and blind, and naked.* Thus the poor, blind, naked, hypocritical Pharisee thought of himself, when God threatened to abase him: Yea, he thought himself thus, and joyed therein, when indeed he was going down to the chambers of death.

Sixth, By these words, the Pharisee *seems to put the goodness of his condition upon the goodness of God*. I am not as other men are, and I thank God for it. God, saith he, I thank thee that I am not as other men are. He thanked God when God had done nothing for him. He thanked God, when the way that he was in was not of God's prescribing, but of his own inventing. So the persecutor thanks God that he was put into that way of roguery that the devil had put him into, when he fell to rending and tearing of the church of God: 'Whose possessors slay them, (saith the prophet,) and hold themselves not guilty: and they that sell them say, Blessed *be* the Lord, for I am rich.'

* To such poor deceived souls, our Lord's words are extremely applicable; 'If therefore the light that is in thee be darkness, how great *is* that darkness!' If poor blind sinners are, through the ignorance of their minds, fully persuaded that the destructive way in which they walk is the road to true happiness, how dangerous is their error, and how deplorable the consequences.—*Ryland*.

Zec. xi. 5. I remember that Luther used to say, 'In the name of God begins all mischief.' All must be fathered upon God: the Pharisee's conversion must be fathered upon God; the right or rather the villany of the outrageous persecution against God's people, must be fathered upon God. God, 'I thank thee,' and blessed be God, must be the burthen of the heretic's song. So again, the free-willer, he will ascribe all to God; the quaker, the ranter, the socinian, &c. will ascribe all to God. 'God, I thank thee,' is in every man's mouth, and must be entailed to every error, delusion, and damnable doctrine that is in the world: But the name of God, and their doctrine, worship, and way, hangeth together, much as doth it and the Pharisee's doctrine; that is to say, nothing at all; for God hath not proposed their principles, nor doth he own them, nor hath he commanded them, nor doth he convey by them the least grace or mercy to them; but rather rejecteth them, and holdeth them for his enemies, and for the destroyers of the world.

Seventh, We come in the next place to *the ground of all this*; and that is, to what the Pharisee had attained. To wit, that he was no extortioner, no unjust man, no adulterer, nor even as this Publican, and for that he fasted twice a-week, and paid tithes of all that he possessed. So that you see he pretendeth to a double foundation for his salvation, a moral and a ceremonial one; but both very lean, weak, and feeble: For the first of his foundations, what is it more, if all be true that he saith, but a being removed a few inches from the vilest men in their vilest actions, a very slender matter to build my confidence for heaven upon.

And for the second part of his ground for life, what is it but a couple of ceremonies, if so good. The first is questioned as a thing not founded in God's law; and the second is such, as is of the remotest sort of ceremonies, that teach and preach the Lord Jesus. But suppose them to be the best, and his conformity to them the thoroughest, they never were ordained to get to heaven by, and so are become but a sandy foundation. But anything will serve some men for a foundation and support for their souls, and to build their hopes of heaven upon. I am not a drunkard, says one, nor a liar, nor a swearer, nor a thief, and therefore, I thank God, I have hopes of heaven and glory. I am not an extortioner, nor an adulterer, nor unjust, nor yet as this Publican; and therefore do hope I shall go to heaven. Alas! poor men! will your being furnished with these things, save you from the thundering claps and vehement batteries, that the wrath of God will make upon sin and sinners in the day that shall burn like an oven? No, no, nothing at that day can shroud a man from the hot rebukes of that vengeance, but the very righteousness of God, which is not the righteousness of the law, however christened, named, or garnished with all those gew-gaws that men's heads and fancies can invent, for that is but the righteousness of man.

[MAN'S RIGHTEOUSNESS REJECTED, AND THE IMPUTED RIGHTEOUSNESS OF CHRIST ALONE TO BE RELIED ON FOR JUSTIFICATION.]

But, O thou blind Pharisee, since thou art so confident that thy state is good, and thy righteousness is that that will stand, when it shall be tried with fire, 1 Co. iii. 13. let me now reason with thee of righteousness. My terror shall not make thee afraid; I am not God, but a man as thou art, we both are formed out of the clay.

First, Prithee when didst thou begin to be righteous? Was it before or after thou hadst been a sinner? Not afore, I dare say; but if after, then the sins that thou pollutedst thyself withal before, have made thee uncapable of acting legal righteousness. For sin, where it is, pollutes, defiles, and makes vile the whole man; therefore thou canst not by after acts of obedience make thyself just in the sight of that God thou pretended now to stand praying unto. Indeed, thou mayest cover thy dirt, and paint thy sepulchre; for that acts of after obedience will do, though sin has gone before. But Pharisee, God can see through the white of this wall, even to the dirt that is within: God also can see through the paint and garnish of thy beauteous sepulchre, to the dead men's bones that are within; nor can any of thy most holy duties, nor all, when put together, blind the eye of the all-seeing majesty from beholding all the uncleanness of thy soul.* Mat. xxiii. 27. Stand not therefore so stoutly to it, now thou art before God; sin is with *thee*, and judgment and justice is before *him*. It becomes thee, therefore, rather to despise and abhor this life of thy hand, and to count all thy doings but dross and dung, and to be content to be justified with another's righteousness instead of thine own. This is the way to be secured. I say, blind Pharisee, this is the way to be secured from the wrath which is to come.

There is nothing more certain than this, that as to justification from the curse of the law, God has rejected man's righteousness, for the weakness and unprofitableness thereof; and hath accepted in the room of that glorious righteousness of his Son; because indeed, that, and that only, is universal, perfect, and equal with his justice and holiness.

* What home-thrusts are here! The two-edged sword of the Spirit, wielded by such a man, pierces—divides—lays bare every refuge of lies to which poor souls vainly fly for succour. It is a solemn and most important subject. May every reader have grace given him to weigh his hopes of heaven in the balances of divine unerring truth.—ED.

This is in a manner the contents of the whole bible, and therefore must needs be most certainly true. Now then, Mr. Pharisee, methinks, what if thou didst this, and that while thou art at thy prayers; to wit, cast in thy mind what doth God love most, and the resolve will be at hand. The BEST righteousness, surely the BEST righteousness; for that thy reason will tell thee: This done, even while thou art at thy devotion, ask thyself again, But WHO has the best righteousness? And that resolve will be at hand also; to wit, he that in person is equal with God; and that is his Son Jesus Christ. He that is separate from sinners, and made higher than the heavens; and that is his Son Jesus Christ. He that did no sin, nor had any guile found in his mouth; and there never was any such HE in all the world but the Son of God, Jesus Christ.

Now Pharisee, when thou hast done this, then as thou art in thy devotion, ask again, But what is this best righteousness, the righteousness of Christ, to do? And the answer will be ready. It is to be made by an act of the sovereign grace of God over to the sinner, that shall dare to trust thereto for justification from the curse of the law. He is made unto us of God, righteousness. 1 Co. i. 30. 'He hath made him to be sin for us, who knew no sin, that we might be made the righteousness of God in him.' 2 Co. v. 21. 'For Christ *is* the end of the law for righteousness to every one that believeth.' Ro. x. 4.

This done, and concluded on, then turn again Pharisee, and say thus with thyself; Is it most safe for me to trust in this righteousness of God? This righteousness of God-man, this righteousness of Christ? Certainly it is. Since, by the text, it is counted the best, and that which best pleaseth God; since it is that which God hath appointed, that sinners shall be justified withal. For in the Lord have we righteousness if we believe: And, in the Lord we are justified, and do glory. Is. xlv. 24, 25.

Nay Pharisee, suppose thine own righteousness should be as long, as broad, as high, as deep, as perfect, as good, even every way as good, as the righteousness of Christ. Yet since God has chosen by Christ, to reconcile us to himself, canst thou attempt to seek by thine own righteousness to reconcile thyself to God, and not be guilty of attempting, at least, to confront this righteousness of Christ before God. Yea, to dare with it, yea, to challenge by it, acceptance of thy person contrary to God's design.

Suppose, that when the king has chosen one to be judge in the land, and has determined that he shall be judge in all cases, and that by his verdict every man's judgment shall stand. I say, suppose, after this another should arise, and of his own head resolve to do his own business himself. Now, though he should be every whit as able as the judge of the king's appointing to do it; yea, and suppose he should do it as justly and righteously too, yet his making of himself a judge, would be an affront to the king, and an act of rebellion, and so a transgression worthy of punishment.

Why Pharisee, God hath appointed, that by the righteousness of his Son, and by that righteousness only, men shall be justified in his sight from the curse of the law. Wherefore, take heed, and at thy peril, whatever thy righteousness is, confront not the righteousness of Christ therewith. I say, bring it not in, let it not plead for thee at the bar of God, nor do thou plead for that in his court of justice; for thou canst not do that and be innocent. If he trusts to his righteousness, he hath sinned, says Ezekiel. Mark the text, 'When I shall say to the righteous, *that* he shall surely live; if he trust to his own righteousness, and commit iniquity, all his righteousnesses shall not be remembered: but for his iniquity that he hath committed, he shall die for it.' ch. xxxiii. 13.

Observe a few things from this text, and they are these that follow.

First, Here is a righteous man; a man, with whom we do not hear that the God of heaven finds fault.

Secondly, Here is a promise made to this man, that 'he shall surely live;' but on THIS condition, that he trusts not to his own righteousness. Whence it is manifest, that the promise of life to this righteous man, is not for the sake of his righteousness, but for the sake of something else, to wit, the righteousness of Christ.

1. Not for the sake of his own righteousness. This is evident, because we are admitted, yea, commanded, to trust in the righteousness that saveth us. The righteousness of God is unto all, and upon all that believe; that is, trust *in it,* and trust *to it* for justification. Now therefore, if thy righteousness, when most perfect, could save thee, thou mightest, yea oughtest most boldly to trust therein. But since thou art forbidden to trust to it, it is evident it cannot save, nor is it for the sake of that, that the righteous man is saved. Ro. iii. 21, 22.

2. But for the sake of something else; to wit, for the sake of the righteousness of Christ, whom God hath set forth to be a propitiation through faith in his blood, to declare his righteousness for the remission of sins that are past, through the forbearance of God. 'To declare, *I say,* at this time his righteousness, that he might be just, and the justifier of him that believeth in Jesus.' Ro. iii. 26. See also Phil. iii. 7—9.

'If he trusts to his own righteousness, and commit iniquity, all his righteousness shall not be remembered; but for his iniquity that he hath committed [in trusting to his own righteousness] he shall die for it.'

Note hence further.

1. That there is more virtue in one sin to destroy, than in all thy righteousness to save thee alive. If he trust, if he trust never so little, if he do at all trust to his own righteousness, all his righteousness shall be forgotten; and *by,* and *for,* and *in,* the sin that he hath committed in trusting to it, he shall die.

2. Take notice also, that there are more damnable sins than those that are against the moral law. By which of the ten commandments is trusting to our own righteousness forbidden? Yet it is a sin. It is a sin therefore forbidden by the gospel, and is included, lurketh close in, yea, is *the,* or *a* root of unbelief itself; 'He that believeth not shall be damned.' But he that trusteth in his own righteousness doth not believe, neither in the truth or sufficiency of the righteousness of Christ to save him, therefore he shall be damned.

But how is it manifest, that he that trusteth to his own righteousness, doth it through a doubt, or unbelief of the truth or sufficiency of the righteousness of Christ?

I answer, Because, even because he trusteth to his own. A man will never willingly choose to trust to the worst of helps, when he believes there is a better as near, and to be had as soon, and that too, upon as easy, if not more easy terms. If he that trusteth to his own righteousness for life, did believe, that there is indeed such a thing as the righteousness of Christ to justify; and that this righteousness of Christ has in it ALL sufficiency to do that blessed work, be sure he would choose that, thereon to lay, lean, and venture his soul, that he saw was the best, and most sufficient to save; especially when he saw also, (and see that he must, when he sees the righteousness of Christ) to wit, that that is to be obtained as soon, because as near, and to be had on as easy terms; nay, upon easier than may man's own righteousness. I say, he would sooner choose it, because of the weight of salvation, of the worth of salvation, and of the fearful sorrow, that to eternity will overtake him, that in this thing shall miscarry. It is for heaven, it is to escape hell, wrath, and damnation, saith the soul; and therefore I will, I must, I dare not but choose that, and that only, that I believe to be the best and most sufficient help in so great a concern, as soul-concern is. So then he that trusteth to his own righteousness, does it of unbelief of the sufficiency of the righteousness of Christ to save him.

Wherefore this sin of trusting to his own righteousness is a most high and damning transgression: because it contemneth the righteousness of Christ, which is the only righteousness that is sufficient to save from the curse of the law. It also disalloweth the design of heaven, and the excellency of the mystery of the wisdom of God, in designing this way of salvation for man. What shall I say, It also seeketh to rob God of the honour of the salvation of man. It seeketh to take the crown from the head of Christ, and to set it upon the hypocrite's head; therefore, no marvel, that this one sin be of that weight, virtue and power, as to sink that man and his righteousness into hell, that leaneth thereon, or that trusteth unto it.

But Pharisee, I need not talk thus unto thee, for thou art not the man that hath that righteousness, that God findeth not fault withal; nor is it to be found, but with him that is ordained to be the Saviour of mankind; nor is there any such one besides Jesus, who is called Christ. Thy righteousness is a poor pittance, a scrap: nay, not so good as a scrap of righteousness. Thine own confession makes thee partial in the law; for here, in the midst of thy boasts, thou hast not, because thou canst not say, thou hast fulfilled all righteousness. What madness then has brought thee into the temple, there in audacious manner to stand and vaunt before God; saying, 'God, I thank thee, I am not as other men are.'

Dost thou not know, that he that breaks one, breaks all the commandments of God; and consequently, that he that keeps not all, keeps none at all of the commandments of God. Say I this of myself? saith not the scriptures the same? 'For whosoever shall keep the whole law, and yet offend in one *point*, he is guilty of all.' Ja. ii. 10. Be confounded then, be confounded.

Dost thou know the God with whom now thou hast to do? He is a God that cannot, no, that cannot, as he is just, accept of an half righteousness for a whole; nor of a lame righteousness for a sound; nor of a sick righteousness for a well and healthy one. Mal. i. 8. And if so, how should he then accept of that which is no righteousness? I say, how should he accept of that which is none at all, save an hypocritical and feigned one, for thine is only such. And if Christ said, when you have done all, say, 'We are unprofitable,' How camest thou to say before thou hadst done one thing well, I am better, more righteous than other men? Didst thou believe, when thou saidst it, That God knew thy heart? Hadst thou said this to the Publican, it had been a high and rampant expression; but to say this before God, to the face of God, when he knew that thou wast vile, and a sinner from the womb, and from the conception, spoils all. It was spoken to put a check to thy arrogancy, when Christ said, 'Ye are they which justify yourselves before men; but God knoweth your hearts.' Lu. xvi. 15.

Hast thou taken notice of this, that God judgeth the fruit by the heart from whence it comes? 'A good man out of the good treasure of his heart bringeth forth that which is good; and an evil man out of the evil treasure of his heart bringeth forth that which is evil.' Lu. vi. 45. Nor can it be otherwise concluded, but that thou art an evil man, and so that all thy supposed good is nought but badness. For that thou hast made it to stand in the room of Jesus, and hast dared to commend thyself to the living God thereby: For thou hast trusted in thy shadow of righteousness, and committed iniquity. Thy sin hath melted away thy righteousness, and turned it to nothing but dross; or, if you will, to the early dew, like to which it goeth away, and so can by no means do thee good, when thou shalt stand in need of salvation and eternal life of God.

But further, thou sayest thou art righteous, but they are but vain words. Knowest thou not that thy zeal, which is the life of thy righteousness, is preposterous in many things. What else means thy madness, and the rage thereof, against men as good as thyself. True, thy being ignorant that they are good, may save thee from the commission of the sin that is unpardonable, but it will never keep thee from spot in God's sight, but will make both thee and thy righteousness culpable.

Paul, who was once as brave a Pharisee as thou canst be, calleth much of that zeal, which he in that estate was possessed with, and lived in the exercise of, madness; yea, exceeding madness, Ac. xxvi. 9—11. Phi. iii. 5, 6. and of the same sort is much of thine, and it must be so; for a lawyer, a man for the law, and that resteth in it, must be a persecutor; yea, a persecutor of righteous men, and that of zeal to God; because by the law is begat, through the weakness that it meeteth with in thee, sourness, bitterness of spirit, and anger against him that rightfully condemneth thee of folly, for choosing to trust to thine own righteousness, when a better is provided of God to save us. Ga. iv. 28—31. Thy righteousness therefore is deficient; yea, thy zeal for the law, and the men of the law, has joined madness with thy moral virtues, and made thy righteousness unrighteousness; How then canst thou be upright before the Lord?

Further, Has not the pride of thy spirit in this hot-headed zeal for thy pharisaical notions, run thee upon thinking that thou art able to do more than God hath enjoined thee, and so able to make thyself more righteous, than God requireth thou shouldest be. What else is the cause of thy adding of laws to God's laws, precepts to God's precepts, and traditions to God's appointments? Mar. vii. 8. Nay, hast thou not by thus doing, condemned the law of want of perfection, and so the God that gave it, of want of wisdom, and faithfulness to himself and thee?

Nay, I say again, hath not thy thus doing charged God with being ignorant of knowing, what rules there needed to be imposed on his creatures to make their obedience complete? And doth not this apish madness of thine intimate, moreover, that if thou hadst not stept in with the bundle of thy traditions, righteousness had been imperfect, not through man's weakness, but through impediment in God, or in his ministering rules of righteousness unto us.

Now, when thou hast thought on these things fairly, answer thyself in these few questions: Is not this arrogancy? Is not this blasphemy? Is not this to condemn God, that thou mightest be righteous? And dost thou think, this is, indeed, the way to be righteous?

But again, what means thy preferring of thine own rules, laws, statutes, ordinances and appointments, before the rules, laws, statutes and appointments of God? Thinkest thou this to be right? Whither will thy zeal, thy pride, and thy folly carry thee? Is there more reason, more equity, more holiness in thy traditions, than in the holy, and just, and good commandments of God? Ro. vii. 12. Why then, I say, dost thou reject the commandment of God, to keep thine own tradition? Yea, Why dost thou rage, and rail, and cry out when men keep not thy law, or the rule of thine order, and tradition of thine elders; and yet shut thine eyes, or wink with them, when thou thyself shalt live in the breach of the law of God? Yea, why wilt thou condemn men, when they keep not thy law, but study for an excuse, yea, plead for them that live in the breach of God's. Mar. vii. 10—13. Will this go for righteousness in the day of God Almighty? Nay rather, will not this, like a millstone about thy neck, drown thee in the deeps of hell? Oh, the blindness, the madness, the pride, and spite, that dwells in the hearts of these pretended righteous men.

Again, What kind of righteousness of thine, is this, that standeth in a misplacing, and so consequently in a misesteeming of God's commands? Some thou settest too high, and some too low; as in the text, thou hast set a ceremony above faith, above love, and above hope in the mercy of God: When, as it is evident, the things last mentioned, are the things of the first rate, the weightier matters. Mat. xxiii. 23.

Again, Thou hast preferred the gold above the temple that sanctifieth the gold, and the gift upon the altar, above the altar that sanctifies the gift. Mat. xxiii. 17.

I say again, What kind of righteousness shall this be called? What back will such a suit of apparel fit, that is set together just cross and thwart to what it should be? Just as if the sleeves should be sewed upon the pocket-holes, and the pockets set on where the sleeves should stand. Nor can other righteousness proceed where a wrong judgment precedeth it.

This misplacing of God's laws cannot, I say, but produce misshaped and misplaced obedience. It indeed produceth a monster, an ill-shapened thing, a mole, a mouse, a pig, all which are things unclean, and an abomination to the Lord. For see, saith he, if thou wilt be making, that thou make all things according to the pattern shewed to thee in the mount. Set faith, where faith should stand, a moral, where a moral should stand; and a ceremony, where a ceremony should stand; for this turning of things upside down shall be esteemed as the potter's clay: And wilt thou call this thy righteousness; yea, wilt thou stand in this, plead for this, and venture an eternal concern in such a piece of linsey-woolsey as this? O fools, and blind!

But further, let us come a little closer to the point. O blind Pharisee. Thou standest to thy righteousness, what dost thou mean? Wouldest thou have MERCY for thy righteousness, or JUSTICE for thy righteousness?

[FIRST MERCY.] If mercy, what mercy? Temporal things God giveth to the unthankful and unholy; nor doth he use to SELL the world to man for righteousness. The earth hath he GIVEN to the children of men. But this is not the thing; thou wouldest have eternal mercy for thy righteousness; thou wouldest have God think upon what an holy, what a good, what a righteous man thou art, and hast been. But Christ died not for the good and righteous, nor did he come to call such to the banquet, that grace hath prepared for the world. 'I came not,' I am not come, saith Christ, 'to call the righteous, but sinners to repentance.' Mar. ii. 27. Ro. v. Yet this is thy plea; Lord God, I am a righteous man, therefore grant me mercy, and a share in thy heavenly kingdom. What else dost thou mean, when thou sayest, 'God I thank thee, that I am not as other men are?' Why dost thou rejoice, why art thou glad that thou art more righteous, if indeed thou art, than thy neighbour, if it is not because thou thinkest, that thou hast got the start of, the better of thy neigbour, with reference to mercy; and that by thy righteousness thou hast insinuated thyself into God's affections, and procured an interest in his eternal favour. But,

What, What hast thou done by thy righteousness? I say, What hast thou given to God thereby? And what hath he received of thy hand? Perhaps thou wilt say, righteousness pleaseth God: But I answer no, not thine, with respect to justification from the curse of the law, unless it be as perfect, as the justice it is yielded to, and as the law that doth command it. But thine is not such a righteousness: no, thine is speckled, thine is spotted, thine makes thee to look like a speckled bird in his eye-sight.

Thy righteousness has added iniquity, to thy iniquity, because it has kept thee from a belief of thy need of repentance, and because it has emboldened thee to thrust thyself audaciously into the presence of God, and made thee there, even before his holy eyes, which are so pure, that they cannot look on iniquity, Hab. i. 13. to vaunt, boast, and brag of thyself, and of thy tottering, ragged, stinking uncleanness; for all our righteousnesses are as menstruous rags, because they flow from a thing, a heart, a man that is unclean. But,

Again, Wouldest thou have mercy for thy righteousness? For who wouldest thou have it; for another, or for thyself? If for another, and it is most proper, that a righteous man should intercede for another by his righteousness, rather than for himself, then thou thrusteth Christ out of his place and office, and makest thyself to be a saviour in his stead; for a mediator there is already, even a mediator between God and man, and he is the man Christ Jesus. There is therefore no need of thine interceding by thy righteousness for the acceptation of any unto justification from the curse.

But dost thou plead by thy righteousness, for mercy for thyself? Why, in so doing thou impliest,

First, That thy righteousness *can prevail with God, more than can thy sins.* I say, that thy righteousness can prevail with God, to preserve thee from death, more than thy sins can prevail with him to condemn thee to it. And if so, what follows? but that thy righteousness is more, and has been done in a fuller spirit than ever were thy sins: but thus to insinuate is to insinuate a lie; for there is no man, but while he is a sinner, sinneth with a more full spirit, than any good man can act righteousness withal.

A sinner when he sinneth, he doth it with all his heart, and with all his mind, and with all his soul, and with all his strength; nor hath he in his ordinary course any thing that bindeth. But with a good man it is not so; all, and every whit of himself, neither is, nor can be, in every good duty that he doth. For when he would do good evil is present with him. And again, 'The flesh lusteth against the Spirit, and the Spirit against the flesh: and these are contrary the one to the other, so that ye cannot do the things that ye would.' Ga. v. 17.

Now if a good man cannot do good things with that wholeness and oneness of soul, with that oneness and universalness of mind, as a wicked man doth sin with, then is his sin heavier to weigh him

VOL. II.

down to hell, than is his righteousness to buoy him up to the heavens.

And again, I say, if the righteousness of a good man comes short of his sin, both in number, weight and measure, as it doth, for a good man shrinks and quakes at the thoughts of God's entering into judgment with him, Ps. cxliii. 2. then is his iniquity more than his righteousness. And I say again, if the sin of one that is truly gracious, and so of one that hath the best of principles, is heavier and mightier to destroy him, than is his righteousness to save him, how can it be, that the Pharisee, that is not gracious, but a mere carnal man, somewhat reformed and painted over with a few, lean, and lousy formalities, should with his empty, partial, hypocritical righteousness, counterpoise his great, mighty, and weighty sins, that have cleaved to him in every state and condition of his, to make him odious in the sight of God?

Second. Dost thou plead by thy righteousness for mercy for thyself? Why in so doing thou impliest, *that mercy thou deservedst;* and that is next door to, or almost as much as to say, God oweth me what I ask for.* The best that can be put upon it, is, thou seekest security from the direful curse of God, as it were by the works of the law, and to be sure betwixt Christ and the law, thou wilt drop into hell. Ro. ix. three last verses. For he that seeks for mercy, as it were, and but as it were, by the works of the law, doth not altogether trust thereto. Nor doth he that seeks for that righteousness, that should save him, as it were, by the works of the law, seek it only, wholly and solely at the hands of mercy.

So then, to seek for that that should save thee, neither at the hands of the law, nor at the hands of mercy, is, to be sure, to seek it where it is not to be found; for there is no medium betwixt the righteousness of the law, and the mercy of God. Thou must have it either at the door of the law, or at the door of grace. But sayest thou, I am for having of it at the hands of both. I will trust solely to neither. I love to have two strings to my bow. If one of them, as you think, can help me by itself, my reason tells me, that both can help me better. Therefore will I be righteous, and good, and will seek by my goodness to be commended to the mercy of God: for surely, he that hath something of his own to ingratiate himself into the favour of his prince withal, shall sooner obtain his mercy and favour, than one that comes to him as stript of all good.

---

* Those who *plead* for mercy, as the reward of their own righteousness, are guilty of gross absurdity. They may claim to *employ* the mercy which they have earned: why plead with the God of justice for that to which they consider themselves in justice entitled? God will *give* to all that to which they are entitled, without being sued for their earnings.—ED.

I answer, But there are not two ways to heaven, not two *living* ways; there is *one* new and *living* way, which Christ hath consecrated for us through the vail, that is to say, his flesh; and besides that one, there is no more. He. x. 19—24. Why then dost thou talk of two strings to thy bow? What became of him that had, and would have, two stools to sit on? Yea, the text says plainly, that therefore they obtained not righteousness, because they sought it not by faith, but, as it were, by the works of the law. See here, they are disowned by the gospel, because they sought it not by faith; that is, by faith only. Again, the law, and the righteousness thereof, flies from them, nor could they attain it, though they followed after it, because they sought it not by faith.

Mercy then is to be found alone in Jesus Christ! Again, the righteousness of the law is to be obtained only by faith of Jesus Christ: that is, in the Son of God is the righteousness of the law to be found; for he, by his obedience to his Father, is become the end of the law for righteousness. And for the sake of his legal righteousness, which is also called the righteousness of God, because it was God in the flesh of the Lord Jesus that did accomplish it, is mercy and grace from God extended, to whoever dependeth by faith upon God by this Jesus his righteousness for it. And hence it is, that we so often read, that this Jesus is the way to the Father: That God, for Christ's sake, forgiveth us: That by the obedience of one, many are made righteous or justified: And that through this man, is preached to us the forgiveness of sins; and that by him all that believe are justified from all things, from which they could not be justified by the law of Moses.

Now, though I here do make mention of righteousness and mercy, yet I hold there is but one way, to wit, to eternal life; which way, as I said, is Jesus Christ; for he is the new, the only new, and living way to the Father of mercies, for mercy to make me capable of abiding with him in the heavens for ever and ever.

But sayest thou, I will be righteous in myself that I may have wherewith to commend me to God, when I go to him for mercy?

I answer, But thou blind Pharisee; I tell thee thou hast no understanding of God's design by the gospel; which is, not to advance man's righteousness, as thou dreamest; but to advance the righteousness of his Son, and his grace by him. Indeed, if God's design by the gospel was to exalt and advance man's righteousness, then that which thou hast said, would be to the purpose. For what greater dignity can be put upon man's righteousness, than to admit it?

I say then, for God to admit it, to be an advocate, an intercessor, a mediator; for all these is that which prevaileth with God to shew me mercy. But this God never thought of, much less could he thus design by the gospel: for the text runs flat against it. Not of works, not of works of righteousness, which we have done; not of works, lest any man should boast, saying, Well, I may thank my own good life for mercy. It was partly for the sake of mine own good deeds that I obtained mercy to be in heaven and glory. Shall *this* be the burden of the song of heaven? Or is this that which is composed by that glittering heavenly host, and which we have read of in the holy book of God! No, no, that song runs upon other feet, standeth in far better strains, being composed of far higher, and truly heavenly matter: For God has 'predestinated us unto the adoption of children by Jesus Christ to himself, according to the good pleasure of his will, to the praise of the glory of his grace, wherein he hath made us accepted in the beloved. In whom we have redemption through his blood, the forgiveness of sins, according to the riches of his grace.' Ep. i. 5—7. And it is requisite, that the song be framed accordingly; wherefore he saith, that the heavenly song runs thus: 'Thou art worthy to take the book, and to open the seals thereof: for thou wast slain, and hast redeemed us to God by thy blood, out of every kindred, and tongue, and people, and nation; and hast made us unto our God kings and priests; and we shall reign on the earth.' Re. v. 9, 10.

He saith not that they have redeemed, or helped to redeem and deliver themselves; but that the Lamb, the Lamb that was slain; the Lamb only was he that had redeemed them. Nor, saith he, that they had made themselves kings and priests unto God to offer any oblation, sacrifice, or offering whatsoever; but that the same Lamb had made them such. For they, as is insinuated by the text, were in, among, one with, and no better, than the kindreds, tongues, nations, and people of the earth. Better! No, in no wise, saith Paul, Ro. iii. 9. therefore their separation from them was of mere mercy, free grace, good will, and distinguishing love: not for, or because of, works of righteousness which any of them have done; no, they were all alike. But these, because beloved, when in their blood, according to Eze. xvi. were separated by free grace. And as another scripture hath it, redeemed from the earth, and from among men by blood. Re. xiv. 3, 4. Wherefore deliverance from the ireful wrath of God, must not, neither in whole, nor in part, be ascribed to the whole law, or to all the righteousness that comes by it; but to this Lamb of God, Jesus, the Saviour of the world; for it is He that delivered us from the wrath to come: and that according to God's appointment; 'For God hath not appointed us to wrath, but to obtain salvation by (or through) our Lord Jesus Christ.' 1 Th. v. 9. Let every man, therefore, take heed what he doth, and whereon he layeth the stress of his salvation, 'For other foundation can no man lay, than that is laid, which is Jesus Christ.' 1 Co. iii. 11.

But dost thou plead still as thou didst before, and wilt thou stand thereto? Why then, thy design must overcome God, or God's design must overcome thee. Thy design is to give thy good life, thy good deeds, a part of the glory of thy justification from the curse. And God's design is to throw all thy righteousness out into the street, into the dirt, and dunghill, as to that. Thou art for glory, and for glorying here before God; yea, thou art for sharing in the glory of justification, when that alone belongeth to God. And he hath said, 'My glory will I not give to another.' Thou wilt not trust wholly to God's grace in Christ for justification; and God will not take thy stinking righteousness in, as a partner in thy acquitment from sin, death, wrath, and hell. Now the question is, who shall prevail? God, or the Pharisee? And whose word shall stand? His, or the Pharisee's?

Alas! The Pharisee here must needs come down, for God is greater than all. Also, he hath said, that no flesh shall glory in his presence; and that he will have mercy, and not sacrifice. And again, that it is not, nor shall be, in him that wills, nor in him that runs, but in God that sheweth mercy. What hope, help, stay, or relief then is there left for the merit-monger? What twig, or straw, or twined thread is left to be a stay for his soul? This besom will sweep away his cobweb: The house that this spider doth so lean upon, will now be overturned, and he in it to hell fire; for nothing less than everlasting damnation is designed by God, and that for this fearful and unbelieving Pharisee: God will prevail against him for ever.

Third. But wilt thou yet plead thy righteousness for mercy? Why, in so doing, *thou takest away from God the power of giving mercy.* For if it be thine as wages, it is no longer his to dispose of at pleasure; for that which another man oweth me, is in equity not at his, but at my disposal. Did I say, that by this thy plea, thou takest away from God the power of giving mercy; I will add, yea, and also of disposing of heaven and life eternal. And then, I pray you, what is left unto God, and what can he call his own? Not mercy; for that by thy good deeds thou hast purchased. Not heaven; for that by thy good deeds thou hast purchased. Not eternal life; for that by thy good deeds thou hast purchased. Thus, Pharisee, O thou self-righteous man, hast thou set up thyself above grace, mercy, heaven, glory; yea, above even God himself, for the purchaser should in reason be esteemed above the purchase.

Awake man! What hast thou done? Thou

hast blasphemed God, thou hast undervalued the glory of his grace; thou hast, what in thee lieth, opposed the glorious design of heaven! Thou hast sought to make thy filthy rags to share in thy justification.

Now, all these are mighty sins; these have made thine iniquity infinite. What wilt thou do? Thou hast created to thyself a world of needless miseries. I call them needless, because thou hadst more than enough before. Thou hast set thyself against God in a way of contending; thou standest upon thy points and pantables:* Thou wilt not bate God an ace, of what thy righteousness is worth, and wilt also make it worth what thyself shalt list. Thou wilt be thine own judge, as to the worth of thy righteousness; thou wilt neither hear what verdict the word has passed about it, nor wilt thou endure, that God should throw it out in the matter of thy justification, but quarrellest with the doctrine of free grace, or else dost wrest it out of its place to serve thy Pharisaical designs; saying, 'God, I thank thee, I am not as other men;' fathering upon thyself, yea, upon God and thyself, a stark lie; for thou art as other men are, though not in *this*, yet in *that*; yea, in a far worse condition than the most of men are. Nor will it help thee any thing to attribute this thy goodness to the God of heaven: for that is but a mere toying; the truth is, the God that thou intendest, is nothing but thy righteousness; and the grace that thou supposest, is nothing but thine own good and honest intentions. So that,

Fourth, In all that thou sayest, thou dost but play the downright hypocrite. *Thou pretendest indeed to mercy, but thou intendest nothing but merit.* Thou seemest to give the glory to God; but at the same time takest it all to thyself. Thou despisest others, and criest up thyself, and in conclusion fatherest all upon God by word, and upon thyself in truth. Nor is there any thing more common among this sort of men, than to make God, his grace, and kindness, the stalking-horse to their own praise, saying, God, I thank thee when they trust to themselves that they are righteous, and have not need of any repentance; when the truth is, they are the worst sort of men in the world, because they put themselves into such a

---

* 'Points and pantables;' quibbles and quirks.
'With periods, *points*, and tropes, he slurs his crimes;
He robb'd not, but he borrowed from the poor.'—*Dryden.*
'Pantable,' from pantoufle, a slipper. To stand upon his pantables, was a contemptuous mode of speech, to express a very dishonourable man's 'standing upon his honour,' which could so easily be slipped from under him. 'What pride is equal to the pope's in making kings kiss his pantables.' *Sir E. Sandys.* 'He standeth upon his pantables, and regardeth greatly his reputation.' *Saker's Character of a Fraudulent Fellow.* Bunyan was peculiarly happy in his use of popular and proverbial expressions.—ED.

state as God hath not put them into, and then impute it to God, saying, God, I thank thee, that thou hast done it; for what greater sin [is there] than to make God a liar, or than to father that upon God which he never meant, intended, or did. And all this under a colour to glorify God; when there is nothing else designed, but to take all glory from him, and to wear [it] on thine own head as a crown, and a diadem in the face of the whole world.

A self-righteous man therefore can come to God for mercy none otherwise than fawningly: For what need of mercy hath a righteous man? Let him then talk of mercy, of grace, and goodness, and come in an hundred times with his, 'God, I thank thee,' in his mouth, all is but words, there is no sense, nor savour, nor relish of mercy and favour; nor doth he in truth, from his very heart, understand the nature of mercy, nor what is an object thereof; but when he thanks God, he praises himself; when he pleads for mercy, he means his own merit; and all this is manifest from what doth follow; for, saith he, 'I am not as this Publican!' Thence clearly insinuating, that not the good, but the bad, should be rejected of the God of heaven: That not the bad but the good; not the sinner, but the self-righteous, are the most proper objects of God's favour. The same thing is done by others in this our day: Favour, mercy, grace, and 'God I thank thee,' is in their mouths, but their own strength, sufficiency, free-will, and the like, they are the things they mean, by all such high and glorious expressions.

[Second Justice.] But, *secondly,* If thy plea be not for mercy, but for justice, then to speak a little to that. Justice has measures and rules to go by; unto which measures and rules, if thou comest not up, justice can do thee no good. Come then, O thou blind Pharisee, let us pass away a few minutes in some discourse about this. Thou demandest justice, because God hath said, that the man that doth these things shall live in and by them. And again, the doers of the law shall be justified; not in a way of mercy, but in a way of justice. He shall live by them. But what hast thou done, O blind Pharisee! What hast thou done, that thou art emboldened to venture, to stand and fall to the most perfect justice of God? Hast thou fulfilled the whole law, and not offended in one point? Hast thou purged thyself from the pollutions and motions of sin that dwell in the flesh, and work in thy own members? Is the very being of sin rooted out of thy tabernacle? And art thou now as perfectly innocent as ever was Jesus Christ? Hast thou, by suffering the uttermost punishment that justice could justly lay upon thee for thy sins, made fair and full satisfaction to God, according to the tenor of his law for thy

transgressions? If thou hast done all these things, then thou mayest plead something, and yet but something for thyself in a way of justice. Nay, in this I will assert nothing, but rather inquire:—What hast thou gained by all this thy righteousness? (we will now suppose what must not be granted) Was not this thy state when thou wast in thy first parents? Wast thou not innocent, perfectly innocent and righteous? And if thou shouldest be so now, what hast thou gained thereby? Suppose that the man, that had forty years ago forty pounds of his own, and had spent it all since, should yet be able now to show his forty pounds again? What has he got thereby, or how much richer is he at last, than he was, when he first set up for himself. Nay, doth not the blot of his ill living betwixt his first and his last, lie as a blemish upon him, unless he should redeem himself also by works of supererogation, from the scandal that justice may lay at his door for that?

But, I say, suppose, O Pharisee, this should be thy case, yet God is not bound to give thee in justice that eternal life, which by his grace he bestoweth upon those, that have redemption from sin, by the blood of his Son. In justice therefore, when all comes to all, thou canst require no more than an endless life in an earthly paradise; for there thou wast set up at first; nor doth it appear from what hath been said, touching all that thou hast done or canst do, that thou deservedst a better place.

Did I say, that thou mayest require justly an endless life in an earthly paradise. Why? I must add to that saying, this proviso: If thou continuest in the law, and in the righteousness thereof, else not.

But how dost thou know that thou shalt continue therein? Thou hast no promise from God's mouth for that, nor is grace or strength ministered to mankind by the covenant that thou art under. So that still thou standest bound to thy good behaviour, and in the day that thou dost give the first, though never so little a trip, or stumble in thy obedience, thou forfeitest thine interest in paradise, and in justice, as to any benefit there.

But alas, what need is there that we should thus talk of things, when it is manifest, that thou hast sinned, not only before thou wast a Pharisee, but when, after the most strictest sect of thy religion, thou livedst also a Pharisee; yea, and now in the temple, in thy prayer there, thou showest thyself to be full of ignorance, pride, self-conceit, and horrible arrogancy, and desire of vain glory, &c., which are none of them the seat or fruits of righteousness, but the seat of the devil, and the fruit of his dwelling, even at this time, in thy heart.

Could it ever have been imagined, that such

audacious impudence could have put itself forth in any mortal man, in his approach unto God by prayer, as has showed itself in thee? 'I am not as other men!' sayest thou; but is this the way to go to God in prayer? Is this the way for a mortal man, that is full of sin, that stands in need of mercy, and that must certainly perish without it, to come to God in prayer? The prayer of the upright is God's delight. But the upright man glorifies God's justice, by confessing to God the vileness and pollution of his state and condition: He glorifies God's mercy by acknowledging, that that, and that only, as communicated of God by Christ to sinners, can save and deliver from the curse of the law.

This, I say, is the sum of the prayer of the just and upright man, Job i. 8; xl. 4. Ac. xiii. 22. Ps. xxxviii.; li. 2 Sa. vi. 21, 22. and not as thou most vain-gloriously vauntest, with thy, 'God, I thank thee, that I am not as other men are.'

True, when a man is accused by his neighbours, by a brother, by an enemy, and the like; if he be clear, and he may be so, as to what they shall lay to his charge, then let him vindicate, justify, and acquit himself, to the utmost that in justice and truth he can; for his name, the preservation whereof is more to be chosen than silver and gold; also his profession, yea, the name of God too, and religion, may now lie at stake, by reason of such false accusations, and perhaps can by no means, as to this man, be recovered, and vindicated from reproach and scandal, but by his justifying of himself. Wherefore in such a work, a man serveth God, and saves religion from hurt; yea, as he that is a professor, and has his profession attended with a scandalous life, hurteth religion thereby: So he that has his profession attended with a good life, and shall suffer it notwithstanding, to lie under blame by false accusations, when it is in the power of his hand to justify himself, hurteth religion also. But the case of the Pharisee is otherwise. He is not here a dealing with men, but God; not seeking to stand clear in the sight of the world, but in the sight of heaven itself; and that too, not with respect to what men or angels, but with respect to what God and his law, could charge him with and justly lay at his door.

This therefore mainly altereth the case; for a man *here* to stand thus upon his points,* it is death; for he affronteth God, he giveth him the lie, he reproveth the law, and in sum, accuseth it of bearing false witness against him; he doth this, I say, even by saying, 'God, I thank thee, that I am not as other men are;' for God hath made none of this difference. The law condemneth all men as sinners, and testifieth, that every imagina-

tion of the thought of the heart of the sons of men is only evil, and that continually. Wherefore they that do as the Pharisee did, to wit, seek to justify themselves before God from the curse of the law, by their own good doings, though they also, as the Pharisee did, seem to give God the thanks for all, yet do most horribly sin, even by their so doing, and shall receive a Pharisee's reward at last. Wherefore, O thou Pharisee, it is a vain thing for thee either to think of, or to ask for, at God's hand, either mercy or justice. Because mercy thou canst not ask for, from sense of want of mercy, because thy righteousness, which is by the law, hath utterly blinded thine eyes, and complimenting with God doth nothing. And as for justice, that can do thee no good, but the more just God is, and the more by that he acteth towards thee, the more miserable and fearful will be thy condition, because of the deficiency of thy, so much by thee, esteemed righteousness.

[*The Pharisee seeth no need of mercy, but thinketh himself righteous before God.*]

What a deplorable condition then is a poor Pharisee in! For mercy he cannot pray, he cannot pray for it with all his heart; for he seeth, indeed, no need thereof. True, the Pharisee, though he was impudent enough, yet would not take all from God; he would still count, that there was due to him a tribute of thanks: 'God, I thank thee,' saith he, but yet not a bit of this, for mercy; but for that he had let him live, for I know not for what he did thank himself, till he had made himself better than other men; but that betterment was a betterment in none other judgment than that of his own, and that was none other but such an one as was false. So then, the Pharisee is by this time quite out of doors; his righteousness is worth nothing, his prayer is worth nothing, his thanks to God are worth nothing; for that what he had was scanty, and imperfect, and it was his pride that made him offer it to God for acceptance; nor could his fawning thanksgiving better his case, or make his matter at all good before God.

But I'll warrant you, the Pharisee was so far off from thinking thus of himself, and of his righteousness, that he thought of nothing so much as of this, that he was a happy man; yea, happier by far than other his fellow rationals. Yea, he plainly declares it when he saith, 'God, I thank thee, that I am not as other men are.'

O what a fool's paradise was the heart of the Pharisee now in, while he stood in the temple praying to God! 'God, I thank thee,' said he, for I am good and holy, I am a righteous man; I have been full of good works; I am no extortioner, unjust, nor adulterer, no nor yet as this wretched

---

* See note on page 235.

Publican. I have kept myself strictly to the rule of mine order, and my order is the most strict of all orders now in being: I fast, I pray, I give tithes of all that I possess. Yea, so forward am I to be a religious man; so ready have I been to listen after my duty, that I have asked both of God and man the ordinances of judgment and justice; I take delight in approaching to God. What less now can be mine than the heavenly kingdom and glory?

Now the Pharisee, like Haman, saith in his heart, To whom would the king delight to do honour, more than to myself? Where is the man that so pleaseth God, and consequently, that in equity and reason should be beloved of God like me? Thus like the prodigal's brother, he pleadeth, saying, 'Lo, these many years do I serve thee, neither transgressed I at any time thy commandment.' Lu. xv. 29. O brave Pharisee! But go on in thine oration: 'Nor yet as this Publican.'

Poor wretch, quoth the Pharisee to the Publican, What comest thou for? Dost think that such a sinner as thou art shall be heard of God? God heareth not sinners; but if any man be a worshipper of God as I am, as I thank God I am, him he heareth. Thou, for thy part, hast been a rebel all thy days: I abhor to come nigh thee, or to touch thy garments. Stand by thyself, come not near me, for I am more holy than thou. Is. lxv. 5.

Hold, stop there, go no further; fie Pharisee, fie; Dost thou know before whom thou standest, to whom thou speakest, and of what the matter of thy silly oration is made? Thou art now before God, thou speakest now to God, and therefore in justice and honesty thou shouldest make mention of his righteousness. not of thine; of his righteousness, and of his only.

I am sure Abraham, of whom thou sayest he is thy father, never had the face to do as thou hast done, though it is to be presumed he had more cause so to do, than thou hast, or canst have. Abraham had whereof to glory, but not before God; yea, he was called God's friend, and yet would not glory before him; but humbled himself, was afraid, and trembled in himself, when he stood before him, acknowledging of himself to be but dust and ashes. Ge. xviii. 27, 30. Ro. iv. 2. But thou, as thou hadst quite forgot, that thou wast framed of that matter, and after the manner of other men, standest and pleadest thy goodness before him. Be ashamed Pharisee! Dost thou think, that God hath eyes of flesh, or that he seeth as man sees? Is not the secrets of thy heart open unto him? Thinkest thou with thyself, that thou, with a few of thy defiled ways canst cover thy rotten wall, that thou hast daubed with untempered mortar, and so hide the dirt thereof from his eyes: Or that these fine, smooth, and oily words, that come

out of thy mouth, will make him forget that thy throat is an open sepulchre, and that thou *within* art full of dead men's bones and all uncleanness? Thy thus cleansing of the outside of the cup and platter, and thy garnishing of the sepulchres of the righteous, is nothing at all in God's eyes, but things that manifest, that thou art an hypocrite, and blind, because thou takest no notice of that which is *within*, which yet is that, which is most abominable to God. For the fruit, alas, what is the fruit to the tree, or what are the streams to the fountain! Thy fountain is defiled; yea, a defiler, and so *that* which maketh thy whole self, with thy works unclean in God's sight.

But Pharisee, how comes it to pass, that the poor Publican is now such a mote in thine eye, that thou canst not forbear, but must accuse him before the judgment of God: for in that thou sayest, 'that thou art not even as this Publican,' thou bringest in an accusation, a charge, a bill against him. What has he done? Has he concealed any of thy righteousness, or has he secretly informed against thee that thou art an hypocrite, and superstitious? I dare say, the poor wretch has neither meddled nor made* with thee in these matters.

But what aileth the Pharisee? Doth the poor Publican stand to vex thee? Doth he touch thee with his dirty garments; or doth he annoy thee with his stinking breath? Doth his posture of standing so like a man condemned offend thee? True, he now standeth with his hand held up at God's bar, he pleads guilty to all that is laid to his charge.

He cannot strut, vapour, and swagger as thou dost? but why offended at this? Oh but he has been a naughty man! and I have been righteous, sayest thou. Well, Pharisee, well, his naughtiness shall not be laid to thy charge, if thou hast chosen none of his ways. But since thou wilt yet bear me down, that thou art righteous, shew now, even now, while thou standest before God with the Publican, some, though they be but small, yea, though but very small fruits of thy righteousness. Let the Publican alone, since he is speaking for his life before God. Or if thou canst not let him alone, yet do not speak against him; for thy so doing will but prove, that thou rememberest the evil that the man has done unto thee; yea, and that thou bearest him a grudge for it too, and that while you stand before God.

But Pharisee, the righteous man is a merciful

* 'Meddle nor make,' to interfere with matters that do not concern us.
  'I think it no sin, to sleep in a whole skin,
  So I neither meddle nor make.'—*Old Play.*
'He that will meddle with all things, may go shoe the goslings.'
'I'll neither meddle nor make, said Bill Heaps, when he spill'd the butter milk.' *Old Proverbs.*—Ed.

man, and while he standeth praying, he forgiveth; yea, and also crieth to God that he will forgive him too. Mar. xi. 25, 26. Ac. vii. 60. Hitherto then thou hast shewed none of the fruits of thy righteousness. Pharisee, righteousness would teach thee to love this Publican, but thou showest that thou hatest him. Love covereth the multitude of sins; but hatred and unfaithfulness revealeth secrets.

Pharisee, thou shouldest have remembered this thy brother in this his day of adversity, and shouldest have shewed, that thou hadst compassion to thy brother in this his deplorable condition; but thou, like the proud, the cruel, and arrogant man, hast taken thy neighbour at the advantage, and that when he is even between the straits, and standing upon the very pinnacle of difficulty, betwixt the heavens and the hells, and hast done what thou couldest, what on thy part lay, to thrust him down to the deep, saying, 'I am not even as this Publican.'

What cruelty can be greater; what rage more furious; and what spite and hatred more damnable and implacable, than to follow, or take a man while he is asking of mercy at God's hands, and to put in a caveat* against his obtaining of it, by exclaiming against him that he is a sinner? The master of righteousness doth not so: 'Do not think,' saith he, 'that I will accuse you to the Father.' Jn. v. 45. The scholars of righteousness do not so. 'But as for me,' said David, 'when they (mine enemies) were sick, (and the Publican here was sick of the most malignant disease) my clothing *was* sackcloth, I humbled my soul with fasting; and my prayer (to wit, that I made for them) returned into mine own bosom. I behaved myself as though *he had been* my friend or brother: I bowed down heavily, as one that mourneth *for his* mother.' Ps. xxxv. 13, 14.

Pharisee, Dost thou see here how contrary thou art to righteous men? Now then, where shall we find out one to parallel thee, but by finding out of him that is called the dragon; for he it is that accuseth poor sinners before God. Zec. iii. Re. xii.

'I am not as this Publican:' Modesty should have commanded thee to have bit thy tongue as to this. What could the angels think, but that revenge was now in thine heart, and but that thou comest up into the temple, rather to boast of thyself and accuse thy neighbour, than to pray to the God of heaven: For what one petition is there in all thy prayer, that gives the least intimation, that thou hast the knowledge of God or thyself? Nay, what petition of any kind is there in thy vain-glo-

rious oration from first to last? only an accusation drawn up, and that against one helpless and forlorn; against a poor man, because he is a sinner; drawn up, I say, against him by thee, who canst not make proof of thyself that thou art righteous: But come to proofs of righteousness, and there thou art wanting also. What though thy raiment is better than his, thy skin may be full as black: Yea, what if thy skin be whiter than his, thy heart may be yet far blacker. Yea, it is so, for the truth hath spoken it; for within you are full of excess and all uncleanness. Mat. xxiii.

Pharisee, there are transgressions against the second table, and the Publican shall be guilty of them: But there are sins also against the first table, and thou thyself art guilty of them.

The Publican, in that he was an extortioner, unjust, and an adulterer, made it thereby manifest that he did not love his neighbour; and thou by making a God, a Saviour, a deliverer, of thy filthy righteousness, doth make it appear, that thou dost not love thy God; for as he that taketh, or that derogateth from his neighbour in that which is his neighbour's due, sinneth against his neighbour, so he that taketh or derogateth from God, sinneth against God.

Now then, though thou hast not, as thou dost imagine, played at that low game as to derogate from thy neighbour; yet thou hast played at that high game as to derogate from thy God; for thou hast robbed God of the glory of salvation; yea, declared, that as to that there is no trust to be put in him. 'Lo, *this is* the man *that* made not God his strength; but trusted in the abundance of his riches, *and* strengthened himself in his wickedness' or substance. Ps. lii. 7.

What else means this great bundle of thy own righteousness, which thou hast brought with thee into the temple? yea, what means else thy commending of thyself because of that, and so thy implicit prayer, that thou for that mightest find acceptance with God?

All this, what does it argue, I say, but thy diffidence of God? and that thou countest salvation safer in thine own righteousness, than in the righteousness of God; and that thy own love to, and care of thy own soul, is far greater, and so much better, than is the care and love of God. And is this to keep the first table; yea, the first branch of that table, which saith, 'Thou shalt love the Lord thy God?' For thy thus doing cannot stand with love to God.

How can that man say, I love God, who from his very heart shrinketh from trusting in him? Or, how can that man say, I would glorify God, who in his very heart refuseth to stand and fall by his mercy?

Suppose a great man should bid all the poor of

---

* The accurate knowledge of Bunyan as to the meaning of law terms is very surprising, and proves him to have been an apt scholar. A caveat is a caution not to admit a will that may injure some other party.—ED.

the parish to his house to dinner, and should more-over send by the mouth of his servant, saying, My lord hath killed his fatlings, hath furnished his table, and prepared his wine, nor is there want of anything, come to the banquet: Would it not be counted as a high affront to, great contempt of, and much distrust in the goodness of the man of the house, if some of these guests should take with them, out of their own poor store, some of their mouldy crusts, and carry them with them, lay them on their trenchers upon the table before the lord of the feast, and the rest of his guests, out of fear that he yet would not provide sufficiently for those he had bidden to his dinner that he made?

Why Pharisee, this is thy very case, Thou hast been called to a banquet, even to the banquet of God's grace, and thou hast been disposed to go; but behold, thou hast not believed, that he would of his own cost make thee a feast, when thou comest; wherefore of thy own store thou hast brought with thee, and hast laid upon thy trencher* on his table, thy mouldy and hoary crusts in the presence of the angels, and of this poor Publican; yea, and hast vauntingly said upon the whole, ' God, I thank thee, that I am not as other men are.' I am no such NEEDY man. Lu. xv. 7. ' I am no extortioner, nor unjust, no adulterer, nor even as this Publican.' I am come indeed to thy feast, for of civility I could do no less; but for thy dainties, I need them not, I have of such things enough of mine own.† Lu. xviii. 9. I thank thee therefore for thy offer of kindness, but I am not as those that have, and stand in need thereof, ' nor yet as this Publican.' And thus feeding upon thine own fare, or by making a com-position of his and thine together, thou condemnest God, thou countest him insufficient or unfaithful; that is, either one that hath not enough, or having it, will not bestow it upon the poor and needy, and therefore, of mere pretence thou goest to his banquest, but yet trustest to thine own, and to that only.

This is to break the first table; and so to make thyself a sinner of the highest form: for the sins against the first table, are sins of an higher nature than are the sins against the second. True, the sins of the second table are also sins against God, because they are sins against the commandments of God: but the sins that are against the first table, are sins not only against the command, but against the very love, strength, holiness, and faith-fulness of God. And herein stands thy condition; thou hast not, thou sayest thou hast not done injury to thy neighbour; but what of that, IF THOU HAST REPROACHED GOD THY MAKER? This is, as if a man should be *in* with his fellow-servant, and *out* with his master.

Pharisee, I will assure thee, thou art besides the saddle; ‡ thy state is not good, thy righteous-ness is so far off from doing of thee any good, that it maketh thee to be a greater sinner than if thou hadst none at all, because it fighteth more imme-diately against the mercy, the love, the grace, and goodness of God, than the sins of other sinners, as to degree, does.

And as they are more odious and abominable in the sight of God, as they needs must, if what is said be true, as it is; so they are more dangerous to the life and soul of man: for that they always appear unto him in whom they dwell, and to him that trusteth in them, not to be sins and trans-gressions, but virtues and excellent things. Not things that set a man further off, but the things, that bring a man nearer to God, than those that want them are or can be.

This therefore is the dangerous estate of those that go about to establish their own righteousness, that neither have, nor can, while they are so doing, submit themselves to the righteousness of God. Ro. x. 3. It is far more easy to persuade a poor wretch, whose life is debauched, and whose sins are written in his forehead, to submit to the righteousness of God, that is, to the righteousness that is of God's providing and giving; than it is to persuade a self-righteous man to do it. For the profane are sooner convinced, as of the necessity of righteousness to save him: so that he has none of his own to do him that pleasure, and therefore most gladly he accepteth of, and submitteth himself to the help and health and salvation that is in the righteous-ness and obedience of another man.

And upon this account it is, that Christ saith, ' The Publicans and the Harlots' enter into the kingdom of heaven before the Scribes and Phari-sees. Mat. xxi. 31. Poor Pharisee, what a loss art thou at? thou art not only a sinner, but a sinner of the highest form. Not a sinner by such sins (by such sins chiefly) as the second table doth make manifest; but a sinner chiefly in that way, as no self-righteous man did ever dream of. For

---

* In this country the introduction of earthenware plates has driven the less cleanly wooden plate, called a trencher, entirely out of use.—ED.

† Sin-sick souls alone seek the Great Physician, and are the proper subjects of Christ's healing power. Pride and unbelief bar the door of mercy and grace; and if not subdued by the blood of the cross, will ruin the soul.—*Ryland.*

‡ ' Thou art besides the saddle.'

                  ' I have no spur
To prick the sides of my intent, but only
Vaulting ambition; which o'erleaps itself,
And falls on the other. - - '   *Macbeth.*

A proud ecclesiastic requested one of his devotees to give him a leg on mounting his horse, which he did so heartily as to throw him to the other side the saddle, and broke his neck. —ED.

when the righteous man or Pharisee shall hear that he is a sinner, he replieth, 'I am not as other men are.'

And because the common and more ordinary description of sin, is the transgression against the second table, he presently replieth again, I am not as this Publican is; and so shrowdeth himself under his own lame endeavours, and ragged, partial patches of moral or civil righteousness. Wherefore when he heareth, that his righteousness is condemned, slighted, and accounted nothing worth, then he fretteth, and fumeth, and chafeth and would kill the man, that so slighteth and disdaineth his goodly righteousness; but Christ and the true gospel-teacher still goeth on, and condemneth all his righteousness to be as menstrous rags, an abomination to God, and nothing but loss and dung.

Now menstrous rags, things that are an abomination, and dung, are not fit matter to make a garment of to wear, when I come to God for life, much less to be made my friend, my advocate, my mediator and spokesman, when I stand betwixt heaven and hell, to plead for me that I might be saved. Is. lxiv. 6. Lu. xvi. 15. Phi. iii. 6—8.

Perhaps some will blame me, and count me also worthy thereof, because I do not distinguish betwixt the matter and the manner of the Pharisee's righteousness. And let them condemn me still; for, saving the holy law, which is neither the matter nor manner of the Pharisee's righteousness, but rather the rules, if he will live thereby, up to which he should completely come in every thing that he doth. And I say again, that the whole of the Pharisee's righteousness is sinful, though not with and to men, yet with and before the God of heaven. Sinful I say it is, and abominable, both in itself, and also in its effects.

[The Pharisee's whole righteousness sinful.]

First, In itself; for that it is imperfect, scanty, and short of the rule by which righteousness is enjoined, and EVEN with which every act should be: For shortness here, even every shortness in these duties, is sin, and sinful weakness; wherefore the curse taketh hold of the man for coming short, but that it could not justly do, if his coming short was not his sin: Cursed is every one that doeth not, and that continueth not to do all things written in the law. De. xxvii. 26. Ga. iii. 10.

Second, It is sinful, because it is wrought by sinful flesh; for all legal righteousness is a work of the flesh. Ro. iv. 1. Phi. iii. 3—8.

A work, I say, of the flesh; even of that flesh, who, or which also committeth the greatest enormities. For the flesh is but one, though its workings are divers: Sometimes in a way most

notoriously sensual and devilish, causing the soul to wallow in wickedness as the sow doth to wallow in the mire.

But these are not all the works of the flesh; the flesh sometimes will attempt to be righteous, and set upon doing actions, that in their perfection would be very glorious and beautiful to behold. But because the law is only commanding words, and yieldeth no help to the man that attempts to perform it; and because the flesh is weak, and cannot do of itself that which it beginneth to meddle with, therefore this most glorious work of the flesh faileth.

But, I say, as it is a work of the flesh, it cannot be good, forasmuch as the hand that worketh it, is defiled with sin: For in a good man, one spiritually good, 'that is in his flesh there dwells no good thing,' but consequently that which is bad; how then can the flesh of a carnal, graceless man, and such a one is every pharisee and self-righteous man in the world, produce, though it joineth itself to the law, to the righteous law of God, that which is good in his sight.

If any shall think that I pinch so hardly, because I call man's righteousness which is of the law, of the righteous law of God, flesh; let them consider that which follows; to wit, That though man by sin, is said to be dead in sin and trespasses, yet not so dead, but that he can act still in his own sphere. That is, to do, and choose to do, either that which by all men is counted base, or that which by some is counted good, though he is not, nor can all the world make him capable of doing anything that may please his God.

Man by nature, as dead as he is, can, and that with the will of his flesh, will his own salvation. Man by nature can, and that by the power of the flesh, pursue and follow after his own salvation; but then he wills it, and pursues or follows after it, not in God's way, but his own. Not by faith in Christ, but by the law of Moses, see Ro. ix. 16, 31; x. 3—7.

Wherefore it is no error to say, that a man naturally has Will, and a Power to pursue his will, and that as to his salvation. But it is a damnable error to say, that he hath will and power to pursue it, and that in God's way. For then we must hold that the mysteries of the gospel are natural; for that natural men, or men by nature, may apprehend and know them; yea, and know them to be the only means by which they must obtain eternal life: for the understanding must act before the will; yea, a man must approve of the way to life by Jesus Christ, before his mind will budge, or stir, or move that way: 'But the natural man receiveth not the things of the Spirit of God; (of the gospel) for they are foolishness unto him, neither can he know them, because they are spiritually discerned.' 1 Co. ii. 14.

He receiveth not these things; that is, his mind and will lie cross unto them, for he counts them foolishness; nor can all the natural wisdom in the world, cause that his will should fall in with them, because it cannot discern them.

Nature discerneth the law, and the righteousness thereof; yea, it discerneth it, and approveth thereof; that is, that the righteousness of it is the best and only way to life, and therefore the natural will and power of the flesh, as here you see in the Pharisee, do steer their course by that for eternal life. 1 Co. ii. 14.

The righteousness of the law therefore is a work of the flesh, a work of sinful flesh, and therefore must needs be as filth and dung, and abominable as to that for which this man hath produced it, and presented it in the temple before God.

Nor is the Pharisee alone entangled in this mischief; many souls are by these works of the flesh flattered, as also the Pharisee was, into an opinion, that their state is good, when there is nothing in it. The most that their conversion amounteth to, is, the Publican is become a Pharisee; the open sinner is become a self-righteous man. Of the black side of the flesh he hath had enough, now therefore with the white side of the flesh he will recreate himself. And now, most wicked must he needs be, that questioneth the goodness of the state of such a man. He, of a drunkard, a swearer, an unclean person, a sabbath-breaker, a liar, and the like, is become reformed; a lover of righteousness, a strict observer, doer, and trader in the formalities of the law, and a herder with men of his complexion. And now he is become a great exclaimer against sin and sinners, defying to acquaint with those that once were his companions, saying, 'I am not even as this Publican.'

To turn therefore from the flesh to the flesh, from sin to man's righteousness: yea, to rejoice in confidence, that thy state is better than is that of the Publican: I mean, better in the eyes of divine justice, and in the judgment of the law; and yet to be found by the law, not in the spirit, but in the flesh; not in Christ, but under the law; not in a state of salvation, but of damnation, is common among men: For they, and they only, are the right men, 'which worship God in the Spirit, and rejoice in Christ Jesus, and have no confidence in the flesh.' Where by flesh, must not be meant the horrible transgressions against the law, though they are also called the works of the flesh, Ga. v. 19. for they minister no occasion unto men, to have confidence in them towards God: but that is that, which is insinuated by Paul, where he saith, he had 'no confidence in the flesh,' though he might have had it, as he said, 'Though I might also have confidence in the flesh. If any other man,' saith he, 'thinketh that he hath whereof he might trust in the flesh, I more:' Phil. iii. 3. 4. And then he re-

peats a two-fold privilege that he had by the flesh.

First, That he was one of the seed of Abraham, and of the tribe of Benjamin, an Hebrew of the Hebrews, &c.

Secondly, That he had fallen in with the strictest men of that religion, which was such after the flesh; to wit, to be a Pharisee, and was the son of a Pharisee, had much fleshly zeal for God, and was 'touching the righteousness which is in the law blameless.' Phil. iii. 6.

But, I say still, there is nothing but flesh, flesh; fleshly privileges, and fleshly righteousness, and so consequently a fleshly confidence, and trust for heaven. This is manifest for these very things, when the man had his eyes enlightened, he counted all but loss and dung, that he might be found in Christ, not having his own righteousness which is of the law, but that which is through the faith of Christ, the righteousness which is of God by faith.

[*Godly men are afraid of their own righteousness.*]

And this leads me to another thing, and that is, to tell thee, O thou blind Pharisee that thou canst not be in a safe condition, because thou hast thy confidence in the flesh, that is, in the righteousness of the flesh. For ' all flesh *is* grass, and all the goodliness thereof *is* as the flower of the field:' and the flesh and the glory of that being as weak as the grass, which to day is, and to morrow is cast into the oven, is but a weak business for a man to venture his eternal salvation upon. Wherefore, as I also hinted before, the godly-wise have been afraid to be found in their righteousness, I mean their own personal righteousness, though that is far better, than can be the righteousness of any carnal man: for the godly man's righteousness is wrought in the spirit and faith of Christ; but the ungodly man's righteousness is of the flesh, and of the law. Yet I say, this godly man is afraid to stand by his righteousness before the tribunal of God, as is manifest in these following particulars.

First, He sees sin in his righteousness, for so the prophet intimates, when he saith, 'All our righteousnesses *are* as filthy rags: Is. lxiv. 6. but there is nothing can make one's righteousness filthy but sin. It is not the poor, the low, the mean, the sickly, the beggarly state of a man, nor yet his being hated of devils, persecuted of men, broken under necessities, reproaches, distresses, or any kind of troubles of this nature, that can make the godly man's righteousness filthy; nothing but sin can do it, and that can, doth, hath, and will do it. Nor can any man, be he who he will, and though he watches, prays, strives, denies himself, and puts his body under what chastisement or hardships he can; yea, though he also shall get his spirit and soul hoisted up to the highest peg, or pin of sanctity, and holy contemplation, and so his lusts to the greatest degree of mortification; but sin will be with him in the best of his performances. With him, I say, to pollute and defile his duties, and to make his righteousness specked and spotted, filthy and menstruous.

I will give you two or three instances for this.

1. Nehemiah was a man, in his day, one that was zealous, very zealous for God, for his house, for his people, and for his ways; and so continued, and that from first to last, as they may see that please to read the relation of his action; yet when he comes seriously to be concerned with God about his duties, he relinquisheth a standing by them. True, he mentioneth them to God, but confesseth that there is imperfections in them, and prayeth that God will not wipe them away: 'Wipe not out my good deeds, O my God, that I have done for the house of my God, and for the offices thereof.' And again, 'Remember me, O my God, concerning this,' also another good deed, 'and spare me according to the greatness of thy mercy: - Remember me, O my God, for good.' Ne. xiii.

I do not think that by these prayers he pleadeth for an acceptation of his person, as touching justification from the curse of the law, as the poor blind Pharisee doth; but that God would accept of his service, as he was a son, and not deny to give him a reward of grace for what he had done, since he was pleased to declare in his testament, that he would reward the labour of love of his saints with an exceeding weight of glory; and therefore prayeth, that God would not wipe away his good deeds, but remember him for good, according to the greatness of his mercy.

2. A second instance is that of David, where he saith, 'Enter not into judgment with thy servant:' O Lord; 'for in thy sight shall no man living be justified.' Ps. cxliii. 2. David, as I also have hinted before, is said to be a man after God's own heart, Ac. xiii. 22. and as here by the Spirit he acknowledges him for his servant; yet behold how he shrinketh, how he draweth back, how he prayeth, and petitioneth, that God would vouchsafe so much as not to enter into judgment with him. Lord, saith he, if thou enterest into judgment with me, I die, because I shall be condemned; for in thy sight I cannot be justified; to wit, by my own good deeds. Lord, at the beginning of thy dealing with me, by thy law and my works I die, therefore do not so much as enter into judgment with me, O Lord. Nor is this my case only, but it is the condition of all the world: 'For in thy sight shall NO man living be justified.'

3. A third instance is, that general conclusion of the apostle, 'But that no man is justified by the law in the sight of God, it is evident: for, The just shall live by faith.' Ga. iii. 11. By this saying of Paul, as he taketh up the sentence of the prophet Habakkuk, ii. 4. so he taketh up this sentence, yea, and the personal justice of David also. No man, saith he, is justified by the law in the sight of God; no, no just man, no holy man, not the strictest and most righteous man. But why not? why? Because the just shall live by faith.

The just man, therefore, must die, if he has not faith in another righteousness, than that which is of the law; called his own: I say, he must die, if he has none other righteousness than that which is his own by the law.* Thus also Paul confesses of himself: I, saith he, know nothing by myself, either before conversion or after; that is, I knew not, that I did anything before conversion, either against the law, or against my conscience; for I was then, touching the righteousness which is of the law, blameless. Also, since my conversion, I know nothing by myself; for 'I have lived in all good conscience before God unto this day.' Ac. xxiii. 1.

A great saying, I promise you. I doubt this is more than our glorious justitiaries can say, except they say and lie. Well, but yet, 'I am not hereby justified.' 1 Co. iv. 4. Phil. iii. 7. Nor will I dare to venture the eternal salvation of my soul upon mine own justice, 'but he that judgeth me is the Lord.' That is, though I, through my dimsightedness, cannot see the imperfections of my righteousness; yet the Lord, who is my judge, and before whose tribunal I must shortly stand, can and will; and if in his sight there shall be found no more but one spot in my righteousness, I must, if I plead my righteousness, fall for that.

Second, That the best of men are afraid to stand before God's tribunal, there to be judged by the law as to life and death, according to the sufficiency or non-sufficiency of their righteousness, is evident, because by casting away their own, in this matter, they make all the means they can for this; that is, that his mercy, by an act of grace, be made over to them, and that they in it may stand before God to be judged.

Hence David cries out so often, 'Lead me, O Lord, in thy righteousness.' Ps. v. 8. 'Deliver me in thy righteousness.' Ps. xxxi. 1. 'Judge me, O Lord my God, according to thy righteousness.' Ps. xxxv. 24. 'Quicken me in thy righteousness.' Ps. cxix. 40. 'O Lord,' says he, 'give ear to my supplications; in thy faithfulness answer me, *and* in thy righteousness. And enter not into judgment with thy servant:' *O Lord:* 'For in thy sight shall no man living be justified.' Ps. cxliii. 1, 2. And David, What if God doth thus? Why then, saith he, 'My

---

* 'For whosoever shall keep the whole law, and yet offend in one *point*, he is guilty of all.' Jam. ii. 10.

tongue shall speak of thy righteousness.' Ps. xxxv. 28. 'My tongue shall sing aloud of thy righteousness.' Ps. li. 14. 'My mouth shall shew forth thy righteousness.' Yea, 'I will make mention of thy righteousness, *even of* thine only.' Ps. lxxi. 15, 16.

Daniel also, when he comes to plead for himself and his people, he first casts away his and their righteousness, saying, 'For we do not present our supplications before thee for our righteousnesses.' And pleads God's righteousness, and that he might have a share and interest in that, saying, 'O Lord, righteousness *belongeth* unto thee,' ix. 7, 18. to wit, that righteousness, for the sake of which, mercy and forgiveness, and so heaven and happiness is extended to us.

Righteousness belongeth to thee, and is thine, as nearly as sin, shame, and confusion, is ours, and belongeth to us, which righteousness he afterwards calleth 'The Lord,' saying, do it, for the Lord's sake; read the 16, 17, verses of the 9th of Daniel. 'O Lord,' saith he, 'according to all thy righteousness, I beseech thee, let thine anger and thy fury be turned away from thy city Jerusalem, thy holy mountain: because for our sins, and for the iniquities of our fathers, Jerusalem and thy people *are become* a reproach to all *that are* about us. Now therefore, O our God, hear the prayer of thy servant, and his supplications, and cause thy face to shine upon thy sanctuary that is desolate, for the Lord's sake.' For the sake of the Lord Jesus Christ; for on him Daniel now had his eye, and through him to the Father he made his supplication; yea, and the answer was according to his prayer, to wit, that God would have mercy on Jerusalem, and that he would in his time send the Lord, the Messias, to bring them in everlasting righteousness for them.

Paul also, as I have hinted before, disclaims his own righteousness, and layeth fast hold on the righteousness of God: seeking to be found in that, or in him that has it, not having his own righteousness; for he knew that when the rain descends, the winds blow, and the floods come down falls on all men, but they that have that righteousness. Phi. iii.

Now the earnest desire of the righteous to be found in God's righteousness, ariseth from strong conviction of the imperfections of their own, and of good knowledge that was given them of the terror that will attend men at the day of the fiery trial; to wit, the day of judgment. For although men can now flatter themselves into a fool's paradise, and persuade themselves that all shall be well with them then, for the sake of their own silly and vain-glorious performances; yet when the day comes that shall burn like an oven, and when all that have done wickedly shall be as stubble, and so will all appear to be that are not found in Christ, then will their righteousness vanish like smoke, or

be like fuel for that burning flame. And hence the righteousness that the godly seek to be found in, is called the name of the Lord, a strong tower, a rock, a shield, a fortress, a buckler, a rock of defence, UNTO which they resort, and INTO which they run and are safe.

The godly wise therefore do not, as this Pharisee, bring their own righteousness into the temple, and there buoy up themselves and spirits by that into a conceit, that for the sake of that, God will be merciful and good unto them: but throwing away their *own*, they make to God for *his*, because they certainly know, even by the word of God, that in the judgment none can stand the trial, but those that are found in the righteousness of God.

Third, That the best of men are afraid to stand before God's tribunal by the law, there to be judged to life and death, according to the sufficiency or non-sufficiency of their righteousness, is evident: for they know, that it is a vain thing to seek by acts of righteousness to make themselves righteous men, as is the way of all them that seek to be justified by the deeds of the law.

And herein lieth the great difference between the Pharisee and the true Christian man. The Pharisee thinks, by acts of righteousness he shall make himself a righteous man, therefore he cometh into the presence of God well furnished, as he thinks, with his negative and positive righteousness.

Grace suffereth not a man to boast it before God, whatever he saith before men: 'His soul *which* is lifted up, is not upright in him:' Hab. ii. 4. And better is the poor in spirit, than the proud in spirit. The Pharisee was a very proud man, a proud, ignorant man, proud of his own righteousness, and ignorant of God's: for had he not, he could not, as he did, have so condemned the Publican, and justified himself.

[*The Pharisee ignorant that he must be righteous before he can do righteousness.*]

And I say again, that all this pride and vain-glorious shew of the Pharisee, did arise from his not being acquainted with this; that a man must be good, before he can do good; he must be righteous, before he can do righteousness. This is evident from Paul, who insinuateth this as the reason, why 'none do good,' even because There is none that is righteous, no, not one. 'There is none righteous,' saith he; and then follows, 'There is none that doeth good.' Ro. iii. 10—12. For it is not possible for a man, that is not first made righteous by the God of heaven, to do anything that in a proper, in a law, or in a gospel-sense may be called righteousness. Meddle with righteous things he may; attempt to make himself a righteous man, by his so meddling with them, he may; but work righteousness, and so by such works of righteousness, make himself a righteous man, he cannot.

The righteousness of a carnal man, is indeed by God called righteousness; but it must be understood, as spoken in the dialect of the world; or with reference to the world's matters. The world indeed calls it righteousness; and it will do no harm, if it bear that term with reference to worldly matters. Hence worldly civilians are called good and righteous men, and so, such as Christ, under that notion, neither died for, nor giveth his grace unto. Ro. v. 7, 8. But we are not now discoursing about any other righteousness, than that which is so accounted either in a law, or in a gospel-sense; and therefore let us a little more touch upon that.

A man then must be righteous in a law-sense, before he can do acts of righteousness, I mean that are such, in a gospel-sense. Hence first, you have true gospel-righteousness made the fruit of a second birth. 'If ye know that he (Christ) is righteous, ye know that every one that doeth righteousness is born of him.' 1 Jn. ii. 29. Not born of him by virtue of his own righteous actions, but born of him by virtue of Christ's mighty working with his word upon the soul; who afterwards, from a principle of life, acteth and worketh righteousness.

And he saith again, 'Little children, let no man deceive you, he that doeth righteousness is righteous, even as he is righteous.' 1 Jn. iii. 7. Upon this scripture, I will a little comment, for the proof of what is urged before; namely, that a man must be righteous in a law-sense, before he can do such things that may be called acts of righteousness in a gospel-sense. And for this, this scripture, ministereth to us two things to be considered by us.

The *first* is, that he that doeth righteousness is righteous.

The *second* is, that he that doeth righteousness is righteous, as Christ is righteous.

First, He that doeth righteousness; that is, righteousness which the gospel calleth so, is righteous; that is, precedent to, or before he doth that righteousness. For he doth not say, he shall make his person righteous by acts of righteousness that he *shall* do; for then an evil tree may bear good fruit: yea, and may make itself good by doing so: But he saith, he that doeth righteousness is righteous; as he saith, he that doeth righteousness is born of him.

So then, a man must be righteous before he can do righteousness, before he can do righteousness in a gospel-sense.

Second, Our second thing then is to inquire, with what righteousness a man must be righteous, before he can do that which in a gospel-sense is called righteousness?

And first, I answer, He must be righteous in a law-sense; that is, he must be righteous in the judgment of the law. This is evident, because he saith, he that doeth righteousness is righteous as he is righteous. That is, in a law-sense; for Christ in no sense is righteous in the judgment of charity only; but in his meanest acts, if it be lawful to make such comparison, he was righteous in a law-sense, or in the judgment of the law. Now the apostle saith, 'That he that doeth righteousness IS righteous, as HE is righteous.' They are the words of God, and therefore I cannot err in quoting of them, though I may not so fully, as I would, make the glory of them shine in speaking to them.

But what righteousness is that, with which a man must stand righteous in the judgment of the law, before he shall or can be found to do acts of righteousness, that by the gospel are so called? I answer

First, It is none of his own which is of the law, you may be sure; for he *hath* this righteousness before he *doeth* any that can be called his own. 'He that doeth righteousness is righteous' already, precedent to, or before he doth that righteousness; yea, he is righteous before, even as HE is righteous.

Second, It cannot be his own which is of the gospel; that is, that which floweth from a principle of grace in the soul: for he is righteous before he doeth this righteousness. He that doeth righteousness, IS righteous. He doth not say he that hath done it, but he that doeth it; respecting the act while it is in doing, he is righteous. He is righteous even then, when he is a doing of the very first act of righteousness; but an act, while it is in doing, cannot, until it is done, be called an act of righteousness; yet, saith the text, 'he is righteous.'

But again, if an act, while it is in doing, cannot be called an act of righteousness; to be sure, it cannot have such influences as to make the actor righteous; to make him righteous, as the Son of God is righteous, and yet the righteousness with which this doer is made righteous, and that before he doeth righteousness, is such; for so saith the text, *that* makes him righteous as he is righteous.

Besides, it cannot be his own, which is gospel-righteousness, flowing from a principle of grace in the soul; for that in its greatest perfection in us, while we live in this world, is accompanied with some imperfections; to wit, our faith, love, and whole course of holiness is wanting, or hath something lacking in it. They neither are apart, nor when put all together, perfect, as to the degree, the uttermost degree of perfection.

But the righteousness under consideration, with which the man, in that of John, is made righteous, is a perfect righteousness; not only with respect to the nature of it, as a penny is as perfect silver as a shilling; nor yet with respect to a comparative degree; for so a shilling arriveth more toward the perfection of the number twenty, than doth a two-penny or a three-penny piece: but it is a righteousness so perfect, that nothing can be added to it, nor can any thing be taken from it: for so implieth the words of the text, 'he is righteous, as Christ is righteous.' Yea, thus righteous before, and in order to his doing of righteousness. And in this he is like unto the Son of God, who was also righteous before he did acts of righteousness referring to a law of commandment: wherefore it is said, that as he is, so are we in this world. As he is or was righteous, before he did acts of righteousness among men by a law, so are HIS righteous, before they act righteousness among men by a law. 'He that doth righteousness is righteous, as HE is righteous.'

Christ was righteous, before he did righteousness, with a two-fold righteousness. He had a righteousness as he was God; his godhead was perfectly righteous; yea, it was righteousness itself. His human nature was perfectly righteous, it was naturally spotless and undefiled. Thus his person was righteous, and so qualified to do that righteousness, that because he was born of a woman, and made under the law, he was bound by the law to perform.

Now, as he is, so are we: not by way of natural righteousness, but by way of resemblance thereunto. Had Christ, in order to his working of righteousness, a two-fold righteousness inherent in himself, the Christian, in order to his working of righteousness, hath belonging to him a two-fold righteousness. Did Christ's two-fold righteousness qualify him for that work of righteousness, that was of God designed for him to do? Why the Christian's two-fold righteousness doth qualify him for that work of righteousness, that God hath ordained, that he should do and walk in in this world.

But you may ask, what is that righteousness, with which a Christian is made righteous before he doth righteousness?

I answer, It is a two-fold righteousness.

I. It is a righteousness put upon him.

II. It is a righteousness put into him.

I. For the first, *It is righteousness put upon him*, with which also he is clothed as with a coat or mantle, Ro. iii. 22. and this is called the robe of righteousness; and this is called the garments of salvation. Is. lxi. 10.* This righteousness is none

other but the obedience of Christ; the which he performed in the days of his flesh, and can properly be called no man's righteousness, but the righteousness of Christ; because no man had a hand therein, but he completed it himself. And hence it is said, That 'by the obedience of one shall many be made righteous.' Ro. v. 19. By the obedience of one, of one man Jesus Christ, as you have it in ver. 15. for he came down into the world to this very end; that is, to make a generation righteous, not by making of them laws, and prescribing unto them rules: for this was the work of Moses, who said, 'And it shall be our righteousness, if we observe to do all these commandments before the Lord our God, as he hath commanded us.' De. vi. 25; xxiv. 13. Nor yet by taking away by his grace the imperfections of their righteousness, and so making of that perfect by additions of his own; but he makes them righteous by his obedience; not in them, but for them, while he personally subjected himself to his Father's law on our behalf, that he might have a righteousness to bestow upon us. And hence we are said to be made righteous, while we work not; and to be justified while ungodly, Ro. iv. 5. which can be done by no other righteousness than that, which is the righteousness of Christ by performance, the righteousness of God by donation, and our righteousness by imputation. For, I say, the person that wrought this righteousness for us, is Christ Jesus; the person that giveth it to us, is the Father; who hath made Christ to be unto us righteousness, and hath given him to us for this very end, that we might be made the righteousness of God in him, 1 Co. i. 30. 2 Co. v. 21. And hence it is so often said, One shall say, surely in the Lord have I righteousness and strength. And again, 'In the Lord shall all the seed of Israel be justified, and shall glory.' 'This is the heritage of the servants of the Lord, and their righteousness *is* of me, saith the Lord.' Is. xlv. 24, 25; liv. 17.

This righteousness is that which justifieth, and which secureth the soul from the curse of the law; by hiding, through its perfection, all the sins and imperfections of the soul. Hence it follows, in that fourth of the Romans, 'Even as David also describeth the blessedness of the man, unto whom God imputeth righteousness without works, *saying*, Blessed *are* they whose iniquities are forgiven, and whose sins are covered. Blessed *is* the man to whom the Lord will not impute sin.'

And this it doth, even while the person that by grace is made a partaker, is without good works, and so ungodly. This is the righteousness of Christ, Christ's personal performances, which he did when he was in this world; that is that, by which the soul while naked, is covered, and so hid as to its nakedness, from the divine sentence of the law;

* When we had no righteousness of our own to cover us, he put on us naked beggars that rich robe, the righteousness of Christ. Though black in ourselves, we are comely in Christ's comeliness; but we never live upon his righteousness, only as we see none in ourselves.—*Ryland.*

'I spread my skirt over thee, and covered thy nakedness.' Eze. xvi. 8.

Now this obediential righteousness of Christ, consisteth of two parts. 1. In a doing of that which the law commanded us to do. 2. In a paying that price for the transgression thereof, which justice hath said, shall be required at the hand of man; and that is the cursed death. In the day that thou eatest thereof, thou shalt die the death; to wit, the death that comes by the curse of the law. So then, Christ having brought in that part of obedience for us, which consisteth in a doing of such obediential acts of righteousness which the law commands; he addeth thereto the spilling of his blood, to be the price of our redemption from that cursed death, that by sin we had brought upon our bodies and souls. And thus are the Christians made perfectly righteous; they have the whole obedience of Christ made over to them; to wit, that obedience that standeth in doing the law, and that obedience that standeth in paying of a price for our transgressions. So then, Doth the law call for righteousness? Here it is. Doth the law call for satisfaction for our sins? Here it is. And what can the law say any more to the sinner but that which is good, when he findeth in the personal obedience of Christ for him, that which answereth to what it can command, that which it can demand of us.

Herein then standeth a Christian's safety, not in a bundle of actions of his own, but in a righteousness which cometh to him by grace and gift; for this righteousness is such as comes by gift, by the gift of God. Hence it is called the gift of righteousness, the gift by grace, the gift of righteousness by grace, which is the righteousness of one, to wit, the obedience of Jesus Christ. Ro. v. 15—19.

And this is the righteousness by which, he that doth righteousness, is righteous as HE is righteous; because it is the very self-same righteousness, that the Son of God hath accomplished by himself. Nor has he any other or more excellent righteousness, of which the law taketh notice, or that it requireth, than this. For as for the righteousness of his god-head, the law is not concerned with that; for as he is such, the law is his creature, and servant, and may not meddle with him.

The righteousness also of his human nature, the law hath nothing to do with that; for that is the workmanship of God, and is as good, as pure, as holy and undefiled, as is the law itself. All then that the law hath to do with, is to exact complete obedience of him that is made under it, and a due satisfaction for the breach thereof, the which, if it hath, then Moses is content.

Now, this is the righteousness, with which the Christian, as to justification, is made righteous;

to wit, a righteousness, that is neither essential to his god-head, nor to his manhood; but such as standeth in that glorious person, who was such, his obedience to the law. Which righteousness himself had, with reference to himself, no need of at all, for his god-head; yea, his manhood was perfectly righteous without it. This righteousness therefore was there, and there only, necessary, where Christ was to be considered as God's servant and our surety, to bring to God Jacob again, and to restore the preserved of Israel. For though Christ was a Son, yet he became a servant to do, not for himself, for he had no need, but for us, the whole law, and so bring in everlasting righteousness for us.

And hence it is said, that Christ did what he did for us: He became the end of the law for righteousness for us; he suffered for us; 1 Pe. ii. 21. he died for us; 1 Th. v. 10. he laid down his life for us, 1 Jn. iii. 16. and he gave himself for us. Ga. i. 4. The righteousness then that Christ did fulfil, when he was in the world, was not for himself simply considered, nor for himself personally considered, for he had no need thereof; but it was for the elect, the members of his body.

Christ then did not fulfil the law for himself, for he had no need thereof. Christ again did fulfil the law for himself, for he had need of the righteousness thereof; he had need thereof for the covering of his body, and the several members thereof; for they, in a good sense, are himself, members of his body, of his flesh, and of his bones; and he owns them as parts of himself in many places of the holy scripture. Ep. v. 30. Ac. ix. 4, 5. Mat. xxv. 45; x. 40. Mar. ix. 37. Lu. x. 16. 1 Co. xii. 12, 27. This righteousness then, even the whole of what Christ did in answer to the law, it was for his, and God hath put it upon them, and they are righteous in it, even righteous as he is righteous. And this they have before they do acts of righteousness.

II. There is righteousness *put into them*, before they act righteous things. A righteousness, I say, put into them; or I had rather that you should call it a principle of righteousness; for it is a principle of life to righteousness. Before man's conversion, there is in him a principle of death by sin; but when he is converted to Christ, there is put into him a principle of righteousness, that he may bring forth fruit unto God. Ro. vii. 4—6.

Hence they are said to be quickened, to be made alive, to be risen from death to life, to have the Spirit of God dwelling in them; not only to make their souls alive, but to quicken their mortal bodies to that which is good. Ro. viii. 11.

Here, as I hinted before, they that do righteousness are said to be born of him, that is, antecedent to their doing of righteousness, 1 Jn. ii. 29. 'born of him,' that is, made alive with new spiritual and heavenly life. Wherefore the exhortation to them is, 'Neither yield ye your members *as* instruments of unrighteousness unto sin: but yield yourselves unto God, as those that are alive from the dead, and your members *as* instruments of righteousness unto God.' Ro. vi. 13.

Now this principle must also be in men, before they can do that which is spiritually and gospelly good: For whatever seeming good thing any man doth, before he has bestowed upon him this heavenly principle from God, it is accounted nothing, it is accounted sin and abomination in the sight of God; for an evil tree cannot bring forth good fruit: Men do not gather grapes of thorns; neither of a bramble gather they figs. Either make the tree good and his fruit good, or the tree evil and his fruit evil. Lu. vi. 43—45 It is not the fruit that makes the tree, but the tree that makes the fruit. A man must be good, before he can do good, and evil before he can do evil.

They be not righteous actions that make a righteous man; nor be they evil actions that make a wicked man: for a tree must be a sweeting tree before it yield sweetings;* and a crab tree before it bring forth crabs. †

This is that which is asserted by the Son of God himself; and it lieth so level with reason and the nature of things, that it cannot be contradicted. Mat. vii. 16—18. 'A good man out of the good treasure of his heart, bringeth forth that which is good; and an evil man out of the evil treasure of his heart, bringeth forth that which is evil.' Lu. vi. 45. But this, notwithstanding all that can be said, seemeth very strange to the carnal world; for they will not be otherwise persuaded, but that they be good deeds that make good men, and evil ones that make evil men: And so by such dotish apprehensions do what in them lieth to fortify their hearts with the mists of darkness against the clear shining of the word, and conviction of the truth.

And thus it was from the beginning: Abel did his first services to God from this principle of righteousness; but Cain would have been made righteous by his deed; but his deed not flowing from the same root of goodness, as did Abel's, notwithstanding he did it with the very best he had, is yet called evil: For he wanted, I say, the principles, to wit, of grace and faith, without which no action can be counted good in a gospel sense.

* 'Sweeting,' an obsolete term for a sweet apple.—Ed.

† This whole paragraph is omitted from all editions subsequent to 1688, when the author died. It is the practical illustration of his whole theory. By their fruit ye shall *know* them; the fruit does not *make* them what they are by nature and sin or by grace and righteousness. The rebuke of the Saviour, Mat. xv. 16, falls heavily on the man who rejected this paragraph.—Ed.

These two things then, *that* man must have that will do righteousness. He must have put upon him the perfect righteousness of Christ; and he must have dwelling in him, as a fruit of the new birth, a principle of righteousness. Then indeed he is a tree of righteousness, and God is like to be glorified in, and by him; but this the Pharisee was utterly ignorant of, and at the remotest distance from it.

[*The righteousness of Christ, unto justification, must be imputed to the Christian before he can attain the principle of righteousness unto sanctification.*]

Quest. You may ask me next, But which of these are first bestowed upon the Christian, the perfect righteousness of Christ unto justification, or this gospel principle of righteousness unto sanctification?

Answ. The perfect righteousness of Christ unto justification, must first be made over to him by an act of grace. This is evident,

1. Because, he is justified as ungodly; that is, whilst he is ungodly: But it must not be said of them, that have this principle of grace in them, that they are ungodly; for they are saints and holy. But this righteousness, by IT God justifieth the ungodly, by imputing it to them, when, and while they, as to a principle of grace, are graceless.

This is further manifested thus: The person must be accepted before the performance of the person can; 'And the Lord had respect unto Abel, and to his offering.' Ge. iv. 4. If he had respect to Abel's person first, yet he must have respect unto it for the sake of some righteousness; but Abel, in that, had no righteousness; for that he acted after that God had had respect unto his person.‡ 'And the LORD had respect unto Abel, and to his offering: But unto Cain, and to his offering, he had not respect.'

The prophet Ezekiel also shows us this; where, by the similitude of the wretched infant, and of the manner of God's receiving it to mercy, he shows how he received the Jews to favour. First, saith he, 'I spread my skirt over thee, and covered thy nakedness.' xvi. 8. There is justification; 'I covered thy nakedness.' But what manner of nakedness was it? Was it utter nakedness, nakedness in its perfection? Yes, it was then as naked as naked could be, even as naked as in the day that it was born. And as thus naked, it was covered, not with *anything*, but with the skirt of Christ; that is, with his robe of righteousness, with his obedience, that he performed by himself

‡ Abel possessed righteousness *before* his offering, which influenced him to make this acceptable sacrifice.—Ed.

for that very purpose. For by the obedience of one many are made righteous.

2. Righteousness unto justification must be first, because the first duty that a Christian performeth to God, must be accepted, not for the sake of the principle from which in the heart it flows, nor yet for the sake of the person that acts it; but for the sake of Christ, whose righteousness it is, by which, before the sinner, he stands just before God. And hence it is said, 'By faith Abel offered unto God a more excellent sacrifice than Cain.' He. xi. 4. By faith he did it; but faith hath respect to the righteousness that justifies. For we are justified by faith, not by faith as it is a grace, nor by faith as it is an acting grace; but by the righteousness of faith; that is, by that righteousness that faith embraceth, layeth hold of, and helpeth the soul to rest upon, and to trust to, for justification of life, which is the obedience of Christ. Besides, it is said, by faith he offered; faith then, faith in Christ, was precedent to his offering.

Now since faith was in being and in act before his offer, and since before his offer, he had no personal goodness of his own, faith must look out from home: I say, it must look out to another than to him in whom it resided for righteousness; and finding the righteousness of Christ to be the righteousness, which by God was designed to be performed for the justification of a sinner, it embraces it, and through it offereth to God a more excellent sacrifice than Cain.

Hence it follows, 'by which he obtained witness that he was righteous.' By which, not by his offering, but by his faith. For his offering, simply as an offering, could not have made him righteous, if he had not been righteous before; 'for an evil tree cannot bring forth good fruit.' Besides, if this be granted, why had not God respect to Cain's offering, as well as to Abel's? For, did Abel offer? so did Cain. Did Abel offer his best? so did Cain his. And if with this, we shall take notice of the order of their offering, Cain seemed to offer first, and so with the frankest will, and forwardest mind; but yet, saith the text, 'The Lord had respect to Abel and to his offering.' But why to Abel? Why, because his person was made righteous before he offered his gift: 'By which he obtained witness that he was righteous.' God testifying of his gifts, that they were good and acceptable, because they declared Abel's acceptation of the righteousness of Christ, for his justice, through the riches of the grace of God.

By faith then, Abel offered to God a more excellent sacrifice than Cain. He shrouded himself under the righteousness of Christ, and so, as out of that righteousness, he offered to God; God also looking and finding him there, where also he could not have been, as to his own apprehension, no

otherwise than by faith, he accepted of his gift; by which acceptation, for so you may understand it also, God testified that he was righteous: For God receiveth not the gifts and offerings of those that are not righteous, for their sacrifices are an abomination unto him. Pr. xxi. 27.

Abel then was righteous before; he was, I say, made righteous first, as he stood ungodly in himself; God justifieth the ungodly. Ro. iv. Now being justified, he was righteous; and being righteous, he offered his sacrifice of praise to God, or other offerings which God accepted, because he believed in his Son, as also other scriptures manifest abundantly. But this our Pharisee understandeth not.

3. Righteousness by imputation must be first, because we are made so, to wit, by another, 'By the obedience of one shall many be made righteous.' Now to be made righteous, implies a passiveness in him that is so made, and the activity of the work to lie in some body else; except he had said, they had made themselves righteous; but that it doth not, nor doth the text leave to any the least countenance so to insinuate: Nay, it plainly affirms the contrary, for it saith, by the obedience of one, of one man Jesus Christ, many are made righteous; by the righteousness of one, Ro. v. So then, if they be MADE righteous by the righteousness of one: I say, if many be made righteous by the righteousness of one, then are they that are so, as to themselves, passive and not active, with reference unto the working out of this righteousness. They have no hand in that; for that is the act of ONE, the righteousness of ONE, the obedience of ONE, the workmanship of ONE, even of Christ Jesus.

Again, if they are made righteous by this righteousness, then also they are passive, as to their first privilege by it; for they are made righteous by it; they do not make themselves righteous; no, they do not make themselves righteous by it.

Imputation is also the act of God. Even as David also describeth the blessedness of the man, unto whom God imputeth righteousness. The righteousness then is the work of Christ, his own obedience to his father's law; the making of it ours, is the act of his father, and of his infinite grace; 'But of him are ye in Christ Jesus, who of God is made unto us wisdom, and righteousness,' 'For he (God) hath made him to be sin for us, who knew no sin, that we might be made the righteousness of God in him.' And both these things God showed to our first parents, when he acted in grace towards them after the fall.

There it is said, the Lord God made unto Adam, and unto his wife, coats of skins, and clothed them. Ge. iii. 21.

Whence note,

2 I

THE PHARISEE AND THE PUBLICAN.

(1.) That Adam and his wife were naked both in God's eye, and in their own. ver. 10, 11.

(2.) That the Lord God made coats of skins.

(3.) That in his making of them, he had respect to Adam and to his wife, that is, he made them for them.

(4.) That when he had made them, he also clothed them therewith.

They made not the coats, nor did God bid them make them; but God did make them himself to cover their nakedness with. Yea, when he had made them, he did not bid them put them on, but he himself did clothe them with them: For thus runs the text; 'Unto Adam also and to his wife did the Lord God make coats of skins, and clothed them.' O! It was the Lord God that made this coat, with which a poor sinner is made righteous! And it is also the Lord God that putteth it upon us. But this our Pharisee understandeth not.

But now, if a man is not righteous before he is made so, before the Lord God has, by the righteousness of another, made him so; then whether this righteousness come first or last, the man is not righteous until it cometh, and if he be not righteous until it cometh, then what works soever are done before it comes, they are not the works of a righteous man, nor the fruits of a good tree, but of a bad. And so again, this righteousness must first come before a man be righteous, and before a man does righteousness. Make the tree good and its fruit will be good.

Now, since a man must be made righteous before he can do righteousness, it is manifest his works of righteousness do not make him righteous, no more than the fig makes its own tree a fig-tree, or than the grape doth make its own vine a vine. Hence those acts of righteousness, that Christian men do perform, are called the fruits of righteousness, which are by Jesus Christ to the glory and praise of God. Phi. i. 11.

The fruits of righteousness they are by Jesus Christ, as the fruits of the tree are by the tree itself. For the truth is, that principle of righteousness, of which mention has been made before, and concerning which I have said, it comes in, in the second place; it is also originally to be found for us no where but in Christ.

Hence it is said to be by Jesus Christ, and again, 'of his fulness have all we received, and grace for grace.' Jn. i. 16. A man must then be united to Christ first, and so being united, he partaketh of this benefit, to wit, a principle that is supernatural, spiritual, and heavenly. Now his being united to Christ, is not of, or from himself, but of, and from the Father, who, as to this work, is the husbandman; even as the twig that is grafted into the tree, officiateth not, that is, grafteth not itself thereinto, but is grafted in by some other, itself being utterly passive as to that. Now being united unto Christ, the soul is first made partaker of justification, or of justifying righteousness, and now no longer beareth the name of an ungodly man, for he is made righteous by the obedience of Christ, he being also united to Christ, partaketh of the root and fatness of Christ; the root, that is, his divine nature; the fatness, that is, that fulness of grace that is laid up in him to be communicated unto us, even as the branch that is grafted into the olive-tree, partaketh of the root and fatness of the olive-tree. Now partaking thereof, it quickeneth, it groweth, it buddeth, and yieldeth fruit to the glory and praise of God. Ro. xi. 17.

But these things, as I have often said, the poor Pharisee was ignorant of, when so swaggeringly he, with his, 'God I thank thee,' came into the temple to pray; and indeed, in that which hath here been said, is something of the mystery of God's will in his way with his elect; and such a mystery it is, that it lieth hid for ever to nature and natural men; for they think of nothing less than of this, nor of nothing more, when they think of their souls and of salvation, than that something must be done by themselves to reconcile them to God. Yea, if through some common convictions their understandings should be swayed to a consenting to that, that justification is of grace by Christ, and not of works by men; yet conscience, reason, and the law of nature, not being as yet subdued by the power and glory of grace unto the obedience of Christ, will rise up in rebellion against this doctrine, and will overrule and bow down the soul again to the law and works thereof for life.

4. Righteousness by imputation must be first, because, else faith, which is a part, yea, a great part, of that which is called a principle of grace in the soul, will have nothing to fix itself upon, nor a motive to work by. Let this therefore be considered by those that are on the contrary side.

Faith, so soon as it has being in the soul, is like the child that has being in the mother's lap, it must have something to feed upon, not something at a distance, afar off, or to be purchased, I speak now as to justification from the curse, but something by promise made over of grace to the soul; something to feed upon to support from the fears of perishing by the curse for sin. Nor can it rest content with all duties and performances, that other graces shall put the soul upon; nor with any of its own works, until it reaches and takes hold of the righteousness of Christ. Faith is like the dove, that found no rest any where in all the world until it returned to Noah into the ark. But this our Pharisee understandeth not.

Objection. Perhaps some may object, That from this way of reasoning it is apparent, that sanctification is first, since the soul may have faith, and so a principle of grace in it; and yet, as yet it cannot find Christ to feed and to refresh the soul withal.

Answ. From this way of reasoning it is not at all apparent, that sanctification, or a principle of grace is in the soul before righteousness is imputed, and the soul made perfectly righteous thereby. And for the clearing up of this let me propose a few things.

(1.) Justifying righteousness, to wit, the obedience of that one man Christ is imputed to the sinner to justify him in God's sight. For his law calls for perfect righteousness, and before that be come TO, and put UPON the poor sinner, God cannot bestow other spiritual blessings upon him; because by the law he has pronounced him accursed; by the which curse, he is also so holden, until a righteousness shall be found upon the sinner, that the law, and so divine justice can alike approve of, and be contented with. So then, as to the justification of the sinner, there must be a righteousness for God; I say, for the sinner, and for God. For the sinner to be clothed with, and for God to look upon, that he may, for the sake thereof in a way of justice, bless the sinner with forgiveness of sins: For forgiveness of sins is the next thing that followeth upon the appearance of the sinner before God in the righteousness of Christ. Ro. iv. 6, 7.

Now, upon this forgiveness, follows the second blessing. Christ hath redeemed us from the curse of the law, being made a curse for us. And so, consequently, hath obtained for us the forgiveness of sins: for he that is delivered from the curse, hath received forgiveness of sins, or rather is made partaker thereof; now being made a partaker thereof, the second blessing immediately follows: to wit, the blessing of *Abraham*, that is, 'the promise of the spirit through faith,' Ga. iii. 13, 14. but this our Pharisee understandeth not.

But now, although it be of absolute necessity that imputed righteousness be first TO the soul; that is, that perfect righteousness be found upon the sinner first by God, that he may bestow other blessings in a way of justice. Yet it is not of absolute necessity that the soul should see this first.

Let God then put righteousness, the righteousness of his Son upon me; and by virtue of that, let the second blessing of God come in to me; and by virtue of that, let me be made to see myself a sinner, and Christ's righteousness, and my need of it, in the doctrine of it, as it is revealed in the scriptures of truth. Let me then believe this doctrine to be true, and be brought by my belief to repentance for my sins, to hungering and thirsting vehemently after this righteousness; for this is

'the kingdom of God and his righteousness.' Yea, let me pray, and cry, and sigh, and groan day and night to the God of this righteousness, that he will of grace make me a partaker: And let me thus prostrate before my God, all the time that in wisdom he shall think fit. And in his own time he shall show me, that I am a justified person, a pardoned person, a person in whom the Spirit of God hath dwelt for some time, though I knew it not.

So then justification before God is one thing; and justification in mine own eyes is another: not that these are two justifications, but the same righteousness by which I stand justified before God, may be seen of God, when I am ignorant of it; yea, for the sake of it I may be received, pardoned, and accounted righteous of him, and yet I may not understand it. Yea, further, he may proceed in the way of blessing, to bless me with additional blessings, and yet I be ignorant of it.

So that the question is not, Do I find that I am righteous? But am I so? Doth God find me so, when he seeth that the righteousness of his Son is upon me, being made over to me by an act of his grace? For I am justified freely by his grace, through the redemption which is in Jesus Christ, whom God hath set forth to be a propitiation through faith in his blood, to declare his righteousness for the redemption of sins that are past, through the forbearance of God. Ro. iii. 25. But this our Pharisee understandeth not.

I am then made righteous first, by the righteousness of another; and because I am thus righteous, God accepteth of my person as such, and bestoweth upon me his grace; the which, at first, for want of skill and experience in the word of righteousness, I make use of but poorly, and have need to be certified that I am made righteous, and that I have eternal life, He. v. 13. not by faith first and immediately, but by the written word, which is called the word of faith; which word declareth unto me, to whom grace, and so faith in the seed of it is given, that I have eternal life; and that I should with boldness, in peace and joy, believe on the Son of God. Ro. xv. 13. 1 Jn. v. 13. But,

Again, I, in the first acts of my faith, when I am come at Christ, do not accept of him, because, I know I am righteous, either with imputed righteousness, or with that which is inherent: both these, as to my present privilege in them, may be hidden from mine eyes, and I only put upon taking of encouragement to close with Christ for life and righteousness, as he is set forth to be a propitiation before mine eyes, in the word of the truth of the gospel; to which word I adhere as, or because I find, I want peace with God in my soul, and because I am convinced, that the means of peace is not to be found any where but in Jesus Christ.

Now, by my thus adhering to him, I find stay for my soul, and peace to my conscience, because the word doth ascertain me, that he that believeth on him hath remission of sins, hath eternal life, and shall be saved from the wrath to come.

But alas! who knows the many streights, and as I may say, the stress of weather, I mean the cold blasts of hell, with which the poor soul is assaulted, betwixt its receiving of grace, and its sensible closing with Jesus Christ?* None, I daresay, but IT and its FELLOWS. 'The heart knoweth his own bitterness; and a stranger doth not intermeddle with his joy.' Pr. xiv. 10. No sooner doth Satan perceive that God is doing with the soul, in a way of grace and mercy, but he endeavoureth what he may, to make the renewing thereof bitter and wearisome work to the sinner. O what mists, what mountains, what clouds, what darkness, what objections, what false apprehensions of God, of Christ, of grace, of the word, and of the soul's condition, doth he now lay before it, and haunt it with; whereby he fighteth, dejecteth, casteth down, daunteth, distresseth, and almost driveth it quite into despair. Now, by the reason of these things, faith, and all the grace that is in the soul, is hard put to it to come at the promise; and by the promise to Christ, as it is said, when the tempest and great danger of shipwreck lay upon the vessel in which Paul was, They 'had much work to come by the boat.' Ac. xxvii. 16. For Satan's design is, if he cannot keep the soul from Christ, to make his coming to him, and closing with him, as hard, difficult, and troublesome, as he by his devices can. But faith, true justifying faith, is a grace, that is not weary by all that Satan can do; but meditateth upon the word, and taketh stomach, and courage, fighteth, and crieth, and by crying and fighting, by help from heaven, its way is made through all the oppositions that appear so mighty, and draweth up at last to Jesus Christ, into whose bosom it putteth the soul, where, for the time, it sweetly resteth after its marvellous tossings to and fro.†

And besides what hath been said, let me yet illustrate this truth unto you by this familiar similitude.

Suppose a man, a traitor, that by the law should

* 'Then was I most distressed with blasphemies, if I have been hearing the word, then uncleanness, blasphemies, and despair would hold me as captive.' 'I blessed the condition of the dog and toad, and counted their state far better than this state of mine.'—*Grace Abounding*, 106 and 184.

† Many are the devices of Satan to keep souls from Christ. The world and the flesh are his grand instruments of seduction, while his temptations and snares drown them in despair. Their wisdom is to resist manfully by faith in the serpent-bruiser, Jesus. He will consummate his victories by a glorious triumph over all the powers of hell and darkness.—*Ryland*.

die for his sin, is yet such an one, that the king hath exceeding kindness for; may not the king pardon this man of his clemency; yea, order that his pardon should be drawn up and sealed, and so in every sense be made sure; and yet, for the present, keep all this close enough from the ears, or the knowledge of the person therein concerned. Yea, may not the king after all leave this person, with others under the same transgression, to sue for, and obtain this pardon with great expence and difficulty, with many tears and heart-achings, with many fears, and dubious cogitations.

Why this is the case between God and the soul that he saveth; he saveth him, pardoneth him, and secur also of David in the fifty-sixth psalm is very pregnant to this purpose; 'Mine enemies,' saith he, 'would daily swallow *me* up, for *they be* many that fight against me, O thou most high.' And what then? Why, 'What time I am afraid,' saith he, 'I will trust in thee.' Thus you see, faith hath an object to work upon to carry the soul unto, and to secure the soul in, in times of difficulty, and that they are almost continually, and that object is Jesus Christ, and his righteousness. But,

Again, as faith hath an object to work upon, so it hath a motive to work by; and that is the love of God in giving of Christ to the soul for righteousness. Nor is there any profession, religion, or duty and performance, that is at all regarded, where this faith, which by such means can work, is wanting. 'For in Jesus Christ neither circumcision availeth any thing, nor uncircumcision; but faith which worketh by love.' Ga. v. 6. So he saith not here, but faith which acteth lovely, or but faith whose fruit is love, though true faith hath love for its offspring, but faith which worketh BY love; that is true saving justifying faith, as it beholdeth the righteousness of Christ, as made over to the soul for justification, so it beholdeth love, love to be the cause of its so being made over. It beholdeth love in the Father, in giving of his Son; and love in the Son, in giving of himself to be made soul-saving righteousness for me. And this *seeing*, it worketh or this apprehending, it worketh by it; that is, it is stirred up to an holy boldness of venturing all eternal concerns upon Christ, and also to an holy endeared affecting love of him for his sweet and blessed redeeming love. Hence the apostle saith, 'The love of Christ constraineth us; because we thus judge, that if one died for all, then were all dead: And *that* he died for all, that they which live should not henceforth live unto themselves, but unto him which died for them, and rose again.' 2 Co. v. 14, 15.

Thus then is the heart united in affection and love to the Father and the Son, for the love that they have shewed to the poor sinner, in their thus delivering him from the wrath to come. Nor doth this love of God cause that the faith of the poor man should work by IT to him alone, no; for by this love faith worketh, in sweet passions and pangs of love, to all that are thus reconciled, as this sinner seeth he is. The motive then, whereby faith worketh, both as to justification, and sanctification, the great motive to them, I say, is love, the love of God, and the love of Christ: 'We love him because he first loved us.' That is, when our faith hath told us so; for so are the words above, 'We have known and believed the love that God hath to us.' And then, 'We love him because he first loved us.' And then, 'This commandment have we from him, That he who loveth God, love

his brother also.' 1 Jn. iv. 16—21. But this our poor Pharisee understandeth not. But,

5. Righteousness by imputation must be first, to cut off boasting from the heart, conceit, and lips of men. Wherefore he saith as also was hinted before, That we are justified freely by the grace of God, not through, or for the sake of an holy gospel principle in us; but 'through the redemption that is in Jesus Christ,' &c. 'Where is boasting then? It is excluded. By what law? of works? Nay: but by the law of faith.' Ro. iii. 24, 27. And this is the law of faith that we are justified as afore [is shewen].

Nor can any man propound such an essential way to cut off boasting as this, which is of God's providing: for what has man here to boast of? No righteousness, nor yet of the application of it to his soul. The righteousness is Christ's, not the sinner's. The imputation is God's, not the sinner's. The cause of imputation is God's grace and love, not the sinner's works of righteousness. The time of God's imputing righteousness, is when the sinner was a sinner, wrapped up in ignorance, and wallowing in his vanity; not when he was good, or when he was seeking of it; for his inward gospel goodness is a fruit of the imputation of justifying righteousness, as has been already shewed. 'Where is boasting then?' Where is our Pharisee then, with his brags of not being as other men are? It is excluded, and he with it, and the poor Publican taken into favour, that boasting might be cut off. 'Not of works, lest any man should boast.' There is no trust to be put in men, those that seem most humble, and that to appearance, are farthest off from pride, it is natural to them to boast; yea, to boast now, now they have no cause to boast. For by grace are we saved through FAITH, and that not of ourselves, it is the gift of God. Not of works, lest any man should boast.

But if man is so prone to boast, when yet there is no ground of boasting in him, nor yet in what he doth, how would he have boasted, had he been permitted by the God of heaven to have done something, though that something had been but a very little something towards his justification. But God has prevented boasting by doing as he has done. Ep. ii. 8, 9. Nay, the apostle addeth further, lest any man should boast, that as to good works, 'we are God's workmanship, created in Christ Jesus unto good works, which God hath before ordained, that we should walk in them.' ver. 10. Can the tree boast, because it is a sweeting tree,* since it was not the tree, but God that made it such: Where is boasting then? 'But of him are ye in Christ

---

* 'A sweeting tree,' a sweet apple, and not a crab apple tree.—ED.

Jesus, who of God is made unto us wisdom, and righteousness, and sanctification, and redemption: That according as it is written, He that glorieth, let him glory in the Lord.' 1 Co. i. 30, 31. Where is boasting then ? Where is our Pharisee then, with all his works of righteousness, and with his boasts of being better than his neighbours ?

Objection. It may be said, If we should be justified for the sake of our inherent righteousness, since that righteousness is the gift of God, will it not follow that boasting is in the occasion thereof, cut off.

Ans. No, for although the principle of inherent righteousness be the gift of God, yet it bringeth forth fruits by man, and through man, and so man having a hand therein, though he should have never so little, he has an occasion offered him to boast. Yea, if a man should be justified before God by the grace, or the working of the grace of faith in him, he would have ground of occasion to boast, because faith, though it be the gift of God, yet as it acteth in man, takes man along with it in its so acting; yea, the acting of faith is as often attributed to the man by whom it is acted, and oftener, than to the grace itself. How then can it be, but that man must have a hand therein, and so a ground therein, or thereof to boast.

But now ! since justification from the curse of the law before God, lieth only and wholly in God's imputing of Christ's righteousness to a man, and that too, while the man to whom it is imputed, is in himself wicked and ungodly, there is no room left for boasting before God, for that is the boasting intended ; but rather an occasion given to shame and confusion of face, and to stop the mouth for ever, since justification comes to him in a way so far above him, so vastly without him, his skill, help, or what else soever. Eze. xvi. 61—63.

6. Righteousness by imputation must be first, that justification may not be of debt, but of mercy and grace. This is evident from reason: It is meet that God should therefore justify us by a righteousness of his own, not of his own prescribing, for that he may do, and yet the righteousness be ours; but of his own providing, that the righteousness may be his. 'Now to him that worketh, is the reward not reckoned of grace, but of debt.' Ro. iv. 4. If I work for justifying righteousness, and that way get righteousness, my justification is not of grace but of debt, God giveth it not unto me, for he oweth it unto me; so then it is no longer his but mine: Mine not of grace, but debt: And if so then, I thank him not for remission of sins, nor for the kingdom of heaven, nor for eternal life; for if justifying righteousness is of debt, then when I have it, and what dependeth thereon, I have but mine own, that which God oweth to me.

Nor will it help at all to say, but I obtain it by God's grace in me, because that doth not cut off my work, nor prevent my having of an hand in my justifying righteousness.

Suppose I give a man materials, even all materials that are necessary to the completing of such or such a thing ; yet if he worketh, though the materials be mine, I am to him a debtor, and he deserveth a reward. Thou sayest, God has given thee his Spirit, his grace, and all other things that are necessary for the working up of a complete righteousness. Well, but is thy work required to the finishing of this righteousness? If so, this is not the righteousness that justifieth, because it is such as has thy hand, thy workmanship therein, and so obtains a reward. And observe it, righteousness, justifying righteousness, consisteth not in a principle of righteousness, but in works of righteousness ; that is, in good duties, in obedience, in a walking in the law to the pleasing of the law, and the content of the justice of God.

I suppose again, that thou shalt conclude with me, that justifying righteousness, I mean that which justifies from the curse of the law, resideth only in the obedience of the Son of God ; and that the principle of grace that is in thee, is none of that righteousness, no, not then when thou hast to the utmost walked with God according to thy gift and grace: Yet if thou concludest that this principle must be in thee, and these works done by thee, before this justifying righteousness is imputed to thee for justification, thou layest in a caveat against justification by grace ; and also concludest, that though thou art not justified by thy righteousness, but by Christ, yet thou art justified by Christ's righteousness, for the sake of thine own, and so makest justification to be still a debt. But here the scripture doth also cut thee off : ' Not for thy righteousness, or for the uprightness of thine heart dost thou go to possess their land ;' which was but a type of heaven, and if our righteousness cannot give us by its excellency a share in the type, be sure, that for it, we shall never be sharers in the antitype itself. ' Understand therefore, that the Lord thy God giveth thee not this good land to possess it, for thy righteousness ; for thou *art* a stiff-necked people.' De. ix. 5, 6.

Gospel-performances therefore are not first; that was first, for the sake of which, God did receive these people into favour with himself, and that was a covenant righteousness ; and where could that covenant righteousness be found but in the prince, mediator, and high priest of the covenant? For it was HE and HE only that was appointed of God, nor could any but himself, bring in everlasting righteousness. Da. ix. 24, 25. This is evident from these texts last mentioned; it was not for their righteousness, that they possessed the land.

Again, As it was not for their righteousness,

that they were made possessors of the land, so it was not for the sake of their righteousness, that they were made partakers of such a righteousness that did make them possess the land. This is plain to reason; for then inherent or inherent and personal righteousness, when by us performed, is of worth to obtain of God a justifying righteousness. But if it be of worth to obtain a justifying righteousness, then it seems, it is more commodious to both parties than is justifying righteousness. First, it is more commodious to him that worketh it, for by it he obtaineth everlasting righteousness; and secondly, it is more commodious unto him that receiveth it, else why doth he for it give us a due debt, and so put upon us the everlasting justifying righteousness.

Perhaps it will be objected, that God doth all this of grace; but I answer, that these are but fallacious words, spake by the tongue of the crafty. For we are not now discoursing of what rewards God can give to the operations of his own grace in us, but whether he can in a way of justice, or how he will, bestow any spiritual blessings upon sinful creatures, against whom, for sin, he has pronounced the curse of the law, before he hath found them in a righteousness, that is proved to be as good justice and righteousness, as is the justice and righteousness of the law, with which we have to do.

I assert he cannot, because he cannot lie, because he cannot deny himself: For if he should first threaten the transgression of the law with death, and yet afterwards receive the transgressor to grace, without a plenary satisfaction, what is this but to lie, and to diminish his truth, righteousness, and faithfulness; yea, and also to overthrow the sanction and perfect holiness of his law. His mercy therefore must act so towards this sinner, that justice may be content, and that can never be, without a justifying righteousness.

Now what this justifying righteousness should be, and when imputed, that is the question. I say, it is the righteousness or the obedience of the Son of God in the flesh, which he assumed, and so his own, and the righteousness of no body else, otherwise than by imputation.

I say again, that this righteousness must be imputed first, that the sinner may stand just in God's sight from the curse, and that God might deal with him both in a way of justice as well as mercy, and yet do the sinner no harm.

But you may ask, How did God deal with sinners before this righteousness was actually in being?

I answer, He did then deal with sinners even as he dealeth with them now; he justifieth them by it, by virtue of the suretiship of him that was to bring it in. Christ became surety for us, and by his suretiship laid himself under an obligation to bring in, in time, for those for whom he became a surety, this everlasting and justifying righteousness, and by virtue of this those of his elect that came into and went out of the world, before he came to perform his work, were saved through the forbearance of God. Wherefore, before the Lord came, they were saved for the Lord's sake, and for the sake of his name. And they that were spiritually wise understood it, and pleaded it as their necessities required, and the Lord for HIS sake also accepted them. He. vii. 22. Ro. iv. 24. Da. ix. 17. Ps. xxv. 11.

7. Righteousness by imputation must be first: that justification may be certain; 'therefore it is of faith, (of the righteousness that faith layeth hold on) that it might be by grace; to the end the promise might be sure to all the seed.' Ro. iv. 16. That the promise, What promise? The promise of remission of sins, &c. might be sure.

Now a promise of remission of sins supposeth a righteousness, a righteousness going before; for there is no forgiveness of sins, nor promise of forgiveness, but for the sake of righteousness: but not for the sake of righteousness that shall be by us, but that IS already found in Christ as head, and so imputed to the elect for their remission. 'God for Christ's sake hath forgiven you.' Ep. iv. 32. For Christ's sake; that is, for the sake of the righteousness of Christ. Therefore imputed righteousness must be first; yea, it must be before forgiveness, and forgiveness is extended by God, then when we lie in our blood, though to us it is manifested afterwards.* Therefore it is OF faith, he saith not BY it, respecting the act of faith; but of, respecting the doctrine or word which presenteth me with this blessed imputed righteousness: 'They that are of faith, are the children of faithful Abraham.' They that are of the doctrine of faith, for all the elect are the sons of that doctrine in which is this righteousness of Christ contained; yea, they are begotten by it of God to this inheritance, to their comfortable enjoyment of the comfort of it by faith.

That 'the promise might be sure to all the seed;' to all them wrapped up in the promise, and so begotten and born. That it might be sure, implying that there is no certain way of salvation for the elect but this, because God can never by

---

* As the disobedience of the first Adam is imputed to all his natural posterity, and brings death upon all; so the righteousness of the second Adam is imputed to all his spiritual progeny, to obtain life for them. As the carnal Adam, lost original righteousness, derives a corrupt nature to all his descendants; so the spiritual Adam, by his obedience, conveys a vital efficacy of grace to us. The same Spirit of holiness which anointed our Redeemer doth quicken all his race, that as they have borne the image of the earthly, THEY may henceforth bear the image of the heavenly Adam.—*Ryland.*

other means reconcile us to himself; for his heavenly eyes perceive through and through the silly cobweb righteousness that we work; yea, they spy faults and sins in the best of our gospel performances. How then can God put any trust in such people, or how can remission be extended to us for the sake of that? Yea, our faith is faulty, and also imperfect; how then should remission be extended to us for the sake of that? But now the righteousness of Christ is perfect, perpetual and stable as the great mountains, wherefore he is called the rock of our salvation, because a man may as soon tumble the mountains before him, as one would tumble a little ball, I say, as soon as sin can make invalid the righteousness of Christ, when, and unto whom, God shall impute it for justice. Ps. xxxvi. 6. In the margin it is said, to be like the mountain of God; to wit, that is called Mount Zion, or that Moriah on which the temple was built, and upon which it stood: All other bottoms are fickle, all other righteousnesses are so feeble, short, narrow, and thin, yea, so specked and full of imperfections. 'For what the law could not do in that it was weak through the flesh,' Christ did for us in the similitude of sinful flesh. But what could not the law do? Why it could not give us righteousness, nor strengthen us to perform it. It could not give us any certain, solid, well-grounded hope of remission of sin and salvation, 'but the bringing in of a better hope did, by the which we draw nigh unto God.'

Wherefore this righteousness being imputed, justice findeth no fault therewith, but consenteth to the extending to the sinner those blessings that tend to perfect his happiness in the heavens.

8. Righteousness by imputation must be first, 'That in all *things* he (Christ) might have the pre-eminence.' Christ is head of the church, and therefore let him have the highest honour in the soul; but how can he have that, if any precede as to justification, before his perfect righteousness be imputed? If it be said, grace may be in the soul, though the soul doth not act it, until the moment that justifying righteousness shall be imputed.

I ask, What should it do there before, or to what purpose is it there, if it be not acted? And again, how came it thither, how got the soul possession of it, while it was unjustified? Or, How could God in justice give it to a person, that by the law stood condemned, before they were quitted from that condemnation? And I say, nothing can set the soul free from that curse, but the perfect obedience of Christ; nor that either, if it be not imputed for that end to the sinner by the grace of God.

Imputed, that is, reckoned, or accounted to him. And why should it not be accounted to him for righteousness? Who did Christ bring it into the world for, for the righteous or for sinners? no doubt for sinners. And how must it be reckoned to them? when in circumcision or in uncircumcision; not in circumcision, but in uncircumcision; not as righteous, but as sinners. And how are they to consider of themselves, even then when they first are apprehensive of their need of this righteousness? Are they to think, that they are righteous or sinners.

And again, How are they to believe concerning themselves, then when they put forth the first act of faith towards this righteousness for justification? Are they to think, that they are righteous or sinners? Sinners, sinners doubtless they are to reckon themselves, and as such to reckon themselves justified by this righteousness. And this is according to the sentence of God, as appeareth by such sayings.

'For when we were yet without strength, in due time Christ died for the ungodly.'

'But God commended his love toward us, in that, while we were yet sinners, Christ died for us.'

'For if when we were enemies, we were reconciled to God by the death of his Son,' &c. Ro. v. 6, 8, 10.

Out of these words I gather these three things.

1. That Christ by God's appointment died for us.

2. That by his death he reconciled us to God.

3. That even then, when the very act of reconciliation was in performing, and also when performed, we were ungodly, sinners, enemies.

Now the act by which we are said to be reconciled to God while ungodly, while sinners, and while enemies, was Christ's offering himself a sacrifice for us, which is, in the words above-mentioned, called his death. Christ died, Christ died for the ungodly, Christ died for us while sinners. Christ reconciled us to God by his death. And just as here Christ is said to die for us, so the Father is said to impute righteousness to us; to wit, as we are without works, as we are ungodly: 'Now to him that worketh not, but believeth on him that justifieth the ungodly, his faith is counted for righteousness.' Ro. iv. 5. He worketh not, but is ungodly, when this gracious act of God, in imputing of the righteousness of Christ to him, is extended, the which when he shall believe, his faith is counted to him for righteousness. And why should we not have the benefit of the righteousness, while we are ungodly, since it was completed for us while we were yet ungodly? Yea, we have the benefit of it: 'For - when we were enemies, we were reconciled to God by the death of his Son.' Ro. v. 10.

When I say, the benefit, I mean that benefit that we are capable of, and that is justification before God; for that a man may be capable of while he is in himself ungodly, because this justice comes to him by the righteousness of another. True, was it to be his own righteousness by which he was to be justified, he should not could not so be, as or while he is ungodly. But the righteousness is Christ's, and that imputed by God, not as a reward for work, or of debt, but freely by his grace, to the glory of it, and therefore may be done, and is so, while the person concerned is without works, ungodly, and a sinner.

And he that denieth that we are capable of this benefit while we are sinners and ungodly, may with like reason deny that we are created beings. For that which is done for a man without him, may be done for him, not only at any time which they that do it shall appoint, but for him while in any condition in this world. While a man is a beggar, may not I make him worth ten thousand a year, if I can and will; yea and yet he shall not know thereof in that moment that I make him so? yet the revenue of that estate shall really be his from the moment that I make him so, and he shall know it too *at the rent-day.*

This is the case, we are sinners and ungodly; there is a righteousness wrought out by Jesus Christ, the which God hath designed we shall be made righteous by; and by it, if he will impute it to us, we shall be righteous in his sight, even then when we are yet ungodly in ourselves; 'for he justifies the ungodly.'

Now though it is irregular and blame-worthy in man to justify the wicked, because he cannot for the wicked provide, and clothe him with a justifying righteousness; yet it is glorious and for ever worthy of praise for God to do it; because it is in his power not only to forgive, but to make a man righteous, even then when he is a sinner, and to justify him, as afore is proved, while he is ungodly.

Objection. But it may be yet objected, That though God has received satisfaction for sin, and so sufficient terms of reconciliation by the obedience and death of his Son, yet he imputeth it not unto us but upon condition of our becoming good.

Answ. This must not be admitted: For,

1. The scripture saith not so; but that we are reconciled to God by the death of his Son, and justified too, and that while, or when we are sinners and ungodly.

2. If this objection carrieth the truth in it, then it follows, that the Holy Ghost, faith, and so all grace, may be given to us, and we may have it dwelling in us, yea, acting in us, before we stand righteous in the judgment of the law before God; for nothing can make us stand just before God in the judgment of the law, but the obedience of the Son of God without us. And if the Holy Ghost,

faith and so consequently the habit of every grace, may be in us, acting in us, before Christ's righteousness be by God imputed to us, then we are not justified as sinners and ungodly: but as persons inherently holy and righteous before.

But I have over and over already shewed you, that this cannot be, therefore righteousness for justification must be imputed first. And here let me present the reader with two or three things.

(1.) That justification before God is one thing; and justification to the understanding and conscience is another. Now, I am treating of justification before God, not of it as to man's understanding and conscience, and I say, a man may be justified before God, even then when himself knoweth nothing thereof, Is. xl. 2. Mat. ix. 2. and so when and while he hath not faith about it, but is ungodly.

(2.) There is a justification by faith, by faith's applying of that righteousness to the understanding and conscience, which God hath afore of his grace imputed for righteousness to the soul for justification in his sight. And this is that by which we, as to sense and feeling, have peace with God: 'Being justified by faith we have peace with God through our Lord Jesus Christ.' Ro. v. 1. And these two the Apostle keepeth distinct, a little lower in this chapter: for after that he had said in the tenth verse, that while 'we were enemies we were reconciled to God by the death of his Son:' He addeth, 'And not only so, but we also joy in God through our Lord Jesus Christ, by whom we have now received the atonement.' ver. 11. Here you see that to be reconciled to God by the death of his Son, is one thing; and for us actually, for that I think he aimeth at, to receive by faith, this reconciliation, is another. That is a thing over and above, and not only so, but we have *received* the atonement.

(3.) Men do not gather their justification from God's single act of imputing of righteousness, that we might stand clear in his sight from the curse and judgment of the law; but from the word, the which they neither see nor understand, till it is brought to their understanding by the light and glory of the Holy Ghost.

We are not therefore in the ministry of the word to pronounce any man justified, from a supposition that God has imputed righteousness to him, since that act is not known to us, until the fruits that follow thereupon do break out before our eyes; to wit, the signs and effects of the Holy Ghost's indwelling in our souls. And then we may conclude it; that is, that such a one stands just before God, yet not for the sake of his inherent righteousness, nor yet for the fruits thereof, and so not for the sake of the act of faith, but for the sake of Jesus Christ his doing and suffering for us.

Nor will it avail to object, That if at first we

stand just before God by his imputing of Christ's righteousness unto us, though faith be not in us to act, we may always stand justified so; and so what need of faith? For therefore are we justified, first, by the imputation of God, as we are ungodly, that thereby we might be made capable of receiving of the Holy Ghost, and his graces in a way of righteousness and justice. Besides, God will have those that he shall justify by his grace through the redemption that is in Jesus Christ, to have the Holy Ghost, and so faith, that they may know and believe the things not only that shall be, but that already ARE, freely given to us of God. Now, says Paul, 'we have received, not the spirit of the world, but the spirit which is of God; that we might know the things that are freely given to us of God.' 1 Co. ii. 12. To know, that is, to believe. It is given to you to believe, who believe according to the working of his mighty power, 'and we have known and believed the love that God hath to us,' preceding to our believing. 1 Jn. iv. 16. He then that is justified by God's imputation, shall believe by the power of the Holy Ghost; for that must come, and work faith, and strengthen the soul to act it, because imputed righteousness has gone before. He then that believeth shall be saved; for his believing is a sign, not a cause, of his being made righteous before God by imputation: And he that believeth not shall be damned, because his non-belief is a sign that he is not righteous, and a cause that his sins abide upon him.

And thus much for the Pharisee, and for his information; and now I come to that part of the text which remains, which part in special respecteth the Publican.

[THE PUBLICAN'S PRAYER.]

AND THE PUBLICAN, STANDING AFAR OFF, WOULD NOT LIFT UP SO MUCH AS HIS EYES UNTO HEAVEN, BUT SMOTE UPON HIS BREAST, SAYING, GOD BE MERCIFUL TO ME A SINNER.

What this Publican was, I have shewed you, both with respect to his nation, office, and disposition. Wherefore I shall not here trouble the reader as to that, with a second rehearsal of these things; we now therefore come to his repentance in the whole and in the parts of it; concerning which I shall take notice of several things, some more remote, and some more near to the matter and life of it.

But first let us see how thwart and cross the Pharisee and the Publican did lie in the temple one to another, while they both were presenting of their prayers to God.

First, The Pharisee he goes in boldly, fears nothing, but trusteth in himself that his state is good, that God loves him, and that there was no doubt to be made but of his good speed in this his religious enterprize. But alas! poor Publican, he sneaks, he lears, he is hardly able to crawl into the temple, and when he comes there, stands behind, a loof off, as one not worthy to approach the divine presence.

Second, The Pharisee at his approach hath his mouth full of something, yea of many fine things, whereby he strokes himself over the head, and in effect calls himself, and that in his presence, one of God's white boys, that always kept close to his will, abode with him; or as the prodigal's brother said, 'Lo, these many years do I serve thee, neither transgressed I at any time thy commandment;' Lu. xv. 29. But alas! poor Publican, thy guilt, as to these pleas, stops thy mouth, thou hast not one good thing to say of thyself, not one rag of righteousness; thy conversation tells thee so, thy conscience tells thee so; yea, and if thou shouldest now attempt to set a good face on it, and for thy credit say something after the Pharisee in way of thine own commendations, yet here is God on the one side, the Pharisee on the other, together with thine own heart to give thee check, to rebuke thee, to condemn thee, and to lay thee even with the ground for thy insolency.

Third, The Pharisee in his approach to God, wipes his fingers of the Publican's enormities, will not come nigh him, lest he should defile him with his beastly rags: 'I am not as other men are, - or even as this Publican.' But the poor Publican, alas for him, his fingers are not clean, nor can he tell how to make them so; besides, he meekly and quietly puts up this reflection of the Pharisee upon him, and by silent behaviour, justifies the severe sentence of that self-righteous man, concluding with him, that for his part, he is wretched, and miserable, and poor, and blind, and naked, and not worthy to come nigh, or to stand by, so good, so virtuous, so holy, and so deserving a man as our spangling Pharisee is.

Fourth, The Pharisee, as at feasts and synagogues, chose the chief and first place for his person, and for his prayer, counting that the Publican was not meet, ought not to presume to let his stinking breath once come out of his polluted lips in the temple, till *he* had made his holy prayer. And poor Publican, how dost thou hear and put up this with all other affronts, counting even as the Pharisee counted of thee, that thou wast but a dog in comparison of him, and therefore not fit to go before, but to come as in chains, behind, and forbear to present thy mournful and *debrorous sup-

---

* 'Debrorous,' probably a misprint for 'dolorous,' sorrowful or dismal.

'Through many a dark and dreary vale
They passed, and many a region dolorous.'—*Milton*.

plication to the holy God, till he had presented him with his, in his own conceit, brave, gay, and fine oration.

Fifth, The Pharisee, as he is numerous in his repeating of his good deeds, so is stiff in standing to them, bearing up himself, that he hath now sufficient foundation on which to bear up his soul against all the attempts of the law, the devil, sin and hell. But alas, poor Publican! Thou standest naked; nay, worse than naked; for thou art clothed with filthy garments, thy sins cover thy face with shame: nor hast thou in, from, or of thyself, any defence from, or shelter against the attempts, assaults, and censures of thy ghostly enemies, but art now in thine own eyes, though in the temple, cast forth into the open field stark naked, to the loathing of thy person, as in the day that thou wast born, and there ready to be devoured or torn in pieces for thy transgressions against thy God.

What wilt thou do Publican! What wilt thou do! Come, let's see, which way wilt thou begin to address thyself to God; bethink thyself man, has thou any thing to say, speak out man, the Pharisee by this time has done, and received his sentence. Make an O yes;* let all the world be silent; yea, let the angels of heaven come near and listen; for the Publican is come to have to do with God! Yea, is come from the receipt of custom into the temple to pray to him.

'And the Publican, standing afar off, would not lift up so much as *his* eyes unto heaven, but smote upon his breast, saying, God be merciful to me a sinner.' And is this thy way poor Publican! O cunning sinner! O crafty Publican! thy wisdom has outdone the Pharisee, for it is better to apply ourselves to God's mercy, than to trust to ourselves that we are righteous. But that the Publican did hit the mark, yea, get nearer *unto,* and more *into* the heart of God and his Son than did the Pharisee, the sequel of the matter will make manifest.

Take notice then of this profound speech of the Publican, every word is heavier than the earth, and has more argument in it, than has ten thousand pharisaical prayers. 'God be merciful to me a sinner.' Yea, the Son of God was so delighted with this prayer, that for the sake of it, he, even as a limner, draweth out the Publican in his manner of standing, behaviour, gestures, &c. while he makes this prayer to God: Wherefore we will take notice both of the one and of the other; for surely his *gestures* put lustre unto his prayer and repentance.

FIRST, His prayer you see is this, 'God be merciful to me a sinner.'

* 'Make an O yes,' alluding to the form of proclamation at sessions of the peace—'Oyer,' the French for 'Hear,' now corrupted to 'O yes.'—ED.

SECOND, His gestures in his prayer were in general three.

First, He stood *afar off.*

Second, He would not lift up *so much as his eyes to heaven.*

Third, He *smote upon his breast,* with his fist, saying, 'God be merciful to me a sinner.'

FIRST, To begin first with his prayer. In his prayer we have two things to consider of. *First,* His confession: I am a sinner. *Second,* His imploring of help against this malady: 'God be merciful to me a sinner.'

[*His Confession.*]

First, In his confession divers things are to be taken notice of. As,

1. The fairness and simplicity of his confession: *A sinner:* I am a sinner; 'God be merciful to me a sinner.' This indeed he was, and this indeed confesses; and this, I say, he doth of godly simplicity. For, for a man to confess himself a sinner, it is to speak all against himself that can be spoken. And man, as degenerate, is too much an hypocrite, and too much a self-flatterer, thus to confess against himself, unless made simple and honest about the thing through the power of conviction upon his heart. And it is yet worth your noting, that he doth not say he was, or had been, but that at that time his state was such, to wit, a sinner. 'God be merciful to me a sinner,' or who am, and now stand before thee a sinner, or, in my sins.

Now a little to shew you what it is to be a sinner; for every one that sinneth may not in a proper sense be called a sinner. Saints, the sanctified in Christ Jesus, do often sin, but it is not proper to call them *sinners:* But here the Publican calls himself a sinner; and therefore in effect, calls himself an evil tree, one that hath neither good nature, nor that beareth good fruit: one whose body and soul is polluted, whose mind and conscience is defiled: one who hath 'walked according to the course of this world, and after the spirit that now worketh in the children of disobedience.' They having their minds at enmity with or against God, and are taken captive by the devil at his will. A sinner, one whose trade hath been in and about sin, and the works of Satan all his days.

Thus he waves all pleas, and shews of pleas, and stoops his neck immediately to the block. Though he was a base man, yet he might have had pleas; pleas, I say, as well as the Pharisee, though not so many, yet as good. He was of the stock of Abraham, a Jew, an Israelite of the Israelites, and so a privileged man in the things and religion of the Jews, else what doth he do in the temple? Yea, why did not the Pharisee, if he was a heathen, lay that to his charge while he stood before

God ? but the truth is, he could not; for the Publican was a Jew as well as the Pharisee, and consequently might, had he been so disposed, have pleaded that before God. But that he would not, he could not, for his conscience was under convictions, the awakenings of God were upon him; wherefore his privileges melt away like grease, and fly from him like the chaff of the summer threshing-floor, which the wind taketh up and scattereth as the dust ; he therefore lets all privileges fall, and pleads only that he is ' a sinner.'

2. In this confession he judges and condemns himself: For, for a man to say, ' I am a sinner,' is as much as to say, I am contrary to the holiness of God, a transgressor of his law, and consequently an object of the curse, and an heir of hell. The Publican therefore goeth very far in this his confession, but this is not all; for, for a man to confess that he is a sinner, is in the

3. Third place, to confess, that there is nothing in him, done, or can be done by him, that should allure, or prevail with God to do any thing for him. For a sinner cannot do good; no, nor work up his heart unto one good thought: no, though he should have heaven itself, if he could; or was sure to burn in hell fire for ever and ever if he could not. For sin, where it is in possession and bears rule, as it doth in every one that we may properly call a sinner, there it hath the mastery of the man, hath bound up his senses in cords and chains, and made nothing so odious to the soul as are the things that be of the Spirit of God. Wherefore it is said of such, that they are enemies in their minds ; that the carnal mind is enmity to God, and that wickedness proceedeth of the wicked; and that the Ethiopian may as well change his skin, or the leopard his spots, as they that are accustomed to do evil may learn to do well. Ep. ii. Ro. viii. 1 Sa. xxiv. 13. Je. xiii. 23.

4. In this confession, he implicitly acknowledgeth, that sin is the worst of things, forasmuch as it layeth the soul without the reach of all remedy that can be found under heaven. Nothing below, or short of the mercy of God, can deliver a poor soul from this fearful malady. This the Pharisee did not see. Doubtless he did conclude, that at some time or other he had sinned; but he never in all his life did arrive to a sight of what sin was: His knowledge of it was but false and counterfeit, as is manifest by his cure; to wit, his own righteousness. For take this for a truth undeniable, that he that thinks himself better before God, because of his reformations, never yet had the true knowledge of his sin: But the poor Publican he had it, he had it in truth, as is manifest, because it drives him to the only sovereign remedy. For indeed, the right knowledge of sin, in the guilt and filth, and damning power thereof, makes a man to

understand, that not any thing but grace and mercy by Christ, can secure him from the hellish ruins thereof.

Suppose a man sick of an apoplexy unto death, and should for his remedy make use only of those things that are good against the second ague, would not this demonstrate that this man was not sensible of the nature and danger of this disease. The same may be said of every sinner, that shall make use only of those means to justify him before God, that can hardly make him go for a good Christian before judicious men. But the poor Publican, he knew the nature of his disease, the danger of his disease; and knew also, that nothing but mercy, infinite mercy could cure him thereof.

5. This confession of the Publican, declareth that he himself was born up now, by an almighty, though invisible hand. For sin, when seen in its colours, and when appearing in its monstrous shape and hue, frighteth all mortals out of their wits, away from God; and if he stops them not, also out of the world. This is manifest by Cain, Judas, Saul, and others, who could not stand up before God under the sense and appearance of their sin, but fly before him, one to one fruit of despair, and one to another. But now this Publican, though he apprehends his sin, and that himself was one that was a sinner, yet he beareth up, cometh into the temple, approaches the presence of an holy and sin-revenging God, stands before him, and confesses that he is that ugly man, that man that sin had defiled, and that had brought himself into the danger of damnation thereby.

This therefore was a mighty act of the Publican. He went against the voice of conscience, against sense and feeling, against the curse and condemning verdict of the law; he went, as I may say, upon hot burning coals to one, that to sin and sinners is nothing but consuming fire.

Now then, did the Publican this of his own head, or from his own mind ? No verily, there was some supernatural power within that did secretly prompt him on, and strengthen him to this most noble venture. True, there is nothing more common among wicked men, than to tick and toy, and play with this saying of the Publican, ' God be merciful to me a sinner ;' not at all being sensible either what sin is, or of their need of mercy. And such sinners shall find their speed in the Publican's prayer, far otherwise than the Publican sped himself; it will happen unto them much as it happened unto the vagabond Jews, exorcists, who took upon them to call over them that had evil spirits, the name of the Lord Jesus; that were beaten by that spirit and made fly out of that house naked and wounded. Ac. xix. 13—16. Poor sinner, dead sinner, thou wilt say the Publican's prayer, and make the

Publican's confession, and say, 'God be merciful to me a sinner.' But hold, dost thou do it with the Publican's heart, sense, dread and simplicity? If not, thou dost but abuse the Publican and his prayer, and thyself, and his God; and shalt find God rejecting of thee and thy prayers, saying, The Publican I know, his prayers, and tears, and godly tears I know; but who or what art thou? And will send thee away naked and wounded. They are the hungry that he filleth with good things, but the rich and the senseless, he sendeth empty away.

For my part, I find it one of the hardest things that I can put my soul upon, even to come to God, when warmly sensible that I am a sinner, for a share in grace and mercy. Oh! methinks it seems to me as if the whole face of the heavens were set against me. Yea, the very thought of God strikes me through, I cannot bear up, I cannot stand before him, I cannot but with a thousand tears say, 'God be merciful to me a sinner.' Ezr. ix. 15.

At another time when my heart is more hard and stupid, and when his terror doth not make me afraid, then I can come before him and talk of my sins, and ask mercy at his hand, and scarce be sensible of sin or grace, or that indeed I am before God: But above all, they are the rare times, when I can go to God as the Publican, sensible of his glorious majesty, sensible of my misery, and bear up, and affectionately cry, 'God be merciful to me a sinner.'

But again, the Publican by his confession, showeth a piece of the highest wisdom that a mortal man can show; because by so doing, he engageth as well as imploreth the grace and mercy of God to save him. You see by the text he imploreth it; and now I will shew you that he engageth it, and makes himself a sharer in it.

'He that covereth his sins shall not prosper: but whoso confesseth and forsaketh *them* shall have mercy.' Pr. xxviii. 13. And again, 'If we confess our sins, he is faithful and just to forgive us *our* sins, and to cleanse us from all unrighteousness.' 1 Jn. i. 9.

[He engageth it]. In the promise of pardon, He shall find mercy; he shall have his sins forgiven. As also Solomon prays, that God will forgive them that know their own sore, and they are indeed, such as are sensible of the plague of their own heart. 2 Ch. vi. 29, 30. 1 Ki. viii. 37, 38. And the reason is, because the sinner is now driven to the farthest point; for confession is the farthest point, and the utmost bound unto which God has appointed the Publican to go, with reference to his work. As it is said of Saul to David, when he was about to give him Micah his daughter to wife, 'The king desireth not any dowry, but an hundred foreskins of the Philistines, to be avenged of the king's enemies.' 1 Sa. xviii. 25.

So says God in this matter, I desire no sacrifices, nor legal righteousness to make thee acceptable to me, only acknowledge and confess thine iniquity that thou hast transgressed against me. Je. iii. 12, 13. And though this by some may be thought to be a very easy way to come at, and partake of, the mercy of God; yet let the sensible sinner try it, and he shall find it one of the hardest things in the world. And there are two things, to which man is prone, that makes confession hard.

I. There is a great incidency in us to be partial, and not thorough and plain in our confessions. We are apt to make half confessions; to confess some, and hide some; or else to make feigned confessions, flattering both ourselves, and also God, while we make confession unto him; or else to confess sin as our own fancies apprehend, and not as the word descries them. These things we are very incident to: Men can confess little sins, while they hide great ones. Men can feign themselves sorry for sin, when they are not, or else in their confessions forget to judge of sin by the word. Hence it is said, They turned to God, not with their whole heart, but as it were feignedly. They spake not aright, saying, what have I done? They flatter him with their lips, and lie unto him with their tongues, and do their wickedness in the dark, and sin against him with a high hand, and then come to him and cover the altar with their tears. These things therefore, demonstrate the difficulty of sincere confession of sin; and that to do it as it should, is no such easy thing.

To right confession of sin, several things must, go. As,

1. There must be found conviction for sin upon the spirit: for before a man shall be convinced of the nature, aggravation, and evil of sin, how shall he make godly confession of it? Now to convince the soul of sin, the law must be set home upon the conscience by the Spirit of God; 'For by the law *is* the knowledge of sin.' Ro. iii. 20. And again, 'I had not known sin except the law had said, Thou shalt not covet.' Ro. vii. 7. This law, now, when it effectually ministereth conviction of sin to the conscience, doth it by putting of life, and strength, and terror into sin. By its working on the conscience, it makes sin revive, 'and the strength of sin *is* the law.' 1 Co. xv. 56. It also increaseth and multiplieth sin, both by the revelation of God's anger against the soul; and also by mustering up, and calling to view sins committed, and forgotten time out of mind. Sin seen in the glass of the law is a terrible thing, no man can behold it and live. 'When the commandment came, sin revived, and I died;' when it came from God to my conscience, as managed by an almighty arm, 'then it slew me.' And now is the time to confess sin, because now a

soul knows what it is, and sees what it is, both in the nature and consequence of it.

2. To right confession of sin, there must be sound knowledge of God, especially as to his justice, holiness, righteousness, and purity; wherefore the Publican here begins his confession by calling upon, or by the acknowledgment of his majesty: 'God be merciful to me a sinner.' As if he should say, God, O God, O great God, O sin-revenging God, I have sinned against thee, I have broken thy law, I have opposed thy holiness, thy justice, thy law, and thy righteous will. O consuming fire! for our God is a consuming fire, I have justly provoked thee to wrath, and to take vengeance of me for my transgressions. But, alas! how few, that make confession of sin, have right apprehension of God, unto whom confession of sin doth belong! Alas, 'tis easy for men to entertain such apprehensions of God as shall please their own humours, and as will admit them without dying, to bear up under their sense of sin, and that shall make their confession rather facile, and fantastical, than solid and heart-breaking. The sight and knowledge of the great God is to the sinful man the most dreadful thing in the world; and is that which makes confession of sin so rare and wonderful a thing. Most men confess their sins behind God's back, but few to his face; and you know there is ofttimes a vast difference in one thus doing among men.

3. To right confession of sin, there must be a deep conviction of the certainty and terribleness of the day of judgment. This John the Baptist inserts, where he insinuates, that the Pharisees' want of sense of, and the true confession of sin, was because they had not been warned, or had not taken the alarm, to flee from the wrath to come. What dread, terror, or frightful apprehension can there be put into a revelation of sin, where there is no sense of a day of judgment, and of our giving there unto God an account for it. Mat. iii. 7. Lu. iii. 7.

I say therefore, to right confession of sin there must be,

(1.) A deep conviction of the certainty of the day of judgment; namely, that such a day is coming, that such a day shall be. This the apostle insinuates, where he saith, 'God commandeth all men every where to repent; Because he hath appointed a day, in the which he will judge the world in righteousness by *that* man whom he hath ordained; *whereof* he hath given assurance unto all *men*, in that he hath raised him from the dead.' Ac. xvii. 30, 31.

This will give a sense of what the soul must expect at that day for sin, and so will drive to an hearty acknowledgment of it, and strong cries for deliverance from it. For thus will the soul argue that expecteth the judgment day, and that believes that he must count for all there. O my heart!

It is in vain now to dissemble, or to hide, or to lessen transgressions; for there is a judgment to come, a day in which God will judge 'the secrets of men by his Son,' and at that day he will bring to light 'the hidden things of darkness, and will make manifest the counsels of the heart.' If it must be so then, to what boot* will it be now to seek to dissemble, or to lessen in this matter. 1 Co. iv. 5. This also is in the Old Testament urged as an argument to cause youth, and persons of all sizes to recal themselves to sobriety, and so to confession of their sin to God; where the Holy Ghost saith ironically, 'Rejoice, O young man, in thy youth; and let thy heart cheer thee in the days of thy youth, and walk in the ways of thine heart, and in the sight of thine eyes: but know thou, that for all these *things* God will bring thee into judgment.' Ec. xi. 9. So again, 'God shall bring every work into judgment, with every secret thing, whether good, or whether evil.' Ec. xii. 14.

The certainty of this, I say, must go to the producing of a sincere confession of sin, and this is intimated by the Publican, who, with his confession, addeth a hearty crave for mercy, 'God be merciful to me a sinner.' As if he should say, if thou art not merciful to me, by thy judgment when thou comest I shall be swallowed up; without thy mercy I shall not stand, but fall by the judgment which thou hast appointed.

(2.) As there must be, for the producing of sincere confession of sin, a deep conviction of the *certainty*, so there must also be of the *terribleness* of the day of judgment. Wherefore the apostle, makes use of the first, so of this to put men upon repentance, an ingredient of which is sincere confession of sin. 'For we must all appear before the judgment seat of Christ; that every one may receive the things *done* in *his* body, according to that he hath done, whether *it be* good or bad. Knowing therefore the terror of the Lord, we persuade men.' 2 Co. v. 10, 11. The terror of the Lord, as we see here, he makes use of *that*, to persuade men to come by confession of sin, and repentance, to God for mercy.

And I am persuaded, that it will be found a truth one day that one reason that *this* day doth so swarm with wanton professors, is, because they have not begun at sound conviction for, nor gone to God at first with sincere confession of sin. And one cause of that has been, for that they did never seriously fall in with, nor yet in heart sink under, either the certainty or terribleness of the day of judgment.

O! the terrors of the Lord! the amazing face that will be put upon all things before the tribunal of God. Yea, the terror that will then be read in

---

* 'Boot,' profit or advantage.—ED.

the face of God, of Christ, of saints and angels, against the ungodly; whoso believes and understands it, cannot live without confession of sin to God, and coming to him for mercy.

Mountains, mountains fall upon us, and cover us, will then the cry of the ungodly be, and 'hide us from the face of him that sitteth upon the throne, and from the wrath of the Lamb: For the great day of his wrath is come, and who shall be able to stand?' This terror is also signified where it is said, 'And I saw a great white throne, and him that sat on it, from whose face the (very) earth and the heaven fled away, and there was found no place for them. And I saw the dead, small and great, stand before God; and the books were opened: and another book was opened, which is *the book* of life: and the dead were judged out of those things which were written in the books, according to their works. And the sea gave up the dead which were in it; and death and hell delivered up the dead which were in them: and they were judged every man according to their works. And death and hell were cast into the lake of fire. This is the second death. And whosoever was not found written in the book of life was cast into the lake of fire. Re. xx. Here is terror, and this terror is revealed afore-hand in the word of the truth of God, that sinners might hear and read and consider it, and so come and confess, and implore God's mercy.

The terror of the Lord, how will it appear, when he 'shall be revealed from heaven with his mighty angels, in flaming fire taking vengeance on them that know not God, and that obey not the gospel of our Lord Jesus Christ.' 2 Th. i. 7—9.

The terror of the Lord, how will it appear, when his wrath shall burn and flame out like an oven, or a fiery furnace before him, while the wicked stand in his sight. Mat. xiii. 50.

The terror of the Lord, how will it appear, while the angels at his commandment shall gather the wicked in bundles to burn them! 'As - the tares are gathered and burned in the fire; so shall it be in the end of this world. The Son of Man shall send forth his angels, and they shall gather out of his kingdom all things that offend, and them which do iniquity; and shall cast them into a furnace of fire: there shall be wailing and gnashing of teeth. Mat. xiii. 40—42. Who can conceive of this terror to its full with his mind? Wherefore much more unable are men to express it with tongue or pen; yet the truly penitent and sin-confessing Publican, hath apprehension so far thereof, by the word of the testimony, that it driveth him to God, with a confession of sin for an interest in God's mercy. But,

4. To right and sincere confession of sin, there must be a good conviction of a probability of mercy. This also is intimated by the Publican in his confession; 'God (saith he) be merciful to me a sinner.' He had some glimmerings of mercy, some conviction of a probability of mercy, or that he might obtain mercy for his pardon, if he went, and with unfeigned lips did confess his sins to God.*

Despair of mercy, shuts up the mouth, makes the heart hard, and drives a man away from God; as is manifest in the case of Adam and the fallen angels. But the least intimation of mercy, if the heart can but touch, feel, taste, or have the least probability of it, that will open the mouth, tend to soften the heart, and to make a very Publican come up to God into the temple and say, 'God be merciful to me a sinner.'

There must then be this holy mixture of things in the heart of a truly confessing Publican. There must be sound sense of sin, sound knowledge of God: deep conviction of the certainty and terribleness of the day of judgment, as also of the probability of obtaining mercy.

But to come to that which remains; I told you that there were two things that did make unfeigned confession hard. The first I have touched upon.

II. And now the second follows: And that is, some private, close leaning to some piece or parcel of goodness, that a man shall conceit that he hath done before, or is doing now, or that he purposeth in his deceitful heart that he will do one of these days, with which he hopes to prevail with God for the pardon of his sins. This man to be sure knows not sin in the nature and evil of it, only he has some false apprehensions about it. For where the right knowledge of sin is in the heart, that man sees so much evil in the least transgression, as that it would, even any one sin, break the backs of all the angels of heaven, should the great God but impute it to them. And he that sees this is far enough off from thinking of doing to mitigate, or assuage the rigour of the law, or to make pardonable his own transgressions thereby. But he that sees not this, cannot confess his transgressions aright; for the confession consisteth in the general, in a man's taking to himself his transgressions, and standing in them, with the acknowledgment of them to be his, and that he cannot stir from under them, nor do any thing to make amends for them, or to palliate the rigour of justice against the soul. And this the Publican did when he cried, 'God be merciful to me a sinner.'

He made his sins his own, he took them to him,

---

* The mercy of God has not only a quick eye to spy out a penitent, but a swift foot to run and embrace him. What infinite condescension! God the Father is said to 'run, fall on the neck of, and kiss' the sinner, whom he has by his Spirit inclined to sue for mercy and peace, which, being obtained, he will withhold from him no manner of thing that is good.— *Ryland.*

he stood before God in them, accounting that he was surely undone for ever if God did not extend forgiveness unto him. And this is to do as the prophet Jeremy bids; to wit, ' only to acknowledge our iniquities,' to acknowledge them and to stand in them at the terrible bar of God's justice, until mercy takes them out of the way; not shifting our shoulders or conscience of them, by doing, or promising to do, either this or that good work, only acknowledge, acknowledge only. And the reason of this kind of confession is,

1. Because this carrieth in it the true nature of confession, to confess, and to abide under the crimes confessed, without shifts and evasions, is the only real simple way of confessions. ' I said, I would confess my transgressions unto the Lord;' and what then, ' and thou forgavest the iniquity of my sin.' Ps. xxxii. 5. Mark, nothing comes in betwixt confession and forgiveness of sin, nothing of works of righteousness, nothing of legal amendments, nothing but an outcry for mercy; and that act is so far off from lessening the offence, that it greatly heighteneth and aggravates it. That is the first reason.

2. A second reason is, because God doth expect that the penitent confessors should for the time that his wisdom shall think meet, not only confess, but bear their shame upon them; yea, saith God, ' be thou confounded also and bear thy shame,' when God takes away thine iniquity, thou shalt be confounded and never open thy mouth more because of thy shame. Eze. xvi. 52, 63. We count it convenient that men, when their crimes and transgressions are to be manifested, that they be set in some open place, with a paper, wherein their transgressions are inserted, pinned upon their back or their forehead, that they may not only confess, but bear their own shame.* And at the penitential confession of sinners, God has something of this kind to do; if not before men, yet before angels, that they may behold, and be affected, and rejoice when they shall see, after the revelation of sin, the sinner taken into the favour and abundant mercy of God. Lu. xv.

3. A third reason is, For that God will in the forgiveness of sin, magnify the riches of his mercy; but this cannot be, if God shall suffer, or accept of such confession of sin, as is yet intermixed with

* The pillory, to which allusion is here made, was a cruel mode of punishment, now out of date. In earlier times, the ears were nailed to the wood, and after an hour's anguish were cut off, and the nose and cheeks slit; thus were treated Leighton and other holy men. In later days, the victims were subjected to the brutality of a mob, and sometimes excited by factious men.

> 'Tell us who 'tis upon the ridge stands there
> So full of fault, and yet so void of fear;
> And from the paper in his hat
> Let all mankind be told for what.'—*Defoe.*

those things that will darken the heinousness of the offence, and that will be darkened either by a partial, feigned, or overly confession: or by a joining with the confession any of the sinners pretended good deeds.

That God in the salvation, and so in the confession of the sinner, designs the magnifying of his mercy, is apparent enough from the whole current of scripture, and that any of the things now mentioned will, if suffered to be done, darken and eclipse this thing, is evident to reason itself.

Suppose a man stand indicted for treason, yet shall so order the matter, that it shall ring in the country, that his offences are but petty crimes; though the king shall forgive this man, much glory shall not thereby redound to the riches and greatness of his mercy. But let all things lie naked, let nothing lie hid or covered, let sin be seen, shewn, and confessed, as it is with and in the sinner himself, and then there will be in his forgiveness a magnifying of mercy.

4. A fourth reason is, for that else God cannot be justified in his sayings, nor overcome when he is judged. Ps. li. Ro. iii. God's word hath told us what sin is, both as to its nature and evil effects. God's word hath told us, that the best of our righteousnesses are no better than filthy rags. God's word has also told us, that sin is forgiven us freely by grace, and not for the sake of our amendments: and all this God will have shewn, not only in the acts of his mercy towards, but even in the humiliations and confessions of the penitent: For God will have his mercy begin to be displayed even there where the sinner hath taken his first step toward him: 'That as sin hath reigned unto death, even so might grace reign through righteousness unto eternal life by Jesus Christ our Lord.' Ro v. 21.

5. A fifth reason is, because God would have by the Publican's conversion, others affected with the displays and discoveries of wonderful grace; but to cloud and cover it with lessening of sin, and the sinful righteousness of man, is not the way to do this. Wherefore the sinner's confession must be such as is *full*, nor must anything of his to lessen sin come in betwixt confession and mercy; and this is the way to affect others [who are] as bad as publicans and sinners, and to make them come in to God for mercy.

For what will such say when sin begins to appear to the conscience, and when the law shall follow it with a voice of words, each one like a clap of thunder? I say, what will such say when they shall read that the Publican did only acknowledge his iniquity, and found grace and favour at the hand of God? But that God is infinitely merciful; merciful indeed, and that to those, or to such, as do in truth stand in need of mercy. Also that he sheweth mercy of his own good pleasure, nothing moving him thereto but the bounty of his own goodness and the misery of his creature.

I say, this is the way to make others be affected with mercy; as he saith, by the apostle Paul, 'But God, who is rich in mercy, for his great love wherewith he loved us, even when we were dead in sins, hath quickened us together with Christ, (by grace ye are saved;) and hath raised *us* up together, and made *us* sit together in heavenly *places* in Christ Jesus: That in the ages to come he might shew the exceeding riches of his grace in his kindness toward us through Christ Jesus. Ep. ii. 4—7. You may also see that 1 Ti. i. 15, 16.

6. Another reason of this is, because this is the way to heighten the comfort and consolation of the soul; and that both here and hereafter. What tendeth more to this, than for sinners to see, and with guilt and amazement to confess what sin is, and so to have pardon extended from God to the sinner as such? This fills the heart; this ravishes the soul! this puts a whole heaven of joy into every one of the thoughts of salvation from sin, and deliverance from wrath to come. 'And the ransomed of the LORD shall return, and come to Zion with songs and everlasting joy upon their heads: they shall obtain joy and gladness, and sorrow and sighing shall flee away.' Is. xxxv. 10. Indeed the belief of this makes joy and gladness endless: I say, it will make it begin here, and make that it shall never have consummation in heaven.

7. Besides, it layeth upon the soul the greatest obligations to holiness; what like the apprehension of free forgiveness, and that apprehension must come in through a sight of the greatness of sin, and of my inability to do anything towards satisfaction, to engage the heart of a rebel and traitor to love his prince, and to submit to his laws.

When Elisha had taken the Syrians captives, some were for using severities towards them; but he said, 'Set bread and water before them, that they may eat and drink, and go to their master;' and they did so. And what follows, 'So the bands of Syria came no more into the land of Israel.' He conquered their malice with his compassion. And it is the love of Christ that constraineth to live to him. 2 Ki. vi. 22, 23. 2 Co. v. 14.

Many other things might possibly be urged, but at present let these be sufficient.

[*His imploring of mercy.*]

Second. The second thing that we made mention of in the Publican's prayer was, an imploring of help against this malady; GOD BE MERCIFUL TO ME A SINNER. In which petition I shall take notice of several things.

I. That a man's help against sins, doth not so absolutely lie in his personal conquest, as in the pardon of them. I suppose a conquest, though there can indeed by man be none, so long as he liveth in this world; I mean, a complete conquest and annihilation of sin.

The Publican, and so every graciously awakened sinner, is doubtless for the subduing of sin; but yet he looketh that the chief help against it doth lie in the pardon of it. Suppose a man should stab his neighbour with his knife, and afterwards burn his knife to nothing in the fire, would this give him help against his murder? No verily, notwithstanding this, his neck is obnoxious to the halter, yea, and his soul to hell fire. But a pardon gives him absolute help: 'It is God that justifies, who shall condemn.' Ro. viii. Suppose a man should live many days in rebellion against God, and after that leave off to live any longer so rebelliously, would this help him against the guilt which he contracted before? No verily, without remission there is no help, but the rebel is undone. Wherefore the first blessedness, yea, and that without which all other things cannot make one blessed, it lies in pardon. 'Blessed *is he whose* transgression is forgiven, *whose* sin *is* covered.' Ps. xxxii. 1. 'Blessed *is* the man to whom the Lord will not impute sin.' Ro. iv. 8.

Suppose a man greatly sanctified and made holy; I say, suppose it; yet if the sins, before committed by him, be not pardoned, he cannot be a blessed man.

Yet again, Suppose a man should be caught up to heaven, not having his sins pardoned, heaven itself cannot make him a blessed man. I suppose these things, not that they can be, but to illustrate my matter. There can be no blessedness upon any man who yet remaineth unforgiven. You see therefore here, that there was much of the wisdom of the Holy Ghost in this prayer of the Publican. He was directed the right, the only, the next* way to shelter, where blessedness begins even to mercy for the pardon of his sins. Alas! What would it advantage a traitor to be taken up into the king's coach, to be clothed with the king's royal robe, to have put upon his finger the king's gold ring, and to be made to wear, for the present, a chain of gold about his neck, if after all this the king should say unto him, but I will not pardon thy rebellion; thou shalt die for thy treason? Pardon then, to him that loves life, is chiefest, is better, and more to be preferred and sought after, than all other things; yea, it is the highest point of wisdom in any sinner to seek after that first.

---

* 'Next,' nighest or nearest. This sentence is highly poetical, as much or more so as any in the writings of the most cultivated scholars.—ED.

This therefore confuteth the blindness of some, and the hypocrisy of others. Some are so silly, and so blind, as quite to forget and look over the pardon of sin, and to lay their happiness in some external amendments; when alas poor wretches, as they are, they abide still under the wrath of God. Or if they be not quite so foolish as utterly to forget the forgiveness of sin, yet they think of it, but in the second place; they are for setting of sanctification before justification, and so seek to confound the order of God; and that which is worse unto them, they by so doing, do what they can to keep themselves indeed from being sharers in that great blessing of forgiveness of sins by grace.

But the Publican here was guided by the wisdom of heaven: He comes into the temple, he confesseth himself a sinner, and forthwith, without any delay, before he removeth his foot from where he stands, craveth help of pardon; for he knew that all other things, if yet he remained as involved in guilt, would not help him against that damnation that belonged to a vile and unforgiven sinner.

This also confuteth the hypocrites, such as is our Pharisee here in the text, that glory in nothing more, or so much, as that they are 'not as other men, - - unjust, adulterers, extortioners, or even as this Publican;' for these men have missed of the beginning of good which is the forgiveness of sin; and if they have missed of the first, of the beginning good, they shall never, as so standing, receive the second, or the third: Justification, sanctification, glorification, they are the three things, but the order of God must not be perverted. Justification must be first, because that comes to man while he is ungodly and a sinner.

Justification cannot be where God has not passed a pardon. A pardon then is the first thing to be looked after by the sinner; this the Pharisee did not, therefore he went down to his house unjustified; he set the stumbling-block of his iniquity before his face when he went to enquire of the Lord; and as he neglected, slighted, scorned, because he thought that he had no need of pardon; therefore it was given to the poor, needy, and miserable Publican, and *he* went away with the blessing of it.

PUBLICANS, since this is so weighty a point, let me exhort you that you do not forget this prayer of your wise and elder brother, to wit, the Publican, that went up into the temple to pray. I say, forget it not, neither suffer any vain-glorious or self-conceited hypocrite to beat you with arguments, or to allure you with their silly and deceitful tongues, from this most wholesome doctrine. Remember that you are sinners, equal to, or as abominable as are the Publicans, wherefore do you, as you have him for your pattern, go to God, and to him confess in all simple, honest, and self-

abasing-wise your great, numerous, and abominable sins; and be sure that in the very next place you forget not to ask for pardon, saying, 'God be merciful to me a sinner.' And remember that heaven itself cannot help you against, nor keep you from, the damnation and misery that comes by sin, if 'twas possible you should go thither, if you miss of pardon and forgiveness.

II. As the Publican imploreth help, so withal he closely approveth, notwithstanding, of the sentence of the law that was gone out against him. This is manifest, for he saith to God, ' be merciful to me;' and also in that he concludes himself ' a sinner.' I say, he justifieth, he approveth of the sentence of the law, that was gone out against him, and by which he now stood condemned in his own conscience before the tribunal of God's justice. He saith not as the hypocrite, ' Because I am innocent, surely his anger shall turn from me ;' Je. ii. 35. or ' What have we spoken *so much* against thee ?' Mal. iii. 13. No, he is none of these murmurers or complainers, but fairly falls before the law, witnesses, judge and jury, and consenteth to the verdict, sentence, and testimony of each of them.

To illustrate this a little, suppose a malefactor should be arraigned before a judge, and that after the witnesses, jury, and judge, have all condemned him to death for his fact, the judge again should ask him what he can say for himself why sentence of death should not pass upon him ? Now if he saith, nothing, but good, my lord, mercy; he in sum confesseth the indictment, justifieth the witnesses, approveth of the verdict of the jury, and consenteth to the judgment of the judge.

The Publican therefore in crying mercy, justifieth the sentence of the law that was gone out against his sins: He wrangleth not with the law, saying, that was too severe, though many men do thus, saying, God forbid, for then woe be to us. He wrangleth not with the witness, which was his own conscience, though some will buffet, smite, and stop its mouth, or command it to be silent. He wrangleth not with the jury, which was the prophets and apostles, though some men cannot abide to hear all that they say. He wrangleth not with the judge, nor sheweth himself irreverently before him, but in all humble-wise, with all manner of gestures that could bespeak him acquiescing with the sentence, he flieth to mercy for relief.

Nor is this alone the way of the Publican; but of other godly men before his time: When David was condemned, he justified the sentence and the judge, out of whose mouth it proceeded, and so fled for succour to the mercy of God. Ps. li. When Shemaiah the prophet pronounced God's judgments against the princes of Judah for their sin, they said, ' The Lord is righteous.' 2 Ch. xii. 6. When the church in the Lamentations had reckoned up several of her grievous afflictions wherewith she had been chastised of her God, she, instead of complaining, doth justify the Lord, and approve of the sentence that was passed upon her, saying, ' The Lord is righteous ; for I have rebelled against his commandment.' La. i. 18. So Daniel, after he had enumerated the evils that befel the church in his day, addeth, ' Therefore hath the LORD - brought it upon us ; for the Lord our God *is* righteous in all his works which he doeth: for we obeyed not his voice.' Da. ix. 14.

I know that all these do justify the judgment of God that was gone out against them, as the Publican did the sentence wherewith he was condemned. And I say, that unless a man doth come hither, his confession and cry for mercy is not right, and so according to the scripture, reason, and nature of things as they ought to be ; for he that has any other plea, why doth he cry God, Mercy ! Surely not because he concludes that what is done, is done justly and righteously against him, but because he is overruled by spite, prejudice, tyranny, or the like.

But this is not the case with our Publican. He has transgressed a law that is holy, just, and good: the witness that accuseth him of this, is God and his conscience ; he is also cast by the verdict of holy men of God ; and all this he knows, and implicitly confesses, even in that he directs his prayer unto his judge for pardon. And it is one of the excellentest sights in the world to see, or understand a sinner thus honestly receiving the sentence of the law that is gone out against him ; to see and hear a Publican thus to justify God.* And this God will have done for these reasons.

1. That it might be conspicuous to all that the Publican has need of mercy. This is for the glory of the justice of God, because it vindicates it in its goings out against the Publican. God loveth to do things in justice and righteousness, when he goeth out against men, though it be but such a going out against them as only tendeth to their conviction and conversion. When he dealt with our father Abraham in this matter, he called him to his foot, as here he doth the Publican. And sinner, if ever God counts thee worthy to inherit the throne of glory, he will bring thee hither. But,

2. The Publican, by the power of conviction stoops to, and falleth under the righteous sentence gone forth against him, that it might be also manifest that what afterward he shall receive is of

the mere grace and sovereign goodness of God. And indeed there is no way that doth more naturally tend to make this manifest than this. For thus ; there is a man proceeded against for life, by the law, and the sentence of death is in conclusion most justly and righteously passed upon him by the judge. Suppose now that after this, this man lives, and is exalted to honour, enjoys great things, and is put into place of trust and power, and that by him that he has offended, even by him that did pass the sentence upon him. What will all say, or what will they conclude, even upon the very first hearing of this story ? Will they not say, well, whoever he was that found himself wrapped up in this strange providence, must thank the mercy of a gracious prince ; for all these things bespeak grace and favour. But,

3. As the Publican falleth willingly under the sentence, and justifieth the passing of it upon him ; so by his flying to mercy for help, he declareth to all that he cannot deliver himself: He putteth help away from himself, or saith, it is not in me.

This, I say, is another thing included in this prayer, and it is a thing distinct from that but now we have been speaking to. For it is possible for a man to justify and fall under the sentence of the judge, and yet retain that with himself that will certainly deliver him from that sentence when it has done its worst. Many have held up their hand, and cried guilty at the bar, and yet have fetched themselves off well enough for all that ; but then they have not pleaded mercy, for he that doth so, puts his life altogether into the hands of another, but privilege or good deeds either done or to be done by them. But the publican in the text puts all out of his own hand ; and in effect saith to that God before whom he went up into the temple to pray ; Lord, I stand here condemned at the bar of thy justice, and that worthily, for the sentence is good, and hath in righteousness gone out against me ; nor can I deliver myself, I heartily and freely confess I cannot ; wherefore I betake myself only to thy mercy, and do pray thee to forgive the transgressions of me a sinner. O how few be there of such kind of Publicans ! I mean of Publicans thus made sensible, that come unto God for mercy.

Mercy with most, is rather a compliment, I mean, while they plead it with God, than a matter of absolute necessity ; they have not awfully, and in judgment and conscience fallen under the sentence, nor put themselves out of all plea but the plea of mercy. Indeed, thus to do, is the effect of the proof of the vanity and emptiness of all experiments made use of before.

Now there is a two-fold proof of experiments ; the one is, the result of practice ; the other is, the result of faith.

---

* A humbling view of our sinful selves is manifested to the soul by the Word and Spirit of God. The gospel of Jesus Christ has all the properties of a great and true light ; it has a piercing power and penetrating virtue ; it enters the darkest recesses of the soul, and detects the errors of men's judgment, as well as discovers the enormities of their lives.—*Ryland.*

The woman with her bloody issue made her proof by practice, when she had spent all that she had upon physicians and was nothing bettered, but rather grew worse. Mar. v. 26. But our Publican here proves the emptiness and vanity of all other helps, by one cast of faith upon the contents of the bible, and by another look upon his present state of condemnation; wherefore he presently, without any more ado, condemneth all other helps, ways, modes, or means of deliverance, and betakes himself only to the mercy of God, saying, 'God be merciful to me a sinner.'

And herein he showeth wonderful wisdom. For,

(1.) By this, He thrusts himself under the shelter and blessing of the promise: and I am sure it is better and safer to do so, than to rely upon the best of excellences that this world can afford. Ho. xiv. 1—4.

(2.) He takes the ready way to please God; for God takes more delight in showing of mercy, than in any thing that we can do. Ho. vi. 6. Mat. ix. 13; & xii. 7. Yea and that also is the man that pleaseth him, even he that hopes in his mercy. Ps. cxlvii. 11. The Publican therefore, whatever the Pharisee might think, stood all this while upon sure ground, and had by far the start of him for heaven. Alas! his dull head could look no further than to the conceit of the pitiful beauty and splendour of his own stinking righteousness.* Nor durst he leave that to trust wholly to the mercy of God; but the Publican comes out, though in his sins, yet like an awakened, enlightened, resolved man, and first abases himself, then gives God the glory of his justice, and after that the glory of his mercy, by saying, 'God be merciful to me a sinner;' and thus in the ears of the angels he did ring the changes of heaven. Again,

(3.) The Publican, in his thus putting himself upon mercy, showeth, that in his opinion there is more virtue in mercy to save, than there is in the law and sin to condemn. And although this is not counted a great matter to do, while men are far from the law, and while their conscience is asleep within them; yet when the law comes near, and conscience is awake, who so tries it, will find it a laboursome work. Cain could not do thus for his heart, no, nor Saul; nor Judas neither. This is another kind of thing than most men think it to be, or shall find it, whenever they shall behold God's angry face, and when they shall hear the words of his law.

However our Publican did it, and ventured his body, soul, and future condition for ever in this bottom, with other the saints and servants of God, leaving of the world to swim over the sea of God's wrath if they will, in their weak and simple vessels of bull-rushes, or to lean upon their cobweb-hold, when he shall arise to the judgment that he hath appointed.

In the mean time pray God awaken us as he did the Publican; pray God enlighten us as he did the Publican; pray God grant us boldness to come to him as the Publican did; and also in that trembling spirit as he did, when he cried in the temple before him, 'God be merciful to me a sinner.'

[His Gestures.]

SECOND. Thus having in brief passed over his prayer, we come in the next place to his gestures; for in my judgment the right understanding of them will give us yet more conviction of the Publican's sense and awakening of spirit under this present action of his.

And I have observed many a poor wretch that has readily had recourse to the Publican's prayer, that never knew what the Publican's GESTURES, in the presence of God, while in prayer before him, did mean. Nor must any man be admitted to think, that those gestures of his were in custom, and a formality among the Jews in those days; for 'tis evident enough by the carriage of the Pharisee, that it was below them and their mode, when they came into the temple, or when they prayed any where else; and they in those days were counted for the best of men, and men too in religious matters they were to imitate and take their examples at the hands of the best, not at the hands of the worst.

The Publican's gestures then, were properly his own, caused by the guilt of sin, and by that dread of the majesty of God that was upon his spirit. And a comely posture it was, else Christ Jesus, the Son of God, would never have taken that particular notice thereof as he did, nor have smiled upon it so much as to take it, and distinctly repeat it as that which made his prayer the more weighty, and the more also to be taken notice of. Yea, in mine opinion, the Lord Jesus has committed it to record, for that he liked it, and for that it shall pass for some kind of touchstone of prayer, that is made in good sense of sin, and of God, and of need of his goodness and mercy. For verily, all these postures signify sense, sight of a lost condition, and a heart in good earnest for mercy.

I know that they may be counterfeited, and Christ Jesus knows who doth so too; but that will not hinder, or make weak or invalid what hath already been spoken about it. But to forbear to make a further prologue, and to come to the handling of particulars.

'And the Publican, standing afar off, would not lift up so much as his eyes unto heaven, but smote upon his breast.'

---

* This sentence is peculiarly striking, and is very illustrative of Bunyan's homely, cutting, faithful phraseology.—ED.

Three things, as I told you already, we may perceive in these words, by which his Publican posture, or gestures are set forth.

First. He stands *afar off*. *Second.* He *would not lift up so much as his eyes to heaven.* *Third.* He *smote upon his breast.*

First. For the first of these, ' He stood afar off.' ' And the Publican standing afar off.' This is, I say, the first thing, the first posture of his with which we are acquainted, and it informeth us of several things.

1. That he came not with senselessness of the majesty of God when he came to pray, as the Pharisee did, and as sinners commonly do. For this standing back, or afar off, declares that the majesty of God had an awful stroke upon his spirit: He saw whither, to whom, and for what, he was now approaching the temple. It is said in that twentieth of Exodus, That when the people saw the thunderings and the lightnings, and the noise of the trumpet, and the mountain smoking, and all these were signs of God's terrible presence, and dreadful majesty, they removed themselves, ' and stood afar off.' Ex. xx. 18. This behaviour therefore of the Publican did well become his present action, especially since, in his own eyes, he was yet an unforgiven sinner. Alas! What is God's majesty to a sinful man, but a consuming fire? And what is a sinful man in himself, or in his approach to God, but as stubble fully dry.

How then could the Publican do otherwise than what he did, than stand *afar off*, if he either thought of God or himself. Indeed the people afore-named, before they saw God in his terrible majesty, could scarce be kept off from the mount with words and bounds, as it is now the case of many: Their blindness gives them boldness; their rudeness gives them confidence; but when they shall see what the Publican saw, and felt, and understood as he, they will pray, and stand afar off, even as these people did. They removed and stood afar off, and then fell to praying of Moses that this dreadful sight and sound might be taken from them. And what if I should say, he stood afar off for fear of a blow, though he came for mercy, as it is said of them, They stood ' afar off for the fear of her torment.' Re. xviii. 10.

I know what it is to go to God for mercy, and what it is to stand all that while in my spirit through fear *afar off*, being possessed with this, will not God now smite me at once to the ground for my sins. David thought something when he said as he prayed, ' Cast me not away from thy presence, and take not thy Holy Spirit from me.' Ps. li. 11.

There is none knows, but those that have them, what turns and returns, what coming on and going off, there is in the spirit of a man that indeed is

awakened, and that stands awakened before the glorious Majesty in prayer.* The prodigal also made his prayer to his Father intentionally, while he was yet a great way off. And so did the lepers too; ' And as he entered into a certain village, there met him ten men that were lepers, which stood AFAR OFF: And they lift up *their* voices and said, Jesus, Master, have mercy on us.' Lu. xvii. 12, 13.

See here, it has been the custom of praying men to keep their distance, and not to be rudely bold in rushing into the presence of the holy and heavenly majesty; especially if they have been sensible of their own vileness and sins, as the prodigal, the lepers, and our Publican was. Yea, Peter himself, when upon a time he perceived more than commonly he did of the majesty of Jesus his Lord, what doth he do! ' When Simon Peter saw *it*,' says the text, ' he fell down at Jesus' knees, saying, Depart from me; for I am a sinful man, O Lord.' Lu. v. 8. Oh! when men see God and themselves, it fills them with holy fear, of the greatness of the majesty of God, as well as with love to, and desire after his mercy.

Besides, by his standing afar off, it might be to intimate that he now had in mind, and with great weight upon his conscience, the infinite distance that was betwixt God, and him. Men should know that, and tremble in the thoughts of it, when they are about to approach the omnipotent presence.

What is poor sorry man! poor dust and ashes, that he should crowd it up, and go jostlingly in the presence of the great God? especially since it is apparent, that besides the disproportion that is betwixt God and him, he is a filthy, leprous, polluted, nasty, stinking, sinful bit of carrion.† Esther, when she went to supplicate the king her husband for her people, made neither use of her beauty, nor relation, nor other privileges of which she might have had temptation to make use, especially at such a time, and in such exigencies, as then did compass her about: But I say, she made not use of them to thrust herself into his presence, but knew, and kept her distance, standing in the inward court of his palace, until he held out the

---

* The newly awakened soul, beholding itself in the glass of the law, is shocked at its own deformity. Sin is truly odious, and an intolerable burthen. So felt the royal penitent when he cried, ' My flesh trembleth for fear of thee; and I am afraid of thy judgments.' God's indignation at sin must be felt on this side the grave, in the conscience of the sinner, if ever he hopes to escape the dreadful punishment of it in the world to come. But blessed be God, the blood of atonement is a sovereign balsam for sick and wounded souls, and is abundantly efficacious for procuring pardon, peace, and reconciliation by the application of the eternal Spirit.—*Ryland.*

† These humbling words, being too rough for ears polite, have been omitted from all the editions of this book published since the author's death, except the 5th, 1702.—ED.

golden sceptre to her; THEN 'Esther drew near, and touched the top of the sceptre.' Es. v. 2.

Men also when they come into the presence of God, should know their distance; yea, and shew that they know it too, by such gestures and carriages, and behaviours that are seemly. A remarkable saying is that of Solomon. 'Keep thy foot when thou goest to the house of God, and be more ready to hear, than to give the sacrifice of fools: for they consider not that they do evil. (And as they should keep their foot, so also he adds) Be not rash with thy mouth, and let not thine heart be hasty to utter *any* thing before God: for God *is* in heaven, and thou upon earth: therefore let thy words be few.' Ec. v. 1, 2.

Three things the Holy Ghost exhorteth to in this text.

The one is, that we look to our *feet*, and not be forward to crowd into God's presence.

Another is, That we should also look well to our *tongues*, that they be not rash in uttering any thing before God.

And the third is, because of the infinite distance that is betwixt God and us, which is intimated by those words, 'for God is in heaven, and thou upon earth.'

The Publican therefore shewed great wisdom, holy shame, and humility, in this brave gesture of his, namely, in his standing *afar off*, when he went up into the temple to pray. But this is not all.

2. The Publican, in standing *afar off*, left room for an advocate, an high priest, a day's-man to come betwixt, to make peace between God and this poor creature. Moses, the great mediator of the Old Testament, was to go nigher to God than the rest of the elders, or of the people were. Ex. xx. 21. Yea, the rest of the people were expressly commanded to worship, standing afar off. xix. 21. No man of the sons of Aaron that hath a blemish was to come nigh. 'No man that hath a blemish of the seed of Aaron the priest, shall come nigh to offer the offerings of the Lord made by fire: He shall not come nigh to offer the bread of his God.' Le. xxi. 21.

The Publican durst not be his own mediator, he knew he had a blemish, and was infirm, and therefore he stands back; for he knew that it was none of him that his God had chosen to come near unto him, to offer the fat and the blood. Eze. xliv. 13—15. The Publican therefore was thus far right: he took not up the room himself, neither with his person, nor his performances, but stood back, and gave place to the high priest that was to be intercessor.

We read, that when Zacharias went into the temple to burn incense, as at that time his lot was, 'The whole multitude of the people were praying without.' Lu. i. 9, 10. They left him where he was,

near to God, between God and them, mediating for them; for the offering of incense by the chief priest was a figurative making of intercession for the people, and they maintained their distance.

It is a great matter in praying to God, not to go too far, nor come too short in that duty. I mean in the duty of prayer, and a man is very apt to do one or the other. The Pharisee went so far, he was too bold, he came into the temple making such a ruffle with his own excellences, there was in his thoughts no need of a Mediator. He also went up so nigh to God, that he took up the room and place of the Mediator himself; but this poor Publican, he knows his distance, and keeps it, and leaves room for the High Priest to come and intercede for him with God. He stood *afar off*, not too far off; for that is the room and place of unbelievers, and in this sense that saying is true, 'For, lo, they that are far from thee shall perish:' Ps. lxxiii. 27. That is, they whose unbelief hath set them in their hearts and affections more upon their idols, and that have been made to cast God behind their backs, to follow and go a whoring after them.

Hitherto therefore it appears, that though the Pharisee had more righteousness than the Publican, yet the Publican had more spiritual righteousness than the Pharisee: And that though the Publican had a baser, and more ugly outside than the Pharisee, yet the Publican knew how to prevail with God for mercy better than he.

As for the Publican's posture of standing in prayer, it is excusable, and that by the very father of the faithful himself: For Abraham stood praying when he made intercession for Sodom. Ge. xviii. 22, 23. Christ also alloweth it where he saith, 'And when ye STAND PRAYING, forgive, if ye have ought against any: that your Father also which is in heaven may forgive you your trespasses.' Mar. xi. 25. Indeed there is no stinted order prescribed for our thus or thus behaving of ourselves in prayer, whether kneeling, or standing, or walking or lying, or sitting; for all these postures have been used by the godly. 'Paul KNEELED down and prayed.' Ac. xx. 36. Abraham and the Publican STOOD and prayed. David prayed as he WALKED. 2 Sa. xv. 30, 31. Abraham prayed LYING upon his face. Ge. xvii. 17, 18. Moses prayed SITTING. Ex. xvii. 12. And indeed prayer, effectual fervent prayer, may be, and often is, made unto God, under all these circumstances of behaviour: for God has not tied us to any of them; and he that shall tie himself, or his people, to any one of these, doth more than he hath warrant for from God; and let such take care of innovating, it is the next way to make men hypocrites and dissemblers in those duties, in which they should be sincere.

True, which of those soever a man shall chose to himself for the present, to perform this solemn duty in, it is required of him, and God expects it, that he should pray to him in truth, and with desire, affection, and hunger, after those things, that with his tongue he maketh mention of before the throne of God. And indeed without this, all is nothing. But alas! how few be there in the world whose heart and mouth in prayer shall go together? Dost thou, when thou askest for the spirit, or faith, or love to God, to holiness, to saints, to the word, and the like, ask for them with love to them, desire of them, hungering after them? Oh! this is a mighty thing! and yet prayer is no more before God, than as it is seasoned with these blessed qualifications. Wherefore it is said, that while men are praying, God is searching of the heart, to see what is the meaning of the spirit, or whether there be the spirit and his meaning in all that the mouth hath uttered, either by words, sighs, or groans; because it is by him, and through his help only that any make prayers according to the will of God. Ro. viii. 26, 27. Whatever thy posture therefore shall be, see that thy prayers be pertinent and fervent, not mocking of thine own soul with words, while thou wantest and art an utter stranger to the very vital and living spirit of prayer.

Now our Publican had, and did exercise, the very spirit of prayer in prayer. He prayed sensibly, seriously, affectionately hungering, thirsting, and with longing after that, for which with his mouth he implored the God of heaven: His heart and soul were in his words, and it was that which made his PRAYER; even because he prayed in PRAYER; he prayed inwardly, as well as outwardly.

David tells us, that God heard the VOICE of his supplication, the voice of his cry, the voice of his tears, and the voice of his roaring. For indeed there are all these without this acceptable sound in them, nor can any thing but sense, and affection, and fervent desire, make them sound well in the ears of God. Tears, supplications, prayers, cries, may be all of them done in formality, hypocrisy, and from other causes, and to other ends than that which is honest and right in God's sight: For God as he had experience of, would search and look after the VOICE of his tears, supplications, roarings, prayers, and cries.

And if men had less care to please men, and more to please God, in the matter and manner of praying, the world would be at a better pass than it is. But this is not in man's power to help, and to amend: When the Holy Ghost comes upon men with greater conviction of their state and condition, and of the use and excellency of the grace of sincerity and humility in prayer, then, and not till then, will the grace of prayer be more prized, and the spacious flouting, complimentary lips of flatterers be more laid aside. I have said it already, and I will say it again, that there is now-a-days a

great deal of wickedness committed in the very duty of prayer; by words, of which men have no sense,* by reaching after such conclusions and clenches therein, as may make their persons to be admired; by studying for, and labouring after such enlargements as the spirit accompanieth not the heart in. O Lord God, O Lord God, make our hearts upright in us, as in all points and parts of our profession, so in this solemn appointment of God, 'If I regard iniquity in my heart,' said David, 'the Lord will not hear me.' But if I be truly sincere he will, and then it is no matter whether I kneel, or stand, or sit, or lie, or walk; for I shall do none of these, nor put up my prayers under any of these circumstances, lightly, foolishly, and idly, but to beautify this gesture with the inward working of my mind and spirit in prayer; that whether I stand or sit, walk or lie down, glory and gravity, humility and sincerity shall make my prayer profitable, and my outward behaviour comely in his eyes, with whom in prayer I now have to do.

And had not our Publican been inwardly seasoned with these, Christ would have taken but little pleasure in his modes and outward behaviour: but being so honest inwardly, and in the matter of his prayer, his gestures by that were made beauteous also; and therefore it is that our Lord so delightfully dilateth upon them, and draweth them out at length before the eyes of others.

I have often observed, that that which is natural, and so comely in one, looks odiously when imitated by another, I speak as to gestures and actions in preaching and prayer. Many, I doubt not, but will imitate the Publican, and that both in the prayer and gestures of the Publican, whose persons and actions will yet stink full foully in the nostrils of him that is holy and just, and that searcheth the heart and the reins.

Well, the Publican STOOD and prayed, he stood *afar off*, and prayed, and his prayers came even to the ears and heart of God.

'AND THE PUBLICAN STANDING AFAR OFF, WOULD NOT LIFT UP SO MUCH AS HIS EYES UNTO HEAVEN.'

Second, We are now come to another of his postures. 'He would not, (says the text) so much as lift up his eyes to heaven.' Here therefore was another gesture added to that which went be-

* A simple-hearted man, at a prayer meeting, used the words, 'Incline our hearts to cast our bread upon the waters, that we may find it after many days.' Upon leaving the prayer meeting, while crossing a bridge, a youth said to him, 'If you were to throw a loaf into the river, what good would it be even if you did find it after many days;' to which his elder replied, 'Oh, it is a scripture expression, though I do not know its meaning!!!' This happened to the editor forty-five years ago, before Sunday schools and the Tract Society had spread their flood of scriptural knowledge over the kingdom.—ED.

fore; and a gesture that a great while before had been condemned by the Holy Ghost himself. 'Is it such a fast that I have chosen? A day for a man to afflict his soul? *Is it* to bow down his head as a bulrush.' Is. lviii. 5.

But why condemned then, and smiled upon now? Why! Because done in hypocrisy then, and in sincerity now. Hypocrisy and a spirit of error will so besmut God's ordinances, that he shall take no pleasure in them: but sincerity, and honesty in duties, will make even those circumstances that in themselves are indifferent, at least comely in the sight of men. May I not say before God? the Rechabites were not commanded of God, but of their father, to do as they did; but, because they were sincere in their obedience thereto, even God himself maketh use of what they did to condemn the disobedience of the Jews; and moreover doth tell the Rechabites, at last, that they should not want a man to stand before him for ever. 'And Jeremiah said unto the house of the Rechabites, Thus saith the LORD of Hosts, the God of Israel; Because ye have obeyed the commandment of Jonadab your father, and kept all his precepts, and done according unto all that he hath commanded you; therefore, thus saith the LORD of Hosts, the God of Israel; Jonadab the son of Rechab shall not want a man to stand before me for ever.' Je. xxxv. 18, 19.

'He would not lift up his eyes to heaven.' Why? Surely because shame had covered his face. Shame will make a man blush and hang his head like a bulrush. Shame for sin is a virtue, a comely thing; yea, a beauty-spot in the face of a sinner that cometh to God for mercy.

God complains of the house of Israel, that they could sin, and that without shame; yea, and threateneth them too with sore and repeated judgments, 'because they were not ashamed,' it is in Je. viii. 12. Their crimes in general were, they turned every one to his course, as the horse runneth into the battle. In particular, they were such as rejected God's word, they loved this world, and set themselves against the prophet's crying peace, peace, peace, when they cried judgment, judgment: 'Were they ashamed when they had committed abomination; nay, they were not at all ashamed, neither could they blush: therefore shall they fall among them that fall: in the time of their visitation they shall be cast down, saith the Lord.' Oh! to stand, or sit, or lie, or kneel, or walk before God in prayer, with blushing cheeks for sin, is one of the excellentest sights- that can be seen in the world. Wherefore the church taketh some kind of heart to herself in that she could lie down in her shame; yea, and makes that a kind of an argument with God, to prove that her prayers did come from her heart, and also that he would hear them. Je iii. 25.

Shame for sin argueth sense of sin, yea, a right sense of sin, a godly sense of sin; Ephraim pleads this when under the hand of God: 'I was,' saith he, 'ashamed, yea, even confounded, because I did bear the reproach of my youth.' But what follows? '*Is* Ephraim my dear son? *is he* a pleasant child? for since I spake against him, I do earnestly remember him still: therefore my bowels are troubled for him: I will surely have mercy upon him, saith the Lord.' Je. xxxi. 19, 20.

I know that there is a shame that is not the spirit of an honest heart; but that rather floweth from sudden surprisal, when the sinner is unawares taken in the act, in the very manner. And thus sometimes the house of Israel was taken, and then when they blushed, their shame is compared to the shame of a thief. 'As the thief is ashamed when he is found, so is the house of Israel ashamed; they, their kings, their princes and their priests, and their prophets.

But where were they taken, or about what were they found? Why they were found 'saying to a stock, Thou art my father; and to a stone, Thou hast brought me forth.' Je. ii. 26, 27. God catched them thus doing, and this made them ashamed, even as the thief is ashamed when the owner doth catch him stealing of his horse.

But this was not the Publican's shame; this shame brings not a man into the temple to pray, to stand willingly, and to take shame before God in prayer. This shame makes one rather to fly from his face, and to count one's self most at ease when they get farthest off from God.

The Publican's shame therefore, which he demonstrateth that he had, even by hanging down of his head, was godly and holy, and much like that of the prodigal, when he said, 'Father, I have sinned against heaven, and in thy sight, and am no more worthy to be called thy son.' Lu. xv. 21. I suppose that his postures were much the same with the Publican's, as were his prayers, for the substance of them. O however grace did work in both to the same end, they were both of them, after a godly manner ashamed of their sins.

He would not lift up so much as his eyes to heaven.

It saith not *he could* not, but he *would* not; which yet more fully makes it appear that it was shame, not guilt, not guilt only or chiefly, though it is manifest enough that he had guilt also by his crying, *God be merciful to me a sinner.* I say, guilt was not the chief cause of hanging down his head, because it saith, he would not; for when guilt is the cause of stooping, it lieth not in the will, or in the power thereof, to help one up.

David tells us, that when he was under guilt, his iniquities were gone over his head: 'As an heavy burden they are too heavy for me.' Ps. xxxviii. 4.

And that with them he was bowed down greatly. Or, as he says in another place, 'Mine iniquities have taken hold upon me, so that I am not able to look up;' Ps. xl. 12. I am not ABLE to do it; guilt disableth the understanding and conscience, shame makes all willingly fall and bare at the feet of Christ.

'He would not.' He knew what he was, what he had been, and should be, if God had not mercy upon him: Yea, he knew also that God knew what he was, had been, and would be, if mercy prevented not; wherefore thought he, Wherefore should I lift up the head? I am no righteous man, no godly man; I have not served God, but Satan; this I know, this God knows, this angels know, wherefore I will not 'lift up the head.' It is as much as to say, I will not be an hypocrite, like the Pharisee; for lifting up of the head signifies innocency and harmlessness of life, or good conscience, and the testimony thereof, under, and in the midst of all accusations. Wherefore this was the counsel of Zophar to Job: 'If thou prepare thine heart, and stretch out thine hands towards him; If iniquity be in thine hand, put it far away, and let not wickedness dwell in thy tabernacles. For then shalt thou lift up thy face without spot; yea, thou shalt be stedfast, and shalt not fear.' Job xi. 13—15.

This was not the Publican's state, he had lived in lewdness and villany all his days; nor had he prepared his heart to seek the Lord God of his fathers, he had not cleansed his heart nor hands from violence, nor done that which was lawful and right. He only had been convinced of his evil ways, and was come into the temple as he was, all foul, and in his filthy garments, and amidst his pollutions; how then could he be innocent, holy or without spot? And consequently how could he lift up his face unto God? I remember what Abner said to Asahel, 'Turn thee aside, from following me; wherefore should I smite thee to the ground? how then should I hold up my face to Joab thy brother?' 2 Sa. ii. 22.

As if he had said, if I kill thee, I shall blush, be ashamed, and hang my head like a bulrush, the next time I come into the company of thy brother.

This was the Publican's case, he was guilty, he had sinned, he had committed a trespass, and now being come into the temple, into the presence of that God whose laws he had broken, and against whom he had sinned, how could he lift up his head? how could he bear the face to do it? No, it better became him to take his shame, and to hang his head in token of guilt; and indeed he did, and did it to purpose too, for he would not lift up, no, not so much as his eyes to heaven.

True, some would have done it, the Pharisee did it; though if he had considered, that hypocrisy,

and leaning to his own righteousness had been sin, he would have found as little cause to have done it, as did the Publican himself. But, I say, he did it, and sped thereafter; he went down to his house as he came up into the temple, a poor unjustified Pharisee, whose person and prayers were both rejected, because, like the whore of whom we read in the Proverbs, after he had practised all manner of hypocrisy, he comes into the temple 'and wipes his mouth, and saith, I have done no wickedness.' Pr. xxx. 20. He lifts up his head, his face, his eyes to heaven; he struts, he vaunts himself; he swaggers, he vapours, and cries up himself, saying, 'God, I thank thee, that I am not as other men are.'

True, had he come and stood before a stock or a stone, he might have said thus, and not have been reprehended; for such are gods that see not, nor hear, neither do they understand. But to come before the true God, the living God, the God that fills heaven and earth by his presence, and that knows the things that come into the mind of man, even every one of them, I say, to come into his house, to stand before him, and thus to lift up his head and eyes in such hypocrisy before him: this was abominable, this was to tempt God, and to prove him; yea, to challenge him to know what was in man if he could, even as those did who said, 'How doth God (see) know? can he judge through the dark cloud? Job xxii. 13. Ps. lxxiii. 11.

But the publican, no the publican could not, durst not, would not do thus: He would not lift up so much as his eyes to heaven. As who should say, O Lord, I have been against thee, a traitor and a rebel, and like a traitor and rebel before thee will I stand. I will bear my shame before thee in the presence of the holy angels; yea, I will prevent thy judging of me by judging myself in thy sight, and will stand as condemned before thee, before thou passest sentence upon me.

This is now for a sinner to go to the end of things. For what is God's design in the work of conviction for sin, and in his awakening of the conscience about it? What is his end I say, but to make the sinner sensible of what he hath done, and that he might unfeignedly judge himself for the same. Now this our Publican doth; his will therefore is now subjected to the word of God, and he justifies him in all his ways and works towards him. Blessed be God for any experience of these things.

'He would not lift up so much as his eyes to heaven.' He knew by his deeds and deservings that he had no portion there; nor would he divert his mind from the remembering, and from being affected with the evil of his ways.

Some men when they are under the guilt and conviction of their evil life, will do what they can to look any ways, and that on purpose to divert their minds, and to call them off from thinking on what they have done; and by their thus doing, they bring many evils more upon their own souls: for this is a kind of striving with God, and a shewing a dislike to his ways. Would not you think, if when you are shewing your son or your servant his faults, if he should do what he could to divert and take off his mind from what you are saying, that he striveth against you, and sheweth dislike of your doings. What else means the complaints of masters and of fathers in this matter? I have a servant, I have a son, that doth contrary to my will. O but why do you not chide them for it: The answer is, so I do; but they do not regard my words; they do what they can, even while I am speaking, to divert their minds from my words and counsels. Why, all men will cry out this is base, this is worthy of great rebuke; such a son, such a servant deserveth to be shut out of doors, and so made to learn better breeding by want and hardship.

But the Publican would not divert his mind from what at present God was about to make him sensible of, no, not by a look on the choicest object, he would not lift up so much as his eyes to heaven. They are but bad scholars, whose eyes, when their master is teaching of them, are wandering off of their books.

God saith unto men, when he is a teaching them to know the evil of their ways, as the angel said to the prophet, when he came to shew him the pattern of the temple; 'Son of man,' says he, 'behold with thine eyes, and hear with thine ears, and set thine heart upon all that I shall shew thee; for to the intent that I might shew *them* unto thee, *art* thou brought hither.' Eze. xl. 4. So to the intent that God might shew to the Publican the evil of his ways, therefore was he brought under the power of convictions, and the terrors of the law; and he also like a good learner gave good heed unto that lesson-that now he was learning of God; for he would not lift up so much as his eyes to heaven.

Looking downwards doth ofttimes bespeak men very ponderous and deep in their cogitations; also that the matter about which in their minds they are now concerned, hath taken great hold of their spirits. The Publican hath now new things, great things, and long-lived things, to concern himself about: His sins, the curse, with death, and hell, began now to stare him in the face; Wherefore it was no time now to let his heart, or his eyes, or his cogitations wander, but to be fixed, and to be vehemently applying of himself as a sinner, to the God of heaven for mercies.

Few know the weight of sin, and how, when the guilt thereof takes hold of the conscience, it commands homewards all the faculties of the soul. No man can go out or off now. Now he is windbound, or as Paul says, caught. Now he is made to possess bitter days, bitter nights, bitter hours, bitter thoughts; nor can he shift them, for his sin is ever before him. As David said, 'For I acknowledge my transgressions: and my sin *is* ever before me,' in mine eye, and sticketh fast in every one of my thoughts. Ps. li. 3.

He would not lift up so much as his eyes to heaven. THIRD, BUT SMOTE UPON HIS BREAST. This was the third and last of his gestures. He smote upon his breast; to wit, with his hand, or with his fist. I read of several gestures with the hand and foot, according to the working and passions of the mind. 'Tis said Balak smote his hands together, being angry because that Balaam had blessed and not cursed for him the children of Israel. Nu. xxiv. 10.

God says also, that he had smitten his hands together, at the sins of the children of Israel. Eze. xxii. 13. God also bids the prophet stamp with his feet, and smite with his hand upon his thigh, upon sundry occasions, and at several enormities, but the Publican here is said to smite upon his breast. ch. vi. 11; xxi. 12. And,

1. Smiting upon the breast betokeneth sorrow for something done, this is an experiment common among men. And indeed, therefore as I take it, doth our Lord Jesus put him under this gesture in the act and exercise of his repentance, because it is that which doth most lively set it forth.

Suppose a man comes to great damage for some folly that he has wrought, and he be made sorrowful for being and doing such folly: There is nothing more common than for such a man, if he may, to walk to and fro in the room where he is, with head hung down, fetching ever and anon a bitter sigh: and smiting himself upon the breast in his dejected condition; 'But smote upon his breast, saying, God be merciful to me a sinner.'

2. Smiting upon the breast is sometimes a token of indignation and abhorrence of something thought upon. I read in Luke, that when Christ was crucified, those spectators that stood to behold the barbarous usage that he endured at the hands of his enemies, 'smote their breasts and returned.' 'And all the people that came together to that sight, beholding the things which were done, smote their breasts, and returned.' Lu. xxiii. 48. smote their breasts; that is, in token of indignation against, and abhorrence of their cruelty, that so grievously used the Son of God.

Here also we have our Publican smiting upon his breast, in token of indignation against, and abhorrence of his former life. And indeed without indignation against, and abhorrence of his former life, his repentance had not been good. Wherefore the apostle doth make indignation against sin, and against ourselves for that, one sign of true repentance, 2 Co. vii. 11. and his indignation against sin in general, and against his former life in particular, was manifested by his smiting upon the breast. Even as Ephraim's smiting upon the thigh was a sign and token of his: 'Surely,' says he, 'after that I was turned, I repented; and after that I was instructed, I smote upon *my* thigh: I was ashamed, yea, even confounded, because I did bear the reproach of my youth.' Je. xxxi. 19. Man when he vehemently dislikes a thing, is very apt to shew that dislike that to that thing he hath, by this or another outward gesture: as in putting the branch to the nose,* in snuffing or snorting at it; Eze. viii. 17. Mal. i. 13. or in deriding; or, as some say, in blowing of their noses at it. Lu. xvi. 14. But the Publican here chooseth rather to use this most solemn posture; for smiting upon the breast, seems to imply a more serious, solemn, grave way or manner of dislike, than any of those last mentioned do.

3. Smiting upon the breast, seems to intimate a quarrel with the heart for beguiling, deluding, flattering, seducing, and enticing of him to sin: For as conviction for sin begets in man, I mean if it be thorough, a sense of the sore and plague of the heart. So repentance, if it be right, begets in the man an outcry against the heart; for as much as by that light, by which repentance takes occasion, the sinner is made to see, that the heart is the fountain, and well-spring of sin. 'For from within, out of the heart of men proceed evil thoughts, adulteries, - covetousness,' &c. Mar. vii. 21, 22. And hence it is, that commonly young converts do complain so of their hearts, calling them wicked, treacherous, deceitful, desperate ones.

Indeed one difference between true and false repentance lieth in this. The man that truly repents crieth out of his heart; but the other, as Eve, upon the serpent, or something else. And that the Publican perceived his heart to be naught I conclude, by his smiting upon his breast.

4. Smiting upon the breast, seems to intimate one apprehensive of some new, sudden, strange and amazing thing: As when a man sees some strange sight in the air, or heareth some sudden or dismal sound in the clouds: Why, as he is struck into a deep damp in his mind, so 'tis a wonder if he can keep or hold back from smiting upon his breast.

Now ofttimes a sight of God and sense of sin, comes to the sinner like a flash of lightning, not for short continuance, but for suddenness, and so for surprisal; so that the sinner is struck, taken

and captivated to his own amazement, with what so unexpectedly is come upon him. It is said of Paul at his conversion, that when conviction of his bad life took fast hold of his conscience, he trembled, and was astonished. Ac. ix. 6. And although we read not of any particular circumstance of his behaviour under his conviction outwardly, yet it is almost impossibly but he must have some, and those of the most solid sort. For there is such a sympathy betwixt the soul and the body, that the one cannot be in distress or comfort, but the other must partake of, and also signify the same. If it be comfort, then 'tis shewn; If comfort of mind, then by leaping, skipping, cheerfulness of the countenance, or some other outward gesture. If it be sorrow or heaviness of spirit, then that is shewed by the body, in weeping, sighing, groaning, softly-going, shaking of the head, a lowering countenance, stamping, smiting upon the thigh or breast as here the Publican did, or somewhat.

We must not therefore look upon these outward actions or gestures of the Publican, to be empty insignificant things; but to be such, that in truth did express and shew the temper, frame, and present complexion of his soul. For Christ, the wisdom of God, hath mentioned them to that very end, that in and by them, might be held forth, and that men might see, as in a glass, the very emblem of a converted, and truly penitent sinner. 'He smote upon his breast.'

5. Smiting upon the breast, is sometimes to signify a mixture of distrust, joined with hope. And indeed in young converts, hope and distrust, or a degree of despair, do work and answer one another, as doth the noise of the balance of the watch in the pocket. Life and death, life and death is always the motion of the mind then, and this noise continues until faith is stronger grown, and until the soul is better acquainted with the methods and ways of God with a sinner. Yea, was but a carnal man in a convert's heart, and could see, he should discern these two, to wit, hope and fear, to have a continual motion in the soul: wrestling and opposing one another, as doth light and darkness, in striving for the victory.

And hence it is that you find such people so fickle and uncertain in their spirits; Now on the mount, then in the valleys; now in the sunshine, then in the shade; now warm, then frozen; now bonny and blithe, then in a moment pensive and sad; as thinking of a portion nowhere but in hell. This will cause smiting on the breast; nor can I imagine that the Publican was as yet farther than thus far in the Christian's progress, since yet he was smiting upon his breast.

6. Smiting upon the breast, seems to intimate, that the party so doing is very apprehensive of some great loss that he has sustained; either by

---

* This is variously interpreted, but may it not mean an ancient mode of mocking, now called taking a sight?—Ed.

negligence, carelessness, foolishness, or the like, and this is the way in which men do lose their souls. Now to lose a thing, a great thing, the only choice thing that a man has, negligently, carelessly, foolishly, or the like, why it puts aggravations into the thoughts of the loss that the man has sustained; and aggravations in the thoughts of them go out of the soul, and come in upon a sudden, even as the bailiff, or the king's sergeant at arms, and at every appearance of them makes the soul start; and starting, it smites upon the breast.

I might multiply particulars; but to be brief, we have before us a sensible soul, a sorrowful soul, a penitent soul: one that prays indeed, that prays sensibly, affectionately, effectually. One that sees his loss, that fears and trembleth before God in consideration of it, and one that knows no way, but the right way, to secure himself from perishing, to wit, by having humble and hearty recourse to the God of heaven for mercy.

I should now come to speak something by way of use and application; but before I do that, I will briefly draw up, and present you with a few conclusions that in my judgment do naturally flow from the text, therefore in this place I will read over the text again.

' Two men went up into the temple to pray; the one a Pharisee, and the other a Publican: The Pharisee stood and prayed thus with himself, God, I thank thee, that I am not as other men are, extortioners, unjust, adulterers, or even as this Publican: I fast twice in the week, I give tithes of all that I possess. And the Publican, standing afar off, would not lift up so much as *his* eyes unto heaven, but smote upon his breast, saying, God be merciful to me a sinner.'

From these words I gather these several conclusions, with these inferences.

Conclusion First, It doth not always follow, that they that pray do know God, or love him, or trust in him. This conclusion is evident by the Pharisee in the text; he prayed, but he knew not God, he loved not God, he trusted not in God; that is, he knew him not in his Son, nor so loved, nor trusted in him. He was, though a praying man, far off from this. Whence it may be inferred, that those that pray not at all cannot be good, cannot know, love, or trust in God. For if the star, though it shines, is not the sun, then surely a clod of dirt cannot be the sun. Why, a praying man doth as far outstrip a non-praying man, as a star outstrips a clod of earth. A non-praying man lives like a beast, nay worse, and with reference to his station, a more sottish life than he. 'The ox knoweth his owner, and the ass his master's crib: but [this man] Israel doth not know, [but this man] my people doth not consider.' Is. i. 3. The prayerless man is therefore of no religion, except he be an Atheist, or an Epicurean. Therefore the non-praying man is numbered among the heathens, and among those that know not God, and is appointed and designed by the sentence of the word to the fearful wrath of God. Ps. lxxix. 6. Je. x. 25.

Conclusion Second, A second conclusion is, That the man that prays, if in his prayer he pleads for acceptance, either in whole or in part, for his own good deeds, is in a miserable state. This also is gathered from the Pharisee here, he prayed, but in his prayer he pleaded his own good deeds for acceptance, that is, of his person, and therefore went down to his house unjustified. Now to be unjustified is the worst condition that a man can be in, and he is in this condition that doth thus. The conclusion is true, forasmuch as the Pharisee mentioned in the parable is not so spoken of, for the only sake of that sect of men, but to caution, forewarn, and bid all men take heed, that they by doing as he, procure not his rejection of God, and be sent away from his presence unjustified. I do therefore infer from hence, that if he that pleadeth his own good doing for personal acceptance with God, be thus miserable; then he that teacheth men so to do, is much more miserable. We always conclude, that a ring-leader in an evil way, is more blame-worthy, than those that are led of him. This falls hard upon the leading Socinians and others, who teach, that men's works make their persons accepted of God.

True, they say, through Christ; but that is brought in as a *blandation, merely to delude the simple with, and is an horrible lie; for we read not in all the word of God, as to personal justification in the sight of God from the curse, and that is the question under consideration, that it must be by man's righteousness, as made prevalent by Christ's, but contrariwise by his, and his only, without the deeds, works, or righteousness of the law which is our righteousness. Wherefore I say, the teachers and leaders of this doctrine have the greater sin.

Conclusion Third, A third conclusion is. They that use high and flaunting language in prayer, their simplicitly and godly sincerity is to be questioned, as to the doing of that duty sincerely. This still flows from our text, the Pharisee greatly used this; for higher and more flaunting language can hardly be found, than in the Pharisee's mouth; nor will ascribing to God by the same mouth laud and praise, help the business at all: For to be sure, where the effect is base and rotten, the cause cannot be good.

The Pharisee would hold himself in hand that he was not as other men, and then gives thanks to

---

* 'Blandation,' a piece of flattery. 'They flattered the Bishop of Ely with this blandation.'—*Camden*.

God for this: But the conclusion was most vilely false, and therefore the praise for it could not but be foolish, vain, and frivolous. Whence I infer, that if to use such language in prayer is dangerous, then to affect the use thereof is yet more dangerous: Prayer must be made with humble hearts, and sensible words, and of that we have treated before, wherefore high, flaunting, swelling words of vanity becomes not a sinner's mouth, no, not at any time, much less when he comes to, and presents himself before God in that solemn duty of prayer. But, I say, there are some that so affect the Pharisee's mode, that they cannot be well if in some sort or other they be not in the practice of it; not knowing what they say, nor whereof they affirm; but these are greatly addicted to hypocrisy, and to desire of vain-glory, especially if the sound of their words be within the reach of other men's ears.

Conclusion Fourth, A fourth conclusion is, that reformation and amendment, though good, with, and before men, are nothing as to justification with God. This is manifest by the condition of our Pharisee; he was a reformed man, a man beyond others for personal righteousness, yet he went out of the temple from God unjustified, his works, came to nothing with God. Hence I infer, that the man that hath nothing to commend him to God of his own, yet stands as fair before God for justification, and so acceptance, as any other man in the world.

Conclusion Fifth, A fifth conclusion is, it is the sensible sinner, the self-bemoaning sinner, the self-judging sinner, the self-abhorring sinner, and the self-condemning sinner, whose prayers prevail with God for mercy. Hence I infer, that one reason why men make so many prayers, and prevail no more with God, is because their prayers are rather the floatings of pharisaical fancies, than the fruits of sound sense of sin, and sincere desire of enjoying God in mercy, and in the fruits of the Holy Ghost.

The use and application we must let alone till another time.

A DEFENCE OF THE DOCTRINE OF JUSTIFICATION,
BY FAITH IN JESUS CHRIST;

SHEWING,

TRUE GOSPEL-HOLINESS FLOWS FROM THENCE;

OR, MR. FOWLER'S PRETENDED DESIGN OF CHRISTIANITY, PROVED TO BE NOTHING MORE THAN TO TRAMPLE UNDER FOOT THE BLOOD OF THE SON OF GOD ; AND THE IDOLIZING OF MAN'S OWN RIGHTEOUSNESS.

AS ALSO,

HOW WHILE HE PRETENDS TO BE A MINISTER OF THE CHURCH OF ENGLAND, HE OVERTHROWETH THE WHOLESOME DOCTRINE CONTAINED IN THE 10TH, 11TH, AND 13TH, OF THE THIRTY-NINE ARTICLES OF THE SAME, AND THAT HE FALLETH IN WITH THE QUAKER AND ROMANIST, AGAINST THEM.

By JOHN BUNYAN.

'Disallowed indeed of men, but chosen of God, and precious.'—1 PET. II. 4.

Printed for Francis Smith, at the Elephant and Castle, without Temple Bar, 1672.

EDITOR'S ADVERTISEMENT.

THIS is one of the least known but most deeply interesting productions of John Bunyan. It has never been reprinted in a separate form ; and once only in any edition of his works—that with notes, by Mason and Ryland, and then with great carelessness, the errata remaining uncorrected, and one leaf being entirely omitted. This treatise was published to counteract the pernicious errors in a very popular volume called 'The Design of Christianity, by Edward Fowler, minister of God's Word at Northill, in Bedfordshire. Printed by the authority of the Bishop of London, April 17th, 1671;' an octavo volume of 308 pages. The whole object proposed by Mr. Fowler was to shew, that Christianity is intended merely to restore man to the original state which he enjoyed before the fall.

Bunyan was at that time suffering his tedious imprisonment for conscience sake in Bedford jail; and having refused to expatriate himself, was in daily fear lest his cruel sentence, ' you must stretch by the neck' for refusing to attend the church service, should be carried into execution.

The fame of Fowler's gross perversion of the design of Christ's gospel reached Bunyan in prison, and its popularity grieved his spirit. At length, on the 13th of the 11th Month (February), a copy of the book was brought to him ; and in the almost incredible space of forty-two short days, on the 27th of the 12th Month (March) 1671-2, he had fully analysed 'The Design,' exposed the sophistry, and scripturally answered the gross errors which abound in every page of this learned and subtle piece of casuistry.

The display of Latin and Greek quotations from the heathens and fathers, those thunderbolts of scholastic warfare, dwindled into mere pop-gun weapons before the sword of the Spirit, which puts all such rabble to utter rout. Never was the homely proverb of Cobbler Howe more fully exemplified, than in this triumphant answer to the subtilties of a man deeply schooled in all human acquirements, by an unlettered mechanic, whose knowledge was drawn from one book, the inspired volume:—

'The Spirit's teaching in a cobbler's shop,
Doth Oxford and Cambridge o'ertop.'

The Babel building of the learned clergyman could not withstand the attack of one who was armed with such irresistible weapons. His words burn 'like a fire,' and consume the wood, hay and stubble ; while they fell with overpowering weight, as ' a hammer that breaketh the rock in pieces.' Je. xxiii. 29. So cunningly was ' the design' constructed, that nothing but the fire and hammer of God's word could have demolished it. Armed with such weapons, he fearlessly from his dungeon made the attack ; and, encouraged by the Spirit which animated the prophet, he was not ' dismayed at their faces,' but became as ' a defenced city, and an iron pillar, and brazen walls against the whole land.' Je. i. 48.

Such internal and powerful support encouraged Bunyan to use the greatest plainness of speech. He was fully aware of his danger, and of the great influence of Mr. Fowler, but he had counted the cost of plain honest dealing, and was undaunted by the perils which surrounded him. With noble bearing, worthy the descendant of the apostles, he declares, 'As for your subtle and close incensing THE POWER to persecute Nonconformists, know that we are willing, God assisting, to overcome you with truth and patience; not sticking to sacrifice our lives, and dearest concerns in a faithful witness-bearing.'* 'Wherefore, sir, laying aside all fear of men, not regarding what you may procure to be inflicted upon me, for this my plain dealing with you, I tell you again, that you are one of them that have closely, privily, and devilishly, by your book, turned the grace of our God into a lascivious doctrine.'† Mr. Fowler's opinions were not only contrary to scripture, but to that which some esteem a more heinous offence, they opposed the thirty-nine articles; and the result was that Bunyan, who vindicated the scriptures and those articles, was kept in prison, while the clergyman who opposed them was soon after consecrated Bishop of Gloucester! It may lead some simple readers to wonder how it could be, that state religion thus made a mockery of itself. The reason is perfectly obvious; Fowler's religion was that of a statesman, which may be comprised in one word, *expediency;* and the man who could publish as truth, that religion consists in obeying the orders made therein by the state, deserved the primacy of the united churches of England and Ireland. His words are, speaking of religious observances, 'Whatsoever of such are commended by the custom of the places we live in, or commanded by superiors, or made by any circumstance convenient to be done; our christian liberty consists in this, that we have leave to do them. And, indeed, it is so far from being a sin, that it would be so to refuse so to do.' Could the state have selected a fitter tool for their purposes?

Mr. Fowler is *somewhat* inconsistent with regard to persecution; in p. 266 he says, 'As for factious hypocrites, they would be with ease *supprest;*' in p. 262 he describes these factious hypocrites, 'Such as preach up free grace,—laying hold on Christ's righteousness and renouncing our own righteousness.' Such are to be suppressed, but for Roman catholics 'imposing their own sense upon the word of God, and their persecuting, burning, and damning men for not subscribing to *theirs* as to *God's* word can be no better than an act of devilish pride and barbarous cruelty,' p. 247. Does not the same pride and cruelty apply equally to the church of Bonner for burning Latimer, of Fowler, for the imprisonment of Bunyan; and of Philpot, for dragging his brother, Shore, from his family, and shutting him up in Exeter jail?

The admirers of Bunyan will feel surprised at his

strictures upon persons calling themselves Quakers. In these severe remarks he does not refer to the Society of Friends; but to some unworthy individuals who assumed the name of Quakers. They will be equally surprised at his freedom of speech with one who he considered to be an enemy to his Lord. He calls Mr. Fowler 'a brutish, beastly man,' 'this thief,' 'a blasphemer,' 'horribly wicked,' 'a learned ignorant Nicodemus,' 'one that would fling heaven's gates off the hinges,' 'a bat,' 'an angel of darkness.' Such epithets sound strangely in our more refined age; but they were then considered essential to faithful dealing. The Bishop in his reply, called 'Dirt wiped off,' beat the tinker in abusive language; he calls Bunyan 'A wretched scribbler,' 'grossly ignorant,' 'most unchristian and wicked,' 'a piece of proud folly,' 'so very dirty a creature that he disdains to dirt his fingers with him,' 'Bunyan can no more disgrace him than a rude creature can eclipse the moon by barking at her; or make palaces contemptible by lifting up their legs against them,' 'a most black-mouthed caluminator,' 'infamous in Bedford for a pestilent schismatic,' and with a heart full of venom he called upon his majesty not to let such a firebrand, impudent, malicious schismatic to enjoy toleration, or *go unpunished,* lest he should subvert all government. Bunyan had then suffered nearly twelve years' incarceration in a miserable jail, and was more zealous and intrepid than ever: and yet this learned fanatic would have added to his privations, because he could not resist the arrows of truth with which this poor prisoner for Christ assailed him, drawn all burning from the furnace of God's holy word.

Bunyan's views of the kingly office of Christ are very striking: not only is he king over the church requiring personal obedience, but over the universe for the benefit of believers. 'Christ is as well a Lord for us, as to, or over us; and it highly concerneth the soul—when it believeth in, or trusteth to, the righteousness of Christ, for justification with God—to see that this righteousness lords it over death and sin, and the devil and hell for us.' 'He led captivity captive, that is, carried them prisoners, whose prisoners we were: He rode to heaven in triumph, having in chains the foes of believers.'

This compendious treatise is upon a most important subject, and detects dangerous errors enveloped in most insinuating sophistry. In preparing this edition for the press, the text has been carefully collated with the original, which is in the editor's possession. The quotations have been verified; those from Fowler by the first edition of his 'Design of Christianity,' 1671. The extracts from 'Penn's Sandy Foundation,' by the second edition, in the Friends' library, Devonshire House. Those from Campian have not been discovered; the

* P. 324. † P. 321.

author's being confined at Bedford, while his book was printing in London, occasioned numerous typographical errors which have been corrected, and all the obsolete words explained.

To assist the reader, a few leading words have been introduced in italics, and between brackets, to distinguish them from the text.

GEORGE OFFOR.

A PREMONITION TO THE READER.

GENTLE READER,

THAT thou mayest not be tired with longing to know what errors, and doctrines destructive to Christianity, Mr. Fowler in his feigned design of Christianity, hath presented the world withal; and that thou mayest even in the entry, see that which more fully is shewn in the house: namely, of the contradiction that is in his book, to the wholesome doctrine of the church of England, while he stands a minister of the same, I have thought convenient, instead of an epistle, to present thee with those doctrines contained in his; and that are refuted by the book that thou hast in thy hand. The which also, I hope, will be a sufficient apology for this my undertaking.

His Doctrines are these:

1. That the first principles of morals, those first written in men's hearts, are the essentials, the indispensable, and fundamental points or doctrines of the gospel, p. 8, 281, 282. 2. That these first principles, are to be followed, principally, as they are made known to us, by the dictates of human nature: and that this obedience is the first, and best sort of obedience, we Christians can perform, p. 8, 9, 10. 3. That there is such a thing as a soundness of soul; and the purity of human nature in the world, p. 6. 4. That the law, in the first principles of it, is far beyond, and more obliging on the hearts of Christians, than is, that of coming to God by Christ, p. 7—10. 5. That the precept of coming to God by Christ, &c. is in its own nature, a thing indifferent, and absolutely considered neither good nor evil, p. 7, 8, 9. 6. That Christ's great errand, in coming into the world, was to put us again in possession of the holiness we had lost, p. 12. 7. That John the Baptist, the Angel that was sent to Zacharias, and Mary, preached this doctrine, and so also did Malachi the prophet, p. 13. 8. That Christ by saving us from sin, is meant, not first, his saving us from the punishment, but from the filth, and from the punishment, as a consequence of that, p. 14, 15. 9. That Christ's work, when he was come, was to establish ONLY an inward real righteousness, p. 16. 10. That Christ's fulfilling the law FOR US, was by giving more perfect, and lighter instances of moral duties, than were before expressly given, p. 17. 11. That Christ's doctrine,

life, actions, miracles, death, resurrection, ascension, and coming again to judgment, is all preached to establish us in this righteousness, chap. 2—8. 12. That it is not possible a wicked man should have God's pardon, p. 119. 13. That it is impossible Christ's righteousness should be imputed to an unrighteous man, p. 120. 14. And that if it were, he boldly affirms, it would signify as little to his happiness, while he continueth so, as would a gorgeous and splendid garment, to one that is almost starved, p. 120. 15. For God to justify a wicked man,* &c., would far more disparage his justice and holiness, than advance his grace and kindness, p. 130. 16. He saith, men are not capable of God's pardoning grace, till they have truly repented them of all their sins, p. 130. 17. The devils, saith he, have a large measure of these attributes of God; as his power, knowledge, &c.† p. 124. 18. That Christ did himself perform, as our example, whatever he required of us to do; yea, that he trod himself EVERY step of our way to heaven, p. 148. 19. The salvation of Christ, first, consists in curing our wounds (our filth) and secondarily, in freeing us from the smart, p. 216. 20. That pardon doth not so much consist in remission, as in healing; [to wit, our filth,] p. 216. 21. Faith justifieth, as it includeth true holiness in the nature of it; it justifieth AS it doth so, p. 221. 22. That faith which entitles a sinner to so high a privilege as that of justification, must needs be such as complieth with *all* the purposes of Christ's coming into the world, &c. And it is no less necessary that it should justify *as* it doth *this*, p. 222. 23. He wonders that any worthy man should be so difficultly persuaded, to embrace THIS account of justifying faith, p. 222. 24. There can be no pretence for a man, to think that faith should be the condition or instrument of justification, as it complieth with, only the precept of relying on Christ's merits for the obtaining of it, p 223. 25. It is, saith he, as clear as the sun at noon-day, that obedience to the other precepts must go before obedience to this, p. 223. 26. He shall be his Apollo, that can give him a sufficient reason, why justifying faith should consist in recumbence‡ and reliance on Christ's merits for the

---

* Fowler's words, in place of, &c., are 'while he continues so (if it were possible for God to do it).'

† Holiness is excepted ! !

‡ 'Recumbence,' depending upon.

pardon of sin,* p. 224. 27. He will take the boldness to tell those who are displeased with this account of justifying faith, that in his opinion it is impossible they should ONCE think of any other, p. 225. 28. The imputation of Christ's righteousness, consisteth in dealing with sincerely righteous persons, as if they were perfectly so, &c. p. 225. 29. The grand intent of the gospel is, to make us partakers of inward real righteousness; and it is but secondary, that we should be accepted as before, p. 226. 30. It is not possible (he saith) that any other notion of this doctrine should have truth in it, p. 226. 31. Whatsoever is commended by the customs of the place we live in, or commanded by superiors, or made by ANY circumstance convenient to be done, our christian liberty consists in this that we have leave to do them, p. 242. 32. For our refusing to comply with these, can hardly proceed from any thing, than a proud affectation of singularity, or at best from superstitious scrupulosity, p. 242. 33. Those ministers hinder the design of Christianity, that preach up free grace, and christian privileges, OTHER WAYS than as motives to obedience, and that scarce ever insist upon any other duties than those of believing, laying hold of Christ's righteousness, applying the promises, &c., p. 262. 34. But to make the christian duties to consist either wholly or *mostly in these*, &c., is the way effectually to harden hypocrites, p. 262. 35. Those ministers do nothing less than promote the design of Christianity, that are never in their element, but when they are talking

* Fowler adds, 'and not also in his power for the mortification of it.'

of the irrespectiveness of God's decrees, the absolute [ness of his] promises, the utter disability, and perfect impotence of natural men, to do any thing towards their own conversion, p. 262. 36. He is the only child of Abraham, who in the purity of his heart obeyeth those substantial laws, that are by God imposed upon him, p. 283. 37. There is NO duty more affectionately commanded in the gospel, than that of almsgiving, p. 284. 38. It is impossible we should not have the design of Christianity accomplished in us, &c., if we make our Saviour's most excellent life, the pattern of our lives, p. 296. 39. To do well is better than believing, p. 299. 40. To be imitators of Christ's righteousness, even of the righteousness we should rely on, is counted by Mr. Fowler, *more* noble, than to rely thereon, or trust thereto, p. 300.

READER,

I have given thee here but a taste of these things; and by my book but a brief reply to the errors that he by his hath divulged to the world: Ay, though many more are by me reflected than the forty thou are here presented with.

God give thee eyes to see, and an heart to shun and escape all these things that may yet come to pass, for hurt, and to stand before the Son of Man.

Thus hoping that this short taste may make Mr. Fowler ashamed, and thee receive satisfaction, touching the truth and state of this man's spirit and principles; I rest,

Thine to serve thee in the gospel of Christ,

J. BUNYAN.

From Prison, the 27th of the
12th Month, 1671.
[27th March, 1672.]

A DEFENCE OF THE DOCTRINE OF JUSTIFICATION BY FAITH IN JESUS CHRIST;

PROVING

THAT GOSPEL-HOLINESS FLOWS FROM THENCE.

SIR,

Having heard of your book, entitled, *The Design of Christianity*; and that in it was contained such principles as gave just offence to christian ears; I was desirous of a view thereof, that from my sight of things I might be the better able to judge. But I could not obtain it till the 13th of this 11th month, which was too soon for you, Sir, a pretended minister of the word, so vilely to expose to public view the rottenness of your heart in principles diametrically opposite to the simplicity of the gospel of Christ. And had it not been for this consideration, that it is not too late to oppose open

blasphemy (such as endangereth the souls of thousands) I had cast by this answer, as a thing out of season.

Two things are the design of your book.

1. To assert and justify a thing which you call inward, real righteousness and holiness.

2. To prove, That the whole, the grand, the only, and ultimate design of the gospel of Christ, is to begin and perfect this righteousness.

Into the truth, or untruth, of both these, as briefly as I may, I shall at this time inquire.

First, Therefore, a little to examine the nature of your holiness and righteousness, as yourself hath described the same.

'It is (say you) so sound a complexion of soul, as maintains in life and vigour, whatsoever is essential to it, and suffereth not anything unnatural to mix with that which is so; by the force and power whereof a man is enabled to behave himself as [becometh] a creature indued with a principle of reason, keeps his supreme faculty in its throne, brings into due subjection all his inferior ones, his sensual imagination, his brutish passions and affections.'

You add farther, 'It is the purity of the human nature, engaging those in whom it resides, to demean themselves suitably in that state in which God hath placed them, and not to act disbecomingly in any condition, circumstance or relation.'

You say, moreover, 'It is a divine, or God-like nature, causing an hearty approbation of, and an affectionate compliance with the eternal laws of righteousness; and a behaviour agreeable to the essential, and immutable differences of good and evil,' p. 6.

Farther, You call it a principle or habit of soul, 'originally dictates of human nature,' p. 8.

'A disposition and temper of the inward man, as powerfully inclines it to regard, and attend to; affectionately to embrace and adhere to; to be actuated by, and under the government of, all those [good] practical principles, that are made known either by revelation, nature, or the use of reason,' p. 11. Which in conclusion you call *that* holiness which already we have lost, p. 12.

Thus, Sir, is your holiness, by you described; which holiness you aver is that, which is the great and only design of Christ to promote both by his life and glorious gospel.

To take therefore your description in pieces, if happily there may be found ought, but naught therein.

1. 'It is (say you) an healthful complexion of soul, the purity of the human nature,' &c.

Ans. These are but words; there is no such thing as the purity of our nature, abstract and distinct from the sinful pollution that dwelleth in us. Ro. vii. 24. It is true, a man may talk of, and by argument distinguish between nature and sin; but that there is such a principle in man (since Adam's fall) a principle by which he may act, or that Christ's whole gospel-design is, the helping forward such a principle, is altogether without scripture or reason. There is no man by nature, that hath any soundness in him, Is. i. 6. no, neither in soul or body; his understanding is darkened, his mind and conscience is defiled, Tit. i. 15. his will is perverted and obstinate. Ep. iv. 18. 'There is no judgment in his goings.' Is. lix. 6–10. Where now is the sound and healthful complexion of soul? Let the best come to the best, when we have mustered up all the excellences of the soul of man, as man,

shall nought we find there, but the lame, the blind, the defiled, the obstinate and misled faculties thereof. And never think to evade me by saying, the graces of the Spirit of God are pure: for with them you have nothing to do; your doctrine is of the sound complexion of soul, the purity of the human nature, a habit of soul, and the holiness we lost in Adam, things a great way off from the spirit of grace, or the gracious workings of the spirit. You talk indeed of a divine or godlike nature,* but this is still the same with your pure human nature, or with your sound complexion, or habit of soul; and so must either respect man, as he was created in the image or likeness of God, or else you have palpable contradiction in this your description. But it must be concluded, that the divine nature you talk of, is that, and no other than the dictates of the human nature, or your feigned purity thereof; because you make it by your words the self same; it is the purity of the human nature, it is a divine or Godlike nature.

2. But you proceed to tell us of a degree, it is so sound and healthful a complexion or temperature of the faculties, qualities, or virtues of soul, 'as maintains in life and vigour whatsoever is essential to it, and suffereth not anything unnatural to mix with that which is so.'†

Ans. If, as was said before, there is no soundness of soul in man, as man, and no such thing as a purity of our nature, abstract from that which is sin; then where shall we find so healthful a complexion, or temperature of soul, as to maintain in life and vigour whatsoever is essential to it, and that suffereth not any thing unnatural to mix with that which is so?

But let us take Paul's definition of a man; 'There is none righteous, no, not one: there is none that understandeth, there is none that seeketh after God. They are all gone out of the way, they are together become unprofitable; there is none that doeth good, no, not one. Their throat *is* an open sepulchre; with their tongues they have used deceit; the poison of asps *is* under their lips: whose mouth *is* full of cursing and bitterness: their feet *are* swift to shed blood: destruction and misery *are* in their ways: and the way of peace have they not known: there is no fear of God before their eyes.' Ro. iii. I the rather give you this of Paul, than any of my own; because it is the *soundest* complexion of soul, that the Holy Ghost himself *could* draw. Here is now no purity of the human nature, nor such sound complexion of soul as can keep itself from mixing with that which is contrary to itself. And note, that this is the state of all men, and that as they stand in themselves before God: wherefore together, even altogether, all the

---

* Fowler's Design, p. 6.　　　　　† Ibid.

men in the world, take them in their most pure naturals, or with all the purity of humanity, which they can make, and together, they still will be unprofitable, and so must come short of doing good, 'that every mouth might be stopped, and all the world become guilty before God.' ver. 19. *

3. But proceeding, you say, that this complexion is so forcible as to 'keep his supreme faculty (I suppose you mean the conscience) in its throne, (and that) brings into due subjection all his inferior ones, (as namely) his sensual imagination, brutish passions and affections.'†

Ans. These words suppose that it is within the power of a man's own soul, always to keep sin out of itself, and so guilt out of the conscience ; albeit the scripture saith, that both the mind and it are defiled with the filth of sin, in all whoever do not believe the gospel, with which belief this description meddleth not. Tit. i. 15.

They suppose that *this* conscience is perfectly clear and light, when the scriptures say they have the understanding darkened; yea and farther, in despite of these your sayings of the sound complexion of soul, of the purity of human nature, and of this supreme faculty, the scriptures teach, that man in his best estate is altogether vanity, that they are darkness and night, &c. Ep. iv. 18, 19. 1 Th. v. Ps. xxxix. 5.

'Yea, (say you) this sound complexion brings into due subjection all his inferior ones.'‡

Ans. Here seems to be a contradiction to the former part of this description, yea, to the nature of the soul itself; for you say before, it suffereth not any thing unnatural to mix itself therewith, when yet here you seem to suggest that part, I say, even part of itself is disobedient and rebellious, 'it brings into subjection all his inferior ones.'

'It brings into due subjection.'

Ans. Due subjection is such as is everlasting, universal, perfect in nature, kind, and manner, such as the most righteous, perfect, comprehensive law, or commandment cannot object against, or find fault therewith. Here's a soul ! here's a

pure human nature ! here are pure dictates of a brutish beastly man, that neither knows himself nor one tittle of the word of God. But ' *There is* a generation *that are* pure in their own eyes, and' *yet* are not washed from their filthiness.' Pr. xxx. 12.

' It is the purity of the human nature, engaging those in whom it resides,' &c. §

Ans. That is, *verily* in none at all; for there is no such thing in any man in this world, as a purity of human nature : 'we are all as an unclean *thing*,' Is. lxiv. 6. and ' Who can bring a clean *thing* out of an unclean ? not one.' Job xiv. 4. Again,

' What *is* man, that he should be clean ? or *he which is* born of a woman, that he should be righteous ? Job xv. 14. These are therefore expressions without the testimony of the word, arising from your own phantasy.

' It is a divine, or Godlike nature.' ‖

Ans. This you seem also to fetch from the similitude or likeness of God that was in us at our first creation, before we sinned; but that similitude being at best but created, and since most unspeakably defiled, defaced and polluted with sin; there is now, no not in the best of men, as men, any sinless likeness, and similitude of God to be found, no such *petty* divine, or Godlike nature to be found, as you imagine.

But having thus stated your holiness in its nature and essence, you come in the next place to tell us, under what considerations it moveth a person to act, also by what rules and laws it squareth its acts and doings.

FIRST, By or under what considerations it acts, and these you scatter here and there in your description of holiness, under these heads. I. To act ' as becomes a creature endued with a principle of reason,' eyeing the state or place in which God hath set him ; approving of, affecting and complying with the eternal laws of righteousness, p. 6. which eternal laws in p. 8. you call ' divine moral laws,' those that were first written in the hearts of men, ' and originally dictates of human nature,' &c. II. ' To do these, from truly generous motives and principles,' p. 7. Such as these, 1. Because ' it is most highly becoming all reasonable creatures (you might have added, and those unreasonable) to obey God in every thing ; (within their spheres) and as much disbecoming them, to disobey him,' p. 8. 2. ' Because it is a base thing to do unjustly,' p. 11.

Now a little to touch upon all these, and then to proceed to what is behind.

I. To act and do the things of the moral law, but as ' creatures endued with a principle of reason,' is but to do things in our sphere as men, as the beast, the hog or horse doth things in his,

---

* Seeing, then, it is evident from scripture, how deeply and dreadfully man is fallen from God, what a folly it is to suppose, in such a depraved creature, conditions previous to his justification ! They who talk at this rate, know not what they say, nor whereof they affirm. In a natural man there is no meetness, but a meetness to sin, and a meetness to be damned. They who know themselves, know this. And there are no pre-requisites to justification, but what God, by his Spirit, is pleased to work in men's hearts. None are meet to obey the gospel, till God implants in their souls a principle of faith and evangelical obedience. Before this is done, there is no meetness in the creature, no disposition to do anything spiritually good ; neither are any of our works, till a change of nature takes place, acceptable and well-pleasing in the sight of Almighty God.—*Mason and Ryland.*

† Fowler, p. 6.   ‡ Ibid.   § Fowler, p. 6.   ‖ Ibid.

as a beast; which is at best, if it could be attained, to act but as pure naturals, which state of man is of at infinite distance from that, in which it is by God expected the man must act, that doth ought that is pleasing in his sight. For,

1. The qualification and consideration by you propounded, is that which is in all men, in men simply as men, they being reasonable creatures, and somewhat, though but somewhat capable of acting as such.

2. This qualification is not only in, but of men; reason is of the man himself, even that which is as essential to him, as is that of his being created or made.

3. The law also, which *you* call divine, moral, and eternal, is that which is naturally seated in the heart, and as you yourself express it, is originally the dictates of humane nature, or that which mankind doth naturally assent to, p. 11.

Now I say, that a man cannot by these principles, and these qualifications, please the God of heaven, is apparent. (1.) Because none of these are faith, 'But without faith *it is* impossible to please *him*.' He. xi. 6. (2.) Because none of these are of the Holy Ghost, but there is nothing accepted of God, under a New Testament consideration, but those which are the fruits of the Spirit. Ga. v. 22—24. (3.) The man and principles you have stated, may be such as are utterly ignorant of Jesus Christ, and of all his New Testament things, as such: 'But the natural man receiveth not the things of the Spirit of God: (the things of his New Testament) for they are foolishness unto him: neither can he know *them*, because they are spiritually discerned.' 1 Co. ii. 14. (4.) Your qualifications and considerations, know nothing at all of the adoption of sons, and of our acting and doing our duty as such. You only content yourself to rest within the confines of the humane nature, acts of reason, as men or creatures only, or in their supposed pure, natural principles.

And Sir, a little by way of digression; I will tell you also of our truly christian righteousness, both as to its original or first principle; and also how, or under what capacity, it puts the person that is acted by it.

First, The principle which is laid within us, it is not the purity of the humane nature, but of the Holy Ghost itself, which we have of God received, by believing in the Son of God, a principle as far above yours of humanity, as is the heavens above the earth; yours being but like those of the first Adam, but ours truly those of the second. 1 Co. vi. 19. 'As *is* the earthy, such *are* they also that are earthy: and as *is* the heavenly, such *are* they also that are heavenly.' 1 Co. xv. 48.

Now whosoever hath not this principle, although he be a creature, and also have the dictates of the humane nature, yea, and also follows them, yet he is not Christ's: 'If any man have not the Spirit of Christ, he is none of his.' Ro. viii. 9. Thus therefore is the christian principle another from, and far above, your heathenish Pagan one. By this Spirit is the Christian qualified with principles, not natural, but spiritual, such as faith, hope, joy, peace, &c. all which are the fruits of the revelation of the forgiveness of sins, freely by grace, Ga. v. 25. 'through the redemption that is in Jesus Christ.' Ro. iii. 24. In this spirit and faith we walk, by this spirit we are led, Ro. viii. 14. even into the joy and peace of the New Testament of our Lord; wherefore our holy actions are the fruits of righteousness, that is by Jesus Christ, not by our humane nature, or the purity of it in us; yea, they are the fruits of the Spirit of God, the qualifications that attend the new covenant, and those that by the work of regeneration are brought within the bounds and privileges thereof. Wherefore,

Second, The capacity that we are in, who act and do from the heavenly principle; it is that of sons, the sons of God by adoption, as the apostle said, 'Because ye are sons, God hath sent forth the Spirit of his Son into your hearts, crying, Abba, Father.' Ga. iv. 6. And again, 'As many as are led by the Spirit of God, they are the sons of God.' Ro. viii. 14. This is a far other than is your human description of acting as a creature, endued with a principle of reason; for here is a man acts as a son, endued with the Holy Spirit of God, who hath, before the world was, predestinated him to this estate, by Jesus Christ, to himself. Ep. i. 4; iv. 6. As a son therefore, the Christian acts and does, because he is endued with that high and heavenly principle mentioned before; by which principle this man hath received a new heart, a new spirit, a new understanding, a good conscience, so made by 'faith in the blood of the Lord Jesus.' He. x. Thus being made again anew and another man, he acts from a new and another principle than yours; a principle as far beyond and above you, as is a man above a brute, and as is grace above nature. 2 Co. v. 14—16.

Third, As the Christian acts and does from a better principle, and under a better capacity or consideration than that you have described; so (to allude to your own notion) the first principles by which they receive this spirit and adoption, are not those principles of morals, or those originally dictates of human nature; but it is through the hearing of faith, Ga. iii. 1—3. by which we understand, that the Son of God became a man, died for our sins, hath saved us from the curse of God, and accounted us to be the righteousness of God in him; this being heard with the gospel, and a New Testament hearing, the Holy Ghost forthwith possesseth us, by the glorious working whereof we are helped, through the Son, to call the God of heaven, our Father.

Now thus being made free from sin, by the only faith of Jesus Christ, 'we have our fruit unto holiness, and the end everlasting life.' Ro. vi. 22.

And here come in those reasonable conclusions, which you would make the very radicals of Christianity, they being only remote, and after conclusions, drawn from the fore-mentioned mercy of God, viz., from predestination, calling, adoption, and justification by Christ's blood, while we in ourselves are sinners. I say these are the things which Paul endeavoured to provoke the Romans, Philippians, and Colossians, to an holy conversation by.

To the Romans, 'I beseech you therefore,' saith he, ' by the mercies of God, (What mercies ? Why those of election, redemption, calling, justification, and adoption, mentioned in the foregoing chapters) that ye present your bodies a living sacrifice, holy, acceptable unto God, *which is* your reasonable service.' Ro. xii. 1.

To the Philippians, 'If *there be* therefore any consolation in Christ, if any comfort of love, if any fellowship of the Spirit, if any bowels and mercies, fulfil ye my joy, that ye be like minded.' Phi. ii. 1, 2.

To the Colossians, 'If ye then be risen with Christ, seek those things which are above, where Christ sitteth on the right hand of God; set your affection on things above, not on things on the earth; for ye are dead, and your life is hid with Christ in God. When Christ, *who is* our life, shall appear, then shall ye also appear with him in glory.' Co. iii. 1—4. Now mark; mortify therefore, therefore ! wherefore ? why, because they were risen with Christ; because they should appear at the end of this world with Christ himself in glory; therefore mortify the deeds of the body, or our members that are upon the earth.

These Sir, are the motives by which we Christians act; because we are forgiven, because we are sons, and if sons, then heirs, and so we act; but to speak to this more anon.

Perhaps you will say I deal not fairly with you, because you treat, as of moral, so of gospel or New Testament laws.

But to that I will answer at present, that in this description of your holy principle, which is the foundation of your book, whether the laws be natural or spiritual, moral or of grace, the principle by which you do them, is no other than the principle of nature, the dictates of the human nature; and so such as can by no means reach the doctrines of the gospel any farther than to make a judgment of them, by that wisdom which is ' enmity with God,' as will farther be seen in my progress through your book.

Indeed you make mention of divine laws, and

that under two heads. 1. Such as are of an indispensable and eternal obligation, as those purely moral, p. 7 and 8. 2. Such which you call positive precepts, in themselves of an indifferent nature, and absolutely considered, are neither good nor evil. Of those of this kind that we have under the gospel, you say you know but three, viz., That of coming to God by Christ, and the institutions of baptism, and the Lord's supper, p. 9.

So then, although you talk of gospel positive laws, and particularly that of coming to God by Christ; yet those which you call first principles of morals, are of higher concern with you, and more indispensible by far than this, this being a thing of an indifferent nature, and in itself absolutely considered, is neither good nor evil; but the other is the life of the matter. But a little to gather you up.

The morals, say you, are indispensable, and good in themselves, but that of coming to God by Christ, a thing indifferent, and in itself neither good nor evil. Wherefore though in this your description, you talk of conforming to all those good and practical principles, that are made known either by revelation, nature, or the use of reason, yet in this your obedience you reckon coming to God by Christ, but an act of a very indifferent nature, a thing if done not good in itself, neither evil in itself, should a man leave it undone; and so consequently a man may have in him the ground and essentials of Christianity without it, may be saved, and go to heaven without it: for this I say, whatsoever is of an indifferent nature in itself, is not essential to the Christian religion; but may or may not be done without the hazard of eternal salvation; but say you, this of coming to God by Christ, is one of the positive precepts, p. 9. which are in themselves things indifferent, and neither good nor evil: therefore not of the substance of Christianity.

But, Sir, where learned you this new doctrine, as to reckon coming to God by Christ, a thing of so indifferent a nature, a thing not good in itself, but with respect to certain circumstances, p. 7. Had you said this of baptism and the Supper of the Lord, I could with some allowance have borne your words, but to count coming to God by Christ a thing indifferent in itself, is a blasphemy that may not be borne by Christians, it being too high a contempt of the blood, and too great a disgrace to the person of the Lord, the king of glory; of which more hereafter, but to return.

II. The intent of this your description is to set before us these two things.

(1.) What are the essentials of the rule of that holiness, which by the gospel we are immediately obliged to, if we would be justified in the sight of God.

(2.) What are the principles by which we act, when we do these works aright.

1. For the first you tell us, 'they are the first principles of morals, such as are self-evident, and therefore not capable of being properly demonstrated; as being no less knowable, and easily assented to, than any proposition that may be brought for the proof of them,' p. 8. Such as are self-evident or evident of themselves; to what? To us as men that know the principles of reason, and that are as easily assented to as any proposition; why said you not such as may be as easily known, as we know there is a day or night, winter and summer, or any other thing that may be brought for the proof of them. This law therefore is none other than that mentioned in Ro. ii. 14, 15. which is the law of our nature, or that which was implanted in us in the day of our creation, and therefore is said to be ourselves, even nature itself. 1 Co. xi. 14.

2. The principle, say you, by which we act, and in the strength of which we do this law, it is the principle of reason, or a reasonable compliance with this law written in our hearts, and originally dictates of human nature, &c. which certain principle, say you, is this, to count it 'most highly becoming all reasonable creatures, to obey God in every thing; and as much disbecoming them, in any thing to disobey him.' p. 8.

The sum is; this your holiness both in root and act is no other than what is common to all the men on earth; I mean so common as that for the first, is in their nature, as the second is also part of themselves, they being creatures whose prime or principal distinction from other, consisteth more in that they are reasonable, and such as have reason as a thing essential to them; wherefore the excellency that you have discoursed of, is none other than the excellency and goodness that is of this world, such as in the first principles of it, is common to Heathens, Pagans, Turks, Infidels: and that as evidently dictates to those that have not heard the gospel (I mean as to the nature the good and evil) as it doth in them that sit under the sound thereof; and is the self-same which our late ungodly heretics the Quakers have made such a stir to promote and exalt, only in the description thereof you seem more ingenious than they: for whereas they erroneously call it Christ, the light of Christ, faith, grace, hope, the spirit, the word that is nigh, &c. you give it the names due thereto, viz. A complexion or complication and combination of all the virtue of the soul, the human nature, the dictates of it, the principles of reason, such as are self-evident, than which there is nothing mankind doth naturally assent to, p. 6—11. Only here, as I have said, you glorify your errors also, with names and titles that are not to be found, but in your own deluded brains: as that the virtues of the souls can keep themselves incommixed, that there is yet in us the purity of the humane nature, or such a disposition, that can both by light and power give a man to see, and powerfully incline him to, and bring him under the government of all those good and practical principles, that are made known either by revelation, nature, or the use of reason.

But I say, these principles thus stated by you, being the principles, and the goodness of this world, and such as have not faith, but the law; not the Holy Ghost, but humane nature in them; they cannot be those which you affirm, was or is the design, the great, the only, and ultimate design of Christ, or his gospel to promote, and propagate in the world; neither with respect to our justification before God from the curse; neither with respect to the workings of his Spirit, and the faith of Jesus in our hearts, the true gospel or evangelical holiness.

First, It is not the righteousness that justifieth us before God from the curse; because it is that which is properly our own; and acted and managed by principles of our own, arising originally in the roots of it, from our own. There is the righteousness of men, and the righteousness of God: that which is the righteousness of men, is that which we do work from matter and principles of our own; but that which is the righteousness of God, is that which is wrought from matter and principles purely divine, and of the nature of God. Again, that which is our own righteousness, is that which is wrought in and by our own persons as men; but that which is the righteousness of God, is that which is wrought in and by the second person in the Trinity, as God and man in one person; and that resideth only in that person of the Son. I speak now of the righteousness by which we stand just before God, from the curse of the law. Now this righteousness of ours, our own righteousness, the apostle always opposeth to the righteousness of God, saying, 'They going about to establish their own righteousness, have not submitted themselves unto the righteousness of God.' Ro. ix. 3. Farther, This righteousness of our own, Paul counts loss and dog's-meat, in comparison of that other, far more glorious righteousness, which he calleth as it is in truth, the righteousness of God, Phi. iii. 7—9. which as I said but now, resideth in the person of the Son. Therefore (saith Paul) I cast away my own righteousness, and do count it loss, and 'but dung, that I may win Christ, and be found in him, not having mine own righteousness, which is of the law, but that which is through the faith of Christ, the righteousness which is of God by faith.' The righteousness therefore, that is our own, that ariseth from matter and principles of our own (such as that which you have described) justifieth us not before God from the curse.

Second, The righteousness that you have described, justifieth us not, as before, because it is the righteousness which is of the moral law, that is, it is wrought by us, as walking in the law. Now it mattereth not, whether you respect the law in its first principles, or as it is revealed in the table of the ten commandments, they are in nature but one and the same, and their substance and matter is written in our hearts, as we are men. Now this righteousness, the apostle casteth away, as was shewn before; ' Not having mine own righteousness (saith he) which is of the law;' why? Because the righteousness that saveth us from the wrath of God, is the righteousness of God; and so a righteousness that is without the law. 'But now the righteousness of God without the law is manifested, being witnessed by the law and the prophets; even the righteousness of God, *which is* by faith of Jesus Christ unto all and upon all them that believe:' Ro. iii. 21, 22. The righteousness of God without the law; the righteousness of Christ who is naturally God; wherefore such a righteousness as was accomplished by him that was Lord, and the very God of the law; whose nature was infinite, and not that which the law could command or condemn; neither was the command of the law, the great and principal argument with him, no, not in its first and highest principles, to do or continue to do it; but even that which the law commanded of us, that he did, not by the law, but by that spirit of life, that eternal spirit, and Godhead, which was essential to his very being: He did naturally and infinitely that which the law required of us, from higher, and more mighty principles than the law could require of him: for I should reckon it a piece of prodigious blasphemy to say, that the law could command his God; the creature, his Lord and Creator: but this Lord God, Jesus Christ, even he hath accomplished righteousness, even righteousness that is without, that is above, higher, and better than that of the law; and that is the righteousness that is given to, and put upon all them that believe. Wherefore the Lord Jesus Christ, in his most blessed life, was neither prompted to actions of holiness, nor managed in them, by the purity of humane nature, or those you call first principles of morals, or as he was simply a reasonable creature; but being the natural Son of God, truly, and essentially, eternal as the Father; by the eternal Spirit, his Godhead, was his manhood governed, and acted, and spirited to do and suffer. ' He through the eternal Spirit offered himself without spot to God;' He. ix. 14. which offering respects not only his act of dying, but also that by which he was capacitated to die without spot in his sight; which was the infinite dignity, and sinlessness of his person; and the perfect justice of his actions. Now this person, thus acting,

is approved of, or justified by the law to be good: for if the righteousness of the law be good, which law is but a creature, the righteousness of the Lord, the God of this law, must needs be much more good; wherefore here is the law, and its perfection swallowed up, even as the light of a candle, or star is swallowed up by the light of the sun. Thus then is the believer made, not the righteousness of the law, ' but the righteousness of God in Christ,' 2 Co. v. 21. because Christ Jesus, who is the righteousness of the Christian, did walk in this world, in, and under the law; not by legal and humane principles, which are the excellences of men, but in, and by those that are divine, even such as were, and are of his own nature, and the essence of his eternal Godhead. This is the righteousness *without* the law, accomplished by a person and principles, far otherwise, than is he, or those you make description of; and therefore yours cannot be that, by which we stand just before the justice of God without the law. Now if it be a righteousness without the law, then it is a righteousness without men, a righteousness that cannot be found in the world; for take away the law, the rule, and you take away, not only the righteousness, but that by which men, as men, work righteousness in the world: ' Mine own righteousness which is of the law.' The righteousness then by which a man must stand just in the sight of God from the curse, is not to be found in men, nor in the law, but in him, and him only, who is greater, and also, without the law; for albeit, for our sakes he became under the law, even to the curse and displeasure of God; yet the principles by which he walked in the world to Godward, they were neither humane, nor legal, but heavenly, and done in the Spirit of the Son. Wherefore it is not the righteousness you have described, by which we stand just before God.

Third, The righteousness you have described, cannot be that which justifieth us before God, because of its imperfections, and that both with respect to the principle, and the power with which it is managed: for though you have talked of a sound complexion of soul, the purity of the humane nature, and that with this addition of power, as to be able to keep itself incommixt with that which is not of itself; yet we Christians know, and that by the words of God, that there is in man, as man, now no soundness at all, but from the crown of the head, to the sole of the foot, botches and boils, putrefactions and sores. Is. i. 6. We are ALL an unclean thing, and our righteousness as filthy ulcerous rags. Is. lxiv. 6. ' If there had been a law given which could have given life, verily righteousness should have been by the law.' Ga. iii. 21. Could a man perform the law to the liking of the justice of the eternal majesty, then would the law give life to that man; but because of the perfection of an infinite justice, and the weakness and unprofitableness of the law through our flesh, Ro. viii. 3, therefore, though you speak yet farther of the excellency of your sound complexion, and of the purity of the human nature, you must fly from yourself, to another righteousness for life, or at the last stick in the jaws of death and everlasting desperation. 'For by the works of the law shall no flesh be justified.' Ga. ii. 16.

It is therefore no better than error, thus to ascribe to poor man, 'that hath drank iniquity like water,' a soundness of soul, a purity of human nature. Wherefore Jude saith of you, and of all such naturalists, 'That even in the things that you know naturally, as the brute, in them you corrupt yourselves,' Jude 10, even in the very principles, the first or original dictates of your nature or humanity. There is none that understandeth or is good, therefore there is none that doth good, no not one: that is, none as continuing in a natural state; none by the power or principles of nature; for he meaneth here, in your own sense, as men by natural principles have to do with the justice of the law.

Fourth, The righteousness which you have described cannot be that which justifieth us before God, because it is that which is not of faith. 'The law is not of faith: but, The man that doeth them shall live in them.' Ga. iii. 12. The apostle also in the 10th chapter of the Romans tells us, that the righteousness that is completed by doing the law is one, and another besides the righteousness of faith. For faith in the justification of a sinner from the curse and wrath of God, respecteth only the mercy of God, and forgiveness of sins for the sake of Christ. 'God for Christ's sake hath forgiven him that is enabled to believe, that is, trust to, and venture the eternal concern of his soul upon the righteousness that is no where to be found, but in the person of the Son of God.' For there is justice more than answerable to all the demands of the law, and equal to the requirements of the eternal justice of God, and he is our justice; he is made unto us of God, righteousness, or justice; that is, the righteousness or justice that is in him, is by God accounted the man's that shall accept thereof by faith, that he might be made the justice or righteousness of God in him. For the righteousness that saveth a sinner from damnation must be equal to that in the eternal Deity: But where can that be found but in him that is naturally God, as is indeed the Son of the Father; in him, therefore, and not in the law, there is a righteousness fit for faith to apply to. Besides, the law is not, neither can be, the object of faith to men; for that which is the object of faith (I speak now as to justifying righteousness) it must be a righteousness already completed, and as I said, a righteousness to be received

and accepted, being now perfected and offered, and given to us by the kindness and mercy of God; but a man may believe long enough in the law, before that performs for him a perfect righteousness. The law can work nothing unless it be wrath. 'No thou must work by, and not believe in, the law.' Ro. iv. Besides, all that cometh out of the mouth of the law is, 'Cursed *is* every one that continueth not in all things which are written in the book of the law to do them,' Ga. iii. 10, which no man is capable of doing, so as to escape the curse by doing, that hath once, or first transgressed the same. Wherefore it is a vain thing, yea an horrible wickedness in you, thus to abuse the law, and the weakness of man, by suggesting that the only, the ultimate, or grand design of Christ Jesus was, or is, the promoting of a righteousness by the law, that is performed by humane principles in us.*

I could double, yea ten times double the number of these arguments against you, but I will pass from this to the second thing. 'The righteousness you have described, is not the true gospel inward holiness.'

I told you before, that the principles which you have described, are not evangelical principles; and now I will add, that as they are not such in themselves, so neither do they fetch in, or obtain by our adhering to them, those things which alone can make, or work in the soul, those truly gospel inward acts of holiness.

[*Things essential to inward gospel holiness.*]

There are three things which are essential to the inward gospel holiness; of which as your description is utterly destitute, so neither can they by that be obtained, or come into the heart. 1. *The Holy Ghost.* 2. *Faith in Christ.* 3. *A new heart, and a new spirit.*

Without these three, there is no such thing as

---

* Man, in his first estate, was holy and righteous; and he continued to be possessed of this righteousness as long as he was obedient to his Creator; but as soon as he disobeyed the divine command, he lost all his holiness and righteousness at once; he emptied himself of every spark of goodness, and was full of all manner of wickedness; he forfeited all his primitive purity, and became a sinful, impure, and unrighteous creature. Hence, all mankind are destitute of original righteousness: there is none of the children of men righteous, 'no not one: there is none that doeth good, no not one,' Rom. iii. 10, 12. What then becomes of the purity and dignity of human nature, so vainly boasted of? or how shall man be righteous before God? To this last question, we answer with Paul, in the above-quoted chapter, ver. 21, 22, 'Now the righteousness of God without the law is manifested, being witnessed by the law and the prophets; even the righteousness of God, *which is* by faith of Jesus Christ, unto all and upon all them that believe.' Without this righteousness, no soul ever was, no soul ever will be, justified before God.—*Mason and Ryland.*

gospel holiness in man, as before I have also hinted at. But now as there are none of these three found in your description of inward holiness; so neither can you, or others, by all your inclinations, either to those you call first principles of natural reason, or the dictates of human nature, obtain or fetch into the soul the least dram of that which is essential, to that which is indeed according to the gospel description of inward gospel holiness, as will further be manifest in this that followeth.

1. *The Holy Ghost* is not obtained by your description, that consisting only in principles of nature, and in putting forth itself in acts of civility and morality. When the apostle would convince the bewitched Galatians, that your doctrine which was also the doctrine of the false apostles, was that, which instead of helping forward, did hinder, and pervert the gospel of Christ; he applieth himself to them in this manner. 'This only would I learn of you, Received ye the Spirit by the works of the law, or by the hearing of faith?' Ga. iii. 2. By the works of the law, that is, by putting of your principles into practice. Nay, may I not add, by putting of your principles into practice, by a more bright and clear rule, than in the beginning of your description is inserted by you; for the law as written and engraven in stones, with the addition of all the Mosaical precepts, was a more ample, and full discovery of the mind of God, than can be obtained by your virtues of soul, your purity of human nature, or the first principles of morals, as they are written in the heart of man; and originally dictates of human nature. Ro. iii. 1—3. Yet by these, by following these, by labouring to live up to the light of these, their own experience told them, that they neither could, nor did obtain the enjoyment of the Holy Ghost; but that rather their now declining the word of faith, by which indeed they receive it at first (whatever pretences of holiness, and godliness were the arguments to prevail with them so to do) was in truth none other but the very witchcraft, and enchantments of the devil.

Farther, The apostle sets this your spirit and principles, and that which indeed is the Spirit of God, in a line diametrically opposite one against another; yea the receiving of the one, opposeth the receiving of the other. 'Now we have received, (saith he) not the spirit of the world,' (that is, your spirit, and principles of humanity) to walk by it, or live in it; 'but the Spirit which is of God; that we may know the things that are freely given to us of God.' 1 Co. ii. 12. But what is the spirit of the world? He tells us in the verse before, it is the spirit of a man; which Solomon calls, 'the candle of the Lord; searching all the inward parts of the belly,' Pr. xx. 27. by human principles, good motions to moral duties, workings of reason, dictates of nature to obey God as Creator. These things flow from the spirit of a man, which is the spirit of all the world. They that preach, or speak by this spirit, they preach or speak of the world, of the virtues of the world; and the world, 'the whole world heareth them,' or know in themselves what they say. 1 Jn. iv. 5.

Now when this spirit is received, embraced, and followed, as the spirit that is of God, then it must be branded with the mark of the spirit of error, and of antichrist; because the act in so doing, is most wicked; yea, and Christ himself is made head against, by it.

But I say, the Holy Ghost is not obtained by these principles, nor by the pursuit of them.

2. *Faith* is not obtained by the pursuit of your principles, but by hearing of another doctrine; he that presseth men to look to, and live by the purity of human nature, principles of natural reason, or by the law, as written in the heart, or bible; he sets the word of faith out of the world; for these doctrines are as opposite, as the spirits I spake of before; 'For Moses describeth the righteousness which is of the law, That the man which doeth those things shall live by them.' Now he that receiveth this law, to do, and live by; he hath set up, and is in pursuit of a doctrine of another nature, than that which is called the righteousness of faith; that being such, as for justification, and deliverance from the curse, maketh no mention at all of hearing the law, or of doing good works; but of hearing of the mercy of God, as extended to sinners; and of its coming to us through the death, and resurrection of Christ Jesus. 'The righteousness which is of faith, speaketh on this wise, Say not in thine heart, Who shall ascend into heaven? (that is, to bring Christ down *from above:*) or, Who shall descend into the deep? (that is, to bring up Christ again from the dead). But what saith it? The word is nigh thee, *even* in thy mouth, and in thy heart: that is, the word of faith, which we preach; That if thou shalt confess with thy mouth the Lord Jesus, and shalt believe in thine heart that God hath raised him from the dead, thou shalt be saved.' Ro. x. 5, 9. This then is the doctrine of faith, or the righteousness with which faith hath to do. Now as old covenant-works are begotten in men by the doctrine of works; so faith is begotten by the doctrine of faith. Therefore after he had said, 'faith cometh by hearing;' he insinuates it to be the hearing the preaching of the gospel of peace (peace by the blood of the cross) and the glad tidings of good things, (ver. 14—17.) of good things promised for the sake of the Lord Jesus; not for the sake of good deeds done of us, by human principles, or the dictates of our nature.

Faith, Then the second essential, comes into the heart, not by the preaching, or the practice of your principles ; but by another, a higher, and far more heavenly doctrine. And hence the apostle completely puts the difference betwixt the worker of good works in the spirit of the law, and the believer that taketh hold of grace by Christ, that he may be saved thereby. The one he calls 'Them that are of the works of the law;' the other, 'They which are of faith.' Ga. iii. This being done, he tells us, that as they differ in the principles, to wit, of faith and works, so they shall differ in conclusion: 'For the law is not of faith, the promise is only made to faith; therefore, they only that are of faith, are blessed with faithful Abraham.'

3. The third essential is, *a new heart, and a new spirit or mind;* and this also comes not by your principle, that being but the old covenant that gendereth to bondage, and that holds its Ishmaels under the curse for ever: there comes no new heart by the law, nor new spirit. It is by the new covenant, even the gospel, that all things are made new. Je. xxxi. 33. Eze. xxxvi. He. viii. 8. 2 Co. v. 17—19.

The apostle, after a large discourse of the two ministrations, and their excellencies, 2 Co. iii. tells us that the heart is nothing changed, so long as it abideth in the works of the law, but remaineth blind and ignorant: 'Nevertheless (saith he) when it shall turn (from the law) to the Lord, the vail shall be taken away.' But what is it to turn from the law to the Lord? Why, even to leave and forsake your spirit and principles, and works from those principles, and fly to the grace and merits; 'the glory of the Lord Jesus Christ.' Now when the heart is turned to Christ, then the vail of Moses is taken off; wherefore then the soul 'with open face beholding as in a glass the glory of the Lord, is changed - from glory to glory, *even* as by the Spirit of the Lord.' 2 Co. iii. 14, 18.

Obj. But it seems a paradox to many, that a man should live to the law, that is, devote himself to the works of the ten commandments, the most perfect rule of life; and yet not be counted one changed, or new.

Ans. Though it seemeth an untruth, yet it is most true, that by the works of the law, no heart is made new, no man made new. A man from principle of nature and reason, (which principles are of himself, and as old) may give up himself to the goodness of the law: yet these principles are so far off from being new, that they are as old as Adam in Paradise; and come into the world with all the children of men. To which principles the law, or the first principles of morals, so equally suit, that, as you have said, p. 8. 'they are self-evident, than which there is nothing mankind doth more naturally assent to,' p. 11. Now nature is no new principle, but an old: even our own, and of ourselves. The law is no new principle, but old,

and one with ourselves (as also you well have called it) 'first written in men's hearts, and originally dictates of human nature.' Let a man then be as devout, as is possible for the law, and the holiness of the law. Yet if the principles from which he acts, be but the habit of soul, the purity (as he feigns) of his own nature; principles of natural reason, or the dictates of human nature; all this is nothing else but the old gentleman in his holiday clothes: the old heart, the old spirit, the spirit of the man, not the spirit of Christ, is here.

And hence the apostle, when he would shew us a man alive, or made a new man indeed; as he talketh of the Holy Ghost and faith, so he tells us such are dead to the law, to the law, as a law of works; to the law as to principles of nature. 'Wherefore, my brethren, ye also are become dead to the law (the moral law, and the ceremonial law) by the body of Christ, that ye should be married to another (another than the law) *even* to him who is raised from the dead, that we should bring forth fruit unto God.' Ro. vii. 4.

Ye are become dead to the law. Dead to the law! Why? That you should be married to another. Married to another! Why? 'That you should bring forth fruit unto God.' But doth not a man bring forth fruit unto God, that walketh orderly according to the ten commandments? No, if he do it before faith make this in the spirit of a man, by the dictates of human nature, respecting the law, as that, by the obeying of which, he must obtain acceptance with God. This is bringing forth fruit unto himself; for all that he doth, he doth it as a man, as a creature, from principles natural, and of himself, his own, and for none other than himself; and therefore he serveth in an old spirit, the oldness of the letter, and for himself. But now (that is, ye being dead to the law, and married to Christ) that (the law) being dead; by which (while in ourselves) we were held; now we are delivered from that law, both as to its curse and impositions, as it stands a law of works in the heart of the world; we serve in newness of the spirit, 'and not *in* the oldness of the letter.' ver. 6. A man must first then be dead to your principles, both of nature and the law; if he will serve in a new spirit, if he would bring forth fruit unto God.[*]

---

[*] Great will be the condemnation of all those who profess to know God, but in works deny him; who are abominable and disobedient, and unto every good work reprobate, Tit. i. 16. A great profession, without a suitable life and conversation, will only procure a greater condemnation. Therefore, up, ye sleepy virgins; up, and be doing; shew your faith by your works. There is no true religion without good works, attended with a godly walk and behaviour. There may be works seemingly good, where there is no true religion. Good works are not the causes, but the fruits and effects of true religion, of justifying faith wrought in the soul by the Holy Ghost; and where true

Wherefore your description of the principle of holiness in man, and also the principles by which this holiness is put forth by him into righteous acts; they are such as are altogether void of the true essentials of inward gospel-holiness and righteousness.

[FOWLER'S ASSERTION THAT THE GRAND, THE ONLY AND ULTIMATE DESIGN OF THE GOSPEL OF CHRIST IS TO RE-PRODUCE MAN'S ORIGINAL RIGHTEOUSNESS EXAMINED AND CONFUTED.]

But there is one thing more in this description, or rather effect thereof, which I shall also inquire into: and that is your saying, 'As it was the errand of Christ to effect our deliverance out of that sinful state we had brought ourselves into: so to put us again into possession of that holiness which we had lost.' p. 12. The proof of this position is now your next business; that is, if I understand your learning, the remaining part of your book, which consisteth of well nigh 300 pages, is spent for proof thereof; which I doubt not but effectually to confute with less than 300 lines. Only first by the way, I would have my reader to take notice that in this last clause, (to put us again into possession of that holiness which we had lost) is the sum of all this large description of his holiness in the foregoing pages; that is, the holiness and righteousness that Mr. Fowler hath been describing; and adds, that Christ's whole business when he came into the world was, as to effect our deliverance from sin; 'so to put us again in possession of that holiness which we had lost.' The holiness therefore that here he contendeth for, is that, and only that which was in Adam before the fall, which he lost by transgression; and we by transgressing in him. A little therefore to inquire into this, if perhaps his reader and mine may come to a right understanding of things.

First then, Adam before the fall, even in his best and most sinless state, was but a pure natural man, consisting of body and soul; these, to use your own terms, were his pure essentials: p. 11. in this man's heart, God also did write the law; that is, as you term them, the first principles of morals, p. 8. This then was the state of Adam, he was a pure natural man; made by God sinless; all the faculties of his soul and members of his body were clean. 'God made man upright.' Ec. vii. 29. But he made him not then a spiritual man; 'the first Adam was made a living soul,' 'howbeit that *was* not first which is spiritual; but that which is

natural, and afterward that which is spiritual: The first man is of the earth, earthy.' 1 Co. xv. 45—47. A living soul he was; yet but a natural man, even in his first and best estate; but earthly, when compared with Christ, or with them that believe in Christ. So then, the holiness of Adam in his best estate, even that which he lost, and we in him, it was none other, than that which was natural, even the sinless state of a natural man. This holiness then was not of the nature of that, which hath for its root the Holy Ghost; for of that we read not at all in him, he only was indued with a living soul; his holiness then could not be gospel, nor that which is a branch of the second covenant: his acts of righteousness, were not by the operations of the Spirit of grace, but the dictates of the law in his own natural heart. But the apostle when he treateth of the christian inherent holiness; first excluding that in Adam, as earthly; he tells us, it is such as is in Christ: 'As is the earthy, such are they that are earthy; and as is the heavenly, such are they that are heavenly.' Let then those that are the sons of Adam, in the state of nature as he, though not so pure, and spotless as he, be reckoned to bear his image and similitude: but let them that are the children of Christ, though not so pure as he, bear the image and similitude of Christ: 'for they are conformable to the image of the Son of God.' Ro. viii 29. The holiness therefore that was in Adam, being but that which was natural, earthly, and not of the Holy Ghost, cannot be that which Christ came into the world to give us possession of.

Second, Adam in his best, and most sinless state, was but a type or figure: 'The figure of him that was to come.' Ro. v. 14. A type in what? A type or figure doubtless, in his sinless and holy estate, a type and figure of the holiness of Christ: But if Christ should come from heaven, to put us in possession of this sinless holiness that was in Adam, or that we lost in him: to what more would his work amount, than to put us into the possession of a natural, figurative, shadowish righteousness or holiness. But this he never intended; therefore it is not the possessing of his people with that holiness, that was the great errand Christ came into the world upon.

Third, The holiness and righteousness that was in, and that we lost by, Adam before the fall; was such as stood in, and was to be managed by his natural perfect compliance with a covenant of works. For, 'Do this and die,' were the terms that was from God to Adam. But Christ at his coming brings in another, a better, a blessed covenant of grace; and likewise possesseth his children, with the holiness, and privileges of that covenant; not with Adam's heart nor Adam's mind; but a new heart, a new spirit, a new principle to act

religion is, good works, of every divine kind and quality, will naturally follow, to the glory and praise of that grace which alone brings salvation to miserable ruined sinners.—*Mason and Ryland.*

by, and walk in a new covenant. Therefore the holiness that was in Adam before, or that we lost in him by the fall, could not be the holiness that Christ at his coming made it his great or only business to put us in possession of.

Fourth, The holiness that was in Adam before, and that we lost in him by the fall, was such as might stand with perfect ignorance of the mediation of Jesus Christ: for Christ was not made known to Adam as a Saviour, before that Adam was a sinner; neither needed he at all to know him to be his Mediator, before he knew he had offended. Ge. iii. But Christ did not come into the world to establish us in, or give us possession of such holiness as might stand with perfect ignorance of his Mediatorship. No; the holiness that we believers have, and the righteous acts that we fulfil, they come to us, and are done by us, through the knowledge of the Lord Jesus, and of his being the Messias promised. Ep. iv. 21, 22. 2 Pe. i. 3.

Fifth, The holiness that was in Adam, was neither given him through the promise, neither encouraged by the promise. Adam had no promise to possess him with a principle of holiness; it came to him by creation; neither had he any promise to strengthen or encourage him in holiness. All he had was instructions concerning his duty, and death threatened if he did it not. Ge. ii. 15—17. But Christ came not to give us possession of an holiness or righteousness, that came to us by our creation, without a promise; and that hath no promise to encourage us to continue therein; but of an holiness that comes to us by the best of promises, and that we are encouraged to by the best of promises. Therefore it was not his great errand when he came from heaven to earth, to put us in possession of that promiseless holiness that Adam had before, and that was lost in him by the fall.

Lastly, In a word; the holiness that Adam had before, and that we lost in him by the fall; it was a natural shadowish old covenant, promiseless holiness; such as stood and might be walked in, while he stood perfectly ignorant of the Mediator Christ. Wherefore it is rather the design of your Apollo the devil,* whom in p. 101. you bring forth to applaud your righteousness; I say, it is rather his design than Christ's, to put men upon an endeavour after a possession of that: for that which is truly evangelical, is the spiritual, substantial, new covenant promised holiness; that which cometh to us by, and standeth in the Spirit, faith and knowledge of the Son of God, not that which we lost in Adam. Wherefore the song which there you learnt of the devil, is true, in the sense he made it, and in the sense for which you bring it; which is, to beget in men, the highest esteem of

* Hierocles, the Greek philosopher.

their own human nature; and to set up this natural, shadowish, promiseless, ignorant holiness, in opposition to that which is truly Christ's.

> To dwell in heaven doth not more please him, than
> Within the souls of pious mortal men.

This is the song; but you find it not in Matthew, Mark, Luke, or John, but among the heathens who were his disciples, and who were wont to inquire at his mouth, and learn of him.

Thus have I razed the foundation of your book, even by overthrowing the holiness, and righteousness, which by you is set up, as that which is the only true gospel, and evangelical. Wherefore it remaineth, that the rest of your book, viz. whatever therein is brought, and urged for the proof of this your description of holiness, &c. it is but the abuse of Christ, of scripture, and reason; it is but a wresting and corrupting the word of God, both to your own destruction, and them that believe you.

[Fowler's insidious errors routed.]

But to pass this, and to come to some other passages in your book; and first to that in p. 5. where you say,

'The holiness, which is the design of the religion of Christ Jesus, - is not such as is subjected in any thing without us, or is made ours by a mere external application,' &c.

Answ. 1. These words secretly smite at the justification that comes by the imputation of that most glorious righteousness that alone resideth in the person of the Lord Jesus; and that is made ours by an act of eternal grace, we resting upon it by the faith of Jesus.

2. But if the holiness of which you speak, be not subjected in any thing without us; then it is not of all that fulness which it pleased the Father should dwell in Christ: for the holiness and righteousness, even the inward holiness that is in saints, it is none other than that which dwelleth in the person of the Son of God in heaven: neither doth any man partake of, or enjoy the least measure thereof, but as he is united by faith to this Son of God, the thing is as true in him as in us; in him as the head, and without measure; 1 Jn. ii. 8. and is originally seated in him, not in us. ' Of his fulness have all we (saints) received, and grace for grace.' Jn. i. 16. Wherefore the holiness that hath its original from us, from the purity of the human nature (which is the thing you aim at) and that originally, as you term it, is the dictates thereof, is the religion of the Socinians, Quakers,* &c., and not the religion of Jesus Christ.

---

* Bunyan must have formed his opinions of the Quakers from some persons who passed as such. No form either of

And now I will come to your indifferent things, viz., those which you call 'positive precepts;' things, say you, 'of an indifferent nature; and absolutely considered, are neither good, nor evil;— but are capable of becoming so; only by reason of certain circumstances:' of these positive indifferent precepts, you say, you know but three in the gospel; but three, that are purely so, viz., 'That of going to God by Christ, and the institutions of baptism, and the Lord's Supper.' This we have in p 7 and 9.

Answ. These words, as I hinted before, are highly derogatory to the Lord, the King of glory; and trample as much upon the blood of the Son of God, as words can likely do. For,

1. If going to God by Christ, be in itself but an indifferent thing, then, as I also hinted before, it is not of the substance of Christianity; but a man may be truly a Christian without it; may be saved, and go to heaven without it; this is in truth the consequence of your words: for things purely of an indifferent nature, do not in themselves either make or mar the righteousness that justifieth us from the curse before God. Wherefore, by your argument, if a man remain ignorant of that positive precept, of 'coming to God by Christ;' he remaineth ignorant but of an indifferent thing, a thing that in itself is neither good nor evil, and therefore not essentially material to his faith or justifying righteousness.

2. An indifferent thing in itself is next to nothing, neither good nor evil then, but a thing betwixt them both.

Then is the blood of the Lord Jesus, in itself, of no value at all; nor faith in him, of itself, any more than a thing of nought; their virtue and goodness only dependeth upon certain circumstances that make them so. For the indifferency of the thing lieth not simply in coming to God, but in coming to him by Christ: coming otherwise to God, even in this man's eyes, being the all in all; but in *this* coming, in coming to him by Christ, there lieth the indifferency. I marvel what injury the Lord Jesus hath done this man, that he should have such indifferent thoughts of coming to God by him?

But hath he no better thoughts of his own good deeds, which are by the law? Yes, doubtless, for those (saith he) 'are of an indispensable, and eternal obligation, which were first written in men's hearts, and originally dictates of human nature,' p. 8. Mark, not a dictate of human nature, or necessary conclusion or deduction from it, is of an indifferent, but of an indispensable; not of a transient, but of

an eternal obligation. It is only going to God by Christ, and two other things that he findeth in the gospel, that of themselves are of an indifferent nature.

But how indifferent? Even as indifferent in itself as the blood of a silly sheep, or the ashes of an heifer; for these are his very words. 'SUCH (that is, such ordinances as in themselves are of an indifferent nature) were all the injunctions and prohibitions of the ceremonial law; and some few such we have under the gospel,' p. 7. Then, in p. 9. he tells you what these positive precepts under the gospel, or things indifferent, are: 'THAT of going to God by Christ, is one; and the other two, are the institutions of baptism, and the Lord's supper.' Such therefore as were the ceremonies of the law, such, even such, saith he, is that of going to God by Christ, &c.

Wherefore, he that shall lay no more stress upon the Lord Jesus to come to God by, than this man doth, would lay as much, were the old ceremonies in force, upon a silly sheep, as upon the Christ of God. For these are all alike positive precepts, such as were the ceremonies of the law, things in themselves neither good nor evil, but absolutely considered of an indifferent nature.

So that to come to God by Christ, is reckoned, of itself, by him, a thing of a very indifferent nature, and therefore this man cannot do it, but with a very *indifferent* heart; his great, and most substantial coming to God, must needs be by some other way. Jn. x. 1. But why should this THIEF love thus to clamber, and seek to go to God by other means; such which he reckoneth of a more indispensable nature, and eternal; seeing Christ only, as indifferent as he is, is the *only* way to the Father. 'I am the way, (saith he) the truth and the life; no man cometh to the Father but by me.' If he be the only way, then there is none other; if he be thus the truth, then is all other the lie; and if he be here the life, then is all other the death; let him call them indispensable and eternal never so often.

So then, how far off this man's doctrine is, of sinning against the Holy Ghost, let him that is wise consider it. For if coming to God by Christ, be in itself but a thing indifferent, and only made a duty upon the account of certain circumstances; then, to come to God by Christ, is a duty incumbent upon us only by reason of certain circumstances; not that the thing in itself is good, or that the nature of sin, and the justice of God, layeth a necessity on us so to do. But what be these certain circumstances? For it is because of these, if you will believe him, that God the Father, yea, the whole Trinity, did consult in eternity, and consent, that Christ should be the way to life: now, I say, it is partly because by him was the

---

greatest safety, he being naturally the justice, wisdom, and power of God; and partly, because it would, we having sinned, be utterly impossible we should come to God by other means and live. He that will call *these* circumstances, that is, things over and above besides the substantials of the gospel, will but discover his unbelief and ignorance, &c.

As for your saying, that Calvin, Peter Martyr, Musculus, Zanchy,* and others, did not question, but that God could have pardoned sin, without any other satisfaction, than the repentance of the sinner, p. 84. It matters nothing to me, I have neither made my creed out of them, nor other, than the holy scriptures of God.

But if Christ was from before all worlds ordained to be the Saviour, then was he from all eternity so appointed and prepared to be. And if God be, as you say, infinitely, p. 136. and I will add, eternally just; how can he pardon without he be presented with that satisfaction for sin, that to all points of the highest perfection doth answer the demands of this infinite, and eternal justice? Unless you will say, that the repentance of a sinner is sufficient to answer whatever could be justly demanded as a satisfaction thereto; which if you should, you would in consequence say, that man is, or may be in himself, just, that is, equal with God; or that the sin of man was not a transgression of the law that was given, and a procurer of the punishment that is threatened, by that eternal God that gave it. (But let me give you a caution, take heed that you belie not these men) Christ cries, 'If it be possible let this cup pass from me.' Mat. xxvi. 39. If what be possible? Why, that sinners should be saved without his blood. He. ix. 22. Lu. xxiv. 26. Ac. xvii. 3. 'Ought not Christ to have suffered?' 'Christ must needs have suffered,' not because of some certain circumstances, but because the eternal justice of God, could not consent to the salvation of the sinner, without a satisfaction for the sin committed.† Of which, more in the next, if you shall think good to reply.

---

* Mr. Fowler gives no reference to any of the works of these learned divines, nor could he!! He traduces these great reformers and the doctrines of his own church, and yet was soon after made a bishop!!!—Ed.

† The saints of God experience a mystery of iniquity, a horrible depth of corruption in their own hearts, and groan under the plague and burden of it. If we rightly know ourselves, and behold our vileness, filthiness, and exceeding sinfulness, in their true colours, we shall be obliged to own that we are very wicked, unholy, ungodly, abominable; and that a principle and inclination to evil is so prevalent in the best of us, that were God to leave us to ourselves, we should greedily commit the most heinous sins. These truly humbled persons, and these alone, are made sensible of the want of the application of the precious atoning blood of Christ to cleanse them from the pollution of sin, and of the sanctifying grace of the Spirit

Now, that my reader may see that I have not abused you in this reply to your sayings, I will repeat your words at large, and leave them upon you to answer it.

You say, 'Actions may become duties or sins 'these two ways; first, as they are compliances 'with, or transgressions of, divine positive precepts: 'These are the declarations of the *arbitrary* will of 'God, whereby he restrains our liberty, for great 'and wise reasons, in things that are of an indifferent 'nature, and absolutely considered are neither good 'nor evil; and so makes things not good in them- 'selves (and capable of becoming so only by reason 'of certain circumstances) *duties*, and things not 'evil in themselves, *sins*. Such were all the in- 'junctions and prohibitions of the ceremonial law, 'and some few such we have under the gospel,' p 7. Then p. 9. you tell us, that 'the reasons of the 'positive laws (that is, concerning things in them- 'selves indifferent) contained in the gospel are de- 'clared; of which (say you) I know not above 'three that are purely so, viz. That of going to God 'by Christ, and the institutions of baptism, and 'the Lord's Supper.'

Here now let the reader note, That the positive precepts, declarations of the arbitrary will of God, in things of an indifferent nature, being such, as absolutely considered, are neither good nor evil; some few such, say you, we have under the gospel, namely, that of coming to God by Christ, &c. I am the more punctual in this thing, because you have confounded your weak reader with a crooked parenthesis in the midst of the paragraph, and also by deferring to spit your intended venom at Christ, till again you had puzzled him, with your mathematics and metaphysics, &c., putting in another page, betwixt the beginning and the end of your blasphemy.

Indeed, in the seventh chapter of your book, you make a great noise of the effects and consequences of the death of Christ, as that it was a sacrifice for sin, an expiatory, and propitiatory sacrifice, p. 83. Yet, he that well shall weigh you, and compare you with yourself, shall find that words and sense, with you are two things; and also, that you have learned of your brethren of old, to dissemble with words, that thereby your own heart-errors, and the snake that lieth in your bosom, may yet there abide the more undiscovered. For in the conclusion of that very chapter, even in and by a word or two, you take away that glory, that of right belongeth to the death and blood of Christ, and lay it upon other things.

For you say, 'The scriptures that frequently affirm, that the end of Christ's death was the for-

---

to deliver them from the dominion and tyranny of it.—*Mason and Ryland.*

giveness of our sins, and the reconciling of us to his Father, we are not so to understand, [those places where this is expressed] as if these blessings were absolutely thereby procured for us any otherwise, than upon condition of our effectual believing.' p. 91.

I answer, By the death of Christ was the forgiveness of sins effectually obtained for all that shall be saved, and they, even while yet enemies, by that were reconciled unto God. So that, as to forgiveness from God, it is purely upon the account of grace in Christ; ' We are justified by his blood, we are reconciled to God by the death of his Son.' Ro. v. 9, 10. Yea peace is made by the blood of his cross, Co. i. 20. and God for Christ's sake hath forgiven us. Ep. iv. 32. So then, our effectual believing is not a procuring cause in the sight of God, or a condition of ours foreseen by God, and the motive that prevaileth with him to forgive us our manifold transgressions : Believing being rather that which makes application of that forgiveness, and that possesseth the soul with that peace that already is made for us with God, by the blood of his Son Christ Jesus; ' Being justified by faith, we have peace with God through our Lord Jesus Christ.' Ro. v. 1. The peace and comfort of it cometh not to the soul, but by believing. Yet the work is finished, pardon procured, justice being satisfied already, or before, by the precious blood of Christ.

Observe, I am commanded to believe, but what should I believe ? Or what should be the object of my faith in the matter of my justification with God ? Why, I am to believe in Christ, I am to have faith in his blood ? But what is it to believe in Christ ? and what to have faith in his blood ? Verily, To believe that while we were yet sinners Christ died for us, that even then, when we were enemies, we were reconciled to God by the death of his Son: To believe that there is a righteousness *already* for us completed.

I had as good give you the apostle's argument and conclusion in his own language. ' But God commendeth his love toward us, in that, while we were yet sinners, Christ died for us. Much more then, being now justified by his blood, we shall be saved from wrath through him.' Ro. v. 8, 9. And note that this word NOW respects the same time with YET that went before. ' For if, when we were enemies, we were reconciled to God by the death of his Son, much more, being reconciled, we shall be saved by his life,' or intercession. Ro. v. 10.

Believing then, as to the business of my deliverance from the curse before God, is an accepting of, 1 Ti. i. 15. a trusting to, Ep. i. 12, 13. or a receiving, Jn. i. 12. the benefit that Christ hath already obtained for me ; by which act of faith, I see my interest in that peace that is made before with God by the blood of his cross: For if peace be

made already by his blood, then is the curse taken away from his sight ; if the curse be taken away from his sight, then there is no sin with the curse of it to be charged from God by the law, for so long as sin is charged by the law, with the curse thereto belonging, the curse, and so the wrath of God remaineth.

' But (say you) Christ died to put us into a capacity of pardon,' p. 91.

Ans. True; but that is not all. He died to put us into the personal possession of pardon: Yea, to put us into a personal possession of it, and that before we know it.

' But (say you) the actual removing of our guilt is not the necessary and immediate result of his death,' p. 91.

Ans. Yea, but it is from before the face of God, and from the judgment and curse of the law; for before God the guilt is taken away, by the death and blood of his Son, immediately, for all them that shall be saved ; else how can it be said we are justified by his blood; he hath made peace by his blood. ' He loved us, and washed us from our sins in his own blood,' Re. i. 5. and that we are reconciled to God by the death of his Son ; which can by no means be ; if, notwithstanding his death and blood, sin in the guilt, and consequently the curse that is due thereto, should yet remain in the sight of God. But what saith the apostle ? ' God was in Christ, reconciling the world to himself, not imputing their trespasses unto them.' 2 Co. v. 19. Those that are but reconciling, are not yet reconciled: I mean, as Paul, not yet come aright over in their own souls by faith ; yet to these he imputeth not their trespasses: Wherefore ? because they have none : or because he forgiveth them as they believe and work: Neither of both; but because he hath first made his Son to be sin for them, and laid all the guilt and curse of their sin upon him, that they might be made the righteousness of God in him. Therefore even because by him their sin and curse is taken off, from before the law of God; therefore, God for the sake of Christ, seeketh for, and beseecheth the sinner to be reconciled; that is, to believe in, and embrace his majesty.

' No (say you) the actual removing of our guilt, is not the necessary and immediate result of his death ; but suspended until such time as the forementioned conditions, by the help of his grace, are performed by us,' p. 92.

Ans. 1. Then may a man have the grace of God within him; yea, the grace and mercy of the new covenant, viz. Faith, and the like, that yet remaineth under the curse of the law ; and so hath yet his sins untaken away from before the face of God; for where the curse is only suspended, it may stand there notwithstanding, in force against the soul. Now, let the soul stand accursed, and his duties must stand accursed: For first the person, and then the offering must be accepted of God. God accepted not the works of Cain, because he had not accepted his person. Ge. iv. 5. But having first accepted Abel's person, he therefore did accept his offering. He. xi. 4. And hence it is said, that Abel offered by faith: He believed that his person was accepted of God, for the sake of the promised Messias, and therefore believed also that his offering should be accepted.

2. Faith, as it respecteth justification in the sight of God, must know nothing to rest upon but the mercy of God, through Christ's blood: But if the curse be not taken away, mercy also hangeth in suspense; yea, lieth as drowned, and hid in the bottom of the sea. This doctrine then of your's overthroweth faith, and rusheth* the soul into the works of the law, the moral law; and so quite involveth it in the fear of the wrath of God, maketh the soul forget Christ, taketh from it the object of faith; and if a miracle of mercy prevent not, the soul must die in everlasting desperation.

'But (say you) it is suspended till such time as the forementioned conditions, by the help of his grace, are performed by us,' p 92.

Ans. Had you said the manifestation of it is kept from us, it might, with some allowance, have been admitted; but yet the revelation of it in the word, which in some sense may be called a manifestation thereof, is first discovered to us by the word; yea, is seen by us, and also believed as a truth recorded; before the enjoyment thereof be with comfort in our own souls. 1 Jn. v. 11.

But you proceed and say, 'Therefore was the death of Christ designed to procure our justification from all sins past, that we might be by this means provoked to become new creatures,' p. 92.

Ans. That the death of Christ is a mighty argument to persuade with the believer, to devote himself to God in Christ, in all things, as becometh one that hath received grace and redemption by his blood, is true; but that it is in our power, as is here insinuated, to become new creatures, is as untrue. The new creature, is of God; yea, immediately of God; man being as incapable to make himself anew, as a child to beget himself. 2 Co. v. 17, 18. Neither is our conformity to the revealed will of God, any thing else, if it be right, than the fruit and effect of that. All things are already, or before, become new in the Christian man. But to return:

After all the flourish you have made about the death of Christ, even as he is an expiatory, and

propitiatory sacrifice; in conclusion, you terminate the business far short of that for which it was intended of God: for you almost make the effects thereof but a bare suspension of present justice and death for sin; or that which hath delivered us at present from a necessity of dying, that we might live unto God; that is, according as you have stated it. 'That we might from principles 'of humanity and reason, act towards the first 'principles of morals, &c. till we put ourselves 'into a capacity of personal and actual pardon.'

Ans. The sum of your doctrine therefore is, that Christ by his death only holds the point of the sword of justice, *not that he received it into his own soul;* that he suspends the curse from us, not that himself was made a curse for us, that the guilt might be remitted by our virtues; not that he was made to be our sin: But Paul and the New Testament, giveth us account far otherwise; viz. 'That Christ was made our sin, our curse, and death, that we by him (not by the principle of pure humanity, or our obedience to your first principles of morals, &c.) should be set free from the law of sin and death.' 2 Co. v. 21. Ga. iii. 13.

If any object that Christ hath designed the purifying our hearts and natures; I answer,

But he hath not designed to promote, or to perfect that righteousness that is founded on, and floweth from, the purity of our human nature; for then he must design the setting up man's righteousness, that which is of the law: and then he must design also the setting up of that which is directly in opposition, both to the righteousness, that of God is designed to justify us; and that by which we are inwardly made holy. As I have shewed before.

You have therefore, Sir, in all that you have yet asserted, shewed no other wisdom than a heathen, or of one that is short, even of a novice in the gospel.

In the next place, I might trace you chapter by chapter; and at large refute, not only the whole design of your book by a particular replication to them; but also sundry and damnable errors, that like venom drop from your pen.

But as before I told you in general, so here I tell you again, That neither the scriptures of God, the promise, or threatenings, the life, or death, resurrection, ascension, or coming again of Christ to judgment; hath the least syllable or tendency in them to set up your heathenish and pagan holiness or righteousness; wherefore your whole discourse is but a mere abuse of, and corrupting the holy scriptures, for the fastening, if it might have been, your errors upon the godly. I conclude then upon the whole, that the gospel hath cast out man's righteousness to the dogs; and conclude that there is no such thing as a purity of human

* 'Rusheth the soul.' To rush is a neuter verb, here used in an active sense;—'precipitateth' gives the correct idea. —ED.

nature, as a principle in us, thereby to work righteousness withal. Farther, It never thought of returning us again to the holiness we lost in Adam, or to make our perfection to consist in the possession of so natural, and ignorant* a principle as that is, in all the things of the holy gospel; but hath declared another and far better way, which you can by no means understand by all the dictates of your humanity.

I will therefore content myself at present with gathering up some few errors, out of those abundance which are in your book; and so leave you to God, who can either pardon these grievous errors, or damn you for your pride and blasphemies.

[*Fowler's false quotations of scripture.*]

You pretend in the beginning of your second chapter, to prove your assertion, viz. 'That the great errand that Christ came upon, was to put us again into possession of that holiness which we had lost.' p. 12. For proof whereof you bring John the Baptist's doctrine, Mat. iii. 1, 2. and the angel's saying to Zacharias, Lu. i. 16, 17. and the prophet Malachi, iii. 1, 2, 3. in which texts there is as much for your purpose, and no more, than there is in a perfect blank; for which of them speak a word of the righteousness or holiness which we have lost? Or where is it said, either by these mentioned, or by the whole scripture, that we are to be restored *to*, and put again into possession of *that* holiness? These are but the dictates of your human nature.

John's ministry was, 'To make ready a people prepared for the Lord Jesus;' not to possess them with themselves and their own, but now lost, holiness. And so the angel told his father, saying, 'Many of the children of Israel shall he turn to the Lord their God:' Not to Adam's innocency, or to the holiness that we lost by him. Neither did the prophet Malachi prophesy that Christ at his coming should put men again in possession of the holiness we had lost. And I say again, as you here fall short of your purpose, so I challenge you to produce but one piece of a text, that in the least looketh to such a thing. The whole tenor of the scripture, that speaks of the errand of Christ Jesus, tells us another lesson, to wit, That he himself came to save us, and that by his *own* righteousness; not *that* in Adam, or which we have lost in him, unless you can say and prove that we had once, even before we were converted, the holiness of Christ within us, or the righteousness of Christ upon us.

But you yet get on, and tell us, 'That this was also the prophesy of the angel to Joseph (p. 14.)

in these words HE (Jesus) shall save his people from their sins.' 'Not (say you) from the punishment of them, although that be a true sense too; but not the primary, but secondary, and implied only, and the consequence of the former salvation,' p. 15.

Ans. Thus Penn the quaker and you run in this, in one and the self same spirit; he affirming that sanctification is antecedent to justification, but not the consequence thereof.

2. But what salvation? Why salvation? say you: First from the filth; for that is the primary and first sense: justification from the guilt, being the never-failing consequence of this. But how then must Jesus Christ, first save us from the filth? You add in p. 16, 'That he shall bring in, instead of the ceremonial observations, a far more noble, viz., An inward substantial righteousness: and by abrogating that (namely of the ceremonies) he shall establish only this inward righteousness.' This is, that holiness, or righteousness you tell us of, in the end of the chapter going before, that you acknowledge we had lost; so that the sum of all that you have said, is, That the way that Christ will take to save his people from their sins, is, first to restore unto them, and give them possession of, the righteousness that they had lost in Adam: and having established this in them, he would acquit them also of guilt. But that this is a shameless error, and blasphemy, is apparent, from which hath already been asserted of the nature of the holiness, or righteousness, that we have lost, viz., That it was only natural of the old covenant, typical: and such as might stand with perfect ignorance of the mediation of Jesus Christ: and now I add, That for Christ to come to establish this righteousness, is alone, as if he should be sent from heaven, to overthrow, and abrogate the eternal purpose of grace, which the Father had purposed should be manifested to the world by Christ. But Christ came not to restore, or to give us possession of that which was once our own holiness, but to make us partakers of that which is in him, 'that we might be made partakers of HIS holiness.' Neither (were it granted that you speak the truth) is it possible for a man to be filled with inward gospel holiness, and righteousness, that yet abideth, as before the face of God, under the curse of the law, or the guilt of his own transgressions. He. xii. The guilt must therefore, first be taken off, and we set free by faith in that blood, that did it, before we can act upon pure Christian principles. Pray tell me the meaning of this one text; which speaking of Christ, saith, 'Who when he had by himself purged our sins, sat down on the right hand of the Majesty on high.' He. i. 3. Tell me, I say, by this text, whether is here intended the sins of all that shall be saved? If so, what kind of a purging is here

---

* 'So natural, and ignorant,' in distinction from that spiritual wisdom which is immortal and illuminating.—ED.

meant, seeing thousands, and thousands of thousands, of the persons intended by this act of purging were not then in being, nor their personal sins in act? And note, he saith, he purged them, before he sat down at the right hand of God: purging then, in this place, cannot first, and primarily, respect the purging of the conscience: but the taking, the complete taking of the guilt, and so the curse from before the face of God, according to other scriptures: 'He hath made him to be sin, and accursed of God for us.' Now he being made the sin which we committed, and the curse which we deserved; there is no more sin nor curse; I mean to be charged by the law, to damn them that shall believe, not that their believing takes away the curse, but puts the soul upon trusting to him, that before purged this guilt, and curse: I say, before he sat down on the right hand of God; not to suspend, as you would have it, but to take away the sin of the world. 'The Lord hath laid upon him the iniquities of us all.' Is. liii. 6. And he bare them in his own body on the tree: 1 Pe. ii. 24, nor yet that he should often offer himself; for then must he often have suffered since the foundation of the world: but now, (and that at once,) in the end of the world hath he appeared, to put away sin, by the sacrifice of himself. He. ix. 24—26. Mark, he did put it away by the sacrifice of his body and soul, when he died on the cross: but he could not then put away the inward filth of those, that then remained unconverted; or those that as yet wanted being in the world. The putting away of sin therefore, that the Holy Ghost here intendeth, is, *such* a putting of it away, as respecteth the guilt, curse, and condemnation thereof, as it stood by the accusations of the law, against all flesh before the face of God; which guilt, curse, and condemnation, Christ himself was made in that day, when he died the death for us. And this is the first and principal intendment of the angel, in that blessed saying to godly Joseph, concerning Christ: 'He shall save his people from their sins;' from the guilt and curse due to them, first: and afterwards from the filth thereof. This is yet manifest, further; because the heart is purified by faith, and hope. Ac. xv. 9. 1 Jn. iii. 3. Now it is not the nature of faith; I mean, of justifying faith, to have any thing for an object; from which it fetcheth peace with God, and holiness before, or besides the Christ of God himself; for he is the way to the Father: and no man can come to the Father, but by him. Come; that is, so as to find acceptance, and peace with him: the reason is, because without his blood, guilt remains. He. ix. 22. He hath made peace by the blood of his cross: so then, faith in the first place seeketh peace. But why peace first? Because till peace is fetched into the soul, by faith's laying hold on the blood of Christ: sin remains in the guilt and

curse, though not in the sight of God, yet upon the conscience, through the power of unbelief. 'He that believeth not, stands yet condemned.' Jn. iii. 18, 19. Now, so long as guilt, and the curse in power remains, there is not purity, but unbelief; not joy, but doubting; not peace, but peevishness; not content; but murmuring, and angering against the Lord himself. 'The law worketh wrath.' Ro. iv. 15. Wherefore, as yet there can be no purity of heart, because that faith yet wants his object. But having once found peace with God by believing what the blood of Christ hath done; joy followeth; so doth peace, quietness, content, and love; which is also the fulfilling of the law: yet not from such dungish principles as yours, for so the apostle calls them. Phi. iii. 8. But from the Holy Ghost itself; which God, by faith, hath granted to be received by them that believe in the blood of his Jesus.

But you add, That Christ giveth, first repentance, and then forgiveness of sins, p. 17.

Answ. 1. This makes nothing for the holiness which we lost in Adam: for the proof of which you bring that text, Ac. v. 31.

2. But for Christ to take away guilt, and the curse, from before the face of God, is one thing; and to make that discovery, is another.

3. Again, Christ doth not give forgiveness for the sake of that repentance, which hath its rise, originally from the dictates of our own nature, which is the thing you are to prove; for that repentance is called the sorrow of this world, and must be again repented of: but the repentance mentioned in the text, is that which comes from Christ: But,

4. It cannot be for the sake of gospel-repentance, that the forgiveness of sins is manifested, because both are his peculiar gift.

5. Therefore, both faith, and repentance, and forgiveness of sins, are given by Christ; and come to us, for the sake of that blessed offering of his body, once for all. For after he arose from the dead, having led captivity captive, and taken the curse from before the face of God: therefore his Father gave him gifts for men, even all the things that are necessary, and effectual, for our conversion, and preservation in this world, &c. Ep. iv. 8.

This text, therefore, with all the rest you bring, falleth short of the least shew of proof, 'That the great errand for which Christ came into the world was—to put us in possession of the holiness that we had lost.'

Your third chapter is as empty of the proof of your design as that through which we have passed: there being not one scripture therein cited, that giveth the least intimation, that ever it entered into the heart of Christ to put us again into possession of that holiness which we had before we were converted: for such was that we lost in Adam.

You tell us the sum of all is, 'that we are commanded to add to our faith, virtue,' &c. p. 25. I suppose you intend a gospel faith, which if you can prove Adam had before the fall, and that we lost this faith in him; and also that this gospel faith is none other, but that which originally ariseth from, or is the dictates of human nature, I will confess you have scripture, and knowledge beyond me. In the mean time you must suffer me to tell you, you are as far in this from the mind of the Holy Ghost, as if you had yet never in all your days heard whether there be a Holy Ghost or no.

Add to your faith. The apostle here lays a gospel principle, viz., Faith in the Son of God: which faith layeth hold of the forgiveness of sins, alone for the sake of Christ; therefore he is a great way off, of laying the purity of the human nature, the law, as written in the heart of natural man, as the principle of holiness; from whence is produced good works in the soul of the godly.

In your fourth chapter also (p. 28.) even in the beginning thereof; even with one text you have overthrown your whole book.

This chapter is to prove, that the only design of the promises, and threatenings of the gospel, is to promote, and put us again in possession of the holiness we had lost. For that the reader must still remember, is the only design of your book, p. 12. Whereas the first text you speak of, 2 Pe. i. 4. maketh mention of the Divine nature, or of the Spirit of the living God, which is also received by the precious faith of Christ, and the revelation of the knowledge of him; this blessed Spirit, and therefore not the dictates of human nature, is the principle that is laid in the godly: but Adam's holiness had neither the knowledge, or faith, or Spirit of the Lord Jesus, as its foundation, or principle: yea, nature was his foundation, even his own nature was the original, from whence his righteousness and good works arose.

The next scriptures also, viz. 2 Co. vii. 1. Ro. xii. 1. overthrow you; for they urge the promises as motives to stir us up to holiness. But Adam had neither the Spirit of Jesus, or faith in him, as a principle: nor any promises to him as motives: wherefore this was not that to which he, or which we Christians are exhorted to seek the possession of; but that which is operated by that Spirit which we receive by the faith of Jesus, and that which is encouraged by those promises, that God hath since given to them that have closed by faith with Jesus.

The rest also, (in p. 29.) not one of them doth promise us the possession of the holiness we have lost, or any mercy to them that have it.

You add: 'And whereas the promises of pardon, and of eternal life are very frequently made to *believing*; there is nothing more evidently declared, than that this *faith* is such as purifieth the heart, and is productive of good works.' p. 30.

Ans. 1. If the promise be made at all to believing, it is not made to us upon the account of the holiness we had lost; for I tell you yet again, that holiness is not of faith, neither was faith the effect thereof. But,

2. The promises of pardon, though they be made to such a faith as is fruitful in good works: yet not to it, as it is fruitful in doing, but in receiving good. Sir, the quality of justifying faith is this, *Not to work, but to believe,* as to the business of pardon of sin: and that not only, because of the sufficiency that this faith sees in Christ to justify, but also for that it knows those whom God thus pardoneth, be justifieth as ungodly. 'But to him that worketh not, but believeth;' (Mark, here faith and works are opposed) 'But to him that worketh not, but believeth on him that justifieth the ungodly, his faith is counted for righteousness.' Ro. iv. 5.

You add farther, 'That the promises may be reduced to these three heads; that of the Holy Spirit, of remission of sins, and eternal happiness, in the enjoyment of God,' p. 30.

Ans. If you can prove that any of these promises were made to the holiness that we had lost, or that by these promises we are to be possessed with that holiness again; I will even now lay down the bucklers. For albeit, the time will come when the saints shall be absolutely, and perfectly sinless; yet then shall they be also spiritual, immortal, and incorruptible, which you cannot prove Adam was, in the best of his holiness, even that which we lost in him.

The threatenings you speak of * are every one made against sin, but not one of them to drive us into a possession of that holiness that we had lost: nay, contrariwise, he that looks to, or seeks after that, is as sure to be damned, and go to hell, as he that transgresseth the law; because that is not the righteousness of God, the righteousness of Christ, the righteousness of faith, nor that to which the promise is made.

And this was manifested to the world betimes, even in that day, when God drove the man and his wife out of Eden, and placed cherubims, and a flaming sword, in the way by which they came out, to the end, that by going back by *that* way, they might rather be killed and die, than lay hold of the 'tree of life.' Ge. iii.

Which the apostle also respects, when he calleth the way of the gospel, the NEW and LIVING way, even that which is made by the blood of Christ; He. x. 20. concluding by this description of the way

---

* Against all ungodliness and unrighteousness of men, such as disbelief, idolatry, adultery, &c., p. 35.

that is by blood, that the other is old, and the way of death, even that which is by the moral law, or the dictates of our nature, or by that fond conceit of the goodly holiness of Adam.

[*Our Lord's object not merely to restore man's natural holiness, but to impart his own infinite and eternal holiness to those that believe.*]

Your fifth chapter tells us, 'That the promoting of holiness was the design of our Saviour's whole life and conversation among men,' p. 36.

Ans. 1. Were this granted, it reacheth nothing at all the design for which you in your way present us with it: For,

2. That which you have asserted is: That the errand about which Christ came, was, as the effecting our deliverance out of that sinful state we had brought ourselves into, so to put us again in possession of that holiness which we had lost; for that, you say, is the business of your book, p. 12. Wherefore you should have told us in the head of this chapter, not so much that our Saviour designed the promoting of holiness in general by his life, but that the whole design of our Saviour's life and conversation, was to put us again into possession of *that* holiness which we had lost, into a possession of that natural, old covenant, figurative, ignorant holiness. But it seems you count that there is no other than that now lost, but never again to be obtained holiness, that was in Adam.

3. Farther, you also falter here, as to the stating of the proposition; for in the beginning of your book, you state it thus: That the enduing men with inward real righteousness, or true holiness, was the ultimate end of our Saviour's coming into the world, still meaning the holiness we lost in Adam. You should therefore in this place also, have minded your reader of this your proposition, and made it manifest if you could, 'that the ultimate end of our Saviour's whole life and conversation, was the enduing men with this Adamitish holiness.' But *holiness*, and *that* holiness, is alone with you; and to make it his end, and whole end; his business, and the whole business of his life; is but the same with you.

But you must know, that the whole life and conversation of our Saviour, was intended for another purpose, than to drive us back to, or to endue us with, such an holiness and righteousness as I have proved this to be.

You have therefore, in this your discourse, put an insufferable affront upon the Son of God, in making all his life and conversation to centre and terminate in the holiness we had lost: As if the Lord Jesus was sent down from heaven, and the word of God made flesh; that by a perfect life and conversation, he might shew us how holy Adam

was before he fell; or what an holiness *that* our holiness was, which we had before we were converted.

Your discourse therefore, of the life and conversation of the Lord Jesus, is none other than heathenish: For you neither treat of the principle, his Godhead, by which he did his works; neither do you in the least, in one syllable, aver the first, the main and prime reason of this his conversation; only you treat of it so far, as a mean man might have considered it. And indeed it stood not with your design to treat aright with these things; for had you mentioned the first, though but once, your Babel had tumbled about your ears; for if in the holy Jesus did ' dwell the word,' one of the three in heaven; or if the Lord and Saviour Jesus Christ, was truly, essentially, and naturally God; then must the principle from whence his works did proceed, be better than the principle from whence proceeded the goodness in Adam; otherwise Adam must be God and man. Also you do, or may know that the self-same act may be done from several principles: and again, that it is the principle from whence the act is done, and not the bare doing of the act, that makes it better or worse accepted, in the eyes either of God or men.

Now then, *to shew you the main, or chief design of the life and conversation of the Lord Jesus.*

First, It was not to shew us what an excellent holiness we once had in Adam, but that thereby God, the Eternal Majesty, according to his promise, might be seen by, and dwell with, mortal men: For the Godhead being altogether in its own nature invisible, and yet desirous to be seen by, and dwell with the children of men; therefore was the Son, who is the self-same substance with the Father, closed with, or tabernacled in our flesh; that in that flesh, the nature and glory of the Godhead might be seen by, and dwell with us: ' The word was made flesh, and dwelt among us, (and we beheld his glory, (what glory? the glory,) as of the only begotten of the Father) full of grace and truth.' Jn. i. 14. Again, ' The life (that is, the life of God, in the works and conversation of Christ) was manifested, and we have seen *it*, and bear witness, and shew unto you that eternal life, which was with the Father, and was manifested unto us;' 1 Jn. i. 2. And hence he is called the image of the invisible God; Col. i. 15. or he by whom the invisible God is most perfectly presented to the sons of men. Did I say before, that the God of glory is desirous to be seen of us? Even so also, have the pure in heart, a desire that it should be so: ' Lord, say they, shew us the Father, and it sufficeth us.' Jn. xiv. 8. And therefore the promise is for their comfort, that ' they shall see God.' Mat. v. 8. But how then must they see him? Why, in the person, and by the life and works of Jesus. When

Philip, under a mistake, thought of seeing God some other way, than in and by this Lord Jesus Christ; What is the answer? 'Have I been so long time with you, (saith Christ) and yet hast thou not known me, Philip? He that hath seen me, hath seen the Father; and how sayest thou *then*, Shew us the Father? Believest thou not that I am in the Father, and the Father in me? The words that I speak unto you I speak not of myself: but the Father, that dwelleth in me, he doth the works. Believe me, that I *am* in the Father, and the Father in me; or else believe me for the very works' sake.' Jn. xiv. 9—11. See here, that both the words and works of the Lord Jesus, were not to shew you, and so to call you back to the holiness that we had lost, but to give us visions of the perfections that are in the Father. He hath given us 'the knowledge of the glory of God, in the face of Jesus Christ.' 2 Co. iv. 6. And hence it is, that the apostle, in that brief collection of the wonderful mystery of godliness, placeth this in the front thereof: 'God was manifest in the flesh.' 1 Ti. iii. 16. Was manifest, viz. In and by the person of Christ, when in the flesh he lived among us; manifest, I say, for this, as one reason, that the pure in heart, who long after nothing more, might see him. 'I beseech thee,' said Moses, 'shew me thy glory.'* 'And will God indeed dwell with men on the earth?' saith Solomon.

Now to fulfil the desires of them that fear him, hath he shewed himself in flesh unto them; which discovery principally is made by the words and works of Christ. But,

Second, Christ by his words and works of righteousness, in the days of his flesh, neither shewed us which was, nor called us back to the possession of the holiness that we had lost; but did perfect, in, and by himself, the law for us, that we had broken. Man being involved in sin and misery, by reason of transgression committed against the law, or ministration of death, and being utterly unable to recover himself therefrom, the Son of God himself assumeth the flesh of man, and for

* How astonishing the mystery! how condescending the love! that the infinite Deity and finite flesh should meet in one person (Christ), in order to display to mankind the glory of God in that divine person! to bring hell-deserving mortals into a nearness, yea, into a oneness with his Creator, that they might be made partakers of his holiness, and adore and admire his perfections for ever! O Christians, know and prize your inestimable privileges, and be instant at the throne of grace, that your souls may be so far assimilated to the image of the ever-blessed and adorable Jesus, that you may be constantly looking and hastening to, and longing for that happy time, when, having dropt the dimning rags of mortality, the veil of sinful flesh, you shall be brought to 'know him even as you are known' of him, because you shall 'see him as he is.'—*Ryland.*

sin condemned sin in that flesh. And that first, by walking, through the power of his eternal Spirit, in the highest perfection to every point of the whole law, in its most exact and full requirements; which was to be done, not only without commixing sin in his doing, but by one that was perfectly without the least being of it in his nature; yea, by one that now was God-Man, because it was God whose law was broken, and whose justice was offended: For, were it now possible to give a man possession of that holiness that he hath lost in Adam, that holiness could neither in the principle nor act deliver from the sin by him before committed. This is evident by many reasons: 1. Because it is not a righteousness able to answer the demands of the law for sin; *that* requiring not only a perfect abiding in the thing commanded, but a satisfaction by death, for the transgression committed against the law. 'The wages of sin *is* death.' Ro. vi. 23. Wherefore he that would undertake the salvation of the world, must be one who can do both these things; one that can perfectly do the demands of the law in thought, word, and deed, without the least commixture of the least sinful thought in the whole course of his life: He must be also able to give by death, even by the death that hath the curse of God in it, a complete satisfaction to the law for the breach thereof. Now this could none but Christ accomplish; none else having power to do it. 'I have power (said he) to lay down my life, and I have power to take it again: And this commandment have I received of my Father.' Jn. x. 18. This work then must be done, not by another earthly Adam, but by the Lord from Heaven; by one that can abolish sin, destroy the devil, kill death, and rule as Lord in heaven and earth. Now the words and works of the Lord Jesus, declared him to be such an one. He was first without sin; then he did no sin; neither could either the devil, the whole world, or the law, find any deceit in his mouth: But by being under the law, and walking in the law, by that Spirit which was the Lord God of the law, he not only did always the things that pleased the Father, but by that means in man's flesh, he did perfectly accomplish and fulfil that law which all flesh stood condemned by. It is a foolish and an heathenish thing, nay worse, to think that the Son of God should only, or specially fulfil, or perfect the law, and the prophets, by giving more and higher instances of moral duties than were before expressly given, p. 17. This would have been but the lading of men with heavy burthens. But know then, whoever thou art that readest, that Christ's exposition of the law was more to shew thee the perfection of his own obedience, than to drive thee back to the holiness thou hadst lost; for God sent him to fulfil it, by doing it, and dying to the most sore sentence it could pronounce: not as he stood a single person, but common,* as Mediator between God and man; making up in himself the breach that was made by sin, betwixt God and the world. For,

Third, He was to die as a lamb, as a lamb without blemish, and without spot, according to the type; 'Your lamb shall be without blemish.' Ex. xii. 5. But because there was none such to be found BY and AMONG all the children of men; therefore God sent HIS from heaven. Hence John calls him the Lamb of God, Jn. i. 29. and Peter him that was without spot, who washed us by his blood. 1 Pe. i. 19. Now wherein doth it appear that he was without spot and blemish, but as he walked in the law? These words therefore *without spot* are the sentence of the law, who searching him could find nothing in him why he should be slain, yet he died because there was sin: Sin! where? Not in him, but in his people; 'For the transgression of my people was he stricken.' Is. liii. 8. He died then for our sins, and qualified himself so to do, by coming sinless into the world, and by going sinless through it; for had he not done both these, he must have died for himself. But being God, even in despite of all that stumble at him, he conquered death, the devil, sin, and the curse, by himself, and then sat down at the right hand of God.

Fourth, And because he hath a second part of his priestly office to do in heaven; therefore it was thus requisite that he should thus manifest himself to be holy and harmless, undefiled, and separate from sinners on the earth. He. vii. 26. As Aaron first put on the holy garments, and then went into the holiest of all. The life, therefore, and conversation of our Lord Jesus, was to shew us with what a curious robe and girdle he went into the holy place; and not to shew us with what an Adamitish holiness he would possess his own. 'Such an high priest became us, *who is* holy, harmless, undefiled, separate from sinners, and made higher than the heavens;' that he might always be accepted, both in person and offering, when he presenteth his blood to God, the atonement for sin. Indeed in some things he was an example to us to follow him; but mark, it was not as he was Mediator, not as he was under the law to God, not as he died for sin, nor as he maketh reconciliation for iniquity. But in these things consist the life of our soul, and the beginning of our happiness. He was then exemplary to us, as he carried it meekly and patiently, and self-denyingly towards the world: But yet not so neither to any but such to whom he first offered justification by the means of his own righteousness; for before he saith 'learn of me,' he saith,

'I will give you rest;' rest from the guilt of sin, and fear of everlasting burnings. Mat. xi. And so Peter first tells us, he died for our sins; and next, that he left us an example. 1 Pe. ii. 21. But should it be granted that the whole of Christ's life and conversation among men was for our example, and for no other end at all, but that we should learn to live by his example, yet it would not follow, but be as far from truth as the ends of the earth are asunder, that by this means he sought to possess us with the holiness we had lost, for that he had not in himself; it is true he was born without sin, yet born God and man; he lived in the world without sin, but he lived as God-Man: he walked in and up to the law, but it was as God-Man. Neither did his manhood, even in those acts of goodness, which as to action, most properly respected it; do ought without, but by and in conjunction with his Godhead: Wherefore all and every whit of the righteousness and good that he did was that of God-Man, the righteousness of God. But this was not Adam's principle, nor any holiness that we had lost.

Your fifth chapter, therefore, consisteth of words spoken to the air.

Your sixth chapter tells us, 'That to make men truly virtuous and holy, was the design of Christ's inimitable actions, or mighty works and miracles, and these did only tend to promote it,' p. 68.

He neither did, nor needed, so much as one small piece of a miracle to persuade men to seek for the holiness which they had lost, or to give them again possession of that; for that as I have shewed, though you would fain have it otherwise, is not at all the Christian or gospel righteousness. Wherefore, in one word, you are as short by this chapter to prove your natural old covenant, promiseless, figurative holiness, to be here designed, as if you had said so much as amounts to nothing. Farther, Christ needed not to work a miracle to persuade men to fall in love with themselves, and their own natural dictates; to persuade them that they have a purity of the human nature in them; or that the holiness which they have lost, is the only true, real, and substantial holiness: These things, both corrupted nature and the devil, have of a long time fastened, and fixed in their minds.

His miracles therefore tend rather to take men off of the pursuit after the righteousness or holiness that we had lost, and to confirm unto us the truth of a far more excellent and blessed thing; to wit, the righteousness of God, of Christ, of faith, of the Spirit, which *that* you speak of never knew; neither is it possible that he should know it who is hunting for your sound complexion, your purity of human nature, or its dictates, as the only true, real, and substantial righteousness. 'They are ignorant of God's righteousness, that go about to establish

---

* 'Common,' as the head of his church, in whom all his people have an equal or *common* right.—ED.

their own righteousness;' and neither have, nor can, without a miracle, submit themselves unto the righteousness of God. They cannot submit *themselves* thereto; talk thereof they may, notion it they may, profess it too they may; but for a man to submit *himself* thereto, is by the mighty power of God.

Miracles and signs are for them that believe not. 1 Co. xiv. 22. Why for them? That they might believe; therefore their state is reckoned fearful that have not yet believed for all his wondrous works. And though he did so many miracles among them, yet they believed him not. Jn. xii. 37—40. But what should they believe? That Jesus is the true Messias, the Christ that should come into the world. Do you say that I blaspheme (saith Christ) because I said I am the Son of God: 'If I do not the works of my Father believe me not; but if I do, though ye believe not me believe the works: that ye may know, and believe that the Father *is* in me, and I in him.' Jn. x. 37, 38. But what is it to believe that he is Messias, or Christ? Even to believe that this man Jesus was ordained and appointed of God (and that before all worlds) to be the Saviour of men, by accomplishing in himself an everlasting righteousness for them, and by bearing their sins in his body on the tree; that it was he that was to reconcile us to God, by the body of his flesh, when he hanged on the cross. This is the doctrine that at the beginning Christ preached to that learned ignorant Nicodemus. 'As Moses (said he) lifted up the serpent in the wilderness, even so must the Son of Man be lifted up, that whosoever believeth in him should not perish, but have eternal life.' Jn. iii. 14, 15. The serpent was lifted up upon a pole: Nu. xxi. 9. 'Christ was hanged on a tree.' The serpent was lifted up for murmurers: Christ was hanged up for sinners: The serpent was lifted up for them that were bitten with fiery serpents, the fruits of their wicked murmuring: Christ was hanged up for them that are bitten with guilt, the rage of the devil, and the fear of death and wrath: The serpent was hanged up to be looked on: Christ was hanged up that we might believe in him, that we might have faith in his blood: They that looked upon the serpent of brass lived: They that believe in Christ shall be saved, and shall never perish. Was the serpent then lifted up for them that were good and godly? No, but for the sinners: 'So God commended his love to us, in that, while we were yet sinners Christ died for us.' But what if they that were stung, could not, because of the swelling of their face, look up to the brazen serpent? then without remedy they die: So he that believeth not in Christ shall be damned. But might they not be healed by humbling themselves? one would think that better than to live by looking up only: No, only looking up did it, when death swallowed up them that looked not. This then is the doctrine,

'Christ came into the world to save sinners:' according to the proclamation of Paul, 'Be it known unto you therefore, men *and* brethren, that through this man is preached unto you the forgiveness of sins; And by him all that believe are justified from all things, from which ye could not be justified by the law of Moses.' The forgiveness of sins: But what is meant by forgiveness? Forgiveness doth strictly respect the debt, or punishment that by sin we have brought upon ourselves. But how are we by this man forgiven this? Because by his blood he hath answered the justice of the law, and so made amends to an offended majesty. Besides, this man's righteousness is made over to him that looks up to him for life; yea, that man is made the righteousness of God in him. This is the doctrine that the miracles were wrought to confirm, and that, both by Christ, and his apostles, and not that holiness and righteousness, that is the fruit of a feigned purity of our nature.

Take two or three instances for all.

First, 'Then came the Jews round about him, and said unto him, How long dost thou make us to doubt? If thou be the Christ, tell us plainly. Jesus answered them, I told you, and ye believed not; the works that I do in my Father's name, they bear witness of me. But ye believe not, because ye are not of my sheep.' Jn. x. 24—26.

By this scripture the Lord Jesus testifies what was the end of his words and wondrous works, viz. That men might know that he was the Christ; that he was sent of God to be the Saviour of the world; and that these miracles required of them, first of all, that they accept of him by *believing;* a thing little set by, by our author, for in p. 299. he preferreth his doing righteousness far before it, and above all things else, his words are verbatim thus, ' Let us exercise ourselves unto real and substantial godliness, (such as he hath described in the first part of his book, viz. That which is the dictates of his human nature, &c.) and in keeping our consciences void of offence, both towards God and towards men, and in studying the gospel to enable us, not to discourse, or only to believe, but also and above all things to *do, well.*' But believing, though not with this man, yet by Christ and his wondrous miracles, is expected first, and above ALL things, from men; and to do well, in the best sense (though his sense is the worst) is that which by the gospel is to come after.

Second, ' Go into all the world, and preach the gospel to every creature. He that believeth and is baptized shall be saved; but he that believeth not shall be damned And these signs shall follow them that believe: In my name shall they cast out devils, they shall speak with new tongues; they shall take up serpents, and if they drink any deadly thing, it shall not hurt them,' &c. Mar. xvi. 15—18.

Mark you here, it is believing, *believing*; It is, I say, believing that is here required by Christ. Believing what? The gospel; even good tidings to sinners by Jesus Christ; good tidings of good, glad tidings of good things. Mark how the apostle hath it; the glad tidings is, 'That through this man [Jesus] is preached unto you the forgiveness of sins; and by him all that believe are justified from all things, from which ye could not be justified by the law of Moses.' Ac. xiii. 38, 39.

These signs shall follow them that believe. Mark, signs before, and signs after, and all to excite to, and confirm the weight of believing. 'And they went forth, and preached everywhere, the Lord working with *them*, and confirming the word with signs following. Amen.' Mar. xvi. 20.

Third, 'Therefore we ought to give the more earnest heed to the things which we have heard, lest at any time we should let *them* slip. For if the word spoken by angels was stedfast, and every transgression and disobedience received a just recompense of reward; How shall we escape, if we neglect so great salvation; which at the first began to be spoken by the Lord, and was confirmed unto us by them that heard *him*; God also bearing *them* witness both with signs and wonders, and with divers miracles, and gifts of the Holy Ghost, according to his own will.' He. ii. 1—4.

Here we are excited to the faith of the Lord Jesus, under these words ' so great salvation.' As if he had said, give earnest heed, the most earnest heed, to the doctrine of the Lord Jesus, because it is ' so great salvation.' What this salvation is, he tells us, it is that which was preached by the Lord himself; ' For God so loved the world, that he gave his only begotten Son, that whosoever believeth in him should not perish, but have everlasting life.' Jn. iii. 16. God so loved, that he gave his Son to be so great salvation. Now as is expressed in the text, to be the better for this salvation, is, to give heed to hear it; for ' Faith *cometh* by hearing.' Ro. x. 17.

He saith not give heed to doing, but to the word you have *heard*; faith, I say, cometh by hearing, and hearing by the word of God. Ro. x. But that this hearing is the hearing of faith, is farther evident:

1. Because he speaketh of a great salvation, accomplished by the love of God in Christ, accomplished by his blood. ' By his own blood he entered in once into the holy place, having obtained eternal redemption *for us*.' He. ix. 12.

2. This salvation is set in opposition to that which was propounded before, by the ministration of angels, which consisted in a law of works; that which Moses received to give to the children of Israel. ' For the law (a command to works and duties) was given by Moses, *but* grace and

truth came by Jesus Christ.' Jn. i. 17. To live by doing works is the doctrine of the law and Moses; but to live by faith and grace, is the doctrine of Christ, and the gospel.

Besides, the threatening being pressed with an ' How shall we escape ?' Respects still a better, a freer, a more gracious way of life, than either the moral or ceremonial law; for both these were long before: But here comes in another way, not that propounded by Moses, or the angels, but since by the Lord himself. ' How shall we escape, if we neglect so great salvation; which at the first began to be spoken by the Lord, and was confirmed unto us by them that heard *him*.'

Now mark, It is this salvation, this *so great* and eternal salvation, that was obtained by the blood of the Lord himself. It was this, even to confirm faith in this, that the God of heaven himself came down to confirm, by signs and wonders; ' God bearing *them* witness, both with signs and wonders, and with divers miracles, and gifts of the Holy Ghost, according to his own will.' He. ii. 4.

Thus we see, that to establish a holiness that came from the first principles of morals in us, or that ariseth from the dictates of our human nature, or to drive us back to that figurative holiness that we had once, but lost in Adam, is little thought on by Jesus Christ, and as little intended by any of the gospel miracles.

A word or two more. The tribute money you mention,* was not as you would clawingly insinuate for no other purpose, than to shew Christ's loyalty to the magistrate: But first, and above all, to shew his godhead, to confirm his gospel, and then to shew his loyalty, the which, Sir, the persons you secretly smite at, have respect for, as much as you.

Again, Also the curse of the barren fig-tree, mentioned, p. 73. was not (if the Lord himself may be believed) to give us an emblem of a person void of good works; but to shew his disciples the power of faith, and what a wonder-working thing that blessed grace is. Wherefore, when the disciples wondered at that sudden blast that was upon the tree, Jesus answered not, behold an emblem of one void of moral virtues; but ' Verily, I say unto you, If ye have faith, and doubt not, ye shall not only do this *which is done* to the fig-tree, but also if ye shall say unto this mountain, Be thou removed, and be thou cast into the sea; it shall be done. And all things, whatsoever ye shall ask in prayer

---

* ' And even that miracle which might seem the most inconsiderable, namely, his causing his disciple Peter to catch a fish with a small piece of money in its mouth, was also instructive of a duty; it being an instance of his loyalty to the supreme magistrate; for the money was expended in paying tribute, and taken out of the sea in that strange manner for no other purpose.'—*Fowler's Design, &c.*, p. 72.

believing, ye shall receive.' Mat. xxi. 21, 22. Again, Mark saith, When Peter saw the fig-tree that the Lord had cursed dried up from the roots, he said to his master, 'behold the fig-tree which thou cursedst is withered away.' xi. 21. Christ now doth not say as you, this tree was an emblem of a professor void of good works; but, 'Have faith in, or the faith of God. For, verily I say unto you, That whosoever shall say unto this mountain, Be thou removed, and be thou cast into the sea, and shall not doubt in his heart, but shall believe that those things which he saith shall come to pass, he shall have whatsoever he saith. Therefore I say unto you, What things soever ye desire, when ye pray, believe that ye receive *them*, and ye shall have *them*.' Christ Jesus therefore had a higher, and a better end, than that which you propound, in his cursing the barren fig-tree, even to shew, as himself expounds it, the mighty power of faith; and how it lays hold of things in heaven, and tumbleth before it things on earth. Wherefore your scriptureless exposition, doth but lay* you even Solomon's proverb, 'The legs of the lame are not equal,' &c. Pr. xxvi. 7.

I might enlarge; but enough of this; only here I add, that the wonders and miracles that attend the gospel, were wrought, and are recorded, to persuade to faith in Christ. By faith in Christ men are justified from the curse, and judgment of the law. This faith worketh by love, by the love of God it brings up the heart to God, and goodness; but not by your covenant, Eze. xvi. 61. not by principles of human nature, but of the Spirit of God; not in a poor, legal, old covenant, promiseless, ignorant, shadowish, natural holiness, but by the Holy Ghost.

[*The death of Christ accomplished an infinitely greater object than the restoring of man to his original temporal holiness.*]

I come now to your seventh chapter; but to that I have spoken briefly already, and therefore here shall be the shorter.

In this chapter you say, 'that to make men holy was the design of Christ's death.' p. 78.

Ans. 1. But not with your described principles of humanity, and dictates of human nature. He designed not, as I have fully proved, neither by his death, nor life, to put us into a possession of the holiness which we had lost, though the proof of that be the business of your book.

2. To make men holy, was doubtless designed by the death and blood of Christ: but the way and manner of the proceeding of the Holy Ghost therein, you write not of; although the first text you mention (p. 78, 79.) doth fairly present you with it. For the way to make men inwardly holy, by the death and blood of Christ, is, first, to possess† them with the knowledge of this, that their sins were crucified with him, or that he did bear them in his body on the tree: 'Knowing this, that our Old Man is crucified with *him*, that the body of sin might be destroyed, that henceforth we should not serve sin.' Ro. vi. 6. So he died for all, that they that live, should not henceforth live unto themselves, as you would have them, nor to the law or dictates of their own nature, as your doctrine would persuade them; 'but to him that died for them, and rose again.' 2 Co. v. 15.

There are two things, in the right stating of the doctrine of the effects of the death and blood of Christ, that do naturally effect in us an holy principle, and also a life becoming such a mercy.

First, For that by it we are set at liberty, by faith therein, from the guilt, and curse that is due to guilt, from death, the devil, and the wrath to come. No encouragement to holiness like this, like the persuasion, and belief of this; because this carrieth in it the greatest expression of love, that we are capable of hearing or believing, and there is nothing that worketh on us so powerfully as love. 'Herein is love, not that we loved God, but that he loved us, and sent his Son *to be* the propitiation for our sins.' 1 Jn. iv. 10. He then that by faith can see that the body of his sin did hang upon the cross, by the body of Christ, and that can see by that action, death and sin, the devil and hell, destroyed for him; it is he that will say, 'Bless the Lord, O my soul, and all that is within me *bless* his holy name,' &c. Ps. ciii. 1—4.

Second, Moreover, the knowledge of this giveth a man to understand this mystery, That Christ and himself are united in one. For faith saith, If our Old Man was crucified with Christ, then were we also reckoned in him, when he hanged on the cross, 'I am crucified with Christ.' Ga. ii. 20. All the Elect did mystically hang upon the cross in Christ. We then are dead to the law, and sin, first, by the body of Christ. Ro. vii. 4. Now he that is dead is free from sin; now if we be dead with Christ, we believe that we shall live with him, knowing that Christ being raised from the dead, dieth no more, death hath no more dominion over him; for in that he died, he died unto sin once; but in that he liveth, he liveth unto God: likewise reckon yourselves also dead unto sin, but alive unto God, through Jesus Christ our Lord. Ro. vi.

---

* 'Lay you,' brings forth to yourself. 'Lay' is here used as in 'a hen lays eggs;' such an application to this proverb is a cutting satire.—ED.

† 'To possess them.' Possess was formerly used as an active verb, but now is only used as a neuter verb; the meaning is 'to fill them with the certainty of the knowledge.'

This also Peter doth lively discourse of, 'Forasmuch then (saith he) as Christ hath suffered for us in the flesh, arm yourselves likewise with the same mind : for he that hath suffered in the flesh hath ceased from sin.' 1 Pe. iv. 1. By which words he insinuateth the mystical union that is between Christ the head, and the Elect his body : arguing from the suffering of a part, there should be a sympathy in the whole. If Christ then suffered for us, we were (even our sins, bodies and souls) reckoned in him when he so suffered. Wherefore, by his sufferings, the wrath of God for us is appeased, the curse is taken from us : for as Adam by his acts of rebellion, made all that were in him guilty of his wickedness ; so Christ by his acts, and doings of goodness, and justice ; made all that were reckoned in him good, and just also : but as Adam's transgression did first, and immediately reside with, and remain in the person of Adam only, and the imputation of that transgression to them that sprang from him ; so the goodness, and justice, that was accomplished by the second Adam, first, and immediately resideth in him, and is made over to his also, by the imputation of God. But again, as they that were in Adam, stood not only guilty of sin, by imputation, but polluted by the filth that possessed him at his fall ; so the children of the second Adam, do not only, though first, stand just by virtue of the imputation of the personal acts of justice, and goodness done by Christ ; but they also receive of that inward quality, the grace, and holiness that was in him, at the day of his rising from the dead.*

Thus therefore come we to be holy, by the death, and blood of the Lord : this also is the contents of those other scriptures, which abusively you cite, to justify your assertion, to wit.

'That the great errand of Christ in coming into the world, was—to put us again into possession of the holiness which we had lost. And that only designed the establishing such a holiness, as is seated originally in our natures, and originally dictates of the human nature.' The rest of the chapter being spoken to already, I pass it, and proceed to the next.

Your eighth chapter tells us, 'That it is only

---

* 'As in Adam all died,' were bereft of every good, and became obnoxious to wrath and endless misery, so 'IN Christ,' by virtue of his life, death, and resurrection, 'shall all be made alive ;' they shall have that incorruptible seed implanted in their hearts, which liveth and abideth for ever. Every grace and blessing is derived to the renewed soul from its union to Christ, as its living head, through the eternal Spirit. Christ hath fulfilled all righteousness for us and in our stead, and this was the end and intent of his coming into the world ; so that Christ is now become the righteousness of all them that do truly believe in him. 'Created IN Christ Jesus unto good works, which God hath before ordained that we should walk in them,' Eph. ii. 10.—*Mason and Ryland.*

the promoting of the design of making men holy, that is aimed at by the apostles insisting on the doctrines of Christ's resurrection, ascension, and coming again to judgment.'

Though this should be granted, as indeed it ought not ; yet there is not one syllable in all their doctrines, that tendeth in the least to drive men back to the possession of the holiness we had lost ; which is still the thing asserted by you, and that, for the proof of which you make this noise, and ado. Neither did Christ at all design the promoting of holiness, by such principles as you have asserted in your book ; neither doth the holy Spirit of God, either help us in, or excite us to our duty, SIMPLY from such natural principles.

But the apostles in these doctrines you mention, had far other glorious designs ; such as were truly gospel, and tended to strengthen our faith yet farther : As,

First, For the resurrection of Christ ; they urge THAT, as an undeniable argument, of his doing away sin, by his sacrifice and death : 'He was delivered for our offences,' because he put himself into the room, and state of the wicked, as undertaking their deliverance from death, and the everlasting wrath of God. Now putting himself into their condition, he bears their sins, and dies their death ; but how shall we know, that by undertaking this work, he did accomplish the thing he intended ? the answer is, 'He was raised again for our justification.' Ro. iv. 25. Even to make it manifest, that by the offering of himself he had purged our sins from before the face of God. For in that he was raised again, and that by him, for the appeasing of whose wrath he was delivered up to death ; it is evident that the work for us, was by him effectually done : for God raised him up again. And hence it is that Paul calls the resurrection of Christ, 'the sure mercies of David. And as concerning that he raised him up from the dead, *now* no more to return to corruption, he said on this wise, I will give you the sure mercies of David.' Ac. xiii. 34. For Christ having conquered and overcome death, sin, the devil, and the curse, by himself, as it is manifest he did, by his rising from the dead ; what now remains for him, for whom he did this, but mercy and goodness for ever ?

Wherefore the resurrection of Christ is that which sealeth the truth of our being delivered from the wrath by his blood.

Second, As to his ascension they [the inspired writers] urge and make use of that, for divers weighty reasons also.

1. As a farther testimony yet, of the sufficiency of his righteousness to justify sinners withal : for if he that undertaketh the work, is yet entertained by him, whose wrath he was to appease thereby : What is it? But that he hath so completed that work.

Wherefore he saith, that the Holy Ghost shall convince the world; that he hath a sufficient righteousness, and that because he went to the Father and they saw him no more, Jn. xvi. because he, when he ascended up to the Father, was there entertained, accepted, and embraced of God. That is an excellent word. 'He is chosen of God, and precious.' Chosen of God to be the righteousness, that his Divine Majesty is pleased with, and takes complacency in; God hath chosen, exalted, and set down Christ at his own right hand; for the sweet savour that he smelled in his blood, when he died for the sins of the world.

2. By his ascension he sheweth how he returned conqueror, and victor over our enemies. His ascension was his going home, from whence he came, to deliver us from death: now it is said, that when he returned home, or ascended, 'he led captivity captive,' Ep. iv. that is, carried them prisoners, whose prisoners we were: He rode to heaven in triumph, having in chains the foes of believers.

3. In that he ascended, it was, that he might perform for us, the second part of his priestly office, or mediatorship. He is gone into heaven itself, there 'now to appear in the presence of God for us.' He. ix. 24. 'Wherefore, he is able also to save them to the uttermost, that come unto God by him, (as indifferent a thing as you make it to be) seeing he ever liveth (viz. in heaven, whither he is ascended) to make intercession for them.' vii. 25.

4. He ascended, that he might be exalted not only above, but be made head over all things to the church. Wherefore now in heaven, as the Lord in whose hand is all power, he ruleth over, both men, and devils, sin, and death, hell, and all calamities, for the good and profit of his body, the church. Ep. i. 19—23.

5. He ascended to prepare a place for us, who shall live and die in the faith of Jesus. Jn. xiv. 1—3.

6. He ascended, because there he was to receive the Holy Ghost, the great promise of the New Testament; that he might communicate of that unto his chosen ones, to give them light to see his wonderful salvation, and to be as a principle of holiness in their souls: 'For the Holy Ghost was not yet given, because that Jesus was not yet glorified.' Jn. vii. 39. But when he ascended on high, even as he led captivity captive, so he received gifts for men; by which gifts he meaneth the Holy Ghost, and the blessed and saving operations thereof. Lu. xxiv. Ac. i. 2.

Third. As to his coming again to judgment, that doctrine is urged, to shew the benefit that the godly will have at that day, when he shall gather together his elect, and chosen, from one end of heaven unto the other. As also to shew you what an end he will make with those who have not obeyed his gospel. Mat. xxv. 2 Th. i. 8. 2 Pe. iii. 7—11.

Now it is true, all these doctrines do forcibly produce an holy, and heavenly life, but neither from your principles, nor to the end you propound; to wit, that we should be put into possession of our first, old covenant righteousness, and act from human and natural principles.

Your ninth chapter is spent, as you suppose, to shew us the nature, and evil of sin; but because you do it more like a heathen philosopher, than a minister of the gospel, I shall not much trouble myself therewith.

Your tenth chapter consisteth in a commendation of virtue, but still of that, and no other, though counterfeited for another, than at first you have described, (chap. i.) even such, which is as much in the heathens you make mention of, as in any other man, being the same both in root, and branches, which is naturally to be found in all men, even as is sin and wickedness itself. And hence you call it here, a living up to your feigned 'highest principle, like a creature possessed of a mind and reason.' Again, 'While we do thus, we act most agreeably to the right frame and constitution of our souls, and consequently most naturally; and all the actions of *nature,* are confessedly very sweet and pleasant;' of which very thing you say, 'the heathens had a great sense.' p. 113, 114.

Answ. No marvel, for it was their work, not to search the deep things of God, but those which be the things of a man, and to discourse of that righteousness, and principle of holiness, which was naturally founded, and found within themselves, as men; or, as you say, 'as creatures possessed with a mind and reason.' But as I have already shewed, all this may be, where the Holy Ghost and faith is absent, even by the dictates, as you call them, of human nature; a principle, and actions, when trusted to that, as much please the devil, as any wickedness that is committed by the sons of men. I should not have thus boldly inserted it, but that yourself did tell me of it, p. 101. But I believe it was only extorted from you; your judgment, and your Apollo, suit not here, though indeed the devil is in the right; for this righteousness and holiness which is our own, and of ourselves, is the greatest enemy to Jesus Christ: the post against his post, and the wall against his wall. 'I came not to call the righteous (puts you quit of the world) but sinners to repentance.'

[*Man in wretched uncertainty if he possessed no better holiness than that of Adam in his creation.*]

Your eleventh chapter is, to shew what a miserable creature that man is, that is destitute of your holiness.

Answ. And I add, as miserable is he, that hath, or knoweth no better. For such an one is under the curse of God, because he abideth in the law of works, or in the principles of his own nature, which neither can cover his sins from the sight of God, nor possess him with faith or the Holy Ghost.

There are two things in this chapter, that proclaim you to be ignorant of Jesus Christ.

First, you say, It is not possible a wicked man should have God's pardon, p. 119, 130.

Secondly, You suppose it to be impossible for Christ's righteousness to be imputed to an unrighteous man, p. 120.

Answ. To both which, a little briefly; God doth not use to pardon *painted* sinners, but such as are really so. Christ died for sinners, 1 Ti. i. 15. and God justifieth the ungodly, Ro. v. 6—9. even him that worketh not, iv. 3—5. nor hath no works to make him godly. ix. 18. Is. xxxiii. 11. Besides, pardon supposes sin; now he that is a sinner is a wicked man; by nature a child of wrath, and, as such, an object of the curse of God, because he hath broken the law of God. But such God pardoneth; not because they have made themselves holy, or have given up themselves to the law of nature, or to the dictates of their human principles, but because he will be gracious, and because he will give to his beloved Son Jesus Christ, the benefit of his blood.

As to the second head, what need is there that the righteousness of Christ should be imputed, where men are righteous first? God useth not thus to do; his righteousness is for the 'stout-hearted, that *are* far from righteousness.' Is. xlvi. 12.

The believing of Abraham was while yet he was uncircumcised; and circumcision was added, not to save him by, but as a seal of the righteousness of that faith, which he had, being yet uncircumcised. Now we know that circumcision in the flesh, was a type of circumcision in the heart; Ro. ii. wherefore the faith that Abraham had, before his outward circumcision, was to shew us, that faith, if it be right, layeth hold upon the righteousness of Christ, before we be circumcised inwardly; and this must needs be so: for if faith doth purify the heart, then it must be there *before* the heart is purified. Now this inward circumcision is a seal, or sign of this: that that is the only saving faith, that layeth hold upon Christ before we be circumcised. But he that believeth before he be inwardly circumcised, must believe in another, in a righteousness without him, and that, as he standeth at present in himself ungodly; for he is not circumcised; which faith, if it be right, approveth itself also so to be, by an after work of circumcising inwardly. But, I say, the soul that *thus* layeth hold on Christ, taketh the only way to please his God, because this is that also, which himself hath determined shall be accomplished upon us. 'Now to him that worketh, is the reward not reckoned of grace, but of debt. But to him that worketh not, but believeth on him that

justifieth THE UNGODLY, his faith is counted for righteousness.' Ro. iv. He that is ungodly, hath a want of righteousness, even of the inward righteousness of works: but what must become of him? Let him believe in him that justifieth the ungodly, because, for that purpose, there is in him a righteousness. We will now return to Paul himself; he had righteousness before he was justified by Christ; yet, he choose to be justified rather as an unrighteous man, than as one endued with so brave a qualification. That I may 'be found in him, not having mine own righteousness,' away with mine own righteousness; I choose rather to be justified as ungodly, by the righteousness of Christ, than by mine own, and his together. Phil. iii.

You argue therefore, like him that desireth to be a teacher of the law, (nay worse,) that neither knoweth what he saith, nor whereof he affirmeth. But you say,

'Were it possible that Christ's righteousness could be imputed to an unrighteous man, I dare boldly affirm that it would signify as little to his happiness, while he continueth so, as would a gorgeous, and splendid garment, to one that is almost starved,' &c. p. 120.

Answ. 1. That Christ's righteousness is imputed to men, while sinners, is sufficiently testified by the word of God. Eze. xvi. 1—8. Zec. iii. 1—5. Ro. iii. 24—25; iv. 1—5; v. 6—9. 2 Co. v. 18—21. Phil. iii. 6—8. 1 Ti. i. 15, 16. Re. i. 5.

2. And that the sinner, or unrighteous man, is happy in this imputation, is also as abundantly evident. For, (1.) The wrath of God, and the curse of the law, are both taken off by this imputation. (2.) The graces and comforts of the Holy Ghost, are all entailed to, and followers of, this imputation. 'Blessed is he to whom the Lord will not impute sin.' It saith not, that he is blessed that hath not sin to be imputed, but he to whom God will not impute them, he saith, therefore the non-imputation of sin, doth not argue a non being thereof in the soul, but a glorious act of grace, imputing the sufficiency of Christ's righteousness, to justify him that is yet ungodly.

But what blessedness doth follow the imputation of the righteousness of Christ, to one that is yet ungodly?

Answ. Even the blessing of Abraham, to wit, grace and eternal life: For Christ was made the curse, and death, that was due to us as sinners; 'That the blessing of Abraham might come on the Gentiles, through [faith in] Jesus Christ; that we might receive the promise of the Spirit through faith.' Ga. iii. 13, 14. Now faith hath its eye upon two things, with respect to its act of justifying. First, it acknowledgeth that the soul is a sinner, and then, that there is a sufficiency in the righteousness of Christ, to justify it in the sight of God, though a sinner.

We have believed in Jesus Christ, that we might be justified by the faith of Christ, and not by the works of the law; therefore they that believe aright, receive righteousness, even the righteousness of another, to justify them, while yet in themselves they are sinners.

Why do they believe in Christ? the answer is: that they *might* be justified, not because in their own eyes they are. They therefore at present stand condemned in themselves, and *therefore* they believe in Jesus Christ, that they *might* be set free from present condemnation. Now being justified by his blood, as ungodly, they shall be saved by his life, that is, by his intercession: for whom he justifieth by his blood, he saveth by his intercession; for by that is given the spirit, faith, and all grace that preserveth the elect unto eternal life and glory.

I conclude therefore, that you argue not gospelly, in that you so *Boldly affirm*, That it would signify as little to the happiness of one, to be justified by Christ's righteousness, while a sinner; as would a gorgeous and splendid garment to one that is ready to perish. For farther, thus to be justified, is meat and drink to the sinner; and so the beginning of eternal life in him. ' My flesh is meat indeed, (said Christ), and my blood is drink indeed; and he that eateth my flesh, and drinketh my blood, hath eternal, or everlasting life.' He affirmeth it once again: ' As the living Father hath sent me, and I live by the Father, so he that eateth me, even he shall live by me.' Jn. vi. 57. Here now is a man an hungered, what must he feed upon? Not his pure humanity, not upon the sound complexion of his soul, nor yet on the dictates of his human nature, nor those neither, which you call truly generous principles: but upon the flesh and blood of the Son of God, which was once given for the sin of the world. Let those then, that would be saved from the devil and hell, and that would find a fountain of grace in themselves, first receive, and feed upon Christ, as sinners and ungodly; let them believe that both his body, and blood, and soul, was offered for them, as they were sinners. The believing of this, is the eating of Christ; this eating of Christ, is the beginning of eternal life, to wit, of all grace and health in the soul; and of glory to be enjoyed most perfectly in the next world.

Your twelfth chapter is to shew, ' That holiness being perfected is blessedness itself; and that the glory of heaven consists chiefly in it.'

Answ. But none of your holiness, none of that inward holiness, which we have lost before conversion, shall ever come to heaven: that being, as I have shewed, a holiness of another nature, and arising from another root, than that we shall in heaven enjoy.

But further, your description of the glory that we shall possess in heaven, is questionable, as to your notion of it; your notion is, that the substance of it consists 'in a perfect resemblance to the divine nature,' p. 123, 124.

Answ. Therefore not in the enjoyment of the divine nature itself: for that which in substance is but a bare resemblance, though it be a most perfect one, is not the thing itself, of which it is a resemblance. But the blessedness that we shall enjoy in heaven, in the very substance of it, consisteth not wholly, nor principally, in a resemblance of, but in the enjoyment of God himself; ' Heirs of God.' Wherefore there shall not be in us a likeness only to, but the very nature of God: ' Heirs of God, and joint heirs with Christ.' Ro. viii. 17. Hence the apostle tells us, that he ' rejoiced in hope of the glory of God.' Ro. v. 2. Not only in hope of a resemblance of it. ' The Lord *is* my portion, saith my soul.' But this is like the rest of your discourse. You are so in love with your Adamitish holiness, that with you it must be God in earth, and heaven.

Who they are that hold, [that] our happiness in heaven shall come by a mere fixing our eyes upon the divine perfections, I know not: But thus I read, ' we shall be like him.' Why? or how? ' For we shall see him as he is.' Our likeness then to God, even in the very heavens, will in great part come by the visions of him. And to speak the truth, our very entrance into eternal life, or the beginnings of it here, they come to us thus, ' But we all, (every one of us that shall be saved, come by it only thus) with open face beholding as in a glass the glory of the Lord, are changed into the same image from glory to glory, *even* as by the Spirit of the Lord.' 2 Co. iii. 18.

And whereas you tell us, p. 124. That the devils themselves have a large measure of some of the attributes of God, as knowledge, power, &c. though themselves are unlike unto them.

In this you most prodigiously blaspheme.

Your thirteenth chapter is to show, ' That our Saviour's preferring the business of making men holy, before any other, witnesseth, that this is to do the best service to God.'

But still respecting the holiness, you have in your first chapter described, which still the reader must have his eye upon, it is false, and a slander of the Son of God. He never intended to promote or prefer your natural old covenant holiness, viz. that which we had lost in Adam, or that which yet from him, in the dregs thereof, remaineth in human nature; but that which is of the Holy Ghost, of faith, of the new covenant.

I shall not here again take notice of your 130th page, nor with the error contained therein, about justification by imputed righteousness.

But one thing I observe, that in all this chapter you have nothing fortified what you say, by any word of God; no, though you insinuate (p. 129 and p. 131.) that some dissent from your opinion. But instead of the holy words of God, being as you feign, conscious to yourself, you cannot do it so well as by another method, viz. The words of Mr. John Smith; therefore you proceed with his, as he with Plato's, and so wrap you up the business.

[*Christ gives a new and spiritual light.*]

You come next to an improvement upon the whole, where you make a comparison between the heathens and the gospel; shewing how far the gospel helpeth the light the heathens had, in their pursuit after your holiness. But still the excellency of the gospel, as you have vainly dreamt, is to make improvement first of the heathen principles; such good principles, say you, ' as were by the light of nature dictated to them,' p. 133. As,

' 1. That there is but one God; that he is infinitely perfect,' &c.

' 2. That we owe our lives, and all the comforts of them to him.'

' 3. That he is our sovereign Lord.'

' 4. That he is to be loved above all things,' p. 136.

Ans. 1. Seeing all these are, and may be known, as you yourself confess, by them that have not the gospel; and I add, nor yet the Holy Ghost, nor any saving knowledge of God, or eternal life: Therefore it cannot be the design of Jesus Christ by the gospel to promote or help forward this knowledge, simply from this principle, viz. Natural light, and the dictates of it. My reason is, because when nature is strained to the highest pin, it is but nature still; and so all the improvement of its light and knowledge is but an increase of that which is but natural. ' But (saith Paul) the natural man receiveth not the things of the Spirit of God: for they are foolishness unto him: neither can he know *them*, because they are spiritually discerned.' 1 Co. ii. 14.

But the gospel is the ministration of the Spirit; a revelation of another thing than is found in, or can be acquired by, heathenish principles of nature.

I say, a revelation of another thing; or rather, another discovery of the same. As, 1. Concerning the Godhead; the gospel giveth us another discovery of it, than is possible to be obtained by the dictates of natural light; even a discovery of a trinity of persons, and yet unity of essence, in the same Deity, 1 Jn. v. 1, 5, 8. 2. The light of nature will not shew us, that God was in Christ, reconciling the world to himself. 3. The light of nature will not shew us, that we owe what we are, and have, to God, because we are the price of the blood of his Son. 4. The light of nature will not

shew, that there is such a thing as election in Christ. 5. Or, that there is such a thing, as the adoption of children to God, through him. 6. Nor, that we are to be saved by faith in his blood. 7. Or, that the man Christ shall come from heaven to judgment. These things, I say, the light of nature teacheth not; but these things are the great and mighty things of the gospel, and those about which it chiefly bendeth itself, touching upon other things, still as those that are knowable, by a spirit inferior to this of the gospel.

Besides, as these things are not known by the light of nature, so the gospel, when it comes, as I also told you before, doth implant in the soul another principle, by which they may be received, and from which the soul should act and do, both towards God and towards men; as namely the Holy Ghost, faith, hope, the joy of the Spirit, &c.

The other things you mention, viz.

1. ' The immortality of the soul,' p. 138.

2. ' The doctrine of rewards and punishments in the life to come,' p. 140.

3. ' Of the forgiveness of sin upon true repentance,' &c. p. 142.

[4. The doctrine of God's readiness to assist men by his special grace in their endeavours after virtue, p. 143.]

Ans. All these things may be assented to, where yet the grace of the gospel is not, but yet the apprehension must be such, as is the light by which they are discovered: but the light of nature cannot discover them, according to the light and nature of the gospel; because the gospel knowledge of them, ariseth also from another principle: So then, These doctrines are not confirmed by the gospel, as the light of nature teacheth them: Wherefore, Paul, speaking of the things of the gospel, and so consequently of these, he saith, ' Which things also we speak, NOT in the WORDS which MAN's wisdom teacheth, but which the HOLY GHOST teacheth ; comparing spiritual things with spiritual.' 1 Co. ii. 13. As if he should say, We speak of God, of the soul, of the life to come, of repentance, of forgiveness of sins, &c. Not as philosophers do, nor yet in their light; but as saints, Christians, and sons of God, as such who have received, not the spirit of the world, but the spirit which is of God; that we may know the things that are freely given to us of God.

But you add (for the glory of the gospel) That we have other things, which no man could, without divine revelation, once have dreamed of. As,

That God hath made miserable sinners the objects of such transcendant love, as to give them his only begotten Son.

Ans. I must confess, If this one head had by you been handled well, you would have written like a worthy gospel minister. But you add, p. 146.

1. That when Christ was sent, it was to shew us upon what terms God was reconcileable to us, viz. By laying 'before us all the parts of that holiness, which is necessary to restore our natures to his own likeness; - and most pathetically, moreover to intreat us to do what lieth in us to put them in practice, that so it may be to eternity well with us.' What these things are, you mention not here; therefore I shall leave them to be spoken to under the third head.

2. A second thing you mention is, 'That this Son of God conversed upon equal terms with men, becoming the Son of Man, born of a woman, (a great demonstration that God hath a liking to the human nature).' But little to the purpose as you have handled it.

3. 'That the Son of God taught men their duty, by his own example, and did himself perform what he required of them; and that himself did tread before us EVERY step of that way, which he hath told us leadeth to eternal life.'

Answ. Now we are come to the point, viz.: 'That the way to eternal life is, First of all to take Christ for our example, treading his step:' And the reason, if it be true, is weighty; 'For he hath trod every step before us, which he hath told us leads to eternal life.'

1. *Every step.* Therefore he went to heaven by virtue of an imputative righteousness. For this is one of our steps thither.

2. *Every step.* Then he must go thither, by faith in his own blood for pardon of sin. For this is another of our steps thither.

3. *Every step.* Then he must go thither by virtue of his own intercession at the right hand of God, before he came thither: For this is one of our steps thither.

4. *Every step.* Then he must come to God, and ask mercy for some great wickedness, which he had committed. For this is also one of our steps thither.

But again, we will consider it the other way.

1. *Every step.* Then we cannot come to heaven, before we first be made accursed of God. For so was he before he came thither.

2. *Every step.* Then we must first make our body and soul an offering for the sin of others. For this did he before he came thither.

3. *Every step.* Then we must go to heaven for the sake of our own righteousness. For that was one of his steps thither.

O, Sir! What will thy gallant, generous mind do here? Indeed you talk of his being an expiatory sacrifice for us, but you put no more trust to that, than to Baptism, or the Lord's Supper; counting that, with the other two, but things indifferent in themselves, p. 6—9.

You add again, 'That this Son of God being raised from the dead, and ascended to heaven, is our high priest there:' But you talk not at all of his sprinkling the mercy seat with his blood, but clap upon him, the heathens demons; negotiating the affairs of men with the supreme God, and so wrap up, with a testification that it is needless to enlarge on the point, p. 149.

But to be plain, and in one word to tell you, about all these things you are heathenishly dark; there hath not in these one hundred and fifty pages one gospel truth been christianly handled by you; but rather a darkening of truth by words without knowledge. What man that ever had read, or assented to the gospel, but would have spoken, yet kept within the bounds of truth, more honourably of Christ, than you have done? His sacrifice must be stept over, as the spider straddleth over the wasp, his intercession is needless to be enlarged upon. But when it falleth in your way to talk of your human nature, of the dictates, of the first principles of morals within you, and of your generous mind to follow it: oh what need is there now of amplifying, enlarging, and pressing it on men's consciences! As if that poor heathenish, pagan principle, was the very spirit of God within us: And as if righteousness done by that, was that, and that only, that would or could fling heaven gates off the hinges.

Yea, a little after you tell us, that 'The doctrine of his sending the Holy Ghost, was to move and excite us to our duty, and to assist, cheer, and comfort us in the performance of it.' Still meaning our close adhering, by the purity of our human nature, to the dictates of the law, as written in our hearts as men. Which is as false as God is true. For the Holy Ghost is sent into our hearts, not to excite us to a compliance with our old and windshaken excellencies, that came into the world with us; but to write new laws in our hearts; even the law of faith, the word of faith and of grace, and the doctrine of remission of sins, through the blood of the Lamb of God, that holiness might flow from thence.

Your 15th chapter is to shew, That the gospel giveth far greater helps to an holy life, than the Jewish ceremonies did of old. I answer,

But the reader must here well weigh, that in the gospel you find also some positive precepts, that are of the same nature with the ceremonies under the law; of which, that of coming to God by Christ, you call one, and baptism, and the Lord's supper, the other two. So then by your doctrine, the excellency of the gospel doth not lie in that we have a Christ to come to God by, but in things as you feign more substantial. What are they? 'Inward principles of holiness,' p. 159. Spiritual precepts, p. 162. That height of virtue, and true goodness, that the gospel designeth to raise us to: all which are general words, falling from a staggering conscience, leaving the world, that are ignorant of his mind, in a muse; but tickling his brethren with the delights of their moral principles, with the dictates of their human nature, and their gallant generous minds. Thus making a very stalking-horse of the Lord Jesus Christ, and of the words of truth and holiness, thereby to slay the silly one; making the Lord of life and glory, instead of a saviour, by his blood, the instructor, and schoolmaster only of human nature, a chacer away of evil affections, and an extinguisher of burning lusts;* and that not so neither, but by giving perfect explications of moral precepts, (p. 17.) and setting himself an example before them to follow him, p. 297.

Your sixteenth chapter, containeth an answer to those that object against the power of the christian religion to make men holy.

Answ. And to speak truth, what you at first render as the cause of the unholiness of the professors thereof (p. 171.) is to the purpose, had it been christianly managed by you, as namely, men's gross unbelief of the truth of it; for it 'effectually worketh in them that believe.' 1 Th. ii. 13. But that you only touch and away, neither showing what is the object of faith, nor the cause of its being so effectual to that purpose; neither do you at all treat of the power of unbelief, and how all men by nature are shut up therein. Ro. xi. 32. But presently, according to your old and natural course, you fall, first, upon a supposed power in men, to embrace the gospel, both by closing with the promise, and shunning the threatening; (p. 172.) farther adding, that 'mankind is endued with a principle of freedom, and that this principle is as essential, as any other to the human nature,' (p. 173.) By all which it is manifest, that however you make mention of unbelief, because the gospel hath laid the same in your way, yet your old doctrine of the purity of the human nature, now broken out into a freedom of will, and that, as an essential of the human nature, is your great principle of faith, and your following of that, as it dictateth to you obedience

to the first principles of morals, the practice of faith, by which you think to be saved. That this is so, must unavoidably be gathered from the good opinion you have yourself of coming to God by Christ; viz., That in the command thereof, it is one of these positive precepts, and a thing in itself absolutely considered indifferent, and neither good nor evil. Now he that looketh upon coming to God by Christ with such an eye as this, cannot lay the stress of his salvation upon the faith, or belief thereof: Indifferent faith, will serve for indifferent things; yea, a man must look beyond that which he believeth is but one with the ceremonial laws, but not the same with baptism, or the Lord's supper; for with those you compare that of coming to God by Christ. Wherefore faith, with you, must be turned into a cheerful and generous complying with the dictates of the human nature; and unbelief, into that which opposeth this, or that makes the heart backward and sluggish therein. This is also gathered from what you aver of the divine moral laws, that they be of an indispensable and eternal obligation, (p. 8.) things that are good in themselves, (p. 9.) considered in an abstracted notion, (p. 10.) Wherefore, things that are good in themselves, must needs be better than those that are in themselves but indifferent; neither can a positive precept make that, which of itself is neither good nor evil, better than that which in its own nature remaineth the essentials of goodness.

I conclude then, by comparing you with yourself, by bringing your book to your book, that you understand neither faith, nor unbelief, any farther than by obeying or disobeying the human nature, and its dictates in chief; and that of coming to God by Christ, as one of the things that is indifferent in itself.

But a little to touch upon your principle of freedom, which in p. 9. you call an understanding and liberty of will.

Answ. First, That there is no such thing in man by nature, as liberty of will, or a principle of freedom, in the saving things of the kingdom of Christ, is apparent by several scriptures. Indeed there is in men, as men, a willingness to be saved their own way, even by following, as you, their own natural principles, as is seen by the Quakers, as well as yourself; but that there is a freedom of will in men, as men, to be saved by the way which God hath prescribed, is neither asserted in the scriptures of God, neither standeth with the nature of the principles of the gospel.

The apostle saith, 'The natural man receiveth not the things of the Spirit of God.' And the reason is, not because, not principally because, he layeth aside a liberty of will, but because 'they are foolishness to him.' 1 Co. ii. 14. Because in his judgment they are things of no moment, but

---

* Would to God this legal, self-exalting, Christ-dishonouring doctrine had been confined to the times in which our author wrote, or had been then banished to hell, from whence it came; but alas! it is but too prevalent in these degenerate times, in which Arianism, Arminianism, Socinianism, &c., &c., so dreadfully infect the multitude even of professors! In the national churches, what do we hear but Moses and the law, 'This do and live;' or, in other words, do your duty as well as you can, and Christ will do the rest: thus making the gospel the sacrifice of Christ, and the work of the Spirit, of no effect. Whereas, on the contrary, unregenerate, depraved, and sinful mortals 'have no power to do good works pleasant and acceptable to God, without the grace of God preventing (or going before) them, that they may have a good will; and working in and by them, when they have that good will;' which is perfectly agreeable to our Lord's declaration, John xv. 5, 'Without me, ye can do nothing.'—*Mason or Ryland.*

things, as you [Mr. Fowler] have imagined of them, that in themselves are but indifferent. And that this judgment that is passed by the natural man, concerning the things of the Spirit of God, of which, that of coming to God by Christ, is the chief, is that which he cannot but do as a man, is evident from that which followeth: 'neither CAN he know *them*, because they are spiritually discerned.' Neither CAN he know them as a man, because they are spiritually discerned. Now, if he cannot know them, from what principle should he will them? For judgment, or knowledge, must be before the will can act. I say, again, a man must know them to be things in chief, that are absolutely, and indispensably necessary, and those in which resteth the greatest glory; or else his *will* will not comply with them, nor centre and terminate in them as such, but still count themselves, as you, though somewhat convinced that he ought to adhere unto them, things that in themselves are only indifferent, and absolutely considered neither good nor evil.

A farther enlargement upon this subject, will be time enough, if you shall contradict.

Another reason, or cause, which you call an immediate one, of the unsuccessfulness of the gospel, is, 'men's [strange and] unaccountable mistaking the design of it, - not to say worse, as to conceive no better of it, than as a science, and a matter of speculation,' &c., p. 173.

Answ. If this be true, you have shewed us the reason, why yourself have so base and unworthy thoughts thereof: for although coming to God by Christ be the very chief, first, the substance, and most essential part of obedience thereto; yet you have reckoned this but like one of the ceremonies of the law, or as baptism with water, and the Lord's supper, p. 7—9. Falling more directly upon the body of the moral law, as written in the heart of men, and inclining more to the teaching, or dictates of human nature, which were neither of them both ever any essential part of the gospel, than upon that which indeed is the gospel of Christ.

And here I may, if God will, timely advertise my reader, that the gospel, and its attendants, are to be accounted things distinct: the gospel, properly taken, being glad tidings of good things; or, the doctrine of the forgiveness of sins freely by grace, through the redemption that is in Christ Jesus. For to speak strictly, neither is the grace of faith, hope, repentance, or newness of life, the gospel; but rather things that are wrought by the preaching thereof, things that are the effects of it; or its inseparable companions, to all them that shall be saved. Wherefore the gospel is said to be preached in all nations, for the obedience of faith. Ro. xvi. 26. Hope also is called the hope of the gospel, not the gospel itself. So again, the gospel

is preached that men should repent, but it is not preached that men should gospel.

But your gospel, which principally or chiefly, centres in the dictates of human nature; and your faith, which is chiefly a subjecting to those dictates, are so far off from being at all any near attendants of the gospel, that they never are urged in the New Testament, but in order to show men they have forgotten to act as men. Ro. i. 19—21; ii. 14, 15. 1 Co. xi. 14.

Your last reason is, because of 'several untoward opinions,' the gospel is very unsuccessful, p. 174.

Ans. But what these opinions are, we hear not; nor how to shun them, you tell us here nothing at all. This I am sure, there are no men in this day have more opposed the light, glory, and lustre of the gospel of Christ, than those, as the Quakers and others, that have set up themselves, and their own humanity, as the essential parts of it.

You in answer to other things, add many other reasons to prove they are mistaken that count the gospel a thing of but mean operation to work holiness in the heart: at which you ought yourself to tremble, seeing the Son himself, who is the Lord of the gospel, is of so little esteem with you, as to make coming to God by him so trivial a business as you have done.

Your large transcript of other men's sayings, to prove the good success of the gospel of old, did better become that people and age, than you and yours; they being a people that lived in the power thereof, but you such bats as cannot see it. That saying you mention of Rigaltias, doth better become you and yours: 'Those now-a-days do retain the name, and society of Christians, which live altogether antichristian lives. Take away publicans, and a wretched rabble, &c. and our Christian churches will be lamentably weak, small, and insignificant things,' p. 181.

I shall add to yours another reason of the unsuccessfulness of the gospel in our days, and that is, because so many ignorant Sir Johns,* on the one hand, and so many that have done violence to their former light, and that have damned themselves in their former anathematizing of others, have now for a long time, as a judgment of God, been permitted to be, and made the mouth to the people: persons whose lives are debauched, and who in the face of the world, after seeming serious detestings of wickedness, have for the love of filthy lucre, and the pampering their idle carcasses, made shipwreck of their former faith, and that feigned good conscience they had. From which number if you, Sir, have kept yourself clear, the less blood of the damned will fall upon your head: I know you not

---

* 'Sir Johns,' formerly the title given to the priests. It was succeeded by the title 'reverend.'—ED.

by face, much less your personal practice; yet I have heard as if blood might pursue you, for your unstable weathercock spirit, which doubtless could not but stumble the weak, and give advantage to the adversary to speak vilifyingly of religion.

[Living faith essential to salvation.]

As to your seventeenth and eighteenth chapters,* I shall say little, only I wish that your eighteenth had been more express in discovering how far a man may go, with a notion of the truth of the gospel, and yet perish because he hath it not in power.

Only in your inveighing so much against the pardon of sin, while you seem so much to cry up healing; you must know that pardon of sin is the beginning of health to the soul: He pardoneth our iniquities, and healeth all our diseases. Ps. ciii. 3. And where he saith, by the stripes of Christ we are healed, it is evident that healing beginneth at pardon, and not pardon after healing, as you would rather have it. 1 Pe. ii. 24. compare Is. liii. As for your comparison of the plaister, and the physician's portion,† I say you do but abuse your reader, and muddy the way of the gospel. For the first thing of which the soul is sick, and by which the conscience receiveth wounding; it is the guilt of sin, and fear of the curse of God for it. For which is provided the wounds and precious blood of Christ, which flesh and blood, if the soul eat thereof by faith, giveth deliverance therefrom. Upon this the filth of sin appears most odious, for that it hath not only at present defiled the soul, but because it keeps it from doing those duties of love, which by the love of Christ it is constrained to endeavour the perfecting of. For filth, appears filth; that is irksome, and odious to a contrary principle now implanted in the soul; which principle had its conveyance thither by faith in the sacrifice and death of Christ going before. 'The love of Christ constraineth us; because we thus judge, that if one died for all, then were all dead: And that he died for all, that they which live should not henceforth live unto themselves, but unto him which died for

* Chap. 17: 'How fearfully the gospel is abused by the papists.' Chap. 18: 'Those sottish, who expect salvation without holiness; and those more so who encourage themselves by the grace of the gospel in unholiness.'—Heads of these Chapters.—ED.

† 'Would that man be accounted any better than a perfect idiot, who, being sorely hurt, should expect from his surgeon perfect ease, when he will not permit him to apply any plaister for the healing of his wound? Or that being deadly sick, should look that his physician should deliver him from his pain, when he will not take any course he prescribes for the removal of the distemper that is the cause of it?'—Fowler's Design, p. 216. How admirably does Bunyan detect and unravel this casuistic sophistry.—ED.

them, and rose again.' 2 Co. v. 14. The man that hath received Christ, desireth to be holy, because the nature of the faith that layeth hold on Christ (although I will not say as you, it is of a generous mind) worketh by love, and longeth, yea, greatly longeth that the soul may be brought, not only into an universal conformity to his will, but into his very likeness; and because that state standeth not with what we are now, but with what we shall be hereafter: therefore 'in this we groan, - being burdened (with that which is of a contrary nature) to be clothed upon - with our house which is from heaven.' 2 Co. v. 1—8. Which state is not that of Adam's innocency; but that which is spiritual and heavenly, even that which is now in the Lord in heaven.

But I will descend to your nineteenth chapter, it may be more may be discovered there.

[Justifying faith and the imputation of Christ's righteousness.]

Your nineteenth chapter is to shew; 'That a right understanding of the design of Christianity (viz. as you have laid it down) will give satisfaction concerning the true notion.' First, 'Of justifying faith.' Second, 'Of the imputation of Christ's righteousness,' p. 221.

First, Of justifying faith; 'It is (say you) such a belief of the truth of the gospel, as includes a sincere resolution of obedience unto all its precepts.'

Ans. To this I shall answer, first, that the faith which we call justifying faith, 'Is like precious faith' with all the elect, 2 Pe i. 1. and that which is most holy: Jude 20. but those acts of it, which respect our justification with God from the curse of the law that is due for sin; are such, as respect not any good work done by us, but the righteousness that resideth in the person of Christ; and is made ours by the imputation of grace. This faith, I say, accounteth him in whom it is, now a sinner, and without works; yea, if he have any that in his own eyes are such, this faith rejects them, and throweth them away; for it seeth a righteousness in the person of Christ sufficient; even such as is verily the righteousness of God. 'Now to him that worketh not, but believeth.' Works and faith are put here in opposition, faith being considered as justifying, in the sight of God from the curse. The reason is, because the righteousness by which the soul must thus stand justified, is a righteousness of God's appointing, not of his prescribing us; a righteousness that entirely is included in the person of Christ. The apostle also, when he speaks of God's saving the election, which hangeth upon the same hinge, as this of justification doth, to wit, on the grace of God; he opposeth it to works; and that, not to this or that sort only, but even to work, in the nature of work, 'If by grace, then *is it* no more of works: otherwise grace is no more grace. But if *it be* of works, then is it no more grace: otherwise work is no more work.' Ro. xi. 6. By this text, I say, the apostle doth so thoroughly distinguish between grace and works as that which soever standeth in the case, the other must be annihilated: If it be by grace, then must works be no more, 'then it is no more of works:' but if it be of works, then is grace no more, 'then it is no more of grace.'

But this, notwithstanding, you urge farther; 'that faith justifieth, as it includes a sincere resolution,' &c.

Ans. Although, as I have said before, the faith which is the justifying faith, is that of the holiest nature, yet in the act, by which it layeth hold of justifying righteousness, it respects it, simply, as a righteousness offered by grace, or given unto the person that by faith layeth hold thereon as he stands yet ungodly and a sinner.

Faith justifieth not separate from the righteousness of Christ as it is a grace in us, nor as it subjecteth the soul to the obedience of the moral law, but as it receiveth a righteousness offered to that sinner, that as such will lay hold on, and accept thereof. Christ Jesus came into the world to save sinners, by being their redemption, and righteousness himself. 1 Co. i. 30.

But you add, 'The faith which entitles a sinner to so high a privilege as that of justification, must needs be such as complieth with *all* the purposes of Christ's coming into the world,' &c. p. 222.

Ans. By this supposition, faith justifieth not by receiving of the righteousness that Christ by himself accomplished for sinners; but by falling in with *all* good works, which because they cannot be known, much less done, by the soul at first, his faith being then, as to the perfection of knowledge of duties, weak, he standeth still before God unjustified, and so must stand until he doth comply with all those purposes of Christ's coming into the world.

But yet again you recal yourself, and distinguish *one* purpose from the rest, as a grand one, p. 222. And that is to receive Christ as Lord, as well as a Saviour.

Ans. 1. Although the soul that in truth receiveth Christ, receiveth him wholly, and entirely as Christ, and not as chopt, and pulled in pieces: yet I distinguish between the act of faith, which layeth hold of Christ for my justification from the curse before God, and the consequences of that act, which are to engage me to newness of life. And indeed, as it is impossible for a man to be a new man, before he be justified in the sight of God; so it is also as impossible, but that when faith hath once laid hold on Christ for life, it should also follow Christ by love. But,

2. Christ may be received at first as Lord, and that in our justification, and yet not at all be considered as a law-giver, for so he is not the object of faith for our justification with God, but a requirer of obedience to laws and statutes, of them that already are justified by the faith that receiveth him as righteousness. But Christ is as well a Lord for us, as to, or over us; and it highly concerneth the soul, when it believeth in, or trusteth to the righteousness of Christ, for justification with God, to see that this righteousness lords it over death, and sin, and the devil, and hell for us: the name wherewith he shall be called, is, 'the Lord our righteousness.' Je. xxiii. 6. Our righteousness, then is Lord, and conqueror over all; and we more than conquerors through this Lord that loved us. Ro. viii. The author to the Hebrews calls him 'King of righteousness,' He. vii. because by his righteousness he ruleth as Lord and King, and can reign and lord it, at all times over all those that seek to separate us from the presence, and glory of God.*

Now, how you will brook this doctrine I know not; I am sure he stands in need thereof, that is lorded over by the curse of the law, the guilt of sin, the rage of the devil, and the fear of death and hell; he, I say, would be glad to know that in Christ there is a righteousness that LORDS IT, or that Christ, as he is righteousness, is LORD.

Wherefore reader, when thou shalt read or hear, that Jesus Christ is Lord, if thou art at the same time under guilt of sin, and fear of hell, then do thou remember that Christ is Lord more ways than one, He is Lord as he is righteousness; he is Lord as he is imputative righteousness; he is 'the Lord our righteousness.' Je. xxiii. 6. Of the same import is that also, 'He is a Prince, and a Saviour,' he is a Prince, as he is a Saviour; because the righteousness by which he saveth, beareth rule in heaven, and earth. And hence we read again, that even when he was in the combat with our sins, the devils, the curse, and death, upon the cross, he even in that place 'made a shew of them openly, triumphing over them.' Col. ii. 15, 16. Now in these

* 'The righteousness of God is revealed from faith to faith;' that is, from one degree of faith to another: therefore increase in faith; live nearer to Christ; and the nearer you live to the Saviour, the farther you will be from sin; yea, he will make you, by precious faith in him, more than conqueror over all your spiritual enemies: therefore venture wholly upon Christ, and see if he will cast you out: indeed, he never will. Trust in him, hope in him, believe in him, and you will never be disappointed. All your fitness is in Christ. Believe in him, and he is yours. In him dwells all fullness. Believe in Christ, and all that Christ has is yours: his blood is yours, his wisdom is yours, his righteousness, his sanctification is yours; yea, Christ Jesus himself is yours—he is yours in this world, and in the world to come; he is yours in time, and in eternity. Even so, Amen.—*Mason and Ryland.*

things he is Lord *for us*, and the Captain of our salvation; as also in that 'He led captivity captive;' Ep. iv. 8. all which places, with many more, being testimonies to us, of the sufficiency of that righteousness which saveth us from the justice of the law and wrath of God. But you respect not this his manner of lording; but will have him be a Saviour, as he giveth laws, especially those you call indispensable, and eternal, the moral law. You would have him a Saviour, as he bringeth us back to the holiness we had lost. But this is none other than barbarous quakerism, the stress of their writing also tending to no other purpose.

But you tell us, 'That you scarcely admired at any thing more in all your life, than that any worthy men especially, should be so difficultly persuaded to embrace this account of justifying faith, and should perplex and make intricate so very plain a doctrine,' p. 222.

Ans. And doubtless they far more *groundedly stand amazed at such as you, who while you pretend to shew the design of the gospel, make the very essential of it, a thing in itself indifferent, and absolutely considered neither good nor evil, p. 7. that makes obedience to the moral laws, p. 8. more essential to salvation, than that of going to God by Christ, p. 9. that maketh it the great design of Christ, to put us into a possession of that promiseless, natural, old covenant holiness which we had lost long since in Adam, that maketh as if Christ, rejecting all other righteousness, or holiness, hath established only this, p. 10—16. Yea, that maketh the very principle of this holiness to consist in 'a sound complexion of soul, the purity of human nature in us, a habit of soul, truly generous motives and principles, divine moral laws which were first written in men's hearts, and originally dictates of human nature.' All this villany against the Son of God, with much more as bad, is comprized within less than the first sixteen pages of your book.

But say you, 'what pretence can there be for thinking, that faith is the condition, or instrument of justification, as it complieth with only the precept of relying upon Christ's merits for the obtaining of it: especially when it is no less manifest than the sun at noon-day, that obedience to the *other precepts* must go before obedience to this; and that a man may not rely upon the merits of Christ for the forgiveness of his sins, and he is most presumptuous in so doing, and puts an affront upon his Saviour too, till he be sincerely willing to be reformed from them.' p. 223.

Ans. That the merits of Christ, for justification, are made over to that faith that receiveth them, while the person that believeth it, stands in his own account, by the law a sinner; hath already been shewed. And that they are not by God appointed for another purpose, is manifest through all the Bible.

1. In the type, when the bloody sacrifices were to be offered, and an atonement made for the soul, the people were only to confess their sins over the head of the bullock, or goat, or lamb, by laying their hands thereon, and so the sacrifice was to be slain. They were only to acknowledge their sins. And observe it, in the day that these offerings were made, they were 'not to work at all; for he that did any work therein, was to be cut off from his people.' Le. iv.; xvi.; xxiii.

2. In the antitype thus it runs; 'Christ died for our sins; Christ gave himself for our sins; he was made to be sin for us; Christ was made a curse for us.'

'Yea, but (say you) What pretence can there be, that faith is the condition, or instrument of justification, as it complieth with only the precepts of relying upon Christ's merits;' that is, first, or before the soul doth other things.

Ans. I say, avoiding your own ambiguous terms, that it is the duty, the indispensable duty of all that would be saved, First, Immediately, now to close in by faith with that work of redemption, which Christ by his blood hath purchased for them, as they are sinners.

1. Because God doth hold it forth, yea, hath set it forth to be received by us, as such. Ro. iii. 23—27.

2. Because God hath commanded us by faith to receive it as such. Ac. xvi.

And I add, If the jailor was altogether ignorant of what he must do to be saved, and Paul yet bids him then, before he knew anything else, 'Believe in the Lord Jesus Christ, and he should be saved,' that then believing, even believing on Christ for a righteousness to justify and save him, must go first, and may, nay ought to be pressed, even then, when the soul stands ignorant of what else he ought to do. Ac. xvi. 30—32.

'But (you say) It is evident as the sun at noon-day, that obedience to the other precepts must go before obedience to this, that is, before faith in Christ.'

Ans. This you say; but Paul said to the ignorant jailor, that knew nothing of the mind of God in the doctrine of justification, that he should first believe on the Lord Jesus Christ, and *so* should be saved. Again, when Paul preached to the Corinthians, the first doctrine that he delivered unto them was, 'That Christ died for their sins, according to the scriptures,' &c. 1 Co. xv. 1—3.

But what be these other precepts? Not Baptism, nor the supper of the Lord; for these you say are, as poor and inconsiderable, as that of coming to God by Christ, even all three, things in

---

* 'More groundedly,' with better foundation.

themselves neither good nor evil, but of an indifferent nature; they must be therefore some more weighty things of the gospel, than these positive precepts. But what things are they? It is good that you tell us, seeing you tacitly forbid all men upon pain of presumption, and of doing affront to Jesus Christ, that they rely not on the merits of Christ for forgiveness till they be sincerely willing to perform *them* first; yet I find not here one particular precept instanced by you: But perhaps we shall hear of them hereafter, therefore now I shall let them pass. You tell us farther, 'That such a reliance (as that of acting faith, first, on the merits of Christ for justification) is ordinarily to be found amongst unregenerate, and even the worst of men,' p. 223.

Ans. This is but a falsehood and a slander, for the unregenerate know him not; how then can they believe on him? 1 Jn. iii. 1. Besides, the worst of men, so far as they pretend religion, set up your idol in their hearts, viz. their own good meanings, their own good nature, the notions and dictates of their nature, living that little which they do live upon the snuff of their own light, the sparks of their own fire, and therefore woe unto them.

But you add, 'How can it be otherwise, than that that act of faith must needs have a hand in justifying, and the special hand too, which distinguisheth it from that which is to be found in such persons.'

Ans. 1. There is no act of faith doth more distinguish true faith from false, and the Christian from the painted hypocrite, than that which first lays hold on Christ, while the person that hath it stands in his own esteem, ungodly; all over like yourself, being fearful and unbelieving Re. xxi. 8. despisers, who wonder, and perish. Ac. xiii. 40, 41.

2. And this faith, by thus acting, doth more subdue sin, though it doth not justify as subduing, but as applying Christ's righteousness, than all the wisdom and purity of human nature, or the dictates of that nature that is found in the whole world.

But you add farther: 'What good ground can men have for this fancy, when as our Saviour hath merited the pardon of sin for this end, that it might be an effectual motive to turn from it?'

Ans. Although you speak this in great derision to faith when it worketh right, yet know that therefore (seeing you would hear it) I say, therefore hath our Saviour merited pardon, and bestowed it on men freely, and bid them believe or receive it, and have it; that thereby they might be encouraged to live to him, and love him, and comply with his commandments. 'For scarcely for a righteous man will one die, yet peradventure for a good man some would even dare to die: But God commendeth his love toward us, in that, while we were yet sin-

ners, Christ died for us. Much more then, being NOW justified by his blood, we shall be saved from wrath through him.' Ro. v. Now, as here we are said to be justified by his blood, that is, as his blood appeaseth the justice of God; so again, it is said that this blood is set forth by God for us to have faith in it, by the term of a propitiation. 'Whom God hath set forth to *be* a propitiation (or a sacrifice to appease the displeasure of God) through faith in his blood. - To declare at this time his righteousness, that he might be just, and the justifier of him which believeth in Jesus.' Ro. iii. 25, 26.

Again, As we are thus justified by blood in the sight of God, by faith in it, so also it is testified of his blood, that it sprinkleth the conscience of the faithful, but still only as it is received by faith. But from what is the conscience sprinkled, but from those dead works that remain in all that have not yet been justified by faith in this blood. Now if faith in this blood doth sprinkle the conscience, and so doth purge it from all dead works, then must faith go first to the blood of Christ for justification, and must bring this home to the defiled conscience, before it be delivered from those dead works that are in it, and made capable of serving the living God. Ro. v. 7—10; iii. 24, 25. He. ix. 14; x. 19—22.

But you say, 'you will never trust your discursive faculty so long as you live, if you are mistaken here,' p. 224.

Tell not me of your discursive faculty: The word of God is plain. And never challenge man, for he that condemneth your way to heaven, to the very pit of hell, as Paul doth, can yet set forth a better.

Second, I come now to the second thing, viz. *the doctrine of the imputation of Christ's righteousness,* which you thus expound.

'It consists in dealing with sincerely righteous persons, as if they were perfectly so, for the sake, and upon the account of Christ's righteousness,' p. 225, 226.

Ans. 1. Any thing but truth; but I would know how sincerely righteous they were that were justified without works? Or how sincerely righteous they were whom God justified as ungodly? Ro iv. 3—5.

2. Your explication of the imputation of Christ's righteousness makes it respect our works rather than our persons: 'It consists (say you) in dealing with sincerely righteous persons, as if they were perfectly so:' That is, it justifieth their imperfect righteousness first, and so secondarily their persons for the sake of that.

But observe a few things from this explication.

1. This concludeth that a man may be sincerely righteous in God's account, WITHOUT the righteousness of Christ; for that is to be imputed to such, and none but such.

2. This concludeth that men may be sincerely righteous, before Christ's righteousness is imputed: For this sincere righteousness is precedent to the imputation of Christ's.

3. This concludeth that a man may have true, yea saving grace in great and mighty action in him, before he hath faith in the righteousness of Christ. For if a man must be sincerely righteous first; then he must not only have that we call the habit, but the powerful acts of grace.

Besides, if the righteousness of Christ is not to be looked to first, but secondarily; not before, but after we be made sincerely righteous; then may not faith be thus acted if a man should have it, until he be first a sincerely righteous person.

4. This concludeth that a man may be brought from under the curse of the law in God's sight, before he have faith in the righteousness of Christ, yea before it be imputed to him: for he that in God's account is reckoned sincerely righteous, is beloved of his God.

5. This concludeth that a man may be from under the curse of God, without the imputation of the righteousness of Christ: For if a man must be sincerely righteous in God's account without it, then he is from under the curse of God without it.

6. This doctrine teacheth farther, that Christ came to call, and justify the righteous, contrary to his express word. In short, by this account of things, first we must be healed, and then the plaister comes.

Yea, so confident is this man in this his assertion, that he saith, 'It is not possible any other notion of this doctrine should have truth in it,' p. 226. O this Jesus! This rock of offence! But he that believeth on him shall not be confounded.

But blessed be God for Jesus Christ, and for that he took our nature, and sin, and curse, and death upon him: And for that he did also by *himself*, by *one* offering purge our sins. We that have believed have found rest, even there where God and his Father hath smelled a sweet savour of rest; because we are presented to God, even now complete in the righteousness of him, and stand discharged of guilt, even by the faith of him: yea, as sins past, so sins to come, were taken up and satisfied for, by that offering of the body of Jesus, we who have had a due sense of sins, and of the nature of the justice of God, we know that no remission of the guilt of any one can be, but by atonement made by blood. He. ix. 22. We also know that where faith in Jesus Christ is wanting, there can be neither good principle, nor good endeavour. For faith is the first of all graces, and without it there is nothing but sin. Ro. xiv. 23. We know also, that faith as a grace in us, severed from the righteousness of Christ, is only a beholder of things, but not a justifier of persons, and that

if it lay not hold of, and applieth not that righteousness which is in Christ, it carrieth us no farther than to the [faith of] devils. We know that this doctrine killeth sin, and curseth it at the very roots; I say we know it, 'who have mourned over him whom WE have pierced,' Zec. xii. 10. and who have been confounded to see that God by his blood should be pacified towards us for all the wickedness we have done. Eze. xvi. 63. Yea, we have a double motive to be holy and humble before him; one because he died for us on earth, another because he now appears for us in heaven, there sprinkling for us the mercy-seat with his blood, there ever-living to make intercession for them that come unto God by him. 'If any man sin, we have an advocate with the Father, Jesus Christ the righteous, and he is the propitiation for our sins.' 1 Ju. ii. 1, 2. Yet this worketh in us no looseness, nor favour to sin, but so much the more an abhorrence of it: 'She loveth much, for much was forgiven her.' Lu. vii. 47. Yea, she weeps, she washeth his feet, and wipeth them with the hairs of her head, to the confounding of Simon the pharisee, and all such ignorant hypocrites.

[The Bible the only measure and standard of truth.]

But I pass this, and come to the twentieth chapter, which is to learn us by what measure and standard we are to judge of doctrines; and that is by the design of Christianity as stated, you must know, by Mr. Fowler. Wherefore it will be requisite here again, that a collection of principles and doctrines be gathered out of this book, that the man that hath a short memory may be helped the better to bear them in mind, and to make them, if he shall be so bewitched by them, instead of the Bible, a standard for truth, and a rule for him to obtain salvation by.

First then, he must know that the principle by which he must walk must be the purity of the human nature, a divine or God-like nature, which yet is but an habit of soul, or more plainly the moral law, as written in the heart, and originally the dictates of human nature, a generous principle, such an one as although it respects law, yet acts in a sphere above it; above it as a written law, that acts even in the first principles of it, p. 7—10.

Second, He must know, that the holiness Christ designed to possess his people with, is that which we had lost in Adam, that which he had before he fell, that natural old covenant Christ-less holiness, p. 12.

Third, He must put a difference between those laws of the gospel that are essential to holiness, and those positive precepts that in themselves are indifferent, and absolutely considered neither good nor evil; but must know also that of these positive precepts, he alloweth but three in the gospel, but three that are purely such; to wit, that of coming to God by Christ, the institutions of baptism, and the Lord's supper, p. 7—9.

Fourth, He must hold for certain, that the faith which entitleth a sinner to so high a privilege as that of justification, must needs be such as complieth with all the purposes of Christ's coming into the world, whether at present it understands them or not, and it is no less necessary it should justify as it doth so, p. 222.

Fifth, He must know, that a man may not rely upon the merits of Christ for the forgiveness of his sins, before he have done other good works first, p. 223.

Sixth, And that the right explication of the imputation of Christ's righteousness is this, that it consisteth in having to do with persons that are sincerely righteous, p. 225. For it is not possible for Christ's righteousness to be imputed to an unrighteous man, p. 120.

These things, with many like to them, being the main points by this man handled, and by him asserted to be the design of Christianity, by these we must, as by a rule and standard, understand how to judge of the truth of doctrines. And, saith he, ' seeing the design of Christianity is to make men holy, (still meaning from principles of humanity, and by possessing us again, with the often repeated holiness which we had lost,) whatsoever opinions do either directly, or in their evident consequences, obstruct the promoting of it, are perfectly false,' p. 227, 228.

Ans. Thus with one word, as if he were Lord and Judge himself, he sendeth to the pit of hell, all things that sanctify or make holy the hearts of men, if they oppose the design of *his* christianity. But what if the Holy Ghost will become a principle in the hearts of the converted, and will not now suffer them to act simply and alone upon the principles of pure humanity; or what now if faith will become a principle to act by, instead of these that are originally dictates of human nature ? Or what if a man should act now as a son, rather than simply as a creature endued with a principle of reason ? I question here whether these things thus doing do not obstruct, put by, yea and take the way* of his pure humanity, dictates of human nature, and instead thereof act and govern the soul by and with their own principles. For albeit, there be the dictates of human nature in the sons of men, yet neither is this nature, nor yet the dictates of it, laid by Jesus Christ as the truly christian principles in his. But you add:

' Those doctrines which in their own nature do evidently tend to the serving of THIS design of

---

* 'Take the way,' occupy the place.—ED.

Christianity, we may conclude are most true and genuine,' p. 229.

Ans. The holiness which you so often call the design of Christianity, being by yourself said to be that which we had lost, for this one sentence is it on which your whole book is built, p. 12. whatsoever doctrine or doctor it be that asserts it, both that doctrine is of the devil, and that doctor an angel of darkness, or rather a minister of Satan, become as a minister of righteousness. For where is it said in all the whole book of God, that ever the Lord Christ designed, yea made it his errand from heaven, to put us again in possession of the holiness which we had lost ? Yet this you affirm, and tell us the business of your book is to prove it. But blessed be God, your shifts are discovered, and your fig-leaves rent from off you, and the righteousness or holiness so much cried up by you, proved to be none of the holiness of the gospel, but that which stood with perfect ignorance thereof. I might speak to what yet remains of falsehood, in the other part of this chapter; but having overthrown the foundation, and broken the head of your Leviathan; what remains falleth of itself, and dieth of its own accord.

What you say of modes or forms, and sticklers for little trifles, such as place their religion in mere externals, you may fasten them where of due they belong: Yet I tell you the least of the commandments of Christ is better than your adamitish holiness.

[*The necessity of a sound foundation.*]

Your twenty-first chapter tells us, if we will believe you, how we shall judge of the necessity of doctrine, to be embraced or rejected; also you say, it giveth us a brief discourse of the nature of fundamentals : But because your discourse of them is general, and not any one particularized, I might leave you in your generals till you dealt more candidly, both with the word of God and your abused reader.

First, Indeed you tell us of *primary fundamentals.* 'Such, as without the knowledge and belief of which it is impossible to acquire that inward righteousness and true holiness which the christian religion aimeth at; - but the particulars of these, say you, I shall not enumerate, because (as will appear from what will be said anon) it is not needful to have a just table of them,' p. 234.

Ans. Deep divinity! (1.) They are such as without the knowledge and belief of them, it is not possible we should acquire your true holiness; and yet for all that, it is not needful that we be told what they are, or that we should have a just table of them. (2.) But if they be things necessary, things without the knowledge of which it is impossible we should be truly holy, then is it needful that we understand what they are: yea, then is it needful that they be written, and presented one by one unto us, that our knowledge of them being distinct and full, we may the better be able to obtain or acquire your glorious (so pretended) holiness.

But I know your primary fundamentals, they are your first principles of morals; not faith in the righteousness of Christ, for that is comprehended in your positive, and in themselves indifferent things: your morals are the things in themselves absolutely necessary; of an indispensable and eternal obligation, p. 8, 9. But,

Second, You tell us of points of faith that are *secondarily fundamental;* the disbelief of which cannot consist with true holiness, in those to whom the gospel is sufficiently made known.

Ans. The secondary fundamentals also, are all kept close and hid, and not otherwise to be understood, but by implication; however, the disbelief of these is not of so sad a consequence as is that of the former, because, say you, ' They are not in their own nature, holiness,' p. 235. Yea, he insinuateth that the disbelief of them may stand with true holiness in those to whom the gospel is not sufficiently made known.

Of these secondary fundamentals therefore, whatever is their number, this is one, even coming to God by Christ; for as in p. 7. and 9. he calleth it a positive precept, a thing that in itself is neither good nor evil; so here he speaks of such as are not in their own nature holy; not such, as that holiness is not in some degree or other attainable without the belief of them.

That one of these secondary fundamentals intended by Mr. Fowler, is, that of coming to God by Christ, I farther gather, because he saith, that ' in the number of these, are all such doctrines, as are with indisputable clearness revealed to us,' that is, by the holy scriptures of the New Testament, p. 235. For therein is this revealed to be a fundamental; but he saith, not a primary one, because, that in itself, it is but indifferent, and not in its own nature good. ' Now the belief of these, saith he, though it is not in itself any more, than in higher or lower degrees, profitable, (confusion! darkness! confusion!) yet it is absolutely necessary from an external cause:' That is, with such abundant clearness, as that nothing can cause men to refuse to admit them, but that which argueth them to be stark naught.

Ans. Then, hence it seems that the reason why you admit these secondary sort of fundamentals, is not from any internal power, but an external declaration only. 2. Nay, and you do but admit them neither, and that too, for some external cause; not because of the worthiness of the nature of the points themselves. 3. And were it not, but that

you are loth to be counted stark naught in the eyes of men, so far as I can discern, you would not at all make profession of them, with pretence as unto God; for, say you, 'We must take notice here, that all such points [as these] (viz. these fundamentals,) are not of equal necessity to be received by all Christians, because, that in regard of the diversity of their capacities, educations, and other means and advantages, some of them may be most plainly perceived by some, to be delivered in the scriptures, which cannot be so by others, with the like ease.'

Ans. From these words I take notice of four things.

1. That by this universal (all Christians) is comprehended the Heathen and Pagan people, they give heed to, and mind to follow that light, that originally, and naturally, stirreth them to moral duties. These be they that want the education, and advantages of others, and are not in such a capacity, as they to whom these things are delivered by the scriptures.

2. That this people, notwithstanding they want a scripture revelation of these secondary fundamentals, yet have the more necessary, the first sort of fundamentals; for the secondary sort, say you, are not in their own nature such, as that holiness is not in some degree or other attainable without the belief of them.

3. That therefore, these secondary sort of fundamentals, are only necessary to be believed by them that have the indisputable (the scripture) revelation of them; and that, in truth, the others may be saved without them.

4. But yet, even those that are made capable, by education and other advantages, to obtain the belief of them, ought, notwithstanding, not to have the same respect for them, as for those of the first sort of fundamentals, because they are not in their own nature such.

But will this man know, that Christ is not only a fundamental, but the very foundation of all other fundamental truths, revealed both in the Old Testament and the New; and that his pure human nature, with the dictates of it, with his feigned adamitish holiness, is no fundamental at all; I mean no fundamental of faith, no gospel fundamental. 1 Co. iii. 14. Ep. ii. 19, 20. Yea, will he know, that from heaven there is none other name given, than the name of Jesus Christ, whereby we must be saved, none other name given under the whole heavens. Ac. iv. 12.

Oh the witchcrafts, by which some men's spirits are intoxicated! and the strength of delusion, by which some are infatuated, and turned aside from the simplicity that is in Jesus Christ! But I proceed:

Your great question, or rather your Urim and Thummim, by which you would have all men make judgment of their saveable, or damnable state.

p. 236. is, according to your description of things, most devilish and destructive. For to obey God and Christ in all things, with you, is to do it from principles purely human in the faith of this: that Christ hath designed to possess us again with that holiness we had lost. Again, to obey God and Christ, with you, is, so to obey all their laws, as respecting the first principles of morals; and our obedience to them, far more indispensable than that of coming to God by Christ. Farther, he that obeys them in all things, with your directions, must not look upon faith in the blood of Christ, and justification by his righteousness, as the main and first, but the second part of our duty; other commands, or precepts, more naturally holy and good, first being embraced, and lived in the practice of, by us.

This, I say, being the doctrine you have asserted, and the foundation on which your Urim and Thummim stands; the foundation, with your trial, are both from the devil and hell, as hath at large been proved, and discovered in this book.

And I now will add, and bid you take your advantage, that should a man with all his might, strive to obey all the moral laws, either as they are contained in the first principles of morals, or in the express decalogue, or Ten Commandments; without faith, first, in the blood, and death, and resurrection of Christ, &c. For his justification with God; his thus doing would be counted wickedness, and he in the end, accounted a rebel against the gospel, and shall be damned for want of faith in the blood of the Lord Jesus.

[*The Christian's great principles.*]

Your twenty-second chapter, saith, 'That the design of Christianity, teacheth us what doctrines and practices we ought, as Christians, to be most zealous for, or against,' p. 237.

Ans. But there is not by that, it being rightly stated, one syllable that tendeth to encourage any man, to have lower thoughts of coming to God by Christ, than of keeping the moral law. For even the first text you bring, doth utterly overthrow it. 'Contend [earnestly], say you, for the faith;' I answer then, not for the law of works, for the law is not of faith; but the man that doth these things, shall live in them, by them. 'Contend earnestly for the faith, for there are certain men crept in unawares, which were before of old, ordained unto this condemnation;' even the condemnation that is to come upon them that contend against the faith; for these ungodly men turn the grace of God into lasciviousness, and deny the only Lord God, and our Lord Jesus Christ. Now these creeping ungodly men, may be divided in three ranks.

1. Such as by principle, and practice both, say, 'Let us do evil, that good may come: whose damnation is just.' Ro. iii. 8.

2. Such as by practice only, appear to be such, denying to profess the principle thereof, such are they that made excuse and delay, when invited to come to the wedding. Mat. xxii. 1—5. Lu. xiv.

3. There is yet another sort; and they are such as seem to deny it, both in principle, and practice also; only they do it covertly, PRIVILY bringing in damnable heresies, even denying the Lord that bought them. These 'bring upon themselves swift destruction.' 2 Pe. ii. 1.

This third sort, made of the doctrine of grace, and of the forgiveness of sins, through the faith of the righteousness of Christ, a loose and licentious doctrine, or a doctrine that giveth liberty to the flesh. By reason of these the way of truth is evil spoken of, and the hearts of innocent ones alienated therefrom. These will not stick to charge it upon the very chief of the brethren, if they shall say, 'As sin abounded, grace hath much more abounded: that they press men to do evil, that good may come of it.' Ro. iii. 8, 9. But, as I said, these vilify Christ, not with open words, but covertly; privily they bring in their blasphemy under a cloak, crying, the law, holiness, strictness, good works, &c. Besides, these clothe their doctrines with names and notions that belong not at all unto them; as of Christ, grace, the spirit, the gospel, when there is only there, the devil, and his angels, and errors; as angels of light, and ministers of righteousness. Of this last sort are you, and the subject matter of your book; for you bring into the world an anti-gospel holiness, anti-gospel principles, and anti-gospel fundamentals; and that these things might be worshipped by your disciples, you give them the name of holiness, the design of Christ, and of Christianity; by which means you remove the Christ of God, from before, and set him behind, forbidding men to believe on him, till they have practised your things first: nay, after they have practised yours, they then must come to God by him, still respecting the principles and dictates of humanity, as things of the greatest weight, things that are good in themselves; still considering that 'coming to God by Christ, is not good in itself, but so only upon the account of certain circumstances; a thing in itself of an indifferent nature, and absolutely considered neither good nor evil.'

Wherefore, Sir, laying aside all fear of men, not regarding what you may procure to be inflicted upon me for this my plain dealing with you, I tell you again, that yourself is one of them, that have closely, privily, and devilishly, by your book, turned the grace of our God into a lascivious doctrine, bespattering it with giving liberty to looseness, and the hardening of the ungodly in wickedness, against whom, shall you persist in your wickedness, I shall not fail, may I live, and know it, and be helped of God to do it, to discover yet farther the rottenness of your doctrine, with the accursed tendencies thereof.

What you say about ' doubtful opinion, alterable modes, rites, and circumstances in religion,' p. 239. I know none so wedded thereto as yourselves, even the whole gang of your rabbling counterfeit clergy; who generally like the ape you speak of,* lie blowing up the applause and glory of your trumpery, and like the tail, with your foolish and sophistical arguings, you cover the filthy parts thereof, as you sweetly argue in the next chapter, p. 242. saying, ' *Whatsoever of such are commended by the custom of the place we live in, or commanded by superiors, or made by any circumstance convenient to be done, our christian liberty consists in this, that we have leave to do them.*'† So that do but call them things indifferent, things that are the customs of the place we live in, or made by ANY circumstance convenient, and a man may not doubt but he hath leave to do them, let him live at Rome or Constantinople, or amidst the greatest corruption of worship and government. These are therefore doubtless, a third sort of fundamentals, by which you can wrestle with conviction of conscience, and stifle it; by which you can suit yourself for every fashion, mode, and way of religion. Here you may hop from Presbyterianism, to a prelatical mode; and if time and chance should serve you, backwards, and forwards again: yea, here you can make use of several consciences, one for this way now, another for that anon; now putting out the light of this by a sophistical delusive argument, then putting out the other, by an argument that best suits the time.‡ Yea, how oft is the candle of the wicked put out, by such glorious learning as this. Nay, I doubt not, but a man of your principles, were he put upon it, would not stick to count those you call gospel-positive precepts, of no value at all in the christian religion; for now, even now, you do not stick to say that, that even *that* of going to God by Christ, is one of these, and that such an one, as if absolutely considered in itself, is neither good nor evil. How then, if God

---

* ' Doubtful opinions, modes and rites, eagerly opposed, is like the apes blowing at a glowworm, which affords neither light nor warmth,' p. 239.

† These sentiments are the essential fundamentals of all state religions, be they heathen, christian, or mohamedan. This plain avowal of them might have been the cause why the author was soon after made a bishop of the Church of England.—ED.

‡ Like the vicar of Bray, near Maidenhead, who boasted of his consistency. He was under Henry VIII. a papist, then a semi-protestant; under Edward, a protestant; under Mary, again a papist; and under Elizabeth, a protestant. Still he had never ceased to be *vicar of Bray.*—ED.

should cast you into Turkey, where Mahomet reigns as Lord ? It is but reckoning that it is the religion, and custom of the country, and that which is authorised by the power that is there; wherefore it is but sticking to your dictates of human nature, and remembering that coming to God by Christ is a thing of an indifferent nature in itself, and then for peace sake, and to sleep in a whole skin, you may comply, and do as your superior commands. Why ? Because in Turkey, are your first sort of fundamentals found: there are men that have human nature, and the law of morals written in their hearts; they have also the dictates thereof written within them, which teach them, those you call the eternal laws of righteousness; wherefore you both would agree in your essential, and immutable differences of good and evil, p. 6. and differ only about these positive laws, indifferent things. Yea, and Mahomet also *for the time*, because by a custom made convenient, might be now accounted worshipful, and the circumstances that attend his worship, especially those of them that clash not with the dictates of your human nature, might also be swallowed down.

Behold you here then, good reader, a glorious Latitudinarian, that can, as to religion, turn and twist like an eel on the angle; or rather like the weather-cock that stands on the steeple.

' For (saith he) our refusing to comply with either of these can hardly proceed from anything better than a proud affectation of singularity, or at best, from superstitious scrupulosity.' p. 242.

Do but believe him therefore in what he saith, and you cannot choose but be ready with him to comply with all modes that may serve for advantage.

Besides, he saith, ' that the word superstition, in the Greek* implieth, a frightful, and over-timorous apprehension of the divine nature; and consequently a base and under-valuing conception of it.'

So that to be tender of conscience, especially in things of divine worship, binding up the soul to the words of the everlasting testament, in such things especially, as a fool can call little, and insignificant trivial matters, rendereth a man such an one as hath a very erroneous conscience.

But he would not be understood (p. 244.) as if he here intended to vilify things that are plainly commanded, or to tolerate that which is plainly forbidden, only he would have all things that may fall within the reach of these two general heads, be examined by this general rule, ' HIS description of the design of Christianity.'

Answ. But I could tell him, that whatsoever is imposed as a part of God's worship, is judged by

---

§ Δεισιδαιμονία.

a better rule than his, both as to its goodness and badness, neither can we account any thing indifferent that is a part thereof. Besides, whatsoever is reputed a part of God's worship, layeth hold on the conscience of the godly: although a ranting Latitudinarian may say, 'If the devil should preach, I would hear him, before I would suffer persecution.' As a brave fellow which I could name, in his zeal was pleased to declare.

But what trust should any man put to the rule to which you direct him for help, and relief therein; seeing that from the beginning to the end, from the top to the bottom, it is a cursed blasphemous book; a book that more vilifieth Jesus Christ, than many of the Quakers themselves: for which of them said worse of him, and make coming to God by him, a more insignificant thing, than you by your pretended design of Christianity have done.

We have therefore a more sure word of the prophets, to the which 'we do well to take heed,' 2 Pe. i. 19. by which, both your doctrine, and practice, is already judged to be naught, as will be farther discovered time enough, when you shall justify or condemn particulars.

Your twenty-fourth chapter I shall now pass by, until I can better compare you and popery, against which you there so stoutly * diggle together.

[The scandalous lives and foolish doctrines of state priests, not the true ground of dissent.]

Your twenty-fifth chapter carrieth in it an hideous outcry against many of *your* ministers and guides, complaining and confessing, 'That no one thing hath so conduced to the prejudice of your church of England, and done the separating parties so much service, as the scandalous lives of some that exercise the ministerial function in her,' p. 258.

Answ. I will grant it, if you respect these poor carnal people, who yet have been shamed from your assemblies, by such vicious persons you mention: but the truly godly, and spiritually judicious have left you from other arguments, of which I shall not here dilate.

But from p. 261. to the end of the chapter, you take upon you to particularize other of your ministers that are an offence to you, and to the design of your Christianity.†

1. 'Such as affect to make people stare at their high flown bombast language, or to please their phantasies with foolish jugglings, and pedantic or boyish wit; or to be admired for their ability in dividing of an hair, their metaphysical acuteness, and scholastic subtilty, or for their doughty dexterity in controversial squabbles.' And I add, had you joined herewith, such as vilify and trample upon the blood of the Lord Jesus, preferring the snivel of their own brains before him, you had herein but drawn your own picture, and given your reader an emblem of yourself.

2. The second sort you blame, are 'such as seek to approve themselves to their auditories to be men of mysteries, and endeavour to make the plain and easy doctrines of the gospel as intricate and obscure as ever they are able.' I will add to these, such as take away the doctrine of faith, and that set themselves and their works in the room thereof: such as have sought to overturn the foundation, Jesus Christ, and have made coming to God by him, in itself of a far more indifferent nature than the dictates of our humanity.

3. Another sort (you say) are 'such as preach upon free grace, and christian privileges, otherwise than as motives to cite to obedience, and never scarce insist upon any duties, but those of believing, laying hold on Christ's righteousness, applying the promises, and renouncing our own righteousness,' which they that have none at all to renounce, have a mighty kindness for.

Answ. (1.) Who they are that preach free grace in your church, to excite men to uncleanness, you may know better than I. But if these words, otherwise than to cite men to obedience, be thus thrust in, of purpose thereby to speak evil of the preachers of free grace, and the exalters of the imputed righteousness of Christ, then look to it; for such venom language as this, doth but involve you within the bowels of that most dreadful prophecy, concerning the false prophets of the last days, that shall privily bring in damnable heresies, even denying the Lord that bought them.

(2.) The preaching of free grace, pressing to believing, and laying hold on Christ's righteousness, is the most available means under heaven, to make men holy, and righteous:‡ 1. Before God. 2. Then before men.

(3.) The preaching of these are first, and principally to beget faith, to beget life, to beget souls to God; yea, to beget in men such a principle, whereby they may serve God acceptably, with reverence and godly fear.

(4.) But to preach free grace, doth much condemn your free will; to preach Christ's righteousness doth utterly curse, and condemn yours; and to preach the promise of grace, doth quite shut

---

* 'Diggle together,' probably from 'degladiation,' a combat, quarrel, or contest; a fencing match between *two friends.* —ED.

† Fowler's picture of the want of uniformity in the preachers of his sect, all being under the 'Act of Uniformity,' is very amusing and instructive!!—ED.

‡ Undoubtedly so; because the good works of a man who is under the influence and power of divine grace, flow from the constraining love of a covenant-reconciled God in Christ Jesus, whom the holy-making Spirit glorifies and renders precious to every true believer in him.—*Mason and Ryland.*

out a covenant of works: therefore no marvel if you, who are so wedded to these things, be such an enemy to free grace, the righteousness of Christ, and the gospel promises, that you make even these things a characteristical note (first abusing the consequences of them) of a church-troubling preacher.

(5.) You tauntingly proceed, saying, 'such preachers also press us to renounce our own righteousness, which they that have none at all to renounce, have a mighty kindness for.'

Answ. Indeed those that have a righteousness of their own, as the pharisees, and hypocrites of old, had never much kindness for the doctrine of grace, and the ministers of Christ, but the publicans and harlots had: and therefore, these, while they that had righteousness stumbled and fell, entered into the kingdom of heaven. 'The publicans and the harlots go into the kingdom of God before you.' But what righteousness have you of your own, to which you so dearly are wedded, that it may not be let go, for the sake of Christ? seeing also so long as you go about to establish it, you submit not yourself 'to the righteousness of God.' Ro. x. 3. Yea, why do you taunt those ministers that persuade us to renounce our own righteousness, and those also that follow their doctrine? Seeing this was both the doctrine and practice of Paul and all others, save only those that had Moses' veil over their hearts.

Another sort of ministers that you say are enemies to the promoting of holiness, are such as 'are never in their element, but when they are talking of the irrespectiveness of God's decrees, the absoluteness of his promises, the utter disability and perfect impotence of natural men, to do any thing towards their own conversion, and that insist with great emphasis, and vehemence, upon such like false, and dangerous opinions,' p. 262.

Answ. The men that preach these things, being rightly stated, preach the truth of God, if the scriptures may bear sway; they having all been proved the truth of the gospel, both by the prophets and apostles: and when you shall think meet by argument to contradict them, either I, or same other may show you the folly of your undertaking. In the mean time let the reader take notice that here you have judged not by scripture, nor by reason, but upon a bare presumption, arising from your pride or ignorance. Wherefore pray you in your next, shew us, (1.) What is in man that the decree of election should respect as a thing foreseen of God, to prevail with him to predestinate him to eternal life by Jesus Christ our Lord. (2.) Make it manifest that in the word of God there neither is, nor can be any absolute promise contained. (3.) Shew us what ability there is in a natural man, as such, to do things

towards his own conversion; I mean things immediately tending to, and that must infallibly consummate therein, and let us see what things they are. And know that when you have well done all this, according to the scriptures of truth, that then it will be time enough to condemn the contrary for false, and dangerous opinions.

But shall I speak the truth for you? The reason of this your presumptuous exclamation, and condemnation of these things; is because they stand in the way of promoting your ignorant, tottering, promiseless, and gospelless holiness; they stand in the way of old Adam, they stand in the way of your dunghill rebellious righteousness, they stand in the way of your freedom of will, and a great rabble more of such like pretended virtues. Yea, they do, and must, and shall stand there, when you and the rest of the Socinians, and Quakers, have said their all against them.

There is yet another sort of preachers whom you condemn, and so do I as well as you, though not in your spirit, nor to advance your pestiferous principles: and they are 'such as make it their great business, to advance the petty interest of any party whatsoever, and concern themselves more about doing this, than about promoting, and carrying on that, wherein consists the chief good of all mankind, and are more zealous to make proselytes to their particular sects, than converts (I will add first to Jesus Christ, and then) to an holy life; and press more exact and rigid conformity to their modes and forms, than to the laws of God, and the essential duties of the christian religion,' p. 263.

Lastly, The caution which you give to ministers, because there wanteth for it, among *you* a foundation, is to be esteemed but an error, and an abuse of the words, and practices of the apostle. And as for your subtil and close incensing the power to persecute Nonconformists, know that we are willing, God assisting, to overcome you with truth and patience, not sticking to sacrifice our lives, and dearest concerns in a faithful witness-bearing against your filthy errors, compiled and foisted into the world, by your devilish design to promote Paganism, against Christianity, p. 265, 266.

[*A compliant temper may prove dangerous.*]

I come now to your twenty-sixth chapter, which is spent to prove, 'That an obedient temper of mind, is a necessary and excellent qualification to prepare men for a firm belief, and a right understanding of the gospel of Christ,' p. 267.

Answ. 1. Forasmuch as the obedient temper you mention, is precedent to, or before, faith, and the right understanding of the gospel, it must needs be also, that which stands with unbelief, and ignorance of the same. Now that this should be an excellent, and necessary qualification, to a firm belief, and right understanding of the gospel, is altogether without proof, and truth. But this is affirmed for the farther promoting of your human nature, and the things that originally are dictates thereof. But,

2. The obedience, or inclination to obedience, that is before faith, or the understanding of the gospel, is so far off from being an excellent preparative, or good qualification for faith, and the knowledge of the gospel, that in its own nature, which is more than in its consequences, it is a great obstruction thereto.

For, while a man remains faithless and ignorant of the gospel, to what doth his obedient temper of mind incline? Not to faith, nor the gospel of Christ; for with these, as yet you suppose he hath not to do; therefore he inclineth to the law of morals, either as it was delivered in tables of stone from Sinai, or as written in the hearts of all the children of men, to it, under the last consideration, which is in truth, the most heathen and pagan to it, as so you intend, your obedient temper of mind should incline, p. 7—10.

Now this doctrine, being in itself of quite another nature than the doctrine of faith, and also, as such, a covenant by itself, it requireth the mind by virtue of its commands, to stand to THAT, and to rest in that; for of necessity, the heart and mind of a man can go no farther than it seeth, and hath learnt, but by this moral doctrine, the heart and mind is bound and limited to itself, by the power of the dictate to obedience, and the promise of obtaining the blessing, when the preceptive part of it is fulfilled. Hence Paul tells us, that though that ministration, that was written, and engraven in stones, (which in nature is the same with this) is glorious, yet these imperfections attended the man that was in it. 2 Co. iii.

1. He was but within the bounds of the ministration of death.

2. In this estate he was blind, and could not see how to be delivered therefrom: 'The vail is over their heart,' so that they could not heretofore, neither can they now, see to the end of that which was commanded, neither to the perfection of the command, nor their own insufficiency to do it, nor to the death and curse of God, that attended him, that in every thing continued not in [all] that was written in the book of the law to do them.

3. Every lecture, or reading of this old law, is as a fresh hood-winking of its disciples, and a doubling of the hindrance of their coming to Christ for life. ' But their minds were blinded, for until this day, remaineth the same vail untaken away in reading of the old testament; which *vail* is done away in Christ. But even unto this day, when Moses is read, the vail is upon their hearts.' 2 Co. iii. 14, 15.

And let the reader note, that all these things attend the doctrine of morals: the ceremonies being in themselves more apt to instruct men in the knowledge of Christ, they being by God's ordination, figures, shadows, representations, and emblems of him; but the morals are not so, neither, as written in our natures, nor as written and engraven in stones. Ga. iii. 24. Wherefore, your so highly commended obedient temper of mind, you intending thereby an hearty compliance before faith, with morals for righteousness, is so far off from being an excellent temper, and a necessary qualification, to help a man to a firm belief, and right understanding of the gospel; that it is the most ready way of all ways in the world, to keep a man perpetually blind, and ignorant thereof. Wherefore the apostle saith, that the vail, the ignorance, cannot be taken away, but when the heart shall turn to the Lord, that is, from the doctrine of morals, as a law and covenant in our natures, or, as it was written and engraven in stones, to Christ for mercy to pardon our transgressions against it, and for imputative righteousness to justify us from it. While Moses is read, the vail is over the heart; that is, while men with their minds stand bending also to do it. But mark, when it, the heart, shall turn to the Lord, or to the word of the gospel, which is the revelation of him, then the vail shall be taken away.

And hence it will not be amiss, if again we consider how the Holy Ghost compareth, or setteth one against another, these two administrations.

The law he calls the letter, even the law of morals, that law that was written and engraven in stones. The other ministration, he calls the ministration of the spirit, even that which Christ offered to the world, upon believing.

Again, he denieth himself to be a minister of the law of morals. He hath made us able ministers of the New Testament, not of the letter, or law; but of the spirit or gospel. The reason is, for the letter, or law, can do nothing but kill, curse, or condemn; but the spirit, or the gospel, giveth life. Farther, in comparing, he calls the law, the ministration of death, or that which layeth death at the doors of all flesh; but the gospel, the ministration of righteousness, because, by this ministry, there is a revelation of *that* righteousness that is fulfilled by the person of Christ; and to be imputed for righteousness to them that believe, that they might be delivered from the ministration of death. How then? Hath the ministration of God no glory? Yes, forasmuch as it is a revelation of the justice of God against sin. But yet again, its glory is turned into no glory, when it is compared with that which excelleth. ' But if the ministration of death, written *and* engraven in stones, was glorious, so that the children of Israel could not stedfastly behold the face of Moses for the glory of his countenance; which *glory* was to be done away; how shall not the ministration of the Spirit be rather glorious? For if the ministration of condemnation *be* glory, much more doth the ministration of righteousness exceed in glory. For even that which was made glorious had no glory in this respect, by reason of the glory that excelleth.' 2 Co. iii. 7—10.

So then, your obedient temper of mind, forasmuch as it respecteth the law of morals, and that too, before faith, or a right understanding of the gospel, is nothing else but an obedience to the law, a living to death, and the ministration of condemnation; and is a persuading the world, that to be obedient to that ministration, that is not the ministration of the gospel, but holdeth its disciples in blindness and ignorance, in which it is impossible Christ should be revealed, is an excellent, yea, a necessary qualification to prepare men for a firm belief, and a right understanding of the gospel of Christ, which yet even blindeth, and holdeth all blind that are the followers of that ministration. I come now to your proof, which indeed is no proof of this anti-gospel assertion, but texts abused, and wrested out of their place, to serve to underprop your erroneous doctrine. The first is, ' If any man will do his will, he shall know of the doctrine, whether it be of God, or *whether* I speak of myself.' Jn. vii. 17. p. 268.

Ans. This scripture respecteth not at all the moral law, or obedience to the dictates of human nature, as an acceptable qualification precedent to faith; or that, for the sake of which God will give men faith in, and a right understanding of the gospel, but is itself an immediate exhortation to believing, with a promise of what shall follow; as who shall say, The Father hath sent me into the world to be salvation to it, through faith in my blood: My Father's will therefore is, ' that men believe in me;' and if any will do his will, he shall know of the doctrine, he shall feel the power thereof, by the peace and comfort that will presently possess the soul, and by the holy effects that follow.

That this is the true exposition of this place will be verified if you consider, that to do the will of God, in a New Testament sense, is to be taken under a double consideration. 1. As it respecteth Christ. 2. Man.

1. *As it respecteth Christ*, so it concerns his completing the redemption of man by himself, by his own personal performances. Jn. vi. 38, 39. He. x. 5—10.

2. *As it respecteth man*, it doth first and immediately respect our believing on him for remission of sins and eternal life. ' And this is the will of him [the Father] which sent me (saith Christ)

that every one that seeth the Son, and believeth on him, may have everlasting life: and I will raise him up at the last day.' Jn. vi. 40. This then is the will of God; that men do believe in Jesus Christ.

Again, when the Jews asked Jesus Christ what they should do, that they might work the works of God, he did not send them first to the moral precept, or to its first principles in the hearts of men; by obeying that, to fit themselves for faith; but immediately he tells them, ' This is the work of God, that ye believe on him whom he hath sent.' Jn. vi. 29. This is the work of God; that is, 'This is his commandment, That we should believe on the name of his Son Jesus Christ, and love one another, as he gave us commandment.' 1 Jn. iii. 23. If any man will do his will, he shall know of the doctrine, that is, as I have said, he shall feel, and have the authority of this faith in his heart, both to give peace and joy in his heart, and assurance, and the sealing of his soul to glory. For all these things come in upon believing *first* in Christ.

1. ' By faith we have peace with God.' Ro. v. 1.

2. ' We have joy and peace through believing.' Ro. xv. 13.

3. ' Assurance comes also through believing.' Jn. vi. 69. He. x. 22.

4. Yea, and the sealings up to eternal life; ' In whom also after that ye believed, ye were sealed with that holy spirit of promise.' Ep. i. 13.

5. Sanctification, and a right obedient temper, is not to be found in men before, but after they have believed; ' He purified their hearts by faith.' Ac. xv. 9. Yea, heaven and eternal happiness is promised to them who are sanctified by faith which is in Christ. ch. xxvi. 18.

This first text, therefore, hath been by you abused, in that you have ungodlily strained it, but in vain, to make it warrant your heathenish preparations to faith.

The second scripture; ' He that is of God heareth God's words: ye therefore hear *them* not, because ye are not of God.' Jn. viii. 47.

Ans. This scripture supposeth men must first be of God, before they can hear God's word; before they can hear it with the hearing of faith; and therefore nothing respecteth those that before they have faith, live in the law of works; and least of all, those that become obedient thereto, that thereby they may obtain everlasting life. For these are not of God, not of him in a New Testament sense; not sons, because they are born of men, of the will of men, of the law, and according to the wisdom of flesh and blood. Jn. i. 12, 13.

Your third scripture is, ' And as many as were ordained to eternal life believed.' Ac. xiii. 48. Which text you thus expound: ' That as many of the Gentiles as were disposed, or in a ready preparedness for eternal life, believed; that is, those which were proselytes of the gate, who were admitted by the Jews to the hope of eternal life, and to have their portion in the age to come, without submitting to their whole law, or any more than owning the God of Israel, and observing the seven precepts of Noah," p. 269.*

Ans. 1. That obedience to the moral law is not a preparative to faith, or an excellent and necessary qualification to the right understanding of the gospel I have proved.

2. That to be a Jewish proselyte was to live in the faith of Messias to come, is the strain of all the scriptures that have to deal with them.

3. But that ordaining men to eternal life respects an act of the Jews, or that the Jews did dispense with the Gentile proselytes, in their casting off all their laws, but the seven precepts of Noah.

4. Or that God counted this a fit, or forerunning qualification to faith in Jesus Christ, neither stands with the word of God, nor the zeal of that people.

5. Besides, the words presently following seem to me to insinuate more, viz. That the Jews and religious proselytes that adhered to Paul at his first sermon, ver. 43. did contradict and blaspheme at his second, ver. 45. and moreover, that it was they that raised persecution upon him, and expelled him out of their coasts, ver. 50. When the Gentiles, even those that were more barbarously ignorant at his coming, when they heard that by Christ there was offered to them the forgiveness of sins, they believed, ver. 48. and glorified the word of the Lord: The wisdom of heaven so disposing such of their hearts, that were before by HIM, not by Jews ordained to life. ' And as many as were ordained to eternal life, believed.'

But you come again, in p. 269. to the scripture first urged by you, ' If any man will do his will,' &c. and you tell us, that this must also needs be implied, he shall rightly understand the doctrine too; which word (understand) you so carry, as may best help you in case you should meet with an adversary. As if any should thus object, that here you have granted that the words make promise of an understanding of the gospel; yea require in it the very first act of the will; then you readily shift it by saying, That this is implied only, suggesting

---

* The Jews were divided into three sections: I. The descendants of Israel; II. Proselytes who conformed to all the Mosaic rites; and, III. Those who were bound to obey the seven precepts of Noah—and these, although they did not conform to the Jewish rites, yet were admitted to the worship of the true God and the hope of the life to come. According to the Talmud these precepts were—1. To renounce idols and all idolatrous worship. 2. To worship the true God, the creator of heaven and earth. 3. Bloodshed, to commit no murder. 4. Not to be defiled with fornication. 5. Rapine, against theft and robbery. 6. To administer justice. 7. Not eating flesh with the blood in it.—ED.

that obedience to morals is expressed, and therefore must first be thought on and done. But if one of your brotherhood stop here, and make the objection; then you add, ' It is knowledge, at least, in all the necessary points thereof, absolutely necessary and essential parts, from among which you long since did cast out, " Coming to God by Jesus Christ." ' Yea you add, ' That by (that which you call) the design of the gospel, it may be presumed, that whosoever considereth it, with a design of being so, (that is, of living up to human principles, and that desireth to be possessed again of the holiness he hath lost, for that is it for the proof of which you have written above 300 pages) he must needs believe the gospel to have come from God, and also be enlightened in the true knowledge of at least the necessary points of it,' viz. All moral duties contained therein, which are never a one of them as such an essential of the gospel, but are such duties as are consequential to the belief thereof.

Wherefore, although you feign it, ' this honest temper,' as you call it, will not help you, 1. To judge of the gospel without prejudice; nor 2. To evidence it with satisfaction; nor 3. Secure those in whom it is from error and delusion; no man being more brutish or heathenish, nor so void of satisfaction about it, nor more involved in error concerning it, than yourself; being truly what you charge upon others; 1. Grossly ignorant; 2. Too highly opinionate; 3. Proud in affectation; 4. Liquorish; 5. A self-lover; 6. And for your blasphemy under the just judgment of God. ' If our gospel be hid, it is hid to them that are lost: In whom the god of this world hath blinded the minds of them which believe not, lest the light of the glorious gospel of Christ, who is the image of God, should shine into them.' 2 Co. iv. 3, 4.

[*' For me to live is Christ' includes in it more than good habits or holy frames of soul.*]

I am come now to your last chapter, which tells us wherein the essence and life of Christianity consisteth, viz. In a good state and habit of mind, in a holy frame and temper of soul, p. 282.

Ans. 1. It consisteth in a life of faith, when I live in the belief of this, that Christ loved me, and gave himself for me. ' The life that I now live in the flesh (saith Paul) I live by the faith of the Son of God, who loved me, and gave himself for me.'

2. And besides, a good state and habit of mind, or an holy frame and temper of soul, in your notion of them, which respecteth purely obedience to morals, from natural impulses, or dictates of our humanity, they are rather heathenish than Christian, and being alone, end in death rather than life. ' As many as are of the works of the

law, are under the curse,' he saith not they that sin against it, but they that are OF the works of it, such as do justice, righteousness, charity, goodness, mercy, patience, and all kind of moral duties, from principles human, natural, or as men, they are under the curse, because they have sinned first, and also are infirm and weak in their pursuit after the perfections they desire. These follow after righteousness, but *that* flies from them; wherefore they do not obtain it, because they seek it not by faith in Christ, but as it were by the works; the righteous, good, and holy works of the law. Ro. ix. 30, 32. But you add,

'It is such a habit of mind, such a frame and temper of soul, as esteemeth God as the chiefest good, and preferreth him and his Son Jesus Christ before all the world, and that prizeth above all things an interest in the divine perfections,' &c. p. 282.

Ans. 1. God must needs be esteemed the chiefest good, by all that have but, and are ruled by, the light of nature, because they see him by his works to be almighty, merciful, and eternal. Ro. i. 20. But this may be where the knowledge of the man, the Mediator is not; therefore this, in this and in your sense, cannot be of the essence of Christianity, for that it is common to all the world. That estimation of God which is common to natural men, cannot be of the essence of Christianity, because they want that knowledge of him that comes by Jesus Christ, and so are not capable to esteem of him under a Christian consideration.

But you say, ' it is that good habit and temper of mind that preferreth God, and his Son Jesus Christ, before all the world.'

Ans. He that esteemeth God above all, must needs, at least in his judgment, so prefer him; but whereas you add, and his Son Jesus Christ, you put in them words but as a cloak, for yourself have not preferred his Son Jesus Christ, no, not before a moral law, no not before your obedience to it, although but by human principles; yea, you have accounted the command of God, by which we are enjoined by him to come to God, a thing in itself but like levitical ceremonies, or as Baptism and the Lord's Supper; a thing in itself indifferent, and absolutely considered neither good nor evil, p. 7, 8, 9.

You add; ' It is such a temper as prizeth above all things, an interest in the divine perfections; such as justice and righteousness, universal charity, goodness, mercy, patience, and all kinds of purity,' p. 282.

Ans. Seeing by these expressions you only intend moral virtues, and those that are inherent in you, and originally operations of humanity, it is evident that you have but impiously and idolatrously attributed to your own goodness so high

and blessed a title. For whatsoever is in your nature, and originally the dictates thereof, and whatsoever proficiency you make therein by human principles, and helps of natural endowments; these things are but of yourself, your own justice, your own righteousness, your own charity, goodness, mercy, patience, kindness, &c. Now to call these the divine perfections, when they are only your own human virtues, bespeaks you, I say, fond, impious, and idolatrous, and shews you, in the midst of all your pretended design to glorify God, such an one who have set up your own goodness with him, yea and given it the title of his blessed grace and favour.

That scripture you mention, Ro. xiv. 17. although by the word righteousness there, is intended obedience to the moral law, yet to it by persons already justified by Christ's righteousness; hence they are said to do it in the joy and peace of the Holy Ghost, or by the joy and peace which they had by faith in Christ's righteousness, as revealed to them by the Spirit of God. Hence again, they are said in IT to serve Christ, or to receive the law at his hand, which he giveth to them to walk after, having first justified them from the curse thereof by his blood.

2. The law was given twice on Sinai, the last time, with a proclamation of mercy going before, and he that receiveth it thus, receiveth it after a gospel manner. For they as justified persons are dead to the law as a covenant of works by the body of Christ, that they might live to another, even to him that is raised from the dead. Ro. vii. Ga. ii. 19. But you by this scripture intend not this doctrine, for you make justification by Christ, come after, not before obedience to the law; yea, you make obedience thereto, the essential, and coming to God by Christ, but a thing of a more remote nature, from true and substantial gospel-righteousness.

In p. 283, you speak again of the old principle, and thus you comment, ' A principle of holiness that respecteth duty, as with respect to the nature of the command, so not with respect to the duty as occasioned by certain external inducements and motives, but from a good temper and disposition of soul.'

Ans. This I say, still respecting your old principle of humanity, and the purity of your nature, the most amounts but to this: Your principle is confined to a liberty of will and affections, with respect to doing of the law of works, which many have professed to have, and do before you, and yet have come short of the glory of God. For as I told you before, I tell you now again, that the gospel-principles are the Holy Ghost and faith, which help that soul in whom they dwell to count believing in Jesus Christ the great and essential part of our Christianity, and our reckoning ourselves pardoned for the sake of him: 'And thus being set free from sin, we become the servants of God, and have our fruit unto holiness, and the end everlasting life.' Ro. vi. 22.

Your description of a child of Abraham, you meaning in a New Testament sense, is quite beside the truth. For albeit, the sons of Abraham will live holy lives, and become obedient to the substantial laws; yet it is not their subjection to morals, but faith in Jesus, that giveth them the denomination of children of Abraham. 'Know ye, therefore, that they that are of faith are the children of faithful Abraham: They that are of faith, the same are the children of Abraham: Yea, they that are of faith are blessed with faithful Abraham.' Ga. iii. 7, 9. In p. 284, you say, 'That there is no one duty more affectionately recommended to us in the gospel than is alms-giving.'

Ans. Yes, That there is, and that which more immediately respecteth our justification with God, than ten thousand such commandments; and that is faith in Christ. Alms-deeds is also a blessed command; yet but one of the second table, such as must flow from faith going before. Faith I mean that layeth hold on Christ's righteousness, if it be accepted of God. For before the heart be good the action must be naught; now the heart is good by faith, because faith, by applying Christ's righteousness, makes over [a] whole Christ to the soul, of whose fulness it receiveth, and grace for grace. Jn. i. 16. Many things in this last chapter are worthy reprehension, but because you tell us, in the last two pages thereof, is the sum of all that need to be said, I will immediately apply myself to what is there contained.

You say, p. 296, 'It is not possible we should not have the design of Christianity accomplished in us, and therefore that we should be destitute of the power of it, if we make our Saviour's most excellent life the pattern of our lives. By our Saviour's life, as by a parenthesis you also express, you mean, as yourself hath in short described it, ch. v. viz., 'The greatest freedom, affability, courtesy, candour, ingenuity, gentleness, meekness, humility, contempt of the world, contentation, charity, tenderness, compassion, patience, submission to the divine will, love of God, devoutest temper of mind towards him, mighty confidence and trust in God,' &c.

Answ. Our Saviour's life, in not only these, but all other duties that respected morals, was not principally or first to be imitated by us, but that the law, even in the preceptive part thereof, might be fully and perfectly fulfilled for us. 'Christ is the end of the law for righteousness;' the end, not only of the ceremonial law, but the ten commandments too; for if the word righteousness, respecteth in special them. 'Jesus increased in favour

VOL. II.

with God.' Lu. ii. 52. Mat. iii. 17. This respecteth him as made under the law, and his pleasing of God in that capacity. So also doth that, 'In him I am well pleased.' Now I say, as Jesus stood in this capacity, he dealt with the law in its greatest force and severity, as it immediately came from God, without the advantage of a Mediator, and stood by his perfect complying with, and fulfilling every tittle thereof. Besides, as Jesus Christ had thus to do with the law, he did it in order to his 'finishing transgression, and putting an end to sin,' Da. ix. 24. and so consequently as Mediator, and undertaker for the world. For his perfect complying withal, and fulfilling every tittle of the law, respected nothing his own private person, that he for himself might be righteous thereby; for in himself he was eternally just and holy, even as the Father, but it respected us, even us. For us he was made under the law, that *we*, by his fulfilling the law, might by him be redeemed from under the law, and also receive the adoption of sons, Ga. iv. 4, 5. For we having sinned, and transgressed the law, and the justice of God, yet requiring obedience thereto, and the law being too weak through our flesh to do it, God therefore sent his own Son in the likeness of sinful flesh, who himself for us did first of all walk in the law, and then for sin suffered also in his flesh, the sentence, and curse pronounced against us by the law. For it was nothing less necessary, when the Son of God became undertaker for the sin of the world, that he should walk in obedience to the whole of the precepts of the law, to deliver us from the judgment of the law; I say it was no less necessary he should so do, than that he should bear our curse and death. For it would have been impossible for him to have overcome the last, if he had not been spotless touching the first. For therefore it was impossible he should be holden of death, because he did nothing worthy of death; no, not in the judgment of the law, to which he immediately stood. Now as Christ Jesus stood thus to, and walked in the law, it is blasphemy for any to presume to imitate him; because thus to do is to turn Mediator and undertaker for the sin of the world. Besides, whoso doth attempt it, undertakes an impossibility; for no man can stand by the moral law, as it immediately comes from the divine majesty; he having sinned first, even before he goeth about to fulfil it. And in this sense is that to be understood, 'as many as are of the works of the law are under the curse,' held accursed, because they have sinned first; accursed in their performances, because of imperfection, and therefore assuredly accursed at last, because they come short of the righteousness thereof.

1. Christ Jesus did never set himself forth for an example, that we by imitating his steps in

2 T

morals should obtain justification with God from the curse of that law; for this would be to overthrow, and utterly abolish the work which himself came into the world to accomplish, which was not to be our example, that we by treading his steps might have remission of sins, but that through the faith of him, through faith in his blood, we might be reconciled to God.

2. Besides, thus to imitate Christ, is to make of him a Saviour, not by sacrifice, but by example. Nay, to speak the whole, this would be to make his mediatorship wholly to center, rather in prescribing of rules, and exacting obedience to morals, than in giving himself a ransom for men; yea, I will add to imitate Christ, as you have prescribed, may be done by him, that yet may be ignorant of the excellency of his person, and the chief end of his being made flesh: For in all these things which you have discoursed in that fifth chapter of him, you have only spoken of that, something of which is apprehended by the light of nature; yea, nature itself will teach that men should trust in God, which is the most excellent particular that there you mention. Wherefore our Lord Jesus himself foreseeing, that in men there will be a proudness, to content themselves with that confidence, he intimateth that it would be in us insignificant, if it stand without faith in himself. 'Ye believe [naturally] in God (saith he) believe also in me.' Jn. xiv. 1. Faith in Jesus is as absolutely necessary as to believe immediately in the divine being. Yea, without faith in Jesus, whosoever believeth in God is sure to perish and burn in hell. 'If you believe not that I am *he*, ye shall die in your sins.' Jn. viii. 24. And to take Jesus in morals for example, is nowhere called believing in him, neither is there one promise of eternal life, annexed to such a practice. But you say, 'If we tread in his blessed steps, and be such, according to our measure and capacity, as we have understood he was in this world.' p. 296.

Answ. I say, for a man to confine himself only to the life of the Lord Jesus, for an example, or to think it enough to make him, in his life, a pattern for us to follow, leaveth us, through our shortness in the end, with the devil and his angels, for want of faith in the doctrine of remission of sins; for Christ did nowhere make another mediator between God and him, nor did he ever trust to another man's righteousness, to be thereby justified from the curse of the law; neither did he at all stand in need thereof, without which, we must be damned and perish. Now I say, these things being nowhere practised by him, he cannot therein be an example to us. And I say again, seeing that in these things, by faith in them, is immediately wrapped up our reconciliation with God; it followeth, that though a man take the Lord Christ

in his whole life, for an example in the end, that notwithstanding, he abideth unreconciled to God. Neither will that clause, 'and be such,' help such a person at all: For justification with God, comes not by imitating Christ as exemplary in morals, but through faith in his precious blood. In the law I read, that the Paschal Lamb was neither to be eaten sodden nor raw, but roast with fire, must it be eaten. Ex. xii. Now to make salvation principally to depend upon imitating Christ's life, it is to feed upon him raw, or at most, as sodden, not sanctified and holy: But the precept is, 'Eat it roast with fire;' is to be the antitype, as accursed of God for sin, and enduring the punishment for it, Ex. xix. De. xxxiii. 2. Mal. iv. 1. The law is compared to fire, and its curse to a burning oven. Now under the curse of this fiery law, was the Lord Jesus afflicted for the sins of the world: wherefore, as so considered, our faith must lay hold upon him, for justification with God. 'This is the law of the burnt-offering: (which was the offering for sin;) It *is* the burnt-offering, because of the burning upon the altar all night unto the morning, and the fire of the altar shall be burning in it.' Le. vi. 9. But now I would inquire: Had Israel done the commandment, if they had eaten the passover raw, or boiled in water? Or if they had offered that offering, that was to be burnt as a sin-offering, otherwise than it was commanded? Even so, to feed upon Christ, as he is holy, and of good life only; and also, as taking him therein for an example to us, to follow his steps for justification with God; this is, to eat the passover raw, and not as roast with fire; this is, to feed upon Jesus, without respecting him as accursed of God for our sin, and so consequently to miss of that eternal life, that by his blood he hath obtained for every one that believeth on him. I have been pleased with this observation: That none of the signs and wonders in Egypt, could deliver the children of Israel thence, till the Lamb was slain, and roast with fire. Ex. xii. 31. And I have been also pleased with this: That the Father, not Moses, gave the manna from heaven, which was a type of the flesh, and blood of Christ, that whoso feedeth on, shall live for ever. Jn. vi. 32. Yea, circumcision also, which was a type of inward, and heart-holiness, was not of Moses, but of the Fathers, and principally a consequence of the faith of Abraham. Jn. vii. 22. Whence I gather, that no wonder, but the blood of Christ can save; that no kindness, but the mercy of God, can give this to us; and that no law, but the law of faith, can make us truly holy in heart. But you add, 'Those that sincerely, and industriously, endeavour to imitate the holy Jesus in his Spirit and actions, can never be ignorant what it is to be truly Christians.' Those that follow Jesus in his Spirit, must first receive that

Spirit from heaven, which Spirit is received, as I have often said, by applying first, by faith, the merits of Christ to the soul, for life and justification with God. The Spirit is not received by the works of the law, but by the hearing of faith; neither comes it in the ministry, or doctrine of morals, but in and by the ministry of faith; and the law is *not* of faith. Wherefore seeing you have, in p. 223. of your book, forbidden sinners to come first to Jesus for justification with God; the Spirit you talk of, however you call it the Spirit of Jesus, can be no other than the spirit of a man; which you also yourself, in p. 7, 8, 9. call 'the purity of human nature, a principle of reason, the first principles of morals, or those that are originally dictates of human nature.' Wherefore by these words, 'in his Spirit,' you do but blaspheme the Holy Ghost, and abuse your ignorant reader; calling now, Quaker-like, the dictates of your humanity, and your Socinian compliances therewith, the Spirit of Holy Jesus. I conclude therefore, that the way of salvation, or the design of Christianity as prescribed by you, is none other than the errors of your own brain, the way of death, the sum and heart of Papistical Quakerism, and is quite denied by the Lord Jesus, and by his blessed Testament. And now go your ways, and imitate the Lord Jesus, and take the whole history of his life for your example, and walk in his steps, and be such as much as you can, yet without faith in his blood, first; yea, and if you stand not just before God through the imputation of his righteousness, your imitating will be found no better than rebellion, because by that, instead of faith in his blood, you hope to obtain remission of sins, thrusting him thereby from his office and work, and setting your dunghill righteousness up in his stead.

[Fowler's false and dangerous conclusions.]

I come now to your conclusion. First, in p. 298. 'You press men to betake themselves to find (that which you call) the design of Christianity, accomplished in their hearts and lives.'

Ans. Seeing that the holiness that your erroneous book has exalted, is none other but that which we have lost; yea, and again, seeing you have set this in the head of, and before the righteousness of Christ, I admonish my reader to tremble at the blasphemy of your book, and account the whole design therein, to be none other but that of an enemy to the Son of God, and salvation of the world. For that holiness as I have shewed, is none other but a shadowish, Christless, graceless holiness; and your so exalting of it, very blasphemy. You proceed, saying, 'Let us exercise ourselves unto real and substantial godliness; (still

meaning your Adamitish holiness) let us study the gospel not to discourse, or only to believe, but also, and above *all* things, to do well.'

Ans. Herein still you manifest, either ignorance of, or malice against, the doctrine of faith; that doctrine, which above all doctrines, is the quintessence of the New Testament, because therein, and not principally, as you feign, by doing well, is the righteousness of God revealed, and that from faith to faith; not from faith to works, nor yet from works to faith. Besides, the gospel is preached in all nations, for the obedience of faith. Ro. xvi. 26. Neither works, the law, the dictates of humanity, nor the first principles of morals, knowing what to do with the righteousness of the gospel, which is a righteousness imputed by God, not wrought by us; a righteousness given, not earned, a righteousness received by believing, not that which floweth from our obedience to laws, a righteousness which comes from God to us, not one that goeth from us to God. Besides, as I also have hinted before, the apostle and you are directly opposite. You cry, 'above all things, do well:' that is, work and do the law; but he, 'above ALL, take the shield of faith, wherewith are quenched all the fiery darts of the wicked.' Ep. vi. 16.

But you add, p. 300. 'Let us do what lieth in us to convince our Atheists, that the religion of the blessed Jesus, is no trick or device; and our wanton and loose Christians, that it is no notional business, or speculative science.'

Ans. This you cannot do by your moral natural principles of humanity: For even some of your brave philosophers, whose godliness you have so much applauded, were even then in the midst of their, and your virtues, atheistically ignorant of the religion of Jesus. And as to the loose Christian; Christ neither hath need of, nor will he bless your blasphemous opinions, nor feigned godliness, but real ungodliness, to make them converts to his faith and grace, neither can it be expected it should, seeing you have not only dirty thoughts, but vilifying words, and sayings of his person, work, and righteousness. You have set your works before his, p. 223. calling them substantial, indispensable, and real; but coming to God by him, a thing in itself indifferent, p. 7–9. You go on, and say, 'Let us declare—that we are not barely reliers on Christ's righteousness, by being imitators of it,' p. 300. You cannot leave off to contemn and blaspheme the Son of God. Do you not yet know that the righteousness of Christ on which the sinner ought to rely for life, is such, as consisted in his standing to, and doing of the law, without a Mediator? And would you be doing this? What know you not, that an essential of the righteousness he accomplished for sinners when he was in the world; is, 'That he was conceived by the

Holy Ghost, born without sin, did all things in the power of, and union with his own eternal Godhead.' And are you able thus to imitate him? Again, the righteousness on which we ought to rely for life, is that which hath in it the merit of blood: we are 'justified by his blood' through faith in his blood. Ro. v. 9. Is this the righteousness you would imitate? Farther, the righteousness on which poor sinners should rely, is that, for the sake of which God forgiveth the sins of him that resteth by faith thereupon. But would you be imitating of, or accomplishing such a righteousness?

Your book, Sir, is begun in ignorance, managed with error, and ended in blasphemy.

Now the God of glory, if it may stand with his glory, give you a sight of your sins, against the Son of God, that you may, as Saul, lie trembling, and being astonished, cry out to be justified, with the righteousness of God without the law, even that which is by faith of Jesus Christ, unto all, and upon all them that believe.

Many other gross absurdities, which I have omitted in your whole book, may perhaps, be more thoroughly gathered up, when you shall have taken the opportunity to reply. In the meantime I shall content myself with this.

Behold the Lamb of God, which taketh away the sin of the world.' Jn. i. 29.

'*Even* Jesus, which delivered us from the wrath to come.' 1 Th. i. 10.

'Who when he had by himself purged our sins, sat down on the right hand of the Majesty on high.' He. i. 3.

'Christ died for our sins.' 1 Co. xv. 3.

'God hath made him *to be* s n for us.' 2 Co. v. 21.

'Christ was made a curse for us.' Ga. iii. 13.

'He bare our sins in his own body on the tree.' 1 Pe. ii. 24.

'He loved us, and washed us from our sins in his own blood.' Re. i. 5.

'God for Christ's sake hath forgiven you.' Ep. iv. 32.

'We have redemption through his blood, the forgiveness of sins, according to the riches of his grace.' Ep. i. 7.

Now unto the King, eternal, immortal, invisible, the only wise God, be honour, and glory, for ever, and ever. Amen.

THE CONCLUSION.

That my reader may farther perceive that Mr. Fowler, even by the chief of the articles of the church of England, is adjudged erroneous; and besides the very fundamentals of the doctrine of Jesus Christ, and that in those very principles that are in the main, I say, and that most immediately concern Christ, faith, and salvation, will be evident to them that compare his design of Christianity, with these articles hereunto recited.

The Article [X.] concerning Free-will.

'The condition of man, after the fall of Adam, is such, that he cannot turn and prepare himself, by his own natural strength and good works, to faith, and calling upon God: wherefore we have no power to do good works, pleasant and acceptable to God, without the grace of God by Christ preventing* us, that we may have a good will, and working with us, when we have that good will.'

The Article [XI.] concerning Justification.

'We are accounted righteous before God, ONLY for the merit of our Lord and Saviour Jesus Christ, by faith; and not for our own works, or deservings. Wherefore that we are justified by faith ONLY, is a most wholesome doctrine, and very full of comfort,' &c.

The Article [XIII.] of Works before Justification.

'Works done before the grace of Christ, and the inspiration of his Spirit, are not pleasant to God, for as much as they spring not of faith in Jesus Christ, - or deserve grace of congruity: yea rather, for that they are not done as God hath willed and commanded them to be done, we doubt not but they have the NATURE of sin.'

These articles, because they respect the points in controversy betwixt Mr. Fowler, and myself; and because they be also fundamental truths of the christian religion, as I do heartily believe, let all men know that I quarrel not with him, about things wherein I dissent from the church of England, but do contend for the truth contained, even in these very articles of theirs, from which he hath so deeply revolted, that he clasheth with every one of them, as may farther be shewn when he shall take heart to reply.

But to wind up this unpleasant scribble, I shall have done when I have farther shewed, how he joineth with papist, and quaker, against these wholesome, and fundamental articles.

Mr. Fowler's Doctrine compared with Campian the Jesuit, upon that question whether Faith only justifieth: saith Campian,

1. *Campian.* 'We (Papists) say, that as grace is put into us in justification, so also our righteousness is enlarged through good works, and is

---

* 'To prevent,' from 'prævenio,' to go before; 'preventing us' was formerly used for 'preparing us.' It is now obsolete in this sense, but frequently occurs in the Bible.—ED.

inherent in us; therefore it is not true that God doth justify by faith ONLY.'

Fowler, p. 221. 'Justifying faith is such a belief of the truth of the gospel, as includes a sincere resolution of obedience unto all its precepts: and that it justifieth *as* it doth so. - In short, is it possible that faith in Christ's blood, for the forgiveness of sins, should be the only act which justifieth a sinner?' p. 224.

2. *Campian.* 'So that faith is urged, but not faith ONLY; again, by faith is meant all Christianity, and the whole religion of Christians.'

Fowler, p. 222. 'For surely the faith which entitles the sinner to so high a privilege, as that of justification, must needs be such as complieth with all the purposes of Christ's coming into the world; especially with his grand purpose, - as Lord, and that it is no less necessary that it should justify as it doth this.'

3. *Campian.* 'Though works void of Christ are nothing; yet through grace they serve to justification.'

Fowler, p. 225, 226. 'Of the imputation of Christ's righteousness, - this is the true explication; it consists in dealing with sincerely righteous persons: as if they were perfectly so, for the sake and upon the account of Christ's righteousness. The grand intent of the gospel being to make us partakers of an inward and real righteousness; and it being but a secondary one, that we should be accepted, and rewarded, as if we were completely righteous.'

4. *Campian.* 'Speaking of faith, hope, and charity, he confesseth; that faith in nature is before them, but it doth not justify before they come.'

Fowler, p. 223. 'What pretence can there be for thinking, that faith is the condition, or instrument of justification, as it complieth with only the precept of relying on Christ's merits, for the obtaining of it: especially when it is no less manifest than the sun at noon-day, that obedience to the other precepts, [or works of love,] must go before obedience to this.' p. 284.

5. *Campian.* 'I deny (that faith ONLY doth justify) for you have not in all the word of God, that faith only doth justify.'

Fowler, p. 225. 'And for my part, I must confess, that I would not willingly be he that should undertake to encounter one of the champions of that foul cause, with the admission of this principle, that faith justifieth, only as it apprehendeth (resteth or relieth on, p. 224.) the merits, and righteousness of Jesus Christ, I must certainly have great luck, or my adversary but little cunning, if I were not forced to repent me of such an engagement.'

6. *Campian.* 'Abraham being a just man, was made more just by a living faith.'

Fowler, p. 283. 'He only is a true child of Abraham, who in the purity of the heart obeyeth those substantial laws, that are imposed by God, upon him.'

7. *Campian.* 'I say that charity and good works, are not excluded (in the causes of our justification.')

Fowler, p. 214, 215. 'For we have shewn, not only that reformation of life from the practice, and purification of heart from the liking of sin, are as plainly as can be asserted in the gospel to be absolutely necessary to give men a right to the promises of it, but also that its great salvation doth even consist in it.'

Mr. Fowler's Doctrine compared with William Penn the Quaker.

1. *Penn's Sandy Foundation,* p. 19. [p. 16. ed. 1684.] 'Life and salvation is to them that follow Christ the light, in all his righteousness, which every man comes only to experiment, as he walks in a holy subjection to that measure of light and grace, wherewith the fulness hath enlightened him.'

Fowler, p. 8. 'That is, those which are of an indispensable, and eternal obligation, which were first written in men's hearts, and originally dictates of human nature.'

2. *Penn,* p. 32. [p. 26. ed 1684.] 'I really confess that Jesus Christ fulfilled the Father's will, and offered up a most satisfactory sacrifice, but not to pay God, or help him [as otherways being unable] to save men.'

Fowler, p. 85. 'Christ was set forth to be a propitiatory sacrifice for sin; I will not say that his Father (who is perfectly *sui juris*) might be put by this means into a capacity of forgiving it.'

3. *Penn,* p. 16. [p. 14. ed. 1684.] 'God's remission is grounded on man's repentance, not that it is impossible for God to pardon without a plenary satisfaction.'

Fowler, p. 84. 'There are many that do not question but that God could have pardoned sin, without any other satisfaction, than the repentance of the sinner,' &c.

4. *Penn,* p. 27. [p. 22. ed. 1684.] 'Justification doth not go before, but is subsequential to the mortification of lusts.'

Fowler, p. 14, 15. 'This blessing of making men holy, was so much the design of Christ's coming, that he had his very name from it:' observe the words are, 'He shall save his people from their sins;' not from the punishment of them. And that is the primary sense of them, which is most plainly expressed in them: 'That he shall save his people from the punishment of sin, is a true sense too; but it is secondary and implied only; as this latter is the never failing and necessary consequent of the former salvation.'

5. *Penn,* p. 25. [p. 21. ed. 1684.] 'Since therefore there

can be no admittance had, without performing that righteous will, and doing those holy, and perfect sayings: alas! to what value will an imputative righteousness amount?' &c.

Fowler, p. 16. 'Christ shall bring in an inward substantial, and everlasting righteousness, and by abrogating the outward (ceremonial) and establishing ONLY this righteousness, he should enlarge the Jewish Church, an accession of the Gentiles, being by that means made unto it.'

6. *Penn*, p. 24, 25. [p. 20. ed. 1684.] 'Since God has prescribed an inoffensive life, as that which only can give acceptance with him; and on the contrary hath determined never to justify the wicked, &c. - - Will not the abomination appear greatest of all, where God shall be found condemning the just, on purpose to justify the wicked; and that he is thereto compelled, or else no salvation, which is the tendency of their doctrine, who imagine the righteous, and merciful God to condemn and punish his [innocent*] righteous Son, that he having satisfied for our sins, we might be justified (while unsanctified) by the imputation of his perfect righteousness. O why should this horrible thing be contended for by Christians!'

Fowler, p. 119. 'If it were possible (as it hath been proved it is not) that a wicked man should have God's pardon, it would not make him cease to be miserable.'

Fowler, p. 120. 'Were it possible that Christ's righteousness could be imputed to an unrighteous man, I dare boldly affirm it would signify as little to his happiness, as would a gorgeous and splendid garment, to one that is almost starved with hunger, or that lieth racked by the torturing diseases of the stone, or colic.

Fowler, p. 130. 'To justify a wicked man, while he continueth so, if it were possible for God to do it, would far more disparage his justice, and holiness, than advance his grace and kindness.'

7. *Penn*, p. 26. [p. 22. ed. 1684.] 'Unless we be[come] doers of that law, which Christ came not to destroy, but as our example to fulfil, we can never be justified before God.'

Fowler, p. 296. 'It is impossible we should not have the design of Christianity accomplished in us, and therefore that we should be destitute of the power of it, if we make our Saviour's most excellent life, the pattern of our lives. Those that sincerely, and industriously endeavour to imitate the holy Jesus in his spirit and actions, can never be ignorant what it is to be truly Christians, nor can they fail to be so.' ·

8. *Penn*, p. 26. 'Nor let any fancy that Christ hath so fulfilled it for them, as to exclude their obedience, from being requisite to their acceptance, but only as their pattern.'

Fowler, p. 148. 'This Son of God taught men their duty, by his own example, and did himself perform among them, what he required of them. Now that he should tread before us EVERY step of that way, which he hath told us leadeth to eternal happiness, and commend those duties which are most ungrateful to our corrupt inclinations, by his own practice; our having so brave an example is no small encouragement, to a cheerful performance of all that is commanded.'

Understandest thou what thou readest?

---

* 'Innocent' instead of 'righteous,' ed. 1684.

REPROBATION ASSERTED:

OR,

THE DOCTRINE OF ETERNAL ELECTION AND REPROBATION PROMISCUOUSLY HANDLED, IN ELEVEN CHAPTERS.

WHEREIN THE MOST MATERIAL OBJECTIONS MADE BY THE OPPOSERS OF THIS DOCTRINE, ARE FULLY ANSWERED; SEVERAL DOUBTS REMOVED, AND SUNDRY CASES OF CONSCIENCE RESOLVED.

BY JOHN BUNYAN OF BEDFORD, A LOVER OF PEACE AND TRUTH.

'*What then? Israel hath not obtained that which he seeketh for; but the election hath obtained it, and the rest were blinded.*'—Rom. xi. 7.

London: Printed for G. L., and are to be sold in Turn-stile-alley, in Holbourn. Small 4to, 44 pages.

THE CONTENTS OF THE CHAPTERS.

EDITOR'S ADVERTISEMENT.

THIS valuable tract was first published without a date, but according to Doe's List, about the year 1674, and has never been reprinted in a separate volume; it appeared in only one edition of the collected works of John Bunyan—that with the notes by Ryland and Mason; and in his select works, published in America in 1832. No man could have been better qualified to write upon the subject of reprobation than Bunyan.—His extraordinary knowledge of, and fervent attachment to, the holy oracles, peculiarly fitted him with unwavering verity to display this doctrine of divine truth. He was incapable of any misrepresentation with a view of concealing what fallen reason might deem a deformity, or to render the doctrines of the cross palatable to mankind. His object is to display the truth, and then humbly to submit to the wisdom of God, and zealously to vindicate it. There is no subject which more fully displays our fallen nature, than that of reprobation. All mankind agree in opinion, that there ever has been an elect, or good class of society; and a reprobate, or worthless and bad class; varying in turpitude or in goodness to a great extent and in almost imperceptible degrees. All must unite in ascribing to God that divine foreknowledge that renders ten thousand years but as one day, or hour, or moment in his sight. All ascribe to his omnipotence the power to ordain or decree what shall come to pass —and where is the spirit that can demonstrate a shade of difference between such foreknowledge and preordination. All agree that in the lower class of animals some of the same species pass their lives in luxury and comfort, while others are cruelly tormented, this world comprising their whole term of existence; and will those who refuse to submit to the sovereignty of God in the doctrine of election dare to arraign his conduct in leaving some out of his electing love? The reprobate or worthless lose nothing by the happiness of others. It is inscrutably hid from mankind who are the elect, until the Holy Spirit influences them with the love of God in Christ Jesus, and this sometimes in the last moments of life. There is every encouragement, nay incentive, to the sinner who feels the burthen of guilt to fly for refuge to the hope set before him in the gospel. 'It *is* a faithful saying, and worthy of all acceptation, that Christ Jesus came into the world to save SINNERS;' even the chief of sinners. The glad tidings are addressed to ALL sin-sick souls; and Bunyan's statement of this truth is clear, scriptural, and reasonable. Very different is the account of reprobation given by R. Resburie in his Stop to the Gangrene of Arminianism, 1651. 'For the reprobate God decrees the permitting of sin in order to hardening, and their hardening in it, in order to their condemnation.'

p. 69. 'As election is the book of life, so reprobation of death; the names of the reprobate are there registered for destruction.' p. 73. It is much to be regretted that sentiments like these have been too commonly uttered. It is as an antidote to such ideas that this little work was written; but, unfortunately, it has never been widely circulated and read. May the divine blessing follow this attempt to spread these important, although to many, unpalatable, doctrines.

GEORGE OFFOR.

REPROBATION ASSERTED.

CHAP. I.

That there is a Reprobation.

IN my discourse upon this subject, I shall study as much brevity as clearness and edification will allow me; not adding words to make the volume swell, but contracting myself within the bounds of few lines, for the profit and commodity of those that shall take the pains to read my labours. And though I might abundantly multiply arguments for the evincing and vindicating this conclusion, yet I shall content myself with some few scripture demonstrations: the first of which I shall gather out of the ninth of the Romans, from that discourse of the apostle's, touching the children of the flesh, and the children of the promise.

1. At the beginning of this chapter, we find the apostle grievously lamenting and bemoaning of the Jews, at the consideration of their miserable state: 'I say the truth in Christ, (saith he) I lie not, my conscience also bearing me witness in the Holy Ghost, that I have great heaviness and continual sorrow in my heart. For I could wish that myself were accursed from Christ for my brethren, my kinsmen according to the flesh:' Poor hearts, saith he, they will perish; they are a miserable sad and helpless people; their eyes are darkened that they may not see, and their back is bowed down alway. Ro. xi. 10. Wherefore? Have they not the means of grace? Yes verily, and that in goodly measure. First they 'are Israelites; to whom *pertaineth* the adoption, and the glory, and the covenants, and the giving of the law, and the service *of God*, and the promises; whose *are* the fathers, and of whom as concerning the flesh Christ *came*, who is over all, God blessed for ever. Amen.' What then should be the reason? Why saith he, though they be the children of Abraham according to the flesh, yet they are the children of Abraham BUT according to the flesh: 'For they *are* not all Israel (in the best sense) which are of

Israel: neither, because they are the seed of Abraham, *are they* all children: but, in Isaac shall thy seed be called.' That is, they that are the children of the flesh, they are not the children of God; but the children of the promise shall be counted for the seed. So then, here you see that they that are only the children of the flesh, as the greatest part of Israel were, they are those that are neither counted for the seed, the children of promise, nor the children of God; but are rejected, and of the reprobation. This therefore shall at this time serve for the first scripture-demonstration.

2. Another scripture you have in the eleventh chapter of this epistle, from these words, 'The election hath obtained it, and the REST were blinded.' Ro. xi. 7. These words are shedding* words, they sever between men and men; the election, the rest; the chosen, the left; the embraced, the refused: 'The election have obtained it, and the *rest* were blinded.' By *rest* here, must needs be understood those not elect, because set one in opposition to the other; and if not elect, what then but reprobate?

3. A third scripture is that in the Acts of the Apostles, 'And as many as were ordained to eternal life, believed.' xiii. 48. 'And as many;' by these words, as by the former, you may see how the Holy Ghost distinguisheth or divideth between men and men; the sons, and the sons of Adam. 'As many as were ordained to eternal life, believed:' If by *many* here, we are to understand every individual, then not only the whole world must at least believe the gospel, of which we see the most fall short, but they must be ordained to eternal life; which other scriptures contradict: for there is the rest, besides the elect; the stubble and chaff, as well as wheat: *many* therefore must here include but some; 'For though - Israel be as the sand

---

* 'Shedding words' means 'scattering or spreading words,' as in Acts ii. 33; now obsolete.—ED.

of the sea, a remnant shall be saved.' Ro. ix. 27. Is. i. 9. and x. 22, 23.

I might here multiply many other texts, but in the mouth of two or three witnesses shall every word be established. Let these therefore for this, suffice to prove that there is a reprobation. · For this I say, though the children of the flesh, the *rest* besides the election, and the like, were not mentioned in the word; yet seeing there is such a thing as the children of the promise, the seed, the children of God, and the like, and that too under several other phrases, as predestinated, foreknown, chosen in Christ, and written in the book of life, and appointed unto life, with many others: I say seeing these things are thus apparent, it is without doubt, that there is such a thing as a reprobation also. Ro. viii. Ep. i. 3, 4. 1 Th. v. 9.

Nay, further, From the very word election, it followeth unavoidably; for whether you take it as relating to this, of distinguishing between persons as touching the world to come, or with reference to God's acts of choosing this or that man to this or that office, work, or employment in this world, it still signifieth such a choosing, as that but some are therein concerned, and that therefore *some* are thence excluded. Are all the elect, the seed, the saved, the vessels of mercy, the chosen and peculiar? Are not some, yea the most, the children of the flesh, the rest, the lost, the vessels of wrath, of dishonour, and the children of perdition? Ro. xi. 9. 1 Pe. ii. 8, 9. Mat. x. 16. 2 Sa. vi. 21. Ps. lxxviii. 67, 68. Jn. xv. 16. 2 Co. iv. 3. Ro. ix. 21, 22. Jn. xvii. 12.

CHAP. II.

What Reprobation is.

Having thus shewed you that there is such a thing as a reprobation, I come now to shew you what it is. Which that I may do to your edification, I shall *First* shew you what this word reprobation signifieth in the general, as it concerneth persons temporary and visibly reprobate: *Second,* more particularly, as it concerneth persons that are eternally and invisibly reprobate.

First, Generally, As it concerneth persons temporarily and visibly reprobate, thus: To be reprobate is to be disapproved, void of judgment, and rejected, &c. To be disapproved, that is, when the word condemns them, either as touching the faith or the holiness of the gospel; the which they must needs be, that are void of spiritual and heavenly judgment in the mysteries of the kingdom; a manifest token [that] they are rejected. And hence it is that they are said to be reprobate or void of judgment concerning the faith; reprobate or void of judgment touching every good work; having a reprobate mind, to do those things that are not convenient, either as to faith or manners.

And hence it is again, that they are also said to be rejected of God, cast away, and the like. 2 Co. xiii. 6, 7. 2 Ti. iii. 8. Tit. i. 16. Ro. i. 28. Je. vi. 30. 1 Co. ix. 27.

I call this temporary visible reprobation, because these appear, and are detected by the word as such that are found under the above-named errors, and so adjudged without the grace of God. Yet it is possible for some of these, however for the present disapproved, through the blessed acts and dispensations of grace, not only to become visible saints, but also saved for ever. Who doubts but that he who now by examining himself, concerning faith, doth find himself, though under profession, graceless, may after that, he seeing his woeful state, not only cry to God for mercy, but find grace, and obtain mercy to help in time of need? though it is true, that for the most part the contrary is fulfilled on them.

Second, But to pass this, and more particularly to touch the eternal invisible reprobation, which I shall thus hold forth: It is to be passed by in, or left out of, God's election; yet so, as considered upright. In which position you have these four things considerable: 1. The act of God's election. 2. The negative of that act. 3. The persons reached by that negative. And, 4. Their qualification when thus reached by it.

1. For the first. This act of God in electing, it is a choosing or fore-appointing of some infallibly unto eternal life, which he also hath determined shall be brought to pass by the means that should be made manifest and efficacious to that very end. Ep. i. 3—5. 1 Pe. i. 2.

2. Now the negative of this act is, a passing by, or a leaving of those not concerned in this act; a leaving of them, I say, without the bounds, and so the saving privileges of this act; as it followeth by natural consequence, that because a man chooseth but some, therefore he chooseth not all, but leaveth, as the negative of that act, all others whatsoever. Wherefore, as I said before, those not contained within this blessed act, are called the *rest* besides the election. 'The election hath obtained it, and the rest were blinded.'

3. The persons then that are contained under the negative of this act, they are those, and those only, that pass through this wicked world without the saving grace of God's elect; those, I say, that miss the most holy faith, which they in time are blest withal, who are fore-appointed unto glory.

4. And now for the qualification they were considered under, when this act of reprobation laid hold upon them; to wit, They were considered upright.

This is evident, From this consideration, that reprobation is God's act, even the negative of his choosing or electing, and none of the acts of God make any man a sinner. It is further evident by

2 U

the similitude that is taken from the carriage of the potter in his making of his pots; for by this comparison the God of heaven is pleased to shew unto us the nature of his determining in the act of reprobation. 'Hath not the potter power over the clay, of the same lump?' &c. Ro. ix. 21. Consider a little, and you shall see that these three things do necessarily fall in, to complete the potter's action in every pot he makes.

(1.) A determination in his own mind what pot to make of this or that piece of clay; a determination, I say, precedent to the fashion of the pot; the which is true in the highest degree, in him that is excellent in working; he determines the end, before the beginning is perfected: Is. xli. 22. xlvi. 10. 'For this *cause* (very purpose) have I raised thee up.' Ex. ix. 16.

(2.) The next thing considerable in the potter; it is the so making of the pot, even as he determined; a vessel to honour, or a vessel to dishonour. There is no confusion nor disappointment under the hand of this eternal God, his work is perfect, and every way doth answer to what he hath determined. De. xxxii 4.

(3.) Observe again, That whether the vessel be to honour or to dishonour, yet the potter makes it good, sound, and fit for service; his fore-determining to make this a vessel to dishonour, hath no persuasion at all with him to break or mar the pot: Which very thing doth well resemble the state of man as under the act of eternal reprobation, for 'God made man upright.' Ec. vii. 29.

From these conclusions then,

Consider, 1. That the simple act of reprobation, it is a leaving or passing by, not a cursing of the creature.

Consider, 2. Neither doth this act alienate the heart of God from the reprobate, nor tie him up from loving, favouring, or blessing of him; no, not from blessing of him with the gift of Christ, of faith, of hope, and many other benefits. It only denieth them that benefit, that will infallibly bring them to eternal life, and that in despite of all opposition; it only denieth so to bless them as the elect themselves are blessed. Abraham loved all the children he had by all his wives, and gave them portions also; but his choice blessing, as the fruit of his chiefest love, he reserved for chosen Isaac. Ge. xxv. 5, 6.

Consider Lastly, The act of reprobation doth harm to no man, neither means him any; nay, it rather decrees him upright, lets him be made upright, and so be turned into the world.*

---

* As election took place before the creation of man—all men in Adam were decreed, made and turned into the world upright.—ED.

CHAP. III.

Of the Antiquity of Reprobation.

Having now proceeded so far as to shew you what reprobation is, it will not be amiss if in this place I briefly shew you its antiquity, even when it began its rise; the which you may gather by these following particulars.

First, Reprobation is before the person cometh into the world, or hath done good or evil: This is evident by that of Paul to the Romans: 'For *the children* being not yet born, neither having done any good or evil, that the purpose of God according to election might stand not of works, but of him that calleth; it was said unto Rebecca, The elder shall serve the younger.' ix. 11. Here you find twain in their mother's womb, and both receiving their destiny, not only before they had done good or evil, but before they were in a capacity to do it, they being yet unborn; their destiny, I say, the one unto, the other not unto, the blessing of eternal life; the one chose, the other refused; the one elect, the other reprobate. The same also might be said of Ishmael and his brother Isaac, both which did also receive their destiny before they came into the world: for the promise that this Isaac should be the heir, it was also before Ishmael was born, though he was elder by fourteen years, or more, than his brother. Ge. xv. 4, 5; xvi. 4, 5, 16; xvii. 25; xxi. 5. And it is yet further evident,

1. Because election is an act of grace; 'There is a remnant according to the election of grace.' Ro. xi. 5. Which act of grace saw no way so fit to discover its purity and independency, as by fastening on the object before it came into the world; that being the state in which at least no good were done, either to procure good from God, or to eclipse and darken this precious act of grace. For though it is true that no good thing that we have done before conversion, can obtain the grace of election; yet the grace of election then appeareth most, when it prevents† our doing good, that we might be loved therefore: wherefore he saith again, 'That the purpose of God according to election might stand, not of works, but of him that calleth; it was said unto her, The elder shall serve the younger.' Ro. ix. 11, 12.

2. This is most agreeable to the nature of the promise of giving seed to Abraham; which promise, as it was made before the child was conceived, so it was fulfilled at the best time, for the discovery of the act of grace, that could have been pitched

---

† 'Prevents our doing good.' Few words in the English language have more altered in their meaning than 'prevent;' it is derived from 'prævenio,' to go before. In Bunyan's time, it meant 'to go before,' 'clear the way,' 'make the way easy' for our doing good. Its present meaning is 'to obstruct,' by going or standing before us.—ED.

upon: At this time will I come (saith God) 'and Sarah shall have a son;' Ge. xviii. 14. which promise, because it carried in its bowels the very grace of electing love, therefore it left out Ishmael, with the children of Keturah: 'For in Isaac shall thy seed be called.' Ro. iv. 16—19; ix. 7.

3. This was the best and fittest way for the decrees to receive sound bottom, even for God both to choose and refuse, before the creature had done good or evil, and so before they came into the world: 'That the purpose of God according to election might stand,' saith he, therefore before *the children* were yet born, or had done any good or evil, it was said unto her, &c. God's decree would for ever want foundation, should it depend at all upon the goodness and holiness either of men or angels; especially if it were to stand upon that good that is wrought before conversion, yea, or after conversion either. We find, by daily experience, how hard and difficult it is, for even the holiest in the world, to bear up and maintain their faith and love to God; yea, so hard, as not at all to do it without continual supplies from heaven. How then is it possible for any so to carry it before God, as to lay, by this his holiness, a foundation for election, as to maintain that foundation, and thereby to procure all those graces that infallibly saveth the sinner? But now the choice, I say, being a choice of grace, as is manifest, it being acted before the creature's birth; here grace hath laid the corner-stone, and determined the means to bring the work to perfection. Thus 'the foundation of God standeth sure, having this seal, The Lord knoweth them that are his.' 2 Ti. ii. 19. That is, who he hath chosen, having excluded works, both good and bad, and founded all in an unchangeable act of grace; the negative whereof, is this harmless reprobation.

Second, But secondly, To step a little backward, and so to make all sure: This act of reprobation was before the world began; which therefore must needs confirm that which was said but now, that they were, before they were born, both destinated before they had done good or evil. This is manifest by that of Paul to the Ephesians, at the beginning of his epistle; where, speaking of Election, whose negative is reprobation, he saith, 'God hath chosen us in Christ before the foundation of the world.' Nay further, if you please, consider, that as Christ was ordained to suffer before the foundation of the world, and as we that are elected were chosen in him before the foundation of the world; so it was also ordained we should know him, before the foundation of the world; ordained that we should be holy before him in love, before the foundation of the world; and that we in time should be created in him to good works, and ordained before that we should walk in them. Wherefore repro-

bation also, it being the negative of electing love; that is, because God elected but some, therefore he left the rest: these rest therefore must needs be of as ancient standing under reprobation, as the chosen are under election; both which, it is also evident, was before the world began. Which serveth yet further to prove that reprobation could not be with respect to this or the other sin, it being only a leaving them, and that before the world, out of that free choice which he was pleased to bless the other with. Even as the clay with which the dishonourable vessel is made, did not provoke the potter, for the sake of this or that impediment, *therefore* to make it so; but the potter of his own will, of the clay of the same lump, of the clay that is full as good as that of which he hath made the vessel to honour, did make this and the other a vessel of dishonour, &c. 1 Pe. i. 20, 21. 1 Co. ii. 7. Ep. i. 3, 4; ii. 10.*

CHAP. IV.

Of the causes of Reprobation.

Having thus in a word or two shewed the antiquity of Reprobation, I now come in this place to shew you the cause thereof; for doubtless this must stand a truth, That whatever God doth, there is sufficient ground therefore, whether by us apprehended, or else without our reach.

First then, It is caused from the very nature of God. There are two things in God, from which, or by the virtue of which, all things have their rise, to wit, the eternity of God in general, and the eternal perfection of every one of his attributes in particular: for as by the first, he must needs be before all things; so by virtue of the second, must all things consist. And as he is before all things, they having consistence by him; so also is he before all states, or their causes, be they either good or bad, of continuance or otherwise, he being the first without beginning, &c., whereas all other things, with their causes, have rise, dependance, or toleration of being from him. Col. i. 17.

Hence it follows, that nothing, either person or cause, &c., can by any means have a being, but first he knows thereof, allows thereof, and decrees it shall be so. 'Who *is* he *that* saith, and it cometh to pass, *when* the Lord commandeth *it* not?' La. iii. 37. Now then, because that reprobation, as well as election, are subordinate to God; his will also, which is eternally perfect, being most imme-

---

* They who diligently attend to the scriptures, will find throughout the whole a vein of election and reprobation. The holy seed may be traced in many instances, and in divers families, in the Bible, from Adam to the birth of our Saviour, whose ancestors, according to the flesh, were of the line of election or the godly; which those who are only born after the flesh, and not after the Spirit, namely, the reprobate, have always despised and persecuted, and will do so to the end of time.—*Mason and Ryland.*

diately herein concerned; it was impossible that any should be reprobate, before God had both willed and decreed it should be so. It is not the being of a thing that administers matter of knowledge or foresight thereof to God, but the perfection of his knowledge, wisdom, and power, &c., that giveth the thing its being: God did not fore-decree there should be a world, because he foresaw there would be one; but there must be one, because he had before decreed there should be one. The same is true as touching the case in hand: 'For this cause [very purpose] have I raised thee up, for to shew *in* thee my power.' Ex. ix. 16. Ro. ix. 17.

Second, A second cause of eternal reprobation, is the exercise of God's sovereignty; for if this is true, that there is nothing either visible or invisible, whether in heaven or earth, but hath its being from him: then it must most reasonably follow, that he is therefore sovereign Lord, &c., and may also according to his own will, as he pleaseth himself, both exercise and manifest the same; being every whit absolute; and can do and may do whatsoever his soul desireth: and indeed, good reason, for he hath not only made them all, but 'for his pleasure they both were and are created.' Re. iv. 11.

Now the very exercise of this sovereignty produceth reprobation: 'Therefore hath he mercy on whom he will *have mercy*, and whom he will he hardeneth.' Ro. ix. 18. 'Hath not the potter power over the clay, of the same lump?' And doth he not make his pots according to his pleasure? Here therefore the mercy, justice, wisdom and power of God, take liberty to do what they will; saying, 'My counsel shall stand, and I will do all my pleasure.' Is. xlvi. 10. Job xxiii. 13. Da. iv. 35. Is. xliii. 13.

Third, Another cause of eternal reprobation, is the act and working of distinguishing love, and everlasting grace. God hath universal love, and particular love; general love, and distinguishing love; and so accordingly doth decree, purpose, and determine: from general love, the extension of general grace and mercy: but from that love that is distinguishing, peculiar grace and mercy: 'Was not Esau Jacob's brother?' saith the Lord, 'yet I loved Jacob.' Mal. i. 2. Yet I loved Jacob, that is, with a better love, or a love that is more distinguishing. As he further makes appear in his answer to our father Abraham, when he prayed to God for Ishmael: 'As for Ishmael, (saith he,) I have heard thee: Behold, I have blessed him, and will make him fruitful. But my covenant will I establish with Isaac, which Sarah shall bear unto thee.' Ge. xvii. 20, 21. Touching which words, there are these things observable.

1. That God had better love for Isaac, than he had for his brother Ishmael. Yet,

2. Not because Isaac had done more worthy and goodly deeds, for Isaac was yet unborn.

3. This choice blessing could not be denied to Ishmael, because he had disinherited himself by sin; for this blessing was entailed to Isaac, before Ishmael had a being also. Ro. iv. 16—19. Ge. xv. 4, 5; xvi.

4. These things therefore must needs fall out through the working of distinguishing love and mercy, which had so cast the business, 'that the purpose of God according to election might stand.'

Further, Should not God decree to shew distinguishing love and mercy, as well as that which is general and common, he must not discover his best love at all to the sons of men. Again, if he should reveal and extend his best love to all the world in general, then there would not be such a thing as love that doth distinguish; for distinguishing love appeareth in separating between Isaac and Ishmael, Jacob and Esau, the many called, and the few chosen. Thus by virtue of distinguishing love, some must be reprobate: for distinguishing love must leave some, both of the angels in heaven, and the inhabitants of the earth; wherefore the decree also that doth establish it, must needs leave some.

Fourth, Another cause of reprobation, Is God's willingness to shew his wrath, and to make his power known. This is one of those arguments that the holy apostle setteth against the most knotty and strong objection that ever was framed against the doctrine of eternal reprobation: 'Thou wilt say then unto me, (saith he,) Why doth he yet find fault?' For if it be his will that some should be rejected, hardened, and perish, why then is he offended that any sin against him; 'for who hath resisted his will?' Hold, saith the apostle; stay a little here; first remember this, Is it meet to say unto God, What doest thou? 'Shall the thing formed say to him that formed *it*, Why hast thou made me thus? Hath not the potter power over the clay, of the same lump,' &c. Besides, when you have thought your worst, to wit, that the effects of reprobation must needs be consummate in the eternal perdition of the creature; yet again consider, 'What if God, willing to shew *his* wrath,' as well as grace and mercy? And what if he, that he may so do, exclude some from having share in that grace that would infallibly, against all resistance, bring us safe unto eternal life? What then? Is he therefore the author of your perishing, or his eternal reprobation either? Do you not know that he may refuse to elect who he will, without abusing of them? Also that he may deny to give them that grace that would preserve them from sin, without being guilty of their damnation? May he not, to shew his wrath, suffer 'with much long-suffering' all that are 'the vessels of wrath,' by their own voluntary will, to fit themselves for wrath and for destruction? Ro. ix. 19—22. Yea, might he not even in the act of reprobation, conclude also to suffer them thus left, to fall from the state he left them in, that is, as they were considered upright; and when fallen, to bind them fast in chains of darkness unto the judgment of the great day, but he must needs be charged foolishly? You shall see in that day what a harmony and what a glory there will be found in all God's judgments in the overthrow of the sinner; also how clear the Lord will shew himself of having any working hand in that which causeth eternal ruin; notwithstanding he hath reprobated such, doth suffer them to sin, and that too, that he might shew his wrath on the vessels of his wrath; the which I also, after this next chapter, shall further clear up to you. As 'the Lord knoweth how to deliver the godly out of temptations,' without approving of their miscarriages; so he also knoweth how 'to reserve the unjust unto the day of judgment to be punished:' 2 Pe. ii. 9. yet never to deserve the least of blame for his so reserving of them; though none herein can see his way, for he alone knows how to do it.*

CHAP. V.

Of the Unchangeableness of Eternal Reprobation.

Many opinions have passed through the hearts of the sons of men concerning reprobation; most of them endeavouring so to hold it forth, as therewith they might, if not heal their conscience slightly, yet maintain their own opinion, in their judgment, of other things; still wringing, now the word this way, and anon again that, for their purpose; also framing within their soul such an imagination of God and his acts in eternity, as would suit with such opinions, and so present all to the world. And the rather they have with greatest labour strained unweariedly at this above many other truths, because of the grim and dreadful face it carrieth in most men's apprehensions. But none of these things, however they may please the creature, can by any means in any measure, either cause God to undo, unsay, or undetermine what he hath concerning this, decreed and established.

First, Because they suit not with his nature, especially in these foundation-acts: 'The foundation of God standeth sure,' 2 Ti. ii. 19. even touching reprobation, 'that the purpose of God according to election might stand.' Ro. ix. 11. 'I know (saith Solomon) that whatsoever God doeth, it shall be

for ever: nothing can be put to it, nor any thing taken from it,' &c. Ec. iii. 14. 'Hath he said, and shall he not do *it*? Hath he spoken, and shall he not make it good?' Nu. xxiii. 19. His decrees are composed according to his eternal wisdom, established upon his unchangeable will, governed by his knowledge, prudence, power, justice, and mercy, and are brought to conclusion, on his part, in perfect holiness, through the abiding of his most blessed truth and faithfulness: '*He is* the rock, his work *is* perfect: for all his ways are judgment: a God of truth and without iniquity, just and right *is* he.' De. xxxii. 4.

Second, This decree is made sure by the number, measure, and bounds of election; for election and reprobation do inclose all reasonable creatures; that is, either the one or the other; election, those that are set apart for glory; and reprobation, those left out of this choice.

Now as touching the elect, they are by this decree confined to that limited number of persons that must amount to the complete making up the fulness of the mystical body of Christ; yea so confined by this eternal purpose, that nothing can be diminished from or added thereunto: and, hence it is that they are called his body and members in particular, 'the fulness of him that filleth all in all.' Ep. i. 23. and 'the measure of the stature of the fulness of Christ.' Ep. iv. 13. Which body, considering him as the head thereof, in conclusion maketh up one perfect man, and holy temple for the Lord. These are called Christ's substance, inheritance and lot; Ps. xvi. and are said to be booked, marked, and sealed with God's most excellent knowledge, approbation and liking. 2 Ti. ii. 19. As Christ said to his Father, 'Thine eyes did see my substance, yet being unperfect; and in thy book all *my members* were written, *which* in continuance were fashioned, when *as yet there was* none of them.' Ps. cxxxix. 16. This being thus, I say, it is in the first place impossible that any of those members should miscarry, for 'Who shall lay any thing to the charge of God's elect?' Ro. viii. 33. and because they are as to number every way sufficient, being his body, and so by their completing to be made a perfect man: therefore all others are rejected, that the 'purpose of God according to election might stand.' Ro. ix. 11. Besides, it would not only argue weakness in the decree, but monstrousness in the body, if after this, any appointed should miscarry, or any besides them be added to them. Mat. xxiv. 24.

Third, Nay further, that all may see how punctual, exact, and to a tittle this decree of election is, God hath not only as to number and quantity confined the persons, but also determined and measured, and that before the world, the number of the gifts and graces that are to be bestowed on

---

* It is of God's mere mercy and grace that any sinners are called and admitted to the privilege of justification and adoption, upon God's own terms. The reason why the sinful and unworthy heathen (of whom Britain is a part) were called to be a people, who were not a people, while the Jews were left out and cast off for their obstinate unbelief, was not because the Gentiles were either more worthy or more willing (for they were all dead in trespasses and sins), but from God's discriminating grace and mercy.—*Mason and Ryland.*

these members in general; and also what graces and gifts to be bestowed on this or that member in particular: He 'hath blessed us with all spiritual blessings - in Christ, according as he hath chosen us in him before the foundation of the word;' Ep. i. 3, 4. And bestoweth them in time upon us, 'According to the eternal purpose which he purposed in Christ Jesus our Lord:' Ep. iii. 11. He hath given to the eye, the grace that belongeth to the eye; and to the hand that which he also hath appointed for it. And so to every other member of the body elect, he doth deal out to them their determined measure of grace and gifts most fit for their place and office. Thus is the decree established, both of the saved, and also the non-elect. Ro. xii. 3. Ep. iv. 16. Col. ii. 19. Ep. iv. 12, 13.

Fourth, But again, another thing that doth establish this decree of eternal reprobation, is the weakness that sin, in the fall, and since, hath brought all reprobates into: For though it be most true, that sin is no cause of eternal reprobation; yet seeing sin hath seized on the reprobate, it cannot be but thereby the decree must needs be the faster fixed. If the king, for this or the other weighty reason, doth decree not to give this or that man, who yet did never offend him, a place in his privy chamber; if this man after this shall be infected with the plague, this rather fastens than loosens the king's decree. As the angels that were left out of God's election, by reason of the sin they committed after, are so far off from being by that received into God's decree, that they are therefore bound for it in chains of everlasting darkness to the judgment of the great day.

CHAP. VI.

Whether to be reprobated be the same with being appointed before-hand unto eternal condemnation? If not, how do they differ? Also whether reprobation be the cause of condemnation?

It hath been the custom of ignorant men much to quarrel at eternal reprobation, concluding, for want of knowledge in the mystery of God's will, that if he reprobate any from eternity, he had as good have said, I will make this man to damn him; I will decree this man, without any consideration, to the everlasting pains of hell. When in very deed, for God to reprobate, and to appoint before-hand to eternal condemnation, are two distinct things, properly relating to two distinct attributes, arising from two distinct causes.

First, They are two distinct things: Reprobation, a simple leaving of the creature out of the bounds of God's election; but to appoint to condemnation is to bind them over to everlasting punishment. Now there is a great difference between my refusing to make of such a tree a pillar in my

house, and of condemning it unto the fire to be burned.

Second, As to the attributes; reprobation respects God's sovereignty; but to appoint to condemnation, his justice. Ro. ix. 18. Ge. xviii. 25.

Third, As to the causes; sovereignty being according to the will of God, but justice according to the sin of man. For God, though he be the only sovereign Lord, and that to the height of perfection; yet he appointeth no man to the pains of everlasting fire, merely from sovereignty, but by the rule of justice: God damneth not the man because he is a man, but a sinner; and fore-appoints him to that place and state, by fore-seeing of him wicked. Ro. i. 18, 19. Col. iii. 6.

Again, As reprobation is not the same with fore-appointing to eternal condemnation; so neither is it the cause thereof.

If it be the cause, then it must either, 1. Leave him infirm. Or, 2. Infuse sin into him. Or, 3. Take from him something that otherwise would keep him upright. 4. Or both license Satan to tempt, and the reprobate to close in with the temptation. But it doth none of these; therefore it is not the cause of the condemnation of the creature.

That it is not the cause of sin, it is evident,

1. Because the elect are as much involved therein, as those that are passed by.

2. It leaveth him not infirm; for he is by an after-act, to wit, of creation, formed perfectly upright.

3. That reprobation infuseth no sin, appeareth, because it is the act of God.

4. That it taketh nothing, that good is, from him, is also manifest, it being only a leaving of him.

5. And that it is not by this act that Satan is permitted to tempt, or the reprobate to sin, is manifest; because as Christ was tempted, so the elect fall as much into the temptation, at least many of them, as many of those that are reprobate: whereas if these things came by reprobation, then the reprobate would be only concerned therein. All which will be further handled in these questions yet behind.

Object. From what hath been said, there is concluded this at least, That God hath infallibly determined, and that before the world, the infallible damnation of some of his creatures: for if God hath before the world [was made] bound some over to eternal punishment, and that as you say, for sin; then this determination must either be fallible or infallible; not fallible, for then your other position of the certainty of the number of God's elect, is shaken; unless you hold that there may be a number that shall neither go to heaven nor hell. Well then, if God hath indeed determined, fore-determined, that some must infallibly perish; doth not this his determination lay a necessity on the reprobate to sin, that he may be damned; for, no sin, no damnation; that is your own argument.

Ans. That God hath ordained, (Jude 4.) the damnation of some of his creatures, it is evident; but whether this his determination be positive and absolute, there is the question: for the better understanding whereof, I shall open unto you the variety of God's determinations, and their nature, as also rise.

The determinations of God touching the destruction of the creature, they are either ordinary or extraordinary: those I count ordinary that were commonly pronounced by the prophets and apostles, &c., in their ordinary way of preaching; to the end men might be affected with the love of their own salvation: now these either bound or loosed, but as the condition or qualification was answered by the creature under sentence, and no otherwise. 1 Sa. xii. 25. Is. i. 20. Mat. xviii. 3. Lu. xiii. 1, 2, 3. Ro. ii. 8, 9; viii. 13; xi. 23. 1 Co. vi. 9—11.

Again, These extraordinary, though they respect the same conditions, yet they are not grounded immediately upon them, but upon the infallible fore-knowledge and fore-sight of God, and are thus distinguished. First the ordinary determination, it stands but at best upon a supposition that the creature may continue in sin, and admits of a possibility that it may not; but the extraordinary stands upon an infallible fore-sight that the creature will continue in sin; wherefore this must needs be positive, and as infallible as God himself.

Again, These two determinations are also distinguished thus: the ordinary is applicable to the elect as well as to the reprobate, but the other to the reprobate only. It is proper to say even to the elect themselves, ' He that believeth shall be saved, and he that believeth not shall be damned;' but not to say to them, These are appointed to UTTER destruction, or that they shall utterly perish in their own corruptions; or that for them is reserved the blackness of darkness for ever. 1 Ki. xx. 42. 2 Pe. ii. 12. Jude 13.

So then, though God by these determinations doth not lay some under irrecoverable condemnation, yet by one of them he doth; as is further made out thus:

1. God most perfectly foreseeth the final impenitency of those that so die, from the beginning to the end of the world. Pr. xv. 11. Ps. cxxxix. 2. Is. xlvi. 10.

2. Now from this infallible foresight, it is most easy and rational to conclude, and that positively, the infallible overthrow of every such creature. Did I infallibly foresee that this or that man would cut out his heart in the morning, I might infallibly determine his death before night.

Object. But still the question is, Whether God

by this his determination doth not lay a necessity on the creature to sin? For, no sin, no condemnation: this is true by your own assertion.

Ans. No, by no means: for,

1. Though it be true, that sin must of absolute necessity go before the infallible condemnation and overthrow of the sinner; and that it must also be pre-considered by God; yet it needs not lay a necessity upon him to sin: for let him but alone to do what he will, and the determination cannot be more infallible than the sin, which is the cause of its execution.

2. As it needs not, so it doth not: for this positive determination is not grounded upon what God will effect, but on what the creature will; and that not through the instigation of God, but the instigation of the devil. What? might not I, if I most undoubtedly foresaw that such a tree in my garden would only cumber the ground, notwithstanding reasonable means, might not I, I say, from hence determine, seven years before, to cut it down, and burn it in the fire, but I must, by so determining, necessitate this tree to be fruitless? the case in hand is the very same. God therefore may most positively determine the infallible damnation of his creature, and yet not at all necessitate the creature to sin, that he might be damned.

Object. But how is this similitude pertinent? For God did not only foresee sin would be the destruction of the creature, but let it come into the world, and so destroy the creature. If you, as you foresee the fruitlessness of your tree, should withal see that which makes it so, and that too before it makes it so, and yet let the impediment come and make it so; are not you now the cause of the unfruitfulness of that tree which you have before condemned to the fire to be burned? for God might have chose whether he would have let Adam sin, and so sin to have got into the world by him.

Ans. Similitudes never answer every way; if they be pertinent to that for which they are intended, it is enough; and to that it answereth well, being brought to prove no more but the natural consequence of a true and infallible foresight. And now as to what is objected further, as that God might have chose whether sin should have come into the world by Adam, to the destruction of so many: to that I shall answer,

1. That sin could not have come into the world without God's permission, it is evident, both from the perfection of his foresight and power.

2. Therefore all the means, motives, and inducements thereunto, must also by him be not only foreseen, but permitted.

3. Yet so, that God will have the timing, proceeding, bounding, and ordering thereof, at his disposal: ' Surely the wrath of man shall praise

thee, and the remainder of wrath shalt thou restrain.' Ps. lxxvi. 10. 1 Ki. xxii 20—22. Jn. viii. 20. Lu. xxii. 51, 52.

4. Therefore it must needs come into the world, not without, but by the knowledge of God; not in despite of him, but by his suffering of it.

Object. But how then is he clear from having a hand in the death of him that perisheth ?

Ans. Nothing is more sure than that God could have kept sin out of the world, if it had been his will; and this is also as true, that it never came into the world with his liking and compliance; and for this, you must consider that sin came into the world by two steps:

1. By being offered.   2. By prevailing.

Touching the first of these, God without the least injury to any creature in heaven or earth, might not only suffer it, but so far countenance the same: that is, so far forth as for trial only: as it is said of Abraham; ' God tempted Abraham ' to slay his only son, Ge. xxii. 1. and led Christ by the Spirit into the wilderness to be tempted of the devil. Mar. i. 12. Lu. iv. 1. This is done without any harm at all; nay, it rather produceth good; for it tends to discover sincerity, to exercise faith in, and love to his Creator; also to put him in mind of the continual need he hath of depending on his God for the continuation of help and strength, and to provoke to prayers to God, whenever so engaged. De. viii. 1—3. 1 Pe. i. 7. He. v. 7. Mat. xxvi. 22, 41.

Object. But God did not only admit that sin should be offered for trial, and there to stay; but did suffer it to prevail, and overcome the world.

Ans. Well, this is granted: but yet consider,

1. God did neither suffer it, nor yet consent it should, but under this consideration; If Adam, upright Adam, gave way thereto, by forsaking his command, ' In the day that thou eatest thereof thou shalt surely die.' Ge. ii. 17; iii. 3. Which Adam did, not because God did compel him or persuade him to it, but voluntarily of his own mind, contrary to his God's command: so then, God by suffering sin to break into the world, did it rather in judgment, as disliking Adam's act, and as a punishment to man for listening to the tempter; and as a discovery of his anger at man's disobedience; than to prove that he is guilty of the misery of his creature.

2. Consider also, that when God permitted sin for trial, it was, when offered first, to them only who were upright, and had sufficient strength to resist it.

3. They were by God's command to the contrary, driven to no strait to tempt them to incline to Satan: ' Of every tree of the garden thou mayest freely eat,' saith God; only let this alone.

4. As touching the beauty and goodness that was in the object unto which they were allured; What was it ? Was it better than God ? Yea, was it better than the tree of life ? For from that they were not exempted till after they had sinned. Did not God know best what was best to do them good?

5. Touching him that persuaded them to do this wicked act; was his word more to be valued for truth, more to be ventured on for safety, or more to be honoured for the worthiness of him that spake, than was his that had forbad it ? The one being the devil, with a lie, and to kill them; the other being God, with his truth, and to preserve them safe.

Quest. But was not Adam unexpectedly surprised ? Had he notice beforehand, and warning of the danger ? For God foresaw the business.

Ans. Doubtless God was fair and faithful to his creature in this thing also; as clearly doth appear from these considerations.

1. The very commandment that God gave him, fore-bespake him well to look about him; and did indeed insinuate that he was likely to be tempted.

2. It is yet more evident, because God doth even tell him of the danger; ' In the day that thou eatest thereof thou shalt surely die.'

3. Nay God by speaking to him of the very tree that was to be forborn, telling him also where it stood, that he might the better know it; did in effect expressly say unto him, Adam, if thou be tempted, it will be about that tree, and the fruit thereof: wherefore if thou findest the tempter there, then beware thy life.

(1.) To conclude then: though sin did not come into the world without God's sufferance, yet it did without his liking: God suffered also Cain to kill his brother, and Ishmael to mock at Isaac, but he did not like the same. Ge. iv. 9—11. Ga. iv. 30.

(2.) Therefore though God was first in concluding sin should be offered to the world; yet man was the first that consented to a being overcome thereby.

(3.) Then, Though God did fore-determine that sin should enter, yet it was not but with respect to certain terms and conditions, which yet was not to be enforced by virtue of the determination, but permitted to be completed by the voluntary inclination of a perfect and upright man. And in that the determination was most perfectly infallible, it was through the foresight of the undoubted inclination of this good and upright person.

Quest. But might not God have kept Adam from inclining, if he would?

Ans. What more certain?   But yet consider,

1. Adam being now an upright man, he was able to have kept himself, had he but looked to it as he should and might.

2. This being so, if God had here stept in, he had either added that which had been needless, and so had not obtained thankfulness; or else had made the strength of Adam useless, yea his own

workmanship in so creating him, superfluous; or else by consequence imperfect.

(3.) If he had done so, he had taken Adam from his duty, which was to trust and believe his Maker; he had also made void the end of the commandment, which was to persuade to watchfulness, diligence, sobriety, and contentedness; yea, and by so doing would not only himself have tempted Adam to transgression, even to lay aside the exercise of that strength that God had already given him; but should have become the pattern, or the first father to all looseness, idleness, and neglect of duty. Which would also not only have been an ill example to Adam to continue to neglect so reasonable and wholesome duties, but would have been to himself an argument of defence to retort upon his God, when he had come at another time to reckon with him for his misdemeanours.*

Many other weighty reasons might here be further added for God's vindication in this particular, but at this time let these suffice.

CHAP. VII.

Whether any under Eternal Reprobation have just cause to quarrel with God for not electing of them?

That the answer to this question may be to edification, recall again what I have before asserted; to wit, That for a man to be left out of God's election, and to be made a sinner, is two things; and again, For a man to be not elect, and to be condemned to hell-fire, is two things also. Now I say, if non-election makes no man a sinner, and if it appoints no man to condemnation neither, then what ground hath any reprobate to quarrel with God for not electing of him? Nay, further, reprobation considereth him upright, leaveth him upright, and so turneth him into the world; what wrong doth God do him, though he hath not elected him? What reason hath he that is left in this case to quarrel against his Maker?

---

* The final condemnation of the wicked does not spring from God's sovereign will to destroy any of his rational creatures; this is evident from the many pressing invitations, declarations, and promises in the word of God: for Jehovah swears by his great self, that he desires not the death of a sinner. Our Lord assigns the cause of reprobation in these words, John v. 40, 'Ye will not come unto me, that ye might have life;' wherefore Christ, the only remedy for their cure, being rejected, the sinner is condemned, and rendered the object of wrath and punishment by the law and justice of God; because the same word of truth which says, 'Whosoever will, let him come, and take of the water of life freely,' also says, 'The soul that sinneth (or lives and dies in sin unpardoned) shall die.' Thus sin is the object of God's hatred, and not the man, abstractedly considered. May we therefore each of us have grace to look to Christ for full and complete salvation, who hath put away sin by the sacrifice of himself, whereby he has perfected for ever them that are sanctified!—*Ryland and Mason.*

If thou say, because God hath not chosen them, as well as chosen others: I answer, ' Nay but, O man, who art thou that repliest against God? Shall the thing formed say to him that formed *it*, Why hast thou made me thus?' Ro. ix. 20. ' Behold, as the clay *is* in the potter's hand, so *are* ye in my hand, O house of Israel,' saith the Lord God. Je. xviii. 6. So then, if I should say no more but that God is the only Lord and Creator, and that by his sovereignty he hath power to dispose of them according to his pleasure, either to choose or to refuse, according to the counsel of his own will, who could object against him and be guiltless? ' He giveth not account of any of his matters.' Job xxxiii. 13. ' And *what* his soul desireth, even *that* he doeth.' Job xxiii. 13.

Again, God is wiser than man, and therefore can shew a reason for what he acts and does, both when and where at present thou seest none. Shall God the only wise, be arraigned at the bar of thy blind reason, and there be judged and condemned for his acts done in eternity? Who hath directed the Spirit of the Lord, ' or who hath been his counsellor?' Ro. xi. 34. Do you not know that he is far more above us, than we are above our horse or mule that is without understanding? ' Great things doeth he, which we cannot comprehend.' Jo. xxxvii. 5. ' Great things and unsearchable, marvellous things without number.' Job v. 9.

But, I say, should we take it well if our beast should call us to account for this and the other righteous act, and judge us unrighteous, and our acts ridiculous, and all because it sees no reason for our so doing? Why, we are as beasts before God. Ps. lxxiii 22.

But again, to come yet more close to the point: the reprobate quarrels with God, because he hath not elected him; well, but is not God the master of his own love? And is not his will the only rule of his mercy? And may he not, without he give offence to thee, lay hold by electing love and mercy on whom himself pleaseth? Must thy reason, nay, thy lust, be the ruler, orderer, and disposer of his grace? ' Is it not lawful for me to do what I will with mine own?' saith he, ' Is thine eye evil, because I am good?' Mat. xx. 15.

Further, What harm doth God to any reprobate, by not electing of him; he was, as hath been said, considered upright, so formed in the act of creation, and so turned into the world: indeed he was not elected, but hath that taken anything from him? No, verily, but leaveth him in good condition: there is good, and better, and best of all; he that is in a good estate, though others through free grace are in a far better, hath not any cause to murmur either with him that gave him such a place, or at him that is placed above him. In a word, reprobation maketh no man personally a sinner, neither doth election make any man personally righteous. It is the consenting to sin that makes a man a sinner; and the imputation of grace and righteousness that makes [men] gospelly and personally just and holy.

But again, seeing it is God's act to leave some out of the bounds of his election, it must needs be, therefore, positively good: Is that then which is good in itself made sin unto thee? God forbid: God doth not evil by leaving this or that man out of his electing grace, though he choose others to eternal life, through Jesus Christ our Lord. Wherefore there is not a reprobate that hath any cause, and therefore no just cause, to quarrel with his Maker, for not electing of him.

And that, besides what hath been spoken, if you consider,

1. For God to elect, is an act of sovereign grace; but to pass by, or to refuse so to do, is an act of sovereign power, not of injustice.

2. God might therefore have chosen whether he would have elected any, or so many or few; and also which and where he would.

3. Seeing then that all things are at his dispose, he may fasten electing mercy where he pleaseth; and other mercy, if he will, to whom and when he will.

4. Seeing also that the least of mercies are not deserved by the best of sinners; men, instead of quarrelling against the God of grace, because they have not what they list, should acknowledge they are unworthy of their breath; and also should confess that God may give mercy where he pleaseth, and that too, both which or what, as also to whom, and when he will; and yet be good, and just, and very gracious still: Nay, Job saith, 'He taketh away, who can hinder him? Who will say unto him, What doest thou?' Job ix. 12.

The will of God is the rule of all righteousness, neither knoweth he any other way by which he governeth and ordereth any of his actions. Whatsoever God doth, it is good because he doth it; whether it be to give grace, or to detain it; whether in choosing or refusing. The consideration of this, made the holy men of old ascribe righteousness to their Maker, even then when yet they could not see the reason of his actions. They would rather stand amazed, and wonder at the heighths and depths of his unsearchable judgments, than quarrel at the strange and most obscure of them. Job xxxiv. 10—12; xxxvi. 3; xxxvii. 23. Je. xii. 1. Ro. xi. 33.

God did not intend that all that ever he would do, should be known to every man, no nor yet to the wise and prudent. It is as much a duty sometimes to stay ourselves and wonder, and to confess our ignorance in many things of God, as it is to do other things that are duty without dispute. So then, let poor dust and ashes forbear to condemn the Lord, because he goeth beyond them; and also they should beware they speak not wickedly for him, though it be, as they think, to justify his actions. 'The Lord is righteous in all his ways, and holy in all his works.'* Ps. cxlv. 17. Mat. xi. 25. 1 Co. ii. 8. Job xiii. 6—8.

CHAP. VIII.

Whether Eternal reprobation in itself, or in its doctrine, be in very deed an hindrance to any man in seeking the salvation of his soul.

In my discourse upon this question, I must entreat the reader to mind well what is premised in the beginning of the former chapter, which is, That reprobation makes no man a sinner, appoints no man to condemnation, but leaveth him upright after all. So then, though God doth leave the most of men without the bounds of his election, his so doing is neither in itself, nor yet its doctrine, in very deed, an hindrance to any man in seeking the salvation of his soul.

First, It hindereth not in itself, as is clear by the ensuing considerations:—

1. That which hindereth him is the weakness that came upon him by reason of sin. Now God only made the man, but man's listening to Satan made him a sinner, which is the cause of all his weakness: this therefore is it that hindereth him, and that also disenableth him in seeking the salvation of his soul. 'Let no man say when he is tempted, I am tempted of God: for God cannot be tempted with evil, neither tempteth he any man.' Ja. i. 13. 'God made man upright; but they have sought out many inventions.' Ec. vii. 29. Eze. xvi. 30. Ho. xiii. 9; xiv. 1. Ge. iii. 8—11.

2. It hindereth not in itself, for it taketh not anything from a man that would help him, might it continue with him; it takes not away the least part of his strength, wisdom, courage, innocency, or will to good; all these were lost by the fall, in that day when he died the death. Nay, reprobation under some consideration did rather establish all these upon the reprobate; for as it decrees him

---

* 'Secret things belong to God, but those that are revealed belong to us.' It is a vain thing for men to cavil at the doctrine of peculiar election, and to quarrel with God for choosing some, and passing by others. Their best way would be to assure themselves of their own election, by using the means, and walking in the ways of God's appointment, as laid down in the word, and then they will find that God cannot deny himself, but will make good to them every promise therein; and thus, by scripture evidence, they will find that they are elected unto life, and will be thankful and humble. They will then find that an hearty affectionate trusting in Christ for all his salvation, as freely promised to us, hath naturally enough in it to work in our souls a natural bent and inclination to, and ability for, the practice of all holiness.— *Ryland and Mason.*

left, so left upright. Wherefore man's hindrance cometh on him from other means, even by the fall, and not by the simple act of eternal reprobation. Ge. iii.

3. As reprobation hindereth not either of these two ways, so neither is it from this simple act that Satan is permitted either to tempt them, that they might be tried, or that they might be overthrown.

(1.) It is not by this act that Satan is permitted to tempt them that they might be tried; because then the Son of God himself must be reached by this reprobation; he being tempted by the devil as much, if not more than any. Yea, and then must every one of the elect be under eternal reprobation; for they also, and that after their conversion, are greatly assaulted by him. 'Many are the troubles of the righteous,' &c. Mat. iv. 1, 2. He. ii. 17; iv. 15.

(2.) Neither is it from the act of reprobation that sin hath entered the world, no more than from election, because those under the power of election did not only fall at first, but do still generally as foully, before conversion, as the reprobate himself. Whereas, if either the temptation, or the fall, were by virtue of reprobation, then the reprobates, and they only, should have been tempted, and have fallen. The temptation then, and the fall, doth come from other means, and so the hinderance of the reprobate, than from eternal reprobation. For the temptation, the fall and hinderance being universal, but the act of reprobation particular, the hinderance must needs come from such a cause as taketh hold on all men, which indeed is the fall; the cause of which was neither election nor reprobation, but man's voluntary listening to the tempter. Ro. iii. 9.

(3.) It is yet far more evident that reprobation hindereth no man from seeking the salvation of his soul: because notwithstanding all that reprobation doth, yet God giveth to divers of the reprobates great encouragements thereto; to wit, the tenders of the gospel in general, not excluding any; great light also to understand it, with many a sweet taste of the good word of God, and the powers of the world to come; he maketh them sometimes also to be partakers of the Holy Ghost, and admitteth many of them into fellowship with his elect; yea, some of them to be rulers, teachers, and governors in his house: all which, without doubt, both are and ought to be great encouragements even to the reprobates themselves, to seek the salvation of their souls. Mat. xi. 28. Re. xxii. 17. He. vi. 4, 5. Mat. xxv. 1, 2. Ac. i. 16, 17.

Second, As it hindereth not in itself, so it hindereth not by its doctrine: for, all that this doctrine saith is, that some are left out of God's election, as considered upright. Now this doctrine cannot hinder any man. For,

1. No man still stands upright.

2. Though it saith some are left, yet it points at no man, it nameth no man, it binds all faces in secret. So then, if it hinder, it hindereth all, even the elect as well as reprobate; for the reprobate hath as much ground to judge himself elect, as the very elect himself hath, before he be converted, being both alike in a state of nature and unbelief, and both alike visibly liable to the curse, for the breach of the commandment. Again, As they are equals here, so also have they ground alike to close in with Christ and live; even the open, free, and full invitation of the gospel, and promise of life and salvation, by the faith of Jesus Christ. Ep. ii. 1, 2. Ro. iii. 9. Jn. iii. 16. 2 Co. v. 19—21. Re. xxi. 6; xxii. 17.

3. It is evident also by experience, that this doctrine doth not, *in deed,* neither can it hinder any (this doctrine I mean, when both rightly stated and rightly used) because many who have been greatly afflicted about this matter, have yet at last had comfort; which comfort, when they have received it, hath been to them as an argument that the thing they feared before, was not because of reprobation rightly stated; but its doctrine much abused was the cause of their affliction: and had they had the same light at first they received afterwards, their troubles then would soon have fled, as also now they do. Wherefore discouragement comes from want of light, because they are not skilful in the word of righteousness: for had the discouragement at first been true, which yet it could not be, unless the person knew by name himself under eternal reprobation, which is indeed impossible, then his light would have pinched him harder; light would rather have fastened this his fear, than at all have rid him of it. He. v. 12—14.

Indeed the scripture saith, the word is to some the savour of death unto death, when to others the savour of life unto life. But mark, it is not this doctrine in particular, if so much as some other, that doth destroy the reprobate. It was respite at which Pharaoh hardened his heart; and the grace of God that the reprobates of old did turn into lasciviousness. Yea, Christ the Saviour of the world, is a stumbling-block unto some, and a rock of offence unto others. But yet again, consider that neither HE, nor any of God's doctrines, are so simply, and in their own true natural force and drift: for they beget no unbelief, they provoke to no wantonness, neither do they in the least encourage to impenitency; all this comes from that ignorance and wickedness that came by the fall: Wherefore it is by reason of that also, that they stumble, and fall, and grow weak, and are discouraged, and split themselves, either at the doctrine of reprobation, or at any other truth of God. Ex. viii. 15. Jude iv. 1. 1 Pe. ii. 8.

Lastly, To conclude as I began, there is no man while in this world, that doth certainly know that he is left out of the electing love of the great God; neither hath he any word in the whole bible, to persuade him so to conclude and believe; for the scriptures hold forth salvation to the greatest of sinners. Wherefore, though the act of reprobation were far more harsh, and its doctrine also more sharp and severe, yet it cannot properly be said to hinder any. It is a foolish thing in any to be troubled with those things which they have no ground to believe concerns themselves; especially when the latitude of their discouragement is touching their own persons only. 'The secret *things belong* unto the Lord our God.' De. xxix. 29. Indeed every one of the words of God ought to put us upon examination, and into a serious enquiry of our present state and condition, and how we now do stand for eternity; to wit, whether we are ready to meet the Lord, or how it is with us. Yet, when search is fully made, and the worst come unto the worst, the party can find himself no more than the chief of sinners, not excluded from the grace of God tendered in the gospel; not from an invitation, nay a promise, to be embraced and blest, if he comes to Jesus Christ. Wherefore he hath no ground to be discouraged by the doctrine of reprobation. 1 Ti. i. 15. Ac. iii. 19. 2 Ch. xxxiii. Jn. vii. 37; vi. 37. Mar. ii. 17.

CHAP. IX.

Whether God would indeed and in truth, that the gospel, with the grace thereof, should be tendered to those that yet he hath bound up under Eternal Reprobation?

To this question I shall answer,

First, In the language of our Lord, 'Go preach the gospel unto every creature;' Mar. xvi. 15. and again, 'Look unto me, and be ye saved; all ye ends of the earth.' Is. xlv. 22. 'And whosoever will, let him take the water of life freely.' Re. xxii. 17. And the reason is, because Christ died for all, 'tasted death for every man;' 2 Co. v. 15. He. ii. 9. is 'the Saviour of the world,' 1 Jn. iv. 14. and the propitiation for the sins of the whole world.

Second, I gather it from those several censures that even every one goeth under, that doth not receive Christ, when offered in the general tenders of the gospel; 'He that believeth not, - shall be damned;' Mar. xvi. 16. 'He that believeth not God hath made him a liar, because he believeth not the record that God gave of his Son;' 1 Jn. v. 10. and, Woe unto thee Capernaum, 'Woe unto thee Chorazin! woe unto thee Bethsaida!' Mat. xi. 21. with many other sayings, all which words, with many other of the same nature, carry in them a very great argument to this very purpose; for if those that perish in the days of the gospel, shall have,

at least, their damnation heightened, because they have neglected and refused to receive the gospel, it must needs be that the gospel was with all faithfulness to be tendered unto them; the which it could not be, unless the death of Christ did extend itself unto them; Jn. iii. 16. He. ii. 3. for the offer of the gospel cannot, with God's allowance, be offered any further than the death of Jesus Christ doth go; because if that be taken away, there is indeed no gospel, nor grace to be extended. Besides, if by every creature, and the like, should be meant only the elect, then are all the persuasions of the gospel to no effect at all; for still the unconverted, who are here condemned for refusing of it, they return it as fast again: I do not know I am elect, and therefore dare not come to Jesus Christ; for if the death of Jesus Christ, and so the general tender of the gospel, concern the elect alone; I, not knowing myself to be one of that number, am at a mighty plunge; nor know I whether is the greater sin, to believe, or to despair: for I say again, if Christ died only for the elect, &c. then, I not knowing myself to be one of that number, dare not believe the gospel, that holds forth his blood to save me; nay, I think with safety may not, until I first do know I am elect of God, and appointed thereunto.

Third, God the Father, and Jesus Christ his Son, would have all men whatever, invited by the gospel to lay hold of life by Christ, whether elect or reprobate; for though it be true, that there is such a thing as election and reprobation, yet God, by the tenders of the gospel in the ministry of his word, looks upon men under another consideration, to wit, as sinners; and as sinners invites them to believe, lay hold of, and embrace the same. He saith not to his ministers, Go preach to the elect, because they are elect; and shut out others, because they are not so: But, Go preach the gospel to sinners as sinners; and as they are such, go bid them come to me and live. And it must needs be so, otherwise the preacher could neither speak in faith, nor the people hear in faith. First, the preacher could not speak in faith, because he knoweth not the elect from the reprobate; nor they again hear in faith, because, as unconverted, they would be always ignorant of that also. So then, the minister neither knowing whom he should offer life unto, nor yet the people which of them are to receive it; how could the word now be preached in faith with power? And how could the people believe and embrace it? But now the preacher offering mercy in the gospel to sinners, as they are sinners, here is way made for the word to be spoke in faith, because his hearers are sinners; yea, and encouragement also for the people to receive and close therewith, they understanding they are sinners: 'Christ Jesus came into the world to save sinners.' 1 Ti. i. 15. Lu. xxiv. 46, 47.

Fourth, The gospel must be preached to sinners as they are sinners, without distinction of elect or reprobate; because neither the one nor yet the other, as considered under these simple acts, are fit subjects to embrace the gospel: for neither the one act, nor yet the other, doth make either of them sinners; but the gospel is to be tendered to men as they are sinners, and personally under the curse of God for sin: wherefore to proffer grace to the elect because they are elect, it is to proffer grace and mercy to them, as not considering them as sinners. And, I say, to deny it to the reprobate, because he is not elected, it is not only a denial of grace to them that have no need thereof, but also before occasion is given on their part, for such a dispensation. And I say again, therefore, to offer Christ and grace to man elect, as simply so considered, this administers to him no comfort at all, he being here no sinner; and so engageth not the heart at all to Jesus Christ; for that comes in, and is effected on them as they are sinners. Yea, to deny the gospel also to the reprobate, because he is not elect, it will not trouble him at all; for saith he, So I am not a sinner, and so do not need a Saviour. But now, because the elect have no need of grace in Christ by the gospel, but as they are sinners; nor the reprobates cause to refuse it, but as they are sinners; therefore Christ by the word of the gospel, is to be proffered to both, without considering elect or reprobate, even as they are sinners. 'The whole have no need of the physician, but they that are sick: I came not to call the righteous, but sinners to repentance.' Mar. ii. 17. 2 Co. v. 14, 15. Lu. vii. 47.

Thus you see the gospel is to be tendered to all in general, as well to the reprobate as to the elect, TO SINNERS AS SINNERS; and so are they to receive it, and to close with the tenders thereof.*

CHAP. X.

Seeing then that the grace of God in the gospel, is by that to be proffered to sinners, as sinners; as well to the reprobate as the elect; Is it possible for those who indeed are not elect, to receive it, and be saved?

To this question I shall answer several things: but *first* I shall shew you what that grace is, that

* None are excluded the benefit of the great and precious salvation procured and finished by the Lord Jesus Christ, but they, who by perverseness, unbelief, and impenitency, exclude themselves. Sinners,—miserable, helpless, and hopeless sinners, are the objects of this salvation: whosoever is enabled to see, in the light of God's Spirit, their wretched and forlorn state; to feel their want of Christ as a suitable Saviour, and to repent and forsake their sins, shall find mercy; for 'God is no respecter of persons,' Acts x. 34.—*Ryland and Mason.*

is tendered in the gospel; and *secondly,* what it is to receive it and be saved.

First then, The grace that is offered to sinners as sinners, without respect to this or that person, it is a sufficiency of righteousness, pardoning grace, and life, laid up in the person of Christ, held forth in the exhortation and word of the gospel, and promised to be theirs that receive it; yea, I say, in so universal a tender, that not one is by it excluded or checked in the least, but rather encouraged, if he hath the least desire to life; yea, it is held forth to beget both desires and longings after the life thus laid up in Christ, and held forth by the gospel. Jn. i. 16. Col. i. 19, 23. 1 Jn. v. 11, 12. Ac. xiii. 38, 39. Ro. x. 12—14.; xvi. 25, 26.

Secondly, To receive this grace thus tendered by the gospel, it is,

1. To believe it is true.

2. To receive it heartily and unfeignedly through faith. And,

3. To let it have its natural sway, course and authority in the soul, and that in that measure, as to bring forth the fruits of good living in heart, word, and life, both before God and man.

Now then to the question.

Is it possible that this tender, thus offered to the reprobate, should by him be thus received and embraced, and he live thereby?

To which I answer in the negative. Nor yet for the elect themselves, I mean as considered dead in trespasses and sins, which is the state of all men, elect as well as reprobate. So then, though there be a sufficiency of life and righteousness laid up in Christ for all men, and this tendered by the gospel to them without exception; yet sin coming in between the soul and the tender of this grace, it hath in truth disabled all men, and so, notwithstanding this tender, they continue to be dead. For the gospel, I say, coming in word only, saveth no man, because of man's impediment; wherefore those that indeed are saved by this gospel, the word comes not to them in word only, but also in power, and in the Holy Ghost; is mixed with faith, even with the faith of the operation of God, by whose exceeding great and mighty power they are raised from this death of sin, and enabled to embrace the gospel. Doubtless, all men being dead in trespasses and sins, and so captivated under the power of the devil, the curse of the law, and shut up in unbelief; it must be the power of God, yea the exceeding greatness of that power that raiseth the soul from this condition, to receive the holy gospel. Ep. ii. 1—3. 1 Th. i. 5, 6. Col. ii. 12. He. iv. 1, 2. Ep. i. 18, 19. &c.

For man by nature, (consider him at best), can see no more, nor do no more than what the principles of nature understands and helps to do; which nature being below the discerning of things truly, spiritually, and savingly good, it must needs fall short of receiving, loving and delighting in them. 'The natural man receiveth not the things of the Spirit of God, for they are foolishness unto him: neither can he know *them*, because they are spiritually discerned.' 1 Co. ii. 14. Now I say, if the natural man at best (for the elect before conversion are no more, if quite so much) cannot do this, how shall they attain thereto, being now not only corrupted and infected, but depraved, bewitched and dead; swallowed up of unbelief, ignorance, confusion, hardness of heart, hatred of God, and the like? When a thorn by nature beareth grapes, and a thistle beareth figs, then may this thing be. Mat. vii. 16—18. To lay hold of and receive the gospel by a true and saving faith, it is an act of the soul as made a new creature, which is the workmanship of God: 'Now he that hath wrought us for the self-same thing *is* God.' 2 Co. v. 5. 'For a corrupt tree cannot bring forth good fruit.' Lu. vi. 43—45. 'Can the Ethiopian change his skin?' Je. xiii. 23.

But yet the cause of this impossibility.

1. Lieth not in reprobation, the elect themselves being as much unable to receive it as the other.

2. Neither is it because the reprobate is excluded in the tender, for that is universal.

3. Neither is it because there wanteth arguments in the tenders of the gospel, for there is not only plenty, but such as be persuasive, clear, and full of rationality.

4. Neither is it because these creatures have no need thereof, for they have broken the law.

5. Wherefore it is, because indeed they are by sin dead, captivated, mad, self-opposers, blind, alienated in their minds, and haters of the Lord. Behold the ruins that sin hath made!

Wherefore whoever receiveth the grace that is tendered in the gospel, they must be quickened by the power of God, their eyes must be opened, their understandings illuminated, their ears unstopped, their hearts circumcised, their wills also rectified, and the Son of God revealed in them. Yet as I said, not because there wanteth argument in these tenders, but because men are dead, and blind, and cannot hear the word. 'Why do ye not understand my speech (saith Christ): *Even* because ye cannot hear my word.' Jn. viii. 43. Ac. ix. 15; xxvi. 9, 10. Ps. cx. 3. Ga. i. 15. Mat. xi. 27.

For otherwise, as I said but now, there is, 1. Rationality enough in the tenders of the gospel. 2. Persuasions of weight enough to provoke to faith. And, 3. Arguments enough to persuade to continue therein.

1. Is it not reasonable that man should believe God in the proffer of the gospel and life by it? Is there not reason, I say, both from the truth and faithfulness of God, from the sufficiency of the

merits of Christ, as also from the freeness and fullness of the promise? What unreasonable thing doth the gospel bid thee credit? Or what falsehood doth it command thee to receive for truth? Indeed in many points the gospel is above reason, but yet in never a one against it; especially in those things wherein it beginneth with the sinner, in order to eternal life.

2. Again, touching its persuasions to provoke to faith: With how many signs and wonders, miracles and mighty deeds, hath it been once and again confirmed, and that to this very end? He. i. 1—3. 1 Co. xiv. 22. With how many oaths, declarations, attestations, and proclamations, is it avouched, confirmed, and established? He. vi. 17, 18. Ac. xiii. 32. Je. i. 12. Ga. iii. 15. And why should not credence be given to that gospel that is confirmed by blood, the blood of the Son of God himself? Yea, that gospel that did never yet fail any that in truth hath cast themselves upon it, since the foundation of the world. He. ix. 16—18. and xii. 1—3.

3. Again, as there is rationality enough, and persuasions sufficient, so there is also argument most prevalent to persuade to continue therein, and that to heartily, cheerfully, and unfeignedly, unto the end: did not, as I have said, blindness, madness, deadness, and wilful rebellion, carry them away in the vanity of their minds, and overcome them. Ep. iv. 17—19.

(1.) For, first, if they could but consider how they have sinned, how they have provoked God, &c., if they could but consider what a dismal state the state of the damned is, and also, that in a moment their condition is like to be the same, would they not cleave to the gospel and live?

(2.) The enjoyment of God, and Christ, and saints, and angels, being the sweetest; the pleasures of heaven the most comfortable, and to live always in the greatest height of light, life, joy, and gladness imaginable, one would think were enough to persuade the very damned now in hell.

There is no man then perisheth for want of sufficient reason in the tenders of the gospel, nor any for want of persuasions to faith; nor yet because there wanteth arguments to provoke to continue therein. But the truth is, the gospel in this hath to do with unreasonable creatures; with such as will not believe it, and that because it is truth: 'And because I tell *you* the truth, (saith Christ,) therefore ye believe me not.' Jn. viii. 45.

Quest. Well, but if this in truth be thus, how then comes it to pass that some receive it and live for ever? For you have said before, that the elect are as dead as the reprobate, and full as unable as they, as men, to close with these tenders, and live.

Answ. Doubtless this is true, and were the elect left to themselves, they, through the wickedness of their heart, would perish as do others. Neither could all the reasonable persuasive prevalent arguments of the gospel of God in Christ, prevail to make any receive it, and live. Wherefore here you must consider, that as there is mercy proclaimed in the general tenders of the gospel, so there is also the grace of election; which grace kindly overruleth and winneth the spirit of the chosen, working in them that unfeigned closing therewith, that makes it effectual to their undoubted salvation; which indeed is the cause that not only in other ages, but also to this day, there is a remnant that receive this grace; they being appointed, I say, thereto, before the world began; preserved in time from that which would undo them, and enabled to embrace the glorious gospel of grace, and peace, and life. 1 Ki. xix. 18. Ro. xi. 5. 1 Th. v. 9.

Now there is a great difference between the grace of election, and the grace that is wrapped up in the general tenders of the gospel; a difference, I say, and that both as to its timing, latituding, and working.

1. Touching its timing; it is before, yea long before, there was either tender of the grace wrapped up in the gospel to any, or any need of such a tender. Ep. i. 4, 5.

2. They also differ in latitude; the tenders of grace in the gospel are common and universal to all, but the extension of that of election special and peculiar to some. 'There is a remnant according to the election of grace.' Ro. xi. 5.

3. Touching the working of the grace of election; it differs much in some things from the working of the grace that is offered in the general tenders of the gospel. As is manifest in these particulars:

(1.) The grace that is offered in the general tenders of the gospel, calleth for faith to lay hold upon, and accept thereof; but the special grace of election, worketh that faith which doth lay hold thereof. Ac. xvi. 31. xiii. 48. Phil. i. 29. 2 Th. i. 11.

(2.) The grace that is offered in the general tenders of the gospel, calleth for faith as a condition in us, without which there is no life; but the special grace of election worketh faith in us without any such condition. Mar. xvi. 15, 16. Ro. xi. 5, 6.

(3.) The grace that is offered in the general tenders of the gospel, promiseth happiness upon the condition of persevering in the faith only; but the special grace of election causeth this perseverance. Col. i. 23. Ep. ii. 10. Ro. xi. 7. 1 Pe. i. 5—7.

(4.) The grace offered in the general tenders of the gospel, when it sparkleth most, leaveth the greatest part of men behind it; but the special grace of election, when it shineth least, doth infallibly bring every soul therein concerned to everlasting life. Ro. x. 16. viii. 33—35.

(5.) A man may overcome and put out all the light and life that is begotten in him by the gene-

ral tenders of the gospel; but none shall overcome, or make void, or frustrate the grace of election. Jude 4. 2 Pe. ii. 20—22. Mat. xxiv. 24. Ro. xi. 1—3, &c.

(6.) The general tenders of the gospel, considered without a concurrence of the grace of election, helps not the elect himself, when sadly fallen. Wherefore, when I say the grace that is offered in the general tenders of the gospel, I mean that grace when offered, as not being accompanied with a special operation of God's eternal love, by way of conjunction therewith. Otherwise the grace that is tendered in the general offers of the gospel, is that which saveth the sinner now, and that brings him to everlasting life; that is, when conjoined with that grace that blesseth and maketh this general tender effectually efficacious. The grace of election worketh not without, but by these tenders generally; neither doth the grace thus tendered, effectually work, but by and with the grace of election: 'As many as were ordained to eternal life believed:' Ac. xiii. 48. The word being then effectual to life, when the hand of the Lord is effectually therewith to that end. Mar. xvi. 20. They 'spake (saith the text) unto the Grecians, preaching the Lord Jesus. And the hand of the Lord was with them; and a great number believed, and turned unto the Lord.' Ac. xi. 20, 21.

We must always put difference between the word of the gospel, and the power that manageth that word; we must put difference between the common and more special operations of that power also; even as there is evidently a difference to be put between those words of Christ that were effectual to do what was said, and of those words of his which were but words only, or at least not so accompanied with power. As for instance: that same Jesus that said to the Leper, 'Say nothing to any man,' said also to Lazarus, 'Come forth;' yet the one obeyed, the other did not; though he that obeyed was least in a capacity to do it, he being now dead, and stunk in his grave. Indeed unbelief hath hindered Christ much, yet not when he putteth forth himself as Almighty, but when he doth suffer himself by them to be abused who are to be dealt with by ordinary means: Otherwise legions of devils, with ten thousand impediments, must fall down before him, and give way unto him. There is a speaking, and a so speaking: 'They so spake, that a great multitude, both of the Jews, and also of the Greeks, believed.' Ac. xiv. 1. Even as I have hinted already, there is a difference between the coming of the word when it is in power, 1 Th. i. 5. and when it is in word only. So then, the blessed grace of election chooseth this man to good, not because he is good; it chooseth him to believe, not because he doth believe; it chooseth him to persevere, not because he doth so; it fore-ordains that this man shall be created in Christ Jesus unto good works, Ep. i. 4—6. not if a man will create himself thereto. 1 Pe. i. 2. Ep. ii. 10.

What shall we say then? Is the fault in God, if any perish? Doubtless no; nor yet in his act of eternal reprobation neither: it is grace that saveth the elect, but sin that damns the rest: it is superabundant grace that causeth the elect to close with the tenders of life, and live; and it is the aboundings of sin that holds off the reprobate from the rational, necessary, and absolute tenders, of grace. To conclude then; the gospel calleth for credence as a condition, and that both from the elect and reprobate; but because none of them both, as dead in sin, will close therewith, and live; therefore grace, by virtue of electing love, puts forth itself to work and do for some beyond reason; and justice cuts off others, for slighting so good, so gracious, and necessary a means of salvation, so full both of kindness, mercy and reason.

CHAP. XI.

Seeing [that] *it is not possible that the reprobate should receive this grace and live, and also seeing* [that] *this is infallibly foreseen of God; and again, seeing God hath fore-determined to suffer it so to be; Why doth he yet will and command that the gospel, and so grace in the general tenders thereof, should be proffered unto them?*

Why then is the gospel offered them? Well, that there is such a thing as eternal reprobation, I have shewed you; also what this eternal reprobation is, I have opened unto you: and shall now shew you also, that though these reprobates will infallibly perish, which God not only foresaw, but fore-determined to suffer them most assuredly so to do; yet there is reason, great reason, why the gospel, and so the grace of God thereby, should be tendered, and that in general terms, to them as well as others.

But before I come to lay the reasons before you, I must mind you afresh of these particulars:

1. That eternal reprobation makes no man a sinner.

2. That the fore-knowledge of God that the reprobate would perish makes no man a sinner.

3. That God's infallibly determining upon the damnation of him that perisheth, makes no man a sinner.

4. God's patience and long-suffering, and forbearance, until the reprobate fits himself for eternal destruction, makes no man a sinner.

So then, God may reprobate, may suffer the reprobate to sin, may fore-determine his infallible damnation, through the pre-consideration of him in sin, and may also forbear to work that effectual work in his soul that would infallibly bring him out of this condition, and yet neither be the au-

author, contriver, nor means of man's sin and misery.

Again, God may infallibly foresee that this reprobate, when he hath sinned, will be an unreasonable opposer of his own salvation; and may also determine to suffer him to sin, and be thus unreasonable to the end, yet be gracious, yea very gracious, if he offer him life, and that only upon reasonable terms, which yet he denieth to close with. Is. i. 18. lv. 12.

The reasons are,

1. Because not God, but sin, hath made him unreasonable; without which, reasonable terms had done his work for him: for reasonable terms are the most equal and righteous terms that can be propounded between parties at difference; yea the terms that most suiteth and agreeth with a reasonable creature, such as man; nay, reasonable terms are, for terms, the most apt to work with that man whose reason is brought into and held captive by very sense itself. Eze. xviii.; xxxiii.

2. God goeth yet further, he addeth promises of mercy, as those that are inseparable to the terms he offereth, even to pour forth his Spirit unto them; 'Turn at my reproof, and behold I will pour forth of my Spirit unto you, and incline your ear; come unto me, hear and your soul shall live.' Pr. i. 23—27.

Now then to the question itself, to wit, that seeing it is impossible the reprobate should be saved; seeing also this is infallibly foreseen of God, and seeing also that God hath beforehand determined to suffer it so to be; yet I shall shew you it is requisite, yea very requisite, that he should both will and command that the gospel, and so grace in the general tenders thereof should be proffered unto them.

FIRST REASON.—And that first, to shew that this reprobation doth not in itself make any man absolutely incapable of salvation: for if God had intended that by the act of reprobation, the persons therein concerned should also by that only act have been made incapable of everlasting life, then this act must also have tied up all the means from them, that tendeth to that end; or at least have debarred the gospel's being offered to them by God's command, for that intent; otherwise who is there but would have charged the Holy One as guilty of guile, and worthy of blame, for commanding that the gospel of grace and salvation should be offered unto this or that man, whom yet he hath made incapable to receive it, by his act of reprobation. Wherefore this very thing, to wit, that the gospel is yet to be tendered to those eternally reprobated, sheweth that it is not simply the act of God's reprobation, but sin, that incapacitateth the creature of live everlasting. Which sin is no branch of this reprobation, as is evident, because the elect and reprobate are both alike defiled therewith.

SECOND REASON.—God also sheweth by this, that the reprobate do not perish for want of the offers of salvation, though he hath offended God, and that upon most righteous terms; according to what is written, 'As I live, saith the Lord GOD, I have no pleasure in the death of the wicked, but that the wicked turn from his way, and live.' Eze. xxxiii. 11; xviii. 31, 32. 'Turn ye unto me, saith the Lord of Hosts, and I will turn unto you, saith the Lord of Hosts.' Zec. i. 3. So then, here lieth the point between God and the reprobate, I mean the reprobate since he hath sinned, God is willing to save him upon reasonable terms, but not upon terms above reason; but no reasonable terms will [go] down with the reprobate, therefore he must perish for his unreasonableness.

That God is willing to save even those that perish for ever, is apparent, both from the consideration of the goodness of his nature, Ps. cxlv. 9. of man's being his creature, and indeed in a miserable state. Job xiv. 15; iii. 16. But I say, as I have also said already, there is a great difference between his being willing to save them, through their complying with these his reasonable terms, and his being resolved to save them, whether they, as men, will close therewith, or no; so only he saveth the elect themselves, even 'according to the riches of his grace.' Ep. i. 7. Even 'according to his riches in glory, by Christ Jesus.' Phi. iv. 19. Working effectually in them, what the gospel, as a condition, calleth for from them. And hence it is that he is said to give faith, Phi. i. 29. yea the most holy faith, for that is the faith of God's elect, to give repentance, Ac. v. 31. to give a new heart, to give his fear, even that fear that may keep them for ever from everlasting ruin; Ep. i. 4. still engaging his mercy and goodness to follow them all the days of their lives, Je. xxxii. 40. Eze. xxxvi. 26, 27. that they may dwell in the house of the Lord for ever, Ps. xxiii. 6. and as another scripture saith, 'Now he that hath wrought us for the selfsame thing, is God.' 2 Co. v. 5. Ro. viii. 26, &c.

But I say, his denying to do thus for every man in the world, cannot properly be said to be because he is not heartily willing they should close with the tenders of the grace held forth in the gospel, and live. Wherefore you must consider that there is a distinction to be put between God's denying grace on reasonable terms, and denying it absolutely; and also that there is a difference between his withholding further grace, and of hindering men from closing with the grace at present offered; also that God may withhold much, when he taketh away nothing; yea, take away much, when once abused, and yet be just and righteous still. Further, God may deny to do this or that absolutely, when

yet he hath promised to do, not only that, but more, conditionally. Which things considered, you may with ease conclude, that he may be willing to save those not elect, upon reasonable terms, though not without them.

It is no unrighteousness in God to offer grace unto the world, though but on these terms only, that they are also foreseen by him infallibly to reject; both because to reject it is unreasonable, especially the terms being so reasonable, as to believe the truth and live; and also because it is grace and mercy in God, so much as once to offer means of reconciliation to a sinner, he being the offender; but the Lord, the God offended; they being but dust and ashes, he the heavenly Majesty. If God, when man had broke the law, had yet with all severity kept the world to the utmost condition of it, had he then been unjust? Had he injured man at all? Was not every tittle of the law reasonable, both in the first and second table? How much more then is he merciful and gracious, even in but mentioning terms of reconciliation? especially seeing he is also willing so to condescend, if they will believe his word, and receive the love of the truth. Though the reprobate then doth voluntarily, and against all strength of reason, run himself upon the rocks of eternal misery, and split himself thereon, he perisheth in his own corruption, by rejecting terms of life. 2 Th. ii. 10. 2 Pe. ii. 12, 13.

Object. But the reprobate is not now in a capacity to fulfil these reasonable terms.

Ans. But I say, suppose it should be granted, is it because reprobation made him incapable, or sin? Not reprobation, but sin: if sin, then before he quarrel, let him consider the case aright, where, in the result, he will find sin, being consented to by his voluntary mind, hath thus disabled him: and because, I say, it was sin by his voluntary consent that did it, let him quarrel with himself for consenting, so as to make himself incapable to close with reasonable terms; yea, with those terms because reasonable, therefore most suitable, as terms, for him notwithstanding his wickedness. And I say again, forasmuch as those reasonable terms have annexed unto them, as their inseparable companions, such wonderful mercy and grace as indeed there is, let even them that perish, yet justify God; yea cry, 'His goodness endureth for ever;' though they, through the wretchedness of their hearts, get no benefit by it.

THIRD REASON.—God may will and command that his gospel, and so the grace thereof, be tendered to those that shall never be saved, (besides what hath been said) to shew to all spectators what an enemy sin, being once embraced, is to the salvation of man. Sin, without the tenders of the grace of the gospel, could never have appeared so exceeding sinful, as by that it both hath and doth:

'If I had not come and spoken unto them, (saith Christ) they had not had sin: but now they have no cloke for their sin.' Jn. xv. 22. As sins that oppose the law, are discovered by the law, that is, by the goodness, and justness, and holiness of the law; Ro. vii. so the sins that oppose the gospel, are made manifest by that, even by the love, and mercy, and forgiveness of the gospel: If 'he that despised Moses' law died without mercy, - of how much sorer punishment, suppose ye, shall he be thought worthy, who hath trodden under foot the Son of God ?' He. x. 28, 29. Who could have thought that sin would have opposed that which is just, but especially mercy and grace, had we not seen it with our eyes ? And how could we have seen it to purpose, had not God left some to themselves ? Here indeed is sin made manifest: 'For all he had done so many miracles amongst them,' (to wit, to persuade them to mercy) 'yet they believed not on him.' Jn. xii. 37. Sin, where it reigneth, is a mortal enemy to the soul; it blinds the eyes, holds the hands, ties the legs, and stops the ears, and makes the heart implacable to resist the Saviour of souls. That man will neither obey the law nor the gospel, who is left unto his sin: which also God is willing should be discovered and made manifest, though it cost the damnation of some: For this very purpose, saith God to Pharaoh, 'have I raised thee up, for to shew in thee my power; and that my name may be declared in all the earth.' Ex. ix. 16. Ro. ix. 17. For God, by raising up Pharaoh to his kingdom, and suffering him to walk to the height, according as his sin did prompt him forward, shewed unto all beholders what a dreadful thing sin is; and that without the special assistance of his Holy Spirit, sin would neither be charmed by law nor gospel. This reason, though it be no profit unto those that are damned; yet it is for the honour of God, and the good of those he hath chosen.

It is for the honour of God, even for the honour of his power and mercy: for his power is now discovered indeed, when nothing can tame sin but that; and his mercy is here seen indeed; because that doth engage him to do it. Read Ro. ix. 22, 23.

FOURTH REASON.—God commandeth that the tender of the gospel, and the grace thereof, be in general offered to all, that means thereby might be sufficiently provided for the elect, both to beget them to faith, and to maintain it in them to the end, in what place, or state, or condition soever they are. Ep. i. God, through the operation of his manifold wisdom, hath an end and an end in his acts and doings amongst the children of men: and, so in that he commandeth that his gospel be tendered to all, an end, I say, to leave the damned without excuse, and to provide sufficiency of means for the gathering all his elect. 'Oh that God

would speak, (saith Zophar,) and open his lips against thee; and - shew thee the secrets of wisdom, that *they are* double to that which is.' Job xi. 5, 6. For though God worketh with and upon the elect, otherwise than with and upon the reprobate; yet he worketh with and upon the elect, with and by the same word he commandeth should be held forth and offered to the reprobate. Now the text thus running in most free and universal terms, the elect then hearing thereof, do through the mighty power of God close in with the tenders therein held forth, and are saved. Thus that word that was offered to the reprobate Jews, and by them most fiercely rejected, even that word became yet effectual to the chosen, and they were saved thereby. They gladly received the word, 'and as many as were ordained to eternal life believed.' Ac. xiii. 48.* 'Not as though the word of God had taken none effect.' Ro. ix. 6. 'God hath not cast away his people whom he foreknew.' xi. 2. The word shall accomplish the thing for which God hath sent it, even the salvation of the few that are chosen, when tendered to all; though rejected by most, through the rebellion of their hearts. Ac. xxviii. 28. IIe. iv. 1—3.

Object. But if God hath elected, as you have said, what need he lay a foundation so general for the begetting faith in his chosen particulars, seeing the same Spirit that worketh in them by such means, could also work in them by other, even by a word, excluding the most, in the first tenders thereof, amongst men ?

Ans. I told you before, that though this be a principal reason of the general tenders of the grace of the gospel, yet it is not all the reason why the tender should be so general, as the three former reasons shew.

But again, in the bowels of God's decree of election, is contained the means that are also ordained for the effectual bringing of those elected to that glory for which they were fore-appointed;

---

* As the same sun which softens the wax, hardens the clay, so it is with the preached gospel, which is to some ' the savour of death unto death, and to others the savour of life unto life,' 2 Cor. ii. 16. The gospel is ineffectual to any saving purpose respecting the reprobate; partly through pride, and in not enduring to be reproved by it; partly through slothfulness, in not coming under the sound of it; and principally through cursed infidelity, in not believing the gracious message it brings. Let it be well attended to, that all who hear the gospel, are obliged to the duty of believing, as well as to all the duties of the moral law, and that before they know their particular election; for we cannot have a certain knowledge of our election to eternal life before we do believe: it is a thing hidden in the unsearchable counsel of God, until it be manifest by our effectual calling, and believing on Christ; therefore we must believe on Christ before we know our election; or else we shall never know it, and shall never believe. All joy, peace, comfort, assurances, are communicated to the soul in the way of believing. May the Lord give and increase saving faith !—*Mason and Ryland.*

even to gather together in one, all the children of God. Jn. xi. 52. 'Whereunto he called you, (saith Paul,) by our gospel, to the obtaining of the glory of our Lord Jesus Christ.' 2 Th. ii. 14. God's decree of election then, destroyeth not the means which his wisdom hath prepared, it rather establisheth, yea ordains and establisheth it; and maketh that means which in the outward sound is indefinite and general, effectual to this and that man, through a special and particular application: Ga. ii. 20, 21. thus *that* Christ that in general was offered to all, is by a special act of faith applied to Paul in particular; 'He loved me, and gave himself for me.'

Further, As the design of the Heavenly Majesty is to bring his elect to glory by means, so by the means thus universal and general, as most behooveful and fit; if we consider not only the way it doth please him to work with some of his chosen, in order to this their glory, but also the trials, temptations, and other calamities they must go through thereto.

1. Touching his working with some, how invisible is it to those in whose souls it is yet begun? How is the word buried under the clods of their hearts for months, yea years together? Only thus much is discovered thereof, it sheweth the soul its sin, the which it doth also so aggravate and apply to the conscience (Jesus still refraining, like Joseph, to make himself known to his brethren) that were there not general tenders of mercy, and that to the worst of sinners, they would soon miscarry, and perish, as do the sons of perdition. But by these the Lord upholdeth and helpeth them, that they stand, when others fall for ever. Ps. cxix. 49.

2. And so likewise for their trials, temptations, and other calamities, because God will not bring them to heaven without, but by them; therefore he hath also provided a word so large, as to lie fair for the support of the soul in all conditions, that it may not die for thirst.

3. I might add also in this place, their imperfect state after grace received, doth call for such a word; yea, many other things which might be named: which God, only wise, hath thought fit should accompany us to the ship, yea in the sea, to our desired haven.

FIFTH REASON.—God willeth and commandeth the gospel should be offered to all, that thereby distinguishing love, as to an inward and spiritual work, might the more appear to be indeed the fruit of special and peculiar love. For in that the gospel is tendered to all in general, when yet but some do receive it; yea, and seeing these some are as unable, unwilling, and by nature, as much averse thereto, as those that refuse it, and perish; it is evident that something more of heaven and the operation of the Spirit of God doth accompany the word thus tendered for their life and salvation

that enjoy it. 1 Th. i. 4—7. Not now as a word barely tendered, but backed by the strength of heaven: 'Behold what manner of love the Father hath bestowed upon us, that we should be called the sons of God!' 1 Jn. iii. 1. even we who believe 'according to the working of his mighty power, which he wrought in Christ, when he raised him from the dead.' Ep. i. 20. This provoketh to distinguishing admiration, yea, and also to a love like that which hath fastened on the called, the preserved, and the glorified: 'He hath not dealt so with any nation: and *as for his* judgments, they have not known them. Praise ye the Lord.' Ps. cxlvii. 20. Now are the sacrifices bound even to the horns of the altar, with a 'Lord, how is it that thou wilt manifest thyself unto us, and not unto the world!' Jn. xiv. 22. He 'sent from above, he took me; he drew me out of many waters; he delivered me from my strong enemy, *and* from them·that hated me; for they were too strong for me.' 2 Sa. xxii. 17. Ps. xviii. 16.

For thus the elect considereth: though we all came alike into the world, and are the children of wrath by nature; Ep. ii. 1—3. yea, though we have alike so weakened ourselves by sin, Ro. iii. 9. that the whole head is sick, and the whole heart faint, Is. i. 5. being altogether gone out of the way, and every one become altogether unprofitable, both to God and ourselves; Ro. iii. 12. yet that God should open mine eyes, convert my soul, give me faith, forgive my sins, raise me, when I fall; fetch me again, when I am gone astray; this is wonderful! Ps. xxxvii. 23. Yea, that he should prepare eternal mansions for me; Ps. xxiii. 6. and also keep me by his blessed and mighty power for that; and that in a way of believing, which without his assistance I am no way able to perform! 2 Co. v. 5. That he should do this notwithstanding my sins, though I had no righteousness! De. ix. 5—7. Yea, that he should do it according to the riches of his grace, through the redemption that is in Jesus Christ our Lord! Even according to an everlasting covenant of grace, which yet the greatest part of the world are void of, and will for ever miss and fall short of! Eze. xvi. 60—63. Besides, that he should mollify my heart! break it, and then delight in it; Ps. li. 17. put his fear in it, and then look to me, Is. lxvi. 2. Ps. cxxxviii. 6. and keep me as the apple of his eye; De. xxxii. 10. yea, resolve to guide me with his counsel, and then receive me to glory! Further, that all this should be the effect of unthought of, undeserved, and undesired love! Mal. i. 2. De. vii. 7, 8. That the Lord should think on this before he made the world, Je. xxxi. 3. and sufficiently ordain the means before he had laid the foundation of the hills! For this he is worthy to be praised: 1 Co. ii. 9. yea, 'Let every thing that hath breath praise the Lord; praise ye the Lord.'

Object. But you have said before, that the reprobate is also blessed with many gospel mercies, as with the knowledge of Christ, faith, light, the gift of the Holy Ghost, and the tastes or relish of the powers of the world to come: if so, then what should be the reason that yet he perisheth? Is it because the grace that he receiveth differeth from the grace that the elect are saved by? If they differ, where lieth the difference? Whether in the nature, or in the degree, or in the management thereof?

Ans. To this objection I might answer many things; but, for brevity, take this reply: That the non-elect may travel very far both in the knowledge, faith, light, and sweetness of Jesus Christ, and may also attain to the partaking of the Holy Ghost; yea, and by the very operation of these things also, escape the pollutions of the world, and become a visible saint, join in church-communion, and be as chief amongst the very elect themselves. This the scriptures every where do shew us.

The question then is, whether the elect and reprobate receive a differing grace? To which I answer, Yes, in some respects, both as to the nature thereof, and also the degree.

1. To begin then with the nature of it.

(1.) The faith that the chosen are blessed with, it goeth under another name than any faith besides, even the faith of God's elect, Tit. i. 1. as of a faith belonging to them only, of which none others do partake; which faith also, for the nature of it, is called faith most holy; Jude 20. to shew it goes beyond all other, and can be fitly matched no where else, but with their most blessed faith who infallibly attain eternal glory: even 'like precious faith with us,' saith Peter; 2 Pe. i. 1. with his elect companions. And so of other things. For if this be true, that they differ in their faith, they must needs therewith differ in other things: for faith being the mother grace, produceth all the rest according to its own nature, to wit, love that abounds, that never fails, and that is never contented till it attain the resurrection of the dead, &c. 2 Th. i. 3. 1 Co. xiii. 8. Phi. iii.

(2.) They differ as to the nature, in this; the faith, and hope, and love, that the chosen receive, it is that which floweth from election itself; he hath blessed us 'according as he hath chosen us,' Ep. i. 4, 5. even with those graces he set apart for us, when he in eternity did appoint us to life before the foundation of the world: which graces, because the decree in itself is most absolute and infallible, they also, that they may completely answer the end, will do the work infallibly likewise, still through the management of Christ: 'I have prayed for thee, that thy faith fail not.' Lu. xxii. 32. But,

2. As they differ in nature, they differ also in degree: for though it be true that the reprobate is blessed with grace, yet this is also as true, that

the elect are blessed with more grace. It is the privilege only of those that are chosen, to be blessed with ALL spiritual blessings, and to have ALL the good pleasure of the goodness of God fulfilled in and upon them. Those who are blessed with ALL spiritual blessings must needs be blessed with eternal life; and those in whom the Lord, not only works all his good pleasure, but fulfilleth all the good pleasure of his goodness upon them, they must needs be preserved to his heavenly kingdom; Ep. i. 4, 5. 1 Th. i. 10. but none of the non-elect have these things conferred upon them; therefore the grace bestowed upon the one, doth differ both in nature and degree from the other.

3. There is a difference as to the management also. The reprobate is principal for the management of the grace he receiveth, but Jesus Christ is principal for the management of the grace the elect receiveth. When I say principal, I mean chief; for though the reprobate is to have the greatest hand in the management of what mercy and goodness the Lord bestoweth on him, yet not so as that the Lord will not help him at all; nay contrariwise he will, if first the reprobate do truly the duty that lieth on him: 'If thou doest well, shalt thou not be accepted? but if thou doest not well, sin lieth at the door.' Ge. iv. 7. Thus it was also with Saul, who was rejected of God upon this account. 1 Sa. xiii. 11—14; xv. 26. And I say, as to the elect themselves, though Jesus Christ our blessed Saviour be chief, as to the management of the grace bestowed on his chosen, yet not so as that he quite excludeth them from 'striving according to his working, which worketh in me mightily.' Col. i. 29. Nay contrariwise, if those who in truth are elect, shall yet be remiss, and do wickedly, they shall feel the stroke of God's rod, it may be till their bones do break. But because the work doth not lie at their door to manage as chief, but as Christ's, therefore though he may perform his work with much bitterness and grief to them; yet he being engaged as the principal, will perform that which concerneth them, even until the day (the coming) of Jesus Christ. Ps. cxxxviii. 8. Phi. i. 6.

From what hath been said, there ariseth this conclusion:

The elect are always under eternal mercy, but those not elect always under eternal justice; for you must consider this: there is eternal mercy and eternal justice, and there is present mercy and present justice. So then, for a man to be in a state of mercy, it may be either a state of mercy present, or both present and eternal also. And so again for a man to be in a state under justice, it may be understood either of present justice only, or of both present and eternal also.

That this may yet further be opened, I shall somewhat enlarge.

I begin with present mercy and present justice. That which I call present mercy, is that faith, light, knowledge, and taste of the good word of God, that a man may have, and perish. This is called in scripture, Believing for a while, during for a while, and rejoicing in the light for a season. He. vi. 4, 5. 2 Pe. ii. 20. Mat. xiii. 22. Lu. viii. 13. Now I call this mercy, both because none, as men, can deserve it, and also because the proper end thereof is to do good to those that have it. But I call it present mercy, because those that are only blessed with that, may sin it away, and perish ; as did some of the Galatians, Hebrews, Alexandrians, with the Asians, and others. Ga. v. 4. He. xii. 15, 16. 1 Ti. i. 20. 2 Ti. ii. 18; i. 15. He. xii. 15. But yet observe again, I do not call this present mercy, because God hath determined it shall last but a while absolutely; but because it is possible for man to lose it, yea determined he shall, conditionally. Jn. v. 35. 1 Co. xii. 7.

Again, as to present justice, it is that which lasteth but a while also ; and as present mercy is properly the portion of those left out of God's election, so present justice chiefly hath to do with God's beloved ; who yet at that time are also under eternal mercy. This is that justice that afflicted Job, ch. vi. 4. David, Ps. lxxxviii.; xxxviii. 3. Heman, and the godly, who notwithstanding do infallibly attain, by virtue of this mercy, eternal life and glory. Am. iii. 2. 1 Co xi. 30, 31. Ps. xxx. 5 ; ciii. 9. 1 Pe. i. 6. I call this justice, because in some sense God dealeth with his children according to the quality of their transgressions ; and I call it also present justice, because though the hand of God for the present be never so heavy on those that are his by election, yet it lasteth but a while ; wherefore though this indeed be called wrath, yet is but a little wrath, wrath for a moment, time, or season. ' In a little wrath I hid my face from thee for a moment ; but with everlasting kindness will I have mercy on thee, saith the LORD thy Redeemer.' Is. liv. 8.

Thus you see there is present mercy and present justice ; also that the elect may be under present justice, when the rest may be under present mercy.

Again, As there is present mercy and present justice, so there is eternal mercy and eternal justice : and I say, as the elect may be under present justice, when the non-elect may be under present mercy; so the elect at that time are also under eternal mercy, but the other under eternal justice.

That the elect are under eternal mercy, and that when under present justice, is evident from what hath been said before, namely, from their being chosen in Christ before the foundation of the world ; as also from the consideration of their sound conversion, and safe preservation quite through this wicked world, even safe unto eternal life ; as he also saith by the prophet Jeremiah,

' Yea, I have loved thee with an everlasting love : therefore with loving kindness have I drawn thee.' ch. xxxi. 3. And hence it is that he calleth the elect his sheep, Jn. x. 16. his children, xi. 52. and people, Ac. xviii. 9, 10. and that before conversion ; for though none of them as yet were his children by calling, yet were they his according to election.

Now the elect being under this eternal grace and mercy, they must needs be under it both before present justice seizeth upon them, while it seizeth them, and also continueth with them longer than present justice can, it being from everlasting to everlasting. This being so, here is the reason why no sin, nor yet temptation of the enemy, with any other evil, can hurt or destroy those thus elect of God : yea this is that which maketh even those things that in themselves are the very bane of men, yet prove very much for good to those within this purpose ; Ro. viii. 28. And as David saith, ' It is good for me that I have been afflicted.' Ps. cxix. 71. And again, ' But when we are judged we are chastened of the Lord, that we should not be condemned with the world.' 1 Co. xi. 32. Now afflictions, &c., in themselves are not only fruitless and unprofitable, but, being unsanctified, are destructive ; ' I smote him, and he went on frowardly:' Is. lvii. 17. But now eternal mercy working with this or that affliction, makes it profitable to the chosen ; ' I have seen his ways, and will heal him, and restore comforts unto him and to his mourners.' ver. 18. As he saith in another place, ' Blessed is the man whom thou chastenest, and teachest him out of thy law.' Ps. xciv. 12. For eternal mercy doth not look on those who are the elect and chosen of God, as poor sinful creatures only, but also as the generation whom the Lord hath blessed, in whom he hath designed to magnify his mercy to the utmost, by pardoning the transgressions of the remnant of his heritage. 1 Pe. ii. 9. Mi. vii. 18, 19. ' Having predestinated us unto the adoption of children by Jesus Christ to himself, - wherein he hath made us accepted in the beloved.' Ep. i. 6. Wherefore, I say, the elect, as they do also receive that grace and mercy that may be sinned away, so they have that grace and mercy which cannot be lost, and that sin cannot deprive them of, even mercy that abounds, and goeth beyond all sin ; such mercy as hath engaged the power of God, the intercession of Christ, and the communication of the blessed Spirit of adoption, which Spirit also engageth the heart, directs it into the love of God, that it may not depart from God after that rate as the reprobates do. Ep. v. 29, 30. ' I will make an everlasting covenant with them, (saith God) that I will not turn away from them, to do them good ; but I will put my fear in their hearts, that they shall not depart from me.' Je. xxxii. 40.

But now I say, God's dealing with the non-elect, is far otherwise, they being under the consideration of eternal justice, even then when in the enjoyment of present grace and mercy. And hence it is that as to their standing before the God of heaven, they are counted dogs, and sows, and devils, even then when before the elect of God themselves they are counted saints and brethren: 'The dog *is* turned to his own vomit again, and the sow that was washed to her wallowing in the mire.' 2 Pe. ii. 22. And the reason is, because notwithstanding all their shew before the world, their old nature and corruptions do still bear sway within, which in time also, according to the ordinary judgment of God, is suffered so to shew itself, that they are visible to saints that are elect, as was the case of Simon Magus, and that wicked apostate Judas, who 'went out from us, but they were not of us; for if they had been of us, they would *no doubt* have continued with us: but *they went out* that they might be made manifest that they were not all of us:' 1 Jn. ii. 19. They were not elect as we, nor were they sanctified as the elect of God themselves; wherefore eternal justice counts them the sons of perdition, when under their profession. And I say, they being under this eternal justice, it must needs have to do with them in the midst of their profession; and because also it is much offended with them for conniving with their lust, it taketh away from them, and that most righteously, those gifts and graces, and benefits and privileges that present mercy gave them; and not only so, but cuts them off for their iniquity, and layeth them under wrath for ever. They 'have forsaken the right way, (saith God) - following the way of Balaam *the son* of Bosor; - these are wells without water, clouds that are carried with a tempest;' trees whose fruit withereth, without fruit, twice dead, plucked up by the roots, 'for whom is reserved the blackness of darkness for ever.' 2 Pe. ii. 5, 16, 17. Jude 11—13. Jn. xvii. 12. Mat. xiii. 12; xxv. 29. Mar. iv. 25. Lu. viii. 18.

These things thus considered, you see,

1. That there is present grace and present mercy, eternal grace and eternal mercy.

2. That the elect are under eternal mercy, and THAT, when under present justice; and that the reprobate is under eternal justice, and THAT when under present mercy.

3. Thus you see again, that the non-elect perish by reason of sin, notwithstanding present mercy, because of eternal justice; and that the elect are preserved from the death, though they sin and are obnoxious to the strokes of present justice, by reason of eternal mercy. What shall we say then? Is there unrighteousness with God? God forbid: 'He hath mercy on whom he will have mercy, and compassion on whom he will have compassion.' Ro. ix. 15.

QUESTIONS ABOUT THE NATURE AND PERPETUITY

OF THE

SEVENTH-DAY SABBATH.

AND PROOF,

THAT THE FIRST DAY OF THE WEEK IS THE TRUE CHRISTIAN SABBATH.

By JOHN BUNYAN.

' The Son of man is lord also of the Sabbath day.'

London: Printed for Nath. Ponder, at the Peacock in the Poultry, 1685.

EDITOR'S ADVERTISEMENT.

ALL our inquiries into divine commands are required to be made personally, solemnly, prayerfully. To ' prove all things,' and ' hold fast' and obey ' that which is good,' is a precept, equally binding upon the clown, as it is upon the philosopher. Satisfied from our observations of nature, that there is a God ; our next inquiry is into the revelation of his will: which, when understood, must be implicitly obeyed, in defiance of any usages of society, and of every erroneous pre-conceived opinion. In this important investigation, we shall find, that the commands of God revealed to man, fall under two classes.

First, Moral and Eternal, being essential to the happiness of all created intelligences, whether pure or sinful. As, the fear and love of the Creator, who preserves and bountifully blesses his creatures; and flowing from this is love to all his creation. He who wantonly destroys life in order that he may glut a demoniac propensity with the agonizing death struggle, is a practical atheist. The Christian will cherish and promote the happiness of all; he dares only to take away life to preserve life.

Second, Ceremonial or Temporal. Those which have been commanded by God, for local, family or national observances, and which, when they have fulfilled their intended object, are removed or suffered gradually to die away.

The well-being of society requires that a portion of time be set apart for divine worship. Individuals are commanded to pray without ceasing. An invaluable custom leads families to unite in morning and evening prayer; and it is an important question whether the Creator having sanctified, and rested on, the seventh day, intended that rest as a pattern to all his rational creatures. If so, *the* seventh day must depend upon our being able to fix upon which day of the week the creation commenced. Again our inquiries will extend to those injunctions, given to the Jews in the wilderness, to sanctify certain days to public worship ; and whether that law was intended for all mankind. In either case it is essential that we ascertain whether those various Sabbaths of weeks—of months or of years—with the ceremonies to be performed on them, were to continue to the end of time or for a limited period.

In all these inquiries we are strictly confined to revelation, for there is no indication in nature, or in any of its laws, of a day of rest; but on the contrary a state of progression marks every day alike. Our Lord has taught us that 'the Sabbath was made for man,' and therefore did not exist among the angels, prior to the creation of man, as all moral or universal obligations must have existed; for they are the same from eternity to eternity; and over this, like other ceremonial or local commands, the Creator claims dominion. ' The Son of man is Lord also of the Sabbath.'

Researches into these questions were made in earlier times, and some curious calculations have appeared to prove, that the work of creation commenced on the day called Monday, so that what is now termed the first day of the week, was originally the rest of God from creation ; as it was his rest from the work of redemption, by rising from the tomb. But the extent of that period called a day, in creation, has never been defined: and the terms ' work' or ' rest,' as applied to the Deity, are used in condescension to our finite powers. The controversy upon this subject assumed a more public and definite form at the Reformation. Sir Thomas More asserted that the seventh day was superseded by the first, in obedience to tradition:* it forms the first of the five commandments of Holy Church—' The Sundays hear thou mass.' William Tyndale, in reply, contends that ' we be lords over the Sabbath;' we may change it for Monday, or any other day, as

---

* Dialogues, 1st chap., xxv.

we see need, or have two every week, if one is not enough to teach the people.* Calvin preferred a daily assembling of the church, but if that was impossible, then at stated intervals: his words are—'Since the Sabbath is abrogate, I do not so rest upon the number of seven, that I would bind the church to the bondage thereof; neither will I condemn those churches that have other solemn days for their meetings.'† Luther considers the observance of the Jewish Sabbath one of the 'weak and beggarly rudiments.'‡

The controversy became still more popular in this country, when James the First and Charles the First put forth the book of sports to be allowed and encouraged on Sundays. The Puritans called Sunday 'The Sabbath,' and a voluminous contest was carried on as to whether it ought not rather to be called 'The Lord's day.' In 1628, Mr. Brabourne, a clergyman of note, kept the Jewish Sabbath, and in a short time several churches, in England, assembled on that day, and were called 'seventh day, or Sabbath keepers'—many of them were Baptists. This led to the controversy in which Bunyan took his part, in this very conclusive and admirable treatise.

The work was first published in the year 1685, and was not reprinted until the year 1806, when it appeared in the third volume of select works by John Bunyan; since then it has been reprinted in two American editions of his works. The reason why it was not republished, probably was, that the churches of the Sabbath keepers died away. At this time only three are known in England; one of these is at Millyard, London, where my talented antiquarian friend, W. H. Black, is elder and pastor. These places of worship are supported by an endowment. Bunyan's book does not appear to have been answered; indeed, it would require genius of no ordinary kind to controvert such conclusive evidence.

His arguments are, that the appearances of nature shew no difference of days—that no Sabbath or other day was set apart for worship before the giving of the Law at Sinai. 'Thou camest down also upon Mount Sinai, and madest KNOWN unto them thy holy Sabbaths, by the hand of Moses.' Ne. ix. 13, 14. 'The seventh day is the Sabbath of the Lord thy God: in it thou shalt not do any work—and remember that thou wast a servant in the land of Egypt, and that the Lord thy God brought thee out thence through a mighty hand and by a stretched out arm, THEREFORE the Lord thy God commanded thee to keep the Sabbath day.' De. v. 14, 15. While many crimes are mentioned in patriarchal times, there is no complaint of Sabbath-breaking. We read of fratricide, drunkenness,

lying, unbelief, theft, idolatry, slave-dealing, and other crimes, but no hint as to sanctifying or desecrating the Sabbath. At length, a few days before the giving of the law, a natural phenomenon announced to the Jews the great change that was at hand—the manna fell in double quantity on Friday, and was not found on Saturday. So new was this that, contrary to the command, the people went out on the seventh day as on other days, and were rebuked but not punished for it. But no sooner is the Sabbath instituted by Moses, than it is broken, and the Sabbath-breaker is punished with a cruel death. It was instituted as a peculiar observance to distinguish the Jews from all other nations—'The Lord hath given you the Sabbath.' Ex. xvi. 39. 'The children of Israel shall keep the Sabbath.' Ex. xxxi. 16, 17. 'I gave them [the Israelites who were delivered from Egypt] my Sabbaths to be a sign between me and them.' Eze. xx. 12. Ceremonies were commanded to be performed as the Sabbath worship, which cannot now be observed, see Le. xxiv. Nu xxviii. Ne. xiii. 22. Eze. xlvi. 4. The Jewish Sabbath was 'a shadow of things to come, but the body is of Christ.' Col. ii. 16, 17. The shadows have fled away; we possess the substance. The covenant of Moses was written on stone—the new covenant is written on our hearts, He. viii. 9, 10. Bunyan admits no uncertainty as to a fixed day for christian worship: the law of nature requires it; the God of nature fixes the day, without borrowing it from the ministration of death. The Jewish passover and Sabbaths are superseded; Christ our passover is slain, and we have not an annual but a perpetual feast. We have an infinitely greater deliverance to commemorate than that of the Jews from Egypt. Released from the dominion and punishment of sin, we have entered into a rest boundless as eternity. Manna, which never fell on the Jewish Sabbath, falls in peculiar and rich abundance on the first day of the week, when it first began to fall. The first day is peculiarly sanctified and honoured of God. On this day the Son rested from His work of redemption, He. iv. 10. He is Lord of the Sabbath, and hath peculiarly blessed his own day. On this day some of the saints that slept arose. Mat. xxvii. 52, 53. On this day Christ was made the head of the corner, and we will rejoice and be glad in it. On the first day God begat his beloved Son from the dead. Ac. xiii. 33. Let all the angels of God worship him. He. i. 6. Hence it is called the Lord's day. Re. i. 10. This day is the only one named upon which Christ appeared to his disciples after his resurrection: it was on the evening of the first day of the week, and on the evening of the following eighth day, that they assembled and Christ appeared in the midst of them. On this day he walked with his disciples to Emmaus, and made their hearts to burn within them with holy

---

* Answer to More.   † Institutes, b. ii. ch. 8.
‡ Com. on Gal. iv. 9.

joy and wonder. The marvels of the day of Pentecost honoured the first day of the week. On *this* day the first great conversion of 'about three thousand souls' took place. On *this* day the disciples at Jerusalem came together to break bread. Ac. xx. 7. Upon THE, not A, first day they broke bread; and upon THE first day, the collections were made for the poor saints. 1 Co. xvi. 1, 2. With such concurrent and ample testimony we must conclude that the seventh day Sabbath, with its Jewish ritual, is dissolved, and the first day has taken its place. The Saviour said, 'It is finished;' and from that moment to the end of the inspired volume, the seventh day is swallowed up in the glories of the first day of the week. Let Jews commemorate their temporal deliverance from Pharaoh and Egypt with their divers ceremonies;

but Christians, blessed with a foretaste of eternal glory, will commemorate the resurrection of their Lord, as the first fruits of an unspeakable rest from the dominion of sin, of Satan, and of hell. Our glorified Redeemer sanctioned and blessed the first day, with his personal appearance in the assemblies of his saints. His inspired apostles kept it, as it is recorded, and thus it is sanctioned by the Holy Ghost; and their descendants are bound to keep it to the end of the world. Go, little treatise, and carry conviction with thee. Emancipate the christian mind from all the beggarly rudiments of Jewish rites and ceremonies. Add to the holy enjoyments of God's saints in public worship, on the day when their eternal redemption is commemorated by the triumphant resurrection of their Lord.—GEO. OFFOR.

TO THE READER.

SOME may think it strange, since God's church has already been so well furnished with sound grounds and reasons by so many wise and godly men, for proof that the first day of the week is our true Christian sabbath, that I should *now* offer this small treatise upon the same account. But when the scales are even by what already is put in, a little more, you know, makes the weight the better.

Or grant we had down weight before, yet something over and above may make his work the harder, that shall by hanging fictions on the other end, endeavour to make things seem too light.

Besides, this book being little, may best suit such as have but shallow purses, short memories, and but little time to spare, which usually is the lot of the mean and poorer sort of men.

I have also written upon this subject, for that I would, as in other gospel truths, be a fellow witness with good men that the day in which our Lord rose from the dead should be much set by of Christians.

I have observed that some, otherwise sound in faith, are apt to be entangled with a Jewish sabbath, &c., and that some also that are afar off from the observation of that, have but little to say for their own practice, though good; and might I help them I should be glad.

A Jewish seventh-day sabbath has no promise of grace belonging to it, if that be true, as to be sure it is, where Paul says, The command to honour parents is the first commandment with promise. Ep. vi. 1—3.

Also it follows from hence, that the sabbath that has a promise annexed to the keeping of it, is rather that which the Lord Jesus shall give to the churches of the Gentiles. Is. lvi.

Perhaps my method here may not in all things keep the common path of argumentation with them that have gone before me: but I trust [that] the godly wise will find a taste of scripture truth in what I present them with as to the sanction of our Christian sabbath.

I have here, by handling four questions, proved, that the seventh day sabbath was not moral. For that must of necessity be done, before it can be made appear that the first day of the week is that which is the sabbath day for Christians. But withal it follows, that if the seventh day sabbath was not moral,* the first day is not so. What is it then? Why, a sabbath for holy worship is moral; but *this* or *that* day appointed for such service, is sanctified by precept or by approved example. The timing then of a sabbath for us lies in God, not man; in grace, not nature; nor in the ministration of death, written and engraven in stones: God always reserving to himself a power to alter and change both *time* and *modes* of worship according to his own will.

A sabbath then, or day of rest from worldly affairs to solemnize worship to God in, all good men do by nature conclude is meet; yea, necessary: yet *that*, not nature, but God reveals.

Nor is that day or time by God so fixed on, in its own nature, better than any other: the holiness then of a sabbath lies, not in the nature or place of a day, but in the ordinance of God.

Nor doth our sanctifying of it, to the ends for

---

* The word 'moral' is here used to mark the difference between obligations binding on all mankind and a positive or limited command: thus, to love God is a moral or universal obligation, but to be baptized is positive and obligatory only on those who believe, Acts viii. 37.—ED.

which it is ordained, lie in a bare confession that it is such ; but in a holy performance of the duty of the day to God by Christ, according to his word. But I will not enlarge to detain the reader longer from the following sheets ; but shall commit both him and them to the wise dispose of God, and rest,

Thine to serve thee,
Joh. Bunyan.

QUESTIONS ABOUT THE

NATURE AND PERPETUITY OF THE SEVENTH-DAY SABBATH.

QUESTION I.

Whether the seventh day sabbath is of, or made known to, man by the law and light of nature ?

SOMETHING must be here premised before I show the grounds of this question. First then, by the law or light of nature, I mean that law which was concreate with man; that which is natural to him, being original with, and essential to, himself; consequently, that which is invariable and unalterable, as is that nature. Secondly, I grant that by this law of nature, man understands that there is one eternal God; that this God is to be worshipped according to his own will; consequently, that *time* must be allowed to do it in: but whether the law or light of nature teacheth, and that of itself, without the help of revelation, that the seventh day of the week is *that* time sanctified of God, and set apart for his worship, that is the question; and the grounds of it are these:

First, Because the law of nature is antecedent to this day, yea completed as a law before it was known or revealed to man, that God either did or would sanctify the seventh day of the week at all.

Now this law, as was said, being natural to a man, for man is a law unto himself, Ro. ii. could only teach the things of a man, and there the Apostle stints it, 1 Co. ii. 11. But to be able to determine, and that about things that were yet without being, either in nature or by revelation, is that which belongs not to a man as a man; and the seventh day sabbath, as yet, was such. For Adam was completely made the day before; and God did not sanctify the seventh day before it was, none otherwise than by his secret decree. Therefore, by the law of nature, Adam understood it not, it was not made known to him thereby.

Second, To affirm the contrary, is to make the law of nature supernatural, which is an impossibility. Yea, they that do so make it a predictor, a prophet; a prophet about divine things to come ; yea, a prophet able to foretel what shall be, and that without a revelation; which is a strain that never yet prophet pretended to.

Besides, to grant this, is to run into a grievous error; for this doth not only make the law of

nature the first of prophets, contrary to Ge. iii. 10. compared with Jn. i. 1. but it seems to make the will of God, made known by revelation, a needless thing. For if the law of nature, as such, can predict, or foretel God's secrets, and that before he reveals them, and this law of nature is universal in every individual man in the world, what need is there of particular prophets, or of their holy writings ? And indeed here the Quakers and others split themselves. For if the law of nature can of itself reveal unto me one thing pertaining to instituted worship, for that we are treating of now, and the exact time which God has not yet sanctified and set apart for the performance thereof, why may it not reveal unto me more, and so still more; and at last all that is requisite for me to know, both as to my salvation, and how God is to be worshipped in the church on earth.

Third, If it be of the law of nature, then all men by nature are convinced of the necessity of keeping it, and that though they never read or heard of the revealed will of God about it; but this we find not in the world.

For though it is true that the law of nature is common to all, and that all men are to this day under the power and command thereof; yet we find not that they are by nature under the conviction of the necessity of keeping of a seventh day sabbath. Yea, the Gentiles, though we read not that they ever despised the law of nature, yet never had, as such, a reverence of a seventh day sabbath, but rather the contrary.

Fourth, If therefore the seventh day sabbath is not of the law of nature, then it should seem not to be obligatory to all. For instituted worship, and the necessary circumstances thereunto belonging, is obligatory but to some. The tree that Adam was forbid to eat of, we read not but that his children might have eat the fruit thereof: and circumcision, the passover, and other parts of instituted worship was enjoined but to some.

Fifth, I doubt the seventh day sabbath is not of the law of nature, and so not moral; because though we read that the law of nature, and that before Moses, was charged upon the world, yet I find not till then, that the profanation of a seventh day sabbath was charged upon the world: and indeed to me this very thing makes a great scruple in the case.

A law, as I said, we read of, and that from Adam to Moses. Ro. v. 13, 14. The transgressions also of *that* law, we read of them, and that particularly, as in Ge. iv. 8. & vi. 5; ix. 21, 22; xii. 13; xiii. 13; xviii. 12—15; xix. 5; (Eze. xvi. 49, 50.*) Ge. xxxi. 30; xxxv. 2; xl. 15; xliv. 8—10. De. viii. 19, 20; xii. 2. Ps. cvi. 35—37. and Romans the first and second chapters.

But in all the scriptures we do not read, that the breach of a seventh day sabbath was charged upon men as men all that time. Whence I gather, that either a seventh day sabbath was not discerned by the light of nature, and so not by that law imposed; or else, that men by the help and assistance of that, for we speak of men as men,† in old time kept it better, than in after ages did the church of God with better assistance by far. For they are there yet found fault with as breakers of the sabbath. Eze. xx. 13.

It follows therefore, that if the law of nature doth not of itself reveal to us, as men, that the seventh day is the holy sabbath of God. That that day, as to the sanction of it, is not moral, but rather arbitrary, to wit, imposed by the will of God upon his people, until the time he thought fit to change it for another day.

And if so, it is hence to be concluded, that though by the light of nature men might see that time must be allowed and set apart for the performance of that worship that God would set up in his house, yet, as such, it could not see what time the Lord would to that end choose. Nature therefore saw *that*, by a positive precept, or a word revealing it, and by no others means.

Nor doth this at all take away a whit of that sanction which God once put upon the seventh day sabbath; unless any will say, and by sufficient argument prove, that an ordinance for divine worship receiveth greater sanction from the law of nature than from a divine precept: or standeth stronger when it is established by a law humane, for such is the law of nature, than when imposed by revelation of God.

But the text will put this controversy to an end. The sanction of the seventh day sabbath, even as it was the rest of God, was not till after the law of nature was completed; God rested the seventh day and sanctified it. Ge. ii. 3. Sanctified it; that is, set it apart to the end there mentioned, to wit, to rest thereon.

Other grounds of this question I might produce, but at present I will stop here, and conclude, That

if a seventh day sabbath was an essential necessary to the instituted worship of God, then itself also as to its sanction for that work, was not founded but by a positive precept; consequently not known of man at first, but by revelation of God.

QUESTION II.

Whether the seventh day sabbath, as to man's keeping of it holy, was ever made known to, or imposed by, a positive precept upon him until the time of Moses? which from Adam was about two thousand years.

Something must also be here premised, in order to my propounding of my grounds for this question; and that is, That the seventh day was sanctified so soon as it had being in the world, unto the rest of God, as it is Ge. ii. 2, 3. and he did rest, from all his works which he had made therein. But the question is, Whether when God did thus sanctify this day to his *own* rest, he did also by the space of time above-mentioned, impose it as an holy sabbath of rest upon men; to the end they might solemnize worship to him in special manner thereon? And I question this,

First, Because we read not that it was. And reading, I mean, of the divine testimony, is ordained of God, for us to find out the mind of God, both as to faith and our performance of acceptable service to him.

In reading also, we are to have regard to two things.

I. To see if we can find a precept: or,

II. A countenanced practice for what we do. For both these ways we are to search, that we may find out what is that good, that acceptable will of God.

For the first of these we have Ge. ii. 16, 17. and for the second, Ge. viii. 20, 21. [as to public worship but not on a stated day.]

Now as to the imposing of a seventh day sabbath upon men from Adam to Moses, of that we find nothing in holy writ either from precept or example. True, we find that solemn worship was performed by the saints that then lived: for both Abel, Noah, Abraham, Isaac, Jacob, sacrificed unto God, Ge. iv. 4; viii. 20, 21; xii. 7; xiii. 4; xxxv. 1. but we read not that the seventh day was the time prefixed of God for their so worshipping, or that they took any notice of it. Some say, that Adam in eating the forbidden fruit, brake also the seventh day sabbath, because he fell on that day;‡ but we

---

* The original edition refers to (Ezek. 49, 50), but it is evidently a typographical error in omitting the chapter.

† Man unaided by revelation.

‡ Adam is supposed by some rabbins not to have passed one night in a state of perfection, (see Ainsworth on Gen. iii. 1; xxviii. 11; and Psal. xlix. 13), and to have fallen on the Sabbath day.

read not that the breach of a sabbath was charged upon him. That which we read is this; 'Hast thou eaten of the tree, whereof I commanded thee that thou shouldest not eat?' Ge. iii. 11. Some say also that Cain killed Abel on a sabbath day;* but we read not that, in his charge, God laid any such thing at his door. This was it of which he stood guilty before God; namely, That his brother's blood cried unto God against him from the ground. Ge. iv. 10.

I therefore take little notice of what a man saith, though he flourisheth his matter with many brave words, if he bring not with him, 'Thus saith the Lord.' For that, and that only, ought to be my ground of faith as to how my God would be worshipped by me. For in the matters material to the worship of God, it is safest that thus I be guided in my judgment: for here only I perceive 'the footsteps of the flock,' Ca. i. 8. Eze. iii. 11. They say further, that for God to sanctify a thing, is to set it apart. This being true; then it follows, that the seventh day sabbath was sanctified, that is, set apart for Adam in paradise; and so, that it was ordained a sabbath of rest to the saints from the beginning.

But I answer, as I hinted before, that God did sanctify it to his own rest. 'The LORD (also) hath set apart him that is godly for himself.' But again, it is one thing for God to sanctify this or that thing to an use, and another thing to command that that thing be forthwith in being to us. As for instance: the land of Canaan was set apart many years for the children of Israel before they possessed that land. Christ Jesus was long sanctified; that is, set apart to be our redeemer before he sent him into the world. De. xxxii. 8. Jn. x. 36.

If then, by God's sanctifying of the seventh day for a sabbath, you understand it for a sabbath for man, (but the text saith not so) yet it might be so set apart for man, long before it should be, as such, made known unto him. And that the seventh day sabbath was not as yet made known to men.

Second, Consider secondly, Moses himself seems to have the knowledge of it at first, not by tradition, but by revelation; as it is. Ex. xvi. 23. 'This *is that* (saith he) which the Lord hath said, (namely to me; for we read not, as yet, that he said it to any body else), To morrow *is* the sabbath of the holy rest unto the Lord.'

Also holy Nehemiah suggesteth this, when he saith of Israel to God, Thou 'madest known unto them thy holy sabbath [by the hand of Moses thy servant]' Ne. ix. 14. The first of these texts shews

us, that tidings of a seventh day sabbath for men, came *first* to Moses from heaven: and the second, that it was to Israel before unknown.

But how could be either the one or the other, if the seventh day sabbath was taught to men by the light of nature, which is the moral law? Or if from the beginning it was given to men by a positive precept for to be kept.

This therefore strengtheneth my doubt about the affirmative of the first question, and also prepareth an argument for what I plead as to this we have now under consideration.

Third, This yet seems to me more scrupulous, because that the punishment due to the breach of the seventh day sabbath was hid from men to the time of Moses; as is clear, for that it is said of the breaker of the sabbath, 'They put him in ward, because it was not [as yet] declared what should be done to him.' Nu. xv. 32—36.

But methinks, had this seventh day sabbath been imposed upon men from the beginning, the penalty or punishment due to the breach thereof had certainly been known before now.

When Adam was forbidden to eat of the tree of the knowledge of good and evil, the penalty was then, if he disobeyed, annexed to the prohibition. So also it was as to circumcision, the passover, and other ordinances for worship. How then can it be thought, that the seventh day sabbath should be imposed upon men from the beginning; and that the punishment for the breach thereof, should be hid with God for the space of two thousand years! Ge. ii. 16, 17; xvii. 13, 14. Ex. xii. 43—48. and the same chapter, ver. 19.

Fourth, God's giving of the seventh day sabbath was with respect to *stated* and *stinted* worship in his church; the which, until the time of Moses, was not set up among his people. Things till then were adding or growing: *now* a sacrifice, *then* circumcision, then again long after that the passover, &c.

But when Israel was come into the wilderness, there to receive as God's congregation, a stated, stinted, limited way of worship, then he appoints them a time, and times, to perform this worship in; but as I said afore, before that it was not so, as the whole five books of Moses plainly shew: wherefore the seventh day sabbath, as such a limited day cannot be moral, or of the law of nature, nor imposed till then.

And methinks Christ Jesus and his apostles do plainly enough declare this very thing. For that when they repeat unto the people, or expound before them the moral law, they quite exclude the seventh day sabbath. Yea, Paul makes that law to us complete without it.

We will first touch upon what Christ doth in this case.

---

* The murder of Abel took place 'at the end of days;' see margin to Gen. iv. 3. Properly rendered 'in process of time;' but by some supposed to mean at the end of the week. See Dr. Gill's Commentary.

As in his sermon upon the mount, Mat. v—vii. In all that large and heavenly discourse upon this law, you have not one syllable about the seventh day sabbath.

So when the young man came running, and kneeling, and asking what good thing he should do to inherit eternal life, Christ bids him keep the commandments; but when the young man asked which; Christ quite leaves out the seventh day, and puts him upon the other. As in Mat. xix. 16—19. As in Mar. x. 17—20. As in Lu. xviii. 18—20.

You will say, he left out the first, and second, and third likewise. To which I say, that was because the young man by his question did presuppose that he had been a doer of them: for he professed in his supplication, that he was a lover of that which is naturally good, which is God, in that his petition was so universal for every thing which he had commanded.

Paul also when he makes mention of the moral law, quite leaves out of that the very name of the seventh day sabbath, and professeth, that to us Christians the law of nature is complete without it. As in Ro. iii. 7—19. As in Ro. xiii. 7—10. As in 1 Ti. i. 8 —11.

'He that loveth another, saith he, hath fulfilled the law. For this, Thou shalt not commit adultery, Thou shalt not kill, Thou shalt not steal, Thou shalt not covet; and if *there be* any other commandment, it is briefly comprehended in this saying, Thou shalt love thy neighbour as thyself. Love worketh no ill to his neighbour: therefore love *is* the fulfilling of the law.'

I make not an argument of this, but take an occasion to mention it as I go. But certainly, had the seventh day sabbath been moral, or of the law of nature, as some would fain persuade themselves, it would not so slenderly have been passed over in all these repetitions of this law, but would by Christ or his apostles have been pressed upon the people, when so fair an opportunity as at these times offered itself unto them. But they knew what they did, and wherefore they were so silent as to the mention of a seventh day sabbath when they so well talked of the law as moral.

Fifth, Moses and the prophet Ezekiel both, do fully confirm what has been insinuated by us; to wit, that the seventh day, as a sabbath, was not imposed upon men until Israel was brought into the wilderness.

1. Moses saith to Israel, 'Remember that thou wast a servant in the land of Egypt, and *that* the Lord thy God brought thee out thence through a mighty hand and by a stretched out arm: THEREFORE the Lord thy God commanded thee to keep the sabbath day.' Yea, he tells us, that the covenant which God made with them in Horeb, that written in stones, was not made with their fore-fathers, to wit, Abraham, Isaac, and Jacob, but with them. De. v. 1—15.

2. Ezekiel also is punctual as to this: I caused them, saith God by that prophet, 'to go forth out of the land of Egypt, and brought them into the wilderness. And I gave them my statutes, and shewed them my judgments, which *if* a man do, he shall even live in them. Moreover also I gave them my sabbaths, to be a sign between me and them, that they might know that I *am* the Lord that sanctify them.' Eze. xx. 10—12. Ex. xx. 8; xxxi. 13; xxxv. 2.

What can be more plain? And these to be sure, are two notable witnesses of God, who, as you see, do jointly concur in this; to wit, That it was not from paradise, nor from the fathers, but from the wilderness, and from Sinai, that men received the seventh day sabbath to keep it holy.

True, it was God's sabbath before: for on the first seventh day we read, that God rested thereon, and sanctified it. Hence he calls it in the first place, My sabbath. I gave them my sabbath: But it seems it was not given to the church till he had brought them into the wilderness.

But I say, if it had been *moral*, it had been natural to man; and by the light of nature men would have understood it, even both before it was, and otherwise. But of this you see we read nothing, either by positive law, or countenanced example, or any other way, but rather the flat contrary; to wit, that Moses had the knowledge of it first from heaven, not by tradition. That Israel had it, not of, or from their fathers, but in the wilderness, from him, to wit, Moses, after he had brought them out of the land of Egypt. And that that whole law in which this seventh day sabbath is placed, was given for the bounding and better ordering of them in their church state for their time, till the Messias should come and put, by a better ministration, this out of his church, as we shall further shew anon.

The seventh day sabbath therefore was not from paradise, nor from nature, nor from the fathers, but from the wilderness, and from Sinai.

QUESTION III.

Whether when the seventh day sabbath was given to Israel in the wilderness the Gentiles, as such, was concerned therein.

Before I shew my ground for this question, I must also first premise, That the Gentiles, as such, were then without the church of God, and pale thereof; consequently had nothing to do with the essentials or necessary circumstances of that worship which God had set up for himself now among the children of Israel.

Now then for the ground of the question.

First, we read not that God gave it to any but to the seed of Jacob. Hence it is said to Israel, and to Israel only, 'The Lord hath given you the sabbath.' Ex. xvi. 29. And again, 'also I gave THEM my sabbath.' Eze. xx. 5, 12.

Now, if the gift of the seventh day sabbath was only to Israel, as these texts do more than seem to say; then to the Gentiles, as such, it was not given. Unless any shall conclude, that God by thus doing preferred the Jew to a state of gentileism; or that he bestowed on them, by thus doing, some high Gentile privilege. But this would be very fictious. For, to lay aside reason, the text always, as to preference, did set the Jew in the first of places. Ro. ii. 10. Nor was his giving the seventh day sabbath to them but a sign and token thereof.

But the great objection is, because the seventh day sabbath is found amongst the rest of those precepts which is so commonly called the moral law; for thence it is concluded to be of a perpetual duration.

But I answer: That neither that as given on Sinai is moral; I mean, as to the manner and ends of its ministration; of which, God permitting, we shall say more in our answer to the fourth question, whither I direct you for satisfaction. But,

Second, The Gentiles could not be concerned, as such, with God's giving of a seventh day sabbath to Israel, because, as I have shewed before, it was given to Israel, considered as a church of God. Ac. vii. 32. Nor was it given to them, as such, but with rites and ceremonies thereto belonging, so Le. xxiv. 5—9. Nu. xxviii. 9, 10. Ne. xiii. 22. Eze. xlvi. 4.

Now, I say, if this sabbath hath ceremonies thereto belonging, and if these ceremonies were essential to the right keeping of the sabbath: and again, if these ceremonies were given to Israel only, excluding all but such as were their proselytes, then this sabbath was given to them as excluding the Gentiles as such. But if it had been moral, the Gentiles could as soon have been deprived of their nature as of a seventh day sabbath, though the Jews should have appropriated it unto themselves only

Again, to say that God gave this seventh day sabbath to the Gentiles, as such, (and yet so he must, if it be of the moral law) is as much as to say, that God hath ordained that *that* sabbath should be kept by the Gentiles *without*; but by the Jews, *not* without her ceremonies. And what conclusion will follow from hence, but that God did at *one* and the *same* time set up two sorts of acceptable worships in the world: one among the Jews, another among the Gentiles! But how ridiculous

such a thought would be, and how repugnant to the wisdom of God, you may easily perceive.

Yea, what a diminution would this be to God's church that then was, for one to say, the Gentiles were to serve God with more liberty than the Jew! For the law was a yoke, and yet the Gentile is called the dog, and said to be without God in the world. De. vii. 7. Ps. cxlvii. 19, 20. Mat. xv. 26. Ep. ii. 11, 12.

Third, When the Gentiles, at the Jews' return from Babylon, came and offered their wares to sell to the children of Israel at Jerusalem on this sabbath; yea, and sold them to them too: yet *not they*, but the *Jews* were rebuked as the only breakers of that sabbath. Nay, there dwelt then at Jerusalem men of Tyre, that on *this* sabbath sold their commodities to the Jews, and men of Judah: yet not they, but the men of Judah, were contended with, as the breakers of this sabbath.

True, good Nehemiah did threaten the Gentiles that were merchants, for lying then about the walls of the city, for that by that means they were a temptation to the Jews to break *their* sabbaths; but still he charged the breach thereof *only* upon his own people. Ne. xiii. 15—20.

But can it be imagined, had the Gentiles now been concerned with this sabbath by law divine, that so holy a man as Nehemiah would have let them escape without a rebuke for so notorious a transgression thereof; especially considering, that now also they were upon God's ground, to wit, within and without the walls of Jerusalem.

Fourth, Wherefore he saith to Israel again, 'Verily my sabbaths YE shall keep.' And again, 'YE shall keep the sabbath.' And again, 'The children of Israel shall keep the sabbath, to observe the sabbath throughout THEIR generations.' Ex. xxxi. 14—16; and xvi. 29.*

What can be more plain, these things thus standing in the testament of God, than that the seventh day sabbath, as such, was given to Israel, to Israel ONLY; and that the Gentiles, as such, were not concerned therein!

Fifth, The very reason also of God's giving of the seventh day sabbath to the Jews, doth exclude the Gentiles, as such, from having any concern therein. For it was given to the Jews, as was said before, as they were considered God's church, and for a sign and token by which they should know that he had chosen and sanctified them to himself for a peculiar people. Ex. xxxi. 13—17. Eze. xx. 12, 13.

And a great token and sign it was that he had so chosen them: for in that he had given to them this sabbath, he had given to them (his own rest) a figure and pledge of his sending his Son into the world to redeem them from the bondage and slavery of the devil: of which indeed this sabbath was a shadow or type. Col. ii. 16, 17.*

Thus have I concluded my ground for this third question. I shall therefore now propound another.

QUESTION IV.

Whether the seventh day sabbath did not fall, as such, with the rest of the Jewish rites and ceremonies? Or whether that day, as a sabbath, was afterwards by the apostles imposed upon the churches of the Gentiles?

I would now also, before I shew the grounds of my proposing this question, premise what is necessary thereunto; to wit, That *time* and *day* were both fixed upon by law, for the solemn performance of divine worship among the Jews; and that *time* and *day* is also by law fixed, for the solemnizing of divine worship to God in the churches of the Gentiles. But that the seventh day sabbath, as such, is *that* time, *that* day, that still I question.

Now before I shew the grounds of my questioning of it, I shall enquire into the nature of that ministration in the bowels of which this seventh day sabbath is placed. And,

First, I say, as to that, the *nature* of that law is moral, but the ministration, and circumstances thereunto belonging, are shadowish and figurative.

By the nature of it, I mean the matter thereof: by the ministration and circumstances thereto belonging, I do mean the giving of it by such hands, at such a place and time, in such a mode, as when it was given to Israel in the wilderness.

The matter therefore, to wit, 'Thou shalt love the Lord thy God with all thy heart, and with all thy soul, and with all thy mind, and with all thy strength:' and 'thy neighbour as thyself,' is everlasting, (Mar. xii. 29—31.) and is not from Sinai, nor from the two tables of stone, but in nature; for this law commenced and took being and place that day in which man was created. Yea, it was concreate with him, and without it he cannot be a rational creature, as he was in the day in which God created him. But for the ministration of it from Sinai, with the circumstances belonging to

* This is a striking application of Col. ii. 17. The sabbath 'a shadow of things to come;' to the Jews it was a shadow of the rest that remaineth to the children of God, reflected from the completion of the work of creation. The day of rest and worship to the Christian, is a much stronger type, yet but a *shadow* of the holy enjoyments of his eternal rest, prefigured from the finishing of the mightier work of redemption.—ED.

that ministration, they are not moral, nor everlasting, but shadowish and figurative only.

That ministration cannot be moral for three reasons. 1. It commenced not when morality commenced, but two thousand years after. 2. It was not universal as the law, as moral, is; it was given only to the church of the Jews in those tables. 3. Its end is past as such a ministration, though the same law as to the morality thereof abides. Where are the tables of stone and this law as therein contained? We only, as to that, have the notice of such a ministration, and a rehearsal of the law, with that mode of giving of it, in the testament of God.

But to come to particulars.

1. The very preface to that ministration carrieth in it a type of our deliverance from the bondage of sin, the devil, and hell. Pharaoh, and Egypt; and Israel's bondage there, being a type of these.

2. The very stones in which this law was engraven, was a figure of the tables of the heart. The first two were a figure of the heart carnal, by which the law was broken: the last two, of the heart spiritual, in which the new law, the law of grace is written and preserved. Ex. xxxiv. 1. 2 Co. iii. 3.

3. The very mount on which this ministration was given, was typical of Mount Zion. See He. xii. where they are compared. ver. 18—22.

4. Yea, the very church to whom that ministration was given, was a figure of the church of the gospel that is on Mount Zion. See the same scripture, and compare it with Ac. vii. 38. Re. xiv. 1—5.

5. That ministration was given in the hand and by the disposition of angels, to prefigure how the new law or ministration of the Spirit was to be given afterwards to the churches under the New Testament by the hands of the angel of God's everlasting covenant of grace, who is his only begotten Son. Is. lxiii. 9. Mal. iii. 1. † Ac. iii. 22, 23.

6. It was given to Israel also in the hand of Moses, as mediator, to shew, or typify out, that the law of grace was in after times to come to the church of Christ by the hand and mediation of Jesus our Lord. Ga. iii. 19. De. v. 5. He. viii. 6. 1 Ti. ii. 5. He. ix. 15; xii. 24.

7. As to this ministration, it was to continue but 'till the seed should come;' and then must, as such, give place to a better ministration. Ga. iii. 19. 'A better covenant, established upon better promises.' He. viii. 6.

From all this therefore I conclude, that there is a difference to be put between the morality of the law, and the ministration of it upon Sinai. The law, as to its morality was before; but as to *this*

† In Bunyan's original edition it is 'Matth. 3, 1,' but this must be a typographical error.—ED.

ministration, it was not till the church was with Moses, and he with the angels on Mount Sinai in the wilderness.

Now in the law, as moral, we conclude a time propounded, but no seventh day sabbath enjoined. But in that law, as thus ministered, which ministration is already out of doors;* we find a seventh day; that seventh day on which God rested, on which God rested from all his works, enjoined. What is it then? Why the whole ministration as written and engraven in stones being removed, the seventh day sabbath must also be removed; for that the *time*, nor yet the *day*, was as to our holy sabbath, or rest, moral; but imposed with that whole ministration, as such, upon the church, until the time of reformation: which time being come, this ministration, as I said, as such, ceaseth; and the whole law, as to the morality of it, is delivered into the hand of Christ, who imposes it now also; but not as a law of works, nor as that ministration written and engraven in stones, but as a rule of life to those that have believed in him. 1 Co. ix. 21.

So then, that law is still moral, and still supposes, since it teaches that there is a God, that time must be set apart for his church to worship him in, according to that will of his that he had revealed in his word. But though by that law *time* is required; yet by that, as moral, the time never was prefixed.

The time then of old was appointed by such a ministration of that law as we have been now discoursing of; and when that ministration ceaseth, that time did also vanish with it. And now by our new law-giver, the Son of God, he being 'lord also of the sabbath day,' we have a time prefixed, as the law of nature requireth, a *new* day, by him who is the lord of it; I say, appointed, wherein we may worship, not in the oldness of that letter written and engraven in stones, but according to, and most agreeing with, his new and holy testament. And this I confirm further by those reasons that now shall follow.

First, Because we find not from the resurrection of Christ to the end of the Bible, anything written by which is imposed that seventh day sabbath upon the churches. *Time*, as I said, the law as moral requires; but *that* time we find no longer imposed. And in all duties pertaining to God and his true worship in his churches, we must be guided by his laws and testaments. By his old laws, when his old worship was in force; and by his new laws, when his new worship is in force. And he hath verily now said, 'Behold, I make all things new.' Re. xxi. 5.

Second, I find, as I have shewed, that this seventh day sabbath is confined, not to the law of nature as such, but to that ministration of it which was given on Sinai: which ministration as it is come to an end as such, so it is rejected by Paul as a ministration no ways capable of abiding in the church now, since the ministration of the Spirit also hath taken its place. 2 Co. iii. Wherefore instead of propounding it to the churches with arguments tending to its reception, he seeks by degrading it of its old lustre and glory, to wean the churches from any †likement thereof:

1. By calling of it the ministration of death, of the letter, and of condemnation, a term most frightful, but no ways alluring to the godly.

2. By calling it a ministration that *now* has no glory, by reason of the exceeding glory of that ministration under which by the Holy Spirit the New Testament churches are. And these are weaning considerations. 2 Co. iii.

3. By telling of them it is a ministration that tendeth to blind the mind, and to veil the heart as to the knowledge of their Christ: so that they cannot, while under that, behold his beauteous face, but as their heart shall turn from it to him. 2 Co. iii.

4. And that they might not be left in the dark, but perfectly know what ministration it is that he means, he saith expressly, it is that 'written *and* engraven in stones.' See again 2 Co. iii. And in that ministration it is that this seventh day sabbath is found.

But shall we think that the apostle speaks any thing of all here said, to wean saints off from the law of nature, as such! No verily, that he retains in the church, as being managed there by Christ: but THIS ministration is dangerous *now*, because it cannot be maintained in the church, but in a way of contempt to the ministration of the Spirit, and is derogatory to the glory of that.

Now these, as I said, are weaning considerations. No man, I do think, that knows himself, or the glory of a gospel ministration, can, if he understands what Paul says here, desire that such a ministration should be retained in the churches.

Third. This seventh day sabbath has lost its ceremonies (those unto which before you are cited by the texts) which was with it imposed upon the old church for her due performance of worship to God thereon. How then can *this* sabbath *now* be kept? Kept, I say, according to law. For if the church on which it was first imposed, was not to keep it, yea, could not keep it legally without the practising of those ceremonies: and if those ceremonies are long ago dead and gone, how will those that pretend to a belief of a continuation of

* 'Out of doors,' no more to be found, quite gone, fairly sent away.—*Locke.* 'Out of court.'—*Law-term.*—ED.

† 'Any likement,' any fondness or partiality.—ED.

the sanction thereof, keep it, I say, according as it is written?

If they say, they retain the day, but change their manner of observation thereof; I ask, who has commanded them so to do? This is one of the laws of *this* sabbath. 'Thou shalt take fine flour, and bake twelve cakes thereof: two tenth deals shall be in one cake. And thou shalt set them in two rows, six on a row, upon the pure table before the Lord. And thou shalt put pure frankincense upon *each* row, that it may be on the bread for a memorial, *even* an offering made by fire unto the Lord. Every sabbath he shall set it in order before the Lord continually, *being taken* from the children of Israel by an everlasting covenant. Le. xxiv. 5—8. You may see also other places, as Nu. xxviii. 9, 10. Ne. xiii. 22 and Eze. xlvi. 4.

Now if these be the laws of the sabbath, this seventh day sabbath; and if God did never command that *this* sabbath should by his church be sanctified without them: and, as was said before, if these ceremonies have been long since dead and buried, *how* must this sabbath be kept?

Let men take heed, lest while they plead for law, and pretend themselves to be the only doers of God's will,* they be not found the biggest transgressors thereof. And why can they not as well keep the other sabbaths? As the sabbaths of months, of years, and the jubilee? For this, as I have shewed, is no moral precept, it is only a branch of the ministration of death and condemnation.

Fourth, The seventh day sabbath, as such, was a sign and shadow of things to come; and a sign cannot be the thing signified and substance too. Wherefore when the thing signified or substance, is come, the sign or thing shadowing ceaseth. And, I say, the seventh day sabbath being so, as a seventh day sabbath it ceaseth also. See again Ex. xxxi. 13, 14. Eze. xx. 12, 21. Col. ii. 14.

Nor do I find that our Protestant writers, notwithstanding their reverence of the sabbath, do conclude otherwise; but that though time as to worshipping God, must needs be contained in the bowels of the moral law, as moral; yet they for good reasons forbear to affix the seventh day as *that* time there too.

They do it, I say, for good reasons; reasons drawn from the scripture; or rather, for that the scripture draws them so to conclude: yet they cast not away the morality of a sabbath of rest to the church. It is to be granted them, that time for God's worship abideth for ever, but the seventh day vanishes as a shadow and sign; because such indeed it was, as the scripture above cited declares as to the sanction thereof as a sabbath.

The law of nature then calls for time; but the God of nature assigns it, and has given power to his Son to continue SUCH time as himself shall by his eternal wisdom judge most meet for the churches of the Gentiles to solemnize worship to God by him in. Hence he is said to be 'Lord even of the sabbath day.' Mat. xii. 8.

Fifth, I find by reading God's word, that Paul by authority apostolical, takes away the sanctions of all the Jews' festivals and sabbaths.

This is manifest, for that he leaves the observation or non-observation of them, as things indifferent, to the mind and discretion of the believers. 'One man esteemeth one day above another: another esteemeth every day *alike.* Let every man be fully persuaded in his own mind.' Ro. xiv. 5.

By this last clause of the verse. 'Let every man be fully persuaded in his own mind,' he doth plainly declare, that *such* days are now stript of their sanction.‡ For none of God's laws, while they retain their sanction, are left to the will and mind of the believers, as to whether they will observe them or no. Men, I say, are not left to their liberty in such a case; for when a stamp of divine authority is upon a law, and abides, so long we are bound, not to *our* mind, but to that law: but when a thing, once sacred, has lost its sanction, then it falls, as to faith and conscience, among other *common* or indifferent things. And so the seventh day sabbath did. Again,

Sixth, Thus Paul writes to the church of Coloss. 'Let no man therefore judge you in meat, or in drink, or in respect of an holyday, or of the new moon, or of the sabbath: which are a shadow of things to come; but the body *is* of Christ.' Col. ii. 16, 17. Here also, as he serveth other holy days, he serveth the sabbath. He gives a liberty to believers to refuse the observation of it, and commands that no man should judge against them for their so doing. And as you read, the reason of his so doing is, because the body, the substance is come. Christ saith he, is the body, or that which these things were a shadow or figure of. 'The body *is* of Christ.'

---

* This spirit is not extinct. Mr. Shenston, in his 'Plea for the Seventh-day,' charges those who keep the Lord's day 'that they yield to the tide—keep their friends—riches—comforts; they believe that the seventh-day is the sabbath, and would greatly prefer keeping it, if the rulers of the nation would alter the day; they imagine that their God is some dumb idol!'† Language most unseemly and insulting — charging all who observe the Lord's day with being hypocrites and the worst of fools. Mr. S. forgot the solemn proverb, 'with what judgment ye judge ye shall be judged.'

† Edit. 1826, pp. 41, 42.

‡ This was the opinion of those great reformers, Tyndale, Calvin, and Luther; see introduction by the Editor. It was a sentiment which led to no practical evil.—Ed.

Nor hath the apostle, since he saith 'or of the sabbath' one would think, left any hole, out at which men's inventions could get: but man has sought out many; and, so, many he will use.

But again, That the apostle by this word 'sabbath' intends the seventh day sabbath, is clear; for that it is by Moses himself counted for a sign, as we have shewed: and for that none of the other sabbaths were a more clear shadow of the Lord Jesus Christ than this. For that, and that alone, is called '*the* rest of God:' in it God rested from all his works. Hence he calls it by way of eminency, 'MY sabbath, and MY holy day.' Is. lvi. 4; lviii. 13.

Yet could that rest be nothing else but typical; for God, never since the world began, really rested, but in his Son. 'This is he,' saith God, 'in whom I am well pleased.' This sabbath then, was God's rest typically, and was given to Israel as a sign of his grace towards them in Christ. Wherefore when Christ was risen, it ceased, and was no longer of obligation to bind the conscience to the observation thereof. [Or of the sabbath.] He distinctly singleth out *this* seventh day, as that which was a most noble shadow, a most exact shadow. And then puts that with the other together; saying, they are a shadow of things to come; and that Christ has answered them all. 'The body *is* of Christ.'

Seventh, No man will, I think, deny but that He. iv. 4. intends the seventh day sabbath, on which God rested from all his works; for the text doth plainly say so: yet may the observing reader easily perceive that both it, and the *rest* of Canaan also, made mention of ver. 5. were typical, as to a day made mention of vers. 7 and 8. which day he calls another. He would not afterwards have made mention of another day. If Joshua had given them rest, he would not. Now if they had not that rest in Joshua's days, be sure they had it not by Moses; for he was still before.

All the rests therefore that Moses gave them, and that Joshua gave them too, were but typical of another day, in which God would give them rest. He. iv. 9, 10. And whether the *day* to come, was Christ, or Heaven, it makes no matter: it is enough that they before did fail, as always shadows do, and that therefore mention by David is, and that afterward, made of another day. 'There remains therefore a rest to the people of God.' A rest to come, of which the seventh day in which God rested, and the land of Canaan, was a type; which rest begins in Christ *now*, and shall be consummated in glory.

And in that he saith 'There remains a rest,' referring to that of David, what is it, if it signifies not, that the other rests remain not? There remains therefore a rest, a rest prefigured by the

seventh day, and by the rest of Canaan, though they are fled and gone.

'There remains a rest;' a rest which stands not now in signs and shadows, in the seventh day, or Canaan, but in the Son of God, and his kingdom, to whom, and to which the weary are invited to come for rest. Is. xxviii. 12. Mat. xi. 20. He. iv. 11.

Yet this casts not out the Christians holiday or sabbath: for that was not ordained to be a type or shadow of things to come, but to sanctify the name of their God in, and to perform that worship to him which was also in a shadow signified by the ceremonies of the law, as the epistle to the Hebrews doth plentifully declare.

And I say again, the seventh day sabbath cannot be it, for the reasons shewed afore.

Eighth, Especially if you add to all this, that nothing of the ministration of death written and engraven in stones, is brought by Jesus, or by his apostles, into the kingdom of Christ, as a part of his instituted worship. Hence it is said of that ministration in the bowels of which this seventh day sabbath is found, that it has now NO glory; that its glory is done away, in or by Christ, and so is laid aside, the ministration of the Spirit that excels in glory, being come in the room thereof.

I will read the text to you. 'But if the ministration of death, written *and* engraven in stones, was glorious, so that the children of Israel could not stedfastly behold the face of Moses for the glory of his countenance; which *glory* was to be done away: (It was given at first with this proviso, that it should not always retain its glory, that sanction, as a ministration.) How shall not the ministration of the Spirit be rather glorious? For if the ministration of condemnation *be* glory, much more doth the ministration of righteousness exceed in glory. For even that which was made glorious had no glory in this respect, by reason of the glory that excelleth. For if that which was done away was glorious, much more that which remaineth *is* glorious.' 2 Co. iii. 7—11.

What can be more plain? The text says expressly, that this ministration doth NOT remain; yea, and insinuates, that in its first institution it was ordained with this proviso, 'It was to be done away.' Now if in its first institution upon Sinai it was thus ordained; and if by the coming in of the ministration of the spirit, this ordination is now executed; that is, if by it, and the apostle saith it, it is done away by a ministration that remains: then where is that seventh day sabbath?

Thus therefore I have discoursed upon this fourth question: And having shewed by this discourse that the old seventh day sabbath is abolished and done away, and that it has nothing to do with the churches of the Gentiles; I am next to shew what day it is that must abide as holy to the Christians, and for them to perform their New Testament church service in.

Take the question thus.

QUESTION V.

Since it is denied that the seventh day sabbath is moral, and it is found that it is not to abide as a sabbath for ever in the church, What time is to be fixed on for New Testament saints to perform together, divine worship to God by Christ in?

Upon this question hangs the stress of all, as to the subject now under consideration: but before I can speak distinctly to it, I must premise, as I have in order to my speaking to the questions before, something for the better clearing of our way—

[Therefore I remark, that] we are not now speaking of all manner of worshipping God, nor of all times in which all manner of worship is to be performed; but of that worship, which is church worship, or worship that is to be performed by the assembly of saints, when by the will of God they in all parts of his dominion assemble together to worship him; which worship hath a prefixed time allotted to, or for its performance, and without which it cannot, according to the mind of God, be done. This is the time, I say, that we are to discourse of, and not of ALL time appointed for all manner of worship.

I do not question but that worship by the godly is performed to God every day of the week; yea, and every night too, and that time is appointed or allowed of God for the performance of such worship. But this time is not fixed to the same moment or hour universally, but is left to the discretion of the believers, as their frame of spirit, or occasions, or exigencies, or temptations, or duty shall require.

We meddle then only with that time that the worship aforesaid is to be performed in; which time the law of nature as such supposes, but the God of nature chooses. And this time as to the churches of the Gentiles, we have proved is not that time which was assigned to the Jews, to wit, THAT seventh day which was imposed upon them by the ministration of death; for, as we have shewed already, that ministration indeed is done away by a better and more glorious ministration, the ministration of the spirit; which ministration surely would be much more inferior than that which has now no glory, was it defective as to this. That is, if it imposed a gospel service, but appointed not time to perform that worship in: or if notwithstanding all its commendation, it should be forced to borrow of a ministration inferior to itself; that, to wit, the time without which by no means its most solemn worship can be performed.

This then is the conclusion, that TIME to wor-

ship God in, is required by the law of nature; but that the law of nature doth, as such, fix it on the seventh day from the creation of the world, that I utterly deny, by what I have said already, and have yet to say on that behalf. Yea, I hope to make it manifest, as I have, that this seventh day is removed; that God, by the ministration of the spirit, has changed the time to another day, to wit, The first day of the week. Therefore we conclude the time is fixed for the worship of the New Testament Christians, or churches of the Gentiles, unto that day.

Now in my discourse upon this subject, I shall,

I. Touch upon those texts that are more close, yet have a divine intimation of this thing in them.

II. And then I shall come to texts more express.

FIRST, for those texts that are more close, yet have a divine intimation of this thing in them.

First, The comparison that the Holy Ghost makes between the rest of God from his works, and the rest of Christ from his, doth intimate such a thing. 'He that is entered into his rest, he also hath ceased from his own works, as God *did* from his.' He. iv. 10.

Now God rested from his works, and sanctified a day of rest to himself, as a signal of that rest, which day he also gave to his church as a day of holy rest likewise. And if Christ thus rested from his own works, and the Holy Ghost says he did thus rest, he also hath sanctified a day to himself, as that in which he hath finished his work, and given it (that day) also to his church to be an everlasting memento of his so doing, and that they should keep it holy for his sake.

And see, as the Father's work was first, so his day went before; and as the Son's work came after, so his day accordingly succeeded. The Father's day was on the seventh day from the creation, the Son's the first day following.

Nor may this be slighted, because the text says, as God finished his work, so Christ finished his; He also hath ceased from his own works as God did from his. He rested, I say, as God did; but God rested on his resting day, and therefore so did Christ. Not that he rested on the Father's resting day; for it is evident, that then he had great part of his work to do; for he had not as then got his conquest over death, but the next day he also entered into his rest, having by his rising again, finished his work, viz., made a conquest over the powers of darkness, and brought life and immortality to light through his so doing.

So then, that being the day of the rest of the Son of God, it must needs be the day of the rest of his churches also. For God gave his resting day to his church to be a sabbath; and Christ rested from his own works as God did from his, therefore he also gave the day in which he rested from his works, a sabbath to the churches, as did the Father. Not that there are TWO sabbaths at once: the Father's was imposed for a time, even until the Son's should come; yea, as I have shewed you, even in the very time of its imposing it was also ordained to be done away. Hence he saith, that ministration ' was to be done away.' 2 Co. iii. 7. Therefore we plead not for two sabbaths to be at one time, but that a succession of time was ordained to the New Testament saints, or churches of the Gentiles, to worship God in; which time is that in which the Son rested from his own works as God did from his.

Second, Hence he calls himself, The ' Lord even of the sabbath day,' as Lu. v. Mat. xii. 8. shews. Now to be a LORD, is to have dominion, dominion over a thing, and so power to alter or change it according to that power; and where is he that dares say Christ has not this absolutely! We will therefore conclude that it is granted on all hands he hath. The question then is, Whether he hath exercised that power to the demolishing or removing of the Jews' seventh day, and establishing another in its room? The which I think is easily answered, in that he did not rest from his own works therein, but chose, for his own rest, to himself another day.

Surely, had the Lord Jesus intended to have established the seventh day to the churches of the Gentiles, he would himself in the first place have rested from his own works therein; but since he passed by that day, and took no notice of it, as to the finishing of his own works, as God took notice of it when he had finished his; it remains that he fixed upon another day, even the first of the week; on which, by his rising again, and shewing himself to his disciples before his passion, he made it manifest that he had chosen, 'as Lord of the sabbath,' that day for his own rest: consequently, and for the rest of his churches, and for his worship to be solemnized in.

Third, And on THIS day some of the saints that slept arose, and began their eternal sabbath. Mat. xxvii. 52, 53. See how the Lord Jesus hath glorified *this* day! Never was such a stamp of divine honour put upon any other day, no not since the world began. ' And the graves were opened; and many bodies of the saints which slept arose, and came out of the graves after his resurrection,' &c. That is, they arose as soon as he was risen. But why was not all this done on the seventh day? No, that day was set apart that saints might adore God for the works of creation, and that saints through that might look for redemption by Christ. But now a work more glorious than that is to be done, and therefore another day is assigned for the doing of it in. A work, I say, of redemption

completed, a day therefore by itself must be assigned for this; and some of the saints to begin their eternal sabbath with God in heaven, therefore a day by itself must be appointed for this. Yea, and that this day might not want that glory that might attract the most dim-sighted Christian to a desire after the sanction of it, the resurrection of Christ, and also of those saints met together on it: yea, they both did begin their eternal rest thereon.

Fourth, The psalmist speaks of a day that the Lord Jehovah, the Son of God, has made; and saith, ' we will rejoice and be glad in it.' But what day is this? Why the day in which Christ was made the 'head of the corner,' which must be applied to the day in which he was raised from the dead, which is the first of the week.

Hence Peter saith to the Jews, when he treateth of Christ before them, and particularly of his resurrection. ' This is the stone which WAS set at nought of you builders, which IS become the head of the corner.' He *was* set at nought by them, the whole course of his ministry unto his death, and was made the head of the corner by God, on *that* day he rose from the dead. This day therefore is the day that the Lord Jehovah has made a day of rejoicing to the church of Christ, and we will rejoice and be glad in it. Ps. cxviii. 24.

For can it be imagined. that the Spirit by the prophet should thus signalise this day for nothing; saying, ' This *is* the day *which* the Lord hath made;' to no purpose? Yes, you may say, for the resurrection of his son.

But I add, that that is not all, it is a day that the Lord has both made for that, and that we might 'rejoice and be glad in it.'* Rejoice, that is before the Lord while solemn divine worship is performed on it, by all the people that shall partake of the redemption accomplished then.

Fifth, God *the Father* again leaves such another stamp of divine note and honour upon this day as he never before did leave upon any; where he saith to our Lord, ' Thou art my Son, this day have I begotten thee.' Ac. xiii. 33. Still, I say, having respect to the first day of the week; for that, and no other, is the day here intended by the apostle. This day, saith God, is the day: ' And as concerning that he raised him up from the dead, *now* no more to return to corruption, he said on this wise, I will give thee the sure mercies of David. Wherefore he saith also in another *Psalm,* Thou shalt not suffer thine Holy One to see corruption.' Wherefore the day in which God did this work, is greater than that in which he finished the work of creation; for his making of the creation saved it not from corruption, but now he hath

---

* Psal. cxviii. 24.

done a work which corruption cannot touch, wherefore the day on which he did this, has this note from his own mouth, THIS day, as a day that doth transcend.

And, as I said, this day is the first of the week; for it was on that day that God begat his beloved Son from the dead. This first day of the week therefore, on it God found that pleasure which he found not in the seventh day from the world's creation, for that in it his Son did live again to him.

Now shall not Christians, when they do read that God saith, ' This day,' and that too with reference to a work done on it by him, so full of delight to him, and so full of life and heaven to them, set also a remark upon it, saying, This was the day of God's pleasure, for that his Son did rise thereon, and shall it not be the day of my delight in him !

This is the day on which his Son was both begotten and born, and became the first fruits to God of them that sleep; yea, and in which also he was made by him the chief, and head of the corner; and shall not we rejoice in it ? Ac. xiii. 33. He. i. 5. Col. i. 18. Re. i. 5.

Shall kings, and princes, and great men set a remark upon the day of their birth and coronation, and expect that both subjects and servants should do them high honour on that day, and shall the day in which Christ was both begotten and born, be a day contemned by Christians! And his name not be but of a common regard on that day?

I say again, shall God, as with his finger, point, and that in the face of the world, at this day, saying, ' Thou art my Son, this day,' &c., and shall not Christians fear, and awake from their employments, to worship the Lord on this day!

If God remembers it, well may I! If God says, and that with all gladness of heart, ' Thou art my Son, this day have I begotten thee!' may not! ought not I also to set this day apart to sing the songs of my redemption in?

THIS day my redemption was finished.

This day my dear Jesus revived.

This day he was declared to be the Son of God with power.

Yea this is the day in which the Lord Jesus finished a greater work than ever yet was done in the world; yea, a work in which the Father himself was more delighted than he was in making of heaven and earth. And shall darkness and the shadow of death stain this day! Or shall a cloud dwell on this day! Shall God regard this day from above! And shall not his light shine upon this day! What shall be done to them that curse this day, and would not that the stars should give their light thereon. This day! After this day was come, God never, that we read of, made mention with delight, of the old seventh day sabbath more.

Sixth, Nor is that altogether to be slighted, when he saith, ' When he bringeth in the first-begotten into the world, Let all the angels of God worship him.' To wit, at that very time and day. He. i. 6.

I know not what our expositors say of this text, but to me it seems to be meant of his resurrection from the dead; both because the apostle is speaking of that, ver. 5, and closes that argument with this text, ' Thou art my Son, this day have I begotten thee? And again, I will be to him a Father, and he shall be to me a Son ? And again, when he bringeth in the first-begotten into the world, he saith, And let all the angels of God worship him.'

So then, for God's bringing of his first-begotten now into the world, was by his raising him again from the dead after they by crucifying of him had turned him out of the same.

Thus then God brought him into the world, never by them to be hurried out of it again. For Christ being now raised from the dead, dies no more; death hath no more dominion over him.

Now, saith the text, when he bringeth him thus into the world, he requireth that worship be done unto HIM. When? That very day, and that by all the angels of God. And if by *all*, then ministers are not excluded; and if not ministers, then not churches; for what is said to the angels, is said to the church itself. Rev. ii. 1—7, 8, 11, 12, 17, 18, 29; iii. 1, 6, 7, 13, 14, and 22.

So then, if the question be asked, when they must worship him: the answer is, when he brought him into the world, which was on the first day of the week; for then he bringeth him again from the dead, and gave the whole world and the government thereof into his holy hand. This text therefore is of weight as to what we have now under consideration, to wit, that the first day of the week, the day in which God brought his first-begotten into the world, should be the day of worshipping him by all the angels of God.

Seventh, Hence this day is called 'the Lord's day,' as John saith, ' I was in the Spirit on the Lord's day,' the day in which Jesus rose from the dead. Re. i. 10.

' The Lord's day.' Every day, say some, is the Lord's day. Indeed this for discourse sake may be granted; but strictly, no day can so properly be called *the* Lord's day, as this first day of the week; for that no day of the week or of the year has those badges of the Lord's glory upon it, nor such divine grace put upon it as has the first day of the week.

This we have already made appear in part, and shall make appear much more before we have done therewith.

There is nothing, as I know of, that bears this title but the Lord's supper, and this day. 1 Co. xi. 20. Re. i. 10. And since Christians count it an abuse to allegorize the first, let them also be ashamed to fantasticalize the last. The Lord's day is doubtless the day in which he rose from the dead. To be sure it is not the old seventh day; for from the day that he arose, to the end of the Bible, we find not that he did hang so much as one twist of glory upon that; but this day is beautified with glory upon glory, and that both by the Father and the Son; by the prophets and those that were raised from the dead thereon; therefore this day must be more than the rest.

But we are as yet but upon divine intimations, drawn from such texts which, if candidly considered, do very much smile upon this great truth; namely, that the first day of the week is to be accounted the Christian sabbath, or holy day for divine worship in the churches of the saints. And SECOND, Now I come to the texts that are more express.

Then *First,* This was the day in the which he did use to shew himself to his people, and to congregate with them after he rose from the dead. On the first first-day, even on the day on which he rose from the dead, he visited his people, both when together and apart, over, and over, and over, as both Luke and John do testify. Lu. xxiv. Jn. xx. And preached such sermons of his resurrection, and gave unto them; yea, and gave them such demonstration of the truth of all, as was never given them from the foundation of the world. Shewing, he shewed them his risen body; opening, he opened their understandings; and dissipating, he so scattered their unbelief on THIS day, as he never had done before. And this continued one way or another even from before day until the evening.

Second, On the next first day following the church was within again; that is, congregated to wait upon their Lord. And John so relates the matter, as to give us to understand that they were not so assembled together again till then. 'After eight days,' saith he, 'again his disciples were within,' clearly concluding, that they were not so on the days that were between, no not on the old seventh day.

Now why should the Holy Ghost thus precisely speak of their assembling together upon the first day, if not to confirm us in this, that the Lord had chosen that day for the *new* sabbath of his church? Surely the Apostles knew what they did in their meeting together upon that day; yea, and the Lord Jesus also; for that he used so to visit them when so assembled, made his practice a law unto them. For practice is enough for us New Testament saints, especially when the Lord Jesus himself is in the head of that practice, and that after he rose from the dead.

Perhaps some may stumble at the word 'after,' after eight days; but the meaning is, at the con-

clusion of the eighth day, or when they had spent in a manner the whole of their sabbath in waiting upon their Lord, then in comes their Lord, and finisheth that their day's service to him with confirming of Thomas's faith, and by letting drop other most heavenly treasure among them. Christ said, he must lie three days and three nights in the heart of the earth, yet it is evident, that he rose the third day. 1 Co. xv. 4.

We must take then a part for the whole, and conclude, that from the time that the Lord Jesus rose from the dead, to the time that he shewed his hands and his side to Thomas, eight days were almost expired; that is, he had sanctified unto them two first days, and had accepted that service they had performed to him therein, as he testified by giving of them so blessed a farewell at the conclusion of both those days.

Hence now we conclude, that this was the custom of the church at this day, to wit, upon the first day of the week to meet together, and to wait upon their Lord therein. For the Holy Ghost counts it needless to make a continued repetition of things; it is enough therefore if we have now and then mention made thereof.

Obj. But Christ shewed himself alive to them at other times also, as in Jn. xxi. &c.

Ans. The names of all those days in which he so did are obliterated and blotted out, that they might not be idolized; for Christ did not set them apart for worship, but *this* day, the first day of the week, by its name is kept alive in the church, the Holy Ghost surely signifying thus much, that how hidden soever other days were, Christ would have *his* day, the *first day* had in everlasting remembrance among saints.

Churches also meet together now on the week days, and have the presence of Christ with them too in their employments; but that takes not off from them the sanction of the first day of the week, no more than it would take away the sanction of the old seventh day, had it still continued holy to them: wherefore this is no let or objection to hinder our sanctifying of the first day of the week to our God. But,

Third, Add to this, that upon Pentecost, which was the first day of the week, mention is made of their being together again: for Pentecost was always the morrow after the sabbath, the old seventh day sabbath. Upon *this* day, I say, the Holy Ghost saith, they were again 'with one accord together in one place.'

But oh! the glory that then attended them, by the presence of the Holy Ghost among them: never was such a thing done as was done on that first day until then. We will read the text, 'And when the day of Pentecost was fully come, they were all with one accord in one place. And suddenly there came a sound from heaven as of a rushing mighty wind, and it filled all the house where they were sitting. And there appeared unto them cloven tongues like as of fire, and it sat upon each of them. And they were all filled with the Holy Ghost.' Ac. ii. 1—4.

Here is a first day glorified! Here's a countenance given to the day of their Christian assembling. But we will note a few things upon it.

1. The church was now, as on other first days, all with one accord in one place. We read not that they came together by virtue of any precedent revelation, nor by accident, but contrariwise by agreement, they were together ' with one accord,' or by appointment, in pursuance of their duty, setting apart *that* day, as they had done the first days afore, to the holy service of their blessed Lord and Saviour Jesus Christ

2. We read that this meeting of theirs was not begun on the old sabbath, but when Pentecost was *fully* come: the Holy Ghost intimating, that they had left now, and began to leave, the seventh day sabbath to the unbelieving Jews.

3. Nor did the Holy Ghost come down upon them till every moment of the old sabbath was past, Pentecost, as was said, was FULLY come first. ' And when the day of Pentecost was fully come, they were all with one accord in one place.' And then, &c.

And why was not this done on the seventh day sabbath? But, possibly, to shew, that the ministration of death and condemnation was not that, by or through which Christ the Lord would communicate so good a gift unto his churches. Ga. iii. 1—5.

This gift must be referred to the Lord's day, the first day of the week, to fulfil the scripture, and to sanctify yet farther this holy day unto the use of all New Testament churches of the saints. For since on the first day of the week our Lord did rise from the dead, and by his special presence, I mean his personal, did accompany his church therein, and so preach as he did, his holy truths unto them, it was most meet that they on the same day also should receive the first fruits of their eternal life most gloriously.

And, I say again, since from the resurrection of Christ to this day, the church then did receive upon the first day, but as we read, upon no other, such glorious things as we have mentioned, it is enough to beget in the hearts of them that love the Son of God, a high esteem of the first day of the week. But how much more, when there shall be joined to these, proof that it was the custom of the first gospel church, the church of Christ at Jerusalem, after our Lord was risen, to assemble together to wait upon God on the first day of the week with their Lord as leader.

To say little more to this head, but only to repeat what is written of this day of old, to wit, that it should be proclaimed the selfsame day, to wit, the morrow after the sabbath, which is the first day of the week, ' *that* it may be an holy convocation unto you; ye shall do no servile work *therein: it shall be* a statute for ever in all your dwellings.' Le. xxiii. 21.

This ceremony was about the sheaf that was to be waved, and bread of first fruits, which was a type of Christ; for he is unto God 'the first fruits of them that slept.' 1 Co. xv. 20.

This sheaf, or bread, must not be waved on the old seventh day, but on the morrow after, which is the first day of the week, the day in which Christ rose from the dead, and waved himself as the first fruits of the elect unto God. Now from this day they were to count seven sabbaths complete, and on the morrow after the seventh sabbath, which was the first day of the week again; and this Pentecost upon which we now are, then they were to have a new meat offering, with meat offerings and drink offerings, &c.

And on the selfsame day they were to proclaim that that first day should be a holy convocation unto them. The which the apostles did, and grounded that their proclamation so on the resurrection of Jesus Christ, not on ceremonies, that at the same day they brought three thousand souls to God. Ac. ii. 41.

Now what another signal [applause] was here put upon the first day of the week! The day in which our Lord rose from the dead, assembled with his disciples, poured out so abundantly of the Spirit, and gathered even by the first draught that his fishermen made by the gospel, such a number of souls to God.

Thus then they proclaimed, and thus they gathered sinners on the first first-day that they preached; for though they had assembled together over and over with their Lord before therein, yet they began not jointly to preach until this first day Pentecost.

Now, after this the apostles to the churches did never make mention of a seventh day sabbath. For as the wave sheaf and the bread of first fruits were a figure of the Lord Jesus, and the waving, of his life from the dead: so that morrow after the sabbath on which the Jews waved their sheaf, was a figure of *that* on which our Lord did rise; consequently, when their morrow after the sabbath ceased, *our* morrow after that began, and so has continued a blessed morrow after their sabbath, as a holy sabbath to Christians from that time ever since.

Fourth, We come yet more close to the custom of churches; I mean, to the custom of the churches of the Gentiles; for as yet we have spoken but of the practice of the church of God which was at Jerusalem; only we will add, that the customs that were laudable and binding with the church at Jerusalem, were with reverence to be imitated by the churches of the Gentiles; for there was but one law of Christ for them both to worship by.

Now then, to come to the point, to wit, that it was the custom of the churches of the Gentiles, on the first day of the week, but upon no other that we read of,* to come together to perform divine worship to their Lord.

Hence it is said ' And upon the first *day* of the week, when the disciples came together to break bread,' &c. Ac. xx. 7. This is a text, that as to matter of fact cannot be contradicted by any, for the text saith plainly they did so, the disciples then came together to break bread, the disciples among the Gentiles, did so.

Thus you see that the solemnizing of a first day to holy uses was not limited to, though first preached by the church that was at Jerusalem. The church at Jerusalem was the mother church, and not that at Rome, as some falsely imagine; for from this church went out the law and the holy word of God to the Gentiles. Wherefore it must be supposed that this meeting of the Gentiles on the first day of the week to break bread, came to them by holy tradition† from the church at Jerusalem, since they were the first that kept the first day as holy unto the Lord their God.

And indeed, they had the best advantage to do it; for they had their Lord in the head of them to back them to it by his presence and preaching thereon.

But we will a little comment upon the text. ' Upon the first *day* of the week.' Thus you see the day is nominated, and so is kept alive among the churches. For in that the day is nominated on which this religious exercise was performed, it is to be supposed that the Holy Ghost would have it live, and be taken notice of by the churches that succeed.

It also may be nominated to shew, that both the church at Jerusalem, and those of the Gentiles did harmonize in their sabbath, jointly concluding to solemnize worship on a [the same] day. And

* ' That we read of' in the New Testament; for this is our sole authority in all inquiries as to a Christian's faith and practice.—ED.

† ' Tradition' is a communication without writing, and when made orally by some apostle or messenger from the first church at Jerusalem, and the message so obeyed as to be *left upon record* by the Holy Ghost, it has the same authority as if it had been commanded in an epistle. It has nothing to do with the vain traditions of the fathers (so called), which were not heard of until after the inspired volume was completed and closed. Any subsequent commands are censures upon God's omniscience, and are deserving only of contempt.—ED.

then again to shew, that they all had left the old sabbath to the unbelievers, and jointly chose to sanctify the day of the rising of their Lord, to this work.

They ' came together to break bread,' to partake of the supper of the Lord. And what day so fit as the Lord's day for this? This was to be the work of that day, to wit, to solemnize that ordinance among themselves, adjoining other solemn worship thereto, to fill up the day, as the following part of the verse shews. This day therefore was designed for this work, the *whole* day, for the text declares it. The first day of the week was set by them apart for this work.

' Upon THE first day;' not upon A first day, or upon *one* first day, or upon *such* a first day; for had he said so, we had had from thence not so strong an argument for our purpose: but when he saith, ' upon the first *day* of the week ' they did it, he insinuates, that it was their custom. [It was] also upon one of these, [that] Paul being among them, preached unto them, ready to depart on the morrow. Upon the first day: what, or which first day of this, or that, of the third or fourth week of the month? No, but upon the first day, every first day; for so the text admits us to judge.

' Upon the first *day* of the week, WHEN the disciples came together,' supposes a custom *when*, or as they were wont to come together to perform such service among themselves to God: *then* Paul preached unto them, &c.

It is a text also that supposes an agreement among themselves as to this thing. They came together then *to* break bread; they had appointed to do it then, for that then was the day of their Lord's resurrection, and that in which he himself congregated after he revived, with the first gospel church, the church at Jerusalem.

Thus you see, that breaking of bread, was the work, the work that by general consent was agreed to be by the churches of the Gentiles performed upon the first day of the week. I say, by the churches; for I doubt not but that the practice here, was also the practice of the rest of the Gentile churches, even as it had been before the practice of the church at Jerusalem.

For this practice now did become universal, and so this text implies; for he speaks here universally of the practice of all disciples as such, though he limits Paul preaching to that church with whom he at present personally was. Upon the first day of the week, ' when the disciples came together to break bread,' Paul being at that time at Troas preached to them on that day.

Thus then you see how the Gentile churches did use to break bread, not on the old sabbath, but on the first day of the week. And, I say, they had it from the church at Jerusalem; where the apostles were first seated, and beheld the way of their Lord with their eyes.

Now, I say, since we have so ample an example, not only of the church at Jerusalem, but also of the churches of the Gentiles, for the keeping of the first day to the Lord, and that as countenanced by Christ and his apostles, we should not be afraid to tread in their steps, for their practice is the same with law and commandmnet. But,

Fifth, We will add to this another text. 'Now (saith Paul) concerning the collection for the saints, as I have given order to the churches of Galatia, even so do ye. Upon the first *day* of the week let every one of you lay by him in store, as *God* hath prospered him, that there be no gatherings when I come.' 1 Cor. xvi. 1, 2.

This text some have greatly sought to evade, counting the duty here, on this day to be done, a duty too inferior for the sanction of an old seventh day sabbath; when yet to show mercy to an ass on the old sabbath, was a work which our Lord no ways condemns. Lu. xiii. 15; xiv. 5.

But to pursue our design, we have a duty enjoined, and that of no inferior sort. If charity be indeed as it is, the very bond of perfectness: and if without it all our doings, yea and sufferings too, are not worthy so much as a rush, 1 Co. xiii. Col. iii. 14. we have here a duty, I say, that a seventh day sabbath, when in force, was not too big for it to be performed in.

The work now to be done, was, as you see, to bestow their charity upon the poor; yea, to provide for time to come. And I say, it must be collected upon the first day of the week. Upon THE first day; not A first day, as signifying one or two, but upon THE first day, even *every* first day; for so your ancient Bibles have it;* also our later must be so understood, or else Paul had left them to whom he did write, utterly at a loss. For if he intended not every first day, and yet did not specify a particular one, it could hardly even have been understood which first day he meant. But we need not stand upon this. This work was a work for A first-day, for EVERY first day of the week.

Note again that we have this duty here commanded and enforced by an apostolical order: 'I have given order,' saith Paul, for this; and his

orders, as he saith in another place, 'are the commandments of the Lord.' You have it in the same epistle, ch. xiv. 37.

Whence it follows, that there was given even by the apostles themselves, a holy respect to the first day of the week above all the days of the week; yea, or of the year besides.

Further, I find also by this text, that this order is universal. I have, saith he, given this order not only to you, but to the churches of Galatia. Consequently to all other that were concerned in this collection. 2 Co. viii.; ix. &c.

Now this, whatever others may think, puts yet more glory upon the first day of the week. For in that all the churches are commanded, as to make their collections, so to make them on *this* day: what is it, but that this day, by reason of the sanction that Christ put upon it, was of virtue to sanctify the offering through and by Christ Jesus, as the altar and temple afore did sanctify the gift and gold that was, and was offered on them. The proverb is, 'The better day, the better deed.' And I believe, that things done on the Lord's day, are better done, than on other days of the week, in his worship.

Obj. But yet, say some, here are no orders to keep this first day holy to the Lord.

Ans. 1. That is supplied; for that by this very text this day is appointed, above all the days of the week, to do this holy duty in.

2. You must understand that this order is but additional, and now enjoined to fill up that which was begun as to holy exercise of religious worship by the churches long before.

3. The universality of the duty being enjoined to this day, supposes that this day was universally kept by the churches as holy already.

4. And let him that scrupleth this, shew me, if he can, that God by the mouth of his apostles did ever command that all the churches should be confined to this or that duty on such a day, and yet put no sanction upon that day; or that he has commanded that this work should be done on the first day of the week, and yet has reserved other church ordinances as a public solemnization of worship to him, to be done of another day, as of a day more fit, more holy.

5. If charity, if a general collection for the saints in the churches is commanded on this day, and on no other day but this day; for church collection is commanded on no other, there must be a reason for it: and if that reason had not respect to the sanction of the day, I know not why the duty should be so strictly confined to it.

6. But for the apostle now to give with this a particular command to the churches to sanctify that day as holy unto the Lord, had been utterly superfluous; for that they already, and that by

---

* The New Testament by Whittingham, 1557; the Genevan or Puritan Bible by Knox, Coverdale, and others, 1560; and the New Testament revised by Tomson, 1576, very frequently reprinted, and very favourite translations among our puritan and pilgrim forefathers in the faith. The marginal note to the Puritan Bible, in Acts xx. 7, 'first day,' is, 'which we call Sunday. Of this place, and also of the 1 Cor. xvi. 2, we gather that the Christians used to have their solemn assemblies this day, laying aside the ceremony of the Jewish sabbath.'—ED.

the countenance of their Lord, and his church at Jerusalem, had done.

Before now, I say, it was become a custom, as by what hath been said already is manifest: wherefore what need that their so solemn a practice be imposed again upon the brethren? An intimation now of a continued respect thereto, by the very naming of the day, is enough to keep the sanctity thereof on foot in the churches. How much more then, when the Lord is still adding holy duty to holy duty, to be performed upon that day. So then, in that the apostle writes to the churches to do this holy duty on the first day of the week, he puts them in mind of the sanction of the day, and insinuates, that he would still have them have a due respect thereto.

Quest. But is there yet another reason why this holy duty should, in special as it is, be commanded to be performed on the first day of the week?

Ans. 1. Yes: for that now the churches were come together in their respective places, the better to agree about collections, and to gather them. You know church worship is a duty, so long as we are in the world, and so long also is this of making collections for the saints. And for as much as the apostle speaks here, as I have hinted afore, of a church collection, when is it more fit to be done, than when the church is come together upon the first day of the week to worship God?

2. This part of worship is most comely to be done upon the first day of the week, and that at the close of that day's work. For thereby the church shows, not only her thankfulness to God for a sabbath day's mercy, but also returneth him, by giving to the poor, that sacrifice for their benefit that is most behoveful to make manifest their professed subjection to Christ. Pr. xix. 17. 2 Co. ix. 12—15. It is therefore necessary, that this work be done on the first day of the week, for a comely close of the worship that we perform to the Lord our God on that day.

3. On the first day of the week, when the church is performing of holy worship unto God, then that of collection for the saints is most meet to be performed; because then, in all likelihood, our hearts will be most warm with the divine presence; consequently most open and free to contribute to the necessity of the saints. You know, that a man when his heart is open, is taken with some excellent thing; then, if at all, it is most free to do something for the promoting thereof.

Why, waiting upon God in the way of his appointments, opens, and makes free, the heart to the poor: and because the first day of the week was it in which now such solemn service to him was done, therefore also the apostle commanded, that upon the same day also, as on a day most fit,

this duty of collecting for the poor should be done. 'For God loveth a cheerful giver.' 2 Co. ix. 6, 7.

Wherefore the apostle by this, takes the churches as it were at the advantage, and as we say, [strikes] while the iron is hot, to the intent he might, what in him lay, make their collections, not sparing nor of a grudging mind, but to flow from cheerfulness. And the first day of the week, though its institution be set aside, doth most naturally tend to this; because it is the day, the only day, on which we received such blessings from God. Ac. iii. 26.

This is the day on which, at first, it rained manna all day long from heaven upon the new testament church, and so continues to do this day. Oh! the resurrection of Christ, which was on this day, and the riches that we receive thereby. Though it should be, and is, I hope thought on every day; yet when the first of the week is *fully* come! Then *to*-day! This day! This is the day to be warmed; this day he was begotten from the dead.

The thought of this, will do much with an honest mind: this is the day, I say, that the first saints did find, and that after saints do find the blessings of God come down upon them; and therefore this is the day here commanded to be set apart for holy duties.

And although what I have said may be but little set by of some, yet, for a closing word as to this, I do think, could but half so much be produced from the day Christ rose from the dead quite down [to the end of revelation], for the sanction of a seventh day sabbath in the churches of the Gentiles, it would much sway with me. But the truth is, neither doth the apostle Paul, nor any of his fellows, so much as once speak one word to the churches that shows the least regard, as to conscience to God, of a seventh day sabbath more. No, the first day, the first day, the first day, is now all the cry in the churches by the apostles, for the performing church worship in to God. Christ began it on THAT day: then the Holy Ghost seconded it on that day: then the churches practised it on that day. And to conclude; the apostle by the command now under consideration, continues the sanction of that day to the churches to the end of the world.

But as to the old seventh day sabbath, as hath been said afore in this treatise, Paul, who is the apostle of the Gentiles, has so taken away that whole ministration in the bowels of which it is; yea, and has so stript it of its old testament grandeur, both by terms and arguments, that it is strange to me it should by any be still kept up in the churches; specially, since the same apostle, and that at the same time, has put a better ministration in its place. 2 Co. iii.

But when the consciences of good men are captivated with an error, none can stop them from a prosecution thereof, as if were itself of the best of truths.

Obj. But Paul preached frequently on the old sabbath, and that after the resurrection of Christ.

Ans. To the unbelieving Jews and their proselytes, I grant he did. But we read not that he did it to any new testament church on that day: nor did he celebrate the instituted worship of Christ in the churches on that day. For Paul, who had before cast out the ministration of death, as that which had no glory, would not now take thereof any part for new testament instituted worship; for he knew that that would veil the heart, and blind the mind from that, which yet instituted worship was ordained to discover.

He preached then on the seventh day sabbath, of a divine and crafty love to the salvation of the unbelieving Jews.

I say, he preached now on that day to them and their proselytes, because that day was theirs by their estimation. He did it, I say, of great love to their souls, that if possible, he might save some of them.

Wherefore, if you observe, you shall still find, that where it is said that he preached on that day, it was to that people, not to the churches of Christ. See Ac. ix. 20; xiii. 14—16; xvi. 13; xvii. 1—3; xviii. 4.

Thus, though he had put away the sanction of that day as to himself, and had left the Christians that were weak to their liberty as to conscience to it, yet he takes occasion upon it to preach to the Jews that still were wedded to it, the faith, that they might be saved by grace.

Paul did also many other things that were Jewish and ceremonial, for which he had, as then, no conscience at all, as to any sanction that he believed was in them.

As his circumcising of Timothy. Ac. xvi. 1—3.

His shaving of his head. Ac. xviii. 18.

His submitting to Jewish purifications. Ac. xxi. 24—26.

His acknowledging of himself a Pharisee. ch. xxiii 6.

His implicitly owning of Ananias for high priest after Christ was risen from the dead. Ac. xxiii. 1—5.

He tells us also that, 'unto the Jews he became as a Jew' that he might save the Jew. And 'without law,' to them that were without law, that also he might gain them. Yea, he became, as he saith, 'all things to all *men*,' that he might gain the more, as it is 1 Co. ix. 19—23.

But these things, as I said, he did not of conscience to the things; for he knew that their sanction was gone. Nor would he suffer them to be imposed upon the churches directly or indirectly; no, not by Peter himself. Ga. ii. 11.

Were I in Turkey with a church of Jesus Christ, I would keep the first day of the week to God, and for the edification of his people: and would also preach the word to the infidels on their sabbath day, which is our Friday; and be glad too, if I might have such opportunity to try to persuade them to a love of their own salvation.

Obj. But if the seventh day sabbath is, as you say, to be laid aside by the churches of the Gentiles, why doth Christ say to his, 'Pray ye that your flight be not in the winter, neither on the sabbath day?' For, say some, by this saying it appears, that the old seventh day sabbath, as you have called it, will as to the sanction of it, abide in force after Christ is ascended into heaven.

Ans. I say first, these words were spoken to the Jewish Christians, not to the Gentile churches. And the reason of this first hint, you will see clearer afterwards.

The Jews had several sabbaths; as, their seventh day sabbath, their monthly sabbaths, their sabbath of years, and their jubilee. Le. xxv.

Now if he means their ordinary sabbaths, or that called the seventh day sabbath, why doth he join the winter thereto? for in that he joineth the winter with *that* sabbath that he exhorteth them to pray their flight might not be in, it should seem that he meaneth rather their sabbath of years, or their jubilee, which did better answer one to another than one day and a winter could.

And I say again, that Christ should suppose that their flight should, or might last some considerable part of a winter, and yet that then they should have their rest on those seventh day sabbaths, is a little beside my reason, if it be considered again, that the Gentiles before whom they were then to fly, were enemies to their sabbath, and consequently would take opportunity at their sabbaths to afflict them so much the more. Wherefore, I would that they who plead for a continuation of the seventh day sabbath from this text, would both better consider it, and the incoherence that seems to be betwixt such a sabbath and a winter.

But again, were it granted that it is the seventh day sabbath that Christ here intendeth; yet, since as we have proved, the sanction before this was taken away; I mean before this flight should be, he did not press them to pray thus because by any law of heaven they should then be commanded to keep it holy; but because some would, through their weakness, have conscience of it till then. And such would, if their flight should happen thereon, be as much grieved and perplexed, as if it yet stood obligatory to them by a law.

This seems to have some truth in it, because among the Jews that believed, there continued a long time many that were wedded yet to the law, to the ceremonial part thereof, and were not so clearly evangelized as the churches of the Gentiles were. 'Thou seest brother,' said James to Paul, 'how many thousands of Jews there are which believe; and they are all zealous of the law.' Ac. xxi. 20; xv. 5.

Of these, and such weak unbelieving Jews, perhaps Christ speaks, when he gives this exhortation to them to pray thus; whose consciences he knew would be weak, and being so, would bind when they were entangled with an error, as fast as if it bound by a law indeed.

Again, though the seventh day sabbath and ceremonies lost their sanction at the resurrection of Christ, yet they retained some kind of being in the church of the Jews, until the desolation spoken of by Daniel should be.

Hence it is said, that then the oblation and sacrifices shall cease. Da. ix. 27. And hence it is, that Jerusalem and the temple are still called the holy place, even until this flight should be. Mat. xxiv. 15.

Now if Jerusalem and the temple are still called holy, even after the body and substance, of which they were shadows, were come; then no marvel though some to that day that believed were entangled therewith, &c. For it may very well be supposed that all conscience of them would not be quite taken away, until all reason for that conscience should be taken away also. But when Jerusalem, and the temple, and the Jews' worship, by the Gentiles was quite extinct by ruins, then in reason that conscience did cease. And it seems by some texts, that all conscience to them was not taken away till then.

Quest. But what kind of being had the seventh day sabbath, and other Jewish rites and ceremonies, that by Christ's resurrection were taken away?

Ans. These things had a virtual and a nominal being. As to their virtual being, that died that day Christ did rise from the dead, they being crucified with him on the cross. Col. ii.

But now, when the virtual being was gone, they still with the weak retained their name, among many of the Jews that believed, until the abomination that maketh desolate stood in the holy place: for in Paul's time they were, as to that, but ready to vanish away.

Now, I say, they still retaining their nominal grandeur, though not by virtue of a law, they could not, till time and dispensation came, be swept out of the way. We will make what hath been said, as to this, out by a familiar similitude.

There is a lord or great man dies; now being dead, he has lost his virtual life. He has now no relation to a wife, to children, virtually; yet his name still abides, and that in that family, to which otherwise he is dead. Wherefore they embalm him, and also keep him above ground for many days. Yea, he is still reverenced by those of the family, and that in several respects. Nor doth

any thing but time and dispensation wear this name away.

Thus then the Old Testament signs and shadows went off the stage in the church of Christ among the Jews. They lost their virtue and signification when Christ nailed them to his cross. Col. ii. But as to their name, and the grandeur that attended that, it continued with many that were weak, and vanished not, but when the abomination that made them desolate came.

The sum then and conclusion of the matter is this; the seventh day sabbath lost its glory when that ministration in which it was, lost its: But yet the name thereof might abide a long time with the Jewish legal Christians, and so might become obligatory still, though not by the law, to their conscience, even as circumcision and other ceremonies did: and to them it would be as grievous to fly on that day, as if by law it was still in force.

For, I say, to a weak conscience, that law which has lost its life, may yet through their ignorance, be as binding as if it stood still upon the authority of God.

Things then become obligatory these two ways. (1.) By an institution of God. (2.) By the overruling power of a man's misinformed conscience. And although by virtue of an institution divine worship is acceptable to God by Christ, yet conscience will make that a man shall have but little ease if such rules and dictates as it imposes be not observed by him.

This is my answer, upon a supposition that the seventh day sabbath is in this text intended: and the answer, I think, stands firm and good.

Also, there remains, notwithstanding this objection, no divine sanction in or upon the old seventh day sabbath.

Some indeed will urge, that Christ here meant the first day of the week, which here he puts under the term of sabbath. But this is foreign to me, so I waive it till I receive more satisfaction in the thing.

Quest. But if indeed the first day of the week be the new christian sabbath, why is there no more spoken of its institution in the testament of Christ?

Ans. No more! What need is there of more than enough! Yea, there is a great deal found in the testament of the Lord Jesus to prove its authority divine.

(1.) For we have shewed from sundry scriptures, that from the very day our Lord did rise from the dead, the church at Jerusalem, in which the the twelve apostles were, did meet together on that day, and had the Lord himself for their preacher, while they were auditors; and thus the day began.

(2.) We have shewed that the Holy Ghost, the third person in the Trinity, did second this of

Christ, in coming down from heaven upon this day to manage the apostles in their preaching; and in that very day so managed them in that work, that by his help they then did bring three thousand souls to God.

(3.) We have shewed also, that after this the gentile churches did solemnize this day for holy worship, and that they had from Paul both countenance and order so to do.

And now I will add, that more need not be spoken: for the practice of the first church, with their Lord in the head of them to manage them in that practice, is as good as many commands. What then shall we say, when we see a first practice turned into holy custom?

I say, moreover, that though a seventh day sabbath is not natural to man as man, yet our christian holy day is natural to us as saints, if our consciences are not clogged before with some old fables, or Jewish customs.

But if an old religion shall get footing and rooting in us, though the grounds thereof be vanished away, yet the man concerned will be hard put to it, should he be saved, to get clear of his clouds, and devote himself to that service of God which is of his own prescribing.

Luther himself, though he saw many things were without ground which he had received for truth, had yet work hard enough, as himself intimates, to get his conscience clear from all those roots and strings of inbred error.

But, I say, to an untainted and well bred Christian, we have good measure, shaken together, and running over, for our christian Lord's day. And I say again, that the first day of the week, and the spirit of such a Christian, suit one another as nature suiteth nature; for there is as it were a natural instinct in Christians, as such, when they understand what in a first day was brought forth, to fall in therewith to keep it holy to their Lord.

1. The first day of the week! Why it was the day of our life. 'After two days he will revive us,' and in the third day 'we shall live in his sight.' 'After two days' there is the Jews' preparation, and seventh day sabbath, quite passed over; and in the third day, that is the first day of the week, which is the day our Lord did rise from the dead, we began to live by him in the sight of God. Ho. vi. 2. Jn. xx. i. 1 Co. xv. 4.

2. The first day of the week! That is the day in which, as I hinted before, our Lord was wont to preach to his disciples after he rose from the dead; in which also he did use to shew them his hands and his feet. Lu. xxiv. 38, 39. Jn. xx. 25. To the end they might be confirmed in the truth of his victory over death and the grave for them. The day in which he made himself known to them in breaking bread. The day in which he so plenti-

fully poured out the Holy Ghost upon them. The day in which the church, both at Jerusalem and those of the Gentiles, did use to perform to God divine worship: all which has before been sufficiently proved. And shall we not imitate our Lord, nor the church that was immediately acted* by him in this, and the churches their fellows? Shall, I say, the Lord Jesus do all this in his church, and they together with him! Shall the churches of the Gentiles also fall in with their Lord and with their mother at Jerusalem herein! And again, shall all this be so punctually committed to sacred story, with the day in which these things were done, under denomination, over and over, saying, These things were done on the first day, on the first day, on the first day of the week, while all other days are, as to name, buried in everlasting oblivion! And shall we not take that notice thereof as to follow the Lord Jesus and the churches herein? Oh stupidity!

3. This day of the week! They that make but observation of what the Lord did of old, to a many sinners, and with his churches on this day, must needs conclude, that in this day the treasures of heaven were broken up, and the richest things therein communicated to his church. Shall the children of this world be, as to this also, wiser in their generations than the children of light, and former saints, upon whose shoulders we pretend to stand, go beyond us here also.

Jacob could by observation gather that the place where he lay down to sleep was no other but the house of God, and the very gate of heaven. Ge. xxviii. 17.

Laban could gather by observation, that the Lord blessed him for Jacob's sake. Ge. xxx. 27.

David could gather by what he met with upon Mount Moriah, that that was the place where God would have the temple builded, therefore he sacrificed there. 1 Ch. xxi. 26—28; xxii. 1, 2. 2 Ch. iii. 1.

Ruth was to mark the place where Boaz lay down to sleep, and shall not Christians also mark the day in which our Lord rose from the dead. Ru. iii. 4.

I say, shall we not mark it, when so many memorable things were done on it, *for* and *to* and *in* the churches of God! Let saints be ashamed to think that such a day should be looked over, or counted common, when tempted to it by Satan, when [it was] kept to religious service of old, and when beautified with so many divine characters of sanctity as we have proved, by Christ, his church, the Holy Ghost, and the command of apostolical authority it was.

But why, I say, is this day, on which our Lord

---

* 'Acted by,' a mode of speech now obsolete; it means 'actuated by' or 'influenced by.'—ED.

rose from the dead, nominated as it is? Why was it not sufficient to say 'he rose again,' or, he rose again the third day? without a specification of the very name of the day. For, as was said afore, Christ appeared to his disciples, after his resurrection, on other days also; yea, and thereon did miracles to. Why then did not these days live? Why was their name, for all that, blotted out, and this day only kept alive in the churches?

The day on which Christ was born of a virgin; the day of his circumcision, the day of his baptism, and of his transfiguration, are not by their names committed by the Holy Ghost to holy writ to be kept alive in the world, nor yet such days in which he did many great and wonderful things. But THIS day, this day is still nominated; the first day of the week is the day. I say, why are things thus left with us? But because we, as saints of old, should gather, and separate, what is of divine authority from the rest. For in that this day is so often nominated while all other days lie dead in their graves, it is as much as if God should say, Remember the first day of the week to keep it holy to the Lord your God.

And set this aside, and I know not what reason can be rendered, or what prophecy should be fulfilled by the bare naming of the day.

When God, of old, did sanctify for the use of his church a day, as he did many, he always called them either by the name of the day of the month, or of the week, or by some other signal by which they might be certainly known, why should it not then be concluded, that for this very reason the first day of the week is thus often nominated by the Holy Ghost in the testament of Christ?

Moreover, he that takes away the first day, as to this service, leaves us now no day, as sanctified of God, for his solemn worship to be by his churches performed in. As for the seventh day sabbath, that, as we have seen, is gone to its grave with the signs and shadows of the Old Testament. Yea, and has such a dash left upon it by apostolical authority, that it is enough to make a Christian fly from it for ever. 2 Co. iii.

Now, I say, since that is removed by God: if we should suffer the first day also to be taken away by man, what day that has a divine stamp upon it, would be left for us to worship God in?

Alas! the first day of the week is the Christian's market day, that which they so solemnly trade in for sole provision for all the week following. This is the day that they gather manna in. To be sure the seventh day sabbath is not that. For of old the people of God could never find manna on that day. 'On the seventh day (said Moses) *which is* the sabbath, in it there shall be none.' Ex. xvi. 26.

Any day of the week manna could be found, but on that day it was not to be found upon the face of the ground. But now our first day is the manna day; the only day that the churches of the New Testament, even of old, did gather manna in. But more of this anon.

Nor will it out of my mind but that it is a very high piece of ingratitude, and of uncomely behaviour, to deny the Son of God his day, the Lord's day, the day that he has made. And as we have shewed already, this first day of the week is it; yea, and a great piece of unmannerliness is it too, for any, notwithstanding the old seventh day is so degraded as it is, to attempt to impose it on the Son of God. To impose a day upon him which yet Paul denies to be a branch of the ministration of the Spirit, and of righteousness. Yea, to impose a part of that ministration which he says plainly 'which was done away,' for that a better ministration stript it of its glory, is a high attempt indeed. 2 Co. iii.

Yet again, the apostle smites the teachers of the law upon the mouth, saying, ' understanding neither what they say, nor whereof they affirm.' 1 Ti. i. 7.

The seventh day sabbath, was indeed God's rest from the works of creation; but yet the rest that he found in what the first day of the week did produce, for Christ was born from the dead on it, more pleased him than did all the seventh days that ever the world brought forth: wherefore, as I said before, it cannot be but that the well-bred Christian must set apart this day for solemn worship to God, and to sanctify his name therein.

Must the church of old be bound to remember that night in which they did come out of Egypt! must Jephtha's daughter have four days for the virgins of Israel yearly to lament her hard case in! Yea, must two days be kept by the church of old, yearly, for their being delivered from Haman's fury! And must not one to the world's end be kept by the saints for the Son of God their Redeemer, for all he has delivered them from a worse than Pharaoh or Haman, even from the devil, and death, and sin, and hell! Oh stupidity! Ex. xii. 24. Judg. xi. 39, 40. Es. ix. 26—32.

A day! say some, God forbid but he should have a day. But what day? Oh! The old day comprised within the bounds and bowels of the ministration of death.

And is this the love that thou hast to thy Redeemer, to keep that day to him for all the service that he hath done for thee, which has a natural tendency in it to draw thee off from the consideration of the works of thy redemption, to the creation of the world! Oh stupidity!

But why must he be imposed upon? Has he chosen that day? Did he finish *his* work thereon? Is there in all the New Testament of our Lord, from the day he rose from the dead, to the end of his holy book, one syllable that signifies in the least the tenth part of such a thing? Where is the scripture that saith that this Lord of the sabbath commanded his church, from that time, to do any part of church service thereon? Where do we find the churches to gather together thereon?

But why the seventh day? What is it? Take but the shadow thereof away. Or what shadow now is left in it since its institution as to divine service is taken long since from it?

Is there any thing in the works that was done in that day, more than shadow, or that in the least tends otherwise to put us in mind of Christ; and he being come, what need have we of that shadow? And I say again, since that day was to be observed by a ceremonial method, and no way else, as we find; and since ceremonies have ceased, what way of divine appointment is there left to keep that old sabbath by Christians in?

If they say, ceremonies have ceased. By the same argument, so is the sanction of the day in which they were to be performed. I would gladly see the place, if it is to be found, where it is said, That day retains its sanction, which yet has lost that method of service which was of God appointed for the performance of worship to him thereon.

When Canaan worship fell, the sanction of Canaan fell. When temple worship, and altar worship, and the sacrifices of the Levitical priesthood fell, down also came the things themselves. Likewise so, when the service, or shadow and ceremonies of the seventh day sabbath fell, the seventh day sabbath fell likewise.

On the seventh day sabbath, as I told you, manna was not to be found. But why? For that *that* day was of Moses and of the ministration of death. But manna was not of him. Moses, saith Christ, 'gave you not that bread of heaven.' Jn. vi. 31, 32. Moses, as was said, gave that sabbath in tables of stone, and God gave that manna from heaven. Christ, nor his Father, gives grace by the law; no not by that law in which is contained the old seventh day sabbath itself.

The law is not of faith, why then should grace be by Christians expected by observation of the law? The law, even the law written and engraven in stones, enjoins perfect obedience thereto on pain of the curse of God. Nor can that part of it now under consideration, according as is required, be fulfilled by any man, was the ceremony thereto belonging, allowed to be laid aside. Is. lviii. 13. Never man yet did keep it perfectly, except he whose name is Jesus Christ: in him therefore we have kept it, and by him are set free from that law, and brought under the ministration of the Spirit.

But why should we be bound to seek manna on that day, on which God says, none shall be found.

Perhaps it will be said, that the sanction of *that* day would not admit that manna should be gathered on it.

But that was not all, for on that day there was none to be found. And might I choose, I had rather sanctify that day to God on which I might gather this bread of God all day long, then set my mind at all upon that in which no such bread was to be had.

The Lord's day, as was said, is to the Christians the principal manna day.

On this day, even on it manna in the morning very early was gathered by the disciples of our Lord, as newly springing out of the ground. The true bread of God: the sheaf of first fruits, which is Christ from the dead, was ordained to be waved before the Lord on the morrow after the sabbath, the day on which our Lord ceased from his *own* work as God did from *his*. Le. xxiii.

Now therefore the disciples found their green ears of corn indeed! Now they read life, both *in* and out of the sepulchre in which the Lord was laid. Now they could not come together nor speak one to another, but either their Lord was with them, or they had heart enflaming tidings from him. *Now* cries one and says, The Lord is risen: And then another and says, He hath appeared to such and such.

Now comes tidings to the eleven that their women were early at the sepulchre, where they had a vision of angels that told them their Lord was risen: Then comes another and says, The Lord is risen indeed. Two also came from Emmaus and cried, We have seen the Lord: and by and by, while they yet were speaking, their Lord shows himself in the midst of them.

Now he calls to their mind some of the eminent passages of his life, and eats and drinks in their presence, and opens the scriptures to them: yea, and opens their understanding too, that their hearing might not be unprofitable to them; all which continued from early in the morning till late at night. Oh! what a manna day was this to the church. And more than all this you will find, if you read but the four evangelists upon this subject.

Thus began the day after the sabbath, and *thus* it has continued through all ages to this very day. Never did the seventh day sabbath yield manna to Christians. A new world was now begun with the poor church of God, for so said the Lord of the sabbath, 'Behold, I make all things new.' A new covenant, and why not then a new resting day to the church? Or why must the old sabbath be joined to this new ministration? let him that can, show a reason for it.

Christians, if I have not been so large upon things as some might expect; know, that my brevity on this subject is, from consideration that must needs not be spoken thereto, and because I may have occasion to write a second part.

Christians, beware of being entangled with old testament ministrations, lest by one you be brought into many inconveniencies.

I have observed, that though the Jewish rites have lost their sanction, yet some that are weak in judgment, do bring themselves into bondage by them. Yea, so high have some been carried as to a pretended conscience to these that they have at last proceeded to circumcision, to many wives, and the observation of many bad things besides.

Yea, I have talked with some pretending to Christianity, who have said, and affirmed, as well as they could, that the Jewish sacrifices must up again.

But do you give no heed to these Jewish fables 'That turn from the truth.' Tit. i. 14. Do you, I say, that love the Lord Jesus, keep close to his testament, his word, his gospel, and observe HIS holy day.

And this caution in conclusion I would give, to put stop to this Jewish ceremony, to wit, That a seventh day sabbath pursued according to its imposition by law, (and I know not that it is imposed by the apostles) leads to blood and stoning to death those that do but gather sticks thereon. Nu. xv. 32—36. A thing which no way becomes the gospel, that ministration of the Spirit and of righteousness. 2 Cor. iii. Nor yet the professors thereof. Lu. ix. 54—56.

Nor can it with fairness be said, that *that* sabbath day remains, although the law thereof is repealed. For confident I am, that there is no more ground to make such a conclusion, than there is to say, that circumcision is still of force, though the law for cutting of the uncircumcised is by the gospel made null and void.

I told you also in the epistle, that if the fifth commandment was the first that was with promise; then it follows, that the fourth, or that seventh day sabbath, had no promise entailed to it. Whence it follows, that where you read in the prophet of a promise annexed to a sabbath, it is best to understand it of our gospel sabbath. Is. lvi.

Now if it be asked, What promise is entailed to our first day sabbath? I answer, The biggest of promises. For,

First, The resurrection of Christ was tied by promise to this day, and to none other. He rose the third day after his death, and that was the first day of the week, 'according' to what was fore-promised in the scriptures. Ho. vi. 1, 2. 1 Co. xv. 3—6.

Second, That we should live before God by him, is a promise to be fulfilled on this day; 'After two days will he revive us: in the third day - we shall live in his sight.' Ho. vi. 2. See also Is. xxvi. 19. and compare them again with 1 Co. xv. 4.

Third, The great promise of the new testament, to wit, the pouring out of the Spirit, fixeth upon these days; and so he began in the most wonderful effusion of it upon Pentecost, which was the first day of the week, that the scriptures might be fulfilled. Ac. ii. 16—19.

Nor could these three promises be fulfilled upon any other days, for that the scripture had fixed them to the first day of the week.

I am of opinion that these things, though but briefly touched upon, cannot be fairly objected against, however they may be disrelished by some.

Nor can I believe, that any part of our religion, as we are Christians, stands in not kindling of fires, and not seething of victuals, or in binding of men not to stir out of those places on the seventh day, in which at the dawning thereof they were found. And yet these are ordinances belonging to that seventh day sabbath. Ex. xvi. 23—29.

Certainly it must needs be an error to impose these things by divine authority upon new testament believers, our worship standing now in things more weighty, spiritual, and heavenly.

Nor can it be proved, as I have hinted before, that this day was, or is to be imposed without those ordinances, with others in other places mentioned and adjoined, for the sanction of that day they being made necessary parts of that worship that was to be performed thereon.

I have charity for those that abuse themselves and their Lord, by their preposterous zeal and affection for the continuing of this day in the churches. For I conclude, that if they did either believe, or think of the incoherence that this day with its rites and ceremonies has with the ministration of the Spirit, our new testament ministration, they would not so stand in their own light as they do, nor so stiffly plead for a place for it in the churches of the Gentiles. But as Paul insinuates in other cases, there is an aptness in men to be under the law because they do not hear it. Ga. iv.

Nor will it out of my mind, but if the seventh day sabbath was by divine authority, and to be kept holy by the churches of the Gentiles, it should not have so remained among the Jews, Christ's deadliest enemies, and have been kept so much hid from the believers, his best friends. For who has retained the pretended sanction of that day from Christ's time, quite down in the world, but the Jews, and a few Jewish Gentiles, I will except some. But, I say, since a sabbath is that without which the great worship of God under the gospel cannot be well performed: how can it be thought, that it should as to the knowledge of it, be confined to so blasphemous a generation of the Jews, with whom that worship is not?

I will rather conclude, that those Gentile professors that adhere thereto are Jewified, legalized, and so far gone back from the authority of God, who from such bondage has set his churches free.

I do at this time but hint upon things, reserving a fuller argument upon them for a time and place more fit; where, and when, I may perhaps also show, some other wild notions of those that so stiffly cleave to this.

Meantime, I entreat those who are captivated with this opinion, not to take it ill at my hand that I thus freely speak my mind. I entreat them also to peruse my book without prejudice to my person. The truth is, one thing that has moved me to this work, is the shame that has covered the face of my soul, when I have thought of the fictions and fancies that are growing among professors. And while I see each fiction turn itself to a faction, to the loss of that good spirit of love, and that oneness that formerly was with good men.

I doubt not but some unto whom this book may

come, have had seal from God, that the first day of the week is to be sanctified by the church to Jesus Christ. Not only from *his* testimony, which is, and should be, the ground of our practice; but also, for that the first conviction that the Holy Ghost made upon their consciences, to make them know that they were sinners, began with them for breaking this sabbath day; which day, by that same spirit was told them, was that now called the first day, and not the day before, and the Holy Ghost doth not use to begin this work with a lie, which first conviction the Spirit has followed so close, with other things tending to complete the same work, that the soul from so good a beginning could not rest until it found rest in Christ. Let this then to such be a second token that the Lord's day is by them to be kept in commemoration of their Lord and his resurrection, and of what he did on this day for their salvation. Amen.

SCRIPTURAL POEMS;

BEING

SEVERAL PORTIONS OF SCRIPTURE DIGESTED INTO ENGLISH VERSE,

VIZ.,

I. THE BOOK OF RUTH.
II. THE HISTORY OF SAMSON.
III. CHRIST'S SERMON ON THE MOUNT.

IV. THE PROPHECY OF JONAH.
V. THE LIFE OF JOSEPH.
VI. THE EPISTLE OF JAMES.

BY JOHN BUNYAN.

LICENSED ACCORDING TO ORDER.

London: Printed for J. Blare, at the Looking Glass, on London Bridge, 1701.

ADVERTISEMENT BY THE EDITOR.

THIS very interesting little volume of poems, we believe, has not been reprinted since the year 1701, nor has it ever been inserted in any edition or catalogue of Bunyan's works. This may have arisen from the author's having sold his entire copyright— a fact which prevented Charles Doe from publishing many other of Bunyan's treatises, when he projected his edition of the entire works, of which the first volume only was printed. With some other of Bunyan's rarest tracts, it escaped the researches of Wilson, who published the works in 1737, and also of Whitefield, Mason, and all other editors of Bunyan's works. Mr. Doe, in his very interesting pages called 'The Struggler, for the Preservation of Mr. John Bunyan's Labours,' gives a catalogue table of his books in the order in which they were published; but he had not discovered these poems, nor the Emblems, nor the Exhortation to Peace and Unity.

The volume from which this edition is printed consists of one hundred pages in crown octavo, with a very rude cut of Ruth and Boaz. It is of extreme rarity, if not unique, in a perfect state. The imprint is—London, for J. Blare, at the Looking Glass, on London Bridge, 1701. It forms part of the Editor's extensive collection of the original or early editions of Bunyan's tracts and treatises; the scarcity of which may be accounted for, from their having been printed on very bad paper, and worn out by use, being so generally and eagerly read by pious persons among the labouring classes of the community.

The style and substance of these scriptural poems are entirely Bunyan's. His veneration for the holy oracles appears through every page, by his close adherence to the text. He fully proves what he asserts in his address to the reader—

'The WORD are for the most part all the same,
For I affected plainness more than fame.'

However uncouth it may appear to use a plural verb after a singular noun, it really expresses his meaning, which is evidently, that portions of the WORD of God are rendered into poetry as nearly as possible, word for word with the original; and he immediately apologises for this rudeness, in neglecting the rules of grammar, by stating his earnest plainness of speech, and his want of education in early life.

'Nor could'st thou hope to have it better done,
For I'm no poet, nor a poet's son,
But a mechanic, guided by no rule,
But what I gained in a grammar school
In my minority.'

How exactly does this agree with his account of himself in boyhood,—'It pleased God to put it into my parent's heart to put me to school, to learn both to read and write; though, to my shame I confess, I did soon lose that I learnt, even almost utterly.'*

Our surprise will be excited, not by little inaccuracies of style or departures from the rules of grammar, but at the talent of a poor mechanic, in so faithfully rendering scripture histories in such simple and striking language. As Mr. Burton says, in commending his Gospel Truths Vindicated, —'This man hath not the learning or wisdom of man, yet through grace he hath received the teaching of God, and the learning of the Spirit of Christ, which is the thing that makes a man both a Christian and a minister of the gospel. Is. l. 4. He was

* Grace Abounding, No. 3.

wherefore fear thou him, and tremble at his word, saying still, with godly suspicion of thine own infirmity, what I see not, teach thou me, and thou art God only wise; but as for me, 'I was *as* a beast before thee.' Ps. lxxiii. 22.

3. Take heed of taking a part of the word only, lest thou thereby go away with the truth as mangled in pieces. For instance, where thou readest, 'The LORD our God *is* one Lord;' De. vi. 4. there take heed that thou dost not thence conclude, Then there are not three persons in the godhead: Or when thou readest of the Father, the Son, and the Holy Spirit, then take heed of concluding, there must therefore either be three Gods, or else that Jesus Christ and the Holy Ghost are not true God, but the Father only. Wherefore to help thee here, observe,

THE SECOND PREPARATIVE.

1. That Christian religion requireth credit concerning every doctrine contained in the word; credit, I say, according to the true relation of every sentence that the Holy Ghost hath revealed for the asserting, maintaining, or vindicating that same truth.

2. And therefore hence it is that a Christian is not called a doer, a reasoner, an objector, and perverse disputer; but a BELIEVER. Be thou an example to the believer. 'And believers were the more added to the Lord,' &c. Ac. v. 14. 1 Ti. iv. 12.

3. Therefore know again that the word, if it saith and expresseth that this or that is so and so, as to the matter in hand, thou art bound and obliged both by the name, profession, and the truth, unto which thou hast joined thyself, to assent to, confess and acknowledge the same, even then when thy carnal reason will not stoop thereto. 'Righteous art thou, O Lord,' saith Jeremiah,

'yet let me talk with thee: *Wherefore* doth the way of the wicked prosper?' Je. xii. 1. Mark, first he acknowledgeth that God's way with the wicked is just and right, even then when yet he could not see the reason of his actings and dispensations towards them. The same reason is good as to our present case. And hence it is that the apostle teacheth, the spiritual armour of Christians should be much exercised against those high-towering and self-exalting imaginations, that within our own bosoms do exalt themselves against the knowledge of God. That every thought, or carnal reasoning, may be not only taken, but brought as captive into obedience to Christ; that is, be made to stoop to the word of God, and to give way and place to the doctrine therein contained, how cross soever our thoughts and the word lie to each other. And it is observable that he here teacheth, They exalt themselves against the knowledge of God, which cannot be understood that our carnal or natural reason doth exalt itself against an eternal deity, simply considered; for that nature itself doth gather from the very things that are made, even his eternal power and godhead; it must be then that they exalt themselves against that God as thus and thus revealed in the word, to wit, against the knowledge of one God consisting of three persons, Father, Son, and Spirit; for this is the doctrine of the scriptures of truth; and therefore it is observable these thoughts must be brought captive, and be made subject in particular to the Lord Jesus Christ, as to the second person in the godhead; for the Father is ever acknowledged by all that profess the least of religion; but the Son is that stumbling-stone, and rock of offence, against which thousands dash themselves in pieces; though in him are hid all the treasures of wisdom and knowledge, and in him dwells the fulness of the godhead bodily.

OF THE LAW AND A CHRISTIAN.

The law was given twice upon mount Sinai, but the appearance of the Lord when he gave it the second time, was wonderfully different from that of his [appearance], when at the first he delivered it to Israel. Ex. xix. and xxxiv.

1. When he gave it the first time, he caused his terror and severity to appear before Moses, to the shaking of his soul, and the dismaying of Israel: Ex. xix. 16. He. xii. 18—20. But when he gave it the second time, he caused all his goodness to pass before Moses, to the comfort of his conscience, and the bowing of his heart. Ex. xxxiv. 8.

2. When he gave it the first time, it was with

thunderings and lightnings, with blackness and darkness, with flame and smoke, and a tearing sound of the trumpet. Ex. xix. 16—18. But when he gave it the second time, it was with a proclamation of his name to be merciful, gracious, long-suffering, and abundant in goodness and truth, keeping mercy for thousands, forgiving iniquity, transgressions and sins. Ex. xxxiv. 6, 7.

3. When he gave it the first time, Moses was called to go up to receive it through the fire, which made him exceedingly fear and quake: Ex. xix. 18. He. xii. 21. But when he went to receive it the second time, he was laid in a clift of the rock. Ex. xxxi. 22.

4. From all which I gather, that, though as to the matter of the law, both as to its being given the first time, and the second, it binds the unbeliever under the pains of eternal damnation, if he close not with Christ by faith ; yet as to the manner of its giving at these two times, I think the first doth more principally intend its force as a covenant of works, not at all respecting the Lord Jesus ; but this second time not, at least in the manner of its being given, respecting such a covenant, but rather as a rule, or directory, to those who already are found in the clift of the rock, Christ: for the saint himself, though he be without law to God, as it is considered the first or old covenant, yet even he is not without law to him as considered under grace, not without law to God, but under the law to Christ. 1 Co. ix. 21.

5. Though therefore it be sad with the unbeliever, because he only and wholly standeth under the law, as it is given in fire, in smoke, in blackness, and darkness, and thunder ; all which threaten him with eternal ruin if he fulfil not the utmost tittle thereof: yet the believer stands to the law under no such consideration, neither is he so at all to hear or regard it, for he is now removed from thence to the blessed mountain of Zion, to grace and forgiveness of sins ; he is now, I say, by faith in the Lord Jesus shrouded under so perfect and blessed a righteousness, that this thundering law of mount Sinai cannot find the least fault or diminution therein ; but rather approveth and alloweth thereof either when, or wherever it find it. He. xii. This is called the righteousness of God without the law, and is also said to be witnessed by both the law and the prophets : even the righteousness of God, which is by faith in Jesus Christ 'unto all and upon all them that believe, for there is no difference.' Ro. iii. 22.

6. Wherefore whenever thou who believest in Jesus, dost hear the law in its thundering and lightning fits, as if it would burn up heaven and earth ; then say thou, I am freed from this law, these thunderings have nothing to do with my soul ; nay even this law, while it thus thunders and roareth, it doth both allow and approve of my righteousness. I know that Hagar would sometimes be domineering and high, even in Sarah's house and against her ; but this she is not to be suffered to do, nay though Sarah herself be barren ; wherefore serve IT also as Sarah served her, and expel her out from thy house. My meaning is, when this law with its thundering threatenings doth

attempt to lay hold on thy conscience, shut it out with a promise of grace ; cry, the inn is took up already, the Lord Jesus is here entertained, and here is no room for the law. Indeed if it will be content with being my informer, and so lovingly leave off to judge me ; I will be content, it shall be in my sight, I will also delight therein ; but otherwise, I being now made upright without it, and that too with that righteousness, which this law speaks well of and approveth ; I may not, will not, cannot, dare not make it my saviour and judge, nor suffer it to set up its government in my conscience ; for by so doing I fall from grace, and Christ Jesus doth profit me nothing. Ga. v. 1—5.

7. Thus therefore the soul that is married to him that is raised up from the dead, both may and ought to deal with this law of God ; yea, it doth greatly dishonour its Lord and refuse its gospel privileges, if it at any time otherwise doth, whatever it seeth or feels. The law hath power over the wife so long as her husband liveth, but if her husband be dead she is freed from that law, so that she is no adulteress though she be married to another man. Ro. vii. 1—3. Indeed so long as thou art alive to sin, and to thy righteousness which is of the law, so long thou hast them for thy husband and they must reign over thee: But when once they are become dead unto thee, as they then most certainly will, when thou closest with the Lord Jesus Christ; then I say, thy former husbands have no more to meddle with thee, thou art freed from their law. Set a case, a woman be cast into prison for a debt of hundreds of pounds, if after this she marry ; yea, though while she is in the gaoler's hand, in the same day that she is joined to her husband, her debt is all become his ; yea, and the law also that arrested and imprisoned this woman, as freely tells her, go, she is freed, saith Paul, from that, and so saith the law of this land.

The sum then of what hath been said is this, the Christian hath now nothing to do with the law, as it thundereth and burneth on Sinai, or as it bindeth the conscience to wrath and the displeasure of God for sin ; for from its thus appearing, it is freed by faith in Christ. Yet it is to have regard thereto, and is to count it holy, just and good; Ro. vii. 12. which that it may do, it is always whenever it seeth or regards it, to remember that he who giveth it to us is 'merciful, and gracious, long-suffering, and abundant in goodness and truth,' &c. Ex. xxxiv. 6.

OF THE TRINITY AND A CHRISTIAN,

AND

OF THE LAW AND A CHRISTIAN.

EDITOR'S ADVERTISEMENT.

THESE two short treatises were found among Mr. Bunyan's papers after his decease. They probably were intended for publication, like his ' Prison Meditations' and his 'Map of Salvation,' on a single page each, in the form of a broadside, or handbill. This was the popular mode in which tracts were distributed; and when posted against a wall, or framed and hung up in a room, they excited notice, and were extensively read. They might also have afforded some trifling profit to aid this *poor* but eminent servant of Christ in his very limited income. They form two pages in that exceedingly interesting volume of ' The Works of Mr. John Bunyan,' in small folio, 1692. To which is added ' The Struggler,' containing some most valuable facts, relative to the various works, imprisonment and sufferings of the author. The titles to these treatises were added by Mr. Doe, the personal friend of Bunyan, who edited the works and wrote ' The Struggler,'the author having left them without any heading or title. They are very unfinished, and may have been intended as a syllabus or outline of more extended treatises.—GEO. OFFOR.

OF THE TRINITY AND A CHRISTIAN.

How a young, or shaken Christian should demean himself under the weighty thoughts of the doctrine of the Trinity, or plurality of persons in the eternal godhead.

THE reason why I say a young, or shaken Christian; it is because some that are not young, but of an ancient standing, may not only be assaulted with violent temptations, concerning gospel principles, but a second time may become a child, a babe, a shallow man, in the things of God; especially, either when by backsliding he hath provoked God to leave him, or when some new, unexpected, and, as to present strength, over-weighty objection doth fall upon the spirit; by means of which, great shakings of mind do commonly attend such a soul, in the most weighty matters of the concerns of faith, which this is one that I have supposed in the above-named question. Wherefore passing other things, I will come directly to that, and briefly propose some helps to a soul in such a case.

THE FIRST PREPARATIVE.

First, then, be sure thou keep close to the word of God; for that is the revelation of the mind and will of God, both as to the truth of what is either in himself or ways; and also as to what he requireth and expecteth of thee, either concerning faith in, or obedience to, what he hath so revealed. Now for thy better performing of this I shall give thee in brief these following directions.

1. Suffer thyself, by the authority of the word, to be persuaded that the scripture indeed is the word of God; the scriptures of truth, the words of the holy one; and that they therefore must be every one true, pure, and for ever settled in heaven.

2. Conclude therefore from the former doctrine, that that God whose words they are, is able to make a reconciliation and most sweet and harmonious agreement with all the sayings therein, how obscure, cross, dark, and contradictory soever they seem to thee. To understand all mysteries, to have all knowledge, to be able to comprehend with all saints, is a great work; enough to crush the spirit, and to stretch the strings of the most capacious and widened soul that breatheth on this side glory, be they notwithstanding exceedingly enlarged by revelation. Paul, when he was caught up to heaven, saw that which was unlawful, because impossible for man to utter. And saith Christ to the reasoning Pharisee, ' If I have told you earthly things, and ye believe not, how shall ye believe, if I tell you of heavenly things?' Jn. iii. 12. It is great lewdness, and also insufferable arrogancy to come to the word of God, as conceiting already that whatever thou readest, must either by thee be understood, or of itself fall to the ground as a senseless error. But God is wiser than man,

not chosen out of an earthly, but out of the heavenly University, and hath taken these three heavenly degrees—Union with Christ—The Anointing of the Spirit, and Experience of the Temptations of Satan ; far better than all the University learning and degrees that can be had.'   May

Bunyan's desire be realized, and his verses prove to all our readers

'As delighting
To thee in reading, as to me in writing.'

GEO. OFFOR.

HACKNEY, August 22, 1849.

SCRIPTURAL POEMS.

TO THE READER.

WHOE'ER thou art that shall peruse this book,
This may inform thee, when I undertook
To write these lines, it was not my design
To publish this imperfect work of mine:
Composed only for diversion's sake.
But being inclin'd to think thou may'st partake
Some benefit thereby, I have thought fit,
Imperfect as it is, to publish it.
The subjects are a part of the contents,
Both of the Old and the New Testaments ;
The word are for the most part all the same,
For I affected plainness more than fame.
Nor could'st thou hope to have it better done:
For I'm no poet, nor a poet's son,
But a mechanic, guided by no rule,
But what I gained in a grammar school
In my minority: I can't commend it,
Such as it is into the world I send it,
And should be glad to see some hand to mend it.

Would but those men whose genius leads them to't,
And who have time and parts wherewith to do't,
Employ their pens in such a task as this,
'Twould be a most delightsome exercise
Of profit to themselves and others too :
If what the learned Herbert says, holds true,
A verse may find him, who a sermon flies,
And turn delight into a sacrifice;*
Thus I conclude, and wish it as delighting
To thee in reading as to me in writing.

JOHN BUNYAN.

* George Herbert, in that admirable poem called 'The Temple,' introduces his reader to the church porch thus :—

'Thou, whose sweet youth and early hopes enhance
Thy rate and price, and mark thee for a treasure;
Hearken unto a verser, who may chance
Rhyme thee to good, and make a bait of pleasure.
A verse may find him, who a sermon flies,
And turn delight into a sacrifice.'

THE BOOK OF RUTH.

A VERY RUDE WOODCUT :—RUTH GLEANING.—RUTH CREEPING TO BOAZ, WHO IS ASLEEP.

CHAP. I.

IN ancient times, e'er Israel knew the way
Of kingly power, when judges bore the sway :
A certain man of Bethlehem Juda fled,
By reason of a famine that o'erspread
The land, into the land of Moab, where
He and his wife, and sons, sojourners were.
His name Elimelech, his eldest son
Was called Mahlon, t'other Chilion,
His wife was Naomi, Ephrathites they were:
They went to Moab and continued there :
Where of her husband Naomi was bereft,
And only she and her two sons were left:
Who took them wives of Moab in their youth.
The name of one was Orpah, t'other Ruth:
And there they died ere twice five years were gone ;
And Naomi was wholly left alone.
Then she arose, and her step-daughters with her,
To leave the land of Moab altogether:
For she had heard the Lord had visited
Her native country, with increase of bread,
Wherefore the land of Moab she forsook,
And to her native place her course she took,

Her daughters with her: whom she did desire,
That to their mother's house they would retire.
The Lord, said she, be kind to you again,
As you to me, and to the dead have been.
God grant you each may be with husbands blest,
And in the enjoyment of them both find rest.
Then she embraced them, and there withal,
Down from their cheeks, the tears began to fall.
They wept aloud, and said, Most surely we
Unto thy people will return with thee.
But Naomi replied, Wherefore will ye,
My daughters, thus resolve to go with me?
Are there yet any more sons in my womb,
That may your husbands be in time to come?
Return again, my daughters, go your way,
For I'm too old to marry: should I say
I've hope?   Should I this night conceive a son?
Would either of you stay till he is grown?
Would you so long without an †husband live?
Nay, nay, my daughters, for it doth me grieve
Exceedingly, even for your sakes, that I
Do under this so great affliction lie.

† 'An husband,' c. i. 12.

And here they wept again. And Orpah kiss'd
Her mother, but Ruth would be not dismiss'd
But clave unto her: unto whom she spake
And said, Behold, thy sister is gone back,
With her own gods, and people to abide,
Go thou along with her. But Ruth replied,
Intreat me not to leave thee, or return:
For where thou goest, I'll go, where thou sojourn,
I'll sojourn also. And what people's thine,
And who thy God, the same shall both be mine.
Where thou shalt die, there will I die likewise,
And I'll be buried where thy body lies.
The Lord do so to me, and more, if I
Do leave thee, or forsake thee till I die.
And when she saw the purpose of her heart,
She left off to desire her to depart.
So they two travelled along together
To Bethlehem, and when they were come thither,
Behold! the people were surprised, and cried,
What, is this Naomi? But she replied,
Oh! call me Mara, and not Naomi;
For I have been afflicted bitterly.
I went out from you full, but now I come,
As it hath pleased God, quite empty home:
Why then call ye me Naomi? Since I
Have been afflicted so exceedingly.
So Naomi return'd, and Ruth together,
Who had come from the land of Moab with her:
And unto Bethlem Judah did they come,
Just as the Barley Harvest was begun.

CHAP. II.

There was a man of kin to Naomi,
One that was of her husband's family,
His name was Boaz, and his wealth was great.
And Ruth, the Moabitess, did intreat
Her Mother's leave, that she might go, and gather
Some ears of corn, where she should most find favour:
Go, daughter, go, said she. She went and came
Near to the reapers, to glean after them:
And lo, it was her hap to light among
The reapers, which to Boaz did belong.
Behold, now Boaz came from Bethlehem
Unto his reapers, and saluted them,
And they bless'd him again: and he enquired
Of him that was set over them he hired,
From whence the damsel was, and was inform'd
She was the Moabitess that return'd
With Naomi: and she did ask, said he,
That here amongst the reapers she might be,
And that she might have liberty to glean
Among the sheaves. And she all day hath been,
Ev'n from the morning until now, with us,
That she hath stay'd a little in the house.
Then Boaz said to Ruth, observe, my daughter,
That thou go not from hence, or follow after
The reapers of another field, but where
My maidens are, see that thou tarry there:
Observe what field they reap, and go thou there,
Have I not charged the young men to forbear
To touch thee? And when thou dost thirst, approach
And drink of what the youths have set *abroach.

Then she fell on her face, and to the ground
She bow'd herself, and said, Why have I found
Such favour in thine eyes; that thou, to me
Who am a stranger, should so courteous be?
And Boaz said, it hath been fully shewn
To me, what to thy mother-in-law thou'st done,
Since of thine husband thou hast been bereft:
How thou thy father and thy mother left,
And thine own native land; to come unto
A land which thou before didst never know:
The Lord, the God of Israel, the defence
Whom now thou'st chosen, be thy recompence.
Then said she, let me in thy sight, my lord,
Find favour in that thou dost thus afford
Me comfort, and since thou so kind to me
Dost speak, though I thereof unworthy be.
And Boaz said, at meal time come thou near,
Eat of the bread, and dip i' th' vinegar.
And by the reapers she sat down to meat,
He gave her parched corn, and she did eat,
And was suffic'd; and left, and rose to glean:
And Boaz gave command to the young men,
Let her come in among the sheaves, said he,
To glean, and let her not reproached be.
Let fall some handfuls also purposely,
And let her take them without injury.
So she till even glean'd, and then beat out
Her barley, being an *ephah or thereabout.
She took it up, and to the city went,
And to her mother-in-law did it present:
And what she had reserv'd to her she gave,
When she had took what she design'd to have.
Then unto her, her mother-in-law did say,
In what field hast thou been to glean to-day?
And where hast thou been working? Blest be he,
That thus hath taken cognizance of thee.
She told with whom, and furthermore did say,
The man's name's Boaz, where I wrought to-day.
And Naomi replied, may he be blest,
Even of the Lord, whose kindness manifest
Unto the living and the dead hath been:
The man's our kinsman, yea, the next of kin.
And Ruth, the Moabitess, said, he gave
Me likewise a commandment not to leave,
Or to depart from following his young men,
Until they had brought all his harvest in.
And Naomi said unto Ruth, my daughter,
'Tis good that thou observe to follow after
His maidens, that they meet thee not elsewhere.
So she to Boaz's maidens still kept near,
Till barley and wheat harvest both, she saw
Were done, and she dwelt with her mother-in law.

CHAP. III.

Then Naomi said, Shall I not, my daughter,
Seek rest for thee, that thou do well hereafter?
And is not Boaz, with whose maids thou wast,
One of the nearest kinsmen that thou hast?
Behold, this night he in his threshing floor
Is winnowing Barley, wash thyself therefore,
Anoint thee, put thy clothes on, and get down
Unto the floor; but make not thyself known,

---

* 'Set abroach,' in a posture to run out, or yield the liquor contained.
—Ed.

* 'An ephah,' a measure containing three pecks and three pints.—
Calmet.

Till he hath eat and drank, and shall prepare
To lie him down; then take good notice where
He goes about to take his night's repose,
And go thou in there, and lift up the clothes
From off his feet, and likewise lay thee down,
And what thou hast to do he will make known.
And she made answer, Whatsoever thou
Hast me commanded, will I gladly do.
And down unto the floor she hasted, and
Forthwith fulfilled her mother-in-law's command.
So now when Boaz had his heart refresh'd,
With meat and drink, he laid him down to rest,
Near to the heap of corn; she softly came,
Uncover'd's feet, and lay down by the same.
And, lo! at midnight, as he turn'd him round,
He was afraid, for at his feet he found
A woman lay. Who art thou? then said he.
I am thine handmaid Ruth, replied she,
Over thine handmaid therefore spread thy skirt,
I pray, because thou a near kinsman art.
Blessed be thou, said he, because thou hast
Made manifest more kindness at the last,
Than at the first, in that thou did'st, my daughter,
No young men, whether poor or rich, go after.
And now, my daughter, be not thou afraid,
I will do to thee all that thou hast said:
For all the city of my people knows,
Thou art a woman truly virtuous;
And now though I am kin undoubtedly,
Yet there is one that's nearer kin than I.
Tarry this night, and when 'tis morning light,
If he will like a kinsman, do thee right,
We'll let him, but if not, I myself will,
As the Lord lives; till morning lie thou still.
And till the morning at his feet she lay,
And then arose about the break of day;
And he gave her a charge, not to declare
That there had any womankind been there.
He also said, bring here thy veil, and hold
To me; she did, and thereinto he told
Six measures full of barley, and did lay
It on her, and she hasted thence away.
And when unto her mother-in-law she came,
Art thou, said she, my daughter come again?
Then what the man had done she told, and said,
He these six measures full of barley laid
Upon me, for said he, This I bestow,
Lest to thy mother thou should'st empty go.
Then, said she, sit still daughter, till thou see
What the event of this intrigue will be;
For till the man this day hath made an end,
No satisfaction will on him attend.

CHAP. IV.

And Boaz went up to the city gate,
And after a short space, while there he sate,
The kinsman of whom he had spoke, came by,
To whom he said, Ho,* such a one, draw nigh,
And sit down here. He came and sat him down.
Then he took ten men, elders of the town,

* Similar to Christian's exclamation, when calling to Faithful to stop
and bear him company. See Pilgrim's Progress, Part 1st.

And caused them to sit down. Then to the man
That was of kin, thus he his speech began,
Naomi, said he, who not long since sojourn'd
Among the Moabites, is now return'd;
And doth intend to sell a piece of ground,
The which Elimelech our brother own'd.
And now to give thee notice, I thought fit,
That if thou pleasest, thou may'st purchase it,
In presence of these men assembled here.
Then if thou wilt redeem it, now declare
Thy mind, but if thou wilt not, then let me,
For thou art next of kin, and I next thee.
Then said the kinsman, I will it redeem.
Boaz reply'd, if good to thee it seem,
To buy it of the hand of Naomi,
Thou also art obliged the same to buy
Of Ruth the Moabitess, wife o' th' dead;
On his inheritance to raise up seed.
The kinsman said, I cannot do this thing
Myself, lest I an inconvenience bring
Upon mine own inheritance, what's mine
By right, therefore I now to thee resign.
Now this in Israel did a custom stand,
Concerning changing and redeeming land;
To put all controversy to an end,
A man pluck'd off his shoe, and gave his friend;
And this in Israel was an evidence,
When e'er they changed an inheritance.
Then said the kinsman unto Boaz, do
Thou take my right. And off he pluck'd his shoe.
Then Boaz to the elders thus did say
And to the people, all of you this day
Appear for me as witnesses, that I
Have bought all of the hand of Naomi,
That was Elimelech's or did belong
Either to Mahlon or to Chilion:
And Ruth the Moabitess, who some time
Was Mahlon's wife, I've purchas'd to be mine,
Still to preserve alive the dead man's name
On his inheritance, lest that the same
Should in the gate where he inhabited,
Or 'mongst his brethren be extinguished:
Behold, this day, my witnesses you are.
Then all the people that were present there,
And elders said, We are thy witnesses:
May God this woman thou hast taken bless,
That she, like Rachel, and like Leah be,
Which two did build up Israel's family:
And thou in Ephratah exalt thy name,
And through the town of Bethl'hem spread thy fame;
And may the seed which God shall give to thee
Of this young woman, full as prosperous be,
As was the house of Pharez heretofore,
(Pharez, whom Tamar unto Judah bore.)
So he took Ruth, and as his wife he knew her,
And God was pleased, when he went in to her
To grant the blessing of conception,
And she accordingly bare him a son.
Then said the woman, Blessed be the Lord!
Bless thou him Naomi, who doth afford
To thee this day a kinsman, which shall be
Famous in Israel; and shall be to thee
As the restorer of thy life again,
And in thy drooping age shall thee sustain:

For that thy daughter-in-law, who loves thee well
And in thy sight doth seven sons excel,
Hath born this child.   Then Naomi took the boy
To nurse; and did him in her bosom lay.

Her neighbours too, gave him a name, for why,
This son, say they, is born to Naomi:
They called him Obed, from whose loins did spring
Jesse, the sire of David, Israel's king.

THE HISTORY OF SAMSON.

JUDGES, CHAP. XIII.

WHEN Israel's sins th' Almighty did provoke,
To make them subject to Philistine yoke
For forty years: in Zorah dwelt a man,
His name Manoah, of the tribe of Dan;
His wife was barren, unto whom appeared
The angel of the Lord, and thus declared:
Though thou, said he, art barren, time shall come
Thou shalt enjoy the blessing of thy womb;
Now therefore I entreat thee to refrain
From wine, strong drink, and things that are unclean,
For lo, thou shalt conceive, and bear a son,
Upon whose head there shall no razor come:
For he to God a Nazarite shall be,
And shall begin to set his people free
From the Philistine yoke.   The woman came
And told her husband, she had seen a man
Of God: his dreadful look made me, said she,
Think him an angel of the Lord to be:
But I inquired not from whence he came,
Neither did he make known to me his name:
But thus he said, Thou shalt conceive a son;
Wherefore strong drink and wine, see that thou shun,
And have a care that thou be not defil'd
With things that are unclean; for why, the child
Shall from his separation from the womb,
Become a Nazarite, ev'n to his tomb.
Manoah then did supplicate the Lord,
And said, O Lord, be pleased to afford
This favour unto me, to send again
The man of God, more fully to explain
Thy will to us, that we may rightly know,
When this child shall be born, what we must do.
And to Manoah's prayer God gave ear,
And to his wife the angel did appear
Again, as she did in the field retire,
At such time as her husband was not nigh her.
And she made haste, and ran, and strait declared
Unto her husband, that the man appeared
Again, whom she had seen the other day.
Manoah then arose, and went his way,
And when he came, he said, Art thou the man
That spakest to my wife?   He said, I am.
Manoah said, Now let thy words be true;
How shall we use the child, What must we do?
Then said the angel of the Lord, let her
Of all that I have charged her beware:
She may not taste of what comes of the vine,
Nor may she drink strong drink, or any wine,
Nor may she eat of things that are unclean,
From all that I have said let her refrain.
Manoah said unto the angel, stay

With us, till we have dress'd a kid, I pray.
But he reply'd, though thou shalt me detain,
I'll eat no bread, but if thou dost design
A sacrifice unto the Lord, then offer:
For ne'er till now, Manoah did discover
It was a man of God he spake unto.
Then said he to the angel, Let me know
Thy name, that when these things shall be perform'd,
The honour due to thee may be return'd.
Whereto the man of God made this reply,
Why askest thou, since 'tis a mystery?
So he a kid, and a meat-off'ring took,
And offer'd to the Lord upon a rock.
And there the man of God did wond'rously,
The whilst Manoah and his wife stood by:
For as the altar did send up the flame,
The man of God ascended in the same.
Manoah and his wife stood looking on,
And on their faces to the ground fell down.
But then the angel did appear no more.
Manoah then knew who he was: therefore
He said unto his wife, most surely we
Shall die, for we the face of God did see.
But she repli'd, If God would such a thing,
He would not now accept our offering,
Or would he have to us these things made known;
Or told us, as at this time he hath done.
And now, according to the angel's word,
The woman bare a son, to whom the Lord
Was pleas'd, his blessing graciously to give:
She call'd him Samson, and the child did thrive.
And lo! the spirit of the Lord began,
At times to move him in the camp of Dan.

CHAP. XIV.

Now down to Timnath Samson's steps incline,
Where seeing the daughter of a Philistine,
He came up and did of his parents crave,
That he in marriage might the woman have.
Then thus his father and his mother said,
'Mongst all thy kin can'st thou find ne'er a maid;
Nor yet among my people, fit to make
A wife, but thou wilt this Philistine take,
Of race uncircumcised?   He replied,
Get her for me, for I'm well satisfied.
But neither of his parents then did know,
It was the Lord that moved him thereto,
To seek a way to accomplish his designs,
Upon the then o'er-ruling Philistines.
Then Samson and his parents both went down
To Timnath, and as they came near the town,
Among the vineyards a young lion roar'd:
Then on him came the spirit of the Lord,

And though unarm'd, he rent him like a kid,
But he discovered not to them the deed.
And he went down, and with the woman treated,
And was well pleas'd to have the match completed.
And in a while as he returned again
To take his wife, behold, where he had slain
The beast, he there a swarm of bees set eye on,
And honey in the carcase of the lion:
He took thereof, and eating, on he went,
And to his parents did a part present:
And they did also eat, but did not know
That from the lion's carcase it did flow.
So down his father went unto the woman,
And Samson made a feast, as it was common
Among young men. The Philistines provide
Thirty companions with him to abide
And Samson said unto them, now behold,
I have a riddle for you to unfold;
Which if you do before the seven days' feast
Be ended, I will give to every guest
A sheet and change of garments; but if ye
Cannot declare it, ye shall give to me
Full thirty sheets, and thirty changes too.
Then said they, What's your riddle, let us know?
And Samson said, The eater sent forth meat,
And from the strong there came a thing most sweet.
And they could not in three days find it out,
Wherefore before the seventh came about,
They said unto his wife, Thou must entice
Thy husband to discover this device
Lest we burn thee, and all thy father's house:
Is it not so, that ye have called us
To make a spoil? And Samson's wife wept sore,
And said, thou dost but hate me, and no more;
To put a riddle to my countrymen
And not tell't me. And he reply'd again,
I have not told my father or my mother,
And shall I now to thee this thing discover.
And she continually before him wept,
During the time the feasting days were kept.
And now behold it came to pass that he,
By reason of her importunity,
Did on the seventh day to her unfold
The riddle, which she to her brethren told;
And e'er the sun went down on that same day,
The Philistines to Samson thus did say,
What is more sweet than honey? What more strong
Than is a lion? And he said, how long
Would it have been, e'er you had understood
This thing, had you not with my heifer plow'd?
Then came the spirit of the Lord upon
Him, and he hasted down to Askelon,
And thirty of the Philistines he slew,
And took their clothes, and gave the garments due.
To every one of them that had disclosed
The meaning of the riddle he proposed;
And towards them his anger fiercely burned,
And he unto his father's house returned.
But Samson's wife was given unto one
That was his friend and chief companion.

CHAP. XV.

But in a while, as Samson visited
His wife, in the wheat harvest with a kid,

To her into her chamber he would go,
The which her father would not let him do;
But said, I thought that thou had'st quite forsook her,
Wherefore I gave consent, and thy friend took her;
Doth not her sister's beauty her's exceed,
Though young? I pray then take her in her stead.
And Samson said, I shall more blameless be
Than they, though I shall do them injury.
And then he caught three hundred foxes, and
Turn'd tail to tail, and put a fiery brand
Between two tails, and setting fire thereto,
Into the standing corn he let them go,
And burnt both shocks and standing corn and vines,
And all the olives of the Philistines.
Then they inquired who this thing had done,
And were inform'd it was the Timnite's son;
Because his father took his wife away,
And gave her his companion to enjoy.
And the Philistines came up, full of wrath,
And burnt with fire, her and her father both.
And Samson said, though you have done this thing,
A further evil I will on you bring;
And my avenging hand shall cease hereafter;
And hip and thigh he smote them with great slaughter.
And he return'd, and came up to the top
Of Etam, and dwelt there upon the rock.
Then the Philistines up to Judah went,
And in the vale of Lehi pitched their tent.
Then said the men of Judah, for what reason
Are you come up against us at this season?
And they made answer, We are come to bind
Samson, to do to him in the same kind
As he hath done to us. Then there went up
Three thousand men of Judah to the top
Of the rock Etam, and to Samson said,
Dost thou not know that we have long obey'd
The Philistines? Wherefore is it that thou
Hast done this thing, to bring this evil now,
Upon us, let us know it? Then said he
I did to them as they have done to me.
Then said they we are come, and have brought bands,
To bind, and give thee up into their hands.
And he made answer, you shall swear unto me,
That you yourselves no injury will do me.
And they reply'd, no no, we will but bind thee,
We will not kill thee, but to them resign thee.
And they took two new cords, and therewith tied him,
And from the rock where he abode convey him:
Whom when they to the camp at Lehi brought,
The Philistines against him gave a shout:
And mightily the Spirit of the Lord
Came on him, and like burning flax each cord
That was upon his arms became; the bands
Were likewise separated from his hands.
And he the jaw-bone of an ass espied,
And took and smote them till a thousand died.
Then said he, with an ass's jaw-bone I
Have made mine enemies in heaps to lie.
Behold I have destroy'd a thousand men
With this same worthless ass's jaw. And when
He made an end to speak, it came to pass
He cast away the jaw-bone of the ass,
And said, Now let the place where this was done
Be by the name of Ramath-Lehi known.

And he was sore athirst, and to the Lord
He cried, and said, O Lord, thou did'st afford
This great deliverance, and now shall I,
By reason of my thirst fall down and die,
And fall into the most accursed hands
Of these uncircumcis'd Philistine bands?
But God was pleas'd to cleave an hollow place,
Within the jaw, from whence did water pass;
Whereof when he had drunk, his spirit came
As heretofore, and he reviv'd again:
Wherefore that place, which is in Lehi, bore
Unto this day the name of En-hakkore.
And in the days the Philistines bore sway,
Israel for twenty years did him obey.

CHAP. XVI.

Then down to Gaza Samson went, and there
Seeing an harlot, went in unto her.
And when the Gazites heard he was come thither:
Straightway they gathered themselves together
To compass him about, and lay in wait
All night, to take him in the city gate;
And they were still all night, for why? Say they,
To-morrow we shall kill him when 'tis day.
And he till midnight lay, and then arose,
And with the city gates away he goes,
Bearing the posts and bar and all away,
And on an hill near Hebron did them lay.
And afterward it came to pass he saw,
And lov'd a woman named Delilah,
Who in the vale of Sorek dwelt, to whom
There did the lords of the Philistines come,
And said, If thou wilt but entice him to reveal
Where lies his strength, and which way we may deal
With him, to bind him, to afflict him, we
Each one will give a great reward to thee.
And she to Samson said, I pray thee, tell
Wherein thy strength doth other men excel,
And how thou may'st be bound. And he replied,
If they with seven green withs that ne'er were dried,
Shall bind me hand and foot, I shall be then
As weak and impotent as other men.
Then the Philistine lords for her provide
The seven green withs which never had been dried,
And she therewith did bind him, (now there were
Men lying in wait whom she had placed there,)
Then she cried out, and said, Now Samson stand
Thy ground, for the Philistines are at hand.
And straight he brake the withs, and they became
Like to a thread of tow when touch'd with flame:
So was his strength not found out. Then said she,
Samson, behold, thou hast deceived me,
And told me lies: therefore no longer blind me,
But tell, I pray thee, wherewith I may bind thee.
Bind me with ropes that ne'er were us'd, said he;
Then weak as other men are, shall I be.
She therefore took new ropes, and bound him, and
Cried, Samson, the Philistines are at hand:
(And in the chamber there were men lay hid)
And from his arms he brake them like a thread.
Then said she, Thou hast mocked me hitherto,
And told me lies: now tell me what to do
To bind thee. He replied, Thou with the web
Must interweave the seven locks of my head.

Then she his locks did fasten with the pin,
And said, The Philistines are coming in,
Shift, Samson, for thyself; then he awoke,
And pin and web, and all away he took.
Then said she, How canst thou pretend to love me,
When thus thy doing towards me disprove thee?
For now, behold, thou hast deceived me thrice,
And hast not told me where thy great strength lies.
At length his soul being vex'd exceedingly,
By reason of her importunity:
He told the secrets of his heart, and said,
Never yet razor on my head was laid;
For I have been to God a Nazarite,
Even from the day that first I saw the light:
Wherefore like other men, if I am shaven,
I shall be weak, and of my strength bereaven.
And when she saw that he had told her all
The secrets of his heart, she sent to call
The lords of the Philistines. Come, said she,
This once, for now he hath made known to me
The very truth. Then they came up together,
And brought the money in their hands to give her.
Then down to sleep upon her knees she laid him,
And call'd a man, who of his locks betray'd him.
And to afflict him she began, and then
His strength became like that of other men.
Then said she, Samson, thy Philistine foes
Are just at hand: and he from sleep arose,
And as at other times went forth to shake him,
Not knowing that the Lord did now forsake him.
But the Philistines seized him, and brought
Him down to Gaza, having first put out
His eyes, and did with brazen fetters bind
And made him in the prison house to grind.
Howbeit the hair upon his head began,
After he had been shaved, to grow again.
Then the Philistine lords together met,
And a thanksgiving-day apart they set,
For to rejoice, and unto Dagon pay
Their highest service; For our God, say they,
Did this: and when the people did behold
Poor captive Samson, they their god extoll'd,
And said, Our God hath given into our hand
Him that destroy'd us, and laid waste our land.
And in their height of mirth they sent to call
Samson, to come and make sport for them all.
And from the prison-house they brought him, and
Between the pillars they set him to stand;
And there he made them sport. Then to the lad
That led him by the hand, thus Samson said;
Let me now feel the pillars that sustain
The house, that I myself thereon may lean.
Now in the house there was a mighty throng
Of men and women gather'd, and among
Them, all the lords of the Philistines were.
Besides, upon the roof there did appear,
About three thousand men and women, who
Beheld, while Samson made them sport below.
And Samson, calling on the Lord, did say,
O Lord, my God, remember me, I pray,
This once give strength, that I aveng'd may be
Of those Philistines who have blinded me.
And with his right hand and his left, he held
Two middle pillars which the house upheld;

And said, Let me with the Philistines die,
And then he bowed himself most mightily :
And down the house fell on the lords, and all
The people that were in't; so that the fall
Thereof, slew at his dying many more
Than he had slain in all his life before.

Then did his brethren and his kinsfolks come
And took him up, and brought him with them home,
And laid him in his father's sepulchre,
When he had judged Israel twenty year.

CHRIST'S SERMON ON THE MOUNT.

MATTHEW, CHAP. V.

AND Jesus, seeing the multitudes, ascended
Up to a mount, where sitting, and attended
By his disciples, he began to preach;
And on this manner following did them teach.
Blessed are all such as are poor in spirit,
For they the heavenly kingdom do inherit.
Blessed are they that mourn; for in the stead
Thereof shall comfort be administred.
Blessed are they, whose meekness doth excel :
For on the earth their portion is to dwell.
Blessed are they, who after righteousness
Hunger and thirst; for they shall it possess.
Blessed are they, for they shall mercy find,
Who to do mercifully are inclin'd.
Blessed are all such as are pure in heart ;
For God his presence shall to them impart.
Blessed are they that do make peace ; for why ?
They shall be call'd the sons of the Most High.
Blessed are they which suffer for the sake
Of righteousness : for they of heav'n partake.
Blessed are ye, when men shall falsely speak
All kind of ill against you for my sake,
And shall revile, and persecute you sore ;
Rejoice, and be exceeding glad therefore :
For your reward in heav'n will be great :
For thus of old they did the prophets treat.
Ye are the salt o' th' earth ; but wherewith must
The earth be season'd when the savour's lost ?
It is from thenceforth good for nothing, but
To be cast out, and trodd'n under foot.
Ye are the light o' th' world; a city set
Upon an hill cannot be hid ; nor yet
Do men a candle with a bushel cover,
But set it where it lights the whole house over.
So shine your light, your good works seen thereby
Men may your heavenly Father glorify.
Think not that to destroy the law I came,
Or prophets ; no, but to fulfil the same.
For till the heav'n and earth shall pass away,
One jot or tittle from the law, I say,
Shall never pass, till all shall be complete.
Whoso therefore presumes to violate,
One of these least commands, and teacheth so,
Shall in God's kingdom be accounted low.
But he that doth, and teacheth them likewise,
Shall in God's kingdom have great dignities.
For I declare unto you, that unless
You shall exceed the scribe and pharisees
In righteousness ; you shall on no condition,
Into the heavenly kingdom gain admission.

Ye've heard 'twas said of old, ' Thou shalt not kill.'
And he incurs the judgment who shall spill
His brother's blood : but I to you declare,
That he that's wroth without a cause, shall bear
The judgment. Likewise of the council he
That sayeth ' racha' shall in danger be.
But whosoe'er shall say, Thou fool, the same
Shall be in danger of eternal flame.
When therefore to the altar thou dost bring
Thy gift, and there rememb'rest any thing
Thy brother hath against thee : leave it there
Before the altar, and come thou not near,
Till thou hast first made reconciliation,
Then may'st thou come and offer thine oblation.
Make an agreement with thine adversary
Whilst thou art in the way, and do not tarry ;
Lest he at any time deliver thee
Unto the judge, and by the judge thou be
Unto the officer forthwith resign'd,
And in imprisonment thou be confin'd;
I do affirm thou shalt not be enlarg'd,
Till thou the utmost farthing hast discharg'd.
Ye've heard that they of old did testify,
That men should not commit adultery :
But I pronounce him an adulterer,
Who views a woman to lust after her.
And if thy right eye shall offensive be,
Pluck thou it out and cast the same from thee ;
For it is better lose one, than that all
Thy members should into hell torments fall.
And if thy right hand doth offend, cut off it,
And cast it from thee, for it will thee profit
Much rather that one of thy members fell,
Than that they should be all condemned to hell.
It hath been said, whoso away shall force
His wife, shall give her a bill of divorce :
But whosoe'er shall put his wife away,
Except for fornication's sake, I say,
Makes her adult'ress, and who marries her,
So put away, is an adulterer.
Again : Ye've heard, Thou shalt not be forsworn,
Was ancient doctrine, but thou shalt perform
Unto the Lord thine oaths: But I declare,
That thou shalt not at all presume to swear ;
Neither by heaven, for it is God's throne ;
Nor by the earth, for his foot stands thereon :
Neither swear by Jerusalem, for why ?
It is the city of the King Most High :
Nor swear thou by thine head, for thou canst make
No hair thereof to be or white or black :
But let yea, yea; nay, nay, in speech suffice,
For what is more from evil doth arise.

Ye've heard, it hath been said; Eye for an eye,
And tooth for tooth: But I do testify,
That you shall not resist; but let him smite
Thy left cheek also, who assaults thy right.
And if that any by a lawsuit shall
Demand thy coat, let them have cloak and all.
And whosoe'er compelleth thee to go
A mile, refuse not to go with him two.
Give him that asketh, and from him that may
Have need to borrow, turn not thou away.
Ye've heard, 'twas said: That thou shalt love thy friend
And hate thy foe: But let your love extend
Unto your enemies: thus I declare,
Bless them that curse, do good to them that bear
Ill will, and for your persecutors pray,
And them that do reproach you; that you may
Be children of your Father that's in heaven;
For he on good and bad alike hath given
His sun to rise, and in like manner doth
Send rain upon the just and unjust both
For what is your reward, if you love them
That love you? Do not publicans the same?
And if your brethren only you salute,
What more than they do ye? They also do't.
I will therefore that you be perfect, ev'n
As is your Father perfect that's in heaven.

CHAP. VI.

Take heed you do not your alms-deeds bestow
Before men, purposely to make a shew;
For then there will no recompence be given
Unto you of your Father that's in heaven:
With sound of trumpet do not thou therefore
Proclaim what thou art giving to the poor;
As is the manner of the hypocrites
To do i' th' synagogues, and in the streets;*
That men may give them praises. Verily
They have their recompence, I testify.
But when thou dost alms, let thy left hand know
Not what thy right hand is about to do:
That giving secretly, thy Father may,
Who sees in secret, openly repay.
And when thou pray'st be not as hypocrites;
For they love in the corners of the streets,
And in the synagogues to stand and pray,
There to be seen: they've their reward I say.
But thou, when thou dost make thy pray'r, go thee
Into thy closet, shut thy door unto thee,
And there in secret to thy Father cry,
Who seeing thee shall reward thee openly.
But when ye pray use not vain repetitions,
As heathens do, for they think their petitions
Prevail; when they the same do multiply:
Be ye not like to them therefore; for why;
Your Father knows what things you need before
You ask him, on this wise pray ye therefore.

Our Father which art in heav'n, thy name alone
Be hallowed. Thy glorious kingdom come.

---

* These lines, and those on the next page, 'The eye's the light o' th'
body,' remind one of Bunyan's style in his Apology for the Pilgrim's
Progress,—

'Dost thou love picking meat? Or would'st thou see
A man i' th' clouds, and hear him speak to thee?'—ED.

Thy will be done on earth as 'tis in heaven.
Give us this day our daily bread. And ev'n
As we remit our debtors, grant remission
To us. And lead us not into temptation,
But from all evil do thou us deliver;
For th' kingdom, power and glory's thine for ever.
Amen.

For if you do forgive men that offend,
Your heavenly Father will to you extend
Forgiveness; but if not, nor will he spare,
At any time when you offenders are.
Moreover when you fast beware lest you
Look sad, as hypocrites are wont to do;
For they disguise their faces, that they may
Appear to fast: they've their reward I say.
But thou, when thou dost fast, anoint thine head
And wash thy face, that undiscovered
Thy fasting may be unto men, but rather
That thou be seen in secret of thy Father:
And then thy Father, who in secresy
Beholds thee, shall reward thee openly.
Lay not up treasure for yourselves in store
Upon the earth, where moth and rust devour,
And where by thieves you may be quite bereaven.
But lay up treasure for yourselves in heaven,
Where neither moth, nor rust, nor thieves can enter:
For where's your treasure there your hearts will centre.
The eye's the light o' th' body, which if right
Then thy whole body will be full of light:
But if thine eye be evil, then there will
A total darkness thy whole body fill.
If therefore all the light that is in thee
Be darkness, how great must that darkness be?
No man can serve two masters, either he
Will hate one, and love t'other, or will be
Faithful to one, and t'other will forego.
Ye cannot serve both God and mammon too.
Take no thought therefore for your life, I say,
What you shall eat or drink; or how you may
Your bodies clothe. Is not the life much more
Than meat; Is not the body far before
The clothes thereof? Behold the fowls o' th' air,
Nor sow nor reap, nor take they any care;
How they provision into barns may gather;
Yet they are nourish'd by your heavenly Father:
Are ye not worth much more? Which of you can
By taking thought add to his height one span?
And why for raiment are ye taking thought?
See how the lilies grow; they labour not,
Nor do they spin; yet Solomon, I say,
In all his pomp, had no such gay array.
If in the field God so doth clothe the grass,
Which is to-day, and doth to-morrow pass
Into the oven, shall he not therefore
O ye of little faith, clothe you much more?
Take no thought therefore, saying, What shall we eat,
Or drink, or where shall we our raiment get:
(For thus the heathen people use to do)
For that you need them doth your Father know.
But seek God's kingdom, and his righteousness
First, and then all these things you shall possess.
Be not then exercis'd with care and sorrow,
In making preparation for the morrow;

The morrow shall things for itself prepare :
Sufficient to the day is each day's care.

CHAP. VII.

Judge not that you may not be judg'd ; for even
As you pass judgment, judgment shall be giv'n :
And with such measure as you mete to men,
It shall be measured unto you again.
And why dost thou take notice of the mote
That's in thy brother's eye ; but dost not note
The beam that's in thine own ? How wilt thou say
Unto thy brother, let me take away
The mote that's in thine eye, when yet 'tis plain
The beam that's in thine own doth still remain ?
First cast away the beam, thou hypocrite,
From thine own eye, so shall thy clearer sight
The better be enabled to descry,
And pluck the mote out of thy brother's eye.
Give not to dogs the things that are divine,
Neith'er cast ye your pearls before the swine
Lest that they should their feet them trample under,
And turn upon you, and rend you asunder.
Ask, and obtain ; seek, and ye shall find ; do ye
Knock, and it shall be opened unto ye :
For he that seeks, shall find ; that asks, obtain,
And he that knocks, shall an admittance gain.
Or what man is there of you, if his son
Shall ask him bread, will he give him a stone?
Or if he ask a fish, will he bestow
A serpent ? If then ye being evil know
To give your children good gifts, how much rather
To them that ask him shall your heav'nly Father.
Then what you wou'd men shou'd to you, so do
To them : for that's the law and prophets too.
Enter in at the strait gate, for the road
That doth unto destruction lead, is broad;
And wide the gate ; and many there be that
Enter therein : because strait is the gate,

And narrow is the way that is inclin'd
To life, and which there are but few that find.
False prophets shun, who in sheep's clothes appear,
But inwardly devouring wolves they are :
Ye by their fruits shall know them. Do men either
Pluck grapes of thorns, or figs of thistles gather ?
Even so each good tree good fruit will produce ;
But a corrupt tree fruit unfit for use :
A good tree cannot bring forth evil food,
Nor can an evil tree bear fruit that's good :
Each tree that bears not good fruit's hewn down
And burnt, thus by their fruits they shall be known.
Not every one that saith Lord, Lord, but he
That doth my heav'nly Father's will shall be
An heir of heaven : many in that day
Will call Lord, Lord, and thus to me will say ;
Have we not prophesied in thy name ?
Cast devils out, done wonders in the same ?
And then will I profess I know you not ;
Depart from me ye that have evil wrought.
Whoso therefore these sayings of mine doth hear,
And doth them, to a wise man I'll compare,
The which upon a rock his building founded,
The rain descended and the floods surrounded,
The winds arose, and gave it many a shock,
And it fell not, being founded on a rock.
And ev'ry one that hears these sayings of mine,
And not to do them doth his heart incline,
Unto a foolish man shall be compar'd ;
Who his foundation on the sand prepar'd :
The rain descended and the floods were great,
The winds did blow, and vehemently beat
Against that house ; and down the building came,
And mighty was the downfall of the same.
And now when Jesus thus had finished
His sayings, the people were astonished
Thereat : for not as do the scribes taught he
Them, but as one that had authority.

THE PROPHECY OF JONAH.

CHAP. I.

Now unto Jonah, old Amittai's son,
Thus did the word of the Almighty come,
And said, Arise, go thou forthwith and cry
'Gainst that great city Nineveh ; for why,
The sins thereof are come up in my sight.
But he arose, that he to Tarshish might
Flee from God's presence ; and went down and found
A ship at Joppa unto Tarshish bound :
He paid the fare, and with them went on board
For Tarshish, from the presence of the Lord.
But the Almighty a great wind did raise,
And sent a mighty tempest on the seas,
So that the ship was likely to be broken.
Then were the mariners with horror stricken ;
And to his God they cried every one ;
And overboard was the ship's lading thrown
To lighten it : but down into the ship
Was Jonah gone, and there lay fast asleep.

So to him came the master and did say,
What meanest thou, O sleeper ! rise and pray
Unto thy God, and he perhaps will hear,
And save us from the danger that we fear.
Then said they to each other, Come let's try,
By casting lots, on whom the fault doth lie,
In bringing all this evil now upon us.
So they cast lots, and the lot fell on Jonas.
Then said they, We entreat thee let us know,
For whose cause we this evil undergo,
Whence comest thou ? What is thine occupation ?
What countryman art thou ? And of what nation ?
And unto them himself he did declare,
And said, I am an Hebrew, and do fear
The living Lord, the God of heaven, who
Alone hath made the sea and dry land too.
Then were the men exceedingly afraid ;
And, wherefore hast thou done this thing ? they said :
(For they did understand he did forego
God's presence, for himself had told them so.)

AND THE SEA CEASED FROM HER RAGING.

TARSHISH

SO THEY TOOK UP JONAH & CAST HIM FORTH INTO THE SEA

JOPPA

JONAH CAST INTO THE SEA

BLACKIE & SON, GLASGOW, EDINBURGH & LONDON.

What shall we do unto thee, then they said,
That so the raging of the sea be stay'd?
(For it did rage and foam.)   Take me, said he,
And cast me overboard into the sea;
So shall the sea be calm, for on my score
I know it is, that thus the waves do roar.
Nevertheless they rowed hard to gain
The land, but all their labour was in vain;
So much against them did the tempest beat.
Wherefore they the Almighty did entreat,
And said, We do beseech thee, and we pray,
O Lord, that thou would'st not upon us lay
The charge of guiltless blood, nor let it be,
That now we perish, on th' account that we
Take this man's life away; for thou alone
As it hath pleased thee, O Lord, hast done.
So they took Jonah up, and to the seas
Committed him, then did the tempest cease.
Then did the dread of the great God on high,
Seize on the mariners exceedingly.
And they did offer up a sacrifice,
And vowed vows unto the Lord likewise.
And now the Lord for Jonah did contrive
A mighty fish, to swallow 'im up alive,
And in the fish's belly for the space
Of three days and three nights, poor Jonah was.

CHAP. II.

Unto the Lord his God then Jonah pray'd
Out of the belly of the fish, and said,
By reason of affliction, which lay sore
Upon me, I the Lord God did implore,
And he gave ear; and from Hell's Belly I
Cry'd unto thee, and thou, Lord, heard'st my cry:
For thou into the deep hadst cast me out,
And there the floods did compass me about;
In the midst of the sea, thy waves were sent,
And all thy billows which my head o'erwent.
Then said I though thy presence hath forsook
Me, to thy holy temple will I look.
The waters compassed about my soul,
And the great deeps did round about me roll,
The weeds were wrapt about my head, I went
Down to the bottom of the element;
The earth with her strong bars surrounded me,
Yet thou, O Lord, from death hast set me free.
When my soul fainted, on the Lord I thought,
And to thee, to thy temple then was brought
My prayer.   They their own mercies do despise,
Who have regard to lying vanities.
But with the voice of my thanksgiving, I
Will offer sacrifice to thee on high,
And pay my vows which I have vow'd, each one,
For why? Salvation's of the Lord alone.
And now the fish, as God did give command,
Did vomit Jonah out upon dry land.

CHAP. III.

And now the second time to Jonah came
God's word, and said, Arise, go and proclaim
To that great city Nineveh, what I
Have heretofore commanded thee to cry.
So Jonah rose up, and prepar'd to go
To Nineveh, as God had bid him do.

(Now was the city Nineveh so great,
That it was three days' journey long complete)
And as into the city Jonah made
His first day's journey, he cry'd out and said,
When forty days shall be expired and past,
This city Nineveh shall be laid waste.
Then did the Ninevites with one accord,
Believe this was the message of the Lord;
And did proclaim a fast, and every one,
From greatest to the least, put sackcloth on:
For to the king this news was quickly flown,
And he arose, and came down from his throne,
And having laid aside his robes of state,
He put on sackcloth, and in ashes sate:
And issuing out his royal proclamation,
And through the city making publication
Thereof (being by the king and council sign'd)
A solemn and a general fast enjoin'd;
And said, I will, that neither man nor beast,
Nor flock, nor herd, shall their provision taste:
But let them all put sackcloth on and cry
Unto the Lord with greatest fervency;
Yea, let them all their evil ways refrain,
And from the violence which they retain.
Who knows if God will yet be pleas'd to spare,
And turn away the evil that we fear?
And God beheld their works, and saw that they
Had turned from the evil of their way.
And God turn'd from his wrath, and did revoke
The dreadful judgment whereof he had spoke.

CHAP. IV.

But hereat Jonah was extremely vext,
And in his mind exceedingly perplext:
And to the Lord his God he pray'd, and said,
O Lord, I pray thee, was not I afraid
Of this, when I was yet at home?   Therefore
I unto Tarshish took my flight before:
For that thou art a gracious God I know,
Of tender mercy, and to anger slow,
Of great compassion, and dost oft recall
The evil thou dost threat mankind withal.
Now therefore, Lord, I earnestly do pray
That thou would'st please to take my life away,
For I had better die than live.   Dost thou
Do well, said God, to be so angry now?
So then out of the city Jonah went,
And on the east side of it made a tent,*
And underneath the shade thereof he sate,
Expecting what would be the city's fate.
And over Jonah's head behold the Lord
Prepar'd, and caused to come up a gourd
To shadow him, and ease him of his grief;
And Jonah was right glad of this relief.
But God a worm sent early the next day,
Which smote the gourd; it withered away:
And when the sun arose, it came to pass,
That God a vehement east wind did raise;
Besides the sun did beat upon his head,
So that he fainted, saying, Would I were dead;
For it is better for me now to die,
Than thus to lead my life in misery.

---

* סֻכָּה, a cover, a booth, bower, or hut made of the boughs of trees.—Ed.

And to distressed Jonah, said the Lord,
Dost thou well to be angry for the gourd?
And he unto the Lord made this reply,
I do well to be angry e'en to die.
Thou hast had pity, Jonah, on the gourd,
For which thou didst not labour, said the Lord,
Nor madest it to grow, which also came
Up in a night, and perish'd in the same.

And should not I extend my gracious pity
To Nineveh, so populous a city,
Where more than six score thousand persons dwell,
Who 'twixt their right hand, and their left can tell
No difference, wherein are also found
Cattle which do in multitudes abound.

THE LIFE OF JOSEPH,

TAKEN OUT OF THE LATTER PART OF THE BOOK OF GENESIS.

CHAP. XXXVII.

WHEN Jacob from his brother Esau fled,
He by the hand of providence was led
To Padan-aram, in Assyria, where
He serv'd his uncle Laban twenty year;
During which time he was in all things blest,
And with a num'rous issue 'mongst the rest:
Amongst whom none so pleasing in his sight
As Joseph was, who was his chief delight:
Who by the time that Jacob was return'd
Into the land, where's fathers had sojourn'd,
Was full arrived at seventeen years of age;
And by his hopefulness did then presage,
He was endued with a noble mind,
That would to virtuous actions be inclin'd;
For being sent to feed his father's flock,
Among his brethren he great notice took
Of what they did, and if in any sort
They did amiss, he thereof made report
Unto his father, and did thus create
His father's favour, but his brethren's hate.
His father loved him better than the rest,
As being the son wherewith his age was blest.
And that his kindness might the more appear,
Made him a party colour'd coat to wear.
But as it often haps, his father's love
Did in his brethren greater hatred move.
But that which most incens'd them was his dreams,
By which, in a prophetic way, he seems
Their low submission, and his future state
Of greatness plainly to prognosticate.
For to his brethren thus his dreams he told,
And said, As we were binding sheaves, behold,
My sheaf arose and stood up in the field,
And all your sheaves stood round about, to yield
Obeisance unto mine: And what, must we
Indeed, say they, be subject unto thee?
Their wrath increas'd, this added to his crime.
And Joseph dreamed yet a second time;
And said, Behold, I saw the sun and moon,
And the eleven stars to me fall down.
At which his father highly was offended,
And for these words, the lad he reprehended,
And said, Fond youth, dost thou pretend to shew
That I, thy mother, and thy brethren too,
Must all submit to thee? Thou dost but dream:
But Jacob kept his words, and thought of them.

Now Jacob's sons did feed their flocks in Shechem,
And he desired Joseph to go seek them,
And find them out, and come again and tell
If all things with them and their flocks were well.
So Joseph went, and wander'd here and there,
But could not find out where his brethren were,
Until a man had told him their intent
Of going to Dothan, where he also went.
And when his brethren at a distance saw him,
They held a consultation how to slay him,
And said, Here comes the dreamer, we shall see
What the event of all his dreams will be;
For we will kill, and in a pit will hide him,
And say some beast or other hath destroy'd him.
But Reuben somewhat tend'rer than the rest,
Endeavour'd to persuade them to desist
From murder, saying, Into this pit let's cast him,
And this he said in hopes to have releas'd him.
And now when Joseph came not dreading ought,
They stript him of his party colour'd coat,
And led him to a pit that was hard by,
And threw him into't, but the pit was dry.
And sitting down to eat, they chanc'd to spy,
A company of Ishmaelites pass by,
Who with balm, myrrh, and spice, their camels lading,
From Gilead came, and were to Egypt trading.
Then Judah said, 'Twill do us little good
To slay our brother, and conceal his blood;
Come therefore, brethren, be advis'd by me,
Let's sell him to these Ishmaelites, for he
Is our own flesh, and 'tis a cruel deed,
To kill him, and to this they all agreed.
Their brother then out of the pit they hale,
And to these merchants offer'd him to sale:
Who, him for twenty silver pieces bought,
And with them to the land of Egypt brought.
But Reuben, ignorant of what was done,
Came to the pit, and seeing the lad was gone,
He rent his clothes in a great consternation,
Returning back with heavy lamentation.
And now that they might make their story good
They kill'd a kid, and dipped in the blood
Their brother Joseph's coat, and home they came,
And to their father's view expos'd the same,
And said, This we have found, now thou dost know
Whether it be thy son's coat, yea or no.
And Jacob knew the coat full well, and said,
Now hath some evil beast devour'd the lad;

Joseph is torn in pieces without doubt,
For, too, too well I know this is his coat.
He rent his clothes, and putting sackcloth on,
He for a long time mourned for his son.
His children striving to assuage his grief
Endeavour'd to administer relief:
But he refus'd, and said, Since he is gone, ⎞
I will in sorrow to the grave go down.   ⎬
Such lamentation made he for his son.   ⎠

CHAP. XXXIX.

And now these merchants, sons of Ishmael,
Again did poor afflicted Joseph sell,
To an Egyptian, named Potiphar,
The captain of King Pharoah's men of war.
And God was with him, and did greatly bless,
And crown his undertakings with success.
Whereof his master being well aware,
Committed all he had to Joseph's care;
And made him overseer of his house,
And, from the time his master us'd him thus,
The Lord was pleas'd to give him to partake,
So many blessings, e'en for Joseph's sake:
Of that with plenty he was hedg'd about,
And prospered within door and without.
Such was his master's love, and he so just,
That all things were committed to his trust.
Now Joseph was grown up to manly stature,
Of goodly presence, and most comely feature.
Wherefore his mistress, with a lustful eye,
Beheld his beauty, and resolv'd to try,
If to unchaste embraces she could gain
The youth, but her endeavours prov'd in vain:
For he refus'd, and said, My master knows ⎞
In all the house of nothing that he owes,*   ⎬
For his concerns are all at my dispose: ⎠
There's not a thing that he hath kept from me
But all is in my hand, save only thee;
Then how can I commit so foul a fact,
And the displeasure of my God contract?
Yet still she sued, and still did he deny her,
Refusing to be with her, or lie by her.
Now on a time when all the men were gone
Out of the house, and she was left alone:
And Joseph at that instant coming in,
About some business he'd to do within;
She took advantage of their being together,
And held his clothes to force him to lie with her.
But Joseph strove, and from her hands got loose,
And left his coat, and fled out of the house.
And when she saw that he had made's escape,
She call'd her servants, and proclaim'd a rape:
Come see now how this Hebrew slave, said she,
Your master's favourite, hath affronted me.
He came to violate my chastity,
And when he heard that I began to cry,
And call for help, afraid lest you should find him,
He's fled, and left his garment here behind him.
And now to give her words the greater credit,
Until her husband's coming home, she hid it,
To whom she spake, and said, Why hast thou brought
This Hebrew here, to set me thus at nought?

* 'He owes,' a contraction for 'he owneth.'—ED.

The slave attempted to defile my bed,
And when I cry'd, he left his coat and fled,
See here it is. Which when he saw, and heard
The heavy accusation she preferr'd,
He was exceeding wroth at his behaviour,
And utterly cashier'd him from his favour;
Nay more, he cast him into prison, where
In fetters bound, King Pharoah's pris'ners were.
But Joseph's God, who never yet forsook
Him in extremity, was pleas'd to look
With great compassion on his injuries,
And gave him favour in the keeper's eyes;
So that he was entrusted with the care
And charge of all the pris'ners that were there:
All were committed unto Joseph's hand,
And what was done, was done at his command.
The prison-keeper took no care at all,
Of ought that he entrusted him withal;
Because he saw that God was with him, and
All things did prosper that he took in hand.

CHAP. XL.

And now, whilst Joseph in confinement lay,
It came to pass upon a certain day,
That Pharoah King of Egypt, being wroth
With his chief butler, and chief baker both,
For their offences, put them both in ward,
In the house of the captain of the guard:
Into the place where Joseph was confin'd,
Unto whose custody they were resign'd;
And he attended on them in the prison.
And there they were continu'd for a season,
During which time it chanced both of them
Did in the same night dream each man his dream:
Which dreams, according to interpretation,
Had to themselves particular relation.
And Joseph coming early the next day,
Into the room where Pharoah's servants lay,
Beheld their countenances much dejected:
Wherefore he said, What evil hath effected
This melancholy frame, what is't that causes
These marks of discontentment in your faces?
Then said they, We have dream'd each man his dream,
And there is no man to interpret them.
Then Joseph said, Your dreams to me make known,
Interpretations are from God alone.
Then unto Joseph the chief butler told
His dream, and said, Methought I did behold
A vine, whereon three branches did appear,
Which seem'd to bud, to blossom, and to bear
Clusters of full ripe grapes, which to my thinking
I press'd into the cup for Pharoah's drinking.
And Joseph said, Thy dream doth signify,
Thou shalt enjoy thy former dignity:
The branches which thou sawest are three days,
In which King Pharoah will his butler raise
And to thy place again will thee restore,
And thou shalt serve him as thou'st done before:
But do not, when it shall be well with thee,
Forget me, but show kindness unto me,
And unto Pharoah represent my case,
That I may be deliver'd from this place;
For I was stol'n out of the Hebrew's land,
And also here am wrongfully detained.

Then the chief baker having understood,
That the interpretation was so good,
He told his dream to Joseph too, and said,
Lo, I had three white baskets on my head,
And in the uppermost there seem'd to be,
Of baked provision, great variety,
Fit for King Pharaoh's table, and there came
A flock of birds, and seem'd to eat the same.
And Joseph said, Thy dream portends thy fall,
For at the end of three days Pharaoh shall
Lift up thy head, and hang thee on a tree,
So that the birds shall feast themselves on thee.
And on the third day Pharaoh made a feast
Unto his servants, and among the rest
The butler and the baker were brought forth,
The day being kept in memory of his birth.
And to his place King Pharaoh did restore
His butler, and he served him as before.
But the chief baker he condemn'd to die,
According unto Joseph's prophecy.
Yet though the butler had regain'd his place,
He was unmindful of poor Joseph's case.

CHAP. XLI.

And now when two years' time was fully past,
And Joseph from confinement not releast,
It came to pass that Pharaoh dream'd, and
He seemed by a river-side to stand,
Whence he seven fat well-favour'd kine beheld,
Come up and grazed in the neighbouring field.
And after them there came up seven more, }
Lean and ill-favour'd, and did soon devour }
The seven fat kine which came up just before. }
So Pharaoh 'woke, and mus'd awhile, and then
Soon as his sleep his dream returned again:
Wherein he saw upon one stalk there stood
Seven ears of corn exceeding rank and good,
And seven others, with the east wind blasted,
And withered, sprang up, and quickly wasted
The seven good ears, and quite devour'd them:
And Pharaoh 'woke, and lo, it was a dream.
And in the morning he was discontent,
And for the wise men and magicians sent,
To ease his mind; but there was none of them
That could interpret to the king his dream.
Then the chief butler, making his address
Unto King Pharaoh, said, I now confess
My former faults, for when the king was wroth
With his chief butler, and chief baker both,
It pleased him, to put us both in ward,
In the house of the captain of the guard:
And in one night we dream'd a dream, each one
According to 's interpretation:
And there was then an Hebrew there in ward,
A youth that serv'd the captain of the guard:
To whom we told whereof we had been dreaming,
And he interpreted to us the meaning;
And what he said fell out accordingly, }
Me he restored to my dignity, }
But told the baker he should surely die. }
Then Pharaoh sent a messenger in haste,
And Joseph from the dungeon was releas'd:

And having shav'd himself and chang'd his clothes,
Into the presence of the king he goes.
To whom king Pharaoh said, I have been told
Thou canst the meaning of a dream unfold:
Now I have dream'd a dream, and there is none
Can give me the interpretation.
And Joseph said, I cannot do this thing
Myself, but God shall answer thee, oh king.
Then Pharaoh said to Joseph, In my dream,
As I stood by a river's side, there came
Up from the river seven well-favour'd kine,
And fed upon the banks, all fat and fine,
And after them there came up seven more,
Lean and ill-favour'd, and exceeding poor:
Such as the land of Egypt never bred,
And on the seven well-favour'd kine they fed,
And eat them up, but 'twas not to be seen
That they had eat them, they look'd still so thin.
So I awoke, and mus'd awhile, and then
Soon as my sleep, my dream return'd again;
Wherein I saw upon one stalk there stood
Seven ears of corn, exceeding rank and good:
Then seven others, with the east wind blasted,
And withered, came up, and quickly wasted
The seven good ears, and quite devoured them.
And being unsatisfied about my dream,
I sought unto the wise men of the nation,
But they could give me no interpretation.
And Joseph said, Thy dream, oh king! is one,
God shews to Pharaoh what he will have done.
The seven fat kine and seven good ears agree
To shew, seven years of plenty there shall be.
The seven lean kine, and seven blasted ears,
Denote there shall be famine seven years.
This I declare to Pharaoh, God doth shew
To thee, oh king! what he's about to do.
Behold seven years of plenty are at hand,
Which shall be very great throughout the land.
And after them seven years of famine shall
Arise, and shall consume the land, and all
The former plenty shall not be perceiv'd,
So much the land with famine shall be griev'd.
And since the dream was doubl'd to the king, }
It is because God hath decreed the thing, }
And on this land the same will shortly bring : }
Now therefore if I may the king advise,
Let him look out a man discreet and wise,
And make him overseer of the land :
And substitute men under his command
To gather a fifth part for public use,
Of what the seven plenteous years produce ;
And in the cities lay it up for store,
Against the famine in the land grows sore ;
And let it be repos'd in Pharaoh's hand,
That so the famine may not waste the land.
And when king Pharaoh and his servants heard
The propositions Joseph had preferr'd,
They were acceptable in Pharaoh's eyes,
And in the eyes of all his court likewise :
So that he said, Can such an one be found ?
A man in whom God's Spirit doth abound.
And Pharaoh said to Joseph, Forasmuch
As God's great kindness unto thee is such,

As to reveal this thing to thee, I know
No man so wise or so discreet as thou.
Be thou therefore the ruler of the land,
And let my people be at thy command ;
Thou shalt in all things be as great as I,
Save only in the royal dignity.
Behold this day I have advanced thee
Said he, to be a man of high degree
Throughout the land.   And therewithal the king
Bestow'd on Joseph his own royal ring ;
And him with robes of state did richly deck,
And put a chain of gold about his neck,
And in his second chariot made him ride,
And as he past, Bow down the knee they cry'd,
With so great honour was he dignifi'd.
And Pharaoh said moreover, I am king,
No man shall dare to purpose any thing,
Or move his hand or foot in all this nation,
Unless it shall be by thy approbation.
He also gave to Joseph a new name,
And for a wife gave him a princely dame,
Who was the daughter of a priest of fame.
(Now Joseph had attained his thirtieth year,
When he before king Pharaoh did appear.)
And he went out from Pharaoh's presence, and
Began his progress over all the land.
Now in the seven plenteous years, the field
Did its increase in great abundance yield.
And Joseph gather'd all that plenteous crop,
And in th' adjacent cities laid it up :
Which like unto the sand upon the shore,
Did so abound that he could count no more,
Such was the plenty that the earth then bore.
And unto Joseph there was born a son,
Even by the daughter of the priest of On,
Before the years of famine were begun ;
The which he call'd Manasseh, for, said he,
God makes me to forget my misery,
And all my father's house.   And after him
Was born another he called Ephraim ;
For God, saith he, hath made me to possess
Abundance in the land of my distress.
And when the seven plenteous years were gone,
The seven years of famine next came on,
As Joseph said, and there was a great dearth
In every nation throughout all the earth ;
But in the land of Egypt there was bread.
And when the people almost famished,
Complained to the king, he bade them go
To Joseph, and whate'er he said to do.
And now the famine daily waxing sore,
Joseph began to bring forth of his store,
Which he had laid up for the public good ;
To whom th' Egyptians came and bought their food.
And people from all countries far and near
To Egypt came to buy provision there ;
For in all lands the famine was severe.

CHAP. XLII.

And now, behold, when Jacob had been told
That there was corn in Egypt to be sold,
He said unto his sons, Why stand ye thus ?
Go down to Egypt and buy corn for us ;

That so our craving stomachs may be fed,
And not be here and die for lack of bread.
Thus Jacob's ten sons were to Egypt sent,
But Joseph's brother Benjamin ne'er went.
For why, his father said, I will not send him,
Lest peradventure some ill chance attend him.
And Joseph's brethren came among the rest
To buy provision, for they were distress'd.
Now he was governor of all the land,
And all the corn of Egypt in his hand.
Wherefore his brethren, when they came to treat
With him for corn, bow'd down e'en at his feet :
And he no sooner saw them but he knew them,
And show'd himself extremely strange unto them :
And very roughly asked who they were,
From whence they came, and what their bus'ness there.
And they made answer, We thy servants from
The land of Canaan to buy food are come.
Now tho' they knew him not, yet he knew them,
And calling now to mind his former dream,
He said, I do suspect ye're come as spies,
To see in what distress our country lies.
But they reply'd again, My lord, we're come
Only to buy some food to carry home.
Think not thy servants spies, but true men rather,
For we are all the children of one father.
Nay, nay, said he, but ye are come to pry
Into the nation's great necessity.
But they reply'd again, Thy servants are
Inhabitants of Canaan, and declare,
That we're twelve brethren, whom one man begot,
The youngest is at home, and one is not
Well then, said Joseph, hereby shall I know,
Whether ye're spies, as I have said, or no ;
Now by the life of Pharaoh do I swear,
Until your brother come I'll keep you here.
Send one of you and fetch the lad to me,
And you shall be confin'd, so shall there be
A proof of what you say before mine eyes,
Or by the life of Pharaoh ye are spies.
Then he for three days put them all in ward,
And on the third day said, I have regard
To equity, therefore if ye are true
And honest men, do this ; let one of you
Be bound in prison here, and let the other
Go carry corn home and bring me your brother ;
So shall ye be approv'd and shall not die.
And they prepared to do accordingly.
And as they were discoursing to each other,
They said, We were in fault about our brother,
In that we saw his soul in great distress,
And yet were so exceeding pitiless,
As not to hearken to his earnest cries :
This is the cause of these our miseries.
And Reuben said, You know I did forewarn,
And beg that you would do the child no harm ;
But you would not do then as I desir'd,
And now his blood is at our hands requir'd.
Thus they discours'd about the cause that brought
Their present trouble, but they little thought
That Joseph knew of what they did confer,
Because he spake by an interpreter.
And he being moved at their words withdrew
To weep, and then returned to renew

His former talk; and choosing Simeon out,
Before them all he bound him hand and foot.
And gave command to fill their sacks with grain,
And to restore their money to 'em again;
And for their journey gave them food to eat;
In such sort Joseph did his brethren treat.
Then with their asses laden towards home
They went, and when into their inn they come
As one of them his sack of corn unty'd,
To give his ass some provender, he spy'd
His money in his sack again return'd;
Wherefore he call'd his brethren and inform'd
Them that his money was returned back.
Behold, said he, it is here in my sack.
On sight whereof their hearts were sore dismay'd,
And being very much affrighted said,
What is the thing that God's about to do,
That we do thus these troubles undergo?
Then coming to their father they related,
After what sort they were in Egypt treated:
And said, the man that's lord of all the land,
And hath the store of corn all in his hand,
Spake roughly to us, and affirm'd that we
Were come the weakness of the land to see.
To whom we said, We are all honest men;
We are twelve brethren, whereof here are ten,
And two elsewhere, all which one man begot,
The youngest's with our father, one is not.
Then said the ruler of the land, Hereby
Shall I make proof of your integrity:
Let one of you continue here with me,
And take provision for your family;
And get you gone and bring the youngest hither,
That so I may be satisfied whether
Ye are true men, as you make protestation, ⎫
Then I'll release him, and give toleration ⎬
To you to come and traffic in the nation. ⎭
And now behold as they their sacks unloos'd
To empty out their corn, there was unclos'd
In each man's sack his money therein bound,
As when they came from home, which when they found,
Both they and their old father were afraid;
And to his sons afflicted Jacob said,
You of my children have bereaved me,
Joseph and Simeon now do cease to be;
And of my Benjamin you would deprive me,
These things do ev'n into distraction drive me.
Then Rueben said, My father I resign
To thy disposing these two sons of mine;
Give me the lad, and let them both be slain,
If I do not return him safe again.
But he reply'd, I will not let him go,
For why his brother is deceas'd you know;
And if upon the way some evil thing
Should happen to the lad, you then will bring
These my grey hairs with sorrow to the grave;
For he's the only comfort that I have.

CHAP. XLIII.

And now the famine still continuing sore, ⎫
And having spent all their late purchas'd store, ⎬
Their father bids them to go down for more ⎭
To whom when Judah had himself address'd,
He said, The man did solemnly protest,

If we without our brother came again,
To seek his face would be for us in vain:
If therefore thou wilt send him, well and good,
Then will we willingly go down for food;
But if thou wilt not, we must let thee know,
We are resolved that we will not go:
For, as I said before, the ruler swore
Without him we should see his face no more.
Then Israel said, Why were you so unkind
To say you had a brother left behind?
The man, said they, was so inquisitive,
He asked if our father were alive,
Or if we had a brother, whereunto ⎫
Accordingly we answer'd, could we know ⎬
If he would bid us bring the lad or no? ⎭
Moreover Judah to his father said,
If thou wilt but entrust me with the lad,
We will begone, that so both thou and we
May be preserved with our family:
I will be surety for him, if I fail
To bring him back, on me the blame entail;
For if we had not lingered, we had been
By this time here the second time again.
Well then, said Isr'el, if it must be so,
My sons, take my advice before you go;
Provide some of the best fruits of the land,
To give the man a present from your hand;
Balm, myrrh, and spices, and a little honey,
Some nuts and almonds, and take double money,
For peradventure it was a mistake,
In that your money was returned back.
And take your brother Benjamin and go,
And God Almighty grant the man may shew
You mercy, that you may bring back again ⎫
Your other brother, and my Benjamin, ⎬
And if I am bereav'd, so have I been. ⎭
Then did the men prepare the present, and
They took their money double in their hand
With Benjamin, and down to Egypt went,
Who unto Joseph did themselves present.
Who, when he saw that Benjamin was come,
Order'd his steward to conduct them home,
And to provide a dinner, for, said he,
I do intend these men shall dine with me.
Then did the steward as his master said,
And brought them home, whereat they were afraid,
And said, The man hath caus'd us to come in,
Because our money was return'd again;
To take occasion now to fall upon us,
And make us slaves, and take our asses from us.
Unto the steward they drew nigh therefore,
And thus communed with him at the door:
O sir, say they, we came at first indeed
To buy provision to supply our need;
And in our inn as we our sacks unloos'd,
We found our money therein all inclos'd
In its full weight, whereat surpris'd with fear,
Not knowing who had put our money there,
We now have brought it in full weight again,
And other money too, to buy more grain.
Peace, peace, said he, let not fear seize upon you
For I had the disposing of your money:
God, unto whom you and your father bow,
Hath giv'n you treasure in your sacks I trow.

And then releasing Simon, who had been
Confin'd in Joseph's house, he brought them in
And set them water, and they wash'd their feet;
And gave their asses provender to eat.
Then they made ready, against Joseph came,
Their gifts, in order to present the same
At noon; for they were told he did design
To have their company with him to dine.
And now when Joseph was returned home,
Into his presence they with rev'rence come,
And brought their presents in and laid before him,
And fell down at his feet for to adore him.
Then he inquired if they all were well,
And said, When you were here I heard you tell
Of an old man, your father, how does he?
Is he in health, or doth he cease to be?
Whereto in humble sort they thus repli'd,
Thy servant, ev'n our father, doth abide
In perfect health, which having said,
They bowed their heads and great obeisance made.
And Joseph viewing Benjamin his brother
(They being both the children of one mother)
He asked if he were the lad of whom
They spake, then said, God give thee grace, my son.
Then making haste to find a secret place
To weep, because his bowels yearn'd apace
Upon his brother, to his chamber went,
Where having giv'n his troubled spirits vent,
He washed his face, and did himself refrain,
And to his brethren then came forth again,
And bade his servants they should set on bread.
At his command the tables were all spread;
One for himself, and for his friends another,
And for the Egyptians one apart from either,
That so they might not eat bread altogether;
For it is held a great abomination
For them to eat among the Hebrew nation.
And they were placed as their age required,
The eldest first, whereat the men admired.
And from his table Joseph sent them messes;
But in a larger manner he expresses
To Benjamin his kindness, which was such,
That he appointed him five times as much
As to the rest: and they drank plenteously,
Till they were merry in his company.

CHAP. XLIV.

And to his steward Joseph spake, and said,
Give these men corn as much as they can lade;
And in their sacks bind each man's money up,
And in the youngest's put my silver cup
Besides his money: and he made haste and did
According as his master had commanded.
And in the morning by the break of day,
With asses laden they were sent away:
And now, e'er they had scarce the town's end pass'd,
He sent his steward after them in haste,
And said, Go, follow them, and ask them why
They have dealt by me so ungratefully?
And say unto them, You have done great evil
To rob my master, who hath been so civil,
And steal the cup wherein he drinks his wine;
Is it not it whereby he doth *divine?

* The word שׁחֵן, translated 'divine,' means to eye subtilly, to search,

Then he pursu'd and quickly overtook
Them, and these very words to them he spoke.
To whom they said, Why hath my lord such thought?
Oh, God forbid that we should be so †naught;
Behold, thou know'st we brought the money back
The which we found bound up in each man's sack,
Which shews that we had no design to cheat;
How then should we now steal your master's plate?
With which of us thy servants it is found
Let him be slain, and we to slavery bound.
Now as you say, said he, so let it be,
He shall be bound, but you shall all go free.
Then they unladed ev'ry man his beast,
And to his view expos'd their sacks in haste.
And he from first to last them searched round,
And lo, the cup on Benjamin was found:
Thereat surpris'd, each man his garment rent,
And lades his beast, and back again they went.
And now when Judah and the rest were come
To Joseph's house, (for he was yet at home)
They fell before him to the ground, to whom
He said, What deed is this that you have done?
Are you not sensible that such a one
As I, can certainly thereof make trial?
Then Judah said, My lord, there's no denial:
We cannot clear ourselves. The Lord hath sent,
For our misdeeds, this heavy punishment.
Behold, to be thy slaves we all are bound,
Both we, and he on whom the cup was found.
Then Joseph said, The Lord forbid that I
Should exercise so great severity:
For he with whom 'tis found, and he alone
Shall be my servant, you may all be gone.
Then unto Joseph, Judah drawing near,
Said, O my lord! I pray be pleas'd to hear
Thy servant speak, and be not angry now,
For as king Pharaoh is ev'n so art thou.
My lord did bid thy servants to discover
Whether we had a father or a brother;
And we made answer that thy servants had
An ancient father and a little lad,
The child of his old age, who was our brother,
And he the only child left of his mother,
His brother being dead; and that this lad
Was all the comfort that our father had.
Then thou wert pleas'd to bid thy servants bring
The lad, that thou might'st have a sight of him.
And we made answer, if the lad should leave
His father, it would bring him to his grave:
And thou didst then protest it was in vain
For us without him to come here again.
Then towards home thy servants went their way,
And told our father what my lord did say.
And in a while, when all our corn was spent,
Thy servant, ev'n our father, would have sent
To buy more food; to whom thy servants said,
We cannot go except thou send the lad.
Because the man did solemnly declare,
Unless we brought him we should not come there.

to try. וְהוּא נַחֵשׁ יְנַחֵשׁ בּוֹ, v. 5, may be rendered, 'And he will search deeply for it; and in v. 15, 'Know ye not that a man like me would search deeply,' alluding to the certainty of detection, but not by divination.—ED.

† 'So naught,' so corrupt, bad, or worthless.—ED.

And then thy servant, ev'n our father, said,
Ye know that by my wife two sons I had,
And one of them went forth and came no more,
Which made me think some beast did him devour.
And if I now should also condescend ⎫
To let this go, and mischief should attend, ⎬
You will with sorrow bring me to my end. ⎭
When to my father I shall come therefore,
And he shall see that I do not restore
The lad again, he certainly will die, ⎫
(Since in his life my father's life doth lie) ⎬
And we shall bring him to his grave thereby. ⎭
For I became a surety for the lad
Unto my father, unto whom I said,
If I do not in safety him deliver,
Then let me bear the blame to thee for ever.
I humbly pray thee, therefore, to accept
Me in his stead, and let me here be kept
My lord's bond-slave, and let the lad go free :
For how can I, thy servant, bear to see
The evil that shall on my father come,
If that the lad return not safely home.

CHAP. XLV.

Then Joseph, who by no means now could hide
His brotherly affection longer, cry'd,
Put all men forth; and he was left alone
When to his brethren he himself made known.
Then Joseph weeping lifted up his voice
So loud, that Pharaoh's servants heard the noise.
And to his brethren did himself discover,
And said, Lo! I am Joseph your own brother;
And doth my father live ?   Whereat amaz'd,
They could not speak, but at each other gaz'd.
Then Joseph said, Come near, I pray, behold,
I am your brother Joseph whom ye sold
To Egypt, be not grieved now therefore,
Nor vex yourselves, for God sent me before
To save life ; for these two years there hath been ⎫
A famine, and five more to come, wherein ⎬
Seed time nor harvest shall at all be seen. ⎭
The Lord, I say, hath sent me to provide
A place, and strangely save your lives beside.
So now ye sent me not, but it was rather
The Lord, and he hath made me as a father
Unto the king, lord of his household, and
A ruler over all this spacious land.
Unto my father, therefore, go your way,
And tell him, Thus doth thy son Joseph say:
The Lord hath rais'd me to a high degree
In Egypt, tarry not, but come to me,
And thou shalt dwell in Goshen and be nigh me,
And with provision there will I supply thee ;
Both thou and thine, flocks, herds, and all thou hast,
(For yet these five years will the famine last)
Lest otherwise, provision being scant,
Thou and thy family may come to want.
Behold, both you and Benjamin my brother
Do see that it is I and not another.
Go tell my father this amazing story,
And bring him hither to behold my glory.
Then falling on his youngest brother's neck,
And he on his, they o'er each other wept.

And to the rest he did likewise, wherefore
They now were more familiar than before.
And now whilst they discoursed, the report
Of their arrival came to Pharaoh's court,
And he was pleas'd thereat, wherefore he said
To Joseph, let thy brethren straightway lade
Their beasts with corn, and thus unto them say,
Unto your native country haste away,
And fetch your father, and your households, and
I'll feed you with the good things of the land ;
And since you are commanded by the king,
Take waggons with you hence wherein to bring
Your wives, your little ones, and come down hither,
Your father, you and yours altogether ;
And never heed to bring your household stuff,
For here in Egypt you shall have enough.
Then did the Isr'elites accordingly :
And Joseph ordering them a large supply
Of necessaries for their journey, sent
Waggons according to the king's intent.
And to each man he gave a suit of clothes,
But on his brother Benjamin bestows
Five suits, and as a token of his love,
A sum of money over and above.
And thus he sent ev'n for his father's use,
Of the best things that Egypt did produce,
Ten asses load, and ten she asses load
Of bread and meat, to spend upon the road.
Then sending them away, he said, I pray
See that you do not fall out by the way.
And leaving Egypt with their num'rous train,
Unto their father they returned again :
To whom, as soon as e'er they did arrive,
They said, Our brother Joseph's yet alive,
And lord of all the land, which sore dismay'd
Him, for he scarce believed what they said.
Then they of all that pass'd gave him relation,
And shewed the waggons for a confirmation
Which being manifest before his eyes,
He rais'd himself, and said, It doth suffice ;
Joseph my son is yet alive, and I
Will go to see him once before I die.

CHAP. XLVI.

Then Isr'el setting forward on his way
With all his household, came to Beersheba;
And offer'd sacrifice there to implore
The God his father Isaac did adore.
And in the visions of the night God spake
To him, and said, Fear not to undertake
This journey into Egypt, for I am
The God of thy forefathers, Abraham
And Isaac ; to the land of Egypt I
Will go with thee, and there will multiply
Thy offspring, and of thee will surely make
A mighty nation, and will bring thee back ;
And thy son Joseph there thine eyes shall close.
After which vision he from thence arose,
And in the waggons which king Pharaoh sent,
He and his family to Egypt went :
His sons, their wives and children, and the rest
Of their concerns, whereof they were possest
When they in Canaan dwelt, and they were then
No more in number but threescore and ten.

And when to Egypt Israel drew near
He sent before him Judah, to prepare
His way to Goshen, which when Joseph heard,
Immediately his chariot he prepar'd;
And unto Goshen he directly went,
And to his father did himself present:
And being over-joy'd fell on his neck,
And for a good while thereupon he wept.
Then Jacob said, Since thou yet liv'st, and I
Have seen thy face once more, now let me die.
And Joseph said, My brethren I will go
Unto king Pharaoh, and will let him know
That you, and all my father's house are come;
And that your occupation when at home,
Hath been in feeding cattle altogether,
And that you've brought your flocks and herds all hither.
Now therefore when you come before the king,
And he should ask you what your trade hath been,
Say thus: Thy servants from our youth till now
Have dealt in cattle, we and our fathers too,
That he may let you dwell in Goshen, for
Th' Egyptians do a shepherd's life abhor.

CHAP. XLVII.

Then to king Pharaoh Joseph went and said,
My father and his sons, with all they had
In their own country, are come down to me,
And in the land of Goshen now they be.
Five of his brethren also with him went,
Whom he unto king Pharaoh did present.
And Pharaoh asked them about their trade,
And they unto the king reply'd and said:
We and our fathers while we were at home
Were shepherds all, and now behold, we come
With all our flocks, to get some pasture here,
For in our land the famine is severe.
We therefore pray thee to appoint a portion
Unto thy servants in the land of Goshen.
And Pharaoh said to Joseph, I empow'r thee
To use thy pleasure, Goshen is before thee;
Settle thy father and thy brethren there, ⎫
And if among them active men there are, ⎬
Commit my cattle to their special care. ⎭
And Joseph brought his aged father in
Before the king, and Jacob blessed him.
And Pharaoh asking him about his age,
He said, The years of my life's pilgrimage
Are but an hundred thirty, very few
And evil, nor have I attain'd unto
The years of my forefathers longer age,
Which they pass'd thro' in this their pilgrimage.
And Jacob bless'd the king again, and then
Out of his presence he return'd again.
And Joseph plac'd his father and relations
In Egypt, and appointed them possessions
In the best of the land, ev'n in the land
Of Rameses, according to the king's command:
And there he nourished them with fit supplies
Of bread, according to their families.
And now the people having spent their store,
And famine still increasing more and more,
Egypt and Canaan too, for want of bread,
Were sore distress'd and almost famished.

And Joseph took the money they did bring
To buy their corn, and kept it for the king.
Wherefore the people came to represent
Their case to him, both corn and coin being spent.
And Joseph said, If money be grown scant,
Bring me your cattle and ye shall not want.
And they brought horses, asses, and their flocks
And herds of cattle, ev'n all their stocks,
And gave to Joseph in exchange for bread,
For which the people he for that year fed:
And when that year was past, the second year
They came again, and said, We can't forbear
To let thee know our want, my lord doth know
Thou hast our money and our cattle too,
And there is nothing left (so hard's our fate)
But only each man's person and estate:
If thou wilt give us bread, into thy hands
Will we resign our persons and our lands:
And be the servants of the king for ever.
From death therefore our hungry souls deliver,
And take some pity on our wretched state,
Lest we die, and the land be desolate.
And the Egyptians sold each man his field,
Because the famine over them prevail'd;
And all their lands became the king's possession,
And Joseph placed them at his own discretion.
But the land of the priests he purchased not,
For Pharaoh had assigned to them their lot:
And they received their food from Pharaoh's hands,
Wherefore they had no need to sell their lands.
And Joseph said unto them, Now behold,
You and your lands are unto Pharaoh sold:
Lo! here is seed to sow in each man's field,
And when the land its ripe increase shall yield,
A fifth part shall belong unto the crown,
And the other four parts shall be your own,
For seed to sow your lands, and for supplies
Of food convenient for your families.
And they said; Thou hast sav'd our lives, my lord, ⎫
Thy gracious favour unto us afford, ⎬
And we will do according to thy word. ⎭
And Joseph made it a decree, to stand
Ev'n to this day throughout th' Egyptian land;
That Pharaoh should have a fifth part, except
The priests' lands, which unto themselves they kept.
And in the land of Egypt ev'n in Goshen,
Did Isr'el dwell, and therein had possession;
And grew and multiply'd exceeding fast.
And Jacob liv'd till seventeen years were past:
So that the sum of Jacob's age appears
To be an hundred forty-seven years.
And when the time approach'd that he must die,
He called Joseph, unto whom he said, If I
Have now found favour in thy sight, I pray,
Swear thou unto me that thou wilt not lay
My bones in Egypt, for I fain would lie
Among my ancestors when e'er I die,
And not be bury'd here; therefore fulfil
This my desire; and he reply'd, I will:
And he said, Swear unto me, which he did:
Then Jacob bow'd himself upon his bed.

CHAP. XLVIII.

And now when Joseph heard his father lay
Even at the point of death he hastes away
To visit him, and took along with him
His son Manasseh, and's son Ephraim.
Whereof when Jacob heard he strength'ned
Himself, and rose and sat upon the bed :
And thus to Joseph said, Lo! God appeared
To me at Luz in Canaan, and declared,
That he would bless, and make me a great nation,
And give my seed that land for a possession :
And Jacob said, Behold, these sons of thine
As Reuben and as Simeon shall be mine ;
And all the rest that shall be born to thee ⎫
Hereafter, shall be thine, and they shall be ⎬
Call'd by the name of their own family. ⎭
Behold thy mother died upon the way,
When I from Padan came, near Ephratah,
The which is in the land of Canaan, where,
To wit, in Bethlem, did I bury her.
And Jacob seeing Joseph's sons were there,
He asked of him who the children were.
And Joseph said, My father, lo! these be
The sons, God in this place hath given me.
Then Jacob said, I pray thee bring them nigh
To me, and I will bless them e'er I die.
(Now Jacob's eyes, by reason of age, were dim)
And Joseph brought his sons near unto him,
And Jacob kissed and embraced them :
And said, I never thought to see thy face,
And lo! the Lord hath shewn me of thy race.
And Joseph from between his knees brought forth
His sons, and bow'd himself even to the earth :
And in his right hand held up Ephraim,
Towards his father's left hand guiding him
And in nis left hand to his father's right,
He held his son Manasseh opposite.
And Isra'l stretching out his right hand, laid
It on the youngest, namely Ephraim's head :
And laid his left hand wittingly upon
Manasseh's head, although the eldest son.
And Jacob blessed Joseph, saying, The God
Of heaven, in whose paths my fathers trod,
Who all my life hath nourish'd me, even he
Who from all evil hath redeemed me,
Bless both the lads, and let them bear my name,
And the name of my fathers Abraham
And Isaac, and let them multiply
In the midst of the earth exceedingly.
And Joseph seeing his father's right hand laid
On Ephraim's head, he was displeas'd, and said,
Not so, my father, lay this hand upon
Manasseh's head, for he's the eldest son :
And therewithal attempted to have laid
His father's right hand on Manasseh's head
But he refus'd and said, I know't my son,
I know't full well, he also shall become
A people, and be mighty: But indeed ⎫
His younger brother shall him far exceed, ⎬
And many nations shall come from his seed. ⎭
Thus Jacob blessed them, and said, In thee
Shall Isra'l bless, and say, God make thee be

Like Ephraim and Manasseh. Thus did he
Prefer the youngest to the first degree.
And Isra'l said to Joseph, Lo! I die,
But God shall visit you, and certainly
Shall bring you back unto your father's land.
And thou shalt have a portion from my hand,
Above thy brethren, which with sword and bow
I took from th' Amorite, my deadly foe.

CHAP. XLIX.

And Jacob called all his sons together,
And said, Ye sons of Jacob come you hither:
And hearken what your aged father says,
Who tells you what shall be in the last days.
Reuben my first born, of my strength the flowrs,
The excellency of dignity and power:
Unstable as water, be for ever vile,
Because thou did thy father's bed defile.
Simeon and Levi 're brethren. Instruments
Of cruelty are lodged in their tents.
Come not, my soul, their secret councils nigh,
My honour, with them have no unity:
For in their wrath they caused a man to fall,
And in their self-will digged down a wall.
Curs'd be their anger, fierce, yea cursed be
Their wrath, for it was full of cruelty.
In Jacob therefore let their seed be spread,
And every where in Israel scattered.
Judah shall have his brethren's praise, and they
Shall bow before him; he his foes shall slay.
Judah's a lion's whelp return'd from prey,
He stoop'd, he couch'd, and as a lion lay;
As an old lion, who shall dare molest,
Or rouse him up, when he lies down to rest.
The sceptre shall from Judah never start,
Nor a lawgiver from his feet depart;
Until the blessed Shiloh come, to whom
The scatter'd people shall from all parts come:
Binding his foal unto the choicest vine,
He wash'd his garments, all of them in wine:
His eyes shall with the blood of th' grapes look red,
And milky whiteness shall his teeth o'erspread.
Lo! Zabulon shall dwell upon the sea, ⎫
An haven for the ship's security, ⎬
And unto Zidon shall his border be. ⎭
And Issachar is a strong ass between
Two burdens crouching, who when he had seen
That rest was pleasant, and the land was good,
His servile neck unto the yoke he bow'd.
Dan as a judge shall over Isra'l sway,
He shall be as a serpent in the way,
To bite the horse, and cast the rider down.
O God! I have look'd for thy salvation.
Gad by a troop shall be o'ercome, but he
Shall at the last obtain the victory.
The bread of Ashur shall be fat indeed,
And royal dainties shall from him proceed.
Like to a hind let loose is Naphtali,
He speaketh all his words acceptably.
Joseph's a fruitful bough, whose branches tall
Grow by a well, and over-top the wall:
By reason of hatred which the archers bore,
They shot at him and griev'd him very sore,

But Joseph's bow in its full strength abode
And by the arm of Jacob's mighty God,
He was indu'd with strength, from whence alone
Is Isra'l's shepherd, and chief corner-stone:
Ev'n by my father's God, who shall assist
Thee, by th' Almighty God shalt thou be blest,
With blessings from above, and from below,
With blessings of the breast, and womb also.
Thy father's blessings have prevail'd beyond
My ancestors.   Unto the utmost bound
Of the perpetual hills, yea let them rest ⎫
On Joseph's head, and let him be possest ⎬
Of all, who was divided from the rest. ⎭
Young Benjamin shall wolf-like take his prey,
And part by night what he hath took by day.
All these are the ten tribes of Israel,
And thus their father did their fate foretel:
And blessed every one of them apart,
According to their personal desert.
Moreover he gave them a charge and said,
Lo! I shall die, but let my bones be laid
Among my ancestors in Canaan, where
Of Ephron, Abraham bought a sepulchre,
Together with a field, to be a place
Of burial, for him and all his race.
(There Abraham and Sarah lie, and there⎫
They Isaac and Rebecca did inter, ⎬
And there when Leah died I buried her.)⎭
The field was purchas'd of the sons of Heth.
Thus having said, resigning up his breath
To him that gave 't, his feet into the bed
He drew, and so was number'd to the dead.

CHAP. L.

And Joseph fell upon his father's face,
And did with tears his lifeless lips embrace:
And sends for his physicians and advises
Them to embalm his father's corpse with spices.
And they did so, and forty days did pass. ⎫
(For so the manner of embalming was) ⎬
And the Egyptians mourned for the space ⎭
Of three score and ten days, which being expired
He spake to Pharaoh's servants and desired,
That they would please to speak in Pharaoh's ear,
And tell him that my father made me swear,
That I should bury him in Canaan, where
He hath provided his own sepulchre.
I therefore pray thee that I may obtain
Thy leave, and I will soon return again.
And Pharaoh said, Since thou hast sworn, fulfil
Thy oath, according to thy father's will.
And Joseph went up to accompany
His father's corpse with great solemnity.
And with him went up Pharaoh's servants, and
The prime nobility of all the land,
And Joseph's houshold, and his brethren all,
Only their flocks, and herds, and children small

Were left behind.   Moreover there went up
Chariots and horsemen, ev'n a mighty troop.
And they came up to Atad's threshing floor
Beyond the river Jordan, where full sore
They mourned for him till seven days were past,
So long their mourning in that place did last.
Which when the Canaanites beheld they said,
Surely some eminent Egyptian's dead.
Wherefore they call'd it Abel-mizraim.*
Thus did his sons as he commanded them.
For to the land of Canaan they convey'd
Him, and in Machpelah near Mamre, laid
His body in the cave which Ephron sold
To Abraham, for him and his to hold.
And thus when Joseph fully had perform'd
His father's will, to Egypt he return'd,
Together with his brethren, and with all
Them that came with him to the funeral.
Now Joseph's brethren being well aware
That they were fatherless, began to fear
That he would hate them, and requite them all
The evil they had treated him withal.
Wherefore to him they sent a messenger
And said, Behold our father did declare
Before he died, that we should come and say,
Forgive thy brethren's trespasses, I pray;
And their misdeeds, for they have been unkind.
And now we humbly pray thee be inclin'd
To pardon our offences, and the rather
For that we serve the God e'en of thy father.
And Joseph wept when they thus spake, and they⎫
Came nearer, and before him prostrate lay, ⎬
And said, We are thy servants all this day. ⎭
And Joseph bad them not to be afraid,
For in the place of God am I he said:
For though you meant me ill, God meant it good,
And sent me hither to provide you food.
Now therefore trouble not yourselves, for I
Will nourish you, and all your family.
After this manner did he satisfy,
And treat them with extreme civility.
And Joseph and his father's house remain'd
In Egypt, and he liv'd till he attain'd
An hundred and ten years, and liv'd to see
Of Ephraim's children to the third degree.
And Macher's children of Manasseh's tribe
Were also born some time before he died.
Then Joseph said, My brethren, lo! I die,
But God will visit you undoubtedly;
And to that land again whereof he spake
Unto our ancestors, will bring you back.
And Joseph also made his brethren swear,
That they would not inter his body there.
And thus he ended his life's pilgrimage,
Being an hundred and ten years of age;
And was embalm'd, and in a coffin laid,
In Egypt, till he could be thence convey'd.

* אֵבֶל מִצְרַיִם, the mourning of Egypt.—ED.

THE GENERAL EPISTLE OF JAMES.

CHAP. I.

UNTO the twelve tribes scattered abroad,
James, an apostle of the living God,
And of the Lord Christ Jesus, salutation.
My brethren, when you fall into temptation
Of divers kinds, rejoice, as men that know
From trial of your faith doth patience flow.
But let your patience have its full effect,
That you may be entire, without defect.
If any of you lack wisdom, let him cry
To God, and he will give it lib'rally,
And not upbraid. But let him ask in faith,
Not wavering, for he that wavereth,
Unto a wave o' th' sea I will compare,
Driv'n with the wind and tossed here and there.
For let not such a man himself deceive,
To think that he shall from the Lord receive.
A double-minded man most surely lacketh
Stability in all he undertaketh.
Let ev'ry brother of a low degree
Rejoice in that he is advanc'd, but he
That's rich in being made low, for he shall pass
Away, as doth the flow'r of the grass.
For as the grass, soon as the sun doth rise,
Is scorch'd by reason of the heat, and dies;
Its flow'r fades, and it retains no more   ⎫
The beauteous comeliness it had before,   ⎬
So fades the rich man, maugre all his store. ⎭
The man is blest that doth endure temptation
For when he's try'd, the crown of God's salvation,
The which the Lord hath promised to give
To them that love him, that man shall receive.
Let no man be possest with a persuasion,
To say, when he falls under a temptation,
That God's the cause; for with no evil can
God be tempted, nor tempts he any man.
But every man is tempted when he's drawn
Away, and by his lusts prevail'd upon;
Then when lust hath conceiv'd, it ushereth
In sin, and sin when finished brings death.
Err not, my brethren, whom I dearly love,
Each good and perfect gift is from above,
Down from th' original of lights descending,
With whom's no change, nor shadow thereto tending,
According to his own good pleasure, he   ⎫
Begat us with the word of truth, that we ⎬
Should as the first fruits of his creatures be. ⎭
Wherefore, beloved brethren, I entreat
You to be swift to hear, and slow to speak,
And slow to wrath, for wrath cannot incline
The sons of men to righteousness divine.
Wherefore avoiding ev'ry filthiness,
And superfluity of naughtiness:
Receive with meekness the engrafted word,
Which can salvation to your souls afford.
But be ye doers of the word each one,
And not deceive yourselves to hear alone;
For he that hears the word and doth it not,
Is like unto a man that hath forgot

What kind of man he was, tho' in a glass
He just before beheld his nat'ral face.
But whoso minds the law of liberty
In its perfection, and continually
Abides therein, forgets not what he's heard,
But doth the work and therein hath reward.
If any man among you seem to be
Religious, he deceives himself if he
Doth not his tongue as with a bit restrain;
And all that man's religion is but vain.
Religion, pure and undefil'd, which is
Acceptable before the Lord, is this:
To visit widows and the fatherless,
In time of their affliction or distress;
And so to regulate his conversation,
As to be spotless in his generation.

CHAP. II.

Faith of the Lord of glory, Jesus Christ,
Doth with respect of persons not consist;
For if, my brethren, when there shall come in
To your assembly one with a gold ring,
In goodly clothes, and there shall also be
Another man that's meanly cloth'd, and ye
Shall have respect to him in rich attire,
And say unto him, come thou, sit up higher;
And bid the poor man stand or sit below, ⎫
Are ye not partial then, and plainly show, ⎬
That you do judge amiss in what you do?   ⎭
Hearken, my brethren, hath not God elected
The poor, who by this world have been rejected;
Yet rich in faith, and of that kingdom heirs,
Which God will give his foll'wers to be theirs?
But you, my brethren, do the poor despise.
Do not the rich men o'er you tyrannise;
And hale ye to their courts; that worthy name
By which you're call'd do not they blaspheme?
Then if ye do the royal law fulfil,
To love thy neighbour as thyself, 'tis well,
According to the scripture; but if ye
Shall have respect to persons, ye shall be
Guilty of sin, and by the law condemn'd,
As such who have its righteousness contemn'd.
For he that shall but in one point offend,
Breaks the whole law, whate'er he may pretend.
For he that doth forbid adultery,
Forbids likewise all acts of cruelty.
Now tho' thou be not an adulterer,
Yet if thou kill, thou shalt thy judgment bear.
So speak and do as those men that shall be
Judg'd by the perfect law of liberty:
For he shall judgment without mercy know; ⎫
That to his neighbour doth no mercy show; ⎬
And mercy triumphs against judgment too.   ⎭
Brethren what profit is't if a man saith
That he hath faith, and hath not works; can faith
Save him? If any of the brotherhood
Be destitute of clothes or daily food,
And one of you shall say, Depart in peace,
Be warmed or be ye fill'd, ne'ertheless,

Ye do not furnish them with what they need,
What boots it ? Thus faith without works is dead.
Yea may a man say, thou dost faith profess,
And I good works, to me thy faith express
Without thy works, and I will plainly show
My faith unto thee by the works I do.
Thou dost believe there is one God, 'tis true,
The devils do believe and tremble too.
But wilt thou know, vain man, that faith is dead,
Which with good works is not accompany'd.
Was not our father Abraham justify'd
By works, and by the same his faith was try'd ;
When he his Isaac to the altar brought ;
Seest thou how with his works his faith then wrought ?
And with his works he perfected his faith ?
And so the scripture was fulfill'd, which saith,
Abraham believed God, and 'twas imputed
For righteousness, and he God's friend reputed.
Thus may you see, that by works ev'ry one
Is justify'd, and not by faith alone.
Thus was the harlot Rahab justify'd }
By works, when she the messengers did hide, }
And by another way their feet did guide. }
For as the body's dead without the spirit,
So faith without works never can inherit.

CHAP. III.

Affect not, brethren, superiority,
As knowing that we shall receive thereby
The greater condemnation in the end :
For we in many things do all offend.
Who doth not with his tongue offend, he can
Guide his whole body, he's a perfect man.
Behold, in horses' mouths we bridles put,
To rule and turn their bodies quite about.
Behold likewise the ships, which tho' they be
Of mighty bulk, and thro' the raging sea
Are driv'n by the strength of winds, yet they
By a small helm the pilot's will obey.
Ev'n so the tongue of man, which tho' it be
But a small member, in a high degree
It boasts of things.   Behold, we may remark
How great a matter's kindled by a spark.
The tongue's a fire, a world of ill, which plac'd
Among the members, often has disgrac'd
All the whole body, firing the whole frame
Of nature, and is kindl'd by hell flame.
All kind of beasts and birds that can be nam'd,
Serpents and fishes, are and have been tam'd
By mankind ; but the tongue can no man tame,
A stubborn evil full of deadly bane.
We therewith God the Father bless, and we
Therewith curse men made like the Deity :
Blessing and cursing from the same mouth flow,
These things, my brethren, ought not to be so.
Is any fountain of so strange a nature,
At once to send forth sweet and bitter water ?
Can olives, brethren, on a fig-tree grow, }
Or figs on vines ? no more can water flow }
From the same fountain sweet and bitter too. }
He that's endu'd with wisdom and discretion
Amongst you, let that man by the profession
Of meekness, wisely give a demonstration,
Of all his works, from a good conversation.

But if your hearts are full of bitterness
And strife, boast not, nor do the truth profess.
This wisdom is not from above descending,
But earthly, sensual, and to evil tending :
For where there's strife and envying there's confusion
And ev'ry evil work in the conclusion.
But the true wisdom that is from above,
Is, in the first place, pure, then full of love,
Then gentle and entreated easily, }
Next merciful, without partiality, }
Full of good fruits, without hypocrisy. }
And what is more, the fruits of righteousness
Is sown in peace, of them that do make peace.

CHAP. IV.

From whence come wars and fights, come they not hence,
Ev'n from th' inordinate concupiscence
That in your members prompts to variance ?
You lust and have not, kill and desire to have ;
But ne'ertheless obtain not what you crave.
With war and fighting ye contend, yet have not
The things which you desire, because you crave not ;
Ye crave but don't receive, the reason's just,
Ye crave amiss to spend it on your lust.
You that live in adultery, know not ye
The friendship of the world is enmity
With God ?   He is God's enemy therefore
That doth the friendship of the world adore.
Do ye think that th' scripture saith in vain,
The spirit that lusts to hate, doth in you reign ?
But he bestows more grace, wherefore he says,
God scorns the proud, but doth the humble raise.
Unto the Lord therefore submissive be,
Resist the devil and he'll from you flee.
Draw nigh to God, and he'll to you draw nigh.
Make clean your hands you sinners, purify
Your hearts you double-minded, weep and mourn,
And be afflicted, let your laughter turn
To sorrow, and your joy to sadness : stoop
Before the Lord, and he will lift you up.
My brethren, speak not evil of each other ;
He that doth judge and speak ill of his brother,
Doth judge and speak ill of the law ; therefore
If thou dost judge the law, thou art no more
A doer of the same, but dost assume
The judgment-seat, and art thyself become
A judge thereof.   There is but one law-giver, }
That's able to destroy and to deliver ; }
Who then art thou that dost condemn thy neighbour ? }
Go to now, you that say, to such a place
To-morrow will we go, and for the space
Of one whole year, or so, will there remain,
And buy and sell, and get great store of gain :
Whereas ye know not what a day may do.
For what's the life of man ? Ev'n like unto
A vapour, which, tho' for a while it may
Appear, it quickly vanisheth away.
So that ye ought to say, If God permit
Us life and health, we will accomplish it.
But now ye glory in your confidence,
Such glorying is of evil consequence.
He therefore that doth know, and doth not act
The thing that's good, doth guilt thereby contract.

CHAP. V.*

Go to now, O ye rich men, howl and cry,
Because of your approaching misery:
Your riches are corrupted, and the moths
Have ent'red, and have eaten up your clothes.
Your gold and silver's canker'd, and the rust
Thereof, shall be an evidence that's just
Against you, and like fire your flesh devour:
Against the last days ye have heap'd up store.
The hire of them that reaped down your field,
The which by you is wrongfully withheld,
Cries, and the voice thereof hath reach'd the ears
Ev'n of the God of sabbath, and he hears.
Your lives in pleasure ye on earth have led,
And as in days of slaughter nourished
Your wanton hearts, and have condemn'd and slain
The just, and he doth not resist again.
Be patient therefore, brethren, ev'n unto
The coming of the Lord: behold, ev'n so
The husbandman expecteth patiently
The precious increase of the earth to see,
With patience waiting till he doth obtain
The showers of early and of latter rain.
So be ye patient, fixing stedfastly
Your hearts, for the coming of the Lord draws nigh.
Grieve not each other, brethren, lest ye bear
The condemnation;† lo! the judge stands near.
The prophets, brethren, who all heretofore
In the name of the Lord their witness bore,

* By a typographical error, in the original edition, it is misprinted
CHAP. XLVI.
† How admirably does Bunyan enlarge upon this in his 'Peaceable
principles yet true.'

Take for examples in their sufferings
And patience: they that endure such things,
Ye know are counted blest.   Have ye not read
Of Job, how patiently he suffered?
Have ye not seen in him what was God's end;
How he doth pity and great love extend?
My brethren, but above all things forbear,
By heav'n or earth, or otherwise to swear;
But let your yea be yea, your nay be nay,
Lest ye become reproveable I say.
Let him sing psalms that's merry; he that's griev'd,
Let him by prayer seek to be reliev'd.
If any of you by sickness be distress'd,
Let him the elders of the church request
That they would come and pray for him a while;
Anointing him in the Lord's name with oil;
So shall the pray'r that is of faith restore
The sick, and God shall raise him as before.
And all th' offences which he hath committed
Shall be forgiv'n, and he shall be acquitted.
Confess your faults each one unto his brother,
And put up supplications for each other,
That so you may be heal'd; the fervency
Of just men's prayers prevails effectually.
Elias was a man as frail as we are,
And he was earnest with the Lord in pray'r,
That there might be no rain, and for the space
Of three years and six months no rain there was:
And afterward, when he again made suit,
The heav'n gave rain, the earth brought forth her fruit.
If any one shall from the truth desert,
And one, my brethren, shall that man convert;
Let him be sure, that he that doth recall
The poor backsliding sinner from his fall,
Shall save a soul from death, and certainly
Shall hide a multitude of sins thereby.

AN EXPOSITION

ON THE

FIRST TEN CHAPTERS OF GENESIS,

AND PART OF THE ELEVENTH;

AN UNFINISHED COMMENTARY ON THE BIBLE, FOUND AMONG THE AUTHOR'S PAPERS AFTER HIS DEATH,
IN HIS OWN HANDWRITING ; AND PUBLISHED IN 1691, BY CHARLES DOE, IN A
FOLIO VOLUME OF THE WORKS OF JOHN BUNYAN.

ADVERTISEMENT BY THE EDITOR.

BEING in company with an enlightened society of Protestant dissenters of the Baptist denomination, I observed to a doctor of divinity, who was advancing towards his seventieth year, that my time had been delightfully engaged with John Bunyan's commentary on Genesis. 'What,' said the D.D., with some appearance of incredulity, 'Bunyan a commentator—upon Genesis!! Impossible! Well, I never heard of that work of the good Bunyan before. Why, where is it to be found?' Yes, it is true that he has commented on that portion of sacred scripture, containing the cosmogony of creation—the fall of man—the first murder—the deluge—and other facts which have puzzled the most learned men of every age; and he has proved to be more learned than all others in his spiritual perceptions. He graduated at a higher university —a university unshackled by human laws, conventional feelings, and preconceived opinions. His intense study of the Bible, guided by the teaching of the Holy Spirit, enabled him to throw a new and beautiful light upon objects which are otherwise obscure. Oh! that young ministers, while attaining valuable book learning, may see the necessity of taking a high degree in, and of never forgetting this Bible university! Reader, is it not surprizing, that such a treatise should have remained comparatively hidden for more than one hundred and fifty years. It has been reprinted in many editions of Bunyan's works: but in all, except the first, with the omission of the scripture references; and with errors of so serious a character as if it was not intended to be read. Even in printing the text of Ge. vii. 7. Noah's three sons do not enter the ark! although in viii. 16. they are commanded to go forth out of the ark. It is now presented to the public exactly as the author left it, with the addition of notes, which it is hoped will illustrate and not encumber the text.

This exposition is evidently the result of long and earnest study of the holy scriptures. It is the history of the creation and of the flood explained and spiritualized, and had it been originally pub-lished in that form and under a proper title, it would most probably have become a very popular work. The author's qualifications for writing this commentary were exclusively limited to his knowledge of holy writ. To book learning he makes no pretensions. He tells us that in his youth ' God put it into my parents' hearts to put me to school, to learn to read and write as other poor men's children ; though, to my shame, I confess, I did soon lose that little I learnt even almost utterly.'* In after life, his time was occupied in obtaining a livelihood by labour. When enduring severe mental conflicts, and while he maintained his family by the work of his hands, he was an acceptable pastor, and extensively useful in itinerant labours of love in the villages round Bedford. His humility, when he had used three common Latin words, prompted him to say in the margin, 'The Latine I borrow.'† And this unlettered mechanic, when he might have improved himself in book wisdom, was shut up within the walls of a prison for nearly thirteen years, for obeying God, only solaced with his Bible and Fox's Book of Martyrs. Yet he made discoveries relative to the creation, which have been very recently again published by a learned philosopher, who surprised and puzzled the world with his vestiges of creation. Omitting the fanciful theories of the vestige philosopher, his two great facts, proved by geological discoveries, are—I. That when the world was created and set in motion, it was upon principles by which it is impelled on to perfection—a state of irresistible progress in improvement. This is the theory of Moses: and Bunyan's exposition is, that all was finished, even to the creation of all the souls which were to animate the human race, and then God *rested* from his work. II. The second geological discovery is that the world was far advanced towards perfection, producing all that was needful for human life, before man was created. Upon this subject, Bunyan's words are—' God

---

* Grace Abounding, No. 3.   † Pilgrim's Progress, Part 2.

shews his respect to this excellent creature, in that he first provideth for him before he giveth him his being. He bringeth him not to an empty house, but to one well furnished with all kind of necessaries, having beautified the heaven and the earth with glory, and all sorts of nourishment for his pleasure and sustenance.'* But the most pious penetration is exhibited in the spiritualizing of the creation and of the flood—every step produces some type of that new creation, or regeneration, without which no soul can be fitted for heaven. The dim twilight before the natural sun was made, is typical of the state of those who believed before Christ, the Sun of righteousness, arose and was manifested. The fixed stars are emblems of the church, whose members all shine, but with different degrees of lustre — sometimes eclipsed, and at others mistaken for transient meteors. The whales and lions are figures of great persecutors. But the most singular idea of all is, that the moral degradation of human nature before the flood, was occasioned by hypocrisy and persecution for conscience sake, arising from governors interfering with matters of faith and worship; in fact, that a STATE CHURCH occasioned the deluge—and since that time has been the fruitful source of the miseries and wretchedness that has afflicted mankind. His prediction of the outpouring of the Spirit in the conversion of sinners, when the church shall be no longer enthralled and persecuted by the state, is remarkable. ' O thou church of God in England, which art now upon the waves of affliction and temptation, when thou comest out of the furnace, if thou come out at the bidding of God, there

shall come out with thee, the fowl, the beast, and abundance of creeping things. O Judah, he hath set an harvest for thee, when I returned the captivity of my people.'† May this prediction soon be verified, and the temporal government no longer vex and torment the church by interfering with spiritual things.

It is remarkable that of the vast number of pious and enlightened mechanics who adorn this country and feed its prosperity, so few read the extraordinary writings of John Bunyan, a brother mechanic; for with the exception of the Pilgrim's Progress and Holy War, they are comparatively little known. His simple but illustrative commentary—his book of Antichrist—his solemn and striking treatise on the resurrection and final judgment—in fact, all his works, are peculiarly calculated to inform the minds of the millions—to reform bad habits, and, under the divine blessing, to purify the soul with that heavenly wisdom which has in it the promise of the life that now is as well as of that which is to come. It is also a fact which ought to be generally known, that those preachers who have edited Bunyan's works and have drunk into his spirit, have been most eminently blessed in their ministry; Wilson, Whitefield, and Ryland, can never be forgotten. If the thousands of godly preachers who are scattered over our comparatively happy island were to take Bunyan's mode of expounding scripture as their pattern, it would increase their usefulness, and consequently their happiness, in the great work of proclaiming and enforcing the doctrines of the gospel.—GEO. OFFOR.

---

* C. i. v. 26.   † C. viii. 16.

AN EXPOSITION ON THE FIRST TEN CHAPTERS OF GENESIS,
AND PART OF THE ELEVENTH.

In the first edition of this commentary, a series of numbers from 1 to 294 were placed in the margin, the use of which the editor could not discover; probably the work was written on as many scraps of paper, thus numbered to direct the printer. They are omitted, lest, among divisions and subdivisions, they should puzzle the reader.

CHAP. I.
I. *Of God.*

GOD *is* a Spirit, Jn. iv. 24. eternal, De. xxxiii. 27. infinite, Ro. i. 17—20. incomprehensible, Job xi. 7. perfect, and unspeakably glorious in his being, attributes, and works. Ge. xvii. li. Is. vi. 3. Ex. xxxiii. 20. ' The eternal God.' ' Do not I fill heaven and earth ? saith the Lord.' Je. xxiii. 24. ' Neither is there any creature that is not manifest in his sight.' He. iv. 13. Pr. xv. 11.

In his attributes of wisdom, power, justice, holiness, mercy, &c., he is also inconceivably perfect

and infinite, not to be comprehended by things in earth, or things in heaven; known in the perfection of his being only to himself. The seraphims cannot behold him, but through a veil; no man can see him in his perfection and live.

His attributes, though apart laid down in the word of God, that we, being weak, might the better conceive of his eternal power and godhead; yet in him they are without division; one glorious and eternal being. Again, though sometimes this, as of wisdom, or that, as of justice and mercy, is most manifest in his works and wonders before men ; yet every such work is begun and completed by the joint concurrence of all his attributes. No act of justice is without his will, power, and wisdom ; no act of mercy is against his justice, holiness and purity.

Besides, no man must conceive of God, as if he consisted of these attributes, as our body doth of its members, one standing here, another there, for the completing personal subsistence. For though by the word we may distinguish, yet may we not divide them, or presume to appoint them their places in the Godhead. Wisdom is in his justice, holiness is in his power, justice is in his mercy, holiness is in his love, power is in his goodness. 1 Jn. i 9. Nu. xiv. 17, 18.

Wherefore, he is in all his attributes almighty, all-wise, holy and powerful. Glory is in his wisdom, glory is in his holiness, glory is in his mercy, justice, and strength ; and 'God is love.' 1 Jn. iv. 16.*

II. Of the Persons or Subsistances in the Godhead.

The Godhead is but one, yet in the Godhead there are three. 'There are three that can bear record in heaven.' 1 Jn. v. 7—9. These three are called 'the Father, the Son [Word], and the Holy Spirit ;' each of which is really, naturally and eternally God : yet there is but one God. But again, because the Father is of himself, the Son by the Father, and the Spirit from them both, therefore to each, the scripture not only applieth, and that truly, the whole nature of the Deity, but again distinguisheth the Father from the Son, and the Spirit from them both ; calling the Father HE, by himself ; the Son HE, by himself ; the Spirit HE, by himself. Yea, the Three of themselves, in their manifesting to the church what she should believe concerning this matter, hath thus expressed the thing : 'Let us make man in our image, after our likeness.' Ge. i. 26. Again, 'The man is become as one of us.' Ge. iii. 22. Again, 'Let us go down, and there confound their language :' Ge. xi. 6, 7. And again, 'Whom shall I send, and who will go for us ?' Is. vi. 8. To these general expressions might be added, That Adam heard the voice of the Lord God walking in the midst of the garden : Ge. iii. 8. Which voice John will have, to be one of the Three, calling that which Moses here saith is the voice, the word of God : 'In the beginning,' saith he, 'was the word :' the voice which Adam heard walking in the midst of the garden. This word, saith John, 'was with God,' this 'word was God. The same was in the beginning with God.' Jn. i. 1, 2.

Marvellous language ! Once asserting the unity of essence, but twice insinuating a distinction of substances therein. 'The word was with God, the word was God, the same was in the beginning with God.' Then follows, 'All things were made by him,' the word, the second of the three.

Now the godly in former ages have called these three, thus in the Godhead, Persons or Subsistances ; the which, though I condemn not, yet choose rather to abide by scripture phrase, knowing, though the other may be good and sound, yet the adversary must needs more shamelessly spurn and reject, when he doth it against the evident text.

To proceed then, *First,* There are Three. *Second,* These three are distinct.

First, By this word Three, is intimated the Father, the Word, and the Holy Ghost, and they are said to be three, 1. Because those appellations that are given them in scripture, demonstrate them so to be, to wit, Father, Son and Holy Ghost. 2. Because their acts one towards another discover them so to be.

Secondly, These three are distinct. 1. So distinct as to be more than one, only : There are three. 2. So distinct as to subsist without depending. The Father is true God, the Son is true God, the Spirit is true God. Yet the Father is one, the Son is one, the Spirit is one : The Father is one of himself, the Son is one by the Father, the Spirit is one from them both. Yet the Father is not above the Son, nor the Spirit inferior to either : The Father is God, the Son is God, the Spirit is God.

Among the three then there is not superiority. 1. Not as to time ; the Father is from everlasting, so is the Son, so is the Spirit. 2. Not as to nature, the Son being of the substance of the Father, and the Spirit of the substance of them both. 3. The fulness of the Godhead is in the Father, is in the Son, and is in the Holy Ghost.

The Godhead then, though it can admit of a Trinity, yet it admitteth not of inferiority in that Trinity : if otherwise, then less or more must be there, and so either plurality of gods, or something that is not God : so then, Father, Son and Spirit are in the Godhead, yet but one God ; each of these is God over all, yet no Trinity of Gods, but one God in the Trinity.

Explication.—The Godhead then is common to the three, but the three themselves abide distinct in that Godhead : Distinct, I say, as Father, and Son, and Holy Spirit. This is manifest further by these several positions.

First, Father and Son are relatives, and must needs therefore have their relation as such : A Father begetteth, a Son is begotten.

Proof.—'Who hath ascended up into heaven, or descended ? Who hath gathered the wind in

* Although no mortal mind can by searching find out the Almighty to perfection, yet Bunyan's views of the Divine Being is an approach to perfection. It is worthy the pen of the most profound christian philosopher.—ED.

his fists? Who hath bound the waters in a garment? What *is* his name, and what *is* his son's name, if thou canst tell?' Pr. xxx. 4.

'God so loved the world, that he gave his only begotten Son,' &c. Jn. iii. 16.

'The Father sent the Son to be the Saviour of the world.' 1 Jn. iv. 14.

Secondly, The Father then cannot be that Son he begat, nor the Son that Father that begat him, but must be distinct as such.

Proof.—'I am one that bear witness of myself, and the Father that sent me beareth witness of me.' Jn. viii. 17, 18.

'I came forth from the Father, and am come into the world:' again, 'I leave the world, and go to the Father.' Jn. xvi. 28.

'The Father judgeth no man, but hath committed all judgment unto the Son: That all *men* should honour the Son, even as they honour the Father.' Jn. v. 22, 23.

Thirdly, The Father must have worship as a Father, and the Son as a Son.

Proof.—They that worship the Father must worship him 'in spirit and in truth: for the Father seeketh such to worship him.' Jn. iv. 23, 24.

And of the Son he saith, and 'when he bringeth in the first begotten into the world, he saith, And let all the angels of God worship him.' He. i. 6.

Fourthly, The Father and Son have really theso distinct, but heavenly, relative properties, that discover them, as such, to be two as well as one.

Proof.—'The Father loveth the Son, and sheweth him all things.' Jn. v. 20.

'Therefore doth my Father love me, because I lay down my life, that I might take it again.' Jn. x. 17. The Father sent the Son; the Father commanded the Son; the Son prayed to the Father, and did always the things that pleased him.

The absurdities that flow from the denial of this are divers, some of which hereunder follow.

1 *Absurdity.*—It maketh void all those scriptures that do affirm the doctrine; some of which you have before.

2 *Absurdity.*—If in the Godhead there be but one, not three, then the Father, Son, or the Spirit, must needs be that one, if any one only: so then the other two are nothing. Again, If the reality of a being be neither in the Father, Son, nor Spirit, as such, but in the eternal deity, without consideration of Father, Son, and Spirit as three; then neither of the three are anything but notions in us, or manifestations of the Godhead; or nominal distinctions; so related by the word; but if so, then when the Father sent the Son, and the Father and Son the Spirit, one notion sent another, one manifestation sent another. This being granted, this unavoidably follows, there was no Father to beget a Son, no Son to be sent to save us, no Holy Ghost to be sent to comfort us, and to guide us into all the truth of the Father and Son, &c. The most amounts but to this, a notion sent a notion, a distinction sent a distinction, or one manifestation sent another. Of this error these are the consequences, we are only to believe in notions and distinctions, when we believe in the Father and the Son; and so shall have no other heaven and glory, than notions and nominal distinctions can furnish us withal.

3 *Absurdity.*—If Father and Son, &c., be no otherwise three, than as notions, names, or nominal distinctions; then to worship these distinctly, or together, as such, is to commit most gross and horrible idolatry: For albeit we are commanded to fear that great and dreadful name, The Lord our God; yet to worship a Father, a Son, and Holy Spirit in the Godhead, as three, as really three as one, is by this doctrine to imagine falsely of God, and so to break the second commandment: but to worship God under the consideration of Father, and Son, and Holy Ghost, and to believe them as really three as one when I worship, being the sum and substance of the doctrine of the scriptures of God, there is really substantially three in the eternal Godhead.

But to help thee a little in thy study on this deep.

1. Thou must take heed when thou readest, there is in the Godhead, Father, and Son, &c., that thou do not imagine about them according to thine own carnal and foolish fancy; for no man can apprehend this doctrine but in the light of the word and Spirit of God. 'No man knoweth the Son, but the Father; neither knoweth any man the Father, save the Son; and *he* to whom the Son will reveal *him*.' Mat. xi. 27. If therefore thou be destitute of the Spirit of God, thou canst not apprehend the truth of this mystery as it is in itself, but will either by thy darkness be driven to a denial thereof; or if thou own it, thou wilt (that thy acknowledgment notwithstanding) falsely imagine about it.

2. If thou feel thy thoughts begin to wrestle about this truth, and to struggle concerning this one against another; take heed of admitting of such a question, How can this thing be? For here is no room for reason to make it out, here is only room to believe it is a truth. You find not one of the prophets propounding an argument to prove it; but asserting it, they let it lie, for faith to take it up and embrace it.

'The grace of the Lord Jesus Christ, and the love of God, and the communion of the Holy Ghost, *be* with you all. Amen.' 2 Co. xiii. 14.

III. *Of the Creation of the World.* Ge. i.

The Apostle saith, That 'to us *there is but* one God, the Father, of whom *are* all things, and we in him, and one Lord Jesus Christ, by whom *are* all things, and we by him.' 1 Co. viii. 6. 'God that made the world.' Ac. xvii. 24. 'All things were made by him; and without him was not any thing made that was made.' Jo. i. 3. This world therefore had a beginning, and was created by the God of heaven. Which work, because it is wonderful, and discovereth much of the greatness, of the wisdom and power of the eternal Godhead, it behoveth such poor mortals as we to behold these works of the mighty God, that thereby we may see how great he is, and be made to cry out, What is man!* Ps. viii. 3, 4.

Now in the creation of the world we may consider several things; as, What was the order of God in this work ? And, whether there was a secret or mystery in this work containing the truth of some higher thing ? For the first of these:

Of the Order of God in Making the World.

[THE HEAVEN.]

Although God be indeed omnipotent, and not only can, but doth do whatsoever he will; and though to do his works he needeth not length of time; yet it pleased him best, in the creation of the world (though it could, had it pleased him, have done all by one only word) to proceed by degrees from one thing to another, to the completing of six days' work in the making thereof.

And forasmuch as this work went on by degrees, now this thing, and then another, it may not be amiss, if in our discourse on this wonderful work, we begin where God began; and if we can, go wondering after him who hath thus wrought.

1. The first thing that God made was time; I say, it was time: All the plain in which he would build this beautiful world; he made nothing before, but in the beginning: 'In the beginning God created the heaven and the earth.' Ge. i. 1. In the beginning of time. 'For *in* six days the LORD made heaven and earth, the sea, and all that in them *is.*' Ex. xx. 11. Therefore the first day must first have a beginning to be. Whatsoever was before time, was eternal; but nothing but God himself is eternal, therefore no creature was before time.

---

* The more extensive our inquiries are into the wonders of creation, the more deeply will our souls be humbled. The answer to the inquiry, 'What is man?' can then, and only then, be made in the language of Isaiah, 'Nothing—vanity—a drop of a bucket—the small dust of the balance,' xl. 15.—ED.

Time, therefore, which was indeed the beginning, was the first of the creatures of God.

2. I think, the second of creatures that the Lord created, were the holy angels of God, they being called the morning stars, as created and shining in the morning of the world; and therefore they are said to be by, when the corner-stone of the universe was laid; that is, when he 'laid the foundations' of the world: Then 'the morning stars sang together, and all the sons of God shouted for joy.' Job v. 4—7.

3. I think the third thing that the Lord created, was these large and copious heavens; The highest for they are mentioned with respect to   heaven. their being before the earth, or any visible creature. 'In the beginning God created the heavens,' Ge. i. 1. &c. Neither do I think that the heavens were made of that confused chaos that afterwards we read of. It is said, he stretched out the heavens as a curtain, and with his hand he hath spanned the heavens; Ps. civ. 2. Is. xl. 22, and xlviii. 13. intimating, that they were not taken out of that formless heap, but were immediately formed by his power. Besides, the Holy Ghost, treating of the creating of heaven and earth, he only saith, The earth was void, and without form; but no such thing of the heavens.

[THE EARTH.]

4. The fourth thing that God created, it was (in mine opinion) that chaos, or first matter, with which he in the six days framed this earth, with its appurtenances; for the visible things that are here below, seem to me to be otherwise put into being and order, than time, the angels, and the heavens, they being created in their own simple essence by themselves: But the things that are visibly here below, whatever their essence and nature be, they were formed of that first deformed chaos. 'In the beginning God created the heaven and the earth, and the earth was without form and void.' Ge. i. 1, 2. He saith not so of the heavens; they, as I said, were at first stretched forth as a curtain; indeed they were afterwards garnished with the beauty which we now behold; but otherwise they had, at their first instant of being, that form which now they have. This seems clear by the antithesis which the Holy Ghost put between them, God created the heaven and the earth, but 'the earth was without form and void.' Ge. i. 2. The earth was without form, &c., without order; things were together on a confused heap; the waters were not divided from the earth, neither did those things appear which are now upon the face of the earth; as man, and beast, fish, fowls, trees, and herbs; all these did afterwards shew themselves, as the word of God gave them being, by commanding their appearance, in what form, order, place and

time he in himself had before determined; but all, I say, took their matter and substance of that first chaos, which he in the first day of the world had commanded to appear, and had given being to: And therefore 'tis said, God said, Let the earth bring forth grass, herbs, trees, &c., ver. 12. and that the waters brought forth the fish, and fowl, yea, even to the mighty whales: ver. 21, 22. Also the earth brought forth cattle, and creeping things: ver. 24. And that God made man of the dust of the ground. iii. 19. All these things therefore were made of, or caused by his word distinctly to appear, and be after its kind, of that first matter which he had before created by his word. Observe therefore, That the matter of all earthly things was made at the same instant, but their forming, &c., was according to the day in which God gave them their being, in their own order and kind. And hence it is said, that after that first matter was created, and found without form and void, that the Spirit of God moved upon the face of the waters; that is to work, and cause those things to appear in their own essence and form, which, as to matter and substance, was before created: Wherefore it follows, And God said, Let there be light; and God divided the light from the darkness, &c. Now he set to putting in frame that which before lay in disorder and confusion: And this was a great part of the six days' work; I say, a great part, but not all; for (as I said) before that time, the angels, and the heavens were made; yea, after the beginning of the morning of the first day. I am of the belief, that other things also, that were formed after, were not made of that first chaos, as the sun, the moon, the stars, the light, the souls of men, and possibly the air, &c. The sun, and moon, and stars, are said to be made the fourth day, yet not of the body of heaven itself, much less, in my opinion, of any earthly matter: God made them, and set them in the firmament of heaven: ver. 16, 17. So the light that was made before, it seems to be a thing created after the heavens and the earth were created: Created, I say, as a thing that wanted a being before, any otherwise than in the decree of God: and God said, Let there be light; Let it have a being: ver. 3. And so, though the body of man was made of the substance of earth, yet as to his soul, it is said, God breathed into his nostrils the breath of life, and man became a living soul. ii. 7.

Whether there was a secret or mystery in this work, containing the truth of some higher thing.

Though God in very deed, by his eternal power, created heaven and earth of things that do not appear, we that are Christians believe: yet in this his wonderful work, neither his will or understand-

ing did here terminate, or make a stop; but being infinite in wisdom, he made them, that both as to matter and manner, they might present unto us, as in a mystery, some higher and more excellent thing; in this wisdom he made them all. And hence it is that other things are also called a creation: As, 1. The essential conversion of a sinner. 2 Co. v. 17. 2. The recovery of the church from a degenerate state. Re. xxi. 5.

And therefore, as Moses begins with the creation of the world, so John begins with the gospel of salvation. Ge. i. 1. Jn. i. 1. There is also besides many excellent things in the manner and order of the creation of the world, held forth to those that have understanding: Some of which I may touch upon by way of observation. But to begin with the first:

The first appearance of this earthy part of the world, is recorded to be but a formless and void heap or chaos; and such is man before a new creation: formless, I mean, as to the order of the Testament of Christ, and void of the holy order thereof: And hence Jeremiah, when he would set forth the condition of a wicked people, he doth it under this metaphor: 'I beheld (saith he) the earth, and, lo, *it was* without form and void.' Je. iv. 23. Indeed, the world would make this a type of Christ; to wit, a man of no form or comeliness: Is. liii. 2. But 'tis only true of themselves; they are without a New Testament impression upon them; they are void of the sovereign grace of God. So then the power of God gave the world a being, but by his word he set it in form and beauty; even as by his power he gives a being to man, but by his word he giveth him New Testament framing and glory. Ep. ii. 10—13. This is still followed by that which follows:

And darkness was upon the face of the deep. ver. 2.

The Deep here, might be a type of the heart of man before conversion; and so Solomon seems to intimate. Now as the darkness of this world did cover the face of this first chaos; so spiritual darkness the heart of the sons of men: and hence they are said to be darkened, to be in darkness, yea, to be very darkness itself.

'And the Spirit of God moved upon the face of the waters.' The first day's work. [ver. 3—5.]

A blessed emblem of the word of God in the matter of regeneration; for as the first chaos remained without form, and void, until the Spirit of God moved to work upon it, and by working, to put this world into frame and order; so man, as he comes into the world, abides a confused lump, an unclean thing; a creature without New Testament order, until by the Spirit of the Lord he is transformed into the image of Jesus Christ. Ga. i. 15.

'And the Spirit of God moved upon the face.'

Solomon compares the heart to a man's face; because as in the face may be discerned whether there is anger or otherwise; so by the inclinations of the heart are discovered the truth of the condition of the man, as to his state either for heaven or hell. And besides, as the Spirit of God moved upon the face of the waters; so in the work of our conversion, the Spirit of God beginneth with the heart of the sons of men; because the heart is the main fort: Ac. ii. 37. Now if the main fort be not taken, the adversary is still capable of making continual resistance. Therefore God first conquers the heart; therefore the Spirit of God moveth upon the face of our heart, when he cometh to convert us from Satan to God.

'And God said, Let there be light.'

This is the first thing with which God began the order of the creation; to wit, light, 'Let there be light:' From which many profitable notes may be gathered, as to the order of God in the salvation of the soul. As,

1. When the Holy Ghost worketh upon us, and in us, in order to a new creation; he first toucheth our understanding, that great peace of the heart, with his spiritual illumination: Mat. iv. 16. His first word, in order to our conversion, is, Let there be light: light, to see their state by nature; light, to see the fruits and effects of sin; light, to see the truth and worth of the merits of Jesus Christ; light, to see the truth and faithfulness of God, in keeping promise and covenant with them that embrace salvation upon the blessed terms of the gospel of peace. He. x. 32. Now that this word, Let there be light, was a semblance of the first work of the Holy Ghost upon the heart, compare it with that of Paul to the Corinthians; 'For God, who commanded the light to shine out of darkness,' that is, at the beginning of the world, 'hath shined in our hearts to *give* the light of the knowledge of the glory of God in the face of Jesus Christ.' 2 Co. iv. 6.

2. 'And God said, Let there be light.' As here, the light of this world; so in conversion, the light of the New Testament of Christ, it comes by the word of God. No word, no light: therefore the apostle saith, He 'hath brought life and immortality to light through the gospel.' 2 Tim. i. 10. And therefore Paul saith again, That salvation is manifest through preaching, through the expounding or opening of the word of faith.

3. 'And God said, Let there be light; and there was light:' He spake the word, and it was done; all that darkness that before did cover the face of the deep, could not now hinder the being of light. So neither can all the blindness and ignorance that is in the heart of man, hinder the light of the knowledge of the glory of God in the face of Jesus Christ. Re. iii. 7. When it pleaseth God to reveal, it is revealed; when he openeth, none can shut: He said, Let there be light, and there was light.

And God saw that the light was good. Truly the light is good (saith Solomon) and a pleasant thing it is for the eye to behold the sun. It was good, because it was God's creature; and so in the work of grace that is wrought in our hearts, that light of the new-covenant, it is good, because it is God's work, the work of his good pleasure; 2 Th. i. 11. that good work which he hath not only begun, but promised to fulfil until the day of Jesus Christ. Phi. i. 6.

God saw that the light was good. The darkness that before did cover the face of the waters, was not a creature of God, but a privation, or that which was caused by reason that light was not as yet in the world: so sin, that darkness that might be felt, is not the workmanship of God in the soul, but that which is the work of the devil; and that taketh occasion to be, by reason that the true light, as yet, doth not shine in the soul.

'And God divided the light from the darkness.' As Paul saith, What communion hath light with darkness? they cannot agree to dwell together. 2 Co. vi. 14. We see the night still flies before the day, and dareth not come upon us again, but as the light diminisheth and conveyeth itself away. So it is in the new creation; before the light of the glorious gospel of Christ appears, there is night, all night, in the soul: Ep. v. 8. but when that indeed doth shine in the soul, then for night there is day in the soul: 'Ye were - darkness (saith Paul) but now *are ye* light in the Lord:' ver. 9. And, 'The darkness is past (saith John) and the true light now shineth.' 1 Jn. ii. 8.

'And God divided the light from the darkness.'

God took part with the light, and preserved it from the darkness. By these words, it seems that darkness and light began the quarrel, before that bloody bout of Cain and Abel. Ga. v. 17. The light and the darkness struggled together, and nothing could divide or part them but God. Darkness is at implacable enmity with light in the creation of the world; and so it is in that rare work of regeneration, the flesh lusteth against the spirit, and the spirit against the flesh; as Peter saith, Fleshly lusts, they war against the soul. This every Christian feels, and also that which I mentioned before, namely, That before he be capable of opposing antichrist, with Abel, in the world, he findeth a struggling in his own soul between the light and the darkness that is there.

'And God called the light Day, and the darkness he called Night.'

God doth not only distinguish by separating,

but also by certain characters; that things which are distinguished and separate, may to us be the better known; he did so here in the work of creating the world, and he doth so also in the great concern of man's eternal happiness. The place of felicity is called heaven: The place of torment is called hell: that which leads to hell is called sin, transgression, iniquity, and wickedness; that which leads to heaven, righteousness, holiness, goodness and uprightness: even as in these types God called the light day, of which the godly are the children; 1 Th. v. 5. but the darkness he called night, of which all ungodly men are the inhabiters and children also. Thus after the Spirit of God had moved upon the face of the waters; after God had commanded the light to shine, and had divided between the light and the darkness, and had characterized them by their proper names, he concludes the first day's work, 'And the evening and the morning were the first day.' In which conclusion there is wrapped up a blessed gospel-mystery; for God, by concluding the first day here, doth shew us how we ought to determine that one is made indeed a Christian: Even then when the Spirit of God hath moved upon the face of the heart, when he hath commanded that light should be there, when he divideth between, or setteth the light at variance with the darkness; and when the soul doth receive the characters of both, to observe them, and carry it to each according to the mouth of God.

The second day's work.   'And God said, Let there be a
[ver. 6—8.]   firmament.' ver. 6.

This firmament he calleth heaven. ver. 8. Now this firmament, or heaven, was to make a separation, or to divide between the waters and the waters; ver. 7. To separate, I say, the waters from the waters; the waters which were under the firmament, from the waters which were above the firmament. Now by waters is signified in the scriptures many things, as afflictions, worldly people, Ps. lxix. 1, 2. and particularly the saints; Re. xix. 6. but in this place is figured forth, all the people in the world, but so as consisting of two parts, the children of God, and the children of the wicked one: They under the heaven, figure out the world, or ungodly: they above the firmament, the elect and chosen of God. And hence in scripture the one is called heaven, and the other is called earth, to signify the separation and difference that there is between the one and the other.

'And God made the firmament, and divided the waters - from the waters.'

Indeed the world think that this separation comes, or is made, through the captiousness of the preacher: But in truth it is the handy work of God; And God made the firmament, and God divided, &c. 'I,' saith he, 'will put enmity

between thee and the woman, and between thy seed and her seed.' Ge. iii. 15. The good seed are the children of the kingdom of God, but the bad are the children of the wicked one. Mat. xiii. 38.

'And God made the firmament, and divided the waters which *were* under the firmament, from the waters which *were* above the firmament: and it was so.' ver. 7.

Whatsoever the Lord doth, it abideth for ever. Ec. iii. 14. And again, What he hath made crooked, who can make straight? Ec. i. 15. He said it in the beginning, and behold how it hath continued! Yea, though there hath been endeavours on Satan's part, to mingle his children with the seed of men; yet it hath not been possible they should ever cleave one to another, 'even as iron is not mixed with clay.' Da. ii. 43. Yea, let me add further, What laws have been made, what blood hath been shed, what cruelty hath been used, and what flatteries and lies invented, and all to make these two waters and people one? And yet all hath failed, and fallen short of producing the desired effect; for the Lord hath made a firmament, even heaven itself hath divided between them.

'And God called the firmament heaven. And the evening and the morning were the second day.' ver. 8.

After the waters were divided from the waters, God called the cause of dividing, heaven; and so concluded the second day's work. And indeed it was a very great work, as in the antitype we feel it to this very day. Dividing work is difficult work, and he that can, according to God, completely end and finish it, he need do no more that day of his life.

'And God said, Let the waters   The third day's work.
under the heaven be gathered to-   [ver. 9—13.]
gether unto one place, and let the dry *land* appear: and it was so.' ver. 9.

Although in the second day's work, the waters above the firmament, and those that be under, are the two peoples, or great families of the world; Pr. viii. 31. yet because God would shew us by things on earth, the flourishing state of those that are his, Ho. x. 12. Joel ii. 21—23. Ps. xci. 1. He. vi. 7. therefore he here doth express his mind by another kind of representation of things: Je. iv. 3, 4. 'And God said, Let the waters under the heaven be gathered together unto one place; and let the dry *land* appear.' The waters here signifying the world; but the fruitful earth, the thrifty church of God. That the fruitful earth is a figure of the thriving church of God in this world, is evident from many scriptures, (and there was nothing but thriftiness till the curse came.) And hence it is said of the church, That she should break the clods of the ground; that she should sow righteousness, and reap it; that she should not sow among thorns; that if this be done, the heart is circumcised, and spiritual fruit shall flow forth, and grow abundantly: And hence again it is that the officers and eminent ones in the church, are called vines, trees, and other fruitful plants. And hence it is said again, When the Lord reigneth, let the earth (that is, the church) rejoice. That earth which bringeth forth fruit meet for him by whom it is dressed, receiveth blessing from God. In all which places, and many more that might be named, the earth is made a figure of the church of God; and so I count it here in this place.

'And God said, Let the waters under the heaven be gathered into one place.

Let them be together: It is not thus of all waters, but of the sea, which is still here a type of the world. Let them be so together, that the earth may appear; that the church may be rid of their rage and tumult, and then she will be fruitful, as it follows in this first book of Genesis. The church is then in a flourishing state, when the world is farthest off from her, and when the roaring of their waves are far away. Now therefore let all the wicked men be far from thence: Ezr. vi. 6. The Lord gather these waters, which in another place are called the doleful creatures, and birds of prey; Let these, O Lord, be gathered together to their own places, and be settled in the land of Shinar upon their own base: Zec. v. 11. Then the wilderness and the solitary places shall be glad for them; that is, for that they are departed thence, the desert shall rejoice and blossom as a rose. Is. xxxiv. and xxxv.

'And God called the dry *land* Earth; and the gathering together of the waters called he seas: and God saw that *it was* good.' ver. 10.

God saw, that to separate the waters from the earth was good: And so it is, for then have the churches rest. Then doth this earth bring forth her fruit, as in the 11th and 12th verses may here be seen.

The fourth day's work. [ver. 14—19.] 'And God said, Let there be lights in the firmament of the heaven.' ver. 14.

The wisdom of God, is there to make use of figures and shadows, even where most fit things, the things under consideration, may be most fitly demonstrated. The dividing the waters from the waters, most fitly doth show the work of God in choosing and refusing; by dividing the waters from the earth, doth show how fruitful God's earth, the church is, when persecutors are made to be far from thence.

Wherefore he speaketh not of garnishing of his church until he comes to this fourth day's work: By his Spirit he hath garnished the heavens, that most fitly showing the glory of the church.

Let there be lights; to wit, the sun, the moon, and the stars.

The sun is in this place a type of Christ, the Sun of Righteousness: The moon is a type of the church, in her uncertain condition in this world: The stars are types of the several saints and officers in this church. And hence it is that the sun is said not only to rule, but it, with the moon and stars, to be set for signs, and for seasons, and for days, and for years, &c. Re. i. 20. But if we take the heaven for the church, then how is she beautified, when the Son of God is placed in the midst of her! Re. i. 12, 13. And how plainly is her condition made out, even by the changing, increasing, and diminishing of the moon! And how excellent is that congregation of men, that for light and glory are figured by the stars! Mat. xxviii. 20.

From this day's work much might be observed.

First, That forasmuch as the sun was not made before the fourth day, it is evident there was light in the world before the sun was created; for in the first day God said, Let there be light, and there was light. This may also teach us thus much, That before Christ came in person, there was spiritual light in the saints of God. And again, That as the sun was not made before the fourth day of the creation, so Christ should not be born before the fourth mystical day of the world; for it is evident, that Christ, the true light of the world, was not born till about four thousand years after the world was made.

Second, As to the moon, there are four things attending her, which fitly may hold forth the state of the church. (1.) In that she changeth from an old to a new, we may conceive, that God by making her so, did it to show he would one day make a change of his church, from a Jewish to a Gentile congregation. (2.) In that she increaseth, she showeth the flourishing state of the church. (3.) In her diminishing, the diminishing state of the church. (4.) The moon is also sometimes made to look as red as blood, to show how dreadful and bloody the suffering of the church is at some certain times.

Third, By the stars, we understand two things. (1.) How innumerable the saints, those spiritual stars shall be. He. xi. 12. (2.) How they shall differ each from other in glory. 1 Co. xv. 41.

'And God said, Let there be lights in the firmament of the heaven, to divide the day from the night.'

For though before the light was divided from the darkness, yet the day and night was not so kept within their bounds, as now by these lights they were: probably signifying, that nothing should be so clearly distinguished and made appear, as by the sun light of the gospel of Christ: for by that it is that 'the shadows flee away.' So. ii. 17. The light of the sun gathers the day to its hours, both longer and shorter, and forceth also the night to keep within his bounds.

'And God made two great lights; the greater light to rule the day, and the lesser light to rule the night.' ver. 16.

Signifying, That Christ should be the light and governor of his church, which are the children of the day; but the church, a light to the children of the night, that by them they might learn the mysteries of the kingdom. Saith Christ to his own, 'Ye are the light of the world:' And again, 'Let your light so shine, - that men may see,' &c., for though they that only walk in the night, cannot see to walk by the sun, yet by the moon they may. Thus the heaven is a type of the church, the moon a type of her uncertain state in this world; the stars are types of her immovable converts; and their glory, of the differing degrees of theirs, both here, and in the other world. Much more might be said, but I pass this.

The fifth day's work. [ver. 20—23.] 'And God said, Let the waters bring forth abundantly the moving creature that hath life.' ver. 20.

The sea, as I said, is a figure of the world; wherefore the creatures that are in it, of the men of the world. Zec. xiii. 8. Is. lx. 5. This sea bringeth forth small and great beasts, even as the world doth yield both small and great persecutors, who like the fishes of prey, eat up and devour what they can of those fish that are of another condition. Now also out of the world that mystical sea, as fishers do out of the natural; both Christ and his servants catch mystical fish, even fish as of the great sea.

In the sea God created great whales, he made them to play therein.

Which whales in the sea are types of the devils in the world: Therefore as the devil is called, the prince of this world; so the whale is called, king over all the children of pride. Job xli. 33, 34.

The sixth day's work. [ver. 24, 25.] 'And God said, Let the earth bring forth the living creature after his kind.' ver. 24.

Of the beginning of this sixth day's work that may be said which is said of the fishes, and the rest of the sea; for as there is variety of fish in the one, so of beasts and cattle in the other, who also make a prey of their fellows, as the fishes do; a most apt representation of the nature and actions of bloody and deceitful men: Hence persecutors are called bulls, bears, lions, wolves, tigers, dragons, dogs, foxes, leopards, and the like.*

'And God said, Let us make man.' ver. 26.

* How sad, but true, is this type of many governments, especially of the olden times; the strong devour the weak—strong in person or by subtilty, or by combination. Should this earth ever be blessed with a christian government, the governors will exclusively seek the welfare and happiness of the governed.—Ed.

I observe, that in the creation of the world, God goeth gradually on, from things less, to things more abundantly glorious; I mean, as to the creation of this earth; and the things that thereto appertain. First he bringeth forth a confused chaos, then he commands matter to appear distinct, then the earth bringeth forth trees, and herbs, and grass; after that beasts; and the sea, fowls; and last of all, Let us make man. Now passing by the doctrine of the trinity, because spoken to before, I come to make some observation upon this wonderful piece of the workmanship of God.

'Let us make man.' Man in whom is also included the woman, was made the last of the creatures. From whence we may gather,

God's respect to this excellent creature, in that he first provideth for him, before he giveth him his being: He bringeth him not to an empty house, but to one well furnished with all kind of necessaries, having beautified the heaven and the earth with glory, and all sorts of nourishment, for his pleasure and sustenance.†

'Let us make man in our image, after our likeness.'

An image, or the likeness of any thing, is not the thing of which it is a figure; so here, Adam is an image, or made in the likeness of God. Now as Adam is the image of God, it must either respect him, as he consisteth of the soul, as a part; or as he consists of a body and soul together: If as he is made a reasonable soul, then he is an excellent image of the eternal Godhead, the attributes of the one being shadowed out by the qualities and passions of the other; for as there is in the Godhead, power, knowledge, love, and righteousness; so a likeness of these is in the soul of man, especially of man before he had sinned: And as there is passions of pity, compassion, affections, and bowels in man; so there are these in a far more infinite way in God.

Again, If this image respect the whole man, then Adam was a figure of God, as incarnate; or of God, as he was to be made afterwards man. And hence it is, that as Adam is called the image of God; Ro. v. 14. so also is Christ himself called and reckoned as the answering antitype of such an image.

† This is one of those beautiful discoveries which modern geology fully confirms. The earth is created, matured, prepared and fitted for him, before man is created. That modern popular work, 'The Vestiges of Creation,' elucidates the same fact from the phenomena of nature: but the philosopher who wrote that curious book little thought that these sublime truths were published more than a century and a half ago, by an unlettered mechanic, whose sole source of knowledge was his being deeply learned in the holy oracles. They discover in a few words that which defies centuries of philosophic researches of the most learned men. A wondrous book is God's book!—Ed.

But again, Though Adam be here called the image or similitude of God; yet but so as that he was the shadow of a more excellent image. Adam was a type of Christ, who only is 'the express image' of his Father's person, and the likeness of his excellent glory. He. i. 3. For those things that were in Adam, were but of a humane, but of a created substance; but those that were in Christ, of the same divine and eternal excellency with the Father.

Is Christ then the image of the Father, simply, as considered of the same divine and eternal excellency with him? Certainly, No: for an image is doubtless inferior to that of which it is a figure. Understand then, that Christ is the image of the Father's glory, as born of the Virgin Mary, yet so, as being very God also: Not that his Godhead in itself was a shadow or image, but by the acts and doing of that man, every act being infinitely perfect by virtue of his Godhead, the Father's perfections were made manifest to flesh. An image is to be looked upon, and by being looked upon, another thing is seen; so by the person and doings of the Lord Jesus, they that indeed could see him as he was, discovered the perfection and glory of the Father.—'Philip, He that hath seen me hath seen the Father; and how sayest thou then, Shew us the Father?' Jn. xiv. 9. Neither the Father nor the Son can by us at all be seen, as they are simply and entirely in their own essence. Therefore the person of the Father must be seen by us, through the Son, as consisting of God and man; the Godhead, by working effectually in the manhood, shewing clearly there through the infinite perfection and glory of the Father: 'The word was made flesh, and - (then) we beheld his glory, the glory as of the only begotten of the Father, (He being in his personal excellencies, infinitely and perfectly, what is recorded of his Father,) full of grace and truth.' Jn. i. 14. So again, he 'is the image of the invisible God.' Col. i. 15. The Godhead is indeed invisible; how then is Christ the image of it? Not by being invisible also; for so is he as much hid as the Father; but being clothed with flesh, that the works of the Son might by us be seen, he thereby presenteth to us, as in a figure, the eternal excellency of the Father. And hence as he is called 'an image,' he is also called 'the first-born' of every creature. Col. i. 18. His being a creature, respecting his manhood, and his birth, and his rising again from the dead. Therefore a little after, he is called, 'the first-born from the dead:' ver. 19. And in another place, 'the first-begotten of the dead:' Re. i. 5. And 'the first-fruits of them that slept.' 1 Co. xv. 20. So then, though Adam was the image of God, yet God's image but as a mere creature: But Christ though a creature as touching his manhood; yet being also God, as the

Father, he shewed forth expressly, in capital characters, by all his works and doings in the world, the beauty and glory of the Father: 'The light of the knowledge of the glory of God,' is given 'in the face of Jesus Christ.' 2 Co. iv. 6. Where by face, we must understand that which is visible, that being open when all else is covered, and that by which most principally we are discovered to others, and known. Now as to the case in hand, this face must signify to us the personal virtues and doings of Christ, by which the glory of the Father is exposed; the glory of his justice, by Christ's exactness of life; the glory of his love, by Christ's compassion to sinners, &c

Ver. 26. 'And God said, Let us make man in our image, after our likeness: and let them have dominion over the fish of the sea, and over the fowl of the air, and over the cattle, and over all the earth, and over every creeping thing that creepeth upon the earth.'

As Adam was a type of Christ, as the image and glory of God; so by these words he further sheweth, that he was a type of his sovereign power; for to him be dominion and power everlasting, He. ii. 8, 9. 'to whom be praise and dominion for ever.' 1 Pe. iv. 11. Jude 25. Now by the fish of the sea, the beasts of the earth, the fowls of the air, and every creeping thing, we may understand all creatures, visible and invisible, whether they be men, angels, or devils; in heaven, earth, or under the earth: also all thrones, authorities and powers, whether in heaven, in earth, or hell: Christ is made head over all; He hath also a name above every name, 'not only in this world, but in that which is to come.' Ep. i. 25.

Ver. 28. 'And God blessed them; and God said unto them, (that is, to the man and his wife) Be fruitful, and multiply, and replenish the earth, and subdue it,' &c.

This in the type doth show, in the antitype, how fruitful Christ and his church shall be; and how he at last shall, all over the earth, have a seed to replenish and subdue it by the power of the immortal seed of the word of God: how his name shall be reverenced from one end of the earth to the other: how the kingdoms of the earth shall ALL at last become the kingdoms of our Lord, and of his Christ.

'And subdue it.' God did put that majesty and dread upon Adam, at his creation, that all the beasts of the field submitted themselves unto him. As God also said to Noah, 'The fear of you and the dread of you shall be upon every beast of the earth, and upon every fowl of the air, upon all that moveth upon the earth, and upon all the fishes of the sea; into your hand are they delivered.' Ge. ix. 2.

'¶ And God said, Behold I have given you

every herb bearing seed, which *is* upon the face of all the earth; and every tree, in the which *is* the fruit of a tree yielding seed; to you it shall be for meat.' Ge. i. 29.

These herbs and trees are types of the wholesome word of the gospel, on which both Christ, his church, and unconverted sinners, ought to feed and be refreshed; and without which there is no subsisting either of one or the other: 'He causeth the grass to grow for the cattle, and herb for the service of man: that he may bring forth food out of the earth; and wine *that* maketh glad the heart of man, *and* oil to make *his* face to shine, and bread *which* strengtheneth man's heart.' Ps. civ. 14, 15.

'And God saw every thing that he had made, and, behold, *it was* very good.' ver. 31.

All things have their natural goodness by creation. Things are not good, because they have a being only, but because God gave them such a being. Neither did God make them, because he saw they would attract a goodness to themselves; but he made them in such kind, as to bring forth that goodness he before determined they should. 'And the evening and the morning were the sixth day.'

CHAP. II.

Ver. 3. 'And God blessed the seventh day, and sanctified it: because that in it he had rested from all his work which God created and made.'

The seventh day did signify two things:

First, Christ Jesus, who is as well the rest of the justice of God, as a rest for sinful man.

Secondly, It was also a type of that glorious rest that saints shall have when the six days of this world are fully ended.

For the first, the apostle makes the sabbath a shadow of Jesus Christ, 'a shadow of things to come; but the body (or substance) *is* of Christ.' Col. ii. 17. And hence it is that he is so often said to be 'a rest' to the Gentiles, a glorious rest, and that he promiseth rest to such as cast their burthen upon him. Mat. xi. 29.

The second also the apostle asserteth in that fourth chapter to the Hebrews, 'There remaineth therefore a rest,' or the keeping of a sabbath, 'to the people of God:' ver. 9. read also ver. 4—11. Which sabbath, as I conceive, will be the seventh thousand of years, which are to follow immediately after the world hath stood six thousand first: for as God was six days in the works of creation, and rested the seventh; so in six thousand years he will perfect his works and providences that concern this world. As also he will finish the toil and travel of his saints, with the burthen of the beasts, and the curse of the ground; and bring all into rest for a thousand years. A day with the Lord, is as a thousand years: wherefore this

blessed and desirable time is also called 'a day,' 'a great day,' 'that great and notable day of the Lord,' Ac. ii. 20. which shall end in the eternal judgment of the world. God hath held forth this by several other shadows, as the sabbath of weeks, the sabbath of years, and the great jubilee, which is to be the year after forty-nine years are expired. Le. xxv. 1—13. Of all which, more in their place, if God permit.

Ver. 4. '¶ These *are* the generations of the heavens and of the earth when they were created, in the day that the LORD God made the earth and the heavens.'

Moses seems by these words, 'In the day,' to insist principally upon them in their first and primitive state, before there was sin or curse in the world; for in the day that they were created, there was a far more glorious lustre and beauty than now can be seen; the heaven, for sin, is, as it were, turned into brass; and the rain into powder and dust, in comparison of what it was as it came from the fingers of God. The earth hath also from that time a curse upon it; yea, the whole creation, by sin, is even 'made subject to vanity,' is in travail, and groans under the burthen that sin hath brought upon it. Ro. viii. 19—23.

Ver. 5. 'And every plant of the field before it was in the earth, and every herb of the field before it grew.'

Thus it was in the first creation; they therefore became neither herbs nor trees, by the course of nature, but by the creation of God. And even so it is in the new creation, men spring not up by nature to be saints: No, not in the church of God, but first they are created in Christ Jesus, and made meet to be partakers of the benefit, and then planted in the church of God; 'planted,' I say, as plants before prepared. Indeed hypocrites, and formal professors, may spring up in the church, by virtue of her forms, and outward services, as thorns and thistles spring up in the earth, by virtue of her moisture and heartiness. But these are but the fruits of the curse, and are determined to be burned at last in the fire: 'Every plant (saith Christ) which my heavenly Father hath not planted, shall be rooted up.' Mat. xv. 13. He. vi. 8.*

'For the Lord God had not caused it to rain upon the earth.' This is the reason that they came not up by nature first, but were first created, then planted, then made to grow. So the reason why men by nature grow not in the church, is, because the Lord doth not cause it to rain upon them, they still abiding and doing according to the course of this world; but he plants them in his house by

---

* In what pointed language are these solemn warnings put. Reader, in the sight of God, let the heart-searching inquiry of the apostle's be yours; Lord. is it I?

the mighty power of his word and Spirit, by which they are created saints, and then they afterwards grow in grace, and in the knowledge of our Lord and Saviour Jesus Christ.

'And *there was* not a man to till the ground.' It seems by this there was a kind of necessity why God should make man, yea, a multitude of men; for otherwise he had made what before he made in vain: that is, his end in making so glorious a creature as this world, which was to shew forth his glory by, had been void, and without effect; for although it was glorious, as it came out of the hand of God; yet it was not of power so to preserve itself, but would, without men to look after and dress it, be turned into a wilderness.

Thus it is with the world of men, if there was not the second Adam to plough them and sow them, they could none of them become saints; No, not the elect themselves; because the means are determined, as well as the end.

By this we may likewise see what a woful condition that people is in, that have no ministers of the word of the gospel: 'My people perish, [are destroyed] for lack of knowledge:' Ho. iv. 6. And again, 'Where *there is* no vision, the people perish.' Pr. xxix. 18. Pray therefore to the Lord of the harvest, that he would send out his ploughers to plough, and his labourers into his harvest.

Ver. 6. 'But there went up a mist from the earth, and watered the whole face of the ground.'

Although as yet there was no ploughman nor rain, yet a mist arose from the earth; so where there is not the word of the gospel, there is yet sufficiency of light, to teach men how to govern themselves in civil and natural society. But this is only 'a mist,' men cannot gospelly grow by this; therefore, as in the next verse, of necessity man must be formed.

But again, I have sometimes thought by this mist, might be held forth that nourishment men had by the doctrine of faith, before the gospel was divulged by Moses, the prophets, or Christ, &c. for before these, that nourishment the church received, was but slender and short, even as short as the nourishing of the mist is to sober and moderate showers of rain; to which both the law and the gospel is compared.

Again, I have also sometimes thought, that by this mist might be typified those excellent proverbs and holy sayings of the men of old, before there was a written word; for it cannot be but the godly did contain in proverbs, and certain sayings, the doctrine of salvation hereafter, and of good living here; [see Ro. ii. 14.] of which we have a touch in Genesis, but more at large by that blessed book of Job; which book, in my opinion, is a holy collection of those proverbs and sayings of the ancients, occasioned by the temptation of that good

man. But whatever this mist did signify (in other men's judgment) certain it is, it was for present necessity, till a man should be made to till the ground, and the fruits thereof watered with 'the bottles of heaven:' Which, so far as I see yet, most aptly presents us with some of all these.

Ver. 7. 'And the Lord God formed man *of* the dust of the ground,' &c.

In the creation of man, God began with his outside; but in the work of regeneration, he first begins within, at the heart. He made him; that is, his body, of the dust of the ground; but he abides a lifeless lump, till the Lord puts forth a second act. 'And [he] breathed into his nostrils the breath of life; and man became a living soul.' Now he lives, now he acts: so it is in the kingdom of Christ, no man can be a living soul in that kingdom by his first creation, he must have life 'breathed' into him, life and spirit from Jesus Christ. Jn. xx. 22.

Now therefore is Adam a type, yet but an earthly one, of things more high and heavenly; 'And as we have borne the image of the earthy, we shall also bear the image of the heavenly.' 1 Co. xv. 49.

Ver. 8. '¶ And the Lord God planted a garden eastward in Eden, and there he put the man whom he had formed.'

'And the Lord God planted a garden.' Thus the Holy Ghost speaks clearer and clearer; for now he presents the church to us under the similitude of a garden, which is taken out of the wide and open field, and inclosed; 'A garden inclosed *is* my sister, *my* spouse;' a garden inclosed, 'a spring shut up, a fountain sealed;' Ca. iv. 12. and there he put the man whom he had formed. An excellent type of the presence of Christ with his church. Re. i. 12, 13.

Ver. 9. 'And out of the ground made the Lord God to grow every tree that is pleasant to the sight,' &c.

These trees, and their pleasurableness, do shew us the beauty of the truly godly, whom the Lord hath beautified with salvation. And hence it is said, the glory of Lebanon, of Sharon, and of Carmel, is given to the church: that is, she is more beautified with gifts and graces than can by types and shadows be expressed. 'The tree of life also in the midst of the garden, and the tree of knowledge of good and evil.'

This 'tree of life,' was another type of Christ, as the bread and healing medicine of the church, that stands 'in the midst of the paradise of God.' Re. ii. 7; xxii. 2.

The tree of the knowledge of good and evil, was a type of the law, or covenant of works, as the sequel of the story clearly manifesteth; for had not Adam eaten thereof, he had enjoyed for ever his first blessedness. As Moses saith, 'It shall be our righteousness, if we observe to do all these commandments before the Lord our God, as he hath commanded us.' De. vi. 25. But both Adam and we have touched, that is, broken the boughs and fruit of this tree, and therefore now for ever, by the law, no man can stand just before God. Ga. ii. 16.

Ver. 10. '¶ And a river went out of Eden to water the garden; and from thence it was parted, and became into four heads.'

This river while it abided in Eden, in the garden, it was the river of God; that is, serviceable to the trees and fruit of the garden, and was herein a type of those watering ministers that water the plants of the Lord. But observe, when it had passed the garden, had gotten without the bound of the garden, from thence it was parted, and became into four heads; from thence it was transformed, or turned into another manner of thing: it now became into four heads; a type of the four great monarchies of the world, of which Babylon, though the first in order of being, yet the last in a gospel or mysterious sense. The fourth is the river Euphrates, that which was the face of the kingdom of Babel of old. Hence note, That how eminent and serviceable soever men are while they abide in the garden of Eden, THE CHURCH; yet when they come out from thence, they evilly seek the great things of the world: one is for compassing the whole land of Havilah, where is gold; another is for compassing this, a third that, and a fourth another thing, according as you see these four heads did. Observe again, That while men abide in the church of God, there is not by them a seeking after the monarchies of this world; but when they depart from thence, then they seek and strive to be heads; as that cursed monster the pope, forsaking the garden of God, became in a manner the prince of all the earth: Of whom Tyrus mentioned by Ezekiel, was a very lively type, 'Thou hast been in Eden, the garden of God; every precious-stone, [that is, doctrine,] was thy covering; as the sardius, topaz, diamond,' &c. 'till iniquity was found in thee;' Eze. xxviii. 13—18. till thou leftest thy station, and place appointed of God, and then thou wast cast as profane out of the mountain of God, yea, though a covering cherub. See it again in Cain, who while he continued in the church, he was a busy sacrificer, as busy as Abel his brother; but when he left off to fear the Lord, and had bloodily butchered his holy brother, then he seeks to be a head, or monarch; then he goeth and buildeth a city to preserve his name and posterity for ever. Ge. iv. 17.

Ver. 15. '¶ And the Lord God took the man, and put him into the garden of Eden, to dress it and to keep it.'

In this also Adam was a figure of our Lord Jesus Christ, as pastor and chief bishop of his church. 'I the Lord, [saith Christ,] do keep it; I will water it every moment, I will keep it night and day.' Is. xxvii. 3.

'And the Lord God took the man.' No man taketh this honour upon him, but he that is called of God, as was Aaron. Blessed is he also that can say as the prophet Amos; 'And the Lord took me (said he) as I followed the flock, and the Lord said unto me, Go, prophesy unto my people Israel.' Am. vii. 15.

'To dress it and to keep it.' He that is not dressed, is not kept: That is a sad judgment, That which dieth, let it die; That which is diseased, let it not be dressed, let it die of that disease. By dressing therefore I understand, pruning, manuring and the like, which the dresser of the vineyard was commanded to do, without which all is overrun with briers and nettles, and is fit for nothing but cursing, and to be burned. Lu. xiii. 6—9. Pr. xxiv. 30 —34. He. vi. 7, 8.

'And the Lord commanded the man, saying, Of every tree of the garden thou mayest freely eat.' ver. 16.

It is God's word that giveth us power to eat, to drink, and do other our works, and without the word we may do nothing. The command gave Adam leave: 'Every creature of God is good, and nothing to be refused, if it be received with thanksgiving; for it is sanctified by the word of God (by the command of the word, and by receiving of it according to the limits thereof,) and prayer.' 1 Ti. iv. 4, 5.

Ver. 17. 'But of the tree of the knowledge of good and evil, thou shalt not eat of it.' I said before, What God's word prohibits, we must take care to shun.

This 'tree of knowledge,' as I said before, was a type of the covenant of works, the which had not Adam touched, (for by touching it he broke that covenant,) he then had lived ever, but touching it he dies. Ge. iii. 3.

Adam going into the garden under these conditions and penalties, was therein a type of the humiliation of Christ; who at his coming into the world, was made under the law, under its command and penalty, even as other men, but without sin. Ga. iv. 4, 5.

'For in the day that thou eatest thereof thou shalt surely die.'

'For in the day.' Adam lived to God no longer than while he kept himself from eating forbidden fruit; in that very day he died; first a spiritual death in his soul; his body also was then made capable of mortality, and all diseases, which two great impediments in time brought him down to dust again.

Ver. 18. ' ¶ And the Lord God said, *It is* not good that man should be alone; I will make him an help meet for him.'

By these words, Adam's state, even in innocency, seems to crave for help; wherefore it is manifest that that state is short of that we attain by the resurrection from the dead; yea, for as much as his need required earthly help, it is apparent his condition was not heavenly: ' The first man *is* of the earth, earthy: the second man *is* the Lord from heaven.' 1 Co. xv. 47. Adam in his first estate was not spiritual: ' That *was* not first which is spiritual, but that which is natural; and afterwards that which is spiritual.' ver. 46. Wherefore those that think it enough to attain to the state of Adam in innocency, think it sufficient to be mere naturalists; think themselves well, without being made spiritual: yea, let me add, they think it safe standing by a covenant of works; they think themselves happy, though not concerned in a covenant of grace; they think they know enough, though ignorant of a mediator, and count they have no need of the intercession of Christ.*

Adam stood by a covenant of works: Adam's kingdom was an earthly paradise; Adam's excellency was, that he had no need of a Saviour; and Adam's knowledge was ignorance of Jesus Christ: Adam in his greatest glory, wanted earthly comforts; Adam in his innocency, was a mere natural man.

Ver. 19. 'And out of the ground the Lord God formed every beast of the field, and every fowl of the air.'

This proveth further what I said at first, That in the first chaos was contained all that was made upon the earth.

' And brought *them* unto Adam, to see what he would call them: and whatsoever Adam called every living creature, that *was* the name thereof.'

In this Adam was a lively type of the Lord Christ's sovereign and glorious power over all flesh: ' Thou hast given him power over all flesh, that he should give eternal life to as many as thou hast given him.' Jn. xvii. 2.

' And brought *them* unto Adam to see what he would call them.'

So Christ nameth the world; whom he will he calleth saints; and whom he will he calleth the world, ' ungodly,' ' serpents,' ' vipers,' and the like. ' I pray for them, I pray not for the world.' Jn. xvii. 9.

' And whatsoever Adam called every living creature, that *was* the name thereof.' Even as Christ passes sentence, so shall their judgment be.

* Bunyan beautifully illustrates this view of divine truth in his controversy with Edward Fowler, Bishop of Gloucester. See ' The Defence of the Doctrine of Justification by Faith in Jesus Christ.'—Ed.

Ver. 20. ' And Adam gave names to all cattle, and to the fowl of the air, and to every beast of the field.' So Christ judgeth of angels, devils, and men.

' But for Adam, there was not found an help meet for him.' All the glory of this world, had not Adam had a wife, could not have completed this man's blessedness; he would yet have been wanting: so all the glory of heaven, considering Christ as mediator, could not, without his church, have made him up complete. The church, I say, ' which is his body, the fulness of him that filleth all in all.'

Ver. 21, 22. ' ¶ And the Lord God caused a deep sleep to fall upon Adam, and he slept: and he took one of his ribs, and closed up the flesh instead thereof; and the rib which the Lord God had taken from man, made he a woman, and brought her unto the man.'

In these words we find an help provided for Adam; also, whence it came. The help was a wife; she came out of his side; she was taken thence while Adam slept. A blessed figure of a further mystery. Adam's wife was a type of the church of Christ; for that she was taken out of his side, it signifies we are flesh of Christ's flesh, and bone of Christ's bone. Ep. v. 30. And in that she was taken thence while Adam slept, it signifies, the church is Christ's, by virtue of his death and blood: ' Feed the church of God, which he hath purchased with his own blood.' Ac. xx. 28.

' And he brought her to the man.' That is, And God brought her to the man. By which he clearly intimates, That as the church is the workmanship of God, and the purchase of the blood of Christ; so yet she cannot come to Christ, unless brought to him of God: ' No man can come to me (saith Christ) except the Father which hath sent me, draw him.' Jn. vi. 44.

Ver. 23. ' And Adam said, This *is* now bone of my bones, and flesh of my flesh: she shall be called Woman, because she was taken out of Man.'

In that Adam doth thus acknowledge his wife to be bone and flesh of his substance, it shews us, that Christ will acknowledge those that are his: ' He is not ashamed to call them brethren, saying, I will declare thy name unto my brethren, in the midst of the church will I sing praise unto thee.' He. ii. 11, 12.

And observe it, He said, ' She is bone of my bone,' &c. before that God, that brought her to him; intimating, that Christ both owns us now at his Father's right hand, and will not be ashamed of us, even in the day of judgment. Mat. x. 33. Lu. xii. 8.

Ver. 24. 'Therefore shall a man leave his father and his mother, and shall cleave unto his wife: and they shall be one flesh.'

This ought to be truly performed in our married

estate in this world. But here endeth not the mystery.

'Therefore shall a man leave his father.' Thus did Christ when he came into the world to save sinners: He came forth from the Father; 'I came forth from the Father, and am come into the world.' Jn. xvi. 28.

'Therefore shall a man leave his father and his mother.' The Jewish church may, in a mystical sense, be called the mother of Christ; for she was indeed God's wife, and of her came his Son Jesus Christ: yet his mother he left and forsook, to be joined to his Gentile spouse, which is now his only wife.

Ver. 25. 'And they were both naked, the man and his wife, and were not ashamed.'

No sin, no shame: Let men stand where God hath set them, and there is no cause of shame, though they be exposed in outward appearance to never so much contempt.

'And they were both naked.' Apparel is the fruits of sin; wherefore let such as pride themselves therein, remember, that they cover one shame with another. But let them that are truly godly have their apparel modest and sober, and with shamefacedness put them on, remembering always the first cause of our covering our nakedness, was the sin and shame of our first parents. [1 Pe. iii. 3.]

CHAP. III.

Ver. 1. 'Now the serpent was more subtil than any beast of the field which the Lord God had made. And he said unto the woman, Yea, hath God said, Ye shall not eat of every tree of the garden?'

In these words we have an entrance of the first great spiritual conflict that was fought between the devil and flesh; and it is worth the observing, how the enemy attempted, engaged, and overcame the world. 2 Co. xi. 3.

1. He tempts by means; he appeareth not in his own shape and hue, but assumeth the body of one of the creatures, the body of the serpent, and so begins the combat. And from hence it is, that in after ages he is spoken of under the name of that creature, 'the dragon, that old serpent which is the devil, and Satan;' Re. xx. 2. because, as the Holy Ghost would have us beware of the devil, so of the means and engines which he useth; for where one is overcome by his own fearful appearance, ten thousand are overcome by the means and engines that he useth.

2. 'The serpent was more subtil.' The devil, in his attempts after our destruction, maketh use of the most suitable means. The serpent was more subtil, therefore the cunning of the devil was least of all discerned. Had he made use of some of the

most foolish of the creatures, Adam had luckily started back, for he knew the nature of all the creatures, and gave them names accordingly; wherefore the serpent, Adam knew, was subtil, therefore Satan useth him, thereby to catch this goodly creature. Hereby the devil least appeared; and least appearing, the temptation soonest took the tinder.*

'Now the serpent was more subtil.' More subtil. Hence the devil is called, 'the serpent with heads,' [with great cunning;] 'the crooked serpent,' [with knotty objections;] 'the piercing serpent,' [for he often wounds;] and his ways are called 'devices,' 'temptations,' 'delusions,' 'wiles,' 'power,' and 'the gates of hell;' because of their mighty prevalency. This is he that undertook our first parents.

But how did he undertake them?

He labours to make them question the simplicity of the word of God, bearing Adam's wife in hand, that there must needs be some meaning that palliates the text; Hath God said ye shall not eat of the tree? Which interrogatory suggested them with a strong doubt that this word would not appear a truth, if you compare it with the 4th verse.

Hence learn, that so long as we retain the simplicity of the word, we have Satan at the end of the staff; for unless we give way to a doubt about that, about the truth and simplicity of it, he gets no ground upon us. And hence the apostle says, He feared lest by some means, as the serpent beguiled Eve through his subtilty, so our minds should be corrupted from the simplicity that is in Christ; 2 Co. xi. 3. that is, lest our minds should be drawn off from the simplicity of the word of the gospel by some devilish and delusive arguments: For mark, Satan doth not first of all deny, but makes a doubt upon the word, whether it is to be taken in this or another sense; and so first corrupting the mind with a doubt about the simplicity of the true sense, he after brings them to a denial thereof; 'Hath God said, Ye shall not eat of every tree of the garden?'

Ver. 2. 'And the woman said unto the serpent, We may eat of the fruit of the trees of the garden.'

'And the woman said.' Indeed, the question was put to her, but the command was not so immediately delivered to her: 'The Lord God commanded the man.' chap. ii. 16. This therefore I reckon a great fault in the woman, an usurpation, to undertake so mighty an adversary, when she was not the principal that was concerned therein; nay,

---

* Christian, you are specially cautioned to 'beware of the flatterer.' The Pilgrim's Christian and Hopeful forgot the caution, and 'a man black of flesh but covered with a *very light robe*, caught them in his net, and they were chastised sore.'—ED.

when her husband who was more able than she, was at hand, to whom also the law was given as chief. But for this act, I think it is, that they are now commanded silence, and also commanded to learn of their husbands: 1 Co. xiv. 34, 35. A command that is necessary enough for that simple and weak sex:* Though they see it was by them that sin came into the world, yet how hardly are some of them to this day dissuaded from attempting unwarrantably to meddle with potent enemies, about the great and weighty matters that concern eternity. 1 Ti. ii. 11—15.

Hence note, That often they who are least able, will first adventure to put in their head to defend that, from whence they return with shame.

'And the woman said unto the serpent, We may eat of the fruit of the trees of the garden.'

This was her prologue to her defence, but that also for which she had no warrant. In time of temptation, it is our wisdom and duty to keep close to the word, that prohibits and forbids the sin; and not to reason with Satan, of how far our outward and worldly privileges go, especially of those privileges that border upon the temptation, as she here did: We may eat of all but one. By this she goeth to the outside of her liberty, and sets herself upon the brink of the danger. Christ might have told the tempter, when he assaulted him, That he could have made stones bread; and that he could have descended from the pinnacle of the temple, as afterwards he did; Mat. iv. 3—7. Lu. iv. but that would have admitted of other questions. Wherefore he chooseth to lay aside such needless and unwarantable reasonings, and resisteth him with a direct word of God, most pertinent to quash the tempter, and also to preserve himself in the way. To go to the outside of privileges, especially when tempted of the devil, is often, if not always very dangerous and hazardous.

By these words therefore, in mine opinion, she spoke at this time too much in favour of the flesh; and made way for what after came upon her, We may eat of all but one.

Ver. 3. 'But of the fruit of the tree which *is* in the midst of the garden, God hath said, Ye shall not eat of it, neither shall ye touch it, lest ye die.'

Now, too late, she urgeth that which should have been her only stay and weapon; to wit, the express word of God; That she should, if she would have disputed with the tempter, have urged at the first that only, and have thought of nothing

else. Thus did the Lord himself: but she looking first into those worthy privileges which God had given her, and dilating delightfully of them before the devil, she lost the dread of the command from off her heart, and retained now but the notion of it: which Satan perceiving, and taking heart therefrom to make his best advantage, he now adds to his former forged doubt, a plain and flat denial, 'Ye shall not surely die.'

Ver. 4. 'And the serpent said unto the woman, Ye shall not surely die.'

When people dally with the devil, and sit too near their outward advantages; when they are tempted to break the command of God, it is usual for them, even by setting their hearts upon things that in themselves are honest and lawful, to fall into temptation: To see a piece of ground, to prove a yoke of oxen, to marry a wife, are doubtless lawful things; but upon the borders of these privileges lay the temptation of the devil; therefore by the love of these, which yet were lawful in themselves, the devil hardened the heart, and so at last made way for, and perfectly produced in them, flatly to deny, as then, to embrace the words of God's salvation. Mat. xxii. 5. Lu. xiv. 16—20. The like befel our first mother; wherefore though at last she freely objected the word; yet because before she had so much reasoned to the pleasing of the flesh, she lost the dread and savour of the command, and having nought but notion left, she found not wherewith to rebuke so plain a lie of the devil, but hearkened to his further reasoning.

'Ye shall not surely die.' Not surely; in the word there is some slight meaning, of which you need not be so afraid. And besides,

Ver. 5. 'God doth know that in the day ye eat thereof, then your eyes shall be opened, and ye shall be as gods, knowing good and evil.'

In these words two privileges are asserted: one, That their eyes should be opened; the other, That they should be as gods, knowing good and evil. The first is very desirable, and was not at all abridged by them; the second, as to their knowing good and evil, was absolutely forbidden; because they could not attain to the knowledge of that which was evil, but by transgressing, or by eating of that forbidden tree.

Hence observe, That it is usual with the devil, in his tempting of poor creatures, to put a good and bad together, that by shew of the good, the tempted might be drawn to do that which in truth is evil. Thus he served Saul; he spared the best of the herd and flock, under pretence of sacrificing to God, and so transgressed the plain command. 1 Sa. xv. 20—22. But this the apostle saw was dangerous, and therefore censureth such, as in a state of condemnation. Ro. iii. 8. Thus he served Adam; he put the desirableness of sight, and a plain trans-

---

* Much allowance must be made for the state of female education in Bunyan's days. Every effort was made to keep women in subordination—a mere drudging, stocking mending help meet for man. Now we feel that the more highly she is cultivated, the more valuable help she becomes, and that in intellect she is on a perfect equality with man.—ED.

gression of God's law together, that by the loveliness of the one, they might the easier be brought to do the other. O poor Eve! Do we wonder at thy folly! Doubtless we had done as bad with half the argument of thy temptation.

'Ye shall be as gods.' In these words he attempts to beget in them a desire to be greater than God had made them. 1 Ti. iii. 6. He knew this was a likely way, for by this means he fell himself; for being puffed up with pride, they left their own estate, or habitation, and so became devils, and were tumbled down to hell, where they are ' reserved in everlasting chains, under darkness, unto the judgment of the great day.' Jude 6.

'Ye shall be as gods.' When souls have begun to hearken to the tempter, that hearkening hath made way for, and given way to so much darkness of mind, and hardness of heart, that now they can listen to anything: as to hear God charged with folly, ' Ye shall not surely die ;' as to hear him made the author of ignorance, and that he delights to have it so, by seeking by a command to prohibit them from knowing what they could ; for God doth know, that in the day ye eat thereof, then your eyes shall be opened ; and therefore he forbids to touch it.

'Ye shall be as gods.' Here is also a pretence of holiness, which he knew they were prone unto ; ' Ye shall be as gods,' as knowing and perfect as God. Oh! Thousands are, even to this day, by such temptations overcome! Thus he wraps his temptations up in such kind of words and suggestions as will carry it either way. But mark his holiness, or the way that he prescribes for holiness; it is, if not point blank against, yet without and besides the word, not by doing what God commands, and abhorring what he forbids, but by following the delusion of the devil, and their own roving fancies ; as Eve here does.

Ver. 6. ' ¶ And when the woman saw that the tree *was* good for food, and that it *was* pleasant to the eyes, and a tree to be desired to make *one* wise, she took of the fruit thereof,' &c.

This verse presents us with the use that Eve made of the reasonings of the serpent; and that was, to take them into consideration ; not by the word of God, but as her flesh and blood did sense them : A way very dangerous and devouring to the soul, from which Paul fled, as from the devil himself : ' Immediately I conferred not with flesh and blood.' Ga. i. 16. Wherefore, pausing upon them, they entangled her as with a threefold cord. 1. ' The lust of the flesh ;' she saw it was good for food. 2. ' The lust of the eye ;' she saw it was pleasant to the eye. 3. ' The pride of life ;' a tree to be desired, to make one wise. 1 Jn. ii. 16. Being taken, I say, with these three snares of the adversary, which are not of the Father, but of the

world, and the devil the prince thereof, forthwith she falls before him : ' And when the woman saw' this, ' she took of the fruit thereof, and did eat.'

' And when the woman saw.' This seeing, as I said, is to be understood of her considering what Satan presented to her, and of her sensing or tasting of his doctrine ; not by the word, which ought to be the touch stone of all, but by and according to her own natural reason without it. Now this makes her forget that very command that but now she had urged against the tempter : This makes her also to consent to that very reason, as an inducement to transgress ; which, because it was the nature of the tree, was by God suggested as a reason why they should forbear ; it was the tree of the knowledge of good and evil, therefore they should not touch it ; it was the tree, that would by touching it, make them know good and evil ; therefore she toucheth, and also eateth thereof. See therefore what specious pretences the devil, and those that are under the power of temptation, will have to transgress the command of God. That which God makes a reason of the prohibition, even that the devil will make a reason of their transgression.

God commands to self-denial, but the world makes that a reason of their standing off from the very grace of God in the gospel. God also commands, That we be sober, chaste, humble, just, and the like ; but the devil, and carnal hearts, make these very things the argument that keeps sinners from the word of salvation. Or rather take it thus ; God forbids wickedness, because it is delightful to the flesh, and draws the heart from God, but therefore carnal men love wickedness and sin : Therefore they go on in sin, and ' therefore they say unto God, Depart from us, for we desire not the knowledge of thy ways.' Job xxi. 14; xxii. 15—17.

She ' did eat, and gave also unto her husband with her, and he did eat.'

The great design of the devil, as he supposed, was now accomplished ; for he had both in the snare, both the man and his wife, and in them, the whole world that should be after. And indeed the chief design of Satan was at the head at first, only he made the weakest the conveyance for his mischief. Hence note again, That Satan by tempting one, may chiefly intend the destruction of another. By tempting the wife, he may aim at the destruction of the husband; by tempting the father, he may design the destruction of the children ; and by tempting the king, he may design the ruin of the subjects. Even as in the case of David : ' Satan stood up against Israel, and provoked David to number the people.' He had a mind to destroy seventy thousand, therefore he tempted David to sin. 1 Ch. xxi. 1.

She gave also to her husband, and he did eat. Sin seldom or never terminates in one person; but the pernicious example of one, doth animate and embolden another; or thus, the beholding of evil in another, doth often allure a stander-by. Adam was the looker-on, he was not in the action as from the serpent: 'Adam was not deceived,' that is, by having to do with the devil, 'but the woman, the woman being deceived, was in the transgression.' 1 Ti. ii. 14. This should exhort all men that they take heed of so much as beholding evil done by others, lest also they should be allured. When Israel went into Canaan, God did command them not so much as to ask, How those nations served their gods? lest by so doing, Satan should get an advantage of their minds, to incline them to do the like. De. xii. 30. Evil acts, as well as evil words, will eat as doth a canker. This then is the reason of that evil-favouredness that you see attending some men's lives and professions; they have been corrupted, as Adam was, either by evil words or bad examples, even till the very face of their lives and professions are disfigured as with the pox or canker. 2 Ti. ii. 17.

Thus have we led you through that woful tragedy that was acted between the woman and the serpent; and have also shewed, how it happened that the serpent went away as victor.

1. The woman admitted of a doubt about the truth of the word that forbad her to eat; for unbelief was the first sin that entered the world.

2. She preferred the privileges of the flesh, before the argument to self-denial; by which means her heart became hardened, and grew senseless of the dread and terror of the words of God.

3. She took Satan's arguments into consideration, and *sensed, or tasted them; not by the word of God, but her own natural, or rather sore-deluded fancy.

4. She had a mind to gratify the lusts of the flesh, the lusts of the eyes, and the pride of life.

Now to speak of the evil consequences that followed this sinful act: That is not in the wisdom of mortal man to do; partly, because we know but in part even the evil and destructive nature of sin; and partly, because much of the evil that will follow this action, is yet to be committed by persons unborn. Yet enough might be said to astonish the heavens, and to make them horribly afraid. Je. ii. 12. 1. By this act of these two, the whole world became guilty of condemnation and eternal judgment. Ro. v. 2. By this came all the blindness,

atheism, ignorance of God, enmity and malice against him, pride, covetousness, adultery, idolatry, and implacableness, &c. that is found in all the world. By this, I say, came all the wars, blood, treachery, tyranny, persecution, with all manner of rapine and outrage that is found among the sons of men. 3. Besides, all the plagues, judgments, and evils that befal us in this world, with those everlasting burnings that will swallow up millions for ever and ever; all and every whit of these came into the world as the portion of mankind, for that first transgression of our first parents.

Ver. 7. 'And the eyes of them both were opened, and they knew that they *were* naked; and they sewed fig-leaves together, and made themselves aprons.'

That their eyes might be opened, was one branch of the temptation, and one of the reasons that prevailed with the woman to forsake the word of God: But she little thought of seeing after this manner, or such things as now she was made to behold. She expected some sweet and pleasant sight, that might tickle and delight her deluded fancy; but behold, sin and the wrath of God appears, to the shaking of their hearts! And thus, even to this very day, doth the devil delude the world: His temptations are gilded with some sweet and fine pretences; either they shall be wiser, richer, more in favour, live merrier, fare better, or something; and that they shall see it, if they will but obey the devil: Which the fools easily are, by these and such like things, allured to do. But behold, when their eyes are opened, instead of seeing what the devil falsely told them, they see themselves involved in sin, made guilty of the breach of God's command, and subject to the wrath of God.†

'And they knew that they *were* naked.' Not only naked of outward clothing, but even destitute of righteousness; they had lost their innocency, their uprightness, and sinless vail, and had made themselves polluted creatures, both in their hearts and in their flesh; this is nakedness indeed; such a kind of nakedness as Aaron made Israel naked with, when he set up his idol calf for them to worship: 'For Aaron had made them naked unto *their* shame.' Ex. xxxii. 25. Naked before the justice of the law.

'And they knew that they *were* naked.' And they knew it: Why, did they not know it before? The text says, They were naked, and were not ashamed. O! they stood not naked before God! they stood not without righteousness, or upright-

---

* 'And sensed.' Not now used as a verb. The meaning is, that Eve, instead of instantly rejecting the temptation, because contrary to God's command, she reasoned upon it, and sought counsel of her carnal *senses.*—Ed.

† This passage would have done honour to Bishop Taylor, or any one of our best English writers. How blessed are we, if our eyes have been thus painfully opened to see and feel the awful state into which sin plunges us.—Ed.

ness before him, and therefore were not ashamed, but now they knew they were naked as to that.

'And they sewed fig-leaves together, and made themselves aprons.' A fit resemblance of what is the inclination of awakened men, who are yet but natural! They neither think of Christ, or of the mercy of God in him for pardon, but presently they betake themselves to their own fig-leaves, to their own inventions, or to the righteousness of the law, and look for healing from means which God did never provide for cure. 'When Ephraim saw his sickness, and Judah saw his wound, then went Ephraim to the Assyrian.' Ho. v. 13. Not to God, and sent to King Jarib, not to Christ, yet could they not heal him, nor cure him of his wound.

'And made themselves aprons.' Not coats, as God did afterwards. A carnal man thinks himself sufficiently clothed with righteousness, if the nakedness which he sees, can be but covered from his own sight: As if God also did see that and only that which they have a sight of by the light of nature; and as if because fig-leaves would hide their nakedness from their sight, that therefore they would hide it from the sight of God. But alas! No man, without the help of another, can bring all his nakedness to the sight of his own eye; much is undiscovered to him, that may yet lie open and bare to a stander-by: So it is with the men that stand without Christ before God, at best they see but some of their nakedness, to wit, their most gross and worst faults, and therefore they seek to cover them; which when they have hid from their own sight, they think them hid also from the sight of God. Thus did Adam, he saw his own most shameful parts, and therefore them he covered: They made themselves aprons, or things to gird about them, not to cover them all over withal. No man by all his own doings can hide all his own nakedness from the sight of the justice of God, and yet, but in vain, as busy as Adam to do it.

'And they sewed fig-leaves together, and made themselves aprons.' Fig-leaves! A poor apron, but it was the best they could get. But was that a sufficient shelter against either thorn or thistle? Or was it possible but that after a while these fig-leaves should have become rotten, and turned to dung? So will it be with all man's own righteousness which is of the law; Paul saw it so, and therefore counted it but loss and dung, that he might win Christ, and be found in him. Phi. iii. 7, 8.

Ver. 8. 'And they heard the voice of the Lord God walking in the garden in the cool of the day: and Adam and his wife hid themselves from the presence of the Lord God, among the trees of the garden.'

'And they heard the voice of the Lord God.'

This voice was not to be understood according, as if it was the effect of a word; as when we speak, the sound remains with a noise for some time after; but by voice here, we are to understand the Lord Christ himself; wherefore this voice is said to walk, not to sound only: 'They heard the voice of the Lord God walking.' This voice John calls the word, the word that was with the Father before he made the world, and that at this very time was heard to walk in the garden of Adam: Therefore John also saith, this voice was in the beginning; that is, in the garden with Adam, at the beginning of his conversion, as well as of the beginning of the world. Jn. i. 1.

'And they heard the voice of the Lord God walking in the garden in the cool of the day.' The gospel of it is, in the season of grace; for by the cool of the day, he here means, in the patience, gentleness, goodness and mercy of the gospel; and it is opposed to the heat, fire, and severity of the law.

'And Adam and his wife hid themselves.' Hence observe, That a man's own righteousness will not fortify his conscience from fear and terror, when God begins to come near to him to judgment. Why did Adam hide himself, but because, as he said, he was naked? But how could he be naked, when before he had made himself an apron? O! the approach of God consumed and burnt off his apron! Though his apron would keep him from the sight of a bird, yet it would not from the eye of the incorruptible God.

Let therefore all self-righteous men beware, for however they at present please themselves with the worthiness of their glorious fig-leaves; yet when God shall come to deal with them for sin, assuredly they will find themselves naked.*

'And they hid themselves.' A man in a natural state, cannot abide the presence of God; yea, though a righteous man. Adam, though adorned with his fig-leaves, flies.

Observe again, That a self-righteous man, a man of the law, takes grace and mercy for his greatest enemy. This is apparent from the carriage of the Pharisees to Jesus Christ, who because they were wedded to the works of their own righteousness, therefore they hated, persecuted, condemned, and crucified the Saviour of the world. As here in the text, though the voice of the Lord

---

* How solemn are these awful facts, and how impressively does Bunyan fix them on our hearts. As Adam and Eve attempted to hide their guilt and themselves by fig-leaves and bushes, so does man now endeavour to screen his guilt from the omniscient eye of God by refuges of lies, which, like the miserable fig-leaf apron, will be burnt up by the presence of God. Oh, sinner! seek shelter in the robe of the Redeemer's righteousness; the presence of your God will add to its lustre, and make it shine brighter and brighter.—ED.

God walked in the garden in the cool of the day, in the time of grace and love, yet how Adam with his fig-leaves flies before him.

'And Adam and his wife hid themselves from the presence of the Lord God.' These latter words are spoken, not to persuade us that men can hide themselves from God, but that Adam, and those that are his by nature, will seek to do it, because they do not know him aright. These words therefore further shew us what a bitter thing sin is to the soul; it is only for hiding work, sometimes under its fig-leaves, sometimes among the trees of the garden. O what a shaking, starting, timorous evil conscience, is a sinful and guilty conscience! especially when 'tis but a little awakened, it could run its head into every hole, first by one fancy, then by another; for the power and goodness of a man's own righteousness, cannot withstand or answer the demands of the justice of God, and his holy law.

'And Adam and his wife hid themselves from the presence of the Lord God, among the trees of the garden.' If you take the trees in a mystical sense as sometimes they may be taken: Eze. xxxi. 8—11. then take them here to signify, or to be a type of the saints of God, and then the gospel of it is, That carnal men, when they are indeed awakened, and roused out of their foolish fig-leaf righteousness; then they would be glad of some shelter with them that are saved and justified freely by grace, as they in the Gospel of Matthew; ' Give us of your oil; for our lamps are gone out.' Mat. xxv. 8. And again, The man without the wedding garment had crowded himself among the wedding guests: Had hid themselves among the trees of the garden. Mat. xxii. 11.

Ver. 9. '¶ And the Lord God called unto Adam, and said unto him, Where *art* thou?'

Adam having eaten of the forbidden tree, doth now fleet his station, is gone to another than where God left him. Wherefore, if God will find Adam, he must now look him where he had hid himself. And indeed so he does with 'Adam, where art thou?'

'And the Lord God called,' &c. Here begins the conversion of Adam, from his sinful state, to God again. But mark, it begins not at Adam's calling upon God, but at God calling upon him: 'And the Lord God called unto Adam.' Wherefore, by these words, we are to understand the beginning of Adam's conversion. And indeed, grace hath gone the same way with the elect, from that time to this day. Thus he dealt with Abraham, Isaac and Jacob; he called them from their native country, the country of their kindred. And hence it is, that, especially in the New Testament, the saints are said to be the Called; 'Called of God,' and ' Called of Jesus Christ.' And hence again it is that Calling is by Paul made the first demonstration of election, and that saints are admonished to prove their election by their calling; for as Adam was in a lost, miserable and perishing condition, until God called him out of those holes into which sin had driven him: so we do lie where sin and the devil hath laid us, until by the word of God we are called to the fellowship of his Son Jesus Christ.

By these words therefore we have the beginning of the discovery of effectual calling or conversion; ' And the Lord God called:' In which call observe three things,

1. God called so that Adam heard him. And so it is in the conversion of the New Testament saints, as Paul says, ' If ye have heard him, and have been taught by him, as the truth is in Jesus.' Ep. iv. 21. That therefore is one discovery of effectual calling, the sinner is made to HEAR him, even to hear him distinctly, singling out the very person, calling, ' Adam, Where art thou?' ' Saul, Saul, why persecutest thou me?' I have called thee by thy name, thou art mine. As he also said to Moses, ' I know thee by name, and thou hast also found grace in my sight.' Ex. xxxiii. 12.

2. God called so, as to fasten sin upon his conscience, and as to force a confession from him of his naked and shameful state.

3. God called so, as to make him tremble under, and be afraid of the judgment of God.

'And the Lord God called unto Adam, and said unto him, Where *art* thou?' Indeed, Where art thou must of necessity be forcibly urged to every man on whose soul God doth work effectual conversion; for until the person is awakened, as to the state and condition he is in, he will not desire, nay, will not endure to be turned to God; but when in truth they are made to see what condition sin hath brought them to, namely, that it hath laid them under the power of sin, the tyranny of the devil, the strength of death, and the curse of God by his holy law; then is mercy sweet.

'Where art thou?' God knew where he was, but foolish Adam thought otherwise; he thought to hide himself from the presence of the Lord, but the Lord found him out. Indeed, deluded sinners think that they can hide themselves and sins from God. ' How doth God know,' say they, ' Can he judge through the thick cloud?' Job xxii. 13. But such shall know he sees them; they shall know it, either to their correction, or to their condemnation. ' Though they dig into hell,' saith God, ' thence shall mine hand take them; though they climb up to heaven, thence will I bring them down: And though they hide themselves in the top of Carmel, I will search and take them out thence,' &c.* Am. ix. 2, 3. ' Can any hide himself in secret

---

* The remaining words of this alarming verse are very

places that I shall not see him, saith the Lord? Do not I fill heaven and earth? saith the Lord.' Je. xxiii. 24.

Ver. 10. 'And he said, I heard thy voice in the garden, and I was afraid, because I *was* naked; and I hid myself.'

This then was the cause of his flying, he heard the voice of God: A wicked and evil conscience saith, every thing is to it as the messenger of death and destruction; for, as was said before, 'the voice of the Lord walked in the garden in the cool of the day,' in the time of grace and mercy. But it mattereth not whether he came with grace or vengeance; guilt was in Adam's heart, therefore he could not endure the presence of God: He 'that doeth evil hateth the light.' Jn. iii. 20. And again, 'The wicked flee when no man pursueth.' Pr. xxviii. 1. Cain thought all that met him, would seek his blood and life.

'I heard thy voice.' Something by the word of God was spoken, that shook the heart of this poor creature; something of justice and holiness, even before they fell into this communication: for observe it, Adam went forthwith from the tree of knowledge of good and evil a convinced man, first to his fig-leaves, but they would not do; therefore he seeks to be hid among the trees. And observe again, That the insufficiency of fig-leaves were discovered by this voice of the Lord God, that at this time walked in the garden: 'I heard thy voice in the garden, and I was afraid, because I *was* naked; and I hid myself.' So then, there was a first and second voice which Adam heard; the first he ran away from, 'I heard thy voice, and hid myself.' The second was this, wherein they commune each with other. The first therefore was the word of justice, severity, and of the vengeance of God; like that in the 19th of Exodus, from the pronouncing of which, a trembling, and almost death, did seize six hundred thousand persons.

'I heard thy voice in the garden.' It is a word from without that doth it. While Adam listened to his own heart, he thought fig-leaves a sufficient remedy, but the voice that walked in the garden shook him out of all such fancies: 'I heard thy voice in the garden, and I was afraid, because I *was* naked; and I hid myself.'

Ver. 11. 'And he said, Who told thee that thou *wast* naked? Hast thou eaten of the tree, whereof I commanded thee that thou shouldest not eat?'

'Who told thee?' This, as I said before, sup-

poseth a third person, a preacher, and that was the Son of God; the voice of the Lord God that walked in the garden.

'Hast thou eaten of the tree?' That is, If thou hast been shewed thy nakedness, thou hast indeed sinnèd; for the voice of the Lord God will not charge guilt, but where and when a law hath been transgressed. God therefore, by these words, driveth Adam to the point, either to confess or deny the truth of the case. If he confess, then he concludes himself under judgment; if he deny, then he addeth to his sin: Therefore he neither denieth nor confesseth, but so as he may lessen and extenuate his sin.

Ver. 12. 'And the man said, The woman whom thou gavest *to be* with me, she gave me of the tree, and I did eat.'

He had endeavoured with fig-leaves to hide his transgressions before, but that being found too scanty and short, he now trieth what he can do with arguments. Indeed he aknowledgeth that he did eat of the tree of which he was forbidden; but mark where he layeth the reason: Not in any infection which was centred in him by reason of his listening to the discourse which was between the woman and the serpent; but because God had given him a woman to be with him: 'The woman whom thou gavest *to be* with me, she gave me of the tree.' The woman was given for an help, not an hindrance: but Satan often maketh that to become our snare, which God hath given us as a blessing. Adam therefore here mixeth truth with falsehood. It is true, he was beguiled by the woman; but she was not intended of God, as he would insinuate, to the end she might be a trap unto him. Here therefore Adam sought to lessen and palliate his offence, as man by nature is prone to do; for if God will needs charge them with the guilt of sin for the breach of the law, they will lay the fault upon anything, even upon God's ordinance, as Adam here doth, rather than they will honestly fall under the guilt, and so the judgment of the law for guilt. It is a rare thing, and it argueth great knowledge of God, and also hope in his mercy, when men shall heartily acknowledge their iniquities, as is evident in the case of David: 'Wash me thoroughly from mine iniquity, and cleanse me from my sin. For I acknowledge my transgressions: and my sin *is* ever before me.' Ps. li. 2, 3. But this knowledge is not at first in young converts; therefore when God begins to awaken, they begin, as sleepy men, to creep further under their carnal covering; which yet is too short to hide them, and too narrow to cover their shame. Is. xxviii. 20.

'The woman whom thou gavest *to be* with me, she gave me of the tree.' Although, as I said, this sinner seeks to hide, or at least to lessen his sin, by laying the cause upon the woman, the gift of God; yet it argueth that his heart was now filled with shame and confusion of face, for that he had broken God's command; for indeed it is the nature of guilt, however men may in appearance ruffle under it, and set the best leg before, for their vindication; yet inwardly to make them blush and fail before their accuser. Indeed their inward shame is the cause of their excuse; even as Aaron, when he had made the golden calf, could not for shame of heart confess in plainness of speech the truth of the fact to his brother Moses, but faulteringly: They gave me their gold, saith he, and 'I cast it into the fire, and there came out this calf.' Ex. xxxii. 24. 'And there came out this calf;' a pitiful fumbling speech: The Holy Ghost saith, Aaron had made them naked; 'had made them naked unto *their* shame,' for he, as also Adam, should, being chief and lord in their place, have stoutly resisted the folly and sin which was to them propounded; and not as persons of a womanish spirit, have listened to wicked proposals.*

Ver. 13. 'And the Lord God said unto the woman, What *is* this *that* thou hast done?' &c.,

Forasmuch as Adam did acknowledge his sin, though with much weakness and infirmity, God accepts thereof; and now applieth himself to the woman, whom Satan had used as his engine to undo the world.

Hence observe, That when God sets to search out sin, he will follow it from the seduced to the seducer, even till he comes to the rise and first author thereof, as in the following words may more clearly appear. Not that he excuseth or acquitteth the seduced, because the seducer was the first cause, as some do vainly imagine; but to lay all under guilt who are concerned therein: the woman was concerned as a principal, therefore he taketh her to examination.

'And the Lord God said unto the woman, What *is* this *that* thou hast done?' What is this? God seems to speak as if he were astonished at the inundation of evil which the woman by her sin had overflowed the world withal: 'What *is* this *that* thou hast done!' Thou hast undone thyself, thou hast undone thy husband, thou hast undone all the world; yea, thou hast brought a curse upon the whole creation, with an overplus of evils, plagues, and distresses.

'What *is* this *that* thou hast done!' Thou hast defiled thy body and soul, thou hast disabled the whole world from serving God; yea, moreover,

thou hast let in the devil at the door of thy heart, and hast also made him the prince of the world. 'What *is* this *that* thou hast done!' Ah! little, little do sinners know what they have done, when they have transgressed the law of the Lord. I say, they little know what death, what plagues, what curse, yea, what hell they, by so doing, have prepared for themselves.

'What *is* this *that* thou hast done!' God therefore, by these words, would fasten upon the woman's heart a deep sense of the evil of her doings. And indeed, for the soul to be brought into a deep sense of its sin, to cry out before God, Ah! what have I done! it is with them the first step towards conversion: 'Acknowledge thy iniquity (saith God) that thou hast transgressed against me.' Je. iii. 13. And again, 'If we confess our sins, he is faithful and just to forgive us *our* sins, and to cleanse us from all unrighteousness.' 1 Jn. i. 9. The want of this is the cause of that obdurate and lasting hardness that continueth to possess so many thousands of sinners, they cry not out before God, What have I done? but foolishly they rush into, and continue in sin, 'till their iniquity be found to be hateful,' yea, their persons, because of their sin.

'What *is* this *that* thou hast done?' By this interrogatory the Lord also implieth an admonition to the woman, to plead for herself, as he also did to her husband. He also makes way for the working of his bowels towards her, which (as will be shewn anon) he flatly denies to the serpent, the devil: I say he made way for the woman to plead for, or bemoan herself; an evident token that he was unwilling to cast her away for her sin: 'I have surely heard Ephraim bemoaning himself; - I will surely have mercy upon him, saith the Lord.' Je. xxxi. 18—20. Again, by these words, he made way for the working or yearning of his own bowels over her; for when we begin to cry out of our miscarriages, and to bewail and bemoan our condition because of sin, forthwith the bowels of God begin to sound, and to move towards his distressed creature, as by the place before alleged appears. 'I have surely heard Ephraim bemoaning himself;—therefore my bowels are troubled for him: I will surely have mercy upon him, saith the Lord.' See also the 11th and 14th chapters of Hosea.

'And the woman said, the serpent beguiled me and I did eat.' A poor excuse, but an heart affecting one; for many times want of wit and cunning to defend ourselves, doth affect and turn the heart of a stander-by to pity us. And thus, as I think, it was with the woman; she had to do with one that was too cunning for her, with one that snapt her by his subtilty or wiles; which also the woman most simply confesses, even to the provoking of God to take vengeance for her.

* How art thou fallen, oh Adam! thus to lay the blame of thy sin upon God,—'the woman whom *thou* gavest me,' she tempted me. Well does Bunyan term these defences—pitiful fumbling speeches, faulteringly made. How would the glorified spirits of Adam and Aaron embrace him, when he entered heaven, for such honest dealing.—ED.

Ver. 14. 'And the Lord God said unto the serpent, Because thou hast done this, thou *art* cursed above all cattle, and above every beast of the field.'

The serpent was the author of the evil; therefore the thunder rolls till it comes over him, the hot burning thunder-bolt falls upon him.

The Lord, you see, doth not with the serpent as with the man and his wife; to wit, minister occasion to commune with him, but directly pronounceth him cursed above all, 'above every beast of the field.' This sheweth us, that as concerning the angels that fell, with them God is at eternal enmity, reserving them in everlasting chains under darkness. Cursed art thou: By these words, I say, they are prevented of a plea for ever, and also excluded a share in the fruits of the Messiah which should afterwards be born into the world. He. ii. 2.

'Because thou hast done this, cursed art thou.' 'Because thou hast done this:' Not as though he was blessed before; for had he not before been wicked, he had not attempted so wicked a design. The meaning then is, That either by this deed the devil did aggravate his misery, and make himself the faster to hang in the everlasting chains under darkness; or else by this he is manifested to us to be indeed a cursed creature.

Further, 'Because thou hast done this,' may also signify how great complacency and content God took in Adam and his wife while they continued without transgression; But how much against his mind and workmanship this wicked work was. 1. Against his mind; for sin so sets itself against the nature of God, that, if possible, it would annihilate and turn him into nothing, it being in its nature point blank against him. 2. It is against his workmanship; for had not the power of the Messias stept in, all had again been brought to confusion, and worse than nothing: as Christ himself expresses it: 'The earth, and all the inhabitants thereof, are dissolved: I bear up the pillars of it.' Ps. lxxv. 3. And again, 'He upholdeth all things by the word of his power.' He. i. 3.

Besides, this being done, man, notwithstanding the grace of God, and the merits of Jesus Christ, doth yet live a miserable life in this world; for albeit that Christ hath most certainly secured the elect and chosen of God from perishing by what Satan hath done; yet the very elect themselves are, by reason of the first transgression, so infested and annoyed with inward filth, and so assaulted still by the devil, and his vassals the proper children of hell, that they groan unutterably under their burthen; yea, all creatures, 'the whole creation groaneth and travaileth in pain together until now.' Ro. viii. 22. And that most principally upon the very account of this first sin of Adam; it must needs be therefore, this being so high an affront to the divine majesty, and so directly destructive to the work of his hands; and the aim of the devil most principally also at the most excellent of his creation (for man was created in God's own image) that he should hereat be so highly offended, had they not sinned at all before, to bind them over for this very fact to the pains of the eternal judgment of God.

Ver. 15. 'And I will put enmity between thee and the woman, and between thy seed and her seed; it shall bruise thy head, and thou shalt bruise his heel.'

The woman may, in this place, be taken either really or figuratively; if really and naturally, then the threatening is also true, as to the very natures of the creatures here under consideration, to wit, the serpent and the woman, and so all that come of human race; for we find that so great an antipathy is between all such deadly beasts, as serpents and human creatures, that they abiding in their own natures, it is not possible they should ever be reconciled: 'I will put enmity:' I will put it. This enmity then was not infused in creation, but afterwards; and that as a punishment for the abuse of the subtlety of the serpent; for before the fall, and before the serpent was assumed by the fallen angels, they were, being God's creatures, 'good,' as the rest in their kind; neither was there any jarring or violence put between them; but after the serpent was become the devils vizor, then was an enmity begot between them.

'I will put enmity between thee and the serpent.' If by woman, we here understand the church, (but then we must understand the devil, not the natural serpent simply,) then also the threatening is most true; for between the church of God, and the devil, from the beginning of the world, hath been maintained most mighty wars and conflicts, to which there is not a like in all the blood shed on the earth. Yea, here there cannot be a reconciliation, (the enmity is still maintained by God:) The reason is, because their natural dispositions and inclinations, together with their ends and purposes, are most repugnant each to other, even full as much as good and evil, righteousness and sin, God's glory, and an endeavour after his utter extirpation.

Indeed, Satan hath tried many ways to be at amity with the church; not because he loves her holiness, but because he hates her welfare, (wherefore such amity must only be dissembled,) and that he might bring about his enterprise, he sometimes hath allured with the dainty delicates of this world, the lusts of the flesh, of the eyes, and the pride of life: This being fruitless, he hath attempted to entangle and bewitch her with his glorious appearance, as an angel of light; and to that end hath made his ministers as the ministers of righteousness, preaching up righteousness, and contending for a divine and holy worship: 2 Co. xi. 12.

—15. but this failing also, he hath taken in hand at length to fright her into friendship with him, by stirring up the hellish rage of tyrants to threaten and molest her; by finding out strange inventions to torment and afflict her children; by making many bloody examples of her own bowels, before her eyes, if by that means he might at last obtain his purpose: But behold! all hath been in vain, there can be no reconciliation. And why, but because God himself maintains the enmity?

And this is the reason why the endeavours of all the princes and potentates of the earth, that have through ignorance or malice managed his design against the church, have fallen to the ground, and been of none effect.

God hath maintained the enmity: doubtless the mighty wonder, that their laws cannot be obeyed;* I mean their laws and statutes, which by the suggestion of the prince of this world they have made against the church: But if they understood but this one sentence, they might a little perceive the reason. God hath put enmity between the devil and the woman; between that old serpent called, The Devil and Satan, and the holy, and beloved, and espoused wife of Christ.

'I will put enmity between thee and the woman, and between thy seed and her seed.' The seeds here are the children of both, but that of the woman, especially Christ. Ga. iii. 16. 'God sent forth his Son made of a woman.' Ga. iv. 4. Whether you take it literally or figuratively; for in a mystery the church is the mother of Jesus Christ, though naturally, or according to His flesh, He was born of the virgin Mary, and proceeded from her womb: But take it either way, the enmity hath been maintained, and most mightily did shew itself against the whole kingdom of the devil, and death, and hell; by the undertaking, engaging, and war which the Son of God did maintain against them, from his conception, to his death and exaltation to the right hand of the Father, as is prophesied of, and promised in the text, 'It shall bruise thy head.'

'It shall bruise thy head.' By head, we are to understand the whole power, subtilty, and destroying nature of the devil; for as in the head of the serpent lieth his power, subtilty, and poisonous nature; so in sin, death, hell, and the wisdom of the flesh, lieth the very strength of the devil himself. Take away sin then, and death is not hurtful: 'The sting of death is sin:' And take away the condemning power of the law, and sin doth cease to be charged, or to have any more hurt in it, so as to destroy the soul: 'The strength of sin

is the law.' 1 Co. xv. 56. Wherefore, the seed, Jesus Christ, in his bruising the head of the serpent, must take away sin, abolish death, and conquer the power of the grave. But how must this be done? Why, he must remove the curse, which makes sin intolerable, and death destructive. But how must he take away the curse? Why, by taking upon Him 'flesh,' as we; Jn. i. 14. by being made 'under the law,' as we; Ga. iv. 4. by being made 'to be sin for us,' 2 Co. v. 21. and by being 'made a curse for us.' Ga. iii. 10—13. He standing therefore in our room, under the law and the justice of God, did both bear, and overcome the curse, and so did bruise the power of the devil.

'It shall bruise thy head.' To bruise is more than to break; he shall quash thy head to death; so he also quashed the heel of Christ; which would, had not his eternal power and Godhead sustained, have caused that he had perished for ever.

'And thou shalt bruise his heel.' By these words, a necessity was laid upon Jesus Christ to assume our flesh, to engage the devil therein; and also because of the curse that was due to us for sin, that he might indeed deliver us therefrom; even for awhile to fall before this curse, and to die that death that the curse inflicteth: 'Christ hath redeemed us from the curse of the law, being made a curse for us.' Thus therefore did Satan, that is, by the fruits and effects of sin, bruise, or kill, the flesh of Christ: But he being God, as the Father, it was not possible he should be overcome. Therefore his head remaineth untouched. A man's life lieth not in his heel, but in his head and heart; but the Godhead being the head and heart of the manhood, it was not possible Satan should meddle with that; he only could bruise his heel; which yet by the power of the Godhead of this eternal Son of the Father, was raised up again from the dead: 'He was delivered for our offences, and was raised again for our justification.' Ro. iv. 25.

In these words therefore the Lord God gave Adam a promise, That notwithstanding Satan had so far brought his design to pass, as to cause them by falling from the command, to lay themselves open to the justice and wrath of God; yet his enterprise by grace, should be made of none effect. As if the Lord had said, 'Adam, thou seest how the devil hath overcome thee; how he, by thy consenting to his temptation, hath made thee a subject of death and hell: but though he hath by this means made thee a spectacle of misery, even an heir of death and damnation: yet I am God, and thy sins have been against me. Now because I have grace and mercy, I will therefore design thy recovery. But how shall I bring it to pass? Why I will give my Son out of my bosom, who shall in your room, and in your nature

---

* A decided Christian *cannot* obey human laws affecting divine worship. All such are of Antichrist; 'Ye *cannot* obey God and mammon.' God requires an undivided allegiance. —ED.

encounter this adversary, and overcome him. But how? Why, by fulfilling my law, and by answering the penalties thereof. He shall bring in a righteousness which shall be "everlasting," by which I will justify you from sin, and the curse of God due thereto: But this work will make him smart, he must be made " a man of sorrows," for upon him will I lay your iniquities; Is. liii. 6. Satan shall bruise his heel.'

Ver. 16. ' ¶ Unto the woman he said, I will greatly multiply thy sorrow and thy conception; in sorrow* shalt thou bring forth children; and thy desire *shall be* to thy husband, and he shall rule over thee.'

' I will greatly multiply thy sorrow,' &c. This is true, whether you respect the woman according to the letter of the text, or as she was a figure of the church; for in both senses their sorrows for sin are great, and multiplied upon them: The whole heap of the female sex know the first,† the church only knows the second.

' In sorrow shalt thou bring forth children.' The more fruitful, the more afflicted is the church in this world; because the rage of hell, and the enmity of the world, are by her righteousness set on fire so much the more.

But again: Forasmuch as the promise is made before this judgment of God for sin is threatened, we must count these afflictions not as coming from the hand of God in a way of vengeance, for want of satisfaction for the breach of the law; but to shew and keep us in mind of his holiness, that henceforth we should not, as at first through ignorance, so now from notions of grace and mercy, presume to continue in sin.

I might add, That by these words it is manifest, that a promise of mercy and forgiveness of sin, and great afflictions and rebukes for the same, may and shall attend the same soul: ' I will greatly multiply thy sorrow,' comes after the promise of grace.

' And thy desire shall be to thy husband, and he shall rule over thee.' Doubtless the woman was, in her first creation, made in subordination to her husband, and ought to have been under obedience to him: Wherefore, still that had remained a duty, had they never transgressed the commandment of God; but observe, the duty is here again not only enjoined, and imposed, but that as the fruit of the woman's sin; wherefore, that duty that before she might do as her natural right by creation, she must now do as the fruits of her disobedience to God. Women therefore,

whenever they would perk it and lord it over their husbands, ought to remember, that both by creation and transgression they are made to be in subjection to their own husbands. This conclusion makes Paul himself: ' Let (saith he) the woman learn in silence with all subjection. But I suffer not a woman to teach, nor to usurp authority over the man, but to be in silence; for Adam was first formed, then Eve; and Adam was not deceived, but the woman being deceived, was in the transgression.' 1 Tim. ii. 11—14.

Ver. 17. ' And unto Adam he said, Because thou hast hearkened unto the voice of thy wife, and hast eaten of the tree of which I commanded thee, saying, Thou shalt not eat of it: cursed *is* the ground for thy sake, in sorrow shalt thou eat *of* it all the days of thy life.'

God having laid his censure upon the woman, he now proceedeth and cometh to her husband, and also layeth his judgment on him: The judgment is, ' Cursed *is* the ground for thy sake,' and in sorrow thou shalt eat thereof. The causes of this judgment are, First, For that ' he hearkened to his wife:' And also, ' For that he had eaten of the tree.'

' Because thou hast hearkened to thy wife.' Why? Because therein he left his station and headship, the condition which God had appointed him, and gave way to his wife to assume it, contrary to the order of creation, of her relation, and of her sex; for God had made Adam lord and chief, who ought to have taught his wife, and not to have become her scholar.

Hence note, That the man that suffereth his wife to take his place, hath already transgressed the order of God.‡

' Because thou hast hearkened to the voice,' &c. Wicked women, such as Eve was now, if hearkened unto, are ' the snares of death ' to their husbands; for, because they are weaker built, and because the devil doth easier fasten with them than with men, therefore they are more prone to vanity and all mis-orders in the matters of God, than they; [the men] and so, if hearkened unto, more dangerous upon many accounts: 'Did not Solomon king of Israel sin by these things? yet among many nations was there no king like him, who was beloved of his God, nevertheless even him did outlandish [wicked] women cause to sin.' Ne. xiii. 26. ' But there was none like unto Ahab, which did sell himself to work wickedness in the

* Genevan or Puritan version.

† Many are the anxieties, sorrows, and pains, that females undergo, from which man is comparatively exempt. How tenderly then ought they to be cherished.—Ed.

‡ Most married men find this to be an exceedingly difficult duty. There are few Eves but whose dominant passion is to rule a husband. Perhaps the only way to govern a wife is to lead her to think that she rules, while in fact she is ruled. One of the late Abraham Booth's maxims to young ministers, was, If you would rule in your church, so act as to allow them to think that they rule you.—Ed.

sight of the Lord, whom Jezebel his wife stirred up.' 1 Ki. xxi. 25.

Hence note further, That if it be thus dangerous for a man to hearken to a wicked wife, how dangerous is it for any to hearken unto wicked whores, who will seldom yield up themselves to the lusts of beastly men, but on condition they will answer their ungodly purposes! What mischief by these things hath come upon souls, countries and kingdoms, will here be too tedious to relate.

'Because thou hast hearkened to the voice of thy wife, and hast eaten of the tree.' That is, From the hand of thy wife; for it was she that gave him to eat: 'Therefore,' &c. Although the scripture doth lay a great blot upon women, and cautioneth man to beware of these fantastical and unstable spirits, yet it limiteth man in his censure: She is only then to be rejected and rebuked, when she doth things unworthy her place and calling. Such a thing may happen, as that the woman, not the man, may be in the right, (I mean, when both are godly,) but ordinarily it is otherwise. Ge. xxi. 12. Therefore the conclusion is, Let God's word judge between the man and his wife, as it ought to have done between Adam and his, and neither of both will do amiss; but contrariwise, they will walk in all the commandments of God without fault. Lu. i. 6.

'Therefore cursed *be* the ground for thy sake.' Behold what arguments are thrust into every corner, thereby to make man remember his sin; for all the toil of man, all the barrenness of the ground, and all the fruitlessness after all; What is it but the fruits of sin? Let not us then find fault with the weed, with the hotness, coldness, or barrenness of the soil; but by seeing these things, remember our sin, Cursed be the ground 'for thy sake;' for this God makes our 'heaven as iron,' and our 'earth as brass.' Ex. xxvi. 19. 'The Lord shall make the rain of thy land powder and dust; from heaven shall it come down upon thee, until thou be destroyed.' De. xxviii. 20—24.

'In sorrow shalt thou eat *of* it all the days of thy life.' He then is much deceived, who thinks to fill his body with the delicates of this world, and not therewith to drink the cruel venom of asps: Yea, 'He shall suck the poison of asps, the viper's tongue shall slay him.' Job xx. 16. The reason is, because he that shall give up himself to the lusts and pleasures of this life, he contracts guilt, because he hath sinned; which guilt will curdle all his pleasures, and make the sweetest of them deadly as poison.

'In sorrow shalt thou eat.' Even thou that hast received the promise of forgiveness: How then can they do it with pleasure, who eat, and forget the Lord? Pr. xxx. 9; xxxi. 5.

Again, Let not the sorrows, crosses, and afflictions, that attend the godly in the things of this life, weaken their faith in the promise of grace, and forgiveness of sins; for such things may befal the dearest Christian.

Ver. 18. 'Thorns also and thistles shall it bring forth to thee; and thou shalt eat the herb of the field.'

This shews us (as I also hinted before), That the thorns and thistles of the ground, are but as the excrements thereof; and the fruits of sin, and the curse for sin. This world, as it dropt from the fingers of God, was far more glorious than it is now: Now it is loaden with a burden of corruption, thorns, thistles, and other annoyances, which Adam knew none of in the days of his innocency. None therefore ever saw this world, as it was in its first creation, but only Adam and his wife; neither shall any ever see it, until the manifestation of the children of God: that is, until the redemption or resurrection of the saints: but then it shall be delivered from the bondage of corruption, into the glorious liberty of the children of God.

'And thou shalt eat the herb of the field.' These words are for his comfort, under all the sorrow sin should bring upon him; 'Thou shalt eat the herb:' The herb was a type of the gospel-comforts which the destroying angels were forbidden to smite. Re. vii. 3. Of these medicinal and healing herbs therefore Adam and his seed are admitted to eat, that their soul may be replenished in the midst of their sorrow.

Ver. 19. 'In the sweat of thy face shalt thou eat bread, till thou return unto the ground; for out of it wast thou taken: for dust thou *art*, and unto dust shalt thou return.'

'In the sweat of thy face.' This is true, whether literally or allegorically understood: For as touching the things that pertain to this life, as they become not ours without toil and labour; so the spiritual comforts of the kingdom of heaven are not obtained without travail and sweat: 'Labour (saith Christ) for the bread and meat which endureth to everlasting life.' Jn vi. 27.

'In the sweat of thy face.' Those that make conscience of walking in the commandments of God, they shall be blessed with the bread of life, when others shall be hunger-bit. That may also be mystically applied, 'On all hills that shall be digged with the mattock, there shall not come thither the fear of briars and thorns; but it shall be for the sending forth of oxen, and for the treading of lesser cattle.' Is. vii. 25. The meaning is, Where people are diligent according to the word of God, especially in spiritual and heavenly things, they shall be fat and flourishing, though sorrow be mixed therewith: 'When *men* are cast down:

then thou shalt say, *there is* lifting up ; and he shall save the humble person.' Job xxii. 29.

' Till thou return to the ground.' A Christian should not leave off sweating labour so long as he is above the ground ; even until he returneth thither, he ought to be diligent in the way and worship of God. Jacob, when sick, would worship God, though so weak as not able to do it, without leaning upon the top of his staff: A blessed example for the diligent, and reproof for those that are slothful. He. xi. 21.

' For out of it wast thou taken.' That is, out of the ground. Behold how the Lord doth mix his doctrine ! Now he tells him of his sin, then he promiseth to give him a Saviour, then again he shews him the fruits of his sin, and immediately after the comforts of the promise; yet again, he would have him remember that he is but a mortal creature, not to live here for ever; neither made of silver nor gold, but even of a clod of dust: ' For dust thou art.' Observe therefore, that in the midst of all our enjoyments, God would have us consider our frame, that we may know how frail we are.

' For out of it was thou taken.' It is hard for us to believe it, though we daily see it is the way even of all the earth, to return thither again : ' For dust thou *art*, and to dust shalt thou return.'

Whether this was spoken to Adam, as a judgment, or a mercy, or both, is not hard to determine, (this first premised, that Adam had received the promise ;) for as it was the fruit of sin, so a judgment and a token of God's displeasure ; ' for the wages of sin is death.' Ro. vi. 23. But as it is made by the wisdom of God, a prevention of further wickedness, and a conveyance through faith in Christ, to a more perfect enjoyment of God in the heavens ; so it is a mercy and blessing of God ; Is. lvii. 1, 2. For thus ' to die is gain.' Wherefore thus we may praise the dead, that are already dead, more than the living, which are yet alive. Ec. iv. 2. This made Paul desire to depart ; for he knew that through death was the way to have more perfect sight of, and more close and higher communion with the Father, and the Son, and the Spirit in the heavens. 2 Co. v. 6. I have a desire to depart, and be with Christ, which is far better. Phi. i. 21—23. Thus therefore those things that in their own nature are the proper fruits and wages of sin, may yet through the wisdom of God be turned about for our good ; Je. xxiv. 5. but let not this embolden to sin, but rather minister occasion to us to magnify the wisdom of God. Ro. viii. 28.

Ver. 20. ' And Adam called his wife's name Eve ; because she was the mother of all living.'

By this act Adam returneth to his first station and authority in which God had placed him, from which he fell when he became a scholar to his wife ; for to name the creatures, was in Adam a note of sovereignty and power: This he attained to, as an effect of his receiving the promise; for before the promise is received, man cannot serve God in his station, because as he wanteth the power of will, so also a good understanding ; but when he hath received the promise, he hath also received the Holy Ghost, which giveth to the godly to know and do his duty in his station: ' The spiritual ' man discerneth, and so ' judgeth all things ;' but he is not discerned nor judged of any. 1 Co. ii. 15.

And he called his wife's name Eve, or Hevah : Because she gave life to, or was the first mother of all mankind. This then admits of two positions. First, That the world was created when Adam was created. And, Secondly, That there were none of the sons of men in the world before Adam, as some have not only vainly, but irreligiously and blasphemously suggested. ' Eve is the mother of all living :' Not a man therefore that is the son of man, but had his being since the woman was made.

Ver. 21. ' ¶ Unto Adam also and to his wife did the Lord God make coats of skins, and clothed them.'

By this action the Lord God did preach to Adam, and to his wife, the meaning of that promise that you read of in ver. 15. Namely, That by the means of Jesus Christ, God himself would provide a sufficient clothing for those that accept of his grace by the gospel: The coats here, being a type of that blessed and durable righteousness.

' The Lord God made the coats.' Not Adam now, because now he is received into a covenant of grace with God: Indeed before he entered into this covenant, he made his own clothing, such as it was, but that could not cover his nakedness ; but now the Lord will make them : And 'unto Adam also and to his wife did the Lord God make coats:' ' Their righteousness *is* of me, saith the Lord.' Is. liv. 17. Of me, that is, of my providing, of my performing. And this is the name whereby he shall be called, THE LORD OUR RIGHTEOUSNESS.' Je. xxiii. 6.

' He made them coats, and clothed them.' As the righteousness by which a sinner stands just in the sight of God from the curse, is a righteousness of God's providing ; so also it is of his putting on. No man can put on the righteousness of Christ, otherwise than by God's imputation: if God reckon it ours then it is ours indeed ; but if he refuseth to shew that mercy, who can impute that righteousness to men ? Blessed are they to whom the Lord imputeth righteousness. Ro. iv. Cursed then must they needs be to whom God hath not imputed the righteousness of his Son. ' The Lord clothed them,' according to that of Paul, ' Christ is made unto us of God wisdom and righteousness,' &c.

1 Co. i. 30. And of that God who hath made him thus to us, even of him are we in Christ Jesus.

Did the Lord God make coats of skins. The coats were made of the skins of beasts, of the skins of the slain, which were slain either for food only, or for sacrifice also: This being so, the effects of that promise mentioned before were by this action the more clearly expounded unto Adam; to wit, That Christ, 'in the fulness of time,' should be born of a woman clothed with flesh; and as so considered, should be made a curse, and so die that cursed death which by sin we had brought upon ourselves; the effects and fruits of which should to us be durable clothing; that is, 'Everlasting righteousness.' Da. ix. 24.

Ver. 22, 23. ' ¶ And the Lord God said, Behold, the man is become as one of us, to know good and evil: and now, [therefore] lest he put forth his hand, and take also of the tree of life, and eat, and live for ever: therefore the Lord God sent him forth from the garden of Eden, to till the ground from whence he was taken.'

'Behold the man is become as one of us.' These words respect the temptation of the devil; the argument that prevailed with Adam; and the fruits of their consenting: And therefore I understand them as spoken ironically, or in derision to Adam. As if God had said, 'Now Adam, you see what a god you are become: The serpent told you "you should be as gods," as one that was infinite in wisdom. But behold, your godhead is horrible wickedness, even pollution of body and soul by sin. A thing you little thought of, when you pleased yourself with the thought of that high attainment; and now if you be not prevented, you will proceed from evil to evil; for notwithstanding I have made promise of sending a Saviour, you will, through the pollution of your mind, forget and set at nought my promise; and seek life and salvation by that tree of life which was never intended for the justification of sinners; therefore I will turn you out of the garden, "to till the ground whence thou wast taken."'

1. Hence observe, That it often falls out, after the promised blessing is come, that God yet maketh us to possess our former sins, not that the guilt thereof might be charged to condemnation, but that remembering of them, we might blush before God, and be the more effectually driven to a continual embracing of the mercy promised.

2. Observe again, That as God would have us to remember our former sins, so he would not that we should feed upon ought but the very mercy promised. We must not rest in shadowish sacraments, as the typical tree of life, but must remember it is our duty to live by faith in the promised seed.

3. Observe also, That even our outward and temporal employments, if they be lawful and honest, are so ordered of God, as that we may gather some heavenly mystery from them: 'To till the ground from whence he was taken:' Mysteriously intimating two things to Adam. (1.) That seeing he was of the earth, he stood in as much need to be ordered and dressed by God, in order to his future happiness, as the ground, in order to its thrift and fruitfulness. (2.) Again, Seeing he was taken from the ground, he is neither God, nor angel, but a poor earthen vessel, such as God can easily knock in pieces, and cause to return to the ground again. These things therefore Adam was to learn from his calling, that he might neither think too highly of himself, nor forget to live by faith, and depending on the Lord God, to be blessed of him.

Ver. 24. 'So he drove out the man; and he placed at the east of the garden of Eden Cherubims, and a flaming sword which turned every way, to keep the way of the tree of life.'

'So he drove out the man.' Adam was loth to forsake this garden of Eden, because there was the tree of life. The promise will hardly satisfy, where faith is weak and low. Had this man with great faith received and retained the gospel preached before, he would not have so hankered after a shadow; but the conscience being awakened, and faith low and weak there, because faith wants the flower or bloom of assurance, the ceremonial or moral law doth with ease engender bondage.

'And he placed at the east of the garden of Eden Cherubims, and a flaming sword.' This shows the truth of what I said before; to wit, That Adam was loth to forsake the garden, loth to forsake his doing of something; but God sets a shaking sword against him, a sword to keep that way, or to prevent that Adam should have life by eating of the tree of life.

Observe, This tree of life, though lawful for Adam to feed on before he had transgressed, yet now is wholly forbidden him; intimating, that that which would have nourished him before he brake the law, will now avail him nothing as to life before the justice of God: the tree of life might have maintained his life before he sinned; but having done that, he hath no ways now but to live by faith in the promise; which that he might effectually do, God takes from him the use of all other things, he driveth him out of the garden, and sets to keep him from the tree of life, 'Cherubims, and a flaming sword.'

'And he placed at the east of the garden Cherubims, and a flaming sword.' These cherubims are one sort of the angels of God, at this time made ministers of justice, shaking the flaming sword of God's severity against Adam for sin, threatening to cut him off thereby, if he ever return by the way that he went.

We read also, that the law was delivered to Israel from Sinai, by the hand and disposition of angels; Ac. vii. the gospel, only by the Son himself. He. i. 2.

To keep the way. Hence the apostle implicitly concludes it a way, that is, to death and damnation; by opposing another against it, even the new and living one; a new, not this the old; a living one, not this the dead one. He. x. For, for that the cherubims are here placed with a flaming, shaking sword, to keep the tree of life, it is evident that death is threatened to him that shall at any time attempt to come at, or that seeks for life that way.

A flaming sword, turning every way to keep,' &c. This still shews us, that man, though he hath already received the promise, is yet exceeding prone to seek life by another way than freegrace by Jesus Christ; to wit, either by the law he hath broken, or by the law and Christ together; and so though not directly, yet ' as it were by the works of the law.' Ro. ix. 32. But all is to no purpose, they are every way prevented. For, forsake the simplicity of the promise in the gospel, and thou shalt meet with the stroke of the justice of God; for that flaming sword of his vengeance, it turneth every way, and therefore will in every way lay wrath upon thee, if thou seek life by ought but Christ.

CHAP. IV.

Ver. 1. ' And Adam knew Eve his wife; and she conceived, and bare Cain, and said, I have gotten a man from the Lord.'

Now we are come to the generation of mankind. ' Adam knew his wife:' A modest expression; and it should teach us, in all such matters where things are discoursed of, that are either the fruits of sin, or the proper effects of man's natural infirmities, there to endeavour the use of such expressions, as neither to provoke to lust, nor infect us with evil and uncivil communication. ' Adam knew his wife;' Jacob, Samson, David, and others, are said to go in unto them. So as to our natural infirmities of the stool, the scripture expression is, ' When thou goest abroad to ease thyself, thou shalt turn again and cover that which cometh from thee:' Modest and bashful expressions, and such as become the godly, being those that are furthest off of occasioning evil, and nearest to an intimation, that such infirmities bespeak us infirm and imperfect creatures.

' And she conceived and bare Cain.' The first sprout of a disobedient couple, a man in shape, but a devil in conditions. This is he that is called elsewhere, The child 'of that wicked one.' 1 Jn. iii. 12.

' And she said, I have gotten a man from the Lord.' If Eve by these words did only ascribe the blessing of children to be the gift of God, then she spake like a godly woman; but if she supposed that this man Cain was indeed the seed promised, then it shows, that she in this was also deceived, and was therein a figure of all such as make false and strange delusions, signs of the mercy of God towards them: The man she thought she had got from the Lord as a mercy, and to be a Saviour, he proved a man of the devil, a curse, and to be a destroyer.

Ver. 2. ' And she again bare his brother Abel, And Abel was a keeper of sheep, but Cain was a tiller of the ground.'

Observe here, That the good child is not the first-born, but Abel, [a breath.] 1 Co. i. 27, 28. God often doth as Jacob did, even cross hands, in bestowing blessings, giving that which is best to him that is least esteemed: For Cain was the man in Eve's esteem; she thought, when she had him, she had got an inheritance; but as for Abel, he was little worth; by his name they showed how little they set by him. It is so with the sincere to this day; they bear not the name of glory with the world: Cain with them is the profitable son; Abel is of no credit with them, neither see they form or comeliness in him; he is the melancholy, or lowering child, whose countenance spoileth the mirth of the world: ' The heart of the wise is in the house of mournings; but the heart of fools is in the house of mirth.' Ec. vii. 4.

' And Abel was a keeper of sheep, but Cain was a tiller of the ground.' By this it seems yet further, that Cain was the man in favour, even him that should, by his Father's intentions, have been heir, and have enjoyed the inheritance: He was nurtured up in his father's employment, but Abel was set in the lower rank.

It was also thus with Isaac and Jacob, Ishmael and Esau, being the eldest, and those that by intention were to be heirs.

Now in the inheritance lay, of old, a great blessing: so that Esau in losing his father's inheritance, lost also the blessing of grace, and moreover the kingdom of heaven. He. xii. 16, 17. Wherefore Cain had by this the better of Abel, even as the Jews by their privileges had the better of the Gentiles. Ro. iii. 1, 2. But mark it, the blessing of grace is not led by outward order, but by electing love: Where the person then is under the blessing of election, be he the first or the second son, the highest or lowest in the family, or whether he be more or less loved of his friends, 'tis he that with Abel hath the everlasting blessing.

Ver. 3. ' And, in process of time, it came to pass

that Cain brought of the fruit of the ground an offering unto the Lord.'

Mark here, That the devil can suffer his children, in outward forms of worship, to be godly and righteous men: Cain, a limb of the devil, and yet the first in order that presents himself and his service to God.

Cain brought of the fruit of the ground, as of wheat, oil, honey, or the like; which things were also clean and good. Hence it is intimated, that his offering was excellent; and I conceive, not at all, as to the matter itself, inferior to that of Abel's; for in that it is said that Abel's was more excellent, it is not with respect to the excellency of the matter or things with which they sacrificed, but with respect to Abel's faith, which gave glory and acceptableness to his offering with God, 'By faith he offered unto God a more excellent sacrifice than Cain.' He. xi. 4.

'And Abel, he also brought of the firstlings of his flock and of the fat thereof.' &c..

Abel, last in appearance, but in truth the first in grace; as it also is at this day: Who do so flutter it out as our ruffling formal worshippers? Alas! the good, the sincere and humble, they seem to be least and last; but the conclusion of the tragedy will make manifest that the first is last, and the last first; for the many are but called, the few are chosen.

'And the Lord had respect unto Abel, and to his offering.' Herein are the true footsteps of grace discovered; to wit, the person must be the first in favour with God, the person first, the performance afterwards.

'And the Lord had respect to Abel.' But how can God respect a man, before he respect his offering? A man's gift (saith Solomon) makes way for him: It should seem therefore that there lies no such stress in the order of words, but that it might as well be read, 'The Lord had respect to Abel, because he respected his offering.'

Answ. Not so: For though it be true among men, that the gift makes way for the acceptance of the person, yet in the order of grace it is after another manner; for if the person be not first accepted, the offering must be abominable; for it is not a good work that makes a good man, but a good man makes a good work. The fruit doth not make a good tree, but 'a good tree bringeth forth good fruit.' Make (saith Christ) the tree good, and his fruit good; or the tree evil, and his fruit evil: Do men gather grapes of thorns, or figs of thistles? Had Abel been a thorn, he had not brought forth grapes; had he been a thistle, he had not brought forth figs. So then, Abel's person must be first accepted, and after that his works.

Object. But God accepteth no man while he remains a sinner, but all men are sinners before they do good works, how then could the person of Abel be accepted first?

Answ. Abel was JUST before he did offer sacrifice. Just, I say, in the sight of God. This God witnessed by testifying of his gift: 'By faith Abel offered unto God a more excellent sacrifice than Cain, by which he obtained witness that he was righteous:' That is, God by accepting of the gift of Abel, did testify that Abel was a righteous man; for we know God 'heareth not sinners:' 'The prayers of the wicked are an abomination unto God.' But Abel was accepted, therefore he was righteous first.

Hence observe, That a man must be righteous before he can do any good work.

Quest. Righteous! 'With what righteousness?'

Answ. With the righteousness of faith. And therefore it is said, that Abel had faith before he offered sacrifice. 'By faith he offered.' He. xi. 4. Where faith is made to precede or go before the work which by faith he offered unto God.

Quest. But are not good works the righteousness of faith?

Answ. They are the fruits of faith: As here in the case of Abel; his faith produced an offering; but before he gave his offering, his faith had made him righteous; for faith respects a promise of grace, not a work of mine: Now the promise of grace, being this, that the seed of the woman, which is Christ, should destroy the power of the devil; by this Abel saw that it was Christ that should abolish sin and death by himself, and bring in 'everlasting righteousness' for sinners. Thus believing, he had accepted of Christ for righteousness, which because he had done, God in truth proclaims him righteous, by accepting of his person and performances when offered.

Abel then presented his person and offering, as shrouding both, by faith, under the righteousness of Christ, which lay wrapped up in the promise; but Cain stands upon his own legs, and so presents his offering. Abel therefore is accepted, both his person and his offering, while Cain remains accursed.

Ver. 5. 'But unto Cain, and to his offering, he [the Lord] had not respect. And Cain was very wroth, and his countenance fell.'

Mark: As first Abel's person is accepted, and then his offering; so first Cain's person is rejected, and afterwards his offering: For God seeth not sin in his own institutions, unless they be defiled by them that worship him; and that they needs must, when persons by * themselves offer sacrifice to God, because then they want the righteousness of faith.

---

* 'By themselves.' This does not mean without human company, but 'without divine aid,' without the sanction and presence of God.—ED.

This then made the difference betwixt Abel and his brother; Abel had faith, but Cain had none. Abel's faith covered him with Jesus Christ, therefore he stood righteous in his person before God: This being so, his offering was accepted, because it was the offering of one that was righteous.

'But unto Cain, and to his offering, the Lord had not respect.' Hence note, That a Christless man is a wicked man, let him be never so full of actions that be righteous; for righteous actions make not a righteous man, the man himself must first be righteous.*

Wherefore, though Cain was the eldest, and first in the worship; yet Abel was the wisest, and the most acceptable therein.

'And Cain was very wroth, and his countenance fell.' From these words it may be gathered, that Cain had some evident token from the observation of God's carriage towards both himself and brother; that his brother was smiled upon, but he rejected: He was wroth: wroth with God, and wroth with his brother. And indeed, before the world hate us, they must needs hate Jesus Christ: 'It hated me (saith he) before *it hated* you.' Jn. xv. 18. He was wroth: and why? Wroth because his sacrifice was not accepted of God: And yet the fault was not in the Lord, but Cain: He came not before the Lord, as already made righteous with the righteousness of Christ, which indeed had been doing well, but as a cursed wicked wretch, he thought that by his own good works he must be just before the Lord.

The difference therefore that was between these worshippers, it lay not in that they worshipped divers gods, but in that they worshipped the same God after a diverse manner: The one in faith, the other without; the one as righteous, the other as wicked.

And even thus it is between us and our adversaries: We worship not divers gods, but the same God in a diverse manner: We according to faith; and they according to their OWN INVENTIONS.†

'And Cain was wroth.' This further shows us the force of the law, and the end of those that would be just by the same; namely, That in conclusion they will quarrel with God; for when the soul in its best performances, and acts of righteousness, shall yet be rejected and cast off by God, it will fret and wrangle, and in its spirit let fly against God. For thus it judgeth, That God is austere and exacting; it hath done what it could to please him, and he is not pleased therewith. This again offendeth God, and makes his justice curse and condemn the soul. Condemn it, I say, for imagining that the righteousness of a poor, sinful, wretched creature, should be sufficient to appease eternal justice for sin. Thus the law worketh wrath, because it always bindeth our transgression to us, and still reckoneth us sinners, and accursed, when we have done our utmost to answer and fulfil it. Ro. iv. 15.

'And his countenance fell.' However, an hypocrite, while God forbeareth to smite him, may triumph and joy in his goodness; yet when God shall pronounce his ·judgment according as he approves of his act, he needs must lower and fall in his countenance; for his person and gift are rejected, and he still counted a sinner.

Ver. 6. 'And the Lord said unto Cain, Why art thou wroth? and why is thy countenance fallen?'

These words are applied to Cain, for a further conviction of his state to be miserable. 'Why art thou wroth?' Is it because I have not accepted thy offering? This is without ground, thy person is yet an abomination to me: Must I be made by thy gift, which is polluted, for and by thy person, to justify thee as righteous? Thou hast not yet done well. Wherefore, Cain had no cause to be wroth; For God rejected only that which was sinful, as was both his person, and gift for the sake thereof: Neither had he grounds to lift up his looks on high, when he came to offer his sacrifice; because he came not as a man in a justify'd state. But '*there is* a generation *that are* pure in their own eyes, and *yet* is not washed from their filthiness. *There is* a generation, - O how lofty are their eyes! and their eyelids are lifted up.' Pr. xxx. 12, 13. Such an one, or the father of these, was Cain; he counted himself clean, and yet was not washed; he lifted up his looks on high, before he was changed from his iniquity.

Ver. 7. 'If thou doest well, shalt thou not be accepted? and if thou doest not well, sin lieth at the door. And unto thee *shall be* his desire, and thou shalt rule over him.'

'If thou do well.' Why, is not worshipping of God, well-doing? It may, and may not, even as the person that worships is found. If he be found righteous at his coming to worship, and if he worship according to rule, then he does well, then he is accepted of God; but if he be not found righteous before, be you sure he cannot do well,

---

* There is no error more universal, nor more fatal, than that which Bunyan here, as well as in other of his treatises, so admirably elucidates and explodes. No sooner does a poor sinner feel the necessity of flying from the wrath to come, than Satan suggests that some good works must be pleaded, instead of casting the soul, burthened with sin, upon the compassion of the Lord, and pleading for unconditional mercy. Good works *must* flow from, but cannot be any *cause* of grace. —ED.

† Adversaries to Christ and his church, although professing to be Christians; worshipping according to 'the traditions of men,' and putting the saints into wretched prisons, and to a frightful death. An awful state of self-delusion; how Cain-like!—ED.

let the matter with which he worshippeth be wrong or right. 'Who can bring a clean *thing* out of an unclean?' Jn. xiv. 4. Let Cain be clean, and his offering will be clean, because brought to God in a vessel that is clean; but if Cain be unclean, all the holy things he toucheth, or layeth up in his skirt, it is made unclean by the uncleanness of his person: 'And so is this nation before me, saith the Lord; and so *is* every work of their hands, and that which they offer there *is* unclean.' Hag. ii. 11—14.*

Men therefore ought to distinguish between doing and well-doing, even in the worship of God. All that worship do not do well, though the matter of worship be good in itself. Cain's offering you find not blamed, as if it had been of a superstitious complexion; but he came not aright to worship. Why? he came not as one made righteous before. Wherefore, as I have already touched, the difference that lay between the gifts of Abel and Cain, was not in the gifts themselves, but the qualifications of the persons. Abel's faith, and Cain's works, made God approve and reject the offering: 'By faith Abel offered to God a more excellent sacrifice than Cain:' For, as I said, Faith in Christ, as promised to come, made him righteous, because thereby he obtained 'the righteousness of God;' for so was Christ in himself, and so to be to him that by faith received and accepted of him: This, I say, Abel did; wherefore now he is righteous or just before God. This being so, his offering is found to be an offering of Abel the just, and is here said to obtain witness even of God, that he was righteous, because he accepted his gift.

Wherefore, he that does well must first be good: 'He that doeth righteousness is [must first be] righteous.' 1 Jn. iii. 7. He is righteous first; he is righteous even as Christ is righteous, because Christ himself is the righteousness of such a person. And so on the contrary; the reason why some men's good deeds are accursed of God, it is because in truth, and according to the law, the Lord finds sin in them; which sins he cannot pardon, because he finds them not in Christ. Thus they being evil for want of the righteousness of the Son of God, they worship God as sinners, according to that of the apostle, Because they are not good, therefore they do not good, no, not one of them. Ro. iii. 10—12.

The way therefore to do well, it is first to receive the mercy of God in Christ; which act of thine will be more pleasing to the Divine Majesty, than all whole burnt-offerings and sacrifices: 'I will have

mercy (saith God) I will have mercy, and not sacrifice.' Mat. ix. 13; xii. 7. This Cain did not understand, therefore he goes to God in his sins, and without faith in the mercy of God through Christ, he offereth his sacrifice. Wherefore because his sacrifice could not take away his sin, therefore it still abode upon him.

But 'if thou doest not well, sin lieth at the door.' This reasoning therefore was much to Cain's condition; he would be wroth, because God did not accept his offering, and yet he did not well: Now, if he had done well, God, by receiving of his brother's sacrifice, shows, he would have accepted him; for this is evident, they were both alike by nature; their offerings also were in themselves one as holy as the other: How then comes it to pass that both were not accepted, they both offered to God? Why, Abel only sacrificed well, because he first by faith in Christ was righteous: This because Cain wanted, 'sin abideth at his door.'

'And to thee *shall be* his desire, and thou shalt rule over him.' That is, if sin abideth at thy door still, to thee shall be his desire; he shall love, pity, pray for thee, and endeavour thy conversion; but thou shalt be lord over him, and shalt put thy yoke upon his neck. This was Jacob's portion also; for after Esau had got head, he broke Jacob's yoke from off his neck, and reigned by nineteen or twenty dukes and princes, before there was any king in Israel. Ge. xxvii. 40.

It is the lot of Cain's brood, to be lords and rulers first, while Abel and his generation have their necks under persecution; yet while they lord it, and thus tyrannically afflict and persecute, our very desire is towards them, wishing their salvation: While they curse, we bless; and while they persecute, we pray.

Ver. 8. '¶ And Cain talked with Abel his brother: and it came to pass, when they were in the field, that Cain rose up against Abel his brother, and slew him.'

When Cain saw that by God's judgment Abel was the better worshipper, and that himself must by no means be admitted for well-doing, his heart began to be more obdurate and hard, and to grow into that height of desperateness, as to endeavour the extirpating of all true religion out of the world; which it seems he did, by killing his brother, mightily accomplish, until the days of Enos; for 'then began men [again] to call upon the name of the Lord.' ver. 26.

Hence see the spite of the children of hell against God: They have slain thy prophets, and digged down thine altars. 1 Ki. xix. 10. If they may have their wills, God must be content with their religion, or none; other they will not endure should have show within their reach, but with Cain, will rather kill their brother; or with the Pharisees,

---

* If it be asked, Why take your unregenerate children, and invite the ungodly, to the place of worship? Our answer is, THERE the Lord is pleased to meet with sinners—convince, convert, and purify them—giving them a good hope that their persons and services are accepted.—ED.

kill their Lord; and with the evil kings of old, will rather kill their sons and subjects. That the truth, I say, may fall to the ground, and their own inventions stand for acceptable sacrifices, they will not only envy, but endeavour to invalidate all the true worship and worshippers of God in the world; the which if they cannot without blood accomplish, they will slay and kill till their cruelty hath destroyed many ten thousands, even as Cain, who slew his brother Abel.*

And Cain talked with his brother. He had not a law whereby to arraign him, but malice enough, and a tongue to set all on fire, of which no doubt, by the goodly replies of his brother, was easily blown up into choler and madness, the end of which was the blood of his brother.

'And Cain talked with Abel,' &c. To wit, about the goodness and truth of his religion. For that the New Testament seems to import, he slew him 'because his works were righteous;' 1 Jn. iii. 12. which Abel, no doubt, had justified before his brother, even then when he most set himself to oppose him. Besides this, the connection of the relation importeth, he talked with him, he slew him; he talked with him and slew him, purely upon a religious account, because his works were righteous.

Hence note, That when wicked men have the head in the world, professors had need be resolved to hazard the worst, before they do enter debate with ungodly men about the things that pertain to the kingdom of God. For behold here, words did not end in words, but from words came blows, and from blows blood. The counsel therefore is, 'That you sit down first, and count up the cost,' before ye talk with Cain of religion. Lu. xiv. 27—33. 'They make a man an offender for a word, and lay a snare for him that reproveth in the gate, and turn aside the just for a thing of nought.' Is. xxix. 21.

'And Cain talked with Abel his brother.' With Abel his only brother, who also was a third part of the world. But tyrants matter nothing, neither nearness of kin, nor how much they destroy: 'The brother shall betray the brother to death,' &c.

'And it came to pass, when they were in the field, that Cain rose up against Abel his brother, and slew him.' When they were in the field, from home, out of the sight, and far from the help of his father: Subtle persecutors love not to bite, till they can make their teeth to meet; for which they observe their time and place. Joseph was

also hated of his brethren, but they durst not meddle till they found him in the field. Ge. xxxvii. 15. Here it is also that the holy virgin falleth: He found her in the field,—and there was none to save her. De. xxii. 27

Hence observe again, That be the danger never so imminent, and the advantage of the adversary never so great, the sincere professor of the truth stands his ground against wind and weather. Bloody Cain daunted not holy Abel; no, though now he have his advantage of him. Da. iii. 16—18.

He rose up against Abel his brother, and slew him. 'And wherefore slew he him? Because his own works were evil,' &c. 1 Jn. iii. 12. It is therefore hence to be observed, That it is a sign of an evil way, be it covered with the name of the worship of God, when it cannot stand without the shedding of innocent blood. 'Wherefore slew he him? Because his own works were evil.' Had his works been good, they had been accepted of God: He had also had the joy thereof in his conscience, as doubtless Abel had; which joy and peace would have produced love and pity to his brother, as it was with his brother towards him; but his works being evil, they minister to him no heavenly joy, neither do they beget in him love to his brother; but contrariwise, his heart fills his eye with evil also; which again provoketh (while it beholdeth the godly carriage of Abel) the heart to more desperate resolutions, even to set upon him with all his might, and to cut him off from the earth. Thus the goodness of God's people provoketh to envy the wicked heart of the hypocrite. As it was betwixt Saul and David; for after Saul had seen that God had rejected him for his wickedness, the more he hated the goodness of David: 'And Saul saw and knew that the Lord was with David.' 1 Sa. xviii. 8—15. 'And Saul was yet the more afraid of David; and Saul became David's enemy continually.' ver. 29.

Ver. 9. 'And the Lord said unto Cain, Where is Abel thy brother? And he said, I know not: Am I my brother's keeper?'

Cain thought it had been no more but to kill his brother, and his intentions and desires must needs be accomplished, and that himself should then be the only man. 'Come, let us kill him, and the inheritance shall be our's.' Mar. xii. 7. But stay, Abel was beloved of his God, who had also justified his offering, and accepted it as a service more excellent than his brother's. So then, because the quarrel arose between them upon this very account, therefore Abel's God doth reckon himself as engaged (seeing he is not) to take up his servant's cause himself.

'And the Lord said unto Cain, Where is Abel thy brother?' A question not grounded on uncertainty, but proposed as a beginning of further

---

* How awfully is this illustrated by acts of uniformity. IF it be lawful to pass such acts, it must be requisite and a duty to enforce them. It was this that filled Europe with tears, and the saints with anguish, especially in Piedmont, France, and England. Mercifully, the tyrant Antichrist's power is curtailed.—ED.

reasoning; and also to make way to this wicked wretch, to discover the desperate wickedness of his bloody heart the more. For questions that stand at first afar off, do draw out more of the heart of another: and also do minister more occasion for matter, than if they had been placed more near to the matter.

'Where is Abel?' God missed the acceptable sacrifices of Abel; Abel was dead, and his sacrifices ceased, which had wont to be savoury in the nostrils of God; Cain could not supply them; his sacrifices were deficient, they were not of faith. Hence note, that if tyrants should have their will, even to the destroying of all the remnant of God, their sacrifices and worship would be yet before God as abominable as they were before.

'And the Lord said unto Cain, Where is Abel?' O dreadful question! The beginning of Cain's hell, for now God entereth into judgment with him. Wherefore, however this wretch endeavoured at first to stifle and choke his conscience, yet this was to him the arrow of death: Abel crieth, but his brother would not hear him while alive, and now being dead God hears the cry of his blood. 'When he maketh inquisition for blood, he remembereth them: he forgetteth not the cry of the humble.' Ps. ix. 12. Blood that is shed for the sake of God's word, shall not be forgotten or disregarded of God: 'Precious in his sight is the death of his saints.' Ps. cxvi. 15. 'And precious shall their blood be in his sight.' Ps. lxxii. 14.

'Where is Abel thy brother?' This word, thy brother, must not be left out, because it doth greatly aggravate his wickedness. He slew 'his brother;' which horrid act the very law and bond of nature forbiddeth. But when a man is given up of God, it is neither this nor another relation that will bind his hands, or make him keep within the bounds of any law. Judas will seek his master's, and Absalom his father's blood. 'Where is Abel thy brother?'

'And he said, I know not.' He knew full well what he had done, and that by his hands his brother's blood was fallen to the ground, but now being called into question for the same, he endeavoureth to plead ignorance before God. 'I know not.' When men have once begun to sin, they know not where they shall end; he slew his brother, and endeavours to cover his fact with a lie. David also little thought his act of adultery would have led him to have spilt the blood of Uriah, and afterwards to have covered all with dissembling lips and a lying tongue. 2 Sa. xi.

'I know not: Am I my brother's keeper?' This is the way of all ungodly men, they will not abide that guilt should be fastened. Sin they love, and the lusts and delights thereof, but to count for it they cannot abide; they will put it off with excuses, or denials: Even like Saul, who though he had spared the cattle and Agag contrary to the command of God, yet would needs bear Samuel down, that he had kept, yea 'performed the commandment of the Lord.' 1 Sa. xv. 13, 20. But they are denials to no boot, and excuses that will not profit, that are made to hide the sin of the soul from the sight and judgment of God. Lies and falsehood will here do nothing.

Ver. 10. 'And he said, What hast thou done? the voice of thy brother's blood crieth unto me from the ground.'

Poor Cain, thy feeble shifts help thee nothing, thy excuses are drowned by the cries of the blood which thou hast shed.

'What hast thou done?' the blood of thy brother cries. Beware persecutors, you think that when you have slain the godly, you are then rid of them; but you are far wide, their blood which you have shed, cries in the ears of God against you. O the cries of blood are strong cries, they are cries that reach to heaven; yea they are cries that have a continual voice, and that never cease to make a noise, until they have procured vengeance from the hands of the Lord of sabbath: Job xvi. 18. And therefore this is the word of the Lord against all those that are for the practice of Cain: 'As I live, saith the Lord God, I will prepare thee unto blood and blood shall pursue thee: sith thou hast not hated blood, (that is, hated to shed it,) even blood shall pursue thee.' Eze. xxxv. 6.

'The voice of thy brother's blood crieth unto me.' The apostle makes this voice of the blood of Abel, a type of the voice of the justice of the law, and so extends it further than merely to the act of murder; intimating that he sheds blood, that breaks any of the commands of God, (and indeed so he doth, 'he layeth wait for his own blood, and privily lurketh for his own life.') Pr. i. 18. Wherefore the apostle compareth the blood of Abel and the blood of Christ together; but so as by the rule of contraries, making betwixt them a contrary voice, even as there is between a broken command and a promise of grace, the one calling for vengeance and damnation; the other calling for forgiveness and salvation; 'the blood of sprinkling it speaketh better things than the blood of Abel;' He. xii. 24. that is, it calls to God to forgive the sinner; but Abel's blood, of the breach of the law, that cries damn them, damn them. Christ also sets his own blood in opposition to the blood of all that was shed before him; concluding that the proper voice of all the blood of the godly, is to call for vengeance on the persecutors, even from the blood of Abel to the blood of Zecharias, that was slain between the altar and the temple. Mat. xxiii. 35. And let me here take leave to propound my private thoughts: namely, that the Zecharias that here is mentioned, might not be he that we find in the book of Chronicles; 2 Ch. xxiv. 21. but one of that name that lived in the days of Christ, possibly John Baptist's father, or some other holy man. My reasons for this conjecture, are, 1. Because the murderers are convict by Christ himself: Zecharias, whom ye slew between the altar and the temple. 2. Because Christ makes a stop at the blood of Zecharias, not at the blood of John the Baptist: wherefore, if the person here mentioned were not murdered after, but before John the Baptist, then Christ seems to excuse them for killing his servant John; for the judgment stops at the including of the guilt of the blood of Zecharias. 3. I think such a thing, because the voice of all holy blood that hath been shed before the law by the adversary, excepting only the blood of Jesus, must needs be included here; the proper voice of his, only being to plead for mercy to the murderers. However, the voice of blood is a very killing voice, and will one day speak with such thunder and terror in the consciences of all the brood of Cain, that their pain and burthen will be for ever insupportable.

Bear with this conjecture.

Ver. 11. 'And now *art* thou cursed from the earth, which hath opened her mouth to receive thy brother's blood from thy hand.'

Here begins the sentence of God against this bloody man; a sentence fearful and terrible, for it containeth a removing of him from all the privileges of grace and mercy, and a binding of him over to the punishment and pains of the damned.

'And now *art* thou cursed from the earth.' Peace on earth, is one branch of those blessed tidings that were brought into the world, at the coming of the Messias. Lu. ii. 14. Again, before Christ was come in the flesh, it is said, He rejoiced 'in the habitable part of his earth.' Pr. viii. 30. Wherefore, by the earth in this place, I understand the state that the men are in, to whom, by the mind of God, the gospel and grace of God is to be tendered. Now, whether it respect the state of man by nature, or the state of those that are saints, from both these privileges Cain is separate, as are all whom the Lord hath utterly rejected. Not but that yet they may live long in the world, but God hath cut them off from the earth, and all the gospel privileges therein, and set them in the condition of devils; so that as to grace and mercy they are separate therefrom, and stand as men, though alive, bound over to eternal judgment. And as to their lives, it matters not how long they live, there is 'no sacrifice for their sins, but a certain fearful looking for of judgment and fiery indignation, which shall devour the adversaries.' He. x. 26, 27. So that I say, as the devils be bound in hell, so such

lie bound in earth; bound I say in the chains of darkness, and their own obstinate heart, over to the day of wrath and revelation of the righteous judgment of God. Cain therefore by these words is denied the blessing of future means of grace, and stands bound over to answer for his brother's blood, which the ground had received from his cruel hand.

Ver. 12. 'When thou tillest the ground, it shall not henceforth yield to thee her strength; a fugitive and a vagabond shalt thou be in the earth.'

This is a branch, or the fruits of this wilful murder. Indeed, sins carry in them not only a curse with respect to eternity, but are also the cause of all the miseries of this life. 'God turneth - a fruitful land into barrenness, for the wickedness of them that dwell therein.' Ps. cvii. 34.

'When thou tillest the ground.' Sin committed doth not always exclude the sinner from an enjoyment of God's mercies, but yet if unrepented of, bringeth a curse upon them. 'I will curse, [saith God,] your blessings: yea, I have cursed them already, because ye do not lay *it* to heart.' Mal. ii. 2. This also is the reason that the table of some is made their snare, their trap, a stumbling-block and a recompence unto them; Ro. xi. 9. men ought not therefore to judge of the goodness of their state, by their enjoyment of God's creatures, but rather should tremble while they enjoy them, lest for sin they should become accursed to them, as were the enjoyments of this wicked man.

'A fugitive and a vagabond shalt thou be in the earth.' The meaning is, thou shalt not have rest in the world, but shalt be continually possessed with a guilty conscience, which shall make thy condition restless, and void of comfort. For the man that indeed is linked in the chains of guilt and damnation, as Cain here was; he cannot rest, but (as we say) fudge up and down from place to place, because his burthen is insupportable. As David said, 'Let their eyes be darkened that they see not, and make their loins continually to shake.' Ps. lxix. 23. A continual shaking and restlessness doth therefore possess such persons as are given up of God, and swallowed up of guilt.

'A fugitive and vagabond shalt thou be in the earth.' Some men certainly know, even while they are in this world, their state to be most miserable, and damnable, as Cain, Saul and Judas did; which knowledge, as I have hinted, puts them besides the very course of other carnal men; who while they behold them at quiet under their enjoyments, these cannot but wonder, fear, and be amazed with the deep cogitations which will abide upon them, of their certain misery and everlasting perdition.

Ver. 13. 'And Cain said unto the Lord, My punishment *is* greater than I can bear.' Or as the margin hath it, 'Mine iniquity is greater than that it may be forgiven.' And both readings are true: for however some men please themselves in lessening sin, and the punishment thereof, yet a burdened conscience judgeth otherwise. And if Cain failed in either, it was in that he counted his sin (if he did so) beyond the reach of God's mercy. But again, when men persecute the worship and people of God, as Cain did his blessed and religious brother, even of spite, and because he envied the goodness of his brother's work; I question whether it be lawful for a minister to urge to such the promise of grace and forgiveness; and also whether it be the mind of God such persons should hope therein. He that sins the sin unto death, is not to be prayed for, 1 Jn. v. 16. but contrariwise he is to be taken from God's altar that he may die. Ex. xxi. 14. This was Cain's case, and now he knew it; therefore as one excluded of God from his mercy and all the means thereof, he breaks out with roaring under the intolerable burden of the judgment of God upon him, concluding his punishment at present 'greater than he could bear,' and that yet his sin should remain unpardonable for ever: As saith our Lord Jesus Christ, He hath neither forgiveness here nor in the world to come. Mat. xii. 32.

Ver. 14. 'Behold, thou hast driven me out this day from the face of the earth; and from thy face shall I be hid; And I shall be a fugitive and a vagabond in the earth, and it shall come to pass, *that* every one that findeth me shall slay me.'

By these words is confirmed what was said before, to wit, to be cursed from the earth, was to be separate from the privileges of the gospel. For Cain was not now to die, neither was he driven into any den or cave; yet driven out from the face of the earth, that is, as I have said, he was excluded from a share in those special mercies that by the gospel were still offered by grace to the others that inhabited the world: The mercies, I say, that are offered by the gospel, as namely, The mercy of eternal life: For as to the blessings of this world, he had yet a notable share thereof. Besides, he groaneth under this judgment, as an insupportable curse: 'Thou hast driven me out this day from the face of the earth.' And indeed, if we take it according as I have laid it down, it is a curse that would break the whole world to pieces; for he that is denied a share in the grace that is now offered, must needs be denied a portion in God's kingdom. And this Cain saw; wherefore he adds in the process of his complaint, 'And from thy face shall I be hid:' ' I shall never come into thy kingdom, I shall never see thy face in heaven.' This is therefore the highest of all complaints; namely, for a man from a certain conviction that his condition must without fail be

damnable, to condole and bemoan his forlorn condition.

'Thou hast driven me out.' O! when God shall bind one over for his sin, to eternal judgment, who then can release him? This was Cain's state, God had bound him over. The blood of his brother was to rest upon him and not to be purged with sacrifice for ever.

'Thou hast driven me out THIS DAY.' He knew by the sentence that fell from heaven upon him, even from that very day that he was made a companion of, and an associate with devils. This day, or for this day's work, I am made an inhabitant of the pit with the devil and his angels. Hence note, That God doth sometimes smite the reprobate so apparently, that himself from that day may make a certain judgment of the certainty of his damnation. Thus did Balaam: 'I shall see him, but not now: I shall behold him, but not nigh.' Nu. xxiv. 17. Where by now, he respects the time of grace; and by nigh, the time or day of judgment: As who should say, 'I, for my sorceries, and wicked divinations, am excluded a portion in the day of grace, and therefore shall not see the Saviour NOW: I am also rejected, as to a portion in the blessed world to come: and therefore when he judgeth, I shall not see him NIGH: Nigh, as a friend, as a saviour to my soul.' I doubt this is the condition of many now alive, who for their perfidiousness and treachery to Christ, and his church, have already received, even 'in themselves, that recompence of their error which was meet.' Ro. i. 27.

Ishmael also, in the day he laughed at Isaac, Ge. xxi. 9. and Esau in the day he sold his birthright, Ge. xxvii., xxviii. might have gathered, the one from God's concurring with the judgment of Sarah, the other, from his father's adhering to his brother; his adhering, I say, in a prophetic spirit; Ga. iv. 29. that from thenceforth they both were excluded grace and glory, as the apostle by the Holy Ghost afterwards doth. He. xii. 16, 17.

'And from thy face shall I be hid.' By face here, we are to understand God's favour, and blessed presence, which is enjoyed by the saints both here, and in the world to come. Ps. iv. 6, 7; xvi. 11. Both which this wicked man, for the murdering of his brother, and his envy to the truth, now knew himself excluded from.

'From thy face shall I be HID.' The pit of hell, to which the damned go, besides the torment that they meet with there, is such a region of darkness, and at such a distance from the heavens, and the glorious comfortable presence of God, that those that shall be found the proper subjects of it, shall for ever be estranged from one glimpse of him: besides, sin shall bind all their faces in secret, and so confound them with horror, shame, and guilt that they shall not be able from thenceforth for ever, so much as once to think of God with comfort.

'From thy FACE.' As it were all the glory of heaven, it lieth in beholding the face of God: A thing the ungodly little think of; yet the men that have received in themselves already the sentence of eternal damnation, they know it after a wonderful rate; and the thoughts of the loss of his face and presence, doth, do what they can, as much torment them, as the thoughts of all the misery they are like to meet withal besides.

'And a fugitive and a vagabond shall I be on the earth.' Even from the present frame of his spirit, Now, having received the sentence, he knew, the judgment past being unrevokable, how it would be with him all his life long; that he should spend his days in trouble and guilt, rolling under the justice of God, being always a terror and burthen to himself, to the day he was to be cut off from the earth, that he might go to the place appointed for him.

'And it shall come to pass, that every one that findeth me shall slay me.' Guilt is a strange thing, it makes a man think that every one that sees him, hath knowledge of his iniquity. It also bringeth such a faintness into the heart, Le. xxvi. 36. that the sound of a shaken leaf doth chase such persons: and above all things, the cries of blood are most fearful in the conscience; the cries of the blood of the poor innocents, which the seed of Cain hath shed on the face of the earth. Je. ii. 34; xix. 4. Thus far of Cain's complaint.

Ver. 15. 'And the Lord said unto him, Therefore whosoever slayeth Cain, vengeance shall be taken on him seven-fold. And the Lord set a mark upon Cain, lest any finding him should kill him.'

By these words, the judgment is confirmed, which Cain, in the verse before, so mournfully pronounced against his own soul. As if the Lord had said, 'Cain, thy judgment is as thou hast said, I have driven thee out this day from a share in my special favour; and when thy life is ended, thou shalt be hid from my face, and blessed presence for ever; and seeing it is thus, therefore I will not suffer that thou die before thy time: Alas, thy glass will be quickly run! Besides, thy days, while thou art here, will sufficiently be filled with vexation and distress; for thou shalt always carry in thy conscience the cries of innocent blood, and the fear of the wrath of God: I have said it, and will perform it: I am not a man, that I should repent: So that thus shall thy judgment be: Therefore he that killeth Cain, I will take vengeance on him.'

Hence note, That none need to add to the sorrows of the persecutors. They above all men are prepared unto wrath. Let them alone (saith Christ) they will quickly fall into the ditch. Besides, God hath taken the revengement of the blood of his servants into his own hand, and will execute his wrath himself. Therefore he saith to his saints (as in this case), 'Dearly beloved, avenge not yourselves, but rather give place unto wrath: for it is written, Vengeance is mine, I will repay, saith the Lord.' Ro. xii. 19. And the reason is, because the quarrel is in special between the prosecutor and God himself. For we are not hated because we are men, nor because we are men of evil and debauched lives; but because we are religious; because we stand to maintain the truth of God. Therefore no man must here intercept, but must leave the enemy in the hand of that God he hath slighted and condemned. This made Moses that he meddled not with Corah and his company, but left them to that new thing which the Lord himself would do unto them, because they had condemned the ordinance of God. Nu. xvi. 25—35. This made David also that he meddled not with Saul, but left him to the vengeance of God, though he had opportunity to have destroyed him. 1 Sa. xxiv. and xxvi. 10—12. Let us learn therefore to be quiet and patient under the hand of wicked and blood-thirsty men. Let us fall before them like holy Abel; it is and will be grief enough to them, that when we are dead, our blood will cry from the ground against them.*

'Therefore he that killeth Cain, vengeance shall be taken,' &c. He now that shall, after this admonition, plead for religious blood with the sword, vengeance shall be taken on him, because he giveth not place to the wrath of God, but intercepts with his own, which 'worketh not the righteousness of God.' Ja. i. 19, 20. Say therefore with David, when you are vexed with the persecutor, Mine hand shall not be upon him; but 'as the Lord liveth, the Lord shall smite him; or, his day shall come to die; or, he shall descend in battle, and perish.'

'Vengeance shall be taken on him seven fold.' It would not be hard to shew how little they have prevailed, who have taken upon them to take vengeance for the blood of saints, on them that have been the spillers of it. But my business here is brevity, therefore I shall not launch into that deep, only shall say to such as shall attempt it hereafter, 'Put up thy sword into his place; for all they that take the sword shall perish with the sword!' Mat. xxvi. 52. And 'here is the patience and faith of the

---

* How solemn are these injunctions, and how opposed to the violent conduct of mankind. A most appalling murder has been committed;—a virtuous and pious young man is brutally murdered by his only brother:—what is the divine judgment? If any man kill him, vengeance shall be taken on him sevenfold: set a mark upon him—drive him from the abodes of man—shut him up in a cage like a wild beast—but shed not his blood.—ED.

saints.' Re. xiii. 10. Let Cain and God alone, and do you mind faith and patience; suffer with Abel, until your righteous blood be spilt: even the work of persecutors, is, for the present, punishment enough; the fruits thereof being the provoking God to jealousy, a denying of them the knowledge of the way of life, and a binding of them over to the pains and punishment of hell.

'And the Lord set a mark upon Cain.' What the opinion of others is about this mark, I know not; to me it seems like those in Timothy, who had 'their conscience seared with a hot iron.' 1 Ti. iv. 2. Which words are an allusion to the way of the magistrates in their dealing with rogues and felons; who that they may be known to all, are either in the hand, shoulder, or cheek branded with a hot iron. So Cain was marked of God for a reprobate, for one that had murdered a righteous man, even of envy to the goodness of his work: But the mark (as it was on those in Timothy) was not on any outward or visible part of his body, but (as there the apostle expresseth it) even upon his very conscience; his conscience then had received the fire-mark of the wrath and displeasure of God, which, as a burning iron doth to the flesh, had left such deep impression therein, that it abode as a scar or brand upon him, in token that good would for ever after hold him for a fugitive rogue or vagabond.

'And the Lord set a mark upon Cain, lest any finding him should kill him.' For though the mark was branded with burning upon his conscience, and so inward and invisible; yet the effects of this hot iron might be visible, and seen of all: the effects, I say, which were, or might be, his restlessness in every place, his dejectedness, the sudden and fearful pangs and agonies of his mind, which might break out into dolorous and amazing complaints; besides, his timorous carriage before all he met, lest they should kill him; gave all to understand, that God had with a vengeance branded him. And indeed this was such a mark as was amazing to all that beheld him, and did ten times more make them afraid of spilling blood, than if any visible mark had been set upon him; for by his trouble and distress of mind, they saw, what was the guilt of blood: and by his continual fear and trembling under the judgment of God, what it was to be in fear of, nay, to have the first fruits of everlasting damnation. Thus therefore God reserved Cain to the judgment which he had appointed for him.

Ver. 16. 'And Cain went out from the presence of the Lord, and dwelt in the land of Nod, on the east of Eden.'

The right carriage of a reprobate, and the infallible fruits of final desperation. For a man that hath received in his mind the stroke of the judg-

ment of God, and that is denied all means of saving and sanctifying grace, (as the great transgressors are,) the presence of God is to such most dreadful; whether we understand the knowledge of him as he is in himself, or as he discovereth himself in his church; for the thought of his being, and eternal majesty, keeps the wound open, and makes terror and guilt revive. To such it would be the best of news, to hear that the Godhead doth cease to be, or that themselves were high above him· But that they are in the hand of the living God, this is the dreadful and fearful thought.

'And Cain went out from the presence of the Lord.' These words may be taken many ways.

1. That he separated himself from the church (the place of God's presence) 2 Co. vi. 16. which then consisted of his father and mother, and of those other children they had. And this appears by the text, 'He went out from the presence of the Lord, and dwelt in the land of Nod.'

2. A man goes out from the presence of God, when he withdraws his thoughts from holy meditations, and employeth the strength of his mind about the things of this life. Job xxi. 14—18. And thus he also did; he went into the land of Nod, and there fell to building a city, and to recreate himself with the pleasures of the flesh what he might.

3. A man goes out from the presence of God, when he throweth up the worship and way of God; and this he did in departing from the church. 2 Ch. xix. 1—3.

4. Besides, his going out from tne presence of the Lord, implieth, that he hardened his heart against him, that he set his spirit against him; that he said to God, Depart from me; He. iii. 12. that he grew an implacable enemy to him, and to every appearance of good in the world. Job xv. 12, 13.

'And Cain went out from the presence of the Lord.' These words may also respect his being thrust out from God, as one anathematized, accursed, or cut off, in effect the same with excommunication. But be it so, the act was extraordinary, being administered by God himself; even as he served Corah and his company, though in kind there was a difference, the one, even Cain, being yet permitted to live for a while in the world; the other being sent down quick into hell; but both, for their villany against the worship and people of God, stand bound over to answer it at the eternal judgment.

Ver. 17 '¶ And Cain knew his wife; and she conceived, and bare Enoch: and he builded a city, and called the name of the city, after the name of his son, Enoch.'

Cain's wife was his sister, or near kinswoman; for she sprang of the same loins with himself; because his mother was 'the mother of all living.' Ge. iii 20.

This wife bare him a son; for whose sake, as it seems, he built the city. Hence note, That men who are shut out of heaven, will yet use some means to be honourable on earth. Cain being accursed of God, yet builds him a city; the renown of which act, that it might not be forgotten, he calleth it after the name of his son. Much like this was that carnal act of blasted Absalom; because he had no child, he would erect a pillar, which must forsooth be called Absalom's place, after the name of Absalom, to keep his name in remembrance upon earth. 2 Sa. xviii. 18.

'And he builded a city,' &c. Note, That it is the design of Satan, and the deceitful heart of man, to labour to quiet a guilty conscience, not by faith in the blood of Christ, but by over much business in the things of this world.

'And called the name of the city, after the name of his son, Enoch.' Although Cain had a mind to keep up his name with fame in the world, yet he would not venture to dedicate the city to his own name; that would have been too gross; and perhaps others would have called it, The City of the Murderer; but he calleth it after the name of his son, his son Enoch; whom he pretended was a man both taught, and dedicate, as it seems his name imports. Hence note again, That men who themselves are accursed of God, will yet put as fair glosses on their actions, as their hypocritical hearts can invent. Who must this city be dedicated to, but to him whom Cain had dedicated and taught. I will not say that in truth he gave him to God, for that his reprobate heart would not suffer; but being given up of God, yet retaining, with Saul, considerations of honour: therefore, as is the custom of ungodly hypocrites, he would put the best show on his ungodly actions.

Thus Saul, when he had received the sentence of the Lord against him; yet, Turn again with me (saith he to Samuel) 'yet honour me now before - the people, and before Israel.' 1 Sa. xv. 30. So the money wherewith the high priests and scribes had bought the life, and obtained the death of Christ; with that they make some shew of godliness, in buying with it a piece of ground to bury strangers in. Mat. xxvii. 3—7.

Ver. 18. 'And unto Enoch was born Irad: and Irad begat Mehujael: and Mehujael begat Methusael: and Methusael begat Lamech.'

These are the offspring of Cain; the English of whose names, if the nature and disposition of the persons were according, they might well be called, with abhorrence, the brood of wicked Cain, even the generation whom the Lord had cursed, notwithstanding Enoch was their father. Enoch begat Irad, a wild ass; Irad begat Mehujael, one presumptuous above measure, his name signifies, one

teaching God. But 'who hath directed the Spirit of the Lord?' Is. xl. 13. Or 'Shall any teach God knowledge?' Job xxi. 22. The son of this man was Methusael, asking death, the true fruit of all such presumptuous ones, 'his confidence shall be rooted out of his tabernacle, and it shall bring him to the king of terrors.' Job xviii. 14. His son was Lamech, one poor or smitten: The first, that, as we read, did break the order of God in the matter of marriage.

Ver. 19. '¶ And Lamech took unto him two wives: the name of the one was Adah, and the name of the other Zillah.'

This man was the first that brake the first institution of God concerning marriage. 'He took unto him two wives.' The New Testament says, Let every man have his own wife. And so said the law in its first institution: therefore plurality of wives first came into practice by the seed of cursed Cain, and for a time was suffered in the world through the hardness of man's heart.

Ver. 20, 21. 'And Adah bare Jabal: he was the father of such as dwell in tents, and of such as have cattle. And his brother's name was Jubal: he was the father of all such as handle the harp and organ.'

Jabal signifies bringing, or budding; Jubal, bringing, or fading. So then in these two sons might be shewed unto us the world, as it is in its utmost glory: that is, it brings buds, it brings fading: to-day in the field, to-morrow in the oven: 'All flesh is grass, and all the goodliness thereof, is as the flower of the field. The grass withereth, the flower fadeth: because the Spirit of the Lord bloweth upon it: surely the people is grass.' Is. xl. 6—8.

And observe in these, the last was the musical one. Indeed, the spirit of the world, after things have budded, is so far off from remembering that they again must fade; that then it begins its Requiem; then it saith to itself, Eat, drink, and be merry; then it is for handling the harp and organ. Lu. xii. 16—20.

Ver. 22. 'And Zillah, she also bare Tubal-Cain, an instructor of every artificer in brass and iron: and the sister of Tubal-Cain was Naamah.'

Tubal-Cain, a worldly possession; and Naamah, one that by her name should be beautiful. Lamech his fruit then was, a budding, fading, worldly possession, with a little deceitful, vain beauty, for 'favour is deceitful, and beauty is vain: but a woman that feareth the Lord, she shall be praised.' Pr. xxxi. 30.

Ver. 23. 'And Lamech said unto his wives, Adah and Zillah, hear my voice; ye wives of Lamech, hearken unto my speech: for I have slain a man to my wounding, and a young man to my hurt.

He that sticks not to exceed in one point, will

not fear to transgress in another. He had hardened his heart, by breaking the modest and orderly bounds of marriage, and so fitted himself to shed blood, or do any other wickedness.

' Hearken to me, ye wives.' Lustful men break their minds to their fleshly companions, sometimes, sooner than to wiser counsellors. Even as Ahab, in the business of the vineyard of Naboth, breaks his mind to that ungodly Jezebel his wife.

' I have slain a man to my wounding.' Who, or what man this murdered person was, therein the word is silent: yet this Lamech being the son of a bloody murderer, it is possible he was some godly man, one of Adam's other children, or of his grandchildren, the son of Seth: for these sons of Cain, and namely this in special, as it seems, took not heed to the mark wherewith God branded Cain; but like Belshazzar, he hardened his heart, though he knew it, and would turn murderer also. Da. v. 18—22.

' I have slain a man to my wounding.' The guilt of blood who can bear? or who can help himself thereby? It is a wounding thing, it is a hurtful thing, he that sheds man's blood wrongfully, cannot establish himself thereby. Mat. xxii. 6, 7. The Jews thought to have preserved themselves and country by killing Jesus Christ; but this so provoked the justice of God, that for this thing's sake he sent the Gentiles upon them to burn up their city; who when they were come, if stories be true, slew of them eleven hundred thousand; and those of them that were taken alive, were sold to who would buy them, Thirty a penny. ' Ye shed blood (says God) and shall ye possess the land? Ye stand upon your sword, ye work abomination, and ye defile every one his neighbour's wife: and shall ye possess the land?' Eze. xxxiii. 25, 26.

Ver. 24. ' If Cain shall be avenged sevenfold, truly Lamech seventy and sevenfold.'

Though wicked men may be willingly ignorant of that part of the judgments of God, that are to premonish them, that they do not that wicked thing for which the judgment was executed; yet if there be anything like favour mixed with the judgment, of that they will take notice, to encourage themselves to evil: even as this ungodly person, he would not be stopped from blood by the judgment of God upon Cain; but rather, as it seems, because the judgment was not speedily executed, his heart was fully set in him to do evil. Ec. viii. 11. Much like that of the Jews, who because Jehoiakim had slain Uriah the prophet, and yet God spared the land; therefore make that an argument to prevail with Zedekiah to kill Jeremiah also. Je. xxvi. 20—23.

' If Cain shall be avenged sevenfold, truly Lamech seventy and sevenfold.' Give wicked men leave to judge of themselves, and they will pass a sentence favourable enough. Though Lamech had not pity when he spilt blood; yea, though the judgment of God upon Cain could not hold his murderous hands: yet now he is guilty, let him but make a law in the case, and woe be to him that killeth Lamech: Vengeance shall be taken of him seventyfold and seven. Joab could with pitiless hands spill the blood of men more righteous than himself, not regarding what became of their souls: but when his blood was by vengeance required for the same, then he would take sanctuary at the horns of the altar. 1 Ki. ii. 28. But judgment is not wholly left to men, the Lord is judge himself; before whom both Cain and Lamech, and all their successors, shall be arraigned, and receive just doom, and that never to be reversed.

Ver. 25. ' ¶ And Adam knew his wife again; and she bare a son, and called his name Seth: for God, *said she*, hath appointed me another seed instead of Abel, whom Cain slew.'

Now we have done, for a while, with Cain, and are come again to the church of God. Cain had slain Abel, and by that means, for a while, had greatly suppressed the flourishing of religion; in which time his own brood began to be mighty upon earth; so encreasing, as if religion was put to an end for ever. But behold their disappointment! ' Adam knew his wife again,' (for Adam's family was then the true church of God;) or take Adam for a type of Christ, and his wife for a type of the church, and then this observation followeth; namely, That so long as Christ and the church hath to do with one another, it is in vain for Cain to think of suppressing religion.

' Adam knew his wife again.' If Eve had now been barren, or Adam had died without farther issue, then Cain might have carried the day; but behold another seed! a seed to stand in Abel's place: therefore she called his name Seth; that is, Set or Put, as namely, in the room of Abel, to stand up for, and to defend the truth against all the army and power of Cain. As Paul also saith of himself, ' I am set, [or put,] for the defence of the gospel.' Phi. i. 17. This man therefore, so far as can be gathered, was the first that put check to the outrage of Cain and his company. But mark some observations about him.

1. He was set in the stead or place of Abel; not an inch behind him, but even at the place where his blood was spilt. So that he that will revive lost religion, must avow it as God's Abels have done before him: every talker cannot do this. The blood that was shed before his face, must not put check to his godly stomach; yea, he must say to religion, as Ruth said once to her mother, ' Where thou diest, I will die, and there will I be buried.' Ru. i. 17. This is the way to revive and to

maintain the ways of God, in despite of bloody Cain.*

2. This Seth that was set to put check to Cain, did not do it of his own brain, but the hand of God was principal in the work. 'God,' said she, 'hath appointed me another seed to be set in the place of Abel.' And indeed it is otherwise in vain, when religion is once suppressed, to think it should ever revive again. Alas! where is the man, if he want God's Spirit, that will care for the flourishing state of religion? and that in truth will make the Lord his delight: 'This *is* Zion, whom no man seeketh [for, or seeketh] after.' Je. xxx. 17. All men here say, 'See to thine own house, David.' 1 Ki. xii. 16. But when Seth comes, then the ground is made good again; then a living saint is found to stand and maintain that truth which but now his brother bled for. When James was killed, Peter stands up, &c. Ac. xii. 1–3. And therefore Seth is said to be another seed, a man of another spirit: One who was principled with a spirit beyond and above the spirit of the world. 'Another seed,' one that was spirited for God's word, and God's worship, and that would maintain his brother's cause.

3. Observe, That when Seth maintains his brother's lot, you hear no more of the brood of Cain. And indeed, the way to weary out God's enemies, it is to maintain and make good the front against them: 'Resist the devil, and he will fly.' Ja. iv. 7. Now if the Captain, their king Apollion, be made to yield, how can his followers stand their ground? 'The dragon, - the devil, Satan, - he was cast out into the earth, and his angels were cast out with him.' Re. xii. 9. But how? It was by fighting: 'Michael and his angels fought against the dragon; - and overcame him by the blood of the Lamb, and by the word of their testimony, and by not loving of their lives unto the death.' Re. xii. 7, 8, 12.

4. Let this, in the last place, serve for persecutors, That when you have cast down many ten thousands, and also the truth to the ground; there is yet a Seth, another seed behind, that God hath appointed to stand in the stead of his brethren, by whom you will certainly be put to flight, and made to cease from oppressing the truth.

Ver. 26. 'And to Seth, to him also there was born a son; and he called his name Enos: Then began men to call upon the name of the Lord.'

The Holy Ghost, in recording the birth of Enos, goeth out of his ordinary style, in that he doubleth the mentioning of his father, with respect to the birth of this son. And indeed it is worth the observing; for it staggereth the faith of some, to think that the man that makes good the ground of a murdered brother, should not leave issue behind him: But ' to Seth, to him was born a son.' Our faithfulness to the truth, shall be no hinderance to the flourishing state of our offspring, take them either for the fleshly or spiritual seed of God's servants, but sons, (especially in the latter sense, if we truly stand by the word of God) shall surely be born unto us.

'And to Seth, to him also there was born a son; and he called his name Enos.' Enos, a man; not a devil, like Cain, but a man; or, a man that was miserable in this world, for the sake and cause of God;† for it seems, as was his father, so was he, even both given up to maintain God's truth; which cannot be done but with great hazard, so long as Cain or his offspring remain. His father therefore, by his very name, did offer him up to bear all hardships for the name and cause of God: 'Behold I send you forth (saith Christ) as lambs in the midst of wolves.' In effect, he called their name Enos, men to be acquainted with grief and miseries: But mark, 'Then began men to call upon the name of the Lord.'

'Then,' when Seth maintained Abel's ground, and when Enos endured all miseries for the same: For indeed this makes spectators believe that religion is more than a fictitious notion: The hardships, miseries, and blood of the saints, will make men, otherwise heedless, consider and ponder their cause aright.

'Then began.' For, as I also before have hinted, the outrage of bloody Cain did put, for a time, a stop to the flourishing state of God's worship; which in all probability was not so little as half a hundred years, even till Seth, and the son of Seth, stood up to maintain the same; but 'then, THEN men began (more men than Seth and Enos) to call upon the name of the Lord.'

Note again, That all true religion beginneth with fervent prayer: Or thus, That when men begin to be servants to God, they begin it with calling upon him. Thus did Saul, 'Behold he prayeth:' Ac. ix. And, 'Lord have mercy upon me,' is the first of the groans of a sanctified heart.

The margin hath it, 'They began to call themselves by the name of the Lord.' As God saith in another place, 'My name is called on them.' The disciples were called Christians, (nay, the

---

* When Bunyan was in prison, under sentence to be hung, all his thoughts were, not how to escape, but, how so to suffer as to glorify God; 'I thought with myself if I should make a scrabbling shift to clamber up the ladder, yet I should either with quaking or other symptoms of faintings, give occasion to the enemy to reproach the way of God and his people for their timorousness. This, therefore, lay with great trouble upon me, for, methought, I was ashamed to die with a pale face and tottering knees for such a cause as this.'— *Grace Abounding*, No. 334.—Ed

† Bunyan has taken the meaning of all these Scripture names from the first table to the Genevan or Puritan version, vulgarly called 'The Breeches Bible,' an invaluable translation. —Ed.

saints are called the anointed ones, and the church is called Christ.) 1 Co. xii. 12. But note, That fervent prayer ends in faith and confidence in God. They called themselves by the name; they counted themselves not from a vain and groundless opinion, but through the faith they had in the mercy of God, The saints and holy people of God.

They began to publish themselves, in contradistinction to the offspring of Cain, the holy people of God. Wherefore, a separation from the wicked began betimes; the one going by the name of 'the sons of God;' the other, 'by the sons and daughters of men:' ch. vi. 1, 2. 'Then began men to call upon the name of the Lord.'

CHAP. V.

Ver. 1. 'This *is* the book of the generations of Adam. In the day that God created man, in the likeness of God made he him.'

The Holy Ghost having thus largely treated of Cain and his offspring, and of the head made against him by Seth and Enos, and of the good success that followed, he now comes to treat of the church in particular, and of the flourishing state of the same.

'This *is* the book.' The Holy Ghost cuts off the genealogy of Cain, accounting him none of the race of the church, although before he was within the pale thereof. John observing this, calls him, 'a child of that wicked one,' 1 Jn. iii. 12. as our Lord also accounted Judas. Wherefore, he here begins his book again, that this wicked race might be quite excluded. 'Let them be blotted out of the book of the living, and not be written with the righteous.' Ps. lxix. 28.

'In the day that God created man, in the likeness of God made he him.' Although by this new beginning the Holy Ghost excludeth Cain, yet he fetcheth the genealogy of the church from the day that man was created; intimating that God, in the very act of creation, had a special intention to plant him a church in the world; and therefore, even before sin was in the world, the image of God was upon man, as a token of his special respect, and of the great delight that he intended to take in that creature above all that he had made. Pr. viii. 30, 31.

Ver. 2. 'Male and female created he them; and blessed them, and called their name Adam, in the day when they were created.'

When Adam was created, the Lord created two in one: So when Christ, the head of the church, was chosen, the church was also chosen in him.

'And blessed them.' With the blessing of generation: A type of the blessing of regeneration that was to be by Christ in the church, according to that which is written, 'So shall thy seed be.' Ep. i. 4.

'And called their name Adam, in the day when they were created.' So that in the man the woman is included: 'Neither is the man without the woman, neither the woman without the man, in the Lord.' 1 Co. xi. 11. For the Holy Ghost, in the work of the new creation, of which this creation was a type, counteth not by male and female, but 'ye are all one in Christ Jesus.' Ga. iii. 28. Wherefore, women are not to be excluded out of the means of salvation; nay, they have, if they believe, a special right to all the promises of grace that God hath made to his saints in all ages: Yea, 'she shall be saved in childbearing, [though she bear children,] if she continue in faith, and charity, and holiness with sobriety.' 1 Tim. ii. 15.

Ver. 3. 'And Adam lived an hundred and thirty years, and begat 'a son in his own likeness, after his image; and called his name Seth.'

Here also by the book of Chronicles, the Holy Ghost carrieth away the genealogy, because Abel had no children, saying Adam, Seth, &c. 1 Ch. i. 1.

'An hundred and thirty years.' Behold the rage of hell! For until Seth stood in Abel's place, religion was greatly hindered, and that was after the world had stood an hundred and thirty years. Indeed, Abel, while he had his breath, did hold it up in the world; but Cain, who was of that wicked one, smote him and religion both to the ground.

'And begat *a son* in his own likeness.' Who can bring a clean *thing* out of an unclean? not one.' Job xiv. 4. If the father be polluted with the inward filth of sin, the son must needs be like him: 'I was shapen in iniquity; (said David) and in sin did my mother conceive me.' Ps. li. 5. Seth then was no better than we by nature, but came into the world in the blood of his mother's filth: 'What *is* man, that he should be clean? and *he which is* born of a woman, that he should be righteous?' Job xv. 14.

This therefore should teach us not to count of our election, and of our effectual calling but by the word of God. Seth by nature was a sinful man, and yet the chosen servant of God; the first that took up God's quarrel after the death of blessed Abel.

This should also help us to hold up the bucklers against the kingdom of the devil and hell. Seth was subject to like infirmities with us, and yet he got ground of the children of iniquity. I know a sense of our own infirmities is apt to weaken our hand in so mighty an undertaking, but it should not: Although we be like old Adam by nature, yet God is able to make us stand.

Ver. 4. 'And the days of Adam, after he had begotten Seth, were eight hundred years: and he begat sons and daughters.'

Adam therefore, as a type of Christ, reigned in the church almost a thousand years. The world therefore beginning thus, doth shew us how it will end ; namely, by the reign of the second Adam, as it began with the reign of the first.

These long-lived men therefore shew us the glory that the church shall have in the latter day, even in the seventh thousand years of the world, that sabbath when Christ shall set up his kingdom on earth, according to that which is written, 'They lived and reigned with Christ a thousand years.' Re. xx. 1—4. They:—Who ? The church of God, according also as it was with Adam. Therefore they are said by John to be holy, as well as blessed: 'Blessed and holy is he that hath part in the first resurrection: on such the second death hath no power, but they shall be priests of God, and of Christ, and shall reign with him a thousand years.' ver. 6. In all which time the wicked in the world shall forbear to persecute, as did also the brood of wicked Cain in the days of Adam, Seth, &c. Hence therefore we find in the first place the dragon chained for these thousand years.

Ver. 5. 'And all the days that Adam lived were nine hundred and thirty years: and he died.'

Adam therefore lived to see the translation of Enoch: In whose translation a conquest was got over all the enemies of his soul and body: So Christ shall reign in and among his saints till all his enemies be destroyed. 'The last enemy that shall be destroyed is death ;' 1 Co. xv. 26. which shall be swallowed up when the members of that glorious head have put on incorruption, and their 'mortal shall have put on immortality.' Adam's reigning therefore until Enoch's translation, looks like a prophecy of the perfection of Christ's kingdom: For he shall reign till he hath 'delivered up the kingdom to God, even the Father:' ver. 24. As Adam, till his Enoch was translated and took up to God.

Ver. 6. '¶ And Seth lived an hundred and five years, and begat Enos.'

Seth therefore stood by the truth of God, a long time, without much help or encouragement from man ; which was a great trial to his spirit, and proof of the truth of his faith, and tended much to the perfection of his patience. Somewhat like this was that of Paul, who had no man stood with him when he stood before Nero.

Seth was set in the stead of Abel, to keep the gap against the children of hell; which, by the grace of God, he faithfully did, even till Enos was sent to his aid and assistance.

Seth therefore was the forlorn hope of the church in those days. So set of God to put check to the enemy, until the church was increased, and more able to defend herself from the outrage.

This therefore should teach the saints of God.

especially those that are sent before, against the offspring of Cain, to stand their ground, and not to shrink like Saul, till God shall send others to take part with them. 1 Sa. x. 8; xiii. 8—14.

Thus David stood, as it were, by himself, against the wicked that was in his day ; which made him cry, 'Who will rise up for me against the evil doers,' or who will stand up for me against the workers of iniquity ? Ps. xciv. 16.

Ver. 7. 'And Seth lived after he begat Enos eight hundred and seven years, and begat sons and daughters.'

Hence also we may gather great encouragement who are set in the front of the army of the Lamb, against the army and regiment of Cain. Seth, saith the Spirit, was set in the stead of Abel, there as forlorn, to defend religion: Must he not now be swallowed up ? Will the blood-hounds let him escape ? Behold, therefore his life must be accounted a wonder ! As was also that of Paul. 1 Co. vi. 9. But for Seth to stand eight hundred years against such a murderous crew, and yet to have his breath in his nostrils ! Our times are in thy hands, and thou, Lord, 'holdeth our soul in life.' Ps. lxvi. 9.

'And all the days of Seth were nine hundred and twelve years, and he died.' ver. 8.

His life was therefore eighteen years shorter than that of Adam ; he lived fifty-five years after Enoch, and died six hundred and fourteen years before the flood.

Ver. 9. '¶ And Enos lived ninety years, and begat Cainan.'

Cainan signifieth a buyer, or owner. Let it be with respect to religion, and then the sense may be, that he had this privilege in religion by the hazard of his father and grandfather's life; they bought it for him, and made him the owner of it: As Paul saith, He gave not place to the false Apostles, 'that the truth of the gospel might continue with the Galatians.' ch. ii. 5. As Jotham also said to Shechem, 'My Father fought for you, and adventured his life far, and delivered you out of the hand of Midian.' Jud. ix. 17. Namely, that they might still be owners of the inheritance that the Lord had given them. This shews us then, that the fruit of a constant standing to the word of God, is, That the generations yet unborn shall be made the possessors and owners of it.

Ver. 10. 'And Enos lived after he begat Cainan eight hundred and fifteen years, and begat sons and daughters.'

He lived then to see his son enjoy the fruits of his own constancy to the truth, so long a time as eight hundred years, &c. as we hope God's people now may do. 'Tis true, they now do own the truth with hazard, and do hold it up by enduring much misery, according to the rage of wicked men;

but, I say, 'tis hoped others will reap the fruits of our travails, and that some of us shall live to see it, as Enos lived to see his Cainan possess religion eight hundred years.*

Ver. 11. 'And all the days of Enos were nine hundred and five years: and he died.'

He lived then one hundred fifty-three years after Enoch, and died five hundred and sixteen years before the flood.

Ver. 12. '¶ And Cainan lived seventy years, and begat Mahalaleel.'

Mahalaleel, signifieth praising God. Wherefore he was born in settled times, wherein religion met with little or no molestation. It began to be as hereditary in the days of blessed Cainan ; wherefore it was requisite that the very next that should possess the truth, should spend their days in praising God. Re. xi. 15. And thus it will be at the downfal of Antichrist: ' After this (saith John) I heard a great voice of much people in heaven, saying Allelujah ; Salvation, and glory, and honour, and power unto the Lord our God. - - - - And a voice came out of the throne saying, Praise our God, all ye his servants ; and ye that fear him, both small and great.' Re. xix. 1—6.

' The whole earth (saith the Prophet) is at rest *and* is quiet, they break forth into singing. Yea, the fir-trees rejoice at thee, (O thou brood of the blood-thirsty Cain,) *and* the cedars of Lebanon, *saying,* Since thou art laid down, no feller is come up against us.' Is. xiv. 7, 8.

Ver. 13. ' And Cainan lived after he begat Mahalaleel eight hundred and forty years, and begat sons and daughters.'

God gave him a long possession and enjoyment of the fruits of his father's labours. They sowed (as Christ said) and he was entered into their labours: They sowed in tears, and he reaped in joy. Mahalaleel, or praise our God, was the language of those times.

Ver. 14. ' And all the days of Cainan were nine hundred and ten years: and he died.'

He lived then two hundred and forty-eight years after Enoch, and died four hundred twenty-one years before the flood.

Ver. 15. '¶ And Mahalaleel lived sixty and five years, and begat Jared.'

Jared signifies ruling, and sheweth us what is the holy fruits of peace and thanksgiving in the church ; to wit, government according to the testament of Christ. Ac. ix. 31. It is hard to have all things according to rule, in the day of the church's

affliction ; because of the weakness and fearfulness of some ; and because possibly those who have most skill in that matter, may for a time be laid up in chains: but now when the church hath rest and quietness, then as she praiseth God, so she conceiveth and bringeth forth governors, and good government and rule among her members. David, a man of blood, could not build that house to the Lord, which peaceable Solomon, that man of rest, afterwards did. 1 Ch. xxviii. 3, 6. When armies are engaged, and hot in battle, 'tis harder to keep them in rank and file, than when they have rest, and time for discipline. Jared therefore is the fruits of thanksgiving, as thanksgiving is the fruits of peace and possession.

Ver. 16. 'And Mahalaleel lived after he begat Jared eight hundred and thirty years, and begat sons and daughters.'

He lived not only to give thanks unto God, but to shew to all that he gave thanks in truth, by submitting his neck the rest of the hundred of years that he lived, to the holy law and word of God.

A good rule to prove people by ; for all that pretend to give thanks for liberty, put not their neck under the yoke, but rather use their liberty as an occasion for the flesh, than by love to serve and advantage one another in the things of the kingdom of Christ. Ga. v. 13. 1 Pe. ii. 16. But as ' the bramble said to the [rest of the] trees,' so saith Christ to such feigned thanksgivers, ' If in truth ye anoint me king over you, *then* come *and* put your trust in my shadow.' Ju. ix. 15. Submit to my law, and be governed by my testament. Let your thanksgiving bring forth Jared, and walk with God in the days of Jared.

Ver. 17. ' And all the days of Mahalaleel were eight hundred ninety and five years: and he died.'

He lived then three hundred and three years after Enoch, and died three hundred and sixty-six years before the flood.

Ver. 18. ' And Jared lived an hundred sixty and two years, and he begat Enoch.'

Enoch, is taught, or dedicate: The true effect of rule or government, be it good or bad: in Cain's posterity it was bad ; ' for an evil tree cannot bring forth good fruit.' By Enoch here, we are to understand, one taught in, and dedicated unto, God. This Enoch therefore was a son that would hear the rules, and submit to the government of his father Jared. ' *As* an ear-ring of gold, and an ornament of fine gold, *so is* a wise reprover upon an obedient ear.' Pr. xxv. 12.

Ver. 19. 'And Jared lived after he begat Enoch eight hundred years, and begat sons and daughters.'

He lived therefore to see the fruit of his good rule and government in the church, even to see his teachable and dedicated son caught up to God, and to his throne. A good encouragement to all rulers

* Bunyan, after suffering much, and witnessing the cruel havoc made with the church of God in his time, fell asleep in peace on the eve of the glorious revolution ;—while many of his cotemporaries did, he did not 'live to see it.' He died August 31, 1688—as James the Second fled and lost his crown on the 11th of December following.—ED.

in the house of God, and also to all godly parents to teach and rule in the fear of God; for that is the way to part with church members, and children with comfort; yea, that is the way, if we shall out-live them, to send them to heaven, and to God before us.

Ver. 20. 'And all the days of Jared were nine hundred sixty and two years: and he died.'

He lived then three hundred thirty-five years after Enoch, and died two hundred thirty-four before the flood.

Ver. 21. 'And Enoch lived sixty and five years, and begat Methuselah.'

Methuselah signifieth, Spoiling his death: This therefore is the true fruits of one that is truly taught in, and dedicate to the service of God, as Enoch was; by this means he spoileth his death: wherefore he adds, 'And Enoch walked with God.' Walking with God, spoileth death, or overcomes it, or it shall be prevented, he shall not be hurt therewith: As Christ saith, 'If a man keep my saying, he shall never taste death.' Jn. viii. 52.

Ver. 22. 'And Enoch walked with God, after he begat Methuselah three hundred years, and begat sons and daughters.'

These words [after he begat Methuselah] may have respect either to his beginning to walk with God, or to the number of the years that he lived after the birth of Methuselah, or both.

If it respect the first, then it sheweth that the only encouragement that a sinner hath to walk with God, it is to see Methuselah, or his death spoiled: for when a man seeth death, and all evils, conquered and overcome, then his soul is encouraged in holiness. 1 Co. xv. 55—58. No encouragement to walking with God like this: 'Enoch walked with God after he begat Methuselah.' As Paul saith, 'Now being made free from sin, - (which indeed is the sting of death) ye have your fruit unto holiness, and the end everlasting life.' Ro. vi. 22.

If it respect the second, then it shews us the invincible nature of true faith, (for by faith Enoch walked with God:) I say, it sheweth us the invincible nature of true faith, in that it would hold up a man in close communion with God for the space of three hundred years.

'He walked with God three hundred years.' How will the conversation of Enoch rise up in judgment with this generation, that walk not with God at all! Or if they do, do it so by fits, as if walking with God was but a work by the by.

'He walked with God and begat sons and daughters.' And kept house, and lived with his wife, according to knowledge. This shews then, that it is sin, not our lawful and honest employment, that hindereth one's walking with God.

Ver. 23, 24. 'And all the days of Enoch were three hundred and sixty and five years: And

Enoch walked with God: and he *was* not; for God took him.' ver. 23, 24.

The New Testament saith, 'By faith Enoch was translated that he should not see death; and was not found, because God had translated him: for before his translation he had this testimony, that he pleased God.'

'And all the days of Enoch were three hundred and sixty and five years.' Enoch therefore lived here but a while; he was too good to live long in this world, the world was not worthy of him; neither would he be spared so long out of heaven, 'for God took him.' The end of walking with God or the path-way thereof, it leads men to heaven, to the enjoyment of the glory of God. Thus also it was with blessed Elijah, he followed God from place to place, till at length he was caught up into heaven. 2 Ki. ii. 1—11.

A word or two more of Enoch. Jude observes, That he was the seventh from Adam: Closely intimating (as I conceive) that by him God prefigured the resurrection and end of the world: And intimated, That in the seventh great day of the world this resurrection should be, each generation from Adam being a type of a thousand years: So that Enoch, the seventh from Adam, was a type of the seventh thousand, in which the Lord will reign with his church a thousand years.

There are two things in Enoch that incline me to this opinion. First, he crieth out, 'Behold the Lord comes!' and then is translated that he should not see death. The right posture and end of those that shall live at the day of God Almighty; and that shall, like Enoch, be found 'walking with God,' when the Lord shall come from heaven. Jude 14, 15.

Ver. 25. '¶ And Methuselah lived an hundred eighty and seven years, and begat Lamech.'

Lamech signifieth poor, or smitten; wherefore I doubt that the apostacy that you read of in the next chapter, began either in the days of, or by, this man: he being, as it seems, more dry and void of grace than those that went before him; poor, or smitten.

Hence note, That faith and godliness, though often it goeth from the father to the son, as from Seth to Enos, and from him to Cainan, yet it is not tied here, but runs according to electing love, as also do the fruits thereof.

Ver. 26, 27. 'And Methuselah lived after he begat Lamech seven hundred eighty and two years, and begat sons and daughters. And all the days of Methuselah were nine hundred sixty and nine years, and he died.'

Methuselah, the spoiling of death, is the longest liver in the world; yet he died in the year that the flood was upon the earth; not by the flood, but by the course of nature, as also did Lamech his son, for the wicked reprobate only was swept away by that, according to the apostle Peter.

Ver. 28, 29. '¶ And Lamech lived an hundred eighty and two years, and begat a son: and he called his name Noah, saying, This *same* shall comfort us concerning our work and toil of our hands, because of the ground which the Lord hath cursed.'

'And he called his name Noah.' Noah signifieth rest; his name was therefore according to his work, for he was a preacher of righteousness, which giveth rest to all that embraceth it. Besides, it was he that prepared the ark, the place of rest to the church of God.

'This *same* shall comfort us concerning our work and toil of our hands, because of the ground which the Lord hath cursed.'

These words seem to carry in them, repentance for the apostacy that before was mentioned. 'This same shall comfort us,' by restoring the church to her former rest, and by delivering us from the 'toil of our hands;' for sin once admitted of in the church, is not without much toil extirpated, and driven forth of the same; yea sometimes it getteth such footing and root, that it cannot again be purged and destroyed, but by breaking the very being of the church where it is. Thus it was as to the case in hand, and is signified also by pulling down the house in which the leprosy was. Le. xiv. 43—45. Yea Ephesus itself was almost thus far infected, had not a threatening prevented. Re. ii. 1—3.

'Because of the ground which the Lord hath cursed.' The Lord did curse it for the sin of Adam: He also renewed the curse to Cain, because he was guilty of the blood of his brother. I incline also to think, that the curse here mentioned, is the first, reiterated for the grievous apostacy of this congregation; according to that which is written, 'If ye walk contrary unto me,' 'I will punish you seven times more:' 'I will bring seven times more plagues upon you, according to your sins.' Le. xxvi. 18—21.

Ver. 30. 'And Lamech lived after he begat Noah, five hundred ninety and five years, and begat sons and daughters.' Wherefore Lamech heard the preaching of Noah, who was the only minister of God in those days, to recover the church to repentance from their apostacy, which also he did in some good measure effect, while he condemned the world for their unbelief. He. xi. 7.

Ver. 31. 'And all the days of Lamech were seven hundred seventy and seven years: and he died.' He died five years before the flood. Methuselah therefore was the longest liver of those godly that fell on the other side the flood, for he died not before the very year the flood came, not by the water, but before. The righteous is taken away

from the evil to come; though, as the prophet saith, no man of the wicked laid it to heart.

Ver. 32. '¶ And Noah was five hundred years old: and Noah begat Shem, Ham, and Japhet.'

CHAP. VI.

Ver. 1. 'And it came to pass, when men began to multiply on the face of the earth, and daughters were born unto them.'

Moses now leaveth the genealogy for a while, and searcheth into the state and condition of the church now after so long a time as its standing upwards of, or above, a thousand years: where he presently findeth two things. 1. The church declined. 2. And God provoked. Wherefore he maketh inquiry into the nature of the church's sin; which he relateth in this following chapter.

'And it came to pass, when men began to multiply.' The men here I understand to be the children of Cain, the church and synagogue of Satan, because they are mentioned by way of antithesis to the church and sons of God.

'And daughters were born unto them.' A snare that was often used in the hand of the devil, to intangle withal the church of God; yea, and doth so usually speed, that it hath often been counted by him as infallible; so that this is the doctrine of his prophet Balaam, and it prevailed, when all the engines of hell beside were prevented. 'The people began to commit whoredom with the daughters of Moab.' Nu. xxv. 1, 2. It may be this child of hell, in this his advice to Balak looked back to the daughters of Cain, and calling to remembrance how of old they intangled the church, advertised him to put the same into practice again. Re. ii. 14.

Ver. 2. 'That the sons of God saw the daughters of men, that they *were* fair; and they took them wives of all which they chose.'

This was the way then of the sons of Cain, to let their fair daughters be shewed to the sons of God. Pr. xxii. 14. For it seems all other their wiles and devices were not able to bring the church and the world together, and to make them live as in one communion. These to the church were such, whose hearts were snares and nets, and whose hands were bands to intangle and hold them from observing the laws and judgments of God. Ec. vii. 26

'And they took them wives.' First their eye saw them, and then their heart lusted after them. Thus the devil deceived the woman, and by this means perished cursed Achan. 'And Achan answered Joshua, and said, Indeed I have sinned against the Lord, and thus have I done: When I saw among the spoils a goodly Babylonish garment,' &c., 'then I coveted them.' Jos. vii. 20, 21.

Note therefore, that it is not good to behold with

the eye that which God hath forbid us to touch with our hand. 'I made a covenant with mine eyes,' saith Job. Job. xxx. 1. And again, if at unawares a thing was cast before him, the beholding of which was of an intangling nature, he forthwith would hold back his heart as with a bridle, lest the design of hell should be effected upon him. ver. 7.

Crush sin then in the conception, lest it bring forth death in thy soul.

Ver. 3. 'And the Lord said, My Spirit shall not always strive with man, for that he also *is* flesh: yet his days shall be an hundred and twenty years.'

By these words is aggravated the sin of the church, that she would attempt to close with, and hold a sinful communion, against the dissuasions of the Spirit of God.

'My Spirit shall not always strive.' To wit, my Spirit in Noah, for he was the only preacher of righteousness to the church in those backsliding times.

By this then, I find, that the doctrine of Noah, was, To declare against a sinful communion, or to command the church, in the name of God, that she still maintain a separation from the cursed children of Cain: As he said to the prophet Jeremiah, If thou separate the precious from the vile, 'thou shalt be as my mouth.' chap. xv. 19.

Noah therefore had a hard task, when he preached this doctrine among them: for this above all is hard to be borne, for by this he condemned the world.

The first great quarrel therefore that God had with his church, it was for their holding unwarrantable communion with others. The church should always 'dwell alone, and not be reckoned among the nations.' Nu. xxiii. 9. The church is 'a chosen generation, a royal priesthood, an holy nation, a peculiar people.' 1 Pe. ii. 9. Therefore the work of the church of God, is not to fall in with any sinful fellowship, or receive into their communion the ungodly world, but to shew forth the praises and virtues of him who hath called them out from among such communicants into his marvellous light.

'My Spirit shall not always strive.' Hence note, that the people that shall continue to grieve the Spirit of God, and to resist the doctrine of Noah, they are appointed for heavy judgments. 'Come out of her, my people, that ye be not partakers of her sins, and that ye receive not of her plagues.' Re. xviii. 4. This because those (finally impenitent) in Noah's time refused to do, therefore the wrath of God overtook them, and swept them off the face of the earth.

'Yet his days shall be an hundred and twenty years.' Noah therefore began his preaching about the four hundred and fourscore year of his life,

which continuing the space of sixscore more, it reached to the day that the flood came.

In which time doubtless his faith was sufficiently tried, both by the hard censures of the hypocrites of the church, and the open profane of the world, against whom he daily pronounced the judgments of God for maintaining their forbidden communion. Ge. iii. 15.

'Yet his days shall be an hundred and twenty years.' God also would yet have patience with these people, if peradventure they would repent that his hand might not be upon them.

Ver. 4. 'There were giants in the earth in those days; and also after that, when the sons of God came in unto the daughters of men, and they bare *children* to them, the same *became* mighty men, which *were* of old, men of renown.'

'There were giants in the earth in those days.' These words seem to be spoken, to shew us the hazards that Noah ran, while he preached the truth of God: He incurred the displeasure of the giants, which doubtless made all men tremble, and kept the whole world in awe. But Noah must engage the giants, he must not fear the face of a giant. This way God took also with Moses, and with his people of Israel, they must go to possess the land of the giants, a people high and tall as the cedars, a people of whom went that proverb, 'Who can stand before the children of Anak?' De. ix. 2. They must not be afraid of Og the king of Bashan, though his head be as high as the ridge of a house, and his bedstead a bedstead of iron. De. iii. 11.

This should teach us then not to fear the faces of men: no, not the faces of the mighty; not to fear them, I say, in the matters of God, though they should run upon us like a giant.

These giants I suppose were the children of Cain, because mentioned as another sort than those that were the fruit of their forbidden and ungodly communion: For he adds, 'And also after that,' or besides them, 'when the sons of God came in unto the daughters of men, and they bare *children* to them, the same, [or they also] *became* mighty men which *were* of old, men of renown.'

Then Noah found giants every where: Giants in the world, and giants in this confused communion. And thus it is at this day; we do not only meet with giants abroad, among the most ungodly and uncircumcised in heart, but even among those that seem to be of the religious, among them we also meet with giants; men mighty to oppose the truth, and very profound to make slaughter: But mark the advice of the Lord, 'Fear not their fear, nor be afraid. Sanctify the Lord of hosts himself, (who is stronger than all the giants that are upon the face of the earth) and *let* him *be* your fear, and *let* him *be* your dread.' Is. viii. 12, 13.

'And when the sons of God came in unto the daughters of men, and they bare *children* to them, the same *became* mighty men;' much like to the giants. The fruit therefore of ungodly communion is monstrous, and of a very strange complexion. They are like unto them that worshipped the Lord, and served their own gods also; 2 Ki. xvii. 24, 41. or like to those of the church, of whom Nehemiah speaks, that had mixed themselves with the children of Ashdod, Ammon and Moab, whose children were a monstrous brood, that spake half the language of Ashdod, and could not speak the Jews' language. Ne. xiii. 23, 24.

By both these sorts of giants was faithful Noah despised, and his work for God condemned. In David's time also Goliah defied Israel, and so did his brethren also. 1 Sa. xvii. 10. Giants, the sons of the giant; but David and his servants must engage them, and fight them, though they were giants. 1 Ch. xx. 4—8.

'Mighty men which were of old.' Persecution therefore, or the appearance of the giants against the servants of God, is no new business; not a thing of yesterday, but of old, even when Noah did minister for God in the world. 'There were giants in the earth in those days,' to oppose him.

'Men of renown.' Not for faith and holiness, but for some other high achievements, may be, mighty to fight, and to shed man's blood; or to find out arts, and the nature of things; both which did render them famous, and men to be noted in their place. Such kind of men might be Corah, Dathan, and their company also; yet they opposed Moses and Aaron, yea, God, his way and worship, and perished after an unheard of manner. Nu. xvi. 1, 2. As also did the opposers of righteous Noah, in the day of the flood.

Ver. 5. 'And God saw that the wickedness of man *was* great in the earth, and *that* every imagination of the thoughts of his heart *was* only evil continually.' The margin saith, 'not only the imagination, but also the purposes and desires.'

These words are to be understood, as still respecting the apostacy that we read of in the first and second verses, and are (in my thoughts) to be taken as the effect of their degeneracy. For though it be true, that the best of men, in their most holy and godly behaviour, have wicked and sinful hearts; yet so long as they walk sincerely according to the rules prescribed of God, there is no such character upon them; especially as it stands related to the words that immediately follow; to wit, 'that it repented the Lord that he made them.'

These evil and wicked purposes then were in special the fruit of their apostacy: for indeed, when men are once fallen from God, they then, as the judgment of God upon them, are given up to all unrighteousness. Again, apostatizing persons are counted abhorrers of God. Zec. xi. 8. Yet persons in this condition will seek their own justification, turning things upside down, traversing their ways like the dromedaries; bearing us still in hand, that they stand not guilty of sin, but that what they do is allowable, or winked at of God. Besides, they say their hearts are still upright with God, and that they have not forsaken the simplicity of his way, of a wicked and ungodly design, with an hundred more the like pretences; all which are condemned of God, and held by him as abominable and vile. Je. ii. 31—37.

And God saw, &c. They covered their shame from men, like the adulterous woman in the Proverbs, and would speak with oily mouths, thereby to cozen the world; Pr. xxx. 20. but God knew their hearts, and had revealed their sin to his servant Noah; he therefore in the Spirit of God, as one alone, cried out against their wickedness.

Hence learn to judge of apostates, not by their words, nor pretences, nor ungodly coverings, whereby they may seek to hide themselves from the stroke of a convincing argument, but judge them by the words of God; for however they think of themselves, or would be accounted of others, God sees their wickedness is great.

'And *that* every imagination of the thoughts of his heart, *was* only evil continually.' If they think they have not sinned; if they think they promote religion; if they think to find out a medium to make peace between the seed of the woman, and the wicked seed of Cain; all is alike ungodly, they have forsaken the right way, they have dissembled the known truth, they have rejected the word of the Lord: And what wisdom or goodness is in them?

Ver. 6. 'And it repented the Lord that he had made man on the earth, and it grieved him at his heart.'

Repentance is in us a change of the mind; but in God, a change of his dispensations; for otherwise he repenteth not, neither can he; because it standeth not with the perfection of his nature: In him 'is no variableness, neither shadow of turning.' Ja. i. 17.

Wherefore, it is man, not God, that turns. When men therefore reject the mercy and ways of God, they cast themselves under his wrath and displeasure; which because it is executed according to the nature of his justice, and the severity of his law, they miss of the mercy promised before. Nu. xxiii. 19. Which that we may know, those shall one day feel that shall continue in final impenitency. Therefore, God speaking to their capacity, he tells them, he hath repented of doing them good. 'The Lord repented that he had made Saul king.' 1 Sa. xv. 35. And yet this repentance was only a change of the dispensation, which Saul by his wickedness had put himself under; otherwise the strength, the eternity of Israel, 'will not lie nor repent.' ver. 29.

The sum is therefore, that men had now by their wickedness put themselves under the justice and law of God; which justice by reason of its perfection, could not endure they should abide on the earth any longer; and therefore now, as a just reward of their deed, they must be swept from the face thereof.

'And it grieved him at his heart.' This is spoken to show, that he did not feign, but was simple and sincere in his promise of remission and forgiveness of sins, had they kept close to his word, according as he had commanded. Wherefore God's heart went not with them in their backsliding, but left them, and was offended with them.

Ver. 7. 'And the Lord said, I will destroy man whom I have created, from the face of the earth, both man, and beast, (or from man to beast,) and the creeping thing, and the fowls of the air; for it repenteth me that I have made them.'

This may be either understood as a threatening, or a determination: if as a threatening then it admitted of time for repentance; but if it was spoken as a determination, then they had stood out the day of grace, and had laid themselves under unavoidable judgment. If it respected the first, then it was in order to the ministry of Noah, or in order to the effecting the ends of its sending; which were either to soften or harden, or bring to repentance, or to leave them utterly and altogether inexcusable. But if it respected the second, as it might, then it was pronounced as an effect of God's displeasure, for their abuse of his patience, his minister, and word. As it also was with Israel of old; 'They mocked the messengers of God, and despised his words, and misused his prophets, until the wrath of the Lord arose against his people, till *there was* no remedy.' 2 Ch. xxxvi. 16.

'And the Lord said, I will destroy man whom I have created.' This word created, is added, on purpose to show that the world is under the power of his hand; for who can destroy, but he that can create? Or who can save alive, when the maker of the world is set against them? 'There is one lawgiver, who is able to save and to destroy.' Ja. iv. 12. And again, 'Fear him which is able to destroy both soul and body in hell.' Mat. x. 28. In both which places power to destroy is insinuated from his power and Godhead: As he saith in another place, 'All souls are mine; - the soul that sinneth, it shall die.' Eze. xviii. 4.

'Both man and beast, and the creeping thing, and the fowls,' &c. Thus it was at first the sin of a man brought a curse and judgment upon other the creatures whom God had made: As Paul says, 'The whole creation groaneth.' Ro. viii. 22.

But again, This threatening upon the beasts, the fowls, and creeping thing, might arise from a double consideration: First, To show, that when God intends the destruction of man, he will also destroy the means of his preservation. Jos. vi. 20. Or, secondly, To shew, that when he is determined to execute his judgments, he will cut off all that stands in his way. 2 Ch. xxxv. 21. He could not destroy the earth without a flood, and preserve the beast, &c., alive; therefore he destroys them also.

'For it repenteth me that I have made them.' This seems to fall under the first consideration, to wit, That God repented that he made the beasts and fowls; because now they were used to sustain his implacable enemies.

Ver. 8. '¶ But Noah found grace in the eyes of the LORD.'

This word GRACE, must in special be observed; for grace is it which delivereth from all deserved judgments and destruction.

Noah, by nature was no better than other men: therefore the reason why he perished not with others, it was because he 'found grace in the eyes of the Lord.' Ye are saved by grace. Ep. ii. 8. And thus was Noah, as is evident, because he was saved by faith. He. xi. 7. For faith respecteth not works, but grace: Ye are saved by grace through faith. As Paul says again, 'Therefore *it is* of faith that *it might be* by grace,' &c. Ro. iv. 16. We must therefore, in our deliverance from all the judgments of God, sing grace, grace, unto it.

Ver. 9. 'These *are* the generations of Noah: Noah was a just man, *and* perfect in his generations; *and* Noah walked with God.'

The Holy Ghost here makes a short digression from his progress, in his relation of the wickedness of the world; and yet not impertinently; for seeing Noah was the man that escaped the judgment, his escape must be for some reason; which was, because God was gracious to him, and because God had justified him. Besides Noah being now made righteous, faithfully walketh with God.

'He was just and perfect in his generations.' But why it is said, Generations? It might be, because he was faithful to God and man, having the armour of righteousness on the right hand, and on the left. It is said in Isaiah, That Christ 'made his grave with the wicked, and with the rich in his death.' liii. 9. To import, That they only have benefit by him to eternal life, that die by his example, as well as live by his blood; for in his death was both merit and example; and they are like to miss in the first, that are not concerned in the second. Phi. viii. 16.

'Perfect in his generations.' In his carriage, doctrines and life, before both God and man. And thus ought every preacher to be; he ought to do in the sight of God, what he commands to men;

by this means he saveth both himself, and them that hear him. 1 Ti. iv. 16.

Besides, Noah was a man, as well as a saint, and in either sense had a generation: to both of which grace made him faithful; and he that shall not serve his generation as a man, will hardly serve his generation as a Christian. But Noah was perfect in both, he was 'perfect in his generations.'

'And Noah walked with God.' This shews he was sincere in his work; for a hypocrite may, as to outward shew, do as the saint of God: but *he* doth it with respect to men, not God, and therefore he is a hypocrite. To walk with God then, is not only to do the duty commanded, but to do it as God requireth it; that is, to do it with faith, and son-like fear, as in God's sight, 'with singleness of heart.'

Ver. 10. 'And Noah begat three sons, Shem, Ham, and Japheth.'

These are the offspring of Noah, and by these was the earth replenished after the flood, as will be further seen hereafter.

Ver. 11. 'The earth also was corrupt before God, and the earth was filled with violence.'

He has now returned to the matter in hand before; to wit, the causes of the flood.

'The earth also was corrupt.' By earth, he may here mean, those that are without the church: and if so, then by corrupt here, we must understand, wicked after a most high manner; for albeit the world and generation of Cain be always sinners before God, yet the Lord cutteth not off the world in general, nor a nation in particular, but because of the commission of eminent outrage and wickedness. Thus it was with those of Sodom, a little before the Lord with fire devoured them. 'The men of Sodom (saith the text) *were* wicked, and sinners before the Lord exceedingly.' Ge. xiii. 13.

Again: As by corrupt, we may understand, corrupt by way of eminency; so again, they were corrupt incurably. This is evident, because they were not brought off from sin by the ministry of Noah, the only appointed means of their conversion.

Hence note, That when men are sinners exceedingly, and when the means of grace appointed of God for their recovery, prove ineffectual, then they are near some signal judgment. 2 Ch. xxxvi. Thus back-sliding Jerusalem, because she was wicked with an high hand, Eze. xxiv. 13, 14. and could not be cured by the ministry of the prophets, therefore her sons must go forth of her into captivity, and the city burned to the ground with fire. Je. xv. 1—3.

'And the earth was filled with violence.' First, they had violated the law of God, in making and maintaining ungodly and wicked communion; according to that of the prophet, 'Her priests have violated my law, and have profaned mine holy things.' But how? 'They have put no difference between the holy and profane, neither have they shewed *difference* between the unclean and the clean.' Eze. xxii. 26.

They also perverted judgment between a man and his neighbour: adhering to their own party, in disaffection to the religious. This is supposed, because of the exceeding latitude of the expression, 'The earth was filled with violence;' that is, all manner of violence, outrage and cruelty was committed by this sort of people. This takes in that saying of Solomon, the oppression of the poor, especially God's poor, is included, in a 'violent perverting of judgment and justice.' Ec. v. 8.

They also shewed violence to the lives of good men, as may be gathered by the act of Lamech, one of the sons of Cain. In a word, 'The earth was filled with violence;' violence of every kind; lust and wickedness was outrageous, there was a world of ungodliness among these ungodly men.

Ver. 12. 'And God looked upon the earth, and, behold, it was corrupt; for all flesh had corrupted his way upon the earth.'

By these words therefore is confirmed the sense of the former verse, 'The earth was corrupt;' for God saw it was so: 'The earth was full of violence,' for they had corrupted God's way.

'And God looked upon the earth.' This shews us, That the Lord doth not with haste, or in a rash inconsiderate way, pour his judgments upon the world; but that with judgment and knowledge, the wickedness first being certain, and of merit deserving the same. This is seen in his way of dealing with Sodom. 'And the Lord said, Because the cry of Sodom and Gomorrah is great, and because their sin is very grievous, I will go down now, and see whether they have done altogether according to the cry of it, which is come unto me; and if not, I will know.' Ge. xviii. 21.

'And, behold, it was corrupt; for all flesh had corrupted his way upon the earth.' It proved, as that of Sodom did, according to the cry thereof; for 'all flesh had corrupted his way.' God's WAY, by violating his law, and perverting of judgment, as was hinted before. All flesh had corrupted it, therefore the evil needed not to be long in searching out: As God saith by the prophet Jeremiah, 'I have not found it by diligent search, but upon all these.' ii. 34. Here upon the whole earth, none exempted but righteous Noah.

Ver. 13. 'And God said unto Noah, The end of all flesh is come before me; for the earth is filled with violence through them; and, behold, I will destroy them with the earth.'

'And God said unto Noah,' or told Noah his purpose: The same way he went with Abraham: 'Shall I hide from Abraham that thing which I do ?' Ge. xviii. 17. ' Surely the Lord will do nothing, but he revealeth his secrets unto his servants the prophets.' Am. iii. 7.

' The end of all flesh is come.' The time or expiration of the world is at hand. God speaks before he smites. Thus he did also by the prophet Ezekiel, saying, ' An end' is come, 'the end is come:' And again, ' An end is come, the end is come: it watcheth for thee; behold, it is come.' vii. 1—6.

' The end of all flesh is come before me.' Sin and wickedness doth not put an end to the ungodly before their own face, yet it brings their end before the face of God. It is said of these very people, ' they knew not' of their destruction, ' until' the day ' the flood came, and took them all away.' Mat. xxiv. 37—39. Indeed, the nature of sin is to blind the mind, that the person concerned may neither see mercy nor judgment; but God sees their end: ' The end of all flesh is come before me.'

' The end of all flesh.' By these words, the souls are left to, and reserved for another judgment: Wherefore, though here we find the flesh consumed; yet Peter saith, their spirits are still in prison, even the souls that Christ once preached to in the days, and by the ministry of Noah: Even the souls ' which sometime were disobedient when once the long-suffering of God waited in the days of Noah, while the ark was a preparing,' &c. 1 Pe. iii. 19, 20.

Ver. 14. ' ¶ Make thee an ark of gopher wood; rooms shalt thou make in the ark, and shalt pitch it within and without with pitch.'

This is the fruits of the grace of God: He said before, That Noah ' found grace in the eyes of the Lord:' Which grace appoints to him the means of his preservation.

' Make THEE an ark.' He saith not, Make one; or, Make one for me: But, Make one; make one for thee: ' Make THEE an ark of gopher wood.'

Noah therefore, from this word THEE, did gather, That God did intend to preserve him from the judgment which he had appointed in this his work: Therein lay his own profit and comfort; not a thought which he had, not a blow that he struck, about the preparing the ark, but he preached, as to others their ruin, to himself, his safeguard and deliverance: He ' prepared an ark, to the saving of his house.' He. xi. 7.

This therefore must needs administer much peace and content to his mind, while he preached to others their overthrow. As the prophet saith, ' The work of righteousness shall be peace; and the effect of righteousness quietness and assurance for ever. And my people shall dwell in a peaceable habitation.' Is. xxxii. 17, 18. Thus did Noah when he dwelt in the ark, and in sure dwellings, and in quiet resting-places.

' Make thee an ark.' The ark was a figure of several things. 1. Of Christ, in whom the church is preserved from the wrath of God. 2. It was a figure of the works of the faith of the godly: ' By faith he prepared an ark;' by which the followers of Christ are preserved from the rage and tyranny of the world (for the rage of the water was a type of that, as I shall shew you hereafter.) So then Noah, by preparing an ark, or by being bid so to do of God, was thereby admonished, First, To live by the faith of Christ, of whom the ark was a type: and hence it is said, that in preparing the ark, he ' became heir of the righteousness which is by faith;' because he understood the mind of God therein, and throughout his figure acted faith upon Christ. But, Secondly, His faith was not to be idle, and therefore he was bid to work. This begat in him an obediential fear of doing ought which God had forbidden: ' By faith Noah, being warned of God of things not seen as yet, moved with fear, prepared an ark, to the saving of his house; by the which he condemned the world, and became heir of the righteousness which is by faith.' He. xi. 7.

' Rooms (nests) shalt thou make in the ark.' To wit, for himself, and the beasts, and birds of the field, &c. Implying, that in the Lord Jesus there is room for Jews and Gentiles. Yea, forasmuch as these rooms were prepared for beasts of every sort, and for fowls of every wing: it informs us, that for all sorts, ranks and qualities of men, there is preservation in Jesus Christ: ' Compel them to come in;' drive them (in a gospel sense as Noah did the beasts of old into the ark, that my house may be full, ' and yet there is room.'* Lu. xiv. 22, 23.

' And thou shalt pitch it within and without with pitch.' This was to secure all from the flood, or to keep them that were in the ark from perishing in the waters.

Ver. 15. ' And this *is the fashion* which thou shalt make it *of*: the length of the ark *shall be* three hundred cubits, the breadth of it fifty cubits, and the height of it thirty cubits.'

A vessel fit to swim upon the waters.

' And this *is the fashion*,' &c. God's ordinances must be according to God's order and appointment, not according to our fancies, ' This *is the fashion*,' to wit, according to what is after expressed.

By these words therefore Noah was limited and bound up, as to a direction from which he must not

* ' And yet there is room.' As in Christ, the ark of his church, so it was in Noah's ark. The best calculations, allowing eighteen inches to a cubit, show that the ark was capable of receiving many more than this selection from all the animals now known, together with their requisite provender. Dr. Hunter estimated the tonnage at 42,413 tons measurement.—ED.

vary; according to that of the angel to the prophet, 'Son of man (saith he) behold with thine eyes, and hear with thine ears, and set thine heart upon all that I shall shew thee: for to the intent that I might shew *them* unto thee, *art* thou brought hither.' Eze. xl. 4. As the Lord said also to his servant Moses, 'In all *things* that I have said unto you, be circumspect.' Ex. xxiii. 13. And so again, about making the tabernacle in the wilderness, which the apostle also takes special notice of, saying, 'See, saith he, *that* thou make all things according to the pattern shewed to thee in the mount.' He. viii. 5.

Hence note, That God's command must be the rule whereby we order all our actions, especially when we pretend to worship that is divine and religious. If our works, orders, and observances, have not this inscription upon them, 'This is the fashion,' or 'This is according to the pattern,' such works and orders will profit us nothing: neither have we any promise when all is done, it wanting the order of God, that we should escape those judgments which those shall assuredly escape, that have their eye in their work to the 'pattern' revealed in the word.*

Ver. 16. 'A window shalt thou make to the ark, and in a cubit shalt thou finish it above; and the door of the ark shalt thou set in the side thereof: *with* lower, second, and third *stories* shalt thou make it.'

I told you before, That the ark was a type of Christ, and also of the works of the faith of the godly. And now he seems to bring in more, and to make it a type of the church of Christ; as indeed the prophet also does, when he calls the church, one afflicted, and tossed with tempests; and compareth her troublers to the waters of Noah, saying, 'This *is as* the waters of Noah.' Is. liv. 9.

Now as the ark was a type of the church, so according to the description of this verse she hath three most excellent things attending her. 1. Light. 2. A door. 3. Stories of a lower and higher rank.

1. She hath a window for light, and that when she was to be tossed upon the waters. Hence note, That the church of Christ wanteth not light, no, not in the worst of times. This light is the Word and Spirit of God which Christ hath given to them that obey him. Jn. xvii.

2. She hath a door. This door was a type of Christ; so was also the door of the tabernacle. And hence it is that you read, That Moses, when

he went to talk with God, would stand to talk in the door of the tabernacle; also that the cloudy pillar stood at the door. Ex. xxxiii. 9, 10. 'I (saith Christ) am the door:' Again, 'I am the door of the sheep.' Jn. x. By this door then, entered all that went into the ark, as by Christ all must enter that enter aright into the church.

3. She had stories in her, of first, second, and third degree: To shew that also in the church of Christ there are some higher than some, both as to persons and states: 1. apostles; 2. evangelists; 3. pastors and teachers. And again, there are in the church degrees of states, as also there are in heaven.

Ver. 17. 'And, behold, I, even I, do bring a flood of waters upon the earth, to destroy all flesh, wherein *is* the breath of life from under heaven; *and* every thing that *is* in the earth shall die.'

This is the reason of the former commandment, of making an ark: But some time was yet to intervene: the flood was hereafter to overflow the world: wherefore, from this it is that those words are inserted, of things not seen as yet: And that the ark was a work, or the fruit of Noah's faith: 'By faith Noah, being warned of God of things not seen as yet,' &c. He. xi.

'And, behold, I, even I,' &c. These words excuse Noah of treason or rebellion, forasmuch as his preparation for himself, and his warning and threatening the whole world with death and judgment for their transgression, was solely grounded upon the word of God: God bid him prepare, God said he would punish the world for their iniquity.

Hence note, That a man is not to be counted an offender, how contrary soever he lieth, either in doctrine or practice, to men, &c. if both have the command of God, and are surely grounded upon the words of his mouth. This made Jeremiah, though he preached, That the city of Jerusalem should be burnt with fire, the king and people should go into captivity; yet stand upon his own vindication before his enemies, and plead his innocency against them that persecuted him. Je. xxvi. 10—15. Daniel also, though he did openly break the king's decree, and refused to stoop to his idolatrous and devilish demand; yet purged himself of both treason and sedition, and justifies his act as innocent and harmless, even in the sight of God. 'My God (saith he) hath sent his angel, and hath shut the lions' mouths, that they have not hurt me: forasmuch as before him innocency was found in me; and also before thee, O king, have I done no hurt.' Da. vi. 22.

Further, Paul also, although by his doctrine he did cry down the ceremonies of the Jews, and the idolatry of the heathen emperor, yet he quits himself of blame from either side: 'Neither against

* How astonishing is the fact, that man dares to introduce his miserable inventions to deform the scriptural simplicity of divine worship; as if HE who makes all things perfect, had, in this important institution, forgotten to direct the use of liturgies—organs—vestments—pomps and ceremonies. When will man, with child-like simplicity, follow gospel rules?—ED.

the law of the Jews, [saith he,] neither against the temple, nor yet against Cæsar, have I offended anything at all.' Ac. xxv. 8. The reason is, because the words of God, how severely soever they threaten sinners, and how sharply soever (the preacher keeping within the bowels of the word) this doctrine be urged on the world, if it destroy, it destroyeth but sin and impenitent sinners, even as the waters of Noah must do.

This then affords us another note worth remarking, to wit, That what God hath said in his word, how offensive soever it be to ungodly men, THAT we that are Christians ought to observe: whether it direct us to declare against others' enormities, or to provide for ourselves against the judgment to come.

'And, behold, I, even I, do bring a flood,' &c. Hence note again, Let us preach and practise well, and let God alone to execute his judgments. It is said of Samuel, That not one of his words did fall to the ground. 1 Sa. iii. 19. He preached, and God, according to his blessing or cursing, did either spare and forgive, or execute his judgments.

'And, behold, I, even I.' Note again, That when sinners have with the utmost contempt slighted and despised the judgment threatened, yet forasmuch as the execution thereof is in the hand of an omnipotent majesty, it must fall with violence upon the head of the wicked. 'I, even I,' therefore, were words of a strong encouragement to Noah, and the godly with him; but black, and like claps of thunder to the pestilent unbelieving world: as the prophet says, 'He is strong that executes his word:' And again, 'Not one of his judgments fail.'

'And, behold, I, even I, do bring a flood.' The flood was a type of three things.

1. A type of the enemies of the church, Is. liv. 9—14.

2. A type of the water baptism under the new testament, 1 Pe. iii. 20, 21.

3. A type of the last and general overthrow of the world by fire and brimstone, 2 Pe. iii. 6, 7.

But here, as it simply respecteth the cause, which (as is afore related) was the sin that before you read of ; so it precisely was a type of the last of these, and to that end put an end to the world that then was. The world that then was, being overflowed with water, perished, to signify, That the heavens and the earth which are now, are reserved unto fire, against the day of judgment, and perdition of ungodly men.

'I bring a flood of waters upon the earth, to destroy all flesh, wherein *is* the breath of life from under heaven ; *and* every thing that *is* in the earth shall die.' By these latter words, as the cause, so the extention of this curse is expressed; and that under a threefold denotation.

1. Every thing that is in the earth.

2. All flesh wherein is the breath of life.

3. Every thing that is under heaven.

So then, this deluge was universal, and extended itself not only to those parts of the world where Noah and that generation lived, which we find repeated before, but even over the face of all the earth ; and it took hold of the life of every living thing that was either on all the earth, or in the air, excepting only those in the ark, as will the general judgment do : 'And Noah only remained *alive,* and they that *were* with him in the ark.' Ge. vii. 23.

Ver. 18. 'But with thee will I establish my covenant ; and thou shalt come into the ark, thou, and thy sons, and thy wife, and thy sons' wives with thee.'

'But with thee,' &c. This concerns what was said before concerning the universality of the flood: As he also said above, 'But Noah found grace in the eyes of the LORD.' This Peter also notes, He 'saved Noah the eighth *person,* a preacher of righteousness, bringing in the flood upon the world of the ungodly.' 1 Pe. ii. 5.

'With thee will I establish my covenant.' My covenant of mercy, or my promise to save thee when I drown the whole world for their iniquity: And therefore he adds, 'And thou shalt come into the ark.'

'I will establish.' Making and establishing of promises are not always the same: He made his promise to Abraham, he seconded it with an oath unto Isaac, and he confirmed, or established it to Jacob ; for by him he multiplied the seed of Abraham as the stars of heaven for multitude. Ps. cv. 8—10.

'With thee will I establish.' Or, unto thee will I perform my promise, 'Thou shalt come into the ark.'

Hence note again, That we ought to look upon signal and great deliverances from sore and imminent dangers, to be confirmations of the promise or covenant of God. Or thus, When God finds means of deliverance, and instateth our souls in a special share of that means, this we should take as a sign, That with us God hath confirmed, or established, his covenant. Lu. i. 68—78.

'Thou, and thy sons, and thy wife, and thy sons' wives with thee.' Because in that family did now reside the whole of the visibility of the church upon the earth ; all the rest were lost, as Peter also intimates, when he calleth Noah the eighth person, or one, and the chief of the eight that made up the visible church, or that maintained the purity of the worship of God upon the face of the whole earth: As he explains it a little after: 'For thee have I seen righteous before me in this generation.' vii. 1.

Ver. 19. 'And of every living thing of all flesh, two of every *sort* shalt thou bring into the ark, to keep *them* alive with thee; they shall be male and female.'

By these words, Noah should seem to be, in this action, a figure or semblance of Christ; who before the Lord shall rain fire and brimstone from heaven, shall gather into his ark, the church, of all kindreds, and tongues, and people, and nations. Lu. xiii. 29; xiv. 21. Even as Noah was to gather of all, of everything, of all flesh, of every sort, with him into the ark.

'Two of every *sort*.' This two, in special, respecteth the unclean, vii. 2. which were a type of the Gentiles, and so further confirms the point.

They shall be male and female. He would not make a full end, he would in judgment remember mercy. Ac. x. 11, 12, 17, 28.

Ver. 20. 'Of fowls after their kind, and of cattle after their kind, of every creeping thing of the earth after his kind: two of every *sort* shall come unto thee, to keep *them* alive.'

'Of fowls after their kind, and of cattle after their kind.' This, still respecting the antitype, may shew us also, how that God, for proof of the prophecy of the spreading of the gospel, doth not only tell us, that the Gentiles were gathered into his ark, but as here the beasts and birds, according to their kind, are specified: so the Gentiles are also denominated according to their several countries, Galatians, Corinthians, Ephesians, Colossians, Thessalonians, Bereans, &c., these, after their country and nation, were gathered unto Jesus to be preserved from the flood of wrath that at last shall fall from God who dwells in heaven, to the burning up of the sinner and ungodly.

'Two of every *sort* shall come unto thee, to keep *them* alive.' If the emphasis lieth in Come, as I am apt to think, and as the eighth verse of the next chapter fairly allows me to judge; then we must observe still, That Noah was not only first in the ark, as our Lord and Christ is the first from the dead; but that the cattle, the fowls, and the creeping things, did come to him into the ark, by a special instinct from heaven of the fruits of a divine election.* Noah therefore, as a man, did not make choice which of every kind; but he went first into the ark, and then of clean beasts by sevens, and of unclean beasts by twos, went in unto Noah into the ark, as the Lord commanded Noah.

* How mysterious are God's ways: some animals of every kind are saved, and all the rest destroyed. So throughout every age some animals have been treated with kindness, and others of the same species cruelly maltreated. Can those who stumble at the doctrine of election, account for this difference. Reason must submit with reverence to the voice of Christ; 'What I do, thou knowest not NOW; but thou shalt know hereafter'—ED.

And thus it is in the antitype: 'Unto thee shall all flesh come,' saith the prophet. Ps. lxv. 2. And again, 'To him *shall* the gathering of the people *be*.' Ge. xlix. 10. But how? Why, by an instinct from heaven, the fruit of a divine election: 'All that the Father giveth me shall come to me; but no man can come to me (saith Christ) except the Father which hath sent me draw him.' Jn. vi. 37, 44.

The beasts therefore which came into the ark, were neither chosen by men, neither came they in by any instinct of nature which was common to them all, but as being by a divine hand singled out and guided thither, so they entered in: the rest were left to the fury of the flood. Like to this also is the antitype, sinners come not to Jesus by any work or choice of flesh and blood, nor yet by any instinct of nature that is common to all the world; but they come, as being by a divine hand singled out from others; and as guided of the Father, so they come to Christ into the ark: The rest are left to the fury of the wrath of God, which, in the day of judgment, shall swallow them up for ever.

'They shall come unto thee to keep them alive.' Indeed, they lived not for their own sakes, they being not better than them that perished; but 'they shall come unto thee to save them:' for, for the sake of Noah they were preserved, when many millions were drowned in the waters. Bring this also to the antitype, and you find them look like one another: for the reason why some are saved from the wrath to come, it is not for that they are better in themselves, for both Jews and Gentiles are all under sin: But it is Christ that saveth by his righteousness, as Noah saved the beasts and fowls, &c. Let us therefore, as the beasts did, go to Jesus Christ, that he may keep us alive from perishing in the day of judgment.

Ver. 21. 'And take thou unto thee of all food that is eaten, and thou shalt gather *it* to thee, and it shall be for food for thee, and for them.'

This therefore was for the preservation of the life of those that were in the ark; by which action there is, as in the former, inclosed a gospel-mystery.

'Take thou unto thee of all food.' This food was not to be at the will and dispose of unruly beasts; but Noah was, as the lord of all that was in the ark, to take it into his own custody: and therefore he doubleth the command, 'Take it unto thee;' Gather it unto thee; to wit, to dispose of after thy discretion and faithfulness. In this therefore he was a type of Christ, whom God hath set as Lord and King in the church, and 'to feed his flock as a shepherd;' for the 'bread of God' is in the hand of Christ, for him to communicate unto his spouses, saints, and children; as Joseph did to Egypt, according to the power committed to him, and trust reposed in him. And hence it is said, as concerning the bread that endureth to everlasting life, 'the Son of man shall give it you; for Him hath God the Father sealed,' or appointed thereunto: Jn. vi. 27. and therefore, that he giveth, we receive, and no more of the bread of God: *That thou givest them, they gather: thou openest thine hand, they are filled with good.* Ps. civ. 28.

'Take unto thee all food.' That is, to be eaten by man and beast; the fowl also, and the creeping thing. This still followed, and brought in to the gospel, it shews us, that, even then, when the church is driven up into a hole, and tossed upon the waves of the rage and fury of the world, as the ark was upon the face of the waters, that even then her Noah hath all food for her, or food of all sorts for her support and refreshment: 'Bread shall be given him; *his* waters *shall be* sure.' Is. xxxiii. 16.

'Take unto thee.' How blessedly was this answered, when the Lion of the tribe of Judah took the book out of the hand of him that sat upon the throne; Re. v. 7. for in the book is contained the words of everlasting life; and the words of God are the food of his church, which this Noah hath received to nourish them withal: Man 'liveth not by bread only,' but by every *word* that proceedeth out of the mouth of the Lord, doth man live. Mat. iv. 4. De. viii. 3.

'And it shall be for food for thee, and for them.' That is, each according to their kind. The same is true also under our present consideration; Christ is the shepherd, we are the sheep, yet He feedeth with us in the ark: 'I will come in to him, and will sup with him, and he with me.' Re. iii. 20. Again, here Christ transcends this action of Noah; for he was to have his food of his own, but Christ feedeth on the same with us, even on the words of God: Yet herein again we differ; he feedeth as a Lord, we as servants; he as a Saviour, we as the saved; but in general, respecting the words of God, we feed all but of one dish, but at one table; the bread therefore that he hath provided, gathered and taken to him, it was food for him, as well as for us.

Ver. 22. 'Thus did Noah; according to all that God commanded him, so did he.'

These words therefore present us with a description of the sincerity and simplicity of the faith of Noah; who received the word at the mouth of God; not to hear only, but to do and live in the same.

'Thus did Noah.' As it is also said of his servant Moses, 'As the Lord commanded Moses, so did he:' As the Lord commanded Moses, so did he, Yea, to shew us how pleasant a thing the Holy Ghost accounteth this holy obedience of faith, he

is not weary with repeating, and repeating again not less than eight times in one chapter, the punctuality of Moses's conformity with the word of God, in this manner, 'Thus did Moses;' 'according to all that the Lord commanded Moses, so did he.' Ex. xl. 16, 19, 21, 23, 25, 27, 29, 32.

'Thus did Noah,' This note therefore is, as it were, a character or mark by which the Lord's people are known from the world: They have special regard to the word. 'All his saints *are* in thy hand: they sat down at thy feet; *every one* shall receive of thy words.' De. xxxiii. 3. As Christ said, 'I have given them thy words and they have received *them:*' Jn. xvii. 5, 6. Yea, 'and they have kept thy word.'

'Thus did Noah.' Let this then be the discriminating character of the saints from the men of this world. It was so in the days of Noah, when all the world went a whoring from their God, and said, 'We desire not the knowledge of thy ways.' Job xxi. 14. Then Noah kept the words of God. 'Thus did Noah; according to all that God commanded him, so did he.'

CHAP. VII.

Ver. 1. 'And the Lord said unto Noah, Come thou and all thy house into the ark; for thee have I seen righteous before me in this generation.'

The ark being now prepared, and the day of God's patience come to an end, he now is resolved to execute his threatening upon the world of ungodly men; but withal, in the first place, to secure his saints, and them that have feared his name. In this therefore we have a semblance of the last judgment, and how God will dispose of his friends and enemies.

'Come thou into the ark.' God, I say, will take care of, and safely provide for us that have feared him, when he most eminently entereth into judgment with the world: As he also saith by Isaiah the prophet, 'Come, my people, enter thou into thy chambers, and shut thy doors about thee: hide thyself as it were for a little moment, until the indignation be over-past.' xxvi. 20. He shall send forth his angels with a great sound of a trumpet, and they shall gather together his elect from the four winds, from one end of heaven to another.'

'Come thou and all thy house.' Not an hoof must be left behind; God will not lose the very dust of his people: Of all that thou hast given me have I lost nothing, but will raise it up at the last day. Jn. vi. 39. God therefore was careful not only of Noah, but of all that were in his house; because they were all of his visible church, they must therefore be preserved from the rage and fury of the deluge. 'Gather my saints together unto me; (saith he) those that have made a covenant with me by sacrifice.' Ps. l. 5.

'For thee have I seen righteous before me.' This is not to be understood as the meritorious cause, but as the characteristical note that distinguisheth them that are gods, from others that are subjects of his wrath and displeasure: wherefore, those that at this time perished, bear the badge of ungodliness, as that which made them obnoxious to this overflowing judgment: As also we have it in the book of Job, 'Hast thou (said Eliphaz) marked the old way which wicked men have trodden? Which were cut down out of time, whose foundation was overflown with a flood.' Job xxii. 15, 16.

Righteousness therefore, is the distinguishing character whereby the good are known from the bad. Thus it was in Ezekiel's time: 'Set a mark (saith God) upon the foreheads of the men that sigh and that cry for all the abominations that be done in the midst of the city.' Eze. ix. 4. Which mark was to distinguish them from those that were profane, and that for their wickedness were to be destroyed by the ministers of God's justice.

'For thee have I seen righteous before me.' These words, before me, are inserted on purpose to shew us, that Noah was no feigned worshipper, but one who did all things in the sight of God. Indeed, there are two things which are of absolute necessity for the obtaining of this approbation of God. 1. All things must be done as to manner according to the word. 2. All things must be done as to the matter of them also according to the word. Both which were found in Noah's performances; and therefore he is said to be perfect in his generations, and that he walked with God. Thus it was also with Zacharias and Elizabeth, 'they were both righteous before God;' that is, sincere and unfeigned in their obedience. Lu. i. 6.

'Righteous before me in this generation.' By this we see, righteousness, or the truth of God's worship in the world, was now come to a low ebb; the devil, and the children of Cain, had bewitched the church of God, and brought the professors thereof so off from the truth of his way, that had they got Noah also, the church had been quite extinct, and gone: wherefore, it now was time for God to work, and to cherish what was left, even by sending a besom of destruction upon all the face of the earth, to sweep away all the workers of iniquity.

Ver. 2, 3. 'Of every clean beast thou shalt take to thee by sevens, the male and his female: and of beasts that are not clean by two, the male and his female.—Of fowls also of the air by sevens, the male and his female; to keep seed alive upon the face of all the earth.'

Something hath been said to this already; only this I will add further, That by this commandment of God, both Noah, and all that were with him, were pre-admonished to look to their hearts; that they continued unfeigned before him. For if God would save unclean beasts, and fowls, from the present and terrible destruction; why also might not some of them, though they partook of this temporal deliverance, be still reputed as unclean in his sight? As indeed it came to pass; for a cursed Ham was there. Wherefore, read not lightly the commands of God, there may be both doctrine and exhortation; both item,* as well as an obligation to a duty contained therein. Circumcision was a duty incumbent as to the letter of the commandment; but there was also doctrine in it, as to a more high and spiritual teaching than the letter simply imported.

Note then from hence, That when you read that unclean beasts, and unclean birds, may be in the ark of Noah: That unclean men, and unclean women, may be in the church of God: 'One of you is a devil,' was an admonition to all the rest: Let this also of the beasts unclean be an admonition to you.

Ver. 4. 'For yet seven days, and I will cause it to rain upon the earth forty days and forty nights; and every living substance that I have made, will I destroy, (or, blot out) from off the face of the earth.'

Now the judgment is at the door; it is time to make haste, and pack into the ark. God doth not love to have his people have much vacancy from employment while they are in this world. Idle times are dangerous; David found it so in the business of Uriah's wife. Wherefore Noah having finished the ark, he hath another work to do, even to get himself, with his family and household, fitly settled in the vessel that was to save him from the deluge, and that at his peril in seven days' time.

'For yet seven days, and I will bring a flood.' Note again, That it hath been the way of God, even when he doth execute the severest judgments, to tell it in the ears of some of his saints sometime before he doth execute the same: Yea, it seems to me, that it will be so even in the great day of God Almighty; for I read, that before the bridegroom came, there was a cry made, 'Behold the bridegroom cometh!' Mat. xxv. 6. Which cry doth not seem to me, to be the ordinary cry of the ministers of the gospel, but a cry that was effected by some sudden and marvellous awakening, the product of some new and extraordinary revelation. That also seems to look like some fore-word to the church, 'Then shall appear the sign of the Son of man in heaven:' Mat. xxiv. 30. Some strange and unusual revelation of that notable day to be near, which in other ages was not made known to the world; upon which sign he presently appears. Now whether this sign will be the appearing of the angels first; or whether the opening of the

---

* 'Item,' a new article added; a caution or warning.—ED.

heavens, or the voice of the arch-angel, and the trump of God, or what; I shall not here presume to determine ; but a fore-word there is like to be, yet so immediately followed with the personal presence of Christ, that they who had not grace before, shall not have time nor means to get it then: And while they went to buy, the bridegroom came ; and they that were ready went in with him, and the door was shut. Mat. xxv.

' And I will cause it to rain forty days and forty nights.' This length of time doth fore-pronounce the completing of the judgment : As who should say, I will cause it to rain until I have blotted out all the creatures, both of men, beasts, and fowls: and so the after-words import ; ' And every living substance that I have made, will I destroy from off the face of the earth.'

Ver. 5. ' And Noah did according to all that the Lord commanded him.'

This note, as already I have said, doth denote him to be a righteous man ; one that might with honour to his God, escape the judgment now to be executed: wherefore, the reiterating of this character is much for the vindicating of God's justice, and for the justification of his overthrowing the world of ungodly sinners.

But again, these words seem to respect in special, what Noah did in the last seven days, in order to the commandment laid before him in the three first verses of this chapter ; and so they signify his faithfulness to the word, and his observance of the law of his God, even to the day that the rain began to fall upon the earth. And therefore they preach unto us, not only that he began well, but that he continued in godly and unfeigned perseverance ; which when perfected, is the most effectual proof, that what before he did, he did with uprightness of heart, and therefore now must escape the judgment. As it is said in the gospel of Matthew, ' He that shall endure unto the end, the same shall be saved.' Mat. xxiv. 13.

Ver. 6. ' And Noah *was* six hundred years old when the flood of waters was upon the earth.'

Four hundred and fourscore of which the world had leisure to study the prophecy that God gave of him by the mouth of his father Lamech ; Ge. v. 29. the other hundred and twenty he spent in a more open testifying, both by word, and his preparing the ark, that God would one day overtake them with judgment ; yet to the day that the flood came, the world was ignorant thereof. Mat. xxiv. 38, 39. (Astonishing is the fruits of sin:) So it came to pass, that in the six hundredth year of Noah's life, which was the one thousand six hundred fifty sixth year of the world's age, the flood of waters were upon the earth, to the utter destruction of all that was found upon the face thereof, Noah only being left alive, and they that were with him in the ark.

Ver. 7. ' ¶ And Noah went in, and his sons,* and his wife, and his sons' wives with him, into the ark, because of the waters of the flood.'

They had hardly done their work in the world, by that it began to rain, by that the first drops of the judgment appeared. They went into the ark, says the text, because of the waters of the flood. This should teach Christians diligence, lest they be called for by God's dispensations, either of death or judgment, before they have served completely their generations, by the will of God. Noah had done it, but it seems he had but done it ; his work was ended just as the judgment came : ' Be ye also ready ; for in such an hour as ye think not the Son of man cometh.' Mat. xxiv. 44.

Ver. 8, 9. ' Of clean beasts, and of beasts that *are* not clean, and of fowls, and of everything that creepeth upon the earth, there went in two and two unto Noah into the ark, the male and the female, as God had commanded Noah.'

By these words it seems (as I also touched before) that the beasts, and fowls, both clean and unclean, did come in to Noah into the ark ; not by Noah's choice, nor by any instinct that was common to all, but by an instinct from above, which so had determined the life and death of these creatures, even to a very sparrow ; for not one of them doth fall to the ground without the providence of our heavenly Father.

' They went in unto Noah. And let no man deride, for that I said, By an instinct from above ; for God hath not only wrought wonders in men, but even in the beasts, and fowls of the air ; to the making of them act both above and against their own nature. How did Baalam's ass speak ! Nu. xxii. 28—30. And the cows that drew the ark, have it right to the place which God had appointed, not regarding their sucking calves ! 1 Sa. vi. 10—14. Yea, how did those ravenous creatures, the ravens, bring the prophet bread and flesh twice a day, but by immediate instinct from heaven ? 1 Ki. xvii. 6. Even by the same did these go in to Noah, into the ark.

Ver. 10. ' ¶ And it came to pass after seven days, that the waters of the flood were upon the earth.'

Just as the Lord had denounced before : Look therefore, what God hath said, shall assuredly come to pass, whether it be believed, or counted an idle tale. The confirmation therefore of what God hath spoken, depended not upon the credence of man, because it came not by the will of man : ' He hath said it, and shall he not make it good ?' It will therefore assuredly come to pass, whatever God hath spoken, be it to save his Noahs, or be it to drown his enemies ; and the reason is, Because

---

* Every edition, but the first, has left out Noah's sons!! from the ark, while they all put in his sons' wives.—ED.

to do otherwise, is inconsistent with his nature. He is faithful, holy and true, and cannot deny himself, that is, the word which he hath spoken.

Ver. 11. 'In the six hundredth year of Noah's life, in the second month, the seventeenth day of the month, the same day were all the fountains of the great deep broken up, and the windows (or flood-gates) of heaven were opened.'

As to the month, and the day of the month I have but little to say: though doubtless, had not there been something worthy of knowing therein, it would not so punctually have been left upon record; for I dare not say this scribe wrote this in vain, or that it was needless thus to punctilio it; a mystery is in it, but my darkness sees it not; I must speak according to the proportion of faith.

'The same day were all the fountains of the great deep broken up.' By these words, it seems that it did not only rain from heaven, but also the springs and fountains were opened; which together with the great rain of his strength, did overflow the world the sooner.

This great deep, in mine opinion, was also a type of the bottomless pit, that mouth and gulf of hell, which at the day of judgment shall gape upon the world of ungodly men, to swallow them up from the face of the earth, and to carry them away from the face and presence of God.

'And the windows (or flood-gates) of heaven were opened.' That is, that the water might descend without measure or order, even in its own natural force, with violence upon the head of the wicked. It came as water out of his buckets upon them, judgment without mercy. Nu. xxiv. 7.

This opening of the flood-gates of heaven, was a type of the way that shall be made for the justice of God upon ungodly men, when Christ hath laid aside his mediatorship; for he indeed is the sluice that stoppeth this justice of God from its dealing according to its infinite power and severity with men. He stands, like Moses, and, as it were, holdeth the hands of God. Oh! but when he shall be taken away! When he shall have finished his mediatory work: then will the flood-gates of heaven be opened, and then will the justice and holiness of God deal with men without stint or diminution, even till it hath filled the vessels of wrath with vengeance till they run over. 'It is a fearful thing to fall into the hands of the living God.'

Ver. 12. 'And the rain was upon the earth forty days and forty nights.'

That is, It rained so long without stop or stint. ver. 4.

Ver. 13. 'In the self same day entered Noah, and Shem, and Ham, and Japheth, the sons of Noah, and Noah's wife, and the three wives of his sons with them, into the ark.'

This therefore more fully approveth of what I said before; to wit, That they had hardly done their work in the world, by that it began to rain; but so soon as they had done, the flood was upon the earth. Much like this is that of Lot; it was not to rain fire and brimstone upon Sodom, till he was got to Zoar: But when Lot was entered, but just entered, 'Then the Lord rained upon Sodom, and upon Gomorrah, brimstone and fire from the LORD out of heaven.' Ge. xix. 21—24.

Hence note, That the reason why God doth forbear to destroy the world for the wickedness of them that dwell therein, it is for the sake of the elect; because his work upon them is not fully perfected. 'The Lord is not slack concerning his promise;' 2 Pe. iii. 9. no, nor as concerning his threatening neither,—but is long-suffering to us-ward who are the elect; not willing that any of us should perish: But when Christ, head and members, are complete in all things, let the world look for patience and forbearance no longer; for in that self same day the trump of God will sound, and the Lord descend with a shout from heaven, to execute his anger with fury, and his rebukes with flames of fire. Behold, he is now 'ready to judge the quick and the dead!' 1 Pe. iv. 5. 'ready to be revealed in the last time!' 1 Pe. i. 5. The judge also stands at the door; Ja. v. 9. it is but opening therefore, and his hand is upon you, which most assuredly he will do when his body is full and complete.

Observe again, that providence sometimes so ordereth it, that as touching the command of the Lord, necessity is as it were the great wheel that brings men into the performances of them, as here the flood drove them into the ark; as he said above, they went in because of the waters of the flood: So concerning the ordinance of unleavened bread, the first institution of that law, was as it were accompanied with an unavoidable necessity, it was unleavened, saith the text, 'because they were thrust out of Egypt, and could not tarry, neither had they prepared for themselves any victual.' Ex. xii. 39.

It will be thus also at the day of judgment: Israel will be sufficiently weary of this world, they will even as it were unexpressibly groan to be taken up from hence; wherefore the Lord will come, as making use of the weariness and groaning of his people, and will take them up into his chambers of rest, and will wipe away all tears from their eyes, as here Noah and his sons, &c. did enter into the ark.

Ver. 14. 'They, and every beast after his kind, and all the cattle after their kind, and every creeping thing that creepeth upon the earth after his kind, and every fowl after his kind, every bird of every sort' or wing.

Without doubt this careful repetition is not without a cause, and have also in the bowels of it some comfortable doctrine for the church of God; every beast, all cattle, every creeping thing that creepeth; every fowl and bird of every wing.

First this sheweth, that God hath respect to the fulfilling of his word in the midst of all his zeal and anger against sin. Ge. xix. He doth not as we, being angry, run headlong upon the offenders, but if there be but three in a kingdom, or one in four cities, he will have respect to them. Eze. xiv. 19, 20.

Secondly, It sheweth that, how inconsiderable soever the persons are, that are within the compass, and care of the love and mercy of God, that inconsiderableness shall not be a let to their safety and preservation: Yea, though they are but as these creeping things, that creep upon the earth, or as the saying is, but as a flea, a dead dog, or a grasshopper, or one of the least of the grains of wheat, not one of them, nay, not a hair of the head of them shall fall to the ground and perish.

Ver. 15, 16. 'And they went in unto Noah into the ark, two and two of all flesh, wherein is the breath of life. And they that went in, went in male and female of all flesh, as God had commanded him: and the Lord shut him in.'

The Holy Ghost in this relation is wonderfully punctual and exact: every beast, all cattle, every creeping thing, every fowl, and every bird, after their kind went in; and saith he again, they that went in, went in two and two; as if there had been an intelligence among these irrational creatures, that the flood was shortly to be upon the earth. Indeed, many among the sensitives have strange instincts, as appendixes to their nature, by which they do, and leave to do, to the astonishment of them that have reason: But that any instinct in nature should put them upon afore providing for shelter from the flood, by going into the ark, (a place to secure them, rather than to save them, had not the occasion and command of God been otherwise) it cannot be once with reason imagined. Wherefore, as their going into the ark, so their going in two by two, and that too male and female, plainly declares that their motion was ordered and governed by heaven, themselves being utterly ignorant thereof.

' And they that went in went in male and female of all flesh, (both man and beast) and the Lord shut him in,' that is Noah; and those that were with him.

These latter words are of great importance, and do shew us the distinguishing grace of God, for by his thus shutting the door of the ark, he not only confirmed his mercy to Noah, but also discovered the bounds and limits thereof. As who should say, Now Noah you have your full tale, just thus many I will save from the flood: and with that he shut the door leaving all other, both man

and beast, &c. to the fury of the waters. God therefore by this act hath shewed how it will go in the day of judgment with men. Those that (like those beasts, and birds, and creeping things) shall come to Christ, into his ark, before it rain fire and brimstone from heaven, those will God shut up in the ark, and they shall live in that day; but those that shall then be found in the world strangers to Jesus Christ, those will God shut out: ' They that were ready went in with him to the marriage: and the door was shut.' Mat. xxv. 10.

And observe, it is not said, that Noah shut the door, but the Lord shut him in: If God shuts in or out, who can alter it? I shut, and no man openeth. Re. iii. 7. Doubtless before the flood had carried off the ark, others besides would with gladness have had there a lodging room, though no better than a dog-kennel; but now it was too late, the Lord had shut the door. Besides, had there been now in the heart of Noah, bowels or compassion to those without the ark, or had he had desire to have received them to him, all had been worth nothing, the Lord had shut him in. This signifying, that at the day of judgment, neither the bowels of Jesus Christ, neither the misery that damned men shall be in, will anything at all avail with God to save one sinner more, ' the door is shut.'

Where you read therefore both in Matthew and Luke of the shutting of the door, understand that by such expressions Christ alludeth to the door in Noah's ark, which door was open while Noah and his attendants were entering into the ark, but they being got in, the Lord shut the door. Then they that stood without and knocked, did weep, and knock, and ask too late. As Christ saith, ' When once the master of the house is risen up, and hath shut to the door, and ye begin to stand without, and to knock at the door, saying, Lord, Lord, open unto us; and he shall answer and say unto you, I know you not whence ye are: Then shall ye begin to say, We have eaten and drunk in thy presence, and thou hast taught in our streets, (as Noah did of old.) But he shall say, I tell you, I know you not whence ye are; depart from me, all ye workers of iniquity. There shall be weeping and gnashing of teeth, when ye shall see Abraham, and Isaac and Jacob, and all the prophets, in the kingdom of God, and you yourselves thrust out.' Lu. xiii. 25—28.

Ver. 17. ' ¶ And the flood was forty days upon the earth, and the waters increased, and bare up the ark, and it was lift up above the earth.'

While the ark rested, and abode in his place, no doubt but the ears of Noah were filled with doleful cries from the wretched and miserable people, whom God had shut without the ark, one while crying, another while knocking, according to what but now was related; which for ought I know might be many of the forty days, but when the waters much increased, and lift up the ark above the earth, this miserable company were soon shaken off.*

It will be thus also in the day of judgment; at the beginning of that day the ears of the godly will sufficiently be filled with the cries and tears of the damned and miserable world; but when the ark shall be taken up, that is, when the godly shall ascend into the clouds, and so go hence with Jesus, they will soon lose this company, and be out of the hearing of their lamentable dolours.

'And the waters increased.' God's judgments have no ears to receive the cries, nor heart to pity the miseries of the damned. They cry, it rains; they increase their cries, and the Lord does increase his judgment. 'And it came to pass, *that* as he cried, and they would not hear; so they cried, and I would not hear, saith the Lord of hosts.' Zec. vii. 13.

Again, As the waters were a type of the wrath of God that in the day of judgment shall fall upon ungodly men: So they were also a type of those afflictions and persecutions that attend the church; for that very water that did drown the ungodly, that did also toss and tumble the ark about; wherefore by the increase of the waters, we may also understand, how mighty and numerous sometimes the afflictions and afflictors of the godly be: As David said, 'Lord, how are they increased that trouble me? many *are* they that rise up against me.' Ps. iii. 1.

'And the waters increased, and bare up the ark.' The higher the rage and tyranny of this world groweth against the church of God, the higher is the ark lifted up towards heaven, the most proud wave lifts it highest: The church is also by persecution more purged and purified from earthly and carnal delights; therefore it is added, 'the waters bare up the ark, and it was lift up above the earth.'

Ver. 18. 'And the waters prevailed, and were increased greatly upon the earth; and the ark went upon the face of the waters.'†

These words are still to be considered under the former double consideration, to wit, both, as they present us with God's wrath at the last judgment, and as they present us with a sign of the rage and malice of ungodly men.

'And the waters prevailed;' that is, over all ungodly sinners; though they were mighty, and stout, and cared for none, yet the waters prevailed against them, as the fire and brimstone will do over all the world at the day and coming of our Lord Jesus Christ. Wherefore, well may it be said to all impenitent sinners, 'Can thy heart endure, or can thy hands be strong, in the days that I shall deal with thee,' Eze. xxii. 14. saith the Lord God? Oh they cannot, the waters of the wrath of God will prevail against, and increase upon them, until they have utterly swallowed them up.

'And the waters prevailed.' Take it now as a type of the nature of persecution, and then it sheweth, that as the waters here did swallow up all but the ark, so when persecution is mighty in the world, it prevaileth to swallow up all but the church; for none else can aright withstand or oppose their wickedness. It is said, when the beast had power to work, 'the whole world wondered after the beast,' Re. xiii. 3. and all men who were not sealed, and that had not the mark of God in their foreheads, fell in with the worship of the beast; as it is said, 'And all that dwell upon the earth shall worship him, whose names are not written in the book of life of the Lamb,' &c. ver. 8. So then it might well be said, 'The waters prevailed and increased.'

'And the ark went upon the face of the waters.' It is said that in the beginning the Spirit of God moved upon the face of the waters, and here that the ark went upon the face of them. Indeed the Spirit of God moveth, and the church, as God, walketh in strange and unthought of stations. It is said, that God hath 'a way in the whirlwind, and in the storm.' Na. i. 3. So he hath upon the very face of the persecution of the day, but none but the church can follow him here; it is the ark that can follow him upon the face of the waters. Deep things are seen by them that are upon the waters: 'They that go down to the sea in ships, that do business in great waters; They see the works of the Lord, and his wonders in the deep.' Ps. cvii. 23, 24. Indeed it oft falls out, that the church seeth more of God in affliction, than when she is at rest and ease; when she is tumbled to and fro in the waters, then she sees the works of God, and his wonders in the deep.

And this makes persecution so pleasant a thing, this makes the ark go upon the face of the waters, she seeth more in this her state, than in all the treasures of Egypt. He. xi. 24, 25.

Ver. 19. 'And the waters prevailed exceedingly upon the earth; and all the high hills, that *were* under the whole heaven, were covered.'

This second repetition of the prevailing of the waters, doth also call for a second consideration.

1. It shews us, that all hope that any ungodly man might have at the beginning of the flood to

---

* They perish in sight of a place of security which they cannot reach; they perish with the bitter remorse of having despised and rejected the means of escape, like the rich man in hell, whose torment was grievously augmented by the sight of Lazarus, afar off, in the bosom of Abraham.—ED.

† Calmet says, 'Apres que l'Arche eut fait le tour du monde pendant l'espace de six mois.'—*Supplement to Dictionary.* He gives no authority for this improbable notion.—ED.

escape the rage thereof, was now swallowed up in death. Indeed it is natural to the creatures, when floods and inundations are upon the earth, to repair to the high places, as they only that are left for preservation of life; where life may be also continued if the waters do not overflow them: but when it comes to pass as here we read, that all the hills under the heavens are covered: then life takes its farewell, and is gone from the world, as was the effect of the waters of Noah.

The hills therefore were types of the hope of the hypocrite, upon which they clamber till their heads do touch the clouds, thinking thereby to escape the judgment of God; but 'though they hide themselves in the top of Carmel, I will search and take them out thence,' saith God. Am. ix. 2, 3. The flood of his wrath will come thither, even over the tops of all the hills. So that safety is only in the ark with Noah, in the church with Christ, all other places must be drowned with the flood.

2. We may also understand by this verse, how God in a time of persecution will cut off the carnal confidence of his people. We are apt to place our hope somewhere else than in God, when persecution ariseth because of the word. We hope that such a man, or that such outward means may prevent our being swept away with this flood. But because this confidence is not after God, but tendeth to weaken our stedfast dependence on him; therefore this flood shall cover all our hills, not one shall be found for us under the whole heaven. Je. ii. 36, 37. When the king of Babylon came up against Jerusalem to war, then Israel, instead of trusting in God, put their confidence in the king of Egypt, but he also was swallowed up by this flood, that Israel might be ashamed of such confidence; and this at last they confessed. 'As for us, [said they,] our eyes as yet failed for our vain help: in our watching, we have watched for a nation *that* could not save *us*.' La. iv. 17.

It was requisite therefore that the hills should be covered, that Noah might not have confidence in them; but surely this dispensation of God was an heart-shaking providence to Noah, and they that were with him; for here indeed was his faith tried, there was no hill left in all the world; now were his carnal helpers gone, there was none shut up or left: Now therefore, if they could rejoice, it must be only in the power of God. As David said, 'Shall I lift up mine eyes to the hills? whence should my help come?' So the margin: 'My help *cometh* from the Lord that made heaven and earth.' Ps. cxxi. 1, 2.

Ver. 20. 'Fifteen cubits upward did the waters prevail; and the mountains were covered.' The height of Goliath was but six cubits and a span, 1 Sa. xvii. 4. neither was Og's bedstead any more than nine. De. iii. 11. Wherefore this flood prevailed far

the highest of those mighty ones: even fifteen cubits above the highest mountains.

Ver. 21, 22, 23. '¶ And all flesh died that moved upon the earth, both of fowl, and of cattle, and of beast, and of every creeping thing that creepeth upon the earth, and every man: All in whose nostrils *was* the breath of life, of all that *was* in the dry *land*, died. And every living substance was destroyed, which was upon the face of the ground, both man, and cattle, and the creeping things, and the fowls of the heaven; and they were destroyed from the earth, and Noah only remained *alive*, and they that *were* with him in the ark.'

In these words you have the effects of the flood, which was punctually according to the judgment threatened. But observe, I pray you, how the Holy Ghost, by repeating, doth amplify the matter. 'All flesh,' 'All in whose nostrils *was* the breath of life;' 'All that *was* in the dry *land*,' 'every living substance,' 'every man;' and they were destroyed from off the earth: By which manner of language doubtless there is insinuated a threatening to them who should afterward live ungodly. And indeed the Holy Ghost affirmeth, that these judgments, with that of Sodom, are but examples set forth before our eyes, to shew us that such sins, such punishment. 'Making *them* an ensample, saith Peter, unto those that after should live ungodly.' 2 Pe. ii. 6. Nay, Jude saith, they are 'set forth' in their overthrow, for that very purpose. ver. 7. Wherefore this careful repeating of this judgment of God, doth carry threatening in it, assuredly foreshewing the doom and downfal of those that shall continue to tread their steps.

Yea, mind how Peter hath it: For if God 'spared not the old world,' &c. 2 Pe. ii. 5. Secretly intimating, that those that then lived, being the first of his workmanship, and far surpassing in magnificence, if he would have spared, he would have spared them; but seeing he so dreadfully swept them away, let no man be so bold to presume that wickedness shall now deliver him that is given to it.

'And Noah only remained *alive*, and they that *were* with him in the ark.' Noah was that man of God that had set himself against a world of ungodly men. The man that had hazarded life and limb for the word of God committed to him; he 'only remained *alive*,' &c. Hence note, That he was the man that outlived the world, that would for God venture life against all the world. Wherefore the saying in the gospel is true, He that will lose his life for my sake, shall save it unto life eternal. Thus did Noah, and passed the end, and went over the bounds, that God had appointed for every living thing. Behold! he was a man in both worlds, yea, the world then to come was given him for a possession.

' ¶ And the waters prevailed upon the earth an hundred and fifty days.' About the same time the scorpions mentioned of John, had power to hurt the earth. Re. ix. 10. Wherefore, the thus prevailing of the water, might be a type of our persecution now in the New Testament days. All which time doubtless Noah was sufficiently tried, while the waves of the water had no pity for him.

CHAP. VIII.

Ver. 1. 'And God remembered Noah, and every living thing, and all the cattle that *was* with him in the ark; and God made a wind to pass over the earth, and the waters asswaged.'

Moses having thus related the judgment of the waters, as they respected the drowning of the world, and so typed forth the last judgment: he now returneth to speak of them more largely, as they were a type of the persecution and afflictions of the church, and so sheweth how God delivered Noah from the merciless violence of the waves thereof.

'And God remembered Noah.' This word remembered is usual in scripture; both when God is about to deliver his people out of affliction, and to grant them the petition which they ask of him. It is said, ' God remembered Abraham; and sent Lot out of Sodom;' Ge. xix. 29. that he remembered Rachel, and hearkened to her; xxx. 22. that he also remembered his covenant with Abraham, when he went to bring Israel out of their bondage. Ex. ii. 24.

Hence note, that Noah was now both in an afflicted and a praying condition; afflicted with the dread of the waters, and prayed for their asswaging. It is a question accompanied with astonishment, How the ark being of no bigger an hull or bulk should contain so many creatures, with sustenance for them? And verily, I think, that Noah himself was put to it, to believe and wait for so long a time. But God remembered him, and also the beasts, and every living thing that was with him, and began to put an end to these mighty afflictions, by causing the waters to assuage.

'And God made a wind to pass over the earth.' The waters being here a type of persecutors and persecution: this wind was a type of the breath of the Lord's mouth, by which he is said to slay the wicked. ' He shall smite the earth with the rod of his mouth, and with the breath of his lips shall he slay the wicked.' Is. xi. 4. It was a wind also that blew away the locusts of Egypt, Ex. x. 19. which locusts were a type of our graceless clergy, that have covered the ground of our land.* Again

the kingdom of Babel was to be destroyed by a destroying wind, which the Lord would send against her, Je. li. 1, 2. which Paul expounds to be by the breath of the Lord's mouth, and by the brightness of his coming. This wind therefore, as I said, was a type of the breathing of the Spirit of the Lord, by which means these tumultuous waves shall be laid lower, and God's ark in a while made to rest upon the top of his mountain. 2 Sa. xxii. 19. For by the breath of the Lord the earth is lightened, and by this lightning coals are kindled; ' yea, he sent out his arrows and scattered them, and he shot out lightnings, and discomfited them. Then the channels of waters were seen, and the foundations of the world were discovered at thy rebuke, O Lord, at the blast of the breath of thy nostrils.' Ps. xviii. 14, 15. 'And God made a wind to pass over the earth, and the waters asswaged.' That is, in New Testament language, the afflictors and afflictions of the church did cease and decay, and came to nought.

'And the waters asswaged:' To wit, by the blowing of this wind, wherefore, as this wind did assault the waters, so it did refresh the spirit of this servant of God, because by it the affliction was driven away. Thus then by the wind of the Lord were these dry bones refreshed, and made to stand upon their feet. Eze. xxxvii. 9, 10.

'And God made a wind to pass over.' And God made it; when God blows, the enemies of his truth shall pass away like waters that fail.

Ver. 2. 'The fountains also of the deep and the windows of heaven were stopped, and the rain from heaven was restrained.'

By these words we see, that when the church of God is afflicted, both heaven and hell have their hand therein, but so as from a differing consideration, and to a diverse end. From heaven it comes, that we may remember we have sinned, and that we may be made white, and tried; Da. xi. 35. but from hell, from the great deep, that we might sin the more, and that we might despair, and be damned. Job i. 11; ii. 5.

'And the fountains of the great deep.' When God begins to slack and abate the afflictions of his church, he rebukes, as it were first, the powers of hell; for should he take off his own hand, while they have leave to do what they list, the church for this would be worse not better: But first he rebuketh them: 'The Lord rebuke thee, O Satan,' that's the first; and then he clothes them ' with change of raiment:' Zec. iii. 1—5. The fountains of the great deep were stopped, and then the bottles of heaven. Ge. xv. 14.

'And the rain from heaven was restrained, or

---

* ' A graceless clergy'!! So numerous as to cover the ground of our land!! How awful a fact—taking the name of God on polluted lips, and professing to teach what they do not comprehend. Men in a state of rebellion against heaven,

calling upon others to submit to God's gospel. Solemn hypocrites, fearful will be your end.—ED.

held back, or made to cease. Afflictions are governed by God, both as to time, number, nature and measure. 'In measure when it shooteth forth, thou wilt debate with it: he stayeth his rough wind in the day of his east wind.' Is. xxvii. 8. Our times therefore, and our conditions in those times, are in the hand of God; yea, and so are our souls and bodies, to be kept and preserved from the evil, while the rod of God is upon us. Je. xv. 1–3.

Ver. 3. 'And the waters returned from off the earth continually: and after the end of the hundred and fifty days the waters were abated.'

The verse before doth treat of the original, the fountains of the deep, and the windows of heaven, that they were shut, or stopped; which being done, the effect beginneth to cease. Hence note, that ease and release from persecution and affliction cometh not by chance, or by the good moods, or gentle dispositions of men, but the Lord doth hold them back from sin, the Lord restraineth them. It is said 'the Lord stirred up the adversaries of Solomon.' 1 Ki. xi. 14, 23. Again, when the Syrians fought against Jehoshaphat, 'the Lord helped him, and God moved them *to depart* from him.' 2 Ch. xviii. 31. The Lord sent the flood, and the Lord took it away.

'And the waters returned from off the earth continually.' When God ceaseth to be angry, the hearts and dispositions of the adversaries shall be palliated, and made more flexible. It is said, when the afflictions of Israel were ended in Egypt, the hearts of the people were turned to pity them; yea, he caused them 'to be pitied of all those that carried them captives.' Ps. cvi. 46.

When you see therefore, that the hearts of kings and governors begin to be moderated toward the church of God, then acknowledge that this is the hand of God. 'I,' saith he, 'will cause the enemy to entreat thee *well* in the time of evil, and in the time of affliction.' Je. xv. 11. For by waters here are typed out the great and mighty of the world, by the flowing of them, their rage; and by their ebbing and returning their stillness and moderation.

'And the waters returned.' That is, to the sea. Ge. i. 9, 10. 'He gathereth the waters of the sea together as an heap: he layeth up the depth in store houses.' Ps. xxxiii. 7.

By 'gathering up,' the persecutors may be understood, his gathering them to their graves, as he did Herod, who stood in the way of Christ. Mat. ii. 19, 20. And as he did those in Ezekiel, who hindered the promotion of truth, and the exaltation of the gospel. xxxi. 14.

'And after the end of the hundred and fifty days the waters were abated.' These words then imply, that for so long time, Noah, and the

church with him, were to exercise patience. They also show us, That when the waters are up, they do not suddenly fall: They were up four hundred years, from Abraham to Moses. Ge. xv. 13. They were up threescore and ten years in the days of the captivity of Babylon; Je. xxv. 12. and Ze. i. 12. They were up ten mystical days in the persecution that was in the days of Antipas. Re. ii. 10. And are to be up forty and two months, in the reign, and under the tyranny of antichrist. xiii. 5. But they will abate; the house of Saul will grow weaker; yea, they shall be gathered to their sea, and shall be laid in the pit; yea, they shall not be on the earth, when God shall set glory in the land of the living. Eze. xxvi. 19—21.

Ver. 4. ¶ 'And the ark rested in the seventh month, on the seventeenth day of the month, upon the mountains of Ararat.'

These instances therefore were a type of Christ, the munition of rocks, Is. xxxiii. 16. who is elsewhere called, the mountain of the Lord's house; Mi. iv. 1. the rock upon which he will build his church, and the gates of hell shall not prevail against it. Mat. xvi. 18. For after the ark had felt the ground, or had got settlement upon the tops of these mountains; however, the waters that came from the great deep, did notwithstanding, for some time, shake, and make it stir, yet off from these mountains they could not get it with all their rage and fury. It rested there; these gates of hell could not prevail. But mark, it did rest on these mountains almost a quarter of a year, before any ground appeared to Noah. A right figure of saving faith; for that maketh not outward observation a ground and foundation for faith, but Christ the rock, who as to sense and feeling is at first quite out of sight. Hence the hope of the godly is compared to the anchor of a ship, which resteth on, or taketh hold of the rock that is now invisible under the water, at the bottom of the sea. He. vi. 19.

This then should learn us to stay on the Lord Jesus, and there to rest when the waters have drowned all the world, and when all the mountains and hills for help are as if they were cast into the midst of the sea.

That is an excellent saying of the prophet, 'God *is* our refuge and strength, a very present help in trouble. Therefore will not we fear, though the earth be removed, (as now it seemed) and though the mountains be carried into the midst of the sea; *Though* the waters thereof roar *and* be troubled; *though* the mountains shake with the swelling thereof. Selah.' Ps. xlvi. 1—3.

Ver. 5. 'And the waters decreased continually until the tenth month: in the tenth *month*, on the first *day* of the month, were the tops of the mountains seen.'

In the third verse we read, that after an hundred and fifty days' flood, the waters returned; that is, began to return, from off the earth: Which beginning of their return, was, because that God had mercifully remembered the prayer and affliction of Noah. Again, in this verse we read, that from the day that the ark did rest upon the mountains of Ararat, the waters decreased continually. Now the resting of the ark on the mountain, was a figure of our trusting on Christ. Hence it follows, that the tumults and raging of the mystical waters, are made to decrease by the power of faith: 'This is the victory, *even* our faith.' 1 Jn. v. 4. As it is also said of Moses, 'By faith they passed through the Red sea.' He. xi. 29. But above all take that as most pertinent, 'Through faith they subdued kingdoms, - stopped the mouths of lions, - and turned to flight the armies of aliens.' He. xi. 33, 34. Here you see faith made the waters decrease; it took away the heat and rage of the adversary.

'And the waters decreased continually until the tenth month, (another period of time,) and in the first day of the tenth month were the tops of the mountains.' These mountains were before the flood, a type of the hope of the hypocrites, and therefore then were swallowed up, fifteen cubits under the waters. But now, methinks, they should be a figure to the church of some visible ground of deliverance from the flood; for almost three months the ark did rest on the invisible mountains of Ararat. But now are the tops of the mountains seen: A further sign that the waters were abated; and a ground, that at length they would be quite dried up. Let these mountains then be types of the high and mighty, which God is used to stir up to deliver his church from the heat and rage of tyranny and persecution, as they are often termed and called in scripture, the mountains of Israel, for this very end. So then, from our thus considering the mountains, Two things we are taught thereby.

1. That when the great ones of this world begin to discover themselves to the church, by way of encouragement, it is a sign that the waters are now decreasing. Or thus: When God lets us see the tops of the mountains, then we may certainly conclude, that the rage of the waters abate.

Doubtless when God made promise of raising up Josias to Israel, in Canaan; 1 Ki. xiii. 1—3. and of raising up for them Cyrus, in Babylon. Is. xlv. and Eze. i. 1—3. The thus appearing of the tops of these mountains, was comfort to the church in her day of affliction.

2. This should teach us while we are in affliction, to look this way and that, if it may be that the tops of the mountains may be seen by us. 1 Sa. xi. 1—3. For though it be too much below a Christian to place his confidence in men, yet when God shall raise up Josias or a Cyrus, we may take

encouragement at this working of God. Therefore is that in the Psalms read both ways, shall I look to the mountains? 'I will lift up mine eyes unto the hills, from whence cometh my help. Yet so, as that he would also conclude his help did come from the Lord.' Ps. cxxi. 1, 2. So then, we must take heed that we look not to the mountains [alone]. Again, it is our wisdom 'to look to the mountains:' only look not to them but when God discovers them. Look unto them if God discovereth them; yet then but so as means of God's appointing. But again, God doth not let us see the hills for our help, before we have first of all seen them drowned. Look not to them therefore while the water is at the rising; but if they begin to cease their raging, if they begin to fall, and with that the tops of the mountains be seen, you may look upon them with comfort, they are tokens of God's deliverance.

Ver. 6. '¶ And it came to pass at the end of forty days, that Noah opened the window of the ark which he had made.'

These forty days seem to commence from the discovery of the tops of the mountains. Wherefore he did not presently go out of the ark, but staid there above fourteen days still, signifying unto us, that we must not be therefore delivered so soon as the tops of the mountains are seen, but may yet be assaulted with the waters of the flood, days, and weeks, and months, &c.

When Moses was sent to deliver Israel, they came not presently out of Egypt; neither seemed their burthens ever the lighter to sense or feeling, though faith indeed did see the end. Ex. v. 15—23. Again, When he had brought them forth of Egypt, they came not in a day, or a month, to Canaan; but, saith the Holy Ghost, 'He brought them out, (or, forth of affliction) after that he had showed wonders and signs in the land of Egypt, and in the Red sea, and in the wilderness forty years.

Let us therefore take heed of a feverish spirit, while we behold 'the tops of the mountains;' possibly, for all they are visible tokens to us of deliverance, themselves may be yet much under water. We see what work Moses, Gideon, Jephthah and Samson had to deliver Israel, even after more than their tops were seen. Be content to stay yet forty days. David stayed, after he was anointed, till years and times went over him, before he could deliver Israel from the tyranny of its opposers.

'At the end of forty days Noah opened the window of the ark.' This opening of the window also, was a type, that now he was preparing to take possession of the world. It also might be a type of the opening the law and testimony, that light might by that come into the church; for we find not that this window had any other use, but to be a conveyance of light into the ark, and as a passage for the raven and the dove, as may be further showed after.   Now much like this, is that of John: 'The temple of God was opened in heaven, and there was seen in his temple the ark of his testament.' Re. xi. 19.   And again, 'I looked, and, behold, the temple of the tabernacle of the testimony in heaven was opened.'   And then, as the raven, and the dove came out of the window of the ark; so 'the angels,' that is, the Lord's executioners, 'came out of the temple' that was opened in heaven. Re. xv. 5, 6.

Hence note, That though men may be borne with, if they lie in their holes in the heighth of the tempest; but to do it when the tops of the mountains were seen, if they then shall forbear to open their window, they are worthy of blame indeed. When the lepers saw the Assyrians were fled, and that liberty from heaven was granted to Samaria, then they feared to conceal the thing any further; They feared, I say, that if they went not to the city to declare it, some judgment of God would befal them. 2 Ki. vii. 9.

Ver. 7, 8. 'And he sent forth a raven, which went forth to and fro, until the waters were dried up from off the earth.   Also he sent forth a dove from him, to see if the waters were abated from off the face of the ground.'

Behold, the raven and dove are now sent out at the window of the ark, as the angels are said to come out of the temple, when it was opened in heaven.   This raven therefore, and the dove, were figures and types of those angels. Re. xv. 5, 6.

But to speak to them both apart.   The raven went forth, but returned not again to the ark. This is intimated by these words, 'She went to and fro, until the waters were abated, and dried up.' This is further evident by that antithesis that the word doth put between the practice of the raven and the dove.   The raven went forth, and went to and fro till the waters were dried up.   But mark it, 'But the dove found no rest for the sole of her foot, and she returned unto him into the ark.' ver. 9.   The raven then did find rest elsewhere, the raven then returned not to him into the ark.

But what did the raven then do?   Why, certainly she made a banquet of the carcases of the giants that were drowned by the flood; it fed upon the flesh of the men that had sinned against the Lord.

The raven therefore was a type of those messengers that God sends out of his temple against Antichrist; that is, for 'eating the flesh of kings, and the flesh of captains, and the flesh of mighty men, and the flesh of horses.'   He was, I say, a type of those professors that God saith he hath a great sacrifice to sacrifice unto, a sort of professors in his church; as the raven was one that had his being in the ark: These are they which Ezekiel mentions, that were to eat flesh, and drink blood;

to eat the fat till they be filled, and to drink blood till they be drunken. xxxix. 17—20.   These also are the guests that Zephaniah mentions, and saith, God hath bidden to the same feast also. i. 7—14.

And let no man be offended that I say these birds are in the church: For one effect of the sixth vial, was that battle of the great day of God Almighty. Re. xvi. 16.   Further, The angel that proclaims this feast, calls to those that are God's guests, by the name of, 'the fowls that fly in the midst of heaven:' That they should 'come and gather together to the supper of the great God: That they may eat the flesh of kings, and the flesh of captains, and the flesh of mighty men,' &c. Re. xix. 17, 18.   Besides, this supper is the effect of the going forth of the King of kings against the Antichristian whore, whose going forth was at the opening of heaven, as the going forth of the raven was at the opening of the window of the ark. ver. 11—16.

Note therefore, That God, in the overthrow of the kingdom of Antichrist, and at the asswaging of the rage of her tumultuous waves, will send forth his birds amongst her fat ones, to partake of the banquet that he hath appointed; who when they shall be tolerated by that angel that standeth in the sun, will come down to their feast Beware of with such greediness, that neither king Noah's raven. nor captain shall keep them from their prey: They will eat flesh, and fat, till they be full, and drink the blood till they be drunk.

'Also he sent forth a dove from him, to see if the waters were abated.'   This dove was a type of another sort of professors in the church, that are of a more gentle nature; Mat. x. 16. for all the saints are not for such work as the raven; they are not all for feeding upon the carcases, the kingdoms and estates of the Antichristian party, but are for spending their time, and for bending their spirits to a more spiritual and retired work; even as the dove is said to be harmless, and to mourn for communion with her companion, Is. xxxvii. 14. and that is content if she hath her nest in the sides of the rock, Christ. Je. xlviii. 28.   Wherefore he adds,

Ver. 9. 'But the dove found no rest for the sole of her foot, and she returned unto him into the ark, for the waters were on the face of the whole earth.' &c.

The dove could not live as the raven; the raven being content, so long as she found the carcases; but the dove found no rest till she returned again to Noah.

The raven therefore, though he was in the ark, was not a type of the most spiritual Christian; nay rather, I think, of the worldly professor, who gets into the church in the time of her affliction, as Ziba did into the army of David, in the day of his trouble; not for love to the grace of David, but that, if time should serve, he might be made the Lord of his master's inheritance. 2 Sa. xvi. 1—4. But David was content to let him go with him, and that too as under such a consideration: as Christ also lets these ravens to herd with his innocent doves; because he hath flesh to give them, which the doves care not for eating.*

'But the dove found no rest.' It seems the raven did, as it is also with some professors, who when they by their profession have advanced themselves to some worldly honour, they have ease and rest, though, like the raven, they have it by going out of the church.

'But the dove found no rest.' Though all the enemies of God lay tumbling in the sea, this could not satisfy a gracious soul: divide her from the ark, and she finds no rest, she is not at ease till she be with Noah.

'And she returned unto him into the ark; - and he put forth his hand, and took her, and pulled her in unto him into the ark.' ver. 9.

Noah here was a type of Christ, who took the dove unto him: And it shows us, That Christ hath a bosom open for the cries and complaints of his people; for the dove returned a-weary with the tidings of this, that the waters still raged. A fit figure of those of the saints that are groaning and weary under the oppression and cruelty of the enemy.

Hence note, That though thou hast no other tidings to Christ but sighs and groans, and weariness, because of the rage of the waters; yet he will not despise thee; yea, he invites thee, as weary, to come. Mat. xi. 28—30.

Ver. 10. 'And he stayed yet other seven days; and again he sent forth the dove out of the ark.'

This staying shows us, That he exercised patience, waiting God's leisure till the flood should be taken away. This grace therefore had yet seven day's work to do, before he obtained any further testimony that the waters were decreasing. O this staying work is hard work! Alas! sometimes patience is accompanied with so much heat and feverishness, that every hour seems seven until the end of the trial, and the blessing promised be possessed by the waiting soul. It may be Noah might not be altogether herein a stranger: I am sure the Psalmist was not, in that he often under affliction, cries, But how long, O Lord! for ever! Ps. vi. 3; lxxix. 5; xiii. 1; lxxiv. 1; lxxxix. 46. Make haste! O Lord, how long! xc. 13; xciv. 3.

'And again he sent forth the dove.' The first time he sent her, she brought no good news, but came panting and weary home; yet he sends her a second time.

This should teach us, not to make conclusions too suddenly about God's dispensation, saying it must be now or never; for it may be the seven days are not out. The men of David said, This is the day that the Lord will give thee the kingdom of Israel: But David perceived otherwise, and therefore adds yet to his temperance, patience. 1 Sa. xxiv. 1—4; xxvi. 8—10. Not sullenly saying like that wicked king, Why should I wait on the Lord any longer? 2 Ki. vi. 32. But comforts himself with the truth of the promise, saying, His time shall come to die, &c. He that believeth, maketh not haste, but waiteth patiently, for the perfecting God's work in God's time. That is excellent in the song: 'I charge you (saith the church) that ye stir not up, nor awake my love, until he please.' Ca. viii. 4. Noah was much for this, wherefore he stayed yet other seven days.

'And again he sent forth the dove.' Elias did much like this, when his servant, at the first sending, brought him no tidings of rain, he gave him his errand again, saying, Go again: go seven times. 1 Ki. xviii. 43—45. As Noah here did with the dove, and again he sent her. Seeming delays are no hindrance to faith; they ought to try it, and put it into exercise: As here it was with this good man about the waters of the flood; he fainted not, but believed to see the goodness of the Lord. That in the prophet is notable as to this, 'The vision is yet for an appointed time, but at the end it shall speak, and not lie: though it tarry, wait for it; because it will surely come, it will not tarry.' Hab. ii. 3.

Ver. 11. 'And the dove came in to him in the evening; and lo! in her mouth was an olive-leaf plucked off: so Noah knew that the waters were abated from off the earth.'

'And the dove came in to him in the evening.' Wherefore his patience was tried this day also. All the day he heard nothing of his dove. Surely she could not keep the wing all the day. Is she drowned I tro? Is she lost? O, no! She comes at last, though she stayed long. Samuel also stayed long before he came to Saul; but Saul could not wait as Noah did, therefore he had not the benefit of the mercy promised.

'The dove came in to him in the evening, and lo, in her mouth was an olive-leaf,' &c. Now he is recompensed for the exercise of patience: As also was Abraham when God gave him Issac; for after he had patiently endured, he obtained the promise.

'And lo, an olive-leaf.' A sign that God was going through with his work of diminishing the waters: A sign, I say, and a good experience of the continued love of God to his servant; according

---

* This should prompt every professing Christian to self-examination—Am I of the raven class, or that of the dove? May my heart, while trembling at the thought that there are ravens in the church, appeal to the heart-searching God, 'Lord, is it I?'—Ed.

to that of Paul, 'patience worketh experience;' that is, it at last obtaineth the blessing promised, and so settleth the soul in a fresh experience of the love and faithfulness of God.

And lo! This word Lo, it is, as it were an appeal to all readers to judge, whether God to Noah was faithful or no. So then, this was not written for his sake only, but for us also that believe in God, that we might now exercise patience, as Noah; and obtain the tokens of God's goodness, as he; for lo the dove, at last, though 'twas night first, came to Noah into the ark, 'and lo in her mouth *was* an olive-leaf plucked off: so Noah knew that the waters were abated.'

'An olive-leaf plucked off.' These words, an olive-leaf plucked off, do intimate, that Noah was now inquisitive and searching how the dove obtained the leaf; that is, whether she found it as dead, and upon the waters; or whether she plucked it off some tree: But he found by the greenness and freshness of the slip, that she plucked it off from the olive. Wherefore, he had good ground now to be comforted; for if this leaf was plucked off from a tree, then the waters could not be deep; especially, because as the story tells us, the olive used also to stand in the bottoms, or valleys.

This should teach us, That not over highly we conclude messages or tokens, to be signs of God's mercy. There are lying visions, and they are causes of banishment; they we should beware of, or else we are not only at present deceived, but our faith is in danger of the rocks; for not a few have cast up all, because the truth of some seeming vision hath failed. Mark how David handleth the messenger that brought him tidings of the death of Saul: says he, How dost thou know that Saul is dead? What proof canst thou make of the truth of this story? 1 Sa. i. 1–10. So should we say of all those visions or messengers that come to persuade us, that either inward or outward deliverance is for us at the door. Prove these stories; look if they be not dead and lifeless fancies; see if you can find that they were plucked off from the tree that is green.

Ver. 12. 'And he stayed yet other seven days; and sent forth the dove; which returned not again unto him any more.'

We read before of forty days' patience, and after that of seven days' patience; and that after the waters began to return from off the earth, and here again of seven days more. Whence note, That the best of God's people, in the times of trials, find their patience too short-winded to hold out the whole length of a trial, unless the time be, as it were, cut in pieces. The prophet when he was to lay siege against Jerusalem, he must rest the one side, by turning him upon the other. Eze. iv. 2–6. It

was with holy Job exceeding hard, when he might not have time to swallow his spittle, when he might not a little sit down and rest him. And if you observe him, he doth not desire an absolute deliverance as yet, but only time to take wind and breathe awhile; and then, if God will, to engage in the combat again:* 'How long (saith he) wilt thou not depart from me.' Depart: what quite? O! No, saith he, I beg not that absolutely, but only so long as till a man might ' swallow down his spittle.' Job vii. 19. This the church in Ezra's time took as an exceeding favour. ' And now (say they) for a little space, grace hath been *shewed* from the Lord our God, to leave us a remnant to escape, and to give us a nail in his holy place, that our God may lighten our eyes, and give us a little reviving in our bondage.' Ezr. ix. 8.

'And he stayed yet other seven days.' Note again, That it is not God's way with his people to shew them all their troubles at once; but first he shews them a part; first forty days, after that seven other days, and yet again seven days more; that, they coming upon them by piecemeal, they may the better be able to travel through them. While Israel was in affliction in Egypt, they knew not the trials that would meet them at the Red Sea. Again, When they had gone through that, they little thought that yet ' for forty years they must be tempted and proved in the wilderness.'

And thus it was with this blessed Noah; he thought that by the first seven days his trials might be ended. But behold, there is yet seven days more behind: 'and he stayed yet other seven days.'

Further: There may also be by these words thus much insinuated, That these periods of time might be also of Noah's prefixing: and if so, then note, That the people of God in these days are not the first that have been under mistake, as to the timing of their afflictions. Noah counted it would end many days before it ended indeed, even seven days, and seven days, and seven days to that; for he sent forth his dove about the beginning of the first month, in which month also were his two seven days' trials. Again, after that he had staid two seven days more, to wit, to the end of that first month. Again, he staid almost four sevens more; for he came not out of the ark till the twenty-seventh day of the second month. A caution.

Hence therefore let Christians beware that they set not times for God, lest all men see their folly.

---

* This may have suggested an idea to Bunyan in writing the second part of his Pilgrim. In the battle between Great Heart and Giant Maul the sophist, after an hour's hard fighting, 'they sat down to rest them, but Mr. Great Heart betook him to prayer. When they had rested them, and taken breath, they both fell to it again.'—ED.

'It is not for you to know the times or the seasons, which the Father hath put in his own power.'

A caution. Ac. i. 7. Yea, I say again, take heed lest that for thy setting of God a seven days' time, he set not thee so many as seven times seven.

'And he sent forth the dove, which returned not again unto him any more.' This is the third time that the dove was sent to see how the waters were abated on the face of the earth. The first time she, by her restlessness, bespake the waters to be high and mighty. The second time, by her olive-leaf, she notifieth that the waters were low and ebbing. But this third time, she seems to be weary of her service, she returned not again to him any more; yet in her so absenting herself, she gives confirmation to Noah, that the waters were even in a manner quite gone. If he will take this for a proof let him, if not, let him hang in suspense with himself. Hence note, that God will not be always testifying, by renewing of his tokens, to that about which we have had sufficient conviction before; for in so doing he should gratify and humour our unbelief. Noah had received already two sufficient testimonies that the waters were decreasing. First by his seeing the tops of the mountains, and then by the olive-leaf; but notwithstanding these two testimonies, his unbelief in part remains; but God will not humour such a groundless mistrust, by giving him any further token, than the very absenting of the dove. Much like this was that of Samson's father; the angel once had told his wife, that she should have a son that should deliver Israel; well, Manoah heard of this, he also desired that he might see that man that had told his wife this happy news. Now God thus far condescends, as to send the angel a second time; but then, this being now a sufficient antidote against their unbelief, the angel after the next departing, was not seen again of them at all. But saith the word, The angel of the Lord did no more appear to Manoah, and to his wife: So that now they must live by faith, or not at all. Ju. xiii. 3, 9, 21.

God's dealing with his people with respect to their spiritual condition, is much like this. The Holy Ghost doth not use to confirm us by new revelations of grace and justification, so often as by our fond doubts or mistrust we call for and desire the same. But having confirmed in us the testimony of Christ, it may be twice or thrice, (for the testimony of two men are true) he then expects we should live by faith. And observe it, if we have after such testimony joyful communion with God, it is either by retreating to former experience, or by arguing according to faith; that because God hath done thus before, he therefore hath given me interest in such and such promises and mercies besides.

I speak now of the first seals of the love of God to the soul, after we have been sufficiently tossed upon the waves of unbelief, as Noah was by the waters of the flood : such seals are few, the Lord gave them to Solomon twice. 1 Ki. xi. 9. And also twice to his servant Paul. Ac. xxii. 6, 18. 'Tis enough that they have seen 'the tops of the mountains,' and have had brought to them the olive-leaf. Let them now believe this confirmation of mercy is sufficient, and if they will not believe now, they shall not be established.

Ver. 13. '¶ And it came to pass in the six hundredth and first year, in the first *month*, the first *day* of the month, the waters were dried up from off the earth: and Noah removed the covering of the ark, and looked, and behold, the face of the ground was dry.'

'And it came to pass.' That is, by the working of God, that the waters were dried up. This came to pass in God's time, to wit, in 'the six hundredth and first year, in the first *month*, the first *day* of the month;' not in the times of Noah's prefixing. God's time is THE time, the best time, because it is the time appointed by him for the proof and trial of our graces, and that in which so much, and so much of the rage of the enemy, and of the power of God's mercy, may the better be discovered unto us; 'I the Lord will hasten it in HIS time,' Is. lx. 22. not before, though we were the signet upon his right hand. Je. xxii. 24.

Noah the only man with God in that generation, could not be restored before the time; no more could Israel from the thraldom of Egypt. Ex. xiii. 4. Yea, the Son of God himself must here give place and be content. And when Satan had ended *all* the temptation, when he 'had ended all, - then he departed from him for a season.' Lu. iv. 13.

'And Noah removed the covering of the ark, and looked.' The failing again of his expected comforter, caused him to be up and doing; probably he had not as yet uncovered the ark, that is, to look round about him, had the dove by returning pleased his humour; but she failing him, he stirs up himself. Thus it should also be with the Christian now: doth the dove forbear to come to thee with a leaf in her bill as before, let not this make thee sullen and mistrustful, but uncover the ark, and look, and by looking thou shalt see a further testimony of what thou receivedst by the first manifestations: 'He looked, and behold the earth was dry.' Paul tells us, that by looking we have a testimony like, or *as* that, which at first was given us by the Spirit of the Lord. 2 Co. iii. 18. 'And behold the face of the earth was dry.'

Ver. 14. 'And in the second month, on the seven and twentieth day of the month, was the earth dried.'

This prospect was like the rain that we read of

in another place, that confirmed God's inheritance when it was weary : It was a comfortable sight to Noah to see that the face of the earth was dry; and now he could wait upon God with less trial and strain to his patience the remaining days, which were fifty and four, to wit, from the first of the first, to the twenty-seventh of the second month, than he could one of the sevens that he met with before. Indeed the path is narrowest just at entrance, as also our nature is then the most untoward; but after we are in, the walk seems to be wider and easy; the flesh is also then more mortified and conformable. The walk is but a cubit wide at the door, but inward ten times as broad. Eze. xlii. 4, 11.

'And in the second month, on the seven and twentieth day of the month, was the earth dried.' So that from the first day it began to rain, which was the seventeenth day of the second month in the year before, unto this day, was Noah in the ark; it was just a year and ten days. That was the time then that God had appointed to try his servant Noah, by the waters of the flood : in which time he was so effectually crucified to the things of this world, that he was as if he was never more to enjoy the same. Wherefore Peter making mention of this estate of his, he tells us, it was even like unto our baptism; wherein we profess ourselves dead to the world, and alive to God by Jesus Christ. 1 Pe. iii. 21.

In the first verse of this chapter, we read that God remembered Noah; but till now we read not, that the face of the earth was dried. Hence note that our being under the rage of the enemy, doth not argue that we are therefore forgotten of God, 'he remembereth us in our low estate,' even when tossed to and fro by the waters of a flood of temptations.

Ver. 15, 16. '¶ And God spake unto Noah, saying, Go forth of the ark, thou, and thy wife, and thy sons, and thy sons' wives with thee.'

Now we are come to the end of the trial, and so to the time of Noah's deliverance, and behold as he went in, so he came out : He went into the ark at the commandment of the Lord. 'And the Lord said unto Noah, Come thou and all thy house into the ark.' Ge. vii. 1. And here again, 'And God spake unto Noah, saying, Go forth of the ark.' Hence note, that notwithstanding the earth was dry about fifty-four days before, yet Noah waited for the word of God for his commission to bring him forth of the ark. Providence seemed to smile before, in that the earth was dry, to which had but Noah added reason, he must have concluded, the time is come for me to go forth of the ark. But Noah knew, that as well the providences of God, as the waters of the flood might be to try his dependance on the word of the Lord : wherefore, though he saw this, yet because he had no answer of God, he will not take the opportunity.

It is dangerous, or at least very difficult, to make the most smiling providence of God our rule to act by : Had David done it, he had killed Saul before the time, but David respected the word of God. 2 Sa. xxiv. 17—20. Elisha also would not suffer the king to make that improvement of the providence of God, which reason should be put in execution, when he rebuked the king's desire that he had to have killed the Syrians, and commanded that bread should be set before them, that they might eat, and go home again to their master. 2 Ki. vi. 19—23. Hear the word of the Lord, ye that tremble at his word. 'At the commandment of the Lord the children of Israel journeyed, and at the commandment of the Lord they pitched. - - At the commandment of the Lord they rested in their tents, and at the commandment of the Lord they journeyed; they kept the charge of the Lord, at the commandment of the Lord, by the hand of Moses.' Nu. ix. 18—23.

'Go forth of the ark, thou, and thy wife, and thy sons, and thy sons' wives with thee.'

When God delivereth, he delivereth completely. Thus Israel also went out of Egypt, they, their wives, their children, with their flocks and herds, not an hoof was left behind. Ex. x. 24—26. When David's time was come to possess the kingdom, he brought along with him those six hundred men that had been his companions in his suffering state, every man with his household. But I say, he went up to possess it, not simply by the voice of providence, though Saul was dead, but 'David enquired of the Lord, saying, Shall I go up into any of the cities of Judah?' Nay, a general answer, even from God, would not satisfy this holy man. 'The Lord said, - Go, but David replied, Whither shall I go? and he said unto Hebron.' 1 Sa. ii. 1. Oh! it is safe to regard the word of the Lord; this makes us all come safe to land. When men wrest themselves from under the hand of God, taking such opportunities for their deliverance, which are laid before them only for trial of obedience to the word : they may, it is probable, have a seeming success; the end will be as with Zedekiah king of Judah, affliction with addition. The Jews that were left in the land of Israel, from the hand of the king of Babylon, would flee to the land of Egypt, Je. xli. 17. that they might have quietness there, but they went without the word of God, and therefore their rest brought them to their ruin. xlii. xliii.

Noah therefore chose the safest way, even to stay in the ark, till God's word came. As it is also said of Joseph, 'The word of the Lord tried him;' till the word of the Lord came to deliver him, and then he had deliverance indeed, Ps. cv. 19. as Noah also and David had safe deliverance for himself and relations.

Ver. 17. 'Bring forth with thee every living thing that *is* with thee, of all flesh, *both* of fowl, and of cattle, and of every creeping thing that creepeth upon the earth; that they may breed abundantly in the earth, and be fruitful, and multiply upon the earth.'

Noah was not only to have in this deliverance, respect to himself and family, but to the good of all the world. Men's spirits are too narrow for the mind of God, when their chief end, or their only design in their enjoying this or the other mercy, is for the sake of their ownselves only. It cannot be according to God, that such desires should be encouraged: 'none of us liveth unto himself,' why then should we desire life only for ourselves.

The church cries thus, 'God be merciful unto us, and bless us; *and* cause his face to shine upon us.' Why? 'That thy way may be known upon earth, thy saving health among all nations.' Ps. lxvii. 1, 2.

So David, 'Restore unto me the joy of thy salvation; and uphold me *with thy* free spirit. *Then* will I teach transgressors thy ways; and sinners shall be converted unto thee.' Ps. li. 12, 13. So then, we must not desire to come out of trials and afflictions alone, or by ourselves, but that in our deliverance the salvation of many may be concerned. It is said, when Israel went up out of Egypt, there went up with them 'a mixed multitude,' to wit, of Egyptians, and other nations: This going out of captivity was right, they carried out with them the fowls, the beasts, and the creeping things; to wit, the heathens of other lands, and so added increase to the church of God. Ex. xii. 37, 38. In Esther's time also, when the Jews came from under the snare of Haman, they brought with them to God many of the people of the provinces. 'Many of the people of the land became Jews.' Es. viii. 17.

These words therefore, 'bring forth with thee every living thing,' &c. are not lightly to be passed over; for they shew us, that we ought in our deliverance to have special respect to the deliverance of others. And if our deliverance be with the word and liking of God, it must needs have this effect. 'When I shall bring again their captivity, the captivity of Sodom and her daughters, and the captivity of Samaria, and her daughters, then *will I bring again* the captivity of thy captives in the midst of them.' Eze. xvii. 53.

And indeed there is reason for this, for in every affliction and persecution, the devil's design is to impair Christ's kingdom: wherefore no marvel, that God designeth in our deliverance, the impairing and lessening the kingdom of sin and Satan. Wherefore, O thou church of God in England, which art now upon the waves of affliction, and temptation, when thou comest out of the furnace, if thou come out at the bidding of God, there shall come out with thee the fowl, the beast, and abundance of creeping things. 'O Judah, he hath set an harvest for thee, when I returned the captivity of my people.' Ho. vi. 11.

'That they may breed abundantly in the earth, and be fruitful, and multiply upon the earth.'

This was God's end in preserving the creatures from the flood, that again the earth might be replenished therewith. The same end he hath in his suffering of the persecutors, and all manner of adversity to take away but 'a part,' some. Am. vii. 4. Some of them they shall kill and crucify, leaving a remnant alive in the world, namely, that they might breed abundantly in the earth, and be fruitful, and multiply upon the earth. As he saith by the prophet Isaiah, 'He shall cause them that come of Jacob to take root: Israel shall blossom and bud, and fill the face of the world with fruit.' Is. xxvii. 6. And this after their deliverance from persecution: According as he saith again, 'The remnant that is escaped of the house of Judah, shall again take root downward, and bear fruit upward: For out of Jerusalem shall go forth a remnant' that is yet to replenish the earth with converts. xxxvii. 32. As Luke observes, that when the churches in Judea, Galilee, and Samaria had rest, they 'walking in the fear of the Lord, and in the comfort of the Holy Ghost, were multiplied.' Ac. ix. 31.

Ver. 18. 'And Noah went forth, and his sons, and his wife, and his sons' wives with him.' Obedience is better than sacrifice. Noah is at the beck of God, what he bid him do, that does he; and indeed this is in truth to worship God, yea, this is to know and worship God. It is said of Abraham, when he went at God's command to offer up Isaac, that he counted it going to worship the Lord. Ge. xxii. 5. And God saith of Hezekiah, that he did 'judgment and justice,' judging the cause of the poor and needy; and then adds, Is not this 'to know me, saith the Lord?' Je. xxii. 15, 16. I bring these to shew, that obedience to the word of God, is the true character of God's people in all ages; and this very text, as also such others before, is on purpose recorded by the Holy Ghost, to shew you, that Noah was obedient in all things; yea, I may add, these commands were to discover the proof of him, whether he would be obedient in all things; and this was also his way with New Testament churches. 2 Co. ii. 9. The sincerity of love, and of the uprightness of the heart, is greatly discovered by the commandments of God. 'He that hath my commandments, and keepeth them,' saith Christ, 'he it is that loveth me.' &c. Jn. xiv. 21.

Ver. 19. 'Every beast, every creeping thing, and every fowl, *and* whatsoever creepeth upon the earth after their kinds, went forth out of the ark.'

These words are yet a further expression of the sincerity of Noah's obedience, for that he at the command of God, did carefully search and seek out every little creeping thing that God had brought to him into the ark. Obedience in little things do ofttimes prove us most; for we through the pride of our hearts are apt to look over little things, because though commanded, they are but little. Je. xxiii. 38. O, but Noah was of another spirit, he carefully looked after little things, even after every thing, 'whatsoever creepeth upon the earth;' and not only so, but sought diligently that they might go out in order, to wit, male and female, according to their kind. Sometimes God would have men exact to a word, sometimes exact to a tache, or pin, or loop; Ex. xxxvi. 12, 13. sometimes to a step: Eze. xl. 3, 4, 37. Be careful then in little things, but yet leave not the other undone. Mat. xxiii. 23.

Indeed the command of God is great; if HE therefore commands us to worship him, though but with a bird, we must not count such ordinances insignificant, or below a human creature. Le. xiv. 52.

Ver. 20. '¶ And Noah builded an altar unto the LORD, and took of every clean beast, and of every clean fowl, and offered burnt-offerings on the altar.'

This is the first work that we read Noah did, when he came forth of the ark; and it shews us, that at this time he had a deep sense of the distinguishing mercy of God. And indeed he had sufficient cause to wonder, for the whole world was drowned, save only himself, and they that were with him in the ark.

But I say, this was the first work, to wit, 'to worship God.' Hence note, That a sense of mercy, of distinguishing mercy, naturally engageth the heart to worship. It is said of Moses, when the name of the Lord was proclaimed before him, as 'merciful and gracious, - and abundant in goodness and truth, - and that he pardoned iniquity, transgression and sin;' that he 'made haste, and bowed his head toward the earth, and worshipped.' Ex. xxxiv. 8.

'And Noah builded an altar.' Although this altar be the first that we read of, yet forasmuch as there was before a blessed church, and also an open profession of godliness, together with offering sacrifice, in all probability this was not the first altar that was builded unto the Lord. Besides, we read not of any immediate revelation, from which Noah had light and instruction to build it. The text only saith, he built an altar unto the Lord; which may be aptly expounded, according as he was wont in the other world.

This altar was a type of Christ, as capacitated to bear the sin of the world (for the altar was it, upon which the sacrifices were burnt;) wherefore it, in mine opinion, in special respected his Godhead, by the power of which he offered himself, that is, his flesh. Again it is said, 'The altar sanctifieth the gift.' Mat. xxiii. 19. So did the Godhead the humanity of Christ, through which 'eternal Spirit, he offered himself without spot to God.' He. ix. 14. By this altar then this blessed man preached to his family the Godhead and eternity of Christ.

'And took of every clean beast, and of every clean fowl.' These beasts and fowls were types of the flesh of the Son of God, as Paul in the ninth and tenth chapters to the Hebrews affirms; wherefore by this act he also preached to his family the incarnation of the Lord Christ, how that 'in the fulness of time' he should in our flesh offer himself a sacrifice for us; for as all the ordinances of the New Testament ministration preach to us, That Christ IS come; so all the ordinances of worship under the Old Testament preached to them that were under it, Christ, as yet TO come.

'Of every clean beast and of every clean fowl.' This was to shew, That when Christ did come, he should not take hold of the Jew, and exclude the Gentile; but that in his flesh he should present unto God EVERY clean beast, and EVERY clean fowl; that is, all the elect, both of Jew and Gentile. Ac. x. 11—16.

And it was requisite that this by Noah should be preached, because the whole world was yet in his family; from whence, at the multiplication of men, if through their rebellion and idolatry they lost not this doctrine, they might to all their offspring preach the Lord Jesus.

Wherefore, the doctrine of the gospel, had the world been faithful, might have been to this day retained amongst them that now are the most barbarous people.*

Ver. 21. 'And the Lord smelled a sweet savour; (a savour of rest;) and the Lord said in his heart, I will not again curse the ground any more for man's sake; for the imagination of man's heart is evil from his youth; neither will I again smite any more every living thing, as I have done.'

These words more fully shew, that this sacrifice of Noah was a type of the offering up of the body of Jesus Christ, he being said to be that blessed sacrifice that is as perfume in the nostrils of God: 'He gave himself for us an offering and a sacrifice to God for a sweet-smelling savour.' Ep. v. 2. Besides, this offering of Noah was a burnt-offering to God; which burning signified, the curse of God, which Christ was made in his death for us. Wherefore, the burnt offerings were all along a type of

---

* Instead of progressing to the meridian sunshine of Christianity, they have retrograded to a darker gloom than the twilight of Judaism. Still, some vestiges of knowledge remain—some idea of a future state, and of sacrifice for sin. Christian, how blessed art thou! How ought your light to shine among men, to the glory of your heavenly Father!—ED.

him; as by reading the epistle to the Hebrews you may see: 'It is the burnt-offering, [saith God,] because of the burning upon the altar all night unto the morning, and the fire of the altar shall be burning in it.' Le. vi. 9. Which was a type of the fire of the law, and the guilt of sin, that Christ, when he offered himself, should undergo for the sins of man.

'And the Lord smelled a sweet savour.' This signifies the content and satisfaction that for the sin of the world, God should have by the offering up of his Son for us upon the cross: Wherefore, he is said to be now 'in Christ, reconciling the world unto himself, not imputing their trespasses unto them.' 2 Co.-v. 19.

Now it is observable, That Noah was a man of faith long before this. Hence note two things.

1. That men, even of eminent faith, have yet need of a continual remembrance of the death and sufferings of Christ; yea, and that in the most plain and easiest manner to understand.

2. They have need also, notwithstanding they have faith before, to present themselves before God, through Jesus Christ our Lord: For as our persons are not accepted, but in and through him, no more are our performances; yea, though they be spiritual services or sacrifices; it is the blood that maketh the atonement, as well for works as persons. Le. xvii. 11. He. ix. 21. as he saith in another place, I will accept you with your sweet savour, but not without it. 1 Pe. ii. 5. Eze. xx. 41. As he also said to his church in Egypt, 'When I see the blood, I will pass over you, and the plague shall not be upon you to destroy *you*, when I smite the land of Egypt.' Ex. xii. 13.

'And the Lord said in his heart, I will not again curse,' &c. By heart here, we may understand two things.

1. That God was altogether unfeigned in this promise. He spake it from his very heart: which we use to count the most sincere expressing of our mind: According to that of the prophet, 'Yea, I will rejoice over them to do them good, and I will plant them in this land assuredly - [in truth, in stability,] with my whole heart, and with my whole soul.' Je. xxxii. 41. Mark, I will rejoice to do it, I will do it assuredly, I will do it in truth, even 'with my whole heart, and with my whole soul.'

2. By his saying, 'In his heart,' we may understand the secrecy of his purpose; for this doctrine, Of not cursing again, it is hid from all but those to whom it is revealed by the Spirit of God. For this purpose, in the heart of God, is one of the depths, or of the deep things of God, which the spirit of a man cannot understand. 'Who hath known the mind of the Lord?' None of all the sons of men, but those that have the Holy Ghost: Therefore Paul applieth that to himself and fellows,

as that which is peculiar to them to know, 'We have the mind of Christ.' 1 Co. ii. 16. It is said, that after Christ had by his parables preached his gospel to the world, he in private 'expounded all things to his disciples.' Mar. iv. 34.

Hence note, That they that will hear God speak this, they must be near his very heart. They that are in his heart, may hear it: but to them that are without, in parables. This secret, in revelation of the gospel, is also expressed in other terms: as, That the Lord spake 'in mine ears,' Is. v. 9. and 'it was revealed in mine ears.' Is. xxii. 14. And again, 'Hear now this word that I speak in thine ears.' Je. xxviii. 7.

'I will not again curse the ground any more.' These words are also under Moses's veil; for in them is contained the sin of the world, and damnation thereof. He said, when he was to bring the flood, that the 'earth was corrupt,' and that he would 'destroy the earth;' vi. 11, 13. but his great meaning, was, of the sinners that dwelt therein; as the effect of that flood declared. So he saith again, he will not bring any more a flood to destroy the earth; and that the bow in the cloud should be a sign of peace between him and the earth: By all which is meant in special, the men that dwell on the earth; Ps. cxiv. 7. De. xxxii. 1. Je. vi. 19; xxii. 29. and they are called, the Ground, and the Earth, because they came from thence. So then, there is, as it were, the foundation of all spiritual blessedness couched under these words, 'I will not curse the ground, I will not destroy man.' And that this must needs be the meaning thereof, consider, that this promise ariseth from the sweet savour that he smelt before in the burnt-offering; which was a figure of Christ, who was 'made a curse for us,' Ga. iii. 13. to deliver us from the curse of the law; that we might through him obtain the blessing of forgiveness of sins; to which the curse stands directly opposite.

'I will not again curse the ground for man's sake; for the imagination of man's heart *is* evil from his youth.' The imagination of man's heart was the ground of this dreadful curse; and the effect of this curse, was, to lay them up in chains in hell: Wherefore Peter saith, These men are 'now in prison.' The curse therefore, in its most eminent extension, reached the souls of those ungodly ones that were swept away with the flood. But it seems a strange argument, or reason rendered of God, why again he would not curse the ground, if it was because of the evil imagination of man's heart, this being the only argument that prevailed with him to send the flood. The meaning therefore is rather this, That because of the satisfaction that Christ hath given to God for sin, therefore he said in his heart, he would 'not again curse the ground,' for the evil imagination of man;

that is, he would not do it, for want of a sacrifice that had in it a sufficient propitiation. Jn. iii. 18, 19.

Hence note, That the great cause now of man's condemnation, is not because of his inherent pollution, but because he accepteth not, with Noah, of the satisfaction made by Christ; for to all them that have so accepted thereof, there is now no curse nor condemnation, Ro. viii. 1. though still the imagination of their heart be evil. 'If any man sin, we have an advocate with the Father, Jesus Christ the righteous.' 1 Jn. ii. 1.

'For the imagination of man's heart is evil from his youth.' These words seem to insinuate the cause of these evil imaginations; and that is, from the corruption of their youth. Now how soon their youth was corrupted, David shows by these words, 'I was shapen in iniquity; and in sin did my mother conceive me.' Ps. li. 5. Ezekiel also shows, we were polluted in the day that we were born. Eze. xvi. 1—8. Further, God to Moses strongly affirms it, in that he commands, That for the first-born, in whom the rest were included, an offering should be offered, by that they were a month old. Ex. xiii. 13; xxxiv. 20. God seems therefore, by this word, to look back to the transgression of our first parents, by whom sin came into our natures; and by so doing, he not only intimateth, yea, promiseth a pardon to personal miscarriages; but assureth us, That neither them, nor yet our inward pollutions, shall destroy us, because of the rest that he found before in Christ. Ro. v

'Neither will I again smite any more every living thing, as I have done.' The creatures therefore also have some kind of benefit by the death and blood of Christ; that is, so as to live, and have a being; for infinite justice is so perfectly just, as that without a sacrifice it could not have suffered the world to stand, after sin was in the world; but must have destroyed, for the sake of sin, the world which he had made.

For although it be foully absurd to say that beasts and fowls are defiled with sin, as man; yet doubtless they received detriment thereby. 'The creature was made subject to vanity, by reason of him who hath subjected the same,' &c. That is, by Adam's sin. Which vanity they also show by divers of their practices; as both in their enmity to man, and one to another, with which they were not created; this came by the sin of man. Now that man lives, yea, that beasts live, it is because of the offering up of Christ: Wherefore it is said in that of the Colossians, The gospel is 'preached to every creature;' in every creature under heaven; to wit, in that they live and have a being. i. 23.

'Neither will I again smite any more every living thing, as I have done.' These words, as I have done, doth not exempt the creature from every judgment of God, but from this, or such as this;

for we know, that other judgments do befal ungodly men now; and if they continue in final impenitence, they shall partake of far greater judgments than to be drowned by the waters of a flood. 'The wicked is reserved unto judgment.' Job xxi. 30. Yea, the heavens and the earth that now are, are 'reserved unto fire, - and perdition of ungodly men.' 2 Pe. iii. 7.

Ver. 22. 'While the earth remaineth, seed time and harvest, and cold and heat, and summer and winter, and day and night, shall not cease.'

'While the earth remaineth.' These words may have respect both to the words before, and to them that follow after. If they respect the words before, then they are as limits to that large promise, of not destroying the world again: not but that the day will come, as I said, in which another general judgment, and that too far more dreadful than this of water, will overflow the world, and every living thing shall again be cut off from the face of all the earth; as *now* by rain of water, *then* by rain of fire and brimstone: Which day and sore judgment, God showed unto men, when he burned Sodom and Gomorrah with 'fire and brimstone from heaven.' But,

'While the earth remaineth,' this shall not be. But in the end, then indeed both it and 'the works that are therein, shall (as Peter saith) be burned up.' 2 Pe. iii. 10. But so long as it remaineth, that is, until it be overtaken with this second, and that too the beginning of eternal judgment, no universal judgment shall overrun the earth: For albeit that since that flood, the earth hath been smitten with many a curse; yet it hath been but here and there, not in every place at once. Famines, and earthquakes, and pestilences, have been in divers places, but yet at the same time hath there been seed time and harvest also. Mar. xiii. 8. Lu. xxi. 11.

'Seed time and harvest, and cold and heat, and summer and winter, and day and night, shall not cease.' These words were some of the first, with that of 'the bow in the cloud,' that prevailed with me to believe that the scriptures were the word of God.

For my reason tells me, they are, and have continued a true prophecy, from the day that they were related; otherwise the world could not have subsisted; for take away seed time and harvest, cold and heat, &c., and an end is put to the * beginning of the universe.

Besides, if these words be taken in a spiritual sense, they have also stood true from that very day; otherwise the church had ceased to have a being long before this: For take away seed time

---

* 'The beginning,' the foundation; that which is essential to the existence, as, 'The fear of the Lord is the beginning of wisdom.' Take away the fear of the Lord, and this heavenly wisdom ceaseth to exist.—Ed.

and harvest from the church, with cold and heat, and day and night, and those ordinances of heaven are taken from her, which were ordained for her begetting and continuation. This head might with much largeness be insisted on; but to pass it, and to come to the next chapter.

CHAP. IX.

Ver. 1. 'And God blessed Noah, and his sons, and said unto them, Be fruitful and multiply, and replenish the earth.'

Noah having thus waded through these great temptations, and being made also to partake of the mercy of God, in preserving and saving him from the evil thereof, and being brought to partake of the beginning of a new world, while the ungodly that were before the flood were perished for their iniquity: he receiveth now from the mouth of the Lord, before whom he walked before the flood, laws and ordinances, as rules by which he should still govern his life before him. But mark, Before he receiveth these rules and commandments, he receiveth blessing from God; blessing, I say, as that which should yet fore-fit him to do his will.

'And God blessed Noah.' Blessed him with spiritual and special grace; for without that, no man can walk, with God's acceptance before him. He blessed him with grace suitable to the work he was now to begin; to wit, for the replenishing and governing the new world God had brought him to: so that Noah did not without precedent qualifications take this work upon him. God also gave Caleb and Joshua another spirit, and then they followed him fully. That of David is for this remarkable, 'Who *am* I, [said he] and what *is* my people, that we should be able to offer so willingly after this sort? for all things *come* of thee, and of thine own have we given thee.' 'O Lord our God, saith he, all this store that we have prepared to build thee an house for thine holy name, *cometh* of thine hand, and *is* all thine own.' 1 Ch. xxix. 10—16. So is faith, love, strength, wisdom, sincerity, and all other good things wherewith and by which we walk with God, worship him, and do his will: all which is comprised in these words, 'I will give them an heart to know me, that I *am* the LORD: and they shall be my people, and I will be their God; for they shall return unto me with their whole heart.' Je. xxiv. 7. 'A new heart also will I give them.' Eze. xxxvi. 25—29. And again, 'I will put my fear in their hearts, that they shall not depart from me.' Je. xxxii. 37—40.

'And God blessed Noah and his sons, and said unto them, Be fruitful, and multiply, and replenish the earth.' After he had blessed him, then he tells him what they should do; namely, 'Be fruitful, and multiply.' This he spake with respect to the seed that he and his sons should beget, therewith to people the world; which was now the remaining part of his work, and he had three arguments to encourage him thereto. First, He was delivered from the wicked and sinners of the old world: II. He was made the heir of a new world; and III. Was to leave it as an heritage to his children.

This therefore should teach us, who are brought into the kingdom of Christ, that new world that hath taken its beginning in the word of the gospel, not to be idle, but to be fruitful, and to labour to fill the world with a spiritual seed to God: for as Noah, so are we made heirs of this blessed kingdom; and shall also, as that good man, leave, when we sleep in Jesus, this spiritual seed to possess the kingdom after us.

Ver. 2. 'And the fear of you and the dread of you shall be upon every beast of the earth, and upon every fowl of the air, upon all that moveth *upon* the earth, and upon all the fishes of the sea; into your hand are they delivered.'

These words seem to be a promise of what shall be a consequence of their putting into practice what was commanded in the verse before; namely, of their being fruitful, and of their 'multiplying in the earth.' Hence note, That the faithful observation of God's word, puts majesty, and dread, and terror upon them that do it: Therefore it is said, that when the church is 'fair as the moon, and clear as the sun, she is terrible as *an army* with banners.' Ca. vi. 4, 10. The presence of godly Samuel made the elders of Bethlehem tremble; yea, when Elisha was sought for by the king of Syria, he durst not engage him, but with chariots and horses, and an heavy host. 2 Ki. vi. 13, 14. Godliness is a wonderful thing, it commandeth reverence, and the stooping of the spirits, even of the world of ungodly ones. Ac. v. 13.

'And the fear of you and the dread of you shall be upon every beast.' This is true in the letter; for because there is upon man, as man, more of the image and similitude of God, than there is upon other creatures; therefore the beasts, and all the creatures, are made to stoop and fall before them; yea, though in themselves they are mighty and fierce. Every kind (or, nature) of birds, and of serpents, and things in the sea, is tamed, and hath been tamed by mankind. Ja. iii. 7.

But to allegorize the word, for by the word, ungodly men are beasts; then, as I said before, godliness puts such a majesty and dread upon the professors of it, that their enemies are afraid of them; yea, even then when they rage against them, and lay heavy afflictions upon them. It is marvellous to see in what fear the ungodly are, even of godly men, and godliness; in that they stir up the mighty, make edicts against them; yea, and raise up armies, and what else can be imagined, to suppress them; while the persons thus opposed, if you consider them as to their state and capacity in this world; they are most inconsiderable; but as a dead dog, or a flea. 1 Sa. xxiv. 14. O but they are clothed with godliness! The image and presence of God is upon them! This makes the beasts of this world afraid. One of you shall chase a thousand.

'Into your hand are they delivered.' That is, the beasts, birds, and fish of the sea (as David saith) to be for the service of man. But again, This is also true in a higher nature; for taking these beasts, &c. for men, even they are delivered into the hand of the church, by whose doctrine, power and faith, they are smitten with severest judgments. 2 Co. ii. 15, 16. Laying all that reject them even in the depth of death, and smiting them 'with all plagues as often as they will.' Re. xi. 6. The world is therefore in our hand, and disposed of by our doctrine, by our faith and prayers, although they think far otherwise, and shall one day feel their judgments are according.

Ver. 3. 'Every moving thing that liveth shall be meat for you; even as the green herb have I given you all things.'

From these words some would insinuate, that before the flood men lived only upon herbs, not eating flesh; as here they have authority granted to do: but, in mine opinion, such should be mistaken, for this reason, if there were no other: because they offered sacrifice before; sacrifices, I say, as types and representatives to the church, of the death and sufferings of Christ. Now, of such sacrifices the offerers used to eat, as is clear by the lamb of the passover, and many other offerings: so that these words seem to be but a renewing of their former privileges, not a granting new liberty to the world.

'Every moving thing.' This must be taken with this restriction, That is wholesome and good for food: for by the law of nature, nothing of that is forbidden to man, though for some significations many such creatures were forbidden us to use for a time. De. xiv.

'Even as the green herb.' For which they expressly had liberty granted them, in the first chapter of this book. ver. 29. And this liberty might afresh be here repeated, from some scruple that might arise in Noah, &c. He remembering that the world before might, for the abuse of the creatures of God, as well as for the abuse of his worship, be drowned with the flood; for sometimes the abuse of that which is lawful to one, may be a snare, abuse and stumbling to another. 1 Co. vii. 1; viii.

Ver. 4. 'But flesh with the life thereof, which is the blood thereof, shall ye not eat.'

This law seems to be ceremonial, although given long before Moses was; as also some sacrifices and circumcision were. Jn. vii. 22. Wherefore we must seek for the reason of this prohibition. 'Whatsoever man (saith God) there be of the house of Israel, - that eateth any manner of blood, I will even set my face against that soul that eateth blood, and will cut him off from among his people.' Why? 'For the life of the flesh is in the blood: and I have given it to you upon the altar to make an atonement for your souls: for it is the blood that maketh an atonement for the soul. Therefore I said unto the children of Israel, No soul of you shall eat blood.' Le. xvii. 10—12. Again, As here the prohibition is only concerning blood; so in another place, the word is as well against our eating the fat: 'It shall be a perpetual statute for your generations, throughout all your dwellings, that ye neither eat fat nor blood.' And the reason rendered, is, For 'all the fat is the LORD's.' Le. iii. 16,17.

So then the meaning, the spiritual meaning, seems to be this, That forasmuch as the blood is the life, and that which maketh the atonement; and the fat, the glory, and the Lord's; therefore they both were to be offered to the Lord. That is, we ought always to offer the merit of our salvation to God, by a continual acknowledgment, that it was through the blood of Christ; and we ought always to give him the glory thereof, and this is the fat of all our performances. Is. xxv. 6. Now this is so blessed a thing, and calleth for that grace, that every professor hath not, every one cannot ascribe to the blood of the Lamb, the whole of his reconciliation to God; nor offer up the fat, the glory, which is God's, to the Lord for so great a benefit: this is the benefit of a peculiar people, even of 'the priests the Levites, the sons of Zadok, [or they that are justified, or just * For so Zadok thereby;*] that kept the charge of   signifies. my sanctuary, when the children of Israel went astray from me; they shall come near to me, to minister unto me, and they shall stand before me to offer unto me the fat and the blood, saith the Lord God.' Eze. xliv. 15.

Wherefore, for men to ascribe to their own works the merit of their salvation, or to take the glory thereof to themselves; it is as eating the blood and the fat themselves, and they shall be cut off from the people of God.

Ver. 5. 'And surely your blood of your lives will I require; at the hand of every beast will I require it, and at the hand of man; at the hand of every man's brother, will I require the life of man.'

These words are spoken to the church, which then resided in this family: Not but that God will avenge the blood that is wrongfully shed, though the person murdered be most carnal and irreligious. 'A man that doeth violence to the blood of *any* person, shall flee to the pit; let no man stay him.' Pr. xxviii. 17.

But I say, these words respect the church in a more special and eminent way. 'Surely (saith God) your blood of your lives will I require.' Thus also David insinuates the thing: 'when he maketh inquisition for blood, he remembereth them: [the saints and godly in special,] he forgetteth not the cry of the humble,' the afflicted. Ps. ix. 12.

'At the hand of every beast will I require it.' The beasts are here also to be taken for men, to whom they are frequently likened in scripture; and that because they have cast off human affections; and, like savage creatures, make a prey of those that are better than themselves. Ignorance therefore or brutishness, O thou wicked man! will not excuse thee in the day of judgment; all the injuries that thou doest to the people of God, shall for certain be required of thee.

At the hand of man will I require it.' By *man* here, we may understand, such as have greater place and shew of reason wherewith they manage their cruelty, than those that are as the natural beast: for all persecutors are not brutish alike; some are in words as smooth as oil; others can shew a semblance of reason of state, why they should sell 'the righteous for silver, and the poor for a pair of shoes.' Am. ii. 6. These act, to carnal reason, like men, as Saul against David, for the safety of his kingdom; but these must give an account of their cruelty, for blood is in their hands.

'At the hand of every man's brother will I require the life of man.' This word *brother* may reach to all the apostatized hypocrites that forsake or betray the godly, for brother shall betray the brother to death. Mat. x. 21. Such are spoken of in Isaiah, 'Your brethren that hated you, [saith God,] and that cast you out for my name's sake, said, Let the LORD be glorified: but he shall appear to your joy, and they shall be ashamed.' Is. lxv. 5. So that let them be as vile as the brute, or as reasonable in appearance as men, or as near in relation as a brother; neither their ignorance, nor their reason, nor their relation to the saints, shall secure them from the stroke of the judgment of God.

Ver. 6. 'Whoso sheddeth man's blood, by man shall his blood be shed: for in the image of God made he man.'

In these words we have both a threatening and a command; and the same words carry both: 'By man shall his blood be shed,' there is the threatening; 'By man shall his blood be shed,' there is the command. For as they threaten, so they instruct us, that he is worthy of the loss of his own blood, that doth wickedly shed the blood of another. Mat. xxvi. 52. Re. xiii. 10. Blood for blood, equal measure: As he also saith elsewhere, An eye for an

eye, a tooth for a tooth, Ex. xxi. 24. wound for wound, burning for burning. Le. xxiv. 20. De. xix. 21.

'For in the image of God made he man.' This seems as the reason of this equal law; because no man can slay his neighbour, but he striketh at the image of God. It is counted a heinous crime for a man to run his sword at the picture of a king, how much more to shed the blood of the image of God? 'He that mocketh, or oppresseth, the poor reproacheth his Maker; but he that honoureth him, hath mercy on the poor.' Pr. xiv. 31; xvii. 5. And if so, how much more do they reproach, yea, despise and abhor their Maker, that slay and murder his image! But most of all those do prove themselves the enemies of God, that make the holiness, the goodness, the religion and sobriety that is found in the people of God, the object of their wrath and hellish cruelty. Hence murder is, in the New Testament, imputed to that man that hated holy and godly man: 'He that hateth his brother, is a murderer; and ye know that no murderer hath eternal life abiding in him.' 1 Jn. iii. 15.

Ver. 7. 'And you, be ye fruitful, and multiply; bring forth abundantly in the earth, and multiply therein.' Thus he doubleth the blessing and command, of multiplying and increasing the church in the earth, for that is the delight of God, and of Christ.

Ver. 8, 9. '¶ And God spake unto Noah, and to his sons with him, saying, And I, behold, I establish my covenant with you, and with your seed after you.'

God having thus blessed them, and given them laws and judgments to walk by, for the further confirmation of their hope in God, he propoundeth to them the immutability of his mind, by the establishing of his covenant with them; for a covenant is that, which not only concludeth the matter concerned between the persons themselves; but it provideth remedy against after temptations, and fears, and mistrusts, as to the faithful performance of that which is spoken of. As Laban said to Jacob, 'Now therefore (said he) come thou, let us make a covenant, I and thou; and let it be for a witness between me and thee.' Ge. xxxi. 44. Thus also the apostle insinuates; where making mention of the promise and oath of God, he saith, this promise and oath are both immutable, that 'we might have a strong consolation, [or always ground for great rejoicing] who have fled for refuge to lay hold upon the hope set before us.' He. vi. 18.

This covenant therefore, it was for the encouragement of Noah and his sons, that they might walk before God without fear. Yea, it was to maintain their hope in his promise of forgiveness, though they should find their after-performances mixed with infirmities; for so he had told them before, namely, 'That he would not again destroy the earth for man's sake, albeit the imagination of man's heart be evil from his youth. I will establish my covenant with you, and with your seed after you.'

Ver. 10. 'And with every living creature that *is* with you: of the fowl, of the cattle, and of every beast of the earth with you; from all that go out of the ark, to every beast of the earth.' These words respect the whole creation;* for all the things in the world, devils only excepted, have a benefit by this covenant of God. And hence it is, that not man only, but ' every thing that hath breath,' is commanded to ' praise the Lord :' Ps. cl. 6. But observe it ; as for the sin of man, they before were destroyed by the flood ; so now by reason of the mercy of God to man, they are spared, and partake of mercy also. This is intimated by these words: ' Every creature that is with you; every beast of the earth with you.'

Ver. 11. 'And I will establish my covenant with you, neither shall all flesh be cut off any more by the waters of a flood ; neither shall there any more be a flood to destroy the earth.'

This is the sum of the covenant, as it respecteth the letter, and the type, and the whole creation in general. But yet as to the spirit and gospel of it, the Holy Ghost must needs have a further reach, an intention of more glorious things, as may further be shewed anon.

' And I will establish my covenant with you.' For you that are men, and especially the members of the church, have the most peculiar share therein.

' Neither shall all flesh be cut off any more by the waters of a flood.' For because of my covenant which I establish with you, I will spare them also, and give them the taste of my mercy and goodness.

' Neither shall there any more be a flood to destroy the earth.' This covenant therefore, is not of that nature as the covenant was which was made with Adam, to wit, a covenant of works, as the only conditions of life; for by that was the ground, for man's sin, accursed, accursed, and accursed again. But now the Lord goeth another way, the way of grace, and forgiveness of sins: Wherefore now, not the curse, but the mercy of God, comes in on the back and neck of sin, still sparing and forgiving man, the great transgressor, and the beast, &c. and the earth, for the sake of him.

Vers. 12, 13. 'And God said, This *is* the token of the covenant which I make between me and you and every living creature that *is* with you, for perpetual generations. I do set my bow in the cloud, and it shall be for a token of a covenant between me and the earth.'

_____
* See chap. viii.

So then, the way to find out the covenant, what that is, it is to see if we can find out this token of it ; to wit, the BOW, of which the rainbow is but a type. I find then by the scriptures, where this BOW is mystically spoken of, that the Lord Jesus Christ himself is encompassed with the bow. The first is this:

' And above the firmament that *was* over their heads *was* the likeness of a throne, as the appearance of a sapphire stone : and upon the likeness of the throne *was* the likeness, as the appearance of a man above upon it. And I saw, as the colour of amber, as the appearance of fire round about within it, from the appearance of his loins even upward, and from the appearance of his loins even downward, I saw as it were the appearance of fire, and it had brightness round about. As the appearance of the bow that is in the cloud in the day of rain, so *was* the appearance of the brightness round about. This *was* the appearance of the likeness of the glory of the LORD.' Eze. i. 26—28. the man, the Lord's Christ, &c.

The second scripture is this. ' I was in the Spirit: and, behold a throne was set in heaven, and *one* sat on the throne. And he that sat was to look upon like a jasper and a sardine stone: and *there was* a rainbow round about the throne, in sight like unto an emerald.' Re. iv. 2, 3. In these two texts there is mention of the rainbow, that was, not to be the covenant, but the token or sign thereof. Now then the covenant itself must needs be the man that was set in the midst of the bow upon the throne; for so he saith by the prophet, ' I the the LORD have called thee in rightousness, and will hold thine hand, and will keep thee, and give thee for a covenant of the people.' Is. xlii. 6. The covenant therefore is Jesus Christ the Saviour, whom the bow in the clouds was a sign or a token of. So then the sum of the text is this, That God, for the sake of the Lord Jesus Christ, will not again all the days of the earth, bring an universal judgment upon the creature, as in the days of Noah, and of the old world he did; for Christ by the worth of his blood and righteousness hath pacified the justice of the law for sin. So then the whole universe standeth not upon a bottom of its own, but by the word and power of Christ. He. i. 2, 3. ' The earth [said he] and all the inhabitants thereof are dissolved: I bear up the pillars of it.' Ps. lxxv. 3.

Quest. But how must Christ be reckoned of God, when he maketh him the poize against all the sin of the world.

The prophet tells us thus: He shall be the covenant of the people, or he shall be accounted the conditions and worth of the world; He shall be the covenant, or works, or righteousness of the people; for, He as the high-priest under the law, is set for the people to Godward; that is, he standeth always in the presence of God, as the complete obedience of the people. So then, so long as the Lord Christ bears up his mediatorship, God in justice will neither destroy the world, nor the things that are therein.

In this covenant therefore, the justice as well as the mercy of God is displayed in its perfection, inasmuch as without the perfection of the mediator Christ, the world could not be saved from judgment.

Ver. 14. 'And it shall come to pass, when I bring a cloud over the earth, that the bow shall be seen in the cloud.'

By these words the Lord looks back to the flood that before had drowned the earth; for in these clouds there was no bow, no token of Christ, or of the mercy of God. But now, saith God, I will do far otherwise; from henceforth when I bring a cloud, and there be showers of rain on the earth, these clouds shall not be as the other. But 'my bow shall be therein.'

The cloud then that here is spoken of, must be understood of the judgment of God for sin, like those before, and at the overthrow of the world; only with this difference, they were clouds, judgments without mercy, but these judgments mixed therewith; and often the clouds are thus to be understood. Job when he curseth his day, saith, 'Let a cloud dwell upon it.' iii. 5. So the judgments of God upon Zion, are called the covering of a cloud. La. ii. 1. So in Joel also, to the darkness of clouds, are the judgments of the church compared; ii. 2. yea, that pillar that went before the children of Israel, it being a judgment to the people of Egypt, goes under this epithet, as a term most fit to express this judgment by, 'it was a cloud and darkness *to them.*' Ex. xiv. 20.

And now to the cloud in hand, the cloud in which is the bow, the cloud of rain, although by the mercy and grace of God it is so great a blessing as it is, yet it sometimes becomes a judgment, it comes for correction, as a rod to afflict the inhabitants of the world withal. Job xxxvii. 13. Thus it was in the days of Ezra, and very often both before and since. x. 12—14.

'The bow shall be seen in the cloud.' This is the mercy of God to the world, and that by which it hath been hitherto preserved; 'The bow shall be seen in the cloud.' You know I told you of the bow before, that it was a sign or token of the covenant of God with the world, and that the covenant itself was Christ, as given of God unto us, with all his good conditions, merit, and worth. So then, in that, God 'set this bow in the cloud,' and especially in the clouds that he sends for judgment, he would have the world remember, that there comes no judgment as yet on the world, but

it is mixed with, or poized by the mercy of God in Christ.

'The bow shall be seen in the cloud.' This may respect God, or the world, that is, the seeing of the bow in the cloud; if it respect God, then it tells us he in judgment will remember mercy; if it respect the world, then it admonisheth us not to despond, or sink in despair under the greatest judgment of God, for the bow, the token of his covenant, is seen in the judgments that he executeth.

When the vision of the ruin of Jerusalem was revealed to the prophet Ezekiel, he saw that yet Christ sat under the bow. i. 28.

When Antichrist was to come against the saints of God, the commission came from Christ, as he sat 'under the bow.' Re. iv. 3. This John did see and relate, of which we should take special notice: for by this token God would have us to know that these clouds, though they come for correction, yet not to destroy the church.

My bow shall be seen in the cloud.

Ver. 15. 'And I will remember my covenant, which *is* between me and you, and every living creature of all flesh; and the waters shall no more become a flood to destroy all flesh.'

'And I will remember my covenant.' Much like this is that of the Lord to Israel, when they are under all, or any of those forty judgments mentioned. Le. xxvi. If they shall confess their iniquity, [saith he,] and the iniquity of their fathers, &c., 'Then will I remember my covenant with Jacob, and also my covenant with Isaac, and also my covenant with Abraham will I remember; and I will remember the land.' Le. xxvi. 40—42. His usual way in other sayings is, to begin with Abraham, but here he ends with him; and the reason is, because there, as it were, the great promise of the Messiah to that people began, 'Saying, in thy seed shall all nations be blessed.'

'And I will remember my covenant which *is* between me and you.' We read not here of any compact or agreement between Noah and God Almighty; wherefore such conditions and compacts could not be the terms between him and us. What then? why that covenant that he calls his, which is his gift to us, 'I will give thee for a covenant,' this is the covenant which is between God and us: 'There is one God, and one mediator between God and man, the man Christ Jesus.' This then is the reason why all the waters, why all the judgments of God, and why all the sins that have provoked those judgments, cannot become a flood to destroy all flesh.

Ver. 16. 'And the bow shall be in the cloud; and I will look upon it, that I may remember the everlasting covenant between God and every living creature of all flesh that *is* upon the earth.'

'And the bow shall be in the cloud.' This is a kind of a repetition; for this he had told us before, saying, 'I do set my bow in the cloud,' and 'the bow shall be seen in the cloud:' which repetition is very needful, for it is hard for us to believe that Christ and grace are wrapped up in the judgments of God. 1 Pe. i. 12. Wherefore it had need be attested twice and thrice. 'To write the same things to you,' saith Paul, 'to me indeed *is* not grievous, but for you *it is* safe.' Phil. iii. 1.

'And I will look upon.' A familiar expression, and suited to our capacity, and spoken to prevent a further ground of mistrust; much like to that of God, when he was to send the plague upon Egypt:

'The blood, saith God, (of the Lamb,) shall be to you for a token upon the houses where ye *are:* and when I see the blood I will pass over you, and the plague shall not be upon you, to destroy *you,* when I smite the land of Egypt.' Ex. xii. 13.

'And I will look upon it that I may remember.' Not that God is forgetful, 'He is ever mindful of his covenant.' But such expressions are used to shew and persuade us that the whole heart and delight of God is in it.

'That I may remember the everlasting covenant.' This word covenant is also the sixth repetition thereof; my covenant, the covenant, a covenant, and the everlasting covenant. O how fain would God beat it into the heads of the world, that he hath for men a covenant of grace.

'The everlasting covenant.' Because the parties on both sides are faithful, perfect, and true; the Father being the one, and the Son of his love the other; for this covenant, as I said before, is not a compact and agreement betwixt God and the world, but his Son, as his gift to men, is set for them to Godward. Zec. ix. 11. So that what conditions there are, they are perfectly found in Christ, by whose blood the covenant is sealed and established, and indeed becomes everlasting, hence it is called 'the blood of the everlasting covenant.' He. xiii. 20. And again, the New Testament is said to be in this blood. Besides, the promises are all in Christ, I mean the promises of this covenant; in him they are yea, and in him amen, to the glory of God the Father: now they being all in him, and yea and amen no where else, the covenant itself must needs be of pure grace and mercy, and the bow in the cloud, not qualifications in us, [but] the proper token of this covenant.

Ver. 17. 'And God said unto Noah, This is the token of the covenant, which I have established between me and all flesh that *is* upon the earth.'

Behold a repetition of all things that were essential either to the covenant itself, or to our faith therein, the *making* of the covenant, the *looking on* the covenant, and the *token* of the covenant; how often are they mentioned, that we might be more fully convinced of the unchangeable nature of it. As Joseph said unto Pharaoh, 'For that the dream was doubled unto Pharaoh twice, *it is* because the thing *is* established by God.' Ge. xli. 32.

'And God said unto Noah.' Where God loveth, he delighteth to apply himself to such, in a more than general way; he singleth out the person, Noah, Abraham, and the like. 'I know thee by name,' saith he to Moses, and 'thou hast found grace in my sight.'

'This is the token of the covenant.' It still wants beating into people's heads, where they should look for the covenant itself, to wit, the throne which the rainbow compasseth round about; for that is the token of the presence of the Messias, and thither we are to look for salvation from all plagues, and from all the judgments that are due to sin: The Lord for Christ's sake forgave you, this is the token of the covenant.

'Of the covenant which I have established.'

This word 'I,' as also hinted before, doth intimate that this covenant is the covenant of grace and mercy, for a covenant of works cannot be established; that is, settled between God and men, before both parties have either by sureties, or performance ratified and confirmed the same. Indeed it may be so established, as that God will appoint no other; but to be so established, as to give us the fruits thereof, that must be the effects of his being well pleased with the conditions of those concerned in the making thereof. But that is not the world, but the Son of God, and therefore it is called his covenant, and he 'as given to us of God,' is so reckoned our condition and worth. Zec. ix. 11.

'Which I have established.' To wit, upon better promises than duties purely commanded, or than the obedience of all the angels in heaven. I have established it in the truth and faithfulness, in the merit and worth of the blood of my Son, of whom the rainbow that you see in the cloud is a token.

Ver. 18. '¶ And the sons of Noah, that went forth of the ark, were Shem, and Ham, and Japheth: and Ham *is* the father of Canaan.'

By these words Moses is returned again to the history of Noah. 'And the sons of Noah that went forth of the ark.' If these words, 'that went forth of the ark,' bear the emphasis of this part of the verse, then it may seem that Noah had more children than these; but they were not accounted of; for they being ungodly, as the rest of the world, they perished with them in their ungodliness. These only went in, and came out of the ark with him;* to wit,

---

* That absurd jumble, called 'The Koran,' mentions a fourth son of Noah, named Kinan, who refused to enter the ark with his family, preferring to trust them on the top of a mountain, where they all perished. See the chapter entitled 'Hod.'—Ed.

'Shem, and Ham, and Japheth.' The names thus placed are not according to their birth; for Japheth was the elder, Ham the younger, and Shem the middlemost of the two.

Shem therefore takes the place, because of his eminency in godliness; ix. 24. also, because from him went the line up to Christ. x. 2. For which cause also the family of the sons of Judah, though he was but the fourth son of Israel, was reckoned before the family of Reuben, Jacob's first born; or before the rest of the sons of his brethren. 1 Ch. ii. 3. Sometimes persons take their place in genealogy, from the fore-sight of the mightiness of their offspring. Thus was Ephraim placed before Manasseh; for ' truly (said Jacob) his younger brother shall be greater than he,' Ge. xliii. 17—20. And he set Ephraim before Manasseh.

Ham is the next in order; not for the sake of his birthright, or because he was much, if anything, now for godliness; but for that he was the next to be eminent in his offspring, for opposing and fighting against the same.

Shem and Ham therefore the two heads, or chief, from whence sprang good and evil men, by way of eminency. ' Ham is the father of Canaan,' or of the Canaanites, the people of God's curse, whom the sons of Shem who afterwards sprang from Abrabraham, Isaac, and Jacob, were to cut off from the earth, for their most high abominations.

Japheth comes in, in the first place, as one that at present was least concerned either in the mercy or displeasure of God; being neither, in his offspring, to be devoutly religious, nor yet incorrigibly wicked, though afterwards he was to be persuaded to dwell in the tents of Shem.

Ver. 19. ' These are the three sons of Noah; and of them was the whole earth overspread.'

Thus though Noah's beginning was small, his latter end did greatly increase.

Ver. 20, 21. ' ¶ And Noah began *to be* an husbandman, and he planted a vineyard:—And he drank of the wine, and was drunken; and he was uncovered within his tent.'

This is the blot in this good man's scutcheon; and a strange blot it is, that such an one as Noah should be thus overtaken with evil! One would have thought that Moses should now have began with a relation of some eminent virtues, and honourable actions of Noah, since now he was saved from the death that overtook the whole world, and was delivered, both he and his children, to possess the whole earth himself. Indeed, he stepped from the earth to the altar; as Israel of old did sing on the shore of the Red Sea: But, as they, he soon forgat; he rendered evil to God for good.*

Neither is Noah alone in this matter: Lot also being delivered from that fire from heaven that burnt up Sodom and Gomorrah, falls soon after into lewdness with the children of his body, and begetteth his own two daughters with child. Ge. xix. 30—36.

Gideon also, after he was delivered out of the hands of his enemies, took that very gold which God had given him, as the spoil of them that hated him, and made himself idols therewith. Ju. viii. 24—27. What shall I say of David ? and of Solomon also, who after he had been twenty years at work for the service of the true God, both in building and preparing for his worship, and in writing of Proverbs by divine inspiration; did, after this, make temples for idols; yea, almost for the gods of all countries ? Yea, he did it when he was old, when he should have been preparing for his grave, and for eternity. ' It came to pass, when Solomon was old, *that* his wives turned away his heart after other gods :—For Solomon went after Ashtoreth, the goddess of the Zidonians; and after Milcom, the abomination of the Ammonites.—He did also build an high place for Chemosh, the abomination of Moab, in the hill that *is* before Jerusalem; and for Molech, the abomination of the children of Ammon. And likewise did he for all his strange wives, which burnt incense and sacrificed unto their gods.' 1 Ki. xi. 4—8.

All these sins were sins against mercies; yea, and doubtless against covenants, and the most solemn resolutions to the contrary. For who can imagine, but that when Noah was tossed with the flood, and Lot within the scent and smell of the fire and brimstone that burnt down Sodom, with his sons, and his daughters; and Gideon, when so fiercely engaged with so great an enemy, and delivered by so strange a hand; should in the most solemn manner both promise and vow to God. But behold! now they in truth are delivered and saved, they recompense all with sin. Lord, what is man! ' How - abominable and filthy is man, which drinketh iniquity like water.' Job xv. 16. Let these things learn us to cease from man, ' whose breath is in his nostrils: for wherein is he to be accounted of ?' Is. ii. 22. Indeed, it is a vain thing to build our faith upon the most godly man in the world, because he is subject to err; yea, far better than He, was so.

If Noah, and Lot, and Gideon, and David, and Solomon, who wanted not matter from arguments, and that of the strongest kind; as arguments that

---

* Faithful is the record of Holy Writ. No excuse is offered for the sin of this great patriarch. Grapes eaten from the vine, or after having been dried, are nutritious, like grain from the ear of corn; pressed out and fermented, they lose that nutriment—acquire a fiery force—mount to the brain—lead reason captive—and triumphs over decency: the most enlightened man becomes the savage.—ED.

are drawn from mercy and goodness be, to engage to holiness, and the fear of God; yet after all, did so foully fall, as we see: let us admire grace, that any stand; let the strongest fear, lest he fearfully fall; and let no man but Jesus Christ himself be the absolute platform and pattern of faith and holiness. As the prophet saith, 'Let us cease from man.' But to return:

'And Noah began *to be* an husbandman.' This trade he took up for want of better employment; or rather, in mine opinion, from some liberty he took to himself, to be remiss in his care and work, as a preacher. For seeing the church was now at rest, and having the world before them, they still retaining outward sobriety, poor Noah, good man, now might think with himself, 'I need not now be so diligent, watchful and painful in my ministry as formerly; the church is but small, without opposition, and also well settled in the truth; I may now take to myself a little time to tamper with worldly things.' So he makes an essay upon husbandry. 'He began *to be* an husbandman.' Ha, Noah! it was better with thee when thou wast better employed! Yea, it was better with thee, when a world of ungodly men set themselves against thee! Yea, when every day thy life was in danger to be destroyed by the giants, against whom thou wast a preacher above a hundred years! For then thou didst walk with God; Then thou wast better than all the world; but now thou art in the relapse!

Hence note, That though the days of affliction, of temptation and distress, are harsh to flesh and blood; yet they are not half so dangerous as are the days of peace and liberty. Wherefore Moses pre-admonished Israel, That when they had received the land of Canaan, and had herds, and silver and gold in abundance, that then their heart be not lifted up to forget the Lord their God. Jesurun kicked when he was fat. O! When provender pricks* us, we are apt to be as the horse or mule, that is without understanding. De. viii. 10—15.

'He planted a vineyard: and he drank of the wine, and was drunken.' Although in the course of godliness, many men have but a speculative knowledge of things; yet it is not so in the ways of this world and sin, the practical part of these things are lived in by all the world. They are sinners indeed, 'He drank of the wine.'

'He drank of the wine, and was drunken.' The Holy Ghost, when it hath to do with sin, it loveth to give it its own name: drunkenness must be drunkenness, murder must be murder, and adultery must bear its own name. Nay, it is neither the

goodness of the man, nor his being in favour with God, that will cause him to lessen or mince his sin. Noah was drunken; Lot lay with his daughters; David killed Uriah; Peter cursed and swore in the garden, and also dissembled at Antioch. But this is not recorded, to the intent that the name of these godly should rot or stink: but to shew, that the best men are nothing without grace; and, 'that he that standeth, should not be high minded, but fear.' Yea, they are also recorded, for the support of the tempted, who when they are fallen, are oft raised up by considering the infirmities of others. 'Whatsoever things were written aforetime were written for our learning, that we through patience, and comfort of the scriptures might have hope.' Ro. xv. 4.

'And he was uncovered within his tent.' That is, he lay like a drunken man, that regarded not who saw his shame. Hence note, how beastly a sin drunkenness is; it bereaveth a man of consideration, and civil behaviour; it makes him as brutish and shameless as a beast; yea, it discovereth his nakedness to all that behold.

'And he was uncovered.' That is, lay naked. Behold ye now, that a little of the fruit of the vine, lays gravity, grey hairs, and a man that for hundreds of years was a lover of faith, holiness, goodness, sobriety, and all righteousness; shamelessly, as the object to the eye of the wicked, with his nakedness in his tent.

'He was uncovered within his tent.' The best place of retirement he had, but it could not hide him from the eye of the ungodly; it is not therefore thy secret chamber, nor thy lurking in holes, that will hide thee from the eye of the reproacher: nothing can do this but righteousness, goodness, sobriety and faithfulness to God; this will hide thee; these are the garments, which, if they be on thee, will keep thee, that the shame of thy nakedness do not appear. Re. xvi. 15.

Ver. 22. 'And Ham, the father of Canaan, saw the nakedness of his father, and told his two brethren without.'

Ham was the unsanctified one, the father of the children of the curse of God. He saw the nakedness of his father, and he blazed abroad the matter. Hence note, That the wicked and ungodly man, is he that doth watch for the infirmities of the godly: as David says, They watched for my halting. Indeed, they know not else how to justify their own ungodliness; but this, instead of excusing them of their wickedness, doth but justify the word against them; for by this they prove themselves graceless, and men that watch for iniquity. 'Let them not say in their hearts (said David) Ah! so would we have it.' Ps. xxxv. 25. Ammon said, 'Aha! against the sanctuary when it was profaned; and against the land of Israel when it was desolate,

---

* To prick—to incite—to spur—to dress one's self for show; thus it was commonly used in Bunyan's time, but in this sense has become obsolete.—Ed.

and against the house of Judah when it went into captivity.' Eze. xxv. 3. The enmity that is in the hearts of ungodly men, will not suffer them to do otherwise; when they see evil befal the saint, they rejoice and skip for joy. Eze. xxvi. 2; xxxvi. 2.

'He saw the nakedness of his father.' Hence note, That saints can rarely slip, but the eyes of the Canaanites will see them. This should make us walk in the world with jealous eyes, with eyes that look round about, not only to what we are and do, but also, how what we do is *resented in the world. Ge. xiii. 7. Abraham was good at this, and so was Isaac and Jacob; xxxiv. 30. for they tendered more the honour and glory of God, than they minded their own concerns.

'He saw the nakedness of his father.' Who was the nearest and dearest relation he had in the world; yet neither relation nor kin, nor all the good that his father had done him, could keep his polluted lips from declaring his father's follies, but out they must go; the sin of his own defiled heart must take place of the fifth commandment, and must rather solace itself in rejoicing in his father's iniquity, than in covering his father's nakedness. Wicked men regard not kindred; and no marvel, for they love not godliness. He that loveth not God, loveth not his brother, or father: nay, he 'wrongeth his own soul.' Pr. viii. 36.

'And told his two brethren without.' He told them, that is, mockingly, reflecting not only upon Noah, but also upon his brethren; to all of whom himself was far inferior, both as to grace and humanity.

Ver. 23. 'And Shem and Japheth took a garment, and laid it upon both their shoulders, and went backward, and covered the nakedness of their father; and their faces were backward, and they saw not their father's nakedness

Shem and Japheth did it: This is recorded for the renown of these, as the action of Ham is for his perpetual infamy.

They 'took a garment, and went backward, and covered their father, and saw not his nakedness.' Love will attempt to do that with difficulty, that it cannot accomplish otherwise. I think it might be from this action, that the wise man gathereth his proverb from. 'Hatred stirreth up strifes; but love covereth all sins.' Pr. x. 12. Indeed, Ham would fain have made variance between his father and his brethren, by presenting the folly of the one, to the shame and provocation of the other. But Shem, and his brother Japheth, they took the course to prevent it; they covered their father's nakedness.

Ver. 24. 'And Noah awoke from his wine,

and knew what his younger son had done unto him.'

By these words more is implied than expressed; for this awaking of Noah, not only informeth us of natural awaking from sleep, but of his spiritual awaking from his sin. He awoke from his wine. As 'Ely said to Hannah, How long wilt thou be drunken? Put away thy wine from thee.' 1 Sa. i. 14. By which words he exhorteth to repentance. It is said of Nabal, That his wine went from him, as many men's sins forsake them, because they are decayed, and want strength and opportunity to perform them. Now this may be done, where the heart remaineth yet unsanctified: but Noah awoke from his wine, put it away, or, repented him of the evil of his doing. 'A just man falleth seven times, and riseth up again: but the wicked shall fall into mischief.' Pr. xxiv. 16. Wherefore they have cause to say to all the Hams in the world, 'Rejoice not against me, O mine enemy: when I fall, I shall arise;' Mi. vii. 8. but your fall, is a fall into mischief.

'He knew what his younger son had done unto him.' Whether this was by revelation from heaven, or through the information of Japheth and Shem, I determine not; but so it was, that the good man had understanding thereof: which might be requisite upon a double account; not only that he might now be ashamed thereof; but take notice, that he had caused the enemies of God to reproach; for this sinks deep into a good man's heart, and afflicteth him so much the more.

Ver. 25. 'And he said, Cursed be Canaan; a servant of servants shall he be unto his brethren.'

By these words one would think that Canaan, the grand-child of Noah, was the first that discovered his nakedness; but of this I am uncertain: I rather think that Noah, in a spirit of prophecy, determined the destruction of Ham's posterity, from the prodigiousness of his wicked action, and of his name, which signifieth indignation, or heat; for names of old were ofttimes given according to the nature and destiny of the persons concerned. 'Is not he rightly called Jacob?' Ge. xxvii. 36. And again, 'As his name is, so is he.' 1 Sa. xxv. 25. Besides, by this act did Ham declare himself void of the grace of God; for he that rejoiceth in iniquity, or that maketh a mock, as being secretly pleased with or at the infirmities of the godly, he is declared already, by the Spirit of God, to be nothing. 1 Co. xiii.

'A servant of servants shall he be unto his brethren.' This was accomplished when Israel took the land of Canaan, and made the offspring of this same Ham, even so many as escaped the edge of the sword, to be captives and bondsmen, and tributers unto them.

Hence note, that the censures of good men are dreadful, and not lightly to be passed over, whether

---

* To resent—to consider as an injury or affront—to take ill.—Ed.

they prophesy of evil or good; because they speak in judgment, and according to the tenor of the word of God.

Ver. 26. 'And he said, Blessed *be* the LORD God of Shem; and Canaan shall be his servant.'

Shem seems by this to be the first in that action of love to his father: and that Japheth did help through his persuasion; for Shem is blessed in a special manner, and Canaan is made his servant.

Hence note, That forwardness in things that are good, is a blessed sign that the Lord is our God: Blessed be the Lord God of Shem. It is said of Hananiah, That ' he *was* a faithful man, and feared God above many.' Ne. vii. 2. Now such men are provocations to good, as I doubt not but Shem's was to Japheth: As Paul saith of some, 'Your zeal hath provoked very many.' 2 Co. ix. 2.

Ver. 27. 'God shall enlarge Japheth, and he shall dwell in the tents of Shem.'

In the margin, it is 'God shall persuade:' And it looks like a confirmation of what I said before, and is a prophecy of that requital of love that God should one day give his posterity, for his kindness to Noah his father. As if Noah had said, ' Well, Japheth, thou wast soon persuaded by Shem to shew kindness to me thy father, and the Lord shall hereafter persuade thy posterity to trust in the God of Shem.'

'God shall enlarge.' This may respect liberty of soul, or how great the church of the Gentiles should be; for Japheth was the father of the Gentiles. Ge. x. 5.

If it respect the first, then it shows that sin is as fetters and chains that holds souls in captivity and thraldom. And hence, when Christ doth come in the gospel, it is ' to preach deliverance to the captives, - and to set at liberty them that are bruised.' Lu. iv. 18.

' God shall persuade.' That is, God shall enlarge him by persuasion; for the gospel knows no other compulsion, but to force by argumentation. Them therefore that God brings into the tents, or churches of Christ, they by the gospel are enlarged from the bondage and thraldom of the devil, and persuaded also to embrace his grace to salvation.

Ver. 28. '¶ And Noah lived after the flood three hundred and fifty years.'

He lived therefore to see Abraham fifty and eight years old: He lived also to see the foundation of Babel laid; nay, the top stone thereof: and also the confusion of tongues. He lived to see of the fruit of his loins, mighty kings and princes. But in all this time he lived not to do one work that the Holy Ghost thought worthy to record for the savour of his name, or the edification and benefit of his church, save only, That he died at nine hundred and fifty years; so great a breach did this drunkenness make upon his spirit.

Ver. 29. 'So all the days of Noah were nine hundred and fifty years: and he died.'

CHAP. X.

Ver. 1. 'Now these *are* the generations of the sons of Noah, Shem, Ham, and Japheth: and unto them were sons born after the flood.'

Having thus passed over the flood, with what Noah and his sons did after; we now come to the second plantation of the world, to wit, by the three sons of Noah; for by these three was the world replenished after the flood. Shem was the father of the Jews; Ham the father of the Canaanites; and Japheth, the father of the Gentiles. So then, of Shem came the then present visible church; of Ham the opposers and enemies of it; but of Japheth came those that should be received into the church afterwards; as also abundance of the haters of the Lord.

Ver. 2. '¶ The sons of Japheth; Gomer, and Magog, and Madai, and Javan, and Tubal, and Meshech, and Tiras.'

Gomer, a consumer; Magog, covering, or melting; Madai, measuring, or judging; Javan, making sad; Tubal, born, brought, or worldly; Meshech, prolonging; Tiras, a destroyer; these are the English of their names.

Gomer, and Magog, and Meshech, and Tubal, are the great persecutors of the church in the latter days. Eze. xxxviii. 2. They shall be persecuted then by consumers, melters, and men of this world. Re. xx. 8. Madai, and Javan, (as some say,) were the fathers of the Medes and Greeks. These therefore did sometimes help, and not always hinder the church.

Ver. 3, 4. 'And the sons of Gomer; Askenaz, and Riphath, and Togarmah. And the sons of Javan; Elishah, and Tarshish, Kittim, and Dodanim.'

Riphath, medicine, or release; Elishah, the Lamb of God; Dodanim, beloved. Either these names were given them by way of prophecy; implying, that of their seed should arise many Gentile churches; or to show us, that when men, as their fathers, have left or lost the power of godliness, yet something of the notion they may yet retain. Is. lx. 9.

Ver. 5. 'By these were the isles of the Gentiles divided in their lands, every one after his tongue, after their families, in their nations.'

But this must be understood to be after the building of, and confusion at Babel; for before they had all but one tongue; and besides, they kept all together. ch. xi. 1, 2.

Ver. 6. '¶ And the sons of Ham; Cush, and Mizraim, and Phut, and Canaan.'

Cush, black. Of Ham and Mizraim came the Ethiopians, or blackamoor: Ps. cv. 23. The land of

Ham was the country about Egypt; wherefore Israel was first afflicted by them.

Ver. 7. 'And the sons of Cush; Seba and Havilah, and Sabtah, and Raamah, and Sabtechah: and the sons of Raamah; Sheba and Dedan.'

Seba and Sheba, sometimes look well upon the church; but when they did not, God gave them for her ransom. Ps. lxxii. 10. Is. xliii. 3.

Ver. 8. 'And Cush begat Nimrod: (or the rebellious one;) he began to be a mighty one in the earth.'

The begetting of Nimrod, is accounted a thing that is over and above, and is laid by the Holy Ghost as a blot upon Cush for ever; for when men would vilify, they used to say, Thou art the son of the rebellious, the son of a murderer. So again, He that begetteth Solomon's fool, (or, wicked one) he begetteth him to his own shame. Pr. xvii. 21.

'Cush begat Nimrod.' So then, the curse came betimes upon the sons of Ham; for he was the father of Cush. For the curse, as it were, begins in rebellion, and a rebellious one was Nimrod, both by name and nature.

'He began to be a mighty one in the earth.' I am apt to think he was the first that in this new world sought after absolute monarchy.

'He began to be a mighty one in the earth,' (or, among the children of men.) I suppose him to be a giant; not only in person, but in disposition; and so, through the pride of his countenance, did scorn that others, or any, should be his equal; nay, could not be content, till all made obeisance to him. He therefore would needs be the author and master of what religion he pleased; and would also subject the rest of his brethren thereto, by what ways his lusts thought best. Wherefore here began a fresh persecution. THAT sin therefore which the other world was drowned for was again revived by this cursed man, even to lord it over the sons of God, and to enforce idolatry and superstition upon them; and hence he is called 'the mighty hunter.'

Ver. 9. 'He was a mighty hunter before the LORD: wherefore it is said, even as Nimrod the mighty hunter before the LORD.'

He was a mighty hunter. That is, a persecutor: Wherefore Saul's persecuting of David is compared to hunting: 1 Sa. xxvi. 20. and so is the persecution of others. La. iv. 18. They hunt every man his brother with a net: Mi. vii. 2. and it may well be compared thereto; for the dog or lion that hunteth, is void of bowels and pity; and if they can but satisfy their doggish and lionish nature, they care neither for innocence, nor goodness, nor life of that they pursue. 1 Sa. xxiv. 11. The life, the blood, the extirpation of the contrary party, is the end of their course of hunting.* Eze. xiii. 18, 22.

'He was a mighty hunter.' As it is said of Jabin, 'He mightily oppressed Israel twenty years;' that is, he did it exceedingly; he went beyond others; he was more cruel and barbarous; he was a mighty hunter. Wherefore the children of blessed Shem, by this monster, had sore affliction. Ju. iv. 2, 3. Noah therefore lived to see Nimrod, the mighty one, make havock of the children of his bowels, to his no little grief and compunction of spirit.

'He was a mighty hunter before the LORD;' or, in the presence of the Lord; or, in defiance to him. This shows, That the hand of God was stretched forth against his work; as also it was against Jeroboam's, by that man of God that from Judah went down to prophesy against him; but he abode obdurate and hard; he regarded not the Lord, nor the operation of his hands. 1 Ki. xiii. 1—3. As he also saith in another place of the cursed brood of Antichrist, 'When they fall upon the sword, they shall not be wounded.' Joel ii. 8. Let them do things never so much against the plain text, they feel not the wounds of conscience; but this is a sore judgment, and that under which this hunter was; and therefore the presence and hand of God would not break him off, nor hinder his hunting of souls. But even before the face of the keeper of the godly, would Nimrod, the rebel, hunt for their precious life to destroy it.

Wherefore it is said, even as Nimrod, the mighty hunter, before the Lord. These words, as it seems, was the proverb that went of him among the godly in after generations; for he had so left his marks in the sides of the church, that she could not quickly forget him. Wherefore, when at any time there arose another that showed cruelty to the ways of God, he was presently compared to Nimrod, that 'hunted before the Lord.' Nimrod therefore was rebellious to a proverb: And as it is said of Ahab, so might it be said of him, 'There was none like' Nimrod, 'which did sell himself to work wickedness in the sight of, [or, before] the LORD.' 1 Ki. xxi. 25.†

Ver. 10. 'And the beginning of his kingdom

* How dreadfully was this exemplified in the cruelties per-

petrated on the dissenters in the valleys of Piedmont, and on the English dissenters in the reign of Mary, of Elizabeth, and of the Stuarts.—ED.

† 'The hunting tribes of air and earth,
  Respect the brethren of their birth;
  The eagle pounces on the lamb;
  The wolf devours the fleecy dam;
  Even tiger fell, and sullen bear,
  Their likeness and their lineage spare.
  Man only mars this household plan,
  And turns the fierce pursuit on man;
  Since Nimrod, Cush's mighty son,
  At first the bloody game begun.'

Scott's Rokeby.

was Babel, and Erech, and Accad, and Calneh, in the land of Shinar.'

By these words, as I suppose, are those in the chapter that followeth expounded: Where it says, 'Let us build us a city, and a tower;' for this work was chiefly the invention of Nimrod, who, with his wicked council, contrived this work; and as one that had made himself head of the people, he enjoined them to set to the work.

'And the beginning of his kingdom was Babel.' Babel therefore was the first great seat of oppressors after the flood; whose situation was in the land of Shinar, in that land which is now called Babylon. By this we may also gather, by whom our mystical Babel was builded; to wit, by those that rebelled (as Nimrod) from the simplicity of the gospel of Christ; for the builders, especially the chief, have a semblance one of another. It was even such as came of the seed of the godly, as these did of blessed Noah; who, in time, apostatizing from the word, and desiring mastership over their brethren; they, as lords, fomented their own conceptions, and then enjoined the people to build. As Rehoboam forsook the counsel of the ancients, that stood before his father Solomon; so these have forsaken the counsel of the old men, the apostles that stood before Jesus Christ; and hearkening to the counsel of a younger sort of wanters of their grace and wisdom, they imagine and build a Babel.*

Ver. 11, 12. 'Out of that land went forth Asshur, and builded Nineveh, and the city Rehoboth, and Calah, and Resen, between Nineveh, and Calah: The same *is* a great city.'

Nimrod having began to exalt himself; others, that were big with desires of ostentation, did soon follow his example, making themselves captains and heads of the people, and built them strong holds for the supportation of their glory. But they did it, as I said, by Nimrod's example; wherefore it is said they went ' out of that land.' Just thus it was at the beginning of mystical Babel: First the tyranny began at Babel itself, where the usurper was seen to sit in his glory, before whose face the world did tremble. Now other inferior persons, inferior, I say, in power, but not in pride, having desire to be lords, as Nimrod himself, they will also go build them cities; by which means Nimrod's invention could not be kept at Rome, but hath spread itself in many and mighty kingdoms.†

'Out of that land went forth Asshur, and builded Nineveh,' &c. Asshur seems to be the second son of Shem, ver. 22. A fit resemblance of those persons that have come from mystical Babel, to build their Ninevehs, and Rehoboths, and Calnehs, in all lands. Still they have pretended religion. That they had their orders from the apostolical see. That they were the true sons of Shem, or disciples of Christ. But the seeing Christian should remember, that some of the children of Shem were in Babel with rebellious Nimrod. That instead of learning humility of their father, through the pride and rebellion of their own vain-glorious fancies, they learned wickedness and rebellion of cursed and prodigious Nimrod.

Hence note, that what cities, that is, churches soever have been builded by persons that have come from Romish Babel, those builders and cities are to be suspected for such as had their founder and foundation from Babel itself. Wherefore let Israel say, 'Asshur shall not save us,' Ho. xiv. 3. for he shall not save himself; Nu. xxiv. 24. but as the star of Jacob ariseth, he shall fade and perish for ever. So perish all the builders and building that hath had its pattern from mystical Babel, unless a miracle of grace prevents.

It was Asshur that carried away the ten tribes; Ezr. iv. 2. it is Asshur that joineth with the enemies of the church; Ps. lxxxiii. 8. it is Asshur that with others upholds the great mart of the nations. Eze. xxvii. 23. Wherefore Asshur and all his company, must at last go down into their pit. Eze. xxxii. 22.

So then, let Augustine the monk, come from Rome into England, and let him build his Nineveh here; let others go also into other countries, and build their Resens and Calahs there; these are all but brats of Babel, and their end shall be, That they perish for ever. John saw it, and the cities, that is, the churches of the nations, or the national churches, fell; and great Babylon, their inventor and founder, ' came into remembrance before God, to give unto her the cup of the wine of the fierceness of his wrath.' Re. xvi. 19.

Ver. 13, 14. 'And Mizraim begat Ludim, and Anamim, and Lehabim, and Naphtuhim, and Pathrusim, and Casluhim, (out of whom came Philistim,) and Caphtorim.'

---

* Great allowances might be made for Bunyan's severe language with respect to state interference in matters of faith and worship, because he so cruelly suffered by it in his own person. But had he escaped persecution, the same awful reflections are just and true. If a christian monarchy robs, imprisons, and murders dissenters, surely a Mohamedan state may do the same to all those who refuse to curse Christ and bless Mahomet. Bunyan appears to consider that the great wickedness of man which caused the flood arose from the state interfering with faith and worship. This is certainly a fruitful source of those dreadful crimes, hypocrisy and persecution, but whether it was the cause of that awful event, the flood, or of that splendid absurdity, the tower of Babel, the reader must judge for himself.—ED.

† First Rome, then the Greek and Russian church; then Henry the VIII. and the church over which that lascivious monster was the supreme head; then the Lutheran church of Germany and Holland; and then . . . . . How admirably true is the genealogy of Antichrist as drawn out by Bunyan. —ED.

Ludim, as I suppose, may be the same with Lubim that came up with the Egyptians and Ethiopians against Israel, 2 Ch. xii. 3; xvi. 8. of whose cruelty Nahum complains; where he saith, They also helped Nineveh against the children of God. iii. 9. The rest of them were of the same disposition, especially the Philistine that came of Casluhim; for they, both in Saul and David's days, were implacable against the church and people of God; they were a giantish people, and trusted in their strength, and seldom overcome but when Israel went against them in the name of the Lord their God.

Ver. 15—18. ' ¶ And Canaan begat Sidon his first born, and Heth, and the Jebusite, and the Amorite, and the Girgasite, and the Hivite, and the Arkite, and the Sinite, and the Arvadite, and the Zemarite, and the Hamathite: And afterward were the families of the Canaanites spread abroad.'

These are the children of Canaan, the son of Ham, the accursed of the Lord. These did chiefly possess the land of Canaan before Israel went out of Egypt: they were a mighty giantish people, yet Israel must fight with them, notwithstanding they were, in comparison to these, but as the grasshopper.

Ver. 19. ' And the border of the Canaanites was from Sidon, as thou comest to Gerar, unto Gaza; as thou goest, unto Sodom, and Gomorrah, and Admah, and Zeboim, even unto Lasha.'

They bordered therefore upon the Philistines on the one side; Ge. xxvi. 15, 18, 19. for Gerar and Gaza belonged to them, and they touched upon Sodom and Gomorrah, &c. on the other. Ju. xvi. 1, 21. They were placed therefore, by the judgment of God, between these two wicked and sinful people, that they might, as a punishment for their former sins, be infected with the sight and infection of their ungodly and monstrous abominations. They that ' turn aside unto their crooked ways, the LORD shall lead them forth with the workers of iniquity.' Ps. cxxv. 5.

Ver. 20. ' These *are* the sons of Ham, after their families, after their tongues, in their countries, *and* in their nations.'

Ham had a mighty offspring; but the judgment of God was, That they should be wicked men, idolaters, persecutors, sinners with a high hand; such as God was resolved to number to the sword, both in this world, and that to come; I mean, for the generality of them.

Ver. 21. ' ¶ Unto Shem also, the father of all the children of Eber, the brother of Japheth the elder, even to him were *children* born.'

The manner of style which the Holy Ghost here useth in his preamble to the genealogy of Shem, is worthy to be taken notice of; as that he is called, ' the father of all the children of Eber,' and ' the brother of Japheth.'

By his being called, ' the father of all the children of Eber,' we may suppose, that from Eber to Abraham, (by whom the reckoning of the genealogy was cut off from Eber, and intailed to the name of Abraham,) all the children of Eber were, as it were, the disciples of Shem, for he lived awhile after Abraham. His doctrine therefore they might profess, though possibly with some mixture of those inventions that came in among men afterwards; which I think were at the greatest about Abraham's time. Besides, he shews by this, that the other children of Shem, as Elam, Asshur, Lud and Aram, with Uz, Hul, Gether and Mash, went away with Nimrod, and the rest of that company, into idolatry, tyranny and other profaneness; so that only the line from Shem to Eber, and from thence to Abraham, &c. were the visible church in those days.

' The brother of Japheth.' So he was of Ham, but because Ham was cut off for his wickedness to his father, therefore both Shem and Japheth did hold him in abomination, and would not own that relation that before was between them, especially in things pertaining to the kingdom of God, and of Christ: Wherefore the Holy Ghost also, in reckoning up the kindred of Shem, excludeth Ham the younger brother, and stops after he had mentioned Japheth: ' The brother of Japheth the elder.'

' Unto him were *children* born,' unto Shem also. Unto him were children born: The Holy Ghost doth secretly here, as he did before in the generation of Seth, insinuate a wonder. For considering the godliness of Shem, and the ungodliness of Ham, and the multitude of his tyrannical brood, it is a wonder that there should such a thing as the offspring of Shem be found upon the face of the earth. For I am apt to think, that Shem, with his posterity, did testify against the actions of Nimrod; as also against the children of Ham, in their wickedness and rebellion against the way of God; as may be hinted after. Wherefore he, with his seed, were in jeopardy, among that tumultuous generation. Yet God preserved him and his seed upon the face of the earth. For let the number and wickedness of men be never so great in the world, there must be also a church, by whose actions the ways of the wicked must be condemned.

Ver. 22. ' The children of Shem; Elam, and Asshur, and Arphaxad, and Lud, and Aram.'

These children were born unto Shem: The book of Chronicles mentions four more, as Uz, and Hul, and Gether, Meshech, or Mash; but these were the natural sons of Aram, Shem being only their father's father.

Elam and Asshur, as also Lud and Aram, notwithstanding they were the sons of Shem, struck off, as I think, with Nimrod, and left their father, for the glory of Babel; yea, they had a province there in the days of Daniel. viii. 2. Wherefore great judgments are threatened against Elam; as, That Elam shall drink the cup of God's fury: That their bow shall be broken: That God would bring upon him the four winds. Je. xlix. 36. And, That there should be no nation whither the captives of Elam should not come: Yet God would save them in the latter days. ver. 39.

As for Lud although through the wickedness of his heart he forsook his father Shem, and so the true religion; yet a promise is made of his conversion, when God calls home the children of Japheth, and persuadeth them to dwell in the tents of Shem. 'I will set a sign among them (saith God,) and I will send those that escape of them, unto the nations to Tarshish, Pul and Lud, - to Tubal and Javan, to the isles afar off, that have not heard my fame. Isa. lxvi. 19. Yea, thus it shall be, although they were once the soldiers of the adversaries of the church, and bare the shield and helmet against her. Eze. xxvii. 10. Of Asshur I have spoken before. Aram became also an heathen, and dwelt among the mountains of the east: Out of him came Balaam the soothsayer that Balak sent for, to curse the children of Israel. Nu. xxiii. 7.

In Arphaxad, though he was not the eldest, remained the line that went from Abraham to David; and from him to Jesus Christ. Lu. iii. 36.

Ver. 23. 'And the children of Aram; Uz, and Hul, and Gether, and Mash.'

Uz went also off from Shem, but yet good men came from his loins; for Job himself was of that land. Job i. 1. Yet the wrath of God was threatened to go forth against them, because they had a hand in the persecution of the children of Israel, &c. Je. xxv. 20; La. iv. 21.

Ver. 24, 25. 'And Arphaxad begat Salah; and Salah begat Eber. And unto Eber were born two sons: the name of one was Peleg; for in his days was the earth divided; and his brother's name was Joktan.'

This Eber was a very godly man, the next after Shem that vigorously stood up to maintain religion. Two things are entailed upon him to his everlasting honour: First, The children of God, even Abraham himself, was not ashamed to own himself one of this man's disciples, or followers; and hence he is called Abraham the Hebrew, or Ebrew. Ge. xiv. 13. Joseph also will have it go there: I was stolen (said he) out of the land of the Hebrews. Ge. xl. 15. Nay, the Lord God himself, to show how he honoured this man's faith and life, doth style himself the God of his fathers, to wit, the God of the Hebrews, the Lord God of the Hebrews. Ex. iii. 18; vii. 16; ix. 1, 13. Secondly, This was the man that kept that language with which

Adam was created, and that in which God spake to the fathers of old, from being corrupted and confounded by the confusion of Babel; and therefore it is for ever called his, the Hebrew tongue, Jn. v. 2; xix. 13, 20. the tongue in which Christ spake from heaven to and by Saul. Ac. xxi. 40; xxii. 2; xxvi. 14. This man therefore, was a stiff opposer of Nimrod; neither had he a hand in the building of Babel; for all that had, had their language confounded by that strange judgment of God.

'And unto Eber were born two sons: the name of the one was Peleg, (or Division,) for in his days was the earth divided; and his brother's name was Joktan.' This division, in mine opinion, was not only that division that was made by the confusion of tongues, but a division also that was made among men by the blessed doctrine of God, which most eminently rested in the bosom of Shem and Eber, neither of which had their hands in that monstrous work.* Wherefore, as Eber by abstaining kept entire the holy language; so Shem, to shew that he was clear from this sin also, is by the Holy Ghost called, 'The father of all the children of Eber.' Implying, that Eber and Shem did mightily labour to preserve a seed from the tyranny and pollution of Nimrod and Babel; and by that means made a division in the earth; unto whom because the rebels would not adhere, therefore did God the Lord smite them with confusion of tongues, and scatter them abroad upon the face of all the earth.

Ver. 26. 'And Joktan begat Almodad, and Sheleph, and Hazarmaveth, and Jerah.'

Here again he hath left the holy line, which is from Eber to Abraham, and makes a stop upon Joktan's genealogy, and so comes down to the building of Babel.

Ver. 27—30. 'These therefore begat Joktan: He also begat 'Hadoram, and Uzal, and Diklah, and Obal, and Abimael, and Sheba; and Ophir, and Havilah, and Johab: all these were the sons of Joktan.—And their dwelling was from Mesha, as thou goest, unto Sephar a mount of the east.'

Ver. 31. 'These are the sons of Shem, after their families, after their tongues, in their lands, after their nations.'

Moses, as I said, by this relation, respecteth, and handleth chiefly those, or them persons, who were at first the planters of the world after the flood; leaving the church, or a relation of that, and its seed, to be discoursed after the building of Babel, unto the tenth verse of the next chapter. Hence methinks one might gather, that these abovementioned, whose genealogies are handled at large, as the families of Japheth, of Ham, and Joktan are, were both, in their persons and offsprings en-

---

* 'That monstrous work,' the attempting to build the tower of Babel.—Ed.

gaged (some few only excepted, who might adhere to Noah, Shem, and Eber) in that foul work, the building of Babel. Now that which inclineth me thus to think, it is because immediately after their thus being reckoned by Moses, even before he taketh up the genealogy of Shem, he bringeth in the building thereof; the which he not only mentioneth, but also enlargeth upon; yea, and also telleth of the cause of the stopping of that work, before he returneth to the church, and the line that went from Shem to Abraham.

Ver. 32. 'These *are* the families of the sons of Noah after their generations, in their nations: and by these were the nations divided in the earth after the flood.'

CHAP. XI.

Ver. 1. 'And the whole earth was of one language, and of one speech.'

Moses having thus briefly passed through the genealogies of Japheth, Ham, and Joktan; in the next place he cometh to shew us their works which they had by this time engaged to do; and that was, to build a Babel, whose tower might reach to heaven. Now, in order to this their work, or rather to his relation thereof, he maketh a short fore-speech, which consisteth of two branches. The first is, That now they had all one language or lip.* The other was, That they yet had kept themselves together, either resting or walking, as an army compact. An excellent resemblance of the state of the church, before she imagined to build her a Babel. For till then, however one might outstrip another in knowledge and love; yet so far as they obtained, their language or lip was but one. Having but one heart, and one soul, they with one mouth did glorify God, even the Father.

'And the whole earth was of one language.' By these words therefore, we may conceive the reason why so great a judgment as that great wickedness, Babel, should be contrived, and endeavoured to be accomplished. The multitude was one. Not but that it is a blessed thing for the church to be one: as Christ saith, 'My beloved is but one.' Jn. xvii. 11. But here was an oneness, not only in the church, but in her mixing with the world. The whole earth, among which, as I suppose, is included Noah, Shem, and others; who being overtopt by Nimrod, the mighty hunter, might company with him until he began to build Babel. Therefore it is said in the next verse, that they companied together from the east, to the land of Shinar.

Hence note, That the first and primitive churches

were safe and secure, so long as they kept entire by themselves; but when once they admitted of a mixture, great Babel, as a judgment of God, was admitted to come into their mind.

Ver. 2. 'And it came to pass, as they journeyed from the east, that they found a plain in the land of Shinar; and they dwelt there.'

By these words, we gather, that the first rest of Noah, and so the inhabiting of his posterity, was still eastward from Babylon, towards the sun rising.

But to gospelise: They journeyed from the east: and so consequently they turned their backs upon the rising of the sun. So did also the primitive church, in the day when she began to decline from her first and purest state. Indeed, so long as she kept close to the doctrine and discipline of the gospel, according to the word and commandment of the Lord Jesus, then she kept her face still towards the sun rising: According to the type in Ezekiel, who saith of the second and mystical temple, Her fore front, or face, did stand towards the east. xlvii. 1. Also he saith, when he saw the glory of God, how it came unto this temple, it came from the way of the east. xliii. 2. Their journeying therefore from the east, was, their turning their backs upon the sun. And to us, in gospel times, it holdeth forth such a mystery as this: That their journey was thus recorded, to show they were now apostatized; for assuredly they had turned their back upon the glorious Sun of Righteousness, as upon that which shineth in the firmament of heaven.

'They found a plain in the land of Shinar.' Shinar is the land of Babylon, Da. i. 2. Zec. v. 11. as those scriptures in the margin declare.

'They found a plain.' Or, place of fatness and plenty, as usually the plains are; and are, upon that account, great content to our flesh: This made Lot separate from Abraham, and choose to dwell with the sinners of Sodom; why, the country was a plain, and therefore fat and plentiful, even like the garden of the Lord, and the land of Egypt. Here therefore they made a stop; here they dwelt and continued together. A right resemblance of the degenerators' course in the days of general apostacy, from the true apostolical doctrine, to the church of our Romish Babel. So long as the church endured hardship, and affliction, she was greatly preserved from revolts and back-slidings; but after she had turned her face from the sun, and had found the plain of Shinar; that is, the fleshly contents that the pleasures, and profits, and honours of this world afford; she forgetting the word and order of God, was content, with Lot, to pitch towards Sodom; or, with the travellers in the text, to dwell in the land of Babel.

---

† 'Language or lip.' שָׂפָה, a lip, is also used for speech. In the figurative language, 'of one lip,' means that they all spoke one language; so in Job xi. 2, אִישׁ שְׂפָתָיִם, literally, 'a man of lips,' is translated 'a man full of talk.'—ED.

Ver. 3. '¶ And they said one to another, Go to, let us make brick, and burn them throughly, (and burn them to a burning). And they had brick for stone, and slime had they for mortar.'

Now they being filled with ease and plenty, they begin to lift up the horn, and to consult one with another what they were best to do: Whereupon, after some time of debate, they came to this conclusion, That they would go build a Babel.

'And they said one to another, Go to.' This manner of phrase is often used in scripture; and is some times, as also here, used to show, That the thing intended, must come to pass, what opinion or contradiction to the contrary soever there be. It argueth that a judgment is made in the case, and proceedings shall be accordingly. Thus it is also to be taken in Ju. vii. 3. Ec. ii. 1. Is. v. 5. Ja.v. 1. &c. Wherefore it shows, that these men had cast off the fear of God, and, like Israel in the days of the prophet Jeremiah, they resolved to follow their own imagination, let God or his judgments speak never so loud to the contrary. And so indeed he says of them at verse the sixth: 'And this they begin to do: (saith God) and now nothing will be restrained from them.'

☞ This is all Mr. Bunyan hath writ of this EXPOSITION, as we perceive by the blank paper following the manuscript.*

---

* That Bunyan intended to have continued this commentary there can be no doubt, not only from the abrupt termination of his labours, and the blank paper following the manuscript, but from an observation he makes on the sabbath—the sabbath of years, the jubilee, &c., 'of all which, more in their place, IF GOD PERMIT.' See Gen. ii. 3.—ED.

A HOLY LIFE THE BEAUTY OF CHRISTIANITY;

OR,

AN EXHORTATION TO CHRISTIANS TO BE HOLY.

'Holiness becometh thine house, O Lord, for ever.'—Psal. xciii. 5.

THE EDITOR'S ADVERTISEMENT.

THIS is the most searching treatise that has ever fallen under our notice. It is an invaluable guide to those sincere Christians, who, under a sense of the infinite importance of the salvation of an immortal soul, and of the deceitfulness of their hearts, sigh and cry, 'O Lord of hosts, that judgest righteously, that triest the reins [most secret thoughts] and the heart.' 'Try MY reins and MY heart,' for it '*is* deceitful above all *things*, and desperately wicked: who can know it? I the Lord search the heart, I try the reins, even to give every man according to his ways, *and* according to the fruit of his doings.' He, in whose heart the Holy Spirit has raised the solemn inquiry, 'What must I do to be saved?' flies from his own estimate of himself, with distrust and fear, and appeals to an infallible and unerring scrutiny. 'Search me, O God, and know my heart: try me, and know my thoughts: And see if *there be any* wicked way in me, and lead me in the way everlasting.' Reader, are *you* desirous of having your hopes of pardon, and of heaven, weighed in the unerring balances of the sanctuary; while you are yet in a state of probation? Meditate and ponder over this faithful little work. If accompanied by the Divine blessing, it will test your faith and practice in the crucible and by the fire of God's word. It is intended to turn your spirit inside out—to lay bare every insidious enemy that may have crept in and lie lurking in the walls of Mansoul. It exhibits sin in all its hideous deformity, stript of its masquerade and disguises; so that it appears, what it really is, the great enemy to human happiness. It is calculated to stir up our pure minds to incessant vigilance, lest we should wander upon tempting, but forbidden paths; and be caught by Giant Despair, to become the objects of his cruelty in Doubting Castle.

This work was first published in 1684, in a pocket volume, comprising nine sheets duodecimo; but became so rare, as to have escaped the researches of Wilson, Whitefield, and other editors of the collected works of Mr. Bunyan,—until about the year 1780, when it was first re-published in an edition of his works, with notes, by Mason and Ryland.

The evident object of this treatise was to aid christian efforts, under the Divine blessing, in stemming the torrent of iniquity, which, like an awful flood, was overspreading this country. The moral and religious restraints, which the government under the Commonwealth had imposed, were dissolved by the accession of a debauched prince to the throne of England; a prince who was bribed, to injure or destroy the best interests of the country, by the voluptuous court of France. He had taken refuge there from the storm; and had been defiled and corrupted beyond ordinary conception. The king and his court were surrounded by pimps, panders, courtesans, and flatterers. The example of the court spread throughout the country—religion became a jest and laughing-stock; and those who were not to be cajoled out of their soul's eternal happiness—whose vital godliness preserved them in the midst of such evil examples and allurements, were persecuted with unrelenting rigour. The virtuous Lord William Russel, and the illustrious Sydney, fell by the hands of the executioner: John Hampden was fined forty thousand pounds. The hand of God was stretched out. An awful pestilence carried off nearly seventy thousand of the inhabitants of London. In the following year, that rich and glorious city, with the cathedral—the churches—public buildings—and warehouses, replenished with merchandize—were reduced to ashes. The Dutch fleet sailed up the Thames and threatened destruction to our navy, and even to the government,—filling the court and country with terror. Still profligacy reigned in the court and country—a fearful persecution raged against all who refused to attend the church service. Thousands perished in prison, and multitudes were condemned to expatriate themselves. The timid and irresolute abandoned the faith,—desolation spread over the church of God. At this time, at imminent risk, John Bunyan not only fearlessly preached, but published his faithful 'Advice to Sufferers;' which was immediately followed by this important work, calling upon every one 'who named the name of Christ,' at all hazards, 'to depart from iniquity.' They were 'words in season,' and were 'good,' '*like* apples of gold in pictures of silver.' Pr. xxv. 11.

The contrast in public manners must have been painfully felt by one, who had seen and enjoyed the general appearances, and doubtless many real proofs of piety, which prevailed under the protectorate of Cromwell. He was now called to witness the effects of open and avowed wickedness among governors and nobles, by which the fountains of iniquity were opened up, and a flood of immorality let loose upon all classes; demoralizing the nation, and distressing the church. It must have been difficult to form any thing like an accurate estimate of the number of those who abandoned their christian profession. The immoral conduct of one bad man is more conspicuous than the unobtrusive holiness of ninety-nine good men; more especially, when a professor becomes profane. Thus Bunyan argues, 'One black sheep is quickly espied among five hundred white ones, and one mangey one will soon infect many. One also, among the saints, that is not clean, is a blemish to the rest, and as Solomon says, "One sinner destroyeth much good."' p. 527. It is more congenial to our fallen nature to notice, and be grieved with, evil conduct, than it is to rejoice over that excellence which may cast the observer into the shade; besides the jaundiced fear that good works *may* arise from improper motives. These principles equally applied to the state of society under the Presbyterian government: but when the restoration to the old system took place, so vast a change passed over society, like a pestilence, 'that sin, through custom, became no sin. The superfluity of naughtiness,' says Bunyan, 'is at this day become no sin with many.' p. 509. 'There are a good many *professors* now in England that have nothing to distinguish them from the worst of men, but their praying, reading, hearing of sermons, baptism, church fellowship, and breaking of bread. Separate them but from these, and every where else they are as black as others, even in their whole life and conversation.' p. 508. 'It is marvellous to me to see sin so high amidst the swarms of professors that are found in every corner of this land.' If the conduct of many professors were so vile, as there can be no doubt but that it was, how gross must have been that of the *openly* profane? It accounts for the wicked wit and raillery of Hudibras, when so many professors threw off the mask and gloried in their hypocrisy—Butler shut his eyes to the cruel sufferings of thousands who perished in jails, the martyrs to the sincerity of their faith and conduct. The falling away was indeed great; and Bunyan, with all earnestness, warns his readers that, 'To depart from iniquity is to shun those examples, those beastly examples to drunkenness—to whoredom—to swearing—to

lying—to stealing—to sabbath-breaking—to pride —to covetousness—to deceit—to hypocrisy, that in every corner of the country present themselves to men.' p. 517. 'O the fruits of repentance thick sown by preachers, come up but thinly! Where are they found? Confession of sin, shame for sin, amendment of life, restitution for cozening, cheating, defrauding, beguiling thy neighbour,—where shall these fruits of repentance be found? Repentance is the bitter pill, without the sound working of which, base and sinful humours rest unstirred, unpurged, undriven out of the soul.' p. 519.

'I would not be austere,' said Bunyan, 'but were wearing of gold, putting on of apparel, dressing up houses, decking of children, learning of compliments, boldness in women, lechery in men, wanton behaviour, lascivious words, and tempting carriages, signs of repentance; then I must say, the fruits of repentance swarm in our land.' 'The tables of God's book are turned upside down. Love, to their doctrine, is gone out of the country.' 'Love is gone, and now coveting, pinching, griping, and such things, are in fashion; now iniquity abounds instead of grace, in many that name the name of Christ.' p. 519, 520. 'Alas! alas! there is a company of half-priests in the world; they dare not teach the people the whole counsel of God, because they would condemn themselves, and their manner of living in the world: where is that minister now to be found, that dare say to his people, walk as you have me for an example, or that dare say, what you see and hear to be in me, do, and the God of peace shall be with you.' p. 520. Such was the general character of the parish priests, after the black Bartholomew Act had driven the pious and godly ministers from the parish churches. It is almost a miracle that Bunyan escaped persecution for his plain dealing. We cannot wonder, that under such teachers, 'Christians learned to be proud one of another, to be covetous, to be treacherous, and false, to be cowardly in God's matters, to be remiss and negligent in christian duties, one of another.' p. 525. A scandal was thus brought upon religion. 'Upon this I write with a sigh; for never more than now. There is no place where the professors of religion are, that is free from offence and scandal. Iniquity is so entailed to religion, and baseness of life to the naming the name of Christ, that 'All places are full of vomit and filthiness.' 'Ah! Lord God, this is a lamentation, that a sore disease is got into the church of God.' p. 529. It was a period when a more awful plague raged as to morals and religion, than that which, about the same time, had ravaged London with temporal death—the plague of hypocrisy—of naming the name of Christ, and still living in sin. 'Hypocrisies are of that nature, that they spread themselves over the mind as the leprosy does over the body. It gets in the pulpit, in conference, in closets, in communion of saints, in faith, in love, in repentance, in zeal, in humility, in alms, in the prison, and in all duties, and makes the whole a loathsome stink in the nostrils of God.' p. 538. 'These licentious times, in which we live, are full of iniquity.' p. 539. 'They change one bad way for another, hopping, as the squirrel, from bough to bough, but not willing to forsake the tree,—from drunkards to be covetous, and from that to pride and lasciviousness—this is a grand deceit, common, and almost a disease epidemical among professors.' p. 532. 'The sins of our day are conspicuous and open as Sodom's were; pride and covetousness, loathing of the gospel, and contemning holiness, have covered the face of the nation.' p. 534. The infection had spread into the households of professors. 'Bless me, saith a servant, are these the religious people! Are these the servants of God, where iniquity is made so much of, and is so highly entertained! And now is his heart filled with prejudice against all religion, or else he turns hypocrite like his master and his mistress, wearing, as they, a cloak of religion to cover all abroad, while all naked and shameful at home.' p. 536. 'He looked for a house full of virtue, and behold nothing but spider-webs; fair and plausible abroad, but like the sow in the mire at home.' The immoral taint infected the young. 'O! it is horrible to behold how irreverently, how saucily, and malapertly, children, yea, professing children, at this day, carry it to their parents; snapping and checking, curbing and rebuking of them, as if they had received a dispensation from God to dishonour and disobey parents.' p. 535. 'This day, a sea and deluge of iniquity has drowned those that have a form of godliness. Now immorality shall, with professors, be in fashion, be pleaded for, be loved and more esteemed than holiness; even those that have a form of godliness, hate the life and power thereof, yea, they despise them that are good.' p. 543.

This melancholy picture of vice and profligacy was drawn by one whose love of truth rendered him incapable of deceit or of exaggeration. It was published at the time, and was unanswered, because unanswerable. It was not painted from imagination by an ascetic; but from life by an enlightened observer—not by the poor preaching mechanic when incarcerated in a jail for his godliness; but when his painful sufferings were past—when his Pilgrim, produced by the folly of persecutors, had rendered him famous through Europe—when his extraordinary pulpit talents were matured and extensively known, so that thousands crowded to hear him preach—when his labours were sought in London and in the country—when his opportu-

nities of observation had become extended far beyond most of his fellow-ministers. The tale is as true as it is full of painful interest. The causes of all this vice are perfectly apparent. Whenever a government abuses its powers by interfering with divine worship—by preferring one sect above all others; whether it be Presbyterian, Independent, or Episcopalian—such a requiring the things that are God's to be rendered unto Cæsar, must be the prolific source of persecution, hypocrisy, and consequent immorality and profaneness. The impure process of immorality is checked by the rival labours of all the sects to promote vital godliness. Can we wonder that such a state of society was not long permitted to exist? In three troublous years from the publication of this book, the licentious monarch was swept away by death, not without suspicion of violence, and his besotted popish successor fled to die in exile. An enlightened monarch was placed upon the vacant throne, and persecution was deprived of its tiger claws and teeth by the act of toleration.

However interesting to the christian historian, and humbling to human pride, the facts may be which are here disclosed; it was not the author's intention thus to entertain his readers. No; this invaluable tract has an object in view of far greater importance. It is an earnest, affectionate, but pungent appeal to all professors of every age, and nation, and sect, to the end of time. The admonition of the text is to you, my reader, and to me; whether we be rich or poor, ministers or ministered unto, it comes home equally to every heart, from the mightiest potentate through every grade of society to the poorest peasant. May the sound ever reverberate in our ears and be engraven upon our hearts, 'Let every one that nameth the name of Christ depart from iniquity.'

The analysis of this book exhibits—How solemn a thing it is to name the name of Christ, as the author and finisher of our faith—God manifest in the flesh, to bear the curse for us, and to work out our everlasting salvation. The hosts of heaven rejoice over the penitent sinner ransomed from the pit of wrath. Is it possible for the soul that has escaped eternal burnings—that has experienced the bitterness and exceeding sinfulness of sin—that has felt the misery of transgression—that has been brought up out of that deep and horrible pit —to backslide and plunge again into misery, with his eyes open to see the smoke of their torments ascending up before him? Is it possible that he should heedlessly enter the vortex, and be again drawn into wretchedness? Yes; it is alas too true. Well may the Lord, by his prophet, use these striking words, 'Be astonished, O ye heavens, at this, and be horribly afraid, be ye very desolate, saith the Lord. For my people have committed two evils; they have forsaken me, the fountain of living waters, *and* hewed out broken cisterns, that can hold no water.' Je. ii. 12, 13.

The extreme folly of such conduct would render the fact almost incredible, did we not too frequently witness it in others, and feel it in our own hearts. This volume places these facts plainly before us, and affectionately exhorts us to be watchful, and diligently to inquire into the causes of such evil, and the remedies which ought to be applied. It shews us the great varieties that are found in the tempers and qualities of God's children, in words calculated to make an indelible impression.

'But in this great house of God there will not only be golden and silver Christians, but wooden and earthly ones. And if any man purge himself from these [earthly ones], from their companies and vices, he shall be a vessel to honour, sanctified, and meet for the master's use, and prepared for every good work.' p. 518. Bunyan earnestly cautions his readers to constant watchfulness, 'for sin is one of the most quick and brisk things that are.' p. 515. And jealousy over ourselves, lest our hearts should deceive us. 'The young man in the gospel that cried to Christ to shew him the way to life, had some love to his salvation; but it was not a love that was strong as death, cruel as the grave, and hotter than coals of juniper.' Ca. viii. 6. It *cost nothing*—no self-denial, no sacrifice. 'Such will love as long as mouth and tongue can wag,' will pray and hear sermons, but will not cut off a darling lust; such deceive their own souls. Some are allured but not changed: 'There is some kind of musicalness in the word; when well handled and fingered by a skilful preacher,' it has a momentary influence; 'they hear thy words, but do them not.' Eze. xxxiii. 30. Above all things, beware of hypocrisy, for when it once enters, it spreads over the soul, as the leprosy does over the body. p. 521. 'He is the same man, though he has got a new mouth.' p. 532. 'Many that shew like saints abroad, yet act the part of devils when they are at home.' Wicked professors are practical atheists. 'The dirty life of a professor lays stumbling blocks in the way of the blind.' p. 545. 'A professor that hath not forsaken his iniquity, is like one that comes out of the pest-house, among the whole, with his plaguey sores running upon him. This is the man that hath the breath of a dragon; he poisons the air round about him. This is the man that slays his children, his kinsmen, his friend, and himself. They are the devil's most stinking tail, with which he casts many a professor into carnal delights, with their filthy conversations.' p. 530. 'Oh! the millstone that God will shortly hang about your necks, when the time is come that you must be drowned in the sea and deluge of God's wrath.' p. 530. Rather

than thus rush upon Jehovah's fiercest anger, 'Tell the world, if you will not depart from iniquity, that Christ and you are parted, and that you have left him to be embraced by them to whom iniquity is an abomination.' p. 530. Thus faithfully and affectionately did Bunyan deal with his hearers and readers. And he takes an occasion, now in his maturer years, to confirm the sentiments which he had formerly published in his 'Differences in Judgment about Water Baptism no Bar to Communion.' 'It is strange to see at this day how, notwithstanding all the threatenings of God, men are wedded to their own opinions, beyond what the law of grace and love will admit. Here is a Presbyterian, here an Independent, here a Baptist, so joined each man to his own opinion, that they cannot have that communion one with another, as by the testament of the Lord Jesus they are commanded and enjoined.' 'To help thee in this, keep thine eye much upon thine own base self, be clothed with humility, and prefer thy brother before thyself; and know that Christianity lieth not in small matters, neither before God nor understanding men.' 'I have often said in my heart, what is the reason that some of the brethren should be so shy of holding communion with those, every whit as good, if not better than themselves? Is it because they think themselves unworthy of their holy fellowship? No, verily; it is because they exalt themselves.' p. 538. He goes on to declare that the difficulties which sin and Satan place in the way of the Christian pilgrim ought never to be concealed. Salvation is to be worked out with fear and trembling. It is only by divine aid, by dependence upon our heavenly Father, that it can be accomplished. 'To depart from iniquity to the utmost degree of requirement, is a copy too fair for mortal flesh exactly to imitate, while we are in this world. But with good paper, good ink, and a good pen, a skilful and willing man may go far.' p. 546, 547. Mr. Ryland's note on the Christian's trials is, 'when the love of sin is subdued in the conscience, then peace will flow in like a river, God will be glorified, Christ exalted; and the happy soul, under the teaching and influence of the all-wise, omnipotent Spirit, will experience sweet peace and joy in believing.' Millions of pilgrims have entered the celestial city, having fought their way to glory; and then, while singing the conqueror's song, all their troubles by the way must have appeared as sufferings but for a moment, which worked out for them an eternal and exceeding weight of glory. And then how blessed the song to him that hath loved us, and washed us from our sins in his own blood, and made us kings and priests unto our God. To him be glory and dominion for ever and ever. Amen.—GEO. OFFOR.

AN INTRODUCTION TO THE FOLLOWING DISCOURSE.

When I write of justification before God from the dreadful curse of the law; then I must speak of nothing but grace, Christ, the promise, and faith. But when I speak of our justification before men, then I must join to these good works. For grace, Christ, and faith, are things invisible, and so not to be seen by another, otherwise than through a life that becomes so blessed a gospel as has declared unto us the remission of our sins for the sake of Jesus Christ. He then that would have forgiveness of sins, and so be delivered from the curse of God, must believe in the righteousness and blood of Christ: but he that would shew to his neighbours that he hath truly received this mercy of God, must do it by good works; for all things else to them is but talk: as for example, a tree is known to be what it is, to wit, whether of this or that kind, by its fruit. A tree it is, without fruit, but so long as it so abideth, there is ministered occasion to doubt what manner of tree it is.

A professor is a professor, though he hath no good works; but that, as such, he is truly godly, he is foolish that so concludeth. Mat. vii. 17, 18. Ja. ii. 18. Not that works *make* a man good; for the fruit maketh not a good tree, it is the principle, to wit, Faith, that makes a man good, and his works that shew him to be so. Mat. vii. 16. Lu. vi. 44.

What then? why, all professors that have not good works flowing from their faith are naught; are bramble bushes; are 'nigh unto cursing, whose end *is* to be burned.' He. vi. 8. For professors by their fruitlessness declare that they are not of the planting of God, nor the wheat, ' but tares and children of the wicked one.' Mat. xiii. 37, 38.

Not that faith needeth good works as an help to justification before God. For in this matter faith will be ignorant of all good works, except those done by the person of Christ. Here, then, the good man ' worketh not, but believeth.' Ro. iv. 5. For he is not now to carry *to* God, but to receive at his hand the matter of his justification by faith; nor is the matter of his justification before God ought else but the good deeds of another man, to wit, Christ Jesus.

But is there, therefore, no need at all of good works, because a man is justified before God without them? or can that be called a justifying faith, that has not for its fruit good works? Job xxii. 3. Ja. ii. 20, 26. Verily good works are necessary, though God need them not; nor is that faith, as to justification with God, worth a rush, that abideth alone, or without them.

There is, therefore, a twofold faith of Christ in the world, and as to the notion of justifying righ-teousness, they both concur and agree, but as to the manner of application, there they vastly differ. The one, to wit, the non-saving faith, standeth in speculation and naked knowledge of Christ, and so abideth idle: but the other truly seeth and receives him, and so becometh fruitful. Jn. i. 12. He. ix. 13. Ro. vi. 16. And hence the true justifying faith is said to receive, to embrace, to obey the Son of God, as tendered in the gospel: by which expression is shewed both the nature of justifying faith, in its actings in point of justification, and also the cause of its being full of good works in the world. A gift is not made mine by my seeing of it, or because I know the nature of the thing so given; but then it is mine if I receive and embrace it, yea, and as to the point in hand, if I yield myself up to stand and fall by it. Now, he that shall not only see, but receive, not only know, but embrace the Son of God, to be justified by him, cannot but bring forth good works, because Christ who is now received and embraced by faith, leavens and seasons the spirit of this sinner, through his faith, to the making of him capable so to be [justified]. Ac. xv. 9. Ge. xviii. 19. He. xi. 11. Faith made Sarah receive strength to conceive seed, and we are sanctified through faith, which is in Christ. For faith hath joined Christ and the soul together, and being so joined, the soul is one spirit with him; not essentially, but in agreement and oneness of design. Besides, when Christ is truly received and embraced to the justifying of the sinner, in that man's heart he dwells by his word and Spirit, through the same faith also. Now Christ by his Spirit and word must needs *season* the soul he thus dwells in: so then the soul being seasoned, it seasoneth the body; and body and soul, the life and conversation.

We know it is not the seeing, but taking of a potion, that maketh it work as it should, nor is the blood of Christ a purge to this or that conscience, except received by faith. He. ix. 14.

Shall that then be counted right believing in Christ unto justification, that amounts to no more than to an idle speculation, or naked knowledge of him? shall that knowledge of him, I say, be counted such, as only causes the soul to behold, but moveth it not to good works? No, verily. For the true beholding of Jesus to justification and life, changes from glory to glory. 2 Co. iii. 18.

Nor can that man that hath so believed, as that by his faith he hath received and embraced Christ for life before God, be destitute of good works: for, as I said, the word and Spirit comes also by this faith, and dwells in the heart and conscience. Now, shall a soul where the word and Spirit of Christ dwells, be a soul without good works? Yea, shall a soul that has received the love, the mercy, the kindness, grace and salvation of God through the sorrows, tears, groans, cross, and cruel death of Christ, be yet a fruitless tree! God forbid. The faith is as the salt which the prophet cast into the spring of bitter water, it makes the soul good and serviceable for ever. 2 Ki. ii. 19—22.

If the receiving of a temporal gift naturally tends to the making of us to move our cap and knee, and binds us to be the servant of the giver, shall we think that faith will leave him who by it has received Christ, to be as unconcerned as a stock or stone, or that its utmost excellency is to provoke the soul to a lip-labour, and to give Christ a few fair words for his pains and grace, and so wrap up the business? No, no; 'the love of Christ constraineth us' thus to judge that it is but reasonable, since he gave his all for us, that we should give our some for him. 2 Co. v. 14, 15,

Let no man, then, deceive himself, as he may and will if he takes not heed with true notions, but examine himself concerning his faith, to wit; Whether he hath any? and if some, Whether of that kind that will turn to account in the day when God shall judge the world.

I told you before that there is a twofold faith, and now I will tell you that there are two sorts of good works; and a man may be shrewdly guessed at with reference to his faith, even by the works that he chooseth to be conversant in.

There are works that cost nothing, and works that are chargeable. And observe it, the unsound faith will choose to itself the most easy works it can find. For example, there is reading, praying, hearing of sermons, baptism, breaking of bread, church fellowship, preaching, and the like; and there is mortification of lusts, charity, simplicity, open-heartedness, with a liberal hand to the poor, and their like also. Now the unsound faith picks and chooses, and takes and leaves, but the true faith does not so.

There are a great many professors now in England that have nothing to distinguish them from the worst of men, but their praying, reading, hearing of sermons, baptism, church-fellowship, and breaking of bread. Separate them but from these, and everywhere else they are as black as others, even in their whole life and conversation. Thus they have chosen to them the most easy things to do them, but love not to be conscionably found in the practice of the other; a certain sign their faith is nought, and that these things, even the things they are conversant in, are things attended to of them, not for the ends for which God has appointed them, but to beguile and undo themselves withal.

Praying, hearing, reading; for what are these things ordained, but that we might by the godly use of them attain to more of the knowledge of God, and be strengthened by his grace to serve him better according to his moral law? Baptism, fellowship, and the Lord's supper, are ordained for these ends also. But there is a vast difference between using of these things, and a using of them for these ends. A man may pray, yea pray for such things, had he them, as would make him better in morals, without desire to be better in morals, or love to the things he prays for. A man may read and hear, not to learn to do, though to know; yea he may be dead to doing moral goodness, and yet be great for reading and hearing all his days. The people then among all professors that are zealous of good works are the peculiar ones to Christ. Tit. ii. 14. What has a man done that is baptized, if he pursues not the ends for which that appointment was ordained. The like I say of fellowship, of breaking of bread, &c. For all these things we should use to support our faith, to mortify the flesh, and strengthen us to walk in newness of life by the rule of the moral law. Nor can that man be esteemed holy whose life is tainted with immoralities, let him be what he can in all things else. I am of that man's mind as to practical righteousness, who said to Christ upon this very question, 'Well, master, thou hast said the truth; - for to love the Lord our God with all the heart, and with all the understanding, and with all the soul, and with all the strength, and to love *his* neighbour as himself, is more than all whole burnt-offerings and sacrifices.' Mar. xii. 28—33. To love my neighbour as myself, to do as I would be done unto, this is the law and the prophets. And he that is altogether a stranger to these things, how dwelleth the love of God in him; or how will he manifest to another that his faith will save him?

Satan is afraid that men should hear of justification by Christ, lest they should embrace it. But yet, if he can prevail with them to keep fingers off, though they do hear and look on, and practise lesser things, he can the better bear it; yea, he will labour to make such professors bold to conclude they shall by that kind of faith enjoy him, though by that they cannot embrace him, nor lay hold of him. For he knows that how far soever a man engages in a profession of Christ with a faith that looks on, but cannot receive nor embrace him, that faith will leave him to nothing but mistakes and disappointments at last.

The gospel comes to some in word only, and the faith of such stands but in a verbal sound; but the apostle was resolved not to know or take notice of such a faith. 1 Th. i. 4, 5. 'For the kingdom of God,' saith he, 'is not in word, but in power.' 1 Co. iv. 18—20. He whose faith stands only in a saying, I believe, has his works in bare words also, and as virtual is the one as the other, and both insignificant enough. ' If a brother or sister be naked, and destitute of daily food, and one of you say unto them, Depart in peace, be *ye* warmed and filled ; notwithstanding ye give them not those things which are needful to the body ; what *doth it* profit ? Even so faith, if it hath not works is dead, being alone.' Ja. ii. 15—17. This faith, therefore, Satan can allow, because it is somewhat of kin to his own. ver. 19.

Besides, what greater contempt can be cast upon Christ than by such wordy professors is cast upon him ? These are the men that by practice say, the gospel is but an empty sound. Yea, the more they profess, the louder they proclaim it thus to be, to his disgrace, while they, notwithstanding their profession of faith, hold and maintain their league with the devil and sin. The Son of God was manifest that he might destroy the works of the devil, but these men profess his faith and keep these works alive in the world. 1 Jn. iii. Shall these pass for such as believe to the saving of the soul ? For a man to be content with this kind of faith, and to look to go to salvation by it, what to God is a greater provocation ?

The devil laugheth here, for he knows he has not lost his vassal by such a faith as this, but that rather he hath made use of the gospel, that glorious word of life, to secure his captive, through his presumption of the right faith, the faster in his shackles.

It is marvellous to me to see sin so high amidst the swarms of professors that are found in every corner of this land. Nor can any other reason be given for it, but because the gospel has lost its wonted virtue, or because professors want faith therein. But do you think it is because of the first ? no, the word of our God shall stand in its strength for ever ; the faith of such therefore is not right; they have for shields of gold, made themselves shields of brass ; or instead of the primitive faith, which was of the operation of God, they have got to themselves a faith that stands by the power, and in the wisdom of man. 2 Ch. xii. 9, 10. Col. ii. 12. 1 Co. ii. 4, 5. And, to say no more to this, for what is God so angry with this land, but for the sin of the professors that dwell therein, while they have polluted his name with their gifts, and with their idols ? God, I say, has been provoked most bitterly by us, while we have profaned his name, making use of his name, his word, and ordinances, to serve ourselves, ' O Lord, what wilt thou do to this land.' We are every one looking for something ; even for something that carrieth terror and dread in the sound of its wings as it comes, though we know not the form nor visage thereof.* One

cries out, another has his hands upon his loins, and a third is made mad with the sight of his eyes, and with what his ears do hear ? and as their faith hath served them about justification, so it now serves them about repentance and reformation : it can do nothing here neither ; for though, as was said, men cry out, and are with their hands upon their loins for fear; yet, where is the church, the house, the man that stands in the gap for the land, to turn away this wrath by repentance, and amendment of life ? Behold the Lord cometh forth out of his place, and will come down and tread upon the places of the earth, and the mountains shall be molten under him, and the valleys shall be cleft, as wax before the fire, and as the waters that are poured down a steep place. But what is the cause of all this ?—For the transgression of Jacob is all this, and for the sins of the house of Israel. Mi. i. 5.

It is that that is observed by them that can make observation, that all that God has done to us already has been ineffectual as to cause that humility and reformation, by which his judgments must be turned away. Repentance is rare this day, and yet without doubt, that without which, things will grow worse and worse. As for them that hope that God will save his people, though but from temporal judgments, whether they repent and reform, or do otherwise, I must leave them and their opinions together : this I have found, that sometimes the repentance, even of the godly, has come too late to divert such judgments. And, how some of the godly should be so indulged as to be saved from punishment without repentance, when the true and unfeigned repentance of others will not deliver them, leaves me, I confess, in a wilderness ! But that which is most of all to be lamented is, that sin, through custom, is become no sin. The superfluity of naughtiness is at this day become no sin with many. Surely this was the case with Israel, else how could they say when the prophets so bitterly denounced God's judgments against them, ' Because we are innocent, surely his anger shall turn from us.' Je. ii. 35. When custom or bad example has taken away the conscience of sin, it is a sign that [that] soul is in a dangerous lethargy; and yet this is the condition of the most that profess amongst us this day. But to leave this and to proceed.

As there is a twofold faith, two sorts of good works, and the like, so there is also a twofold love to Christ ; the one standing, or stopping, in some passions of the mind and affections ; the other is

---

* How clearly is here portrayed the wretched state of this country towards the close of the reign of Charles II. It is

the natural eloquence of one whose very thoughts were governed by scriptural expressions. The martyrdoms of Essex, of Russel, and of Sydney—the uncertainty of the life of a debauched monarch, with the gloomy prospect of a popish successor, filled the country with dismal forebodings.—Ed.

that which breaks through all difficulties to the holy commandment to do it. Of both these there is mention made in the scripture; and though all true love begins at the heart, yet that love is but little set by that breaks not through to practice. How many are there in the world that seem to have the first, but how few shew the second. The young man in the gospel, Mar. x. 17. did by his running, kneeling, crying, inquiring, and entreating of Christ, to shew him the way to life, shew that he had inward love to Christ and his own salvation; but yet it was not a love that was 'strong as death,' 'cruel as the grave,' and hotter than the coals of juniper. Ca. viii. 6. It was a love that stopped in mind and affection, but could not break out into practice. This kind of love, if it be let alone, and not pressed to proceed till it comes into a labouring practising of the commandment, will love as long as you will, to wit, as long as mouth and tongue can wag; but yet you shall not by all your skill drive this love farther than the mouth; 'for with their mouth they shew much love, but their heart goeth after their covetousness.' Eze. xxxiii. 31.

Nor may this love be counted for that of the right kind, because it is in the heart, for the heart knows how to dissemble about love, as much as about other matters. This is feigned love, or love that pretends to dear affections for Christ, but can bestow no cost upon him. Of this kind of love the world is full at this day, especially the professors of this age; but as I said, of this the Lord Jesus makes little or no account, for that it hath in it an essential defectiveness. Thus, therefore, Christ and his servants describe the love that is true and of the right kind, and that with reference to himself and church.

First, with reference to himself. 'If a man love me,' saith he, 'he will keep my words.' Jn. xiv. 23. And again, 'He that hath my commandments, and keepeth them, he it is that loveth me.' And, 'He that loveth me not, keepeth not my sayings.' 'And the word which ye hear is not mine, but the Father's which sent me.' Behold you now where Christ placeth a sign of love, it is not in word nor in tongue, not in great and seemingly affectionate gestures, but in a practical walking in the law of the Lord. Hence such, and such only, are called the undefiled in the way. You know who says, 'I am the way.' 'Blessed,' saith David, '*are* the undefiled in the way, who walk in the law of the Lord.' Ps. cxix. 1.

But here again the hypocrite will give us the slip by betaking himself to exterior matters, as to his 'mint and anise and cummin.' Mat. xxiii. 23. Still neglecting the more weighty matters of the law, to wit, judgment, mercy, faith; or else to the significative ordinances, still neglecting to do to all

men as he would they should do to him. But let such know that God never ordained significative ordinances, such as baptism, the Lord's supper, or the like, for the sake of water, or of bread and wine; nor yet because he takes any delight that we are dipped in water, or eat that bread; but they were ordained to minister to us by the aptness of the elements, through our sincere partaking of them, further knowledge of the death, burial, and resurrection of Christ, and of our death and resurrection by him to newness of life. Wherefore, he that eateth and believeth not, and he that is baptized, and is not dead to sin, and walketh not in newness of life, neither keepeth these ordinances nor pleaseth God. Now to be dead to sin, is to be dead to those things forbidden in the moral law. For sin is the transgression of that, and it availeth not to vaunt that I am a saint and under this or that significative ordinance, if I live in 'the transgression of the law.' 1 Jn. iii. 4. For I am convicted of the law as a transgressor, and so concluded to be one that loveth not Christ, though I make a noise of my obedience to Christ, and of my partaking of his significative ordinances. The Jews of old made a great noise with their significative ordinances, while they lived in the breach of the moral law, but their practice of significative ordinances could not save them from the judgment and displeasure of their God. They could frequent the temple, keep their feasts, slay their sacrifices, and be mighty apt about all their significative things. But they loved idols, and lived in the breach of the second table of the law: wherefore God cast them out of his presence: hark what the prophet saith of them, Am. iv. 4, 5. 'Come to Bethel, and transgress; at Gilgal multiply transgression; and bring your sacrifices every morning, *and* your tithes after three years: and offer a sacrifice of thanksgiving with leaven, and proclaim *and* publish the free offerings: for this liketh you, O ye children of Israel, saith the Lord GOD.' Thus, as I said, the hypocrite gives us the slip; for when he heareth that love is in the keeping of the commandments of God, then he betakes him to the more external parts of worship, and neglecteth the more weighty matters to the provoking of the God of Israel.

Second, As love to God is shewed by keeping of his commandments; so love to my neighbour, is the keeping of the commandments of God likewise. 'By this we know that we love the children of God, when we love God, and keep his commandments. For this is the love of God,' - in us, both to God and man, 'that we keep his commandments: and his commandments are not grievous.' 1 Jn. v. 2, 3. He that keepeth not God's commandments, loves neither God nor men.

Thus then, we must learn to love one another.

He that keepeth God's commandment, doth to his brother what is right, for that is God's commandment. He that keeps God's commandment, doth to his brother even as he would be done unto himself, for that is God's commandment. He that keeps God's commandment, shutteth not up his bowels of compassion from him, for the contrary is his commandment. Further, he that keepeth God's commandment sheweth his brother what he must do to honour the Christ that he professeth, aright: therefore, he that keeps the commandment, loves his brother. Yea, the keeping of the commandment is loving the brethren.

But if all love, which we pretend to have one to another, were tried by this one text, how much of that that we call so, would be found to be nothing less? Preposterous are our spirits in all things, nor can they be guided right, but by the word and Spirit of God; the which, the good Lord grant unto us plentifully, that we may do that which is well pleasing in his sight, through Jesus Christ our Lord. Yea, and that there may, by them, be wrought sound repentance in us for all that hath been done by us amiss, lest he give 'Jacob to the spoil, and Israel to the robbers;' for that they have sinned against him by not walking in his ways, and by not being obedient to his law. Is. xlii. 24.

Let me add, lest God doth not only punish us in the sight, and by the hand of the wicked; but embolden them to say, it was God that set them on; yea, lest they make these sins of ours, which we have not repented of, not only their bye-word against us to after generations, but the argument, one to another, of their justification for all the evil that they shall be suffered to do unto us : saying, when men shall ask them, 'Wherefore hath the Lord done thus unto this land ? what *meaneth* the heat of this great anger ?' De. xxix. 24. 1 Ki. ix. 8. Je. xxii. 8. ' Even because they have forsaken the covenant of the Lord God of their fathers, and walked not in his ways.'

JOHN BUNYAN.

A HOLY LIFE THE BEAUTY OF CHRISTIANITY.

' AND, LET EVERY ONE THAT NAMETH THE NAME OF CHRIST DEPART FROM INIQUITY.'—2 TIM. ii. 19.

TIMOTHY, unto whom this epistle was writ, was an evangelist, that is, inferior to apostles and extraordinary prophets, and above ordinary pastors and teachers. 2 Ti. iv. 5. Ep. iv. 1. And he with the rest of those under his circumstances was to go with the apostles hither and thither, to be disposed of by them as they saw need, for the further edification of those who by the apostolical ministry were converted to the faith: and hence it is, that Titus was left at Crete, and that this Timothy was left at Ephesus. 1 Ti. i. 3 For they were to do a work for Christ in the world, which the apostles were to begin, and leave upon their hands to finish. Now when the apostles departed from places, and had left these evangelists in their stead, usually there did arise some bad spirits among those people, where these were left for the furtherance of the faith. This is manifest by both the epistles to Timothy, and also by that to Titus: wherefore Paul, upon whom these two evangelists waited for the fulfilling of their ministry, writeth unto them while they abode where he left them, concerning those turbulent spirits which they met with, and to teach them how yet further they ought to behave themselves in the house of God, which is the church of the living God, the pillar and ground of truth. And to this purpose he gives them, severally, divers instructions, as the judicious reader may easily understand, by which he encourageth them to the prosecution of that service which for Christ they had to do for those people where he had left them, and also instructeth them how to carry it towards their disturbers, which last he doth, not only doctrinally, but also by shewing them, by his example and practice, what he would have them do.

This done, he laboureth to comfort Timothy with the remembrance of the steadfastness of God's eternal decree of election, because grounded on his foreknowledge; saying, though Hymeneus and Philetus have erred from the faith, and, by their fall, have overthrown the faith of some, ' Yet the foundation of God standeth sure, having this seal, The Lord knoweth them that are his.' Now lest this last hint should still encourage some to be remiss and carnally secure, and foolish, as I suppose this doctrine abused, had encouraged them to be before ; therefore the apostle immediately conjoineth to it this exhortation ; ' And, let every one that nameth the name of Christ depart from iniquity.' Two truths strangely, but necessarily joined together, because so apt to be severed by the children of men; for many, under the pretence of their being elected, neglect to pursue holiness ; and many of them again that pretend to be for holiness, quite exclude the doctrine and motives that election gives thereto. Wherefore the apostle, that he might set men's notions as to these things right, he joins these two together, signifying thereby, that as electing love doth instate a man in the blessing of eternal life ;

so holiness is the path thereto; and, that he that refuseth to depart from iniquity shall be damned; notwithstanding he may think himself secured from hell by the act of God's electing love. For election designeth men not only to eternal glory, but to holiness of life, a means, thereto. Ep. i. 4, 5. And the manner of this connection of truth is the more to be noted by us, because the apostle seems to conjoin* them, in an holy heat of spirit, saying, 'The foundation of God standeth sure, having this seal, The Lord knoweth them that are his.' And, 'let every one that shall but so much as name the name of Christ, depart from iniquity;' or, as who would say, God will be revenged upon them for all, or, notwithstanding, they appropriate unto themselves the benefits of election.

In the text we have, FIRST, An exhortation. SECOND, The extension of that exhortation. The exhortation is, That men depart from iniquity. The extension of it is, to them, all of them, every one of them that name the name of Christ. 'And let every one that nameth the name of Christ, depart from iniquity.'

[FIRST, THE EXHORTATION—THAT MEN DEPART FROM INIQUITY.]

In the exhortation there are several things to be taken notice of, because insinuated by the apostle. The first is, that iniquity is a very dangerous and hurtful thing, as to the souls of sinners in general; so to them that name the name of Christ.

First, Iniquity is a very dangerous and hurtful thing *to men in general;* for it is that which did captivate the world at the beginning, and that made it a bond-slave to the devil. It has also done great hurt to mankind ever since. To instance a few things:

1. It is that which hath stupified and besotted the powers of men's souls, and made them even next to a beast or brute in all matters supernatural and heavenly. 2 Pe. ii. 12. For as the beast minds nothing but his lusts and his belly, by nature, so man minds nothing but things earthly, sensual, and devilish, by reason of iniquity.

2. It has blinded and darkened the powers of the soul, so that it can neither see where it is, nor which is the way out of this besotted condition. Ep. iv. 18.

3. It has hardened the heart against God, and against all admonition and counsel in the things of the gospel of Christ. Ro. ii. 5.

4. It has alienated the will, the mind, and affections, from the choice of the things that should save

it, and wrought them over to an hearty delight in those things that naturally tend to drown it in perdition and destruction. Col. i. 21.

5. It has made man odious in God's eyes, it has provoked the justice of God against him, and made him obnoxious to hell-fire. Eze. xvi. 5.

6. Yea, it so holds him, so binds him, so reserves him to this, that not he himself, nor yet all the angels of heaven, can deliver him from this deplorable condition. Pr. v. 22.

7. To say nothing of the pleasure and delight that it makes him take in that way to hell in which he walketh. Is. lxvi. 3; Pr. vii. 22, 23. Never went fat ox so gamesomely to the shambles, nor fool so merrily to the correction of the stocks, nor silly bird so wantonly to the hidden net, as iniquity makes men go down her steps to the pit of hell and damnation.

O it is amazing, it is astonishing to consider what hurt sin hath done to man, and into how many dangers it has brought him; but let these few hints at this time suffice as to this. I will now speak a word to the other particular, namely,

Second, That as iniquity is dangerous and hurtful to the souls of men in general, so it is *to them that name the name of Christ.* As to the so and so naming of him, to that I shall speak by and by, but at this time take it thus: That religiously name his name. And I say iniquity is hurtful to them.

1. It plucks many a one of them from Christ and the religious profession of him. I have even seen, that men who have devoutly and religiously professed Jesus Christ, have been prevailed withal, by iniquity, to cast him and the profession of his name quite off, and to turn their backs upon him. 'Israel,' saith the prophet, 'hath cast off *the thing that is* good.' Ho. viii. 3. But why? 'Of their silver and their gold have they made them idols.' The sin of idolatry drew their hearts from God; their love to that iniquity made them turn their backs upon him. Wherefore God complains, that of forwardness to their iniquity, and through the prevalence thereof, they had cast him behind their back. Eze. xxiii. 35.

2. As it plucks many a professor from Christ, so it keeps many a one from an effectual closing with him. How many are there that religiously profess and make mention of the name of Christ, that yet of love to, and by the interest that iniquity hath in their affections, never close with him unto salvation, but are like to them, of whom you read in Paul to Timothy, that they are ever learning and never able to come to the knowledge of the truth. 2 Ti. iii. 1—7.

3. And concerning those that have indeed come to him, and that have effectually closed with him, and that name his name to good purpose; yet how hath iniquity hurt and abused many of them. (1.)

---

* This is a solemn truth, which ought ever to be recollected when studying the mysteries of electing love. Election is as much to *a holy life* as it is to eternal glory.—ED.

It has prevailed with God to hide his face from them, a thing more bitter than death. (2.) It has prevailed with God to chastise, and to afflict them sorely, a thing in which he taketh no pleasure. La. iii. 33. (3.) It has provoked God to give them over to the hand of the enemy, and to deliver them to the tormentors. Je. xii. 7. Mat. xviii. 34. (4.) It hath brought them to question their interest in Christ, and whether they ever had grace in their souls. Ps. xxxi. 22. (5.) And for those that have yet believed they were in his favour, this iniquity hath driven them to fear that God would cast them away, and take all his good things from them. Ps. li.

Yea, he that would know the hurt that iniquity hath done to them that name the name of Christ, let him consider the cries, the sighs, the tears, the bemoanings, the bewailings, the lamentations, the sorrows, the confessions, the repentings and griefs wherewith they have been attended, while they have complained that they have been put in the stocks, laid in the dungeon, had their bones broken, suffered the terrors of God, been distressed almost to destruction, and have been fed with gravel, gall, wormwood, and with the wine of astonishment, for days, yea, years together. Job xiii. 27.. Ps. vi. 6; xxxi. 9, 10; xxxviii. 8; lx. 3; lxxxviii; cxvi. 3. Je. viii. 14; xxiii. 15; xxxi. 18. La. iii. 4, 16. Eze. iv. 16. 2 Co. xii. 21. By all which, and many more which might be mentioned, it appears that iniquity is a dangerous and hurtful thing.

[SECOND, THE EXTENSION OF THE EXHORTATION—TO EVERY ONE THAT NAMETH THE NAME OF CHRIST.]

But I proceed, and come in the next place to the extension of the exhortation, namely, that it reacheth to all those that name the name of Christ. 'And let every one that nameth the name of Christ depart from iniquity.'

To handle this a little, and to shew you what the apostle here means by naming of the name of Christ: he meaneth not an irreligious naming of that worthy name, nor those that name it irreligiously. This is evident, because he passed by their manner of naming of it without the least reproof, the which he would not have done had the fault been in their manner of naming of the name of Christ. Now I say, if he intendeth not those that name the name of Christ irreligiously, then, though the exhortation, 'let every one,' seems to extend itself to all, and all manner of persons, that any ways name the name of Christ, yet it is limited by this, to wit, that rightly, religiously, or according to the way of the professors of Christ, name his worthy name. And it must needs be so taken, and that for these reasons:

First, For that, as I said before, the apostle taketh no notice of their manner of naming of his name, so as to reprove any undecency or unseemliness in their naming of him; wherefore he alloweth of the manner of their naming of him.

Second, Because the apostle's design in this exhortation was, and is, that the naming of the name of Christ might be accompanied with such a life of holiness as might put an additional lustre upon that name whenever named in a religious way; but this cannot be applied to every manner of naming the name of our Lord Jesus Christ. For if a man shall name the name of Christ unduly, or irreligiously, though he shall never so much therewithal depart from iniquity, and be circumspect to the utmost in all civility and morality, yet he answers not the apostle's end, which he seeks by this his exhortation. For,

1. Suppose a man should name the name of Christ vainly, idly, in vain mirth, wantonness, false or vain swearing, or the like, and shall back this, his manner of naming the name of Christ, with all manner of justness and uprightness of life, would this answer the apostle's end in this his exhortation? Verily no; for this manner of naming the name is worthy reprehension; 'Thou shalt not take my name in vain,' or vainly make use thereof: and moral goodness attending the so-naming of the name of Christ will do more hurt than good. Ex. xx.

2. There is a reproachful and scandalous naming of the name of Christ, such as the Jews and Pharisees did accustom themselves unto, as to call him Jesus, the deceiver; and Christ, in a way of scorn and contempt. Nor were these men quite destitute of that which put a lustre upon their opinions; for, said the Lord Christ himself unto them, 'Ye indeed appear beautiful outward.' Mat. xxiii. 27.

3. There is such a naming of the name of Christ as to make it a cloak for false and dangerous errors: that men, by the use of that name, and the putting of it upon such errors and delusions, may put off their errors to other the better. 'Many shall come in my name,' to wit, with their delusions, presenting them, in my name, to the world, and shall put them off, in my name, to the destruction of the soul. Mat. xxiv. 5. Now, can any imagine that the apostle should extend his exhortation to such, that they, thus continuing to name the name of Christ, should depart from iniquity. To what end should such be comprehended in this exhortation of his? to no purpose at all: for the more an erroneous person, or a deceiver of souls, shall back his errors with a life that is morally good, the more mischievous, dangerous, and damnable is that man and his delusions; wherefore such a one is not concerned in this exhortation.

4. There is a naming of the name of Christ magically, and after the manner of exorcism, or conjuration; as we read in the Acts of the apostles.

The vagabond Jews, the exorcists, there say, 'We adjure you by Jesus, whom Paul preacheth.' Ac. xix. 13—15. Thus they called over them that had evil spirits, the name of the Lord Jesus. But what if these should clothe this, their devilish art, and devilish way, of using or naming of the name of the Lord Jesus, with departing from iniquity, so as to commend their whole life to by-standers, for such as is morally good: what advantage would Christ, or Paul, or the gospel, get thereby? verily none at all; but rather damage and reproach, as will soon appear to any man's reason, if it be considered that goodness of life, joined to badness of principles is like the devil clothed in white, or Satan transformed into an angel of light. And Paul was grieved in his spirit, when the wench that had a spirit of divination did acknowledge him to be the servant of the most high God, for he knew it would nothing further, or help forward, the Lord's design, but be rather an hinderance thereto. For when witches and devils come once to commend, or make use of the name of Christ, Christ and Paul like it not; therefore Paul's exhortation, which here we are presented with by the text, is not extended to any of the four sorts aforenamed, but,

Third, To those upon whom his name is called, they should depart from iniquity. I say those whom God has so far dignified, as to put the name of Christ upon them. Ac. xv. 17. And I will add, that apply that name to themselves. And the reason is, because God is now concerned. ch. xi. 26. God has changed thy name from Pagan to Christian, and thou choosest to call thyself by that name, saying, 'I belong to Christ.' Now thou must depart from iniquity, for that notice is taken of thee, both by heaven and earth, that thou art become a disciple, and 'let every one that' so 'nameth the name of Christ,' or that nameth it, being himself by God and himself put under such circumstances as these, 'depart from iniquity.' 1 Pe. iv. 16.

Fourth, It is spoken to those that name the name of Christ either in the public or private worship of God, being themselves professed worshippers of him; and the reason is, for that the ordinances, as well as the name of God, is holy, and 'he will be sanctified in them that come nigh him.' Le. x. 3. He therefore that approacheth the presence of Christ in prayer, or any other divine appointment, must take heed of regarding 'iniquity in his heart.' Ps. lxvi. 18. Else the Lord will stop his ears to his prayers, and will shut his eyes, and not take notice of such kind of worship or worshippers.

Fifth, Those that the apostle in this place exhorts to depart from iniquity are such as have taken unto themselves the boldness to say, that they are in him, abide in him, and consequently are made partakers of the benefits that are in him. 'He that saith he abideth in him, ought himself also to walk, even as he walked.' 1 Jn. ii. 6. And the reason is, because Christ is a fruitful root, and a free conveyer of sap into the branches; hence it is written, that 'the trees of the Lord are full *of sap.*' Ps. civ. 16. So then, he that nameth the name of Christ by way of applying to himself his benefits, and as counting that he is found of God in him, and so abideth, ought himself to walk even as he walked, that he may give proof of what he saith to be true, by bearing forth before men that similitude of righteousness that is in his root and stem: for such as the stock or tree is, such let the branches be, but that cannot be known but by the fruit: 'ye shall know them by their fruit.' Mat. vii. 16. So then, he that thus shall name the name of Christ, let him depart from iniquity: yea, let every such man do so.

Sixth, This exhortation is spoken to them that name Christ as their Sovereign Lord and King: let them 'depart from iniquity.' 'The Lord *is* our judge, the Lord *is* our Lawgiver, the Lord *is* our King; he will save us.' Is. xxxiii. 22. [These] are great words; and as they cannot be spoken by every one, so they ought not to be spoken lightly by them that can. Nor may he that claims so high a privilege be but obedient, submissive, apt to learn, conscientiously to put in practice what he hath learnt of his Judge, his Lawgiver, and his King. Lest when some shall hear him say that Christ, by name, is his Lawgiver and his King, and shall yet observe him to do things evil, and to walk in ways that are not good, they shall think evil, and speak so of his King; saying, Learnt you this of Christ your King? or doth your King countenance you in ways that are so bad? or, do you by thus and thus doing submit to the laws of your king? yea, your King, his name and gospel shall bear the burden of the evil, together with the shame thereof, if thou that namest the name of Christ shalt not depart from iniquity.

Lastly, Whatever man he be that by his naming of the name of Christ shall intimate that he hath any reverence of love to, or delight in that Christ, whose name he nameth, that man should depart from iniquity, not only for the reasons that are above mentioned, but for those that may be named afterwards.

But having thus far opened the word, and shewed who and what manner of man the apostle had in his eye, in this his exhortation, I shall come, in the next place, to make some observations upon the text. As,

[OBSERVATION FIRST.]

That it is incident to men to name the name of Christ religiously, that is, rightly as to words and

notions, AND NOT TO *'depart from iniquity.'* This was the occasion of this exhortation, for Paul saw that there were some that did so; to wit, that named the name of Christ well, as to words, but did not depart from iniquity. Some such he also found among them at Corinth, which made him say, 'Awake to righteousness, and sin not.' 1 Co. xv. 34. He found such at Ephesus, and cries out to them most earnestly, saying, 'Awake thou that sleepest, and arise from the dead.' Ep. v. 14. For albeit they were professors of Christ, yet they lived too much like those that were dead in trespasses and sins. This he also found among the Hebrews, wherefore he saith to them, 'Let us lay aside every weight, and the sin which doth so easily beset *us,* and let us run with patience the race that is set before us.' He. xii. 1. These professors were easily beset with sin, yea, it did hang upon them as weights to hinder them from making of that profession of Christ, whose name they named, so beautiful as did become both him and them.

In my discourse upon this subject, I must endeavour to shew you two things. FIRST, What Paul means when he saith, 'depart from iniquity.' SECONDLY, Why some, that as to words, rightly name the name of Christ, do not 'depart from iniquity.'

The first of those doth need some explanation, because in some sense even the best of saints cannot depart from sin, or iniquity.

1. Because as to the being of it, it is seated and rooted in their flesh, and hath its dwelling there. Yea, it hath, and so will have an abiding there, so long as man is on this side that state of perfection, which is not to be enjoyed while we are in the flesh: 'for in me, that is, in my flesh,' sin dwells, Ro. vii. 18. nor doth any thing else but sin dwell there: 'for in me, that is, in my flesh,' said Paul, 'dwelleth no good thing:' therefore the apostle must not be understood as if he intended to insinuate that there was a possibility that the nature and being of sin could be plucked up by the roots, and so cast clean away from us, as to the very nature thereof. No, that will abide with us, for it hath its dwelling in us.

2. And as they cannot depart from the nature of it as such, that is, as they cannot be rid of the being of sin, so neither can they depart from the motions and stirrings of sin, no more than they can stir from the motions or stirrings of their natural senses, or of their natural reason: the motions of sin, which Paul also calls the lusts thereof, will be where the nature and being of sin is, because it is not dead; for that which liveth, what manner of life soever it hath, will have motion according to the manner of life which it hath; and sin being one of the most quick and brisk things that are, it will also have its motions and lusts accordingly.

Hence Paul says, it lusts, and will lust, where it is and dwells; though the very Spirit of God and the utmost diligence of a Christian be also there to oppose it. Ro. vi. 12. Ga. v. 17.

3. Again, as the being and motions of sin will be with us, so also will it in its endeavours. It will endeavour to overcome us, and to make us captives to itself and to Satan; and these endeavours will be with us. Ep. vi. 11, 12. 2 Co. x. 5. He. xii. 4. Nor can we so depart from iniquity, as to be utterly rid of all sense and feeling of what endeavours there are in sin and iniquity to be master and lord, and reign. Sin will endeavour to defile the mind, to defile the conscience, to defile the life and conversation; and this endeavour, as endeavour, we cannot depart from; that is, cause that it should not be in our flesh; for there it will be, since sin in its being is there.

4. As the being, motions, and endeavours of sin will still abide in our flesh, so consequently will its polluting times be upon us; nor doth the apostle mean, when he bids us depart from iniquity, that we should think that we can so be, or so do, in this life, as that our being or doing should not smell of the strong scent of sin. 'Who can bring a clean *thing* out of an unclean? not one.' Job xiv. 4. 'We are all as an unclean *thing,* and' therefore 'all our righteousnesses *are* as filthy rags.' Is. lxiv. 6. The scent, the smell, the rank and odious stink of sins abide upon, yea, and will abide upon us, when most spiritual here, and upon our most spiritual actions too, until they be taken away by Christ. Thus far, therefore, we cannot be concerned in the exhortation. For should Paul exhort us to depart from the being, motion, endeavour, and polluting fumes and scent of sin—I mean so to depart from them, as that there shall no such thing have place, or motion, or striving, or scent in, or upon us—he would exhort us to that which is altogether impossible for us to perform, yea, to perform through that working of the Spirit of God, which is to be with us and in us here. Yea, he must exhort us to that which he could not perform himself. But such exhortations did not stand with the wisdom of an apostle. Wherefore there is a certain meaning in this exhortation, from the which if we swerve, we shall both wrong the apostle and ourselves.

FIRST—Let us inquire then *what Paul should mean when he bids them 'that name the name of Christ depart from iniquity.'* And for our better understanding of him, we must consider that there is an iniquity that is inherent in us, and an iniquity that is apart, and at a distance from us. Now if he means, as certainly he doth, that they that name the name of Christ should depart from that sin and iniquity that is in themselves; then, though he cannot mean that we should separate that from our persons, for that is impossible, yet he would have us,

First, Take off and *withdraw our* MINDS *and* AFFECTIONS *therefrom*. And he tells us that they that are Christ's do so. 'And they that are Christ's have crucified the flesh with the affections and lusts.' Ga. v. 24. Sinful lusts and sinful motions, our minds and affections should depart from them. There are the affections and lusts of sin; and there are the affections and lusts, or desires of the soul; and again, there are the affections and lusts of the new man in saints. Now this is that that the apostle would have, to wit, that the affections and passions of our souls should not choose but depart from the affections and lusts of our old man, and should be renewed and made willing to be led by the Holy Ghost from them. 'This I say,' says he, 'Walk in the Spirit, and ye shall not fulfil the lust of the flesh.' ver. 16.

Wherefore, when he saith, depart from iniquity, if he means from our own inherent iniquity, then he must mean thus, take your mind and your affections off, carry your minds away from them, set your minds and affections upon other objects, and let your minds and affections be yielded up to the conduct of the word and Spirit of God, 'Let not sin therefore reign in your mortal body, that ye should obey it in the lusts thereof.' Ro. vi. 12. Now a man, in mind and affections, *may* depart from that which yet will not depart from him ; yea, a man in mind may depart from that which yet will dwell in him as long as he lives.

For instance, there are many diseases that cleave to men, from which, in their minds, they willingly depart. Yea, their greatest disquietment is, that so bad a distemper will abide by them, and might they but have their desire accomplished, they would be as far therefrom as the ends of the earth are asunder, and while they are found to continue together, the mind departs therefrom, and is gone either to God or to physicians for help and deliverance from it.

And thus it is with the saint, and should be with every one that by way of profession nameth the name of Christ, he should depart from his indwelling sin, with his mind. 'With his mind he should serve the law of God.' Ro. vii. 25. And this is an excellent thing to do, and can be done by none but such as are possessed with an excellent spirit. Ah! to find a man that really departs from *himself*, and that draweth the affections of the soul, from the affections and lusts of his flesh, is a rare thing. Eze. xi. 19—21. The heart of the most of professors goeth after their detestable lusts, and after their inward abominations. But such shall 'of the flesh reap corruption,' notwithstanding they name the name of Christ. Ga. vi. 8.

Sin is sweet to him that is nothing but flesh, or that can savour nothing but what is of the flesh. Job xx. 12. Nor can it be that he that is such should depart from himself, his sweet self. Ro. viii. 5—8. No, they that are after the flesh do mind the things of the flesh ; wherefore they that are in the flesh, though they profess religion and name the name of Christ, cannot please God : for such, instead of walking in and after the Spirit, have put the stumbling-block of their iniquity before their faces, to hinder their departing therefrom. Eze. xiv. 7, 8. nor will all their inquiring of God, nor their seeking and praying to him, keep them from stumbling and falling, and splitting themselves in sunder upon the rocks and ruins that are provided for them, as a reward of the evil of their doings. Job xiv. 16. Yea, they shall suck the poison of asps, and the viper's tongue shall slay them, notwithstanding all their profession.

Quest. But some may say, how shall I know that I do depart from the iniquity of my flesh, from the iniquity that is in me.

Answ. I shall answer this question briefly thus :

(1.) How is iniquity in thine eye, when severed from the guilt and punishment that attends it ? Is it AS separate from these, beauteous, or ill-favoured ? I ask thee how it looks, and how thou likest it, suppose there were no guilt or punishment to attend thy love to, or commission of it ? For if in its own nature it be desirable to thy mind, and only therefore shunned for fear of the punishment that attends the commission of it, without doubt thou art none of them that do depart from it ; all that thou dost is, thou shunnest the sin, not of abhorrence of the sin, but for fear of the punishment that attends it. Like the thief that yet refuseth to take away his neighbour's horse, not of hatred of theft, but for fear of the gallows.

(2.) How dost thou like thyself, as considered possessed with a body of sin, and as feeling and finding that sin worketh in thy members ? doth this yield thee inward pleasedness of mind, and a kind of secret sweetness, or how ? for to be sure, where a sanctified mind is, there is nothing more odious in itself, nor that makes a man so in his own eyes, as doth this sight, the sight of sin in him, of the working of lust in him. Job xlii. 6. Eze. xvi. 63. Ro. vi. 12. It is this that makes the good man ashamed, that makes him blush, and that makes him abhor himself.

(3.) How look thy duties in thine eyes, I mean thy duties which thou doest in the service of God? I say, how look the best of these, the most warm and spiritual of these, since not one of them can be performed, but they do catch the stain of sin, as coming from thee ? or art thou through the ignorance that is in thee as [one] unacquainted with these things ?

(4.) Why wouldst thou go to heaven? Is it because thou wouldst be saved from hell, or because thou wouldst be freed from sin? I say, wouldst thou go to heaven, because it is a place that is holy, or because it is a place remote from the pains of hell? I ask again, wherein dost thou think the blessedness of heaven consists? is it in the holiness that is there, or in the freedom that is there from hell? There is not a man alive but would go to heaven, that he may be saved from hell: but how many would go thither that they might be saved from the pleasures of sin, from the inward pleasure of sin; of that I will be silent, though surely they are those that are out of love with sin, and that do depart from iniquity.

Verily, my brethren, it is a great thing to depart from iniquity; it is a great thing to have my will, my mind, and my affections departing from it. But,

Second, As they that depart from iniquity withdraw their minds and affections from the lusts and motions of it, *so they depart also from the* OCCASIONS *of it;* there are occasions by which sin worketh to bring forth the fruits thereof, and some seek those occasions. Ro. xiv. 13. 1 Ti. v. 4. Ex. xxiii. 7. Pr. v. 8. 2 Ti. ii. 16. But he that hath set himself to depart from sin in himself, will not seek occasions from abroad to *do* it. Such a man as will keep far from an evil matter will not company with a person that pollutes and defiles, nor will he come near the door of the adulteress's house; he will shun profane and vain babbling, for fear of the ungodliness that attends it; he will walk with wise men that he may be wise, knowing that 'a companion of fools shall be destroyed.' Pr. xiii. 20.

Now there are occasions given and occasions taken to sin against the Lord Jesus; but he that departeth from iniquity departeth from them both. He is not for giving any occasion to others to sin; he had rather wrong himself and put up with injuries done, than give occasion to others to do iniquity; and as he is for giving none, so neither is he for taking any: he is for partaking of no man's sins, but for keeping of himself pure. 1 Ti. v. 22.

Third, To depart from iniquity, is to *depart from it in those* EXAMPLES *that are set before us thereto:* occasions and examples are sometimes the same, but there may be occasions to sin where there are no examples thereto, and therefore in that they differ. And to depart from iniquity is to shun and depart from those examples, those beastly examples, that in every corner of the country present themselves to men.

Examples to drunkenness; examples to whoredom; examples to swearing, to lying, to stealing, to sabbath-breaking, to pride, to covetousness, to deceit, to hypocrisy, and to what not, are now-a-days common among men, and he that is to seek in this matter, and that knows not how to be expertly base, may have patterns and examples thereto in every hole. But to depart from iniquity is to depart from sinful examples, to shut the eyes at them, to turn the back upon them, and to cry out to heaven for grace to be kept in the path of life. And, ' Let every one that nameth the name of Christ depart from iniquity.'

Fourth, To depart from iniquity is *to depart from the* ENTICINGS *to iniquity.* There is that in iniquity that is of an enticing nature. Its pleasures, profits, honours, delights, and sweetnesses are enticing, and he that hankers after these is not departed nor departing from iniquity. A man must be weaned from these things, and must find some things somewhere else that are better than these, else he cannot depart from iniquity.

Quest. But some may say, I go from it and it follows me; I reject it and it returns upon me; I have said it nay, a thousand times, and yet it offereth itself and its deceits to me again, what would you have me do?

Answ. I would answer thus; Departing from iniquity is not a work of an hour, or a day, or a week, or a month, or a year; but it is a work that will last thee thy lifetime, and there is the greatness and difficulty of it: were it to be done presently, or were the work to be quickly over, how many are there that would be found to have departed from iniquity; but for that it is a work of continuance, and not worth anything, unless men hold out to the end, therefore it is that so few are found actors or overcomers therein. Departing from iniquity, with many, is but like the falling out of two neighbours, they hate one another for a while, and then renew their old friendship again.

But again, since to depart from iniquity is a work of time—of all thy time, no wonder if it dogs thee, and offereth to return upon thee again and again; for THAT is mischievous, and seeks nothing less than thy ruin: wherefore thou must, in the first place, take it for granted that thus it will be and so cry the harder to God for the continuing of his presence and grace upon thee in this blessed work, that as thou hast begun to call upon the name of the Lord Jesus, and begun to depart from iniquity, so thou mayest have strength to do it to the last gasp of thy life.

And further, for that departing from iniquity is a kind of a warfare with it, for iniquity will hang in thy flesh what it can, and will not be easily kept under; therefore no marvel if thou find it wearisome work, and that the thing that thou wouldest get rid of, is so unwilling to let thee depart from it.

And since the work is so weighty, and that it

makes thee to go groaning on, I will for thy help give thee here a few things to consider of: and [remember],

1. *Remember* that God sees thee, and has his eyes open upon thee, even then when sin and temptation is lying at thee to give it some entertainment. This was that that made Joseph depart from it, when solicited to embrace it by a very powerful argument. Ge. xxxix. 6, 7.

2. *Remember* that God's wrath burns against it, and that he will surely be revenged on it, and on all that give it entertainment. This made Job afraid to countenance it, and put him upon departing from it; 'For destruction *from* God *was* a terror to me, and by reason of his highness I could not endure.' Job xxxi. 23.

3. *Remember* the mischiefs that it has done to those that have embraced it, and what distress it has brought upon others. This made the whole congregation of Israel tremble to think that any of their brethren should give countenance to it. Jos. xxii. 16—18.

4. *Remember* what Christ hath suffered by it, that he might deliver us from the power of it. This made Paul so heartily to depart from it, and wish all Christians to do so as well as he. 2 Co. v. 14.

5. *Remember* that those that are now in hell-fire went thither for that they loved iniquity, and would not depart from it. Ps. ix. 17; xi. 6.

6. *Remember* that a profession is not worth a pin, if they that make it do not depart from iniquity. Ja. ii. 16, 17.

7. *Remember* that thy death-bed will be very uneasy to thee, if thy conscience at that day shall be clogged with the guilt of thy iniquity. Ho. vii. 13, 14.

8. *Remember* that at the judgment-day Christ will say to those, Depart from me, that have not here departed from their sin and iniquity. Lu xiii. 27. Mat. xxv. 41.

Lastly, Remember well, and think much upon what a blessed reward the Son of God will give unto them at that day that have joined to their profession of faith in him a holy and blessed conversation.

Having thus briefly showed you these things, I shall come in the next place,

SECOND, To show you, *why some, that as to words rightly name the name of Christ, do not depart from iniquity.* That it is incident to men to name the name of Christ religiously, and not to depart from iniquity, I have proved already, and now I must show you why it is so, and the reasons are of three sorts:

First, Some profess him, *yet have not saving faith in him, nor yet received grace from him.* That some profess him that have not faith in him, nor received grace from him, I will make appear first;

and then that they do not depart from iniquity, shall be shown afterwards.

That the first is true consider, Christ says to his disciples, 'There are some of you that believe not.' And again, 'For Jesus knew from the beginning who they were that believed not, and who should betray him.' Jn. vi. 64. Now if they believe not, they have none of his grace in them; for faith is the first and head grace, the beginning and leading grace; he, therefore, that is destitute of that is empty of all the rest. Besides, other scriptures also confirm this truth. James calls some of the professors of Christ that were in his day vain or empty men. Ja. ii. 20. That is, men void of grace. And the apostle suggesteth in the very words below the text, that as in God's house there are golden and silver saints, so there are also earthy and wooden ones. For 'in a great house' as God's is, 'are not only vessels of gold and silver, but also of wood and of earth, and some to honour, and some to dishonour.' 2 Ti. ii. 20. That is, some for heaven and some for hell. Ro. ix. 20—23.

Now they are these wooden and earthy professors that he aimeth at in the text; to wit, that they should depart from iniquity, or else their profession would do them no good, and these also that he despaireth of in the next words, saying, But in this great house of God there will not only be golden and silver Christians, but wooden and earthly ones: And if any man purge himself from these, from these men's companies, and from these men's vices, he shall be a vessel to honour, sanctified, and meet for the master's use, and prepared to every good work. From all which it is gathered that there are some that name the name of Christ in a way of profession, that have neither faith nor grace in them, and so, consequently, that do not depart from iniquity. For,

These want that principle, that holy and blessed principle, that should induce them thereunto; to wit, the great and principal graces of the Spirit, and they are four.

1. As I have said, *they want* FAITH, that heart-purifying grace, for the heart is purified by faith. Ac. xv. 9. I have showed you already that departing from iniquity must be with the mind and affections, or with the heart. But how can that be, where the heart is not sanctified and made holy? For an unsanctified mind cannot depart from iniquity, no more than the Ethiopian can change his skin. Je. xiii. 23. But nothing can purify the heart but faith. Therefore nothing can make a professor depart from iniquity where faith is wanting. So then, when men professedly name the name of Christ without having holy faith in him, they still abide by their iniquity; they depart not from their iniquity, but rather make of their profession a cloak for their iniquity, for their malice, and for

their covetousness, and the like. 1 Th. ii. 15. 1 Pe. ii. 16. It is not profession, but faith, that bringeth God and the soul together; and as long as God and the soul are at a distance, whatever profession is made, there is not a departing, not an heart-departing from iniquity. Wherefore to these professors James writeth thus, ' Draw nigh to God, and he will draw nigh to you. Cleanse *your* hands, *ye* sinners : and purify *your* hearts, *ye* double-minded.' Ja. iv. 8. Men, far from God, cannot think reverently of him, nor so speak and profess him, as standeth with the nature of gospel religion ; wherefore God saith, ' draw near hither,' that is, by faith; and again, ' let them come near, then let them speak,' then let them profess. Is. xli. 1. Without faith a man cannot please God, because he cannot without it stand before him in the spotless righteousness of Christ, nor yet depart from iniquity, and live a holy life. He. xi. 6.

There are three things in faith, that directly tend to make a man depart from iniquity. (1.) It apprehendeth the truth of the being and greatness of God, and so it aweth the spirit of a man. (2.) It apprehendeth the love of this God in Christ, and so it conquereth and overcometh the spirit of a man. (3.) It apprehendeth the sweetness and blessedness of the nature of the Godhead, and thence persuadeth the soul to desire here, communion with him, that it may be holy, and the enjoyment of him, when this world is ended, that it may be happy in, and by him, for ever.

But without faith these things cannot be apprehended, and therefore those that want it, whatever their profession is, they will not depart from iniquity.

2. [*They want* REPENTANCE.] Repentance is another of the great and principal graces which the Holy Ghost worketh in the heart. Wherefore, without this also there can be no departing from iniquity. It is in vain to expect it of any man, let his profession be never so stately and great, if he is a stranger to sound repentance. How many are there in our day, since the gospel is grown so common, that catch up a notion of good things, and from that notion make a profession of the name of Christ, get into churches, and obtain the title of a brother, a saint, a member of a gospel congregation, that have clean escaped repentance. I say, they have catched up a notion of good things, and have through that adventured to name the name of Christ, quite forgetting to take repentance with them. Repentance should be, and is one of the first steps into the true gospel profession. Mar. i. 15. Pr. iii. 7; xvi. 6. But some know nothing of it, until they come to the end of all, and their repentance will do them no good. Repentance is not but where the true fear of God is; yea, the fear of God is one ground of repentance. Repentance

is the scouring grace, it is that which purges. Repentance is, as I may call it, that bitter pill without the taking, and sound working of which, base and sinful humours will rest unstirred, unpurged, undriven out of the soul. Can repentance be where godly sorrow is not ? or can repentance be where the fruits of repentance are not ? O the fruits of repentance, thick sown by preachers, but it comes up but thinly ! Mar. i. 4, 5. Ro. vi. 21. Je. vii. 3, 5. Where shall the fruits of repentance be found ? Confession of sin is one fruit of repentance ; shame for sin is another fruit of repentance ; amendment of life is another fruit of repentance ; restitution for couzening, cheating, defrauding, beguiling thy neighbour, is another fruit of repentance. Lu. xix. 5—8 Yea, if you would see the fruits of repentance as described by the Holy Ghost, and put together for the further conviction and shame of the impenitent professor, look into the second epistle to the Corinthians, vii. 9—11.

But this is a day that was never read of, a day wherein conversion is frequent without repentance ; such a conversion as it is, and therefore doth the church of God now swarm with them that religiously name the name of Christ, and yet depart not from iniquity. Alas ! all houses, all tables, all shops, have hanging up in them the sign of the want of repentance. Ec. vii. 27, 28. To say nothing of the talk, of the beds and the backs of most that profess, by which of these is it that one of a thousand for men ; and for women, one of ten thousand, do show that they have repentance ? No marvel then that the name of Christ is so frequently mentioned there, where iniquity dwells, yea, reigns, and that with the consent of the mind.

I would not be austere, but were wearing of gold, putting on of apparel, dressing up houses, decking of children, learning of compliments, boldness in women, lechery in men, wanton behaviour, lascivious words, and tempting carriages, signs of repentance; then I must say, the fruits of repentance swarm in our land ; but if these be none of the fruits of repentance then, O, the multitude of professors, that religiously name the name of Christ, and do not depart from iniquity.* But,

3. [*They want* LOVE.] Love is another of those great and principal graces which the Holy Ghost worketh in the heart; wherefore let profession be never so high, yet if love be wanting there, to be sure such professors ' depart from iniquity,' 1 Co. xiii. Hence all profession, and subjecting to profession, are counted nothing, where love is not. Love is counted a most infallible sign that a man is in a

---

* How much is it to be feared that some towering professors, upon impartial self-examination, will find upon themselves some of these black spots ; all of which are utterly inconsistent with that humility which is the proper and only becoming garb of a Christian.—*Ryland.*—ED.

state of salvation. 'He that loveth dwells in God, is born of God, and knoweth him.' 1 Jn. iv. 7, 16, 21. Love divideth itself, to God, and to my neighbour. Love to God is, that we keep his sayings, his commandments, his laws. 'If a man love me,' saith Christ, 'he will keep my words; - and he that loveth me not, keepeth not my sayings.' Jn. xiv. 23, 24. For this is the love of God, that we keep his commandments: and his commandments are not grievous.' 1 Jn. v. 3. So then, that professor that hath not love, cannot depart from iniquity. (1.) Where no love is, men cannot be tender of the name of God, they are not afflicted because men keep not God's law. Ps. cxix. 136; 1 Co. xiii. 5. (2.) Where no love is, men cannot deny themselves of that which otherwise they might lawfully do, lest the weak should fall, and the world be destroyed. Ro. xiv. 15. (3.) Where love to God is, there is hatred against iniquity; 'ye that love the Lord, hate evil.' Ps. xcvii. 10.

A man cannot love God that loves not holiness; he loves not holiness that loves not God's word; he loves not God's word that doth not do it. It is a common thing to find men partial in God's law, setting much by small things, and neglecting the weightier matters, paying tithe of mint, and anise, and cummin, and neglecting the weightier matters. These turn the tables of God's book upside down; making little laws of great ones; and great ones of little ones; counting half an hour's bodily service better than a moral life. Love! love is gone out of the country; love to the doctrine of the first table, love to the doctrine of the second table. O how many professors, in God's eyes, are accounted of no more than sounding brass, for want of this ornament, love! 1 Co. xiii.

To speak nothing of the first table, where is he that hath his love manifested by the second? where are they that feed the hungry and clothe the naked, and send portions to them, for whom nothing is prepared? Where is Paul that would not eat meat while the world standeth, lest he made his brother offend? 1 Co. viii. 13. Where is Dorcas, with her garments she used to make for the widow, and for the fatherless? Ac. ix. 36—39. Yea, where is that rich man that, to his power, durst say as Job does? as recorded in Job xxx. 25; xxxi. 13, 32. Love! love is gone, and now coveting, pinching, griping, and such things are in fashion: now iniquity abounds, instead of grace, in many that name the name of Christ. They want love, and therefore cannot depart from iniquity.*

4. [*They want* HOPE.] Hope is another of those great and principal graces, which the Holy Ghost

---

* Selfishness is the great enemy to happiness. A heart steeled against *all*, naturally brings upon itself the hostility of all. Love to the Redeemer, for emancipation from that great curse, is the only antidote to selfishness.—ED.

worketh in the heart, and without which, let a man be never so high in profession, and so open in naming the name of Christ, he cannot depart from iniquity. As was said before of faith, so we say now of hope. 'And every man that hath this hope in him purifieth himself, even as he is pure.' 1 Jn. iii. 3. Here is that excellent office, or rather effect of hope made manifest, it purifieth, it cleanseth a man; it makes him make the Lord Jesus his example, as well as his Saviour. He purifieth himself even as he is pure; to wit, in soul, in body, in spirit, in life and conversation. Hope of life, eternal by Christ, makes a man purify himself in obeying the truth through the Spirit. Hope to be with Christ hereafter, will make me strive to believe him here. Hope of being with angels then, will make a man strive to live like an angel here. Alas! alas! there is a company of half-priests in the world, and they cannot, they dare not teach the people the whole counsel of God, because in so doing they will condemn themselves and their manner of living in the world; where is that minister now to be found that dare say to his people, Look on me, and walk as you have me for an example? or that dare say, What you see and hear to be in me, do, 'and the God of peace shall be with you?' Phi. iii. 17; iv. 9. These men had hope, and hope purified them to an example, till they became patterns to others. Is not this now far off from some professors in the world? Are they purified, are they clean that name the name of Christ? are they weaned from that milk, and drawn from the breasts? No, nor their profession is not attended with grace; they name the name of Christ; well, but they do not depart from iniquity. Let a man believe a lie, and according to the reality of his belief, such will his obedience be; let a man hope for that for which he hath no ground to hope, yet his hope will work with him according to the power thereof; and yet we have a generation of men that profess the blessed gospel, which yieldeth the most substantial ground for faith and hope; yea, we have a company of men that will be naming the name of Christ, which is the sweetest, the most taking, and desirable name that is named among the sons of men, and for all that, this gospel, this worthy name, nor yet their naming of it, doth make them depart from iniquity. But what's the reason? why, they have taken up a profession, but want the grace of Christ; the faith, the repentance, the love and hope of the gospel. No marvel then, if they abide among the wooden sort of professors: no marvel then, though the iniquity of their heels still follows them, and that it droppeth from them wherever they go. But so much for the first reason, why men do name the name of Christ and yet do not depart from iniquity.

Second, The second reason, why some that name

the name of Christ, depart not from iniquity, is, for that, though they rest not in bare notions, as those forementioned, yet *they take up as they, short of the saving grace of God.* There are bare notions, there are common workings, and there is a work that is saving, and that will do the soul good to eternity.

1. There are bare notions, and they that have them are such unto whom the gospel comes IN WORD ONLY. 1 Th. i. 5. 1 Co. iv. 19, 20. Such whose religion stands in word only, and is not attended with a power suitable; that is, there goeth not along with the word, a power sufficient to subdue, and work over the heart to a cordial and gracious close with that word that comes to them. Yet such is the noise and sound of the word, that they are willing to become professors thereof; there is some kind of *musicalness* in it, especially when well handled and fingered by a skilful preacher. And lo, saith God unto such preachers, when their auditory is made up of such kind of hearers, ' And lo, thou art unto them as a very lovely song,' or as one that sings a song of loves, ' of one that hath a pleasant voice, and can play well on an instrument: for they hear thy words but they do them not.' Eze. xxxiii. 30—32.

2. But then, besides these, there is another sort, and they go further than these. For to them the word came, not in word only, *but also in* POWER: though not in that or in such a power as is sufficient absolutely against all attempts whatsoever to bring the soul to glory. Of these we read in several places; to wit, that they have tasted of the powers of the world to come; but not so as to bring them safe to glory. Yet thus far they go. (1.) They attain light or illumination, to see much of their state by nature with. He. vi. 4. (2.) This light standeth not in bare speculation, but lets fall upon the conscience convincing arguments to the bowing and humbling of the spirit. 1 Ki. xxi. 27—29. (3.) They submit to these convictions, and reform, and may for a time not only come out from them that live in error, but escape the pollutions of the world, by the knowledge of our Lord and Saviour Jesus Christ. 2 Pe. ii. 18—20. Ga. iii. 4; iv. 20. (4.) Yea, so powerful will this dispensation be, that it will prevail with them to do and suffer many things for the vindication of the truth of that gospel which they profess. For the word will be sweet unto them. Christ, the gift of God, will be relished by them. He. vi. 4, 5. The powers of the world to come will be in them. Some workings of the Holy Ghost will be in them. And joy, which is as oil to the wheels, will be with their souls. Lu. viii. 13.

Thus, I say, it is with some professors, who yet cannot be said to depart from iniquity, that is, for all ado, because the things that now are upon them, abide with them but awhile. ' For awhile they believe: they rejoice in the light for a season.'

Lu. viii. 13. Jn. v. 35. 2 Pe. ii. 21. So they clean escape from them, who live in error for a little, or awhile; and after that return to their old course, and are again entangled with their iniquities and overcome. This is called, ' A turning with the dog to his own vomit again, and with the sow that was washed, to her wallowing in the mire.' And some of these are set forth by this and such like sayings, ' When the unclean spirit is gone out of a man, he walketh through dry places, seeking rest, and finding none. Then he saith, I will return into my house from whence I came out; and when he is come, he findeth *it* empty, swept, and garnished. Then goeth he, and taketh with himself seven other spirits more wicked than himself, and they enter in and dwell there: and the last *state* of that man is worse than the first.' Mat. xii 44, 45.

Now the causes of this declension, returning, or falling away again into iniquity, are many.

First [*Cause of falling away.*] One is for that this work, this work of power that they have been made partakers of, has not been thorough enough upon all the powers of their souls. Their understandings, their judgments and consciences have been dealt with, but the power of God has not been upon their wills and minds, and affections, rightly to subdue them to the grace of the gospel. Ps. cx. 3. Indeed there seems to be a subjection of the will, and an overruling of the mind, and affections also, else they could not for a time lay aside their iniquity, come off from the pollutions of the world, and for a season rejoice in the word and be pleased with the light thereof. But we may consider, that this may be, not for that a sound work of God hath passed upon these powers of the soul, but that rather this was by reason of those reflex acts, that the understanding now enlightened, the judgment now informed, and the conscience now convinced, had upon these other powers of the soul. And I the rather think it so, because willingness, mindfulness of, and affection for, this gospel, lasted no longer than the light shined in their understandings, or than the things were relished by their judgment and conscience. So that when the light of their candle went out, and when the taste of this sugar-plum was out of their mouth, their wills and affections, not being possessed with the fear of God, they returned again to their course, and went away as before with iniquity.

Nor do I by anything here discoursed, lay blame or fault at the door of God. For,

1. He is a free agent to do what he pleaseth, and may, if he please, refuse to give anything, or if he gives something, why may he not give what he pleases also? He may give special grace to one, and that which is not so to another: he may open Balaam's eyes, Nu. xxiv. 3. and open Lydia's heart; Ac. xvi. 14. he may give some but a taste, and **cause**

3 U

some to eat abundantly. He. vi. Ca. v. 1. He may suffer some to fall away, and keep others, by his power, through faith unto salvation.

2. Besides, God's withdrawing, to wit, of those common workings, if they were withdrawn without a cause given—which yet I question—yet why may they not be withdrawn from these, as well as from his own peculiar ones. He knows but little, that doth not know that God ofttimes hides his face from his own, and also withdraws from them the light and great influences of the Holy Ghost: and turns them over, at least in their own apprehensions, to the ungodly, and to fallen angels for their chastisement, or trial, or instruction, &c.

3. And why may not God, since these rebels had such working with them, as that their minds, by their understandings, their will and affections; by their judgment and consciences were somewhat taken and allured, cause a withdrawing of these for trial, and to see if they would cry after him to return.

But we will let these things pass, and call you again to remembrance of what is in hand: we are now shewing that there be them that name the name of Christ, 'that yet depart not from iniquity,' and in shewing the cause of their not so doing, one was for that the gospel came to them in word only; and the other was, for that though it came to others in power, yet not in power, or in that power, that effectually keepeth some to salvation. Upon this second reason I now am, and am shewing how it comes to pass that they that are under the power of the things that we have afore discoursed, should notwithstanding that, return to their vomit again. One cause of this declension, or going back to iniquity, I have just now touched upon, and we have some more behind.

Second [*Cause of falling away.*] Therefore such persons upon the withdrawing of those influences that at present are mighty upon them, do forthwith forget, both what they had, and what work it made upon them. Straightway they forget what manner of men they were. It is said of Israel, they sang his praises, they soon forgot his word. So these they forget.

1. They forget what light and what conviction they had.

2. They forget what sorrow for sin they had.

3. They forget what tastes of Christ and his word they had.

4. They forget what joy and comfort they had.

5. They forget how fair for heaven they were.

6. And they forget how cleansed once they were.

' They have forgotten that they were purged from their old sins.' 2 Pe. i. 9. Now forgetfulness makes things that are past as nothing; and if so, then it can lay no obligations upon the mind, to engage it to the delight of them, and to the enjoying of them,

no not in the thoughts of them, as if they were remembered by us. Forgetfulness is a very dangerous thing: it makes preaching vain, profession vain, faith vain, and all to no purpose. 1 Co. xv. 1, 2. Such profession is but a dream, and the professors but as dreamers: all vanishes in the morning. This made Paul so caution the Corinthians, that they forgot not the preaching; and the author to the Hebrews, so earnestly calls them, in their backsliding, back to the remembrance of former days, and to the recollecting of what it was that then had made them so willingly endure their great fight of affliction. He. x. 32, 33.

Forgetfulness, I say, makes things nothing; it makes us as if things had never been; and so takes away from the soul one great means of stay, support, and encouragement; when choice David was dejected, the remembrance of the hill Hermon was his stay; when he was to go out against Goliah, the remembrance of the lion and the bear was his support: so when those that have had the power of the things of God upon them, can think of this; when they are withdrawn, it will, even the thinking of it, have some kind of operation upon the soul. And therefore you shall find, that the recovering of a backslider usually begins at the remembrance of former things. ' Remember therefore from whence thou art fallen, and repent, and do the first works.' Re. ii. 5.

It is marvellous to see how some men are captivated with this forgetfulness. Those that sometimes have prayed, cried, groaned, and sighed, for eternal life; those that sometimes thought no pains too much, no way too far, no hazards too great to run, for eternal life; those who sometimes were captivated with the word, and with the comforts and joy thereof, and that, had it been possible, could have pulled out their eyes, and have given them to a gospel minister, so dear and sweet were the good tidings which they brought to such. Ga. iv. 14, 15. I say it is marvellous to see how such men are captivated with the forgetfulness of this. They are as if they never had been those men; they are as if they never had had such things; or, as if they never had thought about them. Yea, they are strange, and carry it strangely to all those that still are under the power of that word, and of that mighty hand by which sometimes themselves were guided.

Should one say to some, Art not thou the man that I once saw crying under a sermon, that I once heard cry out, What must I do to be saved? and, that some time ago I heard speak well of the holy word of God? how askew will they look upon one; or if they will acknowledge that such things were with them once, they do it more like images and rejected ghosts, than men. They look as if they were blasted, withered, cast out, and dried to powder, and now fit for nothing but to be cast into the fire, and burned. Jn. xv. 6. The godliness from which they are departed, and the iniquity unto which again they have joined themselves, has so altered, so metamorphosed and changed their heart, and mind, and ways. This therefore is the second thing which shews why some that have been under something of the power of things,* are again with iniquity entangled and overcome.

Third [*Cause of falling away*.] Another thing that makes these enlightened ones, that they continue not to depart from iniquity, is the persecution that always attends the word: for persecution always attends the word, that of the tongue, or that of the sword. Now these men that were once enlightened, though they cannot remember what they were themselves, yet Satan helps them to think that their neighbours remember what they were: and having now lost the savour, the sense of what they once had, and sinned away that Spirit that brought it to them, they grow weak; yea are above all men the most unable to stand up, to abide the shock and trial, that for their profession is coming upon them. Wherefore, by and by they are offended; to wit, with their own profession, and call themselves an hundred fools, for being so heedless, so witless, and unwary, to mind God's holy things in such a time and day. Mat. iv. 16, 17. Lu. viii. 13. Then they bethink with themselves, how to make an honourable retreat, which they suppose they usually do, by finding fault, first with their own unadvisedness, and of the over-persuasiveness of others; they also now begin to say farewell conscience, yea, God and heaven and all, and join in confederacy with the world again. Thus are they in fear, where no fear is; and the sound of a shaken leaf doth chase them. And there are four things that are the cause of this.

1. For that notwithstanding the former power that attended the word to their hearts, their hearts did still abide as hard as a rock, there was no true and sound breaking, nor softening in that; wherefore there the word wanted depth of earth, as our Lord is pleased to call it; and anon when the sun was up, that which remained was presently scorched, and so withered away.

2. Notwithstanding what they had sometimes enjoyed, yet the grace of the fear of God was wanting in them. Ec. vii. 16—18. So wanting that, what should hinder but that they should return to go as they came, and leave Christ, the gospel, and the people of God to shift as well as they can for themselves.

3. All that they enjoyed did not estrange their hearts from their lusts, though when they were in the power of things, they were deader to them than formerly; I say than formerly. Ps. lxxviii. 30, 36, 37. And it is even with such, as with them, who are for a time taken off from what yet they love, by some new employ in which they are engaged. Saul went out to look for David to kill him, but when he came at Naioth, in Ramah, the Spirit of God came upon him, and he prophesied. 1 Sa. xix. 18, 24. But this lasted but for awhile. Saul soon returned to his old envy against the holy man again.

4. It comes upon them even of judgment and wrath, for since they so soon give way to sin, and forget, God suffereth them to fall into the fear of men, and to force their hearts to comply with bad things,—even as Judas and Demas did,—till they are swallowed up of that gulph, into which the ungodly descend. ' As for such as turn aside unto their crooked ways, the Lord shall lead them forth with the workers of iniquity.' Ps. cxxv. 5.

When once God is angry with a people, he can deal with them, he can give them up to those lusts in judgment, that they will not be separated from by mercy. Yea, he can make a way for his anger to overtake them that have made a way, by the deceits of their hearts, to go a-whoring from under him.

And these are the causes why those that were once enlightened, and have tasted the good word of God, and the powers of the world to come, return with the dog to his own vomit again; and so, though they have or do name the name of Christ, yet depart not from iniquity.

Third, A third reason, why they that name the name of Christ do not depart from iniquity, may be, *because* GRACE IS WEAK *and* CORRUPTION STRONG. I speak now of them that are truly gracious; for as those that never had nothing but notion, did never at all depart from iniquity: and as those that never had saving grace, though common workings were with them, do but a little depart from iniquity; so those that yet have the grace of God in them, in truth, do not, as they should, depart from iniquity; wherefore the exhortation is as much to them as it is to any body else; ' and let them that name the name of Christ,' with gracious lips, ' depart from iniquity.' For though there is a great difference betwixt these and the two sorts that I mentioned before,—these having the true principles of holiness in them. but the other nothing thereof,—yet they, even they, also have need of this exhortation; for they do not, as they should, ' depart from iniquity.' Their graces, as I said, are weak, and that is the reason thereof.

That these do not depart from iniquity, as they should, is clear.

1. For that their highest acts of holiness are tainted therewith, and made imperfect thereby. Is. lxiv. 6. Ps. cxliii. 2. He. xii. 15. Mat. vi. 23. This is manifest,

---

* ' Power of things;' the influence of convictions and hopes named in the six divisions on the preceding page.—ED.

because they still are afraid to shew themselves before God in their own works, and because they betake them for acceptation with God, to the priestly office of Christ, and pray by him, ' forgive us our trespasses.'

2. This is clear also, because we are, while in this world, nowhere by the word said to have attained to the mark and point of absolute perfection ; but are bid to grow, to follow on, to press forward, and to perfect holiness in the fear of God. 2 Pe. iii. 18. He. vi. 12. Ph. iii. 12—14. 2 Co. vii. 1.   Yea, the best of us all, even the apostles and prophets, have not only made it manifest by their imperfections, that as yet they have not departed from iniquity as they should ; but they have confessed, and denied not, that they were yet in the pursuit of righteousness, and had not already attained.

3. This is clear also, for that the righteousness, by the which the best of saints are justified in the sight of God, is a righteousness of another, not their own ; the righteousness of another man, for that there is not any upon earth that doth good and sins not.   And what need we pray, ' forgive us our trespasses,' approach God in the perfections of another, and be bid ' to perfect holiness,' if we had already attained, or were already perfect, or were so departed from iniquity as we should.

4. Alas, the complaints of God concerning this matter, doth sufficiently testify the truth of what I say.   When God came to his people in Egypt, and bid them forsake the idols of Egypt, they did not. But they rebelled against me, says he, and would not hearken unto me ; they did not, every man, cast away the abominations of his eyes, neither did they forsake the idols of Egypt.   Well, he saved them out of Egypt, and brought them into the wilderness, and said to them there, Obey my laws, and my commandments ; but the house of Israel rebelled against me in the wilderness, they walked not in my statutes, they despised my judgments. Well, then he had them from the wilderness to Canaan, and then said to them, Keep my laws. Eze. xx.   But when he had brought them into the land, then they also polluted themselves, and sinned against him as before.   Again, when God brought them out of captivity, both they, and every thing that they did, was unclean. Hag. ii. 14.

To be short, what says Paul in the seventh to the Romans ? what says James in the third chapter of his epistle ? ch. iii. 2.   And what says John in his first epistle, and first chapter ? 1 Jn. i. 9.   Do they not all confess, though themselves were apostles, and so for grace and gifts beyond any that breathe in this world, that sin and iniquity was yet with them ; and so consequently, that there was not as yet that departing by them therefrom, as there should.   And the reason, as I have said, is, because grace is weak, weak in the best and most strong

of the saints of God.   Hence the greatest saints use to complain, when much assaulted with corruptions, or attended with very hard service for God, of their weakness and insufficiency, as to a completeness of doing the will of God.

(1.) Moses, when God did but bid him nourish and succour Israel in the wilderness, and carry them in his bosom, as the nursing-father beareth the sucking child, was stricken with such fear of miscarrying, through the weakness of his graces and the power of his corruptions, that he cried to God, saying, ' I am not able to bear all this people alone, because it is too heavy for me.   And if thou deal thus with me, kill me, I pray thee, out of hand, - and let me not see my wretchedness.' Nu. xi. 14, 15.

(2.) Job, when he was, for a proof of his integrity, to be exercised a while with some of the judgments of God, cries out, in a sense of his weakness to bear them, and to go through as he should, ' Is my strength the strength of stones ? or is my flesh of brass ?'   And again, ' Am I a sea, or a whale, that thou settest a watch over me ?   Wilt thou break a leaf driven to and fro ?   And wilt thou pursue the dry stubble ?' Job vi. 12 ; vii. 12 ; xiii. 25.

(3.) So Daniel, when he was but to stand and talk with the angel, how weak did he find himself ; ' There remained,' saith he, ' no strength in me ;' and, ' O my Lord, by the vision my sorrows are turned upon me, and I have retained no strength. For how can the servant of this my Lord talk with this my Lord ? for as for me, straightway there remained no strength in me, neither is there breath left in me.' Da. x.   Some may say, but this is natural weakness.   But I ask, how came nature to be so weak, but through sin ? the remains whereof abiding still upon the best of saints, make them, notwithstanding their graces, uncapable to do any thing as they should.

(4.) Paul, a man of men, who had so much grace, revelation of grace and communion with Christ, that sometimes he knew not whether he was in or out of the body, and yet you find him making bitter complaint of the weakness of his grace, and of the power of his corruptions.   ' I am carnal,' saith he, and what I hate that do I.   ' How to perform that which is good I find not ;' ' when I would do good, evil is present with me.'   ' But I see another law in my members, warring against the law of my mind, and bringing me into captivity to the law of sin, which is in my members.'   ' O wretched man that I am,' &c.   What complaints, what confessions, what bewailing of weakness is here ?   And what need was there of any of this, if Paul could, as he would, have departed from iniquity ? Ro. vii.

I have instanced in these four men, because as to failings and miscarriages they are as free—by what the holy record saith—as any four of whose lives you shall read in all the Bible; but you see that they were too weak to do good and depart from iniquity as they would.

Grace may be said to be weak, either when a lower or less degree thereof is compared with a higher and greater degree of the same; or it may be said to be weak when, in what degree of it you will, it shall be engaged by, or engage itself against sin, &c.

There are degrees of grace in the world, some have less, and some bigger measures thereof, and according to the measure of grace received, so is a Christian capable of action. He that has little, acts but weakly; he that has much, acts more strongly; and he of the saints that has most, acteth best of all: but yet none of these three can act so as they should and would, and, consequently, so depart from iniquity as is their duty. Witness those four that I mentioned but now, for they are among the first-rate of saints, yet you see what they did, and hear what they said.

Sin is a mighty tyrant; it is also installed in our flesh, and has moreover that in it which suiteth with whatever is sensual in us. The flesh relisheth it well, though the spirit of the Christian is against it.

Sin is an active beast, and will not admit that the soul should attempt to put forth itself in any good thing, without opposition and contradiction. 'When I could do good evil is present with me.'*

Sin is of a polluting and defiling nature, and what grace soever it toucheth it staineth, and in staining makes it weaker, than were it not so defiled it would be. Besides, not a grace, nor an act of grace in the soul can escape untouched.

Unbelief stands ready to annoy faith in the grace, as well as in the act of faith.

Hardness of heart will not let love so affectionately and sympathisingly act as it should.

Sense and reason being polluted will not let hope be so stedfastly fixed upon unseen things as it should.

Pride will not let us be so humble as we ought, nor self so self-denying. Passion often interrupts our patience, and angry motions our meekness. By these, and more that might be named, it appears that sin is in us, opposeth our graces, and letteth† them from acting as they should; and because this sin has part of ourself in its possession, therefore though our more noble part be utterly against it, yet we depart not from it as we should.

God chargeth Moses with rash and unadvised

* Plato says that some men are impotent by reason of sin; but Christianity alone developes the awful fact, that sin has poisoned our nature, and that its effects are felt by the holiest of saints. The reference to the experience of Paul in Rom. vii. is conclusive of the fact.—ED.

† 'Letteth;' hindereth or obstructeth: now obsolete.—ED.

words, and so he doth Job also: Daniel did wear the name of an idol god, and Paul freely confesseth himself unfirm. Nu. xx. 12. Ps. cvi. 32. Job xxxviii. 2; xlii. 6. Da. iv. 8. Ro. vii. 24.

Nor may what hath now been said be applied to those that are weak in faith, and so in every other grace; for the strongest grace when acted as well as we can, cannot cause that we depart from iniquity as we should. (1.) Because the strongest grace cannot act without opposition. (2.) Because we that are the actors are lame, infirm, and made weak by sin that dwells in us. (3.) Because grace and a state of grace is not that wherein the perfection designed for us doth lie, for that is in another world. (a.) This is a place to act faith in. (b.) This is a place to labour and travel in. (c.) This is a place to fight and wrestle in. (d.) This is a place to be tried in.

And therefore this is no place of perfection, and consequently no place where God's people can depart from iniquity as they should.

Now there is a *twofold way of departing from iniquity.* I. One is when the mind is set against it, and withdrawn from the love and liking of it. II. The other is when the practice of it is shunned by the whole man.

I. The first of these ways, the saints, though they truly do depart from iniquity, yet depart not from it as they should. (1.) Their understanding sees not the utmost baseness that is in it. (2.) Their judgment is not informed about the vileness of it to perfection. (3.) The conscience has not yet been convinced of all the evil that is in it. Then, (a.) How should the soul abhor it as it should? (b.) How should the desires depart from it with that fervency as they should? (c.) And the will and affections so turn away from it as they should?

II. Second, As to the shunning of the acts of sin, there we also come wonderful short.

We shun not the sins of others as we should. This is made appear, (1.) For that we shun not the company of base men as we should. (2.) Nor shun or refuse to imitate them in their evil, as we should. How easily are good men persuaded to comply with bad men's ways. Yea, Jehoshaphat himself said to Ahab, that base one: Behold, 'I am as thou art, my people as thy people, my horses as thy horses.' 1 Ki. xxii. 4. Joseph could learn in Pharaoh's court, to 'swear by Pharaoh's life,' Ge. xlii. 15, 16. Peter also, when dissembling, was in fashion among the people, could learn to dissemble likewise. Ga. ii. 11—14.

We shun not our own sins, or the sins of our own company as we should. Christians learn to be proud one of another, to be covetous one of another, to be treacherous and false one of another, to be cowardly in God's matters one of another, to be remiss and negligent in christian duties one of another.

Besides, if I should go about to shew here, how Christians will hide iniquity, as David. 2 Sa. xii. 12. How they will excuse it, as did Aaron. Ex. xxxii. 22—24. How they will plead for it, as did the men of the city of Joash for Baal. Ju. vi. 29—31. and the like, I might soon make it abundantly appear, that Christians do not depart from iniquity as they should; and therefore the exhortation stands good, and of use to the best of saints on earth, that they and every of them 'should depart from iniquity.' Yea, the observation also that they do not do it as they should, doth still stand good against us.

Wherefore, as it is true in those that have nothing but notion, and that it is true in those that are wrought upon, but not effectually, so it is true upon those that are truly gracious; observation proves it, fears of damnation prove it, the outcry of the world proves it, and the confession of the best men proves it.

[OBSERVATION SECOND.]

I come now to another observation with which I will present you, and that is this, namely, *that every one that in way of profession and religion names the name of Christ,* 'SHOULD DEPART *from iniquity.*' I say, that every one that in a way of profession and religion, 'nameth the name of Christ, should depart from iniquity.' This truth needs more practice than proof. For I think there are none that have either scripture or reason by them, but will freely consent to this.

Nor is there any thing ambiguous in the observation, that we need now to stand upon the explaining of. For,

What iniquity is, who knows not?

That it cleaves to the best, who knows not?

That it is disgraceful to profession, who knows not? and therefore that it ought to be departed from, who knows not?

But because the motives in particular may not be so much considered as they ought, and because it is Satan's design to tempt us to be unholy, and to keep iniquity and the professing man together; therefore I will in this place spend some arguments upon you that profess, and in a way of profession do name the name of Christ, that you depart from iniquity; to wit, both in the inward thought and in the outward practice of it. And those arguments shall be of *four* sorts, some respecting Christ, some his Father, some ourselves, and some the world.

FIRST, [*Arguments that respect* CHRIST.]

First, The Christ, whom you profess, whose name you name, and whose disciples you pretend

to be, is holy. 'Be ye holy, for I am holy,' 1 Pe. i. 16. This is natural to our discourse; for if Christ be holy, and if we profess him, and in professing of him, declare that we are his disciples, we ought therefore to depart from iniquity, that we may shew the truth of our profession to the world.

Second, They that thus name the name of Christ should depart from iniquity, because this Christ, whose name we name, is loving. Those that have a loving master, a master that is continually extending his love unto his servants, should be forward in doing of his will, that thereby they may shew their sense, and acceptation of the love of their master. Why, this is his will, 'that we depart from iniquity, that we throw sin away; that we fly every appearance of evil.' 1 Th. v. 22.

Third, They that thus name the name of Christ should depart from iniquity, because of the honour and reputation of the Lord. It is a disparagement to Christ, that any of his servants, and that any that name his name, should yet abide by, and continue with, iniquity. 'A son honoureth *his* father, and a servant his master: if then I *be* a Father, where *is* mine honour? and if I *be* a Master, where *is* my fear? saith the Lord of hosts, unto you, O priests, that despise my name. And ye say, Wherein have we despised thy name?' Mal. i. 6.

Fourth, They that name the name of Christ should depart from iniquity, because of his name, that his name may not be evil spoken of by men; for our holiness puts a lustre and a beauty upon the name of Christ, and our not departing from iniquity draws a cloud upon it. Wherefore we ought to depart from iniquity, that the name of the Lord Jesus may be glorified, and not reproached through us.

Fifth, They that name the name of Christ should depart from iniquity, because of the gospel of the Lord Jesus Christ. That the gospel of our Lord Jesus Christ, which they profess, may not be evil spoken of by our neighbours. The gospel is called holy, therefore let them be holy that profess it. 2 Pe. ii. 21. The which they can by no means be, if they depart not from iniquity. Men cannot serve the designs of the gospel, and their own worldly and fleshly designs. But they that profess the name of Christ, they should be tender of his gospel, that they keep that in good esteem and reputation in the world. The which they can by no means do, unless they depart from iniquity.

Sixth, They that name the name of Christ should depart from iniquity, because the very profession of that name is holy. The profession is an holy profession. Be ye clean that bear the vessels of the Lord; the vessels, that is, the profession, for by that is as it were carried about the name and gospel of Jesus Christ. We must therefore lay aside all iniquity, and superfluity of naughtiness, and do as persons professing godliness, as professing a profession, that Christ is the priest of, yea the high-priest of. 1 Ti. ii. 10. He. iii. 1. It is a reproach to any man to be but a bungler at his profession, to be but a sloven in his profession. And it is the honour of a man to be excellent in the managing of his profession. Christians should be excellent in the management of their profession, and should make that which is good in itself, good to the church and to the world, by a sweet and cleanly managing of it.

Seventh, They that profess the name of Christ, or that name it religiously, should to their utmost depart from iniquity, because of the church of Christ which is holy. He that religiously professeth the name of Christ, has put himself into the church of Christ, though not into a particular one, yet into the universal one. Now that is holy. What agreement then hath the temple of God with idols? Ay, or any pillar, or post, or pin, or member of that temple. 2 Co. vi. 16. One black sheep is quickly espied among five hundred white ones, and one mangey one will soon affect many. One also among the saints, that is not clean, is a blemish to the rest, and, as Solomon says, 'one sinner destroyeth much good.' Ec. ix. 18.

Eighth, They that profess the name of Christ, or that name that name religiously, should depart from iniquity, because of the ordinances of Christ, for they are holy. Ex. xxx. 17—31. Men of old before they went in to meddle with holy things, were to wash their hands and their feet in a vessel prepared for that purpose. Now since they that name that name religiously do also meddle with Christ's appointments, they must also wash and be clean; cleanse your hands ye sinners, if you mean to meddle with Christ in his appointment; wash lest God cut you off for your not departing from iniquity.

Ninth, They that name the name of Christ religiously should depart from iniquity, because of Christ's observers. There are many that keep their eye upon Christ, and that watch for an opportunity to speak against him, even through the sides of those that profess him. 'Behold, this *child* is set for the fall and rising again of many in Israel; and for a sign that shall be spoken against.' Lu. ii. 34. Some take occasion to speak against him, because of the meanness of his person; here some again speak against him, because of the plainness of his doctrine; also some speak against him, because of the meanness of his followers; and some speak against him, because of the evil deeds of some that profess him. But if he that gives just occasion of offence to the least

of the saints had better be drowned in the sea with a mill-stone about his neck; what think you shall his judgment be, who, through his mingling of his profession of Christ's name with a wicked life, shall tempt or provoke men to speak against Christ?

SECOND, I come now to *those arguments that respect* GOD THE FATHER.

First, Then, they that profess the name of Christ should depart from iniquity; because of God the Father, because God the Father has made Christ to be to us what he is; to wit, the Apostle and High-priest of our profession. 'He that honoureth not the Son, honoureth not the Father which hath sent him.' 1 Co. i. 30. Jn. v. 23; xv. 8. Nor can the Father be honoured by us, but by our departing from iniquity. All our talk and profession of Christ, adds no glory to his Father, who has made him our King, and Priest, and Prophet, if it be not joined to an holy conversation. Wherefore, if you profess the name of Christ, and would hold the word in hand, that you have believed in him, depart from iniquity, for the Father's sake that hath sent him.

Second, As it is the Father which hath made Christ to us what he is; so it is the Father who hath called us to partake of Christ and all his benefits. 'Wherefore we must depart from iniquity that profess the name of Christ, that we may glorify him for his call.' 1 Co. i. 9. He. iii. 1. He has called us to the fellowship of his Son Jesus Christ; that is, to partake of all that good that is in him, as Mediator, and to be done by him for those that trust in him. Nor had we ever come out of a cursed and condemned condition, to Christ, for life and blessedness, but by the call of the Father; 'For it is not of works, but of him that calleth.' Ro. ix. 11. Now since he has called us to this privilege—even us whom he has called—and left others in their sins to perish by his judgments, it is meet we should depart from iniquity. He. iii. 1. 2 Pe. i. 2, 3. Especially since the call by which he called us is heavenly, and holy, and because he has not only called us to glory, but to virtue.

Third, We that religiously name the name of Christ, should depart from iniquity, because God the Father of our Lord Jesus Christ has commanded us so to do. Wherefore gird up the loins of your minds, be sober, and hope to the end, for the grace that is to be brought unto you at the revelation of Jesus Christ. As obedient children, not fashioning yourselves according to your former lusts in your ignorance; but as he that has called you is holy, so be ye holy in all manner of conversation: because it is written, 'Be ye holy, as I am holy.'

Fourth, They that religiously name the name of Christ should depart from iniquity, that they may answer the end for which they are called to, profess his name. The Father has, therefore, called them to profess his name, that they might be trees of righteousness, the planting of the Lord, that he might be glorified. Dost thou then profess the name of Christ: bring forth those fruits that become that holy profession, that you may be called 'trees of righteousness,' and that God may be glorified for and by your professed subjection to the gospel of his Son. Is. lxi. 3.

Fifth, They that name—as afore—the name of the Lord Jesus Christ, should depart from iniquity, that they may shew to the world the nature and power of those graces, which God the Father has bestowed upon them that do religiously name the name of Christ. And the rather, because he that religiously nameth that name, declareth even by his so naming of him, that he has received grace of the Father, to enable him so to do. Now he cannot declare this by deeds, unless he depart from iniquity; and his declaring of it by words alone, signifies little to God or man. Ti. i. 16.

Sixth, We therefore that religiously name the name of Christ, should also depart from iniquity, because the Spirit of the Father will else be grieved. Ep. iv. 30. The countenancing of iniquity, the not departing therefrom, will grieve the Holy Spirit of God, by which you 'are sealed to the day of redemption;' and that is a sin of a higher nature than men commonly are aware of. He that grieveth the Spirit of God shall smart for it here, or in hell, or both. And that Spirit that sometimes did illuminate, teach, and instruct them, can keep silence, can cause darkness, can withdraw itself, and suffer the soul to sin more and more; and this last is the very judgment of judgments. He that grieves the Spirit, quenches it; and he that quenches it, vexes it; and he that vexes it, sets it against himself, and tempts it to hasten destruction upon himself. 1 Th. v. 19. Wherefore take heed, professors, I say take heed, you that religiously name the name of Christ, that you meddle not with iniquity, that you tempt not the Spirit of the Lord to do such things against you, whose beginnings are dreadful, and whose end in working of judgments is unsearchable. Is. lxiii. 10. Ac. v. 9. A man knows not whither he is going, nor where he shall stop, that is but entering into temptation; nor whether he shall ever turn back, or go out at the gap that is right before him. He that has begun to grieve the Holy Ghost, may be suffered to go on until he has sinned that sin which is called the sin against the Holy Ghost. And if God shall once give thee up to that, then thou art in the iron cage, out of which there is neither deliverance nor redemption. Let every one, therefore, that nameth the name of Christ, depart from iniquity, upon this second consideration.

THIRD, In the next place, I come now to *those arguments that do respect* THYSELF.

First, Those that religiously name the name of Christ should, must, depart from iniquity, because else our profession of him is but a lie. 'If we say that we have fellowship with him, and walk in darkness, we lie.' 1 Jn. i. 6. 'And walk in darkness;' that is, and walk in iniquity, and take part in a life that is according to the course of this world. 'He that saith, I know him, and keepeth not his commandments, is a liar, and the truth is not in him.' ch. ii. 4. The truth that he professes to know, and that he saith he hath experience of, is not in him. Every man that nameth the name of Christ is not therefore a man of God, nor is the word in every man's mouth, truth, though he makes profession of that worthy name. 1 Ki. xvii. 24. It is then truth in him, and to others with reference to him, when his mouth and his life shall agree. Re. ii. 2, 9; iii. 9. Men may say they are apostles, and be liars: they may say they are Jews, that is, Christians, and lie, and be liars, and lie in so saying. Now this is the highest kind of lying, and certainly must therefore work the saddest sort of effects. Thus man's best things are lies. His very saying, I know him, I have fellowship with him, I am a Jew, a Christian, is a lie. His life giveth his mouth the lie: and all knowing men are sure he lies. 1. He lies unto God: he speaks lies in the presence, and to the very face of God. Now this is a daring thing: I know their lies, saith he; and shall he not recompence for this? See Ac. v. 4. Re. xxi. 8, 27; xxii. 15. and take heed. I speak to you that religiously name the name of Christ, and yet do not depart from iniquity. 2. He lies unto men; every knowing man; every man that is able to judge of the tree by the fruit, knows that that man is a liar, and that his whole profession as to himself is a lie, if he doth not depart from iniquity. Thus Paul called the slow bellies,* the unsound professors among the Cretians, liars. They were so in his eyes, for that their profession of the name of Christ was not seconded with such a life as became a people professing godliness. Tit. i. 12—16. They did not depart from iniquity. But again, 3. Such a man is a liar to his own soul. Whatever such an one promiseth to himself, his soul will find it a lie. There be many in the world that profess the name of Christ, and consequently promise their soul the enjoyment of that good, that indeed is wrapt up in him, but they will certainly be mistaken hereabout, and with the greatest terror will find it so, when they shall hear that direful sentence, 'Depart from me, all *ye* workers of iniquity.' Lu. xiii. 27. Christ is resolved

---

* 'Slow bellies;' gluttons, drunkards, slothful, idle, eating the bread of others without working.—ED.

that the loose-lived professor shall not stand in the judgment, nor any such sinners in the congregation of the righteous. They have lied to God, to men, and to themselves; but Jesus then will not lie unto them: he will plainly tell them that he hath not known them, and that they shall not abide in his presence. But,

Second, Those that religiously name the name of Christ should depart from iniquity, else, as they are liars in their profession, so they are self-deceivers. I told you but now such lie to themselves, and so consequently they deceive themselves. 'But be ye doers of the word, and not hearers only, deceiving your ownselves.' Ja. i. 22. It is a sad thing for a man, in and about eternal things, to prove a deceiver of others; but for a man to deceive himself, his ownself of eternal life, this is saddest of all; yet there is in man a propenseness so to do. Hence the apostle says, be not deceived, and let no man deceive himself. And again, ver. 26. ' If any man among you seem to be religious, and bridleth not his tongue, but deceiveth his own heart, this man's religion *is* vain.' These words, ' but deceiveth his own heart,' I have much mused about: for they seem to me to be spoken to show how bold and prodigiously desperate some men are, who yet religiously name the name of Christ: desperate, I say, at self-deceiving. He deceiveth his own heart; he otherwise persuadeth it, than of its ownself it would go: ordinarily men are said to be deceived by their hearts, but here is a man that is said to deceive his own heart, flattering it off from the scent and dread of those convictions, that by the Word, sometimes it hath been under: persuading of it that there needs no such strictness of life be added to a profession of faith in Christ, as by the gospel is called for: or that since Christ has died for us, and rose again, and since salvation is alone in him, we need not be so concerned, or be so strict to matter how we live. This man is a self-deceiver; he deceives his own heart. Self-deceiving, and that about spiritual and eternal things, especially when men do it willingly, is one of the most unnatural, unreasonable, and unaccountable actions in the world. 1. It is one of the most unnatural actions; for here a man seeks his *own* ruin, and privily lurks for his *own* life. Pr. i. 18. We all cry out against him that murders his children, his wife, or his own body, and condemn him to be one of those that has forgot the rules and love of nature. But behold the man under consideration is engaged in such designs as will terminate in his own destruction: he deceiveth his own soul. 2. This is also the most unreasonable act; there can no cause, nor crum of cause that has the least spark or dram of reason, or of anything that looks like reason, be shown why a man should deceive himself, and bereave his soul of eternal life. There-

fore, 3. Such men are usually passed over with astonishment and silence. ' Be astonished, O ye heavens, at this ! and be horribly afraid, for my people have committed two evils; they have forsaken me the fountain of living waters, *and* hewed them out cisterns, broken cisterns, that can hold no water.' Je. ii. 11—13.

But, above all this, as to this head, is the most amazing place, where it is said, that the self-deceiver makes his self-deceiving his sport: ' Sporting themselves with their own deceivings.' 2 Pe. ii. 13. These are a people far gone, to be sure, that are arrived to such a height of negligence, carelessness, wantonness, and desperateness of spirit, as to take pleasure in, and make a sport of, that which will assuredly deceive them for ever. But this is the fruit of professing of Christ, and of not departing from iniquity. The wisdom and judgment of God is such, as to give such over to the sporting of themselves in their own deceivings.

FOURTH. [*Those arguments that respect* THE WORLD.]

First, Those that religiously name the name of Christ should depart from iniquity, because of the scandal that will else assuredly come upon religion, and the things of religion, through them. Upon this head I may begin to write with a sigh, for never more of this kind than now ! There is no place, where the professors of religion are, that is clean and free from offence and scandal. Iniquity is so entailed to religion, and baseness of life to the naming of the name of Christ, that one may say of the professors of this age, as it was said of them of old, ' All tables are full of vomit *and* filthiness, *so that there is* no place *clean.*' Is. xxviii. 8. Where are they even amongst those that strive for the rule, that mind it at all, when it pinches upon their lusts, their pride, avarice, and wantonness? Are not, now-a-days, the bulk of professors like those that ' strain at a gnat and swallow a camel ?' Mat. xxiii. 24. Yea, do not professors teach the wicked ones to be wicked ? Je. ii. 33. Ah ! Lord God, this is a lamentation, and will be for a lamentation. What a sore disease is now got into the church of God, that the generality of professors should walk with scandal !

No fashion, no vanity, no profuseness, and yet no niggardliness, but is found among professors. They pinch the poor, and nip from them their due, to maintain their own pride and vanity. I shall not need to instance particulars; for from the rich to the poor, from the pastor to the people, from the master to his man, and from the mistress to her maiden, all are guilty of scandal, and of reproaching, by their lives, the name of the Lord; for they profess, and name that worthy name of Christ, but are not as they should be, departed from iniquity.

1. Hence the name of God is polluted and

reproached, even till God is weary and cries out, 'Pollute ye my name no more with your gifts and with your idols.' Eze. xx. 39. O do not pollute my name, says God; rather leave off profession, and go every one to his wickedness. Tell the world, if you will not depart from iniquity, that Christ and you are parted, and that you have left him, to be embraced by them to whom iniquity is an abomination. It would far better secure the name of God from scandal and reproach, than for you to name the name of Christ, and yet not to depart from iniquity. Then, though you sin, as now you do, the poor world would not cry out, Ay, this is your religion! Then they would not have occasion to vilify religion because of you, since you tell them that Christ and you are parted. But,

2. If you will not leave off to name the name of Christ, nor yet depart from iniquity, you also scandal the sincere professors of religion, and that is a grievous thing. There are a people in the world that have made it their business, ever since they knew Christ, to cleanse themselves from all filthiness of flesh and spirit, and that desire to perfect holiness in the fear of God; and you scandalous professors mixing yourselves with them, 'make their gold look dim.' La. iv. 1. You are spots and blemishes to them; Jude 12. you are an evil mixing itself with their good, and a scandal to their holy profession. 2 Pe. ii. 13. You are they that make the heart of the righteous sad, whom God would not have sad; you are they that offend his little ones. Oh! the millstone that God will shortly hang about your necks, when the time is come that you must be drowned in the sea and deluge of God's wrath.

3. If you will not leave off to name the name of Christ, nor yet depart from iniquity, you continue to extend your scandal also to the word and doctrine of God. They that name the name of Jesus religiously, should so carry it in the world, that they might adorn the doctrine of God their Saviour; but thou that professest and yet departest not from iniquity, thou causest the name and doctrine which thou professest to be blasphemed and reproached by the men of this world; and that is a sad thing, a thing that will bring so heavy a load upon thee, when God shall open thine eyes, and he will open them either here or in hell-fire, that thou wilt repent it with great bitterness of soul. 1 Ti. vi. 1. Ti. ii. 5, 10. The Lord smite thee to the making of thee sensible to thy shame and conversion, if it be his blessed will. Amen! But,

4. If thou wilt not leave off to name the name of Christ, nor yet depart from iniquity, thou wilt bring reproach, scorn, and contempt upon thyself. For 'sin is a reproach to any people.' Pr. xiv. 34. (1.) These are they that God will hold in great contempt and scorn. Is. i. (2.) These are they that his people shall have in great contempt. 'Therefore,'

saith he, 'have I also made you contemptible and base before all the people, according as ye have not kept my ways,' but have lifted up the face against my law.* Mal. ii. 9. Je. xxv. 9, 18. 3. Such shall also be contemned and had in derision of the men of this world. They shall be a hissing, a byeword, a taunt, and a reproach among all people. 'For them that honour me,' saith God, 'I will honour, and they that despise me shall be lightly esteemed.' 1 Sa. ii. 30. I remember that Philpot used to tell the Papists that they danced with their buttocks uncovered, in a net, because of the evil of their ways; Is. xx. 4. and the Lord bids professors have a care, 'that the shame of thy nakedness do not appear,' or lest they walk naked, and their shame be discovered; for those professors that depart not from iniquity, however they think of themselves, their nakedness is seen of others: and if it be a shame to the modest to have their nakedness seen of others, what bold and brazen brows have they who are not ashamed to show their nakedness, yea, the very shame of it, to all that dwell about them? And yet thus doth every one that religiously names the name of Christ, and yet doth not depart from iniquity.

Second, Those that religiously name the name of Christ, and do not depart from iniquity, they are the cause of the perishing of many. 'Woe,' saith Christ, 'unto the world because of offences,' Mat. xviii. 7. And again, 'Woe to that man by whom the offence cometh!' These are they that cause many to stumble at sin, and fall into hell. Hark, you that are such, what God says to you: 'Ye have caused many to stumble at the law,' and at religion. Mal. ii. 8. Men that are for taking of occasion, you give it them; men that would enter into the kingdom, you puzzle and confound them with your iniquity, while you name the name of Christ, and do not depart therefrom. One sinner destroyeth much good; these are the men that encourage the vile to be yet more vile; these be the men that quench weak desires in others; and these be the men that tempt the ignorant to harden themselves against their own salvation. A professor that hath not forsaken his iniquity, is like one that comes out of the pest-house, among the whole, with his plaguey sores running upon him. This is the man that hath the breath of a dragon, he poisons the air round about him. This is the man that slays his children, his kinsmen, his friends, and himself. What shall I say? A man that nameth the name of Christ, and that departeth not from iniquity, to whom may he be compared? The Pharisees, for that they professed religion, but walked not answerable thereto, unto what doth Christ compare them but to serpents and vipers?

---

* Margin.

What does he call them but hypocrites, whited walls, painted sepulchres, fools, and blind? and tells them that they made men more the children of hell than they were before. Mat. xxiii. Wherefore such an one cannot go out of the world by himself: for as he gave occasion of scandal when he was in the world, so is he the cause of the damnation of many. 'The fruit of the righteous is a tree of life.' Pr. xi. 30. But what is the fruit of the wicked, of the professors that are wicked? why, not to perish alone in their iniquity. Job xxii. 20. These, as the dragon, draw many of the stars of heaven, and cast them to the earth with their most stinking tail. Re. xii. 4. Cast many a professor into earthly and carnal delights, with their most filthy conversations.

The apostle did use to weep when he spake of these professors, such offence he knew they were and would be in the world. Ac. xx. 30. Phi. iii. 18, 19. These are the chief of the engines of Satan, with these he worketh wonders. One Baalam, one Jeroboam, one Ahab. O how many fish bring such to Satan's net! These are the tares that he strives to sow among the wheat, for he knows they are mischief to it. 'Wherefore, let every one that nameth the name of Christ depart from iniquity.'

Fifth, Those that religiously name the name of Christ, and do not depart from iniquity, how will they die; and how will they look that man in the face, unto the profession of whose name they have entailed an unrighteous conversation? Or do they think that he doth not know what they have done, or that they may take him off with a few cries and wringing of hands, when he is on the throne to do judgment against transgressors? Oh! it had been better they had not known, had not professed; yea, better they had never been born; for as Christ said of Judas, so may it be said of these, it had been good for that man if he had never been born; and as Christ says it had been good, so Peter says it had been better. Mar. xiv. 21. 2 Pe. ii. 20, 21. Good they had not been born, and better they had not known and made profession of the name of Christ.

But perhaps some may ask me,

WHAT INIQUITY THEY MUST DEPART FROM THAT RELIGIOUSLY NAME THE NAME OF CHRIST?

First, I answer first, *in general,* those that religiously profess the name of Christ, *must depart from* ALL *iniquity.* They should lay aside every weight; they should fly 'all appearance of evil.' He. xii. 2. 1 Th. v. 22. Many there be that are willing to part with some sins, some pleasures, some unjust profits, if they may be saved; but this selling of all, parting with all, forsaking of all, is a very hard chapter.

And yet the Lord Jesus lays it there, saying so likewise, 'whosoever he be of you,' of any of you that professeth my name, 'that forsaketh not all that he hath, he cannot be my disciple.' Lu. xiv. 33.

Christ by this text requireth more of them that are his than to forsake all iniquity. Wherefore, to be sure, every sin is included. No less than universal obedience will prove a man sincere. A divided heart is a faulty one. Ho. x. 2. He that forsaketh not every sin is partial in the law, nor can he have respect to all God's commandments. Job xx. 13. Jn. xiv. 21–24. There can be no true love to Christ where there are reserves; he that will hide any one sin in his bosom, or that will keep it, as the phrase is, under his tongue, is a secret enemy to Jesus Christ. He loveth not Christ that keepeth not his sayings. To halt between two is naught, and no man can serve two masters. Christ is a master, and sin is a master; yea, and masters are they so opposite, that he that at all shall cleave to the one shall by the other be counted his enemy. If sin at all be countenanced, Christ counts himself despised. What man would count himself beloved of his wife that knows she hath a bosom for another? 'Thou shalt not be for *another* man,' saith he, 'so *will* I *be* for thee.' Ho. iii. 3. Would the king count him a loyal subject who would hide in his house, nourish in his bed, and feed at his table, one that implacably hateth and seeketh to murder his majesty? Why, sin is such an enemy to the Lord Jesus Christ; therefore, as kings command that traitors be delivered up to justice, so Christ commands that we depart from iniquity. 'Take away all iniquity,' is a good prayer, and to 'resist unto blood, striving against sin,' is a good warfare, and he that brings 'every thought to the obedience of Christ' gets a brave victory. Ho. xiv. 2. He. xii. 4. 2 Co. x. 5. Grace leaveneth the whole soul, and so consequently all the parts thereof. Now where the whole is leavened, the taste must needs be the same throughout. Grace leaves no power, faculty, or passion of the soul unsanctified, wherefore there is no corner in a sanctified soul where sin may hide his head, to find rest and abode without control. Consequently, he that has a harbour for this or that sin, and that can find a hiding-place and an abode for it in his heart, is no Christian man. Let them then that christianly name the name of Christ, make it manifest that they do not do it feignedly, by departing from iniquity. But,

Second, And more *particularly,* they that name the name of Christ, as above, *let them depart from their* CONSTITUTION-SIN, or, if you will, the sin that their temper most inclines them to. Every man is not alike inclined to the same sin, but some to one and some to another. Now let the man that professes the name of Christ religiously, consider with himself, unto what sin or vanity am I most inclined; Is it pride? Is it covetousness? Is it fleshly lusts? And let him labour, by all means, to leave off and depart from that. This is that which David called his own iniquity, and saith, 'I was also upright before him, and I kept myself from mine iniquity.' Ps. xviii. 23. Rightly are these two put together, for it is not possible that he should be an upright man that indulgeth or countenanceth his constitution-sin; but on the contrary, he that keeps himself from that will be upright as to all the rest; and the reason is, because if a man has that grace, as to trample upon and mortify his darling, his bosom, his only sin, he will more easily and more heartily abhor and fly the rest.

And, indeed, if a man will depart from iniquity, he must depart from his darling sin first; for as long as that is entertained, the others, at least those that are most suiting with that darling, will always be haunting of him. There is a man that has such and such haunt his house, and spend his substance, and would be rid of them, but cannot; but now, let him rid himself of that, for the sake of which they haunt his house, and then he shall with ease be rid of them. Thus it is with sin. There is a man that is plagued with many sins, perhaps because he embraceth one: well, let him turn that one out of doors, and that is the way to be rid of the rest. Keep thee from thy darling, thy bosom, thy constitution-sin.

Motives to prevail with thee to fall in with this exhortation, are several.

1. There can no great change appear in thee, make what profession of Christ thou wilt, unless thou cast away thy bosom sin. A man's constitution-sin is, as I may call it, his visible sin; it is that by which his neighbours know him and describe him, whether it be pride, covetousness, lightness, or the like. Now if these abide with thee, though thou shouldest be much reformed in thy notions, and in other parts of thy life, yet say thy neighbours, he is the same man still; his faith has not saved him from his darling; he was proud afore, and is proud still; was covetous afore, and is covetous still; was light and wanton afore, and is so still. He is the same man, though he has got a new mouth. But now, if thy constitution-sin be parted with, if thy darling be cast away, thy conversion is apparent, it is seen of all, for the casting away of that is death to the rest, and ordinarily makes a change throughout.

2. So long as thy constitution-sin remains, as winked at by thee, so long thou art an hypocrite before God, let thy profession be what it will; also, when conscience shall awake and be commanded to speak to thee plainly what thou art, it will tell thee so, to thy no little vexation and perplexity.

3. Besides, do what thou canst, so long as thou remainest thus thou wilt be of a scandalous life. No honour is brought to religion by such. But, Again, As they that name the name of Christ

should depart from their constitution-sin, so they should depart from the sins of other men's tempers also. Much harm among professors is done by each others' sins. There is a man that has clean escaped from those who live in error, has shaken off the carnal world and the men thereof, and is come among professors; but, behold, there also he meeteth with wicked men, with men that have not departed from iniquity; and there he is entangled. This is a sad thing, and yet so it is. I doubt there are some in the world, I mean professors, that will curse the day that ever they were acquainted with some professors. There are professors that are defilers, professors that are 'wicked men,' professors of whom a wicked man may learn to sin. Je. v. 26; ii. 33. Take heed of these, lest, having fled from thine own sins, thou shouldest be taken with the sins of others. 'Be not partakers of other men's sins,' is the counsel and caution that Paul giveth to Timothy, if he would keep himself pure. 1 Ti. v. 22.

4. Dost thou profess the name of Christ, and dost thou pretend to be a man departing from iniquity? Then take heed thou dost not deceive thyself, by changing one bad way of sinning for another bad way of sinning. This was a trick that Israel played of old; for when God's prophets followed them hard with demands of repentance and reformation, then they would 'gad about to change their ways.' Je. ii. 36. But, behold, they would not change a bad way for a good, but one bad way for another, hopping, as the squirrel, from bough to bough, but not willing to forsake the tree. Hence they were said to return, but not to the Most High. Take heed, I say, of this. Many leave off to be drunkards, and fall in with covetousness. Many fall off from covetousness to pride and laciviousness: take heed of this. Ho. vii. 16. This is a grand deceit, and a common one too, a deceit of a long standing, and almost a disease epidemical among professors.

Many times men change their darling sins, as some change their wives and servants: that which would serve for such an one this year may not serve to be so for the year ensuing. Hypocrisy would do awhile ago, but now debauchery. Profaneness would do when profaneness was in fashion, but now a deceitful profession. Take heed, professor, that thou dost not throw away thy old darling sin for a new one. Men's tempers alter. Youth is for pride and wantonness; middle age for cunning and craft; old age for the world and covetousness. Take heed, therefore, of deceit in this thing.

5. Dost thou profess the name of Christ, and dost thou pretend to be a man departing from iniquity? take heed, lest thy departing from iniquity should be but for a time. Some do depart from iniquity, as persons in wrangling fits depart from one another; to wit, for a time, but when the

quarrel is over, by means of some intercessor, they are reconciled again. O! Satan is the intercessor between the soul and sin, and though the breach between these two may seem to be irreconcileable; yea, though the soul hath sworn it will never give countenance to so vile a thing as sin is more; yet he can tell how to make up this difference, and to fetch them back to their vomit again, who, one would have thought, had quite escaped his sins, and been gone. 2 Pe. ii. 18—22. Take heed, therefore, O professor. For there is danger of this, and the height of danger lies in it; and I think, that Satan, to do this thing, makes use of those sins again, to begin this rejoinder, which he findeth most suitable to the temper and constitution of the sinner. These are, as I may call them, the master sins; they suit, they jump with the temper of the soul. These, as the little end of the wedge, enter with ease, and so make way for those that come after, with which Satan knows he can rend the soul in pieces. Wherefore,

6. To help this, take heed of parleying with thy sins again, when once thou hast departed from them: sin has a smooth tongue; if thou hearken to its enchanting language, ten thousand to one but thou art entangled. See the saying of the wise man, ' with her much fair speech she caused him to yield, with the flattering of her lips she forced him. He goeth after her straightway, as an ox goeth to the slaughter, or as a fool to the correction of the stocks.' Pr. vii. 21, 22. He heard her charm, and by hearing is noosed, and led away to her house, which is the way to hell, ' going down to the chambers of death.' Take heed, therefore, of listening to the charms wherewith sin enchanteth the soul. In this, be like the deaf adder, stop thine ear, plug it up to sin, and let it only be open to hear the words of God.

Third, Let them that name the name of Christ *depart from the iniquity of* THE TIMES. There are sins that may be called the iniquity of the day. It was thus in Noah's day, it was thus in Lot's day, and it was thus in Christ's day—I mean, in the days of his flesh: and it is a famous thing for professors to keep themselves from the iniquities of the times. Here lay Noah's excellency, here lay Lot's excellency, and here will lie thy excellency, if thou keep thyself from the iniquity of this day. Keep or ' save yourselves from this untoward generation,' is seasonable counsel, Ac. ii. 40, but taken of but few; the sin of the time, or day, being as a strong current or stream that drives all before it. Hence Noah and Lot were found, as it were, alone, in the practice of this excellent piece of righteousness in their generation. Hence it is said of Noah, that he ' was a just man, *and* perfect in his generations.' Ge. vi. 9. And again, the Lord said unto Noah, ' Come thou and all thy house into the ark,

for thee have I seen righteous before me, in this generation.' The meaning is, he kept himself clear of the sin of his day, or of the generation among which he lived. Ge. vii. 1.

The same I say of Lot, he kept himself from the sin of Sodom; and hence Peter cries him up for such a righteous man. ' Just Lot,' saith he, ' that righteous man,' whose righteous soul was vexed with the filthy conversation of the wicked. 2 Pe. ii. 7, 8. Mark, ' a just man,' ' a righteous man,' ' his righteous soul,' &c. But how obtained he this character? Why, he abhorred the sin of his time, he fell not in with the sin of the people, but was afflicted and vexed thereabout; yea, it was to him a daily burden. ' For that righteous man dwelling among them, in seeing and hearing, vexed *his* righteous soul from day to day, with *their* unlawful deeds.' So David, ' I beheld,' saith he, ' the transgressors, and was grieved, because they kept not thy word.' Ps. cxix. 158. The sin of the times is to God the worst of sins; and to fall in with the sin of the times is counted as the highest of transgressions. Consequently, to keep from them, though a man should, through infirmity, be guilty of others, yet he is accounted upright. And hence it is, I think, that David was called a man after God's own heart; to wit, because he served his own generation by the will of God; or, as in Ac. xiii. 22, after he had, in his own age, served the will of God. By the sin of the times Satan, as it were, set up his standard in defiance to God; seeking then to cause his name, in a signal way, to be dishonoured, and that by the professors of that age. And hence it is that the Lord doth manifest such wrath against his people that are guilty of the common sin of their day, and that he shews such special favour to them that abstain therefrom. Was there no more, think you, but Noah, in his generation, that feared God? Yes, several, no doubt; but he was the man that kept clear of the sin of his day, therefore he and his family must be partakers of God's deliverance; the other must die before, and not be permitted to the mercy of the ark, nor to see the new world with Noah. Unbelief was the sin of the day when Israel was going from Egypt to Canaan; therefore all that were guilty of that transgression must be denied to go in to see that good land, yea, though it were Moses himself. ' And the Lord spake unto Moses and Aaron, Because ye believed me not, to sanctify me in the eyes of the children of Israel, therefore ye shall not bring this congregation into the land which I have given them.' Nu. xx. 12.

The sin of the day is an high transgression; from the which, because Caleb and Joshua kept themselves, God kept them from all the blasting plagues that overtook all the rest, and gave them the land which he had promised to their fathers.

'But my servant Caleb, because he had another spirit with him, and hath followed me fully, him will I bring into the land whereinto he went; and his seed shall possess it.' Nu. xiv. 24. Idolatry was the sin of the day just before Israel were carried captive into Babylon. Now those of the priests that went astray then, even they say, God shall bear their iniquity. 'But the priests, the Levites, the sons of Zadok, that kept the charge of my sanctuary when the children of Israel went astray from me, they shall come near unto me, to minister unto me; and they shall stand before me, to offer unto me the fat and the blood, saith the Lord God. They shall enter into my sanctuary, and they shall come near to my table, to minister unto me, and they shall keep my charge.' Eze. xliv. 15, 16.

Great complaints have we now among professors, of deadness in duties, barrenness of the ministry, and of the withdrawing of God from his people; but I can tell you a cause of all this, namely, the sin of the day is got into the church of God, and has defiled that holy place. This is the ground and cause of all these things; nor is it like to be otherwise, till the cause shall be removed. If any should ask me what are the sins of our day, I would say they are conspicuous, they are open, they are declared as Sodom's were. Is. iii. 9. They that have embraced them, are not ashamed of them; yea, they have got the boldness to plead for them, and to count them their enemies that seek to reform them. All tables are full of vomit and filthiness. And for pride and covetousness, for loathing of the gospel, and contemning holiness, as these have covered the face of the nation, so they have infected most of them that now name the name of Christ.

And I say again, when you find out a professor that is not horribly tainted with some of these things, I exclude not the ministers nor their families, let him be as a beacon upon a hill, or as an ensign in our land. But says one, Would you have us singular? and says another, Would you have us make ourselves ridiculous? and says a third, Such and such, more godly-wise than we, do so. But I answer, if God has made you singular, and called you to grace, that is singular; and bid you walk in ways that are singular, and diverse from the ways of all others. Yea, if to depart from iniquity will make you ridiculous, if to be holy in all manner of conversation will make you ridiculous, then be contented to be counted so. As for the godly-wise you speak of, let them manifest themselves to be such by departing from iniquity. I am sure that their being tainted with sins of the day, will not prove them godly-wise. 'Behold, I have taught you,' said Moses, 'statutes and judgments, even as the Lord my God commanded me; that ye should do so in the land whither you go to possess it. Keep therefore, and do them, for this is your wisdom, and your understanding in the sight of the nations, which shall hear of all these statutes, and say, Surely this great nation is a wise and understanding people.' Here then is wisdom, and this is that that manifesteth a people to be understanding, and godly-wise, even the keeping of the commandments of God. And why follow the apish fashions of the world? Hath the God of wisdom set them on foot among us? or is it because the devil and wicked men, the inventors of these vain toys, have outwitted the law of God? 'what nation is there so great, who hath God so nigh unto them' as his people have, and as he 'is in all things that we call upon him for? And what nation is there so great, that hath statutes and judgments so righteous, as all this law,' said Moses, 'which I set before you this day?' De. iv. 5—8. This then is that which declareth us to be godly-wise, when we keep our soul diligently to the holy words of God; and fit not only our tongues and lips, but also our lives thereto.

Fourth, But again, let them that name the name of Christ *depart from the iniquity*, that is, *as I may call it, from* FAMILY INIQUITY. There is a house iniquity; an iniquity that loves not to walk abroad, but to harbour within doors. This the holy man David was aware of, therefore he said that he would behave himself 'wisely, in a perfect way;' yea, saith he, 'I will walk within my house with a perfect heart.' Ps. ci. 2.

Now this house iniquity standeth in these things. (1.) In domestic broils and quarrels. (2.) In domestic chamberings and wantonness. (3.) In domestic misorders of children and servants.

1. For house broils and quarrels, it is an iniquity to be departed from, whether it be betwixt husband and wife, or otherwise. This, as I said, is an iniquity that loves not to walk abroad, but yet it is an horrible plague within doors. And many that shew like saints abroad, yet act the part of devils when they are at home, by giving way to this house iniquity; by cherishing of this house iniquity. This iniquity meeteth the man and his wife at the very threshold of the door, and will not suffer them to enter, no not with one foot into the house in peace, but how far this is from walking together as heirs of the grace of life, is easy to be determined. Men should carry it in love to their wives, as Christ doth to his church; and wives should carry it to their husbands, as the church ought to carry it to her Saviour. Ep. v. 21—28. 1 Pe. iii. 7. And until each relation be managed with respect to these things, this house iniquity will be cherished there. O! God sees within doors as well as without, and will judge too for

the iniquity of the house as well as for that more open.

2. As house iniquity standeth in domestic broils and contentions; so it also standeth in chamberings and wantonness. Ro. xiii. 13. Wherefore the apostle putteth them both together, saying, 'not in chambering and wantonness, not in strife and envying.' This chambering and wantonness is of a more general extent, being entertained by all, insomuch, that sometimes from the head to the foot all are horribly guilty. But, 'it is a shame to speak of those things that are done of some in secret;' for 'through the lusts of their own hearts, they dishonour their own bodies between themselves,' 'working that which is unseemly,' Ep. v. 12. Ro. i. 24, 27. to their ignominy and contempt, if not with their fellows, yet with God, who sees them; for 'the darkness hideth not from him.' Ps. cxxxix. 12. It was for this kind of iniquity with other, that God told Eli that he would 'judge his house for ever.' 1 Sa. iii. 13. also the words that follow are to be trembled at, that say, 'The iniquity of Eli's house shall not be purged with sacrifice nor offering for ever.' ver. 14. Such an evil thing is house iniquity in the eyes of the God that is above.

3. As domestic iniquity standeth in these, so also in the disorders of children and servants. Children's unlawful carriages to their parents is a great house iniquity; yea, and a common one too. 2 Ti. iii. 2, 3. Disobedience to parents is one of the sins of the last days. O! it is horrible to behold how irreverently, how irrespectively, how saucily and malapertly, children, yea, professing children, at this day, carry it to their parents; snapping, and checking, curbing and rebuking of them, as if they had never received their beings by them, or had never been beholden to them for bringing of them up; yea, as if the relation was lost, or as if they had received a dispensation from God to dishonour and disobey parents.

I will add, that this sin reigns in little and great, for not only the small and young, but men, are disobedient to their parents; and indeed, this is the sin with a shame, that men shall be disobedient to parents; the sin of the last times, that men shall be 'disobedient to parents,' and 'without natural affection.' Where now-a-days shall we see children that are come to men and women's estate, carry it as by the word they are bound, to their aged and worn-out parents? I say, where is the honour they should put upon them? who speaks to their aged parents with that due regard to that relation, to their age, to their worn-out condition, as becomes them? Is it not common now-a-days, for parents to be brought into bondage and servitude by their children? For parents to be under, and children above; for parents to be debased, and children to lord it over them. Nor

doth this sin go alone in the families where it is; no, those men are lovers of their ownselves; covetous, boasters, proud, blasphemous, that are disobedient to their parents. This is that the prophet means, when he saith, 'The child shall behave himself proudly against the ancient, and the base against the honourable.' Is. iii. 5. This is a common sin, and a crying sin, and to their shame be it spoken that are guilty; a sin that makes men vile to a high degree, and yet it is the sin of professors. But behold how the apostle brands them; he saith, such have but 'a form of godliness, but denying the power thereof,' and bids the godly shut them out of their fellowship. 2 Ti. iii. 5. This sin also is, I fear, grown to such a height in some, as to make them weary of their parents, and of doing their duty to them. Yea, I wish that some are not 'murderers of fathers and mothers,' by their thoughts, while they secretly long after, and desire their death, that the inheritance may be theirs, and that they may be delivered from obedience to their parents. 1 Ti. i. 9. This is a sin in the house, in the family, a sin that is kept in hugger-mugger, close; but God sees it, and hath declared his dislike against it, by an explicit threatening, to cut them off that are guilty of it. Ep. v. 1—5. Let them then that name the name of Christ, depart from this iniquity.

Disorders of servants is also an house iniquity, and to be departed from by the godly. 'He that worketh deceit shall not dwell within my house;' said David; and 'he that telleth lies shall not tarry in my sight.' Ps. ci. 7. One of the rarities in Solomon's house, and which the queen of Sheba was so taken with, was the goodly order of his servants. 2 Ch. ix. 4.

Some of the disorders of servants are to be imputed to the governors of families, and some to the servants themselves. Those that are to be imputed to the governors of families, are such as these: (1.) When the servant learns his vileness of his master, or of her mistress. (2.) When servants are countenanced by the master against the mistress; or by the mistress against the master; or when in opposition to either, they shall be made equals in things. (3.) When the extravagancies of servants are not discountenanced and rebuked by their superiors, and the contrary taught them by word and life.

Those to be imputed to the servants themselves are: (1.) Their want of reverence to their superiors. (2.) Their backbiting and slandering of them. (3.) Their unfaithfulness in serving of them. (4.) Their murmuring at their lawful commands, &c.

From all these domestic iniquities, let every one depart that religiously nameth the name of Christ. And before I leave this head, let me, to enforce my exhortation, urge upon you a few considerations to work with you yet further to depart from these house iniquities.

Consider 1. A man's house, and his carriage there, doth more bespeak the nature and temper of his mind, than all public profession. If I were to judge of a man for my life, I would not judge of him by his open profession, but by his domestic behaviours. Open profession is like a man's best cloak, the which is worn by him when he walketh abroad, and with many is made but little use of at home. But now what a man is at home, that he is indeed. There is abroad, my behaviour to my friends, and customers, my outward honesty in dealing and avoiding gross sins. There is at home, my house, my closet, my heart; and my house, my closet, shew most what I am: though not to the world, yet to my family, and to angels. And a good report from those most near, and most capable of advantage to judge, is like to be truer than to have it only from that which is gotten by my observers abroad. The outside of the platter and cup may look well, when within they may be full of excess. Mat. xxiii. 25—28. The outward shew and profession may be tolerable, when within doors may be bad enough. I and my house 'will serve the Lord,' is the character of a godly man. Jos. xxiv. 14.

Consider 2. As the best judgment is made upon a man from his house, so that man is like to have the approbation of God for good, that is faithful in all his house. 'I know Abraham,' says God, 'that he will command his children, and his household after him, and they shall keep the way of the Lord.' Ge. xviii. 19. To make religion and the power of godliness the chief of my designs at home, among those among whom God by a special hand has placed me, is that which is pleasing to God, and that obtaineth a good report of him. But to pass these, and to come to other things.

Consider 3. A master of a family, and mistress of the same, are those that are entrusted of God with those under their tuition and care, to be brought up for him, be they children or servants. This is plain from the text last mentioned; wherefore here is a charge committed to thee of God. Look to it, and consider with thyself, whether thou hast done such duty and service for God in this matter, as, setting common frailties aside, thou canst with good conscience lift up thy face unto God; the which to be sure thou canst by no means do, if iniquity, to the utmost, be not banished out of thy house.

Consider 4. And will it not be a sad complaint that thy servant shall take up against thee, before the Judge at the last day, that he learnt the way to destruction in thy house, who art a professor. Servants, though themselves be carnal, expect,

when they come into the house of professors, that there they shall see religion in its spangling colours; but behold, when he enters thy door, he finds sin and wickedness there. There is pride instead of humility, and heighth and *railery instead of meekness and holiness of mind. He looked for a house full of virtue, and behold nothing but spider-webs; fair and plausible abroad, but like the sow in the mire at home. Bless me, saith such a servant, are these the religious people! Are these the servants of God, where iniquity is made so much of, and is so highly entertained! And now is his heart filled with prejudice against all religion, or else he turns hypocrite like his master and his mistress, wearing, as they, a cloak of religion to cover all abroad, while all naked and shameful at home. But perhaps thy heart is so hard, and thy mind so united to the pleasing of thy vile affections, that thou wilt say, 'What care I for my servant? I took him to do my work, not to train him up in religion.' Well, suppose the soul of thy servant be thus little worth in thine eyes; yet what wilt thou say for thy children, who behold all thy ways, and are as capable of drinking up the poison of thy footsteps, as the swine is of drinking up swill: I say, what wilt thou do for them? Children will learn to be naught of parents, of professing parents soonest of all. They will be tempted to think all that they do is right. I say, what wilt thou say to this? Or art thou like the ostrich whom God hath deprived of wisdom, and has hardened her heart against her young? Job xxxix. 13—17. Will it please thee when thou shalt see that thou hast brought forth children to the murderer? or when thou shalt hear them cry, I learnt to go on in the paths of sin by the carriages of professing parents.† Ho. ix. 13. If it was counted of old a sad thing for a man to bring forth children to the sword, as Ephraim did, what will it be for a man to bring up children for hell and damnation? But,

Fifth, Let those that name the name of Christ *depart from the iniquity of* THEIR CLOSET. This may be called part of the iniquity of the house; but because it is not public, but as a retired part, therefore I put it here by itself. There are many closet sins that professors may be guilty of, and from which they have need to depart. As,

1. There is the pride of a library, that is, the study or closet, and I doubt this sin and iniquity to this day is with many great professors, and in

---

* 'Raillery;' jesting, merriment.

† A christian parent has peculiar and solemn duties to perform, in addition to those of every other class of Christians. This ought to lead him perpetually to seek wisdom from his heavenly Father; and in such close communion he becomes as peculiarly blessed as he is burthened.—Ed.

my judgment it is thus manifested. (1.) When men secretely please themselves to think it is known what a stock of books they have, or when they take more pleasure in the number of, than the matter contained in, their books. (2.) When they buy books rather to make up a number than to learn to be good and godly men thereby. (3.) When, though they own their books to be good and godly, yet they will not conform thereto.

This is an iniquity now on foot in this land, and ought to be departed from. It is better to have no books, and depart from iniquity, than to have a thousand, and not to be bettered in my soul thereby.

2. There is an iniquity that attends the closet, which I may call by the name of vacancy. When men have a closet to talk of, not to pray in; a closet to look upon, not to bow before God in: a closet to lay up gold in, but not to mourn in for the sins of my life; a closet that, could it speak, would say, My owner is seldom here upon his knees before the God of heaven; seldom here humbling himself for the iniquity of his heart, or to thank God for the mercies of his life.

3. Then also a man is guilty of closet-iniquity, when though he doth not utterly live in the neglect of duty, he formally, carnally, and without reverence, and godly fear, performs it. Also, when he asketh God for that which he cannot abide should be given him, or when he prayeth for that in his closet, that he cannot abide in his house, nor in his life.

4. Then also a man is guilty of closet-iniquity, when he desireth that the sound of the devotion he doth there, may be heard by them without in the house, the street, or of those that dwell by; for a closet is only for the man and God to do things in secretly. Mat vi. 6.

These things let the professor beware of, lest he add to his iniquity, sin, until he and it comes to be loathsome. The closet is by God appointed for men to wait upon him in, and to do it without hypocrisy; to wait there for his mind and his will, and also for grace to perform it. And how can a man that went last time out of his closet to be naught, have the face to come thither again? If I regard iniquity in my heart, the Lord will not hear my prayer; and if so, then he will not meet me in my closet; and if so, then I shall quickly be weary thereof, being left to myself, and the vanity of my mind.

It is a great thing to be a closet Christian, and to hold it; he must be a close Christian, that will be a closet Christian. When I say a close Christian, I mean one that is so in the hidden part, and that also walks with God. Many there be that profess Christ, who do oftener, in London,* frequent

the coffee-house than their closet; and that sooner in a morning run to make bargains than to pray unto God, and begin the day with him. But for thee, who professest the name of Christ, do thou depart from all these things; do thou make conscience of reading and practising; do thou follow after righteousness; do thou make conscience of beginning the day with God; for he that begins it not with him will hardly end it with him; he that runs from God in the morning will hardly find him at the close of the day; nor will he that begins with the world and the vanities thereof, in the first place, be very capable of walking with God all the day after. It is he that finds God in his closet that will carry the savour of him into his house, his shop, and his more open conversation. When Moses had been with God in the mount his face shone, he brought of that glory into the camp. Ex. xxxiv.

Sixth, I add again, let those that name the name of Christ *depart from the iniquity* THAT CLEAVETH TO OPINIONS. This is a sad age for that; let opinions in themselves be never so good, never so necessary, never so innocent, yet there are spirits in the world that will entail iniquity to them, and will make the vanity so inseparable with the opinion, that it is almost impossible with some to take in the opinion and leave out the iniquity, that by the craft and subtilty of Satan is joined thereto. Nor is this a thing new, and of yesterday; it has been thus almost in all ages of the church of God, and that not only in things small and indifferent, but in things fundamental and most substantial. I need instance in none other for proof hereof, but the doctrine of faith and holiness. If faith be preached as that which is absolutely necessary to justification, then faith fantastical, and looseness and remissness in life, with some, are joined therewith. If holiness of life be preached as necessary to salvation, then [they say that] faith is undervalued, and set below its place, and works as to justification, with God set up and made co-partners with Christ's merits in the remission of sins. Thus iniquity joineth itself with the great and most substantial truths of the gospel, and it is hard to receive any good opinion whatever, but iniquity will join itself thereto. Ep. v. 12, 13. Wicked spirits do not only tempt men to transgress the moral law, but do present themselves in heavenly things, working there, and labouring in them, to wrest the judgment, and turn the understanding and conscience awry in those high and most important things. Wherefore, I say, we must be the more watchful and careful lest we be abused in our notions

---

* Bunyan was in the habit of visiting London, the seat of government, and doubtless saw a sad change in the conduct of many professors, under a profligate monarch, to what it had been under the pious protector.—ED.

and best principles, by the iniquities that join themselves thereto.

It is strange to see at this day how, notwithstanding all the threatenings of God, men are wedded to their own opinions, beyond what the law of grace and love will admit. Here is a Presbyter, here is an Independent, and a Baptist, so joined each man to his own opinion, that they cannot have that communion one with another, as by the testament of the Lord Jesus they are commanded and enjoined. What is the cause? Is the truth? No? God is the author of no confusion in the church of God. 1 Co. xiv. 33. It is, then, because every man makes too much of his own opinion, abounds too much in his own sense, and takes not care to separate his opinion from the iniquity that cleaveth thereto. That this confusion is in the church of Christ, I am of Paul, I of Apollos, I of Cephas, and I of Christ, is too manifest. But what unbecoming language is this for the children of the same father, members of the same body, and heirs of the same glory, to be accustomed to? Whether it is pride, or hypocrisy, or ignorance, or self, or the devil, or the jesuit, or all these jointly working with the church, it makes and maintains these names of distinction. This distance and want of love, this contempt of one another, these base and undervaluing thoughts of brethren, will be better seen, to the shame and confusion of some, in the judgment.

In the meantime, I advise thee with whom I am at this time concerned, to take heed of this mixture, this sinful mixture of truth and iniquity together; and to help thee in this thing, keep thine eye much upon thine own base self, labour also to be sensible of the imperfections that cleave to thy best performances, be clothed with humility, and prefer thy brother before thyself; and know that Christianity lieth not in small matters, neither before God, nor understanding men. And it would be well if those that so stickle by their private and unscriptural notions, which only is iniquity cleaving to truth,— I say, it would be well if such were more sound in faith and morals, and if by their lives they gave better conviction to the world that the truth and grace of Christ is in them.

Sometimes so much iniquity is mixed with good opinions, that it prevails, not only to hurt men in this world, but to drown them in misery everlasting. It was good that the Jews did own and allow the ceremonies of the law, but since the iniquity that joined itself thereto did prevail with them to make those ceremonies copartners with Christ in those matters that pertained to Christ alone, therefore they perished in them. The Galatians also, with many of the Corinthians, had like to have been overthrown by these things. Take heed, therefore, of that iniquity that seeketh to steal with

the truth into thy heart, thy judgment, and understanding.

Nor doth one iniquity come without another; they are linked together, and come by companies, and therefore usually they that are superstitious in one thing, are corrupted in several other. The more a man stands upon his points* to justify himself and to condemn his holy brethren, the more danger he is in of being overcome of diverse evils. And it is the wisdom of God to let it be so, that flesh might not glory in his presence. 'His soul, which is lifted up,' Hab. ii. 4. to wit, with his good doings, with his order and methods in religion, 'his soul is not upright in him.' I have often said in my heart, What is the reason that some of the brethren should be so shy of holding communion with those every whit as good, if not better than themselves? Is it because they think themselves unworthy of their holy fellowship? No, verily; it is because they exalt themselves, they are leavened with some iniquity that hath mixed itself with some good opinions that they hold, and therefore it is that they say to others, 'Stand by thyself, come not near to me, for I am holier than thou.' Is. lxv. 5. But what is the sentence of God concerning those? Why, these are a smoke in my nose, a fire that burneth all the day. Wherefore, as I said before, so I say now again, take heed of the iniquity that cleaveth to good opinions; the which thou wilt in nowise be able to shun unless thou be clothed with humility.† But,

Seventh, Let them that name the name of Christ *depart from* HYPOCRISIES. This exhortation is as the first, general; for hypocrisies are of that nature, that they spread themselves as the leprosy of the body, all over; not the faculties of the soul only, but all the duties of a man. So that here is a great iniquity to be parted from, an over-spreading iniquity. This sin will get into all thy profession, into every whit of it, and will make the whole of it a loathsome stink in the nostrils of God. Hypocrisy will be in the pulpit, in conference, in closets, in communion of saints, in faith, in love, in repentance, in zeal, in humility, in alms, in the prison, and in all duties. Eze. viii. 12. Mal. ii. 18. Mat. vi. 2; vii. 20, 21; xxiii. 15; Lu. xii. 1, 2; xx. 19, 20. 1 Co. xiii. 3. 2 Co. vi. 6. Col. ii. 23. 2 Ti. i. 5. So that here is, for the keeping of thy soul upright and sincere, more than ordinary

* 'His points;' an heraldic term, expressive of the *exact* position of the various bearings on the shield—a scrupulous or superstitious niceness as to points of doctrine.—ED.

† These are faithful words, giving offence to bigots of every sect. The church of England excluded all from her communion except conformists — Independents held no fellowship with Baptists, nor Baptists with Independents. Happily, Christians are coming to their senses. The Test Act is repealed—nor dare we now call that unclean which God has cleansed.—ED.

diligence to be used. Hypocrisy is one of the most abominable of iniquities. It is a sin that dares it with God. It is a sin that saith God is ignorant, or that he delighteth in iniquity. It is a sin that flattereth, that dissembleth, that offereth to hold God, as it were, fair in hand, about that which is neither purposed nor intended. It is also a sin that puts a man upon studying and contriving to beguile and deceive his neighbour as to the bent and intent of the heart, and also as to the cause and end of actions. It is a sin that persuadeth a man to make a show of civility, morality, or Christian religion, as a cloak, a pretence, a guise to deceive withal. It will make a man preach for a place and praise, rather than to glorify God and save souls; it will put a man upon talking, that he may be commended; it will make a man, when he is at prayer in his closet, strive to be heard without door; it will make a man ask for that he desireth not, and show zeal in duties, when his heart is as cold, as senseless, and as much without savour as a clod; it will make a man pray to be seen and heard of men, rather than to be heard of God; it will make a man strive to weep when he repenteth not, and to pretend much friendship when he doth not love; it will make a man pretend to experience and sanctification when he has none, and to faith and sincerity when he knows not what they are. There is opposed to this sin simplicity, innocence, and godly sincerity, without which three graces thou wilt be a hypocrite, let thy notions, thy knowledge, thy profession, and commendations from others, be what they will.

Helps against this sin there are many, some of which I shall now present thee with. Pr. xvi. 2; xxi. 2. Lu. xvi. 15. 1. Believe that God's eye is always upon thy heart, to observe all the ways, all the turnings and windings of it. 2. Believe that he observeth all thy ways and marks thy actions. 'The ways of man *are* before the eyes of the Lord, and he pondereth all his goings.' Pr. v. 21. 3. Believe that there is a day of judgment a-coming, and that then all things shall be revealed and discovered as they are. ' For there is nothing covered that shall not be revealed; neither hid that shall not be known. Therefore whatsoever ye have spoken in darkness shall be heard in the light, and that which ye have spoken in the ear in closets shall be proclaimed upon the house-tops.' Lu. xii. 2, 3. 4. Believe that a hypocrite, with the cunning and shrouds for his hypocrisy, can go unseen no further than the grave, nor can he longer flatter himself with thoughts of life. For ' the triumphing of the wicked *is* short, and the joy of the hypocrite *but* for a moment. Though his excellency mount up to the heavens, and his head reach unto the clouds; *yet* he shall perish for ever, like his own dung: they which have seen him shall say, Where is he? He shall fly away as a dream, and shall not be found; yea, he shall be chased away as a vision of the night.' Job xx. 5—8. 5. Believe that God will not spare a hypocrite in the judgment, no, nor punish him neither with ordinary damnation; but as they have here sinned in a way by themselves, so there they shall receive greater damnation. Lu. xx. 47.

Of all sins, the sin of hypocrisy bespeaks a man most in love with some lust, because he dissembleth both with God and man to keep it.

For a conclusion upon this sevenfold answer to the question above propounded, let me *advise* those that are tender of the name of Christ, to have regard to these things.

Advice First, Be well acquainted with the Word, and with the general rules of holiness; to wit, with the moral law; the want of this is a cause of much unholiness of conversation. These licentious and evil times wherein we live are full of iniquity; nor can we, though we never so much love God, do our duty, as we are enjoined, if we do not know it. The law is cast behind the back of many, when it should be carried in the hand and heart, that we might do it, to the end [that] the gospel which we profess might be glorified in the world. Let then the law be with thee to love it, and do it in the spirit of the gospel, that thou be not unfruitful in thy life. Let the law, I say, be with thee, not as it comes from Moses, but from Christ; for though thou art set free from the law as a covenant of life, yet thou still art under the law to Christ; and it is to be received by thee as out of his hand, to be a rule for thy conversation in the world. 1 Co. ix. 8. What then thou art about to do, do it or leave it undone, as thou shalt find it approved or forbidden by the law. And when ought shall come into thy mind to be done, and thou art at a stand, and at a loss about the lawfulness or unlawfulness thereof, then betake thyself to the law of thy God, which is in thy hand, and ask if this thing be good or to be avoided. If this were practised by professors, there would not be so much iniquity found in their beds, their houses, their shops, and their conversations, as there is.

Advice Second, As thou must be careful to find out the lawfulness or unlawfulness of a thing before thou puttest forth thy hand thereto, so thou must also consider again whether that which is lawful is expedient. A thing may be lawful in itself, and may yet be unlawful to thee; to wit, if there be an inconveniency, or an inexpediency attending the doing of it. ' All things are lawful unto me,' says the apostle, ' but all things are not expedient; all things are lawful for me, but all things edify not.' 1 Co. vi. 12; x. 23. This then thou must consider, and this also thou must practise.

But this is a hard lesson, and impossible to be done, except thou art addicted to self-denial; for this text, and so the practice of what is contained therein, has respect chiefly to another, to wit, to thy neighbour, and his advantage and edification; and it supposeth, yea enjoineth thee, if thou wilt depart from iniquity, to forbear also some things that are lawful, and consequently profitable to thee, for the sake of, and of love to, thy neighbour. But how little of this is found among men? Where is the man that will forbear some lawful things, for fear of hurting the weak thereby? Alas! how many are there that this day profess, that will not forbear palpable wickedness; no, though the salvation of their own souls are endangered thereby; and how then should these forbear things that are lawful, even of godly tenderness to the weakness of their neighbour?

Thus much have I thought good to speak in answer to this question, What iniquity should we depart from that religiously name the name of Christ? And now we will make some use of what hath been spoken.

USE FIRST. And the first shall be *a use of examination.* Art thou a professor? Dost thou religiously name the name of Christ? If so, I ask, dost thou, according to the exhortation here, 'Depart from iniquity?' I say, examine thyself about this matter, and be thou faithful in this work, for the deceit in this will fall upon thine own pate. Deceive thyself thou mayest, but beguile God thou shalt not. 'Be not deceived, God is not mocked: for whatsoever a man soweth, that shall he also reap.' Ga. vi. 7. Wherefore let no man deceive himself, either in professing while he lives viciously, or in examining whether his profession of this name, and his life, and conversation, do answer one another. What departing from iniquity is, I have already showed in the former part of this book; wherefore I shall not here handle that point farther, only press upon thee the necessity of this exhortation, and the danger of the not doing of it faithfully. The necessity of it is urged,

First, From the deceitfulness of man's heart, which will flatter him with promises of peace and life, both now and hereafter, though he live in iniquity while he professeth the name of Christ. For there are that say in their hearts, or that have their hearts say unto them, 'I shall have peace, though I walk in the imagination of mine heart, to add drunkenness to thirst.' De. xxix. 19. And what will become of them that so do, you may see by that which followeth in the text. The heart therefore is not to be trusted, for it will promise a man peace in the way of death and damnation. I doubt not but many are under this fearful judgment to this day. What means else their quietness of mind, their peace and boasts of heaven and glory, though every step they take, as to life and conversation, is an apparent step to hell and damnation.

'The heart is deceitful.' Je. xvii. 9. and, 'He that trusteth in his own heart is a fool.' Pr. xxviii. 26. These sayings were not written without a cause. Let as many, therefore, as would examine themselves about this matter, have a jealous eye over their own heart, and take heed of being beguiled thereby; let them mix hearty prayer with this matter unto God, that he will help them to be faithful to themselves in this so great a matter; yea, let them compare their lives with the holy commandment, and judge by that rather than by the fleshly fondness that men naturally are apt to have for, and of, their own actions; for by the verdict of the Word thou must stand and fall, both now, at death, and in the day of judgment. Take heed, therefore, of thy heart, thy carnal heart, when thou goest into thy life, to make a search for iniquity. Take the Word with thee, and by the Word do thou examine thyself. Jn. xii. 48.

Second, It is urged from the cunning of Satan. Wouldest thou examine thyself faithfully as to this thing, then take heed of the flatteries of the devil: can he help it, thou shalt never find out the iniquity of thy heels. He will labour to blind thy mind, to harden thy heart, to put such virtuous names upon thy foulest vices, that thou shalt never, unless thou stoppest thine ear to him, after a godly sort, truly examine and try thy ways, according as thou art commanded. La. iii. 40. 2 Co. xiii. 5. Wherefore take heed of him, for he will be ready at thy side when thou goest about this work. Now for thy help in this matter, set God, the holy God, the all-seeing God, the sin-revenging God, before thine eyes; 'for our God *is* a consuming fire.' He. xii. 29. And believe that he hath pitched his eyes upon thy heart; also that 'he pondereth all thy goings,' and that thy judgment, as to thy faithfulness, or unfaithfulness, in this work, must proceed out of the mouth of God. Pr. v. 21; xxi. 2. This will be thy help in this thing, that is, if thou usest it faithfully; also this will be thy hindrance, if thou shalt neglect it, and suffer thyself to be abused by the devil.

Third, It is urged from the dangerousness of the latter days. Wouldest thou examine thyself, then make not the lives of others any rule to thee in this matter. It is prophesied long ago, by Christ and by Paul, concerning the latter times, 'that iniquity shall abound, and be very high among professors.' Mat. xxiv. 12. 2 Ti. iii. 1–8. Therefore it will be a rare thing to find an exemplary life among professors. Wherefore cease from man, and learn of the Word, try thyself by the Word, receive conviction from the Word; and to take off thyself from taking of encouragement from others, set the judgment before thine eyes, and that account that God will demand of thee then; and know that it will be but a poor excuse of thee to say, Lord, such a one doth so, did so, would do so: and they professed, &c. Whether thou wilt hear me or not, I know not, yet this I know, 'If thou be wise, thou shalt be wise for thyself: but *if* thou scornest, thou alone shalt bear it.' Pr. ix. 12.

Let me then, to press this use further upon thee, show thee in a few particulars the danger of not doing of it, that is, of not departing from iniquity, since thou professest.

Danger 1. The iniquity that cleaveth to men that profess, if they cast it not away, but countenance it, will all prove nettles and briars to them; and I will assure thee, yea, thou knowest, that nettles and thorns will sting and scratch but ill-favouredly. ' I went,' saith Solomon, ' by the field of the slothful, and by the vineyard of the man void of understanding. And lo, it was all grown over with thorns, *and* nettles had covered the face thereof, and the stone wall thereof was broken down.' Pr. xxiv. 30, 31.

Suppose a man were, after work all day, to be turned into a bed of nettles at night: or after a man had been about such a business, should be rewarded with chastisements of briars and thorns: this would for work be but little help, relief, or comfort to him; why this is the reward of a wicked man, of a wicked professor from God; nettles and thorns are to cover over the face of his vineyard, his field, his profession, and that at the last of all; for this covering over the face of his vineyard, with nettles and thorns, is to show what fruit the slovenly, slothful, careless professor, will reap out of his profession, when reaping time shall come.

Nor can he whose vineyard, whose profession is covered over with these nettles and thorns of iniquity, escape being afflicted with them in his conscience: for look as they cover the face of his vineyard through his sloth now, so will they cover the face of his conscience, in the day of judgment. For profession and conscience cannot be separated long; if a man then shall make profession without conscience of God's honour in his conversation, his profession and conscience will meet in the day of his visitation. Nor will he, whose condition this shall be, be able to ward off the guilt and sting of a slothful and bad conversation, from covering the face of his conscience, by retaining in his profession the name of Jesus Christ: for naming and professing of the name of Christ will, instead of salving such a conscience, put venom, sting, and keenness into those nettles and thorns, that then shall be spread over the face of such consciences. This will be worse than was that cold wet cloth that Hazael took and spread over the face of Benhadad, that he died. 2 Ki. viii. 15. This will sting worse, tear worse, torment worse, kill worse. Therefore look to it!

Danger 2. Nor may men shift this danger by their own neglect of inquiring into the truth of their separation from iniquity, for that God himself will search them. I search the reins and the heart, saith he, ' to give unto every one of you according to your works.' Re. ii. 23.

There are many that wear the name of Christ for a cloak, and so make their advantages by their iniquity; but Christ, at death and judgment, will rend this cloak from off such shoulders, then shall they walk naked, yea, the shame of their nakedness shall then appear. Now since no man can escape the search of God, and so, not his judgment; it will be thy wisdom to search thine own ways, and to prevent judgment by judging of thyself.

Danger 3. Christ will deny those to be his that do not depart from iniquity, though they shall name his name among the rest of his people. ' Depart from me,' saith he, 'all you that departed not from iniquity.' Lu. xiii. 25—27. Yea, they that shall name his name religiously, and not depart from iniquity, are denied by him all along. 1. He alloweth them not now to call him Lord. 'And why call ye me Lord, Lord,' saith he, 'and do not, the things which I say ?' Lu. vi. 46. He cannot abide to be reputed the Lord of those that presume to profess his name, and do not depart from iniquity. Eze. xx. 39. The reason is, for that such do but profane his name, and stave others off from falling in love with him and his ways. Hence he says again, ' Behold, I have sworn by my great name, saith the Lord, that my name shall no more be named in the mouth of any man of Judah.' Je. xliv. 26. Ro. ii. 24. 2. He regardeth not their prayers. ' If I regard iniquity in my heart, the Lord will not hear' my prayer. Ps. lxvi. 18. And if so, then whatever thou hast at the hand of God, thou hast it, not in mercy, but in judgment, and to work out farther thine everlasting misery. 3. He will not regard their soul, but at the last day will cast it from him, as a thing abhorred by him. As is evidently seen by that thirteenth of Luke, but now noted above.

Wherefore, from these few hints, thou, whoever thou art, mayest well perceive what a horrible thing it is to make a profession of the name of Christ, and not to depart from iniquity. Therefore let me exhort thee again to examine thyself, if thou hast, and dost—since thou professest that name— depart from iniquity.

And here I would distinguish, for there is two parts in iniquity, to wit, the guilt and filth. As for the guilt that is contracted by iniquity, I persuade myself, no man who knows it, needs to be bid to desire to depart from that; nay, I do believe that the worst devil in hell would depart from his guilt, if he could, and might: but this is it, to wit, to depart from the sweet, the pleasure, and profit of iniquity. There are that call evil good, iniquity good, and that of professors too: this is that to be departed from, and these are they that are exhorted to forsake it upon the pains and penalties before threatened. Therefore, as I said, let such look to it, that they examine themselves if they depart from iniquity.

And come, now thou art going about this work, let me help thee in this matter. I. Ask thy heart, What evil dost thou see in sin? II. How sick art thou of sin? III. What means dost thou use to mortify thy sins? IV. How much hast thou been grieved to see others break God's law, and to find temptations in thyself to do it?

I. For the first, There is a soul-polluting evil in iniquity. There is a God-provoking evil in iniquity. There is a soul-damning evil in iniquity. And until thou comest experimentally to know these things, thou wilt have neither list, nor will, to depart from iniquity.

II. For the second. I mean not sick with guilt, for so the damned in hell are sick, but I mean sick of the filth, and polluting nature of it. Thus was Moses sick of sin, thus Jabez was sick of sin, and thus was Paul sick of sin. Nu. xi. 14, 15. 1 Ch. iv. 9, 10. Ro. vii. 14. 2 Co. v. 1—3. Phi. iii. 10—14.

III. For the third. You know that those that are sensible of a sickness, will look out after the means to be recovered; there is a means also for this disease, and dost thou know what that means is, and hast thou indeed a desire to it? yea, couldest thou be willing even now to partake of the means that would help thee to that means, that can cure thee of this disease? there are no means can cure a man that is sick of sin, but glory; and the means to come by that is Christ, and to go out of this world by the faith of him. There is no grace can cure this disease; yea, grace doth rather increase it; for the more grace any man has, the more is he sick of sin; the greater an offence is iniquity to him. So then, there is nothing can cure this disease, but glory: but immortal glory. And dost thou desire this medicine? and doth God testify that thy desire is true, not feigned? 2 Co. v. 4. I know that there are many things that do make some even wish to die: but the question is not whether thou dost wish to die: for death can cure many diseases: but is this that that moveth thee to desire to depart: to wit, that thou mightest be rid, quite rid, and stripped of a body of death, because nothing on this side the grave can rid thee and strip thee of it. And is hope, that this day is approaching, a reviving cordial to thee? and doth the hope of this strike arrows into the heart of thy lusts, and draw off thy mind and affections yet farther from iniquity.

IV. To the fourth. How much hast thou been grieved to see others break God's law, and to find temptations in thyself to do it? 'I beheld the transgressors, and was grieved,' said David, 'because men kept not thy word.' Ps. cxix. 158. The

same also had Paul, because of that body of sin and death which was in him. Professor, I beseech thee be thou serious about this thing, because it will be found, when God comes to judge, that those that profess Christ, and yet abide with their iniquity, are but wooden, earthy professors, and none of the silver or golden ones: and so, consequently, such as shall be vessels, not to honour, but to dishonour; not to glory, but to shame.

USE SECOND. My next shall be *a use of terror.* Has God commanded by the mouth of his holy apostles and prophets, that those that name the name of Christ should depart from iniquity: then what will become of those that rebel against his Word. Where the word of a king is, there is power; and if the wrath of a king be as the roaring of a lion, what is, and what will be the wrath of God, when with violence it falls upon the head of the wicked?

Sirs, I beseech you consider this, namely, that the man that professeth the name of Christ, and yet liveth a wicked life, is the greatest enemy that God has in the world, and, consequently, one that God, in a way most eminent, will set his face against. Hence he threateneth such so hotly, saying, 'And the destruction of the transgressors and of the sinner *shall be* together,' and that 'they that forsake the Lord shall be consumed.' Is. i. 28; xxxiii. 14. But what sinners are these? why, the sinners in Zion, the hypocrites in the church. So again the Lord shall 'purge out from among you the rebels, and them that transgress against him.' Eze. xx. 38. 'All the sinners of my people shall die by the sword, which say, The evil shall not overtake nor prevent us.' Am. ix. 10. For though such do think that by professing of the name of Christ, they shall prevent their going down to hell, yet they shall go down thither, with those that have lived openly wicked and profane: Egypt, and Judah, the circumcised with them that are not, for it is not a profession of faith that can save them. Je. ix. 26. 'Whom dost thou pass in beauty,' saith God? wherein art thou bettered by the profession, than the wicked? 'go down, and be thou laid with the uncircumcised.' Eze. xxxii. 19.

This in general; but more particularly, the wrath of God manifesteth itself against such kind of professors.

In that the gospel and means of salvation shall not be effectual for their salvation, but that it shall work rather quite contrary effects. It shall bring forth, as I said, quite contrary effects. 2 Co. ii. 15, 16. As,

First, The preaching of the Word shall be to such the savour of death unto death, and that is a fearful thing.

Second, Yea Christ Jesus himself shall be so far off from being a savour unto them, that he shall be a snare, a trap and a gin to catch them by the heel withal; that they may go and fall backward, 'and be broken, and snared, and taken.' Is. viii. 14, 15; xxviii. 13.

Third, The Lord also will choose out such delusions, or such as will best suit with the workings of their flesh, as will effectually bring them down, with the bullocks and with the bulls to the slaughter: yea, he will lead such forth with the workers of iniquity. Is. lxvi. 3, 4. Ps. cxxv. 5.

Fourth, Such, above all, lie open to the sin against the Holy Ghost, that unpardonable sin, that must never be forgiven. For alas, it is not the poor ignorant world, but the enlightened professor that committeth the sin that shall never be forgiven.

I say, it is one enlightened, one that has tasted the good word of God, and something of the powers of the world to come. He. vi. 4. 1 Jn. v. 16. It is one that was counted a brother, that was with us in our profession: it is such an one that is in danger of committing of that most black and bloody sin. But yet all and every one of those that are such are not in danger of this; but those among these that take pleasure in unrighteousness, and that rather than they will lose that pleasure, will commit it presumptuously. Presumptuously, that is, against light, against convictions, against warnings, against mercies. Or thus, a presumptuous sin is such an one as is committed in the face of the command, in a desperate venturing to run the hazard, or in a presuming upon the mercy of God, through Christ, to be saved notwithstanding: this is a leading sin to that which is unpardonable, and will be found with such professors that do hanker after iniquity. I say, it is designed by the devil, and suffered by the just judgment of God, to catch and overthrow the loose and carnal gospellers. And hence it is that David cries unto God, that he would hold him back from these sort of sins. 'Cleanse thou me from secret *faults,*' says he. And then adds, 'Keep back thy servant also from presumptuous *sins;* let them not have dominion over me: then shall I be upright, and I shall be innocent from the great transgression.' Ps. xix. 12, 13.

If there were any dread of God, or of his word, in the hearts of the men of this generation, the consideration of this one text is enough to shake them in pieces: I speak of those that name the name of Christ, but do not depart from iniquity. But the word of God must be fulfilled: in the last days iniquity must abound; wherefore these days will be perilous and dangerous to professors. 'In the last days perilous times shall come, for men shall be lovers of their ownselves, covetous, boasters, proud, blasphemers, disobedient to parents, unthankful, unholy.' 2 Ti. iii. 1, 2. Mat. xxiv. 12. I do the

oftener harp upon this text at this time, because it is a prediction of what shall be in the latter days, to wit, what a sea and deluge of iniquity shall in the latter days overspread and drown those that then shall have a form of godliness, and of religion. So that this day is more dangerous than were the days that have been before us. Now iniquity, even immorality, shall with professors be in fashion, be pleaded for, be loved and more esteemed than holiness itself. Now godliness and self-denial shall be little set by; even those very men that have a form of godliness hate the life and power thereof; yea, they shall despise them that are good. Now therefore ministers must not think that what they say of the doctrine of self-denial among professors, will be much, if at all regarded. I say, regarded, so as to be loved and put in practice by them that name the name of Christ. For the strong hold that iniquity shall have of their affections will cause that but little effectualness to this end will be found to attend the preaching of the Word unto them.

But what will these kind of men do, when God that is just, God that is holy, and God that is strong to execute his word, shall call them to an account for these things?

Now some may say, But what shall we do to depart from iniquity? I answer,

1. Labour to see the odiousness and unprofitableness thereof, which thou mayest do by the true knowledge of the excellent nature of the holiness of God. For until thou seest a beauty in holiness, thou canst not see odiousness in sin and iniquity. Danger thou mayest see in sin before, but odiousness thou canst not.

2. Be much in the consideration of the power, justice, and faithfulness of God to revenge himself on the workers of iniquity.

3. Be much in the consideration of the greatness and worth of thy soul.

4. Be often asking of thyself what true profit did I ever get by the commission of any sin.

5. Bring thy last day often to thy bedside.

6. Be often thinking of the cries and roarings of the damned in hell.

7. Be often considering the lastingness of the torments of hell.

8. Be often thinking what would those that are now in hell give that they might live their lives over again.

9. Consider often of the frailty of thy life, and that there is no repentance to be found in the grave, whither thou goest.

10. Consider that hell is a doleful place, and that the devils are but uncomfortable companions.

11. Again, consider together with those how the patience of God has been abused by thee; yea, how all his attributes have been despised by thee,

who art a professor, that does not depart from iniquity.

12. Moreover, I would ask with what face thou canst look the Lord Jesus in the face, whose name thou hast profaned by thine iniquity?

13. Also, how thou wilt look on those that are truly godly, whose hearts thou has grieved, while they have beheld the dirt and dung that hath cloven to thee and to thy profession.

14. But especially consider with thyself how thou wilt bear, together with thine own, the guilt of the damnation of others. For as I have often said, a professor, if he perishes, seldom perishes alone, but casteth others down to hell with himself. The reason is, because others, both weak professors and carnal men, are spectators and observers of his ways; yea, and will presume also to follow him especially in evil courses, concluding that he is right. We read that the tail of the dragon, or that the dragon by his tail, did draw and cast down abundance of the stars of heaven to the earth. Re. xii. 4. Is. ix. 14, 15. The tail! ' The prophet that teacheth lies, he is the tail.' The prophet that speaketh lies, either by opinion or practice, he is the tail, the dragon's tail, the serpentine tail of the devil. Is. ix. 14, 15. And so in his order, every professor that by his iniquity draweth both himself and others to hell, he is the tail. The tail, says the Holy Ghost, draws them down; draws down even the stars of heaven; but whither doth he draw them? The answer is, from heaven, the throne of God, to earth, the seat of the dragon; for he is the god of this world. The professor then that is dishonourable in his profession, he is the tail. ' The ancient and honourable, he is the head; and the prophet that teacheth lies, he is the tail.' Nor can Satan work such exploits by any, as he can by unrighteous professors. These he useth in his hand, as the giant useth his club; he, as it were, drives all before him with it. It is said of Behemoth, that ' he moveth his tail like a cedar.' Job xl. 17. Behemoth is a type of the devil, but behold how he handleth his tail, even as if a man should swing about a cedar. Re. ix. 10, 19. This is spoken to shew the hurtfulness of the tail, as it is also said in another place. Better no professor than a wicked professor. Better open profane than a hypocritical namer of the name of Christ; and less hurt shall such an one do to his own soul, to the poor ignorant world, to the name of Christ, and to the church of God.

Let professors, therefore, take heed to themselves, that they join to their naming of the name of Christ an holy and godly conversation; for away they must go else with the workers of iniquity to the pit, with more guilt, and bigger load, and more torment by far than others. But,

USE THIRD. My next word shall be to those that *desire to be true, sincere professors of the name of Christ.*

First, Do you bless God, for that he has put not only his name into your lips, but grace into your hearts, that thereby that profession which thou makest of him may be seasoned with that salt. ' Every sacrifice shall be seasoned with salt.' Mar. ix. 49. Now naming of the name of Christ is a sacrifice, and a sacrifice acceptable, when the salt of the covenant of thy God is not lacking, but mixed therewith. He. xiii. 15. Le. ii. 13. Therefore I say, since God has put his name into thy mouth to profess the same, and grace into thy heart to season that profession with such carriage, such behaviour, such life, and such conversation as doth become the same, thou hast great cause to thank God. A man into whose mouth God has put the name of Christ to profess it, is as a man that is to act his part upon a stage in the market place; if he doth it well, he brings praise both to his master and himself; but if he doth it ill, both are brought into contempt. No greater praise can by man be brought to God, than by joining to the profession of the name of Christ a fruitful life and conversation. ' Herein,' saith Christ, ' is my Father glorified, that ye bear much fruit; so shall ye be my disciples.' Jn. xv. 8. Fruitful lives God expecteth of all that profess the name of Christ. And let every one that nameth the name of Christ depart from iniquity. Bless God, therefore, if he hath kept thee from blotting and blemishing of thy profession; if thy conversation has not been stained with the blots and evils of the times. What thou feelest, fightest with, and groanest under, by reason of the working of thine inward corruptions, with that I meddle not; nor is thy conversation the worse for that, if thou keepest them from breaking out. Thou also shalt be counted holy unto God, through Christ, if thou be of an upright conversation; though plagued every day with the working of thine own corruption.

As God's grace is the salt of saints, so saints are the salt of God. The one is the salt of God in the heart, and the other is the salt of God in the world. ' Ye are the salt of the earth:' Mat. v. 13. that is, the salt of God in the earth. For the earth would be wholly corrupt, and would altogether stink, if professors were not in it. But now if the professor, which is the salt, shall indeed lose his savour, and hath nothing in his conversation to season that part of the earth, in which God has placed him, wherewith shall it be seasoned? The place where he dwells, as well as his profession, will both stink odiously in the nostrils of the Lord, and so both come to ruin and desolation.

Indeed, as I have shewed, the professor will come to the worst of it; for that God doth deny further to give him salt. ' If the salt have lost his savour, wherewith shall it be seasoned?' Lu. xiv. 34. Wherewith shall the salt be salted? with nothing. Therefore it is thenceforth good for nothing. No, not for the dunghill, but to be cast out, and trodden under foot of men. 'He that hath ears to hear let him hear.'

How much, therefore, is the tender-hearted, and he that laboureth to beautify his profession with a gospel conversation, bound to bless God for the salt of his grace, by the which his heart is seasoned, and from his heart, his conversation.

Second, As such Christians should bless God, so let them watch, let them still watch, let them still watch and pray, watch against Satan, and pray yet for more grace, that they may yet more and more beautify their profession of the worthy name of Christ with a suitable conversation. Blessed is he that watcheth and keepeth his garment; that is, his conversation clean, nor is there anything, save the overthrowing of our faith, that Satan seeketh more to destroy. He knows holiness in them that rightly, as to doctrine, name the name of Christ, is a maul and destruction to his kingdom, an allurement to the ignorant, and a cutting off those occasions to stumble, that by the dirty life of a professor is laid in the way of the blind. Le. xix. 14. He knows that holiness of lives, when they shine in those that profess the name of Christ, doth cut off his lies that he seeketh to make the world believe, and slanders that he seeketh to fasten upon the professors of the gospel. Wherefore, as you have begun to glorify God in your body and in your spirit, which are God's; so I beseech you do it more and more.

Third, To this end, shun those professors that are loose of life and conversation: 'From such withdraw thyself,' saith Paul, and follow 'righteousness, faith, charity, peace, with them that call on the Lord out of a pure heart.' 1 Ti. vi. 5. 2 Ti. ii. 22. If a man, if a good man takes not good heed to himself, he shall soon bring his soul into a snare. Loose professors are defilers and corrupters; a man shall get nothing but a blot by having company with them. Is. i. 4. Besides, as a man shall get a blot by having much to do with such; so let him beware that his heart learn none of their ways. Let thy company be the excellent in the earth; even those that are excellent for knowledge and conversation. 'He that walketh with wise men shall be wise; but a companion of fools shall be destroyed.'

Be content to be counted singular, for so thou shalt, if thou shalt follow after righteousness, &c., in good earnest; for holiness is a rare thing now in the world. I told thee before that it is foretold by the Word, that in the last days perilous times shall come, and that men shall walk after their own lusts; yea, professors, to their destruction.

Nor will it be easy to keep thyself therefrom. But even as when the pestilence is come into a place, it infecteth and casteth down the healthful; so the iniquity of the last times will infect and pollute the godly. I mean the generality of them. Were but our times duly compared with those that went before, we should see that which now we are ignorant of. Did we but look back to the Puritans, but especially to those that, but a little before them, suffered for the word of God, in the Marian days, we should see another life than is now among men, another manner of conversation than now is among professors. But, I say, predictions and prophecies must be fulfilled; and since the Word says plainly, that 'in the last days there shall come scoffers, walking after their own lusts,' 2 Pe. iii. 3, 17, and since the Christians shall be endangered thereby, let us look to it, that we acquit ourselves like men, seeing we know these things before; 'lest we, being led away with the error of the wicked, fall from our own steadfastness.'

Singularity in godliness, if it be in godliness, no man should be ashamed of. For that is no more than to be more godly, than to walk more humbly with God than others; and, for my part, I had rather be a pattern and example of piety. I had rather that my life should be instructing to the saints, and condemning to the world, with Noah and Lot, than to hazard myself among the multitude of the drossy.

I know that many professors will fall short of eternal life, and my judgment tells me, that they will be of the slovenly sort of professors that so do. And for my part, I had rather run with the foremost and win the prize, than come behind, and lose that, and my labour, and all. 'If a man also strive for masteries, *yet* is he not crowned, except he strive lawfully.' And when men have said all they can, they are the truly redeemed 'that are zealous of good works.' 1 Co. ix. 24. 2 Ti. ii. 4, 5. Tit. ii. 14.

Not that works do save us, but faith, which layeth hold on Christ's righteousness for justification, sanctifies the heart, and makes men desirous to live in this world, to the glory of that Christ who died in this world to save us from death.

For my part I doubt of the faith of many, and fear that it will prove no better at the day of God than will the faith of devils. For that it standeth in bare speculation, and is without life and soul to that which is good. Where is the man that walketh with his cross upon his shoulder? Where is the man that is zealous of moral holiness? Indeed, for those things that have nothing of the cross of the purse, or of the cross of the belly, or of the cross of the back, or of the cross of the vanity of household affairs; for those things, I find we have many, and those, very busy sticklers; but otherwise, the cross, self-denial, charity, purity in life and conversation, is almost quite out of doors among professors. But, man of God, do thou be singular as to these and as to their conversation. ' Be not ye therefore partakers with them,' Ep. v. 7, in any of their ways, but keep thy soul diligently; for if damage happeneth to thee, thou alone must bear it.

But he that will depart from iniquity must be well fortified with faith, and patience, and the love of God; for iniquity has its beauty spots and its advantages attending on it; hence it is compared to a woman, for it allureth greatly. Zec. v. 7. Wherefore, I say, he that will depart therefrom had need have faith, that being it which will help him to see beyond it, and that will shew him more in things that are invisible, that can be found in sin, were it ten thousand times more entangling than it is. 2 Co. iv. 18. He has need of patience also to hold out in this work of departing from iniquity. For, indeed, to depart from that, is to draw my mind off from that, which will follow me with continual solicitations. Samson withstood his Delilah for a while, but she got the mastery of him at the last; why so? Because he wanted patience, he grew angry and was vexed, and could withstand her solicitation no longer. Ju. xvi. 15—17. Many there be also, that can well enough be contented to shut sin out of doors for a while; but because sin has much fair speech, therefore it overcomes at last. Pr. vii. 21. For sin and iniquity will not be easily said nay; it is like her of whom you read—she has a whore's forehead, and refuses to be ashamed. Je. iii. 3. Wherefore, departing from iniquity is a work for length, as long as life shall last. A work did I say? It is a war; a continual combat; wherefore he that will adventure to set upon this work must needs be armed with faith and patience, a daily exercise he will find himself put upon by the continual attempts of iniquity to be putting forth itself. Mat. xxiv. 13. Re. iii. 10. This is called an enduring to the end, a continuing in the word of Christ, and also a keeping of the word of his patience. But what man in the world can do this whose heart is not seasoned with the love of God and the love of Christ? Therefore, he that will exercise himself in this work must be often considering of the love of God to him in Christ; for the more sense, or apprehension, a man shall have of that, the more easy and pleasant will this work be to him; yea, though the doing thereof should cost him his heart's blood. ' Thy loving-kindness is before mine eyes,' says David, ' and I have walked in thy truth.' Ps. xxvi. 3. Nothing like the sense, sight, or belief of that, to the man of God, to make him depart from iniquity.

But what shall I do, I cannot depart therefrom as I should?

Keep thine eye upon all thy shortnesses, or upon all thy failures, for that that is profitable for thee. 1. The sight of this will make thee base in thine own eyes. 2. It will give thee occasion to see the need and excellency of repentance. 3. It will put thee upon prayer to God for help and pardon. 4. It will make thee weary of this world. 5. It will make grace to persevere the more desirable in thine eyes.

Also, it will help thee in the things which follow:—1. It will make thee see the need of Christ's righteousness. 2. It will make thee see the need of Christ's intercession. 3. It will make thee see thy need of Christ's advocateship. 4. It will make thee see the riches of God's patience. 5. And it will make heaven and eternal life the sweeter to thee when thou comest there.

But to the question. Get more grace, for the more grace thou hast the further is thine heart set off of iniquity, the more, also, set against it, and the better able to depart from it when it cometh to thee, tempteth thee, and entreats thee for entertainment. Now the way to have more grace is to have more knowledge of Christ, and to pray more fervently in his name; also, to subject thy soul and thy lusts, with all thy power, to the authority of that grace thou hast, and to judge and condemn thyself most heartily before God, for every secret inclination that thou findest in thy flesh to sinward.

The improvement of what thou hast is that, as I may say, by which God judges how thou wouldest use, if thou hadst it, more; and according to that so shalt thou have, or not have, a farther measure. He that is faithful in that which is least is faithful, and will be so, also, in much; and he that is unjust in the least, is, and will be, unjust also in much. I know Christ speaks here about the unrighteous mammon, but the same may be applied also unto the thing in hand. Lu. xvi. 10—12.

And if ye have not been faithful in that which is another man's, who will commit unto you that which is your own? That is a remarkable place to this purpose in the Revelation—' Behold,' saith he, ' I have set before thee an open door,' that thou mayest have what thou wilt, as was also said to the improving woman of Canaan, ' and no man can shut it: for thou hast a little strength, and hast kept my word, and hast not denied my name.' Re. iii. 8. Mat. xv. 28.

A good improvement of what we have of the grace of God at present pleases God, and engages him to give us more; but an ill improvement of what we at present have will not do so. ' To him that hath,' that hath an heart to improve what he hath, ' to him shall be given; but to him that hath not, from him shall be taken even that which he hath.' Mat. xxv. 24—30. Well, weigh the place and you shall find it so.

I know that to depart from iniquity so as is

required, that is, to the utmost degree of the requirement, no man can, for it is a copy too fair for mortal flesh exactly to imitate while we are in this world. But with good paper, good ink, and good pen, a skilful and willing man may go far. And it is well for thee if thy complaint be sincere, to wit, that thou art troubled that thou canst not forsake iniquity as thou shouldest; for God accepteth of thy design and desire, and it is counted by him as thy kindness. Pr. xix. 22. But if thy complaint in this matter be true, thou wilt not rest nor content thyself in thy complaints, but wilt, as he that is truly hungry or greatly burdened useth all lawful means to satisfy his hunger and to ease himself of his burden, use all thy skill and power to mortify and keep them under, by the word of God. Nor can it otherwise be but that such a man must be a growing man. 'Every branch that beareth fruit, he purgeth it, that it may bring forth more fruit.' Jn. xv. 2. Such a man shall not be stumbling in religion, nor a scandal to it, in his calling; but shall, according to God's ordinary way with his people, be a fruitful and flourishing bough.

And I would to God this were the sickness of all them that profess in this nation; for then should we soon have a new leaf turned over in most corners of this nation; then would graciousness of heart, and life, and conversation be more prized, more sought after, and better improved and practised than it is; yea, then would the throats of ungodly men be better stopt, and their mouths faster shut up, as to their reproaching of religion, than they are. A Christian man must be the object of the envy of the world; but it is better, if the will of God be so, that we be reproached for well-doing than for evil. 1 Pe. ii.; iii. If we be reproached for evil-doing, it is our shame; but if for well-doing, it is our glory. If we be reproached for our sins, God cannot vindicate us; but if we be reproached for a virtuous life, God himself is concerned, will espouse our quarrel, and, in his good time, will shew our foes our righteousness, and put them to shame and silence. Briefly, a godly life annexed to faith in Christ is so necessary, that a man that professes the name of Christ is worse than a beast without it.

But thou wilt say unto me, Why do men profess the name of Christ that love not to depart from iniquity?

I answer, there are many reasons for it.

1. The preaching of the gospel, and so the publication of the name of Christ, is musical and very taking to the children of men. A Saviour! a Redeemer! a loving, sin-pardoning Jesus! what better words can come from man? what better melody can be heard? 'Son of man,' said God to the prophet, 'Lo, thou *art* unto them as a very lovely song;' or, as a song of loves, 'of one that hath a pleasant voice, and can play well on an instrument.' Eze. xxxiii. 32. The gospel is a most melodious note and sweet tune to any that are not prepossessed with slander, reproach, and enmity against the professors of it. Now, its melodious notes being so sweet, no marvel if it entangle some even of them that yet will not depart from iniquity to take up and profess so lovely a profession. But,

2. There are a generation of men that are and have been frightened with the law, and terrified with fears of perishing for their sins, but yet have not grace to leave them. Now, when the sound of the gospel shall reach such men's ears, because there is by that made public the willingness of Christ to die for sin, and of God to forgive them for his sake; therefore they presently receive and profess those notions as the only ones that can rid them from their frights and terrors, falsely resting themselves content with that faith thereof which standeth in naked knowledge; yea, liking of that faith best that will stand with their pride, covetousness, and lechery, never desiring to hear of practical holiness, because it will disturb them; wherefore they usually cast dirt at such, calling them legal preachers.

3. Here also is a design of Satan set on foot; for these carnal gospellers are his tares, the children of the wicked one; those that he hath sowed among the wheat of purpose, if possible, that that might be rooted up by beholding and learning to be vile and filthy of them. Mat. xiii. 36—43.

4. Another cause hereof is this, the hypocrites that begin to profess find as bad as themselves already in a profession of this worthy name; and, think they, these do so and so, and, therefore, so will I.

5. This comes to pass, also, through the righteous judgment of God, who, through the anger that he has conceived against some men for their sins, will lift them up to heaven before he casts them down to hell, that their fall may be the greater and their punishment the more intolerable. Mat. xi. 20—24. I have now done when I have read to you my text over again—'And, let every one that nameth the name of Christ depart from iniquity.'

CHRISTIAN BEHAVIOUR;

BEING

THE FRUITS OF TRUE CHRISTIANITY:

TEACHING HUSBANDS, WIVES, PARENTS, CHILDREN, MASTERS, SERVANTS, ETC., HOW TO WALK
SO AS TO PLEASE GOD.

WITH A WORD OF DIRECTION TO ALL BACKSLIDERS.

ADVERTISEMENT BY THE EDITOR.

THIS valuable practical treatise, was first published as a pocket volume about the year 1674, soon after the author's final release from his long and dangerous imprisonment. It is evident from the concluding paragraph that he considered his liberty and even his life to be still in a very uncertain state; not from the infirmities of age, for he was then in the prime of life; but from the tyranny of the state church, and probably from the effects of his long incarceration in a damp, unhealthy gaol. It is the best and most scriptural guide that has ever appeared to aid us in the performance of relative duties: written with originality of thought and that peculiar and pious earnestness which so distinguishes all his works.

No one can read this book, without finding in it his own portrait truly and correctly drawn to the life. Many have been the hearers of the word in its public ministration, who have been astonished that a faithful minister has not only opened their outward conduct, but the inward recesses of their hearts—and have inquired with wonder, 'Where could he get such a knowledge of my heart?' The usages and *feelings* of every part of the human family—the rich and poor—outward professors or openly profane—God fearers or God defiers—are displayed in the following pages as accurately as if the author had been present in every family upon earth, and had not only witnessed the conduct of the happy and of the miserable in every grade; but he goes within and unvails that mystery of iniquity the human heart, its secret springs, feelings, and machinations. What mysterious power could this uneducated man have possessed, thus to dive into the most subtle of all secret repositories, the human heart! Could he have left his body at times and his invisible spirit have entered all chambers, as was said of an ancient philosopher,* still time

would have been too short even to have transiently surveyed outward conduct; and then he could not have entered into the thoughts of others. Reader, the fountain of all hidden things was open to him. Shut up for many years in prison, with the key in his possession which unlocks all the mysteries of earth, and heaven, and hell—he diligently used his time and all was revealed to him. He makes the source of his knowledge no secret, but invites you to search, as he did, this storehouse of things new and old. It was the Bible which unfolded to him all the great events of time and of eternity—all the secret springs of states, and families, and individuals—wonderous book! It made an uneducated artizan wiser than all the philosophers who have been contented with Plato, Aristotle, Pliny, Plutarch, and the most renowned of human writers. Not only is the real state of human nature revealed with unerring truth, as suffering under a cruel malady, strangely diverse in its operations, but all tending to the downward, dark, dreary road to misery temporal and eternal: but it also displays the antidote; an infallible remedy against all the subtilties of this tortuous disease. Reader, this treasure is in our hands. How great is the responsibility. How blessed are those who with earnest prayer for divine illumination—read —ponder—and relying upon the aid of the Holy Spirit, understand and instantly obey the sacred precepts which its pages unfold. Weigh well their nature and tendency, as Bunyan opens them in this invaluable treatise. They lead step by step from darkness to light. It may be a tempestuous passage in the dim twilight, as it was with him— but it is safe and leads to the fountain of happiness —the source of blessedness—the presence and smiles of God and the being conformed to his image. In proportion as we are thus transformed in our minds, we shall be able to fulfil all our duties and behaviour as becometh Christians. We dare not seek to avoid these duties because they are full of anxieties. Blessed are those who know and feel the ties of church fellowship—or the nearer

---

* Hermotimus of Lucian. During one of these wanderings his wife thought him dead, and his body was burnt. Whether the poor soul, thus suddenly ejected, obtained another habitation is not narrated.

union of husband and wife, that type of the mystical union of Christ and his church. Happy are those who piously discharge parental and filial duties, that figure of the relationship which the Almighty, in infinite condescension, owns between him and his fallen but renewed creatures. Vows of celibacy disturb all the order and harmonies of creation, and are fleshly, sensual, devilish. The unmarried are strangers to those delightful or painful sensibilities which drive the soul to continual converse with God, either in heart-felt praises or for divine assistance to glorify him in the discharge of domestic duties. They who *vow* celibacy, fly in the face of the infinitely wise eternal, who said, ' It is not good for man to be alone.' He sets up his puny antagonism to omnipotence. It is true, that in the prospect of the desolations which were foretold by the Saviour and were about to be poured out upon Jerusalem, ' for the present distress,' ' the short time ' Paul advised, not commanded, a temporary deviation from the order of nature—like an eclipse of the sun or moon—for a ' short time ' which no one could wish to be prolonged. We are bound, in the expectation of the divine approbation, not to shrink from duties, but to seek wisdom to fulfil them; and in this little work we have a scriptural guide to which we shall do well to take heed. It is a peculiarly solemn legacy — the author's ardent desire is thus expressed; ' Before I die [as the greatest of all the duties he had to perform] let me provoke you to faith and holiness.' Be it our duty and privilege to examine our conduct faithfully by those portions of holy writ, with which this treatise is beautifully adorned. It was written in the prospect of sufferings and death, and yet how serene was his soul. No cloud, no doubts or fears are seen ; his legacy to us as well as to those who survived him is, ' Love one another when I am deceased.' My labours of love to you are limited to this world. ' Though there I shall rest from my labours, and be in paradise, as through grace, I comfortably believe ; yet it is not *there* but *here* I must do you good.' Consider what he has advanced, and the scriptures by which every sentence is confirmed, and may his concluding and fervent prayer be answered to our souls: ' The Lord give us understanding in all things. Farewell.'

GEO. OFFOR.

THE EPISTLE TO THE READER.

COURTEOUS READER,

HAVING formerly writ some small matter touching the doctrine of faith, as justification by grace through the faith of Christ's blood, &c., I do here, as the second to that doctrine, present thee with a few lines touching good works, that I might, as at first I shewed thee the good and glory of the one, so now shew thee the beauty and excellency of the other: for though we are justified freely by grace through Christ before God ; Ro. iii. 24, &c. yet we are justified before men by our works : Ja. ii. 18. nay, a life of holiness flowing from faith in us that are saved by grace, it doth justify that grace before the world, that justifies us before God. 2 Co. vi. 1, 3; ix. 12. 13. 1 Pe. ii. 11, 12.

I have not here only in general treated of this doctrine of good works, but particularly, after some discourse about works flowing from faith, and what makes it truly and gospely good, I discourse of them as we stand under our several relations in this world among men.

As, The duty of the master of a family: Of the husband to his wife; and of hers to him: Of the duty of parents to their children ; and of children to their parents: Of masters also to their servants ; and of the servant again to his master: with a brief touch upon good neighbourhood; and a discovery of covetousness, pride, and uncleanness, which are great obstructions to a truly gospel conversation.

I know there are many that have treated of good works in large and learned discourses; but I doubt all have not so gospelized their discourses as becomes them, and as the doctrine ot the grace of God calleth for. However, I thought it my duty to add this discourse to all that are past; and that for these reasons.

1. To take away those aspersions that the adversaries cast upon our doctrine—as also in the days of Paul—that because we preach justification without the works of the law; therefore they pretend we plead for looseness of life: ' whose damnation is just.' Ro. iii. 8.

2. Because, though there be much discourse about works in general, yet a particular discourse of them, as before is touched, is too much neglected ; and by this means every one too much left at uncertainties (as from them) of their several works under their particular relations ; which I think is one reason of that disorder in families and places where God's people live; to their shame, and the dishonour of God.

3. Because these few books that do particularly treat *thus* of good works, are, I think, now so scarce, or so big, that but few have them, and few

buy them, if they may be had, especially our new converts, for whose sakes principally this short discourse is intended; and indeed, this is one reason of my brevity, that the price might neither be burdensome, nor the reading long and tedious. Multitude of words drown the memory; and an exhortation in few words may yet be so full, that the reader may find *that* in one side of a sheet, which some are forced to hunt for in a whole quire, &c. The Lord teach us this wisdom.

4. I have written this book, to shew that I bear a fellow-testimony and witness, with all that know God, of the operation that grace hath, and will have, in the heart that hath savingly received it.

Lastly, I have thus written, because it is amiable and pleasant to God, when Christians keep their rank, relation, and station, doing all as becometh their quality and calling. When Christians stand every one in their places, and do the work of their relations,* then they are like the flowers in the

garden, that stand and grow where the gardener hath planted them, and then they shall both honour the garden in which they are planted, and the gardener that hath so disposed of them. From the hyssop in the wall, to the cedar in Lebanon, their fruit is their glory.† And seeing the stock into which we are planted, is the fruitfullest stock, the sap conveyed thereout the fruitfullest sap, and the dresser of our souls the wisest husbandman, Jn. xv. 1. how contrary to nature, to example, and expectation, should we be, if we should not be rich in good works!

Wherefore take heed of being painted fire, wherein is no warmth; and painted flowers, which retain no smell; and of being painted trees, whereon is no fruit. 'Whoso boasteth himself of a false gift, is like clouds and wind without rain.' Pr. xxv. 14. Farewell.

The Lord be with thy spirit, that thou mayest profit for time to come. J. BUNYAN.

---

* 'Of their relations,' related or belonging to themselves. —ED.

† 'Also, where the gardener hath set them, there they stand, and quarrel not one with another.'—*Pilgrim*, part 2. *Interpreter's house.*—ED.

CHRISTIAN BEHAVIOUR.

'THAT BEING JUSTIFIED BY HIS GRACE, WE SHOULD BE MADE HEIRS ACCORDING TO THE HOPE OF ETERNAL LIFE. *THIS IS* A FAITHFUL SAYING, AND THESE THINGS I WILL THAT THOU AFFIRM CONSTANTLY, THAT THEY WHICH HAVE BELIEVED IN GOD MIGHT BE CAREFUL TO MAINTAIN GOOD WORKS. THESE THINGS ARE GOOD AND PROFITABLE UNTO MEN.'— TITUS III. 7, 8.

I SHALL not at this time discourse of every particular at large included in these words; but shall briefly fall upon those things that I judge most necessary for the people of God. Neither shall I need to make any great preamble to the words for their explication; they themselves being plain, and without that ambiguity that calleth for such a thing; the general scope being this, THAT THEY WHICH HAVE BELIEVED IN GOD SHOULD BE CAREFUL TO MAINTAIN GOOD WORKS.

But yet, to prosecute what I intend, with what clearness I may, I shall in a word or two make way for what is to be the *main* of this book.

'This is a faithful saying.' This; Which? Why, that which goeth before, namely, 'That being justified by his grace, we should be made heirs according to the hope of eternal life. *This is* a faithful saying, and these things I will that thou affirm constantly.'

Why so?

Why, 'That they which have believed in God, might be careful to maintain good works.' The meaning is, that the way to provoke others to good works, is constantly—in the evidence and demonstration of the spirit—to shew them the certainty of their [these believers] being by grace made heirs of eternal life.

From this scripture, therefore, I do gather these things observable.

FIRST, That good works do flow from faith. Yea,

SECOND, That every one that believeth should be careful that their works be good.

THIRD, That every believer should not only be careful that their works be good, and for the present do them, but should also be careful to maintain them; that is, they should carefully study to keep in a constant course of good works.

FOURTH, and lastly, That the best way to provoke both ourselves and others to this work, it is to be often affirming to others the doctrine of justification by grace, and to believe it ourselves: '*This is* a faithful saying, and these things I will,' saith Paul, 'that thou affirm constantly, that they which have believed in God might be careful to maintain good works.'

FIRST.—I begin with the first. *That good works do flow from faith.* This is evident divers ways.

First, From the impossibility of their flowing from any other thing; they must either flow from faith, or not at all: 'For whatsoever *is* not of faith, is sin.' Ro. xiv. 23. And again, 'Without faith *it is* impossible to please *him.*' He. xi. 6. Every man by nature, before faith, is an evil and a corrupt tree; and a corrupt tree cannot bring forth good fruit: 'Do men gather grapes of thorns, or figs of thistles?' Mat. vii. 16, 17. Now a man is made good by faith, and by that bringeth forth the fruits that are acceptable to God. He. xi. 4. Col. i. 4—6.

Wherefore sinners, before faith, are compared to the wilderness, whose fruits are briars and thorns; and whose hearts are the habitation of dragons; that is, of devils.* Is. xxxv. 6, 7. He. vi. 7, 8.

And hence again it is, that they are said to be Godless, Christless, Spiritless, faithless, hopeless; without the covenant of grace, without strength; enemies in their minds by wicked works, and possessed by the spirit of wickedness, as a castle by a conqueror. Ep. ii. 12. Jude 19. 2 Th. iii. 2. Col. i. 21. Lu. xi. 21.

Now, these things being thus, it is impossible that all the men under heaven, that are unconverted, should be able to bring forth one work rightly good; even as impossible, as for all the briars and thorns under heaven to bring forth one cluster of grapes, or one bunch of figs; for indeed they want the qualification. A thorn bringeth not forth figs, because it wanteth the nature of the fig-tree; and so doth the bramble the nature of the vine. Good works must come from a good heart.

Now, this the unbeliever wanteth, because he wanteth faith; for it is that which purifieth the heart. Lu. vi. 45. Ac. xv. 9. Good works must come from love to the Lord Jesus; but this the unbeliever wanteth also, because he wanteth faith: For faith 'worketh by love,' and by that means doth good. Ga. v. 6.

And hence again it is, that though the carnal man doth never so much which he calleth good, yet it is rejected, slighted, and turned as dirt in his face again; his prayers are abominable, Pr. xv. 8. his ploughing is sin, xxi. 4. and all his righteousness as menstruous rags. Is. lxiv. 6. Thus you see that without faith there are no good works.

Now then, to show you that they flow from faith: and that,

For that FAITH is a principle of life, by which a Christian lives, Ga. ii. 19, 20. a principle of motion, by which it walks towards heaven in the way of holiness. Ro. iv. 12. 2 Co. v. 7. It is also a principle of strength, by which the soul opposeth its lust, the devil, and this world, and overcomes them. 'This is the victory, even our faith.' 1 Jn. v. 4, 5. Faith, in the heart of a Christian, is like the salt that was thrown into the corrupt fountain, that made the naughty waters good, and the barren land fruitful. 2 Ki. ii. 19—22. Faith, when it is wrought in the heart, is like leaven hid in the meal, Mat. xiii. 33. or like perfume that lighteth upon stinking leather, turning the smell of the leather into the savour of the perfume; faith being then planted in the heart, and having its natural inclination to holiness. Hence it is that there followeth an alteration of the life and conversation, and so bringeth forth fruit accordingly. 'A good man out of the good treasure of his heart bringeth forth that which is good.' Lu. vi. 45. Which treasure, I say, is this faith. Ja. ii. 5. 1 Pe. i. 7. And therefore it is that faith is called 'the faith according to godliness,' Tit. i. 1. and the 'most holy faith.' Jude 20.

Second, Good works must needs flow from faith, or no way; because that alone carrieth in it an argument sufficiently prevalent to win upon our natures, to make them comply with holiness.

Faith sheweth us that God loveth us, that he forgiveth us our sins, that he accounteth us for his children, having freely justified us through the blood of his Son. Ro. iii. 24, 25; iv. He. xi. 13. 1 Pe. i. 8.

Faith receiveth the promise, embraceth it, and comforteth the soul unspeakably with it.

Faith is so great an artist in arguing and reasoning with the soul, that it will bring over the hardest heart that it hath to deal with. It will bring to my remembrance at once, both my vileness against God, and his goodness towards me; it will shew me, that though I deserve not to breathe in the air, yet that God will have me an heir of glory.

Now, there is no argument greater than this. This will make a man run through ten thousand difficulties, to answer God, though he never can, for the grace he hath bestowed on him.

Further, FAITH will shew me how distinguishingly this love of God hath set itself upon me; it will shew me, that though Esau was Jacob's brother, yet he loved Jacob. Mal. i. 2. That though there were thousands more besides me that were as good as me, yet I must be the man that must be chosen.

Now this, I say, is a marvellous argument, and unspeakably prevaileth with the sinner, as saith the apostle: 'For the love of Christ constraineth us; because we thus judge, that if one died for all, then were all dead: And *that* he died for all; that they which live,' that is, by faith, 'should not henceforth live unto themselves, but unto him which died for them, and rose again.' 2 Co. v. 14, 15. 'Love,' saith the wise man, '*is* strong as death; Many waters cannot quench love, neither can the floods drown it: if a man would give all the substance of his house for love, it would utterly be contemned.' Ca. viii. 6, 7.

---

* 'Where the great red dragon Satan had his seat.'—*Dr. Gill's Commentary.* See also Rev. xii.—ED.

Oh! when the broken, dying, condemned soul, can but see, by faith, the love of a tender-hearted Saviour, and also see what he underwent to deliver it from under that death, guilt, and hell, that now it feels and fears; which also it knoweth it hath most justly and highly deserved; 'Then bless the Lord, O my soul;' Ps. ciii. 1, 2, 3. and 'What shall I render unto the Lord *for* all his benefits?' Ps. cxvi. 1—14.

Thus is faith a prevailing argument to the sinner, whereby he is fetched off from what he was, and constrained to bend and yield to what before he neither would nor could. 1 Co. ii. 14. Ro. viii. 7.

And hence it is, that gospel obedience is called 'the obedience *of* faith,' as well as obedience *to* the faith. Ro. xvi. 26. For it must be by the faith of Christ in my heart, that I submit to the word of faith in the Bible, otherwise all is to no profit: as saith the apostle, 'The word preached did not profit them, not being mixed with faith in them that heard *it*.' He. iv. 2. For faith alone can see the reality of what the gospel saith; and so I say, argue over the heart to the embracing of it.

Third, Faith is such a grace, as will represent to the soul all things in their proper colours. It doth not, as doth unbelief and ignorance, shew us all things out of order; putting darkness for light, and bitter for sweet; but will set every thing in its proper place before our eyes; God and Christ shall be with it, the chiefest good, the most lovely and amiable; a heavenly life shall be of greater esteem, and more desirable, than all the treasures of Egypt! Righteousness and sanctification will be the thing after which it will most vehemently press; because it seeth not only death and damnation as the fruits of sin, but sin also in itself, distinct from the punishment belonging to it, a detestable, horrible, and odious thing. He. xi. 25—27. Phi. iii. 7—12. Ro. xii. 9.

By faith we see that this world hath no abiding in it for us, nor no satisfaction if it were otherwise. Pr. iii. 35. He. xi. 15, 16; xiii. 14. 1 Co. vii. 29—31. And hence it is, that the people of God have groaned to be gone from hence, into a state that is both sinless and temptationless. And hence it is again that they have run through so many trials, afflictions, and adversities, even because of that love to holiness of life that faith being in their hearts did prompt them to, by shewing them the worth and durableness of that which was good, and the irksomeness and evil of all things else. 2 Co. v. 1—8. He. xi. 33—39.

Fourth, Faith layeth hold of that which is able to help the soul to bring forth good works: it layeth hold of, and engageth the strength of Christ, and by that overcometh that which oppresseth; 'I can do all things through Christ which strengtheneth me.' Phi. iv. 13.

In a word, a life of holiness and godliness in this world, doth so inseparably follow a principle of faith, that it is both monstrous and ridiculous to suppose the contrary. What, shall not he that hath life have motion! Ga. ii. 20.

He that hath by faith received the spirit of holiness, shall not he be holy? Ga. iii. 2. and he that is called to glory and virtue, shall not he add to his faith virtue? 2 Pe. i. 4, 5. We are by faith made good trees, and shall not we bring forth good fruit? Lu. vi. 43. They that believe are created in Christ Jesus unto good works; and God hath, before the world was, ordained that we should walk in them; and shall both our second creation, and God's foreordination be made frustrate? Ep. i. 4; ii. 10. Besides, the children of faith are the children of light, and of the day. 1 Th. v. 5. Lights upon a hill, and candles on a candlestick, and shall not they shine? They are the salt of the earth, shall not they be seasoning? Mat. v. 13—16.

The believer is the alone man, by whom God sheweth to the world the power of his grace, the operation of his people's faith, &c. The unbelievers read indeed of the power of grace; of the faith, hope, love, joy, peace, and sanctification of the heart of the Christian; but they feel nothing of that sin-killing operation that is in these things; these are to them as a story of Rome or Spain. Wherefore to shew them in others, what they find not in themselves, God worketh faith, hope, love, &c., in a generation that shall serve him; and by them they shall see what they cannot find in themselves; and by this means they shall be convinced, that though sin, and the pleasures of this life, be sweet to them, yet there is a people otherwise minded; even such a people, that do indeed see the glory of that which others read of, and from that sight take pleasure in those things which they are most averse unto. To this, I say, are Christians called; herein is God glorified; hereby are sinners convinced; and by this is the world condemned. 1 Th. iv. 7. 1 Pe. ii. 12; iii. 1. He. xi. 7.

Object. But if faith doth so naturally cause good works, what then is the reason that God's people find it so hard a matter to be faithful in good works?

I answer, 1. God's people are fruitful in good works according to the proportion of their faith; if they be slender in good works, it is because they are weak in faith. Little faith is like small candles, or weak fire, which though they shine and have heat; yet but dim shining and small heat, when compared with bigger candles and greater fire. The reason why Sardis had some in it whose works were not perfect before God, it was, because they did not hold fast by faith the word that they have formerly heard and received. Re. iii. 1—3.

2. There may be a great mistake in our judging of our own fruitfulness. The soul that indeed is

candid and right at heart, is taught by grace to judge itself, though fruitful, yet barren upon two accounts. (1.) When it compareth its life to the mercy bestowed upon it: for when a soul doth indeed consider the greatness and riches of the mercy bestowed upon it, then it must needs cry out, ' O wretched man that I am,' Ro. vii. 24. for it seeth itself wonderfully to fall short of a conversation becoming one who hath received so great a benefit. (2.) It may also judge itself barren, because it falleth so far short of that it would attain unto, ' it cannot do the thing that it would.' Ga. v. 17.

3. The heart of a Christian is naturally very barren; upon which, though the seed of grace, that is the fruitfullest of all seeds, be sown, yet the heart is naturally subject to bring forth weeds. Mat. xv. 19. Now, to have a good crop from such ground, doth argue the fruitfulness of the seed. Wherefore I conclude upon these three things, (1.) That the seed of faith is a very fruitful seed, in that it will be fruitful in so barren a soil. (2.) That faith is not beholden to the heart, but the heart to it, for all its fruitfulness. (3.) That therefore the way to be a more fruitful Christian, it is to be stronger in believing.

SECOND—Now for the second thing, to wit, *That every one that believeth should be careful that their works be good.* This followeth from what went just before; to wit, That the heart of a Christian is a heart subject to bring forth weeds.

There is flesh as well as spirit in the best of saints: and as the spirit of grace will be always putting forth something that is good, so the flesh will be putting forth continually that which is evil. ' For the flesh lusteth against the Spirit, and the Spirit against the flesh.' Ga. v. 17.

Now this considered, is the cause why you find so often in the Scriptures so many items and cautions to the Christians to look to their lives and conversations. As, 'Keep thy heart with all diligence.' Pr. iv. 23. ' Watch ye, stand fast in the faith, quit you like men, be strong.' 1 Co. xvi. 13. 'Be not deceived; God is not mocked: for whatsoever a man soweth, that shall he also reap. For he that soweth to his flesh shall of the flesh reap corruption; but he that soweth to the Spirit shall of the Spirit reap life everlasting.' Ga. vi. 7, 8.

All works are not good that seem to be so. It is one thing for a man's ways to be right in his own eye, and another for them to be right in God's. Often ' that which is highly esteemed among men is abomination in the sight of God.' Pr. xxx. 12. Lu. xvi. 15.

Seeing corruption is not yet out of our natures, there is a proneness in us to build [even] upon the right foundation, wood, hay, and stubble, instead of gold and silver, and precious stones. 1 Co. iii. 11—

15. How was both David the king, Nathan the prophet, and Uzza the priest, deceived, touching good works! 1 Ch. xvii. 1—4; xiii. 9—11. Peter also, in both his defending his Master in the garden, and in dissuading of him from his sufferings, though both out of love and affection to his Master, was deceived touching good works. Mat. xvi. 22, 23. Jn. xviii. 10, 11. Many have miscarried both as to *doctrine, worship,* and the *prosecution* of each.

First, For *doctrine.* Christ tells the Jews, that they taught for the doctrines of God the doctrines and traditions of men. Mat. xv. 9. Mar. vii. 7. As also, saith the apostle, They teach ' things they ought not, for filthy lucre's sake.' Tit. i. 11.

Second, Also touching *worship,* we find how frequently men have mistaken, both for time, place, and matter, with which they worshipped.

1. For *time.* It hath been that which man hath devised, not which God hath commanded. 1 Ki. xii. 32. They ' change the ordinance,' saith Isaiah. xxiv. 5. They change God's 'judgments into wickedness,' saith Ezekiel. v. 6.

2. For *place.* When they should have worshipped at Jerusalem, they worshipped at Bethel, at Gilgal and Dan, in gardens, under poplars and elms. 1 Ki. xii. 26—30. Ho. iv. 13—15. Is. lxv. 2—5.

3. For the *matter* with which they worshipped. Instead of bringing according to the commandment, they brought the lame, the torn, and the sick; they would sanctify themselves in gardens, with swine's flesh and mice, when they should have done it at Jerusalem, with bullocks and lambs. Is. lxvi. 17.

Third, Again, touching men's *prosecuting* their zeal for their worship, &c., that they do think right; how hot hath it been, though with no reason at all? Nebuchadnezzar will have his fiery furnace, and Darius his lions' den for Nonconformists. Da. iii. 6; vi. 7, &c. Again, they have persecuted men even to strange cities; have laid traps and snares in every corner, to entrap and to entangle their words; and if they could at any time but kill the persons that dissented from them, they would think they did God good service. Ac. xxvi. 11. Lu. xi. 53, 54. Jn. xix. 1, 2. But what need we look so far from home, were it not that I would seal my sayings with truth. We need look no farther to affirm this position, than to the Papists and their companions. How many have they in all ages hanged, burned, starved, drowned, racked, dismembered, and murdered, both openly and in secret? and all under a pretence of God, his worship, and good works.* Thus you see how wise men and fools,

---

* This manly, bold, and upright statement of truth, was published in 1674, only two years after the author's deliverance from twelve years and a half's incarceration in a damp, miserable jail, for nonconformity! None but those, whose close communion with God inspires them with the confessor's

saints and sinners, Christians and heathens, have erred in the business of good works; wherefore every one should be careful to see that their works BE good.

Now, then, to prevent, if God will, miscarriage in this matter, I shall propound unto you what it is for a work to be rightly good. *First*, A good work must have the word for its authority. *Second*, It must, as afore was said, flow from faith. *Third*, It must be both rightly timed and rightly placed. *Fourth*, It must be done willingly, cheerfully, &c.

First, It must have the word for its authority. Zeal without knowledge is like a mettled horse without eyes, or like a sword in a madman's hand; and there is no knowledge where there is not the word: for if they reject the word of the Lord, and act not by that, 'what wisdom *is* in them?' saith the prophet. Je. viii. 9. Is. viii. 20. Wherefore see thou have the word for what thou dost.

Second, As there must be the word for the authorising of what thou dost, so there must be faith, from which it must flow, as I shewed you before: 'for whatsoever *is* not of faith is sin;' and without faith *it is* impossible to please God.' Now, I say, without the word there is no faith, Ro. x. 17. as without faith there is no good, let men's pretences be what they will.

Third, As it must have these two aforenamed, so also it must have, 1. Right time; and, 2. Right place.

1. It must be *rightly timed*. Every work is not to be done at the same time; every time not being convenient for such a work; There is a time for all things, and every thing is beautiful in its time. Ec. iii. 11. There is a time to pray, a time to hear, a time to read, a time to confer, a time to meditate, a time to do, and a time to suffer. Now, to be hearing when we should be preaching and doing, that is, yielding active obedience to that under which we ought to suffer, is not good. Christ was very wary, that both his doings and sufferings were rightly timed. Jn. ii. 3, 4; xiii. 1, 2. And herein we ought to follow his steps. To be at plough in the field, when I should be hearing the word, is not good; and to be talking abroad, when I should be instructing my family at home, is as bad: 'Whoso keepeth the commandment, shall feel no evil thing: and a wise man's heart discerneth both time and judgment.' Ec. viii. 5. Good things mistimed, are fruitless, unprofitable, and vain.

2. As things must have their right time, so they must be *rightly placed*; for the misplacing of any

work is as bad as the mistiming of it. When I say, things, if good, must be rightly placed, I mean, we should not give to any work more than the word of God alloweth it, neither should we give it less. Mint, anise, and cummin, are not so weighty matters as faith and the love of God; as in Mat. xxiii. 23. For a pastor to be exercising the office of a deacon, instead of the office of a pastor, it is misplacing of works. Ac. vi. 2. For Martha to be making outward provision for Christ, when she should have sat at his feet to hear his word, was the misplacing a work; and for her sister to have done it at her request—though the thing in itself was good—had been her sin also. Lu. x. 39—42.

Now, to prevent the misplacing of good works,

(1.) They misplace them that set them in the room of Christ. Ro. x. 1—3.

(2.) They also misplace them that make them copartners with him. Ro. ix. 31. 32. Ac. xv. 1. This is setting up our post by God's posts, and man's righteousness by the righteousness of Christ. Eze. xliii. 7, 8. These are said to be teachers of the law, not knowing what they say, nor whereof they affirm. 1 Ti. i. 7.

(3.) They also misplace works, who ascribe to a work of less moment that honour that belongeth to a work more noble. And such are (*a*) Those who count the ceremonial part of an ordinance as good as the doctrine and signification of it.* (*b*) Such who account the dictates and impulses of a mere natural conscience, as good, as high, and divine, as the leadings and movings of the Spirit of Christ. (*c*) Those also who count it enough to do something of what God hath commanded, and that something, possibly the least, instead of all, and the things more necessary and weighty. (*d*) They also much misplace them, who count things indifferent as high as those that are absolutely necessary in the worship of God. (*e*) But the grosser, who place men's traditions above them. (*f*) And they greatest of all, who put bitter for sweet, and darkness for light. All these things we must shun and avoid, as things absolutely obstructive to good works.

Wherefore touching good works; obedience is better than sacrifice; that is, to do things according to the word of God, is better than to do them according to my fancy and conceit. 1 Sa. xv. 22. 'Wherefore, let all things be done decently and in order.' 1 Co. xiv. 40.

Fourth, Again, as good works should be ordered and qualified, as before is touched, so they should be done from the heart, willingly, cheerfully, with simplicity and charity, according to what a man

---

courage, can understand the spirit which dictated such language. Had all dissenters used such faithful words, the church would long ago have been emancipated from persecution in this country.—ED.

* This is a very extensive and awful delusion. Baptismal regeneration, as believed by the churches of Rome and of England, and the viaticum, or fitting the soul to appear before God by administering the Lord's supper to a dying sinner, have done infinite mischief to the souls of men.—ED.

hath. 1 Jn. v. 3. 2 Co. ix. 7. Ro. xii. 8. Col. iii. 12. 1 Co. x. 24. 1 Co. viii. 12.

Farther, there are three things that a man should have in his eye in every work he doth. 1. The honour of God. 1 Co. vi. 20. 2. The edification of his neighbour. 1 Co. xiv. 26. 3. The expediency or inexpediency of what I am to do. 1 Co. vi. 12. And always observe it, that the honour of God is wrapped up in the edification of thy neighbour; and the edification of thy neighbour in the expediency of what thou dost.

Again, if thou wouldst walk to the edification of thy neighbour, and so to God's honour, in the midst of thy observers, beware,

1st. That thou in thy words and carriages dost so demean thyself, that Christ in his precious benefits may be with clearness spoken forth by thee; and take heed, that thou dost not enter into doubtful points with them that are weak. Ro. xv. 1. But deal chiefly, lovingly, and wisely, with their consciences about those matters that tend to their establishment in the faith of their justification, and deliverance from death and hell. 'Comfort the feeble-minded,' confirm the weak. 1 Th. v. 14.

2ndly. If thou be stronger than thy brother, take heed that thou do not that before him, that may offend his weak conscience; I mean, things that in themselves may be lawful. All that is lawful is not expedient; all that is lawful edifieth not. 1 Co. vi. 12. Wherefore here is thy wisdom and love, that thou in some things deny thyself for thy brother's sake. 'I will eat no flesh while the world standeth,' saith Paul, 'lest I make my brother to offend.' 1 Co. viii. 13. Wherefore have this faith to thyself before God. Ro. xiv. 22. But if thou walk otherwise, know, thou walkest not charitably, and so not to edification, and so not to Christ's honour, but dost sin against Christ, and wound thy weak brother, for whom Christ died. Ro. xiv. 15. 1 Co. viii. 12.

But I say, all this while keep thy eye upon the word; take heed of going contrary to that under any pretence whatever; for without the word, there is nothing to God's glory, nor thy brother's edification. Wherefore, walk 'wisely in a perfect way.' Ps. ci. 2, 3.

Having thus, in few words, shewed you what are works rightly good, I beseech you in the name of the Lord Jesus Christ, that you put yourselves into a conscientious performance of them, that you may, while you live here, be vessels of honour, and fit for the master's use, and prepared to every good work. 1 Ti. vi. 18. Study to approve things that are excellent, 'that you may be sincere, and without offence, until the day of Christ.' Phi. i. 10. Covet communion with God: 'covet earnestly the best gifts.' 1 Co. xii. 31. Ah! we that are redeemed from among men, Re. xiv. 4, and that rejoice in the hope of the glory of God, Ro. v. 2, we that look, I say, for the blessed hope, and the glorious appearing of the great God and our Saviour Jesus Christ, Tit. ii. 13, 'what manner of *persons* ought we to be in *all* holy conversation and godliness.' 2 Pe. iii. 11.

To conclude, for your farther edification, take a plain rehearsal of your several general duties and works, to which God engageth you in his word, according to your places, callings, and relations in this world;

DUTIES OF THE MASTER OF A FAMILY.

If thou have under thee a family, then thou art to consider the several relations thou standest under; and art to know, that thou in each of them hast a work to do for God, and that he expecteth thy faithful deportment under every one of them. As, in general;

DUTY TO THE FAMILY IN GENERAL.

He that is the master of a family, he hath, as under that relation, a work to do for God; to wit, the right governing of his own family. And his work is twofold. *First*, Touching the *spiritual state thereof. Second*, Touching the *outward state thereof.*

First, As touching the *spiritual state of his family;* he ought to be very diligent and circumspect, doing his utmost endeavour both to increase faith where it is begun, and to begin it where it is not. Wherefore, to this end, he ought diligently and frequently to lay before his household such things of God, out of his word, as are suitable for each particular. And let no man question his rule in the word of God for such a practice; for if the thing itself were but of good report, and a thing tending to civil honesty, it is within the compass and bounds even of nature itself, and ought to be done; much more things of a higher nature; besides, the apostle exhorts us to 'Whatsoever things *are* honest, whatsoever things *are* just, pure, lovely, and of good report, to think of them,' that is, to be mindful to do them. Phi. iv. 8. But to be conversant in this godly exercise in our family, is very worthy of praise, and doth much become all Christians. This is one of the things for which God so highly commended his servant Abraham, and that with which his heart was so much affected. I know Abraham, saith God, 'I know him' to be a good man in very deed, for 'he will command his children, and his household after him, and they shall keep the way of the Lord.' Ge. xviii. 19. This was a thing also which good Joshua designed should be his practice as long as he had a breathing time in this world. 'As for me,' saith he, I 'and my household, we will serve the Lord.' Jos. xxiv. 15.

Further, we find also in the New Testament, that they are looked upon as Christians of an inferior rank that have not a due regard to this duty; yea, so inferior as not fit to be chosen to any office in the church of God. A [bishop or] pastor must be one that ruleth well his own house, having his children in subjection with all gravity; For if a man know not how to rule his own house, how shall he take care of the church of God? 'The deacon' also, saith he, must 'be the husband of one wife, ruling their children, and their own house well.' 1 Ti. iii. Mark a little, the apostle seems to lay down thus much, that a man that governs his family well, hath one qualification belonging to a pastor or deacon in the house of God, for he that knoweth not how to rule his own house, how shall he take care of the church of God? which thing considered, it giveth us light into the work of the master of a family, touching the governing of his house.

1. A pastor must be sound and uncorrupt in his doctrine; and indeed so must the master of a family. Tit. i. 9. Ep. vi. 4.

2. A pastor should be apt to teach, to reprove, and to exhort; and so should the master of a family. 1 Ti. iii. 2. De. vi. 7.

3. A pastor must himself be exemplary in faith and holiness; and so also should the master of a family. 1 Ti. iii. 2—4; iv. 12. 'I,' saith David, 'will behave myself in a perfect way; I will walk in,' or before, 'my house with a perfect heart.' Ps. ci. 2.

4. The pastor is for getting the church together; and when they are so come together, then to pray among them, and to preach unto them. This is also commendable in Christian masters of families.

Object. But my family is ungodly and unruly, touching all that is good. What shall I do?

Answ. I answer,

1. Though this be true, yet thou must rule them, and not they thee! Thou art set over them of God, and thou art to use the authority which God hath given thee, both to rebuke their vice, and to shew them the evil of their rebelling against the Lord. This did Eli, though not enough; and thus did David. 1 Sa. ii. 24, 25. 1 Ch. xxviii. 9. Also, thou must tell them how sad thy state was when thou wast in their condition, and so labour to recover them out of the snare of the devil. Mar. v. 19.

2. Thou oughtest also to labour to draw them forth to God's public worship, if peradventure God may convert their souls. Saith Jacob to his household, and to all that were about him, 'Let us arise and go up to Bethel; and I will make there an altar unto God, who answered me in the day of my distress.' Ge. xxxv. 3. Hannah would carry Samuel to Shiloh, that he might abide with God for ever. 1 Sa. i. 22. Indeed a soul rightly touched,

will labour to draw, not only their families, but a whole city after Jesus Christ. Jn. iv. 28—30.

3. If they are obstinate, and will not go forth with thee, then do thou get godly and sound men to thy house, and there let the word of God be preached, when thou hast, as Cornelius, gathered thy family and friends together. Ac. x.

You know that the jailor, Lydia, Crispus, Gaius, Stephanus, and others, had not only themselves, but their families, made gracious by the word preached, and that some of them, if not all, by the word preached in their houses. Ac. xvi. 14—34; xviii. 7, 8. 1 Co. i. 16. And this, for ought I know, might be one reason among many, why the apostles taught in their day, not only publicly, but from house to house; I say, that they might, if possible, bring in those in some family, which yet remained unconverted, and in their sins. Ac. x. 24; xx. 20, 21. For some, you know how usual it was in the day of Christ, to invite him to their houses, if they had any afflicted, that either would not or could not come unto him. Lu. vii. 2, 3; viii. 41. If this be the way with those that have outward diseases in their families, how much more then, where there are souls that have need of Christ, to save them from death and eternal damnation!

4. Take heed that thou do not neglect family-duties among them thyself; as, reading the word and prayer; if thou hast one in thy family that is gracious, take encouragement; nay, if thou art alone, yet know that thou hast both liberty to go to God through Christ, and also art at that time in a capacity of having the universal church join with thee for the whole number of those that shall be saved.

5. Take heed that thou suffer not any ungodly, profane, or heretical books, or discourse in thy house. 'Evil communications corrupt good manners,' 1 Co. xv. 33. I mean such profane or heretical books, &c., as either tend to provoke to looseness of life, or such as do oppose the fundamentals of the gospel. I know that Christians must be allowed their liberty as to things indifferent; but for those things that strike either at faith or holiness, they ought to be abandoned by all Christians, and especially by the pastors of churches, and masters of families; which practice was figured out by Jacob's commanding his house, and all that was with him, to put away the strange gods from among them, and to change their garments. Ge. xxxv. 2. All those in the Acts set a good example for this, who took their curious books and burned them before all men, though they were worth fifty thousand pieces of silver. Ac. xix. 18, 19. The neglect of this fourth particular hath occasioned ruin in many families, both among children and servants. It is easier for vain talkers, and their deceivable works, to subvert whole households, than many are aware

of. Tit. i. 10, 11. Thus much touching the spiritual state of thy household. And now to its outward.

Second, Touching *the outward state of thy family*, thou art to consider these three things.

I. That it lieth upon thee to care for them that they have a convenient livelihood. 'If any man provide not for his own, and specially for those of his own house, he hath denied the faith, and is worse than an infidel.' 1 Ti. v. 8. But mark, when the Word saith, thou art to provide for thy house, it giveth thee no license to distracting carefulness; neither doth it allow thee to strive to grasp the world in thy heart, or coffers, nor to take care for years or days to come, but so to provide for them, that they may have food and raiment; and if either they or thou be not content with that, you launch out beyond the rule of God. 1 Ti. vi. 8. Mat. vi. 34. This is to labour, that you may have wherewith ' to maintain good works for necessary uses.' Tit. iii. 14. And never object, that unless you reach farther, it will never do; for that is but unbelief. The word saith, ' That God feedeth ravens, careth for sparrows, and clotheth the grass;' in which three, to feed, clothe, and care for, is as much as heart can wish. Lu. xii. 6—28.

2. Therefore though thou shouldest provide for thy family; yet let all thy labour be mixed with moderation; ' Let your moderation be known unto all men.' Phi. iv. 5. Take heed of driving so hard after this world, as to hinder thyself and family from those duties towards God, which thou art by grace obliged to; as private prayer, reading the scriptures, and Christian conference. It is a base thing for men so to spend themselves and families after this world, as that they disengage their heart to God's worship.

Christians, 'The time is short: it remaineth that both they that have wives be as though they had none; and they that weep, as though they wept not; and they that rejoice, as though they rejoiced not ; and they that use this world, as not abusing *it*; for the fashion of this world passeth away.' 1 Co. vii. 29—31. Many Christians live and do in this world, as if religion were but a by-business, and this world the one thing necessary; when indeed all the things of this world are but things by the by; and religion only the one thing needful. Lu. x. 40—42.

3. If thou wouldst be such a master of a family as becomes thee, thou must see that there be that Christian harmony among those under thee, as becomes that house where one ruleth that feareth God.

(1.) Thou must look that thy children and servants be under subjection to the word of God; for though it is of God only to rule the heart, yet he expecteth that thou shouldest rule their outward man; which if thou dost not, he may in a short time cut off all thy stock, [even every male]. 1 Sa. iii. 11—14. See therefore that thou keep them temperate in all things, in apparel, in language, that they be not gluttons, nor drunkards; not suffering either thy children vainly to domineer over thy servants, nor they again to carry themselves foolishly towards each other.

(2.) Learn to distinguish between that injury that in thy family is done to thee, and that which is done to God ; and though thou oughtest to be very zealous for the Lord, and to bear nothing that is open transgression to him ; yet here will be thy wisdom, to pass by personal injuries, and to bury them in oblivion: ' Love covereth a multitude of sins.' Be not then like those that will rage and stare like madmen, when they are injured; and yet either laugh, or at least not soberly rebuke, and warn, when God is dishonoured.

' Rule thy own house well, having thy children —with others in thy family—in subjection, with all gravity.' 1 Ti. iii. 4. Solomon was so excellent sometimes this way, that he made the eyes of his beholders to dazzle. 2 Ch. ix. 3, 4. *

But to break off from this general, and to come to particulars.

[DUTY IN RELATION TO THE WIFE.]

Hast thou a wife ? Thou must consider how thou oughtest to behave thyself under that rela-tion: and to do this aright, thou must consider the condition of thy wife, whether she be one that indeed believeth or not.

First, If she believeth, then,

1. Thou art engaged to bless God for her: ' For her price *is* far above rubies, and she is the gift of God unto thee, and is for thy adorning and glory.' Pr. xii. 4; and xxxi. 10. 1 Co. xi. 7. 'Favour *is* deceitful, and beauty *is* vain: *but* a woman *that* feareth the Lord, she shall be praised.' Pr. xxxi. 30.   The duty of husbands to believing wives.

2. Thou oughtest to love her, under a double consideration : (1.) As she is thy flesh and thy bone : ' For no man ever yet hated his own flesh.' Ep. v. 29. (2.) As she is together with thee an heir of the grace of life. 1 Pe. iii. 7. This, I say, should engage thee to love her with Christian love; to love her, as believing you both are dearly beloved of God and the Lord Jesus Christ, and as those that must be together with him in eternal happiness.

3. Thou oughtest so to carry thyself to and before her, as doth Christ to and before his church; as saith the apostle: So ought men to love their

---

* The queen of Sheba was as much or more delighted with the order, harmony, and happiness of Solomon's household than she was with all his splendour and magnificence. It is to this Bunyan refers in this quotation.—Ed.

wives, ' even as Christ loved the church, and gave himself for it.' Ep. v. 25. When husbands behave themselves like husbands indeed, then will they be not only husbands, but such an ordinance of God to the wife, as will preach to her the carriage of Christ to his spouse. There is a sweet scent wrapped up in the relations of husbands and wives, that believe ; Ep. iv. 32. the wife, I say, signifying the church, and the husband the head and saviour thereof, ' For the husband is the head of the wife, even as Christ is the head of the church.' Ep. v. 23. and he is the Saviour of the body.

This is one of God's chief ends in instituting marriage, that Christ and his church, under a figure, might be wherever there is a couple that believe through grace. Wherefore that husband that carrieth it undiscreetly towards his wife, he doth not only behave himself contrary to the rule, but also maketh his wife lose the benefit of such an ordinance, and crosseth the mystery of his relation. Therefore, I say, ' So ought men to love their wives as their own bodies. He that loveth his wife, loveth himself. For no man ever yet hated his own flesh ; but nourisheth and cherisheth it, even as the Lord the church :' Ep. v. 28, 29. Christ laid out his life for his church, covereth her infirmities, communicates to her his wisdom, protecteth her, and helpeth her in her employments in this world ; and so ought men to do for their wives. Solomon and Pharaoh's daughter had the art of thus doing, as you may see in the book of Canticles. Wherefore bear with their weaknesses, help their infirmities, and honour them as the weaker vessels, and as being of a frailer constitution. 1 Pe. iii. 7.

In a word, be such a husband to thy believing wife, that she may say, God hath not only given me a husband, but such a husband as preacheth to me every day the carriage of Christ to his church.

Second, If thy wife be unbelieving or carnal, then thou hast also a duty lying before thee, which thou art engaged to perform under a double engagement : 1. For that she lieth liable every moment to eternal damnation. 2. That she is thy wife that is in this evil case.

The duty of husbands to unbelieving wives.

Oh ! how little sense of the worth of souls is there in the heart of some husbands ; as is manifest by their unchristian carriage to and before their wives ! Now, to qualify thee for a carriage suitable,

1. Labour seriously after a sense of her miserable state, that thy bowels may yearn towards her soul.

2. Beware that she take no occasion from any unseemly carriage of thine, to proceed in evil. And here thou hast need to double thy diligence, for she lieth in thy bosom, and therefore is capable of espying the least miscarriage in thee.

3. If she behave herself unseemly and unruly, as she is subject to do, being Christless and graceless, then labour thou to overcome her evil with thy goodness, her forwardness with thy patience and meekness. It is a shame for thee, who hast another principle, to do as she.

4. Take fit opportunities to convince her. Observe her disposition, and when she is most likely to bear, then speak to her very heart.

5. When thou speakest, speak to purpose. It is no matter for many words, provided they be pertinent. Job in a few words answers his wife, and takes her off from her foolish talking : ' Thou speakest,' saith he, ' as one of the foolish women ; - shall we receive good at the hand of God. and shall we not receive evil ?' Job ii. 10.

6. Let all be done without rancour, or the least appearance of anger : ' In meekness instructing those that oppose themselves, if - peradventure they may recover themselves out of the snare of the devil, who are taken captive by him at his will.' 2 Ti. ii. 25, 26. ' And how knowest thou, O man, whether thou shalt save thy wife.' 1 Co vii. 16.

DUTY OF PARENTS TO CHILDREN.

If thou art a parent, a father, or a mother, then thou art to consider thy calling under this relation.

Thy children have souls, and they must be begotten of God as well as of thee, or they perish. And know also, that unless thou be very circumspect in thy behaviour to and before them, they may perish through thee : the thoughts of which should provoke thee, both *to instruct,* and also *to correct* them.

First, To *instruct* them as the scripture saith, and to ' bring them up in the nurture and admonition of the Lord ;' and to *do* this diligently, ' when thou sittest in thine house, - when thou liest down, and when thou risest up.' Ep. vi. 4. De. vi. 7.

Now to do this to purpose :

1. Do it in terms and words easy to be understood : affect not high expressions, they will drown your children. Thus God spake to his children, Ho. xii. 10. and Paul to his. 1 Co. iii. 2.

2. Take heed of filling their heads with whimsies, and unprofitable notions, for this will sooner learn them to be malapert and proud, than sober and humble. Open therefore to them the state of man by nature ; discourse with them of sin, of death, and hell ; of a crucified Saviour, and the promise of life through faith : ' Train up a child in the way he should go : and when he is old, he will not depart from it.' Pr. xxii. 6.

3. There must be much gentleness and patience in all thy instructions, ' lest they be discouraged.' Col. iii. 21. And,

4. Labour to convince them by a conversation

answerable, that the things of which thou instructest them are not fables, but realities; yea, and realities so far above what can be here enjoyed, that all things, were they a thousand times better than they are, are not worthy to be compared with the glory and worthiness of these things.*

Isaac was so holy before his children, that when Jacob remembered God, he remembered that he was the Fear of his father Isaac.' Ge. xxxi. 53.

Ah! when children can think of their parents, and bless God for that instruction and good they have received from them, this is not only profitable for children, but honourable, and comfortable to parents: 'The father of the righteous shall greatly rejoice: and he that begetteth a wise *child* shall have joy of him.' Pr. xxiii. 24, 25.

Second, The duty of *correction*.

1. See if fair words will win them from evil. This is God's way with his children. Je. xxv. 4, 5.

2. Let those words you speak to them in your reproof, be both sober, few, and pertinent, adding always some suitable sentence of the scripture therewith; as, if they lie, then such as Re. xxi. 8, 27. If they refuse to hear the word, such as 2 Ch. xxv. 14—16.

3. Look to them, that they be not companions with those that are rude and ungodly; showing with soberness a continual dislike of their naughtiness; often crying out to them, as God did of old unto his, 'Oh, do not this abominable thing that I hate.' Je. xliv. 4.

4. Let all this be mixed with such love, pity, and compunction of spirit, that if possible they may be convinced you dislike not their persons, but their sins. This is God's way. Ps. xcix. 8.

5. Be often endeavouring to fasten on their consciences the day of their death, and judgment to come. Thus also God deals with his. De. xxxii. 29.

6. If thou art driven to the rod, then strike advisedly in cool blood, and soberly show them, (1.) their fault; (2.) how much it is against thy heart thus to deal with them; (3.) and that what thou dost, thou dost in conscience to God, and love to their souls; (4.) and tell them, that if fair means would have done, none of this severity should have been. This, I have proved it, will be a means to afflict their hearts as well as their bodies; and it being the way that God deals with his, it is the most likely to accomplish its end.

7. Follow all this with prayer to God for them, and leave the issue to him: 'Foolishness *is* bound in the heart of a child; *but* the rod of correction shall drive it far from him.' Pr. xxii. 15

Lastly, Observe these *cautions*,

1. Take heed that the misdeeds for which thou correctest thy children be not learned them by thee. Many children learn that wickedness of their parents for which they beat and chastise them.

2. Take heed thou smile not upon them, to encourage them in small faults, lest that thy carriage to them be an encouragement to them to commit greater.

3. Take heed thou use not unsavoury and unseemly words in thy chastising of them, as railing, miscalling, and the like: this is devilish.

4. Take heed thou do not use them to many chiding words and threatenings, mixed with lightness and laughter; this will harden. Speak not much, nor often, but pertinent to them with all gravity.†

DUTIES OF MASTERS TO SERVANTS.

Masters also have a work to do as they stand related to their servants. And,

First, If possibly they can, to get them that fear God: 'He that worketh deceit,' saith David, 'shall not dwell within my house; he that telleth lies, shall not tarry in my sight.' Ps. ci. 7.

Second, But if none at the present but unbelievers can be got to do thy labour, then,

1. Know that it is thy duty so to behave thyself to thy servant, that thy service may not only be for thy good, but for the good of thy servant, and that both in body and soul. Wherefore deal with him, as to admonition, as with thy children; give him the same bread of God thou givest to them; and who knows, but that if thou with spiritual delicates bringest up thy servant, but he may become thy spiritual son in the end. Pr. xxix. 21.

2. Take heed thou do not turn thy servants into slaves, by overcharging them in thy work, through thy greediness. To make men serve with rigour, is more like to Israel's enemies than Christian masters. Ex. i. 14 ‡

3. Take heed thou carry not thyself to thy servant as he of whom it is said, 'He is such a man of Belial, that his servants could not speak to him.' 1 Sa. xxv. 14—17.

And the apostle bids you forbear to threaten them, because you also have a Master in heaven. Ep. vi. 9. As who should say, Your servants cannot be guilty of so many miscarriages against you, as you are guilty of against Christ. Wherefore do

---

* 'Though the words of the wise - are as nails fastened by the master of assemblies, Eccl. xii. 1, yet sure their examples are the hammer to drive them in to take the deeper hold. A father that whipt his son for swearing, and swore himself while he whipt him, did more harm by his example than good by his correction.'—*Fuller's Holy State*, p. 11.—ED.

† How exceedingly admirable are all these scriptural directions, warnings, and cautions. Happy are those parents and their children where such wisdom is manifested in that painful duty of administering counsel and correction.—ED.

‡ One of the Saxon laws was, that if a serf or villain work on Sunday by his lord's command, he shall be a free man.—*Spelman's Concilia, An.* 692.—ED.

with, and to your servants, as you would have your master do with you.

4. Take heed that thou neither circumvent him at his coming in to thy service, nor at his going out.

Servants, at their going into service, may be beguiled two ways.

(1.) By their masters lying unto them, saying, their work is so small and so easy, when it is indeed, if not too burdensome, yet far beyond what at first was said of it. This is beguiling of them.

(2.) The other way is, when masters greedily seek to wire-draw their servants to such wages as indeed is too little and inconsiderable for such work and labour. Both these the apostle opposeth, where he saith, 'Masters give unto *your* servants that which is just,' just labour, and just wages, 'knowing that ye also have a master in heaven.' Col. iv. 1.

As servants may be circumvented at their coming into their labour, so also they may be at their going out: which is done by masters that either change their wages, like heathenish Laban, Ge. xxxi. 7. or by keeping it back, like those against whom God will be a swift witness. Mal. iii. 5.

5. Take heed that thou make not a gain of thy place, because thou art gracious, or livest conveniently for the means of grace.*

Servants that are truly godly they care not how cheap they serve their masters, provided they may get into godly families, or where they may be convenient for the word. But now, if a master or mistress should take this opportunity to make a prey of their servants, this is abominable, this is making a gain of godliness, and merchandise of the things of God, and of the soul of thy brother. 1 Ti. vi. 5.

I have heard some poor servants say, That in some carnal families they have had more liberty to God's things, and more fairness of dealing, than among professors. But this stinketh. And as Jacob said concerning the cruelty of his two sons, so may I say of such masters, they make religion stink before the inhabitants of the land. Ge. xxxiv. 30.

In a word, learn of the Lord Jesus to carry yourselves well to your servants, that your servants also may learn something of the kindness of Christ by your deportment to them. Servants are goers as well as comers; take heed that thou give them no occasion to scandal the gospel when they are gone, for what they observed thee unrighteously to do when they were with thee. Then masters carry it rightly toward their servants, when they labour both in word and life to convince them that the things of God are the one thing necessary. That which servants are commanded to do, touching their fear, their singleness of heart, their doing what they do as to the Lord, and not to men; the master is commanded to do the same things unto them. Ep. vi. 6—9.

THE DUTY OF WIVES.

But passing the master of the family, I shall speak a word or two to those that are under him.

And, first, to the wife: The wife is bound by the law to her husband, so long as her husband liveth. Ro. vii. 2. Wherefore she also hath her work and place in the family, as well as the rest.

Now there are these things considerable in the carriage of a wife toward her husband, which she ought conscientiously to observe.

First, That she look upon him as her head and lord. 'The head of the woman is the man.' 1 Co. xi. 3. And so Sarah called Abraham lord. 1 Pe. iii. 6.

Second, She should therefore be subject to him, as is fit in the Lord. The apostle saith, 'That the wife should submit herself to her husband, as to the Lord.'† 1 Pe. iii. 1. Col. iii. 18. Ep. v. 22. I told you before, that if the husband doth walk towards his wife as becomes him, he will therein be such an ordinance of God to her, besides the relation of a husband, that shall preach to her the carriage of Christ to his church. And now I say also, that the wife, if she walk with her husband as becomes her, she shall preach the obedience of the church to her husband. 'Therefore as the church is subject unto Christ, so *let* the wives *be* to their own husbands in everything.' Ep. v. 24. Now for thy performing of this work, thou must first shun these evils.

1. The evil of a wandering and a gossiping spirit; this is evil in the church, and is evil also in a wife, who is the figure of a church. Christ loveth to have his spouse keep at home; that is, to be with him in the faith and practice of his things, not ranging and meddling with the things of Satan; no more should wives be given to wander and gossip abroad. You know that Pr. vii. 11. saith, 'She *is* loud and stubborn; her feet abide not in her house.' Wives should be about their own husbands' business at home; as the apostle saith, Let them '*be* discreet, chaste, keepers at home, good, obedient to their own husbands.' And why? Because otherwise 'the word of God will be blasphemed.' Tit. ii. 5.

2. Take heed of an idle, talking, or brangling

---

* The rust of money in the rich man's purse, unjustly detained from the labourer, will poison and infect his whole estate.—*Fuller's Holy State*, p. 16.—Ed.

† The apostle Peter, in his solemn injunctions to married persons, commences with the wife. Fuller observes upon this, 'And sure it was fitting that women should first have their lesson given them, because it is harder to be learned,—and therefore they need have the more time to con it.'—*Holy State*, p. 1.—Ed.

tongue. This also is odious, either in maids or wives, to be like parrots, not bridling their tongue; whereas the wife should know, as I said before, that her husband is her lord, and is over her, as Christ is over the church. Do you think it is seemly for the church to *parrot* it against her husband? Is she not to be silent before him, and to look to his laws, rather than her own fictions? Why so, saith the apostle, ought the wife to carry it towards her husband? ' Let the woman,' saith Paul, ' learn in silence with all subjection. But I suffer not a woman to teach, nor to usurp authority over the man, but to be in silence.' 1 Ti. ii. 11, 12. It is an unseemly thing to see a woman so much as once in all her lifetime to offer to overtop her husband; she ought in everything to be in subjection to him, and to do all she doth, as having her warrant, licence, and authority from him. And indeed here is her glory, even to be under him, as the church is under Christ: Now ' she openeth her mouth with wisdom, and in her tongue *is* the law of kindness.' Pr. xxxi. 26.

3. Take heed of affecting immodest apparel, or a wanton gait; this will be evil both abroad and at home; abroad, it will not only give ill example, but also tend to tempt to lust and lasciviousness; and at home it will give an offence to a godly husband, and be cankering to ungodly children, &c. Wherefore, as saith the apostle, Let women's apparel be modest, as becometh women professing godliness, with good works, ' not with broidered hair, or gold, or pearls, or costly array.' 1 Ti. ii. 9, 10. And as it is said again, ' Whose adorning, let it not be that outward *adorning* of plaiting the hair, and of wearing of gold, or of putting on of apparel: But *let it be* the hidden man of the heart, in that which is not corruptible, *even the ornament* of a meek and quiet spirit, which is in the sight of God of great price. For after this manner in the old time the holy women also, who trusted in God, adorned themselves, being in subjection unto their own husbands.' 1 Pe. iii. 3—5.

But yet, do not think that by the subjection I have here mentioned, that I do intend women should be their husbands' slaves. Women are their husbands' yokefellows, their flesh and their bones; and he is not a man that hateth his own flesh, or that is bitter against it. Ep. v. 29. Wherefore, let every man ' love his wife even as himself; and the wife *see* that she reverence *her* husband.' Ep. v. 33. The wife is master next her husband, and is to rule all in his absence;* yea, in his presence she is to guide the house, to bring up the children, provided she so do it, as the adversary have no occasion to speak reproachfully. 1 Ti. v. 10, 13. ' Who can find a

virtuous woman? for her price *is* far above rubies. A gracious woman retaineth honour:' and guideth her affairs with discretion. Pr. xxxi. 10; xi. 16; xii. 4.

Object. But my husband is an unbeliever; what shall I do?

Answ. If so, then what I have said before lieth upon thee with an engagement so much the stronger. For, 1. Thy husband being in this condition, he will be watchful to take thy slips and infirmities, to throw them as dirt in the face of God and thy Saviour. 2. He will be apt to make the worst of every one of thy words, carriages, and gestures. 3. And all this doth tend to the possessing his heart with more hardness, prejudice, and opposition to his own salvation; wherefore, as Peter saith, ' ye wives, *be* in subjection to your own husbands; that, if any obey not the word, they may also without the word be won by the conversation of the wives; while they behold your chaste conversation, *coupled* with fear.' 1 Pe. iii. 1, 2. Thy husband's salvation or damnation lieth much in thy deportment and behaviour before him; wherefore, if there be in thee any fear of God, or love to thy husband, seek, by a carriage full of meekness, modesty, and holiness, and a humble behaviour before him, to win him to the love of his own salvation; and by thus doing, how ' knowest thou, O wife, whether thou shalt save *thy* husband? 1 Co. vii. 16.

Object. But my husband is not only an unbeliever, but one very froward, peevish, and testy, yea, so froward, &c., that I know not how to speak to him, or behave myself before him.

Answ. Indeed there are some wives in great slavery by reason of their ungodly husbands; and as such should be pitied, and prayed for; so they should be so much the more watchful and circumspect in all their ways.

1. Therefore be thou very faithful to him in all the things of this life.

2. Bear with patience his unruly and unconverted behaviour; thou art alive, he is dead; thou art principled with grace, he with sin. Now, then, seeing grace is stronger than sin, and virtue than vice; be not overcome with his vileness, but overcome that with thy virtues, Ro. xii. 21. It is a shame for those that are gracious to be as lavishing in their words, &c., as those that are graceless: They that are ' slow to wrath *are* of great understanding; but *they that are* hasty of spirit, exalteth folly.' Pr. xiv. 29.

3. Thy wisdom, therefore, if at any time thou hast a desire to speak to thy husband for his conviction, concerning anything, either good or evil, it is to observe convenient times and seasons: There is ' a time to keep silence, and a time to speak.' Ec. iii. 7. Now for the right timing thy intentions,

(1.) Consider his disposition; and take him when he is farthest off of those filthy passions that are

* ' In her husband's absence she is wife and deputy husband, which makes her double the files of her diligence. At his return he finds all things so well, that he wonders to see himself at home when he was abroad.'—*Fuller's Holy State*, p. 2.—ED.

thy afflictions. Abigail would not speak a word to her churlish husband till his wine was gone from him, and he in a sober temper. 1 Sa. xxv. 36, 37. The want of this observation is the cause why so much is spoken, and so little effected.*

(2.) Take him at those times when he hath his heart taken with thee, and when he sheweth tokens of love and delight in thee. Thus did Esther with the king her husband, and prevailed. Es. v. 3, 6. vii. 1, 2.

(3.). Observe when convictions seize his conscience, and then follow them with sound and grave sayings of the Scriptures. Somewhat like to this dealt Manoah's wife with her husband. Ju. xiii. 22, 23. Yet then,

(a) Let thy words be few.

(b) And none of them savouring of a lording it over him; but speak thou still as to thy head and lord, by way of entreaty and beseeching.

(c.) And that in such a spirit of sympathy, and bowels of affection after his good, that the manner of thy speech and behaviour in speaking may be to him an argument that thou speakest in love, as being sensible of his misery, and inflamed in thy soul with desire after his conversion.

(d) And follow thy words and behaviour with prayers to God for his soul.

(e) Still keeping thyself in a holy, chaste, and modest behaviour before him.

Object. But my husband is a sot, a fool, and one that hath not wit enough to follow his outward employment in the world.

Answ. 1. Though all this be true, yet thou must know he is thy head, thy lord, and thy husband.

2. Therefore thou must take heed of desiring to usurp authority over him. He was not made for thee; that is, for thee to have dominion over him, but to be thy husband, and to rule over thee. 1 Ti. ii. 12. 1 Co. xi. 3, 8.

3. Wherefore, though in truth thou mayest have more discretion than he, yet thou oughtest to know that thou, with all that is thine, is to be used as under thy husband; even 'every thing.' Ep. v. 24.

Take heed therefore, that what thou dost goes not in thy name, but his; not to thy exaltation, but his; carrying all things so, by thy dexterity and prudence, that not one of thy husband's weaknesses be discovered to others by thee: 'A virtuous woman is a crown to her husband: but she that maketh ashamed, is as rottenness in his bones.' For then, as the wise man sayeth, 'she will do him good and not evil, all the days of her life.' Pr. xii. 4; xxxi. 12.

4. Therefore act, and do still, as being under the power and authority of thy husband.

Now touching thy carriage to thy children and

servants. Thou art a parent, and a mistress, and so thou oughtest to demean thyself. And besides, seeing the believing woman is a figure of the church, she ought, as the church, to nourish and instruct her children, and servants, as the church, that she may answer in that particular also; and truly, the wife being always at home, she hath great advantage that way; wherefore do it, and the Lord prosper your proceeding.

DUTIES OF CHILDREN TO PARENTS.

There lieth also a duty upon children to their parents, which they are bound both by the law of God and nature conscientiously to observe: 'Children, obey your parents in the Lord: for this is right.' And again, 'Children, obey your parents in all things; for this is well pleasing unto the Lord.' Ep. vi. 1. Col. iii. 20.

There are these general things in which children should shew forth that honour that is due to their parents from them.

First, They should always count them better than themselves. I observe a vile spirit among some children, and that is, they are apt to look over their parents, and to have slighting and scornful thoughts of them. This is worse than heathenish; such an one hath got just the heart of a dog or a beast, that will bite those that begot them, and her that brought them forth.

Object. But my father, &c., is now poor, and I am rich, and it will be a disparagement, or at least a hinderance to me, to shew that respect to him as otherwise I might.

Answ. I tell thee thou arguest like an atheist and a beast, and standest in this full flat against the Son of God. Mar. vii. 9—13. Must a gift, and a little of the glory of the butterfly, make thee that thou shalt not do for, and honour to, thy father and mother? 'A wise son maketh a glad father: but a foolish man despiseth his mother.' Pr. xv. 20. Though thy parents be never so low, and thou thyself never so high, yet he is thy father, and she thy mother, and they must be in thy eye in great esteem: 'The eye that mocketh at his father, and despiseth to obey his mother, the ravens of the valley shall pick it out, and the young eagles shall eat it.' Pr. xxx. 17.

Second, Thou oughtest to shew thy honour to thy parents, by a willingness to help them with such necessaries and accommodations which they need. 'If any - have children or nephews, let them learn to shew piety† at home, and to requite their parents:' saith Paul, 'for that is good and acceptable before God.' 1 Ti. v. 4. And this rule Joseph observed

---

* 'She never crosseth her husband in the spring-tide of his anger, but stays till it be ebbing water.'—Fuller's Maxims.—Ed.

† Bunyan's words are 'to show pity,' probably taken from the word 'goodness' in the margin of the Bible; but lest it might be a typographical error, the usual rendering is given in this quotation.—Ed..

to his poor father, though he himself was next the king in Egypt. Ge. xlvii. 12; xli. 39—44.

But mark, let them ' requite their parents.' There are three things for which, as long as thou livest, thou wilt be a debtor to thy parents.

1. For thy being in this world. They are they from whom, immediately under God, thou didst receive it.

2. For their care to preserve thee when thou wast helpless, and couldst neither care for, nor regard thyself.

3. For the pains they have taken with thee to bring thee up. Until thou hast children of thy own, thou wilt not be sensible of the pains, watchings, fears, sorrow, and affliction, that they have gone under to bring thee up; and when thou knowest it, thou wilt not easily yield that thou hast recompensed them for thy favour to thee. How often have they sustained [thee in] thy hunger, clothed thy nakedness? What care have they taken that thou mightest have wherewith to live and do well when they were dead and gone? They possibly have spared it from their own belly and back for thee, and have also impoverished themselves, that thou mightst live like a man.* All these things ought duly, and like a man, to be considered by thee; and care ought to be taken on thy part to requite them. The Scripture saith so, reason saith so, and there be none but dogs and beasts that deny it. It is the duty of parents to lay up for their children; and the duty of children to requite their parents.

Third, Therefore shew, by all humble and son-like carriage, that thou dost to this day, with thy heart, remember the love of thy parents. Thus much for obedience to parents in general.

Again, if thy parents be godly, and thou wicked, as thou art, if thou hast not a second work or birth from God upon thee, then thou art to consider, that thou art more strongly engaged to respect and honour thy parents, not now only as a father in the flesh, but as godly parents; thy father and mother are now made of God thy teachers and instructors in the way of righteousness. Wherefore, to allude to that of Solomon, ' My son, keep thy father's commandment, and forsake not the law of thy mother; bind them continually upon thine heart, *and* tie them about thy neck.' Pr. vi. 20, 21. Now, to provoke thee hereto, consider,

---

* ' What is the child but a piece of the parents wrapped up in another skin.'—*Flavel.*

On seeing a Mother with her Infant asleep in her Arms.

' Thine is the morn of life,
All laughing, unconscious of the evening with her anxious cares,
Thy mother filled with the purest happiness and bliss
Which an indulgent Heaven bestows upon a lower world,
Watches and protects her dearest life, now sleeping in her arms.'
German Poem.—Ed.

1. That this hath been the practice always of those that are and have been obedient children; yea, of Christ himself to Joseph and Mary, though he himself was God blessed for ever. Lu. ii. 51.

2. Thou hast also the severe judgments of God upon those that have been disobedient, to awe thee. As, (1.) Ishmael, for but mocking at one good carriage of his father and mother, was both thrust out of his father's inheritance and the kingdom of heaven, and that with God's approbation. Ge. xxi. 9—14. Ga. iv. 30. (2.) Hophni and Phinehas, for refusing the good counsel of their father, provoked the great God to be their enemy: ' They hearkened not unto the voice of their father, because the Lord would slay them.' 1 Sa. ii. 23—25. (3.) Absalom was hanged, as I may say, by God himself, for rebelling against his father. 2 Sa. xviii. 9.

Besides, little dost thou know how heart-aching a consideration it is to thy parents, when they do but *suppose* thou mayest be damned ! How many prayers, sighs, and tears, are there wrung from their hearts upon this account? Every miscarriage of thine goeth to their heart, for fear God should take an occasion thereat to shut thee up in hardness for ever. How did Abraham groan for Ishmael? ' O,' saith he, to God, ' that Ishmael might live before thee !' Ge. xvii. 18. How was Isaac and Rebecca grieved for the miscarriage of Esau? Ge. xxvi. 34, 35. And how bitterly did David mourn for his son, who died in his wickedness? 2 Sa. xviii. 32, 33.

Lastly, And can any imagine, but that all these carriages of thy godly parents, will be to thee the increase of thy torments in hell, if thou die in thy sins notwithstanding?

Again, if thy parents, and thou also, be godly, how happy a thing is this? How shouldest thou rejoice, that the same faith should dwell both in thy parents and thee? Thy conversion, possibly, is the fruits of thy parents' groans and prayers for thy soul; and they cannot choose but rejoice; do thou rejoice with them. It is true, in the salvation of a natural son, which is mentioned in the parable: ' This my son was dead, and is alive again; he was lost, and is found. And they began to be merry.' Lu. xv. 24. Let therefore the consideration of this, that thy parents have grace, as well as thee, engage thy heart so much the more to honour, reverence, and obey them.

Thou art better able now to consider the pains and care that thy friends have been at, both for thy body and soul; wherefore strive to requite them. Thou hast strength to answer in some measure the command: wherefore do not neglect it. It is a double sin in a gracious son not to remember the commandment, yea, the first commandment with promise. Ep. vi. 1, 2. Take heed of giving thy sweet parents one snappish word, or one unseemly carriage. Love them because they are thy parents, because they are godly, and because thou must be in glory with them.

Again, if thou be godly, and thy parents wicked, as often it sadly falls out; then,

1. Let thy bowels yearn towards them; it is thy parents that are going to hell!

2. As I said before to the wife, touching her unbelieving husband, so now I say to thee, Take heed of a parroting tongue: speak to them wisely, meekly, and humbly; do for them faithfully without repining; and bear, with all child-like modesty, their reproaches, their railing, and evil speaking. Watch fit opportunities to lay their condition before them. O! how happy a thing would it be, if God should use a child to beget his father to the faith! Then indeed might the father say, With the fruit of my own bowels hath God converted my soul. The Lord, if it be his will, convert our poor parents, that they, with us, may be the children of God.*

CONCERNING SERVANTS.

Servants also, they have a work to do for God, in their place and station among men.

The apostles assert masters under a threefold consideration. *First,* The believing master. *Second,* The unbelieving master. *Third,* The froward master.

For all which, servants are furnished with counsel and advice in the word, for the demeaning of themselves, under each of them.

But before I speak in particular to any of these, *I will in general shew you the duty of servants.*

1. Thou art to look upon thyself as thou art; that is, as a servant, not a child, nor a wife; thou art inferior to these; wherefore count thyself under them, and be content with that station. 'For three *things* the earth is disquieted, and for four *which* it cannot bear.' One is 'a servant when he reigneth.' Pr. xxx. 21, 22. It is out of thy place, either to talk or do, as one that reigneth.

2. Consider, that thou being a servant, what is under thy hand is not thy own but thy master's. Now, because it is not thy own thou oughtest not to dispose of it; but because it is thy master's, thou oughtest to be faithful. Thus it was with Joseph. Ge. xxxix. 8, 9. But if thou do otherwise, know that thou shalt receive of God for the wrong that thou dost; and there is with God 'no respect of persons.' Col. iii. 25. Wherefore,

* Bunyan's silence, in all his writings, concerning the state of his parents as to godliness, may lead us to fear that this fervent ejaculation had often been poured forth by his own soul on behalf of his father and mother. All that we know of them is, that they were poor, but gave their children the best education their means afforded; as to their piety he is silent.— ED.

3. Touching thy work and employment, thou art to do it as unto the Lord, and not for man; and, indeed, then servants do their business as becomes them, when they do all in obedience to the Lord, as knowing that the place in which they now are, it is the place where Christ hath put them, and in which he expecteth they should be faithful. 'Servants,' saith Paul, 'be obedient to them that are *your* master's, - with fear and trembling, in singleness of your heart as unto Christ; not with eye-service, as men-pleasers; but as the servants of Christ, doing the will of God from the heart.' Ep. vi. 5, 6.

Observe a little the word of God to servants. 1. Servants must be obedient; yet, 2. Not with that obedience that will serve man only. Servants must have their eye on the Lord, in the work they do for their masters. 3. That their work in this service is the will and ordinance of God. From which I conclude, that thy work in thy place and station, as thou art a servant, is as really God's ordinance, and as acceptable to him, in its kind, as is preaching, or any other work, for God; and that thou art as sure to receive a reward for thy labour, as he that hangs or is burnt for the gospel. Wherefore, saith the apostle to servants, 'Whatsoever ye do, do *it* heartily, as to the Lord, and not unto men, knowing that of the Lord ye shall receive the reward of the inheritance; for ye serve the Lord Christ.' Col. iii. 23, 24.

And now touching the *three sorts of masters mentioned before.*

First, For the *believing* master; saith Paul, 'They that have believing masters, let them not despise *them,* because they are brethren; but rather do *them* service, because they are faithful and beloved, and partakers, with the servants, 'of the' heavenly 'benefit.' 1 Ti. vi. 2. Servants, if they have not a care of their hearts, will be so much in the consideration of the relation that is betwixt their masters and they, as brethren, that they will forget the relation that is between them as masters and servants. Now, though they ought to remember the one, yet let them take heed of forgetting the other. Know thy place, as a servant, while thou considerest that thy master and thee are brethren, and do thy work for him faithfully, humbly, and with meekness, because he is a master faithful and beloved, and partaker of the heavenly benefit. 'If any man teach otherwise,' saith the apostle Paul, 'and consent not to wholesome words, *even* the words of our Lord Jesus Christ, and to the doctrine which is according to godliness; he is proud, knowing nothing, but doting about questions, and strifes of words; whereof cometh envy, strife, railings, evil surmisings, perverse disputings of men of corrupt minds, and destitute of the truth, supposing that

gain is godliness: from such withdraw thyself.'
1 Ti. vi. 3—5.

Second, For the *unbelieving* masters, for of them
Paul speaks in the first verse of the 6th of Timothy,
'Let as many servants,' saith he, 'as are under
the yoke count their own masters worthy of all
honour, that the name of God and *his* doctrine be
not blasphemed.' Servants living with unbelieving
masters, are greatly engaged to be both watchful,
faithful, and trusty. Engaged, I say, 1. From
the consideration of the condition of their master;
for he being unbelieving, will have an evil eye
upon thee, and upon thy doings, and so much the
more because thou professest. As in the case of
Saul and David. 1 Sa. xviii. 8, 9, &c. 2. Thou art
engaged because of the profession thou makest of
the word of God; for by thy profession thou dost
lay both God and his word before thy master,
and he hath no other wit but to blaspheme them,
if thou behave thyself unworthily. Wherefore
Paul bids Titus '*exhort* servants to be obedient to
their own masters, *and* to please *them* well in all
things, not answering again;' not giving parroting
answers, or such as are cross or provoking, 'not
purloining, but shewing all good fidelity, that
they may adorn the doctrine of God our Saviour
in all things.' Tit. ii. 9, 10. That servant, who in an
unbeliever's family doth his work before God, as
God's ordinance, he shall adorn the doctrine of
God, if not save his master by so doing; but if he
doth otherwise, he shall both stumble the unbeliever, dishonour God, offend the faithful, and
bring guilt upon his own soul.

Third, For the *froward* master, though I distinguish him from the unbeliever, yet it is not
because he may not be such, but because every
unbeliever doth not properly go under that name.
Now with this froward and peevish fellow, thou
art to serve as faithfully for the time thou standest
bound, as with the most pleasant and rational master in the world: 'Servants,' saith Peter, '*be*
subject to *your* masters with all fear; not only to
the good and gentle, but also to the froward.'
1 Pe. ii. 18. And if thy peevish master will still be
froward, either out of spite to thy religion, or
because he is without reason concerning thy labour—thou to the utmost of thy power labouring
faithfully—God then reckoneth thee a sufferer for
well-doing, as truly as if thou wert called upon the
stage of this world before men, for the matters of
thy faith. Wherefore Peter adds this encouragement to servants, to the exhortation he gave them
before: 'This *is* thank worthy,' saith he, 'if a
man for conscience toward God endure grief, suffering wrongfully. For what glory *is it*, if when
ye be buffeted for your faults, ye shall take it
patiently? But if when ye do well, and suffer *for
it*, ye take it patiently, this *is* acceptable with God.'
1 Pe. ii. 19, 20. Wherefore be comforted concerning
thy condition, with considering that God looks upon
thee, as on Jacob in the family of Laban; and
will right all thy wrongs, and recompense thee for
thy faithful, wise, and godly behaviour, before,
and in the service of thy froward master. Wherefore, be patient, I say, and abound in faithfulness
in thy place and calling, till God make a way for
thy escape from this place; and when thou mayest
be made free, use it rather. 1 Co. vii. 21.

DUTIES OF NEIGHBOURS EACH TO OTHER.

Having thus in few words shewed you what is
duty under your several relations, I shall now at
last speak, in a word or two, touching good neighbourhood, and then draw towards a conclusion.
Touching neighbourhood, there are these things
to be considered and practised, if thou wilt be
found in the practical part of good neighbourhood.

First, Thou must be of a good and sound conversation in thy own family, place, and station,
shewing to all, the power that the gospel and the
things of another world hath in thy heart, 'That
ye may be blameless, and harmless, the sons of
God, without rebuke, in the midst of a crooked
and perverse nation, among whom ye shine as
lights in the world.' Phi. ii. 15, 16.

Second, As persons must be of good behaviour
at home, that will be good neighbours, so they
must be full of courtesy and charity to them that
have need about them. Lu. x. 36, 37. Right good
neighbourhood is for men readily to communicate,
as of their spirituals, so of their temporalities, as
food, raiment, and help to those that have need;
to be giving to the poor as thou seest them go by
thee, or to inquire after their condition, and according to thy capacity to send unto them. Job
xxxi. 15—17, &c.

Third, Thou must be always humble and meek
among them, as also grave and gracious; not light
and frothy, but by thy words and carriage ministering 'grace to the hearers.' Ep. iv. 29. Thus also
Job honoured God among his neighbours. Job
xxix. 6—12.

Fourth, Thy wisdom will be, rightly to discoun-
tenance sin, and to reprove thy neighbour for the
same, Le. xix. 17. denying thyself in some things, for
the preventing an injury to thy neighbour, that
thou mayest please him for his edification. Ro. xv. 2.

Fifth, If thou wouldest be a good neighbour,
take heed of thy tongue upon two accounts.

1. That thou with it give no offensive language
to thy neighbour, to the provoking of him to
anger. Bear much, put up wrongs, and say little:
'*It is* an honour for a man to cease from strife:
but every fool will be meddling.' Pr. xx. 3. And

again, ' He loveth transgression that loveth strife.'
Pr. xvii. 19.

2. And as thou shouldest take heed that thou
be not the original of contention and anger, so also
take heed that thou be not an instrument to beget
it between parties, by tale-bearing and a gossiping
spirit: ' He that passeth by, *and* meddleth with
strife *belonging* not to him, *is like* one that taketh
a dog by the ears. *As* coals *are* to burning coals,
and wood to fire ; so *is* a contentious man to kindle
strife.' Pr. xxvi. 17—21. I do observe two things very
odious in many professors ; the one is a headstrong and stiff-necked spirit, that will have its
own way ; and the other is, a great deal of tat-
tling and talk about religion, and but a very little,
if anything, of those Christian deeds that carry in
them the cross of a Christian in the doing thereof,
and profit to my neighbour.

(1.) When I say a head-strong and stiff-necked
spirit, I mean, they are for pleasing themselves
and their own fancies, in things of no weight,
though their so doing be as the very slaughter-knife
to the weak conscience of a brother or neighbour.
Now this is base. A Christian, in all such things
as intrench not the matters of faith and worship,
should be full of self-denial, and seek to please
others rather than themselves ; ' Give none offence
- to the Jews, nor to the * Greeks, nor to the
church of God : - not seeking mine own profit, but
the *profit* of many, that they may be saved.' 1 Co. x.
32, 33.

(2.) And the second is as bad, to wit, when
professors are great prattlers and talkers, and dis-
puters, but do little of anything that bespeaketh
love to the poor, or self-denial in outward things.
Some people think religion is made up of words ;
a very wide mistake ! Words without deeds is
but a half-faced religion : ' Pure religion, and undefiled before God and the Father is this, To visit
the fatherless and widows in their affliction, *and*
to keep himself unspotted from the world.' Ja. i. 27.
Again, ' If a brother or sister be naked, and destitute of daily food, and one of you say unto them,
Depart in peace, be warmed and filled,' which are
very fine words, yet if you ' give them not those
things that are needful to the body, what *doth it*
profit ?' Ja. ii. 15, 16.

[*Sins which interfere with the duties of Christian
Brotherhood and Civil Neighbourhood.*]

Now then, before I go any farther, I will here
take an occasion to touch a little upon those sins
that are so rife in many professors in this day : and

they are, covetousness, pride, and uncleanness. I
would speak a word to them in this place, the rather
because they are they which spoil both Christian
brotherhood, and civil neighbourhood, in too great
a measure.

OF COVETOUSNESS.

First, For Covetousness.

1. Covetousness ; it is all one with desire ; he
that desires, covets, whether the thing he desires
be evil or good. Wherefore that which is called
coveting, in Exod. xx. 17, is called *desire*, in Deut.
v. 21. As the apostle also saith, ' I had not
known lust, except the law had said, Thou shalt
not covet.' Ro. vii. 7. That is, I had not known lust
to be a sin, unless the law had forbid it. Wherefore, though lawful desires are good, 1 Co. xii. 31, and
to be commended, yet covetousness, as commonly
understood, is to be fled from, and abhorred, as of
the devil.

2. Covetousness, or evil desire, it is the first
mover, and giveth to every sin its call, as I may
say, both to move and act ; as was said before,
the apostle had not known sin, except the law had
said, Thou shalt not desire or covet ; for where
there is no desire to sin, there appears no sin.

3. Therefore covetousness carrieth in it every
sin—we speak of sins against the second table—
even as a serpent carrieth her young ones in her
belly. This the scripture affirms, where it saith,
' Thou shalt not covet thy neighbour's wife, nor
his man-servant, nor his maid-servant, nor his ox,
nor his ass, nor anything that *is* thy neighbour's.'
Ex. xx. 17. Covetousness will meddle with anything.

Now, there are in my mind at present these
eight notes of covetousness, which hinder good
works, and a Christian conversation among men,
wherever they are harboured.

(1.) When men, to whom God hath given a comfortable livelihood, are yet not content therewith.
This is against the apostle, where he saith, ' *Let
your* conversation *be* without covetousness ; *and be*
content with such things as ye have : for he hath
said, I will never leave thee, nor forsake thee.'
He. xiii. 5.

(2.) It is covetousness in the seller, that puts
him to say of his traffic, it is better than it is,
that he may heighten the price of it ; and covetousness in the buyer, that prompts him to say worse
of a thing than he thinks in his conscience it is,
and that for an abatement of a reasonable price.
This is that which the apostle forbids under the
name of *defraud*, 1 Co. vi. 8, and that which Solomon
condemns. Pr. xx. 14.

(3.) It is through covetousness that men think
much of that which goeth beside their own mouth,
though possibly it goeth to those that have more

---

* ' To the Greeks.' Bunyan in this follows the Puritan
translation. The word ' Greeks' is in the margin of the
authorized Bible.—ED.

need than themselves, and also that better deserve it than they.

(4.) It argueth covetousness, when men will deprive themselves, and those under them, of the privileges of the gospel, for more of this world; and is condemned by Christ. Lu. xiv. 18—20.

(5.) It argueth covetousness, when men that have it, can go by, or hear of the poor, and shut up their bowels and compassions from them. 1 Jn. iii. 17.

(6.) Also when men are convinced it is their duty to communicate to such and such that have need, yet they defer it, and if not quite forget it, yet linger away the time, as being loth to distribute to the necessities of those in want. This is forbidden by the Holy Ghost: 'Withhold not good from them to whom it is due, when it is in the power of thine hand to do it.' Now, it is due from thee to the poor, by the commandment of God, if they want, and thou hast it; 'Say not unto thy neighbour, Go, and come again, and to-morrow I will give; when thou hast it by thee.' Pr. iii. 27, 28.

(7.) It argueth a greedy mind also, when, after men have cast in their minds what to give, they then from that will be pinching and clipping, and taking away; whereas the Holy Ghost saith, 'Every man according as he purposeth in his heart, so let him give, not grudgingly, or of necessity: for God loveth a cheerful giver.' 2 Co. ix. 7.

(8.) And lastly, It argueth a filthy greedy heart also, when a man, after he hath done any good, then in his heart to repent, and secretly wish that he had not so done, or at least, that he had not done so much: this is to be weary of well-doing; (I speak now of communicating,) and carrieth in it two evils, First, It spoileth the work done. And, secondly, It, if entertained, spoileth the heart for doing any more so. 'The vile person shall be no more called liberal, nor the churl said to be bountiful,' for 'the liberal deviseth liberal things; and by liberal things shall he stand.' Is. xxxii. 5, 8.

Now then, to dissuade all from this poisonous sin, observe, that above all sins in the New Testament, this is called idolatry. Ep. v. 5. Col. iii. 5. And therefore God's people should be so far from being taken with it, that they should be much afraid of the naming of it one among another, lest it should, as adulterous thoughts, infect the heart, by the talking of it. Ep. v. 3.

Quest. But why is covetousness called idolatry?
Answ. 1. Because it engageth the very heart of man in it, to mind earthly things; it gets our love, which should be set on God; and sets it upon poor empty creatures; it puts our affections out of heaven, where they should be, and sets them on earth, where they should not be. Eze. xxxiii. 31. Phi. iii. 18, 19. Col. iii. 1—3. Thus it changeth the object on which

the heart should be set, and setteth it on that on which it should not. It makes a man forsake God, 'the fountain of living waters,' and causeth him to hew to himself 'cisterns, broken cisterns, that can hold no water.' Je. ii. 11—13. For,

2. It rejecteth the care, government, and providence of God towards us, and causeth us to make of our care and industry a god, to whom, instead of God, we fly continually, both for the keeping what we have and for getting more. This was Israel's idolatry of old, and the original of all her idolatrous practices. 'For their mother hath played the harlot,' that is, committed idolatry: 'she that conceived them hath done shamefully: for she said, I will go after my lovers, that gave me my bread and my water, my wool and my flax, mine oil and my drink.' Ho. ii. 5.

3. It disalloweth of God's way of disposing his creatures, and would have them ordered and disposed of otherwise than his heavenly wisdom seemeth meet; and hence ariseth all discontents about God's dealing with us. Covetousness never yet said, It is the Lord, let him do what he pleaseth; but is ever objecting, like a god, against everything that goeth against it; and it is that which, like a god, draweth away the heart and soul from the true God, and his Son Jesus Christ: 'And he went away sorrowful; for he had great possessions.' Mat. xix. 16—22. Now then, that which engageth the heart, that rejecteth the providence of God, and that is for ordering and disposing of things contrary to God, and for breaking with God upon these terms, is idolatry; and all these do covetousness. 'The wicked boasteth of his heart's desire, and blesseth the covetous, whom the Lord abhorreth.' Ps. x. 3. Now the way to remedy this disease is, to learn the lesson which Paul had got by heart; to wit, 'In whatsoever state you are, therewith to be content.' Phi. iv. 11.

OF PRIDE.

Second, I come, in the second place, to speak a word of pride, and loftiness of heart and life.

1. Pride, in general, it is that which causeth a man to think of man and his things, above what is written. 1 Co. iv. 6.

2. It hath its seat in the heart among these enormities, fornications, adulteries, lasciviousness, murders, deceit, &c., Mar. vii. 21—23, and sheweth itself in these following particulars.

(1.) When you slight this or that person, though gracious; that is, look over them, and shun them for their poverty in this world, and choose rather to have converse with others, that possibly are less gracious, because of their greatness in this world. This the apostle James writes against, Ja. ii. 1—3. under the name of partiality; 'for indeed the fruits of a puffed-up heart is to deal in this manner with Christians.' 1 Co. iv. 6, 7. Now this branch of pride floweth from ignorance of the vanity of the creature, and of the worth of a gracious heart; wherefore get more of the knowledge of these two, and this sprig will be nipped in the head, and you will learn to condescend to men of low degree. Ro. xii. 16.

(2.) It argues pride of heart, when men will not deny themselves in things that they may, for the good and profit of their neighbours. And it argueth now, that pride has got so much up into self-love and self-pleasing, that they little care who they grieve or offend, so they may have their way. Ob. 12—15.

(3.) It argueth pride of heart, when sober reproofs for sin, and unbeseeming carriages, will not down with thee, but that rather thou snuffest, and givest way to thy spirit to be peevish, and to retain prejudice against those that thus reprove thee. Saith the prophet, 'Hear ye, and give ear; be not proud: for the Lord hath spoken.' That is, hear the reproofs of God for your sins, and break them off by repentance; 'but if ye will not hear it, my soul shall weep in secret for *your* pride,' &c. Je. xiii. 15—17. So also in Hosea, 'They will not frame their doings to turn unto their God: for the spirit of whoredoms *is* in the midst of them, and they have not known the Lord. And the pride of Israel doth testify to his face:' &c. Ho. v. 4, 5. This argueth great senselessness of God, and a heart greatly out of frame.

(4.) It argueth pride also, when a reproof or admonition will not down as well from the poorest saint, as from the greatest doctor; and it argueth a glory in men, 1 Co. iii. 21, and that they would, that their faith should stand in their wisdom, and not 'in the power of God;' that is, of naked truth. 1 Co. ii. 5.

(5.) It argueth pride of heart, when a man that hath this or that in his heart to do, in reference to God, but yet will slight a sober asking counsel and direction of God in this matter: 'The wicked, through the pride of his countenance, will not seek *after God*,' saith David. Ps x. 4.

(6.) It argueth pride of heart, when persons are tickled with thoughts of their own praise, that secretly lust after it; that think of themselves and others above what is written; which those do who do not acknowledge that man in his best estate is altogether vanity: but such kind of people have forgot the exhortation, 'Be not high-minded, but fear:' Ro. xi. 20. And also, That there is a knowledge that puffeth up, and edifieth neither themselves nor others. 1 Co. viii. 1, 2. Wherefore, to such the apostle saith, Be 'not desirous of vain-glory,' but in lowliness of mind 'let each esteem others better than themselves.' Phi. ii. 3. Ga. v. 26.

Pride also there is in outward carriage, behaviour, and gesture, which is odious for Christians to be tainted with; and this pride is discovered by mincing words, a made carriage, and an affecting the toys and baubles that Satan, and every light-headed fool bringeth into the world. As God speaketh of the daughters of Zion, 'they walk with stretched forth necks, and wanton eyes, mincing *as* they go, and making a tinkling with their feet. Is. iii. 16. A very unhandsome carriage for a people that profess godliness, and that use to come before God to confess their sins, and to bemoan themselves for what they have done. How can a sense of thy own baseness, of the vileness of thy heart, and of the holiness of God, stand with such a carriage? Dost thou see the vileness of thy heart, the fruit of sin? And art thou afflicted with that disagreement that is between God and thy heart, that layest the reins on the neck of thy lusts, and lettest them run whither they will? Be not deceived, pride ariseth from ignorance of these things. 1 Ti. vi. 3, 4. A sense of my vileness, of what I have deserved, and of what continually in my heart opposeth God, cannot stand with a foolish, light, and wanton carriage: thou wilt then see there is other things to mind than to imitate the butterfly. Alas, all these kind of things are but a painting the devil, and a setting a carnal gloss upon a castle of his; thou art but making gay the spider: is thy heart ever the sounder for thy fine gait, thy mincing words, and thy lofty looks? Nay, doth not this argue, that thy heart is a rotten, cankered, and besotted heart? Oh! that God would but let thee see a little of thy own inside, as thou hast others to behold thy outside: thou painted sepulchre, thou whited wall, will these things be found virtues in the day of God? Or, is this the way that thou takest to mortify sin? 'An high look, and a proud heart, *and* the plowing of the wicked, *is* sin.' Pr. xxi. 4. Pride is the ringleader of the seven abominations that the wise man nameth, Pr. vi. 16, 17, and is that above all that causeth to fall into the condemnation of the devil. 1 Ti. iii. 6.

OF ADULTERY OR UNCLEANNESS.

Now I come in the last place to touch a word or two of adultery, and then to draw towards a conclusion. Adultery, it hath its place in the heart, among the rest of those filthinesses I mentioned before, Mar. vii. 21, 22, of which sin I observe two things.

1. That almost in every place where the apostle layeth down a catalogue of wickednesses, he layeth down adultery, fornication, and uncleanness in the front; as that in Mar. vii. 21. Ro. i. 29. 1 Co. vi. 9. Ga. v. 19. Ep. v. 3. 1 Th. iv. 3—5. He. xii. 16. Ja. ii. 11. 1 Pe. ii. 11. 2 Pe. ii. 10. From this I gather that the sin of uncleanness is

a very predominant and master sin, easy to overtake the sinner, as being one of the first that is ready to offer itself on all occasions to break the law of God.

2. I observe that this sin is committed unawares to many, even so soon as a man hath but looked upon a woman: 'I say unto you,' saith Christ, 'that whosoever looketh on a woman to lust,' or desire, 'after her, he hath committed adultery with her already in his heart.' Mat. v. 28. This sin of uncleanness, I say, is a very taking sin; it is natural above all sins to mankind; as it is most natural, so it wants not tempting occasions, having objects for to look on in every corner: wherefore there is need of a double and treble watchfulness in the soul against it. It is better here to make a covenant with our eyes, like Job, Job xxxi. 1, than to let them wander to God's dishonour, and our own discomfort.

There are these three things which discover a man or woman too much inclining to the uncleanness of their own hearts.

(1.) The first is a wanton eye, or an eye that doth secretly affect itself with such objects as are tickling of the heart with the thoughts of immodesty and uncleanness. Isaiah calls this a wanton eye: and Peter an eye full of adultery, that cannot cease from sin. 2 Pe. ii. 14. Is. iii. 16. This is that also which Christ calleth an evil eye, and John the lust of the flesh, and of the eyes, and doth defile those who are not very watchful over their own hearts. Mar. vii. 22. 1 Jn. ii. 16. This wanton eye is that which the most holy saints should take heed of, because it is apt to seize upon them also. When Paul bids Timothy beseech the young women to walk as becomes the gospel, he bids him do it with all purity. 1 Ti. v. 1, 2. As, who should say, Take heed that while thou instructest them to holiness, thou thyself be not corrupted with the lust of thy eye. O how many souls, in the day of God, will curse the day that ever they gave way to a wanton eye!

(2.) The second thing that discovereth one much inclining to the lusts of uncleanness, it is wanton and immodest talk; such as that brazen-faced whore in the 7th of the Proverbs had, or such as they in Peter, who allured 'through the lusts of the flesh, through much wantonness, those that were clean escaped from them who live in error.' 2 Pe. ii. 18. 'Out of the abundance of the heart the mouth speaketh,' wherefore if we be saints, let us take heed, as of our eye, so of our tongue, and let not the lust of uncleanness, or of adultery, be once named among us, 'named among us as becometh saints.' Ep. v. 3. Mark, 'Let it not be once named.' This implies, that the lusts of uncleanness are devilishly taking, they will both take the heart with eyes and tongue: 'Let it not be once named among you,' &c.

(3.) Another thing that bespeaks a man or woman inclining to wantonness and uncleanness, it is an adorning themselves in light and wanton apparel. The attire of an harlot is too frequently in our day the attire of professors; a vile thing, and argueth much wantonness and vileness of affections. If those that give way to a wanton eye, wanton words, and immodest apparel, be not whores, &c., in their hearts, I know not what to say. Doth a wanton eye argue shamefacedness? Doth wanton talk argue chastity? And doth immodest apparel, with stretched-out necks, naked breasts, a made speech, and mincing gaits, &c., argue mortification of lusts? If any say, that these things may argue pride as well as carnal lusts; well, but why are they proud? Is it not to trick up the body? And why do they with pride trick up the body, if it be not to provoke both themselves and others to lusts? God knoweth their hearts without their outsides: and we know their hearts by their outsides.

My friends, I am here treating of good works, and persuading you to fly those things that are hindrances to them: wherefore bear with my plainness when I speak against sin. I would strike it through with every word, because else it will strike us through with many sorrows. 1 Ti. vi. 9, 10. I do not treat of good works as if the doing of them would save us, for we are justified by his grace, according to the hope of eternal life; yet our sins and evil works will lay us obnoxious to the judgments both of God and man. He that walketh not uprightly, according to the truth of the gospel, is like to have his peace assaulted often, both by the devil, the law, death, and hell; yea, and is like to have God hide his face from him also, for the iniquity of his covetousness. Is. lvii. 17.

How can he that carrieth himself basely in the sight of men, think he yet well behaveth himself in the sight of God? And if so dim a light as is in man can justly count thee as a transgressor, how shall thy sins be hid from him whose 'eye-lids try the children of men?' Ps. xi. 4.

It is true, faith without works justifies us before God: Ro. iii. 28; iv. 5. yet that faith that is alone, will be found to leave us sinners in the sight both of God and man. Ja. ii. 18. And though thou addest nothing to that which saveth thee by what thou canst do, yet thy righteousness may profit the son of man; as also saith the text: but if thou shalt be so careless as to say, What care I for being righteous to profit others? I tell thee, that the love of God is not in thee. Job xxxv. 8. 1 Jn. iii. 17. 1 Co xiii. 1—3. Walk therefore in God's ways, and do them, for this is your wisdom and your understanding in the sight of the nations, which shall hear of all these statutes, and say, 'This great nation is a wise and understanding people.' De. iv. 6.

THIRD. Observe. Every believer should not only take heed that his works be good, and so for the present do them, *but should carefully study to maintain them; that is, to keep in a continual exercise of them.*

It is an easier matter to begin to do good, than it is to continue therein; and the reason is, there is not so much of a Christian's cross in the beginning of a work, as there is in a continual, hearty, conscientious practice thereof. Therefore Christians have need, as to be pressed to do good, so to continue the work. Man, by nature, is rather a hearer than a doer, Athenian like, continually listening after some new thing; seeing many things, but observing nothing. Ac. xvii. 20. Is. xlii. 20. It is observable, that after Christ had divided his hearers into four parts, he condemned three of them for fruitless hearers. Lu. viii. 5—8. O it is hard continuing believing, continuing loving, continuing resisting all that opposeth; we are subject to be weary of well-doing. Ga. vi. 9. To pluck out right eyes, to cut off right hands and feet, is no pleasant thing to flesh and blood; and yet none but these shall have the promise of life; because none but these will be found to have the effectual work of God's grace in their souls: Mat. xviii. 8, 9. 'If ye continue in my word, then are you my disciples' INDEED. Mat. xxiv. 13. Jn. viii. 31. And hence it is, that you find so many IFS in the Scripture about men's happiness; as, 'if children, then heirs;' and 'if ye continue in the faith;' and 'if we hold the beginning of our confidence steadfast unto the end.' Ro. viii. 17. Col. i. 23. He. iii. 14. Not that their continuing in the way of God is the cause of the work being right; but the work being right causeth the continuance therein. As John saith in another place, 'They went out from us, but they were not of us; for if they had been of us, [saith he] they would, *no doubt,* have continued with us.' 1 Jn. ii. 19. But I say, where the work of God indeed is savingly begun, even there is flesh, corruption, and the body of death to oppose it. Therefore should Christians take heed, and look that against these opposites they maintain a continual course of good works among men.

Besides, as there is that in our own bowels that opposeth goodness, so there is the tempter, the wicked one, both to animate these lusts, and to join with them in every assault against every appearance of God in our souls. And hence it is, that he is called the devil, the enemy, the destroyer, and him that seeks continually to devour us, 1 Pe. v. 8. I need say no more but this. He that will walk like a Christian indeed, as he shall find it is requisite that he continue in good works, so his continuing therein will be opposed; if therefore he will continue therein, he must make it his business to study how to oppose those that oppose such a life, that he may continue therein.

FOURTH. Now then to help in this, here fitly comes in the last observation, to wit, *That the best way both to provoke ourselves and others to good works, it is to be often affirming to others the doctrine of justification by grace, and to believe it ourselves.* '*This is* a faithful saying, and these things I will that thou affirm constantly, that they which have believed in God, might be careful to maintain good works.' Tit. iii. 8.

I told you before, that good works must flow from faith: and now I tell you, that the best way to be fruitful in them, is to be much in the exercise of the doctrine of justification by grace; and they both agree; for as faith animates to good works, so the doctrine of grace animates faith. Wherefore, the way to be rich in good works, it is to be rich in faith; and the way to be rich in faith is to be conscientiously affirming the doctrine of grace to others, and believing it ourselves.

First, To be constantly affirming it to others. Thus Paul tells Timothy, that if he put the brethren in mind of the truths of the gospel, he himself should not only be a good minister of Christ, but should be nourished up in the words of faith and of good doctrine. 1 Ti. iv. 6. It is the ordinance of God, that Christians should be often asserting the things of God each to others; and that by their so doing they should edify one another. He. x. 24, 25. 1 Th. v. 11.

The doctrine of the gospel is like the dew and the small rain that distilleth upon the tender grass, wherewith it doth flourish, and is kept green. De. xxxii. 2. Christians are like the several flowers in a garden, that have upon each of them the dew of heaven, which being shaken with the wind, they let fall their dew at each other's roots, whereby they are jointly nourished, and become nourishers of one another. For Christians to commune savourly of God's matters one with another, it is as if they opened to each other's nostrils boxes of perfume*. Saith Paul to the church at Rome, 'I long to see you, that I may impart unto you some spiritual gift, to the end ye may be established; that is, that I may be comforted together with you, by the mutual faith both of you and me.' Ro. i. 11, 12. Christians should be often affirming the doctrine of grace, and justification by it, one to another.

Second, As they should be thus doing, so they should live in the power of it themselves; they should by faith suck and drink in this doctrine, as the good ground receiveth the rain; which being

---

* This is a most beautiful passage, unequalled by any ancient or modern author. Such a view of church fellowship does honour to the head and heart of the prince of allegorists. It is worthy to be printed in letters of gold, and presented to every candidate for church fellowship among all christian societies of every denomination.—ED.

done, forthwith there is proclaimed good works. Paul to the Colossians saith thus, 'We give thanks to God and the Father of our Lord Jesus Christ, praying always for you, since we heard of your faith in Christ Jesus, and love to all the saints; for the hope which is laid up for you in heaven, whereof ye heard before in the word of the truth of the gospel, which is come unto you, as *it is* in all the world, and bringeth forth fruit, as *it doth* also in you.' But how long ago? Why, ' since the day ye heard it, [saith he,] and knew the grace of God in truth.' Col. i. 3—6.

Apples and flowers are not made by the gardener; but are an effect of the planting and watering. Plant in the sinner good doctrine, and let it be watered with the word of grace; and as the effect of that, there is the fruits of holiness, and the end everlasting life. Ro. vi. 22. Good doctrine is the doctrine of the gospel, which sheweth to men, that God clotheth them with the righteousness of his Son freely, and maketh him with all his benefits over to them; by which free gift the sinner is made righteous before God; and because he is so, therefore there is infused a principle of grace into the heart, whereby it is both quickened, and bringing forth fruit. Ro. iii. 21—26. 1 Co. i. 30. 2 Co. v. 21. Jn. i. 16.

Now then, seeing good works do flow from faith, and seeing faith is nourished by an affirming of the doctrine of the gospel, &c., take here these few considerations from the doctrine of the gospel, for the support of thy faith, that thou mayest be indeed fruitful and rich in good works.

Consider 1. The whole Bible was given for this very end, that thou shouldest both believe this doctrine, and live in the comfort and sweetness of it: ' For whatsoever things were written aforetime were written for our learning, that we through patience and comfort of the Scriptures might have hope.' Ro. xv. 4. Jn. xx. 31.

Consider 2. That therefore every promise in the Bible is thine, to strengthen, quicken, and encourage thy heart in believing.

Consider 3. That there is nothing that thou dost, can so please God as believing; ' The Lord taketh pleasure in them that fear him, in those that hope in his mercy.' Ps. cxlvii. 11. They please him, because they embrace his righteousness, &c.

Consider 4. That all the withdrawings of God from thee, are not for the weakening, but for the trial of thy faith; and also, that whatever he suffers Satan, or thy own heart to do, it is not to weaken faith. Job xxiii. 8—10. 1 Pe. i. 7.

Consider 5. That believing is that which will keep in thy view the things of heaven and glory; and that at which the devil will be discouraged, sin weakened, and thy heart quickened and sweetened. He. xi. 27. Ja. iv. 7. 1 Pe. v. 9. Ep. vi. 16. Ro. xv. 13.

Consider lastly, By believing, the love of God is kept with warmth upon the heart, and that this will provoke thee continually to bless God for Christ, for grace, for faith, hope, and all these things, either in God, or thee, that doth accompany salvation. 2 Co. ii. 14. Ps. ciii. 1—3.

Third, The doctrine of the forgiveness of sins received by faith, will make notable work in the heart of a sinner, to bring forth good works.

But, Forasmuch as there is a body of death and sin in every one that hath the grace of God in this world; and because this body of death will be ever opposing that which is good, as the apostle saith, Ro. vii. 21. therefore take these few particulars further, for the suppressing that which will hinder a fruitful life.

1. Keep a continual watch over the wretchedness of thy own heart, not to be discouraged at the sight of thy vileness, but to prevent its wickedness; for that will labour either to hinder thee from doing good works, or else will hinder thee in the doing thereof; for evil is present with thee for both these purposes. Take heed then, that thou do not listen to that at any time, but deny, though with much struggling, the workings of sin to the contrary.

2. Let this be continually before thy heart, that God's eye is upon thee, and seeth every secret turning of thy heart, either to or from him : 'All things *are* naked and opened unto the eyes of him with whom we have to do.' He. iv. 13.

3. If thou deny to do that good which thou oughtest, with what thy God hath given thee; then consider, that though he love thy soul, yet he can chastise; First, Thy inward man with such troubles, that thy life shall be restless and comfortless. Secondly, And can also so blow upon thy outward man, that all thou gettest shall be put in a bag with holes. Ps. lxxxix. 31—33. Hag. i. 6. And set the case he should licence but one thief among thy substance, or one spark of fire among thy barns, how quickly might that be spent ill, and against God's will, which thou shouldest have spent to God's glory, and with thy will; and I tell thee further, that if thou want a heart to do good when thou *hast* about thee, thou mayest want comfort in such things thyself from others, when thine is taken from thee. See Ju. i. 6, 7.

4. Consider, that a life full of good works is the only way, on thy part, to answer the mercy of God extended to thee; God hath had mercy on thee, and hath saved thee from all thy distresses; God hath not stuck to give thee his Son, his Spirit, and the kingdom of heaven. Saith Paul, ' I beseech you therefore by the mercies of God, that ye present your bodies a living sacrifice, holy, acceptable unto God, *which is* your reasonable service.' Ro. xii. 1. Mat. xviii. 32. 33.

5. Consider, that this is the way to convince all men, that the power of God's things hath taken hold of thy heart—I speak to them that hold the head*—and say what thou wilt, if thy faith be not accompanied with a holy life, thou shalt be judged a withered branch, a wording professor, salt without savour, and as lifeless as a sounding brass, and a tinkling cymbal. Jn. xv. Mat. xiii. 1 Co. xiii. 1, 2. For, say they, shew us your faith by your works, for we cannot see your hearts. Ja. ii. 18. But I say on the contrary, if thou walk as becomes thee who art saved by grace, then thou wilt witness in every man's conscience, that thou art a good tree; now thou leavest guilt on the heart of the wicked. 1 Sa. xxiv. 16, 17. now thou takest off occasion from them that desire occasion; and now thou art clear from the blood of all men. 2 Co. xi. 12. Ac. xx. 26, 31—35. This is the man also that provoketh others to good works. The ear that heareth such a man shall bless him; and the eye that seeth him shall bear witness to him. 'Surely,' saith David, 'he shall not be moved for ever: The righteous shall be in everlasting remembrance.' He. x. 24. Job xxix. 11. Ps. cxii. 6.

6. Again, The heart that is fullest of good works, hath in it at least room for Satan's temptations. And this is the meaning of Peter, where he saith, 'Be sober, be vigilant;' that is, be busying thyself in faith and holiness, 'because, your adversary the devil, as a roaring lion, walketh about, seeking whom he may devour.' 1 Pe. v. 8. 'He that walketh uprightly, walketh safely; and they that add to faith, virtue; to virtue, knowledge; to knowledge, temperance; to temperance, brotherly kindness; and to these charity; and that abounds therein, he shall neither be barren nor unfruitful; he shall never fall; but so an entrance shall be ministered to him abundantly, into the everlasting kingdom of our Lord and Saviour Jesus Christ.' 2 Pe. i. 5—10. Pr. x. 9.

7. The man who is fullest of good works, he is fittest to live and fittest to die: 'I am now,' at any time, 'ready to be offered,' saith fruitful Paul. 2 Ti. iv. 6. Whereas he that is barren, he is neither fit to live, nor fit to die: to die, he himself is convinced he is not fit, and to live God himself saith he is not fit; 'cut him down, why doth he cumber the ground?' Lu. xiii. 7.

Lastly, Consider, to provoke thee to good works, thou shalt have of God when thou comest to glory, a reward for everything thou dost for him on earth. Little do the people of God consider, how richly God will reward, what from a right principle and to a right end, is done for him here; not a bit of bread to the poor, not a draught of water to the meanest of them that belong to Christ, or the loss

* To 'hold the head' is to make a very prominent profession of religion.—Ed.

of a hair of your head, shall in that day go without its reward. Lu. xiv. 13, 14. Mat. x. 42.

'For our light affliction,' and so all other pieces of self-denial, 'which is but for a moment, worketh for us a far more exceeding and eternal weight of glory.' 2 Co. iv. 17. I tell thee, Christian, be but rich in good works, and thou shalt have more than salvation; thy salvation thou hast freely by grace through Christ, without works, Ep. ii. 8—10. but now being justified and saved, and as the fruits hereof, renewed by the Holy Ghost; after this, I say, thou shalt be rewarded for every work that proves good; 'For God is not unrighteous to forget your work and labour of love, which ye have shewed toward his name, in that ye have ministered to the saints, and do minister.' He. vi. 10. 1 Co. iii. 14. Moses counted the reward that he was to have, for a short suffering with the people of God, of greater worth than the treasures of Egypt, the smiles of the king, or the honour of his kingdom. He. xi. 25—27. In a word, let the disappointments that do, and shall most surely befall the fruitless professors, provoke thee to look with all diligence to thy standing. For,

1. Such a one is but deceived and disappointed touching the work of grace he supposeth to be in his heart; he thinks he is a Christian, and hath grace, as faith, hope, and the like, in his soul, yet no fruits of these things manifest themselves in him; indeed his tongue is tipt with a talk and tattle of religion. Poor man, poor empty man! Faith without works is dead; thy hope shall be as the giving up of the ghost; thy gifts with which thy soul is possessed, are but such as are common to reprobates; thou art therefore disappointed; God reputes thee still but wicked, though thou comest and goest to the place of the Holy. Ja. ii. 19, 20. Job xi. 20. 1 Co. xiii. 1—3.

The fruitless professor must meet with disappointments.

2. Therefore all thy joy and comfort must needs fall short of saving comfort, and so leave thee in the suds notwithstanding; thy joy is the joy of the Pharisees, Jn. v. 35. and thy gladness as that of Herod, Mar. vi. 20. and the longest time it can last, it is but a Scripture-moment. Job xx. 5. Alas! in all thy gladness and content with thy religion, thou art but like the boy that plays with brass instead of gold; and with counters instead of that which will go for current coin. Thus, 'if a man think himself to be something when he is nothing, he deceiveth [or disappoints] himself.' Ga. vi. 3.

3. This is not all, but look thou certainly for an eternal disappointment in the day of God; for it must be; thy lamp will out at the first sound the trump of God shall make in thine ears; thou canst not hold up at the appearance of the Son of God in his glory; his very looks will be to thy profession as a strong wind is to a blinking candle, and thou shalt be left only to smoke.

Oh the alteration that will befal a foolish virgin! She thought she was happy, and that she should have received happiness with those that were right at the heart; but behold the contrary, her lamp is going out, she is now to seek for saving grace, when the time of grace is over? Her heaven she thought of, is proved a hell, and her god is proved a devil. God hath cast her out of his presence, and claps the door upon her. She pleads her profession, and the like, and she hath for her answer repulses from heaven. 'So *are* the paths of all that forget God; and the hypocrite's hope shall perish; whose hope shall be cut off, and whose trust *shall be* a spider's web. He shall lean upon his house but it shall not stand; he shall hold it fast, but it shall not endure.' Mat. xxv. 1—10. Lu. xiii. 25, 26. Job viii. 13—15.

Take heed therefore; thy soul, heaven, and eternity, lies at stake; yea, they turn either to thee or from thee upon the hinge of thy faith; if it be right, all is thine: if wrong, then all is lost, however thy hopes and expectations are to the contrary: 'For in Jesus Christ neither circumcision availeth any thing, nor uncircumcision; but faith which worketh by love. Let no man deceive you with vain words: for because of these things cometh the wrath of God upon the children of unbelief.* For the earth which drinketh in the rain that cometh oft upon it, and bringeth forth herbs meet for them by whom it is dressed, receiveth blessing from God: but that which beareth thorns and briars *is* REJECTED, and *is* nigh unto cursing, whose end *is* to be burned.' Ga. v. 6. Ep. v. 3—6. He. vi. 7, 8.

Object. But what shall I do, who am so cold, slothful, and heartless, that I cannot find any heart to do any work for God in this world? Indeed time was when his dew rested all night upon my branches, and when I could with desire, with earnest desire, be doing and working for God; but, alas! now it is otherwise.

Answ. If this be true, thy case is sad, thou art to be pitied; the Lord pity thee. And for thy recovery out of this condition, I would give thee no other counsel than was given to Ephesus when she had lost her first love.

1. 'Remember,' saith Christ, 'from whence thou art fallen, and repent, and do the first works,' &c. Re. ii. 5.

Mark: Thy first work is to enter into a serious considering, and remembrance from whence thou art fallen. Remember that thou hast left thy God, the stay of thy soul, and him without whom there is no stay, comfort, or strength, for thee either to do or suffer anything in this world: 'Without me,' saith he, 'ye can do nothing.' Jn. xv. 5. A sad con-

dition; the remembrance of this, for certain, is the first step to the recovering a backsliding heart; for the right remembrance of this doth bring to mind what loss that soul hath sustained that is in this condition, how it hath lost its former visits, smiles, and consolations of God. When thy conscience was suppled with the blood of thy Saviour; when every step thou tookest was, as it were, in honey and butter; and when thy heart could meditate terror with comfort. Job xxix. 2—6. Is. xxxiii. 14—19. Instead of which, thou feelest darkness, hardness of heart, and the thoughts of God are terrible to thee. Ps. lxxvii. 3. Now God never visits thee; or if he doth, it is but as a wayfaring man, that tarrieth but for a night. Je. xiv. 8, 9.

This also brings to mind how the case is altered with thee, touching thy confidence in God for thy future happiness, how uncertain thou now art of thy hopes for heaven, how much this life doth hang in doubt before thee. De. xxviii. 65, 66.

2. 'Remember therefore from whence thou art fallen, and repent.' These are words well put together; for a solid considering of what I have lost in my declining, will provoke in my heart a sorrow, and godly heaviness, whereby I shall be forced to bemoan my condition, and say, 'I will go and return to my first husband, for then *was it* better with me than now.' Ho. ii. 7.

And believe it, the reason of God's standing off from giving the comfortable communion with himself, it is that thou mightest first see the difference between sticking close to God, and forsaking of him; and next, that thou mightest indeed acknowledge thy offence, and seek his face. Ho. v. 15. He taketh no pleasure in thy forlorn condition; he had rather thou shouldest have him in thy bosom, only he will have it in his own way. 'He looketh upon men, and *if any* say, I have sinned, and perverted *that which was* right, and it profited me not; [then] he will deliver his soul from going into the pit, and his life shall see the light.' Job xxxiii. 27, 28.

3. 'Remember from whence thou art fallen, and repent, and do the first works.'

As there should be a remembering and a repenting so there should be a hearty doing our first works; a believing as before, a laying hold of the things of heaven and glory, as at the first; for now is God returned to thee, as before. Zec. i. 16. And though thou mayest, through the loss of thy locks, with Samson, be weak at the first, yet, in short time, thy hair will grow again; that is, thy former experience will in short space be as long, large, and strong, as in the former times. Indeed at the first thou wilt find all the wheels of thy soul rusty, and all the strings of thine heart out of tune; as also when thou first beginnest to stir, the dust and filth of thy heart will, like smoke, trouble thee

* 'Of unbelief;' see margin of the Bible.—Ed.

from that clear beholding the grace of thy God, and his love to thy soul; but yet wait, and go on, and though thou findest thyself as unable to do anything as thou formerly couldest; yet I say, up, and be doing, and the Lord will be with thee; for he hath not despised the day of thy small things. 1 Ch. xxii. 16. Zec. iv. 10.

I know thou wilt be afflicted with a thousand temptations to drive thee to despair, that thy faith may be faint, &c. But against all them set thou the word of God, the promise of grace, the blood of Christ, and the examples of God's goodness to the great backsliders that are for thy encouragement recorded in the scriptures of truth; and remember, that turning to God after backsliding, is the greatest piece of service thou canst do for him, and the greatest honour thou canst bring to the blood of Christ; and know farther, that God, to shew his willing reception of so unworthy a creature, saith, there shall be joy in heaven at thy conversion to him again. Lu. xv. 7, 10.

TO CONCLUDE.

If thou yet, notwithstanding what hath been said, dost remain a backslider:

1. Then remember that thou must die; and remember also, that when the terrors of God, of death, and a backslidden heart, meet together, there will be sad work in that soul; this is the man that hangeth tilting over the mouth of hell, while death is cutting the thread of his life.

2. Remember, that though God doth sometimes, yea, often, receive backsliders, yet it is not always so. Some draw back into perdition; for, because they have flung up God, and would none of him, he in justice flings up them and their souls for ever. Pr. i. 24—28.

I have observed, that sometimes God, as it were in revenge for injury done him, doth snatch away souls in the very nick of their backsliding, as he served Lot's wife, when he turned her into a pillar of salt, even while she was looking over her shoulder to Sodom. Ge. xix. 26. An example that every backslider should remember with astonishment. Lu. xvii. 32.

Thus have I, in few words, written to you, before I die, a word to provoke you to faith and holiness, because I desire that you may have the life that is laid up for all them that believe in the Lord Jesus, and love one another, when I am deceased. Though there I shall rest from my labours, and be in paradise, as through grace I comfortably believe, yet it is not there, but here, I must do you good. Wherefore, I not knowing the shortness of my life, nor the hinderance that hereafter I may have of serving my God and you, I have taken this opportunity to present these few lines unto you for your edification.

Consider what hath been said; and the Lord give you understanding in all things. Farewell.

A CAUTION

TO STIR UP

TO WATCH AGAINST SIN.

By J. BUNYAN.

ADVERTISEMENT BY THE EDITOR.

This faithful and affectionate appeal to conscience, was originally published on a half-sheet of copy paper, and being only printed on one side of the leaf was called a broadside; probably intended to hang up in the house, or to be pasted inside the cover of the family bible.

Charles Doe gives the date 1685; but a copy of this rare sheet, clean and perfect as when first printed, was lately discovered in the Stowe Library, among a great number of single-sheet poems, songs, and proclamations; a memorandum on it, in the writing of Narcissus Luttrel, shews that he bought it for one penny, on the 8th of April, 1684. By the liberal permission of Mr. Pickering, of Piccadilly, the present owner of that extraordinary collection, I have been able accurately to correct the very numerous alterations and errors which abound in all the later editions.

Reader, whoever thou art, but especially the young, this unassuming poem is most worthy of being committed to memory. It is a striking detection of the devil's sophistry. Strive, as you value your peace and happiness, to escape the depths of moral degradation and misery, by avoiding the FIRST overtures of sin.—GEO. OFFOR.

CAUTION TO STIR UP TO WATCH AGAINST SIN.

The first eight lines one did commend to me,
The rest I thought good to commend to thee:
Reader, in reading be thou rul'd by me,
*With rhimes nor lines, but truths, affected be.**
8. Aprill. 1684.

I.

Sin will at first, just like a beggar, crave
One penny or one half-penny to have;
And if you grant its first suit, 'twill aspire,
From pence to pounds, and so will still mount higher
To the whole soul: but if it makes its moan,
Then say, here is not for you, get you gone.
   For if you give it entrance at the door,
   It will come in, and may go out no more.

II.

Sin, rather than 'twill out of action be,
Will pray to stay, though but a while with thee;
One night, one hour, one moment, will it cry,
Embrace me in thy bosom, else I die:
Time to repent [saith it] I will allow,
And help, if to repent thou know'st not how.
   But if you give it entrance at the door,
   It will come in, and may go out no more.

* This same sentiment is well expressed in Bunyan's verses at the conclusion of the Pilgrim, part First.

   'Nor let my figure or similitude
    Put thee into a laughter or a feud;
    Leave this to boys and fools, but as for thee,
    Do thou the substance of my matter see.'

III.

If begging doth not do, sin promise will
Rewards to those that shall its lusts fulfill:
Penny in hand, yea pounds 'twill offer thee,
If at its beck and motion thou wilt be.
'Twill seem heaven to out-bid, and all to gain
Thy love, and win thee it to entertain.
   But give it not admittance at thy door,
   Lest it comes in, and so goes out no more.

IV.

If begging and promising will not do,
'Twill by its wiles attempt to flatter you.
I'm harmless, mean no ill, be not so shy
Will ev'ry soul-destroying motion cry.
'Twill hide its *sting*, 'twill change its native hue,
Vile 'twill not, but a beauty seem to you.
   But if you give it entrance at the door,
   Its sting will in, and may come out no more.

V.

Rather than fail, sin will itself divide,
Bid thee do this, and lay the rest aside.
Take *little* ones ('twill say) throw *great* ones by,
(As if for little sins men should not die.)
Yea SIN with SIN a quarrel will maintain,
On purpose that thou by it might'st be slain.
   Beware the cheat then, keep it out of door,
   It would come in, and would go out no more.

VI.

Sin, if you will believe it, will accuse,
What is not hurtful and itself excuse:
'Twill make a vice of virtue, and 'twill say
Good is destructive, doth men's souls betray;
'Twill make a law, where God has made man free,
And break those laws by which men bounded be.
   Look to thyself then, keep it out of door,
   Thee 'twould entangle, and enlarge thy score.

VII.

SIN is that beastly thing that will defile
Soul, body, name, and fame in little while;
'Twill make him, who some time God's image was,
Look like the devil, love, and plead his cause;
Like to the plague, poison, or leprosy
Defile 'twill, and infect contagiously.
   Wherefore beware, against it shut the door;
   If not, it will defile thee more and more.

VIII.

SIN, once possessed of the heart, will play
The tyrant, force its vassal to obey:
'Twill make thee thine own happiness oppose
And offer open violence to those
That love thee best; yea make thee to defy
The law and counsel of the deity.
   Beware then, keep this tyrant out of door,
   Lest thou be his, and so thy own no more.

IX.

SIN harden can the heart against its God,
Make it abuse his grace, despise his rod,
'Twill make one run upon the very pikes,
Judgments foreseen bring such to no dislikes
Of sinful hazards; no, they venture shall
For one base lust, their soul, and heav'n and all.
   Take heed then, hold it, crush it at the door,
   It comes to rob thee, and to make thee poor.

X.

SIN is a prison, hath its bolts and chains,
Brings into bondage who it entertains;
Hangs shackles on them, bends them to its will,
Holds them, as *Samson* grinded at the mill,
'Twill blind them, make them deaf; yea, 'twill them gag,
And ride them as the devil rides his hag.
   Wherefore look to it, keep it out of door,
   If once its slave, thou may'st be free no more.

XI.

Though SIN at first its rage dissemble may,
'Twill soon upon thee as a lion prey;
'Twill roar, 'twill rend, 'twill tear, 'twill kill out-right,
Its living death will gnaw thee day and night:

Thy pleasures now to paws and teeth it turns,
In thee its tickling lusts, like brimstone burns.
   Wherefore beware, and keep it out of door,
   Lest it should on thee as a lion roar.

XII

SIN will accuse, will stare thee in the face,
Will for its witnesses quote time and place
Where thou committedst it; and so appeal
To conscience, who thy facts will not conceal;
But on thee as a judge such sentence pass,
As will to thy sweet bits prove bitter sauce.
   Wherefore beware, against it shut thy door,
   Repent what's past, believe and sin no more.

XIII.

SIN is the worm of hell, the lasting fire,
Hell would soon lose its heat, could SIN expire;
Better sinless, in hell, than to be where
Heav'n is, and to be found a sinner there.
One sinless, with infernals might do well,
But SIN would make a very heav'n a hell.
   Look to thyself then, to keep it out of door,
   Lest it gets in, and never leaves thee more.

XIV.

No match has sin save God in all the world,
Men, angels it has from their stations hurl'd:
Holds them in chains, as captives, in despite
Of all that here below is called Might.
Release, help, freedom from it none can give,
But he by whom we also breathe and live.
   Watch therefore, keep this giant out of door
   Lest if once in, thou get him out no more.

XV.

Fools make a mock at SIN, will not believe,
It carries such a dagger in its sleeve;
How can it be (say they) that such a thing,
So full of sweet, should ever wear a sting:
They know not that it is the very SPELL
Of SIN, to make men laugh themselves to hell.
   Look to thyself then, deal with SIN no more,
   Lest he that saves, against thee shuts the door.

XVI.

Now let the God that is above,
That hath for sinners so much love;
These lines so help thee to improve,
That towards him thy heart may move.
   Keep thee from enemies external,
   Help thee to fight with those internal:
   Deliver thee from them infernal,
   And bring thee safe to life eternal.—AMEN.

London: Printed for N. Ponder at the Peacock in the Poultrey.

A DISCOURSE

OF THE

BUILDING, NATURE, EXCELLENCY, AND GOVERNMENT

OF

THE HOUSE OF GOD;

WITH

COUNSELS AND DIRECTIONS TO THE INHABITANTS THEREOF.

BY JOHN BUNYAN, OF BEDFORD.

'*Lord, I have loved the habitation of thy house, and the place where thine honour dwelleth.*'—Psal. xxvi. 8.

ADVERTISEMENT BY THE EDITOR.

BEAUTIFUL in its simplicity is this treatise on the Church of Christ, by John Bunyan. He opens, with profound knowledge and eminent skill, all those portions of sacred writ which illustrate the nature, excellency, and government of the house of God, with the personal and relative duties of its inhabitants. It was originally published in a pocket volume of sixty-three pages, by G. Larkin, 1688, and is now for the first time reprinted. We are deeply indebted to the unknown owner of this rare volume, and to Mr. Creasy, bookseller, Sleaford, through whom the copy was borrowed to enrich this edition.

What is the church? is a question upon which all the subtilty of jesuitic schoolmen and casuists has been exhausted, to mystify and mislead the honest inquirer in every age. The Jews, Papists, Greeks, English, have each claimed the divine favour as being exclusively limited to their respective sects. Apostolic descent has been considered to depend upon human ceremonies, instead of its consisting in a similarity of mind and conduct to that of the apostles, through the powerful influences of the Holy Spirit upon the heart. Judging from this latter mode, we conclude that Bunyan the brazier was very nearly related to, and descended from, Paul the tentmaker, and the other apostles. But we form a very different judgment as to the descent of Bonner and other persecuting bishops.

A visible church of Christ is a congregation of the faithful, who having personally and individually given themselves to the Saviour, unite together to promote each other's spiritual happiness. Such were the churches to whom the epistles in the New Testament were addressed. The instructions given to this spiritual community, in the following treatise, are drawn solely from the sacred volume, and are full of peace and righteousness—tending purely to its happiness and prosperity. If these directions were strictly and constantly followed, our churches, notwithstanding the liability of the members to err, would each present 'a little heaven below.'

The officers in these communities are—I. Bishops, or preaching elders, to dispense the word and ordinances; a plurality in every church, to supply the services of such as suffered under affliction of body, or were imprisoned for conscience-sake. II. Ruling elders, to assist the preachers—to admit the serious inquirer, or shut out the profane backslider, and to re-admit the penitent—to watch over the members, that they be diligent in their worldly callings, that there be no drones or idlers—to heal offences—to feed the church with admonitions, and to visit and comfort the sick. III. Deacons, to manage the temporal affairs—provide for the Lord's table and for that of the bishops and elders—and to distribute the alms to the infirm and needy. IV. Female deacons, to nurse the sick, and direct their attention to that home where there shall be no more sorrow; and generally to aid the deacons and elders.

The duty of the private members is to walk humbly with God, and to be devoted to each other's happiness. In all these particulars Dr. John Cotton of New England, in his 'True Constitution of a Visible Church,'* fully concurs with Bunyan, as does also Dr. John Owen, in his 'Nature of a Gospel Church,' excepting that he is silent as to female deacons. Let every church be thus affec-

---

* 4to, London, 1642. In the editor's library.

tionately and scripturally governed, and in their works of faith and labours of love they will become terrible to the enemy ' as an army with banners.'*

At the present day, great laxity of discipline

* Cant. vi. 4.

has crept in. Some offices have been discontinued, others altered, and it becomes us most solemnly to judge ourselves by the unerring word of the living God, whether we have deviated from the order recorded by the Holy Ghost, and if so, to repent and return to the scriptural model.—GEO. OFFOR.

A DISCOURSE OF THE BUILDING, &c., OF THE HOUSE OF GOD.

I.

BY WHOM THIS HOUSE IS BUILT.

THE builder's God, [a] materials his Elect ;
His Son's the rock[b] on which it is erect ;
The Scripture is his rule, plummet, or line, [c]
Which gives proportion to this house divine,
His working-tools his ordinances are, [d]
By them he doth his stones and timber square,
Affections knit in love, the couplings are ; [e]
Good doctrine like to mortar doth cement
The whole together, schism to prevent: [f]
His compass, his decree ; [g] his hand's the Spirit
By which he frames, what he means to inherit,
A holy temple, [h] which shall far excel
That very place, where now the angels dwell.

Call this a temple or a house of prayer, [i]
A palace, oracle, or spouse most fair ;
Or what you will : God's love is here displayed,
And here his treasure safely up is laid ; [j]
For his own darling none can find a place,
Where he, as here, is wont to show his face.

What though some slight it, it a cottage call,
Give't the reproachful name of beggar's hall ;
Yea, what though to some it an eyesore is,
What though they count it base, and at it hiss,
Call it an alms-house, builded for the poor;
Yet kings of old have begged at the door.

II.

OF THE BEAUTY OF THE CHURCH.

Lo her foundations laid with sapphires are;
Her goodly windows made of agates fair,
Her gates are carbuncles, or pearls ; nor one
Of all her borders but's a precious stone; [k]
None common, nor o' th' baser sort are here,
Nor rough, but squar'd and polish'd everywhere ;
Her beams are cedars, fir her rafters be,
Her terraces are of the algum-tree ; [l]
The thorn or crab-tree here are not of use ;
Who thinks them here utensils, puts abuse
Upon the place, yea, on the builder too ;
Would they be thus controll'd in what they do?

With carved-work of lily, and palm-tree,
With cherubims and chains adorned be
The doors, the walls, and pillars of this place; [m]
Forbidden beasts here must not show their face.
With grace like gold, as with fine painting, he
Will have this house within enriched be;
Fig-leaves nor rags, must here keep out no cold,
This builder covers all with cloth of gold,
Of needle-work, prick'd more than once or twice
(The oft'ner prick'd, still of the higher price) [n]
Wrought by his SON, put on her by his merit,
Applied by faith, revealed by the Spirit. [o]

III.

OF THE CONVENIENCES OF THIS HOUSE.

Within these walls the builder did devise
That there the householders might sacrifice;
Here is an altar, [p] and a laver too, [q]
And priests abundance, [r] temple work to do;
Nor want they living offerings, nor yet fire,
Nor holy garments ; what divine desire
Commands, it has bestowed on this place ;
Here be the censors, here's the throne of grace ;
None of the householders need go elsewhere,
To offer incense, or good news to hear.

A throne for judgment he did here erect, [s]
Virtue to cherish, folly to detect; [t]
Statutes and laws, unto this house he gave,
To teach who to condemn, and who to save :
By things thus wholesome taught is every brother
To fear his God, and to love one another.

And now for pleasure, solace, recreation,
Here's such as helpeth forward man's salvation.
Equal to these none can be found elsewhere,
All else turn to profuseness, sin, and care.
So situate it is, so roomy, fair,
So warm, so blessed, with such wholesome air,
That 'tis enticing : whoso wishes well
To his soul's health, should covet here to dwell.
Here's necessaries, and what will delight
The godly ear, the palate, with the sight
Of each degree and sex ; here's everything
To please a beggar, and delight a king.

---

a 1 Co. iii. 9.
b Is. viii. 14.
c Ro. xvi. 25.
d Ep. iv. 11, 12, 16.
e Col. ii. 2, 19.
f Le. xiv. 42.
g Ac. xiii. 4, 48.
h Ep. ii. 19—22.
i Mat xxi. 13.
j Ps. xxvii. 4.
k Is. liv. 11, 12.
l 2 Ch. ix 11

m 1 Ki. vi. 35.
n Ps. xlv. 13, 14.
o Ro. i. 17.
p He. xiii. 10, 15.
q Tit. iii. 5.
r 1 Pe. ii. 9.
s Re. xvi. 17.
t 1 Co. vi. 3, 4.

Chambers *u* and galleries,*v* he did invent,
Both for a prospect and a retirement.
For such as unto music do incline,
Here are both harps and psalteries divine : *w*
Her cellars and banqueting-house *x* have been,
In former days, a palace for a queen.
O house! what title to thee can be given,
So fit as that which men do give to heaven!

IV.

OF THE STRENGTH AND DEFENCE OF THIS HOUSE.

This house, you may be sure, will always stand;
She's builded on a rock,*y* not on the sand;
Storms, rain, yea floods have oft upon her beat,
Yet stands she,*z* here's a proof she is no cheat;
Fear not therefore in her for to abide,
She keeps her ground, come weather, wind or tide.
Her corner-stone has many times been try'd,
But never could the scorn, or rage, or pride,
Of all her foes, by what force they could make,
Destroy her battlements, or ground-work shake.*a*
Here's God the Lord encamping round about
His dwelling place; *b* nor ought we once to doubt
But that he as a watchman succour will
Those that do dwell upon his holy hill.*c*
A wall of fire about her I will be,
And glory in the midst of her, and she
Shall be the place where I my name record;
Here I will come and bless you, saith the Lord.

The holy watchers at her gates do stand,
With their destroying weapons in their hand,
Those to defend, that in this house do dwell,
From all her enemies in earth and hell; *d*
Safety! where is it, if it is not here?
God dwelleth in her,*e* doth for her appear,
To help her early, *f* and her foes confound,
And unto her will make his grace abound;
Safety is here, and also that advance, *
Will make a beggar sing, a cripple dance.

V.

THE DELICATENESS OF THE SITUATION OF THIS HOUSE.

As her foundation and her beauty's much;
Conveniences, and her defences such
As none can parallel, so doth the field
About her, richest, rarest dainties yield.
Moriah, where Isaac was offered,
Where David from his sin was ransomed;.
Where Solomon the temple did erect,
Compar'd with this is worthy no respect.
Under the very threshold of this place
Arise those goodly springs of lasting grace,

Whose crystal streams minister life to those
That here of love to her, make their repose.*h*
Sweet is her air, (as one may well infer)
'Cause 'tis the breathings of the comforter.*i*
The pomegranates at all her gates do grow,
Mandrakes and vines, with other dainties mo;†
Her gardens yield the chief, the richest spice,
Surpassing them of Adam's paradise: *j*
Here be sweet ointments, and the best of gums;
Here runs the milk, here drops the honey-combs.
Here are perfumes most pleasant to the sense,
Here grows the goodly trees of frankincense;
Her arbours, walks, fountains, and pleasant springs,
Delightful formerly have been to kings.

Such mountains round about this house do stand
As one from thence may see the holy land.*k*
Her fields are fertile, do abound with corn;
The lilies fair, her vallies do adorn.*l*
The birds that do come hither every spring,
For birds, they are the very best that sing.*m*
Her friends, her neighbours too, do call her blest; *n*
Angels do here go by, turn in and rest.*o*
The road to paradise lies by her gate, *p*
Here pilgrims do themselves accommodate
With bed and board, and do such stories tell
As do for truth and profit all excel.
Nor doth the porter here say any nay,
That hither would turn in, that here would stay.
This house is rent-free; here the man may dwell
That loves his landlord, rules his passions well.

VI.

THE WAY OF RECEIVING THOSE THAT WOULD HERE INHABIT.

And wouldst thou know the customs of this place,
How men are here admitted to this grace;
And consequently whether thou mayst be
Made one of this most blest fraternity?
Come hither then, unto me lend an ear;
And what is doubtful to thee, I will clear.
1. This place, as mercy's arms, stands ope to those
That their own happiness us'd to oppose;
Those under hedges, high-way men,*q* or they
That would not God, nor yet good men obey; *r*
Those that among the bushes us'd to browse,
Or under hedges us'd themselves to louze.
The vilest men, of sinners who are chief,
A fornicator, liar, or a thief,
May turn in hither, here take up and dwell
With those who ransom'd are from death and hell. *s*

2. This place, as hospitals, will entertain,
Those which the lofty of this world disdain: *t*
The poor, the lame, the maimed, halt and blind,*u*
The leprous, and possessed *v* too, may find
Free welcome here, as also such relief
As ease them will of trouble, pain and grief.

---

* 'That advance,' preferment, or progress towards perfection.—ED.

u Ca. i. 4.	*z* Lu. vi. 48.	*d* Re. xxi. 12.
v Ca. vii. 5.	*a* Is. xxviii. 16.	*e* Ps xlviii. 3.
w 2 Ch. ix. 11.	*b* Zec. ii. 5. ix. 8.	*f* Ps. xlvi. 1, 5.
x Ca. ii. 4.	*c* Ex. xx. 24.	*g* Ps. cxiii. 7.
v Mat. xvi. 18.		

† 'Mo,' a usual contraction for more in former times, now obsolete.—ED.

h Eze. xlvii. 1.	*m* Ca. ii. 11, 12.	*r* 2 Ti. i. 15.
i Ca. i. 7, 12, 13.	*n* Ps. xlviii. 2.	*s* 1 Co. vi. 9—11.
j Ca. iv. 12—16.	*o* He. xiii. 2.	*t* Eze. xxxiv. 16.
k Ps. cxxv. 2.	*p* Ge. xxviii. 17.	*u* Lu. xiv. 21.
l Ca. ii. 1.	*q* Lu. xiv. 23.	*v* Mar. xvi. 9.

3. This place, as David's heart, with free consent
Opens to th' distressed, and the discontent; *w*
Who is in debt, that has not wherewithal
To quit his scores, may here be free from thrall: *x*
That man that fears the bailiff, or the jail,
May find one here that will become his bail.

4. Art thou bound over to the great assize,
For heark'ning to the devil and his lies;
Art thou afraid thereat to shew thy head,
For fear thou then be sent unto the dead?
Thou may'st come hither, here is room and place,
For such as willingly would live by grace. *y*

5. This place, as father's house in former days,
Is a receptacle for runaways;*
He that, like to the ox,† backslidden is,
Forfeited hath for sin his share of bliss;
May yet come hither, here is room and rest;
Of old such have come hither and been blest.
　Had this been false, O woe had been to David!
Nor Peter *z* had, nor Magdalen, been saved.
Nor Jonah, *a* nor Manasseh, *b* nor the rest;
No runaway from God could been blest
With kind reception at his hands; return
Would here come too late, if nought but burn
Had been the lot of the backsliding man:
But we are told there's no rebellion can
Prevent, or hinder him from being saved,
That mercy heartily of God hath crav'd. *c*
She that went from her God to play the whore, *d*
Returning may be as she was before:
He that refuses to his God to turn,
That is resolved in hell fire to burn;
If he bethinks himself, and turns again,
May find them here that will him entertain. *e*

6. But bring thou with thee a certificate,
To show thou seest thyself most desolate;
Writ by the master, with repentance seal'd, *f*
To shew also that here thou would'st be heal'd,
By those fair leaves of that most blessed tree,
By which alone poor sinners healed be; *g*
And that thou dost abhor thee for thy ways.
And wouldst in holiness spend all thy days; *h*
And here be entertained; or thou wilt find
To entertain thee here are none inclin'd.‡

---

* Probably referring to the parable of the prodigal son, Lu. xv.—ED.
† This may refer to the Levitical law, Ex. xxi. 28—36. The ox that had gored any one to death, 'shall be surely stoned' without possibility of escape, but the backslider or manslayer, although he lie equally under the sentence of death, yet may escape to the city of refuge.—ED.
‡ These stanzas afford an excellent illustration to the meaning of Bunyan in his Pilgrim's Progress, where Christian, before the cross, receives the roll or certificate—loses it for a season in the arbour on the hill Difficulty, when loitering and sleeping on his way to the Interpreter's house, but regains it by repentance and prayer, and eventually, having crossed the river, gives it in at the gate of the Celestial City, and is admitted.—ED.

w 1 Sa. xxii. 2.　　*a* Jonah i.　　　*e* Ro. x. 21.
x Lu. vii. 41, 42.　*b* 2 Ch. xxxiii.　*f* Ac. ix. 26, 27.
y Ac. xvi. 30—32.　*c* Lu. xv. 1 Sa xii.　*g* Re. xxi. 27.
z Lu. xxii. 61.　　　*d* Je. iii. 1—6.　*h* Re. xxii. 2, 14, 15.

VII.

OF THE GOVERNORS OF THIS HOUSE.

The governors that here in office are,
Such be as service do with love and care;
Not swerving from the rule, nor yet intrude
Upon each other's work, nor are they rude
In managing their own: but to their trust
They labour to be honest, faithful, just.
1. The chief is he who is the Lord of all,
The Saviour; *i* some him physician call.
He's cloth'd in shining raiment to the ground,
A golden girdle doth begirt him round;
His head and hairs are white as any snow,
His eyes are like a flame of fire also;
His feet are like fine brass, as if they burn'd
Within a furnace, or to fire were turn'd;
His voice doth like to many waters sound;
In his right hand, seven glittering stars are found.
Out of his mouth goes a two-edged sword,
Sharper than any ('tis his holy word)
And for his countenance, 'tis as the sun
Which shineth in its strength, till day is done. *j*
His name is call'd holy, The WORD OF GOD; *k*
The wine-press of his father's wrath he trod;
At all the power of sin he doth deride,
The keys of hell and death hang at his side. *l*
　This is our governor, this is the chief,
From this physician comes our soul's relief.
He is the tree of life and hidden manna;
'Tis he to whom the children sing hosanna.
The white stone he doth give with a new name;
In heaven and earth he is of worthy fame.
This man hath death destroy'd and slain the devil,
And doth secure all his from damning evil.
He is the prince of life, the prince of peace;
He doth us from the bonds of death release.
His work is properly his own; nor may,
In what he doth, another say him nay.

'Tis he who pays our hospitalian scores,
He's here to search, supple, and bind up sores;
He is our plaster-maker, he applies
Them to our wounds, *m* he wipes our wetted eyes. *n*
　'Tis he that gives us cups of consolation,
'Tis he renews the hopes of our salvation. *o*
　He'll take our parts, oft times to us unknown,
And make as if our failings were his own;
　He'll plead with God his name and doings too,
And save us will, from those would us undo.

His name is as an ointment poured forth;
'Tis sweet from east to west, from south to north.
　He's white and ruddy; yea of all the chief;
His golden head is rich beyond belief.
　His eyes are like the doves which waters wet,
Well wash'd with milk, and also fitly set,
　His cheeks as beds of spices, and sweet flowers.
He us'd to water with those crystal showers,
　Which often flowed from his cloudy eyes;
Better by far than what comes from the skies.

---

i He. iii. 6.　　　*l* Re. i. 18.　　　*n* Mat. viii. 17.
j Re. i. 12—17.　*m* Lu. x. 33—35.　*o* Lu. xxii. 31, 32.
k Re. xix. 13.

His lips like lilies, drop sweet-smelling myrrh,
Scenting as do those of the comforter.
   His hands are as gold rings set with the beryls;
By them we are delivered out of perils;
   His legs like marble, stand in boots of gold,
His countenance is ex'lent to behold.
   His mouth, it is of all a mouth most sweeet, *p*
O kiss me then, Lord, every time we meet! *q*
Thy sugar'd lips, Lord, let them sweeten mine,
With the most blessed scent of things divine.

2. This is one Governor; and next in place,
One call'd the Ghost, in Honour and in Grace
No whit inferior to him; and HE
Will also in this house our helper be,
He 'twas who did at first brood the creation; *r*
And he's the cause of man's regeneration.
'Tis he by whom the heavens were garnished,
With all their host they then abroad did spread
(Like spangles, pearls, diamonds or richest gems)
Far richer than the fairest diadems. *s*
'Twas he who with his cloven tongues of fire
Made all those wise ones of the world admire,
Who heard his breathing in unlearned men. *t*
O blessed ruler! now the same as then!
His work our mind is to illuminate
With things divine, and to accommodate
Us with those graces, which will us adorn,
And make us look like men indeed new-born. *u*
For our inheritance he makes us meet;
He makes us also in this world discreet.
Prudent and wise in what we take in hand,
To do and suffer at our Lord's command. *v*
   'Tis he that leads us to the tomb and cross,
Where Jesus crucified and buried was;
He shews us also, that he did revive,
And doth assure us that he is alive;
And doth improve the merit of his blood,
At grace's throne for our eternal good.
   Dark riddles he doth here to us unfold,
Yea, makes us things invisible behold. *w*
   He sheds abroad God's love in every heart,
Where he doth dwell, yea to them doth impart,
Such tokens of a future happiness,
That's past the tongue of angels to express. *x*
   'Tis he which helpeth us, *that* to perform,
Whether becalm'd, or whether in a storm,
Which God commands: *y* without him we do nought
That's good, either in deed, or word, or thought. *z*

'Tis he that doth with jewels us bedeck,
'Tis he puts chains of gold about our neck;
'Tis he that doth us with fine linen gird, *a*
That maketh us ofttimes live as a bird.
That cureth us of all our doubts and fears, *b*
Puts bracelets on our hands, rings on our ears;
   He sanctifies our persons, *c* he perfumes
Our spirits also; he our lust consumes; *d*

Our stinking breath he sweetens, so that we
To God and all good men sweet-scented be; *e*
He sets God's mark upon us, and doth seal
Us unto life, and life to us reveal.

VIII.

UNDER OFFICERS.

3. Another sort of officers here are,
But such as must not with these first compare;
They're under-officers, but serviceable,
Not only here to rule, but wait at table.
Those clothed are with linen, fine and white,
They glitter as the stars of darksome night. *f*
They have Saint Peter's keys, *g* and Aaron's rod;
They ope and shut, they bind and loose for God.
   The chief of these are watchmen, they have power
To mount on high and to ascend the tower
Of this brave fabric, and from thence to see
Who keeps their ground, and who the stragglers be.
These have their trumpet, when they do it sound
The mountains echo, yea it shakes the ground.
   With it they also sound out an alarm, *h*
When they perceive the least mischief or harm
Is coming, so they do this house secure
There from, or else prepare it to endure
Most manfully the cross, and so attain
The crown which for the victor doth remain.

   This officer is call'd a steward too, *i*
'Cause with his master's cash he has to do,
And has authority it to disburse
To those that want, or for that treasure thirst. *j*
   The distributor of the word of grace
He is, and at his mouth, when he's in place,
They seek the law, he also bids them do it;
He shews them sin, and learns them to eschew it. *k*
By this example too he shews them how
To keep their garments clean, their knees to bow
Before the king, when he comes into place;
And when they do him supplicate for grace. *l*

Another badge this officer doth wear,
Is that of overseer; because the care
Of the whole house is with him, he's to see
They nothing want, nor yet abused be
By false intruders, doctrines, or (perchance)
By the misplacing of an ordinance.*
These also are to see they wander not
From place or duty, lest they get a blot
To their profession, or bring some disease
Upon the whole, or get a trick to lease,
Or lie unto their God, *m* by doing what
By sacred statutes he commanded not.

---

p Ca. v. 10—16. *u* Ep. i. 18—20. *z* 2 Co. iii. 4.
q Ca. i. 2, 3. *v* Mar. xiii. 11. Jn. xvi. 13. *a* Eze. xvi. 10—14.
r Ge. i. 1, 2. *w* 1 Co. xiv. 2. *b* Ro. xv. 13.
s Job xxvi. 13. *x* Ro. v. 5. *c* 1 Co. vi. 11.
t Ac. ii. 1—4. *y* Ro. viii. 26, 27. *d* Is. iv. 4.

e Col. iv. 6. *h* Eze. xxxiii. 3—6. *k* Lu. xii. 42.
f Re. i. 20. *i* 1 Co. iv. 1. *l* Tit. i. 7.
g Mat. xvi. 19. *j* 1 Pe. iv. 10. *m* Acts xx. 28.

Call them your cooks, they're skill'd in dressing food
To nourish weak, and strong, and cleanse the blood :
They've milk for babes, strong meat for men of age;
Food fit for who are simple, who are sage, *n*
When the great pot goes on, as oft it doth,
They put not coloquintida * in broth, *o*
As do those younglings, fondlings of their skill,
Who make not what's so apt to cure as kill.

They are your sub-physicians, and know
What sickness you are incident unto; *p*
Let them but feel your pulse, and they will tell
You quickly whether you are sick or well.
Have you the staggers ?   They can help you there;
Or if the falling-sickness, or do fear
A lethargy, a fever, or the gout,
God blessing of their skill, you need not doubt
A cure, for long experience has made
These officers the masters of their trade.†
Their physic works by purge *q* and vomit too, *r*
Fear not, nor full nor fasting but 'twill do,
Have but a care, and see you catch no cold,
And with their physic then you may be bold.

You may them Prophets call, for they can tell
Of things to come, yea, here they do excel. *s*
They prophesy of man's future event,
Whether to weal or woe his mind is bent,
Yea, so expert are they in their predictions,
Their arguments so full are of convictions,
That none who hear them, but are forced to say,
Woe unto them who wander from the way. *t*
Art bound for hell against all wind and weather ?
Or art thou one a going backward thither ?
Or dost thou wink, because thou would'st not see ?
Or dost thou sideling go, and would'st not be
Suspected ?   Yet these prophets can thee tell,
Which way thou art a going down to hell. *u*
For him that would eternal life attain,
Yet will not part with all, that life to gain,
But keepeth some thing close, he should forsake,
Or slips the time, in which he should awake ;
Or saith he lets go all, yet keepeth some
Of what will make him lose the world to come. *v*
These prophets can tell such a man his state,
And what at last will surely be his fate.

If thou art one who tradeth in both ways,
God's now, the devil's then; or if delays
Thou mak'st of coming to thy God for life ;
Or if thy light, and lusts are at a strife

About who should be master of thy soul,
And lovest one, the other dost control; *w*
These prophets tell thee can, which way thou bendest,
On which thou frown'st, to which a hand thou lendest.
Art one of those whose fears do go beyond
Their faith? when thou should'st hope, dost thou despond ?
Dost keep thine eye upon what thou hast done,
And yet hast licence to look on the sun ? *x*
Dost thou so covet more, as not to be
Affected with the grace bestowed on thee ?
Art like to him, that needs must step a mile
At every stride, *y* or think it not worth while
To follow Christ ?   These prophets they can tell
To cure this thy disease, and make thee well.

This officer is also call'd a guide,
Nor should the people but keep by his side ;
Or tread his steps in all the paths they walk,
By his example they should do and talk.
He is to be to them instead of eyes,
He must before them go in any wise ;
And he must lead them by the water side,
This is the work of this our Faithful Guide.
Since snares, and traps, and gins are for us set,
Since here's a hole, and there is spread a net,
O let no body at my muse deride,
No man can travel here without a guide. *z*
Here's tempting apples, here are baited hooks,
With turning, twisting, cramping, tangling crooks
Close by the way ; woe then to them betide,
That dare to venture here without a guide. *a*
Here haunt the fairies with their chanting voices;
Fiends like to angels, to bewitch our choices ;
Baits for the flesh lie here on every side :
Who dares set here one foot without a guide ?
Master delusion dwelleth by our walks,
Who with confusion, sings and prays and talks ;
He says the straight path's his, and ours the wide : *b*
What then can we do here without a guide ?
Let God then give our leaders always eyes;
Yea, let him make them holy, bold, and wise ;
And help us fast by them for to abide,
And suffer not the blind to be our guide.‡

4. Here are of rulers, yet another sort,
Such as direct our manners to comport
With our professed faith, that we to view,
May let beholders know that we are *new.* *c*
These are our conversations to inspect,
And us in our employments to direct,
That we in faith and love do every thing,
That reacheth from the peasant to the king. *d*

---

* It is a rare thing for Bunyan to use a foreign word; but all pious persons in his time were familiar with, and generally used, the Puritan or Genevan Bible, vulgarly called the Breeches Bible, an extremely valuable book; in the marginal notes of which, on this passage, is the following explanation, ' "wilde gourdes," which the apoticaries call colloquintida, and is most vehement and dangerous in purging.'—ED.

† The university or college in which Bunyan so highly graduated, is the only one where ministers can be instructed in this spiritual physic. It is Christ's college or school, neither at Oxford or Cambridge, but in the Bible.   There, and there *only*, under the teaching of the Holy Spirit, can the Christian bishop or under shepherd receive instruction in the precious remedies against Satan's devices, or in specifics to cure spiritual maladies.—ED.

‡ 'He had in his pocket A MAP of all ways leading to or from the celestial city; wherefore he struck a light, for he never went without his tinder box, and took a view of his book or map; which bid him be careful, in that place, to turn to the right hand way.   And had he not here been careful to look in his map, they had, in all probability, been smothered in the mud; for just before them, and-that in the cleanest way, was a pit, and none knows how deep, full of nothing but mud, there made on purpose to destroy pilgrims in.   Then thought I with myself, who that goeth on pilgrimage, but would have one of these maps about him, that he may look when he is at a stand which is the way he must take.'—*Pilgrim's Progress, Part Second.*

n Luke xii. 42.   *q* He. ix. 14.   *t* 1 Co. xiv. 31.
o 2 Ki. iv. 38—40.   *r* 2 Pe. ii. 22.   *u* Ac. viii. 20—22.
p Mat. x. 8.   *s* Ac. xv. 32.   *v* 2 Ti. iii. 6.

w Tit. i. 16.   *z* Lu. i. 79   *c* Ro. xii. 8.
x Lu. xxii. 32.   *a* Ps. lxxviii. 72.   *d* 1 Co. xii. 28.
y Ca. i. 4.   *b* Mat. xxiii. 16, 24.

That there may be no scandal in our ways,
Nor yet in our profession all our days.*e*
These should after our busy-bodies look,
Tale-bearers also, they have undertook
To keep in order, also they must see
None that can work among us idle be;
Jars, discords, frauds, with grievances and wrongs,
These they're to regulate; to them belongs
The judgment of all matters of this kind,*f*
And happy is the house thus disciplined.*g*

5. Another sort of officers we have,
Deacons we call them 'cause their work's to save
And distribute those crumbs of charity
Unto the poor, for their subsistency,
That contributed is for their relief,
Which of their bus'ness is indeed the chief.*h*
These must be grave, not of a double tongue,
Not given to wine, not apt to do a wrong
Unto the poor, through love to lucre.   (Just
In this their office, faithful to their trust)*i*
The wife must answer here as face doth face;
The husband's fitness to his work and place,
That ground of scandal or of jealousy
Obstructs not proof that he most zealously
Performs his office well, for then shall he
Be bold in faith, and get a good degree
Of credit with the church; yea what is more,
He shall possess the blessings of the poor.

His wisdom teach him will, to find out who
Is poor of idleness, and who comes to
A low estate by sickness, age, or 'cause
The want of limbs, or sight, or work it was
That brought them to it; or such destiny
As sometimes maketh low, who once were high.

They must remember too, that some there are
Who halt before they're lame, while others care
Not to make known their wants, they'll rather die,
Than charge the churches with their poverty.
This done, they must bestow as they see cause;
Making the word the rule, and want the laws
By which they act, and then they need not pause.*j*

The table of the Lord, he also must
Provide for, 'tis his duty and his trust.*k*
The teacher too should have his table spread
By him; thus should his house be clad and fed;
Thus he serves tables with the church's stock,
And so becomes a blessing to the flock.*

I read of widows also that should be
Employed here for further decency;
I dare not say they are in office, though
A service here they are appointed to:

They must be very aged,*l* trusty, meek,
Such who have done much good, that do not seek
Themselves; they must be humble, pitiful,
Or they will make their service void and null.
These are to teach the younger women what
Is proper to their sex and state, what not:
To be discreet, keepers at home, and chaste;
To love their husbands, to be good; shamefac'd:*m*
Children to bear, to love them, and to fly
What to the gospel would be infamy.
I think these to the sick should look also,
A work unfit for younger ones to do.
Wherefore he saith, The younger ones refuse;
Perhaps because their weakness would abuse
Them, and subject them unto great disgrace,*n*
When such a one as Amnon is in place.*o*
And since the good old woman this must do
'Tis fit she should be fed and clothed too,
Out of the deacon's purse, let it so be;
*And let this be her service constantly.*p* †

IX.

THE ORDER AND MANNER OF THE GOVERNMENT HERE.

As I have shew'd you who in office are,
So I will tell you how, and with what care
Those here intrusted with the government,
Keep to the statutes made to that intent.
By rules divine this house is governed;*q*
Not sanguinary ones, nor taught nor fed
By human precepts:*r* for the scripture saith,
The word's our ghostly food; food for our faith.
Nor are all forced to the same degree
In things divine, tho' all exhorted be
To the most absolute proficiency
That law or duty can to them descry.*s*

Alas! here's children, here are great with young;
Here are the sick and weak, as well as strong.
Here are the cedar, shrub, and bruised reed;*u*
Yea, here are such who wounded are, and bleed.
As here are some who in their grammar be,*v*
So here are others in their A, B, C.
Some apt to teach, and others hard to learn;
Some see far off, others can scarce discern
That which is set before them in the glass;
Others forgetful are, and so let pass,
Or slip out of their mind what they did hear *w*
But now; so great our differences appear

---

* These hints to deacons are invaluable. They must have been the result of long intimacy and enlightened watchfulness over the conduct of the poor. To distinguish between the noisy beggar and the unobtrusive sufferer—to administer relief in just proportions, 'the *word* the rule, and *want* the law,' in spite of all that influence which is constantly brought to bear upon those who distribute any common charity fund. It requires much of the fear of God in the heart, and a solemn sense of responsibility at the great day. The terms, 'crumbs of charity,' are beautifully expressive of the general poverty of Christian churches.—ED.

† Bunyan's idea of this scriptural order of female deacons is very striking, and worthy the solemn consideration of all Christian churches. They are to be chosen from such as are 'widows indeed, who trust in God, and continue in supplications and prayers night and day,' 1 Ti. v. 5. They are to devote themselves to the sick—to be patterns of good works—and, if needful, to be fed and clothed at the expense of the church, ver. 16. If to this were added to examine and educate the children, they might be most eminently useful.—ED.

e 1 Th. v. 12—14.	*h* Ac vi. 1—6.	*j* Ac. vi. 1.
f 1 Co. vi. 4.	*i* 1 Ti. iii. 8.	*k* Ac. vi. 2.
g 1 Ti. v. 17.		

l 1 Ti. v. 9.	*p* 1 Ti. v. 16.	*t* Phi. iii. 17.
m Tit. ii. 3—5.	*q* Mat. xxviii. 18—20.	*u* 1 Jn. ii. 1—6.
n 1 Ti. v. 11.	*r* Lu. ix. 54—56.	*v* Ep. iii. 18, 19.
o 2 Sa. xiii. 6—14.	*s* Col. ii. 20—22.	*w* He. v. 12, 13.

Wherefore our Jacob's must have special care
They drive their flocks, but as their flocks can bear; [z]
For if they be o'erdriven, presently
They will be sick, or cast their young, or die. [y]
The laws therefore are more and less of force,
According as they bring us to the source,
Or head, or fountain, or are more remote
To what at first we should ourselves devote.
Be we then wise in handling of the laws,
Not making a confused noise like daws
In chambers, yea let us seek to excel, [z]
To each man's profit; this is ruling well.[a]
With fundamentals then let us begin,
For they strike at the very root of sin.
So the foundation being strongly laid,
Let us go on, as the wise builder said, [b]
For I don't mean, we should at all disdain
Those that are less, we always should maintain
That due respect to either which is meet;
This is the way to sit at Jesus' feet. [c]

Repent I must, or I am cast away; [d]
Believe I must, or nothing I obey: [e]
Love God I must, or nothing I can do,
That's worth so much as loosing of my shoe.
If I do not, bear after Christ, my cross; [f]
If love to holiness is at a loss;
If I my lusts seek not to mortify; [g]
If to myself, my flesh, I do not die;
What law, should I observe't, can do me good?
In little duties life hath never stood.

One reads, he prays, he catechises too;
But doth he nothing else, what doth he do?
I read to know my duty, [h] I do pray
To God to help me do it day by day; [i]
If this be not my end in what I do,
I am a sot, an hypocrite also. [j]
I am baptiz'd, what then? [k] unless I die
To sin, I cover folly with a lie.
At the Lord's table, I do eat; what though?
There some have eat their own damnation too. [l]

I will suppose, I hear, I sing, I pray,
And that I am baptiz'd without delay,
I will suppose I do much knowledge get,
And will also suppose that I am fit
To be a preacher, yet nought profits me
If to the first, poor I a stranger be: [m]
They are more weighty therefore; in compare
These unto them, but mint and anise are. [n]

Not that I would the least of duty slight,
Because the least command, of divine right,
Requires that I myself subject thereto;
Wilful resisters do themselves undo.
But let's keep order, let the first be first;
Repent, believe, and love; and then I trust

I have that right, which is divine, to all
That is enjoined; be they great or small.
Only I must as cautionary speak,
In one word more, a little to the weak;
Thou must not suffer men so to enclose
Thee in their judgments, as to discompose
Thee in that faith and peace thou hast with him;
This would be like the losing of a limb;
Or like to him who thinks he doth not well,
Unless he lose the kernel for the shell.
Thou art no captive, but a child and free;
Thou wast not made for laws, but laws for thee;
And thou must use them as thy light will bear it;
They that say otherwise, do rend and tear it,
More like to wicked tyrants, who are cruel,
And add unto a little fire, more fuel.
But those who are true shepherds of the sheep,
To quench such burnings would most gladly weep.

But I am yet but upon generals;
Particulars our legislator calls
For at our hands, and that in order to
Consummate what we have begun to do.

1. My brother I must love, in very deed.[o]
I'm taught of God to do it: [p] let me heed
This divine duty, and perform it well,
Who loves his brother, God in him doth dwell; [q]
The argument which on me this imposes,
Smells like to ointment, or the sweetest roses. [r]
Shall God love, shall he keep his faith to me?
And shall not I? shall I unfaithful be?
Shall God love me a sinner? and shall I
Not love a saint? [s] Yea, shall my Jesus die
To reconcile me to my God? and shall
I hate his child, nor hear his wants that call
For my little assisting of him? [t] fie
On such a spirit, on such cruelty; [u]
Fie on the thought that would me alienate,
Or tempt me my worst enemy to hate. [v] *

2. He that dwells here, must also be a sharer
In others' griefs; [w] must be a burden-bearer
Among his brethren, or he cannot do
That which the blessed gospel calls him to. [x]
In order hereunto, humility
Must be put on, it is our livery,
We must be clothed with it, if we will
The law obey, our master's mind fulfil. [y]
If this be so, then what should they do here,
Who in their antic pranks of pride appear?
Let lofty men among you bear no sway,
The Lord beholds the proud man far away. [z]
It is not fit that he inhabit there
Where humbleness of mind should have the chair.
Can pride be where a soul for mercy craves? [a]
Shall pride be found among redeemed slaves? [b]

---

* These instructions are like 'apples of gold in pictures of silver.' Thrice happy are those churches whose members act in conformity with these scriptural rules. But is there a member who dares to violate them? Poor wretched creature, the Lord have mercy on thee.—ED.

[z] Is. xl. 11.
[y] Ge. xxxiii. 13.
[z] 1 Co. xiv. 12.
[a] 1 Co. xiv. 26.
[b] He. vi. 1—3.
[c] Mat. xxviii. 19, 20.

[d] Lu. xiii. 1—3.
[e] Mar. xvi. 16.
[f] Lu. xiv. 27.
[g] He. xii. 14.
[h] Jn. v. 39.
[i] Lu. xx. 47.

[j] Mat. vi. 5.
[k] Ac. viii. 13, 23
[l] 1 Co. xi. 29.
[m] 1 Co. xiii. 1—4.
[n] Mat. xxiii. 23.

[o] Jn. xv. 17.
[p] 1 Th. iv. 9.
[q] 1 Jn. iv. 16.
[r] Ps. cxxxiii.
[s] Jn. xv. 17.
[t] 1 Th. iv. 9. 1 Jn. iv. 16. Ps. cxxxiii.
[u] 1 Jn. iv. 20, 21.
[v] Mat. v. 43—48.
[w] Ro. xii. 15.

[x] Ga. vi. 2.
[y] 1 Pe. v. 5.
[z] Ps. cxxxviii. 6.
[a] Lu. xviii. 13.
[b] Is. xlv. 14.

Shall he who mercy from the gallows brought,
Look high, or strut, or entertain a thought
That tends to tempt him to forget that fate,
To which for sin he destin'd was of late,
And could not then at all delivered be,
But by another's death and misery ? [c]
Pride is the unbecoming'st thing of all:
Besides, 'tis the forerunner of a fall.
He that is proud, soon in the dirt will lie,[d]
But honour followeth humility.
Let each then count his brother as his better,
Let each esteem himself another's debtor.
Christ bids us learn of him, humble to be,
Profession's beauty is humility. [e]

3. Forgive, is here another statute law;[f]
To be revenged is not worth a straw,
He that forgives shall also be forgiven,
Who doth not so, *must lose his part in heaven;* [g]
Nor must thou weary of this duty be
'Cause God's not weary of forgiving thee. [h]

Thou livest by forgiveness;[i] should a stop
Be put thereto *one moment,* thou wouldst drop
Into the mouth of hell. Then let this move
Thee thy dear brother to forgive in love.[j]

And we are bid in our forgivenesses
To do as God doth in forgiving his.[k]
  If any have a quarrel against any,
(As quarrels we have oft against a many)
Why then, as God, for Christ's sake, pardons you,
For Christ's sake, pardon thou thy brother too.[l]
We say, What freely comes, doth freely go;
Then let all our forgivenesses be so.
I'm sure God heartily forgiveth thee,[m]
My loving brother, prithee forgive me;
  But then in thy forgiveness be upright;
Do't with thine heart, or thou'rt an hypocrite.[n]

4. As we forgive, so we must watch and pray;[o]
For enemies we have, that night and day,
Should we not watch, would soon our graces spoil,
Should we not pray, would our poor souls defile.
  Without a watch, resist a foe who can?
Who prays not, is not like to play the man?[p]
Complain that he is overcome, he may;
But who would win the field, must watch and pray.
Who watches, should know who and who's together:
Know we not friends from foes, how know we whether
Of them to fight, or which to entertain?[q]
Some have instead of foes,[r] *familiars slain.*
Sometimes a lust will get into the place,
Or work, or office, of some worthy grace;
Till it has brought our souls to great decay.[s]
Unless we diligently watch and pray,
Our pride will our humility precede:
By th' nose, our unbelief our faith will lead.[t]

Self-love will be where self-denial should;
And passion heat, what patience sometime cool'd.
And thus it will be with us night and day, [u]
Unless we diligently watch and pray.[v]

Besides what these domestics do, there are
Abroad such foes as wait us to ensnare;
Yea, they against us stand in battle-'ray,
And will us spoil, unless we *watch and pray.*
There is the world with all its vanities, [w]
There is the devil with a thousand lies;[x]
There are false brethren with their fair collusions,[y]
Also false doctrines with their strong delusions;
These will us take, yea carry us away
From what is good, unless we *watch and pray.*
Long life to many, is a fearful snare;
Of sudden death we also need beware;
The smiles and frowns of men, temptations be;
And there's a bait in all we hear and see.
Let them who can, to any shew a way,
How they should live, that cannot watch and pray.

Nor is't enough to keep all well within,
Nor yet to keep all out that would be sin,
If entertained; I must myself concern
With my dear brother, as I do discern
Him tempted, or a wand'ring from the way;[z]
Else as I should, I do not watch and pray.
Pray then, and watch, be thou no drowsy sleeper,
Grudge, nor refuse, to be thy brother's keeper,[a]
Seest thou thy brother's graces at an ebb?
Is his heel taken in the spider's web?
Pray for thy brother;[b] if that will not do,
To him, and warn him of the present woe
That is upon him; if he shall thee hear
Thou wilt a saviour unto him appear.[c] *

5. Sincerity, to that we are enjoined,
For I do in our blessed law-book find,[d]
That duties, how well done soe'er they seem,
With our great God, are but of small esteem
If not sincerely done; then have a care
For hypocrites are hateful everywhere.[e]
  Things we may do, yea, and may let men see
Us do them too, design but honestly;
Vain-gloriously let us not seek for praise,
Vain-glory's nothing worth in gospel days.[f]
  Sincerity seeks not an open place,
To do, tho' it does all with open face;
It loves no guises, nor disfigurations.
'Tis plain, 'tis simple, hates equivocations.[g]
  Sincerity's that grace by which we poise,
And keep our duties even: nor but toys
Are all we do, if no sincerity[h]
Attend our works, lift it up ne'er so high.

* Happy is that Christian, who, in obedience to his Lord's command, is so humble as to *seek* out the brother who has offended him; 'Go and tell him his fault *between thee and him alone,*' is the divine command. Is it not at the peril of our souls wilfully to violate this self-humiliating but imperative law?—ED.

c Is. liii. 5.
d Pr. xvi. 18.
e Mat. xi. 29.
f Ep. iv. 32.
g Mat. xviii. 34, 35; vi. 15.
h Mat. xviii. 22.
VOL. II.

i Ep. iv. 32.
j Mat. xviii. 34, 35; vi. 15; xviii. 22.
k Mat. xviii. 32, 33.
l 2 Co. ii. 10.
m Je. xxxii. 41.
n Mat. xviii. 35.

o Mat. xxvi. 41.
p 1 Co. xvi. 13.
q Ep. vi. 13—18.
r 1 Pe. v. 8, 9.
s He. xii. 15.
t Lu. xxi. 34, 35. He. iii. 12, 13.

u Ac. xx. 30, 31.
v 1 Th. v. 6. 2 Ti. iv. 5. 1 Pe. iv. 7
w Lu. viii. 14.
x 1 Pe. v. 8.
y Ac. xx. 30. 31.

z He. xii. 15.
a Ge. iv. 9.
b 1 Th. v. 14.
c Ja. v. 20. Mat. xviii. 15.
d Jos. xxiv. 14.

e Mat. xxiii.
f 2 Co. i. 12.
g 2 Co. ii. 17.
h 2 Co. viii. 8. 1 Pe. n. 1, 2. Phi. i. 10.

4 E

Sincerity makes heav'n upon us smile,
Lo, here's a man in whom there is no guile!
Nathaniel, an Israelite indeed! [i]
With duties he sincerely doth proceed;
Under the fig-tree heav'n saw him at prayer,
There is but few do their devotions there.
   Sincerity! Grace is thereto entailed, [j]
The man that was sincere, God never fail'd.
One tear that falleth from sincerity,
Is worth ten thousand from hypocrisy.

6. Meekness is also here imposed by law,
A froward spirit is not worth a straw. [k]
A froward spirit is a bane to rest,
They find it so, who lodge it in their breast. [l]
   A froward spirit suits with self-denial,
With taking up the cross, and ev'ry trial,
As cats and dogs, together by the ears;
As scornful men do suit with *frumps and jeers. [m]
   Meek as a lamb, mute as a fish, is brave,
When anger boils, and passions vent do crave.
   The meek, God will in paths of judgment guide; [n]
Good shall the meek eat, and be satisfied; [o]
The Lord will lift the meek to highest station; [p]
Will beautify the meek with his salvation. [q]
The meek are blest, the earth they shall inherit: [r]
The meek is better than the proud in spirit. [s]
   Meekness will make you quiet, hardy, strong,
To bear a burden, and to put up wrong.
   Meekness, though divers troubles you are in,
Will bridle passion, be a curb to sin.
Thus God sets forth the meek before our eyes;
A meek and quiet spirit God doth prize. [t]

7. Temp'rance also, is on this house imposed, [u]
And whoso has it not, is greatly nosed†
By standers by, for greedy, lustful men:
Nor can all we can say, excuse us, when
Intemp'rance any where to them shall be
Apparent; though we other vices flee. [v]
   Temperance, the mother is of moderation,
The beauty also of our conversation. [w]
   Temperance will our affections moderate,
And keep us from being inordinate
In our embraces, or in our salutes
Of what we have, also in our pursuits
Of more, and in a sedate settlement
Of mind, will make's in all states be content. [x]
Nor want we here an argument to prove
That who, inordinate is, in his love
Of worldly things, doth better things defy,
And slight salvation for the butterfly. [y]

What argument can any man produce,
Why we should be intemperate in the use

Of any worldly good? Do we not see
That all these things from us a fleeting be? [z]
What can we hold? What can we keep from flying
From us? Is not each thing we have a dying? [a]
   My house, my wife, my child, they all grow old,
Nor am I e'er the younger for my gold;
Here's none abiding, all things fade away, [b]
Poor I at best am but a clod of clay. [c]

If that be true, man doth not live by bread,
He that has nothing else, must needs be dead; [d]
Take bread for what can in this world be found,
Yet all that therein is, is but a sound,
An empty sound, there is no life at all,
It cannot save a sparrow from her fall.
Let us then use this world as we are bid,
And as in olden times, the godly did.
   Who buy, should be as if they did possess
None of their purchase, or themselves did bless
In what they have; and he that doth rejoice
In what he hath, should rather out of choice,
Withdraw his mind from what he hath below,
And set his heart on whither he must go. [e]
   For those that weep under their heavy crosses,
Or that are broken with the sense of losses,
Let them remember, all things here are fading,
And as to nature, of a self-degrading
And wasting temper; yea, both we and they
Shall waste, and waste, until we waste away. [f]
Let temperance then, with moderation be
As bounds to our affections, when we see,
Or feel, or taste, or any ways enjoy
Things pleasing to the flesh, lest we destroy
Ourselves therewith, or bring ourselves thereby
To surfeits, guilt, or Satan's slavery. [g]

8. Patience, another duty, as we find
In holy writ, is on this house enjoined; [h]
Her state, while here, is such, that she must have
This grace abounding in her, or a slave
She'll quickly be unto their lusts and will,
That seek the mind of Satan to fulfil.
   He who must bear all wrongs without resistance,
And that with gladness too, must have assistance
Continually from patience, thereunto,
Or he will find such work too hard to do. [i] [squibs,
   Who meets with taunts, with mocks, with flouts and
With raileries, reproaches, checks, and snibs; [j]
Yea, he who for well-doing is abused,
Robb'd, spoiled, and goal'd, and ev'ry way misused;
Has he not patience soon will be offended,
Yea his profession too will soon be ended. [k]
   A Christian for religion must not fight,
But put up wrongs, though he be in the right; [l]
He must be merciful, loving, and meek, [m]
When they smite one, must turn the other cheek. [n]
He must not render railing for reviling
Nor murmur when he sees himself a spoiling, [o]

---

* To 'frump,' to mock or browbeat.—ED.
† 'Greatly nosed,' taken by the nose, ridiculed.—ED.

Jn. i. 47—49.
[j] Ep. vi. 24.
[k] Job v. 13.
[l] Pr. ii. 12; xvi. 28; xvii. 20.
[m] Pr. xxii. 5.

[n] Col. iii. 12. Ps. xxv. 9. Ep. iv. 2.
[o] Ps. xxii. 26.
[p] 1 Ti. vi. 11. Ps. cxlvii. 6.
[q] Ps. cxlix. 4.
[r] Ps. xxxvii. 11.

[s] Is. xxix. 19. Tit. iii. 2.
[t] 1 Pe. iii. 4.
[u] 2 Pe. i. 6.
[v] Phi. iii. 18, 19.
[w] 1 Co. ix. 25.
[x] Phi. iv. 11—13.
[y] Pr. xxiii. 5.

[z] Is. xxviii. 1, 4.
[a] Ja. i. 11.
[b] 1 Jn. ii. 17.
[c] Ge. xviii. 27.
[d] De. viii. 3.
[e] 1 Co. vii. 29—31. Col. iii. 1, 2.

[f] Ge. iii. 19.
[g] Lu. xxi. 34.
[h] Ja. v. 7, 8.
[i] Ro. xii. 12.
[j] He. vi. 15.
[k] Re. xiii. 10; xiv. 12. Mat. xiii. 21.

[l] 2 Co. vi. 4—8.
[m] 1 Co. iv. 12, 13.
[n] Mat. v. 38—41.
[o] 1 Pe. iii. 8, 9. Jn. xviii. 10, 11.

When they shall curse, he must be sure to bless,
And thus with patience must his soul possess.

I doubt our frampered* Christians will not down
With what I say, yet I dare pawn my gown,
Do but compare my notes with sacred story,
And you will find patience the way to glory. *p*

Patience under the cross, a duty is, *q*
Whoso possesses it, belongs to bliss ; *r*
If it its present work accomplisheth ;
If it holds out, and still abideth with
The Truth ; then may we look for that reward, *s*
Promised at the coming of the Lord.

9. To entertain good men let's not forget
Some by so doing have had benefit ;
Yea for to recompense this act of theirs,
Angels have lodged with them unawares. *t*
Yea to encourage such a work as this,
The Lord himself makes it a note of his,
When hungry or when thirsty I have been,
Or when a stranger, you did take me in. *u*
Strangers should not to strangers but be kind
Specially if conferring notes, they find
Themselves, though strangers here, one brotherhood,
And heirs, joint heirs, of everlasting good ;
These should as mother's sons, when they do meet
In a strange country, one another greet
With welcome ; come in, brother, how dost do ?
Whither art wand'ring ? Prithee let me know
Thy state ? Dost want or meat, or drink, or cloth ?
Art weary ? Let me wash thy feet, I'm loth
Thou shouldst depart, abide with me all night ;
Pursue thy journey with the morning light. *v*

X.

THE WAY OF REDUCING WHAT'S AMISS, INTO ORDER HERE.

Although this house thus honourable is,
Yet 'tis not sinless, many things amiss
Do happen here, wherefore them to redress,
We must keep to our rules of righteousness ;
Nor must we think it strange, if sin shall be
Where virtue is ; don't all men plainly see
That in the holy temple there was dust, *w*
That to our very gold, there cleaveth rust ?
In Abraham's family was a derider *x*
I' th' palace of a king will be the spider. *y*
Who saith, we have no sin, doth also say
We have no need at all to watch and pray ;
To live by faith, the flesh to mortify,
Or of more of the spirit to sanctify
Our nature. All this wholly needless is
With him, who as to this, has nought amiss.

But we confess, 'cause we would not be liars, *z*
That we still feel the motions and desires
Of sin within us, and should fall away, *a*
Did not Christ intercede and for us pray. *b*

We therefore do conclude that sin is here,
But that it may not to our shame appear,
We have our rules, thereby with it to deal,
And plaisters too, our deadly wounds to heal.
And seeing idleness gives great occasions
To th' flesh, to make its rude and bold invasions
Upon good orders, 'tis ordained we see,
That none dwell here, but such as workers be :
So plain's the law for this, and so complete,
It bids who will not work, forbear to eat ; *c*
Let then each one be diligent to do
What grace or nature doth oblige them to.

Who have no need to work for meat or clothes,
Should work for those that want. Not that the sloth
Of idleness should be encouraged,
But that those, poor indeed, be clad and fed.
Dorcas did thus, and 'tis to sacred story *d*
Committed for her praise and lasting glory.

This house then is no nurse to idleness ;
Fig-trees are here to keep, *e* and vines to dress ;
Here's work for all ; yea, work that must be done ; *f*
Yet work, like that, to playing in the sun ;
The toil's a pleasure, and the labour sweet, *g*
Like that of David's dancing in the street ; *h*
The work is short, the wages are for ever,
The work like me, the wages like the giver

No drone must hide himself under those eaves :
Who sows not, will in harvest reap no sheaves.
The slothful man himself, may plainly see,
That honey's gotten by the working bee.
But here's no work for life, that's freely given ;
Meat, drink, and cloths, and life, we have from heav'n :
Work's here enjoined, 'cause it is a pleasure,
Vice to suppress, and augment heavenly treasure
Moreover, 'tis to shew, if men profess
The faith, and yet abide in idleness,
Their faith is vain, *i* no man can ever prove
He's right, but by the faith that works by love. *j*

If this good counsel is by thee rejected ;
If work and labour is by thee neglected ;
If thou, like David, lollest on thy bed ; *k*
Or art like to a horse, pamper'd and fed
With what will fire thy lusts, *l* and so lay snares
For thine own soul, when thou shalt be i' th' wars :
Then take what follows, *sin must be detected,*
And thou without repentance quite rejected. *m*

This is the house of God, *n* his dwelling-place,
'Tis here that we behold his lovely face ;
But if it should polluted be with sin,
And so abide, he quickly will begin
To leave it desolate, and then woe to it,
Sin and his absence quickly will undo it. *o*

And since sin is, of things the worst of all,
And watcheth like a serpent on a wall,

---

* 'Frampered' or frampold, peevish, crossgrained, rugged; now obsolete.—Ed.

p He. vi. 15.
q Lu. xxi. 19.
r Ja. i. 3, 4.
s Ja. v. 7—9.
t He. xiii. 1, 2.

u Mat. xxv. 35—40.
v Ju. xix. 16—21
w 2 Ch. xxix. 16, 17.
x Ge. xxi. 9.

y Pr. xxx. 28.
z 1 Jn. i. 8, 10.
a Lu. xxi. 34—36.
b He. vii. 25.

c 2 Th. iii. 10.
d Ac. ix. 36—39.
e Pr. xxvii. 18.
f Mar. xiii. 34.
g 1 Jn. v. 3.

h 2 Sa. vi. 14.
i Ja. ii. 20.
j Ga. v. 6.
k 2 Sa. xi. 1—5.

l Je. v. 8; xiii. 27.
m Lu. xiii. 1—3.
n 1 Co. iii. 16, 17.
o Je. vii. 11—15.

Or flyeth like an eagle in the air,
Or runs as desperate ships, void of all care,
Or, (as great Solomon hath wisely said)
Is as the way of wantons with a maid,
Who tick, and toy, and with a tempting giggle
Provoke to lust, and by degrees, so wriggle
Them into their affections, that they go
The way to death, so do themselves undo:

As it is said, this mischief to prevent,
Let all men watch, yea, and be diligent
Observers of its motions, and then fly,
This is the way to live, and not to die.

☞ He that would never fall, must never slip,
Who would obey the call, must fear the whip.

God would also that every stander by
That in the grass doth see the adder lie,
Should cry as he did, death is in the pot,
That many by its poison perish not.

But if that beastly thing shall hold its hold,
And make the man possessed basely bold
In pleading for it, or shall it deny,
Or it shall seek to cover with a lie;
Then take more aid, and make a fresh assault
At it again, diminish not the fault,
But charge it home. If yet he will not fear,
But still unto his wickedness adhere,
Then tell the house thereof. But if he still
Persist in his abomination will,
Then fly him, 'cause he is a leprous man,
Count him with heathens and the publican. [p]
But if he falls before thee at the first,
Then be thou to him faithful, loving, just,
Forgive his sin, tell it not to a brother, [q]
Lest thou thyself be served so by another. [r]

If he falls not, but in the second charge,
Spread not his wickedness abroad at large. [s]
But, if thou think his sorrow to be sound,
Forgive his sin, and hide it under ground. [t]
If he shall stand the first and second shot;
If he before the church, repenteth not,
Deal with him as the matter shall require,
Let not the house for him be set on fire.
If after all, he shall repent and turn
To God, and you, you must not let him burn
For ever under sense of sin and shame,
You must his sin forgive in Christ his name. [u]

Confirm your love to him in Christ, you must,
By all such ways as honest are, and just.
Shy be not of him, carry't not aloof,
But rather give him of your love such proof,
That he may gather thence, ye do believe
To mercy Christ again doth him receive. [v]

Two things, monish you, as to this, I would;
The first, to shew the church wherein she should
In all her actions so herself behave,
As to convince the faulty, she would save

His soul; and that 'tis for this very thing,
She doth him unto open judgment bring.
Then would I shew the person they reject,
What will, without repentance, be th' effect
Of this tremendous censure, so conclude;
Leaving my judgment to the multitude
Of those who sober and judicious be,
Begging of each of them a prayer for me.

1. This house, in order to this work, must be
Affected with the sin and misery, [w]
Of this poor creature, yea, must mourn and weep,
To think such tares, in your neglect, or sleep,
Should spring up here, nor must they once invent
To think, till he's cast out, you're innocent. [x]

2. Thus leaven, the whole lump has leavened;
Israel was guilty of what Achan did;
And so must stand, until they purged are,
Till Achan doth, for sin, his burden bear. [y]
The reason is, Achan a member was
Of that great body, and by nature's laws,
The hand, foot, eye, tongue, ear, or one of these,
May taint the whole with Achan's foul disease.
The church must too be sensible of this,
Some lep'rous stones make all the house amiss:
And as the stones must thence removed be,
In order to the house's sanctity,
So it must purged be (in any wise)
Before 'tis counted clean (by sacrifice.) [z]

3. Next have a care, lest sin, which you should purge
Becomes not unto you a farther scourge,
The which it will, if such shall judges be,
Which from its spots and freckles are not free;
Pluck thou the beam first out of thine own eye,
Else the condemned will thee vilify [a]
And say, let not the pot the kettle judge; [b]
If otherwise, it will beget a grudge,
A great one 'twixt the church and him that sinned,
Nor by such means, can ever such be winned
To a renew'd embrace of holiness;
More like be tempted further to transgress.

4. Again, let those that loud against it cry,
See they don't entertain it inwardly;
Sin, like to pitch, will to the fingers cleave,
Look to it then, let none himself deceive; [c]
'Tis catching; make resistances afresh,
Abhor the garment spotted by the flesh. [d]
☞ *Some at the dimness of the candle puff,*
Who yet can daub their fingers with the snuff.

5. Beware, likewise, lest rancour should appear
Against the person, do in all things fear:
Bewail the man, while you abhor his sin;
Pity his soul; [e] the flesh you still are in;
Thyself consider thou may'st tempted be, [f]
Hast thou no pity, who will pity thee? [g]

p Mat. xviii. 15—17.   s Ja. v. 20.   u 2 Co. ii. 6.
q Pr. xxv. 9.   t 1 Pe. iv. 8.   v 2 Co. ii. 8—10.
r Mar. iv. 24.

w 1 Co. v. 2.   z Le. xiv. 33—57.   d Jude 23.
x 1 Co. v. 6, 7.   a Mat. vii. 3, 4.   e Jude 20, 23.
y Jos. vii. 10—13.   b Jn. viii. 7.   f Ga. vi. 1.
  xxii. 20.   c Jos. xxii. 17.   g Ja. ii. 13.

6. See that the ground be good on which you go:
Sin, but not virtue show dislike unto.
Take heed of hypocritical intentions,
And quarrel not at various apprehensions
About some smaller matter, lest it breed
Needless debates, and lest that filthy seed
Contention, *h* should o'errun your holy ground, *i*
And lest not love, but nettles there are found. *j*

7. You must likewise allow each man his grains,
For that none perfect are, sin yet remains,
And human frailties do attend the best;
To bear and forbear here, will tend to rest.
Vain janglings, jars, and strifes will there abound,
Where moles are mountains made, or fault is found,
With every little, trivial, petty thing; *k*
This spirit snib, or 'twill much mischief bring *l*
Into this house, and 'tis for want of love, *m*
'Tis entertain'd: *it is not of the dove.* *n*

8. For those that have private opinions too
We must make room, or shall the church undo: *o*
Provided they be such as don't impair
Faith, holiness, nor with good conscience jar: *p*
Provided also those that hold them shall
Such faith hold to themselves, *q* and not let fall
Their fruitless notions in their brother's way, *r*
Do this, and faith and love will not decay.

9. We must also in these our dealings shew
We put a difference 'twixt those sins that do
Clash with the light of nature, and what we
Perceive against the faith of Christ to be.
Those against nature, nature will detect; *s*
Those against faith, faith from them must direct
The judgment, conscience, understanding too,
Or there will be no cure, whate'er you do.
When men are caught in immoralities,
Nature will start, the conscience will arise
To judgment; *t* and if impudence doth recoil,
Yet guilt, and self-condemnings will embroil
The wretch concerned, *u* in such unquietness
Or shame, as will induce him to confess
His fault, and pardon crave of God and man,
Such men with ease therefore we conquer can.

But 'tis not thus with such as swerve in faith
With them, who, as our wise Apostle saith,
Entangled are at unawares, with those
Cunning to trap, to snare, and to impose
By falsifyings, their prevarications: *v*
No, these are slyly taken from their stations,
Unknown to nature; yea, in judgment they
Think they have well done to forsake the way.
Their understanding, and their judgment too
Doth like, or well approve of what they do.
These are, poor souls, beyond their art and skill,
Ta'en captive by the devil, at his will, *w*

Here therefore you must patience exercise,
And suffer long, ye must not tyrannize
It over such, but must all meekness shew;
Still dropping of good doctrine as the dew, *x*
Against their error; so its churlishness
You conquer will, and may their fault redress. *y*

The reason why we must not exercise
That roughness here, as where conviction lies
In nature, is because those thus ensnared
Want nature's light and help to be repair'd.
A spirit hath them taken, they are gone,
Delusions supernat'ral they're on
The wing of; They are out o' th' reach of man
Nothing but God, and gospel reach them can. *z*
Now since we cannot give these people eyes,
Nor regulate their judgment, wherein lies,
Our work with them, if not, as has been said,
In exercising patience. While display'd
The holy word before their faces is,
By which alone they must see what's amiss
With their poor souls, and so convert again,
To him with whom salvation doth remain.

Obj. But they are turbulent, they would confound
The truth, and all in their perdition drown'd.

Ans. If turbulent and mischievous they are,
Imposing their opinions without care
Who they offend, or do destroy thereby. *a*
Then must the church deal with them presently,
Lest tainted be the whole with their delusion,
And brought into disorder and confusion.

XI.

THE PRESENT CONDITION OF THOSE THUS DEALT WITH.

The man that worthily rejected is,
And cast out of this house, his part in bliss
Is lost for ever, turns he not again,
True faith and holiness to entertain.
Nor is it boot, for who are thus cast out,
Themselves to flatter, or to go about
To shift the censure; nothing here will do,
Except a new conversion thou come to.
He that is bound on earth, is bound in heaven,
Nor is his loosing, but the sin forgiven;
Repentance too, forgiveness must precede,
Or thou must still abide among the dead. *b*

XII.

AN EXPOSTULATION WITH SUCH TO RETURN.

O shame! Is't not a shame for men to be
For sin, spu'd out from good society!
For man enlightened to be so base!
To turn his back upon the God of grace!
For one who for his sins has mourn'd and cry'd,
To slight him, who for sin hath bled and died!
What fool would sell his part in paradise,
That has a soul, and that of such a price?

h 1 Co. i. 11.
i Tit. iii. 9. 1 Co. xi.
  16.
j 1 Ti. vi. 3, 6.
k 1 Ti. i. 6, 20.
l 2 Ti. ii. 16.

m Tit. i. 10.
n Ep. iv. 2. Col. iii. 13.
o Ro. xiv. 13.
p Ro. xiv. 16.
q Ro. xiv. 22.
r 1 Co. viii. 9—13.

s Ex. xxxii. 22—24.
  2 Sa. xii. 7—13.
t Jn. viii. 9.
u Ac. v. 1—5.
v Ep. iv. 14.
w 2 Ti. ii. 23—26.

x 2 Ti. iv. 2.
y Tit. i. 13.

z 1 Ti. i. 19, 20.
a 2 Ti. ii. 16—18.

b Mat. xviii. 15—20,
  28—35.

What parallel can suit with such so well,
As those, for sin cast down from heaven to hell!
    But let me tell thee, here is aggravation;
The angels, though they did fall from their station
Had not the caution thou hast had; they fell; [c]
This thou hast seen, and seeing, didst rebel.
    One would a thought, the noise of this their fall,
A warning; yea, a warning, and a call,
Should unto thee have been, to have a care
Of falling too: [d] O how then didst thou dare,
Since God did not spare them, thus to presume
To tempt him in his wrath, thee to consume.
    Nor did the angels from a Jesus fall,
Redeemed they were not, from a state of thrall;
But thou! as one redeem'd, and that by blood,
Redemption hast despised; and the mud
Or mire of thine own filth again embracest:
A dying bleeding Jesus thou disgracest!
What wilt thou do? see'st not how thou hast trod
Under thy foot, the very Son of God? [e]
O fearful hand of God! And fearful will
Thy doom be, when his wrath thy soul shall kill. [f]

    Yea, with a signal these must hear their sin,
☞ This dirty sow from mire has washed been,
Yet there did wallow, after wash'd she was;
So to procure a lust, obtain'd this loss.
    O shame! is't not a shame for man to be,
So much averse to his felicity,
That none can make him leave to play the fool,
Till to the devil he be put to school, [g]
To learn his own salvation to prize?
O fool! must now the devil make thee wise?
O sot! that will in wickedness remain,
Unless the devil drives thee back again. [h]

    Hast quite forgot how thou wast wont to pray,
And cry out for forgiveness night and day?
Or dost thou count they were but painted fears
Which from thine eyes did squeeze so many tears?
Remember man, thy prayers and tears will cry
Thee down to hell, for thine apostacy.
Who will not have what he has prayed for,
Must die the death, his prayers shall him abhor.
    Hast thou forgotten that most solemn vow
Thou mad'st to God, when thou didst crave he bow
His ear unto thee would, and give thee grace,
And would thee also in his arms embrace?
That vow, I say, whereby thou then didst bind
Thyself to him, that now thy roving mind
Recoil against him should, and fling away
From him, and his commandments disobey. [i]
    What has he done? wherein has he offended?
Thou actest now, as if thou wast intended
To prove him guilty of unrighteousness,
Of breach of promise, or that from distress
He could, or would not save thee, or that thou
Hast found a better good than he; but how

Thou wilt come off, or how thou wilt excuse
Thyself, 'cause thou art gone, and did refuse
To wait upon him, that consider well;
Thou art as yet alive, on this side hell.
    Is't not a shame, a stinking shame to be
Cast forth God's vineyard as a barren tree? [j]
To be thrown o'er the pales, and there to lie,
Or be pick'd up by th' next that passeth by?

Well, thou hast turn'd away, return again;
Bethink thyself, thy foot from sin refrain;
Hark! thou art call'd upon, stop not thine ear:
Return, backsliding children, come, draw near
Unto your God; [k] repent, and he will heal
Your base backslidings, to you will reveal
That grace and peace which with him doth remain,
For them that turn away, and turn again. [l]

    Take with thee words, come to the throne of grace
There supplicate thy God, and seek his face;
Like to the prodigal, confess thy sin,
Tell him where, and how vicious thou hast been.
    ☞ Suppose he shall against thee shut the door,
Knock thou the louder, and cry out the more;
What if he makes thee there to stand a while?
Or makes as if he would not reconcile
To thee again? Yet take thee no denial,
Count all such carriages but as a trial
Whether thou art in earnest in thy suit,
As one truly forlorn and destitute;
But hide thou nought of all that thou hast done,
Open thy bosom, make confession
Of all thy wickedness, tell every whit; [m]
Hast thou a secret sin? don't cover it; [n]
Confess, thyself judge, if thou wouldst not die;
Who doth himself judge, God doth justify. [o]

    To sin, and stand in't, is the highest evil;
This makes a man most like unto the devil;
This bids defiance unto God and grace;
This man resists him spitteth in his face,
Scorns at his justice, mocketh at his power,
Tempts him, provokes him, grieves him every hour:
    When he ariseth, he will recompense
This sturdy rebel for his impenitence:
Be not incorrigible then, come back again,
There's hope, beg mercy while life doth remain.

    Obj. But I fear I am lost and cast away,
Sentence is past, and who reverse it may?

    Ans. The sentence past, admitteth of reprieve;
Yea, of a pardon, canst thou but believe. [p]
TURN AGAIN SINNER, NEVER MAKE A DOUBT,
COME, THE LORD JESUS WILL NOT CAST THEE OUT.

---

c 2 Pe. ii. 4.   f 2 Pe. ii. 20—22.   h 1 Ti. i. 20.
d Jude 6.   g Mat. xviii. 34   i Job xv. 6.
e He. x. 29—31.

j Lu. xiii. 7.   m Jer. iii. 13, 23—25.   o 1 Co. xi. 31, 32.
k Jer. iii. 12—14, 22.   n Ps. xxxii. 5.   p Jn. vi. 37.
l Ho. xiv. 1—4.

JOHN BUNYAN ON THE TERMS

OF

COMMUNION AND FELLOWSHIP OF CHRISTIANS

AT THE TABLE OF THE LORD;

COMPRISING

I. HIS CONFESSION OF FAITH, AND REASON OF HIS PRACTICE ;

II. DIFFERENCES ABOUT WATER BAPTISM NO BAR TO COMMUNION; AND

III. PEACEABLE PRINCIPLES AND TRUE.*

ADVERTISEMENT BY THE EDITOR.

READER, these are extraordinary productions that will well repay an attentive perusal. It is the confession of faith of a Christian who had suffered nearly twelve years' imprisonment, under persecution for conscience sake. Shut up with his Bible, you have here the result of a prayerful study of those holy oracles. It produced a difference in practice from his fellow Christians of ALL denominations, the reasons for which are added to this confession; with a defence of his principles and practice, proving them to be peaceable and true. In all this an unlettered man displays the acumen of a thoroughly educated polemical theologian. The author was driven to these publications to defend himself from the slanders which were showered down upon him, by all parties, for nearly eighteen years, and by the attempts which were made to take away his members, injure the peace of his congregation, and alienate him from the church to which he was tenderly attached. His first inquiry is, Who are to be admitted to the Lord's table; and his reply is, Those whom God has received: they have become his children, and are entitled to sit at their Father's table: such only as have examined themselves, and by their conduct lead the church to hope that they have passed from death unto life. The practice of those who admit ungodly persons because they have submitted to some outward ceremonies, he severely condemns. The mixture of the church and the world he deems to be spiritual adultery, the prolific source of sin, and one of the causes of the deluge. The Lord's table is scripturally fenced around: 'Be ye not unequally yoked together with unbelievers;' 'what communion hath light with darkness; Christ with Belial; the temple of God with idols? be ye separate, touch not the unclean thing, and I will receive you.' 'Receive ye one another, as Christ also received us to the glory of God, not to doubtful disputations.' 'Withdraw from them that walk disorderly, working not; but busy bodies; unless with quietness they work and eat their own bread. If any are proud, doting about questions and strifes of words, evil surmisings, perverse disputings, supposing that *gain is godliness;* from such withdraw.' Bunyan rests all upon the word,—the characters are described who are to be excluded from the Lord's table; but in no instance is it upon record that any one was excluded because he had not been baptized in water. And who will dare to make any addition to holy writ?

The practice of making the mode in which water baptism was administered a term of communion, existed among the Independents long before Bunyan's time. Crosby, in his History of the Baptists, makes some long extracts from a book entitled, 'The sin and danger of admitting Anabaptists to continue in the congregational churches, and the inconsistency of such a practice with the principles of both.' In America, Cotton and the Independents severely persecuted their Baptist brethren, even to deportation. As the Baptists increased in numbers, they refused to admit any to the Lord's table, even to occasional communion, who had not been baptized in water upon a profession of faith: in fact, the difference between those who consider baptism to be a *relative* duty to be performed by parents in having their infants sprinkled, and those who deem it a *personal* duty to be immersed in water, as a public putting on of Christ, is so great, as to require the utmost powers of charity to preserve peace. Thus it was in the primitive churches, where great differences prevailed even as to the duty of preaching the gospel to the Gentiles; the

---

* It is much to be regretted that these books, in common with all Mr. Bunyan's Works, were grossly corrupted in the text in all the editions published since 1737,—' poor peace indeed,' was changed to ' pure peace indeed ;' ' here is Rome enough,' meaning popery enough, was altered to ' here is room enough ;' ' Baptist,' was printed ' Papist,' &c., &c. : all the typographical errors have now been carefully corrected by Bunyan's editions.

keeping of days probably extending to the Jewish sabbath, and to the abstaining from certain meats, with other ordinances of the Jewish law.

Bunyan saw all the difficulties of this question: he was satisfied that baptism is a personal duty, in respect to which every individual must be satisfied in his own mind, and over which no church had any control; and that the only inquiry as to the fitness of a candidate for church fellowship should be, whether the regenerating powers of the Holy Ghost had baptized the spirit of the proposed member into newness of life. This is the only *livery* by which a Christian can be known. Bunyan very justly condemns the idea of water baptism being either the Christian's livery or his marriage to the Saviour.

We do well, in our examinations into this subject, to note carefully the various applications of the word baptize, and not always attach the use of water to the term. There is a being baptized in a cloud, and in the sea, to protect God's Israel from their deadly foes; a baptism in sufferings; a baptism in water unto repentance; a baptism in fire, or the Holy Ghost; a baptism into the doctrine of the Trinity. Mat. xxviii. 19. Bunyan had no doubt upon this subject; he deemed water baptism an important personal duty; and that a death to sin, and resurrection to newness of life—a different tint, or dye, given to the character—was best figured by immersion in water: still he left it to every individual to be satisfied in his own mind as to this outward sign of the invisible grace. 'Strange,' he says, 'take two Christians equal on all points but this; nay, let one go far beyond the other for grace and holiness; yet this circumstance of water shall drown and sweep away all his excellencies; not counting him worthy of that reception that with hand and heart shall be given to a novice in religion, because he consents to water.

For these catholic principles he was most roughly handled. Deune, in a pamphlet in the Editor's possession, called him a devil; and likened him to Timri, who slew his master. The most learned of the Baptist ministers entered upon the controversy. They invited him to a grand religious tournament, where he would have stood one against a legion. A great meeting was appointed, in London, for a public disputation—as was common among the puritans—and in which the poor country mechanic was to be overwhelmed with scholastic learning and violence; but Bunyan wisely avoided a collision which could have answered no valuable purpose, and which bid fair to excite angry feelings. He had appealed to the press as the calmest and best mode of controversy; and to that mode of appeal he adhered. Three learned men undertook the cause against Bunyan: these were, D'Anvers, W. Kiffin, and T. Paul. When these

lettered, able, and distinguished disputants published their joint answer, it contained much scurrilous abuse. Their brother, Bunyan, was in prison, and they visited him with gall and wormwood. He closes his reply with these remarkable words, 'Thine to serve thee, Christians, so long as I can look out at those eyes that have had so much dirt thrown at them by many.'

The late Mr. Robert Hall, in his controversy upon this subject with Mr. Kinghorn, in which—having demolished Kinghorn's castle in a few pages—he, in order to make a book, amused the public by kicking the ruins about, thus adverts to these treatises: 'The most virulent reproaches were cast upon the admirable Bunyan, during his own time, for presuming to break the yoke; and whoever impartially examines the spirit of Mr. Booth's Apology, will perceive that its venerable author regards him, together with his successors, much in the light of rebels and insurgents, or, to use the mildest terms, as contumacious despisers of legitimate authority.'*

We cannot have a more decided proof of Bunyan's great powers, and of his being much in advance of his times, than by the opinions of which he was the Christian pioneer having spread so extensively through the Baptist denomination. In this his predictions were fully verified. It is surprising that pious dissenters should ever have made uniformity in outward ceremonies of more importance than inward holiness, as a term of communion. Such sentiments naturally attach to state churches; and ought to be found only with those bodies which exist merely for political purposes, and for it are rewarded with earthly power, pomp, and wealth. I close these observations by quoting the words of Bunyan's learned antagonists, published within a few years of this controversy, and during his lifetime. His sentiments appear to have had a hallowed effect even upon their minds, and produced an apology for their conduct. It is in the appendix to the Baptist confession of faith, republished in 1677: 'We would not be misconstrued, as if the discharge of our consciences did any way disoblige or alienate our affections or conversations from any others that fear the Lord: earnestly desiring to approve ourselves to be such as follow after peace with holiness. We continue our practice, not out of obstinacy, but we do therein *according to the best of our understandings*, in that method which *we* take to be most agreeable to the scriptures. The christening of infants, we find by church history, to have been a very ancient practice; still we leave every one to give an account of himself to God. And if in any case debates between Christians are not plainly determinable by

---

* Reply to Kinghorn. 1818, p. xii.

the scriptures, we leave it to the second coming of Christ.' In 1689, the year after Bunyan's death, this appendix was omitted from the Baptist confession of faith.

May the time soon arrive when water shall not quench love, but when all the churches militant shall form one army, with one object,—that of extending the Redeemer's kingdom.–GEO. OFFOR.

A CONFESSION OF MY FAITH, AND A REASON OF MY PRACTICE:

OR,

WITH WHO, AND WHO NOT, I CAN HOLD CHURCH FELLOWSHIP, OR THE COMMUNION OF SAINTS.

SHEWING, BY DIVERSE ARGUMENTS, THAT THOUGH I DARE NOT COMMUNICATE WITH THE OPENLY PROFANE, YET I CAN WITH THOSE VISIBLE SAINTS THAT DIFFER ABOUT WATER-BAPTISM. WHEREIN IS ALSO DISCOURSED, WHETHER THAT BE THE ENTERING ORDINANCE INTO FELLOWSHIP, OR NO.

'*I believed, therefore have I spoken.*'—Psal. cxvi. 10.

TO THE READER.

SIR,

I MARVEL not that both you and others do think my long imprisonment strange, (or rather strangely of me for the sake of that) for verily I should also have done it myself, had not the Holy Ghost long since forbidden me. 1 Pe. iv. 12. 1 Jn. iii. 13. Nay, verily, that notwithstanding, had the adversary but fastened the supposition of guilt upon me, my long trials might by this time have put it beyond dispute; for I have not hitherto been so sordid, as to stand to a doctrine right or wrong; much less when so weighty an argument as above eleven years' imprisonment, is continually dogging of me to weigh and pause, and pause again, the grounds and foundation of those principles, for which I thus have suffered; *

* King Charles the 2nd, about a year after this time, pardoned near five hundred Quakers, who had been languishing in prison for not attending the church service. Upon this Mr. Bunyan, and his fellow prisoners at Bedford, petitioned for liberty, and at a court of privy council at Whitehall, the 17th May, 1672, present, the King and twenty-four of his councillors, the following minute was made:—'Whereas, by order of the Board of the 8th instant, the humble petition of John Penn, John Bunyan, John Dunn, Thomas Haynes, Simon Haynes, and George Parr, prisoners in the goale of Bedford, convicted upon several statutes for not conforming to the rights and ceremonyes of the church of England, and for being at unlawful meetings, was referred to the Sheriff of the county of Bedford, who was required to certify this Board whether the said persons were committed for the crimes in the said petition mentioned, AND FOR NO OTHER; which he having accordingly done, by his certificate dated the 11th instant. It was thereupon, this day, ordered by his Matie in council, That the said petition and certificate be (and are herewith) sent to his Matie's Attorney-General, who is authorized, and required, to insert them into the general pardon to be passed for the Quakers.' This fully confirms what Bunyan says as to the cause of his long and dangerous imprisonment. It was for being absent from the state church and worshipping God according to His will, as expressed in the Bible. See Introduction to Pilgrim's Progress, Hansard Knollys edition.

but having not only at my trial asserted them, but also since, even all this tedious tract of time, in cool blood, a thousand times, by the word of God, examined them, and found them good; I cannot, I dare not now revolt or deny the same, on pain of eternal damnation.

And that my principles and practice may be open to the view and judgment of all men, though they stand and fall to none but the word of God alone, I have in this small treatise presented to this generation, 'A Confession of my Faith, and a Reason of my Practice in the Worship of God;' by which, although it be brief, candid Christians may, I hope, without a violation to faith or love, judge [that] I may have the root of the matter found in me.

Neither have I in this relation abusively presented my reader, with other doctrines or practices, than what I held, professed, and preached when apprehended, and cast in prison. Nor did I then or now retain a doctrine besides, or which is not thereon grounded. The subject I should have preached upon, even then when the constable came, was, 'Dost thou believe on the Son of God?' From whence I intended to shew, the absolute need of faith in Jesus Christ; and that it was also a thing of the highest concern for men to inquire into, and to ask their own hearts whether they had it or no.

Faith and holiness are my professed principles, with an endeavour, so far as in me lieth, to be at peace with all men. What shall I say, let mine enemies themselves be judges, if anything in these following doctrines, or if ought that any man hath heard me preach, doth [savour], or hath according to the true intent of my words, savoured either of heresy or rebellion. I say again, let they themselves be judges, if ought they find in my writing or preaching, doth render me worthy of almost twelve years' imprisonment, or one that deserveth to be hanged, or banished for ever, according to their tremendous sentence. Indeed my principles are such, as lead me to a denial to communicate in the things of the kingdom of Christ, with the ungodly and openly profane; neither can I in or by the superstitious inventions of this world, consent that my soul should be governed in any of my approaches to God, because commanded to the contrary, and commended for so refusing. Wherefore excepting this one thing, for which I ought not to be rebuked; I shall, I trust, in despite of slander and falsehood, discover myself at all times a peaceable and an obedient subject. But if nothing will do, unless I make of my conscience a continual butchery, and slaughter-shop, unless putting out my own eyes, I commit me to the blind to lead me, as I doubt is desired by some, I have determined, the Almighty God being my help and shield, yet to suffer, if frail life might continue so long, even till the moss shall grow on mine eyebrows, rather than thus to violate my faith and principles. 'Will a man leave the snow of Lebanon, *which cometh* from the rock of the field.? *or* shall the cold flowing waters that come from another place be forsaken?' Je. xviii. 14. 'Hath a nation changed *their* gods, which *are* yet no gods?' Je. ii. 11. 'For all people will walk every one in the name of his god, and we will walk in the name of the LORD our God for ever and ever.' Mi. iv. 5.

Touching my practice as to communion with visible saints, although not baptized with water; I say it is my present judgment so to do, and am willing to render a farther reason thereof, shall I see the leading hand of God thereto.

Thine in bonds for the gospel,

JOHN BUNYAN.

A CONFESSION OF MY FAITH, AND A REASON OF MY PRACTICE, ETC.

'Be *ready always to* give *an answer to every man that asketh you a reason of the hope that is in you with meekness and fear: having a good conscience; that whereas they speak evil of you, as of evil-doers, they may be ashamed that falsely accuse your good conversation in Christ.*']—1 Pet. iii. 15, 16.

1. I BELIEVE, that there is but one only true God, and there is none other but he. 'To us *there is but* one God, the Father, of whom *are* all things.' 1 Co. viii. 6. 'And this is life eternal, that they might know thee the only true God.' &c. Jn. xvii. 3. [see also] Mar. xii. 32. and Ac. xvii. 24.

2. I believe, that this God is almighty, eternal, invisible, incomprehensible, &c. 'I *am* the Almighty God; walk before me, and be thou perfect.' Ge. xvii. 1. 'The eternal God *is thy* refuge.' De. xxxiii. 27. 'Now unto the King eternal, immortal, invisible, the only wise God, *be* honour and glory for ever and ever. 1 Ti. i. 17. [see also] Job xi. 7. and Ro. xi. 33.

3. I believe, that this God is unspeakably perfect in all his attributes of power, wisdom, justice, truth, holiness, mercy, love, &c. his power is said to be *eternal*, Ro. i. 20. his understanding and wisdom *infinite*; Ps. cxlvii. 5. he is called the *just Lord* in opposition to all things. Zep. iii. 5. He is said to be truth itself and the God thereof. 2 Th. ii. 10. De. xxxii. 4. There is none holy as the Lord. 'God is love.' 'Canst thou by searching find out God? canst thou find out the Almighty unto perfection?' Job xi. 7.

4. I believe, that in the Godhead, there are *three persons* or subsistances. 'There are three that bear record in heaven: the Father, the Word, and the Holy Ghost.' 1 Jn. v. 7. [see also] Ge. i. 26. ch. iii. 22. ch. xi. 7. and Is. vi. 8.

5. I believe, that these three are in nature, essence, and eternity, equally one. 'These three are one.' 1 Jn. v. 7.

6. I believe, [that] there is 'a world to come.' He. ii. 5. ch. vi. 5.

7. I believe, that there shall be 'a resurrection of the dead, both of the just and unjust.' Ac. xxiv. 15. 'Many of them that sleep in the dust of the earth shall awake, some to everlasting life, and some to shame *and* everlasting contempt.' Da. xii. 2. 'Marvel not at this: for the hour is coming, in the which all that are in the graves shall hear his voice, and shall come forth; they that have done good, unto the resurrection of life; and they that have done evil, unto the resurrection of damnation.' Jn. v. 28.

8. I believe, that they that 'shall be accounted worthy to obtain that world, and the resurrection from the dead, neither marry nor are given in marriage: neither can they die any more: for they are equal unto the angels; and are the children of God, being the children of the resurrection.' Lu. xx. 34—36. [see also] Jn. x. 27—29. Re. vii. 16. ch. xx. 6.

9. I believe, that those that die impenitent, shall be tormented with the devil and his angels, and shall be cast with them into 'the lake that burneth with fire and brimstone.' Re. xxi. 8. 'Where their worm dieth not, and the fire is not quenched.' Mar. ix. 43, 48. [see also] Mat. xxv. 41, 46. Jn. v. 29.

10. I believe, that because God is naturally holy and just, even, as he is good and merciful; therefore, all having sinned, none can be saved, without the means of a redeemer. 'Then he is gracious unto him, and saith, Deliver him from going down to the pit: I have found a ransom.' Job xxxiii. 24. 'We have redemption through his blood, *even* the

forgiveness of sins.' Col. i. 14. For which 'without shedding of blood, is no remission.' He. ix. 22.

11. I believe that Jesus Christ our Lord himself is the redeemer. 'They remembered that God *was* their rock, and the high God their redeemer.' Ps. lxxviii. 35. 'Forasmuch as ye know that ye were not redeemed with corruptible things, *as* silver and gold, from your vain conversation *received* by tradition from your fathers; but with the precious blood of Christ, as of a lamb without blemish, and without spot.' 1 Pe. i. 18, 19.

12. I believe, that the great reason why the Lord, the second person in the Godhead, did clothe himself with our flesh and blood, was that he might be capable of obtaining the redemption, that before the world, was intended for us. 'Forasmuch then as the children are partakers of flesh and blood, he also himself likewise took part of the same; (mark) that through death he might destroy him that had the power of death, that is, the devil; and deliver them who through fear of death, were all their lifetime subject to bondage.' He. ii. 14, 15. 'When the fulness of time was come, God sent forth his Son, made of a woman, made under the law, to redeem them that were under the law.' Ga. iv. 4, 5. 'Wherefore it behoved him in all things to be made like unto *his* brethren, and that he might be a merciful and faithful high priest in things *pertaining* to God, to make reconciliation for the sins of the people. For in that he himself hath suffered being tempted, he is able to succour them that are tempted.' He. ii. 17, 18. 'Christ hath redeemed us from the curse of the law, being made a curse for us: for it is written, Cursed *is* every one that hangeth on a tree: That the blessing of Abraham might come on the Gentiles through [faith in] Jesus Christ.' Ga. iii. 13, 14.

13. I believe, that the time when he clothed himself with our flesh, was in the days of the reign of *Cæsar Augustus*; then, I say, and not till then, was the Word 'made flesh,' or clothed with our nature. Jn. i. 14. 1 Ti. iii. 16. 'And it came to pass in those days, that there went out a decree from Cæsar Augustus, that all the world should be taxed. And Joseph also went up from Galilee, out of the city of Nazareth, into Judea, unto the city of David, which is called Bethlehem; (because he was of the house and lineage of David:) To be taxed with Mary his espoused wife, being great with child. And so it was, that, while they were there, the days were accomplished that she should be delivered.' Lu. ii. 1, 4—6. This child was he of whom godly Simeon was told by the Holy Ghost, when he said, That he should not see death until he had seen the Lord's Christ. ver. 25—27.

14. I believe, therefore, that this very child, as afore is testified, is both God and man; the Christ of the living God. 'And she brought forth her firstborn son, and wrapped him in swaddling clothes, and laid him in a manger; because there was no room for them in the inn. And there were in the same country shepherds - keeping watch over their flock by night. And, lo, the angel of the Lord came upon them, and the glory of the Lord shone round about them: and they were sore afraid. And the angel said unto them, Fear not: for, behold, I bring you good tidings of great joy, which shall be to all people. For unto you is born this day in the city of David a Saviour, which is Christ the Lord. And this *shall be* a sign unto you; ye shall find the babe wrapped in swaddling clothes lying in a manger.' Lu. ii. 7—12. Again, 'But while he thought on these things, behold, the angel of the Lord appeared unto him; - saying, Joseph, thou son of David, fear not to take unto thee Mary thy wife: for that which is conceived in her is of the Holy Ghost. And she shall bring forth a son, and thou shalt call his name JESUS: for he shall save his people from their sins. Now all this was done, that it might be fulfilled which was spoken of the Lord by the prophet, saying, Behold, a virgin shall be with child, and shall bring forth a son, and they shall call his name Emmanuel, which being interpreted is, God with us.' Mat. i. 21, 22.

15. I believe, therefore, that the righteousness, and redemption, by which we that believe, stand just before God, as saved from the curse of the law, is the righteousness, and redemption, that consists in the personal acts and performances of this child Jesus; this God-man the Lord's Christ: it consisteth, I say, in his personal fulfilling the law for us, to the utmost requirement of the justice of God. 'Think not (saith he) that I am come to destroy the law, or the prophets: I am not come to destroy, but to fulfill.' Mat. v. 17. By which means he became 'the end of the law for righteousness to every one that believeth.' Ro. x. 4. 'For what the law could not do, in that it was weak through the flesh, God sending his own Son in the likeness of sinful flesh, and for sin, condemned sin in the flesh.' Ro. viii. 3. So finishing transgressions, and making an end of sins, and making reconciliation for iniquity, He brought in everlasting righteousness. 1 Jn. iii. 8. 2 Ti. i. 9. He. x. 5—10. Da. ix. 24.

16. I believe, that for the completing of this work, he was always sinless; He. iv. 15. did always the things that pleased God's justice, Jn. viii. 29. that every one of his acts, both of doing and suffering, and rising again from the dead, was really and infinitely perfect, being done by him as God-man: He. vii. 26—28. wherefore his acts before he died, are called, 'the righteousness of God,' Ro. iii. 21, 22. his blood, 'the blood of God,' Ac. xx. 28. and 'hereby perceive we the love *of God*, because he laid down his life for us,' 1 Jn. iii. 16. The Godhead which gave

virtue to all the acts of the human nature, was then in perfect union with it, when he hanged upon the cross for our sins. Ac. x. 36. Jn. xx. 28. Ro. i. 4.

17. I believe then, that the righteousness that saveth the sinner from the wrath to come, is properly and personally Christ's, and ours but as we have union with him; God by grace imputing it to us. ' Yea doubtless, and I count all things *but* loss for the excellency of the knowledge of Christ Jesus my Lord: for whom I have suffered the loss of all things, and do count them *but* dung that I may win Christ, and be found in him, not having mine own righteousness, which is of the law, but that which is through the faith of Christ, the righteousness which is of God by faith.' Phi. iii. 8, 9. ' But of him are ye in Christ Jesus, who of God is made unto us wisdom, and righteousness, and sanctification, and redemption.' 1 Co. i. 30. ' For he hath made him *to be* sin for us, who knew no sin; that we might be made the righteousness of God in him.' 2 Co. v. 21. [' IN the LORD have I righteousness and strength.' Is. xlv. 24.]

18. I believe, that God, as the reward of Christ's undertakings for us, hath exalted him to his own right-hand, as our mediator, and given him a name above every name; and hath made him Lord of all, and judge of quick and dead: and all this that we who believe might take courage to believe, and hope in God. Ep. i. 17—22. ' And being found in fashion as a man, he humbled himself - unto death, even the death of the cross, (where he died for our sins.) Wherefore God also hath highly exalted him; and given him a name - above every name: That at the name of Jesus every knee should bow, of *things* in heaven, and *things* in earth, and *things* under the earth; And *that* every tongue should confess that Jesus Christ *is* Lord, to the glory of God the Father.' Phi. ii. 8—11. ' And he commanded us to preach unto the people, and to testify that it is he which was ordained of God *to be* the Judge of quick and dead.' Ac. x. 42; and xvii. 31. ' Who verily was foreordained before the foundation of the world, but was manifest in these last times for you, who by him do believe in God that raised him up from the dead, and gave him glory; that your faith and hope might be in God.' 1 Pe. i. 19—21.

19. I believe, that being at the right hand of God in heaven, he doth there effectually exercise the offices of his excellent priesthood, and mediatorship, presenting himself continually before God, in the righteousness which is accomplished for us, when he was in the world. For by the efficacy of his blood, he not only went into the holy place, but being there, and having by it obtained eternal redemption for us; now, as receiving the worth and merit thereof from the Father; doth bestow upon us grace, repentance, faith, and the remission of sins: yea he also received for us, the Holy Ghost

to be sent unto us, to ascertain* us of our adoption and glory: ' For if he were on earth, he should not be a 'priest.' He. viii. 4. ' Seeing then that we have a great high priest, that is passed into the heavens, Jesus the Son of God, let us hold fast *our* profession.' He. iv. 14. ' For *there is* one God, and one mediator between God and men, the man Christ Jesus.' 1 Ti. ii. 5. For ' by his own blood he entered in once into the holy place, having obtained eternal redemption *for us*. - For Christ is not entered into the holy places made with hands, *which are* the figures of the true; but into heaven itself, now to appear in the presence of God for us.' He. ix. 12, 24. ' Therefore being by the right hand of God exalted, and having received of the Father the promise of the Holy Ghost, he hath shed forth this, which ye now see and hear.'† Ac. ii. 23; v. 31.

20. I believe, that being there, he shall so continue till the restitution of all things, and then he shall come again in glory, and shall sit in judgment upon all flesh. And I believe, that according to his sentence so shall their judgment be. ' Repent ye therefore and be converted, that your sins may be blotted out, when the times of refreshing shall come from the presence of the Lord; and he shall send Jesus Christ, which before was preached unto you: whom the heaven must receive until the times of restitution of all things, - spoken by the mouth of all his holy prophets since the world began.' Ac. iii. 19—21. For ' this same Jesus, which is taken up from you into heaven, shall so come in like manner as ye have seen him go into heaven.' Ac. i. 11. ' For the Lord himself shall descend from heaven with a shout, with the voice of the archangel, and with the trump of God;' &c. 1 Th. iv. 16. ' When the Son of man shall come in his glory, and all the holy angels with him, then shall he sit upon the throne of his glory: And before him shall be gathered all nations: and he shall separate them one from another, as a shepherd divideth *his* sheep from the goats. And he shall set the sheep on his right hand, but the goats on the left. Then shall the king say unto them on his right hand, Come, ye blessed of my Father, inherit the kingdom prepared for you from the foundation of the world. Then shall he say also unto them on the left hand, Depart from me, ye cursed, into everlasting fire, prepared for the devil and his angels: And these shall go away into everlasting punishment: but the righteous into

---

* ' To ascertain us,' in the 17th century, meant ' to make us confident,' ' to assure us.' ' It ascertaining me that I am one of God's children.'—*Hammond*. ED.

† Eternal blessings on our Emmanuel, who faithfully performed His promise of sending the Comforter to unlock the mysteries of the kingdom of grace, and guide us into all truth: without His powerful aid we can neither know or perform any thing to a good or saving purpose.—*Mason*.

life eternal.' Mat. xxv. 31—33, 41, 46. For 'the day of the Lord will come as a thief in the night, in the which the heavens shall pass away with a great noise, and the elements shall melt with fervent heat, the earth also and the works that are therein shall be burned up. *Seeing* then *that* all these things shall be dissolved, what manner *of persons* ought ye to be in *all* holy conversation and godliness, looking for and hasting unto the coming of the day of God, wherein the heavens being on fire shall be dissolved, and the elements shall melt with fervent heat.' 2 Pe. iii. 10—12.

21. I believe that when he comes, his saints shall have a reward of grace, for all their work and labour of love which they showed to his name in the world. 'And every man shall receive his own reward, according to his own labour.' 1 Co. iii. 8. 'And then shall every man have praise of God.' iv. 5. 'And behold, I come quickly; and my reward *is* with me, to give every man according as his work shall be.' Re. xxii. 12. 'Therefore, my beloved brethren, be ye stedfast, unmoveable, always abounding in the work of the Lord, forasmuch as ye know that your labour is not in vain in the Lord.' 1 Co. xv. 58. 'Knowing that of the Lord ye shall receive the reward of the inheritance : for ye serve the Lord Christ.' Col. iii. 24.

How Christ is made ours ; or by what means this or that man, hath that benefit by him, as to stand just before God now, and in the day of judgment.

Of Justification.

1. I believe, we being sinful creatures in ourselves, that no good thing done by us, can procure of God the imputation of the righteousness of Jesus Christ. But that the imputation thereof is an act of grace, a free gift without our deserving. 'Being justified freely by his grace through the redemption that is in Christ Jesus.' Ro. iii. 24. and v. 17. 'Who hath saved us, and called *us* with an holy calling, not according to our works, but according to his own purpose and grace, which was given us in Christ Jesus.' 2 Ti. i. 9.

2. I believe also, That the power of imputing righteousness resideth only in God by Christ: 1. Sin being the transgression of the law. 2. The soul that hath sinned being his creature, and the righteousness also his, and his only. 'Even as David also describeth the blessedness of the man, unto whom God imputeth righteousness without works, *saying*, Blessed *are* they whose iniquities are forgiven, and whose sins are covered. Blessed *is* the man to whom the Lord will not impute sin.' Ro. iv. 6—8. Hence therefore it is said again, That men 'shall abundantly utter the memory of thy great goodness, and shall sing of thy righteousness.' Ps. cxlv. 7. 'For he saith to Moses, I will have

mercy on whom I will have mercy, and I will have compassion on whom I will have compassion. So then *it is* not of him that willeth, nor of him that runneth, but of God that showeth mercy. Ro. ix. 15, 16.

3. I believe, that the offer of this righteousness, as tendered in the gospel, is to be received by faith ; we still in the very act of receiving it, judging ourselves sinners in ourselves. 'Oh wretched man that I am ! who shall deliver me from the body of this death ? I thank God through Jesus Christ.' Ro. vii. 24, 25. 'Believe on the Lord Jesus Christ, and thou shalt be saved.' Ac. xvi. 31. The gospel is preached in all nations for the obedience of faith. 'Being justified freely by his grace through the redemption that is in Christ Jesus ; whom God hath set forth *to be* a propitiation, (a sacrifice to appease the displeasure of God) through faith in his blood. To declare his righteousness for the remission of sins that are past through the forbearance of God ; to declare *I say*, at this time his righteousness : that he might be just, and the justifier of him which believeth on Jesus.' Ro. iii. 24—26. 'Be it known unto you therefore, men *and* brethren, that through this man is preached unto you the forgiveness of sins: And by him all that believe are justified from all things, from which ye could not be justified by the law of Moses.' Ac. xiii. 38, 39.

4. I believe, that this faith, as it respecteth the imputation of this righteousness, for justification before God, doth put forth itself in such acts, as purely respect the offer of a gift. It receiveth, accepteth of, embraceth, or trusteth to it. 'As many as received him to them gave he power to become the sons of God, *even* to them that believe on his name.' Jn. i. 12. 'This *is* a faithful saying, and worthy of all acceptation, that Christ Jesus came into the world to save sinners ; of whom I am chief.' 1 Ti. i. 15; and He. xi. 13. 'In whom ye also *trusted*, after that ye heard the word of truth, the gospel of your salvation: In whom also after that ye believed, ye were sealed with that holy spirit of promise.' Ep. i. 13. I believe therefore, that as to my justification from the curse of the law, I am, as I stand in myself, ungodly, to receive, accept of, embrace, and trust to the righteousness, that is already provided by, and wrapt up in the personal doings and sufferings of Christ ; it being faith in that, and that only, that can justify a sinner in the sight of God.*

5. I believe, that the faith that so doth, is not to be found with any but those, in whom the Spirit of God by mighty power doth work it: all others being fearful and incredulous, dare not venture

---

* The gracious soul believes in Christ for justification, from a sense of utter inability to obtain justification by works. This is effected by the power of the Holy Spirit, the glorifier of Jesus.—*Mason.*

their souls and eternity upon it.   And hence it is called the faith that is wrought by the exceeding great and mighty power of God; the faith of the operation of God.   And hence it is that others are said to be fearful, and so unbelieving.   These with other ungodly sinners must have their part in the lake of fire, Ep. i. 18, 19. Col. ii. 12. Ep. ii. 8. Phi. i. 19. Re. xxi. 8.

6. I believe, that this faith is effectually wrought in none, but those which before the world were appointed unto glory.   'And as many as were ordained unto eternal life believed.' Ac. xiii. 48.   'That he might make known the riches of his glory on the vessels of mercy, which he had afore prepared unto glory.' Ro. ix. 23.   'We give thanks to God always for you all, making mention of you in our prayers; remembering without ceasing your work of faith, and labour of love, and patience of hope in our Lord Jesus Christ, in the sight of God ; - knowing, brethren beloved, your election of God.' 1 Th. i. 2—4.   But of the rest he saith, 'ye believe not because ye are not of my sheep, as I said,' Jn. x. 26. which latter words relate to the 16th verse, which respecteth the election of God.

'Therefore they could not believe, because that Esaias said again, He hath blinded their eyes, and hardened their heart; that they should not see with *their* eyes, nor understand with *their* heart, and I should heal them.' Jn. xii. 39, 40.

Of Election.

1. I believe that election is free and permanent, being founded in grace, and the unchangeable will of God.   'Even so then at this present time also there is a remnant according to the election of grace.   And if by grace, then *it is* no more of works : otherwise grace is no more grace.   But if *it be* of works, then is it no more of grace : otherwise work is no more work.' Ro. xi. 5, 6.   'Nevertheless the foundation of God standeth sure, having this seal, the Lord knoweth them that are his.' 2 Ti. ii. 19.   'In whom also we have obtained an inheritance, being predestinated according to the purpose of him who worketh all things after the counsel of his own will.' Ep. i. 11.

2. I believe, that this decree, choice or election, was before the foundation of the world; and so before the elect themselves, had being in themselves: For 'God who quickeneth the dead, and calleth those things which be not as though they were,' Ro. iv. 17. stays not for the being of things, to determine his eternal purpose by; but having all things present to him, in his wisdom, he made his choice before the world was. Ep. i. 4. 2 Ti. i. 9.

3. I believe, that the decree of election is so far off from making works in us foreseen, the ground or cause of the choice : that it containeth in the bowels of it, not only the persons, but the graces that accompany their salvation.   And hence it is,

that it is said; we are predestinated '*to be* conformed to the image of his Son ;' Ro. viii. 29. not because we are, but 'that we SHOULD be holy and without blame before him in love.' Ep. i. 4.   'For we are his workmanship, created in Christ Jesus unto good works, which God hath before ordained that we should walk in them.' Ep. ii. 10.   He blessed us according as he chose us in Christ.   And hence it is again that the salvation and calling of which we are now made partakers, is no other than what was given us in Christ Jesus before the world began ; according to his eternal purpose which he purposed in Christ Jesus our Lord. Ep. iii. 8—11. 2 Ti. i. 9. Ro. viii. 29.

4. I believe that Christ Jesus is he in whom the elect are always considered, and that without him there is neither election, grace, nor salvation.   'Having predestinated us unto the adoption of children, by Jesus Christ to himself, according to the good pleasure of his will, to the praise of the glory of his grace: wherein he hath made us accepted in the beloved.   In whom we have redemption through his blood, the forgiveness of sins, according to the riches of his grace. - That in the dispensation of the fulness of times, he might gather together in one all things in Christ, both which are in heaven, and which are in earth, *even* in him.' Ep. i. 5—7, 10.   'Neither is there salvation in any other: for there is none other name under heaven given among men, whereby we must be saved.' Ac. iv. 12.

5. I believe, that there is not any impediment attending the election of God, that can hinder their conversion, and eternal salvation.   'Moreover whom he did predestinate, them he also called: and whom he called, them he also justified : and whom he justified, them he also glorified.   What shall we then say to these things ?   If God *be* for us, who *can be* against us ? - Who shall lay any thing to the charge of God's elect ?   *It is* God that justifieth.   Who *is* he that condemneth ?' &c. Ro. viii. 30—35.   'What then ? Israel hath not obtained that which he seeketh for; but the election hath obtained it, and the rest were blinded.' Ro. xi. 7.   'For Israel *hath* not *been* forsaken, nor Judah of his God, of the LORD of hosts: though their land was filled with sin, against the holy one of Israel,' Je. li. 5.   When Ananias made intercession against Saul, saying, 'Lord, I have heard by many of this man, how much evil he hath done to thy saints at Jerusalem: and here he hath authority from the chief priests to bind all that call on thy name.'   What said God unto him ?   'Go thy way, for he is a chosen vessel unto me, to bear my name before the Gentiles, and kings, and the children of Israel.' Ac. ix. 12—15.

6. I believe that no man can know his election, but by his calling.   The vessels of mercy, which God afore prepared unto glory, do thus claim a

share therein: 'Even us, [say they,] whom he hath called, not of the Jews only, but also of the Gentiles? As he saith also in Hosea; I will call them my people, which were not my people, and her beloved, which was not beloved. Ro. ix. 24, 25.

7. I believe therefore, that election doth not forestal or prevent the means which are of God appointed to bring us to Christ, to grace and glory; but rather putteth a necessity upon the use and effect thereof; because they are chosen to be brought to heaven that way: that is, by the faith of Jesus Christ, which is the end of effectual calling. 'Wherefore the rather, brethren, give diligence to make your calling and election sure.' 2 Pe. i. 10. 2 Th. ii. 13. 1 Pe. ı. 12.

Of Calling.

I believe, that to effectual calling, the Holy Ghost must accompany the word of the gospel, and that with mighty power: I mean that calling, which of God is made to be the fruit of electing love. 'Knowing,' saith Paul to the Thessalonians, 'brethren beloved, your election of God. For our gospel came not unto you in word only, but also in power, and in the Holy Ghost, and in much assurance,' &c. 1 Th. i. 4, 5. Otherwise men will not, cannot, hear and turn. Samuel was called four times, before he knew the voice of him that spake from heaven. 1 Sa. iii. 6–10. It is said of them in Hosea, That as the prophets called them so they went from them; and instead of turning to them, 'sacrificed to Baalim, and burned incense to graven images.' Ho. xi. 2. The reason is, because men by nature are not only dead in sins, but enemies in their minds by reason of wicked works: the call then is, 'Awake thou that sleepest, and arise from the dead, and Christ shall give thee light.' Ep. v. 14. Understand, therefore, that effectual calling is like that word of Christ that raised Lazarus from the dead; a word attended with an arm that was omnipotent. 'Lazarus, come forth.' Jn. xi. 43. It was a word to the dead; but not only so: it was a word for the dead; a word that raised him from the dead; a word that outwent all opposition; and that brought him forth of the grave, though bound hand and foot therein. Ga. i. 15. And hence it is, that calling is sometimes expressed by quickening, Ep. ii. 1, 2. awakening, illuminating, or bringing them forth of darkness to light, that amazeth and astonisheth them. He. x. 32. Ac. ix. 6. For as it is a strange thing for a man that lay long dead, or never saw the light with his eyes, to be raised out of the grave, or to be made to see that which he could not so much as once think of before, so it is with effectual calling. Hence it is that Paul, when called, stood 'trembling and was astonished:' and that Peter saith, 'he hath called us out of darkness into his marvellous light.' 1 Pe. ii. 9. Ep. iv. 24. Ac. ix. 6.

In effectual calling the voice of God is heard, and the gates of heaven are opened: * when God called Abraham, he appeared to him in glory. That of Ananias to Saul is experienced but by few. 'The God of our fathers hath chosen thee, [saith he,] that thou shouldest know his will, and see that just one, and shouldest hear the voice of his mouth.' Ac. xxii. 14. True, Saul's call was out of the ordinary way, but yet as to the matter, and truth of the work, it was no other than all the chosen have, viz.

(1.) An effectual awakening about the evil of sin; and especially of unbelief. Jn. xvi. 9. And therefore when the Lord God called Adam, he also made unto him an effectual discovery of sin; insomuch that he stript him of all his righteousness, Ge. iii. Thus he also served the gaoler. Ac. xvi. 29, 30. Yea it is such an awakening, as by it, he sees he was without Christ, without hope, and a stranger to the commonwealth of Israel, 'and without God in the world.' Ep. ii. 12. Oh the dread and amazement that the guilt of sin brings with it, when it is revealed by the God of heaven; and like to it is the sight of mercy, when it pleaseth God, who calleth us by his grace, to reveal his Son in us.

(2.) In effectual calling there is great awakenings about the world to come, and the glory of unseen things; the resurrection of the dead, and eternal judgment; the salvation that God hath prepared for them that love him; with the blessedness that will attend us, and be upon us, at the coming of our Lord Jesus Christ, are great things in the soul that is under the awakening calls of God. And hence we are said to be called to glory. 1 Th. ii. 12. 'To the obtaining of the glory of our Lord Jesus Christ.' 2 Th. ii. 14.

(3.) In effectual calling there is also a sanctifying virtue; and hence we are said to be called with an holy calling, 1 Th. iv. 7. with an 'heavenly calling.' He. iii. 1. Called to glory and virtue. 'But ye *are* a chosen generation, a royal priesthood, an holy nation, a peculiar people; that ye should show forth the praises of him who hath called you out of darkness into his marvellous light.' 1 Pe. ii. 9. Yea, effectual calling hath annexed to it, as its inseparable companion, the promise of thorough sanctification. 'Faithful *is* he that calleth you, who also will do *it*.' 1 Th. v. 24.

Of Faith.

I believe, that effectual calling doth therefore produce, 1. FAITH; and therefore it is said, that 'faith *cometh* by hearing;' Ro. x. 17. by hearing the

---

* Effectual calling is evidenced by the soul's love to God, in his dear Son; a superior delight in Him, as a reconciled Father, cleaving to Him, His ways, and people; and longing for the full fruition and final enjoyment of Him in glory.— *Mason.*

word that calleth us 'unto the grace of Christ.' Ga. i. 6. For by the word that calleth us, is Jesus Christ held forth to us; and offered to be our righteousness; and therefore the apostle saith again, that God hath called us 'unto the fellowship of his Son Jesus Christ;' 1 Co. i. 9. that is, to be made partakers of the riches of grace, and the righteousness that is in him. 2. It produceth hope. It giveth a ground to hope; and therefore hope is said to be the hope of our calling. Ep. i. 18. And again, 'Even as ye are called in one hope of your calling.' Ep. iv. 4. Now the godly wise know, whoso misseth of effectual calling, misseth of eternal life; because God justifieth none but them whom he calleth; and glorifies none but those whom he justifies: and therefore it is that Peter said before, 'Make your calling, and (so) your election sure:' make it sure, that is, prove your calling right, by the word of God. For whoso staggereth at the certainty of his calling, cannot comfortably hope for a share in eternal life. 'Remember the word unto thy servant, upon which thou hast caused me to hope. My soul fainteth for thy salvation, but I hope in thy word.' Ps. cxix. 49, 81. 3. It produceth repentance; for when a man hath heaven and hell before his eyes (as he will have if he be under the power of effectual calling) or when a man hath a revelation of the mercy and justice of God, with an heart-drawing invitation to lay hold on the tender forgiveness of sins; and being made also to behold the goodly beauty of holiness; it must needs be, that repentance appears, and puts forth itself, unto self-revenging acts, for all its wickedness which in the days of ignorance it delighted in. And hence is that saying, 'I came not to call the righteous, but sinners to repentance.' Mar. ii. 17. For the effecting of which, the preaching of the word of the kingdom, is most proper: 'Repent: for the kingdom of heaven is at hand.' Mat. iv. 17.

Of Repentance.

Repentance is a turning the heart to God in Christ: a turning of it from sin, and the devil, and darkness; to the goodness, and grace, and holiness that is in him. Wherefore, they that of old are said to repent, are said to loath and abhor themselves, for all their abominations. 'I abhor myself,' [said Job,] 'and repent in dust and ashes.' Job xlii. 6. See also Eze. vi. 9; xx. 43; xxxvi. 31; xlii. 6; xvi. 63.

Godly repentance doth not only affect the soul with the loathsome nature of sin that is past; but filleth the heart with godly hatred of sins that yet may come. When Moses feared that through his being overburthened with the care of the children of Israel, some unruly or sinful passions might show themselves in him, what saith he?

'Kill me, I pray thee, out of hand, if I have found favour in thy sight, and let me not see my wretchedness.' Nu. xi. 15. See also how that which Paul calleth godly repentance, wrought in the upright Corinthians, 'Behold,' [saith he,] this self same thing, that ye sorrowed after a godly sort, what carefulness it wrought in you, yea, what clearing of yourselves, yea, what indignation, yea, what fear, yea, what vehement desire, yea, what zeal, yea, what revenge! In all things ye have approved yourselves to be clear in this matter. 2 Co. vii. 11.

Of Love.

It [effectual calling] produceth also love: wherefore Paul, when he had put the church in remembrance that they were called of God, adds, That concerning brotherly love, they had no need that he should write unto them. 1 Th. iv. 9. As who should say, If God be so kind to us, to forgive us our sins, to save our souls, and to give us the kingdom of heaven; let these be motives beyond all other to provoke us to love again. Farther, if we that are thus beloved of God, are made members of one man's body, all partakers of his grace, clothed all, with his glorious righteousness, and are together appointed to be the children of the next world; why should we not love one another? 'Beloved, if God so loved us, we ought also to love one another.' 1 Jn. iv. 11. And truly so we shall, if the true grace of God be upon us; because we also see them to be the called of Jesus. Travellers, that are of the same country, love and take pleasure one in another, when they meet in a strange land.* Why, we sojourn here in a strange country, with them that are heirs together with us of the promised kingdom and glory. He. xi. 9. Now, as I said, this holy love worketh by love: mark, love in God and Christ when discovered, constraineth us to love [one another.] 2 Co. v. 14.

The name, therefore, and word, and truth of God in Christ, together with the sincerity of grace, of faith, and holiness in us, are the delightful objects of this love. Ps. cxix. 47, 127, 132, 159; v. 11; lxix. 36. and ci. 6. For it embraceth with delight and complacency, but as it discerneth the image of God, and of Christ in the soul, his presence in the ministry, and a suitableness in our worship to the word and mind of Christ. Ps. xxvi. 8; xxvii. 4; lxxxiv. 1—4. 1 Th. v. 13. Phil. i. 3—7. Ep. iv. 32.

Love also hath a blessed faculty, and heavenly,

---

* How great is the delight of meeting in a foreign country, after a long absence from home, with one who speaks your own language and sympathizes with your national feelings. How much more strong are those enjoyments arising from the communion of saints, while travelling through an enemy's country, with difficult duties to perform,—animated by a kindred spirit, and seeking the same eternal home.—Ed.

in bearing and suffering afflictions, putting up wrongs, overlooking the infirmities of the brethren, and in serving in all Christian offices the necessities of the saints. 'Charity suffereth long *and* is kind; charity envieth not; charity vaunteth not itself, is not puffed up, doth not behave itself unseemly, seeketh not her own, is not easily provoked, thinketh no evil; rejoiceth not in iniquity, but rejoiceth in the truth; beareth all things, believeth all things, hopeth all things, endureth all things. Charity never faileth.' 1 Co. xiii. 4—8. [also,] 1 Pe. iv. 8. and Ga. v. 13. In a word, it designeth a holy conversation in this world; that God, and Christ, and the word of Christ, 'may be glorified thereby.' 2 Co. xi. 10—12. 1 Pe. i. 12; iii. 16.

Of the Scriptures.

Touching which word of God I thus believe and confess, 1. That all the holy scriptures are the words of God. 'All scripture *is* given by inspiration of God.' 2 Ti. iii. 16. For the prophecy [of the scripture] came not in old time by the will of man: but holy men of God spake *as they were* moved by the Holy Ghost. 2 Pe. i. 21. 2. I believe that the holy scriptures, of themselves, without the addition of human inventions, are able to make the man of God perfect in all things; and 'thoroughly to furnish him unto all good works.' They are able 'to make thee wise unto salvation, through faith which is in Christ Jesus.' 2 Ti. iii. 15. And to instruct thee in all other things, that either respect the worship of God, or thy walking before all men. 2 Ti. iii. 17. 2 Pe. i. 19—21. 3. I believe the great end why God committed the scriptures to writing was; that we might be instructed to Christ, taught how to believe, 1 Jn. v. 13, [and be] encouraged to patience and hope, for the grace that is to be brought unto us at the revelation of Jesus Christ. Jn. xx. 31. Ro. xv. 4. Also that we might understand what is sin, and how to avoid the commission thereof. 'Concerning the works of men (said David) by the word of thy lips, I have kept *me from* the paths of the destroyer.' Ps. xvii. 4. 'Through thy precepts I get understanding: therefore I hate every false way.' Ps. cxix. 104. 'Thy word have I hid in mine heart, that I might not sin against thee.' Ps. cxix. 11. 4. I believe that they cannot be broken, but will certainly be fulfilled in all the prophecies, threatenings, and promises, either to the salvation or damnation of men. They are like that flying roll, that will go over all the earth to cut off and curse. Ze. v. 2—4. In them is contained also the blessing, they preach to us also the way of salvation. Ga. iii. 8. 'Beware, therefore, lest that come upon you, which is spoken of in the prophets; Behold, ye despisers, and wonder, and perish:* for I work a

work in your days, a work which ye shall in no wise believe, though a man declare it unto you.' Ac. xiii. 40, 41. [see also] Jn. x. 35; xii. 37—41; iii. 17—19 5. I believe that Jesus Christ, by the word of the scriptures, will judge all men at the day of doom; for that is the book of the law of the Lord, according to Paul's gospel. Jn. xii. 44—50. Ro. ii. 16. 6. I believe, that this God 'made the world and all things [that are] therein,' Ac. xvii. 24, for 'in six days the Lord made heaven and earth, the sea, and all that in them is.' Ex. xx. 11. Also, that after the time of the making thereof, he disposed of it to the children of men, with a reserve thereof for the children of God, that should in all ages be born thereunto. 'When the Most High divided to the nations their inheritance, when he separated the sons of Adam, he set the bounds of the people according to the number of the children of Israel, De. xxxii. 8. for as he 'made of one blood all nations of men for to dwell on all the face of the earth, [so he] hath determined the times before appointed, and the bounds of their habitation.' Ac. xvii. 26.

Of Magistracy.

I believe, that magistracy is God's ordinance, which he hath appointed for the government of the whole world; and that it is a judgment of God, to be without those ministers of God, which he hath ordained to put wickedness to shame. Ju. xviii. 7. 'Whosoever therefore resisteth the power, resisteth the ordinance of God: and they that resist shall receive to themselves damnation. For rulers are not a terror to good works, but to the evil. Wilt thou not then be afraid of the power? do that which is good, and thou shalt have praise of the same: for he is the minister of God to thee for good. But if thou do that which is evil, be afraid; for he beareth not the sword in vain: for he is the minister of God, a revenger to *execute* wrath upon him that doeth evil. Wherefore *ye* must needs be subject, not only for wrath, but also for conscience sake. For this cause pay ye tribute also: for they are God's ministers, attending continually upon this very thing.' Ro. xiii. 2—6. Many are the mercies we receive, by a well qualified magistrate, and if any shall at any time be otherwise inclined, let us shew our Christianity in a patient suffering, *for well doing*, what it shall please God to inflict by them.†

---

* The despising and disregarding the Holy Scriptures, re-

jecting Jesus and the way of salvation by Him, especially after having attained to the knowledge and conviction of the truth of it by the gospel, is the unpardonable sin, and renders men obdurate and impenitent.—*Mason.*

† How strongly must have been the principle of humble submission to the will of God implanted and rooted in Bunyan's mind. He writes this peaceful advice from his dungeon, after twelve years' cruel imprisonment for his love and obedience to the Saviour. It requires a holy flame of Divine love to enable us to take the spoiling of our goods joyfully; but

A REASON OF MY PRACTICE IN WORSHIP.

Having thus made confession of my faith, I now come to shew you my practice in worship, with the reasons thereof. The which I shall have occasion to touch, under two distinct heads.

I. With whom I dare not hold communion.

II. With whom I dare.

Only, first, note, that by the word communion, I mean fellowship in the things of the kingdom of Christ, or that which is commonly called church communion, the communion of saints. For in civil affairs, and in things of this world that are honest, I am not altogether tied up from the fornicators thereof; 1 Co. v. 9, 10, wherefore in my following discourse understand me in the first sense:—Now, then,

First, I dare not have communion with them that profess not faith and holiness; or that are not visible saints by calling: but note, that by this assertion, I meddle not with the elect; but as he is a visible saint by calling; neither do I exclude the secret hypocrite, if he be hid from me by visible saintship. Wherefore I dare not have communion with men from a single supposition, that they may be elect, neither dare I exclude the other from a single supposing that he may be a secret hypocrite. I meddle not here with these things; I only exclude him that is not a visible saint. Now he that is visibly or openly profane, cannot be then a visible saint; for he that is a visible saint must profess faith, and repentance, and consequently holiness of life: and with none else dare I communicate.

First, Because God himself hath so strictly put the difference, both by word and deed; for from the beginning, he did not only put a difference between the seed of the woman and the children of the wicked, Ge. iii. 15, only the instinct of grace and change of the mind is his own, but did cast out from his presence the father of all the ungodly, even cursed Cain, when he shewed himself openly profane, and banished him to go into the land of the runnagate, or vagabond, where from God's face, and so the privileges of the communion of saints, he was ever after hid. Ge. iv. 8—16.

Besides, when after this, through the policy of Satan, the children of Cain, and the seed of Seth, did commix themselves in worship, and by that means had corrupted the way of God: what followed, but first, God judged it wickedness, raised up Noah to preach against it, and after that, because they would not be reclaimed, he brought the flood upon the whole world of these ungodly; and saved only Noah alive and his, because he had kept himself righteous. Ge. vi. 1—13.* Here I could enlarge abundantly, and add many more instances of a like nature, but I am here only for a touch upon things.

Second, Because it is so often commanded in the scriptures, That all the congregation should be holy. 'I *am* the Lord your God: ye shall therefore sanctify yourselves, and ye shall be holy; for I *am* holy.' Le. xi. 44. 'Ye shall be holy, for I the Lord your God *am* holy.' xix. 2. 'Sanctify yourselves therefore, and be ye holy: for I *am* the Lord your God.' xx. 7. 1 Pe. i. 15, 16. Besides, 1. The gates of the temple were to be shut against all other. 'Open ye the gates, that the righteous nation which keepeth the truth may enter in.' Is. xxvi. 2. 'This gate of the Lord, into which the righteous shall enter.' Ps. cxviii. 20. 'Thus saith the Lord God: No stranger, uncircumcised in heart, nor uncircumcised in flesh, shall enter into my sanctuary, of any stranger that *is* among the children of Israel.' Eze. xliv. 9. 2. Because the things of worship are holy; 'Be ye clean that bear the vessels of the Lord.' Is. lii. 11. 3. Because all the limits and bounds of communion are holy. 'This *is* the law of the house; Upon the top of the mountain, the whole limit thereof - *shall be* most holy. Behold, this *is* the law of the house.' Eze. xliii. 12.†

Third, I dare not have communion with them; because the example of New Testament churches before us, have been a community of visible saints. Paul, to the Romans, writes thus: 'To all that be in Rome, beloved of God, called *to be* saints.' i. 7. And to the rest of the churches thus: 'Unto the church of God which is at Corinth, to them that are sanctified in Christ Jesus; called *to be* saints.' 1 Co. i. 2. 'To the saints which are at Ephesus, and to the faithful in Christ Jesus.' Ep. i. 1. 'To all the saints which are at Philippi, with the bishops and deacons.' Phi. i. 1. 'To the saints and faithful brethren in Christ which are at

---

how much more strongly must this principle pervade the heart to enable us to suffer the loss of liberty, deprived of the society of a much loved wife and family, and in daily fear of an ignominious death! We cannot sufficiently admire the grace of God in the sufferer, nor abhor the tyranny under which he suffered.—Ed.

---

* This idea is found in other of Bunyan's Works. Certainly the mixture of saints and sinners in a national church established for worldly purposes, must engender hypocrisy and pride, intolerance and persecution. Such leaders in Satan's army were calculated mightily to assist, if they were not the original cause, of the overspreading of sin which called forth the flood to wash away.—Ed.

† Bishop Hall describes a Christian indeed as 'having white hands and a clean soul, fit to lodge God in; all the rooms whereof are set apart for his holiness.'—Ed.

Colosse.' Col. i. 2. 'To the church of the Thessalonians, *which is* in God the Father, and *in* the Lord Jesus Christ,' &c. 1 Th. i. 1. Thus you see under what denomination those persons went of old, who were counted worthy to be members of a visible church of Christ. Besides, the members of such churches go under such characters as these.

(1.) 'The called of Christ Jesus.' Ro. i. 6. (2.) Men that have drank into the Spirit of Jesus Christ. 1 Co. xii. 13. (3.) Persons in whom was God the Father. Ep. iv. 6. (4.) They were all made partakers of the joy of the gospel. Phil. i. 7. (5.) Persons that were circumcised inwardly. Col. ii. 11. (6.) Persons that turned from idols to serve the living and true God. 1 Th. i. 9. (7.) Those that were the body of Christ, and members in particular, that is, those that were visibly such; because they made profession of faith, of holiness, of repentance, of love to Christ, and of self-denial, at their receiving into fellowship.

Fourth, I dare not hold communion with the open profane.

(1.) Because it is promised to the church, that she shall dwell by herself; that is, as she is a church, and spiritual; Lo, the people shall dwell alone, and shall not be reckoned among the nations. Nu. xxiii. 9. (2.) Because this is their privilege. 'But ye *are* a chosen generation, a royal priesthood, an holy nation, a peculiar people; that ye should shew forth the praises of him who hath called you out of darkness into his marvellous light.' 1 Pe. ii. 9, 10. (3.) Because this is the fruit of the death of Christ, 'who gave himself for us, that he might redeem us from all iniquity, and purify unto himself a peculiar people, zealous of good works.' Tit. ii. 14. (4.) Because this is the commandment: 'Save yourselves from this untoward generation.' Ac. ii. 40. (5.) Because with such it is not possible we should have true and spiritual communion. Be ye not unequally yoked together with unbelievers: for what fellowship hath righteousness with unrighteousness? and what communion hath light with darkness? And what concord hath Christ with Belial? or what part hath he that believeth with an infidel? And what agreement hath the temple of God with idols? for ye are the temple of the living God, as God hath said, I will dwell in them and walk in *them;* and I will be their God, and they shall be my people. Wherefore come out from among them, and be ye separate, saith the Lord, and touch not the unclean *thing;* and I will receive you, and will be a Father unto you, - saith the Lord Almighty. 2 Co. vi. 14—18.

Fifth, I dare not hold communion with the open profane. Because

(1.) This would be ploughing with an ox, and an ass together: De. xxii. 10. heavenly persons suit best for communion in heavenly matters. (2.) It subjecteth not the nature of our discipline, which is not forced, but free,* in a professed subjection to the will and commandment of Christ: others being excluded by God's own prohibition. Le. i. 3. Ro. vi. 17. 2 Co. viii. 12; ix. 7, 13; viii. 5. Paul also, when he exhorteth Timothy to follow after righteousness, faith, charity, peace, &c., (which are the bowels of church communion,) he saith, do it 'with them that call on the Lord, out of a pure heart.' 2 Ti. ii. 22.

Sixth, In a word, to hold communion with the open profane, is most pernicious and destructive. (1.) 'Twas the wicked multitude that fell a lusting, and that tempted Christ in the desert. Nu. xi. 4. (2.) It was the profane heathen, of whom Israel learned to worship idols. They 'were mingled among the heathen, and learned their works. And served their idols; which were a snare unto them.' Ps. cvi. 35, 36. (3.) It is the mingled people that God hath threatened to plague with those deadly punishments of his, with which he hath threatened to punish Babylon itself; saying, When a sword is upon her liars, her mighty, her chariots, and treasures; a sword also shall be upon the mingled people that are in the midst of her.

And no marvel: for, (1.) Mixed communion polluteth the ordinances of God. Say to the rebels, saith the Lord God, 'Let it suffice you of all your abominations, in that ye have brought *into my sanctuary* strangers, uncircumcised *in heart,* and uncircumcised in flesh, to be in my sanctuary, to pollute it, *even* my house, when ye offer my bread, the fat and the blood, and they have broken my covenant, because of all your abominations.' Eze. xliv. 6, 7. (2.) It violateth the law. 'Her priests have violated my law, and have profaned mine holy things: (how) They have put no difference between the holy and profane, neither have they shewed *difference* between the unclean and the clean.' Eze. xx. 26. (3.) It profaneth the holiness of God. 'Judah hath dealt treacherously, and an abomination is committed in Israel and in Jerusalem; for Judah hath profaned the holiness of the Lord which he loved, and hath married the daughter of a strange god. Mal. ii. 11. (4.) It defileth the truly gracious. 'Know ye not that a little leaven leaveneth the whole lump?' 1 Co. v. 6. Look diligently therefore, 'lest any root of bitterness springing up trouble *you,* and thereby many be defiled.' He. xii. 15.

Lastly, To conclude, it provoketh God to punish with severe judgments: And therefore heed well. (1.) As I said before, The drowning of the whole world was occasioned by the sons of God commixing themselves with the daughters of men; and the corrup-

---

* Submission to the discipline of a Christian church must be voluntary, and not by the constraint of force or hypocrisy. In Christ's church ALL must be free, and not a mixture of freemen and the slaves of sin.—ED.

tion of worship that followed thereupon. Ge. vi ; vii. (2.) He sent a plague upon the children of Israel, for joining themselves unto the people of Moab; and for following their abominations in worship: Nu. xxv. 1—5. Jos. xxii. 17. and let no man think, that now I have altered the state of the question: for it is all one with the church to communicate with the profane; and to sacrifice and offer their gifts to the devil: De. xxxii. 16—19.* Ps. cvi. 36—40. the reason is, because such have by their sin forsaken the protection of heaven, and are given up to their own heart-lusts; and left to be overcome of the wicked, to whom they have joined themselves. De. xii; vii. 1—6. Join not yourselves, said God, to the wicked, neither in religion nor marriages; 'For they will turn away thy son from following me, that they may serve other gods: so will the anger of the Lord be kindled against you, and destroy thee suddenly.' De. vii. 5. 'Did not Solomon king of Israel sin by these things? yet among many nations was there no king like him who was beloved of his God.' Ne. xiii. 26. Hear how Paul handleth the point; 'But I say, that the things which the Gentiles [or openly profane] sacrifice, they sacrifice to devils, and not to God; and I would not that ye should have fellowship with devils. Ye cannot drink the cup of the Lord, and the cup of devils: Ye cannot be partakers of the table of the Lord, and of the table of devils. Do we provoke the Lord to jealousy? Are we stronger than he?' 1 Co. x. 20—22. I conclude, that therefore it is an evil, and a dangerous thing to hold church communion with the openly profane and ungodly. It polluteth his ordinances: it violateth his law: it profaneth his holiness: it defileth his people; and provoketh the Lord to severe and terrible judgments.

Object. But we can prove in all ages [that] there have been the open profane in the church of God.

Answ. In many ages indeed it hath been so: but mark, they appeared not such, when first they were received unto communion, Ex. xii. 48. neither were they with God's liking, as such, to be retained among them, but in order to their admonition, repentance and amendment of life: of which, if they failed, God presently threatened the church; and either cut them off from the church, as he did the idolators, fornicators, murmurers, tempters, sabbath breakers; with Korah, Dathan, Achan, and others: 2 Co. vi. 1 Co. v. Ex. xxxii. 25. Nu. xxv. 1—9; xxi. 5, 6; xiv. 37; xvi; xv. 32—36. Jos. vii. 2 Ki. xvii. Eze. xxii. and xxiii. or else cut off them with the church and all, as he served the ten tribes at one time, and the two tribes at another. 'My God will cast them away,

because they did not hearken unto him: and they shall be wanderers among the nations.' Ho. ix. 17. I might here greatly enlarge, but I intend brevity; yet let me tell you, that when Nehemiah understood by the book of the law of the Lord, that the Ammonite and the Moabite should not come into the congregation of God: 'they separated from Israel all the mixed multitude.' Ne. xiii. 1—3. Many have pleaded for the profane, that they should abide in the church of God; but such hath not considered, that God's wrath at all times hath with great indignation been shewed against such offenders and their conceits. Indeed they like not for to plead for them under that notion, but rather as Korah, and his company: 'All the congregation are holy every one of them.' Nu. xvi. 3. But it maketh no matter by what name they are called; if by their deeds they shew themselves openly wicked: for names and notions sanctify not the heart and nature; they make not virtues of vice, neither can it save such advocates from the heavy curse both of God and men. Pr. xvii. 15; xxiv. 24. 'The righteous men, they shall judge them after the manner of adulteresses, and after the manner of women that shed blood; because they *are* adulteresses, and blood *is* in their hands.' Eze. xxiii. 45.

SECOND, Thus have I shewed you with whom I dare not have communion: and now to shew you with whom I dare. But in order thereto, I desire you

First, To take notice; That touching shadowish, or figurative ordinances; I believe that Christ hath ordained but two in his church, viz., Water baptism and the supper of the Lord: both which are of excellent use to the church in this world; they being to us representations of the death and resurrection of Christ; and are, as God shall make them, helps to our faith therein. But I count them not the fundamentals of our Christianity, nor grounds or rule to communion with saints: servants they are, and our mystical ministers, to teach and instruct us in the most weighty matters of the kingdom of God: I therefore here declare my reverent esteem of them; yet dare not remove them, as some do, from the place and end, where by God they are set and appointed; nor ascribe unto them more than they were ordered to have in their first and primitive institution. It is possible to commit idolatry even with God's own appointments: but I pass this, and come to the thing propounded.

Second, then, I dare have communion, church communion, with those that are visible saints by calling: with those that, by the word of the gospel, have been brought over to faith and holiness: and it maketh no matter to me, what their life was heretofore, if they now be 'washed,' if they be 'sanctified,' if they be 'justified in the name of the Lord Jesus, and by the Spirit of our God.' 1 Co. vi. 11. Now in order to the discovery of this

---

* What faithfulness and plain dealing is here. If any church communicates with the profane it is offering sacrifice to the devil.—ED.

faith and holiness, and so to fellowship in church communion: I hold it requisite that a faithful relation be made thereof by the party thus to be received; yea, if need be, by witnesses also, for the satisfaction of the church, that she may receive in faith and judgment, such as best shall suit her holy profession. Ac. ix. 26—28. 1 Co. xvi. 10. 2 Co. viii. 23. Observe it; these texts do respect extraordinary officers; and yet see, that in order to their reception by the church, there was made to them a faithful relation of the faith and holiness of these very persons; for no man may intrude himself upon, or thrust himself upon, or thrust himself into a church of Christ; without the church have first the knowledge and liking of the person to be received: if otherwise, there is a door opened for all the heretics in the world; yea, for devils also if they appear in human shapes. But Paul shows you the manner of receiving, by pleading (after some disgrace thrown upon him by the false apostles) for his own admission of his companions: 'Receive us, [saith he,] we have wronged no man, we have corrupted no man; we have defrauded no man.' 2 Co. vii. 2. And so concerning Timothy: 'If Timotheus come, (saith he,) see that he may be with you without fear: for he worketh the work of the Lord, as I also do.' 1 Co. xvi. 10. Also, when Paul supposed that Titus might be suspected by some; see how he pleads for him: If *any do enquire* of Titus, *he is* my partner and fellow-helper concerning you: or our brethren *be enquired of, they are* the messengers of the churches, *and the* glory of Christ.' 2 Co. viii. 23. Phebe also, when she was to be received by the church at Rome; see how he speaketh in her behalf: 'I commend unto you Phebe our sister, which is a servant of the church which is at Cenchrea: that ye receive her in the Lord, as becometh saints, and that ye assist her in whatsoever business she hath need of you; for she hath been a succourer of many, and of myself also.' Ro. xvi. 1, 2. Yea, when the apostles

Saul was in Antioch before, but being brought into suspicion by false apostles, he had need of a new commendation.

and brethren sent their epistles from Jerusalem to Antioch; under what characters do those go, that were the messengers to them? 'It seemed good unto [the Holy Ghost and to] us, - to send chosen men unto you with our beloved Barnabas and Paul, men that have hazarded their lives for the name of our Lord Jesus Christ,' &c. Ac. xv. 25—27. Now though the occasions upon which these commendations were written were not simply, or only, in order to church relation, but also for other causes; yet because the persons concerned were of the churches to be received as faithful, and such who would partake of church privileges with them, they have, therefore, their faith and faithfulness related to the churches, as those that were particularly embodied

there. Besides Timothy and Titus being extraordinary officers, stood as members and officers in every church where they were received. Likewise Barnabas and Saul, Judas and Silas, abode as members and officers where they were sent. It was requisite, therefore, that the letters of recommendation should be in substance the same with that relation that ought to be made to the church, by or for the person that is to be embodied there. But to return, I DARE HAVE COMMUNION, CHURCH COMMUNION, WITH THOSE THAT ARE VISIBLE SAINTS BY CALLING.

Quest. But by what rule would you receive them into fellowship with yourselves?

Answ. Even by a discovery of their faith and holiness, and their declaration of willingness to subject themselves to the laws and government of Christ in his church.

Quest. But do you not count that by water baptism, and not otherwise, that being the initiating and entering ordinance; they ought to be received into fellowship?

Answ. No; But tarry, and take my sense with my word. For herein lies the mistake, To think that because in time past baptism was administered upon conversion, that therefore it is the initiating and entering ordinance into church communion: when by the word no such thing is testified of it. Besides, that it is not so will be manifest, if we consider the nature and power of such an ordinance.

That ordinance then, that is, the initiating or entering ordinance [as before] doth give to them that partake thereof a right to, and a being of, membership with that particular church by which it is administered. I say, a right to, and a being of, membership, without the addition of another church act. This is evident by the law of circumcision, which was the initiating law of old; for by the administration of that very ordinance, the partaker thereof was forthwith a member of that congregation, without the addition of another church act. Ge. xvii. This is declared in its first institution, and therefore it is called the token of the covenant. The token or sign of righteousness, of Abraham's faith, and of the visible membership of those that joined themselves to the church with him; the very inlet into church communion that gave a being of membership among them. And thus Moses himself expounds it; 'every man's servant, that is bought for money, when thou hast circumcised him, then shall eat' of the passover, Ex. xii. 44, without the addition of another church act, to empower him thereunto; his circumcision hath already given him a being there, and so a right to, and privilege in church relation: 'A foreigner and an hired servant shall not eat thereof, (because not circumcised). And when a stranger shall sojourn with thee, and will keep the passover to the LORD, let all his males be circumcised, and then let him come near and keep it; (For then he is one of the church) and he shall be as one born in the land: for no uncircumcised person shall eat thereof.' Ex. xii. 48. Neither could any other thing, according to the law of circumcision, give the devoutest person that breathed a being of membership with them. ' He that is born in thy house, and he that is bought with thy money, must needs be circumcised: - and the uncircumcised man child, whose flesh of his foreskin is not circumcised, that soul shall be cut off from his people.' Ge. xvii. 13, 14. Note then, that that which is the initiating ordinance admitteth none into church-communion but these that first partake thereof. The angel sought to kill Moses himself, for attempting to make his child a member without it. Ex. iv. 24—26. Note again, that as it admitteth of none to membership without it; so as I said, the very act of circumcising them, without the addition of another church act, gave them a being of membership with that very church, by whom they were circumcised. But none of this can be said of baptism. First, there is none debarred or threatened to be cut off from the church, if they be not first baptized. Secondly, Neither doth it give to the person baptized a being of membership with this or that church, by whose members he hath been baptized. John gathered no particular church, yet was he the first and great baptizer with water; he preached Christ to come, and baptized with the baptism of repentance, and left his disciples to be gathered by him. Ac. xix. 3—5. ' And unto him *shall* the gathering of the people be.' Ge. xlix. 10. Besides, after Christ's ascension, Philip baptized the eunuch, but made him by that no member of any particular church. We only read, that Philip was caught away from him, and that the eunuch saw him no more, but went on his way rejoicing to his master and country of Ethiopia. Ac. viii. 35—40. Neither was Cornelius made a member of the church at Jerusalem, by his being baptized at Peter's command at Cesarea. Ac. x. and xi. Neither were they that were converted at Antioch, by them that were scattered from the church at Jerusalem, by their baptism, if they were baptized [in water] at all, joined to the church at Jerusalem. Ac. xi. 19. No, they were after gathered and embodied among themselves by other church acts. Ac. xvi. What shall I say? into what particular church was Lydia baptized by Paul, or those first converts at Philippi? Yea even in the second of the Acts, baptizing and adding to the church appear to be acts distinct: but if baptism were the initiating ordinance, then was he that was baptized made a member; made a member of a particular church, by the very act of water baptism. Neither ought any by God's ordinance to

have baptized any, but with respect to the admitting them by that act to a being of membership in this particular church. For if it be the initiating ordinance, it entereth them into the church: What church? Into a visible church. Now there is no church visible but that which is particular; the universal being utterly invisible, and known to none but God. The person then that is baptized stands by that a member of no church at all, neither of the visible, nor yet of the invisible. A visible saint he is, but not made so by baptism; for he must be a visible saint before, else he ought not to be baptized. Ac. viii. 37; ix. 17; xvi. 33.

Take it again; Baptism [in water] makes thee no member of the church, neither particular nor universal: neither doth it make thee a visible saint: It therefore gives thee neither right to nor being of membership at all.

Quest. But why then were they baptized?

Ans. That their own faith by that figure might be strengthened in the death and resurrection of Christ. And that themselves might see, that they have professed themselves dead, and buried, and risen with him to newness of life. Col. ii. 12. Ro. vi. 4. It did not seal to the church that they were so (their satisfaction as to that arose from better arguments) but taught the party himself that he ought so to be. Farther, it confirmed to his own conscience the forgiveness of sins, if by unfeigned faith he laid hold upon Jesus Christ. Ga. iii. 26. 1 Co. xv. 29. Ac. ii. 38; xxii. 16. 1 Pe. iii. 21. Now then, if baptism be not the initiating ordinance, we must seek for entering some other way, by some other appointment of Christ, unless we will say that without rule, without order, and without an appointment of Christ, we may enter into his visible kingdom. The church under the law had its initiating and entering ordinance: it must not therefore be, unless we should think that Moses was more punctual and exact than Christ, but that also our Lord hath his entering appointment. Now that which by Christ is made the door of entrance into the church, by that we may doubtless enter; and seeing baptism is not that ordinance, we ought not to seek to enter thereby, but may with good conscience enter without it.

Quest. But by what rule then would you gather persons into church-communion?

Ans. Even by that rule by which they are discovered to the church to be visible saints; and willing to be gathered into their body and fellowship. By that word of God therefore, by which their faith, experience and conversation, being examined, is found good; by that the church should receive them into fellowship with them. Mark; not as they practise things that are circumstantial, but as their faith is commended by a word of faith, and their conversation by a moral precept. Wherefore that is observable, that after Paul had declared himself sound of faith, he falls down to the body of the law: 'Receive us, [saith he,] we have wronged no man, we have corrupted no man, we have defrauded no man.' He saith not, I am baptized, but I have wronged no man, &c. 2 Co. vii. 2. [see also] v. 18—21. And if churches after the confession of faith made more use of the ten commandments, to judge of the fitness of persons by; they might not exceed by this seeming strictness, Christian tenderness towards them they receive to communion.

I will say therefore, that by the word of faith, and of good works, moral duties gospelized, we ought to judge of the fitness of members by, by which we ought also to receive them to fellowship: For he that in these things proveth sound, he hath the antitype of circumcision, which was before the entering ordinance. 'For he is not a Jew, which is one outwardly; neither is that circumcision, which is outward in the flesh. But he is a Jew, which is one inwardly; and circumcision is that of the heart, in the spirit, - whose praise is not of men, but of God.' Ro. ii. 28, 29. Phi. iii. 1—4. Now a confession of this by word and life, makes this inward circumcision visible; when you know him therefore to be thus circumcised, you ought to admit him to the Lord's passover: he, if any, hath a share not only in church-communion, but a visible right to the kingdom of heaven. Again, 'For the kingdom of God, [or our service to Christ] is not meat and drink, but righteousness, peace and joy in the Holy Ghost. For he that in these things serveth Christ, is acceptable to God, and approved of men.' Ro. xiv. 17, 18. De. xxviii. 47. By which word Righteousness, he meaneth as James doth, the royal law, the perfect law, which is the moral precept evangelized, or delivered to us by the hand of Christ. Ja. ii. 8, 9. The law was given twice on Sinai: the last time it was given with a proclamation of grace and mercy of God, and of the pardon of sins going before. Ex. xix.; and xxxiv. 1—10. The second giving is here intended; for so it cometh after faith, which first receiveth the proclamation of forgiveness; hence we are said to do this righteousness in the joy and peace of the Holy Ghost. Now he that in these things serveth Christ, is accepted of God, and approved of men. For who is he that can justly find fault with him, that fulfilleth the royal law from a principle of faith and love. 'If ye fulfil the royal law according to the scripture, Thou shalt love thy neighbour as thyself, ye do well;' ye are approved of men. Again, he that hath loved another hath fulfilled the law, for love is the fulfilling of the law. He then that serveth Christ according to the royal law, from faith and love going before, he is a fit person for church-communion; God accepteth him, men approve him. Now that the royal law is the moral precept, read the

place. Ja. ii. 8—12. It is also called the law of liberty, because the bondage is taken away by forgiveness going before; and this is it by which we are judged, as is said, meet or unmeet for church-communion, &c.

Therefore I say, the rule by which we receive church-members, it is the word of the faith of Christ, and of the moral precept evangelized, as I said before, I am 'under the law to Christ,' saith Paul. 1 Co. ix. 21. So when he forbiddeth us communion with men, they be such as are destitute of the faith of Christ, and live in the transgression of a moral precept: 'I have written unto you, [saith he,] not to keep company, if any man that is called a brother be a fornicator, or covetous, or an idolater, or a railer, or a drunkard, or an extortioner, with such an one no not to eat.' 1 Co. v. 11. He saith not, if any man be not baptized [in water], have not hands laid on him, or join with the unbaptized, these are fictious, scriptureless notions. 'For this, Thou shalt not commit adultery, Thou shalt not kill, Thou shalt not steal, Thou shalt not bear false witness, Thou shalt not covet; And if there be any other commandment, it is briefly comprehended in this saying, namely, Thou shalt love thy neighbour as thyself. Love worketh no ill to his neighbour: therefore love is the fulfilling of the law.' Ro. xiii. 9, 10. The word of faith, and the moral precept, is that which Paul enjoins the Galatians and Philippians, still avoiding outward circumstances: hence therefore when he had to the Galatians treated of faith, he falls point blank upon moral duties. 'For in Christ Jesus neither circumcision availeth anything, nor uncircumcision, but a new creature. And as many as walk according to this rule, peace be on them, and mercy, and upon the Israel of God.' Ga. vi. 15, 16. As many as walk according to this rule: What rule? The rule by which men are proved new creatures: The word of faith, and the moral precept. Wherefore Paul exhorteth the Ephesians not to walk, 'as other Gentiles, in the vanity of their mind; seeing they had received Christ, and had 'heard him, and had been taught by him as the truth is in Jesus.' That they would put off the old man; what is that? Why, 'the former conversation,' which is 'corrupt according to the deceitful lusts;' lying, anger, sin, giving place to the devil, corrupt communication, all bitterness, wrath, clamour, evil-speaking, with all malice. And that they would 'put on the new man.' What is that? That which is 'created in righteousness and true holiness;' a being 'renewed in the spirit' of their mind, and a putting away all these things. Ep. iv. 'For in Christ Jesus;' these words are put in, on purpose to shew us the nature of New Testament administrations, and how they differ from the old. In Moses an outward conformity to an outward and carnal ordinance, was sufficient to give (they subjecting themselves thereto) a being of membership with the Jews; but in Christ Jesus it is not so; of Abraham's flesh was the national Jewish congregation; but it is Abraham's faith that makes New Testament churches: They that are of faith, are the children of faithful Abraham. They that are of faith, the same are the children of Abraham. Ga. iii. 7—9. So then the seed being now spiritual, the rule must needs be spiritual also, viz. The word of faith and holiness. This is the gospel concision knife, sharper than any two-edged sword; and that by which New Testament saints are circumcised in heart, ears, and lips. 'For in Christ Jesus,' [is] no outward and circumstantial thing, but the new creature; none are subjects of the visible kingdom of *Christ* but visible saints by calling: now that which manifesteth a person to be a visible saint, must be conformity to the word of faith and holiness. 'And they that are Christ's, have crucified the flesh with the affections and lusts.' Ga. v. 24. Hearken how delightfully Paul handleth the point: The new creatures are the Israel of God. The new creature hath a rule by himself to walk by; and as many as walk according to this rule, peace be on them, and mercy, and upon the Israel of God. Paul to the Philippians commandeth as much; where treating of his own practice in the doctrine of faith and holiness, requireth them to walk by the same rule, to mind the same thing. I desire to be found in Christ, saith he, I reach forward toward the things that are before; my conversation is in heaven, and flatly opposite to them whose God is their belly, who glory in their shame, and who mind earthly things. Brethren, saith he, 'be followers together of me, and mark them which walk so.' Ph. iii. 17. Mark them; for what? For persons that are to be received into fellowship, and the choicest communion of saints. And indeed this is the safest way to judge of the meetness of persons by: for take away the confession of faith and holiness; and what can distinguish a Christian from a Turk? He that indeed receiveth faith, and that squareth his life by the royal, perfect, moral precept; and that walketh therein, in the joy and peace of the Holy Ghost, no man can reject him; he cannot be a man if he object against him; not a man in Christ; not a man in understanding. 'The law is not made for a righteous man;' neither to debar him the communion of saints if he desire it, nor to cast him out if he were in. 'But for the lawless and disobedient, for the ungodly and for sinners, for unholy and profane, for murderers of fathers and murderers of mothers, for manslayers, for whoremongers, for them that defile themselves with mankind, for men-stealers, for liars, for perjured persons, and if there be any other thing that is contrary to sound doctrine; according to the glorious gospel of the blessed God, which was committed to my trust.' 1 Ti. i. 9—11. Paul also, when he would leave an everlasting conviction upon the Ephesians, concerning his faith and holiness, treating first of the sufficiency of Christ's blood, and the grace of God to save us; he adds, 'I have coveted no man's silver, or gold, or apparel,' he bringeth them to the the moral precept, to prove the sincerity of his good conversation by. Ac. xx. 33. And when men have juggled what they can, and made never such a prattle about religion; yet if their greatest excellency, as to the visibility of their saintship, lieth in an outward conformity to an outward circumstance in religion, their profession is not worth two mites. 'Let us walk honestly, as in the day; not in rioting and drunkenness, not in chambering and wantonness, not in strife and envying. But put ye on the Lord Jesus Christ, and make not provision for the flesh, to *fulfil* the lusts thereof.' Ro. xiii. 13, 14. And it is observable, that after the apostle had in the 9th and 10th verses of this chapter told us, that the moral precept is the rule of a good conversation, and exhorted us to make no provision for the flesh; he adds, these things provided, we may receive any that believe in Christ Jesus unto communion with us; how weak soever and dark in circumstantials; and chiefly designs the proof thereof in the remaining part of his epistle. For he that is of sound faith, and of conversation honest in the world; no man, however he may fail in circumstantials, may lightly reproach or vilify him. And indeed such persons are the honour of Christian congregations. Indeed he is prejudiced, for want of light in these things about which he is dark, as of baptism, or the like; but seeing that is not the initiating ordinance, or the visible character of a saint; yea, seeing it maketh no breach in a good and holy life: nor intrencheth upon any man's right but his own; and seeing his faith may be effectual without it, and his life approved by the worst of his enemies; why should his friends, while he keeps the law, dishonour God by breaking of the same? 'Speak not evil one of another, brethren. He that speaketh evil of *his* brother, and judgeth his brother, speaketh evil of the law, and judgeth the law: But if thou judge the law, thou art not a doer of the law, but a judge.' Ja. iv. 11. He that is judged, must needs fail somewhere in the apprehension of him that judgeth him, else why is he judged. But he must fail in substance, for then he is worthy to be judged. 1 Co. v. 12. His failure is then in a circumstance, for which he ought not to be judged.

Object. But notwithstanding all that you have said, water baptism ought to go before church-membership; shew me one in all the New Testament, that was received into fellowship without it.

Answ. 1. That water baptism hath formerly gone first is granted: but that it ought of necessity so to do, I never saw proof. 2. None ever received it without light going before, unless they did play the hypocrite: and besides no marvel though in the primitive times it was so generally practised first, for the unconverted themselves know, it belonged to the disciples of Jesus Christ. Jn. i. 24—27. Yet that all that were received into fellowship were even then baptized first, would strain a weak man's wit to prove it, if arguments were closely made upon these three texts of holy scripture, 1 Co. i. 14—16. Ga. iii. 27. Ro. vi. 3. But I pass them, and say, If you can shew me the Christian, that in the primitive times remained dark about it, I will shew you the Christian that was received without it. But should I grant more than can be proved, viz. That baptism was the initiating ordinance; and that it once did, as circumcision of old, give a being of membership to the partakers; yea set the case that men were forbidden then to enter into fellowship without it: yet the case may so be, that these things notwithstanding, men might be received into fellowship without it. All these things intailed to circumcision; that was the initiating ordinance; that gave being of membership; that was it without which it was positively commanded none should be received into fellowship. Jos. v. Yet for all this more than six hundred thousand were received into the church without it, yea received, and also retained there, and that by Moses and Joshua, even those to whom the land was promised, when the uncircumcised were cut off. But why then were they not circumcised? Doubtless there was a reason; either they wanted time, or opportunity, or instruments, or something. But they could not render a bigger reason than this, I have no light therein: which is the cause at this day that many a faithful man denieth to take up the ordinance of baptism: but I say whatever the hindrance was, it mattereth not; our brethren have a manifest one, an invincible one, one that all the men on earth, nor angels in heaven can remove: For it is God that createth light; and for them to do it without light would but prove them unfaithful to themselves, and make them sinners against God; ' For whatsoever is not of faith is sin.' Ro. xiv. 23. If therefore Moses and Joshua thought fit to communicate with six hundred thousand uncircumcised persons; when by the law not one such ought to have been received among them; why may not I have communion, the closest communion with visible saints as afore described, although they want light in, and so cannot submit to that, which of God was never made the wall of division betwixt us. I shall therefore hold communion with such.

First, Because the true visible saint hath already [been] subjected to that which is better; even to the righteousness of God, which is by faith of Jesus Christ; by which he stands just before God; he also

VOL. II.

hath made the most exact and strict rule under heaven, that whereby he squares his life before men. He hath like precious faith with the best of saints, and a conversation according to light received, becoming the gospel of Christ. He is therefore to be received, received I say, not by THY light, not for that in circumstances he jumpeth with thy opinion; but according to his own faith which he ought to keep to himself before God. ' Conscience, I say, not thine own, but of the other; for why is my liberty judged of another *man's* conscience.' 1 Co. x. 29. Some indeed do object, that what the apostles wrote, they wrote to gathered churches, and so to such as were baptized. And therefore the arguments that are in the epistles about things circumstantial, respect not the case in hand. But I will tell such, that as to the first part of their objection, they are utterly under a mistake. The first to the Corinthians, the epistle of James, both them of Peter, and the first epistle of John, were expressly written to all the godly, as well as particular churches. Again; if water baptism, as the circumstances with which the churches were pestered of old, trouble their peace, wound the consciences of the godly, dismember and break their fellowships; it is, although an ordinance, for the present to be prudently shunned; for the edification of the church, as I shall shew anon, is to be preferred before it.

Second, and observe it; ' One Spirit, - one hope, - one Lord, one faith, one baptism (not of water, for by one Spirit are we all baptized into one body) one God and Father of all, who *is* above all, and through all, and in you all.' Ep. iv. 1—6. This is a sufficient rule for us to hold communion by, and also to endeavour the maintaining that communion, and to keep it in unity, within the bond of peace against all attempts whatsoever. 1 Co. xii. 16.

Third, I am bold therefore to have communion with such. He. vi. 1, 2. Because they also have the doctrine of baptisms: I say the doctrine of them. For here you must note, I distinguish between the doctrine and practice of water baptism; The doctrine being that which by the outward sign is presented to us, or which by the outward circumstance of the act is preached to the believer: viz. THE DEATH OF CHRIST; MY DEATH WITH CHRIST; also his resurrection from the dead, and mine with him to newness of life. This is the doctrine which baptism preacheth, or that which by the outward action is signified to the believing receiver. Now I say, he that believeth in Jesus Christ hath richer and better than that [of baptism in water], *viz.* is dead to sin, and that lives to God by him, he hath the HEART, POWER and DOCTRINE of baptism: all then that he wanteth, is but the sign, the shadow, or the outward circumstance thereof. Nor yet is THAT despised but forborne for want of light.

4 H

The best of baptisms he hath; he is baptized by that one Spirit; he hath the heart of water baptism, he wanteth only the outward shew, which if he had would not prove him a truly visible saint; it would not tell me he had grace in his heart. It is no characteristical note to another, of my sonship with God. Indeed it is a sign to the person baptized, and an help to his own faith. He should know by that circumstance, that he hath received remission of sins; if his faith be as true, as his being baptized is felt by him. But if for want of light, he partake not of that sign, his faith can see it in other things, exceeding great and precious promises. Yea, as I also have hinted already, if he appear not a brother before, he appeareth not a brother by that: And those that shall content themselves to make that the note of visible church-membership; I doubt make things not much better, the note of their sonship with God.

Fourth, I am bold to hold communion with visible saints as afore [described]; because God hath communion with them; whose example in the case, we are straitly commanded to follow. 'Receive ye one another as Christ also received us (saith Paul,) to the glory of God.' Ro. xv. 1—7. Yea, though they be saints of opinions contrary to you; though it goeth against the mind of them that are strong. 'We then that are strong ought to bear the infirmities of the weak, and not to please ourselves.' Ro. xv. 1. What infirmities? The strongest may sometimes be out of the way.* Those that are natural are incident to all, they are infirmities then that are sinful, that cause a man, for want of light, to err in circumstantials; And the reason upon which he grounds this admonition is, that 'Christ pleased not himself; but, as it is written, The reproaches of them that reproached thee, fell on me.' You say, to have communion with such weak brethren, reproacheth your opinions, and practice. Grant it, your dulness and deadness, and imperfections also reproach the holiness of God; if you say no, for Christ hath borne our sins; the answer is still the same, Their sins also are fallen upon Christ; he then that hath taken away thy sins from before the throne of God; hath taken away their shortness in conformity to an outward circumstance in religion. Both your infirmities are fallen upon Christ; yea, if notwithstanding thy great sins, thou standest by Christ complete before the throne of God; why may not thy brother, notwithstanding his little ones, stand complete before thee in the church.

Vain man! think not by the straitness of thine

order, in outward and bodily conformity, to outward and shadowish circumstances, that thy peace is maintained with God, for peace with God is by faith in the blood of his cross; who hath borne the reproaches of you both. Wherefore he that hath communion with God for Christ's sake, is as good and as worthy of the communion of saints as thyself. He erreth in A CIRCUMSTANCE, thou errest in A SUBSTANCE; who must bear these errors? Upon whom must these reproaches fall? Phi. i. 10. Some of the things of God that are excellent, have not been approved by some of the saints: What then? must these for this be cast out of the church? No, these reproaches by which the wisdom of heaven is reproached have fallen upon me, saith Christ. But to return; GOD HATH RECEIVED HIM, Christ hath received him, therefore do you receive him. There is more solidity in this argument, than if all the churches of God had received him. This receiving then, because it is set as an example to the church, is such as must needs be visible to them; and is best described by that word which discovereth the visible saint. Whoso, therefore, you can by the word, judge a visible saint, one that walketh with God; you may judge by the selfsame word that God hath received him. Now him that God receiveth and holdeth communion with, him you should receive and hold communion with. Will any say we cannot believe that God hath received any but such as are baptized [in water]? I will not suppose a brother so stupified; and therefore to that I will not answer.

Receive him 'TO THE GLORY OF GOD.' To the glory of God, is put in on purpose, to show what dishonour they bring to God, who despise to have communion with them; who yet they know have communion with God. For how doth this man, or that church, glorify God, or count the wisdom and holiness of heaven beyond them, when they refuse communion with them, concerning whom, they are by the word convinced, that they have communion with God. 'Now the God of patience and consolation grant you to be like minded one towards another according to Christ Jesus.' Ro. xv. 5. By this word patience, Paul insinuateth how many imperfections, the choicest Christians do mingle their best performances with. And by this of consolation, how readily God overlooks, passeth by them, and comforteth you notwithstanding. Now that this mind should be in Christians one to another, is manifest; because Paul prays that it might be so. But this is an heavenly gift, and therefore must be fetched from thence. But let the patience of God, and the willingness of Christ, to bear the reproaches of the weak; and the consolations that they have in God, notwithstanding, moderate your passions, and put you upon prayer, to be minded like Jesus Christ.

* One of the most touching scenes in the Pilgrim's Progress beautifully illustrates this fact. When Christian led Hopeful into Bye-path Meadow, so that they fell into the hands of Giant Despair, Hopeful says, 'I would have spoke plainer, but that you are older than I.' That whole scene manifests the most delicate sensibility and christian feeling.—ED.

Fifth, Because a failure in such a circumstance as water, doth not unchristian us. This must needs be granted, not only from what was said before; but for that thousands of thousands that could not consent thereto as we have, more gloriously than we are like to do, acquitted themselves and their christianity before men, and are now with the innumerable company of angels and the spirits of just men made perfect. What is said of eating, or the contrary, may as to this be said of water baptism. Neither if I be baptized, am I the better, neither if I be not, am I the worse: not the better before God: not the worse before men: still meaning as Paul doth, provided I walk according to my light with God: otherwise it is false; for if a man that seeth it to be his duty shall despisingly neglect it; or if he that hath no faith therein shall foolishly take it up; both these are for this the worse, being convicted in themselves for transgressors. He therefore that doth it according to his light, doth well, and he that doth it not, or dare not do it for want of light, doth not ill; for he approveth his heart to be sincere with God; he dare not do any thing but by light in the word. If therefore he be not by grace a partaker of light, in that circumstance which thou professest; yet he is a partaker of that liberty and mercy by which thou standest. He hath liberty to call God father, as thou: and to believe he shall be saved by Jesus: his faith, as thine, hath purified his heart: he is tender of the glory of God as thou art: and can claim by grace an interest in heaven; which thou must not do because of water: ye are both then Christians before God and men without it: he that can, let him preach to himself by that: he that cannot, let him preach to himself by the promises; but yet let us rejoice in God together: let us exalt his name together. Indeed the baptized can thank God for that, for which another cannot; but may not he that is unbaptized thank God for that which the baptized cannot? Wouldest thou be content that I should judge thee, because thou canst not for my light give thanks with me? why then should he judge me, for that I cannot give thanks with him for his? 'Let us not therefore judge one another any more: but judge this rather, that no man put a stumblingblock or an occasion to fall in *his* brother's way.' Ro. xiv. 13. And seeing the things wherein we exceed each other, are such as neither make nor mar Christianity; let us love one another and walk together by that glorious rule above specified, leaving each other in all such circumstances to our own master, to our own faith. 'Who art thou that judgest another man's servant? to his own master he standeth or falleth. Yea, he shall be holden up: for God is able to make him stand.' Ro. xiv. 4.

Sixth, I am therefore for holding communion

thus, because the edification of souls in the faith and holiness of the gospel, is of greater concernment than an agreement in outward things;* I say, it is of greater concernment with us, and of far more profit to our brother; than our agreeing in, or contesting for the business of water baptism. Jn. xvi. 13. 1 Co. xiv. 26. 2 Co. x. 8; xii. 19. Ep. iv. 12. 2 Ti. iii. 17, 1 Co. viii. 1; xiii. 1—4. That the edification of the soul, is of the greatest concern, is out of measure evident because heaven and eternal happiness are so immediately concerned therein. Besides, this is that for which Christ died, for which the Holy Ghost was given, yea for which the scriptures and the gifts of all the godly are given to the church; yea, and if gifts are not bent to this very work, the persons are said to be proud or uncharitable that have them; and stand but for cyphers or worse among the churches of God. Farther, edification is that that cherisheth all grace, and maketh the Christians quick and lively, and maketh sin lean and dwindling, and filleth the mouth with thanksgiving to God. But to contest with gracious men, with men that walk with God; to shut such out of the churches; because they will not sin against their souls, rendereth thee uncharitable. Ro. xiv. 15, 20. Thou seekest to destroy the word of God; thou begettest contentions, janglings, murmurings, and evil surmisings, thou ministerest occasion for whisperings, backbitings, slanders and the like, rather than godly edifying; contrary to the whole current of the scriptures and peace of all communities. Let us therefore leave off these contentions, 'and follow after the things that make for peace, and things wherewith one may edify another.' Ro. xiv. 19. And know that the edification of the church of God dependeth not upon, neither is tied to this or that circumstance. Especially when there are in the hearts of the godly, different persuasions about it; then it becometh them in the wisdom of God, to take more care for their peace and unity; than to widen or make large their uncomfortable differences.

Although Aaron transgressed the law, because he ate not the sin-offering of the people; yet seeing he could not do it with satisfaction to his own conscience, Moses was content that he left it undone. Le. x. 16—20. Joshua was so zealous against Eldad and Medad, for prophesying in the camp, without first going to the Lord to the door of the tabernacle, as they were commanded, that he desired

---

* How strange that *pious* men should have been prone to punish their *fellows* for non-conformity in an outward sign. They themselves were suffering inconceivable miseries under acts of uniformity in rites and ceremonies. How applicable to the framers of such acts of parliament are our Lord's words, 'Woe unto you, pharisees, who whiten and garnish the outside of a sepulchre, while within it is full of uncleanness, hypocrisy, and iniquity,' Mat. xxiii.—ED.

Moses to forbid them. Nu. xi. 27, 28. But Moses calls his zeal envy, and prays to God for more such prophets; knowing that although they failed in a circumstance, they were right in that which was better. The edification of the people in the camp was that which pleased Moses.

In Hezekiah's time, though the people came to the passover in an undue manner, and 'did eat it otherwise than it was written;' yet the wise king would not forbid them, but rather admitted it, knowing that their edification was of greater concern, than to hold them to a circumstance or two. 2 Ch. xxx. 13—27. Yea, God himself did like the wisdom of the king, and healed, that is, forgave, the people at the prayer of Hezekiah. And observe it, notwithstanding this disorder, as to circumstances, the feast was kept with great gladness; and the Levites and the priests praised the Lord day by day, singing with loud instruments unto the Lord; yea, there was not the like joy in Jerusalem from the time of Solomon unto that same time. What shall we say, all things must give place to the profit of the people of God. Yea, sometimes laws themselves, for their outward preservation, much more for godly edifying. When Christ's disciples plucked the ears of corn on the sabbath, no doubt for very hunger, and were rebuked by the Pharisees for it, as for that which was unlawful; how did their Lord succour them? By excusing them, and rebuking their adversaries. 'Have ye not read,' said he, 'what David did when he was an hungred, and they that were with him; how he entered into the house of God, and did eat the shew bread, which was not lawful for him to eat, neither for them which were with him, but only for the priests? Or have ye not read in the law, how that on the sabbath days the priests in the temple profaned the sabbath, and are blameless?' Mat. xii. 1—5. Why blameless? because they did it in order to the edification of the people. If laws and ordinances of old have been broken, and the breach of them borne with, when yet the observance of outward things was more strictly commanded than now, when the profit and edification of the people came in competition, how much more may not we have communion, church communion, where no law is transgressed thereby.

Seventh, Therefore I am for holding communion thus, because love, which above all things we are commanded to put on, is of much more worth than to break about baptism; Love is also more discovered when it receiveth for the sake of Christ and grace, than when it refuseth for want of water: and observe it, as I have also said before, this exhortation to love is grounded upon the putting on of the new creature; which new creature hath swallowed up all distinctions, that have before been common among the churches.

As I am a Jew, you are a Greek; I am circumcised, you are not: I am free, you are bound. Because Christ was all in all these, ' Put on therefore,' saith he, ' as the elect of God, holy and beloved, bowels of mercies, kindness, humbleness of mind, meekness, long-suffering,' that is, with reference to the infirmities of the weak, 'forbearing one another, and forgiving one another, if any man have a quarrel against any: even as Christ forgave you, so also *do* ye: and above all these things *put on* charity, which is the bond of perfectness.' Col. iii. 12—14. Which forbearing and forgiving respecteth not only private and personal injuries, but also errors in judgment about inclinations and distinctions tending to divisions, and separating upon the grounds laid down in ver. 11. which how little soever they now seem *to* us, who are beyond them, were strong, and of weight to them who in that day were entangled with them. Some saints then were not free to preach to any but the Jews: denying the word of life to the Gentiles, and contending with them who preferred it to them: which was a greater error than this of baptism. Ac. xi. 1—19. But what should we do with such kind of saints? Why love them still, forgive them, bear with them, and maintain church communion with them. Why? because they are new creatures, because they are Christ's: for this swallows up all distinctions. Farther, because they are elect and beloved of God. Divisions and distinctions are of shorter date than election; let not them therefore that are but momentary, and hatched in darkness, break that bond that is from everlasting. It is love, not baptism, that discovereth us to the world to be Christ's disciples. It is love, that is the undoubted character of our interest in, and sonship with God: I mean when we love as saints, and desire communion with others, because they have fellowship one with another, in their fellowship with God the Father, and his Son Jesus Christ. 1 Jn. i. 3. And now though the truth and sincerity of our love to God, be then discovered when we keep his commandments, in love to his name; yet we should remember again, that the two head and chief commandments, are faith in Jesus, and love to the brethren. 1 Jn. iii. 23. So then he that pretendeth to love, and yet seeks not the profit of his brother in chief; he loveth, but they are his own opinions and froward notions. Ja. iv. 11. Ro. xiv. 21. 'Love *is* the fulfilling of the law;' but he fulfils it not who judgeth and setteth at nought his brother; that stumbleth, offendeth, and maketh weak his brother; and all for the sake of a circumstance, that to which he cannot consent, except he sin against his own soul, or Papist like, live by an implicit faith.* Love therefore is sometimes more

* ' An implicit faith ;' faith in things without inquiry, or in things not expressed.—ED.

seen and showed, in forbearing to urge and press what we know, than in publishing and imposing. 'I could not,' (saith Paul, love would not let me) 'speak unto you as unto spiritual, but as unto carnal, *even* as unto babes in Christ. I have fed you with milk, and not with meat: for hitherto ye were not able *to bear it*, neither yet now are ye able.' 1 Co. iii. 1, 2. The apostle considered not only the knowledge that he had in the mysteries of Christ; but the temper, the growth, and strength of the churches, and accordingly kept back, or communicated to them, what might be for their profit. Ac. xx. 18—20. So Christ, 'I have yet many things to say unto you, but ye cannot bear them now.' Jn. xvi. 12. It may be some will count these old and threadbare texts; but such must know, that the word of the Lord must stand for ever. Is. xl. 8. And I should dare to say to such, if the best of thy new shifts, be to slight, and abuse old scriptures; it shews thou art more fond of thy unwarrantable opinion, than swift to hear, and ready to yield to the authority that is infallible.

But to conclude this, when we attempt to force our brother beyond his light, or to break his heart with grief; to thrust him beyond his faith, or to bar him from his privilege: how can we say, I love? What shall I say? To have fellowship one with another for the sake of an outward circumstance, or to make that the door to fellowship which God hath not; yea to make that the including, excluding charter; the bounds, bar, and rule of communion; when by the word of the everlasting testament there is no warrant for it; to speak charitably, if it be not for want of love, it is for want of knowledge in the mysteries of the kingdom of Christ. Strange! take two Christians equal in all points but this, nay, let one go beyond the other far, for grace and holiness; yet this circumstance of water shall drown and sweep away all his excellencies, not counting him worthy of that reception, that with hand and heart shall be given to a novice in religion, because he consents to water.

Eighth, But for God's people to divide into parties, or to shut each other from church communion; though from greater points, and upon higher pretences, than this of water baptism; hath heretofore been counted carnal, and the actors herein babyish Christians. Paul and Apollos, Cephas and Christ, were doubtless higher things than those about which we contend: yet when they made divisions for them; how sharply are they rebuked? Are ye not CARNAL, CARNAL, CARNAL? For whereas there are among you, envyings, strife, divisions, or factions: 'are ye not carnal.' 1 Co. i. 11, 12; iii. 1—4. While one saith, I am of Paul, and another I am of Apollos, are ye not carnal? See therefore from whence arise all thy endeavours, zeal, and labour, to accomplish divisions among the godly: let Paul or Cephas, or Christ himself, be the burthen of thy song, yet the heart from whence they flow is carnal; and thy actions, discoveries of childishness. But, doubtless when these contentions were among the Corinthians, and one man was vilified, that another might be promoted; a lift with a carnal brother, was thought great wisdom to widen the breach. But why should HE be rebuked, that said he was for Christ? Because he was for him in opposition to his holy apostles. Hence he saith, 'Is Christ divided,' or separate from his servants? Note therefore that these divisions are deserted by the persons the divisions were made about; neither Paul, nor Apollos, nor Cephas, nor Christ is here. Let the cry be never so loud, Christ, order, the rule, the command, or the like; carnality is but the bottom, and they are but babes that do it; their zeal is but a puff. 1 Co. iv. 6. And observe it, the great division at Corinth, was helped forward by water baptism: this the apostle intimates by, 'Were ye baptized in the name of Paul?' Ah, brethren! Carnal Christians with outward circumstances, will, if they be let alone, make sad work in the churches of Christ, against the spiritual growth of the same. But '*I thank God*,' saith Paul, '*that I baptized none of you*,' &c. Not but that it was then an ordinance of God, but they abused it, in making parties thereby. 'I baptized none of you, but Crispus and Gaius, - and the household of Stephanus:' men of note among the brethren, men of good judgment, and reverenced by the rest; they can tell you I intended not to make a party to myself thereby. 'Besides, I know not whether I baptized any other.' By this negligent relating, who were baptized by him; he sheweth that he made no such matter of baptism, as some in these days do; nay, that he made no matter at all thereof, with respect to church communion; for if he did not heed who himself had baptized; he much less heeded, who were baptized by others; but if baptism had been the initiating, or entering ordinance, and so appointed of God; no doubt he had made more conscience thereof, than so lightly to pass it over. 'For Christ sent me not to baptize, but to preach the gospel.' The gospel then may be effectually preached, and yet baptism neither administered nor mentioned. The gospel being good tidings to sinners, upon the account of free grace through Christ; but baptism with things of like nature, are duties enjoined such a people who received the gospel before. I speak not this, because I would teach men to break the least of the commandments of God; but to persuade my brethren of the baptized way, not to hold too much thereupon, not to make it an essential of the gospel of Christ, nor yet of communion of saints.

'He sent me not to baptize:' these words are spoken with holy indignation against them that abuse this ordinance of Christ. So when he speaketh of the ministers themselves, which also they had abused; in his speaking, he as it were trampleth upon them, as if they were nothing at all. 'Who then is Paul, and who *is* Apollos?' 'He that planteth is not any thing, neither is he that watereth, but God that giveth the increase.' 1 Co. iii. 5, 7. Yet for all this, the ministers and their ministry are a glorious appointment of God in the world. Baptism also is a holy ordinance, but when Satan abuseth it, and wrencheth it out of its place; making that which was ordained of God for the edification of believers, the only weapon to break in pieces the love, the unity, the concord of saints; then What is baptism? then neither is baptism anything. And this is no new doctrine; for God by the mouth of his prophets of old, cried out against his own institutions, when abused by his people: 'To what purpose *is* the multitude of your sacrifices unto me,' *saith the* LORD: 'I am full of the burnt-offerings of rams, and the fat of fed beasts; and I delight not in the blood of bullocks, or of lambs, or of he goats. When ye come to appear before me, who hath required this at your hands, to tread my courts? Bring no more vain oblations, incense is an abomination to me; the new moons and sabbaths, the calling of assemblies, I cannot away with; *it is* iniquity, even the solemn meeting. Your new moons and your appointed feasts my soul hateth: they are a trouble unto me, I am weary to bear *them.*' Is. i. 11–14. And yet all these were his own appointments. But why then did he thus abhor them? Because they retained the evil of their doings, and used them as they did other of his appointments, viz., 'For strife and debate, and to strike with the fist of wickedness:' ch. lviii. 4. Wherefore when that of God that is great, is overweighed by that which is small; it is the wisdom of them that see it, to put load to the other end of the scale; until the things thus abused, poise in their own place. But to pass this and proceed.

Ninth, If we shall reject visible saints by calling saints that have communion with God, that have received the law at the hand of Christ, that are of an holy conversation among men; they desiring to have communion with us, as much as in us lieth, we take from them their very privileges, and the blessings to which they were born of God. For Paul saith not only to the gathered church at Corinth, but to all scattered saints that in every place call upon the name of the Lord; That Jesus Christ is theirs, That Paul, and Apollos, and the world, and life, and death, and all things are theirs, because they are Christ's, and Christ is God's. But saith he, let no man glory in men, such as

Paul and Cephas, though these were excellent: because this privilege comes to you upon another bottom, even by faith of Jesus Christ, 'Drink you all of this,' is entailed to faith, not baptism: nay, baptized persons may yet be excluded this; when he that discerneth the Lord's body hath right and privilege to it. 1 Co. xi. 28, 29. But to exclude Christians from church communion and to debar them their heaven-born privileges, for the want of that which yet God never made a wall of division between us.

(1.) This looks too like a spirit of persecution. Job xix. 28. (2.) It respecteth more a form, than the spirit and power of godliness. 2 Ti. iii. 5. (3.) This is to make laws, where God hath made none, and to be wise above what is written, contrary to God's word, and our own principles. (4.) It is a directing of the Spirit of God. (5.) It bindeth all men's faith and light to mine opinion. (6.) It taketh away the children's bread. (7.) It withholdeth from them the increase of faith. (8.) It tendeth to harden the hearts of the wicked. (9.) It tendeth to make wicked the hearts of weak Christians. (10.) It setteth open a door to all temptations. (11.) It tempteth the devil to fall upon those that are alone, and have none to help them. (12.) It is the nursery of all vain janglings, back-bitings, and strangeness among the Christians. (13.) It occasioneth the world to reproach us. (14.) It holdeth staggering consciences, in doubt of the right way of the Lord. (15.) It giveth occasion to many to turn aside to most dangerous heresies. (16.) It abuseth the holy scriptures; It wresteth God's ordinances out of their place. (17.) It is a prop to antichrist. (18.) Shall I add, Is it not that which greatly prevailed to bring down these judgments, which at present we feel and groan under;* I will dare to say, it was † a cause thereof.

Tenth, and lastly, Bear with one word farther. What greater contempt can be thrown upon the saints than for their brethren to cast them off, or to debar them church-communion? Think you not that the world may groundly say, Some great iniquity lies hid in the skirts of your brethren; when in truth the transgression is yet your own?

---

* 'These judgments we feel and groan under.' So frightful were the persecutions of the dissenters by the church in 1670, that the narrative says, 'The town [of Bedford] was so thin of people, and the shops shut down, that it seemed like a place visited with the pest, where usually is written upon the door, "Lord, have mercy upon us."' Had the dissenters been united, the church would not have dared to exercise such barbarities—men and women in jails—some hanged for not going to church—all their goods swept away, and their children perishing.—ED.

† The printer had inserted 'the cause;' Bunyan's manuscript was 'a cause.' See marginal note, in his Differences in Judgment, p. 619.—ED.

But I say, what can the church do more to the sinners or open profane? Civil commerce you will have with the worst, and what more have you with these? Perhaps you will say we can pray and preach with these; and hold them Christians, saints, and godly. Well, but let me ask you one word farther: Do you believe, that of very conscience they cannot consent, as you, to that of water baptism? And that if they had light therein, they would as willingly do it as you? Why then, as I have shewed you, our refusal to hold communion with them is without a ground from the word of God. But can you commit your soul to their ministry, and join with them in prayer; and yet not count them meet for other gospel privileges? I would know by what scripture you do it? Perhaps you will say, I commit not my soul to their ministry, only hear them occasionally for trial. If this be all the respect thou hast for them and their ministry, thou mayest have as much for the worst that pisseth against the wall. But if thou canst hear them as God's ministers, and sit under their ministry as God's ordinance; then shew me where God hath such a gospel ministry, as that the persons ministering may not, though desiring it, be admitted with you to the closest communion of saints. But if thou sittest under their ministry for fleshly politic ends, thou hearest the word like an atheist, and art thyself, while thou judgest thy brother, in the practice of the worst of men. But I say, where do you find this piece-meal communion with men that profess faith and holiness as you, and separation from the world. If you object, that my principles lead me to have communion with all; I answer with all as afore described; if they will have communion with me.

Object. Then you may have communion with the members of antichrist.

Answ. If there be a visible saint yet remaining in that church; let him come to us, and we will have communion with him.

Quest. What, though he yet stand a member of that sinful number, and profess himself one of them.

Answ. You suppose an impossibility; for it cannot be that, at the same time, a man should visibly stand a member of two bodies diametrically opposite one to another. Wherefore it must be supposed, that he who professeth himself a member of a church of Christ, must forthwith, nay before, forsake the antichristian one. The which if he refuseth to do, it is evident he doth not sincerely desire to have fellowship with the saints.

[*Quest.*] But he saith he cannot see that that company to which you stand opposite, and conclude antichristian, is indeed the antichristian church.

[*Answ.*] If so, he cannot desire to join with another, if he know them to be professedly and directly opposite. I hold therefore to what I said at first; That if there be any saints in the antichristian church, my heart, and the door of our congregation is open to receive them, into closest fellowship with us.

Object. But how if they yet retain some antichristian principles.

Answ. If they be such as eat out the bowels of a church, so soon as they are detected he must either be kept out, while out, or cast out, if in: for it must be the prudence of every community to preserve its own unity with peace and truth: the which the churches of Christ may do; and yet as I have shewed already, receive such persons as differ upon the point of water baptism. For the doing or not doing of that neither maketh nor marreth the bowels or foundation of church-communion.

Object. But this is receiving for opinion sake; as before you said of us.

Answ. No; we receive him for the sake of Christ, and grace, and for our mutual edification in the faith; and that we respect not opinions, I mean in lesser matters, 'tis evident; for things wherein we differ are no breach of communion among us; we let every man have his own faith in such things to himself before God.

I NOW COME TO A SHORT APPLICATION.

1. Keep a strict separation, I pray you, from communion with the open profane; and let no man use his liberty in church relation as an occasion to the flesh; but in love serve one another. ' Looking diligently - lest any root of bitterness - (any poisonful herb, De. xxix. 18.) springing up trouble *you*, and thereby many be defiled.' He. xii. 15. And let those that before were reasons for my separation, be motives to you to maintain the like: and remember that when men have said what they can for a sinful mixture in the worship of God; the arm of the Lord is made bare against it.

II. In the midst of your zeal for the Lord, remember that the visible saint is his; and is privileged in all those spiritual things that you have in the word and live in the practice of, and that he is to partake thereof, according to his light therein. Quarrel not with him about things that are circumstantial; but receive him in the Lord, as becometh saints: if he will not have communion with you, the neglect is his, not yours. But saith the open profane, why cannot we be reckoned saints also? We have been christened, we go to church, we take the communion.* Poor people!

---

* This is a much more extensive evil than many would credit. I have met with these very expressions not only among the poor but the rich. It is an awful delusion.—Ed.

This will not do; for so long as in life and conversation you appear to be open profane, we cannot, unless we sin, receive you into our fellowship: for by your ungodly lives you shew that you know not Christ; and while you are such by the word, you are reputed but beasts: now then judge yourselves, if it be not a strange community that consisteth of men and beasts: let beasts be with the beasts, you know yourselves do so; you receive not your horse nor your hog to your table, you put them in a room by themselves. Besides I have shewed you before, that for many reasons we cannot have communion with you.

(1.) The church of God must be holy. Le. xi. 44; xix. 2; xx. 7. 1 Pe. i. 15, 16. Is. xxvi. 2. Ps. cxviii. 20. Eze. xliii. 12; xliv. 9. Is. lii. 11.

(2.) The example of the churches of Christ before, hath been a community of visible saints. Ro. i. 7. 1 Co. i. 2. Ep. i. 1. Col. i. 2. 1 Th. i. 1. 2 Th. i. 1—5. Poor carnal man, there are many other reasons urged in this little book, that shew why we cannot have communion with thee: not that we refuse of pride or stoutness, or because we scorn you as men. No, we pity you, and pray to God for you; and could, if you were converted, with joy receive you to fellowship with us: Did you never read in Daniel, That iron is not mixed with miry clay? ii. 43. No more can the saints with you, in the worship of God, and fellowship of the gospel. When those you read of in the fourth of Ezra, attempted to join in temple work with the children of the captivity; what said the children of Judah? 'Ye have nothing to do with us to build an house unto our God; but we ourselves together will build unto the Lord God of Israel,' &c. Eze. iv. 3.

I return now to those that are visible saints by calling, that stand at a distance one from another, upon the accounts before specified: Brethren; CLOSE; CLOSE; be one, as the Father in Christ is one.

1. This is the way to convince the world that you are Christ's, and the subjects of one Lord; whereas the contrary makes them doubt it. Jn. xiii. 34, 35; xvii. 23. 2. This is the way to increase love; that grace so much desired by some, and so little enjoyed by others. 2 Co. vii. 15. 3. This is the way to savour and taste the Spirit of God in each other's experience; for which if you find it in truth you cannot but bless, if you be saints, the name of our Lord Jesus Christ. 1 Th. i. 2—4. 4. This is the way to increase knowledge, or to see more in the word of God: for that may be known by two; that is not seen by one. Is. lii. 8. 5. This is the way to remove secret jealousies and murmurings one against the other: yea this is the way to prevent much sin, and greatly to frustrate that design of hell. Pr. vi. 16—19. 6. This is the way to bring them out of the world into fellowship that now stand off from our gospel privileges, for the sake of our vain janglings. 7. This is the way to make antichrist shake, totter, and tremble. Is. xi. 13, 14. 8. This is the way to leave Babylon as an habitation for devils only; and to make it a hold for foul spirits, and a cage only for every unclean and hateful bird. 9. This is the way to hasten the work of Christ's kingdom in the world; and to forward his coming to the eternal judgment. 10. And this is the way to obtain much of that, WELL DONE, GOOD AND FAITHFUL SERVANT, when you stand before his face. [In the words of Paul] 'I beseech you, brethren, suffer the word of exhortation: for I have written a letter unto you in few words.' He. xiii. 22.

DIFFERENCES IN JUDGMENT ABOUT WATER BAPTISM, NO BAR TO COMMUNION:

OR,

TO COMMUNICATE WITH SAINTS, AS SAINTS, PROVED LAWFUL.

IN ANSWER TO A BOOK WRITTEN BY THE BAPTISTS, AND PUBLISHED BY MR. T. P'AUL] AND MR. W. K[IFFIN], ENTITULED, 'SOME SERIOUS REFLECTIONS ON THAT PART OF MR. BUNYAN'S CONFESSION OF FAITH, TOUCHING CHURCH COMMUNION WITH UNBAPTIZED BELIEVERS.' WHEREIN THEIR OBJECTIONS AND ARGUMENTS ARE ANSWERED, AND THE DOCTRINE OF COMMUNION STILL ASSERTED AND VINDICATED. HERE IS ALSO MR. HENRY JESSE'S JUDGMENT IN THE CASE, FULLY DECLARING THE DOCTRINE I HAVE ASSERTED.

By JOHN BUNYAN.

'Should not the multitude of words be answered? and should a man full of talk be justified? Should thy lies make men hold their peace? and when thou mockest, shall no man make thee an answer [ashamed?]'—Job xi. 2, 3.
'I am for peace; but when I speak, they are for war.'—Psal. cxx. 7.

London: Printed for John Wilkins, and are to be sold at his shop in Exchange Alley, next door to the Exchange Coffee House, over against the Royal Exchange, 1673.

COURTEOUS READER,

BE intreated to believe me, I had not set pen to paper about this controversy, had we been let alone at quiet in our Christian communion. But being assaulted for more than sixteen years, wherein the brethren of the baptized way, as they had their opportunity, have sought to break us in pieces, merely because we are not, in their way, all baptized first: I could not, I durst not, forbear to do a little, if it might be, to settle the brethren, and to arm them against the attempts, which also of late they begin to revive upon us. That I deny the ordinance of baptism, or that I have placed one piece of an argument against it, though they feign it, is quite without colour of truth. All I say is, That the church of Christ hath not warrant to keep out of their communion the Christian that is discovered to be a visible saint by the word, the Christian that walketh according to his light with God. I will not make reflections upon those unhandsome brands that my brethren have laid upon me for this, as that I am a machivilian, a man devilish, proud, insolent, presumptuous, and the like, neither will I say as they, The Lord rebuke thee; Words fitter to be spoken to the devil than a brother. But reader, read and compare; lay aside prejudice and judge. What Mr. Kiffin hath done in the matter I forgive, and love him never the worse, but must stand by my principles because they are peaceable, godly, profitable, and such as tend to the edification of my brother, and as I believe will be justified in the day of judgment.

I have also here presented thee with the opinion of Mr. Henry Jesse, in the case, which providentially I met with as I was coming to London to put my papers to the press; and that it was his judgment is asserted to me, known many years since to some of the Baptists, to whom it was sent, but never yet answered; and will yet be attested if need shall require. Farewell.

Thine in all Christian service, according to my light and power,   JOHN BUNYAN.

DIFFERENCES IN JUDGMENT ABOUT WATER BAPTISM, NO BAR TO COMMUNION.

SIR,

Your seemingly serious reflections upon that part of my plain-hearted confession of faith, which rendereth a reason of my freedom to communicate with those of the saints and faithful who differ from me about water baptism; I have read and considered, and have weighed them so well as my rank and abilities will admit me to do. But finding yours, if I mistake not, far short of a candid replication, I thought [it] convenient, not only to tell you of those impertinencies everywhere scattered up and down in your book; but also, that in my simple opinion, your rigid and church-disquieting principles are not fit for any age and state of the church.

But before I enter the body of your book, give me leave a little to discourse you about your preamble to the same, wherein are two miscarriages unworthy your pretended seriousness, because void of love and humility. The first is, In that you closely disdain my person because of my low descent among men, stigmatising me for a person of THAT rank, that need not to be heeded or attended unto. p. 1.*

Answ. What it is that gives a man reverence with you, I know not; but for certain, He that despiseth the poor reproacheth his Maker; yet, 'a poor man *is* better than a liar.' To have gay clothing, or gold rings, or the persons that wear them in admiration; or to be partial in your judgment, or respects, for the sake, or upon the account of, flesh and blood, doubtless convicteth you to be of the law a transgressor, and not without partiality, &c., in the midst of your seeming sanctity.

Again, you say, ' I had not meddled with the controversy at all, had I found any of parts that would divert themselves to take notice of YOU.' p. 2.

Answ. What need you, before you have shewed one syllable of a reasonable argument in opposition to what I assert, thus trample my person, my Read Ps. i. gifts, and grace, have I any, so disdain-1, 2.† fully under your feet? What kind of a YOU am *I*? And why is MY rank so mean, that the most gracious and godly among you, may not duly and soberly consider of what I have said? Was it not the art of the false apostles of old to

---

* Who is there that reads these revilings of Bunyan for his poverty and mean descent, but must be struck with the unsearchable wisdom of the Almighty. The salvation of the church requires that 'GOD should be manifest in the flesh.' Does he appear in his glory? Does he honour riches, and power, and wisdom, by descending in one of these classes? No; the poor, the despised in this world, claim kindred with him—'Is not this the carpenter's son?' 'Have any of the rulers or pharisees believed on him?' Even with these examples before them, his Baptist ministerial brethren, who sat at his feet when he came to London, and listened to his eloquence, now, in their hot dispute, revile and taunt him with his imprisonment—his poverty—his want of book learning. Refused the communion of some eminent earthly saints, it drove him to closer communion with his God, and the prison became a Bethel—none other than the house of God, and the very gate of heaven; and in a holy, happy frame of soul, he breathes forgiveness: 'What Mr. Kiffin hath done in the matter I forgive, and love him never the worse'!!—ED.

† How do these verses cut down all the carnal pride of man. Who is THE BLESSED? not the rich, or powerful, or worldly wise, but those that delight in the word of God.—ED.

say thus? To bespatter a man, that his doctrine might be disregarded. ' Is not this the carpenter?' And, 'His bodily presence *is* weak and *his* speech contemptible,' 1 Co. x. 10, did not use to be in the mouths of the saints; for they knew that ' the wind bloweth where it listeth.' Jn. iii. 8. Neither is it high birth, worldly breeding, or wealth; but electing love, grace, and the wisdom that comes from heaven, that those who strive for strictness of order in the things and kingdom of Christ, should have in regard and esteem. Ja. iii. 17. Need I read you a lecture? ' Hath not God chosen the foolish, - the weak, - the base, *yea*, and things which are not, to bring to nought things that are?' 1 Co. i. 27, 28. Why then do you despise my rank, my state, and quality in the world?

As for my confession of faith, which you also secretly despise. p. 1. If it be good and godly, why may it not be accepted? If I have spoken evil, bear witness of the evil; but if well, why smitest thou me? If you, and the brethren of your way, did think it convenient to shew to the world what you held; if perhaps by that means you might escape the prison: why might not I, after above eleven years' endurance there, give the world a view of my faith and practice; if peradventure, wrong thoughts, and false judgments of me, might by that means be abated, and removed. But you suggest; I did it, because I was so willing to be known in the world by my SINGULAR faith and practice.* How singular my faith and practice is, may be better known to you hereafter: but that I did it for a popular applause and fame, as your words seem to bear, for they proceed from a taunting spirit, that will be known to you better in the day of God, when your evil surmises of your brother, and my designs in writing my book, will be published upon the house-tops. Lu. xii. 1—4.

And even now, before I go any further, I will give you a touch of the reason of my publishing that part thereof which you so hotly oppose. It was because of those continual assaults that the rigid brethren of your way, made, not only upon this congregation, to rend it; but also upon many others about us. If peradventure they might break us in pieces, and draw from us disciples after them. Assaults, I say, upon this congregation by times, for no less than these sixteen or eighteen years. Yea, myself they have sent for, and endeavoured to persuade me to break communion with my brethren; also with many others they have often tampered, if haply their seeds of division might take. Neither did they altogether fail of their purpose, for some

they did rend and dismember from us; but none but those, of whom now they begin to be ashamed. The judgment of God so following their design, that the persons which then they prevailed upon, are now a stink, and reproach to religion. Neither were these spirits content with that discord they did sow among us, but they proceeded to seize upon others. But to pass these. The wild, and unsound positions they have urged to maintain their practice, would be too large here to insert. Now, Sir, to settle the brethren, the brethren of our community, and to prevent such disorders among others, was the cause of my publishing my papers: and considering my concern in the house of God, I could do no less than to give them warning, ' That every man might deliver his soul.'

You proceed, saying, ' It is my liberty, as well as others into whose hands it falls, to weigh what you have said in truth's balance, and if it be found too light, to reject it whether you will or no.'

Answ. Do but grant me, without mocking of me, the liberty you desire to take, and God helping me, I desire no more [than] to shift for myself among you. As to your saying, that I proudly and imperiously insult, because I say they are ' babes and carnal, that attempt to break the peace and communion of churches, though upon better pretences than water.' You must know I am still of that mind, and shall be, so long as I see the effects that follow, viz. The breach of love, taking off Christians from the more weighty things of God; and to make them quarrel and have heart-burnings one against another.

Where you are pleased to charge me with raging, for laying those eighteen particular crimes to the charge of such who exclude Christians from church communion, and debar them their heaven-born privileges, for the want of that, which yet God never made the wall of division between us. p. 116. I say, when you can prove, That God hath made water baptism that wall, and that the stress of the after eighteen charges lie wholly and only in that; then you may, time enough, call my language such as wanteth charity: but I question though that was granted, whether your saying, I RAGE, will be justified in the day of judgment.

My great noise, as you call it, about an initiating ordinance, you say, you shall take no notice of. p. 3.

Answ. 1. Although you do not, I must: For if baptism be not that, but another; and if visible saints may enter into fellowship by that other, and are nowhere forbidden so to do, because they have not light into water baptism: it is of weight to be considered by me; yea, and of others too who are unprejudiced. 2. How ignorant you are of such as hold it the initiating ordinance I know not: nor how long you have been of that persuasion I

---

* Nearly all the Baptist churches of that day limited communion to them who had been baptized in water on a profession of their faith. It is very different now; Bunyan's principles have spread, are spreading, and must soon become universal.—ED.

know not. This I know, that men of your own party, as serious, godly, and it may be, more learned than yourself, have within less than this twelve-month urged it. Mr. D. in my hearing, did from Ro. vi. 1, 2. in the meeting in *Lothbury* affirm it: also my much esteemed Mr. D. A.* did twice in a conference with me assert it. 3. But whatever you say, whether for, or against, 'tis no matter; for while you deny it be the entering ordinance, you account it the wall, bar, bolt, and door; even that which must separate between the righteous and the righteous; nay, you make want of light therein, a ground to exclude the most godly your communion, when every novice in religion shall be received into your bosom, and be of esteem with you because he hath, and from what ground God knows, submitted to water baptism.

I am glad that in p. 4. you conclude with me what is the initiating ordinance: but withal, give me leave to correct, as I think, one extravagant expression of yours. You say, 'It is CONSENT on all hands and NOTHING else, that makes them members of particular churches, and not faith and baptism.' p. 4. You might have stopped at, and nothing else, you need not in particular have rejected faith: your first error was bad enough: what, NOTHING else but consent? What, not so much as a respect to the matter or end? Why then are not all the communities of all the highwaymen in the land, truly constituted churches of Christ; unless you can prove that they hold together, but not by consent? What? consent and nothing else? But why do YOU throw out FAITH? why, *I* throw out baptism; which because you cannot as to the case in hand fetch in again, therefore out must faith go too. Your action is much like that harlot's, that stood to be judged by Solomon, who because her own child was dead, would have her neighbour's killed also. 1 Ki. iii. 26. Faith, Sir, both in the profession and confession of it, is of immediate and also absolute concern, even in the very act of the church's reception, of this or another member. Throw out faith, and there is no such thing as a Christian, neither visible nor invisible. You ought to receive no man, but upon a comfortable satisfaction to the church, that you are now receiving a believer. Faith, whether it be savingly there or no, is the great argument with the church in receiving any: we receive not men as men, but the man immediately under that supposition; He hath faith, *he* is a Christian. Sir, consent simply, without faith, makes no man a member of the church of God: because then would a church not cease to be a church, whoever they received among them. Yea, by this assertion you have justified the church of Rome itself, to be to this day both good, and godly, unless you can prove that they did at first, and do now receive their unbelieving members, without their own consent. The church hath no such liberty to receive men without respect to faith; yea, faith and holiness must be the essentials, or basis, upon, and for the sake of which you receive them: holiness, I say, yet not such as is circumstantial, but that which is such in the very heart of it: pray you in your next therefore word it better, lest while you slight and trample upon me, you stand before all, blame-worthy yourself.

The scriptures you speak of, I did not in my first (p. 68.) produce to shew persons unbaptized [in water] might hold communion with the church, though I am fully convinced they may, but to shew, that knowledge of those persons, of their faith and holiness in general, ought first to be shewed to the church, before she can lawfully receive them. Ac. ix. 26—31. 1 Co. xvi. 10. 2 Co. viii. 23. As to my answer to a question (p. 70.) which you have at p. 5. of your's corrupted, and then abused: I tell you again, That a discovery of the faith and holiness, and a declaration of the willingness of a person to subject himself to the laws and government of Christ in his church, is a ground sufficient to receive such a member.

But you descant; Is baptism one of the laws of Christ?

Answ. It is none of those laws, neither any part of them, that the church, as a church, should shew her obedience by. For albeit that baptism be given by Christ our Lord to the church, yet not for them to worship him by as a church. Shew me what church-ordinance it is; and when, or where the church, as a church, is to practise it, as one of those laws and appointments that he hath commanded his church to shew to him her obedience by. Again, That submitting to water baptism, is a sign or note, that was ever required by any of the primitive churches, of him that would hold fellowship with them; or that it infuseth such grace and holiness into those that submit thereto, as to capacitate them for such a privilege; or that they did acknowledge it a sign thereof, I find not in all the Bible.

I find not, as I told you in my first, that baptism is a sign to any, but the person that is baptized. Col. ii. 12. Ro. vi. 1—4. 1 Co. xv. 29. Ac. ii. 38; xxii. 16. The church hath her satisfaction of the person, from better proof. 1 Pe. iii. 21.

I told you also, That baptism makes thee no member of the church, neither doth it make thee a visible saint: It giveth thee therefore, neither right to, nor being of membership at all. Why,

---

* Mr. H. D'Anvers: 'A seventh end of baptism is, that the baptized person may orderly thereby have an entrance into the visible church. None were esteemed members, or did partake of its ordinances, before they were baptized, being so God's hedge or boundary.'—*Treatise of Baptism*, p. 20, ed. 1674. —ED.

Sir, did you not answer these things? but slip them with others, as if you were unconcerned; troubling your reader with such kind of insinuations, as must needs be unsavoury to godly ears. You make the moral law none of Christ's but Moses'; not the son's but the servant's; and tell me, because I plead for faith and holiness, according to moral duties gospelized, (they are my words, p. 79.) whereby we ought to judge of the fitness of members; that therefore Moses is more beholden to me than Christ. p. 6.

Sir, know you not yet, that a difference is to be put betwixt those rules that discover the essentials of holiness, and those that in themselves are not such; and that that of faith and the moral law is the one, and baptism, &c. the other. Is not love to God, abhorrence of idols, to forbear blaspheming, to honour our parents, to do no murder, to forbear theft, not to bear false witness, nor covet, &c. are not (I say) these the precepts of the Lord Jesus, because delivered by Moses? Or, are these such as may better be broken, than for want of light to forbear baptism with water? Or, doth a man while he liveth in the neglect of these, and in the mean time bustle about those you call gospel commands, most honour Christ, or best fit himself for fellowship with the saints? Need I tell you, That the faith of Christ, with the ten commandments, are as much now gospel commands as baptism; and ought to be in as much, and far more respect with the holy ones than that, or other the like.*

Yea, shall I tell you, That baptism will neither admit a man into fellowship, nor keep him there, if he be a transgressor of a moral precept; and that a man who believeth in Jesus, and fulfilleth the royal law, doth more glorify God, and honour religion in the world, than he that keepeth, if there were so many, ten thousand figurative laws. As to those commands that respect God's instituted worship in a church, as a church, I have told you that baptism is none of them, and you have been driven to confess it [p. 40. of your book]. The church then must first look to faith, then to good living according to the ten commandments; after that she must respect those appointments of our Lord Jesus that respects her outward order and discipline, and then she walks as becomes her, sinning if she neglecteth either; sinning if she overvalueth either. But why did you not answer those texts I produced for the strengthening of my argument, viz. Ro. xiv. 17, 18. De. xxvii. 47. Ja. ii. 8—12. 1 Co. ix. 21; v. 9—11. Ga. vi. 15, 16. Phi. iii. 1 Ti. i. 9—11. Ac. xx. 28—32. Ro. xiii. 13. Ja. iv. 11. 1 Co. v. 12. Deal fairly; Answer those texts, with the argument made upon

them; and when you have after a godly manner done that, you may the more boldly condemn.

You tell me, that in p. 93. of mine, I say, 'None ever received baptism without light therein.'

What if I did? (as I did not) but you grant it: and now I will ask you, and pray deal fairly in your answer. May a man be a visible saint without light therein? May he have a good conscience without light therein? And seeing that baptism is none of the worship that Christ instituted in his church for them to practice as a church, must he be kept dark about all other things concerning the worship of God in his church, until he receive light therein?

You have answered already, p. 7. 'That they ought to be ashamed, and to repent of that abomination (their sprinkling) BEFORE they come to have a sight of the pattern of the house of God, the goings in and the comings out thereof.' Eze. xliii. 10, 11. But, Sir, where do you find that want of light in water baptism, or because a man hath been sprinkled, that he is to be kept dark in all other temple-institutions, till he be ashamed and repent of that? Pray produce the texts, for Ezekiel helps you nothing: he speaks only of the pattern of the house, the goings out, and comings in thereof. As for the coming in, you have already confessed, That baptism is not the entering ordinance. And as for the worship that Christ hath instituted in his church, as a church, I say, (and you also have said it, p. 40.) baptism is none of the forms thereof, none of the ordinances thereof, none of the laws thereof; for baptism is, as to the practice of it, that which is without the church, without the house of God.† Then by your own text, if a man do repent him of his christening in his childhood, he may be received into fellowship without submitting to baptism: but I will not strain you too far.

You add, 'Is it a person's light that giveth being to a precept?'

Answ. Who said it? Yet it is his light and faith about it, that can make him to do it acceptably.

You ask again, 'Suppose men plead want of light in other commands?'

Answ. If they be not such, the forbearance of which, discapacitates him of membership, he may yet be received to fellowship.

'But what if a man want light in the supper?' p.7.

Answ. There is more to be said in that case than in the other: for that is a part of that worship which Christ hath instituted for his church,

---

* A modern writer, in a critique on Bunyan, says that he did as much justice to grace as his *Calvinism* would allow him!! May all the world be such Calvinists.—Ed.

† 'Without the church,' previous to having entered into the church, a *personal* obedience to the divine command; having repented, then be baptized: neither of these are duties to be performed by the church, as such, but *individually*.—Ed.

to be conversant in as a church; presenting them as such, with their communion with their Head, and with one another as members of him. 'The cup of blessing which we bless, is it not the communion of the blood of Christ? The bread which we break, is it not the communion of the body of Christ? For we *being* many are one bread, *and* one body; for we are all partakers of that one bread.' 1 Co. x. 16, 17. Wherefore this being a duty incumbent on the church, as a church; and on every member of that body as such, they are obliged in that case more closely to deal with the members, than in that wherein they are not so concerned; and with which as such, they have nothing to do. No man baptizeth by virtue of his office in the church; no man is baptized by virtue of his membership there.

'But what if a man want light in his duty to the poor?' p. 8.

Answ. If he doth, God must give it him; I mean to know his duty as a church member. Now I will add, but what if he that can give a shilling, giveth nothing? I suppose all that the church can do in that case, is but to warn, to exhort, and charge him, and to shew him his duty: and if he neglect, to shew him, that 'He which soweth sparingly, shall reap also sparingly.' 2 Co. ix. 6. But to cut a man off for this, as you forwardly urge, p. 8. would argue that church, at least I think so, a little too bold with so high and weighty a censure. I plead not here for the churl, but seek to allay your heat: and should it be granted that such deserve as you would have it, this makes no matter to the case in hand. Now whereas you suggest, 'That moral evils are but sins against men,' p. 8. you are too much unadvised: the moral evil, as you call it, whether you respect the breach of the first or second table, is first and immediately a sin against God; and more insufferable, yea and damnable, than for a man for want of light to forbear either baptism or the Lord's Supper.

But say you, 'We have now found an advocate for sin against God, in the breach of one of HIS holy commands?'

Answ. As if none of the moral precepts were HIS. But, Sir, who have I pleaded for, in the denial of any one ordinance of God? Yea, or for their neglect of it either? What I say, is but that men must have light, that they may not do in darkness, or Papist-like, live by an implicit faith.

But I see you put no difference between an open breach of the law, and a forbearing that which to him is doubtful. But I will suppose a case: There is a man wants light in baptism, yet by his neighbour is pressed to it: he saith he seeth it not to be his duty; the other saith, he sins if he doth it not: now seeing 'whatsoever *is* not of faith is sin;' Ro. xiv. 23. what should this man do?

If you say, let him use the means: I say so too. But what, if when he hath used it, he still continueth dark about it; what will you advise him now? If you bid him wait, do you not encourage him to live in sin, as much as I do? Nay, and seeing you will not let him for want of light in that, obey God in other his institutions; what is it but to say, Seeing you live for want of light in the neglect of baptism, we will make you, while you continue so, live, though quite against your light, in the breach of all the rest. And WHERE you are commanded thus, you may shew the place when you find it.

Now where you urge, that you are one of them that say, 'The epistles were writ to particular churches, and so serve nothing at all for our kind of communion.' Urging further, 'That it will be difficult for me to prove, that they were also directed to particular saints.' p. 9.

Answ. I wish there were nothing harder, that were good for me to do. But what should be the reason that our author, with others of his opinion, should stickle so hard to prove [that] all the epistles were wrote to particular churches? Why, because those members were, as they think, every one baptized; and so the epistles from which we fetch our arguments for the love and concord of saints, to be only proper to themselves.* But if this be true, there is virtue indeed, and more than ever I dreamed of, in partaking of water baptism: for if that shall take away the epistles, and consequently the whole Bible, from all that are not baptized; then are the other churches, and also particular saints, in a very deplorable condition. For he asketh me very devoutly, 'Whether any unbaptized persons were concerned in these epistles?' p. 9. But why would they take from us the Holy Scriptures? Verily, that we might have naught to justify our practice withal: for if the Scriptures belong only to baptized believers, they then belong not to the rest; and in truth, if they could persuade us to yield them this grant, we should but sorrily justify our practice. But I would ask these men, 'If the word of God came out from them? Or if it came to them only?' 1 Co. xiv. 36. Or, whether Christ hath not given his whole word to every one that believeth, whether they be baptized, or in, or out of church fellowship. Jn. xvii. 14. Or, whether every saint in some sort, hath not the keys of the kingdom of heaven, which are the Scriptures and their power? Would to God they had learned more modesty, than thus to take from all others, and appropriate to themselves, and that

---

* 'To themselves,' to the particular churches only to which they were written. Contrary to the word, 'All scripture is given - to be profitable to the man of God' in every church, 2 Tim. iii. 16.—ED.

for the sake of their observing a circumstance in religion, so high, and glorious a privilege.

But we will come a little to proof: what church will this author find in Rome, that time the epistle was sent to the brethren there, besides that church that was in Aquila's house, although many more saints were then in the city? Ro xvi. 5. Yea, the apostle in his salutation at the beginning, embraceth them only as brethren, without the least intimation of their being gathered into fellowship: 'To all that be in Rome, beloved of God, called *to be* saints: Grace to you,' &c. ch. i. 7. To all there, to all in that city, beloved of God, and that are converted to the Lord Jesus Christ. A church there was in Aquila's house, and that there were many more saints besides, is, and that by the text, as manifest. Besides, considering the rules that are given them in the 14th and 15th chapters about their receiving one another, doth yet strongly suggest to me, that they were not yet in fellowship, but as it were now about it, when Paul wrote his epistle to them.

The first epistle written to Corinth, was also wrote to all them '*that in every place call upon the name of Jesus Christ our Lord.*' ch i. 2. But it will be hard work for our author to make it manifest, that none in those days did call on the name of our Lord, but those that were first baptized. The second epistle also, was not only written to the church at Corinth, but also to 'all the saints which were in all Achaia.' 2 Co. i. 1. To the Galatians and Thessalonians indeed, his salutation was only to the churches there: But the three epistles before were as well to all other [saints]: As also that to the Ephesians, Philippians, and Colossians, in which the faithful and SAINTS in Christ Jesus were also every one comprehended. Besides, to what particular church was the epistle to the Hebrews wrote? Or the epistle of James? Both those of Peter, and the first of John? Nay, that of John was wrote to some at that time out of fellowship, 'that also may have fellowship with [us]' the church. ch. i. 1—4. So that these brethren must not have all the scriptures. We have then a like privilege with all saints, to use the scriptures for our godly edifying, and to defend ourselves thereby, from the assaults of those that would make spoil of us. But to pass this, and come to the next.

You object for that I said, 'If water baptism (as the circumstances with which the church was pestered of old) trouble the peace, and wound the consciences of the godly, dismember and break their fellowships; it is, although an ordinance, for the present prudently to be shunned.' p. 86. At this (as I said) you object, p 10, 11. and say, 'Did I ever find baptism a pest or plague to churches? And did ever God send an ordinance to be a pest and plague to his people?'

I answer: I said not that God did send it for any such end at all; God's ordinances are none of this in themselves: nor if used as, and for the end for which God sent them. But yet both baptism, and the supper of the Lord, have, by being wrested out of their place, been a great affliction to the godly both in this and other ages. What say you to breaking of bread, which the devil, by abusing, made an engine in the hand of Papists, to burn, starve, hang and draw thousands? What say you to John of Leyden? What work did he make by the abuse of the ordinance of water baptism? And I wish this age had not given cause, through the church-rending spirits that some are possessed with, to make complaint of this matter; who have also had for their engine the baptism with water. Yea, yourself, Sir, so far as I can perceive, could you get but the opportunity; yourself (I say) under pretence of this innocent ordinance, as you term it, would not stick to make inroads, and outroads too, in all the churches, that suit not your fancy, in the land. For you have already been bold to affirm, 'That all those that have baptized infants, ought to be ashamed and repent, before they be showed the pattern of the house.' And what is this but to threaten, that could you have your will of them, you would quickly take from them their present church privileges, and let them see nothing thereof, till those qualifications, especially subjection to water baptism, was found to attend each of them.

As to the persons you speak of, 'Who have rent churches in pieces, by making preaching by method, doctrine, reason and use, to be anti-christian:' Or, because they could not have other ministrations performed after their fancies (p. 11, 12.) 'the imprudence of such with yourselves, hath been heart-breaking to many a gracious soul; an high occasion of stumbling to the weak, and a reproach to the ways of the Lord.' That it may be prudently shunned, I referred you then for proof, to what should be offered after: but at this you cry out, and so pass it.

And now, reader, although this author hath thus objected against some passages in this my first argument for communion with persons unbaptized; yet the body of my argument he misseth and passeth over, as a thing not worth the answering; whether because he forgot, or because he was conscious to himself, that he knew not what to do therewith, I will not now determine. 1. I effectually prove, 'That baptism is not the initiating ordinance.' p. 71—75. 2. I prove, 'That though it was, yet the case may so fall out, that members might be received without it.' p. 82, 83. 3. I prove, 'That baptism makes no man a visible saint, nor giveth any right to church fellowship.' p. 76. 4. I prove, 'That faith, and a life becoming the law of the ten commandments, should be the chief and most solid argument with true churches to receive saints to fellowship.'* 5. I prove, 'That circumcision in the flesh, which was the entering ordinance of old, was a type of circumcision in the heart,' &c. p. 79, 80. These things, with others, our author letteth pass; although in the proof of them abideth the strength of this first argument; to which I must entreat him in his next, to cast his eye, and give fair answer; as also to the scriptures on which each are built, or he must suffer me to say, I am abused. Further, I make a question upon three scriptures, Whether all the saints, even in the primitive times, were baptized with water? to which also he answereth nothing; whereas he ought to have done it, if he will take in hand to confute. The scriptures are, 1 Co. i. 14—16. Ro. vi. 3. Ga. iii. 27. Yet were they effectually answered, my argument is nothing weakened.

You come to my second argument, drawn from Ep. iv. 4—6. Upon which a little more now to enlarge, and then to take notice of your objection. The apostle then in that fourth of the Ephesians, exhorteth the church there 'with all lowliness and meekness, with long suffering, forbearing one another in love; endeavouring to keep the unity of the spirit in the bond of peace.' ver. 2, 3. This done, he presents them with such arguments, as might fasten his exhortation to purpose upon them.

1. The first is, because the body is ONE; There is 'one body;' therefore they should not divide. For if the church of Christ be a body, there ought not to be a rent or schism among them. 1 Co. xii.

2. His second argument is, There is 'one spirit,' or one quickening principle by which the body is made to live; for having asserted before that Christ hath indeed a body, it was meet that he showed also, that this body hath life, and motion. Now that life, being none other, than that nourishment, or spirit of life, from which 'the whole body fitly joined together and compacted by that which every joint supplieth, according to the effectual working of the measure in every part, maketh increase of the body unto the edifying of itself in love.' Ep. iv 16. Now this spirit, being first, and chiefly, in the head, therefore none other but those that hold the head can have this nourishment ministered to them: besides, this is the

spirit that knits the body together, and makes it increase with the increase of God. Col. ii. 19. This is 'the unity of the spirit' which he before exhorts them to keep.

3. The third argument is, Because their hope is also but one. 'Even as ye are called [saith he] in one hope of your calling:' as who should say, My brethren, if you are called with one calling, if your hope, both as to the grace of hope, and also the object, be but one: if you hope for one heaven, and for one eternal life: then maintain that unity of the spirit, and hope, while here, in love, 'and the bond of peace.' Ep. iv. 3.

4. The fourth argument is, There is 'one Lord,' or husband, or prince, to whom this church belongs: therefore if we have husbands, but one, Lord and prince but one, let us not rend into many parties, as if we had many husbands, lords, and princes, to govern us, as his wife, his house, and kingdom. 'Is Christ divided?' 1 Co. i. 13.

5. The fifth argument is, There is 'one faith,' by which we all stand justified by one Lord Jesus Christ; 'one faith' by which we escape the wrath of God; 'one faith' by which only they that have it are blessed; yea, seeing there is but 'one faith,' by which we are all put into one way of salvation, let us hold together as such.

6. The sixth argument is, There is 'one baptism.' Now we are come to the pinch, viz., Whether it be that of water, or no? which I must positively deny. (1.) Because water baptism hath nothing to do in a church, as a church; it neither bringeth us into the church, nor is any part of our worship when we come there; how then can the peace and unity of the church depend upon water baptism? Besides, he saith expressly, It is the 'unity of the spirit,' not water, that is here intended: and the arguments brought to enforce it, are such as wholly and immediately relate to the duty of the church, as a church. (2.) Further, That other text, that treateth of our being baptized into a body, saith expressly it is done by the spirit: 'For by one spirit are we all baptized into one body.' 1 Co. xii. 13. Here is the church presented as under the notion of 'one body;' here is a baptism mentioned, by which they are brought, or initiated into this body: Now that this is the baptism of water, is utterly against the words of the text; 'For by one spirit are we all baptized into one body.' Besides, if the baptism here be of water, then is it the intiating ordinance; but the contrary I have proved, and this author stands by my doctrine. So then, the baptism here respecting the church as one body, and water, having nothing to do to enter men into the church, nor to command them to practise it as a church, in order to their peace or communion, or respecting the worship of God as such: and (I say again) the baptism in the sixth

---

* To these ten commandments must be added that new command given by the Saviour, 'That ye love one another,' John xii. 34; or rather the evangelical sum of the whole law, 'Thou shalt love the Lord thy God with all thy heart, and thy neighbour as thyself.' This happy state of mind can only be attained by the baptism of the Holy Ghost. How awful the thought that multitudes of professing Christians rely upon outward ceremonies, a fleshly carnal confidence in ordinances, while they are dead as to union with God and to spiritual communion with his saints. Reader, how is it with your own soul.—ED.

argument, being urged precisely for no other purpose, but with respect to the church's peace as a body; it must needs be THAT baptism, by virtue of which, they were initiated, and joined together in one; and that baptism being only that which the Spirit executeth; this therefore is that one baptism.

7. The other argument is also effectual; there is 'One God and Father of all, who *is* above all, and through all, and in you all.' Ep. iv. 6. If we are 'one body;' if to it there be but 'one spirit;' if we have but 'one hope, one faith,' and be all baptized by 'one spirit' into that 'one' body; and if we have but 'one Lord, one God,' and he in every one of us; let us be also 'one:' and let them that are thus qualified, both join together, and hold in one.

But our author against this, objecteth, That, 'now I employ my pen against every man; and give the lie to all expositors, for they hold this one baptism, to be none other than that of water.'* p. 13.

Answ. What if I should also send you to answer those expositors that expound certain scriptures for infant baptism, and that by them brand us for anabaptists; must this drive you from your belief of the truth? EXPOSITORS I reverence, but must live by mine own faith. Hab. ii. 4. God hath no where bound himself to them more than to others, with respect to the revelation of his mind in his word. But it becomes not you to run thus to expositors, who are, as to your notions in many things, but of yesterday: 'to the law, and to the testimony:' Is. viii. 20. for 'Out of the mouth of babes' the Lord hath 'ordained strength.' Ps. viii. 2.

But you bid me tell you, 'What I mean by spirit baptism?'

Answ. Sir, you mistake me, I treat not here of our being baptized with the Spirit, with respect to its coming from heaven into us; but of that act of the spirit, when come, which baptizeth us into a body or church. It is one thing to be baptized with the Spirit in the first sense; and another to be baptized by it in the sense I treat of: for the Spirit to come upon me, is one thing; and for that when come, to implant, embody, or baptize me into the body of Christ, is another. Your question therefore is grounded on a mistake, both of my

judgment, and the words of the apostle. Wherefore thus I soon put an end to your objections, (p. 14.) For the Spirit to come down upon me, is one thing; and for the Spirit to baptize, or implant me into the church, is another: for to be possessed with the spirit, is one thing; and to be led by that spirit, is another. I conclude then; seeing the argument taken from that one baptism, respecteth church fellowship properly; and seeing water baptism meddleth not with it as such; it is the other, even that in 1 Co. xii. 16. that is here intended, and no other.

But you add, 'If nothing but extraordinary gifts are called the baptism of the Spirit in a strict sense; then that baptism, 1 Co. xii. must be water baptism, as well as that in the Ephesians.'

Hold: you make your conclusions before you have cause; first, prove that in the Ephesians to be meant of water baptism, and that the baptism in 1 Co. xii. 16 is the baptism you would have it; and then conclude my argument void. That it is the baptism of the Holy Ghost according to the common notion, I say not; for you to assert it is the baptism of water, gives the lie to the text: but that it is an act of the Holy Ghost, baptizing the saints into a body, or church, you will hardly be able to make the contrary appear to be truth. 'But behold, while here you would have this to be baptism with water, how you contradict and condemn your own notion: you say water baptism is not the entering ordinance; yet the baptism here is such as baptizeth us into a body: wherefore before you say next time that this in 1 Co. xii. 16. is meant of water baptism; affirm that water baptism is the initiating or entering ordinance, that your opinion and doctrine may hang better together.'

We come to my third argument; which is to prove, that it is lawful to hold church communion with the godly sincere believer, though he hath not been baptized with water, because he hath the DOCTRINE of baptisms. He. vi. 2. Which doctrine I distinguish from the practice of it; the doctrine being that which by the outward sign is presented to us; or which by the outward circumstance of the act is preached to the believer, viz., the death of Christ, my death with Christ; also his resurrection from the dead, and mine with him to newness of life. 'This our author calleth one of the strangest paradoxes that he hath LIGHTLY observed.'

Answ. How light he is in his observation of things, I know not; this I am sure, the apostle makes mention of the doctrine of baptisms; now that the doctrine of a man, or ordinance, is the signification of what is preached, is apparent to very sense. What is Christ's doctrine, Paul's doctrine, scripture doctrine, but the truth couched under the words that are spoken? so the doctrine of baptism, yea and the doctrine of the Lord's supper, are

---

* Bunyan's adversaries were wrong in stating that *all* the expositors agreed in referring this 'one baptism' to be that in or with water. John Caime, 1662, refers to 1 Cor. xii. 13, as an illustration of Eph. iv. 5, 'one baptism,' 'by one SPIRIT are we all baptized.' The Assembly's Annotations, 1657, infers that 'one' means 'once,' and refers to the Nicene creed, which says, 'one baptism for the remission of sins;' this surely cannot mean that the application of water remits sins. Diodati, 1648, is silent on this subject. Dr. Hammond, 1653, says, 'the *same vow* to be administered to all.' Very similar to this is the Dutch annotations of Theodore Haak.—ED.

those truths or mysteries that such ordinances preach unto us. And that the doctrine of baptism, in this sense, is the great end for which that, and the Lord's supper, was instituted, is apparent from all the scriptures: it is that which the apostle seeketh for in that eminent sixth of the Romans, ' Know ye not that so many of us as were baptized into Jesus Christ, were baptized into his death ? Therefore we are buried with him by baptism into death : that like as Christ was raised up from the dead by the glory of the Father, even so we also should walk in newness of life. For if we have been planted together in the likeness of his death, we shall be also *in the likeness* of *his* resurrection.' 3—5. What is here discoursed, but the doctrine of or that which baptism teacheth; with an intimation; that that was the chief, for the sake of which that shadow was instituted; as also that they that have the doctrine, or that which is signified thereby, they only must reign with Christ.

Again, This is that which he seeketh for among the Corinthians; 'If the dead rise not at all,' [saith he], 'why then were you baptized for the dead ?' 1 Co. xv. 29. Why then were you baptized ? What did baptism teach you ? What doctrine did it preach to you ? further, ' Buried with him in baptism, wherein also ye are risen with *him* through the faith of the operation of God, who hath raised him from the dead.' Col. ii. 12. What is here in chief asserted, but the doctrine only which water baptism preacheth ? with an intimation, that they, and they only, are the saved of the Lord, that have heard, received, and that live in this doctrine.

The same may be said of the Lord's supper, it also hath its doctrine. But against this our author objecteth, saying, ' That this is called the doctrine of baptism, I am yet to learn.'

Answ. Your ignorance of the truth makes it not an error : but I pray you, what is the doctrine of baptism, if not that which baptism teacheth, even that which is signified thereby? As that is the doctrine of Christ, and the scriptures; which he and they teach as the mind of God.

But you say, ' I took the doctrine of baptism to be the command that a believer should be baptized, for such ends as the gospel expresseth.'

Answ. To assert that a figurative ordinance is of God, is one thing; but the doctrinal signification of that ordinance is another. A man may preach the command, yet none of the doctrine which baptism preacheth. The doctrine lieth not in the command, but the mystery discovered to faith, by the act.

You object, 'If the resurrection be the doctrine of baptism, why doth the apostle make that, and the doctrine of baptism, things distinct, in He. vi.'

Answ. The resurrection simply considered, is not the doctrine of baptism, but Christ's, and mine

by him. Besides, there is more in it than the mystery of this resurrection; there is my death first, and then my rising with him.

But you add, ' Under the law, all the sacrifices of that dispensation, with their sabbaths, were types of that Christ, who was the substance of all those ceremonies. If any of them then that professed faith in the Messias to come, should upon scruples, or want of pretended light, neglect the whole, or part of that typical worship; why may not a man say of them, as this advocate of the practice under debate, they had the richer and better sacrifice.'

Answ. First, that the brethren which refuse to be baptized, as you and I would have them, refuse it for want of pretended light, becomes you not to imagine, unless your boldness will lead you to judge, that all men want sincerity, that come not up to our judgment. Their conscience may be better than either yours or mine; yet God, for purposes best known to himself, may forbear to give them conviction of their duty in this particular. But what, because they are not baptized, have they not Jesus Christ ? Or, must we now be afraid to say that Christ is better than water baptism ?* Yea, God himself for the sake of this better thing, hath suffered in his church a suspension of some of his ordinances, yet owned them for his truly constituted congregation. What say you to the church in the wilderness ? I touched you with it in my first, but perceive you listed not to meddle therewith. That church received members, the way which was not prescribed by, but directly against the revealed mind of God ; yet stood a true church, their members true members; also that church in that state, was such before whom, among whom, and to whom God continually made known himself to be their God, and owned them for his peculiar treasure.

And now I am fallen upon it, let me a little enlarge : this church, according to the then instituted worship of God, had circumcision for their entering ordinance, Ge. xvii. 13, 14. without which it was unlawful to receive any into fellowship with them : yea, he that without it was received, was to be cut off, and cast out again. Further, as to the passover, the uncircumcised were utterly forbidden to eat it. Ex. xii. 48. Now if our brethren had as express prohibition to justify their groundless opinion, as here is to exclude the uncircumcised from the communion of the church and the passover : I say, if they could find it written, ' No unbaptized person shall enter, no unbaptized per-

* Heaven forbid that we should be afraid or ashamed of saying that Christ is better than water baptism. Christ is the heavenly manna, the sweet, pleasant, nourishing food of the soul. Baptism is only once for life, but Christ is our essential food all through the wilderness—every hour of life until we enter the gates of the celestial and eternal city.—ED.

son shall eat of the supper;' what a noise would they make about it? But yet let the reader observe, that although circumcision was the entering ordinance, and our author saith baptism is not; yea, though this church was expressly forbidden to receive the uncircumcised, and we have not a syllable now to forbid the unbaptized, yet this church received members without, and otherwise than by this entering ordinance. They also admitted them to the passover; yea, entertained, retained, and held communion with them so long as forty years without it. I say again, That the number of this sort of communicants was not so few as six hundred thousand. Moreover, to these uncircumcised was the land of Canaan given, yea, a possession of part thereof before they were circumcised; but the old circumcised ones might not enter therein. I am the larger in this, because our author hath overlooked my first mention thereof. And now I ask, What was the reason that God continued his presence with this church notwithstanding this transgression? Was it not because they had that richer and better thing, 'the Lord Jesus Christ?' For they did all eat of that spiritual bread, and drink of that 'spiritual rock that followed them: and that rock was Christ.' 1 Co. x. 3, 4. I confess I find them under rebukes and judgments in the wilderness, and that they were many times threatened to be destroyed; but yet I find not so much as one check for their receiving of members uncircumcised. Further, in the New Testament, where we have a catalogue of their sins, and also of their punishment for them; we find not a word about circumcision, nor the smallest intimation of the least rebuke for neglecting the entering ordinance. 1 Co. x. 5—10. I will therefore say of them, as I have also said of my brethren, 'They had the richer and better thing.'

But you object, 'That this putteth the whole of God's instituted worship both under the law and gospel, to the highest uncertainties.' p. 17. *Answ.* This putteth our opposers out of their road, and quencheth the flame of their unwarrantable zeal. For if the entering ordinance, if the ordinance without which no man might be added to the church, was laid aside for forty years; yea, if more than six hundred thousand did communicate with them without it: I say again, If they did it, and held communion with God, that notwithstanding; yea, and had not, that we read of, all that time one small check for so doing; why may not we now enter communion, hold communion, maintain communion, church communion, without being judged, and condemned by you? because we cannot for want of light be all baptized before; especially considering baptism makes no man a saint, is not the entering ordinance, is no part of the worship of God enjoined the church as a church.

To conclude, although we receive members unbaptized [in water], we leave not God's instituted worship at uncertainties, especially what he hath commanded us as his church; we only profess our want of light in some things; but see no word to warrant the forbearance of our duty in all, for want of persuasion in one.

You object, 'I call baptism a circumstance, an outward-shew I NICKNAME it.'

Answ. Deep reproof! but why did you not shew me my evil in thus calling it, when opposed to the substance, and the thing signified? Is it the substance, is it the thing signified? And why may not I give it the name of a shew; when you call it a symbol, and compare it to a gentleman's livery? p. 52.

But you say, I call it *an* outward *shew.*
Answ. Is it an inward one? What is it?
'It is a command.'
Answ. But doth that install it in that place and dignity, that was never intended for it?

You object further, 'They cannot have the doctrine of baptism that understand not our way of administering it.' p. 18.

This is your mistake, both of the doctrine and thing itself. But if you will not SCORN to take notice of me, I advise you again to consider, That a man may find baptism to be commanded, may be informed who ought to administer it; may also know the proper subject; and that the manner of baptizing is dipping; and may desire to practise it because it is commanded, and yet know nothing of what water baptism preacheth; or of the mystery baptism sheweth to faith. But that the doctrine of baptism is not the practice of it, not the outward act, but the thing signified; and that every believer hath that, must argue you more than too bold to deny it.

But say you, 'Who taught you to divide betwixt Christ and his precepts, that you word it at such a rate? That he that hath the one,' &c.

Answ. To say nothing of faith, and the word; verily reason itself teacheth it. For if Christ be my righteousness, and not water; if Christ be my advocate, and not water; if there be that good and blessedness in Christ, that is not in water; then is Jesus Christ better than water; and also in these to be eternally divided from water; unless we will make them co-saviours, co-advocates, and such as are equally good and profitable to men.

But say you, 'I thought that he that hath Christ, had an orderly right to all Christ's promises and precepts; and that the precepts of Christ, are part of the riches that a believer hath in and by Christ.'

Answ. A believer hath more in Christ than either promise or precept; but all believers know not all things, that of God are given to them by

Christ. But must not they use, and enjoy what they know, because they know not all. Or must they neglect the weightier matters, because they want mint, and anise, and cummin? Your pretended orderly right is your fancy; there is not a syllable in the whole bible, that bids a Christian to forbear his duty in other things, because he wanteth, as you term it, the symbol, or water baptism.

But say you, 'He that despiseth his birthright of ordinances, our church privileges, will be found to be a profane person, as Esau in God's account.'

Baptism is not the privilege of a church as such. But what? are they all Esau's indeed? Must we go to hell, and be damned, for want of faith in water baptism? And take notice, I do not plead for a despising of baptism, but a bearing with our brother, that cannot do it for want of light. The best of baptism he hath, *viz.* the signification thereof: he wanteth only the outward shew, which if he had, would not prove him a truly visible saint; it would not tell me he had the grace of God in his heart; it is no characteristical note to another of my Sonship with God. But why did you not answer these parts of my argument? Why did you only cavil at words? which if they had been left out, the argument yet stands good. 'He that is not baptized [in water], if yet a true believer, hath the DOCTRINE of baptism; yea, he ought to have it before he be convicted, it is his duty to be baptized, or else he playeth the hypocrite. There is therefore no difference between that believer that is, and he that is not yet baptized with water; but only his going down into the water, there to perform an outward ceremony, the substance of which he hath already; which yet he is not commanded to do with respect to membership with the church; but to obtain by that, further understanding of his privilege by Christ, which before he made profession of, and that as a visible believer.'*

But to come to my fourth argument, which you so tenderly touch as if it burnt your fingers: 'I am bold (say I) to have communion with visible saints as before, because God hath communion with them, whose example in the case we are strictly commanded to follow.' 'Receive ye one another, as Christ also received us to the glory of God.' Ro. xv. 7. Yea, though they be saints, in opinion contrary to you, or I. 'We that are strong ought

to bear the infirmities of the weak, and not to please ourselves.' Ro. xv. 1. Infirmities that are sinful: for they that are natural are incident to all. Infirmities therefore they are, that for want of light, cause a man to err in circumstantials: and the reason upon which Paul groundeth this admonition is; 'For even Christ pleased not himself, but, as it is written, The reproaches of them that reproached thee fell on me.' Ro. xv. 3.

You say to this, p. 20. 'That it is Paul's direction to the church at Rome how to receive their brethren church members.' p. 20.

I answer, 1. What? are not the poor saints now in this city? are not they concerned in these instructions? or is not the church by these words at all directed how to carry it to those that were not yet in fellowship? A bold assertion! but grounded upon nothing, but that you would have it so. 2. But how will you prove that there was a church, a rightly constituted church, at Rome, besides that in Aquila's house? ch. xvi. Neither doth this epistle, nor any other in the whole book of God affirm it. Besides, since Paul in this last chapter saluteth the church, as in this man's house, but the other, only as particular saints, it giveth further ground of conviction to you, that those others were not as yet imbodied in such a fellowship. 3. But suppose there was another church besides; it doth not therefore follow, that the apostle exhorteth them only to receive persons already in fellowship; but 'Him,' even every 'Him that is weak in the faith receive ye, *but* not to doubtful disputations.' xiv. 1. 4. Suppose again, the receiving here exhorted to, be such as you would have it, yet the rule by which they are directed to do it, is that by which we perceive that Christ hath received them. But Christ did not receive them by [water] baptism, but as given to him by the Father. Him, therefore, concerning whom we are convinced, that he by the Father is given to Christ, 'Him should we receive.' 5. But what need I grant you, that which cannot be proved? yet if you could prove it, it availeth nothing at all; because you may not, cannot, ought not to dare to limit the exhortation to receiving of one another into each other's affections only; and not also receiving saints into communion.

But you object: 'To make God's receiving the rule of our receiving, in all cases will not hold.' p. 21.

Answ. Keep to the thing, man: if it hold in the case in hand, it is enough, the which you have not denied. And that it holds thus, is plain, because commanded. But let the reader know, that your putting in that way of his receiving which is invisible to us; is but an unhandsome straddling over my argument, which treateth only of a visible receiving; such as is manifest to the church. This you knew, but sought by evading to turn the reader from considering the strength

---

* While we acknowledge the importance of water baptism, to which Christ submitted, yet we do well to consider that it was not intended as a means of purifying his infinite purity; no more does it purify the believer who follows his Redeemer in this ordinance. He was as much a believer before as he is after the ceremony. He submits to it as an act of obedience to the divine command, in the humble hope that his faith may be strengthened and his soul refreshed.—ED.

of this my argument. ' The receiving then (said I. p. 29.) because it is set as an example to the church, is such as must needs be visible unto them; and is best discovered by that word that describeth the visible saint. Whoso then you can judge a visible saint, one that walketh with God, you may, nay ought to judge by the same word, that God hath received him. Now him that God receiveth, him should you receive.' But will any object; they cannot believe that God receiveth the unbaptized saints; I will not suppose you so much stupified, and therefore shall make no answer.

But you seem to be much offended, because I said, 'Vain man! Think not by the straightness of thine order in outward, and bodily conformity to outward and shadowish circumstances, that thy peace is maintained with God?' But why so much offended at this? [It is say you] ' Because you intend by this the brethren of the baptized way.'

Answ. If they be vain men, and set up their OWN order, how straight soever they make it, they are worthy to be reproved; if ' they have rejected the word of the Lord; what wisdom *is* in them?' Je. viii. 9. And as you suggest the first, I affirm the second. But if you would be justified in excluding those, with whom yet you see God hath communion, because they yet see not a shadow with you; produce the scripture for such order, that we may believe it is the order of God. But deal fairly, lest we shew your nakedness, and others see your shame. You tell me of the order of the Colossians. ch. ii. 5. But if you can prove that that church refused to hold communion with that saint whom they knew to be received by Christ, and held communion with him [Christ], or that none but those that are baptized [in water] are received by and hold communion with him, then you justify your order. In the mean while the whole of nine argument stands firm against you; ' You must have communion with visible saints, because God hath communion with them, whose example iu the case we are strictly commanded to follow.'

But you ask me, ' If outward and bodily conformity be become a crime?' p. 23.

Answ. I nowhere said it; but know that to glorify God with our bodies, respecteth chiefly far higher and more weighty things, than that of water baptism; 'Whatsoever *is* not of faith is sin;' Ro. xiv. 23. and to set up an ordinance, though an ordinance of God, that by it the church may be pulled in pieces, or the truly visible saints excluded communion with their brethren; I say again, to make water baptism a bar and division between saint and saint, every whit otherwise gracious and holy alike: This is like fasting ' for strife and debate, and to smite with the fist of wickedness;' Is. lviii. 4. and is not to be found within the whole bible, but is wholly an order of your own devising. As to the peace you

make an objection about (p. 23.) you have granted me what I intended; and now I add further, that for church peace to be founded in water baptism, or any other external rite, not having to do with the church, as a church, is poor peace indeed: Church peace is founded in blood; and love to each other for Jesus' sake. Phi. ii. 1—4. Bearing with, and forbearing one another, in all things circumstantial, that concern not church worship as such. Ep. iv. 31, 32. And in my other [treatise] I have proved that baptism is not such, and therefore ought not to be urged to make rents and divisions among brethren.

But you ask, ' Is my peace maintained in a way of disobedience? and conclude if it be, you fear it is false.' p. 24.

Answ. If the first were true; you need not to doubt of the second; but it may be thought he hath little to say in the controversy, who is forced to stuff out his papers, with such needless prattles as these.

My fifth argument is, ' That a failure in such a circumstance as water baptism, doth not unchristian us;' this you are compelled to grant. p. 25. And I conclude with your words, persons ought to be Christians before visible Christians; such as any congregation in the land may receive to communion with themselves, because God hath shewed us that he has received them. ' Receive him to the glory of God.' To the glory of God, is put in on purpose, to shew what dishonour they bring to him, who despise to have communion with such, whom they know do maintain communion with God. I say again, How doth this man, or that church, glorify God, or count the wisdom and holiness of heaven beyond them, when they refuse communion with them, concerning whom yet they are convinced, that they have communion with God? But my argument you have not denied; nor meddled with the conclusion at all; which is, ' That therefore, even because a failure here, doth not unchristian us, doth not make us insincere;' and I add, doth not lay us open to any revealed judgment or displeasure of God (if it doth, shew where) therefore it should not, it ought not to make us obnoxious to the displeasure of the church of God.

But you say, ' I rank gospel precepts, with Old Testament abrogated ceremonies.' p. 25.

Answ. You should have given your reader my words, that he might have judged from my own mouth: I said then, speaking before of Christianity itself, p. 94. ' that thousands of thousands that could not consent to water, as we, are now with the innumerable company of angels, and the spirits of just men made perfect.' What was said of eating, or the contrary, may as to this be said of water baptism: neither if I be baptized, am I the better? neither if I be not, am I the worse?

not the better before God, not the worse before men: still meaning as Paul, provided I walk according to my light with God; otherwise it is false. For if a man that seeth it to be his duty, shall despisingly neglect it; or if he that hath not faith about it, shall foolishly take it up: both these are for this the worse; I mean, as to their own sense, being convicted in themselves, as transgressors. He therefore that doth it according to his light, doth well; and he that doth it not, for want of light, doth not ill; for he approveth his heart to be sincere with God, even by that his forbearance. And I tell you again, It is nowhere recorded, that this man is under any revealed threatening of God, for his not being baptized with water, he not having light therein, but is admitted through his grace to as many promises as you. If therefore he be not a partaker of that circumstance, yet he is of that liberty, and mercy, by which you stand with God.

But that I practise instituted worship, upon the same account as Paul did circumcision, and shaving, is too bold for you to presume to imagine. What? because I will not suffer water to carry away the epistles from the Christians; and because I will not let water baptism be the rule, the door, the bolt, the bar, the wall of division between the righteous, and the righteous; must I therefore be judged to be a man without conscience to the worship of Jesus Christ? The Lord deliver me from superstitious and idolatrous thoughts about any of the ordinances of Christ and of God. But my fifth argument standeth against you untouched; you have not denied, much less confuted the least syllable thereof.

You tell me my sixth argument is, Edification.

Answ. If it be, why is it not embraced? But my own words are these: 'I am for holding communion thus. Because the edification of souls in the faith and holiness of the gospel, is of greater concern than an agreement in outward things; I say, it is of greater concern with us, and of far more profit to our brother, than our agreeing in, or contesting for, water baptism.' Jn. xvi. 13. 1 Co. xiv. 12. 2 Co. x. 8; xii. 19. Ep. iv. 12. 1 Co. xiii. 1, 2; viii. 1. Now why did you not take this argument in pieces, and answer those scriptures, on which the strength thereof depends; but if to contest, and fall out about water baptism, be better than to edify the house of God, produce the texts, that we may be informed.

You say, 'Edification is the end of all communion, but all things must be done in order, orderly.' p. 26.

Answ. When you have proved that there is no such thing as an orderly edifying of the church, without water baptism precede, then it will be time enough to think you have said something.

You add, 'Edification as to church fellowship being a building up, doth suppose the being of a church; but pray you shew us a church without baptism.' p. 26.

Answ. See here the spirit of these men, who for the want of water baptism, have at once unchurched all such congregations of God in the world; but against this I have, and do urge, That water baptism giveth neither being, nor well-being to a church, neither is any part of that instituted worship of God, that the church, as such, should be found in the practice of. Therefore her edification as a church may, yea and ought to be attained unto without it.

But you say, 'Shew us a New Testament church without baptism.' p. 26.

Answ. What say you to the church all along the Revelation quite through the reign of Antichrist? Was that a New Testament church, or no? Again, If baptism be without the church, as a church, if it hath nothing to do in the constituting of a church; if it be not the door of entrance into the church, if it be no part of church-worship as such; then, although all the members of that church were baptized, yet the church is a church without water baptism. But all the churches in the New Testament were such: therefore, &c. Again, If baptism respect believers, as particular persons only; if it respects their own conscience only; if it make a man no visible believer to me, then it hath nothing to do with church-membership. Because, that which respects my own person only, my own conscience only: that which is no character of my visible saintship to the church, cannot be an argument unto them to receive me into fellowship with themselves. But this is true. Therefore, &c.

You proceed, 'If by edification, be meant the private increase of grace, in one another, in the use of private means, as private Christians in meeting together; how doth the principle you oppose hinder that? Endeavour to make men as holy as you can, that they may be fitted for church-fellowship, when God shall shew them the orderly way to it.' p. 26.

Answ. What a many private things have we now brought out to public view? Private Christians, private means, and a private increase of grace. But, Sir, Are none but those of your way the public Christians? Or, ought none but them that are baptized to have the public means of grace? Or, must their graces be increased by none but private means? Was you awake now? Or, are you become so high in your own phantasies, that none have, or are to have but private means of grace? And, are there no public Christians, or public christian meetings, but them of your way? I did not think that all but baptists, should only abide in holes.

But you find fault because I said, 'Edification is greater than contesting about water baptism.' p. 27.

Answ. If it be not, confute me; if it be, forbear to cavil: water baptism, and all God's ordinances, are to be used to edification; not to beget heats and contentions among the godly, wherefore edification is best.

Object. 'I had thought that the preaching, and opening baptism, might have been reckoned a part of our edification.'

Answ. The act of water baptism hath not place in church worship, neither in whole nor in part; wherefore pressing it upon the church is to no purpose at all.'

Object. 'Why may you not as well say, that edification is greater than breaking of bread.' p. 27.

Answ. So it is, else that should never have been instituted to edify withal; that which serveth, is not greater than he that is served thereby. Baptism and the Lord's supper both, were made for us, not we for them; wherefore both were made for our edification, but no one for our destruction. But again, The Lord's supper, not baptism, is for the church, as a church; therefore as we will maintain the church's edifying, that must be maintained in it; yea, used oft, to shew the Lord's death till he come. 1 Co. xi. 22—26. Besides, because it is a great part of church worship, as such, therefore it is pronounced blessed, the Lord did openly bless it before he gave it; yea and we ought to bless it also; 'The cup of blessing which we bless,' not to say more. Therefore your reasoning from the one to the other will not hold.

Object. 'How comes contesting for water baptism to be so much against you?'

Answ. First, Because weak brethren cannot bear it; whom yet we are commanded to receive, but not to doubtful disputation; doubtful to them, therefore for their sakes, I must forbear it. Ro. xiv. 1. Secondly, Because I have not seen any good effect, but the contrary, wherever such hot spirits have gone before me: 'For where envying and strife *is*, there *is* confusion,' or tumults, 'and every evil work.' Ja. iii. 16.* Thirdly, Because by the example of the Lord, and Paul, we must consider the present state of the church, and not trouble them with what they cannot bear. Jn. xvi. 13. 1 Co. iii. 1—3. I conclude then, edification in the church is to be preferred above what the church, as a church, hath nothing to do withal. 'All things, dearly beloved, are for our edifying.' 1 Co. xiv. 5; xii. 26. 2 Co. xii. 19. Ep. iv. 16. Ro. xv. 2. 1 Co. xiv. 3. 2 Co. x. 8; xiii 10. Ro. xiv. 19. Before I wind up this argument, I present you with several instances, shewing that the breach of [some of] God's precepts have been borne with, when they come in competition with edification.

---

* 'The wrath of man worketh not the righteousness of God,' Ja. i. 20. The angry passions of man work evil. Such fiery zeal is contrary to the spirit of Christ. The ignorant must be won by meekness to embrace the truth.— ED.

As first, That of Aaron, who let the offering for sin be burnt, that should have indeed been eaten. Le. x. 16—20. Yet because he could not do it to his edification, Moses was content. But the law was thereby transgressed, 'The priest that offereth it for sin, shall eat it.' vi. 26.

To this you reply, 'That was not a constant, continued forbearing of God's worship, but a suspending of it for a season.'

Answ. We also suspend it but for a season; when persons can be baptized to their edification, they have the liberty. But, This was not a bare suspension, but a flat transgression of the law. 'Ye should indeed have eaten it.' Yet Moses was content. Le. x. 16—20.

But say you, 'Perhaps it was suspended upon just and legal grounds, though not expressed.'

Answ. The express rule was against it; 'Ye should indeed (said Moses) have eaten it in the holy *place:* as I commanded.' ver. 18. But good Sir, are you now for unwritten verities? for legal grounds, though not expressed? I will not drive you further, here is Rome enough. As for Eldad and Medad, it cannot be denied, but that their edifying of the people, was preferred before their conforming to every circumstance. Nu. xi. 16—26.

You add, 'That Paul for a seeming low thing did withstand Peter.'

Sir, If you make but a seeming low thing of dissembling, and teaching others so to do, especially where the doctrine of justification is endangered, I cannot expect much good conscience from you. Ga. ii. 11—13.

As for your answer to the case of Hezekiah, it is faulty in two respects: 1. For that you make the passover a type of the Lord's supper, when it was only a type of the body and blood of the Lord: 'For even Christ our passover is sacrificed for us.' 1 Co. v. 7. 2. In that you make it an example to you to admit persons unprepared to the Lord's supper. p. 29.

Answ. May you indeed receive persons into the church unprepared for the Lord's supper; yea, unprepared for that, with other solemn appointments? For so you word it, p. 29. O what an engine have you made of water baptism. Thus, gentle reader, while this author teareth us in pieces for not making [water] baptism the orderly rule for receiving the godly and conscientious into communion; he can receive persons if baptized, though unprepared for the supper, and other solemn appointments? I would have thee consult the place, and see if it countenanceth such an act. That a man who pleadeth for water baptism above the peace and edification of the church, ought to be received, although unprepared, into the church to the Lord's supper, and other solemn appointments; especially considering the nature of right church constitution, and the severity of God towards those that came unprepared to his table of old. 1 Co. xi. 28—30. A riddle indeed, That the Lord should, without a word, so severely command, that all which want light in baptism, be excluded church privileges; and yet against his word, admit of persons unprepared, to the Lord's table, and other solemn appointments.

But good Sir, why so short-winded? why could not you make the same work with the other scriptures, as you did with these? I must leave them upon you unanswered: and standing by my argument conclude, That if laws and ordinances of old have been broken, and the breach of them born with, when yet the observation of outward things was more strictly commanded than now, if the profit and edification of the church come in competition; how much more, may not we have communion, church communion, when no law of God is transgressed thereby. And note, That all this while I plead not, as you, for persons unprepared, but godly, and such as walk with God.

We come now to my seventh argument, for communion with the godly, though unbaptized persons; which you say is LOVE, p. 29. My argument is this; 'Therefore I am for communion thus; because love, which above all things we are commanded to put on, is of much more worth than to break about baptism.' And let the reader note, That of this argument you deny not so much as one syllable, but run to another story; but I will follow you. I add further, That love is more discovered when we receive for the sake of Christ, than when we refuse his children for want of water: And tell you again, That this exhortation to love is grounded not upon [water] baptism, but the putting on of the new creature, which hath swallowed up all distinctions. Col. iii. 9—14. Yea, there are ten arguments in this one, which you have not so much as touched; but thus object,

'That man that makes affection the rule of his walking, rather than judgment, it is no wonder if he go out of the way.'

Answ. Love to them, we are persuaded that God hath received, is love that is guided by judgment; and to receive them that are such, because God hath bidden us, Ro. xiv. is judgment guided by rule. My argument therefore hath forestalled all your noise, and standeth still on its legs against you. As to the duties of piety and charity, you boast of, p. 30. sound not a trumpet, tell not your left hand of it; we are talking now of communion of saints, church communion, and I plead, that to love, and hold together as such, is better than to break in pieces for want of water baptism. My reason is, because we are exhorted in all things to put on love; the love of church communion: contrariwise you oppose, Above all things put on water. For

the best saint under heaven that hath not that, with him you refuse communion. Thus you make baptism, though no church ordinance, a bar to shut out the godly, and a trap-door to let the unprepared into churches, to the Lord's supper, and other solemn appointments. p. 29.

But you object, 'Must our love to the unbaptized indulge them in an act of disobedience? Cannot we love their persons, parts, graces, but we must love their sins?' p. 30.

Answ. We plead not for indulging. ' But are there not with you, even with you, sins against the Lord your God?' 2 Ch. xxviii. 10. But why can you indulge the baptists in many acts of disobedience? For to come unprepared into the church, is an act of disobedience: To come unprepared to the supper is an act of disobedience; and to come so also to other solemn appointments, are acts of disobedience.

'But for these things,' you say, ' you do not cast, nor keep any out of the church.'

Answ. But what acts of disobedience do we indulge them in?

' In the sin of infant baptism.'

Answ. We indulge them not; but being commanded to bear with the infirmities of each other, suffer it; it being indeed in our eyes such; but in theirs they say a duty, till God shall otherwise persuade them. If you be without infirmity, do you first throw a stone at them: They keep their faith in that to themselves, and trouble not their brethren therewith: we believe that God hath received them; they do not want to us a proof of their sonship with God; neither hath he made water a wall of division between us, and therefore we do receive them.

Object. 'I take it to be the highest act of friendship to be faithful to these professors, and to tell them they want this one thing in gospel order, which ought not to be left undone.' p. 30.

Answ. If it be the highest piece of friendship, to preach water baptism to unbaptized believers, the lowest act thereof must needs be very low. But contrariwise, I count it so far off from being any act of friendship, to press baptism in our notion on those that cannot bear it; that it is a great abuse of the peace of my brother, the law of love, the law of Christ, or the society of the faithful. Love suffereth long, and is kind, is not easily provoked: let us therefore follow after the things that make for peace, and things wherewith one may edify another: let every one of us please his neighbour, for his good to edification: Bear you one another's burdens, and so fulfil the law of Christ. 1 Co. xiii. Ro. xiv. 19; xv. 2. Ga. vi. 2.

But say you, 'I doubt when this comes to be weighed in God's balance, it will be found no less than flattery, for which you will be reproved.' p. 31.

Answ. It seems you do but doubt it, wherefore the principles from which you doubt it, of that methinks you should not be certain; but this is of little weight to me; for he that will presume to appropriate the epistles to himself and fellows, for the sake of baptism, and that will condemn all the churches of Christ in the land for want of baptism, and that will account his brother as profane Esau (p. 20.) and rejected, as idolatrous Ephraim (p. 32.) because he wanteth his way of water baptism; he acts out of his wonted way, of rigidness, when he doth but doubt, and not affirm his brother to be a flatterer. I leave therefore this your doubt to be resolved at the day of judgment, and in the mean time trample upon your harsh and unchristian surmises. As to our love to Christians in other cases, I hope we shall also endeavour to follow the law of the Lord; but because it respects not the matter in hand, it concerns us not now to treat thereof.

My argument treateth of church communion; in the prosecution of which I prove. 1. That love is grounded upon the new creature. Col. iii. 10—15. 2. Upon our fellowship with the Father and Son. 1 Jn. i. 2, 3. 3. That with respect to this, it is the fulfilling of the royal law. Ja. iv. 11. Ro. xiv. 21. 4. That it shews itself in acts of forbearing, rather than in publishing some truths: communicating only what is profitable, forbearing to publish what cannot be born. 1 Co. iii. 1, 2. Ac. xx. 18—20. Jn. iii. 16, 17. 5. I shew further, That to have fellowship for, to make that the ground of, or to receive one another chiefly upon the account of an outward circumstance; to make baptism the including and excluding charter: the bounds, bar, and rule of communion, when by the word of the everlasting testament, there is no word for it, to speak charitably, if it be not for want of love, it is for want of light in the mysteries of the kingdom of Christ. Strange! Take two Christians equal in all points but this; nay, let one go beyond the other in grace and goodness, as far as a man is beyond a babe, yet water shall turn the scale, shall open the door of communion to the less; and command the other to stand back: yet is no proof to the church of this babe's faith and hope, hath nothing to do with his entering into fellowship, is no part of the worship of the church.* These things should have been answered, seeing you will take upon you so roundly to condemn our practice.

* It becomes all prayerfully to follow divine commands in ALL THINGS. Nothing is indifferent or non-essential that God hath ordained for the believer. But if disciples differ about days, or meats, or water, ought such differences to prevent their communion and fellowship more than differences in personal stature, or beauty, or in mental powers. Uniformity in anything but love to God and to each other is a fool's paradise, contrary to the experience of the apostolic and all ages, and opposed to every law of nature.—ED.

You come now to my eighth argument; which you do not only render falsely, but by so doing abuse your reader. I said not that the church at Corinth did shut each other out of communion; but, for God's people to divide into parties, or to shut each other from church communion, though for greater points, and upon higher pretences, than that of water baptism, hath heretofore been counted carnal, and the actors therein babyish Christians: and then bring in the factions, that was in the church at Corinth. But what! May not the evil of denying church communion now, if proved naught by a less crime in the church at Corinth, be counted carnal and babyish; but the breach of communion must be charged upon them at Corinth also?

That my argument is good you grant, p. 32. saying, 'The divisions of the church at Corinth were about the highest fundamental principles, for which they are often called carnal;' yet you cavil at it. But if they were to be blamed for dividing, though for the highest points; are not you much more for condemning your brethren to perpetual banishment from church communion, though sound in all the great points of the gospel, and right in all church ordinances also, because for want of light they fail only in the point of baptism?

As to your quibble about Paul and Apollos, whether they, or others, were the persons, though I am satisfied you are out, yet it weakeneth not my argument; for if they were blame worthy for dividing, though about the highest fundamental principles, as you say, how ought you to blush for carrying it as you do to persons, perhaps, more godly than ourselves, because they jump not with you in a circumstance? That the divisions at Corinth were helped on by the abuse of baptism, to me is evident, from Paul's so oft suggesting it: 'Were ye baptized in the name of Paul? I thank God that I baptized none of you, - lest any should say, I had baptized in mine own name.' i. 13—15.

I do not say, that they who baptized them designed this, or that baptism in itself effected it; nor yet, though our author feigns it, 'that they were most of them baptized by their factious leaders.' p. 55. But that they had their factious leaders, is evident; and that these leaders made use of the names of Paul, Apollos, and Christ, is as evident; for by these names they were beguiled by the help of ABUSED baptism.

But say you, 'Wherein lies the force of this man's argument against baptism as to its place, worth, and continuance?'

I answer: I have no argument against its place, worth or continuance, although thus you seek to scandalize me. But this kind of sincerity of yours, will never make me one of your disciples. Have not I told you even in this argument, 'That I speak not as I do, to persuade or teach men to break the least of God's commandments; but that my brethren of the baptized way may not hold too much thereupon, may not make it an essential of the gospel, nor yet of the communion of saints.' Yet he feigns that I urge two arguments against it. p. 36. and 38. But reader, thou mayest know I have no such reason in my book. Besides, I should be a fool indeed, were I against it, should I make use of such weak arguments. My words then are these: 'I thank God,' said Paul, 'that I baptized none of you but Crispus,' &c. 'Not but that then it was an ordinance, but they abused it in making parties thereby, as they abused also Paul, and Cephas. Besides, said he, I know not whether I baptized any other. By this negligent relating who were baptized by him, he sheweth that he made no such matter thereof, as some in these days do. Nay, that he made no matter at all thereof with respect to a church communion. For if he did not heed who himself had baptized, much less did he heed who were baptized by others? But if baptism had been the initiating ordinance, and I now add, essential to church communion; then no doubt he had made more conscience of it, than thus lightly to pass it by.'

I add further, where he saith, He 'was not sent to baptize;' that he spake with an holy indignation against those that had abused that ordinance. 'Baptism is an holy ordinance, but when Satan abuseth it, and wrencheth it out of its place, making that which is ordained of God, for the edification of believers, the only weapon to break in pieces the love, unity, and concord of the saints; than as Paul said of himself and fellows. 1 Co. iii. 5—7. What is baptism? Neither is baptism any thing? This is no new doctrine, for God by the mouth of the prophet of old, cried out against his own appointments, when abused by his own people; Is. i. 11—15. because they used them " for strife, and debate, and to smite with the fist of wickedness."' lviii. 4. But to forbear, to take notice thus of these things, my argument stands firm against you: ' For if they at Corinth were blame worthy for dividing, though their divisions were, if you say true, about the highest fundamentals, you ought to be ashamed, thus to banish your brethren from the privileges of church communion for ever, for the want of so low a thing as water baptism.' I call it not low, with respect to God's appointment, though so, it is far from the highest place, but in comparison of those fundamentals, about which you say, 'the Corinthians made their divisions.'

You come next to my ninth argument, and serve it as Hanun served David's servants, 2 Sa. x. 4. you have cut off one half of its beard, and its garments to its buttocks, thinking to send it home with shame. You state it thus: 'That by denying communion with unbaptized believers, you take

VOL. II.

from them their privileges to which they are born.' p. 40.

Answ. Have I such an argument, in all my little book? Are not my words verbatim these? ' If we shall reject visible saints by calling, saints that have communion with God; that have received the law at the hand of Christ; that are of an holy conversation among men, they desiring to have communion with us; as much as in us lieth, we take from them their very privileges, and the blessings to which they were born of God.' This is mine argument: now confute it.

Paul saith, not only to the gathered church at Corinth, but to all scattered saints, that in every place call upon the name of the Lord, 1 Co. i. 2. That if Jesus Christ is theirs; that Paul and Apollos, and Cephas, and the world, and all things else was theirs. iii. 22.

But you answer, ' We take from them nothing, but we keep them from a disorderly practice of gospel ordinances, we offer them their privileges, in the way of gospel order.'

Answ. Where have you one word of God, that forbiddeth a person, so qualified, as is signified in mine argument, the best communion of saints for want of water? There is not a syllable for this in all the book of God. So then, you in this your plausible defence, do make your scriptureless light, which in very deed is darkness, Is. viii. 20. the rule of your brother's faith; and how well you will come off ·for this in the day of God, you might, were you not wedded to your wordless opinion, soon begin to conceive.

I know your reply, 'New Testament saints are all baptized first.'

Answ. Suppose it granted: Were they baptized, that thereby they might be qualified for their right to communion of saints, so that, without their submitting to water, they were to be denied the other? Further, suppose I should grant this groundless notion, Were not the Jews in Old Testament times to enter the church by circumcision? Ge. xvii. Ex. xii. For that, though water is not, was the very entering ordinance. Besides, as I said before, there was a full forbidding of all that were not circumcised from entering into fellowship, with a threatening to cut them off from the church if they entered in 'without it: yet more than six hundred thousand entered that church without it. But how now, if such an one as you had then stood up and objected, Sir Moses, What is the reason that you transgress the order of God, to receive members without circumcision? Is not that the very entering ordinance? Are not you commanded to keep out of the church all that are not circumcised? Yea, and for all those that you thus received, are you not commanded to cast them out again, to cut them off from among this people. Ge. xvii. 13. 14. Ex. xii.

44—46. I say, Would not this man have had a far better argument to have resisted Moses, than you, in your wordless notion, have to shut out men from the church, more holy than many of ourselves? But do you think that Moses and Joshua, and all the elders of Israel, would have thanked this fellow, or have concluded that he spake on God's behalf? Or, that they should then, for the sake of a better than what you call order, have set to the work that you would be doing, even to break the church in pieces for this?

But say you, 'If any will find or force another way into the sheep fold than by the footsteps of the flock, we have no such custom nor the churches of God.' p. 41.

Answ. What was done of old I have shewed you, that Christ, not baptism, is the way to the sheep fold, is apparent: and that the person [who thus enters], in mine argument, is entituled to all these, to wit, Christ, grace, and all the things of the kingdom of Christ in the church, is, upon the scriptures urged, as evident.

But you add, 'That according to mine old confidence, I affirm, That drink ye all of this is entailed to faith, not baptism: a thing,' say you, 'soon said, but yet never proved.'

Answ. 1. That it is entailed to faith, must be confessed of all hands. 2. That it is the privilege of him that discerneth the Lord's body, and that no man is to deny him it, is also by the text as evident, ' and so let him eat,' because he is worthy. Wherefore he, and he only, that discerneth the Lord's body, he is the worthy receiver, the worthy receiver in God's estimation; but that none discern the Lord's body but the baptized [in water], is both fond and ridiculous once to surmise.

Wherefore to exclude Christians, and to debar them their heaven-born privileges, for want of that which yet God never made the wall of division betwixt us: This looks too like a spirit of persecution, Job xix. 28, and carrieth in it those eighteen absurdities which you have so hotly cried out against. And I do still add, 'Is it not that which greatly prevailed with God to bring down those judgments which at present we (the people of God) groan under, I will dare to say it was, *A cause thereof.' Yea, I will yet proceed; I fear, I strongly fear, that the rod of God is not yet to be taken from us; for what [is a] more provoking sin among Christians than to deny one another their rights and privileges, to which they are born of God? And then to father these their doings upon God, when yet he hath not commanded it, neither in the New Testament nor the Old.

But I may not lightly pass this by, for because

* And so it was in my first copy, but for A, the printer put in THE.†

† This typographical error in 'The Reasons of my Practice' is corrected in this edition for the first time.—ED.

I have gathered eighteen absurdities from this abuse of God's ordinances, or from the sin of binding the brethren to observe order, not founded on the command of God; and I am sure you have none to shut out men as good, as holy, and as sound in faith as ourselves, from communion. Therefore you call my conclusion devilish, p. 43, topfull of ignorance and prejudice, p. 41, and me, one of Machiavel's scholars, p. 42, also proud, presumptuous, impeaching the judgment of God.

Answ. But what is there in my proposition, that men, considerate, can be offended at? These are my words: ' But to exclude Christians from church communion, and to debar them their heaven-born privileges, for the want of that which yet God never made a wall of division between us: this looks too like a spirit of persecution: this respecteth more the form than the spirit and power of godliness, &c. Shall I add, Is it not that which greatly prevailed to bring down those judgments which at present we feel and groan under? I will dare to say, it was a cause thereof,' p. 116, 117. *A* was in my copy, instead whereof the printer put in *the*; for this, although I speak only the truth, I will not beg of you belief; besides, the bookseller desired me, because of the printer's haste, to leave the last sheet to be overlooked by him, which was the cause it was not among the erratas. But, I say, wherein is the proposition offensive? Is it not a wicked thing to make bars to communion, where God hath made none? Is it not a wickedness to make that a wall of division betwixt us which God never commanded to be so? If it be not, justify your practice; if it be, take shame. Besides, the proposition is universal, why then should you be the chief intended? But you have in this done like to the lawyers of old, who, when Christ reproved the pharisees of wickedness before them, said, ' Master, thus saying thou reproachest us also.' Lu. xi. 45.

But you feign, and would also that the world should believe, that the eighteen absurdities which naturally flow from the proposition I make, to be the effects of baptism, saying to me, ' None but yourself could find an innocent truth big with so many monstrous absurdities.' p. 42.

I answer: This is but speaking wickedly for God, or rather to justify your wordless practice. I say not that baptism hath any absurdity in it, though your abusing it, hath them all, and many more, while you make it, without warrant from the word, as the flaming sword, to keep the brotherhood out of communion, because they, after your manner, cannot consent thereto. And let no man be offended, for that I suggest that baptism may be abused to the breeding such monstrous absurdities, for greater truths than that have been as much abused. What say you to, ' This is my body?' To instance no more, although I could instance many, are not they the words of our Lord? Are not they part of the scriptures of truth? and yet behold, even with those words, the devil, by abusing them, made an engine to let out the heart-blood of thousands.[*] Baptism also may be abused, and is, when more is laid upon it by us than is commanded by God. And that you do so, is manifest by what I have said already, and shall yet say to your fourteen arguments.

My last argument, you say, is this: 'The world may wonder at your carriage to these unbaptized persons, in keeping them out of communion?'

Answ. You will set up your own words, and then fight against them; but my words are these: 'What greater contempt can be thrown upon the saints, than for their brethren to cut them off from, or to debar them church communion.' And now I add, Is not this to deliver them to the devil, 1 Co. v. or to put them to shame before all that see your acts? There is but one thing can hinder this, and that is, by-standers see that these, your brethren, that you thus abuse, are as holy men as ourselves. Do you more to the openly prophane, yea, to all wizards and witches in the land?[†] For all you can do to them, I speak now as to church acts, is no other than to debar them the communion of saints.

And now I say again, the world may well wonder, when they see you deny holy men of God that liberty of the communion of saints which you monopolise to yourselves: and though they do not understand the grounds of profession, or communion, yet they can both see and say, these holy men of God, in all visible acts of holiness, are not one inch behind you. Yea, I will put it to yourselves, If those many, yea, very many, who thus severely, but with how little ground, is seen by men of God, you deny communion with; are not of as good, as holy, as unblameable in life, and as sound, if not sounder in the faith than many among ourselves: Here only they make the stop, they cannot, without light, be driven into water baptism, I mean after our notion of it: but what if they were, it would be little sign to me, that they were sincere with God.

---

[*] The doctrine of the real presence, called transubstantiation, was the test of adherence to the Romish church, which unless all persons pretended to believe they were sacrificed with brutal ferocity.—ED.

[†] In Bunyan's days, both the laws of the land, the judges, and the commonalty, gave credence to the wicked gambols of wizards and witches. Many a poor iniquitous old woman, from some mysterious hints of her power to tell fortunes, or to gratify the revengeful feelings of her neighbours, was put to a cruel death. More enlightened times have dissipated this illusion, and driven these imaginary imps of darkness into benighted countries.—ED.

To conclude this; when you have proved that water baptism, which you yourself have said is not a church ordinance, p. 40, is essential to church communion, and that the church may, by the word of God, bolt, bar, and for ever shut out those, far better than ourselves, that have not, according to our notion, been baptized with water; then it will be time enough to talk of ground for so doing. In the mean time I must take leave to tell you, 'There is not in all the Bible one syllable for such a practice, wherefore your great cry about your order is wordless, and therefore faithless, and is a mere human invention.'

I COME NOW TO YOUR FOURTEEN ARGUMENTS, AND SHALL IMPARTIALLY CONSIDER THEM.

Your first argument to prove it lawful to reject the unbaptized saint, is, 'Because the great commission of Christ, Mat. xxviii. from which all persons have their authority for their ministry, if any authority at all, doth clearly direct the contrary. By that commission ministers are first to disciple, and then to baptize them so made disciples, and afterwards to teach them to observe all that Christ commanded them, as to other ordinances of worship. If ministers have no other authority to teach them other parts of gospel worship, before they believe and are baptized, it may be strongly supposed they are not to admit them to other ordinances before they have passed this first enjoined in the commission.'

Answ. 1. That the ministers are to disciple and baptize, is granted. But that they are prohibited, by the commission, Mat. xxviii. to teach the disciples other parts of gospel worship that have not light in baptism, remains for you to prove. Shall I add, this position is so absurd and void of truth, that none that have ever read the love of Christ, the nature of faith, the end of the gospel, or of the reason of instituted worship (which is edification) with understanding, should so much as once imagine.

But where are they here forbidden to teach them other truths before they be baptized? This text as fairly denieth to the unbaptized believer heaven and glory. Nay, our author, in the midst of all his flutter about this xxviii. of Matthew, dare venture to gather no more therefrom, but that it may be strongly supposed. Behold therefore, gentle reader, the ground on which these brethren lay the stress of their separation from their fellows, is nothing else but a supposition, without warrant, screwed out of this blessed word of God. Strongly supposed! but may it not be as strongly supposed that the presence and blessing of the Lord Jesus, with his ministers, is laid upon the same ground also? for thus he concludes the text, 'And lo, I am with you alway even unto the end of the world.' But would, I say, any man from these words conclude, that Christ Jesus hath here promised his presence only to them that, after discipling, baptize those that are so made; and that they that do not baptize shall neither have his presence nor his blessing? I say again, should any so conclude hence, would not all experience prove him void of truth? The words therefore must be left, by you, as you found them, they favour not at all your groundless supposition.

To conclude, these words have not laid baptism in the way to debar the saint from fellowship of his brethren, no more than to hinder his inheritance in life and glory. Mark reads it thus: 'He that believeth and is baptized shall be saved; but he that believeth not shall be damned.' Mar. xvi. 16. Letting baptism, which he mentioned in the promise, fall, when he came at the threatening. God also doth thus with respect to his worship in the church, he commands all and every whit of his will to be done, but beareth with our coming short in this, and that, and another duty. But let's go on.

Your second argument is, 'That the order of Christ's commission, as well as the matter therein contained to be observed, may easily be concluded, from God's severity towards them that sought him not according to due order. 1 Ch. xv. 13. Was God so exact with his people then, that all things to a pin must be according to the pattern in the mount, He. viii. 5; ix. 11, whose worship then comparatively, to the gospel, was but after the law of a carnal commandment; and can it be supposed he should be so indifferent now to leave men to their own liberty, to time and place his appointments, contrary to what he had given an express rule for in his word as before? Eze. xliv. 7, 9, 10. It was the priest's sin, formerly to bring the uncircumcised in heart and flesh into his house.'

Answ. That there is no such order in that commission as you feign, I have proved. As for your far-fetch'd instance, 1 Ch. xv. it is quite beside your purpose. The express word was, That the priest, not a cart, should bear the ark of God. Also they were not to touch it, and yet Uzza did, Ex. xxv. 14. 1 Ch. xv. 12—16. Nu. iv. 15. 1 Ch. xiii. Now, if you can make that xxviii. of Matthew say, Receive none that are not baptized first; or that Christ would have them of his, that are not yet baptized, kept ignorant of all other truths that respect church communion; then you say something, else you do but raise a mist before the simple reader: but whoso listeth may hang on your sleeve. As for the pins and tacks of the tabernacle, they were expressly commanded; and when you have proved by the word of God, That you ought to shut saints out of your communion for want of baptism, then you may begin more justly to make your parallel. How

fitly you have urged Eze. xliv. to insinuate that unbaptized believers are like the uncircumcised in heart and flesh, I leave it to all gospel-novices to consider.

Your third argument is, 'The practice of the first gospel-ministers, with them that first trusted in Christ, discovers the truth of what I assert. Certainly they that lived at the spring-head, or fountain of truth, and had the law from Christ's own mouth, knew the meaning of his commission better than we: but their constant practice in conformity to that commission, all along the Acts of the Apostles, discovers that they never arrived to such a latitude as men plead for now-a-days. They that gladly received the word were baptized, and they, yea they only, were received into the church.'

Answ. How well you have proved what you have asserted, is manifest by my answer to the two former arguments. I add, That the ministers and servants of Jesus Christ in the first churches, for that you are to prove, were commanded to forbear to preach other truths to the unbaptized believers; or that they were to keep them out of the church; or that the apostles, and first fathers, have given you to understand by their example, that you ought to keep as good out of churches as yourselves, hath not yet been shewed by the authority of the word. The second of the Acts proveth not, That the three thousand were necessitated to be baptized in order to their fellowship with the church, neither doth it say THEY, yea they only, were received into the church. But suppose all this, as much was done at the first institution of circumcision, &c., yet afterwards thousands were received without it.

Your fourth argument is, 'None of the scripture saints ever attempted this church privilege without baptism, if they did, let it be shewn. The eunuch first desired baptism before anything else; Paul was first baptized before he did essay to join with the church. Our Lord Christ, the great example of the New Testament, entered not upon his public ministry, much less any other gospel ordinance of worship, till he was baptized.'

Answ. That none of the scripture saints, if there be any unscripture ones, so much as attempted this church-privilege first, remains for you to prove. But suppose they were all baptized, because they had light therein, what then? Doth this prove that baptism is essential to church communion? Or, that Christ commanded in the xxviii. of Matthew, or gave his ministers by that, authority, not to make known to believers other parts of gospel-worship, if they shall want light in baptism? The eunuch, Paul, and our blessed Lord Jesus, did none of them, by their baptism, set themselves to us examples how to enter into church communion; what church was the eunuch baptized into, or made a member of; but where is it said, that the unbaptized believer, how excellent soever in faith and holiness, must, for want of water baptism, be shut out from the communion of saints, or be debarred the privilege of his Father's house? This you are to prove.

Your fifth argument is, 'If Christ himself was made manifest to be the SENT of God by baptism, as appears, Mar. i. 9, 10. then why may not baptism, as the first fruits of faith, and the first step of gospel-obedience, as to instituted worship, be a manifesting discovering ordinance upon others who thus follow Christ's steps.'

Answ. That Jesus Christ was manifested as the SENT of God by baptism, or that baptism is the first fruit of faith and the first step to gospel-obedience, as to instituted worship, is both without proof and truth; the text saith not, he was manifest to be the 'sent' of God by baptism; nay it saith not, that by that he was manifest to others to be anything thereby: you have therefore but wronged the text to prove your wordless practice by. Yea, John himself, though he knew him before he was baptized, to be a man of God, for, saith he, 'I have need to be baptized of thee, and comest thou to me.' Mat. iii. 14, and knew him after to be the 'sent' of God; yet not in, or by, but after he was baptized, to wit, by the descending of the Holy Ghost, after he was come out of the water, as he was in prayer, for the heavens were opened to John, Jn. i. 30—34, and he saw, and bare record, because he saw the Spirit descend from heaven, and abide upon Jesus, after his baptism, as he was in prayer. Mat. iii. 13—17. Lu. iii. 21, 22. Thus we find him made known before and after, but not at all by baptism, to be the 'sent' of God.

And that baptism is the fruit of faith, or that faith ought to be tied to take its first step in water baptism, in the instituted worship of God; this you must prove, it is not found expressed within the whole Bible. Faith acts according to its strength and as it sees, it is not tied or bound to any outward circumstance; one believeth he may, and another believeth he may not, either do this or that.

Your sixth argument is, 'If baptism be in any sense any part of the foundation of a church, as to order, He. vi. 1, 2, it must have place here or no where: why are those things called first principles, if not first to be believed and practised? Why are they rendered by the learned the A, B, C, of a Christian, and the beginning of Christianity, milk for babes, if it be no matter whether baptism be practised or no? If it be said water baptism is not there intended, let them shew me how many baptisms there are besides water baptism? Can you build and leave out a stone in the foundation? I intend not baptism a foundation any other ways but in respect of order, and it is either intended for that or nothing.'

Answ. Baptism is in no sense the foundation of a church. I find no foundation of a church but Jesus Christ himself. Mat. xvi. 18. 1 Co. iii. 11. Yea, the foundation mentioned, He. vi. 1, 2, is nothing else but this very Christ. For he is the foundation, not only of the church, but of all that good that at any time is found in her. He is the foundation OF our repentance, and OF our faith towards God. vers. 1, 2. Further, baptisms are not here mentioned with respect to the act in water, but of the doctrine; that is, the signification thereof. 'The doctrine of baptisms.' And observe, neither faith, nor repentance, nor baptisms, are called here foundations: Another thing, for a foundation, is here by the Holy Ghost intended, even a foundation for them all: a foundation of faith, of repentance, of the doctrine of baptisms, of the resurrection of the dead, and of eternal judgment. And this foundation is Jesus Christ himself, and these are the first principles, the milk, the A, B, C, and the beginning of Christian religion in the world. I dare not say, No matter whether water baptism be practised or no. But it is not a stone in the foundation of a church, no not respecting order; it is not, to another, a sign of my sonship with God; it is not the door into fellowship with the saints, it is no church ordinance, as you, yourself, have testified. p. 40. So then as to church work, it hath no place at all therein.

Your seventh argument is, 'If Paul knew the Galatians only upon the account of charity, No other ways to be the sons of God by faith; but by this part of their obedience, as he seems to import, then the same way we judge of the truth of men's profession of faith, when it shows itself by this selfsame obedience. Baptism being an obligation to all following duties.' Ga. iii. 26, 27.

Answ. This your argument, being builded upon no more than a SEEMING import, and having been above ten times overthrown already; I might leave still with you, till your seeming import is come to a real one, and both to a greater persuasion upon your own conscience. But verily Sir, you grossly abuse your reader; must imports, yea, must seeming imports now stand for arguments, thereby to maintain your confident separation from your brethren? Yea, must such things as these, be the basis on which you build those heavy censures and condemnations you raise against your brethren, that cannot comply with you, because you want the word? A seeming import. But are these words of faith? or do the scriptures only help you to seeming imports, and *me-hap-soes** for your practice? No, nor yet to them neither, for

---

* 'Me-hap-soes,' a contraction of 'it may so happen.'—ED.

I dare boldly affirm it, and demand, if you can, to prove, that there is so much as a seeming import in all the word of God, that countenanceth your shutting men, better than ourselves, from the things and privileges of our Father's house. That to the Galatians, saith not, that Paul knew them to be the sons of God by faith, no other way, but by THIS part of their obedience; but puts them upon concluding themselves the sons of God, if they were baptized into the Lord Jesus, which could not, ordinarily, be known but unto themselves alone; because, being thus baptized, respecteth a special act of faith, which only God and him that hath, and acteth it, can be privy to. It is one thing for him that administereth, to baptize in the name of Jesus, and another thing for him that is the subject, by that to be baptized INTO Jesus Christ: Baptizing into Christ, is rather the act of the faith of him that is baptized, than his going into water and coming out again. But that Paul knew this to be the state of the Galatians no other way, but by their external act of being baptized with water, is both wild and unsound, and a miserable IMPORT indeed.

Your eighth argument is, 'If being baptized into Christ, be a putting on of Christ, as Paul expresses, then they have not put on Christ, in that sense he means, that are not baptized; if this putting on of Christ, doth not respect the visibility of Christianity; assign something else as its signification; great men's servants are known by their master's liveries, so are gospel believers by this livery of water baptism, that all that first trusted in Christ submitted unto; which is in itself as much an obligation to all gospel obedience, as circumcision was to keep the whole law.'

Answ. For a reply to the first part of this argument, go back to the answer to the seventh. Now that none have put on Christ in Paul's sense; yea, in a saving, in the best sense; but them that have, as you would have them, gone into water, will be hard for you to prove, yea, is ungodly for you to assert. Your comparing water baptism to a gentleman's livery, by which his name is known to be his, is fantastical. Go you but ten doors from where men have knowledge of you, and see how many of the world, or Christians, will know you by this goodly livery, to be one that hath put on Christ. What! known by water baptism to be one that hath put on Christ, as a gentleman's man is known to be his master's servant, by the gay garment his master gave him. Away fond man, you do quite forget the text. 'By THIS shall all *men* know that ye are my disciples, if ye have *love one to another.*' Jn. xiii. 35. That baptism is in itself obliging, to speak properly, it is false, for set it by itself, and it stands without the stamp of heaven upon it, and without its signification also:

and how, as such, it should be obliging, I see not. Where you insinuate, it comes in the room of, and obligeth as circumcision: you say, you know not what. Ac. xv. 1, 2. Circumcision was the initiating ordinance, but this you have denied to baptism. Further, circumcision *then* bound men to the whole obedience of the law, when urged by the false apostles, and received by an erroneous conscience. Ga. v. 1—4. Would you thus urge water baptism! would you have men to receive it with such consciences? Circumcision in the flesh, was a type of circumcision in the heart, and not of water baptism. Ro. ii. 28, 29. Phi. iii. 3.

Your ninth argument is, 'If it were commendable in the Thessalonians, that they followed the footsteps of the church of Judea, 1 Thes. ii. 14. who it appears followed this order of adding baptized believers unto the church; then they that have found out another way of making church members, are not by that rule praiseworthy, but rather to be blamed; it was not what was since in corrupted times, but that which was from the beginning: the first churches were the purest pattern.'

Answ. That the text saith there was a church of Judea, I find not in 1 Th. ii. 14. And that the Thessalonians are commended for refusing to have communion with the unbaptized believers, for that is our question, prove it by the word, and then you do something. Again, that the commendations, 1 Th. ii. 14. do chiefly, or at all, respect their being baptized: or, because they followed the churches of God, which in Judea were in Christ Jesus, in the example of water baptism is quite beside the word. The verse runs thus: ' For ye, brethren, became followers of the churches of God which in Judea are in Christ Jesus: for ye also have suffered like things of your own countrymen, even as they *have* of the Jews.' This text then commends them, not for that they were baptized with water, but, for that they stood their ground, although baptized with suffering, like them in Judea, for the name of the Lord Jesus. For suffering like things of their own countrymen, as they did of the Jews. Will you not yet leave off to abuse the word of God, and forbear turning it out of its place, to maintain your unchristian practice of rejecting the people of God, and excluding them their blessed privileges. The unbaptized believer, instead of taking shame for entering into fellowship without it, will be ready, I doubt, to put you to shame for bringing scriptures so much beside the purpose, and for stretching them so miserably to uphold you in your fancies.

Your tenth argument is, 'If so be, that any of the members at Corinth, Galatia, Colosse, Rome, or them that Peter wrote to, were not baptized, then Paul's arguments for the resurrection to them, or to press them to holiness from that ground (Ro. vi.;

Col. ii.; 1 Co. xv.) was out of doors, and altogether needless, yea, it bespeaks his ignorance, and throweth contempt upon the Spirit's wisdom. (He. vi. 1 Pe. iii. 21.) by which he wrote; if that must be asserted as a ground to provoke them to such an end, which had no being: and if all the members of all those churches were baptized, why should any plead for an exemption from baptism, for any church member now?'

Answ. Suppose all, if all these churches were baptized, what then? that answereth not our question. We ask where you find it written, that those that are baptized, should keep men as holy, and as much beloved of the Lord Jesus as themselves, out of church communion, for want of light in water baptism. Why we plead for their admission, though they see not yet. that that is their duty, is because we are not forbidden, but commanded to receive them, because God and Christ hath done it. Ro. xiv. and xv.

Your eleventh argument is, 'If unbaptized persons must be received into churches, only because they are believers, though they deny baptism; then why may not others plead for the like privilege, that are negligent in any other gospel ordinance of worship, from the same ground of want of light, let it be what it will. So then as the consequence of this principle, churches may be made up of visible sinners, instead of visible saints.'

Answ. 1. I plead not for believers simply because they are believers, but for such believers of whom we are persuaded by the word, that God hath received them. 2. There are some of the ordinances, that be they neglected, the being of a church, as to her visible gospel constitution, is taken quite away; but baptism is none of them, it being no church ordinance as such, nor any part of faith, nor of that holiness of heart, or life, that sheweth me to the church to be indeed a visible saint. The saint is a saint before, and may walk with God, and be faithful with the saints, and to his own light also though he never be baptized. Therefore to plead for his admission, makes no way at all for the admission of the open prophane, or to receive, as you profess you do, persons unprepared to the Lord's table, and other solemn appointments. p. 29.

Your twelfth argument is, 'Why should professors have more light in breaking of bread, than baptism? That this must be so urged for their excuse: Hath God been more sparing in making out his mind in the one, rather than the other? Is there more precepts or precedents for the supper, than baptism? Hath God been so bountiful in making out himself about the supper, that few or none that own ordinances scruple it? And must baptism be such a rock of offence to professors, that very few will enquire after it, or submit to it?

Hath not man's wisdom interposed to darken this part of God's counsel? By which professors seem willingly led, though against so many plain commands and examples, written as with a sun beam, that he that runs may read? And must an advocate be entertained to plead for so gross a piece of ignorance, that the meanest babes of the first gospel times were never guilty of?'

Answ. Many words to little purpose. 1. Must God be called to an account by you, why he giveth more light about the supper than baptism? May he not shew to, or conceal from this, or another of his servants, which of his truths he pleaseth. Some of the members of the church at Jerusalem had a greater truth than this kept from them, for ought I know, as long as they lived, Ac. xi. 19. yet God was not called in question about it. 2. Breaking of bread, not baptism, being a church ordinance, and that such also as must be often reiterated; yea, it being an ordinance so full of blessedness, as lively to present union and communion with Christ to all the members that worthily eat thereof: I say, the Lord's supper being such, that while the members sit at that feast, they shew to each other the death and blood of the Lord, as they ought to do, till he comes. 1 Co. x. 15—17. and xi. 25, 26. The church as a church, is much more concerned in that, than in water baptism, both as to her faith and comfort; both as to her union and communion. 3. Your supposition, that very few professors will seriously inquire after water baptism, is too rude. What, must all the children of God, that are not baptized for want of light, be still stigmatised with want of serious inquiry after God's mind in it. 4. That I am an advocate, entertained to plead for so gross a piece of ignorance, as want of light in baptism, is but like the rest of your jumbling. I plead for communion with men, godly and faithful, I plead that they may be received, that God hath shewed us he hath received, and commanded we should receive them.

Your thirteenth argument is, ' If obedience must discover the truth of a man's faith to others, why must baptism be shut out, as if it was no part of gospel obedience? Is there no precept for this practice, that it must be thus despised, as a matter of little use? Or shall one of Christ's precious commands be blotted out of a Christian's obedience, to make way for a church fellowship of man's devising.'

Answ. 1. This is but round, round, the same thing over and over. That my obedience to water, is not a discovery of my faith to others, is evident, from the body of the Bible, we find nothing that affirms it. And I will now add, That if a man cannot shew himself a Christian without water baptism; he shall never shew either saint or sinner, that he is a Christian by it. 2. Who [soever] they are that despise it, I know not but that church membership may be without it, (seeing even you yourself have concluded it is no church ordinance, p. 40. nor the entering ordinance, p. 3, 4.) standeth both with scripture and reason, as mine arguments make manifest. So that all your arguments prove no more but this, 'That you are so wedded to your wordless notions, that charity can have no place with you.' Have you all this while so much as given me one small piece of a text to prove it unlawful for the church, to receive those whom she, by the word, perceiveth the Lord God and her Christ hath received? No: and therefore you have said so much as amounts to nothing.

Your last argument is, 'If the baptism of John was so far honoured and dignified, that they that did submit to it, are said to justify God; and those that did it not, are said to reject his counsel against themselves: so that their receiving, or rejecting the whole doctrine of God, hath its denomination from this single practice. And is there not as much to be said of the baptism of Christ, unless you will say it is inferior to John's in worth and use.'

Answ. 1. That our denomination of believers, and of our receiving the doctrine of the Lord Jesus, is not to be reckoned from our baptism, is evident; because according to our notion of it, they only that have before received the doctrine of the gospel, and so shew it us by their confession of faith, they only ought to be baptized. This might serve for an answer for all: but, 2. The baptism of John was 'the baptism of repentance, for the remission of sins,' Mar. i. 4. Mat. iii. 6. Lu. iii. 3. of which water was but an outward signification. Now what is the baptism of repentance, but an unfeigned acknowledgment that they were sinners, and so stood in need of a Saviour, Jesus Christ. This baptism, or baptism under this notion, the Pharisees would not receive, Lu. vii. 29, 30. For they 'trusted in themselves that they were righteous,' that they were 'not as other men,' that they had need of no repentance. Lu. xviii. 9; x. 29; xv. 7. Not but that they would have been baptized with water, might that have been without an acknowledgment that they were sinners; Mat. iii. 7. wherefore seeing the counsel of God respected rather the remission of sins by Jesus Christ, than the outward act of water baptism, ye ought not, as you do, by this your reasoning, to make it rather, at least in the revelation of it, to terminate in the outward act of being baptized, but in unfeigned and sound repentance, and the receiving of Jesus Christ by faith. Ep. i. 7, 8, 11.

Further, A desire to submit to John's water baptism, or of being baptized by him in water, did not demonstrate by that single act, the receiving of the whole doctrine of God as you suggest. 'Why did John reject the Pharisees that would

have been baptized, Mat. iii. 7. and Paul examine them that were?' Ac. xix. 2, 3. If your doctrine be true, why did they not rather say, Oh! seeing you desire to be baptized, seeing you have been baptized, you need not to be questioned any further; your submitting to John's water, to us is a sufficient testimony, even that single act, that you have received the whole doctrine of God. But I say, why did John call them vipers? And Paul asked them, Whether they had yet 'received the Holy Ghost?' Yea, it is evident, that a man may be desirous of water, that a man may be baptized, and neither own the doctrine of repentance, nor know on whom he should believe; evident, I say, and that by the same texts. Mat. iii. 7. Ac. xix. 2—4.

You have grounded therefore this your last argument, as also the rest, upon an utter mistake of things.

I COME NOW TO YOUR *Questions;* WHICH ALTHOUGH THEY BE MIXED WITH GALL, I WILL WITH PATIENCE SEE IF I CAN TURN THEM INTO FOOD.

[*Quest.* 1.] Your first question is, 'I ask your own heart, whether popularity and applause of variety of professors, be not in the bottom of what you have said; that hath been your snare to pervert the right ways of the Lord, and to lead others into a path wherein we can find none of the footsteps of the flock in the first ages?'

Answ. Setting aside a retaliation, like your question, I say, and God knows I speak the truth, I have been tempted to do what I have done, by a provocation of sixteen years long; tempted, I say, by the brethren of your way: who, whenever they saw their opportunity, have made it their business to seek to rend us in pieces; mine ownself they have endeavoured to persuade to forsake the church; some they have rent quite off from us, others they have attempted and attempted to divide and break off from us, but by the mercy of God, have been hitherto prevented. A more large account you may have in my next, if you think good to demand it; but I thank God that I have written what I have written.

Quest. 2. 'Have you dealt brotherly, or like a Christian, to throw so much dirt upon your brethren, in print, in the face of the world, when you had an opportunity to converse with them of reputation amongst us, before printing, being allowed the liberty by them, at the same time for you to speak among them?'

Answ. I have thrown no dirt upon them, nor laid any thing to their charge, if their practice be warrantable by the word; but you have not been offended at the dirt yourselves have thrown at all the godly in the land that are not of our persuasion, in counting them unfit to be communicated with, or to be accompanied with in the house of God. This dirt you never complained of, nor would, I doubt, to this day, might you be still let alone to throw it. As to my book, it was printed before I spake with any of you, or knew whether I might be accepted of you. As to them of reputation among you, I know others not one tittle inferior to them, and have my liberty to consult with who I like best.

Quest. 3. 'Doth your carriage answer the law of love or civility, when the brethren used means to send for you for a conference, and their letter was received by you, that you should go out again from the city after knowledge of their desires, and not vouchsafe a meeting with them, when the glory of God, and the vindication of so many churches is concerned.'

Answ. The reason why I came not amongst you, was partly because I consulted mine own weakness, and counted not myself, being a dull headed man, able to engage so many of the chief of you, as I was then informed intended to meet me. I also feared, in personal disputes, heats and bitter contentions might arise, a thing my spirit hath not pleasure in: I feared also, that both myself and words would be misrepresented; and that not without cause, for if they that answer a book will alter, and screw arguments out of their place, and make my sentences stand in their own words, not mine, when (I say) my words are in a book to be seen, what would you have done, had I in the least, either in matter or manner, though but seemingly miscarried among you. As for the many churches which you say are concerned, as also the glory of God, I doubt not to say they are only your wordless opinions that are concerned; the glory of God is vindicated: We receive him that God hath received, and that 'to the glory of God.' Ro. xv. 7.

Quest. 4. 'Is it not the spirit of Diotrephes of old, in you, who loved to have the pre-eminence, that you are so bold to keep out all the brethren, that are not of your mind in this matter, from having any entertainment in the churches or meetings to which you belong, though you yourself have not been denied the like liberty, among them that are contrary minded to you? Is this the way of your retaliation? Or are you afraid lest the truth should invade your quarters?'

Answ. I can say, I would not have the spirit you talk of; what I have of it, God take it from me. But what was the spirit of Diotrephes? Why, not to receive the brethren into the church, and to forbid them that would. 3 Jn. 9, 10. This do not I; I am for communion with saints, because they are saints: I shut none of the brethren out of the churches, nor forbid them that would receive them. I say again, shew me the man that is a visible believer, and that walketh with God; and
VOL. II.

though he differ with me about baptism, the doors of the church stand open for him, and all our heaven-born privileges he shall be admitted to them. But how came Diotrephes so lately into our parts? Where was he in those days that our brethren of the baptized way, would neither receive into the church, nor pray with men as good as themselves, because they were not baptized; but would either, like Quakers, stand with their hats on their heads, or else withdraw till we had done.

As to our not suffering those you plead for to preach in our assemblies, the reason is, because we cannot yet prevail with them, to repent of their church-rending principles. As to the retaliation, mind the hand of God, and remember Adonibezek. Ju. i. 7. Let the truth come into our quarters and welcome, but sowers of discord, because the Lord hates it, Pr. vi. 19. we also ourselves will AVOID them. Ro. xvi. 17, 18.

Quest. 5. 'Is there no contempt cast upon the brethren, who desired your satisfaction, that at the same time, when you had opportunity to speak to them, instead of that, you committed the letters to others, by way of reflection upon them?'

Answ. It is no contempt at all to consult men more wise and judicious than him that wrote, or myself either. But why not consult with others, Is wisdom to die with you? Or do you count all that yourselves have no hand in, done to your disparagement?

Quest. 6. 'Did not your presumption prompt you to provoke them to printing, in your letter to them, when they desired to be found in no such practice, lest the enemies of truth should take advantage by it?'

Answ. What provoked you to print, will be best known at the day of judgment, whether your fear of losing your wordless opinion, or my plain answer to your letter: The words in my letter are, 'As for my book, never defer its answer till you speak with me, for I strive not for mastery but truth.' Though you did not desire to write, yet with us there was continual labour to rend us to pieces, and to prevent that, was my first book written. And let who will take advantage, so the truth of God, and the edification of my brother be promoted.

Quest. 7. Whether your principle and practice is not equally against others as well as us, viz. Episcopal, Presbyterians, and Independents, who are also of our side, for our practice, though they differ with us about the subject of baptism. Do you delight to have your hand against every man?'

Answ. I own water baptism to be God's ordinance, but I make no idol of it. Where you call now the Episcopal to side with you, and also the Presbyterian, &c. you will not find them easily

4 M

persuaded to conclude with you against me. They are against your manner of dipping, as well as the subject of water baptism; neither do you, for all you flatter them, agree together in all but the subject. Do you allow their sprinkling? Do you allow their signing with the cross? Why then have you so stoutly, an hundred times over, condemned these things as antichristian. I am not against every man, though by your abusive language you would set every one against me; but am for union, concord, and communion with saints, as saints, and for that cause I wrote my book.

To conclude,—1. In all I have said, I put a difference between my brethren of the baptized way; I know some are more moderate than some. 2. When I plead for the unbaptized, I chiefly intend those that are not so baptized as my brethren judge right, according to the first pattern. 3. If any shall count my papers worth the scribbling against, let him deal with my arguments, and things immediately depending upon them, and not conclude that he hath confuted a book, when he hath only quarrelled at words. 4. I have done when I have told you, that I strive not for mastery, nor to shew myself singular; but, if it might be, for union and communion among the godly. And count me not as an enemy, because I tell you the truth. 5. And now, dissenting brethren, I commend you to God, who can pardon your sin, and give you more grace, and an inheritance among them that are sanctified by faith in Jesus Christ. Amen.

HERE FOLLOWETH MR. HENRY JESSEY'S JUDGMENT
UPON THE SAME ARGUMENT.

'*Him that is weak in the faith receive ye,*' &c.—
Rom. xiv. 1.

Whereas some suppose the receiving there mentioned, was but receiving into brotherly affection, such as were in church fellowship; but not a receiving of such as were weak into the church. For answer unto which consider,

That in the texts are two things to be inquired into. *First,* What weakness of faith this is, that must not hinder receiving. *Secondly,* By whom, and to what, he that is weak in the faith is to be received?

First, To the first, What *weakness* of faith this is that must not hinder receiving, whether was it weakness in the graces of faith, or in the doctrine of faith? It is conceived that the first is included, but the second principally intended.

1. That some of the Lord's people are weak in the graces of faith, will be confessed by all; Mar. ix. 24. and Lu. xxiv. 25. and that the Lord would have

his lambs fed as well as his sheep, and his children as well as grown men, and that he hath given the right to gospel privileges, not to degrees of grace, but to the truth; '*him that is weak in the faith receive ye:*' or unto you, as some GOOD translations read it.* Ro. xiv. 1.

2. It is supposed, that this command of receiving him that is weak in the faith, doth principally intend, that is weak in the doctrine of faith, and that not so much in the doctrine of justification, as in gospel institutions, as doth appear by the second and sixth verses: which shew, that it was in matters of practice, wherein some were weak, and at which others were offended; notwithstanding the glorious Lord who bears all his Israel upon his heart receives them (ver. 3.) and commandeth, 'him that is weak in the faith receive ye,' or unto you.

Second, Therefore, here we are to inquire of the receiving in the text, By whom, and to what he that is weak in the faith, should be received. In which inquiry there are two parts. 1. By whom. 2. To what.

1. To the first. The text makes answer, 'Him that is weak in the faith receive ye,' or unto you; which must be the church at Rome, to whom the epistle was writ; as also to all 'beloved of God, called *to be* saints.' Ro. i. 7. And as to them, so unto all churches and saints, Beloved and called throughout the world.

Note, That epistles are as well to direct how churches are to carry things towards saints without, as to saints within; and also toward all men so as to give no offence to Jew or Gentile, nor to the church of God. 1 Co x. 32.

2. The second part of the inquiry is, to what he that is weak in the faith is to be received? whether only unto mutual affection, as some affirm, as if he were in church fellowship before, that were weak in the faith? Or whether the text doth as well, if not rather intend, the receiving such as were, and are weak in the faith, Not only unto mutual affection if in the church, but unto church fellowship also, if they were out. For clearing of which consider, to whom the epistle was written. Ro. i. 7. Not only to the church there, but unto all that were beloved of God, and called to be saints in all ages. And as at Rome it is like there then were, and in other places now are, saints weak in the faith, both in and out of church fellowship; and it is probable there then were, and elsewhere now are, those that will cast such out of

---

* Tyndale, and all the early English translations, render it 'unto you,' until the Elisabethan State Bible, called the Bishop's, in 1568. Do not the words mean that Christians are to receive such as are weak in the faith into their hearts by love, without troubling their heads with perplexing disputes?—ED.

their mutual affection. And if they will cast such out of their mutual affection that are within, no doubt they will keep out of their church fellowship those that are without.

Arg. 1. Whereas the Lord's care extends to all his, and if it were a good argument in the third verse, for them to receive those within, because God hath received them, it would be as good an argument to receive in those without, for God hath received them also: unless it could be proved, that all that were and are weak in the faith, were and are in church fellowship, which is not likely: for if they would cast such out of their affection that are within, they would upon the same account keep them out of church fellowship that were without: therefore as it is a duty to receive those within unto mutual affection, so it is no less a duty, by the text, to receive such weak ones as are without, into church fellowship.

Arg. 2. Is urged from the words themselves, which are, 'Receive him that is weak in the faith;' wherein the Lord puts NO limitation in this text or in any other; and who is he then that can restrain it, unless he will limit the Holy One of Israel? And how would such an interpretation foolishly charge the Lord, as if he took care ONLY of those within, but not like care of those without; whereas he commandeth them to receive them, and useth this motive, he had received them, and he receiveth those that are weak in the faith, if without, as well as those within.

From the example, to wit, That God had received them; whereas had he been of the church, they would have been persuaded of that before the motive was urged: for no true church of Christ's would take in, or keep in any, whom they judged the Lord had not received; but those weak ones were such as they questioned whether the Lord had received them, else the text had not been an answer sufficient for their receiving them: There might have been objected, they hold up Jewish observations of meats and days, which by the death of Christ were abolished, and so did deny some of the effects of his death; yet the Lord who was principally wronged could pass this by, and commandeth others to receive them also. And if it be a good argument to receive such as are weak in any thing, whom the Lord hath received, then there can be no good argument to reject for any thing for which the Lord will not reject them: for else the command in the first verse, and his example in the third verse were insufficient, without some other arguments unto the church, besides his command and example.

☞ Some object, 'Receive ye one another, as Christ also received us to the glory of God.' Ro. xv. 7. And from thence supposing they were all in church fellowship before, whereas the text saith

not so: for if you consider the eighth and ninth verses, you may see he speaks unto Jews and Gentiles in general, that if the Jews had the receiving, they should receive Gentiles; and if the Gentiles had the receiving, they should receive Jews, for had they not been on both sides commanded: the Jews might have said to the Gentiles, you are commanded to receive us, but we are not commanded to receive you; and if the weak had the receiving, they should receive the strong; and if the strong had the receiving, they should not keep out the weak; and the text is reinforced with the example of the Son's receiving us unto the glory of God, that as he receiveth Jews and poor Gentiles, weak and strong, in church fellowship, or out of church fellowship; so should they to the glory of God. And as the Lord Jesus received some, though they held some things more than were commanded, and some things less than were commanded, and as those that were weak and in church fellowship, so those that were weak and out of church fellowship; and that not only into mutual affection, but unto fellowship with himself; and so should they, not only receive such as were weak within into mutual affection, but such as were without, both to mutual affection and to church fellowship: or else such weak ones as were without, had been excluded by the text. Oh! how is the heart of God the Father and the Son set upon this, to have his children in his house, and in one another's hearts as they are in his, and are borne upon the shoulders and breasts of his Son their high priest? and as if all this will not do it, but the devil will divide them still, whose work it properly is; But 'the God of peace' will come in shortly, 'and bruise Satan under their feet,' as in Ro. xvi. 20. And they will agree to be in one house, when they are more of one heart; in the mean time pray, as in ch. xv. 5. 'Now the God of patience and consolation grant you to be like-minded one toward another according to Christ Jesus.'

I shall endeavour the answering of some objections, and leave it unto consideration.

Object. Some say this bearing or receiving, were but in things indifferent.

Answ. That eating, or forbearing upon a civil account, are things indifferent, is true: but not when done upon the account of worship, as keeping of days, and establishing Jewish observations about meats, which by the death of Christ are taken away; and it is not fairly to be imagined the same church at Rome looked so upon them as indifferent; nor that the Lord doth; that it were all alike to him to hold up Jewish observations, or to keep days or no days, right days or wrong days, as indifferent things, which is a great mistake, and no less than to make God's grace little in receiving such. For if it were but in things wherein they had not sinned, it were no great matter for the Lord to receive, and it would have been as good an argument or motive to the church, to say the things were indifferent, as to say the Lord had received them. Whereas the text is to set out the riches of grace to the vessels of mercy, as Ro. ix. 15. That as at first he did freely choose and accept them; so when they fail and miscarry in many things, yea about his worship also, although he be most injured thereby, yet he is first in passing it by, and persuading others to do the like. That as the good Samaritan did in the Old Testament,* so our good Samaritan doth in the New, when priest and Levite passed by, pastor and people pass by, yet he will not, but pours in oil, and carries them to his inn, and calls for receiving, and setting it upon his account.

Object. That this bearing with, and receiving such as are weak in the faith, must be limited to meats and days, and such like things that had been old Jewish observations, but not unto the being ignorant in, or doubting of any New Testament institution.

Answ. Where the Lord puts no limitation, men should be wary how they do it, for they must have a command or example, before they can limit this command; for although the Lord took this occasion from their difference about meats and days to give this command, yet the command is not limited there, no more than Mat. xii. 1—8. That when they made use of his good law rigorously in the letter, he presently published an act of grace in the 7th verse, and tells them, Had they known what this meaneth, 'I will have mercy and not sacrifice,' they would not have condemned the guiltless; as also Mat. ix 13. 'Go ye and learn what *that* meaneth, I will have mercy and not sacrifice,' which is not to be limited unto what was the present occasion of publishing the command, but observed as a general rule upon all occasions, wherein mercy and sacrifice comes in competition, to shew the Lord will rather have a duty omitted that is due to him, than mercy to his creatures omitted by them. So in the text, when some would not receive such as were weak in the faith, as to matters of practice, the Lord was pleased to publish this act of grace: 'Him that is weak in the faith receive ye, *but* not to doubtful disputations.' Now unless it be proved, that no saint can be weak in the faith in any thing but meats and days, or in some Old Testament observations, and that he ought not to be judged a saint that is weak in the faith as it relates to gospel institutions, in matters of practice; you cannot limit the text, and you

must also prove his weakness SUCH, as that the Lord will not receive him; else the command in the first verse, and the reason or motive in the third verse, will both be in force upon you; to wit, 'Him that is weak in the faith receive ye,' or unto you, - 'for God hath received him.'

Object. But some may object from 1 Co. xii. 13. 'For by one spirit are we all baptized into one body, whether *we be* Jews or Gentiles. Some there are that affirm this to be meant of water baptism, and that particular churches are formed thereby, and all persons are to be admitted and joined unto such churches by water baptism.

Answ. That the baptism intended in the text is the Spirit's baptism, and not water baptism; and that the body the text intends, is not principally the church of Corinth, but all believers, both Jews and Gentiles, being baptized into one mystical body, as Ep. iv. 4. '*There is* one body and one Spirit,' wherein there is set out the uniter and the united; therefore in the third verse they are exhorted to keep the unity of the Spirit in the bond of peace. The united are all the faithful in one body; into whom? in the fifth verse, in one Lord Jesus Christ: by what? one faith, one baptism, which CANNOT be meant of water baptism; for water baptism doth not unite all this body, for some of them never had water baptism, and are yet of this body, and by the Spirit gathered into one Lord Jesus Christ, Ep. i. 10. 'both which are in heaven and in earth,' Jew and Gentile, Ep. ii. 16. 'that he might reconcile both unto God in one body by the cross.' The instrument you have in ver. 18. 'by one spirit.' Ep. iii. 6. 'That the Gentiles should be fellow-heirs, and of the same body.' ver. 15. 'Of whom the whole family in heaven and earth is named.' And the reasons of their keeping 'the unity of the Spirit,' in Ep. iv. 3. is laid down in ver. 4, 5. being 'one body,' 'one Spirit,' having 'one hope,' 'one Lord,' 'one faith,' 'one baptism,' whether they were Jews or Gentiles, such as were in heaven or in earth, which CANNOT be meant of water baptism, for in that sense they had not all one baptism, nor admitted and united thereby. So in 1 Co. xii. 13. 'For by one Spirit we are all baptized into one body, whether *we be* Jews or Gentiles, whether *we be* bond or free; and have been all made to drink into one Spirit;' which cannot be meant of water baptism, in regard all the body of Christ, Jews and Gentiles, bond and free, partook not thereof.

Object. But Ep. iv. 5. saith, there is but 'one baptism;' and by what hath been said, if granted, water baptism will be excluded, or else there is more baptisms than one.

Answ. It followeth not that because the Spirit will have no corrival, that therefore other things

---

* Under the Old Testament dispensation; the parable or history is recorded in Luke x.—ED.

may not be in their places. That because the Spirit of God taketh the pre-eminence, therefore other things may not be subservient. 1 Jn. ii. 27. The apostle tells them, That the anointing which they have received of him, abideth in them; and you need not, saith he, 'that any man teach you, but as the same anointing teacheth you of all things.' By this some may think John excludes the ministry; no such matter, though the Holy Ghost had confirmed and instructed them so in the truth of the gospel, as that they were furnished against seducers in ver. 26. yet you see John goes on still teaching them in many things: as also in Ep. iv. 11 —13. 'He gave some, apostles; - some evangelists, and some pastors, and teachers; for the perfecting of the saints, for the work of the ministry, for the edifying of the body of Christ: Till we all come in the unity of the faith, and of the knowledge of the Son of God, unto a perfect man, unto the measure of the stature of the fulness of Christ.' So in the Spirit's baptism, though it have the pre-eminence, and appropriateth some things, as peculiar to itself, it doth not thereby destroy the use and end of water baptism, or any other ordinance in its place: for water baptism is a means to increase grace, and in it, and by it sanctification is forwarded, and remission of sins more cleared and witnessed; yet the giving grace, and regenerating and renewing, is the Holy Spirit's peculiar. Consider Tit. iii. 5. 'By the washing of regeneration, and renewing of the Holy Ghost;' Baptism being the outward sign of the inward graces wrought by the Spirit, a representation or figure, as in 1 Pe. iii. 21. 'The like figure whereunto *even* baptism doth also now save us [not the putting away of the filth of the flesh, but the answer of a good conscience toward God,] by the resurrection of Jesus Christ;' not excluding water baptism; but shewing, That the spiritual part is chiefly to be looked at: though such as slight water baptism, as the Pharisees and lawyers did, Lu. vii. 30. reject the counsel of God against themselves, not being baptized. And such as would set water baptism in the Spirit's place, exalt a duty against the deity and dignity of the Spirit, and do give the glory due unto him, as God blessed for ever, unto a duty.

By which mistake of setting up water baptism in the Spirit's place, and assigning it a work, which was never appointed unto it; of forming the body of Christ, either in general, as in 1 Co. xii. 13. Ep. iv. 5. or as to particular churches of Christ, we may see the fruit; that instead of being the means of uniting as the Spirit doth; that it hath not only rent his seamless coat, but divided his body which he hath purchased with his own blood, and opposed that great design of Father, Son, and Spirit, in uniting poor saints, thereby pulling in pieces what the Spirit hath put together. 'Him that is weak

in the faith receive ye, - for God hath received him;' being such as the Spirit had baptized and admitted of the body of Christ, he would have his churches receive them also: whose baptism is the ☞ ONLY baptism, and so is called the ONE baptism. Therefore consider, whether such a practice, hath a command or an example, that persons must be joined into church fellowship by water baptism; for John baptized many, yet he did not baptize some into one church, and some into another, nor all into one church, as the church of Rome doth. And into what church did Philip baptize the eunuch, or the apostle the jailor and his house? And all the rest they baptized, were they not left free to join themselves for their convenience and edification? All which I leave to consideration. I might have named some inconveniences, if not absurdities that would follow the assertion: as to father the mistakes of the baptizers on the Spirit's act, who is not mistaken in any HE baptizeth; no false brethren creep in unawares into the mystical body by him; and also, how this manner of forming churches would suit a country, where many are converted, and willing to be baptized; but there being no church to be baptized into, how shall such a church state begin? The first must be baptized into no church, and the rest into him as the church, or the work stand still for want of a church.

Object. 'But God is a God of order, and hath ordained order in all the churches of Christ; and for to receive one that holds the baptism he had in his infancy, there is no command nor example for, and by the same rule children will be brought in to be church members.'

Answ. That God is a God of order, and hath ordained orders in all the churches of Christ is true; and that this is one of the orders to receive him that is weak in the faith, is as true. And though there be no example or command, in so many words, receive such an one that holds the baptism he had in his infancy, nor to reject such a one: but there is a command to receive him that is weak in the faith, without limitation, and it is like this might not be a doubt in those days, and so not spoken of in particular.

But the Lord provides a remedy for all times in the text, 'Him that is weak in the faith receive ye;' for else receiving would not be upon the account of saintship; but upon knowing, and doing all things according to rule and order, and that must be perfectly, else for to deny any thing, or to affirm too much is disorderly, and would hinder receiving: but the Lord deals not so with his people, but accounts 'LOVE the fulfilling of the law,' though they be ignorant in many things both as to knowing and doing; and receives them into communion and fellowship with himself, and would have others do the same also. And if he would have so much bearing in the apostle's days, when they had infallible helps to expound truths unto them, much more now, the church hath been so long in the wilderness and in captivity, and not that his people should be driven away in the dark day, though they are sick and weak. Eze. xxxiv. 16, 21. And that it should be supposed such tenderness would bring in children in age to be church members, yea and welcome, if any body could prove them in the faith, though never so weak; for the text is, 'Him that is weak in the faith, receive ye:' It is not He, and his wife and children, unless it can be proved they are IN THE FAITH.

Object. 'By this, some ordinances may be lost or omitted, and is it to be supposed the Lord would suffer any of his ordinances to be lost or omitted in the Old or New Testament, or the right use of them, and yet own such for true churches, and what reason can there be for it ?'

Answ. The Lord hath suffered some ordinances to be omitted and lost in the Old Testament, and yet owned the church. Though circumcision were omitted in the wilderness, yet he owned them to be his church; Ac. vii. 38. and many of the ordinances were lost in the captivity: see Ainsworth upon Ex. xxviii.; xxx. &c. which shewed what the high-priest was to put on, and were not to be omitted upon pain of death, as the Urim and Thummim, yet being lost, and several other ordinances, the ark, with the mercy-seat and cherubims, the fire from heaven, the majesty and divine presence, &c. yet, he owns the second temple, though short of the first, and filled it with his glory, and honoured it with his Son, being a member and a minister therein, Mal. iii. 1. 'The Lord whom ye seek shall suddenly come to his temple:' So in the New Testament, since their wilderness condition, and great and long captivity, there is some darkness and doubts, and want of light in the best of the Lord's people, in many of his ordinances, and that for several ages, and yet how hath the Lord owned them for his churches, wherein he is to have glory and praise 'throughout all ages.' Ep. iii. 21. And so should we own them, unless we will condemn the generation of the just. It must be confessed, That if exact practice be required, and clearness in gospel institutions before communion; who dare be so bold as to say his hands are clean, and that he hath done all the Lord's commands, as to institutions in his worship ? and must not confess the change of times doth necessitate some variation, if not alteration, either in the matter or manner of things according to primitive practice; yet owned for true churches, and received as visible saints, though ignorant either wholly, or in great measure, in laying on of hands, singing, washing of feet, and anointing with oil, in the gifts of the Spirit,

which is the Urim and Thummim of the gospel. And it cannot be proved, that the churches were so ignorant in the primitive times, nor yet that such were received into fellowship; yet now herein it is thought meet their should be bearing, and why not in baptism, especially in such as own it for an ordinance, though in some things miss it, and do yet shew their love unto it, and unto the Lord, and unto his law therein, that they could be willing to die for it rather than to deny it; and to be baptized in their blood; which sheweth, they hold it in conscience their duty, while they have further light from above, and are willing to hear and obey as far as they know, though weak in the faith, as to clearness in gospel institutions: surely the text is on their side, or else it will exclude all the former, 'Him that is weak in the faith receive ye, - but not to doubtful disputations.' Ro. xiv. 5. Let every man be fully persuaded in his own mind, and such the Lord hath received.

As to the query, What reason is there, why the Lord should suffer any of his ordinances to be lost?

Answ. If there were no reason to be shewn, it should teach us silence, for he doth nothing without the highest reason ; and there doth appear some reasons in the Old Testament, why those ordinances of Urim and Thummim, &c. were suffered to be lost in the captivity, that they might long and look for the Lord Jesus, the priest, that was to stand up with Urim and Thummim, Ezr. ii. 63. Ne. vii. 65. which the Lord by this puts them upon the hoping for, and to be in the expectation of so great a mercy, which was the promise of the Old Testament, and all the churches losses in the New Testament By all the dark night of ignorance she hath been in, and long captivity she hath been under, and in her wandering wilderness state, wherein she hath rather been fed with manna from heaven, than by men upon earth ; and after all her crosses and losses, the Lord lets light break in by degrees, and deliverance by little and little ; and she is 'coming out of the wilderness leaning upon her beloved;' and the Lord hath given the valley of Achor for a door of hope, that ere long she may receive the promise of the gospel richly, by the Spirit, to be poured upon us from on high, Is. xxxii. 15. and the wilderness be a fruitful field, and the fruitful field become a forest, and then the Lord will take away the covering cast over all people, Is. xxv. 7. and the vail that is spread over all nations ; Is xi. 9. 'For the earth shall be full of the knowledge of the Lord, as the waters cover the sea.' ver. 13. Then 'Ephraim shall not envy Judah, and Judah shall not vex Ephraim.' Thus will the God of peace bruise Satan under foot shortly ; and one reason why the Lord may suffer all this darkness and differences that have been, and yet are, is, that we might long and look for this blessed promise of the gospel, the pourings out of the Spirit.

Object. But many authors do judge, that the weak and strong were all in church fellowship before, and that the receiving, Ro. xiv. 1. was but into mutual affection.

Answ. It ought to be seriously weighed how any differ from so many worthy authors, is confessed; to whom the world is so much beholden for their help in many things; but it would be of dangerous consequence to take all for granted they say, and unlike the noble Bereans. Ac. xvii. 11. Though they had some infallible teachers, yet they took not their words or doctrine upon trust; and there may be more ground to question expositors on this text, in regard their principles necessitate them to judge that the sense; for if it be in their judgments a duty to compel all to come in, and to receive all, and their children, they must needs judge by that text, they were all of the church, and in fellowship, before their scrupling meats and days, because that is an act of grown persons at years of discretion; and therefore the receiving is judged by them to be only into mutual affection, for it is impossible for them to hold their opinion, and judge otherwise of the text; for in baptism, they judge infants should be received into church fellowship; and then scrupling meats and days must needs be after joining. Their judgments might as well be taken, that it is a duty to baptize infants, as that they can judge of this text rightly, and hold their practice.

Object. But no uncircumcised person was to eat the passover. Ex. xii. And doth not the Lord as well require the sign of baptism now, as of circumcision then? and is there not like reason for it?

Answ. The Lord, in the Old Testament, expressly commanded no uncircumcised person should eat the passover, Ex. xii. 48. and in Eze. xliv. 9. that no stranger, uncircumcised in heart, or uncircumcised in flesh, should enter into his sanctuary.* And

had the Lord commanded, that no unbaptized person should enter into his churches, it had been clear. And no doubt, Christ was as faithful as a son in all his house, as Moses was as a servant; and although there had been little reason, if the Lord had commanded it so to be, yet in God's worship we must not make the likeness of any thing in our reason, but the will of God, the ground of duty; for upon such a foundation some would build the baptizing of infants, because it would be like unto circumcision, and so break the second commandment, in making the likeness of things of their own contrivance, of force with institutions in the worship of God.

The most that I think can be said is, That we have no gospel example for receiving without baptism, or rejecting any for want of it. Therefore it is desired, what hath been said, may be considered; lest while we look for an example, we do not overlook a command upon a mistake, supposing that they were all in church fellowship before; whereas the text saith not so, but, ' Him that is weak in the faith receive ye,' or unto you.

We may see also how the Lord proceeds under the law, though he accounts those things that were done contrary to his law, sinful, though done ignorantly; yet never required the offender to offer sacrifice till he knew thereof. Le. v. 5. comp. with ver. 15, 16. And that may be a man's own sin through his ignorance; that though it may be another's duty to endeavour to inform him in, yet not thereupon to keep him out of his Father's house; for surely the Lord would not have any of his children kept out, without we have a word for it. And though they scruple some meats in their Father's house, yet it may be dangerous for the stronger children to deny them all the rest of the dainties therein, till the weak and sick can eat strong meat; whereas Peter had meat for one, and milk for another; and Peter must feed the poor lambs as well as the sheep; and if others will not do it, the great shepherd will come ere long and look up what hath been driven away. Eze. xxxiv. 4, 11. Is. xl. 11. He will feed his flock like a shepherd; he shall gather the lambs into his bosom, and gently lead those that are with young.

---

* We cannot offer to God any acceptable sacrifice until spiritually baptized. First joined to God by a living faith in the atoning sacrifice of Christ, and then bringing forth the fruits of this internal and purifying baptism, we must give ourselves to his church in the bonds of the gospel.—ED.

PEACEABLE PRINCIPLES AND TRUE:

OR,

A BRIEF ANSWER TO MR. D'ANVER'S AND MR. PAUL'S BOOKS AGAINST MY CONFESSION OF FAITH, AND DIFFERENCES IN JUDGMENT ABOUT BAPTISM NO BAR TO COMMUNION.

WHEREIN THEIR SCRIPTURELESS NOTIONS ARE OVERTHROWN, AND MY PEACEABLE PRINCIPLES STILL MAINTAINED.

'*Do ye indeed speak righteousness, O congregation? do ye judge uprightly, O ye sons of men?*' —Psal. lviii. 1.

SIR,

I HAVE received and considered your short reply to my differences in judgment about water baptism no bar to communion; and observe, that you touch not the argument at all: but rather labour what you can, and beyond what you ought, to throw odiums upon your brother for reproving you for your error, viz. 'That those believers that have been baptized after confession of faith made by themselves, ought and are in duty bound to exclude from their church fellowship, and communion at the table of the Lord, those of their holy brethren that have not been so baptized.' This is your error. Error, I call it, because it is not founded upon the word, but a mere human device; for although I do not deny, but acknowledge, that baptism is God's ordinance; yet I have denied, that baptism was ever ordained of God to be a wall of division between the holy and the holy; the holy that are, and the holy that are not, so baptized with water as we. You, on the Your reflections, p. 7. contrary, both by doctrine and practice, assert that it is; and therefore do separate yourselves from all your brethren that in that matter differ from you; accounting them, notwithstanding their saving faith and holy lives, not fitly qualified for church communion, and all because they have not been, as you, baptized. Further, you count their communion among themselves P. 32. unlawful, and therefore unwarrantable; and have concluded, 'they are joined to idols, and that they ought not to be shewed the pattern of the house of God, until they be ashamed of their sprinkling in their infancy, and accept of and receive baptism as you.' Yea, you count them as they stand, not the churches of God; saying, 'We P. 26. have no such custom, nor the churches of God.' At this I have called for your proofs, the which you have attempted to produce; but in conclusion have shewed none other, but, 'That the P. 41. primitive churches had those they received, baptized before so received.'

I have told you, that this, though it were granted, cometh not up to the question; for we ask not, 'whether they were so baptized? But

whether you find a word in the Bible that justifieth your concluding that it is your duty to exclude those of your holy brethren that have not been so baptized?' From this you cry out, that I take up the arguments of them that plead for infant baptism: I answer, I take up no other argument but your own, viz. 'That there being no precept, precedent, nor example in all the scripture, for our excluding our holy brethren that differ in this point from us, therefore we ought not to dare to do it,' but contrariwise to receive them;* because God hath given us sufficient proof that himself hath received them, whose example in this case he hath commanded us to follow. Ro. xiv. 3, 15. This might serve for an answer to your reply. But because, perhaps, should I thus conclude, some might make an ill use of my brevity; I shall therefore briefly step after you, and examine your short reply; at least, where shew of argument is.

Your first five pages are spent to prove me either proud or a liar; for inserting in the title-page of my 'Differences,' &c. that your book was written by the Baptist, or brethren of your way.

In answer to which; whoso* readeth   * If unbiassed. your second, your fifth and sixth ques- tions to me, may not perhaps be easily persuaded to the contrary; but the two last in your reply, are omitted by you; whether for brevity's sake, or because you were conscious to yourself, that the sight of them would overthrow your insinuations, I leave to the sober to judge. But put the case I had failed herein, Doth this warrant your unlawful practice?

You ask me next, 'How long is it since I P. 5. was a Baptist?' and then add, 'It is an ill bird that bewrays his own nest.'

Answ. I must tell you, avoiding your slovenly language, I know none to whom that title is so proper as to the disciples of John. And since you would know by what name I would be P. 6. distinguished from others; I tell you, I would be,

---

* A tender conscience, jealous of grieving or offending the Holy Spirit, is of an inestimable value. If in our conscientious conclusions we offend others, we must leave to them an equal right to their own conclusions without harsh judgment. —ED.

and hope I am, A CHRISTIAN; and choose, if God should count me worthy, to be called a Christian, a Believer, or other such name which is approved by the Holy Ghost. Ac. xi. 26. And as for those factious titles of Anabaptists, Independents, Presbyterians, or the like, I conclude, that they came neither from Jerusalem, nor Antioch, but rather from hell and Babylon; for they naturally tend to divisions, 'you may know them by their fruits.'

Next, you tell us of your goodly harmony in London; or of the 'amicable christian P. 7. correspondency betwixt those of divers persuasions there, until my turbulent and mutineering spirit got up.'

Answ. The cause of my writing, I told you, which you have neither disapproved in whole, nor in part. And now I ask what kind of christian correspondency you have with them? Is it such as relateth to church communion; or such only as you are commanded to have with every brother that walketh disorderly, that they may be ashamed of their church communion, which you condemn? if so, your great flourish will add no praise to them; and why they should glory in a correspondency with them as Christians, who yet count them under such deadly sin, which will not by any means, as they now stand, suffer you to admit them to their Father's table, to me is not easy to believe.

Farther, Your christian correspondency, as you call it, will not keep you now and then, from fingering some of their members from them; nor from teaching them that you so take away, to judge and condemn them that are left behind: Now who boasteth in this besides yourself, I know not.

Touching Mr. Jesse's judgment in the case in hand, you know it condemneth your practice; and since in your first, you have called for an author's testimony, I have presented you with one, whose arguments you have not condemned.

For your insinuating my abusive and unworthy behaviour, as the cause of the brethren's attempting to break our Christian communion; it is not only false but ridiculous. False; for they have *This attempt attempted to make me also one of their began above disciples, and sent to* me, and for me for sixteen years that purpose. Besides, it is ridiculous; ago. surely their pretended order, and as they call it, our disorder, was the cause; or they must render themselves very malicious, to seek the overthrow of a whole congregation, for, if it had been so, the unworthy behaviour of one.

Now, since you tell me, p. 9, 'That Mr. Kiffin hath no need of my forgiveness for the wrong he hath done me in his epistle.'

I ask, did he tell you so? But let it lie as it doth; I will at this time turn his argument upon him, and desire his direct answer: There being no precept, precedent or example for Mr. Kiffin to

exclude his holy brethren from Christian communion that differ with him about baptism, he ought not to do it; but there is neither precept, precedent, nor example; therefore, &c.

You blame me for writing his name at length: but I know he is not ashamed of his name: and for you, though at the remotest rate, to insinuate it, must needs be damage to him.

Your artificial squibbling* suggestions to the world about myself, imprisonment, and the like, I freely bind unto me as an ornament among the rest of my reproaches, till the Lord shall wipe them off at his coming. But they are no argument that you have a word that binds you to exclude the holy brethren communion.

Now what if, as you suggest, the sober Dr. Owen, though he told me and others at first he would write an epistle to my book, yet waved it afterwards; this is also to my advantage; because it was through the earnest solicitations of several of you that at that time stopped his hand; And perhaps it was more for the glory of God that truth should go naked into the world, than as seconded by so mighty an armour-bearer as he.

You tell me also, that some of the sober Independents have shewed dislike to my writing P. 6. on this subject: What then? If I should also say, as I can without lying, that several of the Baptists have wished yours burnt before it had come to light; is your book ever the worse for that?

In p. 13, You tell us, you meddle not with Presbyterians, Independents, mixed Communionists (a new name), but are for liberty for all according to their light.

Answ. I ask then, suppose an holy man of God, that differeth from you, as those above-named do, in the manner of water baptism; I say, suppose such an one should desire communion with you, yet abiding by his own light, as to the thing in question, Would you receive him to fellowship? If no, do you not dissemble?

But you add, 'If unbaptized believers do not walk with us, they may walk with them with whom they are better agreed.'

Answ. Then it seems you do but flatter them. You are not, for all you pretend to give them their liberty, agreed they should have it with you. Thus do the Papists give the Protestants their liberty, because they can neither will nor choose.

Again, But do you not follow them with clamours and out-cries, that their communion, even amongst themselves, is unwarrantable? Now, how then do you give them their liberty? Nay, do not even these things declare that you would take it away if you could?

'For the time that I have been a Baptist (say

* 'Squibbling,' feeble, ill-natured ridicule; now obsolete.—ED.

you) I do not remember that ever I knew that one unbaptized person did so much as offer themselves to us for church fellowship.'

Answ. This is no proof of your love to your brethren; but rather an argument that your rigidness was from that day to this so apparent, that those good souls despaired to make such attempts; we know they have done it elsewhere, where they hoped to meet with encouragement.

In p. 14, You seem to retract your denial of baptism to be the initiating ordinance. And indeed Mr. D'Anvers told me, that you must retract that opinion, and that he had, or would speak to you to do it; yet by some it is still so acknowledged Denne's Truth outweighing, &c., p. 46. to be; and in particular, by your great helper, Mr. Denne, who strives to maintain it by several arguments; but your denial may be a sufficient confutation to him; so I leave you together to agree about it, and conclude you have overthrown him.

But it seems though you do not now own it to be the inlet into a particular church; yet, as you tell us in p. 14 of your last, 'you never denied that baptism doth not make a believer a member of Treatise of Baptism. the universal, orderly, church visible. And in this Mr. D'Anvers and you agree.' 'Persons enter into the visible church thereby,' saith he.

Answ. Universal, that is, the whole church: This word now comprehendeth all the parts of it, even from Adam to the very world's end, whether in heaven or earth, &c. Now that [water] baptism makes a man a member of this church, I do not yet believe, nor can you shew me why I should. 2. The universal, orderly church. What church this should be, if by orderly you mean harmony or agreement in the outward parts of worship, I do not understand neither.

And yet thus you should mean, because you add the word *visible* to all at the last; 'The universal, orderly, visible church.' Now I would yet learn of this brother where this church is; for if it be visible, he can tell and also shew it. But, to be short, there is no such church: the universal church cannot be visible; a great part of that vast body being already in heaven, and a great part as yet, perhaps, unborn.

But if he should mean by universal, the whole of that part of this church that is on earth, then neither is it 'visible' nor 'orderly.' 1. Not visible; for the part remains always to the best man's eye utterly invisible. 2. This church is not orderly; that is, hath not harmony in its outward and visible parts of worship; some parts opposing and contradicting the other most severely. Yea, would it be uncharitable to believe that some of the members of this body could willingly die in opposing that which others of the members hold to

be a truth of Christ? As for instance at home; could not some of those called Baptists die in opposing infant baptism? And again, some of them that are for infant baptism die for that as a truth? Here therefore is no order, but an evident contradiction: and that too in such parts of worship, as both count visible parts of worship indeed.

So then by 'universal, orderly, visible church,' this brother must mean those of the saints only that have been, or are baptized as we; this is clear, because baptism, saith he, maketh a believer a member of this church; his meaning then is, that there is an universal, orderly, visible church, and they alone are the Baptists; and that every one that is baptized is by that made a member of the universal, orderly, visible church of Baptists, and that the whole number of the rest of saints are utterly excluded.

But now if other men should do as this man, how many universal churches should we have? An 'universal, orderly, visible church of Independents;' an 'universal, orderly, visible church of Presbyterians,' and the like. And who of them, if as much confused in their notions as this brother, might not, they judging by their own light, contend for their universal church, as he for his? But they have more wit.

But suppose that this unheard of fictitious church were the only true universal church; yet whoever they baptize must be a visible saint first, and if a visible saint, then a visible member of Christ; and if so, then a visible member of his body, which is the church, before they be baptized; now he which is a visible member of the church already, that which hath so made him, hath prevented all those claims that by any may be made or imputed to this or that ordinance to make him so. Ac. viii. 37; xix. 17, and xvi. 33. His visibility is already; he is already a visible member of the body of Christ, and after that baptized. His baptism then neither makes him a member nor a visible member of the body of Jesus Christ.

You go on, 'That I said it was consent that makes persons members of particular P. 4 of your first. churches is true.'

Answ. But that it is consent and nothing else, consent without faith, &c., is false. Your afterendeavour to heal your unsound saying will do you no good: 'Faith gives being to, as well as probation for membership.'

What you say now of the epistles, that they were written to particular saints, and those too out of churches as well as in, I always believed: but in your first you were pleased to say, 'You were one of them that objected against our proofs out of the epistles, because they were written to particular churches, (intending these baptized) and that they were written to other saints, Your reflections, p. 9. would be hard for me to prove:' but you do well to give way to the truth.

What I said about baptism's being a PEST, take my words as they lie, and I stand still thereto: 'Knowing that Satan can make any of God's ordinances a PEST and plague to his people, even baptism, the Lord's table, and the holy scriptures; yea, the ministers also of Jesus Christ may be suffered to abuse them, and wrench them out of their place.' Wherefore I pray, if you write again, either consent to, or deny this position, before you proceed in your outcry.

But I must still continue to tell you, though you love not to hear thereof, That supposing your opinion hath hold of your conscience, if you might have your will, you would make inroads and outroads too in all the churches that are not as you in the land. You reckon that church privileges belong not to them who are not baptized as we, saying, 'How can we take these privileges from P. 37 of your reply. them before they have them, we keep them from a disorderly practice of ordinances, especially among ourselves;' intimating you do what you can also among others: and he that shall judge those he walketh not with, or say, as you, that they, like Ephraim, are 'joined to an Your reflections, p. 32. idol, and ought to repent and be ashamed of that idol before they be shewed the pattern of the house;' and then shall back all with P. 26. the citation of a text; doth it either in jest P. 30. or in earnest; if in jest it is abominable; if P. 7. in earnest his conscience is engaged; and being engaged, it putteth him upon doing what he can to extirpate the thing he counteth idolatrous and abominable, out of the churches abroad, as well as that he stands in relation unto. This being thus, it is reasonable to conclude, you want not an heart, but opportunity for your inroads and outroads among them.

Touching those five things I mentioned in my second; you should not have counted they were found no where, because not found under that head which I mention: and now lest you should miss them again, I will present you with them here.

1. 'Baptism is not the initiating ordinance. 2. That though it was, the case may so fall out, that members might be received without it. 3. That baptism makes no man a visible saint. 4. That faith, and a life becoming the ten commandments, should be the chief and most solid argument with churches to receive to fellowship. 5. That circumcision in the flesh was a type of circumcision in the heart, and not of water baptism.' To these you should have given fair answers, then you had done like a workman.

Now we are come to page 22 and 23 of yours;

where you labour to insinuate, 'that a transgression against a positive precept, respecting instituted worship, hath been punished with the utmost severity that God hath executed against men, on record, on this side hell.'

Answ. Mr. D'Anvers says, 'That to Treat. of baptism. transgress a positive precept respecting worship, is a breach of the first and second commandments.' If so, then it is for the breach of them, that these severe rebukes befal the sons of men. 2. But you instance the case of Adam his eating the forbidden fruit; yet to no great purpose. Adam's first transgression was, that he violated the law that was written in his heart; in that he hearkened to the tempting voice of his wife; and after, because he did eat of the tree: he was bad then before he did eat of the tree; which badness was infused over his whole nature; and then he bare this evil fruit of eating things that God hath forbidden. Ge. iii. Either make the tree good, and his fruit good; or the tree bad, and his fruit bad. Mat. vii. 17. Lu. vi. 43, 44. Men must be bad, ere they do evil; and good, ere they do good. Again, which was the greatest judgment, to be defiled and depraved, or to be put out of paradise, do you in your next determine.

But as to the matter in hand, What positive precept do they transgress that will not reject him that God bids us receive, if he want light in baptism?

As for my calling for scripture to prove it lawful thus to exclude them; blame me for it no more; verily I still must do it; and had you but one to give, I had had it long before this. But you wonder I should ask for a scripture to prove a negative. p. 23.

Answ. 1. Are you at that door, my brother? If a drunkard, a swearer, or whoremonger should desire communion with you, and upon your refusal, demand your grounds; would you think his demands such you ought not to answer? would you not readily give him by SCORES? So, doubtless would you deal with us, but that in this you are without the lids* of the Bible. 2. But again, you have acted as those that must produce a positive rule. 'You count it your duty, a part of your obedience to God, to keep those out of church fellowship that are not baptized as you.' I then demand what precept bids you do this? where are you commanded to do it?

You object, p. 24. That in Ep. iv. 5. and 1 Co. xii. 13. is not meant of Spirit baptism: but Mr. Jesse says it is not, cannot be the baptism with water: and you have not at all refuted him. And now for the church in the wilderness; 'You P. 26, 27.

---

* 'Without the lids of the Bible,' not within it; a popular Puritan saying.—ED.

thought, as you say, I would have answered myself in the thing;' but as yet I have not, neither have you. But let us see what you urge for an answer.

I. Say you, 'Though God dispensed with their obedience to circumcision in that time, Ge. xvii. Ex. xii. it follows not that you or I should dispense with the ordinance of water baptism now.'

Answ. God commanded it, and made it the initiating ordinance to church communion. But Moses, and Aaron, and Joshua, and the elders of Israel, dispensed with it for forty years; therefore the dispensing with it was ministerial, and that with God's allowance, as you affirm. Now if they might dispense with circumcision, though the initiating ordinance; why may not we receive God's holy ones into fellowship, since we are not forbidden it, but commanded; yea, why should we make water baptism, which God never ordained to that end, a bar to shut out and let in to church communion?

II. You ask, 'Was circumcision dispensed with for want of light, it being plainly commanded?'

Answ. Whatever was the cause, want of light is as great a cause: and that it must necessarily follow, they must needs see it, because commanded, favours too much of a tang of free will, or of the sufficiency of our understanding, and intrencheth too hard on the glory of the Holy Ghost; whose work it is 'to bring all things to our remembrance, whatsoever Christ hath said to us.' Jn. xiv. 26.

III. You ask, 'Cannot you give yourself a reason, that their moving, travelling state made them incapable, and that God was merciful? Can the same reason, or anything like it, for refusing baptism, be given now?'

Answ. I cannot give myself this reason, nor can you by it give me any satisfaction. Because their travelling state could not hinder; if you consider that they might, and doubtless did lie still in one place years together. 1. They were forty years going from Egypt to Canaan: and they had but forty-two journies thither. 2. They at times went several of these journies in one and the same year. They went, as I take it, eleven of them by the end of the third month after they came out of the land of Egypt. Compare Ex. xix. 1. with Nu. xxxiii. 15. 3. Again, in the fortieth year, we find them in Mount Hor, where Aaron died, and was buried. Now that was the year they went into Canaan; and in that year they had nine journies more, or ten, by that they got over Jordan, Nu. xxxiii. 38, &c. Here then were twenty journies in less than one year and an half. Divide then the rest of the time to the rest of the journies, and they had above thirty-eight years to go their two and twenty journies in. And how this should be such a travelling moving state, as that it should hinder their keeping this ordinance in its season,

to wit, to circumcise their children the eighth day; especially considering to circumcise them in their childhood, as they were born, might be with more security, than to let them live while they were men, I see not.

If you should think that their wars in the wilderness might hinder them; I answer, They had, for ought I can discern, ten times as much fighting in the land of Canaan, where they were circumcised, as in the wilderness where they were not. And if carnal or outward safety had been the argument, doubtless they would not have circumcised themselves in the sight, as it were, of one and thirty kings. Jos. v. xii. I say, they would not have circumcised their six hundred thousand warriors, and have laid them open to the attempts and dangers of their enemies. No such thing, therefore, as you are pleased to suggest, was the cause of their not being as yet circumcised.

IV. 'An extraordinary instance to be brought into a standing rule, are no parallels:' That is the sum of your fourth.

Answ. The rule was ordinary; which was circumcision; the laying aside of this rule became as ordinary, so long a time as forty years, and in the whole church also. But this is a poor shift, to have nothing to say, but that the case was extraordinary, when it was not.

But you ask, 'Might they do so when they came into Canaan?'

Answ. No, no. No more shall we do as we do now 'when that which is perfect is come.'

You add, 'Because the church in the wilderness, Re. xii. could not come by ordinances, &c. therefore when they may be come at, we need not practise them.'

Answ. No body told you so. But are you out of that wilderness mentioned? Re. xii. Is Antichrist down and dead to ought but your faith? Or are we only out of that Egyptian darkness, that in baptism have got the start of our brethren? For shame be silent: yourselves are yet under so great a cloud, as to imagine to yourselves a Rule of Practice not found in the Bible; that is, to count it a sin to receive your holy brethren, though not forbidden but commanded to do it. Ro. xiv. xv.

Your great flourish against my fourth argument, I leave to them that can judge of the weight of your words; as also what you say of the fifth or sixth.

For the instance I give you of Aaron, David, and Hezekiah, who did things not commanded, and that about holy matters, and yet were held excusable; you, nor yet your abettors for you, can by any means overthrow. Aaron transgressed the commandment; Le. vi. 26; x. 18. David did what was not lawful; and they in Hezekiah's time, 'did eat the passover otherwise than it was written,' 2 Ch. xxx. 18. But here I perceive the shoe pincheth;

which makes you glad of Mr. Denne's evasion for help. At this also Mr. D'Anvers cries out, but yet to no purpose, charging me with asserting, that P. 29. ignorance absolves from sin of omission and commission. But, Sirs, fairly take from me the texts, with others that I can urge; and then begin to accuse. You have healed your suggestion of unwritten verities poorly. But any shift to shift off the force of truth. After the same manner also you have helped your asserting, 'that you neither keep out, nor cast out from the church, if baptized, such as come unprepared to the supper, and other solemn appointments.' Let us leave yours and mine to the pondering of wiser men.

P. 31. My seventh argument, as I said, you have not so much as touched; nor the ten in that one, but only derided at the ten. But we will show them to the reader. 1. Love, which above all other things we are commanded to put on, is much more worth, than to break about baptism. Col. iii. 14. 2. Love is more discovered, when we receive for the sake of Christ and grace, than when we refuse for want of water. 3. The church at Colosse was charged to receive and forbear the saints, because they were new creatures. 4. Some saints were in the church at Jerusalem, that opposed the preaching of salvation to the Gentiles; and yet retained their membership. 5. Divisions and distinctions among saints are of later date than election, and the signs of that; and therefore should give place. 6. It is love, not baptism, that discovereth us to the world to be Christ's disciples. Jn. xiii. 35. 7. It is love that is the undoubted character of our interest in, and fellowship with, Christ. Ro. xii. 10; xvi. 10. 8. Fellowship with Christ is sufficient to invite to, and the new creature the great rule of our fellowship with, Christ. 1 Jn. i. 2. 9. Love is the fulfilling of the law, wherefore he that hath it is accepted with God, and ought to be approved of men; but he fulfils it not, who judgeth and setteth at nought his brother. Ga. vi. 16. Phi. iii. 16. Ro. xiv. Ja. iv. 11. 10. Love is sometimes more seen, and showed in forbearing to urge and press what we know, than in publishing and imposing. Jn. xvi. 12. 1 Co. iii. 1, 2. 11. When we attempt to force our brother beyond his light, or to break his heart with grief, to trust him beyond his faith, or bar him from his privileges, how can we say I love? 12. To make that the door to communion which God hath not; to make that the including, excluding charter, the bar, bounds, and rule of communion, is for want of love. Here are two into the bargain.

If any of these, Sir, please you not in this dress; give me a word; and I shall, as well as my wit will serve, give you them in a syllogistical mode.

Now that you say (practically) for some speak with their feet (their walking, Pr. vi. 13.) that water is above love; and all other things are evident; because have they all but water, you refuse them for want of that; yea, and will be so hardy, though without God's word, to refuse communion with them. p. 32.

In our discourse about the carnality that was the cause of the divisions that were at Corinth, you ask, Who must the charge of carnality fall upon, them that defend, or them that oppose the truth? p. 33.

Answ. Perhaps on both; but besure upon them that oppose, wherefore look you to yourselves, 'who without any command of God to warrant you, exclude your brother from communion; your brother whom God hath commanded you to receive.'

My ninth argument, you make yourself merry with in the beginning: but why do you by and by so cut and hack, and cast it as it were in the fire. Those seventeen absurdities you can by no means avoid. For if you have not, as indeed you have not, though you mock me for speaking a word in Latin, one word of God that commands you to shut out your brethren for want of water baptism, from your communion; I say, if you have not one word of God to make this a duty to you, then unavoidably, 1. You do it by a spirit of persecution. 2. With more respect to a form, than the spirit and power of godliness. 3. This also, makes laws, where God makes none; and is to be wise above what is written. 4. It is a directing the Spirit of the Lord. 5. And bindeth all men's consciences to our light and opinion. 6. It taketh away the children's bread. 7. And withholdeth from them the increase of faith. 8. It tendeth to make wicked the hearts of weak Christians. 9. It tendeth to harden the hearts of the wicked. 10. It setteth open a door to all temptations. 11. It tempteth the devil to fall upon them that are alone. 12. It is the nursery of all vain janglings. 13. It occasioneth the world to reproach us. 14. It holdeth staggering consciences in doubt, of the right ways of the Lord. 15. It abuseth the holy scriptures. 16. It is a prop to Antichrist. 17. And giveth occasion to many to turn aside to most dangerous errors.

And though the last is so abhorred by you, that you cannot contain yourselves when you read it; yet do I affirm, as I did in my first (p. 116.) 'That to exclude Christians from church communion, and to debar them their heaven-born privileges, for the want of that which God never yet made a wall of division between us; did, and doth, and will prevail with God to send those judgments we have, or may hereafter feel.' Like me yet as you will.

I come next to what you have said in justification of your fourteen arguments. 'Such as they were,' say you, 'I am willing to stand by them: What I have offered, I have offered modestly: according to the utmost light I had into those scriptures upon which they are bottomed; having not arrived unto such a peremptory way of dictatorship, as what I render must be taken for laws binding to others in faith and practice; and therefore express myself by suppositions, strong pre- Reflections, p. 51. sumptions, and fair seeming conclusions from the premises.

Answ. Your arguments, as you truly say, are builded upon, or drawn from suppositions and presumptions; and all because you want for your help the words of the holy scripture. And let the reader note. For as I have often called for the word, but as yet could never get it, because you have it not, neither in precept, precedent, nor example, therefore come you forth with your seeming imports and presumptions.

The judicious reader will see in this last, that not only here, but in other places, what poor shifts you are driven to, to keep your pen going. But, Sir, since you are not peremptory in your proof; how came you to be so absolute in your practice? For notwithstanding all your seeming modesty, you will neither grant these communion with you; nor allow their communion among themselves, that turn aside from your ' seeming imports;' and that go not with you in your strong presumptions. You P. 30, 31, 32, of your Reflections. must not; you dare not; lest you countenance their idolatry; and nourish them up in sin; they live in the breach of gospel-order; and Ephraim-like are joined to an idol. And as for your love, it amounts to this, you thus deal with them, and withdraw from them, and all because of some strong presumptions and suppositions.

But you tell me, ' I use the arguments of the pædo-baptist, to wit, But where are infants forbidden to be baptized?'

But I ingenuously tell you, I know not what pædo means: and how then should I know his arguments. 1. I take no man's argument but Mr. K.'s, I must not name him farther, I say I take no man's argument but his now, viz. ' That there being no precept, precedent or example, for you to shut your holy brethren out of church communion; therefore you should not do it.' That you have no command to do it, is clear, and you must of necessity grant it. Now where there is no precept for a foundation; it is not what you by all your reasonings can suggest; can deliver you from the guilt of adding to his word. Are you commanded to reject them; If yea, where is it? If nay, for shame be silent.

' Let us say what we will,' say you, ' for our own practice; unless we bring positive scriptures that yours is forbidden, though nowhere written; you will be as a man in a rage without it; and would have it thought you go away with the garland.'

Answ. 1. I am not in a rage, but contend with you earnestly for the truth. And say what you will or can, though with much more squibbing frumps* and taunts than hitherto you have mixed your writing with, Scripture, scripture, we cry still. And it is a bad sign that your cause is naught; when you snap and snarl because I call for scripture. 2. Had you a scripture for this practice, that you ought to shut your brethren out of communion for want of water baptism I had done; but you are left of the word of God, and confess it! 3. And as you have not a text that justifies your own; so neither that condemns our holy and Christian communion. We are commanded also to receive him that is weak in the faith, for God hath received him. I read not of garlands, but those in the Acts; take you them. And I say moreover, that honest and holy Mr. Jesse hath justified our practice, and you have not condemned his arguments. They therefore stand all upon their feet against you.

I leave your 2, 3, 4, 5 and 6 arguments under my answers where they are suppressed. In your seventh you again complain, for that I touch your ' seeming imports;' saying, ' I do not use to say as *John Bunyan*, this I say, and I dare to say. I please myself by commending my apprehensions soberly, and submissively to others much above me.'

Answ. 1. Seeming imports are a base and unworthy foundation for a practice in religion; and therefore I speak against them. 2. Where you say, you submit your apprehensions soberly to those much above you; it is false; unless you conclude none are above you, but those of your own opinion. Have you soberly, and submissively commended your apprehensions to those congregations in London, that are not of your persuasion in the case in hand? and have you consented to stand by their opinion? Have you commended your apprehensions soberly and submissively to those you call Independents and Presbyters? And are you willing to stand by their judgment in the case? Do you not reserve to yourself the liberty of judging what they say? and of choosing what you judge is right, whether they conclude with you or no? If so; why do you so much dissemble with all the world, in print; to pretend you submit to others' judgment, and yet abide to condemn their judgments? you have but one help: perhaps you think they are not above you; and by that proviso secure yourself; but it will not do.

For the offence you take at my comment upon your calling baptism, ' a livery:' and for Reflections, p. 52, 46. your calling it ' the Spirit's metaphorical

* ' Frump,' to mock, flout, scoff. ' You must learn to mock; to frump your own father on occasion.' Ironically used in Ruggle's Ignoramus.—ED.

description of baptism :' both phrases are boldness, without the word. Neither do I find it called a listing ordinance, nor the solemnization of the marriage betwixt Christ and a believer. But perhaps you had this from Mr. D'Anvers, who pleaseth himself with this kind of wording it : and says moreover in justification of you, ' That persons entered into the visible church thereby (by baptism, which is untrue, though Mr. Baxter also saith it) are by consent admitted into particular congregations, where they may claim their privileges due to baptized believers, being orderly put into the body, and put on Christ by their baptismal vow and covenant : for by that public declaration of consent, is the marriage and solemn contract made betwixt Christ and a believer in baptism. And, saith he, if it be preposterous and wicked for a man and woman to cohabit together, and to enjoy the privileges of a married state without the passing of that public solemnity : So it is NO less disorderly upon a spiritual account, for any to claim the privileges of a church, or be admitted to the same, till the passing of this solemnity by them.'

This is in the three last pages of his Treatise of Baptism.

Answ. But these words are very black. First, Here he hath not only implicitly forbidden Jesus Christ to hold communion with the saints that are not yet his by [water] baptism ; but is bold to charge him with being as preposterous and wicked if he do, as a man that liveth with a woman in the privileges of a married state, without passing that public solemnity. Secondly, He here also chargeth him as guilty of the same wickedness, that shall but dare to claim church communion without it; yea, and the whole church too, if they shall admit such members to their fellowship.

And now since cleaving to Christ by vow and covenant, will not do without baptism, after personal confession of faith ; what a state are all those poor saints of Jesus in, that have avowed themselves to be his a thousand times without THIS baptism? Yea, and what a case is Jesus Christ in too, by your argument, to hold that communion with them, that belongeth only unto them that are married to him by this solemnity ! Brother, God give him repentance. I wot that through ignorance and a preposterous zeal he said it : unsay it again with tears, and by a public renunciation of so wicked and horrible words ; but I thus sparingly pass you by.*

---

* Mr. D'Anvers, in a postscript to his History of Baptism, the first edition, 1673, thus violently attacks his brother Bunyan :—' Having read his book, I took myself concerned to give some short return to it, leaving his " manifold absurdities," " contradictions," " unbrotherly tauntings and reflections," " contemptions," " traducings the wisdom of Christ, and his holy appointments," to be called to account by that hand that hath so well begun to reckon with him.' He was

I shall not trouble the world any farther with an answer to the rest of your books : The books are public to the world : let men read and judge. And had it not been for your endeavouring to stigmatize me with reproach and scandal, a thing that doth not become you, I needed not have given you two lines in answer.

And now, my angry brother, if you shall write again, pray keep to the question, namely, ' What precept, precedent, or example have you in God's word to exclude your holy brethren from church communion for want of water baptism.' Mr. Denne's great measure, please yourself with it, and when you shall make his arguments your own, and tell me so, you perhaps may have an answer, but considering him, and comparing his notions with his conversation, I count it will be better for him to be better in morals, before he be worthy of an answer.

THE CONCLUSION.

Reader, when Moses sought to set the brethren that strove against each other, at one, he that did the wrong thrust him away, as unwilling to be hindered in his ungodly attempts ; but Moses continuing to make peace betwixt them, the same person attempted to charge him with a murderous and bloody design, saying, ' Wilt thou kill me as thou didst the Egyptian yesterday ?' Ex. ii. 14. a thing too commonly thrown upon those that seek peace, and ensue it. Ac. vii. 24—29. ' My soul,' saith David, ' hath long dwelt with him that hateth peace. I *am for* peace, [said he] but when I speak, they *are* for war.' Ps. cxx. 6, 7. One would think that even nature itself should count peace and concord a thing of greatest worth among saints, especially since they, above all men, know themselves ; for he that best knoweth himself is best able to pity and bear with another ; He. v. 2. yet even amongst these, such will arise, as will make divisions among their brethren, and seek ' to draw away disciples after them,' Ac. xx. 30. crying still that they, even they are in the right, and all that hold not with them in the wrong, and to be withdrawn from. Ro. xvi. 17. But when every HE, hath said all that he

in prison, and his brother *thus* visits him with gall and wormwood instead of consoling cordials. He goes on to confound water baptism with that of the Spirit, and charges Bunyan with ' ignorance and folly—dangerous and destructive to religion itself,' ' contradicting the authority of Christ,' calls him ' egregiously ignorant,' ' self-condemning.' All this uncharitable vituperation was because Mr. Bunyan would hold communion with all those who had been baptized into, and put on, Christ. The passage quoted is correct, except that ' married estate' should be ' marriage state.' So satisfied was D'Anvers with the just and Christian correction given him for so egregious a blunder, that if he did not repent with tears, he took special care to leave out all this absurd reference to the marriage ceremony *performed in water* from his second edition.— ED.

can, it is one of the things which the Lord hateth, to sow '*discord among brethren.*' Pr. vi. 19.*

Yet many years' experience we have had of these mischievous attempts, as also have others in other places, as may be instanced if occasion requireth it, and that especially by those of the rigid way of our brethren, the Baptists so called, whose principles will neither allow them to admit *to* communion, the saint that differeth from them about baptism, nor consent they should communicate in a church-state among themselves : but take occasion still ever as they can, both to reproach their church-state, and to finger from amongst them who they can to themselves. These things being grievous to those concerned, as we are, though perhaps those at quiet are too little concerned in the matter, therefore when I could no longer forbear, I thought good to present to public view the warrantableness of our holy communion, and the unreasonableness of their seeking to break us to pieces. At this Mr. William K[iffin], Mr. Thomas Paul, and Mr. Henry D'Anvers, and Mr. Denne, fell with might and main upon me ; some comparing me to the devil, others to a bedlam, others to a sot, and the like, for my seeking peace and truth among the godly. Nay, further, they began to cry out murder, as if I intended nothing less than to accuse them to the magistrate, and to render them incapable of a share in the commonwealth, when I only struck at their heart-breaking, church-rending principles and practice ; in their excluding their holy brethren's communion from them, and their condemning of it [even] among themselves. They also follow me with slanders and reproaches, counting, it seems, such things arguments to defend themselves.

But I in the meantime call for proof, scripture proof, to convince me it is a duty to refuse communion with those of the saints that differ from them about baptism : at this Mr. P[aul] takes offence, calling my demanding of proof for their rejecting the unbaptized believer, how excellent soever in faith and holiness, a clamorous calling for proof, with high and swelling words, which he counteth not worthy of answer ; but I know the reason, he by this demand is shut out of the Bible, as himself also suggesteth : wherefore when coming to assault me with arguments, he can do it but by seeming imports, suppositions, and strong presumptions, and tells you farther in his reply, ' That this is the

My 2nd book, p. 34, 78. His reply, p. 42.

utmost of his light in the scriptures urged for his practice ;' p. 41. of which light thou mayest easily judge, good reader, that hast but the common understanding of the mind of God, concerning brotherly love. Strange ! that the scripture that everywhere commandeth and presseth to love, to forbearance, and bearing the burden of our brother ; should yet imply, or implicitly import that we should shut them out of our Father's house ; or that those scriptures that command us to receive the weak, should yet command us to shut out the strong ! Thinkest thou, reader, that the scripture hath two faces, and speaketh with two mouths ? yet it must do so, by these men's doctrine. It saith expressly, ' Receive one another, as Christ also received us to the glory of God.' Ro. xv. 7. But these men say, it is not duty, it is preposterous, and idolatrous ; concluding that to receive this brother, is not a custom of them, not yet of the churches of God : consequently telling thee, that those that receive such a brother are not (let them talk while they will) any of the churches of God : see their charity, their candour and love, in the midst of their great pretensions of love.

Mr. P. Reflections, p. 41.

But be thou assured, christian reader, that for these their uncharitable words and actions, they have not footing in the word of God, neither can they heal themselves with suggesting their amicable correspondence to the world. Church communion I plead for, church communion they deny them, yet church communion is scripture communion, and we read of none other among the saints. True, we are commanded to withdraw ' from every brother that walketh disorderly, - that he may be ashamed, yet not to count *him* as an enemy, but to admonish *him* as a brother.' 2 Th. iii. 6, 14, 15. If this be that they intend, for I know not of another communion, that we ought to have with those, to whom we deny church communion ; then what ground of rejoicing those have that are thus respected by their brethren, I leave it to themselves to consider of.

In the meanwhile, I affirm, ' that baptism with water, is neither a bar nor bolt to communion of saints, nor a door nor inlet to communion of saints.' The same which is the argument of my books ; and as some of the moderate among themselves have affirmed, that neither Mr. K. Mr. P. nor Mr. D'Anvers, have made invalid, though sufficiently they have made their assault.

For Mr. Denne, I suppose they count him none of themselves, though both he, and Mr. Lamb, like to like, are brought for authors and abetters of their practice, and to refel my peaceable principle. For Mr. Denne, if either of the three will make his arguments their own, they may see what their servant can do : but I shall not bestow paper

---

* Strife and contention—evil speaking or surmisings among professors, are tokens of a carnal mind, injurious to spiritual peace, and abominable to God. The envious, discontented, and malicious, are the devil's working tools. If such die unsubdued by divine grace, they plunge themselves into the bottomless pit. True wisdom avoids strife and contention, is moderate in doubtful opinions, patient and cautious in judging others.—ED.

and ink upon him, nor yet upon Mr. Lamb; the one already, having given his profession the lie, and for the other perhaps they that know his life, will see little of conscience in the whole of his religion, and conclude him not worth the taking notice of. Besides Mr. P. hath also concluded against Mr. Denne, That baptism is not the initiating ordinance, and that his utmost strength for the justification of his own practice is, 'suppositions, imports, and strong presumptions,' things that they laugh at, despise and deride, when brought by their brethren to prove infant baptism.

Railing for railing, I will not render, though one of these opposers, Mr. Dan. by name, did tell me, that Mr. Paul's reply when it came out, would sufficiently provoke me to so beastly a work: but what is the reason of his so writing, if not the peevishness of his own spirit, or the want of better matter.

This I thank God for, that some of the brethren of this way, are of late more moderate than formerly, and that those that retain their former sourness still, are left by their brethren, to the vinegar of their own spirits, their brethren ingeniously confessing, that could these of their company bear it, they have liberty in their own souls to communicate with saints as saints, though they differ about water baptism.

Well, God banish bitterness out of the churches, and pardon them that are the maintainers of schisms and divisions among the godly. 'Behold, how good and how pleasant it is for brethren to dwell together in unity! It is like the precious ointment upon the head, that ran down upon the beard, even Aaron's beard: that went down to the skirts of his garments; (farther it is) As the dew of Hermon, that descended upon the mountains of Zion: (Mark) for there the LORD commanded the blessing, even life for evermore.' Ps. cxxxiii.

I was advised by some, who considered the wise man's proverb, not to let Mr. Paul pass with all his bitter invectives, but I consider that the wrath of man worketh not the righteousness of God; therefore I shall leave him to the censure and rebuke of the sober, where I doubt not but his unsavoury ways with me will be seasonably brought to his remembrance. Farewell.

I am thine to serve thee, Christian, so long as I can look out at those eyes, that have had so much dirt thrown at them by many.

J. BUNYAN.

OF THE LOVE OF CHRIST.

THE love of Christ, poor I may touch upon:
But 'tis unsearchable. Oh! there is none
Its large dimensions can comprehend,
Should they dilate thereon, world without end.
    When we had sinned, in his zeal he sware,
That he upon his back our sins would bear.
And since unto sin is entailed death,
He vowed, for our sins he'd lose his breath.
    He did not only say, vow, or resolve,
But to astonishment did so involve
Himself in man's distress and misery,
As for, and with him, both to live and die.
To his eternal fame in sacred story,
We find that he did lay aside his glory,
Stept from the throne of highest dignity;
Became poor man, did in a manger lie;
Yea was beholden upon his, for bread;
Had of his own not where to lay his head:
Though rich, he did, for us, become thus poor,
That he might make us rich for evermore.
    Nor was this but the least of what he did;
But the outside of what he suffered.

God made his blessed Son under the law;
Under the curse, which, like the lion's paw,
Did rend and tear his soul, for mankind's sin,
More than if we for it in hell had been.
His cries, his tears, and bloody agony,
The nature of his death doth testify.
    Nor did he of constraint himself thus give
For sin, to death, that man might with him live.
He did do what he did most willingly,
He sung, and gave God thanks, that he must die.
    But do kings use to die for captive slaves?
Yet we were such, when Jesus died to save us.
    Yea, when he made himself a sacrifice,
It was that he might save his enemies.
And, though he was provoked to retract
His blest resolves, for such, so good an act,
By the abusive carriages of those,
That did both him, his love, and grace oppose:
Yet he, as unconcerned with such things
Goes on, determines to make captives kings
Yea, many of his murderers he takes
Into his favour, and them princes makes.

A CASE OF CONSCIENCE RESOLVED;

VIZ.,

WHETHER, WHERE A CHURCH OF CHRIST IS SITUATE, IT IS THE DUTY OF THE WOMEN OF THAT CONGREGATION,
ORDINARILY, AND BY APPOINTMENT, TO SEPARATE THEMSELVES FROM THEIR BRETHREN, AND
SO TO ASSEMBLE TOGETHER, TO PERFORM SOME PARTS OF DIVINE WORSHIP,
AS PRAYER, ETC., WITHOUT THEIR MEN?

AND THE ARGUMENTS MADE USE OF FOR THAT PRACTICE, EXAMINED.

By JOHN BUNYAN.

London: Printed for Benj. Alsop, at the Angel and Bible in the Poultry, 1683.

EDITOR'S ADVERTISEMENT.

This exceedingly rare tract was first published in a small 4to of thirty-nine pages, in 1683, and was not reprinted, either separately, or in any edition of Bunyan's works. The public are indebted to the owner of a copy in perfect preservation, who kindly lent it, with a painful prohibition that he is to remain unknown; but with full allowance to any one who wishes to collate it with this new edition, by applying to the editor.

At the time this case was drawn and submitted to Mr. Bunyan for his opinion, he was one of the most popular preachers in the kingdom, and universally esteemed in all the churches of Christ, for his profound knowledge of the sacred Scriptures. This may account for such a case being sent to him, in preference to those illustrious divines, who for learning and talent have been unrivalled in any age.

The Reformation had progressed through state impediments so slowly, that the masses of the people were involved in the grossest darkness. So Mr. Keach complained—'The church is but *newly* come out of the wilderness of popish darkness; and not so fully neither as to be as clear as the sun; as in due time she shall.'* The era of the commonwealth let loose a flood of religious light and liberty: those who had just emerged from the darkness of Popery, and those who had received, implicitly, and without investigation, their religion from the formal services of the Liturgy, were now alarmed with the thunder of faithful exhortations, *personally* and prayerfully to examine the sacred Scriptures, upon pain of everlasting death. A light so new, and so marvellous, dazzled and perplexed those who rushed into it, without earnest prayer for divine guidance. They were like men who had been born and brought up in a dark, a deep, a noisome mine, when, suddenly emerging into light, are overpowered by its splendour. Long and sharp was the controversy whether singing ought to be used in public worship; whether the seventh day of the week or the first was to be consecrated; whether ministers were to be paid for their services; and in this case, to define the privileges and duties of women as helpers in the gospel; and it is surprising that this question is almost as *new* now as it was *then*. It is thus stated—'Whether it is the duty of the women of the churches of Christ to separate themselves from their brethren, and, as so separate, to perform divine worship by themselves.'

It appears that some females in Bedford were in the habit of thus meeting, under the advice of a Mr. K. They held prayer meetings for special purposes, at the imminent risk of imprisonment; but whether, in these meetings, they exhorted, or preached to each other, does not appear. John Bunyan was applied to for advice, which he plainly gives. He was a stern advocate for scriptural authority in all things pertaining to divine worship; and one who, in regarding the invaluable virtues of women, most admired retiring modesty as the loveliest adornment of the female character. The terms he uses, and the spirit in which he writes, intimate plainly that his own wife, who was remarkable for her devotion to God and her affectionate attachment to her husband, was also the most obedient of her sex.

In this tract we find no unmeaning gallant fribbling, but the solemn language of one who had death and judgment before his face. He conducts the inquiry with great care, as becomes a subject of such universal interest: and the great majority of Christians remain to this day his disciples. The Society of Friends is an exception, as to females being admitted to the ministry; while the Wesleyan Methodists have gained a most beneficial influence, by embracing, to the full extent, Bunyan's notions of rendering available the tender zeal, in comparatively private labours, of their pious females, in spreading the hallowed influences of Christianity.

* 'Breach Repaired,' a defence of singing in public worship, then newly and partially introduced. 1700, p. 2.

The Society of Friends stands upon high ground in justifying its practice in allowing females to minister in holy things. J. J. Gurney says— 'Friends believe it right, freely and *equally* to allow the ministry of both sexes. His reason is—'That all true ministry is under the immediate spirit of the influence of Christ: therefore we are bound to make way for the exercise of the gift of all persons that the Spirit may direct into this service. We dare not say to the modest and pious female, "Thou shalt not declare the word of the Lord," when we believe that an infinitely higher authority has issued a directly opposite injunction.'*

The difference arises as to the more public work of the ministry in proclaiming or preaching the kingdom of Christ to the world. In the ordinary ministry, by teaching the young—by a godly conversation—by visiting and praying with the sick and afflicted—by encouraging the inquirers and directing their way to the kingdom of heaven,—in these important duties there appears to be neither male nor female in Christ Jesus—all are equal.

John Bunyan would have united to a great degree with John Gurney in these sentiments. But as our Lord appointed no female evangelists,

or apostles, or missionaries; and as the Holy Ghost has directed, that all bishops or elders should be married MEN, it would appear a strange innovation to place a female in the pastoral office. Bunyan believed that God usually commissions men and not women to this important work. J.J. Gurney fully admits that women 'are forbidden to usurp authority over the man,' and therefore no active part is assigned to them in public assemblies for the settlement of the affairs of the church.† The women's meetings were established for the purpose of exercising a wholesome care over their own sex.‡ 'That faithful women should be helps to the men in the service of truth, as they are outwardly in civil and temporal things.'§ And to this who can refuse his hearty AMEN.

There is too much sectarian spirit in all our controversies. Reader, in considering this subject, endeavour to forget for the time those opinions in which you have been trained. Examine the question by the Word alone, and may the Holy Spirit inscribe upon your hearts that divine record, which is to be found only in the christian system: 'There is neither male nor female: for ye are all one in Christ Jesus.' Ga. iii. 28.—G. OFFOR.

---

* Distinguishing Practices of Friends, p. 280-1.

† P. 495. ‡ P. 509. § Sketch of Friends' Discipline, p. 35.

THE EPISTLE DEDICATORY

TO THOSE GODLY WOMEN CONCERNED IN THE FOLLOWING TREATISE.

HONOURED SISTERS,

'TIS far from me to despise you, or to do anything to your reproach. I know you are beloved of God for the sake of Christ, and that you stand fixed for ever by faith upon the same foundation with US. I also know that the Lord doth put no difference betwixt male and female, as to the communications of his saving graces, but hath often made many of your sex eminent for piety; yea, there hath been of you, I speak now of ordinary Christians, that for holiness of life have outgone many of the brethren: Nor can their virtuous lives but be renown and glory to YOU, and conviction to those of US that have come behind you in faith and holiness. The love of women in spirituals, as well as naturals, ofttimes outgoes that of men.

When Christ was upon earth, we read not that any man did to, and for him, as did the woman that was a sinner, Joanna, Susanna, and many others. Lu. vii. 36—38; viii. 1—3. And as they have shewed themselves eminent for piety, so for christian valour and fortitude of mind, when called of God to bear witness to, and for his name in the world: as all histories of that nature doth suffi-

ciently testify. They were WOMEN, as I take it as well as men, that were tortured, and that would not accept of deliverance, that they might obtain a better resurrection. He. xi. 35. Wherefore I honour and praise your eminency in virtue; and desire to be provoked by the exceeding piety of any of you, in all holy conversation and godliness.

And although, as you will find, I have not without a cause, made a question of the lawfulness of your assembling together, by yourselves, to perform, without your men, solemn worship to God: yet I dare not make you yourselves the authors of your own miscarriage in this. I do therefore rather impute it to your leaders, who whether of a fond respect to some seeming abilities they think is in you for this, or from a persuasion that you have been better than themselves in other things; or whether from a preposterous zeal, they have put you upon a work so much too heavy for you: I shall not at this time concern myself to inquire into. But this is certain, at least it is so in my apprehension, that in this matter you are tempted by them to take too much upon you.

I am not insensible but that for my thus writing, though I thereby have designed your honour and good order; I am like enough to run the gauntlet among you, and to partake most smartly of the scourge of the tongues of some, and to be soundly brow-beaten for it by others: specially by our author, who will find himself immediately concerned, for that I have blamed him for what he hath irregularly done, both with the Word, to you, and me. I look also to be sufficiently scandalized, and counted a man not for prayer, and meetings for prayer, and the like; but I will labour to bear them with patience, and seek their good that shall be tempted to abuse me.

I had not, indeed I had not, spoke a word to this question in this manner, had not Mr. K. sent his paper abroad, and amongst us, for the encouraging this practice with us, in opposition to our peace. I do not say he designed our breach, but his arguments tended thereto; and had not our people been of a wise and quiet temper, his paper might have set us into a flame. But thanks be to God, we are at quiet, and walk in love, notwithstanding the LIFTS that have been to make us do otherwise. There are also the mouths of some opened against me for this, who lie at wait for occasions, and shew that they are glad to take them before they are given by me: to whom I now shew by this ensuing discourse, that I had a reason to do what I did.

I commend you to God, and to the word of his grace, which is able to build you up, and to give you an inheritance among them that are sanctified by faith in Jesus Christ: to whom be honour and glory for ever. And remain, your faithful friend and brother to pray for you, to love you in the gospel, and to do you what christian service I can,

JOHN BUNYAN.

A CASE OF CONSCIENCE RESOLVED, &c.

THE occasion of my meddling in this manner with this controversy, is this. After I had, for reasons best known to myself, by searching found, that those called the women's meetings wanted for their support, a bottom in the word: I called them in our fellowship into question. Now having so done, my reasons for so doing, as was but reason, were demanded; and I gave them, to the causing of that practice with us to cease. So subject to the word were our women, and so willing to let go what by that could not be proved a duty for them to be found in the practice of. But when I had so done, by what means I know not, Mr. K., hearing of my proceeding in this matter, though I think he knew little of question or answer, sets pen to paper, and draws up four arguments for the justification of these meetings. The which, when done, were sent down into our parts; not to me, but to some of his own persuasion, who kept them, or sent them, or lent them whither they thought good: And so about two years after, with this note immediately following, they were conveyed to my hand.

Bro: Bunyan, This enclosed, was sent to me from godly women, whose custom for a long time hath been to meet together to pray: who hearing of your contrary opinion, sent this. It came from Mr. K., who would desire to know what objections you have against it: and he is ready to give his further advice. Pray be pleased to give your answer in writing, for Mr. K. expects it.

Your friends in the Lord,
S. B.   S. F.

Pray be pleased to leave your answer with S. F.* in Bedford.

Now having received the papers, and considering the contents thereof: I was at first at a question with myself, whether the thing was feigned, or true; and to that purpose, writ to these women again: but calling to mind, that I had heard something of this before, I concluded there was ground to believe, as I do, [that it was true, and not feigned:] And so resolved to answer his demand and expectation. But to say nothing more as to this, I will next present you with the arguments he sent, and then with my manner of handling of them.

[Mr. K.'s Arguments for Female Prayer Meetings.]

He begins with this question, Whether women fearing God may meet to pray together, and whether it be lawful for them so to do? Which done, he falls to a wonderment, saying, It seems very strange to me, that any who profess the fear of God, can make any question touching the lawfulness thereof: The rule for praying being so

---

* Probably a female branch of the family of John or Samuel Fenn, hatters at Bedford, who, in 1670, were cruelly persecuted for suffering a meeting for religious worship to take place in the house of John Fenn. Not only all their stock of hats, materials, and tools, but the whole of their household furniture was seized and carried off to satisfy ruinous fines. One John Bardolf was also cruelly persecuted for Christ's sake at the same time.—Vide Narrative of Arbitrary Proceedings at Bedford, 4to, 1670, in the editor's possession.

general to all, and there being so many instances for the practice thereof, upon several occasions in the word of God, for their encouragement therein.

He next presents us with his arguments, which are in number *four*, but in verity not one, to prove that thing for the which he urgeth them: as I hope to make appear by that I have done.

First, saith he, If women may praise God together for mercies received for the church of God, or for themselves? then they may pray together: The proof whereof is plain. Ex. xv. 20, 21. If it be objected the case was extraordinary, and that Miriam was a prophetess; To which I answer, That the danger of ruin and destruction, and our deliverance from it, if the Lord grant it, cannot be looked at but as extraordinary. The designs of ruin to the church, and servants of God, being as great as at that time when God delivered his people from the hand of Pharaoh.* And will call for praises, if the Lord please to send it, as then. And whereas it is further objected, that Miriam was an extraordinary person. To which I answer, That the duty itself of praising God for the mercy, was incumbent upon all, in as much as they were partakers of the mercy. And the same spirit of Christ that was in her, is also in all his servants: given for the same end, both to pray for mercies we stand in need of, and to praise God for [them].

Second, If women have in imminent danger to themselves and the church of God, prayed jointly together for deliverance, and God hath answered and approved of the same: then may women jointly pray together. The instance we have is famous. Es. iv. 16. We there see she and her maidens did pray and fast together, and the Lord gave a gracious answer and deliverance.

Third, If God hath in gospel times promised the pouring out of his Spirit to women, to that very end that they may pray together apart from men; then it is not only their liberty, but duty to meet and pray together. But God hath promised his Spirit to that end. Zec. xii. 10–13. Which scripture it is plain is a promise of gospel times. And it is to be noted that the text doth not in the singular number, say, He shall pray apart, and his wife apart; but THEY shall pray apart, and THEIR wives apart. And Mal. iii. 16. God takes notice of all them that speak often together, and call upon his name.

Fourth, If God hath so approved of women's meeting together to pray in gospel times, as then, and at that time to take an advantage to make known to them his mind and will concerning Jesus Christ: then it is lawful for women to pray together. But God hath so approved of their meeting to pray together. Ac. xvi. 13. By which text it appeareth it was a frequent practice for women to meet and pray together.

These are Mr. K.'s arguments; the conclusion of his paper follows. And besides all these particular instances, says he, what means those general rules to build up one another in our most holy faith, and pray in the Holy Ghost. Jude 20. But it extends to all that believe, both men and women; unless any will say women are not to be built up in their most holy faith. Therefore let not any hinder you from a duty so incumbent upon you in a special manner, in such a day as this is. Cannot many women that have used this practice, by experience, say, they have met with the Lord in it, and have found many blessed returns of prayer from God, both to themselves and the church, wherein God hath owned them? Therefore what God hath borne witness to, and approved of, let no man deter you from. Pray turn to the scriptures quoted, which I hope will give you full satisfaction.

[Mr. Bunyan's Answer.]

These are his arguments, and this his conclusion, in which I cannot but say, there is not only boldness, but flattery. Boldness, in fathering of his misunderstanding upon the authority of the word of God: and flattery, in soothing up persons in a way of their own, by making of them the judges in their own cause: the which I hope to make farther appear anon.

For since his women in their letter told me that Mr. K. expects my answer, I count myself called to shew the unsoundness of his opinion. Indeed he would, as they insinuate, confine me to answer by writing. But his papers have been I know not where, and how to put check to his extravagancies, that also, I know not, but by scattering mine [answer] abroad. And as I will not be confined to an answer in writing: so neither to his methods of argumentation. What scholar he is, I know not; for my part, I am not ashamed to confess, that I neither know the mode nor figure of a syllogism, nor scarce which is major or minor. Methinks I perceive but little sense, and far less truth in his

---

* In times of such severe trial and suffering to our pilgrim forefathers, they knew the value of prayer; and at the risk of property, liberty, and even life, held frequent meetings to implore their God and Father to mitigate their sufferings, and to have mercy upon their cruel persecutors. Not only working tools and stock, but commonly all the furniture, was taken from the Christians, while their ministers and members, both men and women, were imprisoned in miserable jails. One of these, Mr. Robert Kalder, dying, was buried in the churchyard; but those furious bigots dug up his naked body, and dragged it to the gates of his former residence, leaving it there, a frightful spectacle to his widow and family. They had meetings for prayer; and how does it become their descendants in the faith to have days of thanksgiving and nights of praise?—See Broadmead Records and Crosby's History of Baptists, vol. ii., p. 240.—ED.

arguments: also I hold that he has stretched and strained the holy Word out of place, to make it, if it might have been, to shore up his fond conceits. I shall therefore, first take these texts from the errors to which he hath joined them, and then fall to picking the bones of his syllogisms.*

But as I shall not confine myself to his mode and way of arguing, so neither shall I take notice of his question upon which he stateth the matter in controversy. But shall propound the same question here, which, for the substance of it, was handled among us, when the thing itself was in doubt among us, namely,

Whether, where a church of Christ is situate, it is the duty of the women of that congregation, ordinarily, and by appointment, to separate themselves from their brethren, and so to assemble together, to perform some parts of divine worship, as prayer, &c. without their men?

This was our question, this we debated, and this Mr. K. might have sent for, and have spoken to, since he will needs be a confuter. And, courteous reader, since I have here presented thee with the question, I will also present thee with the method which I took when I handled it among my brethren.

First, I opened the terms of the question. *Second*, Then shewed what assemblies they were that used to perform divine worship to God. *Third*, And so shewed whose prayers in such worship was used, or by Paul and others desired.

First, By church of Christ, I mean, one gathered or constituted by, and walking after the rule of the Word of God. By situate, I mean, where such church shall happen to be, in whole, or in the parts thereof. By separating, I mean, their meetings together by appointment of their own, and as so met, to attempt to perform divine worship [by] prayer without their men. Having thus explained the question; I, as a preparatory to a solution thereof, come,

Second, To shew what manner of assemblies they were that used to perform divine worship to God of old. Now I find that there have been three sorts of assemblies, in which divine worship has been performed. 1. It has been performed in mixed assemblies; in assemblies made up of saints and sinners. I say divine worship has been performed in such assemblies, for, that there, the saints have been edified, sinners convinced and converted, and made to confess their sins, to the glory of God.

Of these assemblies we read, Mat. v. 1; xiii. 1; xxiii. 1. Mar. iv. 1; ii. 1; vi. 2; x. 1. Lu. v. 1; viii.; xii. 1; xiii. 1; xv. 1; xx. 1. 1 Co. xiv. 23. And in many other scriptures. 2. I also find that the church, by herself, or as distinct from the world, have met together to perform it by themselves. Mar. iv. 34. Ac. ii. 1—4; xiii. 1, 2; xv. 4; xx. 7; Jn. xx. 19—26. 3. I find also that assemblies for divine worship have been made up of the elders, and principal brethren of the church, none of the rest of the congregation being present. Mat. x. 1. Lu. ix. 1. Ac. i. 3; ii. 17, 18. Ga. ii. 1, 2. with several other scriptures beside. But in all the Scripture, I find not that the women of the churches of Christ, did use to separate themselves from their brethren, and as so separate, perform worship together among themselves, or in that *their* congregation: or that they made, by allowance of the Word, appointment so to do. Thus far therefore this must stand for a human invention, and Mr. K. for the promoter thereof.

Third, This done, in the third place, I come to shew you whose prayers, or by whose mouth prayer in such assemblies, as are above proved lawful, used to be made, or by Paul or others were desired. 1. Whose prayers were used, or who was the mouth? and I find them called the prayers of the church in general, or of the principal men thereof in particular. Ju. ii 4, 5; xx. 8, 26; Joel i. 14; ii. 15—17. Ac. xii. 5; xiii. 1—3. 2. Also when Paul, or others, desired that prayers should be made of others for them. They either desired the prayers of the church in general, or of the brethren in particular (but never desireth, or biddeth a woman's meeting, that prayers might there be made for them.) (1.) He desireth the prayers of the church in general. Col. iv. 2. Phi. i. 19; iv. 6. 1 Th. v. 17. He. xiii. 18. (2.) Or if he desireth prayers of certain persons, he only calls upon the men and brethren in particular; but never upon a woman by name nor sex to do it. 1 Th. v. 25. 2 Th. iii. 1. Ro. xv. 30. 1 Ti. ii. 8. Nor was, as I said, the apostle alone in this thing. Christ speaks a parable to this end, that MEN ought always to pray. Lu. xviii. 1. James saith, the effectual fervent prayer of a righteous MAN. v. 16. Moses sent the young men to sacrifice. Ex. xxiv. 5. And the people in the time of Zacharias, sent their MEN to pray before the Lord. Zec. vii. 2. I do not believe that by any of these the prayers of women are despised, but by these we are taught, who, as the mouth in assemblies to pray, is commended unto us.

One word more, The women in the time of Jeremiah the prophet, when they had made their cakes to the queen of heaven, (though the thing which they did was as right in their own eyes, as if they had done true worship indeed) and was questioned by the prophet for what they had done, could not justify what they had done. as to the

---

* 'Syllogism,' a form of reasoning, consisting of three propositions, having this property; that the conclusion necessarily follows from the two premises: so that if the first and second be granted, the conclusion must be granted in like manner. No wonder that Bunyan neither understood nor was awed by this hard word. Armed with holy Writ, he goes to work 'to pick the bones of the syllogism.'—ED.

act, but by pleading, They did it not 'without their men.' Je. xliv. 17—19.

Thus having premised these few things, I shall now come more directly to discourse of the question itself, TO WIT, Whether, where a church of Christ is situate, it is the duty of the women of that congregation, ordinarily, and by appointment, to separate themselves from their brethren, and as so separate, to assemble together to perform divine worship, [by] prayer, without their men?

This was our question, and this I will now give a negative answer unto. For I find not in Christ's testament any command so to do; no nor yet example: and where there is none of these, it cannot be a duty upon them; no, nor yet liberty, but presumption to attempt it.

The command, says Mr. K., is general to all. But I answer, yet limited, and confined to order and manner of performance. Women may, yea ought to pray; what then? Is it their duty to help to carry on prayer in public assemblies with men, as they? Are they to be the audible mouth there, before all, to God? No verily, and yet the command is general to all to pray. Women of the respective churches of Christ, have no command to separate themselves from the men of their congregations, to perform prayer in their own company without them, and yet the command is general to all to pray. We must therefore distinguish of [between] persons and performances, though we may not exclude either. The manner also, and order in which such and such duties must be done, Mr. K. knows is as essential, in some cases, as the very matter of worship. But we will come to my reasons for my dissenting from Mr. K. in this. After which I will consider his arguments, and the scriptures that he would under-prop them with. As for my reasons for my dissenting from him, they are these:—

First, To appoint meetings for divine worship, either in the whole church or in the parts of it, is an act of power: which power, resideth in the elders in particular, or in the church in general. But never in the women as considered by themselves. Mr. K. indeed doth insinuate that this power also resided in them; for he saith, God hath in gospel times promised the Spirit to women to that very end, that they may pray together, apart from men. Now if the Spirit is given them to THIS very end, that they may do it apart from men, then they have a power residing in themselves to call their own sex together to do it. And what brave doings will such a conclusion make, even the blind himself will perceive. But further of this anon; meanwhile we will attend [to] our own assertion. Namely, ' That to call the church, or parts thereof together, to perform divine worship to God, is an ACT of POWER, which power resideth in the church in general, or in the elders in particular.'' We will treat of the last first.

1. For the eldership, Moses and Aaron of old were they, with the priests, that were to call the church together to perform divine worship to God, and that both as to the whole, or as to the parts of it. Nu. x. 7, 8. De. iv. 14; xxxi. 11, 12. Ex. iv. 29; xii. 21; xvii. 5. Also, in after times, they were the elders and chief of the church, that did it. Jos. xxiv. 1. Ezr. x. 5—9. Ac. xiv. 27; xv. 3. Or, 2, if their calling together to perform divine worship, was not by the elders alone: yet it was by the power that resided in the church for that thing, who jointly ordered the same. Ju. xx. 8, 18. Ezr. iii. 1. Zep. ii. 1—3. Ac. xii. 12. 1 Co. v. 4; xi. 20. All these are plain cases. But never, as I ever did read of in the Bible, did women, ordinary believing ones, assume this power of the elders, or of the church, to themselves.

If it be asked, Who did appoint that meeting made mention of in Ac. xii. 12?

I answer, It was appointed by the power of the church, who, for her own conveniency, if she cannot come all into one place at once to perform the duty, as it is not likely four or five thousand should, in times of persecution, which was their case, [they] may meet some here, some there, for their edification and comfort. Compare ver. 5 with 12 and 17. Nor do I question the lawfulness of this or that part of the church's assembling together for prayer: though the elders, and greatest part of the brethren, be absent. If, first, such MEN that call such assemblies are countenanced by the elders, or church, to do it. 1 Ti. ii. 8. 2 Ti. ii. 22. But that the sisters of this or that church, may call their own sex together to perform such worship by themselves to God (for this is the thing in debate) I find no warrant for.

Second, Because this kind of worship, when done in and by a company, is MINISTERIAL to that company, as well as petitionary to God. That is, they that, as the mouth in assemblies pray to God, teach that assembly, as well as beg mercies of him. And I find not that women may assemble to do thus. That such prayer is a kind of ministering in the word to standers by, consider well 1 Co. xiv. 15—19. Wherefore let them keep silence in the church, and in the parts thereof, when assembled to worship God.

In all public worship by prayer, teaching is set on foot, two ways: 1. By propounding to that assembly the things that must, by agreement, be prayed for. 2. And by proving them to suit with the will of God, that prayer may be made in faith. 1 Jn. v. 14.

1. For all such prayer must be made for the things agreed upon first; and consequently for things that by the word are proved good, and suitable for the seasons, persons, or things, for or about which such prayers are made. For they that have meetings for prayer, without this, pray at random, and not by rule.

'If two of you shall agree on earth, as touching anything that they shall ask (according to God's will) it shall be done for them,' saith Christ, 'of my Father which is in heaven.' Mat. xviii. 19. Now, I say, if things prayed for in assemblies must first be jointly agreed upon, then must such things, by some one, or more of that assembly, be first propounded, expounded, and proved to be good by the word. Good for such persons, seasons, or things, for which such prayer is made. And, besides, the gifts required to do this, if this is not teaching I am out. And yet this must first be done to instruct all present, to help their faith, and to quicken their spirits *to*, and *in* that worship. That they may as one man have their eyes unto the Lord. Zec. ix. 1. But that this power is given to women, to ordinary believing ones that are in the highest account in churches, I do not believe. I do not believe they should minister to God in prayer before the whole church, for then I should be a Ranter or a Quaker; nor do I believe they should do it in their own womanish assembly, for the reason urged before. And I will add, if brethren not heretofore called by the church to open scriptures, or to speak in the church to God in prayer,* are not at first to be admitted to do this, but before the elders or principal brethren, that they may hear and judge. 1 Co. xiv. 26—29. How can it be thought to be meet or lawful for women, of whom it must be supposed, that they have received no such gifts, that they should use this power? I say, how can it be imagined that the women should be bound of God to do this in such sort as doth utterly exclude the elders and all the men in the congregation from a possibility of understanding and of judging of what they do? And yet this is the doctrine of Mr. K.; for he saith, 'That the Spirit of God is promised to women to this very end, that they may pray together, apart from men.' But God is not the author of this confusion in the churches.

2. But secondly, As teaching by prayer in assemblies, is thus set on foot; so every one also that shall in such meetings be the mouth of the whole, to God, ministereth so, doctrine to that assembly, as well as presenteth petitions to God. Else how can that assembly say AMEN at their prayer or giving of thanks? For to say AMEN is an effect of conviction, or of edification received of the stander by, from him that now is so ministering in that assembly before God. 1 Co. xiv. 15—17. Yea, I believe that they that pray in assemblies, or that shall give thanks for mercies received there, ought to labour to speak, not only with fervency of words, but with such soundness of doctrine while they mention, urge, or plead the promise with God, that that whole assembly may be enlightened, taught, taken, and carried away in their spirits, on the wing of that prayer, and of faith, to God, whose face they are come to seek, and whose grace they are gathered together to beg. Now this is called praying and praising, to the teaching and edifying of others, as by the scripture afore named is made appear. 1 Co. xiv. 14—19. But by what word of God the sisters of the respective churches may set up this way of teaching of one another in their assemblies, I am ignorant of. For,

Third, The Holy Ghost doth particularly insist upon the inability of women, as to their well managing of the worship *now* under consideration, and therefore it ought not to be presumed upon by them. They are forbidden to teach, yea to speak in the church of God. And why forbidden, but because of their inability. They cannot orderly manage that worship to God, that in assemblies is to be performed before him; I speak now of our ordinary believing ones, and I know none extraordinary among the churches. They are not builded to manage such worship, 'they are not the image and glory of God, as the men are.' 1 Co. xi. 7. They are placed beneath, and are called the glory of the man. Wherefore they are weak, and not permitted to perform public worship to God. When our first mother, who was not attended with those weaknesses, either sinful or natural, as our women now are, stept out of her place but to speak a good word for worship, you see how she was baffled, and befooled therein; she utterly failed in the performance, though she briskly attempted the thing. Yea she so failed thereabout, that at one clap she overthrew, not only, as to that, the reputation of women for ever, but her soul, her husband, and the whole world besides. Ge. iii. 1—7. The fallen angel knew what he did when he made his assault upon the woman. His subtilty told him that the woman was the weaker vessel. He knew also that the man was made the head in worship, and the keeper of the garden of God. The Lord God *took* the man, *said* unto the man, *commanded* the man, and made him keeper of the garden. Ge. ii. 15—17. Wherefore the management of worship belonged to him. This, the serpent, as I said, was aware of. And therefore he comes to the woman, says to the

---

* Much stress was, and is now, laid in many churches upon the necessity of all persons, before praying or preaching in public, being guided by the opinion of the church. The taking advice in so important a step must be proper; but any *pledge* to abide by it, contrary to the conscientious conviction of the individual, would be a violation of the duty of private judgment. If in their ministrations they were false or foolish, the church must exercise discipline; but if they became useful, surely no objection could be urged as to the validity of their call to the ministry, because the church had not been first consulted or had advised them not to proceed. The desire—the ability, by sound views of divine truth, and a happy way of illustrating and enforcing them—with the opportunity of so doing, is the divine call to this holy work.—ED.

woman, and deals with the woman about it, and so overcomes the world. Wherefore it is from this consideration that Paul tells Timothy that he permitted not a woman to teach, nor to usurp authority over the man, but to be in silence. But to call the church or parts thereof together, to perform solemn worship, and in such a call to exclude or shut out the men, is an usurping of that authority over them to a high degree. And he renders the reason of this his prohibition thus, 'For Adam was first formed, then Eve, (and therefore had the headship in worship.) And Adam was not deceived, but the woman being deceived, was in the transgression.' 1 Ti. ii. 13, 14. But again, it should seem, methinks, if women must needs be managers of worship in assemblies, they should do it, as Eve, before Adam, in presence of the men: But that I think none will allow, though that would be the way best to correct miscarriages; how then should it be thought convenient for them to do it alone. If children are not thought fit to help to guide the ship with the mariners, shall they be trusted so much as with a boat at sea alone. The thing in hand is a parallel case. For,

Fourth, If the weightiness of *this* worship be, as indeed it is, so great, that the strongest and best able to perform it do usually come off with blushing, and with repentance for their shortness, as to the well performance thereof; though they engage therein by good and lawful authority; what will they do who are much weaker here, and when, as Eve, they set to it in a way of usurping of authority, and of their own head and will. To offer strange fire with incense, which was a type of prayer, you know what it cost Nadab and Abihu, though men, and the sons of Aaron. [Yet] Mr. K. cries the sisters, the women, the women's meetings, and the like, and how they have prevailed with heaven. Poor man, I am sorry for his weakness, and that he should show that himself is so *nunnish** in such a day as this.

But to return, as all worship in assemblies ought to be performed with the most exact order and solemnity; so this of prayer with that, if possible, that is more than all the rest; and therefore this makes it more heavy still. When men preach they have to do with men, but when they pray in assemblies they have to do both with men and with God at once. And I say, if it be so great a matter to speak to men *before* God; *how* great a matter is it to speak to men and God at once; to God by way of petition, and to men by way of instruction. But I am persuaded if those most fond of the

women's meetings for prayer were to petition the king for their lives, they would not set women to be their advocates to him; specially if the king should declare beforehand by law, that he permitted not a woman in an open auditory to speak before him.

There are also many temptations that attend the duty of praying in assemblies, especially those that are immediately employed therein. These temptations, they awake, are aware of, are forced to wrestle with, and greatly to groan under. Wherefore we put not the weak upon this service; not the weak, though they be men; not they in the presence of the strong. How then should the weakest of all be put upon it, and that when together by themselves. Men, though strong, and though acting by lawful authority in this, are not able, but with unutterable groans, to do it: how then shall all those that attempt it without that authority, perform it as acceptable worship to God? This work, therefore, is as much too heavy for our women now, as that about which Eve engaged in at first, was too heavy for her. But,

Fifth, If this worship may be managed by the sisterhood of the churches, being congregated together in the absence of their men: of what signification is it that man is made head of the woman as well in worship as in nature? 1 Co. xi. 3, 7. Yea more, why are the elders of the churches called watchmen, overseers, guides, teachers, rulers, and the like? If this kind of worship may be performed, without their conduct and government? Eze. iii. 17; xxxiii. 7. Ac. xx. 28. Ep. iv. 11. Ps. xxviii. 72. He. xiii. 17.

1. Why is man made the head of the woman in worship, in the worship now under debate, in that worship that is to be performed in assemblies? And why are the women commanded silence there, if they may congregate by themselves, and set up and manage worship there? Worship was ordained before the woman was made, wherefore the word of God at the first did not immediately come to her, but to him that was first formed, and made the head in worship. Ge. ii. 16--18. 1 Co. xiv. 35, 36. And hence it is that women are so strictly tied up to this headship; that if they will learn, they must ask their husbands at home, ver. 35. not appoint meetings of their own sex to teach one another. 'But what must they do that have unbelieving ones? and what must they do that have none?' Answer, Let them attend upon those ordinances that God has appointed for the building up and perfecting of the body of Christ, Ep. iv. 11--13. and learn as the angels do. Ep. iii. 10. 1 Pe. i. 12

2. But I say, if they must do as Mr. K. says, they are in duty bound, to wit, meet by themselves apart from their men, and as so met, perform this most solemn worship to God: how

---

* 'So nunnish,' a singular mode of expression, alluding to the nuns being separated from the world, and shut up by themselves. They were not permitted to exercise the priestly office. Father confessors and chaplains were appointed for these duties. —Ed.

shall the elders and overseers, the watchmen, rulers, and guides in worship, perform their duty to God, and to the church of God, in this, since from this kind of worship they are quite excluded, and utterly shut out of doors: unless it be said, that to watch, to oversee, and to guide, in the matter and manner of performance of this worship in assemblies, is no part of the watchman or overseer's work; or in their lawful absence, the work of the principal men of the church. Nor will the faithful and dutiful overseer leave worship, no, not in the best part of the congregation assembled to worship, to be performed by every weak brother, though I believe it might with more warrant be left to them, than to the strongest among our ordinary ones of the other sex.

Also our elders and watchmen covet, if we have unbelievers to behold, that our worship be performed by the most able. How then shall it be thought that they should be so silly, to turn a company of weak women loose to be abused by the fallen angels? Can it be thought that their congregation, since they have it without a command, shall fare better among those envious spirits than those that are lawfully called shall fare before the world? Watchman, watchman, see to thy duty, look well to the manner of worship that is to be performed according to thy commission. Trust not Eve, as Adam did, with worship, and with its defence. Look that all things be done in worship as becomes thee—a head, both in nature and by office—and leave not so solemn a part of worship as prayer, in company, is, and ought to be accounted to be done; thou canst by no means tell how. Watch in and over all such worship thyself. Be diligent to know the state of thy flocks, whether they be flocks of men, or women; and look well to thy herds, and thou shalt have milk enough, not only for men and babes, but also for the maintenance and life of thy maidens. So that they need not go with their pitchers to seek water there where their God has not sent them. Pr. xxvii. 23—27. Besides the shepherds' tents is provision sufficient for them. Ca. i. 8. But, for a conclusion of this, I will ask this man, If he doth not, by pleading for these women's meetings, declare, that the women, without their men, are better able by themselves to maintain divine worship, than the men are without their elders? forasmuch as he himself will not allow that the men should always perform worship without his oversight and inspection, and yet will plead for the women to have such worship in their congregation, among themselves, excluding for ever the men therefrom. For, saith he, the Spirit is promised to be given to them to that very end, that they may meet together to pray apart without their men. And now for Mr. K's arguments, which, as I said, are in number four. 1. We will take

the scriptures from them; and, 2. Then pick the bones of their carcasses.

Yet in my taking of the scriptures from his arguments, I will do it in a way that is most to his advantage, making of each of them as formidable an objection as I can against myself.

I. *Object.* Miriam took a timbrel in her hand, and went out, and all the women went out after her, praising God with timbrels and dances for their deliverances. Therefore the women of the churches of Christ may appoint meetings of their own, as separate from their brethren, and then and there perform divine worship, [by] prayer, in that, their congregation, without their men. Ex. xv. 20, 21.

Answ. 1. Miriam was a prophetess: and, I suppose, that none of our women will pretend to be such. And though Mr. K. labours to get over this, by saying that the work of praising was incumbent upon all: yet by his leave, judgment, and discretion, and a spirit of conduct suitable to the duty, as we read of, was found among the women in none but she. Why is it else said, Miriam led them forth; Miriam the prophetess did it. Another, by Mr. K.'s argument, might have done it as well. Thus degrades he the prophetess, that he may get favour with the ordinary women, and prompt them on to a work that he has a superstitious affection for.

2. But his assertion is of no weight. The women were not left in that extraordinary service to the spirit of ordinary believers. Nor can I count it but crooked dealing to bring in extraordinary persons, in their extraordinary acts, to prove it lawful for ordinary persons to do that which is not commanded them.

3. But though Miriam did go forth, or come out with the women, yet not from the men, into some remote place in the wilderness to worship by themselves. She rather went or came out, and the women followed her from the place by the sea, where now they were, after Moses, to sing as her sex became her; for she, though an extraordinary woman, might not make herself an equal with Moses and Aaron, therefore she came behind in worship, yet with the body of the people, as it is said, 'So Moses brought Israel from the Red Sea.' Ex. xv. 22. Women, though prophetesses, must wear some badge or other of inferiority to those that are prophets indeed. 1 Co. xi. 3—9. And I choose to understand that Miriam did this. (1.) Because the text last mentioned says so. (2.) Because Miriam, and all the women, did sing with the words of the men, ver. 1 compared with 21. (3.) For that they did sing them after the men, as taking them from their mouth. For, saith the text, Miriam answered them, and so handed it down to them of her sex, saying, ' Sing ye to the Lord, for he hath triumphed gloriously.' vers. 1 and 21. (4.) For that

she commanded the women that they should sing the same song: hence it is called the song of Moses, not of Miriam. Re. xv. 3. (5.) From all which I conclude, that Miriam did not draw the women away into some such place where neither Moses, nor Aaron, nor the elders of Israel could see, behold, and observe their manner of worship. But that she, as her modesty became her, did lead them out from that place where they were, to sing, and to dance, and to praise God, after the men. (6.) This scripture therefore favoureth not this man's opinion, to wit, 'That it is the duty of the women of the churches of Christ to separate themselves from their brethren, and as so separate, to perform divine worship by themselves.'

II. *Object.* Esther, the queen, performed, with her maidens, this duty of prayer, without their men: therefore the women of gospel churches may separate themselves from their brethren, and perform it among themselves. Es. iv. 16.

Answ. 1. Esther was in the house of the king's chamberlain, and could not at this time come to her brethren; No, not to her uncle, Mordecai, to consult how to prevent an approaching judgment. Yea, Mordecai and she were fain to speak one to another by Hatach, whom the king had appointed to attend upon the queen. ver. 5–9. So she could by no means, at that time, have communion with the church. No marvel, therefore, if she fasted with her maidens alone: for so she must now do, or not do it at all. But I will here ask this, our argumentator, whether Esther did count it a burden or a privilege thus now to be separated from her brethren, and so forced to perform this work as she did? If a privilege, let him prove it. If a burden, he has little cause to make use of it to urge that, her practice then, for a ground to women that are at liberty, to separate from their brethren to perform such worship by themselves in *their* company, without their men. 2. We do not read that she desired that any of the women that were at liberty should come from the men to be with her; whence we may gather, that she preferred their liberty to worship with men, far beyond a woman's meeting. She counted that too many, by herself and her maidens, were in such bondage already. 3. Neither did she attempt to take that unavoidable work upon herself, but as begging of the men that she might, by their faith and prayers, be borne up therein; clearly concluding that she did count such work too hard for women to perform by themselves, without the help of their men. vers. 15, 16. 4. Besides this woman's meeting, as Mr. K. would have it, was made up of none but the queen and her household maids, and with but few of them; nor will we complain of our honest women when the case is so that they cannot go out to the church to do this, if they pray with their maids

at home. 5. But what if Esther did pray with her maids in her closet, because she could not come out to her brethren. Is it fair to make the necessity of a woman in bondage a law to women at liberty? This argument, therefore, is erroneous, and must not have this text to show it up; we therefore take it away from his words and proceed to a sight of his next.

III. *Object.* But it is said by the prophet Zecharias, that the Spirit is promised to be given, in New Testament times, to women, that they may pray together apart from men. Zec. xii. 11—13.

Answ. The text says nothing so, but is greatly abused by this man. Indeed, it says their wives shall mourn apart, but it saith not, they shall do so together. Yea, that they shall separate themselves by the dictate of God, from their brethren, to do so, is that which this text knows nothing of. Sometimes many may be together, apart from others; but why Mr. K., to serve his purpose, should rack and strain this text to justify his woman's meeting, I see no reason at all. My reason against him is, for that the *look here* upon him whom we have pierced, which is to be the cause of this mourning, is to be by an immediate revelation of the Holy Ghost, who doth not use to tell before hand when he will so come down upon us. But such a meeting as Mr. K. intends must be the product of consultation and time. 'I will pour,' saith God, 'upon the house of David - the spirit of grace and of supplications: and then they shall look;' that is, when that spirit so worketh with them as to enable them so to do. Now, I say, I would know, since this mourning is to be the effect of this look, and so before one is aware, Ca. vi. 12, whether Mr. K. can prove that these women were to have an item beforehand, when they should have this look. But as it would be ridiculous thus to conclude, so as ridiculous is it to think to prove his women's meetings from hence.

Nor doth the conclusion that he hath made hereupon prove more but that he is ignorant of the work of the Spirit in this matter, or that his fondness for the women's meetings hath made him forget his own experience. For how can one that never had but one such look upon Jesus Christ, draw such a conclusion from hence. And that all those women should have this look at the same time, even all the women of the house of David and of the inhabitants of Jerusalem, that they might, all of them, by the direction of the Holy Ghost, separate themselves from their men to hold a woman's meeting or meetings by themselves for this, is more fictitious than one would imagine a man should dream. If he says that the women have a promise to have this look when they please, or that they are sure to have it because it is entailed to THEIR meeting, for this seems to come nearest his conclusion: yet what unavoidable inconveniences will flow therefrom, I leave to any to judge. But I take this mourning to be according as another of the prophets says, ' They shall be on the mountains like doves of the valleys, all of them mourning, every one for his iniquity.' Eze. vii. 16. All those souls, therefore, that shall be counted worthy to have *this look* shall mourn apart, or by themselves, when they have it. For though a man cannot appoint to himself when he will repent of his sins, or when the Holy Ghost will work, yet he shall repent indeed; he shall do it, I say, when HE doth so work, not staying till another can do so too. And since our own iniquity will then make us best consider our own case, mourning apart, or every one for their own iniquity, is most naturally proper thereto. And this is the mourning that shall be in the house of David, Jerusalem, the church, both with men and women, at all times when the Holy Ghost shall help us to look upon him whom we have pierced. Pray God give Mr. K. and myself more of these looks upon a crucified Christ, for then we shall understand this and other such like scriptures otherwise than to draw such incoherent inferences from them as he doth.

IV. *Object.* ' Women were wont in gospel times to meet together to pray. Therefore the women in gospel churches may separate themselves from their brethren to perform divine worship by themselves without their men.' Ac. xvi. 13. This is another of his scriptures, brought to uphold this fancy: But,

Answ. 1. It is not said that the women of churches met together alone to pray. But that Paul went down to a river-side where prayer was wont to be made, and spake unto the women that resorted thither. It looks therefore most agreeable to the word, to think that there the law was read by the Jewish priests to the proselyted women of that city, and that prayer, as was their custom in all such service, was intermixed therewith. But this is but conjectural. And yet, for all that, it is better grounded, and hath more reason on its side, than hath any of this man's arguments for the opinion of his women's meetings. But,

2. There was there at that time no gospel church of Christ, nor before that any gospel ministry, consequently no church obedience. Should it then be granted, that there were none but women at that meeting, and that their custom was to meet at that river-side to pray, it doth not therefore follow, that their practice was to be a pattern, a rule, a law to women in churches, to separate from their brethren, to perform divine worship, in their own woman's congregation without their men.

3. There was there no gospel believer. Lydia herself, before Paul came thither, had her heart shut

up against the faith of Jesus Christ; and how a company of strangers to gospel faith, should in that their doing, be a pattern to the women in churches, a pattern of christian worship, I do not understand.

4. If Paul's call to Philippi had been by the vision of a woman, or woman's meeting: what an argument would this man have drawn from thence to have justified his women's meetings? But since it was by a man, he hath lost an argument thereby. Though he, notwithstanding, doth adventure to say, that God so approved of that meeting, as then, and at that time, to take advantage to make known his mind and will to them concerning Jesus Christ.

5. And now I am in, since Mr. K. will needs have this scripture to justify such a practice, I wonder that he so lightly overlooked Paul's going to that meeting, for thither he went to be sure. Ac. xvi. 13—16. Yea how fairly, to his thinking, might he have pleaded, that Paul by this act of his, was a great lover, countenancer and commender of those he calls the women's meetings. Paul went to the women's meeting at Philippi, therefore it is lawful for the women of gospel churches to separate from their brethren, and to congregate by themselves for the performance of some parts of divine worship. I say how easily might he have said this, and then have popt in those two verses above quoted, and so have killed the old one ?* For the word lies liable to be abused by the ignorance of men, and it had been better than it is, if this had been the first time that this man had served it so, for the justification of his rigid principles; but when men, out of a fond conceit of their own abilities, or of prejudice to them that contradict their errors, are tempted to shew their folly, they will not want an opportunity from false glosses put upon the text, to do it.

6. But Paul went to that company to preach Christ's gospel to them, not for that they merited his coming, but of the grace of God, as also did Peter and John, when at the hour of prayer they went up into the temple, and Paul into the synagogue at Antioch. Ac. iii. 1—3; xiii. 14—16. But as fairly might this man have urged, that the healing of the lame man that lay at that time at the gate of the temple, and the conversion of them by Paul at Antioch, was by the procurement of the prayers of the sisters and by their reading of the law in that synagogue at Antioch, as to argue as he has done, that God was so well pleased, or so well approved of that woman's meeting as he feigns it at Philippi, as to send, &c. to them his minister.

7. But again, that this woman's meeting should

---

* To have said that the spirit of divination, which was cast out, was so far killed by virtue of a female prayer meeting, would have been as true as to have said, that these meetings were limited to females only.—ED.

be so deserving, and that while they were without the faith of Christ, as to procure a gospel minister to be sent unto them, that Christ might to them be made known, and yet that so few of them should be converted to the faith, seems a greater paradox to me. For we read not that one of the women then, or of them of the town, that did use to go to that meeting, (for Lydia was of Thyatira, was ever converted to Christ; brethren we read of several, but we hear not of any one more of those women. ver. 40. But Lydia worshipped God, therefore her practice might prevail. Although it is said she worshipped God, yet she was but a proselyte, as those Ac. xiii. were, and knew no more of Christ than the eunuch did. Ac viii. But hold, she had faith, will that make all practice acceptable; yea, law and commandment to others, and the work of those that have none, meritorious? But we must touch upon these things anon.

V. *Object.* 'But (saith Mr. K.) Mal. iii. 16. doth countenance these meetings.'

Answ. Not at all; though Mr. K. has pleased to change a term in the text, to make it speak his mind; for he has put out *thought*, and put in *call*; but all will not do his work; for when he has done what he can, it will be difficult to make that scripture say, It is the duty of women in gospel churches to separate from their brethren, to perform divine worship among themselves.

VI. *Object.* 'But Jude 20. doth justify these meetings, except,' saith he, 'any will say, women are not to be built up in their most holy faith.'

Answ. How fain would the man lay hold on something, only he wants divine help, that is, the word of God, to bottom his things upon. But doth the apostle here at all treat of the women and their meetings, or are they only the beloved; and to be built up, &c. speaks he not there to the church, which consisteth of men and women? and are not men the more noble part in all the churches of Christ? But can women no other way be built up in their most holy faith, but by meetings of their own without their men? But, Building up YOURSELVES, I suppose is the thing he holds by. But cannot the church, and every woman in it, build up themselves without their woman's meetings? wherefore have they the word, their closet, and the grace of meditation, but to build up themselves withal? He saith not, 'Build up one another,' but if he had, it might well have been done without a woman's meeting. But anything to save a drowning man. This text then is written to the church of Christ, by which it is exhorted to faith and prayer; but it speaks not a word of a woman's meeting, and therefore it is fooling with the word to suggest it. I cannot therefore, while I see this impertinent dealing, but think our argumentator dotes, or takes upon him

to be a head of those he thinks to rule over. The woman's letter to me also seems to import the same, when they say, 'Mr. K. would desire to know what objections you have against it (his arguments), and he is ready to give his further advice.'

Thus having taken from his arguments those holy words of God which he has abused, to make them stand; I come next to the arguments themselves, and intend to pick their bones for the crows.

1stly, He saith, 'That the same spirit that was in Miriam, is also in all God's servants for the same end, both to pray for mercies we stand in need of, and to praise God for mercies received.'

Answ. 1. But the question is, whether Miriam did, as she led out the women to dance, act only as an ordinary saint. And if you evade this, you choose the tongue of the crafty, and use the words of deceit; for she managed that work as she was 'Miriam the prophetess;' and in your next, pray tell your women so. 2. But as Miriam the prophetess, she did not lead the women from their men, to worship in some place remote by themselves, as we have shewed before.

2dly, He saith, 'That God hath promised to pour out his Spirit in gospel times to that very end, that women might pray together apart from men.'

Answ. 1. Not mentioning again what was said before: I add, if by *men*, he means the brethren, the prophet will not be his voucher, for he neither saith nor intimates such a thing. 2. And how far short this saying is, of making of God and his holy prophet, the author of schism in worship, and an encouragement unto schism therein, it is best in time that he looks to it. For if they may withdraw to do thus at one time, they may withdraw to do thus at another. And if the Spirit is given to them to this very end, that they may go by themselves from the church, to perform this divine worship at one time, they may, for what bounds this man has set them, go by themselves to do thus always. But, as I said, the whole of this proposition being false, the error is still the greater.

3dly, 'God,' saith he, 'hath so well approved of women meeting together to pray in gospel times, as then, and at that time, to take occasion to make known his mind and will to them concerning Jesus Christ.' Ac. xvi. 13.

Answ. Let the reader consider what was said before, and now it follows; if this assertion be true, then the popish doctrine of merit is good, yea the worst sort of it, which is, works done before faith. For that we read of none of these women save Lydia feared or worshipped God; and yet saith he, God so approved of that meeting as then, and at that time, to send them his gospel, which is one of the richest blessings; nor will it help to lay Cornelius, now in my way, for the deservings here were, for ought we read, of women that feared not God. Here Lydia only bare that character; it is said SHE worshipped God, but she was not *all* the women. But Mr. K. saith thus of them all., I know also there was faith in some in Messias to come, though when he came, they knew not his person; but this is not the case neither; these women, who held up as he feigned, this meeting, were not as we read of, of this people.

4thly, He said, 'That Esther and her maids fasted and prayed, and the Lord gave a gracious return, or answer and deliverance.' That is, to the church, that then was under the rage of Haman.

Answ. Let the reader remember what was said before, and now I ask this man, 1. Whether Mordecai and the good men then did not pray and fast as well as she? And if so, Whether they might not obtain at least, some little of the mercy, as well as those women? If so, 2. Whether Mr. K., in applying the deliverance of this people to the prayer of the queen and her maids, for he lays it only there, be not deceitfully arguing, and do not tend to puff up that sex, to their hurt and damage! Yea whether it doth not tend to make them unruly and headstrong? But if they be more gently inclined to obedience, no thanks to Mr. K. 3. And if I should ask Mr. K. who gave him authority to attribute *thus* the deliverance of this people, to who and what prayers he please, I suppose it would not be easy for him to answer. The text saith not that the prayers of these women procured the blessing. But Mr. K. hath here a woman's meeting to vindicate, and therefore it is that he is thus out in his mind. Prayers were heard and the church was delivered. And I doubt not but that these good women had hand and heart in the work. But should all be admitted that Mr. K. hath said as to this also, yet this scripture, as hath already been proved, will not justify his woman's meeting.

5thly, 'He makes his appeal to the women, if they have not obtained, by their prayers in these their meetings, many blessed returns of prayer from God, both to themselves and the church of God.'

Answ. I count this no whit better than the very worst of his paper, for besides the silliness of his appeal, by which he makes these good women to be judges in their own cause, his words have a direct tendency in them to puff them up to their destruction. I have wondered sometimes, to see when something extraordinary hath happened to the church of God for good, that a few women meeting together to pray, should be possessed with a conceit, that they fetched the benefit down from

heaven, when perhaps ten thousand men in the land prayed for the mercy as hard as they. Yea I have observed, that though the things bestowed, were not so much as thought of by them, yet they have been apt to conclude that their meeting together has done it. But poor women, you are to be pitied; your tempter is to bear the blame, to wit, this man and his fellows.

I come now to some objections that may yet be thought on: and will speak a word to them.

Object. 1. It is said, 'Where two or three are gathered together in my name, there am I in the midst of them.' Mat. xviii. 20.

Answ. To gather together in Christ's name, is to gather together by his authority; That is, by his law and commandment. Ac. iv. 17, 18, 30; v. 28, 40. Col. iii. 17. But we have no law of Christ, nor commandment, that the women of *this* or *that* church, should separate themselves from their brethren, to maintain meetings among themselves, for the performing of divine worship: and therefore such meetings cannot be in his name; that is, by his authority, law, and commandment; and so ought not to be at all.

Object. 2. 'But women may, if sent for by them of their own sex, come to see them when they are sick, and when so come together, pray in that assembly before they part.'

Answ. The law of Christ is, 'Is any sick among you? let him (and the woman is included in the man) call for the elders of the church; and let them pray over him,' &c. And to this injunction there is a threefold promise made. (1.) 'And the prayer of faith shall save the sick.' (2.) 'And the Lord shall raise him up.' (3.) 'And if he have committed sins, they shall be forgiven him.' Ja. v. 14, 15. And considering, that this advice is seconded with so much grace: I think it best in all such cases, as in all other, to make the word of God our rule.

Object. 3. 'But women have sometimes cases, which modesty will not admit should be made known to men, what must they do then?'

Answ. Their husbands and they are one flesh, and are no more to be accounted two. Let them tell their grief to them. Thus Rachel asked children of her husband, and went not to a nest of women to make her complaint to them. Ge. xxx. 1. Or let them betake themselves to their closets, with Rebecca. Ge. xxv. 20—23. Or if they be in the assembly of the saints, let them pray in their hearts, with Hannah. And if their petition be lawful, I doubt not but they may be heard. 1 Sa. i. 13.

Our author, perhaps, will say, I have not spoken to his question; which was, 'Whether women, fearing God, may meet to pray together? And whether it be lawful for them so to do?'

But I answer, I have: with respect to all such

godly women as are in the churches of the saints. 1 Co. xiv. 33—35. compared with ver. 15—17. And when he has told us, that his question respected only those out of churches, then will I confess that I did mistake him. Yet he will get nothing thereby, forasmuch as his question, to be sure, intends those in special. Also his arguments are for the justifying of that their practice. Now the reason why I waved the form of his question, was, because it was both scanty and lean of words, as to the matter of the controversy in hand: Also I thought it best to make it more ample, and distinct, for the edification of our reader. And if after all, Mr. K. is not pleased at what I have done, let him take up the question, and answer it better. The man perhaps may fly to the case of utter necessity, and so bring forth another question, to wit, whether, if the men of a church should all die, be murdered, or cast into prison: the women of that church may not meet together to pray? And whether it be not lawful for them so to do? But when he produceth a necessity for the putting of such a question, and then shall put it to me; I will, as God shall help me, give him an answer thereto.

But, may some say, Our women in this do not what they do of their own heads, they are allowed to do what they do by the church.

I answer, No church allowance is a foundation sufficient to justify that which is neither commanded nor allowed by the word. Besides, who knows not, that have their eyes in their heads, what already has, and what further may, come into the churches, at such a gap as this. And now to give the reader a cautionary conclusion.

Caution 1. Take heed of letting the name, or good show of a thing, beget in thy heart a religious reverence of that thing; but look to the word for thy* bottom, for it is the word that authorizeth, whatever may be done with warrant in worship to God; without the word things are of human invention, of what splendour or beauty soever they may appear to be. Without doubt the Friars and Nuns, and their religious orders, were of a good intent at first, as also compulsive vows of chastity, single life, and the like. But they were all without the word, and therefore, as their bottom wanted divine authority, so the practice wanted sanctity by the Holy Ghost. The word prayer is, of itself, in appearance so holy, that he forthwith seems to be a devil that forbids it. And yet we find that prayers have been out of joint, and disorderly used; and therefore may by one, without incurring the danger of damnation, be called into question; and if found without order by him, he may labour to set them in joint again. Mat. vi. 5—8; xxiii. 14. Ja. iv. 3.

I am not of the number of them that say, 'What

profit should we have if we pray unto God?' Job xxi. 15. But finding no good footing in the word for that kind of service we have treated about above, and knowing that error and human inventions in religion will not offer themselves, but with wiped lips, and a countenance as demure as may be, and also being persuaded that this opinion of Mr. K. is vagrant, yea a mere alien as to the scriptures, I being an officer, have apprehended it, and put it in the stocks, and there will keep it, till I see by what authority it has leave to pass and repass as it lists, among the godly in this land.

Caution 2. Yet by all that I have said, I never meant to intimate in the least, but that believing women are saints as well as men: and members of the body of Christ. And I will add, that as *they*, and *we*, are united to Christ, and made members of his mystical body, the fulness of him that fills all in all, so there is no superiority, as I know of, but we are all one in Christ. For, the man is not without the woman, nor 'the woman without the man, in the Lord,' 1 Co. xi. 11. nor are we counted 'as male or female' in him. Ga. iii. 28. Ep. i. 23. Only we must observe that *this* is spoken of that church which is his true mystical body, and not of every particular congregation of professing Christians. The churches of Christ *here* and there are also called his body. But no church *here*, though never so famous, must be taken for that of which mention was made afore.†

As Christ then has a body mystical, which is called his members, his flesh, and his bones, Ep. v. 30. so he has a body politic, congregations modelled by the skill that his ministers have in his word, for the bearing up of his name, and the preserving of his glory in the world against Antichrist. In *this* church, order and discipline, for the nourishing up of the true mystical body of Christ, has been placed from the foundation of the world. Wherefore in *this*, laws, and statutes, and government, is to be looked after, and given heed unto, for the edification of *that* which is to arrive at last to a perfect man: to the measure of the stature of the fulness of Christ. 1 Co. xii. 27—30. Ep. iv. 11—13.

---

* 'Bottom,' or foundation.

† A dangerous error, originating in the sectarian pride of Antichrist, prevails to a very great extent. It is that some one visible church, or set of united churches, is the mystical body of Christ, and entitled to be called THE CHURCH. Every congregation of pious men and women, united together in the faith, is A church of Christ. But THE church comprises all the saints of God who ever lived—live now, or will live on the earth; until their number is completed, and this creation shall give place to the new heavens and the new earth. Every church is as distinct as it is equal; whether it meet at Corinth, Rome, or Ephesus, at London or Edinburgh. Be it Episcopalian, Independent, Presbyterian, Baptist, or a church of the Society of Friends; each is entitled, according to the New Testament, to equal honour and privileg.—ED.

Now, where there is order and government by laws and statutes, there must, of necessity, be also a distinction of sex, degrees, and age. Yea, offices and officers must also be there, for our furtherance and joy of faith. From which government and rule our ordinary women are excluded by Paul; nor should it, since it is done by the wisdom of God, be any offence unto them.

In this church there are ofttimes many hypocrites, and formal professors, and heresies, 'That they which are approved may be made manifest.' 1 Co. xi. 19. These therefore being there, and being suffered to act as they many times do, provoke the truly godly to contend with them by the word; for that these hypocrites, and formal professors, naturally incline to a denial of the power of godliness, and to set up forms of their own in the stead thereof. Mar. vii 6—9. 2 Ti. iii. 5.

And this is done for the sake and for the good of those that are the true members of the body of Christ, and that are to arrive at his haven of rest: from whom those others at last shall be purged, and with them, all their things that offend. ' Then shall the righteous shine forth as the sun in the kingdom of their Father. Who hath ears to hear let him hear.' Mat. xiii. 43.

This church, that thus consisteth of all righteous, that are so in God's account: they are to have a house in heaven, and to be for God's habitation there. Who, then, shall be governed by their head without those officers and laws that are necessary here. And both at last shall be subject to him, that sometime did put all things under Christ, that God may be all in all. Jn. xiv. 1—3. Ep. ii. 21. 1 Co. xv. 23—27. Wherefore, my beloved sisters, this inferiority of yours will last but a little while. When the day of God's salvation is come, to wit, when our Lord shall descend from heaven, with a shout, with the voice of the archangel, and the trump of God, these distinctions of sexes shall be laid aside, and every pot shall be filled to the brim. For with a *notwithstanding* you shall be saved, and be gathered up to that state of felicity if you continue in faith, and charity, and holiness, with sobriety. 1 Ti. ii. 15.

Caution 3. I doubt not at all of the lawfulness of women's praying, and that, both in private and public: only when they pray publicly, they should not separate from, but join with the church in that work. They should also not be the mouth of the assembly, but in heart, desires, groans, and tears, they should go along with the men. In their closets they are at liberty to *speak* unto their God, who can bear with, and pity them with us; and pardon all our weakness for the sake of Jesus Christ.

And here I will take an occasion to say, there may be a twofold miscarriage in prayer, one in doctrine, the other in the frame of the heart. All are too much subject to the last, women [more easily] to the first. And for this cause it is, at least so I think, that women are not permitted to teach, nor speak in assemblies, for divine worship, but to *be* and to *learn* in silence, 1 Co. xiv. 33—35; xv. 33. For he that faileth as to the frame of his spirit, hurteth only himself: but he that faileth in doctrine corrupteth them that stand by. Let the women be alone with Rebecca in the closet; or, if in company, let her, with Hannah, speak to herself and to God; and not doubt, but if she be humble, and keep within compass, she shall be a sharer with her brethren in the mercy.

Caution 4. Nor are women, by what I have said, debarred from any work or employ, unto which they are enjoined by the word. They have often been called forth to be God's witnesses, and have borne famous testimony for him against the sons of the sorceress and the whore.* I remember many of them with comfort, even of these eminent daughters of Sarah, whose daughters you also are, so long as you do well, and are not afraid with any amazement. 1 Pe. iii. 1—6. What by the word of God, you are called unto, what by the word is enjoined you do; and the Lord be with you.

But this of the women's meetings; since, indeed, there is nothing for its countenance in the word, and since the calling together of assemblies for worship is an act of power, and belongeth to the church, elders, or chief men of the same: let me intreat you to be content, to be under subjection and obedience, as also saith the law. We hold that it is God's word that we are to look to, as to all things pertaining to worship, because it is the word that authorizeth and sanctifieth what we do.

Caution. 5. WOMEN! They are an ornament in the church of God on earth, as the ANGELS are in the church in heaven. Betwixt whom also there is some comparison, for they cover their faces in acts of worship. Is. vi. 2. 1 Co. xi. 10. But as the angels in heaven are not Christ, and so not admitted to the mercy-seat to speak to God, so neither are women on earth, [but] the man; who is to worship with open face before him, and to be the mouth in prayer for the rest. As the angels then cry, Holy, Holy, Holy, with faces covered in heaven: So let the women cry, Holy, Holy, Holy, with their faces covered on earth: Yea, thus they should do, because of the angels. ' For this cause ought the woman to have power,' that is a covering, ' on *her* head, because of the angels.' 1 Co. xi. 10. Not only because the angels are present, but because women and angels, as to their worship, in their respective places, have a semblance. For the angels are inferior to the great man Christ, who is in heaven;

---

* The usual appellations of Popery.—ED.

and the woman is inferior to the man, that truly worships God in the church on earth.

Methinks, holy and beloved sisters, you should be content to wear this power, or badge of your inferiority, since the cause thereof arose at first from yourselves. It was the woman that at first the serpent made use of, and by whom he then overthrew the world: wherefore the woman, to the world's end, must wear tokens of her underlingship in all matters of worship. To say nothing of that which she cannot shake off, to wit, her pains and sorrows in child-bearing, which God has rivetted to her nature, there is her silence, and shame, and a covering for her face, in token of it, which she ought to be exercised with, whenever the church comes together to worship. Ge. iii. 16. 1 Ti. ii. 15. 1 Co. xi. 13. 1 Ti. ii. 9.

Do you think that God gave the woman her hair, that she might deck herself, and set off her fleshly beauty therewith? It was given her to cover her face with, in token of shame and silence, for that by the woman sin came into the world. 1 Ti. ii. 9. And perhaps the reason why the angels cover their faces when they cry, Holy, Holy, Holy, in heaven, is to shew that they still bear in mind, with a kind of abhorrence, the remembrance of their fellows falling from thence. Modesty, and shame-facedness, becomes women at all times, especially in times of public worship, and the more of this is mixed with their grace and personage, the more beautiful they are both to God and men. But why must the women have shame-facedness, since they live honestly as the men? I answer, In remembrance of the fall of Eve, and to that the apostle applies it. For a woman, necessity has no law, to shave her head, and to look with open face in worship, as if she could be a leader there, is so far from doing that which becomes her, that it declares her to have forgot what God would have her for ever with shame remember.

Caution 6. In what I have said about the women's meetings, I have not at all concerned myself about those women, that have been extraordinary ones, such as Miriam, Deborah, Huldah, Anna, or the rest, as the daughters of Philip the evangelist, Priscilla, the women that Paul said laboured with him in the gospel, or such like; for they might teach, prophecy, and had power to call the people together so to do. Though this I must say concerning them, they ought to, and did, notwithstanding so high a calling, still bear about with them the badge of their inferiority to them that were prophets indeed. And hence it is said, under pain of being guilty of disorder, that if they prayed in the church, or prophesied there, with their head uncovered, they then dishonoured their head. 1 Co. xi. 5.

The prophetesses were below the prophets, and their covering for their head was to be worn in token thereof, and perhaps it was for want of regard to this order, that when Miriam began to perk it * before Moses, that God covered her face with a leprous-scab. Nu. xii. 10. Hence these women, when prophets were present, did use to lie still as to acts of power, and leave that to be put forth by them that were higher than they. And even Miriam herself, though she was one indeed, yet she came always behind, not only in name but worship, unless when she was in her own disorders. Nu. xii. 1.

And it is worth your farther noting, that when God tells Israel that they should take heed in the plague of leprosy, that they diligently observed to do what the priest and Levites taught them, that he conjoins with that exhortation, that they should ' remember what God did unto Miriam by the way.' De. xxiv. 8, 9. Intimating surely that they should not give heed to women, that would be perking up in matters of worshipping God. Much less should we invest them with power to call congregations of their own, there to perform worship without their men.

Yet, will I say, notwithstanding all this, that if any of these high women had, but we never read that they did, separate themselves, and others of their own sex with them, apart to worship by themselves: or if they had given out commandment so to do, and had joined God's name to that commandment, I should have freely consented that our women should do so too, when led out, and conducted in worship, by so extraordinary a one. Yea more, If any of these high women had given it out for law, that the women of the churches in New Testament times, ought to separate themselves from their men, and as so separate, perform divine worship among themselves: I should have subscribed thereto. But finding nothing like this in the word of God, for the sanctifying of such a practice: and seeing so many scriptures wrested out of their place to justify so fond a conceit: and all this done by a man of conceit, and of one that, as his sisters say, expects my answer: I found myself engaged to say something for the suppressing of this his opinion.

But to return to the good women in the churches, and to make up my discourse with them.

First, These meetings of yours, honourable women, wherein you attempt to perform divine worship by yourselves, without your men, not having the authority of the word to sanctify them, will be found will-worship, in the day when you, as to that, shall be measured with that golden reed, the law of God. And ' who hath required this at your hand?' may put you to your shifts for an answer, notwithstanding all Mr. K. has said to uphold you. Is. i. 12. Re. xi. 1.

Secondly, These meetings of yours need not be;

---

* ' To perk it,' to hold up her head with affected superiority or spiritual pride.—ED.

there are elders or brethren in all churches, to call to, and manage this worship of God, in the world: if you abide in your subjection and worship as you are commanded.

Thirdly, These meetings of yours, instead of being an ornament to the church in which you are, are a shame and blemish to those churches. For they manifest the unruliness of such women, or that the church wants skill to govern them. 1 Co. xiv. 23. Have you not 'in your flock a male?' Mal. i. 14.

Fourthly, Suppose your meetings in some cases were lawful, yet since by the brethren they may be managed better, you and your meetings ought to give place. That the church together, and the brethren, as the mouth to God, are capable of managing this solemn worship best: consider —1. The gifts for all such service are most to be found in the elders and leading men in the church: and not in the women thereof. 2. The spirit for conduct and government in that worship, is not in the women, but in the men. 3. The men are admitted in such worship, to stand with open face before God, a token of much admittance to liberty and boldness with God, a thing denied to the women. 1 Co. xi. 4, 5. 4. For that when meetings for prayers are commanded, the men, to be the mouth to God, are mentioned, but not in ordinary women, in all the Scriptures. Where the women and children, and them that suck the breasts are called, with the bride and bridegroom, and the whole land, to mourn: yet the ministers, and elders, and chiefest of the brethren, are they, and they only, that are bid to say, 'Spare thy people, O Lord!' and give not thine heritage to reproach.' Joel i. 13, 14; ii. 15—17. 5. The word for encouragement to pray believingly in assemblies is given to men. And it is the word that makes, and that sanctifies an ordinance of God: men, therefore, in all assemblies for worship, should be they that should manage it, and let others join in their places.

Object. But the woman is included in the man, for the same word signifies both.

Answ. 1. If the woman is included here, let her not exclude the man. But the man is [by them] excluded: The man is excluded by this woman's meeting from worship; from worship, though he be the head in worship over the woman, and by God's ordinance appointed to manage it, and this is an excluding of the worst complexion. 1 Co. xi. 3. 2. Though the woman is included, when the man sometimes is named, yet the man is not excluded, when himself as chief is named. But to cut him off from being the chief in all assemblies for worship, is to exclude him, and that when he for that in chief is named. 3. The woman is included when the man is named, yet but in her place, and if she worships in assemblies, her part is to hold her tongue, to learn in silence; and if she speaks, she must do it, I mean as to worship, in her heart to God. 4. Nor, do I think, that any woman that is holy and humble, will take offence at what I have said; for I have not in anything sought to degrade them, or to take from them what either nature or grace, or an appointment of God hath invested them with: but have laboured to keep them in their place. And doubtless to abide where God has put us, is that which not only highly concerns us, but that, which becomes us best. Sisters, I have said what I have said to set you right, and to prevent your attempting to do things in such sort unto which you are not appointed. Remember what God did to Miriam, and be afraid.

Be as often in your closets as you will; the oftener there the better. This is your duty, this is your privilege: this place is sanctified to you for service by the holy Word of God. Here you may be, and not make ordinances interfere, and not presume upon the power of your superiors, and not thrust out your brethren, nor put them behind your backs in worship.

Be also as often as possibly you can, in worship, when the church, or parts thereof, are assembled for that end, according to God's appointment. And when you are there, join with heart and soul with your brethren in all holy petitions to God. Let the men in prayer be the mouth to God, and the women list after with groans and desires. Let the men stand with open face in this worship, for that they are the image and glory of God, and let the women be clothed in modest apparel, with shamefacedness, in token of the remembrance of what has been touched afore.

When women keep their places, and men manage their worshipping of God as they should, we shall have better days for the church of God, in the world. Je. xxix. 10—14. Women are not to be blamed for that they are forward to pray to God, only let them know their bounds; and I wish that idleness in men be not the cause of their putting their good women upon this work. Surely they that can scarce tie their shoes, and their garters, before they arrive at the tavern, or get to the coffee-house door in a morning, can scarce spare time to be a while in their closets with God. Morning closet-prayers are now, by most London professors, thrown away; and what kind of ones they make at night, God doth know, and their conscience, when awake, will know; however I have cause, as to this, to look at home: And God mend me and all his servants about it, and wherein we else are out.

I have done, after I have said, that there are some other things, concerning women, touching which, when I have an opportunity, I may also give my judgment. But at present, I intreat that these lines be taken in good part, for I seek edification, not contention.

INSTRUCTION FOR THE IGNORANT:

BEING

A SALVE TO CURE THAT GREAT WANT OF KNOWLEDGE, WHICH SO MUCH REIGNS BOTH IN YOUNG AND OLD.

PREPARED AND PRESENTED TO THEM IN A PLAIN AND EASY DIALOGUE, FITTED TO THE CAPACITY OF THE WEAKEST.

'My people are destroyed for lack of knowledge.'—Hos. iv. 6.

ADVERTISEMENT BY THE EDITOR.

THIS little catechism is upon a plan perfectly new and unique. It was first published as a pocket volume in 1675, and has been republished in every collection of the author's works; and recently in a separate tract. The earliest edition that has been discovered bears the date of 1691; from which our copy has been prepared for the press. This is the first book of this class that was composed upon the broad basis of Christianity, perfectly free from sectarian bias or peculiarity. It is an exhibition of scriptural truths, before which error falls without the trouble of pulling it down. It is in the world, like the ark of God in the temple of Dagon. It is alike admirably calculated to convey the most important truths to the inmates of a palace or of a workhouse,—to the young or to the aged,—to the ignorant Roman Catholic, or to the equally ignorant Protestant. Its broad catholicity is its distinguishing excellence. In the separate communions included within the general church of Christ are various, and in many respects, inestimable compendiums of Christian truth, arranged for the catechetical instruction of the young and ignorant; but it cannot be denied that these, one and all, exhibit some marks of sectarian feeling and dogmatic teaching in the details that relate to the special views which each communion takes of certain scriptural doctrines. The reason why this should be the case is very obvious: there would be no differences of opinion amongst Christians except from conviction that these differences are essential, and such conviction naturally leads to these points of disagreement being (may we not say?) rather too obtrusively enforced as part and portion of a saving belief. All Bunyan's efforts were to awaken sinners to a sense of their degradation, misery, and danger, and to direct them to the only refuge from the wrath to come—the hope set before them in the gospel; and then leaving the pious convert to the guidance of his Bible in forming his connections in the pilgrimage of life. Bunyan is solemnly in earnest; his desire is, that poor sinners should be relieved from ignorance, darkness, and destruction, and be introduced into the glorious liberty of the sons of God. May his impressive injunction be indelibly fixed upon our souls, 'To read, ponder over, and receive the wholesome medicine as we shall answer in the day of the terrible judgment.'—GEO. OFFOR.

TO THE CHURCH OF CHRIST IN AND ABOUT BEDFORD, WALKING IN THE FAITH AND FELLOWSHIP OF THE GOSPEL, YOUR AFFECTIONATE BROTHER AND COMPANION IN THE KINGDOM AND PATIENCE OF JESUS CHRIST, WISHETH ALL GRACE AND MERCY BY JESUS CHRIST. AMEN.

Holy and beloved,

ALTHOUGH I have designed this little treatise for public and common benefit, yet considering that I am to you a debtor not only in common charity; but by reason of special bonds which the Lord hath laid upon me to you-ward, I could do no less, being driven from you in presence, not affection, but first present you with this little book; not for that you are wanting in the things contained herein, but to put you again in remembrance of first things, and to give you occasion to present something to your carnal relations, that may be, if God will, for their awakening and conversion: accept it therefore as a token of my christian remembrance of you.

Next I present it to all those unconverted, old and young, who have been at any time under my preaching, and yet remain in their sins:* and I

---

* How awful the thought that persons should sit under so faithful and searching a ministry, and still remain in their

entreat them also that they receive it as a token of my love to their immortal souls; yea, I charge them as they will answer it in the day of terrible judgment, that they read, ponder over, and receive this wholesome medicine prepared for them. Now the God of blessing bless it to the awakening of many sinners, and the salvation of their souls by faith in Jesus Christ. Amen.

---

sins. Is is so to the present day under a faithful ministry? then, Oh *my* soul, how is it with thee?—ED.

Yours, to serve you by my ministry, when I can,* to your edification and consolation,

JOHN BUNYAN.

---

* A painful recollection of his long and cruel imprisonment for conscience sake led Bunyan to feel the value of liberty. Still he forcibly appeals to his reader on the *necessity* of private judgment in divine things. His twelve years' converse with God and his word in prison had confirmed his principles; while divine love had swallowed up the fear of man.—ED.

INSTRUCTION FOR THE IGNORANT.

Quest. How many gods are there?—Answ. To the Christians there is but one God, the Father, of whom are all things, and we of him. 1 Co. viii. 6.

Q. Why is not the God of the Christians the God of them that are no Christians?—A. He is their maker and preserver; but they have not chosen him to be their God. Ac. xvii. 24. Ps. xxxvi. 6. Ju. x. 14.

Q. Are there then other gods besides the God of the Christians?—A. There is none other true God but HE; but because they want the grace of Christians, therefore they choose not him, but such gods as will suit with and countenance their lusts. Jn. viii. 44.

Q. What gods are they that countenance the lusts of wicked men?—A. The devil, who is the god of this world; the belly, that god of gluttons, drunkards, and riotous persons; and idle pleasures and vanities, which are, for the most part, the gods of the youth. Job viii. 4. 2 Co. iv. 4. Phil. iii. 19. Ex. xxxii. 6. 1 Co. x. 7. 2 Ti. ii. 22. 1 Jn. v. 21.

Q. Who is a Christian?—A. One that is born again, a new creature; one that sits at Jesus' feet to hear his word; one that hath his heart purified and sanctified by faith,* which is in Christ. Jn. iii. 3, 5, 7. Ac. xi. 24; xv. 9; xxvi. 18. 2 Co. v. 17.

Q. How do you distinguish the God of the Christians from the gods of other people?—A. He is a Spirit. Jn. iv. 24.

Q. Is there no other spirit but the true God?—A. Yes, there are many spirits. 1 Jn. iv. 1.

Q. What spirits are they?—A. The good angels are spirits; the bad angels are spirits; and the souls of men are spirits. He. i. 7, 14. 1 Ki. xxii. 21, 22. Re. xvi. 13, 14. Ac. vii. 59. He. xii. 23.

Q. How then is the true God distinguished from other spirits?—A. Thus: No Spirit is eternal but HE, no Spirit is almighty but HE, no Spirit is incomprehensible and unsearchable but HE: HE is also

---

* Faith is the only principle that, by the power of the Holy Ghost, can purify the heart. It leads the soul into holy communion with a pure and holy God, and thus cleanses the heart.—ED.

most merciful, most just, most holy. De. xxxiii. 27. Ge. xvii. 1. Ps. cxlv. 3. Mi. vii. 18. Job xxxiv. 17. 1 Sa. ii. 2.

Q. Is this God, being a Spirit, to be known?—A. Yes, and that by his works of creation, by his providences, by the judgments that he executeth, and by his word.

Q. Do you understand him by the works of creation?—A. 'The heavens declare the glory of God; and the firmament sheweth his handy work.' Ps. xix. 1. 'For the invisible things of him from the creation of the world are clearly seen, being understood by the things that are made, *even* his eternal power and Godhead.' Ro. i. 20.

Q. Do his works of providence also declare him?—A. They must needs do it, since through his providence the whole creation is kept in such harmony as it is, and that in despite of sin and devils; also, if you consider that from an angel to a sparrow, nothing falls to the ground without the providence of our heavenly Father. Mat. x. 29.

Q. Is he known by his judgments?—A. 'The Lord is known *by* the judgments *which* he executeth; the wicked is snared in the work of his own hands.' Ps. ix. 16.

Q. Is he known by his word?—A. Yes, most clearly: for by that he revealeth his attributes, his decrees, his promises, his way of worship, and how he is to be pleased by us.

Q. Of what did God make the world?—A. 'Things which are seen were not made of things which do appear.' He. xi. 3.

Q. How long was he in making the world?—A. '*In* six days the Lord made heaven and earth, the sea, and all that in them *is*.' Ex. xx. 11. 'And on the seventh day God ended his work which he had made.' Ge. ii. 2.

Q. Of what did God make man?—A. 'The LORD God formed man *of* the dust of the ground, and breathed into his nostrils the breath of life; and man became a living soul.' Ge. ii. 7.

Q. Why doth it say, God breathed into him the breath of life; is man's soul of the very nature of the Godhead?—A. This doth not teach that the soul is of the nature of the Godhead, but sheweth that it is not of the same matter as his body, which is dust. Ge. xviii. 27.

Q. Is not the soul then of the nature of the Godhead ?—A. No, for God cannot sin, but the soul doth; God cannot be destroyed in hell, but the souls of the impenitent shall. Eze. xviii. 4. Mat. x. 28.

Q. How did God make man in the day of his first creation ?—A. God made man upright. Ec. vii. 29. 'In the image of God created he him.' Ge. i. 27.

Q. Did God, when he made man, leave him without a rule to walk by ?—A. No: he gave him a law in his nature, and imposed upon him a positive precept, but he offered violence to them, and brake them both. Ge. iii. 3, 6.

Q. What was the due desert of that transgression ?—A. Spiritual death in the day he did it, temporal death afterwards, and everlasting death last of all. Ge. ii. 17; iii. 19. Mat. xxv. 46.

Q. What is it to be spiritually dead ?—A. To be alienate from God, and to live without him in the world, through the ignorance that is in man, and through the power of their sins. Ep. iv. 18, 19.

Q. Wherein doth this alienation from God appear ?—A. In the love they have to their sins, in their being loth to come to him, in their pleading idle excuses for their sins, and in their ignorance of the excellent mysteries of his blessed gospel. Ep. ii. 2, 3, 11, 12; iv. 18, 19. Ro. i. 28.

Q. What is temporal death ?—A. To have body and soul separated asunder, the body returning to the dust as it was, and the spirit to God that gave it. Ge. iii. 19. Ec. xii. 7.

Q. What is everlasting death ?—A. For body and soul to be separate for ever from God, and to be cast into hell fire. Lu. xiii. 27. Mar. ix. 43.

Q. Do men go body and soul to hell so soon as they die ?—A. The body abideth in the grave till the sound of the last trump; but the soul, if the man dies wicked, goes presently from the face of God into hell, as into a prison, there to be kept till the day of judgment. 1 Co. xv. 52. Is. xxiv. 22. Lu. xii. 20.

Q. Do we come into the world as upright as did our first parent ?—A. No: he came into the world sinless, being made so of God Almighty, but we came into the world sinners, being made so by his pollution.*

Q. How doth it appear that we came into the world polluted ?—A. We are the fruit of an unclean thing, are defiled in our very conception, and are by nature the children of wrath. Job xiv. 4. Ps. li. 5. Ep. ii. 3.

Q. Can you make further proof of this ?—A. Yes, it is said, That by one man came sin, death, judgment, and condemnation upon all men. Ro. v. 12—19.

Q. Do we then come sinners into the world ?—A. Yes, we are transgressors from the womb, and go astray as soon as we are born, speaking lies. Is. xlviii. 8. Ps. lviii. 3.

Q. But as Adam fell with us in him, so did he not by faith rise with us in him ? for he had no seed until he had the promise.—A. He fell as a public person,† but believed the promise as a single person. Adam's faith saved not the world, though Adam's sin overthrew it.

Q. But do not some hold that we are sinners only by imitation ?—A. Yes, being themselves deceived. But God's word saith, we are children of wrath by nature, that is, by birth and generation.

Q. Can you bring further proof of this ?—A. Yes: in that day that we were born, we were polluted in our own blood, and cast out to the loathing of our persons. Again, the children of old that were dedicated unto the Lord, a sacrifice was offered for them at a month old, which was before they were sinners by imitation. Eze. xvi. 4—9. Nu. xviii. 14—16.

Q. Can you make this appear by experience ?—Yes: the first things that bloom and put forth themselves in children, shew their ignorance of God, their disobedience to parents, and their innate enmity to holiness of life; their inclinations naturally run to vanity. Besides little children die, but that they could not, were they not of God counted sinners; for death is the wages of sin. Ro. vi. 23.

Q. What is sin ?—A. It is a transgression of the law. 1 Jn. iii. 4.

Q. A transgression of what law ?—A. Of the law of our nature, and of the law of the ten commandments as written in the holy scriptures. Ro. ii. 12—15. Ex. xx.

Q. When doth one sin against the law of nature ?—A. When you do anything that your conscience tells you is a transgression against God or man. Ro. ii. 14, 15.

Q. When do we sin against the law as written in the ten commandments ?—A. When you do anything that they forbid, although you be ignorant of it. Ps. xix. 12.

Q. How many ways are there to sin against this law ?—A. Three: by sinful thoughts, by sinful words, and also by sinful actions. Ro. vii. 7; ii. 6. Mat. v. 28; xii. 37.

Q. What if we sin but against one of the ten com-

---

* All mankind, as born into the world, show, as soon as the mental powers open, aversion to God, to his purity, his law, his gospel; the doctrines of grace and the work of the Spirit upon the heart. A solemn proof of the universal taint given by original sin.—Ed.

† By the word 'public' is to be understood a federal head, or the representative of all his posterity. Adam's faith can only save his own soul; his sin taints all his seed.—Ed.

mandments ?—A. Whosoever shall keep the whole law, and yet offend in one point, he is guilty of all ; ' For he that said, Do not commit adultery, said also, Do not kill. Now, if thou commit no adultery, yet if thou kill, thou art become a transgressor of the law.' Ja. ii. 10, 11.

Q. Where will God punish sinners for their sins ? —A. Both in this world and in that which is to come. Ge. iii. 24; iv. 10—12. Job xxi. 30.

Q. How are men punished in this world for sin ? —A. Many ways, as with sickness, losses, crosses, disappointments and the like : sometimes also God giveth them up to their own heart's lusts, to blindness of mind also, and hardness of heart ; yea, and sometimes to strong delusions that they might believe lies, and be damned. Le. xxvi. 15, 16. Am. iv. 7, 10. Ro. i. 24, 28. Ex. iv. 21; ix. 12—14. Zep. i. 17. Ro. xi. 7, 8. 2 Th. ii. 11, 12.

Q. How are sinners punished in the world to come ?—A. With a worm that never dies, and with a fire that never shall be quenched. Mar. ix. 44.

Q. Whither do sinners go to receive this punishment?—A. ' The wicked shall be turned into hell, and all the nations that forget God.' Ps. ix. 17.

Q. What is hell ?—A. It is a place and a state most fearful. Lu. xiii. 28; xvi. 28. Ac. i. 25.

Q. Why do you call it a place ?—A. Because in hell shall all the damned be confined as in a prison, in their chains of darkness for ever. Lu. xii. 5, 58; xvi. 26. Jude 6.

Q. What [kind of] a place is hell ?—A. It is a dark bottomless burning lake of fire, large enough to hold all that perish. Mat. xxii. 13. Re xx. 1, 15. Is. xxx. 35. Pr. xxvii. 20.

Q. What do you mean when you say it is a fearful state ?—A. I mean, that it is the lot of those that are cast in thither to be tormented in most fearful manner, to wit, with wrath and fiery indignation. Ro. ii. 9. He. x. 26, 27.

Q. In what parts shall they be thus fearfully tormented ?—A. In body and soul : for hell-fire shall kindle upon both beyond what now can be thought.* Mat. x. 28. Lu. xvi. 24. Ja. v. 3.

Q. How long shall they be in this condition ?— A. ' These shall go away into everlasting punishment.' Mat. xxv. 46. ' And the smoke of their torment ascendeth up for ever and ever, and they have no rest day nor night.' Re. xiv. 11. For they ' shall be punished with everlasting destruction from the presence of the Lord, and from the glory of his power.' 2 Th. i. 9.

Q. But why might not the ungodly be punished with this punishment in this world, that we might have seen it and believe ?—A. If the ungodly should

with punishment have been rewarded in this world, it would in all probability have overthrown the whole order that God hath settled here among men. For who could have endured here to have seen the flames of fire, to have heard the groans, and to have seen the tears, perhaps, of damned relations, as parents or children ? Therefore as Tophet of old was without the city, and as the gallows and gibbets are built without the towns ;† so Christ hath ordered that they who are to be punished with this kind of torment, shall be taken away : ' Take him away,' saith he (out of this world) ' and cast him into outer darkness,' and let him have his punishment there ' there shall be weeping and gnashing of teeth.' Mat. xxii. 13. Besides, faith is not to be wrought by looking into hell, and seeing the damned tormented before our eyes, but by ' hearing the word of God.' Ro. x. 17. For he that shall not believe Moses and the prophets, will not be persuaded should one come from the dead, yea should one come to them in flames to persuade them. Lu. xvi. 27—31.

Q. Are there degrees of torments in hell ?—A. Yes, for God will reward every one according to their works. ' Wo unto the wicked, it shall be ill with him, for the reward of his hands shall be given him.' Is. iii. 11.

Q. Who are like to be most punished there, men or children ?—A. The punishment in hell comes not upon sinners according to age, but sin ; so that whether they be men or children, the greater sin, the greater punishment ; ' For there is no respect of persons with God.' Ro. ii. 11. ‡

Q. How do you distinguish between great sins and little ones ?—A. By their nature, and by the circumstances that attend them.

Q. What do you mean by their nature ?—A. I mean when they are very gross in themselves. 2 Ch. xxxiii. 2. Eze. xvi. 42.

Q. What kind of sins are the greatest ?—A. Adultery, fornication, murder, theft, swearing, lying, covetousness, witchcraft, sedition, heresies, or any the like. 1 Co. vi. 9, 10. Ep. v. 3—6. Col. iii. 5, 6. Ga. v. 19—21. Re. xxi. 8.

Q. What do you mean by circumstances that attend sin ?—I mean light, knowledge, the preaching of the Word, godly acquaintance, timely caution, &c.

---

† It is a very modern custom to have the place of execution within a city—formerly they were always without—their position being still noted by the name ' Gallow Knowe,' the knoll or mound of the gallows ; ' Gallowgate,' the gate or way leading to the gallows ; and so on. Happily for the well-being of society, these exhibitions are less frequent than they formerly were.

‡ ' That servant which knew his lord's will, and prepared not himself, neither did according to his will, shall be beaten with many stripes,' Luke xii. 47.—Ed.

---

* A state of hostility to God plunges the soul into mental darkness, rage, horror, anguish, despair, and endless and unutterable misery and woe. How ought we to love the Lord Jesus for his GREAT salvation !—Ed.

Q. Will these make an alteration in the sin?—A. These things attending sinners, will make little sins great, yea greater than greater sins that are committed in grossest ignorance.

Q. How do you prove that?—A. Sodom and Gomorrah wallowed in all or most of those gross transgressions above mentioned: yea, they were said to be sinners exceedingly, they lived in such sins as may not be spoken of without blushing, and yet God swears that Israel, his church, had done worse than they, Eze. xvi. 48. and the Lord Jesus also seconds it in that threatening of his, 'I say unto you, That it shall be more tolerable for the land of Sodom in the day of judgment than for thee.' Mat. xi. 24. Lu. x. 12.

Q. And was this the reason, namely, because they had such circumstances attending them as Sodom had not?—A. Yes, as will plainly appear, if you read the three chapters above mentioned.

Q. When do I sin against light and knowledge?—A. When you sin against convictions of conscience, when you sin against a known law of God, when you sin against counsels, and dissuasion of friends, then you sin against light and knowledge. Ro. i. 32.

Q. When do I sin against preaching of the word?—A. When you refuse to hear God's ministers, or hearing them, refuse to follow their wholesome doctrine. 2 Ch. xxxvi. 16. Je. xxv. 4—7; xxxv. 15.

Q. When else do I sin against preaching of the Word?—A. When you mock, or despise, or reproach the ministers; also when you raise lies and scandals of them, or receive such lies or scandals raised;* you then also sin against the preaching of the Word, when you persecute them that preach it, or are secretly glad to see them so used. 2 Ch. xxx. 1, 10. Ro. iii. 8. Je. xx. 10. 1 Th. ii. 15, 16.

Q. How will godly acquaintance greaten my sin?—A. When you sin against their counsels, warnings, or persuasions to the contrary; also when their lives and conversations are a reproof to you, and yet against all you will sin. Thus sinned Ishmael, Esau, Eli's sons, Absalom and Judas, they had good company, good counsels, and a good life set before them by their godly acquaintance, but they sinned against all, and their judgment was the greater. Ishmael was cast away, Ge. xxi. 10. Esau hated, Ga. iv. 30. Eli's sons died suddenly, Mal. i. 2. 1 Sa. ii. 25, 34; iv. 11. Absalom and Judas were both strangely hanged. 2 Sa. xviii. Mat. xxvii.

Q. Are sins thus heightened, distinguished from others by any special name?—A. Yes; they are called rebellion, and are compared to the sin of witchcraft, 1 Sa. xv. 23. they are called wilful sins,

He. x. 26. they are called briars and thorns, and they that bring them forth are 'nigh unto cursing, whose end is to be burned.' vi. 7, 8.

Q. Are there any other things that can make little sins great ones?—A. Yes; as when you sin against the judgments of God. As for example, you see the judgments of God come upon some for their transgressions, and you go on in their iniquities; as also when you sin against the patience, long-suffering, and forbearance of God, this will make little sins great ones. Da. v. 21—24. Ro. ii. 4, 5.

Q. Did ever God punish little children for sin against him?—A. Yes; when the flood came, he drowned all the little children that were in the old world: he also burned up all the little children which were in Sodom; and because upon a time the little children at Bethel mocked the prophet as he was a going to worship God, God let loose two she-bears upon them, which tore forty and two of them to pieces. 2 Ki. ii. 23, 24.

Q. Alas! what shall we little children do?†—A. Either go on in your sins, or remember now your Creator in the days of your youth, before the evil days come. Ec. xii. 1.

Q. Why do you mock us, to bid us go on in our sins? you had need pray for us that God would save us.—A. I do not mock you, but as the wise man doth; and besides, I pray for you and wish your salvation.

Q. How doth the wise man mock us?—A. Thus; 'Rejoice, O young man, in thy youth; and let thy heart cheer thee in the days of thy youth, and walk in the ways of thine heart, and in the sight of thine eyes: but know thou, that for all these *things* God will bring thee into judgment.' Ec. xi. 9.

Q. What a kind of mocking is this?—A. Such an one as is mixed with the greatest seriousness; as if he should say, Ay, do, sinners, go on in your sins if you dare; do, live in your vanities, but God will have a time to judge you for them.

Q. Is not this just as when my father bids me be naught if I will: but if I be naught he will beat me for it?—A. Yes; or like that saying of Joshua, 'If it seem evil unto you to serve the Lord, choose you this day whom ye will serve;' serve your sins at your peril. Jos. xxiv. 15.

Q. Is it not best then for me to serve God?—A. Yes; for they that serve the devil must be where he is, and they that serve God and Christ, must be where they are. Jn. xii. 26. Mat. xxv. 41.

---

* Which is the greatest sinner; he who invents scandal, or he who encourages the inventor to retail it? If there were no receivers, there would be no thieves.—ED.

† The terms in which this question is put, shows that the little children here intended were capable of repentance and faith. That Bunyan believed, as Toplady did, the salvation of all that die in infancy by the atonement of Christ, there can be no doubt. 'In my remarks on Dr. Rowell, I testified my firm belief that the souls of all departed infants are with God in glory.' See the Introduction to Toplady's Historic Proof. —ED.

Q. But when had I best begin to serve God ?—
A. Just now: ' Remember NOW thy Creator,' NOW thou hast the gospel before thee, NOW thy heart is tender and will be soonest broken.

Q. But if I follow my play and sports a little longer, may I not come time enough ?—A. I cannot promise thee that, for there be little graves in the churchyard ; and who can tell but that thy young life is short; or if thou dost live, perhaps thy day of grace may be as short as was Ishmael's of old: read also Pr. i. 24—26.

Q. But if I stay a little longer before I turn, I may have more wit to serve God than now I have, may I not ?—A. If thou stayest longer, thou wilt have more sin, and perhaps less wit: for the bigger sinner, the bigger fool. Pr. i. 22.

Q. If I serve God sometimes, and my sin sometimes, how then ?—A. ' No man can serve two masters.' Thou canst not serve God and thy sins. Mat. vi. 24. God saith, ' My Son, give me thine heart.' Pr. xxiii. 26. Also thy soul and body are his ; but the double-minded man is forbidden to think that he shall receive any thing of the Lord. 1 Co. vi. 20. Ja. i. 7, 8.

Q. Do you find many such little children as I am, serve God ?—A. Not many ; yet some I do, Samuel served him being a child. 1 Sa. iii. 1. When Josiah was young he began to seek after the God of his father David. 2 Ch. xxxiv. 3. And how kindly did our Lord Jesus take it, to see the little children run tripping before him, and crying, Hosannah to the Son of David ? Mat. xxi. 15, 16.

Q. Then I am not like to have many companions if I thus young begin to serve God, am I ?—A. ' Strait is the gate, and narrow is the way, which leadeth unto life, and few there be that find it.' Mat. vii. 14. Yet some companions thou wilt have. David counted himself a companion of all them that love God's testimonies. Ps. cxix. 63. All the godly, though grey-headed, will be thy companions; yea, and thou shalt have either one or more of the angels of God in heaven to attend on, and minister for thee. Mat. xviii. 10.

Q. But I am like to be slighted, and despised by other little children, if I begin already to serve God, am I not ?—A. If children be so rude as to mock the prophets and ministers of God, no marvel if they also mock thee ; but it is a poor heaven that is not worth enduring worse things than to be mocked for the seeking and obtaining of. 2 Ki. ii. 23, 24.

Q. But how should I serve God ? I do not know how to worship him.—A. The true worshippers, worship God in spirit and truth. Jn. iv. 24. Phi. iii. 3.

Q. What is meant by worshipping him in the spirit ?—A. To worship him in God's Spirit and in mine own ; that is, to worship him, being wrought over in my very heart by the good Spirit of God,

to an hearty compliance with his will. Ro. i. 9 ; vi. 17. Ps. ci. 1—3.

Q. What is it to worship him in truth ?—A. To do all that we do in his worship according to his word, for his word is truth, and to do it without dissimulation. He. viii. 5. Jn. xvii. 17. Ps. xxvi. 6; cviii. 19, 20. You may take the whole thus, Then do you worship God aright, when in heart and life you walk according to his word.

Q. How must I do to worship him with my spirit and heart.—A. Thou must first get the good knowledge of him. ' And thou, Solomon my son,' said David, ' know thou the God of thy father, and serve him with a perfect heart.' 1 Ch. xxviii. 9. Mind you, he first bids know him, and then serve him with a perfect heart.

Q. Is it easy to get a true knowledge of God ?—A. No ; Thou must cry after knowledge, and lift up thy voice for understanding. ' If thou seekest her as silver, and searchest for her as for hid treasures ; then shalt thou understand the fear of the Lord, and find the knowledge of God.' Pr. ii, 4, 5.

Q. How comes it to be so difficult a thing to attain the true knowledge of God ?—A. By reason of the pride and ignorance that is in us, as also by reason of our wicked ways. Ps. x. 4. Ep. iv. 18, 19. Tit. i. 16.

Q. But do not every one profess that they know God ?—A. Yes ; but their supposed knowledge of him varieth as much as do their faces or complexions, some thinking he is this, and some that.

Q. Will you shew me a little how they vary in their thoughts about him.—A. Yes ; Some count him a kind of an heartless God, that will neither do evil nor good. Zep. i. 12. Some count him a kind of an ignorant and blind God, that can neither know nor see through the clouds. Job xxii. 13. Some again count him an inconsiderable God, not worth the enjoying, if it must not be but with the loss of this world, and their lusts. Job xxi. 9—15. Moreover, some think him to be altogether such an one as themselves, one that hath as little hatred to sin as themselves, and as little love to holiness as themselves. Ps. l. 21.

Q. Are there any more false opinions of God ?—A. Yes ; There are three other false opinions of God. 1. Some think he is all mercy and no justice, and that therefore they may live as they list. Ro. iii. 8. 2. Others think he is all justice and no mercy, and that therefore they had as good go on in their sins and be damned, as turn and be never the better. Je. ii. 25. 3. Others think he is both justice and mercy, but yet think also, that his justice is such as they can pacify with their own good works, and save themselves with their own right hand ; Job. xl. 14. contrary to these scriptures. Ha. i. 13. Is. xlv. 21.

Q. How then shall I know when I have the true

knowledge of God ?—A. When thy knowledge of him and the holy Scriptures agree.

Q. The Scriptures! Do not all false opinions of him flow from the Scriptures ?—A. No, in no wise ; it is true, men father their errors upon the Scriptures, when indeed they flow from the ignorance of their hearts. Ep. iv. 18.

Q. But how if I do not understand the holy Bible, must I then go without the true knowledge of God ?—A. His name is manifested by his Word: the Scriptures are they that testify of him. Jn. xvii. 6—8; v. 39. And they are able to make the man of God perfect in all things, and wise unto salvation through faith in Jesus Christ. 2 Ti. iii. 15, 16.

Q. But what must one that knoweth not God do, to get the knowledge of God ?—A. Let him apply his heart unto the Scriptures. Pr. xxii. 17; xxiii. 12. 'As unto a light that shineth in a dark place,' even this world, 'until the day dawn, and the day star arise in his heart.' 2 Pe. i. 19, 20.

Q. But how shall I know when I have found by the Scriptures the true knowledge of God ?—A. When thou hast also found the true knowledge of thyself. Is. vi. 5. Job xlii. 5.

Q. What is it for me to know myself ?—A. Then thou knowest thyself, when thou art in thine own eyes, a loathsome, polluted, wretched, miserable sinner; and that not anything done by thee, can pacify God unto thee.* Job xlii. 5. Eze. xx. 43, 44. Ro. vii. 24.

Of Confession of Sin.

Q. You have shewed me, if I will indeed worship God, I must first know him aright, now then to the question in hand, pray how must I worship him ?—A. In confessing unto him. Ne. ix. 1—3.

Q. What must I confess ?—A. Thou must confess thy transgressions unto the Lord. Ps. xxxii. 5.

Q. Was this the way of the godly of old ?—A. Yes; Nehemiah confessed his sins. Ne. i. 6. David confessed his sins. Ps. xxxii. 5. Daniel confessed his sins. Da. ix. 4. And they that were baptized by John in Jordan confessed their sins. Mat. iii. 6.

Q. What sins must I confess to God ?—A. All sins whatsoever : for 'He that covereth his sins shall not prosper, but whoso confesseth and forsaketh them shall have mercy.' Pr. xxviii. 13. 1 Jn. i. 9.

Q. But how if I do neither know nor remember all my sins ?—A. Thou must then search and try thy ways by the holy Word of God. La. iii. 40. Ps. lxxvii. 6.

Q. But how if I do not make this search after my sins ?—A. If thou dost not, God will; if thou dost not search them out and confess them, God will search them out and charge them upon thee, and tear thee in pieces for them. Ps. l. 21, 22.

Q. Where must I begin to confess my sins ?—A. Where God beginneth to shew thee them. Observe, then, where God beginneth with conviction for sin, and there begin thou with confession of it. Thus David began to confess, thus Daniel began to confess. 2 Sa. xii. 7—14. Da. ix. 3—9.

Q. What must I do when God hath shewed me any sin, to make right confession thereof ?—A. Thou must follow that conviction until it shall bring thee to the original and fountain of that sin, which is thine own heart. 1 Ki. viii. 38. Ps. lv. 5.

Q. Is my heart then the fountain and original of sin ?—A. Yes; 'For from within, out of the heart of men, proceed evil thoughts, adulteries, fornications, murders, thefts, covetousness, wickedness, deceit, lasciviousness, an evil eye, blasphemy, pride, foolishness. All these evil things come from within, and defile the man.' Mar. vii. 21, 23.

Q. When a man sees this, what will he think of himself ?—A. Then he will not only think but conclude, that he is an unclean thing, that his heart has deceived him, that it is most desperate and wicked, that it may not be trusted by any means, that every imagination and thought of his heart, naturally, is only evil, and that continually. Is. lxiv. 6. Pr. xxviii. 26. Is. xliv. 20. Ge. vi. 5.

Q. You have given me a very bad character of the heart, but how shall I know that it is so bad as you count it ?—A. Both by the text and by experience.

Q. What do you mean by experience ?—A. Keep thine eyes upon thy heart, and also upon God's word, and thou shalt see with thine own eyes, the desperate wickedness that is in thine heart, for thou must know sin by the law, that bidding thee do one thing, and thy heart inclining to another. Ro. vii. 7—10.

Q. May I thus then know my heart ?—A. Yes, that is something of it, especially the carnality of thy mind, 'Because the carnal mind is enmity against God; for it is not subject to the law of God, neither indeed can be.' Ro. viii. 7.

Q. Can you particularize some few things wherein the wickedness of the heart of man shews itself ?—A. Yes; by its secret hankering after sin, although the Word forbids it; by its deferring of repentance ; by its being weary of holy duties; by its aptness to forget God, by its studying to lessen and hide sin ; by its feigning itself to be better than it is; by its being glad when it can sin without being seen of men; by its hardening itself against the threatenings and judgments of God; by its desperate inclinings to unbelief, atheism, and the like.† Pr. i. 24—26. Is. xliii. 22. Mal. i. 12.

---

* The knowledge of ourselves as vile and abominable, hopeless and helpless, is an *essential* step towards our recovery. The next step that leads to heaven, and lands us there, is to 'know the only true God, and Jesus Christ whom he has sent,' as revealed in the word of truth. 'This is eternal life.'—ED.

† The unrenewed heart is the sink of sin, the fountain of

13. Ju. iii. 7. Je. ii. 32. Ps. cvi. 21. Ifo. ii. 13. Pr. xxx. 20. Je. ii. 25. Ro. i. 32; ii. 5. Zep. i. 11—13.

Q. Is there any thing else to be done in order to a right confession of sin ?—A. Yes: Let this conviction sink down into thy heart, that God sees much more wickedness in thee than thou canst see in thyself. 'If our heart condemn us, God is greater than our heart, and knoweth all things ;' 1 Jn. iii. 20. besides, he hath set thy secret sins in the light of his countenance. Ps. xc. 8.

Q. Is there any thing else that must go to a right confession of sin ?—A. Yes; In thy confessions thou must greaten and aggravate thy sin by all just circumstances.

Q. How must I do that ?—A. By considering against how much light and mercy thou hast sinned, against how much patience and forbearance thou hast sinned ; also against what warnings and judgments thou hast sinned ; and against how many of thine own vows, promises and engagements, thou hast sinned: these things heighten and aggravate sin. Ezr. ix. 10—14.

Q. But what need I confess my sins to God, seeing he knows them already ?—A. Confession of sin is necessary, for many reasons.

Q. Will you show me some of those reasons ?—A. Yes; One is, by a sincere and hearty confession of sin thou acknowledgest God to be thy Sovereign Lord, and that he hath right to impose his law upon thee. Ex. xx.

Q. Can you show me another reason ?—A. Yes; By confessing thy sin, thou subscribest to his righteous judgments that are pronounced against it. Ps. li. 3, 4.

Q. Can you show me another reason ?—A. Yes; By confessing of sin, thou showest how little thou deservest the least mercy from God.

Q. Have you yet another reason why I should confess my sins ?—A. Yes; By so doing thou showest whether thy heart loves it, or hates it. He that heartily confesseth his sin, is like him who having a thief or a traitor in his house, brings him out to condign punishment; but he that forbears to confess, is like him who hideth a thief or traitor against the laws and peace of our Lord the King.

Q. Give me one more reason why I should confess my sins to God ?—A. He that confesseth his sin, casteth himself at the feet of God's mercy, utterly condemns and casts away his own righteousness, concludeth there is no way to stand just and acquit before God, but by and through the righteousness of another; whether God is resolved to bring thee, if ever he saves thy soul. Ps. li. 1—3. 1 Jn. i. 9. Phi. iii. 6—8.

Q. What frame of heart should I be in when I confess my sins ?—A. Do it HEARTILY, and to the best of thy power thoroughly. For to feign, in this work, is abominable; to do it by the halves, is wickedness ; to do it without sense of sin cannot be acceptable. And to confess it with the mouth, and to love it with the heart, is a lying unto God, and a provocation of the eyes of his glory.

Q. What do you mean by feigning and dissembling in this work ?—A. When men confess it, yet know not what it is ; or if they think they know it, do not conclude it so bad as it is ; or when men ask pardon of God, but do not see their need of pardon ; this man must needs dissemble.

Q. What do you mean by doing it by the halves ? —A. When men confess some, but not all that they are convinced of ; or if they confess all, yet labour in their confession to lessen it. Pr. xxviii. 13. Job xxxi. 33. Or when in their confession they turn not from all sin to God, but from one sin to another. Ja. iii. 12. They turned, 'but not to the most High,' none of them did exalt him. Ho. vii. 16.

Q. What is it to confess sin without the sense of sin ?—A. To do it through custom, or tradition, when there is no guilt upon the conscience, now this cannot be acceptable.

Q. What is it to confess it with the mouth and to love it with the heart ?—A. When men condemn it with their mouth, but refuse to let it go ; Job xx. 12, 13. Je. viii. 5. when 'with their mouth they show much love, but their heart goeth after their covetousness.' Eze. xxxiii. 31.

Q. But I asked you what frame of heart I should be in, in my confessions ?—A. I have showed you how you should not be. Well, I will show you now what frame of heart becomes you in your confessions of sin. Labour by all means for a sense of the evil that is in sin.

Q. What evil is there in sin ?—A. No man with tongue can express what may by the heart be felt of the evil of sin ;* but this know, it dishonoureth God. Ro. ii. 23. It provoketh him to wrath. Ep. v. 5, 6. It damneth the soul. 2 Th. ii. 12.

Q. What else would you advise me to in this great work ?—A. When we confess sin, tears, shame, and brokenness of heart becomes us. Je. l. 4. Is. xxii. 12. Ps. li. 17. Je. xxxi. 19.

Q. What else becomes me in my confessions of sin ?—A. Great detestation of sin, with unfeigned sighs and groans, that express thou dost it heartily. Job xlii. 6. Eze. ix. 4. Je. xxxi. 9.

Q. Is here all ?—A. No ; Tremble at the word of God ; tremble at every judgment, lest it overtake

---

pollution. 'Out of the heart proceeds evil thoughts, murders, adulteries, fornications, thefts, false witness, blasphemies; these defile a man.' Create in us a clean heart, O God!—ED.

* No poor soul was more severely visited with these feelings than Bunyan. 'Now I beheld the condition of the dog and toad; and counted the state of every thing that God had made far better than this state of mine.'—Grace Abounding, No. 104.—ED.

thee; tremble at every promise, lest thou shouldest miss thereof: for, saith God, 'To this man will I look, *even to him that is* poor and of a contrite spirit, and trembleth at my word.' Is. lxvi. 2. He. iv. 1, 2.

Q. What if I cannot thus confess my sins?—A. Bewail the hardness of thy heart, keep close to the best preachers, remember that thou hangest over hell, by the weak thread of an uncertain life. And know, God counts it a great evil, not to be ashamed of, not to blush at sin. Is. lxiii. 17. Je. vi. 15; viii. 12.

Q. Are there no thanks to be rendered to God in confessions?—A. O Yes. Thank him that he hath let thee see thy sins, thank him that he hath given thee time to acknowledge thy sins; thou mightest now have been confessing in hell: thank him also that he hath so far condescended as to hear the self-bemoaning sinner, and that he hath promised, SURELY to have mercy upon such. Je. xxxi. 18—20.

Of Faith in Christ.

Q. I am glad that you have instructed me into this part of the worship of God, I pray tell me also how else I should worship him?—A. Thou must believe his word.

Q. Is that worshipping of God?—A. Yes; 'After the way which they call heresy, so worship I the God of my fathers, believing all things which are written in the law and in the prophets,' &c. Ac. xxiv. 14.

Q. Why should believing be counted a part of God's worship?—A. Because without faith it is impossible to please him. He. xi. 6.

Q. Why not possible to please him without believing?—A. Because in all true worship, a man 'must believe that God is, and *that* he is a rewarder of them that diligently seek him.' Besides, he that worships God, must also of necessity believe his word, else he cannot worship with that reverence and fear that becomes him, but will do it in a superstitious profane manner: 'For whatsoever *is* not of faith is sin.' Ro. xiv. 23.

Q. But do not all believe as you have said?—A. 'That which is born of the flesh is flesh: and that which is born of the Spirit is Spirit.' Jn. iii. 6. And again 'the children of the flesh, these *are* not the children of God: but the children of the promise are counted for the seed.' Ro. ix. 8.

Q. What do you mean by that?—A. Thou must be born twice before thou canst truly believe once. Jn. iii. 3, 5.

Q. How do you prove that?—A. Because believing is a christian act, and none are true Christians but those that are born again. But I mean by believing, believing unto salvation.

Q. Can you prove this?—A. Yes. They that believe in the name of Christ are such which are born 'not of blood, nor of the will of the flesh, nor of the will of man, but of God.' Jn. i. 13.

Q. What is believing?—A. It is such an act of a gracious soul, as layeth hold on God's mercy through Christ. Ac. xv. 11.

Q. Why do you call it an act of a gracious soul?—A. Because their minds are disposed that way, by 'the power of the Holy Ghost.' Ro. xv. 13.

Q. If such a poor sinner as I am would be saved from the wrath to come, how must I believe?—A. Thy first question should be on whom must I believe? Jn. ix. 35, 36.

Q. On whom then must I believe?—A. On the Lord Jesus Christ. Ac. xvi. 31.

Q. Who is Jesus Christ that I might believe in him?—A. He is the only begotten Son of God. Jn. iii. 16.

Q. Why must I believe on him?—A. Because he is the Saviour of the world. 2 Pe. i. 1. 1 Jn. iv. 14.

Q. How is he the Saviour of the world?—A. By the Father's designation and sending: 'For God sent not his Son into the world to condemn the world, but that the world through him might be saved.' Jn. iii. 17.

Q. How did he come into the world?—A. In man's flesh, in which flesh he fulfilled the law, died for our sins, conquered the devil and death, and obtained eternal redemption for us. Ga. iv. 4. Ro. x. 4; viii. 3. He. ii. 14, 15: vi. 20.

Q. But is there no other way to be saved but by believing in Jesus Christ?—A. 'There is none other name under heaven, given among men, whereby we must be saved;' Ac. iv. 12. and therefore 'he that believeth not, shall be damned.' Mar. xvi. 16. Jn. iii. 18, 36.

Q. What is believing on Jesus Christ?—A. It is a receiving of him with what is in him, as the gift of God to thee a sinner. Jn. i. 12.

Q. What is in Jesus Christ to encourage me to receive him?—A. Infinite righteousness to justify thee, and the Spirit without measure to sanctify thee. Is. xlv. 24, 25. Da. ix. 24. Phi. iii. 7—9. Jn. iii. 34.

Q. Is this made mine if I receive Christ?—A. Yes; If thou receive him as God offereth him to thee. Jn. iii. 16.

Q. How doth God offer him to me?—A. Even as a rich man freely offereth an alms to a beggar, and so must thou receive him. Jn. vi. 32—35.

Q. Hath he indeed made amends for sin? and would he indeed have me accept of what he hath done?—A. That he hath made amends for sin it is evident, because God, for Christ's sake, forgiveth thee. And it is as evident that he would have thee accept thereof, because he offereth it to thee, and hath sworn to give thee the utmost benefit, to wit, eternal life, if thou dost receive it; yea, and hath threatened thee with eternal damnation, if, after all this, thou shalt neglect so great salvation.

Ep. iv. 32. Ro. iii. 24. Mat. xxviii. 18—20. Ac. xiii. 32—39. He. vi. 17, 18; ii. 3. Mar. xvi. 16.

Q. But how must I be qualified before I shall dare to believe in Christ?—A. Come sensible of thy sins, and of the wrath of God due unto them, for thus thou art bid to come. Mat. xi. 28.

Q. Did ever any come thus to Christ?—A. David came thus; Ps. li. 1—3. Paul and the jailor came thus; Ac. ix. 6; xvi. 30. also Christ's murderers came thus. Ac. ii. 37.

Q. But doth it not seem most reasonable that we should first mend and be good?—A. The 'whole have no need of the physician, but they that are sick;' Christ came 'not to call the righteous, but sinners to repentance.' Mar. ii. 17.

Q. But is it not the best way, if one can, to mend first?—A. This is just as if a sick man should say, Is it not best for me to be well before I go to the physician; or as if a wounded man should say, When I am cured I will lay on the plaster.*

Q. But when a poor creature sees its vileness, it is afraid to come to Christ, is it not?—A. Yes; but without ground, for he hath said, 'Say to them *that are* of a fearful heart, Be strong, fear not:' and 'to this *man* will I look, *even to him that is* poor and of a contrite spirit, and trembleth at my word.' Is. xxxv. 4; lxvi. 2.

Q. What encouragement can be given us thus to come?—A. The prodigal came thus, and his father received him, and fell upon his neck and kissed him. Lu. xv. Thus he received the Colossians, and consequently all that are saved. Col. ii. 13.

Q. Will you give me one more encouragement?—A. The promises are so worded, that they that are scarlet sinners, crimson sinners, blasphemous sinners, have encouragement to come to him with hopes of life. Is. i. 18. Mar. iii. 28. Jn. vi. 37. Lu. xxiv. 42, 43. Ac. xiii. 26.

Q. Shall every one that believeth be saved?—A. If they believe as the Scriptures have said, if the Scriptures be fulfilled in their believing. Jn. vii. 38. Ja. ii. 23.

Q. What do you mean by that?—A. When faith, which a man saith he hath, proveth itself to be of the right kind by its acts and operations in the mind of a poor sinner. Ja. ii. 19—23.

Q. Why. are there many kinds of faith?—A. Yes. There is a faith that will stand with a heart as hard as a rock; a short-winded faith, which dureth for a while, and in time of temptation such fall away. Lu. viii. 13.

Q. Is there any other kind of faith?—A. Yes. There is a faith that hath no more life in it than hath the body of a dead man. Ja. ii. 26.

* How pointed and forcible is this illustration of the absurdity of neglecting the Physician of souls, when the malady of sin is felt. The more desperate our disease, the faster we should fly to Christ for cure.—ED.

Q. Is there yet another of these unprofitable faiths?—A. Yes. There is a faith that is of ourselves, and not of the special grace of God. Ep. ii. 8.

Q. Tell me if there be yet another?—A. There is a faith that standeth 'in the wisdom of men,' and not 'in the power of God.' 1 Co. ii. 5.

Q. Is here all?—A. No. There is a faith that seems to be holy, but it will not do, because it is not the most holy faith. 2 Pe. ii. 9. Jude 20.

Q. Alas! if there be so many kinds of faith that will not profit to salvation, how easy is it for me to be deceived?—A. It is easy indeed, and therefore the Holy Ghost doth in this thing so often caution us, 'Be not deceived.' 1 Co. vi. 9. 'Let no man deceive you,' Ep. v. 6. and 'If a man think himself to be something when he is nothing, he deceiveth himself.' Ga. vi. 3.

Q. But is there no way to distinguish the right faith from that which is wrong?—A. Yes; and that by the manner of its coming and operation.

Q. What do you mean by the manner of its coming?—A. Nay, you must make two questions of this one; that is, what is it for faith to come, and in what manner doth it come?

Q. Well then, what is it for faith to come?—A. This word, *faith comes*, supposeth thou wert once without it; it also supposeth that thou didst not fetch it whence it was; it also supposeth it hath a way of coming. Ga. iii. 23—25.

Q. That I was once without it, you intimated before, but must I take it without proof for granted?—A. I will give you a proof or two: 'God hath concluded them all in unbelief.' Ro. xi. 32. And again it is said, 'faith cometh.' Ro. x. 17. And again, the Holy Ghost insinuateth our estate to be dreadful 'before faith came.' Ga. iii. 23.

Q. Why, how is it with men, before faith comes?—A. Without faith, or before faith comes, it is impossible to please God, for whether their actions be civil or religious, they sin in all they do. The sacrifice of the wicked is an abomination, and the ploughing of the wicked is sin. Pr. xxi. 4, 27.

Q. Is not this a very sad condition?—A. Yes; but this is not all, for their present unbelief bindeth them over to wrath, by shutting them up to the law; it also draweth them away from God, and will drown them in everlasting damnation, if the grace of God prevent not. Ga. iii. 23. He. iii. 17, 18. Jn. iii. 36.

Q. What if a man saw himself in this condition?—A. There are many see themselves in this condition.

Q. How came they to see it?—A. By the preaching and hearing the Word of God. Jn. xvi. 8, 9.

Q. And what do such think of themselves?—A. They do not only think, but know that in this condition they are 'without Christ, without hope, and without God in the world.' Ep. ii. 12.

Q. Are not they happy that see not themselves

in this condition ?—A. Yes. If they have seen themselves delivered therefrom by a work of faith in their souls, else not.

Q. How do you mean ?—A. I mean if they have seen themselves delivered from this state, by being by the Word and Spirit of God implanted into the faith of Christ. Ro. xi. 17—19.

Q. Are not they happy that are never troubled with this sad sight of their condition ?—A. They are just so happy as is that man who lieth fast asleep in his house while it is on fire about his ears. Can a man be happy, that is ignorant that he is without God and Christ, and hope ? Can a man be happy that is ignorant that he is hanging over hell by the poor weak thread of an uncertain life ? For this is the state of such an one.*

Q. But may not faith come to a man without he see himself to be first in this condition ?—A. It is God's ordinary way to convince men of this their sad condition before he revealeth to them the righteousness of faith, or work faith in them to lay hold of that righteousness. Jn. xvi. 9—11. Ga. iii. 23—25.

Q. How then do you conclude of them that never saw themselves shut up by unbelief under sin and the curse of God ?—A. I will not judge them for the future, God may convert them before they die; but at present their state is miserable: for because they are shut up and held prisoners by the law, by their lusts, and by the devil, and unbelief; therefore they cannot so much as with their hearts desire that God would have mercy upon them, and bring them out of their snares and chains.

Q. Then do you count it better for a man to see his condition by nature than to be ignorant thereof? —A. Better a thousand times to see it in this world than to see it in hell fire, for he must see it there or here: now if he sees it here, this is the place of prayer; here is the preaching of the word, which is God's ordinance, to beget faith. Besides, here God applieth promises of mercy to the desolate, and Christ also hath protested that he that cometh to him he 'will in no wise cast out.' Jn. vi. 37.

Q. I am convinced that I was once without faith, and also that I cannot fetch it, but pray tell me the way of its coming ?—A. 'Faith *cometh* by hearing, and hearing by the Word of God.' Ro. x. 17.

Q. How by hearing ?—A. God mixeth it with the Word when he absolutely intendeth the salvation of the sinner. He. iv. 2. Ac. xiii. 48.

Q. And how do men hear when faith is mixed with the Word ?—A. They hear the Word, 'not *as* the word of men, but, as it is in truth, the

Word of God, which effectually worketh also in you that believe.' 1 Th. ii. 13.

Q. Pray tell me now the manner of its coming ? —A. It comes through difficulty, it comes gradually.

Q. What are the difficulties which oppose it at its coming ?—A. Sense of unworthiness, guilt of conscience, natural reason, unbelief, and arguments forged in hell, and thence suggested by the devil into the heart against it. Lu. v. 8. Mar. ix. 24. Is. vi. 5. Ro. iv. 18—21.

Q. How doth faith come gradually ?—A. Perhaps at first it is but like a grain of mustard-seed, small, and weak. Mat. xvii. 20.

Q. Will you explain it further ?—A. Faith, at first, perhaps may have its excellency lie in view only, that is, in seeing where justification and salvation is ; after that it may step a degree higher, and be able to say, it may be, or who can tell but I may obtain this salvation ? again, it may perhaps go yet a step higher and arrive to some short and transient assurance.† He. xi. 13. Joel ii. 13, 14. Zep. ii. 3. Ps. xxx. 7.

Q. But doth faith come only by hearing ?—A. It is usually begotten by the word preached, but after it is begotten, it is increased several ways. It is increased by prayer. Lu. xvii. 5. Mar. ix. 24. It is increased by christian conference. Ro. i. 12. It is increased by reading. Ro. xvi. 25, 26. It is increased by meditation. 1 Ti. iv. 12—16. It is increased by the remembrance of former experiences. Mat. xvi. 8, 9.

Q. What do these things teach us ?—A. They teach us, that the men of this world are very ignorant of, and as much without desire after faith : they neither hear, nor pray, confer, nor read, nor meditate for the sake of faith.

Q. But you said even now, that this faith was distinguished from that which profiteth not to salvation, as by the manner of its coming, so by its operation: pray what is its operation ?—A. It causeth the soul to see in the light thereof, that there is no righteousness in this world that can save the sinner. Is. lxiv. 6.

Q. How doth it give the soul this sight ?—A. By giving him to understand the law, and his own inability to fulfil it. Ga. ii. 16.

Q. And doth it always shew the soul where justifying righteousness is ?—A. Yes. It shews that justifying righteousness is only to be found in the Lord Jesus Christ, in what he hath done and suffered in the flesh. Is. xlv. 24, 25. Phi. iii. 3—9.

Q. How doth faith find this righteousness in Christ ?—A. By the word, which is therefore

---

* The awful condition of the unconverted consists in their being in a state of separation from God, insensible of that dismal state, utterly unable to extricate themselves out of it, and loathsome to God while they continue in it. Reader, do you recollect when this was *your* state; if not, what hope is there that you have passed from death unto life ?—Ed.

† The operation of faith is by steps. 'To open their eyes,' 'to turn them from darkness to light,' 'from power of Satan to God,' 'forgiveness of sins,' 'the heavenly inheritance.' Acts xxvi. 18.—Ed.

called the word of faith, because faith, by that, findeth sufficient righteousness in him. Ro. x. 6—9.

Q. How else doth it operate in the soul ?—A. It applieth this righteousness to the sinner, and also helps him to embrace it. Ro. iii. 21, 22. 1 Co. i. 30. Ga. ii. 20.

Q. How else doth it operate ?—A. By this application of Christ, the soul is quickened to life, spiritualized and made heavenly. For right faith quickeneth to spiritual life, purifies and sanctifies the heart; and worketh up the man that hath it, into the image of Jesus Christ. Col. ii. 12, 13. Ac. xv. 9. xxvi. 18. 2 Co. iii. 18.

Q. How else doth it operate ?—A. It giveth the soul peace with God through Jesus Christ. Ro. v. 1.

Q. Surely Christ is of great esteem with them that have this faith in him, is he not ?—A. Yes, Yes. Unto them therefore which believe he is precious, precious in his person, precious in his undertakings, precious in his Word. 1 Pe. ii. 7; i. 18, 19. 2 Pe. i. 3, 4.

Q. Can these people then, that have this faith, endure to have this Christ spoken against ?—A. O! No! This is a sword in their bones, and a burden that they cannot bear.* Ps. xlii. 10. Zep. iii. 19.

Q. Doth it not go near them when they see his ways and people discountenanced ?—A. Yes; and they also choose rather to be despised and persecuted with them, than to enjoy the pleasures of sin for a season. He. xi. 24, 25.

Q. Do they not pray much for his second coming ?—A. Yes, yes; they would fain see him on this side the clouds of heaven, their ' conversation is in heaven, from whence also they look for the Saviour, the Lord Jesus Christ.' Phi. iii. 20.

Q. And do they live in this world as if he were to come presently ?—A. Yes; for his coming will be glorious and dreadful, full of mercy and judgment. ' The day of the Lord will come as a thief in the night; in the which the heavens shall pass away with a great noise, and the elements shall melt with fervent heat, the earth also and the works that are therein shall be burned up. *Seeing* then *that* all these things shall be dissolved, what manner *of persons* ought we to be in *all* holy conversation and godliness.' 2 Pe. iii. 10, 11.

Of Prayer.

Q. Well, I am glad that you have shewed me that I must worship God by confession of sin,

* Under a fear lest he had spoken against Christ, Bunyan thus expresses his misery; ' I fell into a very deep pause about the most fearful state my sin had brought me to; and, lifting up my head, I saw as if the sun did grudge to give me light, and as if the very stones in the street, and tiles upon the houses, did bend themselves against me.'—*Grace Abounding*, No. 186.—Ed.

and faith in Jesus Christ: Is there any other thing a part of the true worship of God ?—A. Yes, several; I will mention only two more at this time.

Q. What are they ?—A. Prayer and self-denial.

Q. Is prayer then a part of the worship of God? —A. Yes; a great part of it.

Q. How do you prove that ?—A. ' O come let us worship and bow down: let us kneel before the Lord our maker.' Ps. xcv. 6.

Q. Is there another scripture proves it ?—A. Yes; ' Then came she and worshipped him, saying, Lord, help me.' Mat. xv. 25.

Q. What is prayer ?—A. A sincere, sensible, affectionate pouring out of the soul to God in the name of Christ for what God hath promised. Pr. xv. 8. Je. xxxi. 18, 19. Ps. xlii. 2—5. Jn. xiv. 13, 14. 1 Jn. v. 14.

Q. Doth not every body pray ?—A. No; ' The wicked, through the pride of his countenance, will not seek *after* God: God *is* not in all his thoughts.' Ps. x. 4.

Q. What will become of them that do not pray ? —A. They do not worship God, and he will destroy them; ' Pour out thy fury (said the prophet) upon the heathen, - and upon the families that call not on thy name.' Je. x. 25. Ps. lxxix. 6.

Q. But seeing God knoweth what we want, why doth he not give us what we need, without praying ?—A. His counsel and wisdom leadeth him otherwise. ' Thus saith the Lord God, I will yet *for* this be enquired of by the house of Israel, to do *it* for them.' Eze. xxxvi. 37.

Q. Why will God have us pray ?—A. Because he would be acknowledged by thee, that he is above thee, and therefore would have thee come to him as the mean come to the mighty. Thus Abraham came unto him. Ge. xviii. 27, 30.

Q. Is there another reason why I should pray ? —A. Yes. For by prayer thou acknowledgest, that help is not in thine own power. 2 Ch. xx. 6, 12.

Q. What reason else have you why I should pray ?—A. By prayer thou confessest that help is only in him. Ps. lxii. 1.

Q. What other reason have you?—A. By prayer thou confessest thou canst not live without his grace and mercy. Mat. xiv. 30. He. iv. 16.

Q. Are all that pray heard of the Lord ?—A. No; ' They looked,' that is prayed, ' but *there was* none to save; *even* unto the Lord, but he answered them not.' 2 Sa. xxii. 42.

Q. To what doth God compare the prayers which he refuseth to answer ?—A. He compareth them to the howling of a dog. Ho. vii. 14.

Q. Who be they whose prayers God will not answer ?—A. Theirs, who think to be heard for their much speaking, and vain repetition. Mat. vi. 7.

Q. Is there any other whose prayer God refuseth ?—A. Yes; There are that ask and have not, because what they ask, they would spend upon their lusts. Ja. iv. 3.

Q. Is there any other whose prayer God refuseth?—A. Yes; 'If I regard iniquity in my heart, the Lord will not hear *me.*'* Ps. lxvi. 18.

Q. Is the regarding of sin in our heart such a deadly hinderance to prayer?—A. 'Son of man,' saith God, 'these men have set up their idols in their heart, and have put the stumblingblock of their iniquity before their face; should I be enquired of at all by them? I will set my face against that man, and will make him a sign and a proverb. And I will cut him off from the midst of my people.' Eze. xiv. 3, 8.

Q. Whose prayers be they that God will hear?—A. The prayers of the poor and needy. Ps. xxxiv. 6. Is. xli. 17.

Q. What do you mean by the poor?—A. Such as have poverty in spirit. Mat. v. 3.

Q. Who are they that are poor in spirit?—A. They that are sensible of the want and necessity of all those things of God, that prepare a man to the kingdom of heaven.

Q. What things are they?—A. Faith, hope, love, joy, peace, a new heart, the Holy Ghost, sanctification. See Ja. ii. 5. 2 Th. ii. 16. Eze. xxxvi. 26, 27.

Q. What do you mean by the needy?—A. Those whose souls long and cannot be satisfied without the enjoyment of these blessed things. Ps. lxiii. 1; cxix. 20.

Q. Will God hear the prayers of such?—A. Yes; 'For he satisfieth the longing soul, and filleth the hungry soul with goodness.' Ps. cvii. 9.

Q. How shall I know that I am one of those to whom God will give these things?—A. If thou seest a beauty in them beyond the beauty of all other things. Ps. cx. 3.

Q. How else shall I know [that] he heareth me?—A. If thou desirest them for their beauty's sake. Ps. xc. 14, 17.

Q. How else should I know I shall have them?—A. When thy groanings after them are beyond expression. Ro. viii. 26.†

Q. How else should I know, and so be encouraged to pray?—A. When thou followest hard after God in all his ordinances for the obtaining of them. Is. iv. 1, 3; lxiv. 5.

Q. How else should I know?—A. When thou makest good use of that little thou hast already. Re. iii. 8.

Q. Are here all the good signs that my prayers shall be heard?—A. No; there is one more without which thou shalt never obtain.

Q. Pray what is that?—A. Thou must plead with God, the name and merits of Jesus Christ, for whose sake only God giveth thee these things. If we ask any thing in his name, he heareth us, and whatsoever you ask the Father in my name, saith Christ I will do it. Jn. xiv. 13, 14.

Q. Doth God always answer presently?—A. Sometimes he doth, and sometimes he doth not. Is. xxx. 19. Da. x. 12.

Q. Is not God's deferring, a sign of his anger?—A. Sometimes it is not, and sometimes it is.

Q. When is it no sign of his anger?—A. When we have not wickedly departed from him by our sins. Lu. xviii. 7.

Q. When is it a sign of his anger?—A. When we have backslidden, when we have not repented some former miscarriages. Ho. v. 14, 15.

Q. Why doth God defer to hear their prayers that hath not wickedly departed from him?—A. He loves to hear their voice, to try their faith, to see their importunity, and to observe how they can wrestle with him for a blessing. Ca. ii. 14. Mat. xv 22—28. Lu. xi. 5—8. Ge. xxxii. 25—28.

Q. But is not deferring to answer prayer a great discouragement to praying?—A. Though it is, because of our unbelief, yet it ought not, because God is faithful. Therefore 'men ought always *to* pray, and not to faint.'‡ Lu. xviii. 1—8.

Of Self-Denial.

Q. I am glad you have thus far granted my request: but you told me that there was another part of God's worship; pray repeat that again?—A. It is self-denial.

Q. Now I remember it well; pray how do you prove that self-denial is called a part of God's worship?—A. It is said of Abraham, that when he went to offer up his son Isaac upon the altar for a burnt-offering, which was to him a very great part of self-denial, that he counted that act of his worshipping God.

Q. Will you be pleased to read the text?—A. Yes; 'And Abraham said unto his young men, Abide ye here with the ass; and I and the lad will go yonder and worship,' &c. This now was when he was a-going to slay Isaac. Ge. xxii. 5.

Q. What is self-denial?—A. It is for a man to forsake his ALL, for the sake of Jesus Christ.

Q. Will you prove this by a scripture or two?—A. Yes; 'Whosoever he be of you that forsaketh not all that he hath, he cannot be my disciple.' Lu. xiv. 33.

---

* 'The sacrifice of the wicked *is* an abomination to the Lord; but the prayer of the upright is his delight. He loveth him that followeth after righteousness,' Prov. xv. 8, 9. That our prayers may be heard, the heart should be right with God, and our souls at peace with him through the Son of his love.—*Mason.*—ED.

† These are parts of a Christian's experience, admirably illustrated in that extraordinary book by Bunyan, 'Grace Abounding to the Chief of Sinners.'—ED.

‡ All-prevailing prayers must be offered up through the mediation of Christ, in obedience to God's command, with an eye to his glory, and for what is agreeable to his will and heavenly wisdom to grant. 'Lifting up holy hands, without wrath and doubting,' 1 Tim. ii. 8. God's service must be in faith, love, and purity of heart.—*Ryland.*—ED.

Q. Indeed this is a full place, can you give me one more ?—A. Yes; 'What things were gain to me, those I counted loss for Christ. Yea, doubtless, and I count all things *but* loss for the excellency of the knowledge of Christ Jesus my Lord: for whom I have suffered the loss of all things, and do count them *but* dung, that I may win Christ,' &c. Phi. iii. 7, 8.

Q. These two are indeed a sufficient answer to my question ; but pray will you now give me some particular instances of the self-denial of them that have heretofore been the followers of Christ?—A. Yes; Abel denied himself to the losing of his blood. Ge. iv. 8. Abraham denied himself to the losing of his country and his father's house. Ge. xii. 1—4. Moses denied himself of a crown and a kingdom, and of ease and tranquillity. He. xi. 24—27. Joseph denied himself of fleshly lusts. Ge. xxxix. 7—9.

Q. But these men each of them denied themselves but of some things, did they?—A. You see Abel lost all, his blood and all; Abraham lost his country to the hazard of his life. Ge. xii. 13. So did Moses in leaving the crown and kingdom. He. xi. 27. And Joseph in denying his mistress. Ge. xxxix. 10—15.

Q. Will you discourse a little particularly of self-denial ?—A. With all my heart.

Q. First then, pray in what spirit must this self-denial be performed ?—A. It must be done in the spirit of faith, of love, and of a sound mind. Otherwise, if a man should sell all that he hath and give to the poor, and his body to be burnt besides, it would profit him nothing. 1 Co. xiii. 1—3.

Q. Who are like to miscarry here ?—A. They whose ends in self-denial are not according to the proposals of the gospel.

Q. Who are they ?—A. They that suffer through strife and vain-glory ; or thus, they who seek in their sufferings the praise of men more than the glory of Christ, and profit of their neighbour.

Q. Who else are like to miscarry here ?—A. They that have designs like Ziba to ingratiate themselves by their pretended self-denial into the affections of the godly, and to enrich themselves by this means. 2 Sa. xvi. 1—4.

Q. Are there any other like to miscarry here ? —A. Yes. They that by denying themselves think with the Pharisee, to make themselves stand more righteous in God's eyes than others. Lu. xviii. 11, 12.

Q. Who else are in danger of miscarrying here? —A. They who have fainted in their works, they whose self-denial hath at last been overcome by self-love. Ga. iii. 4 ; vi. 9.

Q. Shall I propound a few more questions?— A. If you please.

Q. What then if a man promiseth to deny himself hereafter and not now, is not this one step to this kind of worship ?—A. No, by no means ; for the reason why this man refuseth to deny himself now, is because his heart at present sticks closer to his lusts and the world, than to God and Christ.*

Q. Can you give me a Scripture instance to make this out?—A. Yes; Esau never intended for ever to part with the blessing, he intended to have it hereafter ; but God counted his not choosing of it at present, a despising of it, and a preferring of his lusts before it: and therefore when he would, God would not, but reject both him and his tears. Ge. xxv. 30—34. He. xii. 14—16.

Q. How and if a man shall say thus, I am willing to deny myself in many things, though he cannot deny himself in all, is not this one step in this part of this worship of God ?—A. No, in no wise ; for this man doth, just like Saul, he will slay a part, and will keep a part alive ; the kingdom must be taken from him also. 1 Sa. xv.

Q. How if a man be willing to lose all but his life ?—A. He that 'will save his life shall lose it,' but he that 'will lose his life for my sake,' saith Christ, 'shall keep it unto life eternal.' Mat. xvi. 25. Jn. xii. 25.

Q. How if a man has been willing to lose all that he hath, but is not now, will not God accept of his willingness in time past, though he be otherwise now ?—A. No ; for the true disciple must deny himself daily, take up his cross daily, and go after Jesus Christ. Lu. ix. 23.

Q. But how if a man carrieth it well outwardly, so that he doth not dishonour the gospel before men, may not this be counted self-denial ?—A. No, if he be not right at heart ; for though man looketh on the outward appearance, God looketh at the heart. 1 Sa. xvi. 7.

Q. But if I be afraid my heart may deceive me in this great work, if hard things come upon me hereafter, is there no way to find out whether it will deceive me then or no ?—A. I will give you a few answers to this question, and will shew you first whose heart is like to deceive him in this work.

Q. Will you befriend me so much ?—A. Yes. 1. He that makes not daily conscience of self-denial, is very unlike to abide a disciple for times to come, if difficult. Judas did not deny himself daily, and therefore fell when the temptation came. Jn. xii. 6.

Q. Will you give me another sign ?—A. Yes. He that indulgeth any one secret lust under a profession, is not like to deny himself in all things for Christ.

Q. Who are they that indulge their lusts ?—

---

* How debased is the human heart, to delay one moment in giving up its poor all for Christ. In him dwells the fulness of the Godhead ; he has unsearchable riches of wisdom and knowledge to bestow ; all-sufficient grace and strength, to enable us to do and suffer his will ; and everlasting glory at the close of our pilgrimage.—ED.

A. They that make provision for them, either in apparel, or diet, or otherwise. Ro. xiii. 12—14. Is. iii. 6—24. Am. vi. 3—6.

Q. Who else do so ?—A. They that excuse their sins, and keep them disguised that they may not be reprehended, as Saul did, &c. 1 Sa. xv. 18—22.

Q. Who else are they that indulge their lusts ?—A. They that heap up to themselves such teachers as favour their lusts. 2 Ti. iv. 3, 4. Is. xxx. 10.

Q. Who else do indulge their sins ?—A. They that choose rather to walk by the imperfect lives of professors than by the holy Word of God : or thus, they that make the miscarriages of some good men an encouragement unto themselves to forbear to be exact in self-denial, these eat up the sins of God's people as men eat bread. Ho. iv. 7—9.

Q. Will you now shew me who are like to do this part of God's worship acceptably ?—A. Yes ; he whose heart is set against sin as sin, is like to deny himself acceptably. Ro. vii. 13, 14.

Q. Who else ?—A. He that hath the sense and savour of forgiveness of sins upon his heart. 2 Co. v. 14.

Q. Who else is like to deny himself well ?—A. He that hath his affections set upon things above, where Christ sitteth at the right hand of God. Col. iii. 1—5.

Q. Who else is like to deny himself well for Christ ?—A. He that seeth a greater treasure in self-denial, than in self-seeking. 2 Co. xii. 9—11. He. xi. 24—26.

Q. Are there none other signs of one that is like to do this part of God's worship acceptably ?—A. Yes ; he that takes up his cross daily, and makes Christ's doctrine his example. Lu. vi. 47, 48. Jn. xii. 25, 26.

Q. But how do you discover a man to be such a one ?—A. He keepeth his heart with all diligence, he had rather die than sin ; ill carriages of professors break his heart, nothing is so dear to him as the glory of Christ.* Pr. iv. 23. Nu. xi. 15. Phi. iii. 18. Ac. xx. 24.

Q. Pray, can you give me some motive to self-denial ?—A. Yes ; the Lord Jesus denied himself for thee ; what sayest thou to that ?

Q. Wherein did Christ deny himself for me ?—A. He left his heaven for thee, he denied for thy sake to have so much of this world as hath a fox or a bird, and he spilt his most precious blood for thee. Jn. vi. 38. Lu. ix. 58. 2 Co. viii. 9. Re. i. 5.

Q. Can you give another motive to self-denial ?—A. Yes ; 'What shall it profit a man, if he shall gain the whole world, and lose his own soul ?' Mar. viii. 36.

Q. But why doth God require self-denial of them that will be saved ?—A. God doth not require self-denial as the means to obtain salvation, but hath laid it down as a proof of the truth of a man's affections to God and Christ.

Q. How is self-denial a proof of the truth of a man's affections to God ?—A. In that for the sake of his service, he leaveth all his enjoyments in this world. Thus he proved Abraham's affections. Ge. xxii. 12. Thus he proved Peter's affections. Mat. iv. 18—22. and thus he proved their affection that you read of in the gospel. Lu. ix. 57—63.

Q. What reason else can you produce why God requireth self-denial ?—A. Self-denial is one of the distinguishing characters by which true Christians are manifested from the feigned ones : for those that are feigned, flatter God with their mouths, but their hearts seek themselves ; but the sincere, for the love that he hath to Christ, forsaketh all that he hath for his sake.† Ps. lxxviii. 36, 37. Eze. xxxiii. 31, 32.

Q. Is there yet another reason why God requireth self-denial of them that profess his name ?—A. Yes ; because by self-denial the power and goodness of the truths of God are made manifest to the incredulous world. For they cannot see but by the self-denial of God's people, that there is such power, glory, goodness, and desirableness in God's truth as indeed there is. Da. iii. 16, 28. Phi. i. 12, 13.

Q. Have you another reason why God requireth self-denial ?—A. Yes ; because self-denial prepareth a man, though not for the pardon of his sin, yet for that far more exceeding and eternal weight of glory, that is laid up only for them that deny all that they have for the Lord Jesus, his name, and cause in this world. 2 Co. iv. 8—10, 17. 2 Th. i. 5, 6.

Q. Before you conclude, will you give me a few instances of the severity of God's hand upon some professors, that have not denied themselves when called thereto by him ?—A. Yes, willingly ; Lot's wife for but looking behind her towards Sodom, when God called her from it, was stricken from heaven, and turned into a pillar of salt ; therefore remember Lot's wife. Ge. xix. 17, 26. Lu. xvii. 31, 32.

Q. Can you give me another instance ?—A. Yes ; Esau for not denying himself of one morsel of meat was denied a share in the blessing, and could never obtain it after, though he sought it carefully with tears. Ge. xxv. 32—34. He. xii. 16, 17.

Q. Have you at hand another instance ?—A.

---

* No tongue can utter, or heart conceive, the unspeakable reward which an unwearied, unfainting diligence in well-doing, attends the humble believer ; it begins in this world, and is consummated in endless glory.—Ed.

† Christian, you are not your own, you are bought with a price far above all the treasures of the earth. You must not do as you please, but study to do the will of your heavenly Father. The man who is bent upon doing his own will, renounces the name of Christian. Rebel against God is inscribed upon all who do not his will.—Ed.

Yes; Judas for not denying himself, lost Christ, his soul, and heaven: and is continued the great object of God's wrath among all damned souls. Jn. xii. 5, 6. Lu. xxii. 3—6. Mat. xxvi. 14—16. Ac. i. 25.

Q. Will you give me one more instance, and so conclude?—A. Yes; Ananias and Sapphira his wife, did for the want of self-denial, pull upon themselves such wrath of God, that he slew them, while they stood in the midst before the apostles. Ac. v. 1—11.

The Conclusion.

Before I wind up this discourse, I would lay down these few things for you to consider of, and meditate upon.

I. Consider, that seeing every one by nature are accounted sinners; it is no matter whether thy actual sins be little or great, few or many, thy sinful nature hath already lain thee under the curse of the law.

II. Consider, That therefore thou hast already ground for humiliation, sins to repent of, wrath to fly from, or a soul to be damned.

III. Consider, That time stays not for thee, and also that as time goes, sin increaseth; so that at last the end of thy time, and the completing of thy sin, are like to come upon thee in one moment.

IV. Bring thy last day often to thy bedside, and ask thy heart, if this morning thou wast to die, if thou be ready to die or no.

V. Know it is a sad thing to lie a dying, and to be afraid to die; to lie a dying and not to know whither thou art going; to lie a dying, and not to know whether good angels or bad must conduct thee out of this miserable world.

VI. Be often remembering what a blessed thing it is to be saved, to go to heaven, to be made like angels, and to dwell with God and Christ to all eternity.

VII. Consider how sweet the thought of salvation will be to thee when thou seest thyself in heaven, whilst others are roaring in hell.*

The Lord Jesus Christ be with thy spirit.

---

* How blessed is the hope of the Christian; full of life, power, and much assurance. The salvation by Christ is infinitely precious; it redeems the soul from all possible misery, and introduces it to the favour, love, and protection of almighty God, who will save it from the ruins of time, till possessed of the riches of eternity.—Ed.

SEASONABLE COUNSEL:

OR,

ADVICE TO SUFFERERS.

By JOHN BUNYAN.

London: Printed for Benjamin Alsop, at the Angel and Bible in the Poultry, MDCLXXXIV.

ADVERTISEMENT BY THE EDITOR.

THIS valuable treatise was first published in a pocket volume in 1684, and has only been reprinted in Whitfield's edition of Bunyan's works, 2 vols. folio, 1767.

No man could have been better qualified to give advice to sufferers for righteousness' sake, than John Bunyan: and this work is exclusively devoted to that object. Shut up in a noisome jail, under the iron hand of persecution, for nearly thirteen years, in the constant fear of being hanged as a malefactor, for refusing conformity to the national liturgy, he well knew what sufferings were, and equally well did he know the sources of consolation. It was wisely ordered by Divine Providence, that before the king pardoned him, he had a legal return under the hand and seal of the sheriff of Bedfordshire, certifying the reasons of this frightful imprisonment. This is entered in the minutes of the Privy Council on the 8th and 15th of May, 1672; and it proves that he was thus cruelly punished for 'being at conventicles for nonconformity' and for no other cause. In this 'Advice' we find his opinion on the origin of persecution—the instruments—the motives—its cruelty—with cautions, counsels, and support to the persecuted. He considers persecution a strange anomaly,—'The reason is that Christianity is a harmless thing—that be it never so openly professed it hurts no man.' Simple-hearted, honest John, thou dreamest. What wouldst thou have thought of a system by which all would have been taught to tag their laces and mend their own pots and kettles? What would have become of thy trade as a brazier? Christianity teaches all mankind not to trust in those empirics who profess to cure souls for Peter's pence, tithes, mortuaries, and profits; but to go by themselves to the Great Physician, and he will pour in his wine and oil, his infallible remedies for a sin-sick soul, without money and without price. To Bunyan this was not only harmless to others, but the most boundless mercy that God could bestow upon man. What could be more destructive to the blessed hierarchy of popes, cardinals, archbishops, bishops, deans, prebends, canons, and the splendid tribe of mere hireling ministers? A system by which all their services are dispensed with, and priestly and prelatic pride is levelled with the dust. Can we wonder that those who preached the holy, humbling, self-denying doctrines of the cross, were persecuted to the death? Bunyan's opinion is, that Satan is the author of persecution, by which he intended to root out Christianity. The whirlwind and the tempest drives away those who are not rooted and grounded in the faith, some of whom may have stood like stately cedars until the trying time of trial came. But the humble Christian in such a season takes deeper root—a stronger grasp. Faith, his anchor, is sure and steadfast; it enters eternity and heaven, where Satan can find no entrance to disturb its hold. In persecution, men are but the devil's tools, and little think that they are doing his drudgery. p. 696.

The man of God declares the truth in plain terms, 'No one is a Christian except he is born of God by the anointing of the Holy One.' Carnal men cannot endure this; and then 'the game begins,' how such troublesome fellows may be put out of the way, and their families be robbed of their possessions to enrich the persecutors. p. 712. 'The holy places, vestures, gestures—the shows and outward greatness of false religion, are in danger.' Their sumptuous ceremonies, glorious ornaments, new-fashioned carriages,* 'will fall before the simplicity and majesty of truth.' p. 713. The Christian falls out with sin at home, and then with sinful ceremonies in divine worship. With him all that is not prescribed in the word of God is forbidden. Sentiments like these are a blow at the root of superstition with all its fraudful emoluments. Hence the storms of persecution which fall on the faithful followers of Christ. Antichrist declares the excellency of human inventions to supply what he considers defects in God's system.

Such is the mad folly of the human heart! Dust and ashes find fault with a system which is

---

* Not equipages to ride in, but dainty formalities.—ED.

the perfection of wisdom, mercy, and love. And such their infatuation, that 'none must be suffered to live and breathe that refuseth conformity thereto.' p. 713. Mr. Bunyan's cautions and counsels are full of peace—'submission to the powers that be.' Pray for the persecutor—return good for his evil. He is in the hand of God, who will soon level him with the dust, and call his soul to solemn judgment. Although the sufferer's cause is good, do not run yourself into trouble—Christ withdrew himself—Paul escaped by being lowered down the city wall in a basket. If they persecute you in one city, flee to another. 'A minister can quickly pack up and carry his religion with him, and offer what he knows of his God to another people.' p. 714. God is the support of his persecuted ones. 'His power in holding up some, his wrath in leaving of others; his making of shrubs to stand, and his suffering of cedars to fall; his infatuating of the counsels of men, and his making of the devil to outwit himself; his giving of his presence to his people, and his leaving of his foes in the dark;

his discovering the uprightness of the hearts of his sanctified ones, and laying open the hypocrisy of others, is a working of spiritual wonders in the day of his wrath, and of the whirlwind and storm.' p. 694. 'Alas! we have need of these bitter pills at which we so much winch and shuck. The physician has us in hand. May God by these try and judge us as he judges his saints, that we may not be condemned with the world.' Such were the feelings of John Bunyan after his long sufferings; they are the fruits of a sanctified mind. Reader, great are our mercies—the arm of the persecutor is paralysed by the extension of the knowledge of Christ. Still we have to pass through taunts and revilings, and sometimes the loss of goods; but we are saved from those awful trials through which our pilgrim forefathers passed. May our mercies be sanctified, and may grace be bestowed upon us in rich abundance, to enable us to pity and forgive those sects who, in a bye-gone age, were the tools of Satan, and whose habitations were full of cruelty.—GEO. OFFOR.

TO THE CHRISTIAN READER.

BELOVED, I thought it convenient, since many at this day are exposed to sufferings, to give my advice touching *that* to thee. Namely, that thou wouldest take heed to thyself, and keep thy soul diligently, and not suffer thyself to be entangled in those snares that God hath suffered to be laid in the world for some. Beware of 'men' in the counsel of Christ 'for they will deliver you up.' Mat. x. 17. Keep thou therefore within the bounds of uprightness and integrity towards both God and man: for that will fortify, that will preserve thee, if not from, yet under the rage of men, in a comfortable and quiet frame of heart. Wherefore do that, and that only, that will justify thy innocency, and that will help thee, not with forced speech, but with good conscience, when oppressed, to make thy appeals to God, and to the consciences of all men.

This is the advice that, I thank God, I have taken myself: for I find that there is nothing, next to God and his grace by Christ, that can stand one in such stead, as will a good and harmless conscience.*

I hope I can say that God has made me a Christian: and a Christian must be a harmless man, and to that end, must embrace nothing but harmless principles. A Christian's business, as a Christian,

is to believe in Jesus Christ, and in God the Father by him; and to seek the good of all about him, according as his place, state and capacity in this world will admit, not meddling with other men's matters, but ever following that which is good.

A Christian is a child of the kingdom of God, and that kingdom, take it as it begins in grace, or as it is perfected in glory, is not of this world but of that which is to come: and though men of old, as some may now, be afraid of that kingdom: yet that kingdom will hurt no man, neither with its principles, nor by itself. To instance somewhat. Faith in Christ: what harm can that do? A life regulated by a moral law, what hurt is in that? Rejoicing in spirit for the hope of the life to come by Christ, who will that harm? Nor is the instituted worship of our Lord of any evil tendency. Christianity teaches us also to do our enemies good, to 'Bless them that hate us, and to pray for them that despitefully use us and persecute us,' and what evil can be in that? This is the sum of the christian religion, as by the word may be plainly made appear: wherefore I counsel thee to keep close to these things, and touch with nothing that jostleth therewith.

Nor do thou marvel, thou living thus, if some should be so foolish as to seek thy hurt, and to afflict thee, because thy works are good. 1 John iii. 12, 13. For there is need that thou shouldest at sometimes be in manifold temptations, thy good

---

* 'A good and harmless conscience;' not as the procuring cause of confidence in God's tender care of us, but as the strong evidence of our election and regeneration.—ED.

and innocent life notwithstanding. 1 Pe. 1. 6. For, to omit other things, there are some of the graces of God that are in thee, that as to some of their acts, cannot shew themselves, nor their excellency, nor their power, nor what they can do : but as thou art in a suffering state. Faith and patience, in persecution, has that to do, that to shew, and that to perform, that cannot be done, shewed, nor performed any where else but there. There is also a patience of hope ; a rejoicing in hope, when we are in tribulation, that is, over and above that which we have when we are at ease and quiet. That also that all graces can endure, and triumph over, shall not be known, but when, and as we are in a state of affliction. Now these acts of our graces are of that worth and esteem with God, also he so much delighteth in them : that occasion through his righteous judgment, must be ministered for them to shew their beauty, and what bravery* there is in them.

It is also to be considered that those acts of our graces, that cannot be put forth, or shew themselves in their splendour, but when we christianly suffer, will yield such fruit to those whose trials call them to exercise, that will, in the day of God, abound to their comfort, and tend to their perfection in glory. 1 Pe. i. 7. 2 Cor. iv. 17.

Why then should we think that our innocent lives will exempt us from sufferings, or that troubles shall do us such harm ? For verily it is for our present and future good that our God doth send them upon us. I count therefore, that such things are necessary for the health of our souls, as bodily† pains and labour are for [the health of] the body. People that live high, and in idleness, bring diseases upon the body: and they that live in all fulness of gospel-ordinances, and are not exercised with trials, grow gross, are diseased and full of bad humours in their souls. And though this may to some seem strange : yet our day has given us such an experimental proof of the truth thereof, as has not been known for some ages past.

Alas! we have need of those bitter pills, at which we so winch and shuck :‡ and it will be well if at last we be purged as we should thereby. I am sure we are but little the better as yet, though the physician has had us so long in hand. Some bad humours may possibly ere long be driven out: but at present the disease is so high, that it makes some professors fear more a consumption will be made in their purses by these doses, than they

desire to be made better in their souls thereby. I see that I still have need of these trials ; and if God will by these judge me as he judges his saints, that I may not be condemned with the world, I will cry, Grace, grace for ever.

The consideration also that we have deserved these things, much§ silences me as to what may yet happen unto me. I say, to think that we have deserved them of God, though against men we have done nothing, makes me lay my hand upon my mouth, and causes me to hold my tongue. Shall we deserve correction? And be angry because we have it! Or shall it come to save us? and shall we be offended with the hand that brings it! Our sickness is so great that our enemies take notice of it; let them know too that we also take our purges patiently. We are willing to pay for those potions that are given us for the health of our body, how sick soever they make us: and if God will have us pay too for that which is to better our souls, why should we grudge thereat? Those that bring us these medicines have little enough for their pains : for my part, I profess, I would not for a great deal, be bound, for their wages, to do their work. True, physicians are for the most part chargeable, and the niggards are too loth to part with their money to them : but when necessity says they must either take physic, or die : of two evils they desire to choose the least. Why, affliction is better than sin, and if God sends the one to cleanse us from the other, let us thank him, and be also content to pay the messenger.

And thou that art so loth to pay for thy sinning, and for the means that puts thee upon that exercise of thy graces, as will be for thy good hereafter : take heed of tempting of God lest he doubleth this potion unto thee. The child, by eating of raw fruit, stands in need of physic, but the child of a childish humour refuseth to take the potion, what follows but a doubling of the affliction, to wit, frowns, chides, and further threatenings and a forcing of the bitter pills upon him. But let me, to persuade thee to lie down and take thy potion, tell thee, it is of absolute necessity, to wit, for thy spiritual and internal health. For, *First*, Is it better that thou receive judgment in this world, or that thou stay for it to be condemned with the ungodly in the next? *Second*, Is it better that thou shouldest, as to some acts of thy graces, be foreign, and a stranger, and consequently that thou shouldest lose that far more exceeding, and eternal weight of glory that is prepared as the reward thereof ? or that thou shouldest receive it at the hand of God, when the day shall come that every man shall have praise of him for their doings? *Third*, And I say again, since chastisements are a sign of sonship, a

---

* 'Bravery;' magnificence or excellence. 'Like a stately ship, with all her bravery on, and tackle trim, sails filled,' &c. —*Samson Agonistes.*—ED.

† 'Bodily pains;' bodily industry or painstaking.—ED.

‡ 'Winch;' to wince or kick with impatience. 'Shuck;' to shrug up the shoulders, expressive of dislike or aversion. —ED.

§ 'Much;' in a great degree.

token of love: and the contrary a sign of bastardy, and a token of hatred. He. xii. 6—8. Hos. iv. 14. Is it not better that we bear those tokens and marks in our flesh that bespeak us to belong to Christ, than those that declare us to be none of his? For my part, God help me to choose rather to suffer affliction with the people of God, than to enjoy the pleasures of sin for a season: and God of his mercy prepare me for his will. I am not for running myself into sufferings, but if godliness will expose me to them, the Lord God make me more godly still: for I believe there is a world to come.

But, christian reader, I would not detain thee from a sight of those sheets in thy hand: only let me beg of thee, that thou wilt not be offended either with God, or men, if the cross is laid heavy upon thee. Not with God, for he doth nothing without a cause, nor with men, for they are the hand of God: and will they, nill they;* they are the servants of God to thee for good. Ps. xvii. 14. Jer. xxiv. 5. Take therefore what comes to thee from God by them, thankfully. If the messenger that brings it is glad that it is in his power to do thee hurt, and to afflict thee; if he skips for joy at thy calamity: be sorry for him; pity him, and pray to thy Father for him: he is ignorant and understandeth not the judgment of thy God, yea he sheweth by this his behaviour, that though he, as God's ordinance, serveth thee by afflicting of thee: yet means he nothing less than to destroy thee: by the which also he prognosticates before thee that he is working out his own damnation by doing of thee good. Lay therefore the woful state of such to heart, and render him that which is good for his evil; and love for his hatred to thee; then shalt thou shew that thou art acted by a spirit of holiness, and art like thy heavenly Father. And be it so, that thy pity and prayers can do such an one no good, yet they must light some where, or return again, as ships come loaden from the Indies, full of blessings into thine own bosom.

And besides all this, is there nothing in dark providences, for the sake of the sight and observation of which, such a day may be rendered lovely, when it is upon us. Is there nothing of God, of

his wisdom and power and goodness to be seen in thunder, and lightning, in hailstones? in storms? and darkness and tempests? Why then is it said, he 'hath his way in the whirlwind and in the storm.' Na. i. 3. And why have God's servants of old made such notes, and observed from them such excellent and wonderful things. There is that of God to be seen in such a day as cannot be seen in another. His power in holding up some, his wrath in leaving of others; his making of shrubs to stand, and his suffering of cedars to fall; his infatuating of the counsels of men, and his making of the devil to outwit himself; his giving of his presence to his people, and his leaving of his foes in the dark; his discovering the uprightness of the hearts of his sanctified ones, and laying open the hypocrisy of others, is a working of spiritual wonders in the day of his wrath, and of the whirlwind and storm. These days! these days are the days that do most aptly give an occasion to Christians, of any, to take the exactest measures and scantlings of ourselves. We are apt to overshoot, in days that are calm, and to think ourselves far higher, and more strong than we find we be, when the trying day is upon us. The mouth of Gaal and the boasts of Peter were great and high before the trial came, but when that came, they found themselves to fall far short of the courage they thought they had. Jud. ix. 38.

We also, before the temptation comes, think we can walk upon the sea, but when the winds blow, we feel ourselves begin to sink. Hence such a time is rightly said to be a time to try us, or to find out what we are, and is there no good in this? Is it not this that rightly rectifies our judgment about ourselves, that makes us to know ourselves, that tends to cut off those superfluous sprigs of pride and self-conceitedness, wherewith we are subject to be overcome? Is not such a day, the day that bends us, humbleth us, and that makes us bow before God, for our faults committed in our prosperity? and yet doth it yield no good unto us? we could not live without such turnings of the hand of God upon us. We should be overgrown with flesh, if we had not our seasonable winters. It is said that in some countries trees will grow, but will bear no fruit, because there is no winter there. The Lord bless all seasons to his people, and help them rightly to behave themselves, under all the times that go over them.

Farewell. I am thine to serve thee in the gospel,

JOHN BUNYAN.

---

* 'Will they, nill they;' nillan, a Saxon word, meaning 'not will' or contrary to the will—whether with or against their will. 'Neede hath no law; *will I, or nill I,* it must be done.' —*Damon and Pathias,* 1571.

' If now to man and wife to will and nill
The self-same thing, a note of concord be,
I know no couple better can agree.'—*Ben Jonson.*—ED.

ADVICE TO SUFFERERS.

'WHEREFORE LET THEM THAT SUFFER ACCORDING TO THE WILL OF GOD, COMMIT THE KEEPING OF THEIR SOULS *TO HIM* IN WELL DOING, AS UNTO A FAITHFUL CREATOR.'—1 PET. IV. 19.

THIS epistle was written to saints in affliction, specially those of the circumcision, for whom this Peter was an apostle. And it was written to them to counsel, and comfort them in their affliction. To counsel them as to the cause, for which they were in afflictions, and as to the right management of themselves, and their cause, under their affliction. To comfort them also both with respect to their present help from God, and also with reference to the reward that (they faithfully continuing to the end) should of God be bestowed upon them: all which we shall have occasion, more distinctly, to handle in this following discourse.

The text is a conclusion, drawn from the counsel and comfort which the apostle had afore given them in their suffering state. As who should say, my brethren, as you are now afflicted, so sufferings are needful for you, and therefore profitable and advantageous: wherefore be content to bear them. And that you may indeed bear them with such christian contentedness, and patience as becomes you; commit the keeping of your souls to your God as unto a faithful Creator. 'Let them that suffer according to the will of God, commit the keeping of their souls *to him* [in well doing,] as unto a faithful Creator.'

In this conclusion, therefore, we have three things very fit for sufferers to concern themselves with. FIRST, A direction to a duty of absolute necessity. SECOND, A description of the persons, who are unto this, so necessary a duty, directed. THIRD, An insinuation of the good effect that will certainly follow to those that after a due manner shall take this blessed advice.

The duty so absolutely necessary is, that sufferers 'commit the keeping of their souls to God.' The sufferers here intended, are those 'that suffer according to the will of God.' The good insinuated, that will be the effect of our true doing of this, is, we shall find God 'a faithful Creator.'

[FIRST—THE DUTY TO WHICH SUFFERERS ARE DIRECTED.]

We will first begin with the duty, that sufferers are here directed to, namely, the committing of their souls to God. 'Let them - commit the keeping of their souls to him, in well doing.' And I find two things in it that first call for

explaining before I proceed. 1. What we must here understand by 'the soul.' 2. What by 'committing' the soul to God.

1. For the first: 'The soul,' here, is to be taken for that most excellent part of man, that dwelleth in the body; that immortal, spiritual substance, that is, and will be capable of life, and motion, of sense and reason; yea, that will abide a rational being, when the body is returned to the dust as it was. This is that great thing, that our Lord Jesus intends, when he bids his disciples in a day of trial, fear him that can destroy both body and soul in hell. Lu. xii. 5. That great thing, I say, that he there cautions them to take care of. According to Peter here, 'Let them commit the keeping of their soul to him in well doing.'

2. Now to 'commit' this soul to God, is to carry it to him, to lift it to him, upon my bended knees, and to pray him for the Lord Jesus Christ's sake, to take it into his holy care, and to let it be under his keeping. Also, that he will please to deliver it from all those snares that are laid for it, betwixt this and the next world, and that he will see that it be forthcoming, safe and sound, at the great and terrible judgment, notwithstanding so many have engaged themselves against it. Thus David committed his soul to God, when he said 'Arise, O Lord, disappoint him, cast him down: deliver my soul, O Lord, from the wicked, *which is* thy sword.' Ps. xvii. 13. And again, 'Be pleased, O Lord, to deliver me: O Lord, make haste to help me. Let them be ashamed and confounded together that seek after my soul to destroy it.' Ps. xl. 13, 14.

Thus, I have shewed you what the soul is, and what it is to commit the soul to God. This then is the duty that the apostle here exhorteth the sufferers to, namely, to carry their soul to God, and leave it with him while they engage for his name in the world. Now from the apostle's exhortation to this great duty, I will draw these following conclusions.

Conclusion First, That when persecution is raised against a people, there is a design laid for the ruin of those people's souls. This, I say, doth naturally follow from the exhortation. Why else, need they to commit the keeping of their souls to God. For by this word, 'Unto God to keep them,' is suggested; there is that would destroy them, and that *therefore* persecution is raised against them. I am not so uncharitable, as to think, that persecuting men design this.* But I verily believe

---

* How little do persecutors imagine that they are mere

that the devil doth design this, when he stirs them up to so sorry a work. In times of trial, says Peter, 'your adversary the devil walketh about as a roaring lion, seeking whom he may devour.' 1 Pe. v 8.

Alas! men in their acts of this nature, have designs that are lower, and of a more inferior rank. Some of them look no higher than revenge upon the carcass; than the spoiling of their neighbour of his estate, liberty, or life; than the greatening of themselves in this world, by the ruins of those that they have power to spoil. Their 'possessors slay them, and hold themselves not guilty: and they that sell them say, Blessed be the Lord, for I am rich.' Zec. xi. 5.

Ay! But Satan will not be put off thus: it is not a bag of money, or the punishing of the carcass of such a people, that will please or satisfy him. It is the soul that he aims at; the ruin of the precious soul that he hath bent himself to bring to pass. It is this therefore that Peter here hath his heart concerned with. As, who should say, My brethren, are you troubled and persecuted for your faith? look to it, the hand of Satan is in this thing, and whatever men drive at by doing as they do, the devil designs no less than the damnation of your souls. Ware hawk, saith the falconer, when the dogs are coming near her: especially if she be too much minding of her belly, and too forgetful of what the nature of the dog is. Beware Christian, take heed Christian; the devil is desirous to have thee. And who could better give this exhortation than could Peter himself. Who for not taking heed as to this very thing, had like by the devil to have been swallowed up alive: as is manifest to them that heedfully read, and consider how far he was gone, when that persecution was raised against his Master. Lu. xxii.

When a tyrant goes to dispossess a neighbouring prince of what is lawfully his own: the men that he employeth at arms to overcome, and get the land, they fight for half-crowns, and the like, and are content with their wages: But the tyrant is for the kingdom, nothing will serve him but the kingdom.* This is the case: Men when they persecute, are for the stuff, but the devil is for the soul, nor will any thing less than that satisfy him. Let him then that is a sufferer 'commit the

keeping of his soul to God:' lest stuff, and soul, and all be lost at once.

Conclusion Second, A second conclusion that followeth upon these words, is this: That sufferers, if they have not a care, may be too negligent as to the securing of their souls with God, even when persecution is upon them. For these words, as they are an instruction, so they are an awakening instruction; they call as to people in danger; as to people, not so aware of the danger; or as unto a people that forget, too much, that their souls, and the ruin of them, are sought after by Satan, when trouble attends them for the gospel sake. As, who should say, when troubles are upon you for the gospel's sake, then take heed that you forget not to commit your souls to the keeping of God. We are naturally apt with that good man Gideon, to be threshing out our wheat, that we may hide it from the Midianites. Ju. vi. 11. But we are not so naturally apt to be busying ourselves to secure our souls with God. The reason is, for that we are more flesh than spirit, and because the voice of the world makes a bigger sound in our carnal mind, than the word of God doth. Wherefore Peter, here, calls upon us as upon men of forgetful minds, saying, Let them that suffer according to the will of God, have a care of their souls, and take heed, that the fears of the loss of a little of this world, do not make them forget the fear of the losing of their souls. That sufferers are subject to this, may appear by the stir and bustle that at such a time they make to lock all up safe that the hand of man can reach,† while they are cold, chill, remiss, and too indifferent about the committing of their soul to God to keep it. This is seen also, in that many, in a time of trouble for their profession, will study more to deceive themselves by a change of notions, by labouring to persuade their consciences to admit them to walk more at large, by hearkening to opinions that please and gratify the flesh, by adhering to bad examples, and taking evil counsels, than they will to make straight steps for their feet: and to commit the keeping of their souls to God. What shall I say, have there not been many, that so long as peace has lasted, have been great swaggerers for religion, who yet so soon as the sun has waxed warm, have flagged, have been discontented, offended, and turned away from him that speaketh from heaven? All which is because men are naturally apt to be more concerned for their goods, carnal peace, and a temporal life, than they are about

---

tools for the devil to work with, whether they are harassing Christians by taking their goods, or are hunting down their liberties or lives. All works together for good to the Christian, but for unutterable woe to the persecutor. God give them repentance.—ED.

* Wicked men sell themselves to do the devil's work. How degrading to the dignity of man! Enlisting under a foreign prince to destroy their own nation, and in so doing to destroy themselves. For an account of the atrocities and horrors of this war, read the history of the Waldenses.—ED.

† This frequently happened. In Bedford, Nic. Hawkins attended a meeting, and was fined two pounds; but when the harpies went to take away his goods, finding that 'they had been removed beforehand, and his house visited with the small pox, the officers declined entering.'—*Persecution in Bedford,* 1670, p. 6.—ED.

securing of their souls with God. Wherefore I say, these words are spoken to awaken us to the consideration of soul-concerns, and how that should be safely lodged under the care, protection, and mercy of God, by our committing of it to him, for that purpose, by Jesus Christ our Lord.

Conclusion Third, Another conclusion that followeth upon this exhortation, is this: That persecution doth, sometimes, so hotly follow God's people, as to leave them nothing but a soul to care for. They have had no house, no land, no money, no goods, no life, no liberty, left them to care for. ALL IS GONE BUT THE SOUL. Goods have been confiscated, liberty has been in irons, the life condemned, the neck in a halter, or the body in the fire. So then all, to such, has been gone, and they have had nothing left them to care for, but their soul. 'Let them commit the keeping of their soul to God.' This conclusion, I say, doth naturally flow from the words. For that the apostle here doth make mention only of the soul, as of that which is left, as of that which yet remains to the sufferer of all that ever he had. Thus they served Christ; they left him nothing but his soul to care for. Thus they served Stephen; they left him nothing but his soul to care for, and they both cared for that, 'Father, into thy hands I commend my spirit,' said Jesus. Lu. xxiii. 46. And, 'Lord Jesus, receive my spirit,' said Stephen. Ac. vii. 59. As for all other things, they were gone. They parted the very clothes of Christ among themselves before his face, even while he did hang pouring out his life before them, upon the tree. 'They parted my garments among them,' said he, 'and upon my vesture did they cast lots.' Mat. xxvii. 35. Mar. xv. 24. Jn. xix. 24. This also has oftentimes been the condition of later Christians, all has been gone, they have been stript of all, nothing has been left them but 'soul' to care for. Job said that he had escaped with the skin of his teeth; and that is but a little: but he doth not escape with so much, that loses all that he has, life and all, we now except the soul. But,

Conclusion Fourth, Another thing that followeth from the words is this; namely, That when the devil and wicked men have done what they could, in their persecuting of the godly; they have yet had their souls at their own dispose.* They have not been able to rob them of their souls, they are not able to hurt their souls. The soul is not in their power to touch, without the leave of God, and of him whose soul it is. 'And fear not them,' saith Christ, 'which kill the body, but are not able to kill the soul.' Mat. x. 28. This, I say, lies clear also in the text; for the exhortation supposes, that whatever the sufferers, there made mention of, had

lost, they had yet their souls at their own dispose. Let them that suffer, even to the loss of goods, liberty, or life, 'commit the keeping of their souls to God.' As, who should say, though the enemy hath reached them to their all, and stripped them of their all, yet I know, that their soul is not among that all: For their soul is yet free from them, at liberty, and may be disposed of, even as the sufferer will. Wherefore, let him commit the keeping of his soul to God, lest he also through his negligence or carelessness be also spoiled of that. The sufferer, therefore, hath his soul at his own dispose, he may give that away to God Almighty, in spite of all that the devil and the world can do. He may, indeed, see men parting his land, his household stuff, yea, his very raiment among themselves, but they cannot so dispose of his soul.† They 'have no more that they can do.' Lu. xii. 4.

Conclusion Fifth, Another conclusion that followeth from these words is this, That a man, when he is a sufferer, is not able to secure his own soul from the hand of hell by any other means, but by the committing of the keeping thereof to God. Do you suffer? Are you in affliction for your profession? Then keep not your soul in your own hand, for fear of losing that with the rest. For no man 'can keep alive his own soul.' Ps. xxii. 29. No, not in the greatest calm; no, not when the lion is asleep: how then should he do it at such a time, when the horrible blast of the terrible ones shall beat against his wall. The consideration of this was that that made holy Paul, who was a man upon whom persecution continually attended, commit his soul to God. Ac. xx. 22—24. 2 Ti. i. 12. God, as I shall shew you by and by, is he, and he alone that is able to keep the soul, and deliver it from danger. Man is naturally a self-deceiver, and therefore is not to be trusted, any farther than as the watchful eye of God is over him. But as to his soul, he is not to be trusted with that at all, that must be wholly committed to God, left altogether with him; laid at his feet, and he also must take the charge thereof, or else it is gone, will be lost, and will perish for ever and ever. Wherefore it is a dangerous thing for a man that is a sufferer, to be a senseless man, as to the danger that his soul is in, and a prayerless man, as to the committing of the keeping of it to God. For he that is such, has yet his soul, and the keeping thereof, in his own deceitful hand. And so has he also that stays himself upon his friends, upon his know-

---

* 'Dispose;' power, disposal. 'All that is mine, I leave at thy dispose.'—*Shakspeare.*—ED.
VOL. II.

† In Ireland, whole provinces were desolated, both by Protestants and Papists, with a ferocity scarcely credible. In England, the church awfully tormented their Christian dissenters, to whom their Lord's words must have been peculiarly consoling: 'Fear not them which kill the body.' Did they suffer? How holy were their enjoyments!—ED.

4 T

ledge, the promise of men, or the mercy of his enemies, or that has set in his mind a bound to himself, how far he will venture for religion, and where he will stop. This is the man that makes not God his trust, and that therefore will surely fall in the day of his temptation. Satan, who now hunteth for the precious soul to destroy it, has power, as well as policy, beyond what man can think. He has power to blind, harden, and to make insensible, the heart. He also can make truth in the eyes of the suffering man, a poor, little, and insignificant thing. Judas had not committed the keeping of his soul to God, but abode in himself, and was left in his tabernacle: and you by and by see what a worthy price he set upon himself, his Christ, and heaven, and all. All to him was not now worth thirty pieces of silver.

And as he can make truth in thy esteem to be little, so he can make sufferings great, and ten times more terrible, than he that hath committed the keeping of his soul to God shall ever find them. A gaol shall look as black as hell, and the loss of a few stools and chairs, as bad as the loss of so many bags of gold.* Death for the Saviour of the world, shall seem to be a thing both unreasonable and intolerable. Such will choose to run the hazard of the loss of a thousand souls, in the way of the world, rather than the loss of one poor, sorry, transitory life for the holy Word of God. But the reason, as I said, is, they have not committed the keeping of their soul to God. For he that indeed has committed the keeping of his soul to that great one, has shaken his hands of all things here. Has bid adieu to the world, to friends, and life: and waiteth upon God in a way of close keeping to his truth, and walking in his ways, having counted the cost, and been persuaded to take what cup God shall suffer the world to give him for so doing.

Conclusion Sixth, Another conclusion that followeth from these words is, That God is very willing to take the charge and care of the soul (that is committed unto him) of them that suffer for his sake in the world. If this were not true, the exhortation would not answer the end. What is intended by, 'Let him commit the keeping of his soul to God,' but that the sufferer should indeed leave that great care with him; but if God be not willing to be concerned with such a charge, what bottom† is there for the exhortation? But the exhortation

has this for its bottom, therefore God is willing to take the charge and care of the soul of him that suffereth for his name in this world. 'The Lord redeemeth the soul of his servants: and none of them that trust in him shall be desolate.' Ps. xxxiv. 22. 1 Sa. xxv. 28, 29. None, not one that committeth his soul to God's keeping in a way of well doing, but shall find him willing to be concerned therewith.

Ay, this, saith the sufferer, if I could believe this, it would rid me of all my fears. But I find myself engaged for God, for I have made a profession of his name, and cannot arrive to this belief that God is willing to take the charge and care of my soul. Wherefore I fear, that if trials come so high, as that life, as well as estate, must go, that both life, and estate, and soul, and all will be lost at once.

Well, honest heart, these are thy fears, but let them fly away, and consider the text again, 'Let them that suffer according to the will of God, commit the keeping of their souls *to him*, - as unto a faithful creator.' These are God's words, Christ's words, and the invitation of the Holy Ghost. When, therefore, thou readest them, be persuaded that thou hearest the Father, and the Son, and the Holy Ghost, all of them jointly and severally speaking to thee and saying, Poor sinner, thou art engaged for God in the world, thou art suffering for his Word: leave thy soul with him as with one that is more willing to save it, than thou art willing he should: act faith, trust God, believe his Word, and go on in thy way of witness-bearing for him, and thou shalt find all well, and according to the desire of thy heart at last. True, Satan will make it his business to tempt thee to doubt of this, that thy way be made yet more hard and difficult to thee. For he knows that unbelief is a soul-perplexing sin, and makes that which would otherwise be light, pleasant, and easy, unutterably heavy and burdensome to the sufferer. Yea, this he doth in hope to make thee at last, to cast away thy profession, thy cause, thy faith, thy conscience, thy soul, and all. But hear what the Holy Ghost saith again: 'He shall spare the poor and needy, and shall save the souls of the needy. He shall redeem their soul from deceit and violence: and precious shall their blood be in his sight.' Ps. lxxii. 13, 14. These words also are spoken for the comfort of sufferers, ver. 12. 'For he shall deliver the needy when he crieth; the poor also, and *him* that hath no helper.' Wherefore, let them that are God's sufferers, pluck up a good heart; let them not be afraid to trust God with their souls, and with their eternal concerns. Let them cast all their care upon God, for he careth for them. 1 Pe. v. 7.

But I am in the dark.

I answer, never stick at that. It is most bravely done, to trust God with my soul in the

---

* An awful instance occurred soon after the publication of this 'Advice.' John Child, a Baptist minister, one of Bunyan's friends, to escape persecution, conformed, and became terrified with awful compunctions of conscience. His cries were fearful: 'I shall go to hell;' 'I am broken in judgment;' 'I am as it were in a flame.' In a fit of desperation he destroyed himself on the 15th October, 1684.—Ed.

† 'What bottom;' what ground or foundation.—Ed.

dark, and to resolve to serve God for nothing, rather than give out. Not to see, and yet to believe, and to be a follower of the Lamb, and yet to be at uncertainty, what we shall have at last, argues love, fear, faith, and an honest mind, and gives the greatest sign of one that hath true sincerity in his soul. It was this that made Job and Peter so famous, and the want of it that took away much of the glory of the faith of Thomas. Job i. 8—10, 21. Mat. xix. 27. Jn. xx. 29. Wherefore believe, verily, that God is ready, willing, yea, that he looks for, and expects that thou who art a sufferer shouldest commit the keeping of thy soul to him, as unto a faithful Creator.

Conclusion Seventh. Another conclusion that followeth from these words is this, namely, That God is able, as well as willing, to secure the souls of his suffering saints, and to save them from the evil of all their trials, be they never so many, divers, or terrible. ' Let him commit the keeping of his soul to God,' but to what boot, if he be not able to keep it in his hand, and from the power of him that seeks the soul to destroy it? But 'my Father which gave *them* me,' saith Christ, ' is greater than all; and no *man* is able to pluck *them* out of my Father's hand.' Jn. x. 29. So then there can be no sorrow, affliction, or misery invented, by which the devil may so strongly prevail, as thereby to pluck the soul out of the hand of him who has received it, to keep it from falling, and perishing thereby. The text therefore supposeth a sufficiency of power in God to support, and a sufficiency of comfort and goodness to embolden the soul to endure for him: let Satan break out, and his instruments too, to the greatest degree of their rage and cruelty.

1. There is in God *a sufficiency of power to keep them that have laid their soul at his foot to be preserved.* And hence he is called the soul-keeper, the soul-preserver, Pr. xxiv. 12. ' The Lord *is* thy keeper: the Lord *is* thy shade upon thy right hand. The sun shall not smite thee by day, nor the moon by night. The Lord shall preserve thee from all evil: he shall preserve thy soul.' Ps. cxxi. 5—7. ' The sun shall not smite thee:' that is, persecution shall not dry and wither thee away to nothing. Mat. xiii. 6, 21. But that notwithstanding, thou shalt be kept and preserved, carried through and delivered from all evil. Let him therefore commit the keeping of his soul to him, if he is in a suffering condition, that would have it secured and found safe and sound at last. For,

(1.) Then thine own natural weakness, and timorousness shall not overcome thee.—For it shall not be too hard for God. God can make the most soft spirited man as hard as an adamant, harder than flint, yea harder than the northern steel. ' Shall iron break the northern iron and the steel?'

Je. xv. 12. The sword of him is [used] in vain that lays at a Christian, when he is in the way of his duty to God: if God has taken to him the charge and care of his soul, he can shoe him with brass, and make his hoofs of iron. De. xxxiii. 25. ' He can strengthen the spoiled against the strong, so that the spoiled shall come against the fortress.' Am. v. 8. Eze. xiii. 9.

He can turn thee into another man, and make thee that which thou never wast. Timorous Peter, fearful Peter, he could make as bold as a lion. He that at one time was afraid of a sorry girl, he could make at another to stand boldly before the council. Mat. xxvi. Ac. iv. 13. There is nothing too hard for God. He can can say to them that are of a fearful heart, ' Be strong, fear not.' Is. xxxv. 4. He can say, Let the weak say I am strong; by such a word, by which he created the world. Zec. xii. 8.

(2.) Thine own natural darkness and ignorance shall not cause thee to fall; thy want of wit he can supply.—He can say to the fools, be wise; not only by way of correction, but also by way of instruction too. He 'hath chosen the foolish things of the world to confound the wise; - yea, things which are despised, - and things which are not, hath God chosen to bring to nought things that are.' 1 Co. i. 27, 28. Wisdom and might are his: and when, and where he will work, none can at all withstand him. He can give thee the spirit of wisdom and revelation in the knowledge of his Son. Ep. i. 17. Yea, to do this, is that which he challengeth, as that which is peculiar to himself. ' Who hath put wisdom in the inward parts? or who hath given understanding to the heart?' Job xxxviii. 36. And that he will do this that he hath promised, yea, promised to do it to that degree, as to make his, that shall be thus concerned for him, to top, and overtop all men that shall them oppose. I, saith he, ' will give you a mouth and wisdom, that all your adversaries shall not be able to gainsay nor resist.' Lu. xxi. 15.

(3.) Thine own doubts and mistrusts about what he will do, and about whither thou shalt go, when thou for him hast suffered awhile, he can resolve, yea, dissolve, crush, and bring to nothing.—He can make fear flee far away: and place heavenly confidence in its room. He can bring invisible and eternal things to the eye of thy soul, and make thee see that in those things in which thine enemies shall see nothing, that thou shalt count worth the loss of ten thousand lives to enjoy. He can pull such things out of his bosom, and can put such things into thy mouth; yea, can make thee choose to be gone, though through the flames, than to stay here and die in silken sheets. Yea, he can himself come near and bring his heaven and glory to thee. The Spirit of glory and of God resteth upon them that are but reproached for the name of Christ. 1 Pe. iv. 14. And what the Spirit of glory is, and what is his resting upon his sufferers, is quite beyond the knowledge of the world, and is but little felt by saints at peace. They be they that are engaged, and chat are under the lash of Christ; they are they, I say, that have it and that understand something of it.

When Moses went up the first time into the mount to God, the people reproached him for staying with him so long, saying, ' As for this Moses, - we wot not what is become of him.' Ex. xxxii. 1. Well, the next time he went up thither, and came down, the Spirit of glory was upon him; his face shone, though he wist it not, to his honour, and their amazement. Ex. xxxiv. 29—35. Also while Stephen stood before the council to be accused, by suborned men, ' All that sat in the council, looking steadfastly on him, saw his face as it had been the face of an angel.' Ac. vi. 15. Those that honour God, he will honour, yea, will put some of his glory upon them, but they shall be honoured. There is none can tell what God can do. He can make those things that in themselves are most fearful and terrible to behold, the most pleasant, delightful, and desirable things. He can make a gaol more beautiful than a palace; restraint, more sweet by far than liberty. And ' the reproach of Christ greater riches than the treasures in Egypt.' He. xi. 26. It is said of Christ, That ' for the joy that was set before him, he endured the cross, despising the shame.' He. xii. 2. But,

2. As there is in God a sufficiency of power to uphold, so *there is in him also a sufficiency of comfort and goodness to embolden us:* I mean communicative comfort and goodness. Variety of, and the terribleness that attends afflictions, call, not only for the beholding of things, but also a laying hold of them by faith and feeling; now this also is with God to the making of HIS to sing in the night. Paul and Silas sang in prison, the apostles went away from the council rejoicing, when they had shamefully beaten them for their preaching in the temple. Ac. v. But whence came this but from an inward feeling by faith of the love of God, and of Christ, which passeth knowledge? Hence he says to those under afflictions, ' Fear none of those things which thou shalt suffer.' Re. ii. 10. There are things to be suffered, as well as places to suffer in; and there are things to be let into the soul for its emboldening, as well as things to be showed to it. Ro. v. 5.

Now the things to be suffered are many, some of which are thus counted up: ' They were tortured, - had *cruel* mockings and scourgings; - they were stoned, were sawn asunder, were slain with the sword, - were tempted; - they wandered about in sheep-skins, and goat-skins, being destitute, afflicted, tormented.' He. xi. 35—37. These are

some of the things that good men of old have suffered for their profession of the name of Jesus Christ. All which they were enabled by him to bear, to bear with patience; to bear with rejoicing; ' knowing in themselves that they had in heaven a better, and an enduring substance.' He. x. 32—34. And it is upon this account that Paul doth call to mind the most dreadful of his afflictions, which he suffered for the gospel sake with rejoicing; and that he tells us that he was most glad, when he was in such infirmities. Yea, it is upon this account that he boasteth, and vaunteth it over death, life, angels, principalities, powers, things present, things to come, height, depth, and every other creature: for he knew that there was enough in that love of God, which was set on him through Christ, to preserve him, and to carry him through all. 2 Co. xii. 9, 10. Ro. viii. 37—39. That God has done thus, a thousand instances might be given; and that God will still do thus, for that we have his faithful promise. Is. xliii. 2. 1 Co. x. 13.

To the adversaries of the church these things have also sometimes been shewed, to their amazement and confusion. God shewed to the king of Babylon that he was with the three children in the fiery furnace. Da. iii. 24. God shewed to the king of Babylon again, that he would be where HIS were, though in the lion's den. vi. 24.

Also, in later days, whoso reads Mr. Fox's Acts and Monuments, will also find several things to confirm this for truth. God has power over all plagues, and therefore can either heighten, or moderate and lessen them at pleasure. He has power over fire, and can take away the intolerable heat thereof. This those in the Marian days could also testify, namely, Hauks and Bainham, and others, who could shout for joy, and clap their hands in the very flames for joy. God has power over hunger, and can moderate it, and cause that one meal's meat shall go as far as forty were wont to do. This is witnessed in Elias, when he went for his life to the mount of God, being fled from the face of Jezebel. 1 Ki. xix. 8. And what a good night's lodging had Jacob when he fled from the face of his brother Esau: when the earth was his couch, the stone* his pillow, the heavens his canopy, and the shades of the night his curtains.† Ge. xxviii. 12—16.

I can do all things, said Paul, through Christ strengthening me. And again, I take pleasure in

---

* This identical stone is *said* to be in the chair on which our monarchs are crowned in Westminster Abbey.—ED.

† In so unbounded, eternal, and magnificent a mansion, well might he exclaim, 'This is none other but the house of God, and this is the gate of heaven.' Where God meets us with his special presence, we ought to meet Him with the most humble reverence; remembering his justice and holiness, and our own meanness and vileness.—ED.

infirmities, in reproaches, in necessities, in persecutions, in distresses for Christ's sake. But how can that be, since no affliction for the present seems joyous? I answer, though they be not so in themselves, yet Christ, by his presence, can make them so: for then his power rests upon us. When I am weak, saith he, then I am strong; then Christ doth in me mighty things: for my strength, saith Christ, is made perfect in weakness; in affliction, for the gospel sake.

For when my people are afflicted and suffer great distress for me, then they have my comforting, supporting, emboldening, and upholding presence to relieve them: an instance of which you have in the three children and in Daniel, made mention of before. But what, think you, did these servants of the God of Jacob feel, feel in their souls, of his power and comforting presence when they, for his name, were suffering of the rage of their enemies,—while, also, one, like the Son of God, was walking in the fire with the three; and while Daniel sat and saw that the hands of the angels were made muzzles for the lions' mouths.

I say, was it not worth being in the furnace and in the den to see such things as these? O! the grace of God, and his Spirit and power that is with them that suffer for him, if their hearts be upright with him; if they are willing to be faithful to him; if they have learned to say, here am I, whenever he calls them, and whatever he calls them to. 'Wherefore,' when Peter saith, 'let them that suffer according to the will of God, commit the keeping of their souls *to him* in well-doing, as unto a faithful Creator.' He concludes, that how outrageous, furious, merciless, or cruel soever the enemy is, yet there, with him, they shall find help and succour, relief and comfort; for God is able to make such as do so, stand.

Conclusion Eighth. We will now come to touch upon that which may more immediately be called the reason of this exhortation; for, although all these things that have been mentioned before may, or might be called reasons of the point, yet there are those, in my judgment, that may be called reasons, which are yet behind. As,

1. Because, when a man has, by faith and prayer, committed the keeping of his soul to God, he has the advantage of that liberty of soul to do and suffer for God that he cannot otherwise have. He that has committed his soul to God to keep is rid of that care, and is delivered from the fear of its perishing for ever. When the Jews went to stone Stephen they laid their clothes down at a distance from the place, at a young man's feet, whose name was Saul, that they might not be a cumber or a trouble to them, as to their intended work. So we, when we go about to drive sin out of the world, in a way

of suffering for God's truth against it,* we should lay down our souls at the feet of God to care for, that we may not be cumbered with the care of them ourselves; also, that our care of God's truth may not be weakened by such sudden and strong doubts as will cause us faintingly to say, But what will become of my soul? When Paul had told his son Timothy that he had been before that lion Nero, and that he was at present delivered out of his mouth, he adds, And the Lord shall deliver me from every evil work, and will preserve me unto his heavenly kingdom. He shall and will. Here is a man at liberty, here are no cumbersome fears. But how came the apostle by this confidence of his well-being and of his share in another world? Why, 'he had committed the keeping of his soul to God,' compare 2 Ti. i. 12. with iv. 18. For to commit the keeping of the soul to God, if it be done in faith and prayer, it leaves, or rather brings this holy boldness and confidence into the soul. Suppose a man in the country were necessitated to go to London, and had a great charge of money to pay in there; suppose, also, that the way thither was become exceeding dangerous because of the highwaymen that continually abide therein,—what now must this man do to go on his journey cheerfully? Why, let him pay in his money to such an one in the country as will be sure to return it for him at London safely. Why, this is the case, thou art bound for heaven, but the way thither is dangerous. It is beset everywhere with evil angels, who would rob thee of thy soul, What now? Why, if thou wouldest go cheerfully on in thy dangerous journey, commit thy treasure, thy soul, to God to keep; and then thou mayest say, with comfort, Well, that care is over: for whatever I meet with in my way thither, my soul is safe enough: the thieves, if they meet me, can not come at that; I know to whom I have committed my soul, and I am persuaded that he will keep that to my joy and everlasting comfort against the great day.†

This, therefore, is one reason why we should, that suffer for Christ, commit the keeping of our souls to God; because a doubt about the well-being of that will be a clog, a burden, and an

---

* The only way of driving sin out of the world is *to make known* the Saviour. Reader, can you solve Mr. Bunyan's riddle? Burning those who made him known under Mary —hanging, imprisoning, and transporting the most godly preachers for nonconformity under Elizabeth and the Stuarts. How can this be a means of driving much sin out of the world 'in a way of suffering for God's truth against it?'—ED.

† How indescribably blessed is the Christian. It is true that he has to perform his pilgrimage through an enemy's country, beset with snares, pit-falls, and temptations; but in all his buffetings and storms of sorrow, his soul is safe; God is a wall of fire round about it, and the glory in the midst of it. He will guide us by his counsel, and then receive us to his glory. —ED.

affliction to our spirit: yea, the greatest of afflictions, whilst we are taking up our cross and bearing it after Christ. The joy of the Lord is our strength, and the fear of perishing is that which will be weakening to us in the way.

2. We should commit the keeping of our souls to God, because the final conclusion that merciless men do sometimes make with the servants of God is all on a sudden. They give no warning before they strike. We shall not need here to call you to mind about the massacres that were in Ireland, Paris, Piedmont, and other places, where the godly, in the night before they were well awake, had, some of them, their heart blood running on the ground. The savage monsters crying out, Kill, kill, from one end of a street or a place to the other. This was sudden; and he that had not committed his soul to God to keep it was surely very hard put to it now; but he that had done so was ready for such sudden work. Sometimes, indeed, the axe, and halter, or the faggot is shewed first; but sometimes, again, it is without that warning. Up, said Saul to Doeg, the Edomite, and slay the priests of the Lord. 1 Sa. xxii. 11, 18, 19. Here was sudden work: fall on, said Saul, and Doeg fell upon them, 'and slew on that day four score and five persons that did wear a linen ephod.' 'Nob, also, the city of the priests, smote he with the edge of the sword, both men and women, children and sucklings,' &c. Here was but a word and a blow. Thinkest thou not, who readest these lines, that all of these who had before committed their soul to God to keep were the fittest folk to die?

'And immediately the king sent an executioner, and commanded his head to be brought.' Mar. vi. 27. The story is concerning Herod and John the Baptist: Herod's dancing girl had begged John Baptist's head, and nothing but his head must serve her turn; well, girl, thou shalt have it. Have it? Ay, but it will be long first. No; thou shalt have it now, just now, immediately. 'And immediately he sent an executioner, and commanded his head to be brought.'

Here is sudden work for sufferers; here is no intimation beforehand. The executioner comes to John; now, whether he was at dinner, or asleep, or whatever he was about, the bloody man bolts in upon him, and the first word he salutes him with is, Sir, strip, lay down your neck, for I am come to take away your head. But hold, stay; wherefore? pray, let me commit my soul to God. No, I must not stay; I am in haste: slap, says his sword, and off falls the good man's head. This is sudden work; work that stays for no man; work that must be done by and by; immediately, or it is not worth a rush. I will, said she, that thou give me, by and by, in a charger, the head

of John the Baptist. Yea, she came in haste, and hastily the commandment went forth, and immediately his head was brought.

3. Unless a man commits the keeping of his soul to God, it is a question whether he can hold out and stand his ground, and wrestle with all temptations. 'This is the victory,— even our faith;' and 'who is he that overcometh the world, but he that believeth?' And what encouragement has a man to suffer for Christ, whose heart cannot believe, and whose soul he cannot commit to God to keep it? And our Lord Jesus intimates as much when he saith, 'Be thou faithful unto death and I will give thee a crown of life.' Wherefore saith he thus? but to encourage those that suffer for his truth in the world, to commit the keeping of their souls to him, and to believe that he hath taken the charge and care of them. Paul's wisdom was, that he was ready to die before his enemies were ready to kill him. 'I am now ready,' saith he, 'to be offered, and the time of my departure is at hand.' 2 Ti. iv. 6.

This is, therefore, a thing of high concern; to wit, the committing of the soul to God to keep it. It is, I say, of concern to do it now, just now, quickly, whether thou art yet engaged or no; for it is a good preparatory to, as well as profitable in, a time of persecution: consider it, I say. The apostle Paul saith that he and his companions were bold in their God, to profess and stand to the word of God. 1 Th. ii. 2. But how could that be if they had the salvation of their souls to seek, and that to be sure they would have had had they not committed the keeping of their souls to him in well-doing?

Quest. But what is committing of the soul to God?

Answ. I have, in general, briefly spoken to that already, and now, for thy further help, we will a little enlarge. Wherefore,

(1.) To commit is to deliver up to custody to be kept. Hence prisoners, when sent to the gaol, are said to be committed thither. Thus Paul, 'haling men and women, committing them to prison.' Ac. viii. 3. And thus Joseph's master committed all his prisoners to him, to his custody, to be kept there according to the law. Ge. xxxix. 22.

(2.) To commit, is not only to deliver up to custody, but to give in charge; that that which is committed be kept safe, and not suffered to be lost. Lu. xvi. 11. Thus Paul was committed to prison, the jailor being charged to keep him safely. Ac. xvi. 23.

(3.) To commit, is to leave the whole disposal, sometimes, of that which is committed to those to whom such thing is committed. Thus were the shields of the temple committed to the guard. 1 Ki. xiv. 27. And Jeremiah to the hands of Gedaliah. Je. xxxix. 14.

And thus thou must commit thy soul to God and to his care and keeping. It must be delivered up to his care and put under his custody. Thou mayst also, though I would speak modestly, give him a charge to take the care of it. 'Concerning my sons [and concerning my daughters] and concerning the work of my hands, command ye me.' Is. xlv. 11. Thou must also leave all the concerns of thy soul and of thy being an inheritor of the next world wholly to the care of God. He that doth this in the way that God has bid him is safe, though the sky should fall. 'The poor committeth himself unto thee, thou art the helper of the fatherless.' Ps. x. 14.

And for encouragement to do this, the Lord has bidden us, the Lord has commanded us, the Lord expecteth that we should thus do. Yea, thou art also bidden to commit thy way unto him. Ps. xxxvii. 5. Thy work unto him. Pr. xvi. 3. Thy cause unto him. Job v. 8. Thy soul to him, and he will take care of all. And if we do this, as we should, God will not only take care of us and of our souls in the general, but that our work and ways be so ordered that we may not fail in either. 'I have trusted,' said David, 'in the Lord, therefore I shall not slide.' Ps. xxvi. 1.

Before I leave this, I will speak something of the way in which this commitment of the soul to God must be; and that is, 'in a way of well-doing.' Let them commit the keeping of their souls to him 'in well-doing;' or, in a way of well-doing. That is, therefore, the course that a godly man should be found in, at, in, and after he hath committed his soul to God to keep. And, as the apostle says in another place, this is but a 'reasonable service.' Ro. xii. 1. For if God be so gracious as to take care of my soul at my request, why should not I also be so gracious as to be found in a way of well-doing at his bidding? Take care, master, of me for meat and wages, and I will take care, master, that thy work shall be faithfully done. This is honest, and thus should Christians say to God: and he that heartily, in this, shall mean as he saith, shall find that God's ways shall be strength unto him.

A Christian is not to commit his soul unto God to keep, and so to grow remiss, carnal, negligent, cold, and worldly; concluding as if he had now bound God to save him, but sets himself at liberty whether he will longer serve him in trying and troublesome times or no. He must commit the keeping of his soul to him 'in well-doing.' He may not now relinquish God's cause, play the apostate, cast off the cross, and look for heaven notwithstanding. He that doth thus will find himself mistaken, and be made to know at last that God takes the care of no such souls. 'If any man draws back,' saith he, 'my soul shall have no

pleasure in him.' Wherefore, he that committeth the keeping of his soul to God must do it in that way which God has prescribed to him, which is in a way of well-doing. Alas! alas! there is never such a word in it; it must be done in a way of 'well-doing.' You must think of this that would commit your souls to God in suffering and troublesome times. You must do it in well-doing.

'In well-doing,' that is, in persevering in ways of godliness, both with respect to morals and also instituted worship. Thou, therefore, that wouldest have God take care of thy soul, as thou believest, so thou must do well; that is, do good to the poor, to thy neighbour, to all men, especially to the household of faith. Benjamin must have a Benjamin's mess; and all others, as thou art capable, must feel and find the fruit of thy godliness. Thou must thus serve the Lord with much humility of mind, though through many difficulties and much temptation.

Thou must also keep close to gospel worship, public and private; doing of those things that thou hast warrant for from the word, and leaving of that or those things for others that will stick to them—that have no stamp of God upon them. Thou must be found doing of all with all thy heart, and if thou sufferest for so doing, thou must bear it patiently. For what Peter saith to the women he spake to, may be applied to all believers, 'whose daughters ye are,' saith he, meaning Sarah's, 'as long as ye do well, and are not afraid with any amazement.' 1 Pe. iii. 6.

So then, the man that has committed his soul to God to keep has not at all disengaged himself from his duty, or took himself off from a perseverance in that good work that, under a suffering condition, he was bound to do before. No; his very committing of his soul to God to keep it has laid an engagement upon him to abide to God in that calling wherein he is called of God. To commit my soul to God, supposes my sensibleness of hazard and danger; but there is none [no danger] among men when the offence of the cross is ceased. To commit my soul to God to keep, concludes my resolution to go on in that good way of God that is so dangerous to my soul, if God taketh not the charge and care thereof. For he that saith in his heart, I will now commit my soul to God, if he knows what he says, says thus: I am for holding on in a way of bearing of my cross after Christ, though I come to the same end for so doing as he came to before me. This is committing the soul to him in well-doing. Look to yourselves, therefore, whoever you are that talk of leaving your souls with God, but do live loose, idle, profane, and wicked lives. God will not take care of such men's souls; they commit them not unto him as they should. They do but flatter him with their lips, and lie unto him with their tongue, and think to deceive the Lord; but to no purpose. 'He that soweth to the flesh shall of the flesh reap corruption.' It is he that sows to the Spirit that shall 'reap life everlasting.' Ga. vi. 7, 8.

I shall now come to the second thing contained in the text, namely, to give you a more distinct description of the men that are thus bid to commit the keeping of their souls to God. And they are thus described: they that 'suffer according to the will of God.' 'Let them that suffer according to the will of God commit the keeping of their souls to him in well-doing, as unto a faithful Creator.'

Two things are here to be inquired into. FIRST, What the apostle here means by the will of God. SECOND, What suffering according to the will of God is.

FIRST, For the will of God, it is divers ways taken in the scriptures; as, sometimes, for electing, justifying, sanctifying acts of God; sometimes for faith, good life, and sometimes for suffering for his name. Ro. ix. Ep. i. 11. Jn. vii. 17. 1 Jn. iii. 23. 1 Th. iv. 3. Mat. vii. 21. But, by will of God here we must, First, Understand HIS LAW AND TESTAMENT. Second, HIS ORDER AND DESIGNMENT.

[THE WILL OF GOD MEANS HIS LAW AND TESTAMENT.]

First, By his will I understand his law and testament. This is called the revealed will of God, or that by which he has made himself, and how he will be worshipped, known unto the children of men. Now, I, understanding these words thus, must, before I go further, make this distinction, to wit, that there is a difference to be put betwixt them that suffer for the breach and those that suffer for keeping of this law and testament; for though both of them may suffer by the will of God, yet they are not both concerned in this text. A malefactor that suffereth for his evil deeds the due punishment thereof, suffereth, as other texts declare, according to the will of God. But, I say, this text doth not concern itself with them; for both this text and this epistle is writ for the counsel and comfort of those that suffer for keeping the law and testament of God; that suffer for well-doing. 1 Pe. iii. 13, 14, 17; iv. 13, 14.

The man then that is concerned in this advice is he that suffereth from the hands of men for keeping of the word of God; and this is he that has licence, leave, yea, a command to commit the keeping of his soul to God in well-doing, as unto a faithful Creator. We will a little enlarge upon this.

[What it is to suffer according to the will of God, or his law and testament.]

He that keepeth the word of God is such an one that has regard to both the matter and manner thereof. The matter is the truth, the doctrine contained therein; the manner is that comely, godly, humble, faithful way of doing it which becomes a man that has to do with the law and testament of God; and both these are contained in the text. For, first, here is the will of God to be done; and then, secondly, to be done according to his will. 'Let them that suffer according to his will:' which words, I say, take in both matter and manner of doing. So then, the man that here we have to do with, and to discourse of, is a man that, in the sense now given, suffereth. That which makes a martyr, is suffering for the word of God after a right manner; and that is, when he suffereth, not only for righteousness, but for righteousness' sake; not only for truth, but of love to truth; not only for God's word, but according to it, to wit, in that holy, humble, meek manner as the word of God requireth. A man may give his body to be burned for God's truth, and yet be none of God's martyrs. 1 Co. xiii. 1–3. Yea, a man may suffer with a great deal of patience, and yet be none of God's martyrs. 1 Pe. ii. 20. The one, because he wanteth that grace that should poise his heart, and make him right in the manner of doing; the other, because he wanteth that word of the Holy One that alone can make his cause good, as to matter. It is, therefore, matter and manner that makes the martyr; and it is this man that is intended in the text which is aforesaid described. So then, they that suffer for the law and testament of God in that holy and humble manner that the Word requires, they are they that, by this Word of God, are commanded to commit the keeping of their souls to God.

From this consideration, two things present themselves to our sight. 1. That a man may be a Christian, and suffer, and yet not suffer, in the sense last given, according to the will of God. 2. There have been, and may yet be a people in the world that have, and may suffer in the sense of the apostle here, according to the will of God.

[1. A Christian may suffer, but not in the sense of the apostle, according to the will of God.]

A few words to the first of these, namely, that a man may be a Christian, and suffer, and yet not suffer, in the sense of the apostle in the text, 'according to the will of God.' He may be a

Christian and yet not suffer as a Christian. He may want the matter, or, he may want the manner, of suffering as a Christian.

This is evident from what this apostle suggests in several places of this epistle. For,

Saith he, 'If ye be buffeted for your faults.' 1 Pe. ii. 20. This supposeth that a Christian may so be; for he speaketh here to the same people, unto whom he speaketh in the text, though he putteth them not under the same circumstance, as suffering for well doing. If ye be buffeted for your faults, for what God's word calls faults, what thank have you from God, or good men, though you take it patiently?

So again, 'For *it is* better, if the will of God be so, that ye suffer for well doing, than for evil doing.' iii. 17. Here it is plainly supposed that a christian man may suffer for evil doing, yea, that the will of God may be, that he should suffer for evil doing. For God, if Christians do not well, will vindicate himself by punishing of them for their doing ill. Yea, and will not count them worthy, though they be his own, to be put among the number of those that suffer for doing well.

Again, 'But let none of you suffer as a murderer, or *as* a thief, or *as* an evildoer, or as a busybody in other men's matters.' iv. 15. These are cautions to Christians to persuade them to take heed to themselves, their tongues and their actions, that all be kept within the bounds of the Word. For it would be a foolish thing to say, that these are cautions to persuade to take heed of that, into which it is not possible one should fall. It is possible for Christians to suffer for evil doing, and therefore let Christians beware; it is possible for Christians to be brought to public justice for their faults, and therefore let Christians beware. It is possible for Christians to suffer justly by the hand of the magistrate, and therefore let Christians beware. This also is insinuated in the text itself, and therefore let Christians beware.

The causes of this are many, some of which I shall now briefly touch upon.

(1.) Sin is in the best of men: and as long as it is so, without great watchfulness, and humble walking with God, we may be exposed to shame and suffering for it. What sin is it that a child of God is not liable to commit, excepting that which is the sin unpardonable? Nor have we a promise of being kept from any other sin, but on condition that we do watch and pray. Mat. xxvi. 41.

(2.) It is possible for a Christian to have an erroneous conscience in some things, yea, in such things as, if God by his grace prevents not, may bring us to public justice and shame. Abishai, though a good man, would have killed the king, and that of conscience to God, and love to his master. 1 Sa. xxvi. 7, 8. And had David delivered

him up to Saul for his attempt, he had in all likelihood died as a traitor. Peter drew his sword, and would have fought therewith, a thing for which he was blamed of his Master, and bid with a threatening, to put it up again. Mat. xxvi. 52. Besides, oppression makes a wise man mad; and when a man is mad what evils will he not do?

Further, The devil, who is the great enemy of the Christians, can send forth such spirits into the world as shall not only disturb men, but nations, kings, and kingdoms, in raising divisions, distractions and rebellions. And can so manage matters that the looser sort of Christians* may be also dipt and concerned therein. In Absalom's conspiracy against his father, there were two hundred men called out of Jerusalem to follow him, 'and they went in their simplicity, not knowing any thing.' 2 Sa. xv. 11. I thank God I know of no such men, nor thing: but my judgment tells me, that if Christians may be drawn into fornication, adultery, murder, theft, blasphemy or the like, as they may; why should it be thought impossible for them to be drawn in here. Wherefore I say again, watch and pray, fear God, reverence his Word, approve of his appointments, that you may be delivered from every evil work and way.

I said afore that the will of God may be, that a Christian should suffer as an evil doer; but then it is because he keepeth not within the bounds of that, which is also called the will of God. The will of God is, that sin should be punished, though committed by the Christians; punished according to the quality of transgressions: and therefore it is that he hath ordained magistrates. Magistrates, to punish sin, though it be the sin of Christians. They are the ministers of God, revengers, to execute wrath, the wrath of God upon them that do evil. Ro. xiii. Wherefore, though the Christian as a Christian is the only man at liberty, as called thereunto of God; yet his liberty is limited to things that are good: he is not licensed thereby to indulge the flesh. Holiness and liberty are joined together, yea our call to liberty, is a call to holiness.† See, and you shall find, that a quiet and peaceable life, in our respective places, under the government, is that which

---

* 'Looser sort of Christians;' among Christians there are gradations of character. Some are *fixed* upon the Saviour, and can say, 'For me to live is Christ.' Such decision ensures safety and happiness; while the looser sort are subject to many sorrows and continual danger. May we press on towards the mark. 'Lord, I believe, help thou my unbelief.'—ED.

† This truth ought to be imprinted on every heart. As the absence of darkness is light, so liberty from the thraldom of sin, and from the slavery of Satan, essentially induces holiness of life. Thus holiness and liberty are joined together. —ED.

we should pray for, to wit, that we may without molestation, if it were 'the will of God,' spend our days in all godliness and honesty among our neighbours. See 1 Ti. ii. 1—8. 1 Pe. ii. 13—17.

[*First, Caution to Christians as Christians.*]— I would improve this a little, and first, to Christians as Christians: beware the cautions, that are here presented to you, be not neglected by you. The evils are burning hot, as hot as a red hot iron. It is the greatest blemish that can be to a Christian, to suffer as an evil doer. To say nothing of the reproach that such do bring to the name of Christ, their Lord; to his law, their rule; and to the christian profession, which should be their glory: the guilt and shame that evil actions will load the conscience with at such a time, can hardly be stood under. The man that suffereth as an evil doer, and yet weareth the name of a Christian, what stumbling blocks doth he lay in the way of the ignorant in a kingdom? The devil told them before, that a Christian was a mischievous man; and to suffer for evil doing, confirms them in that belief.

Consider also the difficulties that surely such must meet with in the last minutes of their life. For can it be imagined but that such an one must have combats and conflicts at the last, who carry in their consciences the guilt and condemnation that is due to their deeds, to the place which magistrates have appointed for them to receive the reward of their works at. Such an one bereaves not only his own soul of peace, and his name of credit, but himself of life, his friends of all cause of rejoicing, and casteth reproach upon religion, as he is stepping out of the world. What shall I say, Christians as Christians have other things to do than to concern themselves in evil things, or to meddle in other men's matters. Let us mind our own business, and leave the magistrate to his work, office and calling among men also.

I speak now to them that are not by the king called to that employ. A Christian as such has enough to do at home, in his heart, in his house, in his shop, and the like. But if thou must needs be meddling, consider what place, office, calling or relation, God has put thee in, and busy thyself by the rule of the Word to a conscientious performance of that. Nor shalt thou want dignity, though thou art but a private Christian. Every christian man is made a king by Christ. Re. v. 10. But then, his dominion as such, doth reach no further than to himself. He has not dominion over another's faith. 2 Co. i. 24. His office is to govern, and bridle, and keep under, himself; to watch over himself, and to bring his body into subjection to the will of God. The weapons that he has for this purpose are not carnal, but spiri-

tual, and mighty through God. Let him govern then, if he will be a governor, his whole man by the Word. Let him bring down, if he must be bringing down, his own high imaginations, and every high thing that exalts itself against the knowledge of God. If he must be a warrior, let him levy war against his own unruly passions, and let him fight against those lusts that war against his soul.* 2 Co. x. 3—5. Ga. v. 17. Ja. iii. 3—8. 1 Pe. ii. 11.

I say therefore, if thou wilt needs be a ruler, thou hast a tongue, rule that; lusts, rule them; affections, govern them; yea, thou hast excellent graces, manage them, cherish, strengthen and replenish them according to the mind of that great one who has bestowed such power to rule, upon thee. Mortify therefore your members which are upon the earth; fornication, uncleanness, inordinate affection, evil concupiscence, and covetousness, which is idolatry. Col. iii. 5. Nor do I think that murmuring, shrinking, wincing, complaining, and the like, when men, governors, lay a yoke upon our necks, flow from any thing else, but love to our flesh, and distrust of the faithfulness of God to manage men, things, and actions for his church. The powers that be are ordered as well as ordained of God. They are also always in God's hand, as his rod or staff for the good and benefit of his people. Wherefore we ought with all meekness and humbleness of mind to accept of what our God by them shall please to lay upon us. 1 Pe. v. 6.

By what I now say, I do not forbid groaning and crying to God under affliction. I speak against striving to deliver ourselves from the affliction. And since men are, as I said, the rod, staff or sword in God's hand, we should apply ourselves unto him in faith in a way of prayer, intercession, supplication and giving of thanks for governors. For since they are sent of God, they must needs come with some good in their hand for us, also our prayers may make them more profitable to us. And this we ought to do without wrath and doubting; for this is that which is good, and acceptable unto God. 1 Ti. ii.

Besides, it is a sign that we forget ourselves when we complain for the punishment of our sins. If we look into ourselves, and ways, we shall see cause

---

* The whole of this beautiful passage is worthy our careful study and prayerful obedience. Are we ambitious to govern: be it our honour to rule our own spirits and tongues. Are we for war? let it be levied upon our unruly passions. This is laudable ambition. This is honourable war, producing the peace and happiness of man. This is real glory to God and man, the very opposite to those horrors of desolation which gives joy among the devils of hell—the burning cities, the garments rolled in blood, the shrieks of the wounded, and the sickening miseries of the widows and orphans of the slain. —Ed.

of more heavy stripes than yet God by men has laid upon us. What sin has yet been suppressed by all that has happened to us: if pride, covetousness, looseness, treacherous dealing, schisms, and other things, redressed by all the affliction that we have had? Yea, do we not grow worse and worse? Wherefore then should we complain? Where is repentance, reformation, and amendment of life amongst us? Why, then, do we shrink and winch. For my part, I have ofttimes stood amazed both at the mercy of God, and the favour of the Prince towards us; and can give thanks to God for both: and do make it my prayer to God for the king, and that God will help me with meekness and patience to bear whatever shall befall me for my professed subjection to Christ, by men.

We are bid, as I said afore, to give thanks to God for all men, for kings, and for all that are in authority. Because, as I said, there is no man with whom we have to do, we doing as we should, but he bringeth some good thing to us, or doth some good thing for us. We will now descend from them that are supreme in authority, and will come to inferior men: and suppose some of them to act beyond measure, cruelly. What? Can no good thing come to us out of this? Do not even such things as are most bitter to the flesh, tend to awaken christians to faith and prayer, to a sight of the emptiness of this world, and the fadingness of the best it yields? Doth not God by these things ofttimes call our sins to remembrance, and provoke us to amendment of life? how then can we be offended at things by which we reap so much good, and at things that God makes so profitable for us?

Doth not God, ofttimes, even take occasions by the hardest of things that come upon us, to visit our souls with the comforts of his Spirit, to lead us into the glory of his word, and to cause us to savour that love that he has had for us, even from before the world began, till now. A nest of bees and honey did Samson find, even in the belly of that lion that roared upon him. And is all this no good? or can we be without such holy appointments of God? Let these things be considered by us, and let us learn like Christians to kiss the rod, and love it.

I have thought, again, my brethren, since it is required of us that we give thanks to God for all these men, it follows that we do with quietness submit ourselves under what God shall do to us by them. For it seems a paradox to me, to give thanks to God for them, that yet I am not willing should abide in that place that God has set them in for me. I will then love them, bless them, pray for them, and do them good. I speak now of the men that hurt me as was hinted afore. And I will do thus, because it is good so to do, because they do me good by hurting of me, because I am called

to inherit a blessing, and because I would be like my heavenly Father. 'Therefore if mine enemy hunger, let me feed him; if he thirst, let me give him drink.' * Mat. v. 43—48. 1 Pe. iii. 9. Ro. xii. 17—20. (1.) We must see good in that, in which other men can see none. (2.) We must pass by those injuries that other men would revenge. (3.) We must shew we have grace, and that we are made to bear what other men are not acquainted with. (4.) Many of our graces are kept alive by those very things that are the death of other men's souls.

Where can the excellency of our patience, of our meekness, of our long-suffering, of our love, and of our faith appear, if it be not under trials, and in those things that run cross to our flesh? The devil, they say, is good when he is pleased. But Christ and his saints, when displeased. †

Let us therefore covet to imitate Christ and the scripture saints. Let us shew out of a good conversation, our works with meekness of wisdom. Let us take heed of admitting the least thought in our minds of evil, against God, the king, or them that are under him in employ, because, the cup, the king, all men, and things are in the hand of God. Ps. lxxv. 8. Pr. viii. 15; xxi. 1. La. iii. 37. And he can make them better to us, than if they were as our flesh desireth they should.

I have often thought that the best Christians are found in the worst of times: and I have thought again, that one reason why we are no better, is because God purges us no more. Jn. xv. I know these things are against the grain of the flesh, but they are not against the graces of the Spirit. Noah and Lot, who so holy as they, in the day of their affliction? Noah and Lot, who so idle as they in the day of their prosperity? I might have put in David too, who, while he was afflicted, had ways of serving God that were special; but when he was more enlarged, he had ways that were not so good. Wherefore the first ways of David are the ways that God has commended: but the rest of his ways, such as had not pre-eminence. 2 Ch. xvii. 3.

We have need of all, and of more than all that has yet befallen us: and are to thank God, since his word and patience have done no more good to us, that he hath appointed men to make us better. ‡ Wherefore for a conclusion, as we are to receive

---

* If this was our conduct, how soon should we get rid of our enemies: 'for in so doing thou shalt heap coals of fire on his head.' Who would risk such punishment a second time? —ED.

† This old proverb is a very striking illustration of the words of Paul: 'Be not overcome of evil, but overcome evil with good.' —ED.

‡ The saint must be 'made meet for the inheritance.' If he neglects the means given in the Word, his Father, in mercy, 'will chasten him with *the rod of men*, and with the stripes of the children of men,' 2 Sam. vii. 14.—ED.

with meekness the engrafted word of God, so also we are with patience to bear what God, by man, shall lay upon us. O that saying of God to them of old, ' Why criest thou for thine affliction? thy sorrow *is* incurable for the multitude of thine iniquity: *because* thy sins were increased, I have done these things unto thee.' Je. xxx. 15. We have need to consider of, and to sit still and be quiet, and reverence the ordinance of God: I mean affliction. And until we can in truth get hither in our spirits, I neither look to find very right Christianity amongst us, nor much of God among professors. When I think of Mordecai, and Daniel, yea, and of David too, and of the behaviour of them all with respect to the powers that they were under, I cannot but think that a sweet, meek, quiet, loving, godly submission unto men for the Lord's sake, is an excellent token of the grace of God in us. But,

[*Second Caution to Weak Christians.*] — As I cannot but condemn the actions of such Christians as have been touched before, so I would caution weak Christians not to be offended with true religion for the miscarriages of their fellows. There are two things that are very apt to be an occasion of offence to the weak: one is, when the cross attends religion; the other is, when others that profess religion do suffer for evil-doing. To both these I would say this:—

1. Though the cross, indeed, is grievous to the to the flesh, yet we should with grace bear up under it, and not be offended at it.

2. And as to the second, though we should and ought to be offended with such miscarriage; yet not with religion, because of such miscarriage. Some, indeed, when they see these things, take offence against religion itself; yea, perhaps, are glad of the occasion, and so fall out with Jesus Christ, saying to him, because of the evils that attend his ways, as the ten tribes said to Rehoboam, the son of Solomon the king, ' What portion have we in David? neither *have we* inheritance in the son of Jesse; to your tents, O Israel: now see to thine own house, David,' 1 Ki. xii. 16; and so go quite away from him, and cleave no more unto him, to his people, or to his ways: but this is bad. Shun, therefore, the evil ways of Christians, but cleave to the way that is christian: cast away that bad spirit that thou seest in any, but hold fast to thy Head and Lord. Whither canst thou go? the Lord Jesus has the words of eternal life. Jn. vi. 68. Whither wilt thou go? there is not salvation in any other. Ac. iv. 12. Take heed, therefore, of picking a quarrel with Jesus Christ, and with his ways, because of the evil doings of some of his followers. Judas sold him, Peter denied him, and many of his disciples went back and did walk no more with him; but neither himself nor his ways were the worse for that.

Beware, therefore, that thou truly distinguish between the good ways of Jesus Christ and the evil ways of them that profess him; and take not an occasion to throw away thy own soul down the throat of hell, because others have vilely cast away their lives by transgressing of the law of God. Nay, let other men's faults make thee more wary; let other men's falls make thee look better to thy goings: shun the rock that he that went before thee did split his ship against; and cry to God to lead thee in a path that is plain and good, because of thy observers.

Further, Let not opposite Christians rejoice when they see that evil hath taken their brother by the heel. Hate the garment, the thing that is bad, and by which the name, and fame, and life of thy brother is so vilely cast away, thou shouldest; and take good heed lest it also touch thee, but yet thou shouldest pity thy brother, mourn for his hard hap, and grieve that a thing so much unbecoming Christianity should be suffered to show the least part of itself among any of those that profess the gospel.

Directions for the shunning of suffering for evil-doing, are they that come next to hand.

Direction 1. Therefore, wouldest thou not suffer as an evil-doer, then take heed of committing of evil. Evil courses bring to evil ends; shun all appearance of evil, and ever follow that which is good. And if ye be followers of that which is good, who will harm you? 1 Pe. iii. 13. Or if there should be such enemies to goodness in the world as to cause thee for that to suffer, thou needest not be ashamed of thy suffering for well-doing, nor can there be a good man, but he will dare to own and stand by thee in it. Yea, thy sufferings for that will make thee happy, so that thou canst by no means be a loser thereby.

Direction 2. Wouldest thou not suffer for evil-doing, then take heed of the occasions of evil. Take heed of tempting company. Beware of men, for they will deliver thee up. There have been men in the world that have sought to make themselves out of the ruins of other men. This did Judas, and some of the Pharisees. Mat. x. 17. Lu. xx. 19, 20. Take heed to thy mouth: ' A fool's mouth calleth for strokes,—and his lips *are* the snare of his soul.' Pr. xviii. 7. Take heed of indulging, and hearkening to the ease of the flesh, and of carnal reasonings, for that will put thee upon wicked things.

Direction 3. Wouldest thou not suffer as an evil-doer, then take heed of hearing of any thing spoken that is not according to sound doctrine: thou must withdraw thyself from such in whom thou perceivest not the words of knowledge. Let not talk against governors, against powers, against men in authority be admitted; keep thee far from an evil matter. My son, says Solomon, fear thou the Lord, and the King, and meddle not with those that are given to change.

Direction 4. Wouldest thou not suffer as an evil-doer, addict not thyself to play with evil,* to joke and jest, and mock at men in place and power. Gaal mocked at Abimelech, and said, Who is Abimelech, that we should serve him? But he paid for his disdainful language at last. Ju. ix. I have heard of an innkeeper here in England, whose sign was the crown, and he was a merry man. Now he had a boy, of whom he used to say, when he was jovial among his guests, This boy is heir to the crown, or this boy shall be heir to the crown; and if I mistake not the story, for these words he lost his life.† It is bad jesting with great things, with things that are God's ordinance, as kings and governors are. Yea, let them rather have that fear, that honour, that reverence, that worship, that is due to their place, their office, and dignity. How Paul gave honour and respect unto those that were but deputy-kings and heathen magistrates, will greatly appear, if you do but read his trials before them in the book called, The Acts of the Apostles. And what a charge both he and Peter have left behind them to the churches to do so too, may be found to conviction, if we read their epistles.

Direction 5. Wouldest thou not suffer for evil-doing, then take heed of being offended with magistrates, because by their state acts they may cross thy inclinations. It is given to them to bear the sword, and a command is to thee, if thy heart cannot acquiesce with all things with meekness and patience, to suffer. Discontent in the mind sometimes puts discontent into the mouth; and discontent in the mouth doth sometimes also put a halter about the neck. For as a man, by speaking a word in jest may for that be hanged in earnest;† so he that speaks in discontent may die for it in sober sadness. Adonijah's discontent put him upon doing that which cost him his life. 1 Ki. ii. 13, 23. Great peace have they that love thy law, and nothing shall offend them; for they are subjected to the will and foot of God.

Direction 6. But, above all, get thy conscience possessed yet more with this, that the magistrate is God's ordinance, and is ordered of God as such: that he is the minister of God to thee for good,

and that it is thy duty to fear him, and pray for him, to give thanks to God for him, and to be subject to him as both Paul and Peter admonish us; and that not only for wrath, but for conscience sake. Ro. xiii. 5. For all other arguments come short of binding the soul, where this argument is wanting; until we believe that of God we are bound thereto. I speak not these things, as knowing any that are disaffected to the government; for I love to be alone, if not with godly men, in things that are convenient. But because I appear thus in public, and know not into whose hands these lines may come, therefore thus I write. I speak it also to show my loyalty to the king, and my love to my fellow-subjects; and my desire that all Christians should walk in ways of peace and truth.

2. [*That Christians may, and have, suffered according to the will of God.*]

I come now to the second thing propounded to be spoken to, as to suffering, which is this.—That there have been, and yet may be, a people in the world that have, and may, suffer in the sense of the apostle here, according to the will of God, or for righteousness' sake.

That there have been such a people in the world, I think nobody will deny, because many of the prophets, Christ, and his apostles, thus suffered. Besides, since the Scriptures were written, all nations can witness to this, whose histories tell at large of the patience and goodness of the sufferers, and of the cruelty of those that did destroy them. And that the thing will yet happen, or come to pass again, both Scripture and reason affirm.

First, Scripture. The text tells us, That God hath put enmity betwixt the woman and her seed, and the serpent and his seed. Ge. iii. 15. This enmity put, is so fixed that none can remove it so, but that it still will remain in the world. These two seeds have always had, and will have, that which is essentially opposite to one another, and they are 'the spirit of truth and the spirit of error,' 1 Jn. iv. 6; sin and righteousness, iii. 7, 8; light and darkness. 1 Th. v. 5. Hence 'an unjust man *is* an abomination to the just; and *he that is* upright in the way *is* abomination to the wicked.' Pr. xxix. 27. So that unless you could sanctify and regenerate all men, or cause that no more wicked men should any where be in power for ever, you cannot prevent but that sometimes still there must be sufferers for righteousness' sake. 'Yea, and all that will live godly in Christ Jesus shall suffer persecution.' 2 Ti. iii. 12.

Second, To prove this by reason is easy. The devil is not yet shut up in the bottomless pit—Antichrist is yet alive. The government in all kingdoms is not yet managed with such light, and

---

* 'But if you give sin *entrance* at the door,
   It's sting *will* in, and may come out no more.'
                                        Bunyan's Caution.

† An equally cruel scene took place in the presence of Stow, the historian, in the reign of Elizabeth. The bailiff of Romford coming to London, was asked by the curate of Aldgate the news: he replied, 'Many men be up in Essex,' [Qu. not in bed?] For this he was hung the next morning in front of Mr. Stow's house. How grateful ought we to be that such sanguinary laws have fled, with the dark mists of error and cruelty, before the spreading light of the gospel.—ED.

goodness of mind, as to let the saints serve God, as he has said, whatever it is in some. And until then there will be in some places, though for my part I cannot predict where, a people that will yet suffer for well-doing, or for righteousness' sake.

In order to a right handling of this matter, I shall divide this head into these two parts—*A*. Show you what it is to suffer for well-doing, or *for righteousness*. *B*. Show you what it is to suffer *for righteousness' sake*. I put this distinction, because I find that it is one thing to suffer for righteousness, and another to suffer for righteousness' sake.

[*A*. What it is to suffer for righteousness.]

To begin with the first, namely, *to show you what it is to suffer for righteousness*. Now that may be done either passively or actively.

1. *Passively*, as when any suffer for righteousness without their own will, or consent thereto. Thus, the little children at Bethlehem suffered by the hands of bloody Herod, when they died for, or in the room and stead of, Jesus Christ. Mat. ii. 16. Every one of those children died for righteousness, if Christ is righteousness; for they died upon his account, as being supposed to be he himself. Thus also the children of Israel's little ones, that were murdered with their parents, or otherwise, because of the religion of them that begat and bare them, died for righteousness. The same may be said concerning those of them that suffered in the land of the Chaldeans upon the same account. I might here also bring in those poor infants that in Ireland, Piedmont, Paris, and other places, have had their throats cut, and their brains dashed out against the walls, for none other cause but for the religion of their fathers. Many, many have suffered for righteousness after this manner. Their will, nor consent, has been in the suffering, yet they have suffered for religion, for righteousness. And as this hath been, so it may be again; for if men may yet suffer for righteousness, even so, for ought I know, even in this sense, may their children also.

Now, although this is not the chief matter of my text, yet a few words here may do no harm. The children that thus suffer, though their own will and consent be not in what they undergo, may yet, for all that, be accepted as an offering unto the Lord. Their cause is good; it is for religion and righteousness. Their hearts do not recoil against the cause for which they suffer; and although they are children, God can deal with them as with John the Baptist, cause them in a moment to leap for joy of Christ; or else can save them by his grace, as he saveth other his elect infants, and thus comprehend them, though they cannot apprehend him; yea, why may they not only

be saved, but in some sense be called martyrs of Jesus Christ, and those that have suffered for God's cause in the world? God comforted Rachel concerning her children that Herod murdered in the stead, and upon the account of Christ.* He bids her refrain herself from tears, by this promise, that her children should come again from the land of the enemy, from death. And again, saith he, Thy children shall come again to their own border; which I think, if it be meant in a gospel sense, must be to the heavenly inheritance. Compare Je. xxxi. 15–17. with Mat. ii. 18.†

And methinks this should be mentioned, not only for her and their sakes, but to comfort all those that either have had, or yet may have, their children thus suffer for righteousness. None of these things, as shall be further showed anon, happen without the determinate counsel of God. He has ordered the sufferings of little children as well as that of persons more in years. And it is easy to think that God can as well foresee which of his elect shall suffer by violent hands in their infancy, as which of them shall then die a natural death. He has saints small in age as well as in esteem or otherwise; and sometimes the least member of the body suffereth violence, as well as the head or other chief parts. And although I desire not to see these days again, yet methinks it will please me to see those little ones that thus have already suffered for Jesus, to stand in their white robes with the elders of their people, before the throne, to sing unto the Lamb.

2. *Actively*. But to pass this, and to come to that which is more directly intended to be spoken to, namely, to show you who doth actively suffer for righteousness. And,

(1.) *It is he that chooseth by his own will and con-*

* They shed their blood for Him who afterwards shed his blood for them. These were the infantry of the noble army of martyrs. If these infants were thus baptized with blood, though their own, into the church triumphant, it could be said that what they got in heaven abundantly compensated for what they lost on earth.—*Henry.*

† Nearly all Protestants agree as to the salvation of infants dying in their infancy—Toplady and the Calvinists on the ground of their being in the covenant of grace; others because they had not personally transgressed; supposing that the sufferings and death of the body is the penalty of original sin. Holy Scripture appears to settle this question very satisfactorily, by requiring childlike docility as a preparation for the Spirit's working. The language of the Saviour is, 'Suffer little children to come unto me, and forbid them not; for of such is the kingdom of God,' Luke xviii. 16. 'Such' as die in infancy—'such' adults as, with childlike simplicity, search the Scriptures, and fly for refuge to the Saviour. 'It is NOT the will of your Father which is in heaven that *one* of these little ones should perish,' Mat. xviii. 14. 'It were better for him that a milstone* were hanged about his neck, and he cast into the sea, than that he should offend one of these little ones,' Luke xvii. 2.—ED.

* So spelt in the standard edition of the Bible.

sent to suffer for it. All suffering that can be called active suffering, must be by the consent of the will; and that is done when a man shall have sin and suffering set before him, and shall choose suffering rather than sin. He chose 'rather to suffer affliction with the people of God, than to enjoy the pleasures of sin for a season.' He. xi. 25. And again, They did not accept of deliverance, that is, of base and unworthy terms, 'that they might obtain a better resurrection.' ver. 35.

Indeed, no man can force a Christian to suffer as a Christian, without his own consent. All Christians are sufferers of will and consent. Hence it is said, they must take up their cross, by which taking up, an act of their will is intended. Mat. x. 38; xvi. 24. So again, 'Take my yoke upon you,' which also intends an act of the will. xi. 29. This, therefore, is the first thing that I would present you with. Not that an act of the will is enough to declare a man a sufferer for righteousness, it standing alone; for a man, through the strength of delusion, and the power of an erroneous conscience, may be willing to suffer for the grossest opinions in the world. But I bring it to show that actual suffering for righteousness must also be by the consent of the will—the mind of the man must be in it.

(2.) *He that suffereth for righteousness thus, must also have a good cause.* A good cause is that which is essential to suffering for righteousness. A good cause, what is that? Why, verily, it is the truth of God, either in the whole of it, as contained in the Scriptures of truth, or in the parts of it, as set before me to believe, or do, by any part of that holy Word. This may be called the matter for which one suffereth; or, as it is called in another place, 'the word of righteousness.' He. v. 13. It may also be called the form of sound doctrine, or the like. Because without this Word, the matter and nature of God's truths cannot be known. Pilate's question, 'What is truth?' will still abide a question, to those that have not, or regard not the Word, the rule of righteousness. Jn. xviii. 38. See then that thy cause be good, thou that wouldest know what it is to suffer for righteousness; step not an hair's breadth without the bounds of the Word of truth; also take heed of misunderstanding, or of wringing out of its place, any thing that is there. Let the words of the upright stand upright, warp them not, to the end they may comply in show with any crooked notion. And to prevent this, take these three words as a guide, in this matter to thee. They show men their sins, and how to close with a Saviour; they enjoin men to be holy and humble; they command men to submit themselves to authority. And whatever is cross to these, comes from ignorance of, or from wresting, the rule of righteousness out of its place.

But more particularly, the word of righteousness —thy cause, within the bounds of which thou must keep, if thou wilt suffer for righteousness, is to be divided into two parts. (1.) It containeth a revelation of moral righteousness. (2.) It containeth a revelation of evangelical righteousness.

As for moral righteousness, men seldom suffer; only, for that. Because that is the righteousness of the world, and that, simply as such, that sets itself up in every man's conscience, and has a testimony for itself, even in the light of nature. Besides, there is nothing that maketh head against that; but that which every man is ashamed, by words to plead for, and that is immorality. And this is that which Peter intends when he saith, ' And if ye be followers of that which is good, who will harm you?' 1 Pe. iii. 13. If ye be followers of moral goodness. But if it should so happen, for the case is rare, that any man should make you sufferers because you love God, and do good to your neighbour, happy are ye. Though I do not think that the apostle's conclusion terminates there. But more of these things anon. For let a man be a good neighbour in morals; let him feed the hungry, clothe the naked, give freely out of his purse to the poor, and do that which he would another should do to him; and stop there, and not meddle with the name of Christ, and he shall have but few enemies in the world. For it is not the law, but Christ, that is the stumbling-block, and the rock of offence to men. Is. viii. 14, 15. Ro. ix. 31–33.

Wherefore, there is in God's Word a revelation of another righteousness—a righteousness which is not so visible to, yea, and that suiteth not so with, the reason of man as that moral righteousness doth. Wherefore this righteousness makes men righteous in principle, and practise so, as is foreign to natural men. Hence it is said to be foolishness to them. 1 Co. ii. 14. And again, ' Its praise is not of men.' Ro. ii. 29. This righteousness is also revealed in the Scriptures, but the blind cannot see it. It is the work of the Holy Ghost in the heart, and is therefore called the fruits of the Spirit; and the grace, which in the head and fulness of it, is only to be found in Christ. Jn. i. 16. Col. i. 19. 1 Ti. i. 14. This righteousness being planted in the heart, leads a man out by the Word of God, to seek for another righteousness, as invisible to, and foreign from, the natural man, as this. And that righteousness is that which properly is the righteousness of Jesus Christ—a righteousness that standeth in his obedience to his Father's law, as he was considered a common or public person—a righteousness which he brought into the world, not for himself, as considered in a private capacity, but for those that shall by faith venture themselves upon him, to obtain by him life eternal. Ro. v. 19. Ph. iii. 7–10.

Again, This closing by faith, with this righteousness thus found in Christ, and being taken therewith, leads me yet to another righteousness, which is instituted worship, appointed by Christ, for all his followers to be conversant in; this worship is grounded on positive precepts, and so on words of righteousness, called Christ's words, Christ's sayings, &c.

Now, upon this bottom begins the difference betwixt the men of God and the world. For, first, by this inward principle of righteousness we come to see, and say, that men by nature are not Christians, what privileges soever they may account themselves partakers thereof. But whosoever is a Christian, of God's making so, is begotten and born of God, and made a new creature by the anointing received from the Holy One. Ja. i. 18. Jn. iii. 3, 5. 2 Co. v. 17, 18; i. 21. 1 Jn. ii. 20, 24, 27.

Now, this these carnal men cannot endure to hear of; because it quite excludes them, as such, from a share in the kingdom of heaven. To this, again, the Christian stands and backs what he says by the Word of God. Then the game begins, and the men of the world are thoughtful how they may remove such troublesome fellows out of the way. But because the Christians love their neighbours, and will not let them thus easily die in their sins, therefore they contend with them, both by reasonings, writings, sermons, and books of gospel divinity; and stand to what they say. The world, again, are angry with these sayings, sermons, and books, for that by them they are concluded to be persons that are without repentance, and the hope of eternal life. Here again, the carnal world judges that these people are proud, self-willed, pragmatical, contentious, self-conceited, and so unsufferable people. The Christian yet goes on and stands to what he has asserted. Then the poor world at their last shift begins to turn, and overturn the gospel-man's sayings; perverting, forcing, stretching, and dismembering of them; and so making of them speak what was never thought, much less intended by the believer.

Thus they served our Lord; for, not being able to down with* his doctrine, they began to pervert his words, and to make, as also they said afterwards of Luther's, some offensive, some erroneous, some treasonable, and that both against God and Cæsar, and so they hanged him up, hoping there to put an end to things. But this is but the beginning of things; for the christian man, by the word of the gospel, goes further with his censure. For he also findeth fault with all that this man, by the ability of nature, can do for the freeing himself from the law of sin and death. He condemns him by the Word, because he is in a state of nature, and he condemneth also whatever, while in that

state, he doth, as that which by no means can please God. Ro. xiv. 23. He. xi. 6. This now puts him more out; this is a taking of his gods away from him. This is to strip him of his raiment, such as it is, and to turn him naked into the presence of God. This, I say, puts him out and out. These wild-brained fellows, quoth he, are never content, they find fault with us as to our state; they find fault with us as to our works, our best works. They blame us because we are sinners, and they find fault with us, though we mend; they say, by nature we are no Christians, and that our best doings will not make us such. What would they have us do? Thus, therefore, they renew their quarrel; but the christian man cannot help it, unless he would see them go to hell, and saying nothing. For the Word of God doth as assuredly condemn man's righteousness, as it doth condemn man's sin; it condemneth not man's righteousness among men, for there it is good and profitable, Job xxxv. 6–8; but with God, to save the soul, it is no better than filthy rags. Is. lxiv. 6.

Nor will this christian man suffer these carnal ones to delude themselves with a change of terms; for the devil, who is the great manager of carnal men in things that concern their souls, and in the plea that they make for themselves, will help them to tricks and shifts to evade the power of the Word of God. Teaching them to call the beauties of nature grace, and the acts of natural powers the exercise of the graces of the Spirit, he will embolden them also to call man's righteousness the righteousness of Christ, and that by which a sinner may be justified in the sight of God from the law. These tricks the Christian sees, and being faithful to God's truth, and desiring the salvation of his neighbour, he laboureth to discover the fallacy of, and to propound better terms for this poor creature to embrace, and venture his soul upon; which terms are warranted by the New Testament, a stranger to which the natural man is. But, I say, the things which the Christian presseth, being so foreign to nature, and lying so cross to man's best things, are presently judged by the natural man to be fables or foolishness. 1 Co. ii. 14. Wherefore here again, he takes another occasion to maintain his strife, and contention against the righteous man; raising of slanders upon him, and laying things to his charge that he understandeth not; charging also his doctrine with many grievous things. Namely, that he holdeth that man was made to be damned; that man's righteousness is no better than sin; that a man had as good to do ill as well; that we may believe, and do what we list; that holiness pleaseth not God; and that sinning is the way to cause grace to abound. Besides, say they, he condemneth good motions, and all good beginnings of heart to God-

* 'To down with;' to receive, to swallow. 'Probably it will hardly *down* with any body at first hearing.'—*Locke.*—ED.

ward; he casteth away that good we have, and would have us depend upon a justice to save us by, that we can by no means approve of. And thus the quarrel is made yet wider between the men of the world and the christian man. But there is not a stop put here.

For it is possible for the carnal man to be beaten out of all his arguments for himself and his own things, by the power and force of the Word; and to be made to consent to what the Christian has said as to the notion of the truth. I must not speak this of all. But yet the breach doth still abide; for that yet there appears to be no more with the man, but only the notion of things. For though the notion of things are those that of God are made the means of conveying of grace into the heart, yet grace is not always with the notion of things; the Word ofttimes standeth in man's understanding alone, and remaineth there, as not being accompanied with such grace as can make it the power of God to salvation. Now, when it is thus with the soul, the danger is as great as ever, because there is a presumption now begotten in the heart that the man is in a saved condition,—a presumption, I say, instead of faith, which puffeth up, instead of enabling the soul after a godly manner to depend upon God for mercy through Christ. This is called the word of them that are puffed up; the word only, because not accompanied with saving grace. 1 Co. iv. 19; viii. 1. 1 Th. i. 5.

This the Christian also sees, and says it is too weak to conduct the soul to glory. And this, indeed, he says, because he would not that his neighbour should come short home. But neither can this be borne; but here again, the natural man with his notion of things is offended; and takes pet against his friend, because he tells him the truth, and would that he so should digest the truth, that it may prove unto him eternal life. Wherefore he now begins to fall out again, for as yet the enmity is not removed; he therefore counts him an unmerciful man, one that condemneth all to hell but himself; and as to his singularity in things, those he counteth for dreams, for enthusiasms, for allegorical whimsies, vain revelations, and the effects of an erroneous judgment. For the Lord has put such darkness betwixt Egypt and Israel, as will not suffer them to come together. But this is not all.

For it is possible for these carnal men to be so much delighted in the notion of things, as to addict themselves to some kind of worship of Christ, whose notions of truth have by them been received. And because their love is yet but carnal, and because the flesh is swelling, and is pleased with pomp and sumptuousness, therefore, to show how great an esteem such have for Christ, whom they are now about to worship, they will first count his testa-

ment, though good, a thing defective, and not of fulness sufficient to give, in all particular things, direction how they should, to their own content, perform their glorious doctrine. For here and there, and in another place, cry they, there is something wanting. Here, say they, is nothing said of those places, vestures, gestures, shows, and outward greatness that we think seemly to be found in and with those that worship Jesus. Here wants sumptuous ceremonies, glorious ornaments, new-fashioned carriages,* all which are necessary to adorn worship withal.

But now here again, the truly godly, as he comes to see the evil of things, maketh his objections, and findeth fault, and counts them unprofitable and vain. Is. xxix. Mat. xv. Mar. vii. But they again, seeing the things they have made are the very excellencies of human invention, and things added as a supplement to make up what, and wherein, as they think, the man that was faithful over his own house as a son was defective. They are resolved to stand upon their points, and not to budge an inch from the things that are so laudable, so necessary, so convenient, and so comely; the things that have been judged good, by so many wise, learned, pious, holy, reverend, and good men. Nay, if this were all, the godly would make a good shift; but their zeal is so great for what they have invented, and their spirits so hot to make others couch and bend thereto, that none must be suffered to their power to live and breathe, that refuseth to conform thereto.† This has been proved too true, both in France, Spain, Germany, Italy, and other places; and upon this account it is that persecution has been kept alive so many hundred years in some places against the church of God.

From what has been said as to these things, this I collect as the sum—First, That man by nature is in a state of wrath and condemnation. Ep. ii. 1–4. Jn. iii. 18. Secondly, That the natural man, by all his natural abilities, is not able to recover himself from this his condemned condition. Jn. vi. 44. Ep. i. 19, 20. Thirdly, That a man may have right notions of gospel things, that hath no grace in his heart. 1 Co. xiii. 2, 3. Fourthly, That to add human inventions to Christ's institutions, and to make them of the same force and necessity, of the same authority

* 'New-fashioned carriages;' not equipages to ride in, but dainty formalities. 'Nor in my carriage a feigned niceness shown.'—Dryden. 'Trades in the carriage of a holy saint.'—Shakspeare.—Ed.

† Bunyan, when sent to prison, was thus threatened: 'If you do not go to church, or transport yourself, you must stretch by the neck for it.' This led to those painful reflections: 'If I should make a scrabbling shift to clamber up the ladder, yet I should, either with quaking or other symptoms of faintings, give occasion to the enemy to reproach the way of God and his people for their timorousness.'—Grace Abounding, No. 334.—Ed.

and efficacy, is nought; and not to be subjected to. Is. xxix. 13. Mat. xv. 8, 9. Mar. vii. 6, 7.

So then, he that saith these things, saith true; for the Scriptures say the same. This, then, is a good cause to suffer for, if men will that I shall suffer for saying so; because it is that which is founded upon the Word of God; and the Word is the ground and foundation of all true doctrine. Let him, then, that believeth what is here discoursed, and that liveth soberly and peaceably in this belief among his neighbours, stand by what he hath received, and rejoice that he hath found the truth. And if any shall afflict or trouble him for holding of these things, they afflict or trouble him for holding to good things; and he suffereth at their hands because his cause is good.

And such an one may with boldness, as to this, make his appeal to the Bible, which is the foundation of his principles, and to God the author of that foundation, if what he holds is not good. He may say, ' Lord, I have said, that man by nature is in a state of condemnation, and they make me suffer for that. Lord, I have asserted that man, by all his natural abilities, is not able to recover himself from this his condemned state, and they make me suffer for that. Lord, I have said that a natural man may have right notions of the gospel, and yet be without the saving grace thereof, and they make me suffer for that. Lord, I cannot consent that human inventions and doctrines of men should be joined with thy institution as matters of worship, and imposed upon my conscience as such, and they make me suffer for that. Lord, I own the government, pray for my superiors, live quietly among my neighbours, give to all their dues, feed the hungry, clothe the naked, relieve the afflicted, and show myself, by my faith and life, to be a true christian man, and yet my neighbours will not let me alone. True, I cannot comply with all that some men would have me comply with; no more did Daniel, no more did Paul; and yet Daniel said, that he had to the king done no hurt, vi. 22; and Paul said, "neither against the law of the Jews, neither against the temple, nor yet against Cæsar, have I offended anything at all." ' Ac. xxv. 8.

For he that keeps within the compass of God's Word, hurts no man, gives just offence to no man, though he complieth not with all that are modes and ways of worship in the world. Nor can this appeal be judged injurious, if it be not attended with intercessions against them that hate us. But we will pass this, and come to a second thing.

(3.) As he that suffereth for righteousness must have a good cause, so *he that suffereth for righteousness must have a good call.*

A man, though his cause be good, ought not by undue ways to run himself into suffering for it; nature teaches the contrary, and so doth the law

of God. Suffering for a truth ought to be cautiously took in hand, and as warily performed. I know that there are some men that are more concerned here than some; the preacher of the Word is by God's command made the more obnoxious man, for he must come off with a woe, if he preaches not the gospel. 1 Co. ix. 16. He, therefore, I say, doth and ought more to expose himself than other Christians are called to do. Yet it behoveth him also to beware, because that Christ has said to him, ' Behold, I send you forth as sheep, or lambs, in the midst of wolves: be ye therefore wise as serpents, and harmless as doves.' Mat. x. 16. Lu. x. 3. A man is not bound by the law of his Lord, to put himself into the mouth of his enemy. Christ withdrew himself; Paul escaped the governor's hands, by being let down in a basket over the wall of the city. 2 Co. xi. 32, 33. And Christ hath said, If they persecute you in one city, flee ye to another. If they will not let me preach here, I will take up my Bible, and be gone. Perhaps this is because I must preach in some other place. A minister can quickly pack up, and carry his religion with him, and offer what he knows of his God to another people. Ac. xiii. 44–47.* Nor should a minister strive, I think, with the magistrate for place, or time. But let him hearken to hear what God shall say by such opposition. Perhaps the magistrate must drive thee out of this place, because the soul is in another place that is to be converted, or helped by thy sermon to-day. We must also in all things, show ourselves to be such as by our profession we would that men should believe we are, to wit, meek, gentle, not strivers, but take our Lord and our brethren the prophets for our examples.

But I will not here presume to give instructions to ministers; but will speak a few words in the general about what I think may be a sufficient call to a man to suffer for righteousness.

First, Every christian man is bound by God's Word to hold to, or stand by his profession, his profession of faith, and to join to that profession, an holy godly life; because the Apostle and Highpriest of his profession is no less a one than Christ Jesus. He. iii. 1; x. 23. This by Christ himself is expressed thus, Let your light so shine. Mat. v. 16. No man lighteth a candle to put it under a bushel. Let your loins be girded about, and *your* lights burning. Lu. xii. 35. And Paul bids the Philippians hold forth the word of life. Ph. ii. 16.

And more particularly, by all this, this is intended, that we should hide our faith in Christ from no man, but should rather make a discovery of it by a life that will do so; for our profession, thus

---

* This is a truly Bunyanish mode of expression—clear, comprehensive, quaint; but so striking as to make an indelible impression.—ED.

managed, is the badge, and the Lord's livery, by which we are distinguished from other men.* So then, if, while I profess the truth of Christ, and so walk as to make my profession of it more apparent, I be made a sufferer for it, my call is good, and I may be bold in God and in my profession. This, Peter intends when he saith, 'But and if ye suffer for righteousness' sake, happy *are ye*, and be not afraid of their terror, neither be troubled; but sanctify the Lord God in your hearts, and *be* ready always to *give* an answer to every man that asketh you a reason of the hope that is in you, with meekness and fear.' 1 Pe. iii. 14, 15. Here, then, is a call not to meddle with the other, but to mind our own business; to walk in our christian profession, and to adorn it with all good works; and if any man will meddle with me, and ask me a reason of the hope that I have, to give it him with meekness and fear, whatever follows thereupon. This, Peter should have done himself there, where he denied his Master thrice.

The reason is, for that Christianity is so harmless a thing, that, be it never so openly professed, it hurts no man. I believe that Christ will save me; what hurt is this to my neighbour? I love Christ because he will save me; what hurt is this to any? I will for this worship Christ as he has bid me; what hurt is this to anybody? I will also tell my neighbours what a loving one my Christ is, and that he is willing to be good to them as he has been good to me; and what hurt is this to the governor of a kingdom? But and if any man will afflict me for this, my cause is good, and also my call to stand full godly to my profession.

Secondly, There is sometimes a call to suffer for righteousness, even from the voice of necessity. That is, either when, by my silence, the truth must fall to the ground; or when, by my shrinking, the souls of other men are in danger. This, I say, is a call to suffer even by the voice of necessity. The case may be when God's ways may be trodden under foot; yea, his Word, and ways, and name, and people, and all. Thus Goliah did do, for several days together, 1 Sa. xvii., and vaunted in his doing; and there was not a man, no, not in Israel, that durst answer him a word. And now was the spirit of David stirred in him, and he would put his life in his hand, and give this man an answer; and he saw there was reason for it—necessity gave

him a call. Is there not a cause, saith he, lies bleeding upon the ground, and no man of heart or spirit to put a check to the bold blasphemer? I will go fight with him; I will put my life in my hand; if I die, I die.

Consider also what Daniel did when the law was gone out to forbid, for thirty days, petitioning any god or man, save the king only. At that time, also, not a man of Israel peeped. Da. vi. 7. Now necessity walks about the streets, crying, Who is on the Lord's side? Who, &c. And Daniel answers, I am, by opening of his window, and praying, as at other times, three times a day, with his face towards Jerusalem. ver. 10. He heard this voice of necessity, and put his life in his hand, and complied with it, to the hazard of being torn in pieces by the lions.

Much like this was that of the three children; for when that golden image was set up, and worship commanded to be done unto it, not one, that we read of, durst stand upright when the time was come that bowing was the sign of worship. Only the three children would not bow: it was necessary that some should show that there was a God in heaven, and that divine worship was due alone to him. Da. iii. 10—12. But they run the hazard of being turned to ashes, in a burning fiery furnace, for so doing. But necessity has a loud voice, and shrill in the ears of a tender conscience: this voice will awake jealousy and kindle a burning fire within, for the name, and cause, and way, and people, of the God of heaven.

Thirdly, There is sometimes a call to suffer for righteousness by the voice of providence. That is, when, by providence, I am cast for my profession into the hands of the enemies of God and his truth; then I am called to suffer for it what God shall please to let them lay upon me. Only, for the making of my way more clear in this matter, I will deliver what I have to say, with a caution or two. 1. Thou must take heed that thy call be good to this or that place, at which, by providence, thou art delivered up. 2. Thou must also take heed that, when thou art there, thou busiest thyself in nothing but that that good is. 3. Thou must also take heed that thou stay there no longer than while thou mayest do good or receive good there. 4. Thus far a man is in the way of his duty, and therefore may conclude that the providence of God, under which now he is, is such as has mercy and salvation in the bowels of it, whatsoever is by it, at the present, brought upon him.

Christ Jesus, our Lord, though his death was determined, and of absolute necessity, and that chiefly for which he came into the world, chose rather to be taken in the way of his duty than in any other way or anywhere else. Wherefore, when the hour was come, he takes with him

---

* A life of faith and holiness is the Christian's badge and livery. No particular costume, *that* may conceal a carnal heart—not a baptismal profession, *that* may be made by a hypocrite; but it is 'the hidden man of the heart,' evidenced by a 'meek and quiet spirit - in all holy conversation and godliness.' This is the Christian's badge and livery, by which he becomes 'a living epistle, known and read of all men.' —ED.

some of his disciples, and goeth into a garden, a solitary place, to pray; which done, he sets his disciples to watch, and falleth himself to prayer. So he prays once; he prays twice; he prays thrice: and he giveth also good doctrine to his disciples. And now, behold, while he was here, in the way of his duty, busying himself in prayer to God, and in giving of good instruction to his followers, upon him comes Judas and a multitude with swords and staves, and weapons, to take him; to which providence he, in all meekness, submits, for he knew that by it he had a call to suffer. Mat. xxvi. 36—47.

In this way, also, the apostles were called to suffer, even while they were in the way of their duty. Yea, God bid them go into the temple to preach, and there delivered them into the hands of their enemies. Ac. iv. 1—3; v. 20—26.

Be we in the way of our duty, in the place and about the work unto which we are called of God, whether that work be religious or civil, we may, without fear, leave the issue of things to God, who only doth wonderful things. And he who lets not a sparrow fall to the ground without his providence, will not suffer a hair of our head to perish but by his order. Lu. xii. 6, 7. And since he has engaged us in his work, as he has if he has called us to it, we may expect that he will manage, and also bear us out therein; either so as by giving of us a good deliverance by way of restoration to our former liberty and service for him, or so as to carry us well out of this world to them that, under the altar, are crying, How long, holy and true: nor shall we, when we come there, repent that we suffered for him here. Oh! how little do saints, in a suffering condition, think of the robes, the crowns, the harps, and the song that shall be given to them; and that they shall have when they come upon mount Zion. Re. vi. 11; xiv. 1—7.

Fourthly, There is sometimes a call to suffer for righteousness by an immediate and powerful impulse of the Spirit of God upon the heart. This, I say, is sometimes, and but sometimes; for this is not God's ordinary way, nor are many of his servants called after this manner to suffer for righteousness. Moses was called thus to suffer when he went so often unto Pharaoh with the message of God in his mouth. And 'he endured, as seeing him who is invisible.' He. xi. 25—27.

Paul was called thus to suffer, and he obeyed, and went, and performed that work, according to the will of God. This kind of call Paul calls a binding, or a being bound in the Spirit, because the Holy Ghost had laid such a command upon him to do so, that he could not, by any means, get from under the power of it. 'And now, behold,' saith he, 'I go bound in the Spirit unto Jerusalem, not knowing the things that shall befal me there.' Ac. xx. 22. For he that is under this call has, as I

said, bonds laid upon his spirit, which carry him to the place where his testimony is to be borne for God; nor shall he, if he willingly submits and goes, as Paul did, but have an extraordinary presence of God with him, as he. And see what a presence he had; for after the second assault was given him by the enemy, even 'the night following, the Lord stood by him, and said, Be of good cheer, Paul; for as thou hast testified of me in Jerusalem, so must thou bear witness also at Rome.' Ac. xxiii. 11. Thus God meeteth his people in their service for him, when he calls them aloud to do great service for him. The power of such a call as this, I say, is great, and men of ordinary spirits must needs give place thereto, and leave a man thus bound to the God that thus has bound him. All the help such can afford him is to follow him with our prayers, not to judge him or grieve him, or lay stumbling-blocks before him. No; they must not weep nor mourn for him, so as to make him sorrowful. See Ac. xxi. 12—14.

His friends may suggest unto him what is like to attend his present errand, as Agabus did by the Spirit to Paul when he took his girdle and bound himself therewith, to show him how his enemies should serve him whither he went. 'Thus saith the Holy Ghost,' said he, 'so shall the Jews at Jerusalem bind the man that owneth this girdle, and shall deliver *him* into the hands of the Gentiles.' Ac. xxi. But if this call be indeed upon a man, all sorrow is turned into joy before him; for he is ready, not only to be bound, but also to die at Jerusalem for the name of the Lord Jesus. Ac. xxi. 13.

Instances, also, of later times might be given of a call extraordinary to suffer for righteousness. For many, in the first three hundred years' persecution, when nobody knew what they were, would boldly come up to the face of their enemies and tell what they were, and suffer for what they professed, the death. I remember, also, the woman who, when her friends were gone before to suffer, how she came running and panting after, for fear she should not come thither time enough to suffer for Jesus Christ.

But I will give you an instance of later times, even in the beginning of Queen Elizabeth's reign, of an Hertfordshire man that went as far as Rome to bear his testimony for God against the wickedness of that place. This man, when he was arrived there, and had told them wherefore he was come, they took and condemned him to death, to wit, to be burned for an heretic. Now he was to ride from the prison to the place of execution upon an ass, with his face to the beast's tail, and was to be stripped from the shoulders to the waist, that he might be tormented all the way he went with burning torches continually thrust to his sides; but he, nothing at all afraid, spake in his exhortation to the people to fly from their sin and idolatry; he would also catch hold of the torches and put them to his sides, to show how little he esteemed the worst that they could do. Also, when he was come to the place of execution, he suffered there such cruelty, with so unconcerned a mind, and with such burning zeal for God's truth, testified against them while he could speak; that, all amazed, his enemies cried, he could not have suffered as he did but by the help of the devil. His name I have now forgot, but you will find it, with the story at large, in the third volume of Acts and Monuments, at the 1022 page.* But we will pass this, and come to our second particular, namely,

[B. What it is to suffer for righteousness' sake.]

To show when it may be said a man doth not only suffer for righteousness, *but also for righteousness' sake.*

To suffer for righteousness' sake must be either with the intention of the persecutor or else of the persecuted. The persecutor, whatever the person's suffering is, if he afflicteth this person for a supposed good that he thinketh he hath or professeth, he makes him suffer for righteousness' sake. So that, in this sense, a man that hath no grace may not only suffer for righteousness, but also for righteousness' sake. But this I intend not, because the text is not concerned with it.

The thing, therefore, now intended to be spoken to, is this, namely, when a man may be said to suffer what he suffereth upon a religious account, of love to, or for the sake of, that good that he finds in the truths of God, or because his heart is joined and espoused to the good of the truths that he professeth; not that there is any thing in any truth of God that is not good; but a man may profess truth, not for the sake of the goodness that is in it, but upon a remote account. Judas professed truth, not of love to the truth, but of love to the bag, and to the money that was put therein. Men may profess for a wife, for a trade, for friendship, or because profession is at such a time or in such a place, in fashion. I wish that there were no cause to say this. Now there is not any of these that profess the truth for the truth's sake, that profess the truth of love to it; nor shall they, should they suffer as professors, never so

* These awful cruelties were practised upon Richard Atkins, in July, 1581. He went to Rome to reprove the people of idolatry. In St. Peter's Church, he knocked the chalice out of the priest's hand, and spilt the wine; he then endeavoured to seize the host, but was prevented. For these mad pranks he suffered savage torments.—*Fox*, edit. 1631, vol. iii., p. 1022. —ED.

long, never so much, never so grievously, be counted of God among them that suffer for righteousness' sake; that is, of unfeigned love to righteousness. Wherefore, that I may show you who may be said to suffer for righteousness' sake, I will propound and speak to several things.

1. Then, he that suffereth in the apostle's sense, for well-doing, or for righteousness' sake, sets his face against nothing but sin. He resisteth unto blood, striving against sin. Sin is the object of his indignation, because it is an enemy to God, and to his righteous cause in the world. He. xii. 3, 4. Sin, I say, is that which such a man singleth out as his opposite, as his antagonist, and that against which is heart is set. It is a rare thing to suffer aright, and to have my spirit, in my suffering, bent only against God's enemy—sin; sin in doctrine, sin in worship, sin in life, sin in conversation. Now then, he that suffereth for righteousness' sake has singled out sin to pursue it to death, long before he comes to the cross. It is sin, alas, and his hatred to it that have brought him into this condition. He fell out with sin at home, in his own house, in his own heart, before he fell out with sin in the world, or with sin in public worship. For he that can let sin go free and uncontrolled at home within, let him suffer while he will, he shall not suffer for righteousness' sake. And the reason is, because a righteous soul, as the phrase is, 2 Pe. ii. 8, has the greatest antipathy against that sin that is most ready to defile it, and that is, as David calls it, one's own iniquity, or the sin that dwelleth in one's own flesh. I have kept me, says he, from mine iniquity, from mine own sin. People that are afraid of fire are concerned most with that that burneth in their own chimney; they have the most watchful eye against that that is like to burn down their own house first.

He also that suffereth for righteousness' sake, doth it also because he would not that sin should cleave to the worship of God; and, indeed, this is mostly the cause of the sufferings of the godly. They will not have to do with that worship that hath sinful traditions commixed with God's appointments, because they know that God is jealous of his worship; and has given a strict charge that all things be done according to the pattern showed to us in the mount. He knows also that God will not be with that worship, and those worshippers, that have not regard to worship by the rule of the testament of Christ. He is also against the sin that is apt to cleave to himself while he standeth in the presence of God. I will wash mine hands in innocency, so will I compass thine altar, O Lord. This man also chooses to be in the practical parts of worship, if possible, for he knows that to have to do about holy things sincerely is the way to be at the remotest distance from sin. He chooses also to be with those holy ones that are of the same mind with him against sin; for he knows that two are better than one, and that a threefold cord is not easily broken. Wherefore look to yourselves, you that do, or may be called to suffer for religion: if you bend not yourselves against sin, if to be revenged of sin be not the cause of your suffering, you cannot be said to suffer for righteousness' sake. Take heed, therefore, that something else be not an inducement to thee to suffer. A man may suffer to save what he has: there is credit also and an applause; there is shame to conform; there is carnal stoutness of spirit; there is hatred of persecutors and scorn to submit; there is fear of contempt and of the reproach of the people, &c. These may be motives and arguments to a suffering state, and may really be the ground of a man's being in the gaol; though he cries out in the meanwhile of popery, of superstition, and idolatry, and of the errors that attend the common modes of the religions of the world. I charge no man as though I knew any such thing by any; but I suggest these things as things that are possible, and mention them because I would have sufferers have a care of themselves; and watch and pray, because no man can be upright here that is not holy, that cannot pray, and watch, and deny himself for the love that he has to righteousness. I said it before, and will say it again, it is a rare thing to be set in downrightness of heart against sin.

2. Is it for the sake of righteousness that thou sufferest? Then it is because thou wouldest have righteousness promoted, set up, and established in the world; also thou art afflicted at those advantages that iniquity gets upon men, upon things, and against thyself. 'I beheld,' said David, 'the transgressors, and was grieved; because men kept not thy word.' Ps. cxix. 158. And again, These are they that mourn for the abominations that are done among men. Eze. ix. 4. There is a great deal of talk about religion, a great deal of pleading for religion, namely, as to the formalities of this and the other way.* But to choose to be religious, that I might be possessed with holiness, and to choose that religion that is most apt to possess me with it, if I suffer for this, I suffer for righteousness' sake. Wherefore say thus to thy soul, thou that art, like to suffer for righteousness, How is it with the most inward parts of my soul? What is there? What designs, desires, and reachings out are there? Why do I pray? Why do I read? Why do I hear? Why do I haunt and frequent places and ordinances appointed for worship? Is it because I love holiness? would promote righteousness, because I love to see godliness show itself in others, and because I would feel more of the power of it in myself? If so, and if thou sufferest for thy profession, thou sufferest, not only for righteousness, but also for righteousness' sake.

Dost thou thus practise, because thou wouldest be taught to do outward acts of righteousness, and because thou wouldest provoke others to do so too? Dost thou show to others how thou lovest righteousness, by taking opportunities to do righteousness? How is it, dost thou show most mercy to thy dog,† or to thine enemy, to thy swine, or to the poor? Whose naked body hast thou clothed? Whose hungry belly hast thou fed? Hast thou taken delight in being defrauded and beguiled? Hast thou willingly sat down by the loss with quietness, and been as if thou hadst not known, when thou hast been wronged, defamed, abused, and all because thou wast not willing that black-mouthed men should vilify and reproach religion upon thy account? 1 Co. vi. 7.

He that loveth righteousness will do thus, yea, and do it as unto God, and of tenderness to the Word of God which he professeth. And he that thinks to make seeing men believe, that when he suffereth, he suffereth for righteousness' sake, and yet is void in his life of moral goodness, and that has no heart to suffer and bear, and put up, and pass by injuries in his conversation among his enemies at home, is deceived.

There are some Scriptures that are as if they were out of date among some professors, specially such as call for actual holiness and acts of self-denial for God; but it will be found, at the day of judgment, that they only are the peculiar people that are 'zealous of good works.' Tit. ii. 14. God help us, it is hard now to persuade professors to come up to negative holiness, that is, to leave undone that which is bad; and yet this of itself comes far short of ones being found in practical goodness.

But this is the man that suffereth, when he suffereth for righteousness' sake, that makes it his business, by all lawful means, according to the capacity that God has put him in, to promote, set up, and establish righteousness in the world; I say this is the man that suffereth for righteousness' sake, that suffereth for so doing; and I am sure that a life that is moral, when joined to the profession of the faith of the things that are of the Spirit of God, is absolutely necessary to the pro-

---

* Every Christian must be decided in his own conscience as to the formalities of religion; but he who prefers talking of forms and ceremonies to communion in the substance, is in a melancholy state.—Ed.

† What a severe reproach it is to human nature, to see a lovely child in rags and shoeless, running the streets, exposed to the pitiless weather, while a splendid equipage passes, in which a lady holds up her lapdog at the window to give it an airing!! Is not this a greater crime than sends many a poor wretch to the treadmill?—Ed.

moting of righteousness in the world. Hence Peter tells them that suffer for righteousness' sake, that they must have ' a good conscience '—a good conscience towards God, towards men, towards friends, towards enemies. 1 Pe. iii. 14—16. Ac. xxiv. 16 ; xxiii. 1. They must have a good conscience in all things, being willing, ready, desirous to live honestly, godly, and righteously in this world, or else they cannot, though they may suffer for the best doctrine under heaven, suffer for righteousness' sake. He. xiii. 18. Wherefore,

3. Is it for righteousness' sake that thou sufferest? then thy design is the ruin of sin. This depends upon what was said before; for he that strives against sin, that seeks to promote righteousness, he designs the ruin of sin. ' Be not,' said Paul to the suffering Romans, ' overcome of evil, but overcome evil with good.' Ro. xii. 21. To overcome evil with good is a hard task. To rail it down, to cry it down, to pray kings, and parliaments, and men in authority to put it down, this is easier than to use my endeavour to overcome it with good, with doing of good, as I said before.* And sin must be overcome with good at home, before thy good can get forth of doors† to overcome evil abroad.

Abraham overcame evil with good, when he quieted the discontent of Lot and his herdsmen, with allowing of them to feed their cattle in the best of what God had given him. Ge. xiii. 7, 8.

David overcame evil with good, when he saved the life of his bloody enemy that was fallen into his hand; also when he grieved that any hurt should come to them that sought nothing so much as his destruction. ' They rewarded me,' saith he, ' evil for good, to the spoiling of my soul. But as for me, when they were sick, my clothing was sackcloth. I humbled my soul with fasting - I behaved myself as though *he had been* my friend *or* brother; I bowed down heavily, as one that mourneth *for his* mother.' This is to overcome evil with good. Ps. xxxv. 12—14.

Job saith concerning his enemy, that he did not rejoice when evil found him; ' neither have I,' said he, ' suffered my mouth to sin by wishing a curse to his soul.' He means he did the quite contrary, and so overcame evil with good. Job xxxi. 29, 30.

Elisha overcame evil with good, when he received the men that came for his life, and had them where he might feast, and comfort them, and sent them home in peace to their master. 2 Ki. vi. 19—23.

* Revenge naturally rises in the mind of man under a sense of injury. To return good for evil is one of the effects of the new birth. But while this is done, it is also our duty to petition kings and parliaments to remove evils.—Ed.

† ' Forth of doors;' out of doors, public.—Ed.

The New Testament also is full of this, both in exhortations and examples. In exhortations where it is said, resist not evil, that is, with evil, but overcome evil with good. Pr. xxiv. 29. ' But whosoever shall smite thee on thy right cheek, turn to him the other also.—And whosoever shall compel thee to go a mile, go with him twain. Give to him that asketh thee ; and from him that would borrow of thee, turn not thou away.—Love your enemies, bless them that curse you, do good to them that hate you, and pray for them which despitefully use you, and persecute you; that ye may be the children of your Father which is in heaven, for he maketh his sun to rise on the evil, and on the good - on the just, and on the unjust.' Mat. v. 39—45. ' Bless them that persecute you: bless, and curse not.' Ro. xii. 14. ' Not rendering evil for evil, or railing for railing, but contrariwise, blessing; knowing that ye are thereunto called, that ye should inherit a blessing.' 1 Pe. iii. 9. Ro. xii. 14. This is righteousness—these are righteous courses. And as these are preceptively propounded, so they were as practically followed by them that were eminently godly in the primitive church.

' We *are* fools for Christ's sake,' said Paul, ' we are despised, we are hungry, thirsty, naked, and buffeted.—Being reviled, we bless; being persecuted, we suffer it; being defamed, we entreat: we are made as the filth of the earth, *and are* the offscouring of all things unto this day.' 1 Co. iv. 10—13. This is overcoming of evil with good, and he that has chosen to himself that religion that teaches these things, and that loves that religion because it so teacheth him; if he suffereth for it, he suffereth for righteousness' sake.

4. He that suffereth for righteousness' sake, will carry righteousness whithersoever he goes. Neither the enemy, nor thy sufferings, shall be able to take righteousness from thee. Righteousness must be thy chamber mate, thy bed companion, thy walking mate: it is that without which thou wilt be so uncouth, as if thou couldest not live. Ps. xxvi.; xxv. 21.

Paul in his sufferings would have righteousness with him, for it must be as it were his armourbearer; yea, his very armour itself. 2 Co. vi. 7. It is an excellent saying of Job, ' I put on righteousness, and it clothed me; my judgment was as a robe and a diadem. I was eyes to the blind, and feet was I to the lame; I was a father to the poor,' &c. Job xxix. 11—16. ' Princes,' said David also, ' did sit *and* speak against me, *but* thy servant did meditate in thy statutes.' Ps. cxix. 23. A man that loves righteousness doth as Abraham did with his Sarah, carry it every where with him, though he goes, because of that, in danger of his life. Righteousness! It is the only intimate that a Christian has. It is that by which he takes his measures, that with which he consults, with respect to what he doth, or is to do, in the world. 'Thy testimonies,' said David also, '*are* my delight, *and* my counsellors.' The men of my counsel, in the margin. Ps. cxix. 24.

David! He was the man of affliction; the suffering man in his day; but in all places where he came, he had righteousness, the law and godly practice with him. It was his counsellor, as he was a man, a saint, a king. I dare say, for that man that suffers righteousness to be rent away from him by the violence and rage of men, and that casts it away, as David did Saul's armour, that he may secure himself; he has no great love for righteousness, nor to the cross for righteousness' sake. 'My righteousness I hold fast,' said Job, 'and will not let it go: my heart shall not reproach *me* so long as I live.' Job xxvii. 6. What? part with righteousness! A righteous Lord! A righteous Word! A righteous profession! A righteous life! to sleep in a whole skin: the Lord forbid it me, and all that he has counted worthy to be called by his name. Let us carry it with us from the bed to the cross, and then it shall carry us from thence to the crown. Let it be our companion to prison and death, then shall we show that we are lovers of righteousness, and that we choose to suffer for righteousness' sake.

5. Dost thou suffer for righteousness' sake? why then, thy righteousness is not diminished, but rather increased by thy sufferings. Righteousness thriveth best in affliction, the more afflicted, the more holy man; the more persecuted, the more shining man. Ac. vi. 15. The prison is the furnace, thy graces are the silver and the gold; wherefore, as the silver and the gold are refined by the fire, and so made more to show their native brightness, so the Christian that hath, and that loveth righteousness, and that suffereth for its sake, is by his sufferings refined and made more righteous, and made more christian, more godly. Zec. xiii. 9. Some, indeed, when they come there, prove lead, iron, tin, and at the best, but the dross of silver; and so are fit for nothing, but there to be left and consumed, and to bear the badge, if ever they come from thence, of reprobate silver from the mouth and sentence of their neighbours. Eze. xxii. 18—22. Je. vi. 28—30. But when I, says Job, am tried, 'I shall come forth as gold.' xxiii. 10.

When Saul had cast one javelin at David, it made him walk wisely in all his ways. But when he added to his first fury, plots to take away his life, then David behaved himself yet more wisely. 1 Sa. xviii. 10—30. The hotter the rage and fury of men are against righteous ways, the more those that love righteousness grow therein. For they are concerned for it, not to hide it, but to make it spangle; not to extinguish it, but to greaten it,

and to show the excellency of it in all its features, and in all its comely proportion. Now such an one will make straight steps for his feet, 'lest that which is lame be turned out of the way.' He. xii. 13. Now he shows to all men what faith is, by charity, by self-denial, by meekness, by gentleness, by long-suffering, by patience, by love to enemies, and by doing good to them that hate us; now he walketh upon his high places. Yea, will not now admit that so slovenly a conversation should come within his doors, as did use to haunt his house in former times. Now it is Christmas,* now it is suffering time, now we must keep holy day every day. The reason is, for that a man, when he suffereth for Christ, is set upon a hill, upon a stage, as in a theatre, to play a part for God in the world. And you know when men are to play their parts upon a stage, they count themselves, if possible, more bound to circumspection; and that for the credit of their master, the credit of their art, and the credit of themselves. For then the eyes of every body are fixed, they gape and stare upon them. Ps. xxii. 17. And a trip here is as bad as a fall in another place. Also now God himself looks on. Yea, he laugheth, as being pleased to see a good behaviour attending the trial of the innocent.

(1.) He that suffereth for righteousness' sake suffereth for his goodness, and he is now to labour by works and ways to convince the world that he suffereth as such an one. (2.) He that suffereth for righteousness' sake has many that are weak to strengthen by his sweet carriages under the cross, wherefore he had need to exceed in virtue. (3.) He also is by well-doing to put to silence the ignorance of foolish men, he had need be curious and circumspect in all his actions. (4.) He is to come in, and to be a judge, and to condemn, by his faith and patience in his sufferings, the world, with his Lord and fellows, at the appearing of Jesus Christ; he had need be holy himself. This, therefore, is the fit sign of suffering for righteousness' sake. 1 Co. vi. 1—5. He. xi. 7. 2 Th. i. 5, 6. 1 Pe. iv. 3—5.

6. He that suffereth, not only for righteousness, but also for righteousness' sake, will not exchange his cause, though for it in a gaol, for all the ease and pleasure in the world. They that suffered for righteousness' sake of old, were tempted before they were sawn asunder. He. xi. Tempted, that is, allured, to come out of their present sufferings, and leave their faith and profession in irons behind them. Tempted with promises of promotion, of

ease, of friendship, of favour with men. As the Devil said to Christ, so persecutors of old did use to make great promises to sufferers, if they would fall down and worship. But this is alone as if they should say, Butcher, make away with your righteousness,* and a good conscience, and you shall find the friendship of the world. For there is no way to kill a man's righteousness but by his own consent. This, Job's wife knew full well, hence she tempted him to lay violent hands upon his own integrity. Job ii. 9.

The Devil, nor men of the world can kill thy righteousness or love to it, but by thy own hand; or separate that and thee asunder, without thine own act. Nor will he that doth indeed suffer for the sake of it, or of love he bears thereto, be tempted to exhange it for the goods of all the world. It is a sad sight to see a man that has been suffering for righteousness, restored to his former estate, while the righteousness for which he suffered, remains under locks and irons, and is exposed to the scorn, contempt, reproach of the world, and trodden under the foot of men.† 'It is better,' said Paul, 'for me to die, than that any man should make my glorying void.' And it had been a hundred times better for that man, if he had never known the way of righteousness, than after he has known it, to turn from the holy commandment delivered unto him.

The striving is, in persecution, for righteousness; to wit, whether it shall be set up, or pulled down. The sufferer, he is for setting up, and the persecutors are for pulling down. Thus they strive for the mastery. Now, if a man stands by his righteousness, and holds fast his good profession, then is righteousness set up; nor can it, so long, be pulled down. Hence, so long a man is said to overcome; and overcome he doth, though he be killed for his profession. But if he starts back, gives place, submits, recants, or denieth any longer to own that good thing that he professed, and exposed himself to suffering for; then he betrays his cause, his profession, his conscience, his righteousness, his soul, and all; for he has delivered up his profession to be murdered before his face: A righteous man falling down before the wicked, is as a troubled fountain, and a corrupt spring. Pr. xxv. 26. But this, I hope, will not he do that loveth righteousness, and that suffereth for righteousness' sake. I do not say but that a man may slip here, with Peter,

Origen, Hierom, Cranmer, Baynham, Ormis,‡ and other good folk; but be he one of the right kind, a lover of righteousness indeed, he will return, and take revenge upon himself in a godly way, for so ungodly a fact.

7. He that suffereth not only for righteousness, but also for righteousness' sake, is not so wedded to his own notions as to slight or overlook the good that is in his neighbour. But righteousness he loves wherever he finds it, though it be in him that smiteth him. Ps. cxli. 5. Yea, he will own and acknowledge it for the only thing that is of beauty and glory in the world. With the excellent in the earth is all such a man's delight. Wherefore I put a difference betwixt suffering for an opinion and suffering for righteousness; as I put a difference between suffering for righteousness and suffering for righteousness' sake.

If righteousness, if the stamp of God, if divine authority, is not found upon that thing which I hold, let men never suffer for it under the notion of righteousness. If sin, if superstition, if idolatry, if derogation from the wisdom of Christ, and the authority and perfection of his Word, be not found in, nor joined to that thing that I disown in worship, let me never open my mouth against it. I had rather fall in with, and be an associate of a righteous man that has no true grace, than with a professor that has no righteousness. It is said of the young man, though he went away from Christ, that he looked upon him and loved him. Mar. x. 17—22. But it is not said that ever he loved Judas. I know that the righteousness for which a good man suffereth, is not then embraced of the world, for that at such a time it is under a cloud. But yet there is righteousness also in the world, and wherever I see it, it is of a high esteem with me. David acknowledged some of his enemies to be more righteous than he acknowledged some of his servants to be. 2 Sa. iv. 9—11; iii. 31—35. It is a brave thing to have righteousness, as righteousness, to be the top-piece in mine affections. The reason why Christ was anointed with the oil of gladness above his fellows, was, because he loved righteousness, and hated iniquity more than they. He. i. 9. Love to righteousness flows from golden graces, and is that, and that only, that can make a man capable of suffering, in our sense, for righteousness' sake.

8. He that suffereth not only for righteousness, but also for righteousness' sake, will take care that his sufferings be so managed with graciousness of words and actions, that it may live when he is dead; yea, and it will please him too, if righteousness flourishes, though by his loss. Hence it is

---

* A striking expression. If a man's righteousness be killed, it must be by his own will. He must be the butcher to kill himself.—Ed.

† It is indeed sad to see professors, for the sake of paltry pelf, or to escape from persecution, denying the Lord Jesus. It subjects religion to scorn and contempt, and doubles the sorrows and sufferings of real Christians. Bunyan expresses himself here in a most admirable manner.—Ed.

‡ Bunyan's familiarity with these illustrious men was obtained by reading Fox's Acts and Monuments, when in prison.—Ed.

that Paul said, he rejoiced in his suffering, Col. i. 24; namely, because others got good thereby. And that he said, 'Yea, and if I be offered upon the sacrifice and service of your faith, I joy, and rejoice with you all.' Ph. ii. 17. But why rejoice in this? Why, because though his sufferings were to the distressing of his flesh, yet they were to the refreshing, comfort, and stability of others. This was it also that made him jostle with the false brethren among the churches; to wit, 'that the truth of the gospel might continue with them.' Ga. ii. 5.

When a man shall run the hazard of the ruin of what he has, and is, for righteousness, for the good and benefit of the church of God; that man, he managing himself by the rule, if he suffers for so doing, suffers not only for righteousness, but also for righteousness' sake. 'I endure all things,' said Paul, 'for the elect's sake, that they may also obtain the salvation which is in Christ Jesus with eternal glory.' 2 Tim. ii. 10. Here was love, you will say, to persons; and I will say also, to things; to all the righteousnesses of God that are revealed in the world, that all the elect might enjoy them to their eternal comfort and glory, by Christ Jesus. For 'whether we be afflicted,' says he, 'it is for your consolation and salvation, which is effectual in the enduring of the same sufferings which we also suffer: or whether we be comforted, it is for your consolation and salvation. 2 Cor. i. 6.

The end of a man and his design, if that be to promote righteousness, he using lawful means to accomplish it, is greatly accepted of God by Christ; and it is a sign he is a lover of righteousness; and that if he suffereth for so doing, he suffereth not for well-doing, only as to matter of fact, but also for his love to the good thing done, and for its sake.

I have now done with that first head that was to be spoken to, as touching the law and testament; which we have said was to be understood of the will of God spoken of in the text: 'Let them that suffer according to the will of God,' that is, according to his law and testament. Now we have showed what it is to suffer according to that; we come to another thing, namely :—

[THE WILL OF GOD MEANS HIS ORDER AND DESIGNMENT.]

Second, That by the will of God, we also understand his order and designment. For the will of God is active, to dispose of his people, as well as preceptive, to show unto us our duty. He then that suffers for righteousness' sake, as he suffers for that which is good as to the matter of it, and as he suffers for that which is good, after that manner as becomes that truth for which he suffereth; so he that thus suffereth, suffereth by the order and designment of God. That, then, is the next thing that is to be spoken to, namely :—

God is the great orderer of the battle that is managed in the world against antichrist. Hence that battle is called, 'The battle of that great day of God Almighty.' Re. xvi. 14. It is not what enemies will, nor what they are resolved upon, but what God will, and what God appoints; that shall be done. This doctrine Christ teacheth when he saith, 'Are not five sparrows sold for two farthings, and not one of them is forgotten before God? But even the very hairs of your head are all numbered. Fear not therefore: ye are of more value than many sparrows.' Lu. xii. 6, 7. He speaks in the verses before of killing, and bids them that they should not be afraid for that. 'Be not afraid of them that kill the body, and after that have no more that they can do. But I will forewarn you whom ye shall fear: Fear him, which after he hath killed hath power to cast into hell; yea, I say unto you, Fear him.' Then he leads them to the consideration of this, that the will of God governs, and disposes of his [people] to suffering; as well as declares to them for what, and how they should suffer, saying, 'Are not five sparrows sold for two farthings,' &c.

Also in Isa. viii. 9, 10, and in Isa. li. 12, 13, you have in sum the same thing inserted again. But we will not stay upon proof, but will proceed to demonstration hereof.

Pharaoh said he would, ay, that he would, but he could not touch so much as a thread or a rag of Israel, because the will of God was in that thing contrary to him. Saul said that he would have David, and to that end would search for him among the thousands of Judah; but David was designed for another purpose, and therefore Saul must go without him. 1 Sa. xxiii. 25, &c. Rabshakeh said that he was come from Assyria to Jerusalem to make 'Judah eat their own dung, and drink their own piss.' Isa. xxxvi. 12. But God said he should not shoot an arrow there. And it came to pass as God had said. Isa. xxxvii. 33. 2 Ki. xviii. 2 Ch. xxviii. Jeremiah and Baruch's enemies would have killed them, but they could not, for God hid them. How many times had the Jews a mind to have destroyed Jesus Christ; but they could not touch a hair of his head until his hour was come.

Those also that bound themselves in a curse, that they would neither eat nor drink until they had killed Paul, were forced to be foresworn, for the will of God was not that Paul should die as yet. Ac. xxiii. 12. This therefore should be well considered of God's church, in the cloudy and dark day. 'All his saints *are* in thy hand.' De. xxxiii. 3. It is not the way of God to let the enemies of God's church do what they will; no, the devil himself can devour but 'whom he may.' 1 Pe. v. 8. And as no enemy can bring suffering upon a man when the will of God is otherwise, so no man can save himself out of their hands when God will deliver him up for his glory. It remaineth, then, that we be not much afraid of men, nor yet be foolishly bold; but that we wait upon our God in the way of righteousness, and the use of those means which his providence offereth to us for our safety; and that we conclude that our whole dispose, as to liberty or suffering, lieth in the will of God, and that we shall, or shall not suffer, even as it pleaseth him. For,

First, God has appointed WHO shall suffer. Suffering comes not by chance, or by the will of man, but by the will and appointment of God. 'Let no man,' said Paul, 'be moved by these afflictions; for yourselves know that we are appointed thereunto.' 1 Th. iii. 3. We are apt to forget God when affliction comes, and to think it a strange thing that those that fear God should suffer indeed. 1 Pe. iv. 12. But we should not, for we suffer by the will and appointment of God. Hence they under the altar were bid to rest for a while, even until their fellow-servants also, and their brethren that should be killed—mark that—'should be killed, as they *were,* should be fulfilled.' Re. vi. 11. Wherefore, suffering for righteousness and for righteousness' sake, is by the will of God. God has appointed who shall suffer. That is the first.

Second, As God has appointed who shall suffer, so he has appointed WHEN they shall suffer for his truth in the world. Sufferings for such and such a man are timed, as to when he shall be tried for his faith. Hence, when Paul was afraid, at Corinth, that the heathens would fall about his ears, the Lord spake to him by night in a vision, saying, 'Be not afraid, but speak, and hold not thy peace; for I am with thee, and no man shall set on thee to hurt thee.' Ac. xviii. 9, 10. His time of suffering was not yet come there. It is also said concerning Jesus Christ, that even then when 'they sought to take him, no man laid hands on him, because his hour was not yet come.' Jn. vii. 30. The times, then, and the seasons, even for the sufferings of the people of God, are not in the hands of their enemies, but in the hand of God; as David said, 'My times are in thy hand.' By the will of God, then, it is that such shall suffer at, but not until, that time. But,

Third, As God has appointed who and when, so he has appointed WHERE this, that, or the other good man shall suffer. Moses and Elias, when they appeared on the holy mount, told Jesus of the sufferings which he should accomplish at Jerusalem. Jerusalem was the place assigned for Christ to suffer at; also, there must the whole of his sufferings be accomplished. Lu. ix. 30, 31. The saints are sprinkled by the hand of God here and there, as salt is sprinkled upon meat to keep it from stinking. And as they are thus sprinkled, that they may season the earth; so, accordingly, where they must suffer is also appointed for the better confirming of the truth. Christ said, it could not be that a prophet should 'perish out of Jerusalem.' Lu. xiii. 33. But why could it not be that they should perish other where? Were there no enemies but in Jerusalem? Were there no good men but at Jerusalem? No, no; that was not the reason. The reason was, for that God had appointed that they should suffer there. So then, who, when, and where, is at the will of God, and they, accordingly, are ordered by that will.

Fourth, As God has appointed who, when, and where, so he has also appointed WHAT KIND of sufferings this or that saint shall undergo, at this place and at such a time. God said that he would show Paul beforehand how great things he should suffer for his sake. Ac. ix. 16. And it is said that Christ did signify to Peter beforehand 'by what death he should glorify God.' Jn. xxi. 19. When Herod had beheaded John Baptist, and when the Jews had crucified Christ, it is said that they had but fulfilled what was 'written of them.' Mar. ix. 13. Ac. xiii. 29. Our sufferings, as to the nature of them, are all writ down in God's book; and though the writing seem as unknown characters to us, yet God understands them very well. Some of them they shall kill and crucify, and some of them they shall scourge in their synagogue, 'and persecute *them* from city to city.' Mat. xxiii. 34. Shall God, think you, say, some of them they shall serve thus, and some of them they shall do so to; and yet not allot which some to this, and which to that, and which to the other trial?

Doubtless our sufferings fall by the will of God unto us, as they fell of old upon the people of Jerusalem. It was appointed by God who of them should die of hunger, who with the sword, who should go into captivity, and who should be eaten up of beasts. Je. xv. 2, 3. So is the case here, namely, as God has appointed who, when, where, and the like, so he has, also, what manner of sufferings this or that good man shall undergo for his name. Let it then be concluded, that hitherto it appears, that the sufferings of saints are ordered and disposed by the will of God. But,

Fifth, As all this is determined by the will of God, so it is also appointed FOR WHAT TRUTH this or that saint shall suffer this or that kind of affliction. Every saint has his course, his work, and his testimony, as is allotted him of God. Mar. xiii. 34. John had a course, a testimony to fulfil for God, Ac. xiii. 25; and so had holy Paul, 2 Ti. iv. 6, 7; and so has every saint: also, he that is to suffer has his truth appointed him to suffer for. Christ had a truth peculiar to himself to bear witness to in a way of suffering. Mar. xiv. 61, 62. John had a truth peculiar to himself to bear witness to in a way of suffering. Mar. vi. 17, 18. Stephen had also a truth, diverse from them both, to which he bare a holy testimony, and for which he bravely died. Ac. vii. 51–53.

If you read the book of Acts and Monuments, you may see a goodly variety as to this; and yet in all a curious harmony. Some are there said to suffer for the Godhead, some for the manhood, some for the ordinances of Christ, and some laid down their lives for the brethren. And thus far we see that he that suffers for righteousness' sake, suffers, in this sense, according to the will of God.

Sixth, As it is appointed who, when, where, what kind, and for what truth, by the will of God, this and that saint should suffer; so also it is appointed BY WHOSE HAND this or that man shall suffer for this or that truth. It was appointed that Moses and Israel should suffer by the hand of Pharaoh. And for this very purpose, saith God, have I raised thee up, that is, to be a persecutor, and to reap the fruits thereof. Ex. ix. 16. It was also determined that Christ should suffer by the hand of Herod and Pontius Pilate; 'For of a truth,' said they, 'against thy holy child Jesus - both Herod, and Pontius Pilate, with the Gentiles, and the people of Israel, were gathered together, for to do whatsoever thy hand and thy counsel determined before to be done.' Ac. iv. 27.

These are great instances, from which we may gather how all these things are ordered from thence down hitherto. For if a sparrow falls not to the ground without God, she shall not be killed without God; not by he knows not who. And if a christian man is better than many sparrows, it follows, that God concerns himself more with, for, and about him than with, for, or about many sparrows. It follows, therefore, in right reason, that as the person who is appointed to be the sufferer, so the persons who are appointed to be the rod and sword thereby to afflict withal. Thus far, therefore, the will of God is it that ordereth and disposeth of us and of our sufferings.

Seventh, As all these pass through the hand of God, and come not to us but by his will, so HOW is also LONG as really determined as any of them all. It is not in man, but God, to set the time how long the rod of the wicked shall rest upon the lot of the righteous. Abraham must be informed of this. 'Abraham,' says God, 'know of a surety that thy seed shall be a stranger in a land *that is* not theirs, and shall serve them; and they shall afflict them four hundred years.' Ge. xv. 13. So the thraldom of Israel in Babylon was not only in the general appointed, but the time prefixed, how long. Je. xxv. 11, 12; xxix. 10. The time of the beast's reign and of the witnesses walking in sackcloth are punctually fixed, and that beyond which they cannot go. Re. xi. xii. xiii.

I know these are generals, and respect the church in the bulk of it, and not particular persons. But, as was hinted afore, we must argue from the greater to the lesser, that is, from four hundred years to ten days, from ten days to three,

and so from the church in general to each particular member, and to the time and nature of their sufferings. Re. ii. 10. Ho. vi. 2. Ac. xxiii. 11.

And thus, in a word or two, I have finished the first two parts of the text, and showed you what there is in Peter's counsel and advice; and showed you also, to whom his advice is given: in which last, as you see, I have showed you both what the will of God is, and what to suffer according to it. And particularly, I have, in a few words, handled this last, to show you that our sufferings are ordered and disposed by him, that you might always, when you come into trouble for his name, not stagger nor be at a loss, but be stayed, composed, and settled in your minds, and say, 'The will of the Lord be done.' Ac. xxi. 14. I will also say unto you this by the way, that the will of God doth greatly work, even to order and dispose of the spirits of Christians, in order to a willingness, disposedness, readiness, and resignation of ourselves to the mind of God. For with respect to this were those words last recited spoken. Paul saw that he had a call to go up to Jerusalem, there to bear his testimony for Christ and his gospel; but those unto whom he made known his purpose entreated him, with much earnestness, not to go up thither, for that, as they believed, it would endanger his life. But he answereth, What, mean ye to weep, and to break my heart? for I am ready, not to be bound only, but also to die at Jerusalem for the name of the Lord Jesus. And when he would not be persuaded, says Luke, we ceased, saying, 'The will of the Lord be done.'

From what has been thus discoursed, many things will follow; as,

1. That the rod, as well as the child, is God's; persecutors, as well as the persecuted, are his, and he has his own designs upon both. He has raised them up, and he has ordered them for himself, and for that work that he has for them to do. Hence Habakkuk, speaking of the church's enemies, saith, 'Thou hast ordained them for judgment; and, O mighty God, thou hast established them for correction.' Ha. i. 12. And, therefore, they are in other places called the rod of God's anger; his staff, Is. x. 5; his hand; his sword. Ps. xvii. 13, 14.

Indeed, to be thus disposed of, is a sad lot; the lot is not fallen to them in pleasant places, they have not the goodly heritage; but the judgments of God are a great deep. The thing formed may not say to him that formed it, Why hast thou made me thus? To be appointed, to be ordained, to be established to be a persecutor, and a troubler of God's church—O tremendous judgment! O amazing anger!

Three things the people of God should learn from hence.

(1.) Learn to pity and bewail the condition of

the enemy: I know thou canst not alter the counsel of God; appointed they are, established they are for their work, and do it they must and shall. But yet it becomes them that see their state, and that their day is coming, to pity and bewail their condition, yea, and to pray for them too; for who knows whether it is determined that they should remain implacable to the end, as Herod; or whether they may through grace obtain repentance for their doings, with Saul. And I say again, if thy prayer should have a casting hand in the conversion of any of them, it would be sweet to thy thoughts when the scene is over.

(2.) Never grudge them their present advantages. 'Fret not thyself because of evil *men*, neither be thou envious at the workers of iniquity.' Pr. xxiv. 19. Fret not, though they spoil thy resting-place. It is God that has bidden them do it, to try thy faith and patience thereby. Wish them no ill with what they get of thine; it is their wages for their work, and it will appear to them ere long that they have earned it dearly. Their time is to rejoice but as in a moment, in what thus is gotten by them; and then they, not repenting, are to perish for ever, like their own dung. Job xx. 5–7. Poor man, thou that hast thy time to be afflicted by them, that thy golden graces may shine the more, thou art in the fire, and they blow the bellows. But wouldest thou change places with them? Wouldest thou sit upon their place of ease? Dost thou desire to be with them? Pr. xxiv. 1. O rest thyself contented; in thy patience possess thy soul, and pity and bewail them in the condition in which they are.

(3.) Bless God that thy lot did fall on the other side, namely, to be one that should know the truth, profess it, suffer for it, and have grace to bear thee up thereunder, to God's glory, and thy eternal comfort. This honour have not all his saints; all are not counted worthy thus to suffer shame for his name. Do this, I say, though they get all, and leave thee nothing but the shirt on thy back, the skin on thy bones, or an hole in the ground to be put in. He. xi. 23–26.

2. Labour to be patient under this mighty hand of God, and be not hasty to say, When will the rod be laid aside? mind thou thy duty, which is to let patience have its perfect work. And bear the indignation of the Lord, because thou hast sinned against him, until he please to awake, to arise, and to execute judgment for thee. Mi. vii. 9. But to pass this.

Are things thus ordered? then this should teach us that there is a cause. The rod is not gathered without a cause; the rod is fore-determined, because the sin of God's people is foreseen, and ofttimes the nature of the sin, and the anger of the Father, is seen in the fashion of the rod.

The rod of my anger, saith God. A bitter and hasty nation must be brought against Jerusalem; an enemy fierce and cruel must be brought against the land of Israel. Their sins called for such a rod, for their iniquities were grievous. Ha. i. 6.

This should teach us with all earnestness to be sorry for our sins, and to do what we can to prevent these things, by falling upon our face in a way of prayer before God. If we would shorten such days, when they come upon us, let us be lovers of righteousness, and get more of the righteousness of faith, and of compliance with the whole will of God into our hearts. Then I say, the days shall be shortened, or we fare as well, because the more harmless and innocent we are, and suffer, the greater will our wages, our reward, and glory be, when pay-day shall come; and what if we wait a little for that?

These things are sent to better God's people, and to make them white, to refine them as silver, and to purge them as gold, and to cause that they that bear some fruit, may bring forth more: we are afflicted, that we may grow. Jn. xv. 2. It is also the will of God, that they that go to heaven should go thither hardly or with difficulty. The righteous shall scarcely be saved. That is, they shall, but yet with great difficulty, that it may be the sweeter.

Now that which makes the way to heaven so strait, so narrow, so hard, is the rod, the sword, the persecutor, that lies in the way, that marks where our haunt is, that mars our path, digs a pit, and that sets a net, a snare for us in the way. 1 Sa. xxiii. 22. Job xxx. 12–14. Ps. ix. 15; xxxi. 4; xxxv. 7; cxix. 110; cxl. 5; cxlii. 3.

This, I say, is that which puts us to it, but it is to try, as I said, our graces, and to make heaven the sweeter to us. To come frighted and hard pursued thither, will make the safety there the more with exceeding gladness to be embraced. And I say, get thy heart yet more possessed with the power of godliness; that the love of righteousness may be yet more with thee. For this blessedness, this happiness, he shall be sure of, that suffereth for righteousness' sake.

3. Since the rod is God's as well as the child, let us not look upon our troubles as if they came from, and were managed only by hell. It is true, a persecutor has a black mark upon him, but yet the Scriptures say that all the ways of the persecutor are God's. Da. v. 23. Wherefore as we should, so again we should not, be afraid of men: we should be afraid of them, because they will hurt us; but we should not be afraid of them, as if they were let loose to do to us, and with us, what they will. God's bridle is upon them, God's hook is in their nose: yea, and God has determined the bounds of their rage, and if he lets them drive his

church into the sea of troubles, it shall be but up to the neck, and so far it may go, and not be drowned. 2 Ki. xix. 28. Is. xxxvii. 29 ; viii. 7, 8. I say the Lord has hold of them, and orders them ; nor do they at any time come out against his people but by his licence and commission how far to go, and where to stop.

And now for two or three objections :—

1. *Object.* But may we not fly in a time of persecution ? Your pressing upon us, that persecution is ordered and managed by God, makes us afraid to fly.

Answ. First, having regard to what was said afore about a call to suffer; thou mayest do in this even as it is in thy heart. If it is in thy heart to fly, fly: if it be in thy heart to stand, stand. Any thing but a denial of the truth. He that flies, has warrant to do so; he that stands, has warrant to do so. Yea, the same man may both fly and stand, as the call and working of God with his heart may be. Moses fled, Ex. ii. 15; Moses stood. He. xi. 27. David fled, 1 Sa. xix. 12; David stood. xxiv. 8. Jeremiah fled, Je. xxxvii. 11, 12; Jeremiah stood. xxxviii. 17. Christ withdrew himself, Lu. ix. 10; Christ stood. Jn. xviii. 1–8. Paul fled, 2 Co. xi. 33; Paul stood. Ac. xx. 22, 23.

There are therefore few rules in this case. The man himself is best able to judge concerning his present strength, and what weight this or that argument has upon his heart to stand or fly. I should be loath to impose upon any man in these things; only, if thou fliest, take two or three cautions with thee :—

(1.) Do not fly out of a slavish fear, but rather because flying is an ordinance of God, opening a door for the escape of some, which door is opened by God's providence, and the escape countenanced by God's Word. Mat. x. 23.

(2.) When thou art fled, do as much good as thou canst in all quarters where thou comest, for therefore the door was opened to thee, and thou bid to make thy escape. Ac. viii. 1–5.

(3.) Do not think thyself secure when thou art fled; it was providence that opened the door, and the Word that did bid thee escape : but whither. and wherefore, that thou knowest not yet. Uriah the prophet fled into Egypt, because there dwelt men that were to take him, that he might be brought again to Jerusalem to die there. Je. xxvi. 21.

(4.) Shouldest thou fly from where thou art, and be taken in another place; the most that can be made of it—thy taking the opportunity to fly, as was propounded at first—can be but this, thou wast willing to commit thyself to God in the way of his providence, as other good men have done, and thy being now apprehended has made thy call clear to suffer here or there, the which before thou wert in the dark about.

(5.) If, therefore, when thou hast fled, thou art taken, be not offended at God or man: not at God, for thou art his servant, thy life and thy all are his; not at man, for he is but God's rod, and is ordained, in this, to do thee good. Hast thou escaped ? Laugh. Art thou taken ? Laugh. I mean, be pleased which way soever things shall go, for that the scales are still in God's hand.

(6.) But fly not, in flying, from religion; fly not, in flying, for the sake of a trade; fly not, in flying, that thou mayest have ease for the flesh: this is wicked, and will yield neither peace nor profit to thy soul; neither now, nor at death, nor at the day of judgment.

2. *Object.* But if I fly, some will blame me: what must I do now ?

Answ. And so may others if thou standest; fly not, therefore, as was said afore, out of a slavish fear; stand not, of a bravado. Do what thou dost in the fear of God, guiding thyself by his Word and providence; and as for this or that man's judgment, refer thy case to the judgment of God.

3. *Object.* But if I be taken and suffer, my cause is like to be clothed with scandals, slanders, reproaches, and all manner of false, and evil speakings; what must I do ?

Answ. Saul charged David with rebellion. 1 Sa. xxii. 8, 13. Amos was charged with conspiring against the king. Am. vii. 10. Daniel was charged with despising the king; and so also were the three children. Da. vi. 13; iii. 12. Jesus Christ himself was accused of perverting the nation, of forbidding to give tribute to Cæsar, and of saying that himself was Christ a king. Lu. xxiii. 2. These things therefore have been. But,

(1.) Canst thou, after a due examination of thyself, say that as to these things thou art innocent and clear ? I say, will thy conscience justify thee here ? Hast thou made it thy business to give unto God the things that are God's, and unto Cæsar the things that are his, according as God has commanded ? If so, matter not what men shall say, nor with what lies and reproaches they slander thee, but for these things count thyself happy. Blessed are ye, when *men* shall revile you - and shall say all manner of evil against you falsely (lying) for my sake (saith Christ). Rejoice, and be exceeding glad: for great *is* your reward in heaven: for so persecuted they the prophets which were before you. Mat. v. 11, 12. Comfort thyself therefore in the innocency of thy soul, and say, I am counted a rebel, and yet am loyal; I am counted a deceiver, and yet am true. 1 Sa. xxiv. 8–12. 2 Co. vi. 8. Also refer thy cause to the day of judgment; for if thou canst rejoice at the thoughts that thou shalt be cleared of all slanders and evil speakings then, that will bear up thy heart as to what thou mayest suffer now. The answer of a good conscience will carry a man through hell to heaven. Count these slanders part of thy sufferings, and those for which God will give thee a reward, because thou art innocent, and for that they are laid upon thee for thy profession's sake. But if thou be guilty, look to thyself; I am no comforter of such.

[THIRD, THE GOOD EFFECT OF COMMITTING THE SOUL TO GOD'S KEEPING.]

I come now to speak to the third and last part of the text, namely, of the good effect that will certainly follow to those that, after a due manner, shall take the advice afore given. 'Let them that suffer according to the will of God, commit the keeping of their souls to him in well-doing, as unto a faithful Creator.'

Two things from the last clause of the text lie yet before us. And they are they by which will be shown what good effect will follow to those that suffer according to the will of God, and that commit their souls to his keeping. 1. Such will find him to themselves a Creator. 2. They will find him a faithful Creator. 'Let them commit the keeping of their souls to him, as unto a faithful Creator.'

In this phrase, a faithful Creator, behold the wisdom of the Holy Ghost, how fitly and to the purpose he speaketh. King is a great title, and God is sometimes called a King; but he is not set forth by this title here, but by the title of a Creator; for it is not always in the power of a king to succour and relieve his subjects, that are suffering for his crown and dignity. Father is a sweet title—a title that carrieth in it an intimation of a great deal of bowels and compassion, and God is often set forth also by this title in the holy Scriptures. But so he is not here, but rather as a Creator. For a father, a compassionate father, cannot always help, succour, or relieve his children, though he knows they are under affliction! Oh! but a Creator can. Wherefore, I say, he is set forth here under the title of a Creator.

FIRST, A Creator! nothing can die under a Creator's hands. A Creator can sustain all. A Creator can, as a Creator, do what he pleases. 'The Lord, the everlasting God, the Creator of the ends of the earth, fainteth not, neither is weary.' Is. xl. 28.

The cause of God, for which his people suffer, had been dead and buried a thousand years ago, had it not been in the hand of a Creator. The people that have stood by his cause had been out of both as to persons, name, and remembrance, had they not been in the hand of a Creator. Who could have hoped, when Israel was going in, even into the mouth of the Red Sea, that ever his cause, or that people, should have revived again. A huge host of the Egyptians were behind them, and nothing but death before and on every hand of them; but they lived, they flourished, they outlived their enemies, for they were in the hand of a Creator.

Who could have hoped that Israel should have returned again from the land, from the hand, and from under the tyranny of the king of Babylon? They could not deliver themselves from going thither, they could not preserve themselves from being diminished when they came there, their power was gone, they were in captivity, their distance from home was far, their enemies possessed their land, their city of defence was ruined, and their houses burned down to the ground; and yet they came home again: there is nothing impossible to a Creator.

Who could have thought that the three children could have lived in a fiery furnace? that Daniel could have been safe among the lions? that Jonah could have come home to his country, when he was in the whale's belly? or that our Lord should have risen again from the dead? But what is impossible to a Creator?

This, therefore, is a rare consideration for those to let their hearts be acquainted with that suffer according to the will of God, and that have committed the keeping of their souls to him in well-doing. They have a Creator to maintain and uphold their cause, a Creator to oppose its opposers. And hence it is said, all that burden themselves with Jerusalem 'shall be cut in pieces, though all the people of the earth be gathered together against it.' Zec. xii. 3.

SECOND, A Creator! A Creator can not only support a dying cause, but also fainting spirits. For as he fainteth not, nor is weary, so 'he giveth power to the faint, and to *them that have* no might he increaseth strength.' Is. xl. 29. He is the God of the spirits of all flesh, and has the life of the spirit of his people in his own hand. Spirits have their being from him; he is the Father of spirits. Spirits are made strong by him, nor can any crush that spirit that God the Creator will uphold.

Is it not a thing amazing to see one poor inconsiderable man, in a spirit of faith and patience, overcome all the threatenings, cruelties, afflictions, and sorrows, that a whole world can lay upon him? None can quail* him, none can crush him, none can bend down his spirit. None can make him to forsake what he has received of God—a command-

---

* 'Quail;' to overpower. Well might the abettors of Antichrist wonder at the Christian's support under the most cruel tortures. While 'looking unto Jesus' and the bright visions of eternal glory, like Stephen, he can pray for his enemies, and tranquilly fall asleep while undergoing the most frightful sufferings.—ED.

ment to hold fast. His holy, harmless, and profit-able notions, because they are spiced with grace, yield to him more comfort, joy, and peace, and do kindle in his soul so goodly a fire of love to, and zeal for God, that all the waters of the world shall never be able to quench.

Ay, say some, that is because he is headstrong, obstinate, and one that will hear no reason. No, say I, but it is because his spirit is in the hand, under the conduct and preservation, of a Creator. A Creator can make spirits, uphold spirits, and make one spirit stronger to stand, than are all the spirits of the world to cast down. To stand, I say, in a way of patient enduring in well-doing, against all that hell can do to suppress.

THIRD, A Creator! A Creator can bring down the spirits that oppose, and make them weak and unstable as water. The Lord, the everlasting God, the Creator of the ends of the earth, fainteth not, nor is weary; there is no searching of his under-standing. He gives power to the faint, and to those that have no might, he increaseth strength; now mark, even the youth shall faint and be weary, and the young men shall utterly fall. A Creator can dash the spirits of the enemies with fear. God can put them in fear, and make them know that they are men and not God, and that their horses are flesh and not spirit. When the enemy came to take Jesus Christ, their spirits fainted, their hearts died in them; they went backwards, and fell to the ground. They had hard work to strengthen their spirits to a sufficiency of boldness and courage, though they brought halberts, and staves, and swords, and weapons with them, to take a naked* man. Jn. xviii. 3—7.

And although this is that which is not so visible to the world as some other things are, yet I believe that God treads down the spirits of men in a day when they afflict his people, oftener than we are aware of, or than they are willing to confess. How was the hostile spirit of Esau trod down of God, when he came out to meet his poor naked brother, with no less than four hundred armed men? He fainted before his brother, and instead of killing, kissed him. Ge. xxxiii. 4. How was the bloody spirit of Saul trod down, when David met him at the mouth of the cave, and also at the hill Hachilah? 1 Sa. xxiv. xxvi. God is a Creator, and as a Creator, is a spirit maker, a spirit reviver, a spirit destroyer; he can destroy body and soul in hell. Lu. xii. 5.

FOURTH, A Creator! As a Creator, he is over all arts, inventions, and crafts of men that are set on work to destroy God's people, whether they be soldiers, excellent orators, or any other whatso-ever; we will single out one—the smith, that roar-ing fellow, who with his coals and his bellows makes a continual noise. 'I have created the smith,' saith God, 'that bloweth the coals in the fire, and that bringeth forth an instrument for his work; and I have created the waster to destroy.' Is. liv. 16. The smith, what is he? I answer, an idol maker, a promoter of false worship, and one that makes instruments of cruelty, therewith to help to suppress the true [worship]. Is. xli. 7; xliv. 12; xlvi. 6.

'I have created the smith,' saith God, 'that bloweth the coals in the fire.' The idol inventor, the idol maker, the supporter of idol worship, he is my creature, saith God, to teach that he has power to reach him, and to command his sword to approach him at his pleasure, notwithstanding his roaring with his bellows, and his coals in the fire. So then, he cannot do what he will in the fire, nor with his idol when he has made it; the instrument, also that he makes for the defence of his idol, and for the suppressing of God's true worship, shall not do the thing for the which it is designed by him. And so the very next verse saith: 'No weapon that is formed against thee shall prosper, and every tongue *that* shall rise against thee in judgment thou shalt condemn. This is the heri-tage of the servants of the Lord, and their righ-teousness *is* of me, saith the Lord.' Is. liv. 17. And the text saith moreover, I have created the waster to destroy. The waster, what is that? Why, the smith makes an idol, and God has made the rust; the smith makes a sword, and God has made the rust. The rust eats them up, the moth shall eat them up, the fire shall devour them. 'The wicked,' saith the Psalmist, 'have drawn out the sword, and have bent their bow, to cast down the poor and needy, *and* to slay such as be of upright conversa-tion. Their sword shall enter into their own heart, and their bows shall be broken.' Ps. xxxvii. 14, 15.

All this can God do, because he is a Creator, and none but God can do it. Wherefore by this peculiar title of Creator, the apostle prepareth support for suffering saints, and also shows what a good conclusion is like to be made with them that suffer for righteousness' sake, according to his will; and that commit the keeping of their souls to him in well-doing, as unto a faithful Creator.

FIFTH, A Creator! A Creator can make such provision for a suffering people, in all respects, as shall answer all their wants. Have they lost their peace with the world? Have they no more peace with this world? Why, a Creator can make, create peace, can create peace, peace; peace with God, and peace with his conscience; and that is better than all the peace that can be found elsewhere in-

---

* 'A *naked* man;' unarmed, or defenceless.

'Had I but serv'd my God with half the zeal
I serv'd my king, he would not in mine age
Have left me *naked* to mine enemies.'
                              Shakspeare's Wolsey.—ED.

the world. Is. lvii. 19. Have they lost a good frame of heart? Do they want a right frame of spirit? Why, though this is to be had no where in the world, yet a Creator can help them to it. Ps. li. 10. Have they lost their spiritual defence? Do they lie too open to their spiritual foes? Why, this a Creator can help. 'And the Lord will create upon every dwelling place of Mount Zion, and upon her assemblies, a cloud and smoke by day, and the shining of a flaming fire by night: for upon all the glory *shall be* a defence.' Is. iv. 5.

This is the work of the Spirit; for though the Spirit itself be uncreate, yet all the holy works of it in the heart are verily works of creation. Our new man is a creation; our graces are a creation; our joys and comforts are a creation.* 2 Co. v. 17, 18. Ep. iv. 24. Is. lxv. 17–19. Now a creation none can destroy but a Creator; wherefore here is comfort. But again, God hath created us in Christ Jesus; that is another thing. The sun is created in the heavens; the stars are created in the heavens; the moon is created in the heavens. Who can reach them, touch them, destroy them, but the Creator? Why, this is the case of the saint; because he has to do with a Creator, he is fastened to Christ; yea, is in him by an act of creation, Ep. ii. 10; so that unless Christ and the creation of the Holy Ghost can be destroyed, he is safe that is suffering according to the will of God, and that hath committed the keeping of his soul to him in well-doing, as unto a faithful Creator.

And this I would have you consider moreover; the man that suffereth according to the will of God, committeth not such a soul to this Creator as dwells in carnal men—a naked soul, a graceless soul, a soul that has nothing in it but sin; but he commits a converted soul, a regenerate soul, a soul adorned, beautified, and sanctified, with the jewels, and bracelets, earrings, and perfumes of the blessed Spirit of grace.

And I say again, this is the work of a Creator, and a Creator can maintain it in its gallantry,† and he will do so, but he will put forth acts of creating power for it every day.

SIXTH, A Creator! He that can create can turn and alter any thing, to what himself would have it. He that made 'the seven stars and Orion, and turneth the shadow of death into the morning,' Am. v. 8, he can 'make the wilderness a pool of

water, and the dry land springs of water. Is. xli. 18. Our most afflicted and desolate conditions, he can make as a little haven unto us; he can make us sing in the wilderness, and can give us our vineyards from thence. Ho. ii. 14, 15. He can make Paul sing in the stocks, and good Rowland Taylor dance as he goeth to the burning stake. Gaols, and mocks, and scourgings, and flouts, and imprisonments, and hunger, and nakedness, and peril, and sword, and dens, and caves, and rocks, and mountains, God can so sweeten with the honey of his Word, and make so famous for situation by the glory of his presence, and so rich and fruitful by the communications of the Holy Ghost, and so easy by the spreading of his feathers over us, that we shall not be able to say, that in all the world a more commodious place, or comfortable condition, can be found. Some have known this, and have been rather ready to covet to be here, than to shun and fly from it, as a most unsavoury condition.‡

All these things, I say, God doth as a Creator. He hath created antipathies, and he can make antipathies close, and have favour one for another. The lion and the calf, the wolf and the lamb, the little boy and the cockatrice's den he can reconcile, and make to be at agreement. So, sufferings and the saint; the prison and the saint; losses, crosses, and afflictions, and the saint: he can make to lie down sweetly together.

SEVENTH, A Creator! A Creator can make up all that thou hast or shalt lose for the sake of thy profession by the hands of the children of men, be they friends, relations, a world, life, or what you can conceive of.

1. Hast thou lost thy friend for the sake of thy profession? Is the whole world set against thee for thy love to God, to Christ, his cause, and righteousness? Why, a Creator can make up all. Here, therefore, is the advantage that he hath that suffereth for righteousness' sake. Jonathan, the very son of bloody Saul, when David had lost the help of all his own relations, he must fall in with him, stick to him, and love him as he loved his own soul. 1 Sa. xviii. 1–3. Obadiah, Ahab's steward, when the saints were driven even under ground by the rage of Jezebel the queen, he is appointed of God to feed them in caves and holes of the earth. 1 Ki. xviii. 13. Yea, the very raven complied with the will of a Creator to bring the prophet bread and flesh in the morning, and bread and flesh at night. xvii. 6. When Jeremiah the prophet was rejected of all, yea, the church that then was,

---

* How impossible is it for a natural man to understand this new creation—a new heart, a new birth. How different is regeneration to water-baptism. How awful the delusion to be mistaken in this, the foundation of all hope of a blessed immortality. 'Create in me a clean heart, O God!' How consoling the fact: 'Now a creation none can destroy but a Creator!' and 'he changes not, therefore we are not consumed.'—ED.

† 'Gallantry;' splendour of appearance, grandeur, nobleness.—ED.

VOL. II.

‡ 'O happie he who doth possesse
Christ for his fellow-prisoner, who doth gladde
With heavenly sunbeames gaoles that are most sad.'

Written on the prison walls of the Tower of London by William Prynne.—ED.

4 z

could not help him; he was cast into the dungeon, and sunk to a great depth there in the mire. God the Creator, who ruleth the spirits of all men, stirred up the heart of Ebed-melech the Ethiopian both to petition for his liberty, and to put him out of the dungeon by the help of thirty men. Je. xxxviii. 7—13. These now, as Christ says, were both fathers, mothers, brothers, sisters, and as a loving wife or child. Mat. xix. 29.

2. Hast thou, for the sake of thy faith and profession thereof, lost thy part in the world? Why, a Creator can make thee houses as he did for the midwives of Egypt, Ex. i. 20, 21, and can build thee a sure house as he did for David his servant, who ventured all for the love that they had to the fear of God and his way. 2 Sa. vii. David was thrust out of Saul's house, and driven from his own, and God opened the heart of Achish the king of Gath to receive him, and to give him Ziklag. David, when under the tyranny of Saul, knew not what to do with his father and his mother, who were persecuted for his sake, but a Creator inclined the heart of the king of Moab to receive them to house and harbour. 1 Sa. xxvii. 5; xxii. 3, 4.

3. Is thy life at stake—is that like to go for thy profession, for thy harmless profession of the gospel? Why, God the Creator is Lord of life, and to God the Lord belong the issues from death. So then, he can, if he will, hold thy breath in thy nostrils, in spite of all the world; or if he shall suffer them to take away this for his glory, he can give thee another ten times as good for thy comfort. 'He that loveth his life shall lose it; and he that hateth his life in this world shall keep it unto life eternal.' Jn. xii. 25.

4. Is thy body to be disfigured, dismembered, starved, hanged, or burned for the faith and profession of the gospel? Why, a Creator can either prevent it, or, suffering it, can restore it the very same to thee again, with great and manifold advantage. He that made thee to be now what thou art, can make thee to be what thou never yet wast. It doth not yet appear what we shall be, further than only by general words. 1 Jn. iii. 2. Phi. iii. 21.

EIGHTH, A Creator! Peter sets him before us here as a Creator, because he would have us live upon him as such; as well as upon his grace, love, and mercy. In Job's day this was bewailed, that none or but a few said, 'Where is God my maker, who giveth songs in the night?' Job xxxv. 10.

Creator, as was hinted before, is one of God's peculiar titles. It is not given to him above five or six times in all the Book of God; and usually, when given him, it is either to show his greatness, or else to convince us that of duty we ought to depend upon him; and not to faint, if he be on our side, for or under any adversity, according as we

are bidden in the text: 'Let them that suffer according to the will of God, commit the keeping of their souls to him in well-doing, as unto a faithful Creator.' Shall God display his glory before us under the character and title of a Creator, and shall we yet fear man? Shall he do this to us when we are under a suffering condition, and that on purpose that we might commit our souls to him in well-doing, and be quiet, and shall we take no notice of this? 'Who art thou, that thou shouldest be afraid of a man that shall die, and of the son of man which shall be made as grass; and forgettest the Lord thy maker, that hath stretched forth the heavens, and laid the foundations of the earth?' &c. Is. li. 12, 13.

Had God concealed himself, as to his being a Creator, yet since he presenteth himself unto us by his Word under so many excellent titles as are given to no other God besides, methinks it should make us bold in our God; but when, for our relief, he shall add to all other that he verily is a Creator, this should make us rest in hope indeed.

Every nation will have confidence for their own gods, though but gods that are made with hands— though but the work of the smith and carpenter; and shall not we trust in the name of the Lord our God, who is not only a God, but a Creator and former of all things, Mi. iv. 5; consequently, the only living and true God, and one that alone can sustain us? We therefore are to be greatly blamed if we overlook the ground, such ground of support and comfort as presenteth itself unto us under the title of a Creator; but then most of all, if, when we have heard, believed, and known that our God is such, we shall yet be afraid of a man that shall die, and forget the Lord our maker. We, I say, have heard, seen, known, and believed, that our God is the Creator. The heavens declare his glory, and the firmament showeth his handywork, and thus he has showed unto us 'his eternal power and Godhead.' Ro. i. 20.

Behold, then, thou fearful worm, Jacob, the heavens, the sun, the moon, the stars; behold the earth, the sea, the air, the fire, and vapours. Behold, all living things, from leviathan and behemoth to the least that creepeth in the earth and waters. Yea, behold thyself, thy soul, thy body, thy fashion, thy building, and consider; thy God hath made even all these things, and hath given to thee this being; yea, and all this also he made of that which doth not appear. He. xi. 1—3. This is that which thou art called to the consideration of by Peter, in the text; when he letteth fall from his apostolical meditation that thy God is the Creator, and commandeth that thou, in thy suffering for him according to his will, shouldest commit the keeping of thy soul to him as unto a faithful Creator.

He that has the art thus to do, and that can do

it in his straits, shall never be trodden down. His God, his faith; his faith, his God, are able to make him stand. For such a man will thus conclude, that since the Creator of all is with him, what but creatures are there to be against him? So, then, what is the axe, that it should boast itself against him that heweth therewith? or the saw, that it should magnify itself against him that shaketh it? as if the rod should shake itself against him that lifteth it up; or as if the staff should lift up itself as if it were no wood. Is. x. 15. Read also Is. xl. 12—31, and then speak, if God as Creator is not a sure confidence to all the ends of the earth that trust in, and wait upon him. As Creator, he hath formed and upholdeth all things; yea, his hands have formed the crooked serpent, wherefore he also is at his bay. Job xxvi. 13. And thou hast made the dragon in the sea; and therefore it follows that he can cut and wound him, Is. li. 9, and give him for meat to the fowls, and to the beasts inheriting the wilderness, Ps. lxxiv. 13, 14, if he will seek to swallow up and destroy the church and people of God. Eze. xxix. 3, 4.

NINTH, A Creator is God! the God unto whom they that suffer according to his will are to commit the keeping of their souls—the Creator. And doth he take charge of them as a Creator? Then this should teach us to be far off from being dismayed, as the heathens are, at his tokens; for our God, the Lord, is the true God, the living God, the King of eternity. Je. x. 1, 2, 10. We should tremblingly glory and rejoice when we see him in the world, though upon those that are the most terrible of his dispensations. God the Creator will sometimes mount himself and ride through the earth in such majesty and glory, that he will make all to stand in the tent doors to behold him. O how he rode in his chariots of salvation when he went to save his people out of the land of Egypt! How he shook the nations! Then 'his glory covered the heavens, and the earth was full of his praise. And *his* brightness was as the light; he had horns *coming* out of his hand: and there *was* the hiding of his power. Before him went the pestilence, and burning coals went forth at his feet. He stood, and measured the earth: he beheld, and drove asunder the nations; and the everlasting mountains were scattered, the perpetual hills did bow: his ways are everlasting.' Then saith the prophet, ' I saw the tents of Cushan in affliction: *and* the curtains of the land of Midian did tremble. Was the Lord displeased against the rivers? *was* thine anger against the rivers? *was* thy wrath against the sea, that thou didst ride upon thine horses *and* thy chariots of salvation?' Hab. iii. 3—8.

So David: 'The earth shook and trembled,' saith he; ' the foundations also of the hills moved and were shaken, because he was wroth. There

went up a smoke out of his nostrils, and fire out of his mouth devoured: coals were kindled by it. He bowed the heavens also, and came down: and darkness *was* under his feet. And he rode upon a cherub, and did fly: yea, he did fly upon the wings of the wind. He made darkness his secret place; his pavilion round about him *were* dark waters *and* thick clouds of the skies. At the brightness *that was* before him his thick clouds passed, hail *stones* and coals of fire. The Lord also thundered in the heavens, and the Highest gave his voice; hail *stones* and coals of fire. Yea, he sent out his arrows, and scattered them; and he shot out lightnings, and discomfited them. Then the channels of waters were seen, and the foundations of the world were discovered at thy rebuke, O Lord, at the blast of the breath of thy nostrils.' Ps. xviii. 7—15.

These are glorious things, though shaking dispensations. God is worthy to be seen in his dispensations as well as in his Word, though the nations tremble at his presence. ' Oh that thou wouldest rend the heavens, that thou wouldest come down,' saith the prophet, ' that the mountains might flow down at thy presence!' Is. lxiv. 1. We know God, and he is our God, our own God; of whom or of what should we be afraid? Ps. xlvi. When God roars out of Zion, and utters his voice from Jerusalem, when the heavens and the earth do shake, the Lord shall be the hope of his people, and the strength of the children of Israel. Joel iii. 16.

Every man stayeth up, or letteth his spirit fail, according to what he knoweth concerning the nature of a thing. He that knows the sea, knows the waves will toss themselves: he that knows a lion, will not much wonder to see his paw, or to hear the voice of his roaring. And shall we that know our God be stricken with a panic fear, when he cometh out of his holy place to punish the inhabitants of the earth for their iniquity? We should stand like those that are next to angels, and tell the blind world who it is that is thus mounted upon his steed, and that hath the clouds for the dust of his feet, and that thus rideth upon the wings of the wind: we should say unto them, ' This God is our God for ever and ever, and he shall be our guide even unto death.'

Our God! the Creator! He can turn men to destruction, and say, Return, ye children of men. When our God shows himself, it is worth the while to see the sight, though it costs us all that we have to behold it. Some men will bless and admire every rascally juggler that can but make again that which they only seem to mar, or do something that seems to outgo reason; yea, though they make thunderings and noise in the place where they are, as though the devil himself were there. Shall saints, then, like slaves, be afraid of their God, the Creator; of their own God, when he rendeth the heavens, and comes down? When God comes into the world to do great things, he must come like himself—like him that is a Creator: wherefore the heavens and the earth must move at his presence, to signify that they acknowledge him as such, and pay him that homage that is due to him as their God and great Creator.

We that are Christians have been trained up by his Son in his school this many a day, and have been told what a God our Father is, what an arm he has, and with what a voice he can thunder; how he can deck himself with majesty and excellency, and array himself with beauty and glory; how he can cast abroad the rage of his wrath, and behold every one that is proud, and abase him. Job xl. 9—11. Have we not talked of what he did at the Red Sea, and in the land of Ham many years ago, and have we forgot him now? Have we not vaunted and boasted of our God both in church, pulpit, and books; and spake to the praise of them that, instead of stones, attempted to drive Antichrist out of the world with their lives and their blood; and are we afraid of our God? He was God, a Creator, then; and is he not God now? and will he not be as good to us as to them that have gone before us? or would we limit him to appear in such ways as only smile upon our flesh; and have him stay, and not show himself in his heart-shaking dispensations until we are dead and gone? What if we must go now to heaven, and what if he is thus come down to fetch us to himself? If we have been wise as serpents, and innocent as doves—if we can say, Neither against the law of the Jews, neither against the temple, nor against Cæsar, have we offended anything at all, of what should we be afraid? Let heaven and earth come together, I dare say they will not hurt us.

Our Lord Jesus, when dilating upon some of the great and necessary works of our Creator, puts check beforehand to all uncomely fears; to such fears as become not the faith and profession of a Christian. 'Brother,' saith he, 'shall deliver up the brother to death, and the father the child: and the children shall rise up against *their* parents, and cause them to be put to death. And ye shall be hated of all *men* for my name's sake.' What follows? ver. 28, 'Fear them not;' and again, in ver. 31, 'Fear ye not.' Mat. x. 21, 22.

So again, Mat. xxiv.: 'Nation shall rise against nation - there shall be famines, pestilences, and earthquakes, &c. They shall deliver you up to be afflicted, and shall kill you.—Many shall be offended, and shall betray one another.—And many false prophets shall arise, and deceive many.' And yet for all this we are bid not to be afraid, for all these things, with all other are ordered, limited,

enlarged and straitened, bounded and butted by the will, and hand, and power of that God unto whom Peter bids us commit the keeping of our souls, as unto a faithful Creator. ver. 7—11. Mar. xiii. 5—9. To wait for God in the way of his judgments doth well become a Christian.

To believe he loves us when he shows himself terrible to us, is also very much becoming of us. Wherefore has he given us grace? Is it that we should live by sense? Wherefore has he sometimes visited us? Is it that our hearts might be estranged from him, and that we still should love the world? And I say again, wherefore has he so plainly told us of his greatness, and of what he can do? Is it not that we might be still when the world is disturbed; and that we might hope for good things to come out of such providences that, to sense, look as if themselves would eat up and devour all?

Let us wait upon God, walk with God, believe in God, and commit ourselves, our soul, our body, to God, to be kept. Yea, let us be content to be at the disposal of God, and rejoice to see him act according to all his wondrous works. For this is a posture highly becoming them that say of God he is their Father, and that have committed the keeping of their souls to him as unto a Creator. A comely thing it is for the soul that feareth God, to love and reverence him in all his appearances. We should be like the spaniel dog, even lie at the foot of our God, as he at the foot of his master; yea, and should be glad, could we but see his face, though he treads us down with his feet.

Ay, says one son, so I could, if I thought this high God would regard me, and take notice of my laying of my soul at his foot, while I suffer for his Word and truth in the world. Why, do but see now how the Holy Ghost, for our help, doth hedge up that way in at which unbelief would come, that there might, as to this, be no room left for doubting. For as he calleth the God unto whom we are bid to commit the keeping of our soul, a Creator, so he saith that he is A CREATOR THAT IS FAITHFUL. 'Let them commit the keeping of their souls unto him in well-doing, as unto a faithful Creator'—a Creator that will concern himself with the soul committed to his trust, and that will be faithful to it, according to all that he has promised.

This, therefore, of God's faithfulness being added to his might and power, is in itself a ground of great support to those that have in a way of well-doing committed themselves, their souls, to him to keep. A Creator; what is it that a Creator cannot do? A faithful Creator; what is it that one that is faithful will not do, that is, when he is engaged? And now he is engaged, because thou hast committed thy soul to him to keep, and because he has bid thee do so. Let them commit the keeping of their soul to him, as unto a faithful Creator. I have sometimes seen an unfaithful man engaged, when a thing has been committed to him to keep. A man that is a thief, a cheater, a defrauder, will yet be faithful to him that will commit a charge to him to keep. And the reason is, because, though he can steal, cheat, defraud, without being taken notice of; yet he must be seen and known, if he be false in that which is committed to him to keep. I know the comparison is odious, yet such have been made by a holier mouth than mine, and as the case may be, they may be aptest of all to illustrate that which a man is about to explain. Hark what the unjust judge saith, says the Lord Jesus Christ. Lu. xviii.

To commit thy soul to God is to trust him with it; to commit thy soul to God is to engage him to look to it. And if he should not be faithful now, he will not be so in any case. For himself has bidden thee do it; he has also promised to keep it, as has been already showed in the former part of this discourse. Besides, he is here said to be faithful—to be a faithful Creator. He challenges this of faithfulness to himself alone: 'Yea, let God be true, but every man a liar.' Ro. iii. 4. This, therefore, doth still help to encourage them that would be faithful to him, to commit the keeping of our soul to him. A faithful man will encourage one much; how much more should the faithfulness of God encourage us?

Here, therefore, we have a closing word indeed; a word to wrap up the text with that is as full of good as the sun is of light. What can be fitter spoken? What can be added? What now is wanting to the help of him that has committed his soul to God to keep it while he is suffering according to his will in the world? He is engaged, as I said, by the act; thou hast committed thy soul to him to keep; he is engaged by his own Word; he has bidden thee commit thy soul to him to keep. He is engaged by his declaring of himself to be faithful; for that has encouraged thee to commit thy soul to him to keep. Besides, he has promised to do it; he has sworn to do it. 'For when God made promise to Abraham, because he could swear by no greater, he sware by himself, saying, Surely blessing I will bless thee, and multiplying I will multiply thee. And so, after he had patiently endured, (as thou must do,) he obtained the promise. For men verily swear by the greater: and an oath for confirmation *is* to them an end of all strife. Wherein God, willing more abundantly to shew unto the heirs of promise the immutability of his counsel, confirmed *it* by an oath: that by two immutable things, in which *it was* impossible for God to lie, we might have a strong consolation, who have fled for refuge to lay hold upon the hope set before us: which *hope* we

have as an anchor of the soul, both sure and stedfast, and which entereth into that within the veil; whither the forerunner is for us entered, *even* Jesus, made an High-priest for ever after the order of Melchisedec.' He. vi. 13—20.

Thus you see what ground we have who suffer according to the will of God, and that have committed the keeping of our souls to him in welldoing, as unto a faithful Creator. Here, therefore, I might make a stop and conclude as to this advice; but now we are in, we will proceed a little further, and will fall down upon three or four more particulars.

First, then, He will be faithful to us in this: He will keep us from those allurements of the world that a suffering saint is subject to. They that suffer have other kinds of temptations upon this account than other Christians have. The liberty of others, while they are in bonds, is a temptation to them. The peace of others, while they are in trouble, is a temptation to them. The enjoyments of others, while their houses are empty and their goods taking away, while their own water is sold unto them, and while they are buying their own wood, is a great temptation to them. La. v. 4. And this temptation, were it not that we have to do with a God that is faithful, would assuredly be a great snare unto them. But 'God *is* faithful, who will not suffer you to be tempted,' as to this, 'above that ye are able.' 1 Co. x. 13.

Nay, a suffering man has not only these things lying before him as a temptation, but perhaps the wife of the bosom lies at him, saying, O do not cast thyself away; if thou takest this course, what shall I do? Thou hast said thou lovest me; now make it manifest by granting this my small request. Do not still remain in thine integrity. Next to this come the children, all which are like to come to poverty, to beggary, to be undone for want of wherewithal to feed, and clothe, and provide for them for time to come. Now also come kindred, and relations, and acquaintance; some chide, some cry, some argue, some threaten, some promise, some flatter, and some do all, to befool him for so unadvised an act as to cast away himself, and to bring his wife and children to beggary for such a thing as religion. These are sore temptations.*

---

* 'Sore temptations' poor Bunyan found them. When dragged from his home to prison, he speaks of his poor blind daughter in language of impassioned solicitude: 'Poor child, thought I, what sorrow art thou like to have for thy portion in this world! Thou must be beaten, must beg, suffer hunger, cold, nakedness, and a thousand calamities, though I cannot now endure the wind shall blow upon thee! Oh! the hardships I thought my blind one might go under would break my heart to pieces.'—'The parting with my wife and poor children hath oft been to me in this place as the pulling my flesh from my bones.'—*Grace Abounding*, 327, 328.—Ed.

Next to those come the terrors of men, the gripes of the laws, the shadow of death, and no man can tell what. All which are sufficient to pull a man from the gates of life, were he there, if the faithful Creator stands not to him. 'But God is faithful, who will not suffer you to be tempted above that ye are able; but will with the temptation make a way to escape, that ye may be able to bear it.'—'But God is faithful.' It saith not, that thou art: but 'God is faithful'—to his Son, to whom he has given thee; to his promise, the which he has given thee; to his cause, to which he has called thee; and to thy soul, the which thou hast committed to his trust, and the which he also has taken the charge of, as he is a faithful Creator.

'And will not suffer thee to be tempted.' How, not tempted? No; not above what thou art able. He that tempts thee doth not at all consider thy strength, so as to stop when he sees thou art weak; he would have thee overthrown, for therefore it is that he tempteth thee. But God will not suffer that, because he is faithful, and because thou hast committed the keeping of thy soul unto him in well-doing, as unto a faithful Creator.

'Not tempted above that ye are able.' He saith not, above that ye are well able. Indeed, thy strength shall be proportioned to the temptation, but thou mayest have none over and above to spare; thou shalt not have a bigger load than God will give thee shoulders to bear. Christ did bear his burden, but it made him cry out, and sweat as it were great drops of blood, to carry it. Bear thy burden thou shalt, and not be destroyed by it; but perhaps thou mayest sometimes roar under it by reason of the disquietness of thy heart. 'But he will with the temptation make a way of escape.' 'With the temptation,' not without it; thou must be tempted, and must escape too. 'With the temptation.' As sure as Satan is licensed, so sure he is limited; and when Satan has ended all the temptation, he shall depart from thee. Lu. iv. 13. 'He will with the temptation'—by such a managing of it as shall break its own neck. God can admit Satan to tempt, and make the Christian wise to manage the temptation for his own escape.

'Make a way.' It may be thou seest no way of escape. It may be there is no way—no way in all the world, to escape. Well; but God can make a way. When Israel was hemmed in at the Red Sea, there was as then no way—no way in all the world, to escape. O! but God made a way, and a pathway too, and that through the mighty waters. Ex. xv. 8, 16. Ps. cvi. 9; lxxviii. 13. He will make a way with the temptation, or 'will with the temptation make a way to escape, that ye may be able to bear it.' These are the words of the Holy Ghost,

who is God; and they are spoken, yea, committed to record for this very purpose, that those that are under affliction might commit the keeping of their soul to him in well-doing, as unto a faithful Creator. That is the first.

Second, He will also be faithful to us as to this: He will give us a competent measure of wisdom, that in our suffering condition we may in all things be made able to manage our state with discretion. We are perhaps weak of natural abilities, parts of utterance, or the like; and our adversaries are learned, eloquent, and ripe of parts. Thou hast the disadvantage on thy side, and they have what the world can afford to encourage them; thou art weak of spirit, they are bold and strong. The great and the mighty are with thy enemies, but on thy side there is no comforter. Ec. iv. 1.

Why now here is, as to this, and to what else can it be objected, the faithfulness of God engaged. First, in a general promise; I will not fail thee, nor forsake thee. He. xiii. 5, 6. Secondly, we have an invitation to come to this faithful God for wisdom to assist and help. For after he had said, 'My brethren, count it all joy when ye fall into divers temptations - and let patience have *her* perfect work;' he adds, 'If any man lack wisdom, let him ask of God, that giveth to all *men* liberally, and upbraideth not, and it shall be given him.' Ja. i. 2—5. Here is more than an invitation, here is a promise—it shall be given him; and all to show us what a faithful Creator we have committed our souls unto. Doth any lack wisdom to know how to carry it in a time of trial? let them ask it of God—of the God that is wisdom itself; let him ask it of God, the liberal giver, who giveth to all men all that they have, and upbraideth not for their unworthiness.

Nor doth the Holy Ghost stop here, but enlarges himself in a more particular way to those that suffer according to the text, saying, 'But when they deliver you up, take no thought how or what ye shall speak: for it shall be given you in that same hour what ye shall speak.' Mat. x. 19.

I have often been amazed in my mind at this text, for how could Jesus Christ have said such a word if he had not been able to perform it? This text, therefore, declares him to be God. It is also a proof of faithfulness to those that suffer for him.

For it is as if he should say, Try me and trust me; if I stand not by you in a day of distress, never believe me more;—you, suffering according to the will of God, and committing your souls to him in well-doing; 'I will give you a mouth and wisdom, which all your adversaries shall not be able to gainsay or resist,' for so he has it in Lu. xxi. 15. Here is no consideration of what capacity the people might be of, that were to be persecuted;

but what matters what they are? if fools, it is no matter; if wise, it helpeth nothing. A mouth and wisdom is to be given; that of itself shall do. And this is according to that other Scripture mentioned afore, where it saith, 'No weapon that is formed against thee shall prosper; and every tongue *that* shall rise against thee in judgment thou shalt condemn.' Is. liv. 17. Although it may happen in this, as in the former temptation, the devil and his agents may give the saints, in their pleading for the truth, their bellies full both of cross answers, equivocations, sophistications, wrong glosses and erroneous interpretations; but truth shall prevail, shall turn the scale, and bear away the victory.

Third, He will also be faithful to us in this: we shall not want spiritual support to help us to bear up under our particular parts of suffering. I do not say that thou shalt be comforted all the while; but I say he will be to thee so faithful as to comfort thee under those *thodes,** gusts, blasts, or battering storms that beat against thy wall. Is. xxxii. 2.

Look then what present degrees or aggravating appearances are in thy afflictions; to such a degree shalt thou at times be supported. For as surely as ever the Spirit of God moved Samson at times in the camp of Dan, when he lay against the Philistines; so will the Spirit of God move in and upon thee to comfort and to strengthen thee, whilst thou sufferest for his name in the world. As our afflictions abound for Christ, so shall our consolations abound by him. 2 Co. i. 5. I have observed that God lays this, that he useth to comfort his people in a time of sufferings, as an aggravation of sin upon them that did use to shuck† and shrink under sufferings. 'I,' saith he, '*even* I, *am* he that comforteth you: who *art* thou that thou shouldest be afraid of a man *that* shall die?' Is. li. 12.

'God,' says the wise man, 'hath set the one over against the other,' the day of adversity and the day of prosperity, 'to the end that man should find nothing after him' to complain of. Ec. vii. 14. For as certainly as there is a time to mourn, so certainly there is a time to rejoice: set, I say, for them that suffer for God's cause according to God's will. Ec. iii. 4.

There are several degrees of suffering for righteousness; there is the scourge of the tongue, the ruin of an estate, the loss of liberty, a gaol, a gibbet, a stake, a dagger. Now, answerable to

these are the comforts of the Holy Ghost prepared, like to like, part proportioned to part, only the consolations are said to abound. 2 Co. i.

But the lighter the sufferings are, the more difficult it is to judge of the comforts of the Spirit of God, for it is common for a man to be comfortable under sufferings when he suffereth but little, and knows also that his enemy can touch his flesh, his estate, or the like, but little: I say, it is common for such a man to be comfortable in his sufferings, from the consideration that his enemies can touch him no further. And this may be the joy of the flesh—the result of reason, and may be very much, if not altogether, without a mixture of the joy of the Holy Ghost therewith. The more deep, therefore, and the more dreadful the sufferings are, the more clearly are seen the comforts of the Spirit, when a man has comfort where the flesh is dead, stirreth not, and can do nothing. When a man can be comfortable at the loss of all—when he is under the sentence of death, or at the place of execution—when a man's cause, a man's conscience, the promise, and the Holy Ghost, have all one comfortable voice, and do all, together with their trumpets, make one sound in the soul; then the comforts are good, of the right kind, of God and his Spirit.

I told you before that there are several degrees of sufferings; wherefore it is not to be expected that he that suffers but little should partake of the comforts that are prepared for them that suffer much. He that has only the scourge of the tongue, knows not what are the comforts that are prepared for him that meets with the scourge of the whip. And how should a man know what manner of comforts the Holy Ghost doth use to give at the gaol and the gibbet, when himself, for righteousness, never was there?

But whether this or the other Christian knows it, God has his consolations for his suffering people; and those, too, such as are proportioned to the nature or degree of their sufferings; the which shall assuredly be made appear to them that shall after a godly manner stick to his truth, and trust him with their souls. Joseph was cast into prison; but God was with him. John was banished into the isle called Patmos, for the Word of God; but what revelations of God had he there! even such as he was a stranger to all his life before: this, therefore, is to be well heeded. For it is a demonstration of the faithfulness of God to those that, suffering according to his will, do commit the keeping of their souls to him in well-doing, as unto a faithful Creator.

Fourth, He will also be faithful to us in this: He will not let the sharpness, nor keenness, nor venom of the arrows of the enemies of his people, reach so far as to destroy both body and soul at

---

* 'Thodes;' whirlwinds. This word does not occur in any English dictionary or glossary. It gave me much trouble, and a walk of seven miles, to discover its meaning. It is the Saxon for noise, whirlwind, turbulence. This provincial word was probably derived from some Saxon tribe that settled in Bedfordshire.—Ed.

† 'To shuck;' to shake violently—from which is the noun, 'a pea-shuck,' the shell from which peas have been shaken. —Ed.

once: but he will preserve them, when what can be done is done, to his eternal kingdom and glory. Thus being preserved to his eternal kingdom and glory, is a marvellous thing; but it must be so, because God has called them to it. Wherefore, after Peter had told them that the devil their adversary sought to devour them, and had bidden them resist him, stedfast in the faith, he saith, ' But the God of all grace, who hath called us unto his eternal [kingdom and] glory by Christ Jesus, after that ye have suffered a while, make you perfect, stablish, strengthen, settle *you*.' 1 Pe. v. 10.

The truth is, persecution of the godly was, of God, never intended for their destruction, but for their glory, and to make them shine the more when they are beyond this valley of the shadow of death. Indeed, we ofttimes, when we are persecuted, do feel the terrors of our adversaries in our minds. But it is not because they can shoot them thither, nor because they of themselves have power to reach so far, but we, like fools, by our ignorance and unbelief, do admit them thither.

No suffering, nor inflicter of suffering, can reach the peace of the sufferer without his own consent. This is provision of God's making; yea, and if through our folly their terror is admitted to touch us, yet since we are not our own, but are bought with a price, we are not so at our own dispose, but that God will have the butting and bounding of their rage, as also a power to uphold and support our spirits. When I said my foot slipped, thy mercy, O Lord, help me up. And the reason why, by God's ordinance, the spirit is not to be touched in suffering, is, because that is it that is to sustain the infirmity of the sufferer; therefore God will have the spirit of his servants kept sound, and in good health. Pr. xviii. 14. Is. lvii. 16.

The room, therefore, and the ground that the enemy has to play upon, is the body and outward substance of the people of God, but the spirit is reserved, for the reason hinted before, and also that it might be capable of maintaining of communion with God. And how else could they obey that command that bids them rejoice in tribulation, and glorify God in the fires? as it is. Ro. xii. Is. xxiv. 15.

But, I say, if they have not power to touch, much less to destroy body and soul for ever. The body is God's, and he gives that to them to destroy; the spirit is God's, and he keeps that to himself, to show that he has both power to do with us what he pleases, and that he will recover our body also out of their hand; for if the spirit lives, so must the body, when men have done what they can therewith. This is the argument of our Lord Jesus Christ himself. Lu. xx. 37, 38. Therefore the faithfulness of God not only is, but also will be

seen, by them that dare trust him, till the next world, to his glory and their eternal comfort.

We will now conclude with a short word by way of USE. You see how I have opened the text, and what hath naturally followed thereupon; from the whole of which may be gathered:—

Use First, That the people of God are a suffering people—a people subject to trouble for their faith and profession. The reason is, besides what hath been said already, because the power of truth is in their hearts, and shows itself in their lives— a thing which the devil and the world can by no means abide. He that is born after the flesh persecuteth him that is born after the Spirit. Ga. iv. 29. For they cannot agree in religion; the godly are so devout and the other are so profane, that they cannot do. Not but that God's people, as they are commanded, are willing to let them alone; but the other they cannot bear that they should serve God as they have said, Mat. xv. 14; and hence ariseth persecution. The world also would have the religion of the godly to be counted false —a thing that the others can by no means endure, but will stand by and maintain, yet in all peaceable manner, their own ways before them, whatever it costs.

The Christian and the carnal professor are like those two harlots that you read of in the book of Kings, who strove for the living child, whose it should be, whose contest could not be decided until it came to the sword of the king. 1 Ki. iii. O, but when the sword was drawn, under a show as if the living child must now be cut in two, then the true mother was known from the false; for her bowels yearned upon her son. ver. 26, 27. The world, what show soever they have for religion, and however they urge it, that the truth is with them, have no yearning of bowels for it. Let it be neither mine nor thine, said she, but divide it; but the woman whose the living child was, had not a heart to say so. Religion may lie and die in a ditch for all those that are given to their sins; nor doth their zeal appear, except when they are gripping of the godly for his faith towards God. Bowels, yearning of bowels over God's condemned religion, is only found in the souls of those who own God has made it.

Use Second, Is it so? Are God's people a suffering people? Then this should inform them that will be religious, to prepare themselves for what is like to attend them for their religion. To prepare, I say, not with carnal weapons, but with the graces of the Spirit of God; that will help them with meekness and patience to endure. Sit down then, I say, and count up the cost, before for religion thou engagest too far; lest thou take upon thee to meddle with that which thou wilt not know what to do with in the end. Pr. xxv. 8. Lu. xiv. 25—30.

Many there be that are faulty here; they have taken upon them to profess, not considering what what they have taken in hand may cost them. Wherefore, when troubles come indeed, then they start and cry. This they like not, because they looked not for it; and if this be the way to heaven, let who will go on in it for them. Thus they take offence, and leave Christ's cause and people to shift for themselves in the world. Mat. xiii. 20, 21.

Use Third, But let God's people think never the worse of religion, because of the coarse entertainment it meeteth with in the world. It is better to choose God and affliction than the world, and sin, and carnal peace. It is necessary that we should suffer, because that we have sinned. And if God will have us suffer a little while here for his Word, instead of suffering for our sins in hell, let us be content, and count it a mercy with thankfulness.

'The wicked is reserved to the day of destruction: they shall be brought forth to the day of wrath.' Job xxi. 30. How kindly, therefore, doth God deal with us, when he chooses to afflict us but for a little, that with everlasting kindness he may have mercy upon us. Is. liv. 7, 8. And '*it is* better, if the will of God be so, that ye suffer for well-doing than for evil-doing.' 1 Pe. iii. 17.

Use Fourth, Look not, therefore, upon the sufferings of God's people for their religion, to be tokens of God's great anger. It is, to be sure, as our heavenly Father orders it, rather a token of his love; for suffering for the gospel, and for the sincere profession of it, is indeed a dignity put upon us—a dignity that all men are not counted worthy of. Count it, therefore, a favour that God has bestowed upon thee his truth, and graces to enable thee to profess it, though thou be made to suffer for it. Ac. v. 41. Thou mightest have been a sufferer for thy sins in hell, but thou art not; but contrariwise art, perhaps, suffering for conscience to God; this is a dignity. For that thou dost thus by virtue of a heavenly gift, on the behalf of Christ, for the gospel's sake, and according to the will of God. This is a dignity that a persecutor shall not be counted worthy of, until he first convert to Christ. Phi. i. 29.

Use Fifth, Take thy affliction with meekness and patience, though thou endurest grief wrongfully. 'For this *is* thankworthy, if a man for conscience toward God endure grief, suffering wrongfully.' 1 Pe. ii. 19. Lay thy hand, then, upon thy mouth, and speak not a word of ill against him that doth thee wrong; leave thy cause and thy enemy to God; yea, rather pray that his sin may not be laid to his charge; wherefore, as I said before, now show thyself a good man, by loving, pitying, praying for, and by doing good, as thou art commanded, to them that despitefully use thee.

Mat. v. 44. I know thy flesh will be apt to huff, and to be angry, and to wish, would thou mightest revenge thyself. But this is base, carnal, sensual, devilish; cast, therefore, such thoughts from thee, as thoughts that are not fit for a Christian's breast, and betake thee to those weapons that are not carnal. For the artillery of a Christian is the Word, faith, and prayer; and in our patience we must possess our souls. 2 Co. x. 5. Lu. xxi. 16—19.

Use Sixth, Be much in the consideration of the all-sufficiency of thy Father, whose cause thou hast espoused, whose Word thou hast chosen for thy heritage, and whose paths thou delightest to walk in. I say, be much in considering how all the world is sustained by him, and that all life and breath is in his hand, to continue or diminish as he pleases. Think with thyself also how able he is to rescue thee from all affliction, or to uphold thee in it with a quiet mind. Go to him continually, as to a fountain of life that is open for the supply of the needy. Remember also, if he comes not at thy call, and comforteth thee not so soon as thou desirest, it is not of want of love or compassion to thy soul, but to try thy graces, and to show to the fallen angels that thou wilt serve God for nought, rather than give out. Also, if it seemeth to thee, as if God took no care of thee to help thee, but that he hath rather turned thee over to the ungodly; count this also as a sign that he delights to see thee hold fast his name, though thou art laid under the greatest of disadvantages. 'If the scourge slay suddenly, (that is more than it hath done to thee,) he will laugh at the trial of the innocent.' Job ix. 23.

It is a great delight to our God to see his people hold fast their integrity, and not to deny his name, when under such cloudy dispensations and discouraging circumstances. And considerations that thy thus doing is pleasing in his sight through Christ, will be a support unto thee. God sees thee, though thou canst not now see him, and he observeth now thy way, though darkness is round about him; and when he hath tried thee, thou shalt come forth like gold.

Use Seventh, Take heed of setting of thyself a bound and period to thy sufferings, unless that period be the grave. Say not to thy afflicters, Hitherto, and no further, and here shall your proud waves be stayed. I say, take heed of doing thus, for fear God should let them go beyond thee. For a man is not prepared to suffer, further than he thinketh the enemy may be permitted to go. Hence Christ sets their bounds at the loss of life, and no nearer. So then, so far as they go beyond thee, so far they will find thee unprovided, and so not fortified for a reception of their onset with that christian gallantry which becomes thee. Observe Paul; he died daily, he was always delivered unto death, he despaired of life; and this is the way to be prepared for any calamity. When a man thinks he has only to prepare for an assault by footmen, how shall he contend with horses? Or if he looks no further than to horses, what will he do at the swellings of Jordan? Je. xii. 5. Wherefore, set thine enemies no bounds: say not, They shall not pursue me to the death; have the sentence of death in thyself. For though they may but tick and toy with thee at first, their sword may reach thy heart-blood at last. The cat at play with the mouse is sometimes a fit emblem of the way of the wicked with the children of God. Wherefore, as I said, be always dying; die daily: he that is not only ready to be bound, but to die, is fit to encounter any amazement.

Use Eighth, If thine enemies would, or do, put thee under a cloud, if they wrap thee up in a bear's skin, and then set the dogs upon thee, marvel not at the matter; this was Joseph's, David's, Christ's, Stephen's portion, only be thou innocent; say nothing, do nothing that should render thee faulty; yea, say and do always that that should render thee a good neighbour, a good Christian, and a faithful subject. This is the way to help thee to make with boldness thy appeals to God; this is the way to embolden thy face against the faces of thine enemies; this is the way to keep thy conscience quiet and peaceable within thee; and this is the way to provoke God to appear for thy rescue, or to revenge thy blood when thou art gone.

And do this because it is thy duty—we must fear God and honour the king—and because this is the way to make the work of thy enemies hard: few men have that boldness as to say, This I do against you, because you profess Christ. When they persecuted the Lord himself, they said to him, 'For a good work we stone thee not.' Jn. x. 33. Religion that is pure is a hot thing, and it usually burns the fingers of those that fight against it; wherefore it is not common for men to oppose religion under its own naked complexion: wherefore the Jews sought to fasten other matters upon Christ to kill him for them; though the great spite they had against him was for his doctrine and miracles. It was for envy to that that they set themselves against him, and that made them invent to charge him with rebellion and treason. Mat. xxvii. 18. Lu. xxiii. 2.

Use Ninth, Wherefore it becomes all godly men to study to be quiet, to mind their own business, and as much as in them lies, to be at peace with all men; to owe no man any thing but love. Pray, therefore, for all that are in authority; pray for the peace of the country in which thou dwellest; keep company with holy, and quiet, and peaceable men. Seek by all good ways the promotion of godliness,

put up injuries, be good to the poor, do good against evil, be patient towards all men; for ' these things are good and profitable unto men.' Tit. iii. 8.

Be not inclining to injure men behind their backs, speak evil of no man, reproach not the governor nor his actions, as he is set over thee; all his ways are God's, either for thy help or the trial of thy graces. Wherefore he needs thy prayers, not thy revilings; thy peaceable deportment, and not a troublesome life. I know that none of these things can save thee from being devoured by the mouth of the sons of Belial. 1 Ki. xxi. 12, 13. Only, what I say is duty, is profitable, is commendable, is necessary; and that which will, when the devil has done his worst, render thee lovely to thy friends, terrible to thine enemies, serviceable in thy place as a Christian, and will crown the remembrance of thy name, to them that survive thee, with a blessing: ' The memory of the just is blessed: but the name of the wicked shall rot.' Pr. x. 7.

Use Tenth, I will conclude, then, with a word to those professors, if there be any such, that are of an unquiet and troublesome spirit. Friends, I may say to you, as our Lord said once to his disciples, ' Ye know not what manner of spirit ye are of.' To wish the destruction of your enemies doth not become you. If ye be born to, and are called, that you may inherit a blessing, pray be free of your blessing: ' Bless, and curse not.' If you believe that the God whom you serve is supreme governor, and is also wise enough to manage affairs in the world for his church, pray keep fingers off, and refrain from doing evil. If the counsel of Gamaliel was good when given to the enemies of God's people, why not fit to be given to Christians themselves? Therefore refrain from these men, and let them alone. If the work that these men do is that which God will promote and set up for ever, then you cannot disannul it; if not, God has appointed the time of its fall.

A Christian! and of a troublesome spirit; for-shame, forbear; show, out of a good conversation, thy works, with meekness of wisdom; and here let me present thee with three or four things.

1. *Consider*, That though Cain was a very murderer, yet God forbade any man's meddling with him, under a penalty of revenging his so doing upon his own head sevenfold. ' And the Lord said unto him, Therefore, whosoever slayeth Cain, vengeance shall be taken on him sevenfold.' Ge. iv. 15. But why not meddle with Cain, since he was a murderer? The reason is, because he persecuted his brother for righteousness' sake, and so espoused a quarrel against God; for he that persecutes another for righteousness' sake sets himself against God, fights against God, and seeks to overthrow him. Now, such an one the Christian must let alone and stand off from, that God may have his

full blow at him in his time.* Wherefore he saith to his saints, and to all that are forward to revenge themselves, Give place, stand back, let me come, leave such an one to be handled by me. 'Dearly beloved, avenge not yourselves, but *rather* give place unto wrath; for it is written, Vengeance *is* mine, I will repay, saith the Lord.' Ro. xii. 19. Wherefore the Lord set a mark upon Cain, lest any finding him should slay him. You must not, indeed, you must not avenge yourselves of your enemies. Yea, though it was lawful once so to do, it is not lawful now. Ye have heard that it hath been said to them of old time, Thou shalt love thy neighbour and hate thine enemy; but I say, said our Lord, Love them, bless them, do good to them, and pray for them that hate you. Mat. v. 43, 44.

2. *Consider*, Revenge is of the flesh,—I mean this our revenge of ourselves; and it proceeds from anger, wrath, impatience under the cross, unwillingness to suffer, from too much love to carnal ease, to estates, to enjoyments, to relations, and the like. It also flows from a fearful, cowardly spirit; there is nothing of greatness in it, except it be greatness of untowardness. I know there may, for all this, be pretences to justice, to righteousness, to the liberty of the gospel, the suppressing of wickedness, and the promoting of holiness; but these can be but pretences, or, at best, but the fruits of a preposterous zeal. For since, as has been often said in this treatise, the Lord hath forbidden us to do so, it cannot be imagined that he should yet animate any to such a thing by the Holy Ghost and the effects of the graces thereof. Let them, then, if any such be, that are thus minded, be counted the narrow-spirited, carnal, fleshly, angry, waspish-spirited professors—the professors that know more of the Jewish than of the christian religion, and that love rather to countenance the motions, passions, and gross motions of an angry mind, than with meekness to comply with the will of a heavenly Father. Thou art bid to be like unto him, and also thou art showed wherein. Mat. v. 45—48.

There is a man hates God, blasphemes his name, despises his being; yea, says there is no God. And yet the God that he carrieth it thus towards doth give him his breakfast, dinner, and supper; clothes him well, and when night comes, has him to bed, gives him good rest, blesses his field, his corn, his cattle, his children, and raises him to high estate.†

Yea, and this our God doth not only once or twice, but until these transgressors become old; his patience is thus extended, years after years, that we might learn of him to do well.

3. *Consider*, A professor! and unquiet and troublesome, discontented, and seeking to be revenged of thy persecutors; where is, or what kind of graces hast thou got? I dare say, they, even these in which thou thus actest, are none of the graces of the Spirit. The fruits of the Spirit are love, joy, peace, long-suffering, gentleness, goodness, faith, meekness, temperance; against such there is no law; but wrath, strife, seditions, traitors, and inventors of evil things are reckoned with the worst of sins, and sinners, and are plainly called the works of the flesh. Ro. i. 29—31. 2 Ti. iii. 3, 4. Ga. v. 19—21.

But I say, where is thy love to thine enemy? where is thy joy under the cross? where is thy peace when thine anger has put thee upon being unquiet? Where is thy long-suffering? for, as thou actest, not ought but thy waspishness can be seen. Where, also, is thy sweet, meek, and gentle spirit? and is goodness seen in thy seeking the life or the damage of thy enemy? Away, away; thy graces, if thou hast any, are by these, thy passions, so jostled up into corners, and so pent for want of room and liberty to show themselves, that, by the Word of God, thou canst not be known to be of the right kind, what a noise soever thou makest.

A Christian, when he sees trouble coming upon him, should not fly in the face of the instrument that brings it, but in the face of the cause of its coming. Now the cause is thyself, thy base self, thy sinful self, and thy unworthy carriages towards God under all the mercy, patience, and long-suffering that God has bestowed upon thee, and exercised towards thee. Here thou mayest quarrel and be revenged, and spare not, so thou take vengeance in a right way, and then thou wilt do so when thou takest it by godly sorrow. 2 Co. vii. 10, 11.

A Christian, then, should bewail his own doings, his own unworthy doings, by which he has provoked God to bring a cloud upon him, and to cover him with it in anger. A Christian should say, This is my wickedness, when a persecutor touches him; yea, he should say it, and then shut up his mouth, and bear the indignation of the Lord, because he has sinned against him. 'Thy way and thy doings have procured these *things* unto thee; this *is* thy wickedness, because it is bitter, because it reacheth unto thine heart.' Je. iv. 18.

4. *Consider*, What conviction of thy goodness can the actions that flow from such a spirit give

* How correct, but how dismal a picture is here drawn of the persecutor! God has wise and holy ends in protecting and prolonging the lives even of very wicked men. 'Slay them not, lest my people forget; scatter them by thy power.' Comp. Eccl. viii. 10. Pity the persecutor—pray for him; but if he repent not, stand off; 'God will have his full blow at him in his time,' and crush him down into misery and despair.—ED.

† Like a multitude of passages in Bunyan's writings, this passage is exceedingly striking. It illustrates our Lord's words in Mat. v. 44, 45: 'Love your enemies - that ye may be the children of your Father which is in heaven.'—ED.

unto observers? None at all; yea, a spirit of unquietness under sufferings, and that seeketh to be revenged of those that do, for thy faith and the profession thereof, persecute thee, is so far off of giving conviction to beholders that thou art right, that it plainly tells them that thou art wrong. Even Julian the apostate, when he had cast away whatever he could of Christ, had this remaining with him—that a Christian ought to take with patience what affliction fell upon him for his Master's sake; and would hit them in the teeth with an unbecoming behaviour, that complained or that sought redress of them that had abused them for their faith and godly profession. What will men say if you shrink and winch, and take your sufferings unquietly, but that if you yourselves were uppermost, you would persecute also? Much more have they ground to say so, when you will fight lying on your backs. Be quiet, then, and if thine enemy strike thee on one cheek, turn to him the other; and if he also revile and curse thee, down upon thy knees and pray for him. This is the way to convince thy observers that thou art a godly man. Father, forgive them, for they know not what they do, was one of those things that convinced the centurion that Jesus was a righteous man; for he stood by the cross to watch and see how Jesus carried it in these his sufferings, as well as to see execution done. Mat. xxvii. 54. Lu. xxiii. 34—47.

5. *Consider*, A professor, unquiet and turbulent under sufferings, and seeking his own revenge, cannot be a victor over what he should, nor a keeper of God's commandments.

(1.) How can he be a victor over himself that is led up and down by the nose by his own passions? There is no man a christian victor but he that conquers himself, but he that beats down and keeps under his body, his lusts, his passions, in the first place. Is he that is led away with divers lusts a victor? Is he that is a servant to corruption a victor? And if he that is captivated by his anger, wrath, passion, discontent, prejudice, &c., be not led away by them, I am under a mistake. So then, to quarrel with superiors, or with any that are troublesome to thee for thy faith and thy profession, bespeaks thee over-mastered and a captive, rather than a master and a conqueror.

(2.) The same may be said upon the second head. He keepeth not the commandments of God; for those teach him other things, as I have also showed. The great gospel commands terminate in self-denial; but if self-revenge is self-denial, I am besides the Book. Christ, in the book of the Revelation, sets him that keeps the commandments of God a great way off from him that taketh and smiteth with the sword: 'He that killeth with the sword must be killed with the sword. Here is the patience and the faith of the saints.'

Re. xiii. 10. That is, in that they forbear to do thus, and quietly suffer under those that thus take it and afflict the godly with it. Again, 'Here is the patience of the saints, here *are* they that keep the commandments of God and the faith of Jesus.' xiv. 12. A patient continuing in well-doing; and if suffering for righteousness be well-doing, then a patient continuing in that, as in other things, is the way to keep God's commandments. Ro. ii. 7.

So that, I say, he keepeth not God's commandments that is angry with his enemies, and that seeks to be revenged of him that doth him ill. You know the subject I am upon. 'The wrath of man worketh not the righteousness of God.' Ja. i. 20. Wherefore, professors, beware, and take heed to your spirits, and see that you let not out yourselves under your sufferings in such extravagancies of spirit against your enemies as is no way seemly nor convenient.

6. *Consider*, Men that are unquiet and discontented, and that seek revenge upon them that persecute them for their profession, do, by so doing, also put themselves upon the brink of those ruins that others are further from. These men are like the fly that cannot let the candle alone until she hath burned herself in the flame. Magistrates and men in power have fortified themselves from being attacked with turbulent and unruly spirits by many and wholesome laws. And, indeed, should they not do so, one or other, perhaps, would be quickly tempted to seek to disturb them in the due exercise of their authority. Now the angry man, he is the fly that must be tripping and running himself upon the point of these laws; his angry spirit puts him upon quarrelling with his superiors, and his quarrelling brings him, by words spoke in heat, within the reach of the net, and that, with the help of a few more, brings his neck to the halter. Nor is this, whatever men think, but by the just judgment of God. 'Whosoever, therefore, resisteth the power, resisteth the ordinance of God; and they that resist shall receive to themselves damnation.' Ro. xiii. 2. Es. ii. 21—23. Wherefore, let the angry man take heed; let the discontented man take heed. He that has a profession, and has not grace to know, in this matter, to manage it, is like to bring his profession to shame. Wherefore, I say, let such take heed; and the graces afore mentioned, and the due exercise of them, are they and that which can keep us out of all such dangers.

7. *Consider*, And what comfort can such a man have who has, by his discontent and unruly carriages, brought himself, in this manner, to his end; he has brought himself to shame, his profession to shame, his friends to shame, and his name to contempt and scorn. Bad men rejoice at his fall, good men cannot own him, weak men stumble at

him; besides, his cause will not bear him out; his heart will be clogged with guilt; innocency and boldness will take wings and fly from him. Though he talketh of religion upon the stage* or ladder,

that will blush to hear its name mentioned by them that suffer for evil-doing. Wherefore, my brethren, my friends, my enemies, and all men, what religion, profession, or opinion soever you hold, fear God, honour the king, and do that duty to both which is required of you by the Word and law of Christ, and then, to say no more, you shall not suffer by the power for evil-doing.

* 'Stage;' upon which many a Nonconformist stood with his head in the pillory. 'Ladder' to the gallows, upon which victims suffered death by hanging.—ED.

AN

EXHORTATION TO PEACE AND UNITY.

ADVERTISEMENT BY THE EDITOR.

THIS treatise was first published in 1688, after Bunyan's death, at the end of the second edition of the *Barren Fig Tree*, with a black border round the title. It was continued in the third edition 1692, but was subsequently omitted, although the *Barren Fig Tree* was printed for the same publisher. It has been printed in every edition of Bunyan's Works. Respect for the judgment of others leads me to allow it a place in the first complete edition, although I have serious doubts whether it was written by him, for these reasons:—

1. It appears to have been totally unknown to his personal friends, Charles Doe and others, who very carefully gathered up, not only all his published works, but his manuscripts also. An interesting list of these was given in the 'Struggler,' 1691. Nor is it found in any publisher's list of Bunyan's Works.

2. The style is not that of Bunyan, nor is it even Bunyanish. It has none of those striking remarks that render all his treatises so deeply interesting.

3. The author introduces scraps of Latin references to 'Machiavel,' to the '*learned* Stillingfleet,' and to ancient heathen writers. The frequent recurrence of the words, 'as a certain learned man observes,' is very foreign to Bunyan's manner of confirming his sentiments. 'Thus saith the Lord,' is the seal of his testimony.

4. Misapplication of Scripture, Ac. ix. 31, as if the 'rest' was from internal dissensions, when in fact it was from external persecution.

5. The terms 'infallible,' 'excommunication,' and 'reason,' are used in a way not at all Bunyanish.

6. How would his spirit have been grieved at a sentence which occurs on p. 750: 'Would a heathen god refuse to answer such prayers in which the supplicants were not agreed; and shall we think the true God will answer them?' Do stocks or stones answer prayers?

7. Bunyan's peculiar practice of admitting all the Lord's children to the Lord's table; all such as he hoped were spiritually baptized, without reference to water-baptism, is here directly opposed: p. 744. The author refers to 1 Co. xii. 13, on which text he says—'I need not go about to confute that notion that *some of late* have had of this text, viz., that the baptism here spoken of is the baptism of the Spirit, because you have not owned and declared

that notion as your judgment, but on the contrary.' The fact is, that Bunyan is one of those here noticed as '*some of late*,' and his church did hold that judgment. His comment on this text is, 'not of water, for by one SPIRIT are we all baptized into one body.'*—*Reason of my Practice.* And in his 'Differences about Water-Baptism no Bar to Communion,' he thus argues upon that text, 'Here is a baptism mentioned by which they are initiated into one body; now that this is the baptism of water is utterly against the words of the text; for by one SPIRIT we are all baptized into one body.'—'It is the unity of the Spirit, not water, that is intended.'† Bunyan was the great champion for the practice of receiving all to church-communion whom God had received in Christ, without respect to water-baptism; and had he changed his sentiments upon a subject which occasioned him so much hostility, even from his Baptist brethren, it would have been heralded forth as a triumph.

In 1684, four years prior to his death, he re-published these sentiments in the first edition of 'A Holy Life the Beauty of Christianity;'‡ his words are—'Men are wedded to their opinions more than the law of grace and love will permit. Here is a Presbyter, here an Independent, a Baptist, so joined each man to his own opinions, that they cannot have that communion one with another, as by the testament of the Lord Jesus they are commanded and enjoined.' Bunyan, there can be no doubt, lived and died in the conviction, that differences were permitted among Christians to stimulate them to search the Scriptures, and to exercise the grace of forbearance, as was the case in the primitive churches, in their disputes about meats and days, and even as to whether the Gentiles were to be visited with the gospel.

8. Bunyan is ever pressing the duty of private judgment in all the affairs of religion; not to be scared with the taunts of 'schism,' 'division-makers,' 'new separatists,' 'wiser than your teachers,' and similar arrows, drawn from Satan's quiver, which occur in this exhortation.

Judging from the style—the reference to the

---

* See this Edition of his Works, vol. ii., p. 594.
† Works, vol. ii., p. 608.
‡ Works, vol. ii., p. 538.

laying on of hands—the Latin quotations, and those from learned men, it appears somewhat like the pen of D'Anvers, who answered Bunyan upon the question—Whether water-baptism is a scrip-

tural term of communion? It is, however, now faithfully reprinted, that our readers may form their own judgment.

Hackney, New-Year's Day, 1850. GEORGE OFFOR.

AN EXHORTATION TO PEACE AND UNITY.

'ENDEAVOURING TO KEEP THE UNITY OF THE SPIRIT IN THE BOND OF PEACE.'—EPH. iv. 3.

BELOVED, religion is the great bond of human society, and it were well if itself were kept within the bond of unity; and that it may so be, let us, according to the text, use our utmost endeavours 'to keep the unity of the Spirit in the bond of peace.'

These words contain a counsel and a caution: the counsel is, 'That we endeavour the unity of the Spirit;' the caution is, 'That we do it in the bond of peace:' as if he should say, I would have you live in unity; but yet I would have you to be careful that you do not purchase unity with the breach of charity. Let us, therefore, be cautioned that we do not so press after unity in practice and opinion, as to break the bond of peace and affection.

In the handling of these words, I shall observe this method:—*First*, I shall open the sense of the text. *Second*, I shall show wherein this unity and peace consists. *Third*, I shall show you the fruits and benefits of it, together with nine inconveniencies and mischiefs that attend those churches where unity and peace is wanting. *Fourth*, and *lastly*, I shall give you twelve directions and motives for the obtaining of it.

First, As *touching the sense of the text;* when we are counselled to keep the unity of the Spirit, we are not to understand the Spirit of God as personally so considered; because the Spirit of God, in that sense, is not capable of being divided; and so there would be no need for us to endeavour to keep the unity of it.

By the unity of the Spirit, then, we are to understand that unity of mind which the Spirit of God calls for, and requires Christians to endeavour after; hence it is that we are exhorted by 'one spirit, with one mind striving together for the faith of the gospel.' Phi. i. 27.

But farther, the apostle in these words alludes to the state and composition of a natural body; and doth thereby inform us that the mystical body of Christ holds an analogy with the natural body of a man. As,

1. In the natural body there must be a spirit to animate it; for 'the body without the spirit is dead.'

Ja. ii. 26. So it is in the mystical body of Christ; the apostle no sooner tells us of that one body, but he minds us of that 'one spirit.' Ep. iv. 4.

2. The body hath 'joints and bands' to unite all the parts; so hath the mystical body of Christ. Col. ii. 19. This is that bond of peace mentioned in the text, as also in Ep. iv. 16, where 'the whole body' is said to be 'fitly joined together, and compacted by that which every joint supplieth.'

3. The natural body receives counsel and nourishment from the head; so doth the mystical body of Christ. He is their counsellor, and him they must hear; he is their head, and him they must hold; hence it is that the apostle complaineth, Col. ii. 19, of some that did 'not hold the head, from which all the body by joints and bands hath nourishment.'

4. The natural body cannot well subsist, if either the spirit be wounded or the joints broken or dislocated; the body cannot bear a wounded or broken spirit; 'A broken spirit drieth the bones,' Pr. xvii. 22; and 'a wounded spirit who can bear?' Pr. xviii. 14. And on the other hand, how often has the disjointing of the body, and the breakings thereof, occasioned the expiration of the spirit? In like manner it fares with the mystical body of Christ: how do divided spirits break the bonds of peace, which are the joints of this body! And how doth the breakings of the body and church of Christ wound the spirit of Christians, and oftentimes occasion the spirit and life of Christianity to languish, if not to expire! How needful is it, then, that we endeavour 'the unity of the spirit in the bond of peace?'

Second, I now come to show you *wherein this unity and peace consists*, and this I shall demonstrate in five particulars.

1. This unity and peace may consist in the ignorance of many truths, and in the holding of some errors; or else this duty of peace and unity could not be practicable by any on this side perfection. But we must now endeavour the unity of the Spirit, 'till we all come in the unity of the faith, and of the knowledge of the Son of God.' Ep. iv. 13. Because now, as the apostle saith, 'we know in part, and we prophesy in part,' and 'now we see through a glass, darkly.' 1 Co. xiii. 12. And as this is true in general, so we may find it true

if we descend to particular instances : the disciples seemed to be ignorant of that great truth which they had often, and in much plainness, been taught by their Master once and again, viz., that his kingdom was not of this world, and that in the world they should suffer and be persecuted ; yet in Ac. i. 6, we read, that they asked of him if he would ' at this time restore again the kingdom to Israel ?' thereby discovering that Christ's kingdom, as they thought, should consist in his temporal jurisdiction over Israel, which they expected should now commence and take place amongst them. Again, our Lord tells them that he had many things to say, and these were many important truths which they could not now bear. Jn. xvi. 12. And that these were important truths appears by the 10th and 11th verses, where he is discoursing of righteousness and judgment ; and then adds, that he had yet many things to say which they could not bear ; and thereupon promises the Comforter to lead them into ALL TRUTH ; which implies that they were yet ignorant of many truths, and consequently held divers errors ; and yet for all this he prays for, and presses them to their great duty of peace and unity. Jn. xiv. 27, and xvii. 21. To this may be added that of He. v. 11, where the author saith, He had many things to say of the priestly office of Christ, which, by reason of their dulness, they were not capable to receive ; as also that in Ac. x., where Peter seems to be ignorant of that truth, viz., that the gospel was to be preached to all nations ; and contrary hereunto, he erred in thinking it unlawful to preach amongst the Gentiles. I shall add two texts more ; one is Ac. xix. 2, where we read, That those disciples which had been discipled and baptized by John, were yet ignorant of the Holy Ghost, and knew not, as the text tells us, ' whether there be any Holy Ghost,' or no ; though John did teach constantly, that he that should come after him, should baptize with the Holy Ghost and fire. From hence we may easily and plainly infer, that Christians may be ignorant of many truths, by reason of weak and dull capacities, and other such like impediments, even while those truths are with much plainness delivered to them. Again, we read, He. v. 13, of some that were ' unskilful in the word of righteousness,' who nevertheless are called babes in Christ, and with whom unity and peace is to be inviolably kept and maintained.

2. As this unity and peace may consist in the ignorance of many truths, and in the holding some errors, so it must consist with, and it cannot consist without, the believing and practising those things which are necessary to salvation and church communion ; and they are, (1.) Believing that Christ the Son of God died for the sins of men. (2.) That whoever believeth ought to be baptized.

(3.) The third thing essential to this communion is a holy and a blameless conversation.

(1.) That believing that the Son of God died for the sins of men is necessary to salvation, I prove by these texts, which tell us that he that doth not believe shall be damned. Mar. xvi. 16. Jn. iii. 18. 2 Th. ii. 12. Ro. x. 10.

That it is also necessary to church-communion, appears from Mat. xvi. 16—18. Peter having confessed that Christ was the Son of the living God, Christ thereupon assures Peter, that upon this rock, viz., this profession of faith, or this Christ which Peter had confessed, he would build his church, and the gates of hell should not prevail against it. And, 1 Co. iii. 11, the apostle having told the Corinthians they were God's building, presently adds, that they could not be built upon any foundation but upon that which was laid, which was Jesus Christ. All which proves, that christian society is founded upon the profession of Christ ; and not only Scripture, but the laws of right reason, dictate this, that some rules and orders must be observed for the founding all society, which must be consented to by all that will be of it. Hence it comes to pass, that to own Christ as the Lord and head of Christians, is essential to the founding christian society.

(2.) The Scriptures have declared that this faith gives the professors of it a right to baptism, as in the case of the eunuch, Ac. viii., when he demanded why he might not be baptized ? Philip answereth, that if he believed with all his heart, he might ; the eunuch thereupon confessing Christ, was baptized.

Now, that baptism is essential to church-communion, I prove from 1 Co. xii., where we shall find the apostle labouring to prevent an evil use that might be made of spiritual gifts, as thereby to be puffed up ; and to think that such as wanted them, were not of the body, or to be esteemed members ; he thereupon resolves, that whoever did confess Christ, and own him for his head, did it by the Spirit, ver. 3, though they might not have such a visible manifestation of it as others had ; and therefore they ought to be owned as members, as appears, ver. 23. And not only because they have called him Lord by the Spirit, but because they have, by the guidance and direction of the same Spirit, been baptized, ver. 13 : ' For by one Spirit we are all baptized into one body,' &c. I need not go about to confute that notion that some of late have had of this text, viz., that the baptism here spoken of is the baptism of the Spirit, because you have not owned and declared that notion as your judgment ; but on the contrary, all of you that I have ever conversed with, have declared it to be understood of baptism with water, by the direction of the Spirit. If so, then it follows, that men and women are declared members of Christ's body by baptism, and cannot be by Scripture reputed and esteemed so without it; which farther appears from Ro. vi. 5, where men, by baptism, are said to be planted into 'the likeness of his death.' And Col. ii. 12, we are said to be ' buried with him by baptism.' All which, together with the consent of all Christians, (some few in these late times excepted,) do prove that baptism is necessary to the initiating persons into the church of Christ.

(3.) Holiness of life is essential to church-communion, because it seems to be the reason why Christ founded a church in the world, viz., that men might thereby be watched over and kept from falling; and that if any be overtaken with a fault, he that is spiritual might restore him.

That by this means men and women might be preserved, without blame, to the coming of Christ; and ' the grace of God teacheth us to deny ungodliness and worldly lusts, and to live soberly and uprightly in this present evil world.' Tit. ii. 11, 12. ' And let every one that nameth the name of Christ depart from iniquity.' 2 Ti. ii. 19. And James tells us, speaking of the christian religion, that ' pure religion, and undefiled, before God - is to visit the fatherless and widows in their affliction, *and* to keep himself unspotted from the world.' Ja. i. 27. From all which, together with many more texts that might be produced, it appears that an unholy and profane life is inconsistent with christian religion and society, and that holiness is essential to salvation and church-communion; so that these three things—faith, baptism, and a holy life, as I said before, all churches must agree and unite in, as those things which, when wanting, will destroy their being. And let not any think, that when I say believing the Son of God died for the sins of men is essential to salvation and church-communion, that I hereby would exclude all other articles of the christian creed as not necessary, as the belief of the resurrection of the dead and eternal judgment, &c.; which, for want of time, I omit to speak particularly to, and the rather because I understand this great article, of believing the Son of God died for the sins of men, is comprehensive of all others, and is that from whence all other articles may easily be inferred.

And here I would not be mistaken, as though I held there were nothing else for Christians to practise, when I say this is all that is requisite to church-communion; for I very well know that Christ requires many other things of us after we are members of his body, which, if we knowingly or maliciously refuse, may be the cause, not only of excommunication, but damnation. But yet these are such things as relate to the wellbeing, and not to the being, of churches; as laying on of

hands, in the primitive times, upon believers, by which they did receive the gifts of the Spirit—this, I say, was for the increase and edifying of the body, and not that thereby they might become of the body of Christ, for that they were before. And do not think that I believe laying on of hands was no apostolical institution, because I say men are not thereby made members of Christ's body, or because I say that it is not essential to church-communion. Why should I be thought to be against a fire in the chimney, because I say it must not be in the thatch of the house? Consider, then, how pernicious a thing it is to make every doctrine, though true, the bound of communion; this is that which destroys unity; and, by this rule, all men must be perfect before they can be in peace. For do we not see daily, that as soon as men come to a clearer understanding of the mind of God, to say the best of what they hold, that presently all men are excommunicable, if not damnable, that do not agree with them. Do not some believe and see that to be pride and covetousness, which others do not, because, it may be, they have more narrowly and diligently searched into their duty of these things than others have? What then? must all men that have not so large acquaintance of their duty herein be excommunicated? Indeed, it were to be wished that more moderation in apparel and secular concernments were found among churches; but God forbid, that if they should come short herein, that we should say, as one lately said, that he could not communicate with such a people, because they were proud and superfluous in their apparel.

Let me appeal to such, and demand of them, if there was not a time, since they believed and were baptized, wherein they did not believe laying on of hands a duty; and did they not then believe, and do they not still believe, they were members of the body of Christ? And was not there a time when you did not so well understand the nature and extent of pride and covetousness as now you do? And did you not then believe, and do you not still believe, that you were true members of Christ, though less perfect? Why, then, should you not judge of those that differ from you herein, as you judged of yourselves when you were as they now are? How needful, then, is it for Christians to distinguish, if ever they would be at peace and unity, between those truths which are essential to church-communion, and those that are not!

3. Unity and peace consists in our making one shoulder to practise and put in execution the things we do know. ' Nevertheless, whereto we have - attained, let us walk by the same rule, and mind the same thing.' Phi. iii. 16. How sad is it to see our zeal consume us, and our precious time, in

things doubtful and disputable, while we are not concerned nor affected with the practice of those indisputable things we all agree in! We all know charity to be the great command, and yet how few agree to practise it! We all know they that labour in the Word and doctrine are worthy of double honour; and that God hath ordained, that they which preach the gospel should live of the gospel; these duties, however others have cavilled at them, I know you agree in them, and are persuaded of your duty herein; but where is your zeal to practise? O how well would it be with churches if they were but half as zealous for the great, and plain, and indisputable things, and the more chargeable and costly things of religion, as they are for things doubtful or less necessary, or for things that are no charge to them, and cost them nothing but the breath of contention, though that may be too great a price for the small things they purchase with it.

But further: Do we not all agree, that men that preach the gospel should do it like workmen that need not be ashamed? and yet how little is this considered by many preachers, who never consider, before they speak, of what they say, or whereof they affirm! How few give themselves to study that they may be approved! How few meditate, and give themselves to these things, that their profiting may appear to all!

For the Lord's sake, let us unite to practise those things we know; and if we would have more talents, let us all agree to improve those we have.

See the spirit that was among the primitive professors, that knowing and believing how much it concerned them, in the propagating of Christianity, to show forth love to one another, that so all might know them to be Christ's disciples, rather than there should be any complainings among them, they sold all they had. Oh how zealous were these to practise, and, with one shoulder, to do that that was upon their hearts for God! I might further add, how often have we agreed in our judgment? and hath it not been upon our hearts, that this and the other thing is good to be done to enlighten the dark world, and to repair the breaches of churches, and to raise up those churches that now lie agasping, and among whom the soul of religion is expiring? But what do we more than talk of them? Do not most decline these things when they either call for their purses or their persons to help in this and such like works as these? Let us then, in what we know, unite, that we may put it in practice, remembering that, if we know these things, we shall be happy if we do them.

4. This unity and peace consists in our joining and agreeing to pray for, and to press after, those truths we do not know. The disciples in the primitive times were conscious of their imperfections, and, therefore, they, with one accord, continued in prayer and supplications. If we were more in the sense of our own ignorances and imperfections, we should carry it better towards those that differ from us; then we should abound more in the spirit of meekness and forbearance, that thereby we might bring others, or be brought by others, to the knowledge of the truth; this would make us go to God, and say with Elihu, That which we know not, teach thou us. Job xxxiv. 32. Brethren, did we but all agree that we were erring in many things, we should soon agree to go to God, and pray for more wisdom and revelation of his mind and will concerning us.

But here is our misery, that we no sooner receive any thing for truth, but we presently ascend the chair of infallibility with it, as though in this we could not err; hence it is we are impatient of contradiction, and become uncharitable to those that are not of the same mind; but now a consciousness that we may mistake, or that if my brother err in one thing I may err in another—this will unite us in affection, and engage us to press after perfection, according to that of the apostle, 'Brethren, I count not myself to have apprehended: but *this* one thing *I do*, forgetting those things which are behind, and reaching forth to those things which are before, I press toward the mark, for the prize of the high calling of God in Christ Jesus,' 'and if in any thing ye be otherwise minded, God shall reveal even this unto you.' Phi. iii. 13–15. O then, that we could but unite and agree to go to God for one another, in confidence that he will teach us; and that if any one of us want wisdom, as who of us does not, we might agree to ask of God, who giveth to all men liberally, and upbraideth no man. Let us, like those people spoken of in Is. ii., say one to another, Come, let us go to the Lord, for 'he will teach us of his ways, and we will walk in his paths.'

5. This unity and peace mainly consists in unity of love and affection; this is the great and indispensable duty of all Christians; by this they are declared Christ's disciples; and hence it is that love is called the great commandment, the old commandment, and the new commandment—that which was commanded in the beginning, and will remain to the end; yea, and after the end. 'Charity never faileth: but - whether *there be* tongues, they shall cease; whether *there be* knowledge, it shall vanish away.' 1 Co. xiii. 8. 'And now abideth faith, hope, charity - but the greatest of these *is* charity.' ver. 13. 'Above all these things *put on* charity, which is the bond of perfectness.' Col. iii. 14. Because charity is ꞏ the end of the commandment.' 1 Ti. i. 5. Charity is therefore called the royal law; and though it had a superinten-

dency over other laws, and, doubtless, is a law to which other laws must give place when they come in competition with it. 'Above all things, [therefore,] have fervent charity among yourselves, for charity shall cover the multitude of sins.' 1 Pe. iv. 8. Let us, therefore, live in unity and peace, and the God of love and peace will be with us.

That you may so do, let me remember you, in the words of a learned man, that the unity of the church is a unity of love and affection, and not a bare uniformity of practice and opinion.

Third, Having shown you wherein this unity consists, I now come to the third general thing propounded, and that is, *to show you the fruits and benefits of unity and peace; together with the mischiefs and inconveniences that attend those churches where unity and peace are wanting.*

1. Unity and peace is a duty well-pleasing to God, who is styled the author of peace, and not of confusion, in all the churches. God's Spirit rejoiceth in the unity of our spirits; but, on the other hand, where strife and divisions are, there the Spirit of God is grieved. Hence is it that the apostle no sooner calls upon the Ephesians not to grieve the Spirit of God, but he presently subjoins us a remedy against that evil: that they put away bitterness and evil speaking, 'and be ye kind one to another, tender-hearted, forgiving one another, even as God for Christ's sake hath forgiven you.' Ep. iv. 32.

2. As unity and peace is pleasing to God, and rejoiceth his Spirit, so it rejoiceth the hearts and spirits of God's people—unity and peace brings heaven down upon earth among us. Hence it is that the apostle tells us, Ro. xiv. 17, that 'the kingdom of God is not meat and drink; but righteousness, and peace, and joy in the Holy Ghost.' Where unity and peace is, there is heaven upon earth; by this we taste the first fruits of that blessed estate we shall one day live in the fruition of, when we shall come 'to the general assembly and church of the first-born,' whose names are written in heaven, 'and to God, the judge of all, and to the spirits of just men made perfect.' He. xii. 23.

This outward peace of the church, as a learned man observes, distils into peace of conscience, and turns writings and readings of controversy into treatises of mortification and devotion.

And the psalmist tells us, that it is not only good, but pleasant 'for brethren to dwell together in unity,' Ps. cxxxiii; but where unity and peace is wanting, there are storms and troubles; 'where envy and strife *is*, there *is* confusion and every evil work.' Ja. iii. 16. It is the outward peace of the church that increaseth our inward joy, and the peace of God's house gives us occasion to eat our meat with gladness in our own houses. Ac. ii. 46.

3. The unity and peace of the church makes communion of saints desirable. What is it that embitters church-communion, and makes it burdensome, but divisions? Have you not heard many complain that they are weary of church-communion, because of church contention? but now, where unity and peace is, there Christians long for communion.

David saith that he was glad when they said unto him, 'Let us go into the house of the Lord.' Ps. cxxii. 1. Why was this, but because, as the third verse tells us, Jerusalem was a city compact together, where the tribes went up, the tribes of the Lord, to give thanks to his name. And David, speaking of the man that was once his friend, doth thereby let us know the benefit of peace and unity; Ps. lv. 14: 'We,' saith he, 'took sweet counsel together, *and* walked unto the house of God in company.' Where unity is strongest, communion is sweetest and most desirable. You see, then, that peace and union fill the people of God with desires after communion; but, on the other hand, hear how David complains, Ps. cxx. 5, 'Woe is me that I sojourn in Meshech, *that* I dwell in the tents of Kedar!' The psalmist here is thought to allude to a sort of men that dwelt in the deserts of Arabia, that got their livings by contention; and, therefore, he adds, ver. 6, that his soul had long dwelt with them that hated peace: this was that which made him long for the courts of God, and esteem one day in his house better than a thousand. This made his soul even faint for the house of God, because of the peace of it; 'Blessed *are* they,' saith he, 'that dwell in thy house: they will be still praising thee.' Ps. lxxxiv. 4. There is a certain note of concord, as appears, Ac. ii., where we read of primitive Christians, meeting with one accord, praising God.

4. Where unity and peace is, there many mischiefs and inconveniences are prevented which attend those people where peace and unity are wanting; and of those many that might be mentioned, I shall briefly insist upon these nine:—

(1.) Where unity and peace are wanting, there is much precious time spent to no purpose. How many days are spent, and how many fruitless journeys made to no profit, where the people are not in peace! How often have many redeemed time, even in seed-time and harvest, when they could scarce afford it to go to church, and by reason of their divisions, come home worse than they went, repenting they have spent so much precious time to so little benefit! How sad is it to see men spend their precious time, in which they should work out their salvation, by labouring, as in the fire, to prove an uncertain and doubtful proposition, and to trifle away their time, in which they should make their calling and election sure, to make sure of an opinion which, when they have done all, they are not infallibly sure whether it be true or no; because all things necessary to salvation and church-communion are plainly laid down in Scripture, in which we may be infallibly sure of the truth of them; but for other things that we have no plain texts for, but the truth of them depends upon our interpretations, here we must be cautioned that we do not spend much time in imposing those upon others, or venting those among others, unless we can assume infallibility—otherwise, we spend time upon uncertainty; and whoever casts their eyes abroad, and doth open their ears to intelligence, shall both see, and, to their sorrow, hear that many churches spend most of their time in jangling and contending about those things which are neither essential to salvation or church-communion, and that which is worse, about such doubtful questions which they are never able to give an infallible solution of; but now, where unity and peace is, there our time is spent in praising God, and in those great questions—what we should do to be saved? and how we may be more holy and more humble towards God, and more charitable and more serviceable to one another?

(2.) Where unity and peace is wanting, there is evil surmising and evil speaking, to the damage and disgrace, if not to the ruining of one another; Ga. v. 14, 15: 'The whole law is fulfilled in one word, Thou shalt love thy neighbour as thyself; but if ye bite and devour one another, take heed that ye be not consumed one of another.' No sooner the bond of charity is broken, which is as a wall about Christians, but soon they begin to make havoc and spoil of one another; then there is raising evil reports, and taking up evil reports against each other. Hence it is that whispering and backbiting proceeds, and going from house to house to blazon the faults and infirmities of others: hence it is that we watch for the haltings of one another, and do inwardly rejoice at the miscarriages of others, saying in our hearts, Ah, ah, so we would have it; but now, where unity and peace is, there is charity; and where charity is, there we are willing to hide the faults, and cover the nakedness of our brethren. 'Charity thinketh no evil,' 1 Co. xiii. 5; and, therefore, it cannot surmise, neither will it speak evil.

(3.) Where unity and peace is wanting, there can be no great matters enterprised; we cannot do much for God nor much for one another. When the devil would hinder the bringing to pass of good in nations and churches, he divides their councils; and, as one well observes, he divides their heads, that he may divide their hands; when Jacob had prophesied of the cruelty of Simeon and Levi, who were brethren, he threatens them with the consequent of it; Ge. xlix. 7: 'I will divide them in Jacob, and scatter them in Israel.' The devil is not to

learn that maxim he hath taught the Machiavellians of the world, *divide et impera*—divide and rule; it is a united force that is formidable: hence the spouse, in the Canticles, is said to be 'but one,' 'and the *only* one of her mother.' Ca. vi. 9. Hereupon it is said of her, ver. 10, that she is 'terrible as *an army* with banners.' What can a divided army do, or a disordered army, that have lost their banners, or, for fear or shame, thrown them away? In like manner, what can Christians do for Christ, and the enlarging his dominions in the world, in bringing men from darkness to light, while themselves are divided and disordered? Peace is, to Christians, as great rivers are to some cities, which, besides other benefits and commodities, are natural fortifications, by reason whereof those places are made impregnable; but when, by the subtilty of an adversary or the folly of the citizens, these waters come to be divided into little petty rivulets, how soon are they assailed and taken! Thus it fares with churches; when once the devil, or their own folly divides them, they will be so far from resisting of him, that they will be soon subjected by him.

Peace is to churches as walls to cities; nay, unity hath defended cities that had no walls. It was once demanded of Agesilaus why Lacedemon had no walls; he answers, pointing back to the city, that the concord of the citizens was the strength of the city. In like manner, Christians are strong when united; then they are more capable to resist temptation, and to succour such as are tempted. When unity and peace is among the churches, then are they like a walled town; and when peace is the church's walls, salvation will be her bulwarks.

Plutarch tells us of one Silurus that had eighty sons, whom he calls to him as he lay upon his death-bed, and gave them a sheaf of arrows; thereby to signify, that if they lived in unity they might do much; but, if they divided, they would come to nothing. If Christians were all of one piece—if they were all but one lump, or but one sheaf or bundle, how great are the things they might do for Christ and his people in the world, whereas, otherwise, they can do little but dishonour him, and offend his.

It is reported of the leviathan, that his strength is in his scales; Job xli. 15–17: '*His* scales *are his* pride, shut up together, *as with* a close seal. One is so near to another, that no air can come between them. They are joined one to another, they stick together, that they cannot be sundered.' If the church of God were united like the scales of leviathan, it would not be every brain-sick notion, nor angry speculation, that would cause their separation.

Solomon saith, Two are better than one, because if one fail, the other may raise him; then surely twenty are better than two, and an hundred are better than twenty, for the same reason—because they are more capable to help one another. If ever Christians would do any thing to raise up the fallen tabernacles of Jacob, and to strengthen the weak, and comfort the feeble, and to fetch back those that have gone astray, it must be by unity.

We read of the men of Babel, Ge. xi. 6, 'The Lord said, Behold the people is one - And now nothing will be restrained from them which they have imagined to do.'

We learn, by reason, what great things may be done in worldly achievements where unity is. And shall not reason, assisted with the motives of religion, teach us that unity among Christians may enable them to enterprise greater things for Christ? Would not this make Satan fall from heaven like lightning? For as unity built literal Babel, it is unity that must pull down mystical Babel. And, on the other hand, where divisions are, there is confusion; by this means, a Babel hath been built in every age. It hath been observed by a learned man, and I wish I could not say truly observed, that there is most of Babel and confusion among those that cry out most against it.

Would we have a hand to destroy Babylon, let us have a heart to unite one among another.

Our English histories tell us, that after Austin the monk had been some time in England, that he heard of some of the remains of the British Christians, which he convened to a place, which Cambden, in his Britannia, calls Austin's Oak. Here they met to consult about matters of religion; but such was their division, by reason of Austin's imposing spirit, that our stories tell us that synod was only famous for this, that they only met, and did nothing. This is the mischief of divisions, they hinder the doing of much good; and if Christians that are divided be ever famous for any thing, it will be that they have often met together, and talked of this and the other thing, but they did nothing.

(4.) Where unity and peace is wanting, there the weak are wounded, and the wicked are hardened. Unity may well be compared to precious oil. Ps. cxxxiii. 2. It is the nature of oil to heal that which is wounded, and to soften that which is hard. Those men that have hardened themselves against God and his people, when they shall behold unity and peace among them, will say, God is in them indeed; and, on the other hand, are they not ready to say, when they see you divided, that the devil is in you, that you cannot agree?

(5.) Divisions, and want of peace, keep those out of the church that would come in; and cause many to go out that are in.

'The divisions of Christians (as a learned man observes) are a scandal to the Jews, an opprobrium to the Gentiles, and an inlet to atheism and infidelity.' Insomuch that our controversies about religion, especially as they have been of late managed, have made religion itself become a controversy. O, then, how good and pleasant a thing is it for brethren to dwell together in unity! The peace and unity that was among the primitive Christians drew others to them. What hinders the conversion of the Jews, but the divisions of Christians? Must I be a Christian, says the Jew? What Christian must I be; of what sect must I be of? The Jews, as one observes, glossing upon that text in Is. xi. 6, where it is prophesied, that the lion and the lamb shall lie down together, and that there shall be none left to hurt nor destroy in all God's holy mountain; they interpreting these sayings to signify the concord and peace that shall be among the people that shall own the Messiah, do from hence conclude that the Messiah is not yet come, because of the contentions and divisions that are among those that profess him; and the apostle saith, 1 Co. xiv. 23, that if an unbeliever should see their disorders, he would say they were mad; but where unity and peace is, there the churches are multiplied. We read, Ac. ix. 31, that when the churches had rest, they multiplied; and, Ac. ii. 46, 47, when the church was serving God 'with one accord,' the Lord added to them 'daily such as should be saved.'

It is unity brings men into the church, and divisions keep them out. It is reported of an Indian, passing by the house of a Christian, and hearing them contending, being desired to turn in, he refused, saying Habamach dwells there—meaning that the devil dwelt there; but where unity and peace is, there God is; and he that dwells in love, dwells in God. The apostle tells the Corinthians, that if they walked orderly, even the unbeliever would hereby be enforced to come and worship, and say, God was in them indeed; and we read, Zec. viii. 23, of a time when ten men shall take hold of a Jew, and say, 'We will go with you; for we have heard that God is with you.'

And hence it is that Christ prays, Jn. xvii. 21, that his disciples might be one, as the Father and he were one, that the world might believe the Father sent him. As if he should say, you may preach me as long as you will, and to little purpose, if you are not at peace and unity among yourselves. Such was the unity of Christians in former days, that the intelligent heathen would say of them, that though they had many bodies, yet they had but one soul. And we read the same of them, Ac. iv. 32, that 'the multitude of them that believed were of one heart and of one soul.'

And as the learned Stillingfleet observes, in his Irenicum,—'The unity and peace that was then among Christians, made religion amiable in the judgment of impartial heathens. Christians were then known by the benignity and sweetness of their dispositions, by the candour and ingenuity of their spirits, by their mutual love, forbearance, and condescension to one another: but either this is not the practice of Christianity,' viz., a duty that Christians are now bound to observe, ' or else it is not calculated for our meridian, where the spirits of men are of too high an elevation for it; for if pride and uncharitableness, if divisions and strifes, if wrath and envy, if animosities and contentions, were but the marks of true Christians, Diogenes need never light his lamp at noon to find out such among us; but if a spirit of meekness, gentleness, and condescension ; if a stooping to the weaknesses and infirmities of one another; if pursuit after peace, when it flies from us, be the indispensable duties and characteristical notes of Christians, it may possibly prove a difficult inquest to find out such among the crowds of those that shelter themselves under that glorious name.'

It is the unity and peace of churches that brings others to them, and makes Christianity amiable. What is prophesied of the church of the Jews, may in this case be applied to the Gentile church, Is. lxvi. 12, that when once God extends peace to her like a river, the Gentiles shall come in like a flowing stream; then, and not till then, the glory of the Lord shall arise upon his churches, and his glory shall be seen among them; then shall their hearts fear and be enlarged, because the abundance of the nations shall be converted to them.

(6.) As want of unity and peace keeps those out of the church that would come in, so it hinders the growth of those that are in. Jars and divisions, wranglings and prejudices, eat out the growth, if not the life, of religion. These are those waters of Marah that imbitter our spirits, and quench the Spirit of God. Unity and peace is said to be like the dew of Hermon, and as a dew that descended upon Zion, where the Lord commanded his blessing. Ps. cxxxiii. 3.

Divisions run religion into briers and thorns, contentions and parties. Divisions are to churches like wars in countries. Where war is, the ground lieth waste and untilled; none takes care of it. It is love that edifieth, but division pulleth down. Divisions are, as the north-east wind to the fruits, which causeth them to dwindle away to nothing; but when the storms are over, every thing begins to grow. When men are divided, they seldom speak the truth in love; and then, no marvel they grow not up to him in all things, which is the head.

It is a sad presage of an approaching famine, as one well observes, not of bread nor water, but of hearing the Word of God; when the thin ears of corn devour the plump full ones; when the lean kine devour the fat ones; when our controversies about doubtful things, and things of less moment, eat up our zeal for the more indisputable and prac-

tical things in religion ; which may give us cause to fear that this will be the character by which our age will be known to posterity, that it was the age that talked of religion most and loved it least.

Look upon those churches where peace is, and there you shall find prosperity. When the churches had rest, they were not only multiplied, but, walking in the fear of the Lord, and the comforts of the Holy Ghost, they were edified ; it is when the whole body is knit together, as with joints and bands, that they increase with the increase of God.

We are at a stand sometimes why there is so little growth among churches; why men have been so long in learning, and are yet so far from attaining the knowledge of the truth. Some have given one reason, and some another; some say pride is the cause, and others say covetousness is the cause ; I wish I could say these were no causes. But I observe that when God entered his controversy with his people of old, he mainly insisted upon some one sin, as idolatry, and shedding innocent blood, &c., as comprehensive of the rest; not but that they were guilty of other sins, but those that were the most capital are particularly insisted on; in like manner, whoever would but take a review of churches that live in contentions and divisions, may easily find that breach of unity and charity is their capital sin, and the occasion of all other sins. No marvel, then, that the Scripture saith the whole law is fulfilled in love; and if so, then, where love is wanting, it must needs follow the whole law is broken. It is where love grows cold that sin abounds ; and therefore the want of unity and peace is the cause of that leanness and barrenness that is among us: it is true in spirituals as well as temporals, that peace brings plenty.

(7.) Where unity and peace is wanting, our prayers are hindered. The promise is, that what we shall agree to ask shall be given us of our heavenly Father. No marvel we pray and pray, and yet are not answered; it is because we are not agreed what to have.

It is reported that the people in Lacedemonia, coming to make supplications to their idol-god, some of them asked for rain, and others of them asked for fair weather; the oracle returns them this answer, That they should go first and agree among themselves. Would a heathen god refuse to answer such prayers in which the supplicants were not agreed; and shall we think the true God will answer them ?

We see, then, that divisions hinder our prayers, and lay a prohibition on our sacrifice. ' If thou bring thy gift to the altar,' saith Christ, ' and there rememberest that thy brother hath ought against thee; leave there thy gift - and go - and first be reconciled to thy brother, and then come and offer it.' Mat. v. 24. So that want of unity and charity hinders even our particular prayers and devotions.

This hindered the prayers and fastings of the people of old from finding acceptance, Is. lviii. 3; the people ask the reason wherefore they fasted, and God did not see, nor take notice of them. He gives this reason, because they fasted for strife and debate, and hid their face from their own flesh. Again, Is. lix., the Lord saith, His hand was not shortened, that he could not save; nor his ear heavy, that he could not hear: but their sins had separated between their God and them. And among those many sins they stood chargeable with, this was none of the least, viz., that the way of peace they had not known. You see where peace was wanting, prayers were hindered, both under the Old and New Testament.

The sacrifice of the people in Is. lxv., that said, Stand farther off, I am holier than thou, was as smoke in the nostrils of the Lord. On the other hand, we read how acceptable those prayers were that were made ' with one accord,' Ac. iv. 24, compared with ver. 31. They prayed with one accord, and they were all of one heart and of one soul. And see the benefit of it; ' they were all filled with the Holy Ghost, and they spake the Word with boldness:' which was the very thing they prayed for, as appears, ver. 29. And the apostle exhorts the husband to dwell with his wife, that their prayers might not be hindered. 1 Pe. iii. 7. We see, then, want of unity and peace, either in families or churches, is a hinderance of prayers.

(8.) It is a dishonour and disparagement to Christ that his family should be divided. When an army falls into mutiny and division, it reflects disparagement on him that hath the conduct of it. In like manner, the divisions of families are a dishonour to the heads and those that govern them. And if so, then how greatly do we dishonour our Lord and Governor, who gave his body to be broken, to keep his church from breaking, who prayed for their peace and unity, and left peace at his departing from them for a legacy, even a peace which the world could not bestow upon them.

(9.) Where there is peace and unity, there is a sympathy with each other; that which is the want of one will be the want of all,—Who is afflicted, saith the apostle, and I burn not?* we should then remember them that are in bonds, as bound with them; and them which suffer adversity, as being ourselves also of the body. He. xiii. 3. But where the body is broken, or men are not reckoned or esteemed of the body, no marvel we are so little affected with such as are afflicted. Where divisions are, that which is the joy of the one is the

grief of another; but where unity, and peace, and charity abounds, there we shall find Christians in mourning with them that mourn, and rejoicing with them that rejoice; then they will not envy the prosperity of others, nor secretly rejoice at the miseries or miscarriages of any.

Fourth, Last of all, I now come to give you *twelve directions and motives for the obtaining peace and unity.*

If ever we would live in peace and unity, we must pray for it. We are required to seek peace: of whom, then, can we seek it with expectation to find it, but of him who is a God of peace, and hath promised to bless his people with peace ? It is God that hath promised to give his people one heart, and one way; yet for all these things he will be sought unto. O then let us seek peace, and pray for peace, because God shall prosper them that love it.

The peace of churches is that which the apostle prays for in all his epistles; in which his desire is, that grace and peace may be multiplied and increased among them.

1. They that would endeavour the peace of the churches, must be careful who they commit the care and oversight of the churches to; as, first, over and besides those qualifications that should be in all Christians, they that rule the church of God should be men of counsel and understanding; where there is an ignorant ministry, there is commonly an ignorant people,—according as it was of old, Like priest, like people.

How sad is it to see the church of God committed to the care of such that pretend to be teachers of others, that understand not what they say, or whereof they affirm. No marvel the peace of churches is broken, when their watchmen want skill to preserve their unity, which of all other things is as the church's walls; when they are divided, no wonder they crumble to atoms, if there is no skilful physician to heal them. It is sad when there is no balm in Gilead, and when there is no physician there. Hence it is, that the wounds of churches become incurable, like the wounds of God's people of old; either not healed at all, or else slightly healed, and to no purpose. May it not be said of many churches at this day, as God said of the church of Israel, that he sought for a man among them that should stand in the gap, and make up the breach, but he found none?

Remember what was said of old, Mal. ii. 7, The priest's lips should preserve knowledge; and the people ' should seek the law at his mouth.' But when this is wanting, the people will be stumbling and departing from God and one another; therefore God complains, Ho. iv. 6, that his people were ' destroyed for want of knowledge;' that is, for want of knowing guides; for if the light that is

---

* ' Who is weak, and I am not weak? Who is offended, and I burn not?'—Ed.

in them that teach be darkness, how great is that darkness; and if the blind lead the blind, no marvel both fall into the ditch.

How many are there that take upon them to teach others, that had need be taught in the beginning of religion; that instead of multiplying knowledge, multiply words without knowledge; and instead of making known God's counsel, darken counsel by words without knowledge? The apostle speaks of some that did more than darken counsel, for they wrested the counsel of God. 2 Pe. iii. 16. In Paul's epistles, saith he, are 'some things hard to be understood, which they that are unlearned and unstable wrest, as *they do* also the other scriptures unto their own destruction.' Some things in the Scripture are hard to be known, and they are made harder by such unlearned teachers as utter their own notions by words without knowledge.

None are more bold and adventurous to take upon them to expound the dark mysteries and sayings of the prophets and revelations, and the 9th of the Romans,—which, I believe, contains some of those many things which, in Paul's epistles, Peter saith were 'hard to be understood.' I say, none are more forward to dig in these mines than those that can hardly give a sound reason for the first principles of religion; and such as are ignorant of many more weighty things that are easily to be seen in the face and superficies of the Scripture; nothing will serve these but swimming in the deeps, when they have not yet learned to wade through the shallows of the Scriptures. Like the Gnostics of old, who thought they knew all things, though they knew nothing as they ought to know. And as those Gnostics did of old, so do such teachers of late break the unity and peace of churches. How needful, then, is it, that if we desire the peace of churches, that we choose out men of knowledge, who may be able to keep them from being shattered and scattered with every wind of doctrine; and who may be able to convince and stop the mouths of gainsayers!

2. You must not only choose men of counsel; but if you would design the unity and peace of the churches, you must choose men of courage to govern them; for as there must be wisdom to bear with some, so there must be courage to correct others; as some must be instructed meekly, so others must be rebuked sharply, that they may be sound in the faith; there must be wisdom to rebuke some with long-suffering, and there must be courage to suppress and stop the mouths of others. The apostle tells Titus of some 'whose mouths must be stopped,' or else they would 'subvert whole houses.' Tit. i. 11. Where this courage hath been wanting, not only whole houses, but whole churches have been subverted. And Paul

tells the Galatians, that when he saw some endeavour to bring the churches into bondage, that he did not give place to them, 'no, not for an hour,' &c. Ga. ii. 5. If this course had been taken by the rulers of churches, their peace had not been so often invaded by unruly and vain talkers.

In choosing men to rule, if you would endeavour to keep the unity of the spirit and the bond of peace thereby, be careful you choose men of peaceable dispositions. That which hath much annoyed the peace of churches, hath been the froward and perverse spirits of the rulers thereof. Solomon therefore adviseth, that 'with a furious man we should not go, lest we learn his ways, and get a snare to our souls.' Pr. xxii. 24, 25. And with the froward we learn frowardness. How do some men's words eat like a canker; who instead of lifting up their voices like a trumpet, to sound a parley for peace, have rather sounded an alarm to war and contention. If ever we would live in peace, let us reverence the feet of them that bring the glad tidings of it.

O how have some men made it their business to preach contentions, and upon their entertainment of every novel opinion, to preach separation! How hath God's Word been stretched and torn, to furnish these men with arguments to tear churches! Have not our ears heard those texts that saith, 'Come out from among them, and be separate,' &c.; and, 'Withdraw from every brother that walks disorderly?' I say, have we not heard these texts, that were written to prevent disorder, brought to countenance the greatest disorder that ever was in the church of God, even schism and division? whereas one of these exhortations was written to the church of Corinth, to separate themselves from the idol's temple, and the idol's table, in which many of them lived in the participation of, notwithstanding their profession of the true God, as appears 2 Co. vi. 16, 17, compared with 1 Co. viii. 7, and 1 Co. x. 14, 20, 22 recites: and not for some few or more members, who shall make themselves both judges and parties, to make separation, when and as often as they please, from the whole congregation and church of God where they stood related; for by the same rule, and upon the same ground, may others start some new question among these new separatists, and become their own judges of the communicableness of them, and thereupon make another separation from these, till at last two be not left to walk together. And for that other text mentioned, 2 Th. iii. 6, where Paul exhorts the church of Thessalonica to withdraw themselves from every brother that walks disorderly, I cannot but wonder that any should bring this to justify their separation, or withdrawing from the communion of a true, though a disorderly, church. For,

(1.) Consider that this was not writ for a few

members to withdraw from the church, but for the church to withdraw from disorderly members.

(2.) Consider that if any offended members, upon pretence of error, either in doctrine or practice, should by this text become judges, as well as parties, of the grounds and lawfulness of their separation, then it will follow, that half a score notorious heretics, or scandalous livers, when they have walked so as they foresee the church are ready to deal with them, and withdraw from them, shall anticipate the church, and pretend somewhat against them, of which themselves must be judges, and so withdraw from the church, pretending either heresy or disorder; and so condemn the church, to prevent the disgrace of being condemned by the church. How needful, then, is it that men of peaceable dispositions, and not of froward and factious and dividing spirits, be chosen to rule the church of God, for fear lest the whole church be leavened and soured by them.

4. As there must be care used in choosing men to rule the church of God, so there must be a consideration had that there are many things darkly laid down in Scripture; this will temper our spirits, and make us live in peace and unity the more firmly in things in which we agree; this will help us to bear one another's burden, and so fulfil the law of Christ, inasmuch as all things necessary to salvation and church-communion are plainly laid down in Scripture. And where things are more darkly laid down, we should consider that God intended hereby to stir up our diligence, that thereby we might increase our knowledge, and not our divisions; for it may be said of all discoveries of truth we have made in the Scriptures, as it is said of the globe of the earth, that though men have made great searches, and thereupon great discoveries, yet there is still a *terra incognita*—an unknown land; so there is in the Scriptures; for after men have travelled over them, one age after another, yet still there is, as it were, a *terra incognita*, an unknown tract to put us upon farther search and inquiry, and to keep us from censuring and falling out with those who have not yet made the same discoveries; that so we may say with the Psalmist, when we reflect upon our short apprehensions of the mind of God, that we have seen an end of all perfections, but God's commands are exceeding broad; and as one observes, speaking of the Scriptures, that there is a path in them leading to the mind of God, which lieth a great distance from the thoughts and apprehensions of men. And on the other hand, in many other places, God sits, as it were, on the superficies and the face of the letter, where he that runs may discern him speaking plainly, and no parable at all. How should the consideration of this induce us to a peaceable deportment towards those that differ.

5. If we would endeavour peace and unity, we must consider how God hath tempered the body, that so the comely parts should not separate from the uncomely, as having no need of them. 1 Co. xii. 22–25. There is in Christ's body and house some members and vessels less honourable, 2 Ti. ii. 20; and therefore we should not, as some now-a-days do, pour the more abundant disgrace, instead of putting the more abundant honour, upon them. Did we but consider this, we should be covering the weakness and hiding the miscarriages of one another, because we are all members one of another, and the most useless member in his place is useful.

6. If we would live in peace, let us remember our relations to God—as children to a father, and to each other as brethren. Will not the thoughts that we have one Father quiet us, and the thoughts that we are brethren unite us? It was this that made Abraham propose terms of peace to Lot, Ge. xiii.: 'Let there be no strife,' saith he, 'between us, for we are brethren.' And we read of Moses, in Ac. vii. 26, using this argument to reconcile those that strove together, and to set them at one again: 'Sirs,' saith he, 'ye are brethren; why do ye wrong one to another?' A deep sense of this relation, that we are brethren, would keep us from dividing.

7. If we would preserve peace, let us mind the gifts, and graces, and virtues that are in each other; let these be more in our eye than their failings and imperfections. When the apostle exhorted the Philippians to peace, as a means hereunto, that so the peace of God might rule in their hearts, he tells them, ch. iv. 8, that if there were any virtue, or any praise, they should think of these things. While we are always talking and blazoning the faults of one another, and spreading their infirmities, no marvel we are so little in peace and charity; for as charity covereth a multitude of sins, so malice covereth a multitude of virtues, and makes us deal by one another as the heathen persecutors dealt with Christians, viz., put them in bears' skins, that they might the more readily become a prey to those dogs that were designed to devour them.

8. If we would keep unity and peace, let us lay aside provoking and dividing language, and forgive those that use them. Remember that old saying, Evil words corrupt good manners. When men think to carry all afore them, with speaking uncharitably and disgracefully of their brethren or their opinions, may not such be answered as Job answered his unfriendly visitants, Job vi. 25, 'How forcible are right words! But what doth your arguing reprove?' How healing are words fitly spoken! A word in season, how good is it! If we would seek peace, let us clothe all our treaties for peace with acceptable words; and where one word may better accommodate than another, let

that be used to express persons or things by, and let us not, as some do, call the different practices of our brethren will-worship, and their different opinions doctrines of devils, and the doctrine of Balaam, who taught fornication, &c., unless we can plainly, and in expressness of terms, prove it so; such language as this hath strangely divided our spirits, and hardened our hearts one towards another.

9. If we would live in peace, let us make the best constructions of one another's words and actions. Charity judgeth the best, and it thinks no evil; if words and actions may be construed to a good sense, let us never put a bad construction upon them. How much hath the peace of Christians been broken by an uncharitable interpretation of words and actions? As some lay to the charge of others that which they never said, so, by straining men's words, others lay to their charge that they never thought.

10. Be willing to hear and learn, and obey those that God by his providence hath set over you; this is a great means to preserve the unity and peace of churches. But when men, yea, and sometimes women, shall usurp authority, and think themselves wiser than their teachers, no wonder if these people run into contentions and parties, when any shall say they are not free to hear those whom the church thinks fit to speak to them. This is the first step to schism, and is usually attended, if not timely prevented, with a sinful separation.

11. If you would keep the unity of the spirit in the bond of peace, be mindful that the God whom you serve is a God of peace, and your Saviour is a Prince of peace, and that his ways are ways of pleasantness, and all his paths are peace; and that Christ was sent into the world to give light to them that sit in darkness and in the shadow of death, and to guide our feet in the way of peace.

12. Consider the oneness of spirit that is among the enemies of religion; though they differ about other things, yet to persecute religion, and extirpate religion out of the earth, here they will agree: the devils in the air, and the devils in the earth, all the devils in hell, and in the world, make one at this turn. Shall the devil's kingdom be united, and shall Christ's be divided? Shall the devils make one shoulder to drive on the design of damning men, and shall not Christians unite to carry on

the great design of saving of them? Shall the Papists agree and unite to carry on their interest, notwithstanding the multitudes of orders, degrees, and differences that are among them, and shall not those that call themselves reformed churches unite to carry on the common interest of Christ in the world, notwithstanding some petty and disputable differences that are among them? Quarrels about religion, as one observes, were sins not named among the Gentiles. What a shame is it, then, for Christians to abound in them, especially considering the nature of the Christian religion, and what large provisions the author of it hath made to keep the professors of it in peace; insomuch, as one well observes, it is next to a miracle that ever any, especially the professors of it, should fall out about it.

13. Consider and remember that the Judge stands at the door; let this moderate our spirits, that the Lord is at hand. What a sad account will they have to make when he comes, that shall be found to smite their fellow-servants, and to make the way to his kingdom more narrow than ever he made it? Let me close all in the words of that great apostle, 2 Co. xiii. 11: 'Finally, brethren, farewell. Be perfect, be of good comfort, be of one mind, live in peace; and the God of love and peace shall be with you.'

POSTSCRIPT.

Reader, I thought good to advertise thee that I have delivered this to thy hand in the same order and method in which it was preached, and almost in the same words, without any diminishings or considerable enlargings, unless it be in the thirteen last particulars, upon some of which I have made some enlargements, which I could not then do for want of time; but the substance of every one of them was then laid down in the same particular order as here thou hast them: and now I have done, I make no other account, to use the words of a moderate man upon the like occasion, but it will fall out with me, as doth commonly with him that parts a fray, both parties may perhaps drive at me for wishing them no worse than peace. My ambition of the public tranquillity of the church of God, I hope, will carry me through these hazards. Let both beat me, so their quarrels may cease; I shall rejoice in those blows and scars I shall take for the church's safety.

MR. BUNYAN'S LAST SERMON:

PREACHED AUGUST 19TH, 1688.

ADVERTISEMENT BY THE EDITOR.

THIS sermon, although very short, is peculiarly interesting: how it was preserved we are not told; but it bears strong marks of having been published from notes taken by one of the hearers. There is no proof that any memorandum or notes of this sermon was found in the autograph of the preacher.

In the list of Bunyan's works published by Chas. Doe, at the end of the 'Heavenly Footman,' March 1690, it stands No. 44. He professes to give the title-page, word for word, as it was first printed, It is, 'Mr. John Bunyan's last sermon, at London, preached at Mr. Gamman's meeting-house, near Whitechapel, August 19th, 1688, upon John i. 13: showing a resemblance between a natural and a spiritual birth; and how every man and woman may try themselves, and know whether they are born again or not.' Published 1689,

in about one sheet in 12mo. From this it appears to have been preached only two days before his fatal illness, and twelve days before his decease, which took place August 31st, 1688. The disease which terminated his invaluable life, was brought on by a journey to Reading on horseback, undertaken with the benevolent design of reconciling an offended father to his son. Having accomplished his object, he rode to London; on his way home, through a heavy rain, the effects of which appeared soon after this, his last sermon was preached. He bore, with most exemplary patience and resignation, the fever which invaded his body; and, at a distance from his wife and family, in the house of his friend Mr. Strudwick, at Snow Hill, his pilgrimage was ended, and he fell asleep in perfect peace, to awake amidst the harmonies and glory of the celestial city.

GEO. OFFOR.

MR. BUNYAN'S LAST SERMON.

'WHICH WERE BORN, NOT OF BLOOD, NOR OF THE WILL OF THE FLESH, NOR OF THE WILL OF MAN, BUT OF GOD.'—JOHN I. 13.

THE words have a dependence on what goes before, and therefore I must direct you to them for the right understanding of it. You have it thus: 'He came unto his own, and his own received him not; but as many as received him, to them gave he power to become the sons of God, *even* to them that believe on his name: which were born, not of blood, nor of the will of the flesh - but of God.'

In the words before, you have two things. *First,* Some of his own rejecting him, when he offered himself to them. *Second,* Others of his own receiving him, and making him welcome; those that reject him, he also passes by; but those that receive him, he gives them power to become the sons of God.

Now, lest any one should look upon it as good luck or fortune, says he, they 'were born, not of blood, nor of the will of the flesh, nor of the will of man, but of God.' They that did not receive him, they were only born of flesh and blood; but

those that receive him, they have God to their Father; they receive the doctrine of Christ with a vehement desire.

[TO EXPLAIN THE TEXT.]

FIRST, I will show you what he means by blood. They that believe are born to it, as an heir is to an inheritance—they are born of God, not of flesh, nor of the will of man, but of God; not of blood, that is, not by generation, not born to the kingdom of heaven by the flesh, not because I am the son of a godly man or woman—that is meant by blood; Ac. xvii. 26: He 'hath made of one blood all nations.' But when he says here, 'not of blood,' he rejects all carnal privileges they did boast of: they boasted they were Abraham's seed; no, no, says he, it is not of blood; think not to say you have Abraham to your father; you must be born of God, if you go to the kingdom of heaven.

SECOND, 'Nor of the will of the flesh.' What must we understand by that?

It is taken for those vehement inclinations that are in man, to all manner of looseness, fulfilling the desires of the flesh: that must not be understood here; men are not made the children of God by fulfilling their lustful desires. It must be understood here in the best sense: there is not only in carnal men a will to be vile, but there is in them a will to be saved also; a will to go to heaven also. But this it will not do; it will not privilege a man in the things of the kingdom of God: natural desires after the things of another world, they are not an argument to prove a man shall go to heaven whenever he dies. I am not a free-willer, I do abhor it; yet there is not the wickedest man but he desires, some time or other, to be saved; he will read some time or other, or, it may be, pray, but this will not do: ' *It is* not of him that willeth, nor of him that runneth, but of God that sheweth mercy.' There is willing and running, and yet to no purpose. Ro. ix. 16. Israel, which followed after the law of righteousness, have not obtained it. ver. 30. Here, I do not understand, as if the apostle had denied a virtuous course of life to be the way to heaven; but that a man without grace, though he have natural gifts, yet he shall not obtain privilege to go to heaven, and be the son of God. Though a man without grace may have a will to be saved, yet he cannot have that will God's way. Nature, it cannot know any thing but the things of nature—the things of God knows no man but by the Spirit of God; unless the Spirit of God be in you, it will leave you on this side the gates of heaven. ' Not of blood, nor of the will of the flesh, nor of the will of man, but of God.' It may be, some may have a will, a desire that Ishmael may be saved; know this, it will not save thy child. If it was our will, I would have you all go to heaven. How many are there in the world that pray for their children, and cry for them, and are ready to die [for them]? and this will not do. God's will is the rule of all; it is only through Jesus Christ: ' which were born, not of flesh, nor of the will of man, but of God.'

Now I come to the doctrine.

Men that believe in Jesus Christ, to the effectual receiving of Jesus Christ, they are born to it. He does not say they *shall* be born to it, but they *are* born to it—born of God unto God and the things of God, before he receives God to eternal salvation. ' Except a man be born again, he cannot see the kingdom of God.' Now, unless he be born of God, he cannot see it: suppose the kingdom of God be what it will, he cannot see it before he be begotten of God. Suppose it be the gospel, he cannot see it before he be brought into a state of regeneration. Believing is the consequence of the new birth; ' not of blood, nor of the will of man, but of God.'

First, I will give you a clear description of it under one similitude or two. A child, before it be born into the world, is in the dark dungeon of its mother's womb: so a child of God, before he be born again, is in the dark dungeon of sin, sees nothing of the kingdom of God; therefore it is called a new birth: the same soul has love one way in its carnal condition, another way when it is born again.

Second, As it is compared to a birth, resembling a child in his mother's womb, so it is compared to a man being raised out of the grave; and to be born again, is to be raised out of the grave of sin; ' Awake, thou that sleepest, and arise from the dead, and Christ shall give thee light.' To be raised from the grave of sin is to be begotten and born; Re. i. 5: there is a famous instance of Christ; He is ' the first begotten of the dead;' he is the first-born from the dead, unto which our regeneration alludeth; that is, if you be born again by seeking those things that are above, then there is a similitude betwixt Christ's resurrection and the new birth; which was born, which was restored out of this dark world, and translated out of the kingdom of this dark world, into the kingdom of his dear Son, and made us live a new life—this is to be born again: and he that is delivered from the mother's womb, it is the help of the mother; so he that is born of God, it is by the Spirit of God. I must give you a few consequences of a new birth.

(1.) First of all, A child, you know, is incident to cry as soon as it comes into the world; for if there be no noise, they say it is dead. You that are born of God, and Christians, if you be not criers, there is no spiritual life in you—if you be born of God, you are crying ones; as soon as he has raised you out of the dark dungeon of sin, you cannot but cry to God, What must I do to be saved? As soon as ever God had touched the, jailer, he cries out, ' Men and brethren, what must I do to be saved?' Oh! how many prayerless professors is there in London that never pray! Coffee-houses will not let you pray, trades will not let you pray, looking-glasses will not let you pray; but if you was born of God, you would.

(2.) It is not only natural for a child to cry, but it must crave the breast; it cannot live without the breast—therefore Peter makes it the true trial of a new-born babe: the new-born babe desires the sincere milk of the Word, that he may grow thereby: if you be born of God, make it manifest by desiring the breast of God. Do you long for the milk of the promises? A man lives one way when he is in the world, another way when he is brought unto Jesus Christ. Is. lxvi. They shall suck and be satisfied; if you be born again, there is no satisfaction till you get the milk of God's Word into your souls. Is. lxvi. 11. To ' suck and be satisfied with the breasts of her consolation.' Oh! what is a promise to a carnal man? A whore-house, it may be, is more sweet to him; but if you be born again, you cannot live without the milk of God's Word. What is a woman's breast to a horse? But what is it to a child? there is its comfort night and day, there is its succour night and day. O how loath are they it should be taken from them: minding heavenly things, says a carnal man, is but vanity; but to a child of God, there is his comfort.

(3.) A child that is newly born, if it have not other comforts to keep it warm than it had in its mother's womb, it dies; it must have something got for its succour: so Christ had swaddling clothes prepared for him; so those that are born again, they must have some promise of Christ to keep them alive; those that are in a carnal state, they warm themselves with other things; but those that are born again, they cannot live without some promise of Christ to keep them alive; as he did to the poor infant in Eze. xvi. 8: I covered thee with embroidered gold: and when women are with child, what fine things will they prepare for their child! Oh, but what fine things has Christ prepared to wrap all in that are born again! Oh what wrappings of gold has Christ prepared for all that are born again! Women will dress their children, that every one may see them how fine they are; so he in Eze. xvi. 11: 'I decked thee also with ornaments, and I put bracelets upon thine hands, and a chain on thy neck; and I put a jewel on thy forehead, and ear-rings in thine ears, and a beautiful crown upon thine head.' And, says he in ver. 13, 'Thou didst prosper into a kingdom.' This is to set out nothing in the world but the righteousness of Christ and the graces of the Spirit, without which a new-born babe cannot live, unless they have the golden righteousness of Christ.

(4.) A child, when it is in its mother's lap, the mother takes great delight to have that which will be for its comfort; so it is with God's children, they shall be kept on his knee; Is. lxvi. 11: 'They shall suck and be satisfied with the breasts of her consolations;' ver. 13: 'As one whom his mother comforteth, so will I comfort you.' There is a similitude in these things that nobody knows of, but those that are born again.

(5.) There is usually some similitude betwixt the father and the child. It may be the child looks like its father; so those that are born again, they have a new similitude—they have the image of Jesus Christ. Ga. iv. Every one that is born of God has something of the features of heaven upon him. Men love those children that are likest them most usually; so does God his children, therefore they are called the children of God; but others do not look like him, therefore they are called Sodomites.

Christ describes children of the devil by their features—the children of the devil, his works they will do; all works of unrighteousness, they are the devil's works: if you are earthly, you have borne the image of the earthly; if heavenly, you have borne the image of the heavenly.

(6.) When a man has a child, he trains him up to his own liking—they have learned the custom of their father's house; so are those that are born of God—they have learned the custom of the true church of God; there they learn to cry 'My Father' and 'My God;' they are brought up in God's house, they learn the method and form of God's house, for regulating their lives in this world.

(7.) Children, it is natural for them to depend upon their father for what they want; if they want a pair of shoes, they go and tell him; if they want bread, they go and tell him; so should the children of God do. Do you want spiritual bread? go tell God of it. Do you want strength of grace? ask it of God. Do you want strength against Satan's temptations? go and tell God of it. When the devil tempts you, run home and tell your heavenly Father—go, pour out your complaints to God; this is natural to children; if any wrong them, they go and tell their father; so do those that are born of God, when they meet with temptations, go and tell God of them.

[THE APPLICATION.]

The first use is this, To make a strict inquiry whether you be born of God or not; examine by those things I laid down before, of a child of nature and a child of grace. Are you brought out of the dark dungeon of this world into Christ? Have you learned to cry, 'My Father?' Je. iii. 4. 'And I said, Thou shalt call me, My Father.' All God's children are criers—cannot you be quiet without you have a bellyful of the milk of God's Word? cannot you be satisfied without you have peace with God? Pray you, consider it, and be serious with yourselves; if you have not these marks, you will fall short of the kingdom of God—you shall never have an interest there; 'there' is no intruding. They will say, 'Lord, Lord, open to us; and he will say, I know you not.' No child of God, no heavenly inheritance. We sometimes give something to those that are not our children, but [we do] not [give them] our lands. O do not flatter yourselves with a portion among the sons, unless you live like sons. When we see a king's son play with a beggar, this is unbecoming; so if you be the king's children, live like the king's children; if you be risen with Christ, set your affections on things above, and not on things below; when you come together, talk of what your Father promised you; you should all love your Father's will, and be content and pleased with the exercises you meet with in the world. If you are the children of God, live together lovingly; if the world quarrel with you, it is no matter; but it is sad if you quarrel together; if this be amongst you, it is a sign of ill-breeding; it is not according to the rules you have in the Word of God. Dost thou see a soul that has the image of God in him? Love him, love him; say, This man and I must go to heaven one day; serve one another, do good for one another; and if any wrong you, pray to God to right you, and love the brotherhood.

Lastly, If you be the children of God, learn that lesson—Gird up the loins of your mind, as obedient children, not fashioning yourselves according to your former conversation; but be ye holy in all manner of conversation. Consider that the holy God is your Father, and let this oblige you to live like the children of God, that you may look your Father in the face, with comfort, another day.